THE KOSOVO CONFLICT AND INTERNATIONAL LAW

An Analytical Documentation 1974–1999

The Kosovo Conflict and International Law provides international lawyers, scholars and students with access to material on the conflict in Kosovo. As well as the basic material relating to Kosovo's status in Yugoslavia before 1999, this volume reproduces the significant documentation on the following issues: the development of the human rights situation, the diplomatic efforts for the settlement of the crisis, the military action against Yugoslavia and the international community's response, court action with regard to the conflict, and the implementation of the principles for a political solution with an international civil and security presence in Kosovo. An analytical introduction provides the historical and political context as well as an overview of the various legal aspects of the conflict. A chronology and detailed index make the documents more accessible.

Titles available in the Cambridge International Documents Series

The Kuwait Crisis: Basic Documents 0521 46308 4
Iraq and Kuwait: The Hostilities and their Aftermath 0521 46306 8
International Efforts to Combat Money Laundering 0521 46305 X
Regional Peacekeeping and International Enforcemment: The Liberian Crisis 0521 47754 9
The Refugee Convention, 1951: The Travaux Préparatoires with Commentary and Analysis 0521 47295 4
Mutual Assistance in Criminal and Business Regulatory Matters 0521 47297 0
East Timor and the International Community 0521 58134 6
The 'Yugoslav' Crisis in International Law, General Issues 0521 46304 1

This volume may be cited as:

Krieger, H. (ed.),
The Kosovo Conflict and International Law

CAMBRIDGE INTERNATIONAL DOCUMENTS SERIES
VOLUME 11

THE KOSOVO CONFLICT AND INTERNATIONAL LAW

*An Analytical Documentation
1974–1999*

Edited by
HEIKE KRIEGER
Institut für Völkerrecht der Universität Göttingen

CAMBRIDGE UNIVERSITY PRESS
Cambridge, New York, Melbourne, Madrid, Cape Town,
Singapore, São Paulo, Delhi, Tokyo, Mexico City

Cambridge University Press
The Edinburgh Building, Cambridge CB2 8RU, UK

Published in the United States of America by Cambridge University Press, New York

www.cambridge.org
Information on this title: www.cambridge.org/9781107404533

© Heike Krieger 2001

This publication is in copyright. Subject to statutory exception
and to the provisions of relevant collective licensing agreements,
no reproduction of any part may take place without the written
permission of Cambridge University Press.

First published 2001
First paperback edition 2011

A catalogue record for this publication is available from the British Library

ISBN 978-0-521-80071-6 Hardback
ISBN 978-1-107-40453-3 Paperback

Cambridge University Press has no responsibility for the persistence or
accuracy of URLs for external or third-party internet websites referred to in
this publication, and does not guarantee that any content on such websites is,
or will remain, accurate or appropriate.

CONTENTS

Map	*page* xviii
Preface	xix
Chronology	xx
Introduction	xxxi

Chapter 1: Kosovo's Status in Yugoslavia before 1999

1.1 Autonomy of Kosovo

1. Constitution of the Socialist Federal Republic of Yugoslavia, Extracts, 1974	2
2. Constitution of the Socialist Republic of Serbia, Extracts, 1974	5
3. Constitution of the Socialist Autonomous Province of Kosovo, Extracts, 1974	7
4. 1989 Amendments of the Serbian Constitution	8
5. Constitution of the Socialist Republic of Serbia, 28 September 1990	8
6. Constitution of the Federal Republic of Yugoslavia, 27 April 1992	9
7. Speech by Slobodan Milosevic at the Central Celebration Marking the 600th Anniversary of the Battle of Kosovo, Gazimestan, 28 June 1989	10
8. St. Egidio Education Agreement	11
8 a) St. Egidio Education Agreement, 1 September 1996	11
8 b) Agreed Measures for the Implementation of the Agreement on Education of 1 September 1996, Belgrade, 24 March 1998	11

1.2 Unilateral Declaration of Independence

9. Statement Made by the People's Assembly of Albania, 22 October 1991	12
10. Letter from the Charge d'affaires a.i. of the Permanent Mission of Yugoslavia to the United Nations Addressed to the Secretary-General, 18 December 1995	13
11. Letter from the Chargé d'affaires a.i. of the Permanent Mission of Yugoslavia to the United Nations Addressed to the Secretary-General, 11 November 1996	13

Chapter 2: Development of the Human Rights Situation

2.1 Documents of International Organisations

2.1.1 The UN General Assembly

12. Situation of Human Rights in the Territory of the Former Yugoslavia, UN General Assembly Resolution 47/147, 18 December 1992	15
13. Violations of Human Rights in the Republic of Bosnia and Herzegovina, the Republic of Croatia and the FRY (Serbia and Montenegro), UN General Assembly Resolution 48/153, 20 December 1993	15
14. Situation of Human Rights in Kosovo, UN General Assembly Resolution 49/204, 23 December 1994	16
15. Situation of Human Rights in Kosovo, UN General Assembly Resolution 50/190, 22 December 1995	17
16. Situation of Human Rights in Kosovo, UN General Assembly Resolution 51/111, 12 December 1996	18
17. Situation of Human Rights in Bosnia and Herzegovina, the Republic of Croatia and the FRY (Serbia and Montenegro), UN General Assembly Resolution 51/116, 12 December 1996	19
18. Situation of Human Rights in Kosovo, UN General Assembly Resolution 52/139, 12 December 1997	19
19. Situation of Human Rights in Bosnia and Herzegovina, the Republic of Croatia and the FRY (Serbia and Montenegro), UN General Assembly Resolution 52/147, 12 December 1997	20
20. Situation of Human Rights in Bosnia and Herzegovina, the Republic of Croatia and the FRY (Serbia and Montenegro), UN General Assembly Resolution 53/163, 9 December 1998	20
21. Situation of Human Rights in Kosovo, UN General Assembly Resolution 53/164, 9 December 1998	21
22. Situation of Human Rights in Kosovo, UN General Assembly Resolution 54/183, 17 December 1999	23

2.1.2 The UN Commission on Human Rights

23. Report on the Situation of Human Rights in the Former Yugoslavia, E/CN.4/1992/S-1/9, 28 August 1992	25
24. Report on the Situation of Human Rights in the Territory of the Former Yugoslavia Submitted by Mr. Tadeusz Mazowiecki, Special Rapporteur of the Commission on Human Rights, pursuant to Commission Resolution 1992/S-1/1 of 14 August 1992, A/48/92-S/25341, paras. 153-171, 26 February 1993	25
25. Fifth Periodic Report on the Situation of Human Rights in the Territory of the Former Yugoslavia Submitted by Mr. Tadeusz Mazowiecki, Special Rapporteur of the Commission on Human Rights, pursuant to Paragraph 32 of Commission Resolution 1993/7 of 24 February 1993, E/CN.4/1994/47, paras. 188-205, 17 November 1993	27

26. Ninth Periodic Report on the Situation of Human Rights in the Territory of the Former Yugoslavia Submitted by Mr. Tadeusz Mazowiecki, Special Rapporteur of the Commission on Human Rights, pursuant to Commission Resolution 1994/72 of 9 March 1994 and ECOSOC Decision 1994/262 of 22 July 1994, A/49/641-S/1994/1252, paras. 162-203, 4 November 1994   29

27. Situation of Human Rights in the Territory of the Former Yugoslavia, Report Submitted by Ms Elisabeth Rehn, Special Rapporteur of the Commission on Human Rights pursuant to Commission Resolution 1995/89, E/CN.4/1996/63, paras. 140-149, 162-180, 14 March 1996   30

28. Situation of Human Rights in the Territory of the Former Yugoslavia: Two Trials of Kosovo Albanians Charged with Offences against the State in the FRY in 1997, Report Submitted by the Special Rapporteur, Ms Elisabeth Rehn, pursuant to Paragraph 42 (c) of Commission Resolution 1997/57, E/CN.4/1998/9, 10 September 1997   31

29. Situation of Human Rights in the Former Yugoslavia, Report of Mr. Jiri Dienstbier, Special Rapporteur of the Commission on Human Rights on the Situation of Human Rights in Bosnia and Herzegovina, the Republic of Croatia and the FRY, E/CN.4/1999/42, 20 January 1999   38

30. Commission Resolution 1993/7, Situation of Human Rights in the Territory of the Former Yugoslavia, 23 February 1993   40

31. Commission Resolution 1994/76, Situation of Human Rights in Kosovo, 9 March 1994   40

32. Commission Resolution 1998/79, Situation of Human Rights in Bosnia and Herzegovina, the Republic of Croatia and the FRY, 22 April 1998   41

33. Commission Resolution 1999/2, Situation of Human Rights in Kosovo, 13 April 1999   42

34. Commission Resolution 1999/18, The Situation of Human Rights in the FRY (Serbia and Montenegro), the Republic of Croatia and Bosnia and Herzegovina, 23 April 1999   42

2.1.3 The UN High Commissioner for Human Rights

35. Statement by the UN High Commissioner for Human Rights, 26 March 1999   45

36. Briefing on Situation of Human Rights in Kosovo, Geneva, 9 April 1999   45

37. Report on Situation of Human Rights in Kosovo, FRY, HC/K224, Geneva, 22 April 1999   46

38. Report on the Human Rights Situation involving Kosovo, HC/K304, Geneva, 30 April 1999   48

39. Report on the Situation of Human Rights in Kosovo, FRY, E/CN.4/2000/7, 31 May 1999   49

40. Report on the Situation of Human Rights in Kosovo, FRY, E/CN.4/2000/10, 7 September 1999   54

2.1.4 The UN High Commissioner for Refugees (UNHCR)

41. UNHCR Country Updates - Former Yugoslavia: 24 February 1999 - 4 March 1999, UN Inter-Agency Humanitarian Situation Report: Kosovo Population Movements   65

42. UNHCR Country Updates - Former Yugoslavia: 14 - 21 March 1999, UN Inter-Agency Humanitarian Situation Report: Kosovo   66

43. Briefing by Mrs Sadako Ogata to the UN Security Council, New York, 5 May 1999   68

44. Numbers of Refugees Displaced from Kosovo 23 March - 9 June 1999, Geneva, 15 October 1999   70

2.2 U.S. Documents

45. U.S. Department of State: Serbia-Montenegro Country Report on Human Rights Practices for 1998, Released by the Bureau of Democracy, Human Rights, and Labor, 26 February 1999   71

46. U.S., Erasing History: Ethnic Cleansing in Kosovo, Report Released by the U.S. Department of State, Washington, D.C., May 1999   82

2.3 NGO Reports

47. Amnesty International Report 1998: FRY: For the Period January - December 1997   90

48. Human Rights Watch: FRY: Humanitarian Law Violations in Kosovo, Extracts, October 1998   91

49. Medecins Sans Frontieres: Survey Data on Mass Expulsions from Kosovo, A Survey of the Kosovar Refugees at Rosaye, Montenegro, Vincent Brown, MSF/Epicentre, Rosaye, 27 April 1999   111

Chapter 3: Diplomatic Efforts for the Settlement of the Crisis

3.1. Early Attempts to Settle the Crisis

50. The Conference on Yugoslavia 1991/1992   118

50 a) Peace Conference on Yugoslavia, Carrington Draft Paper, "Arrangements for a General Settlement", UN Doc. S/23169, Annex VI, 18 October 1991   118

50 b) Peace Conference on Yugoslavia, Carrington Draft Paper, "Treaty Provisions for the Convention", UN Doc. S/23169, Annex VII, 18 October 1991   118

50 c) Peace Conference on Yugoslavia, Letter from Dr. Rugova to Lord Carrington, 22 December 1991   118

50 d) London International Conference on the Former Yugoslavia, Co-Chairman's Paper on Serbia and Montenegro, 27 August 1992   118

50 e) UN, Report of the Secretary-General on the International Conference on the Former Yugoslavia, UN Doc. S/24795, 11 November 1992   119

50 f) UN, Report of the UN Secretary-General on the International Conference of the Former Yugoslavia, Recent Activities of the Working Groups, UN Doc. S/25490, 30 March 1993   119

51. EU, European Council in Lisbon 26-27 June 1992: Conclusions of the Presidency, DOC/92/3, 27 June 1992   120

Contents

52. UN Security Council Resolution 855 (1993) of 9 August 1993	120
53. EU, 1950th Council Meeting, General Affairs, PRES/96/253, Luxembourg, 1 October 1996	120

3.2 Political Action and Sanctions since 1997

54. Contact Group Foreign Ministers, Statement on Kosovo, New York, 24 September 1997	121
55. Contact Group Meeting, Statement on Kosovo, Moscow, 25 February 1998	121
56. EU, Declaration by the Presidency on behalf of the European Union Concerning the Upsurge of Violence in Kosovo, 98/18/CFSP, Brussels, 3 March 1998	121
57. Contact Group Meeting, Statement on Kosovo, London, 9 March 1998	121
58. Countries of South Eastern Europe, Joint Declaration of the Ministers of Foreign Affairs of Countries of South-Eastern Europe Concerning the Situation in Kosovo, Sofia, 10 March 1998	123
59. FRY, Declaration by Milan Milutinovic, President of the Republic of Serbia on the Political Process Initiated for Kosovo and Metohija, 11 March 1998	123
60. Council of Europe, Parliamentary Assembly, Recommendation 1360 (1998), Crisis in Kosovo, 18 March 1998	125
61. EU, Common Position Defined by the Council on the Basis of Article J.2 of the EU Treaty on Restrictive Measures against the FRY, 98/240/CFSP, 19 March 1998	125
62. FRY, Declaration of the Parliament of Serbia on National Unity, 24 March 1998	126
63. Contact Group, Statement on Kosovo, Bonn, 25 March 1998	126
64. EU, 2078th Council Meeting, General Affairs, PRES/98/86, Brussels, 30/31 March 1998	127
65. UN Security Council Resolution 1160 (1998) of 31 March 1998	128
66. UN, Extracts from the Debates of the Security Council Concerning Security Council Resolution 1160 (1998), UN Doc. S/PV. 3868, 31 March 1998	129
67. FRY, Letter by the President of the FRY to the Presidents of the Republic of Serbia, of the Serbian Government and of the Assembly of Serbia, on the Referendum whether or not Foreign Representatives Should be Involved in Dealing with the Problem of Kosovo, 2 April 1998	137
68. Council of Europe, Parliamentary Assembly, Recommendation 1368 (1998), Latest Developments in the FRY and the Situation in Kosovo, 22 April 1998	138
69. EU, 2085th Council Meeting, General Affairs, PRES/98/109, Luxembourg, 27 April 1998	139
70. EC Council Regulation No 926/98 Concerning the Reduction of Certain Economic Relations with the FRY, 27 April 1998	140
71. Contact Group, Statement, Rome, 29 April 1998	140
72. EU, Common Position Defined by the Council on the Basis of Article J.2 of the EU Treaty Concerning the Freezing of Funds Held Abroad by the FRY and Serbian Governments, 98/326/CFSP, 7 May 1998	141
73. WEU, Ministerial Council, Rhodes Declaration, Rhodes, 12 May 1998	141
74. EU, Common Position Defined by the Council on the Basis of Article J.2 of the EU Treaty Concerning the Prohibition of New Investment in Serbia, 98/374/CFSP, 8 June 1998	142
75. EU, Declaration by the European Union on Kosovo, 98/56/CFSP, 11 June 1998	142
76. Contact Group, Statement Issued Following a Meeting of the Foreign Ministers of the Contact Group and the Foreign Ministers of Canada and Japan, London, 12 June 1998	143
77. EU, Cardiff European Council, Presidency Conclusions, DOC/98/10, 15/16 June 1998	143
78. FRY - Russian Federation, Joint Declaration Signed in Moscow by President Yeltsin and President Milošević, Moscow, 16 June 1998	144
79. EC Council Regulation No. 1295/98 on Freezing of Funds Held Abroad of FRY and Republic of Serbia, 22 June 1998	144
80. Council of Europe, Parliamentary Assembly, Recommendation 1376 (1998), Crisis in Kosovo and the Situation in the FRY, 24 June 1998	145
81. EU, Council Common Position, Ban on Flights by Yugoslav Carriers between FRY and the EC, 29 June 1998	146
82. EU, 2111th Council Meeting, General Affairs, PRES/98/227, Luxembourg, 29 June 1998	147
83. Contact Group, Statement, Bonn, 8 July 1998	147
84. EU, 2113th Council Meeting, General Affairs, PRES/98/240 Brussels, 13 July 1998	148
85. EU, Declaration by the Presidency on behalf of the European Union on Recent Fighting in Kosovo, 98/77/CFSP, Brussels, 20 July 1998	149
86. EC Council Regulation No. 1607/98 on Prohibition of New Investment in Republic of Serbia, 24 July 1998	149
87. UN Security Council, Presidential Statement, S/PRST/1998/25, 24 August 1998	150
88. EC Council Regulation No. 1901/98, Ban on Flights of Yugoslav Carriers between FRY & EC, 7 September 1998	150
89. UN Security Council Resolution 1199 (1998) of 23 September 1998	151
90. UN, Extracts from the Debate of the Security Council Concerning Security Council Resolution 1199 (1998), UN Doc. S/PV. 3930, 23 September 1998	153
91. Council of Europe, Parliamentary Assembly, Recommendation 1384 (1998), Crisis in Kosovo and Situation in the FRY, 24 September 1998	154
92. EU, Declaration by the European Union on a Comprehensive Approach to Kosovo, 98/128/CFSP, Brussels, 27 October 1998	154
93. Hill Proposals for a Settlement in Kosovo, October 1998 - January 1999	155

93 a) First Draft Agreement for a Settlement of the Crisis in Kosovo, 1 October 1998 — 155
93 b) Revised Hill Proposal, 1 November 1998 — 158
93 c) Statement on Fundamental Principles for a Settlement of the Kosovo Question Issued by the Government of the Republic of Kosovo, 3 November 1998 — 165
93 d) FRY, Joint Proposal of the Agreement on the Political Framework of Self-Governance in Kosovo and Metohija, Belgrade, 20 November 1998 — 166
93 e) Third Hill Draft Proposal for a Settlement of the Crisis in Kosovo, 2 December 1998 — 169
93 f) Final Hill Proposal, 27 January 1999 — 176
94. WEU, Ministerial Council, Rome Declaration, Rome, 17 November 1998 — 185
95. FRY, Declaration on Support of the Joint Proposal of the Agreement on the Political Frameworks of Self-Governance in Kosovo and Metohija, Belgrade, 25 November 1998 — 186
96. FRY, Declaration by the Federal Assembly, Belgrade, 3 December 1998 — 186
97. Contact Group Meeting, Statement on Kosovo, Washington, D.C., 8 January 1998 — 187

3.3 International Monitoring of the Developments in Kosovo

3.3.1 The OSCE Kosovo Verification Mission

98. OSCE, Permanent Council, Decision No. 218, PC. DEC/218/98, 11 March 1998 — 187
99. OSCE, Permanent Council, Decision No. 259, PC. DEC/259/98, 15 October 1998 — 188
100. OSCE-FRY, Agreement on the OSCE Kosovo Verification Mission, 16 October 1998 — 188
101. OSCE, Permanent Council, Decision No. 263, PC. DEC/263/98, 25 October 1998 — 189
102. FRY, Government Memorandum on the Situation in the Autonomous Province of Kosovo and Metohija, Belgrade, 1 December 1998 — 190
103. OSCE, Kosovo Verification Mission, Press Release No. 24/99, Oslo, 19 March 1999 — 191

3.3.2 The Racak Incident

104. Human Rights Watch: Report on the Massacre in Racak, January 1999 — 192
105. FRY, Statement by the President of the Republic of Serbia, Milan Milutinovic, 17 January 1999 — 193
106. FRY, Statement by the Federal Government, 18 January 1999 — 194
107. UNHCR Press Release, Kosovo: Ogata Condemns Atrocities, Appeals for Access, 18 January 1999 — 194
108. UN Security Council, Presidential Statement, New York City, UN Doc. S/PRST/1999/2, 19 January 1999 — 195
109. EU, Statement of the Presidency of the European Union on the Racak Massacre, PRES/99/14, Brussels, 20 January 1999 — 195
110. EU, Letter of the German Minister for Foreign Affairs on behalf of the European Union to Milosevic, 20 January 1999 — 195
111. OSCE Troika, Press Release No. 10/99, 21 January 1999 — 196
112. FRY, Statement from the Session of the Federal Government, 21 January 1999 — 196
113. Contact Group, Chairman's Conclusions, London, 22 January 1999 — 197
114. Islamic Group, Statement on the Situation in Kosovo, New York, 26 January 1999 — 197
115. Report of the EU Forensic Expert Team on the Racak Incident, 17 March 1999 — 197

3.3.3 The UN Secretary-General

116. Report of the Secretary-General Prepared pursuant to Security Council Resolution 1160 (1998), UN Doc. S/1998/361, 30 April 1998 — 199
117. Report of the Secretary-General Prepared pursuant to Security Council Resolution 1160 (1998), UN Doc. S/1998/470, 4 June 1998 — 203
118. Report of the Secretary-General Prepared pursuant to Security Council Resolution 1160 (1998), UN Doc. S/1998/608, 2 July 1998 — 207
119. Report of the Secretary-General Prepared pursuant to Security Council Resolution 1160 (1998), UN Doc. S/1998/712, 5 August 1998 — 211
120. Report of the Secretary-General Prepared pursuant to Security Council Resolution 1160 (1998), UN Doc. S/1998/834, 4 September 1998 — 218
121. Report of the Secretary-General Prepared pursuant to Security Council Resolutions 1160 (1998) and 1199 (1998), UN Doc. S/1998/912, 3 October 1998 — 221
122. Report of the Secretary-General Prepared pursuant to Security Council Resolutions 1160 (1998), 1199 (1998) and 1203 (1998), UN Doc. S/1998/1068, 12 November 1998 — 225
123. Report of the Secretary-General Prepared pursuant to Resolutions 1160 (1998), 1199 (1998) and 1203 (1998) UN Doc. S/1998/1147, 4 December 1998 — 233
124. Report of the Secretary-General Prepared pursuant to Security Council Resolutions 1160 (1998), 1199 (1998) and 1203 (1998), UN Doc. S/1998/1221, 24 December 1998 — 238
125. Report of the Secretary-General Prepared pursuant to Security Council Resolutions 1160 (1998), 1199 (1998) and 1203 (1998), UN Doc. S/1999/99, 30 January 1999 — 244
126. Report of the Secretary-General Prepared pursuant to Security Council Resolutions 1160 (1998), 1199 (1998) and 1203 (1998), UN Doc. S/1999/293, 17 March 1999 — 250

Contents

3.4 The Rambouillet Talks
3.4.1 Preparation of the Conference
    127. U.S. Secretary of State Albright and Russian Foreign Minister Ivanov, Joint Statement, Moscow, 26 January 1999 — 253

    128. NATO, Statement to the Press by Secretary General, Press Release (1999)011, Brussels, 28 January 1999 — 254

    129. UN Secretary-General, Statement of Kofi Annan to the North Atlantic Council, Brussels, 28 January 1999 — 254

    130. Contact Group, Chairman's Conclusions, London, 29 January 1999 — 255

    131. UN Security Council, Presidential Statement, UN Doc. S/PRST/1999/5, 29 January 1999 — 256

    132. NATO, Statement by the North Atlantic Council, Press Release 99 (12), 30 January 1999 — 256

    133. Contact Group Negotiators' Proposal, 30 January 1999 — 256

    134. UK, Statement by the Foreign Secretary, Mr. Robin Cook, to the House of Commons, 1 February 1999 — 257

3.4.2 The Rambouillet Conference
    135. Joint Press Conference by Mr. Vedrine and Mr. Cook, Rambouillet, 6 February 1999 — 258

    136. Statement of the Delegation Designated by the Government of the Republic of Serbia, at the Meeting in Rambouillet, 11 February 1999 — 259

    137. Contact Group Meeting, Chairman's Conclusions, Paris, 14 February 1999 — 260

    138. EU, Declaration by the Presidency on behalf of the European Union, 99/15/CFSP, Brussels, 19 February 1999 — 260

    139. NATO, Statement by the Secretary General on behalf of the North Atlantic Council, Press Release (99)020, 19 February 1999 — 260

    140. Conclusions of the Contact Group, Rambouillet, 20 February 1999 — 260

    141. Interim Agreement for Peace and Self-Government in Kosovo, Rambouillet, 23 February 1999 — 261

    142. Contact Group, Rambouillet Accords: Co-Chairmen's Conclusions, Rambouillet, 23 February 1999 — 278

    143. UN Security Council's Statement to the Press, Rambouillet, 23 February 1999 — 278

    144. UN Secretary-General, Press Release, UN Doc. SG/SM/6902, 23 February 1999 — 278

    145. EU, Statement of the Presidency on behalf of the European Union on the Conclusion of the Rambouillet Conference, 23 February 1999 — 279

    146. NATO, Statement by the Secretary General, Press Release (99)21, 23 February 1999 — 279

    147. UK, Statement by the Foreign Secretary, Mr. Robin Cook, House of Commons, 24 February 1999 — 279

3.4.3 The Paris Conference
    148. Kosovo Delegation Letter of Agreement Addressed to the French and British Foreign Ministers, 15 March 1999 — 280

    149. FRY, Agreement for Self-Government in Kosmet, Paris, 18 March 1999 — 280

    150. Declaration of the Co-Chairmen Hubert Vedrine and Robin Cook, Paris, 19 March 1999 — 286

    151. FRY, Letter of Yugoslav President Milosevic to the British and French Foreign Minister, 22 March 1999 — 286

Chapter 4: Military Action against Yugoslavia
4.1 NATO's Threat to Use Force and the Holbrooke Agreement
    152. NATO, Statement on Kosovo Issued at the Ministerial Meeting of the North Atlantic Council, Press Release M-NAC-1(98)61, Luxembourg, 28 May 1998 — 288

    153. NATO, Statement on Kosovo Issued at the Meeting of the North Atlantic Council in Defence Ministers Session, Press Release M-NAC-D-1(98)77, 11 June 1998 — 289

    154. NATO, Statement by the Secretary General following the ACTWARN Decision, Vilamoura, 24 September 1998 — 289

    155. NATO, Statement by the Secretary General Following Decision on the ACTORD, NATO HQ, 13 October 1998 — 289

    156. Holbrooke Agreement — 289

    156 a) FRY, Statement by President of the FRY, Slobodan Milosevic, on the Accords to Resolve the Problems in Kosovo and Metohija in a Peaceful Way and by Political Means, 13 October 1998 — 289

    156 b) FRY, Statement from the Federal Government's Meeting, Belgrade, 14 October 1998 — 290

    156 c) Accord Reached by Slobodan Milosevic, President of the FRY, and the UN Special Envoy, Richard Holbrooke, UN Doc. S/1998/953, Annex, 14 October 1998 — 290

    157. NATO-FRY, Agreement Providing for the Establishment of an Air Verification Mission over Kosovo, Belgrade, 15 October 1998 — 291

    158. UN Security Council Resolution 1203 (1998) of 24 October 1998 — 292

    159. UN, Extract from the Debate of the Security Council Concerning Security Council Resolution 1203 (1998), UN Doc. S/PV. 3937, 24 October 1998 — 293

    160. NATO, Statement by the Secretary General Following the Meeting of the North Atlantic Council, 27 October 1998 — 298

    161. NATO Statement on Kosovo, Meeting of the North Atlantic Council in Foreign Ministers Session, Press Communique M-NAC-2(98)143, 8 December 1998 — 299

    162. FRY, Letter of Federal Foreign Minister Zivadin Jovanovic to the President of the UN Security Council, Mr. Robert Fowler, Belgrade, 1 February 1999 — 299

163. FRY, Statement of the Federal Government Concerning NATO Decisions, Belgrade, 1 February 1999 — 300

164. FRY, Conclusions of the National Assembly of the Republic of Serbia Concerning NATO Threats of Aggression against FRY and the Participation in Talks in France, Belgrade, 4 February 1999 — 300

165. FRY, Letter of the Yugoslav Foreign Minister Z. Jovanovic Addressed to President of the Security Council of the United Nations, Qin Huasun, Belgrade, 17 March 1999 — 302

166. FRY, Letter of the Yugoslav Foreign Minister Z. Jovanovic Addressed to Chairman-in-Office of the OSCE, Minister for Foreign Affairs of the Kingdom of Norway, Knut Vollebaek, Belgrade, 17 March 1999 — 302

167. NATO, Statement by the North Atlantic Council, Press Release (1999)038, 22 March 1999 — 303

168. UK, Statement by Defence Minister, Press Release 083/99, Paris, 22 March 1999 — 303

169. UK, Transcript of Statement Given by the Foreign Secretary, Robin Cook, Brussels, 22 March 1999 — 303

4.2 NATO Air Strikes

170. NATO, Statement by the Secretary General, Press Release (1999)040, 23 March 1999 — 304

171. NATO, Political and Military Objectives of NATO Action with Regard to the Crisis in Kosovo, Press Release (1999)043, 23 March 1999 — 304

172. NATO, Press Statement by the Secretary General following the Commencement of Air Operations, Press Release (1999)041, 24 March 1999 — 304

173. FRY, Statement from the Federal Government's Meeting, Belgrade, 25 March 1999 — 304

174. NATO, Letter from the Secretary General of NATO to the Secretary-General of the UN, 27 March 1999 — 305

175. FRY, The Decree on the Assemblies of Citizens during the State of War, Belgrade, 1 April 1999 — 305

176. NATO, Statement of the North Atlantic Council Following the Meeting between Representatives of the NATO Member States, the EU Member States, the OSCE CIO, the UNHCR, the Council of Europe and the WEU, Press Release (1999)048, Brussels, 4 April 1999 — 305

177. FRY, Statement Carried by Serb Television, 6 April 1999 — 306

178. NATO, Statement by the Secretary General, Press Release (1999)049, 6 April 1999 — 306

179. FRY, The Decree on Internal Affairs during the State of War, 7 April 1999 — 306

180. NATO, Statement Issued at the Extraordinary Ministerial Meeting of the North Atlantic Council held at NATO Headquarters, Press Release M-NAC-1(99)51, Brussels, 12 April 1999 — 307

181. NATO, Statement on Kosovo Issued by the Heads of State and Government Participating in the Meeting of the North Atlantic Council in Washington, D.C. on 23rd and 24th April 1999, Press Release S-1(99)62, 23 April 1999 — 308

182. North Atlantic Council Statement Concerning Bombing of Chinese Embassy, Press Release (1999)076, Brussels, 8 May 1999 — 309

183. NATO, Statement by the NATO Spokesman on the Korisa Incident, Press Release (1999)079, Brussels, 15 May 1999 — 309

184. NATO, Statement by the Secretary General on Suspension of Air Operations, Brussels, 10 June 1999 — 309

4.3 Possible Use of NATO Ground Forces

185. Press Conference Given by the NATO Secretary General, Mr Javier Solana and the British Prime Minister, Mr Tony Blair, Brussels, 20 April 1999 — 310

186. Edited Transcript of Interview Given by the Prime Minister, Tony Blair, for BBC World Service, Tirana, 18 May 1999 — 311

187. Press Conference Given by the NATO Secretary General, Mr Javier Solana and German Chancellor Gerhard Schroeder, Brussels, 19 May 1999 — 311

188. Press Conference Given by the NATO Secretary General, Mr Javier Solana and the Italian Prime Minister, Mr Massimo D'Alema, Brussels, 20 May 1999 — 312

189. Edited Transcript of Interview Given by the Foreign Secretary, Robin Cook, and U.S. Secretary of State, Madeleine Albright, for CNN, Washington, 20 May 1999 — 313

4.4. Land Operations by the KLA

190. Morning Briefing by Jamie Shea, NATO Spokesman, Brussels, 23 May 1999 — 314

191. Morning Briefing by Jamie Shea, NATO Spokesman, Brussels, 30 May 1999 — 315

192. Press Conference by Mr Jamie Shea, NATO Spokesman and Major General Walter Jertz, SHAPE, Brussels, 2 June 1999 — 316

4.5 Reports on the NATO Air Campaign

193. Human Rights Watch, Civilian Deaths in the NATO Air Campaign, February 2000 — 317

194. UK, House of Commons, Foreign Affairs Committee, Fourth Report on Kosovo, 7 June 2000 — 336

195. ICTY, Final Report to the Prosecutor by the Committee Established to Review the NATO Bombing Campaign Against the FRY, PR/P.I.S./510-E, 13 June 2000 — 340

Chapter 5: Settlement of the Crisis

196. Germany, A Stability Pact for South-Eastern Europe, 12 April 1999 — 354

197. U.S. Secretary of State Albright and Russian Foreign Minister Ivanov Joint Press Availability, as Released by the Office of the Spokesman U.S. Department of State, Oslo, 13 April 1999 — 356

198. U.S. Secretary of State Albright and Norwegian Foreign Minister Vollebaek: Joint Press Conference, as Released by the Office of the Spokesman U.S. Department of State, Oslo, 13 April 1999 — 358

Contents

199. Press Statements by Chancellor Mr. Schröder and Russian Special Envoy to the FRY, Mr. Chernomyrdin, Bonn, 29 April 1999 — 358
200. G 8, Statement by the Chairman on the Conclusion of the Meeting of the G 8 Foreign Ministers, Petersberg, 6 May 1999 — 359
201. EU-World Bank Agreement on Economic Co-ordination, IP/99/329, Brussels, 12 May 1999 — 359
202. EU, Common Position Adopted by the Council on the Basis of Article 15 of the EU Treaty Concerning a Stability Pact for South-Eastern Europe, 1999/345/CFSP, 17 May 1999 — 360
203. EU, Statement on Kosovo, Brussels, 31 May 1999 — 360
204. Agreement on the Principles (Peace Plan) to Move towards a Resolution of the Kosovo Crisis Presented to the Leadership of the FRY by the President of Finland, Mr. Ahtisaari, Representing the European Union, and Mr. Chernomyrdin, Special Representative of the President of the Russian Federation, 3 June 1999 — 360
205. FRY, Statement from the Federal Government's Meeting, Belgrade, 3 June 1999 — 361
206. EU, Presidency Conclusions, Cologne European Council, 3 and 4 June 1999 — 361
207. Military-Technical Agreement between the International Security Force (KFOR) and the Governments of the FRY and the Republic of Serbia, 9 June 1999 — 362
208. UN Security Council Resolution 1244 (1999) of 10 June 1999 — 364
209. UN Extracts from the Debates of the Security Council Concerning Security Council Resolution 1244 (1999), UN Doc. S/PV. 4011, 10 June 1999 — 366
210. Stability Pact for South Eastern Europe, Cologne, 10 June 1999 — 374
211. G 8, Proposals of the G 8 Presidency in the Light of the Discussions on Civilian Implementation in Kosovo, Gürzenich, 10 June 1999 — 378
212. NATO, Letter from the Secretary General of the North Atlantic Treaty Organization addressed to the UN Secretary-General, 10 June 1999 — 378
213. FRY, Statement from the Federal Government's Meeting, Belgrade, 11 June 1999 — 379

Chapter 6: Statements by NATO Member States

6.1 Canada

214. Special Debate in the House of Commons, Extracts, 36th Parliament, 1st Session, Hansard 134, 1830-2330, Ottawa/Ontario, 7 October 1998 — 380
215. Notes for a Speech by the Honourable Lloyd Axworthy Minister for Foreign Affairs, Ottawa, Ontario, 24 March 1999 — 390
216. House of Commons Debate on Kosovo, Extracts, 36th Parliament, 1st Session, Hansard 216, 1310-1320, Ottawa/Ontario, 27 April 1999 — 391

6.2 France

217. Statement by M. Lionel Jospin, Prime Minister, in the National Assembly, during Government Question Time, Paris, 23 March 1999 — 392
218. Communiqué by the French Authorities, Paris, 24 March 1999 — 393
219. Statement by M. Jacques Chirac, President of the Republic, Berlin, 24 March 1999 — 393
220. Ministry of Foreign Affairs, Legal Basis for the Action Taken by NATO, 25 March 1999 — 393
221. Speech by M. Lionel Jospin, Prime Minister, to the National Assembly, Paris, 26 March 1999 — 393
222. Speech by M. Lionel Jospin, Prime Minister, during Question Time in the National Assembly, Paris, 27 April 1999 — 395
223. Communique Issued by M. Hubert Vedrine, Minister of Foreign Affairs, Paris, 10 June 1999 — 398

6.3 Germany

224. Deliberations of the *Deutscher Bundestag, BT Plenarprotokolle* 13/248, p. 23127, Extracts, Bonn, 16 October 1998 — 398
225. Statement Made by Federal Chancellor Gerhard Schröder, Bonn, Press Release, Bonn, 24 March 1999 — 399
226. Deliberations of the *Deutscher Bundestag, BT Plenarprotokolle* 14/32, p. 2619, Extracts, Bonn, 15 April 1999 — 400
227. Deliberations of the *Deutscher Bundestag, BT Plenarprotokolle* 14/35, p. 2761, Extracts, Bonn, 22 April 1999 — 402
228. Statement by Federal Chancellor Gerhard Schröder, 1 May 1999 — 404

6.4 Greece

229. Greece and the New Millennium: Signposts to a Point of Departure, Speech by the Greek Prime Minister Costas Simitis, Woodrow Wilson School, United States, April 1999 — 404
230. Press Release by Ministry of Foreign Affairs, Athens, 26 March 1999 — 405
231. Press Release by Ministry of Foreign Affairs, Athens, 29 March 1999 — 405

6.5 Hungary

232. Statement by the Spokesman of the Ministry of Foreign Affairs, Budapest, 24 March 1999 — 405
233. Statement by the Ministry of Foreign Affairs, Budapest, 27 March 1999 — 406

6.6 The Netherlands

234. Statement by the Minister of Foreign Affairs in the Lower House, The Hague, 24 March 1999 — 406

235. Speech by Dick Benschop, Released by the Ministry of Foreign Affairs, State Secretary for Foreign Affairs, College of Europe - Natolin, Warsaw, 12 May 1999 — 406

6.7 United Kingdom

236. Memorandum Submitted by the Foreign and Commonwealth Office, Kosovo: Legal Authority for Military Action, 22 January 1999 — 407

237. Statement by the Prime Minister, Tony Blair, in the House of Commons, Hansard, HC, vol. 328, col. 161, 23 March 1999 — 408

238. Statement by the Deputy Prime Minister, John Prescott, in the House of Commons, Hansard, HC, vol. 328, col. 383, 24 March 1999 — 409

239. Briefing by Mr. George Robertson, Secretary of State for Defence, and Gen Sir Charles Guthrie, Chief of the Defence Staff, 25 March 1999 — 410

240. Statement by the Foreign Secretary, Robin Cook, in the House of Commons, Hansard, HC, vol. 328, col. 526, 25 March 1999 — 410

241. Statement by the Prime Minister, Tony Blair, London, 10 June 1999 — 412

6.8 United States of America

242. Secretary of State Albright, Remarks on Kosovo as Released by the Office of the Spokesman, Department of State, Washington, D.C., 27 October 1998 — 413

243. President Clinton, Address to the Nation, Washington, D.C., 24 March 1999 — 415

244. Secretary of State Albright, Press Conference on "Kosovo" as Released by the Office of the Spokesman, Department of State, Washington, D.C., 25 March 1999 — 416

245. President Clinton and Secretary of Defence Cohen, Statement on Kosovo, Released by the White House Office of the Press Secretary, Washington, D.C., 5 April 1999 — 419

246. Secretary of State Albright: Statement before the Senate Foreign Relations Committee, as Released by the Office of the Spokesman, Department of State, Washington, D.C., 20 April 1999 — 420

247. United States Senate, NATO's 50th Anniversary Summit, Hearing before the Committee on Foreign Relations, One Hundred Sixth Congress, First Session, 21 April 1999 — 422

248. President Clinton, Statement, Released by the White House, Office of the Press Secretary, aboard Air Force One, 25 May 1999 — 423

Chapter 7: International Reactions to the Crisis

7.1 United Nations

249. Statement of the Secretary-General, Press Release, SG/SM/6938, 24 March 1999 — 424

250. Extracts from the Debate of the Security Council Concerning Letter dated 24 March 1999 from the Permanent Representative of the Russian Federation to the UN Addressed to the President of the Security Council (S/1999/320), S/PV. 3988, 24 March 1999 — 424

251. Draft Resolution Submitted by Belarus, the Russian Federation and India, S/1998/328, 26 March 1999 — 432

252. Extracts from the Debates of the Security Council Concerning Draft Resolution S/1999/328, S/PV. 3989, 26 March 1999 — 432

253. Statement of the Secretary-General Concerning Kosovo Transmitted to His Excellency Mr. Milosevic, President of the FRY, and to His Excellency Mr. Solana, Secretary General of NATO, S/1999/402 = SG/SM/6952, 9 April 1999 — 440

254. Security Council Debate Concerning Letter Dated 7 May 1999 from the Permanent Representative of China Addressed to the President of the Security Council (S/1999/523), S/PV. 4000, 8 May 1999 — 440

255. UN Security Council Resolution 1239 (1999) of 14 May 1999 — 444

256. Extracts from the Debate of the Security Council Concerning Security Council Resolution 1239 (1999), S/PV. 4003, 14 May 1999 — 445

257. Extracts of the UN General Assembly General Debate from 20 September 1999 to 2 October 1999 — 451

7.2 EU

258. Presidency Conclusions - Berlin European Council, 24 - 25 March 1999 — 473

259. Special Meeting of the EU General Affairs Council, Conclusions on Kosovo, Luxembourg, 8 April 1999 — 474

260. Chairman's Summary of the Deliberations on Kosovo at the Informal Meeting of the Heads of State and Government of the EU in Brussels, 14 April 1999 — 475

261. Common Position, Defined by the Council on the Basis of Article J.2 of the EU-Treaty Concerning a Ban on the Supply and Sale of Petroleum and Petroleum Products to the FRY, 1999/273/CFSP, 23 April 1999 — 476

262. Conclusions of the 2173rd Council Meeting, General Affairs, Luxembourg, 26 April 1999 — 476

263. Common Position Adopted by the Council on the Basis of Article 15 of the EU-Treaty Concerning Additional Restrictive Measures against the FRY, 1999/318/CFSP, 10 May 1999 — 477

264. Kosovo: Action by the European Commission, IP/99/319, Brussels, 11 May 1999 — 478

Contents

7.3 WEU
- 265. WEU Ministerial Council, Bremen Declaration, Bremen, 11 May 1999 — 479

7.4 Council of Europe
- 266. Council of Europe, Parliamentary Assembly, Resolution 1182 (1999), Crisis in Kosovo and Situation in the FRY, 30 March 1999 — 480
- 267. Council of Europe, Parliamentary Assembly, Recommendation 1403 (1999), Crisis in Kosovo and Situation in the FRY, 28 April 1999 — 481
- 268. Council of Europe, Chairman of the Committee of Ministers, Declaration on the Kosovo Crisis, Budapest, 7 May 1999 — 482

7.5 Russian Federation and CIS States
- 269. Speech Delivered by Minister of Foreign Affairs I. S. Ivanov during the Sitting of the State Duma, 27 March 1999 — 482
- 270. Statement of Ministry of Foreign Affairs, Press-Release, 29 March 1999 — 484
- 271. Press Conference by Russian Federation Foreign Minister Ivanov and Colonel General Baluyevsky, Chief of Main Operational Directorate, General Staff of the Russian Federation Armed Forces, First Deputy Chief of General Staff, Verbatim Report, Ministry of Foreign Affairs, 2 April 1999 — 485
- 272. Declaration Adopted by the Inter-Parliamentary Assembly of States Members of the Commonwealth of Independent States, 3 April 1999 — 487
- 273. Statement by the Official Representative of the Ministry of Foreign Affairs, 3 April 1999 — 487
- 274. Permanent Mission of the Russian Federation to the OSCE, Representation and Request for Information, Vienna, 23 April 1999 — 487
- 275. Permanent Mission of the Russian Federation to the OSCE, Statement by Russian Foreign Ministry Representative, 23 April 1999 — 489
- 276. Statement of the Ministry of Foreign Affairs, 14 May 1999 — 490
- 277. Statement of the Ministry of Foreign Affairs, 20 May 1999 — 490

7.6 China
- 278. Vice Premier and Foreign Minister Qian Qichen on the Question of Kosovo (FRY), PRO 4/98, 13 March 1998 — 491
- 279. Statement by Foreign Ministry Spokesman, PR 12/98, 25 October 1998 — 491
- 280. Ambassador Qin Huasun, Permanent Representative of PRC Talks to the Press at the UN on the Question of Kosovo, 23 March 1999 — 491

7.7 Japan
- 281. Statement by Foreign Minister Masahiko Koumura, 25 March 1999 — 491
- 282. Archives on Press Conferences by the Press Secretary, 27 April 1999 — 492

7.8 Others
- 283. El Salvador, Statement, Press Release 82/99, San Salvador, 24 March 1999 — 492
- 284. India, Official Spokesman's Statement, New Delhi, 24 March 1999 — 492
- 285. Mexico, Statement of Foreign Minister, NUM. 121/99, Tlatelolco, D.F., 24 March 1999 — 492
- 286. The Philippines, Statement, Press Release No. 74-99, 24 March 1999 — 492
- 287. Egypt, Statement by Foreign Minister Moussa, Cairo, 25 March 1999 — 493
- 288. India, Official Spokesman's Statement, New Delhi, 25 March 1999 — 493
- 289. Republic of Korea, Comment by a Foreign Ministry Official, 25 March 1999 — 493
- 290. Rio Group, Communiqué, 25 March 1999 — 493
- 291. Singapore, Response by the Foreign Minister to Questions from Journalists in Rome, 25 March 1999 — 493
- 292. South Africa, Statement Issued by the Department of Foreign Affairs, Pretoria, 25 March 1999 — 493
- 293. Israel, Foreign Minister Sharon, Statement, Communicated by Foreign Minister's Spokesman, 2 April 1999 — 493
- 294. Malaysia, Statement by Datuk Seri Syed Hamid Albar, Minister of Foreign Affairs, Kuala Lumpur, 2 April 1999 — 494
- 295. Islamic Conference on Bosnia and Herzegovina and Kosovo, Statement and Declaration by the Contact Group of the Organization of the Islamic Conference (OIC) on Bosnia and Herzegovina and Kosovo, 7 April 1999 — 494
- 296. Malaysia, Speech by YB Datuk Dr. Leo Michael Toyad, Deputy Minister of Foreign Affairs at the Emergency Ministerial Meeting of the OIC Contact Group, Geneva, 7 April 1999 — 495
- 297. Pakistan, Statement by the Foreign Minister at the Emergency Ministerial Meeting of the OIC Contact Group, Geneva, 7 April 1999 — 495
- 298. Movement of Non-Aligned Countries, Statement, Geneva, 9 April 1999 — 496
- 299. Sri Lanka, Ministry of Foreign Affairs, Press Release, 16 April 1999 — 497
- 300. Islamic Conference on Bosnia and Herzegovina and Kosovo, Statement and Declaration by the Contact Group of the Organization of the Islamic Conference on Bosnia and Herzegovina and Kosovo, 22 April 1999 — 497
- 301. Cuba, Excerpts From the Speech Made by Comrade Fidel Castro at a Mass Rally in the University of Havana, 4 May 1999 — 497
- 302. Egypt, Statement by Foreign Minister Amre Moussa, Cairo, 8 May 1999 — 498
- 303. The Philippines, Statement, Press Release No. 109-99, 10 May 1999 — 498

304. Egypt, Statement by Foreign Minister Moussa, Cairo, 15 May 1999 — 499
305. Zimbabwe, Foreign Affairs Minister, Hon. Mudenge's Address at a Reception in Honour of the Visiting Chinese Foreign Minister, 14 January 2000 — 499

Chapter 8: Court Action with regard to the Kosovo Crisis

8.1 International Court of Justice (ICJ)

306. Request for the Indication of Provisional Measures Concerning the Application of the Federal Republic of Yugoslavia against the Kingdom of Belgium for Violation of the Obligation not to Use Force, Belgrade, 28 April 1999 (Extracts) — 502
307. Legality of Use of Force (Yugoslavia v. Belgium), Application Instituting Proceedings Filed in the Registry of the Court on 29 April 1999 (Extracts) — 503
308. Belgium, Oral Pleading in the Case "Legality of the Use of Force", CR 99/15 (translation), 10 May 1999 — 504
309. ICJ Case Concerning the Legality of Use of Force, Request for the Indication of Provisional Measures, Order, 2 June 1999 — 508
310. Russian Federation, Statement by the Ministry of Foreign Affairs, Press Release, 2 June 1999 — 514
311. FRY, Statement from the Federal Government's Meeting, Belgrade, 6 June 1999 — 514

8.2 International Criminal Tribunal for the Former Yugoslavia (ICTY)

312. ICTY, Statement by the Prosecutor, CC/PIO/302-E, The Hague, 10 March 1998 — 515
313. U.S. Department of State, Office of the Spokesman, Press Statement by James P. Rubin, Spokesman, 15 July 1998 — 515
314. ICTY, Statement by the Office of the Prosecutor, CC/PIU/351-E, The Hague, 7 October 1998 — 515
315. ICTY, Statement by the Prosecutor, CC/PIU/353-E, The Hague, 15 October 1998 — 516
316. UN Security Council Resolution 1207 (1998) of 17 November 1998 — 516
317. ICTY, The Prosecutor v. Slobodan Milosevic, Milan Milutinovic, Nikola Sainovic, Dragoljub Ojdanovic, Vlajko Stojiljkovic, Presentation of an Indictment for Review and Application for Warrants of Arrest and for Related Orders, 22 May 1999 — 516
318. ICTY, The Prosecutor v. Slobodan Milosevic, Milan Milutinovic, Nikola Sainovic, Dragoljub Ojdanovic, Vlajko Stojiljkovic, Decision on Review of Indictment and Application for Consequential Orders, 24 May 1999 — 517
319. ICTY, Indictment of Slobodan Milosevic and others, 24 May 1999 — 521
320. Russian Federation, Statement by the Ministry of Foreign Affairs, 27 May 1999 — 529
321. Russian Federation, Statement of the Ministry of Foreign Affairs, 27 May 1999 — 529
322. ICTY, Statement by the Prosecutor, PR/P.I.S./437-E, The Hague, 29 September 1999 — 529

Chapter 9: Implementation of the Principles for a Political Solution of the Conflict

9.1 International Civil and Security Presence in Kosovo

323. OSCE, Permanent Council, PC. EC/296/Corr., 8 June 1999 — 532
324. UN, Report of the Secretary-General Prepared pursuant to Paragraph 10 of Security Council Resolution 1244 (1999), UN Doc. S/1999/672, 12 June 1999 — 532
325. NATO, Initial Report on the International Security Force (KFOR) Operations (12-15 June 1999), 17 June 1999 — 534
326. US - Russian Federation, Agreement on Russian Participation in KFOR, Helsinki, 18 June 1999 — 534
327. NATO - KLA, Undertaking of Demilitarisation and Transformation by the KLA, 20 June 1999 — 536
328. NATO, Letter from the Secretary General Addressed to the UN Secretary-General, 20 June 1999 — 538
329. Council of Europe, Parliamentary Assembly, Recommendation 1414 (1999), Crisis in Kosovo and Situation in the FRY, 23 June 1999 — 538
330. OSCE, Permanent Council, Decision No. 305, PC. DEC/305, 1 July 1999 — 539
331. OSCE, Permanent Council, Decision No. 306, PC. DEC/306, 1 July 1999 — 539
332. UN, Report of the Secretary-General on the United Nations Interim Administration Mission in Kosovo, UN Doc. S/1999/779, 12 July 1999 — 540
333. EU, Council Joint Action Concerning the Installation of the Structures of the United Nations Mission in Kosovo (UNMIK), 1999/522/CFSP, 29 July 1999 — 548
334. UN, Report of the Secretary-General on the United Nations Interim Administration Mission in Kosovo, UN Doc. S/1999/987, 16 September 1999 — 549
335. Council of Europe, Committee of Ministers, Reply to Recommendation 1414 (1999), 17 September 1999 — 553
336. Council of Europe, Parliamentary Assembly, Recommendation 1422 (1999), Southeastern Europe Following the Kosovo Conflict: Political Situation, 23 September 1999 — 554
337. The Kosovo Protection Corps, Commander Kosovo Force's Statement of Principles, 23 September 1999 — 555
338. UN, Report of the Secretary-General on the United Nations Interim Administration Mission in Kosovo, UN Doc. S/1999/1250, 23 December 1999 — 556

9.2. Regulations of the UN Interim Administration Mission in Kosovo (UNMIK)

339. UNMIK/REG/1999/1, On the Authority of the Interim Administration in Kosovo, 25 July 1999 — 567
340. UNMIK/REG/1999/2, On the Prevention of Access by Individuals and Their Removal to Secure Public Peace and Order, 12 August 1999 — 567

341. UNMIK/REG/1999/5, On the Establishment of an Ad Hoc Court of Final Appeal and an Ad Hoc Office of the Public Prosecutor, 4 September 1999 — 568

342. UNMIK/REG/1999/7, On Appointment and Removal From Office of Judges and Prosecutors, 7 September 1999 — 568

343. UNMIK/REG/1999/8, On the Establishment of the Kosovo Corps, 20 September 1999 — 569

344. UNMIK/REG/1999/14, On the Appointment of Regional and Municipal Administrators, 21 October 1999 — 570

345. UNMIK/REG/1999/16, On the Establishment of the Central Fiscal Authority of Kosovo and Other Related Matters, 6 November 1999 — 570

346. UNMIK/REG/1999/24, On the Law Applicable in Kosovo, 12 December 1999 — 571

9.3 International Contribution to the Implementation of the Kosovo Settlement

347. EC Council Regulation No 1294/1999 Concerning a Freeze of Funds and a Ban on Investment in Relation to the FRY and Repealing Regulations (EC) No 1295/98 and (EC) No 1607/98, 15 June 1999 — 572

348. G-8 Statement on Regional Issues, 20 June 1999 — 575

349. EU, 2192nd Council Meeting, General Affairs, Luxembourg, 21-22 June 1999 — 576

350. EU, Council Common Position Amending Common Position 1999/273/CFSP Concerning a Ban on the Supply and Sale of Petroleum and Petroleum Products to the FRY, and Common Position 1999/318/CFSP Concerning Additional Restrictive Measures against the FRY, 1999/604/CFSP, 3 September 1999 — 578

351. Council of Europe, Parliamentary Assembly, Recommendation 1423 (1999), Southeastern Europe Following the Kosovo Conflict: Economic Reconstruction and Renewal, 23 September 1999 — 578

352. EC Council Regulation No 2111/1999 Prohibiting the Sale and Supply of Petroleum and Certain Petroleum Products to Certain Parts of the FRY and Repealing Regulation (EC) No 900/1999, 4 October 1999 — 579

353. EC Council Regulation No 2151/1999 Imposing a Ban on Flights between the Territories of the Community and the FRY other than the Republic of Montenegro or the Province of Kosovo, and Repealing Regulation (EC) No 1064/1999, 11 October 1999 — 581

354. Council of Europe, Final Communique of the 105th Session of the Committee of Ministers of the Council of Europe, Strasbourg, 4 November 1999 — 583

Chronological List of Documents — 584

Select Bibliography — 595

Index — 598

Kosovo

PREFACE

The Kosovo conflict places international lawyers in the dilemma of choosing between the prohibitions on the use of force and the imperative to avert a humanitarian catastrophe in the face of massive human rights violations. Thus, the conflict qualifies as a hard case under international law which may nevertheless stimulate the development of new legal rules. The aim of this volume is to bring together materials of different origins in order to document the various legal aspects of this crisis.

When using the volume, the following points should be noted. The documents are ordered by subject, as shown in the table of contents. To make individual documents easier to find, a chronological list is provided in the last part of the volume, along with an index. The volume also contains a chronology and a select bibliography. The general introduction provides an overview of the main legal questions arising from the conflict, while the introductions to the chapters place the documents in their historical and political context.

Official texts are reproduced without alteration. Only evident typographical errors have been corrected. In the document headings author, title, source, and date of the document are shown. In some cases source references are made in footnotes to the heading. Comments by the editor in the text or in the footnotes are printed in italics. Extracts from the debates of various international bodies contained in the volume have been selected and annotated according to the following considerations: Only statements which add to a legal analysis or to the factual background have been included. Statements by chairmen have been omitted when not relating to substantive issues. Numbers in square brackets indicate the page number of the original document in which the statement can be found. Documents not translated by the originator have been translated into English by staff members of the Institute of International Law of the University of Göttingen, Germany.

The cut-off date for material is 31 December 1999. However, some outstanding documents on developments after the cut-off date have exceptionally been included.

The volume has been prepared at the Institute of International Law of the University of Göttingen, Germany. The editor wishes to record her thanks to the people who have made the publication of the volume possible. Ms Kathrin Bohl was very helpful in scanning documents. Ms Caroline Fiesser and Ms Sarah Lippke supported the editor in the proofreading. Thanks are due to Mr. Sergey Lagodinsky and Dr. José Martínez Soria for providing translations of Russian and Spanish documents. The editor is also grateful to Mr. Joseph Hayes who helped with certain aspects of the English language. As usual, a special debt of gratitude is owed to Ms Christiane Becker who provided the complete technical support with great enthusiasm. Finally, the editor wishes to thank Professor Dr. Georg Nolte, Director of the Institute, for his critical support. Any shortcomings in the volume are, of course, solely attributable to the editor.

The volume is dedicated to my daughter Helena Luise.

Göttingen, July 2000

CHRONOLOGY

1878	Congress of Berlin; three new countries, Serbia, Montenegro and Romania, are established. League of Prizren is formed.
1882	Proclamation of Serb Kingdom.
1912-13	Two Balkan wars are fought. Serbs, Romanians, Bulgarians, Greeks and Albanians join forces to expel Ottoman forces from the Balkans after several centuries of domination. Serbia gains control over Kosovo, though it was not formally and constitutionally incorporated into Serbia. Ethnic cleansing takes place in Kosovo. Albania becomes independent.
1 December 1918	Yugoslavia, "The Kingdom of Serbs, Croats and Slovenes" is created from territories formerly occupied by the old Turkish and Austrian empires. Kosovo remains within this Kingdom.
1939/45	Kosovo comes first under Italian and since 1943 under German tutelage.
24 October 1944	Josip Broz Tito's communist partisans liberate Belgrade and establish a communist regime in Yugoslavia.
3 September 1945	Serbia creates autonomous region of Kosovo-Metohija as constituent part of Serbia.
1946	Constitution of the Federal People's Republic of Yugoslavia confirms Kosovo's status as an autonomous region with limited self-government.
1953	In the Constitution of the Federal People's Republic of Yugoslavia the status of Kosovo remains unchanged.
1963	Constitution of the Socialist Federal Republic of Yugoslavia (SFRY) is adopted. Kosovo is described as a "social-political community" within the republic. Distinction between autonomous province (Vojvodina) and autonomous region (Kosovo) is removed.
June 1972	Constitutional amendments are adopted which establish a collective presidency of 23 members, including equal numbers from six republics and the two autonomous regions.
1974	New Constitution of the SFRY provides for full equality of republics and autonomous provinces in their participation in the federation as well as for wide-ranging autonomy. Constitutional amendments reduce collective presidency to 9 members consisting of the President of Yugoslavia, Tito, and one representative from each republic and each autonomous province.
1981	Riots in Kosovo lead to declaration of a state of emergency and to renewed accusations and counteraccusations about Albanian and Serbian nationalism.
1986	Memorandum of the Serbian Academy of Arts and Sciences published which is seen as a virtual manifesto for the Greater Serbian policies pursued by Belgrade in the 1990s.
24 April 1987	Serbs launch their first major protest in the town of Kosovo Polje against alleged persecution by the province's majority Albanians. Milosevic reassures Kosovo Serbs in his speech to the crowd at Kosovo Polje.
1989	
23 February	The Serb parliament unanimously approves proposals for amending the Serb constitution. One amendment revokes Kosovo's competence to object to amendments of the Serb Constitution.
3 March	The Yugoslav Government imposes "special measures" assigning responsibility for public security to the Federal Government instead of the Government of Serbia.
22 March	The provincial government of Kosovo approves the constitutional amendments.
23 March	Under dubious circumstances the Kosovo Assembly passes the constitutional amendments granting Serbia control over internal affairs of Kosovo.
28 March	The Serbian National Assembly adopts the final confirmation of the amendments. In Kosovo the decision leads to riots which are answered with harsh reactions by the police.

Chronology

1990

March	The Serbian Assembly promulgates a series of new measures under the title "Programme for the Realization of Peace and Prosperity in Kosovo" attempting to improve the position of the Kosovo Serbs.
18 April	SFRY Presidency ends these "special measures" after Kosovo Albanians have held mass demonstrations.
26 June	Further decrees are made possible by a "Law on the Activities of Organs of the Republic in Exceptional Circumstances". The temporary measures remain permanent. They include the suppression of Albanian language newspapers and the closing of the Kosovo Academy of Arts and Sciences. In addition, the law enables officials of the Serb republic to administer the affairs of Kosovo directly and to nullify public decisions which have been taken in Kosovo.
5 July	Serbia proclaims a law which formally disbands the functioning of the Kosovo Assembly and of its Executive Council.
7 September	The Assembly of Kosovo adopts a new constitution for Kosovo.
28 September	Serbia enacts a new constitution removing elements of sovereignty which Kosovo and Vojvodina have enjoyed under the 1974 Constitution.

1991

	The SFRY breaks up. Wars break out in the former republics of Slovenia, Croatia, and Bosnia-Herzegovina; in the latter two, Serbs ethnically cleanse and seize control of significant parts of the country. In response, the international community imposes sanctions on Yugoslavia.
25 June	Slovenia and Croatia declare independence from Yugoslavia.
7 September	Peace Conference held at The Hague.
22 September	Representatives of Kosovo issue a formal declaration of independence. Only Albania's Parliament recognizes this self-declared Republic.
26-30 September	A secret referendum is held in which the declaration of independence is confirmed. The Kosovo Albanians start non-violent resistance to the oppressive rule from Belgrade.

1992

6 March	Bosnia and Herzegovina proclaims independence from Yugoslavia.
27 April	According to the new federal constitution the autonomous provinces are to be considered as "forms of territorial autonomy". The SFRY is reconstituted as the FRY.
24 May	In defiance of the Serbian authorities, ethnic Albanians elect writer Ibrahim Rugova as president of the self-proclaimed Republic of Kosova and set up a provincial assembly. Serbia declares the election to be illegal.
7 July	CSCE: Suspension of Participation by the FRY.
13/14 August	CSCE: Establishment of Mission of Long Duration to Kosovo, Sandjak and Vojvodina.
26 August	London Conference on Yugoslavia.

1993

26 May	UN Security Council Resolution 827 (1993) establishes the International Criminal Tribunal for the Former Yugoslavia (ICTY).
23 June	Refusal of FRY authorities to allow the CSCE mission of Long Duration to Kosovo, Sandjak and Vojvodina to continue its activities.
28 July	CSCE observer mission withdraws from Kosovo.
9 August	UN Security Council Resolution 855 (1993) calls upon the FRY to reconsider the expulsion of the CSCE mission.

1994

23 February	Closing of the Academy of Arts and Sciences of Kosovo.

16 September	Six Albanians convicted and sentenced to five years imprisonment for belonging to a separatist organisation.
1995	
21 November	Dayton Peace Agreement signed.
22 November	UN and US sanctions against Yugoslavia lifted. UN Security Council votes to phase out arms embargo.
1996	The Kosovo Liberation Army (KLA) begins reprisals, claiming responsibility for a number of bombings and attacks against Serbian police and state officials.
1997	
24 September	Statement of the Contact Group (U.S., Great Britain, France, Germany, Italy, and Russia) on Kosovo.
October	Serb police crush Kosovo-Albanian student demonstrations. The KLA responds by additional attacks against the Serb police.
1998	
January	KLA clashes with Serb police lead to international criticism of Serb brutality.
4 January	KLA announces that it is the armed force of ethnic Albanians and that it will fight for the unification of Kosovo with Albania.
February-March	After four Serb police officers are shot in Likosane, Serbian police conducts a series of raids in the Drenica region of Kosovo. Houses are burned, villages emptied, and dozens of ethnic Albanians are killed.
23 February	U.S. special envoy Gelbard meets Milosevic.
9 March	Contact Group for the Former Yugoslavia meets to discuss Kosovo crisis. The Group's statement includes a deadline of 10 days for Milosevic to withdraw special police units and allow access of international observers.
22 March	Elections in Kosovo despite Serb claims of invalidity.
25 March	Contact Group meeting in Bonn. Deadline is extended another four weeks. Statement calls on Milosevic to begin serious negotiations on Kosovo's status.
31 March	The UN Security Council adopts Resolution 1160 (1998) condemning the excessive use of force by Serbian police force against civilians in Kosovo; also establishes embargo of arms and related *matériel* against the FRY.
22 April	Resolution of UN Human Rights Commission condemns Serb repression in Kosovo.
23 April	95% of Serbs vote in a referendum against international mediation in Kosovo. With the exception of Russia, the Contact Group agrees to re-impose some of the sanctions on Yugoslavia that had been lifted.
29 April	Contact Group members, except Russia, decide to take action to put into effect a freeze of funds held abroad by the FRY and Serbian governments.
May	Ambassador Richard Holbrooke goes to Belgrade and arranges the first meeting between FRY President Slobodan Milosevic and Dr. Rugova.
	Yugoslav President Milosevic invites Rugova for peace talks. Milosevic and Rugova meet once. Milosevic appoints a negotiation team that goes to Pristina to open talks. Following a deliberate Serb offensive in Decani where several dozen Kosovo-Albanians are killed, the dialogue process breaks down.
	The U.S. Ambassador to Macedonia, Christopher Hill, is designated as the U.S. Special Envoy to Kosovo and begins shuttle diplomacy between Belgrade and Pristina in an attempt to negotiate a peaceful, political settlement to the crisis. The European Union later names the Austrian Ambassador to Yugoslavia, Wolfgang Petritsch, as its envoy.
28 May	Ministerial Meeting of the North Atlantic Council issues statement on Kosovo.
8 June	EU bans all foreign investment in Serbia.
12 June	Contact Group calls for cessation of all actions by Serbian security forces and withdrawal of these forces from Kosovo.
15 June	Start of NATO exercise "Determined Falcon" in Macedonia.

Chronology

16 June	Milosevic travels to Moscow to meet President Yeltsin. As result of the meeting, they issue a joint statement on Kosovo, which among other items permits the presence of diplomatic observers in the region.
23 June	U.S. Special Envoy Holbrooke again meets with Milosevic in Belgrade to urge a peaceful end to the conflict.
24 June	Holbrooke meets with KLA commanders in the Kosovo village of Junik.
29 June	EU flight ban.
6 July	The U.S. Charge d'Affaires in Belgrade and his Russian counterpart launch the Kosovo Diplomatic Observer Mission (KDOM), which begins to patrol Kosovo and to report on freedom of movement and security conditions throughout the region.
8 July	Contact Group agrees to recommend basic elements for a resolution of the question of Kosovo's status. The Group stresses that it neither supports the status quo nor independence of the province.
28 July	Christopher Hill meets with Kosovo Albanians to determine members of a Kosovo Albanian delegation to participate in peace talks.
July - September	Serb Forces lead an offensive against the KLA; atrocities committed against civilians leading to about 300.000 refugees.
24 August	The UN Security Council calls for a cease-fire after the village of Junik is overrun by a Serb offensive, but fighting continues.
3 September	Ambassador Hill informs the OSCE Permanent Council that an informal agreement has been reached which includes a three-year stabilisation and normalisation period to allow for the re-establishment of democratic institutions.
16 September	During a massacre at Gornje Obrinje in the Drenica region 16 ethnic Albanians civilians are killed.
23 September	The UN Security Council approves (with China abstaining) Resolution 1199, which demands a cessation of hostilities and warns that, "should the measures demanded in this resolution ... not be taken ... additional measures to maintain or restore peace and stability in the region" will be considered.
24 September	NATO takes the first formal steps toward military intervention in Kosovo and approves 'activation warning', i.e., two contingency operation plans - one for air strikes and the second for monitoring and maintaining a cease-fire agreement if one is reached.
29 September	The UN High Commissioner for Refugees announces that as many as 200,000 civilians have been displaced within Kosovo since fighting began in February. Sixty thousand of them are now living in the open without shelter. The situation threatens to worsen with the onset of winter.
1 October	Presentation of first formal and complete Hill draft. Hill process continues until January 1999.
2 October	Russian State Duma votes against any military action against the FRY.
12 October	Milosevic agrees to an international observer force of 2,000 unarmed civilians under OSCE leadership. He also authorises NATO reconnaissance flights over Kosovo.
13 October	Ambassador Holbrooke, after nearly 10 days of negotiations in Belgrade with Milosevic, informs the North Atlantic Council that progress has been made. NATO approves an activation order ("ACTORD"), placing authority for air strikes in the hands of the Secretary-General, and says execution will begin in approximately 96 hours so Milosevic can sign the accords with the OSCE and NATO.
15 October	Milosevic signs the agreement that allows for NATO forces to carry out the air verification regime to oversee Serbia's compliance with UN Resolution 1199.
16 October	Milosevic signs the agreement that allows 2,000 members of the OSCE Kosovo Verification Mission in Kosovo.
	NATO extends the deadline for the FRY to come into compliance with terms of the accord on Kosovo, giving President Milosevic until 27 October to honour the agreement.
20 October	NATO sends the Supreme Allied Commander Europe (SACEUR), General Wesley Clark, to Belgrade to deliver a message to the Yugoslav military leadership on compliance.

24 October	SACEUR returns to Belgrade to reiterate importance of compliance as deadline nears.
	UN Security Council Resolution 1203 (1998) is passed, which endorses the OSCE agreement and demands full cooperation from both sides.
25 October	Decision of OSCE Permanent Council on the establishment of the Kosovo Verification Mission.
27 October	With hours to go before the deadline expires, 4,000 special police troops depart from Pristina, thus bringing Serbia into compliance with the terms of the agreements it had reached.
	NATO bombing threat "ACTORD" is therefore suspended.
November	The Kosovo Verification Mission, headed by Ambassador William Walker begins to arrive and function. Its mission quickly expands beyond verification to trying to head off armed conflict through negotiations and mediation.
1 November	Revised Hill Proposal.
2 December	Third Hill Draft Proposal.
23-24 December	Heavy fighting in northern Kosovo undermines OSCE mission.

1999

15 January	The bodies of 45 ethnic Albanians are discovered in the village of Racak.
16 January	KVM Chief Walker attributes the Racak massacre to FRY forces. The international community condemns the massacre.
18 January	The international community expresses outrage over the Yugoslav Federal Ministries' decision to expel Ambassador Walker following his comments on Racak. He is given 48 hours to leave the country.
21 January	Under pressure, the Yugoslav government reconsiders and says that it is "suspending" its declaration that Ambassador Walker is persona non grata. He is permitted to stay.
	The UN High Commissioner for Refugees notes that 20,000 people have fled their homes since late December; 5,000 are from the Racak area alone.
22 January	Contact Group meets in London.
26 January	Russian Foreign Minister Ivanov and U.S. Secretary of State Albright meet and issue a joint statement on Kosovo.
27 January	Final Hill proposal issued.
29 - 30 January	The Contact Group meets in London and gives Serbs and ethnic Albanians an ultimatum to attend peace talks in France starting 6 February.
30 January	The North Atlantic Council once again agrees that the Secretary General may authorise air strikes against targets on Yugoslav territory.
6 February	Talks begin in Chateau Rambouillet, in France, under the auspices of the Contact Group and the co-chairmanship of French Foreign Minister Hubert Vedrine and British Foreign Minister Robin Cook. Three co-mediators representing the U.S., the European Union, and the Russian Federation preside.
16/17 February	Hill travels to Belgrade to meet with Milosevic.
23 February	After a further extension of the deadline for 3 days, the talks pause. At the last minute, the ethnic Albanian delegation agrees in principle to sign the political accord but says it first wants to return home to consult further. The Serb delegations says it supports a political agreement but charges that it was changed at the last minute to suit the Albanian side; the delegation continues to reject any discussions of the military annex. The co-chairs announce that talks will resume on 15 March.
26 February	Serb troops mass on the Kosovo border with tanks and heavy artillery.
10 March	Ambassadors Holbrooke and Hill travel to Belgrade to urge Milosevic to accept the interim political accord for Kosovo.
15 March	Talks resume in Paris.
17 March	Report of the EU Forensic Expert Team on the Racak Incident.
18 March	The ethnic Albanian delegation signs the interim agreement.

Chronology

19 March	The Paris peace talks are suspended, as the Serb delegation refuses to budge and even walks back from its earlier positions at Rambouillet.
	In the meantime, one-third of the FRY's total armed forces have massed in and around Kosovo.
	OSCE announces the withdrawal of the Kosovo Verification Mission.
20 March	The Yugoslav armed units launch an offensive, driving thousands of ethnic Albanians out of their homes and villages. Summary executions take place. Kosovo Albanians are displaced and many houses are set on fire.
	KVM leaves Kosovo.
21 March	One last diplomatic effort is made by the international community, which sends Ambassador Holbrooke to Belgrade to deliver a "final warning" to Milosevic.
22 March	The North Atlantic Council authorises Secretary General Solana to decide, upon further consultations, on a broad range of air operations, if necessary.
23 March	Ambassador Holbrooke departs Belgrade having received no concessions of any kind from Milosevic.
	NATO Secretary General announces that he has directed General Clark to begin air operations against the FRY.
24 March	NATO launches air strikes.
	Within three days, ethnic Albanians begin to arrive in neighbouring Albania and the former Yugoslav Republic of Macedonia in huge numbers, on foot, on tractor-trailers and by car. Authorities expel thousands of persons by special 'refugee trains' to Macedonia, virtually emptying all major towns, such as Pristina, of Albanians.
25 March	The Yugoslav government breaks off diplomatic relations with the United States, France, Germany, and the United Kingdom.
26-30 March	North Atlantic Council decisions to escalate air campaign to phase II and then phase II-plus.
27 March	Ethnic Albanians who have fled or been expelled from their homes in Kosovo begin pouring into Albania and Macedonia.
	The Russian Duma adopts a resolution condemning the NATO actions and postponing ratification of the Start II treaty.
29 March	It is reported that refugees are crossing the border from Kosovo at a rate of 4,000 per hour. In Albania there are about 60,000 refugees, half of whom had arrived in the past 48 hours. In Montenegro, the government announces that its "technical and political" limit of 50,000 refugees would be reached imminently.
1 April	Three U.S. soldiers are captured near the Macedonia-FRY border and shown on Serb television.
2 April	Refugee arrivals for the period 24 March to 2 April according to UNHCR: Albania 138,000; The former Yugoslav Republic of Macedonia 43,000; Bosnia and Herzegovina 16,000; Montenegro 50,000.
3 April	NATO missiles strike central Belgrade for the first time and destroy the Yugoslav and Serbian interior ministries.
6 April	NATO air strikes hit the residential area of Aleksinac, killing five persons. FRY declares a unilateral cease-fire to commence at 1200 EDT and last until 1800 EDT 11 April. Belgrade claims that all FRY army and police actions in Kosovo will end and that the government will negotiate with Rugova. NATO rejects the offer, with French President Chirac calling the proposed cease-fire indefensible without a political agreement and security package.
12 April	After reaching a compromise with Russia and Belarus, Hungary releases an aid convoy to the FRY, including some trucks supplying diesel oil.
	UNHCR reports that 309,500 Kosovars have fled to Albania and 118,000 are in Macedonia to date.
	NATO hits a passenger train south of Belgrade, killing 30 according to the FRY. NATO apologizes for the accident.
14 April	Russian President Yeltsin names former Prime Minister Chernomyrdin as FRY peace envoy. NATO airstrikes hit a Kosovar civilian convoy in Kosovo. FRY reports 64 dead.

20 April	NATO Secretary-General Solana directs update of ground force plans.
21 April	NATO missiles in Belgrade hit the headquarters of Milosevic's Serbian Socialist Party and his private residence.
22 April	NATO Summit decision on Kosovo reaffirms Five Points and adds conditions for suspending bombing. NATO announces intensification of air campaign.
23 April	NATO destroys the Serbian state television building in central Belgrade, killing at least 10 people.
	The FRY agrees to accept an international military presence in Kosovo after Chernomyrdin-Milosevic talks in Belgrade.
24 April	Kosovo dominates the NATO 50th anniversary summit in Washington.
25 April	NATO invites Chernomyrdin to talks on Kosovo.
28 April	UNHCR reports 367,000 refugees in Albania, 142,650 in Macedonia, and 63,000 in Montenegro to date.
29 April	The FRY files suit at the International Court of Justice (ICJ) against 10 NATO countries.
	UN Secretary-General Annan arrives in Moscow and meets with Chernomyrdin prior to the Russian envoy's departure for Bonn, Rome and Belgrade.
30 April	NATO hits the headquarters of the Yugoslav Army and the Defence Ministry.
	Russian envoy Chernomyrdin reports progress after 6 hours of talks with Milosevic in Belgrade.
1 May	President Clinton extends U.S. sanctions to ban oil sales and freeze Belgrade's assets in the U.S. Following an agreement with NATO and FRY authorities on modalities, the ICRC announces plans to return to Kosovo.
2 May	NATO bombs hit a power transmission facility at Obrenovac, cutting off power in most FRY cities.
4 May	Russian envoy Chernomyrdin meets with U.S. officials and UN Secretary-General Annan.
6 May	At the G-8 meeting in Bonn, the West and Russia announce agreement over the basic strategy to resolve the conflict.
7 May	NATO planes accidentally hit the Chinese Embassy in Belgrade, killing 3 and wounding 20.
8 May	The UN Security Council convenes in an emergency session to debate the bombing of the Chinese Embassy. China implicitly accuses the U.S. and NATO of a deliberate attack while the alliance apologizes for a "terrible mistake." Thousands demonstrate in front of U.S. diplomatic posts in China. Russian Foreign Minister Ivanov cancels his trip to London in the wake of the attack.
9 May	President Clinton writes to Chinese President Jiang Zemin to offer regrets for the bombing. Chinese demonstrations continue.
	UNHCR announces it is facing a financial crisis in its Kosovo emergency operations.
10 May	Chinese demonstrations continue for a third day. China suspends contacts with the U.S. regarding arms control and human rights. Serbs announce a partial withdrawal from Kosovo.
	The FRY accuses NATO of genocide and demands that the ICJ order an immediate end to NATO air strikes.
11 May	Russian envoy Chernomyrdin meets with President Jiang Zemin in Beijing and labels the Chinese embassy bombing as an act of aggression. China hints that it might hold up Western attempts to achieve a peace deal at the UN unless the bombing stops.
	NATO disputes FRY claims of a troop withdrawal from Kosovo, saying that FRY military and police had actually stepped up their actions against the KLA. Albanian frontier police and FRY forces exchange fire at the FRY-Albania border; two civilians are killed.
	UNHCR says it is running out of cash to deal with the refugee crisis.
12 May	German Chancellor Gerhard Schroeder visits China on a "working visit".

Chronology

14 May	About 87 Kosovar Albanians are killed in the village of Korisa by NATO bombing. NATO says that it hit a military target and suggests that Serb troops were using civilians as human shields. Amnesty International says that Korisa had been under attack by the Yugoslav Army and the Interior Police prior to the bombing.
	The ICRC returns to Kosovo for the first time since 29 March to assess humanitarian needs in and around Pristina.
	The UNHCR receives 20 million Euros from the EC for assistance to Kosovo refugees.
14 May	UN Security Council resolution 1239 (1999) is adopted.
17 May	The EU announces that Finnish President Martti Ahtisaari will serve as the EU's new senior Kosovo envoy.
22 May	NATO bombs army barracks at Kosare, unaware it was captured by Kosovo Liberation Army guerrillas a month earlier.
23 May	NATO begins a bombing campaign of the Yugoslav electricity grid, creating a major disruption of power and water supplies.
27 May	Milosevic and four other Serbian leaders are indicted by the ICTY for crimes against humanity.
1 June	The FRY tells Germany it has accepted G-8 principles for peace and demands an end to NATO bombing.
3 June	The FRY accepts terms brought to Belgrade by EU envoy Ahtisaari and Russian envoy Chernomyrdin. The peace plan requires the withdrawal of all forces from Kosovo and the entry of peacekeepers under a UN mandate.
	NATO announces that NATO raids have killed over 5,000 members of Yugoslav security forces and wounded more than 10,000.
7 June	NATO and Yugoslav commanders fail to agree to terms of pullout from Kosovo and suspend talks. NATO intensifies bombing.
	G 8 foreign ministers in Bonn attempt to finalize UN resolution. The FRY insists on a UN Security Council resolution before any foreign troops enter Kosovo.
8 June	The West and Russia reach an agreement on a draft UN resolution at G8 talks in Cologne. NATO calls on Milosevic to resume military talks on troop withdrawal at once. The resolution, which calls for an "international security presence" under the auspices of the UN, is being studied by Security Council members. Talks between senior NATO and FRY officers on a Serb pullout from Kosovo resume in Macedonia and continue into the night.
9 June	The "Military Technical Agreement" is signed by KFOR and representatives of the Yugoslav Army and Interior Police. This agreement calls for the immediate cessation of hostilities and sets the timelines for the withdrawal of Yugoslav forces from Kosovo. This involves the marking and clearing of mine-fields, booby traps and obstacles.
10 June	NATO confirms the withdrawal of security forces of the FRY from Kosovo, and subsequently suspends air operations against the FRY. The agreement between NATO and FRY is transmitted to the UN Security Council. The Security Council adopts Resolution 1244 (1999), entrusting to the UN Secretary-General establishment of an international civilian administration in Kosovo, under which the people of Kosovo can enjoy substantial autonomy. The Resolution sets up an unprecedented UN operation, the UN Interim Administration Mission in Kosovo (UNMIK), encompassing the activities of three non-UN organisations under the UN's overall jurisdiction. It consists of four substantive components: interim civil administration (UN-led), humanitarian affairs (UNHCR-led), reconstruction (EU-led) and institution building (OSCE-led). A NATO-led force is to provide an international security presence.
	According to UNHCR 862,979 refugees have fled to the neighbouring countries during the crisis.
11 June	The UN Secretary-General names Sergio Vieira de Mello (Brazil) as Acting Special Representative for Kosovo on an interim basis.
	Russian Forces occupy the Pristina airfield.
12 June	KFOR enters Kosovo under the authority of UNSCR 1244 (1999). Within five days 20,000 troops will deploy into the province.

14 June	The UN Secretary-General presents a preliminary operational plan for Kosovo to the Security Council. UNHCR begins distribution of emergency aid.
16 June	The Yugoslav Red Cross reports 24,000 Kosovar Serbs arriving in Serbia and 9,000 in Montenegro on this day.
17 June	Meeting with the Special Representative for Kosovo in Pristina, three Kosovo-Albanian political parties, the LDK, the LDP and the UCK, endorse the UN Mission in Kosovo and commit their support for a multi-party democracy in the territory.
18 June	The Russian Federation agrees to participate in KFOR through the "Helsinki Agreement".
21 June	The Kosovo Liberation Army (KLA) signs an undertaking on demilitarisation and agrees to modalities and schedule for this, to be monitored by KFOR.
25 June	Some 50,000 refugees cross into Kosovo in a single day, bringing the total number of spontaneous returns to 300,000.
28 June	UNHCR begins its organised repatriation of refugees. As the number of returnees overtakes the numbers outside Kosovo, aid operations inside the province are increased.
29 June	UN civilian police are deployed to the five KFOR brigade headquarters in the regions.
1 July	Refugee returns top the half million mark.
2 July	The Secretary-General appoints Bernard Kouchner (France) as his Special Representative in Kosovo.
8 July	Preliminary results of an UNHCR-led survey of 141 villages show 64 per cent of homes to be severely damaged or destroyed, and 40 per cent of water sources to be contaminated, many by household waste and human remains. UNICEF estimates that 40 to 50 per cent of schools have been damaged. A crop assessment mission in Kosovo finds a severe wheat deficit, an 80 per cent fall in corn production, and substantial loss of livestock.
12 July	In his report the UN Secretary-General outlines a comprehensive plan for the civil operation in Kosovo.
14 July	Increasing reports of attacks on Serbs and Roma. The World Health Organization releases estimates that mines and unexploded ordnance in Kosovo caused 130-170 casualties in the period 13 June to 12 July.
16 July	The UN brings together Kosovo-Albanians, Serbs and Turks for the first meeting of the Kosovo Transitional Council. However, Ibrahim Rugova and his political party, the LDK, are absent.
21 July	KFOR reports 200 mass grave sites to UNMIK. The ICTY has several teams of investigators on the ground to pursue the search for evidence.
23 July	Outside the village of Gracko, near Lipljan, 14 Serb farmers are shot dead as they work in their fields.
25 July	A regulation vesting in UNMIK all legislative and executive authority in Kosovo is signed by Kouchner. Under "Regulation No.1", all persons undertaking public duties or holding public office in Kosovo are subject to internationally recognized human rights standards.
27 July	In Geneva, UN humanitarian agencies launch an appeal for $434 million to finance humanitarian operations in Kosovo and neighbouring countries.
28 July	In New York, the General Assembly authorises the Secretary-General to spend up to $200 million on UNMIK operations.
31 July & 1 August	UN civilian police begin customs control at four posts on the international border between Kosovo and Albania, and The former Yugoslav Republic of Macedonia.
3 August	With nearly 90 per cent of the more than 850,000 Kosovar refugees now returned, UNHCR under pressure to reach this population. UNHCR extremely concerned at the standstill in the aid pipeline arising from the imposition of a customs inspection fee on all goods crossing Macedonia.
6 August	The government in Skopje informs UNHCR of its decision to waive the customs fee impeding aid flow across The former Yugoslav Republic of Macedonia since mid July.
13 August	UNMIK Regulation No. 2 aims deter violence, enabling KFOR and UNMIK police to detain or deport instigators of unrest. The move comes after UNMIK determines that recent unrest in Mitrovica was stirred up by both Serb and Albanian agitators brought in from outside.

Chronology

18 August	The Joint Advisory Council on Legislative Matters meets for the first time. Set up by UNMIK and Kosovar legal representatives, the Council's purpose is to eliminate discriminatory laws from Kosovo's legal framework. In a joint statement, UNMIK and KFOR leaders condemn as unacceptable the continuing acts of intimidation and murder of minorities in Kosovo, and say they are together taking extensive measures to protect those communities. UNHCR says it is evacuating Serb minorities in Kosovo only as a last resort in "urgent life-threatening" situations.
23 August	In a first step toward assuming direct responsibility for law and order in Kosovo, UNMIK police take over law enforcement duties in Pristina.
24 August	As an exceptional case, UNHCR evacuates 28 elderly Serbs from Prizren to Serbia where they will be reunited with their families.
30 August	The Security Council issues a statement condemning violence against the civilian population, especially against ethnic minorities, as well as KFOR personnel.
8 September	Kosovo Transitional Council decides that the security situation continues to be worrying and agrees to create a Joint Security Committee to examine related issues in order to improve the security environment.
10 September	Kouchner briefs the Security Council on UNMIK and asks for larger UN civilian police presence.
16 September	Secretary-General's report to the Security Council on UNMIK warns that Kosovo gains "could easily be reversed" if pressing challenges are not resolved.
19 September	Deadline for demilitarisation extended by KFOR for 48 hours to allow for discussions on outstanding issues such as weapons regime, demobilisation and transformation process for the proposed Kosovo Corps.
20 September	Agreement reached on transformation of KLA and final details of demobilisation and weapons regime.
	KLA submits declaration to KFOR that it has complied with 21 June Undertaking on demilitarisation; KFOR confirms that 10,000 weapons and seven million rounds of ammunition have been handed in.
	Kouchner signs regulation creating Kosovo Protection Corps (KPC) as a civilian emergency service to consist of a maximum of 3,000 active members and 2,000 reservists, with at least 10 per cent of recruits to be selected from minority groups.
	Weapons regime agreed upon will allow 200 small arms to the KPC for routine "site guarding", but the use of those weapons will be careful guarded by KFOR and UNMIK.
22 September	Serbs stay away from the weekly KTC meeting in protest against creation of Kosovo Protection Corps.
28 September	Grenade attack in marketplace of town close to Kosovo Polje leaves two people dead, 35 others injured. Members of the Kosovo Transitional Council, including local Albanian leaders, meeting the following day, said they were "determined to stop those cowardly acts of violence against civilians" and pledged their commitment to a multi-ethnic society.
5 October	After funeral service for ethnic Albanians in Mitrovica turns violent, one Serb civilian is killed. Among those injured are eleven Serbs, three UNMIK police and 18 KFOR soldiers.
8 October	The Executive Board of the World Bank approves a $25 million grant as first tranche towards a $60 million strategy to help rebuild Kosovo's infrastructure and develop a modern economy over an 18-month period.
27 October	UNMIK police assumes responsibility for maintaining law and order throughout the Prizren region.
	UNHCR convoy transporting Serb civilians is attacked by crowd of 1,500 Albanian's in town of Pec; 10 to 15 Serbs are injured during incident.
28 October	UN Secretary-General Kofi Annan recommends to the Security Council that the UN international civilian police force in Kosovo be strengthened from a total of 3,110 to 4,718 officers.
31 October	Momcilo Trajkovic, the President of the Serb Resistance Movement and member of the Kosovo Transitional Council, is shot and wounded by unknown assailants in his apartment. UNMIK and KTC subsequently strongly condemn the attack.
8 November	Kouchner approves the 1999 budget for Kosovo totalling 125 million Deutsch Marks (approximately $66.5 million), nearly 70 per cent of which is financed by international donors. The Central Fiscal Authority is established to provide the legal authority to collect revenues and make expenditures.

10 November	The Chief Prosecutor for the ICTY informs the UN Security Council that investigators have exhumed 2,108 bodies from gravesites in Kosovo. She warns this figure did not necessarily reflect the total number of actual victims. Also of 529 gravesites identified only 195 have been examined to date. Kosovo Transitional Council demands from Yugoslavia information on the whereabouts of missing persons.
17 November	Donors at the Second Donors Conference for Kosovo meeting in Brussels pledge over $1 billion to kick-start the first phase of the reconstruction of Kosovo, which covers recovery needs until December 2000.
26 November	The UN Interim Administration in Kosovo (UNMIK) signs an agreement with the German reconstruction loan bank, Kreditanstalt für Wiederaufbau (KfW), pledging 9.3 million Deutsche Marks (approximately $5 million) to rehabilitate water supply systems in five western Kosovo towns.
12 December	UNMIK resolution 1999/24 makes UNMIK regulations the primary law of Kosovo and relegates the the law in force on 22 March 1989 to a subsidiary level. All laws must conform to international human rights standards.
15 December	Three Kosovo Albanian political leaders - Mr. Hashim Thaci of the PPDK (Peoples Democratic Party of Kosovo), Mr. Ibrahim Rugova of the LDK (Democratic League of Kosovo) and Mr. Rexhep Qosja of the LBD (United Democratic Movement) - sign an agreement to set up the Kosovo-UNMIK Joint Interim Structure (JIAS) and to install an Interim Administrative Council. The Council will consist of eight members including the signatories of the agreement and an as of yet unnamed Kosovo Serb, plus four UNMIK members.
23 December	The UN Secretary-General's report to the Security Council notes that UNMIK has made good progress over the past six months in implementing its mandate, but that a worrying level of violence prevails, particularly among minorities.
30 December	Security Council members express concern over continuing violence in Kosovo and urge the communities there to "take a different approach to reconciliation".

INTRODUCTION

A. The Conflict in Kosovo

The province of Kosovo is an administrative unit of 10,887 square kilometres consisting of 29 municipalities in the southwestern part of the Republic of Serbia within the Federal Republic of Yugoslavia (FRY). The last census with nearly universal participation was administered in 1981. The total population of Kosovo was approximately 1,585,000 of which 1,227,000 (77%) were Albanians, and 210,000 (13%) were Serbs. Only estimates are available for the population of Kosovo in 1991 since the Kosovo Albanians boycotted the census that year. General estimates are that the current population of Kosovo is between 1,800,000 and 2,100,000 of which approximately 85-90% are Kosovo Albanians and 5-10% are Serbs (*document no. 319*).

Discussions of the Kosovo conflict often start with the battle of Kosovo Polje (the Field of Blackbirds) in 1389 when the Serbs were defeated by the Ottoman Empire. This victory led to Ottoman rule in the region. This partly legendary battle continues to play an important role in the contemporary politics of Serbia.[1] In the early 19th century, national uprisings in Serbia slowly led to the withdrawal of the Ottoman Empire. In 1878, at the Berlin Congress Montenegro and Serbia obtained formal recognition of independence by the major European powers. The revival of Albanian nationalism, arguably in full flower since the foundation of the League of Prizren in 1878, aimed at uniting the areas of mainly Muslim Albanian-speaking populations. There existed an inherent conflict between the Albanians' long-established wish to unite Kosovo with Albania on the one side and the Serbs' emotional attachment to Kosovo and its holy places, such as the seat of the Serb Patriarchate in Pec. In 1912, as a result of the First Balkan War Serbia won control over Kosovo, while Albania gained independence.

In 1945, Serbia established the autonomous region of Kosovo-Metohija as a constituent part of Serbia and a year later, the new federal constitution endorsed Kosovo's status as an autonomous region with limited self-government.[2] The 1974 Constitution - the third under Tito's rule - was a major step forward in the devolution of government and ceding of economic power to the republics - Bosnia and Herzegovina, Croatia, Macedonia, Montenegro, Serbia, and Slovenia (*document no. 1*). While the constitution defined Kosovo and Vojvodina as autonomous provinces of Serbia, it granted them a status nearly equivalent to that of the republics, however, without the right to secede. Following the death of Tito in 1980, the Kosovo Albanians started to demand the status of a republic. Albanian riots in the province under the starting Serb repression, on the one hand, and the perceived marginalization of Serbs, on the other hand, led to further alienation and conflict between the two ethnic groups.

In 1988, Albanian agitation as well as Serb actions to support the Serbians living in Kosovo culminated. This led to proposals to amend the Serbian constitution to give Belgrade more control over Kosovo. In 1989, Serbia revoked the province's autonomy (*document no. 4*). Changes to the Serb Constitution granted Serbia control over the internal affairs of Kosovo and Vojvodina. Further steps in the revocation of the province's autonomy followed. In the following years Serbian decrees closed publicly funded Albanian language media, ended teaching of Albanian in most secondary schools and reduced it at the University of Pristina. Kosovo Albanians responded by creating a parallel-system of education comprised of teachers who had been sacked from their posts. When the Serb Assembly started to terminate the work of the Kosovo Assembly in 1990, the elected representatives of Kosovo adopted a declaration of sovereignty in response.[3] On 22 September 1991, the Kosovo Albanians issued a formal declaration of independence (*documents no. 9-11*).

The 1991 EC Conference on Yugoslavia aimed at peaceful resolution of the conflicting aspirations of the peoples of Yugoslavia. This Conference, as well as the subsequent London Conference, barely touched upon the issue of Kosovo (*document no. 50*). International attention had turned to the conflict in Bosnia and Herzegovina. In 1995, the General Framework Agreement for Peace in Bosnia and Herzegovina did not deal with the Kosovo problem, either. The Kosovo Albanians were disappointed about this outcome and consequently started to abandon the tactics of non-violent resistance. This led gradually to the forming of the Kosovo Liberation Army (KLA).[4] By 1997, the KLA began hit-and run attacks. Yugoslav forces reacted with large scale and frequently indiscriminate military assaults. In 1998, a major armed conflict erupted in central and western Kosovo between the KLA, regular units of the Yugoslav Army and regular Serbian police as well as three specialized police forces of the Public Security Service within the Ministry of the Interior of the Republic of Serbia.[5] These units forced more than 200,000 Kosovo Albanians to leave their villages and flee into the woods and hills. In February and March 1998, fighting took place in the Drenica region. According to reports of human rights organisations, entire family clans of KLA activists were killed. 85 Kosovo Albanians, mostly civilians, are reported to have been executed (*document no. 48*). This led to UN Security Council resolution 1160 (1998) of 31 March 1998 (*document no. 65*). However, the situation continuously

---

[1] UK, House of Commons, Foreign Affairs Committee, Report on Kosovo, June 200, para. 13.
[2] For a comprehensive account of the history of Kosovo see Noel Malcolm, *Kosovo - A Short History* (London 1998).
[3] Ibid., p. 346.
[4] Stefan Troebst, 'The Kosovo conflict' (1999) *SIPRI Yearbook* at 50.
[5] Ibid., at. 47.

deteriorated while other international actors, such as the Contact Group (consisting of the Foreign Ministers of France, Germany, Italy, the Russian Federation, the UK and the USA) and the European Union, tried to achieve a peaceful resolution of the conflict. In Resolution 1199 of 23 September 1998, the UN Security Council affirmed that the situation constituted a threat to peace in the region, required the FRY, inter alia, to implement a ceasefire, withdraw forces deployed in Kosovo and allow complete access for humanitarian workers *(document no. 89)*. On 24 September 1998, NATO increased pressure on Milosevic by issuing an Activation Warning for a limited air operation and a phased air campaign *(document no. 154)*. On 8 October 1998, the Contact Group sent US Special Envoy Holbrooke to Belgrade to demand the implementation of Resolution 1199 (1998). The mission was supported by a new military threat of NATO *(document no. 155)* Following the Holbrooke Agreement *(document no. 156)*, the Agreement between NATO and the FRY on an Air Verification Mission *(document no. 157)*, and the Agreement between the FRY and the OSCE on an OSCE Verification Mission were concluded *(document no. 100)*. In these agreements Belgrade accepted the presence of international observers in Kosovo to guarantee that Serb police action would not abuse civilians.

UN Security Council resolution 1203 (1998) of 24 October 1998 *(document no. 158)* still under the authority of Chapter VII of the UN Charter welcomed the OSCE and the NATO agreements. However, after NATO's threats to use force it reaffirmed the primacy of the UN Security Council's role in the maintenance of international peace and security. The Security Council expressed its alarm at the impending humanitarian catastrophe.

In his report of 30 January 1999, the UN Secretary-General noted the transformation of the nature of violence in Kosovo *(document no. 125)*. The incident in Racak on 15 and 16 January 1999 *(documents no. 104-115)* in which 45 civilians, including women and children, were reported to have been executed by Serbian Security Forces, highlighted these findings.

By end of January 1999, the Contact Group convened negotiations between the Kosovo Albanians and the Yugoslav Government to create a political framework for Kosovo's autonomy within Serbia for a three-year interim period, while postponing a final settlement. The Contact Group then announced a conference on the future of Kosovo to be held in Rambouillet on 6 February. On 30 January 1999, the North Atlantic Council authorized its Secretary-General to order airstrikes on military objectives in the FRY *(document no. 132)*. At Rambouillet a draft for an Interim Agreement on Peace and Self-government in Kosovo was presented to the parties *(document no. 141)*. Though both sides initially refused to sign, the Kosovo Albanians, after intensive efforts to persuade them, agreed in principle at the end of February and signed it during the Paris conference of 18 March 1999. On 17 March 1999, the UN Secretary-General issued a further report in which he stated that there had been murders of civilians, summary executions, brutality to prisoners and kidnappings. The report informed the Council that 211,000 persons were internally displaced, and stated that about 25,000 had fled to Montenegro. He observed that Serbian forces were blatantly infringing the Security Council resolutions *(document no. 126)*. On 19 March 1999, the Co-Chairmen of the Conference issued a statement which noted that the Kosovo Albanian side had accepted the accords in their entirety while "the Yugoslav delegation has tried to unravel the Rambouillet Accords." *(document no. 150)*. The negotiations were adjourned.

On 19 March, the OSCE ordered its observers to withdraw, and on 22 March Holbrooke travelled to Belgrade, once more, to persuade the FRY to agree to the Rambouillet Accords. However, no agreement was achieved. Upon receiving a briefing by Holbrooke on this final attempt for a peaceful resolution of the conflict, NATO began a bombing campaign against targets in the FRY on 24 March 1999 *(document no. 172)*.

On 26 March, the Russian representative laid before the Security Council a draft resolution condemning NATO's armed intervention as contrary to the United Nations Charter *(document no. 251)*. The Council rejected the proposal by twelve votes to three. NATO's air strikes continued for seventy-seven days until 10 June 1999. NATO Secretary General Solana suspended the air strikes *(documents no 184, 212)* when the Supreme Allied Commander Europe confirmed that Serbian forces had started to withdraw under the peace plan set forth in UN Security Council 1244 (1999) of 10 June 1999 *(document no. 204)*. This peace plan, formally approved by the Serb National Assembly on 3 June, emanated from the continuing efforts for a settlement of the dispute. In its decision taken on 6 May, G-8 had adopted general principles for a peaceful settlement of the conflict which formed the basis for further Russian and European Union mediation *(document no. 200)*.

Following the adoption of resolution 1244 (1999) *(document no. 208)* the deployment of KFOR was synchronised with the departure of the Serb security forces from Kosovo. On 20 June, the Serb withdrawal was complete so that the air campaign was formally terminated *(document no. 328)*. By resolution 1244 (1998) the UN Security Council authorized the UN Secretary-General to establish in Kosovo an interim civilian administration led by the UN. Kofi Annan presented to the Council an operational concept which was implemented as the United Nations Interim Administration Mission in Kosovo (UNMIK). As full partners under UN leadership, other international organisations participate in the international administration of Kosovo. The responsibility for the economic reconstruction of Kosovo and the Balkan region in general lies primarily with the EU which has agreed on a Stability Pact for South-Eastern Europe *(documents no.196, 210)*, while the OSCE is responsible for the creation and maintenance of institutions relating to democratic governance and enforcing human rights *(documents no. 330, 331)*.

Three different issues of public international law are relevant for an evaluation of the conflict: self-determination, humanitarian intervention and humanitarian law:

Introduction

B. Self-Determination and Minority Rights

The Kosovo Albanians' claim to independence as manifested in the declaration of independence of 22 September 1991 is subject to the legal rules of self-determination. The right to self-determination can be considered as one of the essential norms of contemporary international law. It is recognized by the UN Charter and by the jurisprudence of the International Court of Justice. The Court has construed the right of peoples to self-determination, as it has evolved from the Charter and UN practice, to contain an *erga omnes* character.[1] From the historical development of the rule, there are three identifiable recipients of the right: an ethnic minority living in an ethnically different state, peoples seeking decolonisation, and the population of a sovereign state in cases of foreign alien domination.[2] The legal consequences of this right vary for each class of recipient. There are basically two aspects of self-determination: the external self-determination directed against other subjects of international law and the internal self-determination aimed at the situation within a state. External self-determination comprises the right to establish an independent state or to unify with an existing state, especially in cases of decolonisation and secession. However, the prerequisites under which a bearer of the right to self-determination may be entitled to secede are unclear.[3] Internal self-determination has a twofold meaning. On the hand, it describes the right of a people which is organized in a state to decide without external influence on a form of government. On the other hand, it can mean that an ethnic minority living in a state is entitled to claim the observance of certain rights granting a special status in the field of language, religion and education.[4]

The problems of minorities have led to a discussion amongst scholars as to what would be the possible extension of the right to self-determination.[5] After the dissolution of the USSR, the debate was renewed by the minority problems arsing in Yugoslavia and Eastern Europe. Contemporary international law on the protection of minorities is quite rudimentary. It rests on Article 27 of the Covenant on Civil and Political Rights together with the general prohibition on discrimination in customary international law. Most scholars hold that minorities do not enjoy a right to secession under contemporary international law. They are restricted to a right to some form of autonomy within a given state.[6] This conclusion follows from the wording of Article 27 of the Political Covenant which grants only limited rights for minorities to "enjoy their culture, to profess and practise their own religion, or to use their own language." Minorities are not, as such, recognized as subjects of public international law.[7] Thus, the rights in Article 27 have been generally seen as individual rights. This view is also confirmed by an interpretation of Art. 1 of the Covenant which reserves the right of self-determination to peoples. From the plain meaning of the text, a systematic interpretation and the drafting history of this document, writers conclude that external self-determination is not a right of minorities in existing states. This interpretation is supported by later documents, such as the 1970 Friendly Relations Declaration (General Assembly Resolution 2625 (XXV) of 24 October 1970) and the 1992 UN Declaration on Minorities (General Assembly Resolution 47/135 of 18 December 1992). Both Resolutions although giving certain rights to minorities emphasise the territorial integrity of states. However, public international law does not prohibit minorities from trying to secede. The process of secession is legally neutral. The outcome has to be awaited by other states. Only the laws on internal armed conflict and human rights limit the process.

In academic literature, new proposals advocate a re-evaluation of the right to self-determination. Those authors who favour a right of minorities to secession base their arguments on the Friendly Relations Declaration. They maintain that discrimination against ethnic minorities could give rise to a right to secede, if the minority is exposed to flagrant violations of fundamental human rights by the state which is not willing to provide legal remedies or protection by courts. Flagrant violations might consist, inter alia, of murder, unlimited imprisonment without legal protection, of special prohibitions against following religious professions, using one's own language and of destroying family relations. Scholars argue that Art. 1 of the Covenant might include the right to resist such violations as a form of self-defence, and that secession might offer the only possible defensive reaction to brutal oppression.[8]

The international community uniformally rejected the Kosovo Albanians' claim to independence *(documents no. 55, 65)* though the states soon started to demand meaningful self-administration and autonomy for Kosovo. However, as Jennings has observed it seems that the international community has not yet found any clear answer to the question about the ultimate destiny of Kosovo itself.[9]

---

[1] ICJ, East Timor, ICJ Reports 1995, p. 90 para. 29.
[2] Karl Doehring, 'Self-Determination', in: Bruno Simma (ed), *The Charter of the United Nations- A Commentary* (Oxford 1995), paras. 27-31.
[3] Ibid., paras. 35/41/44.
[4] Ibid., para. 32.
[5] See Doehring, 'Self-Determination', paras. 36-40; Daniel Thürer, 'Self-Determination' in Rudolf Bernhard (ed.), Encyclopedia of Public International Law (12 vols. Amsterdam 1985), vol. 8, pp. 470-480; Christian Tomuschat, Modern Law of Self-Determination (Dordrecht 1993).
[6] Peter Malanczuk, *Akehurst's Modern Introduction to International Law* (7th ed., London 1997), p. 338.
[7] Kay Hailbronner, 'Der Staat und der Einzelene als Völkerrechtssubjekt' in Wolfgang Graf Vitzthum (ed.), *Völkerrecht* (Berlin, New York 1997), para. 26.
[8] Doehring, 'Self-Determination', paras. 37-40; Stefan Oeter, 'Selbstbestimmungsrecht im Wandel - Überlegungen zur Debatte um Selbstbestimmungsrecht, Sezession und vorzeitige Anerkennung', (1992) 52 *Zeitschrift für ausländisches öffentliches Recht und Völkerrecht*, 741-780 at 778.
[9] Robert Jennings, 'Kosovo and International Lawyers', (1999) 1 *International Law Forum*, 166-170 at 166.

C. The Legality of NATO Military Action - Humanitarian Intervention under Public International Law

In his report "Kosovo - One Year On" the NATO Secretary-General claims that the Allies were sensitive to the legal basis for their action and elaborates the following justification: The FRY had already failed to comply with numerous demands from the Security Council, even though they were issued under Chapter VII of the UN Charter. The UN Secretary-General had warned in his reports about the dangers of a humanitarian disaster in Kosovo. Considering Yugoslavia's failure to seek a peaceful resolution of the conflict there was a high risk of such a catastrophe. In addition, it was unlikely that a further UN Security Council resolution would be passed in the near future, while a threat to peace and security in the region remained. This conclusion was, inter alia, deduced from the fact that a veto by China on 25 February 1999 hindered the Security Council to authorise a six months extension of the term of the UN Preventive Deployment Force (UNPREDEP) in Macedonia.[1] Thus, the North Atlantic Council agreed that a sufficient legal basis existed for the Alliance to use force against the FRY.[2] On 23 March 1999, NATO Secretary General Javier Solana justified NATO's use of force by reference to the refusal of President Milosevic to accept the Rambouillet proposals and to abide by the limits imposed on the Serb Army and Special Police Forces in Kosovo to which he had agreed in October 1998. More fundamentally, the reason advanced by the Secretary-General was to "prevent more human suffering and more repression and violence against the civilian population of Kosovo" (*document no.170*). Thus, NATO's authorization of air strikes in October 1998 and the actual bombing in spring 1999 renewed the international discussion on the legality of humanitarian intervention.

Humanitarian intervention can be described as a unilateral intervention through military means for humanitarian purposes. Intervention by several states is unilateral if not authorized by the Security Council.[3] The legality of such actions is highly disputed.[4] The cornerstone for judging the legality of the NATO action is Art. 2 (4) of the UN Charter.

I. The Prohibition to Use Force

Art. 2 (4) of the Charter prohibits "the threat or use of force against the territorial integrity or political independence of any state", subject only to the provisions of Chapter VII and Art. 51 of the UN Charter.

Some scholars have advanced the idea that Art. 2 (4) of the Charter does not prohibit humanitarian intervention. Since the Charter does not govern cases in which States commit massive human rights violations, amounting to genocide, states can rely on justifications based on international customary law. This argument rests on the presumption of a changing interpretation of the Charter itself: When drafting the Charter states have focussed on the prohibition of war. The authors of the Charter are said to have presumed that the gravest violations of human rights occur during wartime. Thus, they did not anticipate that in the future massive human rights violations would occur in civil war situations. Scholars point out that by a broader interpretation of Chapter VII the Security Council has assumed competence in such cases so that it has become evident that the Charter does not provide mechanisms for handling massive human rights violations. If the Security Council remains inactive there are no other means in the Charter to prevent such violations, since Art. 51 of the Charter is not applicable. Therefore, customary international law could provide a legal basis.[5]

Others have searched for exceptions to the UN Charter prohibition on the use of force by liberal interpretations of the phrases "territorial integrity" and "inconsistent with the purposes of the Charter". The use of force on strictly humanitarian grounds is said to be neither directed against the territorial integrity nor the political independence of other states.[6] Humanitarian intervention must not be equated with war. Therefore, it is held, that humanitarian intervention does not violate Art. 2. (4) of the UN Charter.[7]

Those scholars who remain opposed to these liberal interpretations emphasise that the two phrases - "territorial integrity" and "inconsistent with the purposes of the Charter" do not restrict the scope of the prohibition of force. Art. 2 (4) is not limited to situations in which a state's territorial existence or the status of its political independence is altered or abolished. The

---

[1] It was commonly believed that China employed its veto because of the establishment of diplomatic relations with Taiwan by Macedonia.
[2] NATO, *Kosovo -One Year On- Achievement and Challenge* (2000), p. 24.
[3] Louis Henkin, 'Kosovo and the law of "Humanitarian Intervention"', (1999) 93 *American Journal of International Law*, 824-828 at 826; Peter Hilpold, 'Sezession und humanitäre Intervention - völkerrechtliche Instrumente zur Bewältigung innerstaatlicher Konflikte', (1999) 54 *Zeitschrift für öffentliches Recht*, 529-602 at 568-571.
[4] In favour of the existence of the right of humanitarian intervention: Karl Doehring, *Völkerrecht* (Heidelberg 1999), paras. 1011-1015; Knut Ipsen, 'Der Kosovo-Einsatz – Illegal? Gerechtfertigt? Entschuldbar?', (1999) 74 *Die Friedens-Warte* 74 19-23 at 20; Christian Tomuschat, 'Völkerrechtliche Aspekte des Kosovo-Konfliktes', (1999) 74 *Die Friedens-Warte* 33-37 at 34; Alain Pellet, 'La guerre du Kosovo – Le fait rattrapé par le droit', (1999) 1 *International Law Forum* 160-165 at 164; Belgium, ICJ, Public Sitting in the Case concerning Legality of Use of Force (Yugoslavia v. Belgium), 10 May 1999, CR 99/15; against humanitarian intervention: Jonathan I. Charney, 'Anticipatory Humanitarian Intervention in Kosovo', (1999) 93 *American Journal of International Law* 834-841 at 835-836; Henkin, 'Kosovo', 826; Hilpold, 'Sezession', 573f.; Christian Lange, 'Zu Fragen der Rechtmäßigkeit des NATO-Einsatzes in Kosovo', 1999 *Europäische Grundrechte-Zeitschrift*, 313-316 at 314; Georg Nolte, 'Kosovo und Konstitutionalisierung: Zur humanitären Intervention der NATO-Staaten', (1999) 59 *Zeitschrift für ausländisches öffentliches Recht und Völkerrecht*, 941-960 at 947; Bruno Simma, 'NATO, the UN and the Use of Force: Legal Aspects', (1999) 10 *European Journal of International Law* 1-22 at 6, also http:// www.ejil.org.
[5] Doehring, *Völkerrecht*, paras. 1013/1014; Karl Doehring, 'Die humanitäre Intervention – Überlegungen zu ihrer Rechtfertigung' in Cancado Trindade (ed.), *Essays in Honour of Thomas Buergenthal* (San José 1996) 549-564 at 555.
[6] Belgium, ICJ, Public Sitting in the Case concerning Legality of Use of Force (Yugoslavia v. Belgium), 10 May 1999, CR 99/15; Michael Reisman/Myres S. McDougal, 'Humanitarian Intervention to protect the Ibos' in Richard Lillich (ed.), *Humanitarian Intervention?* (Charlottesville 1973), pp. 167-195 at 177; Fernando R. Teson, *Humanitarian Intervention: An inquiry into law and morality* (Dobbs Ferry, New York 1988), p. 130-131.
[7] Felix Ermarcora, 'Geiselbefreiung im Licht der UN-Charta' in Heinrich Kipp et al. (ed.), *Festschrift für v.d.Heydte*, (Berlin 1977), pp. 147-171 at 163-164.

Introduction

two modes cover any possible kind of trans-frontier use of armed force.[1] This is underlined by the paramount purpose of the UN, according to Art. 1 (1) of the Charter, which is to maintain international peace and security and "to save succeeding generations from the scourge of war." Rather, the Charter assumes that the use of force, remains itself the most serious violation of human rights.[2] Authors also refer to the travaux preperatoire of the Charter. The phrases "territorial integrity" and "inconsistent with the purposes of the Charter" were added to Art. 2 (4) to close all potential loopholes in its prohibition of the use of force. At the San Francisco Conference, several smaller states succeeded in introducing these variants into the wording of Art. 2 (4) in order to strengthen their position. But there was no intention to restrict the comprehensive prohibition of force put forward in the Dumbarton Oaks Proposals.[3] Therefore, theses authors conclude that the comprehensive validity of Art. 2 (4) of the Charter is not conditioned upon the effectiveness of collective mechanisms for the protection of human rights. The Charter does not give room for any exceptions other than Art. 51 and the rules on collective security.

II. Justifications under the UN Charter

1. Liberal Interpretation of Art. 51 of the Charter

Some writings try to justify humanitarian intervention by a liberal interpretation of Art. 51 of the Charter or by drawing an analogy to that provision. The Council's willingness to expand the reach of Chapter VII to both internal and international conflicts may also justify a broader interpretation of Art. 51 of the UN Charter. Since public international law recognizes the individual as a subject of international law, there is also a presumption for an individual right of self-defence against massive human rights violations. In that case other subjects of international law might be entitled to collective self-defence, as well. This is deduced from the rationale of Art. 51 which guarantees the right of self-defence if the Security Council is unable to react to an act of aggression against a state. Authors apply the same consideration to the comparable situation that the Security Council does not act in case of a genocide.[4] This presumption is also considered to be applicable to minorities since they enjoy increasingly a status as subjects of international law, too.[5]

Other authors consider this argument as a progressive development of international law rather than an existing rule. They claim that this interpretation is doubtful. While they can accept an individual right to self-defence they underline that it is the right to collective self-defence that contravenes the prohibition of the use of force. The aim of the Charter to restrict the exceptions from the prohibition of the use of force to a few strictly defined cases leaves no room for analogies. Use of force by a state against its citizens is a criterion too broad to form a clearly defined exception. Therefore, it is justified to differentiate between an individual right of self-defence and a collective right. Only the latter accelerates the danger of conflict and escalation connected to unprecise definitions of exceptions from the prohibition of the use of force.[6] Furthermore, one has to take into account the problem of representation which does not normally arise in the context of the interstate use of force. It is unclear who represents a minority and, consequently, who is entitled to ask for military support.[7] Finally, some authors argue that collective self-defence for individuals or minorities resembles the rejected exception that support given to wars of national liberation is legal under public international law. Colonialism was considered a permanent aggression against which individual and collective self-defence were allowed.[8] India claimed, for instance, that right when it annexed Goa. However, there were numerous critical reactions from other states, furnishing the conclusion that such a justification is not accepted under international law.[9]

2. Implicit Post Facto Approval by the Security Council

With particular regard to Kosovo some authors take the view that NATO's intervention was not unilateral in a strict sense. In the case before the International Court of Justice Belgium claimed that the Security Council resolutions provided a basis for the armed intervention (*document no. 308*). They are based on Chapter VII of the Charter, under which the Security Council may determine the existence of any threat to international peace and security. NATO intervened to forestall an ongoing humanitarian catastrophe, acknowledged in the Security Council resolutions. In addition, Belgium relied on the need to safeguard the stability of an entire region, for the Security Council resolutions also note that the behaviour of the FRY in Kosovo was generating a threat to international peace and security by deteriorating the stability of the Balkans. Others take the position that the UN Security Council monitored the NATO action and could have ordered NATO to terminated the bombing. UN Security Council resolution 1203 (1998), following the NATO threat of force, does not condemn it, but wel-

---

[1] Albrecht Randelzhofer, 'Art. 2 (4)'in Bruno Simma (ed.), *The Charter of the United Nations- A Commentary* (München 1995) paras. 34/35; Simma, 'NATO', http://www. ejil.org.
[2] Louis Henkin, 'Use of Force: Law and U.S. Policy', in Louis Henkin et. al (ed.), *Right v. Might: International Law and the Use of Force* (2ed., New York 1991) 37-69 at 40.
[3] United Nations Conference on International Organization (UNCIO) VI, pp. 556-558; UNCIO VI, pp. 304, 334-335; Report of the Secretary-General on the "Question of Defining Aggression", UN Doc. A/2211, GAOR (VII), Annexes; Randelzhofer, 'Art. 2 para. 4', para. 35.
[4] Doehring, *Völkerrecht*, para. 1015; Doehring, 'Die humanitäre Intervention', pp. 560-563; Claus Kreß, 'Staat und Individuum in Krieg und Bürgerkrieg', (1999) *Neue Juristische Wochenschrift*, 3077-3084 at 3079/3081-3082; Ruth Wedgwood, 'NATO's Campaign in Yugoslavia', (1999) 93 *American Journal of International Law* 828-834 at 833.
[5] Ipsen, 'Der Kosovo-Einsatz', 22.
[6] Nolte, 'Konstitutionalisierung', 949-950.
[7] On the problem of representation of minorities: Judge Vereshchetin, Separate Opinion, *East Timor* Case, ICJ Reports 1995, p. 90 at 135-138.
[8] Malanczuk, *Introduction*, pp. 336-338.
[9] Antonio Cassese, *Self-Determination of Peoples* (Cambridge 1999), pp. 199-200; James Crawford, *The Creation of States* (Oxford 1979), p. 114.

comes the agreements concluded between the FRY, NATO and the OSCE. The Security Council's silence might be considered as an indirect support of NATO's action. The Security Council rejected the Russian draft resolution which condemns the use of force as illegal (*document no. 158*) by a majority of 12 votes to 3 (*document no. 159*). Some authors hold that Security Council Resolution 1244 (1999) approves the Kosovo settlement, effectively ratifies the NATO action and gives it the Council's support. They take the authorization of the international security presence in Kosovo to exercise "all necessary means" to fulfil its responsibilities as *post facto* approval of the military campaign.[1] Finally, NATO's action might be bolstered by its role as a regional organisation according to Art. 53 of the Charter.[2]

Those scholars who consider NATO's action to be illegal argue that no state should be encouraged to intervene on its own authority in expectation of subsequent approval or acquiescence by the Security Council. Instead of seeking authorization in advance by resolution subject to veto, states would act, and challenge the Council to terminate the action. However, a permanent member favouring the intervention could frustrate the adoption of such a resolution.[3] In addition, Security Council Resolution 1203 (1998) contains a reference to the Security Council's primary responsibility for the maintenance of international peace and security. Scholars consider the reference as an attempt to remind NATO of the Security Council's prerogative.[4] Likewise, it is doubtful that resolution 1244 (1999) really intends to ratify NATO's intervention. The Council stresses its primary responsibility for international peace and security, thus reaffirming its primary competence in this respect. The resolution establishes a regime for a political solution of the conflict. It does not endorse the means by which this solution has been achieved. The authorization *ex post* by the Security Council in the case of Liberia, SC Res. 788 (1992), on the contrary, does expressly state: "The Security Council ... Commends ECOWAS for its efforts to restore peace, security, and stability in Liberia."

Other authors underline that such an interpretation would not necessarily lead to the creation of a new rule of customary international law but to a new interpretation of the United Nations Charter: If the Security Council described a certain situation in a certain manner, it would authorize states to use force in order to implement the aims laid down in the resolution. Thus, a humanitarian intervention would still be linked to a decision of the Security Council. Nonetheless, there would be the danger of increasing legal insecurity when interpreting Security Council resolutions. Additionally, the willingness of important members of the Security Council to name and condemn humanitarian catastrophes could be diminished. It is considered probable that China and the Russian Federation would not be willing to allow the Security Council to determine that violations of human rights were a threat to international peace, if they assumed that such a kind of resolution would ultimately authorize the use of force in that conflict.[5]

Finally, this line of argument brings up questions of legality with regard to NATO's founding treaty. It has long been disputed whether NATO qualifies as a regional organisation according to Chapter VIII of the UN Charter. The opinion that NATO is not a regional agency is, inter alia, supported by the argument that obligations of a military alliance are inconsistent with the prohibition of the use of force. Authors refer to the San Francisco Conference to demonstrate that an offensive or a defensive military alliance *per se* was not a regional arrangement within the meaning of the Charter.[6] The alliances are based on Art. 51 of the UN Charter and the right to self-defence and they come more within the meaning of outwardly directed systems of collective defence.[7] However, the United Nations have extended the notion of regional arrangements. The Security Council has authorized NATO to take specific measures and even armed enforcement actions in Bosnia and Herzegovina.[8] The resolutions are taken as proof that the Security Council considers NATO to be a regional organisation which might carry out specific enforcement actions.

3. General Assembly Resolution 377 (V) - Uniting for Peace

One attempt to make intervention possible under the Charter when the Security Council is paralysed falls back on General Assembly resolution 377 (V) - i.e. the Uniting for Peace procedure.[9] When an item concerning international peace and security is on the Council's agenda and the Council is blocked by veto of one of its permanent members the General Assembly can take up the matter.

Even though Article 24 of the Charter grants the Security Council primary responsibility for the maintenance of international peace and security, it is argued that this does not preclude the General Assembly from exercising a secondary responsibility. The ICJ approved the argument in the Certain Expenses Case.[10] Resolution 377 (V) states that, if the Security Council fails in its primary responsibility of maintaining international peace and security, the General Assembly may consider the matter immediately with a view to making recommendations for collective measures, including the use of armed force. The

---

[1] Pellet, 'La guerre', 164.
[2] Wedgwood, 'NATO's Campaign', 832
[3] Henkin, 'Kosovo', 827.
[4] Christoph Schreuer, 'Is there a legal basis for the NATO Intervention in Kosovo?' (1999) 1 *International Law Forum* 151-154 at 152.
[5] Nolte, 'Konstitutionalisierung', 944; UK, House of Commons, Report on Kosovo, Juni 2000, para. 140.
[6] Waldemar Hummer/ Michael Schweitzer, 'Art. 52', in Bruno Simma (ed), *The Charter of the United Nations - A Commentary* (Oxford 1995), para. 27.
[7] Hummer/ Schweitzer, Art. 52, para. 42.
[8] *Inter alia* UN Doc. S/Res/757 (1992); 770 (1992); 816 (1993); see also 787 (1992).
[9] UK, House of Commons, Foreign Affairs Committe, Report on Kosovo, June 2000, para. 128.
[10] ICJ, Certain Expenses of the United Nations (Art. 17, paragraph 2 of the Charter), Advisory Opinion of 20 July 1962, ICJ Reports 1962, p. 151 at 162-163.

Introduction

Soviet Union's boycott of the Security Council during the Korean crisis of 1951 led to the adoption of the Uniting for Peace resolution which was later used against the UK and France in the Suez crisis in 1956.

However, its legality is open to doubt. Art. 11 (2) of the Charter says that "any ... question on which action is necessary shall be referred to the Security Council by the General Assembly". This gives the Council a monopoly of action.[1] The ICJ preserved the resolution's legality by interpreting action as enforcement action, which allowed the UN Emergency Force in the Middle East created by the General Assembly in 1956 to be considered lawful.[2]

In the Kosovo crisis the UK government is reported to have considered invoking the Uniting for Peace resolution but rejected the option because it was uncertain that the required majority of two thirds could have been achieved.[3] In addition, it remains doubtful that the General Assembly has the legal capacity to authorize enforcement action, i.e. military action against a state.

III. JUSTIFICATIONS UNDER CUSTOMARY INTERNATIONAL LAW

A further string of argument rests on the presumption that there are possibilities under customary international law to justify unilateral military intervention for humanitarian purposes. Several ideas are brought forward:

1. Does a Rule on Humanitarian Intervention exist under Customary International Law?

Belgium, for instance, suggested in the proceedings before the International Court of Justice (*document no. 308*) that a rule on humanitarian intervention existed under customary international law. This has also been debated in the report on Kosovo of the British House of Commons Committee on Foreign Affairs (*document no. 194*). This argument is based on a number of precedents: India's intervention in Eastern Pakistan; Tanzania's intervention in Uganda; Vietnam in Cambodia, the West African countries' interventions first in Liberia and then in Sierra Leone.[4] Belgium claims that while there may have been certain doubts expressed in the doctrine, and among some states, the relevant United Nations bodies have not expressly condemned these interventions.

Other scholars doubt that these cases form sufficient evidence of state practice and opinio juris that would have led to an amendment of the UN Charter, by means of customary international law. They do not consider humanitarian intervention to be a recognized exception to the prohibition laid down in Art. 2 (4). The British Foreign Office, for instance, rejected the existence of a customary international law rule of humanitarian intervention in 1986:[5] "But the overwhelming majority of contemporary legal practice comes down against the existence of a right of humanitarian intervention, for three main reasons: first, the UN Charter and the corpus of modern international law do not seem specifically to incorporate such a right; secondly, state practice in the past two centuries, and especially since 1945, at best provides only a handful of genuine cases of humanitarian intervention, and, on most assessments, none at all; and finally, on prudential grounds, that the scope for abusing such a right argues strongly against its creation." In its report of June 2000 the Foreign Affairs Committee of the House of Commons still holds that "the doctrine of humanitarian intervention has a tenuous legal basis in current international customary law, and that this renders NATO action legally questionable."[6]

2. Humanitarian Intervention as a Lawful Countermeasure under International Law

Some authors advance the idea that humanitarian intervention could be considered a lawful countermeasure under international law against a state committing massive human rights violations and ethnic cleansing. The term countermeasures refers to acts of retaliation, also known as reprisals. If state A is injured by an internationally wrongful act for which state B is responsible, state A is justified in not complying with its legal obligations towards state B.[7] Some authors hold that countermeasures, such as an armed attack, may be allowed under certain circumstances. A genocide could create a comparable threat entitling other states to take countermeasures. Since human rights are rights and duties *erga omnes*, these authors claim that every state would be authorised to take countermeasures in case of genocide.[8]

Other authors are opposed to this line of reasoning, first because they think that from Art. 2 (4) there follows a general prohibition against armed reprisals.[9] Second they doubt that *erga omnes* rights entitle states to take collective countermeasures outside the UN system. This would authorise every state in the world to take countermeasures in response to a breach of fundamental human rights, and to do so on its own separate account. How the principle of proportionality would function in that situation, what the limits and restrictions for collective countermeasures would be, is considered to be very uncertain under contemporary public international law. While the ideas of state responsibility have developed within the framework of bilat-

---

[1] Malanczuk, *Introduction*, pp. 392-393.
[2] ICJ, Certain Expenses of the United Nations (Art. 17, paragraph 2 of the Charter), Advisory Opinion of 20 July 1962, ICJ Reports 1962, p. 151 at 171-172.
[3] UK, House of Commons, Foreign Affairs Committee, Report on Kosovo, June 2000, para. 128.
[4] See also UK, House of Commons, Foreign Affairs Committee, Report on Kosovo, June 2000, para. 131.
[5] FOC, Foreign Policy Document, No. 148, pp. 2-9, reprinted in (1986) 57 *British Yearbook of International Law*, p. 619.
[6] UK, House of Commons, Foreign Affairs Committee, Report on Kosovo, June 2000, para. 132.
[7] Malanczuk, *Introduction*, p. 271.
[8] Doehring, *Völkerrecht*, para. 1037; Ipsen, 'Der Kosovo-Einsatz', 23.
[9] Malanczuk, *Introduction*, p. 271.

eral relations and subjective rights they may not be appropriate for joint obligations, especially obligations to the international community as a whole.¹

3. An Action under State of Necessity?

Another argument put forward classifies humanitarian intervention as an action under a state of necessity (*document no. 308*). The notion of a state of necessity is enshrined in all branches of the law. Therefore, some authors consider it as a general rule of public international law according to Art. 38 (1) lit. c ICJ – Statute.² It is also laid down in draft article 33 of the Draft Articles on State Responsibility proposed by the International Law Commission (ILC). A state of necessity is the cause which justifies the violation of a binding rule in order to safeguard, in face of grave and imminent peril, values which are higher than those protected by the rule which has been breached. The following definition has been adopted by the Drafting Committee of the ILC in 1999³:

1. Necessity may not be invoked by a State as a ground for precluding the wrongfulness of an act not in conformity with an international obligation of that State unless the act:
    (a) Is the only means for the State to safeguard an essential interest against a grave and imminent peril; and
    (b) Does not seriously impair an essential interest of the State or States towards which the obligation exists, or of the international community as a whole.
2. In any case, necessity may not be invoked by a State as a ground for precluding wrongfulness if:
    (a) The international obligation in question arises from a peremptory norm of general international law;
    (b) The international obligation in question excludes the possibility of invoking necessity; or
    (c) The State has contributed to the situation of necessity.

The ILC has dealt with the state of necessity in length for the Draft Articles on State Responsibility. It has examined cases in which governments have invoked a state of necessity in order to justify conduct not in conformity with international obligations relating to the territorial sovereignty of other states. History demonstrates that states have most often abusively invoked a state of necessity as justification for breaches of peremptory rules, especially the prohibition against the use of force. The fears generated by the idea of recognizing this justification have been due to past attempts by states to rely on a state of necessity as justification for acts of aggression, conquest and forcible annexation. However, in the opinion of the Commission, no invocation of a "state of necessity" under international law can preclude the wrongfulness of conduct not in conformity with an obligation of *jus cogens*. It assures that, independent of the extent of the effect of justification by a state of necessity, it can never preclude the wrongfulness of state conduct, constituting an act of aggression against another state, in violation of the obligation banning the use of force. The Commission goes on to state that peremptory rules are so fundamental for the international community as to make it all the more inconceivable that a state should have the right to decide unilaterally, however acute the state of necessity which overtakes it, that it may breach these norms. According to the ILC, state praxis does not provide a sufficient basis for the assumption that a state of necessity is accepted as a general exception to the prohibition on the use of force. ⁴

IV. A POLITICAL APPROACH TO JUSTIFICATION

Especially American authors try to justify humanitarian intervention by a more political approach. These authors presume that international law can and should be read to provide a legal basis for humanitarian intervention. They reject the notion that only a limited number of specific grounds exist to justify the use of force. Instead they evaluate all the circumstances relevant to such an action under the UN Charter and other applicable legal principles.⁵ This idea rests on the proposition that the principles governing the use of force are mere words the meaning of which should be developed through a process of examining and weighing all the facts related to particular uses of force. This approach explains the U.S. strategy with regard to the justification of the use of force. It rejects the proposition that the legality or illegality of an action must be determined using only a few specific rules of international law which are narrowly defined. Instead, it combines the facts concerning all feasible arguments for legality, to establish whether, under the present circumstances, the action was lawful. Thus, this approach explains legality through a process of weighing relevant facts against the standards of the UN Charter rather than by examining whether a situation fulfils the requirements of particular legal norms. Sofaer, a former Legal Adviser of the U.S. government, has described this justification as a rejection of "a view of international law that would have placed the United States at a substantial disadvantage against its competitors in world affairs." Those favouring this pragmatic approach stress that U.S. leaders have never maintained a right to be free to act as they please. Instead, they have consented to the obligation to explain their conduct through established international legal principles. In this manner, the U.S. government is said to have developed

---

¹ "It has the effect, among others, of turning human rights first into collective state rights, and then into individual state powers of reaction, and of doing so *a priori* - which is all rather problematic", James Crawford, The Relationship between Sanctions and Countermeasures, a contribution to the Colloquium of the Graduate Institute of International Studies (Geneva) on United Nations Sanctions and International Law, June 1999, see http://www.law.cam.ac.uk/RCIL/ILCSR/Statresp.htm.
² Ipsen, 'Der Kosovo-Einsatz', 22.
³ E. g. UN Doc. A/CN.4/L.574 as corrected by Corrigenda 1 and 3.
⁴ ILC-Yearbook 1980, vol. II (Part Two), S. 34-52, para. 22.
⁵ Abraham D. Sofaer, 'International Law and Kosovo', (2000) 36 *Stanford Journal of International Law* 1-21 at 9.

a law on the use of force which is in conformity with Charter principles - "based on practice, rather than adhering to the views of states with opposing ideologies and objectives, or of international lawyers having no public authority or responsibility to protect U.S. interests."[1]

V. A NEW RULE OF CUSTOMARY INTERNATIONAL LAW

Some authors who deny that public international law allows for humanitarian intervention argue in favour of the creation of a new rule of customary international law.[2] A proposal of the European Parliament in 1994 demonstrates a certain political desire to create such a norm.[3] The USA argues that the NATO air strikes establish a new doctrine governing military operations for humanitarian intervention - the so-called Clinton Doctrine (*document no. 247*). This doctrine of humanitarian intervention consists of two parts: the use of force on behalf of universal values instead of narrower national interests for which States have traditionally fought; and, in defence of these universal values, military intervention in the internal affairs of sovereign states.[4]

Also scholars have attempted to develop a new law that is clear, limits the potential for abuse and balances the competing interests. An appropriately balanced legal regime asks for certain procedural and factual requirements, among them are:

- Publicly available evidence must establish that widespread and grave international crimes, as defined in the Rome Statute of the International Criminal Court,[5] are being committed in a state and that this state supports these criminal activities, acquiesces in them, or cannot control them. Some authors demand a determination by the Security Council of a grave crisis, threatening international peace and security.

- The intervention must be the act of a group of states, acting within the framework of an alliance, a regional organisation or an ad hoc grouping.

- The group of states must have exhausted all reasonably available peaceful means to stop the massive human rights violations without success, including negotiations, political initiatives, and non-forcible countermeasures, such as economic sanctions.

- If those countermeasures fail, the group of states, acting through its UN member states, must formally bring the matter before the General Assembly or the Security Council on an emergency basis. It should seek authorisation under Chapter VII from the Security Council to take the necessary measures to halt the gross violations of human rights. If the Council does not approve such action and neither it nor the General Assembly adopts a resolution which expressly prohibits further action by the group of states, recourse to a UN remedy will be deemed exhausted. The group of states will be entitled to act.

-In order to stress that international law shall not entail an obligation to intervene some authors add the criterion that the intervention must be likely to achieve its objective.[6]

- Before intervening, the states that are to participate must consent to possible litigation in the ICJ by any directly injured state for violations of international law committed in the course of the humanitarian intervention. Likewise, they must consent to the jurisdiction of the International Criminal Court over their nationals for crimes within that courts jurisdiction that their nationals might commit during the intervention.[7]

- States are allowed to use force only to stop the widespread and massive violations of human rights. To this end, intervening states must limit the targets, minimize collateral damage, avoid unrelated effects on the state's legitimate functions, and observe other requirements of international humanitarian law.

- If the use of force has accomplished the appropriate objectives, the foreign forces must withdraw, except for cases of the state's consent to their remaining or for the authorisation under Chapter VII by the UN Security Council.

Those authors criticising the creation of a new rule stress that the definitions used are too broad and unprecise to effectively limit possible abuses.[8] Even the notion genocide might be open to diverse and unclear interpretations.[9] Since the decision to take action lies with the regional organisation, the problem remains that single states cannot be trusted to judge and act in the common interest.[10] The discretion to determine under which circumstances the parties have exhausted all available diplomatic means remains wide and unlimited.[11] Finally, even the prerequisite only to entitle regional organisations to take action does not necessarily preclude unilateral action. The notion regional organisation has been extended in the course of the time. The

---

[1] Sofaer, 'Kosovo', 11-12.
[2] Antonio Cassese, 'Ex iniuria ius oritur: Are we Moving towards International Legitimation of Forcible Humanitarian Countermeasures in the World Community?', (1999) 10 European Journal of International Law. http:// www.ejil.org; Charney, 'Humanitarian Intervention', 836/838; Hilpold, 'Sezession', 583; Lange, 'Rechtmäßigkeit', 315-316; Wedgwood, 'NATO's Campaign', 828; International Law Association, *Report of the 56th Conference* (New Dehli 1974) pp. 219-220.
[3] Official Journal C 128/225, 20 April 1994.
[4] See Michael Mandelbaum, 'A perfect failure - NATO's war against Yugoslavia', 1999 *Foreign Affairs* 2-8 at 5.
[5] Reprinted in: (1998) 37 *International Legal Materials*, 999-1069.
[6] See UK, House of Commons, Foreign Affairs Committee, Report on Kosovo, June 2000, para. 144.
[7] Charney, 'Humanitarian Intervention', 839.
[8] Nico Schrijver, 'NATO in Kosovo: Humanitarian Intervention turns into Von Clausewitz War (1999) 1 *International Law Forum* 155-159 at 156.
[9] Nolte, 'Konstitutionalisierung', 952.
[10] Henkin, 'Kosovo', 825.
[11] Nolte, 'Konstitutionalisierung', 957-958

intervention in Grenada is said to demonstrate that regional organisations could act in the interest of a leading hegemonial power.[1]

While some scholars hold that there is increasing evidence of the exercise of intervention in defence of human rights,[2] the various reactions and statements of NATO member states and third parties after the Kosovo intervention (*Chapter 6 and 7*) will have to be taken into account as *opinio iuris* for the creation of a rule of customary international law permitting military intervention. Other scholars even favour the conclusion of a treaty regulating the conditions under which humanitarian intervention would be permissible.[3]

In addition, academics put forward certain policy considerations in favour of and against a rule on humanitarian intervention: On the one hand, scholars and states alike (*document no. 257*) take into account that a reform of the Security Council, especially in order to prevent an abuse of the veto power, is not likely to happen in the near future. Likewise, the increasing overload of the work of the Security Council has led to a certain overstrain of the organ.[4] This might necessitate an allocation of certain responsibilities to regional organisations. The assignment of exclusive power to the Council is said to cease to be workable, if the UN's mandate is extended to the protection of human rights and the international control of good governance. On these matters, there are, according to some scholars, deep, possibly unbridgeable differences of opinion between the permanent members of the Security Council.[5]

On the other hand, in the last decade a large number of conflicts stemmed from attempts at secession and subsequent interventions. Authors refer to examples, such as the conflict in Yugoslavia, the dissolution of the Soviet Union, secessionist attempts in Chechnya and the dissolution of the Congo. The examples demonstrate the connection between secession and humanitarian intervention as well as the fact that public international law regulates the two instruments only insufficiently.[6] With regard to potential international conflicts some academics reject the idea that a rule of humanitarian intervention can maintain its asserted character as an exception to the rule. They fear the erosion of Art. 2 (4) of the Charter. A situation which is at present a reality in regard to international conflicts cannot be dismissed as an extreme exception to the rule.[7] In addition, it is uncertain whether legal norms regulating a right to secession and humanitarian intervention might not increase risks for international security, since minorities willing to secede might be tempted to provoke persecution in order to strengthen their claim for a right to secession and to precipitate intervention by third states (*document no. 257*).[8] Observers allege that the KLA has pursued such a policy.

Likewise, it cannot be precluded that states will claim to have a right to intervene without fulfilling the prerequisites of this right. Authors refer to the example of Pakistan which claimed a similarity between the Kosovo conflict and military encounters in Kashmir, shortly after the bombings had stopped.[9] France and Germany underlined this risk of abuse in relation to the notion of international crimes.[10]

Furthermore, authors stress that next to the risk of abuse remains the danger of escalation. Military intervention is subject to a specific dynamic of force and counter-force. States can neither predict nor control its effects and consequences.[11] Escalation of the use of force might have worldwide consequences if a permanent member of the Security Council is concerned in its vital security and strategic interests or if the international balance of power is profoundly disturbed.[12]

Finally, authors point out that that principally a common consent between the permanent members of the Security Council is more likely than ever before. Since the end of the Cold War, the Security Council invoked Chapter VII over 120 times, including situation of massive human rights violations.[13]

The Kosovo crisis qualifies as a hard case under international law. The dilemma international lawyers face when evaluating the action can be described in the words of the UK House of Commons Foreign Affairs Committee: "We believe that, while legal questions in international relations are important, law cannot become a means by which universally acknowledged prin-

---

[1] Nolte, 'Konstitutionalisierung', 954.
[2] See UK, House of Commons, Foreign Affairs Committe, Report on Kosovo, June 2000, para. 130.
[3] See UK, House of Commons, Foreign Affairs Committee, Report on Kosovo, June 2000, para. 139.
[4] Kreß, 'Krieg und Bürgerkrieg', 3083.
[5] Michael Reisman, Kosovo's Antinomies, (1999) 93 *American Journal of International Law* 860-862 at 862.
[6] Hilpold, 'Sezession', 530.
[7] Nolte, 'Konstitutionalisierung', 954.
[8] Liechtenstein, UN Doc. A/54/PV. 13 of 24 September 1999, at 34; Sri Lanka, UN Doc. A/54/PV. 11 of 23 September 1999, at 29,
[9] UN Press Release DCF/370 of 4 June 1999; Nolte, 'Konstitutionalisierung', 956.
[10] France: "(b) Such an article gives rise to numerous difficulties:
By risking encouraging States to have recourse (at times wrongly) to countermeasures in defence of what the draft articles call the "fundamental interests of the international community";
By affording the whole "international community", by virtue of the introduction of the concept of "crime", the possibility of engaging in an actio popularis and reacting collectively to the wrongdoing; this is not without danger. One of the functions of public international law is, in fact, to avoid tension. It is not certain, however, that an actio popularis is the most appropriate mechanism to prevent tension. Draft Articles of the International Law Commission on State Responsibility – Observations of France, see: http://www.law.cam.ac.uk/RCIL/ILCSR/Statresp.htm; see also Germany: Auswärtiges Amt, Bonn, 18 December 1997, Draft Articles on State Responsibility- Comments and observations of the Government of the Federal Republic of Germany, see: http://www.law.cam.ac.uk/RCIL/ILCSR/Statresp.htm.
[11] Gerhard Zimmer, *Rechtsdurchsetzung (Law Enforcement) zum Schutz humanitärer Gemeinschaftsgüter* (Aachen 1998), p. 101-102.
[12] Cassese, 'Ex iniuria', 23.
[13] UK, House of Commons, Foreign Affairs Committee, Report on Kosovo, June 2000, para. 133; Nolte, 'Konstitutionalisierung', 957.

ciples of human rights are undermined. ..., (W)e conclude that NATO's military action, if of dubious legality in the current state of international law, was justified on moral grounds."[1]

VI. THE LEGALITY UNDER THE NATO TREATY

Another issue discussed since the intervention in the FRY is the legality of the action under the NATO treaty. Most scholars maintain that the North Atlantic Treaty does not give a mandate for NATO to act for humanitarian purposes.[2] They refer to Art. 5 of the Treaty which provides for the use of force only in collective self-defence of NATO members. An argument advanced in favour of the legality of the intervention interprets the right to self-defence so broadly as to include the defence of "common interests and values."

However, most authors hold that the wording of Art. 51 of the UN Charter speaks against such an interpretation. Likewise, they maintain that the right to self-defence under customary international law does not justify the NATO action. The International Court of Justice, for instance, in the Nicaragua case takes the content and scope of the customary right to coincide almost completely with the right under Article 51 of the UN Charter. Thus, the right to self-defence may also be resorted to solely in case of an armed attack.[3] Consequently, the Report of the House of Commons on Kosovo of June 2000 recommends "that the Government examine whether any new legal instrument is necessary to allow NATO to take action in future in the same manner as it did in Kosovo." (*document no. 194*). In this context Simma notes that NATO has a capacity to absorb new roles and missions without any formal change considered necessary to the original founding treaty and refers to the expression of a "treaty on wheels". Since NATO arrives at decisions by unanimous vote or a consensual method, transformations of the treaty are considered to be possible without a formal revision of the founding treaty or without using doctrinal instruments such as the implied powers theory.[4] Nonetheless, authors underline the legal limitations of such a transformation. NATO like its member states is subject to peremptory rules of international law, such as the rule banning the use of force. All those authors who consider the UN Charter to be not only a multilateral treaty but more a kind of "Constitution" of the international community will consider UN Charter law as higher law which sets the limits for any feasible self-authorisation of NATO. This is, however, above all disputed by the USA (*document no. 247*).

D. International Humanitarian Law in the Kosovo Conflict

The fact that NATO conducted its military action for humanitarian purposes made it incumbent upon member states to ensure that the targeting decisions were taken in full compliance with international humanitarian law. Member states were aware that the use of force would be subject to close scrutiny of the public opinion. Despite precautions civilian casualties occurred. In the aftermath of the conflict non-governmental organisations, such as Human Rights Watch, issued reports on civilian causalities (*document no. 193*). After numerous requests for investigation during and since the conflict the Prosecutor of the ICTY established a committee to assess the allegations. In June 2000 the committee issued its final report (*document no. 195*). The bombing campaign has attracted criticism alleging the infringement of varying norms of international humanitarian law.

International Humanitarian Law evolved constantly from the 1864 Geneva Convention for the Amelioration of the Conditions of the Wounded in Armies in the Field to the Geneva Conventions of 1949 with their two Additional Protocols of 1977, and further subsequent conventions dealing with the restriction and prohibition of certain weapons, such as anti-personnel mines. 188 states have ratified the Geneva Conventions, 156 states have also ratified Additional Protocol I and 149 Additional Protocol II. The FRY has ratified the Geneva Conventions and both protocols. Out of those NATO states which the FRY has brought before the ICJ only France and the USA have not ratified Protocol I and the USA has neither ratified Protocol II. However, certain provisions of the Additional Protocols reflect customary international law.

I. THE ARMED CONFLICT

According to most international observers, an internal and an international armed conflict overlapped in Kosovo. Chronologically, the first was an internal conflict (as understood in Art. 3 common to all four 1949 Geneva Conventions and in Protocol II) between the FRY and the KLA. The second was an international one between NATO member states and the FRY.[5]

The existence of an internal armed conflict between March 1998 and March 1999 is confirmed by OSCE and by the ICTY. Thus, provisions of international human rights law as well as provisions of international humanitarian law apply to the conflict. The application of humanitarian law follows from Art. 3 of the Geneva Conventions and the Additional Protocol II, dealing with internal conflicts. According to Article 1 para. 1, the Protocol applies to "armed conflicts that take place in the territory of a High Contracting Party between its armed forces and dissident armed forces or other organized armed groups which, under responsible command, exercise such control over a part of the territory as to enable them to carry out sustained and concerted military operations and to implement the Protocol." Thus, the Protocol's provisions place obligations on the KLA, the FRY and Serbian authorities. Even though the parties kept cease-fire in Kosovo for brief periods, the state of an armed conflict persisted according to the ICTY. The Appeals Chamber of the ICTY holds in the *Tadic Case*: "International

---

[1] UK, House of Commons, Foreign Affairs Committee, Report on Kosovo, June 2000, para. 137-138.
[2] See UK, House of Commons, Foreign Affairs Committee, Report on Kosovo, June 2000, para. 135.
[3] ICJ, Nicaragua Case Merits, ICJ Reports 1986, p. 14 (p. 102 para. 193); Simma, 'NATO', http//:www.ejil.org.
[4] Simma, 'NATO', http//:www.ejil.org.
[5] ICRC, International Humanitarian Law and the Conflict on the Balkans: Questions and Answers, 23 April 1999.

humanitarian law applies from the initiation of ... armed conflict and extends beyond the cessation of hostilities until ... a peaceful settlement is achieved. Until that moment, international humanitarian law continues to apply ... in the whole territory under the control of a party, whether or not actual combat takes place there."[1]

In the indictment of Milosevic, the ICTY states that "at all times relevant to this indictment, a state of armed conflict existed in Kosovo." *(document no. 524)*. The question when the "international armed conflict" started was not relevant in this case, since charges were brought under Art. 3 and 5 of the Statute (violations of the laws or customs of war and crimes against humanity). Both articles only require the existence of an "armed conflict" the character of which (international or internal) is not relevant.[2]

The FRY's use of civilian human shields during the international armed conflict between the FRY and the NATO states is described as a violation of humanitarian law according to Art. 51 para. 7 of Protocol I. This is of particular importance when evaluating the Korisa incident where over 80 Kosovo Albanians died, reportedly used as human shields for a military convoy on 14 May 1999.[3]

With regard to NATO's military action against the FRY several questions have received special attention, by the diverse reports issued after the campaign: Do the attacks on certain civilian infrastructure targets, i.e. on dual-use targets, constitute a breach of humanitarian law; did NATO take all the necessary precautions to prevent civilian loss of life and damage to civilian property when attacking; did NATO observe the principle of proportionality when trying to fight a "zero casualty" war for their own side; what does humanitarian law say about the use of certain types of weapons, such as cluster bombs and depleted uranium shells?

II. DUAL USE TARGETS AND THE PRINCIPLE OF PROPORTIONALITY

Supposedly NATO attacks were directed several times against civilian as well as dual use objects. Key incidents, examined by Human Rights Watch and the Committee of the ICTY, include the attack on a civilian passenger train at the Grdelica Gorge on 12 April 1999; the attack on the Djakovica convoy on 14 April 1999; the attack on the Serbian Radio and TV station in Belgrade on 23 April 1999, the attack on the Chinese Embassy on 7 May 1999 and the attack on Korisa village on 13 May 1999 *(documents no. 183, 193, 195, 276)*.

Art. 48 and 51 of Protocol I provide that States shall direct their operations only against military targets. Although the definition of military objects in Art. 52 of Additional Protocol I is disputed in literature,[4] the ICTY, for instance, considers it as the temporary standard for determining the lawfulness of particular attacks.[5] Art. 52 para. 2 of Protocol I limits military objectives to "those objects which by their nature, location, purpose or use make an effective contribution to military action and whose total or partial destruction, capture or neutralization, in the circumstances ruling at the time, offers a definite military advantage." Although the USA and France have not ratified the Protocol, they are bound by the provision insofar as it reflects customary international law.[6] The Committee of the ICTY, however, concludes that most of the targets chosen by NATO were clearly military objectives.

Certain operations by NATO raise the question whether NATO always acted in accordance with the principles of proportionality between civilian damage and military advantage. Pursuant to Art. 35 para. 2, 51 para. 5a, 56, 57 para. 2 (iii), 57 para. 2 (b) of Protocol I, it is prohibited to launch an attack on dual-use objects "which would be excessive in relation to the concrete and direct military advantage anticipated." The provisions require an acceptable relation between the legitimate destructive effect and undesirable collateral effects. The Committee of the ICTY stresses that the application of the principle of proportionality brings up certain unresolved issues, such as the question what are the relative values of a military advantage gained and the injury to non-combatants or the damage to civilian objects; or the question to what extent is a military commander obliged to expose his own forces to danger in order to limit civilian casualties or damage to civilian objects.

The Committee of the ICTY refutes the notion that the mere fact that civilians have been killed amounts to the conclusion that NATO had perpetrated crimes, since collateral casualties can be caused for many reasons. Instead the Committee refers to the jurisprudence of the ICTY in the *Kupreski Judgment*:" ... in case of repeated attacks, all or most of them falling within the grey area between indisputable legality and unlawfulness, it might be warranted to conclude that the cumulative effect of such acts entails that they might not be in keeping with international law."[7] The Committee interprets this formula to stress the need for an overall assessment of the totality of civilian victims in relation to the goals of the military campaign. Comparing the Human Rights Watch report on "Civilian Deaths in the NATO air campaign" to a FRY Ministry of Foreign Affairs publication, the Committee assumes that there were about 500 civilians killed. Comparing the 10,484 strike sorties to the 500

---

[1] ICTY, Tadic Case, Decision on the Defence Motion for Interlocutory Appeal on Jurisdiction, 2 October 1995, No. IT-94-1-AR72.
[2] Sonja Boelaert-Suominen, 'The International Criminal Tribunal for the Former Yugoslavia and the Kosovo conflict', *International Review of the Red Cross* No. 837, pp. 217-252; see http://www.icrc.org. p. 9.
[3] For further violations of humanitarian law by the FRY see Chapter 8.2.
[4] Stefan Oeter, 'Kampfmittel und Kampfmethoden' in Dieter Fleck (ed.), *Handbuch des Völkerrechts in bewaffneten Konflikten* (München 1994), pp. 89-167 at 128-129.
[5] ICTY, *Final Report to the Prosecutor by the Committee Established to Review the NATO Bombing Campaign Against the Federal Republic of Yugoslavia* (Den Haag, June 2000), para. 42.
[6] Thomas Meron, *Human Rights and Humanitarian Norms as Customary Law* (Oxford 1989), pp. 64-65.
[7] ICTY, in: Kupreskic Judgment, Case No: IT-95-16-T of 14 January 2000.

civilian deaths the Committee finds that NATO does not seem to have led the campaign with the aim of causing directly or indirectly substantial civilian casualties.[1]

Moreover, one can argue that the military value of destroying the Serbian television building appears questionable. The media as such is not a traditional military target category. However insofar particular media components are part of the command, control, and communications network, they are considered to be military targets. Otherwise, the qualification depends on their use. The Committee of the ICTY lists prerequisites under which the media may constitute a legitimate target. If the media is used to incite crimes, as in Rwanda, then it is a legitimate target. If it is involved in propaganda to generate support for the war, it is not a legitimate target.[2] According to NATO, the Serbian TV and Radio Station in Belgrade functioned as "radio relay stations and transmitters to support the activities of the FRY military and special police forces."[3] In addition, NATO member states justify the bombing by referring to its propaganda purpose.[4] The legality of this justification is questionable under international humanitarian law. Insofar as the attack was actually directed at disrupting the communications network, it was, according to the Committee, lawful.[5]

Furthermore, the destruction of water-systems is questionable according to Art. 54 para. 2 of Protocol I, providing that "it is prohibited to ... attack drinking water installations and supplies and irrigation works for the specific purpose of denying them for their sustenance value to the civilian population or to the adverse party."

In the eyes of some writers, there is a tension between the reliance on air sorties carried out in altitude above 15,000 ft and certain provisions of the humanitarian law, such as Art. 48, 51, 52 of Protocol I in connection to the obligation to take all necessary precautions to minimise civilian loss of life, as stipulated in Art. 57 para. 2a (ii) of Protocol I.[6] These allegations presuppose that NATO aircraft operated at heights which enabled them to avoid attack by the Yugoslav army, but made it consequently impossible for them to distinguish properly between military and civilian objects on the ground. Some allegations go so far as to accuse NATO of crimes against humanity and genocide. NATO argues that modern weapon systems can strike from great ranges and heights with extreme accuracy. NATO reports refer to the fact that flying above enemy air defences allows the aircraft time to identify targets and even circle them, before striking. In addition, not all strikes have reportedly been conducted from high levels. Some aircraft operated at low levels down to 6,000 feet.[7] Observers suppose that NATO attempted to do everything feasible to verify that the objectives to be attacked were neither civilians or civilian objects, as required by Art. 57 para. 2a (i) of Protocol I.[8] Political arguments stress that the decision to concentrate more on civilian and dual-use targets was only taken after Milosevic failed to comply with basic NATO demands and the FRY began committing severe human rights violations in Kosovo. Military actors argue that the most effective aspect of the bombing campaign involved Serbia rather than directly attacking Serb forces in Kosovo. So some people believe the war might have been shorter had the Alliance adopted such a strategy earlier on.[9] The Committee of the ICTY agrees that with the use of modern technology the obligation to distinguish was effectively carried out in the vast majority of cases during the campaign. Therefore it does not see anything unlawful in flying above the altitude reachable by the enemy air defence.[10]

III. Environmental Damage

Art. 35 and 55 of Protocol I prohibit attacks likely to cause "widespread, long-term and severe damage" to the environment. Consequently attacks on oil installations and chemical plants that lead to grave and long lasting damage of the natural environment could be seen as illegal. The Committee of the ICTY points out that the International Court of Justice in its *Advisory Opinion on the Legality of Nuclear Weapons* appears to suggest that both articles do not reflect customary international law. Thus, they would not be binding upon France and the USA. In addition, the Committee underlines that both articles have a very high threshold of application, covering only very significant long-term damage. For instance, after the 1990/91 Gulf War, there was disagreement whether the oil spills and fires crossed the threshold of Art. 35 and 55 of the Additional Protocol I. Finally, the Committee points out that the actual environmental impact, both present and long-term, of the NATO air strikes in the FRY is presently unknown and difficult to measure.

IV. Use of Certain Weapons

Another issue of controversy of the intervention was the use of cluster bombs and depleted uranium munitions.

1. Use of Cluster Bombs

Cluster bombs such as the CBU-87 and BLU-97 used by the United States and the RBL-755 used by the United Kingdom are bombs which break into a large number of bomblets. These bomblets may penetrate armour or have incendiary capabilities. By subsequently exploding into a large number of fragments they are directed at destroying many different targets over a

---

[1] ICTY, *Report*, paras. 52-54.
[2] ICTY, *Report*, paras. 47/55.
[3] Ibid., para. 73.
[4] See ICTY, *Report*, para. 74.
[5] Ibid., paras. 75-76.
[6] Volker Kröning, 'Kosovo and Internatonal Humanitarian Law' (2000) 13 *Humanitäres Völkerrecht - Informationsschriften* 44-51 at 49.
[7] NATO, *Kosovo*, p. 25.
[8] Kröning, 'International Humanitarian Law', 47.
[9] Ibid., at 48.
[10] ICTY, *Report*, para. 56.

wide area. At least 50% of bomblets do not explode when they reach their target, remaining active for several months. According to U.S. Air Force in densely populated areas the collateral damage may be high due to the fragmentation of these weapons. In addition, the problem with unexploded ordinance remains.[1] It may be doubtful whether civilians can be protected from unnecessary harm when the military uses cluster bombs against a target which may be close to civilian objects. There is, however, no specific treaty provision which prohibits or restricts the use of cluster bombs. Nonetheless, the military must still use these bombs in accordance with the general principles on the use of weapons. Human Rights Watch has condemned the use of cluster bombs by describing them as "indiscriminate in effect - the equivalent of using anti-personnel mines" (*document no. 193*). Even if one disagrees with the comparison of cluster bombs and land mines, the problem of their ability to indiscriminately harm civilians over a longer period of time is left unresolved. Therefore, the ICTY looks at the intention with which such bombs are used. In a decision of Trial Chamber I of the ICTY on 8 March 1996 the Chamber states that "the use of the Orkan rocket (with a cluster bomb warhead) in this case was not designed to hit military targets but to terrorise the civilians of Zagreb" which renders the use illegal.[2] The Committee of the ICTY, however, underlines that there is no indication cluster bombs were deployed in such a way by NATO.

2. Use of Depleted Uranium

Depleted uranium is used on certain types of munition to enhance armour-penetrating effects. Depleted uranium is 0.7 times as radioactive as naturally occurring uranium and has a half-life of 4.5 billion years. Even though the type of radiation emitted by depleted uranium bears little penetrative capabilities to casual human contact, attacks often result in the spreading of fine radioactive dust, which might be inhaled. In addition, it has poisonous characteristics. However, the scientific information about the long-lasting health effects seems to be inconclusive.[3]

There is no specific treaty ban on the use of such projectiles. Due to their poisonous effect, some invoke Art. 23 (a) of the 1907 Hague Convention or state that the use might violate the provision that attacks of an indiscriminate nature shall be avoided (Art. 51 paras. 4 and 5 of Protocol I). The use might also contravene the requirement not to use weapons which have long-term environmental pollution effects. In view of the uncertain state of development of the legal standards governing the use of such weapons, the Committee of the ICTY emphasises that the use of depleted uranium by any adversary to the conflict in the former Yugoslavia since 1991 has not led to any charge by the Prosecutor.

V. THE END OF THE ARMED CONFLICT

The international armed conflict has subsided, since the FRY agreed to KFOR's presence through the agreement annexed to UN Security Council 1244 (1999) and through the Military Technical Agreement of 9 June 1999 (*documents no. 204, 207, 208*). According to Art. 3 of Protocol I, the application of the Conventions and the Protocol ceased on the general close of military operations. However, the temporal scope of applicable rules might reach beyond the actual hostilities, in particular insofar as persons whose final release, repatriation or re-establishment takes place after the cessation of armed conflict (Art. 3 para. B Protocol I). Art. 6 of the Fourth Geneva Convention, for instance, provides that persons whose release, repatriation or re-establishment may take place after such a date shall meanwhile continue to benefit from the convention's protection. Due to these regulations authors hold that the ICTY would be competent to investigate and prosecute crimes committed against persons who continue to be detained at locations in Serbia or Kosovo, such as the ethnic Albanians who were reportedly taken into custody by Serbian forces during the air campaign.[4] Likewise, the question arises whether the ICTY is competent for atrocities committed against minorities after the formal termination of the bombing campaign. Except for the charge of genocide the ICTY Statute requires a connection with the armed conflict in Kosovo, even in the case of a crime against humanity. This might be difficult to evaluate in cases where Albanian civilian perpetrators carry out revenge attacks against the non-Albanian minority. Sofar the ICTY has kept its options open stating that the Prosecutor will continue to examine the factual and legal basis that may link offences to the armed conflict in Kosovo. However, the Prosecutor also underlines that the ICTY has neither the mandate, nor the resources, to function, as the primary agency for all criminal acts committed in Kosovo (*document no. 322*).

E. Conclusion

The conflict in Kosovo highlights old deficiencies and new achievements of public international law. The expected obstruction of the UN Security Council by the veto of a permanent member stresses, once more, the necessity of a reform of the Council. In the UN General Assembly Debate of September 1999 member states focussed on the possibility of such a reform suggesting to endow the UN with independent enforcement capabilities (*document no. 257*). The efficiency of the UN Security Council will be decisive for the question whether the world order will be based on unilateralism or on global governance under a system of collective security. Only the latter option will promote the idea that the UN Charter might serve as a kind of world constitution under which states do not only respect the substantial rules of international law but also the procedural ones. Thus, the question whether humanitarian intervention is or should be legally permitted under international law is also a question in which direction the international legal order will develop.

---

[1] Kröning, 'International Humanitarian Law', 48.
[2] ICTY, Judgment of 8 March 1996, para. 31.
[3] Kröning, 'International Humanitarian Law', 49.
[4] Boelaert, 'The International Criminal Tribunal', 7.

Introduction

The conflict clearly shows that the international community is still unable to deal with secessionist attempts of oppressed minorities. Legal rules as well as policy consideration are still rudimentary. In any case, the Kosovo conflict would serve only as an unfortunate precedent.

The response of international organisations to the human rights violations demonstrates that the international community has moved towards the creation of a strong human rights law, including protection measures which range from observer missions to a system of sanctions. The international community firmly rejected the claim that the Kosovo conflict was an internal affair of the FRY and stressed the limits of the power of governments to adopt repressive and discriminatory measures against parts of their population. All UN human rights bodies monitored the situation in Kosovo closely. However, the conflict also highlighted the shortcomings in the system, especially in regard to implementation. While the human rights bodies clearly named the perpetrator throughout 1998 the international community lacked the determination to enforce these findings when the FRY failed to comply with its international obligations. This lack of determination led, eventually, to the dilemma the international community faced when NATO member states deemed military action to be necessary.

The ICTY's indictment of Milosevic marks an important step forward in regard to the criminal responsibility of heads of states. In this respect it is also important to notice that the Prosecutor did not exclude the possibility from the outset that NATO might have violated norms of international humanitarian law.

Finally, the UN Interim Administration in Kosovo (UNMIK) which combines the efforts of various international organisations proves the UN's capability for post-conflict reconstruction of societies. It also demonstrates that the international community needs permanent instruments in order to turn war-devasted cultures into functioning, democratic societies. The experience in Kosovo already shows that there must be a rapidly deployable reserve of civilian field workers, such as judges, police and administrators.

How the question of the ultimate status of Kosovo will be settled remains yet to be seen.

CHAPTER 1: KOSOVO'S STATUS IN YUGOSLAVIA BEFORE 1999

The 1974 Yugoslav Constitution conferred a status that was a near equivalent of the six republics (Bosnia and Herzegovina, Croatia, Macedonia, Montenegro, Serbia, Slovenia) to the autonomous provinces of Kosovo and Vojvodina *(document no. 1)*. The considerable changes already made by amendments in 1971 were incorporated in the constitution. These changes had created a status for the autonomous provinces equal with the republics in most forms of economic decision-making and even in some areas of foreign policy. The autonomous provinces each had their own central bank and separate police, educational systems, a judiciary, a provincial assembly and representation in the Serbian parliament. The constitution expressly provided for full equality between the republics and autonomous provinces in regard to their participation in the federation, by determining that federal decisions were to be made "according to the principles of agreement among the republics and autonomous provinces." Both provinces also had distinct representation in each federal organ. The federal presidency, as a collective body, was composed of two representatives of each republic and one from each autonomous province. Their leaders thus had separate membership of the rotating collective presidency which took over after the death of Tito. Like all republics, the Kosovo Assembly had the power to veto any amendment to the federal constitution. Moreover, the 1974 constitution added the provinces' right to issue their own constitution. The Yugoslav government, however, did not grant the autonomous provinces the right to secede, which the republics enjoyed. The decision rested on practical political reasons as well as on theoretical ones. The primary fear was that a Kosovo Republic would secede from Yugoslavia in order to unite with Albania. In addition, it was feared that granting the status of a republic to the autonomous provinces could provoke political resentment within Serbia itself, as well as among the Kosovo Serbs.[1] A Communist doctrine developed in the Soviet Union provided the legal foundation: The whole basis of the Yugoslav Federal System rested on the distinction that republics were entities for nations, not for nationalities. A nation was potentially a state-forming unit and therefore kept a right of secession when it formed a republic in a federation. A nationality, on the other hand, was considered as a displaced segment of a nation, the main part of which lived elsewhere. Therefore, it could not be a constituent nation in a federation, and could not create a federal unit of its own. Consequently, the Kosovo Albanians were a nationality, because the nation of Albanians had its own state in Albania.[2]

Serbia's constitution of 1974 granted an equal status to all nations and nationalities in Serbia, establishing that they individually and collectively would enjoy sovereign rights *(document no. 2)*. Kosovo's own constitution stressed that its people had freely organized themselves in the form of a Socialist Autonomous Province on equal basis with the nations and nationalities of Yugoslavia. The Kosovo Assembly had the competence to "directly and exclusively" decide on amendments to the Kosovo constitution, and to approve amendments to the constitution of the Socialist Republic of Serbia *(document no. 3)*.

In 1981, demonstrations and riots by Albanians in Kosovo led to renewed accusations and counteraccusations about Albanian and Serbian nationalism. In Serbia pressure grew to act against the perceived marginalization of Serbs in Kosovo. Complaining of discrimination, of violent attacks upon them going unpunished, and of the domination of political and economic life by the Kosovo Albanian community, Kosovo Serbs had already been migrating from the area in growing numbers since the 1960s. Kosovo Serbs' resentment culminated into protest following the publication of the Memorandum of the Serbian Academy of Arts and Science in September 1986.[3] Milosevic's interest in Kosovo is said to have started during his visit to the province on 24 April 1987. He was met by agitated Serbs, asking for protection from Belgrade against Albanian dominance in Kosovo. Milosevic reassured Kosovo Serbs in his speech to the crowd recorded on camera on that very day *(document no. 7)*.

In 1989, Serbia revoked the province's autonomy. The Serb parliament unanimously approved proposals for amending the Serb constitution. One amendment revoked Kosovo's competence to object to amendments of the Serb Constitution. Only a right of consultation remained *(document no. 4)*. In reaction, the Kosovo Albanian population demonstrated in protest. The Federal State Presidency declared a state of emergency and sent federal armed forces and federal police to Kosovo. On 22 March 1989, the provincial government of Kosovo, which had been set up by Serb political intervention, approved the constitutional amendments. On 23 March 1989, the provincial assembly of Kosovo met under circumstances which remain disputed. Under dubious conditions the Kosovo Assembly passed the constitutional amendments. The Serbian National Assembly adopted the final confirmation of the amendments in Belgrade on 28 March 1989.[4] In Kosovo the decision led to riots which were answered with harsh reactions by the police.

In March 1990, the Serbian Assembly promulgated a series of new measures under the title "Programme for the Realization of Peace and Prosperity in Kosovo" attempting to improve the position of the Kosovo Serbs. The programme created new municipalities for them, concentrated new investment in Serb majority areas and introduced family planning for Albanians. On 26 June 1990, further decrees were made possible by a "Law on the Activities of Organs of the Republic in Exceptional Circumstances". The temporary measures remained permanent. They included the suppression of Albanian language newspapers and the closing of the Kosovo Academy of Arts and Sciences. In addition, the law enabled officials of the Serb republic to administer the affairs of Kosovo directly and to nullify decisions which Kosovar public authorities had taken. These measures included the removal of criminal prosecutions and other judicial functions from the Kosovo courts. On 5 July 1990, Serbia proclaimed a law which formally disbanded the functioning of the Kosovo Assembly and of its Executive Council. In the same year, the Serb authorities dismissed from public service the overwhelming majority of those Albanians, who had any form of state employment in 1990.[5]

On 28 September 1990, Serbia enacted a new constitution *(document no. 5)*. Art. 1 of the 1974 Constitution on the equality of nations and nationalities was abolished, while the Preamble underlined that Serbia was a "democratic State of the Serbian people in

---

[1] Noel Malcolm, *Kosovo - A Short History* (London 1998), pp. 328-329.
[2] Ibid., pp. 327-328.
[3] Ibid., p. 340
[4] Ibid., p. 344.
[5] Ibid., pp. 346/349.

which members of other nations and national minorities will be able to exercise their national rights...". No longer were Kosovo Albanians considered a nationality. Now, they formed a national minority of Serbia. A Statute replaced Kosovo's constitution as the highest legal order of the province. The enactment of this statute was subject to prior approval by the Serbian National Assembly. Eventually according to the new federal constitution of 1992, the Autonomous Provinces were to be considered as "forms of territorial autonomy" *(document no. 6)*.

When the Serb Assembly terminated the work of the Kosovo Assembly in June and July 1990, the elected representatives of Kosovo adopted a declaration of sovereignty in response.[1] On 7 September 1990, the Assembly of Kosovo adopted a new constitution for Kosovo and the Kosovo Albanians issued a formal declaration of independence on 22 September 1991 *(documents no. 9, 10, 11)*. They organized a referendum which reaffirmed this decision. Kosovo Albanian representatives claimed that 87% of eligible voters participated in the referendum and that 99% voted in favour. A year later the Kosovo Albanians privately organized elections, leading to a victory of the Democratic League of Kosovo (LDK) under Ibrahim Rugova.

The Rugova government established a system of parallel administration, whereby, many of the former public sector workers could provide educational, medical and other social services. Albanians organized their own parallel system of schools and clinics, mainly on private premises. The LDK paid employees out of an "income tax" of three percent levied, on a voluntary basis, from Albanians abroad. They arranged teaching for more than 400.000 children. The LDK pursued the basic policy to prevent violent revolt, to internationalise the problem, inviting international political involvement, to deny the legitimacy of the Serbian rule, by boycotting elections and censuses, and by creating the outlines of the state administration of a "Kosovo Republic".[2] However, Rugova's positions were weakened when the 1995 General Framework Agreement for Bosnia and Herzegovina included no provisions for the Kosovo Albanians.

In September 1996, through the mediation of an Italian catholic charity, Rugova and Milosevic negotiated and signed the St' Egidio Educational Agreement under which school and university buildings would be made available to the Albanian parallel education system *(document no. 8)*. However, the Serbian authorities failed to implement the agreement. In 1996/97, began the first signs of genuine terrorist activities, including the shooting of two policemen in Mitrovica. In summer 1997, a spokesman for the "Kosovo Liberation Army" stated openly that his organization was responsible for recent attacks on the Serb authorities.[3] By 1998 the KLA had formed itself into a significant force, challenging the legitimacy of the democratic mandate of the government and engaging in direct military operations.

1.1 AUTONOMY OF KOSOVO

1. The Constitution of the Socialist Federal Republic of Yugoslavia, Extracts, 1974

Basic Principles

The nations of Yugoslavia, proceeding from the right of every nation to self-determination, including the right to secession, on the basis of their will freely expressed in the common struggle of all nations and nationalities in the National Liberation War and Socialist Revolution, and in conformity with their historic aspirations, aware that further consolidation of their brotherhood and unity is in the common interest, have, together with the nationalities with which they live, have united in a federal Republic of free and equal nations and nationalities and founded a socialist federal community of working people - the Socialist Federal Republic of Yugoslavia, in which, in the interest of each nation and nationality separately and of all of them together, they shall realise and ensure;

- socialist social relations based on self-management by working people and the protection of the socialist self-management system;

- national freedom and independence;

- the brotherhood and unity of the nations and nationalities;

- the uniform interests of the working class, and solidarity among workers and all working people;

- possibilities and freedoms for the all-round development of the human personality and for the rapprochement of the nations and nationalities, in conformity with their interests and aspirations on the road to the creation of an ever richer culture and civilisation in a socialist society;

- the unification and adjustment of efforts to develop the economic foundations of a socialist society and the prosperity of the people;

- a system of socio-economic relations and uniform foundations for a political system which will ensure the common interests of the working class and all working people and equality of the nations and nationalities;

- the linking of Yugoslavia's aspirations with the progressive strivings of mankind.

The working people and the nations and nationalities shall exercise their sovereign rights in the Socialist Republics, and in the Socialist Autonomous Provinces in conformity with their constitutional rights, and shall exercise these rights in the Socialist Federal Republic of Yugoslavia when in their common interests it is so specified by the present Constitution.

The working people, nations and nationalities shall make decisions in the Federation according to the principles of agreement among the Republics and Autonomous Provinces, solidarity and reciprocity, equal participation by the Republics and Autonomous Provinces in federal agencies, in line with the present Constitution, and according to the principle of responsibility of the Republics and Autonomous Provinces for their own development and for the development of the socialist community as a whole. [...]

The Socialist Federal Republic of Yugoslavia

Article 1. The Socialist Federal Republic of Yugoslavia is a federal state having the form of a state community of voluntarily united nations and their Socialist Republics, and of the Socialist Autonomous Provinces of Vojvodina and Kosovo, which are constituent parts of the Socialist Republic Serbia, based on the power of an self-management by the working class and all working people; it is at the same time a socialist self-management democratic community of working people and citizens and of nations and nationalities having equal rights.

Article 2. The Socialist Republics are states based on the consists of the Socialist Republic of Croatia, the Socialist Republic of Macedonia, the Socialist Republic of Montenegro, the Socialist Republic of Serbia, the Socialist Autonomous Province of Vojvodina and the Socialist

---
[1] Ibid., p. 346.
[2] OSCE, *Kosovo - As Seen As Told*, Part I, Chapter 1.
[3] Malcolm, *Kosovo*, pp. 353-355.

Article 2. The Socialist Republics are states based on the consists of the Socialist Republic of Croatia, the Socialist Republic of Macedonia, the Socialist Republic of Montenegro, the Socialist Republic of Serbia, the Socialist Autonomous Province of Vojvodina and the Socialist Autonomous Province of Kosovo, which are constituent parts of the Socialist Republic of Slovenia.

Article 3. The Socialist Republics are states based on the sovereignty of the people and the power of self-management by the working class and all working people, and are socialist, self-managing democratic communities of the working people and citizens, and of nations and nationalities having equal rights.

Article 4. The Socialist Autonomous Province are autonomous socialist self-managing democratic socio-political communities based on the power of an self-management by the working class and all working people, in which the working people, nations and nationalities realise their sovereign rights, and when so specified by the Constitution of the Socialist Republic of Serbia in the common interests of the d working people, nations and nationalities of that Republic as a whole, they do so also within the Republic.

Article 5. The territory of the Socialist Federal Republic of Yugoslavia is a single unified whole and consists of the territories of the Socialist Republics.

The territory of a Republic may not be altered without the consent of that Republic, and the territory of an Autonomous province - without the consent of that Autonomous Province.

The frontiers of the Socialist Federal Republic of Yugoslavia may not be altered without the consent of that Autonomous Province.

The frontiers of the Socialist Federal Republic of Yugoslavia may not be altered without the consent of all Republics and Autonomous Provinces.

Boundaries between the Republics may only be altered on the basis of mutual agreement, and if the boundary of an Autonomous province is involved - also on the basis of the latter's agreement. [...]

Article 206. Republican constitutions and the provincial constitutions may not be contrary to the S.F.R.Y. Constitution.

All statutes and other regulations and enactments passed by agencies and organisations of the socio-political communities, and self management enactments of organisations of associated labour and other self-managing organisations and communities, must be in conformity with the S.F.R.Y. Constitution.

Article 207. All regulations and other enactments passed by federal agencies must be in conformity with federal statute.

Republicans and provincial statutes and other regulations and enactments passed by agencies of the socio-political communities, and self-management enactments may not be contrary to federal statute.

If a republican or provincial statute is contrary to federal statute, it will be temporarily applied pending a decision by the constitutional court, and if federal agencies are responsible for their enforcement, the federal statute concerned shall apply.

If an agency which has jurisdiction over individual matters deems that a statute, other regulation or enactment of self-management enactment is not in accord with federal statute, or that it is contrary to federal statute, it shall be bound to institute proceedings before he constitutional court. [...]

Article 245. The nations and nationalities of the Socialist Federal Republic of Yugoslavia shall have equal rights.

Article 246. The languages of the nations and nationalities and their alphabets shall be equal throughout the territory of Yugoslavia. In the Socialist Federal Republic of Yugoslavia the languages of the nations shall be officially used, and the languages of the nationalities shall be used in conformity with the present Constitution and federal statute.

The realisation of the equality of languages and alphabets of the nations and nationalities regarding their official use in areas populated by individual nationalities shall be ensured and the way of and conditions for its realisation regulated by statute, the by-laws of the socio-political communities, and by self-management enactments of a organisations of associated labour and other self-managing organisations and communities.

Article 247. In order to ensure that its right to express its nationality and culture shall be realised, each nationality shall be guaranteed the right freely to use its language and alphabet, to develop its culture and for this purpose to set up organisations and enjoy other constitutionally-established rights. [...]

Article 250. Decisions, documents and individual acts issued by state agencies and authorised organisations in one republic or autonomous province shall be equally valid in other Republics and Autonomous Provinces. [...]

Article 262. The National Bank of Yugoslavia, the National Banks of the Republics and the National Banks of the Autonomous Provinces shall operate deposit accounts of the self-political communities and shall be authorised, on behalf of the socio-political communities and on their account, to perform other banking affairs, if so specified by the constitution.

The National Bank of Yugoslavia shall act as a depository of federal resources, conduct credit and other banking business for the needs of the Yugoslav People's Army and for the needs of national defence, as laid down by the federal statute, and shall carry out other statutorily specified credit and banking operations on account of the Federation.

The National Bank of Yugoslavia, the National Banks of the Republics and the National Banks of the Autonomous Provinces shall not engage in other activities of commercial banks. [...]

Article 263. The status of the National Bank of Yugoslavia and uniform monetary operations of the National Banks of the Republics and Autonomous Provinces shall be regulated by federal statute.

The operations of the National Bank of Yugoslavia concerning the execution of common currency issue, monetary-credit and foreign exchange policy shall be managed by the Board of Governors. In managing these operations the Board of Governors shall make decisions and take measures, and shall be responsible for their implementation.

The Board of Governors shall be composed of the Governor of the National Bank of Yugoslavia, the governors of the National Banks of the Republics and the governors of the National Banks of the Autonomous Provinces. [...]

Article 265. The Republics and Autonomous Provinces shall cooperate in the pursuance of tax policy and shall through compacts adjust the basic principles of tax policy and the tax system whenever it is necessary to ensure the unity and stability of the Yugoslav market.

In order to prevent and eliminate disruptions on the market, federal agencies shall have the right and duty to propose to the Republics and Autonomous Provinces in conformity with mutual compacts to decrease or increase taxes and contributions fixed by the socio-political communities, temporarily to postpone the spending of part of the revenue of the socio-political communities, and to lay down common foundations of the tax policy of the Republics and or Autonomous Provinces. Non-existence of compacts shall not prevent the Republics and Autonomous Provinces from passing regulations and other enactments in the sphere of tax policy and the tax system within the framework of their rights and obligations. [...]

Article 268. In exercising the rights and duties laid down by the present Constitution, federal agencies shall formulate policy and pass federal statutes and other regulations and enactments.

In the sphere regulated by federal statutes, the Republics and Autonomous Provinces may pass statutes within the framework of their rights and duties.

If in areas to be regulated by Federal statute no such statute has been passed, the Republics and/or Autonomous Provinces may pass their own statutes if this is in the interests of the realisation of their rights and duties.

Article 269. Federal statutes and other regulations and enactments shall be promulgated in the Official Gazette of the Socialist Federal Republic of Yugoslavia in authentical texts in the languages of the nations of Yugoslavia specified by the republican constitutions.

Federal statutes and other regulations and enactments shall be promulgated in the Official Gazette of the Socialist Federal Republic of Yugoslavia as authentical texts in the languages of the Albanian and Hungarian nationalities also.

Article 270. Federal statutes and other regulations and enactments shall be binding throughout the entire territory of the Socialist Federal Republic of Yugoslavia, unless their application is restricted by these statutes, regulations or enactments to a narrower territory.

Article 271. International treaties which entail the enactment of new or amendments to existing republican and/or provincial statutes, or which entail special obligations for one or more Republics and/or Autonomous Provinces, shall be concluded in agreement with the competent republican and/or provincial agencies. The procedure for the conclusion of such international treaties shall be regulated by federal statute, in agreement with the republican and provincial assemblies.

In co-operating with agencies and organisations of other states and with international agencies and organisations, the Republics and of Autonomous Provinces shall keep within the established foreign policy of the Socialist Federal Republic of Yugoslavia and international treaties.

In co-operating with appropriate foreign agencies and organisations, international organisations and territorial units of foreign states, Communes, organisations of associated labour and other organisations and communities shall keep within the established foreign policy of the Socialist Federal Republic of Yugoslavia and international treaties.

The principle of the equality of languages of the nations of Yugoslavia, and analogously the principle of the nations and nationalities, shall be applied in international communication.

When international treaties are drawn up in the languages of the signatory countries, the languages of the nations of Yugoslavia shall be equally used.

Article 280. The Socialist Federal Republic of Yugoslavia shall be represented by the federal agencies specified by the present Constitution.

Article 281. The Federation shall through its agencies: [...]

(11) regulate matters concerning settlement of conflicts of law between republicans and/or provincial Autonomous Provinces (conflict rules), and jurisdictional disputes between republican and/or provincial agencies of difference Republics; regulate matters concerning conflicts between domestic laws and legal rules of other countries; [...]

Article 284. The rights and duties of the S.F.R.Y. Assembly shall be exercised by the Federal Chamber and the Chamber of Republics and Provinces in accordance with the provisions of the present Constitution.

The Federal Chamber shall be composed of delegates of self-managing organisations and communities and socio-political organisations in the Republics and Autonomous Provinces.

The Chamber of Republics and Provinces shall be composed of delegations of the Assemblies of the Republics and the Assemblies of the Autonomous Provinces. [...]

Article 291. The Federal Chamber shall be composed of thirty delegates of self-managing organisations and communities and socio-political organisations from each Republic, and of twenty delegates from each Autonomous Province.

The nominating procedure shall be carried out by the Socialist Alliance of the Working People. Candidates for delegates to the Federal Chamber shall be proposed by delegations of basic self-managing organisations and communities from among members of the delegations of these organisations and communities, and also by socio s political communities, within the framework of the Socialist Alliance of the Working People, from among members of their delegations.

The list of candidates for delegates to the Federal Chamber shall be drawn up by the nominating conference of the Socialist Alliance of the Working People of the Republics and Autonomous Provinces.

Delegates to the Federal Chamber shall be elected, on the basis of a list of candidates, by the Commune Assemblies on the territories of the Republics and the Autonomous Provinces, by secret ballot.

The election and recall of delegates to the Federal Chamber shall be regulated by federal statute.

The nominating procedure for the election of delegates of the Federal Chamber to posts of delegates whose tenure has ended before the expiry of their terms shall be regulated by federal statute.

Article 292. The Chamber of Republics and Provinces shall be composed of twelve delegates of each Republican Assembly and eight delegates of each Provincial Assembly.

The delegations to the Chamber of Republics and Provinces shall be elected and recalled by secret ballot by all Chambers of the Assemblies of the respective Republics and of the Assemblies of the respective Autonomous Provinces sitting in joint session.

Delegates elected to the Chamber of Republics and Provinces shall retain their tenure in the assemblies to which they have been elected.

Article 298. The right to introduce bills and other draft enactments falling within the province of work of the Chamber of Republics and Provinces which must be adopted in agreement with the Assemblies of the Republics and the Assemblies of the Autonomous Provinces shall be vested with every delegation to, and working body of, the Chamber, the Assemblies of the Republics and the Assemblies of the Autonomous Provinces, and in the Federal Executive council. [...]

Article 313. The S.F.R.Y. Presidency shall represent the Socialist Federal Republic of Yugoslavia at home and abroad, and shall have other rights and duties as laid down by the present Constitution.

Within the framework of its rights and duties, and in order to realise the equality of the nations and nationalities, the S.F.R.Y. Presidency shall work to achieve adjustment of the common interests of the Republics and Autonomous Provinces, in conformity with their responsibility concerning the realisation of federal rights and duties.

The S.F.R.Y. Presidency is the supreme body in charge of the administration and command of the Armed Forces of the Socialist Federal Republic of Yugoslavia in war and peace.

The S.F.R.Y. Presidency shall consider foreign policy and the safeguard of the order established by the present Constitution (state security), and shall take stands to provide initiative for adopting measures and adjusting the activities of competent agencies in the execution of established policy in these spheres. [...]

Article 321. The S.F.R.Y. Presidency shall be composed of a member from each Republic and Autonomous Province, elected by secret ballot by the Assemblies of the Republics and the Assemblies of the Autonomous Provinces, respectively, at a joint session of all Chambers of the Assemblies, and of the President of the League of Communities of Yugoslavia by virtue of his office. [...]

The Constitutional Court of Yugoslavia

Article 375. The Constitutional Court of Yugoslavia shall:

(I) decide on the conformity of statutes to the Constitution of the Socialist Federal Republic of Yugoslavia;

(2) decide whether or not a republican or provincial statute is contrary to federal statute;

(3) decide disputes involving rights and duties between the Federation and the Republics and/or Autonomous Provinces, between the Republics, between the Republics and the Autonomous Provinces, and between other socio-political communities from the territories of different Republics, if no jurisdiction of another court has been provided by statute for the settlement of such disputes; [...]

Article 396. The federal chamber will decide about the changes of the federal constitution with the consent of the assemblies of all republics and autonomous provinces. [...]

Article 398. Amendments to the S.F.R.Y. Constitution shall be decided upon by the Federal Chamber of the S.F.R.Y. Assembly, in agreement with the Assemblies of all Republics and Autonomous Provinces; if an amendment to the S.F.R.Y. Constitution only concerns the status of the Republics and mutual relations between the Federation and the Republics, it shall be decided upon by the Federal Chamber of the S.F.R.Y. Assembly in agreement with the Assemblies of all Republics.

Article 399. A motion to initiate proceedings for amending the S.F.R.Y. Constitution may be introduced by at least thirty delegates to the Federal Chamber, the S.F.R.Y. Presidency, the Assembly of a Republic, the Assembly of an Autonomous Province, and the Federal Executive Council.

Article 400. A motion to initiate proceedings for amending the S.F.R.Y. Constitution shall be decided upon by the Federal Chamber of the S.F.R.Y. Assembly.

The Federal Chamber may decide to initiate proceedings for amending the S.F.R.Y. Constitution if the motion for the initiation of amendment proceedings has been agreed upon by the Assemblies of all Republics and Autonomous Provinces and the Assemblies of all Republics respectively.

Article 401. Draft amendments to the S.F.R.Y. Constitution shall be drawn up by the Federal Chamber of the S.F.R.Y. Assembly, which shall refer them to the Assemblies of all Republics and Autonomous Provinces for opinion, and shall submit them to public discussion.

Draft amendments to the S.F.R.Y. Constitution shall be debated upon by the Assemblies of all Republics and Autonomous Provinces, which shall give their opinions thereon.

When the opinions of the Assemblies of all Republics and Autonomous Provinces have been obtained and public discussion conducted, the Federal Chamber shall draw up a motion for the amendment of the S.F.R.Y. Constitution and take a vote thereon.

An amendment to the S.F.R.Y. Constitution shall be deemed passed in the Federal Chamber if it has received a two-thirds majority vote from all delegates to the Chamber.

If an amendment to the S.F.R.Y. Constitution has not been adopted in the Federal Chamber, a motion for the same amendment to the S.F.R.Y. Constitution may not be introduced again before the expiry of one year from the day the motion was rejected.

Article 402. An amendment to the S.F.R.Y. Constitution shall be deemed passed when the text adopted by the Federal Chamber of the S.F.R.Y. Assembly has agreed to by the Assemblies of all Republics and Autonomous Provinces and the Assemblies of all Republics respectively.

If the Assembly of one or more Republics or the Assembly of either of the Autonomous Provinces has not agreed with the text of the motion for the amendment of the S.F.R.Y. Constitution passed by the Federal Chamber, the motion for the amendment of the S.F.R.Y. Constitution on which no agreement has been reached may not be placed on the agenda before the expiry of one year from the day the Federal Chamber ruled that no agreement had been reached. [...]

Amendment IV. 1. The SFRY Presidium shall consist of one member from each republic and autonomous province, elected by the assembly of the respective republic or autonomous province by secret ballot at a joint session of all chambers of the assembly, and of the president of the organ of the League of Communists of Yugoslavia specified by the By-Laws of the League of Communists of Yugoslavia, by virtue of his office. [...]

2. Constitution of the Socialist Republic of Serbia, Extracts, 1974

INTRODUCTORY PART: BASIC PRINCIPLES

The Serb nation, together with other nations and nationalities of Yugoslavia, headed by the Communist Party of Yugoslavia in the struggle during the National Liberation War and socialist revolution, overthrew the old class order based on exploitation and national subjugation. [...]

Paragraph 2. Proceeding from the right of every nation to self-determination, including the right of secession, on the basis of the s common struggle and will freely expressed in the National Liberation War and socialist revolution, and in conformity with their historic aspirations, aware that the further consolidation of brotherhood and unity is in the common interest of all nations and nationalities, the Serb nation has, together with nationalities with which it lives, united with other Yugoslav nations in a federal republic of free and equal nations and founded a socialist federal community of working people - the Socialist Federal Republic of Yugoslavia, in which, in the interests of each nation and nationality separately and all together, it shall realise and ensure:

- national freedom and independence
- the brotherhood and unity of the nations and nationalities;
- the uniform interest of the working class and solidarity among worker and all working people;
- possibilities and freedoms for the all-round development of the human personality and for the rapprochement of the nations and nationalities, in conformity with their interests and aspirations on the road to the creation of an ever-richer culture and civilisation in a socialist society; [...]

Paragraph 3. The working people and the nations and nationalities of Serbia shall exercise their sovereign rights in the Socialist Republic of Serbia and in the Socialist Autonomous Provinces in conformity with their constitutional rights, and in the S.F.R.Y. when in their common interest it is so specified by the Constitution of the Socialist Federal Republic of Yugoslavia.

Paragraph 4. The Socialist Republic of Serbia is a self-managing socialist democratic socio-political community of working people and citizens and of equal nations and nationalities.

As the state of the Serb nation, members of other nations of Yugoslavia and nationalities within Serbia, the Socialist Republic of Serbia is based on the sovereignty of the people and by the power of and self-management by the working class and all working people. [...]

Paragraph 6. The Socialist Republic of Serbia comprises the Socialist Autonomous Province of Vojvodina and the Socialist Autonomous Province of Kosovo, which originated in the common struggle of nations and nationalities of Yugoslavia in the National Liberation War and socialist revolution and united, on the basis of the freely expressed will of the population, nations and nationalities of the provinces and Serbia, in the Socialist Republic of Serbia within the Socialist Federal Republic of Yugoslavia.

Paragraph 7. The provinces are autonomous socialist self-managing democratic socio-political communities with a special ethnic composition and other specificities, in which working people and citizens, nations and nationalities exercise their sovereign rights, exercising them also in the Republic as a whole when in the common interest of working people and citizens, nations and nationalities of the Republic it is so specified by the Constitution of the Socialist Republic of Serbia.

Paragraph 8. The working people, nations and nationalities of the Socialist Republic of Serbia shall make decisions on the federal level according to the principles of agreement among the Republics and Autonomous Provinces, solidarity and reciprocity, equal participation by the Republics and Autonomous Provinces in federal agencies consistent with the Constitution of the Socialist Federal Republic of Yugoslavia and the Constitution of the Socialist Republic of Serbia, and according to the principle of responsibility for their own development and for the development of the socialist community as a whole.

The Socialist Republic of Serbia

Article 1. The Socialist Republic of Serbia is a socialist democratic state based on the power of and self-management by the working class and all working people, and a socialist self-managing democratic community of working people and citizens, and equal nations and nationalities, based on the self-management by the working people in associated labour and in other forms of self-management association and free social organisation.

The Socialist Republic of Serbia is a state of the Serb nation and parts of other nations and nationalities, which live and exercise their sovereign rights in it.

The Socialist Autonomous Province of Vojvodina and the Socialist Autonomous Province of Kosovo are parts of the Socialist Republic of Serbia.

The Socialist Republic of Serbia is a part of the Socialist Federal Republic of Yugoslavia.

Article 2. Working people and citizens, nations and nationalities of Serbia shall exercise their sovereign rights in the Socialist Republic of Serbia and in the Socialist Autonomous Provinces consistent with their constitutional rights, and in the Socialist Federal Republic of Yugoslavia when it is so specified by the Constitution of the S.F.R.Y. in the common interest of working people, nations and nationalities of Yugoslavia. [...]

Article 145. In the Socialist Republic of Serbia the nations and nationalities shall be equal.

Every nationality shall be guaranteed the freedom to use its language and alphabet, develop its culture and establish organisations, and enjoy other constitutional rights in the exercise of its right to express its nationality and culture.

Article 146. In the Socialist Republic of Serbia the languages of nations and nationalities and their alphabets shall be equal.

Members of nationalities shall, in conformity with the Constitution and statute, have the right to use their language and alphabet in the exercise of their rights and duties and in proceedings before state agencies and organisations exercising public powers.

The equality of languages and alphabets of nations and nationalities in official use in the areas where individual nationalities live, and the mode of and conditions for the exercise of this equality shall be ensured by law and statutes of the socio-political community and self-management enactments of organisations of associated labour and other self-managing organisations and communities.

Republican law shall lay down the mode of the exercise of the right of members of nationalities to use their language and alphabet in republican agencies and organisations exercising public powers.

Article 147. Members of other nations and nationalities shall have the right to instruction in their language in schools and other institutions of learning in conformity with law and the municipal statute.

In the areas where members of the Serb or other nations of Yugoslavia live together, schools or classes with bilingual instruction may be established. [...]

Article 177. The freedoms and rights of man and citizen, spelled out by the Constitution, shall be realised through solidarity among people and through the fulfillment of duties and responsibilities of everyone towards all and all towards everyone.

The freedoms and rights of man and citizen shall only be restricted by the equal freedoms and rights of others and by the constitutionally specified interests of the socialist community.

Each shall be bound to respect the freedoms and rights of others and shall be responsible therefor.

Article 178. Citizens shall be equal in their rights and duties regardless of nationality, race, sex, language, religion, education, or social status. All shall be equal before the law. [...]

Article 240. The state agencies and organisations exercising public powers shall conduct proceedings in the Serbo-Croatian language.

The state agencies and organisations exercising public powers shall also conduct proceedings in the language of the nationality specified by the municipal statute or the enactment of the organisation of associated labour on other self-managing organisation or community.

The languages in which the proceedings shall be conducted in state agencies and organisations in the territory of the Autonomous Provinces shall be specified by the provincial constitutions. [...]

THE SOCIALIST AUTONOMOUS PROVINCE

Article 291. The Socialist Autonomous Provinces are autonomous, socialist, self-managing democratic socio-political communities based on the power of and self-management by the working class and all working people, in which the working people and the citizens, nations and nationalities exercise their sovereign rights, with the exception of those, which are, in the common interest of the working people, citizens, nations and nationalities of the Republic as a whole, exercised in the Republic.

Article 292. The territory of an autonomous province consists of the territories of the present municipalities as specified by statute.

The territory of an autonomous province may not be altered without the consent of the provincial assembly.

Article 293. In the exercise of their rights and duties the Autonomous Provinces shall regulate autonomously the social relations by statute and other regulations, with the exception of the relations which are by the present Constitution and on the basis thereof regulated uniformly for the whole territory of the Republic by republican statute.

Within the framework of the relations regulated uniformly for the whole territory of the Republic by republican statute, the Autonomous Provinces may regulate matters not regulated by Republican statute.

If a republican law on relations regulated uniformly for the whole territory of the Republic has not been adopted, the Autonomous Provinces may adopt their laws if this is of interest for the exercise of their rights and duties. After the adoption of a republican law on the regulation of these relations, the provisions of the provincial law relative to the matters regulated by the republican law shall be invalidated, unless specified otherwise by this law.

Article 294. Agencies in the Autonomous Provinces shall be responsible for the enforcement and implementation of republican laws and other republican regulations, applied throughout the territory of the Republic, in the territory of the Province.

The regulations for the enforcement of the republican laws applied throughout the territory of the republic, and other acts and measures for the enforcement and implementation of these laws when the Executive Council of the Assembly of the SR Serbia is authorised to pass such acts, shall be adopted by the Executive Council of the Socialist Autonomous Province for the territory of the autonomous province unless otherwise specified by statute.

Provincial administrative agencies shall adopt regulations and other acts for the enforcement and implementation of republican laws and other republican regulations applicable throughout the territory of the Republic when the republican administrative agencies are responsible for the adoption of these acts unless otherwise specified by statute.

The regulations for the enforcement and implementation of laws adopted by consent by the Assembly of the Socialist Republic of Serbia and the Assembly of the Socialist Autonomous Province shall be adopted by provincial agencies.

Article 295. Consistent with the responsibility of the agencies in the Autonomous Provinces for the enforcement and application of republican laws and other republican acts valid throughout the territory of the Republic, the relations between republican agencies and agencies in the Autonomous Provinces bearing on the enforcement of these laws and other regulations shall be based on mutual co-operation, information and agreement, and on the rights and duties laid down by the present Constitution and republican statute.

If agencies in the Autonomous Provinces fail to enforce republican laws or other republican regulations, for the enforcement and application of which they are responsible, the Executive Council of the Assembly of the Socialist Republic of Serbia shall notify the competent agency of the Autonomous Province and take other measures within the framework of its rights and duties. [...]

Article 415. If proceedings have been initiated for the assessment of constitutionality and legality of a regulation or other enactment of an agency of the socio-political community or a self-management enactment, found to be in simultaneous contravention with the Constitution of the Socialist Republic of Serbia or republican law of the provincial constitution or provincial law, the constitutionality and legality shall be assessed by the Constitutional Court of the Province, which shall only assess the conformity of this regulation of other enactment with the provincial constitution or provincial law.

If the Constitutional Court of the Province decides that a regulation or other enactment is in conformity with the provincial Constitution or provincial law, it shall submit the case to the Constitutional Court of Serbia, which shall assess the conformity of the regulation or other enactment with the Constitution of the Socialist Republic of Serbia and republican statute. [...]

Article 423. The uniform implementation of the republican laws by supreme and higher courts in the Republic and settlement of the conflicts of competence between courts in the territory of the Supreme Courts of the Autonomous Provinces and the Supreme Court of Serbia shall be ensured in the Republic.

A special chamber consisting of an equal number of judges of the Supreme Court of Serbia and the Supreme Court of the Autonomous Provinces shall be established at the Supreme Court of Serbia for the discharge of these matters. [...]

Article 427. The Assembly of the SR of Serbia decides about the changes in the constitution of the SR of Serbia. If the change of the constitution of the SR of Serbia is related to questions of interest for the republic as a whole, the Assembly of the SR of Serbia will decide the question with the consent of the Assemblies of the autonomous provinces.

3. Constitution of the Socialist Autonomous Province of Kosovo, Extracts, 1974

INTRODUCTORY PART: BASIC PRINCIPLES

I. United in their past equally by common life and aspirations for freedom and social progress, the Albanians, Montenegrins, Muslims, Serbs, Turks and members of other nations and nationalities of Yugoslavia in the National Liberation War and socialist revolution, headed by the working class and the Communist Party of Yugoslavia, overthrew the old class system based on exploitation, political subjugation and national inequality, have found themselves free, equal and fraternised for the first time in the Socialist Autonomous Province of Kosovo, which has become the political and social form of their close association and mutual equality and their equality with the nations and nationalities of Yugoslavia.

The Socialist Autonomous province of Kosovo emerged from the common struggle of the nations and nationalities in the National Liberation War and socialist revolution of Yugoslavia and, proceeding from the freely expressed will of the population - the nations and nationalities of Kosovo and the freely expressed will of the people of Serbia, has associated itself with the Socialist Republic of Serbia within the framework of the Socialist Federal Republic of Yugoslavia. [...]

Paragraph 3. The working people and the nations and nationalities of Kosovo shall exercise their sovereign rights in the Socialist Autonomous Province of Kosovo and in the Republic when in the common interest of the working people, nations and nationalities of the Republic as a whole it is so specified by the Constitution of the Socialist Republic of Serbia, and in the Socialist Federal Republic of Yugoslavia when in the common interest it is so specified by the Constitution of the Socialist Federal Republic of Yugoslavia.

Paragraph 4. In the exercise of their common interests the working people, nations and nationalities of Kosovo shall make decisions on the federal level according to the principles of agreement among the Republics and Autonomous Provinces, solidarity and reciprocity, equal participation by the Republics and Autonomous Provinces in federal agencies, consistent with the Constitution of the S.F.R.Y. and the Constitution of the S.A.P. Kosovo, and according to the principle of responsibility of the Republics and Autonomous provinces for their own development and the development of the Yugoslav socialist community as a whole. [...]

GENERAL PROVISIONS

Article 1. The Socialist Autonomous Province of Kosovo is an autonomous, socialist, democratic socio-political and self-managing community of working people and citizens, equal Albanians, Montenegrins, Muslims, Serbs, Turks, and members of other nations and nationalities and ethnic groups, based on the power of and self-management by the working class and all working people. The Socialist Autonomous province of Kosovo is a part of the Socialist Republic of Serbia and the Socialist Federal Republic of Yugoslavia.

Article 2. The working people and citizens, nations and nationalities of Kosovo shall exercise their sovereign rights in the SAP Kosovo and in the Republic when in the common interest of the working people, nations and nationalities in the Republic as a whole it is so specified by the Constitution of the SR Serbia, and in the S.F.R.Y. when in their common interest it is so specified by the Constitution of the S.F.R.Y.

Article 3. The territory of the Socialist Autonomous Province of a Kosovo consists of the territory of the present municipalities.

The territory of the Socialist Autonomous Province of Kosovo may not be altered without the consent of the Provincial Assembly.

Article 4. The nations and nationalities in the Socialist Autonomous Province of Kosovo shall be equal in their rights and duties.

To ensure the equality of the nations and nationalities, their right to the free development and expression of national specificities, language, culture, history and other attributes shall be guaranteed.

Article 5. In the Socialist Autonomous Province of Kosovo the equality of the Albanian, Serbo-Croatian and Turkish languages and their alphabets shall be ensured.

The implementation of this principle shall be regulated and ensured by the present Constitution and by provincial statute.

Article 6. Members of all nations and nationalities in the Socialist Autonomous Province of Kosovo shall have the right to use their national flag.

The conditions and manner of the use of the national flag shall be regulated by statute. [...]

THE FREEDOMS, RIGHTS AND DUTIES OF MAN AND CITIZEN

Article 187. Citizens shall be guaranteed the freedom to express their affiliation with a nation or nationality, the freedom to express their national culture and the freedom to use their language and alphabet.

No citizen shall be obliged to state to which nation or nationality he belongs nor to opt for any one nation or nationality.

Citizens shall be guaranteed the freedom to express their affiliation with an ethnic group, the freedom to develop their culture and the freedom to use their language and alphabet.

Propagating or practicing national inequality and any incitement of national, racial or religious hatred and intolerance shall be unconstitutional and punishable. [...]

THE EQUALITY OF LANGUAGES AND ALPHABETS

Article 217. The Albanian and Serbo-Croatian languages and their alphabets shall be equally used in the Socialist Autonomous Province of Kosovo.

The Turkish language and alphabet shall be equally used in the territories where the Turks also live.

Agencies, institutions, work and other organisations in the Province shall be bound to comply in their work with the principle of equality of the languages and alphabets of the nations and nationalities in the Socialist Autonomous Province of Kosovo.

Article 218. In elementary, secondary, high and higher schools of learning, and in their classes conditions shall be ensured for instruction in mother language, that is the Albanian Serbo-Croatian and Turkish languages, in conformity with statute.

Members of other nations and nationalities of Yugoslavia shall have the right to instruction in their languages, in conformity with provincial statute. [...]

Article 292. The National Bank of Kosovo is an establishment of the integral monetary system. The National Bank of Kosovo shall, together with the National Bank of Yugoslavia and the National Banks of the Republics and the Province of Vojvodina, pursue the common policy of issue.

The national Bank of Kosovo, consistent with the Constitution and statue and within the framework of the common policy of issue, shall spell out the conditions and mode of utilisation of monetary resources in the Province and take other measures necessary to implement the credit policy of the Province. [...]

ORGANS OF THE S.A.P. KOSOVO, THE ASSEMBLY OF THE S.A.P. KOSOVO

1. Status and Competence

Article 300. The Assembly of the Socialist Autonomous Province of Kosovo is a body of social self-management and the supreme organ of power within the framework of provincial rights and duties.

The Assembly shall exercise the duties within its competence and on the basis of and within the framework of the Constitution and statute.

Article 301. As the principal subject of the rights and duties of the Province, the Assembly shall directly and exclusively:

1. decide on amendments to the Constitution of the S.A.P. Kosovo and approve the amendments to the Constitution of the S.F.R.Y. and the Constitution of the SR Serbia;

2. lay down the policy and decide on other basic issues of importance for the political, economic, social and cultural life, national defence and social development of the Province;

3. adopt provincial laws and provide authentic interpretation of provincial laws;

4. adopt the social plan, budget and the annual balance sheet of the Province;

5. adopt the regional plan and the plan of the spatial development of the Province;

6. discuss issues of the foreign policy and international relations; consent to the conclusion of international treaties in cases specified by the Constitution of the S.F.R.Y.; ratify agreements concluded by the Province with agencies and organisations of foreign states and international agencies and organisations, within the framework of the specified foreign policy of the S.F.R.Y.; [...]

18. consent to the alteration of the territory of the S.A.P. Kosovo;

19. elect and relieve of office the delegation of the Assembly of the S.A.P. Kosovo to the Chamber of Republics and Provinces of the Assembly of the S.F.R.Y.;

20. elect and relieve of office the member of the Presidency of the S.F.R.Y. from the S.A.P. Kosovo

21. elect and relieve of office the members of the Presidency of the S.A.P. Kosovo [...]

THE PRESIDENCY OF THE S.A.P. KOSOVO

Article 339. The Presidency of the S.A.P. Kosovo shall represent the S.A.P. Kosovo and shall exercise other rights and duties as laid down by the Constitution. [...]

THE EXECUTIVE COUNCIL OF THE S.A.P. KOSOVO

Article 349. The Executive Council shall be the executive body of the S.A.P. Kosovo. The Executive Council shall exercise its rights and duties on the basis of and within the framework of the present Constitution and statute. [...]

THE PROVINICAL ADMINISTRATION

Article 362. Provincial secretariats and other provincial administrative agencies shall be established to perform administrative duties within the framework of the rights and duties of the Province. [...]

THE CONSTITUTIONAL COURT OF KOSOVO

Article 372. The Constitutional Court of Kosovo shall:

1. decide on the conformity of provincial statues to the Constitution of the S.A.P. Kosovo;

2. decide on the conformity of municipal statues to the Constitution of the S.A.P. Kosovo and provincial statutes; [...]

THE SUPREME COURT OF KOSOVO, THE OFFICE OF PROVINCIAL PUBLIC PROSECUTOR, THE OFFICE OF PROVINCIAL SOCIAL ATTORNEY OF SELF-MANAGEMENT

Article 390. The Supreme Court of Kosovo shall:

1. decide on appeals against judgments and other rulings of regular courts, within the framework of its competence as laid down by statute;

2. decide in first instance when so specified by statute;

3. decide on extraordinary legal remedies against valid sentences of regular courts in conformity with statute; [...]

Article 391. The functions of the Office of Public Prosecutor shall be discharged by the Provincial Public Prosecutor within the framework of the rights and duties of the Province.

Article 393. The provincial Social Attorney of Self-Management within the framework of the rights and duties of the Province shall discharge the function of the social attorney of self-management.

The provincial Social Attorney of Self-Management shall be designated and relieved of office by the Assembly of the S.A.P. Kosovo.

4. 1989 Amendments of the Serbian Constitution[1]

Amendment XXCI: 3. Members of the nations and nationalities shall have the right to instruction in their language in schools and other educational institutions in conformity with the Constitution and statute. Item 3 replaces Article 147, paragraph 1 of the Constitution of the SR Serbia.

Amendment XXVII: In the official and public use in the SR Serbia shall be the Serbo-Croatian language and its alphabets - Cyrillic and Latin. In the SR Serbia, in the territories inhabited by individual nationalities, the Serbo-Croatian language and its alphabets and the languages of these nationalities and their alphabets shall be in equal official and public use consistent with the Constitution and statute. The official and public use of the Cyrillic alphabet shall be prescribed by republican statute. State agencies and organisations exercising public powers in the SR Serbia shall use the Cyrillic alphabet unless specified otherwise by republican statute in individual cases. The provincial Constitutions shall specify, consistent with the present Constitution that the languages of nationalities shall be in equal official and public use in the territories of the Autonomous Provinces. The Autonomous Provinces shall ensure the equality of the languages and alphabets of the nationalities and the Serbo-Croatian language and its alphabets. This amendment supplements Article 146 and replaces Article 240, paragraphs 1-3 of the Constitution of the SR Serbia.

Amendment XLVII: The Assembly of the SR of Serbia decides about changes of the Constitution. [...] The Assembly of Serbia, before deciding upon a proposal to adopt changes in the Constitution of Serbia, presents the proposal for consideration *to the assemblies of the autonomous provinces, taking into account the opinion of the assemblies of the autonomous provinces, and takes decisions upon these opinions.*

---

[1] Official Gazette of the SR Serbia, No. 11/89

5. The Constitution of the Socialist Republic of Serbia, 28 September 1990

[...]

Mindful of the centuries-long struggle of the Serbian people for freedom, their freedom-loving, democratic and nation-building traditions, and the historical development and life in common of all the peoples and national minorities in Serbia;

Determined to create a democratic State of the Serbian people in which members of other nations and national minorities will be able to exercise their national rights, based upon observance of the freedoms and rights of man and citizen, sovereignty vested in all citizens, the rule of law, social justice and equal opportunities for the advancement of the individual and society;

The citizens of Serbia have adopted the following:

The Constitution of the Republic of Serbia[1]

SECTION I: BASIC PROVISIONS

[...]

Article 4. The territory of the Republic of Serbia is a single whole, no part of which may be alienated.

Any change in the boundaries of the Republic of Serbia shall be decided upon by the citizens in a referendum. [...]

Article 6. The Republic of Serbia includes the Autonomous Province of Vojvodina and the Autonomous Province of Kosovo and Metohia, these being the forms of territorial autonomy. [...]

Article 8. In the Republic of Serbia the Serbo-Croatian language and the Cyrillic alphabet shall be officially used, while the Latinic alphabet shall be officially used in the manner established by law.

In the regions of the Republic of Serbia inhabited by national minorities, their own languages and alphabets shall be officially used as well, in the manner established by law. [...]

SECTION VI: TERRITORIAL ORGANISATION

1. The Autonomous Province of Voivodina and the Autonomous Province of Kosovo and Metohia

Article 108. The autonomous provinces have been formed in accordance with the particular national, historical, cultural, and other characteristics of their areas.

Citizens within the autonomous province shall autonomously realize the rights and fulfill the duties established by the Constitution and law.

The territory of an autonomous province shall be determined by law

Article 109. The autonomous province shall, through its own agencies:

1. enact the program of economic, scientific, technological, demographic, regional and social development, development of agriculture and rural areas, in accordance with the development plan of the Republic of Serbia, and shall lay down measures for their implementation; 2. adopt a budget and annual balance sheet; 3. enact decisions and general enactments in accordance with the Constitution and law, to regulate matters affecting the citizens in the autonomous province in the areas of: culture; education; official use of the language and alphabet of the national minority; public information; health and social welfare; child welfare; protection and advancement of environment; urban and country planning; and in other areas established by law; 4. enforce laws, other regulations and general enactments of the Republic of Serbia, whose enforcement has been entrusted to the agencies of the autonomous province, and pass regulations necessary for their enforcement if so proved by the law; see to the execution of provincial decisions and general enactments; 5. establish agencies, organisations and services of the autonomous province, and regulate their organisation and work; 6. attend to other business laid down under the Constitution and law, as well as by the statute of the autonomous province.

The Republic of Serbia may entrust by a law an autonomous province with the performance of specific affairs within its own competencies and transfer to it the necessary funds for this purpose.

The autonomous province shall collect revenues as laid down by, law.

Article 110. The statute is the highest legal act of the autonomous province which, on the ground of the Constitution, shall lay down the competencies of the autonomous province, election, organisation and work of its agencies, and other questions pertaining to the autonomous province.

The statute of the autonomous province shall be enacted by its assembly, subject to prior approval of the National Assembly.

Deputies in the assembly of an autonomous province shall not be held responsible for an opinion expressed or for casting a vote in the assembly of the autonomous province. The same immunity shall be enjoyed by the members of the executive council.

Article 111. The agencies of the autonomous province shall be its assembly, executive council, and agencies of administration.

The assembly of an autonomous province shall be composed of deputies elected in direct election by secret ballot.

Article 112. If an agency of an autonomous province, despite a warning of the corresponding republic agency, fails to execute a decision or a general enactment of the autonomous province, the republic agency may provide for its direct execution. [...]

6. The Constitution of the Federal Republic of Yugoslavia, 27 April 1992

Mindful of the freedom-loving, democratic and nation-building traditions, historical ties and shared interests of the state of Serbia and the state of Montenegro.

Arising from the unbroken continuity of Yugoslavia and voluntary association between Serbia and Montenegro.

The Federal Chamber of the Assembly of the Socialist Federal Republic of Yugoslavia, following upon the proposals and consent of the National Assembly of the Republic of Serbia and the Assembly of the Republic of Montenegro.

Hereby adopts and promulgates:

The Constitution of the Federal Republic of Yugoslavia

SECTION I: BASIC PROVISIONS

Article 1. The Federal Republic of Yugoslavia shall be a sovereign federal state, founded on the equality of citizens and the equality of its member republics.

Article 2. The Federal Republic of Yugoslavia shall be composed of the Republic of Serbia and the Republic of Montenegro.

The Federal Republic of Yugoslavia may be joined by other member republics, in accordance with the present Constitution.

Article 3. The territory of the Federal Republic of Yugoslavia shall be a single entity comprising the territories of the member republics.

The frontiers of the Federal Republic of Yugoslavia shall be inviolable.

The boundaries between member republics may be changed only subject to their agreement, in accordance with the constitutions of the member republics. [...]

Article 8. In the Federal Republic of Yugoslavia, power shall be vested in the citizens.

Citizens shall exercise power directly and through freely elected representatives.

Article 9. The Federal Republic of Yugoslavia shall be founded on the rule of law.

Laws must be in conformity with the Constitution.

Executive and judicial powers shall be subject to law.

---

[1] The text of the Constitution of the Republic of Serbia is published in the "Sluzbeni glasnik Republike Srbije", number 1/1990

The rights and freedoms of man and the citizen shall be restricted only by the equal rights and freedoms of others and in instances provided for in the present Constitution.

Article 10. The Federal Republic of Yugoslavia shall recognize and guarantee the rights and freedoms of man and the citizen recognized under international law.

Article 11. The Federal Republic of Yugoslavia shall recognize and guarantee the rights of national minorities to preserve, foster and express their ethnic, cultural, linguistic and other peculiarities, as well as to use their national symbols, in accordance with international law. [...]

Article 15. In the Federal Republic of Yugoslavia, the Serbian language in its ekavian and ijekavian dialects and the Cyrillic script shall be official, while the Latin script shall be in official use as provided for by the Constitution and law.

In regions of the Federal Republic of Yugoslavia inhabited by national minorities, the languages and scripts of these minorities shall also be in official use in the manner prescribed by law.

Article 16. The Federal Republic of Yugoslavia shall fulfill in good faith the obligations contained in international treaties to which it is a contracting party.

International treaties which have been ratified and promulgated in conformity with the present Constitution and generally accepted rules of international law shall be a constituent part of the internal legal order.

Article 17. The Federal Republic of Yugoslavia shall confer Yugoslav citizenship on its inhabitants.

A Yugoslav citizen shall be simultaneously a citizen of one of its member republics.

A Yugoslav citizen may not be deprived of his citizenship, deported from the country, or extradited to another state.

A Yugoslav citizen abroad shall enjoy the protection of the Federal Republic of Yugoslavia.

Yugoslav citizenship shall be regulated by federal law. [...]

SECTION VI: CONSTITUTIONALITY AND LEGALITY

Article 115. The constitutions of the member republics, federal statutes, the legislation of member republics and all other laws and general enactments must be in conformity with the Constitution of the Federal Republic of Yugoslavia.

Statutes, other laws and general enactments in a member republic must be in conformity with federal law.

Regulations and other general enactments adopted by federal agencies must be in conformity with federal law. [...]

7. Speech by Slobodan Milosevic at the Central Celebration Marking the 600th Anniversary of the Battle of Kosovo, Gazimestan, 28 June 1989

By the force of social circumstances this great 600th anniversary of the Battle of Kosovo is taking place in a year in which Serbia, after many years, after many decades, has regained its state, national, and spiritual integrity. Therefore, it is not difficult for us to answer today the old question: how are we going to face Milos. Through the play of history and life, it seems as if Serbia has, precisely in this year, in 1989, regained its state and its dignity and thus has celebrated an event of the distant past which has a great historical and symbolic significance for its future.

Today, it is difficult to say what is the historical truth about the Battle of Kosovo and what is legend. Today this is no longer important. Oppressed by pain and filled with hope, the people used to remember and to forget, as, after all, all people in the world do, and it was ashamed of treachery and glorified heroism. Therefore, it is difficult to say today whether the Battle of Kosovo was a defeat or a victory for the Serbian people, whether thanks to it we fell into slavery or we survived in this slavery. The answers to those questions will be constantly sought by science and the people. What has been certain through all the centuries until our time today is that disharmony struck Kosovo 600 years ago? If we lost the battle, then this was not only the result of social superiority and the armed advantage of the Ottoman Empire but also of the tragic disunity in the leadership of the Serbian state at that time. In that distant 1389, the Ottoman Empire was not only stronger than that of the Serbs but it was also more fortunate than the Serbian kingdom.

The lack of unity and betrayal in Kosovo will continue to follow the Serbian people like an evil fate through the whole of its history. Even in the last war, this lack of unity and betrayal led the Serbian people and Serbia into agony, the consequences of which in the historical and moral sense exceeded fascist aggression.

Even later, when a socialist Yugoslavia was set up, in this new state the Serbian leadership remained divided, prone to compromise to the detriment of its own people. The concessions that many Serbian leaders made at the expense of their people could not be accepted historically and ethically by any nation in the world, especially because the Serbs have never in the whole of their history conquered and exploited others. Their national and historical being has been liberational throughout the whole of history and through two world wars, as it is today. They liberated themselves and when they could they also helped others to liberate themselves. The fact that in this region they are a major nation is not a Serbian sin or shame; this is an advantage which they have not used against others, but I must say that here, in this big, legendary field of Kosovo, the Serbs have not used the advantage of being great for their own benefit either.

Thanks to their leaders and politicians and their vassal mentality they felt guilty before themselves and others. This situation lasted for decades, it lasted for years and here we are now at the field of Kosovo to say that this is no longer the case.

Disunity among Serb officials made Serbia lag behind and their inferiority humiliated Serbia. Therefore, no place in Serbia is better suited for saying this than the field of Kosovo and no place in Serbia is better suited than the field of Kosovo for saying that unity in Serbia will bring prosperity to the Serbian people in Serbia and each one of its citizens, irrespective of his national or religious affiliation.

Serbia of today is united and equal to other republics and prepared to do everything to improve its financial and social position and that of all its citizens. If there is unity, cooperation, and seriousness, it will succeed in doing so. This is why the optimism that is now present in Serbia to a considerable extent regarding the future days is realistic, also because it is based on freedom, which makes it possible for all people to express their positive, creative and humane abilities aimed at furthering social and personal life.

Serbia has never had only Serbs living in it. Today, more than in the past, members of other peoples and nationalities also live in it. This is not a disadvantage for Serbia. I am truly convinced that it is its advantage. National composition of almost all countries in the world today, particularly developed ones, has also been changing in this direction. Citizens of different nationalities, religions, and races have been living together more and more frequently and more and more successfully.

Socialism in particular, being a progressive and just democratic society, should not allow people to be divided in the national and religious respect. The only differences one can and should allow in socialism are between hard working people and idlers and between honest people and dishonest people. Therefore, all people in Serbia who live from their own work, honestly, respecting other people and other nations, are in their own republic.

After all, our entire country should be set up on the basis of such principles. Yugoslavia is a multinational community and it can survive only under the conditions of full equality for all nations that live in it.

The crisis that hit Yugoslavia has brought about national divisions, but also social, cultural, religious and many other less important ones. Among all these divisions, nationalist ones have shown themselves to be the most dramatic. Resolving them will make it easier to remove other divisions and mitigate the consequences they have created.

For as long as multinational communities have existed, their weak point has always been the relations between different nations. The threat is that the question of one nation being endangered by the others can be posed one day - and this can then start a wave of suspicions, accusations, and intolerance, a wave that invariably grows and is difficult to stop. This threat has been hanging like a sword over our heads all the time. Internal and external enemies of multi-national communities are aware of this and therefore they organize their activity against multinational societies mostly by fomenting national conflicts. At this moment, we in Yugoslavia are behaving as if we have never had such an experience and as if in our recent and distant past we have never experienced the worst tragedy of national conflicts that a society can experience and still survive.

Equal and harmonious relations among Yugoslav peoples are a necessary condition for the existence of Yugoslavia and for it to find its way out of the crisis and, in particular, they are a necessary condition for its economic and social prosperity. In this respect Yugoslavia does not stand out from the social milieu of the contemporary, particularly the developed, world. This world is more and more marked by national tolerance, national cooperation, and even national equality. The modern economic and technological, as well as political and cultural development, has guided various peoples toward each other, has made them interdependent and increasingly has made them equal as well. Equal and united people can above all become a part of the civilization toward which mankind is moving. If we cannot be at the head of the column leading to such a civilization, there is certainly no need for us to be at its tail.

At the time when this famous historical battle was fought in Kosovo, the people were looking at the stars, expecting aid from them. Now, 6 centuries later, they are looking at the stars again, waiting to conquer them. On the first occasion, they could allow themselves to be disunited and to have hatred and treason because they lived in smaller, weakly interlinked worlds. Now, as people on this planet, they cannot conquer even their own planet if they are not united, let alone other planets, unless they live in mutual harmony and solidarity.

Therefore, words devoted to unity, solidarity, and cooperation among people have no greater significance anywhere on the soil of our motherland than they have here in the field of Kosovo, which is a symbol of disunity and treason.

In the memory of the Serbian people, this disunity was decisive in causing the loss of the battle and in bringing about the fate which Serbia suffered for a full 6 centuries.

Even if it were not so, from a historical point of view, it remains certain that the people regarded disunity as its greatest disaster. Therefore, it is the obligation of the people to remove disunity, so that they may protect themselves from defeats, failures, and stagnation in the future.

This year, the Serbian people became aware of the necessity of their mutual harmony as the indispensable condition for their present life and further development.

I am convinced that this awareness of harmony and unity will make it possible for Serbia not only to function as a state but to function as a successful state. Therefore I think that it makes sense to say this here in Kosovo, where that disunity once upon a time tragically pushed back Serbia for centuries and endangered it, and where renewed unity may advance it and may return dignity to it. Such an awareness about mutual relations constitutes an elementary necessity for Yugoslavia, too, for its fate is in the joined hands of all its peoples.

The Kosovo heroism has been inspiring our creativity for 6 centuries, and has been feeding our pride and does not allow us to forget that at one time we were an army great, brave, and proud, one of the few that remained undefeated when losing.

Six centuries later, now, we are being again engaged in battles and are facing battles. They are not armed battles, although such things cannot be excluded yet. However, regardless of what kind of battles they are, they cannot be won without resolve, bravery, and sacrifice, without the noble qualities that were present here in the field of Kosovo in the days past. Our chief battle now concerns implementing the economic, political, cultural, and general social prosperity, finding a quicker and more successful approach to a civilization in which people will live in the 21st century. For this battle, we certainly need heroism, of course of a somewhat different kind, but that courage without which nothing serious and great can be achieved remains unchanged and remains urgently necessary.

Six centuries ago, Serbia heroically defended itself in the field of Kosovo, but it also defended Europe. Serbia was at that time the bastion that defended the European culture, religion, and European society in general. Therefore today it appears not only unjust but even unhistorical and completely absurd to talk about Serbia's belonging to Europe. Serbia has been a part of Europe incessantly, now just as much as it was in the past, of course, in its own way, but in a way that in the historical sense never deprived it of dignity. In this spirit we now endeavor to build a society, rich and democratic, and thus to contribute to the prosperity of this beautiful country, this unjustly suffering country, but also to contribute to the efforts of all the progressive people of our age that they make for a better and happier world.

Let the memory of Kosovo heroism live forever! Long live Serbia! Long live Yugoslavia! Long live peace and brotherhood among peoples!

8. St. Egidio Education Agreement

8 a) St. Egidio Education Agreement, 1 September 1996

[The] educational system in Kosovo, from primary to university education, has not been functioning normally for several years.

By signifying their consent, the undersigned, President of Serbia Slobodan Milosevic and Dr. Ibrahim Rugova, have reached agreement to start the normalization of education system for Albanian children and youth in Kosovo.

The agreement envisages the return of Albanian pupils and teachers to schools.

Because of its social and humanitarian importance, this agreement is beyond any political dispute. The mutual concern of the undersigned for the future of Albanian children and youth made them reach this agreement.

They would like to thank their mutual friends from the humanitarian community St. Egidio for their help and support rendered in facilitating their dialogue.

The undersigned are convinced of the readiness of all those who are in charge of implementation of the education system to achieve normalization. For the implementation of this agreement am mixed group (3+3) will be established.

When young people seriously start their educational and cultural improvement, thus becoming responsible citizens, it will be a victory of civilization and not a victory of one over another.

Signed: Dr. Ibrahim Rugova, President of the Republic of Serbia; Slobodan Milosevic, 1 September 1996.

8 b) Agreed Measures for the Implementation of the Agreement on Education of 1 September 1996, Belgrade, 24 March 1998

1. The following measures are temporarily adopted for the implementation of the accord on education, signed by President Slobodan Milosevic and Dr. Ibrahim Rugova on September 1st, 1996.

2. The Institute of Albanology in Prishtina will be re-opened to its previous occupants on March 31st, 1998.

3. By March 31 st 1998, the Community of St. Egidio, taking into account the proposals submitted by the two parties in the "3+3" Commission, will select the first three faculties of the University of Prishtina in which Albanian students and professors will re- enter by

April 30, 1998. In principle, the conditions of the re- entry will be the following: the students who are now normally studying in the premises and Albanian students will alternate in the use of the University spaces and facilities, with the system of double shifts exchanged every semester. In the first semester of implementation of these measures, the students who are now normally studying in the premises will use the facilities in the morning (till 2 p.m) and the Albanians in the afternoon. In the second semester, the shifts will be reversed, with the Albanian students in the morning and the students who are now attending classes in the premises in the afternoon, and so on in the following semesters. Beside the utilization of classrooms for teaching, the Albanian students and professors will have at their disposal adequate facilities in each Faculty for administrative functions and for the teaching staff as well (if this is not possible, other solutions will be devised).

4. By April 30 1998, the Community of St. Egidio, taking into account the proposals submitted by the two parties in the "3+3" Commission, will select the next three faculties of the University of Prishtina in which Albanian students and professors will re- enter by May 31st, 1998. The conditions of this re-entry will be the same as those for the faculties as in the previous point.

5. The remaining Albanian students and professors of the other seven faculties will be able to get back to the facilities of the University of Prishtina by June 30th 1998, according to the same conditions for the previous faculties, stated at points 3 and 4. By September 30th 1998, the Albanian students and professors will have access to the University facilities (dining halls, libraries, dormitories, etc.) in an adequate way. The Community of St. Egidio will provide solutions, after hearing proposals of both sides, to eventual problems which might emerge. Anyway, the academic year must start normally on October 1st 1998.

6. By June 30th 1998, the Albanian students and professors will be able to use the facilities of seven higher schools in Prishtina and in other towns of Kosovo, specializing in pedagogic, economic and technical subjects. Their utilization will be made according to the conditions for the re-use of the University facilities, as in point 3, if these schools are used.

7. The "3+3" Commission, assisted by the Community of St. Egidio, underlines the necessity of fund raising to build new facilities quickly, in order to increase space for teaching, research and administration at the disposal of all. New University buildings, that could be quickly built, will be able to house, on equal terms, all the structures of the University. This will be subject of a special program, containing the timetable and financing for its realization in accordance with real needs and material possibilities.

8. Similarly, by March 31st 1998, the Albanian students and pupils will get back to high and elementary school buildings which actually are not used, according to the list prepared by the "3+3" Commission. The Community of St. Egidio will provide solutions to eventual problems that might emerge. The Albanian students and pupils will get back to high and elementary school buildings which are partially used by April 30th 1998. Their utilization will be made according to the conditions for the re-use of University facilities, set in point 3, or in another mutually accepted mode.

9. The meeting of the "3+3" Commission, with the assistance of members of St. Egidio Community, will begin not later than March 30th to guarantee the implementation of the transitional measures of normalization. The "3+3" Commission will immediately form working groups for each faculty. The "3+3" Commission will study other problems concerning the normalization of the education system (financing, administration, languages, diplomas, programs, degrees, status issues of the staff).

The measures were signed by Ratomir Vico, Goran Percevic, Dobrosav Bjeletic, Fehmi Agani, Abdulj Rama and Redzep Osmani.

Present were the members of the St. Egidio Community - Monsignor Vicenzo Paglia, Professor Roberto Moroco della Roca and Dr. Mario Giro.

1.2 UNILATERAL DECLARATION OF INDEPENDENCE

9. Statement Made by the People's Assembly of Albania, 22 October 1991

Letter dated 23 October 1995 from the Charge d'affaires of the Permanent Mission of the Federal Republic of Yugoslavia to the United Nations addressed to the Secretary General, UN Doc. A/C.1/50/4, 26 October 1995

Upon the instructions of my Government, I am writing to you concerning the information submitted by the Government of Albania regarding the agenda item of the General Assembly entitled "Maintenance of international security". The Government of the Federal Republic of Yugoslavia has taken note in particular of the statements contained in paragraphs 21 and 22 of the addendum to the report of the Secretary-General on the development of good-neighbourly relations among Balkan States (A/50/412/Add.1), where it is stated that Albania "has always implemented and will continue to implement the principles of the Charter of the United Nations" and that its "policy aims at respecting sovereignty, territorial integrity, political independence and not changing borders by force".

Without any attempt to dwell upon other parts of the information submitted by Albania, the Government of the Federal Republic of Yugoslavia underlines the political significance of the statements contained therein and expects that consequently Albania shall revoke, as a matter of urgency, the decision of the People's Assembly of the Republic of Albania of 22 October 1991, enclosed herewith (see annex), on the recognition of the Province of Kosovo and Metohija, an integral part of the Republic of Serbia and the Federal Republic of Yugoslavia, as a sovereign and independent state.

I should be grateful if you would have the present letter and its annex circulated as an official document of the General Assembly under agenda item 81.

(Signed) Vladislav Jovanovic, Chargé d'affaires a.i.

Annex

STATEMENT MADE ON 22 OCTOBER 1991 BY THE PEOPLE'S ASSEMBLY OF ALBANIA

The People's Assembly of the Republic of Albania learned of the result declared by the Central Commission of the Assembly of Kosova, namely, the full success of the referendum for the approval of the resolution of this Assembly, through which the Republic of Kosova is defined as a sovereign and independent State, on the basis of freedom and complete equality with all other peoples. The People's Assembly of the Republic of Albania considers the resolution completely right, legitimate and based on fundamental international democratic principles such a those enshrined in the Charter of the United Nations, the Helsinki Final Act and the Charter of Paris. The People's Assembly of the Republic of Albania has also noted the decision to create a new provisional government of the Republic of Kosova, with Dr. Bujar Bukushi as its Chairman.

Through this historic act, the People of Kosova, as the most ancient people and the third as regards number of people living in their territories in Yugoslavia, and their legitimate organ of State power, the Assembly of Kosova, will go on making their contribution to the solution of the Yugoslav crisis through democratic means and to the consolidation of the democratic spirit, security and stability of the Balkans and Europe.

The People's Assembly of the Republic of Albania recognizes the Republic of Kosova as a sovereign and independent state, on the basis of freedom and complete equality with all other peoples. It also recognizes as legitimate the new provisional government of the Republic of Kosova under the direction of Dr. Bujar Bukushi. It appeals to democratic international opinion and the member countries of the conference on Security and Cooperation in Europe to recognize and observe the legitimate will of the Albanian people of Kosova. This would be another proof of their sincere engagement and without prejudice to a correct resolution of the Yugoslav crisis.

10. Letter from the Charge d'affaires a.i. of the Permanent Mission of Yugoslavia to the United Nations Addressed to the Secretary-General, 18 December 1995[1]

I am writing to you in connection with the draft resolution entitled "Situation of the human rights in Kosovo", prepared by Albania, which was adopted by the Third Committee of the United Nations General Assembly on 11 December 1995 (A/50/635/Add.1, para. 16 and para. 76, draft resolution III) and, upon instructions of my Government, I have the honour to make the following comments.

The draft resolution addresses only one aspect of the situation in the Autonomous Province of Kosovo and Metohija and does so in a highly biased, unbalanced and unconstructive manner. At the same time, the draft resolution ignores the root cause of the problems in Kosovo and Metohija, which is the unbridled separatism of parts of the Albanian minority.

The leadership of the Albanian minority in Kosovo and Metohija illegally declared an independent state in 1991 in contravention of the Charter of the United Nations, the International Covenant on Civil and Political Rights, the Final Act of the Conference on Security and Cooperation in Europe (CSCE) and the Paris Charter of the CSCE as well as the Convention of the Council of Europe on National Minorities.

The People's Assembly of the Republic of Albania recognized "the Republic of Kosovo" as a sovereign and independent state on 22 October 1991 (A/C.1/50/4, Annex), in contravention of the Charter of the United Nations and international legal instruments.

How is it possible that the draft resolution on the situation of human rights in Kosovo blatantly ignores the said fundamental facts? We hope that all Member States shall take into account the said facts when deciding whether it is appropriate to support the draft resolution.

I should be grateful if you would have the text of the present letter circulated as an official document of the General Assembly under agenda item 112 (c).

(Signed) Vladislav Jovanovic, Chargé d'affairs a.i.

11. Letter from the Chargé d'affaires a.i. of the Permanent Mission of Yugoslavia to the United Nations Addressed to the Secretary-General, 11 November 1996[2]

I am writing to you in connection with the statement made in the Third Committee by the Permanent Representative of Albania to the United Nations, Mr. Pellumb Kulla, on 6 November 1996 during the consideration of the item entitled "The right of peoples to self-determination".

The representative of Albania has once again abused the debate on this agenda item to manifest that his Government openly interferes into the internal affairs to the Federal Republic of Yugoslavia. Mr. Kulla misrepresents the situation in the Autonomous Province of Kosovo and Metohija, especially the status of the Albanian national minority. He claims that the Albanians in the Autonomous Province of Kosovo and Metohija are a "people" and that they are entitled to the right to self-determination. However, the facts are different. The Republic of Albania is a country of the Albanian people. The Albanians of Kosovo and Metohija are by every definition of recognized international law a national minority. They are granted the highest standards of human and minority rights envisaged by the international legal instruments and political documents, but are not entitled to the right to self-determination. Under the Charter of the United Nations and other international documents, this right belongs only to peoples. Otherwise, the existence of a national minority in sizeable numbers in various countries could entitle them to a claim to the right of self-determination and would bring about chaos not only in Europe but all over the world.

In accordance with the present constitutions of Yugoslavia and Serbia, the Autonomous Province of Kosovo and Metohija is an integral part of the Republic of Serbia and the Federal Republic of Yugoslavia. Numerous institutional changes did not affect the autonomous status of the Autonomous Province of Kosovo and Metohija.

Time and again we have to emphasize that members of the Albanian national minority enjoy equal rights with all other citizens of the Federal Republic of Yugoslavia. In addition, the Province has a very large degree of autonomy. Their individual rights, as well as their collective rights stemming from their status of national minority, are not jeopardized in any way. Recently, a memorandum of understanding has been reached on the normalization of education in the Autonomous Province of Kosovo and Metohija, which was commended internationally, even in Albania. This shows that it is possible to solve any question through dialogue and by political means, despite numerous terrorist acts committed in the Province this year by Albanian extremists and the thinly disguised "sabre rattling" in the statement of the Permanent Representative of Albania.

In assessing the situation in the Autonomous Province of Kosovo and Metohija, one has to bear in mind that the prerequisite of the realization of the rights of national minorities is, first and foremost, their loyalty towards the country in which they live. That is also the basic position contained in all international documents regulating this matter, such as the Copenhagen Document of the Organization for Security and Cooperation on national minorities. However, a large portion of the Albanian national minority persistently boycotts the public life in the Province, the Republic of Serbia and the Federal Republic of Yugoslavia. The underlying reason for the boycott is that the political leaders of this minority are preventing members of the Albanian national minority from exercising their constitutional minority and democratic rights, including the right to vote and cooperate in the conduct of the official census.

Yugoslavia is committed to good-neighbourly relations with all the Balkan countries. However, Albania's policy towards Yugoslavia has not changed during the entire period since the second World War. Both past-Communist- and present regimes in Tirana have been consistent in their endeavours to dismember the former and present Yugoslavia and steadfast in their support for those forces in the Autonomous Province of Kosovo and Metohija calling for secession of the Province from the Republic of Serbia and the Federal Republic of Yugoslavia. In this connection, we particularly note that the decision of the People's Assembly of the Republic of Albania of 22 October 1991 recognizing the Autonomous Province of Kosovo and Metohija as a sovereign and independent State in contravention of the basis principles contained in the Charter of the United Nations, the OSCE Helsinki Final Act and the Paris Charter and the Declaration on Principles of International Law concerning Friendly Relations and Cooperation among States in accordance with the Charter of the United Nations, has not yet been revoked.

[...]

(Signed) Vladislav Jovanovic, Chargé d'affairs a.i.

---

[1] UN Doc. A/50/854, 29 December 1995
[2] UN Doc. A/C.3/51/14, 13 November 1996

CHAPTER 2: DEVELOPMENT OF THE HUMAN RIGHTS SITUATION

The Socialist Federation Republic of Yugoslavia (SFRY) was bound by human rights obligations contained in general international law and in human rights conventions. It was party to the 1966 Covenant on Civil and Political Rights, the 1966 Covenant on Economic, Social and Cultural Rights, the Genocide Convention, the Convention Against Torture and Other Cruel Inhuman or Degrading Treatment or Punishment, the Convention on the Rights of the Child, the Convention on the Elimination of Racial Discrimination and the Convention on the Elimination of All Forms of Discrimination against Women. It has signed Optional Protocol I to the Covenant on Civil and Political Rights. The FRY is still listed as party to these conventions. After the UN organs determined that Yugoslavia was not to be regarded as the automatic successor of the rights of the SFRY but would have to apply anew for membership in the UN,[1] the FRY refused to participate in the work of the human rights treaty bodies. In a letter the chairman of the Committee on the Elimination of Racial Discrimination stated that the Committee has always considered the FRY duty bound as a state party to the International Convention on the Elimination of All Forms of Racial Discrimination.[2]

In regard to domestic standards, the 1992 FRY Constitution provides that the FRY is a democratic state founded on the rule of law. The Constitution includes 49 articles guaranteeing basic political, civil, economic, social and cultural rights and freedom for all citizens without discrimination.

Yugoslavia claimed that the events in Kosovo fell entirely within the internal affairs of the FRY *(documents no. 66, 164)*. The international community, however, did not accept this view, but criticised the substantive violations of the Albanian minority's human rights from the outset *(documents no. 12, 23)*: In order to respond to the human rights situation in the former Yugoslavia, the UN Commission on Human Rights convened in a special session in August 1992 where it appointed a Special Rapporteur for Yugoslavia to investigate first hand the human rights situation in the territory. The first Rapporteur was Tadeusz Mazowiecki who was later replaced by Elisabeth Rehn upon his resignation in 1995 *(documents no. 23-29)*. Thematic Rapporteurs, inter alia those on arbitrary detention and on extrajudicial, summary and arbitrary executions supported the Special Rapporteur during his investigations. In 1994, the General Assembly requested the UN Secretary-General to "seek ways and means to establish an adequate international monitoring presence in Kosovo and to report thereon to the General Assembly" *(document no. 14)*. Since numerous human rights bodies were involved in the monitoring of the human rights crisis the resolution asked the Secretary-General to ensure the full and effective coordination of the activities of all UN bodies. He reported on the efforts to establish a human rights monitoring presence and on the issue of access by the monitoring missions to the General Assembly.[3] In this period questions of access for international observers of human rights preoccupied the concern for Kosovo because the FRY had expelled the CSCE Mission of Long Duration to Kosovo, Sandjak and Vojvodina in the summer of 1993 *(document no. 52)*.

The increasing attention that UN bodies paid to the continuously evolving conflict in Kosovo reflects the gradual escalation of the situation. By the end of 1995, 340,700 Kosovo Albanians had sought political asylum outside the FRY.[4] In 1998, the clashes between the KLA and the Serb security forces led to a disproportionate use of force on the part of the Yugoslav authorities which resulted in a humanitarian emergency situation and a refugee crisis in the region *(document no. 20)*. 98,100 Kosovo Albanians left the country while 200 000 were internally displaced.[5]

The UN High Commissioner for Refugees (UNHCR) coordinated international humanitarian efforts to address the crisis. Since 1998 UNHCR led aid convoys throughout Kosovo. By March 1999, UNHCR was providing assistance to 400,000 people displaced or otherwise affected by fighting inside Kosovo and to 90,000 refugees and displaced persons outside Kosovo *(document no. 41, 42)*. On 23 March 1999, UNHCR had to leave Kosovo following a decision of the United Nations Security Coordinator. The emergency developed in the wake of NATO air strikes against the FRY. In the following weeks there was a refugee outflow from Kosovo the size and speed of which the international aid organisations did not foresee. 862,979 refugees had been displaced from Kosovo between 23 March and 9 June 1999. In addition, more than 100,000 Serb internally displaced persons are estimated to have left Kosovo and to have been registered in Serbia and Montenegro *(document no. 44)*. During and since the conflict international humanitarian organisations have attracted harsh criticism when they appeared unprepared for the massive movement of refugees from Kosovo into neighbouring countries.

Pursuant to UN Security Council Resolution 1244 (1999) UNHCR is part of one of the four sectors involved with implementing the civilian aspects of rebuilding Kosovo.[6] UNHCR is in charge of humanitarian assistance. It is reported that more than 810,000 people have returned to Kosovo after residing in camps or with host families in Albania, the Former Yugoslav Republic of Macedonia, Montenegro (FRY), Bosnia and Herzegovina and other countries during the NATO air campaign.

On 31 March 1999, the UN High Commissioner for Human Rights decided to deploy human rights monitors to the FYR Macedonia, Albania and Montenegro - in an operation called the Kosovo Emergency Operation. In addition, the Commissioner dispatched a Personal Envoy to the area along with the new Special Rapporteur of the Human Rights Commission, Jiri Dienstbier. The purpose of this mission was to record the human rights situation and gather first-hand information about violations. The UN Commission for Human Rights welcomed the dispatch of human rights monitors and requested the UN High Commissioner for Human Rights to inform the Commission as soon as possible on the human rights situation and the humanitarian crisis relating to Kosovo *(document no. 33)*. In response the High Commissioner issued several reports on the human rights situation *(documents no. 39, 40)*.

---

[1] UN SC Res 777 (1992) of 19 September 1992.
[2] UN Doc. A/50/18 of 22 September 1995, para. 227.
[3] UN Doc. A/50/767 of 20 November 1995; A/51/556 of 25 October 1996, A/52/502 of 17 October 1997, A/53/563 of 30 October 1998.
[4] Council of Europe, Parliamentary Assembly, 1996 Ordinary Session, 5th Sitting, Resolution 1077 (1996) on Albanian asylum seekers from Kosovo, Strasbourg, 24 January 1996, para. 3.
[5] UNHCR, UN inter-agency update on Kosovo situation report covered: 14 - 20 October 1998, Pristina, 22 October 1998, p. 4.
[6] See Chapter 9.

Following UN Security Council resolution 1244 (1999), and in light of the return of refugees to Kosovo, the Kosovo Emergency Operation was officially terminated and staff members of the Office of the High Commissioner for Human Rights (OHCHR) returned to Kosovo with the advance team of UNMIK. The OHCHR carries out the following tasks for the reconstruction of Kosovo: following up on investigations initiated in Albania, the former Yugoslav Republic of Macedonia and Montenegro (FRY); sharing information, through the OHCHR database, with the United Nations human rights mechanisms for follow-up action; maintaining institutional representation in bodies advising on the re-establishment of a judiciary in Kosovo; maintaining institutional representation in the Task Force on Minority Issues with responsibilities for assessing the situation in the field and devising protection response mechanisms and legal regulatory policies; gathering information, in cooperation with the ICRC, on the circumstances of arrest of prisoners transferred to Serbia, for follow-up outside of Kosovo; gathering information, in cooperation with KFOR, UNMIK, OSCE, UNHCR and ICRC, on persons kidnapped in Kosovo by KLA "police" and "military police" and other non-State actors; participating in the subcommission of the Kosovo Transitional Council on detainees and prisoners; liasing with human rights NGOs; and cooperating with OSCE on the possible establishment of an ombudsman's office.

2.1 DOCUMENTS OF INTERNATIONAL ORGANISATIONS

2.1.1 THE UN GENERAL ASSEMBLY

12. Situation of Human Rights in the Territory of the Former Yugoslavia, UN General Assembly Resolution 47/147, 18 December 1992

[Parts not referring to the situation in Kosovo have been omitted.]
The General Assembly, [...]

Welcoming the efforts by the Conference on Security and Cooperation in Europe to prevent further human rights violations and its missions dispatched to the territory of the former Yugoslavia, including missions of long duration to Kosovo, Voyvodina and Sandjak, where the human rights situation remains a cause of great concern; [...]

14. *Expresses its grave concern* at the report of the Special Rapporteur on the dangerous situation in Kosovo, Sandjak and Voyvodina, urges all parties there to engage in a meaningful dialogue under the auspices of the International Conference on the Former Yugoslavia, to act with utmost restraint and to settle disputes in full compliance with human rights and fundamental freedoms, and calls upon the Serbian authorities to refrain from the use of force, to stop immediately the practice of "ethnic cleansing" and to respect fully the rights of persons belonging to ethnic communities or minorities, in order to prevent the extension of the conflict to other parts of the former Yugoslavia;[...]

21. *Also requests* the Secretary-General, within the overall budgetary framework of the United Nations, to make all necessary resources available for the Special Rapporteur to carry out his mandate and in particular to provide him with a number of staff based in the territories of the former Yugoslavia adequate to ensure effective continous monitoring of the human rights situation there and coordination with other Unitd Nations bodies involved, including the United Nations Protection Force; [...]

92nd plenary meeting 18 December 1992; adopted without a vote.

13. Violations of Human Rights in the Republic of Bosnia and Herzegovina, the Republic of Croatia and the FRY (Serbia and Montenegro), UN General Assembly Resolution 48/153, 20 December 1993

[Parts not referring to the situation in Kosovo have been omitted.]
The General Assembly, [...]

Welcoming the ongoing efforts of the Conference on Security and Cooperation in Europe to re-establish its presence in the Federal Republic of Yugoslavia (Serbia and Montenegro) in order to prevent further human rights violations, and deeply concerned about the decision of the authorities in the Federal Republic of Yugoslavia (Serbia and Montenegro) to expel the monitoring missions of long duration of the Conference on Security and Cooperation in Europe and the European Union to Kosovo, Sandjak and Vojvodina, where the human rights situation remains a cause of great concern,

Welcoming also the efforts of the European Union, inter alia, through its monitoring missions, to promote respect for human rights and fundamental freedoms in the territory of the former Yugoslavia, [...]

Noting the discriminatory policies, measures and violent actions committed against ethnic Albanians in Kosovo, and aware of the possible escalation of the situation into a violent conflict there, [...]

17. *Expresses* its grave concern at the deteriorating human rights situation in the Federal Republic of Yugoslavia (Serbia and Montenegro), particularly in Kosovo, as described in the reports of the Special Rapporteur, and strongly condemns the violations of human rights occurring there;

18. *Strongly condemns* in particular the measures and practices of discrimination and the violations of the human rights of the ethnic Albanians of Kosovo, as well as the large-scale repression committed by the Serbian authorities, including:

(a) Police brutality against ethnic Albanians, arbitrary searches, seizures and arrests, torture and ill-treatment during detention and discrimination in the administration of justice, which leads to a climate of lawlessness in which criminal acts, particularly against ethnic Albanians, take place with impunity;

(b) The discriminatory removal of ethnic Albanian officials, especially from the police and judiciary, the mass dismissal of ethnic Albanians from professional, administrative and other skilled positions in State-owned enterprises and public institutions, including teachers from the Serb-run school system, and the closure of Albanian high schools and universities;

(c) Arbitrary imprisonment of ethnic Albanian journalists, the closure of Albanian-language mass media and the discriminatory removal of ethnic Albanian staff from local radio and television stations;

(d) Repression by the Serbian police and military;

19. *Urges* the authorities in the Federal Republic of Yugoslavia (Serbia and Montenegro):

(a) To take all necessary measures to bring to an immediate end the human rights violations inflicted on the ethnic Albanians in Kosovo, including, in particular, discriminatory measures and practices, arbitrary detention and the use of torture and other cruel, inhuman or degrading treatment and the occurrence of summary executions;

(b) To revoke all discriminatory legislation, in particular that which has entered into force since 1989;

(c) To re-establish the democratic institutions of Kosovo, including the Parliament and the judiciary;

(d) To resume dialogue with the ethnic Albanians in Kosovo, including under the auspices of the International Conference on the Former Yugoslavia;

20. *Also urges* the authorities of the Federal Republic of Yugoslavia (Serbia and Montenegro) to respect the human rights and fundamental freedoms of ethnic Albanians in Kosovo, and expresses the view that the best means to safeguard human rights in Kosovo is to restore its autonomy;

[...]

22. *Calls upon* the authorities of the Federal Republic of Yugoslavia (Serbia and Montenegro) to allow the immediate entry of an international human rights monitoring presence into the country, particularly into Kosovo, and strongly urges them to reconsider their refusal to allow the continuation of the activities of the missions of the Conference on Security and Cooperation in Europe in Kosovo, Sandjak and Vojvodina and to cooperate with the Conference by taking the practical steps needed for the resumption of the activities of those missions, called for by the Security Council in its resolution 855 (1993) of 22 February 1993, in order to prevent the extension of the conflict to those areas;

[...]

85th plenary meeting, 20 December 1993, adopted unanimously.

14. Situation of Human Rights in Kosovo, UN General Assembly Resolution 49/204, 23 December 1994

The General Assembly,

Guided by the Charter of the United Nations, the Universal Declaration of Human Rights,[1] the International Covenants on Human Rights,[2] the International Convention on the Elimination of All Forms of Racial Discrimination,[3] the Convention on the Prevention and Punishment of the Crime of Genocide[4] and the Convention against Torture and Other Cruel, Inhuman or Degrading Treatment or Punishment,[5]

Recalling its resolution 48/153 of 20 December 1993,

Taking note of Commission on Human Rights resolution 1994/76 of 9 March 1994,[6] and recalling Commission resolutions 1992/S-1/1 of 14 August 1992,[7] 1992/S-2/1 of 1 December 1992[8] and 1993/7 of 23 February 1993,[9]

Taking note of the report of the Special Rapporteur of the Commission on Human Rights on the situation of human rights in the territory of the former Yugoslavia,[10] in which he stated that the situation in Kosovo had deteriorated further in the course of the past six months, as well as his earlier reports,[11] in which he described the various discriminatory measures taken in the legislative, administrative and judicial areas, acts of violence and arbitrary arrests perpetrated against ethnic Albanians in Kosovo and the continuing deterioration of the human rights situation in Kosovo, including:

(a) Police brutality against ethnic Albanians, the killing of ethnic Albanians resulting from such violence, arbitrary searches, seizures and arrests, forced evictions, torture and ill-treatment of detainees and discrimination in the administration of justice;

(b) Discriminatory and arbitrary dismissals of ethnic Albanian civil servants, notably from the ranks of the police and the judiciary, mass dismissals of ethnic Albanians, confiscation and expropriation of their properties, discrimination against Albanian pupils and teachers, the closing of Albanian-language secondary schools and university, as well as the closing of all Albanian cultural and scientific institutions;

(c) The harassment and persecution of political parties and associations of ethnic Albanians and their leaders and activities, maltreating and imprisoning them;

(d) The intimidation and imprisonment of ethnic Albanian journalists and the systematic harassment and disruption of the news media in the Albanian language;

(e) The dismissals from clinics and hospitals of doctors and members of other categories of the medical profession of Albanian origin;

(f) The elimination in practice of the Albanian language, particularly in public administration and services;

(g) The serious and massive occurrence of discriminatory and repressive practices aimed at Albanians in Kosovo, as a whole, resulting in widespread involuntary migration; and noting also that the Subcommission on Prevention of Discrimination and Protection of Minorities, in its resolution 1993/9 of 20 August 1993,[12] considered that these measures and practices constituted a form of ethnic cleansing,

Recognizing that the long-term mission of the Organization for Security and Cooperation in Europe to Kosovo played a positive role in monitoring the human rights situation and in preventing an escalation of conflict there and recalling in this context Security Council resolution 855 (1993) of 9 August 1993,

Considering that the re-establishment of the international presence in Kosovo to monitor and investigate the situation of human rights is of great importance in preventing the situation in Kosovo from deteriorating into a violent conflict,

1. *Strongly condemns* the measures and practices of discrimination and the violations of human rights of ethnic Albanians in Kosovo committed by the authorities of the Federal Republic of Yugoslavia (Serbia and Montenegro);

2. *Condemns* the large-scale repression by the police and military of the Federal Republic of Yugoslavia (Serbia and Montenegro) against the defenceless ethnic Albanian population and the discrimination against the ethnic Albanians in the administrative and judiciary branches of government, education, health care and employment, aimed at forcing ethnic Albanians to leave;

3. *Demands* that the authorities of the Federal Republic of Yugoslavia (Serbia and Montenegro):

(a) Take all necessary measures to bring to an immediate end all human rights violations against ethnic Albanians in Kosovo, including, in particular, the discriminatory measures and practices, arbitrary searches and detention, the violation of the right to a fair trial and the practice of torture and other cruel, inhuman or degrading treatment;

(b) Revoke all discriminatory legislation, in particular that which has entered into force since 1989;

(c) Establish genuine democratic institutions in Kosovo, including the parliament and the judiciary, and respect the will of its inhabitants as the best means of preventing the escalation of the conflict there;

(d) Reopen the cultural and scientific institutions of the ethnic Albanians;

(e) Pursue dialogue with the representatives of ethnic Albanians in Kosovo, including under the auspices of the International Conference on the Former Yugoslavia;

4. *Demands* that the authorities of the Federal Republic of Yugoslavia (Serbia and Montenegro) cooperate fully and immediately with the Special Rapporteur of the Commission on Human Rights on the situation of human rights in the territory of the former Yugoslavia in the

---

[1] Resolution 217 A (III).
[2] Resolution 2200 A (XXI), annex.
[3] Resolution 2106 A (XX), annex.
[4] Resolution 260 A (III).
[5] Resolution 39/46, annex.
[6] See Official Records of the Economic and Social Council, 1994, Supplement No. 4 and corrigendum (E/1994/24 and Corr.1), chap. II, sect. A.
[7] Ibid., 1992, Supplement No. 2A (E/1992/22/Add.1/Rev.1), chap. II.
[8] See E/1992/22/Add.2-E/CN.4/1992/84/Add.2.
[9] See Official Records of the Economic and Social Council, 1993, Supplement No. 3 (E/1993/23), chap. II, sect. A.
[10] A/49/641-S/1994/1252, annex.
[11] E/CN.4/1993/50 and E/CN.4/1994/110.

[12] E/CN.4/1994/2-E/CN.4/Sub.2/1993/45 and Corr.1, chap. II, sect. A.

discharge of his functions as requested by the Commission by its resolution 1994/76 and other relevant resolutions;

5. *Encourages* the Secretary-General to pursue his humanitarian efforts in the former Yugoslavia, in liaison with the Office of the United Nations High Commissioner for Refugees, the United Nations Children's Fund and other appropriate humanitarian organizations, with a view to taking urgent practical steps to tackle the critical needs of the people in Kosovo, especially of the most vulnerable groups affected by the conflict, and to assist in the voluntary return of displaced persons to their homes;

6. *Urges* the authorities of the Federal Republic of Yugoslavia (Serbia and Montenegro) to allow the immediate unconditional return of the long-term mission of the Organization for Security and Cooperation in Europe to Kosovo, called for in Security Council resolution 855 (1993);

7. *Requests* the Secretary-General to seek ways and means, including through consultations with the United Nations High Commissioner for Human Rights and relevant regional organizations, to establish an adequate international monitoring presence in Kosovo and to report thereon to the General Assembly;

8. *Calls upon* the Special Rapporteur to continue to monitor closely the human rights situation in Kosovo and to pay special attention to this matter in his reporting;

9. *Decides* to continue examination of the human rights situation in Kosovo at its fiftieth session under the item entitled "Human rights questions".

94th plenary meeting, 23 December 1994

15. Situation of Human Rights in Kosovo, UN General Assembly Resolution 50/190, 22 December 1995

The General Assembly,

Guided by the Charter of the United Nations, the Universal Declaration of Human Rights,[1] the International Covenants on Human Rights,[2] the International Convention on the Elimination of All Forms of Racial Discrimination,[3] the Convention on the Prevention and Punishment of the Crime of Genocide[4] and the Convention against Torture and Other Cruel, Inhuman or Degrading Treatment or Punishment,[5]

Welcoming the General Framework Agreement for Peace in Bosnia and Herzegovina[6] reached on 21 November 1995 at Dayton, Ohio, and hoping that it will have a positive impact also on the human rights situation in Kosovo,

Recalling its resolution 49/204 of 23 December 1994 and other relevant resolutions,

Taking note of Commission on Human Rights resolution 1995/89 of 8 March 1995[7] and recalling previous Commission resolutions 1992/S-1/1 of 14 August 1992,[8] 1992/S-2/1 of 1 December 1992,[9] 1993/7 of 23 February 1993 [10] and 1994/76 of 9 March 1994,[11]

Taking note also of the reports of the Special Rapporteurs of the Commission on Human Rights on the situation of human rights in the territory of the former Yugoslavia, in which they describe the situation in Kosovo, the various discriminatory measures taken in the legislative, administrative and judicial areas, acts of violence and arbitrary arrests perpetrated against ethnic Albanians in Kosovo and the continuing deterioration of the human rights situation in Kosovo, including:

(a) Police brutality against ethnic Albanians, the killing of ethnic Albanians resulting from such violence, arbitrary searches, seizures and arrests, forced evictions, torture and ill-treatment of detainees and discrimination in the administration of justice, including the recent trials of ethnic Albanian former policemen;

(b) Discriminatory and arbitrary dismissals of ethnic Albanian civil servants, notably from the ranks of the police and the judiciary, mass dismissals of ethnic Albanians, confiscation and expropriation of their properties, discrimination against ethnic Albanian pupils and teachers, the closing of Albanian-language secondary schools and the university, as well as the closing of all Albanian cultural and scientific institutions;

(c) The harassment and persecution of political parties and associations of ethnic Albanians and their leaders and activities, their maltreatment and imprisonment;

(d) The intimidation and imprisonment of ethnic Albanian journalists and the systematic harassment and disruption of the news media in the Albanian language;

(e) The dismissals from clinics and hospitals of doctors and members of other categories of the medical profession of Albanian origin;

(f) The elimination in practice of the Albanian language, particularly in public administration and services;

(g) The serious and massive occurrence of discriminatory and repressive practices aimed at ethnic Albanians in Kosovo, as a whole, resulting in widespread involuntary migration;

and *noting* that the Subcommission on Prevention of Discrimination and Protection of Minorities, in its resolutions 1993/9 of 20 August 1993[12] and 1995/10 of 18 August 1995,[13] considered that those measures and practices constituted a form of ethnic cleansing,

Concerned at any attempt to use Serb refugees and other means to alter the ethnic balance in Kosovo, thus further suppressing the enjoyment of human rights there, and, in this context, noting with concern the new citizenship law awaiting approval by the Parliament of the Federal Republic of Yugoslavia (Serbia and Montenegro),

Reaffirming that the long-term mission of the Organization for Security and Cooperation in Europe to Kosovo played a positive role in monitoring the human rights situation and in preventing an escalation of conflict there, and recalling in this context Security Council resolution 855 (1993) of 9 August 1993,

Considering that the re-establishment of the international presence in Kosovo to monitor and investigate the situation of human rights is of great importance in preventing the situation in Kosovo from deteriorating into violent conflict, and, in this context, taking note of the report of the Secretary-General submitted pursuant to General Assembly resolution 49/204,[14]

1. *Strongly condemns* the measures and practices of discrimination and the violations of the human rights of ethnic Albanians in Kosovo committed by the authorities of the Federal Republic of Yugoslavia (Serbia and Montenegro);

2. *Condemns* the large-scale repression by the police and military of the Federal Republic of Yugoslavia (Serbia and Montenegro) against the defenceless ethnic Albanian population and the discrimination against the ethnic Albanians in the administrative and judiciary branches of government, education, health care and employment, aimed at forcing ethnic Albanians to leave;

3. *Urgently demands* that the authorities of the Federal Republic of Yugoslavia (Serbia and Montenegro):

---

[1] Resolution 217 A (III).
[2] Resolution 2200 A (XXI), annex.
[3] Resolution 2106 A (XX), annex.
[4] Resolution 260 A (III).
[5] Resolution 39/46, annex.
[6] See A/50/790-S/1995/999.
[7] See Official Records of the Economic and Social Council, 1995, Supplement No.3 and corrigenda (E/1995/23 and Corr. 1 and 2), chap. II, sect. A.
[8] Ibid., 1992, Supplement No. 2A (E/1992/22/Add.1/Rev.1), chap.II. sect. A.
[9] Ibid., Supplement No. 2B (E/1992/22/Add.2), chap. II, sect. A.
[10] Ibid., 1993, Supplement No. 3 (E/1993/23), chap. II, sect. A.
[11] Ibid., 1994, Supplement No. 4 and corrigendum (E/1994/24 and Corr. 1), chap. II, sect. A.
[12] See E/CN.4/1994/2-E/CN.4/Sub.2/1993/45 and Corr.1, chap. II, sect. A.
[13] See E/CN.4/1996/2-E/CN.4/Sub.2/1995/51, chap. II, sect. A.
[14] A/50/767.

(a) Take all necessary measures to bring to an immediate end all human rights violations against ethnic Albanians in Kosovo, including, in particular, the discriminatory measures and practices, arbitrary searches and detention, the violation of the right to a fair trial and the practice of torture and other cruel, inhuman or degrading treatment, and to revoke all discriminatory legislation, in particular that which has entered into force since 1989;

(b) Release all political prisoners and cease the persecution of political leaders and members of local human rights organizations;

(c) Allow the establishment of genuine democratic institutions in Kosovo, including the parliament and the judiciary, and respect the will of its inhabitants as the best means of preventing the escalation of the conflict there;

(d) Abrogate the official settlement policy as far as it is conducive to the heightening of ethnic tensions in Kosovo;

(e) Reopen the cultural and scientific institutions of the ethnic Albanians;

(f) Pursue dialogue with the representatives of ethnic Albanians in Kosovo, including under the auspices of the International Conference on the Former Yugoslavia;

4. *Demands once again* that the authorities of the Federal Republic of Yugoslavia (Serbia and Montenegro) cooperate fully and immediately with the Special Rapporteur of the Commission on Human Rights on the situation of human rights in the territory of the former Yugoslavia in the discharge of her functions, as requested by the Commission in its resolution 1994/76 and in other relevant resolutions;

5. *Encourages* the Secretary-General to pursue his humanitarian efforts in the former Yugoslavia, in liaison with the Office of the United Nations High Commissioner for Refugees, the United Nations Children's Fund and other appropriate humanitarian organizations, with a view to taking urgent practical steps to tackle the critical needs of the people in Kosovo, especially of the most vulnerable groups affected by the conflict, and to assist in the voluntary return of displaced persons to their homes;

6. *Urges* the authorities of the Federal Republic of Yugoslavia (Serbia and Montenegro) to allow the immediate unconditional return of the long-term mission of the Organization for Security and Cooperation in Europe to Kosovo, called for in Security Council resolution 855 (1993);

7. *Welcomes* the report of the Secretary-General submitted pursuant to General Assembly resolution 49/204;

8. *Requests* the Secretary-General to continue to seek ways and means, including through consultations with the United Nations High Commissioner for Human Rights and relevant regional organizations, to establish an adequate international monitoring presence in Kosovo and to report thereon to the General Assembly at its fifty-first session;

9. *Emphasizes* the importance of laws and regulations concerning citizenship applied by the authorities of the Federal Republic of Yugoslavia (Serbia and Montenegro) being in accordance with the standards and principles of non-discrimination, equal protection before the law and the reduction and avoidance of statelessness, as set out in the relevant international human rights instruments;

10. *Calls upon* the Special Rapporteur to continue to monitor closely the situation of human rights in Kosovo and to continue to pay due attention to this matter in her reporting;

11. *Decides* to continue examination of the human rights situation in Kosovo at its fifty-first session under the item entitled "Human rights questions".

99th plenary meeting 22 December 1995

16. Situation of Human Rights in Kosovo, UN General Assembly Resolution 51/111, 12 December 1996

The General Assembly,

Guided by the Charter of the United Nations, the Universal Declaration of Human Rights,[1] the International Covenants on Human Rights,[2] the International Convention on the Elimination of All Forms of Racial Discrimination,[3] the Convention on the Prevention and Punishment of the Crime of Genocide[4] and the Convention against Torture and Other Cruel, Inhuman or Degrading Treatment or Punishment,[5]

Taking note with concern of the reports of the Special Rapporteur of the Commission on Human Rights on the situation of human rights in the territory of the former Yugoslavia, which describe the continuing grave human rights situation in Kosovo, including in particular police brutality, killings resulting from such violence, arbitrary searches and arrests, torture and ill-treatment of detainees, the deliberate maltreatment, persecution and imprisonment of political and human rights activists, the mass dismissals of civil servants and discrimination against pupils and teachers, acts which are mainly perpetrated against ethnic Albanians,

Welcoming, as a first step, the recent signature of a memorandum of understanding concerning the educational system in the Albanian language in Kosovo, and calling for the proper implementation of that memorandum,

Appreciating efforts to monitor the situation in Kosovo, but at the same time expressing regret that the establishment of an adequate international monitoring presence in Kosovo has not yet been achieved,

Recalling its resolution 50/190 of 22 December 1995 and other relevant resolutions, and taking note of the resolutions on the matter adopted by the Commission on Human Rights and the resolution adopted by the Subcommission on Prevention of Discrimination and Protection of Minorities at its forty-eighth session,[6]

1. *Condemns* all violations of human rights in Kosovo, in particular repression of the ethnic Albanian population and discrimination against them, as well as all acts of violence in Kosovo;

2. *Demands* that the authorities of the Federal Republic of Yugoslavia (Serbia and Montenegro):

(a) Take all necessary measures to bring to an immediate end all human rights violations against ethnic Albanians in Kosovo, in particular the discriminatory measures and practices, arbitrary searches and detention, the violation of the right to a fair trial and the practice of torture and other cruel, inhuman or degrading treatment, and to revoke all discriminatory legislation, in particular that which has entered into force since 1989;

(b) Release all political prisoners and cease the persecution of political leaders and members of local human rights organizations;

(c) Allow the establishment of genuine democratic institutions in Kosovo, including the parliament and the judiciary, and respect the will of its inhabitants as the best means of preventing the escalation of the conflict there;

(d) Allow the reopening of educational, cultural and scientific institutions of the ethnic Albanians;

(e) Pursue constructive dialogue with the representatives of ethnic Albanians of Kosovo;

3. *Welcomes* the visits to Kosovo of the Special Rapporteur of the Commission on Human Rights on the situation of human rights in the territory of the former Yugoslavia and her relevant reports, and calls upon her to continue to monitor closely the human rights situation in Kosovo and to continue to pay due attention to this matter in her reporting;

4. *Urges* the authorities of the Federal Republic of Yugoslavia (Serbia and Montenegro) to allow the immediate unconditional return of

---

[1] Resolution 217 A (III).
[2] Resolution 2200 A (XXI), annex.
[3] Resolution 2106 A (XX), annex.
[4] Resolution 260 A (III).
[5] Resolution 39/46, annex.
[6] E/CN.4/1997/2-E/CN.4/Sub.2/1996/41, chap. II, sect. A, resolution 1996/2.

the mission of long duration of the Organization for Security and Cooperation in Europe to Kosovo, called for in Security Council resolution 855 (1993) of 9 August 1993;

5. *Welcomes* the report of the Secretary-General submitted pursuant to resolution 50/190,[1] and requests him to continue his efforts to seek ways and means, including through consultations with the United Nations High Commissioner for Human Rights and relevant regional organizations, to establish an adequate international monitoring presence in Kosovo and to report thereon to the General Assembly at its fifty-second session;

6. *Encourages* the Secretary-General to pursue his humanitarian efforts in the former Yugoslavia, in liaison with the Office of the United Nations High Commissioner for Refugees, the United Nations Children's Fund and other appropriate humanitarian organizations, with a view to taking urgent practical steps to tackle the critical needs of the people in Kosovo, especially of the most vulnerable groups affected by the conflict, and to assist in the voluntary return of displaced persons to their homes in conditions of safety and dignity;

7. *Emphasizes* the importance of laws and regulations concerning citizenship applied by the authorities of the Federal Republic of Yugoslavia (Serbia and Montenegro) being in accordance with the standards and principles of non-discrimination, equal protection before the law and the reduction and avoidance of statelessness, as set out in the relevant international human rights instruments;

8. *Decides* to continue examination of the human rights situation in Kosovo at its fifty-second session under the item entitled "Human rights questions".

82nd plenary meeting 12 December 1996

17. Situation of Human Rights in Bosnia and Herzegovina, the Republic of Croatia and the FRY (Serbia and Montenegro), UN General Assembly Resolution 51/116, 12 December 1996

[Part not referring to the situation in Kosovo have been omitted.]

The General Assembly, [...]

Gravely concerned nonetheless at the continuing evidence of violations of human rights and fundamental freedoms taking place in Bosnia and Herzegovina, the Republic of Croatia and the Federal Republic of Yugoslavia (Serbia and Montenegro), [...]

8. *Calls upon* the Government of the Federal Republic of Yugoslavia (Serbia and Montenegro) to undertake substantially greater efforts to institute democratic norms, especially in regard to the protection of free and independent media, and full respect for human rights and fundamental freedoms;

9. *Strongly urges* the Government of the Federal Republic of Yugoslavia (Serbia and Montenegro) to revoke all discriminatory legislation and to apply all other legislation without discrimination and to take urgent action to prevent arbitrary evictions and dismissals and discrimination against any ethnic or national, religious or linguistic group;

10. *Urgently demands* that the authorities of the Federal Republic of Yugoslavia (Serbia and Montenegro) take immediate action to put an end to the repression of, and to prevent violence against, non-Serb populations in Kosovo, including acts of harassment, beatings, torture, warrantless searches, arbitrary detention and unfair trials, and also to respect the rights of persons belonging to minority groups in the Sandjak and Vojvodina and of persons belonging to the Bulgarian minority;

11. *Calls upon* the Government of the Federal Republic of Yugoslavia (Serbia and Montenegro) to act immediately to allow all residents in Kosovo to participate freely and fully in the political, economic, social and cultural life of the region, particularly in the areas of education and health care, and to ensure that all the residents of the region are guaranteed equal treatment and protection regardless of ethnic affiliation;

[...]

82nd plenary meeting 12 December 1996

18. Situation of Human Rights in Kosovo, UN General Assembly Resolution 52/139, 12 December 1997

The General Assembly,

Guided by the Charter of the United Nations, the Universal Declaration of Human Rights,[2] the International Covenants on Human Rights[3] and other human rights instruments,

Taking note with concern of the reports on the situation of human rights in Bosnia and Herzegovina,[4] the Republic of Croatia[5] and the Federal Republic of Yugoslavia[6] submitted by the Special Rapporteur of the Commission on Human Rights on the situation of human rights in the territory of the former Yugoslavia, which describe the continuing grave human rights situation in Kosovo,

Noting with regret that a memorandum of understanding on the educational system in Kosovo, signed in 1996, has not yet been implemented, and calling for full and immediate implementation of that memorandum,

Noting with concern the use of force by Serbian police against peaceful Albanian student protesters of Kosovo on 1 October 1997 and the failure of the Government of the Federal Republic of Yugoslavia to make reasonable accommodation to address the legitimate grievances of the students,

1. *Expresses* its deep concern about all violations of human rights and fundamental freedoms in Kosovo, in particular the repression of the ethnic Albanian population and discrimination against it, as well as acts of violence in Kosovo;

2. *Calls upon* the authorities of the Federal Republic of Yugoslavia:

(a) To take all necessary measures to bring to an immediate end all human rights violations against ethnic Albanians in Kosovo, including, in particular, discriminatory measures and practices, arbitrary searches and detention, the violation of the right to a fair trial and the practice of torture and other cruel, inhuman or degrading treatment, and to revoke all discriminatory legislation, in particular that which has entered into force since 1989;

(b) To release all political prisoners and to cease the persecution of political leaders and members of local human rights organizations;

(c) To allow the return in safety and dignity of Albanian refugees from Kosovo to their homes;

(d) To allow the establishment of genuine democratic institutions in Kosovo, including the parliament and the judiciary, and to respect the will of its inhabitants as the best means of preventing the escalation of the conflict there;

(e) To allow the reopening of the educational, cultural and scientific institutions of the ethnic Albanians;

3. *Urges* the authorities of the Federal Republic of Yugoslavia to pursue constructive dialogue with the representatives of the ethnic Albanians of Kosovo;

4. *Welcomes* the visits to Kosovo of the Special Rapporteur of the Commission on Human Rights on the situation of human rights in the territory of the former Yugoslavia and her relevant reports,[7] and calls upon her to continue to monitor closely the human rights situation in Kosovo and to continue to pay due attention to that matter in her reporting;

---

[1] A/51/556.
[2] Resolution 217 A (III).
[3] Resolution 2200 A (XXI), annex.
[4] E/CN.4/1998/13; see also A/52/490.
[5] E/CN.4/1998/14; see also A/52/490.
[6] E/CN.4/1998/15; see also A/52/490.
[7] Ibid.

5. *Urges* the authorities of the Federal Republic of Yugoslavia to allow the immediate unconditional return of the mission of long duration of the Organization for Security and Cooperation in Europe to Kosovo, as called for in Security Council resolution 855 (1993) of 9 August 1993;

6. *Welcomes* the report of the Secretary-General on the situation of human rights in Kosovo,[1] submitted pursuant to General Assembly resolution 51/111 of 12 December 1996, and requests him to continue his efforts to seek ways and means, including through consultations with the United Nations High Commissioner for Human Rights and relevant regional organizations, to establish an adequate international monitoring presence in Kosovo and to report thereon to the Assembly at its fifty-third session;

7. *Encourages* the Secretary-General to pursue his humanitarian efforts in the former Yugoslavia, in liaison with the Office of the United Nations High Commissioner for Refugees, the United Nations Children's Fund and other appropriate humanitarian organizations, with a view to taking urgent practical steps to tackle the critical needs of the people in Kosovo, and to assist in the voluntary return of displaced persons to their homes in conditions of safety and dignity;

8. *Emphasizes* the importance of laws and regulations concerning citizenship applied by the authorities of the Federal Republic of Yugoslavia being in accordance with the standards and principles of non-discrimination, equal protection before the law and the reduction and avoidance of statelessness, as set out in the relevant international human rights instruments;

9. *Also emphasizes* that improvements in the promotion and protection of human rights and fundamental freedoms in Kosovo will assist the Federal Republic of Yugoslavia to establish the full range of relations with the international community;

10. *Decides* to continue the examination of the situation of human rights in Kosovo at its fifty-third session under the item entitled "Human rights questions".

70th plenary meeting 12 December 1997; vote: 106-2-56

19. Situation of Human Rights in Bosnia and Herzegovina, the Republic of Croatia and the FRY (Serbia and Montenegro), UN General Assembly Resolution 52/147, 12 December 1997

[Parts not referring to the situation in the situation in Kosovo have been omitted.]

The General Assembly, [...]

12. *Calls upon* the Government of the Federal Republic of Yugoslavia to undertake substantially greater efforts to institute democratic norms, especially in regard to the promotion and protection of free and independent media, and full respect for human rights and fundamental freedoms; [...]

15. *Urgently demands* that the authorities of the Federal Republic of Yugoslavia take immediate action to put an end to the repression of, and prevent violence against, non-Serb populations in Kosovo, including acts of harassment, beatings, torture, warrantless searches, arbitrary detention and unfair trials, and also to respect the rights of persons belonging to minority groups in the Sandjak and Vojvodina and of persons belonging to the Bulgarian minority and to allow the immediate, unconditional return of the long-term mission of the Organization for Security and Cooperation in Europe to Kosovo, the Sandjak and Vojvodina, as called for in Security Council resolution 855 (1993) of 9 August 1993;

16. *Calls upon* the Government of the Federal Republic of Yugoslavia to respect the democratic process and to act immediately to allow freedom of expression and assembly and full and free participation by all residents in Kosovo in the political, economic, social and cultural life of the region, particularly in the areas of education and health care, and to ensure that all the residents of the region are guaranteed equal treatment and protection regardless of ethnic affiliation;

17. *Strongly urges* the Government of the Federal Republic of Yugoslavia to revoke all discriminatory legislation and to apply all other legislation without discrimination and to take urgent action to prevent arbitrary evictions and dismissals and discrimination against any ethnic or national, religious or linguistic group; [...]

70th plenary meeting 12 December 1997; vote: 133-2-27

20. Situation of Human Rights in Bosnia and Herzegovina, the Republic of Croatia and the FRY (Serbia and Montenegro), UN General Assembly Resolution 53/163, 9 December 1998

[Parts not referring to the situation in Kosovo have been omitted.]

The General Assembly, [...]

III. FEDERAL REPUBLIC OF YUGOSLAVIA (SERBIA AND MONTENEGRO)

31. *Calls upon* the authorities of the Federal Republic of Yugoslavia (Serbia and Montenegro) to end any torture and other cruel, inhuman or degrading treatment or punishment of persons in detention, as described in the report of the Special Rapporteur of the Commission on Human Rights on the situation of human rights in Bosnia and Herzegovina, the Republic of Croatia and the Federal Republic of Yugoslavia (Serbia and Montenegro),[2] and to bring those responsible to justice;

32. *Strongly urges* the Government of the Federal Republic of Yugoslavia (Serbia and Montenegro) to institutionalize democratic norms, especially in regard to respect for the principle of free and fair elections, the rule of law, the administration of justice, the promotion and protection of free and independent media, and full respect for human rights and fundamental freedoms, and calls upon the authorities in the Federal Republic of Yugoslavia (Serbia and Montenegro) specifically to repeal repressive laws on universities and the media;

33. *Demands* that the Government of the Federal Republic of Yugoslavia (Serbia and Montenegro) immediately cease all harassment and hindrance of journalists, whatever their ethnicity or national origin and wherever within the Federal Republic of Yugoslavia (Serbia and Montenegro) they may be practising their profession, repeal repressive laws on universities and the media, which suppress any and all internal dissent or expression of independent views, and concomitantly respect the right of free speech;

34. *Urges* all parties, groups and individuals in the Federal Republic of Yugoslavia (Serbia and Montenegro) to act with full respect for human rights, to refrain from all acts of violence and to act with respect for the rights and dignity of all persons belonging to minority groups;

35. *Strongly urges* the authorities of the Federal Republic of Yugoslavia (Serbia and Montenegro) immediately to bring to justice any persons, in particular those among its personnel, who have engaged in or authorized human rights abuses against the civilian population, including summary executions, indiscriminate attacks on civilians, indiscriminate destruction of property, mass forced displacement of civilians, the taking of civilian hostages, torture and other cruel, inhuman or degrading treatment or punishment, and in this context reminds the Government of the Federal Republic of Yugoslavia (Serbia and Montenegro) of its obligations to cooperate fully with the International Tribunal and the United Nations High Commissioner for Human Rights;

36. *Calls upon* the Government of the Federal Republic of Yugoslavia (Serbia and Montenegro) to revoke all discriminatory legislation and to apply all other legislation without discrimination against any ethnic, national, religious or linguistic group, to ensure the speedy and consistent investigation of acts of discrimination and violence against refugees and internally displaced persons, and to ensure the arrest and punishment of those responsible for acts of discrimination and violence;

---

[1] A/52/502.

[2] See A/53/322 and Add.1.

37. *Also calls upon* the Government of the Federal Republic of Yugoslavia (Serbia and Montenegro) to respect the rights of all persons belonging to minority groups especially in the Sandjak and Vojvodina, and of persons belonging to the Bulgarian minority, and supports the unconditional return of the long-term missions of the Organization for Security and Cooperation in Europe, as called for by the Security Council in its resolutions 855 (1993) of 9 August 1993 and 1160 (1998) of 31 March 1998;

38. *Further calls upon* the Government of the Federal Republic of Yugoslavia (Serbia and Montenegro) to respect the democratic process and to act immediately to make possible the establishment of genuine democratic self-governance in Kosovo, through a negotiated political settlement with representatives of the ethnic Albanian community, to cease all restrictions on freedom of expression or assembly, to ensure that all the residents of the region are guaranteed equal treatment and protection regardless of ethnic affiliation, and calls upon all individuals or groups in Kosovo to resolve the crisis there through peaceful means;

39. *Demands* that the Government of the Federal Republic of Yugoslavia (Serbia and Montenegro) take immediate steps to allow for and to create conditions for the return of internally displaced persons and refugees in safety and dignity;

40. *Calls upon* the authorities of the Federal Republic of Yugoslavia (Serbia and Montenegro) to cooperate fully with the Office of the United Nations High Commissioner for Refugees and other humanitarian organizations to alleviate the suffering of refugees and internally displaced persons and to assist in their unimpeded return to their homes;

41. *Takes note* of the report of the Special Rapporteur,[1] in which concern is expressed about the continuing grave situation of human rights in Kosovo, as well as the report of the Secretary-General on the situation of human rights in Kosovo,[2] while noting that the Federal Republic of Yugoslavia (Serbia and Montenegro) is allowing international verifiers into Kosovo;

42. *Welcomes* the establishment of a sub-office of the United Nations High Commissioner for Human Rights in Pristina in the context of the United Nations Field Operation in the Former Yugoslavia;

43. *Calls upon* States to consider additional voluntary contributions to meet the pressing human rights and humanitarian needs in the area, and underlines the need for continuing coordination among States, international organizations and non-governmental organizations of initiatives and programmes with the aim of avoiding duplication, overlap and working at cross-purposes;

44. *Decides* to continue its consideration of this question at its fifty-fourth session under the item entitled "Human rights questions".

85th plenary meeting 9 December 1998; vote: 141-0-21

21. Situation of Human Rights in Kosovo, UN General Assembly Resolution 53/164, 9 December 1998

The General Assembly,

Guided by the Charter of the United Nations, the Universal Declaration of Human Rights,[3] the International Covenants on Human Rights[4] and other human rights instruments,

Taking note of Security Council resolutions 1160 (1998) of 31 March 1998, 1199 (1998) of 23 September 1998 and 1203 (1998) of 24 October 1998, as well as the statement made on 24 March 1998 by the Chairman of the Commission on Human Rights at its fifty-fourth session[5] and Commission resolution 1998/79 of 22 April 1998,[6]

Taking fully into account the regional dimensions of the crisis in Kosovo, particularly with regard to the human rights and the humanitarian situation, and deeply concerned at the potential adverse consequences thereof,

Taking note with concern of the report of the Secretary-General on the situation of human rights in Kosovo[7] and the report of the Special Rapporteur of the Commission on Human Rights on the situation of human rights in Bosnia and Herzegovina, the Republic of Croatia and the Federal Republic of Yugoslavia (Serbia and Montenegro),[8] which describe the persistent and grave violations and abuse of human rights and humanitarian law in Kosovo,

Gravely concerned about the systematic terrorization of ethnic Albanians, as demonstrated in the many reports, inter alia, of torture of ethnic Albanians, through indiscriminate and widespread shelling, mass forced displacement of civilians, summary executions and illegal detention of ethnic Albanian citizens of the Federal Republic of Yugoslavia (Serbia and Montenegro) by the police and military,

Concerned about reports of violence committed by armed ethnic Albanian groups against non-combatants and the illegal detention of individuals, primarily ethnic Serbs, by those groups,

Stressing, in this context, the importance of the International Tribunal for the Prosecution of Persons Responsible for Serious Violations of International Humanitarian Law Committed in the Territory of the Former Yugoslavia since 1991,

Distressed by the lack of due process in the trials of those ethnic Albanians who have been detained, charged or brought to trial in relation to the crisis in Kosovo,

Concerned by the grave infringements upon the freedom of expression in the Federal Republic of Yugoslavia (Serbia and Montenegro), in particular the adoption of the new law on public information by the Serbian Parliament and the recent closure of several independent newspapers and radio stations in the Federal Republic of Yugoslavia (Serbia and Montenegro),

1. *Welcomes* the commitment made by the authorities of the Federal Republic of Yugoslavia (Serbia and Montenegro) to address the conflict and the ongoing human rights violations in Kosovo, as manifested by agreements signed by the Organization for Security and Cooperation in Europe and the North Atlantic Treaty Organization, and the international supervision of elections and verification of the implementation of human rights commitments;

2. *Welcomes* also the withdrawal and return to garrison of a number of military and police units, as demanded by the Security Council in its resolution 1199 (1998), but cautions that such withdrawals must be genuine, complete and lasting;

3. *Welcomes further* the establishment by the Organization for Security and Cooperation in Europe of the Kosovo Verification Mission, and calls upon all parties in Kosovo to cooperate fully with the Mission and ensure the protection, freedom of movement and unrestricted access within Kosovo of its personnel;

4. *Welcomes* the conclusion of a memorandum of understanding with the United Nations High Commissioner for Human Rights, in accordance with the statement by the Chairman of the Commission on Human Rights,[9] regarding the status of the office in Belgrade, leading the way to the establishment of office premises for the Office of the High Commissioner and the deployment of additional human rights officers in Kosovo;

5. *Calls upon* the Government of the Federal Republic of Yugoslavia (Serbia and Montenegro) to respect all human rights and fundamental freedoms fully and to abide by democratic norms, especially in regard to respect for the principle of free and fair elections, the rule of law, the

---

[1] See A/53/322 and Add.1.
[2] A/53/563.
[3] Resolution 217 A (III).
[4] Resolution 2200 A (XXI), annex.
[5] See Official Records of the Economic and Social Council, 1998, Supplement No. 3 (E/1998/23), chap. III, sect. E, para. 28.
[6] Ibid., chap. II, sect. A.

[7] A/53/563.
[8] See A/53/322 and Add.1.
[9] See Official Records of the Economic and Social Council, 1998, Supplement No. 3 (E/1998/23), chap. III, sect. E, para. 28.

administration of justice, free and fair trials and the promotion and protection of free and independent media;

6. *Calls upon* the authorities of the Federal Republic of Yugoslavia (Serbia and Montenegro) and the ethnic Albanian leadership in Kosovo to condemn acts of terrorism, denounce and refrain from all acts of violence, encourage the pursuit of goals through peaceful means, and respect international humanitarian law and international human rights standards;

7. *Urges* the authorities of the Federal Republic of Yugoslavia (Serbia and Montenegro) and the Kosovo Albanian leadership to enter immediately into a meaningful dialogue, without preconditions and with international involvement, and to commit themselves both to a clear timetable, leading to an end of the crisis, and to a negotiated political settlement of the issue of Kosovo, and welcomes the current efforts aimed at facilitating such a dialogue;

8. *Strongly condemns* the overwhelming number of human rights violations committed by the authorities of the Federal Republic of Yugoslavia (Serbia and Montenegro), the police and military authorities in Kosovo, including summary executions, indiscriminate and widespread attacks on civilians, indiscriminate and widespread destruction of property, mass forced displacement of civilians, the taking of civilian hostages, torture and other cruel, inhuman or degrading treatment, in breach of international humanitarian law including article 3 common to the Geneva Conventions of 12 August 1949[1] and Additional Protocol II to the Conventions, relating to the protection of victims of non-international armed conflicts,[2] and calls upon the authorities of the Federal Republic of Yugoslavia (Serbia and Montenegro) to take all measures necessary to eliminate these unacceptable practices;

9. *Condemns* the acts of violence, including kidnappings, by armed ethnic Albanian groups, in particular against non- combatants;

10. *Strongly condemns* the denial of appropriate access to Kosovo of non-governmental organizations, the manipulation and denial of relief and basic foodstuffs, and the denial of medical care to wounded civilians, calls upon the authorities of the Federal Republic of Yugoslavia (Serbia and Montenegro) to take all measures necessary to eliminate these unacceptable practices forthwith, and recalls the commitment to allow unhindered access to humanitarian organizations and the need to facilitate the immediate return of internally displaced persons to their homes;

11. *Deeply deplores* the killing of humanitarian aid workers, as reported by the Secretary-General;[3]

12. *Calls upon* all parties, in particular those of the Federal Republic of Yugoslavia (Serbia and Montenegro), to clear the area forthwith of all landmines and booby-traps and to work with the relevant international bodies to this end;

13. *Calls upon* the authorities of the Federal Republic of Yugoslavia (Serbia and Montenegro) to comply with and build on the commitments made by the President of the Republic of Serbia in his statement of 13 October 1998, which were subsequently endorsed by the Government of the Federal Republic of Yugoslavia (Serbia and Montenegro);

14. *Also calls upon* the authorities of the Federal Republic of Yugoslavia (Serbia and Montenegro):

(a) To establish a local police force in Kosovo under local or communal direction, which will be representative of the local population;

(b) To abide by the principle that no person will be prosecuted in state courts for crimes related to the conflict in Kosovo, except for crimes against humanity, war crimes and other crimes covered by international law;

(c) To allow the International Tribunal for the Prosecution of Persons Responsible for Serious Violations of International Humanitarian Law Committed in the Territory of the Former Yugoslavia since 1991and its forensic experts complete, unimpeded access to Kosovo to examine the recently alleged atrocities against civilians;

(d) To mitigate the punishments of and where appropriate to amnesty the ethnic Albanians in Kosovo sentenced for criminal offences motivated by political aims;

(e) To respect fully all the rights of individuals in Kosovo, whatever their ethnic, cultural or religious backgrounds, so as to guarantee equitable treatment of their values and historic patrimony and so as to preserve and permit expression of their national, cultural, religious and linguistic identities in accordance with international standards and the Final Act of Helsinki of 1 August 1975;

15. *Further calls upon* the authorities of the Federal Republic of Yugoslavia (Serbia and Montenegro) to open to public observation all trials or criminal prosecutions against all those charged in relation to the conflict in Kosovo;

16. *Calls upon* the authorities of the Federal Republic of Yugoslavia (Serbia and Montenegro) to make possible the establishment of genuine democratic self-governance in Kosovo, through a negotiated political settlement with representatives of the ethnic Albanian community, as called for by the Security Council in its resolutions 1160 (1998), 1199 (1998) and 1203 (1998), to include executive, legislative and judicial bodies and police, and in so doing to respect the rights of Kosovar Albanians and all who live in Kosovo, and expresses its support for an enhanced status for Kosovo, which would include a substantially greater degree of autonomy;

17. *Also calls upon* the authorities of the Federal Republic of Yugoslavia (Serbia and Montenegro) to grant access to and free and unaccompanied movement within Kosovo for all humanitarian aid workers and international monitors;

18. *Further calls upon* the authorities of the Federal Republic of Yugoslavia (Serbia and Montenegro):

(a) To promote and respect fully freedom of expression and freedom of the press, without discrimination;

(b) To repeal those legal measures used to discriminate against ethnic Albanians, including repressive laws on universities;

19. *Calls upon* the authorities of the Federal Republic of Yugoslavia (Serbia and Montenegro) and armed Albanian groups to refrain from any harassment and intimidation of journalists;

20. *Calls upon* the authorities of the Federal Republic of Yugoslavia (Serbia and Montenegro) to work closely with and support the mission to Kosovo of the personal representative of the Chairman-in-Office of the Organization for Security and Cooperation in Europe, and with the Kosovo Verification Mission;

21. *Also calls upon* the authorities of the Federal Republic of Yugoslavia (Serbia and Montenegro) to investigate and prosecute in all cases where so warranted, notably those cases concerning its personnel, anyone suspected of torture and ill-treatment of persons held in detention;

22. *Further calls upon* the authorities of the Federal Republic of Yugoslavia (Serbia and Montenegro) to release all political prisoners, to allow unimpeded access by non-governmental organizations and international observers to those prisoners who remain in detention, and to cease the persecution of political leaders and members of local human rights organizations;

23. *Calls upon* the authorities of the Federal Republic of Yugoslavia (Serbia and Montenegro) and ethnic Albanian leaders to allow for and facilitate the free and unhindered return to their homes, in safety and with dignity, of all internally displaced persons and refugees, and expresses its concern about reports of continuing harassment or other impediments in this regard;

24. *Calls upon* the Government of the Federal Republic of Yugoslavia (Serbia and Montenegro) and all others concerned to guarantee the unrestricted access of humanitarian organizations and the United Na-

---

[1] United Nations, Treaty Series, vol. 75, Nos. 970-973.
[2] Ibid., vol. 1125, No. 17513.
[3] See A/53/563, para. 6.

tions High Commissioner for Human Rights to Kosovo, and to allow the unhindered delivery of relief items and ensure the safety and security of humanitarian, diplomatic and other affected personnel accredited to the Federal Republic of Yugoslavia (Serbia and Montenegro), including members of the Verification Mission of the Organization for Security and Cooperation in Europe;

25. *Encourages* the useful cooperation of the United Nations and the Organization for Security and Cooperation in Europe on the ground, in the light of the report of the Secretary-General on the situation of human rights in Kosovo;[1]

26. *Requests* the Secretary-General to pursue his humanitarian efforts in the Federal Republic of Yugoslavia (Serbia and Montenegro), working through the Office of the United Nations High Commissioner for Refugees, the World Food Programme, the United Nations Children's Fund, other appropriate humanitarian organizations and the Office of the United Nations High Commissioner for Human Rights, with a view to taking urgent practical steps to meet the critical needs of the people in Kosovo, and to assist in the voluntary return of the displaced persons to their homes in conditions of safety and dignity;

27. *Encourages* the Office of the Prosecutor of the International Tribunal to continue investigations at all levels on serious violations of international humanitarian law committed in Kosovo, and reaffirms that such crimes fall within its jurisdiction;

28. *Demands* that the authorities of the Federal Republic of Yugoslavia (Serbia and Montenegro) and the Kosovo Albanian leadership and all others concerned cooperate fully with the International Tribunal and honour all their obligations towards it by, inter alia, providing full and free access to Kosovo for the investigators of the Tribunal;

29. *Reiterates* its call upon the authorities of the Federal Republic of Yugoslavia (Serbia and Montenegro) to live up to their commitment to provide financial and material assistance to those residents of Kosovo whose homes have been damaged;

30. *Emphasizes* that legislation on citizenship of the Federal Republic of Yugoslavia (Serbia and Montenegro) should be applied in accordance with the principles set out in relevant international instruments, in particular with regard to the standards and principles of the reduction and avoidance of statelessness;

31. *Also emphasizes* that improvement in the promotion and protection of human rights and fundamental freedoms in the Federal Republic of Yugoslavia (Serbia and Montenegro) will assist in establishing a full range of relations with the international community;

32. *Requests* the Special Rapporteur of the Commission on Human Rights on the situation of human rights in the territories of Bosnia and Herzegovina, the Republic of Croatia and the Federal Republic of Yugoslavia (Serbia and Montenegro) to continue to monitor closely the situation of human rights in Kosovo, to pay special attention to Kosovo in his reporting and to report his findings to the Commission on Human Rights at its fifty-fifth session and to the General Assembly at its fifty-fourth session;

33. *Decides* to continue its consideration of the situation of human rights in Kosovo at its fifty-fourth session under the item entitled "Human rights questions".

85th plenary meeting 9 December 1998, vote: 122-3-34

22. Situation of Human Rights in Kosovo, UN General Assembly Resolution 54/183, 17 December 1999

The General Assembly,

Guided by the Charter of the United Nations, the Universal Declaration of Human Rights, Resolution 217 A (III), the International Covenants on Human Rights Resolution 2200 A (XXI), Annex, and other human rights instruments,

Bearing in mind Security Council resolutions 1160 (1998) of 31 March 1998, 1199 (1998) of 23 September 1998, 1203 (1998) of 24 October 1998, 1239 (1999) of 14 May 1999 and 1244 (1999) of 10 June 1999, and the general principles annexed to that resolution, as well as the statement made on 24 March 1998 by the Chairman of the Commission on Human Rights at the fifty-fourth session of the Commission,[2] Commission on Human Rights resolutions 1998/79 of 22 April 1998[3] and the report of the United Nations High Commissioner for Human Rights to the Bureau of the Commission on the situation of human rights in Kosovo of 7 September 1999,

Recalling, against the background of years of repression, intolerance and violence in Kosovo, the challenge to build a multi-ethnic society on the basis of substantial autonomy, respecting the sovereignty and territorial integrity of the Federal Republic of Yugoslavia (Serbia and Montenegro), pending final settlement in accordance with Security Council resolution 1244 (1999),

Taking fully into account the regional dimensions of the crisis in Kosovo, in particular with regard to the human rights and humanitarian situation and the continuing problems in that regard, and noting that the return of refugees to their homes has contributed to the easing of this crisis,

Taking note with concern of the report of the Special Rapporteur of the Commission on Human Rights on the situation of human rights in Bosnia and Herzegovina, the Republic of Croatia and the Federal Republic of Yugoslavia (Serbia and Montenegro), A/54/396-S/1999/1000 and Add.1. which describes the persistent and grave violations and abuses of human rights and international humanitarian law in Kosovo,

Condemning the grave violations of human rights in Kosovo that affected ethnic Albanians prior to the arrival of personnel of the United Nations Interim Administration Mission in Kosovo and troops of the international security presence, the Kosovo Force, as demonstrated in the many reports of torture, indiscriminate and widespread shelling, mass forced displacement of civilians, summary executions and illegal detention of ethnic Albanians in Kosovo by the Yugoslav police and military,

Deeply concerned, in spite of the efforts of the Mission and the Force, about the frequent instances of harassment, periodic kidnapping and murder of ethnic Serb, Roma and other minorities of Kosovo by ethnic Albanian extremists,

Expressing concern that the entire population of Kosovo has been affected by the conflict, and stressing that all of the national minorities there must benefit from their full and equal rights,

Stressing, in this context, the importance of the International Tribunal for the Prosecution of Persons Responsible for Serious Violations of International Humanitarian Law Committed in the Territory of the Former Yugoslavia since 1991,

Distressed by the lack of due process in the trials in Serbia of the ethnic Albanians who have been detained, charged or brought to trial in relation to the crisis in Kosovo in violation of international human rights standards,

Stressing the urgent need to implement effective measures to stop trafficking in women and children,

1. *Underlines* the obligation of the authorities of the Federal Republic of Yugoslavia (Serbia and Montenegro) to abide by the terms of Security Council resolution 1244 (1999) and the general principles on the political solution to the Kosovo crisis adopted on 6 May 1999 and annexed to that resolution;

2. *Reaffirms* that the human rights and humanitarian crisis in Kosovo shall be addressed within the framework of a political solution based

---

[1] A/53/563.

[2] See Official Records of the Economic and Social Council, 1998, Supplement No. 3 (E/1998/23), chap. III, sect. E, para. 28.

[3] Ibid., chap. II, sect. A. and 1999/2 of 13 April 1999 Ibid., 1999, Supplement No. 3 (E/1999/23), chap. II, sect. A.

upon the general principles annexed to Security Council resolution 1244 (1999);

3. *Welcomes* the establishment of the United Nations Interim Administration Mission in Kosovo and the Kosovo Force, and calls upon all parties in Kosovo and the authorities of the Federal Republic of Yugoslavia (Serbia and Montenegro) to cooperate fully with the Mission and the Force in the fulfilment of their respective mandates;

4. *Also welcomes* the work of the Office of the United Nations High Commissioner for Human Rights in Kosovo and the Office of the United Nations High Commissioner for Refugees and the efforts of the Organization for Security and Cooperation in Europe;

5. *Calls upon* all parties in Kosovo to cooperate with the Mission in ensuring full respect for all human rights and fundamental freedoms and democratic norms in Kosovo;

6. *Calls upon* all authorities in the Federal Republic of Yugoslavia (Serbia and Montenegro), the local Serb leaders in Kosovo and the leaders of the Albanian community in Kosovo to condemn all acts of terrorism, sequestration or kidnapping and forced eviction from homes or places of work of any resident of Kosovo, whatever the ethnic background of the victim and whoever the perpetrators, to refrain from all acts of violence and to use their influence and leadership to cooperate with the Force and the Mission in stopping these incidents and in bringing the perpetrators to justice;

7. *Expresses* its concern about the forced division of any part of Kosovo into ethnic cantons or ethnically based divisions of any type, which is counter to Security Council resolution 1244 (1999) and to the guiding principles of Rambouillet,[1] and stresses the need for all parties in Kosovo to take all necessary measures to stop or reverse any action that de facto or de jure permits such ethnic cantonization;

8. *Calls upon* all parties, in particular the authorities and representatives of the Federal Republic of Yugoslavia (Serbia and Montenegro) and the Kosovar Serb and Albanian leaderships, to cooperate with the Mine Action Coordination Centre;

9. *Demands* that the Government of the Federal Republic of Yugoslavia (Serbia and Montenegro) provide an updated list of all persons detained and transferred from Kosovo to other parts of the Federal Republic of Yugoslavia (Serbia and Montenegro), specifying the charge, if any, under which each individual is detained, and that it guarantee their families and non-governmental organizations and international observers unimpeded and regular access to those who remain in detention and release all individuals detained and transferred from Kosovo prior to July 1999 in violation of international humanitarian and human rights standards;

10. *Calls upon* the authorities of the Federal Republic of Yugoslavia (Serbia and Montenegro) to open to public observation trials or criminal prosecutions against all those charged in relation to the conflict in Kosovo;

11. *Calls upon* the authorities of the Federal Republic of Yugoslavia (Serbia and Montenegro) and ethnic Kosovar Serb and Albanian representatives to allow for and to facilitate the free and unhindered return to their homes, in safety and with dignity, of all displaced persons and refugees, of whichever ethnic background, and expresses its concern about reports of continuing harassment or other impediments in this regard;

12. *Calls upon* the authorities of the Federal Republic of Yugoslavia (Serbia and Montenegro) to return or to facilitate the fair, unbiased and accurate restoration or reconstruction of Kosovar documentation and legal records taken or destroyed during the conflict;

13. *Stresses* the importance of and the responsibility of all parties to create a secure environment in Kosovo that will allow refugees and displaced persons to return and allow all those who wish to remain in Kosovo a genuine possibility to do so, irrespective of their ethnic origin;

14. *Requests* the Secretary-General to pursue his humanitarian efforts in Kosovo through the Office of the United Nations High Commissioner for Refugees, the World Food Programme, the United Nations Children's Fund, other appropriate humanitarian organizations and the Office of the United Nations High Commissioner for Human Rights and to continue to take the urgent practical steps to meet the critical needs of the people in Kosovo and to assist in the voluntary return of displaced persons to their homes in conditions of safety and dignity;

15. *Encourages* the Office of the Prosecutor of the International Tribunal for the Prosecution of Persons Responsible for Serious Violations of International Humanitarian Law Committed in the Territory of the Former Yugoslavia since 1991 to continue investigations at all levels concerning official individuals or private citizens with regard to serious violations of international humanitarian law committed in Kosovo, and reaffirms that the investigation of such crimes falls within the jurisdiction of the Office;

16. *Demands* that the authorities of the Federal Republic of Yugoslavia (Serbia and Montenegro) and the Kosovar Serb and Albanian leaderships and all others concerned cooperate fully with the International Tribunal for the Former Yugoslavia and honour all obligations towards it;

17. *Reiterates* its call upon the authorities of the Federal Republic of Yugoslavia (Serbia and Montenegro) to live up to their commitment to provide financial and material assistance to those residents of Kosovo whose homes have been damaged;

18. *Calls upon* the authorities of the Federal Republic of Yugoslavia (Serbia and Montenegro) to provide information on the fate and the whereabouts of the high number of missing persons from Kosovo, and encourages the International Committee of the Red Cross to pursue its clarification efforts in this regard, in cooperation with other organizations such as the Organization for Security and Cooperation in Europe;

19. *Encourages* the ongoing cooperation provided by the Federal Republic of Yugoslavia (Serbia and Montenegro) regarding the visits to some two thousand prisoners, mainly of Kosovar Albanian origin, carried out by the International Committee of the Red Cross and held under the authority of the Ministry of Justice of Serbia;

20. *Welcomes* the efforts made by the international community, and calls for continuing support for the Office of the United Nations High Commissioner for Refugees and other agencies engaged in the effort to provide those in need in Kosovo with proper accommodation, in particular with a view to facilitating the preparation and provision of adequate winter accommodation;

21. *Urges all* parties involved in Kosovo to support the efforts of the United Nations Children's Fund to ensure that all children in Kosovo return to school as soon as possible and to contribute to the rebuilding and repair of schools destroyed or damaged during the conflict in Kosovo;

22. *Calls* for the most rapid and full deployment of United Nations police and for the creation of a multi-ethnic local police force throughout Kosovo, as a key step towards guaranteeing respect for law and order and for creating a safe environment for all inhabitants of Kosovo;

23. *Condemns* any effort, on behalf of any ethnic group, to create any sort of parallel institutions for Kosovar Serb and Albanian populations, be they police, school, administrative or other institutions, and calls upon the Mission and the Force to prevent any such institutions from being formed;

24. *Requests* the Special Rapporteur of the Commission on Human Rights on the situation of human rights in Bosnia and Herzegovina, the Republic of Croatia and the Federal Republic of Yugoslavia (Serbia and Montenegro) to continue to monitor closely the situation of human rights in Kosovo, to pay special attention to Kosovo in his reporting and to report his findings to the Commission on Human Rights at its fifty-sixth session and to the General Assembly at its fifty-fifth session.

83rd plenary meeting 17 December 1999

---

[1] See S/1999/648, Annex.

2.1.2 THE UN COMMISSION ON HUMAN RIGHTS

23. Report on the Situation of Human Rights in the Former Yugoslavia, E/CN.4/1992/S-1/9, 28 August 1992

[Parts not referring to the situation in Kosovo have been omitted.]

Introduction

[...]

I. Observations Concerning the Situation of Human Rights in the Areas Visited

A. THE POLICY OF ETHNIC CLEANSING

[...]

1. Ethnic cleansing directed against Muslims and ethnic Croatians in the territories of Bosnia and Herzegovina and Croatia under the control of ethnic Serbs

[...]

2. The situation elsewhere in Bosnia and Herzegovina

[...]

3. The flight of ethnic Serbs from Croatia

[...]

4. The situation in Serbia and Montenegro

31. The leadership of the Federal Republic of Yugoslavia, which comprises the Republics of Serbia and Montenegro, does not openly endorse the policy of ethnic cleansing. In a statement made to the Special Rapporteur, the President of the Federal Republic of Yugoslavia condemned ethnic cleansing. He also stated that the solution to the ethnic conflict in Bosnia and Herzegovina is "cantonization", which he defined as the establishment of ethnically mixed units within Bosnia and Herzegovina with reciprocal guarantees for the rights of ethnic Serbs, ethnic Croatians and Muslims. The President of Serbia also repudiated the policy of ethnic cleansing in statements to the Special Rapporteur. However, the Federal Republic of Yugoslavia and Serbia clearly exercise very great influence on the "Serbian Republic of Bosnia and Herzegovina" which, without their cooperation, would be completely cut off from the rest of the world. There is thus far no evidence that the Federal Republic of Yugoslavia and Serbia have taken effective measures to use their influence to put a stop to ethnic cleansing in Bosnia.

32. In addition, there is some evidence that ethnic cleansing may be imminent in certain parts of Serbia and Montenegro where there are large communities of persons not of Serbian origin. In Kosovo, where the population of Albanian origin has complained of discrimination and oppression for many years, non-governmental organizations presented evidence of an increasing number of torture and killings. In Vojvodina, in the north of Serbia, where there are large numbers of persons of Hungarian, Croatian and other origins, an increase in the harassment and intimidation of the non-Serbian population has been reported. Thousands of persons are already reported to be fleeing the region of Sandzac, on the border of Serbia and Montenegro, where the population is largely Muslim. It was not possible to visit any of these areas during the mission, and the Special Rapporteur intends to explore these aspects of his mandate further during future missions.

[...]

II. Recommendations

[...]

61. The United Nations should continue firmly to call upon the competent authorities to abandon the policy of ethnic cleansing in all its forms. Every victim of this policy should be guaranteed the possibility of claiming his/her rights under international supervision. This should also be the case in regard to those persons who have been forced to consent to "voluntary" displacement. No norms or decisions issued by the authorities conducting the policy of ethnic cleansing can make this policy and its consequences legal.

62. There is a real possibility that the most violent forms of the policy of ethnic cleansing will spread to Kosovo, Sandzak and Vojvodina. This danger requires the immediate creation of an international mechanism to monitor the human rights situation on those territories. It would be highly advisable to secure the cooperation of the Conference on Security and Cooperation in Europe in this respect. [...]

24. Report on the Situation of Human Rights in the Territory of the Former Yugoslavia Submitted by Mr. Tadeusz Mazowiecki, Special Rapporteur of the Commission on Human Rights, pursuant to Commission Resolution 1992/S-1/1 of 14 August 1992, A/48/92-S/25341, paras. 153-171, 26 February 1993

[Parts not referring to the situation in Kosovo have been omitted.]

[...]

153. In his report to the General Assembly at its forty-seventh session (A/47/666), the Special Rapporteur expressed his concern about the situation of human rights in Kosovo following a brief visit to Prishtina. The main issues raised concern the mass dismissal of Albanians from the public sector, police brutality, the lack of freedom of the media and problems concerning education. The situation of human rights has been constantly worsening since Kosovo lost its status as an autonomous province in July 1990. The Albanian population has been enduring various forms of discrimination as a result of new laws adopted by the Republic of Serbia and the economic situation has deteriorated to the extent that even the subsistence of many Albanian families is threatened.

154. Since his visit, the Special Rapporteur has continued to receive information from international monitors, in particular the CSCE mission, concerning the human rights situation in Kosovo.

Legal Aspects

155. The Special Rapporteur has received a list of laws reportedly discriminating against Albanians. The following paragraphs describe some of these laws.

156. Reportedly, a number of laws, programmes and decrees adopted by the authorities of Serbia contributed to the dismissal of Albanians and the appointment of Serbs and Montenegrins in their places. To this effect the Albanians cited:

(a) The Programme for the establishment of peace, liberty, equality, democracy and prosperity in the autonomous province of Kosovo (Official 5 Gazette of Serbia 15/90 of 30 March 1990), paragraph 3 of which envisages assistance to Serbs and Montenegrins who want to move to Kosovo. Paragraph 9 of the programme implies the dismissal of Albanians from the police force, which was carried out at the time of the abolishment of the Secretariat (i.e. Ministry) of the Interior of Kosovo on 16 April 1990. The places of the dismissed Albanian policemen were taken by Serbs and Montenegrins;

(b) The Law on police institutions (Official Gazette of Serbia 44/91 of 25 July 1991) was used as the legal basis for taking policemen from all over former Yugoslavia to replace the dismissed Albanians,

(c) The Law on the creation of a fund to finance the return of Serbs and Montenegrins to Kosovo (Official Gazette of Serbia 35/90 of 14 July 1990), and

(d) The Programme for the development of the Autonomous Province of Kosovo and Metohia, aiming at the return of Serbs and Montenegrins to Kosovo and Metohia, for 1992 (Official Gazette of Serbia 54/92 of 8 August 1992) provides for assistance to Serbs for building houses, setting up private firms and enterprises, and creating cultural establishments, schools, communications and infrastructure;

(e) The Law on labour relations in special circumstances (Official Gazette of Serbia 40/90 of 26 July 1990) provides for the right of the directors of enterprises to impose on the workers disciplinary measures envisaged by the laws. Given the fact that in a large number of cases directors are Serbs, Albanians complain that this law leads to arbitrary dismissals of Albanians. The introduction of special measures in many enterprises and social institutions led to the discontinuation of their activities and many Albanians lost their jobs as a consequence:

(f) The Law on the conditions, ways and means for distributing agricultural land to citizens who would like to live and work on the territory of the Autonomous Province of Kosovo and Metohia (Official Gazette of Serbia 43/91 of 20 July 1991) envisages making credit available to Serbs who want to move to Kosovo;

(g) The Law on the health service (Official Gazette of Serbia 17/92 of 31 March 1992) allegedly led to the dismissal of many Albanians working in the health sector;

(h) The Law on public information (Official Gazette of Serbia 19/91 of 29 March 1991) led to the dismissal of many journalists and other staff of the Albanian nationality from newspapers, radio and television in Prishtina;

(i) The Law abolishing the Kosovo Law on the educational service (Official Gazette of Serbia 75/91 of 17 December 1991) is said to be the reason that many Albanian teachers lost their jobs.

157. Other discriminatory legal acts against the Albanians in Kosovo concerning education, cultural institutions and the use of the Albanian language were reported as follows:

(a) The laws abolishing those adopted earlier by the legislature of the Socialist Autonomous Province of Kosovo (Law on higher education, Law on university education, Law on the Pedagogical Academy, Law on primary education, the Law on secondary education (Official Gazette of Serbia 45/90 of 7 August 1990) and the law abolishing the Law on the Educational Council of the Socialist Autonomous Province of Kosovo (Official Gazette of Serbia 75/91 of 17 December 1991) destroyed the established system of education for the Albanians in Kosovo on all levels;

(b) The Law establishing the publishing house "Panorama" (Official Gazette of Serbia 80/92 of 6 November 1992) and the above-cited law on public information (Official Gazette of Serbia 19/91 from 29 March 1991) contributed to the enforcement of state control over the mass media in Kosovo. The new agency incorporates the newspaper Rilindja which has been published in Albanian for more than 50 years;

(c) The Law on the official use of the language and the alphabet (Official Gazette of Serbia 45/91 of 27 July 1991) gives priority to the official use of the Serbian language in public institutions;

(d) The Law abolishing the Kosovo Law on the Institute of the History of Kosovo (Official Gazette of Serbia 49/92 of 21 July 1992) hampers the -development of knowledge about the national history and culture of the Albanians in Kosovo. To acquire such knowledge Kosovars must address themselves to the respective Serbian institutions;

(e) The Law on the Serbian Academy of Sciences (Official Gazette of Serbia 49/92 of 21 July 1992) served as a basis for the Serbian Academy of Sciences to take over the property of the Academy of Sciences of Kosovo;

(f) The Law on the universities (Official Gazette of Serbia 54/92 of 8 August 1992) envisages in its article 10 that education should be given in Serbo-Croatian. It can be given in the languages of the minorities if the board of the corresponding university or faculty agrees on this. The Albanians claim that this discriminates against them because the boards of the universities are nominated by the Serbian authorities.

158. Albanians see discrimination in the sphere of population policies: (a) Paragraph 91 of the Programme for the establishment of peace, liberty, equality, democracy and prosperity in the Autonomous Province of Kosovo (Official Gazette of Serbia 15/90 of 30 March 1990) envisages measures for the decrease of the birth rate in Kosovo, which is among the highest in Europe;

(b) The law on public care for children (Official Gazette of Serbia 49/92 of 21 July 1992) provides for families with more than three children 5 (and these are typically Albanian families) to receive from the State much lower allowances for the younger children. Albanians regard these provisions as discriminatory as Serbs usually have small families and thus all their children receive allowances.

159. A Declaration on human rights and the rights of persons belonging to national minorities was adopted by the Serbian authorities and published in the Official Gazette of Serbia 89,Y2 of 7 December 1992. The Albanians, however, consider that this declaration is in total contradiction with the real facts of violations of minority and human rights in Kosovo.

Police Brutality

160. Several reports indicate that, before and after the elections of 20 December 1992, the police adopted a more severe and aggressive attitude towards the Albanian population. It has been reported that searches without warrants of the houses of Albanians have been carried out on a regular basis, and that at least 70 people, including five Serbs, were arrested. According to a recent report by the CSCE mission "the President of the Assembly of the Muslim Community of Serbia, Kosovo, Sandzak and Vojvodina 86 well as other Muslim personalities have been arrested". According to official sources some of those arrested have been released.

161. Police action has gone beyond arrest and imprisonment and cases of death as a result of shooting or brutality by the police have been reported. During the first two weeks of December 1992, four incidents were reported from Prishtina and three other small towns during which four Albanians were said to have been killed, and two others and a policeman wounded. It has been asserted that the armed forces also participated in the recent incidents. In two clashes with the Albanian community, the armed forces have allegedly killed two people. Furthermore, the following incidents have also been reported:

(a) On 3 December 1992, in the market of Prishtina, a 19-year-old Albanian was shot dead by the police and his older brother wounded in both legs, presumably while selling goods on the black market;

(b) On 18 December 1992, in Dakovica, a young man was beaten to death;

(c) On 19 December 1992, a 32-year-old Albanian from Brovina died in the hospital in Prishtina as a result of police brutality and beatings:

(d) On 24 December 1992, the police arrested a group of Albanians in Prishtina outside the Great Mosque, allegedly without giving any reason for the arrest;

(e) On 25 December 1992, in two villages between Prishtina and Pec, police abuse, maltreatment of the inhabitants and destruction of their food supply have been alleged. According to the information received, police brutality and harassment has increased in the town of Pec and the surrounding area with the pretext of seizing and collecting arms held illegally by civilians.

162. According to the Albanians the police have adopted a variety of repressive measures in Kosovo with the aim of provoking the Albanian population.

The Situation of the Mass Media

163. With regard to freedom of press, the Special Rapporteur has been informed of a new Press Law adopted by the Serbian Parliament at the beginning of November 1992 to be applied in Kosovo. The federal authorities of Yugoslavia did not approve the law and declared it unconstitutional. This law has established a State-owned publishing house, Panorama, in charge of printing. publishing and distributing all newspapers, periodicals, graphics and books in the three languages, Serbian, Albanian and Turkish. Allegedly, the main objective of Panorama is to absorb all the assets and staff of the exiting Albanian Publishing House run by Albanians, as well as the Serbian daily and Turkish weekly. The Government of Serbia is the only authority empowered to nominate and dismiss the members of the Administrative

Council, Supervisory Board and the General Manager as well as to approve all the internal regulations of Panorama. Independent and private publications have not been banned by the law but, due to the high cost of printing and distribution, it is highly improbable that independent enterprises can survive. Panorama is considered by Albanian journalists, who until recently have still been able to express the Albanian point of view, as a means of censorship.

164. Since the visit by the Special Rapporteur to Prishtina all Albanian staff of the local radio and television stations have been removed from their posts. The surviving 15-minute daily television programme in Albanian is allegedly produced and presented by Serbian journalists who speak Albanian.

Dismissals

165. The Special Rapporteur was recently informed by the CSCE mission that in accordance with a law adopted by the Serbian Parliament nine regional medical departments and the hospital of Dakovica Medical Centre were closed and integrated into the Pec Medical Centre. The authorities claimed that this decision was taken on the basis of the difficult economical situation, while Albanian physicians asserted that the reason for this law was political. The Dakovica Medical Centre was among the rare organizations where the overwhelming majority of staff was still Albanian, and thus was the preferred place of treatment by the entire Albanian community of the province.

166. With regard to the judiciary, the Special Rapporteur has been informed that since his visit to Kosovo, all remaining Albanian judges or magistrates have been dismissed. Under such conditions the right to a fair trial and the impartiality of the judiciary can hardly be guaranteed with regard to the Albanian population of Kosovo.

Economic Situation

167. With regard to the economic situation in Kosovo the Special Rapporteur has been informed that the regression is such that even Serbian refugees are unwilling to move there. Albanians work mostly in the private sector, mainly in small grocery stores, which allows the owners to meet their basic needs. A large number of Albanians, mainly dismissed civil servants, live in extremely poor conditions. The rate of inflation is very high and rising continuously. The few Albanians who have the opportunity to do so leave Kosovo.

168. A charitable organization, the Financial Council, financed by voluntary donations mostly from Albanians living in Western countries, has been set up by the Albanians of Kosovo. Welfare cases are taken care of by the Financial Council and about 80,000 families registered by the organization are receiving material help.

Education System

169. The Special Rapporteur was informed that the problems outlined in his previous report concerning the education system have not yet been solved. Albanian high schools and the university are closed. Some 70 per cent of the primary schools are operating following Albanian-language curricula; however, Albanian teachers do not receive any salary since they refuse to teach according to the Serbian programme and are helped by the above-mentioned Financial Council.

Elections

170. As regards the elections of 20 December 1992, the CSCE reported that "in Kosovo Albanians generally did abstain, although there are reports that some - maybe between 5 to 10 per cent - did nevertheless take part. The Mission in Prishtina has reported the presence of armed police inside some polling stations and confused and disorganized arrangements for the completion of ballots". The CSCE Mission observed that "the electoral law did not provide for envelopes in which the voters should insert the ballot papers, before throwing them into the ballot boxes ... . The lack of visually protected sites (with curtains) where the voters would secretly make their choice violated the secrecy of voting, as voters openly were making their choice and even cooperated with each other". According to the CSCE report, "the outcome of the 20 December 1992 elections has caused concern among Albanians in Kosovo ... . The presence of Arkan, an alleged war criminal, in the Serbian Assembly is viewed with great concern". Therefore, according to the CSCE, "on the Serbian side the rhetoric has grown harsher after the hard-liner won the elections and more moderate forces no longer are represented among the elected legislators from Kosovo", which could in the long term entail more deprivation of rights for the Albanians.

Conclusion

171. The conclusion to be drawn on the basis of the recent information gathered is that the human rights situation in Kosovo has not improved. On the contrary, the police has intensified their repression of the Albanian population since 1990. The Albanians continue to be deprived of their basic rights, their education system has been largely destroyed, they are victims of dismissal for political reasons and they face a very difficult economic situation. However, it must be stressed that until now they have resisted peacefully.

[...]

25. Fifth Periodic Report on the Situation of Human Rights in the Territory of the Former Yugoslavia Submitted by Mr. Tadeusz Mazowiecki, Special Rapporteur of the Commission on Human Rights, pursuant to Paragraph 32 of Commission Resolution 1993/7 of 24 February 1993, E/CN.4/1994/47, paras. 188-205, 17 November 1993

[Parts not referring to the situation in Kosovo have been omitted.]
[...]

C. The Situation in Kosovo

188. The polarization of the Albanian and Serb populations in Kosovo continues. One area affected by this polarization is the judicial system. Albanians lack confidence in the will and ability of the courts to provide an independent and effective remedy and point to the small number of Albanian judges. The CSCE monitors investigated this issue and commented:

"A major reason for the lack of Albanian judges is the refusal of most Albanians to serve in the courts. Judges must take an oath to the government, which most Albanians feel would give recognition to what they see as an illegal Serb regime."

However, the situation is in reality more complex and is illustrated by the experience of the Prizren District Court. Three Albanian judges have refused to serve as judges, but in June 1993, two others, both well qualified, were rejected by the Serbian Assembly in June 1993 after being described as "separatist murderers".

Ill-Treatment and Torture

189. The Special Rapporteur has continued to receive reports that the Serbian police and state security services act in excess of their powers and in breach of the law in their dealings with the Albanian population in Kosovo. These reports have increased significantly since July 1993.

190. In May 1993, some 30 Albanian prisoners were serving sentences for offences involving illegal political activities; this figure does not include those given administrative sentences of up to 60 days. New trials have since taken place and are continuing; most frequently the defendants are charged under article 116 of the Serbian Criminal Code with acts against the territorial integrity of Yugoslavia. In October 1993 Albanian sources reported that 93 people had been detained since July and were in custody; they included former officers of the Yugoslav National Army, as well as members of the Democratic League of Kosovo.

191. Two former detainees told the Special Rapporteur's staff that in August 1993 they had been systematically beaten to induce them to confess to membership of illegal Albanian separatist movements and to provide information about armaments. In each case, the individual was

asked whether he had arms himself. When this was denied, he was told to obtain gun(s) and produce them to the police.

192. Albanian human rights organizations have reported deaths following detention and ill-treatment by the police. One such case, that of Adem Zeqiraj from Dakovica, was investigated by the CSCE monitors. Mr. Zeqiraj was arrested on 17 December 1992 during a search for firearms at his father's house. The next day he was admitted to the Dakovica hospital and then transferred to Pristina hospital, where he died on 19 December. A medical report from Dakovica hospital recorded that he had been admitted with traumatic shock, internal bleeding and a serious kidney condition.

193. The Special Rapporteur's staff were told by the Serbian Ministry of the Interior that 52 attacks against the police had taken place between 1 January and 30 September 1993. Two police had been killed and 15 wounded. The Deputy Minister denied that Albanians who had been in contact with CSCE monitors had been arrested. However, this denial is inconsistent with statements made to the Special Rapporteur's staff by four people who were questioned by police after the departure of the CSCE monitors.

194. The Special Rapporteur has also received reports of police abuse in the course of searches for illegal arms. Such searches are frequent. There is frequently damage to property, including the destruction of national flags, symbols and teaching materials and removal of money and valuables.

HOUSING EVICTIONS

195. The Special Rapporteur's staff have received information about the eviction of Albanians from apartments in which they were lawfully resident, often without legal proceedings, in order to accommodate Serb families. In one case, a worker from the JP Elektropower enterprise of Kosovo, was evicted from the apartment of which he was the legal tenant, by two police on 7 December 1992. He remains employed, has held his job for 20 years and occupied the apartment as a member of his workers' association. The apartment was then occupied by a Serb family. Legal proceedings have commenced in the Pristina court.

USE OF LANGUAGE

196. Albanians are a "national minority" under the federal Constitution and have a constitutional right to use their language in the areas in which they live and in court proceedings. The 1991 Serbian Law on the Official Use of Language and Alphabets gives municipalities the discretion to decide which languages shall be in official use. Given the use of Albanian before 1990 and the fact that Albanians represent around 90 per cent of the Kosovo population, the Special Rapporteur believes the use of Albanian in all official matters should be normal practice, regardless of Albanian representation on municipal bodies. In practice, there has been a decline in the official use of the Albanian language.

197. The Special Rapporteur notes the issue of identity cards, birth and marriage certificates and other public documents in the Serbian language. The Special Rapporteur's staff took copies of identity cards issued in Pristina: in 1984 the cards were in three languages (Albanian, Serbo-Croat and Turkish); in 1990 in two languages (Serbo-Croat and Albanian) and in 1993 in Serbian only.

198. In the Prizren District Court proceedings are now held only in Serbian, although 95 per cent of criminal defendants are Albanian. Before 1990, Albanian and Serbo-Croat were of equal status, the criterion being the language of the defendant. While in principle a complaint may be made in Albanian, in practice it will not be dealt with because there is only one translator. A complaint made by an Albanian to the Prosecutor of the Pristina District Court, alleging ill-treatment at the hands of the police, with a medical certificate attached, was returned the same day (27 August 1993) by the Deputy Prosecutor, with a note saying: "We return your complaint ... so it may be translated into the Serbo-Croat language".

199. Throughout the territories of the former Yugoslavia, street names continued to be changed in 1993 to reflect recent political changes. While in many areas this is not controversial, the Special Rapporteur's staff were told of changes in Pristina and Prizren which had the effect of giving a Serbian character to areas in which the overwhelming majority of the population is Albanian. In Prizren, he is informed that 90 per cent of names have been changed since 1991. For example: "Bayran Curri" (an Albanian leader) to "27 March" (the date of the 1992 Serbian constitution); "League of Prizren" (Liohja e Prizreni) to "Car Dushani" (a Serb king). Similar changes have been made in the Hungarian areas of Vojvodina.

EDUCATION

200. The Special Rapporteur has received reports of continuing harassment and use of force by the police against teachers and pupils working in the "parallel" education system.

201. According to the President of the Association of Albanian Teachers, during the 1992-1993 school year, 274,280 pupils attended primary "parallel" schools. This figure contrasts with official statistics showing that in 1990, more than 295,000 Albanian pupils were enrolled in state primary, secondary and tertiary education. It will be recalled that the "parallel" schools started after August 1990, when teachers refused to accept a new curriculum drawn up by the Ministry of Education in Belgrade and some 18,000 of them lost their jobs. The new curriculum is compulsory throughout Serbia and replaces, inter alia, curricula prepared by the educational councils of Kosovo and Vojvojdina. The councils were abolished as part of a broad centralisation process and with the aim of creating a common teaching system for all schools in Serbia. The "parallel" system functions at the primary, secondary and tertiary levels. Teaching is in Albanian, according to a curriculum which is not recognized by the Serbian Ministry of Education. The schools issue their own diplomas, which are, in turn, not recognized by the Serbian educational authorities. Though teachers receive no official salary, teaching at the primary level (which is compulsory under Serbian law) largely continues to take place in school buildings, the expenses of which are paid by the education authorities. Secondary and tertiary education takes place in private houses and premises.

202. The Serbian Minister of Education told the Special Rapporteur's staff that teaching in the Albanian language is available in the state system and both the Serbian Constitution and Serbian education laws give national minorities a right to education in their own languages. The Minister said that the teachers had refused to accept curricula decided in Belgrade. In June 1990 all national minorities had been invited to propose their own teaching programmes in certain culturally specific subjects to be included in a "core" Serbian curriculum: literature, history, applied arts and music. The minorities in, for example, Vojvodina had done so, but the Albanians had not.

203. In March 1993, the former Rector of the University of Pristina, Professor Ejup Statovci, was arrested to serve a sentence imposed in 1992, when he was convicted on a public order charge after writing a letter to the current Rector asking for the university buildings "which were taken by force" to be returned to Albanian teaching staff and students. The Special Rapporteur notes with concern that the conflict surrounding the University of Pristina continues and is contributing to the prevailing climate of tension.

204. Views expressed recently by the Minister of Education and by the current Rector of the University of Pristina illustrate the intellectual climate. The Minister described education as the "sphere in which a country manifests its identity" and criticized the University of Pristina and the former Kosovo Academy of Sciences before 1990 as "centres of actual and theoretical separatism". The Rector of the University, Professor Radivoje Popovic, speaking in May 1993, referred to changes in the university since 1990 in these terms:

"Our first task was to remove the hatred for all that is Serbian which had been accumulated here for decades ... This factory of evil, established with the basic intention of destroying Serbia and the Serbian name ... is now destroyed thanks to the coordinated action of the Government and university personnel ... Our university has the ultimate object of renewing Serbian thought in Kosovo and Metohija."

205. Throughout 1993 the police have entered "parallel" schools, questioned teachers and students and in some instances threatened or used violence. On 21 June, the CSCE monitoring team in Pec reported a "campaign" against the parallel schools to coincide with the end of the school year. Eight schools were searched for graduation certificates issued in the name of the Republic of Kosovo. In Klina, the police searched the school and then went to the local Democratic League of Kosovo (LDK) office where a meeting was in progress which included a number of teachers. The 12 people present were arrested; 8 were beaten on the head and arms and 2 were beaten more severely, while being questioned about the school system. Similar police actions marked the start of the new school year in September 1993.

26. Ninth Periodic Report on the Situation of Human Rights in the Territory of the Former Yugoslavia Submitted by Mr. Tadeusz Mazowiecki, Special Rapporteur of the Commission on Human Rights, pursuant to Commission Resolution 1994/72 of 9 March 1994 and ECOSOC Decision 1994/262 of 22 July 1994, A/49/641-S/1994/1252, paras. 162-203, 4 November 1994

[Parts not referring to the situation in Kosovo have been omitted.]
[...]

III. Federal Republic of Yugoslavia (Serbia and Montenegro)

A. INTRODUCTORY REMARKS

162. The Special Rapporteur notes the fact that, owing to the refusal of the Government to permit the establishment of a field office in the Federal Republic of Yugoslavia (Serbia and Montenegro), he has been unable to collect firsthand information concerning the human rights situation in that country. In view of this fact, the Special Rapporteur finds it even more discouraging to note that the Government has, since the submission of his sixth periodic report, rejected all his requests to send missions to the country in order to investigate recent allegations of human rights abuses.

163. It should further be noted that the Government's reluctance to cooperage with the Special Rapporteur is in contravention of paragraph 30 of Commission on Human Rights resolution 1994/72, in which the Commission Demands that the Federal Republic of Yugoslavia (Serbia and Montenegro) permit entry into Kosovo, Sandjak and Vojvodina of United Nations observer missions and field officers of the Special Rapporteur and resumption of the missions of long duration of the Conference on Security and Cooperation in Europe.

[...]

1. The situation in Kosovo

182. Regular and consistent reports indicate that the situation in Kosovo has deteriorated further in the course of the past six months. The Special Rapporteur has taken note of some particularly disturbing reports according to which, during the period January to June 1994, more than 2,000 persons were taken to police stations for so-called "informative talks", lasting from hours to several days. A majority of these persons were allegedly subjected to severe ill-treatment and torture while detained by the police.

183. During the past month, there has reportedly been a drastic increase in the number of violent house searches, raids and arbitrary arrests by the law enforcement authorities. Most of the violence has reportedly occurred when the police, under the pretext of looking for hidden arms or wanted persons, raided homes or entire neighbourhoods. During these searches, minors, women and elderly people have reportedly also been ill-treated, apparently because of their relationship to persons wanted by the police. These attacks appear to be controlled or at least condoned by the leadership of the law enforcement authorities. According to recent reports, in the period 1 January to 30 June 1994, more than 3,000 homes were searched and more than 1,700 persons subjected to police abuse in connection with the raids. A particularly brutal incident was reported from Podujevo, where the police, while conducting an identity check on 15 September 1994, violently forced the passers-by to lie down on the ground. Fourteen of these people were subsequently beaten brutally by police using truncheons.

184. Undue delays and serious irregularities have been reported in connection with court proceedings against a large number of ethnic Albanians accused of posing a threat to the territorial integrity of the Federal Republic of Yugoslavia (Serbia and Montenegro). The majority of the accused appear to be members of the Democratic League of Kosovo (LDK). One of the latest of these trials reportedly started in Prizren on 16 September 1994 against four ethnic Albanians, members of the League. It is alleged that two of the defendants were arrested as early as 24 May 1994, and that they have been kept in detention since that date. Moreover, it appears that these persons have been subjected to severe ill-treatment during interrogations by the police.

185. Another cause for concern are the extremely difficult circumstances under which schools and other educational institutions work in Kosovo. It has been reported that, on 22 February 1994, the Government discontinued the activities of the Academy of Sciences and Arts of Kosovo and confiscated its building. Moreover, it is with great concern that the Special Rapporteur has taken note of reports according to which several Albanian primary and secondary schools have been forced to interrupt their work because of police harassment. Shortly after the beginning of the school year in early September 1994, it was reported that police entered the premises of several elementary schools. A particularly brutal incident was reported to have taken place in connection with a police raid on 1 September 1994 at the "Ibrahim Pervizi" elementary school in Mitrovica. During the raid, several teachers were reportedly severely beaten and kicked in front of their pupils by police officers. Two of the teachers allegedly had to seek medical care after the incident.

[...]

D. CONCLUSIONS AND RECOMMENDATIONS

198. The Special Rapporteur finds it discouraging to note that the police forces in the Federal Republic of Yugoslavia (Serbia and Montenegro) appear reluctant to prevent and control acts of violence and harassment. The acquiescence in such acts shows evidence of an unacceptable disregard for fundamental human rights on the part of those authorities which are primarily responsible for the security of the citizens of their country.

199. It is with great concern that the Special Rapporteur takes note of the numerous occasions on which police units are reported to have used excessive force when carrying out their duties. He, therefore, urges the Government to improve discipline in the country's police forces and to prevent further cases of police abuse.

200. The Special Rapporteur requests the Government to investigate and prevent all cases of evictions and dismissals that may be of a discriminatory nature.

201. The Special Rapporteur further urges the Government to put an end to the police abuse and violent house searches in the province of Kosovo and the region of Sandzak. He also calls upon the Government to ensure that persons detained or under investigation are not subjected to ill-treatment or torture, and that their trials are conducted in a fair manner without undue delay.

202. The Special Rapporteur urges third States to proceed with great caution in deciding whether to return externally displaced persons to the Federal Republic of Yugoslavia (Serbia and Montenegro) in cases where human rights abuses are known to occur in or near their home places.

203. The Special Rapporteur urges the Government to reconsider its refusal to allow international monitors to conduct missions to the territories of the Federal Republic of Yugoslavia (Serbia and Montenegro) and its refusal to permit the opening of a field office of the Centre for Human Rights.

27. Situation of Human Rights in the Territory of the Former Yugoslavia, Report Submitted by Ms Elisabeth Rehn, Special Rapporteur of the Commission on Human Rights pursuant to Commission Resolution 1995/89, E/CN.4/1996/63, paras. 140-149, 162-180, 14 March 1996

[Parts not referring to the situation in Kosovo have been omitted.]

[...]

140. There are a number of concerns regarding the protection of minorities in the Federal Republic of Yugoslavia. Widespread discrimination against particular ethnic and religious groups continues to be reported in the areas of Kosovo, Vojvodina and Sandzak.

141. It is acknowledged that the Federal Republic of Yugoslavia has had severe strains placed upon its resources by the influx of refugees, particularly from the Krajina region of Croatia in 1995, and that insufficient support has been provided by the international community compared with other former Yugoslav territories. Such difficulties have also been exacerbated by the transition to a market-orientated economy. However, these obstacles should not preclude the authorities' compliance with international standards governing minority rights. The relocation of the displaced Serbian population within the territory of the Federal Republic of Yugoslavia should be exercised with caution to preserve as much as possible existing ethnic composition.

142. Ethnic Albanians in the Kosovo region constitute 90 per cent of the population; between 1.1 and 1.5 million people. On 27 November 1995, during her visit to the Federal Republic of Yugoslavia, the Special Rapporteur had meetings with Serb officials and representatives of the ethnic Albanian population in Kosovo. In her discussions, the Special Rapporteur requested clarification of the situation in Kosovo, as information she has received has often been contradictory.

143. It should be noted that the ethnic Albanian population has established operations of a parallel administrative system in response to the suspension of Kosovo as a federal unit in 1989-1990. The educational system for ethnic Albanian children in Kosovo, however, is far from adequate, since there is an insufficient number of trained teachers and a lack of adequate school premises and educational materials. Albanian children also suffer intimidation when not on school premises.

144. At its eleventh session, the Committee on the Rights of the Child, having considered the reports of State parties, expressed grave concern about the situation of Albanian-speaking children in Kosovo, especially with regard to their health and education. It would appear that the rejection by the Albanian population of the Government's decision to apply a uniform education system and curriculum have resulted in the summary dismissal of a large number of schoolteachers, therefore preventing some 300,000 school-age children from attending classes (CRC/C/15/Add.49, para 7).

145. Medical services are boycotted by the Albanian population due to mistrust stemming in part from an alleged poisoning incident which occurred in March 1990 during a vaccination programme carried out by Serb medical teams. Consequently, children, who are especially susceptible to illness, are not provided with adequate medical care, and inoculations against epidemic diseases have stopped. Infant mortality is high and incidents of tuberculosis have generally increased for both the young and the aged. It is of grave concern to the Special Rapporteur that it is children and the elderly who pay the price for adult mistrust.

146. The Special Rapporteur has received reports of systematic torture and ill-treatment committed by the police in Kosovo. Those who have experienced such incidents have often been refused medical assistance. Permanent disabilities have been reported by those who have been subjected to electric-shock treatment and beatings. Information provided by the Humanitarian Law Fund in Belgrade, which defended 120 cases of this nature in court, indicates that only 10 detainees were spared ill-treatment or torture whilst in detention.

147. The Special Rapporteur raised the above issue with the authorities through the Secretariat. The Minister of Justice stated that, although some incidents of abuse of power and authority had been registered in the area of Kosovo, those incidents were isolated and the perpetrators were brought to justice. The Ministry promised to forward to the Special Rapporteur the results of the proceedings and the actual number of officials charged by the court, as well as the number of those serving sentences.

148. The Special Rapporteur welcomes this initiative of the Ministry of Justice. The Special Rapporteur may consider this action as a possible mechanism for reporting human rights violations; this method could also be envisaged for establishing a dialogue with the authorities for future corrective actions.

149. A practice which appears to be widespread throughout the territory of the Federal Republic of Yugoslavia is the phenomenon of so-called "informative talks". It has been alleged that a special unit of the police entrusted with political matters invites people suspected of political involvement to report to the police stations and respond to questioning on their activities. In many instances people have been detained soon after these talks and placed in incommunicado detention. Accusations have also indicated that in some cases people have been detained for a month without their families' knowledge.

[...]

Conclusions

162. The human rights situation in the Federal Republic of Yugoslavia remains a serious concern.

163. Current legislation dealing with freedom of expression, freedom of movement and freedom of association should be examined with a view to the enactment of new laws.

164. The present system dealing with the question of citizenship is subjective and open to abuse.

165. The media in the Federal Republic of Yugoslavia is not assured of its independence, nor is the State-funded media impartial.

166. The education system in Kosovo is in a dire situation. Education in children's mother tongues can be beneficial, but only if different ethnic groups are provided with equivalent resources. Failing to do so can only serve to exacerbate community tensions.

167. Medical services in Kosovo are a source of mistrust for ethnic Albanians. This, coupled with the effect of sanctions on the general health of the population, has caused children and the elderly to suffer.

168. There are random home searches, arbitrary arrests and systematic beating of detainees whilst in custody in the Kosovo and Sandzak regions.

169. The Special Rapporteur acknowledges the efforts of the Government to facilitate the temporary settlement of refugees.

170. The right to express ethnic culture, language and religion could be undermined in the areas of Kosovo, Vojvodina and Sandzak if the Government does not undertake concrete measures to make effective the enjoyment of the guarantees enshrined in the Constitution.

Recommendations

171. Human rights law and standards for the population of the Federal Republic of Yugoslavia must be ensured and enforced, regardless of ethnic status.

172. Individuals should enjoy the right to fair trial and freedom from arbitrary arrest and detention.

173. The practice of so-called "informative talks" by the police should be discontinued.

174. A mechanism should be established with the relevant authorities of the Federal Republic of Yugoslavia for reporting human rights violations and for providing the Special Rapporteur with prompt responses on corrective actions undertaken by the Government.

175. Legislation regarding citizenship should take into account the provisions contained in the Universal Declaration of Human Rights and the International Covenant on Civil and Political Rights, as well as any other international legislation regarding this question.

176. Interference in broadcasting and publishing must be discontinued. Improvements must be introduced to the legislation of the Federal Republic of Yugoslavia to protect the freedom of the media, as this is a crucial indicator of democracy. Freedom of the media will be especially important in the context of the forthcoming elections. International governmental and non-governmental organizations must assist the implementation of media freedom through financial, technical or professional support.

177. The freedom of independent trade unions must be protected and enforced by the Government. The development of independent trade unions must be furthered by the development of social and political freedoms, as the two are inextricably linked.

178. Dialogue must be established between the leaders of the ethnic Albanian population in Kosovo and the Government of the Federal Republic of Yugoslavia. The cycle of mistrust must be discontinued in order to achieve a peaceful settlement of differences.

179. Refugees now in Vojvodina must be allowed to return to their homes of their own free will and with dignity. Those who choose to remain in the Federal Republic of Yugoslavia should be allowed to do so.

180. The freedom of culture, religion, education, language, and other expressions of ethnicity must be protected and defended by the Constitution of the Federal Republic of Yugoslavia.

28. Situation of Human Rights in the Territory of the Former Yugoslavia: Two Trials of Kosovo Albanians Charged with Offences against the State in the FRY in 1997, Report Submitted by the Special Rapporteur, Ms Elisabeth Rehn, pursuant to Paragraph 42 (c) of Commission Resolution 1997/57, E/CN.4/1998/9, 10 September 1997

Introduction

1. At the request of the Special Rapporteur on the situation of human rights in the territory of the former Yugoslavia, an observer from the Belgrade office of the High Commissioner/Centre for Human Rights attended major parts of two trials held in Pristina of 35 Kosovo Albanians. The present report is based on first-hand information gathered by the observer in Pristina, as well as on study of the charges and the trial transcripts. Furthermore, the observer spoke to the president of the court, introduced herself to the two presiding judges, and also spoke on various occasions to the Deputy Prosecutor conducting the prosecution and to lawyers for the defence.

2. This report reviews the two trials, which were held in May 1997 and in June/July 1997. They are assessed on the basis of international standards for fair trial provided in United Nations human rights instruments, in particular article 14 of the International Covenant on Civil and Political Rights. The Federal Republic of Yugoslavia is a party to that Covenant and also to the Convention against Torture and Other Cruel, Inhuman or Degrading Treatment or Punishment (The Convention against Torture), which contains several provisions in articles 12 and 15 which are particularly relevant to the trials held in Pristina. The report ends with a set of conclusions and recommendations submitted to the Government by the Special Rapporteur of the Federal Republic of Yugoslavia on the basis of the report of the trial observer.

I. The First Trial of 20 Persons, Held in Pristina in May 1997

3. Between 19 and 30 May 1997, 20 Kosovo Albanian men and women were tried and sentenced by the Pristina District Court. Two were tried in absentia. All the accused were charged with preparing to conspire to participate in activities endangering the territorial integrity of the Federal Republic of Yugoslavia under article 136 in connection with article 116 of the Penal Code. The offences carry a maximum sentence of 10 years' imprisonment in the case of forming a group with the above aims (article 136 (1)) or of five years' imprisonment in the case of membership in such a group (article 136 (2)). Six of the defendants were in addition charged with using dangerous or violent means in attempts to threaten the constitutional order or security of the Federal Republic of Yugoslavia, acts which article 125 of the Penal Code defines as terrorism, punishable with a minimum of three years' imprisonment.

4. According to the indictment, the accused formed or belonged to a secret association called the National Movement for the Liberation of Kosovo (NMLK) aiming to attempt, by the use of force, to sever Kosovo and Metohija from the Federal Republic of Yugoslavia and unite it with Albania. The organization's main aims, according to the indictment, are increasing its membership, preparing armed rebellion by collecting various weapons and obtaining maps and blueprints of official buildings and distributing the movement's magazine Qllirimi (Liberation). The statute of the organization, of which only a photocopy was presented in court, advocates what it calls the liberation of all Albanians living in Serbia, Montenegro and Macedonia, an aim to be achieved, as a last resort, by armed struggle. It describes NMLK as an illegal organization, which, however, uses every opportunity to resort to legal means in pursuit of its aim.

5. The trial, which lasted six days, is the first of three involving Kosovo Albanians charged this year with having committed offences against national security. The charges in the first trial were limited to attempts and planning. Unlike the accused in the other trials, none were charged with actually having carried out acts of violence threatening the security of the State, which was the case in the second trial against 15 persons, reviewed in Section II below. Since then, 21 Kosovo Albanians, 18 of whom are in custody, have been indicted for forming what the indictment describes as a hostile terrorist organization, the Liberation Army of Kosovo, carrying out acts of violence in order to separate Kosovo from the Federal Republic of Yugoslavia. That trial has yet to take place.

6. All the accused, many of whom denied the charges against them or parts thereof, in particular the charge of terrorism, were found guilty. The main accused, who admitted to being a leader of NMLK and the editor of its magazine, was sentenced to the maximum punishment under article 136 of the Penal Code: 10 years' imprisonment. The other defendants, who included two women, one of them a 20-year-old student, were sentenced to prison terms of between two and nine years. Ten defendants claimed they had done no more than distribute the monthly magazine of the organization or write articles for it; five of them denied that they ever were members of NMLK.

A. BACKGROUND

7. The trial took place following a series of armed attacks which had occurred in Kosovo during the previous year directed against several police officers, local government employees and persons whom the attackers have labelled "collaborators with the Serbian authorities". A previously unknown organization, the "Liberation Army of Kosovo", has claimed responsibility for most of these attacks, which started in April 1996, when six persons were killed and five others were wounded. The Special Rapporteur has repeatedly condemned these attacks. Similar incidents have been reported on a monthly basis. In reaction, the Serbian police initiated a wave of arrests on 22 January 1997, detaining around 100 people. The Belgrade office of the High Commissioner/Centre for Human Rights received testimony indicating that the police used excessive force in the course of making a number of these arrests and during subsequent interrogation of suspects.

B. GENERAL OBSERVATIONS

8. The trial was held in the District Court in Pristina. At the opening of the trial the 13 defence lawyers did not have enough space to sit and write, but the situation was promptly remedied on orders of the presiding judge the following day.

9. The presiding judge was firm but courteous to all parties, including the defendants and their lawyers. He invariably informed the defendants of their right to remain silent, a right which several defendants exercised. The judge scrupulously summarized statements from the defendants for the record, including details given by 11 defendants alleging that they were tortured, ill-treated or threatened into making

"confessions" before the investigative judge and, sometimes, afterwards. This contrasts sharply with reports of lack of accurate record keeping by judicial officials during the period of pre-trial detention.

C. SPECIFIC OBSERVATIONS

1. Independence and impartiality of the tribunal

10. Article 14, paragraph 1 of the International Covenant on Civil and Political Rights specifies that "everyone shall be entitled to a fair and public hearing by a competent, independent and impartial tribunal". The aim of this provision is to ensure that charges are brought before an independent court, established independently of a particular case and not especially for the trial of the offence in question. The United Nations observer, however, was informed by court officials in Pristina that it is customary for trials involving State security in one district in Kosovo to be brought by one public prosecutor and to be heard by one bench. The appearance of impartiality and independence of judicial and prosecution officials involved in trying political prisoners would be strengthened if these cases, like others, were heard by rotating benches and prosecutors.

11. The Pristina trial chamber consisted of a presiding judge sitting with two lay judges. Yugoslav law - in article 23.1 of the Code of Criminal Procedure - does not specify the latter's qualifications. The observer was told by lawyers that, in this case, the two lay judges were retired policemen, one of them reportedly a former head of the Criminal Investigation Department. Such a background could create an appearance of lack of impartiality. Furthermore, lawyers informed the observer that consultations between the prosecution and judges before and during trials involving political prisoners were not uncommon, and that this happened in this and the second trial.

12. Independence presupposes the judiciary to be institutionally protected from undue influence by the executive branch. The independence and impartiality of a court can be called into question when one or more of its judges are perceived to be close to one of the parties, in this case to the prosecution.

2. The publicity of hearings

13. The publicity of hearings is also a requirement of article 14 of the International Covenant on Civil and Political Rights. In the Pristina District Court there was little space in the public gallery. Nevertheless, many representatives of the press, embassies and non-governmental and intergovernmental organizations were present. Only one member of the family of each of the accused was permitted to attend court proceedings, but this was prompted by space limitations. The requirements of publicity were fully complied with.

3. The right to adequate time and facilities to prepare a defence and to communicate with counsel of one's own choosing

14. The right to adequate time and facilities is one of the most important minimum guarantees for fair trial provided in article 14.3 of the International Covenant on Civil and Political Rights. It is the most important of all the facilities which a defendant must be provided with and is of particular concern to the United Nations in this case.

(a) Adequate time and facilities

15. The Special Rapporteur concludes that a number of defendants were denied an adequate defence for a variety of reasons. First, several lawyers met their clients for the first time after the investigative judge had already concluded the crucial stage of investigation, the results of which the prosecution relied upon. Lawyers experienced legal and practical difficulties in obtaining access to clients at an early stage (see below under (b) and (c)).

16. Second, some defendants had lawyers assigned to them only after they entered the courtroom and thus did not have an effective opportunity to prepare a defence, although they appear to have waived their right to have a week to do so (see below under (c)).

17. Third, access to nearly all relevant trial documents was denied to defence lawyers until shortly before the start of the trial, leaving them insufficient time to prepare a defence. On 14 February 1997 the investigative judge of the District Court in Pristina, Ms. Danica Marinkovic, made the following ruling applicable to all indicted persons and their defence lawyers. She ruled that, for reasons of State security: "all documents and records, as well as objects gathered as evidence, and presence during certain stages of the investigation, namely during the examination of the indicted, and confrontation and examination of witnesses, will be denied to the defence". In practice, the order prohibited defence lawyers from having access to any trial documents other than the statement made by their own client to the investigative judge and also prevented their being present during the investigation of other accused persons. Consequently, access to any statements by the co-accused or essential documentary evidence for the preparation of a defence was only granted to the defence about one or at most two weeks before the start of the trial.

18. Article 73 (2) of the Code of Criminal Procedure, on which the judge's ruling is based, permits, by way of exception, that "during preliminary proceedings, before the indictment has been brought, examination of certain documents or certain items of physical evidence by the defence counsel may be temporarily restricted if particular reasons of national defence or national security so require". However, that provision does not appear to permit the exclusion of virtually all evidence as happened in this case. Authoritative legal commentary (by Dr. Branco Petric) explains that this provision should only be used in a very restricted manner. This did not happen. The restrictions applied to the defence regarding timely access to relevant trial documents in this case put them at such a disadvantage as to result in a violation of the important fair trial principle of "equality of arms", namely the procedural equality of the accused with the prosecutor.

(b) The right to communicate with counsel

19. Current legal standards in Yugoslavia prohibit a lawyer access to his client until he or she is brought before an investigative judge, which has to happen not later than 72 hours after arrest (article 196 of the Code of Criminal Procedure). The Constitution of the Federal Republic of Yugoslavia, in article 23, sets a higher degree of protection: it requires that arrested persons should have prompt access to counsel. However, in practice the Constitution's higher standards are not enforced, as the federal Constitution, in article 67, permits ordinary legal standards to prevail. As a result, lawyers are in practice often not granted access to their clients until three days after their arrest, that is to say when they are brought before the investigative judge. In fact most allegations of torture and ill-treatment concern that three-day period preceding the defendants' appearance before the investigative judge, when they are interrogated and denied access to a lawyer.

20. All the lawyers to whom the United Nations observer spoke stated that, when they were allowed to meet their clients, they were not permitted to communicate with them in private and to discuss their defence confidentiality. One or two prison guards were always present. One lawyer told the observer that the first time he was allowed to meet his client in private was at the opening of the trial itself. Another lawyer said that because of the constant presence of guards his client only felt able to tell him at their third meeting that he had been subjected to torture.

21. Yugoslav law in fact permits wide restrictions to be imposed on free communication between legal counsel and their clients. Article 74 (2) of the Code of Criminal Procedure permits the investigative judge to order "that the accused may converse with defence counsel only in his (the investigative judge's) presence or in the presence of some particular official". Even where free communication without surveillance between lawyers and clients is permitted and indeed when, in accordance with article 74 (3) of the Code, it is obligatory - i.e. in the period after the examination by the investigative judge has been completed or the indictment has been served - several lawyers maintained that such free communication continues to be denied in practice.

22. One experienced lawyer told the United Nations observer that he had referred to this legal provision when he met his client in prison after the initial investigation was concluded. The guard present at the meeting informed him that he was aware of the law. However, he also told the lawyer that he had nevertheless strict instructions from the

State Security service to remain present throughout the interview between the lawyer and his client.

23. The apparent practice of not permitting defendants to communicate with their legal counsel in private is a clear violation of international human rights standards for fair trial. The Human Rights Committee, in its General Comment 13 on article 14 of the International Covenant on the Civil and Political Rights, states that article 14.3 (b) "requires counsel to communicate with the accused in conditions giving full respect for the confidentiality of their communications. Lawyers should be able to counsel and to represent their clients in accordance with their professional standards and judgement without any restrictions, influences, pressures and undue interference from any quarter". Principle 18 of the Body of Principles for the Protection of All Persons under Any Form of Detention or Imprisonment provides that, save in exceptional circumstances, the right to confidential communication between legal counsel and his or her client may not be suspended. It also provides that "Interviews between a detained or imprisoned person and his legal counsel may be within sight, but not within the hearing, of a law enforcement official."

(c) The right to defend oneself in person or through legal assistance of one's own choosing and to have legal assistance assigned in all cases where the interests of justice so require

24. The Prosecutor assured the United Nations observer that all the defendants had access to a lawyer at relevant stages of the proceedings. However, several defendants complained that when they were brought before the investigative judge they had no access to a lawyer to provide them with legal assistance. Enver Dugoli, for example, stated in court that he had been subjected to physical and mental torture that had resulted in visible injuries on his face, hands and other parts of his body, and denied the prosecution's claim that he had agreed to being questioned by the investigative judge without a lawyer. He told the judge that access to a lawyer had been forbidden to him when he had been brought before the investigative judge. One lawyer told the United Nations observer that interrogations of virtually all the defendants in this case started in the evening, when it was difficult for them to obtain the services of a lawyer. In this case, most defendants retracted in court the statements which they had previously made, often without having received legal advice, before the investigative judge, on the grounds that their statements had been extracted under torture, ill-treatment or duress. Nevertheless, the prosecution relied upon these statements as important evidence.

25. Some defendants did not have a lawyer when they entered the courtroom. Ragip Berisa, charged with an offence carrying a maximum of five years' imprisonment, had no lawyer. He explained that the lawyer who had visited him previously had not turned up in court. Although Yugoslav law does not oblige the court to appoint a lawyer in cases where offences carry a maximum punishment of five years' imprisonment, the presiding judge nevertheless proceeded to arrange for him to choose a lawyer on the spot from among the 13 legal counsel present. Mr. Berisa chose a lawyer, but he must have waived his right to postpone examination because the trial proceeded without the lawyer having time to prepare his client's defence. (Mr. Berisa was sentenced to two years' imprisonment.)

26. The main defendant, Avni Klinaku, had no lawyer when he appeared in court. Mr. Klinaku explained that he had not accepted the lawyer appointed by his family and that he would conduct his own defence. However, since he was charged with a serious offence punishable by 10 years' imprisonment, Yugoslav law requires that the accused in such a case should have defence counsel if necessary, assigned to him. The presiding judge promptly arranged for a lawyer present in court to defend the accused, who waived his right to have eight days to prepare his defence. However, article 70 (2) of the Code of Criminal Procedure requires that the accused in cases of such a serious nature "must have defence counsel at the time when the indictment is delivered". As far as can be established, this obligation was not honoured in the case of Mr. Klinaku.

4. The right to trial without undue delay

27. Sixteen of the accused were arrested between 26 and 31 January 1997, and two more on 24 April 1997. The trial started on 19 May 1997 and thus was held without delay.

5. The right to the free assistance of an interpreter if the court language cannot be understood

28. The court proceedings were held in Serbian, but most of the defendants spoke only Albanian. A court interpreter translated questions from the judge or the prosecutor to the defendants, and the latter's answers. However, discussions between the parties in court not addressed to the defendants were not translated to the defendant, who thus remained unaware of questions put and answers given concerning them in the course of the trial. It would be better if all discussions between the parties were translated to defendants in their own language throughout court proceedings, a matter which is particularly important for those defendants conducting their own defence.

6. The right not to be compelled to testify against oneself and not to be subjected to torture

29. Many defendants, when brought to court, retracted the statements which they had made previously before the investigative judge, on the grounds that had been forced to make them because they had been tortured, ill treated or had been subjected to other forms of duress.

30. The United Nations delegation received several allegations from lawyers and defendants who stated in court that the investigative judge did not wish to read their claims that defendants' statements had been extracted under torture or duress into the record, even though such statements are an essential component of testimony, which the Code of Criminal Procedure requires to be entered into the record (art. 80).

31. Eleven defendants claimed they had been subjected to torture, ill-treatment or duress. The lawyer of Duljah Salahu claims that he saw bruises on the face of his client and wanted to draw the attention of the investigative judge to other injuries on his client's body. However, the investigative judge reportedly said she did not wish him to do so. The lawyer also claimed that the investigative judge was reluctant to enter Mr. Salahu's claims of torture into the 1 February 1997 record of examination. He said that she only did so, and then only in very general terms, after Mr. Salahu had insisted that he would otherwise not sign the statement he had made before her. Evidence of beatings was still visible when Mr. Salahu was admitted to Pristina prison. The prison doctor stated on 26 February 1997: "after a detailed clinical examination we found, on admission, bruises on both hands (post contusion)". The lawyer said he requested an independent medical examination of his client, but the request was apparently not granted.

32. Ljiburn Aliju said that he was beaten with batons over the course of three days before being brought before the investigative judge. He also told his lawyer that the men whom he claimed had beaten him had visited him again in the week before the start of the trial and had threatened him that he should repeat in court what he had been made to say before the investigative judge. Hajzer Betulahu also said that his interrogators had subjected him to physical and mental torture and had threatened him by saying: "if you refuse to say in court what you told the investigative judge, we will break your bones".

33. Gani Baljija stated that he had been punched and kicked. A medical report drawn up during his detention was read out in court. Enver Dugoli alleged that his lawyer, the investigative judge and prison officials could see, when he was brought before them, the injuries on his face and hands resulting from beatings. His medical report was read out in court. A detailed statement of torture was given by Emin Salahi, who claimed that a gas mask had been put over his head, that paper had been stuffed into his mouth and that he had been given electric shocks and had been hit on the arms, legs and kidneys. He stated that he had asked for medical assistance, which had been denied.

34. Arsim Ratkoceri said that he had been beaten with batons on the hands and genitals and denied food for 24 hours. Muja Prekupi's lawyer alleged that he had been subjected to physical and mental torture for three days. Nebih Tahiri made a general statement that he had been

"coerced" into making his statement and Ragip Berisa said he had done so under "duress". Sukrije Redza told the court that she had been interrogated late at night by State Security personnel and claimed she had been subjected to "mental and physical terror". In court, the prosecutor did not deny that interrogations had taken place late at night, pointing out that there were no rules regulating the court's working hours.

35. To the Special Rapporteur's knowledge, no prompt and impartial investigations were carried out into any of the allegations that statements had been extracted by various forms of torture, ill-treatment or duress, as required under article 12 of the Convention against Torture. Nor are attempts known to have been made to comply with the requirement of article 15 of the Convention against Torture that "any statement, which is established to have been made as a result of torture, shall not be invoked as evidence in any proceedings". No such investigations were made prima facie evidence thereof in their medical records. The above allegations were carefully recorded during trial; however, it appears that the statements apparently extracted by such methods - which Yugoslav law specifically prohibits - were admitted in evidence in contravention of the requirements of the Convention against Torture and articles 83 and 219 of the Yugoslav Code of Criminal Procedure.

7. Non-compliance with several procedural requirements of Yugoslav law

36. The Code of Criminal Procedure provides a number of safeguards to protect the authenticity of legal records and the quality of evidence. Lawyers alleged in court that several of these procedural requirements had not been met. It appears that all their requests to have the evidence in question removed from the record on that ground were rejected by the court.

37. One lawyer stated that the times of beginning and ending of the interrogation of his client, Gani Baljija, had not been recorded, as the Code of Criminal Procedure requires in article 82 (2). He said that his client had been questioned for a long time in the evening and without a break. Hajzer Bejtulahu's lawyer drew the attention of the court to the fact that the interpreter had not signed the record of the interrogation, a fact not contested by the Prosecutor, who maintained, however, that such a failure was not sufficient ground to declare the statement in question inadmissible. It appears that the unsigned statement was indeed admitted in evidence, notwithstanding the clear requirement in article 82 (3) of the Code of Criminal Procedure that "the record shall be signed at the end by the interpreter if there was one".

38. Yugoslav law provides that the examining magistrate has a duty to inform all parties, including defence counsel, of the time and place of investigative procedures. Article 168 (6) of the Code of Criminal Procedure specifies that if the accused has a defence counsel, the examining magistrate shall ordinarily inform only the defence counsel. However, State Security personnel took several accused persons for further investigation, without the knowledge of the lawyers concerned, after the investigative judge had completed the initial investigation.

39. For example, after the investigative judge had completed the interrogation of Gani Baljija, he was reportedly taken back nine times to the Kosovska Mitrovica security police for further interrogation. Saban Beka stated that he had been questioned once after his investigation by the investigative judge. Majlinda Sinani stated that she had been taken out as many as 12 times after the completion of her investigation, which had usually taken place at night, between 7 and 12 p.m. Her lawyer had no knowledge of these subsequent interrogations and therefore was not present to defend her client. Since any such further interrogations cannot take place without the prior permission of the investigative judge, the judge either failed to inform the defence lawyer in accordance with the legal procedures or else these interrogations were carried out in breach of the law, without the knowledge of the investigative judge. What is clear is that Majlinda Sinani's lawyer was unable to assist her client in the course of these interrogations, when Ms. Sinani was repeatedly pressed to admit to membership of NMLK.

8. Evidence

40. The main evidence on which the prosecution relied was statements made by the defendants in the course of investigation, parts or all of which many of them subsequently retracted in court on the grounds that these statements were the result of torture or other forms of duress. Observers from organizations other than the United Nations who were in court when other evidence was presented have pointed out that no witness testimony was presented and that the only material evidence produced was a machine-gun. Lawyers and the main accused argued that there was no proof that plans of buildings and other documents or material produced or referred to in court in support of the charges were in fact taken from the defendants, since the confiscated objects were not specified in the receipts issued after the search of the defendants' homes. Consequently, they argued, there was no evidence that the confiscated objects were in fact those produced in court and relied upon by the prosecution. Lawyers also observed that key documents presented in court, such as the Statute and the monthly magazine Qllirimi, were only presented in the form of photocopies which could not be accepted in evidence since they had not been properly authenticated. Nevertheless, this material appears to have remained on the court record and to have been used in evidence.

41. Although the United Nations observer was not able to study all the relevant documents, a review of the main evidence and a reading of the trial transcript, as well as consideration of comments made by observers present throughout the proceedings, indicate that the serious charges against the defendants were supported by little credible material evidence.

9. Trials in absentia

42. Two of the defendants were tried in absentia and sentenced to up to nine years' imprisonment. A strict interpretation of article 14.3 (d) of the International Covenant on Civil and Political Rights appears to prohibit trials in absentia, although the Human Rights Committee has held that such trials are permissible, but in strictly limited circumstances. Further observations about such trials are made in paragraph 66 below.

II. The Second Trial of 15 Persons, Held in Pristina in June/July 1997

43. For five days in June/July 1997 the District Court in Pristina tried 15 Kosovo Albanian men, 12 of them in absentia. According to the indictment, the accused had received military training in Albania and had subsequently formed a terrorist organization active in Kosovo with the aim of endangering the constitutional order and security of the State and of forming a separate state to be joined to Albania. Unlike the first trial held in May 1997, the accused were not only charged with preparing acts of violence, but also with responsibility for carrying out several attacks, killing 4 persons and attempting to kill 16 others. The attacks were said to have been carried out by the accused as members of the "Liberation Army of Kosovo", which had claimed responsibility for these acts.

44. All three accused who stood trial - Besim Rama, Idriz Aslani and Avni Nura - were charged under article 125 of the Penal Code with using dangerous or violent means in attempts to threaten the constitutional order or security of the Federal Republic of Yugoslavia ("terrorism"), an offence carrying a maximum penalty of three years' imprisonment. They were also charged with premeditated murder of one or more people, carrying a minimum penalty of 10 and a maximum of 20 years' imprisonment. One or more of the accused were also said to have been involved in the following incidents: the shooting of two policemen at Glogovac in an ambush in May 1993; an attack on a police car in April 1996 in which a policeman was wounded and a female convict travelling in the car was killed; the shooting of a policeman in Kosovska Mitrovica in June 1996; the throwing of two hand grenades - which did not explode - in February 1996 at a refugee camp in Vucitrn; and the throwing of bombs, which did explode but without causing casualties, in September 1996 at military barracks in Vucitrn.

45. Twelve of the 15 persons charged - including the chief defendant Besim Rama - received the maximum sentence of 20 years' imprisonment. Two defendants were sentenced to 15 years, one to 10 years and the remaining defendant, Avni Nura, had the charge of "terrorism" altered to unauthorized possession of arms and received the shortest sentence, of four years' imprisonment.

46. The observations concerning this trial should be read together with the observations made above about the first trial of political prisoners involving 20 Kosovo Albanians who were tried in May 1997 and convicted for lesser offences involving State security. Nearly all the issues and concerns raised there which stem from an assessment of international standards for fair trial provided in United Nations instruments apply equally to the trial of the 15 men in June/July 1997.

1. SPECIFIC OBSERVATIONS

1. Independence and impartiality and conduct of the court

47. The bench consisted of 5 judges, including the same 3 judges who had tried the 20 accused in the first case. The same prosecutor argued for the prosecution. For reasons stated above with regard to the first trial, the appearance of independence and impartiality of the bench is not enhanced if the same judicial and prosecution officials appear to conduct all cases of a political nature; a concern compounded by the fact that several lay judges reportedly were former policemen.

48. Unlike in the first trial, the judge who presided in this trial did not promptly read into the record the claims by defendants that they had been subjected to torture. However, when this omission was pointed out to her, the presiding judge did include in the record a summary of the defendants' claims.

2. The right to be brought promptly before a judge and not to be held in unacknowledged detention

49. Article 9 of the International Covenant on Civil and Political Rights provides every person arrested on a criminal charge with the right to be brought promptly before a judge. Two defendants, Besim Rama and Avni Nura, told the court that between 16/17 September and 2 October 1996 they were held in an unknown place in unacknowledged detention, without access to anyone. Besim Rama was kept in a cell alone, but said he could hear Avni Nura being beaten. In court, Avni Nura stated that he had been arrested on 16 September 1996 and not on 29 September, the date wrongly recorded in the official records. Both men appeared before the investigative judge on 2 October 1996. Therefore, they were held for 16 days in unacknowledged detention and in breach of international human rights law and of Yugoslav law, which requires that no arrested persons can be kept longer than 72 hours without being brought before a judge.

50. For two weeks, these men had effectively "disappeared". The seriousness of any such detentions which the authorities refuse to acknowledge is underlined in article 1 of the Declaration on the Protection of All Persons from Enforced Disappearance, which states:

"Any act of enforced disappearance is an offence to human dignity. It is condemned as a denial of the purposes of the Charter of the United Nations and as a grave and flagrant violation of the human rights and fundamental freedoms proclaimed in the Universal Declaration of Human Rights ... Any act of enforced disappearance places the persons subjected thereto outside the protection of the law and inflicts severe suffering on them and their families. It constitutes a violation of the rules of international law guaranteeing, inter alia, the right to recognition as a person before the law, the right to liberty and security of the person and the right not to be subjected to torture ... ."

3. The right to access to counsel

51. International human rights standards require that such access should be prompt and that free communication between lawyer and client should be permitted. However, Idriz Aslani told the court that he had been kept for over six months without access to legal counsel to discuss his case. The first time he was allowed to meet his counsel freely to discuss his defence was on 30 May, three days before the start of the trial and then only for one minute, after which a guard came and free communication between counsel and client was made impossible.

52. The investigative judge interrogated Avni Nura and Idriz Aslani twice, on 2 and 7 October, without a lawyer even though, according to their lawyer, they had asked for legal assistance. Before that the two men had been held in unacknowledged detention, their lawyer making every effort to locate them, but obviously unable to meet them. The first day that their lawyer got permission to meet them was 8 October, but then only in the presence of a guard. However, when the lawyer showed the written authorization from the authorities, the guard reportedly informed the lawyer that he had received instructions from the investigative judge that any discussion between lawyer and client was forbidden. When the lawyer attempted nevertheless to speak with his client, asking his client about the treatment he was given in police custody, the guard said he would terminate the visit. When the United Nations observer raised these reports with the prosecutor appearing in the case, he did not deny that guards had instructions to be present when lawyers met their clients, adding that this was done because lawyers had abused their powers in the past. However, the prosecutor did not make any specific allegation of abuse concerning the lawyers involved in this case.

53. Orders for the supervision by a guard of lawyer-client meetings, if they were indeed given, constitute not only a violation of international legal standards, but also breach article 74 (3) of the Code of Criminal Procedure, which makes free communication between a lawyer and his or her client at the conclusion of the investigation by the investigative judge mandatory. On 10 October 1997, the lawyer for the two men requested that this law be observed and that free communication be permitted, but he never received a response. The first time that their lawyer was allowed to meet his clients to discuss their defence was when the indictment was actually raised, according to the lawyer this only happened one week before the start of the trial. Given the seriousness and variety of the charges and the large number of defendants, this short period was clearly insufficient to prepare an effective defence.

4. Adequate time and facilities to prepare a defence

54. As in the previous trial, the investigative judge denied the defence lawyers access to all files, with the exception of their own client's file, and the possibility of being present during the interrogation of other accused persons. The order read: "Because of security reasons, the defence lawyers ... are denied presence during the investigation, during interrogation of the accused (except their client), the hearing and confrontation, and the examination of the file and records (except the ones relating to their client)". The defence lawyers appealed against the ruling, arguing that it was unnecessarily restrictive and went beyond the limits set in article 73 of the Code of Criminal Procedure (which permits restrictions on access to certain documents and items only), thus making it impossible for them to conduct a professional defence. However, the appeal was rejected by the President of the District Court, on 17 February 1997.

55. As observed in the first case, such broad restrictions on access to crucial documents and other evidence violates the principle of "equality of arms" between the defence and the prosecution which underlies the fair trial guarantees provided in article 14 of the International Covenant on Civil and Political Rights.

56. During the trial, defence lawyers pointed out that Besim Rama had been dismissed from military service on the grounds, as Besim Rama put it, of "pains in his head". They requested that the military service report be submitted to the court (which was done but did not prove to be conclusive) and that Besim Rama be examined by experts to establish whether he was in full possession of his mental capacities and aware of his actions at the time the crime in question was committed. The court ordered Besim Rama to be examined by three psychiatric/psychological specialists from the Belgrade prison hospital. Their report, subsequently presented in court, did not show that Besim Rama was suffering from a mental illness or backwardness and found that his capacity to understand the meaning of his acts was unimpaired. How-

ever, defence lawyers objected to the findings on the grounds that the period of examination had been too short, that the conclusions of the report did not match the examination's findings and that the findings by psychiatrists who were part of a penal establishment were biased. They requested a second examination by an independent institution or, failing that, the opportunity to question the experts in court. However, the court denied both requests. The credibility of the findings of the experts would have been enhanced if the defence lawyers had been able to question the experts in court.

5. The right not to be compelled to testify against oneself and not to be subjected to torture

57. In court the main defendant, Besim Rama, stated on 3 June 1997 that from the moment that he was arrested, until the time that he was brought before the investigative judge, the police did not stop beating him. He said that his statement before the investigative judge - acknowledging his participation in a number of the crimes with which he was charged - was made under duress, because he had been tortured and because the police who had beaten him stood outside the judge's office, overhearing what he said. He claimed that his face was visibly swollen at the time. The reason for his distinct fear of the police was, he said, that he had been tortured to such an extent that he wanted to commit suicide. He said that he had informed the prison warden of the torture by his investigators, but that he had not been tortured while in prison.

58. In court Besim Rama initially acknowledged his participation in one incident, the firing on a police car in June 1996 in which one policeman was killed. Although he also admitted possessing several weapons, he denied his involvement in the other crimes with which he was charged and also that he had received military training or had gone to Albania. However, when the trial resumed on 9 July, Besim Rama retracted his statement acknowledging his involvement in the June 1996 shooting, claiming that he had made that statement out of fear of the police.

59. Besim Rama explained that he had been visited three times by police while in prison after the investigative judge had completed the investigation. He said that on 1 June, just before the start of the trial, an official, whom he identified in court as the public prosecutor in this case, had threatened him that he "would lose his head" if he failed to repeat in court what he had admitted to the police. Besim Rama maintained that two people had witnessed that threat. The public prosecutor was not in court that day and therefore could not be asked to confirm or deny this specific allegation. The court, however, is not known to have investigated this or other allegations by Besim Rama that his statement had been obtained through torture or duress, as required by the Convention against Torture. It was thus admitted in evidence, notwithstanding the provisions of international and Yugoslav law which exclude evidence being relied upon if it is established to have been extracted by such illegal methods. The same was the case for the other two defendants.

60. In court, Idriz Aslani denied all the charges against him, including possession of weapons or planning any of the attacks with which he was charged. He stated that he did not know any of the other accused. He added that all his statements to the police had been made under duress and threats and that medicines had had to be provided to him to help him recover from police torture. At one stage he had been told that he could leave the room in which he was being interrogated but not alive. The statement he had given to the investigative judge was also entirely false because he felt threatened. He saw that the same policemen, who had threatened and tortured him for three days previously, telling him what to say before the investigative judge, were standing outside the courtroom where he could see them when he made his statement to the judge.

61. Avni Nura told the court that he had been continually beaten for 10 days after arrest, after which a second group of interrogators had arrived who treated him "extremely inhumanely". He had been made to strip naked and sit on an electric heater until he fainted, then hit again. This apparently happened twice. At one stage, he had had to lean against the wall, standing one metre away from it for a prolonged period and only allowed to touch the wall with two fingers, while being beaten on the back. He had then had to do push-ups and kneel on batons, after which, he said, he had been unable to walk. He had been tied to a bed for most of the time and at night prevented from sleeping. He had been unable to eat for several days. He claimed he had been beaten mainly on the stomach, hands and legs and had had electricity applied to parts of his body so that the marks would not be clearly visible. However, his face had swollen, and he had had visible scars. On 2 October 1996, 16 days after his arrest and after these injuries had become less visible, he was taken before the investigative judge.

62. In court, he admitted possessing weapons and bombs, but claimed this was because he had been a fugitive from justice since wounding a person in a blood feud and because he had to stand guard for his brother who was an arms dealer. Of the three defendants, he alone admitted to having visited Albania, but claimed this was to escape from the blood feud.

63. On 10 October 1996 the defence lawyer requested a medical examination of Avni Nura and Idriz Aslani at the Institute of Forensic Medicine "to establish the degree and extent of physical injuries". He added that this should be done as soon as possible lest the wounds and traces of the injuries disappeared. However, he received no response and no such examination, which could have provided important evidence of torture or ill treatment, or the lack thereof, was carried out.

6. Evidence

64. Unlike in the previous trial, a number of witnesses appeared, all of them called by the prosecution. The United Nations observer was not in court on the day of their appearance, nor has the observer been able to review the many documents referred to in court on that day. However, a reading of the trial transcript and discussions with other local and international observers about the witnesses' evidence produced in court that day indicate that none of the witnesses called produced credible material evidence to link the accused with the charges against them.

65. As in the previous case, the main evidence produced by the prosecution was the stated confessions of the accused before the investigative judge, and the admission made in court by the main accused, Besim Rama, which he subsequently retracted. There is strong evidence, however, that the statements to the investigative judge were made under torture and should therefore, according to international human rights standards which apply in the Federal Republic of Yugoslavia, not be accepted in evidence.

7. Trials in absentia

66. The majority of the accused (12 out of 15) were tried in absentia, as Yugoslav law permits. Several lawyers were present in court to represent the accused in their absence. The commentary of the Human Rights Committee on the Covenant permits trials in absentia in restricted circumstances: "When exceptionally for justified reasons trials in absentia are held, strict observance of the right of the defence is all the more necessary" (General Comment 13 (21) (d) (art. 14)). The United Nations observer was not in a position to establish whether the defendants' rights were strictly observed but the Special Rapporteur wishes to draw attention to the growing body of international opinion that such trials in absentia are no longer acceptable.

III. Conclusions and Recommendations

CONCLUSIONS

67. The trials were conducted in public, without delay, as international standards require. International and local observers had full access to the trial. During the two main trials the courts generally respected, with few exceptions, Yugoslav procedural rules for trial conduct. Major breaches, however, occurred during the period of pre-trial detention. Furthermore, both trials failed to meet important minimum guarantees for fair trial provided in United Nations standards, notably the International Covenant on Civil and Political Rights and the Convention against Torture, which the Federal Republic of Yugoslavia is bound to uphold.

68. As regards the evidence presented in court, the fact that several procedural requirements of Yugoslav law regarding the authentication and production of evidence were not met - apparently with impunity - seems unfortunately not to have prevented such evidence from being admitted in court. The apparent absence of credible material evidence linking the accused to the crimes they allegedly committed is a matter of grave concern. Serious doubts remain as to whether, on the basis of the nature of the evidence presented and the illegal manner in which many statements were apparently extracted, the accused should have been found guilty as charged. By the international standards provided in human rights instruments to which the Federal Republic of Yugoslavia is a party, the accused were definitely denied a fair trial. In particular:

Defendants and their lawyers were given totally inadequate time and facilities to prepare a defence and to communicate freely;

The broad restrictions applied to defence lawyers regarding access to relevant documents and even in some cases regarding questioning their clients violated the important fair trial principle of "equality of arms";

Many statements which defendants retracted in court on the grounds that they had been extracted under torture, ill-treatment or duress were not removed from the record and were apparently admitted in evidence (despite injuries reportedly being visible to judicial officials and despite the presence of other prima facie evidence in medical reports);

Prompt and impartial investigations into allegations of such unlawful treatment are not known to have been ordered by any authority;

Requests for independent medical examinations which could have confirmed or denied torture allegations were refused;

Two defendants in the second trial were held for two weeks in secret detention, which the authorities refused to acknowledge, denying them their rights to personal security, to be brought promptly before a judge and to have access to a lawyer.

69. The Special Rapporteur is concerned that basic human rights standards were not met in the two trials of 35 persons convicted to very long terms of imprisonment for offences against state security. In addition questions can be raised about the independence and impartiality of the judicial process.

She expresses the hope that the Government will review the issues and concerns raised in the present report and that officials and others concerned will take them into account in the course of appeals, where appropriate, as well as in future trials involving similar offences.

Recommendations

70. The Special Rapporteur makes the following recommendations to the Government on the basis of the United Nations trial observer's report:

(a) The Government should promptly order an impartial investigation into the claims of defendants and their lawyers that statements relied upon by the prosecution were extracted under torture or duress. If confirmed, the accused should be retried solely on the basis of evidence obtained by legal means.

(b) The appropriate authorities should ensure that any statements obtained by such methods are not admitted in evidence and are removed from the record.

(c) Trials of political prisoners for offences involving state security should be held by courts consisting of judges, including lay judges, whose background and qualifications fully meet established criteria of impartiality and independence. Such trials should be held, as is customary in other cases, before rotating benches and prosecutors.

(d) The Government should ensure that constitutional standards which provide arrested persons with prompt access to a lawyer should be immediately enforced (art. 23 of the federal Constitution). The legal provisions in the Code of Criminal Procedure which still do not permit such access effectively until 72 hours after arrest and which are currently being revised by the Ministry of Justice should be promptly brought into line with these constitutional standards.

(e) The Government should review legal provisions which permit broad restrictions to be imposed on free communication between lawyers and their clients (art. 74 (2) of the Code of Criminal Procedure), and ensure that they comply with international human rights standards which stipulate that all communication between lawyers and their clients should normally be conducted in private in full confidentiality, at most within sight but not within the hearing of any officials.

(f) The Government should introduce clear rules for the duration of interrogation of arrested persons, for the intervals between interrogations and for the recording of the identity of the persons conducting the interrogation. Late evening or night interrogations should be the exception. Sanctions should be provided for disobeying such rules.

(g) An independent investigation should be undertaken into allegations that the authorities refused to acknowledge that two defendants in the second trial were held for 16 days in September 1996 in secret detention and tortured. If the allegations are confirmed, those responsible should be brought to justice.

(h) If the impartial investigation into the allegations of torture, ill-treatment or duress described in this report confirms that these methods have been used, the Government should ensure that those responsible are brought to justice.

(i) Instructions should be given to investigative judges that torture allegations are essential elements of the testimony which should invariably be read into the record at all stages of the criminal proceedings. If there is credible evidence that statements were extracted under torture or duress, the allegations should be properly investigated and the statements concerned should not be admitted in evidence. The Government should introduce a mechanism to ensure that statements obtained from an accused person in violation of the law are forthwith invariably removed from the record and not admitted in evidence, as article 83 and 219 of the Code of Criminal Procedure and article 15 of the Convention against Torture require.

(j) Broadly phrased legal provisions permitting wide restrictions to be imposed on lawyers' access to relevant trial documents and interrogations - such as article 73 (2) of the Code of Criminal Procedure - should be restrictively interpreted to ensure that their application does not unduly favour the prosecution and result in violations of the important fair trial principle of "equality of arms" between defence and prosecution.

(k) Lawyers should have unhindered access to medical records of the examination of their clients in custody.

(l) The Government should introduce a mechanism to ensure that sanctions are invariably imposed when procedural requirements regarding the taking and recording of evidence are not met. Failure to meet such requirements should automatically result in the statements or documents concerned being excluded as evidence, unless supported by corroborative evidence.

(m) In all cases where the accused does not speak the language of the court, arrangements should be made to provide that the court interpreter translates the entire proceedings for the defendant, and not only the questions addressed to him or her by the judge and the prosecutor and his or her answers thereto. This is particularly important for those defendants conducting their own defence.

(n) The Government should ensure that, if trials have to take place in absentia, the defendants so tried are guaranteed the strictest possible observance of their rights.

29. Situation of Human Rights in the Former Yugoslavia, Report of Mr. Jiri Dienstbier, Special Rapporteur of the Commission on Human Rights on the Situation of Human Rights in Bosnia and Herzegovina, the Republic of Croatia and the FRY, E/CN.4/1999/42, 20 January 1999

[...]

E. Kosovo

83. The ongoing crisis in the province of Kosovo has dominated international attention to the situation of human rights in the FRY, and the Special Rapporteur has devoted special attention to its nature and consequences. He stresses that the crisis in Kosovo is not new or isolated. The immediate crisis of politics, diplomacy and human rights engendered by the violence in Kosovo is based on long-standing systemic causes within the FRY which, if not addressed throughout the country, threaten national and regional security.

84. Though violence in Kosovo decreased since the Special Rapporteur's October mission, no political agreement had been reached by late 1998 to implement the general framework set out in the 13 October accord. Representatives of an enlarged Kosovo Diplomatic Observer Mission (KDOM) continued to monitor events and, at this writing, the OSCE announced that the Kosovo Verification Mission (KVM), which had deployed its advance team, was to begin operations in mid-January 1999. In this environment, violations of human rights that had characterized the crisis in Kosovo for many months were continuing to occur. Violations threatening security of the person continued unchecked in detention and arbitrary detention. There were new allegations and reports of summary execution. Other serious violations assumed a pattern of attack and retaliation resembling events in February, March and early April 1998. Violations were attributed to Serbian security forces, the Kosovo Liberation Army and armed persons representing paramilitary groups and village defence units.

85. Accurate information about the statistical scope of conflict in Kosovo has been difficult to obtain. The elusive nature of the numbers has affected events on the ground and attempts to defuse them. New and often conflicting numbers of persons killed, wounded, abducted, arrested and alleged missing, as well as those displaced from the areas of conflict or returning to the region, have appeared every day. The numbers in any category cannot be exhaustively confirmed, and security considerations have often prevented access to areas of concern. After the 16 June "Moscow declaration", diplomatic missions accredited in the FRY increased their presence in Kosovo. Diplomatic monitors concentrated on patrolling conflict areas and gathering general information on the scope and nature of armed activity, but have had no single mandate and no specific human rights monitoring responsibilities. At this writing, the OSCE verification mission was defining an understanding of the "human dimension" of the 16 October agreement, to include democratization and the organization and conduct of elections. As a result, specialized information from intergovernmental sources on the situation of human rights in Kosovo was coming principally from United Nations field presences.

86. In his letter of 8 April, the Special Rapporteur focused on human rights concerns related to operations carried out by the Serbian Ministry of Internal Affairs in the Drenica region during late February and March 1998 and to the activity of armed Kosovo Albanians during that same period. In the following months, the increased intensity of armed hostilities between government forces and armed groups of the "Kosovo Liberation Army" (KLA) and gross violations attributed to all sides lessened only in October after days of negotiations under threat of NATO intervention. In the first week of December, violence reached its highest level since the 13 October accord. After a long period of sustained armed confrontation along fluid front lines, the nature of the conflict had returned to a stage of isolated attacks and retaliations, dramatically illustrated by cases of abduction, arbitrary detention, and reports of summary executions. Testimonies gathered by the Special Rapporteur in the field suggest that, throughout the conflict, government forces have used excessive force, including deliberate destruction of property, leading to extensive civilian casualties. Concerns raised in the Special Rapporteur's 8 April letter, as well as in his report to the fifty-third session of the General Assembly, remain unaddressed.

87. Recent months have been marked by more discoveries of concentrations of corpses and evidence of massacres, including the massacre of civilians. Serbian authorities announced that, on 27 August, in the village of Klecka, they discovered in a makeshift crematorium what they believed to be the remains of civilians abducted and then killed by the KLA. The exact number, identity, age, and sex of the persons who died at Klecka has yet to be determined. Shortly after the discovery of the Klecka site, the remains of at least 39 persons were discovered in nearby Glodjane where exhumation was continuing at year's end. On 29 September, the badly mutilated bodies of 14 Kosovo Albanians, including six women, six children and two elderly men, were found in a forest near Gornje Obrinje in the Drenica region. There are reports that on 26 September 1998 another 14 Kosovo Albanian men were killed in Golubovac, near Gornje Obrinje. In early October, police discovered the remains of four persons, believed to have been abducted by the KLA, in a pit close to the copper mine in Volujak near Klina. Two more bodies were found on 4 October near Gremnik, and returning displaced persons continue to report coming upon human remains.

88. As a result of efforts by the European Union and other international organizations, including OHCHR and ICTY, and the Government of the FRY, some progress has been made in initiating independent investigations into these alleged arbitrary killings. On 20 October, a team of experts from the Institute of Forensic Medicine at Helsinki University arrived in Belgrade, following clarification of the experts' terms of reference in contacts between the Finnish and FRY ministries for foreign affairs. The team has authorization from government authorities to investigate grave sites in Glodjane, Golubovac, Gornje Obrinje, Volujak, Klecka and Orahovac; it began work at Gornje Obrinje on 10 December. Information gathered by the team will be shared with the Serbian Government and the European Union. The team has also been asked by both Kosovo Albanian and Serb non-governmental sources to investigate perhaps as many as a dozen other sites. Despite official authorization, the team has encountered delays and obstacles in its cooperation with authorities and found its investigations complicated by ongoing Serbian forensic examinations in certain cases. Preliminary examinations, as well as contemporary media reports and first-hand observations, suggest that some sites have been tampered with, compromising and complicating forensic investigation. Considering the nature of these crimes, the Special Rapporteur stresses the importance of full cooperation with the International Criminal Tribunal for the Former Yugoslavia.

89. The Special Rapporteur remains concerned about the fate of the Serb, Kosovo Albanian and Roma civilians and Serbian police officers abducted by armed Kosovo Albanians, believed to be KLA. He has appealed directly for their release. Efforts continue to determine whether any newly discovered grave sites contain the remains of those believed abducted. According to information received from the FRY authorities, as of 7 December 1998, 282 civilians and police had been abducted by Kosovo Albanians. Of these, the fate and whereabouts of 136 persons were still unknown; others were released, escaped, or had been identified as killed.

90. Information on the activity of Kosovo Albanian paramilitary "tribunals" has become public since the 13 October accord. The activity of the "tribunals" suggests a pattern of arbitrary arrest. On 30 October, two Kosovo Albanian activists associated with the Democratic League of Kosovo were arrested by the KLA in Malisevo and placed under interrogation before being released on 1 December. A KLA communiqué also acknowledged that two additional individuals had been executed. On 31 October, according to a communiqué, the KLA arrested three men and killed a fourth near Podujevo for "alleged criminal activity". On 1 November, a KLA "military court" sentenced two abducted Tanjug journalists to 60 days of detention for having committed violations of KLA regulations, respectively "the military

police book of regulations, chapter VIII, item 5, page 27". Representatives of international agencies, including ICRC and OHCHR, were not allowed to visit the abductees who were released to the KVM after 41 days of arbitrary detention. On 9 November, in Srbica, KLA forces abducted the third and fourth Serb civilians taken since mid-October. Family members of the victims and villagers from Leposavic organized the arbitrary detention of roughly 25 Kosovo Albanian passengers from an intercity bus. All of them were released on 11 and 12 November in exchange for the two abducted Serbs. On 17 November, near Podujevo, KLA members abducted a Serbian police officer. On 23 November, the KLA issued a communiqué stating that it had "arrested" the police officer and other Albanian "collaborators". On 24 November, through the actions of the United States element of the Kosovo Diplomatic Observer Mission, the officer was released. The Special Rapporteur denounces these abductions as grave violations of basic principles of international human rights and humanitarian law.

91. The Serbian Ministry of Justice has confirmed to the Special Rapporteur that more than 1,500 persons, including 500 in absentia, are currently being investigated under suspicion of involvement in anti-State activities and in activities of the KLA. The number of persons in actual custody is difficult to obtain, as "custody" includes persons in pre-arraignment police detention, under the auspices of the Ministry of Interior and in investigative or post-sentencing detention, under the auspices of the Ministry of Justice. Serbian security officials in Kosovo have arrested and held in police detention large numbers of individuals for periods ranging from several hours to several days. The routine police "screening" of male returnees, however, had abated in the aftermath of the 13 October accord. Persons in police detention are routinely held incommunicado, without access to attorneys, longer than the three-plus-one days of pre-arraignment detention allowed by law. Their families are not informed of their arrest or of their release from police detention. The number of persons subsequently arraigned and held in investigative detention is unclear, as the ICRC is not routinely and regularly informed of arraignments by the Ministry of Justice. As a result, the Special Rapporteur can only estimate, as have the Serbian Minister of Justice and defence attorneys, that from 1,500 to 1,900 cases were pending in late 1998 on charges related to terrorism, anti-State activity or aiding and abetting such activity. This does not include persons in police detention or persons called for "informative talks" by the police, whose number is absolutely unknown and whose names are known only anecdotally or when reported on a case-by-case basis by NGOs or family members.

92. The Special Rapporteur notes that, two months after the 13 October accord, implementation of the last two points of the accord, which concern prosecution in State courts, remained unclear. The Serbian Minister of Justice had sent teams of prosecutors to district courts in Kosovo to examine individual cases, and court officials confirmed to the Special Rapporteur that they had participated in working sessions with representatives of the Serbian Ministry of Justice and the office of the President of Serbia. The Ministry of Justice, together with the federal Ministry for Foreign Affairs and the office of the President of Serbia, have solicited OHCHR's cooperation in resolution of individual cases and categories of cases pending in Kosovo to which OHCHR or the Special Rapporteur have drawn particular attention. These efforts resulted in the release of several individuals from pre-trial detention and/or pending appeal. Those released include some medical and humanitarian workers and juveniles on whose behalf the Special Rapporteur had appealed. New arrests, trials, and sentencing continued. The Special Rapporteur and OHCHR continue to raise individual cases of alleged human rights violations of detainees and, in early December alone, submitted to the Serbian Ministry of Justice over 50 requests for clarification of alleged violations regarding persons in Ministry custody, including elderly and infirm detainees.

93. Arrests, trials and sentencing are most numerous in the districts of Prizren and Pec, in which the bulk of armed activity has occurred and where a total of approximately 1,350 cases were pending at the end of the year, far exceeding the number of cases in the courts of Kosovska Mitrovica, Pristina, Prokuplje and Gnjilane combined. The district court in Prizren, which had been holding trials related to allegations of terrorism and anti-State activity on a regular daily basis, suspended trials from 31 October through 9 November so that, according to the court president, case review could be conducted. The district court in Pec, however, continued to hold up to four trials a day, except when weather or security conditions prevented transport of defendants to court. At this writing, the Special Rapporteur had recorded 92 completed decisions of courts of first instance throughout Kosovo, but that figure was by no means comprehensive and only included court documents at hand. Of that number, nearly all decisions had been convictions, with only eight acquittals. Sentences ranged from 60 days to 13 years, with the majority of sentences from two to five years. For sentences of less than five years, until they have been confirmed by a court of final instance, detention is not mandatory during the appeals process, but most so sentenced have been detained nonetheless.

94. The Special Rapporteur is alarmed at consistent disregard by Serbian State security forces of both domestic and international standards pertaining to police conduct and treatment of detainees, illustrated by a growing number of cases of arbitrary detention and systematic ill-treatment, abuse and torture, including five deaths in custody. Throughout Serbia, persons are arbitrarily detained by the police for questioning or held in pre-trial detention longer than the period mandated by law. Their families are not informed of their arrest or of their release from police detention. Lawyers report that they experience serious difficulties in gaining access to their clients and are generally not allowed to consult their clients in private. In practice, pre-trial detainees in police (investigative) and court (post-arraignment) custody are not permitted access to their own physicians, but only to official physicians provided by the police or court. Official physicians do not report injuries sustained by detainees during police interrogations, even when those injuries are obvious, and do not provide adequate medical treatment. These serious violations occur when persons are held in pre-arraignment custody under the auspices of the Ministry of the Interior, or in investigative detention and after court sentencing under the auspices of the Ministry of Justice. In his discussions with the Serbian Minister of Justice, the Serbian Minister of the Interior, and the FRY Foreign Minister, the Special Rapporteur strongly emphasized the urgent need to end impunity for security officials and others responsible for human rights abuses.

95. As an illustrative example of arbitrary process by police and judicial officials, disregard for the rule of law and violation of domestic and international standards, the Special Rapporteur notes the case of attorney Destan Rukiqi, arrested in his office in Pristina on 23 July. The same day Rukiqi was arrested, he was tried and sentenced to the maximum 60 days in prison for "disturbing public order". The Serbian Ministry of Internal Affairs brought charges against Rukiqi based on an investigative judge's claim that Rukiqi had insulted her by saying she had behaved like a policeman. Rukiqi made the remark after the judge had denied him his right as a defence attorney, guaranteed under the Law on Criminal Procedure, to unconditional review of court files relating to a client. Six days after sentencing, Rukiqi was taken to hospital suffering from kidney injuries allegedly inflicted in the Pristina prison. Rukiqi was finally transferred to the prison hospital in Belgrade, where he stayed till 22 August when he was released by a decision of the Supreme Court of Serbia overturning the sentence on procedural grounds. The court did not enter into the merits of Rukiqi's arrest, conviction, or treatment during detention, but argued that the maximum sentence was unmerited. The Special Rapporteur has spoken with the hospital administrator of the Belgrade prison hospital and with Rukiqi himself; both attested to Rukiqi's medical condition on arrival in Belgrade and adequate medical treatment provided him in the Belgrade prison hospital.

96. The Special Rapporteur is concerned at widespread abuse of the investigative procedure of "informative talks", which has amounted to harassment of targeted or vulnerable populations and individuals. Summons to such talks can by law be issued only in the event of criminal conduct or to gather direct information on criminal activity under investigation. [...]

30. Commission Resolution 1993/7, Situation of Human Rights in the Territory of the Former Yugoslavia, 23 February 1993

[Parts not referring to the situation in Kosovo have been omitted.]
The Commission on Human Rights,
[...]
Deeply concerned about the situation of human rights in Serbia, particularly in Kosovo, as well as in Sandzak and Vojvodina,
[...]

24. *Expresses* its grave concern at the deteriorating human rights situation in Serbia, particularly in Kosovo, as described in the report of the Special Rapporteur, and condemns the violations of human rights occurring there, including:

(a) Police brutality against ethnic Albanians, arbitrary searches, seizures and arrests, torture and ill-treatment during detention and discrimination in the administration of justice which leads to a climate of lawlessness in which criminal acts, particularly against ethnic Albanians, take place with impunity;

(b) The discriminatory removal of ethnic Albanian officials, especially from the police and judiciary, the mass dismissal of ethnic Albanians from professional, administrative and other skilled positions in State-owned enterprises and public institutions, including teachers from the Serb-run school system, and the closure of Albanian high schools and universities;

(c) Arbitrary imprisonment of ethnic Albanian journalists, the closure of Albanian-language mass media and the discriminatory removal of ethnic Albanian staff from local radio and television stations;

25. *Demands* that the authorities of the Federal Republic of Yugoslavia (Serbia and Montenegro) respect the human rights and fundamental freedoms of ethnic Albanians in Kosovo, and expresses its view that the best means to safeguard human rights in Kosovo is to restore its autonomy with a view to an overall political settlement of the situation in the former Yugoslavia;

26. *Expresses* its grave concern at the report by the Special Rapporteur of violations of human rights occurring in Sandjak and Vojvodina, particularly acts of physical harassment, abductions, the burning of homes, warrantless searches, confiscation of property and other practices intended to change the ethnic structure in favour of the Serbian population;

27. *Recognizes* the courage and sacrifice of many Serbs who have refused to participate in these violations;

28. *Urges* all parties in Serbia, particularly in Kosovo, Sandjak and Vojvodina, to engage in a substantive dialogue, act with the utmost restraint and settle disputes in full compliance with human rights and fundamental freedoms, and calls on the Serbian authorities to refrain from the use of force and the practice of ethnic cleansing and to respect fully the rights of persons belonging to minority groups in Serbia, in order to prevent the extension of the conflict to other parts of the former Yugoslavia and other States;

29. *Invites* the Security Council to consider establishing a United Nations observer mission, in coordination with the Special Rapporteur and the Conference on Security and Cooperation in Europe and its missions of long duration, to be deployed as soon as possible to investigate and report on alleged human rights violations in Kosovo, Sandjak and Vojvodina;
[...]

34th meeting 23 February 1993 [Adopted without a vote]

31. Commission Resolution 1994/76, Situation of Human Rights in Kosovo, 9 March 1994

The Commission on Human Rights,

Guided by the Charter of the United Nations, the Universal Declaration of Human Rights, the International Covenants on Human Rights and other international human rights instruments,

Recalling its resolutions 1992/S-1/1 of 14 August 1992 and 1993/7 of 23 February 1993 and its decision 1992/103 of 13 August 1992,

Recalling also Security Council resolution 855 (1993) of 9 August 1993,

Noting in the report of the Special Rapporteur on the situation of human rights in the former Yugoslavia (E/CN.4/1994/110) the continuing deterioration of the human rights situation in Kosovo including:

(a) Police brutality against ethnic Albanians, arbitrary searches, seizures and arrests, forced evictions, torture and ill-treatment of detainees and discrimination in the administration of justice;

(b) Discriminatory and arbitrary dismissals of ethnic Albanian civil servants, notably from the ranks of the police and the judiciary, mass dismissals of ethnic Albanians, discrimination against Albanian pupils and teachers of primary schools, the closing of the Albanian-language secondary schools and university, as well as the closing of Albanian cultural and scientific institutions;

(c) The intimidation and imprisonment of ethnic Albanian journalists and the systematic harassment and disruption of the news media in the Albanian language;

(d) The dismissals of doctors and members of other categories of the medical profession of Albanian origin from clinics and hospitals;

(e) The elimination in practice of the Albanian language, particularly in public administration and services;

(f) The serious and massive occurrence of discriminatory and repressive practices aimed at Kosovo Albanians as a whole, resulting in widespread involuntary emigration;

1. *Strongly condemns* the discriminatory measures and practices, as well as the violations of human rights, committed by the authorities of the Federal Republic of Yugoslavia (Serbia and Montenegro) against ethnic Albanians in Kosovo;

2. *Urgently demands* that the authorities of the Federal Republic of Yugoslavia (Serbia and Montenegro):

(a) Cease all human rights violations, discriminatory measures and practices against ethnic Albanians in Kosovo, in particular arbitrary detention and violation of the right to a fair trial and the practice of torture and other cruel, inhuman and degrading treatment;

(b) Release all political prisoners and cease all persecution of political leaders and members of local human rights organizations;

(c) Establish democratic institutions in Kosovo and respect the will of its inhabitants as the best means of preventing the escalation of the conflict there;

(d) Cooperate with the Conference on Security and Cooperation in Europe to enable the long-term mission to resume its activities immediately, inter alia, by permitting its return to Kosovo;

3. *Urges* the Secretary-General to explore ways and means to establish an adequate international monitoring presence in Kosovo;

4. *Calls upon* the Special Rapporteur to continue to monitor closely the human rights situation in Kosovo and to pay special attention to this matter in his reporting;

5. *Decides* to remain seized of this matter.

65th meeting 9 March 1994 [Adopted without a vote]

32. Commission Resolution 1998/79, Situation of Human Rights in Bosnia and Herzegovina, the Republic of Croatia and the FRY, 22 April 1998

[Parts not referring to the situation in Kosovo have been omitted.]
The Commission on Human Rights,
[...]

IV. Federal Republic of Yugoslavia

16. *Welcomes* the cooperation by the Federal Republic of Yugoslavia with the former Special Rapporteur on the situation of human rights in Bosnia and Herzegovina, the Republic of Croatia and the Federal Republic of Yugoslavia, Ms. Elisabeth Rehn;

17. *Also welcomes* the recent visit to the Federal Republic of Yugoslavia by the new Special Rapporteur, Mr. Jiri Dienstbier;

18. *Further welcomes* the deployment of additional human rights officers in Kosovo;

19. *Endorses* the recommendations of the Special Rapporteur as contained in his report on his visit to the Federal Republic of Yugoslavia, including Kosovo (E/CN.4/1998/164), in particular:

(a) That the Federal Republic of Yugoslavia should permit forensic investigation by independent experts concerning the 28 February 1998 operations in Likosani and Cirez and the 5 March 1998 operations in Prekaz, and should also conduct its own investigation of these events;

(b) That the Kosovo Albanian leadership should commit itself to ensure that the Kosovo Albanian community shall pursue their goals only by peaceful means;

(c) That all parties should allow free access for international and humanitarian organizations and the establishment of a temporarily expanded office of the United Nations High Commissioner for Human Rights operating out of the permanent premises to be established in Kosovo;

20. *Regrets* that the Federal Republic Yugoslavia has complied only partially with the recommendations of the Chairman in Office of the Organization for Security and Cooperation in Europe regarding fostering democracy and the rule of law;

21. *Also regrets* the express refusal of the Federal Republic of Yugoslavia to allow a visit by the Special Rapporteur on extrajudicial, summary or arbitrary executions;

22. *Calls upon* authorities in the Federal Republic of Yugoslavia:

(a) To comply with the recommendations contained in the reports of the Special Rapporteur;

(b) To comply also with its obligation to cooperate with the Tribunal;

(c) To undertake substantially greater efforts to strengthen and implement fully democratic norms, especially in regard to respect for the principle of free and fair elections, the rule of law, and full respect for human rights and fundamental freedoms, and to improve its performance in the area of the administration of justice;

(d) To protect and expand opportunities for free and independent media, institute non-partisan management of the State-owned media and cease efforts to restrict press and broadcast journalism;

(e) To put an end to torture and ill-treatment of persons in detention as described in the reports of the Special Rapporteur, and to bring those responsible to justice;

(f) To repeal the 1989 Law on Special Conditions for Real Property Transactions and to apply all other legislation without discrimination;

(g) To respect the rights of persons belonging to minority groups, especially in Sandjak and Vojvodina, and of persons belonging to the Bulgarian and Croatian minorities;

23. *Condemns* violent repression of non-violent expression of political views in Kosovo, in particular the brutal police actions and the excessive use of force against the civilian population, including demonstrators and journalists among the Albanian population, condemns as well the killing of innocent civilians, equally condemns terrorism in all its forms and from any quarter, and underscores the grave concern of member States regarding the increasingly serious situation there;

24. *Urges* all parties in the Federal Republic of Yugoslavia to act with the utmost restraint and with full respect for human rights, and to refrain from acts of violence;

25. *Insists* that the Government of the Federal Republic of Yugoslavia:

(a) Take immediate action, in view of the deteriorating situation in Kosovo and the danger of escalating violence there, to put an end to the continuing repression of and prevent violence against the ethnic Albanian population, as well as other communities living in Kosovo, including acts of harassment, beatings, brutality, torture, warrantless searches, arbitrary detention, unfair trials and arbitrary, unjustified evictions and dismissals;

(b) Ensure the complete withdrawal of its special police from Kosovo;

(c) Release all political detainees, allow the return in safety and in dignity of ethnic Albanian refugees to Kosovo and respect fully all human rights and fundamental freedoms, including freedom of the press, freedom of movement and freedom from discrimination in the field of education and information, and, in particular, improve the situation of ethnic Albanian women and children;

(d) Allow the establishment of democratic institutions in Kosovo;

(e) Agree to the establishment of an office of the High Commissioner for Human Rights in Pristina;

(f) Broaden cooperation with other regional and international actors, including by allowing the return of the long-term missions of the Organization for Security and Cooperation in Europe, visits by the personal representative of the Chairman-in-Office of the Organization for Security and Cooperation in Europe and the establishment of a European Union presence in Kosovo;

(g) Implement the September 1996 "Sant'Egidio" memorandum of understanding on education in Kosovo immediately and without conditions, including at the university level, as an important first step towards reducing regional tensions, while welcoming efforts made in that regard;

26. *Emphasizes* the importance of a substantive, unconditional dialogue between authorities in Belgrade and the Kosovo Albanian leadership aimed at achieving a lasting solution to the problems of Kosovo consistent with the territorial integrity of the Federal Republic of Yugoslavia, and notes the proposals made by the Government of the Federal Republic of Yugoslavia in that direction;

27. *Also emphasizes* that improvements in the promotion and protection of human rights and political freedoms in Kosovo and the rest of its territory as well as cooperation with the Tribunal, will assist the Federal Republic of Yugoslavia to improve relations with the international community;

28. *Welcomes* positive developments in Montenegro, including in the areas of freedom of the media and the treatment of ethnic minorities, and also welcomes the formation of a multi-ethnic coalition government;

29. *Calls upon* the international community:

(a) To establish appropriate safeguards to ensure the security and fair treatment upon return of those who sought temporary protection and asylum, including appropriate measures by Governments, such as legal guarantees and follow-up mechanisms, to allow those persons to return to their homes in the Federal Republic of Yugoslavia in safety and in dignity;

(b) To continue to support existing national democratic forces and non-governmental organizations in their efforts to build a civil society and achieve multi-party democracy in the Federal Republic of Yugoslavia;

V. International Criminal Tribunal for the Former Yugoslavia

[...]

33. *Calls upon* authorities in the Federal Republic of Yugoslavia to comply with their obligation to cooperate with the Tribunal, including with regard to events in Kosovo, on the basis of Security Council resolution 1160 (1998) of 31 March 1998, and strongly recommends that the Office of the Prosecutor of the Tribunal begin gathering information relating to the violence in Kosovo that may fall within its jurisdiction; [...]

VII. Special Rapporteur

[...]

48. Decides to renew the mandate of the Special Rapporteur for one year and welcomes the appointment of a new Special Rapporteur on the situation of human rights in Bosnia and Herzegovina, the Republic of Croatia and the Federal Republic of Yugoslavia;

49. Requests the new Special Rapporteur, in addition to the activities mandated in Commission resolutions 1994/72 of 9 March 1994, 1996/71 of 23 April 1996 and 1997/57 of 15 April 1997:

(a) To work with the High Commissioner for Human Rights on behalf of the United Nations in dealing with the question of missing persons, including by participation in the International Commission on Missing Persons advisory group and other groups involved in missing persons issues, such as those chaired by the Office of the High Representative and the International Committee of the Red Cross, and to include in his report to the Commission on Human Rights information about activities concerning missing persons in the former Yugoslavia;

(b) To pay particular attention to the situation of persons belonging to ethnic minorities, displaced persons, refugees and returnees who fall within his mandate;

(c) To address human rights issues that transcend the borders between the States covered by his mandate and which can be addressed only through concerted action in more than one country;

50. Requests that the Special Rapporteur carry out missions to:

(a) Bosnia and Herzegovina;

(b) The Republic of Croatia, including Eastern Slavonia, Baranja and Western Sirmium;

(c) The Federal Republic of Yugoslavia, including to Kosovo, as well as to Sandjak and Vojvodina;

[...]

59th meeting, 22 April 1998 [Adopted by a roll-call vote of 41 votes to none, with 12 abstentions]

33. Commission Resolution 1999/2, Situation of Human Rights in Kosovo, 13 April 1999

The Commission on Human Rights,

Guided by the purposes and principles of the Charter of the United Nations, the Universal Declaration of Human Rights, the international covenants and conventions on human rights, the Convention relating to the Status of Refugees, the Geneva Conventions of 12 August 1949 and the Additional Protocols thereto of 1977, as well as other instruments of international humanitarian law,

Expressing deep concern at the continued campaign of repression and the gross and systematic violations of the human rights of the Kosovars following the revocation of autonomy by the Serbian authorities,

Strongly condemning the policy of ethnic cleansing against the Kosovars being perpetrated by the Belgrade and Serbian authorities,

Condemning also the massive military operations launched by the Serbian authorities against the unarmed civilians in Kosovo, resulting in large-scale killings, systematic and planned massacres, destruction of homes and property, and forced mass exoduses to neighbouring countries, as well as internal displacement,

Alarmed by the reports of recent enforced and involuntary disappearances of large numbers of Kosovars, as well as by reports of detention and execution of several members of the Kosovar political leadership,

Recognizing that the people of Kosovo must be allowed to determine freely their own future as envisaged in the provisions of the Rambouillet agreement,

1. *Condemns* strongly the widespread and systematic practice of ethnic cleansing perpetrated by the Belgrade and Serbian authorities against the Kosovars, and the risk of destabilization of neighbouring countries;

2. *Demands* an immediate halt to all repressive actions undertaken in Kosovo by the Serbian authorities which have led to further ethnic cleansing in the region, massive criminal violations of international human rights and humanitarian law inflicted against the Kosovars, including summary executions, mass forced exoduses, destruction of personal identity documents, records, homes and property, as well as their agricultural capacity, with the aim of preventing their return, and also demands the immediate and complete withdrawal of the Belgrade army and the Serbian military and paramilitary forces from Kosovo;

3. *Calls upon* the international community and the International Criminal Tribunal for the former Yugoslavia to bring to justice the perpetrators of international war crimes and crimes against humanity, in particular those responsible for acts of ethnic cleansing and identity elimination in Kosovo;

4. *Demands* that the Serbian authorities immediately sign and implement all aspects of the Rambouillet agreement;

5. *Welcomes* the decision of the United Nations High Commissioner for Human Rights, in view of the gravity of the situation, to dispatch human rights monitors immediately to the region to assess the human rights and humanitarian crisis caused by the Serbian policy and practice of ethnic cleansing and to ensure compliance with international human rights and international humanitarian law;

6. Appeals to the international community, including the United Nations High Commissioner for Refugees, to extend urgently humanitarian assistance to refugees from Kosovo and the internally displaced, and in this context commends the efforts being made by the High Commissioner;

7. *Underscores* the right of all refugees and internally displaced persons to return to their homes in safety and honour;

8. *Requests* the United Nations High Commissioner for Human Rights to report to the Commission urgently on the situation of human rights and the humanitarian crisis relating to Kosovo and on the implementation of the provisions of the present resolution.

30th meeting 13 April 1999 [Adopted by a roll-call vote of 44 votes to 1, with 6 abstentions]

34. Commission Resolution 1999/18, The Situation of Human Rights in the FRY (Serbia and Montenegro), the Republic of Croatia and Bosnia and Herzegovina, 23 April 1999[1]

[Parts not referring to the situation in Kosovo have been omitted.]

The Commission on Human Rights,

[...]

Reaffirming the territorial integrity of all States in the region, within their internationally recognized borders,

[...]

Shocked and horrified by ongoing massacres and other brutal repressive measures committed by Serbian security and paramilitary forces in Kosovo with the intent of ethnic cleansing, in clear violation of international human rights standards and international humanitarian law and

---

[1] E/CN.4/RES/1999/18.

resulting in the loss of lives and a massive humanitarian tragedy affecting the entire region,

Mindful in this context that development of early warning procedures to identify patterns of gross and persistent violations of human rights in a systematic way could contribute to conflict prevention and the full enjoyment of all human rights by all,

I. Introduction

[...]

2. *Stresses* the need to focus international human rights efforts in the countries of the mandate on the core problems of:

(a) Lack of full respect for the human rights of all individuals, without any distinction;

(b) Massive forced expulsions and obstruction of return of refugees and displaced persons to their homes in safety and in dignity, and return to them of property and occupancy rights of which they were deprived;

(c) Lack of resources for capacitybuilding in the areas of rule of law and administration of justice, and lack of independence of the judiciary;

(d) Lack of respect for the freedoms of expression and association and for the freedom and independence of the media;

(e) Continuing obstruction of the work of the International Criminal Tribunal for the Former Yugoslavia;

(f) Missing persons;

3. *Appeals* once more to the international community to support such efforts in the promotion and protection of human rights and insists that the parties act to promote and protect democratic institutions of government, the rule of law and effective administration of justice at all levels in their respective countries, to further ensure freedom of expression and of the media, to allow and encourage freedom of association, including with respect to political parties, to provide appropriate protection and assistance to refugees and displaced persons until they are able to return to their homes in safety and in dignity and to foster a culture of respect for human rights;

4. *Requests* the United Nations High Commissioner for Human Rights and the Secretary-General to take concerted action with the assistance of the international community to develop earlywarning procedures in the field of human rights with a view to identifying situations that could lead to conflict or humanitarian tragedy, and requests the High Commissioner and the Secretary-General to report to the Commission on Human Rights at its fifty-sixth session on their efforts;

II. Federal Republic of Yugoslavia (Serbia and Montenegro)

5. *Expresses* its grave concern at the ongoing serious violations of human rights and the deteriorating human rights and humanitarian situation in the Federal Republic of Yugoslavia (Serbia and Montenegro) caused by the repressive policies and measures of the authorities of the Federal Republic of Yugoslavia (Serbia and Montenegro) at all levels, including the highest leaders, and also of authorities at all levels in Serbia;

6. *Condemns* the continued repression of the independent media, the passage of the Serbian Law on Public Information and, in particular, the slaying of Mr. Slavko Curuvija, publisher and director of the Belgrade Dnevni Telegraf, and also the forcible closing of independent newspapers and radio stations;

7. *Regrets* that the Federal Republic of Yugoslavia (Serbia and Montenegro) has not complied with the recommendations of the Personal Representative of the Chairman-in-Office of the Organization for Security and Cooperation in Europe regarding fostering democracy and the rule of law;

8. *Also regrets* the express refusal of the Federal Republic of Yugoslavia (Serbia and Montenegro) to allow a visit by the Special Rapporteur on extrajudicial, summary or arbitrary executions;

9. *Calls upon* authorities in the Federal Republic of Yugoslavia (Serbia and Montenegro):

(a) To comply with all previous resolutions of the Commission and with the recommendations contained in the reports of the Special Rapporteur and to cooperate with other relevant mechanisms of the Commission;

(b) To comply fully with its obligation to cooperate with the International Criminal Tribunal for the Former Yugoslavia;

(c) To institutionalize democratic norms of governance, especially in regard to respect for the principle of free and fair elections, the rule of law, the administration of justice, the promotion and protection of free and independent media and full respect for human rights and fundamental freedoms, and calls upon the authorities in the Federal Republic of Yugoslavia (Serbia and Montenegro) specifically to repeal repressive laws on universities and the media;

(d) To end torture and other cruel, inhuman or degrading treatment or punishment of persons in detention, as documented in the reports of the Special Rapporteur and other reports, and to bring those responsible to justice;

(e) To repeal the 1989 Serbian Law on Special Conditions for Real Property Transactions and the 1998 Serbian Law on Public Information and to apply all other legislation without discrimination;

(f) To respect the rights of all persons belonging to minority groups, especially in the Sandjak and Vojvodina, including the Hungarian and Croatian national minorities, and equally of persons belonging to the Muslim minority and to the Bulgarian national minority, and to support the unconditional return of the long-term missions of the Organization for Security and Cooperation in Europe, as called for by the Security Council in its resolutions 855 (1993) of 9 August 1993 and 1160 (1998) of 31 March 1998;

10. *Welcomes* positive developments in Montenegro with regard to the democratic process, in particular to the freedom of the media and to the efforts to give shelter to Kosovars;

11. *Also welcomes* the selection by the Office of the United Nations High Commissioner for Human Rights of nine organizations from civil society to participate in the Assisting Communities Together Programme;

12. *Calls upon* the international community:

(a) To help the countries of the mandate establish appropriate safeguards to ensure the security and fair treatment upon return of those who sought temporary protection and asylum, including appropriate measures by Governments, such as legal guarantees and follow-up mechanisms, to ensure the right of all those persons to return to their homes in the Federal Republic of Yugoslavia (Serbia and Montenegro) in safety and dignity;

(b) To continue to support existing national democratic forces and non-governmental organizations in their efforts to build a civil society and achieve multi-party democracy in the Federal Republic of Yugoslavia (Serbia and Montenegro), and to provide resources for capacitybuilding in the administration of justice;

III. Kosovo

13. *Calls upon* the authorities of the Federal Republic of Yugoslavia (Serbia and Montenegro), especially its President and the political leadership:

(a) To ensure a verifiable stop to all military action and the immediate ending of violence and repression against the civilian population of Kosovo;

(b) To ensure the withdrawal from Kosovo of all military, Ministry of Interior police and paramilitary forces;

(c) To agree to the stationing of an international military peacekeeping presence;

(d) To agree to the voluntary, unconditional return of all internally displaced persons and refugees in safety and dignity and to provide unhindered access to them by humanitarian aid organizations;

(e) To work, on the basis of the Rambouillet agreements, on the establishment of a political framework agreement for Kosovo, in conformity with international law and the Charter of the United Nations;

14. *Condemns* the grave, horrendous and ongoing war crimes and abuses of human rights in Kosovo, especially the violent repression of non-violent expression of political views, systematic terrorization of ethnic Albanians and others, torture, deaths in detention, summary executions and illegal detention of ethnic Albanian citizens, widespread destruction of homes, property and villages, and systematic targeting of the civilian population of Kosovo by Serbian forces, resulting in mass forced displacement, expulsion, rape and harsh living conditions of the civilian population, as well as the harassment, intimidation and closure of independent media outlets in Kosovo by the Serbian authorities;

15. *Also condemns* the escalation of the Serbian military offensive against the civilian population of Kosovo in recent weeks, which has led to further ethnic cleansing in the region, massacres and gross violations of international human rights and international humanitarian law inflicted upon the Kosovars, including destruction of personal identity documents, records, further destruction of houses and property, as well as agricultural capacity, with the aim of preventing their return, deplores the recent discovery of mass graves and condemns harassment and obstruction of humanitarian aid delivery from any quarter;

16. *Underscores* the grave concern of Member States regarding ethnic cleansing, war crimes and crimes against humanity;

17. *Condemns* abuses by elements of the Kosovo Liberation Army, in particular killings in violation of international humanitarian law, enforced disappearances and abduction and detention of Serbian police, as well as Serb and Albanian civilians;

18. *Emphasizes* that those found responsible for serious violations of international humanitarian law, other war crimes and crimes against humanity will be held accountable by the international community and will not escape justice;

19. *Insists* that the authorities of the Federal Republic of Yugoslavia (Serbia and Montenegro) and the ethnic Albanian leadership in Kosovo condemn acts of terrorism, refrain from all acts of violence, encourage the pursuit of political ends through peaceful means, act with respect for the rights and dignity of all persons belonging to minority groups and respect international human rights standards and international humanitarian law;

20. Also insists that the Government of the Federal Republic of Yugoslavia (Serbia and Montenegro) implement a ceasefire, demilitarize the province and cooperate with the implementation force as demanded by the Contact Group, respect the democratic process and act immediately to make possible the establishment of genuine democratic self-governance in Kosovo, especially by acceptance of a settlement on the basis of the Rambouillet agreements, with representatives of the ethnic Albanian community, and ensure that all the residents of *the region are guaranteed equal treatment and protection regardless of* ethnic affiliation, and calls upon all individuals or groups in Kosovo to resolve the crisis there through peaceful means;

21. Insists that the Government of the Federal Republic of Yugoslavia (Serbia and Montenegro):

(a) Take immediate action, in view of the escalating violence in Kosovo, to put an end to the continuing repression of and prevent violence against the ethnic Albanian population and other communities living in Kosovo, as well as to end torture, beatings, brutality, warrantless searches, arbitrary detention, unfair trials and arbitrary, unjustified evictions and dismissals, largescale demolition of houses and scorched earth tactics;

(b) Release all political detainees, guarantee the right to voluntary return in safety and dignity of all refugees and displaced persons to Kosovo and respect fully all human rights and fundamental freedoms, including freedom of the press, including for the Albanian language media, freedom of expression or assembly, freedom of movement and freedom from discrimination in the field of education and information and, in particular, improve the situation of ethnic Albanian women and children;

(c) Allow the establishment of democratic institutions in Kosovo;

(d) Abide by its international obligations under common article 3 of the Geneva Conventions of 12 August 1949;

(e) Cooperate with international humanitarian organizations in dealing with the issue of missing persons in Kosovo and also ensure that non-governmental organizations may operate freely without harassment or unduly burdensome requirements;

22. *Welcomes* the recent initiative of the High Commissioner to investigate human rights violations and atrocities committed in Kosovo, and requests that the Special Rapporteur, the Personal Representative of the High Commissioner and the Office of the United Nations High Commissioner for Human Rights investigative teams cooperate to the extent appropriate with the international bodies charged with bringing those responsible for these crimes to justice;

23. *Calls upon* the authorities in Belgrade to work closely with and support the mission to Kosovo of the personal representative of the Chairmanin-Office of the Organization for Security and Cooperation in Europe;

24. *Emphasizes* once again that improvement in the promotion and protection of human rights and fundamental freedoms in Kosovo, as well as in the rest of its territory, will assist the Federal Republic of Yugoslavia (Serbia and Montenegro) in establishing a full range of relations with the international community;

25. *Expresses* grave concern over the overwhelming humanitarian crisis in Kosovo and the forced expulsion of hundreds of thousands of Kosovar Albanians, which has placed a massive burden on the surrounding countries, calls upon the international community to take immediate efforts to relieve this burden, expresses its appreciation to those countries that have offered assistance or that have offered to accept refugees, commends the Office of the United Nations High Commissioner for Refugees and other humanitarian organizations for their response to this crisis and encourages the international community to strengthen its actions, especially in the field of coordination of all humanitarian efforts;

[...]

VI. International Criminal Tribunal for the Former Yugoslavia

[...]

45. *Stresses* the evidence that the most senior leaders of the Government of the Federal Republic of Yugoslavia (Serbia and Montenegro) are responsible for the continuing refusal of the Federal Republic of Yugoslavia (Serbia and Montenegro) to meet its obligations to cooperate with the Tribunal and demands that the authorities in the Federal Republic of Yugoslavia (Serbia and Montenegro) comply with their obligation to cooperate with the Tribunal, including with regard to events in Kosovo, on the basis of resolution 1160 (1998) of the Security Council and all its subsequent resolutions on the subject, including 1207 (1998) of 17 November 1998, and commends the Office of the Prosecutor of the Tribunal for its efforts to gather information relating to the violence in Kosovo;

46. *Demands*, in accordance with Security Council resolution 827 (1993) and the Statute of the International Criminal Tribunal for the former Yugoslavia, that the Federal Republic of Yugoslavia (Serbia and Montenegro) cooperate fully with the International Criminal Tribunal for the former Yugoslavia and, in particular, permit immediate access to all parts of the Federal Republic of Yugoslavia (Serbia and Montenegro) including Kosovo, including by the prompt issuance of requested visas to officials of the Tribunal to conduct investigations into atrocities there and for any other purpose allowed under the Tribunal's Statute;

[...]

48. *Calls upon* the international community to give the Tribunal every appropriate help to bring into custody suspects indicted by it;

VII. Missing Persons

[...]

51. *Insists* that the Federal Republic of Yugoslavia (Serbia and Montenegro) authorities and Kosovar Albanians cooperate with international humanitarian organizations in dealing with the issue of missing persons in Kosovo;

VIII. Special Rapporteur

[...]

53. *Decides* to renew for one year the mandate of the Special Rapporteur on the situation of human rights in Bosnia and Herzegovina, Croatia and the Federal Republic of Yugoslavia;

54. *Requests* the Special Rapporteur, in addition to the activities mandated in its resolutions 1994/72 of 9 March 1994, 1996/71 of 23 April 1996 and 1997/57 of 15 April 1997:

(a) To work vigorously in support of the initiative of the United Nations High Commissioner for Human Rights to investigate human rights violations and atrocities committed in Kosovo;

(b) To pay particular attention to discrimination against persons belonging to ethnic minorities and displaced persons, refugees and returnees who fall within his mandate, with specific reference to their economic, social and cultural rights;

(c) To address human rights issues that transcend the borders between the States covered by his mandate and which can be addressed only through concerted action in more than one country;

(d) To work with the High Commissioner for Human Rights on behalf of the United Nations in dealing with the question of missing persons and to include in his report to the Commission information about activities concerning missing persons in the former Yugoslavia;

55. *Requests* that the Special Rapporteur carry out missions to:

(a) Bosnia and Herzegovina, including the Republika Srpska;

(b) The Republic of Croatia, including Eastern Slavonia, Baranja and Western Sirmium;

(c) The Federal Republic of Yugoslavia (Serbia and Montenegro), including to Kosovo, as well as to Sandjak and Vojvodina;

56. *Requests* the Special Rapporteur to report to the Commission at its fifty-sixth session on the work carried out in fulfilment of his mandate, and to make interim reports as appropriate about his work in support of the Kosovo initiative of the High Commissioner, and to present interim reports to the General Assembly at its fifty-fourth session;

[...]

58. *Urges* the Secretary-General, within existing resources, to make all necessary resources available for the Special Rapporteur to carry out his mandate successfully and, in particular, to provide him with adequate staff based in those territories to ensure effective continuous monitoring of the human rights situation in the countries of the mandate and coordination with other international organizations involved.

52nd meeting, 23 April 1999 [Adopted by a rollcall vote of 46 votes to 1 with 6 abstentions.]

2.1.3 THE UN HIGH COMMISSIONER FOR HUMAN RIGHTS

35. Statement by the UN High Commissioner for Human Rights, 26 March 1999

My office has been following the situation of human rights in the Federal Republic of Yugoslavia closely for some time and, after conclusion of the Dayton accords, has sought to work with other international partners to help nurture peace with respect for human rights. Pursuant to a Memorandum I signed with the Yugoslav authorities last November, I established an office in the Federal Republic of Yugoslavia that has been gathering information about human rights developments on the ground and making representations, particularly in Kosovo, regarding matters such as the right to life, to protection of the law, and to a fair trial. My office has also worked closely with other international institutions following the situation of human rights in the Federal Republic of Yugoslavia including in Kosovo.

At different times I have had occasion to express serious concern about lack of respect for human rights, particularly in Kosovo. I have also written to the Yugoslav authorities about these matters.

Now, at a perilous time for the international community and for the peoples of the Federal Republic of Yugoslavia, particularly the people of Kosovo, I have followed with dismay and deep anguish the developments on the ground that have occasioned massive violations of the right to life and have caused such human suffering.

I deeply regret the turn of events that has led to the current military actions in Yugoslavia. As High Commissioner for Human Rights, I should like to stress that it is imperative on everyone concerned to do their utmost to protect the right to life, to physical and mental integrity, and to protect from the threat of harm or of being forced to flee from their homes and neighbourhoods.

I strongly appeal to all concerned to exercise maximum vigilance and to do their utmost to protect the right to life and other basic human rights. This, after all, is the year in which we mark the fiftieth anniversary of the Geneva Conventions and the one hundredth anniversary of the Hague Conventions. I also strongly appeal to everyone concerned to make a special effort to help turn the current situation around so that the peoples of the Federal Republic of Yugoslavia, particularly the people of Kosovo, can enjoy their inalienable human rights in peace and dignity.

36. Briefing on Situation of Human Rights in Kosovo, Geneva, 9 April 1999

Mme Chairperson, Distinguished delegates,

One week ago, this Commission discussed the human rights situation in the Federal Republic of Yugoslavia, particularly in and around Kosovo. The Special Rapporteur, Mr. Dienstbier, and my personal representative, Mr. Michel Moussali, are now in Skopje at my request, accompanied by my staff, talking to the authorities, international agencies and refugees to obtain accurate information on the human rights situation. Our staff from OHCHR FRY has been redeployed to Skopje, Tirana and Montenegro with the following objectives:

establish a human rights presence as close as possible to actual developments; consult and liaise with institutional partners; gather information about human rights violations; and provide information gathered to this Commission, its Special Rapporteurs, and its other mechanisms as appropriate.

The Governments of Norway and Switzerland have already indicated to me their willingness to support the deployment of additional human rights monitors in Albania, Montenegro (FRY) and FYR Macedonia to seek to verify allegations of grave human rights violations which have taken place in recent weeks in Kosovo. The mission, which will build on the OHCHR's human rights monitoring capacity previously based in the FRY, will coordinate its activities closely with both humanitarian actors on the ground.

I would now like to brief you on human rights developments since you discussed the situation a week ago. This briefing is based on information provided by institutional partners, by colleagues on the ground and by OHCHR staff in Geneva. It aims to provide a factual summary of the main developments on the ground as we have been able to assemble them through the sources I have mentioned. I shall, in cooperation with the Special Rapporteur, provide periodic updates about what is happening on the ground during the course of the present session of the Commission.

Refugees and Displaced Persons

As of today, UNHCR estimates that, over five hundred thousand people have fled the Kosovo province, of which at least 304,000 are in Albania, 122,000 are in former Yugoslav Republic of Macedonia, 59,000 in Montenegro, 24,300 in Bosnia and 7,612 in Turkey. According to Yugoslav Government sources, 50,000 are in Serbia. The number of internally displaced people within Kosovo is estimated at several hundred thousand.

On top of this, in recent days Kosovars have faced considerable obstacles in fleeing the province. Preliminary indications are that the Serb authorities have in some cases prevented the departure of fleeing refugees at the border. We have now received reports that the borders have been closed and all movement stopped.

Forcible Displacement of Population

Ethnic Albanians tell of extreme and cruel violence; of people forced to leave their homes, towns and villages at gunpoint. Many women and children have arrived at the borders separated from their husbands, fathers and sons. Refugees have complained that they were displaced through intimidation, expulsion and under direct orders to leave by Serb security forces, police and paramilitaries.

Numerous persons fleeing Kosovo have also affirmed that the destruction set in motion by the Serbian authorities has affected almost every part of the Kosovo region. Much of the area is reportedly under Serb arms, the clearance of ethnic Albanians reportedly being systematic, deliberate and methodical. Whole towns and villages have reportedly been emptied of their people.

A large number of refugees entering Albania have complained that they have been stripped of their passports, ID cards, vehicle number plates and other kinds of identifying documents before leaving the FRY.

Arbitrary and Summary Executions

There are numerous reports of arbitrary and summary executions. On 28 March, the OSCE KVM reported the alleged murder of civilians, including women and children, near Orahovac. On the same day, the OSCE informed that the bodies of 35 people, who had died of gunshot wounds, were reportedly found next to the Klina-Prizren railway line. OSCE also reported that on 2 and 3 April, human rights organizations and the media collected statements from refugees about an alleged massacre in Elika Krusa.

According to the International Criminal Tribunal for the former Yugoslavia in the Hague, investigators from the Tribunal have received numerous reports from refugees fleeing Kosovo of four lorries filled with dead bodies being dumped into mass graves. Other reports backed up by numerous eyewitnesses refer to trucks and tractors pulling wagons carrying Kosovars which are being stopped near the Macedonian border. Women refugees are being asked by Serb soldiers to pay 2,000 DM in order to pass the border. If they are not able to pay, they are being removed from the trucks and taken to a near by building where they are allegedly being raped.

Enforced or Involuntary Disappearances

These are reported cases of forced disappearances of Kosovars, particularly groups of men and boys. Refugees fleeing from Kosovo claim that numerous Kosovo Albanian males have been separated from their families by the Serbian army and police. Their fate is unknown.

Treatment of Women and Children

Women and children have suffered terribly in this situation. We are also concerned about the rising number of unaccompanied children refugees, who are moving away from the border areas. Accurate figures are still unavailable. UNICEF and ICRC are setting up a registration system of unaccompanied children.

But I would like to remind the Commission that such events are not unusual on the territory of the former Yugoslavia. Women have been the target of reprisals in the former Yugoslavia. Cases of mass sexual assault perpetrated against young women and girls during the conflict are well known to the international community and, in particular, to the International Criminal Tribunal. At this point in time, we are beginning to receive acurate information from the field about such occurrences. I am deeply concerned about the particular situation of women and young girls who have been subjected in the past to such despicable practices.

Right to Health and Right to Food

A major concern is over the health conditions of the refugees, mainly children and women. According to the WHO, the major health threat to the refugees is communicable diseases, such as measles and cholera. Many of those attempting to leave Kosovo, mainly women, children and elderly people, have been waiting to cross for days, and are weak from lack of food and exhaustion.

Civilians Affected by Military Actions

There are reliable reports of civilians killed and injured, and of civilian establishments destroyed or damaged in the course of the ongoing military action.

Conclusion

We are remaining in touch with our institutional partners and are continuing to gather information. I have just come from a meeting of the ACC here in Geneva, where, under the chairmanship of the Secretary-General, the heads of the humanitarian agencies have been reflecting their deep concerns about the immediate desperate plight of those who have fled from Kosovo and also about the longer term implications, including the impact on the neighbouring countries. I shall keep the Commission informed in the coming weeks.

37. Report on Situation of Human Rights in Kosovo, FRY, HC/K224, Geneva, 22 April 1999

Mme. Chairperson, Distinguished Delegates,

Last week, I reported to the Commission on the latest developments in the Kosovo crisis and its human rights aspects. Today, I would like to give you an update on the situation.

At present, there are six OHCHR staff in Skopje, five in Tirana and three in Podgorica. Five human rights officers contributed by the Government of Switzerland will reinforce the OHCHR field office in Tirana in the coming week, while two data-processing experts from the NORDEM programme of the Government of Norway are already in Geneva to help OHCHR set up a database. Another three human rights officers from NORDEM will arrive in Geneva this weekend and will subsequently be deployed in Skopje.

The Special Rapporteur, Mr. Jiri Dienstbier, is arranging a mission to the Federal Republic of Yugoslavia shortly.

Let me now give you an account of the latest developments in the region:

1. Refugees and Displaced Persons

The number of persons dislocated by the crisis in Kosovo has continued to grow. The latest statistics, as provided by UNHCR, are as follows:

32,300 in Bosnia; 68,200 in Montenegro; 132,100 in the Former Yugoslav Republic of Macedonia; 359,000 in Albania; Figures for Serbia are not available.

This brings the total to 591,600.

In the last few days, the number of refugees who have managed to cross international borders has fluctuated substantially. Earlier in the week many refugees, including women and children, were turned back at the FYROM border crossing by Yugoslav officials. Those who were allowed to pass reportedly obtained permission to enter FYROM only after showing border officials identity documents.

The World Food Programme has estimated that there are some 800,000 internally-displaced persons inside Kosovo. Some refugees who made it to the border reported that they had been hiding for weeks in the hills and in some cases had to walk for days in order to reach the border. Our Office has received accounts of children and elderly people dying of exposure on their way out of Kosovo. Several refugees have reported being forced to pay substantial bribes to border officials in order to cross the frontier.

Some refugees who have arrived during the last week in Macedonia and Albania are reported to have shown signs of mistreatment and beatings, such as scars and bruises, while others, including children, had bullet or shrapnel wounds. Relief agencies also reported the first cases of malnutrition among refugees.

On 17 April, five Kosovo Albanian refugees, including three children, died in a landmine explosion in the "no-man's land" between a Serbian checkpoint and the Albanian border. UNHCR expects that thousands of refugees will flee the region in the next few days.

2. Forced Displacement and Ethnic Cleansing

One of the objectives of our mission is to determine patterns or trends. Testimonies received so far confirm that, in many cases, inhabitants were forced to leave after their towns or villages were shelled or set on fire by Serb military or paramilitary forces or by police. Several persons from Llashtice have reported that their village was shelled by heavy artillery on 17 March and the population obliged to hide in the nearby woods for 15 days. They said their houses were burned by paramilitaries and regular Yugoslav army troops. When one group of IDPs attempted to flee, they were surrounded by paramilitary forces who opened fire on them. They later encountered a group of Serb regular forces who took their ID papers and robbed them. Several young men were beaten. Men were ordered to fetch their tractors and the IDPs were ordered to go to the border. These witnesses reported that on 14 April, about 100 persons were similarly expelled from Presheva. Many villages along the road from Gnjiliane to Presheva have reportedly been burned and the population forcibly expelled in similar manner.

OHCHR staff in Tirana interviewed three refugee families from different villages in the Prizren municipality. All three families reported that they were forcibly evicted from their homes by Serbian police forces. In each village, the Serbian forces surrounded the village and police went from house to house, ordering the occupants to leave within a short time ranging from 15 minutes to one hour. They reported that the police arrived in tanks, armoured vehicles, as well as what appeared to be confiscated civilian vehicles. In each case, the police either had masks over their faces or their faces were painted. The families reported that their identity cards, car registration plates and valuables were confiscated or destroyed. My personnel in the field have provided me with numerous similar accounts of forcible displacement.

In one incident, it was reported that six ethnic Albanians were killed by Yugoslav Army fire in the village of Kaluderski Laz, Montenegro. As a consequence of increasing violence, many Kosovar IDPs, as well as ethnic Albanians from Montenegro, have been leaving for Albania, fearing a spill-over of ethnic-cleansing.

3. Summary and Arbitrary Executions

OHCHR staff in the field and other sources continue to receive accounts of mass executions and killings in Kosovo. Serbs reportedly kill those who hesitate to leave their houses and villages when ordered to do so.

Witnesses reported, for example, that the bodies of three persons were found after the forced displacement of the population of a village close to Gnjiliane. They had been shot in the head. Other witnesses reported that, on 15 April, paramilitary and regular forces expelled the residents of the village of Rahovia, in the outskirts of Peresheva. During this operation, two persons were allegedly executed. One witness interviewed on 18 April related that after being ordered out of his home by the police, he hid for four days in a nearby house. When the witness finally left his village, near Djakovica, he said he saw 15 to 20 corpses with their throats slit. In another interview, a refugee family stated that they witnessed the killing of 10 relatives by Serbian police. The victims allegedly were shot dead by machine gun fire on 25 March in Celin.

4. Children and other Vulnerable Groups

UNHCR reports that among refugees there is a significant number of handicapped children and adults requiring special care.

The International Committee of the Red Cross has already registered 251 unaccompanied children and has recorded 826 parents claiming one or more missing children.

5. Arbitrary Detention

Newly-arrived refugees have stated that thousands of Kosovo Albanians are "detained" between Mitrovica and Djakovica and that they are being used as forced labour. We are seeking more information on this allegation.

6. Enforced or Involuntary Disappearances

Different sources have reported that as many as 100,000 Kosovo Albanian men of fighting age are unaccounted for.

7. Treatment of Women

OHCHR staff in the field have contacted a number of local organizations to seek information concerning the situation of women refugees. OSCE staff have interviewed a number of women refugees, the majority of whom experienced the same treatment as men: forced expulsion, deportation or flight to the border, confiscation of possessions including documents and money etc. Where police have demanded money and women have refused, the women have been beaten or treated roughly. In addition, women have witnessed the ill-treatment of male family members including the execution in front of their eyes of husbands or sons and the separation or abduction of male family members or men from the community. There have also been accounts of alleged sexual assaults.

8. Economic, Social and Cultural Rights

OHCHR staff report that patients from the Pristina hospital who arrived at the Radusha camp in Macedonia told Médecins du Monde that the hospital in Pristina had been closed and all patients expelled. The consequence of the month-long NATO bombing on economic and social rights in the FRY are not known. I have written to the FRY authorities giving them the opportunity to provide me with information for my reports to the Commission.

9. Civilians Killed or Wounded

Last week I reported on civilian casualties resulting from the NATO military action. It is clear that civilians are being killed and injured in these bombings. As I said, I offered the FRY authorities the opportunity to provide me with information and they have responded as follows:

"As a consequence of the NATO action, the living conditions of the eleven million citizens of the FRY have dramatically changed. Hundreds of thousands of workers have become jobless due to the destruction of industrial facilities. Hundreds of families were left roofless after destruction of residential buildings. The destruction of heating plants has left half the citizens of Belgrade without any heating. After the destruction of a bridge on the Danube river in Novi Sad, 600,000 residents were cut off from safe drinking water supply.

"Over 190 schools and education facilities have been destroyed and many hospitals and care institutions have been either damaged or destroyed.

"To date, over 500 civilians have been reported killed. Over 4,000 have sustained severe injuries, particularly in Kursumlija, Pancevo, Cacak, Pristina, Orahovac."

Conclusion

I would like to call again on the responsible authorities in the Federal Republic of Yugoslavia and in the international community to increase their efforts to reach a peaceful resolution of the situation in order to put an end to the suffering of the people of Kosovo and FRY. I would like also to take the opportunity to commend the valuable work carried out by international organizations, especially UNHCR, and international and local NGOs on the ground in Albania, the former Yugoslav Republic of Macedonia, and Montenegro, FRY, as well as the prompt response of the international community to this humanitarian tragedy. Finally, I would like to pay special tribute to the memory of the three humanitarian aid workers, including two staff members of Refugees International, who lost their lives this week in a car accident while bringing aid to refugees in northern Albania.

38. Report on the Human Rights Situation involving Kosovo, HC/K304, Geneva, 30 April 1999

Introduction

This report is submitted in virtue of my mandate as High Commissioner and pursuant to Commission resolution 1999/2 on the situation in Kosovo. It follows on the two public statements I have issued on the situation, my statement to the Commission on 1 April, and the preceding three weekly reports I have made to the Commission. The sources of information used for this report are as I have previously stated them: information gathered by our personnel on the ground and in Geneva, information provided by institutional partners, and information submitted by Governments directly involved, including the authorities of the Federal Republic of Yugoslavia. As before, I have contacted a number of institutions offering them the possibility of providing me with information to help me prepare my report.

The Background

To set this report in perspective, it is helpful to summarise the background to the situation. The key elements are the following:

(a) An internal conflict in Kosovo resulted in disproportionate use of force on the part of the Yugoslav authorities, widespread loss of life, human suffering, and forced displacement of the population.

(b) A group of countries sought to broker a peace agreement; laid down a blueprint which was accepted by one side to the conflict but not the Government of the Federal Republic of Yugoslavia.

(c) On the basis that the conflict could not be permitted to continue because of the massive gross violations of human rights involved, NATO began a bombing campaign in the Federal Republic of Yugoslavia which has thus far lasted five weeks.

(d) NATO asserts that it has legal authority for its actions while this is contested by others, including the authorities of the Federal Republic of Yugoslavia, who contend that the use of force in such a situation must be explicitly approved beforehand by the United Nations Security Council. These two sets of views were canvassed in the debate that led to the adoption of Commission resolution 1999/2.

(e) In its resolution 1999/2, the Commission condemned gross violations of human rights taking place in Kosovo and called for the deployment of human rights monitors.

The Facts

Some essential facts are beyond dispute in the situation:

(a) Over half a million people have fled Kosovo into neighbouring countries.

(b) Thousands of people are internally displaced inside Kosovo.

(c) Numerous women and children have reached refuge outside Kosovo separated from their men-folk, whose whereabouts and fate are unknown.

(d) There is widespread fear for the fate of these thousands of missing Kosovar men-folk.

(e) There is overwhelming evidence from numerous thousands of refugees that they were forced to flee by military and security personnel of the Federal Republic of Yugoslavia. The Government of the Federal Republic of Yugoslavia asserts that the NATO bombing campaign has caused people to flee.

(f) Refugees arriving in neighbouring countries have in overwhelming numbers complained that they were stripped of all identity papers, car registration papers or plates. This is widely interpreted as intended to prevent them from returning to their places of residence. It is hard to avoid the conclusion of premeditation in the expulsion of the refugees and in the intention to keep them out for good.

(g) Children, women, and the elderly have been mistreated in the most callous manner. Vivid reports of women being raped and of young and old people hobbling bare-feet across the borders into safety have riven our consciences.

(h) From the reports of the deliberate destruction of the homes of the Kosovar Albanians, the destruction of their property, and the looting of their personal belongings, it is hard to avoid the conclusion of a pattern of ethnic cleansing carried out with cold-blooded determination.

(i) In the NATO bombing of the Federal Republic of Yugoslavia, large numbers of civilians have incontestably been killed, civilian installations targeted on the basis that they are or could be of military application, and NATO remains the sole judge of what is or is not acceptable to bomb. In this situation, the principle of proportionality must be adhered to by those carrying out the bombing campaign.

Issues of Principle

We face, as a matter of conscience, various issues of principle in this situation:

The principle of justice: In the closing year of this century, we must surely agree on one thing: that those responsible for the deliberate ethnic cleansing that has gone on in Kosovo must be brought to justice.

The Prosecutor of the ICTY has made it clear that, as a matter of international law, the International Tribunal has jurisdiction over continuing events in the Federal Republic of Yugoslavia, including the territory of Kosovo. Under the Tribunal's statute, the Prosecutor may investigate war crimes committed by any of the parties to the armed conflict. The actions of individuals belonging to Serb forces, the KLA, or NATO may therefore come under scrutiny, if it appears that serious violations of international humanitarian law have occurred. The investigations of the Office of the Prosecutor are currently focusing on two main areas: first, the crimes themselves; and second, the persons responsible for their commission. The Prosecutor also wishes to do as much as possible to deter the commission of crimes by those involved in the conflict.

The principle of human rights protection: The right of the refugees and displaced persons to return to their homes and to be compensated for the losses and damage they have suffered must be vindicated if we are to be true to the principle of human rights protection.

The principle of proportionality: It surely must be right to ask those carrying out the bombing campaign to weigh the consequences of their campaign for civilians in the Federal Republic of Yugoslavia.

As Secretary-General Kofi Annan said in Berlin on Wednesday, "Since the beginning of the conflict, we've all been consumed with the tragedy of the Kosovo Albanians. But as the conflict escalates, we see its negative impact spreading through the sub-region, claiming victims throughout the Federal Republic of Yugoslavia. The human cost of the violence is unacceptably high."

The principle of legality: It surely must be right for the Security Council of the United Nations to have a say in whether a prolonged bombing campaign in which the bombers choose their targets at will is consistent with the principle of legality under the Charter of the United Nations.

The ends and means of peacemaking: What we are in effect seeing is that war-making has become the tool of peacemaking. There must surely be cause for us to pause and to think where this will lead us. The Secretary-General made this appeal in Berlin: "Each day's delay in the search for a political solution means more deaths, more displacement and more destruction.

Once again, innocent civilians are paying the price for unresolved political conflict. We must be bold and imaginative in the search for a lasting political solution, which cannot be won on the battlefield."

Conclusion

You will have a separate briefing from UNHCR on the humanitarian dimensions of this unfolding tragedy. In presenting this report to you, I thought it important for us to take a view of the salient facts, to give expression to the voice of conscience, to underline the issues of principle at stake, and at the same time to raise some issues for reflection. The objectivity that is required of me as High Commissioner requires that in reporting on a situation such as this, I have in mind the Charter of the United Nations, the norms of international human rights and humanitarian law, my mandate, the sentiments of this Commission, and the plight of the innocent children, women and men caught up in the conflict.

Regrettably, the conflict victimizes innocent people on all sides, Serbs as well as Kosovars, and other nationalities too. It is therefore all the more crucial and pressing that diplomacy and peacemaking be stepped up to bring about a peaceful resolution of the situation respectful of human rights precepts. Unless diplomacy succeeds, Kosovo will be thoroughly cleansed of Albanians while Serbs will, on present performance, be bombed without end. There must be a better way. I call for reason to prevail on all sides and for a return to diplomacy and peacemaking. I call for an immediate end to ethnic cleansing. I call on the authorities of the Federal Republic of Yugoslavia to declare unequivocally that every refugee and displaced person will be entitled to return to his or her home in safety.

39. Report on the Situation of Human Rights in Kosovo, FRY, E/CN.4/2000/7, 31 May 1999

Introduction

1. In its resolution 1999/2 the Commission on Human Rights requested the High Commissioner for Human Rights to report to the Commission urgently on the situation of human rights and the humanitarian crisis relating to Kosovo and on implementation of the provisions of the resolution. The present report is based on information gathered by the Kosovo Emergency Operation of the Office of the High Commissioner for Human rights (OHCHR) and on information obtained by the High Commissioner for Human Rights during her mission to the region from 2 to 13 May 1999.

I. The Response of OHCHR to the Kosovo Crisis

2. On 31 March 1999 the High Commissioner for Human Rights decided to deploy human rights monitors to the former Yugoslav Republic of Macedonia, Albania and Montenegro (Federal Republic of Yugoslavia). The objectives of the Kosovo Emergency Operation are: (i) to establish a human rights presence as close as possible to the actual developments in Kosovo; (ii) to interview refugees and seek impartial verification about alleged human rights violations; (iii) to seek to identify patterns and trends in human rights violations; (iv) to consult and help coordinate among international partners the assembling and analysis of information relating to human rights violations in Kosovo; (v) to assemble information in reports to the High Commissioner for Human Rights, the Special Rapporteur and other United Nations mechanisms including the International Criminal Tribunal for the Former Yugoslavia; and (vi) to explore opportunities for technical cooperation for the future reconstruction and security of the region.

3. At the outset of the crisis, the High Commissioner for Human Rights appointed Mr. Michel Moussalli her Personal Representative and asked him and the Special Rapporteur of the Commission on Human Rights, Mr. Jiri Dienstbier, to travel urgently to the region with a view to monitoring the human rights situation. At the conclusion of his mission, Mr. Moussalli submitted a report to the High Commissioner.

4. The dispatch of human rights monitors to the region was welcomed by the Commission on Human Rights in its resolution 1999/2. In its resolution 1999/18, adopted on 23 April 1999, the Commission requested the Special Rapporteur, the High Commissioner for Human Rights and OHCHR to cooperate to the extent appropriate with the international bodies charged with bringing those responsible for human rights violations and atrocities committed in Kosovo to justice.

5. From 2 to 13 May, the High Commissioner for Human Rights travelled to the former Yugoslav Republic of Macedonia, Albania, Bosnia and Herzegovina, Croatia and the Federal Republic of Yugoslavia, including stops in Serbia and in Montenegro. The High Commissioner met government officials, refugees from Kosovo and representatives of international organizations and local and international NGOs. In addition to reviewing OHCHR monitoring activities and the overall human rights situation, the High Commissioner took the opportunity to discuss with Governments long-term strategies to develop a human rights culture and thereby assist in preventing future conflicts. Discussions on technical cooperation projects, which could involve human rights training, the development of national plans of action and improved cooperation with the treaty bodies, were held with authorities in the former Yugoslav Republic of Macedonia, Albania, Bosnia and Herzegovina and the Federal Republic of Yugoslavia, while in Croatia a programme of technical cooperation was formally agreed upon with the Government.

II. Methodology

6. The present report is based principally on the work of the Kosovo Emergency Operation. Interviews in the field are conducted by OHCHR staff on the basis of guidelines prepared at headquarters with a view to ensuring the reliability of information on the human rights situation in Kosovo.

7. Questionnaires have been developed in consultation with the International Criminal Tribunal for the Former Yugoslavia and other agencies in order to ensure their compatibility with forms used by other organizations involved in information-gathering. The forms will be regularly reviewed and revised as necessary on the basis of input received from the field.

8. Nine additional human rights officers were inducted in Geneva on the objectives and methodology of the OHCHR Kosovo Emergency Operation and have been deployed to Tirana and Skopje to join OHCHR staff there. Two data-processing experts have initiated a database for the management of the information gathered by the three OHCHR field presences, including ensuring the safe transmission of information to OHCHR headquarters in Geneva. The experts have travelled to the field to assess the needs of the field offices and to consolidate standard procedures for interviewing refugees and preparing reports. The analysed data will be shared with the thematic and country mechanisms of the Commission on Human Rights and with the human rights treaty bodies for further action.

III. Cooperation with Others in the Field

9. The three OHCHR field presences cooperate closely with other United Nations agencies and with regional organizations, including the Organization for Security and Cooperation in Europe (OSCE) and the Council of Europe. One of the priorities is to ensure a coordinated approach to monitoring activities in refugee camps in the former Yugoslav Republic of Macedonia and in Albania. Information on human rights violations is shared between organizations as appropriate in the light of their respective mandates. During her mission, the High Commissioner met officials of OSCE, including the Kosovo Verification Mission, and discussed cooperation regarding information on human

rights violations gathered from refugees, with a view to channelling the information to United Nations human rights mechanisms.

10. OHCHR acceded to a request from the International Criminal Tribunal for the Former Yugoslavia that important witnesses to crimes committed in the region, including violations perpetrated during the deportation or expulsion of refugees from Kosovo, be identified. In the field, OHCHR staff are in contact with the Tribunal. On 10 May 1999, the High Commissioner met its Chief Prosecutor, Louise Arbour, and discussed ways to strengthen cooperation between OHCHR and the Tribunal. OHCHR is coordinating its activities and reporting with the Tribunal, in order not to interfere with ongoing investigations and to ensure, as appropriate, the confidentiality of OHCHR interviews.

11. Coordination has also been established with international and national NGOs which are responding to the Kosovo crisis. In refugee camps, OHCHR staff are in close contact with humanitarian NGOs. The Office has further established contact with NGOs which formerly worked in Kosovo. In the former Yugoslav Republic of Macedonia and Albania OHCHR is working with local NGOs on issues concerning the human rights of refugees. For example, in Tirana, the Albania field presence trained local NGOs, in cooperation with the Council of Europe.

IV. Information Gathered

12. Accounts received by the High Commissioner and OHCHR staff in the former Yugoslav Republic of Macedonia, Albania and Montenegro (Federal Republic of Yugoslavia) provide substantial evidence of gross human rights violations which have been committed in Kosovo, including summary executions, forcible displacement, rape, physical abuse, and the destruction of property and identity documents.

A. FORCIBLE DISPLACEMENT

13. Forced displacement and expulsions of ethnic Albanians from Kosovo have increased dramatically in scale, swiftness and brutality.

14. A large number of corroborating reports from the field indicate that Serbian military and police forces and paramilitary units have conducted a well planned and implemented programme of forcible expulsion of ethnic Albanians from Kosovo. More than 750,000 Kosovars are refugees or displaced persons in neighbouring countries and territories, while according to various sources there are hundreds of thousands of internally displaced persons (IDPs) inside Kosovo. This displacement appears to have affected virtually all areas of Kosovo as well as villages in southern Serbia, including places never targeted by NATO air strikes or in which the so-called Kosovo Liberation Army (KLA) has never been present.

15. This last fact strengthens indications that refugees are not fleeing NATO air strikes, as is often alleged by the Yugoslav authorities. The deliberateness of the programme to expel ethnic Albanians from Kosovo is further supported by statements made by the Serbian authorities and paramilitaries at the time of eviction, such as telling people to go to Albania or to have a last look at their land because they would never see it again. However, in the light of the deteriorating security situation, some persons have apparently decided to flee before being ordered to leave. A number of refugees, particularly intellectuals, fled after receiving threatening phone calls from unidentified persons with detailed knowledge of their activities.

16. The High Commissioner for Human Rights visited the Blace border crossing on 2 May 1999 and spoke to some of the thousands of Kosovars waiting to be registered and granted permission to enter the former Yugoslav Republic of Macedonia. Several persons described how they had been compelled to abandon their homes, leaving all their possessions behind, because of violence, threats or the prevailing threatening atmosphere. In several cases, males had been separated from their families and taken away. One victim showed a gunshot wound to his knee, while several others displayed fresh marks of beatings inflicted by members of the Serbian police force. Some refugees had spent weeks in the forest before leaving Kosovo.

17. From testimonies gathered so far, it appears that the majority of refugees have been expelled from their homes by force or under threat of the use of force by the Yugoslav army and/or paramilitary forces. Many witnesses spoke of the involvement of Serbian civilians, often known to the victim, or local police in the displacement campaign. Police, military and paramilitary forces taking part in these operations were often described as wearing masks and gloves in order not to be identified.

18. Refugees have arrived at border locations in waves from particular areas. According to accounts received, villages have been systematically emptied of their inhabitants, who were either transported - in some cases escorted - to the border or told to leave Kosovo. In many cases, refugees reported witnessing the looting and destruction of their homes, mostly by shelling and burning. En route to the border or during the evictions, some refugees were stripped of valuables and money and their cars were taken. In many cases identity papers and other official documents, such as property documents, were confiscated by the Yugoslav police or border officials.

19. Villages were emptied in house-to-house operations. Accounts indicate that, in many cases, populations were grouped together or driven to certain assembly points where transport had been prearranged, or from which they were escorted out of the area. OHCHR received accounts of the local Hoxha - the religious leader of the community - being ordered by Yugoslav Army commanders to act as an intermediary to instruct inhabitants how and when to leave the village.

B. ENFORCED OR INVOLUNTARY DISAPPEARANCES

20. OHCHR has documented cases of persons who have been taken away by the Serbian authorities and whose whereabouts and fate remain unknown. In some cases persons were taken from their homes while others, predominantly men, were taken from cars or from lines of refugees and led away.

21. In some instances, a number of persons were held back when the remainder of the village community was forced to leave. Such cases have included men, but also women and children. It is difficult at this stage to confirm whether such persons were later expelled and might have arrived at a different refugee location than the rest of the group or whether, and under what conditions, they remain in Kosovo.

22. Information gathered will be shared with the Working Group on Enforced or Involuntary Disappearances for further action.

C. SUMMARY EXECUTIONS

23. A number of refugees interviewed by OHCHR witnessed or confirmed accounts of summary executions, while others reported having seen mass graves. Summary executions have taken place in different circumstances. There are confirmed reports of the singling out and killing by the Serbian authorities of well-known intellectuals or activists, the most recent being the case of Mr. Fehmet Agani. Mr. Agani was taken off a train that was sent back to Pristina on 7 (or 6) May 1999, after the closure of the Macedonian border at Blace. His family was informed to pick up the body on Saturday 8 May and he was buried the next day. OHCHR is seeking more detailed accounts of the reported killing of Mr. Agani.

24. Other killings occurred when Serbian forces opened fire on groups of Kosovars in the process of departure. OHCHR has received reports of soldiers or paramilitary forces shooting at groups of refugees after they were rounded up in a village and were waiting to depart. Similar accounts have been given by refugees who hid in the forest after having fled from their village. During her visit to a refugee camp in Albania the High Commissioner talked with two survivors of a mass execution and with the widow of a man who had been summarily killed. Some refugees reported that they had been told to run for their lives and had then been targeted by gunfire. This might have been done with the intention of giving the Serbian authorities the possibility to claim that the victims died as a result of military operations.

25. OHCHR has also received accounts from refugees who witnessed a number of men being ordered to line up or lie on the ground and subsequently being shot. Paramilitary forces have entered houses and summarily killed inhabitants. Other refugees witnessed a family being ordered out of their house and then being shot while they were

fleeing. The perpetrators have been identified as belonging to several paramilitary forces, the Yugoslav army or police (MUP), or as being armed (Serb) civilians.

26. Finally it seems to have been the practice of Serbian forces in some cases to burn the corpses of executed ethnic Albanians in an attempt to destroy evidence of atrocities.

27. Detailed accounts collected by OHCHR will be shared with the Special Rapporteur on extrajudicial, summary or arbitrary executions, who was in Skopje and Tirana from 23 to 28 May 1999.

D. TORTURE/ILL-TREATMENT

28. Refugees interviewed by OHCHR have experienced various forms of ill-treatment at the hands of the Serbian paramilitary and police, as well as Yugoslav Army soldiers. Forms of ill-treatment have included beatings with fists and rifle butts, cruel treatment, rape and other forms of sexual assault, mutilation, shooting and threats of violence. In the former Yugoslav Republic of Macedonia, the High Commissioner spoke with a refugee whose ear had been mutilated by paramilitary forces; others reported physical abuse to her, including beatings with batons inflicted by the Serbian authorities just before the refugees reached the border crossing at Blace. In one reported incident a number of persons were shot dead and a survivor was ordered by paramilitary forces to lie on top of them. Ill-treatment has occurred mostly outside of detention facilities, in streets, homes, the forest and on the road to the border. Refugees have also been mistreated by (Serb) civilians.

29. OHCHR does not have information about the treatment and fate of more than 1,000 prisoners who faced trial on terrorist charges in various courts in Kosovo before the beginning of the NATO attack.

30. The findings of the Kosovo Emergency Operation will be passed on to the Special Rapporteur on torture and to the Committee against Torture for follow-up action.

E. VIOLATIONS OF THE RIGHTS OF WOMEN

31. In general, women have experienced and witnessed the same violations as men, such as forced expulsion from their homes and ill-treatment at the hands of the paramilitary and police. Women have been searched and stripped to detect hidden valuables or money. Women have also experienced separation from, and in some cases witnessed the execution of, male family members.

32. Other organizations have received detailed accounts of rape and sexual assaults of individual and groups of women. OSCE has interviewed witnesses as well as victims of rape. In some instances, women have been taken away from a group for short periods of time, raped and later returned. There are reports of women having been mutilated and killed after having been raped. A number of women have confirmed that they attempted to commit suicide after having been raped. While there are confirmed reports of rape and sexual assault of women, there is no evidence to support allegations of the existence of rape camps.

33. On 25 May 1999, the United Nations Population Fund (UNFPA) published a report on sexual violence based on interviews with Kosovar refugee women. The report indicates widespread sexual violence by Serbian forces against Kosovo Albanian women and raises serious concerns about the well-being of women still inside Kosovo.

34. It is premature to assess whether the sexual assault and rape of women in Kosovo form part of a deliberate strategy to harm the Kosovo Albanian population or are acts perpetrated in a general environment of lawlessness and disregard for human rights.

35. The information gathered will be shared with the Special Rapporteur on violence against women.

F. VIOLATIONS OF THE RIGHTS OF CHILDREN

36. A number of children have been separated from their family members. In addition, children have witnessed and experienced the same events as adults. OHCHR has received reports of children being beaten when the parent holding the child was also beaten.

37. The information gathered by the Kosovo Emergency Operation will be passed on to the Committee on the Rights of the Child and to the Special Representative of the Secretary-General on children affected by armed conflict, for further action.

G. ARBITRARY DETENTIONS

38. Newly-arrived refugees have reported that ethnic Albanians are being used as human shields to protect military convoys from NATO air strikes. Young ethnic Albanian men have allegedly been forced to wear Serbian military uniforms and to walk alongside convoys. Several locations within Kosovo are reportedly used as mass detention centres for ethnic Albanians.

39. The data collected by OHCHR will be shared with the Working Group on Arbitrary Detention for follow-up action.

H. ECONOMIC, SOCIAL AND CULTURAL RIGHTS

40. Violations of economic, social and cultural rights concern particularly those remaining in Kosovo. Refugees who have recently arrived from Kosovo, and particularly those from urban centres, have reported shortages and denial of access to food as a reason compelling them to leave. For instance, in Pristina, where State bakeries supply bread to the remaining population, Albanian refugees said they had only received bread after all Serbs waiting in line had been served. Albanian shops have been looted and essential supplies are scarce. Access to medical care for Albanians in Kosovo has become very difficult. The hospital in Pristina is reportedly closed to ethnic Albanians. The Albanian-language university closed two days before the start of the NATO bombing and schools throughout Kosovo are no longer functioning.

V. Impact on Civilians of the Armed Conflict

41. According to the Serbian authorities, more than 1,200 civilians have died in the Federal Republic of Yugoslavia as a result of the NATO air strikes, and about 4,500 have been seriously injured. Several civilian targets have been hit by NATO: on 12 April 1999 a train was hit in the bombing of a railroad bridge, killing at least 10 civilians; on 14 April, NATO bombed a refugee convoy near Dakovica, killing 72 civilians; on 23 April, NATO attacked the Serbian State television headquarters, killing 15 civilians; on 1 May, NATO bombed a bridge near Luzane and hit a passenger bus, killing 23 people; on 7 May, NATO bombed a civilian market and a hospital in Nis, killing 15 civilians; on 8 May, the bombing of the Chinese Embassy resulted in the deaths of three civilians; and, on 15 May, 80 civilians were killed when the village of Korisa, near Prizren, was bombed.

42. The High Commissioner was in Nis shortly after NATO bombs struck a civilian area. She saw the damage caused by cluster bombs and the danger of unexploded bombs. The Mayor of Nis, who arrived on the scene, referred to the bombing of the hospital the previous day, which had caused the death of 15 civilians.

43. Bridges have been damaged and communications disrupted. The suspension of navigation on the Danube is causing serious damage to the economy of the Federal Republic of Yugoslavia. The NATO campaign has destroyed or partially damaged schools, hospitals and places of worship. According to Yugoslav sources, the total or partial destruction of economic facilities has left more than half a million people without jobs.

44. The air strikes have also caused serious environmental damage to agricultural land, plants, cattle and wildlife. Furthermore the destruction of petrochemical installations and the bombing of warehouses storing products of the chemical industry raise serious concerns for health.

45. The destruction of private radio and television stations has created a serious impediment to freedom of expression and freedom of information for the people of Serbia.

46. The use of graphite bombs by NATO has caused short circuits on long-distance power lines and left areas of the Federal Republic of Yugoslavia without water and electricity, causing enormous hardship to civilians. Those most severely affected are patients in hospitals, especially emergency cases in need of intensive care. NATO is also using cluster bombs in the air campaign against the Federal Republic

of Yugoslavia. The submunitions inside cluster bombs have a high failure rate and can leave unexploded ordnance across wide areas, capable of detonation on contact.

VI. Humanitarian Situation

A. ALBANIA

47. According to figures of the Government of Albania, as of 20 May 1999, Albania was hosting more than 400,000 refugees from Kosovo. The daily influx of refugees varies widely, sometimes being as high as 13,000, at other times dwindling almost to none. Given the harsh terrain and lack of infrastructure at the border crossing areas, there has been a major effort to relocate refugees from the north near Kukes to other points in central and southern Albania where it is easier to establish facilities for accommodation. The border areas remain tense and there are increasing incursions and shelling by Yugoslav forces into Albanian territory. This military action, as well as training activity by the KLA, particularly in the north, has fueled interest in relocating refugees.

48. Refugees are accommodated in a variety of facilities. Some two thirds of the refugee population, approximately 305,000 persons, are accommodated in the homes of Albanian families. Past experience forewarns of potential future problems. Only six weeks into the massive refugee influx, host families were experiencing difficulties meeting the additional financial burden. These will only increase if the refugees do not return soon, possibly leading to tension between the domestic and refugee populations. This phenomenon has a precedent in Serbia, where refugees who were taken in from Croatia and Bosnia and Herzegovina remained years longer than expected. This together with the direction (or the perception thereof) of international aid primarily towards the refugee population, rather than its being balanced between the domestic and refugee populations, can sow seeds of conflict between the two communities. An agreement for financial aid to host families has been reached between the Office of the High Commissioner for Refugees (UNHCR) and the Albanian Ministry of Local Government, the ministry responsible for refugees. However, the mechanism for families to obtain the financial benefit appears not yet to be in place.

49. Conditions at many collective centres and tented camps are deteriorating. Poor sanitary conditions and warm weather are causing increasing health problems. In Kukes, NGOs report an increase of 30 to 40 per cent in the incidence of diarrhoeal diseases. Children are especially vulnerable in the face of traumatic dislocation, in some cases having been separated from their families. During her visit to a refugee camp in Albania, the High Commissioner met a young refugee school teacher who, despite the lack of materials, has an open-air school, the walls of which are defined by clothes lines, for children in the camp.

1. Registration of Refugees

50. Given the wide-scale loss by the refugee population of their documents, efforts to provide identity documentation have been undertaken. Some camps provide camp identity documentation in an effort to control who has access to the camp. The International Organization for Migration (IOM), UNHCR and the Government of Albania have designed a programme for the registration of refugees, one by-product of which will be a picture-identity document. IOM will also maintain a database of all refugees registered.

2. Refugee Security Issues

51. Security for refugees from various criminal elements is becoming an increasing concern and conditions in some camps, particularly in the north of Albania, are deteriorating. Criminal activities pose a threat to the human rights of refugees in their current accommodation. Major issues include trafficking and prostitution, abduction of children, recruitment and training for the KLA and illegal immigration.

B. THE FORMER YUGOSLAV REPUBLIC OF MACEDONIA

52. According to official government sources, the former Yugoslav Republic of Macedonia harbours more than 200,000 refugees from Kosovo.

53. Poor hygiene, inadequate medical attention and overcrowding of camps put the health of refugees at risk. The lack of space is also affecting school programmes. The number of reported security incidents in the camps is low; in several cases refugees have been arrested and taken away to local police stations for attempting to leave the camp without authorization.

54. There is a need to provide follow-up care and counselling to victims or witnesses traumatized by serious human rights violations. Often such cases are identified during human rights interviews conducted by OHCHR. In some camps, mental-care facilities exist, but in other camps, such as Cegrane, such services are currently lacking.

55. There is also concern about the presence of members of the KLA in the camps and the possible (forced) recruitment of refugees into the KLA.

1. Status of Refugees

56. UNHCR considers those displaced outside the Federal Republic of Yugoslavia in the context of the current conflict as prima facie refugees and has not generally conducted status determination interviews. However, the Macedonian authorities reportedly have granted the status of "humanitarian assisted persons" (HAP) to those refugees accommodated with host families, excluding the automatic extension of all rights incumbent on recognized "Convention" refugees.

57. The HAP status is a temporary protection status granting the right to remain temporarily in the former Yugoslav Republic of Macedonia, with renewal linked to the situation in Kosovo. According to government instructions, persons with HAP status are "entitled to accommodation, food, health care, education of children and youth and other humanitarian rights".

58. Persons with HAP status are limited in their movement to the municipality of registration. At the outskirts of towns and along the main highways, police have established checkpoints and control the movement of refugees. To visit the camps, a person with HAP status must obtain permission, which applies for one visit, from the Ministry of Labour or the local Macedonian Red Cross. Children with HAP status are not legally entitled to education, although the Ministry of Education has issued a statement that children can attend schools on a local basis. In fact, children have joined local schools and in some cases, additional classes have been organized.

59. Rudimentary registration of refugees inside the camps is taking place. However, as camps are considered transit centres from which refugees are expected to move to third countries, camp residents are not granted HAP status. Despite registration, which is entered into an IOM database, refugees have not received identity documents nor a copy of the registration form. UNHCR intends to issue some form of picture ID cards in the near future and to initiate registration of children born in the camps.

60. Camp refugees are restricted in their movements. They are not permitted to leave the camps unless they have a medical referral or have obtained permission on other humanitarian grounds, to be determined by UNHCR in coordination with the Macedonian police. The refugees receive humanitarian assistance in the camps.

2. Violations of the Rights of Refugees

61. Incidents of refoulement as well as denial of entry to refugees have occurred on various occasions and in various locations. Refugees attempting to cross at illegal border crossings are regularly refouled.

62. Allegations of beating of refugees in a refugee camp have led to demands that the Macedonian police stay out of the camps. After negotiations with UNHCR, the Macedonian police agreed to increase the number of ethnic Albanian policemen in the camps. OHCHR has not been able to confirm allegations of beating of refugees by Macedonian police in the camps. There are a number of reports of ill-treatment by Macedonian military police of refugees who crossed the border illegally. There are unconfirmed reports of prostitution, trafficking and abuse of women and children in camps and host families. An incident of an attempt to traffic some 30 children was reported by one embassy in Skopje.

63. Families have been split up in the process of forced expulsion and deportation from Kosovo, and in some cases again at the border crossing. Further separation has occurred during the first wave of humanitarian evacuation. Procedures at the border-crossing of Blace now are intended to ensure that family units are maintained.

3. Impact of the Crisis on the Economy and Social Structure

64. The fragile economy of the former Yugoslav Republic of Macedonia has been put under great strain by the current crisis. Yugoslavia was among its main markets and many of its industrial plants were dependent on imports from Yugoslavia of raw materials and production components. As a result, exports have dropped by 40 per cent and some 40,000 workers have been laid off. In addition, the main transport route from the former Yugoslav Republic of Macedonia to Europe has been cut off.

65. In the social and demographic sphere, unemployment is rising - it is currently close to 50 per cent according to official sources - and the number of people on compulsory leave increasing. Health institutions function for urgent cases only as medical stocks have been exhausted by treatment of refugee patients. Refugees now make up 15 per cent of the total population of the former Yugoslav Republic of Macedonia, altering the ethnic balance in the country. The fact that the large majority of the refugees are of ethnic Albanian origin and the fear among some that most of the refugees will remain have increased inter-ethnic tensions in the former Yugoslav Republic of Macedonia.

VII. Republic of Montenegro (Federal Republic of Yugoslavia)

66. The Republic of Montenegro presently hosts more than 60,000 IDPs from Kosovo. Some IDPs are accommodated in Ulcinj, on the coast, with host families or in camps, while others are housed in camps and other ad hoc arrangements in Rozaje, near the border with Kosovo. The conditions at Rozaje in particular have been described as unacceptable and raise serious health concerns due to lack of hygiene.

67. The arrival of a large number of IDPs from Kosovo has put great pressure on the authorities of the Republic of Montenegro, who are responsible for responding to the humanitarian needs of the IDPs and ensuring their security. The blockade by the federal authorities on humanitarian assistance arriving through the port of Bar has placed the well-being of IDPs at risk. Furthermore, the relative scarcity of international representatives has left Montenegro without necessary support, including for resettlement, leading many IDPs to cross the border into Albania.

VIII. Republic of Serbia (Federal Republic of Yugoslavia)

68. According to the findings of the United Nations Needs Assessment Mission, which travelled throughout the Federal Republic of Yugoslavia from 16 to 28 May, the situation in that country is so grave that in each republic and province, without exception, people, regardless of ethnic group, political affiliation, socioeconomic status, gender or age, fear for their survival.

69. Apart from the city centres where one can see very few people and practically no vehicles on the streets, Kosovo is a panorama of burned houses, untended farms, wandering livestock, empty villages and looted shops.

70. In the Republic of Serbia the air campaign, which has been especially intensive in densely populated centres of Vojvodina and southern Serbia, has led as-yet-uncalculated numbers of persons to seek shelter in what are perceived to be "safe" locations outside the cities. Children, in particular, are being sent away from their parents and have not attended school since the start of the NATO campaign. Parents in Belgrade and Stimlje complained of the effects on their children of unhygienic and psychologically unhealthy conditions in air raid shelters. Severe restrictions on fuel have effectively brought civilian Serbia to a standstill and many parts are often without electricity and water.

IX. IDPs In Kosovo

71. Ethnic Albanians who remain in Kosovo are reportedly suffering from hunger and lack of medical attention. In the mountains, where many IDPs are reported to be hiding, food, shelter and basic provisions are lacking.

72. Certain villages have become refuges for large numbers of IDPs. In such overwhelmed villages, food is lacking, sanitation is poor and severe overcrowding facilitates the spread of disease. Cattle have been killed, shops closed and in certain towns and villages Serb merchants have allegedly refused to sell food to ethnic Albanians. Numerous refugees reported that relatives and friends hit by bullets or mortar fire have died for lack of medical care.

X. Conclusions and Recommendations

73. The grave humanitarian tragedy taking place in Kosovo, the Federal Republic of Yugoslavia and neighbouring countries has its roots in a human rights crisis. By 20 May 1999 more than 750,000 persons had left or been forcibly displaced from Kosovo, while an unknown, reportedly large number of IDPs remained in the region. Credible allegations of severe and ongoing human rights violations have been reported by refugees and IDPs to international and national organizations in the former Yugoslav Republic of Macedonia, Albania and the Republic of Montenegro (Federal Republic of Yugoslavia).

74. The High Commissioner calls on the responsible authorities of the Federal Republic of Yugoslavia to put an end to human rights violations and to respect the principles of international human rights and the four Geneva Conventions and Optional Protocols to which the Federal Republic of Yugoslavia is a party. The High Commissioner also urges the Government of the Federal Republic of Yugoslavia to withdraw immediately and unconditionally all the army and police (MUP) units from Kosovo, as well as federal police and paramilitary forces responsible for gross violations of human rights in the region.

75. The High Commissioner for Human Rights calls on all concerned to intensify political negotiations and find a solution to the current crisis.

76. The High Commissioner calls on NATO to respect the principles of international humanitarian law, including the principle of proportionality, in its military actions against the Federal Republic of Yugoslavia.

77. The High Commissioner calls on the Government of the Federal Republic of Yugoslavia to allow humanitarian agencies to bring aid and support to the internally-displaced persons still inside the territory of the Federal Republic of Yugoslavia, particularly in Kosovo, as well as to the Serb civilian population severely affected by the war.

78. The High Commissioner calls on all the agencies committed to information-gathering activities relating to human rights violations in Kosovo to ensure that the necessary efforts are made to bring to justice the perpetrators of gross human rights violations and crimes against humanity.

79. The High Commissioner believes the indictment of Mr. Slobodan Milosevic and four other Serbian leaders is a major step in the process of addressing impunity. The five persons indicted are charged with crimes against humanity, detailed specifically as murders, deportation and persecutions, and with violations of the laws and customs of war.

80. The High Commissioner urges the international community to increase its efforts to improve the living conditions of refugees and IDPs in the former Yugoslav Republic of Macedonia, Albania and Montenegro (Federal Republic of Yugoslavia). The High Commissioner underlines that the refugee burden must be shared among more countries in order to alleviate the pressure placed on the economies, social life and inter-ethnic relations of the countries and territories bordering on Kosovo.

81. The High Commissioner underlines that the registration of refugees and the issuing of identity papers undertaken by UNHCR and IOM should be considered by the responsible authorities of the Federal

Republic of Yugoslavia as valid identification and proof of the refugees' former habitual residence in the Federal Republic of Yugoslavia and thus a sufficient basis for establishing the right to return. The High Commissioner also calls on the responsible authorities to create the conditions for a secure and peaceful return of refugees to their homes. Their return should be monitored by an international peace-keeping force.

82. Any durable solution to the crisis in Kosovo will have to be built on a solid foundation of respect for human rights, on strong national and local human rights infrastructures and on a culture of respect for human rights and tolerance. It must provide an adequate basis for the future observance of human rights and the establishment of effective human rights institutions in Kosovo and throughout the Federal Republic of Yugoslavia, as well as for the support of long-term programmes that would create or strengthen national human rights capacities.

83. There should be a key human rights component in any future United Nations presence in Kosovo, the objectives of which should be: to monitor and promote respect for human rights and the rule of law; to follow up individual cases of human rights violations and to determine patterns of continuing violations; to investigate complaints of human rights abuses, in cooperation with international civilian police; and to continue providing support to United Nations human rights mechanisms, including the Special Rapporteur of the Commission on Human Rights, thematic mechanisms and treaty bodies.

84. In the event of the deployment of a United Nations mission in Kosovo, OHCHR will contribute to the design and implementation of human rights training programmes for international peacekeepers and police monitors.

85. As a component of a United Nations presence in Kosovo, OHCHR will work with the local the authorities to improve capacities to ensure respect for human rights. Special attention should be given to bringing legislation (at the federal, republican and local levels) into conformity with international standards. OHCHR will also endeavour to work with the Government of the Federal Republic of Yugoslavia on the elaboration of a national plan of action for human rights and on the establishment of a national human rights institution. Training of key professional groups such as lawyers, judges, local police, prison officials and educators, should be a priority.

86. Concerning civil society, once back in Kosovo OHCHR will strive to design and implement programmes to strengthen NGOs, human rights programmes in education, independent media and other sectors. Workshops and seminars will be arranged in order to increase awareness of international human rights standards and better ensure their implementation. Emphasis should be placed on the development of a culture of tolerance which embodies the principles of international human rights and non-discrimination. A human rights education campaign involving schools and the media will be pursued.

87. The High Commissioner stresses the need to strengthen democracy and the rule of law, economic and social development and respect for human rights and fundamental freedoms throughout the region. In this perspective, the High Commissioner hopes that the presence of OHCHR in Albania, the former Yugoslav Republic of Macedonia, Croatia, Bosnia and Herzegovina, Montenegro (Federal Republic of Yugoslavia) and eventually again throughout the entire territory of the Federal Republic of Yugoslavia will offer the opportunity to support longer-term technical cooperation programmes to create or strengthen national human rights capacities and assist in the development and implementation of national plans of action for human rights and human rights education.

88. The High Commissioner is prepared to report further in due course on human rights violations and the humanitarian situation in and around Kosovo.

40. Report on the Situation of Human Rights in Kosovo, FRY, E/CN.4/2000/10, 7 September 1999

Introduction

1. The situation of human rights in Kosovo has lately been the subject of continuous attention of the members of the Commission on Human Rights and the international community. At the outset of the crisis, in March 1999, the High Commissioner dispatched a personal envoy to the area along with Mr. Jiri Dienstbier, the Special Rapporteur. The High Commissioner also established the Kosovo Emergency Operation (KEO) with deployments in Albania, the former Yugoslav Republic of Macedonia and Podgorica (Montenegro, Federal Republic of Yugoslavia (FRY)). The purpose of these deployments was to register concern for the human rights situation then prevailing in Kosovo and to gather first-hand information about those violations for the purpose of accountability. During the fifty-fifth session of the Commission, the High Commissioner submitted weekly reports as the situation evolved. Since the end of the Commission, she has also visited the area on two occasions.

2. In its resolution 1999/2, the Commission requested the High Commissioner to report to it urgently on the situation of human rights and the humanitarian crisis relating to Kosovo and on the implementation of the provisions of its resolution. Pursuant to this request, the High Commissioner submitted a report to the Commission on 31 May (E/CN.4/2000/7). The High Commissioner is now submitting a consolidated report which has a triple purpose: to present to the Commission the major findings of the Kosovo Emergency Operation, drawing on its database for the collection and analysis of information; to update the Commission on the evolving human rights situation in Kosovo; and to offer some observations and recommendations for consideration. The first part of the report deals with the situation prior to the withdrawal of Serb forces from Kosovo on 10 June; the second part deals with the situation from June to August 1999.

I. Findings of the Kosovo Emergency Operation

A. METHODOLOGY

3. OHCHR-KEO sought to interview refugees of diverse geographic backgrounds, with a view to achieving an overall picture of the human rights situation in Kosovo. In order to be able to verify facts and reports of violations, corroborate testimonies and reconstruct patterns of violations, efforts were made also to interview a reasonable number of refugees from each geographic location.

4. Priority was given to quality as opposed to quantity. OHCHR staff, including human rights monitors provided by the Governments of Switzerland and Norway, conducted a total of 273 in-depth interviews in Albania and the former Yugoslav Republic of Macedonia, while another OHCHR team gathered information in Montenegro. Considerable time was spent in each interview in order to build trust and get the witnesses/victims to provide many details which, in turn, were useful to assess the reliability of the information provided.

5. From the moment they left their houses to the moment they crossed the border to the former Yugoslav Republic of Macedonia or Albania, refugees lived an odyssey through the mountains and villages of Kosovo, witnessing and/or suffering countless human rights violations. By conducting in-depth interviews, OHCHR has sought to obtain full accounts of the events witnessed and abuses suffered by the interviewees.

6. The use of the database has been crucial to identifying all the interview records referring to the same events, comparing them with each other and obtaining a reliable reconstruction of the facts.

B. DISPLACEMENT AND DEPORTATION OF ETHNIC ALBANIANS FROM KOSOVO

7. Human rights violations were among the root causes of the mass exodus of more than 1 million ethnic Albanians from Kosovo. Out of 273 refugees interviewed, only 1 reportedly left his village out of fear of North Atlantic Treaty Organization (NATO) bombs, while all the

others described how they were compelled, either by direct violence or by intimidation, to leave their homes.

8. Different patterns of displacement and deportation emerged from the interviews conducted by OHCHR-KEO. Trends of displacement vary considerably from area to area. Cases which are particularly significant both for the number of people involved and for the events which accompanied the displacement and deportation are reported below.

1. Pristina

9. Twenty-six per cent of refugees interviewed by OHCHR-KEO were habitual residents of the municipality of Pristina. After NATO launched the air campaign, the security situation in the streets of Pristina deteriorated rapidly and some of the inhabitants decided to leave owing to the general lack of security. However, numerous interviewees also reported that a comprehensive and systematic expulsion campaign was begun at the end of March by Serb military and police units in predominantly Albanian neighbourhoods of Pristina / Dragodan, Vranjevac, the hospital neighbourhood, etc./ and adjacent villages. / Maticane, Zlatare and Kojlovica./

10. In the majority of cases Albanians were expelled from their apartments during house-to-house raids conducted by Serb forces. Many interviewees reported being escorted to the railway station and then forced onto trains heading for the border. It appears that a corridor was left open by Serb forces for people to flee to the Golak and Lap regions, with some people even being ordered to flee in that direction. Some interviewees estimated that more than 100,000 internally displaced persons (IDPs) headed for these regions from the municipalities of Pristina and Podujevo. In mid-April, Serb forces undertook a major offensive in these regions, well known for being strongholds of the Kosovo Liberation Army (KLA). The inhabitants and the large IDP population were targeted directly and the attacks resulted in a large number of civilian casualties. / In Mramor and Kolic villages many civilians died as a result of this offensive. /

11. The inhabitants of the Golak and Lap regions, together with IDPs, were forced by these attacks to head for Pristina. When IDPs reached Pristina, the police ordered Podujevo residents to go back to their homes while the other IDPs were allowed to remain. Many of them eventually decided to go by train or by bus from Kosovo Polje to the border of the former Yugoslav Republic of Macedonia owing to harassment, intimidation and abuse by groups of Serb police and paramilitary personnel.

2. Podujevo

12. Ethnic Albanians were forcibly displaced from Podujevo municipality by methods similar to those used in the municipality of Pristina. In the town of Podujevo, Serb troops evicted Albanians from their homes at gunpoint, while a significant number of villages with predominantly Albanian populations / Bradas, Donja Dubnica, Donja Pakastica, Hrtica, Majance, etc./ were shelled and later entered and destroyed by infantry forces. These operations were systematically undertaken in the period March/April and caused a large influx of IDPs to the Lap and Golak regions. Many people from Podujevo were sheltering in the villages of Kolic and Mramor at the time when Serb forces attacked these villages in mid-April.

3. Mitrovica

13. In Mitrovica, Albanian intellectuals and political activists were targeted, soon after the beginning of the NATO bombing campaign, according to a list allegedly prepared by the police with the help of Serb civilians. Some were evicted from their homes by the police while others went into hiding after receiving reports of deliberate killings of Albanian intellectuals.

14. The Ibar river divides the town of Mitrovica in half: the northern side was predominantly Serb, the southern predominantly Albanian. IDPs interviewed by OHCHR described a system of ill-treatment of Mitrovica's Albanian population that combined wholesale violence, harassment, and a uniquely strategic process to support intimidation and forced expulsion. During the war food was available only on the northern or "Serb" side of the city, and the road to obtain food, narrowed to one path because of the bridge, was a gauntlet of attack and humiliation.

15. Serb police and paramilitary forces launched an extensive ethnic cleansing operation in Mitrovica town and surrounding villages on 15 April. Some 70,000 Albanians were rounded up in the centre of Mitrovica and eventually forced to walk for several days towards the Albanian border, escorted by paramilitary troops. When the convoy reached Gremnik, the paramilitary troops ordered thousands of IDPs back to Mitrovica, while the rest were deported to Albania.

16. From the beginning of May onwards, paramilitary troops started raiding Albanian homes in Mitrovica and surrounding villages. People were rounded up in large numbers and young men were arrested, detained, interrogated, and some eventually deported by bus to Albania.

4. Orahovac

17. A few days before the beginning of the NATO air campaign, paramilitary groups launched an offensive against several villages in the municipality of Orahovac. Attacks intensified towards the end of March. During the offensive inhabitants and IDPs sheltering in the area were forcibly evicted from their homes and, in some instances, ordered under threat to leave for Albania. IDPs were then escorted to the border or forced into buses going to Prizren, from where they were ordered to walk the remaining distance to the border.

18. Reportedly, several thousand / Estimates given by interviewees of the number of IDPs ranged from 20,000 to 40,000./ IDPs were rounded up in the town of Belanica and prevented from escaping by encircling attacks on villages / Malisevo, Dragobilje, Ostrozub among other villages./ in adjacent areas. At the beginning of April, Serb forces eventually entered Belanica and forced residents and IDPs to walk towards the Albanian border. Some days later, paramilitary and police forces undertook a brutal military offensive in the village of Pusto Selo. All the remaining villagers and IDPs, mostly women and children, were expelled from their homes and rounded up in a field. Women and children were ordered to walk to Ratkovac and from there to Albania.

5. Lipljan

19. In mid-April, army and police forces together with local Serbs started an offensive against several villages in the area. / Smolusa, Marevc, Glavica, Oklap and Slovinje./ Serb forces systematically burned down Albanian houses. Local Serbs painted the symbol of Serb unity / A cross with a Cyrillic C in each angle./ on the walls of Serb-owned houses in Slovinje to have them spared from arson.

6. Urosevac

20. In Urosevac the police targeted Albanian intellectuals, such as trade union leaders, journalists, prominent members of the Democratic League of Kosovo (LDK) and civil rights activists. Some of them were forced to flee to avoid persecution. Upon their departure their houses were destroyed. The office of the LDK, the non-governmental organization "Mother Theresa", and the former office of the Organization for Security and Cooperation in Europe (OSCE) were blown up. At the end of March some of the neighbourhoods of Urosevac were shelled by regular army (VJ) forces, while Serb military troops undertook house searches in another part of the town, evicting people and subsequently setting their houses on fire.

21. At the beginning of April, VJ troops together with paramilitary forces undertook a massive offensive against a considerable number of villages / Kamena Glava, Zlatare, Staro Selo, Biba and Varos Selo, among others./ in the municipality. Some villages were shelled / Four civilians were killed and eight wounded by a grenade in Zlatare./ and then entered by paramilitary infantry who set abandoned houses on fire. Inhabitants of these villages / Inhabitants of Zlatare fled to Slatina, Kacanik municipality, from where, in mid-May, they were further expelled by the police and escorted to the border. / fled to Urosevac town, where Albanians were allegedly denied the right to buy food in

shops. The lack of food further pushed IDPs to leave by train or by bus for the border.

7. Suva Reka

22. Immediately after the beginning of the NATO campaign, paramilitary forces undertook a brutal offensive against the Albanian population in the city of Suva Reka. People were systematically driven from their homes during a three-day offensive and many houses were destroyed. Paramilitary troops forced most of the population to leave in different directions. / Allegedly IDPs were escorted by paramilitary troops to the villages of Musutiste and Selograzde and to Prizren./ Serb forces repeatedly attacked the villages of the municipality in April and at the beginning of May. During these attacks, inhabitants were displaced and gathered in KLA-controlled areas in the mountains. / Like the village of Grejcevce./ Serb forces repeatedly shelled these positions forcing the KLA to withdraw and to leave the group of IDPs behind. Serb forces entered the area in the middle of May and IDPs were forced to move to Suva Reka. The arrivals were directed to the bus station and taken by bus to the Albanian border. / People walked from Zur, municipality of Prizren, to Morina, Albania./

8. Glogovac

23. VJ and special police, together with paramilitary groups, started a large-scale offensive throughout the municipality of Glogovac some days before the beginning of the NATO campaign. People from a number of villages / Dobrosevac, Gladno Selo, Novo Cikatovo, Godance, Gradica, Likosane, Stutica, among others. / fled and gathered in the village of Cirez, Srbica municipality. The forces rounded up IDPs in Cirez, separated men from women and children, and ordered people to walk towards Glogovac town. The column was escorted by tanks and troops. Later, IDPs decided to return to their villages in search of food, not available in Glogovac. In another brutal offensive villagers were rounded up and again forced back to Glogovac town. In May, paramilitary groups conducted several house-to-house raids during which many people were robbed and some killed. The police denied the requested protection to the residents and the IDP population sheltering in town. Due to these circumstances, inhabitants and IDPs boarded buses heading for the border.

9. Srbica

24. At the end of March, Serb military forces undertook joint offensives throughout the municipality of Srbica. Villages were shelled by military forces and then entered and set on fire by police and paramilitary groups. Inhabitants of several villages / Baks, Donje Prekaze, Gornje Prekaze./ fled to Cirez, where a large number of IDPs from the municipality of Glogovac had already taken shelter. Serb forces surrounded, shelled and eventually entered Cirez. IDPs were gathered into columns and forced to head for Glogovac escorted by Serb forces.

25. Serb forces used the same tactics in other villages / Izbica, Rudnik, Ozrim, Leocina, Kladernica./ of Srbica municipality: inhabitants were forced to the mountains and to the villages of Rakitnica and Tusilje. At the end of March, Serb forces entered these villages and forced a group of IDPs to Prizren, from where they were taken to Albania by bus, while another group of IDPs was ordered to head back to Tusilje. The IDP population continued to increase in Tusilje. In mid-April, Serb forces once again stormed the village and forced inhabitants and IDPs to walk in columns to Prizren, from where they were brought to the border by bus. A large number of men from the municipality were brought to Mitrovica for interrogation before being eventually taken to the Albanian border-crossing point.

10. Kacanik

26. In Kacanik, before 24 March, army groups shelled several villages. / Palivodenica, Gajre, Kotlina, Bob./ Most of the villagers fled to Kacanik town or took temporary shelter in the mountains. At the end of May, the intensive shelling and the build-up of Serb forces in the area of Vate made the population flee the village in a long convoy. Serb forces let the convoy proceed, through their checkpoints, to the border. As they left, IDPs witnessed Serb forces enter Vate and set houses on fire.

27. The KLA was reportedly present in the town of Kacanik when the NATO campaign was launched. Serb police forces and paramilitary groups searched the town for KLA activists and other Albanian intellectuals. As a result of these activities and the general climate of violence in town, a large / Allegedly around 1,000 persons./ number of people fled to a KLA-controlled area north of Kacanik. At the end of March, Kacanik was attacked from the north and south by the army and the police. The attack lasted for some days and resulted in a large number of civilian casualties and in a mass exodus of civilians to the former Yugoslav Republic of Macedonia.

11. Djakovica

28. From 24 March until 2 April, special police action, originating from Djakovica itself, drove Albanian residents towards the periphery and towards villages in the south, as well as towards Prizren. From 3 April until 6 May, IDPs were driven further towards Albania by the police. On 7 May, a Serbian offensive began in Cabrat, which eyewitness testimony described as a combination of special police and paramilitary activity, characterized by mass arrests and detention of military-age men, including teenagers, burning of homes, and summary executions in house-to-house actions. From 7 May until 14 June, Djakovica was completely blockaded, its population driven into concentrated areas within the city, whereupon the police conducted mass registration of residents and began selected arrests.

C. KILLINGS/EXECUTIONS

29. The displacement and expulsion of ethnic Albanians from Kosovo occurred in a climate of lawlessness and total disregard for human life and dignity which resulted in an extremely high level of violence.

30. According to several sources, and to the appalling discoveries made by the international security force in Kosovo (KFOR) and the United Nations Mission in Kosovo (UNMIK) upon the return to Kosovo, as many as 10,000 Kosovo Albanians died during the period of the NATO campaign and several thousand remain missing. The majority of refugees interviewed by OHCHR indicated having witnessed at least one incident in which one or more individuals died a violent death.

31. In some instances, civilians died as a result of military actions and indiscriminate shelling against towns and villages. It was especially vulnerable and elderly people, incapable of leaving their homes or unwilling to do so, who died in these circumstances. / In the municipality of Podujevo, for example, Serbian aircraft reportedly launched two rockets on a village killing 30 civilians; in March eight people died as a result of a grenade explosion in Prizren./ However, only a small number of cases reported refer to incidents of this nature.

32. About 10 per cent of the cases reported refer to orchestrated actions conducted by military, police and paramilitary forces in order to gather crowds of fleeing Kosovo Albanians in specific locations where the latter were subsequently robbed and executed. / On 27 March, in Belanica, Suva Reka municipality, Serb forces reportedly surrounded the village, precluding any escape, and then gathered the villagers in an open space to extort money and valuables from them. Those who had no money were taken to a private house and shot dead. Similar cases are reported in Celina, Orahovac municipality, and in Slovinje, Lipljan municipality./

33. Almost one third of the cases reported refer to random executions of civilians perpetrated mainly by police and paramilitary forces. In many instances, men of military age were killed at police checkpoints upon presentation of their identification documents, because they had come from areas believed to be KLA strongholds. When villages and towns were besieged, civilians became victims of appalling acts of violence at the hands of Serbian military, police and paramilitary forces. In these circumstances, many individuals were reportedly robbed, questioned, tortured and, in some cases, killed in their own houses. / Some of these incidents allegedly took place in Maticane, Urosevac, Glogovac and Staro Selo. In Mramor, a man who had been previously wounded by a grenade was executed in his house because he was suspected of having been injured while fighting against Serbian forces./

34. Kosovo Albanians were also targeted by virtue of their real or supposed affiliation with political associations or because they were believed to support NATO intervention in Kosovo. / In Kacanik, local Serbs and police officers prepared a list of all Albanians affiliated with different political organizations and went house to house to question them. Some men were killed in the process. An interviewee indicated that in Djakovica, in the early stage of the bombing campaign, postal workers provided lists of addresses of targeted groups and individuals. Concerning Pristina, OHCHR interviewed an eyewitness to the murder of the Kosovo Albanian lawyer Bajram Kelmendi and his two sons. They were seen being taken out of two white police jeeps. Mr. Kelmendi was asked to kill one of his sons and refused to do it, then his older son was asked to kill his father and he also refused. Then police officers asked Bajram Kelmendi whom they should kill first, and in spite of the desperate appeal of the lawyer they shot his two sons dead in front of him, and 30 seconds later they shot him as well. In Stimlje, a father and son were killed because they had rented their house to an OSCE officer. In Kosovo Polje two men were stopped at a police checkpoint while going to repair their television and killed because they were accused of wanting to watch "NATO air strikes". In Orahovac a young man was killed because he had a KLA emblem in his wallet./

35. Many displaced Kosovo Albanians decided to return to their villages in search of food, valuables or relatives and friends they had left behind and were killed by Serbian soldiers who had resettled in their homes and/or established control over the village. / In the municipality of Gnjilane, on 6 April, five men who had returned to their village were ordered to lie face down by paramilitary forces and then shot dead. In Lipljan municipality (Smolusa), after a first round of forced displacement, a group of inhabitants decided to go back to their homes. Paramilitary groups and police forces returned to the village and killed them. Similar events were reported in Vitina, Verban and Stagova./

36. Many of the reported killings occurred in the process of displacement itself, in what seemed to be an attempt to gather and keep under control crowds of terrified civilians and to speed up the process of departure, as well as to show determination and to intimidate those who were reluctant to leave. Reportedly, in many cases, shots were fired into crowds of civilians, houses were set on fire and those who tried to escape were shot at and killed. / In the village of Gladno Selo, Glogovac municipality, paramilitaries set houses on fire killing as many as 45 civilians, mainly elderly women. In Suva Reka as many as 350 civilians were allegedly killed in the process of displacement. In Pristina, while forcing people to the railway station the police killed several civilians./

37. A considerable number of the killings reported to the KEO refer to incidents in which police and/or paramilitary and/or army forces attacked groups of IDPs hiding in the mountains or proceeding to the border in convoys. Sometimes fire was opened against civilian convoys, while in other instances individuals were picked out of the crowd and executed. / In Grastica, 30 young men were taken out of a convoy and shot dead; in Kralan, two wounded women were asked to get off a tractor and, since they couldn't because of their injuries, they were burned alive on the tractor; in Kolic, Serb forces fired into a group of IDPs, allegedly killing 91 civilians./

38. A small number of the executions reportedly appear to have been perpetrated by Serb forces in response to KLA activities or by way of revenge or reprisal against KLA offensives. In some instances it also appears that civilians who had sought KLA protection in the mountains died as a result of fighting between KLA and Serb forces, or were captured and killed by Serb forces upon retreat of the KLA. / In the village of Vrbovac, Glogovac municipality, upon retreat of KLA, a group of about 50 civilians was caught, ordered to gather in rows, tortured and executed by paramilitary forces. In Srbica, after a KLA offensive and subsequent withdrawal, 5 old men were killed. In Pusto Selo after fighting between KLA and Serbs in the area, Serb forces by way of reprisal allegedly executed 106 persons after having humiliated and mistreated them./

39. One case of execution of an ethnic Albanian by the KLA was reported to OHCHR-KEO. The man was suspected of collaborating with Serb forces and was killed at a KLA checkpoint close to Kacanik the day after he had allegedly buried bodies of KLA soldiers killed in fighting against Serb forces.

40. The corpses of executed Kosovo Albanians were either buried by civilians (sometimes upon explicit demand by the perpetrators) or KLA soldiers, or taken away by Serbian forces. In other instances Serb forces reportedly returned to the place of massacres, dug out bodies previously buried in secret by civilians and took them away. Many refugees declared having observed tractors or trucks carrying piles of dead bodies driven by Serbian police to unknown destinations. OHCHR heard testimonies and saw evidence of deliberate burning of bodies, while on different occasions Serb forces were observed digging mass graves. / The police were seen transporting some 40 bodies in Kosovo Polje in early April. In Kacanik paramilitary groups and some Romas were observed digging holes with bulldozers after the massacre at "Racak stream". In Slovinje, Lipljan municipality, Serbian forces buried 16 bodies and the day after ordered the relatives of the executed to exhume the bodies and re-bury them in a cemetery./ Romas were reportedly often involved in the transport and burial of corpses. / For example, Romas were allegedly observed burying bodies of Kosovo Albanians executed in Rezala, Srbica municipality, after Serb forces had exhumed them. In Vucitrn, Romas allegedly buried some 100 Kosovo Albanians who had been killed by "snipers". In Grastica, Pristina municipality, some Romas were reportedly observed loading a tractor with dead bodies./

41. The majority of the killings documented were allegedly carried out by paramilitary and police forces with the cooperation or complicity of the army. However, in a few cases, police officers reportedly stopped paramilitary forces from committing crimes and cruelties against ethnic Albanians. / For example, in Kisnica/Pristina, on 25 March, paramilitary groups wearing red bandanas, black masks and camouflage uniforms entered a house and started robbing and killing the inhabitants one by one, until a police officer arrived and stopped them./ Paramilitary groups and special police units were described as wearing camouflage or black uniforms, gloves, black masks, and some of them wore red scarfs and had shaved heads and wore a red insignia with a white eagle on their uniforms. Some refugees have explicitly described the paramilitaries as "Arkan's troops", while others have reported the involvement of "Seselj" troops in the killings. Some ethnic Albanians claimed that Serbs from neighbouring villages participated in abuses against them. Russian mercenaries have also been reported to be present and active in Kosovo on the side of Serb forces. / Russian mercenaries were reportedly present among other places, in Glogovac, Djakovica, Srbica. /

42. It appears that the action of paramilitary troops was characterized by a very high level of violence and cruelty. Paramilitaries were allegedly responsible for the killings of women and children, for stabbing people and for mutilating dead bodies.

D. VIOLENCE AGAINST WOMEN AND CHILDREN

43. Twenty-two per cent of the incidents reported involved children, while 17.5 per cent of the cases referred to violence against women.

44. Both women and children were victims of killings and executions. In particular, several cases were reported in which women died as a result of indiscriminate shootings into crowds of civilians, while in a few reported cases women were picked out of convoys and executed. Children have been deliberately targeted in several circumstances. / In Kacanik, boys as young as 17 were killed; in Bela Crkva three children, respectively six, four and three years old, were shot dead by Serb forces./

45. Twenty per cent of refugees interviewed reported incidents in which women and children were separated from male relatives and exposed to mistreatment. / In Grastica, for example, children were threatened with knives./ In several instances, women and children were beaten by the police during house-to-house raids. / Cases of this nature reportedly took place in Miratovc and Preshevo. In Staro Selo, para-

military groups went house to house to question suspected KLA supporters and killed several males in the process, including a 15-year-old boy./ Incidents of forced labour have also been reported in which boys as young as 15 have been obliged by Serbian forces to dig trenches. Furthermore, it appears that young boys suspected of being KLA members were questioned, tortured and sometimes killed regardless of their age. / Cases of this nature were reported in Vrani Do, Lipljan and Krusha e Made. /

46. Children and women have also been victims of episodes of discrimination: for example, women giving birth were denied medical assistance and injured children were refused treatment.

47. Fourteen interviewees spoke of confirmed or suspected rape and several cases of sexual assault. Considering the cultural stigma attached to sexual violence in the Albanian culture, it is reasonable to assume that the number of incidents of this nature may be higher than reflected in public reports. / On 30 June 1999, in Pristina, the High Commissioner for Human Rights met the Chairperson of the Centre for Protection of Women and Children. The Chairperson said that the number of unreported cases of rape in Kosovo was very high. She also said that in Kosovo two different forms of rape were common: biological rape and gun-rape and that both women and men were allegedly victims of rape before and during the war. /

48. In some instances, women were reportedly raped in their houses when their villages were under siege. / In Cirez, when IDPs were surrounded young women and girls were taken away for one night by army soldiers. In Vranjevac, a woman was raped in her house and her husband was killed while trying to protect her. In Kolic, paramilitary troops, allegedly Arkan's, during the attack against the village abducted a number of women. In Ponesh, paramilitaries entered a house and raped a 20-year-old woman in front of her mother./ In other cases women were taken away and raped by Serb soldiers after attacks on groups of IDPs. Cases of rape on the train to the border or at the railway station in Pristina / In Pristina, the departure of one train was delayed for six hours. During this time, many paramilitaries boarded the train and raped 10-15 young girls in front of all, including young children. / were also reported. Allegedly a woman was raped by a paramilitary soldier at the hospital in Gnjilane where she was being treated for injuries suffered in a grenade explosion. In several reported cases women were asked to hand over money and other valuables in order not to be sexually abused.

49. OHCHR-KEO also recorded accounts of immoral and intimidating behaviour towards Albanian women by Serb military and police personnel. For example, women have been ordered to undress during confiscation of valuables, addressed with sexual language and sometimes touched and fondled in an intimidating manner.

50. According to numerous reports, there appear to have been a pattern of mutilating women by cutting off their ears and fingers. / In Gladno Selo, for example, when the village was attacked, many women were allegedly killed and their ears cut off. In Celine, IDPs were surrounded, women and men separated, young women separated from older women, and then beaten and obliged to undress. The ears of at least 20 women were allegedly mutilated while a lesser number had their fingers severed. / At this stage it is difficult to determine whether this macabre ritual had a particular significance or was merely an act of sadism.

E. ARBITRARY ARREST AND DETENTION

51. Twenty-three per cent of refugees interviewed suffered or directly witnessed incidents of arbitrary arrest and detention. Arbitrary arrests and detentions occurred according to a similar pattern throughout Kosovo. However, the frequency and circumstances of the incidents varied according to the overall situation in the area of apprehension and adjacent areas.

52. Men of military age throughout Kosovo were often separated from their families and detained on mere speculation of being KLA members, KLA collaborators, or with the simple aim of obtaining information. In many cases, mass arrests of men followed Serb military offensives against Albanian villages. Inhabitants and IDPs were encircled by Serb forces in their villages, or intercepted as they tried to flee, and captured. They were detained for a brief period at assembly points, sometimes transported to detention centres and eventually jailed for longer periods in regional prisons.

53. Large numbers of men were captured by paramilitary groups and special police forces during mopping-up operations against villages / Gladno Selo, Vrbovac, Baks, Donje Prekaze, Gornje Prekaze. / in the municipalities of Glogovac and Srbica. The mosque in Cirez / Nearly 200 men were detained in the mosque at one point./ functioned as an assembly point. At the end of April, these men were escorted by Serb troops to Glogovac, transported to the police station in Pristina and then to a location known as "Building 92". Prisoners were eventually transferred to the prison in Lipljan. Some men were released and deported to the former Yugoslav Republic of Macedonia on 30 May.

54. Some of the detainees stated that they were charged with terrorism while still in Pristina, while others claim to have been forced to sign confessions.

55. The arrest and detention of men from the municipalities of Podujevo, Pristina and eastern parts of Vucitrn followed a slightly different pattern, although the purposes of detention seem to have been the same as mentioned above. Mass arrests of men occurred in locations where large convoys of IDPs were expected to move in an attempt to escape heavy bombardment or mopping-up operations. Especially during the month of April, large numbers of men were arrested and detained in the villages of Lukare and Grastica. / IDPs escaping offensives in the Golak and Lap region./ Large IDP convoys / Some interviewees describe convoys 2-3 km long./ were at that time heading for Pristina escorted by paramilitary groups. Convoys were blocked by special police and detained for hours, sometimes for days. During this time paramilitary troops searched people for valuables and interrogated men. Many men were not released and their fate is unknown.

56. Serb special police troops maintained a checkpoint near Pristina, in the village of Vrani Do, where Albanian men were separated from their families and held back in large numbers. / Two hundred men detained on 30 April./ Interrogation of the detainees took place in a designated house near the road. Family members were forced by the police to continue towards Pristina. After hours of interrogation the prisoners were taken in buses to Pristina and detained further in "Building 92" or released. Eventually some detainees were transferred to the prison in Lipljan.

57. The Albanian population of Vucitrn town and adjacent villages was forcibly gathered in a field, where men were separated from women, children and the elderly and taken by bus to a jail in the village of Smrekovnica. In a similar incident inhabitants were gathered in an agricultural cooperative and subsequently taken to the same detention centre.

58. Men abducted in Mitrovica and adjacent areas in the municipality of Srbica were transferred, after interrogation in Smrekovnica, to an improvised prison in the technical school in Mitrovica for further questioning. After being detained for up to a month, a group of prisoners were deported to the Albanian border in buses at the end of May.

59. Albanian intellectuals, human rights lawyers and activists, politicians and others were arbitrarily arrested and detained throughout Kosovo. Some were killed in detention while many others are still missing.

60. A group of young men were reportedly captured after an offensive against a village in the municipality of Urosevac. The men were subjected to forced labour and detained near Serb troops as human shields. Ethnic Albanians were allegedly used as human shields also in the village of Stutica, near Glogovac town, in mid-April. In some villages in the municipality of Vitina, there were reports of people held in "house arrest" as human shields to protect Serb military vehicles and tanks. Reportedly, large columns of IDPs were escorted by Serb paramilitary troops and police from Mitrovica to Albania and then some of the IDPs were compelled to head back in order to "protect" with their bodies military convoys from NATO bombs.

F. TORTURE AND MISTREATMENT

61. Sixty-nine per cent of the refugees interviewed stated that they had witnessed or personally suffered torture or other cruel, inhuman and degrading treatment at the hands of Serb forces.

62. The vast majority of cases of torture reportedly occurred in detention, with the purpose of extracting information or confessions from the detainees. OHCHR-KEO interviewed some of the prisoners who were released and deported to Albania and the former Yugoslav Republic of Macedonia towards the end of the NATO campaign. They stated that they had been separated from their families and temporarily detained at different locations until they were transferred to a regular prison. Torture occurred at the place of apprehension and at assembly points where men were detained pending transfer to a detention centre or prison. / Three young men were abducted by Serb paramilitary troops in the hills near Vrbovac in Glogovac. They were interrogated on the spot and accused of being KLA members. One of the interviewees was hit on the head with a rifle, the second victim was stabbed in the arms and the third was shot dead. The two survivors were later detained in the mosque at Cirez, where the interviewee and others were severely hit in their kidneys with a wooden stick. In the city hall, detainees were severely beaten with police batons and metal bars. Shortly afterwards, they were transported to the police station in Pristina and detained in "Building 92". The inhabitants of Vucitrn were rounded up in a square at the end of May, whereupon some 250 men were separated from the rest and detained in a sports hall for three days. They were denied food and water, forced to sit for 10 hours on steps with the upper part of the body bent down, and given water mixed with diesel fuel./

63. Several refugees reported severe beatings with wooden and metal poles in "Building 92" in Pristina. Detainees were taken to different locations in Pristina for questioning and reportedly torture occurred during interrogation. / Prisoners were taken in turns to a private house in the city, where their hands were tested for gun smoke and powder. They were forced to face the wall with legs spread and kicked in the genitals. They were furthermore hit with police batons in the limbs and kidneys. Similar treatment occurred in "Building 92" and the city jail./ Detainees were regularly beaten by guards. Reportedly some were put in a cell with cold water up to their knees for a night.

64. Some of the detainees were transferred to the prison in Lipljan, where similar treatment was inflicted on them. Corroborating statements describe how a former Serb criminal, working as a barber in the prison of Lipljan, continuously beat and harassed the prisoners.

65. Refugees reported that prison conditions in Smrekovnica, Pristina and Lipljan were inhumane. Men were detained in cold cells without beds or blankets. Cells were overcrowded and prisoners were only given bread and far too little water. / In Smirkovnica, detainees were given food once a day: 500 g of bread and some cookies for six persons and 50 litres of water for 500 prisoners. The interviewee stayed in a cell of 4 x 4 metres together with eight other men, but having 50 men in one cell was not uncommon. Prisoners were held in cells for up to 24 hours without being allowed to use the toilet./

66. Some of the most serious cases of torture reportedly occurred in Urosevac, in a private house previously used as a café. Young Albanian men were detained in the cellar of the house and occasionally brought to the upper floors for interrogation about KLA activity. Some victims were reportedly held for several days in the cellar immersed in water up to the knees. During interrogations, detainees were severely beaten with wooden sticks and some were allegedly given electric shocks. Some of the victims were hospitalized in refugee camps in the former Yugoslav Republic of Macedonia for injuries received as a result of the beatings.

67. A few cases of mock executions were reported to OHCHR-KEO. / For example, in Cirez at the end of March./ In other instances the systematic confiscation of valuables by paramilitary groups from IDP convoys was accompanied by particularly sadistic and brutal acts. In Grastica, through which 100,000 people passed in mid-April, paramilitary personnel indiscriminately stabbed people's arms and legs.

G. DESTRUCTION OF PROPERTY

68. About half of the refugees interviewed reported large-scale destruction of property at the hands of Serb forces, especially burning of Albanian-owned houses. Towns and cities were not heavily affected by the destruction, although Albanian neighbourhoods were in some instances attacked and houses burned down. More often, premises and properties of intellectuals, political activists and suspected KLA collaborators were preferred targets, as well as houses and apartments which had been rented by officers of the OSCE Kosovo Verification Mission.

69. Following military offensives, villages with predominantly Albanian populations were systematically burnt down by Serb troops. In many cases interviewees observed from hiding places in the hills Serb troops entering villages and setting houses on fire. Along with houses, barns with hay, remaining tractors and agricultural equipment were burnt as well. Villagers who returned after the withdrawal of Serb forces found livestock killed or disappeared, while corpses were sometimes thrown into wells to contaminate drinking water.

70. Many Kosovo Albanians had their personal documents torn apart by Serb troops during the eviction, at police checkpoints, at the border or elsewhere in the course of searches by police, army or paramilitary forces. It appears that all of these acts of destruction were aimed at preventing Albanians from returning to and resuming life in their places of residence. The destruction of property was apparently not solely an act of vandalism but an attempt at wiping out signs of the presence of the Albanian population in Kosovo, as well as its national and cultural identity.

H. CONFISCATION OF PROPERTY

71. The majority of interviewees also reported confiscation of property by Serb forces. Confiscation took place during raids into Albanian homes: Serb troops went from house to house in villages and towns, people present in the houses were searched and deprived of money and other valuables, and cars and tractors were confiscated.

72. Serb police and paramilitary groups intercepted large groups of IDPs and forced them to surrender money, jewellery, cars, tractors and other valuables at gunpoint. Paramilitary groups occasionally stabbed or shot IDPs who failed to meet their demands and threatened to kill hostages captured on the spot if family members could not pay the demanded amount of money. / IDP convoys targeted by paramilitary groups in Grastica were brutally robbed and many persons allegedly killed or injured because they failed to provide the demanded amount, which in some cases was as high as DM 1,000./

73. A few cases of extortion of money from Albanians at border crossing points were also reported. Furthermore, IDPs were often ordered to abandon their vehicles before they were allowed across the border. Car documents and license plates were in some cases confiscated. Numerous cars were allegedly stripped and parts transported away in trucks to be sold elsewhere. Personal documents were also confiscated at border crossing points.

74. Abandoned Albanian houses were systematically and extensively looted for movable property. As the Albanian population fled their villages, Serb infantry systematically loaded goods onto trucks before setting houses on fire. In some instances Roma civilians allegedly assisted Serb forces in transporting confiscated goods.

I. THE KLA FACTOR

75. OHCHR has to date been unable to gather reliable and impartial information on the role played by the KLA during the 11 weeks of the NATO campaign. However, from interviews conducted by OHCHR-KEO it appears that during that period, the KLA was actively involved in fighting against Serbian forces in several areas of Kosovo. Moreover, in some instances civilians allegedly sought KLA protection by resettling close to KLA positions, and KLA soldiers moved to urban areas or fled the country by mingling with crowds of displaced civilians. This circumstance might have negatively affected the attitude of Serbian forces towards civilians. At this stage it is impossible to deter-

mine whether and to what extent the "KLA factor" weighed upon the events which took place in Kosovo.

J. Impact of the Armed Conflict on Civilians

76. Outside Kosovo, the NATO air strikes were especially intensive in and around the densely populated centres of Vojvodina, southern Serbia, and in Belgrade itself. Several city centres suffered from missile or cluster bombs attacks. Repeated attacks on Nis resulted on 7 May in the deaths of 15 civilians when cluster bombs exploded over the city market and central hospital. In Aleksinac, 12 civilians were killed and more than 40 wounded when bombs struck downtown housing blocks and commercial premises on 5 April. In Novi Pazar, 13 were killed and 35 wounded in an attack that destroyed 25 buildings in the city's residential centre. Many civilians, including 27 children, died in repeated strikes to Surdulica and Kursumlija. / The Ministry of Foreign Affairs of the Federal Republic of Yugoslavia has published two volumes of a survey of civilian casualties provoked by NATO intervention: NATO Crimes in Yugoslavia, Documentary Evidence. / Strikes on bridges and means of transportation resulted in the deaths of 55 persons on a passenger train travelling through Grdelica gorge (12 April); 60 persons when a bus was hit on a bridge near Luzani (1 May); 20 persons when a bus travelling between Pec and Rozaje was hit (3-4 May). Large convoys moving through Kosovo were attacked by air, resulting in the deaths of 87 IDPs at Korisa on 14 May; exactly one month earlier, 75 persons, including 19 children, died when missiles struck refugee columns on the Djakovica-Prizren road.

77. Following NATO attacks on fuel reserves, severe restrictions on fuel imposed by the authorities brought civilian life to a standstill. Fuel is now being rationed in Serbia. Many parts of the country were often without electricity and water, and restrictions and shortages continue. Throughout the FRY, damage done to the infrastructure of public utilities threatens an extremely difficult winter.

78. During the war, the formal declaration of martial law gave men in uniform, specifically officials of the Ministry of the Interior, vast powers over most areas of civil activity. Moreover, even in areas where such power was not formally extended to the military by the civil authorities, OHCHR noted that Yugoslav Army and Serbian police either took or were granted effective control. The Republic of Montenegro did not recognize the declaration of martial law, but actions by the Yugoslav Army on the territory of Montenegro challenged and threatened civil authority in that Republic. / On 18 April, eight people were killed by Yugoslav Army fire in Kaluderski Laz, near Rozaje. OHCHR received several reports of military police and reservists within or immediately outside northern Montenegro stopping civilian buses and taking away large groups of men before permitting women and children in the buses to go further. One such group of approximately 102 men was taken away at Bozaj on 30 May and, after a media and international organization outcry, was returned to Montenegro along with 56 others the same day. Some of the men described being robbed and beaten along a gauntlet of army reservists, after which a group of 10 were forced to engage in sexual acts while others were made to watch./

79. Within the FRY, restrictions on information inherent in martial law placed the army in control of public information management. Radio and television towers were bombed, as were the Belgrade headquarters of Radio Television Serbia. Throughout the FRY, foreign and domestic journalists were brought to "informative talks", detained, imprisoned, and charged in proceedings before military courts. In Montenegro, the Yugoslav Army attempted forcibly to conscript journalists from independent media.

80. In the Republic of Serbia federal authorities were denied the immunity of elected or appointed officials by attempts to mobilize them, and the army further moved to arrest several officials in Serbia and Montenegro for refusing mobilization notices. Changes to the Law on Criminal Procedure removed many legal protections of the accused and substituted expedited procedures that allowed, for example, for searches without prior warrants, and police investigations without prior request of the court or State prosecutor.

81. In many towns in south-eastern Serbia-Preshevo, in particular, but also Leskovac and Vranja-Albanian inhabitants were arrested en masse during the war but were cut off from advocacy, as Serbian human rights and media activists from those regions were also targeted before and after 24 March. The Albanian advocacy network, which is so strong throughout Kosovo, effectively stops at the border. / Albanians from south-eastern Serbia are still particularly susceptible to charges of "collaborationism" from more extreme elements within the Kosovo Albanian community. /

II. Re-Establishment of the Role of OHCHR in Kosovo after 10 June 1999

A. Return to Kosovo

82. On 10 June 1999, following confirmation by NATO of the withdrawal of security forces of the FRY from Kosovo and the subsequent suspension of NATO air operations against the FRY, the Security Council adopted resolution 1244 (1999) of 10 June 1999 which authorized the Secretary-General, "with the assistance of relevant international organizations, to establish an international civil presence in Kosovo in order to provide an interim administration for Kosovo". The resolution also provided for the establishment of an international security presence.

83. Following these developments, and in light of the return of refugees to Kosovo, the Kosovo Emergency Operation was officially terminated and OHCHR-FRY staff members returned to Kosovo with the advance team of the United Nations Interim Administration Mission in Kosovo (UNMIK). The head of OHCHR-FRY had already been in Kosovo since May under a temporary secondment as special adviser on human rights to the acting Special Representative of the Secretary-General.

B. Cooperation and Coordination with Other Actors

84. On 21 June, the High Commissioner convened an informal consultative meeting assembling international organizations with an interest in human rights to commence the process of discussion of long-term strategies for the promotion and protection of human rights in the Balkan region, with a special focus on Kosovo. Following the interest expressed by all the participants in continuing consultations and in increasing cooperation between different organizations on the ground, a second consultation was held in Geneva on 28 July 1999. Similar meetings will be held in the future.

C. Visits to Kosovo by the High Commissioner and the Special Rapporteur

85. On 30 June the High Commissioner travelled to Pristina for a one-day visit to Kosovo. In Pristina the High Commissioner met the KFOR Commander, the acting Special Representative of the Secretary-General and other representatives of United Nations agencies. The High Commissioner also chaired a meeting with representatives of the Council for the Defence of Human Rights and Freedoms and the Centre for the Protection of Women and Children. She visited a massacre site at Maticane and met with a Serbian Orthodox clergyman in Kosovo Polje. In Kosovo Polje she also visited a school housing 4,000 Roma fleeing persecution. On several occasions during this visit, the High Commissioner was urged to increase the number of human rights personnel on the ground. In response to this request, additional OHCHR officers were deployed to Kosovo at the beginning of July.

86. Mr. Jiri Dienstbier, United Nations Special Rapporteur on the situation of human rights in Bosnia and Herzegovina, the Republic of Croatia and the Federal Republic of Yugoslavia, visited Kosovo from 7 to 12 July 1999. During his visit, the Special Rapporteur met with representatives of the newly established United Nations Interim Administration in Kosovo, and OSCE and KFOR personnel in the various districts. *He also discussed the situation with representatives of the KLA, the LDK, local Albanian NGOs, the Serbian Orthodox Church and other ethnic communities in Kosovo.*

D. HUMAN RIGHTS ADVISORY UNIT OF THE OFFICE OF THE SPECIAL REPRESENTATIVE OF THE SECRETARY-GENERAL

87. The report of the Secretary-General to the Security Council of 12 July 1999 (S/1999/779) on the structure of UNMIK provided for the appointment of a senior human rights adviser in the office of the Special Representative of the Secretary-General. The human rights adviser should ensure a pro-active approach on human rights in all UNMIK activities and the compatibility of regulations issued by UNMIK with international human rights standards. OHCHR consulted with the Department of Peacekeeping Operations on the establishment and staffing of the unit, and identified the person appointed as senior human rights adviser.

88. The senior human rights adviser, Mr. William O'Neill, who arrived in Pristina on 2 September 1999, will ensure that priority is given to the establishment of institutions and infrastructures for the promotion and protection of human rights in Kosovo, especially the rights of minority groups.

E. OHCHR-KOSOVO

89. As of 24 August 1999, OHCHR had 12 international officers in Pristina and had reopened offices in Belgrade and Podgorica. In Kosovo, building on its country-wide mandate and on long-standing experience in the area, OHCHR will carry out the following tasks:

Following up on investigations initiated in Albania, the former Yugoslav Republic of Macedonia and Montenegro (FRY);

Sharing information, through the OHCHR database, with the United Nations human rights mechanisms for follow-up action;

Maintaining institutional representation in bodies advising on re-establishment of a judiciary in Kosovo;

Maintaining institutional representation in the Task Force on Minority Issues with responsibilities for assessing the situation in the field and devising protection response mechanisms and legal regulatory policies;

Gathering information, in cooperation with ICRC, on the circumstances of arrest of prisoners transferred to Serbia, for follow-up outside of Kosovo;

Gathering information, in cooperation with KFOR, UNMIK, OSCE, UNHCR and ICRC, on persons kidnapped in Kosovo by KLA "police" and "military police" and other non-State actors;

Participating in the subcommission of the Kosovo Transitional Council on detainees and prisoners;

Liaising with human rights NGOs;

Cooperating with OSCE on the possible establishment of an ombudsman's office.

III. The Situation of Human Rights in Kosovo after the Establishment of UNMIK

A. RETURN OF REFUGEES

90. Immediately after the withdrawal of Serb forces from Kosovo and the end of NATO bombardments, Kosovo refugees spontaneously and massively started returning to their homes. According to UNHCR figures, as of 24 August 1999, more than 761,000 Kosovars had returned to Kosovo while 6,800 Kosovars remained in Albania, 19,000 in the former Yugoslav Republic of Macedonia, 8,000 in Montenegro and 11,400 in Bosnia and Herzegovina.

91. UNHCR estimates that about 50,000 refugees in the region are awaiting repatriation and that of the returned refugees, 500,000 lack appropriate accommodation for the winter.

B. EXODUS OF ETHNIC MINORITIES FROM KOSOVO AND "ETHNIC CONCENTRATION"

92. When the return of refugees to Kosovo began, it became clear immediately that Serbs, Roma and other ethnic minorities in Kosovo, as well as Albanians perceived as "collaborators", would be the new victims of revenge and ethnic hatred. / OHCHR has received reports that "politically suspect" Albanians are being called in by KLA "police" for "informative talks". / It also soon appeared that KFOR and UNMIK would face immense difficulties in protecting these new vulnerable groups.

93. According to Yugoslav sources and still incomplete data, as many as 165,000 Serbs and Montenegrins have left Kosovo since the arrival of the international force, while more than half of Kosovo's estimated 120,000-150,000 Roma population has also fled Kosovo since mid-June. UNHCR reported that as of mid-August, there were only 50,000 non-Albanians left in Kosovo.

94. The reason for this exodus lies in fear, killings, kidnapping, looting of properties, evictions, widespread burning of villages as well as cultural, historical and religious monuments, and other forms of intimidation.

95. Muslim Slavs, including Bosniaks, have also been subjected to harassment, destruction of property and killings. Apparently, at least some of the violence is predicated on or provoked by the use of the Bosniak/Serbian language, instead of Albanian. / It has been reported to OHCHR that some 10 Bosniaks, primarily elderly, have been killed by ethnic Albanians, some reportedly in KLA uniforms, in the vicinity of Pec. There are also reports that Bosniaks have simply gone missing in the region of Prizren and Klina./

96. In Gnjilane municipality there is an ongoing "ethnic concentration process" in which Serbs and Albanians are leaving ethnically mixed villages for ethnically "pure" enclaves, adding to the new group of internally displaced persons. Even within towns, Serbs are retreating to ethnic enclaves. This is similar to the patterns observed in Prizren, Pec, Djakovica and other areas where Serbs, often elderly, are retreating to Orthodox Church institutions after harassment, looting or attempted burning of their property.

97. In Mitrovica, Serbs are concentrating in the northern part of town and further north towards Serbia proper in the municipality of Leposavic. All Roma are reported to have left the Albanian part of Mitrovica. Continuing tension in Mitrovica, which presents a Mostar-style divided city patrolled by French units of KFOR, has resulted in repeated confrontations between Serbs and Albanians, apparently fueled, at least in part, by excessive media presence.

C. HUMANITARIAN EVACUATION FROM KOSOVO

98. Given the precarious security situation, many Serbs and Romas have virtually no freedom of movement and are essentially prisoners in their own homes, unable to go out for food, medical care or other needs. This desperate situation has resulted, in some circumstances, in the need for humanitarian evacuation out of Kosovo.

99. OHCHR visited the Orthodox seminary in the centre of Prizren where approximately 180 local Serbs including injured persons, had taken refuge, some more than a month previously. Some Albanians in mixed marriages and about 30 Roma had also taken refuge there. The seminary is heavily guarded by KFOR. On 2 August, UNHCR evacuated 88 Kosovo Serbs to Serbia. UNHCR and KFOR are transporting Serbs still living in their homes to the seminary, and in some cases advising others to move there. Approximately 120 Serbs remain living in their own homes in Prizren. Of those sheltering in monasteries, some are waiting to see if the situation calms down, while others have already decided to be evacuated if international agencies agree that their case meets the criteria for humanitarian evacuation.

100. OHCHR receives frequent requests from family or friends in Belgrade and other areas of Serbia for information about the whereabouts and assistance with evacuation of Serbs, particularly elderly parents, from Kosovo to Serbia proper. Serbs and Montenegrins in Kosovo who want to visit family in Serbia or Montenegro are fearful of travelling either by public transport or private vehicle owing to security concerns. Family members from outside Kosovo are similarly fearful of visiting their relatives in Kosovo owing to the tense security situation.

D. VIOLATIONS OF HUMAN RIGHTS OF MINORITY GROUPS

101. Minority ethnic groups have become victims of human rights abuses in today's Kosovo. From a first assessment of the situation made by OHCHR, it appears that some individuals have been carefully

targeted for revenge -indeed, that life and career histories have, over time, been assembled, based on rumour or fact or unsubstantiated allegation, in a systematic selection of individual victims or groups of victims. This follows the same pattern used by Serbian authorities in targeting influential members of the Kosovo Albanian community. Other individuals are being targeted on suspicion of "complicity" in gross violations of human rights, / The High Commissioner during her visit to Kosovo visited a Roma camp in Kosovo Polje where she met a man who had been repeatedly beaten for his supposed support to the ethnic-cleansing campaign carried out by Yugoslav police, military and paramilitary forces./ while some of the reported incidents seem to be fishing operations directed at Serbs for being Serbs. / According to several reports, KLA "parallel" civil administration has issued instructions to its representatives to report the whereabouts of Serb-owned houses and the number of Serbs still living in them./ However, violence and harassment are not limited to inter-ethnic conflict. As of mid-August, Albanians made up nearly half the casualty figures for violent deaths.

102. The KLA reportedly has been threatening employees of international organizations who are seen intervening on behalf of minorities, accusing them of collaboration. Some victims of ethnic violence have reported that their assailants included men in KLA uniforms, although it is possible that much of the violence is simply the work of criminal elements masquerading in uniforms of the KLA. Open borders have in fact allowed the large-scale arrival of criminal elements, particularly from Albania. It has also been noted that KLA uniforms are available for about DM 50 in Albania and that Albanian-national men with no relationship at all to the KLA can use the uniform as a passport through the German KFOR sector of Kosovo.

1. Murder

103. As of 14 August, 280 murders had been confirmed by KFOR to have been committed in Kosovo since 15 June. The brutal massacre of 14 Serbian farmers, women and children in the village of Staro Gracko, Lipljan municipality, on 23 July 1999 represents the most appalling crime committed since KFOR and UNMIK were deployed in Kosovo. In Klokot, unidentified attackers fired mortar rounds in August killing a 14-year-old girl and a 16-year-old boy. On 15 August, an elderly woman was beaten to death in her flat in the centre of Pristina; on 2 August, a woman and her 10-year-old daughter witnessed the murder of her elderly father in their flat in Pristina.

2. Evictions

104. Kosovar Serbs and other minorities continue to be forcibly evicted from their places of residence. The methods employed vary from physical force and harassment to those which evidence an attempt to ensure the legal loss of the property under a subsequent property scheme. One such example in Pristina, which unfortunately echoes schemes used in other parts of the Balkans, is the forced signature of a document transferring the property ownership or occupancy to person or persons who seize the property under threat. / In Pristina, in early August, four Serb women were forced under threat to sign contracts giving their flats to Albanian families. / KLA "military police" are called to respond to cases of eviction and in the absence of clear civil law and ownership use their own methods for resolving the dispute.

105. In Pristina and Prizren, houses presumably owned by Serbs / The apartments that are being taken over first are empty apartments and those with Serb nameplates on the doors. However, just because an apartment has a Serb nameplate does not mean that the property actually belongs to a Serb. The Serbian Law on Real Property forbids the cross-ethnic sale of property by Serbs to Albanians without the prior approval of a government body in Belgrade. Such approval was virtually never granted, so individuals entered into private transactions, retaining normal registration and external identification with the Serb "owner". Marauding and desperate Kosovo Albanian apartment-occupiers, seizing property with Serb nameplates, are displacing Kosovo Albanian residents./ which have been destroyed either by fire or explosion have been razed and all traces removed within days of the destruction. This complete destruction of the housing structure not only eliminates evidence of a crime, but will likely frustrate the ability of the owner to make a property claim, particularly given the likelihood that a new structure will be constructed on the lot in the interim. Such activities appear to go on outside the effective control of UNMIK as the civil authority and under normal circumstances could only be sanctioned by the local governing authorities. In Prizren, however, UNMIK is attempting to exert its authority by taking action against illegal construction.

3. Rape

106. Several cases of rape, including of elderly women, have been reported to OHCHR. OHCHR visited a 61-year-old Serb woman who had been raped in Pristina. She stated that she remained in Pristina because she believed that her honesty and her age would be respected. On 15 July, one person entered her flat, grabbed her by the hair and put a pistol to her head. Three other men also entered the apartment. She was pushed to the floor of her kitchen and hit with a gun several times, and she was raped by two of the men.

4. Kidnapping

107. Kidnapping, primarily of ethnic Serbs and some Roma, continues in numerous areas including Gnjilane, Pristina, Prizren and Djakovica. Approximately 110 new kidnapping cases have reportedly occurred since the arrival of UNMIK, and OHCHR has received a list of 80 names of specific persons (43 from Pristina alone) kidnapped since 15 June. The military police in Pristina and Mitrovica report that unless kidnap victims are found quickly, i.e. within a matter of hours, they will most likely be found dead.

108. In Pristina, the bodies of kidnap and subsequent murder victims tend to be found in the same parts of town and evidence similar forensic patterns, leading police to believe that the same perpetrators are involved. In Mitrovica, the military police report that none of the recent kidnap victims have been found alive. OHCHR has conducted interviews with several women who have taken refuge in the Orthodox Church Patriarchy in Pec concerning the kidnapping of their male family members. In the Djakovica area, OHCHR conducted similar interviews with family members, including an interview concerning the abduction of a 16-year-old mentally disabled Roma boy. According to OSCE, / Weekly mission report, 29 July-4 August 1999./ kidnappings in the Gnjilane and Orahovac areas "are beginning to form a disturbing pattern".

109. KFOR has located some detention centres maintained and controlled by the KLA. At least two of them, in Prizren and Gnijlane, were described as containing instruments of torture.

110. KFOR has also reported that young Albanian women have been abducted near Gnjilane, by what is believed to be a trafficking ring which forces the women into prostitution.

E. MISSING PERSONS AND THE IDENTIFICATION OF DEAD BODIES

111. Special problems are posed regarding missing persons. It is still unknown how many persons are buried throughout Kosovo, where such graves might be, and who is buried in them. Reports come in daily to KFOR, OSCE, UNHCR and ICRC field offices of discovered bodies. Agencies have developed a standard form for identification of the bodies which, when completed, is centralized with the ICRC, so as to support its lead role in tracing. At the same time, local doctors and hospitals, largely under the broad KLA "civil administration" / Parallel institutions which existed during the past 10 years have quickly resurfaced and present a constant challenge to the assertion of UNMIK authority. Indeed, there is no way that UNMIK can compete in terms of speed of development of institutions, given the Kosovar Albanians' past experience of running parallel institutions separate from those of the "official government", language, staff, etc. An alternative civil administration is firmly established in most or all locales in which OHCHR is working or has visited such as Gnjilane, Drenica, Djakovica and Malisevo. This civil administration affects all levels of civic life including police, who have identification cards permitting them to carry weapons and detain people. In an effort to assert control in the different UNMIK regions, UNMIK Regional Administrators

have convened the Transitional Municipal Authorities which are chaired by the Regional Administrator and composed of Kosovar members./ are issuing ad hoc death certificates, but it is questionable whether these have a legal character.

112. Although the International Criminal Tribunal for the Former Yugoslavia (ICTY), the International Commission on Missing Persons in the Former Yugoslavia, ICRC and others have been working together to provide information to families, a special effort will be needed not just to gather information that can be useful for identification purposes, but to provide counselling and support to family members.

F. ADMINISTRATION OF JUSTICE - THE JUDICIARY

113. In response to the arrest and detention of persons by KFOR, and in the absence of a functioning judiciary in Kosovo, the Special Representative of the Secretary-General, Mr. Bernard Kouchner, adopted emergency decrees establishing a Joint Advisory Council on Provisional Judicial Appointments (JAC). JAC is composed of four national judges, including two ethnic Albanians, one Serb and one Turk, and three international lawyers, including one from OHCHR. JAC advises the Special Representative on the provisional appointment of judges, judicial personnel and prosecutors in order to re-establish an independent and multi-ethnic judiciary.

114. The Pristina district court has travelled around Kosovo to review the legality of continued detention of persons held by KFOR on suspicion of theft, looting, arson, murder, rape and other crimes. Since there is only one court level so far, it is responsible for adjudicating all types of criminal offences, from minor to serious.

115. As of mid-August, the judges and prosecutors had conducted hearings in 144 cases involving 263 individuals, 120 of whom have been released. Prior to the detention hearings before the provisional judiciary, KFOR legal personnel had reviewed the detentions in hearings based on a KFOR regulation and varying procedures based on contingent national laws. Decisions of the investigating judge can be appealed to a panel of three judges.

116. The significant number of releases may be a result of the fact that many persons appear before the tribunals charged with relatively minor offences and their continued detention is deemed unnecessary, although the criminal proceeding will continue. There is a concern, however, among KFOR legal personnel that the judges are overly lenient in granting release. The problem of KFOR locating witnesses, which it is required to do for detention hearings, also makes it more likely that release will be ordered or charges dropped.

117. OHCHR has monitored the initial reviews conducted by the mobile judiciary and visited KFOR detention centres and examined the workings of the recently appointed judiciary in Pec, Lipjane, Bondsteel (at the United States KFOR base) and Prizren, attending detention hearings as well as meeting with court personnel and KFOR military police. As of mid-August, the Prizren court had heard 17 cases; the proceedings related to the review of the legality of the detention of persons, mainly Albanians, arrested by KFOR.

118. Three judges have refused to begin their work, protesting the continued application of Yugoslav law under UNMIK regulation No. 1. Under this regulation, the law applicable in Kosovo before 24 March 1999 continues to apply insofar as it does not conflict with internationally recognized standards, UNMIK regulations or Security Council resolution 1244 (1999). The three judges and others contend that the Kosovo Criminal Code, in effect until the late 1980s, should be applied. In a related matter, some ethnic Albanian defendants in Bondsteel (where detainees from Gnjilane region are detained) refuse to speak to the Serbian judge who was assigned for their hearing.

G. DETAINEES

119. Allegedly, some 5,000 detainees in various phases of court proceedings on terrorism charges were moved by Serbian authorities to prisons in Serbia during the war.

120. In July, the Government of Serbia provided the names of over 2,000 individuals who were transferred from prisons in Kosovo to prisons in Serbia proper. The information indicates only the names of individuals and the place of detention; it does not specify the criminal basis for detention. / Some of these cases were brought to the attention of the High Commissioner during her last visit to Kosovo. In particular, the High Commissioner met with the husband of Dr. Flora Brovina, a human rights activist transferred to a prison in Serbia during the war. Allegedly, her lawyer was denied access to her and she was not being provided with necessary medical care. The High Commissioner, upon return to Geneva, transmitted the information on this case to the special procedures of the Commission on Human Rights for follow-up action. /

121. The issue of transferred detainees is an extremely potent and emotional one for family members in Kosovo and is the subject of frequent demonstrations making demands for action by UNMIK and the international community. Groups representing detainees contend that there are many more persons who were last seen in the custody of Serbian military and police than those named on the lists.

122. Family members in Kosovo have difficulty visiting detainees in Serbia given the fears for the security of Albanians in some parts of Serbia. Some family members have also reported being denied access to their family members in detention. Family members who have succeeded in visiting their relatives in detention have expressed concern about the conditions of detention in prisons such as Srmeska Mitrovica and Pozaravac. Groups representing the detainees seek the release of these prisoners or at least their transfer back to prison facilities in Kosovo. / Of 420 prisoners from Prizren charged with terrorist crimes before 24 March 1999, 320 have been identified by local lawyers as being included on the list made public by the FRY Ministry of Justice. Lawyers from Prizren have requested the United Nations to demand the transfer of the Kosovar prisoners back to Kosovo and the jurisdiction of UNMIK. In Gnjilane, OHCHR interviewed an individual who had been transferred from detention in Gnjilane to Vranja prison (inside Serbia proper) in mid-June along with a full busload of detainees (approximately 45). He was, however, released within a few days of the end of NATO hostilities and returned to Gnjilane. He provided information about mistreatment during his detention./

H. HUMAN RIGHTS CONSEQUENCES OF THE WAR OUTSIDE OF KOSOVO

123. Several hundred Albanians have been expelled from southern Serbia into the Gnjilane district of Kosovo. In the east, ethnic Albanians from the Serbian towns of Medvedja, Bujanoc and Preshevo, which lie just beyond the Kosovo boundary, continue to arrive in Gnjilane. According to the provisional authorities in Gnjilane, 320 families (3,227 persons) have arrived from these towns, reporting that they were evicted by Serb police and the Yugoslav Army.

124. Reciprocally, UNHCR reports that approximately 4,000 Serb displaced from the Gnjilane area have now been registered in the adjoining area of Serbia. Reportedly, there are some 170,000 Kosovo Serb IDPs inside the FRY. They are disliked by the Government because they represent the failure of the Government's policy in Kosovo and allegedly are being herded around Serbia, prevented from settling in Belgrade and from registering their children in school.

125. In the past 10 years 20,000 refugees went to Montenegro from Bosnia and Herzegovina, 10,000 from Croatia and 70,000 IDPs from Kosovo. Of the 70,000 from Kosovo, 20,000 remain of those who went last year and 8,000 still remain from the recent war. Montenegro has taken in far more persons than its capacities allow. In addition, it has not received the necessary support from the international community.

126. According to a census done in 1991, Albanians constitute about 7 per cent of the entire population in Montenegro. They are living in five municipalities: Ulcinj, Bar, Podgorica, Plav and Rozaje. Two Albanian political parties have called for a special status for Albanians in Montenegro and to have representatives in the Montenegrin Parliament. However, the prevailing opinion among all relevant political parties in Montenegro, except the two Albanian parties, is that Albanians have no need for any kind of special status. On the other hand, neither Albanian political leaders nor their representatives in Government are sure what the term "special status" should mean. From discus-

sions of the Special Rapporteur and the High Commissioner with Montenegrin authorities, it emerged that in the north there is a fear of a repetition of what happened in other areas, as part of an established strategy of disrupting multi-ethnic communities.

127. During the NATO campaign, the Government of President Milo Djukanovic criticized and opposed Serbia's ethnic cleansing in Kosovo and, despite intense pressure from Belgrade, hosted Kosovo refugees. International observers warn that Montenegro seems to be moving towards independence / The Government of Montenegro adopted a platform proposing substantially diminished authority of the federal State in an "association" of Serbia and Montenegro./ from Serbia and that an important minority of Montenegrins would resist this. For these reasons, the Republic of Montenegro is increasingly considered to be the likely next site of instability in the Balkans.

128. In the Republic of Serbia, with the lifting of martial law, public political activity has resumed. Hundreds of thousands of persons have participated in peaceful demonstrations and petition campaigns in several locations in Serbia, demanding the ouster of President Milosevic.

IV. Concluding Observations

129. This report once again confirms that Serb forces committed shocking crimes during the NATO air campaign which commenced on 24 March 1999. The High Commissioner continues to believe that it is essential that those responsible for such criminal violations be brought to justice. In this respect, OHCHR supports fully the ongoing investigations of the International Criminal Tribunal for the Former Yugoslavia. In submitting this consolidated report, the High Commissioner wishes to stress that the international community cannot accept that those who are responsible for such terrible atrocities would go unpunished.

130. As the present report has shown that, alas, the situation of the Serb, Roma and other minority communities since the withdrawal of Serb forces has been a painful one. Killings, oppression, harassment, intimidation, expulsion, rape and other violations continue to take place at an alarming rate, particularly targeting the non-Albanian communities of Kosovo. This is a distressing situation for a number of reasons. In the first place, it cannot be accepted that a campaign to vindicate the rights of the Kosovar Albanians would be followed by a campaign of atrocities against the Serb, Roma and other minority communities. In the second place, it is a matter of deep anguish that international forces present in Kosovo have not yet been able to extend effective protection to these endangered communities. The fact that these communities are effectively disappearing from Kosovo raises serious concerns. In the third place, there is no Government as such to which the international community can address itself, and human rights special rapporteurs and working groups are left to address themselves to the Special Representative of the Secretary-General. As is well known, the Special Representative and his staff are dependent on the physical protection that can be extended to these endangered communities by the international forces present on the ground.

131. The High Commissioner considered it a matter of conscience to bring this situation to the attention of the Commission on Human Rights because what is involved is, in fact, a situation of endangered communities without adequate protection. The High Commissioner should like to invite the members of the Commission on Human Rights to consider how the international community can discharge its duty of protecting endangered communities in a situation that is unfolding in full view of the international community. The Commission on Human Rights may wish, after considering this situation, to address appropriate recommendations to the Security Council and to others directly involved with a view to urgent measures being taken to respond to the duty of protection that is incumbent upon the international community.

V. Recommendations

132. The High Commissioner attaches the highest importance to investigation of the crimes committed by the Serbian forces during the conflict in Kosovo and to efforts to bring the perpetrators of such crimes to justice. In this context, the High Commissioner urges Member States to provide the ICTY with the support and resources necessary to carry out this essential task.

133. The High Commissioner calls upon the ICTY, ICRC and OSCE to maintain their efforts to investigate the fate and whereabouts of missing persons.

134. The international community should support UNHCR and other agencies engaged in the effort of providing 500,000 Kosovars with proper accommodation before the onset of winter.

135. The High Commissioner supports UNICEF's efforts to ensure that all Kosovar children will be back in school as soon as possible and stresses the necessity of rebuilding damaged and partially destroyed schools and speeding up the process of demining.

136. The High Commissioner recommends the rapid deployment of United Nations police as the key step in guaranteeing respect for law and order and creating a safe environment for all inhabitants of Kosovo.

137. Particular importance should be given to the re-establishment of customs control at the borders so as to avoid the free access of criminal elements to the territory of Kosovo and to combat the phenomenon of trafficking of women and children.

138. The High Commissioner attaches the highest importance to the preservation of a multi-ethnic Kosovo in which human rights of all inhabitants are respected. However, the High Commissioner recognizes that priority must be given to the effort of saving lives of people at risk. In this respect she supports the humanitarian evacuation programme undertaken by UNHCR but stresses the necessity of preparing conditions for the safe return of all displaced Kosovars.

139. The High Commissioner calls upon the population of Kosovo to refrain from violence and to put an end to attacks against Serbs, Roma and other minority groups. The High Commissioner calls upon the Albanian leaders to condemn these acts of violence and invites the KLA to cooperate with UNMIK and KFOR in investigating such crimes.

140. The High Commissioner calls upon neighbouring countries to provide the appropriate protection to those fleeing Kosovo in fear of persecution and upon the Government of FRY to respect the rights of Kosovar IDPs, in accordance with the Guiding Principles on Internal Displacement, and to protect the rights of Albanian minority groups.

141. The High Commissioner calls upon the Government of Serbia to provide an updated list of all detainees transferred from Kosovo, specifying the charges, if any, under which persons are detained, and to guarantee their families access to them.

142. The High Commissioner stresses the need to investigate swiftly allegations of KLA detention centres, killings, rape, torture, arson, expulsion, looting, theft and other violations of the rights of all inhabitants of Kosovo, regardless of their ethnicity.

143. As part of the measures necessary to the creation of a safe and secure environment for all Kosovars, the High Commissioner urges UNMIK to proceed to the complete demilitarization and disarmament of the KLA.

144. The High Commissioner stresses the importance of involving Kosovars in civil reconstruction and in United Nations decision-making processes.

145. The High Commissioner urges the international community to take all necessary steps to assess and redress from a broad humanitarian perspective the effects of the NATO campaign on the civilian population of FRY. In particular, the High Commissioner urges that similar efforts to those undertaken in Kosovo be made to ensure that Serbian children can return safely to school.

146. The High Commissioner also calls upon the international community to pay particular attention to the situation of human rights in the Republics of Serbia and Montenegro and to take all the necessary steps to prevent the outbreak of violence and to strengthen democracy in the region. In this context, the High Commissioner stresses the importance of designing long-term strategies for the promotion and protection of human rights in the Balkan region and of improving coordination and cooperation among international actors to promote a culture of respect for human rights and tolerance.

2.1.4 THE UN HIGH COMMISSIONER FOR REFUGEES (UNHCR)

41. UNHCR Country Updates - Former Yugoslavia: 24 February 1999 - 4 March 1999, UN Inter-Agency Humanitarian Situation Report: Kosovo Population Movements

1. The most recent displacement is along Kosovo's Southeastern region bordering the former Yugoslav Republic of Macedonia an area previously unaffected by violence. To date UNHCR reports that more than 5,000 people have fled six villages in this area. On 2 March UNHCR brought plastic sheeting, sleeping bags, blankets, hygienic kits and canned food to 250 displaced staying in a school in Kacanik town. The displaced had previously been evacuated by UNHCR after spending two days under plastic sheeting in the mountains.

2. On 3 March UNHCR saw about 200 IDPs living rough on a mountainside at Kodra Ljacit. They had been there five days, fearing fighting between security forces and the Kosovo Liberation Army. UNHCR brought food for the these IDPs (mostly women, children and elderly) who on 26 February fled from their homes at nearby Pustenik, a village of about 600.

3. Elsewhere, UNHCR staff said on 3 March that they continued to hear shelling and gunfire overnight in the Vucitrn region. More than 11,000 people left their homes there after fighting broke out two weeks ago. Some 1,500 residents of Prcevo near Klina fled their homes at 03:00h 2 March when troops conducted military exercises there, but returned to their houses six hours later after troops withdrew. Most of the 4,000 residents of Studencane, near Suva Reka, returned home in this period.

4. UNHCR currently estimates that there are at least 211,000 displaced within Kosovo. Some 63,000 people have been forced to leave their homes during the past two and a half months due to clashes between Government security forces and the KLA, kidnappings, street violence and, more recently, military exercises by the Yugoslav army. In places where there is no violence, and especially where KVM has a continuing presence, returns have continued.

Protection

5. On 3 March UNHCR discussed with local authorities in Pristina and Kacanik the possibility of facilitating the issuance of travel papers for people who wished to go to Macedonia. The authorities appear willing to help within the law, and have provided a focal point for UNHCR to work with. However, as applicants must present citizenship, birth and residence certificates, the process inevitably will be delayed because most of those who want to leave have evacuated villages engulfed in fighting. UNHCR also urged the KLA to allow villagers to secure documentation.

Relief Distribution

6. During the period under review UNHCR continued to lead inter-agency convoys delivering food and non-food items to the municipalities of Djakovica, Srbica, Urosevac, Kosovska Mitrovica, Glogovac, Lipljan, Pec, Prizren, Klina, Orahovac, Suva Reka and Kacanik. Agencies supplying relief items include UNHCR, WFP, Mercy Corps International, Mother Teresa Society, Doctors of the World, Children's Aid Direct, Caritas and Catholic Relief Services.

Education

7. According to UNICEF, distribution of firewood for schools started last week in the municipality of Glogovac. In 15 schools 395 cubic metres of firewood were distributed. Some 900 cubic metres of wood has been distributed to Albanian-run and State schools in the municipality of Klina and in the Malisevo area.

8. 17,000 school kits have been distributed thus far. Distribution of the remaining 24,500 school kits (17,000 provided by UNHCR, 7,500 provided by UNICEF) continues for children in the municipalities of Glogovac, Suva Reka and Orahovac. UNICEF has coordinated the distribution of school kits in other municipalities through UNHCR-led convoys.

Food Aid Programme Related to the Kosovo Crisis

9. Stocks for full WFP distributions in Kosovo, Montenegro and Albania are available and a further 7,500 MT of mixed WFP, CRS and MCI commodities are awaiting clearance in the Montenegrin port of Bar which acts as the main supply point for food aid programmes in the region. On 27 February two new vessels containing wheat flour, oil and pulses for WFP, CRS and MCI arrived in Bar. There are now sufficient quantities of food in the region to meet the needs of people affected by the Kosovo crisis in FRY for a period of approximately four months.

10. Food dispatches resumed from Bar to Kosovo on 25 February, following the temporary one-week suspension due to insecurity. Nonetheless, distributions in Kosovo were not significantly disrupted with convoys leaving Pristina daily. A loan of oil from CRS enabled WFP to continue distributions with a full food basket. February was the first month that WFP included sugar in the monthly food basket in Kosovo. WFP estimates that current stocks of sugar in Pristina will last for at least three months.

11. WFP continues to mill wheat grain in Kosovo and Montenegro thereby supporting local industry. In Kosovo, WFP has signed agreements with an additional three mills in Lipljan and Vucitrn for the milling of 3,500 MT of wheat grain currently awaiting clearance in Bar.

12. In Montenegro food aid distributions to the caseload of 32,100 have been completed for the month of February. February was the first month that distributions were made to host families and the Montenegrin Red Cross identified 4,389 host families for whom MCI and CRS provided food aid.

Montenegro

13. UNICEF has identified a total of 14 schools with an estimated 1,700 displaced students in Plav, Gusinje, Rozaje, Tuzi and Ulcinj. Classes have begun in nearly all locations. Agencies involved will include Danish Refugee Council for provision of desks and chairs, CRS for provision of firewood, CARE for coal and heating fuel, heating stoves by UNHCR, rehabilitation of premises by Swiss Disaster Relief and UNHCR, transportation of students by Danish Refugee Council and textbooks and school supplies by UNICEF.

14. WHO and the Institute of Public Health report that there are no major health problems among the displaced population in Montenegro although it is becoming apparent that there are strains being placed on the health system. The availability of drugs is inadequate to provide sufficient coverage. The outbreak of cases of hepatitis A are part of a regular cyclical occurrence and affect both the displaced and local population. No other serious illnesses have been identified among the displaced population.

Former Yugoslav Republic of Macedonia

15. Some 1,500 asylum seekers from Kosovo entered the former Yugoslav Republic of Macedonia during the period under review, fleeing fighting between Serbian security forces and the KLA in border villages in the municipality of Kacanik. The new influx were registered by the Macedonian Red Cross (MRC) assisted by UNHCR, the International Federation of the Red Cross (IFRC) and ICRC. Most of those

entering the former Yugoslav Republic of Macedonia were met by friends and relatives but some of the refugees were accommodated in villages near the border and provided with emergency assistance in the form of wheat flour, beans, oil, blankets and soap.

16. The United Nations Preventive Deployment Force (UNPREDEP) ceased its monitoring activities in the former Yugoslav Republic of Macedonia on 1 March 1999 after a draft resolution to extend its mandate by six months was vetoed by China, a permanent member of the UN Security Council. China considered that UNPREDEP had achieved its original objective of securing stability in the country and therefore did not require its mandate to be extended. China did not accept the arguments linking UNPREDEP to the situation in Kosovo which it considered to be an internal issue for the Federal Republic of Yugoslavia. Discussions are ongoing to determine whether other agencies might be able to fulfil elements of UNPREDEP's mandate.

Albania
CONTINGENCY PLANNING

17. UNHCR is collaborating with the Government to develop contingency plans in the event of a further influx of refugees from Kosovo into Albania. A preliminary planning refugee caseload of some 50,000 is being used and efforts are underway to identify sites to accommodate a possible new influx in Western Albania.

HUMANITARIAN ASSISTANCE

18. During the last week of February IFRC and UNHCR, through its implementing partner Humanitarian Cargo Carriers, distributed shoes, *jackets, underwear and trousers to some 500 Kosovo refugees still* living in Tropoje district. This was a significant achievement as humanitarian operations have been constrained in recent months in Northern Albania due to insecurity. The distribution took place without incident. The only other humanitarian intervention to have taken place in Tropoje in recent months was a food distribution which took place one month ago.

19. Efforts are underway to address drug shortages in refugee centres in Velipoje and Shengjin in North-west Albania. Food agencies are also trying to standardise the food basket to ensure equitable distribution throughout the country. The relief community is also working jointly to provide community and social services to the most vulnerable, regardless of whether they are refugees or members of the local population.

Bosnia and Herzegovina

20. According to UNHCR approximately 10,000 refugees from Kosovo have arrived in Bosnia and Herzegovina since January 1998. Some 8,500 are living in private accommodation, mainly in Sarajevo canton, and 1,500 are living in transit or collective centres.

21. It is planned that refugees currently living in collective accommodation will ultimately be accommodated in four different centres (1 in Srednje, 3 in Bosanski Petrovac) with a total capacity of some 2,000 persons. An additional centre with a capacity of some 1,000 persons is expected to be completed by June 1999 as a contingency measure in the event of a small-scale influx of refugees from Kosovo. If a large number of Kosovo refugees arrive in Bosnia and Hercegovina tented accommodation will be used.

22. The Coca Cola factory in Hadzici on the outskirts of Sarajevo has now been closed following the transfer of the 330 Kosovo refugees living in the factory to the new refugee reception centre in Bosanski Petrovac and the nearby Rakovica centre. The transfer was organised by UNHCR with security being provided by the NATO Stabilisation Force (SFOR) and the United Nations International Police Task Force (IPTF). The closure of the camp is a welcome development as the refugees had been living in poor conditions for a period of nearly six months. The closure of the "Coca Cola camp" marks the end of UNHCR's direct operational involvement in the management of refugee centres in Bosnia and Herzegovina which are now all entirely managed by Government personnel with support and advice from UNHCR and NGOs.

23. Refugees from Kosovo living in collective accommodation continue to benefit from humanitarian assistance as food and non-food items are provided by relief agencies to those in need. Primary health care is also available to those living in transit centres. However, successful integration of Kosovo Albanian children into the Bosnian school system remains a challenge.

42. UNHCR Country Updates - Former Yugoslavia: 14 - 21 March 1999, UN Inter-Agency Humanitarian Situation Report: Kosovo

Population Movements

1. The humanitarian situation has continued to deteriorate during the past week due to ongoing and increasing clashes between Government security forces and the Kosovo Liberation Army (KLA). Displacement has been accompanied by renewed burning of villages and destruction of means of livelihood, thus preventing return.

2. Since the breakdown of peace talks and the subsequent withdrawal of the Organisation for Security and Cooperation Kosovo Verification Mission (KVM) from Kosovo on 20 March, conflict between the two sides has intensified. Casualties on both sides have been sustained. On Sunday evening four policemen were shot dead and one badly wounded while on patrol in Pristina, the most serious event in the capital since the start of the conflict. The police immediately mounted a search for the culprits.

3. On 20 and 21 March the Government launched a campaign against the KLA in Srbica, 35 kilometres northwest of Pristina. On Sunday afternoon UNHCR saw houses burning and large parts of Srbica were empty. Heavy gunfire could be heard and small groups of people – totaling about 500 – were on the road waiting for a bus ride to nearby Kosovska Mitrovica. Srbica had a population of about 11,000 and was hosting some 10,000 evacuees – half of whom had gone there only last week from nearby villages after Serbian security forces deployed there. UNHCR estimates that about 15,000 of the people in Srbica town had fled. Shops in the main town had broken windows and the warehouse of Mother Teresa Society was vandalized and looted.

4. In Glogovac, about 4,000 IDPs were reported to be on the move on the afternoon of Sunday 21 March. They included an estimated 1,000 displaced many of whom were travelling in tractor-trailers, which UNHCR saw, from villages west of Srbica where tank and armour movements had been seen. At nearby Cikotovo, UNHCR was told that 700 people had gone there from eight villages west of Srbica over the last 24 hours.

5. On 20 March, UNHCR saw houses on fire in the villages of Barilevo and Prugovac just outside Pristina at noon. The sound of firing from automatic weapons and anti-aircraft guns could be heard during the time UNHCR was in the villages. UNHCR and other aid agencies evacuated to Pristina some 200 people, mostly elderly men, women and children caught in the fighting in these two villages with a combined population of 3,700. The villages were practically empty, except for a few elderly men who refused to leave. Several tanks were deployed around the area near the main Pristina-Belgrade road which had been sealed off.

6. On 17 March some 7,000 people fled their homes in Korisa in Prizren municipality after security forces shelled a KLA base at nearby Kabas. This was the biggest one-day evacuation so far this year. UNHCR reported that at least five shells overshot Kabas and hit neighbouring Grejkovac where some of the evacuees had taken shelter. The evacuees moved to houses in neighbouring villages. Some 5,000 of the civilians who fled Korisa have since returned.

7. From 14-16 March security forces, in an offensive against Kosovo Liberation Army positions, bombarded villages in at least four municipalities prompting more than 10,000 people to flee their homes. More than 5,000 have fled fighting in Klina, 2,000 in Kosovska Mitrovica and 2,000 in Srbica. On 16 March some 1,500 people abandoned Sibovac in Obilic municipality just outside Pristina. In Glogovac mu-

nicipality, UNHCR visited Gradica, where it was told by Mother Teresa Society that evacuees from the Vucitrn-Kosovska Mitrovica region had reached more than 1,600 in the last few days.

8. Many displaced and host families are living in extremely overcrowded conditions. For example, in the town of Gradica in Glogovac municipality UNHCR saw a household of 20 members which had taken in 60 evacuees, mostly women and children. They were crammed in three rooms in appalling conditions in a house that was severely damaged in fighting last summer. There were no sanitation facilities there, few blankets or mattresses to sleep on in the harsh winter nights and little food. UNHCR was told that the condition of the evacuees was the same in other host families in the area.

9. UNHCR estimates that there are 235,000 internally displaced within Kosovo as at 18 March. This overall total includes the 60,000 of the 100,000 displaced since 24 December who have not returned to their homes in Kacanik, Vucitrn, Mitrovica and Podujevo regions. They are staying in the houses of friends and relatives in the major towns in Kosovo. More than 20,000 were believed to have been displaced in the Drenica region alone in the week to 18 March, 1999. This weekend has seen further displacement but UNHCR has no accurate count as yet.

10. Estimated population movements since 24 December 1999 are summarised by municipality below (Source: UNHCR as at 18 March, 1999):

	Displacement	Returns
Podujevo	20,000	5,700
Suva Reka	6,100	5,600
Stimlje	5,500	
Decane	4,000	4,000
Prizren	16,400*	12,000
Vucitrn/Mitrovica	22,700*	5,000
Klina	6,200*	1,000
Obilic	1,500*	
Srbica	4,600*	
Kacanik	13,350*	2,000
TOTAL	100,450	40,300

* Displacement after 23 February

Humanitarian Assistance

11. UNHCR has continued to lead interagency convoys delivering relief supplies to displaced, host families and returnees on a daily basis throughout Kosovo. Municipalities targeted during the past week include Orahovac, Klina, Urosevac, Obilic, Lipljan, Stimlje, Decane, Lipljan, Prizren Suva Reka and Kacanik. Agencies providing relief items include UNHCR, UNICEF, WFP, Catholic Relief Services, Children's Aid Direct, Doctors of the World and Mother Teresa Society. UNICEF reports that 470 cubic metres of firewood have now been distributed to schools in Malisevo.

12. Rising insecurity, coupled with the withdrawal of KVM, has prompted most humanitarian agencies to reduce their presence in Kosovo during the weekend of 20-21 March. Nevertheless, the provision of humanitarian assistance has continued, albeit at a reduced level. On 20 March a convoy brought blankets, mattresses and food parcels to Kosovska Mitrovica and Obilic. On 21 March UNHCR led multi-agency convoys that delivered relief aid for some 10,000 people in Glogovac and Cikatovo. The supplies included wheat flour, rice, salt, food parcels, mattresses, blankets and hygienic kits. The supplies came from UNHCR, WFP, Mother Teresa Society and Doctors of the World.

Montenegro

13. UNHCR reports that there continues to be no major new arrivals of displaced into Montenegro. The only report received was from the office in Rozaje which said that one family with 7 members arrived by bus through the Dacici checkpoint on 14 March.

14. Food distribution by WFP, ICRC, Catholic Relief Services and Mercy Corps International for displaced from Kosovo has started for the month of March. The planning figure for assistance is 32,000 displaced. WFP's contribution consists of 139 MT of wheat flour and 18.5 MT of pulses, stored in UNHCR warehouse. WFP is waiting for beneficiaries figures from the Montenegrin Red Cross before authorising the release of allocation for refugees in March.

15. 600 hygienic parcels were delivered to the Danish Refugee Council for education activities for displaced from Kosovo in Plav, Berane and Rozaje. Distribution of baby parcels to refugees and displaced is ongoing in Red Cross branches. Equipment for new Collective Centres in Ulcinj and in Rozaje were received. The distribution of hygiene items (soap and sanitary napkins) for March to refugees in collective centres and private accommodation continues. Procurement authorisation was received for 2 months cleaning supply items to schools attended by displaced children.

16. UNICEF has completed distribution of 1,967 sets of textbooks and 2,000 student kits to the 14 schools in Montenegro involved in the non-formal education programme for displaced children from Kosovo. The Ministry of Education has donated a stock of chalk which will be reimbursed by UNICEF. Contributions from other humanitarian agencies include the following: stoves from UNHCR, wood from CRS, cleaning costs from World Vision International, desks and chairs from the Danish Refugee Council which has also provided financial support to enable those living in the more remote areas to gain access to schools.

Albania

17. UNHCR reports that the situation in Kukes Commune (located in Northern Albania near the border with Kosovo) is generally calm although small groups have continued to cross the border. 33 refugees from Kosovo have reportedly entered into Kukes during the period under review. They were given collective accommodation in Kruma and received humanitarian assistance.

Former Yugoslav Republic of Macedonia

18. As at 20 March 1999 the Macedonian Red Cross has registered some 10,400 refugees from Kosovo (9,100 since 25 February 1999). Most of the refugees originated from the villages along the border and crossed into the former Yugoslav Republic of Macedonia at Jacince (towards Tetovo) and Blace (towards Skopje). At the time of writing the influx into the former Yugoslav Republic of Macedonia has dwindled to a few crossings per day.

19. The Government of the former Yugoslav Republic of Macedonia has clarified its position on refugee issues. The status of Humanitarian Assisted Persons will be given to all asylum seekers from Kosovo for a period of 3 months with the further possibility of extension. The procedure for obtaining this status comprises three phases:

A) RECEPTION AND ACCOMMODATION UPON ARRIVAL

Upon arrival in Macedonia refugees are received by the border police and the Macedonian Red Cross where they are registered and directed to host families. They receive an Emergency package consisting of food, soap and blankets which will allow them to wait until they are processed and put on the regular distribution lists.

B) REGISTRATION OF THE ADDRESS

When the refugees are accommodated, they have five days to declare their final address to the police. At this stage, they are under the Law on Movement of Foreigners which allows them to stay for two months.

C) REQUEST FOR ASYLUM

Those seeking asylum must register themselves at specific police stations for the status which is granted through the issuance of a special "green card."

20. The Ministry of Interior has launched a registration campaign with mobile teams going through the villages. The Government has decided that the registration exercise should be completed by 30 March 1999.

43. Briefing by Mrs Sadako Ogata to the UN Security Council, New York, 5 May 1999

Mr President,

In my briefing to the Council today I shall focus on the plight of refugees in the southern Balkans. The situation of women, men and children fleeing the Province of Kosovo and Metohija, in the Federal Republic of Yugoslavia, is increasingly desperate. Kosovo is being emptied – brutally and methodically – of its ethnic Albanian population. In the last three days alone, about 37,000 new refugees and internally displaced people have arrived in Albania, the former Yugoslav Republic of Macedonia, and the Republic of Montenegro. More trains with thousands of refugees have arrived last night at the Yugoslav/Macedonian border. Ethnic cleansing and mass forced expulsions are yielding their tragic results faster than we can respond – faster than anybody's response. Fragile and unprepared countries are bearing the brunt of one of the largest refugee flows Europe has seen in the 20th century. 700,000 people have already been forced to leave their homes.

The Refugee Crisis

In spite of this, the response is gaining momentum. But let me say at the outset that with the outflow continuing at the current rate and speed, the ability of the international community to deal with it has already been severely tested. The fundamental problem of this crisis, however, has not been an inadequate humanitarian response: its root cause is the systematic and intolerable violence being waged against an entire population, and the failure to prevent it; and its immediate effect is that the capacity of countries receiving refugees has been stretched to its limit, and beyond.

This refugee crisis is not new. Last year, more than a quarter of all asylum requests in Europe were by people from Kosovo. Up to 23 March, when UNHCR had to reluctantly leave the province following a decision of the United Nations Security Coordinator, it was providing assistance to 400,000 people displaced or otherwise affected by fighting inside the province, and to 90,000 refugees and displaced people outside Kosovo. The efforts of verifiers and humanitarian workers were containing, albeit in a limited way, the crisis that was to follow our departure.

Figures are dry, but telling. Last night, there were 404,000 refugees from Kosovo in Albania, 211,000 in The former Yugoslav Republic of Macedonia and 62,000 internally displaced people in Montenegro. Refugees from the Federal Republic of Yugoslavia have also fled to Bosnia and Herzegovina – 17,000 from Kosovo and about 20,000 from the Sandjak, among others. According to unverified government estimates, 60,000 displaced people from Kosovo have fled to other parts of Serbia. Tens of thousands – any estimate is a guess in the absence of credible intelligence – are displaced inside the province. Tens of thousands have fled or are seeking asylum further afield, particularly in Western European countries. By tonight, all these figures will have to be revised upwards.

The Response

In spite of previous tragic experiences with ethnic cleansing in this region, nobody foresaw deportations, and a refugee outflow from Kosovo, on such a massive scale, and at such a speed.

It took a few days for UNHCR and other humanitarian agencies to step up their activities and deal with tens of thousands of people streaming through borders. I wish we – all of us – could have reacted faster. But with the indispensable help of other partners, the response has become more organized. I could see it myself when I visited Albania and The former Yugoslav Republic of Macedonia in early April. Refugees are, in spite of all difficulties, relatively well assisted.

The response to the refugee crisis can be described as consisting of four elements.

The first is the reception of refugees at borders and their temporary accommodation in transit camps. This is perhaps the biggest challenge, given the uninterrupted stream of refugees, which compels us to constantly review contingency figures and plans. Host countries have kept their borders open for the most part, in spite of the enormous burden placed upon them by the influx. In recent weeks, however, we have seen some countries waver in their commitment to admit refugees to their territory. It is essential that they continue to keep borders open, facilitate safe access to refugees by humanitarian agencies, and allow refugees to move immediately to secure, adequately equipped camps. Providing asylum is literally vital, since preventing them from crossing the border would expose them to violence and death. On our part, we will continue to mobilize international support in order to ease the burden on asylum countries.

The second element of the response is the search for more suitable accommodation beyond transit camps. Many – about half of those in The former Yugoslav Republic of Macedonia, for example – are hosted by families, and I wish to praise the people in all countries of asylum, who are sharing their meagre resources with refugees. Were it not for their generosity, this would be an even greater tragedy. UNHCR is coordinating projects with governments and NGOs to provide host families with cash grants and food assistance. For the other refugees, UNHCR and its partners are setting up camps away from insecure border areas. I may add that very soon, unless an early political solution creates conditions for refugees to return home, we shall have to make plans to equip refugee camps and public buildings for the bitter Balkan winter. This will require additional, substantial resources.

The third and fourth elements of the response are related to the situation in The former Yugoslav Republic of Macedonia, where the reception capacity of transit centers, camps and host families, in a country with a fragile ethnic and social balance, has reached breaking point.

As a third response element, therefore, in cooperation with the International Organization for Migration, UNHCR has initiated a Humanitarian Evacuation Programme, under which refugees, on a voluntary basis, are flown from the former Yugoslav Republic of Macedonia to third countries offering to host them temporarily. This programme has no precedent in UNHCR's history. Initially, we were hoping to evacuate refugees only to Europe, a more obvious choice since the eventual solution for those evacuated is to return to Kosovo. But of the 85,000 slots offered by European countries so far, only 28,000 have been filled to date. On 30 April I have therefore requested extra-European countries to activate their own quotas. I regret that the pace of evacuations to Europe, with some exceptions, has been slow, and I would urge once again European governments to fill their quotas as rapidly as possible.

The fourth element of the response is to further relieve pressure on The former Yugoslav Republic of Macedonia by carrying out a "humanitarian transfer" of some refugees to Albania, with the agreement of the governments of the two countries. Let me stress that such transfers should only be carried out on a voluntary basis.

Humanitarian transfers are not without operational consequences in Albania. Given that this country will also continue to receive refugees directly from Kosovo, as well as via Montenegro, camp construction in Albania has become the most crucial element of the response. I am concerned, however, that it is not progressing as fast as it should. There are two problems: site availability and actual construction. I urge the government of Albania to make available more rapidly a larger number of suitable sites. I also urge governments that have offered to set up new camps, to speed up the pace of construction. If shelter facilities in Albania are not improved soon, there may be little incentive for refugees to accept the transfer from The former Yugoslav Republic of Macedonia.

Mr President, I also wish to share with the Council my deep concerns with respect to the protection and security of refugees. Human traffickers are a serious threat, especially in Albania. They have already started smuggling refugees across the Adriatic into Italy and the European Union. Young women, often forced into prostitution, and children, are frequent victims, particularly when they are hosted in families, and are thus more vulnerable to these threats. This phenomenon will increase if it is not addressed more forcefully, and immediately. There is also a very real risk of forced recruitment of refugees by the Kosovo Liberation Army. I strongly urge governments to discourage this practice.

UNHCR is coordinating efforts to improve refugee protection, through some basic measures such as setting up camps away from dangerous border areas, or promoting tracing and family reunification schemes. To ensure the protection of refugees, the security of local communities and the safety of humanitarian staff, however, it will also be indispensable to provide international support – material, training, funds – to police and other law enforcement institutions, especially in Albania. This is a most urgent task to which I would like to draw the attention of the Council.

Registration of refugees is another priority, particularly with the reported destruction of identification papers and population civil records in Kosovo. Registration is also essential to conduct tracing activities and bring back together thousands of separated families, as well as for the preparations for voluntary return, when refugees will have to reclaim their properties. In Albania, logistical problems have hampered a proper refugee registration but I am pleased to inform you that – with the support of IOM and the Organization for Security and Cooperation in Europe – the exercise is now beginning.

Because refugees continue to arrive in large numbers, the four elements of the relief operation, which I described earlier, must be carried out simultaneously. Needless to say, UNHCR could not be leading the humanitarian response without support from its traditional partners – UNICEF, the World Food Programme, the World Health Organisation, national and international NGOs. We have received valuable help, especially in the coordinating, reporting and fund raising functions, by the Office of the Coordinator of Humanitarian Affairs. A crucial partnership has been established with the OSCE Kosovo Verification Mission. Its staff have played an essential role, especially in the first few days of the emergency.

I wish also to clarify the nature of the assistance we have sought from military contingents. As in all such situations, we insist that protection and assistance of refugees must absolutely remain civilian and strictly humanitarian in character. I can assure you that the fundamental principle of non-militarization of refugee activities has been and will be upheld. Let me remind you that in response to NATO Secretary-General Solana's letter of 2 April offering support to humanitarian activities, I wrote on 3 April defining precisely the four areas in which we required assistance: management of the airlift operation; offloading and immediate storage of aid at airports and ports; logistics support in setting up camps; and air evacuation of refugees from The former Yugoslav Republic of Macedonia. This cooperation was expanded to some other logistical functions in a further exchange of letters on 20-21 April, related to operation "Allied Harbour" in Albania. Let me also add that my appeal for support was not and is not limited to NATO member states. Finally, I wish to stress that military involvement in humanitarian activities will continue only as long as, and wherever, extraordinary circumstances prevail. Should it become unnecessary, it will be terminated, as shown by the hand-over to UNHCR of camp management in Brazda and Kukes. We need logistical support from the military to alleviate refugee suffering, but at the same time we must maintain a clear distinction between the humanitarian operation led by UNHCR and military operations, especially as long as NATO forces are engaged in military action in the Federal Republic of Yugoslavia.

I am extremely worried about the humanitarian situation inside the Federal Republic of Yugoslavia. Until we had to considerably reduce our presence in the country at the end of March, we were helping the Yugoslav government assist over half a million ethnic Serb refugees from Croatia and Bosnia and Herzegovina. Our assistance has had to be drastically curtailed. The office of the Serbian Commissioner for Refugees has continued its work, albeit with limited means, and under understandably difficult circumstances. And I wish to express my deepest concern for the plight of all civilians affected by conflict in the Federal Republic of Yugoslavia. Civilians have also been victims of air raids, including people trying to flee Kosovo. I wish to take this opportunity to make a plea to the parties, including NATO, to exert their utmost to avoid civilian casualties.

Of great concern is of course the fate of civilians, and particularly displaced people, in the province of Kosovo, which is still by and large off limits to humanitarian agencies. Refugees increasingly report that civilians are being subjected to violence, forced eviction from their homes, deportations and arbitrary detention. Clearly, we only hear of a fraction of the violations taking place. From the beginning of the conflict, I have expressed my strongest protest against this intolerable situation, as has the High Commissioner for Human Rights.

The Secretary-General, at his briefing to the Council yesterday, announced the plan to send a humanitarian assessment mission to the Federal Republic of Yugoslavia, proposing that the team start by examining the situation in Kosovo. UNHCR has been invited to participate in the assessment. This mission, as the Secretary-General and various Council members pointed out, must be given all necessary security assurances to be able to function effectively, and in safety.

The Future

Mr President, the response to the refugee crisis is taking up much of our resources, energy and time. This should not prevent us from looking to the future. We must eventually help refugees return home and live in security – security, I should add, that can be sustained over time; and that is not just safety from physical threats, but that will be included in a broader rehabilitation framework, and reinforced by appropriate legal guarantees, and formal assurances of respect for the rights of those who return. It is not too early for planning.

Planning for return, on which we have already engaged, is made difficult by the on-going outflow, and by the uncertainty about what kind of peace will eventually be implemented. In the meantime, we must plan along two different tracks. On the one hand, as I have already described, we have to continuously review preparedness plans to meet further outflows of refugees. On the other, we must start planning for their return to Kosovo. I foresee a "mixed" scenario eventually prevailing, with some refugees returning, and others remaining in host countries. For this reason, we must adopt, and be funded for, a flexible approach, allowing for preparedness resources to be utilized either to respond to new outflows, or to support return, or both.

Voluntary return is not only the best solution for refugees – it is also the hope of a majority of them. This said, I can assure you that it is very unlikely that any refugee will return to Kosovo unless Serbian forces withdraw, and international armed forces are deployed in the province to keep peace. I have to insist on this point. Until March, the international community attempted to maintain a fragile agreement between the parties with an unarmed mission. Such an option, already facing difficulty in February and March, will prove inadequate when hundreds of thousands of refugees, who have been forced out of their homes, return to Kosovo. However, if people feel that adequate security is provided to all civilians, I am confident that a majority will choose to return, probably very quickly. My Office, Mr President, will play its mandated role in leading a repatriation operation. This must – and I stress must – be based on internationally recognized standards of voluntariness, and provided that security conditions are fully re-established.

The return of refugees, obviously, will not just be a logistical operation. A major reconstruction programme must be carried out in Kosovo, with extraordinary means and the intervention of bilateral donors and financial institutions. Many refugees may not even return if such a programme does not start in earnest, as soon as repatriation becomes possible. I am not referring simply to the rebuilding of infrastructure – houses, roads, water and electricity – but also to the reconstruction of institutions, the re-establishment of the rule of law and respect for basic human rights, and the rehabilitation of a traumatized society. The Secretary-General yesterday in his briefing outlined a structure for a transitional civilian administration of Kosovo, which I welcome. Let me also add that reconstruction should extend to the Federal Republic of Yugoslavia as a whole. Economic, social and environmental programmes will have to be carried out also in the regions as a whole, and especially in those countries hosting large numbers of refugees.

In conclusion, a return plan will be carried out only if adequate security measures guarantee a solid, lasting peace, that requires more than just physical safety; and if the international community will implement a comprehensive, regional rehabilitation plan in the southern Balkans. There should not be a "gap" left between immediate humanitarian and medium to long-term development efforts if recurring conflicts are to be prevented and an inevitably fragile peace is to be reinforced. Our goal should not just to bring refugees back, but to create durable conditions for them to stay, in safety and peace.

Mr President, having experienced the world's indifference to many refugee crises, I welcome the sense of solidarity – almost of international ownership – that has developed around the Kosovo crisis. I hope it will foster a heightened sense of determination to reach a political solution in the very near future. Faced with an increasing tide of human suffering, I join my voice to that of the Secretary-General of the United Nations, and urge governments to multiply efforts to re-establish peace soon. I count very much on the leadership and detemination of the Security Council.

In the meantime, I pledge that UNHCR, with support from partner agencies, will continue to lead efforts to protect and assist refugees and internally displaced persons. I welcome the help of governments. I also welcome their scrutiny and constructive comments about our work. But I shall be frank again. Direct support should not become direct management. We appreciate the need for visible bilateral efforts, but to be effective, they must be integrated into a larger multilateral effort, that my Office is mandated to lead. Failure to uphold this system, for which my Office exists, will ultimately make relief efforts less effective, and will also seriously weaken the international refugee protection regime worldwide established by the member states of the United Nations almost 50 years ago. And I should add that for efforts to succeed, we also need immediate better financial support, and we need such support to be sustained while the crisis continues, even if it disappears from the headlines. Since the crisis began, we have received 50% of the required resources foreseen until the end of June.

Mr President, I would like to conclude this briefing by appealing to the Security Council not to overlook other refugee crises around the world. Unresolved conflicts continue to make victims and force people to flee their homes in many African countries – the Democratic Republic of the Congo, Sierra Leone, Angola and Sudan, just to mention a few; the situation in Liberia is fragile and the return of refugees is threatened; Burundi refugees are still hosted in Tanzanian camps; Western Sahara is an unresolved issue, and the potential for further displacement in the Horn of Africa is very real. Beyond Africa, Afghanistan remains of great concern – there are more than three times as many Afghan refugees as there are from Kosovo. Most of them have been away from home for over twenty years. The situation in Indonesia is fragile, with great potential for massive displacement.

Huge means are desperately required to respond to the Kosovo refugee crisis. I am worried, however, that this may result in decreasing resources to resolve other, equally grave and destabilizing refugee situations, that humanitarian agencies continue to tackle alone, far from the spotlights of media and the preoccupation of governments. I trust that the Security Council will ensure that in addition to the efforts currently made to address and resolve the Kosovo emergency, adequate political attention and material resources continue to be devoted to the solution of all other such crises.

44. Numbers of Refugees Displaced from Kosovo 23 March - 9 June 1999, Geneva, 15 October 1999

Numbers of refugees displaced from Kosovo 23 March-9 June 1999
(Figures represent total arrivals on each given date)

	Montenegro	B-H	FYROM	Albania	HEP	Total
23 March	25,000	10,000	16,000	18,500		69,500
30 March	32,500	13,000	20,500	78,500		144,500
31 March	35,000	14,000	28,000	103,500		180,500
1 April	40,000	15,000	43,000	103,500		201,500
2 April	50,000	16,000	43,000	138,000		247,000
3 April	52,000	17,000	108,000	200,000		377,000
4 April	54,000	18,000	109,000	247,000		428,000
5 April	55,000	20,000	110,125	254,813		439,938
6 April	58,000	21,000	111,250	262,625		452,875
7 April	60,000	22,000	112,375	270,438		464,813
8 April	61,000	23,000	113,500	278,250		475,750
9 April	62,000	24,000	114,625	286,063		486,688
10 April	63,000	25,000	115,750	293,875		497,625
11 April	64,000	26,000	116,875	301,688		508,563
12 April	63,000	27,300	118,000	309,500	7,987	525,787
13 April	65,500	27,400	116,500	314,300	9,351	533,051
14 April	67,200	27,700	116,000	314,300	10,780	535,980
21 April	70,000	32,300	130,000	357,000	16,911	606,211
28 April	63,300	15,000	142,650	367,200	22,084	610,234
5 May	61,700	17,600	211,340	404,200	28,654	723,494
12 May	64,400	18,500	231,200	427,000	40,518	781,618
19 May	64,000	20,000	226,800	433,300	52,643	796,743
26 May	64,700	21,500	252,600	439,600	63,575	841,975
2 June	68,400	21,700	248,900	442,600	74,014	855,614
9 June	69,700	21,700	247,400	444,200	79,979	862,979

B-H: Bosnia-Herzegovina.
FYROM: the former Yugoslav Republic of Macedonia.
HEP: Humanitarian Evacuation Programme.
In addition, more than 100,000 Serb IDPs are estimated to have left Kosovo and to have been registered in Serbia and Montenegro.

2.2 U.S. DOCUMENTS

45. U.S. Department of State: Serbia-Montenegro Country Report on Human Rights Practices for 1998, Released by the Bureau of Democracy, Human Rights, and Labor, 26 February 1999

Serbia - Montenegro, a constitutional republic, is dominated by Federal President Slobodan Milosevic. President Milosevic continues to control the country through his role as President of the Socialist Party of Serbia (SPS) - a dual role arrangement proscribed by the federal Constitution - and his domination of other formal and informal institutions. Although the SPS lacks majorities in both the Federal and Serbian Parliaments, it controls governing coalitions and holds the key administrative positions. The Milosevic regime effectively controls the judiciary and respects the country's legal framework only when it suits the regime's immediate political interests.

Serbia abolished the political autonomy of Kosovo and Vojvodina in 1990, and all significant decisionmaking since that time has been centralized under Milosevic in Belgrade. The Milosevic regime's repressive policies quashed any prospect of interethnic cooperation with Kosovo's ethnic Albanians and led to a full - fledged separatist insurgency that erupted early in the year. The regime undertook a brutal police and military crackdown against separatist insurgents in Kosovo - a crackdown that by some measures resulted in the deaths of about 2,000 persons by year's end, the vast majority of whom were ethnic Albanians.

The international community does not recognize the Federal Republic of Yugoslavia (FRY) - Serbia - Montenegro - as the sole successor state to the former Yugoslavia. Accordingly, the "FRY" still is not permitted to participate in the United Nations (U.N.), the Organization for Security and Cooperation in Europe (OSCE), or other international organizations and financial organizations.

As a key element of his hold on power, President Milosevic effectively controls the Serbian police, a heavily armed force of some 100,000 officers that is responsible for internal security. Serbian police committed numerous serious and systematic human rights abuses.

Despite the suspension of certain U.N. economic sanctions, economic performance was anemic due to the imposition of new sanctions as a response to the situation in Kosovo and the FRY's continued exclusion from international financial institutions. Unemployment and underemployment remained high (about 60 percent), since the Government was unable or unwilling to introduce necessary restructuring measures. The Government failed to implement needed sweeping economic reforms, including privatization, which would help the economy but could undermine the regime's crony system.

The Government's human rights record worsened significantly, and there were problems in many areas. Serbian police committed numerous serious abuses including extrajudicial killings, disappearances, torture, brutal beatings, and arbitrary arrests and detentions. The judicial system is not independent of the Government, suffers from corruption, and does not ensure fair trials. The authorities infringed on citizens' right to privacy. The Government severely restricted freedom of speech and of the press, and used overbearing police intimidation and economic pressure to control tightly the independent press and media. The Government restricted freedom of assembly and association. While under the Constitution citizens have a right to stage peaceful demonstrations, in practice the police seriously beat scores of protesters throughout the republic of Serbia, sending many to hospitals. The Government infringed on freedom of worship by minority religions and restricted freedom of movement. The Milosevic regime used its continued domination of Parliament and the media to enact legislation to manipulate the electoral process. In practice citizens cannot exercise the right to change their government. The most recent electoral manipulation by the regime was in the Serbian parliamentary and presidential elections in the fall of 1997. The Federal and Serbian Governments' record of cooperation with international human rights and monitoring organizations was poor. The Federal Government remained uncooperative with the International Criminal Tribunal for the Former Yugoslavia (ICTY): it failed to meet its obligations under numerous U.N. Security Council Resolutions to comply fully with the Tribunal's orders, failed to issue visas to allow ICTY investigators into Kosovo (and, in the last quarter of the year, even into the rest of Serbia), and failed to transfer or facilitate the surrender to the Tribunal of persons on Serbian territory indicted for war crimes or other crimes against humanity under the jurisdiction of the Tribunal. Instead, the Milosevic Government openly harbored indicted war criminals - three of whom the Government openly acknowledged were present on Serbian territory - and publicly rejected the Tribunal's jurisdiction over events in Kosovo. Discrimination and violence against women remained serious problems. Discrimination against ethnic Albanians, Muslims, Roma, and other religious and ethnic minorities worsened during the year. Police repression continued to be directed against ethnic minorities, and police committed the most widespread and worst abuses against Kosovo's 90 percent ethnic Albanian population. Police repression also was directed against Muslims in the Sandzak region and other citizens who protested against the Government. The regime limits unions not affiliated with the Government in their attempts to advance worker rights.

Montenegro continued to be the only bright spot in the FRY, although Milosevic's influence threatens to complicate the Republic's efforts at democratization. In January 1998, Milo Djukanovic became Montenegro's President after November 1997 elections judged by international monitors to be free and fair, and his reform coalition won parliamentary elections in May. The Milosevic regime continued a relentless campaign to undermine Djukanovic's popular support, including by refusing to accept his choice of delegates to the upper house of the Federal Parliament; refusing to accept a Montenegrin Government choice for the new Federal Prime Minister; and withholding financial contributions owed to the Montenegrin pension system. Moreover, the Milosevic regime was believed to be behind a violent campaign to wreak havoc at the time of Djukanovic's inauguration. In his effort to crush Montenegrin democratization, Milosevic violated the Federal and Montenegrin Constitutions by persuading the federal Constitutional Court to review Montenegrin electoral legislation and by using his influence over Federal judges to have Montenegrin legislation declared unconstitutional.

Elements of the Kosovo Liberation Army (KLA, an armed ethnic Albanian group that seeks independence for Kosovo) were also responsible for abuses. They committed killings, were responsible for disappearances, abducted and detained Serbian police, as well as Serb and Albanian civilians (those suspected of loyalty to the Serbian Government), and in a few isolated cases "tried" suspects without due process. There are also credible reports of instances of torture by the KLA.

Respect for Human Rights

SECTION 1: RESPECT FOR THE INTEGRITY OF THE PERSON, INCLUDING FREEDOM FROM:

a. Political and Other Extrajudicial Killing

Political violence, including killings by police, became a significant problem during the year as a result of the conflict in Kosovo (see Section 1.g.). Beginning in the early spring and again throughout the year, Serbian police killed scores of ethnic Albanians often in brutal fashion. In Likosane in early March police entered the family compound of the Ahmeti family, rounded up the male members of the clan plus one acquaintance - 12 individuals - and summarily executed them.

Development of the Human Rights Situation

A few days later, in Donji Prekaz, police surrounded the family compound of Adem Jashari, whom they believed to be well armed and a member of the KLA, and destroyed it. Over 80 persons died in the siege, including women and children.

On May 25, police in Ljubenic entered the compound of the Hamzaj clan and allegedly executed at least five male members of the family. According to witnesses who spoke to the Humanitarian Law Center, police lined up the victims and forced them to strip down to their underpants before killing them. News of the atrocities committed by the police spread rapidly in Kosovo, fed the separatist insurgency, and led to more violence.

Rexhep Bislimi, an activist of the Urosevac chapter of the Pristina - based Council for the Defense of Human Rights and Freedoms, died as a result of injuries inflicted by Serbian security forces while in detention in July. Serbian authorities denied Bislimi's family access to him, both while he was in detention and after he was transferred to Pristina hospital with serious injuries (see Section 4). Three humanitarian aid workers were killed by Serbian mortar fire while trying to deliver food near Kijevo on August 24 (see Section 1.g.).

On September 26 in Gornje Obrinje, Serbian special police allegedly killed 18 members of an ethnic Albanian family, including women and infants. In December Serbian and FRY officials blocked access for a team of independent international forensic experts to the site of the grave where those killed in Gornje Obrinje were buried. On May 31, Serbian security forces attacked the village of Novi Poklek, near Glogovac. Police seized 10 ethnic Albanian men in the raid, one of whom was found dead later that day. The other nine were still missing at year's end and presumed dead. According to eyewitness accounts of international human rights groups, Serbian special police summarily executed 13 ethnic Albanian men in Golubovac on September 26.

The FRY, in contravention of repeated U.N. Security Council Resolutions, denied investigators from the ICTY access to any part of Kosovo, preventing them from undertaking a thorough and independent investigation into these and other atrocities committed in the province that fall under the Tribunal's jurisdiction (see Section 4).

On December 29 the bodies of five Kosovo Albanians were found alongside roads or bridges, two in Prizren, two in Kosovska Mitrovica, and one on the Pec - Decani road. On December 30 a Kosovo Albanian was killed near the village of Dremnjak. By year's end according to credible reports, about 2,000 persons were dead as a result of the conflict in Kosovo, the vast majority of whom were ethnic Albanians. The domestic Pristina - based Council for the Defense of Human Rights and Freedoms reported in late December that the bulk of casualties among ethnic Albanians were unarmed civilians.

According to an international human rights NGO, at least five persons died from abuse in prison during the year in Serbia (see Section 1.c.).

There were reports of many extrajudicial killings by members of the armed ethnic Albanian insurgency, including of several so - called ethnic Albanian "collaborators" and several Serb civilians near one of the strongholds of the KLA in Glodjane in the late summer (see Section 1.g.). Forces alleged to be from the KLA kidnaped and killed the deputy mayor of Kosovo Polje, Zvonko Bojanic, on December 17. According to international observers, two masked persons entered a cafe in Pec during the night of December 14 and began firing at customers. Six Serbs were killed in the attack, and three others were hospitalized. Police identified 14 suspects and arrested 3 between December 15 and 17. In late December, a local police inspector was killed in central Podujevo, an elderly Serb man was shot dead in the village of Obranza, and a Serb janitor was killed in Urosevac, all in circumstances that led to suspicion that the KLA was responsible for the killings.

On December 27, three Roma were found dead in Kosovska Mitrovica. The Roma community reportedly attributed responsibility for the deaths to the KLA. On December 31 a Serb janitor in the Urosevac agricultural school was found dead on the outskirts of town.

b. Disappearance

There were unconfirmed reports of hundreds of disappearances. According to Human Rights Watch, at least a hundred ethnic Albanians disappeared in Kosovo during the worst fighting between February and September, about half of whom were last seen in police custody.

In one instance several corpses were found hastily buried by Serbian forces in a garbage dump near Orahovac in July. There were also reports of mass graves, which Serbian authorities strongly denied. However, Serbian and federal authorities failed to grant investigators from the ICTY access to the gravesites. Among the persons who disappeared was Dr. Hafir Shala, a medical doctor, who was apprehended on April 10 by police near Glogovac, taken to the central police station in Pristina, and never heard from again. The Belgrade-based Humanitarian Law Center documented numerous cases of ethnic Albanians who were apprehended by police over the summer months and were still missing at year's end. Access for international humanitarian organizations such as the International Committee of the Red Cross (ICRC) to those detained was impeded by the Serbian Government throughout most of the year, but slightly improved after October.

The fate of some 136 Serbs and Montenegrins reported missing and presumed to have been abducted by the KLA or other ethnic Albanian insurgent fighters was still unknown at year's end, according to international intergovernmental organizations, based on reports from family members of the missing. Up to 280 Serbs were reported missing throughout the year. Several Serbs reported cases of family members - mostly civilians - taken hostage by separatist fighters and not heard from again, including many reportedly taken after fighting between police and insurgent forces at Orahovac in July. Many of those still missing are believed to have been killed; others are presumed to be still alive. The KLA kidnaped a Serb policeman on November 19 in the Podujevo area; after intervention by the Kosovo Diplomatic Observer Mission (KDOM) the KLA released the policeman on November 24. International organizations and diplomatic observers had very little success in winning access to those believed to be detained by armed Albanian groups.

c. Torture and Other Cruel, Inhuman, or Degrading Treatment or Punishment

The law prohibits torture and other cruel forms of punishment; however, Serbian security forces regularly and systematically used torture, beatings in detention, and other forms of abuse against the ethnic Albanian population after fighting erupted in Kosovo early in the year. There were several police roundups in Kosovo during the year of ethnic Albanians charged by the Serb authorities with supporting terrorism. The worst police brutality takes place during the 3 to 4 day period of incommunicado detention allowed by law. According to credible reports, police also used electric shock and sleep deprivation to torture detainees. In one incident, Serbian police took into custody Sokol Rugovci, an ethnic Albanian from Montenegro. According to the Helsinki Committee for Human Rights in Sandzak, when Rugovci admitted during an interrogation that he supported the reform government of Milo Djukanovic, the police used a welding machine to brand "Milo" on his chest. In another incident, police carved a cross on the chest of Arsim Krasnici, an ethnic Albanian, in a Pristina hospital. In another incident, an ethnic Serb woman reported to authorities that police threatened to carve off her genitals because she worked in a Muslim restaurant. One of three policemen involved in the incident was sentenced to 20 days in prison but by year's end had not served his sentence. According to the Center for the Protection of Women and Children in Pristina, Serb security forces reportedly engaged in the rape of Albanian women in Kosovo. Two girls who reportedly were raped by Yugoslav Army members committed suicide near the end of the year (see Section 1.c.). At least five Kosovo Albanian males died in custody during the year - all individuals who were in good health prior to their detention by Serbian police, according to international human rights groups. Evidence of torture in detention is widespread.

Human rights lawyer Destan Rukiqi, who defended dozens of ethnic Albanian political prisoners in Kosovo in recent years, was arrested on

July 23 and then severely beaten by the police. On his third day of detention he was beaten with rubber batons on the kidneys and spent 2 weeks on dialysis. On July 30, he was taken from Lipljan prison to Pristina hospital with serious injuries to his kidneys. Rukiqi was sentenced the same day in an expedited procedure to the maximum 60 days in prison for the misdemeanor offense of disturbing public order. His arrest was related to an incident in which he raised his voice to a judge who refused to let him review the case file of his client. Serb authorities denied Rukiqi's wife and his lawyers, as well as diplomatic and human rights observers, access to him in prison and in the hospital. Rukiqi was released on August 22 after 30 days in prison.

Ethnic Albanians continued to suffer at the hands of security forces conducting searches for weapons, ammunition, and explosives. The police, without following proper legal procedures, frequently extract "confessions" during interrogations that routinely include the beating of suspects' feet, hands, genital areas, and sometimes heads. The police use their fists, nightsticks, and occasionally electric shocks. Apparently confident that there would be no reprisals, and in an attempt to intimidate the wider community, police often beat persons in front of their families. There has been virtually no prosecution of those responsible, despite a public commitment from the President of the Government of Serbia in October to do so and despite repeated demands from the international community calling on the Milosevic Government to cooperate in the investigation and prosecution of those responsible. According to various sources, ethnic Albanians are frequently too terrified to ask police to follow proper legal procedures - such as having them provide written notice of witness interrogation. In some cases, Serbian police also used threats and violence against family members of suspects and held them as hostages. Local human rights monitors report that Serbian police threatened and intimidated doctors working in Kosovo to prevent them from treating KLA members. One doctor reported that police entered his private clinic, held him at gunpoint, and threatened him for treating suspected terrorists. According to Albanian and foreign observers, the worst abuses against ethnic Albanians took place not in big towns but in rural enclaves - a pattern which, according to many observers, increased separatist sentiment and provided the basis for the strong support for the KLA in these areas.

On December 15, police in Belgrade detained and beat a student activist from the "Student Resistance Movement" Otpor, Srdjan Popovic. On December 29, unknown thugs (possibly special police forces) beat another prominent Otpor activist, Boris Karajcic, just weeks after considerable media exposure of his trip abroad to publicize the Milosevic regime's human rights abuses (see Section 2.a.).

Police beat an APTV cameraman in Pristina in October (see Section 2.a.). Police occasionally attacked Roma (also see Section 5). Police used truncheons, tear gas, and water canons against student demonstrators in Belgrade (see Section 2.b.).

The police harassed persons connected with the distribution of the Belgrade independent newspaper Dnevni Telegraf. Kiosk owners were approached and told that if they sold the newspaper the financial police would look into their operations. Throughout the year the police systematically intimidated printing houses - including in November the Forum of Novi Sad - to prevent them from printing independent newspapers (see Section 2.a.).

In a country where many of the adult males are armed, the Serbian government and police, according to some members of ethnic minorities, selectively enforced the laws regulating the possession and registration of firearms during the year so as to harass and intimidate ethnic minorities, particularly Kosovo Albanians and Bosniak Muslims. The most frequent justification given for searches of homes and arrests was the illegal possession of weapons. Observers allege that in Kosovo the police use the pretext of searching for weapons when in fact they are also searching for hard currency. It is reported that local police authorities more easily approve the registration of legal weapons for Kosovo Serbs and frequently turn a blind eye to Serbs' possession of illegal weapons. In fact, the Serbian police in some cases reportedly actively promoted the arming of local Kosovo Serb civilians.

Prison conditions meet minimum international standards. According to human rights monitors based in Belgrade, prison conditions deteriorated in recent years. However, there were few confirmed reports of the abuse of prisoners once they were sentenced and serving time. The vast majority of cases of torture occur before the detainees are charged with offenses or during the period between the filing of charges and the commencement of the trial.

The Government generally permits prison visits by human rights monitors, although access is sporadic and subject to the whim of local officials. Access was poor for much of the year but improved slightly by October. On several occasions, outside monitors, including representatives of the ICRC, were denied access to individuals held by Serbian police. For example, in September although the Government agreed to allow access to the 523 persons it acknowledged to have in custody then, the ICRC gained access to less than 30 of them.

After poor cooperation between the ICRC and the Serbian authorities, relations improved significantly after Milosevic reached agreements with international interlocutors in June and October. At year's end the Ministry of Justice improved its record in notifying the ICRC of detainees. According to Ministry of Justice statistics, 771 persons were detained on charges relating to the conflict in Kosovo at year's end. The ICRC visited 421 of those detained; 276 of the 771 had been in detention since October. However, the ICRC was denied access to persons detained by the Ministry of Defense, which only has heightened international concern for the condition and treatment of those prisoners. The ICRC estimates that the Ministry of Defense had 40 persons in custody. Access to those civilians alleged by the Government or by family members to be detained by the KLA has been almost nonexistent.

d. Arbitrary Arrest, Detention, or Exile

Police use of arbitrary arrest and detention was concentrated primarily in Kosovo and, to a lesser degree, in Sandzak. Serbian police often apply certain laws only against ethnic minorities and used force with relative impunity. Sandzak Muslims as well as Kosovo Albanians were subjected to trumped up or exaggerated charges, ranging from unlawful possession of firearms to willfully undermining the country's territorial integrity. According to Serbian Ministry of Justice statistics, the authorities were in the process of charging or trying approximately 1,500 persons for activities related to the Kosovo conflict. Serbian security forces arrested Sylejman Bytyci, a member of the local leadership of the LDK (Democratic League of Kosovo) Party, as well as Milaim Jashari, a senior member of the local chapter of the Council for the Defense of Human Rights and Freedoms, and his 21-year - old son, Zylbehar Jashari, during a large - scale raid in Urosevac. In July Serbian police arrested several seasonal workers from Kosovo in Novi Pazar without cause and kept them overnight before releasing them the following day. According to the Helsinki Committee in Sandzak, the police feared demonstrations on the first anniversary of appointed rule, July 10 in Novi Pazar, which marked the date when the Milosevic regime forcibly removed the elected local government in the predominantly Muslim municipality. The police arrested many non-Serbs to avoid problems. Earlier, without cause, the police on June 16 arrested student activists in Novi Pazar who were involved in a national antiwar campaign against the regime's Kosovo policy.

Laws regarding conspiracy, threats to the integrity of the government, and state secrets are so vague as to allow easy abuse by the regime.

Federal statutes permit the police to detain criminal suspects without a warrant and hold them incommunicado for up to 3 days without charging them or granting them access to an attorney. Serbian law separately provides for a 24-hour detention period. The police often combine the two for a total 4-day detention period. After this period, police must turn a suspect over to an investigative judge, who may order a 30-day extension and, under certain legal procedures, subsequent extensions of investigative detention up to 6 months. In Kosovo, Serbian police often detain and beat persons without ever officially charging them and routinely hold suspects well beyond the 3-day statutory period. Bail rarely is granted.

Defense lawyers and human rights workers complained of excessive delays by Serbian authorities in filing formal charges and opening investigations. The ability of defense attorneys to challenge the legal basis of their clients' detention often was hampered further by difficulties in gaining access to detainees or acquiring copies of official indictments and decisions to remand defendants into custody. In some cases, judges prevented defense attorneys from reading the court file. Investigative judges in Serbia often delegated their responsibility for carrying out investigations to the police or members of the state security service and rarely questioned their accounts of the investigation - even when it was obvious that confessions were coerced from the accused. Results of such sham investigations were then used in court to convict defendants on trumped up charges.

The regime ignored its pledge to grant amnesty for "crimes related to the conflict in Kosovo," a pledge that was part of Milosevic's October agreement to end the repression there. Humanitarian organizations reported in December that there were no reported cases of amnesty for individuals charged with terrorist acts. As a result, about 1,500 ethnic Albanians remained in custody at year's end charged with committing terrorist acts or with "anti-State activities" related to the conflict in Kosovo. According to an international human rights NGO, prosecutors in the Pec district in Kosovo were increasing the charges in many cases to crimes against humanity in an effort to circumvent the Serbian government's own pledge in October to grant an amnesty for conflict-related crimes.

Four members of the "Student Resistance Movement" protesting Serbia's repressive new information law and the removal of faculty from a university for political reasons were arrested in late fall for spraying anti-Fascist graffiti (see Section 2.a.). In November three of the four students were sentenced to 10 days in jail and were released from custody. The four were convicted in a hastily staged trial, and their sentences were considered harsh for first-time offenders. Also unusual in such cases, the sentences were served before the appeal was heard.

According to the Ministry of Justice, at year's end 771 persons were detained on charges relating to the conflict on Kosovo.

The KLA kidnaped two journalists of the state-run news agency Tanjug on October 18. On October 30 the "military court" of the KLA sentenced them to 60 days in prison for violating the civilian and military regulations of the KLA and the regulations of the KLA "police." The journalists were given 7 days to appeal their sentences, according to the KLA. The ICRC announced that it was unsuccessful in its repeated attempts to visit the two (see Section 2.a.). The KLA finally released the pair in late November. In October the KLA detained 13 Albanian politicians, including members of the Kosovo Albanian Shadow Parliament, in Cirez for 2 days. The KLA forces are reported to have repeatedly tortured 6 of the 13 detainees, whom they considered to be too close to the Serbian Government. International intergovernmental human rights organizations believe that the KLA held at most a relatively small number of hostages/prisoners at year's end.

Exile is not permitted legally, and no instances of its use are known to have occurred. However, the practical effect of police repression in Kosovo and Sandzak has been to accentuate political instability, which in turn has limited economic opportunity. As a result, many ethnic Albanians and Bosniak Muslims go abroad to escape persecution, although only in a few cases could direct links to police actions be identified.

e. Denial of Fair Public Trial

The Constitution provides for an independent judiciary, but in practice, Federal and Serbian courts largely are controlled by the Government and rarely challenge the will of the state security apparatus. Judicial corruption is also widespread. While judges are elected for fixed terms, they may be subjected to governmental pressure. Serbian authorities frequently deny fair public trial to non-Serbs and to persons whom they believe oppose the regime. The fraud that followed the November 1996 municipal elections was perpetrated mainly through the regime's misuse of the judicial system. In Milosevic's FRY, the key perpetrator of that fraud, president of the First Belgrade Municipal Court Dragoljub Jankovic, became the Serbian Justice Minister. Another perpetrator, Balsa Grovedarica, at the time the presiding judge of the Serbian Supreme Court, was awarded an extra official position: he became president of the Serbian Electoral Commission.

The court system comprises local, district, and supreme courts at the republic level, as well as a Federal Court and Federal Constitutional Court to which republic supreme court decisions, depending on the subject, may be appealed. There is also a military court system. According to the Federal Constitution, the Federal Constitutional Court rules on the constitutionality of laws and regulations and relies on the constituent republic authorities to enforce its rulings.

The Federal Criminal Code of the former Socialist Federal Republic of Yugoslavia remains in force. Considerable confusion and room for abuse remain in the legal system because the 1990 Constitution of Serbia has not yet been brought into conformity with the 1992 Constitution of the Federal Republic of Yugoslavia. Under federal law, defendants have the right to be present at their trial and to have an attorney represent them, at public expense if needed. The courts also must provide interpreters. The presiding judge decides what is read into the record of the proceedings. Either the defendant or the prosecutor may appeal the verdict.

Although generally respected in form, defense lawyers in Kosovo and Sandzak have filed numerous complaints about flagrant breaches of standard procedure, which they believed undermined their clients' rights. Even when individual judges admitted that the lawyers were correct, the courts ignored or dismissed the complaints.

Human rights lawyer Destan Rukiqi, who defended dozens of ethnic Albanian political prisoners in Kosovo in recent years, was arrested on July 23 and severely beaten by Serbian police (see Section 1.c.). His arrest was related to an incident in which he raised his voice to a judge who refused to let him review the case file of his client.

In November police in Belgrade arrested four students with the Otpor student resistance movement, and a court sentenced them to 10-day prison terms in a summary trial with no right of appeal (see Section 2.a.).

The Government continues to pursue cases previously brought against targeted minority groups under the Yugoslav Criminal Code for jeopardizing the territorial integrity of the country and for conspiring or forming a group with intent to commit subversive activities - that is, undermining the "constitutional order." Numerous questionable trials took place in Kosovo during the year involving almost 500 ethnic Albanians. Over 90 percent of the cases involved alleged violations under the Federal Penal Code of Article 136 related to "association to conduct enemy activity," or Article 125 concerning "terrorism." According to the Ministry of Justice, as of December some 1,500 Kosovo Albanians were being charged or tried for crimes related to the Kosovo conflict. According to the ICRC, the Justice Ministry stated that some 500 were being tried in absentia. The Office of the U.N. High Commissioner for Human Rights was monitoring the cases of 1,350 prisoners in the Pec and Prizren regional courts at year's end.

Generally, the evidence in these cases was inadequate, and the defendants largely were denied timely access to their attorneys. According to international civilian verifiers from the OSCE Kosovo Verification Mission (KVM) office in Pec, some 80 "nonprofessional" judges work in the district and municipal courts there, of whom the vast majority are former police officers. Although there are two courtrooms in the court building, many trials are held in the offices of the judges on the upper floors where no members of the public are present. International human rights monitors observed a lack of impartiality by Serb judges in the municipal and district court system in the province. They also noted the absence of legal counsel for the defense, the absence of witnesses or experts during proceedings, and a failure to provide medical care during proceedings to defendants obviously in need of immediate attention. Continuing a common pattern of abuse, independent observers reported that several defendants met their defense attorneys for the first time only after the investigative judge already concluded the crucial investigation stage, while other defendants had defense counsel assigned after they entered the courtroom. Much evidence appeared to have been obtained by authorities through forced confessions of defendants under duress. Other evidence was kept from defense attorneys until just before the trial. Other international observers monitoring the trials of alleged terrorists in Pristina complained of irregularities in the process involving evidentiary standards, the nonuse of native languages, and the failure to respect the presumption of innocence.

Many legal scholars expressed concern in July over the passage of the Act on Lawyers, which is said to be an attempt to restrict the freedoms of lawyers and to interfere with the independence of lawyers in their dealings with clients. In particular, according to an analysis done by the Helsinki Committee for Human Rights in Serbia, the law is said to give too much authority to the lawyers' chambers - both at the republic and federal levels - which the Helsinki Committee alleges would enable the regime to exercise stricter control over the profession. According to a Serbian Constitutional Court Judge, the law will also enable the regime to interfere with the lawyer - client relationship, which, even during the Communist era, was upheld to a greater degree.

Ulsin Hoti, leader of UNIKOM, a political party that advocates Kosovo's unification with Albania, was in detention for the entire year. Hoti was in a Nis jail and was reportedly in poor health. His lawyers have been denied access to him since February.

The Government introduced a constitutional initiative in July to rein in republic-level judges by discarding the provision that gives them their mandates for life and requiring that they seek office periodically through election. This process would involve obtaining Justice Ministry approval for each judge's candidacy. Local observers fear that the provision would in effect make judges functionaries of the regime, easily removed if they do not cooperate.

The Government continues to hold some ethnic Albanians as political prisoners.

f. Arbitrary Interference With Privacy, Family, Home, or Correspondence

The authorities infringed on citizens' privacy rights. Federal law gives republic ministries of the interior sole control over the decision to monitor potential criminal activities, a power that routinely is abused. It is widely believed that authorities monitor opposition and dissident activity, eavesdrop on conversations, read mail, and tap telephones. Although illegal under provisions of Federal and Serbian law, the Federal post office registers all mail from abroad, ostensibly to protect mail carriers from charges of theft.

Although the law includes restrictions on searches, officials often ignored them. In Kosovo and Sandzak, Serbian police systematically subjected ethnic Albanians and Bosniak Muslims to random searches of their homes, vehicles, shops, and offices, asserting that they were searching for weapons. According to the Kosovo Council for the Defense of Human Rights and Freedoms, the police carried out scores of raids on homes, including in areas not affected by the fighting. Police used threats and violence against family members of suspects.

Serbian security forces systematically destroyed entire villages in Kosovo by burning and shelling houses, contaminating water wells, and killing livestock (see Section 1.g.).

A government law requiring universal military service is enforced only sporadically; it was not vigorously enforced during the year. The informal practice of the military has been not to call up ethnic Albanians. Of approximately 100,000 draft evaders living abroad to avoid punishment, 40 percent were estimated to be ethnic Albanian. This number in part reflects the large number of conscription-age men in the FRY's Albanian community. Leaders of Kosovo's Albanian and Sandzak's Muslim communities maintained that forced compliance of these ethnic groups with universal military service was an attempt to induce young men to flee the country. According to an amnesty bill passed in 1996, up to 12,000 young men for whom criminal prosecution for draft evasion already had started were granted amnesty. Others who did not fall into this category were told that if they returned to the FRY their cases would be reviewed on a "case by case" basis, a policy that has not inspired confidence among offenders. Another law passed in October stated that draft dodgers who did not report for military service would forfeit their right to inheritance.

In a related development, under a 1996 agreement with Germany, ethnic Albanian refugees repatriated to the FRY were not supposed to be prosecuted for fleeing the draft. However, according to the Humanitarian Law Center, many returning ethnic Albanians faced irregular procedures on returning to the FRY. The Center reported many misdeeds by authorities against returned asylum seekers, including physical abuse, threats of imprisonment, deportation, confiscation of identification cards, and a requirement that persons report to their local police stations on a daily basis. Returning ethnic Albanians and Sandzak Muslims are detained routinely on their arrival at local airports. In many cases FRY officials have refused to issue proper travel documents to children born to asylum seekers.

g. Use of Excessive Force and Violations of Humanitarian Law in Internal Conflicts

The conflict in Kosovo placed civilian populations on both sides of the ethnic divide in an unusually vulnerable position. The excessive and indiscriminate use of force by Serbian police forces and the Yugoslav Army (VJ) resulted in widespread civilian casualties and the mass forced displacement of up to 250,000 persons by September, the vast majority of whom were displaced within Kosovo while tens of thousands sought refuge in Montenegro. The Milosevic Government's actions and the ensuing humanitarian crisis nearly resulted in a humanitarian catastrophe in the fall.

In Likosane in early March police entered the family compound of the Ahmeti family, rounded up the male members of the clan plus one acquaintance - 12 individuals - and summarily executed them. A few days later, in Donji Prekaz, police surrounded the family compound of Adem Jashari, whom they believed to be well armed and a member of the KLA, and destroyed it. Over 80 persons died in the siege, including women and children.

On September 26 in Gornje Obrinje, Serbian special police allegedly killed 18 members of an ethnic Albanian family, including women and infants. In December Serbian and FRY officials blocked access for a team of independent international forensic experts to the gravesites of those killed in Gornje Obrinje. On May 31, Serbian security forces attacked the village of Novi Poklek, near Glogovac. Police seized 10 ethnic Albanian men in the raid, one of whom was found dead later that day. The other nine were still missing at year's end and presumed dead. According to eyewitness accounts of international human rights groups, Serbian special police summarily executed 13 ethnic Albanian men in Golubovac on September 26. The FRY, in contravention of repeated U.N. Security Council Resolutions, denied investigators from the ICTY access to any part of Kosovo, preventing them from undertaking a thorough and independent investigation into these and other atrocities committed in the province that fall under the Tribunal's jurisdiction (see Section 4).

According to international observers, two masked persons entered a cafe in Pec during the night of December 14 and began firing at customers. Six Serbs were killed in the attack, and three others were hospitalized. Police identified 14 suspects and arrested 3 between December 15 and 17. In late December, a local police inspector was killed in central Podujevo, an elderly Serb man was shot dead in the village of Obranza, and a Serb janitor was killed in Urosevac, all in circumstances that led to suspicion that the KLA was responsible for the killings.

On December 27, three Roma were found dead in Kosovska Mitrovica. The Roma community reportedly attributed responsibility for the deaths to the KLA.

Development of the Human Rights Situation

The international community was engaged continuously during the year in an effort to compel Milosevic to act constructively to find a peaceful solution to the Kosovo crisis. After police killed scores of civilians in late February in the process of trying to eliminate what the regime alleged was a "terrorist" cell, the international community imposed further sanctions, including an investment ban, which went into effect in the summer. However, further violence followed, and the North Atlantic Treaty Organization (NATO) allies stepped up pressure on the regime in the fall. In the face of the threat of NATO air raids, Milosevic agreed to steps aimed at mitigating the humanitarian disaster unfolding in the province. He undertook to comply fully with the terms of U.N. Security Council Resolution (UNSCR) 1199 (adopted in September), which included demands that the FRY cease all action by the security forces affecting the civilian population, order the withdrawal of security forces used for civilian repression, cooperate with the ICTY, and allow full and unimpeded access for all international humanitarian aid organizations to Kosovo, including the U.N. High Commissioner for Refugees (UNHCR) and the ICRC. Milosevic also agreed to allow a NATO air verification mission to verify compliance with UNSCR 1199 from the air and to allow 2,000 unarmed civilian "verifiers" of the OSCE KVM to verify compliance on the ground in Kosovo. Agreements establishing these missions were signed separately by the FRY, with NATO and the OSCE respectively, in mid-October. In subsequent meetings with NATO representatives, Milosevic agreed to specific limits on Serbian police and Yugoslav Army presence in Kosovo.

According to a resolution adopted by the U.N. Third Committee in November, Serbian security forces damaged by arson or artillery over 20,000 houses in Kosovo, and the fighting resulted in over 1,000 documented deaths, including many small children and the elderly. International diplomatic observers witnessed Serbian armed forces purposefully destroying civilian property: police systematically looted, trashed, and burned villages and shot livestock with the intention of depopulating certain regions, especially the villages near the border with Albania. In the summer, international diplomatic observers and members of intergovernmental organizations witnessed Serbian security forces torching and vandalizing homes of ethnic Albanians after fighting between police forces and insurgents had already ceased in those villages. Other NGO's reported that areas that were occupied by Serbian security forces were at high risk for well water contamination. The security forces used the wells for waste disposal (i.e., garbage, animal remains, and other contaminants) when they departed. Numerous credible incidents were reported in which civilians were seized from intercity buses and held hostage by both Serbian security forces and Albanian insurgents. By year's end, the UNHCR estimated that there were still over 180,000 internally displaced persons (IDP's) as a result of the conflict in Kosovo. According to the Pristina-based Center for the Protection of Women and children, 89 percent of the IDP's are women and children.

In addition to the terror tactics employed by Serbian security forces against the ethnic Albanian civilian population of Kosovo, credible sources indicated that the Milosevic regime sought to block some shipments of food into the province. When presented with a list alleged to have been prepared by Belgrade authorities of products to be stopped from entering the province, Serbian police in Kosovo did not deny the operation, but stated that it was part of a countrywide campaign to stop "tax avoidance." At the same time, the Milosevic regime compiled at best an uneven record of cooperation and hostility toward non-governmental organizations that sought to deliver humanitarian shipments to the needy in Kosovo, including to IDP's forcibly displaced by the police campaign of shelling, looting, and burning ethnic Albanians' homes after fighting had concluded.

Three local humanitarian aid workers were killed by mortar fire from Serbian forces in the summer, and others were harassed and detained on trumped up charges of "aiding and abetting" terrorist groups. On September 30 one ICRC employee was killed and three others were wounded after their vehicle hit a land mine at Gornje Obrinje. On September 14 a KDOM vehicle also struck a land mine in the area.

Separatist fighters set up roadblocks and denied passage to Serbs, including civilians attempting to get to and from work. In Kijevo over the summer, the KLA blockaded the Pristina - Pec road, forcing Serbian police to extract some Serbian civilians - including a pregnant woman - from the village by helicopter. Separatist fighters harassed Serbian journalists and took some hostage. In addition to credible cases in which so-called "collaborators" were killed, some ethnic Albanians employed by state-owned enterprises were threatened.

SECTION 2: RESPECT FOR CIVIL LIBERTIES, INCLUDING:

a. Freedom of Speech and the Press

Federal law provides for freedom of speech and of the press; however, the Serbian and Federal Governments severely restricted this right in practice. The Milosevic regime's assault on these freedoms during the year was the most pronounced since Milosevic came to power over a decade ago.

In October, after NATO threatened to intervene because of the deteriorating humanitarian situation in Kosovo, the Serbian Government issued a decree effectively allowing press censorship, possibly as a response to the perceived threat to the regime of the free flow of information and ideas. It later passed a new information law, which incorporated many of the decree's strict provisions that left the country's independent media severely constrained. Under the law, private citizens or organizations can bring suit against media outlets for printing materials not sufficiently patriotic, or "against the territorial integrity, sovereignty and independence of the country." Media outlets also can be fined for publishing items of a personal nature without the consent of the individual concerned (an apparent reference to political cartoons). The rebroadcast of foreign news programs, including from the British Broadcasting Corporation and the Voice of America, was banned. Media outlets whose practices do not conform to the new law may be subjected to exorbitant fines, which must be paid within a 24-hour period. Two independent radio stations, Radio Indeks and Radio Senta, were shut down. On October 28, criminal charges were filed against Nenad Cekic, the editor in chief of Radio Indeks. In October independent radio stations Radio/Television Kursumlija, Radio Globus Kraljevo, and Radio Velika Kikinda stopped broadcasting altogether after government pressure to stop broadcasting foreign programs. According to its management, the Government froze the bank accounts of Belgrade City Television Studio B in early December, although the station was associated with a coalition partner in the Government. The Government annulled existing contracts with Studio B on frequencies and offered new contracts effective retroactively to June, which offered fewer frequencies at a significantly increased cost: $100,000 per month. Since Studio B refused to sign the contracts, according to the director, the station was already operating illegally, effectively providing the Government with grounds for closing the station.

The Government shut down several other stations during the year, using confusing regulations governing frequency allocations, including Radio Kontact in Pristina in July, the independent city radio in Nis in August, and STV Negotin in September. A problem that often renders independent electronic media outlets vulnerable is the deliberate vagueness of the relevant laws. Radio and television stations, depending on their political dispositions, can be harassed bureaucratically. Instead of obtaining long-term licenses to broadcast, stations receive only 1-year temporary licenses if they are approved at all. The bureaucratic procedures are so difficult that stations frequently cannot possibly fulfill the requirements - leaving them at the mercy of the regime. For example, under current law, to obtain a license to broadcast, a station must obtain approval of a government "construction inspector" on its office space. But to obtain a construction inspector's approval, a station needs a broadcast license. In another example, in the spring authorities closed Feman, a newly opened television station in Jagodina and justified their action by the fact that the station was operating without a license. The station editor in chief claimed that the Federal Telecommunications Ministry had informed him that he did not need a license prior to opening the station and led him to believe that there was a grace period during which to obtain proper documentation. Two other private television stations in Jagodina operate without licenses. The day after the station broadcast a program critical of the Government's financial policies, an inspector from the Telecommunications Ministry, escorted by five police officers, closed the station. According to the NGO Fund for Humanitarian Law, in the spring authorities closed down Radio Lazarevac, Radio/Television Studio M in Vranje, and Radio Herc in Zitoradje, much in the same manner as the Feman television station.

In addition to license problems, those stations that do obtain licenses are forced to pay exorbitantly high fees, the nonpayment of which is enforced selectively by Serbian authorities to close down those stations that do not adhere to the Government's line.

Although there are many independent television and radio stations operating throughout the country, their broadcasts typically cannot be received beyond the major cities. The only network that covers the entire country is the Serbian State Television and Radio Network RTS. An estimated one-third of the population of Serbia only receives RTS, the official voice of President Milosevic.

In October police beat an APTV cameraman in Pristina (see Section 1.c).

According to independent journalists, most journalists started practicing self-censorship in an effort to avoid a violation under the media law. Journalists had been informed that printing anything that was not true - even an advertisement or a death announcement - could be punished under the information law. One independent newspaper reported that it was publishing half as many articles as usual, in view of the new need to check extensively the facts in every article. The weekly Zrenjanin decided not to publish public statements after it was sued for publishing false statements made at a press conference, since such comments cannot be verified easily.

The police harassed persons connected with the distribution of the widely circulated Belgrade independent daily Dnevni Telegraf. Kiosk owners were approached and told that if they sold the newspaper the financial police would look into their operations. Days after the repressive new Serbian information law was passed in late October, it was used to justify the imposition of an exorbitant fine on Slavko Curuvija, the newspaper's publisher. Police barged into the paper's offices, confiscated property, and prompted the publisher to move his operations to Podgorica, the capital of Montenegro. According to the newspaper's management, it wanted to pay the fine and return operations to something like the conditions that prevailed before the crackdown, but the regime was more interested in keeping the newspaper off the streets. As a result of the media crackdown and its changed circumstances, the daily circulation of Dnevni Telegraf dropped from 60,000 to 70,000 copies to 10,000 to 12,000 copies.

Dnevni Telegraf's experience had a chilling effect on other independent dailies, including Danas and Nasa Borba. Both newspapers, less financially secure than Dnevni Telegraf, suspended operations to avoid fines that could destroy them. By year's end, Danas was publishing using a printing house in Montenegro. In November Serbian authorities confiscated shipments of Montenegro's only weekly independent newsmagazine, Monitor. Although the magazine is completely Montenegrin-owned, Serbian authorities claimed that the law on information covered distribution channels as well. In November the regime attempted to levy a large fine under the Serbian information law on the publisher of Monitor. The Federal Government issued a decree in November that the independent magazine Ekonomska Politika would from that point on be part of the Borba publishing house. Borba's first act was to replace the director and managing director of Ekonomska Politika with individuals close to the Yugoslav Left Party (JUL), the neo-Communist Party headed by Mira Markovic, wife of FRY President Milosevic. Publication of the magazine was stopped completely just as an issue highly critical of the Government's economic planning policies was going to press in late December. Nasa Borba and NT Plus, another independent daily, were still shut down at year's end.

After the media law went into effect the Serbian Government started prosecuting the owner and editor of the newsmagazine Evropljanin. On December 17, Serbia's Ministry of Information issued threatening letters to five Albanian-language newspapers and magazines in Kosovo to the effect that they were in violation of the new public information law. Shortly thereafter, the newspaper Bujku was effectively closed down. Editors from Koha Ditore, the leading Albanian-language daily, Zeri, an intellectual Albanian weekly, and Kosovo Sot, a new Albanian daily, reported that threats against the Albanian language media, which began with warning letters from the Serbian Ministry of Information, were escalating.

Throughout the year Serbian police systematically intimidated printing houses - including in November the Forum of Novi Sad - to prevent them from printing independent newspapers.

Before the Montenegrin parliamentary elections in 1998, state-controlled RTS openly campaigned on behalf of Momir Bulatovic's Socialist Peoples Party (SNP), considered to be Milosevic's surrogate political party in the republic of Montenegro.

In March Belgrade public prosecutor Miodrag Tmusic called on police to investigate five major independent newspapers (Nasa Borba, Blic, Danas, Dnevni Telegraf, and Demokratija) along with some unidentified television stations to determine whether there were elements of "biased reporting" that incited terrorist acts or condoned terrorism

On December 10, the new government-appointed Dean of Belgrade University's School of Electrical Engineering Vlada Teodosic, ordered "filters" to prevent users of the academic Internet network from accessing the OpenNet web site, a major source of independent news and information. The measure also affects the independent media and NGO's in the country, many of which access OpenNet through the university. According to Human Rights Watch, the filters appeared to have been prompted by a link on the web site to a political cartoon that showed Teodosic in a Nazi uniform and portrayed Milos Laban, another newly appointed administrator, as a monkey.

Montenegrin newspaper publishers not friendly to the Belgrade regime frequently had their papers removed from trains and buses entering Serbia (see Section 2.d.).

The KLA kidnaped two Serbian journalists for the state-run news agency Tanjug on October 13. The KLA finally released the two journalists in late November (see Section 1.d.) after a "trial."

In May the Serbian Parliament passed the new Universities Law. It severely curtails academic freedom by allowing the Government to appoint rectors and governing boards and hire and fire deans of faculties. Deans in turn under the new law can hire and fire professors-in effect taking away tenure and promoting regime loyalists inside the universities. The law also discourages political activism among students, who were a mainstay of the antigovernment protests of 1996-97. According to the Belgrade Center for Human Rights, some 22 professors were fired and 30 were suspended after the law went into effect for refusing to sign new contracts, as required by the law. By year's end, protests over the law were gathering force. In November police arrested four students affiliated with the Student Resistance Movement Otpor, and a court sentenced them to 10-day prison terms in a summary trial with no right of appeal (see Section 1.e.). In one incident on December 29, unknown thugs (allegedly special police forces) beat a prominent student activist from the Otpor movement, Boris Karajcic, after considerable media exposure and his trip abroad to publicize human rights abuses in Serbia. Serbian police detained and beat another Otpor activist, Srdjan Popovic, in Belgrade on December 15 (see Section 1.c.).

b. Freedom of Peaceful Assembly and Association

The Federal and republic-level Constitutions provide for freedom of peaceful assembly and association; however, the Serbian and Federal Governments restricted this right. In Belgrade in May the police beat university protesters over passage of the new universities law. In November four students with the Otpor movement were arrested and convicted and given 10-day prison sentences in a summary trial with no right of appeal (see Section 1.e.). In Kosovo the regime cracked down on peaceful demonstrators during the 1997-98 academic year. When ethnic Albanian students in Kosovo staged peaceful protest marches in Pristina during the 1997-98 academic year, they were accused by the state-controlled media of instigating violence in one clash during the winter when police moved in with truncheons, tear gas, and water cannons. The regime cited the student protesters' unwillingness to apply for demonstration permits from the authorities. Moreover, the state-controlled media took advantage of the protests to accuse the Belgrade opposition of being in league with "Albanian separatists." In Sandzak the Milosevic regime banned all outdoor rallies, even for election campaigning.

According to the president of the Presevo city assembly, police officers in Presevo (southern Serbia, bordering Kosovo and Macedonia) beat peaceful protestors demonstrating against the Serbian police campaign against Kosovo Albanians in the Drenica region of Kosovo. The police reportedly attacked the ethnic Albanian political leaders who were attempting to control the crowds. The police arrested and detained several ethnic Albanian leaders for 5 hours in connection with the protest. The Assembly of Presevo issued a declaration against the police action. The Assembly claimed that one leader was denied medical treatment and that an ethnic Albanian journalist was given a 15-day prison sentence.

In response to the passage of the new law on universities (see Section 2.a.), between 2,000 and 3,000 students protested in Belgrade on May 27, but police blocked the students from marching to the Parliament. No violence was reported. According to Serb authorities, the students blocked traffic and police were required to ensure that traffic through the city was undisturbed.

The Federal and republic level Constitutions provide for freedom of association, but the Serbian and Federal Governments restricted this right. Prior to the most recent Serbian elections, in the fall of 1997, officials blocked the coalition Sandzak - Dr. Rasim Ljajic from forming an alliance with the Kosovo-based Democratic Reform Party of Muslims, a move that protected regime candidates from additional competition. During the year Serb authorities obstructed the registration of an NGO, the Independent Jurists' Association.

c. Freedom of Religion

There is no state religion, but the Milosevic regime gives preferential treatment, including access to state-run television for major religious events, to the Serbian Orthodox Church to which the majority of Serbs belong. The regime subjected religious communities in Kosovo to harassment. For example, in 1998 a Roman Catholic parish in Klina had the money, property, and permission (including up to the supreme court of Serbia) to build a church for its 6,000 member parish. However, the local chapter of Milosevic's Socialist Party of Serbia continued to block construction. Other Catholic and Muslim communities in the province had similar experiences.

The Serbian Government made no progress in the restitution of property that belonged to the Jewish community, despite President Milosevic's promises to resolve the disputes. The Orthodox and Catholic Churches have had similar difficulties with the restitution of their property.

d. Freedom of Movement Within the Country, Foreign Travel, Emigration, and Repatriation

The Constitution provides for freedom of movement; however, the Federal and Serbian Governments restrict this right in practice. The FRY Government makes passports available to most citizens; however, the authorities frequently bar FRY citizens from reentering the country. The Milosevic regime also continues to restrict the right of Kosovo Albanians and Sandzak Muslims to travel by holding up the issuance or renewal of passports for an unusually long period of time and reserves the option of prosecuting individuals charged previously with violating exit visa requirements. Kosovo Albanians also have problems with the issuance and renewal of passports and are sometimes called in for interrogation by state security officers before passports are issued.

Citizens reported difficulties at borders and the occasional confiscation of their passports. Ethnic Albanians, Sandzak Muslims, and Vojvodina Croats frequently complained of harassment at border crossings. There were numerous reports that border guards confiscated foreign currency or passports from travelers, as well as occasional complaints of physical mistreatment. The authorities generally allowed political opposition leaders to leave the country and return. FRY embassies overseas generally are considered to apply a double standard in issuing passports to their citizens; ethnic Serbs have a much easier time obtaining passports than members of ethnic minorities.

Many inhabitants of Serbia-Montenegro who were born in other parts of the former Yugoslavia, as well as large numbers of refugees, have not been able to establish their citizenship in the FRY, leaving them in a stateless limbo.

The FRY Government has been very slow to issue passports to refugees. This is a particular problem for asylum-seeking parents. For example, German authorities issue such children born in Germany a document certifying their birth. FRY officials in Germany refuse to issue passports to such children. When these asylum seekers who have been refused in Germany return to the FRY with their children, the children travel on the basis of this document. FRY authorities take the paper at the port of entry and issue a receipt for it. Then the children have no documentation in a country where documentation is a basic requirement. In January 1997 a new citizenship law entered into force, which, when fully implemented, is expected to affect adversely the rights of many inhabitants, including those born in other parts of the former Yugoslavia, refugees, and citizens who migrated to other countries to work or seek asylum.

The U.N. Special Rapporteur for the former Yugoslavia noted in 1997 that the new law would give the Ministry of Interior almost complete control over the granting of citizenship. The Government served notice that it plans to limit severely the granting of citizenship to refugees from the conflicts in Bosnia and Croatia. The Government also plans to revise the eligibility status of a large number of persons; refugees who have been granted citizenship since 1992 may stand to lose their FRY citizenship if they have acquired the citizenship of a former Yugoslav republic.

Observers in the Sandzak region also noted that Muslim residents who were forced to flee to Bosnia from Sandzak in 1992 and 1993 may not be permitted to return to Serbia, particularly if they obtained Bosnian passports in the interim. In violation of the Dayton Accords, Muslims from Sandzak frequently have been harassed on attempting to reenter Serbia after visits to Sarajevo or elsewhere in the Federation entity of Bosnia and Herzegovina.

As part of its campaign to undermine the reform government in Montenegro, the Milosevic regime also implemented a commercial blockade against the FRY's junior republic, a direct violation of the FRY Constitution's protection of the free flow of goods. Businesses frequently had their goods confiscated without cause by Serbian police. Newspaper publishers not friendly to the regime frequently had their papers removed from trains and buses entering Serbia (see Section 2.a.).

The FRY Government cooperated to a large extent with the Office of the UNHCR in assisting (predominantly Serb) refugees who fled to the FRY from neighboring Croatia and Bosnia-Herzegovina.

In sharp contrast to the record of the Federal and Serbian governments in this area, the Government of the Republic of Montenegro actually accepted tens of thousands of IDP's fleeing the fighting in the neighboring Kosovo province in Serbia. The international community contributed financial support to the IDP's in Montenegro through the UNHCR and other intergovernmental and non-governmental humanitarian organizations. In September the Montenegrin Government temporarily closed its border to Kosovo Albanian IDP's after almost 50,000 had entered the republic. The Montenegrin Government stated that the IDP's, when combined with 30,000 refugees from Croatia and

Bosnia, put too much pressure on the infrastructure of the junior republic, where the total population is only 600,000. Many speculated that the Milosevic regime deliberately channeled the IDP's in the direction of Montenegro to undermine its multiethnic reform government. The issue of first asylum did not arise during the year.

There were no reports of the forced return of persons to a country where they feared persecution during the year.

SECTION 3: RESPECT FOR POLITICAL RIGHTS: THE RIGHT OF CITIZENS TO CHANGE THEIR GOVERNMENT

The three Constitutions - the Federal constitution and those of the Serbian and Montenegrin Republics - provide for this right, but in practice citizens in Serbia are prevented from exercising it by the Milosevic regime's domination of the mass media and manipulation of the electoral process. Through its control of the purse strings at the Serbian republic level, the regime sought to undermine the effectiveness of the opposition leadership of most major cities. Only Montenegro's electoral system showed marked improvement, with the Government of then-Prime Minister Djukanovic holding a roundtable with the political opposition, including ethnic minorities, in September 1997. The Montenegrin government invited the OSCE to take part in preparing election legislation in time for Montenegrin parliamentary elections in May. Montenegrin presidential elections in late 1997 and the subsequent May parliamentary elections were judged by the OSCE to be free and fair. Djukanovic's invitation to outside observers came in stark contrast to the grudging last-minute acceptance of monitors by Milosevic during the fall 1997 Serbian elections. In February the Montenegrin Parliament approved a third law changing the electoral process and fulfilled the major recommendations of the OSCE. The law lowered the threshold for party representation from 4 percent to 3 percent of votes cast and established strict procedures to prevent vote fraud. The other two laws concerned voter lists and the media. The law also granted Albanians special status in accordance with an agreement reached by a consensus among all parties in the Montenegrin Parliament. The law combined regions where Albanians constitute a majority that are spread out among different cities into one parliamentary district that elects 5 of the 78 seats in Parliament. Minorities won seats both in the Republic's Assembly and in the Republic's coalition government.

The most recent Serbian elections, held in the fall of 1997, were seriously flawed. According to a 1998 study by the Belgrade-based Center for Free Elections and Democracy, both rounds of the Serbian presidential elections in September and December 1997 involved widespread fraud. In the latter campaign, the Center estimated that 500,000 votes were stolen to give the victory for the Serbian presidency to Milosevic ally Milan Milutinovic. Several disaffected SRS members charged in the fall that the Milosevic regime extracted mandates from the Radical Party of Serbia in exchange for giving the Radical Party a role in the Government.

Earlier, in July 1997, the regime gerrymandered electoral districts to smooth the way for candidates in the ruling coalition, expanding the number of districts in Serbia from 9 to 29. Most opposition politicians charged that changes in the election law, including the redrawing of districts, were designed specifically to favor the ruling party. The redistricting was one factor that compelled a number of opposition parties to boycott the last Serbian elections.

Slobodan Milosevic dominates the country's political system and is attempting to consolidate institutional power at the federal level as a result of his move from the Serbian republic-level presidency to the federal presidency. This precipitated a clash with authorities in Montenegro, who were intent on protecting that republic's rights under constitutional arrangements and its position within the FRY, which is made up of Serbia and Montenegro. Manipulating power within the federation based on the comparative size of the Serbian and Montenegrin populations and economies, Milosevic has been able to circumscribe the Montenegrin Government's capacity for independent action. As a result of Serbia's political crisis during the winter of 1996-97, Montenegro's then Prime Minister, Milo Djukanovic, began to take a steadily more assertive, reformist course. Djukanovic's victory in November 1997 presidential elections and his coalition's victory in the May parliamentary elections over forces led by incumbent Montenegrin president and Milosevic crony Momir Bulatovic threatened Milosevic's complete control over the institutions of power in the FRY and prompted a standoff. Bulatovic's supporters - likely with the backing of the Milosevic regime - attempted to thwart Djukanovic's victory by staging violent protests against Djukanovic's inauguration as President in January.

Despite the Montenegrin Government's legal rights under the FRY Constitution, federal authorities under Milosevic's control by year's end had not recognized the 20 Montenegrin members to the upper chamber of the Federal Assembly designtaed by the Montenegrin President. The Montenegrins in the federal body, including the speaker of the upper house, were not changed to reflect the results of Montenegrin elections. Moreover, in violation of the law, Milosevic installed Momir Bulatovic as Federal Prime Minister and ignored the Montenegrin Government's wish to have some voice in who was picked for this key position in the Federal power structure. Milosevic's antidemocratic control over Federal courts was demonstrated when the Federal Constitutional Court ruled against the Montenegrin Government late in the year in disallowing the Montenegrin president's attempt to select all 20 Montenegrin representatives to the Federal Assembly's Chamber of the Republics. The ruling was a complete reversal of a 1994 decision, which allowed Milosevic's ruling coalition in Serbia at the time to name all 20 Serbian representatives to the upper chamber while he was the President of the Serbian republic.

No legal restrictions exist on women's participation in government and politics, and women are active in political organizations. However, they are greatly underrepresented in party and government offices, holding less than 10 percent of ministerial-level positions in the Serbian and Federal Governments. An exception is the controversial Mira Markovic, wife of Federal President Milosevic. She is the leading force in the neo-Communist Yugoslav Left Party (JUL), through which she exerts extraordinary and disproportionate influence on policy makers. (In Montenegrin elections in May, JUL obtained 0.1 percent of the vote, which according to press reports was less than the Party of Universal Flying Yogis. To avoid humiliation, the Party pulled out of the race at the last moment.) In Kosovo, a woman leads one wing of the Social Democratic Party of Kosovo, and the LDK has three women in its 12-member presidency. However, according to Albanian women's groups, those women are exceptional in their political participation, and few Albanian women enter Kosovo politics because of a lack of interest, money, and family support.

No legal restrictions affect the role of minorities in government and politics, but ethnic Serbs and Montenegrins dominate the country's political leadership. Few members of other ethnic groups play any role at the top levels of government or the state-run economy. Ethnic Albanians in Kosovo refused to take part in the electoral process at the Serbian republic and federal level, including most recently in Serbian elections in 1997. They have virtually no representation in the Serbian republic and FRY government structures. However, this situation is not the case in Montenegro.

Ethnic Albanians' refusal to participate in FRY and Serbian elections has the practical effect of increasing the political influence of President Milosevic and his supporters. Ultranationalist parties, including Milosevic's coalition partner the Radical Party of Serbia, also have taken advantage of the ethnic Albanian boycott to garner representation beyond their numbers. Ethnic Albanians in the republic of Montenegro do participate in the political process. Albanian parties, candidates, and voters participated to a large degree in the republic's parliamentary elections in May and won a handful of seats in the republic's assembly. Several towns in Montenegro have Albanian mayors. Montenegro's current ruling coalition is multiethnic. Albanians and Muslims hold posts at the ministerial and deputy ministerial levels in the new Government formed in July.

Development of the Human Rights Situation

SECTION 4: GOVERNMENTAL ATTITUDE REGARDING INTERNATIONAL AND NON-GOVERNMENTAL INVESTIGATION OF ALLEGED VIOLATIONS OF HUMAN RIGHTS

The Governments of the republics of Serbia and Montenegro formally maintain that they have no objection to international organizations conducting human rights investigations on their territories. However, the Serbian regime routinely hindered the activities of and regularly rejected the findings of human rights groups. With some exceptions, the Milosevic Government's Federal Ministry of Foreign Affairs systematically denied visas to international non-governmental human rights organizations and denied entry visas to investigators from the ICTY who wished to conduct impartial investigations into allegations of atrocities committed by Serbian forces and Albanian paramilitary groups in Kosovo. In October the Government agreed to the establishment of the OSCE Kosovo Verification Mission (KVM). By year's end, the KVM had expanded to several hundred international verifiers, including human rights personnel, who verified civilian aspects of implementation of U.N. Security Council Resolution 1199. The Montenegrin Government's record toward outside investigations was much more cooperative, with the then Prime Minister taking the initiative to invite OSCE observers well in advance of presidential and parliamentary elections in the Republic.

The Milosevic regime repeatedly has ignored the ICTY's orders to transfer indicted war criminals known to be living in Serbia, in blatant defiance of the U.N. Security Council, which created the Tribunal. It also publicly rejected the Tribunals' mandate in Kosovo and obstructed all efforts by the ICTY to investigate allegations of crimes in Kosovo.

A number of independent human rights organizations operate in the country, researching and gathering information on abuses, and publicizing such cases. The Belgrade-based Humanitarian Law Center and Center for Antiwar Action researches human rights abuses throughout Serbia-Montenegro and, on occasion, elsewhere in the former Yugoslavia. The Belgrade-based Helsinki Committee for Human Rights in Serbia publishes studies on human rights issues and cooperates with the Pristina-based Helsinki Committee in monitoring human rights abuses in Kosovo. In Kosovo the Council for the Defense of Human Rights and Freedoms (CDHRF) collects and collates data on human rights abuses and publishes newsletters. A number of reliable international human rights monitors reported that one worker of the CDHRF was missing at year's end, and all the organization's workers are routinely and severely harassed and distrusted by Serbian authorities. In the Sandzak region, two committees monitor abuses against the local Muslim population and produce comprehensive reports. Most of these organizations offer advice and help to victims of abuse.

Local human rights monitors (Serbs as well as members of ethnic minorities) and NGO's worked under difficult circumstances. Human Rights Watch reports that three humanitarian aid workers were killed by mortar fire from Serbian forces while trying to deliver food near Kijevo on August 24. Rexhep Bislimi, an activist of the Urosevac chapter of the Pristina-based CDHRF died as the result of injuries inflicted by Serbian security forces while in detention (see Section 1.a.). Police arrested Bislimi on July 6 and later took him to Pristina hospital in critical condition, with several broken ribs. He underwent surgery on his kidneys and died after several days in a coma.

In May according to the ethnic Albanian Kosovo Information Center, Serbian police raided the premises of the local LDK party branch and the local chapter of the CDHRF in Glogovac. Police broke into the offices, destroyed furniture, and seized written materials. The Council reported that the police seized written materials, including copies of all recent human rights reports.

Serbian police arrested a local human rights activist, Zahrida Podrimcaku, in Pristina in June. She had been investigating events on May 31 in the village of Poklek, where police detained 10 ethnic Albanian men during an attack on the village. The body of one of the men was found the next day; the other nine are missing and presumed dead. Podrimcaku was charged with supporting terrorists and was awaiting trial as of the end of September.

NGO's reported several blockages to the delivery of humanitarian commodities. The Mother Teresa Society, a local humanitarian aid NGO, reported consistent harassment and detention of its staff. NGO's and the press reported that some 50 humanitarian aid workers were missing from Prizren. Mercy Corps-Pristina reported that police raided the warehouse of the Mother Teresa Society in Vucitrn in July. Serbian police confiscated 12.5 metric tons of flour and about 350 pounds (800 kg) of detergent during the distribution of relief supplies. Police also beat two aid workers and their driver.

ICRC officials complained in September of difficulties in securing access to detainees. However, by year's end ICRC officials reported that access to detainees improved (see Section 1.d.).

On December 10, Serbian police in armored vehicles prevented a Finnish forensic team from visiting the site of an alleged massacre of ethnic Albanians at Gornje Obrinje. Serbian authorities insisted on accompanying the team but would not permit ethnic Albanian observers to participate as well. Serbian authorities also failed to allow access to ICTY investigators to the Kosovo province, preventing the ICTY from carrying out independent and objective investigations into crimes within the Tribunal's jurisdiction.

Several NGO's and international organizations reported to international observers in December that they were experiencing unacceptable delays of up to a month or more in obtaining Serbian government approval of visas for international humanitarian aid workers for Kosovo.

As a signatory of the 1995 Dayton Accords that ended the war in Bosnia and Herzegovina, Serbia-Montenegro is obliged to cooperate fully with the ICTY by turning over to the Tribunal the persons on its territory who were indicted for war crimes or other crimes against humanity under the jurisdiction of the Tribunal.

In December, in open defiance of UNSCR 1207 and previous resolutions that demanded that the FRY turn over all indicted war criminals on its territory, a Belgrade military court invited three Yugoslav generals, two retired and one active, who were indicted by the ICTY to "hearings." The "Vukovar Three" as they are known - Veselin Sljivancanin, Mile Mrksic, and Miroslav Radic - were indicted by the Tribunal in 1995 for their role in the murder of over 200 unarmed men at Vukovar Hospital in Croatia 1991. They appeared at the hearings in Belgrade in late December, in open defiance of the Tribunal's request for deferment of the case to its jurisdiction. The Milosevic government's actions constituted an open acknowledgment that it harbors indicted war criminals. In the 5 years since the Tribunal was established, the Milosevic regime has yet to transfer one Serbian or Bosnian Serb indictee to the Hague, in violation of its obligations under repeated U.N. Security Council resolutions and its commitments under the Dayton Accords. Some of those indicted live openly in Serbia, and others travel freely in and out of Serbia. It is widely alleged that Ratko Mladic, who was indicted by the Tribunal in 1995 for his command and responsibility role in crimes against humanity, grave breaches of the Geneva Conventions, and violations of the laws and customs of war committed during the conflict in Bosnia and Herzegovina, continues to travel in and out of the country. In August indicted war crimes suspect Slobodan Miljkovic was killed in a barroom brawl in the Serbian city of Kragujevac.

The Milosevic regime's brutal crackdown in Kosovo prompted calls for the ICTY to conduct investigations into alleged atrocities committed there. *The ICTY's jurisdiction also is delineated clearly under UNSCR 827 of 1993 and many subsequent resolutions.* The regime so far has been uncooperative, claiming that the violence in Kosovo does not constitute an "armed conflict." In contrast, authorities in Montenegro have cooperated with the ICTY.

SECTION 5: DISCRIMINATION BASED ON RACE, SEX, RELIGION, DISABILITY, LANGUAGE, OR SOCIAL STATUS

While Federal and republic laws provide for equal rights for all citizens, *regardless of ethnic group, religion, language, or social status,* and prohibit discrimination against women, in reality the legal system provides little protection to such groups.

Women

The traditionally high level of domestic violence persisted. The few official agencies dedicated to coping with family violence have inadequate resources and are limited in their activity by social pressure to keep families together at all costs. Few victims of spousal abuse ever file complaints with the authorities. The Center for Autonomous Women's Rights offers a rape and spousal abuse hot line, as well as sponsors a number of self-help groups. The Center also offered help to refugee women, many of whom experienced extreme abuse or rape during the conflict in the former Yugoslavia. However, tradition prevents much discussion of the topic of rape among Albanians, since the act is seen as dishonoring the entire family. According to the Center for the Protection of Women and Children in Pristina, rape is not recognized as a crime in Albanian society, making the subject even more secretive.

Women do not enjoy status equal to men in the FRY, and relatively few women obtain upper level management positions in commerce. Traditional patriarchal ideas of gender roles, which hold that women should be subservient to the male members of their family, have long subjected women to discrimination. In some rural areas, particularly among minority communities, women are little more than serfs without the ability to exercise their right to control property and children. However, women in the FRY legally are entitled to equal pay for equal work and are granted maternity leave for 1 year, with an additional 6 months available. Moreover, the lack of job opportunities for women in Kosovo has reinforced the traditional culture in which women remain at home. The cost of an education in Kosovo - fees for enrollment in the parallel system, transportation, clothes, and school supplies - made families reluctant to send girls to school since the prospect of future employment was slim. Women are active in political and human rights organizations. Women's rights groups continue to operate with little or no official acknowledgment.

Children

The State attempts to meet the health and educational needs of children. The educational system provides 8 years of mandatory schooling. Montenegrin authorities at one point denied the children of IDP's from Kosovo basic education, claiming that the republic lacked sufficient resources to educate this group. Montenegrin officials were working with international organizations in the second half of the year to seek assistance that would allow them to ensure education benefits to the IDP's.

The current division of Kosovo into parallel administrative systems results in Serb and Albanian Kosovar elementary age children being taught in separate areas of divided schools, or attending classes in shifts. Older Albanian Kosovar children attend school in private homes. The quality of the education thus was uneven before the conflict started, and the tension and division of society in general has been replicated to the detriment of the children.

An agreement negotiated under the auspices of the Rome-based Sant-Egidio community and signed in 1996 by President Milosevic and Dr. Ibrahim Rugova, the leader of the Democratic League of Kosovo, sought to resolve the division of the educational system and lend impetus to efforts to normalize the situation within Kosovo. An "implementation" agreement was signed in March, but it unraveled as a result of the outbreak of conflict in Kosovo at about the same time. Small gains remain, including the turnover of a large classroom facility to the ethnic Albanian parallel university in Pristina. In November the U.N. Children's Fund estimated that between 55,000 and 60,000 Albanian children were not in school in the Albanian parallel educational system because schools were not functioning in Decane, Klina, Glogovac, Srbica, and Djakovica. According to ethnic Albanian educational authorities, there were 100 destroyed or damaged schools throughout Kosovo. In December international observers reported multiple incidents of police being stationed near schools in Kosovo. Albanian villagers claimed that they were intimidated by the police presence and that consequently children would not return to those schools.

Economic distress spilled over into the health care system, adversely affecting children. In Kosovo the health situation for children remained particularly poor. Humanitarian aid officials blamed the high rate of infant and childhood mortality, as well as increasing epidemics of preventable diseases, primarily on poverty that led to malnutrition and poor hygiene and to the deterioration of public sanitation. Ethnic minorities in some cases fear Serb state-run medical facilities, which results in a low rate of immunization and a reluctance to seek timely medical attention. According to the Center for Protection of Women and Children in Pristina, 63 percent of Kosovo IDP's are children.

There is no societal pattern of abuse of children.

People With Disabilities

Facilities for persons with disabilities are inadequate, but the Government made some effort to address the problem. The law prohibits discrimination against persons with disabilities in employment, education, or in the provision of other state services. The law mandates access to new official buildings, and the Government enforces these provisions in practice.

Religious Minorities

Religion and ethnicity are so closely intertwined as to be inseparable. Serious discrimination against, and harassment of, religious minorities continued, especially in Kosovo and Serbian Sandzak. Violence against the Catholic minority in Vojvodina, largely made up of ethnic Hungarians and Croats, also was reported.

National/Racial/Ethnic Minorities

There were credible reports that ethnic Albanians and Muslims in Serbia continued to be driven from their homes or fired from their jobs on the basis of religion or ethnicity. Other ethnic minorities, including ethnic Hungarians in Vojvodina, also allege discrimination. Vojvodina Croats reported no progress during the year on their demand for separate curriculums in the schools or programs in the media in the Croatian language. However, an hour was set aside for programs in Croatian on the local radio station, Radio Subotica.

The Romani population generally is tolerated, and there is no official discrimination. Roma have the right to vote, and there are two small Romani parties. However, prejudice against Roma is widespread. Local authorities often ignore or condone societal intimidation of the Romani community. Skinheads and police occasionally violently attacked Roma (see Section 1.c.).

SECTION 6: WORKER RIGHTS

a. The Right of Association

All workers except military and police personnel have the legal right to join or form unions. Unions are either official (government affiliated) or independent. The total labor force is approximately 2.3 million. The government-controlled Alliance of Independent Labor Unions (Samostalni Sindikati) claims 1.8 million members but probably numbers closer to 1 million in reality. The largest independent union is the United Branch Independent Labor Unions (Nezavisnost), which has about 170,000 members. Most other independent unions are sector specific, for example, the Independent Union of Bank Employees (12,000 members). Due to the poor state of the economy, over one-half of union workers are on long-term mandatory leave from their firms pending increases in production. The independent unions, while active in recruiting new members, have not yet reached the size needed to enable countrywide strikes. The independent unions also claim that the Government prevents effective recruiting through a number of tactics, which include preventing the busing of workers to strikes, threatening the job security of members, and failing to grant visas to foreign visitors who support independent unions. Some foreign union organizers managed to secure visas during the year after long delays.

The largely splintered approach of the independent unions left them little to show in terms of increased wages or improved working conditions. The Nezavisnost union gained new members as a result of its well-organized and tough bargaining positions during strikes of teachers and health workers in the spring. The official union lost credibility with some of its members because it ultimately accommodated the government's position on these strikes. The ability of unions to affiliate internationally remains constrained.

b. The Right to Organize and Bargain Collectively

While this right is provided for under law, collective bargaining remains at a rudimentary level of development. Individual unions tend to be very narrow and pragmatic in their aims, unable to join with unions in other sectors to bargain for common purposes. The history of trade unionism in the country has centered not on bargaining for the collective needs of all workers but rather for the specific needs of a given group of workers. Thus, coal workers, teachers, health workers, and electric power industry employees have been ineffective in finding common denominators (e.g., job security protection, minimum safety standards, universal workers' benefits, etc.) on which to negotiate. The overall result is a highly fragmented labor structure composed of workers who relate to the needs of their individual union but rarely to those of other workers. Additionally, job security fears, which stem from the high rate of unemployment, limited workers' militancy.

The Government still is seeking to develop free trade zones.

c. Prohibition of Forced or Compulsory Labor

Forced labor, including that performed by children, is prohibited by law and is not known to occur.

d. Status of Child Labor Practices and Minimum Age for Employment

The minimum age for employment is 16 years, although in villages and farming communities it is not unusual to find younger children at work assisting their families. With an actual unemployment rate (registered unemployed plus redundant workers who show up at the workplace but perform only minimal work) in excess of 60 percent, real employment opportunities for children are nonexistent. Forced and bonded labor by children is prohibited by law and is not known to occur (see Section 6.c.). However, children can be found in a variety of unofficial "retail" jobs, typically washing car windows or selling small items such as cigarettes.

e. Acceptable Conditions of Work

Large government enterprises, including all the major banks, industrial, and trading companies generally observe minimum wage standards. The monthly minimum wage is approximately $20 to $40 (Din 250 to 500). However, this figure is roughly comparable to unemployment benefits and (at least theoretically) is paid to workers who have been placed in a mandatory leave status. The actual minimum wage is at the low end of the range of average net salaries, $85 to $106 (Din 700 to 1,200). The minimum wage is insufficient to provide a decent standard of living for a worker and family. The cost of food and utilities alone for a family of four is estimated to be $230 (Din 2,150) per month. Private enterprises use the minimum wage as a guide but tend to pay somewhat higher average wages.

Reports of sweatshops operating in the country are rare, although some privately owned textile factories operate in very poor conditions. The official workweek, listed as 40 hours, had little meaning in an economy with massive underemployment and unemployment. Neither employers nor employees tended to give high priority to the enforcement of established occupational safety and health regulations, focusing their efforts instead on economic survival. In light of the competition for employment, and the high degree of government control over the economy, workers are not free to leave hazardous work situations without risking the loss of their employment.

46. U.S., Erasing History: Ethnic Cleansing in Kosovo, Report Released by the U.S. Department of State, Washington, D.C., May 1999

[All figures have been omitted]

Executive Summary

This report is part of a larger international effort to lay out the contours of the ethnic cleansing in Kosovo, which dramatically accelerated in mid-March, 1999. In preparing this report, the United States Government has drawn on its own resources, as well as reports received from international organizations and non-governmental organizations (NGOs) to date. We encourage others to make their own contributions to record these events, get the facts out, and ultimately, hold the perpetrators of these crimes accountable.

This document provides a chronology of events after the departure of the OSCE's Kosovo Verification Mission on March 19, 1999, which prior to its departure had been regularly issuing human rights reporting. It is compiled from hundreds, if not thousands, of reported violations of human rights and humanitarian law since late March 1999. Due to lack of outside access to Kosovo, this report represents only a partial account of the ethnic cleansing.

The term "ethnic cleansing" generally entails the systematic and forced removal of members of an ethnic group from their communities to change the ethnic composition of a region. Although we are still gaining information on all aspects of Serbian efforts to ethnically cleanse Kosovo, reports of human rights and humanitarian law violations we have received fall under seven broad categories:

1. Forced expulsions: The regime of Slobodan Milosevic is conducting a campaign of forced migration on a scale not seen in Europe since the Second World War. More than 90 percent of all ethnic Albanians have been expelled from their homes in Kosovo. In contrast to last fall, when attacks on civilians by Serb security forces generally occurred in small villages, this spring Yugoslav Army and Special Police units have joined with recently-armed Serb civilians to expel their neighbors from almost all towns and villages in Kosovo:

An estimated 600,000 internally displaced persons are now struggling to survive in Kosovo. They are scattered throughout the province, often taking shelter in isolated forests and mountain valleys. Approximately 700,000 Kosovars have taken refuge in Albania, Bosnia-Herzegovina, the Former Yugoslav Republic of Macedonia, and the Republic of Montenegro since hostilities commenced in March 1998. Over three-fourths of these people have arrived since late March.

2. Looting and Burning: Some 500 residential areas have been at least partially burned since late March, including over 300 villages burned since April 4, according to overhead imagery. Besides houses and apartments, mosques, churches, schools, and medical facilities have also been targeted and destroyed. Many settlements have been totally destroyed in an attempt to ensure that the ethnic Albanian residents do not return.

3. Detentions: There are consistent refugee reports that Serbian forces are separating military-aged men from their families in a systematic pattern. At the time of writing, the total number of missing men and their fate is unknown.

4. Summary Execution: Refugees have provided accounts of summary executions in at least 70 towns and villages throughout Kosovo. In addition to random executions, Serbian authorities are targeting intellectuals, professionals, and community leaders.

5. Rape: Ethnic Albanian women are reportedly being raped in increasing numbers. Refugee accounts indicate systematic and organized mass rapes in Djakovica and Pec. We believe that many crimes of gender violence have not been reported due to the cultural stigma attached to these offenses in Kosovar society.

6. Violations of Medical Neutrality: NGOs report that since late March, violations of medical neutrality in Kosovo have accelerated dramatically. Serb authorities have looted and destroyed dozens of medical facilities, murdered Kosovar Albanian physicians, expelled ethnic Albanian patients and care providers from hospitals, and have used large numbers of health facilities as protective cover for military activities. The apparent goal is to effectively deny health care to ethnic Albanians and extinguish the community base that Kosovo's health professionals provide.

7. Identity Cleansing: Refugees report that Serbian authorities have confiscated passports and other identity papers, systematically destroyed voter registers and other aspects of Kosovo's civil registry, and

even removed license plates from departing vehicles as part of a policy to prevent returns to Kosovo. Reports of identity cleansing are prevalent in refugee camps in Macedonia and Albania.

Introduction

With this report, the United States offers a documentary record of the war crimes, crimes against humanity, and human rights violations that underpin the current tragedy of ethnic cleansing in Kosovo. At this writing, the forces of Yugoslav President Slobodan Milosevic continue to burn, loot, rape, shell, and de-populate Kosovo, and thousands of refugees continue to flee into neighboring Albania and Macedonia. Although we do not yet know all the details, the fact that this crisis has happened so quickly, methodically, and so savagely, strongly suggests that Serb forces acted based on plans drawn up long before NATO intervened.

The refugees coming out of Kosovo are only now beginning to tell their stories. Yet even these fragmented accounts portray a systematic policy of ethnic cleansing:

- Serbian forces have made Pristina, the capital of Kosovo, a ghost town. Serbian military, police, and paramilitary forces reportedly expelled between 100,000 to 120,000 persons from Pristina in only four days. Kosovars now in Macedonia have claimed that only 100 ethnic Albanians remain in Pristina. Serbian forces reportedly had been taking furniture from abandoned homes.

- In Pec, Serbian forces allegedly herded young Albanian women to the Hotel Karagac, and raped them repeatedly. The commander of the local base reportedly used a roster of soldiers' names to allow his troops to visit the hotel on a rotating basis. The Hotel Karagac is only one example of the gender violence that plays such a large role in Serbian actions in Kosovo.

- Reports indicate that the violence in western Kosovo is stronger than in any other region of the province. Serbian forces emptied Pec of ethnic Albanians in 24 hours. In Djakovica's old city, Serbian forces allegedly burned 200 to 600 homes the day after NATO airstrikes began. By the next day, the rest of the old city had been torched.

- Serbian forces have forced thousands of Kosovars onto trains and sent them to border crossings in Macedonia. Some refugees reported arriving at train stations in buses arranged by the Serb Army. Others reported a mass of humanity - thousands - waiting for trains at gunpoint.

- Based on consistent refugee accounts, the UN High Commissioner for Refugees reported that the Djakovica region "undoubtedly has been one of the most violent and cruel in the whole of Kosovo, turning it at times into a virtual killing field."

The United States had hoped to resolve the crisis in Kosovo through the use of diplomacy backed by the threat of force. Only after Belgrade repeatedly rejected the diplomatic solution offered and re-offered at Rambouillet - and only after it became clear that the Milosevic regime launched attacks on the civilian population in Kosovo and demonstrated its determination to have its way in Kosovo no matter what the consequences - did NATO pursue a policy of force backed by diplomacy, justified by law and humanitarian necessity.

We have made it clear to the government of Serbia what it will take to end NATO intervention: an immediate halt to all violence and repression in Kosovo; the withdrawal of Serbian military, paramilitary, and police forces; the unconditional safe return of all refugees and internally displaced; the stationing of an international security force; and the establishment of a political framework for Kosovo based on the Rambouillet accords.

In the meantime, we will continue to seek justice for the hundreds of thousands of Kosovo's ethnic Albanians who have suffered at the hands of Serbian forces. We are working closely with the International Criminal Tribunal for the Former Yugoslavia (ICTY), the Organization for Security and Cooperation in Europe (OSCE), and the appropriate United Nations human rights and refugee mechanisms to address, document, and ultimately reverse the damage created by these crimes. As part of this effort, non-governmental organizations working in Macedonia and Albania have joined international organizations in an unprecedented alliance to document abuses, supply evidence to the ICTY, and get the story of ethnic cleansing out to the public at large. We wish to thank the American Bar Association's Central and East European Law Initiative, Physicians for Human Rights, and the Coalition for International Justice for their contributions to this effort.

We also have secured general agreement among the ICTY, the OSCE, the Council of Europe, the major UN human rights institutions, and many of the leading NGOs in-theater to use a standard form for refugee accounts (see figure 1) that will allow for the coherent collection and packaging of refugee accounts. Refugees are participating in this effort on a voluntary basis. In response to requests from the ICTY, the U.S. Government is ensuring that refugees who have been selected for residence in the United States are properly interviewed for ICTY purposes. By standardizing the refugee interview process, not only will we ensure that the ICTY has information in a usable form for future investigations and prosecutions, but the resulting data can be aggregated and used as the basis for future reports and updates on war crimes, crimes against humanity and human right violations in Kosovo.

This report chronicles some of the history of the recent ethnic cleansing in Kosovo, beginning with the withdrawal of the OSCE's Kosovo Verification Mission (KVM) on March 19, 1999. The KVM had been issuing reports on human rights conditions until its departure. With the crisis still taking place, it is not yet possible to provide a complete appraisal. Furthermore, the Serbian government's refusal to cooperate with the ICTY or to allow any independent monitors or media into Kosovo since the withdrawal of the KVM has limited efforts to document the scope and extent of ethnic cleansing. Due to limited access to Serbia, the report also does not address the situation of Serb refugees from Kosovo. Thus the report should be regarded only as a snapshot of the tragic events and incidents that have unfolded in recent weeks. A more comprehensive accounting, built in part on refugee interviews and in part on on-site investigations, still must take place, hopefully in the near future.

Staff in the Bureaus of Intelligence and Research and Democracy, Human Rights, and Labor at the Department of State, working in conjunction with staff from the Bureau of Population, Refugees and Migration, the Bureau of European Affairs, and the Office of War Crimes Issues, undertook the research and writing of this report. It is based on multiple sources, including foreign governments, international organizations, non-governmental human rights and humanitarian relief organizations, refugees, combatants, and the press.

This report begins the process of telling the world a story it has heard thus far only in bits and pieces. Although incomplete, it already has taught us much. We have watched families, uprooted and torn asunder, stagger across Kosovo's borders. We have seen the locked trains on one-way missions of despair. We have consoled children weeping for parents they cannot find. We have listened to the stories of people whose fathers, brothers, sons, and husbands were led away. We have reached out to rape victims struck mute by savagery. We have seen ominous overhead photos of freshly-upturned earth and burned-out towns. Already we can testify to the horror. Already we are witnesses.

We - as a people, as a nation, as a world - cannot let such outrageous violations of human rights stand. That is why NATO continues to fight for the victims of Belgrade's ethnic cleansing.

Overview

What began in late February 1998 as a Serb government campaign against the separatist Kosovo Liberation Army (KLA) has evolved into a comprehensive, premeditated, and systematic program to ethnically cleanse the Serbian province of Kosovo of its roughly 1.7 million ethnic Albanian residents (also referred to as Kosovar Albanians). Because Serbian authorities have denied access to international monitors, documentation efforts have been too fragmented to estimate definitively the number of missing and dead.

Serb military, paramilitary, and police forces have forcibly expelled over 1 million Kosovars from their homes. Since March 1998, approximately 700,000 Kosovars have fled to neighboring states, including Albania, Bosnia-Herzegovina, the Former Yugoslav Republic of Macedonia, and the Republic of Montenegro. As many as an additional 600,000 Kosovars could be internally displaced. In the process, Serbian forces have conducted summary executions, separated military-age men from their families, raped women and girls, destroyed mosques and churches, converted medical facilities to military outposts, and looted and burned homes and villages.

The term "ethnic cleansing" first came into use during the mass expulsions of ethnic Muslims from towns in eastern Bosnia-Herzegovina in 1992; since then, media outlets, human rights groups and governments have used it on enough occasions to require careful definition. As used in this report, ethnic cleansing is defined as the systematic and forced removal of the members of an ethnic group from a community or communities in order to change the ethnic composition of a given region. In Bosnia, many ethnically cleansed towns and regions were eventually reoccupied by members of another ethnic group (who themselves often had been cleansed).

From the beginning, the regime in Belgrade has deliberately misled the international community and its own people about its ethnic cleansing campaign. Counterinsurgency operations against the KLA began in late February and early March 1998, when Serbian Ministry of Internal Affairs Police (MUP) attacked the villages of Likosane and Cirez. These attacks resulted in the death of 25 Kosovar Albanians, of which as many as 14 may have been summarily executed. Since then, the MUP, Yugoslav Army (VJ) forces, and paramilitary units have made little effort to distinguish between KLA fighters and civilians.

In late March 1999, Serbian forces dramatically increased the scope and pace of their efforts, moving away from selective targeting of towns and regions suspected of KLA sympathies toward a sustained and systematic effort to ethnically cleanse the entire province of Kosovo. To date, Serb forces conducting ethnic cleansing operations have not yet tried to repopulate the over 500 towns and villages from which residents have been evicted. Some villages are now used as cover for Serb military emplacements. Many, however, remain depopulated. NATO is committed to ensuring the return of all Kosovars to their homes.

Since the March 19, 1999 departure of the OSCE Kosovo Verification Mission, the Office of the United Nations High Commissioner for Refugees (UNHCR) estimates that over 700,000 Kosovars have fled to the Former Yugoslav Republic of Macedonia (211,000), Albania (404,000), Bosnia-Herzegovina (17,000) the Republic of Montenegro (62,000), and elsewhere (as of May 5, 1999). The Governments of Macedonia, Albania, Bosnia, and Montenegro have provided land for camps, logistical support, and protection. NATO forces in Macedonia and Albania have helped establish transit camps. Other governments have begun to accept varying numbers of refugees to ease the pressure on the so-called "front-line" states. Even with such support, however, the front-line states will continue to bear the brunt of these mass expulsions, which has badly burdened the economies and upset the political balances of these states.

Although the media has focused almost exclusively on the story of the hundreds of thousands of exhausted refugees arriving at camps in Macedonia and Albania, another story has escaped their attention, in large part because Serbian authorities have not permitted entry into Kosovo. Those left behind in Kosovo - known as internally displaced persons, or IDPs - suffer under much worse conditions than even those faced by refugees. While independent sources have not been able to confirm reports of starvation among IDPs in Kosovo many in all likelihood are experiencing food shortages, malnutrition, health problems, and other types of deprivation as a result of having to hide from Serbian forces for weeks in neighboring mountains and forests. Needless to say, they also likely face attack by Serbian forces. According to some reports, VJ units have thrown grenades from helicopters at fleeing IDPs. Shelling of civilians reportedly has been used to herd groups of refugees for later deportation.

Reports of the detention and summary execution of military-aged men continue to increase. In recent weeks, refugees have reported that Serbian forces have undertaken mass executions and individual summary executions in at least 70 towns and villages throughout the province. Overhead imagery confirms the presence of mass grave sites in Pusto Selo and Izbica (see figure 2 and figure 3); there may be other sites in Drenica, Kaaniku, Malisevo, Rezala, and the Pagarusa valley. Anecdotal refugee accounts suggest that Serbian forces have executed at least 4,000 Kosovars. This number is likely to increase with the collection of additional data as will the already much larger number of persons unaccounted for.

In recent weeks, refugees have reported a new method of execution: Serbian forces order unarmed ethnic Albanian men to run away, and then shoot them. Serb authorities apparently favor this method so that they can portray the murders as collateral casualties of military operations.

There are increasing numbers of reports of the rape of ethnic Albanian women by Serbian security forces, both on an organized basis and by individual members of Serbian forces. According to refugees, organized rape has occurred in Djakovica and at the Hotel Karagac in Pec.

Documenting the Abuses

Since the withdrawal of the KVM on March 19, 1999, Serbian military, paramilitary, and police forces in Kosovo have committed a wide range of war crimes, crimes against humanity, and other violations of international humanitarian and human rights law. This report briefly reviews seven categories of such crimes: forced expulsion of Kosovars from their homes; burning and looting of homes, schools, religious sites and healthcare facilities; detention, particularly of military-age men; summary execution; rape; violations of medical neutrality; and identity cleansing.

1) FORCED EXPULSIONS

The regime of President Slobodan Milosevic is conducting a campaign of forced migration on a scale not seen in Europe since the Second World War. Serbian forces appear to have driven the vast majority of Kosovars from their homes, trapping many within Kosovo, while pushing even larger numbers over Kosovo's borders. The Serbian authorities' claim that the refugee crisis is the result of popular fear of NATO airstrikes is belied by the regime's redeployment of its military forces in the weeks prior to its rejection of the Rambouillet settlement. Refugees consistently report that they fled their homes not because of any concern about NATO airstrikes, but because Serbian forces threatened them at gunpoint.

In contrast to last fall, when attacks on civilians by Serbian security forces generally occurred in small villages, this spring VJ and MUP units have apparently joined with recently armed Serb civilians to expel their neighbors from both villages and the larger towns of Kosovo. Serbian forces reportedly have been going house-to-house to rob Kosovars before looting and burning their homes. Before allowing ethnic Albanians to flee Kosovo, some Serbian officials have forced them to sign disclaimers saying that they left voluntarily. The fact that many of the places targeted reportedly had not been the scene of any previous fighting or KLA activity, indicates that these expulsions were part of a systematic effort to depopulate the region of Kosovar Albanians.

Current status of IDPs. About 600,000 internally displaced persons are now struggling to survive in Kosovo. They are scattered throughout the province, often seeking shelter in isolated forests and mountain valleys. Many have not been able to move very far from their home villages. Typically, they are found in encampments with a combination of tents, crude shelters, tractors, flat-bed trailers, farm tractors, and automobiles. In some areas, there are reports of severe shortages and hunger, particularly in the mountain encampments.

Major clusters of IDPs can be found at the following sites (see figure 4): Tusilje-Tica camp; Obrinje camp; Novo Selo-Crnoljevo camp; Kijevo camp; Studenica camp; Bradas camp; Duz-Kolic camp.

Current status of refugees. Almost 700,000 Kosovars have fled to Albania, Macedonia, Montenegro, and Bosnia and Herzegovina (see figure 5) since hostilities commenced in March 1998. The number of displaced outside of Kosovo but in Serbia proper is unknown. Over three-fourths of the 700,000 refugees have arrived since late March. At the peak of the exodus, refugees attempting to enter Albania and Macedonia formed lines many miles in length from the border. While Serbian authorities have caused this mass exodus to take place, they have alternately allowed refugees to cross the border, and then prevented them from doing so. This has made the efforts by refugee and relief agencies to accommodate refugees even more difficult by creating confusion and uncertainty. Serbian authorities overseeing the expulsion seem to systematically expel Kosovar Albanians, distributing the movements among crossing points so as to manage the expulsions to achieve a political result.

According to the UNHCR, some 65,000 refugees left Kosovo during a one week period in mid-April and various sources indicate that tens of thousands more are moving toward the Albanian and Macedonian borders. The UN has more recently reported that thousands of additional refugees have arrived in Macedonia, and that the situation in the refugee camps there has reached a critical point. Macedonian camps are overcrowded and tensions are rising. The health and sanitation situation is quickly deteriorating, leading relief workers to fear the outbreak of epidemics in the camps with the onset of warmer weather.

As of May 5, an estimated 1.5 million Kosovar Albanians have been displaced from their homes:

Kosovo (IDPs): 600,000

Albania: 404,000

Montenegro: 62,000

Macedonia: 211,000

Bosnia: 38,000 (includes 20,000 Sandzak Muslims)

Other countries: 160,000 (includes 30,000 ethnic Serbs)

2) LOOTING AND BURNING

More than 600 settlements have been at least partially damaged since October, 1998 (see figure 6), including over 300 villages burned since April 4, according to overhead imagery. Most Serb homes and stores reportedly have remained intact, and according to refugee reports, Serb civilians in the town of Vucitrn painted a Cyrillic "S" on their doors so that Serbian forces would not attack their homes by mistake. The destruction appears to be much more extensive and thorough than occurred last summer. Many settlements were totally destroyed in an apparent attempt to ensure that the ethnic Albanian population could not return. Serbian forces have reportedly burned all houses previously rented to OSCE observers in Vucitrn, Stimlje, and Mitrovica.

Refugees report that mosques and religious sites have been attacked or destroyed in at least 21 villages and towns. Refugees also report that schools have been attacked or destroyed in at least 14 villages and towns.

Imagery confirms that the following villages have been burned or largely destroyed:

Bajcina, Bajgora, Banja, Batlava, Bela Crkva, Bradas, Celine, Crebnik, Crni Lug, Dobri Do, Donja Penduha, Donja Lapistica, Donji Retimlje, Donji Streoci, Dumos, Gajrak, Gedje, Godisnjak, Gornja Zakut, Gornje Pakastica, Gornji Crnobreg, Gornji Streoci, Jablanica, Jovic, Kacandol, Klincina, Letance, Lipovac, Luzane, Mamusa, Madare, Mala Hoca, Malisevo, Mirusa, Neprebiste, Novo Selo Begova, Pantina, Pasoma, Radoste, Randubrava Retimlje, Rogovo, Skorosnik, Slatina, Smac, Sopnic, Stanica Donje Ljupce, Suvi Do, Vlaski Drenovac, Vucitrn, Vujitun, Zrze

3) DETENTION

There are consistent refugee reports that Serbian forces are separating military-aged men from their families, in what appears to be a systematic pattern. A disproportionate percentage of refugees allowed to flee Kosovo, especially into Albania, are women, the elderly, and children. At this writing, the number of missing men and their fate are unknown. Mass detention sites include:

- Djeneral Jankovic: A cement factory in this town is reportedly being used as a detention center for 5,000 ethnic Albanians.

- Glogovac: The Ferro-Nickel factory in this town was reportedly being used as a detention center for a large number of Kosovars; it was allegedly used as a detention and execution site during last year's security operation.

- Srbica: Press sources report that as many as 20,000 ethnic Albanians-including women and children - were taken by forced march from the town of Cirez to Srbica as human shields for Serbian tanks before being detained in a munitions factory.

- Vucitrn: An unknown number of ethnic Albanians were reportedly herded into a school in this town.

4) SUMMARY EXECUTION

Refugees have provided accounts of summary executions in at least 70 towns and villages throughout Kosovo. Kosovar Albanian refugees from throughout the province continue to report mass executions. In addition, there are reports of mass graves in Drenica, Kaaniku, Rezalla, Malisevo, Pusto Selo, Izbica, and the Pagarusa valley. Serbian security forces reportedly locked an entire family into a house in a village in Drenica and burned them alive. Overhead imagery has provided evidence that corroborates at least two reports-the summary executions at Izbica and Pusto Selo (see figure 2 and figure 3). In addition to random executions, the Serbian authorities appear to be targeting Kosovar intellectuals, professionals, and leaders.

5) RAPE

Ethnic Albanian women are reportedly being raped in increasing numbers; according to refugees, Serbian forces have raped women in an organized and systematic fashion in Djakovica and Pec. Rape victims were reportedly separated from their families and sent to an army camp near Djakovica where Serbian soldiers repeatedly raped them. In Pec, refugees alleged that Serbian forces rounded up young Albanian women and took them to the Hotel Karagac, where they were raped repeatedly. The commander of the local base reportedly uses a roster of soldiers' names to allow all of his troops an evening in the hotel. In addition to these specific accounts, refugees claim that during Serbian forces' raids on their villages, young women have been gang raped in homes and on the sides of roads. We believe that there may be many more incidents that have not been reported because of the cultural stigma attached to this offense in traditional Kosovar society.

6) VIOLATIONS OF MEDICAL NEUTRALITY

Refugees have reported that Serbian forces systematically attacked ethnic Albanian physicians, patients, and Kosovar medical facilities. Reports indicate that violations of medical neutrality by Serbian forces include killings, torture, detention, imprisonment, and forced disappearances of Kosovar physicians - one NGO has documented the killings of seven ethnic Albanian doctors within the past year. In addition to targeting individuals, Serbian forces reportedly have looted and destroyed numerous clinics, private health centers, pharmacies, and other medical facilities run by ethnic Albanian medical personnel. According to reports, since late March, violations of medical neutrality have accelerated dramatically, and have been directed against the entire ethnic Albanian population throughout Kosovo, effectively depriving them of medical and health care altogether. In the past month, Serbian healthcare providers, police and military reportedly have expelled ethnic Albanian patients and healthcare providers from health facilities, and then used a number of these health facilities as protective cover for military activities. In late March the Serbian medical directors of the state hospitals of Pristina and Pec allegedly dismissed all ethnic Albanian physicians from their staffs and expelled all ethnic Albanian patients, including those critically ill.

Refugees have reported that government and private clinics, pharmacies, and other healthcare structures in the following cities and villages are among those that have been damaged or destroyed: Cirez; Decani; Glogovac; Gnjilane; Gornja Klina; Grebno; Kacanik; Kamena Glava; Klina; Kosovska Mitrovica; Lipljan; Magura; Malisevo; Nevoljane; Orahovac; Obilic; Pristina; Shtimlje; Srbica; Urosevac; Vucitrn.

7) IDENTITY CLEANSING

In addition to reports of Serbian VJ, MUP, and paramilitary forces looting Kosovar homes and businesses, refugees report that Serbian forces robbed them of their remaining personal belongings before they allowed them to leave Kosovo. Reports of Serbian forces confiscating documentation, including national identity papers, and told them that they would never be allowed to return to their villages. The destruction of voter registers and other aspects of Kosovo's civil registry along with the removal of license plates from departing vehicles have also been reported. The United States and others are in the process of fully documenting the scope of Belgrade's identity cleansing.

Atrocities and War Crimes by Location

The following is a partial list of alleged war crimes and violations of international humanitarian law committed in Kosovo since late March 1999. These are fragmentary accounts that are being investigated and documented:

Bela Crkva

Serbian forces reportedly killed 35 people, then dumped their bodies near the Bellaja River (between the Rogova and Bela Crvka railroad). By March 28, Serbian forces reportedly had killed as many as 500 civilians in this town.

Belenica

Serbian forces reportedly executed 60 young male Kosovar Albanians on April 1.

Brusnik

Serbian forces reportedly burned down this village near Vucitrn in early April. A Kosovar refugee claimed that Serbian forces killed 100 ethnic Albanians there following the Rambouillet conference.

Cecelija

On May 4, refugees arriving in Albania from the Kosovo village of Shale reported that they were stopped in the village of Cecelija, where Serbian forces removed all the men from a tractor convoy and killed them. Also on May 4, Albanian TV in Tirana reported by telephone from Shale on the burial of 63 bodies of individuals killed by Serbian forces on May 2. These may be the bodies of those killed in Cecelija.

Cirez

20,000 Albanian Kosovars were reportedly used as human shields against NATO bombings.

Djakovica

Armed Serb civilians have been active in the town and reportedly burned a building while a group of ethnic Albanians were taking cover in it during a NATO airstrike. Kosovars in the town were warned to leave by March 29. Serbian forces began burning their homes and businesses. Men reportedly were separated from women and children. In addition, MUP and paramilitary units in this city reportedly executed over 100 ethnic Albanians. Seventy bodies reportedly were found in two houses and 33 were found in a nearby river. Nearly 14,000 refugees from Djakovica fled to the Albanian border crossing point at Prushit on April 5. According to refugee reports, on April 27, Serbian forces executed 200 military aged ethnic Albanian men.

Djeneral Jankovic

Several refugees claim that Serbian security forces have detained as many as 5,000 ethnic Albanians in a cement factory in this border town.

Glodane

In early April a large concentration of displaced Kosovars was observed in this town under guard by Serbian forces. Eight hours later they were no longer there and the village was ablaze.

Glogovac

The Albanian residential area has been burned, sending IDPs into the Cicavica Mountains. On April 12, Serbian forces reportedly executed 50 ethnic Albanian refugees as they were leaving town. Glogovac also reportedly houses a mass detention center for Kosovar men.

Gnjilane

Between April 7 and 15, Serbian VJ and paramilitary forces reportedly physically abused and extorted money from ethnic Albanians in this town. On April 16, the paramilitary units allegedly ordered that all ethnic Albanians leave the town, or be killed. At least 1,000 IDPs departed and were reportedly harassed by Serbian forces along the way. Men were reportedly separated from the convoy of refugees and killed; Serbian forces reportedly ordered other refugees to bury the bodies of at least six ethnic Albanians. Two of the bodies allegedly had been burned, while the other four had bullet wounds to the back of the head.

Goden

On March 25, Serbian forces allegedly executed 20 men, including schoolteachers, before burning the village.

Gornje Obrinje

A refugee claimed that Serbian forces executed 12 ethnic Albanians on April 5.

Hade

Serbian forces reportedly expelled all 1400 villagers and five men were reportedly executed.

Istok

One thousand refugees from this town arrived at the border with Macedonia on April 8. Some refugees reported that an unknown number of people had died en route and that others were turned back by Serbian police near Raska and Novi Pazar.

Izbica

Serbian forces reportedly killed approximately 150 ethnic Albanians since mid-March. Refugees reportedly saw bodies that appeared to have been tortured and burned.

Jovic

Serbian forces reportedly separated men from the columns of ethnic Albanian civilians, and a refugee claimed that he saw 34 corpses in the town.

Kaaniku

Refugees claim that Serbian forces killed 45 ethnic Albanians on April 9 and buried their bodies in a mass grave.

Kacanik

A refugee claimed that as many as 300 masked VJ and MUP soldiers forcibly expelled ethnic Albanian villagers towards Prizren. On April 14, Serbian paramilitaries reportedly separated men from women and children, drove them into a pasture, and forced them to kneel and pledge allegiance to Serbia. The paramilitaries then fired at them, killing at least twelve, according to refugee reports.

Kamena Glava

On April 6, Serbian paramilitary units reportedly looted homes and burned the village. After driving the villagers into the woods for 10 days, VJ forces reportedly ordered all of them to leave the area on April 17.

Klina

The expulsion of the town's ethnic Albanian population began on March 28, with Serbian forces removing residents from their homes and ordering them out of the country. Serbian forces reportedly used 500 Kosovar men as human shields during fighting with KLA forces.

A refugee who survived the fighting claimed that the men were robbed of their possessions and forced to strip naked and lie in a field for two hours while Serbian artillery fired on nearby KLA positions.

Kosovska Mitrovica

Serbian forces have reportedly expelled all Kosovar Albanians from this city since March 23. In addition, over 200 Albanian homes and shops reportedly have been torched, and Serbian forces reportedly have killed prominent Kosovars. Latif Berisha, a poet and president of the Democratic Alliance of the Mitrovica municipality, allegedly was executed in his home, and Agim Hajrizi, chairman of the assembly of the Independent Workers' Union, reportedly was murdered along with his mother and 12-year-old son. Serbian forces reportedly looted Kosovar Albanian shops and burned Albanian homes near a barracks that was targeted by NATO air strikes in an apparent attempt to blame NATO for the damage. Serb forces reportedly were continuing to burn villages around this town as of April 2.

A refugee claimed that Serbian forces separated out young ethnic Albanian men, tied their hands together, and led them into the street. Although the refugee did not witness any mass executions, she claimed to have witnessed one VJ soldier shooting an ethnic Albanian while he sat in a car. A refugee from a nearby village claims to have witnessed Serb civilians executing a young ethnic Albanian boy. The ethnic Albanians who were expelled from nearby villages remain in the Cicavica Mountains, east of the town.

Kosovo Polje

Serbian forces reportedly forced ethnic Albanians into their homes and then threw hand grenades inside. According to other refugee reports, ethnic Albanians were burned alive in their homes, and on March 28, Serbian paramilitary forces killed at least 70 Kosovar civilians. Refugees traveling from Pristina by train reported that Serbian paramilitary units boarded the cars and stole all of their valuables. Serbian forces reportedly entered the village on April 4, collected all the villagers, confiscated their personal documents and car keys, and then transported them to the border by train.

Kotlina

According to refugees from this town near Kacanik, between 50 and 60 ethnic Albanian men remain missing. The rest of the Kosovar inhabitants were reportedly loaded onto trains and sent to Macedonia. On April 8, ethnic Albanians discovered a mass grave, which it is suspected contains the bodies of some 26 persons, according to refugee reports. The victims allegedly were murdered in mid-March by a Serbian paramilitary group, which had reportedly entered the town and separated the ethnic Albanian men from their families.

Kraljane

Kosovar Albanian refugees claim that Serbian forces executed 100 ethnic Albanian civilians on April 4.

Kuraz

Serbian forces reportedly killed 21 schoolteachers in this village near Srbica. Refugees also claim that as many as 200 ethnic Albanians were detained there by Serbian security forces as of April 5.

Likovac

Serbian forces reportedly burned this village south of Srbica on March 30.

Lipjan

Serbian forces reportedly forced ethnic Albanian villagers out of the area on April 20. In addition, they looted and burned Albanian residences. Serbian paramilitary forces allegedly shot more than 50 civilians in three surrounding villages.

Ljubenic

Refugees reported that on April 8 Serbian forces murdered at least 100 ethnic Albanians from this village in western Kosovo.

Mala Krusa

One hundred and twelve men were shot and their bodies burned in an apparent attempt to conceal the evidence, according to a wounded and burned survivor of the executions.

Malisevo

Serbian forces reportedly destroyed most of the town and its surrounding villages. Refugees from the town claim to have witnessed Serbian forces burning ethnic Albanians alive. Female refugees claim that Serbian forces were separating men from the groups of refugees. Serbian forces reportedly executed approximately 50 men in this town on March 27. Part of the town was set on fire on March 30. By April 1 the Serbian forces appeared to have emptied the town. Refugees reported that the 50,000 to 140,000 IDPs in the Malisevo-Dulje area had been bombed and strafed by Serbian aircraft and helicopters.

Morina

Refugees claim that on April 7 Serbian security forces laid mines at this main border post between Kosovo and Albania to prevent refugees from crossing.

Negrovce

According to refugee reports, Serbian forces executed five ethnic Albanians on April 5.

Orahovac

Refugees reported that an unknown number of ethnic Albanian civilians were killed during the ethnic cleansing of the city. Members of a group of Roma who arrived at the Albanian border on April 8 claimed that they were expelled because Serbian authorities said that they were originally from Albania and were not "true" Kosovars. The group also reported that Serbian forces killed some 50 ethnic Albanians, including women, children, and the elderly.

According to refugees, as many as 700 men were used as human shields in early April. The ethnic Albanian men reportedly were forced to stand in front of tanks in the rain for two days with their hands tied behind their backs. A few of them reported that they eventually escaped by paying the soldiers 10,000 German marks.

Orlate

According to refugees, buildings in this small village located on the crossroads between Pristina, Pec, and Malisevo were set on fire by Serbian forces on March 30 after some 200 ethnic Albanian men had been executed.

Ovcareva

Serbian forces reportedly burned this village in the Drenica region on March 30.

Pec

It was reported that at least 50 ethnic Albanians were killed and then buried in the yards of their homes on the evening of March 27. On the same day, many ethnic Albanians were reportedly herded into a five-story building in the center of town. MUP forces then loaded them on buses and transported them out of the city. On March 28, 200 ethnic Albanians who sought sanctuary in a Catholic church in Pec were removed and forced out of town. Serbian forces reportedly looted and burned homes and shops throughout the town. Refugees claim that the indicted war criminal Zeljko Raznjatovic (aka "Arkan") was responsible for these abuses. Serbian forces may have expelled 50,000 Kosovars from Pec, and reportedly attacked a column of refugees leaving Pec on April 6.

Podujevo

Serbian forces reportedly were continuing to burn villages east and southeast of this town as of April 5. Serbian forces allegedly executed 200 Kosovar Albanian men of military age. In addition, Serbian forces reportedly removed ethnic Albanians from their cars and shot them on the spot. Ninety percent of the buildings in the town reportedly have been burned. On April 19, Serbian forces allegedly used ethnic Albanians as human shields along the road between Podujevo and Pristina.

Development of the Human Rights Situation

Pristina

Serbian forces appear to have completed military operations in the city and began expelling residents and internally displaced persons (IDPs) as of April 4. According to refugee reports, ethnic Albanians were forcibly expelled first from their homes and then from Pristina via train. Approximately 25,000 ethnic Albanians were sent by rail from Pristina to Macedonia on April 1, and over 200,000 reportedly were detained pending transport. According to refugee reports, most of these IDPs were without food, water, medicine, or shelter. Several refugees claim that Serbian forces used loudspeakers and distributed pamphlets to warn ethnic Albanians to leave town or be killed. A Kosovar claimed to have seen three truckloads of dead bodies accompanied by three or four armored vehicles in a graveyard in Pristina on April 2.

Pristina police reportedly arrested as many as 20 former OSCE/KVM local employees, and authorities were said to have searched for ethnic Albanians who held official government positions, worked for international organizations, or worked with foreign journalists. Male ethnic Albanians, including prominent human rights lawyer Bajram Kelmendi and his two sons, reportedly were executed. Serbian paramilitary units reportedly burned and looted Albanian homes and stores throughout the city. Mixed Serbian police and paramilitary units allegedly separated men from women and children.

Kosovar civilians reportedly were processed at the Pristina Sports Complex and then marched to the train station. However, we have received conflicting reports on processing at the Pristina Sports Complex. Buses and large cargo trucks also reportedly were used to transport IDPs to within three to six miles of the border, where they were left to make their way on foot. Refugees reported that the ethnic Albanian neighborhoods of Pristina had been emptied.

Prizren

Serbian forces reportedly executed between 20 and 30 civilians and transported ethnic Albanians to the border. Serbian paramilitary units operated freely throughout the town, according to refugee accounts. At the border, Serbian forces reportedly confiscated all personal documentation, removed license plates from vehicles, and warned the refugees never to return to Kosovo.

A Kosovar Albanian who traveled to Prizren for a funeral on April 2 claimed to have witnessed ethnic Albanian civilians being forcibly evicted from their homes. He alleged that the families were given two hours to vacate their property and that the houses were then either burned or used to shelter Serbian forces. Another refugee from Prizren reportedly witnessed Serbian forces burying numerous ethnic Albanian bodies and burning homes throughout the town. According to refugee reports, many ethnic Albanians remain in hiding because they fear Serb reprisals.

Popovo

Serbian aircraft reportedly bombed this village southwest of Podujevo, killing 10 ethnic Albanians.

Pusto Selo

The bodies of some 70 ethnic Albanians ranging in age from 14 to 50 were reportedly discovered by IDPs on April 1. Serbian authorities reportedly executed a survivor who sought medical treatment nearby. Overhead imagery confirms the presence of a mass burial site.

Rezala

Serbian forces reportedly burned this village south of Srbica on March 30. According to refugees, a mass grave containing approximately 70 bodies was discovered on April 14.

Rugovo

Serbian forces reportedly executed at least 50 ethnic Albanians.

Sojevo

Serbian snipers reportedly killed eight ethnic Albanians, and security forces allegedly expelled the remaining villagers into a nearby field in early April.

Srbica

Serbian forces reportedly emptied the town of its Kosovar inhabitants and executed approximately 115 ethnic Albanian males over the age of 18. Serbian authorities reportedly are holding detainees in an ammunition factory in the town.

Stari Trg

On April 23, Albanian press reported that Serbian forces dumped the bodies of numerous ethnic Albanians from trucks into crematorium furnaces, apparently to eliminate evidence of these deaths.

Stimlje

Serbian forces reportedly burned the headquarters of a human rights committee and the Democratic League of Kosovo. Serbian forces also reportedly burned Kosovar homes, stores, and vehicles, and drove some 25,000 civilians out of the city to villages to the south. In addition, the building housing the former OSCE mission reportedly was burned.

Suva Reka

On March 25, Serbian forces reportedly killed at least 30 Kosovar Albanians, most allegedly by burning them alive in their homes. By March 28, Serbian forces reportedly had burned 60 percent of the buildings in the town. A refugee from the town claimed that Serbian forces killed 40 men on April 4 and dumped their bodies into two mass graves. Serbian military and police forces reportedly killed as many as 350 ethnic Albanians in this town. According to refugee reports, a group of Serbian police officers and civilians robbed and killed an ethnic Albanian family living in a former OSCE office. The Serbian forces then reportedly burned the bodies of their victims. The entire ethnic Albanian population has reportedly been forced from the town.

Urosevac

Serbian forces reportedly forcibly expelled Kosovar civilians from their homes on April 10, and are now using some of the homes as barracks. Former Kosovar shops and homes were reportedly given to Serb villagers. Serbian police officers allegedly transported the civilians to Blace by train. Serbian forces reportedly are targeting the homes of prominent politicians and intellectuals. As many as 40 ethnic Albanians allegedly have been killed. Refugees report the raping of young Albanian girls. According to a refugee, Serbian paramilitary units are forcing Albanian males to dig defensive positions on the southeast side of the city. Nearly 50 paramilitary members reportedly forced 25 civilians from the nearby town of Starosello to dig trenches for three days from April 10 to 12.

Varos Selo

According to refugee reports, Serbian paramilitary forces reportedly entered ethnic Albanian homes, forcibly expelled the residents at knifepoint, and stole their belongings. They reportedly killed an unknown number of Kosovars and carried their bodies away.

Vataj

According to refugee reports, Serbian forces killed 14 ethnic Albanians on April 13. One refugee claimed that he was forced to bury the bodies, and that the corpses had gunshot wounds to the back of the head.

Velika Hoca

Two paramilitary units, Arkan's "Tigers" and the "White Eagles," are reportedly based in a housing complex in the town and control the area between Orahovac and Suva Reka.

Velika Krusa

There were reports from refugees in late March that Serbian forces killed between 150 and 160 ethnic Albanian men, after separating them from women and children, and dumped 50 bodies in a mass grave. These reports appear to be corroborated by a videotape shot by a survivor, who stated that about 100 Kosovars had been shot; he gave the names of two dozen of the victims. The BBC aired the refugee's video showing several dead bodies lying in ditches and in the streets. According to the refugee, all of the victims had single bullet wounds in the back of the head or neck. A female refugee from the same village claimed that approximately 40 men were executed by Serbian forces, while other refugees claim that homes were burned, resulting in the deaths of over 60 Kosovars - including women and children, who were in them at the time. Police reportedly told residents of the nearby villages of Lashec, Kobanje, and Atmadja that "as a gift, we will only kill ten of you," and then told the survivors to "go to NATO."

Vrsevac
Serbian police reportedly used ethnic Albanians as human shields on April 7.

Vucitrn
Serbian forces reportedly burned all houses previously rented by the OSCE and looted Kosovar homes. Refugees from the town also claim that men were separated from their families. On March 27, Serbian forces reportedly killed four young ethnic Albanians, including a 14-year-old girl. By March 29, Serbian forces reportedly had herded Kosovars into a school in the city, and refugees from the town claim that the men were being separated from their families. On May 4, a newly arrived refugee in Albania reported that he had seen at least 50 dead bodies.

Zegra
Serbian forces reportedly expelled all ethnic Albanians from this village, then burned all the buildings on April 13.

Zur
On March 28, local police reportedly ordered all ethnic Albanians to leave town. As many as 7,000 Albanian Kosovars may have been displaced as a result.

Zulfaj
Serbian forces reportedly expelled all ethnic Albanians from this village, then burned all the buildings.

Zjum
Serbian forces reportedly burned this southern Kosovo town.

Chronology of Recent Ethnic Cleansing in Kosovo

March 19: Withdrawal of the Kosovo Verification Mission (KVM).

Extensive mobilization of Serbian security forces beyond earlier force deployments began several days prior to the March 19 withdrawal of the KVM monitors and most NGOs following the failure of the Paris talks and in anticipation of NATO airstrikes. By the time OSCE Chairman-in-Office Knut Vollebaek authorized departure of the monitors for Macedonia, additional Serbian forces and VJ reinforcements had deployed to Kosovo to secure major transport routes, and appeared to be poised for larger scale operations. The speed with which the campaign was conducted and the breadth of the operation appear to indicate that there was a plan to ethnically cleanse at least the KLA strongholds, if not the entire province, of its ethnic Albanian population.

The humanitarian situation, which had improved somewhat in February, significantly deteriorated by mid-March - including the outflow of refugees and displaced persons - due to the widespread activities of Serbian forces. For example, a MUP/VJ force of 200 entered a village west of Djakovica on March 18, and engaged in looting and shooting, which resulted in the death of one person. The MUP was also active in Orahovac and Kacanik, and paramilitary forces were active near Gnjilane. Serbian spokesmen claimed that they were responding to KLA provocations, although KVM observers did not observe such incidents. In another example, Serbian forces on March 20 attacked three key towns - Srbica, Glogovac, and Luzane - on the pretense that the KLA had attacked police stations there on March 19. There is no evidence currently available to support the Serbian government claim of the earlier KLA attacks.

On March 19, the UNHCR reported a total of 333,000 displaced Kosovars: 250,000 IDPs within Kosovo, 30,000 elsewhere in Serbia, 25,000 in Montenegro, as well as almost 10,000 refugees in Macedonia and 18,000 in Albania.

March 20: VJ and MUP forces launched a significant operation against KLA forces in northeastern and north-central Kosovo to secure key lines of communication and the Cicavica mountains area apparently as a prelude to initiating their broader offensive against the KLA. One sector of the attack, between Vucitrn and Pristina, had seen no recently reported KLA activity. The Podujevo-Pristina road was blocked by Serbian forces activity, which forced civilians to flee to the hills.

March 21: By this date, 25,000 Kosovars were newly displaced in the Drenica region where Serbian forces were reportedly looting and burning homes; civilian executions were reported by the KLA in Srbica.

March 23: By this time, most major cities were targeted by Serbian forces for ethnic cleansing: Pec, Prizren, Djakovica, Pristina, Urosevac, Podujevo, and Kacanik. The emptying of Kosovska Mitrovica had began.

March 24: Beginning on or shortly after the commencement of the NATO airstrikes, VJ forces reportedly joined police and paramilitary units in systematically expelling ethnic Albanians from both villages and larger towns. Population centers that had not been targeted before and had no KLA presence were being emptied. Thousands of dwellings reportedly were looted and torched. Serbian forces allegedly significantly accelerated their large-scale confiscation and destruction of documents. Reports of atrocities increased significantly.

March 25: Yugoslavia broke off diplomatic relations with France, Germany, the United Kingdom, and the United States.

March 26: The OSCE office in Tirana reported the burning of villages in Kosovo.

March 27: Ethnic Albanians, fleeing or expelled from Kosovo, began to pour into Albania and Macedonia, leading to a refugee crisis.

March 29: By this time there were reports that the majority of the 1.6 million ethnic Albanians in Kosovo may have been displaced from their homes. Whole towns and villages had been emptied. UNHCR reports estimated that Serbian forces had forcibly expelled upwards of 70,000 persons into Albania over the weekend. Refugees reported the forced separation of military-aged men from groups, summary executions in at least 20 towns and villages, and the widespread looting and burning of homes.

March 30: There were reports from an NGO that Albanian men may have been herded into the Sports Stadium Complex in Pristina for detention, while press and refugees reports indicated that as many as ethnic Albanians were taken by forced march from the town of Cirez to Srbica and were being detained in a factory.

March 31: Trains carried Kosovar refugees to the Macedonian border. The UNHCR reported that 125,000 refugees had fled since March 24.

April 2: The governments of Albania and Macedonia reported that they were overwhelmed by refugees. Some 25,000 ethnic Albanians reportedly were forcibly transported by trains from Pristina to Macedonia

April 4: Western leaders proposed an airlift to take another 100,000 Kosovars to NATO countries. Macedonia agreed to let NATO set up camps for another 100,000.

April 5: At least 560,000 Kosovar Albanians - over one-quarter of the province's pre-conflict population - had left Kosovo since the Serb crackdown that began in March of last year. Over half are in neighboring countries. NATO released imagery of 500 people surrounded by Serb forces in the town of Glodane.

April 6: Refugees reported the existence of mass graves in Drenica, Malisevo, and Pagarusa. Approximately 150 bodies reportedly were discovered in Drenica and 34 in Malisevo. Serbian forces reportedly locked the members of an entire family into a house in a village in Drenica and burned them alive. About 150 Kosovo refugees were flown to Turkey, the first flight of the proposed airlift.

April 9: An estimated 700,000 ethnic Albanians were reportedly displaced within Kosovo at this point. Refugee reports claimed that over 3,200 ethnic Albanians died as a result of executions by Serbian forces. The UNHCR recommended that refugees should stay close to Kosovo; most NATO airlift plans were put on hold.

April 12: The Yugoslav parliament voted to join a union with Russia and Belarus

April 13: Publicly-released NATO imagery corroborates refugee reports of mass burials at Pusto Selo.

April 16: The refugee exodus returned to the crisis level of 20,000 new arrivals per day. Governments, international organizations, and NGOS were challenged to expand the camps to meet the need.

April 17: The UNHCR reported that it might have to revive plans for a mass airlift of refugees to distant countries. NATO released imagery of a mass grave at Izbica.

April 18: NATO reported that 850,000 uprooted ethnic Albanians were being herded or attacked by Serbian forces in Kosovo. The government of Yugoslavia broke diplomatic relations with Albania.

April 21: Press reports indicated that some 3,300 ethnic Albanians fled into Albania from Montenegro, probably in reaction to the killing of a group of Kosovar IDPs and a Montenegrin near Rozaj by VJ reservists on April 19.

April 22: According to the UNHCR, the Bosnian government was preparing to handle up to 100,000 more refugees from Kosovo in the event of a worst-case scenario. At this time, Bosnia hosted around 32,000 refugees from Serbia-Montenegro. Such a new influx would severely strain Bosnia's resources.

April 23: The UNHCR estimated that some 1.2 to 1.5 million Kosovar Albanians were displaced from their homes since the conflict escalated in March of last year. Some 400 towns and villages were reportedly damaged or destroyed by Serbian forces since mid-March 1999.

April 27: According to refugee reports, Serbian forces killed 200 military-aged ethnic Albanian men along a road near Djakovica. About a hundred Kosovar Albanians were observed fleeing from Serb forces in Dobros.

April 30: The UNHCR reported over 3,000 refugees entering Albania and over 5,000 entering Macedonia from Kosovo. The UNHCR also reported that 6,000 to 8,000 refugees arrived from the southern Serbian town of Presevo, indicating that ethnic Albanian refugees are beginning to leave parts of Serbia outside of Kosovo. Refugees claimed that they left the Presevo area because they were either being conscripted or forced into military barracks by paramilitaries. Refugees also claimed that Serbian forces were storing military equipment in villages. The U.S. Government released imagery of refugees fleeing Dobros.

May 5: The UNHCR reported over 7,000 refugees entering Albania and 8,400 entering Macedonia from Kosovo. Many of the refugees entering Albania told stories of widespread abduction of hundreds of young men and the killings of some of those abducted. The UNHCR estimated that the number of Kosovars who have fled to neighboring areas reached a total of almost 700,000, including 404,000 in Albania, 211,000 in Macedonia, and 62,000 in Montenegro. The refugees entering Albania from the Djakovica region reported stories consistent with earlier reports. Based on these accounts the UNHCR reported that the Djakovica region "undoubtedly has been one of the most violent and cruel in the whole of Kosovo, turning it at times into a virtual killing field."

2.3 NGO REPORTS

47. Amnesty International Report 1998: FRY: For the Period January - December 1997

Approximately 34 ethnic Albanian political prisoners were convicted, mostly after unfair trials. Scores of others remained in prison. Some may have been prisoners of conscience. Police routinely tortured or ill-treated detainees and peaceful demonstrators. Most victims were ethnic Albanians from Kosovo province, but some were Serbs. At least three people died in police custody. At least three people were sentenced to death.

At the start of the year, demonstrations led by supporters of the Zajedno (Together) coalition of opposition parties continued in Belgrade and other towns, as the authorities refused to reinstate local election results which they had overturned in late 1996 (see Amnesty International Report 1997). After continued international pressure, the authorities conceded the opposition victories in February.

In Kosovo province, ethnic Albanian political parties continued to demand independence for the province by peaceful means. However, violent attacks against police stations, police officers, Serb civilians and ethnic Albanians working for or with the authorities occurred throughout the year. Among dozens of victims were two police officers who were shot near Srbica in August and an ethnic Albanian civilian who was travelling in their car. Responsibility for many of the attacks was claimed by a clandestine organization called the Ushtria Clirimitare e Kosovës (UCK), Kosovo Liberation Army. Police responses to the violent attacks included what appeared to be indiscriminate arrests and house searches.

In July the President of Serbia, Slobodan Milosevic, stood down. He was subsequently elected President of the Federal Republic of Yugoslavia (FRY) by the Federal Parliament. Milan Milutinovic was elected President of Serbia in December. Some Serbian opposition parties and all ethnic Albanian parties from Kosovo province boycotted the election. In October students and opposition supporters staged demonstrations against the ousting of the Mayor of Belgrade. In October Milo Djukanovic, an opponent of Slobodan Milosevic, was elected President of Montenegro.

In October and December ethnic Albanian students from the unofficial Albanian-language university staged peaceful demonstrations demanding access to state university facilities in Pristina.

The Federal and Serbian authorities continued to fail to cooperate fully with the International Criminal Tribunal for the former Yugoslavia. However, the authorities in Montenegro met Tribunal officials and expressed a desire to cooperate. In February a Belgrade military court reportedly sentenced an adherent of the Jehovah's Witnesses, a religious group, to six months' imprisonment for refusing, on conscientious grounds, to do military service. He was a prisoner of conscience.

Courts in Kosovo province held a number of political trials during the year involving ethnic Albanians. Among the most significant cases was that of Avni Klinaku and 19 other ethnic Albanians who were sentenced in Pristina in May to between two and 10 years' imprisonment. They were convicted of "conspiring to endanger the territorial integrity of the FRY" and other similar charges. Two were tried and sentenced in absentia. They were accused of belonging to a secret association called the Levizje Kombëtare për Clirimin e Kosovës (LKCK), National Movement for the Liberation of Kosovo. The trial was unfair: the conviction was based largely on self-incriminating statements which were not substantiated in court and 11 of the accused alleged that the statements had only been given as a result of torture in custody.

In a similar trial in July, 15 ethnic Albanian men were convicted - 12 in absentia - of having formed a terrorist organization - the UCK - and of responsibility for attacks between 1993 and 1996 on police and civilians resulting in the death of four people. Twelve of the accused, including Besim Rama (see Amnesty International Report 1997), received the maximum sentence of 20 years' imprisonment. The trial was unfair. Statements from the three detained defendants were reportedly extracted by means of torture during unacknowledged detention. One of the defendants told the court that he was denied access to his defence lawyer for six months, only being allowed a brief private consultation with his lawyer three days before the trial. In December Nait Hasani and 16 other ethnic Albanians were sentenced to prison terms of up to 20 years after a similar unfair trial.

Scores of ethnic Albanians remained in prison after being convicted in largely unfair political trials between 1994 and 1997. Most of them had been charged with seeking the secession of Kosovo province by means of violence. However, evidence of the use or advocacy of violence was not presented in all cases and some may have been prisoners of conscience.

Incidents in which police beat and ill-treated ethnic Albanians, including women, children and elderly people, took place almost daily throughout the year. Victims were often beaten in their homes during searches for arms. The most severe ill-treatment took place in police stations where victims were often taken for questioning. Ethnic Albanians engaged in political parties or ethnic Albanian "parallel" institutions, such as Albanian-language schools, were often targeted.

Many of the instances of torture or ill-treatment occurred in the context of police operations in response to the violent attacks on police and Serbian civilians. For example, Nait Hasani (see above) was arrested by police on 28 January and was transferred the next day to hospital, reportedly to treat injuries sustained from torture during interrogation. On 31 January he "disappeared" after being taken from hospital by people who were later identified as police officers. Despite repeated requests from his family and lawyer, the police and judicial authorities refused to provide any information about his whereabouts or confirm that he was in detention until he was brought before an investigating magistrate on 28 February. He was reportedly further tortured during his time in unacknowledged detention.

In January and February police beat hundreds of opposition supporters who were demonstrating peacefully in Belgrade, Kragujevac and other towns in Serbia. For example, Zoran Simonovic, a paediatrician and opposition member of the Federal Parliament, was reportedly beaten unconscious in Kragujevac when police beat demonstrators surrounding the town radio station. The new opposition-controlled authorities had appointed a new managerial board, but police reportedly stormed the radio station building in an attempt to overturn the decision. In February Vesna Peßic, leader of the political party Gradjanski Savez, Civic Alliance, was beaten by police along with other peaceful demonstrators on a bridge in Belgrade.

At least three people, all ethnic Albanians, died in police custody, allegedly as a result of torture, ill-treatment or shooting. For example, Ismet Gjocaj died after being shot by police in November. Despite police claims that he had been shot while participating in an armed attack on a police station, there was clear evidence that at the time of his death he was already in custody and had been tortured.

Despite the abolition of the death penalty in federal law in 1992, at least three people were sentenced to death during the year for aggravated murder under the criminal codes of the FRY's two constituent republics. No executions were reported to have been carried out during the year.

Refugees who had returned to the FRY from abroad, either voluntarily or under duress, were allegedly ill-treated by police. For example, in May Azem Hali Haxolli, who had returned voluntarily from Germany, was allegedly denied food and ill-treated after being held in detention by police in Belgrade. He was subsequently returned to Germany.

Amnesty International appealed repeatedly to the authorities for thorough, independent and impartial investigations into allegations of "disappearance", torture and ill-treatment and for the perpetrators to be brought to justice. The organization also appealed for the immediate and unconditional release of prisoners of conscience and for other political prisoners to receive fair and prompt trials.

Annual Report Update: From January to June 1998

More than 250 ethnic Albanians have been reported as killed since the conflict began in February this year between police and armed ethnic Albanians, including the Kosovo Liberation Army (KLA), in the Kosovo province of Yugoslavia. This number grows each day. The police have killed, tortured and ill-treated ethnic Albanians in response to attacks upon them. Around 40 Serbs, 14 of them police officers, were reported to have been killed by armed ethnic Albanians since the beginning of the year. More than 50,000 ethnic Albanians were reported to have been displaced from their homes.

Between 28 February and 6 March police killed at least 80 ethnic Albanians in the villages of Likosane, Cirez and Donji Prekaz in the Drenica region of Kosovo. Although evidence was incomplete, it was clear that many of the victims - who included at least 12 women and 11 children - had no connection with the attacks. Indeed, Amnesty International visited the country in March and collected testimonies describing police officers killing a number of the victims.

Police beat ethnic Albanian demonstrators, including women, who protested about the killings and the increasing police violence. In March one such demonstrator was shot dead in Pec and five others were wounded by police. Clashes with police and the Yugoslav Army continued after these incidents and reports continued to come in of possible unlawful killings. In late March, for example, three unarmed ethnic Albanian men were reportedly shot as they fled the village of Glodjane near De...ani. Children were used as human shields in the same incident. There were also reports of the abduction and ill-treatment of Serbs by the KLA.

Although in many cases it appeared that the police policy was to shoot rather than take prisoners, police arrested dozens of men who were accused of "terrorism". Some men, who were reportedly abducted by police, remain missing. In May, Amnesty International demanded justice and not "trial by truncheon" as detainees faced convictions in unfair trials after being tortured during interrogation.

48. Human Rights Watch: FRY: Humanitarian Law Violations in Kosovo, Extracts, October 1998[1]

Summary

This report documents serious breaches of international humanitarian law, the rules of war, committed in Kosovo from February to early September 1998. Future Human Rights Watch reports will provide evidence about atrocities in villages such as Donja Obrinja, Golubovac, and Vranic, the details of which were just emerging as this report went to press. (See appendices A,B and C). The vast majority of these abuses were committed by Yugoslav government forces of the Serbian special police (MUP) and the Yugoslav Army (VJ). Under the command of Yugoslav President Slobodan Milošević, government troops have committed extrajudicial executions and other unlawful killings, systematically destroyed civilian property, and attacked humanitarian aid workers, all of which are violations of the rules of war.

The Albanian insurgency, known as the Kosova Liberation Army (KLA, or UCK in Albanian), has also violated the laws of war by such actions as the taking of civilian hostages and by summary executions. Although on a lesser scale than the government abuses, these too are violations of international standards, and should be condemned.

---

[1] *Used with the permission of HRW. Cannot be reused or reprinted without the expressed written consent of HRW.*

The primary responsibility for gross government abuses lies with Slobodan Milošević, who rode to power in the late eighties by inciting Serbian nationalist chauvinism around the Kosovo issue. Now, after wars in Bosnia and Croatia, he has returned to the place where his post-communist career began.

The first atrocities took place in late February and early March in the Drenica region of central Kosovo, a stronghold of the KLA. Special police forces attacked three villages with artillery, helicopters, and armored vehicles, killing at least eighty-three people, twenty-four of them women and children. Although it is unclear to what extent the KLA was offering resistance, the evidence strongly suggests that at least seventeen people were executed after they had been detained or surrendered.

The police attack in Drenica was a watershed in the Kosovo conflict; thousands of outraged Albanians who had been committed to the nonviolent politics of Ibrahim Rugova decided to join the KLA. In the ensuing months, the KLA, called a "liberation movement" by most ethnic Albanians and a "terrorist organization" by the Yugoslav government, took control of an estimated 40 percent of Kosovo's territory.

The first major government offensive began in mid-May, a few days after Milošević agreed to U.S. demands that he meet with Rugova. The special police together with the Yugoslav Army attacked a string of towns and villages along the border with Albania in the west, with the specific intent of depopulating the region. Until then, the KLA had been receiving arms and fresh recruits from across the border.

Many villages from Pec in the north to Dakovica in the south were shelled while civilians were still present. Noncombatants who fled the attacks were sometimes fired on by snipers, and a still undetermined number of people were taken into detention. In three cases, helicopters marked with the Red Cross emblem reportedly fired on civilians. Landmines were placed in strategic points along the border, as well as along the southern border with Macedonia. Most villages in the region were looted and systematically destroyed, and farmers' livestock was shot, to ensure that no one could return in the short-run. Fifteen thousand people fled to Albania and an estimated 30,000 went north to Montenegro.

The KLA's first major offensive began on July 19 when it attempted to capture the town of Orahovac. The offensive failed, as the police recaptured the town two days later. In the fighting at least forty-two people were killed. Witnesses reported summary executions and the use of human shields by the police. Foreign journalists reported on mass graves, although these reports have not been confirmed. The extent of the abuses in Orahovac may remain unknown until the government allows an international forensics team to inspect the site.

The government forces intensified their offensive throughout July, August and September, despite promises from Milošević that it had stopped. By mid-August, the government had retaken much of the territory held by the KLA, including their stronghold Mališevo. Unable to protect the civilian population, the KLA retreated into Drenica and some pockets in the West.

The government offensive, still ongoing, is an apparent attempt to crush civilian support for the rebels. Government forces have attacked civilians, systematically destroyed towns, and forced thousands of people to flee their homes. One attack killed seventeen civilians who were hiding in the woods, and another killed three humanitarian aid workers who were trying to deliver food. The police have been seen looting homes, destroying already abandoned villages, burning crops, and killing farm animals.

The majority of those killed and injured have been civilians. At least 250,000 people are currently displaced, many of them women and children now living without shelter in the mountains and woods. They face dire conditions with winter approaching. Many are too afraid to return to their homes, or have no homes to which they can return.

Despite some improvements, the government still restricts the ability of humanitarian aid agencies adequately to treat the internally displaced. On various occasions, the police have restricted access to needy populations, confiscated supplies, harassed and even attacked humanitarian aid workers. The government has justified the restricted access by arguing that some humanitarian organizations had distributed supplies, including arms, to the KLA.

The Yugoslav government has also restricted the work of domestic and foreign journalists who seek to report the atrocities. Some ethnic Albanian journalists have been threatened, detained, or beaten by the police. Independent radio and television stations in the Albanian language are denied licenses or, in one case, closed down.

The independent Serbian-language media is not exempt from state pressure. News wires, newspapers, and radio stations that report objectively on Kosovo are labeled "traitors" and sometimes threatened with legal action. A complex and contradictory legal framework has made it virtually impossible for independent radio or television stations to obtain a broadcast frequency. As was the case during the wars in Bosnia and Croatia, the state-run radio and television purposefully spreads disinformation and promotes images of "the enemy" intended to inflame the conflict.

The international media covering Kosovo also faces a number of restrictions on its work, starting with the denial of visas to critical journalists whom the state considers "anti-Serb." One journalist was declared persona non grata. A number of foreign journalists have been beaten and fired upon by the police.

At least one hundred ethnic Albanians have "disappeared" in Kosovo since February 1998, about half of whom were last seen in the custody of the police. The precise number is impossible to determine since the Yugoslav authorities do not make public the number of people they have in detention. Some of the "disappeared" may be in prison, others may be dead. Others unaccounted for in the conflict may be in hiding, have fled Kosovo, or have joined the KLA.

According to the government, 538 ethnic Albanians have been arrested and charged with committing "terrorist acts." In July and August, detained individuals increasingly included human rights activists, humanitarian aid workers, political party members, doctors, and lawyers, many of whom were physically abused. The use of torture against detainees is widespread, and five people are known to have died from abuse in prison.

The KLA has also committed serious violations of international humanitarian law, including the taking of hostages and extrajudicial executions. An estimated 138 ethnic Serbs, and a number of ethnic Albanians and Roma, are missing in circumstances in which KLA involvement is suspected: at least thirty-nine of them were last seen in KLA custody. In some villages the KLA tried to drive ethnic Serbs from their homes. In some cases, elderly Serbs stayed behind, either too old to flee or unwilling to abandon their homes. Some of these people are currently missing and feared dead.

On September 9, the police announced that they had found a number of bodies of people reportedly killed by the KLA near Glodjane. By September 16, the authorities had gathered thirty-four bodies, eleven of whom were identified, including some ethnic Albanians. Before that, the most serious KLA abuse involved the reported execution of twenty-two Serbian civilians in the village of Klecka, where the police claimed to have discovered human remains and a kiln used to cremate the bodies. The manner in which the allegations were made, however, raises serious questions and underlines the importance of an investigation by an impartial forensic investigations team, which should examine Klecka, as well as the other areas where summary executions have been reported.

Despite the seriousness of these abuses, the international community has failed to take any serious action to stop the killing. Milošević continues to be viewed by many as a legitimate and trustworthy negotiating partner.

The U.S. government, European Union, United Nations, and NATO have all issued strong warnings, including participating in military maneuvers in neighboring Macedonia and Albania in June and September. But threats have come and gone as the abuses mounted. Punitive measures have been slow, weak, and rapidly rescinded when Milošević offered the slightest concession. The tentative international response has been driven by fear of either endorsing Kosovo independence or being drawn into a long-term commitment of forces to maintain a peaceful settlement within former Yugoslavia.

The consequences of this policy will be catastrophic, not only for the Albanians and Serbs in Kosovo. An ongoing conflict will have a direct and destabilizing impact on the neighboring republic of Montenegro, and on the bordering countries of Bosnia and Albania, already fragile, as well as Macedonia, where fighting could draw in Greece, Bulgaria, and Turkey. It also ensures that Milošević will remain the head of a corrupt and authoritarian Yugoslavia that will continue to be a threat to the region's stability.

Recommendations

[...]

Violations of the Rules of War by Government Forces

VIOLATIONS IN THE DRENICA REGION

Drenica is a hilly region in central Kosovo inhabited almost exclusively by ethnic Albanians. The region has a tradition of strong resistance to outside powers, dating back to Turkish rule in the Balkans. By 1997, Albanians had begun to refer to Drenica as "liberated territory" because of the local KLA presence, which forced Serbian policemen to abandon their checkpoints at night. The government considered Drenica the hotbed of "Albanian terrorism."

A focal point of police attention in Drenica was the village of Donji Prekaz, and especially the family compound of Adem Jashari, who was gaining repute in 1997 as a local KLA leader. In January and then again in March 1998, the police mounted attacks on the compound, the second involving a large-scale force based at the nearby ammunition factory. Jashari's entire family, save an eleven-year-old girl, was killed in the attack. Of fifty-eight bodies later buried, eighteen were women and ten were children sixteen years old or younger (see below).

On February 28 and March 1, the police mounted a major attack on two other villages in Drenica: Cirez and Likošane. In both cases, special police forces attacked without warning, firing indiscriminately at women, children and other non-combatants. Helicopters and military vehicles sprayed village rooftops with gunfire before police forces entered the village on foot, firing into private homes. A pregnant woman, Rukia Nebihi, was shot in the face, and four brothers from one family were killed, apparently while in police custody. Ten members of the Ahmeti family were summarily executed by the police (see below).

The Serbian police denied any wrongdoing in the attacks and claimed they were pursuing "terrorists" who had attacked the police. A police spokesman denied the "lies and inventions" about torture carried by some local and foreign media and said "the police has never resorted to such methods and never will."[1]

These events in Drenica, in which eighty-three people died, including at least twenty-four women and children, were the turning point in the Kosovo crisis. Although it is unknown precisely how large the KLA was up to that point and what its exact structure was, there is no question that the brutal and indiscriminate attacks on women and children greatly radicalized the ethnic Albanian population and swelled the ranks of the KLA. Whether Milošević thought he could crush the KLA in Drenica, or whether he intended for the KLA to grow and become overly confident and more aggressive is a question for debate.

THE ATTACK ON LIKOŠANE

The first large-scale police attacks in Drenica were on Likošane and Cirez, small villages that lie about two kilometers apart from one another, on February 28 and March 1. From the testimonies of victims, witnesses, and those who visited the villages just after the attack, it is clear that the special police forces used at least one attack helicopter, armored personnel carriers (APCs), mortars and automatic machine guns in the attack.

Twenty-five Albanians died in the attack. Although it is unknown how much resistance was mounted by the local villagers and the KLA, most of the Albanians who died were clearly not offering any resistance at the time of their death. Evidence strongly suggests that the police summarily executed at least fourteen people.

It is still not clear how and why the attack began. According to police reports, a police patrol was attacked by armed Albanians near Likošane on February 28; four policemen were killed and two seriously injured.[2] A fight ensued over the next two days, in which sixteen "terrorists" and two policemen were killed. Albanians from Likošane and Cirez told Human Rights Watch that they heard shooting near Likošane, at the place called "Six Oaks," around 11:00 a.m. on February 28, and some had heard that the police had been ambushed there. There were also unconfirmed reports that armed Albanians had attacked the ammunition plant near Donji Prekaz, where the police were based, on February 27. When the police chased the Albanians, they were ambushed near Likošane.

Regardless of what triggered the incident, there is no question that the special police forces acted in a quick and well-organized manner, which suggests that the police may have been planning to attack. There is also no doubt that the police used arbitrary and excessive force against the villagers long after resistance ceased.

Some articles in the Western press cited anonymous Serbian police sources who said that, while the Albanians had fired first, the situation had then gotten "out of hand."[3] One article cited an unnamed Serbian police officer as saying that only intervention by a Belgrade commander had limited the slaughter of villagers.[4]

According to those present in Likošane, the police arrived in the village between 11:30 and 12:00 p.m., about half an hour after the shots had been heard near Six Oaks. An attack helicopter was firing overhead while APCs and many armed special police surrounded the village. Villagers told Human Rights Watch that there was no KLA presence, but it is possible that someone was firing at the police.

Two neighboring households were the focus of police attacks: the families Gjeli and Ahmeti. Two men were killed by gunshots in the former, eleven in the latter, apparently while in police custody.

At around 3:30 p.m. the police burst into the compound of the Ahmeti family, which was the richest family in Likošane. There is some speculation that a KLA member may have entered the house and then left, but it remains unclear why the Ahmeti house was targeted. Interviews conducted by Human Rights Watch, the Humanitarian Law Center, the Council for the Defense of Human Rights and Freedoms, and journalists corroborate a story of beatings and, ultimately, the extrajudicial executions of ten Ahmeti men, aged between sixteen and fifty, as well as one family guest, Bajram Fazliu.

According to two women in the Ahmeti family interviewed by the Humanitarian Law Center, the police, dressed in green and blue camouflage uniforms, broke down the family compound gate with an armored vehicle and then broke into the house. The police ordered everyone to lie down on the floor, and then the men were taken out-

---

[1] "Interior Ministry Spokesman Gives Press Conference," Tanjug, March 7, 1998.

[2] "Interior Ministry Spokesman Gives Press Conference," Tanjug March 7, 1998.
[3] Reuters, March 2, 1998.
[4] Guy Dinmore, "Serbian Forces Accused of Slaughter," Financial Times, March 3, 1998.

side the compound, where they were beaten. Two neighbors of the Ahmeti family, Ilir Islami and Haxhi Hasani, told the Council for the Defense of Human Rights and Freedoms that they heard the screams of the Ahmeti men from the front yard until the evening.

One woman in the house, Merci Ahmeti, told a journalist from the Times:

"All of our men walked out to protect the rest of us. The police beat them unconscious. Then they told us to lie on the ground and kept some policemen to watch over us for the next four hours. We heard screams outside and shots. We do not know what happened, but I knew then they were no longer alive."[1]

The only brother to survive the attack, Xhevdet Ahmeti, was by chance in Priština on February 28. The next day, having learned of the incident, he returned to Likošane and watched from a hill overlooking the village as the police continued their attack. He told Human Rights Watch:

"I arrived around 8 a.m. on March 1. There was an APC in our compound and another outside. A third was behind. There was artillery all over and the police were shooting everywhere."[2]

According to Xhevdet Ahmeti, the police withdrew around 3:30 p.m. He immediately went to his house and was told that the police had taken ten male members of his family and Bajram Fazliu into custody. He told Human Rights Watch that the doors and furniture of the house had been destroyed, and that the police had taken most of the family's valuables, such as the television satellite dish, clothing, and shoes that their uncle had just brought back from Switzerland, as well as some gold and 50,000 Swiss francs.

Xhevdet and the rest of the Ahmeti family did not learn that the eleven men in custody had been killed until March 2, when their bodies were seen by chance in the Priština morgue by another Likošane resident, Kadri Gjeli, who had gone to collect two members of his family who had been killed (see below). An Ahmeti cousin then went to the morgue himself to collect the bodies. On his return, he was blocked by the police in Komoran and was forced to take a circuitous route by unpaved roads.

The eleven men were buried on March 3, along with the fifteen other victims from Likošane and Cirez. A journalist from the United States who saw the Ahmeti corpses on May 2 told Human Rights Watch that they bore clear signs of torture, including gouged out eyes and slash wounds.[3] Autopsies were not performed on any of the victims, even though Article 252 of the Yugoslav Criminal Code mandates autopsies in cases where the death may have been related to a criminal act. On April 3, lawyers for the Ahmeti family asked the local prosecutor and investigating judge to investigate why the autopsies had never been performed but, as of September 1998, they had received no answer. As of September 1998, the Ahmeti family had still not received death certificates from the local authorities despite repeated requests by their lawyers.

It is not clear whether the Ahmeti men and Bahram Fazliu were killed in Likošane in front of the Ahmeti family compound or after they had been taken away by the police. A researcher for the Humanitarian Law Center, who was in Likošane on March 2, saw blood, teeth, and what looked like brain tissue near the bushes in front of the front gates, which suggests some or all of the men were either killed or severely beaten in front of the compound. Human Rights Watch spoke separately with two journalists, an ethnic Albanian and an American, who both saw the same blood and human remains in front of the Ahmeti's gates on March 2, as well as Serbian writing on the compound wall that said: "This is what will happen next time too."[4]

The other household in Likošane targeted by the police was that of seventy-year-old Muhamet Gjeli, who, according to the Albanian-language media, had been deported from Germany on December 17, 1998.[5] Muhamet and his son Naser were apparently killed by gunshots, Muhamet in a small dairy next to his house and Naser inside the house in front of his wife and two children, aged two and four. It is not known whether the two men were shooting at the police or whether the police warned them to surrender before shooting.

Naser's wife, Ganimete Islami, told the Council for the Defense of Human Rights and Freedoms that she first heard shooting from Six Oaks around 12:00 p.m., so she took her children into the bathroom while her husband joined them with a hunting rifle and put a mattress over the window. She said:

At one moment, bullets got through the windows and shot my husband dead. Bullets came through the door, too. The firing stopped and the room was full of steam and dust...

Muhamet was apparently killed in the small dairy next to the house. Journalists who visited the scene saw an axe, a cap, and a blood smear indicating that the body had been dragged out of the dairy.[6] According to Ganimete Islami, the police took Naser and Muhamet's bodies, as well as 6,500 DM from the house. They also destroyed the family's tractor and Zastava car.

THE ATTACK ON CIREZ

According to those present on February 28, the police arrived in Cirez around 12:30 p.m., after the shooting near Six Oaks. Three witnesses independently told Human Rights Watch that at least seven APCs were present, as well as a helicopter which was firing down on rooftops.[7] Damage of the buildings in Cirez seen by Human Rights Watch was consistent with those claims.

The most brutal incident was the killing of Rukia Nebihu, a twenty-seven-year-old woman who was seven months pregnant. Her father-in-law, Sefer Nebihu, was present with his wife, eldest son, Xhemsil, and five children when the police shot Rukia in the face, killing her instantly. Xhemsil was also killed. Sefer Nebihu told Human Rights Watch:

"The police destroyed my front gate with two tanks and came up to the windows of my house. About seventeen policemen came out of the tanks. They wore military camouflage, green and yellow, with a police sign on their chests. No masks. The tank came up to the window. One policeman broke the window with the butt of his gun and started shouting. They said "stand up" and I said "don't shoot because there are only women and children here." They cursed me and then one fired at me."[8]

Sefer Nebihu was hit three times in the right leg and one time in the left. Human Rights Watch saw the bullet marks, which were consistent with an automatic gun having been sprayed at about thigh level. All of the bullet scars were between the knees and groin. According to Sefer, he fell back and Rukia grabbed his leg while he was on the ground. He said:

"Rukia grabbed my leg and saw what happened as they smashed the side door. When the door was smashed, Rukia was holding my leg.

---

[1] Tom Walker, "Massacre by the 'Ethnic Cleansers'," Times (London), March 4, 1998.
[2] Human Rights Watch interview with Xhevdet Ahmeti, Likošane, May 24, 1998.
[3] Human Rights Watch telephone interview with Chris Hedges, June 16, 1998. See Chris Hedges, "Albanians Bury 24 Villagers Slain by the Serbs," New York Times, March 3, 1998.

[4] Humanitarian Law Center, Spotlight Report No. 26, "Kosovo: Human Rights in Times of Armed Conflict," May 1998. See also Philip Smucker, "Evidence Grows that Serb Police Units Carried Out Summary Executions," The Daily Telegraph, March 4, 1998.
[5] "Viktima e Likoshanit ishte debuar nga Gjermania gjate dhjetori te vjetme," Koha Ditore, May 1998.
[6] See, for example, Guy Dinmore, "Serbian Forces Accused of Slaughter," Financial Times, March 3, 1998.
[7] In a press conference on March 7, Ministry of Internal Affairs spokesman Colonel Ljubinko Cvetic told journalists that helicopters were only used for humanitarian purposes, such as for evacuating the injured.
[8] Human Rights Watch interview with Sefer Nebihu, Cirez, May 24, 1998.

They shot her and hit her in the face... After they shot Rukia, they said "What is he doing here?" and they fired at Xhemsil. I think there were fifteen to seventeen bullet holes in his stomach. He [the policeman] kept shooting until the magazine was empty. Then they [the police] entered all of the rooms checking everything. Seventeen policemen were inside, one was outside with a Motorola [radio]. I heard him say 'where now'?"

After the shooting, the police took Sefer to the house next door where his other son, twenty-one-year-old Zahir, was hiding. Sefer was told to call his son, which he did. He said:

"One [policeman] tried to hit him [Zahir] with the butt of his gun in the head but he ducked and it hit him in the chest. They told him to lie down. They forced me to open all the rooms in the house and they searched everything.

They took me to my brother's house and they asked who lives there. Inside the house were twenty-three women and children. I told them to come out. They came out and were told to lay down on the grass. One policeman came running up and said 'kill them all.' They started arguing amongst themselves and some of them said 'we can't shoot them'."

Sefer's other son, Ilir, who was the husband of Rukia, was also taken by the police from somewhere in the village during the attack in Cirez. His corpse was returned to Cirez on March 2 along with the other twenty-five victims from Likošane and Cirez. It is not known when or how he died.

Four other victims from Cirez were the sons of the Sejdiu family, Bekim, Nazmi, Bedri, and Beqir, who were apparently executed by the police outside of their home. According to Abida Sejdiu, the mother of the household, her sons came back from working in the fields when they heard the shooting near Likošane around 12:00 p.m.. Around 3:30 p.m. some APCs slammed open the family's front gates. Visibly disturbed, she told Human Rights Watch:

They [her sons] came from the field and we sat in one room. My daughter-in-law, two kids and my sons. They [the police] surrounded the house. We heard fighting in Likošane around noon. My sons were killed around 4 p.m. The tanks came in the garden, they broke the gates and two tanks were outside the compound and two behind. Two helicopters were constantly firing. Some seven to ten policemen broke into the house and our room. I stepped in front of the police and put my hands out in front of my sons. They took all of us into the garden. They said lie on the ground. They hit Bekim and I shouted "Don't you have any sons!" They hit me on the head with the end of the gun. They took all of my sons then I took the kids inside...[1]

At this point, Mrs. Sejdiu could say no more and left the room. Her husband, Sheremet said that she had witnessed her sons being killed. According to him, the police killed Nazmi first. Then they took Bekim outside and shot him in the garden, followed by Bedri and Beqir. He told Human Rights Watch that Beqir had seventeen bullets in his chest. The police didn't take the bodies. Human Rights Watch saw photographs of two of the Sejdiu brothers, each with bullet wounds, although it was not possible to determine from this the circumstances of their deaths.

Also killed in Cirez on March 1 in unknown circumstances were Ibish Rama, Smail Bajrami, Rexhep Rexhepi, Beqir Rexhepi, and Shaban Muja. Ibish Rama and Smail Bajrami were last seen in police custody.

According to Liman Ademi, a local villager, he, Ibish Rama, and Smail Bajrami, were hiding along with three others in a warehouse in the center of Cirez when the police attack began around 12:30 p.m.. After one hour with machine gun fire and a helicopter shooting over head, the three of them decided to leave the warehouse and hide in the village. Liman Ademi told Human Rights Watch what happened next:

"Three of us went in one direction. Me and Ibish went towards our homes. Smail came with us because his sister lives in the same village. But the three of us found ourselves in front of an APC. They [the police] said lie down and one policeman got out of the APC. We were handcuffed together and guns were pointed at us. They took us inside the APC and we drove to the main road. One policeman went out of the APC and called some other policeman. I was closest to the door. They untied me and I went outside with one policeman and he told me to wait there, but the other one was aiming his gun at me. Then the APC started to move slowly [because there was a disturbance somewhere else]. The other cop started to move away from me slowly. At that moment, the other cop aiming at me turned away. I took the chance and ran away. My two friends were still tied inside the APC. Three days later I found out that my two friends were massacred along with twelve others."[2]

On March 3, all twenty-six people killed in Likošane and Cirez were buried in a field near the two villages. An estimated 30,000 people attended the ceremony. Police checkpoints on the major road from Komoran prohibited many more from coming. Visitors from outside the area and journalists had to circumvent the police by back roads and walking through fields.

POLICE ATTACKS IN DONJI PREKAZ

Human Rights Watch was not able to visit Donji Prekaz, a village with a pre-war population of approximately 1,000 people, due to continued fighting. It is, therefore, the case from Drenica on which the least direct testimony was available to Human Rights Watch. This notwithstanding, Human Rights Watch has concluded that serious violations of international humanitarian law were committed by the Serbian special police: notably, indiscriminate attacks on non-combatants, the systematic destruction of civilian property, and the summary and arbitrary executions of those in detention.[3] Although it appears that some Albanian villagers in Donji Prekaz were armed and defending themselves against the police, the evidence is overwhelming that the police used excessive and indiscriminate force, and that the police executed at least three people after they had been detained or had surrendered.

The first attack on Donji Prekaz took place on January 22, 1998, and was focused on the compound of Shaban Jashari, whose son Adem was known as a local KLA leader. Adem Jashari had already been convicted in absentia by a Priština court on July 11, 1997, for "terrorist acts" along with fourteen other ethnic Albanians, in a trial that clearly failed to conform to international standards.[4]

According to the Serbian Ministry of Internal Affairs, the January 22 incident was a shoot-out between local gangs. However, according to Adem Shaban Jashari, who was interviewed a few days after the first incident by the Humanitarian Law Center and was killed in the second police attack, the police attacked his home around 5:20 a.m. but were repelled when Adem's friends "from the woods" came to help.[5]

Others were also victims of what appears to have been execution-style killings after detention or in unknown circumstances. Hysen

---

[1] Human Rights Watch interview with Abida Sejdiu, Cirez, May 24, 1998.

[2] Human Rights Watch interview with Liman Ademi, Cirez, May 24, 1998.

[3] This conclusion is founded on Human Rights Watch interviews with journalists and human rights researchers, reports by other human rights organizations, notably Amnesty International and the Humanitarian Law Center, as well as newspaper reports and the analysis of photographs. See Amnesty International, "A Human Rights Crisis in Kosovo Province, Document Series A: Violence in Drenica, February-April 1998," London, June 1998, and Humanitarian Law Center, Spotlight Report No.26.

[4] See press release, "Human Rights Watch/Helsinki Condemns Political Trial in Kosovo," July 15, 1997. The three defendants that were present for the trial, Besim Rama, Idriz Asllani, and Avni Nura, all stated that they had "confessed" after being tortured. All of the defendants were sentenced to prison terms ranging between four and twenty years.

[5] Humanitarian Law Center, Spotlight Report No. 26, Kosovo.

Manxholli, a fifty-two-year-old ethnic Albanian from the nearby town of Srbica was killed on January 22 in unknown circumstances. His body was found the same day near the ammunition factory. According to the Council for the Defense of Human Rights and Freedoms and the Humanitarian Law Center, Idriz Idrizi was seized by the police on January 23 near the ammunition factory and, as of September 1998, was still missing.[1]

The police attacked Prekaz and the Jashari compound again on March 5, 1998, this time in a more prepared and determined manner. All evidence suggests that the attack was not intended to apprehend armed Albanians, considered "terrorists" by the government, but, as Amnesty International concluded in its report on violence in Drenica, "to eliminate the suspects and their families."[2] Testimonies collected by human rights groups and journalists indicate several cases of extra-judicial executions and unlawful killings from excessive force.

An estimated fifty-eight ethnic Albanians were killed in the attack, including eighteen women and ten children under the age of sixteen, and then summarily buried by the police before autopsies could be performed. The exact number and identities of the dead reported by different sources varies slightly, a consequence of the manner in which the burial was conducted (see below) and because some of the bodies were burned beyond recognition.[3] Among those buried were at least six Albanians who were killed in unclear circumstances in the nearby village of Lausa and buried together with the dead from Donji Prekaz.

According to the Serbian police, the attack on Donji Prekaz was in response to KLA attacks on nearby police patrols. According to witnesses, however, the attack was well orchestrated and included APCs, artillery shelling from the nearby ammunition factory, and special police forces in camouflage and face paint. The first target was the Ljushtaku family compound, which is between the Jashari compound and the ammunition factory. The Ljushtaku family members fled their home as the police turned the focus of their attack on the compound of Shaban Jashari.

Based on interviews with witnesses, the Humanitarian Law Center confirmed that inside the house were, at least, Shaban Jashari (74), his wife Zaha (72), and their sons Rifat, Hamza (47), and Adem (42) with their families, including four girls, Blerina (7), Fatime (8), Besarte (11) and Lirije (14), and four boys, Blerim (12), Besim (16), Afete (17), and Selvete (20). All of these people died except Besarte, who hid under a marble slab used for kneading dough during the attack. Besarte was later captured by the police, taken to the nearby ammunition factory and then released. Interviewed later by a foreign journalist, Besarte told of hours-long shelling which killed her seven brothers and sisters, her mother and uncle Adem inside the house. "I tried to pretend I was dead," she told a journalist from the Sunday Times. "But one of the soldiers put his hand on my chest and he felt I was alive."[4]

Also killed in the attack, and probably in Shaban Jashari's house, were Adem Jashari's wife Adilje, their son Kushtrim (13), Rifat Jashari's wife, Zafire Batir, and their daughter Igballe (11), and Hamza Jashari's wife Feride Ramadan and their child Fatusha (8).

The police also attacked the homes of other Jashari family members in the village, including those of Sherif, Zuk, Qazim, Fejzija, and Beqir Jashari (43). The daughter of Serif Jashari, who was hiding in the house of Beqir Jashari together with twenty-four children, five women, and six men told the Humanitarian Law Center that the police surrounded the house with APCs, shelled the roof and then fired tear gas into the house. She told the center:

The soldiers shouted for us to come out one by one or they would kill us. When my cousin Qazim (47) came out with his hands up, they killed him on the steps. I was in the middle of the yard when it happened. We ran and had just gone through the first cordon when the soldiers caught my cousin Nazim (27) who was helping his mother Bahtije along. They grabbed him, tore off the woman's dress we had given him to wear, ordered him to lie down on the ground and then to get up. He had to do this many times. They fired into the back of his head and back and I saw his body jerking from the bullets.[5]

Bahtije Jashari, who also witnessed the killing of Qazim Jashari, told center staff about her son's death:

"My son Nazim took a child of one and a half years to hide him from the police and tried to help me along because I didn't have my crutch. The police grabbed him by both arms and stopped him from helping me. I begged them to let him go. They ordered my son to lie down and then searched him for guns. Then they ordered him to stand up with his hands in the air. It lasted only a few seconds. I clutched my head and started screaming. All of a sudden, the police ordered Nazim to lie down again and emptied a whole magazine into his back. They didn't let me turn him face up. A policeman told me to get away from there but I didn't. I looked at my son for the last time and said good-bye to him."[6]

The Humanitarian Law Center interviewed three people who witnessed Qazim and Nazim's executions. A forensic pathologist who examined a photograph of Nazim Jashari's body for Amnesty International found injuries "broadly consistent with the accounts of him having been extrajudicially executed."[7]

Amnesty International also interviewed most of the family groups that hid in Beqir Jashari's house and found their testimonies largely corroborated details of the attack and the extrajudicial execution of three of the six men who were with them, as well as the wounding of a fourth.

SUMMARY BURIAL

On March 8, 1998, the police contacted the local Council for the Defense of Human Rights and Freedoms in Srbica and told them to take the bodies of those killed in Donji Prekaz. The council asked for the list of people killed and the appropriate documentation but were provided nothing. According to the Council, the police had transferred forty-six of the corpses to the Priština hospital morgue on March 7, and then brought them back to Srbica the next day, where they were eventually placed in a warehouse without walls on the outskirts of town.[8] Among the fifty-eight bodies were those of eight children aged seven to sixteen, and thirteen women, as well as a number of elderly. Ten corpses remained unidentifiable.[9]

Photographs taken at this time of the corpses reveal serious disfigurement and deep burns, probably from explosions. Shaban Jashari had a large hole in his chest with burn marks and was missing his right hand. There were a number of dead children, including a baby, some

---

[1] "Enforced Disappearances in Kosovo January-May 1998," Humanitarian Law Center.
[2] Amnesty International, "A Human Rights Crisis in Kosovo Province, Document Series A: Violence in Drenica, February-April 1998," London, June 1998.
[3] According to Amnesty International, fifty-six bodies were buried on March 11, forty-one of which were identified. Of these, twelve were women, eleven were children under sixteen, and at least two people came from Lausa. According to the Humanitarian Law Center, at least fifty-five people were buried, thirty-seven identified and eighteen unidentified. Among these were seven women, eleven children and five people from Lausa. The Albanian-language daily Koha Ditore wrote on March 9 that, in Donji Prekaz alone, forty-six people died, including eleven children, eleven women and five elderly (above seventy years old). The account of the local Council for the Defense of Human Rights and Freedoms is the most detailed, and is cited further below.
[4] Marie Colvin, "Kosovo's Silent Houses of the Dead," Sunday Times, March 15, 1998.

[5] Humanitarian Law Center, Spotlight Report No. 26, Kosovo.
[6] Ibid.
[7] Amnesty International, "A Human Rights Crisis in Kosovo Province, Document Series A: Violence in Drenica, February-April 1998."
[8] Council for Defense of Human Rights and Freedoms, "Appeal on the Latest Events in Skenderaj," Priština, March 9, 1998.
[9] Council for Defense of Human Rights and Freedoms, "Quarterly Report January-March, 1998," Priština, April 17, 1998.

of them burned almost beyond recognition. Adem Jashari had a bullet wound in his neck.

On March 9, the police warned publicly that they would bury the victims themselves if they were not buried by family members quickly. Family members waited in the hope that autopsies would be conducted so, on March 10, the police dug a large grave with a bulldozer near Donji Prekaz and buried fifty-six people, ten of them still unidentified.

That same day, relatives of the deceased, a group of Albanian doctors from Priština, religious leaders from the Islamic community and the Catholic church, and international aid agencies like the ICRC were denied access to Drenica by the police. ICRC also tried to act as an intermediary between the police and the families but was turned down by the authorities.[1] Police spokesman Ljubinko Cvetic, in a press conference in Priština, told reporters that humanitarian aid agencies had been turned back because they had been caught with weapons in the past. The head of the Secretary of Information in Kosovo, Bosko Drobnjak, later told Human Rights Watch the same story.[2]

The next day, March 11, the bodies were disinterred by relatives and reburied in accordance with Islamic tradition, with the heads pointed towards Mecca. None of the bodies showed signs that autopsies had been performed, even though Yugoslav law stipulates that autopsies should be conducted when there is reason to believe that the death was connected to a criminal act.[3]

On March 13, the United States-based human rights group Physicians for Human Rights (PHR), which conducted autopsies in Bosnia, requested twelve visas from the Yugoslav authorities for an international team of forensics experts it had assembled to investigate the deaths in Donji Prekaz, Likošane and Cirez. In addition, the prosecutor for the ICTY requested visas for PHR and asked that its staff accompany the team to Kosovo.[4] In mid-April, the Yugoslav government responded to PHR, via the U.S. State Department, that three U.S. citizens could travel to the region as long as they were accompanied by "experts" designated by the Yugoslav government, an offer that PHR did not accept.[5]

The Council for the Defense of Human Rights and Freedoms later compiled a list of those who were identified as having died in Donji Prekaz from March 5-7, as well as some Albanians killed in unclear circumstances in the nearby village of Lausha. They are:

From Donji Prekaz
Shaban Murat Jashari (74), Zahide Jashari (72), Hamëz Shaban ashari (47), Adem Shaban Jashari (42), Zarife Bahtir Jashari (49), eride Jashari (43), Adile Bahtir Jashari (40), Hidajete Rifat Jashari 18), Igballe Rifat Jashari (13), Igballe Rifat Jashari (11), Valdete fat Jashari (14), Selvete Hamëz Jashari (20), Besim Hamëz Jashari 16), Afete Hamëz Jashari (17), Blerim Hamëz Jashari (12), Fatime amëz Jashari (8), Blerina Hamëz Jashari (7), Lirije Hamëz Jashari 14), Fitim Adem Jashari (17), Kushtrim Adem Jashari (13), Elheme ashari (57), Blerim Zenë Jashari (16), Bujar Zenë Jashari (12), Abullah Zenë Jashari, Hajzer Zymer Jashari (20), Halit Imer Jashari 65), Qazim Osman Jashari (47), Nazmi Zukë Jashari (26), Sinan amadan Jashari (66), Ali Ramadan Jashari (68), Feride Ramadan ashari (43), Beqir Bajram Jashari (43), Halil Bajram Jashari (35), herif Brahim Jashari (47), Bahtije Muharrem Jashari (45), Murtez ymber Jashari (22), Faik Tahir Jashari (30), Qerim Husë Jashari (54), alë Hajzer Jashari (60), Kajtaz Jashari (44), Hamit H. Jashari (65), sak Halili (35)

From Lauša
Osman Shaban Geci, Sadik Miran Kackini (38), Miftar Rreci (43), Fatime Gashi (46), Gazmend Bajram Gashi (16), Makfirete Bajram Gashi (13)

ATTACK ON NOVI POKLEK

On May 31, an estimated 300 special police forces attacked Novi Poklek, a relatively wealthy village next to the small city of Glogovac. Ten men were seized by the police during the attack; one of them was found dead later that day and the other nine are still missing and are presumed dead. An eyewitness claims he saw five of these men being shot by the police, although this could not be confirmed.

How the attack began remains unclear. According to ethnic Albanians from Novi Poklek who spoke with Human Rights Watch, a car with two policemen had an accident near the village. Two villagers, Ajet Gashi and Shefqit Bytyci, went to give the plainclothes policemen some help. One of them reportedly heard the policeman in the car radio for help, saying that they had come under attack. While Human Rights Watch was not able to confirm this story, and it thus remains unclear why the police attacked Novi Poklek, there is no question of the abuses that followed.

According to three separate eyewitnesses, the police attack lasted from 12:15 p.m. to 8:00 p.m. and involved an estimated twenty-two vehicles, both APCs and jeeps, from a base at the nearby ferrous-nickel plant. The witnesses told Human Rights Watch that the police went from house to house and gathered the men and women of the village. About sixty women and children and ten men were then forced into the house of Sahit Qorri. The women and children were later released and told to run for the neighboring village of Vasiljevo. One of the ten men, seventeen-year-old Ardian Deliu, was found dead that evening after the police had left, while the other nine men are still missing.

One man from Novi Poklek claimed to have witnessed most of the attack from behind a stone wall about 200 meters from the center of the village. He testified that he saw the police shoot five people from behind, but Human Rights Watch was not able to corroborate the story. He said:

"The village was surrounded by about three hundred policemen with artillery. I saw it with my own eyes, about twenty-two vehicles were in the village. Four to five policemen entered each house and I saw the police forcing people out of their homes. They gathered them together in front of one house [Sahit Qorri's] at the entrance of the village and made them go into the house. Ten men and I don't know how many women and children, probably between sixty or seventy.

They burned one house in the center of the village. I don't know whose house because I only saw the flames. After one hour they led the women and children out of the village and forced them to Vasiljevo. Then they burned two or three more houses. And then the shooting began from all directions. It was about 4:00 or 4:30 p.m.

Then two men, Ahmet Berisha and Hajjriz Hajdini, were taken out of the house. They told them to walk in the other direction from the women and children. While they were walking, it was sixty or seventy meters away, they started shooting. I just saw them falling, and I could see their backs, and they didn't get up. Ten minutes later another neighbor [Sefer Qorri] was told to leave the house and he was also told to walk in the same direction, and at about the same point they shot him too.

After that many other houses were burned. Smoke was rising and it kept me from seeing but I saw two more silhouettes walking and falling but I could not see who it was.[6]

According to this witness, twenty-eight houses were burned and many were looted. This number was confirmed by Zahrije Podrimcaku, an activist from Glogovac for the Council for the Defense of Human Rights and Freedoms, who witnessed the attack from her balcony about 500 meters away. According to her, twenty-nine houses

---

[1] Associated Press, March 10, 1998.
Human Rights Watch interview with Bosko Drobnjak, Priština, June 11, 1998.
Yugoslav Code of Criminal Procedure, Article 252.
According to the Dayton Accords, signed by the Federal Republic of Yugoslavia, the Yugoslav government is obliged to cooperate fully with ICTY and to comply with requests for investigations into alleged war crimes.
Physicians for Human Rights press release, April 28, 1998.

[6] Human Rights Watch interview, Vasiljevo, June 7, 1998.

were burned and she saw the police taking away television sets and video recorders."[1]

A woman from Novi Poklek, who was among the women and children taken into Sefer Qorri's house, largely corroborated the other witness' story. According to her, the police, who were familiar with Albanian customs, went from house to house ordering the men of the households to hand over their guns. She said:

"One [policeman] approached us and said that the head of the household should come out. He said give me your gun. My husband said that he had no gun and that he only works for his family. He said just give it. "You have a good house, you are wealthy so it is not possible that you don't have a gun." He had green eyes and a thin gold chain. He was not tall and was dirty blond. He wore black gloves and was in a policeman's uniform. They told my husband to go on and take the weapon and they made the children and women go outside and lie down."

According to this woman, her husband emerged from the house with some policemen holding a cloth on his bleeding head. One policeman allegedly said, "How could you not have guns if you have this?" - waving an Albanian state flag. Another policeman then came and held a gun to her husband's mouth ordering him to lie down. Then they told all of them to walk to the house of Safit Qorri. She said:

All of us were told to go in the house and we were led to a room. When we entered there was a guy watching us and he spoke Serbian and Albanian. There were ten men and fifty or sixty women. They asked the men where their sons were. One old man didn't understand Serbian and they hit him. One policeman pulled out his knife and threatened him saying, 'I'll show you now'. My husband said to the police "In God's name, don't do it." The policeman stopped and said I'll leave you alone, but you'll see what happens when Lutka[2] comes.

Another guy then came with a green uniform. He had black gloves and a black vest with thinning, short blond hair. He told the other policemen to separate the men and the women. He asked my husband where he is from. The men were in the other room but I heard him say he is from Vasiljevo, so he decided to send us [the women and children] in that direction. We went outside and they ordered us to walk and not to stop. When we started to walk we heard shooting. We were running and bullets were flying all around, even at us, so we kept going. The men were still in the house."[3]

Zahrije Podrimcaku was in Novi Poklek on June 1 and saw the body of Ardian Deliu with a bullet wound in his left cheek and one in the left side of his neck. She told Human Rights Watch that she saw nine spots of blood, and shoes, a belt, and coat buttons near the blood marks.[4] Human Rights Watch spoke with two foreign journalists who were in Novi Poklek that week. Carsten Ingemann, a Danish photographer, said:

"I saw several blood stains on the ground. They looked similar. In some of the places you could see that there was shooting there because there were holes in the ground. I saw three or four blood splotches. One was from the same person. You could see the blood spot and then a trail of blood, like the body had been dragged, and then another blood spot with a bullet hole in the ground."[5]

An American journalist, Philip Smucker, was also in Novi Poklek that week. He told Human Rights Watch that he saw blood in eight places in the area where villagers said the men had been shot, as well as bullet casings next to the blood stains.[6]

---

[1] Human Rights Watch interview with Zahrije Podrimcaku, Priština, June 9, 1998.
[2] "Lutka" means "doll" in Serbian.
[3] Human Rights Watch interview, Vasiljevo, June 7, 1998.
[4] Human Rights Watch interview with Zahrije Podrimcaku, Priština, June 9, 1998.
[5] Human Rights Watch interview with Carsten Ingemann, Priština, June 7, 1998.
[6] Human Rights Watch interview with Philip Smucker, Priština, June 7, 1998. See also Philip Smucker, "Villagers Tell of Ouster, Mass Executions," The Washington Times, June 5, 1998, and Tim Butcher, "Hidden Massacre is Uncovered in Kosovo Village," Sunday Telegraph, June 28, 1998.

What remains unclear in the Novi Poklek attack is whether the police faced any resistance from the Albanians prior to the concentration of villagers in Safit Qorri's house. One villager claimed that she saw a dead policeman and heard the police speaking on a walkie-talkie that one policeman had been killed. But she, like all the other villagers interviewed by Human Rights Watch, strenuously asserted that "there was no resistance."

All evidence points to at least one summary execution after police gathered Poklek's villagers together, that of Ardian Deliu, and the detention and possible execution of nine others. As of September 1998, the police had not offered any information about the nine men last seen being taken away by the police, despite requests from the families and their lawyers.[7] The nine missing are: Ahmet Berisha (40), Hajriz Hajdini (48), Muhamet Hajdini (45), Sahit Qorri (60), Sefer Qorri, (55), Ferat Hoti (39), Rama Asllani (60), Fidel Berisha (17), and Blerim Shishani (15).

Villagers told Human Rights Watch that one man from the army in a military camouflage uniform was leading the action, while the others were in police uniforms. One villager said that the leader was about 165 cm tall, well-built, and had short, blond hair and a reddish face. The name of Lutka, the vice-commander of the Glogovac police station, was also mentioned a number of times as someone who was present. Some villagers also claim that they saw Pero Damjarac, the police chief in Glogovac, entering the village in a white Volkswagen during the action.

Zahrije Podrimcaku, an activist for the Council for Defense of Human Rights and Freedoms who investigated the incident, was arrested by the police in Priština on June 9, 1998, about one hour after she told Human Rights Watch about her findings in Novi Poklek. On June 13 she was charged with "terrorist acts," according to Articles 125 and 136 of the Yugoslav Penal Code, and is currently in the Lipljan prison.

Violations in the Yugoslav-Albania Border Region

After a period of intense shuttle diplomacy by American diplomat Richard Holbrooke, on May 15, 1998, Yugoslav President Slobodan Milošević met the president of the shadow Kosovar Albanian state Ibrahim Rugova for the first time in almost ten years. The talks were heralded by Western governments as "a positive first step" that could lead to a negotiated settlement of the conflict. On May 25, the E.U. member states rewarded Milošević by deciding not to go forward with an earlier decision to impose a ban on investment in Serbia. (See section Response of the International Community.)

That week, the Serbian police together with forces of the Yugoslav Army began the largest offensive to date against a series of villages on Kosovo's border with Albania. The offensive was apparently intended to create a cordon sanitaire along the border in order to cut off the supply routes of the KLA. Up until that point, small arms and new recruits had been arriving in large numbers from northern Albania, a region that is largely out of the control of the Albanian government.

While KLA troops were definitely in the area, and at times were attacking the police and army, many villages from Pec in the north to Dakovica in the south were shelled while civilians were still present. Noncombatants who fled the attacks weresometimes fired on by snipers, and a still undetermined number of people were taken into detention. Afterwards, most villages in the region were systematically destroyed, and farmers' livestock was shot, to ensure that no one could return in the short run. Human Rights Watch conducted an investigation in the area in September and saw clear indications that houses had been set on fire where there was no evidence that combat had occurred.

The offensive was clearly intended to depopulate the region. Approximately 15,000 people fled over the mountains into Albania,

---

[7] Letter submitted to the district court in Priština by the lawyers Fazli Balaj, Bajram Kelmendi, Destan Rukiqi, Lirije Osmani, and Nekibe Kelmendi, June 11, 1998.

sometimes under fire from the police and army, and an estimated 30,000 escaped northwards into Montenegro. An unknown number went east towards the then-KLA held territory in Drenica.

Human Rights Watch spent four days interviewing refugees in northern Albania and Tirana, Albania's capital, in late June, and two weeks interviewing refugees in Montenegro in September. A clear pattern emerged of detentions, beatings, indiscriminate shelling, excessive force, and the systematic destruction of villages. One refugee claimed to have witnessed the rape of six people, two of them thirteen-year-old girls. On three occasions, refugees said, helicopters marked with the red cross fired on refugees heading for the border.[1]

Based on interviews with refugees in Albania, Human Rights Watch heard of shelling in the following villages and towns: Decan, Junik, Bakaj, Bokez, Carabrec, Prelep, Ljocan, Vokš, Drenovac, Slup, Dobroš, Rastevica, Ljbuša, Nivokaz, Ponoševac, Poberz, Smolic, Jasic, Isnic, Strelc, Polac, Polluz, Obri, and Likovac.

USE OF INDISCRIMINATE FORCE AND ATTACKS ON CIVILIANS

Refugees interviewed by Human Rights Watch in Albania and Montenegro told strikingly similar stories about the shelling of their villages. Most often the attacks began in the early morning, around 5:00 a.m., without warning. The villagers would flee into the woods or the mountains until the shelling subsided. Many civilians were reportedly killed during the shelling and as they attempted to flee their villages.

Civilians, predominantly women, children, and elderly people, would travel from village to village, sometimes under the escort of armed male family members or the KLA. When there was no place left to go, they crossed the mountains into Albania. Along the way, the police or army sometimes fired in their direction, and occasionally at them directly.

Shkurta Bacaj from Drenovac said she left her village on May 25 and went to her uncle's home in Junik because they were shelling:

"At 7 a.m. they began [shelling] and it went on all day. In the evening we left the village. When they shelled, every person in the village went to a village where they had family. We had no other solution but to go to the mountain. The place where they shell from is Hulaj village, where the police are based. They shell from there and we had to be careful because the police were shooting at us too. We were lots of children, old women and men."[2]

She and her family stayed four days in Junik, until the shelling began there too on May 30.

According to Ms. Bacaj, everybody in Junik left the village, in total some 7,000 Junik inhabitants and 5,000 people who had come to Junik from nearby villages. Ms. Bacaj went to Dubrosh. Along the way, snipers injured her grandmother, Time Gazheraj, and six others, including Hate Shalaj, who later died, Caush Cestaj, Osman Gazheraj, and Shkelzen Kukaj. Then Ms. Bacaj herself was injured. She told Human Rights Watch:

"While I was walking they saw us and they shot at us in order to kill. The police shot at us and hit me in the leg. We lay down on the ground, then they kept on shooting. The bullet entered my left leg and right arm. We were a group of eight [her father, two sisters, a niece, younger brother and two uncles]. Only I was hit. We stayed there [in a ditch at a place called Shkoze] for fifteen hours not daring to move because they were shooting. From 7 a.m. to 10 p.m. we didn't dare to move. We returned to Junik when it got dark. Then they took me by car to Dobrosh, where I stayed for ten days."

Ms. Bacaj walked twelve hours through the mountains into Albania on June 9 without incident. Human Rights Watch visited her in the Bajram Curri hospital and saw two bullet scars. One bullet apparently entered her lower left shin and exited above the knee; the other bullet grazed the right shoulder.

Other refugees said that they were shot at as they tried to cross the border. Human Rights Watch interviewed the Selmanaj family just as they arrived in Bajram Curri directly from the mountains. Two women and one man escorted ten children, ranging in age from a baby to twelve years old. The children and the adults looked worn and dazed, having just walked for two days and two nights through the mountains. One of the women said:

"We left my village [Rastavica] three months ago when there was the attack on Glodjane. We have been moving for three months. Two nights ago we left and we have been traveling for two days and two nights. In the night they tried to shoot us. They were shelling us in the forest. They put lights on us and fired. They were shooting at us with helicopters near the border."[3]

One woman from the village of Slup said:

"We left Jasic at 6 a.m. for the border. We were lucky that no one shot at us. While we were coming, an airplane came and was shooting. An airplane was following us and bombing. We were 300 people all spread out. They shot with automatic guns and bombs. They shot for two hours near the border. We hid in some caves. I don't know if there were injured people because we all hid in the caves."[4]

On June 21, Human Rights Watch interviewed Dr. Imra Vishi, a doctor from Kosovo who was working in the Bajram Curri hospital. He said that, since the refugees began arriving in early June, the hospital had treated twenty-two refugees in the department of surgery with gunshot wounds, shrapnel, or other similar injuries. Eight people with gunshot wounds were in the hospital at that moment, one of them, a twenty-three-year-old man, with multiple wounds believed to have been from a single projectile in Smolic on June 8.[5] According to Dr. Vishi, most of the twenty-two injuries since June 1 were incurred during the shelling of villages, but some people, he said, were injured in battle. Two people were injured by grenades while trying to cross the border. Human Rights Watch interviewed one seventy-year-old woman in the hospital, Time Maserekaj from Voks, who had bullet wound scars on her right forearm and left wrist from what she claimed was sniper fire.[6]

Some of the wounded interviewed were most likely injured while fighting with the police and army; as combatants, they do not have protected status under international humanitarian law unless hors de combat. However, non-combatants too were systematically attacked in their villages during indiscriminate shelling or deliberately targeted as they were fleeing. Common Article 3 of the Geneva Conventions clearly states that, in internal armed conflicts, civilians and others who have ceased to be combatants are protected persons who must be treated humanely, with specific prohibitions on murder, torture, or cruel, humiliating or degrading treatment. In addition, there is clear evidence that livestock was killed and villages were destroyed beyond any possible military need, which is also a violation of the rules of war (see section Legal Standards and the Kosovo Conflict).

Finally, refugees reported three incidents where helicopters marked with the Red Cross emblem fired on civilians. Two cases were reported by journalist Roy Gutman in an article published on June 22, 1998, in Newsday. Mr. Gutman told Human Rights Watch that he had spoken with four individuals who described observing a Red Cross

---

[1] See also a report by Physicians for Human Rights based on a mission to northern Albania in June. The report documents "serious human rights violations, including detentions, arbitrary arrests, violent beatings and rape, throughout Kosovo during the past six months." Physicians for Human Rights, "Medical Group Recounts Individual Testimony of Human Rights Abuses in Kosovo," June 24, 1998.

[2] Human Rights Watch interview with Shkurta Bacaj, Bajram Curri, Albania, June 16, 1998.

[3] Human Rights Watch interview with members of the Selmanaj family, Bajram Curri, Albania, June 19, 1998.

[4] Human Rights Watch interview with man from Slup, Bajram Curri, Albania, June 21, 1998.

[5] Dr. Vishi said that the patient had eight shrapnel-like wounds but claimed he had been struck by only one bullet.

[6] Human Rights Watch interview with Dr. Imra Vishi, Bajram Curri, Albania, June 21, 1998.

helicopter firing on people near Rrasa e Zogut (in Albanian) on June 13 and 14. He also spoke with one witness who said he saw the same thing at Baba I Bokes (in Albanian) on June 11.[1]

Human Rights Watch interviewed one witness who claimed to have seen a Red Cross helicopter engaged in military activity: this, however, was a KLA soldier who said that the helicopter fired on civilians in Smolic on approximately June 2, 1998.[2]

SUMMARY EXECUTIONS IN LJUBENIC

There is still no clear picture of what happened in Ljubenic on May 25, 1998. But interviews with six witnesses conducted by six different organizations suggest that at least eight, ethnic Albanians were executed there by the Serbian special police.

The first account of the executions was made by the Kosova Information Center (KIC), a news service close to Ibrahim Rugova's Democratic League of Kosovo. In its May 26 bulletin, KIC reported that police killed the following nine people in Ljubenic: Zeqe Hamzaj (68), Brahim Hamzaj (64), Dervish Hamzaj (51), Ymer Hamzaj (53), Gani Hamzaj (25), Rifat Hamzaj (24), Bashkim Hamzaj (23), Hysen Alimehaj (40), and Haxhi Goga (24). One eye witness, Mehmet Gogaj, reportedly told KIC:

Around 1:15 p.m., the Serb army started shelling Albanian homes. A bit later, many policemen in buses and armored personnel carriers surrounded the Ljubenic village. The Serb forces raided houses of local Albanians, killing and massacring people. Men were forced out in the yards and executed in front of their family members. The Serbs also took my three sons and my nephew. They were forced to stand against the outside wall of the house. Then, the Serbs walked several meters back and started firing rallies from automatic rifle on them. The four boys fell to the ground. There was nothing I could do.[3]

Two human rights organizations, the Humanitarian Law Center and Amnesty International, subsequently interviewed witnesses who had slightly different stories, but were able to confirm some executions. According to the Amnesty International report on the incident, a civilian car possibly carrying reserve policemen was fired upon on the road between Decan and Pec near Ljubenic, on the morning of May 25. Ostensibly in retaliation, police with armored cars attacked Ljubenic from a distance with artillery for thirty minutes and then entered the village around 1:30 p.m. A group of police reportedly entered one house where fourteen people were sheltered and separated the men from the women and children. The women and children were told to run away, while the men were beaten. The men were then also ordered to run away and, as they were running, they were shot in the back. Ymer Hamzaj, Brahim Hamzaj, and Bashkim Hamzaj were killed; one man was injured but survived.

According to Amnesty International, a group of policemen also entered the house of Zeqe Hamzaj, who was taken away with his sons, Gani and Rifat. The three, together with a guest, Haxhi Goga (24), were reportedly told to strip to their underwear, beaten and then killed.[4]

The Helsinki Committee for Human Rights in Serbia interviewed one witness from Ljubenic, identified as N.N., who arrived in Plav, Montenegro, on June 3, 1998, with six other men. He told the Helsinki Committee that he saw the police kill nine of his neighbors, aged twenty-three to sixty-five, in front of their house, although no names were provided.[5]

Finally, the Council for the Defense of Human Rights and Freedoms interviewed Ardeshir Gogaj, who was wounded by the police in Ljubenic. He told the council:

At about 12:30 p.m., after several shots, we saw the Serbian army and police from Peja [Pec] heading for Decan [Decan]. They entered the village of Ljubenic and beat women, children, elderly, and adults. Then they went into the house of Shaban Husku, where ten citizens from Decan had hidden. They took women and children and lined them up to execute them. We could see what the Serbian army was doing to them. They came and took us out into the yard. They lined us up to execute us and opened fire towards us. My brother Haxhi Mehmet Goga was killed, whereas I was wounded. Later on, I went towards the place called "Zagerlla", where I saw many killed, about twenty-nine. On the way to the mosque, I saw many killed and wounded near the house of Rame Huskaj. I saw that Zeqe Misini and his two sons were killed. As I was wounded, I could not go further, so I went back home where my brother's corpse was. Then I passed out and I have no idea what happened later on. Once again, I point out that I have seen tens of killed and wounded who remained in the fields, as well as tens of houses that were ruined and burned. Our village has become ruins.[6]

In northern Albania, Human Rights Watch interviewed a refugee, T.H., from the village of Slup who had been in Ljubenic for four days prior to the morning of the attack, and gave a slightly different account of the attack. She said that police dressed in blue uniforms arrived in Ljubenic around 4:00 a.m. wearing masks. She told Human Rights Watch that she watched from a house about twenty meters away where she was staying with her three children:

Four policemen came around 4:00 a.m. They wore masks. We were in the basement of M.D.'s house.... I saw from the window. The police took nineteen people from a house. It was three men, four woman and twelve children. They took an old man with twin daughters, thirteen years old. They pushed the old man against the wall of the garden. They took off the girls' clothes and four policemen raped the two daughters ... It was all between 4:00 and 6:00 a.m..[7]

T.H. claimed to have seen the police shoot those in the yard, but Human Rights Watch was unable to confirm her account. However, taken together with the testimonies collected by the other human rights groups, the evidence is overwhelming that at least nine summary executions took place. Human Rights Watch also saw a photograph, allegedly of the Hamzaj family, which showed the bodies of four older men, ranging in age from forty to sixty, all of them in their underwear on the ground with bullet wounds to their bodies.

THE USE OF LANDMINES

The Federal Republic of Yugoslavia has not signed the Convention on the Prohibition of the Use, Stockpiling, Production and Transfer of Anti-Personnel Mines and On their Destruction, known as the 1997 Mine Ban Treaty. At a regional conference on the treaty held in March 1998, the Yugoslav Ministry of Defense defended the decision by arguing that, "through no fault of her own," Yugoslavia had been, "excluded from the work of a number of international organizations, and been subjected to additional political, economic, and psychological pressure."[8]

---

[1] Human Rights Watch interview with Roy Gutman, Bajram Curri, Albania, June 21, 1998.

[2] Human Rights Watch interview with KLA soldier, Tirana, Albania, June 23, 1998.

[3] KIC, May 26, 1998.

[4] Amnesty International, "A Human Rights Crisis in Kosovo Province, Document Series A: Events to June 1998, 5: Ljubenic and Poklek: A Pattern Repeated," July 1998.

[5] Helsinki Committee for Human Rights in Serbia, "Report on Refugees from Kosovo Situated in Montenegro," Belgrade, June 18, 1998.

[6] Council for the Defense of Human Rights and Freedoms, "Human Rights Violations in the Course of June-July 1998."

[7] Human Rights Watch interview with woman from Slop, Markaj, Albania, June 19, 1998.

[8] Basic Points of the Statement by the Representative of the Federal Republic of Yugoslavia at the International Seminar on Anti-Personnel Mines, Budapest, March 26-28, 1998. The Yugoslav government's justifications for not signing the landmines treaty are worth noting. At the regional seminar, the Yugoslav delegate said:
(I) Through no fault of her own, the Federal Republic of Yugoslavia has been, for a longer period in a very specific international situation, excluded from the work of a number of international organizations, and been subjected to additional political, economic, and psychological pressure, (II) It is evident that due to the above the Federal Republic of

The FRY representative to the seminar told the delegates that Yugoslavia was maintaining its stock of landmines only for the purposes of training. He said:

By maintaining her stock of anti-personnel mines for a certain period, the Federal Republic of Yugoslavia does not threaten anybody, she does not use the mines, does not develop them, neither does she distribute, nor export them to other countries but rather uses them for educational purposes in a very restricted way, primarily in teaching de-mining techniques.[1]

Despite this, the United Nations, through information from the Kosovo Diplomatic Observer Mission (KDOM), has confirmed that either the Serbian police or the Yugoslav Army has placed anti-personnel and anti-tank mines on Yugoslavia's borders with Albania in the west and Macedonia in the south, as well as in some places in central Kosovo.

An August 25, 1998, security alert issued by UNICEF said:

"While the United Nations High Commissioner for Refugees (UNHCR) cannot confirm various reports about mines in Kosovo, it is confirmed that mines have been laid along the Albanian and Macedonian border with Kosovo and in the areas of Lapusnik, Iglrevo, Rakovina and the road between Rakovina and Klina. Landmines are confirmed in the areas of:

Junik and surroundings, particularly a dirt road which goes to the north from the village of Junik
Yugoslav-Albanian border
South of Grevnik (south of Dolac checkpoint in Klina municipality)
Southwest of Komerane."[2]

Human Rights Watch spoke with two people who claimed to have seen mines inside Kosovo but did not find anyone who claimed to have been injured by a mine, or to have witnessed a mine-related injury. One of them, a KLA fighter who identified himself as Gazmend, said that in early June he saw eight mines about ten meters from the border with Albania at a place called Qafe e Morines.[3] As of June 21, 1998, however, no mine-related injuries had been reported in the hospital in Bajram Curri, the Albanian town closest to Qafe e Morines or to the international humanitarian agencies, like ICRC and UNHCR, working in northern Albania.

According to the Anti-mining Friends Committee/Shoqata Anti-Mina, the Albanian branch of the International Campaign to Ban Landmines, approximately twenty refugees, including some KLA fighters, arrived in a hospital in Tirana, Albania, with wounds from landmines around July 18, 1998. Most had fled Kosovo after the police overran the border town of Junik, which had been a stronghold of the KLA. Those still in the hospital on August 1 told a member of the Anti-mining Friends Committee that they knew of eleven deaths from landmines in the villages of Ponashec, Mulliq and Rrasa e Zogut, but Human Rights Watch was not able to confirm these cases.[4]

On August 20, 1998, U.S. State Department spokesman James Rubin accused Serbian forces of laying land mines around the town of Junik: "Reports indicate that the Serbs have mined paths around the village and refugees from the Junik area are entering Albania and have been treated for injuries consistent with anti-personnel land mines."[5]

According to the United Nations Preventive Deployment Force (UNPREDEP), the U.N. mission based in Macedonia, and the Macedonian Ministry of Defense, landmines have also been placed along the Yugoslav border with Macedonia, ostensibly to hinder the flow of arms coming into Kosovo from Albania through Macedonia. On August 5, an UNPREDEP spokesman said that the U.N. had spotted mines along the border and the Macedonian Ministry of Defense announced that mines had been placed near the Jazince and Blace border crossings.[6] The Macedonian media speculated whether the mines had been placed inside Macedonian territory, since the Macedonian and Yugoslav governments have not yet agreed on the exact location of their common border, which was an unmarked internal boundary until Macedonia's independence in 1991.

On August 5, the Anti-mining Friends Committee in Albania cited witnesses who had seen mines near five villages along the Yugoslav-Macedonia border: Gorance, Krivenik, Secishte, Dimce, and Dermja. According to the organization, signs marking landmine fields had been placed in these areas, and the Yugoslav Army had asked the local religious organizations to inform the local population of the mine fields.[7]

On September 14, an armored car carrying the KDOM team from Canada and an Albanian translator hit an anti-tank mine on a road just south of Likovac in Drenica. The car flipped over but nobody was seriously hurt.

Forcible Disappearances

Well over one hundred ethnic Albanians have "disappeared" in Kosovo since February 1998, approximately half of whom were last seen in the custody of the police. The precise number, however, is impossible to determine since the Yugoslav authorities do not make public the number of people they have in detention, despite requests from Human Rights Watch and other organizations.[8] Some of the "disappeared" may be in prison, while others are in hiding, have fled Kosovo, or joined the KLA; others may have been secretly executed.

The most comprehensive report on missing persons, both Albanians and Serbs, was published in August 1998 by the Humanitarian Law Center.[9] According to the center, 119 ethnic Albanians have "disappeared" in the Kosovo conflict. Forty-four of these "disappearances" are directly attributable to the police, while seventy-two occurred in unclear circumstances. The Humanitarian Law Center documented three cases of ethnic Albanians who were detained and held without acknowledgment by the KLA; the actual number is believed to be much higher. The center also documented 112 cases of ethnic Serbs

---

Yugoslavia has failed to participate in the process from the outset, therefore she has been unable to participate in the negotiations on the elaboration of the Convention's text on equal footing with other states, (III) During last year's second semester, over a period of accelerated work to prepare the Convention for signing, the Federal Republic of Yugoslavia was engaged with other priorities, in particular, in striving to contribute to the strengthening of the region's stability, coming to terms with the Dayton Agreement, then to successfully implement her obligations under the Agreement on the sub-regional control of armaments, to integrate herself in the institutions of the international community, and last by not least, to solve the humanitarian and social problems of refugees and to ameliorate the consequences of the war in her neighborhood, (IV) The experience we have gained in the course of implementing the obligations under the Agreement on the sub-regional control of armaments shows that - despite certain difficulties and being without any outside assistance - the Federal Republic of Yugoslavia can bear the costs related to the destruction of mines, and she can honor other financial obligations deriving from the Convention, too, (V) By maintaining her stock of anti-personnel mines for a certain period the Federal Republic of Yugoslavia does not threaten anybody, she does not use the mines, does not develop them, neither does she distribute, no export them to other countries but rather uses them for educational purposes in a very restricted way, primarily in teaching de-mining techniques.

1 Ibid.
2 UNICEF, Security Alert: Landmine Information on Kosovo, August 25, 1998.
3 Human Rights Watch interview with KLA soldier, Tirana, June 23, 1998.

4 Correspondence with Dhimiter Haxhimihali, August 1, 1998.
5 U.S. State Department press briefing, Washington D.C., August 22, 1998.
6 "Yugoslavia mines its border with Macedonia," Associated Press, August 5, 1998, and "Minefields near Jazince and Blace," Macedonian Information Center, August 5, 1998.
7 Letter from Besnik Alibali, head of the Anti-mining Friends Committee/Shoqata Anti-Mina, August 5, 1998.
8 Human Rights Watch letters to Yugoslav Minister of Internal Affairs Zoran Sikolovic and Yugoslav Minister of Justice Zoran Knezevic, July 20, 1998.
9 Humanitarian Law Center, "Disappearances in Times of Armed Conflict," Spotlight Report Number 27, August 5, 1998.

who are unaccounted for and may have been seized - or killed - by the KLA. (See section on Abuses by the KLA.)

Below are some cases of "disappearances" of ethnic Albanians believed to have been carried out by government forces:

DR. HAFIR SHALA

On April 10, 1998, Dr. Hafir Shala, a doctor with the Health Care Center in Glogovac, was taken into detention by the police, along with two friends, Hetem Sinani and Shaban Neziri. The latter two were interrogated and released but Mr. Shala was held. He has not been seen or heard from since.

The three men were traveling in Shaban Neziri's car to Priština when the traffic police stopped the car near Slatina village around 8:00 a.m. As the police were checking their identification, three men in plain clothes emerged from a black jeep that was parked nearby and told Dr. Shala to come with them to Priština, while Mr. Sinani and Mr. Neziri were instructed to follow in their car. All three men were taken to the police station in Priština and interrogated in separate rooms until 2:00 p.m.. At that time, Mr. Sinani and Mr. Neziri were released. They told their lawyer, Destan Rukiqi, that they heard Dr. Shala screaming from pain from an unknown room in the police station as they left.[1]

Mr. Rukiqi told Human Rights Watch that he had taken various measures to locate Dr. Shala, all to no avail. On April 16, he wrote to the Serbian Ministry of Justice, the Serbian Prosecutor's office, and the district prosecutor in Priština. The next day, the Priština prosecutor, Slavko Stevanovic, said the State Security office in Priština had no information on Shala's whereabouts. Letters written by Human Rights Watch to the Serbian and Yugoslav Ministries of Interior and Justice on July 20, 1998, on Dr. Shala's case remain unanswered.

FOURTEEN MEMBERS OF THE JASHARI FAMILY

Fourteen members of the Jashari family remained unaccounted for after the March 5 police attack on their family compound in Donji Prekaz (see section on Abuses in Drenica). Ten people were buried by the police on March 10 without proper identification, so it is possible that the missing Jashari family members are among those buried at that time.

JAKUP QERIMI

According to the Council for the Defense of Human Rights and Freedoms, the police detained Jakup Qerimi, a twenty-seven-year-old ethnic Albanian who is mentally handicapped, in Urosevac on June 20, and he has not been seen since. The police allegedly told his mother that she would never see her son again.

IDRIZ IDRIZI

According the Council for the Defense of Human Rights and Freedoms and the Humanitarian Law Center, Idriz Idrizi from Srbica was taken by the police on January 23 from near the ammunition factory outside of Donji Prekaz. As of September 1998, he was still unaccounted for.[2] (See section on Abuses in Drenica.)

NINE MEN FROM NOVI POKLEK

On May 31, 1998, Serbian special police forces attacked the village of Novi Poklek near Glogovac. Ten men were taken by the police: the body of one of them, Ardian Deliu, was found the next day. The other nine men are still "disappeared."

A witness told Human Rights Watch that he saw the police shoot five men dead, three of whom he identified as Sefer Qorri, Hajriz Hajdini, and Ahmet Berisha, although his account could not be confirmed by Human Rights Watch. The nine missing men from Poklek are: Ahmet Berisha (40), Hajriz Hajdini (48), Muhamet Hajdini (45), Sahit Qorri (60), Sefer Qorri (55), Ferat Hoti (39), Rama Asllani (60), Fidel Berisha (17), and Blerim Shishani (15). (See section on Novi Poklek.)

---

[1] Human Rights Watch interview with Destan Rukiqi, Priština, June 3, 1998.
[2] Spotlight Report Number 27, "Disappearances in Times of Armed Conflict," Humanitarian Law Center, August 5, 1998.

Detentions and Arrests

Arbitrary detentions and arrests of ethnic Albanians have escalated rapidly throughout 1998. Until late September, the precise number of individuals in custody at any given time had been impossible to determine since the Yugoslav authorities refused to provide detailed information, despite specific inquiries from Human Rights Watch.[3] On September 23, Serbian Minister of Justice Drogulub Jankovic stated that criminal investigations had been opened against 927 individuals in five local courts of Kosovo and one court in Prokuple - all of them on charges of terrorism or enemy activities against the state. According to the minister, 538 of these people are currently in detention.[4] It was later reported that as many as 325 ethnic Albanians had been arrested between September 22 and 26, although it was unclear how many of these individuals remained in custody as of this writing.

In July and August, detained individuals increasingly included human rights activists, humanitarian aid workers, political party members, doctors, and lawyers, many of whom were physically abused in custody. Human Rights Watch has substantial credible evidence from lawyers and family members of detainees that detainees are routinely tortured and ill-treated. From March to August 1998, five people are known to have died while in police custody; hundreds of others have been beaten. Human rights and humanitarian agencies, including the International Committee of the Red Cross, report restricted access to detainees.[5]

According to the Yugoslav government, a round of trials will begin in October, and eight judges will be sent to Kosovo to deal with the high case load.[6] In the past, terrorism-related trials have been marred by serious procedural irregularities, as well as the use of torture to extract confessions.[7]

Human Rights Watch obtained the following general information on arrests:

According to Adem Bajri, a lawyer in Pec who works with the Council for the Defense of Human Rights and Freedoms, as of September 21, 251 ethnic Albanians were in the Pec jail facing charges of terrorist activity. Criminal charges had been filed against 510 others who remain at large. Mr. Bajri told Human Rights Watch that he has twenty-four clients in prison, all of whom are facing charges of terrorism. Mr. Bajri has been allowed to visit his clients and said that virtually all show signs of torture, including injuries such as bruises on the body and broken bones.[8]

According to Albanian press reports, on July 20 the police stopped a bus near Podujevo that was traveling to Kosovo from Slovenia. Fifty-four ethnic Albanians who had been working in Slovenia were initially arrested. On August 17, thirty-nine were released. A lawyer who visited them on July 29 in Prokuple prison, which lies about

---

[3] Human Rights Watch letters to Yugoslav Minister of Internal Affairs Zoran Sikolovic and Yugoslav Minister of Justice Zoran Knezevic, July 20, 1998.
[4] Blic, September 23, 1998.
[5] ICRC Position on the Crisis in Kosovo, International Committee of the Red Cross, September 1998.
[6] NT Plus, September 18, 1998.
[7] See Human Rights Watch/Helsinki, "Persecution Persists: Human Rights Violations in Kosovo," December 1996, and "Human Rights Watch/Helsinki Condemns Political Trial in Kosovo," Press Release, July 15, 1997. Yugoslav laws guarantees all defendants the right to due process. Article 23 of the federal constitution forbids arbitrary detention and obliges the authorities to inform a detainee immediately of the reason for his or her detention and to grant that person access to a lawyer. Article 24 obliges the authorities to inform the detainee in writing of the reason for his or her arrest within twenty-four hours. Detention ordered by a lower court may not exceed three months, unless extended by a higher court to a maximum of six months. Article 25 outlaws torture against a detainee, as well as any forcible extraction of confessions or statements. The use of force against a detainee is also a criminal offence.
[8] Human Rights Watch interview with Aden Bajri, Pec, September 21, 1998.

twenty-five miles outside Kosovo in Serbia proper, told Human Rights Watch that he saw clear signs that they had been beaten.[1] The other fifteen remain in detention charged with terrorist acts based on Articles 125 and 136 of the Serbian Penal Code.[2] At the time of arrest, the police took from them a total of 352,018 DM.

On May 23, eight students from the Pedagogical High School "Xhevdet Doda" in Prizren and one student from the University of Pristina, all of them members of the Students' Independent Union, were arrested in Prizren. On June 8, they were charged with KLA membership and committing terrorist acts. On August 24, they were convicted of "enemy activity" against the state because they had organized first aid courses in Prizen and sentenced to prison terms ranging from one to seven and a half years. Four of the students were also charged with having contacted the KLA. The lawyer for some of the students, Hazer Susuri, told Human Rights Watch that two of his clients, Bylbyl Duraku and Sejdi Bullanica, had been beaten in pre-trial detention. According to Mr. Susuri and an international observer who monitored the trial, the entire proceedings lasted four and a half hours. The conviction was based entirely on the confessions of the students. Their sentences were as follows:[3]

Nijazi Kryeziu (aged twenty-one; sentenced to seven and a half years imprisonment); Aqif Iljazi (aged twenty-one; sentenced to six and a half years imprisonment); Bylbyl Duraku (aged twenty-two; sentenced to five and a half years imprisonment); Sejdi Bellanica (aged twenty-three; sentenced to three and a half years imprisonment); Defrim Rifaj (aged twenty-two; sentenced to two and a half years imprisonment); Behare Tafallari (aged twenty-two; sentenced to two years imprisonment); Jehona Krasniqi (aged twenty-two; sentenced to two years imprisonment); Leonora Morina (aged twenty-one; sentenced to two years imprisonment); Sherif Iljazi (aged twenty; sentenced to one year imprisonment).

According to the Serbian police, after intense fighting with the KLA in Orahovac, they arrested 223 ethnic Albanians suspected of "terrorism." All of them except twenty-six were reportedly released after questioning.[4]

On September 4 and 5, the Serbian police detained more than 600 ethnic Albanians from around the villages of Ponorac, Ratkovac, and Drenovac who had been internally displaced because of fighting.[5] According to diplomatic sources who spoke with witnesses, the women and children were released and the men were taken to the Ponorac schoolhouse, where they were filmed by Serbian state television as "captured terrorists." Most of the men were reportedly released on September 5 but an estimated forty people remained in police custody. Human Rights Watch saw photographs of the alleged "terrorists" which showed a large group of men on their knees with the hands behind their heads being guarded by armed police officers.

On September 24, the Media Center in Priština reported that, according to the police, 194 ethnic Albanians had been arrested on September 22 and 23 during a police action in the Cicavica Mountains northwest of Priština. The authorities have opened investigations against those arrested. In contrast, on September 26, the Albanian daily Koha Ditore cited Ministry of Interior spokesman Bozidar Filic as saying that 325 Albanians had been arrested.[6]

SOME INDIVIDUAL CASES ARE OUTLINED BELOW:

Destan Rukiqi

Destan Rukiqi, a lawyer in Priština who has defended dozens of ethnic Albanian political prisoners in Kosovo in recent years, was arrested on July 23, 1998, and sentenced that same day in a summary proceeding to the maximum sixty days in prison for disturbing public order (under Article 6, paragraph 3 of the Serbian Law on Public Order). The arrest was related to an incident that morning, when Rukiqi had raised his voice at a district judge in Priština, Ms. Danica Marinkovic,[7] telling her, "I am in the court but you are acting like the police," after she had refused to let Rukiqi take notes while reviewing the case file of his client, Cen Dugolli (see below).

Mr. Rukiqi was severely beaten on his third day in detention by policemen at the Priština prison. He told Human Rights Watch that he was held down and beaten on his hands, feet and kidneys with a three-foot long rubber baton. Over the next two weeks, he underwent dialysis eleven times.[8] Mr. Rukiqi's sentence was reduced by the Serbian Supreme Court to thirty days, and he was released on August 22.

Rukiqi had been involved in a number of human rights related cases, and had provided information on war crimes committed by Serbian special police forces in Kosovo to the ICTY in the Hague.

Zahrida Podrimcaku

Ms. Zahrida Podrimcaku, an activist with the Council for the Defense of Human Rights and Freedoms in Glogovac, was detained by police in Priština on June 8, 1998, together with Ibrahim Makolli, who works at the council's offices in Priština.[9] Mr. Makolli was released after a few hours of questioning, but Ms. Podrimcaku remained in custody and was denied contact with a lawyer or her family for several days. On June 12, she was charged with committing "terrorist acts" (Articles 125 and 136 of the Serbian Penal Code). Ms. Podrimcaku had been investigating what happened on May 31, 1998, in the village of Novi Poklek, when police detained ten ethnic Albanian men during an attack on the village. The body of one of the men, Ardian Deliu, was found the next day, while the other nine men remain missing and are presumed dead. Podrimcaku was charged with supporting terrorists and is awaiting trial in Lipljan prison. Her lawyer, Mrs. Lirije Osmani, has been allowed to visit, and reported that Ms. Podrimcaku had been physically maltreatment.[10]

LDK Activists from Urosevac

On July 31, 1998, seven activists of the Democratic League of Kosovo (LDK) in Urosevac were detained, interrogated, and beaten by the police, according to the LDK. Milazim Haliti and Fatmir Sylejmani, members of the LDK presidency were arrested at their offices in the morning. Adem Salija, chairman of the local LDK presidency and member of the Kosovo Parliament, was arrested in the afternoon, as was Agim Recica, chairman of the local LDK sub-branch in Urosevac.

Besa Arllati

Mrs. Besa Arllati, chairwoman of the LDK information commission in Dakovica, was arrested on May 26 and brought to the police station in Dakovica, where she was interrogated and beaten by police chief

---

[1] Human Rights Watch interview with Bajram Krasniqi, September 19, 1998.
[2] Republic of Serbia Prosecutor's Office, Kt. Nr. 55/98, July 23, 1998, Prokuple, signed by District Prosecutor Miroslav Nikiolic.
[3] Human Rights Watch Interview with Hazer Susuri in Prizren on September 21, 1998.
[4] United Nations Office of the High Commissioner for Human Rights, "Report from the Human Rights Field Operation in Bosnia and Herzegovina, the Republic of Croatia, and the Federal Republic of Yugoslavia," August 7, 1998.
[5] Ljubomir Milasin, "Hundreds of Kosovars Detained, UNHCR Warns of Bosnia Spectre," AFP, September 8, 1998, and Tanjug, September 6, 1998.
[6] Koha Ditore, "PB e Serbise: Ka perfunduar aksioni ne Qyqavice, jane arrestuar 325 shqiptare," September 26, 1998.
[7] Judge Marinkovic has presided over a number of political trials against ethnic Albanians in Kosovo in which the defendants were tortured. See Human Rights Watch/Helsinki, "Persecution Persists: Human Rights Violations in Kosovo," December 1996, pg 22.
[8] Human Rights Watch telephone interview with Destan Rukiqi, August 23, 1998.
[9] Podrimcaku's arrest occurred about one hour after she had spoken with a Human Rights Watch researcher about her investigations in Novi Poklek.
[10] Letter to Human Rights Watch from Behxhet Shala, executive secretary of the Council for the Defense of Human Rights and Freedoms, August 21, 1998.

Sreten Camatovic.[1] Police reportedly wanted to know about two Serbian policemen, Nikola Jovanovic and Rade Popadic, who they believed had been seized by the KLA. Arllati was detained and interrogated on and off for the next few days, until June 1, about the work of the KLA and the activities of Albanians in the area.

Dr. Fehmi Vula

Dr. Fehmi Vula, a surgeon at the Dakovica hospital, member of the Dakovica LDK presidency and member of the shadow Kosovo Parliament, was arrested on May 29, 1998. On June 3, a Prizren court extended his detention to thirty days to investigate possible "terrorist acts" as defined in Article 136 of the Serbian penal code. As of September 1, Dr. Vula was in detention awaiting trial.

Mevlude Sarraqi

Mrs. Mevlude Sarraqi, member of the LDK presidency, head of the LDK Women's Forum, and a member of the Kosovo Parliament, was arrested on June 1 and charged with "Association for the purpose of hostile activity" under Article 136 of the Serbian penal code. She was arrested in advance of a rally organized by the Women's Forum to protest the detention of LDK activists, such as Dr. Vula and Besa Arllati. She is currently in Lipljan prison.

DEATHS IN DETENTION

Cen Dugolli, an activist with the Democratic League of Kosovo in Urosevac, died on August 17, 1998, in Priština Hospital, from beatings sustained while in detention. According to his family, the police arrested Cen and his neighbor, Haxhi Bytyqi, at 8:00 a.m. on June 21, 1998, from their homes in Urosevac. Cen was taken to the Gnjilane prison a few days later and then transferred to the Priština prison. He was taken by police to the Priština hospital on August 16 and died the next day from internal injuries, according to the official autopsy report seen by Human Rights Watch. Dugolli's family told Human Rights Watch that they first visited Cen on July 1 in Priština prison and that he showed signs of physical abuse, such as bruises on the face. The family was supposed to visit Cen on August 17 but was not allowed in by the prison guards. That night they learned from the Albanian Satellite Television News from Albania that Cen had died.[2] Human Rights Watch saw photographs of Mr. Dugolli that showed severe signs of torture, including deep bruising that covered large parts of his body.

Dugolli's lawyer, Destan Rukiqi, was arrested on July 23 for "insulting" Judge Danica Marinkovic while trying to review Dugolli's case file. Rukiqi himself spent thirty days in prison and was severely beaten on the kidneys while in the Lipljan prison (see above).

Rexhep Bislimi, an activist with the Council for the Defense of Human Rights and Freedoms in Urosevac was arrested on July 6, 1998, from the street in Urosevac, and died on July 22, from beatings he sustained while in detention. According to Bislimi's family, the police brought Rexhep back to his house on July 7 and made him dig some holes in the garden to look for weapons they thought he had hidden there, but they found nothing. Members of the family told Human Rights Watch that Rexhep had bruises on his face, as well as blood.[3] Three days later, the family learned that Rexhep was in Gnjilane prison, but they were never allowed to see him. On July 19, the family learned that Rexhep had been taken to the Priština hospital, but they were again not able to see him because two policemen were guarding his hospital room. Rexhep died on July 21 due to, according to the official autopsy report, "constusio capitis et corporis." Human Rights Watch saw a photograph of Mr. Bislimi that showed severe bruising on large sections of his legs and torso that were consistent with allegations of torture.

According to the Council for the Defense of Human Rights and Freedoms, Adem Berisha from Bruc village, died on August 18, 1998, in the Prizren hospital reportedly from injuries inflicted by police during his detention in Prizren. He had been arrested on the Dragas-Prizren road on August 16.

According to Albanian media reports, on August 29, around 11:00 p.m. forty-seven-year-old Bilall Shala from Uroševac died while in police custody. Shala was arrested in Uroševac on August 28 together with his son, Agron, who was released later that day, reportedly after having been beaten by the police. Bilall's brother, Zenel Shala, told the Albanian media that he was informed on the evening of August 28 that his brother had died and was in the Priština city morgue.[4]

According to the Council for the Defense of Human Rights and Freedoms, on August 23 Maksut Qafleshi from Belobrade died as a result of police torture he sustained in Uroševac.[5] Maksut's brother told the Council that Maksut was arrested and beaten by the police on the road between Prizren and Uroševac, and was then taken to the police station in Urosevac, where he was denied medical treatment. He was later transferred to the hospital in Priština, where he died.

Attacks and Restrictions on Medical and Relief Personnel

By September 1998, at least 300,000 people had been displaced in Kosovo, the vast majority of them ethnic Albanians. According to the United Nations High Commissioner for Refugees (UNHCR), as of August 31, 40,000 ethnic Albanians from Kosovo were in Montenegro, 15,000 were in Albania, and 20,000 were in Macedonia. At least 50,000 displaced persons are considered "exposed," meaning they are without any shelter in the open mountains or woods. Humanitarian aid agencies and top government officials warn of a human catastrophe once winter arrives if shelter cannot be found for these people. U.S. Assistant Secretary of State for Population, Refugees, and Migration Julia Taft, who visited Kosovo in late August, said of her trip:

It was one of the most heart-wrenching experiences I have had in twenty-five years of working in humanitarian relief. We have a catastrophe looming, and we only have as a world humanitarian community six weeks to help the government of Serbia respond to this crisis.[6] The snows come early, I understand, to this part of the world. With the snow may come the death of many of the more than 300,000 people who have been displaced from their homes because of the conflict in Kosovo.[7]

Despite this, the Yugoslav government has posed a number of obstacles to the delivery of aid for internally displaced persons (IDPs), ignoring promises to allow unimpeded access for humanitarian agencies.[8] Moreover, it continues to carry out a military offensive that results in further displacement and a security environment not conducive to return. First and foremost among these are the continued attacks on villages and the burning of settlements in excess of any possible military necessity, deliberately damaging or systematically destroying homes, which keep civilians from returning. Scattered in valleys and forests, many of the displaced are unreachable by the aid agencies working out of Priština. In addition, direct restrictions on the aid agencies, and even attacks, severely hinder their ability to reach those in need.

Albanian and foreign relief workers have faced a series of obstacles from the government in their attempts to deliver food to the internally

---

[1] Humanitarian Law Center, "Kosovo - Disappearances in Times of Armed Conflict," Spotlight Report No. 27, August 5, 1998.
[2] Human Rights Watch interview with the Dugolli family, Urosevac, September 25, 1998.
[3] Human Rights Watch interview with the Bislimi family, Urosevac, September 25, 1998.

[4] "One More Albanian Dead From Prison Torture," Arta, August 30, 1998, and "Another Albanian Detainee Dies of Police Torture," KIC, August 30, 1998.
[5] "Within Two Months Five Albanians Die in Serbian Prisons," Council for the Defense of Human Rights and Freedoms, September 1998.
[6] Press conference of Assistant Secretary of State Julia Taft, Belgrade, August 28, 1998.
[7] Press conference of Assistant Secretary of State Julia Taft, Belgrade, August 28, 1998.
[8] Following a June 16, 1998, meeting between Presidents Miloševic and Boris Yeltsin in Moscow, the Yugoslav government agreed, among other things, to allow diplomats and humanitarian agencies full access throughout Kosovo.

displaced, including restricted access to needy populations, confiscation of supplies, harassment and, in the case of the Mother Theresa Society, the largest and most important local relief organization, occasional arrests and attacks.

The most serious attack on humanitarian aid workers, local or international, was the August 24 attack by Serbian police on an aid convoy that killed three ethnic Albanians working with the Mother Theresa Society. According to the New York Times, the August 24 attack occurred at mid-afternoon in an open field in the village of Vlaski Drenovac near Kijevo, when police fired upon an aid convoy of tractors with cannon-fire from about half a mile away. The wagons were reportedly filled with boxes clearly marked "Doctors of the World," the relief agency that had donated the food supplies. Sadri Ramadan Gashi (61), Adem Isuf Morina (40), and Hajriz Haxhi Morina (24) were killed. Local and international press reported that the convoy had previously been allowed through a Serb checkpoint.[1] According to the New York Times, the government explained the barrage by saying that the police in an armored personnel carrier could not see what was in the wagons and became suspicious and opened fire. U.S. Department of State spokesman James Foley contradicted this by saying "the evidence indicates that the workers' vehicle was deliberately targeted by a Serbian armored vehicle less than a kilometer away in broad daylight."[2] Diplomats in Belgrade told Human Rights Watch that they were convinced the Serbian police had fired directly on the convoy from a nearby hill.[3]

In an August 28 press conference held in Priština after her brief visit to Kosovo, U.S. Assistant Secretary of State Julia Taft said she had raised the attack on the Mother Theresa Society convoy with the Yugoslav authorities. "I must say I was very reassured by the regret and the apology by the authorities that these people had been killed," she said. "And there is going to be an inspection."[4]

The Mother Theresa Society has reported attacks on its activists before, but this was the first reported death. On July 11, two Mother Theresa Society activists in Dakovica, Fatime Boshnjaku and Uran Luxha, were arrested while delivering supplies in town. Many others have reported harassment and interrogations.

Also on July 11, three activists of the Mother Theresa Society were fired upon by people believed to be the police while returning from an aid delivery in the village of Cibovc. Xhevdet Stulcaku, vice president of the Mother Theresa Society in Obilic, was struck in the head and is currently paralyzed on his right side.[5] Selatin Hashani, secretary of the Society in Obilic, was also wounded.

On August 31, more than 200 ethnic Serb women demonstrated in front of the United States Information Agency office in Priština to protest reported executions of Serbian civilians by the KLA in Klecka (see section on Abuses by the KLA). They threw stones at the building shouting "Fascists!" and "Murderers!" as the police watched from a distance.[6] The crowd then moved to the office of the ICRC, where they pelted the building with stones and beat up an ethnic Albanian guard while accusing the ICRC of "bringing humanitarian aid to the terrorists." According to one press report, the women then got on two buses that Serb policemen had brought for them.[7]

A fundamental problem for all humanitarian aid organizations working in Kosovo is restricted access to civilians in need. On numerous occasions, the Serbian police have blocked aid convoys on main roads. Some medical supplies and food stuffs have been confiscated by the police on the grounds that it was intended for "Albanian terrorists."

Human Rights Watch raised the issue with Bosko Drobnjak, head of the Secretary of Information in Kosovo. He said that the police had occasionally blocked aid convoys because "some humanitarian organization have been helping terrorists. Not necessarily with weapons, but with military equipment."[8]

Humanitarian aid agencies working in Kosovo told Human Rights Watch that they are frequently denied access to areas where fighting is taking place. From May 20 to approximately June 21, for example, the ICRC was denied access to the Decan area where a large police and army offensive was under way. An ICRC press release said that they had been denied access, "despite a number of previous assurances from the highest authorities in Belgrade that the ICRC would be able to work unhindered in Kosovo."[9]

In early July, the police forced an aid convoy from Medecin San Frontiers (MSF) to deliver its supplies to a collective center with ethnic Serbian refugees in Dakovica, rather than give it to the Mother Theresa Society for distribution, as MSF had intended.[10] On August 27, a Serbian police checkpoint at Slatina turned back an eight-truck convoy of the United Nations High Commissioner for Refugees (UNHCR) that was carrying one month's worth of food for more than 30,000 families.[11]

The police also blocked aid deliveries during the police attacks in Drenica from February 28 to March 1. Doctors were also not allowed into the Drenica villages of Likošane, Cirez and Prekaz to perform autopsies on those killed, although there was strong evidence to suggest summary executions (see section on Abuses in Drenica). In a press conference held on March 7 to explain the police actions in Drenica, Police Colonel Ljubinki Cvetic said that humanitarian organizations had been denied access to the area because some of them had supplied arms and equipment to terrorists.[12]

In August, international relief agencies reported continued obstructions by the government, such as the denial of visas for foreign staff, lengthy customs procedures for imported relief supplies, and the slow processing of licences for hand-held radios used by relief agencies to communicate with their staffs in the field.

The KLA has reportedly also blocked some relief convoys (see section Abuses by the KLA).

Government Restrictions on the Media

Since the armed conflict began in February 1998, the Yugoslav government has placed a number of serious restrictions on the work of local journalists, including threats, detentions, and beatings by the police. Independent radio and television stations in the Albanian language are denied broadcast licenses or, in one case, closed down.

The independent Serbian-language media is not exempt from state pressure. News wires, newspapers, and radio stations that report objectively on Kosovo are labeled "traitors" and sometimes threatened with legal action. A complex and contradictory legal framework has made it virtually impossible for independent radio or television stations to obtain a broadcast frequency.

The international media covering Kosovo also faces a number restrictions on its work, starting with the denial of visas to journalists

---

[1] U.S. State Department Press Briefing, Washington D.C., August 27, 1998.
[2] Arta, Priština, Kosovo, August 24, 1998, and The Guardian, London, August 26, 1998.
[3] Human Rights Watch interview, Belgrade, September 1, 1998.
[4] Press conference of U.S. Assistant Secretary Julia Taft, Priština, August 28, 1998.
[5] Human Rights Watch interview with Xhevdet Stulcaku in Obilic, September 22, 1998.
[6] "Serb Women Stone US Building In Protest; Yugoslavia Refuses Visa to US Envoy," AP, August 31, 1998.
[7] "Serb Women Stone US Center, ICRC in Kosovo," AFP, August 31, 1998.
[8] Human Rights Watch interview with Bosko Drobnjak, June 11, 1998, Priština.
[9] "Kosovo: ICRC Urgently Requests Access to Affected Areas," ICRC press release 98/21, June 3, 1998.
[10] Human Rights Watch interview with Francois Fille, Priština, June 10, 1998.
[11] "UNHCR Aid Convoy Repulsed Near Kosovo Capital Priština," AFP, August 27, 1998, and UN Inter-Agency Update on Kosovo, August 28, 1998.
[12] "Interior Ministry Spokesman Gives Press Conference," Tanjug, March 7, 1998.

the state considers critical of its policies. A number of foreign journalists have been beaten at demonstrations and fired upon by the police.

RESTRICTIONS ON THE ALBANIAN-LANGUAGE MEDIA

At least five ethnic Albanian journalists were beaten by the police in March 1998 during street demonstrations in Priština. On March 2, the police beat Veton Surroi, editor-in-chief of the daily Koha Ditore, Ibrahim Osmani, a journalist with Agence France Presse and the Voice of America, Avni Spahiu, editor-in-chief of the daily Bujku, Agron Bajrami, a journalist at Koha Ditore, and Sherif Kunjufca, a journalist with Albanian Television. Police forces also broke into the offices of Koha Ditore and beat people who had taken refuge inside; a photographer, Fatos Berisha, jumped from a second story window and broke his leg. Police also broke into the offices of Bujku.[1]

Since then, at least two other ethnic Albanian journalists have been beaten by the police. According to the Koha Ditore editorial offices in Priština, on August 19, five policemen in Dakovica entered the home of their local correspondent, Musa Kurhasku, and confiscated articles, documents, his telephone book, and a telex machine. Kurhasku was reportedly ordered to the local police station where the police allegedly told him to go to another city, Orahovac, in order to negotiate the release of an ethnic Serb who had been captured by members of the KLA. Mr. Kurhasku reportedly refused to go, saying that it was not a journalist's responsibility to act as a broker or to do the work of the Red Cross, and was beaten.[2] He has gone into hiding, as has another Koha Ditore correspondent, Adem Metaj, from Srbica.

On August 4, an editor with Bujku, Zeke Gecaj, was stopped by the police near the center of Priština. The police took Mr. Gecaj to the local station around 11:00 p.m. where he was questioned and told to report again the next morning. On August 5, he was interrogated for four hours and reportedly threatened.[3]

THE BROADCAST MEDIA IN KOSOVO

The Yugoslav government does not allow any domestic independent radio or television stations to broadcast in Kosovo. Two start-up stations, Radio Koha and Radio 21 were denied frequency licenses in a public tender announced in February 1998. Radio 21 currently broadcasts over the Internet in Albanian and English (http://www.radio21.net).

Ethnic Albanians in Kosovo can receive the Albanian-language radio programs of the BBC, Deutsche Welle, and the Voice of America. A satellite television program from Tirana, Albania is also broadcast a few hours every day.

On July 1, 1998, the government shut down Radio Kontakt, an independent, multi-ethnic radio station in Kosovo, that strived, in its own words, to be a radio of "good-will and reconciliation" by providing objective news in both Albanian andSerbian. An inspector of the Yugoslav Telecommunications Ministry, accompanied by armed policemen in four police cars, entered the station's offices in Priština and confiscated part of the transmitter.[4]

In a press conference on July 3 in Belgrade, Yugoslav Secretary of Information Goran Matic said that Radio Kontakt had been closed "because it did not tender in the competition for frequency allocation... this is a technical issue rather than a political one."[5] But Radio Kontakt had submitted all of the necessary documentation for the second round of the frequency tender and had received confirmation from the Ministry of Telecommunications that it would soon be granted a license. The station had been broadcasting only music during an experimental period beginning on June 19, 1998. The confiscation of its transmitter occurred two days after the station had begun rebroadcasting Radio B92, the BBC, and VOA.

RESTRICTION ON THE SERBIAN-LANGUAGE MEDIA

The Yugoslav government maintains direct control of the state radio and television, Radio Television Serbia (RTS), which provides news for the majority of the population. State programs blatantly glorify the government's accomplishments (real or imagined), conceal its failures and, most importantly, manipulate the fears of the ethnic Serbian population. During the fighting in Bosnia and Croatia, and now with war in Kosovo, state radio and television have purposefully spread disinformation and promoted an atmosphere of nationalist hysteria that has encouraged conflict.

Coupled with this is an ongoing attempt to hinder or make illegal the work of the private, independent media that has been struggling to break the information blockade. Conscious of the threat that objective news poses to its power, the Yugoslav government places various restrictions on Yugoslavia's independent newspapers, magazines, television and radio stations. Censorship is not blatant but is effectively applied through financial controls, legal manipulation, and police harassment.

Independent newspapers and magazines are faced with a host of problems, specifically restrictions on printing and distribution, both industries controlled by the state. Newspaper editors and journalists are sometimes subjected to harassment and, on occasion, physical violence by the police.

On March 6, 1998, the editors of five independent newspapers were charged with disseminating misinformation because of their Kosovo coverage. The Belgrade city prosecutor, Mjedrak Tmusic, accused the editors of Danas, Blic, Dnevni Telegraf, Demokratiya, and Naša Borba "because they published articles, editorials and headlines and broadcast programs which encouraged actions of terrorist gangs in Kosovo and misrepresented measures taken by the Serbian Interior Ministry against terrorists in Kosovo-Metohija."[6] The charges were later dropped.

Independent radio and television stations face even more restraints, including the confiscation of radio equipment and arbitrary bans. The least obvious but most effective restriction is the deliberate lack of a coherent legal framework for the establishment of private radio and television stations, which the government uses to justify the denial of broadcast licenses.[7]

---

[1] Human Rights Watch interview with Agron Bajrami and Veton Surroi, Priština, May 22, 1998.
[2] Although Human Rights Watch could not confirm this account, it is consistent with other reports of Serbian police ordering ethnic Albanian civilians to negotiate with the KLA, such as the cases of Besa Arllati and Dr. Fehmi Vula, also from Dakovica.
[3] "IFJ Condemns Attacks on Journalists in Kosova," Press Release of the International Federation of Journalists, August 5, 1998, and "Bujku Editor in Serb Custody on Tuesday and Wednesday," KIC, August 4, 1998.
[4] IFEX Action Alert, July 7, 1998.
[5] ANEM Alert, July 3, 1998.
[6] "Prosecutor Takes Action Against Media Over Coverage of Clashes," Tanjug, March 6, 1998.
[7] The broadcast media in Serbia is regulated by the following laws: A) Federal laws: 1. Law on Telecommunications of the Socialist Federal Republic of Yugoslavia (SFRY) 2. Law on Mass Media of SFRY; B) Laws of the Republic of Serbia: 1. Law on the System of Communication 2. Law on Mass Media 3. Law on Radio and Television A number of other state bodies are involved in media regulation, including the Ministry of Transport and Telecommunications, the Ministry of Information, and the commercial courts. Relevant laws include the Law on Companies, the Law on Procedure for Entry into the Court Register, the Law on Unified Classification of Operation and Units ofClassification, as well as a series of regulations for the implementation of these laws. When viewed together, these law and regulations create an unnavigable maze of legal obstructions for private media outlets. For example, under current regulations, the Yugoslav Ministry of Transport and Telecommunications requires applicants for a broadcast license to prove that the station has been registered as a media company at the Ministry of Information and at the appropriate commercial court. But these documents cannot be obtained without first having a license from the Ministry of Transport and Telecommunications. Even taken individually, Serbia and Yugoslavia's media law and regulations do not guarantee that broadcast licenses will be allocated on a non-discriminatory basis. Article 5 of Serbia's Law on Radio and Television, for example, gives the government a very broad right to grant licenses, while Article 10 (6) of the same law allows the government to revoke licenses under vague terms.

The complex and contradictory set of media laws at the Serbian republic and the federal level has made it exceedingly difficult, if not impossible, for independent radio or television stations to obtain a frequency license. At the same time, stations that were either blatantly pro-Milošević or, at least, strictly commercial and wholly uncritical, have regularly obtained licenses for broadcasts in large parts of the country. Despite numerous promises, the government has failed to introduce legislation that would allow private stations to obtain broadcast licenses, satellite link-ups, or Internet connections in a fair and apolitical manner.

An estimated 400 private radio and television stations have generally been allowed to broadcast, but they are prone to summary closure by the government, as happened to seventy-seven stations in mid-1997, and to four stations in 1998. Most often the state justifies such a closure by claiming that the station in question did not have the proper license to broadcast. This is usually true, but the lack of a license is due to the government's persistent refusal to grant licenses to any station that broadcasts independent or critical news.

The most recent government action against the independent electronic media was a public tender for radio and television stations to obtain temporary broadcast licenses. According to the government, it was intended to "create order in the airwaves" since "pirate" stations had proliferated. But the questionable legality of the tender, and the secretive and misleading manner in which it was administered, suggested that the government was devising another legal ruse to hinder the free press. The results of the tender, announced on May 16, 1998, proved these fears to be true: the vast majority of independent radio and television stations that applied were denied licenses, while numerous stations with close business or political ties to the ruling elite were granted permission to broadcast, including a radio station owned by Milošević's son, Marko, and a television station connected with his daughter, Marija. For the stations that did get licenses, the government imposed exorbitantly high licensing fees, as much as U.S.$40,000 per month for a television station in Belgrade. The fees were later reduced, but they are still prohibitively high for most stations, especially in Montenegro. Six Yugoslav non-governmental organizations have challenged the legality of the fees before the Yugoslav Constitutional Court.

The second stage of the tender process is officially still open, since stations were granted an opportunity to resubmit their applications. But the behavior of the government again suggests that most independent stations will be denied licenses. Some stations were not informed of the results from the first round. Other stations that did not get a frequency because of "missing documents" have been denied those documents (such as building permits) by their local authorities.

The frequency tender and the court cases against newspaper editors are consistent with the Yugoslav government's media policy over the past decade. Milošević regularly applies particular pressure on the independent media in times of conflict, as there is now with Kosovo.

RESTRICTIONS ON THE FOREIGN MEDIA

The first problem faced by foreign journalists covering Kosovo is in obtaining a visa for the Federal Republic of Yugoslavia. Many journalists have either had to wait long periods to get a visa, or have been denied outright, especially if they have a reputation for critical reporting and are, therefore, considered "anti-Serb" in the eyes of the government.[1] Some foreign journalists have also been attacked in the state-run media, accused of "biased" and "anti-Serb" reporting.[2]

The government has repeatedly complained about the foreign media's "one-sided" reporting in the Kosovo crisis. In a letter sent to the international press on August 31, Serbian Secretary of Information Alexander Vucic said:

After a deluge of sensational and false reports blaming only one side for everything that happened in the former Yugoslavia - the Serbian people - many reporters and media are directly accountable for the political moves of their governments, and indirectly for the death, persecution and living-on-the-verge-of-death of the Serbs.[3]

On August 12, the Yugoslav government declared a journalist with the German newspaper "Die Tageszeitung" persona non grata because he "created and spread evil lies." Erich Rathfelder, who had been covering Kosovo since 1987, had reported witness statements about mass graves of Albanians killed by the police in Orahovac, which have not been confirmed.[4] Rathfelder also claims he was threatened by the police during his last trip to Kosovo on August 2. In an opinion piece published in his newspaper, he said:

I was stopped by five policemen who, after the remark, "You were in Drenica after all," pointed their weapons at me. They threatened to confiscate my car and to arrest me. The intervention of a Dutch journalist who was following behind me in his car resulted in a calming of tempers.[5]

On August 14, Friedhelm Brebeck and his two cameramen with the German television station ARD were expelled from the Federal Republic of Yugoslavia and barred from entry into the country for three years. The government accused Brebeck of inciting Albanians to set a house in Junik on fire - an accusation Brebeck has categorically denied.[6] According to Brebeck, the Yugoslav Army checked his footage of Junik and returned it, leading him to believe it was acceptable. On the morning of August 14, however, the police arrived at the Grand Hotel in Priština, demanded the passports of Brebeck and his two colleagues, and told them that they would be escorted to the border with Macedonia.[7]

Foreign journalists also report increased difficulty in obtaining accreditation from the Secretary of Information in Priština, which is necessary to get through checkpoints throughout Kosovo. In August, the Secretary of Information's office reduced its working hours to two hours a day, and began demanding a photo identification from every applicant. The office also stopped putting translators' names on the accreditation document, which made it more difficult for them to get through police checkpoints.

Some foreign journalists have been physically assaulted or shot at by the police. On June 22, 1998, two journalists from the Danish television TV2, Neils Brinch and Heinrik Gram, and their Albanian interpreter were fired upon while in their armored car by the Serbian police near Glogovac.[8] No one was injured.

On March 6, a BBC cameraman and an Albanian translator were secretly filming the demolition of houses in Prekaz by the police, one day after the large-scale police attack on the village (see section on Abuses in Drenica). The police fired at them with automatic weapons from a distance as they tried to leave. Both men lay down for about five minutes, but were shot at again when they got up to run away. A bullet hit the journalist's cell phone which was hanging on his waist, causing a large bruise. The Albanian translator, who wished to remain anonymous, was hit in the shoulder, but the bullet did not penetrate his bullet proof vest. After some time, they managed to get away safely.[9]

---

[1] According to Freimut Duve, the Media Representative of the OSCE, Milada Jedrysik and Jerzy Gumowski from the Polish newspaper Gazeta Wyborcza, an Austrian cameraman Friedrich Wedan and a German television reporter, Hasim Hosny, have been denied visas. "Duve Kritisiert Serbiens Regierung," Die Tageszeitung, August 28, 1998.

[2] See Politika, August 4, 1998, for an article attacking the journalist Halim Hosny, with the German television station ZDF, and Roy Gutman, a reporter for the American newspaper Newsday.

[3] "Serb Information minister complains of biased reports," Reuters, August 31, 1998.

[4] "Taz-Korrespondent erhält Einreiseverbot in Jugoslavien," Die Tageszeitung, August 13, 1998

[5] "Man wollte mich loswerden," Die Tageszeitung, August 17, 1998.

[6] IFEX Action Alert, August 18, 1998.

[7] "Serben Erobern Verlassene Stadt im Kosovo," Die Tageszeitung, August 17, 1998, and "Jugoslavien Weist ARD-Journalisten Aus," Die Tageszeitung, August 15, 1998.

[8] IFEX Action Alert, June 23, 1998.

[9] Human Rights Watch interview, Priština, May 22, 1998.

Taras Protsyuk, a Ukrainian cameraman working for Reuters TV, was knocked to the ground from behind by plainclothes policemen as he filmed a street protest in Priština on March 19, 1998. On the same day, a Belgian cameraman working for RTBF in Belgium, Michel Rousez, was beaten by the police near the university.[1]

On July 6, 1998, two correspondents traveling with a convoy of foreign diplomats were assaulted by men believed to be plainclothes policemen. Kurt Schork of Reuters reportedly shouted at the driver of a car he thought had been driving recklessly. The driver hit Schork in the face, sending his glasses flying. Anthony Lloyd from the Times of London came to his assistance and was kicked in the ribs.[2]

Violations of the Rules of War by Insurgent Forces

Abuses by the KLA

The rules of internal armed conflict, outlined in Common Article 3 and Protocol II of the Geneva Conventions, are binding on both governments and armed insurgencies. As such, the KLA is legally obliged to respect the provisions of international humanitarian law, such as the protection of non-combatants and the prohibition of hostage taking. (See section on Legal Standards and the Kosovo Conflict.)

Despite these obligations, the KLA has committed violations of international humanitarian law, including the taking of hostages and, by their own apparent admission, summary executions (see below). Over one hundred people, mostly ethnic Serbs (but also some ethnic Albanians and Roma) are feared abducted by the KLA.

Some KLA operations were apparently intended to drive ethnic Serbs out of their villages. Human Rights Watch heard credible reports of ethnic Serbs being forced to leave the villages of Jelovac, Kijevo, Leocina, Gorni Ratiš, Maznik, Dašinovac, Veliki Djurdjevak, Mlecane, Dubrava, Boksic, and Lugodjija. In a number of cases, elderly Serbs refused to leave, either too old to flee or unwilling to abandon their homes. Some of these people are currently missing and feared dead (see below).

The KLA has attacked and seized some ethnic Albanians and Roma who it considers "collaborators" with the Yugoslav government. According to the Serbian Ministry of Internal Affairs, from January to May 1998, the KLA attacked twenty-eight ethnic Albanians, killing four and injuring five.[3]

Spokesmen for the KLA have repeatedly stressed the KLA's willingness to respect the rules of war, although their statements raise doubts about their interpretation of these norms. The prohibition on summary executions appears to be misunderstood, particularly in the case of ethnic Albanians suspected of collaboration with government forces, and Serbian civilians considered a part of the local security apparatus.

In an interview given to the Albanian-language newspaper Koha Ditore on July 11, 1998, KLA spokesman Jakup Krasniqi said:

"[T]he KLA has never dealt with civilians, or only if they have been in the service of the army and the police and have done serious harm to the people and the Albanian national cause. There have been cases in which they have been kidnaped, but in this event they have been handed over to international organizations, of course when they have been innocent.

First of all, all Serbian forces, whether the police, the military, or armed civilians, are our enemy. From the start, we had our own internal rules for our operations. These clearly lay down that the KLA recognizes the Geneva Conventions and the conventions governing the conduct of war, even though it has not been offered the chance of signing them, as it would have done. We do not go in for kidnaping.

Even if some people have suffered, these have been more Albanian collaborators than Serbian civilians. We do not deal with civilians, and we return those whom we take as prisoners of war. A few days ago we handed over two Serbs originating from Croatia to the International Red Cross. Those we have kidnaped are either announced in a list or reported to be executed, but we do not behave in a base fashion like Serbia."[4]

Shaban Shala, a KLA commander who used to be an activist with the Council for the Defense of Human Rights and Freedoms in Glogovac, said that the KLA General Headquarters would not order human rights abuses, but that some fighters may "make mistakes":

"I say this with complete responsibility - the KLA is called as such because it really is a liberation army. It is not engaged in conflict to harm others. It never made any attempts to usurp property, to destroy property that belongs to others; it did not abduct or massacre innocent children, women, or elderly. We are at war with the Serbian police and military forces, as well as other Serb paramilitary formations. We are not at war with civilians, innocent people, with children and the handicapped. I can add in this context that the KLA General Headquarters has not and will not issue an order to pursue, kill, or massacre innocent people, or loot or destroy Serbian property. However, not everything can be controlled during a war. There are cases when individuals make mistakes, but such cases are punished by the KLA, even if its soldiers conducted them."[5]

More recently, the KLA's newly-appointed political representative, Adem Demaqi,[6] told Radio B92 from Belgrade:

"When I talked to certain people from the headquarters, I saw that there was a united view on one thing: we do not deal in kidnapings. If some groups do it on their own, and if we have influence on them, we always intervene and kidnaped persons are released.[7]"

On September 9, the police announced that they had found the bodies of people they claimed had been killed by the KLA near Glodjane in a canal near Lake Radonjic. By September 16, they had gathered thirty-four bodies, eleven of whom were identified, including some ethnic Albanians. As of September 23, the identification process was ongoing.[8]

The most serious allegation made against the KLA prior to the September 9 announcement was the Yugoslav government's accusation that in the village of Klecka the KLA had executed twenty-two civilians, including women and children, and burned the bodies. The police claimed to have discovered human remains and a kiln used to cremate the bodies when they recaptured Klecka from the KLA around August 28. The details of the execution-style killings were provided by two ethnic Albanians who the Yugoslav authorities said were KLA fighters. One of them, Bekim Mazreku, was presented to foreign reporters while in police custody and then questioned by Danica Marinkovic,[9] an investigating judge from Priština who has been involved in a number of political trials in which ethnic Albanians were tortured. Mazreku was not allowed to speak independently to the journalists.[10] According to the New York Times, "one man, whose videotaped interrogation was made available to the New York Times

---

[1] Letter to President Slobodan Miloševic from the Committee to Protect Journalists, March 20, 1998.
[2] Committee to Protect Journalists, "British Correspondents Roughed Up in Kosovo," New York, July 8, 1998.
[3] "Terrorism in Kosmet in Numbers and Pictures," taken from the website of the Serbian Secretary of Information (www.serbia-info.com).
[4] "Spokesman Explains Structure of Rebel Army," BBC Summary of World Broadcasts, from Koha Ditore in Albanian, July 12, 1998, and "Koha Ditore Interview with Jakup Krasniqi, KLA Spokesman - Part II," Arta, July 12, 1998.
[5] "Koha Ditore Interview with KLA Commander," Arta, July 25, 1998.
[6] Demaqi resigned from his position as the KLA's political representative on September 21, 1998.
[7] "Demaqi Will Contact Main Headquarters of KLA," Radio B92, August 26, 1998.
[8] Among those identified were: Ilire Frakaj, Jusuf Hoxha, Milos Radunovic and Slobodan Radosevic.
[9] See, for example, the case of Destan Rukiqi in the section on Detentions and Arrests and "Persecution Persist: Human Rights Violations in Kosovo," Human Rights Watch/Helsinki report, December 1996.
[10] Reuters, August 29, 1998.

today, gave accounts that did not make sense and which the police say they cannot corroborate."[1]

KLA spokesmen rejected the charges, saying that the KLA, "has not killed a single Serb civilian."[2] The two ethnic Albanians presented by the police and interviewed by Danica Marinkovic were not members of the KLA, they claimed.

As of September 1, 1998, Human Rights Watch was not able to confirm the charges about Klecka. The manner in which the allegations were made raise serious questions about their validity and underline the importance of an investigation by an impartial forensics team.

Abductions of Ethnic Serbs by the KLA

The precise number of people held by the KLA is difficult to determine since the KLA does not provide public information on those in its custody, and a number of people have been held hostage and then released. Estimates of human rights and humanitarian organizations working on the ground range from one hundred to 140. According to the International Committee for the Red Cross, 138 ethnic Serbs are believed to have been taken by the KLA.

The Humanitarian Law Center, which has been monitoring detentions and abductions by the police and the KLA, has documented 103 ethnic Serbs who were unaccounted for as of August 1998, thirty-nine of whom were last seen in KLA custody. The center also documented the cases of three ethnic Albanians abducted by the KLA, ostensibly because they were considered "collaborators" with the Yugoslav government, whose whereabouts are currently unknown.[3]

According to a statement from the Yugoslav Ministry of Foreign Affairs issued on August 31, 1998, Albanian "terrorists" had abducted 178 individuals in Kosovo, including 128 ethnic Serbs and Montenegrins, forty-two ethnic Albanians, and six ethnic Roma. Out of this group, thirty-nine were released, seven escaped, and sixteen had been killed, leaving 114 people still in KLA detention.[4]

BELOW ARE SOME SPECIFIC CASES:

Abductions in Orahovac

On July 19, the KLA began its first major attack on a larger city: Orahovac. An estimated eighty-five ethnic Serbs were taken into custody by the KLA, although thirty-five of them were subsequently released. As of August 1998, at least forty people were still unaccounted for.

During the attack, approximately thirty elderly Serbs took shelter in the Monastery of Saints Cosmas and Damian in Zociste village together with seven monks and one nun. According to the Serbian Orthodox Church, the monastery was attacked for forty-five minutes with light artillery and machine guns and the guest house was damaged by two grenades.[5] Local Serbs told the Humanitarian Law Center, however, that the monks had resisted for two hours with four rifles before they realized a defense was futile and surrendered.[6] Everyone inside the monastery was taken to a school in nearby Semetište.

According to the ICRC and numerous media sources, the KLA handed thirty-five of these people over to the ICRC unharmed on July 22, including the seven Orthodox monks, one nun and twenty-five elderly people.[7] According to the Humanitarian Law Center, another ten people detained in the Orahovac offensive were released on the night of July 29-30, including Slavka, Snezana, and Ninoslav Baljoševic.[8]

The fate of an estimated forty other people taken from the Orahovac area, however, remains unknown. They include: Tomislav Baljoševic and his son Saša, Duško Dolasevic, Srdjan and Srecko Vitosevic, Djordje Djoric, Duško Djonovic, Sinisa Lukic, Veselin Lazic, Dusko Patranogic, Predrag Djurdjic, Jovan Vasic and Rajko Nikolic, plus five members of the Bozanic family: Mladen, Nemanja, Tihomir, Novica and Boško, and eight members of the Kostic family: Lazar, Todor, Saska, Miroljub, Vekoslav, Srecko, Svetomir, and Vitko. There are also reports of seventeen other people abducted by the KLA from the village of Retimlje near Orahovac.

Jovan Lukic

According to Tanjug and the Humanitarian Law Center, Jovan Lukic was detained by a group of armed Albanians while driving near Orahovac. Tanjug reported that Lukic was detained on July 19 along with Veselin Lazic, but the center mentions only Lukic being detained on July 17.[9]

Lukic told the center that he was held in Mališevo with a group of prisoners, including Srdjan and Srecko Vitoševic, a Roma man named Azem with his wife and daughter, a man named Duško from Orahovac, a man named Toma and his son, two doctors from Orahovac, and a doctor from Velika Hoca. The male detainees, he said, were taken out in small groups by a van that returned empty. Lukic was eventually taken in the van with some others, their hands tied, to a place in the woods. He succeeded in freeing his hands, however, and after struggling with one of the armed Albanians, managed to escape. He told the center that he does not know what happened to the other prisoners.

Ratko and Branko Staletic

The police found the bodies of Ratko Staletic and his son Branko on July 30 near Orlate village on the Priština-Pec road, according to the Humanitarian Law Center. The two residents of Mlecane village had reportedly been taken by ethnic Albanians in military uniforms on June 20, 1998.[10]

Vojko and Ivan Bakrac

Vojko and Ivan Bakrac, two ethnic Serb refugees from Croatia, and two other ethnic Serbs were taken off a bus on the Prizren-Štimlje road by armed ethnic Albanians on June 29. Vojko and Ivan Bakrac were on their way to the UNHCR offices in Priština, because they had been accepted in a United States resettlement program for ethnic Serb refugees in Kosovo.[11] According to the Humanitarian Law Center, they were released on July 8 or 9, although the two other Serbs, whose identities are unknown, remain unaccounted for.[12]

Ten Employees of the Belacavac Mine

On June 22, the KLA took control of the Belacavac mine, a large coal mine near the town of Obilic. The police recaptured the mine a few days later. The KLA reportedly captured nine ethnic Serbs in Obilic on July 22 as they were on their way to work at the mine; they were Dušan Andjancic, Pero Andjancic, Zoran Andjancic, Mirko Buha, Filip Gojkovic, Bozidar Lempic, Srboljub Savic, Mirko Trifunovic and Dragan Vukmirovic. None of them has been heard from since. The Times of London cites a senior Serbian policeman as saying that negotiations between the police and the KLA over the nine workers had "broken down" before the police retook control of the mine. A local miner, Nebojsa Jankovic was reportedly told that his

---

1 Mike O'Connor, "Rebel Terror Forcing Minority Serbs Out of Kosovo," The New York Times, August 30, 1998.
2 Agence France Press, August 30, 1998.
3 Humanitarian Law Center, "Kosovo - Disappearances in Times of Armed Conflict," Spotlight Report No. 27, August 5, 1998.
4 Statement Yugoslav Ministry of Foreign Affairs, Belgrade, August 31, 1998.
5 Press Release of the Serbian Orthodox Diocese of Raska and Prizren, July 22, 1998.
6 Humanitarian Law Center, "Kosovo - Disappearances in Times of Armed Conflict," Spotlight Report No. 27, August 5, 1998.
7 "Federal Republic of Yugoslavia/Kosovo: ICRC Aid for Conflict Victims," ICRC News 98/30, July 29, 1998, and "Kidnaped Serbs Released," AFP, July 22, 1998.

8 Humanitarian Law Center, "Kosovo - Disappearances in Times of Armed Conflict."
9 "Terrorist Abduct Two Serbs," Tanjug, July 20, 1998, and Humanitarian Law Center, "Kosovo - Disappearances in Times of Armed Conflict."
10 Humanitarian Law Center, "Kosovo - Disappearances in Times of Armed Conflict."
11 Human Rights Watch interview with UNHCR, Brussels, June 15, 1998.
12 Humanitarian Law Center, "Kosovo - Disappearances in Times of Armed Conflict."

nine colleagues had been "executed," but this could not be confirmed.[1]

Oliver Zalic

On June 22, the New York Times reported the death of Oliver Zalic, an ethnic Serb from Bica village who, according to his family, was killed by ethnic Albanians in front of his house while defending his sister and mother.[2]

Milosav, Sultana, Radomir, Aleksandra, and Dostana Šmigic

By May 1998, most ethnic Serbs in Leocina had left their homes after threats from local Albanians. Five members of the Šmigic family, however, four of them over seventy years old, decided not to leave their village. One of them, Krstiva Šmigic, told the Humanitarian Law Center that ethnic Albanians in military uniforms entered their yard around 10 a.m. on July 9. She managed to escape but Milosav (75), Sultana (72), Radomir (54), Aleksandra (c. 75), and Dostana (42) have not been heard from since:

Us three women [Sultana, Aleksandra and Dostana] left the house and went into the fields. After a while, Sultana and Lenka said they wanted to go back. Sultana went to her husband, and me and Lenka went back to her house, to Radomir. But about thirty of them [ethnic Albanians] were going into the yard and, when they saw us, they came toward us. They were armed, some in uniform and some in civilian clothes. Ten of them went into Radomir's house. They found him upstairs. We heard screams and Lenka rushed upstairs. I stayed below. I heard terrible screams and moaning from above. I couldn't bear it any more and went out again. I heard three rifle shots before I got into some high grass.[3]

Krstiva said she saw Milosav's house in flames from her hiding spot. After two days, she made it to the town of Rudnik, where she reported the incident to the police. On May 19, Krstiva Šmigic's daughter, Dostana, went back to Leocina to get her mother and three relatives. She was then abducted, reportedly in Ozrim, and has not been heard from since.[4]

Zivorad Spasic

Zivorad Spasic, a driver for the Mitrovica power plant, was last seen on May 10, 1998. His father, from a village near Obilic, asked the Council for the Defense of Human Rights and Freedoms and the Democratic League of Kosovo for help in finding his son.

Slobodan, Milica and Miloš Radoševic

Slobodan (64), Milica (59), and Miloš (60) Radoševic were the only ethnic Serbs to stay behind in Dašinovac village when the KLA took control on April 22. On September 16, the police announced that the bodies of Miloš and Slobodan Radoševic had been found in a canal that feeds into Lake Radonic near Glodjane.

According to the Humanitarian Law Center and Amnesty International, Rosa Radoševic tried to go back to Dašinovac the next day with her son Staniša to look for her husband Slobodan. They were stopped in Pozar village at a KLA checkpoint and taken to KLA headquarters in Glodjane, where Staniša was reportedly beaten.[5]

Dara and Vukosava Vujoševic, Milka, and Milovan Vlahovic

According to both the Humanitarian Law Center and Amnesty International, most ethnic Serbs fled their homes in Gornji Ratiš on April 21 when the KLA took control of the village. Dara (69) and Vukosava (65) Vujoševic and Milka (62) and Milovan (60) Vlahovic decided to stay and their whereabouts are currently unknown.[6]

Abductions of Roma by the KLA

According to the Humanitarian Law Center and the newspaper Blic, Gurim Bejta and Agron Beriša, both Roma, and Ivan Zaric, an ethnic Serb, left Dolac on May 20 for the village of Grabanica. As of August 1998, their whereabouts were still unknown.[7]

Human Rights Watch heard unconfirmed reports that four armed ethnic Albanians dragged Ramadan Uka and his wife, both Roma, from their homes in Budisavci near Pec at the end of March 1998. According to a center researcher who spoke with Mr. Uka, the Albanians, whom Ramadan knew, beat him and raped his wife, but his story could not be confirmed.[8]

Abductions of Ethnic Albanians by the KLA

Since the intensification of it activities in 1996, the KLA has targeted ethnic Albanians it considers "collaborators" with the Yugoslav government.

According to the Serbian Orthodox Monastery at Visoki Decani near Decan, two elderly ethnic Albanians, Hajdar Kuci and Beki Cacaj, were killed near the Bistrica river outside of Decan on May 7. The next day, unknown armed individuals attacked a van from the nearby power plant. An ethnic Albanian, Vehbi Mustafa (65), was killed, while four ethnic Serbs, Boško Vlahovic, Esad Muminovic, Miso Mijovic, and Dragan Djurisic were injured.[9]

According to the pro-government Priština Media Center, the KLA abducted three ethnic Albanians from Donji Godanc on June 26: Agim Ademi, Veselj Ahmeti and Shucrija Zumeri.

As of September 16, forensics experts were still conducting investigations on the thirty-two bodies found near Lake Radonjic. Two ethnic Albanians had been identified: Ilire Frakaj and Jusuf Hoxha.

Restrictions on the Media by the KLA

The KLA has periodically restricted the domestic and international media in Kosovo by denying access to certain areas, detaining and, on a few occasions, physically attacking journalists. On August 21, 1998, an ethnic Serbian journalist with the state-run Radio Priština, Djuro Slavuj, and his driver, Ranko Perinic, went missing near the city of Orahovac, and were feared abducted by the KLA. According to the Radio Priština office, the two left Orahovac for the nearby town of Malisevo in a blue Zastava car, but never arrived.[10] As of September 1, 1998, their whereabouts were still unknown.

On August 26, the KLA's newly appointed political representative, Adem Demaqi, said that he would try to secure the journalists' release, although he didn't know if the group that abducted the journalists was under the control of "KLA headquarters."[11] Six days later, KLA spokesman Jakup Krasniqi said the KLA knows nothing about the journalists' abduction. In an interview with the Albanian-language Koha Ditore, he said:

---

[1] Tom Walker, "Guerrillas in Kosovo 'Killed Mine Hostages'," Times (London), July 2, 1998.

[2] Mike O'Connor, "Kosovo Rebels' New Tactic: Attack Serb Civilians," the New York Times, June 24, 1998.

[3] Humanitarian Law Center, "Kosovo - Disappearances in Times of Armed Conflict."

[4] See Mike O'Connor, "Rebel Terror Forcing Minority Serbs Out of Kosovo," the New York Times, August 30, 1998, and Blic newspaper, May 21, 1998.

[5] Amnesty International, "Human Rights Violations Against Women in Kosovo Province," and Humanitarian Law Center, "Kosovo - Disappearances in Times of Armed Conflict."

[6] "Human Rights Violations Against Women in Kosovo Province," A Human Rights Crisis in Kosovo Province, Document Series B 1, Amnesty International, August 1998, and Humanitarian Law Center, "Kosovo - Disappearances in Times of Armed Conflict."

[7] Blic newspaper, May 21, 1991, and Humanitarian Law Center, "Kosovo - Disappearances in Times of Armed Conflict."

[8] Human Rights Watch interview with Humanitarian Law Center researcher, Priština, May 21, 1998.

[9] Press Release of the Brotherhood of the Serbian Orthodox Monastery at Visoki Decani, May 9, 1998, Decan. The Council for the Defense of Human Rights and Freedoms also reported on Mustafa's death, but implied that he had been shot by police or the military. "Another Albanian Killed in Deçan," Press Release of the Council for the Defense of Human Rights and Freedoms, May 8, 1998.

[10] Human Rights Watch telephone interview with editor at Radio Priština, August 26, 1998.

[11] "Demaqi Will Contact Main Headquarters of UCK," Radio B92, August 26, 1998.

We know nothing about the arrest or the kidnaping of any Serb resident or journalist. The KLA did not pick up weapons to fight Serb residents or journalists, but to fight against Serb terrorists and soldiers, that turned Kosova into a burnt land. After all this terror and destruction seen in Kosova, it is impossible to control the feelings of hate and revenge that have been planted by the enemy itself, despite our insistence that the Albanian war does not take the features of the barbarous war conducted by the enemy.[1]

In July, three Russian journalists were reportedly detained by members of the KLA. According to Reporters San Frontieres, on July 18, Sergei Mitim from the newspaper Izvestia was detained and reportedly beaten by members of a KLA patrol on the Glogovac-Srbica road. He was released after several hours, but his film and rented car were taken.[2] On July 20, Oleg Safiulin and Oleg Galanov, with the TV program Vesti, were reportedly interrogated for several hours by the KLA and then released.[3]

On August 14, freelance journalist Stacy Sullivan was in Glodjane interviewing ethnic Albanian civilians with two KLA escorts present. According to Sullivan, another KLA member drove up and demanded she stop. He grabbed her notebook and burned some pages that contained interviews of ethnic Albanian refugees she had taken over the past three days. Later, this KLA member and her two escorts drove to the regional command headquarters near Vranoc. The commander in charge apologized to Sullivan for the soldier's actions and said that he had stripped the soldier of his weapons, although whether this happened could not be confirmed.[4]

Restrictions on Humanitarian Aid Workers

On July 23, 1998, KLA fighters at a checkpoint in Lodja near Pec confiscated a vehicle belonging to Medecins Sans Frontieres, but the vehicle was returned some days later.[5]

In early September 1998, a KLA checkpoint turned back a UNHCR convoy for the first time. According to UNHCR, a convoy with five tons of ready-to-eat meals was blocked while heading to the village of Golubach. UNHCR spokesman Kris Janowski said that KLA soldiers blocked the convoy because of shelling, which could be heard a short distance away. But the rebels also suggested that the UNHCR convoy leader and driver were spies.[6]

According to diplomatic sources, the KLA turned back a truck at an undisclosed location with five tons of food from the World Food Program on September 7, 1998, because the driver of the truck was an ethnic Serb.

Legal Standards and the Kosovo Conflict

[...]

The International War Crimes Tribunal for the Former Yugoslavia

[...]

Role of the International Community

[...]

---

[1] Koha Ditore, September 1, 1998.
[2] IFEX Action Alert, July 21, 1998.
[3] "Two Russian Journalists Taken Hostage by Albanian Militants," Itar-Tass, July 21, 1998.
[4] Human Rights Watch interview with Stacy Sullivan, New York, September 3, 1998.
[5] "Kosovo Rebels Confiscate an MSF Vehicle," Agence France Presse, July 24, 1998.
[6] Wendy Lubetkin, "UN Appeals for Funds to Avert Catastrophe in Kosovo this Winter," September 8, 1998, USIA European Correspondent.

49. Medecins Sans Frontieres: Survey Data on Mass Expulsions from Kosovo, A Survey of the Kosovar Refugees at Rosaye, Montenegro, Vincent Brown, MSF/Epicentre, Rosaye, 27 April 1999[7]

A Summary of Results from a Randomised Survey of 201 Kosovar Refugee Families at Rosaye, Montenegro, 14-15 April 1999

Results	Number	% families
1. DESCRIPTION OF THE SAMPLE AND HISTORY OF DEPORTATION		
Families surveyed Size of the sample = 1537 Number of people per family = 7.6 Male/Female Ratio (15-55 years) = 0.88 (400/453)	201	100.0 %
Families homeless for more than 5 years Average length of exodus = 7.6 days (extremes:<1 to 23 days)	94	46.7 %
Families from "Villages"	89	94.0%
Families who fled on foot	187	93.0%
Without Kosovar identity papers	92	45.8%
Length of stay at Rosaye > 5days	93	46.3%
Reason for departure = direct threats/armed men	94	46.5%
2. IMPACT OF THE WAR		
Families with >1 member remaining in Kosovo Total for the sample = 169 people remaining in Kosovo (9.9%)	56	27.8 %
With at least one death/war (24/03-15/04/99)	3	1.5 %
With one missing person Total for the sample = 28 missing persons	10	5.0 %
With at least one wounded member (Total wounded = 14)	9	4.5 %
3. BASIC NEEDS		
Without blankets global average for the sample = 1.7 people / blanket	17	8.5 %
Without mattresses global average for the sample = 6.7 people / mattress	87	3 %
Without bread for at least 24 hours global average for the sample = 200 grams of bread per person/24hrs.	19	9.5 %
4. OUTLOOK FOR THE IMMEDIATE FUTURE		
"Staying in Rosaye" or"Do not know" 24 families (11.9%) are planning move on to Albania	159	79 %

Introduction

Nato air raids in the region began on 24 March 1999 and have continued up to now. The raids have been immediately followed by attacks lead by the Serbian army (and/or paramilitary groups, and /or the special police) on the Albanian majority of the Kosovar population. For over a month, these systematic attacks on towns and villages have forced the civilian population of Kosovo into the neighbouring countries or regions of Macedonia, Albania and Montenegro. More than half a million people have fled to these countries and over 70 000 are now in Montenegro (Source UNHCR: 73 000 refugees in Montenegro as of 19/04/1999).

At the request of Medecins Sans Frontieres, a survey was carried out among Kosovar refugees in Rosaye, Montenegro. It is intended to describe the situation of the refugees and to evaluate their urgent needs.

The refugee population living with residents in Rosaye has been estimated at over 15 000. This population and a further population of refugees housed in the mosques do not feature in the survey.

---

[7] *Used with permission of Medecins Sans Frontieres.*

Development of the Human Rights Situation

Survey Objectives

1. To establish demographic data on the refugee population (and the history of the exodus). 2. To evaluate the impact of exactions on the civilian population. 3. To evaluate the refugees' most urgent needs. 4. To envision immediate plans for the future.

Method

A sample was established by drawing at random in the three factories, Kristal, Liego-Biele, and Dekor. These sites are located in the most eastern part of Rosaye. They were chosen with the intention of evaluating the situation of the population which is considered to be "the most in need."

From the outset it was decided that the survey would focus on a random sample of 150 to 200 families. The proportional distribution of the refugees between the three factories was taken into account in establishing the sample.

In order for the sample to be as representative as possible, each of the three factories was divided into ten sections (or rooms). The population of each of the 10 rooms was estimated before the draw was made.

When randomly selecting families from each room, the four teams conducting the survey (each team was made up of one MSF member and one translator speaking Albanian) followed the same procedure. The team stood in the centre of the room and chose one family at random and then proceeded with every second family counting from this initial choice.

A "family" was defined as "all of the members of a closely knit group living under the same roof in Kosovo (in an apartment, or in a house)".

Results

A total of 201 families, in all 1537 people were chosen to participate in the survey.

All of the families responded to the questions on the individual questionnaire.

Number of people per family = 7.6

Description of the refugee population:
- For the entire population, Male/Female ratio = 0.99 (768/769)
- For the 15-55 age group, Male/Female ratio = 0.88 (400/453)

Table 1: Distribution of the 1537 Refugees into 4 Age Groups, and by Gender, Rosaye, Montenegro, 15 April 1999

Age	Men	(%)	Women	(%)	Total	(%)
0-4	82	(10.6)	77	(10.0)	159	(10.5)
5-14	220	(28.7)	159	(20.7)	379	(24.5)
15-55	400	(52.1)	453	(58.9)	853	(55.5)
+55	66	(8.6)	80	(10.4)	146	(9.5)
TOTAL	768	(100.0)	769	(100.0)	1537	(100.0)

Towns/villages distribution:

Villages =189 families/201 = 94.0% (56 villages counted + list of names)

Towns = 12 families/ 201 = 6.0% (mostly from Pec and Ishtok).

Duration of the exodus:

- The average duration of the exodus for the 201 families in the sample was 7.6 days (extremes: <1 day to 23 days). Among these families, a proportion of 53.2% (107/201) reached Rosaye in 5 days (see Table 2).

- Most of the families had to flee on foot across the mountains = 187/201 (93.0%).

- A total of 45/201 families (22.3%) reached Rosaye in less than 24 hours. Among these 45 families, 33 (73.3%) made their way on foot (some of them made a short part of their journey by tractor).

- For the 156 families for whom the duration of exodus was more than 24 hours (> 1 day) the average was 9.8 days (extremes: 1 to 23 days).

Table 2: Duration of Exodus for 201 Refugee Families in three Factories: Rosaye, Montenegro, 15 April 1999.

Days on the road	No. Families	(%)
< 5 days	107	(53.2)
5-10 days	25	(12.5)
11-23 days	69	(34.3)
Total	201	(100.0)

IDENTITY

- The names of a majority of refugees have been registered on lists established by 'Mother Theresa' (NGO).

- Only one family (1 / 201) has received an official registration form (which recognises its status as a refugee family).

- A total of 92/201 families (45.8%) have no Kosovar identity papers.

LENGTH OF STAY

- On average, surveyed families have already spent 6 days at Rosaye (extremes 1 - 16 days).

- At the time of the survey, 46.3%(93/201) of families have been in Rosaye for at least 5 days (see Table 3).

Table 3: Length of stay for 201 refugee families in three factories, Rosaye, Montenegro, 15 April 1999.

Length of stay	No. Families	(%)
< 5 days	108	(54.0)
5-10 days	54	(27.0)
11-16 days	39	(19.0)
Total	201	(100.0)

IMPACT OF THE WAR

- A total of 56/201 (27.8%) families left "at least" one member behind when they left Kosovo.

- The number of persons left behind in this manner comes to a total of 169 representing a proportion of 9.9% percent of the overall sample. [169 / (1537 + 169)].

- The three main causes cited for fleeing from Kosovo: 1) attacks on towns/villages (bombs, grenades,..), 2) direct physical threats from armed men, 3) to avoid reprisals which had already begun in their region: among 201 families these reasons respectively represented 89 (44.5%), 94 (46.5%), and 18 (9.0%) of the 201 families.

- A total of 6 deaths (civilians) were reported for the period from 24 March to 14 April 1999. Of these six deaths, 4 were violent (caused by bullets,..) and 2 were caused by "exhaustion" which occurred while the refugees were on the run (a child of 7 months and a woman of 80).

- A total of 14 people were wounded during the expulsion. Wounded or injured members were reported by 9/201 of the families (4.5%).

BASIC NEEDS

- A total of 17/201 families do not have blankets, 8.5% of the sample.

- The other 184 families surveyed, have a total of 880 blankets, an average of 4.8 per family [or 1.7 (1537/880) people per blanket].

- 43.3% of the families (87/201) have no mattresses.

- A total of 228 mattresses was recorded for the 1537 people in the sample (= 6.7 persons per mattress).

- 9.5% of the families (19/201) had not received a ration of bread (distributed = once a day). These 19 families all belonged to a group of 45 families who had arrived at Rosaye less than 24 hours earlier.

- A total of 525 loaves of bread (600 grams each) were distributed to the 1537 persons in the sample.

SHORT TERM PROSPECTS

The refugee families were asked what they thought they would do in the following week.

For now, 2/3 of the sample thought they would remain in the factories at Rosaye.

Table 4: Short term prospects ("a week") for 201 refugee families, in three factories at Rosaye, Montenegro, 15 April 1999.

Prospect	Number	(%)
Remain here	137	(68.2)
Another town[1]	8	(4.0)
Another country[2]	34	(16.9)
Do not know	22	(10.9)
Total	201	(100.0)

INTERPRETATION AND ANALYSIS OF RESULTS

The sample selected for the survey can be considered as quite representative of the refugee population the most in need, however the survey could not take into account the most recent arrivals who were settled under tents in difficult conditions (night temperatures hovering at close to 0°C, windy area, lack of basic necessities...).

The overall sex distribution within the sample appears to be "normal", although the figure for males in the 15 to 55 age group is underrepresented. This may indicate that a proportion of men have stayed on to fight, or are dead. A further possibility is that they were taken prisoner. During the survey it was reported that some civilians were taken prisoner.

The proportion of children aged under 15 (36%) seems higher than the expected figure for this type of population in peace time. Due to a lack of reliable reference data, no conclusions can be drawn for the moment.

Nearly 46% of the families surveyed no longer have their Kosovar identity papers. Neither did they receive papers when they were recorded on the lists maintained by "Mother Theresa" (NGO) or by the local police. Given that this population is officially considered to be displaced in Montenegro (Republic of Serbia), and given that under current conditions the UNHCR is unable to grant them the status of refugees, official recognition of their identity and status is now a serious problem.

More than half of the surveyed population arrived in Rosaye less than five days ago. They had fled to avoid the recent series of exactions which took place in the villages around Ishtok. Now that a list of the names of the villages which produced this wave of refugees has been established, it is possible to determine the order of successive attacks launched by Serbian forces.

The survey has also facilitated the documentation of military strategies used against villages: mortar or grenade attacks, followed by heavy gunfire or firebomb attacks, and then the pursuit of the fleeing population (direct fire on civilians, including women and children). The reports of this kind of attack are corroborated by accounts of shootings and wounded civilians which were reported in the survey. Furthermore, almost half of the refugee families questioned in the course of the survey report having their lives threatened in their own homes.

If we extrapolate the results of the survey to the entire refugee population of Rosaye (at least 25,000 people), almost one hundred violent deaths are likely to have occurred in this population, over the period from 24 March to 15 April 1999. In the same period, the number of those wounded by bullets and mortar grenade shrapnel is likely to represent more than 200 cases.

Since 24 March 1999, the refugee population has also been affected by the separation of families. About a third of families report being separated from at least one close family member - either "left behind" in Kosovo (28.0%), or "missing" (5.0%). Extrapolating from this data, the figure for those left behind or missing for the 25,000 refugee population in Rosaye may be as high as 3,000.

Figures for dead and wounded as well as "missing persons" and persons "left behind" were also reported for the period from 28 February 1998 (attacks on Drenica) to 23 March 1999. These 1998 figures are lower than those reported for the period from 24 March to 15 April 1999, and they are not analysed in this report.

Regarding basic needs, the refugees living in the factories, under tents or in the mosques brought virtually nothing with them to Rosaye, and sanitary conditions are very precarious (before the survey was conducted a rapid evaluation of basic needs in the three refugee sites was undertaken). The results of the survey confirm the findings of the rapid evaluation particularly with regard to food and bedding (blankets and mattresses).

The survey attempted to establish the effectiveness of the last distribution of bread rations on the preceding day. The survey found that the average individual bread ration per refugee was around 200g (instead of the 300g officially announced planned).

It is possible that some families are still living on their meagre savings, but from now on it is important to envision that the nutritional situation could deteriorate. With the constant influx of new arrivals, the limited resources of NGOs and the local community may soon prove to be insufficient.

In terms of basic needs, the question of the living conditions of the refugee population must be addressed immediately. Sanitary problems pose a serious threat in the short term. Usual indicators (number of square metres/person, number of litres of water/day, the ratio of refugees/latrines) show that recommended norms are not being respected and that there is a real risk of epidemics.

Despite registered departures for Albania (over 20 000 departures registered at the border post in Tuzi, for the period 24 March to 22 April 1999), it is likely that the global needs of refugees will remain more or less constant in the following weeks. The influx of refugees arriving from Kosovo to Rosaye can reach 1000 - 2000 per day (confirmed from 13 to 20 April 1999). One must keep in mind that thousands of other refugees, blocked in Kosovo because of security reasons, can still arrive.

Given that Rosaye is only 20km from a war zone, the question of security is one of the most urgent issues.

Since its arrival in the municipality of Rosaye, Montenegro, the Kosovar refugee community has lived in fear. Refugees are frightened by the possibility of exactions perpetrated by groups of armed men crossing the border from Kosovo (since 15 April, non-identified cars with armed men were met on several occasions between Rosaye and the border). On 20 April 1999, two refugees were killed only 7km south east of Rosaye. Others have reported being insulted and beaten by paramilitaries, the Serbian army or the special police. The wounded avoid seeking treatment in Rosaye because they are afraid of drawing attention to themselves. All of these facts confirm the existence of the current repressive policy which has been adopted with regard to the Kosovar refugees.

RECOMMENDATIONS

Obviously a long term solution to the problem of the Kosovar refugees in Montenegro will be some time in the making. In the interim, it is imperative that they should be provided with living conditions which correspond to acceptable levels of security and sanitation. Urgent measures to be taken are as follows:

1. Take measures ensuring usual security conditions in refugee situation
    - Register each family and provide them with an individual registration document.
    - Inform the international community of any exactions perpetrated on refugees.

---

[1] A total of 4/201 (2.0%) families wanted to go to Ulcinj.
[2] A total of 24/201 (11.9%) families wanted to move on to Albania.

- Relocate refugees to sites which are at a sufficient distance from the border (the usual recommended distance = at least 50km from the border).
- Settle a security perimeter around the sites.
- Maintain security during transport of refugees from one site to another.
- Monitor and defend cases of murdered, missing, imprisoned and wounded refugees.

2. Ensure a minimum scale of decent living conditions for refugees in exile in Montenegro:
- Install refugees in accommodation providing a minimum of 3.5 square metres per person (at the moment, this figure is usually < 1 square metre per person).
- Set up a water supply system. It is recommended in refugee situations to provide a minimum of twenty litres per person per day, the usual recommended level, and at least one tap for every 250 people. (At the moment the refugees in Montenegro have less than 10 litres/person/day; and a tap of water for several hundred refugees).
- Ensure a minimal individual ration of 2300 Kcal / person / day "during cold weather". (At the moment there is no reliable data on the refugees' diet).
- Provide a sufficient number of WCs and latrines ; the norm is 1 WC / 20 people (the current estimate = 1 WC / 200 - 300 people).
- Ensure a minimal provision for protection from the cold (mattresses, blankets and clothing).
- Ensure minimal conditions for personal hygiene and group hygiene are maintained (soap, hot water, privacy/showers, diapers, sanitary towels, flea treatment...).

3. Medical services: as access to medical services is complicated by security issues, overworked staff and lack of means, the following must be monitored closely:

- Ensure basic treatments are available (necessary means should be given to Kosovar doctors working on the refugee sites, and support of the Montenegrin health service should be encouraged).
- Ensure the management of medical and surgical cases (heart problems/HTA, endocrinous problems/diabetes, war wounds..).
- Vaccinate children under five with the five antigens (children under five are known to have low vaccine coverage in Kosovo).
- Evaluate the extent of psychiatric problems so that the management of particular cases can be envisioned. .
- Set up the surveillance of common diseases, and also monitor "deaths" and "wounded" (c.f. appendix), alert in case of any outbreak.

CONCLUSION

The survey has allowed to describe the drama suffered by Kosovar refugees since 24 March. It also sheds light on the particular difficulties the refugees face in Montenegro, particularly in the Rosaye municipal area.

When the refugees are asked about their immediate plans (see Survey), only a small percentage of families envision to leave Rosaye for another Montenegrin town (e.g. Ulcinj) or to move on to another country (Albania).

One of the main reasons for this is that the refugee population living in the factories (and also in the mosques and under tents) has very limited finances or no finances whatsoever.

The current situation is characterised by issues of security and sanitary priorities. The NGOs are unable to deal with these problems alone. In as much as this situation is likely to continue, the international community in agreement with the local national government ought to seek medium term solutions for the Kosovar refugees.

CHAPTER 3: DIPLOMATIC EFFORTS FOR THE SETTLEMENT OF THE CRISIS

3.1. Early Attempts to Settle the Crisis

While the constitutional crisis in Kosovo has been worsening since 1988, the international community did not act before the dissolution of the SFRY. However, when armed conflict broke out in Croatia and subsequently in Bosnia and Herzegovina this conflict dominated the international agenda. In June 1991, Slovania and Croatia declared their independence. Fighting broke out in Slovenia and continued in Croatia. The European Union condemned the use of force by the Federation and urged the parties to agree to a peace conference sponsored by the EU. The conference was convened in The Hague on 7 September 1991 under the chairmanship of Lord Carrington with the aim to create a peaceful resolution of the conflict. During the conference a framework for the settlement of the Yugoslav crisis as a whole was drafted. The proposal suggested the forming of autonomous regions or special status areas, applying, "in particular, to the Serbs living in areas in Croatia where they form a majority." Without mentioning Kosovo and Vojvodina, the draft also proposed that "the republics will apply fully and in good faith established provisions for the benefit of ethnic and national groups, and for autonomous provinces which were given a special constitutional status" (*document no. 50 a*). Thus, however, it was not clear whether the constitutional changes of 1989/90 were accepted by the international community because they were not mentioned. The second draft of the Carrington plan became more precise in its refutation of the constitutional amendments stressing that " the republics shall apply fully and in good faith the provisions existing prior to 1990 for autonomous provinces" (*document no. 50 b*).

When Serbia rejected the peace plan for all Yugoslavia the EU changed its policy and offered recognition to the republics seeking independence in exchange for their commitment to several conditions, such as their compliance with international standards for human and minority rights.[1] The attempt to resolve issues arising from the dissolution of the SFRY comprehensively had failed. The republics were invited to notify whether they would opt for independence by 23 December 1991. The decision on recognition was based on an assessment of the implementation of the republics' commitments to the conditions set out by the EC member states for recognition. The "Badinter Commission", an arbitration commission headed by Robert Badinter and attached to the peace conference, undertook the assessment. Kosovo formally applied for recognition in a letter by Dr. Rugova to the Chairman of the Conference (*document no. 50 c*). The Commission, however, did not considered the request unlike the requests of the Bosnia and Herzegovina, Croatia, Macedonia and Slovenia.

By summer 1992, international concern focused on the armed conflict in Bosnia and Herzegovina. The international community made a second major attempt for a solution of the conflict through the London Conference on Yugoslavia in August 1992. The conference failed to invite a Kosovo Albanian delegation. However in a letter addressed to Dr. Rugova, the Chairman informed him that he would have access to the conference building, though not to the conference chamber itself. The proceedings were transmitted to a separate room reserved to the Kosovo Albanian delegation.[2]

The Conference did not resolve the issues it had addressed, but the parties continued the process through follow-up meetings. They established a "Special Group" on Kosovo. This working group concentrated on the issue of education, since progress in this area was deemed to be possible. However, the group reached no result (*documents no. 50 e, 50 f*). In 1996, Rugova and Milosevic signed an educational agreement after the mediation of a non-governmental organisation, but the FRY did not implement the agreement. A final attempt undertaken in 1998 failed due to the escalating violence in the area (*document no. 8*).

The CSCE started an early action with regard to Kosovo by establishing a Mission of Long Duration to Kosovo, Sandjak and Vojvodina on 13/14 August 1992. Yugoslavia terminated the operation of the mission by withdrawing its consent in June 1993. This was done in response to the CSCE's decision to suspend Yugoslavia from participation in the CSCE due to the events in Bosnia and Herzegovina which violated the CSCE principles. The international community criticised strongly the termination of the operation. The criticism culminated in UN Security Council resolution 855 (1993) (*document no. 52*).

3.2 Political Actions and Sanctions since 1997

The Contact Group was formally established in April 1994 as the Contact Group on Bosnia and Herzegovina and consisted originally of the Foreign Ministers of France, Germany, the Russian Federation, the UK and the USA. In May 1996, it was enlarged to include Italy. By autumn 1997, the Contact Group emerged as the main coordinating body for handling the Kosovo crisis (*document no. 54*). At its London meeting of 9 March 1998 (*document no. 57*) the group was unable to agree on a unanimous position. While the USA and the UK favoured a quick and harsh reaction, France, Italy and Russia were opposed to such a move. Germany tried to mediate.[3] The Contact Group, in its statement, proposed UN Security Council considerations of a comprehensive arms embargo, denial of visas for senior FRY representatives and a moratorium on government financed export. However, the Contact Group had to note that the Russian Federation could not support the latter measures. The statement included a deadline of ten days in which Milosevic was required to withdraw special police units, allow international observers into Kosovo, commit himself to a process of dialogue, and to cooperate with the Contact Group. This led to UN Security Council Resolution 1160 of 31 March 1998 taken under Chapter VII of the UN Charter (*document no. 65*). The resolution condemned "the use of excessive force by Serbian police forces against civilians and peaceful demonstrators in Kosovo, as well as acts of terrorism by the KLA." The Security Council called for a political solution of the conflict, and demanded greater autonomy for Kosovo with meaningful self-administration." Above all, it

---

[1] European Political Cooperation, Guidelines on Recognition of New States in Eastern Europe and in the Soviet Union, 16 December 1991 and European Political Cooperation, Declaration on Yugoslavia, 16 December 1991.
[2] Letter from Lord Carrington to Dr. Rugova, 17 August 1992.
[3] Stefan Troebst, 'The Kosovo conflict' (1999) *SIPRI Yearbook* at 52.

included an arms embargo against the FRY. The Security Council established a committee to monitor compliance with the embargo. The UN Secretary-General reported on the implementation of the embargo drawing on the reports of European institutions, such as the EU, the WEU or NATO (*documents no. 116-126*). The embargo became necessary because the UN had terminated sanctions directed against the FRY during the conflict in Bosnia and Herzegovina, when the FRY implemented the 1995 General Framework Agreement for Peace in Bosnia and Herzegovina.[1]

When the Contact Group met in Bonn on 25 March 1998 the deadline, set by the Contact Group, for Yugoslav actions to stop the violence and engage in political negotiations had expired, but was extended another four weeks (*document no. 63*). At a meeting held in Rome on 29 April 1998 (*document no. 71*), the Contact Group stated that "crucial requirements set out in the Contact Group's statements of 9 and 25 March 1999 have not yet been met." They decided to take action by freezing the funds held abroad in bank accounts by the FRY and Serbian governments. By 9 May the Contact Group would take action to stop new investment in Serbia if the FRY should not comply. When Milosevic met with Rugova on 15 May 1999, ostensibly demonstrating his willingness to find a political solution to the conflict, the Contact Group refrained from imposing a ban on investment in the FRY.[2]

When Milosevic started once again to attack Kosovo Albanian villages in May, the UK and the USA shifted their focus away from the Contact Group which was obstructed by the Russian Federation and started acting through NATO and the EU. Unlike the UN, the European Union had not lifted its sanctions against Yugoslavia. On 19 March 1998, the EU imposed further sanctions. In addition to arms, the EU barred non-lethal police equipment and issued a moratorium on government financed export, credit support for trade and investment, including financing for privatisation, in Serbia. The regulation prohibited the granting of visas for senior FRY and Serbian representatives (*document no. 61*). There was also a freezing of Yugoslav and Serb state funds and of investment in Serbia when the FRY did not comply with the UN Security Council resolution (*document no. 72*). A flight ban was added on 29 June 1998 (*document no. 81*). The EU had also appointed Felipe Gonzalez as its Special Representative for a mission to the region in June 1998 (*documents no. 64, 66, 68, 71*). However, the government denied Felipe Gonzalez entrance into the FRY (*documents no. 75, 77*).

On 8 June 1998, the EU banned new investment in Serbia (*document no. 74*) while NATO was increasing its military presence in Albania and Macedonia (*document no. 153*). Milosevic responded by paying an official visit to the Russian Federation. His meeting with President Yeltsin resulted in an announcement that diplomats accredited by the FRY as well as representatives of humanitarian non-governmental organisations would be given unhindered access to Kosovo, that the FRY would not impede the return of refugees, and that the Serbian security forces and army would refrain from any oppressive action against the Kosovo Albanian population (*document no. 78*).

However, when the KLA started to set up temporary checkpoints on the Pristina-Pec road the parties resumed fighting. NATO, taken by surprise by the KLA forays, reduced its pressure on Belgrade.[3] On 6 July, the Kosovo Diplomatic Observer Mission (KDOM) became operational. The mission was led by a coordinating group composed of the ambassadors of the Contact Group countries in Belgrade as well as the ambassadors of Austria, representing the EU Presidency, and Poland, representing the OSCE Chairman-in-Office.

Fighting still continued on a massive scale. The Serbian forces were so successful in their new campaign so that on 17 August 1998 regional KLA leaders in the Pec area and Serbian forces agreed on a ceasefire mediated by KDOM in order to enable international aid agencies to assist civilians being displaced or wounded in the conflict.[4] The humanitarian catastrophe caused by the internal displacement of some 200,000 Kosovar Albanians kept the attention of the international community focused on Kosovo. News of a massacre at Gornje Obrinje in the Drenica region, in which 16 ethnic Albanians civilians had been killed on 25 September 1998, had the same galvanizing effect on world opinion.

In response to a report of the UN Secretary-General (*document no. 120*), the UN Security Council adopted resolution 1199 (1998) of 23 September 1998 (*document no. 89*) condemning the indiscriminate use of force. It reaffirmed that the situation in Kosovo constituted a threat to peace and security in the region. The Security Council was alarmed "at the impending humanitarian catastrophe". Taken under Chapter VII of the UN Charter, the resolution repeated the demands of resolution 1160 (1998). On 24 September, NATO increased its pressure on the FRY by issuing an Activation Warning for both a limited air operation and a phased air campaign (*document no. 154; see Chapter 4*). On 13 October 1989, the Serb government announced the acceptance of an 11-point political framework for the settlement of the Kosovo issue - the Holbrooke Agreement (*document no. 156*).[5]

Simultaneous to these actions the Contact Group directed a diplomatic effort to achieve a settlement. US Ambassador to Macedonia, Chris Hill, led this mission. At its Bonn meeting of 8 July 1998, the Contact Group recommended to its negotiators basic elements for a resolution of the status of Kosovo (*document no. 83*). The Group stressed that it neither supported the status quo nor independence of the province. The initial efforts of the Hill mission, carried out through shuttle diplomacy between the FRY/Serbian government and representatives of the Kosovo Albanians, soon turned into a different direction. When it became evident that the parties could not achieve an agreement on Kosovo's status, they sought for an interim solution. On 3 September 1998, Ambassador Hill informed the OSCE Permanent Council that the parties had reached an informal agreement which included a three-year stabilisation and normalisation period to provide for the re-establishment of democratic institutions. After this period, new approaches would be attempted. He underlined the crucial importance of the international presence in Kosovo during the implementation period (*document no. 121*). It appeared that the drafts for a settlement emanated from Ambassador Hill and the legal advisor Jim O'Brian, although the Contact Group retained considerable influence over the contents of the drafts. On 1 October 1998, the Hill team presented the first formal and complete draft to the parties (*document no. 93 a*). While negotiations were underway Milosevic and Holbrooke concluded the Holbrooke Agreement (*document no. 156*). A unilateral statement of the Serbian government was part of this agreement. The statement outlined the principles for a political solution on which agreement had allegedly been reached. On 2

---

[1] UN Doc. S/Res/ 1074 (1996) of 1 October 1996.
[2] Stefan Troebst, 'The Kosovo conflict' (1999) *SIPRI Yearbook* at 54.
[3] Ibid., at 56.
[4] Ibid., at 57.
[5] See Chapter 4.1.

November, an agreement was to be completed using the first Hill Draft as a starting point. Unlike the Hill Draft the Serbian statement included a reference to the territorial integrity of the FRY. However, the Kosovo Albanians were not involved in the Holbrooke negotiations. Therefore, the Kosovo Albanians issued their own statement on fundamental principles for a political settlement (*document no. 93 c*). On 2 November 1998, a new far more detailed Hill draft was presented to the parties (*document no. 93 b*). While the first Hill draft allocated authority to different levels of administration, i.e. individual communes or local districts, without granting any significant element of legal personality to Kosovo as such, the second draft enhanced Kosovo's status. However, Serbia did not accept the draft in November, but issued a counter-proposal supported by the FRY, Serbia and Kosovo Serb, Gorani, Egyptian, Romani, Turk and Muslim national communities. While rejecting the Serb proposal the Kosovo Albanians embraced the Hill draft. However, the Hill team issued a third proposal on 2 December 1998 (*document no. 93 e*) granting Serbia express powers over Kosovo. Both sides rejected this new draft ending the negotiation period. The Hill team produced the final draft two days before the Contact Group's decision to convene talks in Rambouillet (*document no. 93 f*).

3.3 International Monitoring of the Developments in Kosovo

As a result of the Milosevic-Holbrooke agreement, on 16 October 1998, the OSCE Chairman-in-Office signed an agreement with the FRY on an OSCE Kosovo Verification Mission (KVM) (*document no. 100*). The mission's aim was "to verify compliance by all parties in Kosovo with UN Security Council Resolution 1199, and report instances of progress and/or non-compliance to the OSCE Permanent Council, the UN Security Council and other organisations" (Part. II, Article 1). Therefore, the agreement enabled the mission to "travel throughout Kosovo to verify the maintenance the ceasefire by all elements. It will investigate reports of ceasefire violations. Mission personnel will have full freedom of movement and access throughout Kosovo at all times." (Part III, Article 1) The mission was composed of unarmed observers from OSCE member states and could "be augmented with technical experts provided by OSCE" (Part IV, Article 2). Its headquarters was to be Pristina, and outside Pristina, the mission was entitled to set up coordination centres in the capital of each municipality as well as sub-stations in other towns and villages (Part IV, Article 3 and Part V, Article 1 and 2). On 17 October, the OSCE Chairman-in-Office appointed US diplomat William Walker as head of the KVM. The mere presence of KVM is said to have improved the human rights situation in Kosovo. After its withdrawal from Kosovo on 20 March 1999 its human rights division continued to monitor the human rights situation in Kosovo by collecting information through interviewing refugees. The UN Security Council endorsed the KVM through its Resolution 1203 (1998) of 24 October 1998 (*document no. 158*).

By the end of the year it became evident that the reduction in the fighting had only been temporary. The KLA had used the time to rearm and retrain, while substantial Serbian forces were being assembled outside the province. Atrocities against unarmed civilians had not ceased. In this respect the Racak incident was of great importance to the international community (*documents no. 104 - 115*). When Ambassador Walker, the head of the OSCE-KVM, publicly accused the Serbian authorities of responsibility for the incident they ordered him to leave the country. He had rejected their claim that the KLA had rearranged bodies of dead fighters to look like civilian victims. Ambassador Walker refused to leave while NATO threatened military action against the FRY, unless the cease-fire was restored. The Contact Group then announced a conference on the future of Kosovo, to be held in Rambouillet on 6 February 1999 (*document no. 130*).

3.4 The Rambouillet Talks

In preparation of the meeting, the Contact Group developed certain non-negotiable principles structuring any final agreement (*document no. 133*): Key points were that the interim agreement was to be concluded for a period of three years, during which a final settlement would be negotiated; that the territorial integrity of the FRY was to be respected; that the rights of all ethnic communities were to be respected; and that the interim agreement was to be implemented through international participation. While the FRY/Serb delegation first accepted these principles as a basis for a settlement, the KLA, now dominating the Kosovar delegation, was unwilling to agree to the draft as there was no commitment to an option of independence. The FRY/Serb delegation, however, rejected provisions on the implementation, above all the insistence that the 28,000 strong implementation force KFOR would be a NATO force.[1] Likewise, the scope of operations and authority of NATO created an obstacle. According to para. 8 Appendix B of the Agreement on the Status of Multi-National Military Implementation Force "NATO shall enjoy, together with their vehicles, vessels, aircraft, and equipment, free and unrestricted passage and unimpeded access throughout the FRY including associated airspace and territorial waters. This shall include, but not be limited to, the right of bivouac, manoeuvre, billet, and utilization of any areas or facilities as required for support, training, and operations." According to para. 3 of Appendix B, NATO personnel had the right to enter and exit the FRY on production of an identity document.

On 23 February, due to both parties refusal to agree to the interim agreement, the negotiations were adjourned until 15 March in Paris. After difficult negotiations the Kosovar Albanians signed the agreement on 18 March during the Paris Conference. The FRY/Serb delegation, however, rejected it. The co-chairmen of the conference terminated the negotiations on 19 March, on the same day OSCE ordered its observers to withdraw, on 22 March the Serbs launched an offensive in Kosovo, and on 24 March NATO began the bombing campaign against targets in the FRY.

---

[1] Michael MccGwire, 'Why did we bomb Belgrade' (1999) 76 *International Affairs* 1-23 at 7.

3.1. EARLY ATTEMPTS TO SETTLE THE CRISIS

50. The Conference on Yugoslavia 1991/1992

50 a) Peace Conference on Yugoslavia, Carrington Draft Paper, "Arrangements for a General Settlement", UN Doc. S/23169, Annex VI, 18 October 1991

[Parts not referring to the situation in Kosovo have been omitted.]
[...]

C. Special Status

2.5 In addition, areas in which persons belonging to a national or ethnic group form a majority, will enjoy a special status (autonomy).

Such status will provide for:

(a) The right to have and show the national emblems of that group;

(b) The right to a second nationality for members of that group in addition to the nationality of the republic;

(c) An educational system which respects the values and needs of that group;

(d) (i) A legislative body,

(ii) An administrative structure, including a regional police force,

(iii) And a judiciary

responsible for matters concerning the area which reflects the composition of the population of the area;

(e) Provisions for appropriate international monitoring.

The status set out above will apply, in particular, to the Serbs living in areas in Croatia where they form a majority.

D. General Provisions

2.6 It is recognized that persons belonging to a national or ethnic group, in exercising their rights, must respect the rights of the majority and of persons belonging to other groups.

2.7 Without prejudice to the implementation of the arrangements set forth in paragraph 2.5, the republics will apply fully and in good faith established provisions for the benefit of ethnic and national groups, and for autonomous provinces which were given a special constitutional status. [...]

50 b) Peace Conference on Yugoslavia, Carrington Draft Paper, "Treaty Provisions for the Convention", UN Doc. S/23169, Annex VII, 18 October 1991

[Parts not referring to the situation in Kosovo have been omitted.]
[...]

C. Special Status

5. In addition, areas in which persons belonging to a national or ethnic group form a majority, shall enjoy a special status of autonomy.

Such a status will provide for:

(a) The right to have and show the national emblems of that group;

(b) The right to a second nationality for members of that group in addition to the nationality of the republic;

(c) An educational system which respects the values and needs of that group;

(d) (i) A legislative body,

(ii) An administrative structure, including a regional police force,

(iii) And a judiciary

responsible for matters concerning the area, which reflects the composition of the population of the area;

(e) Provisions for appropriate international monitoring.

These areas are listed in annex ...

5A Such areas, unless they are defined in part by an international frontier with a State not party to this Convention, shall be permanently demilitarized and no military forces, exercises or activities on land or in the air shall be permitted in those areas.

5B (a) The republics shall provide for international monitoring of the implementation of the special status of autonomy. To this end, they shall conclude agreements which would provide for a permanent international body to monitor implementation of this paragraph.

(b) The monitoring missions thus established shall:

- Report to the republics in question as well as to the other parties to the agreement, and

- As appropriate formulate recommendations on the implementation of the special status.

(c) The republics shall give effect to such recommendations through legislation or otherwise. In case of dispute, the Court of Human Rights shall be requested to give its decision.

6. Without prejudice to the implementation of the arrangements set forth in this paragraph, the republics shall apply fully and in good faith the provisions existing prior to 1990 for autonomous provinces. [...]

50 c) Peace Conference on Yugoslavia, Letter from Dr. Rugova to Lord Carrington, 22 December 1991

Your Excellency,

In accordance with the Declaration on Yugoslavia adopted December 16, 1991 in an Extraordinary EPC Ministerial Meeting I, Dr. Ibrahim Rugova, President of the Coordinative Body of Albanian Political Parties in Kosova urge you to grant your full and immediate consideration of the request of Prime Minister Bujar Bukoshi and Chairman of the Assembly of the Republic of Kosova Ilaz Rmajli that the Republic of Kosova be recognised as a sovereign and independent state. I support their request absolutely and unconditionally.

Thank you for your consideration and support.

Sincerely,

Dr. Ibrahim Rugova, President of the Coordinative Body of Albanian Political Parties of Kosova

P.S. The Coordinative Body of Albanian Political Parties of Kosova represents over 1 million Albanians and other various ethnic nationals that are members of eleven unique political parties in the republic.

50 d) London International Conference on the Former Yugoslavia, Co-Chairman's Paper on Serbia and Montenegro, 27 August 1992

We welcome the fact that all participants in the Conference have subscribed to the Statement on Bosnia and Herzegovina. All participants must fulfil the obligations to which they have agreed. In particular, Serbia and Montenegro face a clear choice. They have undertaken to:

- cease intervention across their border with Bosnia and Croatia;

- to the best of their ability restrain the Bosnian Serbs from taking territory by force and expelling the local population;

- restore in full the civil and constitutional rights of the inhabitants of the Kosovo and Vojvodina and also to ensure the civil rights of the inhabitants of the Sandjak;

- use their influence with the Bosnian Serbs to obtain the closure of their detention camps, to comply with their obligations under international humanitarian law and in particular the Geneva Conventions, and to permit the return of refugees to their homes. The Bosnian Croats and Muslims have given similar undertakings;

- fully observe the relevant resolutions of the UN Security Council;

- declare that they fully respect the integrity of present frontiers;
- guarantee the right of ethnic and national communities and minorities within the borders of Serbia and Montenegro in accordance with the UN Charter, the CSCE and the draft convention of the EC Conference on Yugoslavia;
- work for the normalization of the situation in Croatia, for implementation of the Vance plan and for acceptance by the Serbs in the Kajina of special status as forseen in the draft convention of the EC Conference on Yugoslavia;
- respect all relevant international treaties and agreements.

If, as suggested by Mr. Panic's letter to the President of the Security Council of the UN, Serbia and Montenegro do intend to fulfil these obligations in deed as well as word they will resume a respected position in the international community. They will be enabled to trade, to receive assistance and to enjoy the full cooperation of all members of the international community. If they do not comply the Security Council will be invited to apply stringent sanctions leading to their total international isolation.

50 e) UN, Report of the Secretary-General on the International Conference on the Former Yugoslavia, UN Doc. S/24795, 11 November 1992

[Parts not referring to the situation in Kosovo have been omitted.]
[...]

90. Intensive work was done in the Special Group on Kosovo. The basic approach agreed to by both sides is to try a pragmatic breakthrough in one important sector - the ethnic Albanians chose education - in order to improve the political atmosphere for talks on more fundamental issues where positions are at present irreconcilable. After difficult and tedious preparations, in which the release of the Chairman of the Albanian Teachers Association from prison could be achieved, the first Conference-sponsored talks between the Federal and the Serbian Governments from Belgrade on one side and ethnic Albanian representatives from Kosovo on the other took place. On 14 October, all parties agreed to the following statement:

"1. Representatives of the Government of the FRY and Serbia led by the Federal Minister of Education, Mr. Ivic, and representatives of the Albanians met in Pristina on 13 and 14 October with the participation of the Geneva Conference Special Group on Kosovo, under the Chairmanship of Ambassador Ahrens. A representative of the CSCE mission was also present.

"2. After detailed discussion of the problems of education in the Albanian language, the participants agreed that the present situation must be changed. They further agreed on the urgent desirability of the return to normal working conditions for schools and other educational institutions.

"3. It was agreed that, to achieve this, it would be necessary to adopt a pragmatic approach requiring urgent resolution, without prejudice to the positions of the parties on broader political issues.

"4. The Albanian representatives agreed to provide a list of schools and other educational institutions to be covered by the measures mentioned in (2); as well as a list of teaching plans and programmes.

"5. The Group agreed to meet again in Belgrade on 22 October. At that meeting discussions will be held on all the issues mentioned above and on the equal working status of teaching and educational personnel with the aim of reaching the necessary decisions for immediate action."

91. These talks were continued accordingly on 22 October in Belgrade, after meetings with both President Cosic and Mr. Rugova. The participants reaffirmed their commitment to the necessity of changing the existing situation in the field of education, and the urgent need for a return to normal conditions in schools and other educational institutions in Kosovo, as set out in their statement of 14 October. They agreed that this commitment refers to all four levels of education: pre-school, elementary school, secondary school and higher education. On Albanian insistence, there was agreement that all problems related to education in Albania at all levels are related and must be treated as a whole. The Serbian and Federal representative made plain the material and financial constraints affecting their areas of responsibility. Within those constraints, there will be no discrimination as between the support which they will provide for instruction in both the Albanian and the Serbian languages. However, no agreement could be reached so far on conditions under which school buildings should be opened, teachers should be reinstated and entrance examinations should be handled. The Working Group has done its best to arrange proper coordination with the CSCE efforts in former Yugoslavia. A representative of the CSCE participated in both of the Kosovo talks, in Pristina on 13 October and in Belgrade on 22 October. On 21 October there was also a conversation with the leader of the CSCE mission in Belgrade. The activities of the CSCE observers on the ground complement the negotiating endeavours of the International Conference. [...]

Kosova, Vojvodina, Sandzak

The next potential flashpoint concerns the minorities in Serbia - by far and away the most important of which is Kosova, where nearly 2 million Albanians live and 200,000 Serbs, or thereabouts. The Albanians living in Kosova have had an election of their own and declared their independence from Serbia. But this, as in the Krajina, is not a solution, since existing borders must be maintained, and it is certainly not one which the Serbs would ever accept, since Kosova is perceived as the birthplace of Serbian nationhood.

The Kosovans have recently shown willingness to negotiate without pre-judging the outcome but have, given the general antipathy between Kosovan and Serb, asked the conference to mediate. Regrettably, the Serbs have so far refused to accept EC Conference participation. I believe it is essential for the Peace Conference to be involved in seeking a settlement between the Kosovans and the Serbian Government. The dangers there are infinitely great and it is overwhelmingly in the interest of both sides to come to the negotiating table and hammer out a solution on the basis of real autonomy.

50 f) UN, Report of the UN Secretary-General on the International Conference of the Former Yugoslavia, Recent Activities of the Working Groups, UN Doc. S/25490, 30 March 1993

[Parts not pertinent to the situation in Kosovo have been omitted.]
[...]

III. Working Group on Ethnic and National Communities and Minorities

[...]

SPECIAL GROUP ON KOSOVO

17. The Special Group on Kosovo met at Geneva from 26 to 28 January and in Belgrade on 17 and 18 February. As in past meetings, the talks were limited to the subject of education, on which the Group still endeavours to reach pragmatic solutions in the hope of improving the overall climate between the parties, which continues to be far from positive.

18. The Kosovar Albanians presented their teaching plans. These were rejected by the Government on the ground that they contained an underlying assumption of independence for Kosovo. The Government made new proposals on the reinstatement of teachers and on the recognition of years spent in the parallel school system run by the Albanians. They were rejected by the Kosovar Albanian side, which insists on the "unconditional" reopening of school premises before they would be ready to address other issues.

19. In the talks on Kosovo, fundamental issues are constantly hindering the pragmatic approach for solutions in the field of education. The Group will pursue its efforts, but at the same time it is necessary to address fundamental issues in the light of the principles agreed upon at the London Conference.

20. When in Belgrade on 10 March, the Chair emphasized to Mr. Jovanovic, the Federal Minister for Foreign Affairs, the necessity of this double-track approach. While agreeing in principle, the Foreign Minister stressed the desirability for sucess on the educational issue as a first step before other issues were approached. On 17 March, Ambassador Ahrens had a discussion with Mr. Bukoshi, who spoke on behalf of Albanians from Kosovo. There was agreement that everything should be tried to achieve progress in the ongoing talks. Mr. Bukoshi informed Ambassador Ahrens that authorities in Kosovo had taken away the passport of Professor Statovci, a member of the Kosovar Albanian negotiating team since the beginning, on whose participation the Kosovar Albanians had to insist. [...]

51. EU, European Council in Lisbon 26-27 June 1992: Conclusions of the Presidency, DOC/92/3, 27 June 1992

[Parts not pertinent to the situation in Kosovo have been omitted.]
[...]

Annex II - European Council Declaration on Former Yugoslavia

[...]

With regard to Kosovo, the European Council expects the Serbian leadership to refrain from further repression and to engage in serious dialogue with representatives of this territory.

The European Council reminds the inhabitants of Kosovo that their legitimate quest for autonomy should be dealt with in the framework of the Conference on Yugoslavia.

It stresses the need to immediately dispatch observers to Kosovo as well as to neighbouring countries in order to prevent the use of violence and with a view to contributing to the restoration of confidence.

The Community and its member States call upon the CSCE to take the necessary steps to that effect and stand ready, as far as they are concerned, to take part in such a mission. [...]

The European Community and its Member States will not recognise the new federal entity comprising Serbia and Montenegro as the successor State of the former Yugoslavia until the moment that decision has been taken by the qualified international institutions.

They have decided to demand the suspension of the delegation of Yugoslavia in the proceedings at the CSCE and other international fora and organisations.

The European Council states its determination to help the peoples of the former Yugoslavia in their quest for a peaceful future in Europe and reiterates that the EC Conference on Yugoslavia chaired by Lord Carrington is the only forum capable of ensuring a durable and equitable solution to the outstanding problems of the former Yugoslavia, including constitutional arrangements for Bosnia and Hercegovina.

The European Council urges all parties involved in the peace process to participate fully and without further delay in the negotiations sponsored by the Conference.

52. UN Security Council Resolution 855 (1993) of 9 August 1993

The Security Council,

Taking note of the letters of 2 July 1993 (S/26121) and 23 July 1993 (S/26148) from the Chairman-in-Office of the Council of Ministers of the Conference on Security and Cooperation in Europe (CSCE),

Further taking note of the letters of 28 July 1993 (S/26210) and 3 August 1993 (S/26234) circulated by the authorities of the Federal Republic of Yugoslavia (Serbia and Montenegro),

Deeply concerned at the refusal of the authorities in the Federal Republic of Yugoslavia (Serbia and Montenegro) to allow the CSCE missions of long duration to continue their activities,

Bearing in mind that the CSCE missions of long duration are an example of preventive diplomacy undertaken within the framework of the CSCE, and have greatly contributed to promoting stability and counteracting the risk of violence in Kosovo, Sandjak and Vojvodina, the Federal Republic of Yugoslavia (Serbia and Montenegro),

Reaffirming its relevant resolutions aimed at putting an end to conflict in the former Yugoslavia,

Determined to avoid any extension of the conflict in the former Yugoslavia and, in this context, *attaching* great importance to the work of the CSCE missions and to the continued ability of the international community to monitor the situation in Kosovo, Sandjak and Vojvodina, the Federal Republic of Yugoslavia (Serbia and Montenegro),

Stressing its commitment to the territorial integrity and political independence of all States in the region,

1. *Endorses* the efforts of the CSCE as described in the letters noted above from the Chairman-in-Office of the Council of Ministers of the Conference on Security and Cooperation in Europe (CSCE);

2. *Calls upon* the authorities in the Federal Republic of Yugoslavia (Serbia and Montenegro) to reconsider their refusal to allow the continuation of the activities of the CSCE missions in Kosovo, Sandjak and Vojvodina, the Federal Republic of Yugoslavia (Serbia and Montenegro), to cooperate with the CSCE by taking the practical steps needed for the resumption of the activities of these missions and to agree to an increase in the number of monitors as decided by the CSCE;

3. *Further calls upon* the authorities in the Federal Republic of Yugoslavia (Serbia and Montenegro) to assure the monitors' safety and security, and to allow them free and unimpeded access necessary to accomplish their mission in full;

4. *Decides* to remain seized of the matter.

Adopted by the Security Council at its 3262nd meeting, on 9 August 1993 with 14 votes to none and China abstaining.

53. EU, 1950th Council Meeting, General Affairs, PRES/96/253, Luxembourg, 1 October 1996

[Parts not referring to Kosovo have been omitted.]
[...]

Ex-Yugoslavia: Council Conclusions

[...]

The Council discussed the question of Kosovo in the Federal Republic of Yugoslavia, noting that this was an important and sensitive issue which had international dimensions and implications for wider regional efforts to promote lasting stability, and which remains a cause of grave concern for the EU. Ministers welcomed the progress on education issues which has been made in talks between the Belgrade authorities and the Albanian community in Kosovo, as a first step in the direction of a comprehensive dialogue on the status of the region, urging early implementation of the measures agreed upon and recalling the EU position that a large degree of autonomy must be granted to the region within the Federal Republic of Yugoslavia. The Ministers underlined the importance of an increased international presence in Kosovo which has the potential to reduce conflicts. Ministers believe that progress on this issue would represent another positive step in the context of finding an acceptable solution to the question of the status of Kosovo within the FRY which is a crucial factor in determining the Union's attitude towards the FRY. The Council reiterated the Union's strong and unequivocal support for the work of the International Criminal Tribunal for former Yugoslavia and stressed that full cooperation by all parties with the Tribunal in the effort to bring war criminals to justice was a fundamental obligation which must be honoured if genuine stability and lasting peace is to be consolidated. Achieving progress in this area was more important than ever following the elections in Bosnia and Herzegovina. The Council stressed that the governments of Croatia and the Federal Republic of Yugoslavia, as well as the central government and entity administrations in Bosnia and Herzegovina, must abide by the commitments which they have made to hand over indicted suspects. They also agreed that international organisations and agencies active on the ground should examine how they can make a more effective contribution to the efforts of ICTY in this regard.

Arms control is another crucially important factor in the effort to secure lasting peace and stability. In this regard, the Council stressed the importance which the EU attaches to full implementation of the Agreement on sub-regional arms control which was signed in Florence on 14 June. Ministers also emphasised the urgency of opening discussions on the establishment of a regional balance, as called for under article V of Annex 1B of the General Framework Agreement.

[...]

3.2 POLITICAL ACTION AND SANCTIONS SINCE 1997

54. Contact Group Foreign Ministers, Statement on Kosovo, New York, 24 September 1997

We, the Foreign Ministers of the Contact Group countries (France, Germany, Italy, Russian Federation, United Kingdom, and the United States) meeting at the United Nations in New York on September 24 together with representatives of Luxembourg EU Presidency, EU Commission and the Office of the High Representative, discussed the situation in Kosovo, the Federal Republic of Yugoslavia.

We voiced our deep concern over tensions in Kosovo. We call on the authorities in Belgrade and the leadership of the Kosovar Albanian community to join in a peaceful dialogue. We urge the two sides to create the conditions necessary for refugees from Kosovo to return home. As a first step, we call on all concerned to implement the Education Agreement without delay and to follow this up with additional confidence-building measures.

We warn against any resort to violence to press political demands and urge all sides to exercise maximum restraint.

Regarding the dispute over Kosovo's status, the position of the Contact Group countries is clear: we do not support independence and we do not support maintenance of the status quo. We support an enhanced status for Kosovo within the FRY. Such a status should fully protect the rights of the Albanian population in accordance with OSCE standards and the UN Charter. As a first step to reduce tensions, it is essential that dialogue begins.

55. Contact Group Meeting, Statement on Kosovo, Moscow, 25 February 1998

At its Moscow meeting on February 25, 1998, the Contact Group confirmed its position on Kosovo, FRY, expressed in the New York Declaration of Foreign Ministers of September 24, 1997, as well as in the Washington Contact Group Declaration of January 8, 1998. It noted that since that time, despite repeated calls for dialogue to resolve the problems in Kosovo, there had been little progress on this vitally important issue. It also shared the valid expressions of concern by those in the region about the implication of the situation in Kosovo for regional security.

The Contact Group reaffirmed its commitment to uphold human rights values, and their condemnation of both violent repression of non-violent expressions of political views, including peaceful demonstrations, as well as terrorist actions, including those of the so-called Kosovo Liberation Army.

The Contact Group agreed that both sides should be reasonable and flexible and focus on immediate steps to reduce tensions - bearing in mind the overriding need to avoid conflict and violence. It expressed continuing support for full and rapid implementation of the Education Agreement, recognizing its importance as a step for the promotion of stability in the region. It called on the authorities in Belgrade and leadership of the Kosovar Albanian community to enter without preconditions into a full and constructive dialogue to deal with the underlying social, economic and status problems.

The Contact Group reiterated that it supported neither independence nor the maintenance of the status quo. The principles of the solution of the Kosovo problem should be based on the territorial integrity of the Federal Republic of Yugoslavia, taking into account the rights of the Kosovo Albanians and all those who live in Kosovo in accordance with OSCE standards, Helsinki principles and the UN Charter. The Contact Group supports an enhanced status for Kosovo within the FRY and recognizes that this must include meaningful self-administration.

The Contact Group reiterated their view that the FRY needs to address this question urgently, and that making progress to resolve the serious political and human rights issues in Kosovo is critical for Belgrade to improve its international position and relations with the international community. The Contact Group expressed its readiness to facilitate dialogue.

The Contact Group reaffirmed its intention to continue to pay close attention to the problem of Kosovo.

56. EU, Declaration by the Presidency on behalf of the European Union Concerning the Upsurge of Violence in Kosovo, 98/18/CFSP, Brussels, 3 March 1998

The EU is deeply concerned by the violent incidents in Kosovo over the past few days. The EU unreservedly condemns the violent repression of non-violent expressions of political views, including peaceful demonstrations as well as the use of violence and terrorism to achieve political goals. It regrets that police action led directly to civilian casualties. The EU urges all sides to exercise restraint and refrain from further violence, and calls on the Serbian law enforcement agencies to respect fully human rights and the rule of law in the pursuit of their duties. The EU reiterates its call as a matter of urgency for the authorities in Belgrade and leaders of the Kosovar Albanian community to resolve the situation peacefully through a full and constructive dialogue.

57. Contact Group Meeting, Statement on Kosovo, London, 9 March 1998

1. We the Foreign Ministers of Contact Group countries, together with representatives of the European Commission and the Office of the High Representative, met in London on 9 March to discuss the increasingly tense situation in Kosovo, Federal Republic of Yugoslavia (FRY), and the unacceptable use of force over recent days. The Balkans region has seen too much bloodshed in recent years for the international community to stand aside.

2. We recalled that when we met in New York on 24 September 1997, we voiced deep concern over developments in Kosovo and called on the authorities in Belgrade and the leadership of the Kosovar Albanian community to join in a peaceful dialogue. We are dismayed that in the period since September, rather than taking steps to reduce tensions or to enter without preconditions into dialogue toward a political solution, the Belgrade authorities have applied repressive measures in Kosovo. We note with particular concern the recent violence in

Kosovo resulting in at least 80 fatalities and condemn the use of excessive force by Serbian police against civilians, and against peaceful demonstrators in Pristina on 2 March.

3. Our condemnation of the actions of the Serbian police should not in any way be mistaken for an endorsement of terrorism. Our position on this is clear. We wholly condemn terrorist actions by the Kosovo Liberation Army or any other group or individual. Those in the Kosovar Albanian community who speak for the different political constituencies should make it clear that they, too, abhor terrorism. We insist likewise that those outside the FRY who are supplying finance, arms or training for terrorist activity in Kosovo should immediately cease doing so.

4. We condemn the large-scale police actions of the last 10 days that further inflamed an already volatile situation. The violent repression of non-violent expression of political views is completely indefensible. We call upon the authorities in Belgrade to invite independent forensic experts to investigate the very serious allegations of extrajudicial killings. If these accusations are borne out, we expect the FRY authorities to prosecute and punish those responsible.

5. Our commitment to human rights values means that we cannot ignore such disproportionate methods of control. Government authorities have a special responsibility to protect the human and civil rights of all citizens and to ensure that public security forces act judiciously and with restraint.

6. In the light of the deplorable violence in Kosovo, we feel compelled to take steps to demonstrate to the authorities in Belgrade that they cannot defy international standards without facing severe consequences. The Contact Group has decided to take a broad range of action to address the current situation on an urgent basis. The Contact Group welcomes the continuation of consultations in the United Nations Security Council, in view of the implications of the situation in Kosovo for regional security. Against that background, the Contact Group:

- requests a mission to Kosovo by the United Nations High Commissioner for Human Rights,

- urges the office of the Prosecutor of the ICTY to begin gathering information related to the violence in Kosovo that may fall within its jurisdiction. The FRY authorities have an obligation to cooperate with the ICTY. Contact Group countries will make available to the ICTY substantiated relevant information in their possession,

- supports the proposal for a new mission by Felipe Gonzalez as the Personal Representative of the OSCE Chairman-in-Office for the FRY that would include a new and specific mandate for addressing the problems in Kosovo,

- supports the return of the OSCE long-term missions to Kosovo, the Sandzak and Vojvodina,

- recommends that the Special Session of the OSCE Permanent Council meeting on 11 March arrange for Embassies in Belgrade, of OSCE participating states to intensify their visits to Kosovo so as to provide for a continuous presence,

- will continue vigorously to support Sant'Egidio's efforts to secure implementation of the Education Agreement, and identify resources to assist a fair and acceptable arrangement,

- proposes the establishment of an international consortium including non-Governmental Organisations that would promote civil-society building in Kosovo and the distribution of humanitarian assistance,

- recognising that neighbouring countries of the FRY have legitimate security concerns stemming from violence and unrest in Kosovo, will arrange an urgent meeting of the Contact Group with representatives of governments in the region to discuss the grave consequences of an inter-ethnic conflict and its possible spillover to other parts of the region. We expect them to do all in their power to prevent support for terrorism. The meeting will in particular address:

- the possible despatch of a short-term OSCE monitoring group to enhance the ability of the Albania mission's Shkodra field office to monitor the FRY (Kosovo) border,

- the possible strengthening of the present OSCE mission in Skopje

- recommends that consideration be given to adapting the current UNPREDEP mandate, and would support the maintenance of an international military presence on the ground in the former Yugoslav Republic of Macedonia when the current mandate of UNPREDEP expires,

- will monitor the situation in Kosovo by frequent joint visits to Pristina by Contact Group and other representatives.

7. At the same time, it is not enough for the killing to stop; too much damage has already been done to human life and to the FRY's credibility. Because of the gravity of the situation, we endorse the following measures to be pursued immediately:

a) UN Security Council consideration of a comprehensive arms embargo against the FRY, including Kosovo;

b) Refusal to supply equipment to the FRY which might be used for internal repression, or for terrorism;

c) Denial of visas for senior FRY and Serbian representatives responsible for repressive action by FRY security forces in Kosovo;

d) A moratorium on government financed export credit support for trade and investment, including government financing for privatisations, in Serbia.

The Contact Group notes that the Russian Federation cannot support measures c) and d) above for immediate imposition. But if there is no progress towards the steps called for by the Contact Group, the Russian Federation will then be willing to discuss all the above measures.

We call upon President Milosevic to take rapid and effective steps to stop the violence and engage in a commitment to find a political solution to the issue of Kosovo through dialogue. Specifically, he should within 10 days:

- Withdraw the special police units and cease action by the security forces affecting the civilian population.

- Allow access to Kosovo for the ICRC and other humanitarian organisations as well as by representatives of the Contact Group and other Embassies.

- Commit himself publicly to begin a process of dialogue, along the lines in paragraph 10, with the leadership of the Kosovar Albanian community.

- Cooperate in a constructive manner with the Contact Group in the implementation of the actions specified in paragraph 6 above which require action by the FRY government.

If President Milosevic takes these steps, we will immediately reconsider the measures we have now adopted. If he fails to take these steps, and repression continues in Kosovo, the Contact Group will move to further international measures, and specifically to pursue a freeze on the funds held abroad by the FRY and Serbian governments.

The Contact Group has decided to meet again on 25 March to assess the response of the government of the FRY.

8. Belgrade's own actions have seriously set back the process of normalisation of the FRY's relations with the international community. Unless the FRY takes steps to resolve the serious political and human rights issues in Kosovo, there is no prospect of any improvement in its international standing. On the other hand, concrete progress to resolve the serious political and human rights issues in Kosovo will improve the international position of the FRY and prospects for normalisation of its international relationships and full rehabilitation in international institutions.

9. No one should misunderstand our position on the core issue involved. We support neither independence nor the maintenance of the status quo. As we have set out clearly, the principles for a solution of the Kosovo problem should be based on the territorial integrity of the Federal Republic of Yugoslavia, and be in accordance with OSCE standards, Helsinki principles, and the UN Charter. Such a solution also must take into account the rights of the Kosovo Albanians and all those who live in Kosovo. We support an enhanced status for Kosovo

within the FRY which a substantially greater degree of autonomy would bring and recognise that this must include meaningful self-determination.

10. The way to defeat terrorism in Kosovo is for Belgrade to offer the Kosovar Albanian community a genuine political process. The authorities in Belgrade and the leadership of the Kosovar Albanian community must assume their responsibility to enter without preconditions into a meaningful dialogue on political status issues. The Contact Group stands ready to facilitate such a dialogue.

58. Countries of South Eastern Europe, Joint Declaration of the Ministers of Foreign Affairs of Countries of South-Eastern Europe Concerning the Situation in Kosovo, Sofia, 10 March 1998[1]

The Ministers of Foreign Affairs of countries of South-Eastern Europe, Mr. Andrei Plesu, Mr. Blagoi Handziski, Mr. Ismail Cem, Mrs. Nadezhda Mihaylova and Mr. Theodoros Pangalos, express their serious concern with the deteriorating situation in Kosovo and with the grave consequences of an inter-ethnic conflict and its possible spillover in the region.

The Ministers declare the commitment of their States to take all appropriate steps in order to prevent such a development in the region of south-eastern Europe.

The Ministers reiterate that a first step to reduce tensions in Kosovo is the initiation of a genuine dialogue between the Serb authorities and the ethnic Albanians, and call on both parties to take prompt measures to that end. Both parties should condemn and refrain from use of violence as a means to resolve their conflict.

They deeply regret the suppression by the Serbian police of peaceful demonstrations in Kosovo and the subsequent unrestrained use of force that has resulted in fatalities. At the same time, they urge all organizations of the Kosovo Albanian community to make clear their opposition to violence and terrorism as tools to seek change. They condemn terrorist actions to achieve political goals, as well as violence as a means to repress political views.

The Ministers call for the full respect of the human rights and fundamental freedoms of the ethnic Albanian population. They declare that a lasting solution to the Kosovo problem can be based only on the full protection of the rights of Albanians, Serbs and all others living in Kosovo in accordance with the Charter of the United Nations, the Helsinki principles and the Organization for Security and Cooperation in Europe (OSCE) standards.

The Ministers call for the immediate and full implementation of the agreement on education concluded in 1996 between President Milosevic and Mr. Rugova, leader of the Albanians in Kosovo.

The Ministers underline that the solution to the Kosovo problem should be sought with full respect to the existing borders. They call on all organizations of the ethnic Albanians to deny any secessionist policies and to respect fully the territorial integrity of the Federal Republic of Yugoslavia.

The Ministers call on Belgrade to face the problems with utmost responsibility and to search for mutually acceptable solutions based on granting a large autonomy for Kosovo within the Federal Republic of Yugoslavia.

The Ministers believe that the integration of the Federal Republic of Yugoslavia into the international community would be to the benefit of that country and would strengthen the stability of the region. They also recognize that considerable progress towards the solution of the Kosovo issue will contribute to this end.

The Ministers call on the Federal Republic of Yugoslavia to enable the return of the international monitors in Kosovo as a means of preventive diplomacy.

The Ministers declare the readiness of their States to play an active role in the efforts to find a peaceful and political solution to all issues related to the Kosovo problem. Within this framework, they also welcome the initiatives of the United States of America, the European Union and the Contact Group. The Ministers call on all States in the region and beyond to support this declaration and to join the efforts towards preserving peace, stability and security in south-eastern Europe.

59. FRY, Declaration by Milan Milutinovic, President of the Republic of Serbia on the Political Process Initiated for Kosovo and Metohija, 11 March 1998

Hesitation and delays in commencing direct political dialogue between representatives of the Government of the Republic of Serbia and of the Albanian political parties of Kosovo and Metohija are unjustified and destructive. It thwarts the removal of tensions and blocks political processes for the solution of issues upon which the attainment of equality for all citizens and the affirmation of peace, tolerance and mutual respect in Kosovo and Metohija depends.

I call upon leaders of the political parties of the Albanian national minority of Kosovo and Metohija to begin a political dialogue without delay or preconditions. As President of the Republic of Serbia, I am prepared to be guarantor of these talks on the principle that our territorial integrity will be preserved and that the agenda will include the question of self-government in Kosovo and Metohija within the framework of Serbia.

Political means and peaceful ways are the only acceptable manner for the solution of the problem of Kosovo and Metohija. It is only through dialogue that lasting solutions can be attained for all the problems in hand, wherewith the basis approach to the achievement of principles of equality for all citizens, including equal rights for national minorities will be those of the highest international standards prescribed by the UN, the OSCE and the European Council.

I wish to emphasize the significance of the continued engagement and presence of the International Committee of the Red Cross in the performance of its humanitarian tasks. The relevant authorities will continue to guarantee all conditions for their normal performance.

It is my conviction that the international community, particularly countries of the region, should, in conformity with standard international practice, refrain from everything that can contribute to raising tensions and encouraging separatism, or whatever may constitute interference in our internal affairs.

As a European country, the Federal Republic of Yugoslavia is dedicated to the values and principles of the United Nations Charter, the Helsinki Acts and the Charter of Paris, and is committed to active participation in the current integration processes, and, thus, within the framework of FR Yugoslavia, Serbia is interested and open for cooperation with the OSCE, assuming that the membership rights and obligations of our country, the Federal Republic, are renewed. Cooperation with a mission of the OSCE must therefore be revived on a long-term basis and be the subject of an agreement similar to that for the previous mission whose work in 1992 had shown positive results and had, with considerable objectivity, presented to the international public what the state of affairs was in Kosovo and Metohija.

Education of the young generations happens to be one of the most vital questions. I therefore call upon the Group of 3-plus-3 to immediately commence implementing the Agreement on the Normalization of Education. This will give impetus to the solution of other matters and the successful realization of the rights and interests of all the citizens of Kosovo and Metohija.

May I emphasize my conviction that the future of the citizens of Kosovo and Metohija, as in Serbia and our country as a whole, is not in ethnic, religious or cultural containment and division, but in peace, equality, association and life together.

---

[1] UN Doc. S/1998/234, Annex, 13 March 1998

I believe that all the citizens and responsible political forces of Serbia and our country as a whole, are in favour of the policy of the equality of our citizens, the preservation of our sovereignty and territorial integrity and of open equitable cooperation with other countries and the international community.

The Government of the Republic of Serbia Invites Responsible Albanian National Minority Representatives to Open Dialogue for the Solution of Pertinent Issues

The Government of the Republic of Serbia reviewed the reports of its ministries about the situation in Kosovo and Metohija at a meeting held 10 March 1998, including that of the Ministry of International Affairs (MIA) on the measures taken to confront terrorism, submitted by Col.Gen. Vlastimir Djordjević, Head of the Department of Public Security and Dragiša Ristivojević, Deputy Head of the Department of State Security.

The Government assessed that the action taken recently by the MIA of Serbia in Kosovo and Metohija had been executed solely in counter-action against the escalated terrorism in the preceding months which had caused the injury and death of many innocent people - Serbs, Albanians and people in the service of the Ministry of Internal Affairs.

The Government likewise assessed that the measures taken had been strictly limited and defensive in character, targeted against the imprudent attacks of terrorists and at eradicating terrorist nests, and were executed in line with regulations and proper regard for the safety of other citizens and their property.

The Government of the Republic of Serbia most profoundly condemns the terrorism carried on by Albanian separatists in Kosovo and Metohija and confirms the resolve of all the organs of the Government of Serbia to ensure respect for the law, complete equality and the peace and safety of every citizen regardless of nationality.

Serbia makes a clear difference between terrorists and terrorism, on the one hand, and members of the Albanian national minority, on the other, and invites pertinent representatives of the Albanian national minority to dissociate themselves from terrorism and join the collective international condemnation of that evil.

The MIA had informed the public on all the measures it had taken against the terrorists. The diplomatic corps in Belgrade and foreign journalists had occasion to visit villages of the Drenica area where the anti-terrorist actions were carried out, and thus were personally assured that the actions of the MIA of Serbia had been directed exclusively at arresting and preventing the operation of terrorist bands.

Considering their having witnessed the actual state of affairs on the spot and been assured that the authorities have nothing to hide, the Government feels it would be most useful if the whole truth were to be asserted and that a group of experts of the International Red Cross Committee should, therefore, visit Kosovo and Metohija and, in cooperation with the Yugoslav Red Cross establish whether there had been any ground for the news placed in certain media and, to that end, is extending such an invitation.

Serbia's standing policy is not to divide her citizens along national, religious or any other lines. The Government of Serbia and all the Organs of authority of the Republic are devoting equal attention to all citizens of the Republic of Serbia and shall neither now nor in the future permit injustices to be made against any of them, not even against members of the national minorities whose rights are protected in the Republic of Serbia in conformance with the highest of international standards.

The Government confirms, most resolutely, that all matters relating to Kosovo and Metohija, must be resolved within the framework of Serbia by political means according to international standards pertaining to the protection of the rights of national minorities. There is consensus with regard to this among all the influential political forces and parties of the Republic, as well as the stance of relevant international factors as the best guarantee of its successful solution.

The Government likewise asserts, on this occasion, its openness for the solution of all matters relating to the fulfillment of civil and human rights for all the citizens of Kosovo and Metohija, as well as questions regarding their speedier economic and cultural development as the Constitution of the Republic of Serbia, of European and international standards, OSCE principles, the Charter of Paris and the United Nations Charter require, namely through dialogue and by political means. The Government furthermore points out its acceptance of all the rights and principles laid down by the Framework Convention of the European Council on the Protection of National Minorities.

Through its overall policy and concrete measures, the Government shall secure conditions for stable political, economic and cultural development, the building of relations of tolerance and confidence among all the citizens of Kosovo and Metohija. The Government confirms this resolve in that its representatives of the Group of 3-plus-3 have already submitted their proposal of operative measures for implementation of the Agreement for Normalization of the Education System of Kosovo and Metohija, in the prescribed manner.

"In accordance with the aforesaid, the Government of the Republic of Serbia invites responsible representatives of the Albanian national minority to an open dialogue for the sake of resolving all pertinent issues, considering that this is the only way of promoting political processes aimed at resolving the vital issued of the citizens of this province of ours.

As the statement of the Ministry of Information relates: "The Government of the Republic of Serbia points out, once again, the only prospect of Kosovo and Metohija lies in peace, development, tolerance, equality and life together.

Serbian Government's Selected Representatives for Talks with the Leaders of Albanian Parties and Associations on Kosovo and Metohija

"Pursuant to the conclusion reached at its meeting of 10 March 1998, the Government of the Republic of Serbia has selected its representatives for talks with the leaders of Albanian parties and associations as well as representatives of the public and cultural life of Kosovo and Metohija and persons who are considered to be representatives of the Albanian national minority, towards the promotion of political processes and the solution of specific issues pertaining to the life of the citizens of Kosovo and Metohija.

"Participants at these talks on behalf of the Government of the Republic of Serbia, will be Prof. Dr. Ratko Marković, Vice-President of the Government, and Ratomir Vico, Andrea Milosavljević and Ivan Sedlak, ministers in the Government of Serbia.

"On this occasion, also, the Government expresses its openness for dialogue in order to resolve all matters upon which the fulfillment of the human and civil rights of all the citizens of Kosovo and Metohija depends, as well as questions relating to speedier economic and cultural development, by political means in accordance with the Constitution of the Republic of Serbia, of European and international standards, the principles of the OSCE, the Charter of Paris and the United Nations Charter, as well as in line with the principles laid down in the Framework Convention of the European Council on the Protection of national Minorities.

"The Government of Serbia invites all parliamentary parties of the National Assembly of the Republic of Serbia to appoint one of their parliamentary members to participate in talks to establish the common approach of the National Assembly of the solution of issues pertaining to Kosovo and Metohija.

"Representatives of the Government of the Republic of Serbia will on this day, Thursday, 12 March, at 11:00 hrs. initiate open, public talks with representatives of the Albanian National minority on the premises of the Government in Priština at 2, Vidovdanska Street.

"The Government of the Republic of Serbia issues this statement as a public invitation to tomorrow's talks in Priština," it is said in this announcement.

60. Council of Europe, Parliamentary Assembly, Recommendation 1360 (1998), Crisis in Kosovo, 18 March 1998

[Text adopted by the Standing Committee, acting on behalf of the Assembly, on 18 March 1998.]

1. The Assembly is deeply concerned about the escalation of violence in Kosovo in recent weeks. While rejecting violence as a means to achieve the political goals of the Albanian community in Kosovo, it strongly condemns the excessive and indiscriminate use of force by the Serbian security forces during the recent events in the Drenica region, which caused many civilian casualties.

2. The Assembly stresses that the human rights situation in Kosovo and threats to the stability of the region are a legitimate concern of the international community, and cannot be declared an internal matter of the Federal Republic of Yugoslavia or of Serbia.

3. The Assembly notes the conclusions of its high level mission, headed by its President and composed of the Chairmen of the Political Groups and the Chairman of the Political Affairs Committee, which visited Belgrade and Pristina on 12 and 13 March 1998 to discuss the crisis in Kosovo in the context of relations between the Federal Republic of Yugoslavia and the Council of Europe.

4. The Assembly fully supports the decisions taken at the ministerial meeting of the Contact Group for the former Yugoslavia in London on 9 March 1998.

5. The Assembly reiterates its demand for the instant and full restoration of human rights and fundamental freedoms of the Albanian community in Kosovo. It expects the Yugoslav authorities to implement forthwith the agreement on education concluded in September 1996 between Mr Milosevic, then President of Serbia, and Mr Rugova, leader of the Albanian community in Kosovo.

6. The Assembly calls for the establishment of an international monitoring presence in Kosovo, and for an independent inquiry into the recent events in the Drenica region.

7. The Assembly believes that a long-term solution to the crisis can only be found on the basis of a greater autonomy for Kosovo within the Federal Republic of Yugoslavia, and calls for an immediate start to genuine negotiations on this issue between the Yugoslav authorities and representatives of the Albanian community in Kosovo.

8. The Assembly reiterates its offer to assist in contacts between the Yugoslav authorities and representatives of the Albanian community. The Council of Europe has considerable expertise in the relevant areas, such as human rights, minority rights, local and regional democracy and education, which it could put at the disposal of the parties.

9. The Assembly welcomes the existence of political dialogue in Montenegro between the authorities of this republic and the Albanian, as well as Muslim, communities, which has led to the participation of representatives of these communities in the new Montenegro government.

10. The Assembly calls on the authorities of the Federal Republic of Yugoslavia to :

i. make every effort to de-escalate the situation;

ii. establish dialogue without any preconditions with representatives of the Albanian community to examine ways for a greater autonomy for Kosovo within the Federal Republic of Yugoslavia;

iii. enable the international community to establish a monitoring presence in Kosovo;

iv. agree to an independent inquiry into the recent events;

v. implement the education agreement concluded between Mr Milosevic and Mr Rugova in September 1996;

vi. comply with the recommendations made by Mr Felipe González on behalf of the OSCE in December 1996 and accept his role as a mediator for the opening of a dialogue with the Kosovo Albanians;

11. The Assembly expects the leaders of the Albanian community in Kosovo to condemn and refrain from the use of violence, and agree to a dialogue with the Yugoslav government.

12. The Assembly calls on the international community to re-establish, and, if necessary, reinforce its sanctions with regard to the Federal Republic of Yugoslavia, if its requests concerning the peaceful resolution of the Kosovo crisis are not complied with.

13. The Assembly reaffirms its position that the development of relations between the Council of Europe and the Federal Republic of Yugoslavia will depend on compliance by the latter with the requests of the international community.

14. The Assembly recommends the Committee of Ministers deal with the Kosovo crisis as a matter of priority within the framework of its political dialogue and in close co-ordination with the OSCE and the European Union.

61. EU, Common Position Defined by the Council on the Basis of Article J.2 of the EU Treaty on Restrictive Measures against the FRY, 98/240/CFSP, 19 March 1998[1]

The Council of the European Union,

Having regard to the Treaty on European Union, and in particular Article J.2 thereof,

Whereas recent events in the Federal Republic of Yugoslavia (FRY), and in particular the use of force against the Kosovar Albanian Community in Kosovo, represent an unacceptable violation of human rights and put the security of the region at risk;

Whereas the European Union strongly condemns terrorism and violent acts committed by the Kosovo Liberation Army, or any group or individual;

Whereas the Union strongly condemns the violent repression of the non-violent expression of political views;

Whereas the Union endorsed on 12 March 1998 the statement issued by the Contact Group on 9 March 1998;

Whereas the Union demands that the Government of the FRY take effective steps to stop the violence and engage in a commitment to find a political solution to the issue of Kosovo through a peaceful dialogue with the Kosovar Albanian Community, in particular by:

- withdrawing the special police units and ceasing action by the security forces affecting the civilian population,

- allowing access to Kosovo for the International Committee of the Red Cross and other humanitarian organisations as well as by representatives of the Union and other Embassies,

- committing itself publicly to begin a process of dialogue with the leadership of the Kosovar Albanian Community,

- cooperating in a constructive manner in order to implement the action set out in paragraph 6 of the Contact Group statement;

Whereas the restrictive measures in Articles 1 to 4, including the reduction of economic and/or financial relations, are deemed necessary; whereas such measures will be reconsidered immediately if the Government of the FRY takes the steps referred to in the previous recital;

Whereas the Union will move to further international measures, and specifically to pursue a freezing of the funds held abroad by the FRY and the Serbian Governments, should the above steps not be implemented and repression continue in Kosovo,

has defined this common position:

Article 1

The European Union confirms the embargo on arms exports to the former Yugoslavia established by Common Position 96/184/CFSP[2].

---

[1] OJ L 95, 27/03/1998 p. 0001 - 0003, 498X0240.
[2] OJ L 58, 07/03/1996, p. 1.

Article 2

No equipment which might be used for internal repression or for terrorism will be supplied to the Federal Republic of Yugoslavia.

Article 3

A moratorium will be implemented on government-financed export credit support for trade and investment, including government financing for privatisations, in Serbia.

Article 4

1. No visas shall be issued for senior FRY and Serbian representatives responsible for repressive action by FRY security forces in Kosovo.

2. The persons listed in the Annex, who have been identified as having clear security responsibilities, shall be reported for the purpose of non-admission in the territories of the Member States. Other senior FRY and Serbian representatives responsible for repressive action in Kosovo would be added in the case of a failure by the FRY authorities to respond to the demands of the International Community. In exceptional cases, exemptions may be made if this would further vital Union objectives. The Council shall update the list in the light of developments in Kosovo.

Article 5

This Common Position shall take effect on the date of its adoption.

Article 6

This Common Position shall be published in the Official Journal.

Done at Brussels, 19 March 1998. For the Council: The President J. Straw

Annex

Vlajko Stojlkovic (Serbian Minister for the Interior)

Vlastimir Djordjevic (Head of Public Security Department)

Dragisa Ristivojevic (Deputy Head of Public Security Department)

Obrad Stevanovic (Assistant Minister for the Interior)

Jovica Stanisic (Assistant Minister for the Interior: Head of Serbian State Security)

Radomir Markovic (Assistant Minister for the Interior: Deputy Head of State Security)

Frenki Simatovic (Chief of Special Forces of State Security)

David Gajic (Head of Security in Kosovo)

Lubinko Cvetic (Deputy Head of Security in Kosovo)

Veljko Odalovic (Deputy Head of the Kosovo Okrug)

62. FRY, Declaration of the Parliament of Serbia on National Unity, 24 March 1998

Give the need to unite all the human, material and spiritual forces for the good of Serbia and her citizens, and committed to development under the principles of freedom democracy, justice, equality and solidarity, the National Assembly of the Republic of Serbia, at a session held 24 March 1998, passed a Declaration on National Unity, stating:

1. Responsibility for fulfillment of the vital interests of the nation and the State, for Serbia's present and future, imposes the need for commitment to national unity in relation to the fundamental requirements of the State and the nation.

Serbia and the well-being of its people and citizens must be everyone's common concern and supreme interest, regardless of their affiliation or other alignment.

As historical circumstances have in the past caused the Serbian nation to split, the present calls for accord and unity.

Serbia needs accord and unity. Conscious, therefore, of this responsibility as well as the demands of the time and expectations of the nation and its citizens for Serbia's development and advancement in peace, we relinquish all these division of the past to history.

Universal principles for freedom, justice and democracy are the foundation of strong and stable States and constitute the firmest bulwark against dispersion.

The attributes and commemorative days of our State shall constitute thy symbols and dated imbued in the traditions of our State and nation, uniting us in patriotic faith and dedication to the State and people.

2. The history of our nation is intertwined with struggles for freedom and independence. We are rightly proud for this. Consequently we shall persist in defending our freedom and safeguarding the independence of our State.

The Serbian nation has never founded its rights nor will it ever do so at the detriment of the rights of others, but shall likewise never accept that anyone should threaten the rights of the Serbian people and the sovereignty and integrity of Serbia.

3. We resolutely refute all attempts at ideological, religious and national exclusiveness and self-indulgence.

While respecting human rights and freedoms and the rights of the national minorities living in Serbia in line with the highest international standards, we shall at the same time protect the civil and national rights and wealth of our nation.

4. We further undertake to develop and strengthen our democratic order by competing in learning and zealousness through our party programmes which should aim the common good of Serbia and her citizens.

Political differences must not present an obstacle to accelerated development and reforms, but should afford stimulus to reach the best possible solutions and State governance on the principle of market economy, parliamentary democracy, and the full affirmation and implementation of human and civil rights and freedoms.

5. Serbia and Montenegro are two names for a synonymous root and historical aspiration and destiny. Never has one been nor shall be more or less superior.

Serbia and Montenegro, along with the Republic of Srpska, are therefore not merely the pillars of national unity, but expression of national aspiration towards a redemption of everything that historically, politically, economically, spiritually, ethnically, culturally and in whatever other way cannot be separated much less be opposed to one another.

The Federal Republic of Yugoslavia represents our statehood and the fullest confirmation of our national unity.

6. United around the objectives for the comprehensive advancement of the people and the State, we wish and want the Republic of Serbia and FR Yugoslavia to be the firmest pillar of peace and cooperation with our neighbours and equal and respected members of the European and world community of nations and States.

Today, more than ever before, our destiny lies in our own hands and through this Declaration we affirm our ability to successfully meet up with it. These are decisions that concern the future. Our vision of Serbia is that of a modern, democratic, economic and culturally developed country that holds the respect of all others.

A strong and democratic Serbia, the guarantor of a democratic, stable and strong Federal Republic of Yugoslavia, is a lasting commitment.

In times like this, our State and national interests require that all our political parties and every other subject should pass decisions that will unite, mobilize and steer the national potential towards Serbia's advancement and for the good of all in Serbia the Declaration states.

63. Contact Group, Statement on Kosovo, Bonn, 25 March 1998[1]

1. We, the Foreign Ministers of Contact Group countries, together with the Deputy Chairman in Office of the Organization for Security

---

[1] UN Doc. S/1998/272

and Cooperation in Europe, the Chairman in Office's personal representative for the Federal Republic of Yugoslavia and the European Union Special Representative, the High Representative and the representatives of the European Commission met in Bonn on 25 March to review developments in Kosovo and to follow up decisions reached at our 9 March London meeting.

2. In London, we called upon President Milosevic to take rapid and effective steps to end the violence in Kosovo and commit himself to a political solution through unconditional dialogue. We adopted an action plan to advance these goals, decided on a series of concrete measures, and agreed to reconsider these measures if President Milosevic took the steps required by the Contact Group.

3. We insist that an urgent start be made in the process of unconditional dialogue with the leadership of the Kosovar Albanian community, involving federal and republic levels of government. Neither party should attempt to predetermine the outcome. We expect President Milosevic to implement the process of unconditional dialogue and to take political responsibility for ensuring that Belgrade engages in serious negotiations on Kosovo's status.

4. Today we have reviewed the situation in Kosovo, including the degree of compliance by President Milosevic, the Federal Republic of Yugoslavia and Serbian authorities with the requirements of the London statement.

5. Since our meeting in London, there has been progress in some areas of concern, notably, some movement in Belgrade's position on dialogue on a range of issues, including the autonomy of Kosovo and the conclusion of the long-overdue agreement on implementation of the education accord.

6. Our overall assessment is that further progress by Belgrade on certain points in paragraphs 6 and 7 of the London statement requiring action by the Federal Republic of Yugoslavia and Serbian governments is necessary. Therefore, we have agreed to maintain and implement the measures announced on 9 March, including seeking adoption by 31 March of the arms embargo resolution currently under consideration in the United Nations Security Council. We call upon President Milosevic again to implement fully all the relevant steps in the London statement.

7. We demand that authoritative delegations from both sides convene rapidly in order to agree upon a framework for a substantive negotiation process and agree to the participation in the negotiating process of an outside representative or representatives. We will accept no pretext for delaying such a process. We affirm the willingness of the Contact Group to facilitate talks, recognizing that international engagement in support of dialogue is essential to the achievement of a political solution.

8. We agree that the Contact Group will meet again in four weeks' time to reassess the situation. Our assessment and subsequent decision will take account of a report on compliance to be submitted to the Contact Group by the Troika of OSCE, if they agree to our request to prepare such a report. If President Milosevic takes the steps specified in London, we will reconsider existing measures, including action in the Security Council, to terminate the arms embargo. If Belgrade fails to meet the London Benchmarks, and if the dialogue does not get under way within the next four weeks because of the position of the Federal Republic of Yugoslavia or Serbian authorities, we shall take steps to apply further measures as announced in London.

9. Unless the Federal Republic of Yugoslavia takes steps to resolve the serious political and human rights issues in Kosovo, there is no prospect of any improvement in its international standing. On the other hand, concrete progress to resolve the serious political and human rights issues in Kosovo will improve the international position of the Federal Republic of Yugoslavia and prospects for normalization of its international relationships and full rehabilitation in international institutions. We urge President Milosevic to cooperate fully with the mission of Mr. Felipe González as the Personal Representative of Chairman-in-Office of OSCE and Special Representative of the European Union. Once the González mission is under way, it will certainly be possible to address the potential for participation of the Federal Republic of Yugoslavia in the work of OSCE.

10. We take this opportunity to reaffirm our strong opposition to all terrorist actions. Violence does not contribute to the search for a solution in Kosovo. This applies equally to Serbian police and Kosovar Albanian extremists. We will use all appropriate elements of pressure and influence with both sides to ensure that violence does not escalate and that the serious dispute over Kosovo's status between Belgrade and the Kosovar Albanian community is resolved strictly through peaceful means. We urge those outside the Federal Republic of Yugoslavia who are supplying financial support, arms or training for terrorist activity in Kosovo to cease doing so immediately.

11. We welcome Dr. Rugova's clear commitment to non-violence and urge others in the leadership of the Kosovar Albanian community to make their opposition to violence and terrorism both clear and public. Belgrade authorities cannot, however, justify their repression and violence in Kosovo in the name of anti-terrorist activities. We repeat that the way to combat terrorism is for Belgrade to offer the Kosovar Albanian community a genuine political process.

12. We applaud the work of Sant' Egidio and of the 3+3 commission in reaching agreement on measures to implement the 1996 Education Agreement. We call upon all sides to ensure that implementation proceeds smoothly and without delay, according to the agreed timetable. We are considering what assistance we can provide to facilitate implementation. We will also consider measures if either party blocks implementation. We urge all sides to cooperate with Sant' Egidio in efforts to reduce tensions in other social sectors as well.

13. The fundamental position of the Contact Group remains the same. We support neither independence nor the maintenance of the status quo as the end result of negotiations between the Belgrade authorities and the Kosovo Albanian leadership on the status of Kosovo. Without prejudging what that result may be, we base the principles for a solution to the Kosovo problem on the territorial integrity of the Federal Republic of Yugoslavia and on OSCE standards, the Helsinki principles, and the Charter of the United Nations. Such a solution must also take into account the rights of the Kosovar Albanians and all those who live in Kosovo. We support a substantially greater degree of autonomy for Kosovo which must include meaningful self-administration.

64. EU, 2078th Council Meeting, General Affairs, PRES/98/86, Brussels, 30/31 March 1998

[Parts not referring to the situation in Kosovo have been omitted.]
[...]

Relations with the Western Balkans - Conclusions
KOSOVO

The Council discussed the continuing tension in Kosovo, underlining its concern at the further incidents of violence in the province within the last few days. It reaffirmed its insistence that the Serbian special police force be immediately withdrawn and that FRY and Serbian security forces should act with restraint and in accordance with internationally accepted standards. It also condemned all terrorist acts, notably those by the Kosovo Liberation Army, and called on those outside the FRY who are supplying financial support, arms or training for terrorist activity in Kosovo to cease doing so immediately.

The Council welcomed the statement of 25 March by the Foreign Ministers of the Contact Group. It expressed the view that the steps taken by the FRY and Serbian authorities since 9 March were insufficient to meet the full range of requirements set out on that date and reiterated on 25 March. It underlined that the measures set out in its Common Position of 19 March would not be lifted, and others would need to be considered unless these requirements had been met in full.

The Council reaffirmed its conviction that meaningful dialogue without preconditions must begin urgently between the parties. It supports neither independence nor the maintenance of the status quo as the end-result of negotiations between the Belgrade authorities and the Kosovo Albanian leadership on the status of Kosovo. It welcomed the steps already taken by Dr Rugova to prepare for negotiations and encouraged him to announce his negotiating team without delay.

The Council welcomed the agreement reached in the 3+3 Commission on the implementation of the Education Agreement and thanked Monsignor Paglia of Sant' Egidio for all his efforts in this field. Noting that the Contact Group urged all sides to cooperate with Sant'Egidio to reduce tensions in other social sectors as well, the Council called for rapid implementation by both sides of this new agreement and affirmed the European Union's readiness to give substantial assistance to this process. It asked for a rapid follow-up to the recommendations of the Presidency/Commission factfinding team currently in Kosovo.

The Council expressed its full support for the mission of Mr Felipe Gonzalez as Personal Representative for the Federal Republic of Yugoslavia of the OSCE Chairman in Office and Special Representative of the European Union. It called upon President Milosevic to cooperate with this mission, which would constitute an important element in the future course of relations between the European Union and the Federal Republic of Yugoslavia.

The Council underlined its intention to continue to follow developments closely and asked the competent instances to develop further the European Union's line on this issue within the framework of the European Union's regional approach. It underlined that concrete progress to resolve the serious political and human rights issue in Kosovo will improve the international position of the FRY and prospects for normalisation of its international relationships and full rehabilitation in international institutions.

[...]

65. UN Security Council Resolution 1160 (1998) of 31 March 1998

The Security Council,

Noting with appreciation the statements of the Foreign Ministers of France, Germany, Italy, the Russian Federation, the United Kingdom of Great Britain and Northern Ireland and the United States of America (the Contact Group) of 9 and 25 March 1998 (S/1998/223 and S/1998/272), including the proposal on a comprehensive arms embargo on the Federal Republic of Yugoslavia, including Kosovo,

Welcoming the decision of the Special Session of the Permanent Council of the Organization for Security and Cooperation in Europe (OSCE) of 11 March 1998 (S/1998/246),

Condemning the use of excessive force by Serbian police forces against civilians and peaceful demonstrators in Kosovo, as well as all acts of terrorism by the Kosovo Liberation Army or any other group or individual and all external support for terrorist activity in Kosovo, including finance, arms and training,

Noting the declaration of 18 March 1998 by the President of the Republic of Serbia on the political process in Kosovo and Metohija (S/1998/250),

Noting also the clear commitment of senior representatives of the Kosovar Albanian community to non-violence,

Noting that there has been some progress in implementing the actions indicated in the Contact Group statement of 9 March 1998, but stressing that further progress is required,

Affirming the commitment of all Member States to the sovereignty and territorial integrity of the Federal Republic of Yugoslavia,

Acting under Chapter VII of the Charter of the United Nations,

1. *Calls upon* the Federal Republic of Yugoslavia immediately to take the further necessary steps to achieve a political solution to the issue of Kosovo through dialogue and to implement the actions indicated in the Contact Group statements of 9 and 25 March 1998;

2. *Calls also upon* the Kosovar Albanian leadership to condemn all terrorist action, and emphasizes that all elements in the Kosovar Albanian community should pursue their goals by peaceful means only;

3. *Underlines* that the way to defeat violence and terrorism in Kosovo is for the authorities in Belgrade to offer the Kosovar Albanian community a genuine political process;

4. *Calls upon* the authorities in Belgrade and the leadership of the Kosovar Albanian community urgently to enter without preconditions into a meaningful dialogue on political status issues, and notes the readiness of the Contact Group to facilitate such a dialogue;

5. *Agrees*, without prejudging the outcome of that dialogue, with the proposal in the Contact Group statements of 9 and 25 March 1998 that the principles for a solution of the Kosovo problem should be based on the territorial integrity of the Federal Republic of Yugoslavia and should be in accordance with OSCE standards, including those set out in the Helsinki Final Act of the Conference on Security and Cooperation in Europe of 1975, and the Charter of the United Nations, and that such a solution must also take into account the rights of the Kosovar Albanians and all who live in Kosovo, and expresses its support for an enhanced status for Kosovo which would include a substantially greater degree of autonomy and meaningful self-administration;

6. *Welcomes* the signature on 23 March 1998 of an agreement on measures to implement the 1996 Education Agreement, *calls upon* all parties to ensure that its implementation proceeds smoothly and without delay according to the agreed timetable and *expresses* its readiness to consider measures if either party blocks implementation;

7. *Expresses* its support for the efforts of the OSCE for a peaceful resolution of the crisis in Kosovo, including through the Personal Representative of the Chairman-in-Office for the Federal Republic of Yugoslavia, who is also the Special Representative of the European Union, and the return of the OSCE long-term missions;

8. *Decides* that all States shall, for the purposes of fostering peace and stability in Kosovo, prevent the sale or supply to the Federal Republic of Yugoslavia, including Kosovo, by their nationals or from their territories or using their flag vessels and aircraft, of arms and related matériel of all types, such as weapons and ammunition, military vehicles and equipment and spare parts for the aforementioned, and shall prevent arming and training for terrorist activities there;

9. *Decides* to establish, in accordance with rule 28 of its provisional rules of procedure, a committee of the Security Council, consisting of all the members of the Council, to undertake the following tasks and to report on its work to the Council with its observations and recommendations:

(a) to seek from all States information regarding the action taken by them concerning the effective implementation of the prohibitions imposed by this resolution;

(b) to consider any information brought to its attention by any State concerning violations of the prohibitions imposed by this resolution and to recommend appropriate measures in response thereto;

(c) to make periodic reports to the Security Council on information submitted to it regarding alleged violations of the prohibitions imposed by this resolution;

(d) to promulgate such guidelines as may be necessary to facilitate the implementation of the prohibitions imposed by this resolution;

(e) to examine the reports submitted pursuant to paragraph 12 below;

10. *Calls upon* all States and all international and regional organizations to act strictly in conformity with this resolution, notwithstanding the existence of any rights granted or obligations conferred or imposed by any international agreement or of any contract entered into or any license or permit granted prior to the entry into force of the prohibitions imposed by this resolution, and *stresses* in this context the importance of continuing implementation of the Agreement on Subregional Arms Control signed in Florence on 14 June 1996;

11. *Requests* the Secretary-General to provide all necessary assistance to the committee established by paragraph 9 above and to make the necessary arrangements in the Secretariat for this purpose;

12. *Requests* States to report to the committee established by paragraph 9 above within 30 days of adoption of this resolution on the steps they have taken to give effect to the prohibitions imposed by this resolution;

13. *Invites* the OSCE to keep the Secretary-General informed on the situation in Kosovo and on measures taken by that organization in this regard;

14. *Requests* the Secretary-General to keep the Council regularly informed and to report on the situation in Kosovo and the implementation of this resolution no later than 30 days following the adoption of this resolution and every 30 days thereafter;

15. *Further requests* that the Secretary-General, in consultation with appropriate regional organizations, include in his first report recommendations for the establishment of a comprehensive regime to monitor the implementation of the prohibitions imposed by this resolution, and calls upon all States, in particular neighbouring States, to extend full cooperation in this regard;

16. *Decides* to review the situation on the basis of the reports of the Secretary-General, which will take into account the assessments of, inter alia, the Contact Group, the OSCE and the European Union, and *decides also* to reconsider the prohibitions imposed by this resolution, including action to terminate them, following receipt of the assessment of the Secretary-General that the Government of the Federal Republic of Yugoslavia, cooperating in a constructive manner with the Contact Group, have:

(a) begun a substantive dialogue in accordance with paragraph 4 above, including the participation of an outside representative or representatives, unless any failure to do so is not because of the position of the Federal Republic of Yugoslavia or Serbian authorities;

(b) withdrawn the special police units and ceased action by the security forces affecting the civilian population;

(c) allowed access to Kosovo by humanitarian organizations as well as representatives of Contact Group and other embassies;

(d) accepted a mission by the Personal Representative of the OSCE Chairman-in-Office for the Federal Republic of Yugoslavia that would include a new and specific mandate for addressing the problems in Kosovo, as well as the return of the OSCE long-term missions;

(e) facilitated a mission to Kosovo by the United Nations High Commissioner for Human Rights;

17. *Urges* the Office of the Prosecutor of the International Tribunal established pursuant to resolution 827 (1993) of 25 May 1993 to begin gathering information related to the violence in Kosovo that may fall within its jurisdiction, and *notes* that the authorities of the Federal Republic of Yugoslavia have an obligation to cooperate with the Tribunal and that the Contact Group countries will make available to the Tribunal substantiated relevant information in their possession;

18. *Affirms* that concrete progress to resolve the serious political and human rights issues in Kosovo will improve the international position of the Federal Republic of Yugoslavia and prospects for normalization of its international relationships and full participation in international institutions;

19. *Emphasizes* that failure to make constructive progress towards the peaceful resolution of the situation in Kosovo will lead to the consideration of additional measures;

20. *Decides* to remain seized of the matter.

[Adopted at the 3868th meeting with 14 votes to none with China abstaining.]

66. UN, Extracts from the Debates of the Security Council Concerning Security Council Resolution 1160 (1998), UN Doc. S/PV. 3868, 31 March 1998[1]

[Members had before them, inter alia, the text of a draft resolution UN Doc. S/1998/284 submitted by France, Germany, Italy, Japan, Portugal, Sweden, the United Kingdom of Great Britain and Northern Ireland and the United States of America] [2]

[3] **Mr. Owada** (Japan): The Government of Japan is deeply concerned about the recent deterioration of the situation in Kosovo, which, tragically, has resulted in a mounting death toll. Japan strongly condemns both the use of excessive force by the Serbian police against civilians in Kosovo and the use of violence, especially acts of terrorism, by the Kosovo Liberation Army or anyone else as a means to achieve political goals. My delegation recognizes that the current situation in Kosovo poses a threat to international peace and security in the region and that the further spread of violence there might lead to the destabilization of the entire Balkans.

Against this background, the draft resolution before us is intended to send a clear and concerted message by the Security Council that the parties concerned must stop this violence in Kosovo in the Federal Republic of Yugoslavia and begin the process of finding a solution to the serious political and human rights problems there. We are convinced that this draft resolution, which includes a decision to impose an arms embargo against the Federal Republic of Yugoslavia, including Kosovo, will be, upon its adoption, an effective instrument to prevent the further spread of such violence.

The basic position of Japan on the problem of Kosovo, which I believe it shares with the rest of the international community, is that neither the repression of the human and political rights of the Albanian population in Kosovo nor the separation and independence of Kosovo is acceptable. My Government urges the authorities in Belgrade and the leadership of the Albanian community in Kosovo to immediately enter into a substantive dialogue without precondition, so that the citizens of Kosovo may enjoy a sufficient degree of autonomy with meaningful selfadministration, as well as complete respect for their human rights within the border of the Federal Republic of Yugoslavia. Japan is of the view that the participation of an outside representative or representatives will be important in order to ensure that such a dialogue can be promoted in a meaningful way.

The Government of Japan fully supports the efforts of the relevant international organizations and other bodies, especially the Organization for Security and Cooperation in Europe (OSCE) and the Contact Group, in their cooperation for the resolution of the crisis in Kosovo. My Government urges the authorities in Belgrade to fully cooperate with the OSCE and to take steps to implement without delay the actions set out in the statement of the Contact Group of 9 March 1998. While my delegation recognizes that some positive steps have been taken by the authorities in Belgrade during the past few weeks, such as the declaration of 18 March by the President of the Republic of Serbia and the signature on 23 March of an agreement to implement the 1996 Education Agreement, further progress must be made without delay by the authorities of both the Republic of Serbia and the Federal Republic of Yugoslavia. At the same time, the Government of Japan calls upon all elements of the Albanian community in Kosovo to immediately

---

[1] *Only statements which add to a legal analysis or to the factual background have been included. Presidential statements not related to substantive issues have also been omitted.*

[2] *In 1998, membership of the Security Council was as follows: Bahrain, Brazil, China, Costa Rica, France, Gabon, Gambia, Japan, Kenya, Portugal, Russian Federation, Slovenia, Sweden, the United Kingdom of Great Britain and Northern Ireland, the United States of America.*
At the invitation of the President representatives of Albania, Bosnia and Herzegovina, Canada, Croatia, Egypt, Germany, Greece, Hungary, Italy, Pakistan, Poland, Turkey and Ukraine participated, without vote, in the discussion in accordance with the Charter and rule 37 of the Council's provisional rules of procedure. Mr. Jovanovic (FRY) was also invited.

accept the dialogue and to categorically denounce terrorist activities and external support for such activities.

For these reasons, my delegation will vote in favour of the draft resolution now before us, which sets out in a balanced manner all these points that I have emphasized as important.

I should like to close my statement by expressing the readiness of the Government of Japan to actively participate in the efforts of the Security Council and of the international community as a whole to assist in the peaceful resolution of the crisis in Kosovo.

[A statement by the representative of Costa Rica has been omitted.]

[4] **Mr. Dejammet** (France) *(interpretation from French)*: The situation in Kosovo in the Federal Republic of Yugoslavia calls for a response from the Security Council. The tragic events that have marked the former Yugoslavia in recent years have indeed demonstrated the need for a rapid and appropriate response to crisis situations in the region.

The States that make up what has been called the Contact Group, as well as the European Union, the 26 countries that participated in the European conference held in London and the neighbouring Balkan States, have been involved since the beginning of the crisis. They have emphasized the need for a cessation of violence and the withdrawal of the special police forces, their condemnation of terrorism and the importance of achieving a political solution to the Kosovo crisis through dialogue and with respect for the territorial integrity of the Federal Republic of Yugoslavia. That solution should include substantially greater autonomy for Kosovo.

During the London Contact Group meeting, on 9 March 1998, specific requirements were defined, deadlines were set and measures for immediate implementation were decided on. Meeting again on 25 March at Bonn, the States of the Contact Group noted that progress had been achieved since the London meeting.

The joint visit of the German and French Foreign Ministers to Belgrade on 19 March made it possible to appreciate positive developments in the position of the authorities in the Federal Republic of Yugoslavia. The agreement reached on 23 March between the parties regarding measures to implement the 1996 Education Agreement also demonstrates that it is possible to achieve a negotiated solution to delicate issues.

That progress, however important, is still not enough. Additional steps must be taken by the Belgrade authorities and the representatives of the Kosovar Albanians in order for substantive dialogue to commence without preconditions.

The draft resolution before the Security Council today is part of this context. By this draft resolution, the Security Council would decide on an embargo on the sale or supply of arms to the Federal Republic of Yugoslavia, including Kosovo. France already supports such a measure, in accordance with the embargo decided on by the European Union in 1991 and reconfirmed on 19 March 1998.

The measures stipulated in the draft resolution should first and foremost be seen as a means to achieve a negotiated settlement of the current crisis. The text provides that the Security Council will review the prohibitions that have been decided on and will be able to lift them as soon as the Government of the Federal Republic of Yugoslavia has met the conditions set out in [5] the draft resolution. The prohibitions can thus be lifted when the Secretary-General, in one of the periodic reports he must submit to the Security Council every 30 days, deems that the Government of the Federal Republic of Yugoslavia has fulfilled the specific requirements set by the Security Council.

The draft resolution also provides that specific progress on certain difficult issues related to Kosovo will make it possible for the Federal Republic of Yugoslavia to improve its prospects for normalizing its international relations and for full participation in international institutions.

My country therefore considers this draft resolution to be a balanced text that can contribute to a peaceful political settlement of the current crisis in Kosovo. That is why France will vote in favour of the draft resolution.

[A statement by the representative of Kenya has been omitted.]

Mr. Lidén (Sweden): The situation in Kosovo remains serious and clearly constitutes a threat to international peace and security. We are pleased to see the Council today discharging its duty in accordance with the Charter of the United Nations in an effort to prevent a flare-up of new armed violence in the Balkans. We will therefore welcome the adoption of the draft resolution before us, imposing an arms embargo on the Federal Republic of Yugoslavia, including Kosovo. For Sweden, peace and stability in the Balkans are necessary prerequisites for European security.

We condemn the excessive use of force by the Serbian special police in Kosovo, which has caused several deaths and injuries to unarmed civilians. We also condemn all acts of terrorism. Both sides must exercise restraint and enter into a serious political dialogue on how to settle their differences through exclusively peaceful means and on the basis of human rights and the rule of law.

Sweden fully supports the declarations made by the Contact Group ministers on 9 and 25 March in response to the developments in Kosovo. We agree with the measures recommended in order to persuade the authorities in Belgrade to take necessary steps towards an acceptable solution. It is also incumbent upon the Kosovar Albanian leadership to act responsibly and facilitate the beginning of a constructive dialogue.

While Belgrade has recently taken some positive steps, much remains to be done. The concrete steps the authorities in Belgrade must take are clearly spelt out in paragraph 16 of the draft resolution. These steps include, first, initiating a substantive dialogue on Kosovo with the participation of an outside representative or representatives; secondly, withdrawal of the special police; thirdly, allowing access to Kosovo by humanitarian organizations and others; fourthly, accepting a mission by the Organization for Security and Cooperation in Europe (OSCE) and the European Union representative, Mr. Felipe Gonzalez, as well as the return of the OSCE long-term missions; and, fifthly, facilitating a mission to Kosovo by the United Nations High Commissioner for Human Rights.

Hopefully, Belgrade will listen to the international community and take these steps, which would enable the Council to reconsider the sanctions. Together with progress in resolving human rights issues and in cooperating with the International Tribunal, this would also enhance the prospects for the normalization of the Federal Republic of Yugoslavia's international relations, which we look forward to. If Belgrade does not comply, however, additional measures will be considered.

The arms embargo that we are about to impose must be immediately and strictly implemented by all States. As a member of the European Union, Sweden has already decided to implement not only the arms embargo but also the other sanctions recommended by the Contact Group, [6] including refusal to supply equipment which can be used for internal repression or for terrorism, denial of visas for officials responsible for the repression and a moratorium on Government-financed export credits. [...]

Mr. Valle (Brazil): Given the tragic background of inter-ethnic violence in the recent history of the Balkans, the international community has not been unjustified in reacting with disquiet to the recent events in the Kosovo region of the Federal Republic of Yugoslavia. I do not wish to minimize the complex threats to internal security posed by clandestine terrorist activity, but the fact remains that the repressive measures taken against civilians in Kosovo by Serbian police forces have provoked indignation throughout the world.

Significantly, the Ministers for Foreign Affairs of the countries of South-Eastern Europe, meeting in Sofia on March 10, circulated a declaration expressing their

"concern with the deteriorating situation in Kosovo and with the grave consequences of an inter-ethnic conflict and its possible spillover in the region."

In addition to the Sofia meeting, there have been a number of important encounters and declarations dealing with these new episodes of Balkan instability, which have all seemed to converge towards the need for the international community to avoid the mistakes of the past by articulating a quick and effective response which will help stem the violence and create the conditions for improved dialogue and cooperation between the parties.

We have welcomed the many joint and individual diplomatic initiatives taken by those who would be potentially most affected by a new wave of unrest in the Balkans, and have remained attentive to their strategies for dealing with what might best be described as a very delicate situation. It is from this intense diplomatic mobilization that a decision has seemed to emerge in favour of an arms embargo, as a measure capable of putting pressure on the parties to negotiate while placing a limit on the presence of weapons in an already heavily armed and volatile region.

As a matter of principle, it has seemed important for my delegation to emphasize the need for clear provisions regarding the conditions for lifting the sanctions in the draft before us. We note that paragraph 16 addresses this problem in a manner which we consider satisfactory, although we would stress the need for the Secretary-General to base the assessments he is to make under that paragraph on as wide a spectrum of information as possible, and in close cooperation with the region, the countries which meet as the Contact Group-France, Germany, Italy, the Russian Federation, the United Kingdom and the United States-the Organization for Security and Cooperation in Europe and the European Union.

While concurring with the imposition of an embargo, we cannot fail to stress that these measures will not yield the desired effect if they are not accompanied by parallel diplomatic efforts aimed at the promotion of a safer and more harmonious environment for those who have been most directly affected by the unrest.

Furthermore, if there is movement in a positive direction, the Security Council should acknowledge it promptly. The declaration by the President of the Republic of Serbia on the political process in Kosovo has been received by the international community as an auspicious sign. In the face of further and sustained progress, there should be no reason to doubt that the Security Council will respond accordingly. At this stage we should confine ourselves to the measures contained in the draft, in the expectation that developments will render needless the consideration of additional restrictions.

Although the Charter enshrines the principle of non-intervention in matters which are essentially within the domestic jurisdiction of any State, we are all aware that this principle does not prejudice the application of enforcement measures under Chapter VII, in accordance with Article 2, paragraph 7. Perhaps it is not by coincidence that the proliferation of decisions authorized by the Security Council under Chapter VII since the end of the cold war, and of sanctions in particular, has come about in a world where conflict has often seemed to break out within the internal borders of States. Some observers have gone as far as to suggest that there may have been a tendency to frame emergencies under Chapter VII in recent years so as to circumvent the non-intervention principle. If this were indeed the case, we would be witnessing a distortion in the waiver provided by Article 2, paragraph 7, which would seem to be incompatible with its original purpose.

On the other hand, as stated in General Assembly resolution 51/242, annex II, on the question of sanctions [7] imposed by the United Nations, sanctions are a matter of the utmost seriousness and concern. That text, adopted by consensus, declares in paragraph I that

"Sanctions should be resorted to only with the utmost caution, when other peaceful options provided by the Charter are inadequate."

By concluding my statement with these references to an important General Assembly resolution and to the United Nations Charter, I wish to emphasize my delegation's commitment to the pacific settlement of disputes within a context of respect for sovereignty and territorial integrity. We believe that by exercising caution in resorting to coercive measures we are actually strengthening the authority of the Security Council in the face of serious and otherwise intractable situations.

[Statements by the representatives of Slovenia, Bahrain and Portugal have been omitted.]

[10] **Mr. Fedotov** (Russian Federation) *(interpretation from Russian)*: From the very outset, the Russian Federation has viewed the recent events in Kosovo as the internal affair of the Federal Republic of Yugoslavia. We strongly believe that the basic principle for a settlement of the situation in Kosovo is that that autonomous region must remain within Serbia on the basis of unswerving compliance with the principle of the territorial integrity of the Federal Republic of Yugoslavia and of the republics that make it up.

Only within this legal framework is an effective settlement of the Kosovo problem possible through peaceful political dialogue without preconditions or unilateral approaches. It is precisely in support of such a political process that the decisions of the international Contact Group, adopted at London and Bonn, are directed.

While we condemn the use of excessive force by the Serbian police, we also strongly condemn any terrorist acts on the part of the Kosovar Albanians, including the so-called the Kosovo Liberation Army, and other manifestations of extremism, which seriously destabilize the situation and complicate the search for a mutually acceptable and effective political settlement of the situation. This approach is based on a key principle of Russian foreign policy: Terrorism is categorically unacceptable in any form or manifestation and calls for the most decisive condemnation of the international community. Clearly, any foreign support for terrorism must be nipped in the bud, which requires a coordinated international effort.

Unfortunately, the events in Kosovo have an adverse regional impact. At the same time, the situation in Kosovo, despite its complexity, does not constitute a threat to regional, much less international peace and security. It is precisely this understanding that is reflected in the draft resolution before us today.

[11] It was extremely difficult for Russia to agree with such a measure as the introduction of a military embargo. We embarked on this step only on the understanding - which is now embedded in the draft resolution - that the issue is not about punishing anyone, Belgrade in particular, but about specific measures designed to prevent an increase in tensions, to erect an obstacle to external terrorism, and to foster the political process with a view to a speedy and lasting settlement. The prospects for such a settlement depend on the political will and willingness to take a constructive approach of both sides - the Serbian leadership of the Federal Republic of Yugoslavia and the Kosovar Albanians.

One of the most important conditions for the viability of the embargo is an effective monitoring regime for its implementation, particularly on the Albanian-Macedonian border. The illegal arms traffic must be reliably impeded and mere declarations on that subject do not suffice. It is precisely from this perspective that we must consider the mandate of the United Nations Preventive Deployment Force. It may be useful in this context for the Secretary-General, in preparing the reports contemplated in the draft resolution, to conduct investigations on the supply of weapons, training, and financial and other support for the Kosovo terrorists from the territories of neighbouring and other countries.

Russia's position has been and continues to be that the Security Council's establishment of a military embargo, like any military sanctions, is possible only with a clear exit strategy. In the future, we will continue to advocate the need to limit the sanctions with a clear schedule, following the expiration of which the Council will have to decide whether or not the sanctions should be extended.

Unfortunately, our approach has not, for the time being, received sufficient support in the Security Council. Nevertheless, the draft resolution has been able to define strict criteria; if Belgrade complies with these, the Security Council will decide to lift the embargo. We note that the Governments of the Federal Republic of Yugoslavia and

Serbia have already taken important steps in that direction. They have announced the withdrawal of police units; the International Committee of the Red Cross and other humanitarian organizations have been given access to Kosovo; the President of Serbia, Mr. Milutinovic, officially announced his readiness for a political dialogue with the Kosovar Albanians, without preconditions. We encourage Belgrade to intensify these positive efforts. As the draft resolution confirms, concrete progress to resolve the issues relating to the situation in Kosovo will improve the international position of the Federal Republic of Yugoslavia and prospects for normalization of its full participation in international institutions. Russia sincerely hopes that this will happen as soon as possible.

It is also important that the draft resolution clearly links the restrictions it imposes to existing agreements in the region on the levels of armaments, inter alia, the Florence Agreement on Subregional Arms Control.

We see the main task of the international community to be the full promotion of the consolidation of progress made in the situation around Kosovo. This must not be done by increasing sanction measures, which may have the most adverse repercussions for the entire Balkan region and many other States besides. The efforts of all interested countries and international organizations must be directed to encouraging and supporting the political process, fostering dialogue to the greatest extent possible, and preventing any deterioration of the situation. Russia will continue to work precisely to that end.

Mr. Shen Guofang (China) *(interpretation from Chinese)*: The Chinese delegation is concerned about the current situation in Kosovo, in the Federal Republic of Yugoslavia. Kosovo is an integral part of the territory of the Federal Republic of Yugoslavia. The question of Kosovo is, in its essence, an internal matter of the Federal Republic. It should be resolved properly through negotiations between both parties concerned on the basis of the principle of respect for the sovereignty and territorial integrity of the Federal Republic of Yugoslavia.

We have noted that the Government of the Federal Republic of Yugoslavia has taken a series of positive measures in this regard and that the situation on the ground is moving towards stability. We do not think that the situation in Kosovo endangers regional and international peace and security.

Ethnic issues are extremely complicated and sensitive, especially in the Balkans. On the one hand, the legitimate rights and interests of all ethnic groups should be protected; on the other, secessionist activities by various extremist elements should be prevented.

Many countries in the region are multiethnic. If the Council is to get involved in a dispute without a request from the country concerned, it may set a bad precedent [12] and have wider negative implications. Therefore, the Council should be cautious when addressing these issues.

The priority issue in solving the question of Kosovo in the Federal Republic of Yugoslavia is for the parties to start the political talks as soon as possible. However, the draft resolution before us would not help move the parties to negotiations. Furthermore, it is neither appropriate to bring before the Council the differences between the Organization for Security and Cooperation in Europe and the Federal Republic of Yugoslavia, as well as the human rights issues in Kosovo, nor proper to link the Federal Republic of Yugoslavia's return to the international community with the question of Kosovo.

The Chinese delegation has stated its principled position repeatedly in the Council's consultations. Since the contents of the draft resolution do not conform to our principled position, we have no choice but to abstain in the voting. The Chinese delegation requests that its position be placed on record.

[The President put to the vote draft resolution S/1998/284, which was adopted as Security Council Resolution 1160 (1998) with 14 votes to none with China abstaining.]

Mr. Richmond (United Kingdom): The United Kingdom shares the deep concern expressed around this table about the violence and bloodshed which, in recent weeks, have once again visited this troubled part of the world. The resolution which the Council has adopted today is one element in a concerted international effort to prevent a repetition in Kosovo of the cycle of violence we have already seen elsewhere in the region.

On 9 March the United Kingdom hosted a meeting of Foreign Ministers of Contact Group countries in London. The Group agreed a plan of action aimed at putting a stop to further violence and paving the way for a serious political dialogue between the authorities in Belgrade and representatives of the Kosovar Albanian community.

Meeting again in Bonn on 25 March, the Contact Group concluded that while there had been some progress in the intervening period, included the belated agreement to implement the 1996 Education Agreement, the steps taken by the Belgrade authorities towards meeting the requirements set out in London did not go far enough.

In adopting this resolution, the Security Council sends an unmistakable message: that by acting under Chapter VII of the Charter, the Council considers that the situation in Kosovo constitutes a threat to international peace and security in the Balkans region. It says to Belgrade that repression in Kosovo will not be tolerated by the international community; and to the Kosovar side, it says that terrorism - in whatever guise and for whatever purpose - is unacceptable.

The United Kingdom's record against terrorism is firm. But terrorism cannot be a pretext for the use of force against a civilian population. Belgrade cannot pass off the repressive acts of recent weeks as purely an internal affair. Human rights abuses are a matter for us all. And we have a particular responsibility to reduce tension in the region before it causes instability in neighbouring countries.

The United Kingdom does not support separatism or independence in Kosovo. But we expect Belgrade to grant Kosovo an enhanced status including self-administration. Getting the authorities in Belgrade and the Kosovar Albanian community to start a constructive dialogue without preconditions about the differences between them is the only chance of reaching a peaceful settlement. Repressive police actions of the kind we have witnessed in recent weeks serve merely to undermine the moderates on both sides and to increase support for terrorists.

The United Kingdom looks forward to the day when we can welcome the Federal Republic of Yugoslavia into the family of democratic nations of Europe. But we cannot do so while Belgrade fails to meet the standards [13] that the rest of Europe has set itself. President Milosevic has a choice: he must decide whether he wishes to consign the future of his State and its people to further isolation and mounting international pressure, or whether he wants to see progress in the Federal Republic of Yugoslavia's relations with the European Union and the rest of the international community of the kind already being made by its neighbours.

Mr. Richardson (United States of America): Today the Security Council is taking a clear stand for peace and security in the Balkans. The United States strongly supports this resolution imposing an arms embargo on the Federal Republic of Yugoslavia. In so doing, the Council sends an unambiguous message that the international community will not tolerate violence and "ethnic cleansing" in the region of the former Yugoslavia. We must avoid the mistakes of the past, when the international community waited too long before taking decisive action. We fully recognize that the security of the region directly affects broader international interests and that deterioration of the situation in Kosovo constitutes a threat to international peace and security.

Over the last few years, this Council and the international community have worked hard to promote ethnic reconciliation in Bosnia and Croatia. The United States and our partners in the peace effort must not now watch years of peace-building in the Balkans destroyed by repressive violence or by terrorist activity in Kosovo.

The Foreign Ministers of the Contact Group, meeting in London on March 9 and in Bonn on March 25, agreed that the situation in Kosovo is not simply an internal matter, but also has a direct impact on the stability of neighbouring countries and jeopardizes peace in the Balkans. As Secretary Albright said in Bonn, the international community has not faced a problem in the former Yugoslavia as dangerous as the situation in Kosovo since the last war in the region began.

President Milosevic knows what he must do to have the arms embargo and other sanctions lifted and to avoid further measures. As a necessary and crucial step, President Milosevic must begin an unconditional dialogue on political status issues with the Kosovar Albanian leadership. The United States joins the Council in expressing support for an enhanced status for Kosovo, including greater autonomy and meaningful self-administration. The United States believes this is the only way to achieve long-term peace and a satisfactory resolution to the conflict in the region. The United States strongly welcomes the clear commitment of Mr. Rugova and other senior representatives of the Kosovar Albanian leadership to non-violence and a negotiated solution to the crisis in Kosovo. We will not countenance terrorist activity or external support for terrorist activity. The Kosovar Albanian community should pursue their goals through peaceful means.

This resolution also underlines the important role of the Office of the Prosecutor of the International Tribunal in gathering evidence about the violence in Kosovo which may fall within its jurisdiction. We remind the authorities of the Federal Republic of Yugoslavia of their obligation to extend full cooperation in this effort, as well as of their commitments under the Bosnia peace agreement to cooperate fully with the International Tribunal.

Of key importance is urgent action by the Federal Republic of Yugoslavia to stop the violence and other provocative action by its police and paramilitary security forces. In spite of assurances by the authorities to the contrary, these special police remain in Kosovo in force. They must be withdrawn immediately, in keeping with the London Contact Group statement. Civilians and members of the international community, including international humanitarian workers in the region, have been harassed, threatened, arrested and even beaten by these police.

We believe that only sustained international pressure will ensure continued progress towards the goal of a peacefully negotiated solution in Kosovo. This resolution confirms that the international community will hold President Milosevic firmly to meeting in full the benchmarks of the London Contact Group. Otherwise, as the Bonn Contact Group recognized, additional measures may be needed.

[A statement by the President made in his capacity as representative of Gambia has been omitted.]

[14] **Mr. Richmond** (United Kingdom): I would like to make a statement on behalf of the European Union. The Central and Eastern European countries associated with the European Union - the Czech Republic, Hungary, Lithuania, Poland and Romania - as well as the European Free Trade Association country, Norway, a member of the European Economic Area, align themselves with this statement.

The European Union is deeply concerned at the threat to regional peace and security posed by the situation in Kosovo. The international community must send a clear message to the Federal Republic of Yugoslavia and the Serbian authorities that the excessive violence by military police units, involving deaths and injury among the civilian population, is unacceptable. Equally, we condemn unreservedly all terrorist acts and call on those supplying financial support, arms or training to cease to do so. We urge both sides to engage immediately in genuine and unconditional dialogue, including with the participation of an outside representative.

The European Union fully supports the statement made by the Contact Group Foreign Ministers in Bonn on 25 March. It endorses their assessment that while some positive developments have occurred - notably the deal on the implementation of the Education Agreement, which is a particularly welcome step forward - progress has not been sufficient to meet the requirements set out by the [15] meeting of Contact Group Foreign Ministers in London on 9 March.

The European Union has nominated Mr. Felipe Gonzalez as European Union Special Representative, with a view to enhancing the effectiveness of the European Union's contribution to resolving the problems in the Federal Republic of Yugoslavia, including Kosovo, and the European Union strongly supports the mission by Mr. Gonzalez as Personal Representative of the Organization for Security and Cooperation in Europe Chairman-in-Office for the Federal Republic of Yugoslavia.

The European Union believes that pressure must be maintained to bring the Belgrade authorities to the negotiating table. That means implementing forthwith the measures agreed at the London Contact Group meeting.

Against this background, the European Union strongly supports the resolution which has just been adopted by the Council. The Union already has a comprehensive arms embargo in place against the countries of the former Yugoslavia. We wish to see all other Member States taking an equally stringent position. This resolution is an expression of the international community's rejection of the policy of violence, whether carried out by military police or by terrorists.

It is essential also that the international response to the crisis be a united and coherent one. We know, to our cost, from the early days of the Bosnian war, that international divisions undermine our efforts. The resolution we have adopted today sends a powerful signal to the authorities in Belgrade that the international community is united in its desire to see real progress on Kosovo and is monitoring events there closely. Neighbouring States have already expressed concern that further turmoil in Kosovo might spread instability beyond the borders of the Federal Republic of Yugoslavia. We owe it to them to take a firm line.

The European Union favours granting a large degree of autonomy to Kosovo within the Federal Republic of Yugoslavia. This must include meaningful self-administration for the local population. But the key is getting both sides to talk, and we will support a settlement on Kosovo's status reached by mutual agreement. [...]

Mr. Jovanovic: At the very outset, let me eliminate every risk of perceptive mistakes: Kosovo and Metohija is a Serbian province that has always been, and is today, an integral part of the Republic of Serbia. That territory has never been part of any other State. It is the cradle of the Serbian State, one of the oldest European States, the birthplace of Serbian culture and civilization.

Besides the Serbs and Montenegrins, and besides the members of the Albanian national minority, members of other national minorities and ethnic communities - such as Muslims, numbering over 150,000; Romanies, numbering 150,000; Turks, Croats and others - have for centuries also lived in Kosovo and Metohija.

Under the constitution and laws, all of them are granted the same civil and human rights: to their language, culture, media and religion; to elect and to be elected; and to participate in genuine political processes, from self-rule to republican and federal parliaments. All these rights are based on the highest European standards, including the standards of the Organization for Security and Cooperation in Europe and the Council of Europe Framework Convention.

The members of the Albanian national minority are granted the same rights that are granted to other citizens. However, whereas all other citizens exercise their rights, a large part of the Albanian national minority boycott some of those rights - under pressure from and because of blackmail by their separatist representatives - and exercise others. For instance, they boycott municipal and local elections, the official census and political institutions, yet they are very active in exercising the right to private property, pensions and social benefits and the right to employment, passports, freedom of movement and private enterprise. The exercise of the right to information, for instance, is attested to by the fact that over 50 private dailies, weeklies and periodicals are printed in the Albanian language, the aggregate circulation of which amounts to 2.5 million copies.

The selective boycott of some, and the exercise of other, rights is not the result of the free will of the members of the Albanian national minority, most of whom are responsible, loyal and law-abiding citizens. It is the result of pressure and blackmail by some leaders of the political parties in Kosovo and Metohija whose public programme is secession from Serbia. Terrorist actions, the killing of Albanians loyal to Serbia, the assassination of public officials, attacks on public institutions and the ambushing of police officers such as took place on 28 [16] February 1998, when four policemen were killed, are designed to intimidate ethnic Albanians into closing ranks, increase tension, attract the attention of the international public and "substantiate" the requests for mediation and internationalization. The ultimate goal is the secession of this Serbian land from Serbia. Simply put, Serbia cannot and will not allow that to happen under any conditions.

I trust and believe that it is apparent that the problems in Kosovo and Metohija are rooted in a separatism which, at this very moment, is publicly advocated by the representatives of some political parties of the Albanian national minority. This underpins terrorism, which has so far claimed dozens of human lives. It is the right of every State to defend itself from this evil, to protect its territorial integrity, public peace and order and the safety of its citizens. This right is not denied anywhere in the world and it cannot be denied to Serbia and the Federal Republic of Yugoslavia.

Today's meeting of the Security Council and the adoption of a resolution are not acceptable to the Government of the Federal Republic of Yugoslavia, since questions that represent an internal matter for Serbia and the Federal Republic of Yugoslavia are at stake. We consider that this internal question cannot be the subject of deliberation in any international forum without the consent of the Government of the Federal Republic of Yugoslavia. Such consent has not been granted.

The pretext for this unprecedented action by the Security Council has been found in two anti-terrorist police actions in Kosovo and Metohija, the autonomous province of Serbia. The first was carried out on 28 February in self defence following the killing of four police officers in an ambush, and the second was carried out on 5 March against a terrorist stronghold.

There is not, nor has there been, any armed conflict in Kosovo and Metohija. Hence, there is no danger of a spillover, there is no threat to peace and security and there is no basis for invoking Chapter VII of the Charter of the United Nations.

There have been many much larger instances all over the world of not only police, but also military action against terrorists in which civilians have been frequent victims. Yet neither the Security Council nor any other international forum has ever seen fit to raise, in any way whatever, the responsibility of States that are defending themselves against terrorism and protecting their territorial integrity and sovereignty. The Council would be ill advised to do it this time. Were the Council to recognize the right of some States to fight terrorism and deny that right to others in one way or another, or were it even to threaten punitive measures, it would then formally legalize the practice of double standards. It would have catastrophic consequences for the struggle against terrorism in general, erode trust in the Security Council and the entire United Nations system and allow international relations to be governed by the right of might instead of by law and principle.

The positions taken by the Contact Group in London on 9 March 1998 and in Bonn on 25 March 1998 are tantamount to the pursuit of a policy of force and socalled gunboat diplomacy. Under the pressure of certain Powers, the Contact Group, by its policy, places itself above every Government and every principle. Those Powers dictate solutions to internal questions and decide who can and who cannot defend himself against terrorism and separatism. They even determine who must cooperate in the destruction of the integrity of the territory of one's own State. Sanctions are threatened, as well as military intervention, and the normal economic development and lives of millions of people are hampered - and all in the name of democracy and human rights. The Contact Group, by its policy, places itself over and above the Charter of the United Nations in an attempt to transform the Security Council, before the eyes of the world, into a body that merely executes decisions taken at some other place, and with a motivation that is different from the goals and objectives of the Charter.

It is with regret and deep concern that we note that, by their activities, representatives of some permanent members of the Security Council encourage the separatism of the leaders of the Albanian national minority in Kosovo and Metohija. They are currently causing enormous damage to Serbia and the Federal Republic of Yugoslavia. However, that policy will bring no good to their own countries either, or to Europe or the world. On the contrary, it is counterproductive and dangerous for the international legal system and for all the countries and peoples of the world at the threshold of the third millennium.

It is stated in the statements of the Contact Group and the resolution of the Security Council that the situation in Kosovo and Metohija threatens international peace and security in the region. This position is not based on facts, nor on law. It is designed to justify support for separatism and flagrant interference in the internal affairs of a sovereign country, a Member State of the United Nations. The arbitrary pressure on Serbia and [17] the Federal Republic of Yugoslavia is aimed at imposing a solution that is a direct threat to the territorial integrity of Serbia and the Federal Republic of Yugoslavia. A local anti-terrorist police action can never be qualified as a threat to international peace and security. The situation in Kosovo and Metohija is stable and does not threaten, nor can it threaten, in any way the peace and security of neighbouring countries or the region. There are no armed conflicts in Kosovo and Metohija.

It is therefore very clear that there is no basis for invoking Chapter VII of the United Nations Charter or for taking any measure by invoking any other principle or document.

The Contact Group is not authorized to create, by its statements, obligations, legal or factual, for the Security Council to establish the calendar of its meetings and decisions or to determine the content of those decisions. That would deal a serious blow to the dignity of the Security Council.

The real threat to regional peace and security is the overt or covert support that, under the influence of Albanian lobbies in some countries, certain circles - permanent members of the Security Council - render to secessionism and to the leaders of the political parties of the Albanian minority in Kosovo and Metohija. This is contrary to the principles of the Charter of the United Nations and the Final Act of the Conference on Security and Cooperation in Europe (OSCE), and contrary to the interests of peace and security in Southeast Europe. It causes great damage to the lasting interests of the members of the Albanian national minority themselves in Serbia and Yugoslavia, as well as in other countries of the region.

We recall that the Government of the Republic of Serbia has addressed a number of public and direct calls to the representatives of the political parties of the Albanian national minority for an unconditional, direct and genuine political dialogue. The representatives of all other minorities that have lived in Kosovo and Metohija for centuries - the Muslims, Romanies, Turks, Croats and others - requested to take part in the dialogue themselves, since questions relative to their rights as well have been raised. Those requests are legitimate and have been accepted. The members of those minorities have publicly condemned terrorism; their lasting desire is to live in Serbia - a State of their own - and to solve all questions relating to the realization of their rights within Serbia and by political means. A considerable number of influential Albanians in Kosovo and Metohija have also distanced themselves from separatism, condemned terrorism and displayed interest in seeking solutions through dialogue to all outstanding questions, as well as better living conditions in Serbia, alongside all other citizens.

The leaders of some political parties of the Albanian national minority are the only ones who have not heeded the invitation of the Government of the Republic of Serbia to unconditional dialogue. They continue to turn a deaf ear to the appeals of the international community to condemn terrorism publicly and to give up the idea of independence.

Consequently, who is responsible for separatism and terrorism in Kosovo and Metohija or for the procrastination and delay of the dialogue? Serbia, which, by its Constitution and laws, guarantees all rights to the members of all national minorities under the highest European standards - rights that are exercised by the members of 26 out of the total of 27 national minorities in its territory? Or is it the leaders of separatism who - by pressure, blackmail and even by recourse to terrorism - force the boycott of those rights?

Since the Republic of Serbia is deeply convinced that procrastination and the delay of the beginning of a direct political dialogue are unjustified and harmful and that they block the genuine political process in Kosovo and Metohija, the President of the Republic of Serbia, Milan Milutinovic, issued on 18 March 1998 the declaration on the political process in Kosovo and Metohija, calling on the leaders of the political parties of the Albanian national minority in Kosovo and Metohija to embark upon a political dialogue without delay or conditions. The President of the Federal Republic of Yugoslavia, Slobodan Milosevic, fully supported the declaration and designated his personal envoy to conduct dialogue with the representatives of the Albanian and other national minorities in Kosovo and Metohija.

By its declaration of 31 March 1998, the new Government of the Republic of Serbia further reaffirmed the initiative and its openness to a genuine and unconditional dialogue and renewed its invitation to the leaders of the Albanian political parties to dialogue, for it is clear that no other solution is available.

The agreement on the implementation of the Education Agreement is an important positive accomplishment. Besides, the Institute of Albanology in Pristina was officially opened yesterday by the representatives of the Government of the Republic of [18] Serbia and made available to its Albanian users. This is the only institution of its kind for the Albanian minority in South-East Europe, and it is unique in Europe in the context of the exercise of minority rights by any national minority.

Upholding its principled position that it is necessary to regularize Yugoslavia's full-fledged membership in the OSCE, the Federal Republic of Yugoslavia has expressed its readiness to receive, on a contractual basis, an OSCE mission of longer duration. We would like to trust, in the objectivity of this mission, for we believe that it could contribute to spreading the truth about the situation in Kosovo and Metohija. The Federal Republic of Yugoslavia is also ready to receive a personal representative of the OSCE Chairman-in-Office and of the European Community to conduct talks with the representatives of the Government on questions of cooperation and normalization of relations.

Considering that the limited action in the area of Drenica has ended and that the situation is stable, the special anti-terrorist unit, with its equipment and means, has been withdrawn to its permanent base outside the region. This has been affirmed also in the declaration of the new Government of the Republic of Serbia of 31 March 1998.

The official judicial authorities have opened an inquiry aimed at establishing facts relative to the allegations that the police exceeded their authority during the anti-terrorist actions.

Serbia and the Government of the Federal Republic of Yugoslavia are quite open to cooperation with the International Committee of the Red Cross (ICRC), which we consider the key humanitarian organization. This was borne out also by the letter of 24 March 1998 to the ICRC President from the Federal Minister for Foreign Affairs, Zivadin Jovanovic. Representatives of the ICRC and other humanitarian organizations operate freely in Kosovo and Metohija, which was confirmed also by the ICRC representative in the Federal Republic of Yugoslavia. On 15 March 1998 the Government of the Republic of Serbia also extended an invitation to Comelio Sommaruga, ICRC President, to send an ad hoc group of expert pathologists, composed of representatives of various countries, to Kosovo and Metohija to establish facts relative, in particular, to the allegations that civilians have been killed in the aforementioned anti-terrorist actions. Separate invitations have also been extended to a number of countries to send their independent experts, who, alongside the Yugoslav pathologists and judicial authorities, would carry out that task.

Official Yugoslav representatives have reaffirmed their readiness to cooperate with the United Nations High Commissioner for Human Rights, whose office in Belgrade carries out its activities on the entire territory of Yugoslavia undisturbed.

Terrorist actions and secessionist goals cannot be equated with the legitimate struggle against terrorism: the defence of a State, its sovereignty, its integrity and the safety of its citizens.

Serbia and the Federal Republic of Yugoslavia have nothing to hide in Kosovo and Metohija. Foreign diplomats and other representatives, and hundreds of foreign journalists and parliamentarians visit and travel up and down Yugoslavia and Serbia every day. Besides, the International Committee of the Red Cross and other international humanitarian organizations and governmental and non-governmental organizations operate in Kosovo and Metohija undisturbed. These are facts that cannot be denied.

Kosovo and Metohija is an integral part of Serbia, and every problem arising in that Serbian province is an internal matter. Serbia is firmly committed to an unconditional dialogue with the members of the Albanian minority and to the solution of all questions through political means in accordance with European standards.

As a signatory of the Helsinki Final Act and as a European country, the Federal Republic of Yugoslavia accepts all standards of the Organization for Security and Cooperation in Europe and of the Council of Europe relative to the rights of national minorities, and is open to full and constructive cooperation. However, questions of constitutional and State organization, relations between various levels of government and relations between government and self-rule belong to the internal jurisdiction of States. Such questions are internal matters for each sovereign State and hence for Serbia and the Federal Republic of Yugoslavia. Such questions brook no foreign intervention or internationalization. It is my firm belief that this position is in full conformity with the Charter of the United Nations.

The call of some countries for solutions to be sought outside Serbia - or, as they say, within the Federal Republic of Yugoslavia - constitutes a violation of the territorial integrity of Serbia, a State which has been in existence for more than 13 centuries, much longer than even the first ideas of "Yugoslavness". The United Nations must not allow itself to be a confederate of those who [19] loath the idea of one integrated Serbia as a republic of equal citizens. The Security Council should continue to uphold the noble principle that all countries, big or small, are equal. It should not harbour policies of force and double standards. [...]

Mr. Eitel (Germany): [...] In the Kosovo region of the Federal Republic of Yugoslavia, tension has been building up over several years. Repression of the Kosovar Albanian community and serious violations of human rights contributed to this, along with increasing doubts within that community about the success of the Kosovar Albanian leadership's course of non-violent opposition. Guerrilla attacks on police stations and the excessive use of force by Yugoslav security forces, resulting in at least 80 fatalities, were the latest steps in that escalation. My country is deeply concerned about this political state of affairs, as well as about the resulting humanitarian situation.

More than many other States, Germany is affected by this situation. Germany is the refuge of an estimated 300,000 ethnic Albanians, most of them from Kosovo, out of the total of an estimated 1.3 million persons from the former Yugoslavia currently living in Germany. When on 25 March, the Foreign Ministers of the Contact Group met in Bonn to discuss the situation in Kosovo, some 40,000 Kosovar Albanians also met in Bonn - for a peaceful demonstration. [...]

The explosive situation in the Kosovo region constitutes a clear threat to international peace and security. The genesis of the war in Bosnia and Herzegovina, which in the beginning was considered by some to be an internal matter, is still very much alive in our memories.

The outside world cannot simply stand by and watch a new, potentially even more devastating conflict develop in the region. [...]

[A statement by the representative of Italy has been omitted.]

[21] **Mr. Tanç** (Turkey): [...] Turkey is gravely concerned at the situation in Kosovo and the wider implications it may have for peace, security and stability in the region and beyond. Unless appropriate measures are taken in time, the conflict in Kosovo will intensify and may drag the Balkans into serious turmoil. The tragic consequences of the international community's not having shown a sufficient and timely response to such a crisis were witnessed in Bosnia and Herzegovina.

The dangers inherent in the situation in Kosovo have been visible since at least 1989, when the acquired rights of autonomy and self-administration of the people of Kosovo were suddenly abrogated. Moreover, the economic hardships and deprivation faced by the people of Kosovo following the disintegration of the Socialist Federal Republic of Yugoslavia put unbearable strain on their endurance. The restrictions on the right of education also added fuel to the feeling of deep resentment, as, over the years, children have been deprived of adequate education.

Consequently, as a reaction, the desire for independence in Kosovo has grown. And the new Federal Republic of Yugoslavia (Serbia and Montenegro), instead of reinstating the rights of the people of Kosovo, has resorted to repression and agitation. The reaction of the Kosovar Albanians to all this has reached the point of explosion.

The rights taken away from the people of Kosovo should be restored to them urgently. Unless an agreed solution is found, the explosion in Kosovo may shake all the neighbouring countries, including all the Balkan countries, and lead to a wider international crisis.

The democratic and pluralistic nature of Kosovo is of the utmost importance. The presence of a Turkish community in Kosovo, the large number of Turkish citizens of Balkan origin and Turkey's geographic location will further explain our close attention to this crisis. Turkey is keenly interested in the finding of a satisfactory solution to the plight of the people of Kosovo and in the protection of their acquired and human rights.

In this context, since tensions escalated in the Kosovo region and violence broke out on 28 February, [22] resulting in loss of life, Turkey has been in contact with many concerned parties and with the Federal Republic of Yugoslavia authorities with a view to seeing an end to the violence and the commencement of a political process. The Turkish Minister for Foreign Affairs visited Belgrade on 7 and 8 March. We participated in the adoption of the declaration of the Ministers for Foreign Affairs of countries of South-Eastern Europe, which set out the elements of a political process. We support the efforts of the Contact Group, the Organization for Security and Cooperation in Europe (OSCE) and the Organization of the Islamic Conference (OIC).

My Government has formulated the following proposals towards finding a concrete solution to the Kosovo problem.

A solution to the dispute must be found through comprehensive dialogue between the parties and within the framework of the territorial integrity of the Federal Republic of Yugoslavia (Serbia and Montenegro). Any resort to acts of terrorism or violence must be avoided.

It should be possible for a third party, which will be decided on by the two sides, to assume a function that would facilitate reaching a settlement.

The dialogue aimed at reinstating all the rights of all the ethnic minorities in Kosovo should begin immediately. These minorities, including the Turkish community, should be represented in the talks concerning the future of Kosovo. The solution to be found should guarantee the rights of all the ethnic minority groups, together with the Albanian majority.

Effective measures against the possibility of violence and repression in Kosovo should be taken with the participation of the international community, which should also contribute to meeting the urgent economic and humanitarian needs of the people of Kosovo and displaced persons.

The gravity of the situation is of such dimensions as to warrant the urgent action taken by the Security Council. We hope that the determined efforts of the international community will not only help resolve this problem through peaceful means but also set a lasting precedent both for the region and beyond.

[Statements by the representative of Pakistan, Albania, Poland, Hungary and Croatia have been omitted.]

[27] **Mr. Zacharakis** (Greece): [...] My country firmly believes that a solution in Kosovo must be sought only through peaceful means, namely through dialogue between the Government in Belgrade and the Kosovar Albanian leadership. Terrorism must be wholly condemned and so must the excessive use of force insofar as it stifles the free exercise of human rights.

On the other hand, Greece particularly insists upon the need to safeguard the inviolability of existing international borders, which is a fundamental and sine qua non condition for peace and stability in the Balkans. In this respect, Greece fully supports the sovereignty and territorial integrity of the Federal Republic of Yugoslavia and categorically rejects any secessionist claims.

Finally, I wish to express my country's support for the resolution adopted by the Council today, which in our view is balanced and should be implemented by all parties concerned. But I would also like to point out that any measures against the Federal Republic of Yugoslavia should also take into account the stability of south-eastern Europe and should not unduly harm States in the region, which were particularly hit by the negative consequences of the sanctions regime in the years 1992 through 1996.

[...]

Mr. Sacirbey (Bosnia and Herzegovina): [...] The development of the peace process in Bosnia and Herzegovina, both in spirit and substance, cannot help but be impacted by the situation in Kosovo and our neighbour in general, the Federal Republic of Yugoslavia (Serbia and Montenegro). Many formulate that the disintegration of the former Yugoslavia started with the unilateral repudiation of Kosovo's autonomous status within the ex-Yugoslavia and that the circle will be completed only with the just and stable resolution of this situation. The commitment of the Stabilization Force, the Office of the High Representative and other international factors, including the United Nations, have given the peace process in Bosnia and Herzegovina a more stable foundation, minimizing the risk of spill-over.

Nonetheless, the longer-term developments and solutions for Kosovo can only have a substantial impact [28] on peace, stability and the development of democracy, human rights and minority and national rights in the region as a whole. In this context, my delegation believes that it is imperative that the following fundamentals be incorporated into any process designed to produce immediate and longer-term solutions.

First, we welcome the Security Council's role, as well as that of other relevant international factors, in this process, and emphasize the determinative importance of the Security Council's remaining seized of the matter. The situation in Kosovo does have more than a passing impact upon stability and peace in the region and international security as a whole.

Second, in the same vein, the authority and active role of the International Criminal Tribunal for the Former Yugoslavia is unquestionable and necessary in this situation, despite the prolonged attempt of certain parties to negate its jurisdiction. Bosnia and Herzegovina itself cannot morally, politically or legally remain silent; as our former colleague, Secretary of State Madeleine Albright, so appropriately put it, the Belgrade authorities will not be allowed to do in Kosovo with what they can no longer get away with in Bosnia and Herzegovina. "Ethnic cleansing" is intolerable for all, but those of us who have been victims and overcome must be especially clear and add our voices to the vigilant chorus of "Never Again". We are not dealing with ethnic madness, but with the political manipulation of differences for crude, selfish power.

Third, Bosnia and Herzegovina stresses the territorial integrity and sovereignty of all the States in the region, without any prejudice to the eventual solution.

Fourth, at the same time we must emphasize that the basis for solution, not only in Kosovo, but in Sandjak and Vojvodina, lies with full respect for the democratic, human, national and minority rights of all the citizens of the Federal Republic of Yugoslavia (Serbia and Montenegro).

Fifth, the role of the Federal Republic of Yugoslavia (Serbia and Montenegro) in the situation in Bosnia and Herzegovina has been frequently addressed before this body. I do not need to remind the Council of the context of those references. However, we must emphasize that the health of our neighbour also reflects upon our own.

Sixth, let me draw the Council's attention to paragraphs 8, 9, 10 and 15 of the resolution before us. Paragraph 15 in particular addresses the neighbours of the Federal Republic of Yugoslavia (Serbia and Montenegro). Of course, that means us. Again, the role of the Federal Republic of Yugoslavia (Serbia and Montenegro) reflected a military relationship in its dealings with our country in the past. We would like to stress the importance of the arms-control arrangements negotiated under the authority of the Organization for Security and Cooperation in Europe, both within the region and in our country. Here, the heightened vigilance of monitors can be helpful in assuring that new abuses are not invented and old abuses not repeated. Arms monitors ensuring compliance and deterring cross-border transfers should receive our most active support. [...]

Mr. Elaraby (Egypt) *(interpretation from Arabic)*: Today, the Security Council adopted a resolution reimposing an international embargo on the export of arms to the Federal Republic of Yugoslavia. There is no doubt that this is a step, though it may be regarded as a step backward with regard to the developments in the area in general, yet it is a realistic reflection of the recent deterioration of the situation in Kosovo.

Egypt considers the content of today's resolution as a preventive message, which we hope that the concerned parties will fully understand in a way that will prevent the situation in the area from further deterioration and protect the lives of the innocent Albanian civilians in the region. This is especially so since the resolution adopted today clearly condemns the excessive use of force by the Serbian police against the civilians of Kosovo and clearly [29] defines the steps that the Government of the Federal Republic of Yugoslavia should take in order to open the way for the Security Council to review the sanctions imposed on it today.

Our delegation has noted that the Security Council candidly refers to the fact that this resolution has been adopted under the provisions of Chapter VII of the Charter without a prior reference to a determination by the Security Council that there exists a threat to international peace and security as required by the provisions of Article 39 of the Charter. Of course, it may be said that the Council is the master of its own procedures, and this is correct with regard to procedures. However, in principle, the constitutional requirements in the Charter should in general be scrupulously followed and respected. The delegation of Egypt would like to record this observation with regard to the future work of the Council.

At the same time, Egypt supports the call contained in the resolution for the authorities in Belgrade and the leadership of the Kosovar Albanian communityand to enter urgently without preconditions into a serious dialogue in order to reach a political settlement of the situation in Kosovo. Such a settlement should take into consideration the interests and the aspirations of the Albanian community, which accounts for 90 per cent of the population of the region, which has long had a special status.

The situation in Kosovo represents a source of grave concern to public opinion the world over. For this reason, the Foreign Ministers of the Organization of the Islamic Conference adopted, at their latest meeting in Qatar in March, a resolution in which they condemned the wideranging acts of suppression, the discriminatory measures and the human rights violations against the Albanian inhabitants. They also called on the international community to take the necessary steps to immediately end these violations and to set up democratic institutions in Kosovo. The adoption by the Council today of this resolution is a step towards the achievement of what the Foreign Ministers of the Organization of the Islamic Conference called for two weeks ago.

In conclusion, my delegation hopes that the parties concerned would exercise their authority responsibly through the desired dialogue in order to reach a just solution that would restore stability, security and peace to the region.

[A statement by the representative of Ukraine has been omitted.

The President invited the representative of Iran to participate, without vote, in the discussion in accordance with rule 37 of the Council's provisional rules of procedure.]

[30] **Mr. Nejad Hosseinian** (Islamic Republic of Iran): [...] The situation in Kosovo has caused considerable international outrage because of the excessive use of force by Serbian police against the ethnic Albanians in Kosovo, which has resulted in considerable loss of life and material damage. This international outrage finds further grounds and is duly increased because it is reminder of an unholy and dark experience in Bosnia that has yet to be fully resolved. The experience of Bosnia cannot and should not be allowed to be repeated.

The Islamic Republic of Iran has repeatedly raised deep concern about the deteriorating situation in Kosovo and condemned the suppression of and the use of force against the Kosovar Albanians by Serbian Special Police, which has led to the death of many civilians, including women and children. The use of force and violence must be rejected, and the authorities in Belgrade should take the necessary steps so that the rights of the Kosovar Albanian community are fully guaranteed. Furthermore, the Government of the Federal Republic of Yugoslavia should be persuaded that as far as the international community is concerned, the solution to the problem can be found only in a genuine and serious process of political negotiations with the ethnic minority in Kosovo.

The Islamic Republic of Iran believes that the solution to the problem in Kosovo lies in respecting the territorial integrity of the Federal Republic of Yugoslavia on the one hand, and finding an agreed formula for the political future of the Kosovar Albanian community through political dialogue on the other.

The twenty-fifth ministerial meeting of the Organization of the Islamic Conference, held in Qatar from 15 to 17 March 1998, expressed deep concern about the violation of the political and human rights of the Kosovar Albanian community, which constitutes about 90 per cent of the entire population in Kosovo. The meeting condemned the use of force by Serbian police against the Albanian minority and called for the withdrawal of military forces from Kosovo.

The Islamic Republic of Iran supports the resolution just adopted in the context of the international efforts to curb further bloodshed in Kosovo and bring a political solution to the conflict. We call upon both sides to exercise restraint and engage in serious political negotiations without preconditions on the political status of Kosovo. [...]

67. FRY, Letter by the President of the FRY to the Presidents of the Republic of Serbia, of the Serbian Government and of the Assembly of Serbia, on the Referendum whether or not Foreign Representatives Should be Involved in Dealing with the Problem of Kosovo, 2 April 1998

It is public knowledge that we have rejected the participation of foreign representatives in dealing with the internal questions of our country, particularly in the solving of the problem in Kosovo and Metohija which is an internal issue for Serbia.

I believe that our stance is of a crucial significance for the preservation of our country's sovereignty and territorial integrity. Our country is running the risk of being again subjected on this account to all kinds of pressure. The stance taken to our firm attitude that as a sovereign state we should deal with our own problems is highly negative and aggressive on the part of those who pretend to dictate to the whole world how they should live, and even more than that, how they should think.

We have recently been given to understand that they have nothing against our people as such, that they even love our people and regret that our people should be subjected to pressures on account of the stand taken by their leadership. I think we cannot accept such a cynicism which serves as a excuse for the armtwisting in the name of democracy. I believe that throughout the time of crisis in what was former Yugoslavia we conducted a national policy and not a personal or even party policy. In this matter, too, our rejection of involvement of a foreign factor in what is an internal affair of the Republic of Serbia - the problem of Kosovo and Metohija, is part of a national policy and not personal or party policy. Whether or not this is true, will be answered by our citizens themselves.

I, therefore, suggest that you, in accordance with the Constitution and laws of Serbia, should start the procedure for the organizing of a referendum that would answer the question: 'Do you agree to the participation by foreign representatives in solving the problem of Kosovo and Metohija?

I wish to point out that at the same time an intensive work should be carried on to successfully resolve the problems bedevilling Kosovo and Metohija. This calls for an urgent start of a dialogue and steps leading to an equitable affirmation of interests of all those who live in Kosovo and Metohija.

68. Council of Europe, Parliamentary Assembly, Recommendation 1368 (1998), Latest Developments in the FRY and the Situation in Kosovo, 22 April 1998

[Text adopted by the Assembly on 22 April 1998 (13th Sitting).]

1. The latest political developments in the Federal Republic of Yugoslavia - and in particular the situation in Kosovo - represent a threat to the stability of the country and of the Balkan region as a whole.

2. The Assembly reiterates its position expressed in Recommendation 1360 (1998) on the crisis in Kosovo and in Resolution 1146 (1998) on recent developments in the Federal Republic of Yugoslavia and their implications for the Balkan region.

3. The Assembly is concerned about the growing influence of political extremists in the Federal Republic of Yugoslavia, as demonstrated by the participation of the Serb Radical Party of Mr Seselj in the new Serbian Government.

4. The continuing tensions in Montenegro should be resolved through political dialogue. The parliamentary elections in Montenegro, scheduled for 31 May 1998, will be an important indicator of respect for democratic standards.

5. The Assembly deplores the growing repression by the Yugoslav authorities of media that are trying objectively to report on the situation in Kosovo, namely the violence used by the police against the independent local media and foreign journalists covering events in Kosovo and the threats of legal prosecution.

6. The Assembly reaffirms its position that, without pre-judging the outcome of the negotiations, a long-term solution to the crisis in Kosovo can only be found on the basis of a mutually agreed solution. The Assembly believes that the solution could be greater autonomy for Kosovo, within a democratically reformed Federal Republic of Yugoslavia. Such autonomy should guarantee respect for the rights of all ethnic groups in Kosovo. The Assembly repeats its call for an immediate start to unconditional negotiations.

7. It welcomes the beginning of the implementation in Kosovo of the 1996 education agreement, which should contribute to a more favourable political climate for any future talks.

8. The Assembly welcomes the constitution of the delegation of the Serbian Government, which includes a special envoy of President Milosevic, for talks with representatives of the Kosovo Albanian community. The delegation should be authorised to discuss solutions going beyond the existing Serbian Constitution. The international community should be represented at these talks.

9. The Assembly also welcomes the constitution of a negotiating team representing the Kosovo Albanian community. It should agree to open talks with the Belgrade authorities forthwith.

10. The Assembly reiterates its offer to assist in contacts between the Yugoslav authorities and representatives of the Kosovo Albanian community. The Council of Europe has considerable expertise in the relevant areas, such as human rights, minority rights, education and the media, which it could put at the disposal of the parties.

11. The Assembly considers that the referendum decided by the Serbian Parliament, following a proposal by President Milosevic, on the acceptability of foreign mediation does not contribute to a solution to the Kosovo crisis. The Yugoslav authorities should comply with the requests of the international community, including the mission of Mr Felipe González on behalf of the OSCE and the European Union.

12. The Assembly fully endorses Resolution 1160 of the United Nations Security Council on the crisis in Kosovo, adopted on 31 March 1998. In the light of the request by the Federal Republic of Yugoslavia for membership of the Council of Europe, the Council of Europe should be included in consultations between the United Nations, the Contact Group, the OSCE and the European Union.

13. The Assembly takes note of the Yugoslav Government's request for Council of Europe membership of 18 March 1998. However, this request can only be considered if the Federal Republic of Yugoslavia respects the principles and values on which the Council of Europe is based, and complies with the requests of the international community, notably with regard to Kosovo.

14. The Assembly calls on the authorities of the Federal Republic of Yugoslavia to:

i. empower the delegation for talks with the Albanian Kosovo community to discuss all options for the autonomy of Kosovo within the Federal Republic of Yugoslavia;

ii. agree to the presence of a foreign representative or representatives to facilitate talks;

iii. comply with other requests of the international community concerning Kosovo and the democratic reforms in the country, as contained in the relevant documents of the United Nations, the OSCE, the European Union, the Contact Group and the Council of Europe.

15. The Assembly calls on the leadership of the Kosovo Albanians:

i. to condemn and do their utmost to prevent the use of violence and arms-trafficking;

ii. to enter into talks with the delegation of the Serbian Government and the special envoy of President Milosevic.

16. The Assembly recommends that the Committee of Ministers:

i. continue to deal with the situation in Kosovo as a matter of priority within the framework of its political dialogue;

ii. verify, in particular, the further implementation of the education agreement regarding Kosovo;

iii. examine, in close co-ordination with the United Nations, the OSCE, the European Union and the Contact Group, ways in which the Council of Europe could facilitate contacts and assist in talks between the Yugoslav authorities and the Kosovo Albanian community;

iv. call on both sides to ensure implementation of any agreement reached;

v. decide on the follow-up to be given to the Yugoslav request for Council of Europe membership in the light of progress made by the Federal Republic of Yugoslavia authorities in complying with the requests by the international community, notably with regard to Kosovo.

17. The Assembly resolves to remain actively seized on the issue and to send a delegation to visit Belgrade, Pristina and Podgorica as soon as possible.

69. EU, 2085th Council Meeting, General Affairs, PRES/98/109, Luxembourg, 27 April 1998

[Parts not referring to the FRY have been omitted.]

[...]

Western Balkans - Conclusions
KOSOVO

The Council expressed its deep concern at the mounting violence in Kosovo and called on both parties to act with restraint. It reaffirmed its insistence that the FRY and Serbian security forces conform to internationally accepted standards. It also reiterated its condemnation of all terrorist acts and called on those outside the FRY who are providing support for terrorist activity in Kosovo to cease doing so immediately.

The Council underlined the fundamental importance of an urgent start to a meaningful dialogue without preconditions between the parties if further bloodshed is to be avoided. It expressed its disappointment that time had passed without material progress in this respect, but welcomed indications that both sides were now trying to address the need to settle the modalities for substantive discussions. The Council considered that the assistance by the international community in the process would be necessary to establish a climate of confidence between the parties. It welcomed the intention of Mr. Gonzalez to arrange an early visit to Belgrade, taking up his mission on behalf of the EU and the OSCE jointly.

The Council reiterated its support for the territorial integrity of the FRY. It emphasised in this context the particular responsibility that President Milosevic has to promote a peaceful settlement to the problems of Kosovo. It regretted that he had so far declined to shoulder fully this responsibility and agreed that additional measures against Belgrade would be taken in the case of continued failure to meet the international community's requirements. In this context, it noted the contingency technical work which was being taken forward by the Council instances on such measures. The Council recalled that if, on the other hand, the FRY Government were to show a real willingness to cooperate with the international community and engage in meaningful dialogue, the European Union would be prepared to consider positively the FRY's participation in the mechanisms of European cooperation.

The Council underlined the importance of a cohesive international approach to this crisis. It welcomed the recent Troika visit at senior official level to Bulgaria, Romania and Hungary and will continue to cooperate closely with the countries in the region, not least, where appropriate, on the question of border security.

MONTENEGRO

The Council welcomed the continuing commitment shown by President Djukanovic to political and economic reforms in Montenegro and agreed that the EU should send a clear and immediate signal of its support for the reform process. It therefore agreed to allocate an initial amount of ECU 3 million in financial assistance to the Montenegrin government to help it meet outstanding social welfare payments, and instructed the appropriate Council bodies to finalise urgently the necessary Joint Action. It asked the Commission to ensure that the funds are disbursed with the minimum of delay.

The Council endorsed the proposed mission by the Troika at senior official level to Montenegro on 5 May in order to assess further how the EU might assist the process of democratic reform. In particular it saw this visit as a good chance to identify opportunities for Community assistance such as in the field of independent media.

CROATIA

[...]

Western Balkans: Conditionality
CONCLUSIONS (ADOPTED WITHOUT DEBATE)

1. The Council discussed the performance of Albania, Bosnia, Croatia, FRY and the former Yugoslav Republic of Macedonia in meeting the criteria, set out in its 29 April 1997 conclusions, for developing EC relations (autonomous trade measures, PHARE and contractual relations) with the countries in question. The Council's assessment of each country follows.

2. The Council declared itself in broad agreement with the conclusions suggested by the Commission on this subject, namely, that the present level of relations with the countries covered by the Regional Approach should continue. The Council remained keen to develop relations with the countries concerned, but the speed of the development of the relationship depended upon them. If they moved quickly to fulfil the necessary (and clearly stated) criteria, then there could be a corresponding deepening of ties with the EC. But any country which showed itself to be moving backwards with respect to the criteria, would similarly jeopardise its existing level of relationship with the EC. The onus, therefore, lay with each of the states to demonstrate that it was fitted to maintain and move forward in its relations with Europe. The Council recalled that its next review would take place in October 1998: it hoped that by then further progress would be possible.

3. The Presidency and the Commission will ensure that this assessment is brought to the attention of the countries concerned.

BOSNIA AND HERZEGOVINA

[...]

FEDERAL REPUBLIC OF YUGOSLAVIA

The Council considered the FRY's performance as a whole, given the nature of the instruments covered by the regional approach, which can only apply to states. It will examine other means of responding appropriately to progress made in an individual constituent republic.

The Council remains gravely concerned about the situation in Kosovo, as made clear by its recent statements and acts (eg 19 March Common Position). No progress has been made towards granting Kosovo a large degree of autonomy within the borders of the FRY. The position of the authorities in Belgrade and the Kosovar Albanians continue to fall short of satisfying the demands of the EU and the international community. Progress on the Education Agreement is a first step, but there is an urgent need for a dialogue without preconditions to begin.

On internal democracy, the recommendations set out in the Gonzalez report remain largely unfulfilled in Serbia. In Montenegro, the OSCE judged the October 1997 Presidential election to reflect the will of the voters, and since his inauguration, President Djukanovic has provided evidence of a credible commitment to democratic reforms.

Little progress has been made in the FRY on market economy reform. Some steps have been taken in trade liberalisation (eg reduction of customs duties) and Serbia has passed a privatisation law (although no company has yet been privatised under it).

FRY attitude to Dayton/Paris has been mixed. There has been no change to the negative position of the FRY authorities on cooperation with the ICTY, although President Djukanovic has stated Montenegro's commitment to implement all FRY's obligations under Dayton/Paris including on the ICTY. The FRY still has to make its agreement on special relations with the RS compatible with Dayton/Paris. The FRY has, however, played a constructive role in developments in the RS, including the formation of the new government.

On regional cooperation, there had been some improvement in relations with neighbouring countries such as Albania and the former Yugoslav Republic of Macedonia. Normalisation of relations with Croatia has come nearer, although currently further progress appears blocked and relations with all the ex-Yugoslav republics remain hampered by lack of progress on the succession issue.

CONCLUSION

The current situation allows no progress in relations with the EC. The Council wishes to see development of relations with the FRY, once the conditions established by the Council on 29 April 1997 are met. Progress in advancing the process of dialogue on Kosovo, with a view to reaching a satisfactory solution to the current crisis, and in addressing grave problems of internal democracy should be undertaken as a matter of priority. [...]

70. EC Council Regulation No 926/98 Concerning the Reduction of Certain Economic Relations with the FRY, 27 April 1998[1]

The Council of the European Union,

Having regard to the Treaty establishing the European Community, and in particular Articles 73g and 228a thereof,

Having regard to Common Position 98/240/CFSP of 19 March 1998 defined by the Council on the basis of Article J.2 of the Treaty on European Union on restrictive measures against the Federal Republic of Yugoslavia[2],

Having regard to the proposal from the Commission,

Whereas the said Common Position 98/240/CFSP provides for restrictive measures against the Federal Republic of Yugoslavia, including action by the Community to reduce certain economic relations;

Whereas certain of these measures fall within the scope of the Treaty establishing the European Community;

Whereas, therefore, and notably with a view to avoiding distortion of competition, Community legislation is necessary for the implementation of these measures, as far as the territory of the Community is concerned; whereas such territory is deemed to encompass, for the purposes of this Regulation, all the territories of the Member States to which the Treaty establishing the European Community is applicable, under the conditions laid down in that Treaty;

Whereas a procedure should be provided to amend, if necessary, the list of equipment which might be used for internal repression or terrorism;

Whereas there is a need for the Commission and the Member States to inform each other of the measures taken under this Regulation and of other relevant information at their disposal in connection with this Regulation, without prejudice to existing obligations with regard to certain items concerned,

has adopted this Regulation:

Article 1

The supply or sale, directly or indirectly, to the Federal Republic of Yugoslavia of equipment which might be used for internal repression or terrorism such as that set out in the Annex hereto shall be prohibited, except under the conditions laid down therein. The Annex shall not include items specially designed or modified for military use already subject to the arms embargo established on the basis of Common Positions 96/184/CFSP[3] and 98/240/CFSP.

Article 2

As laid down in Article 3 of Common Position 98/240/CFSP, the following shall be prohibited:

(a) the provision and/or use of government and/or other official financial support, insurance and/or guarantees in respect of new export credit for trade with or investment in the Republic of Serbia or in relation to the renewal or extension of existing export credit, if the execution of the contract or transaction for which the export credit has been provided has not yet been started;

(b) the provision or use of government and/or other official financing for privatisations in the Republic of Serbia in respect of which no legally binding commitments have been entered into so far.

Article 3

The participation, knowingly and intentionally, in related activities the object or effect of which is, directly or indirectly, to promote the transactions or activities referred to in Articles 1 and 2 shall also be prohibited.

Article 4

The Council shall adopt by qualified majority amendments to the list set out in the Annex on the basis of a proposal from the Commission in conformity with Article 1.

Article 5

Each Member State shall determine the sanctions to be imposed where the provisions of this Regulation are infringed.

Article 6

The Commission and the Member States shall, insofar as they are not otherwise obliged to do so, inform each other of the measures taken under this Regulation and supply each other with other relevant information at their disposal in connection with this Regulation, such as breaches and enforcement problems, judgments handed down by national courts or decisions of relevant international fora.

Article 7

This Regulation shall apply:

- within the territory of the Community including its airspace,

- on board any aircraft or any vessel under the jurisdiction of a Member State,

- to any person elsewhere who is a national of a Member State,

- to any body which is incorporated or constituted under the law of a Member State.

Article 8

This Regulation shall enter into force on the day of its publication in the Official Journal of the European Communities.

This Regulation shall be binding in its entirety and directly applicable in all Member States.

Done at Luxembourg, 27 April 1998. For the Council: The President R. Cook

[The Annex: Equipment for Internal Repression or Terrorism, envisaged by Article 1 has been omitted.]

71. Contact Group, Statement, Rome, 29 April 1998

1. The Contact Group met in Rome on April 29 to decide on next steps regarding the increasingly dangerous situation in Kosovo, taking into account the report of the OSCE Troika on developments since the Bonn Contact Group Ministerial. They considered the report an important and balanced contribution to the assessment of the situation. The Contact Group believes that the current situation is untenable. The risk of an escalating conflict requires immediate action.

2. All members of the Contact Group are firmly opposed to independence for Kosovo and to a continuation of the unacceptable status quo. Immediate steps by the parties to reduce tension and to begin an unconditional dialogue are indispensable, and the only way to reverse the deterioration in the situation and bring about a political solution.

3. The Contact Group condemns the increase in violence in recent days in Kosovo, in particular the excessive use of force by the Yugoslav Army, and the proliferation of arms in the territory. The Contact Group rejects absolutely terrorism as a means of bringing about political change as well as all other violence to suppress political dissent. The Contact Group calls on political leaders in the FRY and in the countries of the region to exercise maximum restraint, full respect for human rights, to prevent the introduction of arms and of armed groups from outside, and to condemn terrorism. It also calls on the countries of the region to confirm the respect for territorial integrity and for the inviolability of internationally recognised borders.

4. The Contact Group is not seeking to impose any particular outcome for the resolution of the differences between Belgrade and Kosovo Albanian leadership. It is for the parties themselves to determine a solution to the political status of Kosovo through negotiations. The Contact Group notes that representatives of Belgrade and Pristina have

---

[1] OJ L 130, 01/05/1998 p. 0001 - 0004, 398R0926
[2] OJ L 95, 27/03/1998, p. 1.
[3] OJ L 58, 07/03/1996, p. 1.

recently stated their general willingness to open unconditional dialogue. But the two sides have yet to agree with full authority on modalities for talks, particularly on the issue of international participation.

5. The Contact Group regards an appropriate international involvement as an essential factor to establish confidence between the parties and to facilitate talks.

6. To begin the urgent process of dialogue, the Contact Group recommends, and urges both Belgrade and Kosovo Albanian leadership to adopt, a framework for dialogue and a stabilisation package:

a. The framework should be based on fundamental principles that the parties must accept, such as rejection of violence for achieving political goals, no preconditions, mutual respect, accordance with standards and principles of the OSCE and of the UN Charter, mutually agreed modalities, and protection of all individuals and ethnic groups. There should be mutual assurances, which the Contact Group itself will support, that the parties will not abandon nor seek to undermine an agreement once it is reached. The framework for dialogue must be formally endorsed by the top leadership in Belgrade and the leadership of the Kosovo Albanians. The respective leaders must take political responsibility for initiating good-faith talks. The framework must provide for international involvement in facilitating substantive negotiations.

b. The stabilisation package must include, as the minimum:

Cessation of repression by the Authorities in Belgrade, as specified in UNSCR 1160, and a strong condemnation of terrorism by the Kosovo Albanian leadership.

Reopening of the OSCE missions in the FRY, including Kosovo.

Concrete inter-communal confidence building measures, including implementation of the education agreement according to the agreed timetable. The Contact Group appreciates and encourages the work of Sant'Egidio Community in this field.

7. The Contact Group attaches the highest priority to the immediate launching of the Gonzalez mission, which is essential for substantial progress in the relationship between FRY and the international community. This mission is also meant to reduce tension, restore confidence and improve general prospects for dialogue. The top leadership in Belgrade should therefore immediately invite the Gonzalez mission to start its work. The Contact Group fully supports the OSCE Chairman-in-Office in his efforts to facilitate this mission.

8. If the leadership in Belgrade agrees to the framework for dialogue, the stabilisation measures listed in para. 6 are implemented, the Gonzalez mission is launched, and substantive talks begin, the Contact Group will promote a clear and achievable path towards Belgrade's full integration in the international community, including participation in the OSCE. We want the FRY to reap the benefits of membership in international financial and political institutions.

9. Crucial requirements set out in the Contact Group's statements of 9 and 25 March have not yet been met. We have therefore decided to take action to put into effect a freeze on the funds held abroad by the FRY and Serbian Governments. If Belgrade takes the steps in paragraph six to bring about negotiations, we will immediately reverse this decision. We have also decided that if dialogue is blocked because of Belgrade's non-compliance we will, by the 9th of May, take action to stop new investment in Serbia. The Russian Federation does not associate itself with these measures.

10. If unresolved, the situation in Kosovo threatens to spill over to other parts of the region. The Contact Group attaches high priority to supporting the security interests of the neighbouring States and to ensuring security of borders. It is of particular importance that developments in Kosovo should not disrupt progress in implementing the Dayton/Paris peace agreement in Bosnia, to which the Government in Belgrade is committed. The Contact Group will contribute to the strict implementation of Res. 1160, working also with the UN and other relevant international fora.

11. The next meeting of the Contact Group will take place in Paris in May.

72. EU, Common Position Defined by the Council on the Basis of Article J.2 of the EU Treaty Concerning the Freezing of Funds Held Abroad by the FRY and Serbian Governments, 98/326/CFSP, 7 May 1998 [1]

The Council of the European Union,

Having regard to the Treaty on European Union, and in particular Article J.2 thereof,

Whereas on 19 March 1998 the Council adopted Common Position 98/240/CFSP[2] on restrictive measures against the FRY;

Whereas further measures, and in particular the freezing of funds, were contemplated in Common Position 98/240/CFSP, should the conditions set out therein not be met and repression continue in Kosovo; whereas those conditions have not been met and therefore a further reduction of financial relations with the FRY should be foreseen;

Whereas, the restrictive measures set out in Article 1 will be reconsidered immediately if the FRY and Serbian Governments move to adopt a framework for dialogue and a stabilisation package;

Whereas the European Union will move to further restrictive measures, and specifically to take action to stop new investment in Serbia, if by 9 May 1998 dialogue between the parties is blocked because of the FRY and Serbian Government's non-compliance,

Has defined this common position:

Article 1

Funds held abroad by the Federal Republic of Yugoslavia and Serbian Governments will be frozen.

Article 2

This common position shall take effect from the date of its adoption.

Article 3

This common position shall be reviewed not later than six months after its adoption.

Article 4

This common position shall be published in the Official Journal.

Done at Brussels, 7 May 1998. For the Council, The President, M. Beckett

73. WEU, Ministerial Council, Rhodes Declaration, Rhodes, 12 May 1998

[Parts not pertinent to the situation in Kosovo have been omitted.]
[...]

V. Kosovo and Regional Stability

25. Ministers held an extensive exchange of views on the situation in Kosovo. They expressed their strong concern about the increasing violence and growing polarisation in Kosovo. They condemned the excessive use of force by FRY and Serbian security forces and insisted that these forces should conform with internationally accepted standards, whilst condemning all terrorist acts, calling on those who are providing support for terrorist activity in Kosovo to cease immediately. They reiterated their support for the territorial integrity of the FRY, whilst underlining that the status quo in Kosovo was unacceptable. They agreed that the crisis in Kosovo constituted a risk to the stability of the surrounding region. They insisted that immediate steps by the parties to reduce tension and to begin an unconditional dialogue are indispensable. Ministers expressed their readiness to promote a clear and achievable path towards Belgrade's full integration in the international community, should Belgrade take the steps needed to launch substantive talks on Kosovo's political status. They also expressed their support for the efforts of the international community, including the United Nations, the OSCE, the G8, the Contact Group and countries of

---

[1] OJ L 143, 14/05/1998 p. 0001 - 0002, 498X0326.
[2] OJ L 95, 27/03/1998, p. 1.

the region; and welcomed the recent declarations of the EU General Affairs Council, North Atlantic Council and of the Ministers of Foreign Affairs of countries of South-Eastern Europe. They deeply regretted that President Milosevic had, nonetheless, so far failed to create the conditions for a meaningful dialogue without preconditions. They noted that insufficient action by Belgrade could only lead to the deepening isolation of the FRY.

26. Ministers considered that WEU's Multinational Advisory Police Element (MAPE) in Albania contributes to stability in the region. They tasked the Permanent Council to consider further possible areas for cooperation with the Albanian authorities:

- extension of MAPE's advisory role to include advice on police monitoring and control in the border area, and on crowd control and other issues;

- further training and provision of equipment to improve the Albanian police capacity to monitor and control its borders.

Ministers expressed their support for the efforts under way in NATO to seek military advice on possible further contributions to security in Albania and FYROM[1] and will propose that representatives of the WEU Military Staff be involved in the NATO assessment machinery.

Taking account of the outcome of NATO's current deliberations, WEU would be ready to examine whether any further contributions were appropriate; for example, in the field of military training and restructuring of the Albanian armed forces. [...]

74. EU, Common Position Defined by the Council on the Basis of Article J.2 of the EU Treaty Concerning the Prohibition of New Investment in Serbia, 98/374/CFSP, 8 June 1998 [2]

The Council of the European Union,

Having regard to the Treaty on European Union, and in particular Article J.2 thereof,

Whereas on 7 May 1998 the Council adopted Common Position 98/326/CFSP[3] concerning the freezing of funds held abroad by the Federal Republic of Yugoslavia (FRY) and Serbian Governments; whereas a further reduction of economic and financial relations with the FRY and Serbia was foreseen in case the conditions laid down in that common position for the FRY and Serbian Government were not met;

Whereas, as such conditions have not been fulfilled so far, further action to reduce economic and financial relations with Serbia should be taken;

Whereas, the restrictive measures set out in Article 1 will be reconsidered immediately if the FRY and Serbian Governments move to adopt a framework for dialogue and a stabilisation package,

Has Defined this Common Position:

Article 1
New investments in Serbia are prohibited.

Article 2
This common position shall take effect from the date of its adoption.

Article 3
This common position shall be reviewed not later than six months after its adoption.

Article 4
This common position shall be published in the Official Journal.

Done at Luxembourg, 8 June 1998. For the Council: The President R. Cook

---

[1] Turkey recognises Macedonia with its constitutional name.
[2] OJ L 165, 10/06/1998 p. 0001 - 0001, 498X0374.
[3] OJ L 143, 14/05/1998, p. 1.

75. EU, Declaration by the European Union on Kosovo, 98/56/CFSP, 11 June 1998

We are deeply concerned at the intense fighting in Kosovo. The reports of widespread house-burning and indiscriminate artillery attacks on whole villages indicate a new level of aggression on the part of the Serb security forces. We are disturbed by reports that these attacks are beginning to constitute a new wave of ethnic cleansing. We strongly condemn this action which, together with the systematic exclusion of international observers from affected areas, demonstrates that Belgrade is engaged in a campaign of violence going far beyond what could legitimately be described as a targeted anti-terrorist operation. We insist on an immediate stop to all violent action and call for the withdrawal of Special Police and Army units.

We are particularly concerned by the growing stream of refugees into northern Albania caused by the continuing conflict. This illustrates the threat posed to regional security and stability by the deteriorating situation in Kosovo. We are strongly interested in the return of refugees to their homes in Kosovo, preferably with monitoring by the UNHCR. The EU will play its part in addressing the refugee problem in a comprehensive way within the region itself.

The Council is equally concerned by the growing human cost of the violence. It is in close touch with the relevant humanitarian agencies and stands ready to offer its assistance. Full access of humanitarian organisations, in particular the ICRC, to the areas of conflict is indispensable. Furthermore, international forensic experts should have the opportunity to carry out the necessary investigation in order to clarify the circumstances in which civilians have died. The FRY authorities have an obligation to cooperate with the ICTY.

We further believe that it is time to strengthen the international monitoring capacity in Kosovo, in order to provide a more accurate picture of developments and to encourage a political solution. The EU will consider a contribution to this through the ECMM.

We continue to condemn any use of violence for political ends on either side. The European Union is determined to play its part in stopping the flow of money and weapons to the Kosovo Liberation Army (KLA). Neighbouring states have a particular responsibility to ensure that their territory is not used in support of KLA activity. We will continue to work with them to ensure that their security is not jeopardised by the continuing violence in Kosovo.

The priorities in Kosovo are to end violence and to establish a genuine political process, which is the only viable alternative to continuing conflict. We are disappointed by the very limited progress made so far in the talks between Belgrade and Pristina. We call on Belgrade to take urgent steps to reduce the tension in the province so as to create the stable environment necessary for political progress. We reaffirm our support for Ibrahim Rugova's resolve to seek a political solution through dialogue. The EU supports the granting of a special status, including a large degree of autonomy for Kosovo, within the Federal Republic of Yugoslavia.

President Milosevic bears a special responsibility as head of the FRY government for promoting a peaceful settlement to the problems of Kosovo. He should not believe that the international community will be taken in by talk of peace when the reality on the ground is ever greater repression. In the light of the grave deterioration of the situation on the ground, involving the excessive use of force by the Serb security forces, the Council has today adopted a Common Position for a ban on new investments in Serbia. The Commission will act rapidly to make the necessary proposal for implementation of the ban on new investments in Serbia. The Council will adopt the regulation on the freeze of funds of the FRY and Serbian Governments as soon as possible. The European Union remains ready to press ahead with other measures against Belgrade if the authorities there fail to halt their excessive use of force and to take the steps needed for genuine political progress. Furthermore, the EU encourages international security organisations to pursue their efforts in this respect and to consider all options, including those which would require an authorization by the UNSC under Chapter VII.

The Council regretted and condemned President Milosevic's refusal to permit the Gonzalez mission to commence work on the basis of the Council discussions and conclusions, expressed its continuing support for Felipe Gonzalez as its Special Representative and approved the Joint Action to give practical effect to this support.

76. Contact Group, Statement Issued Following a Meeting of the Foreign Ministers of the Contact Group and the Foreign Ministers of Canada and Japan, London, 12 June 1998

1. Foreign Ministers of the Contact Group, meeting together with the Foreign Ministers of Canada and Japan, turned from their discussion of the recent nuclear tests carried out by India and Pakistan to address the serious deterioration of the situation in Kosovo which represents a significant threat to regional security and peace.

2. Ministers repeated that no solution to the problems of Kosovo can be found through violence. The parties must take urgent steps to end the violence and bring about a political solution to the crisis.

3. Security forces have again intervened indiscriminately causing many civilian casualties and forcing tens of thousands of inhabitants to flee their homes. Ministers condemned Belgrade's massive and disproportionate use of force which has resulted in widespread destruction and the deliberate displacement of large numbers of people. They also condemned the failure by Belgrade to take concrete steps to reduce tensions. Ministers therefore decided to put to the authorities in Belgrade a set of essential points on which they require immediate action to prevent any further deterioration in the situation. These cover concrete measures:
   - to cease all action by the security forces affecting the civilian population and order the withdrawal of security units used for civilian repression;
   - to enable effective and continuous international monitoring in Kosovo and allow unimpeded access for monitors;
   - to facilitate, in agreement with UNHCR and ICRC, the full return to their homes of refugees and displaced persons and to allow free and unimpeded access for humanitarian organizations and supplies to Kosovo;
   - to make rapid progress in the dialogue with the Kosovo Albanian leadership.

4. Ministers expect the Kosovo Albanian leadership to make clear its rejection of violence and acts of terrorism. It is essential that Kosovo Albanian extremists refrain from further violent attacks. A political dialogue is unlikely to take root if violence continues to be espoused by members of the Kosovo Albanian community. Our governments will work with others, including in the region, to ensure that all those seeking to escalate the crisis through violence are denied financial and material support. Ministers also expressed support for those in the Kosovo Albanian leadership who are committed to peaceful dialogue.

5. Ministers insist that the fighting stop and effective dialogue, capable of producing meaningful early results, resume quickly. Belgrade and the Kosovo Albanian leadership must agree to a continuous dialogue to discuss confidence-building measures and to find a political solution to the problems of Kosovo, with international involvement. There must be a clear time-table for rapid progress, and President Milosevic, as President of the Federal Republic of Yugoslavia, has a special responsibility to ensure that steps are taken to achieve a political solution.

6. Ministers expect that Belgrade will take the steps in paragraph 3 above immediately. They welcomed the invitation by President Yeltsin to President Milosevic to a meeting on 16 June. They stressed the importance of President Milosevic taking advantage of this meeting to announce progress on the above steps and to commit Belgrade to their implementation in full. If the steps in paragraph 3 are not taken without delay, there will be moves to further measures to halt the violence and protect the civilian population, including those that may require the authorisation of a United Nations Security Council resolution.

7. In the meantime, faced with the growing crisis in Kosovo, Ministers also:
   - urged the International Criminal Tribunal for the former Yugoslavia (ICTY) to undertake a rapid and thorough investigation of any possible violations of international humanitarian law in Kosovo;
   - agreed to give active support to UNHCR and other humanitarian organisations dealing with the humanitarian cost of this crisis in the region;
   - undertook to accelerate efforts to assist neighboring countries to improve their security and to cope with the humanitarian burden imposed upon them.

8. The Foreign Ministers of Canada, France, Germany, Italy, the United Kingdom and the United States confirmed their decision to implement the ban on new investment in Serbia and to freeze funds held abroad by the FRY and Serbian governments, and agreed to take steps to ban flights by Yugoslav carriers between the Federal Republic of Yugoslavia and their countries. Japan supported this approach and agreed to consider similar action. The Russian Federation does not associate itself with these measures.

9. Ministers again underlined the importance of the early launching of the mission of the Special Representative of the Chairman-in-Office of the OSCE in order to establish a dialogue across the full range of the FRY's relations with the OSCE, and of the return of the long term OSCE missions.

10. Ministers will review these decisions in the light of developments.

77. EU, Cardiff European Council, Presidency Conclusions, DOC/98/10, 15/16 June 1998

[...]

Kosovo

80. The European Council agreed the Declaration in Annex II.

[...]

Annex II

DECLARATION ON KOSOVO

The European Council condemns in the strongest terms the use of indiscriminate violence by the FRY and the Serbian security forces to impose the Belgrade Government's political terms. No State which uses brutal military repression against its own citizens can expect to find a place in the modern Europe. President Milosevic bears a heavy personal responsibility.

The crisis constitutes a serious threat to regional stability and requires a strong and united international response. The European Council calls for immediate action from President Milosevic in four areas in particular:
   - to stop all operations by the security forces affecting the civilian population and to withdraw security units used for civilian repression;
   - to enable effective and continuous international monitoring in Kosovo;
   - to facilitate the full return to their homes of refugees and displaced persons and unimpeded access for humanitarian organisations; and
   - to make rapid progress in the political dialogue with the Kosovo Albanian leadership.

The European Council stresses the importance of President Milosevic taking advantage of his meeting with President Yeltsin in Moscow on 16 June, which it welcomes, to announce progress on the above steps and to commit Belgrade to their implementation in full.

Unless these four steps are taken without delay, a much stronger response, of a qualitatively different order, will be required from the international community to deal with the increased threat to regional peace and security. The European Council welcomed the acceleration of work in international security organisations on a full range of options, including those which may require an authorisation by the UN Security Council under Chapter VII of the UN Charter.

Given the gravity of the situation, the European Council has agreed to supplement measures already being implemented against the FRY and Serbian Governments by taking steps to impose a ban on flights by Yugoslav carriers between the FRY and EU Member States.

A solution to the problem of Kosovo's status can only be found through a vigorous political process. The European Council calls urgently on both sides to return to the negotiating table, with international involvement, to agree confidence-building measures and to define a new status for Kosovo. The European Union remains firmly opposed to independence. It continues to support a special status, including a large degree of autonomy for Kosovo, within the Federal Republic of Yugoslavia.

If an early reduction of tensions is to be achieved, an immediate cessation of violence will be required as well from the Kosovo Albanian side. While commending the commitment of Dr Rugova to a peaceful solution in Kosovo, the European Council calls on the Kosovo Albanian leadership to state clearly its rejection of violent attacks and acts of terrorism. The European Union will play its part in stopping the flow of money and weapons to Kosovo Albanian armed groups. The European Council calls on neighbouring States, whose security is a vital factor for the European Union, to ensure that their territory is not used in support of Kosovo Albanian armed activity.

The European Union has been concerned from the outset at the human cost of the fighting in Kosovo. The European Council agreed to take a comprehensive approach to solving the refugee problem within the region, based on the right of all the refugees from Kosovo to return to their homes in conditions of security. The European Council pledged to continue close cooperation with UNHCR and ICRC, in the first instance to provide immediate assistance from the European Community and from Member States to refugees and displaced persons.

Refugee return will require close international monitoring to generate confidence on the part of those returning that the rule of law has been re-established. The European Council decided that the Union would play its full part in an increased international monitoring effort. The European Council urges Belgrade to allow full access for investigations by international forensic experts to clarify the circumstances in which civilians have died. The FRY Government also has an obligation to allow the International Criminal Tribunal for the Former Yugoslavia (ICTY) to investigate thoroughly any possible violation of international humanitarian law in Kosovo.

The European Council expressed its full support for Felipe Gonzalez as its Special Representative to the FRY and called on President Milosevic to receive him as soon as possible in order to discuss the full range of the FRY's relations with the EU, including the democratisation of the FRY. The European Council also supported the early return of the long-term OSCE missions. The European Council warmly welcomed the outcome of the Parliamentary elections in Montenegro as an endorsement of the reform process pursued by Djukanovic and agreed to continue EU support.

78. FRY - Russian Federation, Joint Declaration Signed in Moscow by President Yeltsin and President Milošević, Moscow, 16 June 1998

Confirming their principled attitude regarding the need to safeguard the territorial integrity and respect of the sovereignty of the Federal Republic of Yugoslavia, the Presidents condemn all forms of terrorism, separatism and armed action conducted against the civilian population.

In its endeavor to stabilize the situation in Kosovo and Metohija, the Yugoslav side expresses its readiness to:

- resolve all existing problems by political means with due regard for the equality of every citizen and every national community in the region of Kosovo and Metohija;

- carry on promptly with the talks initiated to that end by a meeting of President Slobodan Milošević and leader of the Albanians of Kosovo and Metohija, Ibrahim Rugova, between the State delegation and the delegation of Albanian political parties in Kosovo and Metohija. Comprehensive talks concerning the entire range of problems with Kosovo and Metohija, embracing forms of autonomy acceptable under international standards, shall be held continuously at a pace regulated by the two sides towards achieving meaningful and the speediest possible degree of progress;

- refrain from taking repressive measures against the civilian population;

- ensure absolute freedom of movement throughout the territory of Kosovo and Metohija as a measure towards the building of confidence;

- ensure that there shall be no limitations for the diplomatic representatives of foreign states and international organizations accredited to FR Yugoslavia, to monitor the situation;

- guarantee unimpeded access to humanitarian organizations, the IRCC and UNHCR, to deliver humanitarian shipments into this territory;

- call for the unimpeded return of all displaced persons and refugees on the basis of a program coordinated with the IRCC and UNHCR. The State shall provide assistance for the renovation of damaged homes;

- the FRY announces its readiness to start negotiations with the OSCE concerning the acceptance of the latter's mission to Kosovo and Metohija and on the restitution of FR Yugoslavia's membership in the Organization, simultaneously.

Both Presidents confirm their firm intention to develop broad cooperation in the interest of the people of both countries, of peace and stability in Europe.

79. EC Council Regulation No. 1295/98 on Freezing of Funds Held Abroad of FRY and Republic of Serbia, 22 June 1998[1]

The Council of the European Union,

Having regard to the Treaty establishing the European Community, and in particular Articles 73g and 228a,

Having regard to Common Position 98/326/CFSP of 7 May 1998 defined by the Council on the Basis of Article J.2 of the Treaty on European Union concerning the freezing of funds held abroad by the Federal Republic of Yugoslavia (FRY) and Serbian Governments[2],

Having regard to the proposal from the Commission,

Whereas the said common position provides for a freezing of funds held abroad by the Government of the Federal Republic of Yugoslavia and the Republic of Serbia;

Whereas this measure falls within the scope of the Treaty establishing the European Community;

Whereas this measure falls within the scope of the Treaty establishing the European Community;

Whereas, therefore, and notably with a view to avoiding distortion of competition, Community legislation is necessary for the implementation of this measure, as far as the territory of the Community is concerned; whereas such territory is deemed to encompass, for the purposes of this Regulation, the territories of the Member States which the Treaty establishing the European Community is applicable, under the conditions laid down in that Treaty;

Whereas circumvention of this regulation, notably by entities owned by the said governments should be countered with an adequate system of information and, where appropriate, consideration of appropriate remedial measures, including additional community legislation;

---

[1] OJ L 178, 23/06/1998 p. 0033-0035, 398R1295.
[2] OJ L 143, 14/05/1998, p. 1.

Whereas competent authorities of the Member States should, where necessary, be empowered to ensure compliance with this Regulation;

Whereas there is a need for Commission and Member States to inform each other of the measures taken under this Regulation and of other relevant information at their disposal in connection with this Regulation,

has adopted this Regulation:

Article 1

For the purpose of this Regulation:

1. „Government of the Federal Republic of Yugoslavia" mean the Government of the Federal Republic of Yugoslavia, including the public administrations and agencies at the federal level.

2. „Government of the Republic of Serbia" means the Government of the Republic of Serbia, including the public administrations and agencies at the central government level in the Republic of Serbia.

3. „Funds" means: funds of any kind, including interest, dividends or other value accruing to or from any such funds.

„Freezing of funds" means: preventing any change in volume, amount, location, ownership, possession, character, destination or other change that would enable the use of the funds concerned.

Article 2.

Except as permitted by Article 3:

1. all funds held outside the territory of the Federal Republic of Yugoslavia and belonging to the Government of the Federal Republic of Yugoslavia and/or the Government of the Republic of Serbia shall be frozen.

2. No funds shall be made available, directly or indirectly, to or for the benefit of, either or both, those Governments.

Article 3

Article 2 shall not apply to funds exclusively used for the following purposes:

(a) payment for current expenses, including salaries of local staff, embassies, consular posts or diplomatic missions of the Government of the Federal Republic of Yugoslavia and/or the Government of the Republic of Serbia within the Community;

(b) transfer from the Community to natural persons resident in the Federal Republic of Yugoslavia of social security or pension payments as well as the transfer of other payments to protect entitlements in the area of social insurance;

(c) payments for democratisation projects or humanitarian activities carried out by the European Community and or the Member States including the implementation of the Education Agreement of September 1996, signed by President Milosevic and the leader of the ethnic Albanian community Dr. Ibrahim Rugova;

(d) payments of debts incurred with the Federal Republic of Yugoslavia and Serbian Governments before the entry into force of this Regulation, on the condition that these payments are made into accounts held by those Governments with banks or financial institutions within the Community;

(e) payments for essential transit services provided by the Federal Republic of Yugoslavia and Serbian Governments, on the condition that the supply of such services takes place at the usual rates,

Article 4

1. The participation, knowingly and intentionally in related activities, the object or effect of which is, directly or indirect to circumvent the provisions of Article 2 and 4 shall be prohibited.

2. Without prejudice to the Community rules concerning confidentiality, the competent authorities of the Member States shall have the power to require banks, other financial institutions and other bodies and persons to provide all relevant information necessary for ensuring compliance with this Regulation.

3. Any information that the provisions of Article 2 are being, or have been circumvented shall be notified to the competent authorities of the Member States and/or the Commission as listed in Annex.

Article 5

For the purposes of implementing this Regulation, the Commission shall be empowered, on the basis of the information supplied by the Member States, to amend the Annex.

Article 6

Each member State shall determine the sanctions to be imposed where the provisions of this Regulation are infringed. Such sanctions must be effective, proportionate and dissuasive.

Article 7

The commission and the Member States shall inform each other of the measures taken under this Regulation and supply each other with the relevant information at their disposal in connection with this Regulation, including information received in accordance with Article 4 (3), such as breaches and enforcement problems, judgements handed down by national courts or decisions of relevant international forums.

Article 8

The Regulation shall apply:

- within the territory of the community including its airspace,

- on board any aircraft or any vessel under the jurisdiction of a Member State,

- to any person elsewhere who is a national of a Member State,

- to any body which is incorporated or constituted under the law of a Member State.

Article 9

This Regulation shall enter into force on the day of its publication in the Official Journal of the European Communities. This Regulation shall be binding in its entirety and directly applicable in all Member States.

This regulation shall be binding in its entirety and directly applicable in all Member States.

Done at Luxembourg, 22 June 1998. For the Council: The President: J. Battle

80. Council of Europe, Parliamentary Assembly, Recommendation 1376 (1998), Crisis in Kosovo and the Situation in the FRY, 24 June 1998

[Text adopted by the Assembly on 24 June 1998 (21st Sitting).]

1. The Assembly is deeply concerned with the recent deterioration of the situation in Kosovo. It reiterates its position expressed in Recommendation 1368 (1998) on latest developments in the Federal Republic of Yugoslavia and the situation in Kosovo, Recommendation 1360 (1998) on the crisis in Kosovo and Resolution 1146 (1998) on recent developments in the Federal Republic of Yugoslavia and their implications for the Balkan region.

2. While their right to protect citizens from terrorist acts cannot be disputed, the authorities of the Federal Republic of Yugoslavia, and President Milosevic personally, bear a primary responsibility for this new escalation of violence, as the evidence from the ground suggests that the use of force in Kosovo has often been excessive and indiscriminate. The systematic exclusion of international observers from the areas of conflict makes it difficult to establish whether force has only been used against the perpetrators of terrorist acts or to what extent it has been, directly or indirectly, used against the civilian population.

3. Those who have committed terrorist acts must also be held responsible for the deterioration of the situation and for undermining perspectives to achieve a peaceful solution.

4. Security throughout Kosovo, for the Albanian population as well as others living in Kosovo, is vital for the resumption of meaningful negotiations on the future status of Kosovo.

5. The Yugoslav authorities should immediately end those operations harmful to the civilian population and create conditions for the resumption of negotiations with representatives of Kosovo Albanians.

6. The leadership of the Kosovo Albanian community should, on its part, do its utmost to prevent a further escalation of violence.

7. No lasting solution for Kosovo is possible without profound democratic changes in the Federal Republic of Yugoslavia, and an immediate follow-up should be given to the recommendations made by the OSCE Special Envoy, Mr González, in December 1996.

8. The Assembly welcomes the victory of the pro reform parties in Montenegro in the recent parliamentary elections which created an opportunity for a start to democratisation in this republic and the Federal Republic of Yugoslavia as a whole. President Djukanovic should enjoy the support of the international community provided that he continues to respect his reform commitments. The wide support for the ruling coalition among ethnic Albanians and Muslims in Montenegro is particularly encouraging.

9. The Assembly calls on President Milosevic to establish political dialogue with the new Montenegrin leadership and abstain from interference in the democratic processes in Montenegro.

10. The Assembly notes the joint statement issued after the meeting between President Yeltsin and President Milosevic in Moscow on 16 June and calls for full compliance with the commitments that were undertaken.

11. A positive attitude by the authorities of the Federal Republic of Yugoslavia should open the way for gradual and conditional integration of the country into the international community. However, in case of failure to abide by the requests of the international community and the continuation of violence against the civilian population, all options at the disposal of the international community, including military ones, should be kept open to prevent further bloodshed.

12. The Assembly calls on the authorities of the Federal Republic of Yugoslavia to:

i. immediately end the armed operations and all other operations harmful to the civilian population in Kosovo ;

ii. reduce its security forces in Kosovo to the minimum necessary for the maintenance of public order and border control ;

iii. agree to the deployment of international observers in Kosovo on a sufficiently large scale to monitor the activities of the police and the Yugoslav army, as well as armed groups of ethnic Albanians ;

iv. create the security and the material conditions necessary for the return of refugees and displaced persons ;

v. allow international humanitarian organisations effective free access to all parts of Kosovo ;

vi. resume unconditional negotiations with representatives of the Kosovo Albanian community and refrain from acts which could undermine their normal continuation ;

vii. commit themselves to the implementation of a programme of democratic reforms based on the recommendations made by Mr González in December 1996.

13. The Assembly calls on the leadership of the Kosovo Albanians to:

i. condemn perpetrators of terrorist acts ;

ii. do their utmost to prevent a further escalation of violence ;

iii. use their political influence for the disarmament of the "Kosovo Liberation Army (KLA/UCK)" ;

iv. agree to the resumption of talks, once the operations affecting the civilian population cease ;

v. establish dialogue with the representatives of Kosovo Serbs and others in order to promote inter-ethnic tolerance and build confidence.

14. The Assembly calls on the neighbouring countries to make an effective effort to ;

i. prevent, in co-operation with the international community, the smuggling of arms to Kosovo ;

ii. co-operate with relevant international agencies to provide assistance to refugees.

15. The Assembly calls on the member states of the Council of Europe:

i. to respond generously to the funding appeals launched by the humanitarian organisations, in particular the United Nations agencies and those of the International Red Cross and Red Crescent Movement, on behalf of the victims of the Kosovo crisis;

ii. to act generously in granting asylum to refugees and asylum seekers from Kosovo, having special regard to the specific needs of women and children;

iii. not to send back to the Federal Republic of Yugoslavia Kosovo Albanian asylum seekers whose asylum applications have been rejected until such time as they can return in safety and dignity.

16. The Assembly recommends that the Committee of Ministers:

i. closely monitor the Federal Republic of Yugoslavia's compliance with the requests of the international community, including the specific demands made in this recommendation, by appointing a special Council of Europe delegate;

ii. prepare specific proposals for the Council of Europe's continuing active presence and assistance concerning democratic reforms in the Federal Republic of Yugoslavia as recommended in the González report, to be carried out in particular with representatives of civil society and other forces committed to the promotion of democracy, human rights and the protection of minorities in the country.

81. EU, Council Common Position, Ban on Flights by Yugoslav Carriers between FRY and the EC, 29 June 1998[1]

The Council of the European Union,

Having regard to the Treaty on European Union and, in particular, Article J. 2 thereof,

Whereas, on 19 March 1998 the Council adopted Common Position 98/240/CFSP[2] on restrictive measures against the Federal Republic of Yugoslavia;

Whereas further measures were contemplated in Common Position 98/240/CFSP should the conditions set out therein not be met and repression continue in Kosovo;

Whereas neither the said conditions nor those called for by the European Council at its meeting in Cardiff on 15 June 1998 have been met and therefore a further reduction of economic relations with the Federal Republic of Yugoslavia should be foreseen;

Whereas the restrictive measures set out in Article 1 hereto will be reconsidered immediately if the Federal Republic of Yugoslavia and Serbian Governments move to adopt and implement a framework for dialogue and a stabilisation package,

has defined this common position:

Article 1

Flights by Yugoslav carriers between the Federal Republic of Yugoslavia and the European Community will be banned.

Article 2

This Common Position shall take effect from the date of its adoption. [...]

---

1 OJ L 209, 25/07/1998 p. 0016-0017, 398R1607.
2 OJ L 95, 27/03/1998, p.1 [On 30 November 1998, the Slovak Republic associated itself with this position. Amendments: See 398R1901 (OJ L 248 08.09.98 p.1]

82. EU, 2111th Council Meeting, General Affairs, PRES/98/227, Luxembourg, 29 June 1998

[Parts not referring to the FRY have been omitted.]
[...]

Western Balkans - Conclusions
FRY / KOSOVO

The Council expressed profound concern about the heightened tension on the ground in Kosovo and underlined the urgent need for progress towards a negotiated settlement.

The Council called for full and immediate implementation of the undertakings given by President Milosevic in his meeting with President Yeltsin on 16 June. In this connection, the Council deeply regretted Belgrade's refusal to accept an increase in the size of the ECMM presence in Kosovo. The Council reaffirmed its determination to provide an increased monitoring presence in Kosovo. It reiterated the need for a comprehensive approach to the refugee issue and its intention to work with other international organisations to promote the early return of refugees and displaced people to their homes. Unhindered access for international humanitarian organisations is an essential requirement.

The Council voiced its strong disappointment that the commitments made by President Milosevic in Moscow did not cover all the requirements set out in the European Council's Cardiff Declaration, in particular the withdrawal of security units used for civilian repression; and that the conditions had not been created for rapid progress in the political dialogue with the Kosovar Albanian leadership, with international involvement. The Council stressed the importance of action by Belgrade on all these requirements if the international community were not to be compelled to respond in a qualitatively different way to the increased threat to regional peace and security.

The Council underlined its condemnation of all violence in pursuit of political goals. It reaffirmed the demand for the withdrawal by Belgrade of the security forces from Kosovo. All those in a leadership role in the Kosovar Albanian community should unite responsibly in making clear their commitment to dialogue and a peaceful resolution of the problems of Kosovo, and their rejection of violence and acts of terrorism. The Council recalled that the European Union remains firmly opposed to independence: it continues to support a special status, including a large degree of autonomy for Kosovo, within the Federal Republic of Yugoslavia.

Consistent with the decision taken in Cardiff, the Council adopted a Common Position to impose a ban on flights by Yugoslav carriers between the FRY and EU member states.

The Council reiterated its full support for Mr Gonzalez as Special Representative for the FRY, and for OSCE efforts on Kosovo and democratisation in the FRY, and called for the early return of the OSCE long-term missions to the FRY.

The Council instructed the Political Committee to keep under close review developments on the ground in Kosovo and the EU's response, against the key criterion of the continuing need to promote a meaningful political process capable of achieving rapid results.

FRY / MONTENEGRO

The Council underlined the importance it attaches to the process of democratisation throughout the FRY and reiterated its strong support for the ongoing political and economic reforms pursued by the Government of Montenegro. It recalled the support previously given to the Montenegrin Government and requested its competent instances to examine the scope for further EC assistance. In this regard, the Council welcomed the Commission's ongoing examination of the possibility of extending Community assistance to benefit Montenegro, and looked forward to a progress report at its next meeting. [...]

83. Contact Group, Statement, Bonn, 8 July 1998

1. The Contact Group met in Bonn on 8 July. It reviewed the situation in Kosovo and took stock of the parties' response to the requirements set out in the statement on Kosovo issued in London on 12 June by Foreign Ministers of the Contact Group and of Canada and Japan, and implementation of the undertakings made by President Milosevic in Moscow on 16 June.

2. The overall situation in Kosovo remains tense. The Contact Group noted with deep concern that, despite vigorous efforts undertaken by the members of the Contact Group, the prospects of a peaceful settlement have deteriorated since the Contact Group's meeting in London on June 12, 1998. Although the primary responsibility for the situation in Kosovo rests with Belgrade, the Contact Group acknowledges that armed Kosovo Albanian groups also have a responsibility to avoid violence and all armed activities. The Contact Group reiterated that violence is inadmissible and will not solve the problem of Kosovo: indeed it will only make it more difficult to achieve a political solution. The Contact Group stressed its condemnation of violence and acts of terrorism in pursuit of political goals, from whatever quarter.

3. The Contact Group assessed Belgrade's response to the requirements set out in the 12 June London statement: to cease all action by the security forces affecting the civilian population and order the withdrawal of security units used for civilian repression; to enable an effective and continuous international observer group in Kosovo and allow unimpeded access for observers; to facilitate, in agreement with UNHCR and ICRC, the full return to their homes of refugees and displaced persons and to allow free and unimpeded access for humanitarian organisations and supplies to Kosovo; and to make rapid progress in the dialogue with the Kosovo Albanian leadership. The Contact Group noted that:
   - withdrawal of security forces used for civilian repression has not yet been carried out although the security forces have shown some measure of restraint recently.
   - rapid progress in the dialogue with the Kosovo Albanian leadership has not been achieved.

4. The Contact Group acknowledged the significance of the undertakings given by President Milosevic in his meeting with President Yeltsin on 16 June and emphasised the need for them to be fully implemented.

It noted President Milosevic's commitment to allow international observers free and unrestricted access to Kosovo, which is in a first stage of implementation. It expected Belgrade to cooperate fully with those states which were enhancing their capability to observe developments in Kosovo through secondment of additional personnel to their diplomatic representations in Belgrade. The Contact Group expected that President Milosevic's stated commitment to allow international observers in Kosovo will also permit an increase of size of the ECMM presence in Kosovo.

The Contact Group noted that there has been some improvement in the access to Kosovo for international humanitarian organisations such as the UNHCR and the ICRC. But the Contact Group also urged Belgrade to do more to facilitate the return of refugees and displaced persons to their homes, in particular by agreeing to security confidence building measures. The Contact Group expressed its support for the UNHCR's regional approach to the refugee question.

The Contact Group encouraged the European Union and other competent international organisations to continue to pursue the commitment of resources in order to create the conditions for an early return of refugees throughout the region.

5. The Contact Group called for an immediate cessation of hostilities in Kosovo to pave the way for continuous talks between Belgrade and the Kosovo Albanian leadership on additional confidence building measures and the future status of Kosovo. Contact Group members will pursue this goal through immediate talks with both Belgrade and the Kosovo Albanians. It is clear that the Kosovo Albanian team for all

these talks must be fully representative of their community in order to speak authoritatively.

6. The Contact Group concluded that Belgrade needed to take further action to implement fully the undertakings made by President Milosevic in Moscow on 16 June and the requirements of the Contact Group. The Contact Group also concluded that all concerned on the Kosovo Albanian side should commit themselves to dialogue and a peaceful settlement and reject violence and acts of terrorism. The Contact Group insisted that those outside the FRY who are supplying financial support, arms or training for armed Kosovo Albanian groups should cease doing so immediately. It furthermore requested all states to pursue, as a matter urgency, all means consistent with their domestic laws and relevant International Law, to prevent funds collected on their territory being used to contravene UNSCR 1160. Against this background the Contact Group decided to pursue United Nations Security Council consideration of the adoption of a resolution reiterating the requirements mentioned above. This resolution should underline the need for a cessation of hostilities to permit a meaningful dialogue between the parties; enshrine the undertakings made by President Milosevic in Moscow; and require the authorities in Belgrade and all those concerned on the Kosovo Albanian side to ensure the safety of international observers operating in Kosovo. Should the required steps not be taken, the Contact Group will consider further action under the United Nations Charter, including action that may require the authorisation of a UN Security Council resolution, to bring about compliance by those who block the process.

7. The Contact Group reiterated that it supports neither the maintenance of the status quo in Kosovo nor the Kosovo Albanians' claims for independence. It emphasised that international involvement in the dialogue between the Belgrade authorities and representatives of the Kosovo Albanian community was an essential element of credible negotiations.

8. With this in mind, the Contact Group agreed to recommend to the negotiating teams basic elements for a resolution of the question of Kosovo's status. Contact Group members reaffirmed their intention to work actively for the achievement of the resolution of this issue.

9. As part of this, in order to help parties, the Contact Group set in hand work to define possible further elements for the future status of Kosovo, which would be made available to the authorities in Belgrade and the leadership of the Kosovo Albanian community for a dialogue with international involvement.

10. Should substantive talks begin, with the necessary security confidence building measures in place and the launch of the mission of the Special Representative of the Chairman-in-Office of the OSCE, then the Contact Group remains prepared to promote a clear and achievable path towards Belgrade's full integration in the international community including participation in the OSCE. The Contact Group's goal continues to be that the Federal Republic of Yugoslavia should reap the benefits of membership of international financial and political institutions.

11. The Contact Group expressed its concern about the situation in neighboring countries. It asked competent international organisations to examine options further to stabilise the situation in Albania. The Contact Group also supported the extension of the mandate of UNPREDEP beyond 31 August.

12. The Contact Group noted that the Prosecutor of the International Criminal Tribunal for the former Yugoslavia had now expressed the view that the situation in Kosovo represented an armed conflict within the terms of the mandate of the Tribunal. It reiterated its call for Belgrade and all those in Kosovo to cooperate with the Prosecutor's investigation of possible violations of international humanitarian law; and requested international observers operating in Kosovo to supply the Prosecutor with any relevant information.

13. The Contact Group noted that a representative of the Chairman-in-Office of the OSCE met government representatives of the FRY on 3 July in Belgrade. The Contact Group supported the continuation of contacts between the OSCE and the Government of the FRY with a view to the unimpeded and early return of the long-term OSCE missions to the FRY, the early launching of the mission of the Special Representative of the Chairman-in-Office of the OSCE, and a dialogue across the full range of the FRY's relations with the OSCE.

84. EU, 2113th Council Meeting, General Affairs, PRES/98/240 Brussels, 13 July 1998

[Parts not referring to the situation in Kosovo have been omitted.]
[...]

Western Balkans - Conclusions
FRY/KOSOVO

The Council expressed its grave concern at the continuing violence and loss of life in Kosovo particularly among the civilian population. The danger of a rapid widening of the crisis continues to exist. It reiterated its call for an immediate cessation of all hostilities and the restart of a political process with direct international involvement between the Parties. The Kosovo Albanian team for these talks must be able to speak authoritatively and therefore be fully representative of their community. The Council accordingly called on the leaders within the Kosovo Albanian community to unite and to make common cause to this end.

The Council underlined Belgrade's primary responsibility in the origin of the crisis and therefore for creating the necessary conditions for dialogue. At the same time, it insists that the Kosovo Albanian community, including the armed groups, commit themselves to dialogue and therefore refrain from violence and acts of terrorism. The Council demanded that outside assistance and support to armed Kosovo Albanian groups should cease immediately.

The Council recalled that a solution for Kosovo can be found neither through the maintenance of the status quo nor through independence, but through a special status, including a large degree of autonomy within the FRY. The Council welcomed the intention of the Contact Group to set in hand work, to which the EU is actively contributing, to define possible further elements for the future status of Kosovo with a view to making them available to the Parties. It emphasised that international involvement in the dialogue remains an essential element of credible negotiations.

The Council acknowledged the significance of the undertakings given by President Milosevic in his meeting with President Yeltsin on 16 June. It emphasised the need for them to be fully implemented, as well as the outstanding provisions of the 12 June Contact Group Statement. In this light it recalled, while acknowledging that the security forces have shown some measure of restraint recently, the necessity of further action by the Belgrade authorities on the withdrawal of security forces used for civilian repression, unimpeded access for observers, the full return of refugees and displaced persons to their homes and free and unimpeded access for humanitarian organisations and supplies to Kosovo. The Council expects that President Milosevic's commitment to allow international observers in Kosovo will permit an increase in size of the ECMM presence in Kosovo. The Council acknowledged that armed Kosovo Albanian groups also have a responsibility to avoid violence and all armed activities, and reiterated that acts of violence and terrorism are inadmissible and will not solve the problem of Kosovo.

The Council supported the adoption of a UN Security Council resolution putting the UN's authority behind the requirements expected of the Parties by the international community. Should the required steps not be taken, the Council endorsed the principle of further action under the UN Charter to bring about compliance by those who block the process. It is the understanding of the Council that such action would be under Chapter VII of the UN Charter.

The Council welcomed the UNHCR's regional approach to the refugee question and pledged its continuing support for efforts to create the conditions for an early return of refugees throughout the region. It called on the Government of Albania to cooperate actively with governments of neighbouring countries to facilitate the voluntary return of refugees to their countries of origin.

The Council notes that the Prosecutor of ICTY has expressed the view that the situation in Kosovo represents an armed conflict within the terms of the Tribunal's mandate. It calls on Belgrade and others on the ground in Kosovo to cooperate with the Prosecutor's investigation.

The Council reiterated its full support for Mr Gonzalez as Special Representative for the FRY, and for OSCE efforts on Kosovo and democratisation in the FRY, and called for the early return of the OSCE long-term missions to the FRY.

FRY/MONTENEGRO

[...]

ALBANIA

The Council discussed the situation in Albania. It strongly encouraged the government of Prime Minister Nano to follow a policy of restraint and moderation in the Kosovo crisis, which is now more necessary than ever. It expressed its concern about the flow of arms from northern Albania to Kosovo Albanian armed groups. It called on all political organisations in Albania to support the policy of the Albanian government and to associate themselves with the line taken by the European Union on the Kosovo issue. At the same time it called upon the Albanian government to increase its efforts to stop the flow of weapons from Albania to Kosovo.

The Council called on the international community to find ways to support the Albanian government in this endeavour. It noted the decision of the WEU Permanent Council to prepare a feasibility study on possible options for an international police operation in Albania.

The Council encouraged the government of Albania to continue progress towards the democratic stabilisation of the country. It emphasised the need for further efforts by the Albanian government to fight corruption and to restore law and order and urged it to continue and strengthen this policy. The Council underlined its conviction that political questions in Albania should be discussed and solved in the structures of the Albanian state, in particular in the Albanian parliament, and urged all political organisations to play a constructive role in the democratic process. In this connection it expresses concern at the decision by the opposition Democratic Party to begin a second boycott of parliament and urges the Democratic Party to reconsider its decision and return to parliament.

The Council supported the Albanian government's proposal for an Albania conference at the appropriate time and confirmed the European Union's willingness to continue to make a particular effort to support the rebuilding of Albania. It re-emphasised the closeness of the link between strong EU support for Albania and close co-operation of Albania with the European Union and the international community in its efforts to solve the Kosovo problem.

85. EU, Declaration by the Presidency on behalf of the European Union on Recent Fighting in Kosovo, 98/77/CFSP, Brussels, 20 July 1998

The European Union is appalled and dismayed by reports on intensified hostilities in Kosovo over the last weekend which have - according to reports - left up to 450 people unaccounted for, several dozens of whom seem to have been killed.

The EU condemns the alleged recent infiltrations of several hundred fighters from Albania into Kosovo territory as well as the violence in the Albanian-Yugoslav border area and at Orahovac/Rahovec, and calls urgently on both the armed Kosovar groups and the Serbian authorities to exercise restraint and to cease hostilities immediately. The EU is particularly concerned that VJ shelling has allegedly violated the international border and demands from the Serbian and Yugoslav authorities an immediate halt to such action. It calls on the FRY and the Albanian governments to do all in their power to reduce tensions over Kosovo.

The EU recalls that violent action will not enhance the prospects for a negotiated solution of the Kosovo problem. Indeed, each individual casualty will render an early solution more difficult.

The priorities now are a cessation of hostilities and a start of a meaningful political process.

86. EC Council Regulation No. 1607/98 on Prohibition of New Investment in Republic of Serbia, 24 July 1998[1]

The Council of the European Union,

Having regard to the Treaty establishing the European Community, and in particular Articles 73g and 228a,

Having regard to Common Position 98/374/CFSP of 8 June 198 defined by the Council on the basis of Article J.2 of the Treaty on European Union concerning the prohibition of new investment in Serbia[2],

Having regard to the proposal from the Commission,

Whereas this prohibition measure falls under the scope of the Treaty establishing the European Community;

Whereas, therefore, and notably with a view to avoiding distortion of competition, Community legislation is necessary for the implementation of this measure, as far as the territory of the community is concerned; whereas such territories deemed to encompass, for the purposes of this Regulation the terrritories of the Member States to which the Treaty establishing the European Community is applicable, under the conditions laid down in that Treaty;

Whereas the competent authorities of the Member States should, where necessary, be empowered to ensure compliance with this Regulation;

Whereas there is a need for the Commission and the Member States to inform each other of the measures taken under this Regulation and of other relevant information at their disposal in connection with this Regulation,

has adopted this Regulation:

Article 1

1. It shall be prohibited, as from the date of entry into force of this Regulation, to transfer funds or other financial assets to:

- the State or Government of the Federal Republic of Yugoslavia and of the Republic of Serbia,

- any person in, or resident in, the Republic of Serbia,

- any body carrying out business in, incorporated or constituted under the law of the Republic of Serbia,

- any body owned or controlled by any of the governments, persons or bodies referred to in this paragraph,

- any person acting on behalf of any of the above governments, persons or bodies,

in so far as such funds or other financial assets are transferred for the purposes of establishing a lasting economic link with the Republic of Serbia, including, the acquisition of real establish there.

2. For the purposes of paragraph 1, „funds and other financial assets" shall be understood to mean cash, liquid assets, dividends, interest or other income on shares, bonds, debt obligations and any other securities, are amounts derived from an interest in, or the sale or other disposal of, or any other dealing with tangible and intangible assets, including property rights.

3. The prohibition of paragraph 1 is without prejudice to the execution of contracts concluded before the entry into force of this Regulation and without prejudice to the execution of trade contracts for the supply of goods or services on usual commercial payment conditions.

---

[1] OJ L 209, 27/05/1998, p. 0016-0017, 39R1607.
[2] OJ L 165, 10/06/1998, p. 1.

Article 2

Notwithstanding Article 1, the competent authorities of the Member States may authorise the release of the funds or other financial assets on a case-by-base basis, where those funds or other financial assets are to be used solely for projects in support of democratisation, humanitarian and educational activities and independent media.

Article 3

Each Member State shall determine the sanctions to be imposed where the provisions of this Regulation are infringed. Such sanctions must be effective, proportionate and dissuasive.

Article 4

Without prejudice to the Community rules of confidentiality, the competent authorities of the Member States shall have the power to require banks, other financial institutions and other bodies and persons to provide all relevant information necessary for ensuring compliance with this Regulation.

Article 5

The Commission and the Member States shall inform each other of the measures taken under this Regulation and supply each other with other relevant information at their disposal in connection with this Regulation, such as breaches and enforcement problems, judgements handed down by national courts or decisions of relevant international fora.

Article 6

This Regulation shall apply:

- within the territory of the Community including its airspace,
- on board any aircraft or any vessel under the jurisdiction of a Member State,
- to any person elsewhere who is a national of a Member State,
- to any body which is incorporated or constituted under the law of a Member State.

Article 7

This Regulation shall enter into force on the day of its publication in the Official Journal of the European Communities. This Regulation shall be binding in its entirety and directly applicable in all Member States.

This Regulation shall be binding in its entirety and directly applicable in all Member States.

Done at Brussels, 24 July 1998. For the Council: The President W. Schüssel

87. UN Security Council, Presidential Statement, S/PRST/1998/25, 24 August 1998

[At the 3918th meeting of the Security Council, held on 24 August 1998, the President of the Security Council made the following statement on behalf of the Council:]

"The Security Council has considered the report of the Secretary-General of 5 August 1998 (S/1998/712) submitted pursuant to its resolution 1160 (1998) of 31 March 1998.

"The Security Council remains gravely concerned about the recent intense fighting in Kosovo which has had a devastating impact on the civilian population and has greatly increased the numbers of refugees and displaced persons.

"The Security Council shares the concern of the Secretary-General that the continuation or further escalation of the conflict in Kosovo has dangerous implications for the stability of the region. In particular, the Council is gravely concerned that given the increasing numbers of displaced persons, coupled with the approaching winter, the situation in Kosovo has the potential to become an even greater humanitarian disaster. The Council affirms the right of all refugees and displaced persons to return to their homes. In particular, the Council emphasizes the importance of unhindered and continuous access of humanitarian organizations to the affected population. The Council is concerned over reports of increasing violations of international humanitarian law.

"The Security Council calls for an immediate ceasefire. The Council emphasizes that the authorities of the Federal Republic of Yugoslavia and the Kosovo Albanians must achieve a political solution to the issue of Kosovo and that all violence and acts of terrorism from whatever quarter are unacceptable, and reiterates the importance of the implementation of its resolution 1160 (1998). The Council reaffirms the commitment of all Member States to the sovereignty and territorial integrity of the Federal Republic of Yugoslavia, and urges the authorities of the Federal Republic of Yugoslavia and the Kosovo Albanian leadership to enter immediately into a meaningful dialogue leading to an end to the violence and a negotiated political solution to the issue of Kosovo. It supports in this context the efforts of the Contact Group, including its initiatives to engage the authorities of the Federal Republic of Yugoslavia and the Kosovo Albanian leadership in discussions on the future status of Kosovo.

"In this regard, the Security Council welcomes the announcement by Dr. Ibrahim Rugova, the leader of the Kosovo Albanian community, of the formation of a negotiating team to represent the interests of the Kosovo Albanian community. The formation of the Kosovo Albanian negotiating team should lead to the early commencement of a substantial dialogue with the authorities of the Federal Republic of Yugoslavia, with the aim of ending the violence and achieving a peaceful settlement, including the safe and permanent return of all internally displaced persons and refugees to their homes.

"It remains essential that the authorities of the Federal Republic of Yugoslavia and the Kosovo Albanians accept responsibility for ending the violence in Kosovo, for allowing the people of Kosovo to resume their normal lives and for moving the political process forward.

"The Security Council will continue to follow the situation in Kosovo closely and will remain seized of the matter."

88. EC Council Regulation No. 1901/98, Ban on Flights of Yugoslav Carriers between FRY & EC, 7 September 1998[1]

The Council of the European Union,

Having regard, to the Treaty establishing the European Community and in particular Article 228A thereof,

Having regard to Common Position 98/426/CFSP of 29 June 1998 defined by the Council on the basis of Article J.2 of the Treaty on European Union, concerning a ban on flights by Yugoslav carriers between the Federal Republic of Yugoslavia and the European Community[2]

Having regard to the proposal from the Commission,

Whereas the developments regarding Kosovo have already led the Security Council of the United Nations to impose an arms embargo against the Federal Republic of Yugoslavia (FRY) under Chapter VII of the Charter of the United Nations, and to the consideration of additional measures in case of failure to make constructive progress towards the peaceful resolution of the situation in Kosovo;

Whereas the European Union has already decided on additional measures as envisaged by Common Positions 98/240/CSFP[3], 98/326/CFSP[4] and 98/374/CFSP[5] and the ensuing Council Regulations (EC) Nos. 926/98[6] and 1607/98[7];

---

1 OJ L 248, 08/09/1998, p. 0001, 398R1901.
2 OJ L 190, 04/07/1998, p.3.
3 OJ L 95, 27/03/1998, p. 1
4 OJ L 143, 14/05/1998, p. 1
5 OJ L 165, 10/06/1998, p. 1
6 OJ L 178, 23/06/1998, p. 33
7 OJL 209, 25/07/1998, p.16.

Whereas the Government of the FRY has not stopped the use of indiscriminate violence and brutal repression against its own citizens, which constitute serious violations of human rights and international humanitarian law, and has not taken effective steps to find a political solution to the issue of Kosovo through a process of peaceful dialogue with the Kosovar Albanian Community in order to maintain the regional peace and security;

Whereas, therefore, Common Position 98/426/CFSP foresees a ban of flights by Yugoslav carriers between the Federal Republic of Yugoslavia (FRY) and the European Community as a further measure to obtain from the Government of the FRY the fulfilment of the requirements of UNSC Resolution 1160 (1998) and of the said Common Positions;

Whereas this further measure falls under the scope of the Treaty establishing the European Community;

Whereas, therefore, and notably with a view to avoiding distortion of competition, Community legislation is necessary for the implementation of these measures, as far as the territory of the Community is concerned; whereas such territory is deemed to encompass, for the purposes of this Regulation, the territories of the Member States to which the Treaty establishing the European Community is applicable, under the conditions laid down in that Treaty;

Whereas there is a need to provide for certain specific exemptions;

Whereas there is a need for the Commission and Member States to inform each other of the measures taken under this Regulation and of other relevant information at their disposal in connection with his Regulation;

has adopted this Regulation:

Article 1

1. Aircraft operated directly or indirectly by a Yugoslav carrier, that is a carrier having its principal place of business or office in the Federal Republic of Yugoslavia, shall be prohibited from flying between the Federal Republic of Yugoslavia and The European Community.

2. All operating authorisations granted to Yugoslav carriers are hereby revoked.

Article 2

No new operating authorisations shall be granted or existing ones renewed enabling aircraft registered in the Federal Republic of Yugoslavia to fly to or from airports in the Community.

Article 3

1. Articles 1 and 2 shall not apply to

(a) emergency landings on the territory of the Community and ensuing take-offs;

(b) authorisations for charter series flights between Leipzig and Tivat by Montenegro Airlines.

2. Nothing in this Regulation shall be construed as limiting any existing rights of Yugoslav carriers and aircraft registered in the FRY other than rights to land in or to take off from the territory of the Community.

Article 4

The participation, knowingly and intentionally, in related activities, the object or effect of which is, directly or indirectly, to circumvent the provisions of Articles 1 and 2 shall be prohibited.

Article 5

Each Member State shall determine the sanctions to be imposed where the provisions of this Regulation are infringed. Such sanctions must be effective, proportionate and dissuasive.

Article 6

The Commission and the Member States shall inform each other of the measures taken under this regulation and supply each other with any other relevant information at their disposal in connection judgements handed down by national courts or decisions of relevant international fora.

Article 7

This Regulation shall apply:

- within the territory of the Community including its airspace,

- on board any aircraft or any vessel under the jurisdiction of a Member State,

- to any person elsewhere who is a national of a Member State,

- to any body which is incorporated or constituted under the law of a Member State.

Article 8

This Regulation shall enter into force on the day of its publication in the Official Journal of the European Communities. This Regulation shall be binding in its entirety and directly applicable in all Member States.

This Regulation shall be binding in its entirety and directly applicable in all Member States.

Done at Brussels, 7 September 1998. For the Council: The President W. Schüssel.

89. UN Security Council Resolution 1199 (1998) of 23 September 1998

The Security Council,

Recalling its resolution 1160 (1998) of 31 March 1998,

Having considered the reports of the Secretary-General pursuant to that resolution, and in particular his report of 4 September 1998 (S/1998/834 and Add.1),

Noting with appreciation the statement of the Foreign Ministers of France, Germany, Italy, the Russian Federation, the United Kingdom of Great Britain and Northern Ireland and the United States of America (the Contact Group) of 12 June 1998 at the conclusion of the Contact Group's meeting with the Foreign Ministers of Canada and Japan (S/1998/567, annex), and the further statement of the Contact Group made in Bonn on 8 July 1998 (S/1998/657),

Noting also with appreciation the joint statement by the Presidents of the Russian Federation and the Federal Republic of Yugoslavia of 16 June 1998 (S/1998/526),

Noting further the communication by the Prosecutor of the International Tribunal for the Former Yugoslavia to the Contact Group on 7 July 1998, expressing the view that the situation in Kosovo represents an armed conflict within the terms of the mandate of the Tribunal,

Gravely concerned at the recent intense fighting in Kosovo and in particular the excessive and indiscriminate use of force by Serbian security forces and the Yugoslav Army which have resulted in numerous civilian casualties and, according to the estimate of the Secretary-General, the displacement of over 230,000 persons from their homes,

Deeply concerned by the flow of refugees into northern Albania, Bosnia and Herzegovina and other European countries as a result of the use of force in Kosovo, as well as by the increasing numbers of displaced persons within Kosovo, and other parts of the Federal Republic of Yugoslavia, up to 50,000 of whom the United Nations High Commissioner for Refugees has estimated are without shelter and other basic necessities,

Reaffirming the right of all refugees and displaced persons to return to their homes in safety, and underlining the responsibility of the Federal Republic of Yugoslavia for creating the conditions which allow them to do so,

Condemning all acts of violence by any party, as well as terrorism in pursuit of political goals by any group or individual, and all external support for such activities in Kosovo, including the supply of arms and training for terrorist activities in Kosovo and expressing concern at the reports of continuing violations of the prohibitions imposed by resolution 1160 (1998),

Deeply concerned by the rapid deterioration in the humanitarian situation throughout Kosovo, alarmed at the impending humanitarian catastrophe as described in the report of the Secretary-General, and emphasizing the need to prevent this from happening,

Deeply concerned also by reports of increasing violations of human rights and of international humanitarian law, and emphasizing the need to ensure that the rights of all inhabitants of Kosovo are respected,

Reaffirming the objectives of resolution 1160 (1998), in which the Council expressed support for a peaceful resolution of the Kosovo problem which would include an enhanced status for Kosovo, a substantially greater degree of autonomy, and meaningful self-administration,

Reaffirming also the commitment of all Member States to the sovereignty and territorial integrity of the Federal Republic of Yugoslavia,

Affirming that the deterioration of the situation in Kosovo, Federal Republic of Yugoslavia, constitutes a threat to peace and security in the region,

Acting under Chapter VII of the Charter of the United Nations,

1. *Demands* that all parties, groups and individuals immediately cease hostilities and maintain a ceasefire in Kosovo, Federal Republic of Yugoslavia, which would enhance the prospects for a meaningful dialogue between the authorities of the Federal Republic of Yugoslavia and the Kosovo Albanian leadership and reduce the risks of a humanitarian catastrophe;

2. *Demands also* that the authorities of the Federal Republic of Yugoslavia and the Kosovo Albanian leadership take immediate steps to improve the humanitarian situation and to avert the impending humanitarian catastrophe;

3. *Calls upon* the authorities in the Federal Republic of Yugoslavia and the Kosovo Albanian leadership to enter immediately into a meaningful dialogue without preconditions and with international involvement, and to a clear timetable, leading to an end of the crisis and to a negotiated political solution to the issue of Kosovo, and welcomes the current efforts aimed at facilitating such a dialogue;

4. *Demands further* that the Federal Republic of Yugoslavia, in addition to the measures called for under resolution 1160 (1998), implement immediately the following concrete measures towards achieving a political solution to the situation in Kosovo as contained in the Contact Group statement of 12 June 1998:

(a) cease all action by the security forces affecting the civilian population and order the withdrawal of security units used for civilian repression;

(b) enable effective and continuous international monitoring in Kosovo by the European Community Monitoring Mission and diplomatic missions accredited to the Federal Republic of Yugoslavia, including access and complete freedom of movement of such monitors to, from and within Kosovo unimpeded by government authorities, and expeditious issuance of appropriate travel documents to international personnel contributing to the monitoring;

(c) facilitate, in agreement with the UNHCR and the International Committee of the Red Cross (ICRC), the safe return of refugees and displaced persons to their homes and allow free and unimpeded access for humanitarian organizations and supplies to Kosovo;

(d) make rapid progress to a clear timetable, in the dialogue referred to in paragraph 3 with the Kosovo Albanian community called for in resolution 1160 (1998), with the aim of agreeing confidence-building measures and finding a political solution to the problems of Kosovo;

5. *Notes*, in this connection, the commitments of the President of the Federal Republic of Yugoslavia, in his joint statement with the President of the Russian Federation of 16 June 1998:

(a) to resolve existing problems by political means on the basis of equality for all citizens and ethnic communities in Kosovo;

(b) not to carry out any repressive actions against the peaceful population;

(c) to provide full freedom of movement for and ensure that there will be no restrictions on representatives of foreign States and international institutions accredited to the Federal Republic of Yugoslavia monitoring the situation in Kosovo;

(d) to ensure full and unimpeded access for humanitarian organizations, the ICRC and the UNHCR, and delivery of humanitarian supplies;

(e) to facilitate the unimpeded return of refugees and displaced persons under programmes agreed with the UNHCR and the ICRC, providing State aid for the reconstruction of destroyed homes,

and calls for the full implementation of these commitments;

6. *Insists* that the Kosovo Albanian leadership condemn all terrorist action, and emphasizes that all elements in the Kosovo Albanian community should pursue their goals by peaceful means only;

7. *Recalls* the obligations of all States to implement fully the prohibitions imposed by resolution 1160 (1998);

8. *Endorses* the steps taken to establish effective international monitoring of the situation in Kosovo, and in this connection welcomes the establishment of the Kosovo Diplomatic Observer Mission;

9. *Urges* States and international organizations represented in the Federal Republic of Yugoslavia to make available personnel to fulfil the responsibility of carrying out effective and continuous international monitoring in Kosovo until the objectives of this resolution and those of resolution 1160 (1998) are achieved;

10. *Reminds* the Federal Republic of Yugoslavia that it has the primary responsibility for the security of all diplomatic personnel accredited to the Federal Republic of Yugoslavia as well as the safety and security of all international and non-governmental humanitarian personnel in the Federal Republic of Yugoslavia and calls upon the authorities of the Federal Republic of Yugoslavia and all others concerned in the Federal Republic of Yugoslavia to take all appropriate steps to ensure that monitoring personnel performing functions under this resolution are not subject to the threat or use of force or interference of any kind;

11. *Requests* States to pursue all means consistent with their domestic legislation and relevant international law to prevent funds collected on their territory being used to contravene resolution 1160 (1998);

12. *Calls upon* Member States and others concerned to provide adequate resources for humanitarian assistance in the region and to respond promptly and generously to the United Nations Consolidated Inter-Agency Appeal for Humanitarian Assistance Related to the Kosovo Crisis;

13. *Calls upon* the authorities of the Federal Republic of Yugoslavia, the leaders of the Kosovo Albanian community and all others concerned to cooperate fully with the Prosecutor of the International Tribunal for the Former Yugoslavia in the investigation of possible violations within the jurisdiction of the Tribunal;

14. *Underlines* also the need for the authorities of the Federal Republic of Yugoslavia to bring to justice those members of the security forces who have been involved in the mistreatment of civilians and the deliberate destruction of property;

15. *Requests* the Secretary-General to provide regular reports to the Council as necessary on his assessment of compliance with this resolution by the authorities of the Federal Republic of Yugoslavia and all elements in the Kosovo Albanian community, including through his regular reports on compliance with resolution 1160 (1998);

16. *Decides*, should the concrete measures demanded in this resolution and resolution 1160 (1998) not be taken, to consider further action and additional measures to maintain or restore peace and stability in the region;

17. *Decides* to remain seized of the matter.

[Adopted by the Security Council at its 3930th meeting on 23 September 1998 with 14 votes to none and China abstaining.]

90. UN, Extracts from the Debate of the Security Council Concerning Security Council Resolution 1199 (1998), UN Doc. S/PV. 3930, 23 September 1998[1]

[Members of the Council had before them the report of the Secretary-General prepared pursuant to resolution 1160 (1998) of the Security Council, documents S/1998/834 and addendum 1, as well as a draft resolution submitted by France, Germany, Italy, Japan, Portugal, Slovenia, Sweden, the United Kingdom of Great Britain and Northern Ireland and the United States of America (S/1998/882).][2]

[...]

Mr. Lavrov (Russian Federation) *(interpretation from Russian)*: [...] The situation in and around Kosovo, Federal Republic of Yugoslavia, remains extremely difficult. As a result of the continued armed confrontations, including some in which heavy weapons are used, there is a steady flow of refugees and displaced persons, which, under conditions of the onset of winter, is fraught with grave humanitarian consequences. In violation of Security Council resolution 1160 (1998), material and financial support from abroad continues to be provided to Kosovo extremists, first and foremost from the territory of Albania, which is seriously destabilizing the situation and provoking tensions in Kosovo. Despite the efforts undertaken, it has to date been impossible to establish a direct political dialogue between the Serbian authorities, the Federal Republic of Yugoslavia and the leadership of the Kosovo Albanians.

Under these circumstances, an urgent need has arisen to give additional impetus to international efforts to facilitate a political settlement and the normalization of the humanitarian situation in the area.

Such an impetus should be given by the draft resolution that the Security Council will be adopting today. That draft resolution explicitly reaffirms the sovereignty and territorial integrity of the Federal Republic of Yugoslavia, and calls once again upon Belgrade and the Kosovo Albanians to cease hostilities immediately and maintain a ceasefire in Kosovo in order to create favourable conditions for the launching of a political dialogue and to avert a humanitarian disaster.

The Security Council demands also that the authorities in the Federal Republic of Yugoslavia and the Kosovo Albanian leadership take immediate steps to improve the humanitarian situation. It calls upon them once again to enter immediately into a meaningful dialogue leading to a negotiated political settlement to the issue of Kosovo, and endorses the agreements reached by the Presidents of Russia and the Federal Republic of Yugoslavia at their June meeting in Moscow.

It insists that the Kosovo Albanian leadership condemn all terrorist action and rely on peaceful means only. The draft resolution reaffirms the provisions of Security Council resolution 1160 (1998), inter alia, on assistance to Kosovo separatists from abroad. It condemns the continuing promotion from abroad of terrorist activities in Kosovo. Recalling the obligations of all States to implement fully the prohibitions imposed by resolution 1160 (1998), the Security Council expresses concern over reports of their continuing violation. The draft resolution also contains a reference to Chapter VII of the Charter of the United Nations, as did resolution 1160 (1998).

The Security Council maintains that if the demands set forth in resolution 1160 (1998) and in the draft resolution before us today - which apply both to Belgrade and the Albanians living in Kosovo - are not met, the Council will consider further actions and necessary additional measures. No use of force and no sanctions are being imposed by the Council at the present stage.

The basic provisions of the draft resolution correspond to the fundamental stance taken by the Russian Federation which favours settlement of the conflict in Kosovo exclusively through peaceful and political means on the basis of granting broad autonomy to Kosovo, with strict respect for the territorial integrity of the Federal Republic of Yugoslavia. We are convinced that there is no reasonable alternative to such an approach. In particular, the use of unilateral measures of force in order to settle this conflict is fraught with the risk of destabilizing the Balkan region and of all of Europe and would have long-term adverse consequences for the international system, which relies on the central role of the United Nations.

The Russian Federation, in voting in favour of today's draft resolution, will continue to make an active to contribution to international efforts to foster a peaceful settlement of the Kosovo conflict.

Mr. Qin Huasun (China) *(interpretation from Chinese)*: [...] China has always been of the view that the question of Kosovo is an internal matter of the Federal Republic of Yugoslavia. Proceeding from the principle, recognized by the whole international community, of respect for and maintenance of the sovereignty and territorial integrity of the Federal Republic of Yugoslavia, we believe that the question of Kosovo should and can only be solved by the Yugoslav people themselves in their own way. Ultimately, it is for the Yugoslav people themselves to come to a resolution.

We appreciate the position of the Government of the Federal Republic of Yugoslavia regarding settling the Kosovo issue through unconditional dialogue. The situation in the Kosovo region is now stabilizing. There is no large-scale armed conflict, still less any escalation of the conflict. The Government of the Federal Republic of Yugoslavia has also taken a series of positive measures to encourage the refugees to return home and provide facilities for humanitarian relief work.

However, at the same time, we are gravely concerned about the action - pointed out in the Secretary-General's report of 4 September - of blocking, for political purposes, the return of refugees and prolonging the humanitarian crisis so as to keep the attention of the international community on this region.

We believe that the international community should view the current situation in Kosovo as it really is and evaluate the positive efforts by the Government of the Federal Republic of Yugoslavia in an objective and just manner. We do not see the situation in Kosovo as a threat to international peace and security.

I would like to reiterate here that many countries in the region are multi-ethnic. If the Security Council becomes involved in a dispute without being requested to do so by the countries of the region - or goes even further and unfairly applies pressure on or threatens actions against the Government of the country concerned - it would create a bad precedent and have wider negative implications.

Unfortunately the draft resolution before us has not taken into full consideration the situation in Kosovo and the legitimate rights of the Federal Republic of Yugoslavia within its sphere of sovereignty. It has invoked Chapter VII of the United Nations Charter all too indiscreetly in order to threaten the Federal Republic of Yugoslavia. This will not help bring about the fundamental settlement of the Kosovo issue. It may, on the contrary, reinforce the separatist and terrorist forces in the region and increase the tension there.

In view of the above, the Chinese delegation cannot support the draft resolution before us and will be compelled to abstain.

[The President put to the vote the draft resolution S/1998/882, which was adopted with 14 votes to none and China abstaining. The draft resolution has been adopted as resolution 1199 (1998).]

[...]

Sir Jeremy Greenstock (United Kingdom): [...] Despite the efforts of the international community to help find a settlement, the security forces of President Milosevic are continuing to inflict brutality and repression on those they claim to see as their fellow citizens. The so-

---

[1] Only statements which add to the legal analysis or factual background have been included. Presidential statements not related to substantive issues have also been omitted.

[2] In 1998 membership of the Council was as follows: Bahrain, Brazil, China, Costa Rica, France, Gabon, Gambia, Japan, Kenya, Portugal, Russian Federation, Slovenia, Sweden, the United Kingdom of Great Britain and Northern Ireland and the United States of America. The President invited the representatives of Albania, Bosnia and Herzegovina, Germany and Italy to participate in the discussion, without the right to vote in accordance with the Charter and rule 37 of the Council's provisional rules of procedure.

called Kosovo Liberation Army has contributed to the present crisis. Terrorism in whatever guise and for whatever end is unacceptable. But as the British Prime Minister said in his speech to the General Assembly two days ago:

"Nothing can justify scorched earth tactics and forcible creation of hundreds of thousands of refugees".

This resolution, co-sponsored and strongly supported by the United Kingdom, does three things. First, it calls for an immediate ceasefire and for the two parties to begin a political dialogue - the only route to a political and lasting solution. Secondly, it sets out clearly President Milosevic's obligations and commitments, including to put an end to repression and to facilitate the return of refugees. Thirdly, and most important, it makes clear that the international community's patience is exhausted.

President Milosevic carries a direct responsibility. If he ignores those obligations and continues to pursue military repression, the international community will respond and will respond vigorously. By acting under Chapter VII of the United Nations Charter and by explicitly characterizing the deterioration of the situation in Kosovo as a threat to peace and security in the region, the Security Council is putting President Milosevic on notice that he will be held accountable for his actions. He would be wise to take heed.

Mr. Burleigh (United States of America): [...] My Government strongly supports this important resolution on Kosovo. It underscores our growing concern that Belgrade's repressive actions have created a potentially catastrophic humanitarian situation as winter approaches. It increases pressure on Belgrade to negotiate seriously with the Kosovo Albanians to achieve a political settlement that provides for democratic self-government for the people of Kosovo and avoids the devastating consequences of continued conflict. It also affirms that the situation constitutes a serious threat to peace and security in the region.

To date, approximately a quarter of a million people have been displaced by the offensive actions of the Serb security forces. At least 50,000 Kosovo Albanians are living in open valleys and forests, without shelter or basic necessities. The international community must act to prevent a disaster this fall.

The best way to stem this crisis is for Belgrade to heed our demands for an immediate cessation of offensive actions and the pull-back of its security forces. We also call for a meaningful dialogue, without preconditions and with international involvement, leading to a solution to the Kosovo question, as set out in this resolution. My Government is continuing its efforts to assist in such a dialogue and to coordinate with members of the Contact Group and others in this effort.

In particular, the authorities in Belgrade must be held to account for creating the current crisis. It is their responsibility to create the conditions to allow all refugees and displaced persons to return to their homes in safety. Belgrade is responsible for the well-being of the people of Kosovo, as well as for the security of all diplomatic personnel and non-governmental humanitarian personnel on the ground.

This resolution endorses international monitoring and humanitarian efforts and demands that there be full and unimpeded access, without interference in international monitoring or delivery of assistance and humanitarian supplies.

Adequate resources for humanitarian assistance in the region are vital. My Government has earmarked $20 million in assistance, in addition to $11 million previously identified, as well as other donations. We appreciate the very important contributions of others, including Members of this Council, and urge all United Nations Member States to respond to the urgent appeal by the United Nations High Commissioner for Refugees.

We also underline the importance of full cooperation with the International Tribunal for the Former Yugoslavia.

We all hope that this resolution and the ongoing efforts to reach a settlement will convince Belgrade to comply with the demands of the international community. Planning at the North Atlantic Treaty Organization for military operations if these efforts do not succeed is nearing completion. The international community will not stand idly by as the situation in Kosovo deteriorates.

Today the Security Council sends a strong, unequivocal message. The Council will not tolerate the continued violence, lawlessness, repression, and violation of human rights in Kosovo. [...]

91. Council of Europe, Parliamentary Assembly, Recommendation 1384 (1998), Crisis in Kosovo and Situation in the FRY, 24 September 1998

[Text adopted by the Assembly on 24 September 1998 (31st Sitting).]

1. The Assembly strongly condemns the continuing escalation of violence in Kosovo, which has already driven more than 280 000 people from their homes and brought the region to the brink of war.

2. The Assembly reiterates its position expressed in Resolution 1146 and Recommendations 1360, 1368 and 1374 (1998), adopted since January this year. It calls for an immediate ceasefire and the creation of conditions permitting the voluntary return of refugees and displaced persons. International observers should have unimpeded access to all parts of Kosovo, to assess the situation and investigate allegations of war crimes and other violations of human rights.

3. The Assembly considers the following elements to be essential in reaching a lasting peaceful solution to the crisis:

i. security guaranteed to all people living in Kosovo and achieved through the withdrawal of the Serbian security forces, the disarmament of armed groups of ethnic Albanians and the deployment of an international peace force;

ii. a new political status for Kosovo based on a high level of autonomy within the Yugoslav federation and including:

a. the highest possible form of self-government for Kosovo in the fields of law-making and the executive, the judiciary, public order, the economy, education and culture;

b. respect for the rights of Serbs and other minorities living in Kosovo;

c. direct participation of Kosovo representatives in the federal institutions;

iii. democratic reforms implemented throughout the Federal Republic of Yugoslavia and guaranteeing full compliance with Council of Europe standards concerning the functioning of a democratic political system, the rule of law and the protection of human rights and the rights of national minorities, notably in Kosovo, Vojvodina and Sanjak;

iv. international guarantees ensuring respect for the future agreement and preventing any attempts to return to the status quo or to secede.

4. The Assembly considers that, in the absence of a clear and unequivocal position of the international community on the future status of Kosovo, the political and military pressure exerted on both sides to engage in negotiations remains largely ineffective.

5. The Assembly strongly supports the resolution of the United Nations Security Council of 23 September 1998 and underlines the necessity for an immediate ceasefire.

6. The Assembly therefore recommends that the Committee of Ministers organise an international conference on the future status of Kosovo as soon as possible, with the participation of all interested parties, governments and all relevant international bodies.

92. EU, Declaration by the European Union on a Comprehensive Approach to Kosovo, 98/128/CFSP, Brussels, 27 October 1998

The EU remains gravely concerned at the situation in Kosovo, in particular regarding the plight of the civilian population, refugees and displaced persons. Tens of thousands of people may still be without permanent shelter in Kosovo as winter approaches. The EU will continue to engage substantial resources towards alleviating this plight.

The EU fully supports the agreements signed in Belgrade on 16 October 1998 between the FRY and the OSCE, and on 15 October 1998 between the FRY and NATO through negotiations mandated by the Contact Group on the basis of relevant SCRs, as an important step towards a political solution to the Kosovo crisis. It welcomed UN Security Council Resolution 1203 of 24 October conferring the authority of the UN to the demand for full and immediate compliance by all parties concerned with these agreements, the unilateral commitments and UNSCRs 1160 and 1199. The focus is now on full and immediate compliance, by all Parties concerned.

Although some progress has been made, the FRY is still not respecting the provisions of UNSCR 1199, in particular with regard to the withdrawal of security forces to their positions prior to March 1998. The EU calls on all parties, and in particular on President Milosevic, to live up to their obligations and commitments, to refrain from further acts of violence in the region and to engage in immediate political negotiations. It welcomes the statement of Ibrahim Rugova on 22 October in response to the efforts of the EU Special Envoy Petritsch calling on the armed Kosovo Albanian groups to refrain from action which could be used as a provocation for new attacks by Serb/Yugoslav security forces, and expressing his support for the Milosevic-Holbrooke agreement. The need remains for pressure to be maintained to ensure compliance and to prevent a return to violence and repression. In this respect the EU will take the necessary steps to enhance the effective implementation of its own sanctions.

The EU pledges its full support for the OSCE and for the Kosovo Verification mission, to which Member States will contribute very substantially in personnel and resources. It commends the efforts of Poland, as chair-in-office of the OSCE, and Norway in this respect. Clear and effective lines of responsibility within the KVM are essential. The substantial overall European contribution to the KVM should be fully reflected in the positions of responsibility to be filled by EU nationals. The Presidency has conveyed this point to the OSCE Chairman in Office. Financial provisions should be based on the principle of equitable burden-sharing and on established OSCE procedures.

The EU welcomes the ECMM plans to considerably and quickly increase its presence in Kosovo in order to facilitate the early start of KVM. The ECMM should maintain a liaison presence in KVM HQs in Pristina for reporting purposes.

The effectiveness and security of the OSCE KVM mission are paramount concerns. The EU expects President Milosevic and those responsible in the Kosovo Albanian community to ensure the safety of the verifiers and international humanitarian personnel. The EU supports the provision of a rapid reaction capability.

The EU also supports NATO's air verification mission, and would welcome the participation of Russia and other non-NATO countries. Good coordination between air and ground verification are essential in verifying compliance.

It is urgent for the Parties to start real negotiations on the future status of Kosovo. President Milosevic must stand by his unilateral statement, which is a constitutive element in his overall agreement with Ambassador Holbrooke. The Kosovo Albanian leadership must engage in serious dialogue without preconditions, and with the widest possible representation in its negotiating team. The EU as a major factor in the stability of the Balkans will continue its efforts to restore peace in Kosovo. As part of these efforts, the EU will remain actively involved in supporting the negotiating process, notably through the activity of the EU Special Envoy, Ambassador Petritsch, on the basis of the US proposal as amended and endorsed by the Contact Group and the EU.

The EU is already contributing very substantially in Kosovo, and is prepared to continue contributing, not least in the framework of the KVM. The Commission is already urgently analysing all possibilities in the different fields of assistance to Kosovo. Member States will provide substantial assistance directly and through UN agencies, international organizations and NGOs. EU Member States are ready, in accordance with EU priorities, to make available additional financial resources to support the OSCE KVM mission and EC and Member States will consider this for humanitarian programmes. The EU will address the issues of refugee return, winterization and reconstruction, within a plan of action, on the basis of the assessment by the Belgrade and Geneva working groups on humanitarian issues.

The EU will consider ways in which it can contribute, under the right conditions, to implementing confidence building measures among the various communities in Kosovo and to further civil society building, including community support for the implementation of the Education Agreement.

The Council has invited the Commission and competent Council bodies to prepare further proposals within this comprehensive approach for early presentation to the General Affairs Council.

93. Hill Proposals for a Settlement in Kosovo, October1998 - January 1999

93 a) First Draft Agreement for a Settlement of the Crisis in Kosovo, 1 October 1998

I. 1. All citizens in Kosovo have equal rights and duties as set forth in this Agreement in Kosovo, members of each national community have additional rights as set forth below.

2. Nothing in this Agreement shall be interpreted as authority or Federal and Republic organs to intervene in the work of the organs of Kosovo. The areas of competence of the respective organs shall be defined in this Agreement.

3. The organs of Kosovo shall follow principles of full respect for human rights, democracy, and national communities.

4. Citizens in Kosovo shall enjoy, without limitation, human and democratic rights and shall be given the opportunity to be represented in all organs of authority.

5. Every person in Kosovo shall have the right to apply to international institutions, including the European Court of Human Rights, for the protection of their rights in accordance with the procedures of such institutions.

6. Each side will implement the Agreement in accordance with its procedures including for the Republic of Serbia and the Federal Republic of Yugoslavia their respective legal systems, and international standards, including the Helsinki Final Act.

II. Rights and Duties of Citizens in Kosovo

1. Kosovo shall retain its current boundaries.

2. Persons in Kosovo shall concern themselves democratically through legislative, executive, and judicial organs established in this Agreement. The rights and duties of citizens in Kosovo will include the right to democratic-government and to participate in free and fair elections.

3. The basic unit of government will be the communes. All responsibilities not expressly assigned elsewhere by this Agreement will be the responsibility of the communes.

4. The Federal authorities will have responsibility in Kosovo for territorial integrity, maintaining a common market within the Federal Republic of Yugoslavia, monetary policy, defense, foreign policy consistent with the Constitution of the Federal Republic of Yugoslavia, customs services, and other functions specified in the Agreement.

5. The organs of Kosovo shall not interfere in the additional rights described in Part 3 of this Agreement.

III. Rights of National Communities

1. Members of the national communities shall have additional rights determined by this Agreement in order to preserve and express their national, cultural, religious, and linguistic identities in accordance with international standards and the Helsinki Final Act.

2. The national communities shall be legally equal and shall not use their additional rights as to endanger the rights of other national communities or the rights of citizens.

3. Each national community shall select through democratic means, in accordance with procedures it shall decide, a National Council to administer the affairs of the community in Kosovo. Each Council will establish its own executive organs and procedures.

4. The national communities shall be subject to decisions of the Assembly of Kosovo, provided that any decisions concerning national communities must be non-discriminatory. The Assembly shall decide upon a procedure for resolving disputes between national communities.

5. The additional rights of the national communities are to:

(i) preserve and protect their national cultures, including by: using their languages and alphabets. inscribing local names of towns and villages, of squares and streets, and of other topographic names in the language and alphabet of the national community, consistent with decisions about style made by the communal organs. providing information in the language and alphabet of the national community. establishing educational, cultural and religious associations, for which relevant authorities will provide financial assistance. enjoying unhindered contacts with their respective national communities outside of the Federal Republic of Yugoslavia. using and displaying national symbols. providing for education, in particular for schooling in their own language and alphabet and in national culture and history. protecting national practices on family law by, if the community decides, arranging rules in the field of heritage, family, and matrimonial relations; tutorship and adoption. the preservation of sites or religious, historical, or cultural importance. implementing public health and social services. operating religious institutions in cooperation with religious authorities.

(ii) adopt procedures for dispute resolution, as provided in Article V(1)(b) of this Agreement;

(iii) be guaranteed at least one radio and TV frequency, which it shall administer subject to non-discriminatory, technical standards;

(iv) finance activities of the national communities by collecting charges a National Council decides to levy on members of its own community.

6. Members of national communities will also be guaranteed: the right to participate in regional and international non-governmental organizations in accordance with procedures of these organizations; and equal access to employment in public services.

IV. The Organs of Kosovo
PART I: GENERAL

1. The organs of Kosovo are the Assembly, the Chairman, the Government, the Administrative Organs, and the Ombudsman.

The Assembly

2. The Assembly

(a) (i) The Assembly shall comprise ( ) Members, of which ( ) Members shall be directly elected in accordance with Article VII(4). (ii) The remaining) Members shall be allocated among the national communities with at least)% of the population, each of which shall elect Members democratically according to its own procedure.

(b) The Assembly shall he responsible for enacting all decisions of Kosovo, including those regulating relations in political, economic, social, and cultural areas consistent with this Agreement. Its areas of responsibility include:

The adoption of the organic documents of Kosovo;

The adoption of regulations on the organization and procedures of the organs of Kosovo;

The adoption of budgets and annual accounts of the Organs of the Government;

Cooperation with Federal and Republic authorities;

Ensuring freedom of movement;

Financing activities of the Organs of the Provisional Government;

Coordination among communes or national communities when necessary, including the enactment of laws or decisions necessary and property for inter-communal issues; and Confirmation of the members of the Governing Board and judges of the courts.

(c) Decisions of the Assembly shall be taken by majority of those present and voting, except as provided in paragraph (d).

(d) When a majority of the Members of a national community covered by paragraph (a)(ii) assert that a proposed decision affects the vital interests of their national community, that decision shall require for approval a majority that includes the majority of the Members present and voting from the affected national community. If a majority of Members from the asserting community is not present and voting, the regular voting rule shall apply.

(e) A procedure for resolving disputes over the sue of the procedure established in paragraph (d) will be agreed.

(f) A majority of Members present shall constitute a quorum.

(g) The Assembly will decide its own rules of procedure and select its officers. Each national community covered by paragraph (a)(ii) shall be represented in the leadership. The Presidency of the Assembly shall rotate each term of office among those national communities in alphabetical order but may not be from the same national community as the Chairman.

The Chairman

3. There shall be a Chairman, who shall be directly elected. The Chairman shall be responsible for: Chairing meetings of the Government -

Representing all persons in Kosovo before any international Federal, or

Republic body, with the President of the Assembly when required by this Agreement.

Meeting regularly with the National Councils and with other representatives of the national communities and other persons.

Conducting foreign relations consistent with the Constitution of the Federal Republic of Yugoslavia.

Signing agreements on behalf of Kosovo after they are approved by the Assembly.

Serving on the Joint Implementation Commission established by this Agreement. Meeting regularly with the president of the Federal Republic of Yugoslavia, the President of Montenegro, and the President of Serbia to discuss issues of mutual concern.

Government

4. Executive power shall be exercised by the Government.(a) The Government shall comprise ( ) Members, including at less one person from each national community.(b) The Government shall be responsible for implementing an enforcing decisions of the Assembly and, when devolved to the competences, of other governmental organs.

(c) Decisions of the Government shall require a majority of members present and voting. The Government shall otherwise decide its own rules of procedure.

Ombudsman

6. (a) There shall be an Ombudsman of Kosovo, who shall monitor the implementation of this Agreement, particularly with regard to the right of the national communities.

(b) The selection, term, and termination of the Ombudsman shall be set forth in the Agreement.

(a) The Ombudsman shall have complete, unimpeded and immediate access to any person, place, or information upon his on her request. He or she shall have the right to intervene before any Federal or other domestic authority upon his or her request.

PART II: THE COMMUNES

1. Kosovo shall have ( ) communes, with boundaries determined by

2. Communes may by mutual agreement form self-administering regions comprising multiple communes.

3. Each commune shall have a Council and such executive bodies as each Council may establish. Each national community with at least ( )% of the population of the commune shall be represented on the Council in proportion to its share of the regional population or by one member, whichever is greater.

4. The communes shall have exclusive responsibility for carrying out typical function of local and regional government, including: Providing law enforcement, including criminal investigations, prosecution, and punishment. Regulating and, when appropriate, providing childcare. Establishing and regulating the work of medical institutions and hospitals. Special arrangements will be made for institutions owned by government entities. Protecting the environment. Regulating commerce and privately owned stores. Regulating hunting and fishing. Planning and carrying out public works of communal or Kosovo wide territorial importance, including roads and water supplies. Regulating land use, town planning, building regulations and housing construction. Designing and implementing programs of economic, scientific, technological, demographic, regional and social development, and programs for the development of agriculture and of rural areas. Developing programs for tourism, the hotel industry, catering, and sport. Organizing fairs and local markets. Organizing public services of communal importance, including fire, emergency response, and police. Financing the work of communal organs, including raising revenues, taxes, and preparing budgets.

4. Each commune shall conduct its business in public and shall maintain publicly available records of its deliberations and decisions.

Part 3. Representation of Kosovo in Federal and Republic Bodies.

(a) The participation of Kosovo in Federal institutions shall be discussed, in particular to obtain appropriate representation in Federal organs responsible for developing and implementing defense and economic policies and to take into account developments in Yugoslavia since 1991.

(b) The following is without prejudice to the rights of persons in Kosovo to decide whether to accept the offer and to the review described in section VIII(3):

Kosovo shall be offered at least (ten) deputies in the House of Citizens of the Federal Assembly and (twenty) deputies in the National Assembly of the Republic of Serbia. Each national community in Kosovo shall be offered at least one place in the Federal Government and in the Government of the Republic of Serbia. Each national community in Kosovo shall be offered at least one judge on the Federal Court of the Federal Republic and three judges on the Supreme Court of Serbia.

(c) In order to monitor the protection of additional rights of the national communities, a Council for the protection of members of the national communities shall be established.

V. RESOLVING CONFLICTS AND MAINTAINING PUBLIC ORDER

(I) Dispute Resolution

(a) Courts in Kosovo.

The Assembly shall establish common and supreme courts for Kosovo with jurisdiction over constitutional, civil, and criminal matters. Appeals from these courts?

(b) National Communities. Each community may establish procedures for resolving conflicts concerning inheritance, family law, matrimonial relations, tutorship, adoption, civil lawsuits as decided by the Assembly of Kosovo, and criminal cases for which imprisonment of up to one year is prescribed in the currently applicable penal code. These procedures must ensure that practices are consistent with internationally recognized human rights. They shall have jurisdiction only when all parties to a dispute agree.

Decisions of the national community dispute resolution mechanism shall be honored by other courts in Kosovo and the Federal Republic of Yugoslavia in accordance with applicable rules.

(2) Police.

(a) Police shall be sworn to uphold the law impartially, fairly, and with equal treatment for all persons.

(b) All police operating in Kosovo must be trained to internationally accepted standards for police operations, in particular with regard to human rights.

Paragraphs (c) and (d) to be developed further

(c) Each commune shall establish local police, which shall have membership representative of the commune. Police (such as customs police) from other governmental levels shall recruit members of national communities so that the composition of such police forces in Kosovo will be representative of the population there.

(d) The local police shall be exclusively responsible for maintaining public order and peace. Federal and Republic police shall not carry out this responsibility. Federal and Republic authorities, in accordance with their respective responsibilities, shall retain responsibility for external security, border police, and the investigation of international and extra-Kosovo crime.

(e) Each commune shall establish commission to review and make recommendations on all matters concerning the police, including in particular complaints about violations of human rights. Every national community in the commune will have the right to participate on the commission. These commissions shall have the complete cooperation of both sides and unimpeded access to any person, place. document, and information it requests.

VI. FINANCING

1. The bodies established in Sections II-IV shall have the right to keep revenues from their own taxes or other charges. They shall also have part of revenue otherwise derived in Kosovo (including duties or fees). The organs of Kosovo shall participate in the collection of customs and other duties within Kosovo according to procedures to be agreed.

2. In recognition of the fact that this Agreement confers new responsibilities upon bodies in Kosovo, Republic and the Federal authorities shall examine how to provide resources necessary for the conduct of its responsibilities. These resources shall include funds (including tax remission), equipment, and training.

3. Federal and Republic authorities shall also facilitate, to the extent of their respective authorities, the delivery of resources from international sources to Kosovo.

VII. IMPLEMENTATION PERIOD

1. This Agreement shall be implemented as quickly as possible. The signatories of this Agreement take the obligation to allow, insofar as possible, it's adequate implementation even before the adoption and undertaking of all acts and measures fixed in the Agreement.

2. All sides will start without delay an any and all legal changes, necessary for the full implementation of this Agreement. They acknowledge that complete implementation will require the adoption of necessary state regulations and other general acts of the organic document of Kosovo, political acts and measures, and the elections of establishment of institutions and bodies established by this Agreement.

3. Each national community in Kosovo is authorized to start exercising the additional rights determined by this Agreement, to the extent possible, immediately upon signature.

4. Within ( ) months, there will be elections for all bodies established by this Agreement. The Government of the FRY hereby invites the Organization for Security and Cooperation in Rome (OSCE) to conduct those elections.

5. Under international supervision, an objective and free census of the population in Kosovo shall be carried out when the international supervisor determines that conditions allow an accurate census.

6. All relevant governmental institutions shall provide the organs of Kosovo with all necessary records about the places of residence, citizenship, voters' lists, and other data.

7. The signatories of this Agreement shall provide active support, cooperation, and participation for the successful implementation of the Agreement.

8. Laws and institutions currently in place in Kosovo shall remain until replaced by a decision of a competent body established by this Agreement.

VIII. AMENDMENTS

1. Amendments to the Agreement shall be adopted by signature of the parties.

2. Each signatory may propose amendments at any time and will consider and consult with the other with regard to proposed amendments.

3. In three years, the sides will undertake a comprehensive assessment of the Agreement, with the aim of improving its implementation and considering proposals by either side for additional steps, which will require mutual agreement for adoption.

IX. FINAL PROVISIONS

1. This Agreement is concluded in the ( ) languages.

2. This Agreement shall enter into force upon the competition of the internal process of each side.

FOR Federal Republic of Yugoslavia; Republic of Serbia; Kosovo

93 b) Revised Hill Proposal, 1 November 1998

I. Introduction

1. All citizens in Kosovo have equal rights and duties as set forth in this Agreement and the international agreements specified in Annex 1. In Kosovo, members of each national community have additional rights as set forth below.

2. The authorities of Kosovo, acting in accordance with this Agreement, are autonomous. The Parties accept and will abide by the principle that their powers and authorities in Kosovo are as specified by this Agreement, which shall prevail over contradictory legal authority of any Party. The Parties shall take all necessary legal steps within their respective systems to carry out this Agreement.

3. The authorities of Kosovo shall follow principles of full respect for human rights, democracy, and national communities.

4. Citizens in Kosovo shall enjoy, without limitation, human and democratic rights and shall be given the opportunity to be represented in all institutions of authority.

5. Every person in Kosovo shall have the right to apply to international institutions [, including the European Court of Human Rights,] for the protection of their rights in accordance with the procedure of such institutions.

6. Each side will implement the Agreement in accordance with its procedures and international standards, including the Helsinki Final Act.

II. Governance in Kosovo

PART I: GENERAL

1. Citizens in Kosovo shall govern themselves democratically through legislative, executive, judicial, and other institutions established in this Agreement. The rights and duties of citizens in Kosovo will include the right to democratic self-government and to participate in free and fair elections.

2. The basic [territorial] unit of [local] government will be the communes. All responsibilities not expressly assigned elsewhere by this Agreement will be the responsibility of the communes.

[Option 1: 3. The authorities of Kosovo shall have responsibility for all areas except the following, which shall be within the competence of the Federal Republic save as specified in paragraph four: (a) territorial integrity, (b) maintaining a common market within the Federal Republic of Yugoslavia, which power shall be exercised in a manner that does not discriminate against any particular region or area of the Federal Republic, (c) monetary policy, (d) defense, (e) foreign policy consistent with the Constitution of the Federal Republic of Yugoslavia, (f) customs services, and (g) other functions specified in the Constitution of the Federal Republic of Yugoslavia][1].Citizens in Kosovo shall continue to participate in areas reserved for the Federal Republic through their representation in Federal institutions.

4. Kosovo shall retain the following powers in the areas otherwise reserved for the Federal Republic:

(a) No change to the borders of Kosovo shall be made without the consent of the Kosovo Assembly and [President] [Presidency];

(b) No armed attacks shall be launched from the territory of Kosovo without the prior consent of the [President] [Presidency] of Kosovo. Deployment and use of force in Kosovo shall be governed by Annex 2 of this Agreement;

(c) Kosovo officers and institutions shall have the authority to conduct foreign relations [in cultural, economic, and other fields] consistent with the present Constitution of the Federal Republic of Yugoslavia;

(d) Citizens in Kosovo serving as Federal customs officers shall play a role in carrying out customs activities in Kosovo. Customs officers shall be representative of the national communities of Kosovo.]

[Option 2:

3. The authorities of Kosovo will not have responsibility in Kosovo for the following areas: (a) territorial integrity, (b) maintaining a common market within the Federal Republic of Yugoslavia, (c) monetary policy, (d) defense, (e) foreign policy except as consistent with the Constitution of the Federal Republic of Yugoslavia, (f) customs services, and (g) other functions specified in the Constitution of the Federal Republic of Yugoslavia][2].It is understood that Federal authorities will carry out these responsibilities. Citizens in Kosovo shall continue to participate in areas reserved for the Federal Republic through their representation in Federal institutions.

The authorities of Kosovo shall not interfere in the additional rights described in Part V of this Agreement.

PART II: ASSEMBLY, [PRESIDENT] [PRESIDENCY], COUNCIL OF MINISTERS, AND ADMINISTRATIVE BODIES

The Assembly

1. There shall be an Assembly, which shall comprise [ ] Members.

(a) [ ] Members shall be directly elected in accordance with Article X (4) and Annex 4.

(b) The remaining [ ] Members shall be allocated [equally] by the formula set forth in Annex 5] among the international communities with at least [ ] % of the population of Kosovo, each of which shall elect Members democratically according to its own procedure. Each national community recognized under the principle set forth in Annex 5 shall have at least one Member in the Assembly.

2. The Assembly shall be responsible for enacting [Decisions] [laws] of Kosovo, including those regulating relations in political, economic, social, and cultural areas consistent with this Agreement. Its areas of responsibility shall include:

- The adoption of the [Basic Law] [Constitution] of Kosovo consistent with this Agreement, which shall not be subject to change or modification by authorities of the Republics or the Federal Republic of Yugoslavia;

- The adoption of regulations concerning the organization, procedures, and functioning of the administrative bodies of Kosovo;

- The adoption of budgets and annual accounts of the Administrative bodies and other institutions of Kosovo, with the exception of communal and national community institutions unless otherwise specified by this Agreement;

- Cooperation with Federal Assemblies, and with the Assemblies of the Republics;

---

[1] A proposal may be made to expand the list of Federal responsibilities.
[2] see supra note.

- Ensuring freedom of movement of goods, services, and persons inside Kosovo and between Kosovo and other parts of the Federal Republic of Yugoslavia, consistent with Federal responsibilities;

- Financing activities of Kosovo institutions, including by levying taxes or other charges;

- Conduct of relations with foreign entities consistent with this Agreement and the [Basic Law] [Constitution] of Kosovo;

- Coordination among communes or national communities when necessary, including the enactment of [Decisions] [laws] concerning inter-communal issues;

- Designing programs for regional development;

- Protection of the environment where inter-communal issues are involved; and

- Confirmation of the Ministers and Justices of the Supreme Court and the Constitutional Court.

3. [Decisions] [Laws] of the Assembly shall be taken by majority of those present and voting, except as provided in paragraph 4.

4. When a majority of the Members of a national community selected pursuant to paragraph 1(b) assert that a proposed decision affects the vital interests of their national community, that decision shall require for approval, in addition to the majority specified in paragraph 3, a majority of the Members present and voting from that national community. If a majority of Members from the asserting community is not present and voting, the regular voting rule shall apply. Any other national community wishing to assert that the same proposed decision also affects its vital interests must make its claim within two days after the privilege is first asserted. After that two day period has elapsed, no national community may assert the privilege set forth in this paragraph with respect to the same proposed decision.

5. The following procedure shall be used to resolve disputes regarding the exercise of the national community privilege set forth in paragraph 4:

(a) The national community or communities asserting the privilege will give reasons to the Assembly explaining its concerns. Members of the Assembly supporting the proposed decision will given an opportunity to respond. The [President] [Presidency] of Kosovo shall mediate the dispute and attempt to reach a settlement agreeable to all affected national communities.

[Option 1:

(b) If mediation does not produce a mutually agreeable result within seven days, there shall be a vote of the Assembly. The proposed decision shall take effect if it receives the support of [4/5] of the Members of the whole Assembly.]

[Option 2:

(b) If mediation does not produce a mutually agreeable result within seven days, the matter will be given to the Constitutional Court for decision. The Court shall determine whether as a matter of law the vital national interests of national community or communities asserting the privilege set forth in paragraph 4 are [affected] [substantially harmed] by the proposed decision. The Court shall hear argument and rule within ten days.

(c) The decision of the Court may be appealed to the [President of the European Court of Human Rights] [Special Court provided for in this Agreement].]

6. A majority of Members shall constitute a quorum. The Assembly will decide its own rules of procedure. Members of Assembly shall be immune from civil or criminal proceedings on the basis of opinions expressed or votes cast in the Assembly.

7. The Assembly shall elect from among its Members a President, two Vice-Presidents, and other leaders as it deems proper. Each national community covered by paragraph 1(b) shall be represented in the leadership.

(a) The President of the Assembly shall represent the Assembly, call its sessions to order, chair its meetings, coordinate the work of any Committees it may establish, and perform other tasks prescribed by the rules of procedure of the Assembly.

[Option 1:

8. The President of the Assembly may not be from the same national community as the [President] [Chair of the Presidency] of Kosovo.]

[Option 2: No text.]

[President] [Presidency] of Kosovo

[Option 1:

9. There shall be a President of Kosovo.

(a) The President shall be selected for a [three] year term. No person may serve more than two terms as President. The President shall be elected directly by the people of Kosovo.]

[Option 2:

9. There shall be a President of Kosovo.

(a) The President shall be elected for a [three] year term. No person may serve more than two terms as President. The President shall be elected [by vote of the Assembly.] [by majority vote of the communal governments. Each commune shall receive one vote, and shall cast that vote as it decides by a majority vote of the communal assembly.]

[Option 3:

9. Kosovo shall have a collective Presidency, which shall consist of one Serbian of Kosovo, one Albanian of Kosovo [and others].

(a) Each member of the Presidency shall be elected for a [three] year term. No person may serve more than two terms as a member of the presidency. Candidates for the Presidency shall run for office together on interethnic states. A state shall be selected for the Presidency directly by the people of Kosovo.

(i) There shall be a Chair of the Presidency, who shall be selected from among the members of the Presidency by majority vote of the Assembly.

(ii) The Presidency shall decide its own rules of procedure. It shall endeavour to act by consensus. Subject to the privilege set forth in section (a) (iii) of this paragraph, decisions may be taken [by the Chair] [by majority vote] where all efforts to achieve consensus have failed.

(iii) Within four days of the adoption of a Decision of the Presidency, a Member of the Presidency may assert that the Decision affects a vital interest of his or her national community. The issue shall be promptly referred to [the National Council on his or her national community. If the national community affirms within ten days by a decision taken under its own democratic procedures that its vital interests are affected, the Decision shall be rescinded.[1] [Dissenting Members of the Presidency may petition the Constitutional Court to have a

(iv) Decision reinstated. The Court shall decide within ten days whether the vital interests of the national community are [substantially] affected as a matter of law. [The decision of the Constitutional Court may be further appealed by either party to the Special Court, which shall rule within ten days.]]

(b) The [President] [Presidency] shall be responsible for:

- Representing all citizens in Kosovo before any international or Federal body, or any body of the Republics.

- Proposing to the Assembly candidates for Prime Minister and Justices of the Supreme Court and the Constitutional Court

- Meeting regularly with [the National Councils and with other] democratically selected representatives of the national communities and other persons.

- Conducting foreign relations consistent with the Constitution of the Federal Republic of Yugoslavia.

- Concluding agreements on behalf of Kosovo, consistent with the Constitution of the Federal Republic of Yugoslavia, after they are approved by the Assembly.

---

[1] The privilege to block a Decision of the Presidency as affecting a vital interest could be limited to certain categories of important Decisions. This will be a subject for further discussion.

- Serving or designating a representative to serve on the Joint Commission and Joint Council established by Article VIII of this Agreement.

- Meeting regularly with the President of the Federal Republic of Yugoslavia, the President of Montenegro, and the President of Serbia.

Council of Ministers

10. Executive power shall be exercised by the Council of Ministers.

(a) The Council of Ministers shall consist of a Prime Minister and [ ] Ministers, including at least one person from each national community.

(b) The candidate for Prime Minister shall put forward a list of Ministers to the Assembly. The Prime Minister and his or her proposed Ministers shall be approved by a majority of those Members present and voting in the Assembly. In the event that the Prime Minister is not able to obtain a majority for the Council of Ministers, the [President] [Presidency] shall propose a new candidate for Prime Minister within ten days.

(c) The Council of Ministers shall be responsible for implementing and enforcing [Decisions] [laws] of the Assembly and actions of other government authorities when such responsibilities are devolved by those authorities. Ministers of the Council shall head the Administrative Bodies of Kosovo, and shall also have independent authority to propose [laws] [Decisions] to the Assembly.

(d) The Prime Minister shall call meetings of the Council of Ministers, represent the Council of Ministers in appropriate settings, and organize its work. Decisions of the Council shall require a majority of Members present and voting. The Prime Minister shall cast the deciding vote if the Ministers are equally divided. The Council shall otherwise decide its own rules of procedure.

Administrative Bodies

11. Administrative Bodies shall be responsible for implementing [Decisions] [laws] of Kosovo and, where devolved to them, of other authorities. (a) Employees of administrative bodies shall be fairly representative of the population of Kosovo.

(b) Any citizen of Kosovo claiming to have been aggrieved by the decision of an administrative body shall have the right to judicial review of that decision. The Assembly shall enact administrative law to regulate this review.

(c) An administrative body of Kosovo shall have responsibility for all enforcement matters in Kosovo, in accordance with Annex 2 to this Agreement.

PART III: COURTS IN KOSOVO

General

1. Kosovo and its Communes shall establish courts for Kosovo. There shall be a Constitutional Court, a Supreme Court, and Communal Courts. [There shall also be a special Court for purposes of monitoring the implementation of this Agreement.] Justices and judges of the Kosovo courts shall not be held criminally or civilly liable for any acts carried out within the scope of their duties.

2. The courts of Kosovo shall have jurisdiction over all legal matters arising under the [Basic Law] [Constitution] of Kosovo and [Decisions] [laws] of the Assembly, and international law to be applied in Kosovo including, but not limited to, matters relating to the application and interpretation of the international human rights agreements listed in Annex 1.

3. The courts of Kosovo shall also have jurisdiction as specified in this paragraph over matters arising under federal law or raising questions of federal law.

(a) Kosovo courts shall adjudicate all civil cases in Kosovo arising under Federal law or raising federal law questions in the first instance. Unless otherwise specified in this Agreement, Kosovo courts shall also adjudicate criminal cases in Kosovo arising under federal law. Disputes presenting federal questions may be appealed to the Federal courts after all appeals available under the Kosovo system have been exhausted. Kosovo courts shall be the final authority as to the meaning of Kosovo legal authorities.

[Option 1:

(b) Those federal criminal matters specified in [ ][1] shall be adjudicated entirely by the courts of the Federal Republic of Yugoslavia. Appropriate Federal courts of first instance shall be established in Kosovo for this purpose. The courts of the Federal Republic shall conduct these proceedings in a manner fully in keeping with all international human rights standards.]

[Option 2:

(b) Those federal criminal matters specified in [ ][2] shall be adjudicated in the first instance by the courts of the Republic of Serbia, with appeal to the Federal courts. The Courts of the Republic of Serbia and the Federal Republic shall conduct these proceedings in a manner fully in keeping with all international human rights standards.]

Constitutional Court and Supreme Court

4. Composition. The Constitutional Court shall consist of [five] Justices. The supreme Court shall consist of [nine] Judges. (a) The Justices and Judges shall be distinguished jurists of the highest moral character. The two tribunals shall be broadly representative of the national communities of Kosovo. [Each national community representing at least [ ] % of the population of Kosovo shall have at least one Justice and one Judge on each of the two tribunals.] [Another procedure to allocate seats.]

(b) The Justices and Judges shall each be selected for a term of five years, and may not be reappointed. They shall be required to retire at age 70, and may resign at any time. Justices and Judges may otherwise be removed only for cause. Removal for cause shall require the consensus of the other Justices or Judges of the tribunal.

5. Jurisdiction of the Constitutional Court

The Constitutional Court shall have sole authority to resolve disputes relating to the [Basic Law] [Constitution] of Kosovo. That authority shall include, but is not limited to, determining whether decisions or actions of the [President] [Presidency], the Assembly, the Council of Ministers, the Communes, and the National Communities are compatible with the [Basic Law] [Constitution] of Kosovo. The Court shall also have jurisdiction to decide whether the actions of any official or institution are compatible with the European Convention for Human Rights and its Protocols, and with the other human rights agreements listed in Annex 1, and with the Human Rights and Fundamental Freedoms and rights of National Communities set forth in this Agreement.

(a) Matters may be referred to the court by the [President] [Presidency] of Kosovo, the President or Vice-Presidents of the Assembly, the Prime Minister, the Ombudsman, the communal assemblies and councils, and any national community acting according to its democratic procedures.

(b) Any Kosovo court, which finds in the course of adjudicating a matter that the dispute depends on the answer to a question within the Court's jurisdiction, may refer the issue to the Court for a preliminary decision.

(c) The Court shall have appellate jurisdiction over cases raising matters within its authority after all other avenues for appeal have been exhausted, including the Supreme Court.

(d) Questions relating to the compatibility of official actions with the European Convention for Human Rights and its Protocols may be further appealed to the European Court of Human Rights. In such matters, the decisions of the European Court shall be final.][Where a matter falls within the jurisdiction of the Special Court, appeals may also be taken to that tribunal consistent with this agreement. Questions of Federal law may be appealed to the courts of the Federal Republic of Yugoslavia.

---

[1] This section of the Agreement will set forth a list of serious crimes with cross border implications, such as counterfeiting of money and narcotics trafficking. The list will be a subject for negotiation between the parties.
[2] Id.

6. Jurisdiction of the Supreme Court. The Supreme Court shall hear appeals from the Communal Courts. It shall be the final appellate tribunal of Kosovo for all matters of Kosovo law falling outside the jurisdiction of the Constitutional Court [and the Special Court]. Questions of Federal law may be appealed to the courts of the Federal Republic of Yugoslavia.

7. Functioning. The two tribunals shall adopt decisions by majority vote of all the Justices or Judges. They shall hold public proceedings and issue published opinions setting forth the reasons for their decisions along with any dissenting views.

Communal Courts

8. The Communes shall establish such tribunals of first instance as they deem proper to address matters falling within the jurisdiction of the Kosovo courts. Judges shall be unbased, and a representative percentage shall be selected from each national community in the Commune after consultations with the national communities.

National Community Dispute Settlement Mechanism

9. Each national community may establish procedures for resolving conflicts concerning inheritance. Family law, matrimonial relations tutorship, adoption, civil lawsuits as decided by the Assembly of Kosovo, and criminal cases for which imprisonment of up to one year is prescribed in the currently applicable penal code.

(a) These procedures must ensure that practices are consistent with internationally recognized human rights. They shall have jurisdiction only when all parties to a dispute agree.

(b) Decisions of the national community dispute resolution mechanism shall be honored by other courts in Kosovo and the Federal Republic of Yugoslavia in accordance with applicable rules.

[Special Court

10. General.

A Special Court shall be established to ensure compliance with this Agreement. Three judges of the Special Court shall be elected by the Chamber of Citizens of the Federal Republic of Yugoslavia and three by the Assembly of Kosovo. During a period of [twenty] years from the entry into force of the Agreement, three judges appointed by the European Court of Human Rights following consultations with the Government of the Federal Republic of Yugoslavia and Kosovo Council of Ministers shall sit on the Court. These judges shall not be citizens of the Federal Republic of Yugoslavia or any neighboring state. The Special Court shall establish its own rules of procedure.

11. Jurisdiction and Powers.

The Special Court shall have jurisdiction to decide matters arising under this Agreement and its Annexes. In particular, it shall hear cases under the following circumstances:

(a) At the request of the President, the Government, the Chamber of the Republics, or the Chamber of the Citizens of the Federal Republic of Yugoslavia; of the President, the Government, or the National Assembly of the Republic of Serbia, of the [President] [Chairman of the Presidency], the Council of Ministers, the Assembly, or the Ombudsman of Kosovo; or the Chair of the Joint Commission:

(i) In case of disagreement as to the compatibility of Federal Republic of Serbia, or Kosovo legislation or of the Federal Republic of Serbia Constitution or the [Basic Law] [Constitution] of Kosovo with this Agreement; or

(ii) In case of disagreement as to the rights and obligations of the Federation, the Republic of Serbia, or Kosovo under this Agreement.

(b) At the request of the [President] [Chair of the Presidency] the Council of Ministers, the Assembly, the Ombudsman, a National Community, a Commune, or the Chair of the Joint Commission in the case of a disagreement as to the rights or obligations of the requesting body under the Agreement.

(c) Upon appeal from a ruling of the Constitutional Court as to whether a proposed Decision [or law] of the Assembly [substantially] affects the vital interest of a national community.

(d) Following the exhaustion of other legal remedies, at the request of any natural or legal person or association on a compliant that any rights granted by this Agreement, including by the provisions of international treaties incorporated herein, have been violated by a public authority.

12. If a court on the territory of the Federal Republic of Yugoslavia considers that a law, on whose validity its ruling in a case before it disputes, may be inconsistent with this Agreement, it shall stay the proceedings and seek a ruling from the Special Court as to the compatibility of the law with this Agreement.

13. If the Constitutional Court of the Federal Republic of Yugoslavia considers that a provision of the Federal Republic of Yugoslavia Constitution, on whose validity its ruling in a case before it depends, may be inconsistent with this Agreement, or if the Constitutional Court of the Republic of Serbia considers that a provision of the Constitution of the Republic of Serbia on whose validity its ruling in the case before it depends, may be inconsistent with this Agreement, it shall stay the proceedings and ask for a ruling by the Special Court.

14. Decisions of the Special Court shall be final and binding, and shall be executed by all public authorities on the territory of the Federal Republic of Yugoslavia.]

PART IV: THE OMBUDSMAN

GENERAL

1. There shall be an Ombudsman of Kosovo, who shall monitor the protection of human rights and fundamental freedoms and the protection of the rights of national communities under this Agreement.

(a) The Ombudsman shall be an eminent person of high moral standing who possesses a demonstrated commitment to human rights. He or she shall be appointed for a non renewable [four] year term. The Ombudsman shall be independently responsible for choosing his or her own staff. He shall have two Deputies, one drawn each of the two national communities representing the largest percentage of the population of Kosovo.

(b) The first Ombudsman shall be appointed by the Federal Republic of Yugoslavia from a list of candidates prepared by [the Chairman-in-Office of the Organization for Security and Cooperation in Europe (OSCE).] [the President of the European Court of Human Rights.] Federal authorities shall consult with the other parties to this Agreement and the National Communities of Kosovo to guide their selection. The initial appointee may not be a citizen of the Federal Republic of Yugoslavia or of any neighboring state.

(c) Subsequent appointees shall be selected on the basis of consensus between the [President] [Presidency] of Kosovo and the President of the Federal Republic of Yugoslavia, after consultation with the national communities of Kosovo.

2. The Office of the Ombudsman shall be an independent agency of Kosovo. In carrying out its mandate, no person, institution, or entity of the Parties may interfere with its functions.

3. The salaries and expenses of the Ombudsman and his or her staff shall be determined jointly by the Federal republic of Yugoslavia and Kosovo. The salaries and expenses shall be fully adequate to implement the Ombudsman's mandate.

4. The Ombudsman and members of his or her staff shall not be held criminally or civilly liable for any acts carried out within the scope of their duties. When the Ombudsman and members of the staff are not citizens of the Federal Republic of Yugoslavia, they and their families shall be accorded the same privileges and immunities as are enjoyed by diplomatic agents and their families under the Vienna Convention on Diplomatic relations.

Jurisdiction

5. The Ombudsman shall consider:

(a) alleged or apparent violations of human rights and fundamental freedoms in Kosovo, as provided in the European Convention for the Protection of Human Rights and Fundamental Freedoms and the Protocols thereto, the international agreements listed in Annex I of this Agreement, and Article IV of this Agreement, and

(b) alleged or apparent discrimination on any ground such as sex, race, color, language, religion, political or other opinion, national or social origin, association with a national minority, property, birth or other status arising in the enjoyment of any of the rights and freedoms provided for in the international agreements listed in Annex I of this Agreement, where such violation is alleged or appears to have been committed by the Parties, including by any official, institution, or entity of the Parties, or any individual acting under the authority of such an official, institution, or entity, and

(c) violations of the rights of National Communities specified in this Agreement.

6. All citizens in Kosovo shall have the right to submit complaints to the Ombudsman. The Parties agree not to take any measures to punish persons who intend to submit or who have submitted such allegations, or in any other way to deter the exercise of this right.

Powers and Authorities

7. The Ombudsman shall investigate alleged violation falling within the jurisdiction set forth in paragraph five. He may act either on his own initiative or in response to an allegation presented by any Party or person, non-governmental organization, or group of individuals claiming to be the victim of a violation or acting on behalf of alleged victims who are deceased or missing. The work of the Ombudsman shall be free of charge to the person concerned.

8. The Ombudsman shall determine which allegations warrant investigation and in what priority, giving particular priority to allegations of especially severe or systematic violations.

9. The Ombudsman shall have complete, unimpeded, and immediate access to any person, place, or information upon his or her request. (a) He shall have access to and may examine all official documents, including classified documents, and he can require any person, including officials of Kosovo, the Republics and the Federal Republic of Yugoslavia to cooperate by providing relevant information, documents and files.

(b) The Ombudsman may attend administrative hearings, meetings of other Kosovo institutions, and meetings and proceedings of the Republics and the Federal Republic of Yugoslavia in order to gather information.

(c) He may examine facilities and places where persons deprived of their liberty are detained, work, or are otherwise located.

(d) The Ombudsman and staff shall maintain the confidentiality of all confidential information obtained by them, unless the Ombudsman determines that such information is evidence of a violation of rights falling within his or her jurisdiction, in which case that information may be revealed in public reports or appropriate legal proceedings.

(e) Where an official impedes an investigation by refusing to provide necessary information, the Ombudsman shall contact the official's superior or the public prosecutor for appropriate penal action to be taken in accordance with the law. Where the competent authority fails to take action, the Ombudsman may, in substitution for that authority, institute disciplinary proceedings against the official responsible or where appropriate before a criminal court.

10. The Ombudsman shall issue finding and conclusions in the form of a published report promptly after concluding an investigation.

(a) A Party institution, or official in Kosovo identified by the Ombudsman as a violator shall, within a period specified by the Ombudsman, explain in writing how it will comply with any prescriptions the Ombudsman may put forth for remedial measures.

(b) In the event that a person or entity does not comply with the conclusions and recommendations of the Ombudsman, the report shall be forwarded for further action to the Joint commission set forth in Article VIII of this Agreement, to the Presidency of the appropriate Party, and to any other officials or institution that the Ombudsman deems appropriate.

11. The Ombudsman shall have the right to appear and intervene before any Federal, domestic, or (consistent with the rules of such bodies) international authority upon his or he request [including the Special Court].

(a) The right of intervention shall include the power to appear in support of the application of any person claiming violation of the rights set forth in paragraph five before any tribunal or proceeding of Kosovo, the Republic, or the Federal Republic of Yugoslavia.

(b) The Ombudsman may support appropriate applications to [the European court of Human rights and other] international bodies.

(c) The Ombudsman shall promptly report to the International Criminal Tribunal for the Former Yugoslavia evidence of war crimes, crimes against humanity, and other fundamental violations of international humanitarian law that may fall within the jurisdiction of that tribunal.

PART V: COMMUNES

[Option 1:1. Kosovo shall have the existing communes.]

[Option 2:1. Kosovo shall have [ ] communes within the boundaries specified in annex 6 of this Agreement.]

[Option 1:

2. Communes may by mutual agreement form self-administering regions comprising multiple communes. These regions shall have the authorities of communes, unless the agreement establishing them expressly determines otherwise.]

[Option 2:

2. Communes may develop relationships among themselves for their mutual benefit.]

3. Each Commune shall have an Assembly, a Council, and such executive bodies as the commune may establish. Each national community with at least [ ]% of the population of the commune shall be represented on the Council in proportion to its share of the regional population or by one member, whichever is greater.

4. The communes shall have exclusive responsibility for:

- Law enforcement, as specified in annex 2 of this Agreement. Regulating and, when appropriate, providing childcare.

- Establishing and regulation the work of medical institutions and hospitals. Special arrangements will be made for institutions owned by government entities.

- Providing and regulating education, consistent with the rights and duties of national communities.

- Protecting the communal environment.

- Regulating commerce and privately owned stores.

- Regulating hunting and fishing.

- Planning and carrying out public works of communal importance, including roads and water supplies, and participating in the planning and carrying out Kosovo-wide public works projects in coordination with other communes and Kosovo authorities.

- Regulating land use, town planning, building regulations, and housing construction.

- Designing and implementing programs of economic, scientific, technological, demographic, and social development, and programs for the development of agriculture and of rural areas.

- Developing programs for tourism, the hotel industry, catering, and sport.

- Organizing fairs and local markets.

- Organizing public services of communal importance, including fire, emergency response, and police consistent with Annex 2 of this Agreement.

- Financing the work of communal institutions, including raising revenue, taxes, and preparing budgets.

5. Each commune shall conduct its business in public and shall maintain publicly available records of its deliberations and decisions.

6. Members of national communities may avail themselves of Federal institutions and institutions of the Republics, in accordance with the procedures of those institutions and without prejudice to the ability of communes to carry out their responsibilities.

IV. Human Rights Fundamental Freedoms

1. The Parties shall ensure that the highest level of intenationally recognized human rights and fundamental freedoms is secured for the people of Kosova. The Parties shall take every measure to ensure the protection and preservation of these rights.

(a) Applicable rights and freedoms shall include those specified in the European Convention for the Protection of Human Rights and Fundamental Freedoms and its protocols, and the other international agreements listed in Annex I of this Agreement including, but not limited to, those to which the Federal republic of Yugoslavia is already a party. (b) All competent authorities shall cooperate with and provide unrestricted access to the supervisory bodies established by any of the international agreements listed in Annex I of this Agreement and the international Criminal Tribunal for the Former Yugoslavia.

2. The rights referred to in paragraph I shall be directly applicable in Kosovo and in any matter involving a person of Kosovo, and shall take precedence over all other law of the Parties. All courts, agencies government institutions, and instrumentality's of the Parties and all of their officials and employees shall conform to these human rights and fundamental freedoms. Applicable rights include:

(a) The right to life.

(b) The right not to be subjected to torture or to inhuman or degrading treatment or punishment.

(c) The right not to be held in slavery or servitude or to perform forced or compulsory labor.

(d) The right to peacefully assemble and freely associate with others.

(e) The right to liberty and security of person.

(f) Freedom of thought, conscience and religion.

(g) Freedom of expression, and the right to freely receive information and ideas without interference or threats.

(h) The right to a fair hearing in civil and criminal matters, and other rights relating to criminal proceedings. (i) The right to liberty and security of person.

J) The right to marry and found a family.

(k) The right to property.

(l) The right to education.

(m) The right to liberty of movement and residence.

3. The rights and freedoms provided for in this Article and detailed in the international agreements listed in Annex 1 shall be enjoyed without discrimination on any ground such as race, color, language, religion, political or other opinion, national or social origin or membership in a particular national community, property, birth, or other status.

V. Rights and Duties of Members of National Communities

1. Members of the national communities shall have additional rights determined by this Agreement in order to preserve and express their national, cultural, religious, and linguistic identities in accordance with international standards and the Helsinki final Act.

2. The national communities shall be legally equal and shall not use their additional rights so as to endanger the rights of other national communities or the rights of citizens.

[Option 1:

3. Each national community shall select through democratic means, in accordance with procedures it shall decide, institutions to administer its affairs in Kosovo.]

[Option 2:

3. Each national community shall select through democratic means, in accordance with procedures it shall decide, a National Council to administer the affairs of the community in Kosovo. Each Council will establish its own executive institutions and procedures.]

4. The national communities shall be subject to [Decisions] [laws] of the Assembly of Kosovo, provided that any action concerning national communities must be nondiscriminatory. The Assembly shall decide upon procedure for resolving disputes between national communities.

5. The additional rights of the national communities are to:

(a) preserve and protect their national culture, including by:

- using their language and alphabets,

- inscribing local names of towns and villages, of squares and streets, and of other topographic names in the language and alphabet of the national community [in addition to signs in Serbian,] consistent with decisions about style made by the communal institutions,

- providing information in the language and alphabet of the national community,

- establishing educational, cultural and religious associations, for which relevant authorities will provide financial assistance,

- enjoying unhindered contacts with their respective national communities outside the Federal Republic of Yugoslavia.

- Using and displaying national symbols [as well as the symbols of the Federal Republic of Yugoslavia and Serbia],

- providing for education, in particular for schooling in their own language and alphabet and in national culture and history,

- protecting national practices on family law by, if the community decides, arranging rules in the field of inheritance, family and matrimonial relations; tutorship; and adoption,

- the preservation of sites of religious, historical, or cultural importance

- implementing public health and social services;

- operating religious institutions in cooperation with religious authorities.

(b) adopt procedures for dispute resolution, as provided in Article II. Part 3(g) of this Agreement.

(c) be guaranteed at least one radio and TV frequency, which it shall administer subject to non-discriminatory, technical standards; (d) finance activities of the national communities by collecting charges [a National Council] [the national community] decides to levy on members of its own community.

6. Each national community may exercise these additional rights through Federal institutions, or institutions of the Republics.

7. Members of national communities will also be guaranteed:

- the right to participate in regional and international non-governmental organizations in accordance with procedures of these organizations; and

- equal access to employment in public services

VI. Representation of Kosovo in Federal Institutions

1. The participation of Kosovo in Federal institutions shall be discussed in accordance with Article XI (3);

2. The following is without prejudice to the rights of persons in Kosovo to decide whether to accept the offer and to the review described in section XI (3);

- Kosovo shall be offered at least [thirty] deputies in the House of Citizens of the Federal Assembly.

- Each national community in Kosovo shall be offered at least one place in the Federal Government.

- Each national community in Kosovo shall be offered at least one judge on the Federal court of the Federal Republic.

- The [President] [Presidency] of Kosovo shall be a full member of the Supreme Defense Council of the Federal Republic of Yugoslavia.

VII. Financing and Other Economic Issues

FINANCING

1. The authorities established to levy and collect taxes and other charges are set forth in this Agreement. Except if otherwise expressly provided in this Agreement, those bodies have the right to keep all revenues from their own taxes or other charges.

2. In recognition of the fact that this Agreement confers new responsibilities upon authorities in Kosovo, [Republic and] Federal authorities shall examine how to provide resources necessary for the conduct of the new responsibilities. These resources shall include funds (including tax remission), equipment, and training.

3. The authorities of Kosovo shall have part of revenue otherwise derived in Kosovo including duties or fees. Authorities collecting such revenue shall be representative of the population in Kosovo. Federal taxation and revenue collection in Kosovo, and the rules governing any additional contribution to Federal Republic of Yugoslavia institutions from which Kosovo benefits, shall be governed by the terms and conditions specified in Annex 3 of this Agreement.

4. Federal and other authorities shall also facilitate, to the extent of their respective powers, the delivery of resources from international sources to Kosovo.

OTHER ECONOMIC ISSUES

5. Annex 3 of this Agreement shall specify, in terms consistent with this Agreement, arrangements for the disposition of government owned assets in Kosovo; the resolution of disputes over pension and social insurance contributions; and the resolution of other matter relating to economic relations between the parties.[1]

VIII. Joint Commission and Joint Council

JOINT COMMISSION

1. A Joint Commission will serve as the central mechanism for monitoring and coordination the implementation of this Agreement. It will be comprised of Federal [and Republic] representatives, representatives of the national communities in Kosova, representatives of Kosovo political institutions including the [President] [Presidency] of Kosovo and the Ombudsman, and international representatives (including the Kosovo Verification Mission), the Contact Group, and others as agreed).

[Option 1:
2. The members of the Joint Commission shall select a Chair to organize its work.]

[Option 2:
2. A person of high moral character will be selected to serve as Chair of the Joint Commission. The Chair will coordinate the work of the Joint Commission, and shall have other powers and authorities as set forth in this Agreement.

(a) For [ten] years following the entry into force of this Agreement, the Chair shall be a person chosen by the Chair in Office of the 4 OSCE after consultation with the Parties. During this initial period, the Chair of the Joint Commission shall not be citizen of the Federal republic of Yugoslavia or a surrounding state. The Chair: l shall organize the work of the Joint Commission, and supervise the overall implementation of this Agreement.

(b) After the initial period, the Chair shall be elected by consensus between the President of the Federal Republic of Yugoslavia, and the [President] [Presidency] of Kosovo.]

3. The sides shall cooperate completely with the Commission and its Chair.

The Joint Commission as a whole and the Chair individually on his or her own initiative shall have safe, complete, and unimpeded access to all places, persons, and information (including documents and other records) both within Kosovo and, where the Joint Commission or the Chair deem it relevant, within the Federal Republic.

JOINT COUNCIL

4. The national communities shall establish a Joint Council to coordinate their activities under this Agreement, and to provide an informal mechanism for the resolution of disputes. The Joint council shall consist of one member from each of the national communities. It shall meet no less than once each month. The Joint Council shall encourage the creation of similar mechanisms at the communal level, building on the example of local commissions established pursuant to Article IX(5) of this Agreement.

IX. Confidence Building Measures

1. Violence in Kosova shall cease. Alleged violations of the cease-fire shall be reported to international observers and will not be used to justify violence in response. All persons held by the Parties without charge shall be released.

2. [An agreement on the status of security forces in Kosovo, to be added after expert consultations.]

3. [An agreement on the status of police forces in Kosovo, to be added after expert consultations.]

4. Each side shall encourage all persons displaced during the conflict to return to their homes as the security situation permits. There will be no Impediments to the normal flow of goods in Kosovo. International humanitarian organizations will be freely permitted to provide building materials and other assistance to persons returning to their homes in Kosovo.

5. In each community a local commission, representative of all national communities there, will assist international humanitarian agencies in the delivery and distribution of food, medicine, clothes, construction materials, the restoration of electricity and water supply, and in encouraging return.

6. International personnel, including the Kosovo Verification Mission and members of non-governmental organizations, shall be allowed unfettered access, at any time, throughout Kosovo. It is expected that international personnel will be present at all times in selected communities.

7. Each side shall respect its obligation to cooperate in the investigation and prosecution of war crimes, crimes against humanity, and other violations of international humanitarian law. In acknowledgement that allegations of atrocities cannot be resolved to the satisfaction of the other, each side will allow complete, unimpeded, and unfettered access to international experts including forensics experts-authorized to investigate such allegations. Each side will provide fully support and cooperation to the activities of the International Criminal Tribunal for the Former Yugoslavia.

[Option 1:
8. Republic and Federal authorities shall re-examine, for extraordinary mitigation of punishments, all sentences pronounced on members of national communities from Kosovo for acts motivated by political goals.]

[Option 2:
8. There shall be a general amnesty for all persons in Kosovo accused or convicted of committing politically motivated crimes. The amnesty shall not apply to those accused for or convicted of committing war crimes, crimes against humanity, or other fundamental violations of international humanitarian law.]

X. Implementation Period

1. This Agreement shall be implemented as quickly as possible. The signatories of this Agreement take the obligation to allow, insofar as possible, its adequate implementation even before the adoption and undertaking of all acts and measures fixed in the Agreement.

2. The sides will start without delay on any and all legal changes necessary for the full implementation of this Agreement. They acknowledge that complete implementation will require the adoption of necessary state regulations and other general acts, of the [Basic Law] [Constitution] of Kosovo, political acts and measures, and the election

---

[1] The Parties are encouraged to convene expert working groups forthwith to examine these technical issues in detail.

and establishment of institutions and bodies set forth in the Agreement. This Agreement shall take precedence over all existing legal authorities of the parties.

3. Each national community in Kosovo is authorized to start exercising the additional rights determined by this Agreement, to the extent possible, immediately upon signature.

4. Within [nine] months, there shall be elections in accordance with Annex 4 of this Agreement for all authorities established by this Agreement, according to an electoral list prepared to international standards. The Government of the Federal Republic of Yugoslavia hereby invites the organisation for Security and Cooperation in Europe (OSCE) to supervise those elections to ensure openness and fairness.

5. Under the supervision of the OSCE and with the participation of Kosovo authorities, Federal authorities shall conduct an objective and free census of the population in Kosovo, which shall be carried out when the OSCE determines that conditions allow an accurate census.

(a) The first census shall be limited to name, place of birth, address, gender, age, citizenship, nationality, and religion.

(b) The institutions and authorities of the parties shall provide the institutions of Kosovo with all records necessary to conduct the census, including data about places of residence, citizenship, voters' lists, and other information.

6. The signatories of this Agreement shall provide active support, cooperation, and participation for the successful implementation of the Agreement.

7. Laws and institutions currently in place in Kosovo shall remain until replaced by a decision of a competent body established by this Agreement. The initial elections called for in paragraph four of this Article will be conducted pursuant to the procedures in Annex 4.

XI. Amendments

Amendments to this Agreement shall be adopted by signature of all the parties.

2. Each signatory may propose amendments at any time and will consider and consult with the other with regard to proposed amendments.

3. In three years, the sides will undertake a comprehensive assessment of the Agreement, with the aim of improving the implementation and considering proposals by either side for additional steps, which will require mutual agreement for adoption.

XII. FINAL PROVISIONS

1. This Agreement is concluded in [ ] languages.

2. This Agreement shall enter into force upon the completion of the internal process of each side.

For Federal Republic of Yugoslavia; Republic of Kosovo; Republic of Serbia

Annex 1: Human Rights and Fundamental Freedoms

Human Rights Agreements

- 1948 Convention on the Prevention and Punishment of the Crime of Genocide
- 1949 Geneva Conventions l-IV on the Protection of the Victims of War, and the 1977 Geneva Protocols 1-11 thereto
- 1950 European Convention for the Protection of Human Rights and Fundamental Freedoms, and the Protocols thereto
- 1951 Convention relating to the Status of Refugees and the
- 1966 Protocol thereto
- 1957 Convention on the Nationality of Married Women
- 1961 Convention on the Reduction of Statelessness
- 1965 International Convention on the Elimination of All Forms of Racial Discrimination
- 1966 International Covenant on Civil and Political Rights and the 1966 and 1989 Optional Protocols thereto
- 1966 Covenant on Economic, Social, and Cultural Rights
- 1979 Convention on the Elimination of All Forms of Discrimination Against Women
- 1984 Convention Against Torture and Other Cruel, Inhuman or Degrading Treatment or Punishment
- 1987 European Convention on the Prevention of Torture and Inhuman or Degrading Treatment or Punishment
- 1989 Convention on the Rights of the Child
- 1990 Convention on the Protection of the Rights of All Migrant Workers and Members of Their Families
- 1992 European Charter for Regional or Minority Languages
- 1994 Framework Convention for the Protection of National Minorities Other Annexes The following additional annexes will be a part of the completed Agreement:

The following annexes will be part of the completed Agreement: Annex 2: Police and Security Matters; Annex 3: Financing and Other Economic Issues; Annex 4: Conduct and Supervision of Elections; Annex 5: National Communities [Annex 6: Communal Boundaries]

93 c) Statement on Fundamental Principles for a Settlement of the Kosovo Question Issued by the Government of the Republic of Kosovo, 3 November 1998

The Government of the Republic of Kosova has studied with interest the proposals for a settlement put forward by Ambassador Hill. On the basis of expert advice received, this proposal has been found to be fundamentally incompatible with the democratic mandate bestowed upon the Government of the Republic of Kosova by the people of Kosova. The Government of the Republic of Kosova declares that it cannot furnish basis for discussion.

Despite the outrages suffered by the population of Kosova at the hands of FRY/Serb armed forces, special police forces and other instrumentalities of the Belgrade regime, the Government of the Republic of Kosova remains committed to the search for a peaceful solution of the crisis in the region. However, the terms of a possible settlement, and the path towards it, must obviously be influenced by these latest atrocities which have resulted the death of thousands, in immense suffering by tens of thousands, and in over 400,000 displaced members of the civilian population a large number of whom are dwelling at the edge of death through exposure and starvation.

The Government of the Republic of Kosova will engage in further talks once all the demands made by the United Nations Security Council in legally binding resolutions, adopted under Chapter VII, have been implemented by the FRY. It must be noted that it is not for any delegation, or group of states, unilaterally to relieve the FRY from the mandatory demands of the Security Council. Instead, in its latest resolution 1203 (1998), adopted in response to the so-called Holbrooke agreement of 12/13 October, the Security Council expressly reiterated its demand that the FRY must comply fully and swiftly with its previous resolutions 1160 (1998) and 1199 (1998). This further resolution was also expressly adopted under Chapter VII of the UN Charter.

The Government of the Republic of Kosova was not consulted about the terms of the so-called Holbrooke agreement. Despite serious reservations relating to the arrangement, it has consented (for an initial period of three month, to be automatically extended for further periods of three months unless revoked by the Government of the Republic of Kosova) to the presence of the proposed verification force on its territory, and to the overflight of monitoring aircraft. It is also actively participating in the administration of the humanitarian operations which are now being conducted.

The Government of the State of Kosova has, for its part, fully implemented all aspects of Resolutions 1160 (1998), 1199 (1998) and 1203 (1998). Matters of compliance which are outstanding on the FRY/Serb side, and which must be resolved before talks can progress, include:

- The cessation of the campaign of violence and intimidation by the FRY/Serb forces, principally directed against the civilian population;

- The full withdrawal of FRY/Serb armed forces and special police forces, as required by mandatory Security Council resolution;

- The establishment of freedom of movement, including free and unhindered access for humanitarian aid;

- The creation of conditions necessary for the protection and safe return in dignity of the displaced;

- Full access to all areas of Kosova to international monitors, including human rights monitors, and war crimes investigators;

- Full acceptance by the FRY of its duty to cooperate with the ICTFY war-crimes investigation, including the furnishing of full access to all persons and materials that may be requested.

The Government of the Republic of Kosova proposes the creation of a neutral Implementation Commission, composed of two representatives nominated by the Government of the Republic of Kosova, two nominated by the FRY, and three individuals from outside of the region, to be nominated by the UN Secretary-General acting jointly with the Presidency of the European Union. The members of the Commission will evaluate the extent to which the parties have complied with the mandatory demands of the Security Council and will, by a majority decision, advise the parties, the United Nations Security Council and other relevant bodies of its findings.

The Implementation Commission will adopt its initial report on compliance within two weeks of its coming into being. It is entitled to receive information from all sources, and will be given access to the reports of the verification mission and others, and will enjoy full freedom of movement and access to all individuals and places it might deem relevant. The decisions of the Commission shall be reasoned and public.

Once compliance has been certified by the Commission, negotiations on an interim settlement will commence. The Commission will remain active to monitor continued compliance during the negotiating period. In cases of substantial violations of the demands imposed upon the parties under mandatory Security Council Resolutions, it will adopt a decision to this effect by a simple majority and will so report publicly to the Security Council, the EU Presidency and other relevant bodies within a week of having obtained knowledge of significant alleged violations.

Either of the parties shall be entitled to submit to the Commission allegations of violations, together with the relevant evidence. The Commission shall immediately seek the views of the party which is alleged to have committed the allegation and mount an investigation. It shall publish its findings within one week of having received the allegation and bring them to the attention of the relevant international bodies to which reference is made above.

Once it has been established that the parties have achieved substantive compliance, negotiations about an interim agreement shall commence. These talks shall be conduced in Geneva, starting seven days after certification of compliance has occurred. In addition to the delegations of the Republic of Kosova and of the FRY, there will be international involvement in the talks, in the form of three guarantor states and representatives of implementing organizations to be designated.

1. There will be no pre-conditions for the substantive outcome of such talks. Instead, each party will be free to formulate its views as to a desirable interim arrangement adopted at the level of international law. Without prejudice to its legal position, and reserving the right to amend and modify its views in the light of subsequent developments, the Government of the Republic of Kosova will seek an agreement on the basis of the following principles:

2. The Republic of Kosova is a self-determination entity through which the people of Kosova have actualized their international and constitutional right to obtain independence upon the dissolution of the Socialist Federal Republic of Yugoslavia, and in the light of the repression suffered at the hands of an unrepresentative regime. An interim agreement need not expressly confirm the status of Kosova as an independent state, but it must not prejudice it. An interim agreement must recognize the inalienable right to self-determination.

3. The Republic of Kosova's territorial definition shall be the same as under the 1974 SFRY constitution. The Republic of Kosova has no territorial claims in relation to the other states of the region, and, unless this is provided in an overall regional settlement, it will not seek to merge with other states. It exercises foreign affairs powers.

4. The Republic of Kosova is a multi-ethnic state. Public authority is exercised on the basis of parliamentary democracy based on the equality of all citizens.

5. Kosova has already adopted its own constitution and has re-established indigenous structures of public authority. An interim agreement must be based on the legal personality of Kosova as a whole, and on the exercise of principal public authority through the organs of Kosova on the basis of its own legal order. Kosova is willing to subject its constitutional structure to a further internal referendum, internationally monitored, and will hold parliamentary and local elections with international involvement.

6. The exercise by FRY or other non-indigenous public organs of any remaining authority in the territory of the Republic of Kosova or in relation to it will be progressively reduced and removed. As this phasing out process takes place, the Republic of Kosova will engage in certain co-operative arrangements in relation to issues of common concern.

7. The transfer of all aspects of state activity to the organs of Kosova will be conducted in a way to ensure that public authority is exercised at a national and local level in a way which is representative of the population. To reassure minority populations, there will occur joint police patrols with international involvement in certain locations to be agreed during the interim period.

8. Kosova has already embraced international standards on the treatment of minorities, religious and cultural freedoms and other international human rights standards. It is willing to reiterate its commitment to these standards in a legally binding way, along with the FRY. It will also accept significant international involvement in the interpretation and application of these standards.

9. The organs of the Republic of Kosova will give full effect to and vigorously enforce human rights and minority rights provisions on the basis of full equally. All parties will collaborate with the relevant international organs in the pursuit of war criminals who have committed offences against the civilian population and others, whatever their religious or ethnic appurtenance.

10. At the conclusion of the interim period, the future status of Kosova will be determined or confirmed in accordance with the principle of self-determination of the people of the Republic of Kosova. A referendum will be conducted with international involvement.

11. The interim agreement will be subject to international guarantees and will be implemented with strong international involvement, also on the ground.

93 d) FRY, Joint Proposal of the Agreement on the Political Framework of Self-Governance in Kosovo and Metohija, Belgrade, 20 November 1998

Signatories to this Agreement,

Considering that, in view of the complex national structure in Kosovo and Metohija, it is necessary to protect the development and existence of each individual national community;

Firm in their commitment to the position that all national communities, regardless of their numbers, are mutually equal and that, therefore, in relations among them there can be no discrimination;

Considering that persons belonging to all national communities in Kosovo and Metohija should be enabled to exercise fully their ethnic, cultural, linguistic and religious identity, in accordance with the highest international standards and basic documents of the United Nations, Organization on Security and Cooperation in Europe, Council of

Europe (the Charter of the United Nations, Universal Declaration on Human Rights, Helsinki Final Act, Paris Charter, European Convention on Human Rights, Council of Europe Framework Convention on the Rights of the Persons belonging to National Minorities), etc;

Considering that it is necessary to set up appropriate democratic institutions in order to create the atmosphere of tolerance and dialogue;

Determined in their position that broad self-governance within national communities and in the territory of Kosovo and Metohija is a precondition for overcoming inter-ethnic tensions and conflicts;

Bearing in mind the most positive experience and legal solutions developed through long-standing common life;

Have agreed as follows:

I. PRINCIPLES

1. Political approach and peaceful solution of problems in Kosovo and Metohija achieved through dialogue are the only acceptable way to reach a lasting, just and humane solution to all outstanding questions;

2. All solutions for Kosovo and Metohija must respect the territorial integrity and sovereignty and internationally recognized borders of the Federal Republic of Yugoslavia, in compliance with the basic principles of the UN Charter, the Helsinki Final Act and the Paris Charter of the OSCE.

3. The solution has to be based on full respect of equality of all citizens and national communities in Kosovo and Metohija. Full affirmation and equal treatment of their national, religious, cultural values as well as historic heritage shall be guaranteed;

4. The future of Kosovo and Metohija lies in peace, equality, integration, economic prosperity and free and common existence, not in ethnic, religious, cultural or any divisions and isolation;

5. The legal arrangements establishing self-governance in Kosovo and Metohija should be in line with legal systems of the Republic of Serbia and of the FR of Yugoslavia, and with international standards and basic documents;

6. Citizens of Kosovo and Metohija shall exercise their rights democratically through assembly, executive, and judicial organs.

7. Citizens and members of each national community in Kosovo and Metohija shall enjoy, without limitations, human and democratic rights and shall have the opportunity to be represented in all organs of authority.

8. Members of national communities shall have additional rights, in order to be able to express and preserve their national, cultural, religious, and linguistic identity, in accordance with international standards and fundamental international documents.

The national communities and their members shall be equal before the law, they shall abide by all State laws and shall not use their additional rights to endanger the rights of other national communities or other rights of citizens, especially territorial integrity and state sovereignty of the Federal Republic of Yugoslavia.

9. The responsibilities of organs in Kosovo and Metohija shall be set forth in this Agreement. The organs in Kosovo and Metohija acting within their competencies, shall be independent.

10. All citizens of Kosovo and Metohija shall have the right to apply to international institutions, including the European Court of Human Rights, for the protection of their rights, after all legal means envisaged by domestic legislation are exhausted.

II. RIGHTS OF CITIZENS

1. The rights of citizens of Kosovo and Metohija shall be realized through assembly, executive and judicial organs established by this Agreement. These rights make up democratic self-governance, including:

- the adoption of the Statute of Kosovo and Metohija;
- the adoption of regulations on the organization and procedures of organs of Kosovo and Metohija;
- adoption of the budget and annual accounts;
- regulation and provision of child care;
- establishment and regulation of the functioning of health institutions and hospitals, except those owned by the State;
- protection of environment;
- regulation of trade and private stores in accordance with republican and federal laws;
- regulation of hunting and fishing;
- planning and execution of public works of communal importance or of importance to Kosovo and Metohija;
- regulation of the land use, town planning and civil engineering, in accordance with republican and federal regulations;
- adoption and implementation of programs of economic, scientific, technological, demographic, regional and social development, as well as programs for development of agriculture and rural areas;
- adoption of tourism development programs, catering and sports;
- organization of fairs and local markets;
- setting up of public services of communal importance and of importance to Kosovo and Metohja;
- financing of the activities of communal organs and organs of Kosovo and Metohija.

2. The organs of Kosovo and Metohija shall not interfere with the additional rights of the members of national communities.

3. A commune shall be the basic unit of local self-governance.

III. ADDITIONAL RIGHTS OF MEMBERS OF NATIONAL COMMUNITIES

1. The members of national communities shall have additional rights set forth this Agreement. The additional rights shall preserve and express national, cultural, religious, and linguistic and other characteristics of members of national communities, in accordance with international standards and the Helsinki Final Act.

2. National communities shall be equal in terms of law and may not use their additional rights to threaten additional rights of other national communities or rights of citizens of the Republic of Serbia or of the Federal Republic of Yugoslavia.

3. Each national community shall select, in accordance with procedures it shall establish, a National Council which will make decisions on additional rights of national communities in Kosovo and Metohija. Each Council shall establish its own executive organs.

4. Additional rights of the national communities include:

- Using their language and alphabet;
- Inscribing local names of towns and villages, squares and streets, and of other topographic names, in the language and alphabet of the national community, along with inscriptions in Serbian;
- Providing information in the language and alphabet of the national community;
- Establishment of educational, cultural and religious associations, to which the State authorities will provide financial assistance;
- Maintenance of unimpeded contacts with their respective national communities outside the Federal Republic of Yugoslavia;
- Using and displaying national symbols, along with the State symbols of Serbia and the FR of Yugoslavia;
- Providing education, in particular for schooling in their own language and alphabet, in subjects related to national culture and history. National communities are encouraged to coordinate curricula with the republican authorities concerning some subjects (for example to ensure that pupils satisfy certain standards in subjects like math or science);
- Protection of national customs in the field of family law, if a community so decides, by establishing regulations in the field of heritage, family and matrimonial relations, adoption and tutorship;
- Each commune shall be able to establish a procedure for resolving disputes in these areas, with the consent of the parties to a dispute. These regulations have to be in accordance with internationally recognized human rights;
- Protecting the sites of religious, historical, or cultural importance to national communities;

- Setting up public health and social services;
- Operation of religious institutions in cooperation with religious authorities;
- Determining procedures of the courts of national communities as provided for in this Agreement and ensure the funds for the implementation of the decisions of those courts;
- Guaranteeing the right to at least one radio and TV frequency, which it shall administer subject to non-discriminatory technical standards;
- Financing activities of national communities by collecting duties which the National Council decides to levy on members of its own community;
- Participating in regional and international non-governmental organizations in accordance with the procedures of these organizations;
- Having equal access to employment in public services.

IV. THE ORGANS OF KOSOVO AND METOHIJA

1. The Assembly

1. The Assembly shall be elected directly. The Assembly shall have two Chambers: Chamber of Citizens and Chamber of National Communities.

2. Members of the Chamber of Citizens shall be elected directly in line with the principle one citizen - one vote.

3. Members of the Chamber of National Communities shall be elected democratically, within each national community. Each national community shall have a delegation with equal number of members in the Chamber.

4. The Assembly shall be responsible for:
- the adoption of the Statute of Kosovo and Metohija;
- making decisions and adoption of other acts regulating some questions related to rights of citizens of Kosovo and Metohija;
- the adoption of budgets and annual accounts;
- cooperation with Federal and Republic Assemblies;
- financing activities of the organs established by this Agreement;
- coordination among communes or national communities when necessary, including decisions concerning inter-communal issues, and
- election of members of the organs set forth in this Agreement.

5. Decisions of the Assembly shall be taken by majority in both Chambers, except as provided for in paragraph (6).

6. If members of one national community assert that a proposed decision affects the vital interests of this national community, such decision shall require majority vote, which includes the majority among the members of that national community delegation in the Council of National Communities.

7. If a decision cannot be taken on account of reasons referred to in paragraph 6, but needs to be taken, the National Assembly of Serbia shall make an interim decision pending the one taken pursuant to paragraph 5.

8. The Assembly shall elect the Presidency of the Assembly which shall consist of one representative from each national community. The Presidency shall have a President, which function shall rotate among members of Presidency each year, in alphabetical order.

The Presidency shall be responsible for:
- calling the meetings of the Assembly and proposing the agenda;
- representing the Assembly;
- regular contacts with National Councils and other representatives of the national communities in order to facilitate the work of the Assembly.

Each national community shall be represented in the leadership of the Assembly. The President of the Presidency of the Assembly cannot be a member of the same national community as the President of the Executive Council and Ombudsman.

2. Executive Council

Executive Council shall exercise executive power.

The Council shall comprise at least one person from each national community. Members shall be proposed by the Presidency of the Assembly and shall be elected by both Assembly Chambers on the basis of equality.

The Executive Council shall be responsible for implementing the decisions of the Assembly and regulations of the State authorities, when authorized for their implementation.

Decisions of the Council shall be adopted by majority vote of Members present and voting, except on questions affecting vital interests of a certain national community. In that case, the principle valid for voting in the Assembly shall apply.

3. Administrative Organs

The administrative organs of Kosovo and Metohija shall have responsibility for the implementation of decisions and general acts, in accordance with this Agreement.

Executives in administrative organs in Kosovo and Metohija shall be representative of the local population.

4. Ombudsman

The Ombudsman shall monitor the realization of the rights of members of national communities.

The Ombudsman shall be nominated by the Presidency of Assembly and shall be elected by the Assembly, each term from another national community.

The Ombudsman shall have a right to review the acts and unimpeded access to any person or place and shall have the right to appear before any domestic organ.

V. THE COMMUNES

1. Communes shall be basic units of self-governance.

2. Each commune shall have an Assembly and Executive Council and such administrative organs established by Executive Council. The organs of a commune shall be organized along the same principles as the organs of Kosovo and Metohija.

3. The duties of local self-governance in a commune include:
- Providing child-care;
- Health institutions and hospitals, except those owned by the State;
- Educational institutions except those State-owned;
- Protection of environment;
- Public works of communal or regional importance, including roads and water supplies;
- Land use;
- Tourism, hotel industry, catering, and sport;
- Fairs and local markets;
- Public services of communal importance, including fire department, emergency response, and local police;
- Financing the work of communal organs, levying duties in accordance with the law.

VI. REPRESENTATION OF THE CITIZENS OF KOSOVO AND METOHIJA IN FEDERAL AND REPUBLIC BODIES

1. Citizens of Kosovo and Metohija shall be represented by at least ten deputies in the Chamber of Citizens of the Federal Assembly and at least twenty deputies in the National Assembly of the Republic of Serbia.

2. From among the citizens of Kosovo and Metohija at least one member shall be elected to the Federal Government and the Government of the Republic of Serbia.

3. From among the citizens of Kosovo and Metohija at least one judge in the Federal Court and three judges in the Supreme Court of Serbia shall be elected.

4. There shall be a Council of the Republic of Serbia for the protection of the rights of the members of national communities. The Presi-

dent of the Republic of Serbia shall preside over the Council of the Republic of Serbia for the protection of the rights of members of national communities.

VII. COURTS AND LOCAL POLICE

1. Courts of National Communities

Each national community may establish, in accordance with the law, courts and determine procedures for resolving disputes concerning inheritance, family law, matrimonial relations, tutorship, adoption and trials for which imprisonment of up to one year is prescribed by the Penal Code. The competence of these courts may be established only if parties to a dispute agree.

The judges shall be appointed by the National Councils and approved by the Assembly. The judges of these courts have to meet criteria necessary for the selection of judges in the corresponding State courts.

2. Local police

Each commune may, if it so decides, establish its local police representative of the population in the commune.

The local police shall be trained in specialized state police schools to respect human rights, particularly the rights of national communities.

The members of local police shall be sworn in to uphold the law impartially, fairly, equally treating all persons.

The local police shall be responsible for the maintenance of public order.

The members of the local police may use, as means of coercion, only guns, rubber truncheons and handcuffs and passenger transportation vehicles and adequate means for communication. The members of the local police cannot use means of coercion against the members of another national community.

If necessary, local police shall be obliged to place itself under control of the State police in fulfilling its tasks in accordance with the law.

A commune may establish a commission to monitor the work of local police. Each national community in a commune shall have the right to participate in the work of the commission.

VIII. FINANCING

1. The organs established in Sections II-IV shall be entitled to income from their own duties and to a share of State taxes.

2. In view of the fact that this Agreement establishes new responsibilities for the organs of Kosovo and Metohija, the Republic and Federal authorities shall consider possibilities to ensure additional resources to exercise the competencies of the organs in Kosovo and Metohija established by this Agreement. These resources shall include funds (plus tax deductions), equipment and training.

IX. CONFIDENCE-BUILDING MEASURES

1. No person shall be prosecuted for acts related to the conflicts in Kosovo and Metohija except for crimes against humanity and international law as set forth in Chapter XVI of the Federal Penal Code. In order to facilitate transparency, the State shall grant access to foreign experts (including forensics), along with state investigators.

2. The competent organs shall, through the relevant judicial procedure based on the law, grant amnesty to persons for whom it is proved that they had not committed crimes against humanity and international law, mitigate the sentences to those who cooperated with investigative authorities, those who had been forcibly drafted or voluntarily handed over weapons.

X. IMPLEMENTATION OF THE AGREEMENT

1. The signatories to this Agreement undertake the obligation to implement it as soon as possible.

2. The State authorities shall undertake the amending of regulations necessary for the implementation of the Agreement, without delay.

3. The competent State organs shall organize, as soon as possible, an objective and free census of the population in Kosovo and Metohija, under the OSCE supervision. The census shall provide necessary information on the places of residence, citizenship, voter lists, and other data relevant for conducting elections.

4. Within nine months, there shall be free and fair elections for all organs in Kosovo and Metohija. The Government of the FR of Yugoslavia invites the OSCE to monitor the elections.

5. The signatories to this Agreement shall extend active support and cooperation to, and shall participate in the implementation of the Agreement.

6. The State authorities shall ensure initial and necessary conditions for the functioning of organs established by this Agreement.

XI. AMENDMENTS

1. Amendments to this Agreement shall be made by agreement of the signatories.

2. Each signatory may propose amendments to this Agreement. The signatories undertake to duly consider proposed amendments.

3. After three years, the signatories shall comprehensively review this Agreement with a view to improving its implementation and shall consider the proposals of any signatory for additional measures, whose adoption shall require the consent of all signatories.

XII. FINAL PROVISIONS

1. This Agreement is concluded in the Serbian language and the languages of national communities (Albanian, Romany, and Turkish) in Kosovo and Metohija.

2. This Agreement shall enter into force on the day of its signature.

For the Republic of Serbia

For the National Communities in Kosovo and Metohija (in alphabetical order)

For the FR of Yugoslavia

93 e) Third Hill Draft Proposal for a Settlement of the Crisis in Kosovo, 2 December 1998

I. Introduction

1. All citizens and peoples in Kosovo have equal rights and duties as set forth in this Agreement. Members of each national community shall have additional rights as set forth below. The national communities shall be legally equal and shall not use their additional rights so as to endanger the rights of other national communities or the rights of citizens.

2. The authorities of Kosovo shall follow principles of full respect of human rights and democracy, and for the equality of all citizens and national communities. Citizens in Kosovo shall enjoy human and democratic rights and shall be given the opportunity to be represented in all institutions in Kosovo. All citizens and national communities in Kosovo shall be guaranteed full affirmation and equal treatment of the international, confessional, and cultural values and historic patrimony.

3. The authorities in Kosovo, acting in accordance with this Agreement, shall be independent. Citizens in Kosovo shall have the right to democratic self-government through assemblies, executive, judicial, and other institutions established in accordance with this Agreement. The right of democratic self-government shall include the right to participate in free and fair elections.

4. Every person in Kosovo shall have the right to apply to international institutions for the protection of their rights in accordance with the procedures of such institutions. The Parties accept and will abide by the principle that their powers and authorities in Kosovo are as specified by this Agreement, which shall prevail over any other legal provisions of the Parties. In implementing this Agreement in accordance with their procedures and international standards, the parties shall harmonize their governing practices and documents. All parties shall make the necessary political and legal commitments to implement this Agreement fully.

II. Governance in Kosovo
PART I: GENERAL

1. The basic territorial unit of local government will be the communes. All responsibilities of government and public authority affecting Kosovo not expressly assigned elsewhere by this Agreement will be the responsibility of the communes.

2. The Federal Republic's authority in Kosovo over the following areas shall not be affected by this Agreement, except as specified in paragraph 3: (a) territorial integrity; (b) maintaining a common market within the Federal Republic of Yugoslavia; c) monetary police; (d) defense; (e) foreign policy; (f) federal taxation; (g) customs services; and (h) [ ].[1]

3. The Federal Republic of Yugoslavia shall act in Kosovo in a manner consistent with Kosovo's democratic self-governance. This includes, but is not limited to, the following undertakings:

a) No change to the external or international borders of Kosovo shall be made without the consent of the Kosovo Assembly and Presidency.

b) Deployment and use of Federal military forces in Kosovo shall be governed by Annex 2 of this Agreement.

c) Kosovo officers and institutions shall have the authority to conduct foreign relations within the areas for which they are responsible, subject to respect for the sovereignty and territorial integrity of the Federal Republic of Yugoslavia and Article 109 (6) of the Constitution of the Republic of Serbia.

d) Citizens in Kosovo will have the opportunity to participate in carrying out customs activities in Kosovo. They shall serve this function as Federal customs officers. Custom officers in Kosovo shall be representative of the national communities of Kosovo.

e) All Federal taxes and duties applicable within Kosovo shall be set in a non-discriminatory way at uniform rates applicable for the whole territory of the Federation.

f) Martial law shall not be declared in Kosovo without the consent of the Kosovo Presidency.

g) Federal measures having a differential, disproportionate, or discriminatory impact on Kosovo shall not take effect in Kosovo without the consent of the Kosovo Presidency.

h) The institutions and officers of the Federal Republic shall abide by this Agreement in its entirety.

4. Within Kosovo the institutions established by this Agreement shall exercise all competencies currently exercised by the Republic, except for the following and any other competencies expressly reserved for the Republic by this Agreement:

a) The Republic may continue to maintain a system of health care, of education, and of care for war veterans and disabled persons, which shall be available equally to the members of all national communities. This authority shall not be interpreted to limit the authority of Kosovo institutions to establish similar systems in their areas. Arrangements will be made in Annex 3 for the treatment of existing health care and educational facilities.

b) The Republic shall have the authority to enact measures relating to the protection of workers' safety and health, provided that all such measures shall be administered in a nondiscriminatory manner throughout the Republic.

c) The Republic may maintain systems of social protection and social security and provide other public services to citizens in Kosovo. These programs shall not discriminate on the basis of membership in a particular National Community, and participation and use (including payment of any taxes necessary to fund participation in or use of such services) shall be on a voluntary basis. This authority shall not be interpreted to limit the authority of Kosovo institutions to establish systems and provide services in these areas. 5. Kosovo, Federal and Republic authorities shall not interfere with the exercise of the additional rights described in Article IV of this Agreement.

PART II: ASSEMBLY, PRESIDENCY, AND ADMINISTRATIVE BODIES
The Assembly

1. There shall be an Assembly, which shall comprise [ ] Members.

(a) [ ] Members shall be directly elected in accordance with Article IX (4) and Annex 4.

(b) The remaining [ ] Members shall be allocated equally among the national communities with at least [ ] % of the population of Kosovo, each of which shall elect Members democratically according to its own procedure. Each applicable national community shall have at least one Member in the Assembly.

2. The Assembly shall be responsible for adopting the Constitution of Kosovo and enacting Decisions of Kosovo, including those regulating relations in political, economic, social, and cultural areas. The Constitution and Decisions of the Kosovo Assembly shall not be subject to change or modification by authorities of the Republics or the Federation so long as they are consistent with this Agreement and within the scope of the jurisdiction herein provided for Kosovo.

a) The Assembly's areas of responsibility shall include:
- Financing activities of Kosovo institutions, including by levying taxes and duties on sources within Kosovo;
- The adoption of budgets and mutual accounts of the Administrative bodies and other institutions of Kosovo, with the exception of communal and national community institutions unless otherwise specified by this Agreement;
- The adoption of regulations concerning the organization, procedures, and functioning of the Administrative Bodies of Kosovo;
- Approving candidates put forward by the Kosovo Presidency for Kosovo judicial offices;
Ensuring freedom of movement of goods, services, and persons consistent with the responsibilities of other authorities;
- Conducting relations with foreign entities and approving agreements within its areas of responsibility, consistent with the authorities of Kosovo institutions under this Agreement;
- Cooperating with the Federal Assembly, and with the Assemblies of the Republics;
Establishing, in accordance with this Agreement, the main rules of local self-government, including in particular rules on elections, finance, the status of elected local officials, and on local government employees;
- Coordination among communes or national communities when necessary, including the enactment of Decisions concerning inter-communal issues;
- Protection of the environment where inter-communal issues are involved; and
- Designing and implementing programs of economic, scientific, technological, demographic, regional, and social development of agriculture and of rural areas.

b) The Assembly shall also have authority to enact Decisions on areas within the responsibility of the Communes if the matter cannot be effectively regulated by the Communes or if regulation by individual Communes might prejudice the rights of other Communes or if uniform legislation is necessary to ensure throughout Kosovo the equality of rights granted by this Agreement to individuals. In the absence of a specific Decision by the Assembly validly taken within this authority that preempts communal action, the Communes shall retain their authority.

3. Decisions of the Assembly shall be taken by majority of those and voting, except as provided in paragraph 4.

[Option 1:

4. When a majority of the Members of a national community selected pursuant to paragraph 1 (b) assert that a proposed decision affects the vital interests of their national community, that decision shall require for approval, in addition to the majority specified in paragraph 3, a majority of the Members present and voting from that

---

[1] Note: A proposal may be made to expand the list of Federal responsibilities to include other matters.

national community. If a majority of Members from the asserting community is not present and voting, the regular voting rule shall apply. Any other national community wishing to assert that the same proposed decision also affects its vital interests must make its claim within two days aft the privilege is first asserted. After that two day period has elapsed, no national community may assert the privilege set forth in this paragraph with respect to the same proposed decision.

5. The following procedure shall be used to resolve disputes regarding the exercise of the national community privilege set forth in paragraph 4:

(a) The national community or communities asserting the privilege will give reasons to the Assembly explaining its concerns. Members of the Assembly supporting the proposed decision will given an opportunity to respond. The Presidency of Kosovo shall mediate the dispute and attempt to reach a settlement agreeable to all affected national communities.

[Option 1 a:

(b) If mediation does not produce a mutually agreeable result within seven days, there shall be a vote of the Assembly. The proposed decision shall take effect if it receives the support of [4/5] of the Members of the whole Assembly, including a simple majority of the members representing each of at least two national communities selected pursuant to paragraph l(b).]

[Option 1 b:

(b) If mediation does not produce a mutually agreable result within seven days, the matter will be given to the Constitutional Court. The Court shall determine whether as a matter of law the vital national interests of the community or communities asserting the privilege set forth in paragraph 4 are affected by the proposed decision. The Court shall hear argument and rule within ten days.

(c) The decision of the Court may be appealed by either party to the [Director of the Kosovo Verification Mission so long as the mission remains in place, or alternatively the designee of the OSCE Chair in Office] [Chair of the Joint Commission], who shall resolve the matter acting in a quasi-judicial capacity. He or she shall rule within ten days. The judgement shall be final.]]

[Option 2:

Decisions of the Assembly are presumed valid. If a majority of the members from any national community delegation selected pursuant to paragraph I (b) believes that its vital interests are adversely affected by a Decision, the delegation may seek review of the Decision before the Constitutional Court and, on appeal, the [Director of the Kosovo Verification Mission so long as the mission remains in place, or alternatively the designee of the OSCE Chair in Office] [Chair of the Joint Commission]. Decisions determined to affect adversely a national community's vital interests will be set aside.]

6. A majority of Members shall constitute a quorum. The Assembly will decide its own rules of procedure. Members of Assembly shall be immune from civil or criminal proceedings on the basis of opinions expressed or votes cast in the Assembly.

7. The Assembly shall elect from among its Members a President, two Vice-Presidents, and other leaders in accordance with the procedures of the Assembly. Each national community covered by paragraph l(b) shall be represented in the leadership.

(a) The President of the Assembly shall represent the Assembly, call its sessions to order, chair its meetings, coordinate the work of any Committees it may establish, and perform other tasks prescribed by the rules of procedure of the Assembly.

[Option 1

b) The President of the Assembly may not be from the same national community as the Chair of the Kosovo Presidency.]

[Option 2: No text.]

Presidency

8. Executive power shall be exercised by the Presidency, which shall consist of one representative from each National Community qualifying under the terms set forth in Annex 5.

(a) Each member of the Presidency shall be selected by the Assembly for a [three] year term. No person may serve more than two terms as a member of the presidency.

(i) There shall be a Chair of the Presidency, who shall be selected from among the members of the Presidency by majority vote of the Assembly. The Chair shall call meetings of the Presidency, represent it in areas within its competence, and organize its work.

(ii) The Presidency shall decide its own rules of procedure. It shall endeavor to act by consensus. Subject to the privilege set forth in section (a) (iii) of this paragraph, decisions may be taken by the Chair where all efforts to achieve consensus have failed.

(iii) Within four days of the adoption of a Decision of the Presidency, a Member of the Presidency may assert that the Decision affects a vital interest of his or her national community.

a) The issue shall be promptly referred to his or her national community. If the national community affirms within ten days by a decision taken under its own democratic procedures that its vital interests are affected, the Decision shall be rescinded.[1]

b) Dissenting Members of the Presidency may petition the Constitutional Court to have a Decision reinstated on the grounds that the vital interests of the national community asserting the privilege are not adversely affected. The Court shall decide within ten days.

c) The ruling of the Constitutional Court may be further appealed by either party to the [Director of the Kosovo Verification Mission so long as the mission remains in place, or alternatively the designee of the OSCE Chair in Office] [Chair of the Joint Commission] who shall resolve the matter acting in a quasi-judicial capacity. The decision shall be final.

b) The Presidency shall be responsible for:

Representing all citizens in Kosovo before any international or Federal body, or any body of the Republics.

- Implementing the Decisions of the Assembly and of other authorities when authorized by those authorities.

- Selecting officers of the Administrative Bodies to assist in carrying out these executive responsibilities.

- Proposing to the Assembly candidates for the Constitutional Court, the Supreme Court, and other Kosovo judicial offices.

- Proposing Decisions to the Assembly.

- Meeting regularly with the democratically selected representatives of the national communities and other persons.

- Conducting foreign relations and concluding agreements on behalf of Kosovo

- after they are approved by the Assembly, consistent with the authorities of Kosovo institutions under this Agreement.

- Serving or designating a representative to serve on the Joint Commission and Joint Council established by Article VII of this Agreement.

- Meeting regularly with the President of the Federal Republic of Yugoslavia, the President of Montenegro, and the President of Serbia.

- Other duties specified in this Agreement.

Administrative Bodies

9. Administrative Bodies shall be responsible for assisting the Presidency in implementing Decisions of Kosovo and, where authorized, of other authorities.

(a) Employees of administrative bodies shall be fairly representative of the population and national communities of Kosovo.

---

[1] Note: The privilege to block a Decision of the Presidency as affecting a vital interest could be limited to certain categories of important matters. This will be a subject for further discussion.

(b) Any citizen of Kosovo claiming to have been directly and adversely affected by the decision of an executive or administrative body shall have the right to judicial review of that decision after exhausting any avenues for administrative review. The Assembly shall enact administrative law to regulate this review.

(c) An administrative body of Kosovo shall have primary responsibility for all criminal law enforcement matters in Kosovo, in accordance with Annex 2 to this Agreement.

PART III: COURTS IN KOSOVO

General

1. Kosovo shall have a Constitutional Court, a Supreme Court, District Courts, and Communal Courts. The Kosovo Supreme Court shall, upon approval by the Kosovo Assembly, promulgate rules of procedure consistent with this Agreement to guide the courts' activities.

[Option:

a) Until such time as the parties mutually agree to discontinue this arrangement or the Federal Republic becomes member of the Council of Europe and appeals are possible under its rules to the European Court of Human Rights, a majority of judges on the Constitutional Court shall be selected from a list presented by the Committee of Ministers of the Council of Europe pursuant to Council Resolution (93) 6.]

2. The Kosovo courts shall have jurisdiction over all legal matters arising under the Constitution of Kosovo, Decisions of the Assembly, and laws of the Republic of Serbia. Disputes presenting solely questions of Republic law may be appealed to the Supreme Court of Serbia after all appeals available in the Kosovo courts have been exhausted.

3. The Kosovo courts shall also have jurisdiction as specified in this paragraph over matters arising under federal law or raising questions of federal law. Disputes presenting federal questions may be appealed to the Federal courts after all appeals available under the Kosovo system have been exhausted.

(a) Kosovo courts shall adjudicate all civil and administrative cases in Kosovo arising under Federal law or raising federal law questions in the first instance. Except as specified in Section 3 (b) of this Part, Kosovo courts shall also adjudicate criminal cases in Kosovo arising under federal law.

(b) Those federal criminal matters specified in [ ][1] shall be adjudicated entirely by the courts of the Federal Republic of Yugoslavia. An appropriate branch of the Federal Court shall be established in Kosovo for this purpose.

4. The Republic of Serbia shall continue to maintain separate courts in Kosovo. Citizens in Kosovo may opt to have civil and administrative disputes to which they are a party adjudicated by the Republic courts, which shall apply applicable Kosovo legal authorities and shall refer matters falling within paragraph 6 (b) to the Constitutional Court. Criminal defendants may opt to have their cases decided by a Republic court pursuant to the same provisions applicable to civil and administrative cases, except with respect to these cases involving federal matters specified in Section 3 (b) of this Part.

Members of the Judiciary

5. Composition. The Constitutional Court shall consist of [nine] judges. The Supreme Court shall consist of [nine] judges. The Assembly shall determine the number of other judges necessary to meet current needs.

(a) The judges shall be distinguished jurists of the highest moral character.

(b) The judges shall be broadly representative of the national communities of Kosovo. There shall be a least one Constitutional Court judge and one Supreme Court judge from each national community representing at least []% of the population of Kosovo.

(c) Removal of a Kosovo judge shall require the consensus of the judges of the Constitutional Court. A Constitutional Court judge whose dismissal is in question shall not participate in the deliberations on his case.

6. Jurisdiction of the Constitutional Court

The Constitutional Court shall have sole authority to resolve disputes relating to the meaning of the Kosovo Constitution. That authority shall include, but is not limited to, determining whether decisions or actions of the Presidency, the Assembly, the Council of Ministers, the Communes, and the national communities are compatible with the Kosovo Constitution.

(a) Matters may be referred to the court by the Presidency of Kosovo, the President or Vice-Presidents of the Assembly, the Ombudsman, the communal assemblies and councils, and any national community acting according to its democratic procedures.

(b) Any court, which finds in the course of adjudicating a matter that the dispute depends on the answer to a question within the Court's jurisdiction, shall refer the issue to the Court for a preliminary decision.

(c) Following the exhaustion of other legal remedies, the Court shall at the request of any natural or legal person or association have jurisdiction over complaints that human rights and fundamental freedoms and the rights of members of national communities set forth in this Agreement have been violated by a public authority.

(d) The Constitution of Kosovo may provide that the Court shall have jurisdiction over other questions arising under it. The Constitutional Court shall have such other authorities and jurisdiction as may be specified elsewhere in this Agreement.

7. Jurisdiction of the Supreme Court. The Supreme Court shall hear appeals from the District Courts and the Communal Courts. Subject to the specific powers of the Constitutional Court, and to paragraphs 2, 3, and 4 of this Part, the Supreme Court shall take the final decision in all cases arising within Kosovo. Its decisions shall be recognized and executed by all public authorities on the territory of the Federal republic of Yugoslavia.

8. Functioning of the Courts. The Constitutional and Supreme Courts shall each adopt decisions by majority vote of their members. All Kosovo courts shall hold public proceedings, and issue published options setting forth the reasons for their decisions along with any dissenting views.

National Community Dispute Settlement Mechanism

9. Each national community may establish procedures for resolving conflicts concerning inheritance, family law, matrimonial relations tutorship, adoption, civil lawsuits as decided by the Assembly of Kosovo, and criminal cases for which a monetary fine is prescribed as punishment in the currently applicable penal code.

a) Dispute settlement mechanisms established under this provision shall have jurisdiction only when all parties consent.

b) Within the framework of these procedures, no decisions on arrest or detention of a person may be taken. If a competent authority established under this provision considers during its review of a criminal case that a sentence of imprisonment might be appropriate, it shall refer the case to the competent court.

c) Procedures established under this provision must maintain practices consistent with intentionally recognized human rights. At the request of one of the parties, the Constitutional Court of Kosovo shall review whether any decision taken within this framework respects the provisions of this Agreement, including in particular the human rights guarantees set forth in Article III.

d) Decisions of the national community dispute resolution mechanism shall be honored in accordance with applicable rules by Kosovo courts, Republic courts, and the courts of the Federal Republic of Yugoslavia.

---

[1] This section of the Agreement will set forth a list of serious crimes with gross-border implications, such as counterfeiting of money and narcotics trafficking. The list will be a subject for negotiation between the parties.

PART IV: THE OMBUDSMAN

1. There shall be an Ombudsman, who shall monitor the realization of the rights of members of national communities and the protection of human rights and fundamental freedoms in Kosovo.

(a) The Ombudsman shall be an eminent person of high moral standing who possesses a demonstrated commitment to human rights and the rights of the national communities.

(b) He or she shall be nominated by the Presidency and shall be elected by the Assembly from a list of candidates prepared by the President of the European Court for Human Rights for a non renewable [four] year term.

2. The Ombudsman shall be independently responsible for choosing his or her staff. He or she shall have two Deputies. The Deputies shall each be drawn from different national communities and neither shall be from the same national community as the Ombudsman if he or she is a member of a national community in Kosovo.

3. The Ombudsman shall have a right to review the acts and shall have unimpeded access to any person or place and shall have the right to appear and intervene before any domestic, Federal, or (consistent with the rules of such bodies) international authority upon his or her request. The Ombudsman shall have other powers and jurisdiction as set forth in Annex 1.

PART V: COMMUNES

[Option 1: 1. Kosovo shall have the existing communes.]

[Option 2: 1. Kosovo shall have [ ] communes within the boundaries specified in annex 6 of this Agreement.]

2. Communes may develop relationships among themselves for their mutual benefit.]

3. Each Commune shall have an Assembly, a Council, and such executive bodies as the commune may establish. Each national community with at least [ ]% of the population of the commune shall be represented on the Council in proportion to its share of the regional population or by one member, whichever is greater.

4. The communes shall have exclusive responsibility for:

- Law enforcement, as specified in annex 2 of this Agreement.

- Regulating and, when appropriate, providing childcare.

- Establishing and regulating the work of medical institutions and hospitals.

- Providing and regulating education, consistent with the rights and duties of national communities.

- Protecting the communal environment. Regulating commerce and privately owned stores.

- Regulating hunting and fishing.

- Planning and carrying out public works of communal importance, including roads and water supplies, and participating in the planning and carrying out Kosovo-wide public works projects in coordination with other communes and Kosovo authorities.

- Regulating land use, town planning, building regulations, and housing construction.

- Developing programs for tourism, the hotel industry, catering, and sport.

- Organizing fairs and local markets.

- Organizing public services of communal importance, including fire, emergency response, and police consistent with Annex 2 of this Agreement.

- Financing the work of communal institutions, including raising revenues, taxes, and preparing budgets.

5. The commune shall also have responsibility for all other areas not expressly assigned elsewhere by this Agreement, subject to the provisions of Article II, Part II.2 (b).

6. Each commune shall conduct its business in public and shall maintain publicly available records of its deliberations and decisions.

III. Human Rights and Fundamental Freedoms

1. The Parties shall ensure that the highest level of internationally recognized human rights and fundamental freedoms is secured for all persons in Kosovo.

2. Applicable rights and freedoms shall include those specified in the European Convention for the Protection of Human Rights and Fundamental Freedoms and its protocols.

a) The European Convention shall be directly applicable in Kosovo and in any matter involving a person of Kosovo, and shall take precedence over all other law.

b) All courts, agencies, government institutions, and instrumentalities of the Parties and all of their officials and employees shall conform to these human rights and fundamental freedoms.

IV. Rights and Duties of Members of National Communities

1. Members of the national communities shall have additional rights determined by this Agreement in order to preserve and express their national, cultural, religious, and linguistic identities in accordance with international standards and the Helsinki Final Act.

2. Each national community shall select through democratic means, in accordance with procedures it shall decide, institutions to administer its affairs in Kosovo.

3. The national communities shall be subject to Decisions of the Assembly of Kosovo, provided that any action concerning national communities must be nondiscriminatory. The Assembly shall decide upon procedure for resolving disputes between national communities.

4. The additional rights of the national communities, acting through their democratically selected institutions, are to:

(a) preserve and protect their national culture, including by:

- inscribing local names of towns and villages, of squares and streets, and of other topographic names in the language and alphabet of the national community in addition to signs in Serbian, consistent with decisions about style made by the communal institutions.

- providing information in the language and alphabet of the national community.

- establishing cultural and religious associations, for which relevant authorities will provide financial assistance.

- providing for education and establishing educational institutions, in particular for schooling in their own language and alphabet and in national.

- culture and history, for which relevant authorities will provide financial assistance. National communities are encouraged to coordinate curricula with Republic authorities concerning some subjects (for example, to ensure that pupils satisfy common standards in subjects such as math and science).

- enjoying unhindered contacts with representatives of their respective national communities, within the Federal Republic of Yugoslavia and abroad.

- using and displaying national symbols, along with symbols of the Federal Republic of Yugoslavia and the Republic of Serbia.

- protecting national practices on family law by, if the community decides, arranging rules in the field of inheritance, family and matrimonial relations; tutorship and adoption.

- the preservation of sites of religious, historical, or cultural importance to the national community, in cooperation with other authorities.

- implementing public health and social services.

- operating religious institutions in cooperation with religious authorities.

- participating in regional and international non-governmental organizations in accordance with procedures of these organizations.

(b) adopt procedures for dispute resolution, as provided in Article 11, Part III (g) of this Agreement.

(c) be guaranteed at least one radio and television frequency, which they shall each administer subject to non-discriminatory, technical standards;

(d) finance their activities by collecting charges the national communities may decide to levy on members of their own communities.

5. Members of national communities shall also be individually guaranteed:

the right to enjoy unhindered contacts with members of their respective national communities elsewhere in the Federal Republic of Yugoslavia and abroad,

- equal access to employment in public services at all levels,
- the right to use their languages and alphabets,
- the right to use and display national community symbols on private occasions,
- the right to participate in democratic institutions that will determine the national community's exercise of the collective rights set forth in this Article,

6. Each national community and, where appropriate, their members acting individually may exercise these additional rights through Federal institutions and institutions of the Republics, in accordance with the procedures of those institutions and without prejudice to the ability of Kosovo institutions to carry out their responsibilities.

V. Representation of Kosovo in Federal Institutions

1. Kosovo shall be offered the following representation, without prejudice to the rights of persons in Kosovo to decide whether to accept this offer;

a) At least [ ] deputies in the House of Citizens of the Federal Assembly.

b) At least [ ] deputies in the National Assembly of the Republic of Serbia.

c) The opportunity for the Kosovo Assembly to present to the appropriate authorities a list of candidates from which shall be drawn:

(i) at least one citizen in Kosovo to serve in the Federal Government, and at least one citizen to serve in the Government of the Republic of Serbia.

(ii) at least one judge on the Federal Constitutional Court, one judge in the Federal Court, and three judges on the Supreme Court of Serbia.

2. There shall be a Council of the Republic of Serbia for the protection of the rights of the members of national communities. The President of the Republic of Serbia shall preside over this Council.

VI. Financing and Other Economic Issues

FINANCING

1. The authorities established to levy and collect taxes and other charges are set forth in this Agreement. Except if otherwise expressly provided in this Agreement, those bodies have the right to keep all revenues from their own taxes or other charges.

2. In accordance with the provisions of Annex 3, the authorities of Kosovo shall forward to Federal authorities a fair share of revenue collected within Kosovo if necessary for funding of Federal responsibilities within Kosovo and not covered by revenue from Federal taxes from Kosovo.

3. In accordance with the provisions of Annex 3, revenue from certain Kosovo taxes and duties shall accrue to the Communes, taking into account the need for an equalization of revenues between the Communes based on objective criteria. The Communes shall also be able to levy local taxes, in accordance with the provisions of Annex 3.

4. Federal and other authorities shall also ensure, to the extent of their respective powers, the delivery of resources from international sources to Kosovo.

OTHER ECONOMIC ISSUES

5. Annex 3 of this Agreement shall specify in terms consistent with this Agreement, arrangements for the disposition of government owned assets in Kosovo; the resolution of disputes over pension and social insurance contributions: and the resolution of other matters relating to economic relations between the parties.

VII. Joint Commission and Joint Council.

JOINT COMMISSION

1. A Joint Commission will serve as the central mechanism for monitoring and coordinating the implementation of this Agreement. It will be comprised of Federal and Republic representatives, representatives of the national communities in Kosovo, representatives of Kosovo political institutions including the Presidency and the Ombudsman, and international representatives (including the Kosovo Verification Mission and Contact Group).

2. A person of high moral character will be selected to serve as Chair of the Joint Commission. The Chair will coordinate and organize the work of the Joint Commission, supervise the overall implementation of this Agreement, and shall have other powers, authorities, and duties as set forth herein or as may be later agreed by the Parties.

(a) For [ten] years following the entry into force of this Agreement, the Chair shall be a person chosen by the Chair in Office of the OSCE after consultation with the Parties. During this initial period, the Chair of the Joint Commission shall not be citizen of the Federal Republic of Yugoslavia or a surrounding state.

(b) After the initial period, the Chair shall be selected by consensus between the President of the Federal Republic of Yugoslavia, and the Presidency of Kosovo. In the event the parties cannot reach an agreement, the Chair shall be a person selected by the Chair in Office of the OSCE after consultations with the Parties.

3. The Parties shall cooperate with the Commission and its Chair. The Joint Commission as a whole and the Chair individually on his or her own initiative shall have safe, complete, and unimpeded access to all places, persons, and information (including documents and other records) both within Kosovo and, where the Joint Commission or the Chair deem it relevant, within the Federal Republic.

4. In the event of disagreement as to the meaning of any provision of this Agreement a Party may petition the Chair of the Join Commission, who shall have final authority to resolve such disputes. The Parties agree to abide by the Chair's decision.

JOINT COUNCIL

5. The national communities shall establish a Joint Council to coordinate their activities under this Agreement, and to provide an informal mechanism for the resolution of disputes. The Joint Council shall consist of one member from each of the national communities. Its activities shall be founded equally by the once each month. The Joint Council shall encourage the creation of similar mechanisms at the communal level, building on the example of local commissions established pursuant to Article VIII(5) of this Agreement.

VIII. Confidence - Building Measures

1. Violence in Kosova shall cease. Alleged violations of the ceasefire shall be reported to international observers and will not be used to justify violence in response. All persons held by the Parties without charge shall be released.

2. [An agreement on the status of security forces in Kosovo, to be added after expert consultations.]

3. [An agreement on the status of police forces in Kosovo, to be added after expert consultations.]

4. Each side will encourage all persons displaced during the conflict to return to their homes as the security situation permits. There will be no impediments to the normal flow of goods in Kosovo. International humanitarian organizations will be freely permitted to provide building materials and other assistance to persons returning to their homes in Kosovo.

5. In each community a local commission, representative of all national communities there, will assist international humanitarian agencies in the delivery and distribution of food, medicine, clothes, con-

struction materials, the restoration of electricity and water supply, and in encouraging returns.

6. International personnel, including the Kosovo Verification Mission and members of non-governmental organizations, shall be allowed unfettered access, at any time, throughout Kosovo. It is expected that international personnel will be present at all times in selected communities.

7. Each side shall respect its obligation to cooperate in the investigation and prosecution of war crimes, crimes against humanity, and other violations of international humanitarian law. In acknowledgement that allegations of atrocities cannot be resolved to the satisfaction of the other, each side will allow complete, unimpeded, and unfettered access to international experts - including forensics experts - authorized to investigate such allegations. Each side will provide full support and cooperation to the activities of the International Criminal Tribunal for the Former Yugoslavia.

8. No person shall be prosecuted for crimes related to the conflict in Kosovo, except for those who have committed war crimes, crimes against humanity, and other fundamental violations of international humanitarian law.

[Option 1:
Republic and Federal authorities shall reexamine, for extraordinary mitigation of punishments, all sentences pronounced on members of national communities from Kosovo for acts motivated by political goals.]

[Option 2:
There shall be a general amnesty for all persons in Kosovo convicted of committing politically motivated crimes related to the conflict in Kosovo.

This amnesty shall not apply to those properly convicted of committing war crimes, crimes against humanity, or other fundamental violations of international humanitarian law.]

IX. Implementation Period

1. This Agreement shall be implemented as quickly as possible. The parties undertake to allow, insofar as possible, its adequate implementation even before the adoption and undertaking of all acts and measures required to implement this Agreement.

2. The Parties will start without delay on any and all legal changes necessary for the full implementation of this Agreement. They acknowledge that complete implementation will require the adoption of necessary state regulations and other general acts, of the Constitution of Kosovo, political acts and measures, and the election and establishment of institutions and bodies set forth in the Agreement. This Agreement shall take precedence over all existing legal authorities of the parties.

3. Each national community in Kosovo is authorized to start exercising the additional rights determined by this Agreement, to the extent possible, immediately upon signature.

4. Within [nine] months, there shall be elections in accordance with and pursuant to procedures specified in Annex 4 of this Agreement for all authorities established herein, according to an electoral list prepared to international standards. The Government of the Federal Republic of Yugoslavia hereby invites the Organization for Security and Cooperation in Europe (OSCE) to supervise those elections to ensure openess and fairness.

5. Under the supervision of the OSCE and with the participation of Kosovo authorities, Federal authorities shall conduct an objective and free census of the population in Kosovo, which shall be carried out when the OSCE determines that conditions allow an accurate census.

(a) The first census shall be limited to name, place of birth, address, gender, age, citizenship, nationality, and religion.

(b) The institutions and authorities of the Parties shall provide the institutions of Kosovo with all records necessary to conduct the census, including data about places of residence, citizenship, voters' lists, and other information.

6. The Parties shall provide active support, cooperation, and participation for the successful implementation of the Agreement.

7. Institutions currently in place in Kosovo shall remain until the establishment of the bodies created by this Agreement.

8. Martial law shall be repealed. Laws compatible with this Agreement shall remain in force until replaced by the decision of a competent body established herein.

X. Amendments

1. Amendments to the Agreement shall be adopted by agreement of all the parties.

2. Each Party may propose amendments at any time and will consider and consult with the other with regard to proposed amendments.

3. In three years, the Parties will undertake a comprehensive assessment of the Agreement, with the aim of improving its implementation and considering proposals by either side for additional steps, which will require mutual agreement for adoption.

XI. Final Provisions

1. This Agreement is concluded in [ ] languages.
[?]

6. This Agreement shall enter into force when each Party has notified the others of the completion of its internal process.

For Federal Republic of Yugoslavia; Republic of Serbia; Kosovo

Annex 1: The Ombudsman

GENERAL

1. The Office of the Ombudsman shall be an independent agency of Kosovo. In carrying out its mandate, no person, institution, or entity of the Parties may interfere with its functions.

2. The salaries and expenses of the Ombudsman and his or her staff shall be determined and paid by the Kosovo Assembly. The salaries and expenses shall be fully adequate to implement the Ombudsman's mandate.

3. The Ombudsman and members of his or her staff shall not be held criminally or civilly liable for any acts carried out within the scope of their duties.

JURISDICTION

4. The Ombudsman shall consider:

a) alleged or apparent violations of human rights and fundamental freedoms in Kosovo, as provided in the Constitutions of the Federal Republic and the Republic of Serbia, and the European Convention for the Protection of Human Rights and Fundamental Freedoms and the Protocols thereto; and

b) alleged or apparent violations of the rights of national communities specified in this Agreement.

5. All citizens in Kosovo shall have the right to submit complaints to the Ombudsman. The Parties agree not to take any measures to punish persons who intend to submit or who have submitted such allegations, or in any other way to deter the exercise of this right.

POWERS AND AUTHORITY

6. The Ombudsman shall investigate alleged violations falling within the jurisdiction set forth in paragraph five. He may act either on his own initiative or in response to an allegation presented by any Party or person, non-governmental organization, or group of individuals claiming to be the victim of a violation or acting on behalf of alleged victims who are deceased or missing. The work of the Ombudsman shall be free of charge to the person concerned.

7. The Ombudsman shall have complete, unimpeded, and immediate access to any person, place, or information upon his or her request.

a) He shall have access to and may examine all official documents, and he can require any person, including officials in Kosovo, the Republic of Serbia, and the Federal Republic of Yugoslavia to cooperate by providing relevant information, documents, and files.

b) The Ombudsman may attend administrative hearings, meetings of other Kosovo institutions, and meetings and proceedings of the Republics and the Federal Republic of Yugoslavia in order to gather information.

c) He may examine facilities and places where persons deprived of their liberty are detained, work, or are otherwise located.

d) The Ombudsman and staff shall maintain the confidentiality of all confidential information obtained by them, unless the Ombudsman determines that such information is evidence of a violation of rights falling within his or her jurisdiction, in which case that information may be revealed in public reports or appropriate legal proceedings.

e) The Parties undertake to ensure cooperation with the Ombudsman's investigation. Willful and knowing failure to comply shall be a criminal offense prosecutable in any jurisdiction of the Parties. Where an official impedes an investigation by refusing to provide necessary information, the Ombudsman shall contact that official's superior or the public prosecutor for appropriate penal action to be taken in accordance with the law.

8. The Ombudsman shall issue findings and conclusions in the form of a published report promptly after concluding an investigation.

a) A Party, institution, or official identified by the Ombudsman as a violator shall, within a period specified by the Ombudsman, explain in writing how it will comply with any prescriptions the Ombudsman may put forth for remedial measures.

b) In the event that a person or entity does not comply with the conclusions and recommendations of the Ombudsman, the report shall be forwarded for further action to the Joint Commission set forth in Article VII of this Agreement, to the Presidency of the appropriate Party, and to any other officials or institutions that the Ombudsman deems proper.

9. The Ombudsman shall promptly report to the International Criminal Tribunal for the Former Yugoslavia evidence of war crimes, crimes against humanity, and other fundamental violations of international humanitarian law that may fall within the jurisdiction of that tribunal.

Other Annexes: The following additional annexes will be a part of the completed Agreement: Annex 2: Police and Security Matters; Annex 3: Financing and Other Economic Issues; Annex 4: Conduct and Supervision of Election; Annex 5: National Communities; [Annex 6: Communal Boundaries]

93 f) Final Hill Proposal, 27 January 1999

I. Introduction

1. All citizens in Kosovo have equal rights and duties as set forth in this Agreement. National communities and their members shall have additional rights as set forth below. The national communities shall be legally equal and shall not use their additional rights so as to endanger the rights of other national communities or the rights of citizens.

2. All authorities in Kosovo shall fully respect principles of human rights, democracy, and the equality of citizens and national communities.

3. Citizens in Kosovo shall have the right to democratic self-government through legislative, executive, judicial, and other institutions established in accordance with this Agreement. They shall have the opportunity to be represented in all institutions in Kosovo. The right of democratic self-government shall include the right to participate in free and fair elections.

4. Every person in Kosovo shall have the right to apply to international institutions for the protection of their rights in accordance with the procedures of such institutions.

5. The Parties accept that their powers and authorities in Kosovo are as specified by this Agreement, which shall prevail over any other legal provisions and shall be directly applicable. In implementing this Agreement in accordance with their procedures and international standards, the parties shall harmonize their governing practices and documents. All parties commit to implement this Agreement fully.

6. The Parties invite the OSCE to carry out the functions set forth in this Agreement. They agree to cooperate fully with all international organizations working in Kosovo on the implementation of this Agreement. The Kosovo Verification mission shall have the authority to call upon international organizations for additional assistance as necessary.

II. Governance in Kosovo
PART I: GENERAL

1. The basic territorial unit of local government in Kosovo will be the communes. All responsibilities not expressly assigned elsewhere by this Agreement will be the responsibility of the communes.

2. The authorities of Kosovo shall have responsibility for all areas except the following, which shall be within the competence of the Federal Republic of Yugoslavia save as specified in paragraph three:

(a) territorial integrity (b) maintaining a common market within the Federal Republic of Yugoslavia, which power shall be exercised in a manner that does not discriminate against any particular region or area of the Federal Republic of Yugoslavia (c) monetary policy (d) defense (e) foreign policy (f) customs services, and (g) federal taxation.

Citizens in Kosovo shall continue to participate in areas reserved for the Federal Republic of Yugoslavia through their representation in Federal institutions.

3. Kosovo shall retain the following powers in the areas otherwise reserved for the Federal Republic of Yugoslavia:

(a) No changes to the borders of Kosovo shall be made without the consent of the Kosovo Assembly and President;

(b) Deployment and use of police and public security forces in Kosovo shall be governed by Annex 2 of this Agreement;

(c) Citizens in Kosovo shall not be conscripted for Federal military service without the consent of the President of Kosovo;

(d) Kosovo officers and institutions shall have authority to conduct foreign relations within their areas of responsibility equivalent to the power provided to Republics under Article 7 of the Constitution of the Federal Republic of Yugoslavia;

(e) Martial law shall not be declared in Kosovo without the consent of the President of Kosovo;

(f) Federal measures having a differential, disproportionate, or discriminatory impact on Kosovo shall not take effect in Kosovo without the consent of the Kosovo President.

4. There shall be no interference with the right of citizens and national communities in Kosovo to call upon institutions of the Republic of Serbia for the following purposes on a purely voluntary basis:

(a) assistance in designing school curricula and standards;

(b) participation in social benefits programs, such as care for war veterans, pensioners, and disabled persons; and

(c) other voluntarily received services, provided that these services are not be related to police and security matters which shall be governed by Annex 2, and that any Republic personnel serving in Kosovo pursuant to this paragraph shall be unarmed social service providers acting at the invitation of a national community in Kosovo; the Chair of the Joint Commission shall have the authority to limit the exercise of this right to ensure the protection of all national communities.

5. Kosovo, Federal, and Republic authorities shall not interfere with the exercise of the additional rights described in Article IV of this Agreement.

6. All candidates for appointed, elective, or other public office in Kosovo, and all office holders in Kosovo, shall meet the following criteria:

a) No person who is serving a sentence imposed by the International Criminal Tribunal for the Former Yugoslavia and no person who is under indictment by the Tribunal and who has failed to comply with an order to appear before the Tribunal, may stand as a candidate or hold any office; and

b) All candidates and office holders shall renounce violence as a mechanism for achieving political goals; past political or resistance activities shall not be a bar to holding office in Kosovo.

PART II: ASSEMBLY, PRESIDENT, GOVERNMENT, AND ADMINISTRATIVE BODIES

The Assembly

1. There shall be an Assembly, which shall be comprised of one hundred Members.

(a) Sixty Members shall be directly elected.

(b) The remaining forty Members shall be elected by the members of qualifying national communities. The seats shall be divided equally among the national communities meeting a threshold determined as follows:

(i) After the completion of the census specified in Article IX.5, those national communities representing at least five percent of the population of Kosovo as determined by the census shall be eligible for seats allocated under this paragraph.

(ii) Prior to the completion of the census, the national communities eligible for seats in the Assembly under this paragraph shall be decided by the Head of the Kosovo Verification Mission based on his estimation of which national communities meet the five percent population threshold. His decision shall take into account previous census data and other information.

(iii) The Serbian and Albanian national communities shall be presumed to meet the necessary population threshold.

(c) Elections for all Members, whether under paragraph 1 (a) or 1 (b), shall be conducted democratically, consistent with the provisions of Article IX.4 and Annex 3.

2. The Assembly shall be responsible for adopting the Constitution of Kosovo and enacting laws of Kosovo, including those regulating relations in political, economic, social, and cultural areas. The Constitution and laws of the Kosovo Assembly shall not be subject to change or modification by authorities of the Republics or the Federation.

(a) The Assembly's areas of responsibility shall include:

- Financing activities of Kosovo institutions, including by levying taxes and duties on sources within Kosovo;

- The adoption of budgets and annual accounts of the Administrative Bodies and other institutions of Kosovo, with the exception of communal and national community institutions unless otherwise specified by this Agreement;

- The adoption of regulations concerning the organization, procedures, and functioning of the Administrative Bodies of Kosovo;

- Approving the Government proposed by the President of Kosovo; Approving candidates put forward by the Kosovo President for Kosovo judicial offices;

- Adoption of laws ensuring free movement of goods, services, and persons in Kosovo consistent with the responsibilities of other authorities;

- Conducting relations with foreign entities and approving agreements within its areas of responsibility, consistent with the authorities of Kosovo institutions under this Agreement;

- Cooperating with the Federal Assembly, and with the Assemblies of the Republics;

- Establishing, in accordance with this Agreement, the main rules of local self-government, including in particular rules on elections consistent with the rules and regulations of the Central Election Commission, finance, the status of elected local officials, and on local government employees;

- Coordination among communes or national communities when necessary, including the enactment of laws concerning inter-communal issues;

- Protection of the environment where inter-communal issues are involved; and

- Designing and implementing programs of economic, scientific, technological, demographic, regional, and social development, as well as programs for the development of agriculture and of rural areas.

(b) The Assembly shall also have authority to enact laws in areas within the responsibility of the Communes if the matter cannot be effectively regulated by the Communes or if regulation by individual Communes might prejudice the rights of other Communes or if uniform legislation is necessary to ensure throughout Kosovo the equality of rights granted by this Agreement to citizens in Kosovo. In the absence of a law enacted by the Assembly validly taken within this authority that preempts communal action, the Communes shall retain their authority.

3. Laws shall be enacted by majority of those present and voting, except as provided in paragraph 4.

4. If a majority of the Members of a national community present and voting elected pursuant to paragraph 1(b) make a motion that a law adversely affects the vital interests of their national community, that law shall remain in force subject to completion of the dispute settlement procedure in paragraph 5. Vital interest motions shall be made within five days of a law's enactment.

5. The following procedure shall be used in the event of a motion asserting that the vital interest of a national community has been adversely affected:

(a) The national community or communities asserting that its vital interest has been adversely affected will give reasons explaining its concerns to the President of Kosovo. Members of the Assembly supporting the law will be given an opportunity to respond. The President of Kosovo shall mediate the dispute and attempt to reach a settlement agreeable to all affected national communities.

(b) If mediation does not produce a mutually agreeable result within seven days, the matter shall be given to the Constitutional Court. The Court shall determine whether as a matter of law the vital interests of the national community or communities asserting the privilege set forth in paragraph 4 are adversely affected by the law. The Court shall hear argument and rule within fifteen days. Its judgment shall be final.

(c) A law determined by the President of Kosovo or, if applicable, the Constitutional Court to adversely affect the vital interests of a national community shall be void. The law shall stay in effect pending the completion of any appeal to the Constitutional Court.

6. A majority of Members shall constitute a quorum. The Assembly will decide its own rules of procedure. Members of the Assembly shall be immune from all civil or criminal proceedings on the basis of opinions expressed or other acts performed in their capacity as Members of the Assembly.

7. The Assembly shall elect from among its Members a President, two Vice-Presidents, and other leaders in accordance with the procedures of the Assembly.

8. Each national community meeting the threshold specified in paragraph 1(b) shall be represented in the leadership. The President of the Assembly shall not be from the same National Community as the President of Kosovo.

9. The President of the Assembly shall represent the Assembly, call its sessions to order, chair its meetings, coordinate the work of any Committees it may establish, and perform other tasks prescribed by the rules of procedure of the Assembly.

President of Kosovo

10. There shall be a President of Kosovo, who shall be selected by the Assembly for a three year term. No person may serve more than two terms as President of Kosovo.

11. The President of Kosovo shall be responsible for:

- Representing Kosovo before any international or Federal body, or any body of the Republics.

- Proposing to the Assembly candidates for Prime Minister, the Constitutional Court, the Supreme Court. and other Kosovo judicial offices. Meeting regularly with the democratically elected representatives of the national communities and other persons.

- Conducting foreign relations and concluding agreements on behalf of Kosovo after they are approved by the Assembly, consistent with the authorities of Kosovo institutions under this Agreement.

- Serving or designating a representative to serve on the Joint Commission and Joint Council established by Article VII of this Agreement.

- Meeting regularly with the President of the Federal Republic of Yugoslavia, the President of Montenegro, and the President of Serbia.

- Other duties specified in this Agreement.

Government

12. Executive power shall be exercised by the Government. The Government shall be responsible for implementing and enforcing the laws of Kosovo, and of other government authorities when such responsibilities are devolved by those authorities. The Government shall also have the authority to propose laws to the Assembly.

(a) The Government shall consist of a Prime Minister and Ministers, including at least one person from each national community meeting the threshold specified in paragraph l(b). Ministers shall head the Administrative Bodies of Kosovo.

(b) The candidate for Prime Minister proposed by the President shall put forward a list of Ministers to the Assembly. The Prime Minister and the proposed Ministers shall be approved by a majority of those present and voting in the Assembly. In the event that the Prime Minister is not able to obtain a majority for the Government, the President shall propose a new candidate for Prime Minister within ten days.

(c) The Government shall serve at the confidence of the Assembly, and may be dissolved by majority vote of the Assembly. In the event of dissolution of the Government by the Assembly or because of resignation by the Prime Minister, the President shall select a new candidate for Prime Minister who shall seek to form a Government under the rules set forth in paragraph 12(b) of this Part.

(d) The Prime Minister shall call meetings of the Government, represent it in appropriate settings, and coordinate its work. Decisions of the Government shall require a majority of Ministers present and voting. The Prime Minister shall cast the deciding vote in the event Ministers are equally divided. The Government shall other vise decide its own rules of procedure.

Administrative Bodies

13. Administrative Bodies shall be responsible for assisting the Government in carrying out its duties.

(a) Employees of administrative bodies shall be fairly representative of the population and national communities of Kosovo.

(b) Any citizen of Kosovo claiming to have been directly and adversely affected by the decision of an executive or administrative body shall have the right to judicial review of that decision after exhausting all avenues for Administrative review. The Assembly shall enact administrative law to regulate this review.

(c) An administrative body of Kosovo shall have primary responsibility for all criminal law enforcement matters in Kosovo, in accordance with Annex 2 to this Agreement.

PART III: COURTS IN KOSOVO

General

1. Kosovo shall have a Constitutional Court, a Supreme Court, District Courts, and Communal Courts. The Kosovo Supreme Court shall, upon approval by the Kosovo Assembly, promulgate rules of procedure consistent with this Agreement to guide the courts' activities.

2. The Kosovo courts shall have jurisdiction over all matters arising in Kosovo under the Constitution and laws of Kosovo and laws of the Assembly except as specified in paragraph 4.

3. The Kosovo courts shall also have jurisdiction over matters arising in Kosovo under federal law or raising questions of federal law. Disputes resenting questions of federal law may be appealed to the Federal courts on those federal legal questions after all appeals available under the Kosovo system have been exhausted.

4. Citizens in Kosovo may opt to have civil disputes to which they are a party adjudicated by the Republic courts, which shall apply applicable Kosovo law and shall refer matters falling within paragraph 6(b) to the Constitutional Court of Kosovo. Criminal defendants may seek access to and participation of Republic of officials in Kosovo proceedings.

Members of the Judiciary

5. Composition. The Constitutional Court shall consist of nine judges. The Supreme Court shall consist of nine judges. The Assembly shall determine the number of other judges necessary to meet current needs.

(a) The judges shall be distinguished jurists of the highest moral character,

(b) The judges shall be broadly representative of the national communities of Kosovo. There shall be a least one Constitutional Court judge and one Supreme Court judge from each national community qualifying for seats in the Kosovo Assembly under paragraph l(b) of this Part.

(c) Until such time as the parties mutually agree to discontinue this arrangement or the Federal Republic of Yugoslavia becomes a party to the European Convention for the Protection of Human Rights and Fundamental Freedoms, a majority of judges on the Constitutional Court shall be selected from a list presented by the Committee of Ministers of the Council of Europe pursuant to Council Resolution (93)6.

(d) Removal of a Kosovo judge shall require the consensus of the judges of the Constitutional Court. A Constitutional Court judge whose dismissal is in question shall not participate in the deliberations on his case.

6. *Jurisdiction of the Constitutional Court*

The Constitutional Court shall have sole authority to resolve disputes relating to the meaning of the Kosovo Constitution. That authority shall include, but is not limited to, determining whether decisions or actions of the President, the Assembly, the Government, the Communes, and the national communities are compatible with the Kosovo Constitution.

(a) Matters may be referred to the Court by the President of Kosovo, the President or Vice-Presidents of the Assembly, the Ombudsman, the communal assemblies and councils, and any national community acting according to its democratic procedures.

(b) Any court which finds in the course of adjudicating a matter that the dispute depends on the answer to a question within the Court's jurisdiction shall refer the issue to the Court for a preliminary decision.

(c) Following the exhaustion of other legal remedies, the Court shall at the request of any natural or legal person or association have jurisdiction over complaints that human rights and fundamental freedoms and the rights of members of national communities set forth in this Agreement have been violated by a public authority.

(d) The Constitution of Kosovo may provide that the Court shall have jurisdiction over other questions arising under it. The Constitutional Court shall have such other authorities and jurisdiction as may be specified elsewhere in this Agreement.

7. Jurisdiction of the Supreme Court. The Supreme Court shall hear appeals from the District Courts and the Communal Courts. Subject to the specific powers of the Constitutional Court, and to paragraph 4 of this Part, the Supreme Court shall take the final decision in all cases arising within Kosovo. Its decisions shall be recognized and executed by all public authorities on the territory of the Federal Republic of Yugoslavia.

8. Functioning of the Courts. The Constitutional and Supreme Courts shall each adopt decisions by majority vote of their members. All Kosovo courts shall hold public proceedings, and issue published opinions setting forth the reasons for their decisions along with any dissenting views.

PART IV: THE OMBUDSMAN

1. There shall be an Ombudsman, who shall monitor the realization of the rights of members of national communities and the Protection of human rights and fundamental freedoms in Kosovo.

(a) The Ombudsman shall be an eminent person of high moral standing who possesses a demonstrated commitment to human rights and the rights of the national communities.

(b) He or she shall be nominated by the President and shall be elected by the Assembly from a list of candidates prepared by the President of the European Court for Human Rights for a non-renewable three year term.

2. The Ombudsman shall be independently responsible for choosing his or her own staff. He or she shall have two Deputies. The Deputies shall each be drawn from different national communities, and neither shall be from the same national community as the Ombudsman if he or she is a member of a national community in Kosovo.

3. The Ombudsman shall have unimpeded access to any person or place and shall have the right to appear and intervene before any domestic, Federal, or (consistent with the rules of such bodies) international authority upon his or her request. The Ombudsman shall have other powers and jurisdiction as set forth in Annex 1.

PART V: COMMUNES

1. Kosovo shall have the existing communes. Changes may be made to communal boundaries by act of the Kosovo Assembly.

2. Communes may develop relationships among themselves for their mutual benefit.

3. Each commune shall have an Assembly, a Council, and such executive bodies as the commune may establish.

(a) Each national community whose membership constitutes at least five percent of the population of the commune shall be represented on the Council in proportion to its share of the communal population or by one member, whichever is greater.

(b) Prior to the completion of a census, disputes over communal population percentages for purposes of this paragraph shall be resolved by the Head of the Kosovo Verification Mission or his designee taking into account past census data and other information.

4. The communes shall have responsibility for:

- Law enforcement, as specified in Annex 2 of this Agreement.
- Regulating and, when appropriate, providing child care.
- Establishing and regulating the work of medical institutions and hospitals.
- Providing education, consistent with the rights and duties of national communities, and in a spirit of tolerance between national communities and respect for the rights of the members of all national communities in accordance with international standards.
- Protecting the communal environment.
- Regulating commerce and privately owned stores.
- Regulating hunting and fishing.
- Planning and carrying out public works of communal importance, including roads and water supplies, and participating in the planning and carrying out of Kosovo-wide public works projects in coordination with other communes and Kosovo authorities.
- Regulating land use, town planning, building regulations, and housing construction.
- Developing programs for tourism, the hotel industry, catering, and sport.
- Organizing fairs and local markets.
- Organizing public services of communal importance,
- including fire, emergency response, and police consistent with Annex 2 of this Agreement.
- Financing the work of communal institutions, including raising revenues, taxes, and preparing budgets.

5. The communes shall exercise the authorities specified in paragraph 4 and shall also have responsibility for all other areas not expressly assigned elsewhere by this Agreement, subject to the provisions of Article II, Part II.2(b).

6. Each commune shall conduct its business in public and shall maintain publicly available records of its deliberations and decisions.

III. Human Rights and Fundamental Freedoms

1. The Parties shall ensure respect for internationally recognized human rights and fundamental freedoms in Kosovo.

2. Applicable rights and freedoms shall include those specified in the European Convention for the Protection of Human Rights and Fundamental Freedoms and its Protocols.

(a) The rights and freedoms set forth in the European Convention for the Protection of Human Rights and Fundamental Freedoms and its Protocols shall apply directly in Kosovo. These shall have priority over all other law.

(b) All courts, agencies Government institutions, and instrumentalities of the Parties and all of their officials and employees shall conform to these human rights and fundamental freedoms.

IV. Rights and Duties of National Communities and Their Members

1. National communities and their members shall have additional rights determined by this Agreement in order to preserve and express their national, cultural, religious, and linguistic identities in accordance with international standards and the Helsinki Final Act.

They shall have these rights without regard to their representation as a percentage of the Kosovo population.

2. Each national community shall elect through democratic means in a manner consistent with the provisions of Annex 3 institutions to administer its affairs in Kosovo.

3. The national communities shall be subject to the laws enacted by the Kosovo Assembly, provided that any action concerning national communities must be nondiscriminatory. The Assembly shall decide upon a procedure for resolving disputes between national communities.

4. The additional rights of the national communities, acting through their democratically elected institutions are to:

(a) preserve and protect their national cultures, including by:

- inscribing local names of towns and villages, of squares and streets, and of other topographic names in the language and alphabet of the national community, consistent with decisions about style made by the communal institutions;
- providing information in the language and alphabet of the national community;
- providing for education and establishing educational institutions, in particular for schooling in their own language and alphabet and in national culture and history, for which relevant authorities will provide financial assistance; curricula shall reflect a spirit of tolerance between national communities and respect for the rights of members of all national communities in accordance with international standards;
- enjoying unhindered contacts with representatives of their respective national communities, within the Federal Republic of Yugoslavia and abroad;
- using and displaying national symbols, including symbols of the Federal Republic of Yugoslavia and the Republic of Serbia;
- protecting national practices on family law by, if the community decides, arranging rules in the field of inheritance, family, and matrimonial relations; tutorship; and adoption;

- the preservation of sites of religious, historical, or cultural importance to the national community, in cooperation with other authorities. implementing public health and social services;

- operating religious institutions in cooperation with religious authorities;

- participating in regional and international non-Government all organizations in accordance with procedures of these organizations.

(b) be guaranteed at least one radio and one television frequency, which they shall each administer subject to non-discriminatory, technical standards;

(c) finance their activities by collecting charges the national communities may decide to levy on members of their own communities.

5. Members of national communities shall also be individually guaranteed:

- the right to enjoy unhindered contacts with members of their respective national communities elsewhere in the Federal Republic of Yugoslavia and abroad.
- equal access to employment in public services at all levels.
- the right to use their languages and alphabets.
- the right to use and display national community symbols.
- the right to participate in democratic institutions that will determine the national community's exercise of the collective rights set forth in this Article.
- the right to establish cultural and religious associations, for which relevant authorities will provide financial assistance.

6. Each national community and, where appropriate, their members acting individually may exercise these additional rights through Federal institutions and institutions of the Republics, in accordance with the procedures of those institutions and without prejudice to the ability of Kosovo institutions to carry out their responsibilities.

V. Representation of Kosovo in Federal and Republic Institutions

1. Kosovo shall be offered the following representation, without prejudice to the rights of persons in Kosovo to decide whether to accept this offer:

(a) At least 10 deputies in the House of Citizens of the Federal Assembly.

(b) At least 20 deputies in the National Assembly of the Republic of Serbia.

(c) The opportunity for the Kosovo Assembly to present to the appropriate authorities a list of candidates from which shall be drawn:

(i) at least one citizen in Kosovo to serve in the Federal Government, and at least one citizen to serve in the Government of the Republic of Serbia.

(ii) at least one judge on the Federal Constitutional Court, one judge on the Federal Court, and three judges on the Supreme Court of Serbia.

VI. Financing and Other Economic Issues
FINANCING

1. The authorities established to levy and collect taxes and other charges are set forth in this Agreement. Except if otherwise expressly provided in this Agreement, those bodies have the right to keep all revenues from their own taxes or other charges. In particular, Republic authorities shall have no right to levy or collect taxes on Kosovo sources.

2. Revenue from certain Kosovo taxes and duties shall accrue to the Communes, taking into account the need for an equalization of revenues between the Communes based on objective criteria. The Assembly shall enact appropriate nondiscriminatory legislation for this purpose. The Communes shall also have authority to levy local taxes in accordance with this Agreement.

3. Federal and other authorities shall facilitate the delivery of resources from international sources to Kosovo to the extent of their respective powers, and in particular shall allow unfettered access of persons delivering such resources.

OTHER ECONOMIC ISSUES

4. The Parties agree to the following arrangements for: the disposition of government owned assets in Kosovo (including educational institutions and hospitals); the resolution of disputes over pension and social insurance contributions; and the resolution of any other matters relating to economic relations between the parties not covered by this Agreement.

(a) The Parties shall make a good faith effort to mediate these disputes under the auspices of the Head of the Kosovo Verification Mission or his designee.

(b) In the event the Parties cannot reach agreement, the Head of the Kosovo Verification Mission shall arbitrate the disputed issues. His decision shall be final and binding on the Parties.

VII. Joint Council and Joint Commission
JOINT COUNCIL

1. The national communities shall establish a Joint Council to coordinate their activities under this Agreement, and to provide an informal mechanism for the resolution of disputes. The Joint Council shall consist of one member from each of the national communities. Its activities shall be funded equally by the participating national communities. It shall meet no less than once each month. The Joint Council shall encourage the creation of similar mechanisms at the communal level, building on the example of local commissions established pursuant to Article VIII-5 of this Agreement.

JOINT COMMISSION

2. A Joint Commission will serve as the central mechanism for monitoring and coordinating the implementation of this Agreement. It will be comprised of Federal and Republic representatives, representatives of the national communities in Kosovo, representatives of Kosovo political institutions including the President and the Ombudsman, and international representatives of the Kosovo Verification Mission.

3. The head of the Kosovo Verification Mission shall serve as the Chair of the Joint Commission. The Chair will coordinate and organize the work of the Joint Commission, supervise the overall implementation of this Agreement, and shall have other powers, authorities, and duties as set forth herein or as may be later agreed by the Parties.

4. The Parties shall cooperate with the Commission and its Chair. The Joint Commission as a whole and the Chair individually on his own initiative shall have safe, complete, and unimpeded access to all places, persons, and information (including documents and other records) both within Kosovo and, where the Joint Commission or the Chair deem it relevant, within the Federal Republic of Yugoslavia.

5. In the event of disagreement as to the meaning of any provision of this Agreement a Party may petition the Chair of the Joint Commission, who shall have final authority to resolve such disputes. The Parties agree to abide by his decisions.

VIII. Confidence-Building Measures

1. Violence in Kosovo shall cease. Alleged violations of the cease-fire shall be reported to international observers and will not be used to justify violence in response. All persons held by the Parties without charge shall be released. The Parties shall grant full and immediate access by the ICRC to all detainees, wherever they might be held.

2. The status of police and security forces in Kosovo shall be governed by the terms set forth in Annex 2. The parties shall abide by its provisions completely. The existence of any paramilitary or irregular force in Kosovo is incompatible with the spirit and terms of this Agreement.

3. The Parties shall facilitate the safe return of refugees and displaced persons to their homes. The Parties shall allow free and unimpeded access for humanitarian organizations and supplies to Kosovo, including materials for the reconstruction of homes and structures damaged during the conflict.

4. In each community a local commission, representative of all national communities there, will assist international humanitarian agen-

cies in the delivery and distribution of food, medicine, clothes, construction materials, the restoration of electricity and water supply, and in encouraging returns.

5. There will be no impediments to the normal flow of goods into Kosovo. All goods and materials entering Kosovo at an international border or transiting the Federal Republic of Yugoslavia for entry into Kosovo to be used by international organizations (whether governmental or non governmental) assisting in the reconstruction and development of Kosovo or the implementation of this Agreement shall enter without duties or taxes of any kind.

6. International personnel, including the Kosovo Verification Mission, shall be allowed unfettered entry, movement, and access to any place at any time throughout Kosovo. The Federal Republic of Yugoslavia shall waive all visa, customs, or licensing requirements of persons or things for the Kosovo Verification Mission, UNHCR, and other international organizations and NGO's working in Kosovo. The FRY shall provide all necessary facilities, including frequencies for radio communications, to all humanitarian organizations responsible for delivering aid in the region. It is expected that international personnel will be present at all times in selected communities.

7. The Parties shall immediately comply with all Kosovo Verification Mission support requests. KVM shall have its own broadcast frequencies for radio and television programming in Kosovo.

8. All Parties shall comply with their obligation to cooperate in the investigation and prosecution of war crimes, crimes against humanity, and other serious violations of international humanitarian law. The parties will allow complete, unimpeded, and unfettered access to international experts-including forensics experts and investigators from the International Criminal. Tribunal for the Former Yugoslavia (ICTY) to investigate such allegations. Pursuant to the terms of UN Security Council resolution 827 and subsequent resolutions, the Parties shall provide full support and cooperation for the activities of the ICTY, including complying with its orders and requests for information, and facilitating its investigations.

9. The Parties shall not prosecute anyone for crimes related to the conflict in Kosovo, except for those who have committed war crimes, crimes against humanity, and other serious violations of international humanitarian law.

10. With respect to persons already convicted, there shall be a general amnesty for all persons in Kosovo convicted of committing politically motivated crimes related to the conflict in Kosovo. This amnesty shall not apply to those properly convicted of committing war crimes, crimes against humanity, or other serious violations of international humanitarian law at a fair and open trial conducted pursuant to international standards.

11. Recognizing the importance of free and independent media to the development of a political climate necessary for the reconstruction and development of Kosovo, the Parties shall ensure the widest possible press freedoms in all mediums, including print, television, and radio. Prior to the election of Kosovo officials pursuant to this Agreement, the head of the KVM shall promulgate such rules as may be necessary to ensure the flourishing of independent media in keeping with international standards, including allocation of radio and television frequencies.

IX. Implementation Period

1. This Agreement shall be implemented as quickly as possible, under the supervision of the head of the KVM pursuant to a schedule that he shall specify. The Parties undertake to allow insofar as possible implementation of individual elements, not conditioned on the adoption and undertaking of other acts and measures required to implement this Agreement.

2. The Parties acknowledge that complete implementation will require political acts and measures, and the election and establishment of institutions and bodies set forth in this Agreement. The Parties agree to proceed expeditiously with this task under the supervision and direction of the head of the KVM.

3. Each national community in Kosovo is authorized to start exercising the additional rights determined by this Agreement, to the extent possible, immediately upon signature.

4. Within nine months, there shall be elections in accordance with and pursuant to procedures specified in Annex 3 of this Agreement for authorities established herein, according to a voter registry prepared to international standards by the Central Election Commission. The Government of the Federal Republic of Yugoslavia hereby invites the Organization for Security and Cooperation in Europe (OSCE) to supervise those elections to ensure openness and fairness.

5. Under the supervision of the OSCE and with the participation of Kosovo authorities and experts nominated by and belonging to the major national communities of Kosovo, Federal authorities shall conduct an objective and free census of the population in Kosovo under rules and regulations agreed with the OSCE in accordance with international standards. The census shall be carried out when the OSCE determines that conditions allow an objective and accurate enumeration.

(a) The first census shall be limited to name, place of birth, place of usual residence and address, gender, age, citizenship, national community, and religion.

(b) The institutions and authorities of the Parties shall provide each other and the OSCE with all records necessary to conduct the census, including data about places of residence, citizenship, voters' lists, and other information.

6. The Parties shall provide active support, cooperation, and participation for the successful implementation of the Agreement.

7. Unless otherwise specified herein or in any Annex hereto, institutions currently in place in Kosovo shall remain until the establishment of the bodies created by this Agreement. The head of the KVM may order existing institutions to cease operations on the grounds that they are functioning in a manner contrary to the spirit or terms of this Agreement. During this transitional period, the KVM head may also designate persons to serve on an interim basis in administrative and judicial capacities and shall also have the authority to remove officials from office.

8. Martial law shall be repealed. Laws compatible with this Agreement shall remain in force until replaced by the decision of a competent body established herein, and shall become part of the law of the entity responsible according to this Agreement.

X. Amendments

1. Amendments to the Agreement shall be adopted by agreement of all the parties.

2. Each Party may propose amendments at any time and will consider and consult with the other with regard to proposed amendments.

3. [In three years, there shall be a comprehensive assessment of this Agreement under international auspices with the aim of improving its implementation and determining whether to implement proposals by either side for additional steps, by a procedure to be Determined taking into account the Parties' roles in and compliance with this Agreement.]

XI. Final Provisions

1. This Agreement is concluded in the Albanian, English, and Serbian languages. Each version shall be equally authentic, but in the event of a conflict the English text shall be definitive.

2. This Agreement shall enter into force upon conclusion of the document.

Federal Republic of Yugoslavia; Serbia; Kosovo

Annex 1: The Ombudsman

GENERAL

1. The Office of the Ombudsman shall be an independent agency of Kosovo. In carrying out its mandate, no person, institution, or entity of the Parties may interfere with its functions.

2. The salaries and expenses of the Ombudsman and his or her staff shall be determined and paid by the Kosovo Assembly. The salaries and expenses shall be fully adequate to implement the Ombudsman's mandate.

3. The Ombudsman and members of his or her staff shall not be held criminally or civilly liable for any acts carried out within the scope of their duties.

JURISDICTION

4. The Ombudsman shall consider:

(a) alleged or apparent violations of human rights and fundamental freedoms in Kosovo, as provided in the Constitutions of the Federal Republic of Yugoslavia and the Republic of Serbia, and the European Convention for the Protection of Human Rights and Fundamental Freedoms and the Protocols thereto; and

(b) alleged or apparent violations of the rights of national communities specified in this Agreement.

5. All persons in Kosovo shall have the right to submit complaints to the Ombudsman. The Parties agree not to take any measures to punish persons who intend to submit or who have submitted such allegations, or in any other way to deter the exercise of this right.

POWERS AND AUTHORITY

6. The Ombudsman shall investigate alleged violations falling within the jurisdiction set forth in paragraph five. He may act either on his own initiative or in response to an allegation presented by any Party or person, non-governmental organization, or group of individuals claiming to be the victim of a violation or acting on behalf of alleged victims who are deceased or missing. The work of the Ombudsman shall, be free of charge to the person concerned.

7. The Ombudsman shall have complete, unimpeded, and immediate access to any person, space, or information upon his or her request.

(a) He shall have access to and may examine all official documents, and he can require any person, including officials of Kosovo, the Republic of Serbia, and the Federal Republic of Yugoslavia to cooperate by providing relevant information, documents, and files.

(b) The Ombudsman may attend administrative hearings, meetings of other Kosovo institutions, and meetings and proceedings of the Republics and the Federal Republic of Yugoslavia in order to gather information.

(c) He may examine facilities and places where persons deprived of their liberty are detained, work, or are otherwise located.

(d) The Ombudsman and staff shall maintain the confidentiality of all confidential information obtained by them, unless the Ombudsman determines that such information is evidence of a violation of rights falling within his or her jurisdiction, in which case that information may be revealed in public reports or appropriate legal proceedings.

(e) The Parties undertake to ensure cooperation with the Ombudsman's investigations. Willful and knowing failure to comply shall be a criminal offense prosecutable in any jurisdiction of the Parties. Where an official impedes an investigation by refusing to provide necessary information, the Ombudsman shall contact that official's superior or the public prosecutor for appropriate penal action to be taken in accordance with the law.

8. The Ombudsman shall issue findings and conclusions in the form of a published report promptly after concluding an investigation.

(a) A Party, institution, or official identified by the Ombudsman as a violator shall, within a period specified by the Ombudsman, explain in writing how it will comply with any prescriptions the Ombudsman may put forth for remedial measures.

(b) In the event that a person or entity does not comply with the conclusions and recommendations of the Ombudsman, the report shall be forwarded for further action to the Joint Commission set forth in Article VII of this Agreement, to the President of the appropriate Party, and to any other officials or institutions that the Ombudsman deems proper.

9. The Ombudsman shall promptly report to the International Criminal Tribunal for the Former Yugoslavia evidence of war crimes, crimes against humanity, and other serious violations of international humanitarian law that may fall within the jurisdiction of that tribunal.

Annex 2: Police and Security

I. GENERAL PRINCIPLES

A. In exercising authorities under this Annex, all law enforcement and military components shall act in compliance with this Agreement and shall observe internationally recognized standards of human rights, due process, and fundamental fairness.

B. The KVM shall monitor the enforcement of this Annex and related provisions of the Agreement, and supervise their implementation. The Parties agree to cooperate fully with the KVM and to comply with its directives.

C. In addition to other responsibilities specified in this Annex and the Agreement, the KVM shall have the authority to:

1. Monitor, observe, and inspect law enforcement activities, personnel, and facilities, including associated judicial organizations, structures, and proceedings;

2. Advise law enforcement personnel and forces and, when necessary to bring them into compliance with this Agreement and Annex, issue appropriate binding directives;

3. Participate in and guide the training of law enforcement personnel;

4. Assess threats to public order and advise on the capability of law enforcement agencies to deal with such threats;

5. Advise and provide guidance to governmental authorities on the organization of effective civilian law enforcement agencies; and

6. Accompany the Parties' law enforcement personnel as they carry out their responsibilities, as the KVM deems appropriate.

D. All Kosovo, Republic and Federal law enforcement and military authorities shall be obligated, in their respective areas of authority to ensure freedom of movement and safe passage for all persons, vehicles and goods. This obligation includes a duty to permit the unobstructed passage into Kosovo of police equipment which has been approved by the KVM for use by Kosovo police.

E. The Parties undertake to provide one another mutual assistance in the extradition of those accused of committing criminal acts within a Party's jurisdiction, and in the investigation and prosecution of cross-border offenses. The Parties shall develop agreed procedures and mechanisms for responding to these requests. The head of the KVM or his designee shall resolve disputes on these matters.

II. LAW ENFORCEMENT COMPONENTS

A. Communal Police Units

1. Communal police units, organized and stationed at the communal and municipal levels, shall have primary responsibility for law enforcement in Kosovo. The specific responsibilities of the communal police will include:

a. Police patrols and crime prevention

b. Criminal investigations

c. Arrest and detention of criminal suspects

d. Crowd control

e. Traffic control

2. Number. The total number of communal police operating within Kosovo shall not exceed 2,700 active duty law enforcement officers.

3. Criminal Justice Administration. Communal police units shall be coordinated by the Criminal Justice Administration (CJA), which shall be an Administrative Body of Kosovo. The CJA shall report to the Government of Kosovo.

4. Communal Commanders. Each commune will appoint, and may remove for cause, a communal police commander with responsibility for police operations within the commune.

5. Service in Police.

a. Communal police recruitment will be conducted primarily at the local level. Local and communal governments, upon consultation with communal security commissions, will nominate officer candidates to attend the Kosovo Police Academy. Offers of employment will be made by communal police commanders, with the concurrence of the academy director, only after the candidate has successfully completed the academy basic recruit course.

b. Recruitment, selection and training of communal police officers shall be conducted under the direction of the KVM during the period of its operation.

c. There shall be no bar to service in the communal police based on prior political activities. Members of the police shall not, however, be permitted while they hold this public office to participate in partisan Political activities other than belonging to a political party and voting for candidates at elections.

d. Continued service in the police is dependent upon behavior consistent with the terms of this Annex and the Agreement. The KVM shall supervise regular reviews of officer performance, which shall be conducted in accordance with international due process norms. The KVM shall have the authority to dismiss or discipline officers for cause.

6. Uniforms and Equipment

a. All communal police officers, with the exception of officers participating in crowd control functions, will wear a standard dark blue uniform. Uniforms will include a badge, picture identification, and name tag.

b. Communal police Officers will be equipped with a sidearm, handcuffs, a baton, and a radio.

c. Each commune may maintain, either at the communal headquarters or at municipal stations, no more than 20 long-barreled weapons.

i. Long-barreled weapons may be carried or used only with the permission of the communal police commander in response to serious law enforcement problems clearly justifying their release from storage. When no--- in use, all weapons will be securely stored and each commune will keep a registry of all weapons assigned to it.

ii. If the head of the KVM determines that a long barreled weapon has been used by a communal police force in a manner contrary to this Annex, he may take appropriate corrective measures; such measures may include reducing the number of such weapons that the communal police force is allowed to possess.

d. Communal police officers engaged in crowd controls functions will receive equipment appropriate to their task, including batons, helmets and shields.

B. Interim Police Academy

1. Under the supervision of the KVM, the Kosovo CJA shall establish an interim Police Academy that will offer mandatory and professional development training for all communal police officers. All police candidates will be required to successfully complete a course of police studies before serving as communal police officers.

2. The Academy shall be headed by a Director appointed and removed by the CJA in consultation with the Kosovo Security Commission and the KVM. The Director shall consult closely with the KVM and comply fully with its recommendations and guidance.

III. SECURITY COMMISSIONS

A. The parties shall establish a Kosovo Security Commission and Communal Security Commissions. The Commissions shall be forums for cooperation, coordination and the resolution of disputes concerning law enforcement and security in Kosovo.

B. The functions of the Commissions shall include the following:

a. Monitor, reviews and make recommendations regarding the operation of law enforcement personnel and policies in Kosovo, including communal police units.

b. Review, and make recommendations regarding the recruitment, selection and training of communal police officers and commanders.

c. Consider complaints regarding police practices filed by individuals or national communities, and provide information and recommendations to the head of the KVM for consideration in its reviews of officer performance.

d. In the Kosovo Security Commission only: In consultation with designated local, Republic and Federal police liaisons, monitor jurisdiction sharing in cases of overlapping criminal jurisdiction between Kosovo, Republic and Federal authorities.

C. The membership of the Kosovo Security Commission and each Communal Security Commission shall be representative of the population and shall include:

1. In the Kosovo Security Commission:

a. a representative of each commune.

b. the head of the Kosovo CJA.

c. a representative of each Republic and Federal law enforcement component operating in Kosovo (for example, Customs police and Border police).

d. a representative of each national community.

e. a representative of the KVM, during its period of operation in Kosovo.

f. a representative of the VJ.

2. In the Communal Security Commissions:

a. the communal police commander.

b. a representative of any Republic and Federal law enforcement component operating in the commune.

c. a representative of each national community.

d. a civilian representative of the communal government.

e. a representative of the KVM, during its period of operation in Kosovo.

f. a representative of the VJ, who shall have observer status. D. Each Security Commission shall meet at least monthly, or at the request of any Commission member.

IV. POLICE OPERATIONS IN KOSOVO

A. The communal police established by this Agreement shall have exclusive law enforcement authority and jurisdiction and shall be the only police or security presence in Kosovo, with the exceptions set forth in this Article and Article V of this Annex.

1. The Republic of Serbia shall immediately withdraw its security forces in Kosovo (hereinafter referred to as "MUP") to 2,500 officers, and shall in no event exceed that level of deployment with the exception of separate provisions for border police in Article V.A of this Annex. All anti-terror forces, special forces, special police, armored vehicles - including APC's, self-propelled Air Defense Artillery (ADA), and armored reconnaissance vehicles weighing more than six tons - and all weapon systems of 12.7 millimeters and above shall be withdrawn from Kosovo immediately.

2. The remaining MUP shall carry out only normal policing duties at the direction of the head of the KVM, and shall withdraw according to a progressive schedule to be determined by the KVM head. As communal police are trained and become available for deployment, law enforcement responsibility shall be transferred to the local police. It is expected that this transfer will occur in phases. The head of the KVM may specify particular regions or localities for withdrawal of all MUP and early transfer to local policing during this transitional period.

3. During the period of phased withdrawal, MUP in Kosovo shall serve under the supervision and direction of the head of the KVM. The head of KVM shall have the authority to order Individual MUP officers or units to leave Kosovo at any time, and to take, or refrain from taking, any action he deems necessary to effect the implementation of this Agreement.

4. Notwithstanding paragraph 2, all MUP shall be withdrawn no later than 12 months after the entry into force of this Agreement with the exception of Border Police as specified in Article V.A. The head of KVM shall have the discretion to extend this deadline for up to na additional 12 months if necessary to meet operational needs.

B. Concurrent Law Enforcement in Kosovo

1. With the exception of IV.A above, Federal and Republic law enforcement officials may only act within Kosovo in cases of:

a) Hot pursuit of a person suspected of committing a felony criminal offense who has entered Kosovo in order to flee arrest.

(i) Federal and Republic authorities shall as soon as practicable, but in no event later than one hour after their entry into Kosovo, notify the nearest Kosovo law enforcement officials that the pursuit has crossed into Kosovo. Once notification has been made, further pursuit and apprehension shall be coordinated with Kosovo law enforcement. Following apprehension, suspects shall be placed into the custody of the authorities originating the pursuit. If the suspect has not been apprehended within four hours, the original pursuing authorities shall cease their pursuit and immediately depart Kosovo unless invited to continue their pursuit by the CJA or the head of the KVM.

(ii) In the event the pursuit is of such short duration as to preclude notification, Kosovo law enforcement officials shall be notified that an apprehension has been made and shall be informed prior to the detained person being moved.

(iii) The same rules will apply to hot pursuit of suspects by Kosovo law enforcement authorities to Federal territory outside of Kosovo.

b) The President of Kosovo may on a purely voluntary basis request that Federal and Republic law enforcement officials assist in law enforcement matters in Kosovo. Federal and Republic officials shall comply with reasonable requests for assistance.

V. SECURITY ON THE INTERNATIONAL BORDERS

The Government of the FRY will maintain official border crossings on its international borders (Albania and FYROM). Personnel from the organizations listed below may be present along Kosovo's international borders and at international border crossings, and may not act outside the scope of the authorities specified in this

ANNEX. A. REPUBLIC BORDER POLICE

1. The Border Police shall continue to exercise authority at Kosovo's international border crossings and in connection with the enforcement of Federal Republic of Yugoslavia immigration laws. The total number of border police shall be limited to 75. All border police in excess of this figure shall immediately leave Kosovo.

2. Membership. While maintaining the personnel threshold specified in paragraph one, the ranks of the existing Border Police units operating in Kosovo shall be supplemented by new recruits so that they are representative of the Kosovo population.

3. Training. All Border Police stationed in Kosovo must attend police training at the Kosovo police academy.

B. THE FEDERAL ARMY (VJ)

1. VJ garrisons shall be limited to pre-February 1998 Border Guard Battalions located in Djakovica, Prizren, and Urosevac and subordinate facilities within 5 km of the FRY-Albania and FRY-FYROM border (specified on the attached map). There shall be no more than 1,506 members of the VJ present at any time in Kosovo. Border Guard units at the above locations shall be limited to weapons of 82 millimeters and below. Border Guard units shall not maintain armored vehicles above six tons - including APC'S, BOV's, and BRDM's - or Air Defense Artillery weapons in Kosovo. The VJ shall immediately withdraw from Kosovo all forces and equipment above this level. VJ units shall not deploy mines.

2. VJ units shall be permitted to patrol in Kosovo only within 5 km of the international border, and solely for the purposes of defending the borders against external attack and maintaining their integrity.

3. The VJ may travel through the territory of Kosovo to reach its duty stations and garrisons only along routes that have been agreed upon between the VJ and communal police commanders. In the event that they are unable to agree, the head of the KVM shall have binding authority to resolve disputes. VJ forces transiting and deployed in Kosovo shall be permitted to act only in response to direct threat to life or property, pursuant to rules of engagement agreed with the head of the KVM.

C. CUSTOMS OFFICERS

1. The FRY Customs Service will continue to exercise customs jurisdiction at Kosovo's official international border crossings and in such customs warehouses as may be necessary within Kosovo. The total number of customs personnel shall be limited to 50. All customs personnel in excess of this figure shall immediately leave Kosovo.

2. While maintaining the personnel threshold specified in paragraph 1, the FRY Customs Service shall recruit persons of Kosovar Albanian ethnicity to work as officers within the Customs Service. Within eight months of the effective date of this agreement, each unit of Customs officers working at an international border or elsewhere within Kosovo shall include at least one officer of Kosovar Albanian ethnicity.

3. Kosovar Albanian officers of the Customs Service shall be trained and compensated by the FRY. The FRY shall receive all customs duties collected at Kosovo's international borders.

VI. OTHER SECURITY ISSUES

1. No Party shall deploy mines anywhere in Kosovo. The Parties shall provide the KVM with all information in their possession as to the location of existing minefields to, facilitate humanitarian demining efforts.

2. Within three months of the conclusion of this Agreement, all existing paramilitary and irregular forces in Kosovo shall disband in accordance with the timetable and rules to be promulgated by the KVM director. The KVM will supervise the disbandment of paramilitary and irregular forces, which shall turn in to the KVM all weapons having a caliber of greater than 7.62 millimeters. The KVM will arrange for the destruction of these weapons. No new paramilitary and irregular forces will be permitted while this Agreement is in force.

VI. ARREST AND DETENTION

A. Except as noted in Article IV of this Annex and in the following paragraphs, only officers of the communal police shall have authority to arrest and detain individuals in the territory of Kosovo. Officers may use reasonable and necessary force proportionate to the circumstances for these purposes. Immediately upon making such arrests, communal police authorities shall notify the detention, and the location of the detainee, to the appropriate communal security commission.

B. Border Police officers shall have authority within Kosovo to arrest and detain individuals who have violated criminal provisions of the immigration laws. Immediately upon arrest, Border Police officers shall notify the detention, and the location of the detainee to the appropriate communal security commission.

C. Officers of the Customs Service shall have authority within Kosovo to arrest and detain individuals for criminal violations of the customs laws. Immediately upon arrest, Customs Service officers shall notify the detention, and the location of the detainee, to the appropriate communal security commission.

VII. ADMINISTRATION OF JUSTICE

A. Authorities

1. Except in accordance with paragraph 2, any person arrested within Kosovo shall be subject to the jurisdiction of the Kosovo courts.

2. Any person arrested within Kosovo, in accordance with the law and with this Agreement, by the Border Police or Customs Police shall be subject to the jurisdiction of Federal Republic of Yugoslavia courts. If there is no applicable court of the Federal Republic of Yugoslavia to hear the case, then the Kosovo courts shall have jurisdiction.

B. Prosecution of Crimes

1. Kosovo shall create an Office of the Prosecutor responsible for prosecuting individuals who violate the criminal laws of Kosovo before the criminal courts of Kosovo.

2. The CJA shall appoint, and have the authority to remove, a Chief Prosecutor with responsibility for the Office of the Prosecutor.

C. Prisons

1. Kosovo and its constituent communes shall establish jails and risons to accommodate the detention of criminal suspects and the imprisonment of individuals convicted of violating the laws of Kosovo.

2. Prisons shall be operated consistent with international standards. Access shall be provided to international personnel, including the ICRC.

Annex 3: Conduct and Supervision of Elections
CONDITIONS FOR ELECTIONS

1. The Parties shall ensure that conditions exist for the organization of free and fair elections, which include but are not limited to:

a) freedom of movement for all citizens;

b) an open and free political environment;

c) an environment conducive to the return of displaced persons;

d) a safe and secure environment that ensures freedom of assembly, association, and expression;

e) an electoral legal framework of rules and regulations complying with OSCE commitments, which will be implemented by a Central Election Commission representative of the population of Kosovo in terms of national communities and political parties;

f) free media, effectively accessible to all registered political parties and candidates, and available to voters throughout Kosovo;

2. The Parties request the OSCE to certify when elections will be effective under current conditions in Kosovo, and to provide assistance to the Parties to create conditions for free and fair elections.

3. The Parties shall comply fully with Paragraphs 7 and 8 of the OSCE Copenhagen Document, which are attached to this Agreement.

THE OSCE ROLE

4. The Parties request the OSCE to adopt and put in place an elections program for Kosovo and supervise elections is set forth in this Agreement.

5. The Parties request the OSCE to supervise, in a manner to be determined by the OSCE and in cooperation with other international organizations the OSCE deems necessary, the preparation and conduct of elections for:

a. Members of the Kosovo Assembly;

b. Members of Communal Assemblies;

c. other officials popularly elected in Kosovo under this Agreement and the laws and Constitution of Kosovo at the discretion of the OSCE.

6. The Parties request the OSCE to establish a Central Election Commission in Kosovo ("the Commission").

7. Consistent with Article IX.4, the first elections shall be held within nine months of the entry into force of this Agreement. The President of the Commission shall decide, in consultation with the Parties, the exact timing and order of elections for Kosovo political offices.

THE CENTRAL ELECTION COMMISSION

8. The Commission shall adopt electoral Rules and Regulations on all matters necessary for the conduct of free and fair elections in Kosovo, including rules relating to: the eligibility of candidates, parties, and voters; ensuring a free and fair elections campaign; administrative and technical preparation for elections including the establishment, publication, and certification of election results; and the role of international and domestic election observers.

9. The responsibilities of the Commission, as provided in the electoral Rules and Regulations, shall include:

a) the preparation, conduct, and supervision of all aspects of the electoral process, including development and supervision of political party and voter registration, and creation of secure and transparent procedures for production and dissemination of ballots and sensitive election materials, vote counts, tabulations, and publication of elections results;

b) ensuring compliance with the electoral Rules and Regulations, established pursuant to this Agreement;

c) ensuring that action is taken to remedy any violation of any provision of this Agreement, including imposing penalties such as removal from candidate or party lists, against any person, candidate, political party, or body that violates such provisions; and

d) accrediting observers, including personnel from international organizations and foreign and domestic non-Government al organizations, and ensuring that the Parties grant the accredited observers unimpeded access and movement.

10. The Commission shall consist of the Head of the OSCE Kosovo Verification Mission or his representative, representatives of national communities and political parties in Kosovo, and any such other persons as the Head of the Kosovo Verification Mission may decide. The Head of the Kosovo Verification Mission shall act as the President of the Commission. In the event of disputes within the Commission, the decision of the President shall be final.

11. The Commission shall enjoy the right to establish communication facilities, and to engage local and administrative staff.

94. WEU, Ministerial Council, Rome Declaration, Rome, 17 November 1998

[Parts not referring to Kosovo have been omitted.]
[...]

WEU's Operational Role

[...]

To help in defining its own contribution while supporting those of others, WEU has taken part in NATO's planning for the emergency in Kosovo, and has kept in touch with the developing international responses to other aspects of the crisis including the acute human problem of displaced persons and refugees. WEU supports the missions of the OSCE and NATO and the efforts of the EU and calls on all parties to live up to their obligations and commitments, to refrain from further acts of violence in the region and to engage in immediate political negotiations.

5. Ministers noted with appreciation that the general institutional framework and conditions for WEU to fulfil its operational role are being steadily strengthened. WEU Ministers at this meeting have confirmed WEU's readiness to organize a mine-clearance assistance mission in Croatia in response to a request from the European Union under Article J.4.2 of the Maastricht Treaty and have welcomed the recent J.4.2 decision concerning the use of the WEU Satellite Centre to contribute to monitoring the situation in Kosovo. Work by the EU and WEU on illustrative profiles will clarify how WEU can help meet future EU needs and complement the EU's own work on crisis management. At the same time, WEU, together with NATO, is considering how to mobilize and manage the assets and capabilities which NATO might put at its disposal for missions under WEU political control and strategic direction. [...]

Programme of German Presidency

11. Ministers welcomed the statement presented by Germany on its programme for its forthcoming Presidency of WEU during the first semester of 1999. The programme includes: [...]

- [...] to train and supervise mine clearance specialists and mine clearance instructors in Croatia and to contribute to the international verification mission in Kosovo by making available the capabilities of the WEU Satellite Centre; [...]

WEU'S PRESENCE IN ALBANIA AND CONTRIBUTION TO PEACE AND STABILITY IN THE REGION

[...]

11. In view of the grave developments in Kosovo and their consequences for the region, MAPE was tasked in June to give special priority to training, advice and assistance for Albanian border police,

including the assessment of their material needs. Representatives of the WEU Military Staff have meanwhile participated in the Alliance's assessment and planning work related to the Kosovo emergency. Responding to impulsions from the European Union in the context of a comprehensive European strategy for support to Albania - including a J.4.2 decision adopted by the EU Council - WEU has studied ways to widen and better focus the geographic and functional scope of its support for the maintenance of law and order, given the necessary security conditions and material and financial support. In this context, Ministers welcomed the outcome of the Feasibility Study on international police operations in Albania and the subsequent production of a contingency plan by the Military Staff and stressed the importance of the ongoing work of the Permanent Council on that basis. [...]

REINFORCING RELATIONS WITH NATO

[...]

34. They welcomed the arrangements made, pursuant to paragraph 26 of the Rhodos Declaration, for representatives of the WEU Military Staff to be involved in NATO's assessment and planning work related to Kosovo and regional stability. The exchange of information on plans and concepts as well as the secondment of a WEU liaison officer to the International Military Staff have not only helped to maintain transparency and complementarity of institutional approaches in the specific instance but also to deepen the working relations, confidence and understanding between WEU and the Alliance. [...]

95. FRY, Declaration on Support of the Joint Proposal of the Agreement on the Political Frameworks of Self-Governance in Kosovo and Metohija, Belgrade, 25 November 1998

1. The signatories to the Declaration assess that the joint proposal of the Agreement on the political frameworks for self-governance in Kosovo and Metohija represents a just and democratic political solution to the problems in Kosmet and emphasize that its adoption and implementation will be of key importance to peace, stability and development of this Province.

2. The signatories to the Declaration assess that the Joint Agreement on political frameworks for self-governance in Kosovo and Metohija entirely affirms full equality of all national communities, as well as that all legal solutions for the establishment of self-governance in Kosovo and Metohija should be in accordance with the legal systems of the Republic of Serbia and the FR of Yugoslavia, as well as with the international standards and basic documents.

It was jointly assessed that broad self-governance, based on the equality of national communities, is a cornerstone for the political solution and a condition for overcoming tensions and conflicts.

3. The signatories to the Declaration particularly point out that the proposed Agreement defines principles, creates institutional prerequisites of the broad democratic self-governance of national communities in Kosmet, sets forth the rights and obligations and ensures that they be efficiently realized and protected within the rule of law - in the interest of every national community and all citizens in Kosovo and Metohija.

They point out that the proposed Agreement provides a new atmosphere of tolerance, dialogue, trust and life and work in peace, freedom and equality.

4. The signatories to the Declaration decide to establish a single Commission to organize the elaboration of legal documents and undertake necessary acts and procedures in the process of realization of the jointly proposed Agreement.

The Joint Commission will be composed of members of the State delegation, representatives of national communities and representatives of political parties in Kosovo and Metohija.

5. The signatories to this Declaration invite all other political parties from Kosovo and Metohija to join the Agreement, i.e. to consider the Agreement open for accession by all other parties, and as an invitation to make their full contribution (through observations, suggestions and in other ways) to its elaboration and realization in the interest of all people living in Kosmet, in the interest of peace, development and prosperity.

6. This Declaration has been signed in Serbian and in the languages of the members of national communities (Albanian, Turkish) in Kosovo and Metohija.

For the Republic of Serbia: Dr Ratko Markovic
For the national and political parties in Kosovo and Metohija:
Kosovo Democratic Initiative - Faik Jasari
National Party of Kosovo - Agron Abazi
National Community of Goranies - Ibro Vait
National Community of Egyptians - Cerim Abazi
National Community of Muslims - Refik Senadovic
National Community of Romanies - Ljuan Koka
National Community of Turks - Zejnelabedin Kurejs
Democratic Party of the Turks - Sadik Tanjol
Parliamentary parties from Kosovo and Metohija - Radenko Krulj
For the FR of Yugoslavia: Dr Vladan Kutlesic

96. FRY, Declaration by the Federal Assembly, Belgrade, 3 December 1998

The Federal Assembly of the Federal Republic of Yugoslavia notes with indignation

That recently there has been a series of flagrant attacks by the representatives of the US administration against the Federal Republic of Yugoslavia, its vital State and national interests and constitutional institutions.

That new American pressures ensued after it became clear that Serbia and Yugoslavia do not accept the thesis about the so called "dislocation of Serbia from Kosovo and Metohija", i.e. that it will defend at any cost the sovereignty and territorial integrity of the Republic of Serbia and the Federal Republic of Yugoslavia, and in Kosmet, the solution on the basis of equality of all citizens, national and ethnic communities.

In that connection, the Federal Assembly of the Federal Republic of Yugoslavia

Declares

1. All present, as well as former US pressures, in fact represent support to separatism and terrorism in Kosovo and Metohija and cause destabilization in the region.

2. The Federal Assembly resolutely rejects and condemns all instruments of pressure, threats and flagrant interference of USA in the internal affairs of the FRY. In order to achieve their destructive goals in the Balkans, the United States of America, its official representatives and agencies, render direct support and assistance to separatism and terrorism and finance those opposing the independence, stability and progress of the FRY. In that way the USA, as a super power, at the same time places itself in the service of terrorists and separatists, of those forces whose declared goal is the recharting of international borders, the creation of the so called "Greater Albania" to the detriment of territories of sovereign States in the region. This constitutes a violation of basic principles of the UN Charter and UN Security Council Resolutions, which condemned terrorism and separatism and threats to lasting peace and stability in the region.

3. It calls on the US representatives to stop deceiving the American and world general public that they, through their policy of threats and blackmail against Yugoslavia, allegedly work for human rights, protection of national minorities and democracy.

4. It energetically condemns contacts and cooperation of the high representatives of the USA with the Albanian terrorists, murderers, kidnappers and confirmed bandits of the Albanian narco-mafia and organized international crime in general. In this way, American representatives give an open support to separatism and terrorism in Kosovo and Metohija, in spite of their proven connection with terrorist organi-

zations in Asia, the Gulf, in the Eastern and Northern Africa, which is very well known to the competent American authorities.

5. The fact that high American representatives state that they cannot dislocate Kosovo and Metohija from Serbia, that they cannot detach and annex it to some "Greater Albania" as long as the Yugoslav President Slobodan Milosevic is in power, is in fact a recognition of the policy of Yugoslavia and its President to defend the territorial integrity and sovereignty of the country. The Federal Assembly gives its full support to the President of the FR of Yugoslavia, Mr. Slobodan Milosevic, to persist on the defense of vital national and State interests, on a peaceful and just solution to the problems in Kosovo and Metohija in the interest of all national communities living in Kosmet as well as in the interest of all the citizens of our country.

6. The will citizens expressed at the elections is a sovereign will, and this principle, on which modern democracies, including the USA, are based, equally applies to Serbia and the FR of Yugoslavia. Constitutional organs of Serbia and Yugoslavia cannot be dismissed and established to please any foreign factor, nor can the will of the people be questioned. It is the duty of democratically elected organs and institutions to efficiently protect, by all available means, the sovereignty, independence and integrity of the country, to defend its dignity, and at this time above all to resolutely put an end to every form of separatism and terrorism. Kosovo and Metohija has always been, still is and will remain the integral part of the Republic of Serbia and the FR of Yugoslavia. We expect that the American public and the United States of America will realize and accept this truth, and not provoke crises, orchestrate pressures to achieve goals which they hide from their own as well as the international public.

7. If the USA truly want a democratic Serbia and the FR of Yugoslavia, than they will assist it in the best way by lifting economic sanctions and pressures against Serbia and the FRY, as well as by a resolute and principled position on Albanian separatism and terrorism in Kosovo and Metohija, in accordance with the UN Charter, international law and principles of modern democracy. The outer wall of sanctions and direct or indirect support to the Albanian separatists, do not encourage democratic processes, but rather seriously obstruct them.

8. The Federal Assembly points out that peace, stability and relations can be built exclusively on the principles of equality, independence, non-interference in the internal affairs and strict respect of sovereignty and territorial integrity. Any other approach would result in inconceivable threats not only to the region, but also to international relations in general.

97. Contact Group Meeting, Statement on Kosovo, Washington, D.C., 8 January 1998

Foreign Ministers of the Contact Group countries meeting in New York on 24 September voiced their deep concern over tensions in Kosovo and called on the authorities in Belgrade and the leadership of the Kosovar Albanian community to join in a peaceful dialogue.

At the Bonn Peace Implementation Council on 9/10 December, the Council took note with increasing concern of escalating tensions in Kosovo. The decision by the delegation of the FRY to leave the PIC meeting did nothing to diminish this concern.

Against this background, Contact Group Political Directors, meeting in Washington on 8 January, indicated that the Contact Group would continue to focus on Kosovo as a matter of high priority. The following principles underlay the Contact Group's continued interest in the situation in Kosovo:

It is for the authorities in Belgrade and the leadership of Kosovar Albanian community to assume their responsibility to promote stability and a solution to the problems between them in order to ensure a peaceful and prosperous future for their people. The Contact Group will support a mutually agreed solution that respects democratic standards; as a first step to reduce tensions, it is essential that dialogue begins; the Contact Group supports neither independence nor the maintenance of the status quo. It supports an enhanced status for Kosovo within the FRY. Such a status should fully protect the rights of the Albanian, Serb, and other residents of Kosovo in accordance with OSCE standards, Helsinki principles and the UN Charter; the Contact Group condemns both violent repression of non-violent expressions of political views and terrorist actions to achieve political goals, and strongly urges all sides to seek peaceful solutions to their difficulties; we call on the FRY to address this question urgently. Making concrete progress to resolve the serious political and human rights issues in Kosovo is critical for Belgrade to improve its international position and relations with the international community.

To facilitate dialogue, the Contact Group has decided to consider further the Kosovo issue and, in particular, how to support existing efforts to implement the Education Agreement, which would be an important first step towards the promotion of stability. It will draw on the views of all those that have been working to resolve the problems of Kosovo.

3.3 INTERNATIONAL MONITORING OF THE DEVELOPMENTS IN KOSOVO

3.3.1 THE OSCE KOSOVO VERIFICATION MISSION

98. OSCE, Permanent Council, Decision No. 218, PC. DEC/218/98, 11 March 1998

The Permanent Council meeting in a special session,

Deeply concerned about the crisis in Kosovo, Federal Republic of Yugoslavia (FRY), and *urging* those involved to cease unconditionally any form of violence,

Condemning the excessive and indiscriminate use of force during Serb police actions in Kosovo, which have led to the death of some 80 people over the past week,

Stressing the unacceptability of any terrorist action and calling on all concerned actively to oppose the use of violence to achieve political aims,

Recalling the statements of the Chairman-in-Office of 2 March and 10 March 1998 on the situation in Kosovo,

Recognizing that the crisis is not solely an internal affair of the FRY because of violations of OSCE principles and commitments on human rights and because it has a significant impact on the security of a region, as well as taking into account the need for immediate efforts by the international community to prevent further escalation,

Calling on the authorities in Belgrade and the leadership of the Kosovar Albanians to assume their responsibility to enter without preconditions into meaningful dialogue, based on full observance of the OSCE principles and commitments, including those of the Helsinki Final Act, and expressing the readiness of the OSCE to assist in this process,

1. *Takes positive note* of the activities of the Chairman-in-Office undertaken with regard to the crisis in Kosovo and encourages him to continue efforts aimed at an effective OSCE contribution to its peaceful resolution;

2. *Supports* a new mission by Mr. Felipe Gonzales as the Personal Representative of the Chairman-in-Office for the FRY which would include a mandate for addressing the problems in Kosovo;

3. *Expresses* gratitude for the work of Mr. Max van der Stoel, whose experience and expertise remain invaluable in helping the OSCE in its efforts to resolve the problems in the region;

4. *Authorizes* the following operational measures to be taken to allow adequate observation of the borders with Kosovo, FRY, and prevention of possible crisis spillover effects, as already requested by the Chairman-in-Office:

- The monitoring capabilities of the OSCE Presence in Albania and, as appropriate, the OSCE Spillover Monitor Mission to Skopje will be temporarily enhanced for the fulfillment of those tasks;

- The respective Heads of Mission will report regularly on their observations;

5. *Requests* the representative of OSCE Troika members accredited in Belgrade to co-ordinate arrangements for continuous monitoring of the situation in Kosovo by diplomatic representatives in Belgrade of the OSCE participating States. The Permanent Council will be kept informed about relevant findings;

6. *Calls* on FRY authorities:

- To halt excessive use of force in Kosovo, to vigorously investigate and accept international investigation and reported summary executions and to bring to justice those found responsible;

- To co-operate fully with the OSCE Chairman-in-Office's Personal Representative to the FRY, Mr. Felipe Gonzales;

- To initiate a meaningful dialogue with Kosovar Albanian representatives which will lead to concrete steps towards the resolution of ongoing political problems in the region;

- To allow access to Kosovo for the International Committee of the Red Cross and other humanitarian organizations;

- To implement without delay the Education Agreement and seek agreements on further confidence-building measures;

- To accept without preconditions, an immediate return of the OSCE missions of long duration to Kosovo, Sandjak and Vojvodina, noting the return of these missions as essential for future participation in the OSCE by the FRY.

156th plenary meeting, PC Journal No.156, Agenda item 3

99. OSCE, Permanent Council, Decision No. 259, PC. DEC/259/98, 15 October 1998

The Permanent Council,

Acting within the framework of the United Nations Security Council Resolution No. 1199,

Recalling the Permanent Council Decision No. 218 paragraph 1, and the statement of the Chairman-in-Office of 7 October 1998 confirming the OSCE's long-standing readiness to give its contribution to the peaceful solution of the crisis in Kosovo,

1. *Declares* the preparedness of the OSCE to embark upon verification activities related to compliance of all parties in Kosovo with the requirements set forth by the international community with regard to the solution of the crisis in Kosovo;

2. *Supports* the Chairman-in-Office's efforts to arrange with the FRY authorities for the OSCE to make such contribution;

3. *Expresses* its readiness to consider in an urgent manner any further specific steps necessary to meet the requirements for efficient verification in Kosovo.

189th plenary meeting, PC Journal No.189, Agenda item 2

100. OSCE-FRY, Agreement on the OSCE Kosovo Verification Mission, 16 October 1998

Devoted to the respect of the principles of the UN Charter and to the Principles of the Helsinki Final Act on peace, stability and cooperation in Europe, as well as to the Paris Charter,

Considering in particular the importance of reaching a peaceful, democratic and lasting solution of all existing problems in the Province of Kosovo and Metohija, based on the equality of all citizens and national and ethnic communities,

Devoted to the respect of the sovereignty and territorial integrity of all states in the region,

Agreeing to comply with and willing to contribute to the FRY implementation of Resolutions 1160 and 1199 of the UN Security Council,

The Federal Government of the FR of Yugoslavia, on one side, and, The OSCE, on the other, have reached the following

Agreement
I. ESTABLISHMENT AND TERMINATION

1. The OSCE Kosovo Verification Mission will be established by the OSCE Permanent Council pursuant to a resolution of the United Nations Security Council calling upon the OSCE to establish the Mission.

2. The FRY government has informed the OSCE Chairman-in-Office of its endorsement of the establishment of the Mission.

3. OSCE will request member states to contribute personnel and funding for the Verification Mission in accordance with established procedures.

4. OSCE will establish coordination with other organizations it may deem appropriate to allow the Verification Mission to accomplish all its objectives most effectively.

5. KDOM will act in place of the OSCE Verification Mission pending its establishment. Once OSCE is operational, KDOM will be absorbed by the Verification Mission.

6. The FRY government hereby guarantees the safety and security of the Verification Mission and all its members.

7. In the event of an emergency situation in Kosovo which in the judgement of the Mission Director threatens the safety of members of the Verification Mission, the FRY shall permit and cooperate in the evacuation of Verification Mission members.

8. The FRY government will accept the OSCE Verification Mission as a diplomatic entity in terms of the Vienna Convention on Diplomatic Relations. The Mission will enjoy the privileges and immunities conferred by such status, as will its members, in accordance with the Vienna Convention.

9. The FRY government and its entities will designate formal liaison officers to work with the Verification Mission in Belgrade, Pristina and field locations. The FRY, Serbian and Kosovo authorities will undertake to provide full cooperation and support to the Verification Mission. This will include, but not be limited to, billets, frequency or frequencies, visas and documentation, customs facilities, vehicle registration, fuel, medical support, airspace access for support aircraft and access to Belgrade, Pristina and other airports in accordance with normal procedures.

10. The OSCE and the FRY agree on a Verification Mission for one year, with extensions upon request of either the OSCE Chairman-in-Office or the FRY government.

II. GENERAL RESPONSIBILITIES, ROLES AND MISSIONS

1. To verify compliance by all parties in Kosovo with UN Security Council Resolution 1199, and report instances of progress and/or non-compliance to the OSCE Permanent Council, the United Nations Security Council and other organizations. These reports will also be provided to the authorities of the FRY.

2. To establish permanent presences at as many locations throughout Kosovo as it deems necessary to fulfil its responsibilities;

3. To maintain close liaison with FRY, Serbian and, as appropriate, other Kosovo authorities, political parties and other organizations in Kosovo and accredited international and non-government organizations to assist in fulfilling its responsibilities;

4. To supervise elections in Kosovo to ensure their openness and fairness in accordance with regulations and procedures to be agreed. For the elections, the Mission may be augmented with election support personnel;

5. To report and make recommendations to the OSCE Permanent Council, the UN Security Council and other organizations on areas covered by UN Security Council Resolution 1199.

III. SPECIFIC TERMS OF REFERENCE

1. The Verification Mission will travel throughout Kosovo to verify the maintenance of the cease-fire by all elements. It will investigate reports of cease-fire violations. Mission personnel will have full freedom of movement and access throughout Kosovo at all times.

2. The Verification Mission will receive weekly information from relevant FRY/Serbian military/police headquarters in Kosovo regarding movements of forces during the preceding week into, out of or within Kosovo. Upon request of the Verification Mission Director, Mission personnel may be invited to accompany police within Kosovo.

3. The Verification Mission will look for and report on roadblocks and other emplacements which influence lines of communication erected for purposes other than traffic or crime control. The Mission Director will contact the relevant authorities upon receipt of such reports. These authorities will explain the reasons for the emplacements or else direct that the emplacements be removed immediately. The Verification Mission will also receive notification should emergent circumstances lead to the establishment of a roadblock for other than traffic or crime control-related reasons. The Mission Director may request the removal of any roadblocks.

4. The Verification Mission will maintain liaison with FRY authorities about border control activities and movements by units with border control responsibilities through areas of Kosovo away from the border. The Verification Mission, when invited by the FRY authorities or upon its request, will visit border control units and accompany them as they perform their normal border control roles.

5. When invited or upon request, the Verification mission will accompany police units in Kosovo as they perform their normal policing roles.

6. The Verification Mission will, to the extent possible, assist UNHCR, ICRC and other international organizations in facilitating the return of displaced persons to their homes, the provision of facilitative and humanitarian assistance to them by the FRY, Serbian and Kosovo authorities as well as the humanitarian organizations and NGOs. The Mission will verify the level of cooperation and support provided by the FRY and its entities to the humanitarian organizations and accredited NGOs in facilitating procedural requirements such as issuance of travel documentation, expedited customs clearance for humanitarian shipments and radio frequencies. The Mission will make such representations as it deems necessary to resolve problems it observes.

7. As the political settlement defining Kosovo's self-government is achieved and implementation begins, the Mission Director will assist, both with his own resources and with augmented OSCE implementation support, in areas such as election supervision, assistance in the establishment of Kosovo institutions and police force development in Kosovo.

8. The Mission Director will receive periodic updates from the relevant authorities concerning eventual allegations of abusive actions by military or police personnel and status of disciplinary or legal actions against individuals implicated in such abuses.

9. The Verification Mission will maintain liaison with FRY, Serbian and, as appropriate, Kosovo authorities and with ICRC regarding ICRC access to detained persons.

10. The Mission Director will, as required, convene representatives of national communities and authorities to exchange information and provide guidance on implementation of the agreement establishing the Verification Mission.

11. The Mission Director will report instances of progress and/or non-compliance or lack of full cooperation from any side to the OSCE and other organizations.

IV. COMPOSITION AND FACILITIES

1. A Director, together with headquarters staff to be determined by Verification Mission requirements.

2. 2000 unarmed verifiers from OSCE member states will be permitted. Headquarters and support staff included in this total. The Mission may be augmented with technical experts provided by OSCE.

3. A headquarters in Pristina.

4. Field presence in locations around Kosovo to be determined by the Mission Director.

5. A small liaison office in Belgrade.

6. Vehicles, communications and other equipment along with locally-hired interpreters and support staff which the Director deems to be required for the performance of the responsibilities of the Mission.

V. FIELD PRESENCE

1. Coordination centers will be established in the capital of each opstina in Kosovo with specific areas of responsibility, under the Mission Director in Pristina.

2. Many opstina coordination centers will have one or more sub-stations in smaller towns/villages in the opstina. The number and location of sub-stations will vary from opstina to opstina, depending on the verification environment and past conflict situation.

3. The chief of each coordination center will maintain a liaison relationship with the opstina authorities and the local leadership of the ethnic Albanian and other communities. Each sub-station will be responsible for coordination with the local authorities, including the local leadership of main ethnic groups.

4. The number of verification personnel assigned to each coordination center and sub-station would depend on the complexity of verification issues in the particular area.

5. Each coordination center and sub-station would have appropriately configured vehicles with which to patrol its assigned area of responsibility.

Done at Belgrade on 16 October 1998 in two original copies in the English and Serbian languages.

For the Organization for Cooperation and Security in Europe: H.E. Bronislaw Geremek, Chairman-in-Office

For the Federal Republic of Yugoslavia: H.E. Zivadin Jovanovic, Minister of Foreign Affairs

101. OSCE, Permanent Council, Decision No. 263, PC. DEC/263/98, 25 October 1998

The Permanent Council,

Acting in accordance with its Decision No.259 (PC.DEC/259) and the agreement signed by the Chairman-in-Office (CiO) of the OSCE and the Foreign Minister of the FRY (CIO.GAL/65/98),

Noting the United Nations Security Council Resolution No.1203,

Decides:

1. To establish the Kosovo Verification Mission (KVM) in accordance with the mandate contained in the agreement signed by the CiO (CIO.GAL/65/98);

2. To authorize immediate start-up deployment of the KVM;

3. To establish the KVM for one year, with extensions upon the request of either the OSCE Chairman-in-Office or the FRY government;

4. To request hereby OSCE States to contribute personnel and funding for the KVM in accordance with established procedures;

5. To task the Secretary General, taking account of offers of voluntary contributions, to establish urgently the budget for the KVM for the approval of the Council.

193rd plenary meeting, PC Journal No.193, Agenda item 1

102. FRY, Government Memorandum on the Situation in the Autonomous Province of Kosovo and Metohija, Belgrade, 1 December 1998

I

Cooperation between the state authorities and the OSCE Verification Mission in Kosovo and Metohija (hereinafter: Kosmet) and international humanitarian organizations (UNHCR, ICRC, UNHCHR) is successful, with regular and constructive contacts at all levels, guaranteeing full security, freedom of movement and access. The Government of the FR of Yugoslavia and all state authorities consistently implement all the provisions of the Agreement of 16 October 1998, in the spirit of cooperation and mutual respect, as is expected from the OSCE (KVM). This has been a special task entrusted to the Federal Government Commission for Cooperation with KVM headed by Deputy Federal Prime Minister Nikola Sainovic and to the Federal Ministry of Foreign Affairs.

So far, around 600 visas were granted to the OSCE representatives (about 100 to the members of the Preparatory Mission and 500 to the verifiers). Currently, there is more than 820 foreign diplomatic representatives in Kosmet: 500 KVM members, approximately 70 members of the Preparatory Mission and about 250 KDOM members.

The overall situation in Kosmet is one of stabilization and normalization. Seventeen humanitarian and more than a hundred distribution centres have been set up throughout the Province which operate successfully. There are no people without shelter, in the open. The security forces of the Republic of Serbia and the units of the Army of Yugoslavia have been deployed at the levels before the start of terrorist actions. Local police forces representative of the will and ethnic structure of each settlement have been set up in 115 villages throughout the Autonomous Province. There are no special actions of the security forces whatsoever in the Province, except those related to the maintenance of public law and order, protection of citizens and of course, legitimate response to attacks and provocations by terrorists.

These positive developments have also been confirmed by foreign representatives in their reports on the situation in Kosmet (see weekly KDOM report for the period 9-16 November 1998, the interim KVM report of 16 November 1998).

The report by UN Secretary-General Kofi Annan of 20 November 1998 contains much more objective assessments than some of the previous ones, compiled on the basis of indirect knowledge, characterized by incomplete and extremely one-sided observations.

II

The Governments of the Republic of Serbia and the FRY are determined to pursue the policy of a peaceful political solution in Kosmet, on the basis of equality of all citizens and all national and ethnic communities, consistent with international standards. It was along these lines that they initiated an unconditional political dialogue.

The Declaration on the joint draft Agreement on the Political Frameworks for Self-Governance in Kosmet of 25 November 1998, reflects its multi-cultural and multi-confessional character, as an integral part of the Republic of Serbia and the FRY, and it has received the support of all ethnic and national communities, including some parties of citizens of the Albanian national minority - who taken together represent about 600,000-800,000 citizens of all nationalities and confessions in Kosmet (around 250,000 Serbs and Montenegrins, 150,000 Muslims, 150,000 Romanies and more than 100,000 members of other national communities - Turkish, Goranies, Croat, Egyptian and others).

The joint draft Agreement on the Political Frameworks for Self-Governance in Kosmet adopted by the state delegation and the delegations of national and ethnic communities in Kosmet proceeds from the political framework outlined as 11 points proposed by the Government of Serbia, supported as annex of the UN Security Council Resolution 1203 of 24 October 1998 (operative paragraph 2 of the resolution). Its main characteristic is that it elaborates upon and guarantees the equality of all ethnic and national communities and of all citizens in Kosmet. This draft incorporates at the same time the highest international standards of human rights and rights of persons belonging to national minorities, in particular it takes over the standards set forth in the Council of Europe Framework Convention for the Protection of Minorities.

In that sense, the Proposal guarantees ethnic, cultural, linguistic and religious identity of national minorities, without any discrimination, as well as freedom to maintain one's own culture, language, religion and customs, equally before the law. It guarantees autonomy and local self-governance, appropriate participation of ethnic and national communities at all levels of democratically elected authorities, while respecting the sovereignty and territorial integrity of the Republic of Serbia and the FRY.

This approach of the joint draft Agreement essentially relies on the agreements reached between FRY President Slobodan Milosevic and Special US Representative Ambassador Richard Holbrooke.

The joint proposal of 25 November 1998 is also open for discussion with representatives of other Albanian political parties. Regrettably, the political parties of Kosmet Albanians rallied around the Democratic Alliance of Kosmet have not still accepted to participate in the resumption of a political dialogue which, inter alia, implies granting of extensive autonomy rights to Kosmet Albanians, about which there is a consensus of the entire international community.

While the leaders of certain political parties of Kosmet Albanians refuse or postpone the dialogue on various pretexts, the terrorists of the self-proclaimed "KLA" are buying time to commit new crimes, murders, to kidnap innocent civilians and officers protecting public law and order. At the same time, the measures and sanctions imposed on the FR of Yugoslavia and its citizens are kept in place or even tightened, in order to economically and socially cripple the country and its population.

III

An obstacle to the political process in Kosovo and Metohija is presented by impudent, criminal actions and a provocative behaviour of Albanian terrorists, who abuse the newly-created situation to launch daily terrorist attacks and to commit crimes - defying both the state authorities and the calls of the international community.

From 13 October through 30 November 1998, Albanian terrorists carried out 310 terrorist attacks and provocations, killing nine police officers from ambushes and inflicting serious and light wounds on 30 officers. Three police officers have been kidnapped, two of whom were tortured and then brutally killed. Eighty-seven attacks were launched against civilians (43 Serbs, 42 ethnic Albanians, members of Roma and Muslim ethnic community). These attacks claimed six lives (one Serb, four ethnic Albanians and one Muslim), while 14 civilians were either seriously or slightly injured. Also, 13 Serb and Montenegrin villages came under attack in order to intimidate and expel them from Kosmet.

Only in the past month and a half from the signing of the Agreement between the FRY and OSCE, the terrorists abducted eleven persons (six Serbs, three ethnic Albanians, one Roma and one Muslim), thus bringing the total number of abducted persons to 282.

The above facts clearly indicate that all national communities in Kosmet are equally cruelly victimized by terrorists and their Nazi-like obsession of creating the so called "Greater Albania".

The FRY Government reiterates that it is of the utmost importance that the international community as a whole and all countries individually -pursuant to UNSC resolutions - condemn clearly and strongly terrorist attacks, provocations, murders and abductions and that they cuts off resolutely, all channels through which the terrorists continue to receive money, weapons and equipment from abroad to commit their crimes. Short of a strong condemnation and appropriate measures, the separatists and terrorists will continue with the crimes against innocent population of all nationalities, which the state will not allow at any cost. The goal of terrorists and separatists is no political solution, least of all a democratic one in accordance with European standards - it is terror, violence and recharting of borders in a Nazi-like fashion.

IV

Over the past eight months, there have been over 170 border incidents provoked from the territory of Albania. Some of them were virtual invasions of several hundred to one thousand of armed terrorists and bandits in one attempt. Ever since the FRY-OSCE Agreement began to be implemented, 31 armed attacks were staged against the VJ from the territory of the Republic of Albania. During that period, 18 armed attacks from the territory of the Republic of Albania were recorded against the VJ border units; there were 13 attempts of grave violation of the territorial integrity and sovereignty of the FRY; and VJ prevented 233 attempted illegal crossings to the state territory of the FR Yugoslavia. Two VJ soldiers were killed in these attacks and nine were wounded.

What causes concern is that armed incidents from the territory of Albania have become more serious and frequent in the last few days. These incidents coincide with the increased efforts to set in motion the political process. This testifies to the fact that the goals of those inspiring and organizing the incidents is to divert attention, generate tension and derail dialogue and peaceful resolution in Kosmet. This is confirmed by serious border incidents provoked from the territory of Albania on 27 and 28 November in the area of Goro'up and Liken border posts, when groups of terrorists carrying arms and equipment attempted to illegally cross to the territory of the FR of Yugoslavia, opening fire and threatening the lives of Yugoslav border guards.

Such a behaviour on the part of Albania represents a flagrant violation of the territorial integrity and sovereignty of the FRY and a breach of the principles of both the United Nations Charter and the OSCE. The failure of Albanian representatives to carry out on-site investigations, implies the violation of the mechanism of verification of border incidents and avoiding responsibility. All this represents a part of the policy of systematic assistance and support to terrorism and banditry in Kosovo and Metohija and seriously undermines the efforts towards a peaceful political settlement and permanent stability.

The fact that a chaotic situation prevails in Albania, that it became the center where all international terrorist organizations and other criminal organizations in the world are based, including Mujaheedin, drug cartels and others, cannot diminish the international legal responsibility of that country for systematically threatening the sovereignty and integrity of any neighbouring country. All the more so, since its official representatives not only fail to condemn terrorism and separatism but by their statements and otherwise in many ways fuel the senseless idea of "Greater Albania" at the expense of territories of neighbouring countries.

All this clearly indicates that Albania, by its negative role, situation and conduct of its leaders, became a serious source of actual danger to peace and security in the region.

V

The FRY Government recognizes and implements in good faith all the agreements reached, written down and signed as part of the Agreement between the FRY and the OSCE. Any other arrangements among third parties affecting the FRY and parts of its territory and its national and state interests - are considered contrary to the Agreement and may not either directly or indirectly imply any obligations for the FR of Yugoslavia and its authorities. Under the Agreement, the FRY Government has assumed the sole responsibility for the safety of verifiers and it is capable and ready to fulfil this commitment.

The FRY-OSCE Agreement (Section II, para. 1) envisages that the OSCE verification mission in Kosmet submits its reports to the FRY authorities. Accordingly, the Government of the FR of Yugoslavia expects consistent implementation in practice.

The FRY Government strongly condemns the contacts of representatives of various countries and some organizations maintained with terrorists, killers, kidnappers and other criminals calling themselves "KLA". These contacts are part of the policy of double standards aimed at supporting and gradually legalizing this terrorist organization, which is contrary to the basic principles and standards of international practice and is in violation of UNSC resolutions condemning terrorism pursued by Albanian separatists. Such actions undermine a genuine political process and peaceful solution. It is particularly worrisome that the representatives of exactly those countries knowing full well the criminal terrorist character of the so called KLA, its direct connections with international terrorism, extreme Islamism, narco-mafia and organized crime in general, maintain the contacts and oblige others do the same.

Such behaviour is dangerous for the political process in Kosmet, it affects the combat against international terrorism in general and may backfire against those practising it.

VI

The Governments of the FRY and the Republic of Serbia are firmly committed to a peaceful political solution in Kosmet. The ultimate text of the agreement may be reached solely in dialogue between the state delegations and representatives on an equal footing of representatives of all national and ethnic communities, and it should not be the outcome of imposition, prejudging or overruling. The respect of political frameworks contained in 11 points and of international standards, the Helsinki Final Act and the OSCE Paris Charter, and above all of the principles of equality of citizens and all national and ethnic communities - are key preconditions for a peaceful and lasting solution in the Serb province of Kosovo and Metohija.

103. OSCE, Kosovo Verification Mission, Press Release No. 24/99, Oslo, 19 March 1999

The OSCE Chairman-in-Office, Norwegian Foreign Minister Knut Vollebaek, today made the decision to withdraw the OSCE mission (the Kosovo Verification Mission) from Kosovo immediately. The decision has been made in the light of the unsuccessful negotiations in Paris and following extensive consultations with the foreign ministers of the Contact Group and the other members of the OSCE troika: Austria and Poland.

The OSCE Chairman-in-Office says that the situation for the unarmed OSCE verifiers has gradually deteriorated. Conditions have made it increasingly difficult for the Mission to carry out its tasks, and it is at present not justifiable to keep the personnel in Kosovo.

Vollebaek emphasizes the responsibility of the Yugoslav authorities for the safety of the OSCE personnel and calls on the parties to show restraint and refrain from any action that can put the personnel at risk. "The OSCE Mission has made an important contribution to stability in Kosovo under very difficult conditions. But as OSCE Chairman-in-Office, responsible for the safety of approximately 1400 verifiers from many different countries in Kosovo, I have no other choice in the present situation than to withdraw the OSCE personnel", says Foreign Minister Vollebaek.

The Norwegian Foreign Minister deplored the negative outcome of the Paris negotiations. "The Yugoslav authorities have taken on a heavy responsibility in refusing to sign the peace agreement, says Vollebaek. "This may lead to a further escalation of the conflict, with much human suffering as a result."

3.3.2 THE RACAK INCIDENT

104. Human Rights Watch: Report on the Massacre in Racak, January 1999[1]

Background

The village of Racak, about half a kilometer from the town of Stimlje, had a pre-conflict population of approximately 2,000 people. During the large-scale government offensive in August 1998, the Serbian police shelled Racak, and several family compounds were looted and burned. Since then, most of the population has lived in Stimlje or nearby Urosevac. On the day before the January 15 attack, less then four hundred people were in the village. The KLA was also in Racak, with a base near the power plant. A number of ethnic Serbs were kidnapped in the Stimlje region, mostly during the summer.

The January 15 attack might have been provoked by a well-prepared KLA ambush near Dulje (west of Stimlje) on January 8, in which three Serbian policeman were killed and one was wounded. On January 10, the KLA ambushed another police patrol in Slivovo (south of Stimlje), killing one policeman. A Yugoslav Army buildup in the area around Stimlje ensued over the next four days, especially on the mountain road between Dulje and Caraljevo villages.

The Police Action in Racak

Witnesses told Human Rights Watch that they heard automatic weapons fire beginning around 6:30 a.m. on January 15, when the police reportedly exchanged fire with the KLA from a hill called Cesta. Half an hour later, army tanks and armored cars came as backup and shelled the forest near the neighboring village of Petrovo, where some KLA units were positioned. They also fired at some family compounds in Racak. Some families managed to escape Racak, fleeing towards Petrovo, which was also affected along with the villages of Malopoljce and Belinca.

Around 7:00 a.m., Racak was surrounded by the Serbian police. Several witnesses told Human Rights Watch that they saw seven blue armored vehicles on Cesta hill, as well as three VJ tanks (type T-55). The police were shooting and some heavy artillery was fired directly into some houses near Malopoljce and Petrovo from a position in the nearby forest called, in Albanian, Pishat.

The extent of the fighting in Racak that morning remains somewhat unclear. According to one Serbian policeman, the KLA's resistance around Racak lasted almost four hours, and when they were finally able to enter the village the police confiscated three mounted machine guns. Villagers, however, said that the police had entered the village by 9:00 a.m. They said that there was shooting and some artillery until 4:00 p.m. By 4:30 p.m., the police had left the village.

Deliberate Killings of the Beqa Family Members

Ten households of the Beqa family live in the part of Racak called Upper Mahalla on the edge of the village. According to one member of the family, whose son and husband were both killed, at around 7:00 a.m. thirty members of the Beqa family tried to run toward the nearby forest when they heard the police. She told Human Rights Watch that more then forty policemen wearing blue uniforms and without masks began shooting at them from a distance of twenty meters from the top of the hill. She said: My son H.B. was running on my left side, maybe two meters from me. He had his trousers in his hands, we did not have time to dress properly. He was warning me to move aside and suddenly he fell down. The bullet hit him in the neck. In front of me my husband fell as well. He didn't move any more.

Another person in the same group, aged seventy, told Human Rights Watch how he saw his twenty-two-year-old grandson shot dead, while his eighteen-year-old granddaughter and her mother were both wounded.

The other members of the Beqa family ran back to a house and hid under the steps until nightfall. Nobody dared to help the wounded, who spent two hours crawling for shelter from the police. One young women said that the police stayed on the hill singing songs and calling her relative by name in the Albanian language ("Aziz, come here to see your dead relatives!"), which suggests that local policemen from Stimlje who were familiar with the residents of Racak may have participated in the attack.

Killed by Grenade

According to M.B., who was hiding in his home, Bajram Mehmeti and his daughter Hanumshahe were killed by a grenade early in the morning of January 15 as they were running through the center of the village. He said: My cousins were lying twenty meters from the water well. He was hit in the head and she was hit in the chest. One man pulled her in the house and she died in his hands.

Searching for Weapons and the Killing of Nazmi Ymeri (76)

According to eleven different witnesses interviewed separately, groups of about thirty policemen each were entering Racak from different directions beginning around 7:00 a.m. By 9:00 a.m., most of them had gathered in the village center near the mosque. These policemen also wore blue uniforms but they had masks on their faces with slits for their eyes and mouth, and they wore helmets. Some of them had "rocket propelled grenades" strapped to their backs. These police searched house by house, witnesses said, looking for people and weapons. Most of the hidden civilians, upon seeing the police in the village center, ran in the opposite direction towards another part of the village.

One witness, S.A. (46), was hiding with his wife and the five children of his neighbor between the house and stable of Hyrzi Bilalli. From this spot, he said he overheard a discussion held by a group of policemen. He told Human Rights Watch: I heard clearly when one said, "Release everybody under the age of fifteen. You know what to do with the others." I heard when another one gave the order to pick up the bodies from the yards in plastic bags and put them in the cars. They took away the body of Ahmet's wife who was shot on the street while she was trying to run from one house to another. I later saw the place where her body was. It was just a pool of blood.

The same witness said that the same group of policeman went into the next door house of the elderly Nazmi Imeri, who lived alone, and was later found dead. He said: I heard shooting and a scream. In the evening I went in his [Imeri's] yard and took his body to our yard. The top of the head was blown off.

Torture in the Yard of Sadik Osmani

As the police were in the Racak, many villager made their way, running and hiding, to the large house of Sadik Osmani near the place called, in Albanian, Kodra e Bebushit. One boy who was present, aged twelve, told Human Rights Watch that approximately thirty men and four boys, himself included, decided to hide in Osmani's stable. A group of approximately twenty women and children hid in the cellar of Osmani's three-storey house. The police later detained, beat, and executed the men in the stable (see below), but the women and children in the cellar were left unharmed.

According to the boy, the police entered Osmani's yard sometime before noon. One tall policeman wearing a black mask and a helmet

---

[1] Used with the permission of HRW. Cannot be reused or reprinted without the expressed written consent of HRW.

with a blue police uniform kicked in the door and immediately began to shoot over the heads of the thirty men lying on the ground, who were screaming "Don't shoot! We are civilians!"

All of the men were taken outside into the yard, where they were forced to lie on the ground and searched for weapons. The four boys were taken out of this group, including the twelve-year-old who spoke with Human Rights Watch, and were locked up together with the women and other children in Osmani's cellar. The police also took four men from the cellar - Sadik Osmani, Burim Osmani, Rama Shabani, and Mufail Hajrizi - and put them with the other men in the yard. Burim Osmani, who is a teenager around fifteen years old, was later put back into the cellar, apparently because he was too young. The conscious decision to return him, while later executing the others, suggests that the police had a clear order to kill the adult males of the village.

Before the twelve-year-old boy was sent to the cellar, however, he saw how the police beat the men in the yard, including his father and some other relatives. The boy told Human Rights Watch: Two or three policeman beat them with wooden sticks. One was kicking them in the face with his boots. The others were just watching. It was terrible. The men were screaming, and their heads were covered with blood. A policeman locked me in the cellar with the women, but I could hear screaming for the next half an hour.

This version of events was corroborated by three other women locked in the cellar who spoke with Human Rights Watch in two separate interviews, although they could not see the men in the yard. All of them believed that the police had only arrested their male relatives and taken them away to the police station in Stimlje. It was only the next day when they realized that the twenty-three men had been killed.

Extrajudicial Executions

Some time around 1:00 p.m. the police led the twenty-three men out of Osmani's yard. One witness, S. A., was hidden at that time behind a compound wall fifty meters from the Osmani house. He told Human Rights Watch that he heard the police leading the detained men through the Racak streets. He said: I heard the police ask them [the men] where is the headquarters of our army [the KLA], and they answered where it was. Then they went together toward the power station in the direction of our army. I think it was maybe 3:00 p.m. when I heard shooting, but I did not know that they were killed.

Members of the OSCE's Kosovo Verification Mission (KVM) entered Racak late in the afternoon of January 15, after having been prevented from entering the area during the day by VJ and police forces. The KVM took five wounded persons, including a woman and a boy suffering from gunshot wounds, and left. During the night, the remaining men of the village searched for the wounded, still thinking that the twenty-three men were in the Stimlje police station. One person who participated in the search told Human Rights Watch that they found the bodies on the hill called Kodri e Bebushit, in Albanian, around 4:00 a.m.. He said: I saw Mufail Hajrizi. He was slashed on the chest. Then we found Haqif, the guest from Petrovo. His body was lying on his side with the hands as if he wanted to defend himself. His throat and half his face had been cut by a knife. On the top of his head was a wooden stick with some paper. Something was written on that paper but I can't remember what it was. There were more than twenty bodies, almost all of them were my relatives. We wanted to cover the bodies with blankets, or something else, but one man said not to touch anything before KVM comes tomorrow.

One woman, L.S., told Human Rights Watch that her son and husband had survived the execution. She told Human Rights Watch: In the morning I got information that the men from the stable were found dead. But soon I saw my husband and son coming toward me - like they were standing up from the grave. My son told me that the group of policeman had pushed them with their hands behind their heads to go towards the hill. My son was in front with Sadik, and the others were behind. When he came to the top of the hill, he saw another group of policeman waiting for them with rifles. He turned his head and shouted to the others to run away. He ran toward the village of Rance, and didn't turn his head. One bullet crossed through his pocket, and another one is still in his belt.

Precisely how the twenty-three men were killed by the police on the hill outside of Racak remains somewhat unclear. But witness testimony, as provided here, and the physical evidence found at the site by journalists and KVM monitors, makes it clear that most of these men were fired upon from close range as they offered no resistance. Some of them were apparently shot while trying to run away.

Journalists at the scene early on January 16 told Human Rights Watch that many of these twenty-three men also had signs of torture, such as missing finger nails. Their clothes were bloody, with slashes and holes at the same spots as their bullet entry and exits wounds, which argues against government claims that the victims were KLA soldiers who were dressed in civilian clothes after they had been killed. All of them were wearing rubber boots typical of Kosovo farmers rather than military footwear. It is possible that some of these men were defending their village in the morning and then went to the Osmani house once they saw the police entering the village. However, they clearly did not resist the police at the time of their capture or execution. They were tortured and arbitrarily killed - crimes that can never be justified in times of war or peace.

The Forensic Investigation

After a thorough inspection of the bodies by KVM, villagers collected the bodies and transported them to the Racak mosque. Two days later, however, under heavy arm, the police entered the village and took the corpses to the morgue in Prishtina.

On January 25, head of the Institute of Forensic Medicine in Prishtina, Slavisa Dobricanin, announced that autopsies had been conducted on twenty-one bodies, some of them conducted in the presence of OSCE personnel. None of the bodies bore the signs of a massacre, he said. The OSCE did not comment on its impressions of the procedures or the announced results.

A Finnish pathology team subsequently took over for the OSCE, and began to participate in the autopsy procedures together with the government authorities. The team distanced itself from Dobricanin's statements and, on January 26, expressed concern that there had been a tampering with the evidence, although they did not clarify by whom or when. The results of the Finns' investigations should be made public in early February.

The International War Crimes Tribunal for the Former Yugoslavia (ICTY)

[...] On January 18, Chief Prosecutor of the ICTY, Louise Arbour, attempted to enter Kosovo through Macedonia in order to "investigate the reported atrocities in Racak." She did not have a Yugoslav visa, having been denied one by the authorities, and was refused entry into the country. Back in The Hague, Arbour stated unequivocally that she will be investigating the massacre in Racak "with or without access to the territory." Regarding the fears of evidence tampering, she said: Evidence of tampering - should such evidence become available, is, in fact, excellent circumstantial evidence of guilt. If one can trace where the order to tamper came from, it permits a pretty strong inference that it was done for the purpose of hiding the truth, which demonstrates consciences of guilt.

Western governments and the Contact Group, including Russia, have called on President Milosevic to cooperate with the ICTY. More than just a visa for Arbour, this should mean unrestricted access for ICTY's investigators to Racak and the sites of other humanitarian law violations in Kosovo committed by both the KLA and the government.

105. FRY, Statement by the President of the Republic of Serbia, Milan Milutinovic, 17 January 1999

During the search for terrorists undertaken by the police the day before yesterday (15 January 1999) in connection with the murder in a terrorist attack of the policeman Svetislav Przić near the village of Račak, municipality of Štimlje, the terrorists opened fire at the police from automatic weapons, bazookas and mortars. Such a brutal terrorist assault forced the police to respond in conformity with its powers under the law. The OSCE Mission and Ambassador Walker were duly informed of the impending action for arrest of perpetrators. Shortly after the conflict, the investigation team headed by the investigating judge of the District Court in Priština and by the Deputy District Public Prosecutor came to the scene of the event; however, the terrorists who were concentrated on the surrounding hills opened fire making impossible the conduct of the investigation.

Yesterday, on 16 January 1999, the investigation was repeatedly prevented, because William Walker demanded that the investigating judge, Mrs. Danica Marinković, should go to the ground without police protection, thus obstructing the organs of justice in discharging their duties under the law. At the same time, however, Ambassador Walker, accompanied by foreign and Albanian journalists from separatist newspapers of his own choice, visited the scene of the event taking advantage of the absence of the judicial and other state organs. Immediately after that he made a statement containing falsified facts and his own, completely groundless assessment. Moreover, he allowed himself to assess by himself what had really happened, to pass judgement and even to issue orders as to what should be done next - all this in a sovereign country.

In this act calculated to mislead the world public, using the known patterns, and exerting himself to stage some new Markale, Ambassador Walker ensured the full cooperation of his proteges from the terrorist so-called KLA. Resorting to a pack of lies and fabrications he accused our state organs, in an obvious attempt to divert the attention from the terrorists, murderers and kidnappers and once again to take them under his protection as he did so many times before. Throughout the period since his arrival he turned a blind eye only to the crimes of terrorists. The safety of citizens, the safety and responsibilities of the police are of no concern to him; in his today's statement he passed judgement on the authorities of Serbia and the FRY, on their competent organs, accusing them of "violating cease-fire" for no other reason but to protect the terrorists whose wrongdoings he skips in silence.

The attacks of terrorists even when they carried out with mortars and other heavy weapons are not considered illegal by him. It is not the first time that such a conduct on his part has found expression in his statement and in the prevention of the investigating judge to perform her duties in her own country under the relevant laws. He probable forgot that he is no governor, prosecutor or judge in Serbia and the FRY, but a representative of the organization of 54 equal member countries and the head of a mission whose task is not to administer a part of the territory of a sovereign country but to monitor the situation and to report on it correctly. In this yesterday's statement he was carried away because the role of being at the same time the prosecutor and the judge seems to suit him best.

Although it is crystal clear that the police were provoked and forced to defend themselves with weapons from the terrorist acts, Mr. Walker today overlooked this fact and proclaimed it a conflict with civilian population. In this context, astonishing is Walker's reaction to all the facts presented by the authorities in Kosovo and Metohija to the effect that "the world will believe him" and not heed our arguments and facts.

At the same time he visited Račak even without informing the Yugoslav authorities, obviously seeking to ensure in this way the monopoly of interpretation of what had really happened. Thus he violated both his mandate of head of the Verification Mission and the Agreement with OSCE.

This is yet another glaring example not only of a biased behaviour but also of protecting terrorism and a terrorist organization which calls itself the KLA.

Such a conduct on the part of William Walker shows that he did not comport himself as a representative of an international organization but as a representative and protector of separatists and terrorists. And to them manipulation and lies are always more important than facts and truth. For such lies the Serbian people has already paid a high price, and such and similar behaviour will no longer be tolerated.

106. FRY, Statement by the Federal Government, 18 January 1999

At its session of 18 January 1999, presided over by Prime Minister Momir Bulatović, the Federal Government considered the latest developments in Kosovo and Metohija and the stepped up pressures from abroad on the Federal Republic of Yugoslavia.

The Federal Government noted that a new campaign by a part of the international community is involved, and strongly denied as unfounded, untrue and ill-intentioned the assertions associated with the events in the village of Račak, calculated to place the blame on the authorities.

As special item on the agenda the Federal Government considered the activities of William Walker, head of the OSCE Verification Mission for Kosovo and Metohija, and assessed that they are in flagrant contravention of the provisions of the agreement on OEB Mission. His activities are going far beyond the framework of the mandate of the head of Mission, as defined by the Agreement on OSCE Mission. The Agreement implies (Article 8 of its Part One) compliance with the obligations established by the 1961 Vienna Convention on Diplomatic Relations.

Proceeding from the observance of the provisions of the Vienna Convention, the Federal Government, on the basis of the Agreement on OSCE Verification Mission in Kosovo and Metohija (Part One, Article 8) which clearly defines that the Mission has a diplomatic status on the basis of the Vienna Convention and Article 9 of the Vienna Convention on Diplomatic Relations, decided to declare William Walker persona non grata, which implies the obligation to leave the territory of the FR of Yugoslavia within 48 hours.

In regard to the question of cooperation with the Hague Tribunal, the Federal Government confirmed the readiness of the Federal Republic of Yugoslavia to fully implement the Agreement signed with that institution. However, the Hague Tribunal has no jurisdiction in Kosovo and Methoija and cannot have any, since it is not a matter of war conflict, but of terrorism, and of the country's legitimate right to fight it.

Representatives of the Hague Tribunal can freely visit our country to talk about the implementation of the existing agreement, but they are not entitled to engage in any inspection or investigation in Kosovo and Metohija.

The Federal Government recalls that the openness of our country for cooperation in this domain has also been demonstrated by the cooperation realized so far with the independent forensic experts from Finland and other countries, says the statement from the extraordinary session of the Federal Government.

The Federal Government reiterated this time again its determination to continue cooperation with the Verification Mission, as well as with OSCE in general, and to consistently implement all agreements through co-operation, in the conviction that it is in the mutual interest of the FR of Yugoslavia and OSCE. It is in full harmony with the efforts to bring about a durable political solution in Kosovo and Metohija, which is the main objective of the FR of Yugoslavia.

107. UNHCR Press Release, Kosovo: Ogata Condemns Atrocities, Appeals for Access, 18 January 1999

The UN High Commissioner for Refugees Sadako Ogata on Monday called for the immediate cessation of hostilities in Kosovo, warning that fighting in the Stimlje area has once again forced people to flee into the hills and that children are reported to be dying in the cold.

"There are hundreds of people who have spent the past three nights in the woods in freezing weather. Most of them are women and children. My staff are trying to help them, but the only way to do this is for the two sides to stop fighting and allow these people to seek shelter," Ogata said.

Renewed fighting since Christmas Eve has forced more than 20,000 people to flee at least 23 villages in the municipalities of Decane, Podujevo, Stimlje, and Suva Reka. UNHCR staff report that the conflict area in Kosovo seems to be widening. Field workers in the Stimlje area on Monday could hear gunfire and artillery rounds coming from the surrounding villages. They met a group of displaced people who told them that two babies had died in the woods during the night.

"It is devastating that the current round of fighting is happening just when the presence of the Kosovo Verification Mission was clearly starting to make a difference. I was shocked to learn of the massacre at Racak and I condemn it in the strongest possible terms," Ogata said.

The cease fire called in October averted a humanitarian catastrophe in Kosovo. The tens of thousands of people who were living out in the open in the wooded hills at that time came down to seek warm shelter before winter.

"I was encouraged by that development, but now we are again seeing people in the hundreds encamped in the woods. A new upsurge of violence will undermine what we have accomplished to date," said the High Commissioner. She said there would be "dramatic consequences" for both Serbian and Albanian civilians in Kosovo, unless the fighting stops.

UNHCR has been leading aid convoys throughout Kosovo since the beginning of the crisis last year. A UNHCR team which tried to deliver food and blankets to Racak on Sunday, 17 January, was blocked by Serbian security forces from entering the village. The convoy unloaded its supplies at Stimlje, one kilometer from Racak, in the hope that the aid would reach the neediest people. By Sunday evening, however, most of the 2,000 residents of Racak had fled, heading for the woods and for the town of Stimlje. Aid workers in Stimlje on Sunday evening said there was a steady stream of displaced people arriving on foot, in horse-drawn carts and tractors. UNHCR workers reported that around 3,500 villagers had also left the nearby areas of Petrovo, Malopolje and Rance.

108. UN Security Council, Presidential Statement, New York City, UN Doc. S/PRST/1999/2, 19 January 1999

[At the 3967th meeting of the Security Council, held on 19 January 1999 the President of the Security Council made the following statement on behalf of the Council:]

The Security Council strongly condemns the massacre of Kosovo Albanians in the village of Racak in southern Kosovo, Federal Republic of Yugoslavia, on 15 January 1999, as reported by the Organization for Security and Cooperation in Europe (OSCE) Kosovo Verification Mission (KVM). It notes with deep concern that the report of the KVM states that the victims were civilians, including women and at least one child. The Council also takes note of the statement by the Head of the KVM that the responsibility for the massacre lay with Federal Republic of Yugoslavia security forces, and that uniformed members of both the Federal Republic of Yugoslavia armed forces and Serbian special police had been involved. The Council emphasizes the need for an urgent and full investigation of the facts and urgently calls upon the Federal Republic of Yugoslavia to work with the International Tribunal for the former Yugoslavia and KVM to ensure that those responsible are brought to justice.

The Security Council deplores the decision by Belgrade to declare KVM head of Mission Walker persona non grata and reaffirms its full support for Mr. Walker and the efforts of the OSCE to facilitate a peaceful settlement. It calls upon Belgrade to rescind this decision and to cooperate fully with Mr. Walker and the KVM.

The Security Council deplores the decision by the Federal Republic of Yugoslavia to refuse access to the prosecutor of the International Tribunal and calls upon the Federal Republic of Yugoslavia to cooperate fully with the International Tribunal in carrying out an investigation in Kosovo, in line with the call for cooperation with the International Tribunal in its resolutions 1160 (1998) of 31 March 1998, 1199 (1998) of 23 September 1998 and 1203 (1998) of 24 October 1998.

The Security Council notes that, against clear KVM advice, Serb forces returned to Racak on 17 January 1999 and that fighting broke out.

The Security Council considers that the events in Racak constitute the latest in a series of threats to the efforts to settle this conflict through negotiation and peaceful means.

The Security Council condemns the shooting of personnel of the KVM on 15 January 1999 and all actions endangering KVM and international personnel. It reaffirms its full commitment to the safety and security of the KVM personnel. It reiterates its demands that the Federal Republic of Yugoslavia and the Kosovo Albanians cooperate fully with the KVM.

The Security Council calls upon the parties to cease immediately all acts of violence and to engage in talks on a lasting settlement.

The Security Council also strongly warns the "Kosovo Liberation Army" against actions that are contributing to tensions.

The Security Council considers all of these events to be violations of its resolutions and of relevant agreements and commitments calling for restraint. It calls upon all parties to respect fully their commitments under the relevant resolutions and affirms once again its full support for international efforts to facilitate a peaceful settlement on the basis of equality for all citizens and ethnic communities in Kosovo. The Council reaffirms its commitment to the sovereignty and territorial integrity of the Federal Republic of Yugoslavia.

The Security Council takes note with concern of the report of the United Nations High Commissioner for Refugees that five and a half thousand civilians fled the Racak area following the massacre, showing how rapidly a humanitarian crisis could again develop if steps are not taken by the parties to reduce tensions.

The Security Council will remain actively seized of the matter.

109. EU, Statement of the Presidency of the European Union on the Racak Massacre, PRES/99/14, Brussels, 20 January 1999

The Political Committee reviewed recent developments on Kosovo. It concluded:

- The EU condemns the recent Racak massacre in the strongest possible terms. Belgrade's response to the massacre is totally inadequate.

- The parties to the conflict must refrain from any further acts of violence.

- Belgrade's decision to expel Ambassador Walker is entirely unacceptable and must be rescinded.

- Belgrade must fully cooperate with the Kosovo Verification Mission in accordance with existing Security Council Resolutions and agreements.

- Belgrade must fulfil its obligations under Security Council Resolutions fully to cooperate with the International Criminal Tribunal for the former Yugoslavia, in particular to grant entry to the Tribunal's chief prosecutor Mrs Arbour in order to carry out a proper investigation.

- The EU remains fully determined to work towards a political settlement for the Kosovo and will use every means at its disposal to remove obstacles on that way created by the parties to the conflict.

110. EU, Letter of the German Minister for Foreign Affairs on behalf of the European Union to Milosevic, 20 January 1999[1]

Mr. President,

I write to you on behalf of the European Union, in order to explain the attitude of the European Union concerning the shocking events in Kosovo.

---

[1] *Unofficial translation by the editor.*

The massacre in Racak is unacceptable and has been publicly condemned by the European Union and other members of the international community. Such kind of atrocities elicited appropriately a common feeling of repulsion. It is unthinkable that the relations between the FRY and the European Union could improve as long as such atrocities happen.

I know that the Kosovo-Albanian side must be reproached with their mistakes, too. I have no doubts that the KLA has also breached the ceasefire und has attempted to provoke your security forces. However, this is no excuse for the mass executions, which have been perpetrated in Racak.

I know that your government has maintained that the victims have been members of the KLA. However, this contradicts the common contents of the reports we have heard from KVM observers, anyway in no instance would that justify the execution of 45 unarmed individuals, including women and children, by the security forces. There is an urgent neccessity for independent investigations. I expect from you the full implementation of the demands of UN Security Council Resolutions 1160, 1199, 1203 and 1207 with regard to the co-operation with the ICTY.

Likewise, the decision to expel the head of the OSCE verification mission, Ambassador Walker, is unacceptable. KVM has played a decisive role in the reduction of tensions in the region. It is not true to assert that the members of KVM have acted in an unbalanced manner. As you know, KVM has been partly responsible for the release of members of the Yugoslav security forces, who were taken as hostages by the KLA. Your lack of co-operation with the KVM continues to undermine the possibility of reaching a political solution through negotiations acceptable to both sides.

I expect from you to take immediately the following actions:

- retraction of the decision to declare the head of the OSCE verification mission, Ambassador Walker, persona non grata;

- full compliance with the provisions of the OCSE-FRY and the NATO-FRY agreements and with all pertinent UN Security Council Resolutions;

- unconditional co-operation with the KVM and guarantee of the security of all KVM-personnel;

- full co-operation with the ICTY's investigations of the events in Racak, especially the permission for chief prosecutor Arbour to enter and enjoy unrestricted movement in Kosovo. The same applies to the EU Forensic Team so that they can fulfill their role in the investigations;

- guarantee that those responsible for the massacre in Racak will be held responsible under criminal law. The names of the persons who have participated in the murders as well as those in command must be immediately handed over to the Tribunal;

- suspend from service those officers of the army and police unit, who were employed in Racak at 15 January 1999, for the duration of the investigations of the killings;

- constructively support efforts by the European Union and the Contact Group to engage the Yugoslav government and the Kosovo-Albanian leadership in negotiations with direct international participation in the near future.

The European Union, together with other members of the international community and the parties involved, remains determined to strive for a permanent solution of the Kosovo question through negotiation. The aid programmes of the European Union and their contributions to KDOM and KVM demonstrate that they are willing to prove their words by action. A peaceful solution of the Kosovo problem is urgently necessary in the interest of peace and stability in Europe and would clear a path for us, wich I believe we are already on, to normalize between the European Union and the FRY. In Kosovo, the constant use of force and disregard of the international community will only exacerbate FRY's international isolation and lead to further measures by the international community.

In highest esteem, Joschka Fischer, Minister of Foreign Affairs of the Federal Republic of Germany

111. OSCE Troika, Press Release No. 10/99, . 21 January 1999

The OSCE Ministerial Troika, Foreign Ministers Knut Vollebæk of Norway, Wolfgang Schüssel of Austria and Bronislaw Geremek of Poland, met today in Vienna under Norwegian Chairmanship. The Secretary General of OSCE also took part in the meeting. The Ministers discussed a broad range of OSCE-related issues, with a special emphasis on the situation in Kosovo. The Ministers called for an immediate cease-fire in Kosovo and full compliance with existing agreements.

They rejected as totally unacceptable the decision of the government of the Federal Republic of Yugoslavia to declare Ambassador William Walker, head of the Kosovo Verification Mission, persona non grata. This decision has led to a further worsening of the Kosovo crisis and has thus complicated the efforts to bring about a political settlement. The Ministers stressed that Yugoslav authorities must rescind their decision to expel Ambassador Walker and co-operate fully with the OSCE.

The Ministers condemned the recent killing of more than forty Kosovo Albanian civilians in Racak. They stressed the need to bring those responsible for the atrocity to justice. A full investigation should be carried out by international experts. To this end they demanded that Yugoslav authorities must give free access to the site of the crime to the International Criminal Tribunal for Former Yugoslavia, under the leadership of Judge Louise Arbour.

The killings in Racak and the unwillingness of the Yugoslav leadership to co-operate with the OSCE represents a serious instance of non-compliance with UN Resolutions and with the Agreement signed between Ministers Geremek and Jovanovic.

The Ministers underlined that the escalation of violence in Kosovo seriously undermines the broad international effort to bring about a political solution to the conflict. The danger of a new humanitarian crisis is growing. Ministers appealed to the parties to abstain from violence and show restraint in order to create the necessary conditions for a political solution to the conflict in Kosovo.

The Ministers referred to the visit to Belgrade of Generals Clark and Naumann and expressed their disappointment at the continued lack of cooperation on the part of the Yugoslav authorities. They reemphasized the close coordination and cooperation between the OSCE and NATO.

The Ministers also discussed a wide range of pressing issues facing the OSCE. The agenda included discussions on the situation in Bosnia and Herzegovina, Croatia, Albania, Moldova, Ukraine, Chechnya and Central Asia. The Ministers also reviewed the status of the Document-Charter on European Security and the relationship with the OSCE's Mediterranean Partners for Cooperation.

Also taking part in the meeting were the President of the OSCE Parliamentary Assembly, Helle Degn, the OSCE Representative on Freedom of the Media, Mr. Freimut Duve and a representative of the OSCE High Commissioner on National Minorities.

112. FRY, Statement from the Session of the Federal Government, 21 January 1999

At its session held on 21 January 1999, presided over by Prime Minister Momir Bulatović, the Federal Government decided to freeze the enforcement of the decision on the expulsion of William Walker. The decision remains in force and will be frozen until full clarification of the consequences of his conduct.

The Federal Government made this decision at the proposal of the Federal Ministry of Foreign Affairs after detailed talks which the Federal Minister for Foreign Affairs, Živadin Jovanović, had with the

OSCE Chairman in Office, Knut Vollebaek, directly concerned with these issues.

Since the adoption of the Federal Government's decision on the expulsion of Walker the leadership of the Federal Republic of Yugoslavia has been contacted by senior representatives of a number of countries and international organizations seeking re-consideration of the decision.

In adopting its decision the Federal Government heeded in particular the arguments of Russia's President Boris Yeltsin and Prime Minister Yevgeny Primakov, contained in the message handed to the President of the Federal Republic of Yugoslavia by the First Deputy to the Russian Minister for Foreign Affairs, Alexander Avdeyev the other day.

The Federal Government also had in mind the appeal of the United Nations Secretary General, Kofi Annan, during his yesterday's telephone conversation with the Federal Minister for Foreign Affairs, Živadin Jovanović.

113. Contact Group, Chairman's Conclusions, London, 22 January 1999

Members of the Contact Group met in London on 22 January to discuss the grave situation in Kosovo. It reaffirmed its united commitment to achieve an early political solution to the present crisis, and its determination to intensify its efforts to that end.

The Contact Group unreservedly condemns the massacre of Kosovo Albanians in Racak on 15 January. All members expressed their revulsion at this act of mass murder. No amount of provocation could justify it. The Contact Group condemns UCK provocations which can only contribute to rising tensions and further violence. It deplores the taking of hostages and calls for the unconditional release of any hostages currently held. The Contact Group calls on both sides to comply fully with relevant SCRs.

The Contact Group also condemns the decisions by the FRY authorities to refuse entry into Kosovo by ICTY Chief Prosecutor Judge Arbour.

The Contact Group looks to the FRY to:

stop all offensive actions/repression in Kosovo;

promote the safe return home of those persons displaced in the past few days from the Racak area and take all steps to avoid a humanitarian catastrophe;

permit the KVM and its Chief of Mission to carry out their responsibilities unimpeded;

co-operate fully with ICTY, in particular by allowing unimpeded access for its investigators to Kosovo;

work with the International Tribunal to ensure that those responsible for Racak are brought to justice;

suspend those VJ/MUP officers operating in Racak on 15 Janaury pending the results of this investigation becoming available;

comply fully with the OSCE/FRY and NATO/FRY agreements and relevant SCRs.

The Contact Group set a goal of early negotiations on a political settlement with direct international involvement.

The Contact Group is assuming its responsibilities and has identified the basic elements for these negotiations.

All members of the Contact Group, and in particular Chris Hill and Wolfgang Petritsch, will intensify pressure on the parties in order for these negotiations to be successful. It expects the parties to engage constructively in these negotiations.

Robin Cook will now consult his colleagues in order to arrange an early Ministerial meeting.

114. Islamic Group, Statement on the Situation in Kosovo, New York, 26 January 1999[1]

The Islamic Group at the United Nations is gravely concerned about the developments in Kosovo, in particular the cold-blooded and premeditated massacre of 45 innocent Muslim civilians on 15 January 1999 in the village of Racak, during the holy month of Ramadan.

The Islamic Group expresses deep shock and anger over the Racak massacre, which was reminiscent of the widespread crimes of genocide and ethnic cleansing witnessed in Bosnia and Herzegovina, and strongly condemns the massacre of innocent civilians and the ongoing Serbian policy of ethnic cleansing in Kosovo.

The Islamic Group expresses its full solidarity with the people of Kosovo.

The Group:

(a) Strongly condemns crimes against humanity being committed by the Serbian security forces in Kosovo;

(b) Takes note of the statement by the President of the Security Council of 19 January 1999 (S/PRST/1999/2), which has been ignored by Belgrade;

(c) Urges the Security Council to take action under Chapter VII of the Charter of the United Nations to ensure the safety and security of all inhabitants of Kosovo, implementation by Belgrade of its undertakings and implementation of the demands of the Albanian leadership of Kosovo;

(d) Notes, with grave concern, the failure of the Belgrade authorities to cooperate with the International Tribunal for the Prosecution of Persons Responsible for Serious Violations of International Humanitarian Law Committed in the Territory of the Former Yugoslavia since 1991, a further indication of their continuing violation of international law, of the relevant resolutions of the Security Council and of the General Framework Agreement for Peace in Bosnia and Herzegovina and the annexes thereto (collectively the "Peace Agreement"), initialled at Dayton, United States of America;

(e) Demands full cooperation by Belgrade with the investigations being conducted by the International Tribunal into the Racak massacre, as well as into other crimes against humanity being committed by Serbian forces, and in bringing the criminals to justice;

(f) Also demands that Belgrade adhere to the need for the full protection of lives, and that it respect the rights and property of all inhabitants of Kosovo;

(g) Further demands the cessation of all atrocities and crimes against humanity by the Serbian forces;

(h) Further demands the withdrawal of all Serbian forces from Kosovo;

(i) Urges the international community to extend every possible form of humanitarian assistance to the oppressed people of Kosovo;

(j) Urges a just, comprehensive and peaceful solution of the crisis through dialogue, which should include representatives of all national communities of Kosovo.

115. Report of the EU Forensic Expert Team on the Racak Incident, 17 March 1999

These comments are based on the medicolegal investigations by the EU Forensic Expert Team in Pristina as locally authorised by the District Court of Pristina in accordance with the Yugoslav Law on Criminal Procedure. It should be emphasized, that medicolegal investigations constitute only a part - but do not cover the whole spectrum - of criminal investigations. The comments represent the personal view of the author, Dr. Helena Ranta, and should not in any manner be construed as an authorised communication on behalf of the Department of

---

[1] UN Doc. S/1999/76, Annex.

Forensic Medicine, University of Helsinki or the EU Forensic Expert Team.

1. Terms of Reference of the EU Forensic Expert Team

The EU Forensic Expert Team consisting of Finnish experts has been involved in the investigation of alleged atrocities in Kosovo since October 1998. When the Racak tragedy was discovered on 16 January 1999, the OSCE turned to the European Union for assistance. Since an EU Forensic Team was already available, it was decided that the Team should also embark on the investigation of the Racak victims.

It should be emphasized that the terms of reference of the EU Forensic Team cover solely the medicolegal autopsies of the 40 victims brought to the hospital. They do not concern the full scale of criminal investigations. Accordingly, to mention one important example - there was no possibility to conduct scene investigations at the actual site of the presumed crime - which could have rendered important additional information concerning the manner of death of the victims. The findings by the experts are therefore based almost entirely on information derived by investigating the bodies at the morgue. Furthermore, the investigation of the bodies at the hospital was greatly complicated by the fact that the start of autopsies by the EU experts became possible only approximately a week from the estimated time of death of the victims. More importantly, there was no chain of custody by the EU forensic experts of the bodies from the moment of death until the time the investigations started on 22 January 1999 in Pristina. What may or may not have happened to the bodies during that time is difficult to establish in connection with the autopsies with absolute certainty.

It should be noted that the EU experts now have completed only a part of the overall investigations concerning the events in Racak - namely the medicolegal investigation of the victims. For a more complete picture of what took place in Racak a full criminal investigation into the events would be required, combining scene investigations, interrogation of witnesses and analysis of the evidence with the autopsy findings of the EU experts.

The original mission of the EU forensic experts was authorised to investigate in an impartial and independent manner, sites of alleged killings of civilians in Kosovo, i.a. in Glodjane, Golubovac, Gornje Obrinje, Klecka, Orahovac and Volujak. The investigations concerning Klecka and Volujak, initiated last year, are to be completed by the end of March 1999 when the DNA analysis will be available. Thereafter, the Team will as soon as possible resume preparations for the investigations with respect to Glodjane, Golubovac, Gornje Obrinje and Orahovac.

The first crucial step that one would normally expect to be implemented at any alleged crime scene would be the isolation of the area and the exclusion of unauthorized access. The scene should then be photographed and videotaped, any evidence be collected and victims localized and marked at site. This step should also include sampling for a gunshot residue (GSR) analysis. Victims should then be placed in individual body bags for transport to the morgue. With respect to Racak none of this was done at all - or was done only partially or improperly. Therefore, important information at the site may have been lost.

2. Details of the Racak Incident

According to various sources of information, the incident in Racak most probably took place on or around 15 January 1999. The EU forensic experts only started working in Pristina on 22 January when the bodies had already been brought to the morgue. The Team therefore has no first hand information on the events at Racak. Concerning the site of the events and the circumstances surrounding the deaths of the victims the Team has to rely entirely on the information from the OSCE/KVM and EU/KDOM observers who visited the site on 16 January 1999, and from reports in the media. According to these sources altogether some 45 bodies were found in Racak. Yet, only 40 were taken to the Department of Forensic Medicine, University of Pristina to be investigated.

Based on the information obtained from the KVM and KDOM observers the total of 22 men were found in a gully close to the village of Racak. They were most likely shot where found. Most of them have been turned over at some stage. The rest of the victims were found at or close to the village and had either been turned over or moved after death into houses in the village.

The more time elapses, the more difficult it usually becomes to establish the assumed time of death. When the Finnish experts had the possibility to start investigations, more than a week had already passed since the discovery of the bodies at Racak. However, the temperature both at the mosque in Racak, where the bodies were first brought, and at the Pristina hospital morgue was close to 0° C, which has contributed to their preservation. Most that can be said is that the victims appear to have died approximately at the same time.

Most of the victims wore several warm jackets and pullovers. No ammunition was found in the pockets. It is likely that no looting of the bodies has occurred, because money (bank notes) was found on them. The clothing bore no identifying badges or insignia of any military unit. No indication of removal of badges or insignia was evident. Based on autopsy findings (e.g. bullet holes, coagulated blood) and photographs of the scenes, it is highly unlikely that clothes could have been changed or removed. Shoes of some of the victims, however, had been taken off, possibly before the bodies were carried inside the mosque. Among those autopsied, there were several elderly men and only one woman. There were no indications of the people being other than unarmed civilians.

The Racak events have been described as a "massacre". However, such a conclusion does not fall within the competence of the EU Forensic Team or any other person having participated solely in the investigation of the bodies. The term "massacre" cannot be based on medicolegal facts only but is a legal description of the circumstances surrounding the death of persons as judged from a comprehensive analysis of all available information. Thus, the use of this term is better suited to be used by organs conducting criminal investigations for the purpose of initiating legal proceedings. Moreover, medicolegal investigations cannot give a conclusive answer to the question whether there was a battle or whether the victims died under some other circumstances. A full criminal investigation combined with the interrogation of witnesses by appropriate investigative entities could shed more light on the circumstances prior to and at the time of the death.

It should be noted that especially persons not familiar with criminal investigations may have a natural tendency to interpret some observations made at the site of the tragedy as signs of post-mortem mutilation. These, however, are most likely related to animal activity - such as stray dogs, which are in abundance in the area, and other wild animals - or traces on the dead bodies caused by the high pressure of projectiles. No indication of tampering or fabrication of evidence was detected. Traditionally, a paraffin test has been used in gunshot residue analysis (GSR). To remove residues from the hand, casting with paraffin has been suggested. This test lacks specificity, however, and at the Interpol meeting in 1968 it was officially stated that it no longer should be used. The most successful technique to date for the analysis of GSR analysis is without doubt the Scanning Electron Microscope with an Energy Dispersive X-Ray Analyzer (SEM-EDX). Only this method has the ability of determining the metallic content without concern about environmental contamination. With the SEM-EDX, the sample is virtually unaffected by the analysis and can be re-examined, if necessary, many times. The sample for the GSR analysis is collected by means of a tape-lift taking into consideration routine precautions (contamination). Paraffin test was for the above reasons not used by the Finnish Team. Test samples for SEM-EDX were taken and they proved to be negative.

3. Co-operation between Organs and Technical Arrangements

At the professional level, the Team experienced no problems in collaboration with Yugoslavian or Belorussian pathologists. After a demonstration autopsy, all agreed upon common methods and procedures.

Furthermore, local criminal and autopsy technicians contributed to the cooperative working atmosphere. The Team was able to complete its investigations without any outside pressure put upon it in Yugoslavia or elsewhere.

In Finland, the presence of media in autopsy theatres is unacceptable. Prior to initiating the autopsies it was agreed that media coverage should be minimised. Nevertheless, the Head of the Pristina Institute of Forensic Medicine, Professor Dobricanin, allowed television teams and photographers to enter the premises. When asked, he confirmed that this was in accordance with his instructions. Confusion has been caused by statements and premature conclusions drawn by local experts while the investigations were not completed. In Finland, on-going investigations are not commented upon. After the completion of the autopsies in January, the Serbian and Belorussian pathologists decided to draw up common reports summarising their findings. The Finnish Team declined to sign these which was erroneously interpreted as disagreement on the findings between the local experts and the Finnish Team. The view of the Finnish Team is that no professional conclusions on the basis of the autopsies should be made without a comprehensive analysis of the data gathered from the corpses. The analysis and tests were conducted at the Helsinki University Department of Forensic Medicine only after the Team returned from Kosovo.Therefore, arriving at conclusions or signing of reports in January would have been premature and thus out of place.

Bearing in mind the complex nature of the investigations, it is the view of the Finnish experts that nothing could have been achieved by unnecessarily speeding up procedure. The involvement of the Team began after 16 autopsies had already been performed by local pathologists. With respect to these corpses, the EU experts were in the position only to verify that the work had been done properly. There was no information available from the scene of the alleged crime at the time when autopsies were being performed, which further complicated a systematic approach. All histological, toxicological, and DNA analysis had to be performed afterwards in Helsinki. For safety reasons films had to be developed in Helsinki. All radiographs were digitized and incorporated into a data base. In all, more than 3000 photos were taken and 10 hrs of videofilm taped. There is court order by the Investigative Judge authorising the Team to conduct the medicolegal autopsies. According to Yugoslav law the autopsy reports will therefore have to be handed over to the District Court of Pristina. A copy of the autopsy reports will also be conveyed to the Department of Forensic Medicine, University of Pristina. The European Union Presidency will be notified of the results of the investigations accordingly.

It should be emphasized that the medicolegal investigations undertaken by the EU forensic experts constitute only part of the normal investigation of alleged crimes. Comprehensive picture over the sequence of events in Racak can only be achieved by combining the medicolegal findings of the EU Forensic Team with other possible information from different sources eventually available at a later stage.

3.3.3 THE UN SECRETARY-GENERAL

116. Report of the Secretary-General Prepared pursuant to Security Council Resolution 1160 (1998), UN Doc. S/1998/361, 30 April 1998

I. Introduction

1. On 31 March 1998, acting under chapter VII of the Charter of the United Nations, the Security Council adopted resolution 1160 (1998) by which it decided that all States would prevent the sale or supply to the Federal Republic of Yugoslavia, including Kosovo, of arms and related matériel of all types and spare parts thereof, as well as the arming and training for terrorist activities there.

2. By paragraph 9 of Security Council resolution 1160, the Security Council decided to establish a sanctions committee to undertake the following tasks and to submit reports on its work, with its observations and recommendations, to the Council:

(a) To seek from all States information regarding the action taken by them concerning the effective implementation of the prohibitions imposed by the resolution;

(b) To consider any information brought to its attention by any State concerning violations of the prohibitions imposed by the resolution and to recommend appropriate measures in response thereto;

(c) To make periodic reports to the Security Council on information submitted to it regarding alleged violations of the prohibitions imposed by the resolution;

(d) To promulgate such guidelines as may be necessary to facilitate the implementation of the prohibitions imposed by the resolution;

(e) To examine the reports submitted pursuant to paragraph 12 of the resolution.

3. At its first meeting, on 3 April 1998, the Committee elected Mr. Celso L. N. Amorim of Brazil as its Chairman. Kenya and Portugal were elected to serve as Vice-Chairmen. The Committee is currently considering draft guidelines for the conduct of its work.

4. In paragraph 14 of Security Council resolution 1160 (1998), the Security Council requested me to keep it regularly informed and to report on the situation in Kosovo and the implementation of the resolution no later than 30 days following its adoption and every 30 days thereafter.

5. In paragraph 15 of the resolution, the Security Council requested that, in consultation with appropriate regional organizations, I include in my first report recommendations for the establishment of a comprehensive regime to monitor the implementation of the prohibitions imposed by the resolution.

II. Comprehensive Regime to Monitor the Implementation of the Prohibitions Imposed by the Security Council Resolution 1160 (1998)

6. The establishment of a comprehensive regime to monitor the implementation of the prohibitions imposed by Security Council resolution 1160 (1998) would require the deployment of teams composed of qualified experts. The teams should be supported by a fully equipped communications centre. These teams would provide advice and assistance to the authorities of neighbouring and other States that bear the responsibility for enforcement of the mandatory measures in accordance with the provisions of the above resolution. In accordance with its mandate and the guidelines to be adopted by it, the Committee established by Security Council resolution 1160 (1998) would be responsible for considering reports from national authorities and regional organizations and for providing policy guidance to them. It should be noted that the United Nations is unable, within existing budgetary resources, to establish and administer the requested comprehensive monitoring regime.

7. Security Council resolution 1160 (1998) acknowledges the positive role the Organization for Security and Cooperation in Europe (OSCE) and other appropriate regional organizations could play in facilitating the implementation of the prohibitions imposed by the resolution. I believe that OSCE, with contributions and assistance from other regional organizations, as necessary, would be in a position to carry out the requested monitoring functions effectively. Those regional organizations might include the European Union, the North Atlantic Treaty Organization, and the Western European Union. They, along with the Danube Commission, contributed to the success of the former sanctions regime. The above arrangement would also facilitate

the central role of the Committee established by Security Council resolution 1160 (1998).

8. If the members of the Security Council are in agreement with the concept outlined in paragraph 7 above, I would propose to explore with OSCE and other regional organizations as appropriate, their readiness to participate in a comprehensive monitoring regime with a view to submitting a more detailed proposal to the Security Council.

III. Situation in Kosovo

9. I am concerned about the deteriorating situation in Kosovo and the absence of progress in negotiations between the parties concerned. There are also alarming reports about incidents on the border with Albania. The Secretariat, however, has no political presence in Kosovo that would enable it to obtain first-hand information on the situation in the area. Such United Nations personnel as are located in the area are devoted to humanitarian assistance. In this regard, I informed the President of the Security Council in my letter dated 9 April 1998 that the Secretariat was not in a position to make an independent assessment of the situation on the ground. Therefore, in discharging this part of my mandate, as well as in assessing whether the Government of the Federal Republic of Yugoslavia has complied in a constructive manner with conditions put forward by the Contact Group, I have had to rely on information and assessments provided by the Contact Group, OSCE and the European Union, as foreseen in paragraph 16 of Security Council resolution 1160 (1998).

10. Accordingly, I sent requests for information and assessments to the Coordinator of the Contact Group, to the Chairman-in-Office of the Organization for Security and Cooperation in Europe and to the Presidency of the European Union. As of 24 April 1998, in response to my request, I had received information on the situation in Kosovo from the Presidency of the European Union (annex I) and the Chairman-in-Office of the OSCE (annex II). Whereas no information has been received to date from the coordinator of the Contact Group, one of its members, the Russian Federation, submitted its own assessment (annex III). The Chairman-in-Office further informed me that the Organization for Security and Cooperation in Europe was working on a substantive report on the crisis in Kosovo, to be submitted to the Contact Group at the end of April, and would be prepared to provide the United Nations with regular updates on the situation in Kosovo.

11. I shall endeavour to continue to present assessments to the Security Council on the basis of information obtained from various sources.

Annex I: European Union Report on the Situation in Kosovo, 21 April 1998

1. Paragraph 16 of Security Council resolution 1160 (1998) calls for an assessment by the Secretary-General of whether the Government of the Federal Republic of Yugoslavia, cooperating in a constructive manner with the Contact Group, has:

"16. (a) begun a substantive dialogue in accordance with paragraph 4 above, including the participation of an outside representative or representatives, unless any failure to do so is not because of the position of the Federal Republic of Yugoslavia or Serbian authorities;"

2. The Government of the Republic of Serbia has issued several public invitations to representatives of "national minorities" in Kosovo, including the Kosovar Albanian community, to attend talks in Pristina. The Government has established a team, headed by Serbian Deputy Prime Minister Mr. Ratko Markovic, which has travelled to Pristina for the talks. On one occasion, the delegation of the Republic of Serbia was led by the President of the Republic, Mr. Milan Milutinovic. On 19 March, Federal President Milosevic appointed Deputy Federal Prime Minister Vladan Kutlesic as his Special Envoy for talks with the Kosovar Albanians and since then he has been a member of the team. The President of the Federal Republic of Yugoslavia has stated that he is ready to be the sponsor of the dialogue. Although representatives of some of the numerically smaller minorities have attended meetings with the Serbian Government team, the Kosovar Albanians have refused to participate.

3. The Security Council requirement on beginning a dialogue is explicitly directed at the Government of the Federal Republic of Yugoslavia. An invitation to begin a dialogue has been issued by the Serbian Government, with the inclusion of a Federal representative. The inclusion of such a representative in a Serbian Government delegation, while a positive step in itself, does not meet the requirement. This is reinforced by the decision to issue the invitation solely in the name of the Republic of Serbia. Furthermore, the Republic of Serbia has offered to hold talks in Serbian Government offices. Moreover, although the Serbian authorities have insisted that the dialogue can take place without preconditions, the stipulation that a solution must be found within the Republic of Serbia (rather than leaving this question open) amounts to the establishment of a precondition.

4. The Serbian Government has also refused to accept the participation of an outside representative or representatives, as required by paragraph 16 (a). Acting on a proposal by the President of the Federal Republic of Yugoslavia, Mr. Slobodan Milosevic, the Serbian Government intends to hold a referendum on 23 April on the participation of foreign representatives in the solution of the Kosovo crisis. This is an attempt by the Serbian Government to seek popular confirmation of its rejection of foreign involvement.

5. Although the Kosovar Albanian parties have not attended the offered talks with the Serbian Government, their representatives have made clear their willingness to enter into dialogue without preconditions with the Government of the Federal Republic of Yugoslavia in the presence of a third party. Mr. Ibrahim Rugova, President of the Democratic League of Kosovo, has established both a 15-member team of advisers and a 4-member negotiating team in preparation for talks. The members of the advisory board have not yet agreed on a programme and some, including Mr. Rugova, continue to insist on maintaining, as an objective, independence for Kosovo. This would be in conflict with the principle of the territorial integrity of the Federal Republic of Yugoslavia affirmed in paragraph 7 of Security Council resolution 1160 (1998). On 17 April, Mr. Rugova reconfirmed the commitment of the Kosovar Albanian leadership to the dialogue. He urged that the Belgrade team meet with the Kosovar negotiating team in a neutral country/venue, with international participation, as called for by the Contact Group Ministerial meeting in Bonn, and indeed the international community.

"16. (b) withdrawn the special police units and ceased action by the security forces affecting the civilian population;"

6. The atmosphere throughout Kosovo remains extremely tense, in particular in Drenica and surrounding areas. The activities of the security forces continue, albeit at a reduced level from that of a few weeks ago, impeding the freedom of movement of the civilian population along the main routes. A major contributory factor is the presence of approximately 16 vehicle checkpoints, situated mainly on the roads going through the Drenica triangle or those bordering it and on the Pristina-Pec road. These checkpoints were set up in early March and are in addition to the long-established vehicle control points at the entry to many towns in Kosovo. Initially the new checkpoints were manned by special police forces (PJP) and Ministry of Interior Police (MUP), supported by armoured personnel carriers and heavy machine-guns. Weapon calibres included .5", 20 mm and 30 mm cannon and 2x60 mm mortars. These checkpoints have been fortified and are now of a semi-permanent nature.

7. Until 9 April, PJP forces were effectively in control of all vehicle checkpoints. Since then, there has been no evidence of uniformed PJP forces at these points. However, the armoured personnel carriers and heavy machine-guns are still present. The current strength of uniformed security forces on duty at any given time at these vehicle checkpoints is around 300. At checkpoints in the more sensitive areas, men, apparently part of the police complement, but who are not wearing normal uniform and whose role is not immediately identifiable, have been observed.

8. In some areas, the population has returned and appears to be resuming normal life. However, there are reports of harassment of civil-

ians at checkpoints, including physical and verbal attacks and long delays apparently without good reason. Many residents of the affected areas claim that they now choose not to travel outside their home towns for fear of harassment or delay at checkpoints. On the other hand, the police have not recently sought to prevent regular demonstrations in Pristina and other towns and, although there have been isolated confrontations, have generally refrained from excessive use of force.

9. In this connection, it should be noted that the Kosovar Albanian political representatives have not yet unreservedly condemned all terrorist activity as required by paragraph 2. There have also been continuing Kosovar Albanian attacks on Serb police positions and, although responsibility has not been acknowledged, other attacks on alleged Kosovar Albanian collaborators.

"16. (c) allowed access to Kosovo by humanitarian organizations as well as representatives of Contact Group and other embassies;"

10. In contrast to the situation in the period immediately after the first incidents in the Drenica area, neither European Union (EU) embassies nor the humanitarian organizations have recently reported any specific problems in obtaining access to parts of Kosovo.

"16. (d) accepted a mission by the Personal Representative of the OSCE Chairman-in-Office for the Federal Republic of Yugoslavia that would include a new and specific mandate for addressing the problems in Kosovo, as well as the return of the OSCE long-term missions;"

11. The Federal Republic of Yugoslavia has indicated willingness to accept a mission by a Personal Representative of the EU and the OSCE Chairman-in-Office to discuss relations between the Federal Republic of Yugoslavia and the EU/OSCE, but has not agreed that the mission should include a new and specific mandate for addressing the problems in Kosovo. The Federal Republic of Yugoslavia has also sought to impose conditions on the return of the OSCE long-term missions. Informal discussions on this matter are continuing.

"16. (e) facilitated a mission to Kosovo by the United Nations High Commissioner for Human Rights;"

12. The Federal Republic of Yugoslavia has not granted the requested visa to the United Nations High Commissioner for Human Rights Special Rapporteur on extrajudicial, summary or arbitrary executions, although visas were granted for visits by the Special Rapporteur on the Former Yugoslavia and three human rights officers.

13. In addition, paragraph 17 of Security Council resolution 1160 (1998) "Urges the Office of the Prosecutor of the International Tribunal established pursuant to resolution 827 (1993) of 25 May 1993 to begin gathering information related to the violence in Kosovo that may fall within its jurisdiction, and notes that the authorities of the Federal Republic of Yugoslavia have an obligation to cooperate with the Tribunal ..."

14. The Prosecutor wrote in March to the Minister of Justice in Belgrade seeking information to help the Court assess whether the incidents in Kosovo justified an investigation. The EU understands that the Minister's preliminary response was to dispute that the International Tribunal for the Former Yugoslavia has jurisdiction in this matter. The EU further understands that the Prosecutor has sent a second letter to Belgrade upholding the Tribunal's rights of jurisdiction, reiterating her request for information and warning the authorities of the Federal Republic of Yugoslavia that their initial response did not meet the demand in Security Council resolution 1160 (1998) for full cooperation with the Tribunal.

15. With reference to paragraph 6 of Security Council resolution 1160 (1998), the parties have begun implementation of the Education Agreement. Discussions on this matter are continuing.

Annex II: Information on the Situation in Kosovo and on Measures Taken by the Organization for Security and Cooperation in Europe, Submitted Pursuant to Paragraphs 13 and 16 of Security Council Resolution 1160 (1998), Warsaw, 20 April 1998

I. SITUATION IN KOSOVO

1. The situation on the ground remains relatively calm but very tense. A heavy Serbian police presence, which includes special police forces, instils in the population a sense of being under siege.

2. While there was no further large-scale violence on the scale of that reported in February and at the beginning of March, there were separate violent incidents causing a number of casualties in late March and in April.

3. There were several street demonstrations in Pristina and other towns in Kosovo in March and April, most of them organized by the Kosovar Albanians and some by the Serbian population. While all were conducted peacefully, some were dispersed by the Serbian police.

4. There has been no progress on beginning a political dialogue between the Belgrade authorities and the Kosovar Albanian community, although both sides declared their readiness to enter into such a dialogue. A delegation from Belgrade travelled to Pristina on several occasions declaring a readiness to begin a dialogue. The Kosovar Albanians declined to participate because there was no agreement on a framework and procedure for the talks. Moreover, this invitation for dialogue was issued by the Serbian Government in their Pristina offices and with the requirement that the question of the status of Kosovo be discussed only in the framework of the Republic of Serbia. This has been interpreted by the Albanian side as a precondition. At the same time, the request of the Kosovar Albanians and the international community to allow participation of an outside representative or representatives has been rejected by Belgrade. In spite of these factors, the Kosovar Albanians have formed a 15-member advisory team to prepare a platform for the talks as well as a 4-member group to participate in the talks once they begin. The longer the talks are delayed, however, the farther apart the political sides will drift.

5. Offers by the Organization for Security and Cooperation in Europe (OSCE) to the Federal Republic of Yugoslavia to facilitate the dialogue have been rejected.

6. Adding to the deadlock between the parties, the Serbian Government, acting on the proposal of President Milosevic, decided to hold a referendum on 23 April on the question of accepting or not accepting "the participation of foreign representatives in the settlement of the problem of Kosovo and Metohija". This decision was criticized by OSCE as being a diversionary tactic and having "a disruptive effect on an already inflamed situation" (statement of the OSCE Troika, 8 April 1998). The Chairman-in-Office declined a subsequent invitation by the Minister for Foreign Affairs of the Federal Republic of Yugoslavia to observe the referendum replying that the invitation was "rather rhetorical than a meaningful effort to contribute to the improvement of the situation".

7. Access for international humanitarian organizations has improved. Also, representatives of the embassies of OSCE participating States have not reported particular obstacles to their trips to Kosovo. However, the tense atmosphere prevalent throughout Kosovo due to heavy police presence and checkpoints makes travel in the region difficult.

8. The beginning of implementation of the Education Agreement was a positive step forward, although there is a long way to go towards full reintegration of Albanians into the State system of education.

9. The situation along the borders of Albania and the former Yugoslav Republic of Macedonia is relatively normal. No evidence of a refugee flow has been reported. The danger of refugees cannot, however, be excluded in the case of renewed violence.

II. MEASURES TAKEN BY THE ORGANIZATION FOR SECURITY AND COOPERATION IN EUROPE

10. On 2 March 1998, the Chairman-in-Office issued a statement on Kosovo in which he expressed his deep concern over armed clashes and appealed to the sides to refrain from any further acts of violence and to start a meaningful dialogue.

11 On 10 March 1998, the Chairman-in-Office presented an action plan on Kosovo in which he requested the authorities of the Federal Republic of Yugoslavia to decrease police presence in Kosovo and for both sides to refrain from violence and prepare for dialogue. He also expressed his will to immediately dispatch Mr. Felipe Gonzalez as his Personal Representative to the Federal Republic of Yugoslavia. He called upon the Federal Republic of Yugoslavia to accept the return of the OSCE long-term missions in Kosovo, the Sandjak and Vojvodina.

12. At a special session, the OSCE Permanent Council, on 11 March, adopted Decision No. 218 which, along the lines of the Chairman-in-Office's action plan, called for the sending of Mr. Gonzalez as Personal Representative, the return of OSCE missions and the urgent beginning of a meaningful dialogue without preconditions and with the participation of an outside representative or representatives. The decision fully supported the position of the Contact Group statement adopted in London on 9 March 1998.

13. On 18 March, the Chairman-in-Office presented the mandate for his Personal Representative, Mr. Gonzalez, after consultations with the Presidency of the European Union and the members of the Contact Group. The mandate requests Mr. Gonzalez to represent OSCE in all specific areas of concern, including democratization, human rights, treatment of national minorities and the problem of the future participation of the Federal Republic of Yugoslavia in OSCE. The mandate also asks Mr. Gonzalez to address the conflict in Kosovo.

14. On 19-20 March, the Chairman-in-Office travelled to Tirana and Skopje. The main goal of his visit was to see what measures OSCE could take to prevent spillover of the Kosovo crisis. The highest authorities in both countries declared their cooperative approach to international efforts to finding a peaceful solution to the conflict.

15. Both the OSCE presence in Albania as well as the OSCE mission in Skopje have been enhanced in order to provide for monitoring of the situation on the Kosovo border.

16. At their meeting in Bonn on 25 March, the Contact Group requested the OSCE Troika (Poland, Denmark and Norway) to submit to their next meeting a "report on compliance" of the Federal Republic of Yugoslavia on Kosovo to the Contact Group demands. The work on this report is currently under way and the final document will be presented to the Contact Group at the end of April 1998.

17. On 27 March, the Chairman-in-Office visited the Federal Republic of Yugoslavia where he met authorities in Belgrade, Pristina and Podgorica.

18. During his talks with President Milosevic in Belgrade, the Chairman-in-Office reiterated the points of his plan of action and the decision of the Permanent Council. President Milosevic responded that the Federal Republic of Yugoslavia would not be ready to accept OSCE "demands" before "taking back its seat in the Organization". He indicated that Mr. Gonzalez would be welcome under the condition that his mandate would be limited to the question of readmittance of the Federal Republic of Yugoslavia to OSCE. The authorities of the Federal Republic of Yugoslavia strongly rejected any outside participation in a dialogue on Kosovo.

19. In Pristina, the Chairman-in-Office met with Mr. Ibrahim Rugova, President of the Democratic League of Kosovo, and other leaders of the Kosovar Albanians. Mr. Rugova reiterated his position that a peaceful solution to the conflict must be found through dialogue with the participation of an outside representative. He continues to maintain his objective of achieving independent status for Kosovo, a demand that may contradict the OSCE principle of territorial integrity of States.

20. In Podgorica, President Djukanovic of Montenegro presented the Chairman-in-Office with an open-minded position on the OSCE's offer to assist the Federal Republic of Yugoslavia in the democratization process and with regard to Kosovo.

21. On 26 March, a special meeting of the Permanent Council on Kosovo took place in Vienna to discuss the status of implementation of its Decision 218. In the meantime, representatives of the embassies to the Federal Republic of Yugoslavia of the OSCE participating States have continued their visits to Kosovo to monitor the situation firsthand.

22. The Ministers of the OSCE Troika met in Warsaw on 8 April and reiterated the importance of carrying out OSCE demands leading to unconditional dialogue as the only solution to bringing about a peaceful solution to the ongoing crisis in Kosovo.

III. CONCLUSION

23. The basic demands of OSCE have not been sufficiently considered by the authorities of the Federal Republic of Yugoslavia. The conditions required for bringing about a meaningful dialogue have not been improved and a resolution of the crisis is not in sight.

24. The existing tensions could easily escalate into new clashes with unforeseen consequences. The potential that the conflict will continue unabated threatens the stability of the Federal Republic of Yugoslavia, the region and Europe as a whole. Intensified international efforts, therefore, are indispensable, not only to prevent a further escalation of violence, but to advance a peaceful solution to the conflict. The OSCE stands ready to participate in these efforts.

Annex III: Memorandum by the Russian Federation, 14 April 1998

1. As a result of the joint efforts of the Contact Group countries, there has lately been serious progress in the implementation of the requirements of the Security Council and the Contact Group on the stabilization of the situation in Kosovo. The basis for the comprehensive dialogue, including on the issue of meaningful self-administration in Kosovo within Serbia, the Federal Republic of Yugoslavia, has been laid down.

2. The Government of Serbia has set up a delegation to participate in negotiations without preconditions. The delegation includes a special representative of the President of the Federal Republic of Yugoslavia, Deputy Premier of the Federal Government, Mr. Kutlesic. The President of the Federal Republic of Yugoslavia, Slobodan Milosevic, whose involvement in the negotiations process has been sought by all members of the Contact Group, has confirmed his intention to sponsor the dialogue.

3. The implementation of the Educational Agreement of September 1996 has begun in accordance with the document on educational issues of 23 March 1998.

4. The situation regarding the access of international representatives to Kosovo has significantly improved. The International Committee of the Red Cross, the United Nations High Commissioner for Human Rights and the field office of the United Nations High Commissioner for Refugees in Pristina have no complaints against the authorities of Serbia and the Federal Republic of Yugoslavia in this regard.

5. In accordance with the agreement of the Contact Group of 6 April 1998, in the event that foreign representatives encounter problems with trips to Kosovo or in their other activities, a respective embassy will immediately inform the embassies of the other members of the Contact Group and the OSCE "Troika" countries in order to quickly resolve those problems with the authorities in Belgrade and Pristina.

6. We have received unambiguous assurances from the high-level authorities of the Federal Republic of Yugoslavia and Serbia that the special police units have been withdrawn from Kosovo and that the overall strength of the law enforcement personnel, including anti-terrorist forces, does not exceed the level of a year ago and is defined by the crime rate and the general crime situation in the area. Our representatives in the field confirm this information.

7. In this context, new terrorist actions by the extremist forces in Kosovo and continued external support for terrorist activities there cause deep concern. We believe that, in the recommendations on the establishment of a comprehensive regime of monitoring of the implementation of measures contained in Security Council monitoring of the implementation of measures contained in Security Council resolution 1160 (1998), which the Secretary-General is to submit to the Security Council, it is necessary to clearly outline measures aimed at prevention by the States of the arming and training of terrorists, as well as providing financial support for terrorist activities. In view of this objective, such recommendations should specifically refer to ensuring effective monitoring on the borders of Albania and Macedonia with the Kosovo region.

8. The main task now is to make the parties begin negotiations. In this connection, we are disappointed by the fact that the Kosovar Albanian side has once again ignored Belgrade's proposal to begin the dialogue, all the more so now that the President of Serbia, Mr. Milutinovic, and a Deputy Premier of the Federal Republic of Yugoslavia have arrived in Pristina for that purpose. Contrary to the requirements of the Contact Group to immediately begin the dialogue without preconditions, it is the leadership of the Kosovar Albanians who set forth such preconditions, demanding the presence of international mediators and a conduct of negotiations solely with the representative of the President of the Federal Republic of Yugoslavia.

9. The issue of an international presence at the negotiations is of significant importance. In our view, there should be no direct mediation in the process of the negotiations per se. It is important to achieve the main goal which is to ensure necessary political support for the dialogue.

10. The Chairman-in-Office of the Organization for Security and Cooperation in Europe should agree with Belgrade on the mandate of his special representative as soon as possible. We believe that such a mandate should be formulated flexibly enough to provide the special representative with the opportunity to promote the solutions acceptable to both parties. The authorities of the Federal Republic of Yugoslavia should get a clear message that the successful mission of the special representative of the Chairman-in-Office will be conducive to the return of the Federal Republic of Yugoslavia to the Organization for Security and Cooperation in Europe. Such an assumption should be reflected in the special representative's mandate.

117. Report of the Secretary-General Prepared pursuant to Security Council Resolution 1160 (1998), UN Doc. S/1998/470, 4 June 1998

I. Introduction

1. The present report is submitted pursuant to Security Council resolution 1160 (1998) of 31 March 1998. It covers the period since my last report, dated 30 April 1998 (S/1998/361).

2. Acting under Chapter VII of the Charter, the Security Council adopted resolution 1160 (1998) by which, inter alia, it decided that all States should prevent the sale or supply to the Federal Republic of Yugoslavia, including Kosovo, of arms and related matériel of all types and spare parts for them, and prevent arming and training for terrorist activities there.

II. Security Council Committee Established Pursuant to Resolution 1160 (1998)

3. At its second meeting, on 6 May 1998, the Security Council Committee established pursuant to resolution 1160 (1998) adopted the guidelines for the conduct of its work to assist it in discharging its mandate pursuant to paragraph 9 of resolution 1160 (1998). The text of the guidelines was transmitted to all States and appropriate international organizations.

4. On 7 May 1998, Ambassador Celso L. N. Amorium (Brazil), Chairman of the Committee, issued an appeal on behalf of the members of the Committee to all States and international and regional organizations to provide information regarding violations or suspected violations of the prohibitions imposed by the Security Council in resolution 1160 (1998).

5. As at 29 May 1998, the following 34 States had reported pursuant to paragraph 12 of resolution 1160 (1998) to the Committee on the steps they had taken to give effect to the prohibitions imposed by the resolution: Armenia, Austria, Bahrain, Belarus, Brazil, Bulgaria, Cyprus, Czech Republic, Fiji, Finland, France, Hungary, Iran (Islamic Republic of), Italy, Japan, Malta, Monaco, Norway, Poland, Portugal, Romania, Saudi Arabia, Singapore, Slovakia, Slovenia, South Africa, Spain, Sweden, Switzerland, the former Yugoslav Republic of Macedonia, Turkey, Ukraine, United Kingdom of Great Britain and Northern Ireland, Uruguay.

III. Comprehensive Regime to Monitor the Implementation of the Prohibitions Imposed by Resolution 1160 (1998)

6. In my first report (S/1998/361) dated 30 April 1998, I outlined in general terms the concept of the comprehensive regime to monitor the implementation of the prohibitions imposed by resolution 1160 (1998). Following the informal consultations of the Security Council held on 8 May 1998 to consider the report, I was informed by the President of the Security Council of the Council's wish that in exploring the establishment of a comprehensive regime to monitor the implementation of the prohibitions imposed by resolution 1160 (1998), I should take into account the existing capacities and potentials, in particular of the United Nations and the Organization for Security and Cooperation in Europe (OSCE). Accordingly, on 15 May, I addressed a letter to Mr. Bronislaw Geremek, Minister for Foreign Affairs of Poland, in his capacity as Chairman-in-Office of OSCE, in which I invited him to provide me, at his earliest convenience, with the views of OSCE on how to establish the comprehensive monitoring regime. I stated that, in doing so, OSCE could benefit from advice and support from other regional organizations which might be in a position to contribute to the success of the monitoring regime. The full text of the letter is contained in annex I to the present report.

7. In a letter dated 1 June 1998, the Chairman-in-Office of OSCE conveyed the views of his Organization on the establishment of a comprehensive monitoring regime. He confirmed the readiness of OSCE to contribute to the monitoring of the arms embargo within its capabilities. He stated that the particular comparative advantage of OSCE was its ongoing presence in the region through its missions deployed in Bosnia and Herzegovina, Croatia, Albania and the former Yugoslav Republic of Macedonia. He stated further that the monitoring activities, carried out currently by OSCE, along the border between Albania and the Federal Republic of Yugoslavia as well as the border between the former Yugoslav Republic of Macedonia and the Federal Republic of Yugoslavia, can usefully contribute to an overall arms embargo monitoring effort, under the overall responsibility of the United Nations. He added that the border monitoring capabilities of the OSCE presence in Albania were being strengthened. He concluded that, while not being able to assume a leading coordinating role with regard to an arms embargo monitoring effort undertaken by other regional organizations, OSCE might offer a flexible coordinating framework for monitoring activities in the field if so desired by participants in the effort. The full text of the letter is attached to the present report as annex II.

8. In the light of the response from OSCE and in accordance with the provisions of paragraph 15 of Security Council resolution 1160 (1998), I have written to the Secretary-General of the North Atlantic Treaty Organization (NATO) the Presidency of the European Union, the Secretary-General of the Western European Union and the Executive Director of the Danube Commission with a view to exploring their readiness to participate in the comprehensive regime, and to submit to me, on the basis of information that may be available to them, reports on suspected violations of the prohibitions imposed by the resolution, for consideration by the Security Council Committee established pursuant to resolution 1160 (1998).

9. Upon receipt of the views of the above-mentioned organizations, I shall submit my recommendation to the Security Council for a comprehensive monitoring regime, taking into account the existing potential within the United Nations and the views expressed by those organizations.

10. In accordance with the request of the President of the Security Council, I am looking into the possibility of utilizing the existing potential within the United Nations for the purposes of establishing a comprehensive monitoring regime. I have, in my latest report on the United Nations Preventive Deployment Force (UNPREDEP) in the former Yugoslav Republic of Macedonia (S/1998/454 of 1 June 1998), concluded that it would seem to be premature to proceed with a decision to withdraw UNPREDEP after 31 August 1998. I have suggested that the Council may wish to consider extending the mandate of UNPREDEP for an additional six months, until 28 February 1999, on the understanding that the Council could review its decision, should the ongoing discussions at the international level on the possible need for an expanded military presence in the region and on the establishment of a comprehensive monitoring regime result in decisions which would affect UNPREDEP's role and responsibilities. Meanwhile, UNPREDEP will, in accordance with its mandate, continue to monitor and report on developments along the border with Albania and the Federal Republic of Yugoslavia. However, within its current strength, UNPREDEP will not be able to sustain intensive monitoring and reporting on activities at the borders. Consequently, it would be my intention, should the Council so wish, to submit before 15 July specific proposals on a possible strengthening of the Force's overall capacity, taking into consideration the situation in the region and the relevant Security Council resolutions, including 795 (1992) and 1160 (1998).

IV. Situation in Kosovo

11. The Security Council, in resolution 1160 (1998), requested me to keep it regularly informed on the situation in Kosovo and to provide an assessment on whether the Federal Republic of Yugoslavia had complied in a constructive manner with conditions put forward by the Contact Group. As the Council is aware, the situation in Kosovo is evolving daily. This report describes the situation up to the time of writing.

12. As I indicated in my first report, the United Nations Secretariat has no political presence in Kosovo. Consequently, this part of my report draws primarily on information received from a variety of non-United Nations sources, including the Chairman-in-Office of OSCE and the United States of America, as a member of the Contact Group, in response to requests from the Secretariat for information. Where indicated, it also includes specific data obtained from other sources, such as NATO. The information collected is summarized below in the remainder of section IV.

SECURITY SITUATION

13. Since my last report to the Security Council, the situation in Kosovo has continued to remain tense and security conditions have been steadily deteriorating. Almost daily violent clashes have occurred along the borders with Albania and in other parts of Kosovo. The authorities of the Federal Republic of Yugoslavia assert that a total of 356 terrorist assaults were perpetrated between 1 January and 27 May 1998 in Kosovo; and that the main targets were police officers, police premises and civilians, both ethnic Serbs and Albanians. The highest number of incidents was reported in the Glodovac, Decani, Srbica, Djakovica and Klina areas.

14. The Serbian special police maintain a strong presence in Kosovo. They have consolidated their positions and reinforced checkpoints, particularly in Drenica. Police heavy equipment is still in place. Special police units have been responsible for armed action against civilians, although they also have suffered casualties as a result of attacks by armed Kosovo Albanians. The Government of Serbia recently announced that it was undertaking what it termed more effective measures against terrorism in Kosovo, which entails the deployment of forces from urban barracks to field camps to restrict the manoeuvrability of the Kosovo Liberation Army (KLA) and to counter the increased sophistication of KLA weaponry. The Government reportedly does not plan to reduce its police force in Kosovo.

15. The activities of the Yugoslav Army, which maintains a large presence in Kosovo, have centred on securing the borders. Fighting continues between the Government forces and armed Kosovo Albanians in several areas, including Drenica and the Ponosevac region, near the border with Albania.

16. The upsurge in violence since mid-May has been characterized by an increase in civilian casualties and the use of heavy weapons against non-combatants. Security incidents have spread beyond Srbica and Glodovac to Klina in the Drenica region, and to the west and south into Decani and Djakovica municipalities, bordering Albania. Fighting between Serbian police and Kosovo Albanians, and KLA attacks on the Pristina-pec road, caused the Serbian authorities to close this main east-west highway for several days beginning on 11 May. This reportedly led to severe food shortages in the western part of Kosovo. During recent police operations in Klina, Ponosevac and Decani municipalities, a number of casualties on both sides were reported. According to Government sources, the clashes were provoked by the KLA attacks. Several villages were reportedly razed or burned, and there are reports that police summarily executed a number of ethnic Albanians. Total casualties in the Kosovo crisis are estimated at approximately 200 since fighting broke out there last February.

17. The Kosovo Liberation Army has increased its attacks in recent weeks, and has shown an increased propensity and ability to attack government security forces. It has issued threats against police and military, as well as against Kosovo Albanians who allegedly cooperate with the authorities of the Federal Republic of Yugoslavia. Killing and abductions of civilians and police personnel are reportedly continuing on a daily basis in different parts of Kosovo. There are also reports of attacks directed against civilian population centres.

18. Various sources report that both Serbs and Kosovo Albanians have been maltreated, harassed and beaten by police and/or unknown perpetrators at various locations. Security incidents have reportedly affected not only ethnic Albanians and Serbs, but also Montenegrins, Roma and Muslims. In a troubling new development, there have been reports of a rise in the number of incidents involving civilians attacking other civilians for ethnically motivated reasons.

19. The increased number of acts of violence on both sides and the heavy presence of the Serbian police, including special police units, as well as military forces, have been generating insecurity among the local population. According to some estimates, the number of internally displaced persons, including Kosovo Albanians and ethnic Serbs, exceeded 42,000 by the end of May.

20. The intensity of the conflict significantly increased in recent days as a result of a major Serbian police offensive operation in the south-western part of Kosovo, adjacent to the Albanian border. The most recent reports indicate extremely heavy fighting between the Serbian police and armed groups, believed to be KLA, resulting in the loss of dozens of lives. Some observers indicate that the Serbian forces used heavy weaponry, including mortars and possibly artillery. There are also reports that several villages in the area and a number of houses in the town of Decani have been burnt and destroyed. It was not possible to verify these reports as access to the area has been restricted. This new wave of violence in Kosovo caused, for the first time, a significant flow of refugees to Albania. As at 4 June, the Office of the United Nations High Commissioner for Refugees (UNHCR) registered some 6,500 refugees and the number was gradually increasing. Therefore, UNHCR has increased its planning figures to 20,000.

21. The latest fighting represents a worrying trend. There is strong apprehension that with the further escalation of hostilities the situation may get out of control and draw neighbouring States into the conflict.

22. Tension has increased along the border with Albania. Both the Federal Republic of Yugoslavia and Albania have reported a number of incidents at the border, ranging from illegal border crossings to violations of airspace.

23. No evidence was found of large-scale arms trafficking across the border between Albania and the Federal Republic of Yugoslavia, involving the transfer of heavy weapons or bulk transfers of small arms. The arms trafficking which is occurring appears to be primarily smaller-scale transfers across that border. Because of the topography of the region, the porous border and the limited monitoring, estimates of total amounts are difficult. The Government of Albania reportedly has set up checkpoints on roads leading to the border to prevent vehicles transporting weapons from reaching the border area. Albanian authorities have acknowledged difficulty in controlling the border with Kosovo, and that checkpoints could serve to prevent weapons from reaching the area of conflict.

24. In support of efforts aimed at preventing the spread of the current conflict beyond the Federal Republic of Yugoslavia, OSCE has developed its border-monitoring capacities in Albania and the former Yugoslav Republic of Macedonia. Proposals to increase the number of monitors are being considered. In Albania, temporary field offices are now established in Bajram Curri and Kukes. The OSCE mission in Albania (19 personnel) cooperates closely with local authorities, the European Community Monitor Mission (22 personnel), UNHCR, the Spillover Monitor Mission to Skopje, and also with UNPREDEP.

25. The situation along the Federal Republic of Yugoslavia border with the former Yugoslav Republic of Macedonia is calm and relatively normal. There does not appear to be significant arms trafficking across that border. The former Yugoslav Republic of Macedonia has redeployed troops and stepped up patrols along its border with the Federal Republic of Yugoslavia. UNPREDEP conducts daily patrols along the border and reports on incidents it observes, including smuggling. UNPREDEP has not reported any incidents of arms smuggling since the adoption of resolution 1160 (1998).

26. On 2 June, NATO Secretary-General Javier Solana informed me about the discussion of the situation in Kosovo by the NATO Foreign Minister at a meeting of the North Atlantic Council held on 28 May in Luxembourg. The Foreign Ministers strongly supported the continuation of an international military presence in the former Yugoslav Republic of Macedonia after the end of the current mandate of UNPREDEP. They also supported the continuation of the mandate of UNPREDEP that contributed significantly to the stability in the region. Mr. Solana told me that NATO has two major objectives with respect to the situation in Kosovo: first, to help achieve a peaceful resolution of the crisis by contributing to the response of the international community; and secondly, to promote stability and security in neighbouring countries, with particular emphasis on Albania and the former Yugoslav Republic of Macedonia. To that end, the Foreign Ministers decided to enhance and supplement NATO's Partnership for Peace activities in both Albania and the former Yugoslav Republic of Macedonia, so as to promote security and stability in these Partner countries and to signal NATO's interest in containing the crisis and in seeking a peaceful resolution.

27. In addition, so as to have options available for possible later decisions and to confirm NATO's willingness to take further steps if necessary, the Foreign Ministers have commissioned military advice on support for United Nations and OSCE monitoring activity, as well as on NATO preventive deployments in Albania and the former Yugoslav Republic of Macedonia, on a relevant legal basis, in order to help achieve a peaceful resolution of the crisis and to strengthen security and stability in the region.

ACCESS TO KOSOVO

28. Foreign diplomats and journalists have encountered some restrictions in their visits to Kosovo. In some cases the police of the Federal Republic of Yugoslavia said diplomats could not enter as roads were impassable because of fighting. Following the Serbian police offensive of 22 May, monitors of the European Community Monitor Mission were reportedly harassed and prevented from reaching the areas under siege.

29. There are concerns regarding deterioration of the humanitarian situation. The ability of humanitarian non-governmental organizations to provide relief to internally displaced persons in Kosovo has reportedly been hampered by incidents of harassment by Serbian police and by blocked access to areas with large humanitarian needs. Various sources reported that, beginning on 15 May, the authorities of the Federal Republic of Yugoslavia impeded food deliveries into Kosovo by blocking the passage of trucks carrying commercial shipments of food and supplies arriving by road. Some 200 trucks were reportedly turned back between 15 and 17 May. The Federal Republic authorities denied that a ban was in place, and stated that certain shipments had been denied entry because of incomplete or false documentation. Meanwhile, UNHCR goods from Belgrade were delivered as usual.

30. Information on the blockade caused panic among the local population, which emptied the local stores to stock up on essential foodstuffs. Almost immediately, shortages of staple foodstuffs began to appear in Kosovo. These shortages were alleviated on 21 May, when Federal Republic authorities lifted the blockade, allowing some 80 trucks into Kosovo.

31. Reacting to these worrying reports, the NATO Foreign Ministers on 28 May 1998 expressed particular concern "that the recent resurgence of violence has been accompanied by the creation of obstacles denying access by international observers and humanitarian organizations to the affected areas in Kosovo".

DIALOGUE BETWEEN THE PARTIES CONCERNED

32. Following intensive diplomatic efforts by European regional organizations and individual States, Ambassador Richard Holbrooke and United States Special Representative Robert S. Gelbard were able to overcome obstacles on both sides to gain agreement for the start of substantive dialogue without preconditions on Kosovo. The dialogue began in Belgrade on 15 May, with a meeting between President Slobodan Milosevic and Dr. Ibrahim Rugova, along with their respective teams. The two sides discussed the modalities of the follow-up negotiations process.

33. The Heads of State of the group of eight industrialized countries, meeting at Birmingham on 16 May, noted in their statement on the Federal Republic of Yugoslavia/Kosovo that the 15 May meeting was a "positive first step". The leaders urged both sides "to ensure that the dialogue now begun leads rapidly to the adoption of concrete measures to lower tensions and stop violence". The group of eight further noted that "it is particularly important that President Milosevic has assumed personal responsibility in the search for a resolution of the problems of Kosovo, including its future status".

34. At the meeting held on 22 May in Pristina, groups of six experts from each side discussed the framework for future talks and confidence-building measures. The initial meetings were an important first step in the dialogue process. The distance between the two parties remains great, however, and it will be important to reinforce that process. The United States has informed me that it will continue to play an active role in the negotiating process and that Special Representative Gelbard and Ambassador Holbrooke have agreed to facilitate the dialogue if called upon by the parties to do so.

35. The NATO Foreign Ministers, in their statement of 28 May 1998, expressed their conviction that the problems of Kosovo can best be resolved through a process of open and unconditional dialogue between the authorities in Belgrade and the Kosovo Albanian leadership. They acknowledged that the status quo is unsustainable and supported a political solution which provides an enhanced status for Kosovo, preserving the territorial integrity of the Federal Republic of Yugoslavia and safeguarding the human and civil rights of all inhabitants of Kosovo, whatever their ethnic origin.

36. The Federal Republic of Yugoslavia, however, has continued to reject the engagement of outside representatives in the dialogue. The referendum held in the Federal Republic of Yugoslavia on 23 April created a hurdle to direct third-party participation. I discussed this matter and the current situation in Kosovo during my meeting with Mr. Felipe González on 1 June 1998.

MEASURES TAKEN BY THE ORGANIZATION FOR SECURITY AND COOPERATION IN EUROPE

37. The situation in Kosovo has been the subject of discussion at the weekly meetings of the OSCE Permanent Council and the Watch Group focusing on developments in Kosovo. Furthermore, OSCE has been closely following developments in Kosovo through monitoring visits conducted by diplomatic personnel of OSCE participating States accredited to Belgrade.

38. The OSCE Troika prepared a "report on compliance" with the requirements to be met by the Federal Republic of Yugoslavia, forwarded to the Group's meeting in Rome on 29 April. The report noted, inter alia, no positive development on such central issues as the opening of unconditional dialogue, cessation of violence and the acceptance of the mission of Mr. González.

39. In a letter to President Milosevic, dated 4 May, the OSCE Chairman-in-Office noted that the situation in Kosovo was deteriorating rather than improving and urged the Federal Republic of Yugoslavia to accept the mission of Mr. González. A reply dated 7 May from Foreign Minister Jovanovic reiterated that the mission would be welcome only to discuss the relationship between the Federal Republic of Yugoslavia and OSCE, and the possible return of the OSCE missions of long duration to Kosovo, Sandjak and Vojvodina would not be considered before the participation of the Federal Republic of Yugoslavia in OSCE was restored. The Chairman-in-Office, replying to Mr. Jovanovic on 8 May, insisted on the importance of launching the mission of Mr. González to talk on all issues dealing with relations between OSCE and the Federal Republic of Yugoslavia.

40. In a statement issued on 13 May, the Chairman-in-Office welcomed the announced meeting between President Milosevic and Dr. Rugova and characterized it as an important first step and an opportunity for the two sides to agree on a format for dialogue. The Chairman-in-Office reiterated that an international representative would greatly facilitate such talks.

41. A representative of the Chairman-in-Office participated in an informal meeting of the Contact Group organized on the margins of the meeting of the group of eight at Birmingham on 16 May. On the previous day, the group of eight leaders in their final communiqué underlined the importance of cooperation with the González mission. They expressed their readiness to promote a clear and achievable path towards the full integration of the Federal Republic of Yugoslavia into the international community. At the same time the statement warned that "if Belgrade fails to build on recent progress and a genuine political process does not get under way, its isolation will deepen".

42. The NATO Foreign Ministers on 28 May also called upon President Milosevic "to agree to the readmission of the OSCE long-term mission, and to accept the mission of Mr. Felipe González, the Personal Representative of the OSCE Chairman-in-Office and the Special Representative of the European Union".

43. The Organization for Security and Cooperation in Europe remains ready to assist in the process aimed at peaceful solution of the conflict in Kosovo and maintains its expectation that the Federal Republic of Yugoslavia will accept the mission of Mr. González as OSCE and European Union representative, as well as three missions of long duration, including that in Pristina.

IMPLEMENTATION OF THE KOSOVO EDUCATION AGREEMENT

44. There has been progress in the implementation of the agreement signed by Serbian and Kosovo Albanian members of the "3 plus 3" commission on 23 March. In compliance with the agreement, the Institute of Albanology opened in Pristina on 31 March. The authorities of the Federal Republic of Yugoslavia turned over three faculties of the University of Pristina to the Kosovo Albanians on 15 May. Ethnic Serb protesters attempted to block the transfer, and government forces intervened to evict the protesters after they damaged the facilities.

V. Observations

45. I have welcomed the beginning of a political dialogue as an important step forward in the search for a just and lasting solution of the problems in Kosovo. Convinced that a non-violent approach is the way to reach a mutually accepted settlement in Kosovo, I strongly support the efforts of those committed to peaceful means. In this regard, I urge the parties concerned to continue the negotiations started in Pristina on 22 May with the aim of lowering tensions, stopping the spread of violence and opening the way for peaceful resolution of the crisis.

46. However, the situation in Kosovo continues to be extremely volatile and shows marked signs of deterioration. The armed confrontation in Kosovo has led to loss of life and there is a serious risk of a humanitarian and refugee crisis in the area. In this regard, the most recent Serbian police offensive in Kosovo is particular cause for alarm. I am gravely concerned that the mounting violence in Kosovo might overwhelm political efforts to prevent further escalation of the crisis. I deplore the excessive use of force by the Serbian police in Kosovo and call upon all parties concerned to demonstrate restraint and commit themselves to a peaceful solution. The use of violence to suppress political dissent or in pursuit of political goals is inadmissible. Terrorist activities from whatever quarter contribute to the deadly spiral of violence that jeopardizes stability in the region.

47. During a meeting with Dr. Rugova on 2 June 1998, I welcomed his non-violent approach and encouraged him to continue the search for a peaceful and mutually acceptable settlement short of independence. I reiterated that the current situation in Kosovo is unacceptable and assured Dr. Rugova that he may count on international support in his quest for such a solution.

48. I commend efforts by regional and other organizations, coalitions of States and individual Governments aimed at achieving a political solution in Kosovo. I invite all parties to cooperate fully with them. I am ready to support the efforts of the international community to resolve the Kosovo crisis with the means at my disposal.

Annex I: Letter Dated 15 May from the Secretary-General Addressed to the Chairman-in-Office of the Organization for Security and Cooperation in Europe

I have the honour to refer to Security Council resolution 1160 (1998) of 31 March 1998, by operative paragraph 15 of which the Council requested me "in consultation with appropriate regional organizations to include in my first report recommendations for the establishment of a comprehensive regime to monitor implementation of the prohibitions imposed by this resolution, and calls upon all States, in particular neighbouring States, to extend full cooperation in this regard". As you may be aware, the Council decided by the above resolution that "all States should, for the purposes of fostering peace and stability in Kosovo, prevent the sale or supply to the Federal Republic of Yugoslavia, including Kosovo, by their nationals or from their territories or using their flag vessels and aircraft, of arms and related matériel of all types, such as weapons and ammunition, military vehicles and equipment and spare parts for the aforementioned, and should prevent arming and training for terrorist activities there".

In my report to the Security Council dated 30 April 1998 (S/1998/361), I expressed the belief that the Organization for Security and Cooperation in Europe (OSCE), with contributions and assistance from other organizations, as necessary, would be in a position to carry out the requested monitoring functions effectively. In this connection, I was referring to the European Union, the North Atlantic Treaty Organization, the Western European Union and the Danube Commission, bearing in mind their contribution to the success of the sanctions regime in the case of the former Yugoslavia and the Bosnian Serb party.

Following the informal consultations of the Security Council held on 8 May 1998 to consider my first report, the President of the Council informed me of the Council's wish that, in exploring the establishment of a comprehensive regime to monitor the implementation of the prohibitions imposed by Security Council resolution 1160 (1998), I should take into account the existing capacities and potentials, in particular of the United Nations and OSCE.

I would be grateful, in particular, if in your capacity as Chairman-in-Office of OSCE, you could provide me, at your earliest convenience, with the views of your Organization for the establishment of the comprehensive monitoring regime. In doing so, you may wish to seek advice and support from other regional organizations which may be in a position to contribute to the success of the monitoring regime. In the meantime, I am looking into the possibility of utilizing existing potential within the United Nations, in accordance with the request of the President of the Security Council.
(Signed) Kofi A. Annan

Annex II: Letter Dated 1 June 1998 from the Chairman-in-Office of the Organization for Security and Cooperation in Europe Addressed to the Secretary-General

Thank you for your letter of 15 May 1998, requesting my views - in my capacity as Chairman-in-Office of the Organization for Security and Cooperation in Europe (OSCE) - in regard to a possible OSCE role in enforcing the United Nations Arms Embargo against the Federal Republic of Yugoslavia in accordance with Security Council resolution 1160 (1998) of 31 March 1998.

I would begin by noting that OSCE stands ready to contribute to the monitoring of an arms embargo within its capabilities. This has been confirmed in the course of consultations carried out among the representatives of the OSCE member States in Vienna.

In my view, resolution 1160 (1998) places primary responsibility for enforcing the arms embargo on States. This burden falls particularly on neighbouring States and those with existing arms supplier relationships with the Federal Republic of Yugoslavia.

Within that scope, OSCE is prepared to contribute to the monitoring of an arms embargo under the overall responsibility of the United Nations. Unfortunately, OSCE has rather limited capabilities and does not have the required resources for the establishment of a comprehensive arms embargo-monitoring regime. It is my understanding of the mentioned resolution 1160 (1998) that any enforcement mechanism must relate to the entire border of the Federal Republic of Yugoslavia, and not simply to borders with the former Yugoslav Republic of Macedonia and Albania, where OSCE has a presence. This would require comprehensive monitoring of all border crossings, airports, sea- and riverports. Indeed, OSCE experience in enforcing the previous arms embargo indicates that the majority of large-scale arms shipments to the Federal Republic of Yugoslavia have entered by air or sea, rather than overland. Since OSCE does not have missions in Hungary, Bulgaria or Romania, the Federal Republic of Yugoslavia authorities are unlikely to welcome OSCE monitors to carry out this function within the Federal Republic of Yugoslavia, comprehensive enforcement of resolution 1160 (1998) appears to be out of the reach of our Organization.

Executing a less-than-comprehensive enforcement effort would be in my view problematic. Comprehensive border monitoring in Albania and the Former Yugoslav Republic of Macedonia alone would be extremely resource-intensive, and would result in the unequal application of the embargo. Clearly, the intent of the resolution was not to place a selective arms embargo on Kosovo alone.

The Organization for Security and Cooperation in Europe can, however, play a useful part in such a regime. This Organization's particular comparative advantage is its presence on the ground in the region, through the missions deployed in Bosnia and Herzegovina, Croatia, Albania and the Former Yugoslav Republic of Macedonia.

Monitoring activities along the borders between Albania and the Federal Republic of Yugoslavia, as well as the Former Yugoslav Republic of Macedonia and the Federal Republic of Yugoslavia carried out currently by OSCE, can usefully contribute to an overall arms embargo monitoring effort, under the mentioned overall United Nations responsibility, as a possible early warning indicator. I would note that the border-monitoring capabilities of the OSCE presence in Albania are undergoing a process of strengthening.

The OSCE presence in Albania provides important early warning of large-scale movements of people and weapons, and balanced reporting from the border area. It also serves as a visible symbol of the international community's abiding interest in promoting a peaceful resolution to this crisis.

The OSCE is ready to share the relevant information available as a result of its current monitoring activities with the United Nations, including its bodies responsible for arms embargo monitoring.

In conclusion, I would summarize my reaction to your request by saying that, while not able to assume a leading coordinating role with regard to an arms embargo monitoring effort undertaken by other regional organizations, OSCE may offer a flexible coordinating framework for monitoring activities in the field if so desired by the participants in the effort.
(Signed) Bronislaw Geremek

118. Report of the Secretary-General Prepared pursuant to Security Council Resolution 1160 (1998), UN Doc. S/1998/608, 2 July 1998

I. Introduction

1. The present report is submitted pursuant to Security Council resolution 1160 (1998) of 31 March 1998. It covers the period since my last report of 4 June 1998 (S/1998/470).

II. Security Council Committee Established Pursuant to Resolution 1160 (1998)

2. As at 30 June 1998, the following 43 States had reported to the Committee, pursuant to paragraph 12 of resolution 1160 (1998) on the steps they had taken to give effect to the prohibitions imposed by the resolution: Armenia, Australia, Austria, Bahrain, Belarus, Belgium, Brazil, Bulgaria, Cyprus, Czech Republic, Fiji, Finland, France, Hungary, Iran (Islamic Republic of), Italy, Japan, Kenya, Latvia, Lithuania, Malaysia, Malta, Monaco, New Zealand, Norway, Poland, Portugal, Romania, Saudi Arabia, Singapore, Slovakia, Slovenia, South Africa, Spain, Sweden, Switzerland, Thailand, the former Yugoslav Republic of Macedonia, Turkey, Ukraine, United Kingdom of Great Britain and Northern Ireland, United States of America and Uruguay.

III. Comprehensive Regime to Monitor the Implementation of the Prohibitions Imposed by the Security Council Resolution 1160 (1998)

3. In my last report (S/1998/470) dated 4 June 1998, I informed the Security Council that, in the light of the response from the Chairman-in-Office of the Organization for Security and Cooperation in Europe (OSCE) dated 1 June 1998 and in accordance with the provisions of paragraph 15 of Security Council resolution 1160 (1998), I had written to the Secretary-General of the North Atlantic Treaty Organization (NATO), the Presidency of the European Union (EU), the Secretary-General of the Western European Union (WEU) and the Executive Director of the Danube Commission with a view to exploring their readiness to participate in the comprehensive regime and to submit to me, on the basis of information that may be available to them, reports on suspected violations of the prohibitions imposed by the resolution for consideration by the Security Council Committee established pursuant to resolution 1160 (1998).

4. As at 30 June, I had received an interim reply from the Secretary-General of NATO dated 11 June, as well as replies from the Secretary-General of WEU dated 18 June, the Acting President and the Secretary of the Danube Commission dated 23 June 1998 and the Presidency of the European Union dated 30 June 1998. The full text of those replies is annexed to the present report (annexes I-IV).

5. The Secretary-General of NATO informed me that a study by the NATO Military Authorities on possible support for the monitoring regime would be completed shortly, and, once it had been considered

by the North Atlantic Council, the Secretary-General would contact me again. He stated that in the meantime, the NATO-led Stabilization Force (SFOR) in Bosnia and Herzegovina was using its authority under Annex 1A of the 1995 Peace Agreement to step up its efforts, within the existing mission and capabilities, to monitor the Bosnian border with the Federal Republic of Yugoslavia to prevent the transfer of weapons. He expressed the readiness of NATO to share SFOR findings with the United Nations.

6. WEU expressed its readiness to provide any useful information that comes to its notice on the implementation of the measures imposed by resolution 1160 (1998), in particular through its Multinational Advisory Police Element (MAPE) established in Albania at the request and with the cooperation of the Albanian authorities. WEU also stated that it was in the process of considering its role with regard to the very serious developments in Kosovo and their implications for regional stability. While seeking further information on the nature of a comprehensive regime for enforcement of the prohibitions contained in resolution 1160 (1998), WEU expressed its interest in taking any relevant action in full transparency and partnership with other organizations, including EU and NATO, and in agreement with the neighbouring countries on whose territories any relevant operation would take place.

7. The Danube Commission stated that in the event that OSCE or another international organization should offer the framework for coordinating the monitoring under resolution 1160 (1998), the Commission would be prepared to contribute, within the areas of its competence and expertise, to the accomplishment of this task through its support and advice concerning navigation on the Danube and the facilitation of transit of vessels, goods and passengers in compliance with resolution 1160 (1998). At the same time, the Commission suggested that a well-defined mechanism should be devised in due course to deal with cooperation between the authorities responsible for conducting inspections under the sanctions system and organizations and representatives of the shipowners, shippers and consignees of goods on the Danube.

8. The Presidency of EU welcomed my initiative to seek its views, as well as those of other organizations, on the enforcement of Security Council resolution 1160 (1998). The member States of EU agreed to assist the Committee established pursuant to paragraph 9 of Security Council resolution 1160 (1998) by providing information on the action taken by them to implement the resolution and by making available information on alleged violations of the arms embargo. The Presidency also expressed the readiness of EU members to contribute to international efforts to monitor the embargo by asking the European Community Monitoring Mission (ECMM) to report to the Committee any relevant information on the movement of arms that should come into its possession as a result of its operations in Albania, Bosnia, Croatia, the Federal Republic of Yugoslavia and the former Yugoslav Republic of Macedonia. EU is seeking a significant increase in the number of monitors in the Federal Republic of Yugoslavia/Kosovo, in line with President Milosevic's undertaking in Moscow on increased international monitoring, and has increased the number of its monitors in northern Albania. The monitors would be tasked to be alert for any evidence relevant to the implementation of resolution 1160 (1998).

9. I will submit my recommendation, as required in paragraph 15 of the above-mentioned resolution once I have received all necessary information.

IV. Situation in Kosovo

10. As the Council is aware, the situation in Kosovo has deteriorated significantly since the submission of my last report. A new outbreak of violence in early June led to an influx of refugees to Albania and to an increase in internally displaced persons in Kosovo and Montenegro. The number of registered refugees in Albania at the end of June was 6,900. In addition, an estimated 3,150 have departed to southern Albania. It is estimated, however, that there may be as many as 13,000 refugees more in Albania. As of 19 June, the Montenegrin authorities had registered another 10,177 internally displaced persons from Kosovo. According to estimates of the Office of the United Nations High Commissioner for Refugees (UNHCR), some 45,000 people have been displaced within Kosovo itself. UNHCR is unable to assess the situation on the ground more precisely, since it cannot gain access to the affected areas.

11. Anticipating that further deterioration of the situation might lead to a major humanitarian and refugee crisis in the area, United Nations agencies expanded their activities in the region. In addition to the UNHCR office in northern Albania, the World Food Programme (WFP) also opened an emergency office there on 17 June. UNHCR continues to lead inter-agency contingency planning in the region. On 15 June, the Office of the Coordinator for Humanitarian Affairs, the United Nations Development Programme (UNDP), the United Nations Children's Fund (UNICEF), UNHCR, WFP and the World Health Organization (WHO) launched the consolidated inter-agency flash appeal for humanitarian assistance needs related to the Kosovo crisis: 1 June-31 August 1998. The appeal is aimed at obtaining US$ 18 million for multisectoral assistance for the United Nations system, of which UNHCR is seeking US$ 12.9 million. Coordinating mechanisms are operating in Pristina, Belgrade, Podgorica, Tirana and Skopje. WFP is stockpiling food in Pristina - rations are now sufficient to feed 35,000 for one month. In northern Albania, WFP is ready to start distribution of 500 tons of food assistance, which would cover existing needs until September.

12. In its resolution 1160 (1998), the Security Council requested me to keep it regularly informed on the situation in Kosovo and to provide an assessment of whether the Federal Republic of Yugoslavia had complied in a constructive manner with conditions put forward by the Contact Group. By the time of writing of the present report, I had received the relevant information from the Chairman-in-Office of OSCE, which I attach in annex V.

V. Observations

13. The international community is appalled by the continued violence in Kosovo. The parties concerned must demonstrate restraint and resume negotiations to find a peaceful solution to the conflict. I am increasingly concerned that, unless hostilities in Kosovo are stopped, tensions could spill across borders and destabilize the entire region. Kosovo therefore becomes a key issue for the overall stability of the Balkan region. I welcome the diplomatic efforts being made at the international level to address fundamental aspects of the situation which can only be resolved through negotiation.

14. It has been widely reported that authorities of the Federal Republic of Yugoslavia have agreed to allow foreign diplomats and accredited international organizations in Belgrade to monitor the situation in Kosovo. The process of establishing that monitoring presence is reportedly under way. Such a monitoring mission would improve the ability of the international community to assess directly the situation on the ground and could better serve the desire of the international community and the Security Council for impartial and substantive information regarding Kosovo. Should this come about, the Council may wish to review the continued need for reporting by the United Nations on the situation in Kosovo, as requested in paragraph 14 of resolution 1160 (1998), in view of the absence of a United Nations presence in Kosovo to provide an independent assessment of that situation.

Annex I: Letter Dated 11 June 1998 from the Secretary-General of the North Atlantic Treaty Organization Addressed to the Secretary-General

Thank you for your letter of 4 June 1998 in which you sought the views of the North Atlantic Treaty Organization (NATO) on the establishment of a comprehensive monitoring regime for the prohibitions imposed on the Federal Republic of Yugoslavia by Security Council resolution 1160 (1998) of 31 March 1998.

As I informed you in my letter of 29 May, the North Atlantic Council has tasked the NATO Military Authorities to study possible support for the monitoring regime. This study will be completed shortly, and I will write to you again once it has been considered by the North Atlantic Council.

In the meantime, the NATO-led Stabilization Force (SFOR) in Bosnia and Herzegovina is using its authority under Annex 1A of the 1995 Peace Agreement to step up its efforts, within the existing mission and capabilities, to monitor the Bosnian border with the Federal Republic of Yugoslavia to prevent the transfer of weapons. We are making the necessary arrangements to forward any information on suspected violations in the SFOR area of operations to NATO headquarters for onward transmission to the United Nations Secretariat, via the monthly SFOR reports or on an ad hoc basis as necessary.
(Signed) Javier Solana

Annex II: Letter Dated 18 June 1998 from the Secretary-General of the Western European Union Addressed to the Secretary-General

I have the honour to thank you for your letter of 4 June in pursuance of Security Council resolution 1160 (1998) of 31 March 1998, which I have drawn to the attention of the Permanent Council. I am now replying on the Council's behalf.

The Western European Union (WEU) welcomes your initiative to include our organization in your consultations on this important matter. WEU has repeatedly made clear its readiness to act in support of and - as appropriate - under mandates from the United Nations, as well as the Organization for Security and Cooperation in Europe.

At present, as you know, the only mission being conducted by WEU in the region concerned is the Multinational Advisory Police Element (MAPE) established in Albania at the request and with the cooperation of the Albanian authorities. MAPE is a training and advisory mission whose mandate includes assistance with the training of all Albanian police forces and advice on their future organization; its activities thus contribute to the development of the capacity of the Albanian authorities themselves, inter alia, for implementation of the embargo. WEU is ready to provide immediately, by the appropriate means, any useful information that comes to its notice on the conditions of implementation of the embargo.

WEU shares your concern for the effective implementation of resolution 1160 (1998). As indicated in the declaration recently adopted by our Ministers at their meeting in Rhodes, we are in the process of considering the role of our organization in relation to the very serious developments in Kosovo and their implications for regional stability. To make sure that the WEU Council can include in its deliberations any possible practical contributions that might be appropriate for us in that context, we would be happy to receive further information or proposals on the nature of a "comprehensive monitoring regime" for enforcement, as mentioned in your letter. I might add that we would expect to take any relevant action in full transparency and partnership with other institutions, including the European Union and the North Atlantic Treaty Organization, and in agreement with the neighbouring countries on whose territory any relevant operations would take place.
(Signed) Jose Cutileiro

Annex III: Letter Dated 23 June 1998 from the Acting President and the Secretary of the Danube Commission Addressed to the Secretary-General

Allow us to thank you for your letter of 4 June 1998, in which you included the Danube Commission in the consultations pursuant to paragraph 15 of Security Council resolution 1160 (1998) of 31 March 1998, thus recognizing the role of our international intergovernmental organization in the Danube region.

One of the main tasks of the Danube Commission is to ensure implementation of the provisions of the Convention concerning the regime for navigation on the Danube, which provide that "navigation on the Danube shall be free and open for the nationals, vessels of commerce and goods of all States, on a footing of equality". Hence the Danube Commission believes that any monitoring system to be established under the above-mentioned resolution and to be operated by the appropriate institutions must respect this fundamental principle of navigation on the Danube, which is based on international law and recognized by the entire international community.

Without prejudice to the provisions of resolution 1160 (1998), which must be applied in full, or to the Charter of the United Nations, it must be ensured that, when sanctions are applied by the United Nations, the interests of "innocent and neutral" transit navigation on the Danube of countries that are not the object of the sanctions are respected and protected. Not only is this navigation essential to the economies of the landlocked Danubian countries, it is also important for some 40 nations that use the Danube each year as a major European waterway.

In the event that the Organization for Security and Cooperation in Europe (OSCE) or another international organization should offer the framework for coordinating the monitoring, the Danube Commission would be prepared to contribute, within the areas of its competence, to the accomplishment of this task through its support and advice concerning navigation on the Danube and the facilitation of "innocent" transit of vessels, goods and passengers. To the extent that a control system becomes inevitable, the Danube Commission hopes that the institutions responsible for this task will take advantage of the experience of the experts of the Commission and the Danubian countries in matters related to navigation on the Danube.

At the same time, a well-defined mechanism should be devised in due course to deal with cooperation between the authorities responsible for conducting inspections under the sanctions system and organizations and representatives of the shipowners, shippers and consignees of goods on the Danube.

If the implementation of such a monitoring system causes losses to the navigation on the Danube of countries that are not the object of the sanctions but experience their consequences, a mechanism for compensating for those losses should be devised as soon as possible.

(Signed) Petru Cordos, Acting President of the Danube Commission, Representative of Romania on the Danube Commission

(Signed) Felix P. Bogdanov, Secretary of the Danube Commission, Representative of the Russian Federation on the Danube Commission

Annex IV: Letter Dated 30 June 1998 from the Secretary of State for Foreign and Commonwealth Affairs of the United Kingdom of Great Britain and Northern Ireland Addressed to the Secretary-General

Thank you for your letter of 4 June, addressed to me in my capacity as President of the European Union, seeking the views of the States members of the European Union on the establishment of a regime to monitor the arms embargo on the Federal Government of Yugoslavia imposed by Security Council resolution 1160 (1998).

The European Union welcomes your initiative in seeking its views, as well as those of other regional organizations, on the enforcement of Security Council resolution 1160 (1998), the aim of which we strongly support. The States members of the European Union have agreed to assist the committee established under paragraph 9 of resolution 1160 (1998) in its work by providing information on the action taken by member States to implement the resolution and by making available to the Committee any information available to member States on alleged violations of the embargo. I have asked member States to pool such information so that the Presidency of the day can pass this on to the committee.

The EU and its member States also stand ready to contribute to international efforts to monitor the embargo by asking the European Community Monitoring Mission (ECMM) to report to the Sanctions Committee any relevant information on the movement of arms that should come into its possession as a result of its operations in Albania, Bosnia, Croatia, the Federal Republic of Yugoslavia and the former Yugoslav Republic of Macedonia.

The European Union is seeking a significant increase in the number of monitors in the Federal Republic of Yugoslavia/Kosovo, in line with President Milosevic's undertaking in Moscow on increased interna-

tional monitoring. The European Union has also increased the number of its monitors in northern Albania. The European Union will ensure that its monitors are tasked to be alert for any evidence relevant to implementation of resolution 1160 (1998). The European Union would also be willing to consider any further proposals from the Secretary-General or other regional organizations on a monitoring regime.
Robin Cook

Annex V: Information on the Situation in Kosovo and on Measures Taken by the Organization for Security and Cooperation in Europe, Submitted Pursuant to Paragraphs 13 and 16 of Security Council Resolution 1160 (1998)

I. INTRODUCTION

The further deterioration of the situation in Kosovo and along the border between the Federal Republic of Yugoslavia and Albania since the May report to the Secretary-General has prompted the Contact Group to impose a package of economic sanctions on both the Federal Republic of Yugoslavia and Serbia to induce them to seek a political solution to the problem. For its part, the North Atlantic Treaty Organization (NATO) produced an array of crisis scenarios, and on 15 June staged a display of air power in the airspace of Albania and the former Yugoslav Republic of Macedonia, along the border with Kosovo.

II. THE DIALOGUE

On 15 May in Belgrade, President Milosevic and Dr. Rugova agreed on weekly working contacts between the two sides. However, so far only one such meeting has been held, in Pristina (on 22 May). The Albanian side contended that the military-cum-police operation unleashed on south-west Kosovo by Belgrade in late May and the whole of June precluded its participation in further meetings of this kind.

Those of the Kosovo Albanians who do not count among the supporters of Rugova's policy line have made known their displeasure with his meeting with Milosevic. Representatives of the so-called Kosovo Liberation Army (KLA) have strongly reiterated their direct objective, namely, the independence of Kosovo.

By 16 June 1998, no signs had emerged of a possibility of resumption of the Belgrade-Pristina dialogue. The issue was taken up during the Milosevic-Yeltsin meeting in Moscow on 16 June.

The two sides to the Kosovo conflict have had numerous contacts over the past month with representatives of foreign countries visiting Yugoslavia, and also with diplomats posted in Belgrade. Dr. Rugova has visited the United States of America, Italy and France and has met with the Secretary-General of the United Nations.

III. VIOLENCE

A further deterioration of the situation was recorded in Kosovo soon after the Milosevic-Rugova meeting, notably in the Yugoslav-Albanian borderland and along the Pec-Dechani, Djakovica-Prizren and Pristina-Pec highways. Serious armed clashes were noted in those areas.

The wholesale destruction visited upon the Albanian villages in the process sent consecutive waves of refugees streaming out of the area. Casualty figures released by both sides differ considerably. The Serbs maintain that their actions had a purely anti-terrorist character and claim only a "negligible" number of victims, while the Albanians insist scores have been killed (no credible data about the number of victims are available, but some unofficial sources indicate there might be over 200 dead). Many observers agree that the range and scope of combat operations validates the contention that a guerilla war is now under way in Kosovo.

More people these days are prepared to cross illegally into the war-torn Yugoslav province from Albania, and contraband weapons are pouring into Kosovo, brought there by armed groups of ethnic Albanians.

The media quote the Belgrade office of the Office of the United Nations High Commissioner for Refugees to the effect that the combat operations in Kosovo have displaced 30,000 to 40,000 Albanians, who have now established temporary residence in other parts of the province or left for Albania (around 12,000) or Montenegro. On the other hand, there has been no confirmation of the earlier Albanian reports of their countrymen streaming into the former Yugoslav Republic of Macedonia. The Serbians argue that the Albanians overstate the facts and inflate the figures, but they do not counter them with their own information.

In the opinion of A. Demaci, Chairman of the Parliamentary Party of Kosovo, carried by the media in early June, the Kosovo Liberation Army allegedly controlled an area of 3,000 square kilometres, including some 250 villages, with a total population of 700,000 to 800,000, most of them in the Drenica region.

IV. EDUCATION

Serb students and professors in Pristina do not agree to hand over to the Albanian side a part of the premises of the local university. A student demonstration was recently dispersed by the police, while the Serb educational authorities made a hasty decision to end the academic year ahead of schedule.

V. ACCESS TO KOSOVO

The armed clashes resulted in a temporary closure in May and June of the Pristina-Pec and Pec-Decani-Djakovica-Prizren sections of the highway, with telecommunication lines severed partially within this area and a news blackout of several days imposed by the authorities. Instances of Serb troops stopping food transports and other supplies being sent from the north to Kosovo have been noted. In early June, the Serb side regained control over the aforesaid sections of the highway, which were then reopened to traffic.

Members of the KLA stop travellers in KLA-controlled areas (notably in the Drenica region), check their identification documents and often confiscate items they find of use. For instance, Japanese and American television crews were relieved of their bullet-proof vests.

The Ministry of Foreign Affairs of the Federal Republic of Yugoslavia, on 7 June, conducted a tour of Kosovo for diplomats posted in Belgrade, who reported on the widespread destruction of housing in the now-abandoned villages affected by the hostilities at the end of May/beginning of June. However, those diplomats did not confirm the allegations of some Kosovo Albanians that the Serb authorities had subjected the area to heavy artillery and aerial bombardment.

VI. RISKS OF SPILLOVER

According to the reports of the OSCE presence in Albania, the situation on the Albanian border with Kosovo remains volatile. There has been almost daily military activity in western Kosovo since the end of May, causing large-scale displacement of civilians. Over 10,000 of them have fled to Albania, most of them women, children and the elderly. The violence has caused a drastic increase in militancy on both sides of the border. Armed resistance has become very visible, including cross-border movement of arms and men. Border incidents have increased, pointing to efforts on the part of the Federal Republic of Yugoslavia to clamp down on this movement. Recent incidents also involved border violations. There is increasing evidence of mines being laid, and there have also been a number of accounts from refugees of detention of men of military age.

The refugees have been accommodated by the local population in the border region, the poorest part of Albania. For the moment, their immediate needs are being met, but the totally inadequate infrastructure makes the long-term outlook grim.

Politically, the conflict causes problems for the Government in Tirana, in that it must take into account both national sentiments of indignation and solidarity, echoed by the opposition, and international calls for restraint.

The overriding priority is to secure an early end to the fighting, followed by the deployment of a large-scale international monitoring force. This would not only enable a meaningful dialogue to take place, but also facilitate an early return of the refugees.

The OSCE mission in Skopje reports that "spillover" from the current crisis in Kosovo in the territory of the former Yugoslav Republic of Macedonia may take physical form (movement of individuals whether seeking refuge privately or coming as refugees) or political form (an adverse effect on ethnic relations in local politics). Hitherto the risks of physical "spillover" have been contained: there have been no refugees and no identifiable net inflow based on family ties; border areas are stable and calm, with life proceeding normally, albeit with increased anxiety among the local population; and there has been no serious incident, in recent months, on the country's border with Kosovo and the rest of Serbia, with reduced smuggling and illegal crossings. Any significant number of Kosovars arriving would be resented by the majority population. The key to continuing stability remains the policy approach of the Yugoslav border authorities on the northern side of the border. Should similar operations be launched to those in the Decani area, movement of refugees would be very likely, but the area has traditionally been relatively quiet.

In terms of risks of political "spillover", ethnic Albanian demonstrations in Skopje and other towns, showing solidarity with Kosovars and voicing support for the KLA, although peaceful, have caused disquiet and resentment among the ethnic Macedonian population, complicating the political scene, which is otherwise dominated by forthcoming parliamentary elections.

VII. MEASURES TAKEN BY THE ORGANIZATION FOR SECURITY AND COOPERATION IN EUROPE

Kosovo continues to be in the forefront of OSCE activities. It has become one of the priorities of its Chairmanship.

The latest developments in Kosovo have clearly demonstrated the necessity of participation by international organizations in solving the humanitarian problems in the region as well. This is why the OSCE Permanent Council stressed on 4 June the importance of free access for the International Committee of the Red Cross and other humanitarian organizations to the areas affected by fighting. The major influx of refugees arriving in Albania from Kosovo is being observed by OSCE.

At the end of May, the Chairman of the Parliamentary Assembly of OSCE, Mr. Javier Ruperez, visited the Federal Republic of Yugoslavia for talks in Belgrade and Pristina. He did not register any change in the position of the Federal Republic of Yugoslavia vis-à-vis the Gonzalez mission or a prospective OSCE mission, including one in Kosovo.

OSCE has developed relatively modest but effective monitoring capabilities in Albania. The Organization decided on 4 June to increase the number of OSCE monitors on Albania's border with Kosovo to 30.

Addressing the Central Europe Initiative meeting in Brioni on 6 June, the OSCE Chairman-in-Office came forward with the idea of a special status for Kosovo. In his opinion, it should be elaborated through the dialogue between the authorities of the Federal Republic of Yugoslavia and Kosovo Albanians. He suggested that a round table dialogue concentrating on special status for Kosovo would help resolve the dichotomy between independence and autonomy. This could be helpful in moving away from political rhetoric and turning to concrete matters, such as the functioning of legislative and executive powers there, assuring local identity, development of local government and education.

On 11 June, the Chairman-in-Office condemned violence by either side in the strongest possible terms and urged an immediate cessation of hostilities. He expressed his deep concern about the continued flow of refugees driven across the border into Albania by the violence. He called on the Belgrade authorities to facilitate the return of displaced persons and refugees.

In his address to the Permanent Council in Vienna on 17 June, the Chairman-in-Office stated that a political solution to the crisis required not only that hostilities in Kosovo be stopped and talks resumed, but also that democracy and full respect for human rights and minorities be introduced in the Federal Republic of Yugoslavia, and that the participation of that country in international organizations, including OSCE, be ensured once it applies international standards to its behaviour. The Chairman-in-Office repeated that the OSCE platform for a political solution is still available and that the Organization would be ready to dispatch a mission to Kosovo without delay, if and when it proved to be possible.

In his letter of 19 June to President Milosevic, the Chairman-in-Office showed interest in the suggestion by the Federal Republic of Yugoslavia to hold talks with OSCE on the acceptance of the OSCE mission in Kosovo and on the participation of the Federal Republic of Yugoslavia in OSCE (this proposal was made by the Yugoslav side after the Milosevic-Yeltsin talks in Moscow on 16 June and included in the joint statement).

119. Report of the Secretary-General Prepared pursuant to Security Council Resolution 1160 (1998), UN Doc. S/1998/712, 5 August 1998

I. Introduction

1. The present report is submitted pursuant to Security Council resolution 1160 (1998) of 31 March 1998. It covers the period since my last report of 2 July 1998 (S/1998/608). As at 31 July 1998, I had received several communications from Member States and regional organizations relating to developments in Kosovo, as well as to the steps they had taken to give effect to the prohibitions imposed by resolution 1160 (1998). By a letter dated 9 July 1998 (S/1998/657), the Acting Permanent Representative of Germany to the United Nations conveyed a statement issued on 8 July 1998 by the Contact Group regarding the situation in Kosovo. I also received a letter dated 21 July from the Permanent Representative of Austria to the United Nations (S/1998/675) which contained the Declaration of the Presidency of the European Union of 20 July 1998. In a letter dated 16 July 1998 (S/1998/654), the Permanent Mission of the Federal Republic of Yugoslavia transmitted remarks of the Federal Republic of Yugoslavia in connection with my previous report. On 24 July 1998, the Chairman-in-Office of the Organization for Security and Cooperation in Europe (OSCE) conveyed to me updated information on the situation in Kosovo, which I attach in annex I to the present report.

II. Security Council Committee Established Pursuant to Resolution 1160 (1998)

2. As of 31 July, in addition to those States listed in my earlier report (S/1998/608), Greece, Germany and Liechtenstein reported to the Committee pursuant to paragraph 12 of resolution 1160 (1998) on the steps they had taken to give effect to the prohibitions imposed by that resolution.

III. Comprehensive Regime to Monitor the Implementation of the Prohibitions Imposed by Security Council Resolution 1160 (1998)

3. In paragraph 15 of resolution 1160 (1998), the Security Council requested that, in consultation with appropriate regional organizations, I include in my first report to the Council recommendations for the establishment of a comprehensive regime to monitor the implementation of the prohibitions imposed by that resolution. It also called upon all States, in particular neighbouring States, to extend full cooperation in that regard.

4. In my report to the Council dated 30 April 1998 (S/1998/361), I provided a general outline of the concept for a comprehensive monitoring regime and stated that the United Nations was unable, within existing budgetary resources, to establish and administer such a regime. I reiterate my view expressed therein that for a monitoring regime to be comprehensive, it would require the deployment at key points of teams composed of qualified experts, as well as the setting up of a fully equipped communications centre to support the work of the monitoring teams and to interact with the Sanctions Committee and its secretariat. These teams would provide advice and assistance to the authorities of neighbouring and other States that bear the responsibility for enforcement of the mandatory measures in accordance with the provisions of Security Council resolution 1160 (1998).

Diplomatic Efforts for the Settlement of the Crisis

5. In my second report pursuant to resolution 1160 (1998), dated 4 June 1998 (S/1998/470), I stated that upon receipt of the views of the organizations I had contacted, I would submit my recommendations to the Security Council for a comprehensive monitoring regime, taking into account the existing potential within the United Nations and the views expressed by those organizations.

6. In addition to OSCE, replies were received from the European Union (EU), the North Atlantic Treaty Organization (NATO), the Western European Union (WEU) and the Danube Commission. Those communications were annexed to my earlier reports (S/1998/470, S/1998/608). On 14 July 1998, the Secretary-General of NATO informed me of his organization's decision at the current stage to proceed with the "Stabilization Force (SFOR) option" to step up its efforts to monitor the Bosnian border with the Federal Republic of Yugoslavia, and to forward to me any relevant information on suspected violations of resolution 1160 (1998) in SFOR's area of operations. The text of the letter from the Secretary-General of NATO is contained in annex II to the present report.

7. All the organizations I contacted have stated their readiness to contribute actively to the monitoring of the prohibitions imposed by resolution 1160 (1998). At this stage, however, the overall resources pledged by those organizations would not allow for the establishment of a comprehensive monitoring regime as envisaged in resolution 1160 (1998). Nonetheless, their proposed contributions, coupled with that of the United Nations Preventive Deployment Force (UNPREDEP), as outlined in my reports to the Security Council dated 1 June and 14 July 1998 (S/1998/454 and S/1998/644 respectively), provide a useful framework for reporting on violations of the prohibitions imposed by the above resolution and for assisting the Committee established pursuant to Security Council resolution 1160 (1998) in discharging its mandate.

8. Accordingly, I propose to invite the organizations mentioned in paragraph 6 above to forward to the Secretariat, for consideration by the Security Council Committee established pursuant to Security Council resolution 1160 (1998), relevant information based on reports of their own monitors or any other information that may be available to them, concerning violations or allegations of violations of the prohibitions imposed by Security Council resolution 1160 (1998).

9. On 21 July 1998, the Security Council adopted resolution 1186 (1998), by which it decided to authorize an increase in the troop strength of UNPREDEP and to extend its current mandate for a period of six months until 28 February 1999, including the tasks of monitoring the border areas and reporting to me on illicit arms flows and other activities that are prohibited under resolution 1160 (1998).

10. In the absence of an integrated coordinating mechanism, it would *be essential for representatives of participating organizations, UN-PREDEP and the Secretariat to hold*, as necessary, periodic meetings in order to exchange information on the monitoring of the prohibitions established by resolution 1160 (1998) and to address practical issues arising in that connection.

IV. Situation in Kosovo

11. In early July, efforts by the members of the Contact Group, EU and OSCE offered hopeful signs that meaningful dialogue might be possible between the parties to the conflict. Regrettably, those hopes were not realized. I must therefore report that, as the Security Council is already aware, the situation in Kosovo continues to deteriorate. Increased heavy fighting between the security forces of the Federal Republic of Yugoslavia and the so-called Kosovo Liberation Army (KLA) has been reported from several areas in Kosovo. The numbers of civilian and military casualties are at their highest point since the outbreak of the conflict. The attitudes of the two sides appear to be hardening with every day of fighting. There is no progress on renewal of dialogue. Most disturbing are reports of increased tensions along the border between the Federal Republic of Yugoslavia and Albania. In this regard, I share the concerns expressed in the Declaration of the Presidency of the European Union of 20 July 1998 (S/1998/675).

12. The unrelenting violence has led to a dramatic increase in internally displaced persons in Kosovo and Montenegro since my last report. According to estimates by the Office of the United Nations High Commissioner for Refugees (UNHCR), more than 100,000 people have been driven from their homes by the conflict. Between 70,000 and 80,000 people were internally displaced in Kosovo by the end of July. Authorities in Montenegro had recorded 22,000 internally displaced persons from Kosovo by 22 July. As local food production has come to a standstill, food shortages could worsen sharply. With the increasing number of displaced persons and the approaching winter, Kosovo has the potential of becoming a humanitarian disaster.

13. The number of refugees in northern Albania remains approximately the same (estimated at around 13,500) with 10,300 registered refugees. The majority (some 10,000) arrived in Albania between 29 May and 9 June. While one of the main refugee locations, Tropoje, lies just 7 kilometres from the border, the proximity of the border has not created a security risk for refugees at this stage. However, with the increasing militarization of the border region and the escalation of tensions in Kosovo, destabilization of the Albanian border region is possible.

14. United Nations agencies are intensifying their efforts to prevent a major humanitarian and refugee crisis. In response to the consolidated inter-agency flash appeal for humanitarian assistance needs related to the Kosovo crisis: 1 June-31 August 1998, however, only 9.7 per cent of assistance requirements (US$ 1.7 million) had been pledged by donors as of 14 July. Most of the funding, provided by Denmark, Germany, Luxembourg, Sweden and Switzerland, was intended for UNHCR assistance programmes for refugees and internally displaced persons in Albania and Montenegro. The World Health Organization (WHO) and the United Nations Children's Fund (UNICEF) continue to jointly assess all possible means for assisting the networks and facilities to provide vaccination for children. WHO is intensifying its coordination with health-related non-governmental organizations (NGOs) to properly address the donations of medicine. UNICEF and UNHCR are to meet with the Ministry of Education of Montenegro in order to explore ways of supporting schools hosting classes with internally displaced children. WHO is also planning an assessment of the medical and psychosocial needs of the displaced population in Montenegro.

V. Observations

15. The limitations on my capacity to report on the situation in Kosovo, as requested in paragraph 14 of resolution 1160 (1998), remain unchanged. At the same time, it is my understanding that there has been an increase in the presence of diplomatic observers from European and Contact Group countries in general who, as I suggested in my last report, *might be better placed to provide the Security Council with a reliable flow of information concerning the situation on the ground.*

16. The continuing infiltration from outside the borders of the Federal Republic of Yugoslavia of weapons and fighting men is a source of continuing widespread concern. The sharp escalation of violence and the reported use of excessive force by security forces against civilians as part of the government operations against the KLA are cause for both distress and alarm. A particularly dangerous element in the situation is the move in certain quarters away from a willingness to search for compromise on a basis of multi-ethnic communities. Centrifugal tendencies appear to be gaining ground. As indicated in paragraphs 12 and 13, the continuing conflict has led to a growing number of internally displaced persons and refugees. This in turn causes further instability. The international community risks once against being placed in a position where it is only dealing with the symptoms of a conflict through its humanitarian agencies.

17. This situation is aggravated by the failure of the authorities of the Federal Republic of Yugoslavia and the Albanian Kosovars to enter into serious negotiations on the future status of Kosovo. The continuation or further escalation of this conflict has dangerous implications for the stability of the region. Given the responsibilities of the United Nations in the wider region and the ethnic makeup in neighbouring countries, I cannot but express my alarm at this prospect. Several

Security Council-mandated or Security Council-authorized operations in the region are playing a useful role in promoting dialogue and harmony among different ethnic groups. I wish to record before the Security Council my strong hope that the question of Kosovo will be examined not in isolation but in a manner that fully takes into account and embraces the broad, regional context and the principles of the Charter of the United Nations.

Annex I: Information on the Situation in Kosovo and on Measures Taken by the Organization for Security and Cooperation in Europe, Submitted Pursuant to Paragraphs 13 and 16 of Security Council Resolution 1160 (1998)

SUMMARY

Since mid-June, there has been further escalation of the conflict in Kosovo, with the hostilities spreading to engulf the entire southwestern part of the province.

By mid-July, the crisis had reached new levels of intensity. As the fighting drew nearer Pristina, the "Kosovo Liberation Army" (KLA) removed any ambiguity as to its intention to bring the province under its control.

Numerous armed clashes were reported from the regions of Kosovo bordering Albania.

All appeals of the international community for talks and a cessation of the hostilities have remained unanswered. Prospects for a negotiated settlement appear dim and time is running out for the attainment of a peaceful solution. The Kosovo crisis entered into a phase of unpredictable consequences for regional stability and is therefore a source of deep concern for the Chairman-in-Office as it is for the entire Organization for Security and Cooperation in Europe (OSCE).

VIOLENCE AND THE USE OF FORCE

1. The period between the 16 June meeting between President Miloevi of the Federal Republic of Yugoslavia and President Yeltsin of the Russian Federation and the end of the month was marked by a drop in the number of combat operations in Kosovo. However, units of the Yugoslav Army remained active in the border region. Isolated incidents also took place along Yugoslavia's border with the former Yugoslav Republic of Macedonia.

2. Shortly thereafter the KLA became more active, moving on from defensive actions to sporadic attacks on the Yugoslav security forces. New information continued to be received on the fighting between the KLA and the Serb security forces around Pec, Cecanice and Djakovic. Offensive operations, with heavy fighting and casualties, have been the hallmarks of the period since 20 July. The civilian population has also suffered losses and the numbers of the refugees from the area have grown.

3. Meanwhile, the OSCE presence (mission) in Albania has reported a number of serious armed clashes inside Kosovo, close to the border with Albania, with the number of such incidents increasing after 15 July. OSCE observers witnessed stepped-up military activities in the Decani area. Increased cross-border transit of KLA troops as well as shipments of arms and ammunition were recorded, as was a flare-up of the fighting on the border region on 18 July.

SITUATION ON THE ALBANIAN/KOSOVO BORDER

4. Military activity by the Federal Republic of Yugoslavia has continued unabated since mid-May. In the border areas close to Albania, many villages and hamlets have been targeted. More recently, the larger town of Orahovac has also been the scene of fighting. This has caused an increase in the number of internally displaced persons. The refugee movement to Albania, however, has come to a virtual halt. This is probably a result of the deterrent measures by forces of the Federal Republic of Yugoslavia, including the laying of mines and increased patrols at the border.

5. The continued violence in Kosovo has reinforced overall militancy among ethnic Albanians on both sides of the border. KLA transborder activities have become increasingly overt. Regular movement of KLA arms/ammunition and manpower has been observed by OSCE across known refugee routes. There are strong indications that some of these routes have been mined on the Federal Republic of Yugoslavia side, and are targeted by direct and indirect fire. OSCE observers have recently sighted fresh shell craters 25 metres from the border on the Albanian side.

6. The increased levels of tension and armed confrontation have led to further destabilization of the north-east region of Albania. There are indications that the vital ferry link on the main supply route to the border area is under the control of the KLA.

ACCESS TO KOSOVO

7. The number of visits to Kosovo by foreign diplomats posted in Belgrade has grown since the meeting between President Milosevic and President Yeltsin.

8. However, regions hit by heavy fighting and those preparing for armed operations were virtually impossible to visit. In danger zones Serbian police did grant individual passage permits while warning prospective travellers of considerable risk.

9. Units and outposts of the KLA continued to stop individuals for ID checks and sometimes refused to give access to some areas of Kosovo under its control.

10. On 6 July, the International Kosovo Diplomatic Observer Mission started work in the war-torn province, with the participation of the OSCE Troika. Observers from the United States of America, the Russian Federation and the European Union have set up offices in Pristina and operate from there.

11. On 21 July, at Belgrade, the heads of the diplomatic observer missions, representing Contact Group countries, the European Union (EU) Troika and the OSCE Chairman-in-Office, presented their first report on the situation in Kosovo.

DIALOGUE

12. Despite strenuous diplomatic efforts, the international community has so far failed to bring about a resumption of the dialogue between the country's authorities and representatives of the Kosovo Albanians. The Serbian side has reiterated its understanding that a dialogue should be conducted within the framework of Serbia and the Federal Republic of Yugoslavia and that the territorial integrity of Yugoslavia would first be guaranteed. Units of the Serb special forces remained in Kosovo.

13. Representatives of the Albanian negotiating team and the Chairman of the Kosovo Democratic League are of the opinion that the present-day conditions of conflict are not conducive to dialogue. In their view, a withdrawal from Kosovo of the Serb special forces, a cessation of the operations aimed against the Albanian civilian population and putting the idea of Kosovo's independence on the agenda of the negotiations would be their preconditions before a resumption of the dialogue.

14. The emergence on the Kosovar Albanian political scene of the KLA, as a force commanding considerable influence throughout the Albanian community, has introduced a new element into the idea of negotiations. Representatives of the KLA believe that the political parties should accept the existence and importance of the armed organization and that none of the parties represents the KLA. Neither do they recognize the leadership of Ibrahim Rugova. The KLA further rules out the possibility of declaring a ceasefire should the talks resume without them being accepted as one of the negotiating parties.

15. The commitment of the international community is of immense importance for the ongoing efforts to defuse the threat of a further escalation of the conflict. During their visits to both Belgrade and Pristina, international visitors have tried to pressure the two belligerent parties to stop the use of violence. The string of measures adopted with the purpose of bringing more pressure to bear on the Belgrade authorities includes the 8 June European Union decision (which went into force on 23 June) to freeze within the boundaries of the European Union all the fixed assets and financial resources of both the Federal

Republic of Yugoslavia and Serbia, and the 29 June resolution of the Council of Ministers banning all flights by JAT airlines as well as other Yugoslav carriers to EU destinations.

OSCE ACTIVITIES

16. Following the communiqué released in Moscow on 16 June at the close of the meeting between President Yeltsin and President Miloevi, Mr. Bronislaw Geremek, Minister of Foreign Affairs of Poland and Chairman-in-Office of OSCE, wrote a letter to Mr. Milosevic requesting clarification of some points of the communiqué's paragraph dealing with OSCE. The letter elicited a response from Mr. Z. Jovanovic, Minister for Foreign Affairs of the Federal Republic of Yugoslavia, who wrote to Mr. Geremek inviting a delegation of political directors to Belgrade "to start negotiations simultaneously on the acceptance of the OSCE mission in Kosovo and Metohija and the regulation of the membership rights of the Federal Republic of Yugoslavia in the organization". In his reply Mr. Geremek proclaimed his "readiness to begin exploratory talks" between OSCE and the Federal Republic of Yugoslavia.

17. The exploratory talks, which were held at Belgrade on 3 July, revealed that the Federal Republic of Yugoslavia did not accept a return of the Gonzalez Mission and/or the OSCE Long-term Mission unless the problem of the Federal Republic's participation in OSCE had first been resolved. Moreover, the Federal Republic also rejected the idea of a step-by-step "re-establishment" of its membership. As a gesture of "good will", the Federal Republic invited an "OSCE assessment mission" to visit the Federal Republic of Yugoslavia without any preconditions.

18. As a result of the above invitation, an OSCE technical assessment mission visited the Federal Republic of Yugoslavia from 14 to 22 July 1998. Its report and conclusions are attached to the present report as a source of additional information.

Chairman-in-Office of the Organization for Security and Cooperation in Europe, Warsaw, 24 July 1998.

Enclosure: Organization for Security and Cooperation in Europe:
Report of the Technical Assessment Mission on its Visit to the Federal Republic of Yugoslavia from 14 to 22 July 1998

I. MISSION OBJECTIVE

1. The mission had the task set by the OSCE Chairman-in-Office to go to the Federal Republic of Yugoslavia to make a preliminary assessment of the relations between OSCE and the Federal Republic of Yugoslavia, with a view to facilitating the mission of Mr. Felipe Gonzalez (as Personal Representative of the OSCE Chairman-in-Office) and a comprehensive resolution of these issues, including the re-establishment of the OSCE Long-term Mission to the Federal Republic of Yugoslavia on the basis of OSCE Permanent Council decision 218 of 11 March 1998.

II. FRAMEWORK

2. In Belgrade, the 12-member delegation, headed by Ambassador Hansjorg Eiff of Germany, met with the Foreign Minister of the Federal Republic of Yugoslavia at the outset as well as towards the end of the visit, and had discussions with Federal and/or Serbian ministers responsible for the media, national and minority rights, and culture; the Chairman and three other members of the Foreign Relations Committee of the Parliament of the Federal Republic of Yugoslavia (representing predominantly government opinion); the Serbian Commissioner for Refugees; leaders of the political opposition; non-governmental organizations (NGOs) (including human rights groups); representatives of the independent media; and international organizations. In Belgrade it also met with representatives of regional parties from the Sandjak and Vojvodina. The Head of Mission met twice with the foreign policy adviser of President Milosevic.

3. In Kosovo, the mission met the local Serb authorities; political representatives of Kosovo Albanians (including several members of the negotiating team); the Albanian Students Union; the Helsinki Committee; and the Kosovo Diplomatic Observer Mission.

4. In Montenegro, the mission was received by President Djukanovi and met with: the Prime Minister; the Chairman of the National Assembly; the Foreign Minister and the Minister responsible for ethnic minorities; and representatives of the media and of human rights organizations.

5. The Yugoslav authorities cooperated fully with the mission and provided assistance to facilitate its work.

6. The mission focused its work on the following issues:
- The possible return of the long-term missions to Kosovo, Sandjak and Vojvodina;
- The mission of the Personal Representative of the Chairman-in-Office for the Federal Republic of Yugoslavia;
- The situation on the ground in Kosovo, Sandjak and Vojvodina insofar as it would affect the work of the returned missions and the mission by the Personal Representative of the Chairman-in-Office;
- Recent developments in the areas of concern (e.g. media, judiciary, legal and electoral systems) highlighted by Mr. Gonzalez in his 1996 report;
- Possible participation of the Federal Republic of Yugoslavia in the work of OSCE.

III. RETURN OF THE LONG TERM MISSIONS TO KOSOVO, SANDJAK AND VOJVODINA

7. There was a general recognition of the usefulness of the work of the three missions prior to their interruption in 1993. All regional groupings favoured a return of the missions to their areas. One Vojvodina representative suggested that that region might be covered from a base located more centrally in Belgrade, if a mission was to be established there. While some Albanians expressed reservations as to whether the mission in Kosovo could have prevented the serious deterioration of the situation, they believed that its presence could have served as a partial check on the violence. Many interlocutors noted that the missions generally could help to bridge the gap between the communities, and serve as a reassurance, and point of contact for the minorities. It was suggested that the missions could be given the mandate of an ombudsman, to receive and assess complaints about human rights violations submitted to them.

8. The Government of the Federal Republic of Yugoslavia side, both in Belgrade and in Pristina, also acknowledged the fairness and accuracy of the missions' reporting and recognized that, in the current situation, a mission could play a useful role in Kosovo. It was clear they would consider the possibility of a mission returning to Kosovo alone. They noted that OSCE missions were only dispatched to OSCE participating States. They placed the return of the mission to Kosovo firmly in the context of the agreement between President Milosevic and President Yeltsin in Moscow on 16 June and linked it to what they described as the simultaneous readmission of the Federal Republic of Yugoslavia to OSCE. The OSCE delegation stressed that the return of the missions was insufficient to secure the participation of the Federal Republic of Yugoslavia in the organization, which would require a consensus decision of all OSCE member States.

IV. ATTITUDE EXPRESSED TOWARDS THE MISSION OF THE PERSONAL REPRESENTATIVE OF THE OSCE CHAIRMAN-IN-OFFICE

9. The assessment mission emphasized to all its interlocutors its role of preparing the ground for the mission by the Personal Representative of the OSCE Chairman-in-Office, Mr. Felipe Gonzalez, and made it clear that it was no substitute for that mission. It also stressed that Mr. Gonzalez's mandate covered the whole of the Federal Republic of Yugoslavia, including Kosovo. The Foreign Minister said the Gonzalez mission of 1996 had been completed. The Federal Republic of Yugoslavia had not been consulted on the second mission. The Federal Republic was ready to discuss this once the question of its participation in the OSCE was settled. The Chairman of the Federal Parliament Foreign Relations Committee went further, stating that the mandate could not cover internal issues and criticizing the earlier report of Mr. Gonzalez.

10. All opposition political parties to whom the mission spoke as well as all representatives of the ethnic minorities, the independent media and human rights groups favoured a continuation of the Gonzalez mission. Many said so publicly during the visit. Among the most keen were those parties which had boycotted the Serbian Republic and presidential elections in 1997 because they had believed the electoral conditions were unacceptable. Some of the Albanian representatives noted that any international mediator on Kosovo would need strong international backing, and that there were already others involved in that field.

V. KOSOVO

11. Federal Foreign Minister Jovanovic, like other government representatives, emphasized the official view that the Kosovo problem was one of separatism and terrorism, and not of national and minority rights. The Government of the Federal Republic of Yugoslavia needed to defend the interests of all the residents of Kosovo. The situation could be resolved only through direct dialogue between the parties on a series of confidence-building measures and forms of self-governance for the province, including different forms of autonomy. The outcome must respect the territorial integrity of Serbia and the Federal Republic of Yugoslavia and the rights of all nationalities and minorities, according to European standards. The Minister also highlighted the progress he said the Federal Republic had made on humanitarian issues. He called for European countries to stop what he claimed was the provision of assistance to Albanian extremists in Kosovo from groups based on their territory.

12. The mission's visit to Pristina was depressing. The total lack of trust between the two communities, which was reflected both in an absence of everyday human contact and a lack of communication between representatives of the two communities, was striking. This was one of the key reasons for the failure of the two sides to negotiate. It was very obvious that the most pressing need was for an immediate cessation of hostilities. The representatives of the local Serb authorities insisted that the Serb security forces only responded to attacks made on them by the so-called Kosovo Liberation Army (KLA). They claimed that the continuing presence of Serbian special units in the province was only necessary because of KLA attacks. They also denied that the Serbs had used disproportionate force in their engagements with the KLA. They handed the mission lists of names of 30 Albanians and 14 Serbs who they said had been killed by the KLA, together with a list of 111 Serbs, Albanians and other minority nationals who they claimed had been kidnapped since the beginning of the year. They said they were ready to continue the dialogue which had begun with the meeting between President Milosevic and Mr. Rugova on 15 May. But the Albanian side had failed to appear for the scheduled meetings since 22 May.

13. Representatives of the Kosovar Albanian political parties and community emphasized the need to find a rapid solution to the situation. They insisted that the KLA was a defensive grouping of Albanians who had taken up arms to protect themselves against the Serbian security forces. They highlighted the growing popularity of the KLA and the diminishing support for political parties as a whole. Some openly admitted that they had offered to serve as that body's political wing. But to date no party was fulfilling that role. Most significantly, no political personality distanced himself from the KLA.

14. The Albanians insisted that no dialogue could begin while, they maintained, Serb security forces continued attacking the Kosovar Albanian population. They stressed the importance of international involvement in the process, into which they said the KLA needed to be brought. All agreed that Kosovo's rights as set out in the 1974 Constitution were non-negotiable and constituted the starting point for any dialogue. Some believed that there should be an interim arrangement, including confidence-building measures, before talks on a final settlement could begin. In this context some parties looked to intervention by the North Atlantic Treaty Organization (NATO) to guarantee the security environment in the region. While some said the outcome of this dialogue should not be prejudged, it was clear that all interlocutors saw independence as the final goal. None were prepared to accept autonomy, to whatever degree, as the final outcome. There seemed to be no readiness either to accept a moratorium on the status issue.

15. The Kosovo Albanians told the mission that some 300 Albanians had been killed, and 150,000 displaced, since the beginning of the year. The Office of the United Nations High Commissioner for Refugees (UNHCR) said it had identified the whereabouts of some 57,000 internally displaced persons in the province but believed the total number was over 100,000. UNHCR said that, since mid-June, it had in principle been given free access to all areas by both the Serb authorities and the KLA. For the time being, food supplies seemed to be adequate. However, if the situation continued to deteriorate, the international community should be aware that the supply of food to the population could become very difficult once winter came. The Government of the Federal Republic of Yugoslavia said it had asked the Albanian Government to allow the Serbian Commissioner for Refugees to visit northern Albania, to meet the Kosovo refugees and to encourage them to return. So far the Federal Republic had not received any direct reply from Tirana. (This issue is being pursued by the Austrian European Union (EU) Presidency.) If a bilateral agreement could be reached, UNHCR would provide the logistics.

16. The Government of the Federal Republic of Yugoslavia said that it favoured a census held under OSCE auspices in Kosovo to establish the ethnic breakdown in the province.

VI. SANDJAK

17. The mission's interlocutors placed the problems in the Sandjak in the context of the loss by the Muslims of their status as a nation (which they had held under the former Socialist Federal Republic of Yugoslavia) with the creation of the Federal Republic of Yugoslavia in 1992. Stress was placed upon the polarization between Muslims and Serbs, which encouraged voters to opt for parties representing more extreme ethnic options, and the resulting increase in tension between the two communities. The mission was told that Muslims were not adequately represented in key positions in State institutions, such as those of senior police officer and school headmaster. While the most serious human rights violations in the areas had occurred in the early 1990s, the mission was told that in July 1997, the Government had removed the elected Muslim local authorities in Novi Pazar on questionable legal grounds. It was noted that, since that action, no fresh elections had been called. Nor had appeals to the Constitutional and Supreme courts produced any response. This had led people to lose faith in the parliamentary system and the country's institutions. It could also encourage the radicalization of the population.

18. The attention of the mission was also drawn to the problems caused by the arrival in the Sandjak of refugees from Kosovo.

VII. VOJVODINA

19. The mission noted that none of the Serbian and Hungarian regional party interlocutors from Vojvodina said they were seeking territorial autonomy. However, the representatives of one non-ethnic party pointed out that the return of territorial autonomy to Kosovo could lead to similar demands for Vojvodina and to unrest among the population. Most interlocutors were seeking increased personal rights (and in the case of some Serbs, a political decentralization of power to the Province of Vojvodina). One Hungarian party had had contracts with the Government to try to improve the community's position. This had led to the establishment of a consultative body for the province's main minority groups and the return of the teaching faculty from Sombor to the town of Subotica. While most interlocutors said the situation had improved since 1992, they pointed out that there were still outstanding concerns. These included State interference in local government (most recently in Titel) and the need for greater personal autonomy in fields such as education and social affairs.

20. The Croats claimed that as a "new minority" they did not enjoy any internationally recognized rights. They also asserted that when the citizenship documents from the former Socialist Federal Republic of Yugoslavia (which gave "Croat" as the nationality) of some Croats had

expired, they had been refused new citizenship documents for the Federal Republic of Yugoslavia.

VIII. MONTENEGRO

21. In Montenegro the mission's discussions centred on the conflict in Kosovo, the constitutional position of the Republic of Montenegro and the problems of democracy-building in the Republic. The Montenegrin leadership underlined strongly that their Republic and people had no part in the conflict in Kosovo. They quoted a Montenegrin National Assembly resolution stating that neither Montenegrin territory nor Montenegrin conscripts should be used in the conflict. They also highlighted the difficult situation created by the flow of refugees (an estimated 20,000) from the conflict area to the Republic, and they called for an increase in international relief assistance. The President stressed that the full involvement of an international mediator, and in particular OSCE, would be crucial, especially to re-establish mutual trust.

22. On the future status of Kosovo, the President ruled out both the options of retaining the status quo or making insignificant changes on the one hand, and independence on the other. He also rejected the option of giving Kosovo the status of a third republic in the Federation. If the latter occurred, Montenegro would reconsider its own place within that body. He seemed to favour some sort of far-reaching autonomy for Kosovo within Serbia, although he recognized the Kosovar Albanian dislike of any connection with Serbia.

23. President Djukanovic also set out Montenegro's current difficulties within the Federation, which he had discussed with Federal President Milosevic in the course of two recent meetings. Montenegro insisted on the right to nominate the Federal Prime Minister (in place of Bulatovic, who although a Montenegrin, was now Djukanovic's main opponent); and to appoint half of the judges to the Federal Supreme and Constitutional courts; as well as to have equal rights with Serbia in the Central Bank.

24. The government representatives painted a positive picture of developments in the field of human rights, freedom of the media, the rule of law and the independence of the judiciary. Other representatives of human rights groups and the independent media gave a more critical assessment. Nevertheless, there was an impression that definite progress had been made, especially since the last presidential election. The mission was told that there was still room for improvement, especially in the attitude of magistrates, civil servants and the police. Both government and non-government representatives had high expectations of what could be achieved in this respect through continued cooperation with the Office for Democratic Institutions and Human Rights.

IX. RECENT DEVELOPMENTS IN THE FIELDS OF HUMAN RIGHTS, THE MEDIA, AND JUDICIARY, LEGAL AND ELECTORAL SYSTEMS

25. The mission's findings on these issues are necessarily incomplete as it could not cover in depth the full range of questions in the time available.

A. The media

Summary. While the situation of the print media had improved and a network of independent radio and TV stations had been set up outside Belgrade, serious concern still remained in respect of the State media, the overall legislative framework governing the information sector and the Government's implementation of that legislation.

26. In the print media field, the mission noted that the number of independent publications had grown over the last two years. There is now a wide range of dailies as well as some weekly magazines, reflecting a diversity of opinion. These include a variety of publications, among them some dailies, in the Albanian language. But the mission was told that sales of newspapers were dropping and that the Yugoslav population looked mainly to the electronic media, in particular television, as its main source of information. It was also informed that the only factory producing roto-press paper in Serbia gave priority to pro-Government newspapers, which meant that many independent outlets had to import paper at higher prices.

27. In the electronic media field, the ANEM network of 33 independent local radio stations (including some stations run by municipalities in which the opposition had been victorious in the 1996 local elections) was established in 1997. The network is centred on Radio B 92 in Belgrade and covers some 60 per cent of the country. Opposition politicians said that this enabled them to gain access to the electronic media outside Belgrade. But serious problems with the legal framework governing the electronic media remain. Frequency allocation is in the hands of the Government; there is no independent regulatory council. The mission was told that the recent frequency competition (the first in five years, although it was said legislation prescribed annual competitions) was neither transparent nor strictly in accordance with the law. The Government had rejected the applications of a number of independent stations on technical grounds and had signed easily broken contracts, rather than issuing permits for the frequency licences. The media environment was governed by a series of laws and ministries at both the Federal and Republic levels, whose requirements and actions were often mutually contradictory. The Government had recently closed down independent stations (two of which were ANEM members) on the grounds that they were broadcasting without a licence, even though hundreds of others were doing likewise. These included the first attempt to establish a multi-ethnic radio station in Kosovo.

28. Concern was also expressed over the domination of the Serbian State television system, which constitutes the main source of information for the population as a whole. Its output totally supports the government line. It is the only TV network covering the whole of Serbia. Opposition leaders told the mission that they had no access to State TV and radio apart from the legally required appearances during election campaign. Independent analysis of its coverage of events during the 1997 elections showed a clear bias in favour of Government candidates. All independent media interlocutors said that Serbian State radio and TV and other pro-Government media were given preferential access to the Government's central information system, with independent outlets mainly being denied access to official press conferences, press releases, etc. This was denied by the Government.

B. Elections

Summary. There is still a lack of confidence in the electoral system in opposition and other non-governmental circles.

29. A number of interlocutors, and in particular those members of the opposition who had boycotted the 1997 Serbian Republic and presidential elections, expressed their lack of faith in the electoral system, which the OSCE observer mission saw as flawed in many respects. The critics focused in particular on the Government's decision fundamentally to change the number of constitutional units shortly before the elections without gaining the agreement of all the main political parties; the bias of the State media; and the election process in Kosovo. The mission was unable to examine the electoral system in detail. It will be necessary to follow up these concerns in advance of the next round of elections.

C. The Legal Process

Summary. There is a lack of confidence in non-official circles in the legal system.

30. A large majority of non-governmental interlocutors expressed a lack of confidence in the legal institutions and processes. The mission was told that all key positions in the main institutions, including the judiciary, were filled by Government supporters. This made it difficult to seek redress against the executive branch through the judicial system. On those occasions when verdicts against the Government were handed down, they were often not implemented by the State institutions, e.g. the court decision to overrule the expulsion of a Croat family from their house in the Radical Party-controlled municipality of Zemun; and the failure by the Government to return to Radio Pirot its equipment in accordance with a court order to that effect.

31. The Serbian Parliament in May 1998 adopted a law regulating the status of universities which reduced the status of all universities to economic enterprises. The post of Rector is identical to that of a company director. He and all the deans are appointed by the Government.

Each university is run by a 15-member board, including 9 nominated (6 professors, 3 students) individuals from the university, and 6 political appointees. Heads of departments are appointed by the Dean, while other teaching staff are nominated by the Dean after consulting the Education Minister. Students are not allowed to form any political, religious or ethnic organizations at the university and are separated into three groups: those paid for from the budget; those partly financed from the budget; and those self-financed.

32. The Government justified the universities' loss of autonomy on the grounds that their financier (the State) had the right to administer them. It also claimed that the law gave the universities autonomy in respect of education and scientific and research work.

X. ATTITUDE TO THE PARTICIPATION OF THE FEDERAL REPUBLIC OF YUGOSLAVIA IN OSCE

33. There was general support from both the Government of the Federal Republic of Yugoslavia and the Serbian opposition for future participation by the Federal Republic in OSCE, but a widely diverging range of views on the conditionality which it needed to satisfy to secure full participation. The Foreign Minister of the Federal Republic expressed his Government's interest in full participation in OSCE at as early a date as possible. It was wrong that the Federal Republic was the only European country excluded. He claimed that it was already applying the organization's standards despite its non-participation. He insisted on the linkage he said had been established in the Milosevic/Yeltsin agreement between the start of simultaneous talks on the return of the long-term missions and the simultaneous membership of the organization by the Federal Republic of Yugoslavia (the text actually speaks of readiness to start negotiations with OSCE simultaneously on receiving its mission to Kosovo and on the restoration of the membership of the Federal Republic in OSCE). He said that the Federal Republic did not maintain it was the sole successor State of the former Socialist Federal Republic of Yugoslavia, but it did claim to be the continuing State thereof, and indeed of Serbia and Montenegro as established by the Congress of Berlin in 1878.

34. The degree of conditionality for participation sought by interlocutors in Belgrade varied from those who thought immediate membership was necessary, to those who believed membership would play into the hands of the Government and therefore favoured greater conditionality, e.g. the return of the Gonzalez mission and a commitment to make progress on the issues it addressed.

35. For the Kosovar Albanians, this did not appear to be a major issue. But all who expressed a view on the subject linked significant progress on Kosovo, including in one case the complete solution of the Kosovo problem, to OSCE membership. Of those advocating independence, one at least would like to see an independent Kosovo in OSCE.

36. The President of Montenegro was against participation by the Federal Republic of Yugoslavia in OSCE unless it demonstrated a cooperative attitude, not only in words but also in deeds. He reminded the mission of the Federal Republic's conduct following the suspension of Kosovo-related sanctions in May.

XI. CONCLUSIONS

37. The perceptibly deteriorating situation in Kosovo, together with the relative lack of progress on issues identified by Mr. Gonzalez in his December 1996 report, underlined the need for a rapid re-establishment of the Long-term Missions to Kosovo, Sandjak and Vojvodina and the return of the Personal Representative of the OSCE Chairman-in-Office to the Federal Republic of Yugoslavia. The Federal Republic was only prepared to consider discussing the terms of the mandate of the OSCE Chairman-in-Office's Personal Representative, Mr. Gonzalez, once the question of its participation in OSCE had been settled. There seemed to be a general willingness on all sides within the Federal Republic of Yugoslavia that the country should participate in the work of OSCE. But the degree of conditionality which it would have to satisfy to achieve this varied considerably.

38. The mission believed that its visit strongly underlined the need for the return of the Long-term Mission. Care would have to be taken that the work of the mission and other international efforts, such as the Kosovo Diplomatic Observer Mission, were not duplicated, and an assessment made, in the light of the situation at the time, of the extent to which the existing mandate was still valid. It could address issues such as the stimulation of dialogue between the two communities, serve as an ombudsman on human rights matters and provide some form of coordinating role for international activities in the area.

39. The lack of trust between the two communities in Kosovo, against the background of increasing violence, and the distance between the political positions as to how the conflict could be resolved, strongly reinforced the need for a committed high-level international involvement in the negotiation process.

40. The humanitarian situation needed to be observed carefully, as the supply of food to the population in winter could become very difficult, in particular if the situation in the province continued to deteriorate.

41. Although the scale of the problems of the Muslims in Sandjak was of a different magnitude from those of Kosovo, there was a case for a renewed presence of a long-term mission there.

42. The mission believed that the conditions in Vojvodina were such as to warrant coverage by the Long-term Mission.

43. A case can be made for the Long-term Mission to have its headquarters in Belgrade, with a sizeable presence in Kosovo and perhaps a branch office in the Sandjak.

Since the visit of Mr. Gonzalez in 1996, the situation regarding the media and the judiciary, legal and electoral systems did not appear to have improved significantly, apart from some progress in the field of print media. There was a continuing lack of confidence in non-official circles in the legal system, including the legislation relating to the election process. Developments in these fields needed to be monitored with a view to an ongoing dialogue with the authorities, including offering expertise on how progress could be made.

44. The Law on the University gave great cause for concern, as it provided for government control over the administration and teaching staff and limited the possibility of political expression by students. It fell short of relevant European standards.

45. While the Federal Republic of Yugoslavia indicated its readiness to accept the return of the Long-term Mission to Kosovo, it was only prepared to do so in return for the simultaneous participation of the Federal Republic in OSCE.

46. The mission recommends the continuation of talks between the Chairman-in-Office and the Federal Republic of Yugoslavia on issues of relevance to relations between OSCE and the Federal Republic.

Annex II: Letter Dated 14 July 1998 from the Secretary-General of the North Atlantic Treaty Organization Addressed to the Secretary-General

I am writing to inform you that the military authorities of the North Atlantic Treaty Organization (NATO) have completed their assessment of possible support for a monitoring regime in connection with Security Council resolution 1160 (1998), as noted in my previous letter to you of 11 June 1998. Having considered a variety of options, the North Atlantic Council has decided at this stage to proceed with the SFOR option to step up its efforts, within its existing mission and capabilities, to monitor the Bosnian border with the Federal Republic of Yugoslavia. In this context I can confirm that the necessary arrangements have been put in place to forward any relevant information on suspected violations in the SFOR area of operations via the monthly report to the United Nations or on an ad hoc basis as necessary.

Should circumstances change I will write to you again. In the meantime allow me to take this opportunity to assure you of our continuing close cooperation.
(Signed) Javier Solana

120. Report of the Secretary-General Prepared pursuant to Security Council Resolution 1160 (1998), UN Doc. S/1998/834, 4 September 1998

I. Introduction

1. The present report is submitted pursuant to Security Council resolution 1160 (1998) of 31 March 1998. It covers the period since my last report, of 5 August 1998 (S/1998/712).

II. Security Council Committee Established Pursuant to Resolution 1160 (1998)

2. As at 31 August 1998, in addition to those States listed in my earlier reports (S/1998/608 and S/1998/712), Albania, Chile, Croatia and the Republic of Korea reported to the Committee established pursuant to paragraph 12 of resolution 1160 (1998) on the steps they had taken to give effect to the prohibitions imposed by that resolution.

3. In a letter dated 18 August, the Permanent Representative of Austria to the United Nations, in his capacity as the representative of the Presidency of the European Union, transmitted to the Chairman of the Committee the first monthly report of the European Community Monitoring Mission containing observations on violations of Security Council resolution 1160 (1998). The report covered the Mission's activities in July and early August and was submitted in accordance with the European Union's earlier pledge to contribute to international efforts to monitor the embargo and to report to the Committee any relevant information. The Mission has instructed its regional centres in Tirana, Belgrade and Skopje, as well as its coordination centres in Pristina and Podgorica, to be particularly alert to the possibility of weapons transfers from their respective areas of responsibility into the Federal Republic of Yugoslavia.

4. At its 3rd meeting, held on 19 August 1998, the Committee decided, inter alia, to renew its appeal of 7 May 1998 to all States, international organizations and regional organizations to provide information on violations or suspected violations of the prohibitions imposed by Security Council resolution 1160 (1998). That appeal was issued on 26 August 1998 by the Chairman of the Committee, Mr. Celso L. N. Amorim (Brazil), on behalf of the Committee (SC/6564).

5. In my previous report (S/1998/712), I submitted, in accordance with paragraph 15 of Security Council resolution 1160 (1998), my observations and recommendations for the establishment of a comprehensive regime to monitor the implementation of the prohibitions imposed in paragraph 8 of the resolution. If the Council concurs with the suggested arrangements, I will proceed accordingly.

III. Situation in Kosovo

6. Continued international efforts to facilitate a political solution to the Kosovo crisis have had limited results. As the Security Council is aware, the situation in Kosovo remains volatile. In mid-July and early August, heavy fighting occurred in the towns of Orahovac and Malisevo, as well as in the Suva Reka and Stimlje areas. By mid-August, fierce fighting was raging in the western parts of Djakovica, Decani and Pec. Towards the end of August, fighting continued in several areas: west of Pec in Rugovska Klisura area, along the Stimlje-Suva Reka road, on the Komorane-Kijevo stretch of the Pristina-Pec Road and near the Pristina airport. Although the scale of fighting between the security forces of the Federal Republic of Yugoslavia and the Kosovo Liberation Army (KLA) has decreased, and the Government has announced that life is returning to normal, it is evident that the conflict continues and any prediction of its end would be premature. The negotiating process has not been renewed and tensions along the border between the Federal Republic of Yugoslavia and Albania have been evident.

HUMANITARIAN CONCERNS

7. An estimated 600 to 700 civilians have been killed in the fighting in Kosovo since March. The conflict has resulted in the estimated cumulative displacement of over 230,000 persons. This is a nearly tenfold increase compared to the figure of 25,000 persons estimated by the Office of the United Nations High Commissioner for Refugees (UNHCR) to have been displaced during the first four months of 1998. The vast majority of those currently displaced by the conflict are within Kosovo (170,000). Others have moved to locations in Montenegro (33,500) and Serbia (20,000). Some 14,000 refugees are currently in Albania. Deserted towns and villages, as well as destroyed houses, slaughtered livestock and burned fields, bear witness to the scale of displacement and destruction in Kosovo. However, it has not always been possible fully to gauge the level of population movement inside Kosovo, owing to the increasingly insecure environment, impediments to access and the fluidity of the population movements. Thousands of civilians are constantly in flight to escape attacks by government forces.

8. According to UNHCR estimates, there could be up to 50,000 displaced people in Kosovo who have been forced from their homes into the woods and mountains. These people are the most vulnerable and are in need of urgent help. Despite assurances from the authorities, access is hindered, and the immediate priority of the humanitarian agencies is to find these groups and to deliver essential relief. It is clear that if these people remain in their current locations over the winter, they will be at serious risk of death. It remains a priority to assist them to return to their homes, or to move them to host families, or, as a last resort, into collective centres where assistance can be more reliably provided.

9. The authorities of the Federal Republic of Yugoslavia have committed themselves to the creation of conditions for the return of refugees and displaced persons to their homes in Kosovo. The reality on the ground, however, is that inadequate security conditions and the continued destruction of homes are making return to many areas virtually impossible. There are disturbing reports that some returnees, mostly young men, were taken by police for "informative talks". In some cases, the police have prevented returnees from harvesting crops. The Assistant High Commissioner for Refugees, Mr. Soren Jessen-Petersen, who visited the area from 18 to 22 August, reported one instance when the police, occupying the house of the potential returnee, vandalized it and did not allow the owner to move back in. Such practices, as well as any potential attempts to change the ethnic balance in Kosovo, are unacceptable. I am also concerned by unconfirmed reports that some Kosovo Albanian groups, in pursuit of their political interests, may be blocking the return process in order to prolong the humanitarian crisis and maintain international attention on Kosovo.

10. In order to expedite the return process and to facilitate political progress on the Kosovo issue, there is a critical need to promote confidence-building measures between the parties in conflict. As most refugees and internally displaced persons have no trust in the willingness or ability of the Serbian or federal authorities to protect them, all necessary measures should be taken to bridge the confidence gap. In this connection, UNHCR strongly argues the urgent need to strengthen the international presence in Kosovo. The government authorities in the Federal Republic of Yugoslavia, who bear primary responsibility for the well-being and security of all its citizens, should unambiguously commit themselves to guaranteeing the safety of those returnees not proved to have participated in terrorist activities. The authorities must undertake to prosecute any member of the security forces involved in the mistreatment of innocent civilians. Another important factor is that many internally displaced persons have no place to go, since a significant number of houses have been destroyed or burned. The authorities must bring to justice all those involved in the deliberate destruction of property. They must also make every effort to provide assistance for the reconstruction of damaged and destroyed homes.

11. A prolongation of the Government's present policies is likely to result in further displacement of the wider population. This is particularly worrying because of the approaching winter, which could transform what is currently a humanitarian crisis into a humanitarian catastrophe. It is likely that most of the displacement will continue to be concentrated within Kosovo itself, although an increasing number of those displaced appear to be electing to move to other areas within the Federal Republic of Yugoslavia (Montenegro in particular) and abroad.

12. At the beginning of 1998, there were 1,800 refugees from Croatia and Bosnia and Herzegovina housed in 28 collective centres in Kosovo. UNHCR has requested the federal authorities to transfer the refugees to safe locations outside the conflict areas, but this has not yet been done. Regular visits to the collective centres reveal that the numbers of refugees therein have dropped, as most refugees with the health and means to do so have made their own way out; their present location and condition are unknown. The options of voluntary repatriation and resettlement are being pursued. So far some 600 are being assisted to return to Croatia at their request. Interest in repatriation, especially among the elderly, is increasing and it is expected that the number of requests for return will grow in the near future. More than 1,000 refugees have now requested resettlement abroad.

13. In response to the crisis, the humanitarian agencies continue to identify the location and needs of the displaced, to provide protection when possible, and to deliver assistance from available resources. At the time of writing, the municipalities in Kosovo affected by the conflict include Decane, Djakovica, Glogovac, Istok, Klina, Lipljan, Orahovac, Pec, Srbica, Stimlje and Suva Reka. Most of the displaced within Kosovo are staying within these areas, though some have moved to other municipalities. Populations in other areas, while not directly involved in the fighting, are increasingly affected by the conflict. Many have little or no access to food supplies, as stocks in shops have, for the most part, not been replenished, and medical facilities face major supply problems. Livestock has been lost or slaughtered, crops lie unharvested in the fields, and fodder is scarce, rendered inaccessible or destroyed. It is feared that many wounded in the conflict areas have no access to medical services.

14. The most worrying problem in Montenegro is the impact of internally displaced persons on the demographic balance and the high burden they place on that Republic of the Federal Republic of Yugoslavia, since they already represent more than 10 per cent of its population. In Montenegro, UNHCR is increasing its budget to cope with the needs of new arrivals from Kosovo. The focus in the short term is on assisting the most vulnerable host families and to winterize public buildings used to shelter the internally displaced. A similar approach is required in northern Albania, although in the medium term those refugees willing to go there should be relocated to the south in order to decongest Bajram Curri and to move the refugees away from the area, which has become a KLA base. The security situation has become a major concern for the humanitarian agencies in northern Albania.

HUMAN RIGHTS

15. The human rights situation in Kosovo has been marked by widespread violations. Acting under the mandates of the United Nations High Commissioner for Human Rights and the Special Rapporteur on the situation of human rights in Bosnia and Herzegovina, the Republic of Croatia and the Federal Republic of Yugoslavia, the Office of the United Nations High Commissioner for Human Rights is engaged in monitoring and reporting on the human rights situation in the whole of the Federal Republic of Yugoslavia. The Office of the High Commissioner opened its office in Belgrade in March 1996 and has in addition maintained a continuous monitoring presence in Pristina since March 1998.

16. The Office of the High Commissioner has received increasing reports of persons being arbitrarily arrested for questioning and kept in pre-trial detention for periods well beyond the legal time limit. It has registered more than 200 persons who are reported to be in police detention, and another 200 or more are reported by various sources as "missing". Some persons are believed to be in unacknowledged detention. While most of these people have been arrested in connection with police operations in the field, there is a growing number of cases in which Kosovo Albanian political activists, lawyers, humanitarian workers and medical personnel are being arrested and interrogated by the police. The Office of the High Commissioner has been informed that detainees have recently been transferred to Belgrade from prisons in Kosovo. Lawyers and family members say that they encounter serious problems in obtaining permission to see those detained. Lawyers have reportedly been prevented from speaking with their clients in private for longer than five minutes and have not been allowed by the police to speak with their clients in the Albanian language. There are many reports of torture and ill-treatment during pre-trial detention, including at least four alleged cases of death in custody. The Office of the High Commissioner has on several occasions written to the Serbian Ministry of the Interior inquiring about cases brought to its attention. In Kosovo, the Office is monitoring trials of persons charged with crimes against the state, including "terrorism". Some defendants have reportedly been tortured while under interrogation. In these politically sensitive trials there are serious concerns regarding the independence of the courts and defendants' access to legal counsel.

17. Also a serious cause for concern are reports that a number of Serb, Kosovo Albanian and Roma civilians, as well as Serbian police officers, have been abducted since early April by armed Kosovo Albanians, believed to be KLA members. The Office of the High Commissioner has interviewed relatives and family members of abductees as well as eyewitnesses to abductions. The Yugoslav authorities have indicated that more than 179 civilians and police were abducted since the beginning of the conflict. On 26 and 27 August, in Klecka, 22 persons believed to be abductees reportedly were killed and their bodies burned in a makeshift crematorium. The precise number of victims and the circumstances of their death are being investigated. International monitors have also visited the site.

IV. Humanitarian Activities

18. The provision of humanitarian assistance is of great urgency, particularly with the onset of the harsh winter months in the Balkans. In cooperation with the International Committee of the Red Cross, international non-governmental organizations and local organizations, United Nations agencies are attempting to deal with the crisis in the face of difficult conditions and limited funding. Within Kosovo, UNHCR has been escorting multi-agency convoys to deliver humanitarian assistance to internally displaced persons; the first priority in this regard has been to help those living in the open, who are, unfortunately, the most difficult to reach.

19. Given the growing crisis in Kosovo and the commensurate increase in humanitarian needs, the international humanitarian assistance programme has become an indispensable factor in ensuring the provision of efficacious and cost-effective relief assistance at the local, national and regional level. UNHCR continues to act as the focal point for inter-agency coordination on issues pertaining to the crisis in Kosovo. Capacity for inter-agency and interregional information flow and coordination continues to be undertaken by UNHCR with support from the Office for the Coordination of Humanitarian Affairs. A purpose of the recent visit to Kosovo by the Assistant High Commissioner for Refugees was to assess the humanitarian situation on the ground, including issues of access, security and other operational concerns and constraints.

20. Pursuant to its mandated role as lead agency in the region, UNHCR maintains close liaison with representatives of the Government of the Federal Republic of Yugoslavia as well as with members of the Kosovo Albanian community and the respective Red Cross Societies to share relevant information on population movements and assistance needs. In this connection, it is worth noting that UNHCR has worked out a division of labour for humanitarian assistance in Kosovo. It also liaises with the diplomatic community and human rights organizations in Belgrade, Pristina and Montenegro as well as with the Kosovo Diplomatic Observer Mission, the European Community Monitoring Mission and relevant diplomatic missions. Regular briefings are provided on current developments and the monitoring of the safety of displaced persons and refugees.

21. The military operations and civil strife of the past months, resulting in the mass displacement of civilian populations, coupled with the disruption of trade and the failure to harvest crops, have also worsened the food security situation of internally displaced persons and other affected populations. The World Food Programme's intervention in the food sector has been designed to prevent hunger and malnutrition

among refugees and displaced persons, as well as among affected populations in conflict areas. UNHCR has a small provision in its budget to cover special dietary food requirements and supplementary food, to assist the most needy during the winter months of 1998 especially. A number of non-governmental organizations and the International Committee of the Red Cross/ International Federation of Red Cross Societies have funding to provide food assistance to the affected population in Kosovo as well as to internally displaced persons in Kosovo and Montenegro.

22. In the non-food sector, UNHCR provides such items as blankets, mattresses, hygienic items, heating/cooking stoves and firewood, with special emphasis on the needs of women and children. Winter clothing will be essential in the coming months. UNHCR will make clothing and footwear available from its stocks in the region; non-governmental organizations are expected to supply substantial quantities of clothing and footwear. The United Nations Children's Fund (UNICEF) will complement the activities of UNHCR and its partners through the provision of children's garments, basic household supplies and essential hygiene items required by displaced children and women. These supplies will improve the general health status of the internally displaced persons and help to prevent the outbreak of water-borne and food-borne diseases, lice infestation and other conditions related to living in deprived circumstances.

23. The conflict and population displacement in Kosovo has led to a shortage of essential drugs and to the collapse of basic health services. Children in temporary and inadequate shelter are at risk from common diseases and there is a serious threat of a measles epidemic in the coming months. The World Health Organization (WHO) maintains a coordination role in the public health sector and provides technical guidance to agencies involved in this sector. Activities include the procurement of emergency water supply and chlorination systems, the establishment or improvement of sanitary facilities, the improvement of the emergency health surveillance system and its management, and the strengthening of the management of drugs donations and distribution. Preventive health-care activities, in particular immunization programmes and prenatal care, will be undertaken to compensate for local services which have been severely curtailed because of shortages of trained staff and essential medical supplies. In addition to the activities of WHO, UNICEF will continue to provide special paediatric essential drug kits, together with guidelines for health workers on their use. UNICEF also promotes community health and hygiene education, sound infant-feeding practices and, in collaboration with WHO, assists in the monitoring of the general health and nutritional status of the affected population. Building on the work which began in April this year, UNICEF will seek to re-establish the network of trained care providers in Kosovo, in order to provide trauma screening and psychosocial support for children and families seriously affected by the violence and conflict. WHO continues its activities of psycho-social emergency assistance to the internally displaced persons in Montenegro.

24. Accommodation is one of the major concerns in relation to the well-being of internally displaced persons and affected populations. UNHCR will provide material for emergency repairs; more substantial repairs can be carried out only once relative peace has been restored, and it is hoped that reconstruction may be possible immediately after the 1998/1999 winter. In Montenegro, where a different type of shelter assistance is required, some basic repair and maintenance of the collective centres is foreseen. Assistance will also be provided to host families in an effort to support them and encourage them to continue to extend their hospitality, as resources have already started to dwindle. However, if fighting continues in Kosovo and it is impossible for those now living outside to reach their homes, they may seek to reach Montenegro. This would necessitate the urgent provision of greater resources for collective accommodation.

25. The current conflict has taken a serious toll on education services in Kosovo. UNICEF plans to assist up to 100,000 internally displaced children in Kosovo and other parts of Serbia and up to 20,000 internally displaced children in Montenegro, so that they can start school promptly in September. In Montenegro, UNICEF will concentrate its assistance on providing necessary school materials and basic textbooks for the start of the new school year, and on providing teacher training. In areas of Kosovo with a high influx of internally displaced persons, existing schools will not have the capacity to provide classroom space for all children and alternative arrangements will have to be made. Finally, as a precautionary measure, UNICEF will prepare and print a teachers' manual and posters for use in mine awareness education in primary schools in certain parts of Kosovo. UNHCR will support UNICEF activities and will, in consultation with the Government of Montenegro, provide assistance to carry out sanitation and rehabilitation work at school buildings in Montenegro to increase their capacity. Activities in this sector in Kosovo will depend on the local situation but are expected to be limited at this stage. Working with the legal community and non-governmental organizations, the Office of the United Nations High Commissioner for Human Rights is attempting to produce educational materials that link international human rights standards with domestic law and procedures, particularly in the area of police and judicial procedures. In August, the Office began its first small grants programme for communities and organizations involved in human rights education.

26. Humanitarian agencies can continue to operate only in areas where security conditions permit and access is granted by the relevant authorities. Although access has generally improved, insecurity resulting from fighting often prevents or delays the delivery of aid. In recent weeks, the incidence of cases of restriction of movement and denial of access for humanitarian agencies to certain areas, detention of relief personnel and attacks on relief workers has increased. On 25 August, three relief workers of a local non-governmental organization, the Mother Theresa Society, were killed under fire in a Serbian offensive. In late August, a UNHCR driver of ethnic Serb background was threatened by a KLA member at a KLA checkpoint near Pagarusa while escorting a humanitarian convoy. Humanitarian aid workers must cross numerous checkpoints established by both the police and KLA, often one after another; sometimes relief workers are sandwiched between two checkpoints as neither group will allow them to pass through. Reports of landmines also give cause for concern. While guarantees of access have been given, the security and safety of aid workers remains a real issue and must be addressed by the parties.

27. The most disappointing problem is a lack of resources. Three humanitarian convoys per week do not meet the needs of the affected people. An extension of the United Nations Consolidated Inter-agency Appeal for Humanitarian Assistance Related to the Crisis in Kosovo will be launched by UNHCR and the Office for the Coordination of Humanitarian Affairs in September. It is vital that the international community responds generously to this new appeal so that United Nations agencies may meet the expanding emergency humanitarian needs. The support of donors is critical to enhance the response capacity of agencies participating in this appeal, and to allow them to do their utmost to alleviate the human suffering caused by the conflict in Kosovo.

V. Observations

28. I am alarmed by the lack of progress towards a political settlement in Kosovo and by the further loss of life, displacement of civilian population and destruction of property resulting from the ongoing conflict. It is essential that negotiations get under way so as to break the cycle of disproportionate use of force by the Serbian forces and acts of violence by the Kosovo Albanian paramilitary units by promoting a political resolution of the conflict. On 1 September, I wrote to President Milosevic to underline my alarm at the excessive use of force by Serbian military and police forces, noting that Kosovo Albanian extremists also bear responsibility for their acts of provocation. Persistent tensions on the border between the Federal Republic of Yugoslavia and Albania, including reports of border violations and cross-border shelling, are a further cause of serious concern. As I have indicated, this escalation of tensions risks detrimental consequences for the stability

in the region. In this regard, I wish to reiterate the concern, expressed in my previous report, that United Nations operations in the region could be negatively affected by developments in Kosovo.

29. I continue to believe strongly that there can be no military solution for the crisis. I urge both parties to demonstrate restraint and to start the negotiating process as soon as possible. Efforts by the Contact Group, regional organizations and individual States to put an end to the violence and to create appropriate conditions for a political settlement of the conflict have my full support. For my part, I remain prepared to contribute to these efforts through all resources available to me.

30. As I have outlined above, recent clashes in Kosovo have led to further displacement of civilian population which have borne the brunt of the fighting since March 1998. I urge parties in the Federal Republic of Yugoslavia to assure unhindered humanitarian access to all affected areas and to ensure the security of the relief personnel. I call also on international humanitarian organizations to intensify their efforts to provide relief to Kosovo's population. To achieve this, the international community must support these efforts by providing urgently the necessary resources for assistance in Kosovo, in order to prevent a major humanitarian disaster in the region.

121. Report of the Secretary-General Prepared pursuant to Security Council Resolutions 1160 (1998) and 1199 (1998), UN Doc. S/1998/912, 3 October 1998

I. Introduction

1. The present report is submitted pursuant to Security Council resolutions 1160 (1998) of 31 March 1998 and 1199 (1998) of 23 September 1998. In its resolution 1160 (1998), the Council requested me to keep it regularly informed on the situation in Kosovo and to provide an assessment on whether the Federal Republic of Yugoslavia had complied in a constructive manner with conditions put forward by the Contact Group. In its resolution 1199 (1998), the Council further requested me to provide regular reports to it as necessary on my assessment of compliance with that resolution by the authorities of the Federal Republic of Yugoslavia and all elements in the Kosovo Albanian community, including through my regular reports on compliance with resolution 1160 (1998). The present report covers the period since my previous report, dated 4 September 1998, prepared pursuant to resolution 1160 (1998) (S/1998/834).

II. Security Council Committee Established Pursuant to Resolution 1160 (1998)

2. As at 2 October 1998, a total of 51 States, listed in my earlier reports (S/1998/608, S/1998/712 and S/1998/834), as well as Ireland and the Russian Federation, had reported to the Committee established pursuant to paragraph 9 of Security Council resolution 1160 (1998), in accordance with paragraph 12 of that resolution, on the steps they had taken to give effect to the prohibitions imposed by the same resolution. In a note verbale dated 15 September 1998, the Permanent Mission of Austria to the United Nations, on behalf of the European Union, transmitted to the Chairman of the Committee the second special report from the European Community Monitoring Mission containing its observations pertaining to the Albania/Kosovo border.

3. It will be recalled that on 21 July 1998, the Security Council adopted resolution 1186 (1998), by which it mandated the United Nations Preventive Deployment Force (UNPREDEP) to perform tasks of monitoring the border areas and to report to me on illicit arms flows and other activities that are prohibited under resolution 1160 (1998). In this connection I would like to refer to paragraph 5 of my previous report (S/1998/834) and to inform the Council that I have not yet received any suggestions on the establishment of an integrated coordinating mechanism of which UNPREDEP would form a part.

III. Situation in Kosovo

4. The present report is based on information regarding the situation on the ground from the Chairman-in-Office of the Organization for Security and Cooperation in Europe (OSCE), the European Union, the North Atlantic Treaty Organization (NATO), the Contact Group and individual Member States. My Special Representative for Children and Armed Conflict, Olara A. Otunnu, and the United Nations High Commissioner for Refugees, Sadako Ogata, visited the region from 10 to 12 September and from 24 to 29 September respectively and reported to me on their findings. As the present report was being finalized, the Secretariat received a factual report from NATO on the military situation in Kosovo following the adoption of resolution 1199 (1998). The information provided therein is reflected in the report. Reports have also been received from the Kosovo Diplomatic Observer Mission. In addition to other information provided (see annex), the Chairman-in-Office of OSCE indicated to me that, despite a number of approaches, the authorities of the Federal Republic of Yugoslavia had not changed their position vis-à-vis the earlier requests of OSCE, including the acceptance of the mission of Felipe González or prospective OSCE missions, including one in Kosovo.

HOSTILITIES

5. During the reporting period, fighting in Kosovo continued unabated. Government security forces conducted offensives in the various parts of Kosovo, including the areas of Licovac, Glogovac and Cicavica. In the week following the adoption, on 23 September 1998, of resolution 1199 (1998), the forces in fact intensified their operations, launching another offensive in the Drenica region and in the Suva Reka-Stimlje-Urosevac triangle. Those operations have reportedly resulted in the displacement of some 20,000 additional people. Smaller operations were conducted by the Serbian security forces in the Prizren area. Fighting continued on 28 and 29 September, contrary to the statement of the Serbian Prime Minister, Mr. Marjanovic, on 28 September, that anti-insurgency operations in Kosovo had been completed and that peace reigned in Kosovo.

6. Military activity seemed to wind down in the last days of September. There was evidence of heavily armoured formations returning to their barracks. On 29 September, Federal Minister for Foreign Affairs Zivadin Jovanovic assured me that troops were returning to the places of their permanent location. According to the most recent reports, military forces withdrew from the Drenica and Prizren areas on 1 October and observers indicated a decrease in activities of the security forces. However, the Secretariat is still receiving information that the Government's armed presence remains significant and that the operations of the special police continue.

7. The desperate situation of the civilian population remains the most disturbing aspect of the hostilities in Kosovo. I am particularly concerned that civilians increasingly have become the main target in the conflict. Fighting in Kosovo has resulted in a mass displacement of civilian populations, the extensive destruction of villages and means of livelihood and the deep trauma and despair of displaced populations. Many villages have been destroyed by shelling and burning following operations conducted by federal and Serbian government forces. There are concerns that the disproportionate use of force and actions of the security forces are designed to terrorize and subjugate the population, a collective punishment to teach them that the price of supporting the Kosovo Albanian paramilitary units is too high and will be even higher in future. The Serbian security forces have demanded the surrender of weapons and have been reported to use terror and violence against civilians to force people to flee their homes or the places where they had sought refuge, under the guise of separating them from fighters of the Kosovo Albanian paramilitary units. The tactics include shelling, detentions and threats to life, and finally short-notice demands to leave or face the consequences. There have been disruptions in electricity and other services, and empty dwellings have been burned and looted, abandoned farm vehicles have been destroyed, and farm animals have been burned in their barns or shot in the fields. For example, international observers witnessed Serb troops looting and burning houses in the Suva Reka area on 27 September.

8. The level of destruction points clearly to an indiscriminate and disproportionate use of force against civilian populations. As of mid-

September, an estimated 6,000 to 7,000 buildings in 269 villages had been severely damaged or destroyed by shelling and deliberate burning in the Serb forces' main areas of operations. Information available to me from reliable sources covered only villages - not cities - in western and central Kosovo. If the rate of destruction observed in the first two weeks of September were to continue, an estimated total of 9,000 homes in nearly 300 settlements would be uninhabitable (without significant reconstruction) by early November.

HUMAN RIGHTS

9. I am outraged by reports of mass killings of civilians in Kosovo, which recall the atrocities committed in Bosnia and Herzegovina. Following reports concerning the killing of 20 Kosovo Albanian internally displaced persons in Gornje Obrinje in the central Drenica area on 28 September, a Kosovo Diplomatic Observer Mission team witnessed at least 14 bodies, some severely mutilated. Most were children and women at ages ranging from 18 months to 95 years. The Serb authorities denied any involvement of the police force in those atrocities. However, further killings of Kosovo civilians were reported, including the alleged summary execution of some 12 to 23 males (accounts vary) in the Golubovac area on 27 September. The Kosovo Diplomatic Observer Mission conducted a preliminary investigation in the area and observed pools of blood in the dirt, tools presumably used to stab the victims and small-calibre shell casings.

10. While the victims of the conflict are overwhelmingly ethnic Albanians, Kosovo Serbs are suffering as well. There have been a number of reports of the kidnapping and killing of Serbian and Albanian civilians by Kosovo Albanian paramilitary units. The village of Zocite, which was once half-Serb and half-Kosovo Albanian, now has only 30 Serbs, and 80 per cent of the houses were burned and destroyed during the period of several months when the village was under the control of Kosovo Albanian paramilitary units. Mass graves of Serbs were discovered in Klecka, Glodjane and Ratis. The Kosovo Diplomatic Observer Mission investigated the latest mass grave in Glodjane. The ambushing of members of the security forces by the Kosovo Albanian paramilitary units has led to reprisals, not only by the Serbian authorities, but also by armed Serb civilians, against the innocent population.

HUMANITARIAN SITUATION

11. The pattern of displacement is fast-changing and unpredictable as people flee in response to the actions and real or perceived threats of the security forces. Even though there have been some returns, the Office of the United Nations High Commissioner for Refugees (UNHCR) estimates that more than 200,000 persons remain displaced in Kosovo and some 80,000 are in neighbouring countries and other parts of Serbia. Shifting operations by Serb security forces and the Yugoslav army have continued to uproot new groups of Kosovars and to keep relief efforts off-balance. Although reporting indicated that approximately 30,000 to 50,000 internally displaced persons in Kosovo had recently returned to their homes, the total number of internally displaced persons remains unchanged, offset by the most recent government offensives. International monitors have been told that displaced persons are refusing to return home because of their fear of reprisals, and a number of displaced people have been arrested by the security forces upon returning home.

12. In Albania, while the estimated number of refugees is relatively small (some 20,000), the political and economic impact of their presence is clearly felt. The poor infrastructure and rampant lawlessness in some areas magnify the impact of the arrival of refugees. The harsh winter and insecurity in Bajram Curri led to the closure of the UNHCR office there, where only 2,500 refugees remain. The High Commissioner requested a quick decision on the allocation of land and buildings for collective accommodation in more suitable locations. The internal situation in Albania, however, is likely to delay this allocation and the adoption of legislation on refugees.

13. With 45,000 recent arrivals from Kosovo, Montenegro now has about the same number of displaced persons as at the height of the war in 1993 - some 12 per cent of the population. The High Commissioner for Refugees told President Djukanovic that while the reasons for the closure of the border with Kosovo announced on 11 September were understandable, she urged him to reverse the decision. President Djukanovic gave assurances that the decision would be implemented flexibly, with individual situations considered. He also gave assurances that there would be no more forced returns to Kosovo or expulsions to Albania. The High Commissioner pledged additional support for assistance programmes and noted a positive response to the August 1998 inter-agency appeal for the Kosovo crisis.

14. There are some 7,000 Kosovo Albanian asylum-seekers in Bosnia and Herzegovina, and the number continues to rise. The Government has finally adopted an instruction on the treatment of asylum-seekers. Finding satisfactory accommodation is now the main problem, given the already very heavy pressure on housing.

15. In the former Yugoslav Republic of Macedonia there are an estimated 3,000 to 5,000 Kosovo Albanians whose presence is directly linked to the conflict. Citizens of the Federal Republic of Yugoslavia do not need an entry visa for a two-month stay, and the Government has just formally agreed to regularize the status of those who have exceeded this period. Some 500 persons have approached UNHCR and its partners for assistance. A large-scale influx is thought unlikely but cannot be excluded.

16. The Government claims that some 100,000 refugees have returned to their homes (independent estimates are some 30,000 to 50,000) and has pledged to facilitate the process of returns. At present, the authorities have opened 12 centres around Kosovo to provide assistance to internally displaced persons. In some of them, ethnic Albanians are employed. An immediate and fundamental change in the Serbian authorities' approach is, however, essential. Without it, indicators of different stages in the underlying cycle of violence and repression - for example, the end of one offensive, fluctuations in the number of those affected, displaced or without shelter or returnees - will have only short-term significance. The current policy and methods used by the authorities predictably cause large-scale and often repeated displacement and a well-founded fear of mistreatment by the security forces upon return. Many internally displaced persons were reportedly prevented from returning to their homes and were forced to move elsewhere. There are a number of reports of detentions and arrests of able-bodied men, some of whom are still unaccounted for. Such an attitude, combined with information about atrocities committed against civilians, has generated fear among many internally displaced persons, preventing them from returning. Thus, the absence of adequate security remains the main obstacle to return.

17. With only a few weeks before the onset of winter, the issue of the return of displaced persons and refugees remains one of the most pressing issues. Some 50,000 internally displaced persons currently lack shelter or any support network, and are ill-prepared for inclement winter weather that may arrive as early as next month. The priority of any humanitarian strategy should be to assist these people. Children and the elderly will almost certainly risk death from exposure if they remain at their current locations - especially the ones at higher elevations - into the winter.

18. While the major focus is on immediate needs, such as the return of internally displaced persons and the provision of urgent assistance to those still living in the open air, it is also necessary to address broader humanitarian issues. As most of the displaced persons in Kosovo are staying with families, assistance has to be provided to a much broader segment of the population. The host families that support most of them are beginning to deplete their personal food stocks. In this regard, an important element, in addition to providing assistance to local host families, is the removal of an unofficial blockade of Kosovo by the Serbian authorities.

19. The Government has appealed to internally displaced persons, encouraging them to return. However, after six months of hostilities, mere declarations appear to be insufficient to ensure their return. The Government of the Federal Republic of Yugoslavia must be made to assume its full responsibility of guaranteeing security for returnees as

well as punishing those responsible for previous abuses and destruction.

20. I welcome the good intentions contained in the conclusions of the National Assembly of the Republic of Serbia, adopted on 28 September, regarding the speedy resolution of all humanitarian problems in Kosovo, including the reconstruction of damaged houses and the adoption of concrete measures for health care as well as the overall normalization of the economy and supply. The National Assembly also indicated that the Government of Serbia would continue to cooperate fully with the International Committee of the Red Cross (ICRC) and UNHCR with the basic goal of reducing as much as possible humanitarian problems and eliminating them soon through joint and concerted efforts, and would ensure the ability of humanitarian agencies to work unhindered. I am looking forward to seeing these assurances implemented in the most expeditious and effective way.

21. The United Nations High Commissioner for Refugees urged President Milosevic to stop the violence against civilians, the destruction and looting of deserted property and the random detention of able-bodied males. She stressed the importance of confidence-building measures such as amnesty, a reduction in the presence of a highly visible and intimidating security force, an end to the de facto commercial blockade imposed in Kosovo and the restoration of essential services. However, even those measures would have little impact without evidence of a real change of heart and approach.

THE HUMANITARIAN RESPONSE

22. There has been a significant increase in operational capacity, and coordination is good on the ground. UNHCR has strengthened both this capacity and its presence in order to discharge its lead agency responsibilities effectively. Coordination with UNHCR non-governmental organization partners, with ICRC and with the Kosovo Diplomatic Observer Mission is of particular importance. UNHCR has a full-time liaison officer with the Mission.

23. Coordination with the provincial and local authorities and with representatives of the Kosovo Albanian community is no less important. The High Commissioner for Refugees underlined to President Milosevic that the beneficiaries must have confidence in the delivery of humanitarian assistance and that a key role had to be played by such agencies as the Mother Theresa Society.

24. Although aid agencies have significantly expanded their operations in Kosovo, total requirements are not being met because of the restrictive environment in which aid agencies operate. The security operations have continued to delay relief convoys travelling to populations in need until they have deemed an area "secure", have carried out protracted shelling of targets in close proximity to large groups of internally displaced persons and have displayed extremely heavy-handed behaviour when dealing with displaced persons. While overall freedom of movement for humanitarian agencies and international observers has improved, it does not apply to internally displaced persons or, in certain cases, to journalists. Moreover, continued fighting and security operations in the area have impeded the access of monitors and the delivery of humanitarian aid. There is an urgent need for non-governmental organizations to be given access and for clearance to be granted for humanitarian supplies. To date, non-governmental organizations have been denied radio clearance, thereby jeopardizing the coordination of life-saving operations and personal security.

25. It has been reported that the Federal Republic of Yugoslavia has undertaken the systematic deployment of both anti-personnel and anti-tank landmines in the border areas with Albania and the former Yugoslav Republic of Macedonia. In the areas of fighting within Kosovo itself, however, there have so far been only isolated reports of the use of anti-personnel landmines. However, a Kosovo Diplomatic Observer Mission vehicle recently hit a mine, and on 1 October an ICRC vehicle ran into an anti-tank mine in the same area. Since the laying of landmines could become a trend, the early deployment of a United Nations Mine Action Service team could become necessary. It should be given clearance to assess the situation of landmines in conflict areas. This will be fundamental to the return process and will also help to ensure the safe and free movement of humanitarian personnel and international observers.

POLITICAL SETTLEMENT

26. There is a need to create a favourable climate for the process of negotiating a political settlement of the Kosovo crisis. I welcome in this regard the efforts of the international community to bring about a political solution to the problem and support the efforts of the Contact Group, and in particular Ambassador Christopher Hill, to negotiate a political settlement between the Serb authorities and Kosovo Albanian leaders, of whom Dr. Rugova remains the most prominent figure, although his leadership is contested by the Albanian opposition and Kosovar paramilitary units. Following the discussion of the Kosovo issue at the meeting of the Contact Group in London on 2 October, the Chairman communicated to me his conclusions:

"The Contact Group is united and intends to be united. We expect full and immediate compliance with Security Council resolution 1199. This has not so far been achieved.

"We heard a report on the work of the U.S. facilitator, Ambassador Hill, on the negotiating track. We endorsed a revised paper which will now be put to the parties on behalf of the Contact Group.

"We are united in condemning what is happening on the ground and in support for humanitarian efforts.

"We all concluded that time is running out."

27. I support the Chairman's conclusions and believe that there is no alternative to a direct dialogue in search of a mutually acceptable settlement in the interest of all people of Kosovo and the Federal Republic of Yugoslavia. The consequences of the current repressive approach not only affect the immediate humanitarian situation, they also have a direct and major adverse impact on the prospects for a just and lasting political solution. Even once there is a fundamentally new approach by Belgrade, the task of correcting the very deep-rooted damage of the last years, and in particular the last months, will be enormous.

IV. Observations

28. In the last few weeks, the international community has witnessed appalling atrocities in Kosovo, reminiscent of the recent past elsewhere in the Balkans. These have been borne out by reporting by the Kosovo Diplomatic Observer Mission and other reliable sources. I reiterate my utter condemnation of such wanton killing and destruction. It is clear beyond any reasonable doubt that the great majority of such acts have been committed by security forces in Kosovo acting under the authority of the Federal Republic of Yugoslavia. But Kosovar Albanian paramilitary units have engaged in armed action also, and there is good reason to believe that they too have committed atrocities. All those involved in the killing and mistreatment of civilians and in the destruction of property must be brought to justice. There is a need for a thorough investigation, under effective international control or with international participation, of all reported cases of atrocities and violations of human rights.

29. The Security Council has reaffirmed the commitment of all Member States to the sovereignty and territorial integrity of the Federal Republic of Yugoslavia. The authorities of the Federal Republic of Yugoslavia have the inherent right, as well as the duty, to maintain public order and security and to respond to violent acts of provocation. However, this can in no way justify the systematic terror inflicted on civilians these past few days and weeks. It is the duty of security forces to give equal protection to all citizens, not to intimidate or murder them. It is equally necessary, as called for by the Security Council, for terrorist action, including the taking of hostages by Kosovar Albanian elements, to cease.

30. If the present state of affairs persists, thousands could die in the winter. In my earlier statements on the situation in Kosovo, I have emphasized this danger repeatedly and appealed to the international community to undertake urgent steps in order to prevent a humanitarian disaster. The possibilities of asylum outside Kosovo are ever more limited, and much of the shelter available clearly is inadequate for

winter. Conditions must be created that would allow for the return of a significant number of internally displaced persons. This requires a radical change of policy and behaviour and the introduction of confidence-building measures - such as a withdrawal of police units, a declaration of amnesty and a release of prisoners. The Federal Republic of Yugoslavia authorities assert that such steps have already been taken. According to reports from the field, the withdrawal so far appears limited, and it would seem that the fear that led civilians to flee remains. For all internally displaced persons, the first priority is the restoration of security. The Government must restrain police excesses and give police instructions to respect international human rights conventions. Greater efforts are also required to improve access to prisoners taken by the authorities and to secure the release of, or accounting for, hostages taken by the Kosovar Albanian side.

31. It is my earnest hope that the negotiations between the Federal Republic of Yugoslavia and the Kosovo Albanian leadership will be resumed without delay and produce early agreements, and that they will result in the restoration of confidence that is needed for a return and resettlement of all those who have fled their homes in fear. Such agreements might also envisage more far-reaching steps, possibly even institutional reforms, to address long-term needs. If there is to be a role for the international community in assisting in the implementation of such agreements, it will require a proper assessment of needs that would take humanitarian as well as rehabilitation and reconstruction requirements fully into account. The necessary operational planning must be conducted, including an appropriate division of labour, and effective implementation and coordination mechanisms. I would like to express my hope that these considerations will be borne in mind by those involved in the negotiations. It would in my view be useful, in this regard, to initiate consultations amongst international actors to prepare to face such a challenge, without necessarily awaiting the agreements. The United Nations is prepared to play an active role in such consultations.

32. I believe that action is urgently required on several fronts. The violence on all sides has to be brought to a halt. Full humanitarian access must be granted. Conditions need to be created that will enable refugees and internally displaced persons to return to their homes with confidence that they will not face harassment or worse. It is imperative that the international presence be strengthened and made more effective. In particular, it would be helpful if, in the immediate term, the Kosovo Diplomatic Observer Mission were brought to its full strength and if the presence of human rights observers were enhanced. Also, it will be essential to ensure the closest possible coordination of international efforts in the political, humanitarian and other fields. A broad range of options could be considered in that regard.

33. In the present report, as in previous ones issued pursuant to Security Council resolution 1160 (1998), I have had to rely largely on information and analysis from sources external to the United Nations. I am grateful for these contributions, which carry conviction and are reflected in the body of the report. But, unlike reports to the Council on missions or operations where the United Nations has a direct political presence on the ground, I do not have the means necessary to provide an independent assessment of compliance, as required by the Security Council in paragraph 15 of resolution 1199 (1998), other than on the humanitarian situation. Therefore, the Council may wish to make its own judgement in this respect on the basis of the present report. As the Council has affirmed in its resolution 1199 (1998), the deterioration in the situation in Kosovo, Federal Republic of Yugoslavia, constitutes a threat to peace and security in the region. It is widely recognized in the international community that the humanitarian crisis is a consequence of what is fundamentally a political problem, which requires a comprehensive political solution through a negotiated settlement.

34. While I fully share the sense of indignation and revulsion at what has been happening in Kosovo, the international community must never lose sight of the ultimate need for a comprehensive political solution. Otherwise, we shall be treating only the symptoms of the problem, and not its causes.

Annex: Information on the Situation in Kosovo and Measures Taken by the Organization for Security and Cooperation in Europe, Submitted Pursuant to Paragraphs 13 and 16 of Security Council Resolution 1160 (1998)

GENERAL SITUATION

The period since the previous report (S/1998/834/Add.1) has been characterized by a decrease in military operations after the offensive against armed groups of Kosovo Albanians launched by Serb forces in August.

During the second half of August only limited military actions were observed. However, house-to-house searches were carried out and the number of mine accidents increased. In the first week of September the area of Kosovo bordering north-eastern Albania was relatively calm, but continued fighting was observed towards the south, on the outskirts of Djakovica and in villages nearby. During September Yugoslav forces continued to pound villages to stamp out any traces of resistance, the burning of houses continued in the area south of Prizren and military operations commenced in the area of Orahovac with a starting line at Zrze-Orahovac and moving west.

At the end of August, Kosovo Liberation Army (KLA) fighters admitted that because of serious setbacks and lack of success with previous tactics they would resort to "hit and run" operations. Similar views were presented by Adem Demaci, leader of the Parliamentary Party of Kosovo and recently appointed political representative of the Kosovo Liberation Army. In late August, he stated to the media that the group would now adopt classic guerrilla warfare tactics against Yugoslav targets after losing territory during the recent Serbian offensive.

At the beginning of September, the United States Ambassador to the former Yugoslav Republic of Macedonia and Peace Envoy, Christopher Hill, announced that an outline agreement had been reached between the Kosovo Albanians and the Belgrade authorities on the future of Kosovo. The agreement, based on options featured in the document of the Contact Group, envisages a three-year stabilization and normalization period to allow for the re-establishment of democratic institutions. It was also agreed that indirect talks should continue, despite the fact that indirect talks had as yet been fruitless.

Still, there is confusion as to just who the Kosovo Albanians making such an agreement represent. Hitherto, there has been little success in the attempts to persuade the Albanian Democratic Movement (LDS), a party created in late June 1998 and led by Mr. Rexhep Qosja, a former ally of Rugova, to join the negotiations. Moreover, the political representative of KLA, Mr. Demaci, sees any temporary agreement as a capitulation and has pledged to continue the fighting. But the fact that some returnees have handed over their weapons to Serb forces is seen as an indication that segments of the Albanian population are prepared to accept whatever interim political agreement is reached.

In this respect there are increasing indications of splits among Albanian fighting groups. With sharp divisions within the Kosovo Albanian ranks, the problem of just who represents them will likely continue and the prospects of a ceasefire called by KLA and the Serbian authorities currently appear remote.

MONITORING ACTIVITIES IN KOSOVO

The Kosovo Diplomatic Observer Mission has continued its activity despite the growing aversion on the part of Serb security forces and KLA. The Mission is composed of several tens of people representing European Union (EU) States, the United States of America, the Russian Federation and Canada. Every week there are about 50 to 60 observation trips and a report on the situation is presented and further accepted in Belgrade by the ambassadors of the Contact Group States (the United Kingdom of Great Britain and Northern Ireland, France, Italy, Germany, Russian Federation and the United States of America) and Austria (EU Presidency) and Poland (Chairmanship of the Organization for Security and Cooperation in Europe (OSCE)).

Regardless of the missions, Kosovo has been regularly visited by employees of embassies accredited to Belgrade. Also, politicians and diplomats on a visit to the Federal Republic of Yugoslavia used to go to Kosovo.

THE SITUATION OF THE CIVILIAN POPULATION

Fighting has forced more than 200,000 people to flee their homes. The situation is made worse by large-scale destruction of houses, food shortages and the risk of epidemic. The threat of humanitarian catastrophe is becoming ever more real. According to the Office of the United Nations High Commissioner for Refugees (UNHCR), large numbers of displaced persons, as many as 50,000, are today living out in the open in Kosovo. Many others are living in desperate conditions as entire villages have been destroyed, livestock slaughtered and fields burned.

Although great emphasis has been given recently to the return of displaced persons, the return process is hampered by the level of destruction in some villages, and, for those who can return to relatively undamaged areas, the issue of security is paramount. The presence of Serb security forces in many areas continues to create a feeling of insecurity on the part of those wishing to return.

Several cases of large-scale detentions have been reported on different occasions where men of fighting age suspected of being separatist guerrillas were separated from the women, children and elderly by police, backed by armoured vehicles, and taken to places of detention for interrogation.

ANALYSIS OF THE KOSOVO CONFLICT SPILLOVER POTENTIAL

As at 1 September, UNHCR was reporting a total of 14,000 refugees in Albania of which 7,000 remained in the Tropoja district, the rest having left for other parts of the country. Still, reliable statistics are difficult to compile owing to the fluid nature of the situation. According to Albanian sources there are about 7,500 registered refugees in the Bajram Curri area and 7,500 in central Albania, particularly in the Durrës area. Out of a total of 15,000 persons (6,100 families), about 1,000 live in accommodations provided by the Government and the rest live with ordinary families.

The relative decrease in incoming refugees during the summer in the Tropoja and Has districts was caused by the tightening of the border by Yugoslav forces: the creation of a cordon sanitaire along the border west of Djakovica (Deane-Ponoevac-Djakovica road and Deane-Skrivljan-Djakovica road), heavier controls by the Yugoslav authorities on the routes over the mountains and the laying of mines. The need for refugees to find more arduous routes through this area in order to avoid detection resulted in many refugees trying to enter Albania through Montenegro. It was estimated that, by the end of August, approximately 100 to 120 refugees a day were entering the Shkodr-Koplik area through Montenegro. During the first two weeks of September, the number of refugees crossing into Albania increased steadily, indicating an opening of safe corridors through the border.

The readiness of the local population to accommodate a vast majority of the refugees, mainly elderly people, women and children, largely facilitated the immediate handling of the major influx. However, it put further strain on the local Albanian population already living under difficult or even harsh economic and social conditions. Evidence suggests that the absorption capacities are exhausted. This underlines the importance of establishing appropriate shelter facilities, preferably in other parts of Albania, in order to alleviate current and potential needs before the winter.

In this respect, in the first week of September, the Kosovo refugee issue was discussed in the Albanian Parliament, and the respective parliamentary commissions severely criticized the Government for failing to take measures to accommodate the refugees from Kosovo, particularly with winter approaching.

According to the latest figures, the number of refugees in Montenegro (640,000 inhabitants) exceeds 45,000, which have to be added to the 30,000 refugees from Bosnia and Herzegovina and Croatia. The Podgorïca authorities have begun the organized transport of about 3,000 refugees from Kosovo to Albania across the unofficial Vrmos border crossing some three kilometres from Plav (south-east of Montenegro).

Numerous incidents between KLA units and the Yugoslav army and Serb police have been reported in the border areas. Many attempts have been recorded of the illegal crossing of the border by armed Albanians. The Federal Republic of Yugoslavia and Albania have accused one another of causing incidents on the border and of shooting in the other State's territory.

MEASURES TAKEN BY THE ORGANIZATION FOR SECURITY AND COOPERATION IN EUROPE

On 18 August 1998, in a letter addressed to the Foreign Minister of the Federal Republic of Yugoslavia, Mr. Jovanovic, the OSCE Representative on Freedom of the Media, Mr. Duve, expressed his concerns over lack of access for foreign journalists intending to cover events in Yugoslavia in a number of instances, considered as serious incidents and not consistent with OSCE principles and commitments. On 27 August, Mr. Duve addressed the Permanent Council of OSCE, recalling the letters sent to the Yugoslav Foreign Minister and urging the Belgrade authorities to allow unimpeded access to the media to cover the events in the country, especially in Kosovo.

On 3 September 1998, Ambassador Hill addressed the OSCE Permanent Council in Vienna and assessed the current situation in the region, elaborating on the prospects for a negotiated settlement to the crisis in Kosovo. He made it very clear that violence must stop and that there can only be a peaceful solution to the problems of Kosovo, but emphasizing also that the search for political solutions should not be conditioned by the continued violence and that pursuing diplomatic action cannot wait until a ceasefire is called.

On the political negotiations, Ambassador Hill informed the Permanent Council that a new Albanian negotiating team composed of moderate and more radical Albanian participants had reached an agreement based on options featured in the document of the Contact Group. The agreement envisages a three-year stabilization and normalization period to allow for the re-establishment of democratic institutions, and after this period new approaches could be envisaged. He stressed the crucial importance of the international presence in Kosovo during the implementation period and the important role OSCE had to play in the area.

In her address to the Permanent Council on the same day, United States Secretary of State Madeleine Albright elaborated on the same issue, stating that she foresaw a special role for OSCE in a possible negotiated settlement of the Kosovo conflict, especially with regard to elections.

In its continued efforts to monitor the situation on the borders of Albania and the former Yugoslav Republic of Macedonia with the Federal Republic of Yugoslavia, on 10 September the OSCE Permanent Council approved supplementary budgets for the continued enhancement of the OSCE presence in Albania and the OSCE Spillover Monitor Mission to Skopje.

122. Report of the Secretary-General Prepared pursuant to Security Council Resolutions 1160 (1998), 1199 (1998) and 1203 (1998), UN Doc. S/1998/1068, 12 November 1998

I. Introduction

1. The present report is submitted pursuant to Security Council resolutions 1160 (1998) of 31 March 1998, 1199 (1998) of 23 September 1998 and 1203 (1998) of 24 October 1998 and covers the period since my previous report of 3 October 1998 prepared pursuant to resolutions 1160 (1998) and 1199 (1998) (S/1998/912).

II. Security Council Committee Established pursuant to Resolution 1160 (1998)

2. As of 31 October 1998, in addition to the 53 States listed in my earlier reports (S/1998/608, S/1998/712, S/1998/834 and S/1998/912),

Diplomatic Efforts for the Settlement of the Crisis

Israel reported to the Security Council Committee established pursuant to resolution 1160 (1998), in accordance with paragraph 12 of that resolution, on steps taken to give effect to the prohibitions imposed by the resolution. In a note verbale dated 3 November 1998, the Permanent Mission of Austria to the United Nations, on behalf of the European Union, transmitted to the Chairman of the Committee the third special report from the European Community Monitoring Mission containing its observations pertaining to the Committee's mandate.

3. At its fourth meeting, on 15 October 1998, the Committee considered information gathered by the Secretariat from public sources on violations of the prohibitions imposed by resolution 1160 (1998) in conjunction with information of the same nature received from relevant regional organizations. The Committee acknowledged that concentrated efforts by States were needed for the effective implementation of the arms embargo, especially by those countries neighbouring the Federal Republic of Yugoslavia. The Committee authorized its Chairman, Celso L. N. Amorim (Brazil), to renew his appeal to those States that had not yet fulfilled their obligations under paragraph 12 of Security Council resolution 1160 (1998) to adopt the necessary measures as soon as possible and to inform the Committee accordingly. States, as well as international and regional organizations, were urged to provide to the Committee information that might be available to them concerning violations or suspected violations of the imposed prohibitions. The appeal was addressed especially to States in the region, as well as to other States that could play a significant role in achieving the objectives of resolutions 1160 (1998) and 1199 (1998).

III. Comprehensive Regime to Monitor the Implementation of the Prohibitions Imposed by Security Council Resolution 1160 (1998)

4. The first consultative meeting of organizations participating in the comprehensive monitoring regime was convened at United Nations Headquarters in New York on 19 October 1998. Representatives from the Danube Commission, the European Union, the North Atlantic Treaty Organization (NATO), the Organization for Security and Cooperation in Europe (OSCE), the Western European Union and the Secretariat exchanged information on the monitoring of the prohibitions established by resolution 1160 (1998) and addressed practical issues arising in that regard. The participants also met with the Chairman of the Security Council Committee established pursuant to resolution 1160 (1998), with whom they discussed their contributions to the monitoring of the arms embargo.

IV. Situation in Kosovo

5. This section of the report is based on information provided by the Chairman-in-Office of OSCE (annex I), the European Union, NATO (annex II), the Kosovo Diplomatic Observer Mission and individual Member States. It also draws upon the report of a United Nations mission to the Federal Republic of Yugoslavia that visited the region from 17 to 27 October 1998 (hereinafter referred to as the United Nations mission; see sect. V), as well as contributions provided by the Office of the United Nations High Commissioner for Refugees and the United Nations High Commissioner for Human Rights.

POLITICAL FRAMEWORK

6. The accord reached by the President of the Federal Republic of Yugoslavia, Slobodan Milosevic, and the United States Special Envoy, Richard Holbrooke, on 13 October 1998 (see S/1998/953, annex), as well as the agreements signed in Belgrade on 15 October 1998 between the Federal Republic of Yugoslavia and NATO, and on 16 October 1998 between the Federal Republic of Yugoslavia and OSCE, have contributed towards defusing the immediate crisis situation in Kosovo and have created more favourable conditions for a political settlement.

7. The authorities of the Federal Republic of Yugoslavia welcomed the Agreement of 16 October establishing the Kosovo Verification Mission and indicated their readiness to cooperate fully with the Mission. They pledged to ensure full freedom of movement for the Kosovo Verification Mission monitors and undertook to inform them of possible dangers. The Minister of the Interior of Serbia, in particular, indicated the Government's intention to inform the Mission promptly of all incidents that might occur in the region excluding, however, incidents that the authorities might classify as "criminal activity".

8. Government officials informed the United Nations mission that they were considering holding elections in Kosovo in about nine months. The Kosovo Executive Council, that is, the local administration established by the Government, had recently became functional, albeit with no Kosovo Albanian participation. The Deputy Prime Minister of the Federal Republic of Yugoslavia indicated to the United Nations mission the need for joint national and international efforts to address the humanitarian situation in Kosovo and pledged to promote active cooperation with humanitarian organizations on the ground to that end.

9. The Kosovo Albanian leaders, in their contacts with the United Nations mission, expressed reservations about the 13 October accord and the 16 October agreement, although they appreciated the fact that Kosovo was no longer considered to be exclusively an internal problem of the Federal Republic of Yugoslavia. They still insisted on their right to self-determination and signalled their continuing wish for an international armed presence on the ground.

10. The position of Kosovo Albanian paramilitary units remained unclear. The authorities of the Federal Republic of Yugoslavia expressed concern that members of those units might try to provoke the police and military in Kosovo and trigger a reaction from the Government. The Kosovo Albanian leaders indicated, with various degrees of certainty, that Kosovo Albanian paramilitary units would respect the 13 October accord by and large. Nonetheless, they could not rule out the possibility that some small splinter armed groups might continue attacks, thus giving the authorities of the Federal Republic of Yugoslavia a pretext for violent retaliation.

RECENT MILITARY SITUATION

11. Both the parties to the conflict and the international observers on the ground acknowledge that the military situation has stabilized recently and that, despite some serious but isolated incidents, there has been no major fighting since 1 October. Many local people indicated to the United Nations mission that the situation had improved in the two weeks following the ceasefire, although several villages had reportedly been destroyed recently by the Serbian police. Tensions persist, however, in many areas dominated by Kosovo Albanian paramilitary units, with guerrilla-style attacks on police and military positions and frequent reports of sporadic gunfire exchanges and shelling by Government forces.

12. Between 28 September and 19 October 1998, the Ministry of the Interior reported a total of 117 attacks of varying intensity, in which a total of 10 policemen were killed and 22 were injured. Seven members of the Yugoslav army were also reported killed and two injured during the incidents. The demarcation between police and Kosovo Albanian paramilitary units was not always clear at the time of the visit of the United Nations mission; in some cases their respective positions were only several hundred metres apart. Accordingly, in almost all cases, it was difficult to determine which side had initiated hostilities.

13. Recent attacks by Kosovo Albanian paramilitary units have indicated their readiness, capability and intention to actively pursue the advantage gained by the partial withdrawal of the police and military formations. Reports of new weapons, ammunition and equipment indicate that the capacity of those units to resupply themselves is still fairly good.

14. The army and police presence in Kosovo has been significantly reduced since early October. The presence and disposition of the remaining Government forces indicate a strategy based on containing pockets of resistance and on control of high ground and the main arterial routes in areas dominated by Kosovo Albanian paramilitary units. Tripwires and anti-personnel mines have reportedly been laid at the approaches to some police positions as an early warning measure. Since 27 October, there has been a continued withdrawal of the Serbian security forces from Kosovo and numerous checkpoints and fortified positions have been dismantled. The Serbian police retain control over

key roads. Mobile police checkpoints have been established on major roads in some areas.

15. Kosovo Albanian paramilitary units are asserting their own authority to supplant that of the Serbian police in areas from which the police have withdrawn, and have established their own checkpoints on a number of secondary roads.

16. While the ceasefire is generally holding, there are continued reports of sporadic violations, including armed provocations against police and police harassment of ethnic Albanians. The presence of Kosovo Albanian paramilitary units is reportedly on the increase in several areas, and they appear to be responsible for some of the reported violations, including attacks on civilians. Serbian police raised security measures around a coal mine and power plant outside Pristina following an attack by Kosovo Albanian paramilitary units on 3 November in which three Serbian workers were injured.

17. Kosovo Albanian paramilitary units denied access to Kosovo Diplomatic Observer Mission teams to some areas, requesting a letter from their political representative. On 5 November, a clearly marked OSCE vehicle was fired on as it drove close behind a Federal Republic of Yugoslavia military convoy between Suva Reka and Stimlje.

SECURITY

18. The overriding concern of both ethnic Serbs and Albanians is the security of their families. While the Serbian authorities told the United Nations mission that they needed a large police presence in designated parts of Kosovo to protect ethnic Serbs living in the province and to ensure that at least main highways remained safe and free for travel, the Kosovo Albanian representatives stated that police units were used as another arm of the military, intent on intimidating local Albanians. Police and military personnel have occupied some village homes, making their owners' return impossible. Furthermore, many deserted villages have a presence of some five to eight police, who remain purportedly to prevent or give early warning of attempts by Kosovo Albanian paramilitary units to reoccupy territory previously taken by Government forces. This presence was cited almost universally by the internally displaced persons as the primary reason for people not returning to their homes.

19. Government authorities informed the mission that they had established local police units with Kosovo Albanian participation in some 100 "secured" villages. The only ethnic Albanian police officers met by the mission were three elderly officers involved in food distribution near Dakovica.

HUMANITARIAN SITUATION

20. As of mid-October, the United Nations High Commissioner for Refugees (UNHCR) estimated that some 200,000 persons were still displaced inside Kosovo. The number of people who had fled to other areas was estimated at 42,000 in Montenegro, 20,500 in Albania, 3,000 in the former Yugoslav Republic of Macedonia, 10,000 in Bosnia and Herzegovina and some 20,000 in Serbia. In 11 European countries recently surveyed by UNHCR, the total number of applications by asylum-seekers from the Federal Republic of Yugoslavia increased from 11,000 in the first quarter of 1998 to 28,000 in the third. Some 80 to 90 per cent of the applicants are asylum-seekers from Kosovo.

21. Significant progress was made in the return of displaced persons in Kosovo following the ceasefire and the 13 October accord. UNHCR estimates that up to 50,000 people have returned to their original villages, including 2,000 internally displaced persons from Montenegro. Since the military withdrawal on 27 October, thousands of displaced persons have returned to their villages. Many of the returnees whose houses were intact indicated that they would stay and would shelter neighbours who had lost their homes. Others are repairing homes to bring back their families. In some areas, villagers were preparing to plant the winter crop of wheat. Although there were some reports of harassment and obstruction by security forces, most returnees encountered few problems.

22. As of mid-October, people living in the open presented one of the major concerns to the international community. Of the 10,000 internally displaced persons estimated to be living under plastic sheeting before the 27 October military withdrawal, almost all had either returned to their villages or were staying with host families. There were still, however, a number of villages that remained deserted.

23. There are still many displaced families remaining with host families and in towns that have been untouched by the hostilities. This, in turn, has created problems. In many towns private dwellings are packed to three or four times their normal capacity, creating serious sanitary hazards.

24. UNHCR estimates that there are some 20,000 damaged houses, of which approximately 60 per cent are currently inhabitable. From 2 to 4 November, United Nations agencies, non-governmental organizations and the Kosovo Diplomatic Observer Mission conducted a village-by-village survey in order to get an accurate picture of the number of returnees and the condition of houses. The results of the survey are expected to help aid agencies in planning emergency shelter assistance and relief supplies. Preliminary indications are that some 370 villages have suffered varying degrees of damage. UNHCR, together with non-governmental organizations, is currently distributing 3,000 emergency shelter kits, pending a more systematic distribution of shelter materials upon completion of the inter-agency survey.

25. Access by humanitarian agencies to internally displaced persons has generally improved since the time of my previous report, although delays in obtaining entry visas from the authorities of the Federal Republic of Yugoslavia for their staff and difficulties in obtaining radio licences persist.

26. The encouraging response from donors to the current United Nations Consolidated Inter-agency Appeal for Humanitarian Assistance to Kosovo has enabled United Nations humanitarian agencies to step up emergency assistance to the victims of the conflict. From 28 October to 4 November, UNHCR escorted multi-agency convoys that delivered relief aid for 208,700 people in various parts of Kosovo. Supplies came from UNHCR, the World Food Programme (WFP), Mercy Corps International, Children's Aid Direct, Catholic Relief Services and Oxfam. Convoys are currently running three times a day, six days a week.

27. The initiative of the authorities of the Federal Republic of Yugoslavia to establish distribution centres throughout Kosovo has been welcomed by United Nations agencies as a constructive step. However, many potential beneficiaries interviewed by the mission stressed that the decision to delegate management of the centres to the local police is likely to dissuade Albanian internally displaced persons from taking advantage of such facilities. In line with the United Nations principle that assistance should be delivered where it is most needed, most agencies have so far opted to continue to distribute aid mainly through the Mother Teresa Society, which has a wide network and enjoys the trust of the Albanian population. Since it is questionable whether any Serb in need in Kosovo would be in a position to use the Albanian-managed Mother Teresa centres, assistance to needy Serbs is channelled through the Yugoslav Red Cross Society.

28. The situation of refugees and internally displaced persons in Montenegro, which hosts the biggest number of internally displaced persons outside Kosovo, remains of concern. The decision by the Government of Montenegro to close its border to internally displaced persons from Kosovo on 11 September is still in force. The authorities have justified this decision on economic and security grounds, voicing particular concern about potential destabilization in Montenegro as a result of the situation in Kosovo.

29. With almost half of the Montenegrin population living under the poverty line and with refugees and internally displaced persons comprising up to 12 per cent of the total population, Montenegro may indeed face a lack of capacity to cope with the problem. Economic sanctions against the Federal Republic of Yugoslavia and the general downturn in Montenegro's economy have made it virtually impossible for the Government, through the local Red Cross, to continue on its own to provide comprehensive assistance to the 42,000 new arrivals from Kosovo, in addition to a refugee caseload of 25,000 from the

former Yugoslavia. However, considerable assistance is being provided by the international community to these persons.

30. A recent assessment mission by the Food and Agriculture Organization of the United Nations (FAO) to the Federal Republic of Yugoslavia concluded that the conflict in Kosovo was affecting the agricultural sector through uncertain access by returnees to their land, the collapse of local cereal production, a shortage of farming equipment and a decline in livestock. FAO will appeal for essential agricultural inputs to enable basic food production activities.

MINES

31. There have been many reports of mines being laid in Kosovo by both the Government forces and the Kosovo Albanian paramilitary units. The Deputy Chief of the General Staff of the Federal Republic of Yugoslavia asserted that the Yugoslav army had laid mines only on the borders with Albania and the former Yugoslav Republic of Macedonia, but not in the interior; that they were properly and accurately recorded in accordance with international conventions; and that the army was in a position to lift all mines without the assistance of the United Nations or other agencies. There are, however, some reports of small protective minefields being laid by police around their positions in central Kosovo. Reports of mined areas in the territories dominated by Kosovo Albanian paramilitary units are mostly undetailed.

32. Landmines and booby traps are becoming a growing problem in Kosovo, both for displaced persons returning to their homes and for humanitarian personnel. As internally displaced persons returned to their villages, several people were reportedly killed by anti-personnel mines or booby traps laid around houses, buildings and wells. Vehicle mines are also present on a number of dirt roads in the province. The reported presence of mines has restricted humanitarian access in several areas. This situation will be exacerbated by the onset of winter, when snow will cover traces of landmine locations. Humanitarian agencies have asked local communities to seek the assistance of Kosovo Albanian paramilitary units in removing landmines in the areas that they control. Efforts are under way to train relief staff in mine awareness and first aid. In the absence of a technical mine survey mission, the general uncertainty regarding mined areas poses a particular threat.

HUMAN RIGHTS

33. The Office of the United Nations High Commissioner for Human Rights continues its monitoring presence in Kosovo and reports regularly to the United Nations High Commissioner for Human Rights and the Special Rapporteur of the Commission on Human Rights, Jiri Dienstbier. From 21 to 29 October, the Special Rapporteur conducted his third visit to the Federal Republic of Yugoslavia. His report on human rights in Bosnia and Herzegovina, Croatia and the Federal Republic of Yugoslavia, including Kosovo, is contained in documents A/53/322 and Add.1.

34. Reports on the situation of human rights are consistent with the categories of serious violations of human rights that have characterized the crisis in Kosovo for many months. The human rights situation appears not to have changed significantly since the signing of the 16 October agreement. Violations have been attributed to Serbian security forces, Kosovo Albanian paramilitary units and village defence groups. Retaliatory and armed action, torture and ill-treatment, arbitrary detention, forced disappearances, harassment and discriminatory treatment are widely reported.

35. Religious and cultural monuments have been damaged and vandalized, both in conflict-affected areas and in urban areas where no fighting has taken place. In discussions with the Special Rapporteur and the staff of the Office of the United Nations High Commissioner for Human Rights, Government representatives in Pristina confirmed that in some locations Government forces had been responsible for deliberate and retaliatory destruction of property owned by Kosovo Albanians. Returning internally displaced persons and Government officials have also confirmed the practice of the "screening" of internally displaced persons, in which men are separated from women and children and then held for questioning for periods ranging from hours to several days. It is reported that many of those detained are beaten and ill-treated during interrogation.

36. The Serbian Ministry of Justice has also confirmed that more than 1,500 persons, including 500 in absentia, are currently being investigated under suspicion of involvement in anti-state activities and in activities of the Kosovo Albanian paramilitary units. Some persons have already been convicted and sentenced. Five cases of death in custody have been reported so far. The Office of the United Nations High Commissioner for Human Rights monitors these trials, the first of which began on 22 October in Prizren. The Serbian Minister of the Interior has observed that an amnesty law can be discussed only after a political agreement has been finalized, a census and elections held, and new organs of local government subsequently formed.

37. The need for independent investigations into alleged arbitrary executions gained renewed urgency with the discovery of additional concentrations of corpses in several locations in Kosovo. The United Nations mission also received reports of alleged extra-judicial killings and massacres at Gornje Obrinje, Klecka, Golubovac, Volujak, Malisevo, Rausic, Glogovac and Gremnik. As a result of efforts by the European Union and other international organizations, including OHCHR, and initiatives by the Government of the Federal Republic of Yugoslavia, a group of Finnish forensic experts arrived in the Federal Republic of Yugoslavia on 20 October to assist the authorities in investigations into alleged arbitrary killings and mass graves. According to the Finnish Ministry for Foreign Affairs, the group also intended to carry out independent investigations as necessary. Unfortunately, the Government of the Federal Republic of Yugoslavia failed to cooperate fully with the International Tribunal for the Former Yugoslavia. A team of Tribunal officials, led by Chief Prosecutor Louise Arbour, was unable to visit Kosovo since the requested visas were not issued by the Federal Republic of Yugoslavia.

38. There are growing concerns as to the fate and whereabouts of the 140 to 150 civilians and police officers who are still missing after having been abducted by the Kosovo Albanian paramilitary units. The authorities of the Federal Republic of Yugoslavia report that 249 civilians and police have been abducted by Kosovo Albanian paramilitary units. The most recent of these cases involves two journalists of the state news agency, who went missing on 18 October; despite assurances about their well-being and imminent release, reports now indicate that they have been "sentenced" to 60 days' imprisonment. During his visit to Kosovo, the Special Rapporteur has appealed for the release of all abductees.

V. United Nations Mission to the Federal Republic of Yugoslavia

39. In a statement to the press on 6 October 1998 on behalf of the Security Council, the President of the Council requested me to consider how the Secretariat might be ensured a first-hand capability to assess developments on the ground, and to continue reporting to the Council on compliance with its resolutions 1160 (1998) and 1199 (1998). In response to that request, and following consultations with the authorities of the Federal Republic of Yugoslavia, I dispatched a United Nations interdepartmental mission, headed by Staffan de Mistura, Director of the United Nations Information Centre in Rome, to the Federal Republic of Yugoslavia to look into those matters. In view of the expected deployment by OSCE of the Kosovo Verification Mission, the United Nations mission also assessed possible modalities for the coordination of activities between OSCE and United Nations agencies on the ground.

40. Between 17 and 27 October, the mission visited the Federal Republic of Yugoslavia, including Kosovo and Montenegro, as well as the OSCE secretariat in Vienna. Members of the mission met with a number of government and local officials, as well as with representatives of the Kosovo Albanian community. They also held consultations with international organizations, international and local non-governmental organizations and members of the diplomatic community in the Federal Republic of Yugoslavia. The mission visited various parts of Kosovo (see map), and interviewed a number of local citizens

of different ethnic backgrounds. The head of the mission held consultations with senior OSCE and Kosovo Verification Mission officials.

41. So far, the Secretariat's capability to assess developments on the ground has been limited mainly to the humanitarian and human rights situation. Information in these areas has effectively been provided on a regular basis by UNHCR in its capacity as lead agency, and OHCHR, which has contributed to the Secretary-General's monthly reports prepared pursuant to resolution 1160 (1998). The Office of the High Commissioner for Human Rights, through the Special Rapporteur, has a separate mandate to report to the General Assembly and the Commission on Human Rights on human rights violations in the former Yugoslavia. Although the United Nations liaison office in Belgrade informs the Secretariat on political and military developments in the Federal Republic of Yugoslavia, including in Kosovo, it does not have a mandate to report to the Security Council on these issues, nor does it have a presence in Kosovo. It thus does not have the capacity to provide to the Council consistent, comprehensive first-hand information on the situation on the ground. Meanwhile, OSCE and NATO confirmed to the United Nations mission their preparedness to report to the Security Council on the situation in Kosovo in accordance with their newly approved mandates. Having explored various modalities for providing the Council with first-hand information on the situation in Kosovo, Mr. de Mistura prepared several alternatives for my consideration.

42. In doing so, he has taken into account that UNHCR, as the lead humanitarian agency in the region, has enhanced its coordinating role with arrangements to encompass other humanitarian partners operating in Kosovo and the increasing number of international and national non-governmental organizations represented on the ground. Weekly meetings chaired by UNHCR are held to coordinate the provision of assistance and to avoid the duplication of activities between partners. UNHCR also has good working relations with federal and local authorities. Effective coordination arrangements are thus in place to ensure comprehensive reporting on the humanitarian situation. The activities of the Office of the High Commissioner for Human Rights in the Federal Republic of Yugoslavia, in particular in Kosovo, are to be strengthened in the fields of monitoring, training and capacity-building, by increasing the number of Office personnel in the field. The memorandum of understanding between OHCHR and the Government of the Federal Republic of Yugoslavia was concluded on 9 November 1998.

43. It is self-evident that OSCE, with 2,000 Kosovo Verification Mission monitors due to be deployed on the ground, is becoming the lead political organization dealing with the Kosovo crisis. The principal task of the Mission will be to monitor compliance with Security Council resolution 1199 (1998). The Mission will not enforce compliance, nor will it respond to local disturbances, react to hostilities or enforce access by relief organizations.

44. Pending the establishment of the OSCE Kosovo Verification Mission, United Nations agencies, through the UNHCR liaison office with the Kosovo Diplomatic Observer Mission in Pristina, will continue to cooperate with the Kosovo Diplomatic Observer Mission, which is expected in the transitional period to start acting as the Kosovo Verification Mission and eventually to be absorbed by it. Initial consultations by Mr. de Mistura with the head of the Kosovo Verification Mission, William Walker, and with the pre-deployment logistical team for the Mission, as well as with OSCE Secretary-General Giancarlo Aragona and the central planning team of the Mission, reflected a strong desire on the part of both organizations to ensure that there is early agreement on coordination issues, in order to avoid the danger of overlapping or any misconception of the roles of each organization, and to ensure the optimal use of the international community's resources.

45. To this end, it is envisaged that the United Nations role in Kosovo will focus on humanitarian and human rights issues and UNHCR is thus expected to remain the lead agency in the humanitarian field and OHCHR in the field of human rights. In order to facilitate coordination between the Kosovo Verification Mission and UNHCR on the ground, UNHCR has established close liaison with OSCE in Vienna, and with the Kosovo Verification Mission advance party in the field. The Office for the Coordination of Humanitarian Affairs is also expected to establish a presence in Pristina, under the UNHCR umbrella, to assist in coordination efforts and longer-term reconstruction/post-conflict development plans in Kosovo. For its part, OHCHR is planning to open a sub-office in Pristina and, with the Kosovo Verification Mission and UNHCR, will establish an effective system of information sharing on cases of human rights violations in Kosovo. While liaison with NATO is expected to be maintained primarily through the NATO liaison office at United Nations Headquarters, it is anticipated that coordination on the ground will be established in Pristina.

VI. Observations and Recommendations

46. I welcome the accord reached by the President of the Federal Republic of Yugoslavia and the United States Special Envoy on 13 October 1998 and the agreements of 15 October between the Federal Republic of Yugoslavia and NATO and of 16 October between the Federal Republic of Yugoslavia and the OSCE. I believe the establishment of the Kosovo Verification Mission can contribute to the peaceful settlement of the Kosovo crisis, and I call upon all parties concerned to cooperate with the mission. For its part, the United Nations will continue its humanitarian and human rights activities and will support the efforts of the Kosovo Verification Mission, regional organizations and individual Member States aimed at restoring peace and stability to the region. The complexity and the scope of tasks in Kosovo require coordinated and concerted efforts by all organisations on the ground. All United Nations agencies operating there will establish their lines of communication with the Kosovo Verification Mission to this end. Moreover, the United Nations is prepared to provide assistance to the Mission operation through the United Nations Logistics Base at Brindisi and the United Nations Staff College in Turin.

47. I also welcome the efforts of Christopher Hill of the United States of America, supported by European Union Envoy Wolfgang Petrisch of Austria, in promoting a political dialogue between the Serbian authorities and the representatives of the Albanian community in Kosovo and I call on all parties to cooperate with them in their endeavours.

48. While welcoming reports of the withdrawal of Government forces in Kosovo to agreed levels, I urge all the parties concerned to honour their commitments and to comply fully with the Security Council resolutions. In this regard, reports of the return of Kosovo Albanian paramilitary units to positions vacated by Government forces and particularly by their continued attacks against security forces and civilians are disturbing. This situation makes it all the more urgent that early deployment of Kosovo Verification Mission monitors take place, with a 24-hour presence in order to restore stability and confidence and to enable continuous verification of events on the ground.

49. I am also disturbed by the denial of cooperation on the part of the Government of the Federal Republic of Yugoslavia with the International Tribunal for the Former Yugoslavia. I urge the authorities of the Federal Republic of Yugoslavia to comply with the demands of the international community including, inter alia, paragraph 14 of Security Council resolution 1203 (1998).

50. Despite the beginning of the mass return of internally displaced persons to their homes, the situation on the ground indicates that their needs must be further addressed at the international, regional and local levels. In this connection, the effective and well-established coordinating role played by UNHCR as the lead agency for humanitarian activities in Kosovo should be maintained and reflected in a formal agreement with OSCE. The coordinating role of UNHCR will be further reinforced by the larger involvement of the Office for the Coordination of Humanitarian Affairs in facilitation of coordination efforts and longer-term reconstruction and post-conflict development plans in Kosovo. More attention will also need to be paid to the humanitarian needs of refugees in Montenegro, as well as to those of the half a million refugees in Serbia.

51. Given the fact that legitimate personal security fears were the overriding obstacle to the return of internally displaced persons, political action to ensure real security to the people is a requisite for any solution to the humanitarian crisis. Such a process would be facilitated if the authorities of the Federal Republic of Yugoslavia were to extend guarantees to all returning civilians so as to avoid the blanket interrogation of male internally displaced persons. The issuance of appropriate amnesty legislation to permit this to happen would be crucial in this regard. Likewise, Kosovo Albanian paramilitary units must stop any armed actions to provoke the Federal Republic of Yugoslavia security forces and must put an immediate end to abductions and other violent activities.

52. The persistent fear expressed about returnees' security highlights the need to actively monitor the activities of and to train local police forces, particularly in the area of human rights. Unless this issue is addressed on an urgent basis, the return process will be seriously undermined by a lack of confidence in the ability or the desire of the local police to protect returnees. If requested and deemed appropriate, the United Nations Civilian Police Unit would be prepared to provide advice in this area. The Office of the High Commissioner for Human Rights will provide existing manuals and other training resources on the subject.

53. The establishment of a United Nations human rights sub-office in Kosovo will allow OHCHR to perform its expanded monitoring and promotional tasks in close cooperation with the Kosovo Verification Mission and UNHCR and other international and national institutions and organizations. Early, effective and coordinated action in cases of human rights abuses will be critical in building confidence for the return of refugees and displaced persons.

54. It is necessary to establish a capability to initiate a comprehensive and integrated mine action plan, including mine awareness, education, information, mine-marking and mine clearance. The United Nations Mine Action Centre will study the possibility of providing assistance in this area.

55. The immediate crisis in Kosovo should not overshadow the necessity to assess the medium-term rehabilitation and reconstruction needs of the Federal Republic of Yugoslavia. As conditions allow, the World Bank, the United Nations Development Programme and bilateral donors should play a major role in this process, particularly in post-conflict projects in Kosovo.

56. With regard to the issue of a first-hand capability to assess the situation on the ground (see sect. V above), it is recalled that subsequent to its request to me, the Security Council endorsed the establishment of the Kosovo Verification Mission by OSCE. Under the 16 October agreement between the Federal Republic of Yugoslavia and OSCE, the Kosovo Verification Mission has been assigned, inter alia, the responsibility of reporting to the Council. In my view, this should subsume the reporting on the situation in Kosovo from a political perspective, a function that the Secretariat has been carrying out with considerable difficulty, for lack of an independent presence on the ground in the past few months. It is quite obvious that any need that might have existed for such a presence has been superseded by the decision to establish the Kosovo Verification Mission. Taking this into account and having considered the options presented by Mr. de Mistura, I have decided against recommending a United Nations political presence in Kosovo, thus avoiding parallel reporting channels that might lead to confusion and overlapping in the field, as well as unnecessary financial expenditure. I consider it important at this stage, therefore, to develop clear channels of communication between the United Nations and OSCE on this issue. If necessary, short-term missions could be sent to the region to look into specific aspects at the Council's request. Should the future situation require an expanded United Nations presence on the ground, the Council could revert to this issue at a later stage.

57. In its resolution 1203 (1998), the Security Council requested me, in consultation with the parties concerned with the agreements signed in Belgrade on 16 October 1998 between the Federal Republic of Yugoslavia and OSCE, and on 15 October 1998 between the Federal Republic of Yugoslavia and NATO, to report regularly to the Council regarding implementation of that resolution. The agreement between the Federal Republic of Yugoslavia and OSCE, however, indicates that the latter will report directly to the Council. I suggest that OSCE and NATO report to the Council through me (as do the Stabilization Force and the Office of the High Representative), while I would continue to report to the Council on the humanitarian and human rights situation in Kosovo. As to the frequency of these reports, this should be determined in consultation with the Kosovo Verification Mission and NATO. It is my opinion, however, that under the present circumstances and in view of the stability achieved on the ground, quarterly reports would suffice, unless otherwise requested by the Council or necessitated by events in the area.

Annex I: Information on the Situation in Kosovo and Measures Taken by the Organization for Security and Cooperation in Europe, Submitted pursuant to Paragraphs 13 and 16 of Security Council Resolution 1160 (1998) (September/October 1998)

GENERAL SITUATION

1. The period since the previous report of 21 September 1998 has been characterized by relative calm, with sporadic fighting throughout Kosovo and specific operations launched by Yugoslav security forces in several locations. Burning and looting of houses, destruction of property and shelling of villages continued, especially in the Djakovica and Prizren areas.

2. By the end of September, for the first time since the conflict erupted, Serb security forces launched operations not only in central Kosovo and along the border to Albania, but also in an area north of Pristina, between Mitrovica and Podujevo, the so-called Shala region (triangle between Kosovska Mitrovica, Podujevo and Vuitrn), causing the displacement of numerous persons, who moved to Vuitrn and Pristina. This operation was later extended to several villages along the foot of the iavica mountain (the edge of the Drenica region).

3. During the second week of October, armed forces of the Federal Republic of Yugoslavia were observed redeploying personnel and equipment away from some of the larger Kosovo towns to locations near the border.

4. Despite announcements by both the Serbian Government and the Kosovo Liberation Army (KLA), declaring their readiness to show "self-restraint" in response to a call from the Security Council last month, cases of fighting, as well as destruction of property, continue to be reported.

MONITORING ACTIVITIES IN KOSOVO

5. The Kosovo Diplomatic Observer Mission continued its activity in the province, monitoring the situation and compliance with Security Council resolutions 1160 (1998) and 1199 (1998).

6. At the beginning of October, the most noticeable response to international demands was the partial withdrawal of units, in particular those of the Yugoslav army. The security forces behaved in a more discrete fashion, but with still noticeable presence. Observers deemed this presence necessary given the likelihood that KLA, emboldened by the circumstances, could take advantage of the depleted security arrangements.

THE SITUATION OF THE CIVILIAN POPULATION

7. According to the Office of the United Nations High Commissioner for Refugees (UNHCR), the continued crackdown by the Serbian police and military against KLA strongholds has forced an estimated 300,000 people to flee their homes. Out of these, 200,000 are displaced within Kosovo and an estimated 50,000 internally displaced persons still remain in the open. Fear is still a major factor inhibiting their return and an additional concern is the destruction of housing, which raises the question of what they can return to.

8. Generally, the conflict has continued to cause more displaced persons and refugees than returnees. In addition, internally displaced Kosovars have experienced increasing difficulties in entering Montenegro from Serbia.

INFLUX OF REFUGEES

9. As at 13 October, UNHCR was reporting a total of 20,500 refugees in Albania, out of which 7,000 remain in the Tropoje district. During the reporting period, the major flow of refugees entering Albania came from Montenegro, as crossing the border with the Federal Republic of Yugoslavia Province of Kosovo became more hazardous for refugees.

10. A critical juncture was reached during the second half of September, when a sudden large influx of more than 4,500 Kosovar refugees expelled from Montenegro were driven by Montenegrin authorities to the border crossing point of Bashkim, in the remote northern valley of Vermosh, from which the refugees tried to make their way to Shkodra. Most of them came from the Decane area, reflecting the ongoing fighting there. The refugees found a much deteriorated security situation, suffering several ambushes, which only added to the very difficult conditions of the roads.

11. At other parts of the border between Albania and the Federal Republic of Yugoslavia, refugees continued to enter Albania, although in smaller numbers than before, since the first snows in mountainous areas created additional difficulties for those trying to cross the border. During the first week of October, limited numbers of refugees continued to enter Albania through the Has district and via Shkodra lake. UNHCR has estimated that some 3,000 remain in the Tropoje district and around 900 in the Kukes/Has district.

SPILLOVER POTENTIAL OF THE KOSOVO CONFLICT

12. The missions of the Organization for Security and Cooperation in Europe (OSCE) in Tirana, Skopje and Sarajevo were instructed to follow closely the spillover potential of the Kosovo conflict.

13. The refugee situation in Albania during the reporting period became even gloomier following the influx in the north, making it very difficult for the Albanian authorities to handle. UNHCR expressed its readiness to declare a humanitarian state of emergency if the authorities were unable to provide sufficient accommodation.

14. The problem of refugees in Albania acquired much wider political dimensions because it appeared impossible to hold all the refugees in the north-east. Of the perhaps 25,000 refugees that have crossed into Albania, many have moved abroad, and significant numbers have taken refuge in Tirana and Durres. A few of this latter group will be persuaded to move to collective accommodation.

15. Enforcement of law and order in the north-east of Albania remained extremely weak and very much depended on family ties, giving the international community continued cause for concern. The unpredictable security situation, along with deteriorating weather conditions, caused most international agencies to abandon the area.

16. In Shkodra, despite high tension connected to events in Tirana, the situation remained relatively calm during the reporting period, although the local police apparently teamed up with ex-police related to the Democratic Party. In Bajram Curri, ongoing lawlessness resulted in the heavy looting of the UNHCR warehouse, and most humanitarian agencies working in the area decided either to cease activities in the region or severely cut back on their operations.

17. As regards border incidents, by the end of September, a serious clash took place near the Morina border post, as about 30 soldiers of the Federal Republic of Yugoslavia opened fire on Albanian territory after a truck of the Federal Republic of Yugoslavia struck a mine believed to have been laid by KLA. This incident was followed by the shelling of the Albanian village of Padesh from the Federal Republic of Yugoslavia. By mid-October it was reported that units of the Federal Republic of Yugoslavia in the areas bordering Albania were reinforced far beyond normal staffing just before threats of air strikes by the North Atlantic Treaty Organization (NATO).

18. During the first week of October, an increase in KLA activities in the Has and Tropoje districts was observed, with KLA moving openly in some border areas. Internationals observed what appeared to be a training facility in Babine and a KLA logistics base at Papaj. The Padesh plateau and the town of Tropoje, both former strongholds of KLA, are virtually empty of irregular fighters.

19. The political crisis in Albania in mid-September, which deteriorated into a situation of violence, with shooting and looting of official buildings and private property in Tirana, did not help to enhance the already weak State presence in northern Albania and thus the control by Albanian authorities of the border with the Federal Republic of Yugoslavia.

20. Prime Minister Nano received considerable criticism from all political parties concerning a declaration he made in Lisbon in early September, a few days before his resignation, calling for a Kosovo within a democratic Yugoslav Federation.

21. It remains clear that an unresolved Kosovo problem will continue to link Albania to the crisis in the Yugoslav province and that an unstable Albania, used as a base or housing numbers of disenchanted former fighters, will only add to the difficulties of finding a long-term solution. Therefore, initiatives like the Friends of Albania Group serve as stabilization, not only in Albania, but in the region as a whole.

22. In the former Yugoslav Republic of Macedonia, the situation at the northern border remained calm during the first half of October, without substantive incidents and with all border crossings open and functioning normally. There have been no significant incidents; illegal crossings and smuggling have been less than at any time since independence, attributable in large part to the presence of Yugoslav security forces on the northern side of the border and the increased risks of illegal crossing during the Kosovo crisis. On the western border with Albania there has been no substantive change in the pattern of activity. Periodic incidents continue to occur of attempted illegal entry, sometimes armed, of small groups from Albania. These groups sometimes engage security forces of the former Yugoslav Republic of Macedonia, and are sometimes fired upon.

23. According to UNHCR there are 3,000 people in the former Yugoslav Republic of Macedonia whose presence is directly linked to the conflict in Kosovo.

24. The potential risks of spillover from Kosovo to the former Yugoslav Republic of Macedonia seem to be dividing public opinion along ethnic lines as the ethnic population of the former Yugoslav Republic of Macedonia fears the consequences of military action and an implicit endorsement of such action by many in the ethnic Albanian community. The leader of the principal political party representing the Serb minority, the Democratic Party of Serbs in the former Yugoslav Republic of Macedonia, warned that an attack on Serbia would be interpreted as an attack on Serbs generally. Still, during the parliamentary election campaign, Kosovo was not a major issue, attracting minimal public comment.

25. By the second week of October, an estimated 7,800 refugees from Kosovo had settled in Bosnia and Herzegovina, the great majority of whom have come to the Sarajevo area. The peak rate of this inflow came in mid-September (approximately 800 weekly arrivals) and it has declined rapidly since. Almost all the refugees are Muslim, ethnic Albanians; only a handful of Serb refugees from Kosovo have been reported. Limited preparations have been made to provide refugee camps. Only three are currently operational, and another three are planned. Some 1,000 are sheltered at a Coca Cola plant in the Sarajevo suburb of Hadzici, while the other two camps house around 100 each. The remaining refugees have dispersed throughout Bosnia and Herzegovina finding shelter most often through the hospitality of relatives.

26. Though no specific incidents have been reported, OSCE field staff have noticed a "domino effect" on the general level of reconciliation in those areas experiencing inflows of refugees from Kosovo. In areas already struggling with return issues, the additional presence of refugees from Kosovo has added tension. In those areas, other return-

ees regard the new arrivals from Kosovo as competitors for precious available accommodations.

MEASURES TAKEN BY THE ORGANIZATION FOR SECURITY AND COOPERATION IN EUROPE

27. On 6 October, the Minister for Foreign Affairs of the Republic of Yugoslavia, Zivadin Jovanovic, sent a letter to the OSCE Chairman-in-Office, Polish Foreign Minister Bronislav Geremek, inviting OSCE "to witness first-hand the positive evolution of the most crucial processes in Kosovo and Metohija". In a press release issued the following day, the Chairman-in-Office emphasized that the best conditions for accepting this invitation would appear when the Federal Republic of Yugoslavia satisfied the requirements contained in decision No. 218 of the OSCE Permanent Council, as well as Security Council resolutions 1160 (1998) and 1199 (1998). He underlined that it was up to the Federal Republic of Yugoslavia, through full compliance with the terms of the above-mentioned documents, to enable OSCE to make its contribution to the resolution of the crisis over Kosovo.

28. On 15 October 1998, the OSCE Permanent Council, recalling paragraph 1 of its decision No. 218 and the statement of the Chairman-in-Office of 7 October 1998 confirming the long-standing readiness of OSCE to give its contribution to the peaceful solution of the crisis in Kosovo, adopted decision No. 259 supporting the efforts of the Chairman-in-Office to arrange with the authorities of the Federal Republic of Yugoslavia for OSCE to make such contribution.

29. Based on arrangements reached by Richard Holbrooke, United States Special Envoy and representing also the Contact Group, and Yugoslav President Miloevic, the OSCE Chairman-in-Office, and the Minister for Foreign Affairs of the Federal Republic of Yugoslavia signed an agreement on the establishment of an OSCE Kosovo Verification Mission in Belgrade on 16 October 1998.

30. The overall task of the Verification Mission will be to verify compliance by all parties in Kosovo with Security Council resolution 1199 (1998) and to report instances of progress and/or non-compliance to the OSCE Permanent Council, the Security Council and other organizations. Further, the Verification Mission will be tasked to supervise elections in Kosovo in order to ensure their openness and fairness.

31. The Verification Mission, unprecedented in size, will be composed of up to 2000 unarmed verifiers and will establish a permanent presence at as many locations throughout Kosovo as it deems necessary to fulfil its responsibilities. The current Kosovo Diplomatic Observer Mission will act in place of the OSCE Verification Mission pending its establishment, and will subsequently be absorbed by the new Mission.

32. During the talks on 16 October in Belgrade, the Minister for Foreign Affairs of the Federal Republic of Yugoslavia made a number of promises to the effect that the Federal Government would do its best to implement the agreement and expressed hope that the Verification Mission would contribute to assessing the situation "in an objective, truthful and unbiased manner". He also made a solemn promise to care for the security of the personnel of the Verification Mission in accordance with the Vienna Conventions. He confirmed that the Verification Mission would have all possibilities of movement and access to desired information on the ground.

33. On the same day, the OSCE Chairman-in-Office met in Pristina with Ibrahim Rugova. The leader of the Albanian community in Kosovo expressed the view that the agreement signed in Belgrade contained many weak points that could cause disappointment in the Albanian community. He also voiced disappointment that no representatives of the Albanian community from Kosovo had been a party to the negotiations.

34. In spite of these critical moments, Mr. Rugova welcomed the agreement and unequivocally expressed the view that the Albanian community in Kosovo would cooperate with the Verification Mission. He sees this act as an important step towards enlarging the international presence in Kosovo, which should facilitate negotiations for a political solution to the crisis, recognition of the Albanian community institutions, including local police, and deciding over the future of Kosovo.

35. The agreement on the OSCE Kosovo Verification Mission and the agreement on the NATO-Kosovo air verification regime, signed on 15 October in Belgrade, are aimed at supporting international efforts to solve the crisis in Kosovo and constitute an important step towards development of a political framework to ensure compliance with the demands set out in Security Council resolution 1199 (1998). The agreements highlight the verification of compliance with the said resolution, as stipulated in paragraph 16 thereof.

36. Once this important political support is secured, the OSCE Chairman-in-Office would be ready to begin immediately deployment of the Verification Mission on the ground. It has already been decided to dispatch to the Federal Republic of Yugoslavia a small OSCE technical advance mission to start preparation of the operation, the scope of which goes beyond previous OSCE experience. Consequently, the 13-member OSCE technical advance mission arrived on 17 October in Belgrade and started talks with the authorities of the Federal Republic of Yugoslavia regarding the preparations for establishing the OSCE Kosovo Verification Mission. On 18 October, the OSCE technical advance mission arrived in Pristina to assess conditions for deployment of the Verification Mission.

37. Acting as OSCE Chairman-in-Office, Mr. Geremek decided to appoint William Graham Walker as Head of the OSCE Kosovo Verification Mission, effective 17 October 1998. Mr. Walker has recently served as Special Representative of the Secretary-General as Transitional Administrator for the United Nations Transitional Administration for Eastern Slavonia, Baranja and Western Sirmium (UNTAES), in Croatia.

38. On 17 October, the OSCE Chairman-in-Office sent a letter to the Secretary-General informing him of the signing of the agreement with the authorities of the Federal Republic of Yugoslavia and expressing his hope that the agreements would be acknowledged and supported by the Security Council in an appropriate resolution in order to make these acts effective and to ensure the safety and security of international verifiers.

39. The OSCE Chairman-in-Office and the OSCE Representative of the Freedom of the Media, Helmut Duve, have on several occasions expressed their concern over the treatment of foreign journalists, as well as domestic, independent media, by the authorities of the Federal Republic of Yugoslavia. In a press release issued on 16 October, Mr. Duve called upon the Belgrade Government to stop repression of the media. Reacting to a government decree leading to the closure of Nasa Borba, a leading independent newspaper, the previous day, he noted that "a free media is one of the elements that will ensure the success of the difficult task of bringing peace to Kosovo".

Annex II: Letter Dated 27 October 1998 from the Secretary-General of the North Atlantic Treaty Organization Addressed to the Secretary-General

Thank you for your letter of 21 October, in which you apprised me of United Nations efforts with regard to the crisis in Kosovo.

Further to my letter of 22 October, I am writing to inform you that the North Atlantic Council today decided to maintain the activation order for the limited air response on the understanding that execution would be subject to a further Council decision and assessments that the Federal Republic of Yugoslavia was not in substantial compliance with Security Council resolution 1199 (1998). The Council also decided to continue the present air activities as part of the phased air campaign.

This decision was reached by the North Atlantic Treaty Organization (NATO) after a thorough assessment by NATO of the level of compliance by the Federal Republic of Yugoslavia with the provisions of Security Council resolution 1199 (1998). NATO aerial surveillance assets and the Kosovo Diplomatic Observer Mission have confirmed that Federal Republic of Yugoslavia and Serb security forces have withdrawn in substantial numbers towards pre-March levels. Also, the necessary conditions are being established for the return of refugees and displaced persons. However, NATO will continue to monitor the situation very closely.

In this context, NATO welcomes the recent adoption of Security Council resolution 1203 (1998), which, inter alia, endorses and supports the verification agreements signed between the Federal Republic of Yugoslavia and NATO and OSCE, respectively. We are continuing our work to ensure close coordination between NATO and OSCE and hope that both missions can be fully operational in the very near future. Our military authorities are developing planning for the possible extraction of OSCE verifiers in an emergency.

Meanwhile, NATO military authorities have begun technical discussions with some nations within the Partnership for Peace about associating the latter with the NATO air surveillance mission.

I will continue to keep you informed of further important developments.
(Signed) Javier Solana

123. Report of the Secretary-General Prepared pursuant to Resolutions 1160 (1998), 1199 (1998) and 1203 (1998) UN Doc. S/1998/1147, 4 December 1998

I. Introduction

1. The present report is submitted pursuant to Security Council resolutions 1160 (1998) of 31 March 1998, 1199 (1998) of 23 September 1998 and 1203 (1998) of 24 October 1998. It covers the period since my last report of 12 November 1998 (S/1998/1068).

II. Security Council Committee Established Pursuant to Resolution 1160 (1998)

2. As at 30 November 1998, a total of 53 States listed in my earlier reports (S/1998/608, S/1998/712, S/1998/834, S/1998/912 and S/1998/1068) had reported to the Committee, in accordance with paragraph 12 of resolution 1160 (1998), on the steps they had taken to give effect to the prohibitions imposed by that resolution.

3. At its meeting held on 12 November 1998, the Committee considered reports on violations of the prohibitions established by the Security Council in its resolutions 1160 (1998) and 1199 (1998) received from relevant international organizations, together with information of the same kind gathered by the Secretariat from public sources. The Committee expressed its concern at continuing serious violations of the arms embargo and other prohibitions imposed by resolutions 1160 (1998) and 1199 (1998). The Committee urged States, in particular States neighbouring the Federal Republic of Yugoslavia, to make every effort to comply fully with resolutions 1160 (1998) and 1199 (1998) in seeking to prevent the sale or supply to the Federal Republic of Yugoslavia, including Kosovo, of arms and related matériel of all types and prevent any arming, training and financing of terrorist activities there. The Committee reiterated the responsibility of all States to support international efforts aimed at stabilizing the situation in Kosovo and enhancing the prospect of peace in the region by strictly observing the prohibitions contained in resolutions 1160 (1998) and 1199 (1998) and acting promptly upon their violations.

4. At its meeting on 3 December 1998, the Committee continued consideration of violations reported by regional organizations and information received from public sources. The Committee also decided to hold informal consultations in order to submit, as appropriate, its report to the Security Council in accordance with paragraph 9 (c) of Security Council resolution 1160 (1998) and paragraph 11 of the Committee's revised guidelines for the conduct of its work.

III. Comprehensive Regime to Monitor the Implementation of the Prohibitions Imposed by Security Council Resolution 1160 (1998)

5. The Committee was briefed on the first consultation meeting of organizations participating in the comprehensive monitoring regime, which was convened at United Nations Headquarters on 19 October 1998. Members supported holding such meetings periodically and considered that, in the absence of a comprehensive coordinating mechanism, they could provide a useful framework for exchanging information on the monitoring of the established prohibitions and addressing practical issues arising in that connection.

IV. Situation in Kosovo

6. This section of the report deals with humanitarian and human rights aspects of the situation in Kosovo, as I recommended to the Council in my previous report. It is based on information provided by the Chairman-in-Office of the Organization for Security and Cooperation in Europe (OSCE) (see annex), the Kosovo Diplomatic Observer Mission and individual Member States, as well as contributions provided by the Office of the United Nations High Commissioner for Refugees (UNHCR) and the Office of the United Nations High Commissioner for Human Rights.

HUMANITARIAN SITUATION

7. No major combat between military forces has occurred in Kosovo since the time of my last report, but the situation on the ground is still far from peaceful. Sporadic ceasefire violations were reported by both the Serbian authorities and Kosovo Albanian sources. In most cases it was impossible to identify who initiated the clashes.

8. Since the withdrawal of the Serbian police and Yugoslav military forces on 27 October the return of internally displaced persons to their homes has significantly increased. With the onset of winter, villages across Kosovo are being repopulated, as people uprooted by eight months of fighting are looking for better shelter than plastic tents in the woods, the crammed houses of friends or relatives in urban centres and rented space they could no longer afford in neighbouring countries and territories. As at 24 November, UNHCR estimates that some 75,000 displaced persons have gone back to their villages in hard-hit central and western Kosovo. About 175,000 people remained displaced within Kosovo. Many of them have returned to their villages to find their homes reduced to rubble. These returnees are forced to stay in the houses of their more fortunate neighbours and thus are still displaced, albeit within their own villages.

9. A trickle of several refugee families from northern Albania have returned to Kosovo's western frontier villages. Albania hosts some 24,000 refugees from Kosovo. Lawlessness and bandit attacks on aid agencies in the northern Albanian district of Tropoja have created a precarious security situation, in view of which some of the approximately 2,500 refugees located there decided to return home for lack of other options. UNHCR is working to relocate such refugees to safer areas within Albania, thus avoiding involuntary returns.

10. The Montenegrin Red Cross reported that, as at 24 November, it had provided assistance to some 34,000 internally displaced persons; however, UNHCR believes that the number is now closer to 30,000. Some 10,000 to 12,000 internally displaced persons have returned from Montenegro to Kosovo, but it is impossible to estimate at this time how many have remained there. Many internally displaced persons have returned again to Montenegro, others have gone to Albania or have moved to Western Europe. Only upon receiving the November distribution figures will it be possible to have a more accurate count of the displaced persons still in Montenegro. It will also take a few weeks to establish with more certainty the whereabouts of those displaced persons that have departed from Montenegro.

11. The return process is fragile, and those returning home often sleep with their belongings still packed beside them. Many families come only during the daylight hours, returning to their host families each evening. The fluidity of the movement back makes it almost impossible for the humanitarian organizations to accurately assess the number of people returning at present, but it appears that the number of returnees is growing and that the number living with host families will continue to decrease.

12. At the end of each month, UNHCR and the humanitarian organizations in Kosovo will hold meetings to assess the number of internally displaced persons and returnees inside Kosovo. These meetings will be

attended by UNHCR staff from Montenegro and Albania, where information can be shared and the actual numbers more accurately counted.

OBSTACLES TO RETURNS

13. Uncertainty and continuing danger appear to be the main deterrent to returns. People who have returned spontaneously have done so mainly in search of survival during the expected harsh winter months. In the villages where internally displaced persons have gone back, many have prepared just one room to endure winter conditions.

14. Returns continue to be tentative and little permanent reconstruction is being undertaken. Returnees hesitate to put money into something that they fear they may well lose later. In the towns, businessmen appear to be holding back on investments, awaiting signs that a political settlement may be forthcoming.

15. In many cases, the internally displaced persons have returned to find their houses totally destroyed, prompting them to remain in the towns, where they feel they can at least be assured of continuing relief aid. Another major factor preventing returns is damaged infrastructure - lack of schools, no electricity and polluted wells.

16. International monitors observe increased returns of displaced persons to areas located in Malisevo, Orahovac, Suva Reka, Djakovica, Decani and Drenica municipalities. However, during the reporting period, in the wake of skirmishes between the government forces and Kosovo Albanian paramilitary units, renewed displacement was reported in areas such as Malisevo, south of Komorane and Lapusnik.

CONFIDENCE-BUILDING FOR RETURNEES

17. Most returnees say they will feel more secure when teams of the Kosovo Diplomatic Observer Mission are around them. They anxiously await the arrival of the monitors of the OSCE Kosovo Verification Mission.

18. Where the presence of the Observer Mission is most visible, substantial returns have taken place. For example, between 70 and 100 per cent returns have been reported in the villages of Dragobilje, Ostrozub, Banja, Dobrodeljane and Pagarusa. The Mission has either maintained an outpost or conducted regular patrols in those villages, which have a combined population of more than 10,000. The same is true of seven villages in the Suva Reka region. Since the Mission began to deploy there, 13,000 of the 30,000 residents have returned.

AID AND SHELTER PROGRAMMES

19. UNHCR, together with the World Food Programme and the non-governmental organization community, is continuing to provide aid to the displaced and returnee populations. The frequency of UNHCR-escorted convoys has increased to six days per week. During the third week of November, 120 trucks provided food and non-food assistance for 100,000 beneficiaries in 21 different locations.

20. UNHCR has satellite offices in Pec, Prizren and Mitrovica. Coordination of food and non-food assistance will be decentralized and the number of convoys per week is expected to increase to over 150 trucks by the beginning of December.

21. The UNHCR-non-governmental organization shelter assessment of 2-4 November covered 285 villages, of which 210 had been damaged by the conflict. Nearly 40 per cent of the homes were found to be habitable, requiring basic shelter materials - tiles, bricks, windows - which the Government of the Federal Republic of Yugoslavia should provide, pursuant to Security Council resolution 1199 (1998).

SECURITY

22. A ceasefire called last month has generally held, although there have been arbitrary detentions, killings and kidnappings blamed on both Serbian security forces and the Kosovo Albanian paramilitary units. For the first time in the conflict, self-appointed groups on both sides of the ethnic divide have taken part in these actions, threatening to unravel the fragile peace.

23. Although security checkpoints were dismantled following the 27 October pullback, police continued to control checkpoints on highways, moving to less visible positions on strategic hills. Mobile checkpoints have been established by Serbian security forces and Kosovo Albanian paramilitary units. These have not impeded the access of staff or vehicles of the office of the United Nations High Commissioner for Human Rights during this reporting period. However, at traffic checkpoints established by Serbian police, the Office has both directly observed and received reports of the questioning and search of passengers on regular intercity bus lines. While the pullback has resulted in freer movement, fear of being accosted on the street by police remains.

24. Security remains tight in villages along the border with Albania, where illegal traffic in arms and movement of members of Kosovo Albanian paramilitary units continue. Recently, troops detained an entire village population for 24 hours while they conducted a house-to-house search for weapons.

25. In the meantime, Kosovo Albanian paramilitary units have taken over checkpoints left by Serbian police in the interior villages, provoking incursions by Serbian armoured vehicles and triggering occasional gun battles. In many villages, members of Kosovo Albanian paramilitary units returned with the villagers - often their own family members - and acted as protectors. However, they seem to be in no mood to resume full-scale fighting and are battening down for the winter, as are the Serbian police.

HUMAN RIGHTS

26. The situation of human rights in Kosovo continues to be characterized by the abduction and arbitrary detention of persons, as well as reports of summary execution of persons detained. Reports of systematic severe ill-treatment of persons in police detention and pre-trial detention continue.

27. In November the Office of the High Commissioner for Human Rights devoted all its country-wide staff resources to monitoring court proceedings in Kosovo against persons charged with terrorism, violating or endangering constitutional order or contributing to anti-state activity. Over a month after the accord of 13 October between the President of the Federal Republic of Yugoslavia, Slobodan Milosevic, and the United States Special Envoy, Richard Holbrooke, implementation of the last two points of the accord, which concern prosecution in state courts, remains unclear. The Serbian Minister of Justice has sent teams of prosecutors to district courts in Kosovo to examine individual cases, and court officials have confirmed to the Office of the High Commissioner that they have participated in working sessions with representatives of the Serbian Ministry of Justice and the office of the President of Serbia. The Ministry of Justice, together with the Federal Ministry for Foreign Affairs and the office of the President of Serbia, have solicited the cooperation of the Office of the High Commissioner in the ongoing resolution of individual cases and categories of cases pending in Kosovo to which the Office or the Special Rapporteur have drawn particular attention. These efforts have resulted in the release of several individuals from pre-trial detention and/or detention pending appeal, but new arrests, trials and sentencing continue. Kosovo Albanian media have taken an intense interest in reports of the ill-treatment of detainees and in the court proceedings themselves, particularly the potential application of "paraffin glove evidence". To the knowledge of the Office of the High Commissioner, however, no clear position has been enunciated by the Kosovo Albanian political leadership on amnesty or pardon for detainees. The Kosovo Albanian defence attorneys continue to pursue strongly the interest of their individual clients, as cases come up for trial.

28. The Office of the High Commissioner concentrated its efforts in the district courts of Prizren and Pec, where the bulk of armed activity has occurred and approximately 1,350 cases are pending, far exceeding the number of cases in the courts of Kosovska Mitrovica, Pristina and Gnjilane combined. The district court in Prizren, which had been holding trials related to allegations of terrorism and anti-state activity on a regular daily basis, suspended trials from 31 October to 9 November so that, according to the court president, case review could be conducted. The district court in Pec, however, has continued to hold up to four trials a day, except when weather or security conditions have prevented the transport of defendants to court. The Office of the High

Commissioner has to date recorded 92 completed decisions of courts of first instance throughout Kosovo, but that figure is by no means comprehensive and only includes court documents at hand. Of that number, nearly all decisions have been convictions, with eight acquittals. Sentences range from 60 days to 13 years, with the majority of sentences from two to five years. For sentences of less than five years, until they have been confirmed by a court of a final instance, detention is not mandatory during the appeal process, but most so sentenced have been detained.

29. The number of persons in actual custody is difficult to obtain, as "custody" includes persons in pre-arraignment detention by Serbian police, under the auspices of the Ministry of Interior, and investigative or post-sentencing detention, under the auspices of the Ministry of Justice. On a massive scale, Serbian security officials in Kosovo have arrested and held in police detention large numbers of individuals for periods ranging from several hours to several days. The routine police "screening" of male returnees, however, has abated in recent weeks. Persons in police detention are routinely held incommunicado, without access to attorneys, longer than the three-plus-one days of pre-arraignment detention allowed by law. Their families are not informed of their arrest or of their release from police detention. The number of persons subsequently arraigned and held in investigative detention is unclear, as the International Committee of the Red Cross (ICRC) is not routinely and regularly informed of arraignments by the Ministry of Justice. As a result, the Office of the High Commissioner can only estimate, as have the Serbian Minister of Justice and defence attorneys, that from 1,500 to 1,900 cases are pending on charges related to terrorism, anti-state activity and/or aiding and abetting such activity. This does not include persons in police detention or persons called for "informative talks" by the police, whose number is absolutely unknown and whose names are known only anecdotally or when reported by non-governmental organizations.

30. Since the accord of 13 October and the Agreement of 16 October, information on the activity of Kosovo Albanian paramilitary "tribunals" has become public. The activity of the "tribunals" suggests a pattern of arbitrary arrest and summary execution. On 30 October, two League of Democratic Kosova activists were "arrested" by the Kosovo Albanian paramilitaries in Malisevo and have been "charged" with advocating the surrender of weapons to Serbian authorities. On 3 November, the "KLA Military Police Directorate" issued a communiqué stating that the two men had been arrested and were "under interrogation". The communiqué also acknowledged that two additional individuals had been executed and that Kosovo Albanian paramilitary units were seeking to arrest a member of the presidency of the League of Democratic Kosova. On 31 October, in "policing" activities, members of Kosovo Albanian paramilitary units arrested three men and killed a fourth near Podujevo for "alleged criminal activity".

31. On 1 November, a "Military Court" of Kosovo Albanian paramilitary units sentenced two abducted Tanjug journalists to 60 days of detention for "having committed violations and ignorance of the internal regular civilian-military book of regulations of the KLA, chapter VIII, respectively the military police book of regulations, item 5, page 27". Representatives of international agencies, including ICRC and the Office of the High Commissioner in the Federal Republic of Yugoslavia, have not been allowed to visit the abductees.

32. On 9 November, in Srbica, Kosovo Albanian paramilitary units abducted the third and fourth Serb civilians taken since mid-October, Zlatan Ivanovic and Bojan Pavlovic. In retaliation, on the evening of 11 November, family members of the victims and villagers from Leposavic organized the arbitrary detention of roughly 25 Kosovo Albanian passengers from an intercity bus. It is reported that the detention occurred with the knowledge of Serbian police who, at a minimum, did not intervene to stop it. During the night of 11 November, all but seven of the passengers were released; the seven were held in exchange for the two abducted Serbs. On 12 November, through the intervention of the Kosovo Diplomatic Observer Mission, an exchange took place.

33. On 17 November, near Podujevo, members of Kosovo Albanian paramilitary units abducted a Serbian police officer, Goran Zbiljic. In the same area on the same day, a Kosovo Albanian, Hakif Hoti, was also abducted. On 23 November, Kosovo Albanian paramilitary units issued a communiqué stating that it had "arrested" Mr. Zbiljic and other Albanian "collaborators". On 24 November, through the actions of the Observer Mission, Mr. Zbiljic was released. Nothing is known about the fate of Mr. Hoti or other Serb, Albanian and Roma civilians and police officers abducted by armed Kosovo Albanians.

34. The Yugoslav authorities have reportedly authorized the team of Finnish experts acting under the European Union auspices to start investigations at six locations in Kosovo and in any other locations where forensic investigation proves to be justified. The choice of places, however, remains the prerogative of the Serb authorities since the forensic investigation, as part of the criminal investigation in general, can be initiated only on the basis of a Court order issued by an investigating judge.

V. Observations

35. After eight months of fighting, there are indications that displaced persons and refugees from Kosovo have begun returning to their homes, many destroyed. This is a difficult process and the United Nations agencies on the ground are making every effort to assist in the restoration of normal life in Kosovo. These activities, however, require close cooperation with the Kosovo Verification Mission and the support of the international community.

36. The extent to which the internally displaced persons and refugees are willing to return to their homes still varies by area. The reluctance to return permanently is mainly due to Kosovo Albanian paramilitary units and security forces remaining concentrated in certain areas, thus posing the potential of continuing clashes. Among other constraints hampering the return process are mines and booby traps and the destruction of utilities and dwellings. However, it is to be hoped that, as a result of the ceasefire, the increased international presence in the region and unhindered humanitarian assistance, the rate of returns will accelerate.

37. Nevertheless, humanitarian efforts cannot be an alternative to the political process. I am therefore concerned that, after the end of major hostilities in Kosovo, the advance towards a political solution remains slow. I commend the efforts of Ambassador Christopher Hill of the United States and of the Contact Group, and call upon the parties to engage in a meaningful dialogue aimed at finding a peaceful settlement in Kosovo to benefit all its people.

38. It is evident that the relative tranquillity in Kosovo is very deceptive. It is neither stable, nor irreversible. According to various reports, members of the Kosovo Albanian paramilitary units, which have been reappearing in greater numbers throughout Kosovo, seem to be motivated, well armed and ready for renewed action. The Government has enough security forces in the area to launch a new crack-down should these units engage in provocative actions. I urge all parties concerned to show restraint so as not to undermine the efforts for a political settlement.

39. Abductions and arbitrary arrests, coupled with fear of such actions, pose the most dangerous potential threats to the security and human rights of all persons in Kosovo. I strongly urge the Serbian authorities to stop the practice of arbitrary arrests and to cooperate fully with the international community in the field of human rights. I also urge Kosovo Albanian paramilitary units to immediately release all abductees without any preconditions.

40. As earlier stated, it is expected that the early deployment of the OSCE Kosovo Verification Mission will be a critical factor in building the confidence necessary for the return of those who fled their homes in the past months. It will also greatly assist in providing the Security Council with cogent information on the situation in the region. I hope that the Verification Mission will have taken over the reporting responsibility on the situation in Kosovo, other than on humanitarian and human rights questions, by the time another report is due.

Annex
Information on the Situation in Kosovo and Measures Taken by the Organization for Security and Cooperation in Europe, Submitted Pursuant to Paragraph 13 of Security Council Resolution 1160 (1998)
(October/November 1998)

GENERAL SITUATION

1. The period since the last report, of 20 October, has been calm, without major operations being undertaken by Federal Republic of Yugoslavia or Kosovo Liberation Army (KLA) forces. Sporadic skirmishes and incidents of hostage-taking have occurred and tension has increased accordingly in many areas.

2. During the early part of the period, military activity was observed in western Kosovo between the towns of Pec, Gjakova and Dakovica. This area, adjacent to the Albanian border, has been an area of heavy fighting since the beginning of June. On 16 October, amid clear indications of withdrawal of Federal Republic of Yugoslavia security forces, the KLA "General Staff" announced a unilateral ceasefire but stated that it would also respond to any provocation.

3. Special Yugoslav police units were still present all over the province mostly on main roads, in the Drenica and Maljiševo areas, but in significantly decreased numbers. Federal Republic of Yugoslavia forces adopted a more discreet stance with troops hiding in the woods and mobile patrols. Many checkpoints were still in place and manned, particularly south-east of Kosovo and in the Drenica region. Freedom of movement was affected in some areas:

Kosovo Diplomatic Observer Mission staff were prevented from entering a military base near Kosovska Mitrovica, and denied access to western regions by KLA forces near Glogovac. In the Shala region (the triangle between Kosovska, Mitrovica, Podujevo and Vucitrn) an Observer Mission team was stopped and denied onward access by the KLA.

4. KLA presence has become more significant in many areas over the last fortnight. KLA fighters were allegedly reported in the Orahovac area and in the Rugova Canyon, west of Pec. KLA seem to be filling the vacuum left by departing Federal Republic of Yugoslavia forces: many of them were spotted in abandoned MUP positions.

5. The ceasefire was violated several times in November through incidents such as an attack on mineworkers in Grabovac, a shoot-out between a heavily-armed KLA patrol and police resulting in five dead KLA members, attacks on the Maljiševo and Orahovac police stations and the burning of a school in Sipitula (west of Priština) with mutual accusations flying between Serb security forces and local Albanian population.

6. During the reporting period, the presence of large numbers of security forces, increasing tension and clashes were reported in the Dragobilje area, although it appeared difficult to establish who was responsible. The situation in Maljiševo remained tense with Serb security forces and Kosovo Albanians blaming each other for sporadic shootings. The situation was complicated by the arrest of two leading members of the League of Democratic Kosova chapter in Maljiševo by KLA on 30 October. In small villages in the area of Pec an increasing number of cases of harassment, arbitrary arrest and intimidation were reported.

7. The situation on the northern border of the former Yugoslav Republic of Macedonia with the Federal Republic of Yugoslavia (Kosovo) has remained stable and calm throughout the reporting period. All border crossings have continued to function normally. There have been no significant incidents; illegal crossing and smuggling have remained at a lower level than at any time since independence, attributable in large part to the presence of Yugoslav security forces on the northern part of the border of the former Yugoslav Republic of Macedonia. On the western border with Albania there has been no substantive change in the pattern of activity. Periodic incidents continue to occur of attempted illegal entry by small groups from Albania, sometimes armed, which sometimes engage Macedonian security forces, and are sometimes fired upon. The arrival of the first winter snow can be expected to dampen activity.

THE SITUATION OF THE CIVILIAN POPULATION

8. By the end of October, the Head of the Office of the United Nations High Commissioner for Refugees (UNHCR) in the Federal Republic of Yugoslavia indicated that the fear of winter had forced some 30,000 internally displaced persons to return to their homes and repair them before the winter, in spite of security fears. It is estimated that some 10,000 internally displaced persons still remain exposed in the open on high ground. Internally displaced persons accommodated in other people's homes are estimated at 60,000 in Priština, 42,000 in Kosovska Mitrovica and 20,636 in the Pec area. In some cases, such as a camp in the area of Kormorane with an estimated 1,500 internally displaced persons, people spend the day in their villages rebuilding, returning to the camp at night.

9. Refugee returns are occurring but trends vary according to region. In some villages south-east of Maljiševo approximately 90 per cent of the population has returned; but the area closest to the Albanian border and to Junik remains deserted, as do all the small villages to the east. There are no signs of spontaneous return of refugees.

10. Urgently required aid has been delivered by UNHCR and all other agencies at a rate of 14 convoys a week, supplying some 100,000 internally displaced persons. Humanitarian agencies have encountered considerable problems, many of which centre on security fears and trust among the internally displaced persons. An incident that typifies the precarious situation occurred on 23 October, when, for the first time in the experience of UNHCR in Kosovo, an aid convoy came under KLA fire in a case of mistaken identity.

11. A medical team assessed the general health situation of people living in Kosovo as very poor. Owing to the conflict situation and subsequent collapse of medical supplies and availability of treatment, especially in the rural areas, a significant increase of various infectious diseases is to be expected.

12. Another issue of concern is that of missing persons, whether ethnic Albanians or Serbs. In this respect the International Committee of the Red Cross in Kosovo has drawn attention to 119 missing Serbs.

REFUGEE INFLUX

13. A significant number of refugees have continued to enter Albania via Montenegro, while in the north-east of Albania very few refugees were reported to have crossed into the country. This is thought to be a result of the first heavy snowfalls, which are making for very harsh winter conditions, the increased number of Federal Republic of Yugoslavia patrols in the area and reports of newly laid mines.

14. By the end of October, UNHCR claimed that an average 12 refugees were still crossing the border each day and the number of refugees in Kukes, Has and Zogaj was 1,106. The deployment of the Kosovo Verification Mission has brought demands for early repatriation from refugees who remain in the north of the country who are extremely wary of returning without solid guarantees for their security. Still, some of the registered refugees voiced their intention to stay in Albania during the winter months.

15. The inadequate security situation in the Tropoje district continues to seriously hamper the registration process of refugees, a prerequisite for their continued aid. The situation of refugees in the area is deteriorating, little aid has arrived in the district since September, and locals have stolen previous supplies. Action to improve the security situation in the district by the appropriate Albanian authorities is considered grossly inadequate.

16. The current number of refugees from Kosovo in the former Yugoslav Republic of Macedonia is 2,800, although the figure is difficult to verify. The number of Kosovars visiting and staying on a temporary or extended footing with friends or relatives has remained broadly stable. The great majority of those staying wish to remain out of public view, shun officialdom and appear to wish to return to Kos-

ovo as soon as they judge it is safe to do so. There has been little sign to date of any significant number returning.

KOSOVO CONFLICT SPILLOVER POTENTIAL

17. The OSCE presence in Albania, the OSCE spillover mission to Skopje and the OSCE missions to Bosnia and Herzegovina and to Croatia have been instructed to continue to follow closely the spillover potential of the Kosovo conflict.

18. OSCE monitors in Albania observed convoys of Federal Republic of Yugoslavia security vehicles regrouping and moving in the border area, suggesting that some elements have withdrawn from there. Despite these withdrawals heavy border patrolling continued, especially in traditional refugee crossing points, in the north-east and north of the country.

19. Additional mines have been laid by Federal Republic of Yugoslavia forces and an increased number of people have been killed or injured by newly laid mines. Laying of mines is seen as an attempt to limit the activity of the KLA, and is regarded as provocative at a time when the peace process is at an embryonic stage and does nothing to instill hope in the refugees who wish to return to their homes.

20. Movement and training of fighters continue to be observed in the north-eastern border areas of Albania, and it is apparent that cross-border activity is continuing, albeit more limited than in the past, owing to the heavy presence of Federal Republic of Yugoslavia forces. There have been a number of actions inside the Federal Republic of Yugoslavia, and some wounded fighters were being treated later in local Albanian hospitals.

21. A number of border incidents have occurred during the reporting period, sometimes triggered by KLA activity. One incursion by a Federal Republic of Yugoslavia patrol was reported as being a kilometre inside Albanian territory. Another border incident occurred on 1 November when the Serb forces fired several mortar rounds at Koshara BP and one round landed on the Albanian side of the border.

22. Albanian Prime Minister Majko, while following the policy established by his predecessor, Mr. Nano, has been introducing some changes in the Government's public approach to the Kosovo issue. Pointing out that the Albanian State will not play an active role in giving advice to the Kosovo Albanian people to find their political identity, Mr. Majko stressed indirectly the idea of an ethnic Albanian solution as an offer for the Albanians in Kosovo. Nevertheless, the Kosovo crisis is far from being the dominant topic in Albanian politics, which focused on the International Conference on Albania, called by the Government of Albania under the auspices of "Friends of Albania" (a group co-chaired by OSCE and European Union), held on 30 October, the first large gathering of this nature since the traumatic events of early 1997.

23. Law and order enforcement in the north-east of Albania remained extremely weak and the continuing lack of government control in the region is still a source of serious concern also in the context of the Kosovo crisis.

24. In the former Yugoslav Republic of Macedonia, the situation in the northern border with the Federal Republic of Yugoslavia remained mostly calm during the reporting period. In a shooting on 11 November, a Macedonian border patrol killed an Albanian male on the border between the former Yugoslav Republic of Macedonia and Albania. The potential risks of spillover from Kosovo to the former Yugoslav Republic of Macedonia are, however, at the moment regarded as slight, in particular in view of the increase in troops of the United Nations Preventive Deployment Force from 850 to 1,050 and the stationing of the NATO "Extraction Force" on Macedonian territory in support of the Kosovo Verification Mission.

25. During the campaign for the second round of the parliamentary elections, the crisis in Kosovo was a dominant issue and the leading coalition, VMRO-DPMNE/DA, continue to stress its commitment to dealing with the problems of the economy as a first priority. Macedonian officials said that the government had a basic policy of an "equal relationship" with all neighbours and that regional cooperation was to be promoted to achieve its objectives. Speaking of rumours of Macedonian Albanians joining the KLA, an official stated that Albanians were well integrated in the former Yugoslav Republic of Macedonia.

The attitude of people in the former Yugoslav Republic of Macedonia can best be described as "apprehensive", owing to the problems in neighbouring countries, but neither of the ethnic groups is militant.

26. Referring to the explosions in Gostivar, Skopje, Kumanovo and Prilep, the Minister of the Interior reported that 12 persons of Albanian origin were arrested and that direct material evidence had been found, as well as supplies of weapons. Press speculation was that the KLA were responsible but the Interior Ministry confirmed that the 12 were members of an interior group associated to radical political parties inside the former Yugoslav Republic of Macedonia and connected with foreign countries. Measures taken by the Organization for Security and Cooperation in Europe

27. Following negotiations between Ambassador Holbrooke and President Milosevic, the Government of the Federal Republic of Yugoslavia signed two agreements designed to verify compliance with Security Council resolution 1199 (1998) of 23 September which called, inter alia, for a cessation of hostilities in Kosovo. On 15 October an agreement was concluded between the authorities of the Federal Republic of Yugoslavia and NATO that permitted unarmed NATO aircraft to fly over Kosovo. An agreement between OSCE and the Federal Republic of Yugoslavia was then signed on 16 October between the Chairman-in-Office, Bronislaw Geremek, and Federal Republic of Yugoslavia Minister of Foreign Affairs Jovanovic, agreeing to the establishment of an OSCE Verification Mission. The Permanent Council of OSCE declared "the preparedness of OSCE to embark on verification duties related to compliance of all parties in Kosovo" in its decision 259.

28. OSCE study teams have since undertaken detailed examinations to establish the operational requirements of the OSCE Kosovo Verification Mission. The Verification Mission Support Unit, consisting of planning, personnel, logistics and communications cells, was formed in Vienna. The working groups produced the concept of operations document, which was approved by the Head of Mission, Ambassador William Walker, who first visited Pristina on 22 October and permanently took up his duties there on 11 November 1998.

29. The Verification Mission's immediate financial requirements were covered by the OSCE Contingency Fund and a spending authority allocated by the Secretary-General. The OSCE Permanent Council, in its decision 266 of 11 November, authorized the 1998 budget for the Mission in the amount of ATS 756,530,264. This enabled the Mission to make the major investments required this year; it additionally enabled augmentation of the secretariat's departments in Vienna.

30. The Verification Mission's advance headquarters has been established in Pristina, and Norway has assumed the responsibility for providing initial staffing and communications links. The Activation Unit has been replaced by Mission staff. A training location (the Kosovo Verification Mission Induction Centre) has been identified in Brezovica, outside Pristina, where three-day training courses will begin on 23 November for OSCE verifiers.

31. Cooperation between the OSCE Kosovo Verification Mission, humanitarian and other international organizations is a key ingredient of the Mission's concept of operations. The successful outcome of the Mission depends largely on coordination at headquarters level and close collaboration in the field.

32. NATO has a pivotal role in supporting the implementation of the mandate and underpinning the Mission's security plan; a number of meetings have taken place between the two organizations in Brussels and in Vienna.

33. An early example of this kind of cooperation is the target-oriented meeting organized by the OSCE Office of Democratic Institutions and Human Rights in Warsaw on 5 November 1998 to bring together international and humanitarian organizations, non-

governmental organizations and OSCE institutions for an exchange of views on this subject.

34. On 5 November the Chairman-in-Office of OSCE, Bronislaw Geremek, received in Warsaw Ambassador William Graham Walker, head of the OSCE Kosovo Verification Mission. During the meeting it was agreed that, at this stage of Verification Mission planning, the main concern is to assure the security of Mission personnel on the ground. Minister Geremek emphasized his strong support to Ambassador Walker and provided him with his view on the major problems regarding deployment of the OSCE verifiers in Kosovo. He underlined the need for cooperation with the authorities of the Federal Republic of Yugoslavia and NATO, as well as immediate deployment of the personnel in Kosovo.

35. The same day the Chairman-in-Office of OSCE, accompanied by Ambassador Walker, met with the deputies of the Kosovo Verification Mission and delivered them their nominations.

36. Preparations for the deployment of the Mission were going relatively well. By the date of the OSCE Ministerial Meeting in Oslo, that is by 2 December, the aim is to have around 800 verifiers on the ground in Kosovo, with further deployment capacity of 200 to 250 a week. Allowing for Christmas and the New Year, by mid-January the Mission should reach 1,500 to 1,600 personnel. By mid-November, the leadership group of the Mission was already in the field.

37. The following international Kosovo Verification Mission and Kosovo Diplomatic Observer Mission personnel are already present on the ground in Kosovo:

Kosovo Verification Mission headquarters: 50 personnel and 11 soft-skinned vehicles

Kosovo Diplomatic Observer Mission:

United States: 183 personnel and 13 armoured vehicles

European Union: 30 personnel and 13 armoured vehicles

Russian Federation: 17 personnel and 3 soft-skinned vehicles

United Kingdom: 50 personnel and 20 armoured vehicles

France: 15 personnel and 8 armoured vehicles

Kosovo Verification Mission 12 personnel and 2 soft-Induction Centre: skinned vehicles

38. The Organization for Security and Cooperation in Europe is making all efforts to verify Yugoslav compliance with Security Council resolutions 1160 (1998), 1199 (1998) and 1203 (1998), as well as in supporting the establishment of proper political conditions to start unconditional peace negotiations between the parties to the conflict.

124. Report of the Secretary-General Prepared pursuant to Security Council Resolutions 1160 (1998), 1199 (1998) and 1203 (1998), UN Doc. S/1998/1221, 24 December 1998

I. Introduction

1. The present report is submitted pursuant to Security Council resolutions 1160 (1998) of 31 March 1998, 1199 (1998) of 23 September 1998 and 1203 (1998) of 24 October 1998. It covers the period since my most recent report of 4 December 1998 (S/1998/1147).

II. Comprehensive Regime to Monitor the Implementation of the Prohibitions Imposed by the Security Council in Resolution 1160 (1998)

2. The second consultative meeting of organizations participating in the comprehensive monitoring regime was held on 14 December 1998 in Vienna. Representatives of the Danube Commission, the European Union, the North Atlantic Treaty Organization (NATO), the Organization for Security and Cooperation in Europe (OSCE), the Western European Union and the United Nations Preventive Deployment Force (UNPREDEP) Force Commander exchanged information on the monitoring of the prohibitions established by the Council in resolutions 1160 (1998) and 1199 (1998) and addressed practical issues arising in that regard.

III. Situation in Kosovo

3. This section of the report is based on information provided by the Office of the United Nations High Commissioner for Refugees (UNHCR) and the Office of the United Nations High Commissioner for Human Rights, the Kosovo Diplomatic Observer Mission and individual Member States. The report also includes information submitted by the Chairman-in-Office of OSCE (see annex I).

4. Since my last report was issued, the situation in Kosovo has not significantly improved and there are alarming signs of potential deterioration. While various sources report that the ceasefire is still holding, there are indications of growing tensions on the ground. During the first half of December, violence reached its highest level since the 16 October Agreement; more than 50 persons have died in violent attacks.

5. Meanwhile, despite the efforts of Ambassador Christopher Hill of the United States of America and the European Union Envoy, Ambassador Wolfgang Petritsch of Austria, to bring the parties concerned to the negotiation table, there has been no progress in the political dialogue in Kosovo. Recent statements by both sides regarding the draft agreement proposed by Ambassador Hill indicate that there is considerable distance between the positions of the parties and that they are far from engaging in meaningful negotiations.

6. Though no additional abduction cases have been reported since mid-November, the fate and whereabouts of abducted persons remain unknown and family members and others have begun to organize public protests and appeals to representatives of OSCE. These protests, which have also addressed arbitrary detentions, have failed to obtain satisfactory results or information. Reports continue to be received concerning arbitrary detention and systematic ill-treatment of persons in police detention and pre-trial detention.

RETURNS

7. Despite tensions, displaced persons continue to return to their homes. UNHCR estimates that some 100,000 people have now returned, while some 200,000 remained displaced within Kosovo. The estimated number of internally displaced persons has increased based on the evidence obtained from the first phase of the shelter survey, and on figures cited by the Yugoslav state media on 14 December.

8. As winter's cold weather has arrived, more people are seeking to return home, encouraged in part by the growing presence of humanitarian agencies and the Kosovo Verification Mission. Returns began even to such "sensitive" locations as Junik, near the Albanian border; the Djakovica area; and Lodja, a village near Pec. Potential returnees have made tentative visits even to the Malisevo area. According to UNHCR, some 1,300 of the 6,000 residents of Junik who had fled during the Government offensive in August have returned, although the army and police have maintained a heavy presence in the area as they consider it one of the key routes in trafficking of illegal weapons and personnel of Kosovo Albanian paramilitary units. On 11 December, UNHCR and the Observer Mission escorted the first group of 16 displaced persons back to Lodja. They had expressed a wish to rebuild their houses which had been severely damaged last August. The return was preceded by assurances from police officials in Pec that returnees would not be harmed. Since the area has been almost totally destroyed, the repair of the local school will take priority so that it can be used as a temporary shelter while returnees rebuild their homes.

9. These returns indicate the genuine desire of many displaced persons to return home. However, the process is impeded by the lack of housing and adequate security mechanisms to monitor returnees' reintegration into their respective communities. Other returns, however, have taken place in situations of continued tension and sporadic clashes and under far from ideal conditions, apparently as a result of desperation and the lack of other options. Difficulties in paying for accommodation in the places of refuge and the worsening winter weather prompted many of the displaced to opt for return.

10. Among those who have returned are some 10,000 who previously sought safety in Montenegro. The number of displaced in Montenegro is at present estimated at 27,000. Bosnia and Herzegovina now hosts an estimated 10,000 refugees from Kosovo, of whom 6,700 have registered with UNHCR. Some of them have already requested assistance to repatriate. According to the latest registration of refugees from Kosovo in Albania, there are some 24,000 persons there. In addition, it is estimated that there are still some 20,000 displaced persons from Kosovo in other areas of Serbia. The latter figure might be growing, as there are some indications of fear among the Serbian inhabitants of remote villages as Kosovo Albanians return.

OBSTACLES TO RETURNS/SECURITY

11. On 20 November, two policemen were killed and three injured in a suspected ambush by Kosovo Albanian paramilitaries in Prilep. On 3 December, 12 Albanians were killed in separate incidents, 8 by Yugoslav Army border guards in the area of the Gorozup watchtower, 1 by Kosovo Albanian paramilitaries along the Pristina-Pec road and 3 others on a main street in downtown Pristina under circumstances which are unclear.

12. Not only has the number of persons killed increased dramatically, but during the reporting period there were violent incidents in heavily populated urban centres. On 4 December, an armed confrontation between Serbian security personnel and Kosovo Albanian paramilitaries occurred in the hospital compound in Pec, resulting in the death of one of the Kosovo Albanians. On 11 December, three Kosovo Albanian men - a policeman, and two state company employees - were killed in Glogovac. On 14 December, 34 violent deaths occurred in two separate incidents. Thirty Albanians were killed and 12 wounded near the Gorozup and Liken border posts in fighting between Yugoslav border guards and a group of armed Albanians. That same day, two masked men entered and attacked patrons in a cafe in Pec, killing six Serbs. On 18 December, the Deputy Mayor of Kosovo Polje was kidnapped and murdered.

13. Following the 13 October accord between President Slobodan Milosevic and United States Special Envoy Richard Holbrooke, Kosovo Albanian paramilitary units have taken advantage of the lull in the fighting to re-establish their control over many villages in Kosovo, as well as over some areas near urban centres and highways. These actions by Kosovo Albanian paramilitary units have only served to provoke the Serbian authorities, leading to statements that if the Kosovo Verification Mission cannot control these units the Government would. The local authorities have indicated to UNHCR that they would not allow "terrorists to take over Kosovo". Government officials have warned that recent incidents, particularly attempts by the armed groups to cross into Kosovo from Albania and killings of civilians, would justify a renewal of operations against Kosovo Albanian paramilitary units.

14. In this regard, serious apprehension of a new cycle of major hostilities has been expressed by different sources. While Kosovo Albanian paramilitary units are taking an increasingly bold stance, the Serbian police force is responding by increasing patrols and the use of mobile checkpoints. Some reports suggest that the number of Yugoslav Army and Serbian special police units deployed in Kosovo may exceed agreed figures.

15. The persistent insecurity reinforces UNHCR's position of not promoting return from areas outside Kosovo. However, where individuals clearly express their wish to repatriate, UNHCR will facilitate their return, seeking clearance, ensuring that they possess the necessary documentation and providing transport assistance, if appropriate. UNHCR will monitor the security situation of returnees and of those who remain displaced within Kosovo and will assess their material needs.

ABDUCTIONS

16. The lack of information about the fate of persons abducted by Kosovo Albanian paramilitaries has given rise to growing impatience among the families and their affected communities. According to information received from the authorities of the Federal Republic of Yugoslavia, as of 7 December, 282 civilians and police have been abducted by Kosovo Albanian paramilitary units, 136 of whom are sill unaccounted for. On 9 December, the political spokesperson of the Kosovo Albanian paramilitary units, Adem Demaqi, noted publicly that he had made efforts to release abducted Serb civilians and that he expected "the Serbian side" to do the same. However, Mr. Demaqi admitted that he feared that many persons listed as missing had been killed in clashes between the police and Kosovo Albanian paramilitary units during the summer offensive. On 10 December, Kosovo Serbs from Orahovac organized a march to the Kosovo Albanian paramilitary-controlled area of Dragobilje, demanding information about the fate of the missing. The march proceeded without incident, owing mainly to the mediation of the Kosovo Diplomatic Observer Mission, and concluded with a meeting between Serb and Kosovo Albanian representatives. On 11 December, Serb civilians from the Urosevac area held a group of five national and international humanitarian workers for approximately eight hours, demanding that they be exchanged for two Serbs abducted in July. The group was released through the intervention of the Observer Mission. On 14 December, relatives and supporters of abducted Serbs demonstrated outside the OSCE headquarters in Pristina; a letter was submitted to Ambassador Walker requesting OSCE to take concrete steps to resolve the issue.

VISIT OF THE UNITED NATIONS HIGH COMMISSIONER FOR REFUGEES TO THE FEDERAL REPUBLIC OF YUGOSLAVIA

17. The purpose of the visit of the High Commissioner for Refugees to the Federal Republic of Yugoslavia from 20 to 22 December was to review the effectiveness of the United Nations humanitarian action in the new situation and to ensure that there was a solid foundation for close cooperation between the Kosovo Verification Mission and the humanitarian action led by UNHCR. In Kosovo she met senior government officials and Ambassador William Walker, the Head of the Verification Mission, with whom she visited returnees who in some cases were repairing their homes, and met Croatian refugees at a collection centre. In Belgrade, the High Commissioner met with President Milosevic and other senior officials.

18. In her meeting with the President at the end of her mission, the High Commissioner reviewed the assistance programme and discussed possible solutions for the problem of over 500,000 refugees from earlier conflicts in the region as well as the humanitarian situation in Kosovo. With regard to the latter issue, the High Commissioner noted significant positive changes that had occurred since her last meeting with the President three months ago. The conflict which had caused large-scale displacement had effectively ceased in October and many persons had returned to their villages, if not to their homes. The humanitarian operation was now able to meet the challenge and an immediate humanitarian catastrophe had been averted.

19. The High Commissioner strongly condemned acts of violence and intimidation against all civilians. She noted that many Kosovo Albanians feared detention on suspicion of having been involved in the conflict and that this was adversely affecting the prospects for the return of those still displaced, as well as the sustainability of the returns that had occurred. A number of those she had met had asked her about an amnesty and she recalled earlier exchanges on the subject with President Milosevic and the authorities. The High Commissioner expressed her concern that the necessary safeguards on return would not be in place at the time they were most needed, and requested the President to adopt an amnesty law as soon as possible. Such an amnesty was a key component of confidence-building in any post-conflict return and would contribute to the declared aim of the authorities of finding a political solution without delay.

20. The High Commissioner also underlined the importance of the restoration of essential services, such as electricity, and the need to help health and education services recover from the effects of the conflict. President Milosevic said that the restoration of such services was a high priority, but adversely affected by acts of violence committed by "terrorists".

AID/SHELTER PROGRAMMES

21. UNHCR and non-governmental organizations (NGOs) are conducting the second phase of the shelter survey, which will cover some 500 more villages in western and central Kosovo.

22. At the same time, UNHCR is providing assistance to those returnees undertaking major repairs of their houses. Some 450 houses in 31 villages are currently undergoing repairs using startup kits from UNHCR and other aid agencies, including heavy-duty tarpaulin and wooden beams and fillets, battens for window and door frames, boards, nails and tools. UNHCR has also distributed 4,500 shelter kits for minor repairs, which include plastic sheets, wood, nails and hammers, thus facilitating the preparation of at least one room in the house for the winter.

23. One of the most significant problems in Kosovo facing people affected by the fighting has been the lack of food. Wheat flour stored for the winter has often been either looted or burned. Thousands of livestock have been killed. Farmers missed the October planting season. Thus many displaced persons will depend on donated food supplies well into 1999.

24. In addition to the six-days-per-week deliveries of food and other humanitarian assistance coordinated by UNHCR from Pristina, aid distribution has begun in Pec. Convoys from Pec will deliver assistance to nearby villages and remote areas in Decane and Klina. Another distribution centre is scheduled to begin operations from Prizren and will distribute food supplies to 10 municipalities in southern Kosovo. These decentralized distribution centres will expand the capacity of UNHCR and other humanitarian organizations to deliver needed relief supplies to a larger group of people, targeting more areas.

SECURITY OF THE HUMANITARIAN PERSONNEL

25. Humanitarian agencies in general have unhindered access to all areas of Kosovo. Although Kosovo Albanian paramilitary units have not directly posed a threat or any obstacles to the delivery of humanitarian aid, their practice of laying mines and engaging in sporadic clashes with the Serbian police clearly create a risk for humanitarian workers. No harassment of aid workers by the Government forces has been reported.

COORDINATION WITH THE KOSOVO VERIFICATION MISSION

26. Although the Kosovo Diplomatic Observer Mission has significantly increased in size and presence, the operational date and deployment of the Verification Mission remain delayed and expectations of large-scale presence of international verifiers on the ground have not been met. OHCHR field staff report that civilians in urban areas and villages are pointing increasingly to unfulfilled expectations and to even further delays in deployment likely to be caused by the traditional winter holidays. The combination of unfulfilled expectations of international confidence-building, dramatic incidents of urban-area violence and border clashes is exacerbating an already grave human rights situation.

27. UNHCR has systematically continued briefings for the incoming observers of the Verification Mission at their induction sessions. With four liaison officers now in place, UNHCR maintains daily contact between the Mission and the humanitarian agencies on staff security and humanitarian issues. The basis is being laid for a functional and effective working relationship, similar to the one developed with the Diplomatic Observer Mission. As with the Observer Mission, UNHCR, on behalf of all humanitarian agencies, is establishing a mechanism for exchange of information with the Verification Mission to promote conditions that would spur returns to those areas where return is feasible.

28. The Head of the Verification Mission assured the High Commissioner for Refugees during their meeting that the Mission would support the humanitarian action in every way possible consistent with its mandate and primary task. The High Commissioner assured him of close coordination on the part of UNHCR in order to make the best possible use of the potential of the Mission to contribute, with its rapidly expanding field presence, to creating conditions that allowed sustainable return and in helping identify humanitarian needs. They recognized that a good foundation for this cooperation had already been laid, including, for example, with information provided for the humanitarian actors by the Verification Mission Mine Action and Information Centre, with which UNHCR works very closely.

TRIALS AND DETAINEES

29. The trials reported upon at length in my previous report continue on a daily basis, according to a regular court schedule. Trials have now been scheduled additionally in the court districts of Gnjilane and Prokuplje. Several proceedings were delayed or rescheduled for the period of the traditional December holidays, which are not observed as holidays in the Federal Republic of Yugoslavia. The Office of the United Nations High Commissioner for Human Rights observes that the proceedings so rescheduled involve especially large groups of defendants or incidents and operations of an especially sensitive nature. The Office's complement of trial monitors will not decrease during the December holiday period and the Office continues to meet with court officials, prosecutors and defence attorneys, and to monitor proceedings.

30. The absence of an amnesty law continues to be a major hindrance to confidence among the population. While paragraph 10 of the Serbian Government's statement of 13 October on the accord between President Milosevic and United States Special Envoy Richard Holbrooke envisaged an amnesty, the present practice of the Serbian authorities contradicts it. UNHCR expressed its concern over this situation in a letter dated 9 December addressed to the Deputy Federal Prime Minister, highlighting the importance of an amnesty in the context of confidence-building and requesting an opportunity to discuss with the competent officials the specific provisions of such a law while it was still in draft form.

31. In view of regular reports of ill-treatment of detainees and of the continuing absence of an elaborated policy to implement paragraphs 10 and 11 of the 13 October accord, the Office of the High Commissioner for Human Rights pursued its efforts to review implementation options. To that end, the Office met with representatives of the Kosovo Albanian political leadership and continues to correspond with the Serbian Ministry of Justice. On 18 November, the Ministry responded in writing to inquiries by the Office regarding the whereabouts and status of named detainees, largely humanitarian and medical workers and juveniles. On 27 November, the Office asked the ministry about 46 additional cases of reported human rights violations, largely of the elderly, young persons and invalids.

FORENSIC INVESTIGATION

32. On 10 December, Serbian security forces refused to allow a team of Finnish forensic investigators, accompanied by the Ambassador of Finland to the Federal Republic of Yugoslavia, to proceed without a police escort to the site of Gornje Obrinje. Serbian authorities pointed to a provision of the forensic investigators' terms of reference which permits Serbian Government presence during the investigations. The Finnish team noted, however, that the excessive police and military presence (two buses of security forces, two armed personnel carriers and six armoured vehicles) was likely to provoke action by Kosovo Albanian paramilitary units and would thus endanger the team. After a formal protest, the chief of the forensic team met with the Minister of Justice of Serbia. The Minister reportedly assured him that such an incident would not be repeated and proposed that only one investigative judge and two Serbian forensic experts accompany the team.

IV. Observations

33. It bears repeating that the problems in Kosovo can be resolved only by political means through negotiations between the parties directly concerned. I urge all parties concerned to engage without delay in such negotiations; the lack of agreement so far has a direct bearing on the current volatility. The tireless efforts of Ambassador Christopher Hill of the United States and of the European Union Envoy, Ambassador Wolfgang Petritsch, aimed at finding a peaceful political settlement in Kosovo merit the support of all those wishing to set

Kosovo on a positive course. Progress in this direction is all the more pressing in view of the increased levels of violence in Kosovo in December and its spread to urban areas, which earlier remained relatively untouched by the hostilities. These actions put at risk the entire peace process and could trigger a renewal of fighting in the coming months.

34. Should the worst happen, it would be very difficult for the humanitarian action to meet the resulting needs, still less encourage those affected to return and rebuild their homes and lives once more, which reinforces my conviction that those in a position to influence developments must spare no effort to find a negotiated settlement in early 1999, before it is too late.

35. I urge all the parties concerned to honour their obligations under the 16 October Agreement and to refrain from actions that could provoke resumed hostilities that would only lead to the further suffering of civilians. Continued instability in Kosovo impedes the return process and has the potential to jeopardize humanitarian efforts.

36. In this regard, the completion of the full deployment of the Kosovo Verification Mission should become a decisive factor for stability and confidence-building in Kosovo. The United Nations agencies that have a presence on the ground will continue developing their cooperation with the Verification Mission in order to coordinate efforts aimed at the restoration of normal life in Kosovo. It is my hope that the Verification Mission will soon be fully deployed and that it will be in a position to provide the Security Council with information on the compliance by the parties by the time of my next report as well as on the situation in Kosovo in accordance with the Security Council request in resolutions 1160 (1998) and 1199 (1998). With regard to the absence of a field capacity on the ground, except in the humanitarian and human rights field, I would hope that the Kosovo Verification Mission would assume such reporting by early February and would accordingly discontinue it, except as concerns the humanitarian and human rights situation, in order to eliminate duplication.

Annex I: Information on the Situation in Kosovo and Measures Taken by the Organization for Security and Cooperation in Europe, Submitted Pursuant to Paragraph 13 of Security Council Resolution 1160 (1998) (November/December 1998)

GENERAL SITUATION

1. Low-intensity conflict with incidents and moments of increased tension has continued in Kosovo since 20 November. A single armed clash in mid-December between armed Kosovo Albanians, later described as "our soldiers" by the Kosovo Liberation Army (KLA), and forces of the Federal Republic of Yugoslavia near Prizren was a significant exception to this trend.

2. The principal area of concern continues to be the western region of Kosovo, centred on the triangle formed by Malisevo and the border zone adjacent to the towns of Pec, Dakovica and Prizren. KLA activity in the area of Podujevo to the north of Pristina is an emergent source of tension. The number of demonstrations by members of the Serb community is increasing. There are indications that they may be politically motivated and that the Kosovo Albanian community is poised to follow suit.

3. There have been a number of violations of the ceasefire during the reporting period. These include KLA attacks on Serb police (MUP) vehicles, typically carried out with rocket-propelled grenades and small arms fire. Incidents like these were reported in Prilep, Dolovo, Klina and Zociste. Police also invited the Kosovo Diplomatic Observer Mission (KDOM) to investigate two other incidents on the Decani-Djakovica road in which police vehicles had been destroyed. A joint patrol of MUP and KDOM was fired upon in the general area of Belanci.

4. Armed clashes between uniformed groups of Kosovo Albanians and the Serbian security force continue to occur. The most significant of these occurred on 14 December where 31 Kosovo Albanians were killed in the border region near Prizren and 9 were taken prisoner. An attack by two gunmen in a Pec bar later that day killed six Serb youths and worsened a tense situation. The Serb authorities blamed the KLA; the KLA blamed criminals. Further reports of clashes were investigated by KDOM during the reporting period, notably in Planeja, west of Prizren, where eight corpses and ammunition were found at the scene. The funeral that followed in Velika Krusa was attended by 2,000 to 3,000 people and 25 uniformed members of the KLA.

5. Incidents of kidnap and abduction continue to create tension and division in Kosovo. KDOM successfully negotiated the release of a Serbian policeman held by the KLA since 19 November and two Tanjug journalists who had been held by the KLA for two months. Demonstrations and protests by members of the Serbian community about the missing have increased, with activity centred on the Serb town of Orahovac, east of Dakovica. The area encompassed by such protests has begun to spread. A group of 700 protestors, led by the mayor of Orahovac, marched from Orahovac to the KLA-dominated town of Dragobilja in a potentially tense confrontation largely defused by members of the Organization for Security and Cooperation in Europe (OSCE) Kosovo Verification Mission (KVM). Demonstrations have taken place twice outside the KVM headquarters at Pristina in which the crowd requested action to release Serb abductees.

6. Local agreements brokered by KDOM have proved useful in decreasing tension in some areas but levels of KLA cooperation differ; some local commanders agree to maintain a discreet posture in their areas of operation, while others are more assertive. Central control and unified political and military strategy are increasingly visible aspects of KLA activity and it remains true that KLA forces seek to fill the vacuum left by the withdrawal of Serb forces. This trend has created perceptible frustrations among the Serb authorities and an unwillingness to further cede "control" of territory. This is now marked in Podujevo, a town north of Pristina astride the principal road into Kosovo from northern Serbia, where the KLA have been seen constructing bunkers overlooking the route.

7. Isolated incidents of vandalism directed at the international community were reported, resulting in minor damage to parked vehicles. Occasional verbal abuse and stone throwing was also reported by KVM and NGO staff.

SITUATION OF THE CIVILIAN POPULATION

8. Sources of the Office of the United Nations High Commissioner for Refugees (UNHCR) estimate that 75,000 internally displaced persons (IDPs) have returned to their homes in central and western Kosovo. There are now no refugees known to be living in the open in the region but serious sheltering problems remain. Uncertainty or fear in the minds of IDPs remains the principal factor affecting returns. Where KVM and KDOM presence has been frequent, permanent returns have been substantial; in areas where such presence has been less visible, or where MUP presence has continued, the pace of return has been affected. Return trends continue to vary by region. In Decari and Junik, south of Pec, significant returns have occurred; returns to areas close to the Albanian border have been more tentative; and there have been few returns to the area of Malisevo, north of Prizren, though many of the houses in the area remain habitable.

9. MUP presence, particularly in Malisevo, continues to hamper the refugee return process. Examples include complaints by the villagers of Semetesite (north-west of Suva Reka) of harassment at a MUP checkpoint, and returnee concern about the proximity of a MUP observation point in Vitak (south-east of Klina). In the Serb village of Svinjare (south of Mitrovica), KDOM officials were informed that some members of the Serb community were refugees from neighbouring areas and were afraid to return home because of KLA threats. KDOM received complaints about a MUP checkpoint in the area of Movjalne (north-west of Prizren). MUP maintained it was vital for the protection of 15 Serb families living there; Kosovar Albanians complained that it was preventing the return of Kosovo Albanians to an essentially Albanian area. KDOM members patrolling Podujevo (north of Pristina) were informed that the KLA had been denying Serb IDPs access to villages in the area to the north of the town.

10. UNHCR published a survey of the shelter situation in 20 of the 29 municipalities of Kosovo, which, in conjunction with other NGOs, assessed the needs of 285 villages in those areas. Two hundred ten of them were found to have been affected by the conflict, with 30 per cent of the houses destroyed, a further 30 per cent of houses suffering minor to major damage and 40 per cent left undamaged. Whereas the pre-conflict population of the villages was 349,657, the current population was 88,950 and the IDP population was 24,177, some 24 per cent of the total.

11. UNHCR has reorganized its regional structure to reflect that of the OSCE Kosovo Verification Mission, with distribution points now decentralized to the main towns of Pec, Prizren and Mitrovica. Food delivery responsibilities have been divided by area with Catholic Relief Services, Mercy Corps International and the World Food Programme (WFP). Aid delivery operations by humanitarian organizations have been hampered by winter weather and food supply shortages. The International Committee of the Red Cross (ICRC) has assisted with the shortfall. Kosovo's current food requirement stands at 3,600 tons per month, to feed 300,000 IDP returnees and host families.

REFUGEE INFLUX

12. The situation of refugees in Albania is closely followed by the OSCE presence in Tirana. There was a slight improvement during the reporting period. The number of refugees currently in Albania remains unclear but is estimated to be 23,000. The registration process, crucial for accurate and targeted supplies, is not properly under way. This has caused instances of food shortages and of oversupply and has made the calculation of future needs difficult.

13. The situation of refugees is especially difficult in the north-east of Albania where the number of refugees is estimated at 3,000. Refugees in the Tropoje District, numbering up to 1,500, have not received aid for almost two months owing to the lack of security for aid agencies in the area. These refugees have been offered transport to other locations where the security situation permits aid agencies to supply them on a regular basis. OSCE gave initial assistance in providing administrative arrangements for their transport. A large number of the refugees who decided to leave Bajram Curri chose to go to Tirana and Durres and not to collection centres.

14. Refugees in the districts of Kukes and Has suffered food shortages owing to miscalculation of the number of refugees in the area (1,100), coupled with the fact that supplies were delayed in reaching the districts. Relief agencies are unwilling to stockpile food because of the security situation. The appalling road conditions, together with the weather and the scarcity of transport, are additional difficulties faced in determining whether refugees received aid.

15. The number of crossings from Kosovo into Albania during the reporting period was estimated to be very low, with most taking place in the area of Dobruna.

16. The Holbrooke Agreement raised expectations that a safe return to Kosovo would be feasible in the near future and resulted in a number of representatives of refugees in Albania approaching OSCE field offices requesting that their return be facilitated as soon as possible. It was initially feared that many refugees would try to return on their own initiative, running the risk of entering minefields or being mistaken by Federal Republic of Yugoslavia forces as KLA infiltrators. By mid-November, only a limited number of refugees had crossed using this dangerous route and the message that they should wait a few more months before returning in an orderly manner seems to have been accepted, not least because many are still unhappy with the current security situation in Kosovo. The issue of refugee return is one that will need to be addressed between the relevant authorities in Albania and the Federal Republic of Yugoslavia.

KOSOVO CONFLICT SPILLOVER POTENTIAL

17. The OSCE presence in Albania, the OSCE spillover mission to Skopje and the OSCE missions to Bosnia and Herzegovina and to Croatia continue to follow closely the spillover potential of the Kosovo conflict.

18. During the reporting period, the situation on the Albanian border with Kosovo (Federal Republic of Yugoslavia) was relatively calm. Some isolated incidents occurred. Bad weather and poor road conditions continued to hamper movement and monitoring along the border areas. By mid-December, tension had increased at the border between Albania and Kosovo (Federal Republic of Yugoslavia) after several border incidents. This was seen as an indication that the KLA had become more active after a quieter preparatory period.

19. Very limited KLA movement was observed in the Has District, although the existence of a KLA training camp with about 10 fighters near the border was reported at the beginning of December. Overall activity remains limited and is probably constrained by poor weather.

20. During December, poor weather conditions limited OSCE Mission members' movement, precluding accurate observation, but no movement of any kind could be seen within the immediate areas of Kosovo adjacent to the border.

21. Few border incidents occurred during the period but previous incidents had led the Albanian Foreign Minister in mid-December to state that the Federal Republic of Yugoslavia authorities were ignoring an agreement on border incidents signed by both countries obliging the parties to verify and confirm any border incidents through a bilateral commission.

22. In his address to the OSCE Ministerial Council Meeting in Oslo on 2 December, Foreign Minister Milo of Albania said that his Government is ready "to cooperate with OSCE and other international organizations committed to Kosovo". He added that pressure should continue to be applied on Belgrade to find a satisfactory political solution and welcomed the new flexibility that, in his view, the KLA was showing with regard to demands for independence, stating that Albania was working with the KLA to convince them to be more realistic.

23. Speaking in Brussels on 7 December, Foreign Minister Milo voiced pessimism over a solution to the crisis, reaffirmed that Tirana did not subscribe to the idea of a greater Albania and rejected allegations that armed groups were being trained in its territory and sent to Kosovo.

24. The security situation remained tense during the campaign for the referendum on the Constitution held on 22 November. Media distortion and veiled threats of violence, some directed at the international community, and at OSCE in particular, were the main cause.

25. In northern Albania, in a letter sent to central government officials, the Tropoja District Council, the Mayor of Bajram Curri and political parties described the security situation as one of total lawlessness and chaos brought about by the absence of working judicial institutions and effective policing and called upon the Government to take urgent measures.

26. The situation on the northern border between the former Yugoslav Republic of Macedonia and the Federal Republic of Yugoslavia remained stable and calm during the reporting period, without substantive incident. All border crossings remained open and functioned normally. Similarly, the western border has been quiet.

27. The Federal Republic of Yugoslavia objected strongly to the intention of the North Atlantic Treaty Organization (NATO) to deploy an extraction force in the former Yugoslav Republic of Macedonia in relation to the Kosovo Verification Mission and sought to put pressure on the new Government over the issue. However, shortly after its endorsement by Parliament, the Government approved the stationing of NATO forces on Macedonian territory. Prime Minister Georgievski announced that the basis of the decision was the country's wish to achieve NATO membership as soon as possible, in addition to its commitments under the Partnership for Peace and certain status-of-forces agreements.

MEASURES TAKEN BY THE ORGANIZATION FOR SECURITY AND COOPERATION IN EUROPE

28. The process of fully establishing the Kosovo Verification Mission has continued since the Agreement between OSCE and the Fed-

eral Republic of Yugoslavia of 16 October 1998 and OSCE Permanent Council Decision 263 of 25 October 1998 that formally established the Mission. Its strength on 19 December stood at 888, including 392 local staff, with 180 international staff in headquarters in Pristina and 111 in Regional Centre One (RC1), Prizren. Two coordination centres are established as RC1 sub-stations, in the towns of Orahovac and in Suva Reka. KDOM strength is now at 217. Prizren Regional Centre became fully operational on 11 December; Regional Centre 2 (Mitrovica) became operational on 19 December. All five regional centres will be fully established by the end of January 1999. Staff have now been selected for all regional centres. Liaison offices have been established in Belgrade and Tirana.

29. Patrols by KVM personnel have begun and are coordinated closely with KDOM. KVM submits a regular interim report, instituted as a temporary measure in order to inform OSCE participating States and other international organizations of developments in the Mission area pending full establishment of the Mission. Reporting will subsequently reflect the full range of KVM's verification tasks.

30. Training of KVM verifiers began on 23 November at the Kosovo Verification Mission's induction centre in Hotel Narcis in Brezovica, outside Pristina. Five training courses have been completed; they were conducted by a KVM training team with support from other OSCE missions, OSCE institutions, UNHCR and ICRC. The syllabus consists of a four-day course with a capacity of up to 125 per course. Subjects taught include communications, policing issues, security, the human dimension and reporting procedures.

31. KVM and OSCE institutions continue to work in close cooperation with other international and humanitarian organizations in Kosovo. A fact-finding visit to Belgrade and Kosovo, led by Ambassador Stoudmann of the Office for Democratic Institutions and Human Rights, was conducted from 22 to 26 November in order to carry out a preliminary assessment of conditions for elections in the region. The group included representatives from the European Commission, the Council of Europe and the International Foundation for Election Systems. KVM and UNHCR hosted a meeting of key humanitarian agencies on 14 December in Pristina to discuss the outlook for the civil population of Kosovo over the winter period.

32. The OSCE Ministerial Meeting was held at Oslo on 2 December and issued a consensus-based statement declaring that "security, human rights, democracy and fundamental freedoms are inseparable". It went on to say that "the ten basic principles of the Helsinki Final Act, together with the current operational capabilities the OSCE has gained throughout the years, have contributed to making this Organization one of the best-suited instruments to address the crisis in Kosovo" (see annex II). Ambassador William Walker, the head of KVM, briefed the OSCE Ministerial Meeting about the situation regarding the KVM. He also briefed the North Atlantic Council in Brussels.

33. Discussions between members of KVM and the Government of the former Yugoslav Republic of Macedonia took place on 8 December to determine arrangements concerning the Mission. The Government agreed to allow KVM members to make emergency use of medical facilities in Skopje and allowed emergency access by air and road under these conditions.

34. KVM carried out its first verification at the barracks of the Yugoslav Army's 549th Motorized Brigade in Prizren on 11 December. This consisted of a meeting at the base followed by an inspection of a company team position in Dobruste, west of Prizren. KVM officials were prevented from conducting an inspection inside the barracks as planned and lodged an official complaint.

35. NATO has begun deployment of an advance force in the former Yugoslav Republic of Macedonia. Secure communications links have been established between KVM headquarters and the Kosovo Verification Coordination Centre in Skopje.

STRUCTURE

36. The Prizren Regional Centre has temporarily extended its area of operations to include the Djakovica municipality. Although this falls outside the boundaries of the Prizren political district, there is an operational need for KVM to patrol the area. When the Pec Regional Centre is established, it will undertake KVM patrolling of Djakovica.

37. KVM headquarters received 11 orange-coloured cargo vehicles during the period. There has been a delay in the arrival of armoured vehicles. The first were scheduled to be in Pristina on 18 December.

38. Current strength of KVM and KDOM on the ground in Kosovo is as follows:

KVM

Headquarters mission members: 179 personnel and 2 armoured vehicles[1]

Headquarters temporary mission members: 20 personnel

Induction centre: 33 instructing personnel

Prizren: 108 personnel and 21 armoured vehicles

Mitrovica: 56 personnel

Belgrade: 8 personnel

Pec (embryonic regional centre): 38 personnel

Gujilane (embryonic regional centre): 8 personnel

Pristina (embryonic regional centre): 13 personnel

KVM Local Staff (all locations): 445 personnel

Total: 908

KDOM

United States: 143 personnel[2] and 37 armoured vehicles

European Union: 33 personnel and 14 armoured vehicles

Russian Federation: 11 personnel

Canada: 3 personnel and one armoured vehicle

Annex II: Oslo Ministerial Draft Statement on Kosovo

1. Involvement in Kosovo represents both a test and an opportunity for the Organization for Security and Cooperation in Europe (OSCE). The challenge of Kosovo shows that security, human rights, democracy and fundamental freedoms are inseparable.

2. The plight of the people of Kosovo caught up in violent confrontation and fleeing their homes in fear has moved us all.

3. Thanks to vigorous efforts by the international community, including OSCE, there is now a ceasefire. It is still fragile, but it marks a great step forward for the people of Kosovo. Now further diplomatic efforts are under way to find a political solution. They have our strong support.

4. There is still violence in Kosovo, and this is of deep concern to us. We urge all parties involved to stop the violence and to resolve their differences by peaceful means. We urge them to negotiate a settlement as soon as possible. The international community is determined to help. But only the parties can overcome their differences. The sooner they do so, the sooner the reconstruction and development of Kosovo can make headway.

5. The 10 basic principles of the Helsinki Final Act, together with the current operational capabilities OSCE has gained throughout the years, have contributed to making this Organization one of the best suited instruments to address the crisis in Kosovo. We do not take this challenge lightly. From the very beginning of the conflict in the former Yugoslavia, including Kosovo, we have made every possible effort to contribute to its solution, without reservation.

6. Security Council resolutions 1160 (1998) and 1199 (1998) set out what is required of the parties to bring the confrontation to an end. OSCE has taken on the task of verifying that all parties are complying with these resolutions. OSCE is setting up its largest operation ever, the Kosovo Verification Mission (KVM). Besides verifying compli-

---

[1] Plus 30 armoured vehicles on loan from the United Kingdom of Great Britain and Northern Ireland, and 1 from Sweden; 70 soft-skinned vehicles.

[2] Thirty-three of these are in Belgrade or Skopje.

ance, KVM will help to implement the political settlement to be reached by the parties by supervising elections, providing support in building up democratic institutions and assisting with police force development in Kosovo.

7. The OSCE verifiers come to Kosovo as friends of all those attached to the idea of a peaceful, long-lasting political settlement, and to provide assistance where required. In good faith, we will do all we can on our part to help ensure that this endeavour is realized through the coordinated effort of the international community.

8. The Head of KVM, Ambassador Walker, and his team have worked very hard in the past few weeks to establish the Mission. Numbers are building up quickly. We encourage all those involved to continue their excellent work. OSCE will continue to work closely with other international organizations and NGOs involved in the international effort in Kosovo.

9. The staff of KVM must be able to carry out their duties safely. We urge all parties to the conflict to respect the ceasefire, to comply fully with relevant resolutions of the Security Council, and to cooperate closely with KVM so that it can carry out its duties unimpeded throughout Kosovo.

10. The OSCE verifiers are not a fighting force. Their true protection is the terms of agreement notion of pacta sunt servanda. In case it is required, OSCE welcomes the commitment of other organizations to provide assistance and to protect OSCE and its verifiers in its mission in Kosovo.

11. It is our hope and belief that the Kosovo Verification Mission will make the path to a settlement of the conflict in Kosovo easier. We will continue to give it our full support. But it is for the parties themselves to go down that path and to ensure that the people of Kosovo can look forward to a peaceful future.

125. Report of the Secretary-General Prepared pursuant to Security Council Resolutions 1160 (1998), 1199 (1998) and 1203 (1998), UN Doc. S/1999/99, 30 January 1999

I. Introduction

1. The present report is submitted pursuant to Security Council resolutions 1160 (1998) of 31 March 1998, 1199 (1998) of 23 September 1998 and 1203 (1998) of 24 October 1998. It covers the period since my previous report of 24 December 1998 (S/1998/1221).

II. Situation in Kosovo

2. The present report addresses humanitarian and human rights aspects of the situation in Kosovo. It is based on contributions provided by the Office of the United Nations High Commissioner for Refugees (UNHCR) and the Office of the United Nations High Commissioner for Human Rights, as well as by individual Member States. Information provided by the Chairman-in-Office of the Organization for Security and Cooperation in Europe (OSCE) and by the Secretary-General of the North Atlantic Treaty Organization (NATO) is contained in annexes I and II respectively. This information, submitted by organizations directly involved in the monitoring of the situation in Kosovo, should be read as complementing that contained in the present report.

VIOLENCE

3. The human rights situation in Kosovo has remained consistently grave for nearly 11 months. The October 1998 ceasefire did reduce the number of internally displaced persons and civilian casualties, the use of heavy weaponry, and the destruction of property and means of livelihood. However, during the reporting period, violence in Kosovo, including violations of the ceasefire, has continued, and the situation of human rights has further deteriorated, culminating with the massacre of Kosovo Albanian civilians in Racak.

4. The most disturbing new element is the spread of violence in Kosovo and the transformation of the nature of that violence. Prior to the ceasefire hostilities were limited to certain geographic locations, with fluid lines of engagement, although sniper fire did occur sporadically outside the discrete areas of encounter. In many cases, the civilian population fled from threatened locations to areas of perceived relative safety, some to urban areas within Kosovo but many others to exposed conditions with poor access to shelter and food. Following the ceasefire, many internally displaced persons began returning to their homes, but many continue to express fear of government forces and paramilitary units in and around villages. Calculated acts of violence followed by retaliatory measures now occur frequently in cities that, until winter, had been notably exempt from violence, even during the influx of internally displaced persons into urban areas whose social resources were already overtaxed. With the exception of some isolated incidents, the resident communities of Kosovo's large multi-ethnic cities, where most of its population resides, have not turned violently upon each other. However, targeted acts of violence and growing expressions of public rage during the past month might seriously threaten peace in urban areas.

5. In December, field staff of the Office of the United Nations High Commissioner for Human Rights in the Federal Republic of Yugoslavia attempted to follow up acts of discriminate violence, interviewing victims, families and community leaders, not only in the immediate aftermath of incidents but long after them. While some violent acts were widely publicized, it would appear that most were less well known, particularly in cases in which the perpetrators, be they Serb police or Kosovo Albanian paramilitary units, still maintained positions or control in or near the area. The Office of the United Nations High Commissioner for Human Rights observed that the transformation of the nature of violence in Kosovo had reduced the geographic area of perceived safety and had resulted in a real increase in the number of persons who live in apprehension of direct experience of violence or arbitrary treatment. During this period, assailants have selectively fired directly upon urban sidewalks and cafés, as well as civilian passenger vehicles - in at least one instance, on a car clearly transporting a family group.

6. The violence and arbitrary treatment characterizing this period have surgically targeted influential individuals and localities known for open-mindedness and flexibility in community relations. The Office of the United Nations High Commissioner for Human Rights concluded with concern that a message was being transmitted throughout Kosovo, where codes based on individual reputation have for generations governed social relations within and among all regional communities, that a reputation for open-minded and flexible behaviour was no guarantee of personal safety. The responsibility for targeted killings is increasingly a matter of attribution by one side or another. Frequently, assailants have been identified simply as "masked men", and witness interviews by the Office of the United Nations High Commissioner for Human Rights have indicated that the "masked men" have exhibited signs of unfamiliarity with their immediate surroundings. Moreover, public responsibility is rarely claimed for acts of violence, further fuelling polarization and fear. Perpetrators of acts of violence, gross official misconduct and crimes against humanity committed throughout the crisis still have not been brought to justice, suggesting that such acts are committed with impunity.

7. A brief summary of casualty figures is insufficient to illustrate how the nature of violence against civilians has been transformed or to suggest how it has fuelled an atmosphere of fear. A narrative of the time and place of major incidents better suggests how tensions have spread.

8. The abduction and murder on 16-17 December of the deputy mayor of Kosovo Polje, noted in my last report, sparked several days of public protests from the Serb community. On 22 December, armed assailants attacked a café in Kosovska Mitrovica, killing one Kosovo Albanian immediately, while another, who was reportedly a member of the newly created municipal government's local security force, died later of his wounds. On 27 December, Kosovo Albanian paramilitary units claimed responsibility for the 26 December killing of an elderly Serb from the village of Obranza, shot on the doorstep of his home. On

27 December, three Roma were found dead in Kosovska Mitrovica. On 29 December, the bodies of five Kosovo Albanians were found, left alongside roads or bridges, in three municipalities, two in Prizren, two in Kosovska Mitrovica and one on the Pec-Decani road. On 30 December, a Kosovo Albanian was killed near the village of Dremnjak. On 31 December, a Serb janitor in the Urosevac agricultural school was found dead on the outskirts of the town.

9. On 2 January, the bodies of several Serbs were demonstrably left in the Roma neighbourhood of Kosovska Mitrovica. The same day, unknown assailants killed a Kosovo Albanian in front of his house in Stimlje. During the night of 4-5 January, two Kosovo Albanians were killed at a gasoline station in Vitina, south-west of Gnjilane, a region of comparatively little violence. On 5 January, a grenade exploded outside a Serbian café in Pristina, followed by shooting in Pristina, as well as vandalism directed at cafés frequented by Pristina's Albanian community. The 6 January killing outside Pristina of a Serb electric company employee from Kosovo Polje sparked angry armed demonstrations by Serb civilians, who effectively sealed all roads in and out of Pristina on 7 January. On 9 January, one Kosovo Albanian was killed and another wounded by unknown attackers who opened fire on them from a car.

10. On 11 January, the director of the Kosovo Information Centre, Enver Maloku, was killed by unknown assailants while getting out of his car in a Pristina suburb. On the same day, a Kosovo Albanian man was shot and killed in a car near Pec. On 13 January, one Kosovo Albanian man was shot and killed in front of his house in Kosovska Mitrovica by unknown assailants and another was reported to have been killed in Urosevac. Also on 13 January, the mutilated body of a local forest caretaker, a Serb, was discovered at the same spot on a highway outside Pristina where the dead body of Kosovo Polje's deputy mayor had been left less than one month before.

THE RACAK MASSACRE

11. During the period from 15 to 18 January, fighting occurred in and around the village of Racak, near Stimlje. On 15 January, the Serb police and, as indicated in some reports, paramilitary units entered Racak. On 16 January, the Kosovo Verification Mission reported that the bodies of 45 Kosovo civilians, including 3 women, at least 1 child and several elderly men, were found, 11 in houses, 23 on a rise behind the village and others in various locations in the immediate vicinity of the village. Many of the dead appeared to have been summarily executed, shot at close range in the head and neck. The Council is aware of the developments in the aftermath of the Racak massacre that prompted the presidential statement of 19 January 1999 (S/PRST/1999/2). Detailed information on this incident was contained in the special report by the Kosovo Verification Mission attached to my letter of 17 January 1999 addressed to the President of the Security Council and in the report of the Kosovo Verification Mission attached to my letter of 20 January 1999 addressed to the President of the Security Council.

12. The Special Rapporteur on human rights in the territory of the former Yugoslavia, in a statement issued on 16 January from Prague, and the United Nations High Commissioner for Human Rights, in a letter of 19 January to President Milosevic, condemned the massacre and called for an immediate investigation of the Racak deaths. However, investigative and forensic efforts in the wake of this massacre have been wilfully obstructed by the lack of cooperation by the authorities of the Federal Republic of Yugoslavia with the international community. In an attempt to enter the Federal Republic of Yugoslavia to investigate the Racak deaths, the Chief Prosecutor of the International Tribunal for the Former Yugoslavia, Louise Arbour, was turned back, without a visa, at the border of the Federal Republic of Yugoslavia on 18 January 1999; the Government of the Federal Republic of Yugoslavia continues to assert that the International Tribunal for the Former Yugoslavia does not have jurisdiction to investigate alleged war crimes in Kosovo. In order to resolve this problem, the Chief Prosecutor proposed to the authorities of the Federal Republic of Yugoslavia that she would publicly state that her access to Kosovo would not prejudice the position of the Federal Republic of Yugoslavia on jurisdiction, nor would she use the access as evidence that the Federal Republic of Yugoslavia has voluntarily submitted to the jurisdiction of the Tribunal. The authorities, however, continued to deny the Chief Prosecutor's entry to Kosovo.

13. Meanwhile, on 18 January, the bodies of the victims were moved from the site to Pristina, where autopsies were performed in the presence of monitors of the Kosovo Verification Mission. The authorities of the Federal Republic of Yugoslavia, however, failed to respond to the appeal of the head of a Finnish forensic team to postpone examinations until the arrival of Finnish experts. The forensic team arrived in Pristina on 21 January. By that time, 16 autopsies had been carried out without the Finnish experts being present. The Finnish team, together with Serb and other foreign experts, performed autopsies on the remaining bodies and examined the autopsies performed earlier.

ABDUCTIONS AND TAKING OF HOSTAGES

14. During this period, no new information emerged or was volunteered on the whereabouts or fate of persons abducted or reported missing. On 26 December, after the Head of the Kosovo Verification Mission, William Walker, met with the families of persons abducted from Orahovac, the Mission announced that it had opened a special office to investigate reports of abductions. The office, staffed in shifts by two international verifiers, takes testimony on reported abductions.

15. From 24 December to 2 January, during fighting around Podujevo, it was reported that 11 Serbs and Kosovo Albanians were captured by Kosovo Albanian paramilitaries and released with the intervention of the Kosovo Verification Mission and the Kosovo Diplomatic Observer Mission.

16. On 8 January, as the OSCE Chairman-in-Office, Knut Vollebaek, began his visit to Albania and the Federal Republic of Yugoslavia, Kosovo Albanian paramilitary units attacked a Yugoslav Army convoy north-east of Kosovska Mitrovica, capturing eight army personnel, including several conscripts. This action led to the largest build-up of infantry, armour and artillery since the deployment of the Kosovo Verification Mission. Representatives of the Verification Mission initiated negotiations for the captives' release, which continued intensively throughout the Chairman's visit, and, on 13 January, the eight were released. The release did not, however, lead to a reduction of forces of the Federal Republic of Yugoslavia deployed throughout the area. Yugoslav Deputy Prime Minister Sainovic and all Serbian government officials emphasized that the release of the army personnel had been absolutely unconditional. On 14 January, a communiqué issued by Kosovo Albanian paramilitary units asserted that the eight had been released as part of an exchange for nine "prisoners".

DETENTION AND TRIALS

17. Reports of arbitrary detention and systematic ill-treatment of persons in police detention and under the jurisdiction of the Ministry of Justice continue. Measures that would build confidence among communities are not forthcoming. Of particular importance would be implementation of points 10 and 11 of the 13 October accord between President Slobodan Milosevic and United States Special Envoy Richard Holbrooke, release of information as to the whereabouts of those reported abducted and missing, and full cooperation by all parties with the International Committee of the Red Cross regarding persons held in detention.

18. Court proceedings on criminal charges of alleged terrorist and anti-State activity, as well as conspiracy to aid and abet such activity, continue to be held regularly in all district courts in Kosovo. Related proceedings have also begun in the military courts of Belgrade and Nis. The Office of the United Nations High Commissioner for Human Rights continues to monitor proceedings directly and to obtain court records of proceedings it cannot physically attend. The efforts of the Office to illuminate the legal and procedural issues raised by the proceedings have expanded informal working exchanges between and among court officials, prosecutors, defence attorneys, defendants and national and international organizations interested in the administration of justice. As part of this process, the Office makes repeated inquiries into judicial practice in the area of detention. Its consultations have

contributed to a re-evaluation of detention decisions in cases throughout Serbia and, in some proceedings in Kosovo, to critical evaluation of evidence previously used to bring criminal charges or to justify continued detention. A small but growing body of precedent is being established as courts have released from detention, or dropped charges against, roughly 40 persons who were the specific subject of inquiry by the Office of the United Nations High Commissioner for Human Rights. However, hundreds of Kosovo Albanians remain in detention and the wave of violence described in this and my previous report has led to sweep arrests, police detentions, or "informative talks" in the search for perpetrators. As of 18 January, the Serbian Ministry of Justice had not responded to the Office on approximately 50 inquiries pending since late November. At the political level, no policy on implementation of points 10 and 11 has been enunciated, although existing federal and Serbian laws and procedures already include means for implementing, inter alia, federal and republic-level executive amnesty, termination of proceedings, suspension of charges, mitigation of sentences and release from detention.

19. Several proceedings involving especially large groups of defendants or incidents and operations of an especially sensitive nature were scheduled during the traditional December and January holidays. In monitoring many trials, the Office of the United Nations High Commissioner for Human Rights has observed violations of domestic judicial procedure in the treatment of selected groups of Kosovo Albanians. Courtroom observation also indicates obvious differences in the physical condition and demeanour of prisoners held in Lipljan and Gnjilane prisons, both under the jurisdiction of the Pristina district prison administration, from those held in the jurisdiction of the Prizren district prison administration. Reports of ill-treatment at Lipljan are received regularly, and two prisoners have already died in custody in Gnjilane. During this period, the Office repeatedly observed the transport of Lipljan prisoners in the 40-member Kosovo Albanian "Orahovac group" by heavily armed special police, who, holding automatic weapons, were permitted by the presiding judge to remain in the courtroom, at a ratio of one policeman to one defendant, instead of regular court guards. Such prisoners were chained on arrival in the courtroom, remained in a submissive head-down position throughout the proceeding, looked to individual police guards before answering even cursory questions put to them by the court and were rechained on removal from the courtroom. In contrast, imprisoned Kosovo Albanians kept in the Prizren prison jurisdiction were transported in handcuffs by prison guards who carried light arms and handguns; prisoners did not appear ill or malnourished, and they looked attorneys, judges and even family members in the eye during court proceedings.

20. The Office of the United Nations High Commissioner for Human Rights monitored several trials during this period that included the conviction and sentencing of persons in absentia. As a general rule, persons convicted in absentia received higher sentences than those present for trial.

21. The Office of the United Nations High Commissioner for Human Rights monitored trials in which several Kosovo Albanian defendants, in open court testimony, indicated that their statements during police detention and after arraignment before an investigative judge were made under ill-treatment or torture. Of the 26-member "Urosevac group" arrested in June 1998 and brought before the Pristina district court in late December and mid-January, two defendants had died while in police custody, and all nine standing trial (the others were in absentia) claimed that they had been tortured and still had visible traces of injuries inflicted by police and State security officials, including after arraignment. Of the 15-member "Kacanik group" arrested in August 1998 and tried in Pristina in mid-December, all present (eight were in absentia) testified to having been subjected to ill-treatment ranging from beatings to electric shock. Neither the presiding judge nor the prosecutor made further inquiry into these allegations. All members of the group were convicted of sentences ranging from three to nine years, and those sentenced to less than three years were not released pending appeal, even though such provision exists in domestic law for sentences of under five years.

FORENSIC INVESTIGATION OF MASS GRAVES

22. Following the incident at Gornje Obrinje referred to in my previous report, the Finnish forensic team discussed the matter with the Serb authorities and representatives of Kosovo Albanian paramilitary units. Both parties suggested independently that since for the moment it was dangerous to carry out investigations at Gornje Obrinje (and also Golubovac), the Finnish team should instead start work at other locations currently not under the control of Kosovo Albanian paramilitary units, investigating in the first instance sites at Glodjane and Orahovac. The team, however, did not consider it possible to continue its field work at any other locations and therefore decided to leave Pristina on 20 December for a Christmas break. Under the prevailing circumstances, it remains uncertain whether in the foreseeable future there will be any prospect of making another attempt at Gornje Obrinje.

23. The difficulties experienced by the Finnish forensic team in performing their task were discussed at a meeting with the European Union Heads of Mission, and the Federal Republic of Yugoslavia Vice-Prime Minister and Head of the Government Commission for Cooperation with the Kosovo Verification Mission, Mr. Sainovic, on 29 December 1998 in Belgrade. Mr. Sainovic indicated his Government's readiness to discuss the problems, but only once the Finnish team was back in the Federal Republic of Yugoslavia.

COORDINATION WITH THE KOSOVO VERIFICATION MISSION

24. Since the arrival of the Technical Assessment Team and throughout the build-up of the Kosovo Verification Mission, the Office of the United Nations High Commissioner for Human Rights has briefed representatives of OSCE and the Kosovo Verification Mission on the situation of human rights and has provided regular introductions to human rights issues to Verification Mission inductees. In December, the Office of the United Nations High Commissioner for Human Rights provided the services of a consultant on mission to the Kosovo Verification Mission, who advised the Mission on plans for sustained human rights training of its verifiers. UNHCR and the Office of the United Nations High Commissioner for Human Rights also met with the OSCE Chairman-in-Office and the OSCE secretariat delegation during its mission to the Federal Republic of Yugoslavia.

HUMANITARIAN SITUATION

25. Since late December, more than 20,000 people have fled from some 23 villages in the four municipalities of Decane, Podujevo, Stimlje and Suva Reka. The four days of fighting in late December at Podujevo led to the flight from the suburbs and surrounding villages of an estimated 5,000 people. As little damage was done to buildings, return to the villages started as soon as a ceasefire was brokered. However, following the capture of eight Yugoslav soldiers, tension rose again, leading to new displacement. From a total of 11 villages in the Podujevo-Mitrovica area some 15,000 inhabitants fled, of whom over 5,000 people later returned.

26. In the second week of January, clashes in the Decane municipality prompted some 4,000 people to flee from five villages. UNHCR estimates that over 500 of these have now returned to two of the villages. As a result of serious fighting in Stimlje/Suva Reka and following the massacre in Racak on 15 January, 6,400 Kosovo Albanian civilians fled from six villages.

27. Meanwhile, from some 90 villages, principally in central and western Kosovo, all Serbian inhabitants have left, estimated to total some 1,500 people.

28. Where peace has held, there have been continuing returns, usually slow and gradual. For example, in Malisevo more than half of the 3,000 who left in July have come back, returns are continuing and some normalcy is being established. At Lodja near Pec, work stopped on the school that is to serve as a home for some families while they repair their houses following the murders in the Pec café, but is now expected to start again. Representatives of 20 families from Opertusa, a village in Suva Reka, have asked UNHCR for assistance to return home. At Junik, a village from which 10,000 fled in August, there have been 1,500 returns; however, some trouble between the villagers and

the police last week prompted about 200 to flee the village again. Returns to Junik appear to be from Albania and Djakovica and, despite the recent incident, appear to be continuing.

29. At the start of 1999, UNHCR estimated that some 180,000 civilians remained displaced within Kosovo, the vast majority of whom are Kosovo Albanians, including some 5,000 displaced in the last days of 1998. Some 110,000 were thought to have returned to their villages, if not their homes, in the last quarter of 1998. The great majority of these returns were from displacement within Kosovo, but included were some 12,000 returnees from Montenegro. No other significant returns were reported from outside Kosovo.

30. With regard to those still displaced or refugees outside Kosovo as a result of the conflict, at least 20,000 from Kosovo are thought to have moved to other parts of Serbia, and there are indications that the figure may be higher. Some 25,000 displaced persons are in Montenegro. Numbers in neighbouring countries are estimated as follows: Albania, 22,000 (of whom only some 500 remain in the Tropoje district); Bosnia and Herzegovina, 10,000; and the former Yugoslav Republic of Macedonia, 3,000. It is estimated that some 93,890 persons from the Federal Republic of Yugoslavia sought asylum in other countries in Europe in 1998, of whom 85 to 90 per cent are Kosovo Albanians.

31. In the first three weeks of 1999, some 20,000 persons are thought to have fled their homes for reasons of insecurity. Of these and those displaced at the end of 1998, some 7,000 have already been able to return, and a further 3,000 have returned to areas not affected by recent conflict. As at 20 January, UNHCR therefore estimated that some 190,000 remained displaced within Kosovo.

III. OBSERVATIONS

32. I am shocked and dismayed by reports of the atrocities committed in Racak on 15 January and urge the Yugoslav authorities to launch an urgent investigation of this crime with the participation of international experts. Sadly, the massacre and events surrounding it appear indicative of the pattern of disproportionate use of force by the authorities of the Federal Republic of Yugoslavia in retaliation for provocations by Kosovo Albanian paramilitaries. It is imperative that the perpetrators be brought to justice in order to deter further violence and to give peace in Kosovo a chance. Any appearance of impunity for the perpetrators could become a real obstacle to the process of finding a peaceful solution to the conflict through negotiation. In this regard, I urge that unconditional respect be given to the authority of the International Tribunal for the Former Yugoslavia throughout all of the territory of the former Yugoslavia.

33. The violence since 24 December, and in particular the massacre at Racak on 15 January and subsequent events, has been a major setback for the humanitarian operation, just when the deployment of the Kosovo Verification Mission was beginning to help create and consolidate conditions for return of the internally displaced, even to the most difficult areas such as Malisevo. Civilians have once again had to flee for their lives; many have had to spend bitter nights in the open. Continued violence would undermine what has been achieved by the humanitarian operation to date.

34. Fear of fighting between the security forces and Kosovo Albanian paramilitary units and continued violence against civilians are the overriding obstacle to return and to the sustainability of those returns that have taken place. The humanitarian operation has demonstrated its capacity to deliver large-scale assistance, but without an end to violence and the establishment of a climate of security this will not suffice. I am deeply concerned about the risk of a return to the situation that existed in Kosovo before October 1998, and I urge those in positions of public authority to put an end to the spiral of violence and to seek the path of constructive dialogue.

35. I am increasingly concerned that the spread of violence and the nature of the attacks could lead to a situation of all-out civil war in Kosovo, which might have unpredictable repercussions for the entire region. Violence, from whatever quarter, can only lead to further suffering for the civilian population in Kosovo, which has been the main target and victim of the conflict. Full and unconditional acceptance of peaceful negotiations is the only way to resolve the crisis in Kosovo. I therefore once again urge the parties to engage in negotiations on a peaceful settlement in Kosovo without further delay and without preconditions, as demanded by the international community and, in particular, by the Security Council in its resolutions 1160 (1998), 1199 (1998) and 1203 (1998).

36. I support the efforts of OSCE and of the Head of the Kosovo Verification Mission, Mr. Walker, to facilitate such a settlement and call upon the Yugoslav authorities to honour their obligations under the 16 October agreement and to cooperate fully with Mr. Walker and the Kosovo Verification Mission. I also call upon the authorities of the Federal Republic of Yugoslavia to honour their obligation to cooperate fully with the Prosecutor of the International Tribunal for the Former Yugoslavia as requested in Security Council resolutions 1160 (1998), 1199 (1998) and 1203 (1998).

37. I expect that the OSCE Chairman-in-Office, in consultation with the Head of the Kosovo Verification Mission, will henceforth be in a position to provide the Council with regular information on the political aspects of the situation in Kosovo.

Annex: Letter Dated 22 January 1999 from the Secretary-General of the North Atlantic Treaty Organization Addressed to the Secretary-General

I am writing to bring you up to date with regard to the actions and decisions of the North Atlantic Treaty Organization (NATO) in the Kosovo crisis. As you know, the situation has deteriorated significantly in recent weeks culminating in the massacre of Kosovar Albanians in the village of Racak last Friday.

Following its meeting on 17 January to assess the situation, the North Atlantic Council called on the Yugoslav authorities to cooperate fully with the International Tribunal for the Former Yugoslavia, in accordance with United Nations resolutions, and to take immediate steps to bring those responsible for the massacre to justice. It also expressed its full support for the mission of the Organization for Security and Cooperation in Europe (OSCE) in Kosovo, as established by Security Council resolution 1203 (1998), and called on President Milosevic to comply fully with his commitments to NATO and OSCE, based on Security Council resolution 1199 (1998) and the undertakings provided to the Alliance last October on force levels and posture.

At the request of the Council, NATO's senior military authorities, the Chairman of the Military Committee, General Klaus Naumann, and the Supreme Allied Commander Europe (SACEUR), General Wesley K. Clark, visited President Milosevic personally on 19 January to underline its concern and reinforce the need for him to honour his obligations. Regrettably, until now, he has failed to do so. The North Atlantic Council is accordingly now assessing the situation and considering how best to help the international community achieve a political solution to the crisis.

The North Atlantic Council also agreed on 20 January 1999 that I would provide a report to the United Nations on compliance by the parties to the conflict. Accordingly I enclose, for your information and for distribution as you deem appropriate, an assessment of compliance trends derived from various public and official Alliance sources. The report covers significant trends and incidents over the past month, but is not intended as a complete compilation. As you will see from the report, neither side in the conflict has respected the ceasefire; and there have been a number of cases of kidnappings and attacks by Kosovar armed elements. The activities of the Yugoslav Army (VJ) and the Special Police (MUP), however, have been wholly disproportionate and excessive, particularly bearing in mind the operations conducted during the period from 10 to 16 January 1999.

I will keep you informed of any further important developments and am looking forward to an exchange of views on these and other issues with you on 28 January.

I am sending a copy of this letter to the Chairman-in-Office of the Organization for Security and Cooperation in Europe.

(Signed) Javier Solana

Enclosure
North Atlantic Treaty Organization Compliance Report for Kosovo
13 December 1998 - 19 January 1999

North Atlantic Treaty Organization compliance report for Kosovo
13 December 1998 - 19 January 1999

TABLE 1*
UNITED NATIONS SECURITY COUNCIL RESOLUTION 1199 (1998)

Resolution tenet	Related activity
1. Federal Republic of Yugoslavia and Kosovo Albanians: Cease hostilities and maintain ceasefire	13-19 Dec.: VJ units begin deployment to Podujevo area. VJ kills 31 Kosovo Albanians crossing border. UCK, in separate incidents, kill 8 Serb civilians, 1 MUP officer. UCK kidnap and kill Deputy Mayor of Kosovo Polje. 20-26 Dec.: UCK attack MUP patrol; 2 UCK killed. UCK kill MUP officer in Podujevo, local security official in a café in Kosovska Mitrovica. VJ forces, reinforced with armour and artillery, attack villages in and around Podujevo. 27 Dec.- VJ continue shelling civilian 2 Jan. facilities and UCK positions in and around Podujevo resulting in the deaths of at least 15 Kosovo Albanians. UCK kill Serb judge in Podujevo. 3-9 Jan.: UCK kill 3 MUP officers in ambush. UCK blamed for grenade attack against Serb bar, death of Serb official in Polje, Serb guard at a power plant and 6 MUP. UCK capture 8 VJ soldiers (later released, unharmed). VJ/MUP shell villages in Podujevo area; attack UCK positions. 10-16 Jan.: VJ tanks fire on Lapastika. VJ/MUP operations with artillery support in Decane area. VJ/MUP operations in Suva Reka and Stimlje. VJ heavy shelling in Racak. VJ/MUP believed (including by Head of the Organization for Security and Cooperation in Europe (OSCE) Kosovo Verification Mission) to be responsible for 45 civilian deaths in Racak.
2. Federal Republic of Yugoslavia: Take steps to improve humanitarian situation.	On 17 December, the Government of the Federal Republic of Yugoslavia has announced but has not yet implemented plans to build humanitarian centres and new houses and to reconstruct damaged houses. Federal Republic of Yugoslavia operations around Podujevo, Suva Reka have displaced over 7,000 persons.
3. Federal Republic of Yugoslavia and Albanian-Kosovars: Enter into dialogue, with international involvement, to end crisis.	Nothing significant to report.
4. Federal Republic of Yugoslavia: Cease all action by security forces affecting the civilian population and order the withdrawal of security units used for civilian repression.	3-9 Jan.: MUP accused by civilians of firing on villages of Djakavica, Sipitula and Belince. 10-16 Jan.: MUP/VJ forces conduct counter-insurgency operations in Stimlje, Decane, Suva Reka and Racak; see entry 1 above.
5. Federal Republic of Yugoslavia: Enable effective and continuous international monitoring, including access and complete freedom of movement.	Throughout the reporting period, VJ and MUP forces have denied access, in selected areas, to Kosovo Diplomatic Observer Mission and OSCE personnel.
6. Federal Republic of Yugoslavia: Facilitate with the Office of the United Nations High Commissioner for Refugees (UNHCR) and the International Committee of the Red Cross safe return of refugees and internally displaced persons to their homes.	There is no overt example of cooperation by the Federal Republic of Yugoslavia with UNHCR to assist in the safe return of refugees and internally displaced persons. The most recent fighting in the Stimlje area has created a new situation with estimates of up to 6,000 internally displaced persons fleeing their homes in the Stimlje/Racak regions. Many of these people are without shelter.
7. Federal Republic of Yugoslavia and Kosovo Albanians: Set a timetable aimed at confidence-building measures and political solutions.	Nothing significant to report.
8. Federal Republic of Yugoslavia: Cooperate with the International Tribunal for the Former Yugoslavia in the investigation of possible violations.	10 Dec.: Serb police blocked the Finnish forensics team from carrying out the first exhumations of Kosovo massacre victims in a dispute over Serb access to a UCK-controlled area. A Serb contingent, consisting of an associate police commander and nearly two dozen policemen wearing flak jackets and carrying automatic weapons, stopped the Finnish convoy on the road to Trstenik. The UCK in the area said that the police were unwelcome but that the Finnish team could proceed. The Serb police were not satisfied with this arrangement and therefore prohibited the investigators from proceeding to the grave site. The Finnish team leader has accused the Serb side of obstruction, adding that the Serb action violated the diplomatic immunity of the Finnish Ambassador for Human Rights who accompanied the team.

Resolution tenet	Related activity
	19 Jan.: The Government of the Federal Republic of Yugoslavia denied the chief of the International Tribunal for the Former Yugoslavia, Louise Arbour, entry to Kosovo to evaluate the alleged massacre of 45 civilians in Racak. The authorities of the Federal Republic of Yugoslavia have moved the bodies from a mosque in Racak to Pristina and have begun their own autopsies.
9. Federal Republic of Yugoslavia: Bring to justice security force members involved in mistreatment of civilians and the deliberate destruction of property.	There is no indication that the Government of the Federal Republic of Yugoslavia has assisted in this effort. See entry 8 above.
10. Kosovo Albanian leadership: Condemn all terrorist activity.	There has been no public declaration by either the political or the military leadership to denounce alleged UCK acts of terrorism during the reporting period.

* MUP = Special Police;
UCK = Kosovo Liberation Army;
VJ = Yugoslav Army.

Table 2*
Modalities for Kosovo Federal Republic of Yugoslavia Security Force Reductions and Operations Agreed to by the North Atlantic Treaty Organization and the Federal Republic of Yugoslavia on 25 October 1998

Modality	Actions by the Federal Republic of Yugoslavia
1. Special Police units deployed to Kosovo after February 1998 will be withdrawn from Kosovo. Combined police/Special Police strength in Kosovo will be reduced to their February 1998 duty level.	There is strong evidence that Special Police detachments from Serbia proper continue to operate within Kosovo. There are no indications that externally based detachments are being withdrawn.
2. Any heavy weapons (12.7 mm and above) or equipment brought into Kosovo or transferred from the VJ to the police/Special Police after February 1998 will be withdrawn from Kosovo or returned to the VJ.	In violation of this provision, MUP has and is employing heavy weaponry in Kosovo.
3. Police/Special Police will resume their normal peacetime activities. Heavy weapons and equipment remaining under MUP control in Kosovo will be returned to cantonments and police stations.	See table 1, entry 4. Excessive traffic patrolling, fortification of observation posts and unauthorized checkpoints continue.
4. All VJ units and additional equipment brought into Kosovo after February 1998 will be withdrawn from Kosovo.	VJ forces may have been reinforced with personnel from outside Kosovo.
5. Except for those VJ currently augmenting border guards, all VJ elements remaining in Kosovo will return to garrison, with agreed exceptions.	VJ units clearly began to violate this requirement in mid-December and continue to deploy units above the agreed-to limits in size and location.
6. VJ and MUP commanders will provide to the Kosovo Diplomatic Observer Mission/OSCE detailed weekly reports on manning, weapons and activities of their forces and will provide immediate notification and explanation to the Kosovo Diplomatic Observer Mission/OSCE of any deployment contrary to these provisions.	VJ and MUP reporting has been inaccurate and misleading. VJ and MUP units have failed to account for equipment and personnel numbers and activities.
Federal Republic of Yugoslavia-Kosovo Diplomatic Observer Mission verification modalities	
7. All checkpoints will be dismantled.	MUP continue to maintain and build unauthorized checkpoints throughout Kosovo. Some include kitchens and sleeping facilities.
8. In case of incidents of increased tension, the police will have the right, upon notifying the Kosovo Diplomatic Observer Mission/OSCE, to perform patrol duties in armoured vehicles.	See entry 6 above. Notification is usually relayed after the fact as a statement of action already carried out.

* MUP = Special Police;
VJ = Yugoslav Army.

Table 3*
United Nations Security Council Resolution 1203 (1998)

Resolution tenet	Related activity
1. Federal Republic of Yugoslavia: Cooperate fully with the Organization for Security and Cooperation in Europe (OSCE) Kosovo Verification Mission and Air Verification Mission.	Kosovo Air Verification Mission continues uninhibited with full support of the Federal Republic of Yugoslavia. On 18 January, the Government of the Federal Republic of Yugoslavia declared the Head of the OSCE Kosovo Verification Mission, Ambassador William Walker, "persona non grata" and ordered him to leave the Federal Republic of Yugoslavia within 48 hours.
2. Federal Republic of Yugoslavia: Comply immediately with	Offensive operations conducted by VJ and MUP forces, inter alia, from 23 to

Resolution tenet	Related activity
Security Council resolutions 1160 (1998) and 1199 (1998).	27 December in the Podujevo area and, from 15 to 21 January in the Stimlje region. See table 1, entries 1 and 4.
3. Federal Republic of Yugoslavia and Kosovo Albanians: Respect freedom of movement of OSCE Kosovo Verification Mission and other international personnel.	Both parties prohibit access in some areas and at some facilities. To date, the Federal Republic of Yugoslavia has not allowed Kosovo Verification Mission personnel access to border operations nor to some MUP facilities.
4. Federal Republic of Yugoslavia: Ensure the safety and security of all diplomatic personnel, including OSCE Kosovo Verification Mission personnel and all international and non-governmental organization humanitarian personnel.	On 17 January, without warning, MUP began mortar and automatic weapons fire in Racak, seriously endangering Kosovo Verification Mission personnel in the vicinity.
5. Federal Republic of Yugoslavia and Kosovo Albanians: Ensure personnel are not subject to the threat or use of force or interference of any kind.	On 15 January, UCK small arms fire wounded two Kosovo Verification Mission personnel. UCK claims firing was not intentional.
6. Federal Republic of Yugoslavia and Kosovo Albanians: Cooperate with international efforts to improve the humanitarian situation and avert pending humanitarian crisis.	Nothing significant to report.
7. Federal Republic of Yugoslavia: Create the conditions that allow internally displaced persons to return home.	See table 1, entry 6.
8. Federal Republic of Yugoslavia: Conduct prompt and complete investigation of all atrocities committed against civilians through the Hague-based International Tribunal for the Former Yugoslavia.	See table 1, entry 8.

- MUP = Special Police;
UCK = Kosovo Liberation Army;
VJ = Yugoslav Army.

126. Report of the Secretary-General Prepared pursuant to Security Council Resolutions 1160 (1998), 1199 (1998) and 1203 (1998), UN Doc. S/1999/293, 17 March 1999

I. Introduction

1. The present report is submitted pursuant to Security Council resolutions 1160 (1998) of 31 March 1998, 1199 (1998) of 23 September 1998 and 1203 (1998) of 24 October 1998. It addresses the comprehensive monitoring regime established under Security Council resolution 1160 (1998) and humanitarian and human rights aspects of the situation in Kosovo covering the period since my previous report of 30 January 1999 (S/1999/99). Information contained in this report complements that provided by the Chairman-in-Office of the Organization for Security and Cooperation in Europe (OSCE) in his report to the Council of 26 February 1999 (S/1999/214). As I indicated in my letter of transmittal to that report, I have discontinued comprehensive reporting on the situation in Kosovo, which is being covered by OSCE in compliance with the Council's wish to be kept informed about the situation there.

II. Comprehensive Regime to Monitor the Implementation of the Prohibitions Imposed by the Security Council Resolution 1160 (1998)

2. As stated in my report of 5 August 1998 (S/1998/712), the overall resources pledged by organizations willing to participate in the monitoring of the prohibitions imposed by resolution 1160 (1998) did not allow for the establishment of a comprehensive monitoring regime as envisaged by that resolution. I also stated that, nonetheless, their proposed contributions, coupled with that of the United Nations Preventive Deployment Force (UNPREDEP), could provide a useful framework for reporting on violations and for assisting the Committee established by resolution 1160 (1998) in discharging its mandate. These organizations, as well as UNPREDEP, have provided useful information in their reports to the above Committee.

3. The termination of the mandate of UNPREDEP will affect efforts to monitor the implementation of the prohibitions established by Security Council resolution 1160 (1998). Accordingly, the Security Council may wish to reconsider the modalities for the monitoring regime. In the meantime, it would be necessary for representatives of participating organizations and the Secretariat to continue to hold periodic meetings in order to exchange information and address practical issues arising in connection with their monitoring activities.

III. Humanitarian and Human Rights Situation in Kosovo

VIOLENCE

4. The humanitarian and human rights situation in Kosovo remains grave. The general insecurity, combined with continuing and unpredictable outbreaks of violence, has resulted in a cycle of displacement and return throughout Kosovo. During the reporting period, targeted killings of civilians, summary executions, mistreatment of detainees and new abduction cases were reported almost daily. Since 20 January, the Office of the United Nations High Commissioner for Human Rights (UNHCHR) has registered more than 65 cases of violent death, including one in custody. The Office's background investigations of targeted violence further confirmed the observations expressed in my previous report that the nature of violent activity in Kosovo, which has now spread to urban areas, has increased the number of persons who live in fear of being directly affected by violence or arbitrary treatment.

5. While clashes between the Serbian security forces and Kosovo Albanian paramilitary units continued at a relatively lower level, civilians in Kosovo are increasingly becoming the main target of violent acts. An increasingly common pattern of individual killings throughout the region accounts for the majority of deaths. Most violent incidents have remained unclaimed. This has contributed to the climate of fear and insecurity, causing deep distrust among communities and adding to the humanitarian and social problems in Kosovo.

6. The following narrative of when and where major incidents occurred suggests how violence against civilians in Kosovo continues to spread. On 18 January 1999, a Serb man was killed after reportedly failing to stop at a Kosovo Liberation Army's (KLA) roadblock in Nedakovac, near Kosovska Mitrovica. On 19 January, the body of a Kosovo Albanian teacher was discovered near Istok. On 20 January, two Serbian women (mother and daughter) were wounded after unidentified persons opened fire on their house, apparently targeting the father. On 21 January, a Kosovo Albanian man and woman were killed when their car was fired upon at an intersection outside Orahovac. The same day, the body of a Kosovo Albanian doctor was found near the Pec-Mitrovica highway.

8. On 25 January, a Kosovo Albanian was killed and his son severely wounded near Decani when masked assailants fired a reported 55 rounds into their car. On 26 January, a Serb man was severely wounded in an attack directed at his house in the Istok municipality. The body of a 23-year-old Serb was found under a driveway in the outskirts of Kosovska Mitrovica on 27 January; the body may have been moved to that location after the victim was killed elsewhere.

9. On 29 January, Kosovo Albanian sources reported that the body of a Kosovo Albanian was found in Bistrazin village and that another Albanian, close to the Democratic League of Kosovo (LDK), was seriously wounded in front of his apartment by two shots fired by unknown persons. On 30 January, a 36-year-old Kosovo Albanian from Pec was found shot in the head on the Pec-Pristina road. That same day, the body of another reputed "Kosovo Albanian loyalist", a physics teacher from Djakovica, was found in the village of Gradis. In Istok municipality, an elderly Serb was killed and his 72-year-old wife was injured when unidentified persons threw a grenade into their house in the village of Rakos.

10. On 31 January, the body of a Kosovo Albanian from the village of Begov Vukovac was found, shot in the head, south of Istok. That same day, in Stimlje municipality, masked gunmen reportedly broke into a house in the village of Donje Godance and wounded one man and two boys.

11. Attacks and killings in urban areas continued during the first half of February. On 4 February, bodies of three Kosovo Albanians were found in a car between the villages of Istinic and Gornja Lika, in Decani municipality, and the body of a Serb was found near the village of Rastavica. All had been shot. On 4 February, a Serb male was killed by automatic weapon fire while travelling on the Pec-Djakovica highway.

12. On 7 February, bodies of two Kosovo Albanians reported missing since 3 January were found in Kacanik, south of Urosevac. During the night of 7-8 February, the body of an unidentified man aged about 30 was found in the village of Livadja in Lipljan municipality. At this writing, UNHCHR is attempting to clarify several reports of bodies found in or around Djakovica on 8 February. The bodies of two young persons, one a 17-year-old boy and one a 20-year-old woman, were reported found in two different locations in a Djakovica suburb. The body of a Kosovo Albanian male, dead from gunshot wounds, was found in his car in the Djakovica area, near the village of Trakanic. The same day, again in Djakovica, bodies of a male and an elderly woman were also found. Both victims, who are believed to be from the Roma community, died of gunshot wounds to the neck. Bodies of two Kosovo Albanians from the village of Goden near Djakovica were found on 10 February.

13. On 11 February, four more bodies were discovered in different areas of Kosovo. According to media reports, the body of the Kosovo Albanian owner of an Istok tea room was found on the Zac-Zablace road; he had been shot in the head. Two men, one a Kosovo Albanian shot in the head, the other, as-yet-unidentified, were found in separate locations in Novo Selo, near Pec. The body of an unidentified male was found in a pond in Klina.

14. Targeted violence against civilians in Kosovo is taking new, even more dangerous, forms. In particular, recently increased terrorist acts against Serb and Albanian establishments in urban areas, including grenade attacks on cafes and shops, are a cause of serious concern. Since the end of January, at least 10 such incidents in Pristina, Pec, Kosovska Mitrovica and Urosevac have been reported. The investigation by UNHCHR indicated that in many cases these establishments had been frequented by Serbs and Albanians and no incidents between them had previously been reported. The latest attack, on 13 February in the main town square in Urosevac, was particularly horrible: 12 people were wounded and about 20 neighbouring shops and several cars parked nearby heavily damaged. On 17 February, another explosive device planted at the Urosevac market was discovered and deactivated by the Kosovo Verification Mission. The result of these attacks is the growing alienation of the Serb and Albanian communities, a pervasive feeling of insecurity and the shrinking of the remaining ground for coexistence.

15. Following these grenade attacks and a number of killings in Pristina and in the areas of Pec and Djakovica, UNHCHR field staff have expressed concern that, particularly in these three urban areas, civilians known for open-mindedness and flexibility in community relations, as well as professionals, intellectuals and moderate community activists, have been targeted. Increasing pressure on the urban elite in Pristina, Pec and Djakovica has also frequently been cited to UNHCHR staff as a source of tension and apprehension in Prizren.

RACAK INVESTIGATION

16. On 10 February 1999, the 40 remaining bodies of the Kosovo Albanian victims of the Racak massacre were handed over to their families. A funeral was held in Racak on 11 February. The release of the bodies had become a point of contention between the Government of the Federal Republic of Yugoslavia and the Kosovo Verification Mission. As of 1 February, the team of Finnish forensic experts had completed or monitored autopsies on 24 of the 40 bodies brought from the Racak mosque to Pristina. Sixteen bodies had been autopsied by Serbian forensic specialists before the arrival of the Finnish team. Five bodies of the total of 45 dead at Racak were reportedly removed from the village by families and were not autopsied. The Finnish team stressed, during its two-week stay in the Federal Republic of Yugoslavia, that it was not carrying out an investigation into the events at Racak, but an examination of the bodies moved from the place of death to the mosque in Racak and then to the Pristina morgue. After the events at Racak, the scene was not isolated; the circumstances of evidence-gathering and the chain of custody of evidence remain unclear. The Finnish team indicated that it would release the results of its examination in Racak to the European Union and to the Pristina district court in early March. There is no indication at this time of action by the authorities of the Federal Republic of Yugoslavia to bring the perpetrators of the Racak massacre to justice.

ABDUCTIONS AND TAKING OF HOSTAGES

17. During this period, no new information emerged or was volunteered on the whereabouts and fate of persons abducted or reported missing. Eleven persons were abducted, 10 Serbs, among whom five were released and one escaped, and one Kosovo Albanian, who was found dead. On 21 January, five Serb civilians (three men and two women) were abducted in the village of Nevoljane, Vucitrn municipality, and released on 23 January through mediation by the Kosovo Verification Mission. The KLA spokesman in Pristina stated that the five were not kidnapped. Instead, he claimed that "stopping, disarming and the arrest of the five members of the Serb nationality ... were performed in accordance with the international conventions and norms, and for the reason of public security and order in that village".

18. During the night of 8-9 February, one Serb civilian went missing near Kosovska Mitrovica. The following night, two Serb civilians were abducted near Novo Selo on the Pristina-Vucitrn road. One managed to escape and reported that he was kidnapped by persons wearing KLA uniforms and insignia. On 10 February, the body of a Kosovo Albanian from Urosevac, who had been kidnapped the day before, was discovered. On 11 February, Serbian sources reported that two plainclothes police officers were abducted the night before, after having last been seen off-duty in Kosovo Polje, outside Pristina.

DETENTION AND TRIALS

19. Reports of arbitrary detention and systematic ill-treatment of Kosovo Albanians in police detention and under the jurisdiction of the Ministry of Justice continue to emerge from UNHCHR field interviews and during court testimony. According to information released by Serbian Public Prosecutor, Dragica Krsmanovic, 2,007 persons in Kosovo have been charged with criminal offences of terrorism, endangering the territorial integrity of the country and seditious activity. Of those, 1,060 are currently in detention and 824 are under indictment. As earlier reported, the number of Kosovo Albanians detained, questioned, subjected to "informative talks" or arrested and subsequently released by police is not known.

20. On 16 January it was reported that Halit Aliaj, aged 48, who was arrested the day before, died while in police custody in the Djakovica police station. UNHCHR is making further inquiry into this case. Three other persons are known by UNHCHR to have died in 1998 while in police custody in Djakovica.

21. UNHCHR staff continue to monitor proceedings in which Kosovo Albanian defendants are accused of alleged terrorist or anti-state activity. The number of persons already sentenced in courts of first instance is relatively small. Most proceedings are still pending. Regardless of the size of the group of defendants or the number of witnesses to be called, most proceedings monitored by the Office have been discontinued after a hearing lasting only one working day or less, and subsequent hearings in the same case are frequently postponed for only a few days short of the maximum postponement allowed by law. As a result, defendants remain in detention indefinitely. On 8 February, proceedings against 24 "Orahovac group" defendants were once again postponed until 10 March. The group was arrested on or about 21 July 1998 and has been in detention, under systematic abuse, at Lipljan prison ever since. The hearing on 8 February was the first time any of the accused gave court testimony after more than six months' detention and after repeated postponements.

22. During this reporting period, sentences were handed over on 5 February in the "Urosevac group" case. Of the 28-member Urosevac group, 11 were arrested in June 1998; two of those defendants died while in police custody, allegedly as a result of torture. The nine remaining defendants were first brought before the Pristina district court in late December and mid-January. Seventeen defendants were tried in absentia. All nine standing trial claimed they had been tortured and still had visible traces of injuries allegedly inflicted by police and state security officials, including after their arraignment before an investigative judge. The defendants, including those tried in absentia, were sentenced to periods ranging from two and a half to 15 years.

23. On 10 February, the district court of Prizren sentenced eight men from Orahovac municipality to five years' imprisonment on charges of terrorism. The accused had all been charged with membership in the "so-called 'KLA'". Individual charges included providing medicine, food and fuel to KLA, possession of weapons, carrying out patrols and opening fire on patrols of the Ministry of the Interior. The decision of the court relied on confessions of the accused made before the investigating judge and photocopies of alleged lists of KLA membership. No originals of these documents were submitted by the prosecution as evidence. In earlier proceedings, defendants had maintained that their statements were made under coercion and torture, allegations not examined by the court. In explaining why the court did not consider these allegations, the presiding judge, on pronouncing his sentence, stated that the court would have considered these allegations seriously were it not for the fact that some of the accused had admitted they were KLA members. The court's final judgement did not indicate which acts had been proved to have been committed by each individual accused. The presiding judge did indicate in his explanation of his judgement that the strategy of defence attorneys had compelled him to issue heavy sentences.

DISPLACEMENTS

24. To keep count of the numbers of displaced is difficult, but the Office of the United Nations High Commissioner for Refugees (UNHCR), in consultation with non-governmental organization (NGO) partners, believes the number inside Kosovo stands at some 211,000, while there are an estimated 25,000 displaced in Montenegro. To assess the numbers of returns is even more difficult, given the long-term displacement of some, the short-term and sometimes repeated displacement, combined with return, of others. Therefore, UNHCR believes that it is more appropriate at this stage to address the humanitarian needs of the war-affected, including displaced, returnees, host families and those who never moved but lost their property and means of livelihood. The United Nations humanitarian agencies and NGOs are together providing relief assistance to some 420,000 persons in Kosovo and Montenegro.

25. A resumption of hostilities in Kosovo in January and February resulted in new displacement of population. Clashes between Kosovo Albanian paramilitary units and Serbian forces in the Podujevo area have prevented the return of some 15,000 displaced from about 17 villages. Serb and Albanian homes along the main Pristina-Podujevo road remain deserted, as intermittent fighting occurs some 3 kilometres to the west. This area has witnessed a pattern of displacement, return and fresh displacement. In Drenica, Suva Reka, Stimlje, Prizren and Vucitrn similar clashes also led to a new displacement of population. In some cases return took place, at least of some of the displaced, as soon as the violence passed; in other places, where the presence of Serbian security forces or Kosovo Albanian paramilitary units continued, fear prevented early return.

26. February was also marked by the continuing departure of the Serbian population from towns and villages where they had been in the minority, or where clashes between Kosovo Albanian paramilitary units and security forces occurred. According to information provided by the Serbian Commissioner for Refugees, some 90 villages in central and western Kosovo have lost their entire Serbian population in recent months, while towns like Podujevo and Kosovska Mitrovica have seen a reduction of the Serbian population. The estimated number of displaced Serbs within Kosovo is 10,000 while 30,000 more have moved to other parts of Serbia. In contrast, Kosovo Albanians who have lost or never had identity documents are afraid to move from their villages for fear of harassment by the security forces. UNHCR is seeking to prevent further displacement and to facilitate visits of persons without documentation to the appropriate police stations in order to secure identity documents.

RETURN MOVEMENTS

27. Throughout the reporting period, some returns have continued to take place, especially where the OSCE/Kosovo Verification Mission has established a continuing presence. In Slapuzane, south of Pristina, for example, 1,200 formerly displaced persons have returned. In Malisevo more than half of the former 3,000 residents are back in their village, while in Junik, more than 1,500 of the inhabitants are back in their homes. Following the burial, on 13 February, of 40 of those killed at Racak, the OSCE/Kosovo Verification Mission established a continuing presence there and some villagers have since returned. In Lodja, a village on the outskirts of Pec that was almost totally destroyed last summer, UNHCR and NGOs are assisting a group of about 16 families in repairing the largely undamaged school building. These families are now living in the school while undertaking the major task of rebuilding their homes.

HUMANITARIAN ASSISTANCE

28. Delivery of humanitarian assistance has continued almost uninterrupted throughout the month of February, despite the violence and severe weather. UNHCR has coordinated and led three multi-agency convoys six days per week, bringing systematic assistance to the displaced, the returned and to the war-affected population. Some relief assistance by NGOs working outside the escorted convoy system has been disrupted. There were reports of confiscation by the Serbian security forces of local trucks contracted by an NGO and of relief items belonging to another. Moreover, cases of harassment of relief NGOs were also reported. Some NGOs have been repeatedly visited by the regular and the financial police and questioned about their activities, others reported aggressive behaviour by KLA members.

SHELTER SURVEY

29. UNHCR and UNICEF worked with 14 NGOs from November 1998 to February 1999 to undertake a shelter survey covering 654 villages in 19 municipalities affected by the conflict in Kosovo, 440 villages were directly affected by the conflict, with damage ranging from slight to complete destruction. These villages had a total of 66,686 family houses before the conflict. Half of these houses have differing degrees of damage and 22,239 houses require major reconstruction. The resulting Shelter Report catalogues the extent of damage, village by village, for each of the 19 municipalities surveyed, and

differing degrees of damage and 22,239 houses require major reconstruction. The resulting Shelter Report catalogues the extent of damage, village by village, for each of the 19 municipalities surveyed, and will prove an important document in the planning of priorities for repair and reconstruction.

30. UNICEF, in cooperation with five international NGOs, has conducted a school damage assessment survey in 13 municipalities. The survey indicated that out of 900 schools, 163 have been destroyed or seriously damaged, while the remaining have minor damages or have been looted.

IV. Observations

31. UNHCR and its United Nations and NGOs partners will continue their efforts, in these risky conditions, to protect and assist the large number of refugees and displaced persons, and to support the population affected by the 12 months of conflict in Kosovo. There is strong apprehension, however, that violence against civilians and clashes between Serbian security forces and Kosovo Albanian paramilitary units will continue, with the resultant displacement of the civilian population. Cooperation between UNHCR and the Kosovo Verification Mission will remain crucial in monitoring developments and reacting rapidly in order to meet the needs of the displaced and their host communities. UNHCR and its partners have updated contingency and preparedness plans, but it is clear that any break in the continuity of humanitarian action would create further suffering.

32. I share the strong concerns of the UNHCHR about the spread of violence against civilians in Kosovo. Beyond the unacceptable actions of the Serbian security forces, the recent dangerous terrorist bombings are causing a growing number of victims. Terror tactics by Government forces, ethnically motivated violence, arbitrary treatment, targeted killings, abductions and bomb attacks must be halted by those responsible.

33. It is obvious that the humanitarian problems in Kosovo are a consequence of the armed conflict and the political crisis and they are difficult to separate from security issues. I am increasingly alarmed that continued confrontation in Kosovo, including persistent breaches of the ceasefire, has led to a substantial aggravation of the situation. According to OSCE, the current security environment in Kosovo is characterized by disproportionate use of force, including mortar and tank fire, by the Yugoslav authorities in response to persistent attacks and provocations by the Kosovo Albanian paramilitaries. As tensions mount in Kosovo, the number of Yugoslav troops deployed in the field exceeds the agreed level by a factor of five. Kosovo Albanian paramilitary units are consolidating their presence throughout Kosovo, including areas they did not control before. As a result, fighting now affects areas previously untouched by hostilities, leading to further deterioration of the situation and new displacements of civilian population.

34. Further fighting has rendered the October 1998 ceasefire agreement almost meaningless. I urge both parties to halt military activities in Kosovo, to comply fully with relevant Security Council resolutions and honour their commitments under the October 1998 agreements. In particular, the Yugoslav authorities should immediately reduce the number of troops deployed in the field to the level established in October 1998 and Kosovo Albanian paramilitary units should refrain from any provocative actions.

35. I strongly support efforts by the Contact Group to provide a political framework for a settlement of the crisis. I encourage the parties to seize this opportunity to achieve peace and autonomy for the people of Kosovo by negotiation, while respecting the national sovereignty and territorial integrity of the Federal Republic of Yugoslavia.

3.4 THE RAMBOUILLET TALKS

3.4.1 PREPARATION OF THE CONFERENCE

127. U.S. Secretary of State Albright and Russian Foreign Minister Ivanov, Joint Statement, Moscow, 26 January 1999

Secretary Albright and Foreign Minister Ivanov expressed their preoccupation with the recent deterioration in the situation in Kosovo. They noted positively the outcome of the Contact Group Political Directors meeting in London January 22. The sides in Kosovo must work harder to achieve an interim political settlement providing substantial autonomy for Kosovo and should engage in meaningful intensive negotiations for that purpose. Such a settlement should respect the territorial integrity and sovereignty of the FRY. Russia and the United States, backing the efforts of Ambassadors Hill and Petritsch, will continue to press the sides to agree on such a political settlement, and will collaborate in the Contact Group toward that end.

Secretary Albright and Foreign Minister Ivanov expressed their complete commitment to the unimpeded functioning of the OSCE Kosovo Verification Mission under the leadership of Ambassador William Walker. All attacks on and threats to the OSCE KVM must cease immediately. It is incumbent upon everyone in Kosovo to ensure the safety of KVM and other international personnel. They call on FRY authorities and media to create a supportive atmosphere for the activities of the KVM and its Head of Mission. The FRY authorities should facilitate the work of the KVM by fulfilling the Head of Mission's requests for adequate security arrangements and other measures to make fully effective the agreement between the OSCE and the FRY.

The United States and Russia firmly demand that the FRY comply fully with the resolutions of the UN Security Council, particularly with regard to police and military units, and its agreements with the OSCE and other international entities. They call on the FRY to do so without delay.

The United States and Russia reiterate their indignation at the massacre of Kosovar Albanians in Racak, which cannot be justified. Those responsible must be brought to justice.

The FRY authorities must give their full cooperation to the International Criminal Tribunal for the Former Yugoslavia, as required by resolutions of the UN Security Council. The FRY authorities must conduct a fully investigaiton of what happened at Racak with the participation of the Tribunal. Judge Louise Arbour and ICTY investigatory should be allowed to enter and work in Kosovo, to participate in the investigation of the massacre at Racak. The FRY authorities should identify the officers operating in Racak at the time of the massacre and suspend them until the results of the investigation become available.

The United States and Russia urge the Kosovo Albanians to fulfill all their obligations and commitments. "Kosovo Liberation Army" provocations have contributed significantly to the renewed deep tensions in Kosovo. The United States and Russia condemn such provocations and demand they end immediately. Measures should be developed to discourage such activity whenever feasible, in the interest of ensuring full compliance with the commitments and obligations undertaken by the sides, including implementing the arms embargo under the relevant UN Security Council resolutions.

Hostage taking must cease. All hostages should be released. Secretary Albright and Foreign Minister Ivanov appreciated the work of the KVM in such situations. They called upon the Serbian authorities to carry out the commitments in their 11 point Statement of Principles of a Political Settlement of October 13, 1998, in particular to mitigate the sentences of persons detained in connection with the Kosovo conflict and to provide due process to all detainees. Such steps would contribute to easing tensions.

Recent escalated hostilities in Kosovo have displaced thousands more civilians. This has put at risk progress made since last year in averting a humanitarian catastrophe. The sides must avoid actions that affect the civilian population and must facilitate the work of international and non-governmental organizations providing humanitarian assistance. The FRY authorities should provide all necessary facilities including radio communication to humanitarian organizations and remove impediments they have encountered.

Secretary Albright and Foreign Minister Ivanov decided to maintain close contacts on the matter of Kosovo in order to coordinate U.S. and Russian support for a resolution of the crisis.

128. NATO, Statement to the Press by Secretary General, Press Release (1999)011, Brussels, 28 January 1999

Good Evening Ladies and Gentlemen,

I would like to make the following statement on behalf of the North Atlantic Council:

1. NATO fully supports the early conclusion of a political settlement under the mediation of the Contact Group, which will provide an enhanced status for Kosovo, preserve the territorial integrity of the Federal Republic of Yugoslavia and protect the rights of all ethnic groups.

2. The Federal Republic of Yugoslavia authorities must immediately bring the Yugoslav Army and the Special Police force levels, posture and actions into strict compliance with their commitments to NATO on 25 October 1998 and end the excessive and disproportionate use of force in accordance with these commitments. All Kosovar armed elements must immediately cease hostilities and any provocative actions, including hostage taking. All parties must end violence and pursue their goals by peaceful means only.

3. The appropriate authorities in Belgrade and representatives of the Kosovo Albanian leadership must agree to the proposals to be issued by the Contact Group for completing an interim political settlement within the timeframe to be established.

4. NATO demands that the parties to the conflict in Kosovo cooperate fully with the Organisation for Security and Cooperation in Europe Verification Mission, ensure the security of its personnel and provide full freedom of movement and lift all restrictions on institutions monitoring the situation in Kosovo. We demand that the Federal Republic of Yugoslavia authorities fully respect all commitments undertaken in relation to the Organisation of Security and Cooperation in Europe, and ensure that Ambassador Walker is able to continue to carry out his responsibilities fully as Head of the Kosovo Verification Mission.

5. NATO fully supports and shares the demands of the international community that the parties must cooperate fully with the International Criminal Tribunal for the former Yugoslavia including by granting immediate and unrestricted access to its representatives to carry out their investigation of the Racak massacre and by ensuring the safety of its personnel. We also demand that the Federal Republic of Yugoslavia authorities take immediate steps to ensure that those responsible for the massacre are brought to justice.

6. We reaffirm our support to international efforts to bring peace to Kosovo and to avoid a humanitarian catastrophe, including by the Security Council of the United Nations, Organisation for Security and Cooperation in Europe, the European Union, the countries of the region, and the current efforts of the Contact Group. NATO stands ready to act and rules out no option to ensure full respect by both sides of the demands of the international community, and in particular observance of all relevant Security Council Resolutions. NATO is also intensively studying how to support measures to curb arms smuggling into Kosovo. It calls upon the international community, particularly neighbouring countries, to take all necessary steps to prevent the smuggling of arms and will work with other international bodies to this end.

7. In addition to the measures implemented last week, the North Atlantic Council has decided to increase its military preparedness to ensure that the demands of the international community are met. The North Atlantic Council will follow developments closely and will decide on further measures in the light of both parties' compliance with international commitments and requirements and their response to the Contact Group's demands.

That concludes the statement of the North Atlantic Council.

I would like to add for my own part that we are at a critical turning point in the Kosovo crisis. The next few days will be decisive. What we have seen in Yugoslavia during the past decade is that it is very difficult to stop internal conflicts if the international community is not willing to use force - and when all other means have failed. We may be reaching that limit, once again, in the Former Yugoslavia.

The Contact Group meeting in London tomorrow will launch an important initiative. It will be fully backed by NATO's military capabilities. We are ready to act, if necessary. The parties must seize this opportunity. It is the only way to overcome the Kosovo conflict and prevent a humanitarian catastrophe. The entire international community has come together to push for a diplomatic solution. You have seen from the visit of the United Nations Secretary-General to NATO earlier today that the United Nations shares our determination and objectives. In this endeavour, NATO has a key role to play and will make a full contribution - but the parties must finally face up to their responsibilities. We will keep them under strong pressure until they do so. The North Atlantic Council will be meeting round the clock and we will be ready to take further measures as the situation develops.

129. UN Secretary-General, Statement of Kofi Annan to the North Atlantic Council, Brussels, 28 January 1999

Secretary-General Solana, Ambassadors, Friends,

Let me begin by saying how pleased I am to meet with you today. Ever since my time as Special Envoy to NATO, I have greatly valued the bonds between our two organizations.

As we enter a new century of challenges and inevitable crises, it is critically important for us to draw on each other's strengths in pursuit of peace and security.

We must create a new architecture of preventive, pro-active policies for peace - designed not for the wars of the past, but for those of the future. We must seek and find new ways to prevent instability from any source, even as we advance reconciliation in post-conflict societies to prevent the all-too frequent relapses into war and violence.

We must build on the remarkable cooperation between the UN and SFOR in Bosnia to further refine the combination of force and diplomacy that is the key to peace in the Balkans, as everywhere. The success of the NATO-led mission operation under a United Nations mandate is surely a model for future endeavours. No one, however, can expect our future tasks to be easy in execution or brief in duration.

The bloody wars of the last decade have left us with no illusions about the difficulty of halting internal conflicts - by reason or by force - particularly against the wishes of the government of a sovereign state. But nor have they left us with any illusions about the need to use force, when all other means have failed. We may be reaching that limit, once again, in the former Yugoslavia.

Friends,

I have looked forward to this meeting as an exchange of views, and so I will only briefly outline three areas of common interest that I believe will affect our relations in the years to come.

Let me begin with Kosovo. When I addressed the NATO Conference in Rome last June, I expressed the hope that we were beginning to draw the right lessons from our experience in the Bosnian war - about such critical factors as credibility, legitimacy and the morality of intervention and non-intervention. But I added that there is only one way in which we can prove that we have done this; by applying those lessons practically and emphatically where horror threatens.

Alas, the horror no longer threatens. It is present, in the lives of hundreds of thousands of the people of Kosovo whose lives have been disrupted violently. And now, Racak has been added to the list of crimes against humanity committed in the former Yugoslavia.

I know that you and your member states are engaged in intense consultations - in the Contact Group and elsewhere - in order to restore the fragile agreement that halted the killings last time round and bring the parties to the negotiating table. Therefore, let me ask only that we all - particularly those with the capacity to act - recall the lessons of Bosnia.

That means full and unconditional respect for the human rights of all citizens in Kosovo; full and unconditional acceptance of peaceful negotiation as the only way to resolve the conflict in Kosovo; and full and unconditional respect for the authority of the United Nations War Crimes Tribunal throughout all of the territory of the Former Yugoslavia.

Ultimately, however, it means providing the people of Kosovo with the degree of autonomy that is consistent with their need to live lives free from terror and violence. What form such autonomy will take will depend not only on the wishes of the Kosovars, but also on the actions of the Yugoslav authorities. We can only hope that they, too, have learned the lessons of Bosnia.

Second, let me say that the cooperation between the UN and SFOR in Bosnia remains essential to its prospects for lasting peace. In every area - from security to the return of refugees to restoring schools and roads and hospitals - we are working together. Still, we need to ensure that IPTF and SFOR communication remains clear and effective, so that all threats to the peace can be contained in concert.

Let me conclude by congratulating you - a bit early - on the upcoming 50th anniversary of the alliance, and wish you all success in your deliverations on devising a new strategic concept for the next century. How you define your role, and where and how you decide to pursue it, is of vital interest to the United Nations, given the long tradition of cooperation and coordination between NATO and the UN in matters of war and peace. I look forward to hearing your views on this matter.

Thank you.

130. Contact Group, Chairman's Conclusions, London, 29 January 1999

1. Contact Group Ministers met in London on 29 January to consider the critical situation in Kosovo, which remains a threat to peace and security in the region, raising the prospect of a humanitarian catastrophe.

2. Despite the intensive efforts of the international community, violence remains a daily occurrence in Kosovo. Ministers unreservedly condemned the massacre of Kosovo Albanians at Racak which resulted in several thousand people fleeing their homes. The escalation in violence - for which both Belgrade's security forces and the KLA are responsible - must be stopped. Repression of civilians by the security forces must end and those forces must be withdrawn. Ministers of the Contact Group deplore the failure of the parties to make progress towards a political settlement, and cannot accept that this should permit the crisis to continue. Time is of the essence in reaching a solution, and the Contact Group is therefore assuming its responsibility.

3. Ministers called on both sides to end the cycle of violence and to commit themselves to a process of negotiation leading to a political settlement. To that end, the Contact Group:

- insisted that the parties accept that the basis for a fair settlement must include the principles set out by the Contact Group;

- considered that the proposals drafted by the negotiators contained the elements for a substantial autonomy for Kosovo and asked the negotiators to refine them further to serve as the framework for agreement between the parties;

- recognised that the work done by the negotiators had identified the limited number of points which required final negotiation between the parties;

- agreed to summon representatives from the Federal Yugoslav and Serbian Governments and representatives of the Kosovo Albanians to Rambouillet by 6 February, under the co-Chairmanship of Hubert Vedrine and Robin Cook, to begin negotiations with the direct involvement of the Contact Group. The Contact Group recognised the legitimate rights of other communities within Kosovo. In the context of these negotiations, it will work to ensure their interests are fully reflected in a settlement;

- agreed that the participants should work to conclude negotiations within seven days. The negotiators should then report to Contact Group Ministers who will assess whether the progress made justifies a further period of less than one week to bring the negotiations to a successful conclusion.

4. The Contact Group demanded that the parties seize this opportunity to reach a settlement offering peace to the people of Kosovo. The Contact Group praised the present role of the OSCE Kosovo Verification Mission in working to reduce tensions in Kosovo and create the conditions for political dialogue, and recognised the continuing role of KVM. The Contact Group recognised that continuing international engagement would be necessary to help the parties implement a settlement and rebuild the shattered province. It required that the parties accept the level and nature of international presence deemed appropriate by the international community.

5. In the meantime, the Contact Group demands that the FRY:

- stop all offensive actions/repression in Kosovo;

- comply fully with the OSCE/FRY and NATO/FRY agreements and relevant SCRs;

- promote the safe return of all those who have been forced to flee their homes as a result of the conflict. This includes full cooperation with humanitarian agencies and NGOs bringing much needed relief to Kosovo;

- cooperate fully with the OSCE and permit the KVM and its Chief of Mission to continue to carry out their responsibilities unhindered;

- cooperate fully with ICTY as required by relevant SCRs;

- conduct a full investigation of Racak with participation of ICTY, allowing the Chief Prosecutor and ICTY investigators to enter and work in Kosovo to participate in the investigation of the massacre;

- identify and suspend the VJ/MUP officers operating in Racak at the time of the massacre until the results of the investigation become available;

- mitigate the sentences of those imprisoned in connection with the conflict and provide due process to all detainees.

6. The Contact Group emphasised that compliance with SCRs 1160, 1199 and 1203 applied equally to the Kosovo Albanians. It condemned all provocations by the UCK which could only fuel the cycle of violence, and insisted that all hostages should be released. The Contact Group believes that the framework it has set out meets the legitimate aspirations of the Kosovo Albanians and demanded that their leaders rally behind negotiations to reach a settlement and end provocative actions which would impede the political process.

7. The Contact Group asked Robin Cook to travel to Belgrade and Pristina to transmit these messages to the parties.

8. The future of the people of Kosovo is in the hands of leaders in Belgrade and Kosovo. They must commit themselves now to complete the negotiations on a political settlement within 21 days to bring peace to Kosovo. The Contact Group will hold both sides accountable if they fail to take the opportunity now offered to them, just as the Group stands ready to work with both sides to realise the benefits for them of a peaceful solution.

131. UN Security Council, Presidential Statement, UN Doc. S/PRST/1999/5, 29 January 1999

The Security Council expresses its deep concern at the escalating violence in Kosovo, Federal Republic of Yugoslavia. It underlines the risk of a further deterioration in the humanitarian situation if steps are not taken by the parties to reduce tensions. The Council reiterates its concern about attacks on civilians and underlines the need for a full and unhindered investigation of such actions. It calls once again upon the parties to respect fully their obligations under the relevant resolutions and to cease immediately all acts of violence and provocations.

The Security Council

welcomes and supports the decisions of the Foreign Ministers of France, Germany, Italy, the Russian Federation, the United Kingdom of Great Britain and Northern Ireland and the United States of America (the Contact Group), following their meeting in London on 29 January 1999 (S/1999/96), which aim at reaching a political settlement between the parties and establish a framework and timetable for that purpose. The Council demands that the parties should accept their responsibilities and comply fully with these decisions and requirements, as with its relevant resolutions.

The Security Council reiterates its full support for international efforts, including those of the Contact Group and the Organization for Security and Cooperation in Europe Kosovo Verification Mission, to reduce tensions in Kosovo and facilitate a political settlement on the basis of substantial autonomy and equality for all citizens and ethnic communities in Kosovo and the recognition of the legitimate rights of the Kosovo Albanians and other communities in Kosovo. It reaffirms its commitment to the sovereignty and territorial integrity of the Federal Republic of Yugoslavia.

The Security Council will follow the negotiations closely and would welcome members of the Contact Group keeping it informed about the progress reached therein.

The Security Council will remain actively seized of the matter.

132. NATO, Statement by the North Atlantic Council, Press Release 99 (12), 30 January 1999

1. NATO reaffirms the demands set out in its statement of 28th January 1999. It stands ready to act and rules out no option to ensure full respect by both sides in Kosovo for the requirements of the international community, and observance of all relevant Security Council Resolutions, in particular the provisions of Resolutions 1160, 1199 and 1203.

2. NATO gives full support to the Contact Group strategy of negotiations on an interim political settlement which are to be completed within the specified timeframe. It welcomes the Presidential Statement of the United Nations Security Council of 29th January 1999.

3. NATO recalls that those responsible for the massacre at Racak must be brought to justice and that the FRY authorities must cooperate fully with ICTY. They must also cooperate fully with the OSCE Kosovo Verification Mission and ensure the security of its personnel.

4. The crisis in Kosovo remains a threat to peace and security in the region. NATO's strategy is to halt the violence and support the completion of negotiations on an interim political settlement for Kosovo, thus averting a humanitarian catastrophe. Steps to this end must include acceptance by both parties of the summons to begin negotiations at Rambouillet by 6 February 1999 and the completion of the negotiations on an interim political settlement within the specified timeframe; full and immediate observance by both parties of the cease-fire and by the FRY authorities of their commitments to NATO, including by bringing VJ and Police/Special Police force levels, force posture and activities into strict compliance with the NATO/FRY agreement of 25 October 1998; and the ending of excessive and disproportionate use of force in accordance with these commitments.

5. If these steps are not taken, NATO is ready to take whatever measures are necessary in the light of both parties' compliance with international commitments and requirements, including in particular assessment by the Contact Group of the response to its demands, to avert a humanitarian catastrophe, by compelling compliance with the demands of the international community and the achievement of a political settlement. The Council has therefore agreed today that the NATO Secretary General may authorise air strikes against targets on FRY territory. The NATO Secretary General will take full account of the position and actions of the Kosovar leadership and all Kosovar armed elements in and around Kosovo in reaching his decision on military action. NATO will take all appropriate measures in case of a failure by the Kosovar Albanian side to comply with the demands of the international community.

6. NATO is also studying how to support measures to curb arms smuggling into Kosovo.

7. NATO's decisions today contribute to creating the conditions for a rapid and successful negotiation on an interim political settlement which provides for an enhanced status for Kosovo, preserves the territorial integrity of the FRY and protects the rights of all ethnic groups. NATO is resolved to persevere until the violence in Kosovo has ended, and a political solution has been reached.

133. Contact Group Negotiators' Proposal, 30 January 1999

General Elements

Necessity of immediate end of violence and respect of cease-fire

Peaceful solution through dialogue

Interim agreement: a mechanism for a final settlement after an interim period of three years

No unilateral change of interim status

Territorial integrity of the FRY and neighbouring countries

Protection of rights of the members of all national communities (preservation of identity, language and education; special protection for their religious institutions)

Free and fair elections in Kosovo (municipal and Kosovo wide) under supervision of the OSCE

Neither party shall prosecute anyone for crimes related to the Kosovo conflict (exceptions: crimes against humanity, war crimes, and other serious violations of international law)

Amnesty and release of political prisoners

International involvement and full co-operation by the parties on implementation

Governance in Kosovo

People of Kosovo to be self-governed by democratically accountable Kosovo Institutions

High degree of self-governance realized through own legislative, executive and judiciary bodies (with authority over, inter alia, taxes, financing, police, economic development, judicial system, health care, education and culture (subject to the rights of the members of national communities), communications, roads and transport, protection of the environment

Legislative: Assembly

Executive: President of Kosovo, Government, Administrative bodies

Judiciary: Kosovo court system

Clear definition of competencies at communal level

Members of all national communities to be fairly represented at all levels of administration and elected government

Local police representative of ethnic make-up with coordination on Kosovo level

Harmonization of Serbian and Federal legal frameworks with Kosovo Interim agreement

Kosovo consent required inter alia for changes to borders and declaration of marial law

Human Rights

Judicial protection of human rights enshrined in international conventions and rights of members of national communities

Ombudsman selected under international auspices

Role of OSCE and other relevant ISO

Implementation

Dispute resolution mechanism

Establishment of a joint commission to supervise implementation

Participation of OSCE and other international bodies as necessary

134. UK, Statement by the Foreign Secretary, Mr. Robin Cook, to the House of Commons, 1 February 1999

The situation on the ground remains tense. On Friday - over twenty Kosovar Albanians were shot in Rugovo. On Saturday - a hand grenade was lobbed into a cafe in Pristina frequented by Serbs, injuring eight including one Albanian. Yesterday two Serb policemen were injured when a grenade was fired into their van while they were returning from the funeral of a casualty of earlier conflict. Over 200 people have been killed since the Holbrooke agreement last October provided for a cease-fire.

At its meeting in London last Friday, the Contact Group called on both sides to end hostilities now. They insisted on full compliance by Belgrade with its undertakings of last October and real cooperation with both the Verification Mission and the War Crimes Tribunal.

The main focus of the meeting was on the urgent need to put momentum into the political process. Since last October, Ambassadors Hill and Petritsch have developed the Contact Group's framework document for a political settlement. It reflects extensive consultation with both sides.

Their detailed document provides for an interim accord for three years. That period would provide the opportunity for the creation of democratic self-government in Kosovo through free and fair elections supervised by the OSCE. The new institutions of Kosovo would enjoy a wide range of self-government, including control of its own police and internal security.

The Federal Republic of Yugoslavia would retain competence only for foreign policy, external defence, monetary policy, single market, customs and federal taxation. Both Serb and Albanian communities would be fully protected with the right to elected institutions preserving their national cultures, language and education.

The framework document also provides that at the end of three years the future status of Kosovo would be reviewed under international auspices.

Despite the extensive consultation and the detailed work which has gone into the framework document by representatives of the Contact Group, in three months there has not been one negotiating meeting on it between Belgrade and the Kosovo Albanians. On Friday, the Contact Group resolved on a programme of action to break that stalemate.

We agreed to summon both sides to negotiations on the basis of the framework document. We set a tight timetable which requires both sides to attend talks by this Saturday and to conclude negotiations within less than two further weeks. France has offered to provide a venue for the talks which will take place under the joint chairmanship of myself and Hubert Vedrine, the French Foreign Minister.

Also on Friday the United Nations Security Council welcomed the strategy of the Contact Group and demanded that both parties should comply with it.

On Saturday the North Atlantic Council also gave its full support to the strategy of the Contact Group, and warned that 'NATO is ready to take whatever measures are necessary' to avert the humanitarian catastrophe by compelling compliance with the demands of the international community. In the meantime the North Atlantic Council delegated to its Secretary-General, Javier Solana, authority to order military action in the light of the responses of both parties.

My Right Honourable Friend the Prime Minister discussed Kosovo with President Chirac during his visit last Thursday. They agreed that both Britain and France would be willing to consider the deployment, with their Allies of ground troops in Kosovo to provide a period of stability and peace during which a political settlement could take root.

I was instructed by the Contact Group to convey our demands to both parties and on Saturday I visited Belgrade and Skopje.

I was accompanied throughout by Bill Walker, Chief of the Verification Mission. The visit increased my respect for the valuable work of the Verification Mission. They have provided instant and reliable information on the atrocities which invariably occur in places where they are absent, and have undoubtedly deterred further atrocities where they are present.

In Belgrade, I met jointly with President Milosevic of the Federal Republic of Yugoslavia, and President Milutinovic of the Republic of Serbia. I stressed to them that I came with the mandate of the united Contact Group, and also backed by the authority of the North Atlantic Council. Our requirement of them to take part in negotiations under international chairmanship is the best opportunity Belgrade will get to extricate itself from a conflict that it cannot win.

President Milosevic undertook to study the Contact Group proposals and to reply within a few days.

In Skopje I met with Dr Rugova, Mr Demaqi and Mr Qosja, who between them represent a broad spectrum of Kosovar opinion.

I stressed in all my conversations with the Kosovar Albanians that the proposals of the Contact Group offered a democratic, self-governing Kosovo free from the bloodshed of recent months.

Dr Rugova, who was elected overwhelmingly last year as leader of the Kosovar Albanians, welcomed the opportunity for talks and committed his party to participate fully in them.

I also spoke by phone to Mr Surroi, an independent publisher and a leading political figure in Pristina, who gave his full support to the proposals and expressed his willingness to participate.

Mr Demaqi who acts as political spokesman for the Kosovo Liberation Army and Mr Qosja, leader of the third largest Kosovo Albanian party, both undertook to consult their colleagues and to let me have their response within days.

Madam Speaker, I cannot confirm that the talks which we seek will take place. Nor can I guarantee that if they take place, they will succeed. There remain serious issues of difference between the two sides which it will take hard negotiation to resolve - such as the nature of the review to take place in three years time, and the relationship between a self-governing Kosovo and Serbia.

But I can confirm that the meeting of the Contact Group showed real unity and a common determination to provide for progress towards a political settlement of the conflict.

It is now for both parties to show the same commitment to finding a political solution. Neither of them can win the conflict by military means. Both of them would benefit from a political settlement. The offer of these talks, brokered by the Contact Group, and backed by the Security Council and NATO, provides the best opportunity they will ever get to achieve a political settlement through dialogue.

I urge both of them now to seize that opportunity and to give the people of Kosovo hope for their future in place of their fear of the present bloodshed.

3.4.2 THE RAMBOUILLET CONFERENCE

135. Joint Press Conference by Mr. Vedrine and Mr. Cook, Rambouillet, 6 February 1999

Mr. Védrine: Ladies and gentlemen, good evening. As you know, Robin Cook and I were chosen by our American, Russian, German and Italian Contact Group partners to chair the negotiations which are starting now.

The President of the French Republic, Mr. Jacques Chirac, made a statement and spoke to the two delegations, after which we opened the negotiations as co-chairmen. Naturally, we will remain available and attentive to every aspect as the talks move forward, and ready to intervene at any time;

Right up to the last moment, before the talks, as co-chairmen, we'd already had to overcome a number of difficulties. But as a result of international pressure, unprecedented on this matter of Kosovo, the negotiations are now beginning at Rambouillet;

We believe you know the texts of the three short statements which have just been made so we're here now to supplement them by answering your questions

Mr. Cook: I'd like to add to what Hubert has just said that so far everything is going well. We've managed three stages. We managed to achieve unanimity in the Contact Group and international community on looking for an agreement and bringing pressure to bear to that end. Second, we obtained a commitment from the two sides to participate and reached a situation in which the two parties are actually present. And we overcame the first obstacle to the talks which was to make sure that the two parties could participate. And this afternoon, the talks duly got off to a start. The negotiations will not be easy but we are approaching them with real determination to ensure that they succeed. This is the best chance the people of Kosovo and the Federal Republic of Yugoslavia will have to reach an agreement and implement it successfully. Hubert Védrine and myself are working in close collaboration with the mediators so that it actually produces results.

Q. - Mr. Minister, is the international deployment being discussed during the conference and if yes, how? How would you assess the role that Russia has played and is playing in the conference?

Mr. Cook: If you mean by that deployment of forces on the ground, that presupposes first achieving a political settlement. So that's the first point to reach. Russia is fully engaged in the talks. I talked with the Russian foreign minister this morning, as did Hubert, and he is wholeheartedly supporting the negotiations. Russia is part of the troika of three ambassadors with representatives of Russia, the United States and the European Union who are therefore going to be working as a team.

Mr. Védrine: On the question of deployment, I can confirm that this matter will be examined when the time comes along with the possibility of achieving a political agreement. As for Russia, it is a very important partner in the Contact Group; it has been fully involved in the entire process which led up to the meeting at Rambouillet and we were able to verify only a short while ago that it intends to participate fully in the search for a solution;

Q. - Mr. Minister, Albanian public opinion and world opinion in general expects a great deal from the conference. Why wasn't it held a year ago and then the tragedy in Kosovo could have been avoided? The Contact Group and NATO have the means. Can we say this evening that after the Rambouillet conference there will be no more terrible images of the tragedy in Kosovo?

Mr. Védrine: The aim of the Rambouillet conference, as the Contact Group wanted, is precisely to stop the never-ending cycle of tragedy We invited the two parties to come to the meeting and they came. So I'd like to think that they came because they share that goal.

Q. - It's been reported that certain delegations were not able to come with all their advisers and also that a number of issues for discussion have been imposed by the international community. Is that true?

Mr. Védrine: With regard to the second point, a format had to be defined for each delegation if only for reasons of place and for the negotiations to be efficient and direct. The two parties had originally decided on delegations that were too large and the two parties adjusted to the conditions that we had set for the negotiations. As for the issues under discussion, over the course of the past several weeks the Contact Group worked out a number of basic principles which form the core of the possible solution. The discussions around these central principles should make it possible to complete and make clear what still hasn't been settled.

Q. - Mr. Minister, why did Mr. Milosevic not come to the international conference on Kosovo today? As you know, Karadjic said that Mr. Milosevic had not been out of Yugoslavia for two or three years?

Mr. Védrine: The Rambouillet meeting was not convened or organized at head-of-state level.

Q. - Mr. Minister, you mentioned international pressure. What kind of international pressure are you going to put on the two parties to reach a solution? Are we talking about military pressure when the time comes?

Mr. Cook: Let's be clear. We've brought the parties together so that they can be here for seven days. The seven day deadline has been agreed to, and so you've got international pressure for reaching a settlement. It is planned for the two sides to get down to business immediately. They have seven days to reach an agreement. After the seven days, we will review the situation with our Contact Group colleagues, and if necessary, with the authority of the Security Council, the OSCE and NATO we will support the negotiations with international pressure so that they produce results.

Q. - Can you give us some details about the famous basic principles you mentioned, the main lines set out by the Contact Group? And do the two delegations agree on how the discussions are going to take place? Will there be direct discussions between the two delegations?

Mr. Védrine: I can't exactly go into the detail about the principles because I'm keeping all possibilities open for the talks to move forward and conclude successfully. But I would remind you that we've proposed substantial autonomy which already says a great deal. It means autonomy that goes very far in the framework of respect for existing and recognized international borders. As for the method, all methods are good when they allow things to move forward.

Mr. Cook: I'd simply like to add that the framework document which has been prepared wasn't drafted in an empty room miles from Belgrade. It was discussed intensively with the two sides. Three quarters of the solution is already there in this framework document. But we've done enough shuttling back and forth. In order to complete the work and fill in the remaining 25% we have to have the parties together, which is the purpose of this meeting.

Q. - The first part of the question concerns the NATO summit in Washington in two months: is there an objective with a view to this summit or is it really, as President Chirac said in his speech, to achieve genuine stability in the region? Supposing an agreement is obtained this time, what's going to happen at the end of three years? Is there going to be a second Rambouillet to gain independence for Kosovo?

Mr. Védrine: Regarding your first point. You'll have seen that it is by getting all the institutions and all the international organizations to pull together that the international community took back the initiative in the tragedy of Kosovo. And among the various organizations, there is NATO. Even though the general political line was decided in the

Contact Group, all that has no particular link to the table at a summit. All organizations have regular summit meetings. The two things are not linked. As for the second point: what is to happen at the end of a certain period of time? Well, that is precisely the purpose of the negotiations. So as co-chairmen, we can't give you an answer this evening. But the purpose of all these tremendous efforts everyone is making is to reach a political solution.

Mr. Cook: Indeed, I can't tell you if there will be a Rambouillet 2, but our putting this effort into it implies obtaining a success in achieving an interim agreement, and that has to be the thrust of our efforts.

Q. - You mentioned the framework document which refers to autonomy, to self-government for Kosovo. These are strong words, does that mean in the long run independence for Kosovo?

Mr. Cook: The point of our efforts is to show the importance of reaching an interim agreement with powers devolving on the assemblies and local administrations so they can handle their own defense, their own single market and do so in the context of their own authority from parliament. So these are strong words which have been used deliberately. The document provides for the devolution of basic democratic rights so as to protect communities having their own language and culture in order to make Kosovo still more democratic at local government level, and only those who are against the democratic process should oppose this agreement.

Q. - In the case of an international deployment, would the eventual deployment of troops take place in a matter of days or weeks, and are the Europeans satisfied with U.S. guarantees in such an event?

Mr. Védrine: I think it is positive to observe that several very important countries, in Europe and also the United States, have already expressed their readiness to this end, and a converging readiness. But nothing has been negotiated yet, nothing is decided yet.

Mr. Cook: We have begun contingency planning and we are trying to make sure that if plans go as scheduled, the interval is as brief as possible. Of course, if the two parties reach an agreement tomorrow, then we'd be taken up short. But it is a problem we'll consider with pleasure once the talks have ended.

Q. - Do you think that Montenegro will be the sole loser in the conference? Can the European Union guarantee that this will not be the result for Montenegro?

Mr. Cook: The principles which Montenegro refers to have been fully explained and applied. Montenegro has absolutely no reason to be worried about results coming out of this conference that would go against it.

Mr. Védrine: I would like to add that to my mind, the continuation of the tragedy in Kosovo is much more threatening than the prospect of a solution. And I would like to say after Robin that no country in the Contact Group, and especially not us, will be looking for a solution that would in any way be injurious to Montenegro.

Q. - In the days prior to the opening of the conference, the Slav party kept on insisting that it would refuse to talk to the Kosovo Liberation Army, calling it a terrorist organization. How do the mediators intend to overcome the problem and how meaningful would an agreement be if the Kosovo Liberation Army were not a party to it?

Mr. Védrine: You will certainly have noticed that in every conflict of this kind the moment negotiations start to draw close, every party states its positions of principle rather firmly--and they appear to be absolutely incompatible. It is the negotiators' task to manage to get the work started in spite of that and to see that it is successfully concluded. And one result has been achieved already in that they are here, not far from us.

Mr. Cook: I agree with Hubert. Look at the ground that we've covered. The two parties agreed to come, they met in the same room. We've just had the opening meeting, and that is real progress. But in the end, negotiating peace means you have to negotiate with those making war. You don't talk peace with your friends.

Q. - When you talk about substantial autonomy, one gets the impression that the decisions, if decision there is in these negotiations, have been made in advance. What are the margins for the negotiations, what can the negotiators say yes and no to?

Mr. Védrine: Autonomy is a general principle but if you look around the world, especially at a number of places where tragedies have been resolved by this approach, there is very great diversity in the forms of autonomy. It's an area for negotiation just like the one mentioned earlier by Robin Cook in response to a question on the interim period. But admittedly the Contact Group has shouldered its responsibilities by proposing a body of principles because it was impossible to leave matters as they were.

Mr. Cook: To be more specific about what I said a moment ago, the FRY retains responsibility for foreign policy, defense, customs and the single market. The other responsibilities will therefore be under the authority of the assemblies, local administrations and elected offices in Kosovo. Of course, these responsibilities may be discussed further by the various parties as to the breakdown, but don't forget that it is a document which is the result of three months of talks, it didn't simply fall out of the sky. So there remains the responsibilities to be settled by the parties, not simply by this constant shuttling back and forth between the cities.

Q. - There are reportedly differences of views among the Albanian leaders. Do you think that this my have some bearing on the success of the conference?

Mr. Védrine: It is one of the many problems that have to be addressed, that have to be resolved, that the negotiators have to surmount. There are an infinite number of them. There are matters on either side, problems that must be worked out to be successful in spite of everything.

Mr. Cook: No one is saying that things will be easy. We all recognize that there are problems. The important thing is not to see these problems as obstacles but as challenges that we can overcome. But that presupposes that each party comes with the goodwill to overcome these challenges and to reach a solution.

136. Statement of the Delegation Designated by the Government of the Republic of Serbia, at the Meeting in Rambouillet, 11 February 1999

The Delegation designated by the Government of the Republic of Serbia, at the Meeting in Ramouillet, at the suggestion of the Co-Chairman of the Meeting, Mr. Robin Cook, Secretary of State for Foreign and Commonwealth Affairs of the United Kingdom of Great Britain and Northern Ireland, makes the following

Statement

1. The Delegation accepts the following general elements set by the Contact Group as a basis for finding a political solution for self-government in Kosovo and Metohija:

- Necessity of immediate end of violence and respect of cease-fire;

- Peaceful solution through dialogue;

- Interim agreement; a mechanism for a final settlement after an interim period of three years;

- No unilateral change of interim status;

- Sovereignty and territorial integrity of the FRY and its neighbouring countries;

- Protection of rights of the members of all national communities (preservation of identity, language and education; special protection for their religious institutions);

- Free and fair elections in Kosovo (municipal and Kosovo-wide) under supervision of the OSCE;

- Neither party shall prosecute anyone for crimes related to the Kosovo conflict (exceptions: crimes against humanity, war crimes and other serious violations of international law);

- Amnesty and release of political prisoners;

- International involvement and full co-operation by the parties on implementation.

2. Convinced that it will contribute to the successful work of the Meeting, the Delegation calls upon the Delegation of the Kosmet Albanians to sign also the above elements.[1]

137. Contact Group Meeting, Chairman's Conclusions, Paris, 14 February 1999

Contact Group Foreign Ministers met at Paris on 14 February following a week of negotiations for an interim political settlement in Kosovo on the basis of the principles and basic elements agreed in London on 29 February. On the basis of a report from our three negotiators, Ambassadors Hill, Petritsch and Mayorsky, we assessed the state of the negotiations. Progress has been slower than we had hoped when we met in London on 29 January, but essential ground clearing work has been carried out. It is now crucial that the parties immediately reach agreement on the hard issues outstanding. On this basis we have decided, as provided for in the conclusions of our last meeting, to continue the negotiations. They must be concluded by 1200 noon on Saturday 20 February.

We agreed that this is a decisive moment for peace efforts over Kosovo. Time is now very short to reach a negotiated settlement, which is the only way to avoid further large scale violence leading to humanitarian catastrophe. We consider that the Contact Group approach and the documents being tabled to the parties, provide the basis for the interim political settlement. We therefore expect both parties to use the few remaining days to:

- agree very rapidly on the Contact Group's detailed proposals for self-government in Kosovo which have now been under negotiation for a week.

- accept the implementation arrangements needed to establish this self-government, including the development of a local police force, and measures to end the military confrontation in Kosovo.

We underlined our total support for our three negotiators. We endorsed their determination to intensify the peace of negotiations so as to conclude them within a week at the latest. The two Co-Chairmen, Hubert Vedrine and Robin Cook, made clear their readiness to return to Rambouillet whenever necessary to work with the negotiators in pushing the talks forward. We agreed that the negotiators have discretion to table the remaining annexes on the implementation of a settlement. Provided that the parties are ready to live up to their responsibilities to reach an interim political settlement, the international community is willing to devote significant civilian and military resources to helping all the people of Kosovo to rebuild their lives in conditions of security. But we reiterate what we said at London: we will hold both sides accountable if they fail to take this opportunity.

138. EU, Declaration by the Presidency on behalf of the European Union, 99/15/CFSP, Brussels, 19 February 1999

Given a still outstanding breakthrough in Rambouillet, and in case this cannot be achieved, the EU presidency points out that action is in hand for a coordinated and phased withdrawal of staff from EU diplomatic missions in the FRY, according to the specific needs and priorities of each mission.

The EU is taking this action in the context of, and in full accordance with, its repeatedly underlined determination that a peaceful outcome should be achieved in the Rambouillet negotiations concerning Kosovo.

---

[1] Members of the Delegation: Prof. Dr. Ratko Markovic Nikola Sainovic, M.Sc., Prof. Dr. Vladan Kutlesic, Prof. Dr. Vladimir Stambuk, Zejnelabidin Kurejs, Ibro Vait, Refik Senadovic, Ljuan Koka, Sokolj Cuse, Guljbehar Sabovic, Faik Jasari.

139. NATO, Statement by the Secretary General on behalf of the North Atlantic Council, Press Release (99)020, 19 February 1999

The Alliance today recalls the demands set out in its statement of 30 January 1999, including the necessity of compliance by all parties involved with the appropriate UN Security Council Resolutions.

It expresses its full support to the efforts of the Contact Group to secure an interim political settlement for Kosovo at Rambouillet which provides for a substantially greater degree of autonomy for Kosovo, reaffirms the sovereignty and territorial integrity of the FRY, protects the rights of all national communities, and contains effective measures for its implementation including an international military presence.

The deadline set by the Contact Group for the parties to come to an agreement is approaching fast, underlining the urgency of finding a peaceful solution. They must therefore accept their responsibilities and show the maximum flexibility and political will to bring the negotiations to a successful conclusion.

The crisis in Kosovo remains a threat to peace and security in the region. NATO's strategy is to halt the violence and support the completion of negotiations on an interim political settlement for Kosovo, thus averting a humanitarian catastrophe.

A viable political settlement must be guaranteed by an international military presence. Accordingly, the Alliance is prepared, following acceptance by the parties, to lead a multinational peacekeeping force with broad participation, to implement and enforce the military aspects of an interim agreement, which include specific commitments by both parties, and to contribute to an environment which supports the OSCE and other organisations in the implementation of the civil aspects.

As clearly spelled out in the statement by the North Atlantic Council of 30 January and if no agreement is reached by the deadline set by the Contact Group, NATO is ready to take whatever measures are necessary - in the light of both parties' compliance with international commitments and requirements, including in particular assessment by the Contact Group of the response to its demands - to avert a humanitarian catastrophe by compelling compliance with the demands of the international community and the achievement of a political settlement. These include the use of air strikes as well as other appropriate measures.

NATO has taken appropriate steps to prepare its forces to ensure that they are ready in the event that military action is necessary.

140. Conclusions of the Contact Group, Rambouillet, 20 February 1999

A fortnight ago, the FRY and Serb delegation and the Kosovar delegation, summoned by the Contact Group to meet, agreed to come to Rambouillet. The aim of these negotiations was to reach an interim agreement on substantial autonomy for Kosovo while respecting the FRY's national sovereignty and territorial integrity. The purpose was to allow the inhabitants of Kosovo to live again in peace. Last week, in Paris, we decided to extend these negotiations by one additional week. They were to end at noon today. No effort has been spared either by the three negotiators or by the member states of the Contact Group to achieve this goal. Today, Contact Group ministers heard the Parties and the report of the negotiators. Very substantial progress has been made in reaching agreement on the Framework and Political Chapters of the Interim Agreement for Peace and Self-Government in Kosovo. At the request of the Parties, we believe that this justifies an ultimate effort to finalise as a whole the Interim Agreement and the proposed arrangements for an international military and civilian presence in Kosovo, if so agreed by the Parties, to implement and guarantee the Interim Agreement. This work must be completed by 15.00 on Tuesday 23 February 1999. Ministers recalled that they had spelt out in London on 29 January and Paris on 14 February, that those responsible for the failure of the talks would be held accountable.

141. Interim Agreement for Peace and Self-Government in Kosovo, Rambouillet, 23 February 1999

The Parties to the present Agreement,

Convinced of the need for a peaceful and political solution in Kosovo as a prerequisite for stability and democracy,

Determined to establish a peaceful environment in Kosovo,

Reaffirming their commitment to the Purposes and Principles of the United Nations, as well as to OSCE principles, including the Helsinki Final Act and the Charter of Paris for a new Europe,

Recalling the commitment of the international community to the sovereignty and territorial integrity of the Federal Republic of Yugoslavia,

Recalling the basic elements/principles adopted by the Contact Group at its ministerial meeting in London on January 29, 1999,

Recognizing the need for democratic self-government in Kosovo, including full participation of the members of all national communities in political decision-making,

Desiring to ensure the protection of the human rights of all persons in Kosovo, as well as the rights of the members of all national communities,

Recognizing the ongoing contribution of the OSCE to peace and stability in Kosovo,

Noting that the present Agreement has been concluded under the auspices of the members of the Contact Group and the European Union and undertaking with respect to these members and the European Union to abide by this Agreement,

Aware that full respect for the present Agreement will be central for the development of relations with European institutions, Have agreed as follows:

Framework
ARTICLE I: PRINCIPLES

1. All citizens in Kosovo shall enjoy, without discrimination, the equal rights and freedoms set forth in this Agreement.

2. National communities and their members shall have additional rights specified in Chapter 1. Kosovo, Federal, and Republic authorities shall not interfere with the exercise of these additional rights. The national communities shall be legally equal as specified herein, and shall not use their additional rights to endanger the rights of other national communities or the rights of citizens, the sovereignty and territorial integrity of the Federal Republic of Yugoslavia, or the functioning of representative democratic government in Kosovo.

3. All authorities in Kosovo shall fully respect human rights, democracy, and the equality of citizens and national communities.

4. Citizens in Kosovo shall have the right to democratic self-government through legislative, executive, judicial, and other institutions established in accordance with this Agreement. They shall have the opportunity to be represented in all institutions in Kosovo. The right to democratic self-government shall include the right to participate in free and fair elections.

5. Every person in Kosovo may have access to international institutions for the protection of their rights in accordance with the procedures of such institutions.

6. The Parties accept that they will act only within their powers and responsibilities in Kosovo as specified by this Agreement. Acts outside those powers and responsibilities shall be null and void. Kosovo shall have all rights and powers set forth herein, including in particular as specified in the Constitution at Chapter 1. This Agreement shall prevail over any other legal provisions of the Parties and shall be directly applicable. The Parties shall harmonize their governing practices and documents with this Agreement.

7. The Parties agree to cooperate fully with all international organizations working in Kosovo on the implementation of this Agreement.

ARTICLE II: CONFIDENCE-BUILDING MEASURES
End of Use of Force

1. Use of force in Kosovo shall cease immediately. In accordance with this Agreement, alleged violations of the cease-fire shall be reported to international observers and shall not be used to justify use of force in response.

2. The status of police and security forces in Kosovo, including withdrawal of forces, shall be governed by the terms of this Agreement. Paramilitary and irregular forces in Kosovo are incompatible with the terms of this Agreement.

Return

3. The Parties recognize that all persons have the right to return to their homes. Appropriate authorities shall take all measures necessary to facilitate the safe return of persons, including issuing necessary documents. All persons shall have the right to reoccupy their real property, assert their occupancy rights in state-owned property, and recover their other property and personal possessions. The Parties shall take all measures necessary to readmit returning persons to Kosovo.

4. The Parties shall cooperate fully with all efforts by the United Nations High Commissioner for Refugees, (UNHCR) and other international and non-governmental organizations concerning the repatriation and return of persons, including those organizations, monitoring of the treatment of persons following their return.

Access for International Assistance

5. There shall be no impediments to the normal flow of goods into Kosovo, including materials for the reconstruction of homes and structures. The Federal Republic of Yugoslavia shall not require visas, customs, or licensing for persons or things for the Implementation Mission (IM), the UNHCR, and other international organizations, as well as for non- governmental organizations working in Kosovo as determined by the Chief of the Implementation Mission (CIM).

6. All staff, whether national or international, working with international or non-governmental organizations including with the Yugoslav Red Cross, shall be allowed unrestricted access to the Kosovo population for purposes of international assistance. All persons in Kosovo shall similarly have safe, unhindered, and direct access to the staff of such organizations.

Other Issues

7. Federal organs shall not take any decisions that have a differential, disproportionate, injurious, or discriminatory effect on Kosovo. Such decisions, if any, shall be void with regard to Kosovo.

8. Martial law shall not be declared in Kosovo.

9. The Parties shall immediately comply with all requests for support from the implementation Mission (IM). The IM shall have its own broadcast frequencies for radio and television programming in Kosovo. The Federal Republic of Yugoslavia shall provide all necessary facilities, including frequencies for radio communications, to all humanitarian organizations responsible for delivering aid in Kosovo.

Detention of Combatants and Justice Issues

10. All abducted persons or other persons held without charge shall be released. The Parties shall also release and transfer in accordance with this Agreement all persons held in connection with the conflict. The Parties shall cooperate fully with the International Committee of the Red Cross (ICRC) to facilitate its work in accordance with its mandate, including ensuring full access to all such persons, irrespective of their status, wherever they might be held, for visits in accordance with the ICRC's standard operating procedures.

11. The Parties shall provide information, through tracing mechanisms of the ICRC, to families of all persons who are unaccounted for. The Parties shall cooperate fully with the ICRC and the International Commission on Missing Persons in their efforts to determine the identity, whereabouts, and fate of those unaccounted for.

12. Each Party:

(a) shall not prosecute anyone for crimes related to the conflict in Kosovo, except for persons accused of having committed serious violations of international humanitarian law. In order to facilitate transparency, the Parties shall grant access to foreign experts (including forensics experts) along with state investigators;

(b) shall grant a general amnesty for all persons already convicted of committing politically motivated crimes related to the conflict in Kosovo. This amnesty shall not apply to those properly convicted of committing serious violations of international humanitarian law at a fair and open trial conducted pursuant to international standards.

13. All Parties shall comply with their obligation to cooperate in the investigation and prosecution of serious violations of international humanitarian law.

(a) As required by United Nations Security Council resolution 827 (1993) and subsequent resolutions, the Parties shall fully cooperate with the International Criminal Tribunal for the Former Yugoslavia in its investigations and prosecutions, including complying with its requests for assistance and its orders.

(b) The Parties shall also allow complete, unimpeded, and unfettered access to international experts- including forensics experts and investigators-to investigate allegations of serious violations of international humanitarian law.

Independent Media

14. Recognizing the importance of free and independent media for the development of a democratic political climate necessary for the reconstruction and development of Kosovo, the Parties shall ensure the widest possible press freedoms in Kosovo in all media, public and private, including print, television, radio, and Internet.

Chapter 1: Constitution

Affirming their belief in a peaceful society, justice, tolerance, and reconciliation,

Resolved to ensure respect for human rights and the equality of all citizens and national communities,

Recognizing that the preservation and promotion of the national, cultural, and linguistic identity of each national community in Kosovo are necessary for the harmonious development of a peaceful society,

Desiring through this interim Constitution to establish institutions of democratic self-government in Kosovo grounded in respect for the territorial integrity and sovereignty of the Federal Republic of Yugoslavia and from this Agreement, from which the authorities of governance set forth herein originate,

Recognizing that the institutions of Kosovo should fairly represent the national communities in Kosovo and foster the exercise of their rights and those of their members,

Recalling and endorsing the principles/basic elements adopted by the Contact Group at its ministerial meeting in London on January 29, 1999,

ARTICLE I: PRINCIPLES OF DEMOCRATIC SELF-GOVERNMENT IN KOSOVO

1. Kosovo shall govern itself democratically through the legislative, executive, judicial, and other organs and institutions specified herein. Organs and institutions of Kosovo shall exercise their authorities consistent with the terms of this Agreement.

2. All authorities in Kosovo shall fully respect human rights, democracy, and the equality of citizens and national communities.

3. The Federal Republic of Yugoslavia has competence in Kosovo over the following areas, except as specified elsewhere in this Agreement: (a) territorial integrity, (b) maintaining a common market within the Federal Republic of Yugoslavia, which power shall be exercised in a manner that does not discriminate against Kosovo, (c) monetary policy, (d) defense, (e) foreign policy, (f) customs services, (g) federal taxation, (h) federal elections, and (i) other areas specified in this Agreement.

4. The Republic of Serbia shall have competence in Kosovo as specified in this Agreement, including in relation to Republic elections.

5. Citizens in Kosovo-may continue to participate in areas in which the Federal Republic of Yugoslavia and the Republic of Serbia have competence through their representation in relevant institutions, without prejudice to the exercise of competence by Kosovo authorities set forth in this Agreement.

6. With respect to Kosovo:

(a) There shall be no changes to the borders of Kosovo;

(b) Deployment and use of police and security forces shall be governed by Chapters 2 and 7 of this Agreement; and

(c) Kosovo shall have authority to conduct foreign relations within its areas of responsibility equivalent to the power provided to Republics under Article 7 of the Constitution of the Federal Republic of Yugoslavia.

7. There shall be no interference with the right of citizens and national communities in Kosovo to call upon appropriate institutions of the Republic of Serbia for the following purposes:

(a) assistance in designing school curricula and standards;

(b) participation in social benefits programs, such as care for war veterans, pensioners, and disabled persons; and

(c) other voluntarily received services, provided that these services are not related to police and security matters governed by Chapters 2 and 7 of this Agreement, and that any Republic personnel serving in Kosovo pursuant to this paragraph shall be unarmed service providers acting at the invitation of a national community in Kosovo.

The Republic shall have the authority to levy taxes or charges on those citizens requesting services pursuant to this paragraph, as necessary to support the provision of such services.

8. The basic territorial unit of local self-government in Kosovo shall be the commune. All responsibilities in 7Kosovo not expressly assigned elsewhere shall be the responsibility of the communes.

9. To preserve and promote democratic self-government in Kosovo, all candidates for appointed, elective, or other public office, and all office holders, shall meet the following criteria:

(a) No person who is serving a sentence imposed by the International Criminal Tribunal for the Former Yugoslavia, and no person who is under indictment by the Tribunal and who has failed to comply with an order to appear before the Tribunal, may stand as a candidate or hold any office; and

(b) All candidates and office holders shall renounce violence as a mechanism for achieving political goals; past political or resistance activities shall not be a bar to holding office in Kosovo.

ARTICLE II: THE ASSEMBLY

General

1. Kosovo shall have an Assembly, which shall be comprised of 120 Members.

(a) Eighty members shall be directly elected.

(b) A further 40 Members shall be elected by the members of qualifying national communities.

(i) Communities whose members constitute more than 0.5 per cent of the Kosovo population but less than 5 per cent shall have ten of these seats, to be divided among them in accordance with their proportion of the overall population.

(ii) communities whose members constitute more than 5 per cent of the Kosovo population shall divide the remaining thirty seats equally. The Serb and Albanian national communities shall be presumed to meet the 5 per cent population threshold.

Other Provisions

2. Elections for all Members shall be conducted democratically, consistent with the provisions of Chapter 3 of this Agreement. Members shall be elected for a term of three years.

3. Allocation of seats in the Assembly shall be based on data gathered in the census referred to in Chapter 5 of this Agreement. Prior to the completion of the census, for purposes of this Article declarations of national community membership made during voter registration

shall be used to determine the percentage of the Kosovo population that each national community represents.

4. Members of the Assembly shall be immune from all civil or criminal proceedings on the basis of words expressed or other acts performed in their capacity as Members of the Assembly.

Powers of the Assembly

5. The Assembly shall be responsible for enacting laws of Kosovo, including in political, security, economic, social, educational, scientific, and cultural areas as set out below and elsewhere in this Agreement. This Constitution and the laws of the Kosovo Assembly shall not be subject to change or modification by authorities of the Republics or the Federation.

(a) The Assembly shall be responsible for:

(i) Financing activities of Kosovo institutions, including by levying taxes and duties on sources within Kosovo;

(ii) Adopting budgets of the Administrative organs and other institutions of Kosovo, with the exception of communal and national community institutions unless otherwise specified herein;

(iii) Adopting regulations concerning the organization and procedures of the Administrative organs of Kosovo;

(iv) Approving the list of Ministers of the Government, including the Prime minister;

(v) Coordinating educational arrangements in Kosovo, with respect for the authorities of national communities and Communes;

(vi) Electing candidates for judicial office put forward by the President of Kosovo;

(vii) Enacting laws ensuring free movement of goods, services, and persons in Kosovo consistent with this Agreement;

(viii) Approving agreements concluded by the President within the areas of responsibility of Kosovo;

(ix) Cooperating with the Federal Assembly, and with the Assemblies of the Republics, and conducting relations with foreign legislative bodies;

(x) Establishing a framework for local self-government;

(xi) Enacting laws concerning inter-communal issues and relations between national communities, when necessary;

(xii) Enacting laws regulating the work of medical institutions and hospitals;

(xiii) Protecting the environment, where inter-communal issues are involved;

(xiv) Adopting programs of economic, scientific, technological, demographic, regional, and social development, as well as urban planning;

(xv) Adopting programs for the development of agriculture and of rural areas;

(xvi) Regulating elections consistent with Chapters 3 and 5;

(xvii) Regulating Kosovo-owned property; and

(xviii) Regulating land registries.

(b) The Assembly shall also have authority to enact laws in areas within the responsibility of the Communes if the matter cannot be effectively regulated by the Communes or if regulation by individual Communes might prejudice the rights of other Communes. In the absence of a law enacted by the Assembly under this subparagraph that preempts communal action, the Communes shall retain their authority.

Procedure

6. Laws and other decisions of the Assembly shall be adopted by majority of Members present and voting.

7. A majority of the Members of a single national community elected to the Assembly pursuant to paragraph 1(b) may adopt a motion that a law or other decision adversely affects the vital interests of their national community. The challenged law or decision shall be suspended with regard to that national community until the dispute settlement procedure in paragraph 8 is completed.

8. The following procedure shall be used in the event of a motion under paragraph 7:

(a) The Members making the vital interest motion shall give reasons for their motion. The proposers of the legislation shall be given an opportunity to respond.

(b) The Members making the motion shall appoint within one day a mediator of their choice to assist in reaching an agreement with those proposing the legislation.

(c) If mediation does not produce an agreement within seven days, the matter may be submitted for a binding ruling. The decision shall be rendered by a panel comprising three Members of the Assembly: one Albanian and one Serb, each appointed by his or her national community delegation; and a third Member, who will be of a third nationality and will be selected within two days by consensus of the Presidency of the Assembly.

(i) A vital interest motion shall be upheld if the legislation challenged adversely affects the community's fundamental constitutional rights, additional rights as set forth in Article VII, or the principle of fair treatment.

(ii) If the motion is not upheld, the challenged legislation shall enter into force for that community.

(d) Paragraph (c) shall not apply to the selection of Assembly officials.

(e) The Assembly may exclude other decisions from this procedure by means of a law enacted by a majority that includes a majority of each national community elected pursuant to paragraph 1(b).

9. A majority of the Members shall constitute a quorum. The Assembly shall otherwise decide its own rules of procedure.

Leadership

10. The Assembly shall elect from among its Members a Presidency, which shall consist of a President, two Vice-Presidents, and other leaders in accordance with the Assembly's rules of procedure. Each national community meeting the threshold specified in paragraph 1(b)(ii) shall, be represented in the leadership. The President of the Assembly shall not be from the same national community as the President of Kosovo.

11. The President of the Assembly shall represent it, call its sessions to order, chair its meetings, coordinate the work of any committees it may establish, and perform other tasks prescribed by the rules of procedure of the Assembly.

ARTICLE III: PRESIDENT OF KOSOVO

1. There shall be a President of Kosovo, who shall be elected by the Assembly by vote of a majority of its members. The President of Kosovo shall serve for a three-year term. No person may serve more than two terms as President of Kosovo.

2. The President of Kosovo shall be responsible for:

(i) Representing Kosovo, including before any international or Federal body or any body of the Republics;

(ii) Proposing to the Assembly candidates for Prime Minister, the Constitutional Court, the Supreme Court, and other Kosovo judicial offices;

(iii) Meeting regularly with the democratically elected representatives of the national communities;

(iv) Conducting foreign relations and concluding agreements within this power consistent with the authorities of Kosovo institutions under this Agreement. Such agreements shall only enter into force upon approval by the Assembly;

(v) Designating a representative to serve on the Joint Commission established by Article I.2 of Chapter 5 of this Agreement;

(vi) Meeting regularly with the Federal and Republic Presidents; and

(vii) other functions specified herein or by law.

ARTICLE IV: GOVERNMENT AND ADMINISTRATIVE ORGANS

1. Executive power shall be exercised by the Government.

The Government shall be responsible for implementing the laws of Kosovo, and of other government authorities when such responsibilities are devolved by those authorities.

The Government shall also have competence to propose laws to the Assembly.

(a) The Government shall consist of a Prime Minister and Ministers, including at least one person from each national community meeting the threshold specified in paragraph 1(b)(ii) of Article II. Ministers shall head the Administrative Organs of Kosovo.

(b) The candidate for Prime Minister proposed by the President shall put forward a list of Ministers to the Assembly. The Prime Minister, together with the list of Ministers, shall be approved by a majority of those present and voting in the Assembly. In the event that the Prime Minister is not able to obtain a majority for the Government, the President shall propose a new candidate for Prime Minister within ten days.

(c) The Government shall resign if a no confidence motion is adopted by a vote of a majority of the members of the Assembly. If the Prime Minister or the Government resigns, the President shall select a new candidate for Prime Minister who shall seek to form a Government.

(d) The Prime Minister shall call meetings of the Government, represent it as appropriate, and coordinate its work. Decisions of the Government shall require a majority of Ministers present and voting. The Prime Minister shall cast the deciding vote in the event Ministers are equally divided. The Government shall otherwise decide its own rules of procedure.

2. Administrative organs shall be responsible for assisting the Government in carrying out its duties.

(a) National communities shall be fairly represented at all levels in the Administrative Organs.

(b) Any citizen in Kosovo claiming to have been directly and adversely affected by the decision of an executive or administrative body shall have the right to-judicial review of the legality of that decision after exhausting all avenues for administrative review. The Assembly shall enact a law to regulate this review.

3. There shall be a Chief Prosecutor who shall be responsible for prosecuting individuals who violate the criminal laws of Kosovo. He shall head an Office of the Prosecutor, which shall at all levels have staff representative of the population of Kosovo.

ARTICLE V: JUDICIARY

General

1. Kosovo shall have a Constitutional Court, a Supreme Court, District Courts, and Communal Courts.

2. The Kosovo courts shall have jurisdiction over all matters arising under this Constitution or the laws of Kosovo except as specified in paragraph 3. The Kosovo courts shall also have jurisdiction over questions of federal law, subject to appeal to the Federal courts on these questions after all appeals available under the Kosovo system have been exhausted.

3. Citizens in Kosovo may opt to have civil disputes to which they are party adjudicated by other courts in the Federal Republic of Yugoslavia, which shall apply the law applicable in Kosovo.

4. The following rules will apply to criminal cases:

(a) At the start of criminal proceedings, the defendant is entitled to have his or her trial transferred to another Kosovo court that he or she designates.

(b) In criminal cases in which all defendants and victims are members of the same national community, all members of the judicial council will be from a national community of their choice if any party so requests.

(c) A defendant in a criminal case tried in Kosovo courts is entitled to have at least one member of the judicial council hearing the case to be from his or her national community. Kosovo authorities will consider and allow judges of other courts in the Federal Republic of Yugoslavia to serve as Kosovo judges for these purposes.

Constitutional Court

5. The Constitutional Court shall consist of nine judges.

There shall be at least one Constitutional Court judge from each national community meeting the threshold specified in paragraph 1(b)(ii) of Article II. Until such time as the Parties agree to discontinue this arrangement, 5 judges of the Constitutional Court shall be selected from a list drawn up by the President of the European Court of Human Rights.

6. The Constitutional Court shall have authority to resolve disputes relating to the meaning of this Constitution. That authority shall include, but is not limited to, determining whether laws applicable in Kosovo, decisions or acts of the President, the Assembly, the Government, the Communes, and the national communities are compatible with this Constitution.

(a) Matters may be referred to the Constitutional Court by the President of Kosovo, the President or Vice-Presidents of the Assembly, the Ombudsman, the communal assemblies and councils, and any national community acting according to its democratic procedures.

(b) Any court which finds in the course of adjudicating a matter that the dispute depends on the answer to a question within the Constitutional Court's jurisdiction shall refer the issue to the Constitutional Court for a preliminary decision.

7. Following the exhaustion of other legal remedies, the Constitutional Court shall at the request of any person claiming to be a victim have jurisdiction over complaints that human rights and fundamental freedoms and the rights of members of national communities set forth in this Constitution have been violated by a public authority.

8. The Constitutional Court shall have such other jurisdiction as may be specified elsewhere in this Agreement or by law.

Supreme Court

9. The Supreme Court shall consist of nine judges. There shall be at least one Supreme Court judge from each national community meeting the threshold specified in paragraph 1(b)(ii) of Article II.

10. The Supreme Court shall hear appeals from the District Courts and the Communal Courts. Except as otherwise provided in this Constitution, the Supreme Court shall be the court of final appeal for all cases arising under law applicable in Kosovo. Its decisions shall be recognized and executed by all authorities in the Federal Republic of Yugoslavia.

Functioning of the Courts

11. The Assembly shall determine the number of District and Communal Court judges necessary to meet current needs.

12. Judges of all courts in Kosovo shall be distinguished jurists of the highest moral character. They shall be broadly representative of the national communities of Kosovo.

13. Removal of a Kosovo judge shall require the consensus of the judges of the Constitutional Court. A Constitutional Court judge whose removal is in question shall not participate in the decision on his case.

14. The Constitutional Court shall adopt rules for itself and for other courts in Kosovo. The Constitutional and Supreme Courts shall each adopt decisions by majority vote of their members.

15. Except as otherwise specified in their rules, all Kosovo courts shall hold public proceedings. They shall issue published opinions setting forth the reasons for their decisions.

ARTICLE VI: HUMAN RIGHTS AND FUNDAMENTAL FREEDOMS

1. All authorities in Kosovo shall ensure internationally recognized human rights and fundamental freedoms.

2. The rights and freedoms set forth in the European Convention for the Protection of Human Rights and Fundamental Freedoms and its Protocols shall apply directly in Kosovo. Other internationally recognized human rights instruments enacted into law by the Kosovo Assembly shall also apply. These rights and freedoms shall have priority over all other law.

3. All courts, agencies, governmental institutions, and other public institutions of Kosovo or operating in relation to Kosovo shall conform to these human rights and fundamental freedoms.

ARTICLE VII: NATIONAL COMMUNITIES

1. National communities and their members shall have additional rights as set forth below in order to preserve and express their national, cultural, religious, and linguistic identities in accordance with international standards and the Helsinki Final Act.

Such rights shall be exercised in conformity with human rights and fundamental freedoms.

2. Each national community may elect, through democratic means and in a manner consistent with the principles of Chapter 3 of this Agreement, institutions to administer its affairs in Kosovo.

3. The national communities shall be subject to the laws applicable in Kosovo, provided that any act or decision concerning national communities must be non-discriminatory. The Assembly shall decide upon a procedure for resolving disputes between national communities.

4. The additional rights of the national communities, acting through their democratically elected institutions, are to:

(a) preserve and protect their national, cultural, religious, and linguistic identities, including by:

(i) inscribing local names of towns and villages, of squares and streets, and of other topographic names in the language and alphabet of the national community in addition to signs in Albanian and Serbian, consistent with decisions about style made by the communal institutions;

(ii) providing information in the language and alphabet of the national community;

(iii) providing for education and establishing educational institutions, in particular for schooling in their own language and alphabet and in national culture and history, for which relevant authorities will provide financial assistance; curricula shall reflect a spirit of tolerance between national communities and respect for the rights of members of all national communities in accordance with international standards;

(iv) enjoying unhindered contacts with representatives of their respective national communities, within the Federal Republic of Yugoslavia and abroad;

(v) using and displaying national symbols, including symbols of the Federal Republic of Yugoslavia and the Republic of Serbia;

(vi) protecting national traditions on family law by, if the community decides, arranging rules in the field of inheritance; family and matrimonial relations; tutorship; and adoption;

(vii) the preservation of sites of religious, historical, or cultural importance to the national community in cooperation with other authorities;

(viii) implementing public health and social services on a non-discriminatory basis as to citizens and national communities;

(ix) operating religious institutions in cooperation with religious authorities; and

(x) participating in regional and international non-governmental organizations in accordance with procedures of these organizations;

(b) be guaranteed access to, and representation in, public broadcast media, including provisions for separate programming in relevant languages under the direction of those nominated by the respective national community on a fair and equitable basis; and

(c) finance their activities by collecting contributions the national communities may decide to levy on members of their own communities.

5. Members of national communities shall also be individually guaranteed:

(a) the right to enjoy unhindered contacts with members of their respective national communities elsewhere in the Federal Republic of Yugoslavia and abroad;

(b) equal access to employment in public services at all levels;

(c) the right to use their languages and alphabets;

(d) the right to use and display national community symbols;

(e) the right to participate in democratic institutions that will determine the national community's exercise of the collective rights set forth in this Article; and

(f) the right to establish cultural and religious associations, for which relevant authorities willprovide financial assistance.

6. Each national community and, where appropriate, their members acting individually may exercise these additional rights through Federal institutions and institutions of the Republics, in accordance with the procedures of those institutions and without prejudice to the ability of Kosovo institutions to carry out their responsibilities.

7. Every person shall have the right freely to choose to be treated or not to be treated as belonging to a national community, and no disadvantage shall result from that choice or from the exercise of the rights connected to that choice.

ARTICLE VIII: COMMUNES

1. Kosovo shall have the existing communes. Changes may be made to communal boundaries by act of the Kosovo Assembly after consultation with the authorities of the communes concerned.

2. Communes may develop relationships among themselves for their mutual benefit.

3. Each commune shall have an Assembly, an Executive Council, and such administrative bodies as the commune may establish.

(a) Each national community whose membership constitutes at least three percent of the population of the commune shall be represented on the Council in proportion to its share of the communal population or by one member, whichever is greater.

(b) Prior to the completion of a census, disputes over communal population percentages for purposes of this paragraph shall be resolved by reference to declarations of national community membership in the voter registry.

4. The communes shall have responsibility for:

(a) law enforcement, as specified in Chapter 2 of this Agreement;

(b) regulating and, when appropriate, providing child care;

(c) providing education, consistent with the rights and duties of national communities, and in a spirit of tolerance between national communities and respect for the rights of the members of all national communities in accordance with international standards;

(d) protecting the communal environment;

(e) regulating commerce and privately-owned stores;

(f) regulating hunting and fishing;

(g) planning and carrying out public works of communal importance, including roads and water supplies, and participating in the planning and carrying out of Kosovo-wide public works projects in coordination with other communes and Kosovo authorities;

(h) regulating land use, town planning, building regulations, and housing construction-

(i) developing programs for tourism, the hotel industry, catering, and sport;

(j) organizing fairs and local markets;

(k) organizing public services of communal importance, including fire, emergency response, and police consistent with Chapter 2 of this Agreement; and

(l) financing the work of communal institutions, including raising revenues, taxes, and preparing budgets.

5. The communes shall also have responsibility for all other areas within Kosovo's authority not expressly assigned elsewhere herein, subject to the provisions of Article II.5(b) of this Constitution.

6. Each commune shall conduct its business in public and shall maintain publicly available records of its deliberations and decisions.

ARTICLE IX: REPRESENTATION

1. Citizens in Kosovo shall have the right to participate in the election of:

(a) At least 10 deputies in the House of Citizens of the Federal Assembly; and

(b) At least 20 deputies in the National Assembly of the Republic of Serbia.

2. The modalities of elections for the deputies specified in paragraph 1 shall be determined by the Federal Republic of Yugoslavia and the Republic of Serbia respectively, under procedures to be agreed with the Chief of the Implementation Mission.

3. The Assembly shall have the opportunity to present to the appropriate authorities a list of candidates from which shall be drawn:

(a) At least one citizen in Kosovo to serve in the Federal Government, and at least one citizen in Kosovo to serve in the Government of the Republic of Serbia; and

(b) At least one judge on the Federal Constitutional Court, one judge on the Federal Court, and three judges on the Supreme Court of Serbia.

ARTICLE X: AMENDMENT

1. The Assembly may by a majority of two-thirds of its Members, which majority must include a majority of the Members elected from each national community pursuant to Article II.1(b)(ii), adopt amendments to this Constitution.

2. There shall, however, be no amendments to Article I.3-8 or to this Article, nor shall any amendment diminish the rights granted by Articles VI and VII.

ARTICLE XI: ENTRY INTO FORCE

This Constitution shall enter into force upon signature of this Agreement.

Chapter 2: Police and Civil Public Security

ARTICLE I: GENERAL PRINCIPLES

1. All law enforcement agencies, organizations and personnel of the Parties, which for purposes of this Chapter will include customs and border police operating in Kosovo, shall act in compliance with this Agreement and shall observe internationally recognized standards of human rights and due process. In exercising their functions, law enforcement personnel shall not discriminate on any ground, such as sex, race, color, language, religion, political or other opinion, national or social origin, association with a national community, property, birth or other status.

2. The Parties invite the organization for Security and Cooperation in Europe (OSCE) through its Implementation Mission (IM) to monitor and supervise implementation of this Chapter and related provisions of this Agreement. The Chief of the Implementation Mission (CIM) or his designee shall have the authority to issue binding directives to the Parties and subsidiary bodies on police and civil public security matters to obtain compliance by the Parties with the terms of this Chapter. The Parties agree to cooperate fully with the IM and to comply with its directives. Personnel assigned to police-related duties within the IM shall be permitted to wear a uniform while serving in this part of the mission.

3. In carrying out his responsibilities, the CIM will inform and consult KFOR as appropriate.

4. The IM shall have the authority to:

(a) Monitor, observe, and inspect law enforcement activities, personnel, and facilities, including border police and customs units, as well as associated judicial organizations, structures, and proceedings;

(b) Advise law enforcement personnel and forces, including border police and customs units, and, when necessary to bring them into compliance with this Agreement, including this Chapter, issue appropriate binding directions in coordination with KFOR;

(c) Participate in and guide the training of law enforcement personnel;

(d) In coordination with KFOR, assess threats to public order;

(e) Advise and provide guidance to governmental authorities on how to deal with threats to public order and on the organization of effective civilian law enforcement agencies;

(f) Accompany the Parties, law enforcement personnel as they carry out their responsibilities, as the IM deems appropriate;

(g) Dismiss or discipline public security personnel of the Parties for cause; and

(h) Request appropriate law enforcement support from the international community to enable IM to carry out the duties assigned in this Chapter.

5. All Kosovo, Republic and Federal law enforcement and Federal military authorities shall be obligated, in their respective areas of authority, to ensure freedom of movement and safe passage for all persons, vehicles and goods. This obligation includes a duty to permit the unobstructed passage into Kosovo of police equipment which has been approved by the CIM and COMKFOR for use by Kosovo police, and of any other support provided under subparagraph 4(h) above.

6. The Parties undertake to provide one another mutual assistance, when requested, in the surrender of those accused of committing criminal acts within a Party's jurisdiction, and in the investigation and prosecution of offenses across the boundary of Kosovo with other parts of the FRY. The Parties shall develop agreed procedures and mechanisms for responding to these requests. The CIM or his designee shall resolve disputes on these matters.

7. The IM shall aim to transfer law enforcement responsibilities described in Article II below to the law enforcement officials and organizations described in Article II at the earliest practical time consistent with civil public security.

ARTICLE II: COMMUNAL POLICE

1. As they build up, Communal police units, organized and stationed at the communal and municipal levels, shall assume primary responsibility for law enforcement in Kosovo. The specific responsibilities of the communal police will include police patrols and crime prevention, criminal investigations, arrest and detention of criminal suspects, crowd control, and traffic control.

2. *Number and Composition.* The total number of communal police established by this Agreement operating within Kosovo shall not exceed 3,000 active duty law enforcement officers. However, the CIM shall have the authority to increase or decrease this personnel coiling if he determines such action is necessary to meet operational needs. Prior to taking any such action, the CIM shall consult with the Criminal Justice Administration and other officials as appropriate. The national communities in each commune shall be fairly represented in the communal police unit.

3. *Criminal Justice Administration.*

a. A Criminal Justice Administration (CJA) shall be established. It shall be an Administrative Organ of Kosovo, reporting to an appropriate member of the Government of Kosovo as determined by the Government.

The CJA shall provide general coordination of law enforcement operations in Kosovo. Specific functions of the CJA shall include general supervision over, and providing guidance to, communal police forces through their commanders, assisting in the coordination between separate communal police forces, and oversight of the operations of the police academy. In carrying out these responsibilities, the CJA may issue directives, which shall be binding on communal police commanders and personnel. In the exercise of its functions, the CJA shall be subject to any directions given by CIM.

b. Within twelve months of the establishment of the CJA, the CJA shall submit for review by the CIM a plan for the coordination and development of law enforcement bodies and personnel in Kosovo within its jurisdiction. This plan shall serve as the framework for law enforcement coordination and development in Kosovo and be subject to modification by the CIM.

c. The IM will endeavor to develop the capacities of the CJA as quickly as possible. Prior to the point when the CJA is able to properly carry out the functions described in the preceding paragraph, as determined by the CIM, the IM shall carry out these functions.

4. *Communal Commanders.* Subject to review by the CIM, each commune will appoint, and may remove for cause, by majority vote of the communal council, a communal police commander with responsibility for police operations within the commune.

5. *Service in Police.*

(a) Recruitment for public security personnel will be conducted primarily at the local level. Local and communal governments, upon consultation with communal Criminal Justice Commissions, will nominate officer candidates to attend the Kosovo Police Academy. Offers of employment will be made by communal police commanders, with the concurrence of the academy director, only after the candidate has successfully completed the academy basic recruit course.

(b) Recruitment, selection and training of communal police officers shall be conducted under the direction of the IM during the period of its operation.

(c) There shall be no bar to service in the communal police based on prior political activities. Members of the police shall not, however, be permitted while they hold this public office to participate in party political activities other than membership in such a party.

(d) Continued service in the police is dependent upon behavior consistent with the terms of this Agreement, including this Chapter. The IM shall supervise regular reviews of officer performance, which shall be conducted in accordance with international due process norms.

6. *Uniforms and Equipment.*

(a) All communal police officers, with the exception of officers participating in crowd control functions, shall wear a standard uniform. Uniforms shall include a badge, picture identification, and name tag.

(b) Communal police officers may be equipped with a sidearm, handcuffs, a baton, and a radio.

(c) Subject to authorization or modification by the CIM, each commune may maintain, either at the communal headquarters or at municipal stations, no more than one long-barreled weapon not to exceed 7.62 mm for every fifteen police officers assigned to the commune. Each such weapon must be approved by and registered with the IM and KFOR pursuant to procedures established by the CIM and COMKFOR. When not in use, all such weapons will be securely stored and each commune will keep a registry of these weapons.

(i) In the event of a serious law enforcement threat that would justify the use of these weapons, the communal police commander shall obtain IM approval before employing these weapons.

(ii) The communal police commander may authorize the use of these weapons without prior approval of the IM for the sole purpose of self-defense. In such cases, he must report the incident no later than one hour after it occurs to the IM and KFOR.

(iii) If the CIM determines that a weapon has been used by a member of a communal police force in a manner contrary to this Chapter, he may take appropriate corrective measures; such measures may include reducing the number of such weapons that the communal police force is allowed to possess or dismissing or disciplining the law enforcement personnel involved.

(d) Communal police officers engaged in crowd control functions will receive equipment appropriate to their task, including batons, helmets and shields, subject to IM approval.

ARTICLE III: INTERIM POLICE ACADEMY

1. Under the supervision of the IM, the CJA shall establish an interim Police Academy that will offer mandatory and professional development training for all public security personnel, including border police. Until the interim police academy is established, IM will oversee a temporary training program for public security personnel including border police.

2. All public security personnel shall be required to complete a course of police studies successfully before serving as communal police officers.

3. The Academy shall be headed by a Director appointed and removed by the CJA in consultation with the Kosovo Criminal Justice Commission and the IM. The Director shall consult closely with the IM and comply fully with its recommendations and guidance.

4. All Republic and Federal police training facilities in Kosovo, including the academy at Vucitrn, will cease operations within 6 months of the entry into force of, this Agreement.

ARTICLE IV: CRIMINAL JUSTICE COMMISSIONS

1. The parties shall establish a Kosovo Criminal Justice Commission and Communal Criminal Justice Commissions.

The CIM or his designee shall chair meetings of these Commissions. They shall be forums for cooperation, coordination and the resolution of disputes concerning law enforcement and civil public security in Kosovo.

2. The functions of the Commissions shall include the following:

(a) Monitor, review, and make recommendations regarding the operation of law enforcement personnel and policies in Kosovo, including communal police units;

(b) Review, and make recommendations regarding the recruitment, selection and training of communal police officers and commanders;

(c) Consider complaints regarding police practices filed by individuals or national communities, and provide information and recommendations to communal police commanders and the CIM for consideration in their reviews of officer performance; and

(d) In the Kosovo Criminal Justice Commission only: In consultation with designated local, Republic and Federal police liaisons, monitor jurisdiction sharing in cases of overlapping criminal jurisdiction between Kosovo, Republic and Federal authorities.

3. The membership of the Kosovo Criminal Justice Commission and each Communal Criminal Justice Commission shall be representative of the population and shall include:

(a) In the Kosovo Criminal Justice Commission:

(i) a representative of each commune;

(ii) the head of the Kosovo CJA;

(iii) a representative of each Republic and

Federal law enforcement component operating in Kosovo (for example, Customs police and Border police);

(iv) a representative of each national community;

(v) a representative of the IM, during its period of operation in Kosovo;

(vi) a representative of the VJ border guard, as appropriate;

(vii) a representative of the MUP, as appropriate, while present in Kosovo; and

(viii) A representative of KFOR, as appropriate.

(b) In the Communal Criminal Justice Commissions:

(i) the communal police commander;

(ii) a representative of any Republic and Federal law enforcement component operating in the commune;

(iii) a representative of each national community;

(iv) a civilian representative of the communal government;

(v) a representative of the IM, during its period of operation in Kosovo;

(vi) a representative of the VJ border guard, who shall have observer status, as appropriate; and

(vii) A representative of KFOR, as appropriate.

4. Each Criminal Justice Commission shall meet at least monthly, or at the request of any Commission member.

ARTICLE V: POLICE OPERATIONS IN KOSOVO

1. The communal police established by this Agreement shall have exclusive law enforcement authority and jurisdiction and shall be the only police presence in Kosovo following the reduction and eventual withdrawal from Kosovo by the MUP, with the exception of border police as specified in Article VI and any support provided pursuant to Article I(3)(h).

(a) During the transition to communal police, the remaining MTJP shall carry out only normal policing duties, and shall draw down, pursuant to the schedule described in Chapter 7.

(b) During the period of the phased drawdown of the MUP, the MUP in Kosovo shall have authority to conduct only civil police functions and shall be under the supervision and control of the CIM. The IM may dismiss from service, or take other appropriate disciplinary action against, MUP personnel who obstruct implementation of this Agreement.

2. Concurrent Law Enforcement in Kosovo.

(a) Except as provided in Article V.1 and Article VI, Federal and Republic law enforcement officials may only act within Kosovo in cases of hot pursuit of a person suspected of committing a serious criminal offense.

(i) Federal and Republic authorities shall as soon as practicable, but in no event later than one hour after their entry into Kosovo while engaged in a hot pursuit, notify the nearest Kosovo law enforcement officials that the pursuit has crossed into Kosovo. Once notification has been made, further pursuit and apprehension shall be coordinated with Kosovo law enforcement. Following apprehension, suspects shall be placed into the custody of the authorities originating the pursuit. If the suspect has not been apprehended within four hours, the original pursuing authorities shall cease their pursuit and immediately depart Kosovo unless invited to continue their pursuit by the CJA or the CIM.

(ii) In the event the pursuit is of such short duration as to preclude notification, Kosovo law enforcement officials shall be notified that an apprehension has been made and shall be given access to the detainee prior to his removal from Kosovo.

(iii) Personnel engaged in hot pursuit under the provisions of this Article may only be civilian police, may only carry weapons appropriate for normal civilian police duties (sidearms, and long-barreled weapons not to exceed 7.62mm), may only travel in officially marked police vehicles, and may not exceed a total of eight personnel at any one time. Travel in armored personnel carriers by police engaged in hot pursuit is strictly prohibited.

(iv) The same rules shall apply to hot pursuit of suspects by Kosovo law enforcement authorities to Federal territory outside of Kosovo.

(b) All Parties shall provide the highest degree of mutual assistance in law enforcement matters in response to reasonable requests.

ARTICLE VI: SECURITY ON INTERNATIONAL BORDERS

1. The Government of the FRY will maintain official border crossings on its international borders (Albania and FYROM).

2. Personnel from the organizations listed below may be present along Kosovo's international borders and at international border crossings, and may not act outside the scope of the authorities specified in this Chapter.

(a) Republic of Serbia Border Police

(i) The Border Police shall continue to exercise authority at Kosovo's international border crossings and in connection with the enforcement of Federal Republic of Yugoslavia immigration laws. The total number of border police shall be drawn down to 75 within 14 days of entry into force of this Agreement.

(ii) while maintaining the personnel threshold specified in subparagraph (i), the ranks of the existing Border Police units operating in Kosovo shall be supplemented by new recruits so that they are representative of the Kosovo population.

(iii) All Border Police stationed in Kosovo must attend police training at the Kosovo police academy within 18 months of the entry into force of this Agreement.

(b) Customs Officers

(i) The FRY Customs Service will continue to exercise customs jurisdiction at Kosovo's official international border crossings and in such customs warehouses as may be necessary within Kosovo. The total number of customs personnel shall be drawn down to 50 within 14 days of the entry into force of this Agreement.

(ii) Kosovar Albanian officers of the Customs Service shall be trained and compensated by the FRY.

(c) The CIM shall conduct a periodic review of customs and border police requirements and shall have the authority to increase or decrease the personnel ceilings described in paragraphs (a)(i) and (b)(i) above to reflect operational needs and to adjust the composition of individual customs units.

ARTICLE VII: ARREST AND DETENTION

1. Except pursuant to Article V, Article I(3)(h), and sections (a)-(b) of this paragraph, only officers of the communal police shall have authority to arrest and detain individuals in Kosovo.

(a) Border Police officers shall have authority within Kosovo to arrest and detain individuals who have violated criminal provisions of the immigration laws.

(b) Officers of the Customs Service shall have authority within Kosovo to arrest and detain individuals for criminal violations of the customs laws.

2. Immediately upon making an arrest, the arresting officer shall notify the nearest Communal Criminal Justice Commission of the detention and the location of the detainee. He subsequently shall transfer the detainee to the nearest appropriate jail in Kosovo at the earliest opportunity.

3. Officers may use reasonable and necessary force proportionate to the circumstances to effect arrests and keep suspects in custody.

4. Kosovo and its constituent communes shall establish jails and prisons to accommodate the detention of criminal suspects and the imprisonment of individuals convicted of violating the laws applicable in Kosovo. Prisons shall be operated consistent with international standards. Access shall be provided to international personnel, including representatives of the International Committee of the Red Cross.

ARTICLE VIII: ADMINISTRATION OF JUSTICE

1. Criminal Jurisdiction over Persons Arrested within Kosovo.

(a) Except in accordance with Article V and subparagraph

(b) of this paragraph, any person arrested within Kosovo shall be subject to the jurisdiction of the Kosovo courts.

(b) Any person arrested within Kosovo, in accordance with the law and with this Agreement, by the Border Police or Customs Police shall be subject to the jurisdiction of the FRY courts. If there is no applicable court of the FRY to hear the case, the Kosovo courts shall have jurisdiction.

2. Prosecution of Crimes.

(a) The CJA shall, in consultation with the CIM, appoint and have the authority to remove the Chief Prosecutor.

(b) The IM shall have the authority to monitor, observe, inspect, and when necessary, direct the operations of the office of the Prosecutor and any and all related staff.

ARTICLE IX: FINAL AUTHORITY TO INTERPRET

The CIM is the final authority regarding interpretation of this Chapter and his determinations are binding on all Parties and persons.

Chapter 3: Conduct and Supervision of Elections

ARTICLE I: CONDITIONS FOR ELECTIONS

1. The Parties shall ensure that conditions exist for the organization of free and fair elections, which include but are not limited to:

a) freedom of movement for all citizens;

b) an open and free political environment;

c) an environment conducive to the return of displaced persons;

d) a safe and secure environment that ensures freedom of assembly, association, and expression;

e) an electoral legal framework of rules and regulations complying with OSCE commitments, which will be implemented by a Central Election Commission, as set forth in Article III, which is representative of the population of Kosovo in terms of national communities and political parties; and

f) free media, effectively accessible to registered political parties and candidates, and available to voters throughout Kosovo.

2. The Parties request the OSCE to certify when elections will be effective under current conditions in Kosovo, and to provide assistance to the Parties to create conditions for free and fair elections.

3. The Parties shall comply fully with Paragraphs 7 and 8 of the OSCE Copenhagen Document, which are attached to this Chapter.

ARTICLE II: ROLE OF THE OSCE

1. The Parties request the OSCE to adopt and put in place an elections program for Kosovo and supervise elections as set forth in this Agreement.

2. The Parties request the OSCE to supervise, in a manner to be determined by the OSCE and in cooperation with other international organizations the OSCE deems necessary, the preparation and conduct of elections for: a) Members of the Kosovo Assembly; b) Members of Communal Assemblies;

c) other officials popularly elected in Kosovo under this Agreement and the laws and Constitution of Kosovo at the discretion of the OSCE.

3. The Parties request the OSCE to establish a Central Election Commission in Kosovo ("the Commission").

4. Consistent with Article IV of Chapter 5, the first elections shall be held within nine months of the entry into force of this Agreement. The President of the Commission shall decide, in consultation with the Parties, the exact timing and order of elections for Kosovo political offices.

ARTICLE III: CENTRAL ELECTION COMMISSION

1. The Commission shall adopt electoral Rules and Regulations on all matters necessary for the conduct of free and fair elections in Kosovo, including rules relating to: the eligibility and registration of candidates, parties, and voters, including displaced persons and refugees; ensuring a free and fair elections campaign; administrative and technical preparation for elections including the establishment, publication, and certification of election results; and the role of international and domestic election observers.

2. The responsibilities of the Commission, as provided in the electoral Rules and Regulations, shall include:

a) the preparation, conduct, and supervision of all aspects of the electoral process, including development and supervision of political party and voter registration, and creation of secure and transparent procedures for production and dissemination of ballots and sensitive election materials, vote counts, tabulations, and publication of elections results;

b) ensuring compliance with the electoral Rules and Regulations established pursuant to this Agreement, including establishing auxiliary bodies for this purpose as necessary;

c) ensuring that action is taken to remedy any violation of any provision of this Agreement, including imposing penalties such as removal from candidate or party lists, against any person, candidate, political party, or body that violates such provisions; and

d) accrediting observers, including personnel from international organizations and foreign and domestic non-governmental organizations, and ensuring that the Parties grant the accredited observers unimpeded access and movement.

3. The Commission shall consist of a person appointed by the Chairman-in-office (CIO) of the OSCE, representatives of all national communities, and representatives of political parties in Kosovo selected by criteria to be determined by the Commission. The person appointed by the CIO shall act as the President of the Commission. The rules of procedure of the Commission shall provide that in the exceptional circumstance of an unresolved dispute within the Commission, the decision of the President shall be final and binding.

4. The Commission shall enjoy the right to establish communication facilities, and to engage local and administrative staff.

Chapter 4a: Economic Issues
ARTICLE I

1. The economy of Kosovo shall function in accordance with free market principles.

2. The authorities established to levy and collect taxes and other charges are set forth in this Agreement. Except as otherwise expressly provided, all authorities have the right to keep all revenues from their own taxes or other charges consistent with this Agreement.

3. Certain revenue from Kosovo taxes and duties shall accrue to the Communes, taking into account the need for an equalization of revenues between the Communes based on objective criteria. The Assembly of Kosovo shall enact appropriate non-discriminatory legislation for this purpose. The Communes may also levy local taxes in accordance with this Agreement.

4. The Federal Republic of Yugoslavia shall be responsible for the collection of all customs duties at international borders in Kosovo. There shall be no impediments to the free movement of persons, goods, services, and capital to and from Kosovo.

5. Federal authorities shall ensure that Kosovo receives a proportionate and equitable share-of benefits that may be derived from international agreements concluded by the Federal Republic and of Federal resources.

6. Federal and other authorities shall within their respective powers and responsibilities ensure the free movement of persons, goods, services, and capital to Kosovo, including from international sources. They shall in particular allow access to Kosovo without discrimination for persons delivering such goods and services.

7. If expressly required by an international donor or lender, international contracts for reconstruction projects shall be concluded by the authorities of the Federal Republic of Yugoslavia, which shall establish appropriate mechanisms to make such funds available to Kosovo authorities. Unless precluded by the terms of contracts, all reconstruction projects that exclusively concern Kosovo shall be managed and implemented by the appropriate Kosovo authority.

ARTICLE II

1. The Parties agree to reallocate ownership and resources in accordance insofar as possible with the distribution of powers and responsibilities set forth in this Agreement, in the following areas:

(a) government-owned assets (including educational institutions, hospitals, natural resources, and production facilities);

(b) pension and social insurance contributions;

(c) revenues to be distributed under Article I.5; and

(d) any other matters relating to economic relations between the Parties not covered by this Agreement.

2. The Parties agree to the creation of a Claim Settlement Commission (CSC) to resolve all disputes between them on matters referred to in paragraph 1.

(a) The CSC shall consist of three experts designated by Kosovo, three experts designated jointly by the Federal Republic of Yugoslavia and the Republic of Serbia, and three independent experts designated by the CIM.

(b) The decisions of the CSC, which shall be taken by majority vote, shall be final and binding. The Parties shall implement them without delay.

3. Authorities receiving ownership of public facilities shall have the power to operate such facilities.

Chapter 4b: Humanitarian Assistance, Reconstruction and Economic Development

1. In parallel with the continuing full implementation of this Agreement, urgent attention must be focused on meeting the real humanitarian and economic needs of Kosovo in order to help create the conditions for reconstruction and lasting economic recovery. International assistance will be provided without discrimination between national communities.

2. The Parties welcome the willingness of the European Commission working with the international community to co-ordinate international support for the parties' efforts. Specifically, the European Commission will organize an international donors, conference within one month of entry into force of this Agreement.

3. The international community will provide immediate and unconditional humanitarian assistance, focusing primarily on refugees and internally displaced persons returning to their former homes. The Parties welcome and endorse the UNHCR's lead role in co-ordination of this effort, and endorse its intention, in close co-operation with the Implementation Mission, to plan an early, peaceful, orderly and phased return of refugees and displaced persons in conditions of safety and dignity.

4. The international community will provide the means for the rapid improvement of living conditions for the population of Kosovo through the reconstruction and rehabilitation of housing and local infrastructure (including water, energy, health and local education infrastructure) based on damage assessment surveys.

5. Assistance will also be provided to support the establishment and development of the institutional and legislative framework laid down in this Agreement, including local governance and tax settlement, and to reinforce civil society, culture and education ' Social welfare will also be addressed, with priority given to the protection of vulnerable social groups.

6. It will also be vital to lay the foundations for sustained development, based on a revival of the local economy. This must take account of the need to address unemployment, and to stimulate the economy by a range of mechanisms. The European Commission will be giving urgent attention to this.

7. International assistance, with the exception of humanitarian aid, will be subject to full compliance with this Agreement as well as other conditionalities defined in advance by the donors and the absorptive capacity of Kosovo.

Chapter 5: Implementation I

ARTICLE I: INSTITUTIONS

Implementation Mission

1. The Parties invite the OSCE, in cooperation with the European Union, to constitute an Implementation Mission in Kosovo. All responsibilities and powers previously vested in the Kosovo Verification Mission and its Head by prior agreements shall be continued in the Implementation Mission and its Chief.

Joint Commission

2. A Joint Commission shall serve as the central mechanism for monitoring and coordinating the civilian implementation of this Agreement. It shall consist of the Chief of the Implementation Mission (CIM), one Federal and one Republic representative, one representative of each national community in Kosovo, the President of the Assembly, and a representative of the President of Kosovo. Meetings of the Joint Commission may be attended by other representatives of organizations specified in this Agreement or needed for its implementation.

3. The CIM shall serve as the Chair of the Joint Commission. The Chair shall coordinate and organize the work of the Joint Commission and decide the time and place of its meetings. The Parties shall abide by and fully implement the decisions of the Joint Commission. The Joint Commission shall operate on the basis of consensus, but in the event consensus cannot be reached, the Chair's decision shall be final.

4. The Chair shall have full and unimpeded access to all places, persons, and information (including documents and other records) within Kosovo that in his judgment are necessary to his responsibilities with regard to the civilian aspects of this Agreement.

Joint Council and Local Councils

5. The CIM may, as necessary, establish a Kosovo Joint Council and Local Councils, for informal dispute resolution and cooperation. The Kosovo Joint Council would consist of one member from each of the national communities in Kosovo. Local Councils would consist of representatives of each national community living in the locality where the Local Council is established.

ARTICLE II: RESPONSIBILITIES AND POWERS

1. The CIM shall:

(a) supervise and direct the implementation of the civilian aspects of this Agreement pursuant to a schedule that he shall specify;

(b) maintain close contact with the Parties to promote full compliance with those aspects of this Agreement;

(c) facilitate, as he deems necessary, the resolution of difficulties arising in connection with such implementation;

(d) participate in meetings of donor organizations, including on issues of rehabilitation and reconstruction, in particular by putting forward proposals and identifying priorities for their consideration as appropriate;

(e) coordinate the activities of civilian organizations and agencies in Kosovo assisting in the implementation of the civilian aspects of this Agreement, respecting fully their specific organizational procedures;

(f) report periodically to the bodies responsible for constituting the Mission on progress in the implementation of the civilian aspects of this Agreement; and

(g) carry out the functions specified in this Agreement pertaining to police and security forces.

2. The CIM shall also carry out other responsibilities set forth in this Agreement or as may he later agreed.

ARTICLE III: STATUS OF IMPLEMENTATION MISSION

1. Implementation Mission personnel shall be allowed unrestricted movement and access into and throughout Kosovo at any time.

2. The Parties shall facilitate the operations of the Implementation Mission, including by the provision of assistance as requested with regard to transportation, subsistence, accommodation, communication, and other facilities.

3. The Implementation Mission shall enjoy such legal capacity as may be necessary for the exercise of its functions under the laws and regulations of Kosovo, the Federal Republic of Yugoslavia, and the Republic of Serbia. Such legal capacity shall include the capacity to contract, and to acquire and dispose of real and personal property.

4. Privileges and immunities are hereby accorded as follows to the Implementation Mission and associated personnel:

(a) the Implementation Mission and its premises, archives, and other property shall enjoy the same privileges and immunities as a diplomatic mission under the Vienna Convention on Diplomatic Relations;

(b) the CIM and professional members of his staff and their families shall enjoy the same privileges and immunities as are enjoyed by diplomatic agents and their families under the Vienna Convention on Diplomatic Relations; and

(c) other members of the Implementation Mission staff and their families shall enjoy the same privileges and immunities as are enjoyed by members of the administrative and technical staff and their families under the Vienna Convention on Diplomatic Relations.

ARTICLE IV: PROCESS OF IMPLEMENTATION

General

1. The Parties acknowledge that complete implementation will require political acts and measures, and the election and establishment of institutions and bodies set forth in this Agreement. The Parties agree to proceed expeditiously with these tasks on a schedule set by the Joint Commission. The Parties shall provide active support, cooperation, and participation for the successful implementation of this Agreement.

Elections and Census

2. Within nine months of the entry into force of this Agreement, there shall be elections in accordance with and pursuant to procedures specified in Chapter 3 of this Agreement for authorities established herein, according to a voter list prepared to international standards by the Central Election Commission. The Organization for Security and Cooperation in Europe (OSCE) shall supervise those elections to ensure that they are free and fair.

3. Under the supervision of the OSCE and with the participation of Kosovo authorities and experts nominated by and belonging to the national communities of Kosovo, Federal authorities shall conduct an objective and free census of the population in Kosovo under rules and regulations agreed with the OSCE in accordance with international standards. The census shall be carried out when the OSCE determines that conditions allow an objective and accurate enumeration.

(a) The first census shall be limited to name, place of birth, place of usual residence and address, gender, age, citizenship, national community, and religion.

(b) The authorities of the Parties shall provide each other and the OSCE with all records necessary to conduct the census, including data about places of residence, citizenship, voters, lists, and other information.

Transitional Provisions

4. All laws and regulations in effect in Kosovo when this Agreement enters into force shall remain in effect unless and until replaced by laws or regulations adopted by a competent body. All laws and regulations applicable in Kosovo that are incompatible with this Agreement shall be presumed to have been harmonized with this Agreement. In particular, martial law in Kosovo is hereby revoked.

5. Institutions currently in place in Kosovo shall remain until superseded by bodies created by or in accordance with this Agreement. The CIM may recommend to the appropriate authorities the removal and appointment of officials and the curtailment of operations of existing institutions in Kosovo if he deems it necessary for the effective implementation of this Agreement. If the action recommended is not taken in the time requested, the Joint Commission may decide to take the recommended action.

6. Prior to the election of Kosovo officials pursuant to this Agreement, the CIM shall take the measures necessary to ensure the development and functioning of independent media in keeping with international standards, including allocation of radio and television frequencies.

ARTICLE V: AUTHORITY TO INTERPRET

The CIM shall be the final authority in theater regarding interpretation of the civilian aspects of this Agreement, and the Parties agree to abide by his determinations as binding on all Parties and persons.

Chapter 6: The Ombudsman

ARTICLE I: GENERAL

1. There shall be an Ombudsman, who shall monitor the realization of the rights of members of national communities and the protection of human rights and fundamental freedoms in Kosovo. The Ombudsman shall have unimpeded access to any person or place and shall have the right to appear and intervene before any domestic, Federal, or (consistent with the rules of such bodies) international authority upon his or her request. No person, institution, or entity of the Parties may interfere with the functions of the Ombudsman.

2. The Ombudsman shall be an eminent person of high moral standing who possesses a demonstrated commitment to human rights and the rights of members of national communities. He or she shall be nominated by the President of Kosovo and shall be elected by the Assembly from a list of candidates prepared by the President of the European Court of Human Rights for a non-renewable three-year term. The Ombudsman shall not be a citizen of any State or entity that was a part of the former Yugoslavia, or of any neighboring State. Pending the election of the President and the Assembly, the CIM shall designate a person to serve as Ombudsman on an interim basis who shall be succeeded by a person selected pursuant to the procedure set forth in this paragraph.

3. The Ombudsman shall be independently responsible for choosing his or her own staff. He or she shall have two Deputies. The Deputies shall each be drawn from different national communities.

(a) The salaries and expenses of the Ombudsman and his or her staff shall be determined and paid by the Kosovo Assembly. The salaries and expenses shall be fully adequate to implement the Ombudsman's mandate.

(b) The Ombudsman and members of his or her staff shall not be held criminally or civilly liable for any acts carried out within the scope of their duties.

ARTICLE II: JURISDICTION

The Ombudsman shall consider:

(a) alleged or apparent violations of human rights and fundamental freedoms in Kosovo, as provided in the Constitutions of the Federal Republic of Yugoslavia and the Republic of Serbia, and the European Convention for the Protection of Human Rights and Fundamental Freedoms and the Protocols thereto; and

(b) alleged or apparent violations of the rights of members of national communities specified in this Agreement.

2. All persons in Kosovo shall have the right to submit complaints to the Ombudsman. The Parties agree not to take any measures to punish persons who intend to submit or who have submitted such allegations, or in any other way to deter the exercise of this right.

ARTICLE III: POWERS AND DUTIES

1. The Ombudsman shall investigate alleged violations falling within the jurisdiction set forth in Article II.1. He or she may act either on his or her own initiative or in response to an allegation presented by any Party or person, non-governmental organization, or group of individuals claiming to be the victim of a violation or acting on behalf of alleged victims who are deceased or missing. The work of the Ombudsman shall be free of charge to the person concerned.

2. The Ombudsman shall have complete, unimpeded, and immediate access to any person, place, or information upon his or her request.

(a) The Ombudsman shall have access to and may examine all official documents, and he or she can require any person, including officials of Kosovo, to cooperate by providing relevant information, documents, and files.

(b) The Ombudsman may attend administrative hearings and meetings of other Kosovo institutions in order to gather information.

(c) The Ombudsman may examine facilities and places where persons deprived of their liberty are detained, work, or are otherwise located.

(d) The Ombudsman and staff shall maintain the confidentiality of all confidential information obtained by them, unless the Ombudsman determines that such information is evidence of a violation of rights falling within his or her jurisdiction, in which case that information may be revealed in public reports or appropriate legal proceedings.

(e) The Parties undertake to ensure cooperation with the ombudsman's investigations. Willful and knowing failure to comply shall be a criminal offense prosecutable in any Jurisdiction of the Parties. Where an official impedes an investigation by refusing to provide necessary information, the Ombudsman shall contact that officials superior or the public prosecutor for appropriate penal action to be taken in accordance with the law.

3. The Ombudsman shall issue findings and conclusions in the form of a published report promptly after concluding an investigation.

(a) A Party, institution, or official identified by the Ombudsman as a violator shall, within a period specified by the Ombudsman, explain in writing how it will comply with any prescriptions the Ombudsman may put forth for remedial measures.

(b) In the event that a person or entity does not comply with the conclusions and recommendations of the Ombudsman, the report shall be forwarded for further action to the Joint Commission established by Chapter 5 of this Agreement, to the President of the appropriate Party, and to any other officials or institutions that the Ombudsman deems proper.

Chapter 7: Implementation II
ARTICLE I: GENERAL OBLIGATIONS

1. The Parties undertake to recreate, as quickly as possible, normal conditions of life in Kosovo and to co-operate fully with each other and with all international organizations, agencies, and non-governmental organizations involved in the implementation of this Agreement. They welcome the willingness of the international community to send to the region a force to assist in the implementation of this Agreement.

a. The United Nations Security Council is invited to pass a resolution under Chapter VII of the Charter endorsing and adopting the arrangements set forth in this Chapter, including the establishment of a multinational military implementation force in Kosovo. The Parties invite NATO to constitute and lead a military force to help ensure compliance with the provisions of this Chapter. They also reaffirm the sovereignty and territorial integrity of the Federal Republic of Yugoslavia (FRY).

b. The Parties agree that NATO will establish and deploy a force (hereinafter IIKFORII) which may be composed of ground, air, and maritime units from NATO and non-NATO nations, operating under the authority and subject to the direction and the political control of the North Atlantic Council (NAC) through the NATO chain of command. The Parties agree to facilitate the deployment and operations of this force and agree also to comply fully with all the obligations of this Chapter.

c. it is agreed that other States may assist in implementing this Chapter. The Parties agree that the modalities of those States' participation will be the subject of agreement between such participating States and NATO.

2. The purposes of these obligations are as follows:

a. to establish a durable cessation of hostilities.

Other than those Forces provided for in this Chapter, under no circumstances shall any armed Forces enter, reenter, or remain within Kosovo without the prior express consent of the KFOR Commander (COMKFOR). For the purposes of this Chapter, the term "Forces" includes all personnel and organizations with military capability, including regular army, armed civilian groups, paramilitary groups, air forces, national guards, border police, army reserves, military police, intelligence services, Ministry of Internal Affairs, Local, Special, Riot and Anti-Terrorist Police, and any other groups or individuals so designated by COMKFOP. The only exception to the provisions of this paragraph is for civilian police engaged in hot pursuit of a person suspected of committing a serious criminal offense, as provided for in Chapter 2;

b. to provide for the support and authorization of the KFOR and in particular to authorize the KFOR to take such actions as are required, including the use of necessary force, to ensure compliance with this Chapter and the protection of the KFOR, Implementation Mission (IM), and other international organizations, agencies, and non- governmental organizations involved in the implementation of this Agreement, and to contribute to a secure environment;

c. to provide, at no cost, the use of all facilities and services required for the deployment, operations and support of the KFOR.

3. The Parties understand and agree that the obligations undertaken in this Chapter shall apply equally to each Party. Each Party shall be held individually responsible for compliance with its obligations, and each agrees that delay or failure to comply by one Party shall not constitute cause for any other Party to fail to carry out its own obligations. All Parties shall be equally subject to such enforcement action by the KFOR as may be necessary to ensure implementation of this Chapter in Kosovo and the protection of the KFOR, IM, and other international organizations, agencies, and non-governmental organizations involved in the implementation of this Agreement.

ARTICLE II: CESSATION OF HOSTILITIES

1. The Parties shall, immediately upon entry into force of this Agreement (EIF), refrain from committing any hostile or provocative acts of any type against each other or against any person in Kosovo. They shall not encourage or organize hostile or provocative demonstrations.

2. In carrying out the obligations set forth in paragraph 1, the Parties undertake in particular to cease the firing of all weapons and explosive devices except as authorized by COMKFOR. They shall not place any mines, barriers, unauthorized checkpoints, observation posts (with the exception of COMKFOR-approved border observation posts and crossing points), or protective obstacles. Except as provided in Chapter 2, the Parties shall not engage in any military, security, or training-related activities, including ground, air, or air defense operations, in or over Kosovo, without the prior express approval of COMKFOR.

3. Except for Border Guard forces (as provided for in Article IV), no Party shall have Forces present within a 5 kilometer zone inward from the international border of the FRY that is also the border of Kosovo (hereinafter "the Border Zone"). The Border Zone will be marked on the ground by EIF + 14 days by VJ Border Guard personnel in accordance with direction from IM. COMKFOR may determine small scale reconfigurations for operational reasons.

4. a. With the exception of civilian police performing normal police duties as determined by the CIM, no Party shall have Forces present within 5 kilometers of the Kosovo side of the boundary of Kosovo with other parts of the FRY.

b. The presence of any Forces within 5 kilometers of the other side of that boundary shall be notified to COMKFOR; if, in the judgment of COMKFOR, such presence threatens or would threaten implementation of this Chapter in Kosovo, he shall contact the authorities responsible for the Forces in question and may require those Forces to withdraw from or remain outside that area.

5. No Party shall conduct any reprisals, counter-attacks, or any unilateral actions in response to violations of this Chapter by another Party. The Parties shall respond to alleged violations of this Chapter through the procedures provided in Article XI.

ARTICLE III: REDEPLOVMENT, WITHDRAWAL, AND DEMILITARIZATION OF FORCES

In order to disengage their Forces and to avoid any further conflict, the Parties shall immediately upon EIF begin to re-deploy, withdraw, or demilitarize their Forces in accordance with Articles IV, V, and VI.

ARTICLE IV: VJ FORCES

1. VJ Army Units

a. By K-Day + 5 days, all VJ Army units in Kosovo (with the exception of those Forces specified in paragraph 2 of this Article) shall have completed redeployment to the approved cantonment sites listed at Appendix A to this Chapter. The senior vi commander in Kosovo shall confirm in writing to COMKFOR by K-Day + 5 days that the VJ is in compliance and provide the information required in Article VII below to take account of withdrawals or other changes made during the redeployment. This information shall be updated weekly.

b. By K-Day + 30 days, the Chief of the VJ General Staff, through the senior VJ commander in Kosovo, shall provide for approval by

COMKFOR a detailed plan for the phased withdrawal of Vi Forces from Kosovo to other locations in Serbia to ensure the following timelines are met:

1) By K-Day + 90 days, VJ authorities must, to the satisfaction of COMKFOR, withdraw from Kosovo to other locations in Serbia 50% of men and materiel and all designated offensive assets. Such assets are taken to be: main battle tanks; all other armored vehicles mounting weapons greater than 12.7mm; and, all heavy weapons (vehicle mounted or not) of over 82mm.

2) By K-Day + 180 days, all VJ Army personnel and equipment (with the exception of those Forces specified in paragraph 2 of this Article) shall be withdrawn from Kosovo to other locations in Serbia.

2. VJ Border Guard Forces

a. VJ Border Guard forces shall be permitted but limited to a structure of 1500 members at pre-February 1998 Border Guard Battalion facilities located in Djakovica, Prizren, and Urosevac and subordinate facilities within the 5 kilometer Border Zone, or at a limited number of existing facilities in the immediate proximity of the Border Zone subject to the prior approval of COMKFOR, with that number to be reached by K-Day + 14 days. An additional number of VJ personnel - totaling no more than 1000 C2 and logistics forces - will be permitted to remain in the approved cantonment sites listed at Appendix A to fulfill brigade-level functions related only to border security. After an initial 90 day period from K-Day, COMKFOR may at any time review the deployments of VJ personnel and may require further adjustments to force levels, with the objective of reaching the minimum force structure required for legitimate border security, as the security situation and the conduct of the Parties warrant.

b. VJ elements in Kosovo shall be limited to weapons of 82mm and below. They shall possess neither armored vehicles (other than wheeled vehicles mounting weapons of 12.7mm or less) nor air defense weapons.

c. VJ Border Guard units shall be permitted to patrol in Kosovo only within the Border Zone and solely for the purpose of defending the border against external attack and maintaining its integrity by preventing illicit border crossings. Geographic terrain considerations may require Border Guard maneuver inward of the Border Zone; any such maneuver shall be coordinated with and approved by COMKFOR.

d. With the exception of the Border Zone, VJ units may travel through Kosovo only to reach duty stations and garrisons in the Border Zone or approved cantonment sites. Such travel may only be along routes and in accordance with procedures that have been determined by COMKFOR after consultation with the CIM, VJ unit commanders, communal government authorities, and police commanders. These routes and procedures will be determined by K-Day + 14 days, subject to re- determination by COMKFOR at any time. VJ forces in Kosovo but outside the Border Zone shall be permitted to act only in self-defense in response to a hostile act pursuant to Rules of Engagement (ROE) which will be approved by COMKFOR in consultation with the CIM. When deployed in the Border Zone, they will act in accordance with ROE established under control of COMKFOR.

e. VJ Border Guard forces may conduct training activities only within the S kilometer Border Zone, and only with the prior express approval of COMKFOR.

3. Yugoslav Air and Air Defense Forces (YAADF)

All aircraft, radars, surface-to-air missiles (including man-portable air defense systems (MANPADS) and anti-aircraft artillery in Kosovo shall immediately upon EIF begin withdrawing from Kosovo to other locations in Serbia outside the 25 kilometer Mutual Safety Zone as defined in Article X. This withdrawal shall be completed and reported by the senior VJ commander in Kosovo to the appropriate NATO commander not more than 10 days after EIF.

The appropriate NATO commander shall control and coordinate use of airspace over Kosovo commencing at EIF as further specified in Article X. No air defense systems, target tracking radars, or anti-aircraft artillery shall be positioned or operated within Kosovo or the 25 kilometer Mutual Safety Zone without the prior express approval of the appropriate NATO commander.

ARTICLE V: OTHER FORCES

1. The actions of Forces in Kosovo other than KFOR, VJ, MUP, or local police forces provided for in Chapter 2 (hereinafter referred to as "Other Forces") shall be in accordance with this Article. Upon EIF, all Other Forces in Kosovo must immediately observe the provisions of Article I, paragraph 2, Article II, paragraph 1, and Article III and "in addition refrain from all hostile intent, military training and formations, organization of demonstrations, and any movement in either direction or smuggling across international borders or the boundary between Kosovo and other parts of the FRY. Furthermore, upon EIF, all Other Forces in Kosovo must publicly commit themselves to demilitarize on terms to be determined by COMKFOR, renounce violence, guarantee security of international personnel, and respect the international borders of the FRY and all terms of this Chapter.

2. Except as approved by COMKFOR, from K-Day, all other Forces in Kosovo must not carry weapons:

a. within 1 kilometer of VJ and MUP cantonments listed at Appendix A;

b. within 1 kilometer of the main roads as follows:
1) Pec - Lapusnik - Pristina
2) border - Djakovica - Klina
3) border - Prizren - Suva Rika - Pristina
4) Djakovica - Orahovac - Lapusnik - Pristina
5) Pec-Djakovica - Prizren - Urosevac - border
6) border - Urosevac - Pristina - Podujevo - border
7) Pristina - Kosovska Mitrovica - border
8) Kosovka Mitrovica - (Rakos) - Pec
9) Pec - Border with Montenegro (through Pozaj)
10) Pristina - Lisica - border with Serbia
11) Pristina - Gnjilane - Urosevac
12) Gnjilane - Veliki Trnovac - border with Serbia;
13) Prizren - Doganovic

c. within 1 kilometer of the Border Zone;

d. in any other areas designated by COMKFOR.

3. By K-Day + 5 days, all Other Forces must abandon and close all fighting positions, entrenchments, and checkpoints.

4. By K-Day + 5 days, all Other Forces' commanders designated by COMKFOR shall report completion of the above requirements in the format at Article VII to COMKFOR and continue to provide weekly detailed status reports until demilitarization is complete.

5. COMKFOR will establish procedures for demilitarization and monitoring of Other Forces in Kosovo and for the further regulation of their activities. These procedures will be established to facilitate a phased demilitarization program as follows:

a. By K-Day + 5 days, all Other Forces shall establish secure weapons storage sites, which shall be registered with and verified by the KFOR;

b. By K-Day + 30 days, all other Forces shall store all prohibited weapons (any weapon 12.7mm or larger, any anti-tank or anti-aircraft weapons, grenades, mines or explosives) and automatic weapons in the registered weapons storage sites. Other Forces commanders shall confirm completion of weapons storage to COMKFOR no later than K-Day + 30 days;

c. By K-Day + 30 days, all Other Forces shall cease wearing military uniforms and insignia, and cease carrying prohibited weapons and automatic weapons;

d. By K-Day + 90 days, authority for storage sites shall pass to the KFOR. After this date, it shall be illegal for Other Forces to possess prohibited weapons and automatic weapons, and such weapons shall be subject to confiscation by the KFOR;

e. By K-Day + 120 days, demilitarization of all Other Forces shall be completed.

6. By EIF + 30 days, subject to arrangements by COMKFOR if necessary, all Other Forces personnel who are not of local origin, whether or not they are legally within Kosovo, including individual advisors, freedom fighters, trainers, volunteers, and personnel from neighboring and other States, shall be withdrawn from Kosovo.

ARTICLE VI: MUP

1. Ministry of Interior Police (MUP) is defined as all police and public security units and personnel under the control of Federal or Republic authorities except for the border police referred to in Chapter 2 and police academy students and personnel at the training school in Vucitrn referred to in Chapter 2. The CIM, in consultation with COMKFOR, shall have the discretion to exempt any public security units from this definition if he determines that it is in the public interest (e.g. firefighters).

a. By K-Day + 5 days, all MUP units in Kosovo (with the exception of the border police referred to in Chapter 2) shall have completed redeployment to the approved cantonment sites listed at Appendix A to this Chapter or to garrisons outside Kosovo. The senior MUP commander in Kosovo or his representative shall confirm in writing by K-Day + 5 days to COMKFOR and the CIM that the MUP is in compliance and update the information required in Article VII to take account of withdrawals or other changes made during the redeployment. This information shall be updated weekly. Resumption of normal communal police patrolling will be permitted under the supervision and control of the IM and as specifically approved by the CIM in consultation with COMKFOR, and will be contingent on compliance with the terms of this Agreement.

b. Immediately upon EIF, the following withdrawals shall begin:

1) By K-Day + 5 days, those MUP units not assigned to Kosovo prior to 1 February 1998 shall withdraw all personnel and equipment from Kosovo to other locations in Serbia.

2) By K-Day + 20 days, all Special Police, including PJP, SAJ, and JSO forces, and their equipment shall be withdrawn from their cantonment sites out of Kosovo to other locations in Serbia. Additionally, all MUP offensive assets (designated as armored vehicles mounting weapons 12.7mm or larger, and all heavy weapons (vehicle mounted or not) of over 82mm) shall be withdrawn.

c. By K-Day + 30 days, the senior MUP commander shall provide for approval by COMKFOR, in consultation with the CIM, a detailed plan for the phased drawdown of the remainder of MUP forces. In the event that COMKFOR, in consultation with the CIM, does not approve the plan, he has the authority to issue his own binding plan for further MUP drawdowns. The CIM will decide at the same time when the remaining MUP units will wear new insignia. In any case, the following time-table must be met:

1) by K-Day + 60 days, 50% drawdown of the remaining MUP units including reservists. The CIM after consultations with COMKFOR shall have the discretion to extend this deadline for up to K-Day + 90 days if he judges there to be a risk of a law enforcement vacuum;

2) by K-Day + 120 days, further drawdown to 2500 MUP. The CIM after consultations with COMKFOR shall have the discretion to extend this deadline for up to K-Day + 180 days to meet operational needs;

3) transition to communal police force shall begin as Kosovar police are trained and able to assume their duties. The CIM shall organize this transition between MUP and communal police;

4) in any event, by EIF + one year, all Ministry of Interior Civil Police shall be drawn down to zero. The CIM shall have the discretion to extend this deadline for up to an additional 12 months to meet operational needs.

d. The 2500 MUP allowed by this Chapter and referred to in Article V.1(a) of Chapter 2 shall have authority only for civil police functions and be under the supervision and control of the CIM.

ARTICLE VII: NOTIFICATIONS

1. By K-Day + 5 days, the Parties shall furnish the following specific information regarding the status of all conventional military; all police, including military police, Department of Public Security Police, special police; paramilitary; and all Other Forces in Kosovo, and shall update the COMKFOR weekly on changes in this information:

a. location, disposition, and strengths of all military and special police units referred to above;

b. quantity and type of weaponry of 12.7 mm and above, and ammunition for such weaponry, including location of cantonments and supply depots and storage sites;

c. positions and descriptions of any surface-to-air missiles/launchers, including mobile systems, anti-aircraft artillery, supporting radars, and associated command and control systems;

d. positions and descriptions of all mines, unexploded ordnance, explosive devices, demolitions, obstacles, booby traps, wire entanglements, physical or military hazards to the safe movement of any personnel in Kosovo, weapons systems, vehicles, or any other military equipment; and

e. any further information of a military or security nature requested by the COMKFOR.

ARTICLE VIII: OPERATIONS AND AUTHORITY OF THE KFOR

1. Consistent with the general obligations of Article I, the Parties understand and agree that the KFOR will deploy and operate without hindrance and with the authority to take all necessary action to help ensure compliance with this Chapter.

2. The Parties understand and agree that the KFOR shall have the right:

a. to monitor and help ensure compliance by all Parties with this Chapter and to respond promptly to any violations and restore compliance, using military force if required. This includes necessary action to:

1) enforce VJ and MUP reductions;

2) enforce demilitarization of Other Forces;

3) enforce restrictions on all VJ, MUP and Other Forces' activities, movement and training in Kosovo;

b. to establish liaison arrangements with IM, and support IM as appropriate;

c. to establish liaison arrangements with local Kosovo authorities, with Other Forces, and with FRY and Serbian civil and military authorities;

d. to observe, monitor, and inspect any and all facilities or activities in Kosovo, including within the Border Zone, that the COMKFOR believes has or may have military capability, or are or may be associated with the employment of military or police capabilities, or are otherwise relevant to compliance with this Chapter;

e. to require the Parties to mark and clear minefields and obstacles and to monitor their performance;

f. to require the Parties to participate in the Joint Military Commission and its subordinate military commissions as described in Article XI.

3. The Parties understand and agree that the KFOR shall have the right to fulfill its supporting tasks, within the limits of its assigned principal tasks, its capabilities, and available resources, and as directed by the NAC, which include the following:

a. to help create secure conditions for the conduct by others of other tasks associated with this Agreement, including free and fair elections;

b. to assist the movement of organizations in the accomplishment of humanitarian missions;

c. to assist international agencies in fulfilling their responsibilities in Kosovo;

d. to observe and prevent interference with the movement of civilian populations, refugees, and displaced persons, and to respond appropriately to deliberate threat to life and person.

4. The Parties understand and agree that further directives from the NAC may establish additional duties and responsibilities for the KFOR in implementing this Chapter.

5. KFOR operations shall be governed by the following provisions:

a. KFOR and its personnel shall have the legal status, rights, and obligations specified in Appendix 13 to this Chapter;

b. The KFOR shall have the right to use all necessary means to ensure its full ability to communicate and shall have the right to the unrestricted use of the entire electromagnetic spectrum. In implementing this right, the KFOR shall make reasonable efforts to coordinate with the appropriate authorities of the Parties;

c. The KFOR shall have the right to control and regulate surface traffic throughout Kosovo including the movement of the Forces of the Parties. All military training activities and movements in Kosovo must be authorized in advance by COMKFOR;

d. The KFOR shall have complete and unimpeded freedom of movement by ground, air, and water into and throughout Kosovo. It shall in Kosovo have the right to bivouac, maneuver, billet, and utilize any areas or facilities to carry out its responsibilities as required for its support, training, and operations, with such advance notice as may be practicable. Neither the KFOR nor any of its personnel shall be liable for any damages to public or private property that they may cause in the course of duties related to the implementation of this Chapter. Roadblocks, checkpoints, or other impediments to KFOR freedom of movement shall constitute a breach of this Chapter and the violating Party shall be subject to military action by the KFOR, including the use of necessary force to ensure compliance with this Chapter.

6. The Parties understand and agree that COMKFOR shall have the authority, without interference or permission of any Party, to do all that he judges necessary and proper, including the use of military force, to protect the KFOR and the IM, and to carry out the responsibilities listed in this Chapter. The Parties shall comply in all respects with KFOR instructions and requirements.

7. Notwithstanding any other provisions of this Chapter, the Parties understand and agree that OMKFOR has the right and is authorized to compel the removal, withdrawal, or relocation of specific Forces and weapons, and to order the cessation of any activities whenever the COMKFOR determines such Forces, weapons, or activities to constitute a threat or potential threat to either the KFOR or its mission, or to another Party. Forces failing to redeploy, withdraw, relocate, or to cease threatening or potentially threatening activities following such a demand by the KFOR shall be subject to military action by the KFOR, including the use of necessary force, to ensure compliance, consistent with the terms set forth in Article I, paragraph 3.

ARTICLE IX: BORDER CONTROL

The Parties understand and agree that, until other arrangements are established, and subject to provisions of this Chapter and Chapter 2, controls along the international border of the FRY that is also the border of Kosovo will be maintained by the existing institutions normally assigned to such tasks, subject to supervision by the KFOR and the IM, which shall have the right to review and approve all personnel and units, to monitor their performance, and to remove and replace any personnel for behavior inconsistent with this Chapter.

ARTICLE X: CONTROL OF AIR MOVEMENTS

The appropriate NATO commander shall have sole authority to establish-rules and procedures governing command and control of the airspace over Kosovo as well as within a 25 kilometer Mutual Safety Zone (MSZ). This MSZ shall consist of FRY airspace within 25 kilometers outward from the boundary of Kosovo with other parts of the FRY. This Chapter supersedes the NATO Kosovo Verification Mission Agreement of October 12, 1998 on any matter or area in which they may contradict each other. No military air traffic, fixed or rotary wing, of any Party shall be permitted to fly over Kosovo or in the MSZ without the prior express approval of the appropriate NATO commander. Violations of any of the provisions above, including the appropriate NATO commander's rules and procedures governing the airspace over Kosovo, as well as unauthorized flight or activation of FRY Integrated Air Defense within the MSZ, shall be subject to military action by the KFOR, including the use of necessary force. The KFOR shall have a liaison team at the FRY Air Force HQ and a YAADF liaison shall be established with the KFOR. The Parties understand and agree that the appropriate NATO commander may delegate control of normal civilian air activities to appropriate FRY institutions to monitor operations, deconflict KFOR air traffic movements, and ensure smooth and safe operation of the air traffic system.

ARTICLE XI: ESTABLISHMENT OF A JOINT MILITARY COMMISSION

1. A Joint Military Commission (JMC) shall be established with the deployment of the KFOR to Kosovo.

2. The JMC shall be chaired by COMKFOR or his representative and consist of the following members:

a. the senior Yugoslav military commander of the Forces of the FRY or his representative;

b. the Ministers of Interior of the FRY and Republic of Serbia or their representatives;

c. a senior military representative of all other Forces;

d. a representative of the IM;

e. other persons as COMKFOR shall determine, including one or more representatives of the Kosovo civilian leadership.

3. The JMC shall:

a. serve as the central body for all Parties to address any military complaints, questions, or problems that require resolution by the COMKFOR, such as allegations of cease-fire violations or other allegations of non-compliance with this Chapter;

b. receive reports and make recommendations for specific actions to COMKFOR to ensure compliance by the Parties with the provisions of this Chapter;

c. assist COMKFOR in determining and implementing local transparency measures between the Parties.

4. The JMC shall not include any persons publicly indicted by the International Criminal Tribunal for the Former Yugoslavia.

5. The JMC shall function as a consultative body to advise COMKFOR. However, all final decisions shall be made by COMKFOR and shall be binding on the Parties.

6. The JMC shall meet at the call of COMKFOR. Any Party may request COMKFOR to convene a meeting.

7. The JMC shall establish subordinate military commissions for the purpose of providing assistance in carrying out the functions described above. Such commissions shall be at an appropriate level, as COMKFOR shall direct. Composition of such commissions shall be determined by COMKFOR.

ARTICLE XII: PRISONER RELEASE

1. By EIF + 21 days, the Parties shall release and transfer, in accordance with international humanitarian standards, all persons held in connection with the conflict (hereinafter "prisoners"). In addition, the Parties shall cooperate fully with the International Committee of the Red Cross (ICRC) to facilitate its work, in accordance with its mandate, to implement and monitor a plan for the release and transfer of prisoners in accordance with the above deadline. In preparation for compliance with this requirement, the Parties shall:

a. grant the ICRC full access to all persons, irrespective of their status, who are being held by them in connection with the conflict, for visits in accordance with the ICRC's standard operating procedures;

b. provide to the ICRC any and all information concerning prisoners, as requested by the ICRC, by EIF + 14 days.

2. The Parties shall provide information, through the tracing mechanisms of the ICRC, to the families of all persons who are unaccounted for. The Parties shall cooperate fully with the ICRC in its efforts to determine the identity, whereabouts, and fate of those unaccounted for.

ARTICLE XIII: COOPERATION

The Parties shall cooperate fully with all entities involved in implementation of this settlement, as described in the Framework Agreement, or which are otherwise authorized by the United Nations Security Council, including the International Criminal Tribunal for the former Yugoslavia.

ARTICLE XIV: NOTIFICATION TO MILITARY COMMANDS

Each Party shall ensure that the terms of this Chapter and written orders requiring compliance are immediately communicated to all of its Forces.

ARTICLE XV: FINAL AUTHORITY TO INTERPRET

1. Subject to paragraph 2, the KFOR Commander is the final authority in theater regarding interpretation of this Chapter and his determinations are binding on all Parties and persons.

2. The CIM is the final authority in theater regarding interpretation of the references in this Chapter to his functions (directing the VJ Border Guards under Article II, paragraph 3; his functions concerning the MUP under Article VI) and his determinations are binding on all Parties and persons.

ARTICLE XVI: K-DAY

The date of activation of KFOR - to be known as K-Day - shall be determined by NATO.

Appendix A: Approved VJ/MUP Cantonment Sites

1. There are 13 approved cantonment sites in Kosovo for all VJ units, weapons, equipment, and ammunition. Movement to cantonment sites, and subsequent withdrawal from Kosovo, will occur in accordance with this Chapter. As the phased withdrawal of VJ units progresses along the timeline as specified in this Chapter, COMKFOR will close selected cantonment sites.

2. Initial approved VJ cantonment sites:
a) Pristina SW 423913NO210819E
b) Pristina Airfield 423412NO210040E
c) Vuctrin North 424936NO20575SE
d) Kosovska Mitrovica 425315NO2OS227E
e) Gnjilane NE 422807NO21284SE
f) Urosevac 422233NO2107S3E
g) Prizren 421315NO204SO4E
h) Djakovica SW 422212NO202530E
i) Pec 4239ION020172SE
j) Pristina Explosive Storage Fac 423636NO211225E
k) Pristina Ammo Depot SW 423518NO205923E
l) Pristina Ammo Depot 510 424211NO211056E
m) Pristina Headquarters facility 423938NO210934E

3. Within each cantonment site, VJ units are required to canton all heavy weapons and vehicles outside of storage facilities.

4. After EIF + 180 days, the remaining 2500 VJ forces dedicated to border security functions provided for in this Agreement will be garrisoned and cantoned at the following locations: Djakovica, Prizren, and Ursoevac; subordinate border posts within the Border Zone; a limited number of existing facilities in the immediate proximity of the Border zone subject to the prior approval of COMKFOR; and headquarters/C2 and logistic support facilities in Pristina.

5. There are 37 approved cantonment sites for all MUP and Special Police force units in Kosovo. There are seven (7) approved regional SUPS. Each of the 37 approved cantonment sites will fall under the administrative control of one of the regional SUPS. Movement to cantonment sites, and subsequent withdrawal of MUP from Kosovo, will occur in accordance with this Chapter.

6. Approved MUP regional SUPs and cantonment sites:
a) Kosovska Mitrovica SUP 42530ON0205200E
1) Kosovska Mitrovica (2 locations)
2) Leposavic
3) Srbica
4) Vucitrn
5) Zubin Potok
b) Pristina SUP 42400ON0211000E
1) Pristina (6 locations)
2) Glogovac
3) Kosovo Polje
4) Lipjan
5) Obilic
6) Podujevo
c) Pec SUP 42390ON0201600E
1) Pec (2 locations)
2) Klina
3) Istok
4) Malisevo
d) Djakovica SUP 42230ON0202600E
1) Djakovica (2 locations)
2) Decani
e) Urosevac SUP 42220ON0211000E
1) Urosevac (2 locations)
2) Stimlje
3) Strpce
4) Kacanik
f) Gnjilane SUP 42280ON0212900E
1) Gnjilane (2 locations)
2) Kamenica
3) Vitina
4) Kosovska
5) Novo Brdo
g) Prizren SUP 42130ON0204500E
1) Prizren (2 locations)
2) Orahovac
3) Suva Reka
4) Gora

7. Within each cantonment site, MUP units are required to canton all vehicles above 6 tons, including APCs and BOVs, and all heavy weapons outside of storage facilities.

8. KFOR will have the exclusive right to inspect any cantonment site or any other location, at any time, without interference from any Party.

Appendix B: Status of Multi-National Military Implementation Force

1. For the purposes of this Appendix, the following expressions shall have the meanings hereunder assigned to them:

a. "NATO" means the North Atlantic Treaty Organization (NATO), its subsidiary bodies, its military Headquarters, the NATO-led KFOR, and any elements/units forming any part of KFOR or supporting KFOR, whether or not they are from a NATO member country and whether or not they are under NATO or national command and control, when acting in furtherance of this Agreement.

b. "Authorities in the FRY" means appropriate authorities, whether Federal, Republic, Kosovo or other.

c. "NATO personnel" means the military, civilian, and contractor personnel assigned or attached to or employed by NATO, including the military, civilian, and contractor personnel from non-NATO states participating in the Operation, with the exception of personnel locally hired.

d. "the Operation" means the support, implementation, preparation, and participation by NATO and NATO personnel in furtherance of this Chapter.

e. "Military Headquarters" means any entity, whatever its denomination, consisting of or constituted in part by NATO military personnel established in order to fulfill the Operation.

f. "Authorities" means the appropriate responsible individual, agency, or organization of the Parties.

g. "Contractor personnel" means the technical experts or functional specialists whose services are required by NATO and who are in the territory of the FRY exclusively to serve NATO either in an advisory capacity in technical matters, or for the setting up, operation, or maintenance of equipment, unless they are:

(1) nationals of the FRY; or

(2) persons ordinarily resident in the FRY.

h. "Official use" means any use of goods purchased, or of the services received and intended for the performance of any function as required by the operation of the Headquarters.

i. "Facilities" means all buildings, structures, premises, and land required for conducting the operational, training, and administrative activities by NATO for the Operation as well as for accommodation-of NATO personnel.

2. Without prejudice to their privileges and immunities under this Appendix, all NATO personnel shall respect the laws applicable in the FRY, whether Federal, Republic, Kosovo, or other, insofar as compliance with those laws is compatible with the entrusted tasks/mandate and shall refrain from activities not compatible with the nature of the Operation.

3. The Parties recognize the need for expeditious departure and entry procedures for NATO personnel. Such personnel shall be exempt from passport and visa regulations and the registration requirements applicable to aliens. At all entry and exit points to/from the FRY, NATO personnel shall be permitted to enter/exit the FRY on production of a national identification (ID) card. NATO personnel shall carry identification which they may be requested to produce for the authorities in the FRY, but operations, training, and movement shall not be allowed to be impeded or delayed by such requests.

4. NATO military personnel shall normally wear uniforms, and NATO personnel may possess and carry arms if authorized to do so by their orders. The Parties shall accept as valid, without tax or fee, drivers, licenses and permits issued to NATO personnel by their respective national authorities.

5. NATO shall be permitted to display the NATO flag and/or national flags of its constituent national elements/units on any NATO uniform, means of transport, or facility.

6. a. NATO shall be immune from all legal process, whether civil, administrative, or criminal.

b. NATO personnel, under all circumstances and at all times, shall be immune from the Parties, jurisdiction in respect of any civil, administrative, criminal, or disciplinary offenses which may be committed by them in the FRY. The Parties shall assist States participating in the operation in the exercise of their jurisdiction over their own nationals.

c. Notwithstanding the above, and with the NATO Commander's express agreement in each case, the authorities in the FRY may exceptionally exercise jurisdiction in such matters, but only in respect of Contractor personnel who are not subject to the jurisdiction of their nation of citizenship.

7. NATO personnel shall be immune from any form of arrest, investigation, or detention by the authorities in the FRY. NATO personnel erroneously arrested or detained shall immediately be turned over to NATO authorities.

8. NATO personnel shall enjoy, together with their vehicles, vessels, aircraft, and equipment, free and unrestricted passage and unimpeded access throughout the FRY including associated airspace and territorial waters. This shall include, but not be limited to, the right of bivouac, maneuver, billet, and utilization of any areas or facilities as required for support, training, and operations.

9. NATO shall be exempt from duties, taxes, and other charges and inspections and custom regulations including providing inventories or other routine customs documentation, for personnel, vehicles, vessels, aircraft, equipment, supplies, and provisions entering, exiting, or transiting the territory of the FRY in support of the Operation.

10. The authorities in the FRY shall facilitate, on a priority basis and with all appropriate means, all movement of personnel, vehicles, vessels, aircraft, equipment, or supplies, through or in the airspace, ports, airports, or roads used. No charges may be assessed against NATO for air navigation, landing, or takeoff of aircraft, whether government-owned or chartered. Similarly, no duties, dues, tolls or charges may be assessed against NATO ships, whether government-owned or chartered, for the mere entry and exit of ports. Vehicles, vessels, and aircraft used in support of the operation shall not be subject to licensing or registration requirements, nor commercial insurance.

11. NATO is granted the use of airports, roads, rails, and ports without payment of fees, duties, dues, tolls, or charges occasioned by mere use. NATO shall not, however, claim exemption from reasonable charges for specific services requested and received, but operations/movement and access shall not be allowed to be impeded pending payment for such services.

12. NATO personnel shall be exempt from taxation by the Parties on the salaries and emoluments received from NATO and on any income received from outside the FRY.

13. NATO personnel and their tangible moveable property imported into, acquired in, or exported from the FRY shall be exempt from all duties, taxes, and other charges and inspections and custom regulations.

14. NATO shall be allowed to import and to export, free of duty, taxes and other charges, such equipment, provisions, and supplies as NATO shall require for the operation, provided such goods are for the official use of NATO or for sale to NATO personnel. Goods sold shall be solely for the use of NATO personnel and not transferable to unauthorized persons.

15. The Parties recognize that the use of communications channels is necessary for the Operation. NATO shall be allowed to operate its own internal mail services. The Parties shall, upon simple request, grant all telecommunications services, including broadcast services, needed for the Operation, as determined by NATO. This shall include the right to utilize such means and services as required to assure full ability to communicate, and the right to use all of the electromagnetic spectrum for this purpose, free of cost. In implementing this right, NATO shall make every reasonable effort to coordinate with and take into account the needs and requirements of appropriate authorities in the FRY.

16. The Parties shall provide, free of cost, such public facilities as NATO shall require to prepare for and execute the Operation. The Parties shall assist NATO in obtaining, at the lowest rate, the necessary utilities, such as electricity, water, gas and other resources, as NATO shall require for the Operation.

17. NATO and NATO personnel shall be immune from claims of any sort which arise out of activities in pursuance of the operation; however, NATO will entertain claims on an ex gratia basis.

18. NATO shall be allowed to contract directly for the acquisition of goods, services, and construction from any source within and outside the FRY. Such contracts, goods, services, and construction shall not be subject to the payment of duties, taxes, or other charges. NATO may also carry out construction works with their own personnel.

19. Commercial undertakings operating in the FRY only in the service of NATO shall be exempt from local laws and regulations with respect to the terms and conditions of their employment and licensing and registration of employees, businesses, and corporations.

20. NATO may hire local personnel who on an individual basis shall remain subject to local laws and regulations with the exception of labor/employment laws. However, local personnel hired by NATO shall:

a. be immune from legal process in respect of words spoken or written and all acts performed by them in their official capacity;

b. be immune from national services and/or national military service obligations;

c. be subject only to employment terms and conditions established by NATO; and

d. be exempt from taxation on the salaries and emoluments paid to them by NATO.

21. In carrying out its authorities under this Chapter, NATO is authorized to detain individuals and, as quickly as possible, turn them over to appropriate officials.

22. NATO may, in the conduct of the Operation, have need to make improvements or modifications to certain infrastructure in the FRY,

such as roads, bridges, tunnels, buildings, and utility systems. Any such improvements or modifications of a non-temporary nature shall become part of and in the same ownership as that infrastructure. Temporary improvements or modifications may be removed at the discretion of the NATO Commander, and the infrastructure returned to as near its original condition as possible, fair wear and tear excepted.

23. Failing any prior settlement, disputes with the regard to the interpretation or application of this Appendix shall be settled between NATO and the appropriate authorities in the FRY.

24. Supplementary arrangements with any of the Parties may be concluded to facilitate any details connected with the Operation.

25. The provisions of this Appendix shall remain in force until completion of the Operation or as the Parties and NATO otherwise agree.

Chapter 8: Amendment, Comprehensive Assessment, and Final Clauses

ARTICLE I: AMENDMENT AND COMPREHENSIVE ASSESSMENT

1. Amendments to this Agreement shall be adopted by agreement of all the Parties, except as otherwise provided by Article X of Chapter 1.

2. Each Party may propose amendments at any time and will consider and consult with the other Parties with regard to proposed amendments.

3. Three years after the entry into force of this Agreement, an international meeting shall be convened to determine a mechanism for a final settlement for Kosovo, on the basis of the will of the people, opinions of relevant authorities, each Party's efforts regarding the implementation of this Agreement, and the Helsinki Final Act, and to undertake a comprehensive assessment of the implementation of this Agreement and to consider proposals by any Party for additional measures.

ARTICLE II: FINAL CLAUSES

1. This Agreement is signed in the English language. After signature of this Agreement, translations will be made into Serbian, Albanian, and other languages of the national communities of Kosovo, and attached to the English text.

2. This Agreement shall enter into force upon signature.
For the Federal Republic of Yugoslavia
For the Republic of Serbia
For Kosovo
Witnessed by:
For the European Union
For the Russian Federation
For the United States of America

142. Contact Group, Rambouillet Accords: Co-Chairmen's Conclusions, Rambouillet, 23 February 1999

1. Contact Group Ministers met in Rambouillet on 23 February at the end of more than two weeks of intensive efforts to reach an agreement on substantial autonomy for Kosovo, while respecting the national sovereignty and territorial integrity of the Federal Republic of Yugoslavia.

2. Ministers noted the historic nature of the Rambouillet Conference, which launched a process on the basis of the principles and basic elements adopted by the Contact Group in London on 29 January, bringing together those long divided by deep and bitter differences.

3. These have been complex and difficult negotiations, as we expected. The important efforts of the parties and the unstinting commitment of our negotiators Ambassadors Hill, Petritsch and Mayorsky, have led to a consensus on substantial autonomy for Kosovo, including on mechanisms for free and fair elections to democratic institutions, for the governance of Kosovo, for the protection of human rights and the rights of members of national communities; and for the establishment of a fair judicial system.

4. A political framework is now in place, as set out in the Rambouillet Accords, and the groundwork has thereby been laid for finalising the implementation Chapters of the Agreement, including the modalities of the invited international civilian and military presence in Kosovo. It is essential that the agreement on the interim accord be completed and signed as a whole. In this spirit, the parties committed themselves to attend a conference, covering all aspects of implementation, in France on 15 March, following consultations with the parties and relevant international organisations. We are determined to monitor closely that this commitment is fully respected, in order to complete the Rambouillet process.

5. The parties must abstain from any action which would undermine the achievements of Rambouillet. In particular, we expect the parties to honour fully and immediately the cease-fire which should be in place throughout Kosovo, to abstain from all provocative actions and to abide fully by their commitments of October 1998 and to comply with the relevant Security Council Resolutions. We fully support the mission and personnel of the OSCE's Kosovo Verification Mission, and we insist that the parties provide for the security of KVM and other international personnel, for which they will be held responsible.

6. We pledge ourselves to work together to achieve a settlement meeting the legitimate aspirations of all the people of Kosovo. Only such a settlement can create the conditions in which a humanitarian catastrophe can be avoided. Those who prevent the completion of the interim agreement for Kosovo, or who provoke further hostilities or who threaten the security of KVM, will be held fully accountable for their actions.

143. UN Security Council's Statement to the Press, Rambouillet, 23 February 1999

Members of the Security Council took note of the conclusions of the co-chairmen of the Rambouillet Conference at the end of the two weeks of intensive efforts aimed at reaching an agreement on substantial autonomy for Kosovo, which respects the national sovereignty and territorial integrity of the FRY. Members of the council noted with satisfaction that, with the Rambouillet Agreements, a political framework for substantial autonomy has been set out. Members of the coucil noted the commitment of the parties to attend a conference covering all aspects of the implementation of these agreements, in France on 15 March. Members of the Council encouraged the parties to work constructively to this end. Members of the Council underlined that it was essential for all the parties to refrain from any action which could jeopardise the achievements of the Rambouillet negotiations, and to fully comply with their commitments of October 1998 and the relevant security council resolutions. Members of the Council will continue to follow closely the situation.

144. UN Secretary-General, Press Release, UN Doc. SG/SM/6902, 23 February 1999

The Secretary-General welcomes the conclusion of negotiations led by the Contact Group in Rambouillet, France, that have led to an agreement on substantial autonomy for Kosovo, while respecting the national sovereignty and territorial integrity of the Federal Republic of Yugoslavia. He is encouraged to note in the Co-Chairmen's conclusions following the talks that they have provided for a political framework, thereby laying the groundwork for finalizing the implementation Chapters of the Agreement, including the modalities of the invited international civilian and military presence in Kosovo. The Secretary-General is pleased that there is a commitment to attend a conference, covering all aspects of implementation, on 15 March, and hopes that it will result in a comprehensive interim agreement. He wishes to congratulate the members of the Contact Group for their persistence and initiative in forging this framework, and trusts that its fulfilment will provide genuine autonomy for the long-suffering people of Kosovo. The Secretary-General strongly supports the appeal made by the Contact Group to the parties to abstain from any actions which could undermine the achievements of Rambouillet, to honour fully and immediately the ceasefire which should be in place throughout Kosovo, to abstain from all provocative actions, to provide for the security of all international personnel, and to abide fully by their commitments of October 1998 and to comply with all relevant Security Council resolutions.

145. EU, Statement of the Presidency on behalf of the European Union on the Conclusion of the Rambouillet Conference, 23 February 1999[1]

The Presidency on behalf of the European Union takes note of the decision of the Contact Group that the parties have time until the 15 March 1999 to sign the agreement negotiated in Rambouillet.

Having settled the basic principles during the Kosovo peace talks in Rabouillet both sides must fully take advantage of their chance to finally conclude the agreement, especially the chapters on implementation, for the benefit of all ethnic communities living in Kosovo. By signing the whole agreement, the possibility now exists for peace and the full observance of the rights of all peoples living in Kosovo. The European Union will hold President Milosevic and the leadership of the Kosovo Albanians personally responsible for a failure of the signature of the agreement. The European Union will take the necessary steps to stop a further escalation of the conflict and it calls upon both sides to refrain from any measures that could endanger the results of Rambouillet.

The Presidency acknowledges in the highest possible manner the considerable accomplishments of the Contact Group, of the Co-chairmen Cook and Védrine, and of the three negotiators: the EU Special Envoy Petritsch, the U.S. Special Envoy Hill, and the Special Envoy of the Russian Federation Majorski.

The signing of the agreement will contribute to the creation of a new beginning for Kosovo and the rest of the FRY and will open a new chapter in the relations between the FRY and the community of European states. The European Union calls upon both sides to seize this last opportunity in order to reach a peaceful regulation of the Kosovo conflict and to avoid the gravest consequences levied by the international community. The European Union has emphasized her willingness to play a substantial role in the reconstruction efforts and in the implementation of the agreement. Based upon the successful inplementation, the sanctions against the FRY for its actions in Kosovo will gradually be lifted.

146. NATO, Statement by the Secretary General, Press Release (99)21, 23 February 1999

NATO welcomes the substantial progress made in the Kosovo Peace Talks in Rambouillet towards a political settlement which will give Kosovo a significant degree of autonomy and help bring stability to the region. However, a final agreement has not yet been reached. I appeal to the parties to accept rapidly the Contact Group Peace Plan in its entirety, including its military aspects, and at the very latest by the time of the implementation conference in France on 15th March.

During the period until the 15th March, NATO expects the parties to work constructively to bring about a peace settlement. In particular they must respect the cease fire, refrain from all provocations and carry out all of the provisions of the UNSC Resolutions on Kosovo. The Federal Republic of Yugoslavia must comply fully with all of its commitments under its agreement of October 25th, 1998 with NATO. The OSCE Kosovo Verification Mission must be allowed to carry out its work and both parties must ensure the safety of its personnel.

NATO will continue to watch the situation on the ground very closely. We are very concerned by the violence in Kosovo in recent days. We remain ready to use whatever means are necessary to bring about a peaceful solution to the crisis in Kosovo and to prevent further human suffering. Those who prevent the achievement of an interim agreement, provoke violent incidents or threaten the security of the Kosovo Verification Mission personnel will be held fully responsible for their actions.

Since the beginning of the crisis, NATO has fully supported the efforts of the international community to bring peace to Kosovo and to help achieve a negotiated political solution. Our stance in putting the threat of force at the service of diplomacy has helped to create the conditions for the Rambouillet talks to make progress. The Alliance remains ready to lead an international military force in Kosovo which would guarantee the implementation of an interim political settlement. I call on both parties to build on the considerable progress that has been achieved at Rambouillet and to seize this opportunity to achieve a lasting settlement for the benefit of all the peoples of the region. NATO stands ready to help them in this endeavour.

147. UK, Statement by the Foreign Secretary, Mr. Robin Cook, House of Commons, 24 February 1999

Madam Speaker, with permission I would like to make a statement on the Kosovo talks.

In my statement three weeks ago I reported that the Contact Group had agreed to summon both sides to negotiations for a political settlement on the basis of the documents tabled by the Contact Group.

Both sides responded to that summons and took part in peace talks held until yesterday at Rambouillet. As co-Chair of the talks, the United Kingdom was fully engaged in brokering agreement between the two parties, and the House will wish to recognise the immense effort put in by officials, some of whom have worked without break and occasionally without sleep. I would record the appreciation of all the British team for the close cooperation of France, both as co-Chair and host of the talks.

At the outset both parties to the talks had a large number of reservations to the Contact Group proposals for the constitution of a self-governing Kosovo. The great majority of them were resolved.

But the Yugoslav delegation still have some difficulties, such as the limited role of the Serbian Courts. The Albanian side are still particularly concerned by the absence of a commitment to a referendum on independence at the end of the three year period.

These problems remain, but nevertheless we obtained consensus from both sides to a democratic, self-governing Kosovo, and agreement to the main elements in the detailed texts on its constitution.

These texts provide for Kosovo its own Assembly, constitution, President, government, taxes, laws, and police and security. They provide a sweeping measure of autonomy for Kosovo, including the right to conduct foreign relations in respect of the areas within the competence of the Kosovar Assembly.

The Constitution also provides full protection for the national communities within Kosovo, including the right of both Serb and Albanian communities to representative bodies to protect and promote their respective language, culture, religion and educational curriculum.

There was broad agreement on both sides to a major international presence in support of the political settlement. Elections to the Assembly, local communes, and community bodies are to be supervised by the OSCE. Both parties agreed to the appointment of an international ombudsman to monitor human rights and fundamental freedoms, and the texts provides for the European Commission to take the lead role in coordinating the economic reconstruction of Kosovo.

The most difficult issue of all was the proposal for an international military presence in Kosovo. The Yugoslav delegation refused to accept that the presence of foreign troops was consistent with their national sovereignty. There were also serious difficulties on the Albanian side, among whom the representatives of the Kosovo Liberation Army found it hard to accept that a condition of an international military force was that they must demilitarise and surrender their weapons.

---

[1] *Unofficial Translation by the editor.*

Throughout the talks I made clear the willingness of Britain to provide ground troops to underpin the interim settlement, but that there could be no question of us or our Allies doing so without a clear commitment to such a cease-fire and to the withdrawal or disarmament on both sides necessary to make it a reality.

Both parties agreed to meet again on March 15th, to discuss all aspects of the implementation of the new constitution of Kosovo, including the civilian and military international presence.

My colleague Hubert Vedrine and I are considering how we can use the interval between now and then to convince the wider public in Kosovo and Serbia that the outcome is a good bargain for both, and the best deal they will have to end the conflict.

I regret to inform the House that violent conflict continues in Kosovo. On Monday there was fighting near Vucitrn. Yesterday there was further fighting at Bukos, in which we know that at least one Serb was killed and five injured. We do not yet have figures for casualties on the Albanian side. Today there have been further exchanges of fire near Suva Reka.

Last night Javier Solana confirmed that NATO expects both sides to respect the cease-fire, and remains ready to use whatever means are necessary in support of it. Yesterday all the NATO members of the Contact Group repeated their support for decisive NATO action if Belgrade makes a disproportionate response or takes violent reprisals against the civilian population. We also hold the Kosovo Liberation Army responsible for their part in maintaining a cease-fire.

Both sides should use the next three weeks to build on the new agreement for peace, not to break down the existing agreement for a cease-fire.

When I spoke to the House last on this issue, I ended by saying that I could not confirm that the talks which we were seeking would take place, nor guarantee that they would succeed.

We were successful in getting both sides to take part in the talks. As a result, we have created a peace process, and the end of the Rambouillet talks is not the end of that process, but only the conclusion of its first phase. Both sides have committed themselves to taking part in its next phase.

I cannot report to the House that we have yet reached complete agreement to the Contact Group texts, but we have secured agreement to the overwhelming majority of them.

That result proves that we were right to try for peace by summoning these talks. But it also demonstrates the extra mile we still have to travel. I can assure the House that we will maintain our pressure on both sides to end the conflict through negotiations.

Neither side is going to end this conflict through military action. Neither side can gain from prolonging it. The longer Belgrade continues to try to resolve the conflict by military repression, the more difficult it makes any final outcome that stops short of independence for Kosovo. And the longer the Kosovo Liberation Army continue to provoke conflict, the more difficult they make it for the international community to stop the bloodshed among their people.

Both sides have recognised the value of the Contact Group proposals. I urge them now to work with us in implementing those proposals, and to turn their commitments on paper into the reality on the ground of a Kosovo free from fear and governed by free elections.

3.4.3 THE PARIS CONFERENCE

148. Kosovo Delegation Letter of Agreement Addressed to the French and British Foreign Ministers, 15 March 1999

Dear Messrs Vedrine and Cook,

After the consultations of the Kosova delegation with political and military factors, as well as with the people of Kosova, concerning the agreement for peace and self-government (dated February 23, 1999) from the Rambouillet meeting, this delegation and I personally say "yes" to this agreement.

We would be honoured to sign the agreement in your presence at a time and place of your choosing.

The agreement creates a chance and a perspective for Kosova and its people.

Our consultations in Kosova were necessary and very important. Now that a positive mood on behalf of the agreement has been created within the political and military structures, the Kosova delegation is able to sign the agreement.

In this success of ours, your contribution as well as the contribution of the administration of your countries was great. The fate of the Albanian people of Kosova is at a historical turning point and the Kosova delegation has a big responsibility. You have shown attention and patience concerning this fact.

Our delegation, and I, are very thankful for this.

We will expect your help, as well as the help of your governments, in the future. The people of Kosova have been and will continue to be allies of your countries, and you can count on this. Kosova needs freedom and democracy. Your personal contribution and that of your countries are essential and respected.

Sincerely, The Kosova delegation Chairman, Hashim Thaci

149. FRY, Agreement for Self-Government in Kosmet, Paris, 18 March 1999

The Signatories to the present Agreement,

Convinced of the need for a peaceful and political solution in Kosmet as a prerequisite for stability and democracy,

Determined to establish a peaceful environment in Kosmet,

Reaffirming their commitment to the Purposes and Principles of the United Nations as well as to the OSCE principles, including the Helsinki Final Act and the Charter of Paris for a new Europe,

Recalling the commitment of the international community to the sovereignty and territorial integrity of the Federal Republic of Yugoslavia,

Recalling the basic elements/principles adopted by the Contact Group at its ministerial meeting in London of January 29, 1999,

Recognizing the need for democratic self-government in Kosmet, including full participation of the members of all national communities in political decision-making,

Desiring to ensure the protection of the human rights of all persons in Kosmet, as well as the rights of the members of all national communities,

Noting that the present Agreement has been concluded under the auspices of the members of the Contact Group and the European Union and undertaking with respect to these members and the European Union to abide by this Agreement,

Aware that full respect for the present Agreement will be central for the development of relations with European institutions,

Have agreed as follows:

Framework
ARTICLE I: PRINCIPLES

1. All citizens in Kosmet shall enjoy, without discrimination, the equal rights and freedoms set forth in this Agreement.

2. National communities and their members shall have additional rights specified in Chapter 1. Kosmet, Federal, and Republic authorities shall not interfere with the exercise of these additional rights. The national communities shall be legally equal as specified herein, and shall not use their additional rights to endanger the rights of other national communities or the rights of citizens, the sovereignty and territorial integrity of the Federal Republic of Yugoslavia, or the functioning of representative democratic government in Kosmet.

3. All authorities in Kosmet shall fully respect human rights, democracy, and the equality of citizens and national communities.

4. Citizens in Kosmet shall have the right to democratic self-government through normative, executive, judicial, and other institutions established in accordance with this Agreement. They shall have the opportunity to be represented in all institutions in Kosmet. The right to democratic self-government shall include the right to participate in free and fair elections.

5. Every person in Kosmet may have access to international institutions for the protection of their rights in accordance with the procedures of such institutions.

6. The Signatories accept that they will act only within their powers and responsibilities in Kosmet as specified by this Agreement. Acts outside those powers and responsibilities shall be null and void. Kosmet shall have all rights and powers set forth herein, including in particular as specified in the Basic Act at Chapter 1.

7. The Signatories agree to cooperate fully with all international organizations working in Kosmet on the implementation of this Agreement.

ARTICLE II. CONFIDENCE BUILDING MEASURES

End of Use of Force

1) Use of force in Kosmet shall cease immediately.

2) The status of police and security forces in Kosmet, shall be governed by the terms of this Agreement. Paramilitary and irregular forces in Kosmet are incompatible with the terms of this Agreement.

Return

3) The Signatories recognize that all persons have the right to return to their homes. Appropriate authorities shall take all measures necessary to facilitate the safe return of persons, including issuing necessary documents under the condition that they are the citizens of the FRY. The Signatories shall take all measures necessary to readmit returning persons to Kosmet.

4) The Signatories shall cooperate fully with all efforts by the United Nations High Commissioner for Refuges (UNHCR) and other international and non-governmental organizations acting under auspices of the UNHCR concerning the repatriation and return of persons, including those organizations' monitoring of the treatment of persons following their return.

Access for International Assistance

5) There shall be no impediments to the normal flow of the goods into Kosmet including materials for the reconstruction of homes and structures.

6) All staff, whether national or international, working with international or non-governmental organizations including with the Yugoslav Red Cross, shall be allowed unrestricted access to the Kosmet population for purposes of international assistance. All persons in Kosmet shall similarly have safe, unhindered, and direct access to the staff of such organizations.

Other Issues

7) The Federal Republic of Yugoslavia shall provide all necessary facilities including frequencies for radio communications, to all humanitarian organizations responsible for delivering aid in Kosmet.

8) All abducted persons or other persons held without charge shall be released. The Signatories shall cooperate fully with the International Committee of the Red Cross (ICRC) to facilitate its work in accordance with its mandate, including ensuring full access to all such persons, irrespective of their status, wherever they might be held, for visits in accordance with the ICRC's standard operating procedures.

1. All Signatories shall provide information, through tracing mechanisms of the ICRC, to families of all persons who are unaccounted for. The Signatories shall cooperate fully with the ICRC and the International Commission on Missing persons in their efforts to determine the identity, whereabouts, and fate of those unaccounted for.

2. Each Signatory:

(a) shall not prosecute anyone for crimes related to the conflict in Kosmet, except for persons accused of crimes against humanity and international law. The Signatories shall grant access to foreign experts (including forensics experts) along with state investigators;

(b) shall grant a general amnesty for all persons already convicted of committing politically motivated crimes related to the conflict in Kosmet. This amnesty shall not apply to those properly convicted of committing crimes against humanity and international law at a fair and open trial conducted pursuant to international standards.

Independent Media

11. Recognizing the importance of free and independent media for the development of a democratic political climate necessary for the reconstruction and development of Kosmet, the parties shall insure the widest possible press freedoms in Kosmet in all media, public and private, including print, television, radio and internet.

Chapter 1: Basic Act

Affirming their belief in a peaceful society, justice, tolerance, and reconciliation,

Resolved to ensure respect for human rights and the equality of all citizens and national communities,

Recognizing that the preservation and promotion of the national, cultural, and linguistic identity of each national community in Kosmet are necessary for the harmonious development of a peaceful society,

Desiring through this Basic Act to establish institutions of democratic self-government in Kosmet grounded in respect for the territorial integrity and sovereignty of the Federal Republic of Yugoslavia and from this Agreement, from which the authorities of governance set forth herein originate,

Recognizing that the institutions of Kosmet should fairly represent the national communities in Kosmet and foster the exercise of their rights and those of their members,

Recalling and endorsing the principles/ basic elements adopted by the Contact group at its ministerial meeting in London on January 29, 1999.

ARTICLE I: PRINCIPLES OF DEMOCRATIC SELF-GOVERNMENT IN KOSOVO

1. Recognizing multi-ethnic character of Kosmet, substantial self-government shall be based on self-government of citizens in Kosmet and self-government of national communities in Kosmet.

2. Respecting the sovereignty and territorial integrity of the Federal Republic of Yugoslavia and of the Republic of Serbia, substantial self-government in Kosmet shall be based on broadest powers and rights of Kosmet organs and national communities in Kosmet. However, federal organs and organs of the Republic of Serbia shall also exercise their powers and rights in Kosmet.

3. All federal laws shall be valid and implemented, in accordance with the Constitution of the FRY, in the entire territory of the FRY, including the territory of Kosmet.

4. All republican laws enacted in accordance with the Constitution of the Republic of Serbia, whose validity and implementation are possible in line with personal principle, shall be valid and implemented in Kosmet for those physical and legal persons who chose to have these

regulations implemented in their case or those laws shall be valid and implemented in the institutions, services and organizations founded by the Republic of Serbia, or whose functioning it regulated or whose work it finances (for example the laws in the field of education, science, culture, health-care, marital and family relations, adoption, tutorship, child and youth care, veterans' and disabled persons' protection, heritage, labour relations, social protection, social insurance and other).

In the fields listed above, the Assembly of Kosmet shall enact its regulations with legal force which shall be valid and implemented for those physical and legal persons in Kosmet who opt for them. They shall also be valid and implemented in the institutions, services and organizations founded by Kosmet, or whose work it regulated or finances.

5. In the fields in which validity and implementation of republican laws are not possible along the personal principle, the Assembly of Kosmet shall enact its regulations with legal effect which will be valid for all physical and legal persons in Kosmet. However, decision-making within each national community shall ensure protection from discrimination or endangering on the basis of nationality (for example, agriculture, environment, protection of plants and animals, hunting and fishing, use and management of land, public information, urban planning and construction, organization and work of the organs of Kosmet, public services of importance for Kosmet and other fields).

6. Each national community may enact separate rules for its members, in order to protect their specific national characteristics, subject to their approval (for example in the field of matrimonial and family relations, adoption, tutorship and heritage).

7. Federal laws, in the entire territory of the FRY, including in Kosmet, in accordance with the Constitution of the FRY, shall be directly enforced by the federal organs through their regional organs (they shall enact enforcement regulations, individual legal acts and carry out administration control and inspection duties);

8. Republican laws, which on the basis of personal principle, are valid and implemented in Kosmet, shall be enforced, as in the entire territory of the Republic of Serbia, including in Kosmet, by republican organs (they shall enact enforcement regulations, individual legal acts, carry out administration control and inspection duties).

9. Provincial regulations with legal effect implemented on the basis of personal principle, as well as provincial regulations with legal effect which are valid and implemented for all physical and legal persons in Kosmet, shall be enforced by the organs of Kosmet (they shall enact enforcement regulations, individual legal acts, carry out administration control and inspection duties).

10. Individual regulations of national communities shall be enforced by the organs of that national community.

11. Kosmet shall govern itself democratically through the normative, executive, judicial, and other organs and institutions specified herein. Organs and institutions of Kosmet shall exercise their authorities consistent with the terms of this Agreement.

12. All authorities in Kosmet shall fully respect human rights, democracy, and the equality of citizens and national communities.

13. The basic territorial unit of local self-government in Kosmet shall be the commune. All responsibilities in Kosmet not expressly assigned elsewhere shall be the responsibility of the communes.

14. To preserve and promote democratic self-government in Kosmet, all candidates for appointed, elective, or other public office, and all office holders, shall meet the following criteria:

All candidates and office holders shall renounce violence as a mechanism for achieving political goals; past political activities shall not be a bar to holding office in Kosmet.

ARTICLE II: THE ASSEMBLY

1. Kosmet shall have an Assembly which shall comprise 130 members. Ninety-five members shall be elected directly by citizens, through the system of proportionate representation. Kosmet shall be one electoral unit and thirty-five shall be elected by the national communities of Albanians, Serbs, Turks, Romanies, Egyptians, Goranies and Muslims, five members each.

The Assembly of Kosmet shall make decisions from its competencies by majority vote of those present and voting, unless otherwise stipulated by this Basic Act.

When the Assembly of Kosovo enacts regulations which are valid and implemented in relation to all physical and legal persons in Kosmet (when no option exists for the regulations of the Republic of Serbia), such regulations shall be enacted by majority vote of those members present and voting. At least three members from the same national community, elected by the national community, may in relation to the proposed regulation initiate a separate procedure for the protection of their vital national interests in the following cases:

- regarding the election of organs of Kosmet and equal representation of all national communities in them;
- regarding resettlement of population;
- regarding impediments to the exercise of rights;
- regarding endangering security;
- regarding worsening of conditions of life;
- regarding the adoption of the Kosmet budget.

In a separate proceeding managed by the President of the Assembly of Kosmet, together with the Vice-Presidents of the Assembly of Kosmet, those proposing the regulations and the representatives of national communities elected by the national community, shall endeavor to eliminate the causes affecting vital national interests. Those taking part in this proceeding have to take account equally of the protection of general interests and vital national interests.

Should this procedure prove to be unsuccessful (within 30 days of its initiation) and the regulation is not enacted, a proposal for its adoption may again be placed on the agenda of the Assembly of Kosmet, if at least six months have elapsed since it was asserted that the causes affecting vital national interests have not been eliminated.

2. The Assembly of Kosmet shall elect President and 6 Vice-Presidents, at least one from each national community, at the proposal of the members elected by national communities, for a four-year term. No one shall be elected as President or Vice-Presidents of the Assembly of Kosmet for more than two terms.

The President and Vice-Presidents shall decide among themselves who will exercise which competency of the President of the Assembly of Kosmet.

The President of the Assembly promulgates the regulations enacted by the Assembly of Kosmet, represents the Assembly of Kosmet, proposes agenda for the meetings of the Assembly of Kosmet and chairs its meetings, holds regular meetings with the President of the National Assembly of Serbia and Presidents of the Chambers of the Federal Assembly, maintains contacts with the organs of national communities, proposes candidates for the President of the Council of Minister, proposes candidates for judges of courts in Kosmet and performs other duties set forth in the Basic Act and other regulations.

Powers of the Assembly

3. The Assembly shall be responsible for enacting decisions and regulations with legal force of Kosmet, including in political, economic, social, educational, scientific and cultural areas as set out bellow and elsewhere in this Agreement.

a) The Assembly shall be responsible for:

(i) Financing activities of Kosmet institutions, including by levying taxes and duties on sources within Kosmet;

(ii) Adopting of budgets of the Administrative organs and other institutions of Kosmet, with the exception of communal and national community institutions unless otherwise specified herein;

(iii) Adopting regulations concerning the organization and procedures of the Administrative organs of Kosmet;

(iv) Approving the list of Ministers of the Council of Ministers, including the Prime Minister;

(v) Coordinating educational arrangements in Kosmet, with respect for the authorities of national communities and Communes;

(vi) Electing candidates for judicial office put forward by the President of Assembly of Kosmet;

(vii) Establishing a framework for local self-government;

(viii) Enacting regulations concerning inter-communal issues and relations between national communities when necessary;

(ix) Enacting regulations regulating the work of medical institutions and hospitals;

(x) Protecting the environment, where intercommunal issues are involved;

(xi) Adopting programs of economic, scientific, technological, demographic, regional, and social development, as well as urban planning;

(xii) Adopting programs for the development of agriculture and of rural areas;

(xiii) Regulating elections;

(xiv) Regulating Kosmet -owned property; and

(xv) Regulating land registries.

(b) The Assembly shall also have authority to enact decisions and regulations with force of law in areas within the responsibility of the Communes if the matter cannot be effectively regulated by the Communes or if regulation by individual Communes might prejudice the rights of other Communes on the basis of the agreement of these communes. In the absence of decisions enacted by the Assembly under this subparagraph that preempts communal action, the Communes shall retain their authority.

ARTICLE III: COUNCIL OF MINISTERS AND ADMINISTRATIVE ORGANS

The Council of Ministers shall perform executive functions. It shall be responsible for the enforcement of the regulations of Kosmet and shall make proposals for their adoption to the Assembly of Kosmet.

The Council of Ministers shall be composed of the President and Ministers. The candidate for the President of the Council of Ministers shall be proposed by the President of the Assembly of Kosmet. The candidate for the President of the Council of Ministers shall make a list of candidates for Ministers making sure that each national community is represented with at least one candidate and shall submit it to the Assembly for adoption. The President of the Council of Ministers cannot be from the same national community as the President of the Assembly of Kosmet. The Council of Ministers shall be elected when it receives majority of the total number of the members of the Assembly of Kosmet, i.e. when it receives majority by representatives of each individual national community.

Administrative Organs shall be responsible for assisting the Council of Ministers in carrying out its duties.

The administration organs of Kosmet shall be responsible for direct implementation of laws and decision-making in administration matters. Public officials working in the administration organs shall be fairly representative of each national community.

ARTICLE IV: COURTS AND ENFORCEMENT

1. The functions of the courts in Kosmet shall be performed by the courts of the Republic of Serbia, Kosmet courts and the courts of national communities.

The courts in Kosmet, except the courts of national communities, shall implement the federal and republican laws, and provincial decisions and regulations with legal force.

2. Citizens and legal persons in Kosmet shall have the right to choose the court which will try their case. Any citizen and legal person in Kosmet may, at the start of court proceedings (litigation, out-of-court proceedings and criminal) as a plaintiff, petitioner or accused, choose to be tried either by the Court of the Republic of Serbia or Kosmet court.

If other participants in the proceedings (defendant or the wronged party) are not members of the same national community as plaintiff or the defendant, they may request that the members of the panel be chosen from their national community. They are also entitled to other rights in the proceedings, specified by the laws on proceedings.

The courts of national communities may be established by those national communities which established the separate rules for the settlement of disputes among the members of that national community, who accepted those rules and who agreed to the competencies of these courts.

3. The Kosmet courts shall be established, organized and their judges and jurors elected by the Assembly of Kosmet. The Kosmet courts shall be established as first instance, second instance and the High Court of Kosmet.

The High Court of Kosmet, in addition to the competencies related to trials according to regular and extraordinary legal means, in a separate permanent council composed of five judges, shall ensure that all regulations enacted by the organs of Kosmet are in line with the Basic Act of Kosmet, as well as that other regulations and general acts of organs of Kosmet are in line with the regulations with legal force enacted by the Assembly of Kosmet. In exercising this authority, this council may revoke any regulation or general act of the organs of Kosmet.

All regulations and general acts of Kosmet enacted from the competencies of the federal and republican organs set forth in the Constitution of the Federal Republic of Yugoslavia and the Constitution of the Republic of Serbia, shall be null and void. The federal and republican laws and other general acts of the federal and republican organs enacted in the fields in which Kosmet enacts regulations with legal force, implemented for all citizens and legal persons in Kosmet, shall be null and void.

4. The function of the Public Prosecutor in Kosmet shall be performed by the Federal, Republican and Kosmet Public Prosecutor. The Federal and republican prosecutor shall act before the republican and Kosmet courts, whereas the Kosmet prosecutor shall act before the Kosmet courts. The establishment, organization and competencies of Kosmet Public Prosecutor shall be specified by the regulation adopted by the Assembly of Kosmet.

5. A citizen in Kosmet who, by legally effective and enforceable ruling of the Court of the Republic of Serbia or the Kosmet court, is sentenced to an unconditional prisonterm in a prison set up by the Republic of Serbia according to enforcement regulations of the Republic of Serbia, if he is convicted by the republican court in the prison set up by the Assembly of Kosmet and according to enforcement regulations enacted by it, if he is sentenced by the Kosmet court.

Local Police

6. In the communes in Kosmet, local police may be established as an organ performing certain police duties in the territory of a commune.

Heads and chiefs of departments of local police shall be appointed by an organ of communal government in charge of internal affairs with the approval of all national communities living in that commune.

Local police shall be representative of the national composition of the residents of the commune.

In communes with mixed population, local police departments shall be set up comprising police officers, members of the same national community. These departments shall carry out the tasks of local police in relation to members of the same national community.

In relation to members of different national communities, the duties of local police shall be jointly performed by local police officers from each department of local police.

7. Local police shall be responsible for preventing smaller violations of public order, investigation and other functions of police related to offences, traffic and patrol activities, fire protection, safety of traffic in local roads, prevention and suppression of offences, recording and controlling residence of citizens, establishment of a unique identification number and issuance of identity cards.

Other duties of police (State security, aliens, borders, serious criminal acts, arms, ammunition, explosives and other hazardous substances, traffic in regional main roads, passports, etc) in the communes where local police has been set up and all police duties in the communes where local police has not been set up, shall be performed by the state police. In larger places with mixed population traffic and patrol duties, in addition to local police, shall be performed by the State police, comprising police officers of different nationalities.

Relations between local and state police shall be based on mutual cooperation and they shall provide information to each other on all issues of importance to the performance of their duties.

8. The members of local police may use, as means of coercion, guns, rubber truncheons, handcuffs and passenger transport vehicles as well as appropriate communications means.

Local police shall be trained in appropriate police schools and its members shall be specifically trained to perform police duties in areas with mixed population.

The commune where local police has been established shall set up a commission to oversee its work. It will be composed of the representatives of all national communities living in the commune.

ARTICLE V: HUMAN RIGHTS AND FUNDAMENTAL FREEDOMS

1. All authorities in Kosmet shall ensure internationally recognized human rights and fundamental freedoms in Kosmet.

2. The rights and freedoms set forth in the European Convention for the Protection of Human Rights and Fundamental Freedoms and its Protocols shall apply directly in Kosmet. Other internationally recognized human rights instruments enacted into its regulations by the Kosmet Assembly shall also apply. These rights and freedoms shall have priority over all other law.

3. All courts, agencies, government institutions, and other public institutions of Kosmet or operating in relation to Kosmet shall conform to these human rights and fundamental freedoms.

ARTICLE VI: NATIONAL COMMUNITIES

1. National communities and their members shall have additional rights as set forth below in order to preserve and express their national, cultural, religious, and linguistic identities in accordance with international standards and the Helsinki Final Act. Such rights shall be exercised in conformity with human rights and fundamental freedoms.

2. Each national community may elect through democratic means institutions to administer its affairs in Kosmet.

3. The additional rights of the national communities are to:

(a) preserve and protect their national, cultural, religious, and linguistic identities, including by:

- inscribing local names of towns and villages, of squares and streets, and of other topographic names in the language and alphabet of the national community in addition to signs in Albanian and Serbian, consistent with decisions about style made by the communal institutions.

- providing information in the language and alphabet of the national community.

- providing for education and establishing educational institutions, in particular for schooling in their own language and alphabet and in national culture and history, for which relevant authorities will provide financial assistance; curricula shall reflect a spirit of tolerance between national communities and respect for the rights of members of all national communities in accordance with international standards.

- enjoying unhindered contacts with representatives of their respective national communities, within the Federal Republic of Yugoslavia and abroad.

- using and displaying national symbols, including symbols of the Federal Republic of Yugoslavia and the Republic of Serbia;

- protecting national traditions on family law by, if the community decides, arranging rules in the field of inheritance, family, and matrimonial relations; tutorship; and adoption.

- the preservation of sites of religious, historical, or cultural importance to the national community, in cooperation with other authorities.

- operating religious institutions in cooperation with religious authorities; and

- participating in regional and international non-governmental organizations in accordance with procedures of these organizations.

- be guaranteed access to, and representation in, public broadcast media, including provisions for separate programming in relevant languages under the direction of those nominated by the respective national community on a fair and equitable basis; and

- finance their activities by collecting contributions the national communities may decide to levy on members of their own communities.

- the right to enjoy unhindered contacts with members of their respective national communities elsewhere in the Federal Republic of Yugoslavia and abroad.

- equal access to employment in public services at all levels.

- the right to use their languages and alphabets.

4. Each national community and, where appropriate, their members acting individually may exercise these additional rights through Federal institutions and institutions of the Republic, in accordance with the procedures of those institutions and without prejudice to the ability of Kosovo institutions to carry out their responsibilities.

5. Every person shall have the right freely to choose to be treated or not to be treated as belonging to a national community, and no disadvantage shall result from that choice or from the exercise of the rights connected to that choice.

ARTICLE VII: COMMUNES

1. Communes shall be units of local self-government.

The Assembly of Kosmet may change the present borders of the existing communes only with their prior consent.

2. Each commune shall have an Assembly, Executive Board and administration authorities. The organs of commune shall be set up in accordance with the principles that the organs of Kosmet have been set up.

3. Through its organs, in accordance with the legal powers of the Assembly of Kosmet, a commune shall be responsible for:

- making development plans, town planning, budget and annual accounts

- regulating and ensuring and development of communal activities;

- regulating and ensuring the use of city construction land and business space;

- taking care of construction, maintenance and use of local roads and streets and other public facilities of communal importance;

- establishing organs, organizations and services for communal needs and regulating their work.

The Assembly of Kosmet may devolve some of the duties from its competencies to a certain commune and transfer the funds to it to carry out that work.

ARTICLE VIII: REPRESENTATION

1. The citizens in Kosmet shall be represented by at least 10 representatives in the Chamber of Citizens of the Federal Assembly and at least 20 representatives in the National Assembly of the Republic of Serbia.

2. At least one citizen in Kosmet shall be elected to the Federal Government and to the Government of the Republic of Serbia.

3. At least one citizen in Kosmet shall be elected as judge of the Federal Court and three judges in the Supreme Court of Serbia.

ARTICLE IX: AMENDMENT

1. The Assembly may by a majority of two-thirds of its members, which majority must include a majority of the Members elected by the national community, adopt amendments to this Basic Act.

ARTICLE X: ENTRY INTO FORCE

This Basic Act shall enter into force upon entering into force of this Agreement.

Chapter 3: Conduct and Supervision of Elections[1]

CENSUS AND THE FIRST PARLIAMENTARY ELECTIONS

1. The competent state authorities shall organize, together with the OSCE, as soon as possible, an objective and free census of the population in Kosmet. The census shall include information on places of residence, citizenship, nationality and other data relevant to the conduct of elections.

2. Free and fair elections for organs of Kosmet shall be held within nine months of the signing of the Agreement on Kosmet, under the supervision of OSCE.

3. The rules for the first elections for the Assembly of Kosmet, communal assemblies in Kosmet, harmonization of candidates on the basis of the OSCE electoral standards, shall be determined by the representatives of all national communities and all political parties in Kosmet.

Chapter 4: Economic Issues

ARTICLE I

1. The economy of Kosmet shall function in accordance with free market principles.

2. The authorities established to levy and collect taxes and other charges are set forth in the Agreement. Except as otherwise expressly provided, all authorities have the right to keep all revenues from their own taxes or other charges consistent with the Agreement.

3. Certain revenue from Kosmet taxes and duties shall accrue to the Communes, taking into account the need for an equalization of revenues between the Communes based on objective criteria. The Assembly of Kosmet shall enact appropriate non-discriminatory regulations for this purpose. The Communes may also levy local taxes in accordance with the Agreement.

4. If expressly required by an international donor or lender, international contracts for reconstruction projects shall be concluded by the authorities of the Federal Republic of Yugoslavia which shall establish appropriate mechanisms to make such funds available to Kosmet authorities. Unless precluded by the terms of contracts, all reconstruction projects that exclusively concern Kosmet shall be managed and implemented by the appropriate Kosmet authority.

Chapter 6: The Ombudsman[2]

ARTICLE I: GENERAL

1. There shall be an Ombudsman, who shall monitor the realization of the rights of members of national communities and the protection of human rights and fundamental freedoms in Kosmet. The Ombudsman shall have unimpeded access to any person or place and shall have the right to appear and intervene before any domestic, Federal, or (consistent with the rules of such bodies) international authority upon his or her request. No person, institution, or entity of the Signatories may interfere with the functions of the Ombudsman.

2. The Ombudsman shall be an eminent person of high moral standing who possesses a demonstrated commitment to human rights and the rights of members of national communities. He or she shall be nominated by the President of the Assembly of Kosmet and shall be elected by the Assembly

3. The Ombudsman shall be independently responsible for choosing his or her own staff. He or she shall have six Deputies. One deputy shall be elected from each national community.

---

[1] The document on the Yugoslav government server did not contain chapter 2.

[2] The document on the Yugoslav government server did not contain chapter 5.

The salaries and expenses of the Ombudsman and his or her staff shall be determined and paid by the Kosovo Assembly. The salaries and expenses shall be fully adequate to implement the Ombudsman's mandate.

The Ombudsman and his or her deputies shall have immunity equal to the immunity of the members of the Assembly.

ARTICLE II: JURISDICTION

1. The Ombudsman shall consider:

(a) alleged or apparent violations of human rights and fundamental freedoms in Kosmet, as provided in the Constitutions of the Federal Republic of Yugoslavia and the Republic of Serbia, and the European Convention for the Protection of Human Rights and Fundamental Freedoms and the Protocols thereto; and

(b) alleged or apparent violations of the rights of members of national communities specified in this Agreement.

2. All persons in Kosmet shall have the right to submit complaints to the Ombudsman. The Signatories agree not to take any measures to punish persons who intend to submit or who have submitted such allegations, or in any other way to deter the exercise of this right.

ARTICLE III: POWERS AND DUTIES

1. The Ombudsman shall investigate alleged violations falling within the jurisdiction set forth in Article II.1. He or she may act either on his or her own initiative or in response to an allegation presented by any Party or person, non-governmental organization, or group of individuals claiming to be the victim of a violation or acting on behalf of alleged victims who are deceased or missing. The work of the Ombudsman shall be free of charge to the person concerned.

2. The Ombudsman shall have complete, unimpeded, and immediate access to any person, place, or information upon his or her request.

(a) The Ombudsman shall have access to and may examine all official documents, and he or she can require any person, including officials of Kosmet to cooperate by providing relevant information, documents, and files.

(b) The Ombudsman may attend administrative hearings and meetings of other Kosmet institutions in order to gather information.

(c) The Ombudsman may examine facilities and places where persons deprived of their liberty are detained, work, or are otherwise located.

(d) The Ombudsman and staff shall maintain the confidentiality of all confidential information obtained by them, unless the Ombudsman determines that such information is evidence of a violation of rights falling within his or her jurisdiction, in which case that information may be revealed in public reports or appropriate legal proceedings.

(e) The Signatories undertake to ensure cooperation with the Ombudsman's investigations.

3. The Ombudsman shall issue findings and conclusions in the form of a published report promptly after concluding an investigation. Chapter 8

AMENDMENT, COMPREHENSIVE ASSESSMENT, AND FINAL CLAUSES

ARTICLE I: AMENDMENT AND COMPREHENSIVE ASSESSMENT

1. Amendments to this Agreement shall be adopted by agreement of all the Signatories, except as otherwise provided by Article X of Chapter 1.

2. Each Signatory may propose amendments at any time and will consider and consult with the other Signatories with regard to proposed amendments.

3. After three years, the signatories shall comprehensively review this Agreement with a view to improving its implementation and shall consider the proposals of any signatory for additional measures, whose adoption shall require the consent of all signatories.

ARTICLE II: FINAL CLAUSES

1. This Agreement is signed in the Albanian, English, Romany, Serbian and Turkish language.

2. This Agreement shall enter into forces after each signatory informs the other that it completed its internal procedure.

For Republic of Serbia: Prof. Dr. Ratko Markovic, Vice-President of the Government of theRepublic of Serbia and Head of the Delegation of the Republic of Serbia

For Kosovo and Metohija

For national community of Albanians: Sokolj Cuse Democratic Reform Party of Albanians, Faik Jashari, Kosovo Democratic Initiative

For Federal Republic of Yugoslavia: Prof. Dr. Vladan Kutlesic, Vice-President of the Federal Government

For national community of Serbs and Montenegrins: Vojislav Zivkovic

For national community of Turks: Zeynelabidin Kureys, Guljbehar Sabovic

For national community of Goranies: Ibro Vait

For national community of Muslims: Refik Senadovic

For national community of Romanies: Ljuan Koka

For national community of Egyptians: Cerim Abazi

150. Declaration of the Co-Chairmen Hubert Vedrine and Robin Cook, Paris, 19 March 1999

1) The Rambouillet Accords are the only peaceful solution to the Kosovo problem

2) In Paris, the Kosova delegation seized this opportunity and, by their signature, have committed themselves to the Accords as a whole.

3) Far from seizing this opportunity, the Yugoslav delegation has tried to unravel the Rambouillet Accords.

4) Therefore, after consultation with our partners in the Contact Group (Germany, Italy, the Russian Federation, the United States, the European Union, the Chairman in Office of the OSCE), we consider there is no purpose in extending the talks any further. The negotiations are ajourned. The talks will not resume unless the Serbs express their acceptance of the accords.

5) We will immediately engage in consultations with our partners and allies to be ready to act. We will be in contact with the Secretary General of NATO. We ask the Chairman in office of the OSCE to take all appropriate measures for the safety of the KVM. The Contact Group will remain seized of the issue.

6) We solemnly warn the authorities in Belgrade against any military offensive on the ground and any impediment to the freedom of movement and of action of the KVM, which would contrevene their commitments. Such violations would have the gravest consequences.

151. FRY, Letter of Yugoslav President Milosevic to the British and French Foreign Minister, 22 March 1999

Gentlemen Ministers,

This is my reply to the message you have sent me.

The talks in Paris, which you called adjourned, did not take place at all. The delegation of the Government of the Republic of Serbia and the representatives of the Albanian separatist and terrorist movement never met to talk.

As concerns the signed "Agreement", two documents were signed in Paris.

One of the documents was signed by the representatives of all national communities from Kosovo, and these are the representatives of Kosovo. The other document was signed by the representatives of the Albanian separatist and terrorist movement, and they, of course, are not the representatives of Kosovo.

That other document, which you call the Rambouillet Agreement, however, is not the Rambouillet Agreement. For neither in Ramouillet, nor in Paris, people who came to negotiate, did not negotiate. There were no talks between them, therefore there could be no common document to be accepted or rejected.

Otherwise, the text you call the Rambouillet Agreement, was published in the Kosovo press (the Albanian paper "Koha Ditore") before the start of the Rambouilet talks.

Belgrade is tolerant, but not stupid. Thanks to the stupidity of someone else, the document which should have been the result of the talks which were still to take place, was published.

Of course, we have nothing against preparing a draft document before the start of the talks. But we are strongly against not having talks at all, and being asked to sign something which could eventually be a draft agreement as an agreement, never meeting those with whom we should have agreed.

Therefore, my reply to your sentence "the agreement is on the table", is the following: Only a draft agreement could be at the table. But an empty table does not bring about an agreement. Nor can an agreement be reached only if one side of the table is filled. Those concerned with the agreement must sit at the table.

Regarding your threats with NATO military intervention, your peoples should be ashamed of them, for you prepare yourselves to use force against a small European nation, just because it protects its territory from separatism, protects its citizens from terrorism, and its historical dignity against rats who know nothing about history or dignity.

You say that large movements of our security forces are a matter of great concern. If you think they are a matter of concern for the separatists who would like to take away a part of the territory of Serbia and Yugoslavia, they, of course, should be concerned. If you have in mind some possible aggressors outside Yugoslavia, this should be a matter of concern for them, too.

It is really possible for a normal person to think that somebody who is being threatened will not show the intention to defend himself.

You are, Gentlemen, Ministers of Foreign Affairs of two European countries, and as such are distinguished diplomats. In such a capacity, you have the right to mediate, to negotiate, to advocate goodwill, to strive for peace in Europe, for better relations among nations. But you do not have the right to threaten other countries and other citizens, nor to arrange life in other countries.

We stay with our strong opinion to solve the problems in Kosovo and Metohija by peaceful means, through negotiations. The fact that negotiations did not take place in Rambouillet and in Paris does not mean that we should give up negotiations. At least from our peaceful and democratic standpoint.

Slobodan Milošević

CHAPTER 4: MILITARY ACTION AGAINST YUGOSLAVIA

In 1998, open military conflict escalated in Kosovo. On 28 May 1998, the North Atlantic Council stated NATO's major aims in regard to Kosovo: to achieve a peaceful resolution to the crisis by contributing to the response of the international community and to promote stability and security in neighbouring countries with particular emphasis on Albania and the former Yugoslav Republic of Macedonia (*document no. 152*). On 11 June 1998, the North Atlantic Council asked for an assessment of possible further measures that NATO might take considering the developing crisis (*document no. 153*). This led to a consideration of a large number of military options.

On 24 September 1998, NATO first decided to have recourse to a threat to use force in order to resolve the Kosovo conflict and issued an Activation Warning for both a limited air operation and a phased air campaign (*document no. 154*). In autumn 1998, the approaching winter with the threat of a humanitarian catastrophe among the internally displaced people caused the international community to demand a ceasefire. On 8 October 1998, the Contact Group decided to send US Special Envoy Richard Holbrooke to Belgrade "with the full authority of the Contact Group" to demand compliance with UN Security Council Resolution 1199 (1998). His mission was accompanied by a renewed military threat by NATO and by Russian approval of an OSCE verification mission on the ground. This combination caused Milosevic to accept the Contact Group's mediation and negotiate with Holbrooke. On 12 October 1998, at the peak of military pressure by NATO, Milosevic agreed to a ceasefire, to an OSCE presence of 2000 unarmed observers in Kosovo combined with unarmed NATO aerial reconnaissance, as well as to a political solution of the conflict in the form of an increased degree of internal self-determination (*document no. 156*). However, no formal document seems to have been signed by Milosevic; at least, none was made public.

On 13 October, after having been briefed by Holbrooke on the agreement, NATO decided to turn the Activation Warning of 24 September 1998 into Activation Orders for both limited air strikes and a phased air campaign in Yugoslavia (*document no. 155*). Following Holbrooke's request, NATO extended a 48-hour deadline to 96 hours. This new deadline corresponded to the deadline Holbrooke had issued for Milosevic to comply with the ceasefire agreement. On 15 October, NATO and the FRY signed an agreement on the establishment of a NATO Air Verification Mission over Kosovo (*document no. 157*). The agreement set up a Mutual Safety Zone composed of Kosovo and a 25-km corridor extending beyond Kosovo's boundaries. Unarmed NATO aircraft were entitled to free rein over Kosovo. Consequently on 16 October, NATO extended its previous deadline another ten days. The deadline then was temporarily suspended, while the ACTORD remained in force.

On the same day, the OSCE Chairman-in-Office signed an agreement with the FRY on an OSCE Kosovo Verification Mission (KVM) (*document no. 100; see Chapter 3.3.*). In support of the OSCE, the Alliance set up a special military task force to help with the emergency evacuation of members of KVM, if renewed conflict should endanger them. This task force was deployed in the former Yugoslav Republic of Macedonia under the overall direction of NATO's Supreme Allied Commander Europe.

When in January 1999 international efforts for a peaceful solution of the conflict intensified, NATO supported and reinforced the Contact Group efforts by agreeing on 30 January to the use of air strikes if required, and by warning both sides to the conflict of this decision (*document no. 132*). These initiatives accompanied the negotiations in Rambouillet from 6 to 23 February which were followed by a second round of talks in Paris from 15 to 18 March 1999. When the peace talks in Paris broke up without a signature of the FRY/Serb delegation,[1] the FRY's military forces increased the intensity of their operations, moving extra troops and tanks into the region. On 19 March 1999, the OSCE announced the withdrawal of the Kosovo Verification Mission and, on 22 March US Ambassador Holbrooke flew to Belgrade in a final attempt to reach a peaceful solution. When the attempt failed, NATO commenced air strikes on 23 March 1999.

During the bombing campaign NATO aircraft flew 38,400 combat sorties, including 10,484 strike sorties. The air campaign lasted 77 days. The concept for Operation Allied Forces envisaged a phased air campaign. According to NATO the phases ranged from a show of force in the initial stages, to operations against Serb forces in Kosovo, expanding, if necessary, to targets throughout the FRY that supported the FRY's ability to attack the civilian population of Kosovo.[2] NATO set out its objectives in relation to the conflict in a statement issued at the Extraordinary Meeting of the North Atlantic Council held on 12 April 1999 (*document no. 180*). The Heads of State and Government reaffirmed these objectives in Washington on 23 April 1999 (*document no. 181*). They considered the following principles as prerequisites for bringing an end to violence in Kosovo: a verifiable stop to all military action and the immediate ending of violence and repression; the withdrawal from Kosovo of the military, police and paramilitary forces; the stationing in Kosovo of an international military presence; the unconditional and safe return of all refugees and displaced persons and unhindered access to them by humanitarian aid organisations; the establishment of a political framework agreement for Kosovo on the basis of the Rambouillet Accords, in conformity with international law and the UN Charter.

In the course of the campaign, discussions among NATO member States emerged on the possible use of ground forces (*documents no. 185 - 189*). Milosevic's acceptance of the peace plan presented by the President of Finland, Ahtisaari, and the Special Representative of the Russian Government, Chernomyrdin (*documents no. 204, 205; see Chapter 5*) is said to have been influenced by the fact that especially Britain and France were actively contemplating a ground force deployment.[3] President Clinton, however, had rejected this strategy from the very outset. In his Address to the Nation of 24 March 1999 (*document no. 243*) he stated that he did not "intend to put our troops in Kosovo to fight a war." During the campaign land operations by the KLA continued, leading to questions about the cooperation between NATO and KLA (*documents no. 190 - 192*).

On 10 June 1999, NATO Secretary-General Solana announced that he had instructed the Supreme Allied Commander Europe, temporarily to suspend NATO's air operations. He took the decision after consultations with the North Atlantic Council and after confirmation from the Supreme Allied Commander Europe that the full withdrawal of Yugoslav forces from Kosovo had begun (*document no. 184, 212*).

---

[1] See Chapter 3.
[2] NATO, *Kosovo - One Year On - Achievement and Challenge* (2000), p. 13.
[3] Ibid., at p. 26.

During and after the bombing campaign NATO was accused of certain violations of international humanitarian law[1] leading to reports by non-governmental organisations, such as Human Rights Watch (document no. 193). The Prosecutor of the ICTY had received requests asking for investigations into whether senior political and military representatives of NATO member States committed serious violations of international humanitarian law during the air strikes. She was asked to prepare indictments pursuant to Art. 18 para. 1 and para. 4 of the Statute. On 14 May 1999, the Prosecutor established a committee to assess the allegations and the material presented. The committee's purpose was to advise the Prosecutor whether there existed a sufficient basis to proceed with an investigation. In its report the committee recommended that no investigation be commenced by the Office of the Prosecutor in relation to the NATO bombing campaign (document no. 195). The committee has not addressed in detail the question of the basic legality of the use of force since, if such action were unlawful, it could be considered as a crime against peace, over which the ICTY has no jurisdiction.

4.1 NATO'S THREAT TO USE FORCE AND THE HOLBROOKE AGREEMENT

152. NATO, Statement on Kosovo Issued at the Ministerial Meeting of the North Atlantic Council, Press Release M-NAC-1(98)61, Luxembourg, 28 May 1998

1. We are deeply concerned by the situation in Kosovo. We deplore the continuing use of violence in suppressing political dissent or in pursuit of political change. The violence and the associated instability risk jeopardising the Peace Agreement in Bosnia and Herzegovina and endangering security and stability in Albania and the former Yugoslav Republic of Macedonia.[2] It is particularly worrying that the recent resurgence of violence has been accompanied by the creation of obstacles denying access by international observers and humanitarian organisations to the affected areas in Kosovo.

2. We are firmly convinced that the problems of Kosovo can best be resolved through a process of open and unconditional dialogue between authorities in Belgrade and the Kosovar Albanian leadership. The status quo is unsustainable. We support a political solution which provides an enhanced status for Kosovo, preserves the territorial integrity of the Federal Republic of Yugoslavia (FRY), and safeguards the human and civil rights of all inhabitants of Kosovo, whatever their ethnic origin. President Milosevic has a special responsibility to ensure that steps are taken to achieve a political solution in Kosovo. The Kosovar Albanian leadership, represented by Dr. Rugova, also has a crucial part to play in bringing about a political solution. We therefore urge both sides to ensure that the dialogue that has now begun leads rapidly to the adoption of concrete measures to lower tensions, stop the spread of violence and open the way to a peaceful resolution of the crisis. The dialogue process should take into account the views of all communities in Kosovo. We welcome all efforts of the international community to these ends.

3. We support strongly the continuation of an international military presence in the former Yugoslav Republic of Macedonia after the end of the current mandate of UNPREDEP. We support the continuation of the mandate of UNPREDEP, which has contributed significantly to stability in the region.

4. We have two major objectives with respect to the situation in Kosovo: to help achieve a peaceful resolution of the crisis by contributing to the response of the international community; and to promote stability and security in neighbouring countries, with particular emphasis on Albania and the former Yugoslav Republic of Macedonia.

5. We have decided to enhance and supplement PfP activities in both Albania and the former Yugoslav Republic of Macedonia to promote security and stability in these Partner countries and to signal NATO's interest in containing the crisis and in seeking a peaceful resolution: We are launching NATO-led assistance programmes to help Albania and the former Yugoslav Republic of Macedonia to secure their borders, based on enhanced PfP activities and on bilateral assistance. We are upgrading a PfP exercise in the former Yugoslav Republic of Macedonia, scheduled to take place in September. We are scheduling by the end of August a PfP exercise in Albania involving ground and air forces. We are establishing a NATO/PfP Cell in Tirana, which will play a direct role in the implementation of Albania's Individual Partnership Programme and which, with the other measures we are taking, will help to enhance the capabilities of Albania's armed forces to ensure the security of its borders. We are elaborating a concept for the establishment of PfP training centres, including the possible future use of the Krivolak training area in the former Yugoslav Republic of Macedonia. We are authorising the visit of NATO's Standing Force Mediterranean (STANAVFORMED) to the port of Durres in early July. We will prepare to support the UNHCR in the event of a humanitarian crisis in the area.

6. In addition, in order to have options available for possible later decisions and to confirm our willingness to take further steps if necessary, we have commissioned military advice on support for UN and OSCE monitoring activity as well as on NATO preventive deployments in Albania and the former Yugoslav Republic of Macedonia, on a relevant legal basis, in order to help achieve a peaceful resolution of the crisis and to strengthen security and stability in the region.

7. We will continue to monitor closely the situation in and around Kosovo and we task the Council in Permanent Session to consider the political, legal and, as necessary, military implications of possible further deterrent measures, if the situation so requires.

8. We are in close consultation with the governments of Albania and the former Yugoslav Republic of Macedonia about the measures involving their countries. We have informed Partners of the development of NATO's thinking prior to this meeting. With Russia, we have consulted in a special meeting of the PJC. We will use the meetings of the NATO-Russia Permanent Joint Council, the NATO-Ukraine Commission and the Euro-Atlantic Partnership Council, both here in Luxembourg and in the future, with a view to seeking the cooperation of Russia, Ukraine and our other Partners with our efforts to help achieve a peaceful resolution of the crisis in Kosovo. We have invited the Secretary General to inform the UN Secretary-General, the OSCE Chairman-in-Office, the WEU Secretary General and other appropriate international organisations with a view to suggesting the coordination of the activities of the various international organisations involved in Albania and the former Yugoslav Republic of Macedonia.

9. We call upon President Milosevic to agree to the re-admission of the OSCE Long-Term Mission, and to accept the mission of Mr. Felipe González, the Personal Representative of the OSCE Chairman-in-Office and the EU Special Representative.

10. We are determined, through the ongoing activities of the Alliance through Partnership for Peace and the additional measures we have decided today, to contribute to the international efforts to solve the crisis in Kosovo and to promote regional security and stability.

---

[1] See Introduction, part E.
[2] Turkey recognises the Republic of Macedonia with its constitutional name.

153. NATO, Statement on Kosovo Issued at the Meeting of the North Atlantic Council in Defence Ministers Session, Press Release M-NAC-D-1(98)77, 11 June 1998

1. We are deeply concerned by the situation in Kosovo which has deteriorated seriously in recent days. Reports have indicated a new level of violence on the part of the Serb security forces. We condemn any use of violence for political ends by either the authorities in Belgrade or Kosovar Albanian extremists. We are particularly concerned by the number of refugees and displaced persons.

2. We call upon all parties to avoid actions which prolong the violence. NATO continues to support a political solution which brings an end to the violence, provides an enhanced status for Kosovo, preserves the territorial integrity of the Federal Republic of Yugoslavia, and safeguards the human and civil rights of all inhabitants of Kosovo, whatever their ethnic origin. On this basis, we intend to contribute to the response of the international community.

3. NATO also remains determined to contribute to efforts promoting stability and security in neighbouring countries, with particular emphasis on Albania and the former Yugoslav Republic of Macedonia. In this regard, we support the continuation of UNPREDEP following the end of its current mandate and reviewed the progress made in implementing the measures agreed by Foreign Ministers in Luxembourg to enhance and supplement PfP activities in the two Partner countries.

4. We reviewed the serious security situation, drawing also on a report from the assessment team which is currently in Albania and the former Yugoslav Republic of Macedonia. Against this background, we, as Defence Ministers, took the following additional decisions: We directed the NATO Military Authorities, subject to the agreement of the governments of Albania and the former Yugoslav Republic of Macedonia, to conduct an appropriate air exercise in these two countries as quickly as possible, with the aim of demonstrating NATO's capability to project power rapidly into the region. We directed the NATO Military Authorities as soon as possible to assess and develop for further Council consideration and decisions as appropriate a full range of options with the mission, based on the relevant legal basis, of halting or disrupting a systematic campaign of violent repression and expulsion in Kosovo; supporting international efforts to secure the agreement of the parties to a cessation of violence and disengagement; and helping to create the conditions for serious negotiations toward a political settlement. The study will give priority to options which are effective and readily available. Together with the measures already commissioned in Luxembourg, these new options should also contribute to preventing spillover of violence into neighbouring states.

5. We also decided to accelerate the provision of advice mandated by NATO Foreign Ministers on possible support for UN and OSCE monitoring activity and on possible NATO preventive deployments in Albania and the former Yugoslav Republic of Macedonia, on a relevant legal basis; agreed the details of the PfP exercise to take place in Albania in August; and we recommend that the Euro-Atlantic Disaster Response Coordination Centre support the UNHCR and other international organizations by the coordination of national humanitarian assistance.

6. We will use the occasion of tomorrow's meetings of the NATO-Russia Permanent Joint Council, the NATO-Ukraine Commission and the Euro-Atlantic Partnership Council to consult with our Partners on measures being undertaken. NATO is also consulting directly with the governments of Albania and the former Yugoslav Republic of Macedonia.

7. NATO will continue to monitor closely the situation in and around Kosovo. We are determined to play our part as Defence Ministers in helping to achieve a resolution of the conflict by the international community and in providing stability and security in the region.

154. NATO, Statement by the Secretary General following the ACTWARN Decision, Vilamoura, 24 September 1998

Just a few moments ago, the North Atlantic Council approved the issuing of an ACTWARN for both a limited air option and a phased air campaign in Kosovo.

The ACTWARN will take NATO to an increased level of military preparedness. In particular, the ACTWARN will allow NATO Commanders to identify the assets required for these NATO air operations.

Let me stress that the use of force will require further decisions by the North Atlantic Council. But today's decision is an important political signal of NATO's readiness to use force, if it becomes necessary to do so.

Finally, let me express the strong support of all Allies for firm Resolution that was adopted in New York last night by the UN Security Council. This Resolution makes it clear what President Milosevic must do:

- he must stop his repressive actions against the population;
- he must seek a political solution to the Kosovo crisis based on negotiations, as must the Kosovar Albanians;
- and he must take immediate steps to alleviate the humanitarian situation.

The Resolution and today's decision by NATO underline the unity of the international community and our resolve to find a solution to the Kosovo crisis.

155. NATO, Statement by the Secretary General Following Decision on the ACTORD, NATO HQ, 13 October 1998

A few hours ago we were briefed by Ambassador Holbrooke on his efforts to resolve the crisis in Kosovo. Ambassador Holbrooke reported that there has been progress. He stressed that the process was largely due to the pressure of the Alliance in the last few days and that we have to maintain this pressure in order to ensure that the process continues.

In response, just a few moments ago, the North Atlantic Council decided to issue activation orders - ACTORDs - for both limited air strikes and a phased air campaign in Yugoslavia, execution of which will begin in approximately 96 hours. We took this decision after a thorough review of the situation in Kosovo. The Federal Republic of Yugoslavia has still not complied fully with UNSCR 1199 and time is running out. Even at this final hour, I still believe diplomacy can succeed and the use of military force can be avoided.

The responsibility is on President Milosevic's shoulders. He knows what he has to do.

156. Holbrooke Agreement

156 a) FRY, Statement by President of the FRY, Slobodan Milosevic, on the Accords to Resolve the Problems in Kosovo and Metohija in a Peaceful Way and by Political Means, 13 October 1998

"Honorable citizens, I wish to inform you about the talks we have had in the past several days. Accord has been reached that problems Kosovo and Metohija and in connection with Kosovo and Metohija resolved by peaceful means, by political means. The accords we have reached eliminate the danger of military intervention against our country. As for the political solution, it will be directed towards the affirmation of the national equality of all citizens and all nation communities in Kosovo and Metohija. In the immense pressures we have been exposed to, I would say, for years and, especially, in the past weeks and days, the commitment that good solutions can be reached only by peaceful means has nevertheless prevailed. The accords we have reached are fully in keeping with the interests of our country, the interests of the Republic of Serbia and all its citizens, and with the interests of all citizens and national communities in Kosovo an Metohija. The next task is to step up the political process and to step u the economic recovery of our country as a whole. In conclusion, I wish to thank all the citizens at home and abroad who were sending me all this time messages of strong support. These messages also contained the duty to preserve our country's sovereignty and territorial integrity in other words to preserve its dignity. And, on the other hand, to secure that problems which burden life in Serbia's southern Province be peacefully resolved. I believe that we have accomplished this. I thank you all."

156 b) FRY, Statement from the Federal Government's Meeting, Belgrade, 14 October 1998

At today's meeting, chaired by Prime Minister Momir Bulatovic, the Federal Government fully supported the agreement concluded by the President of the Federal Republic of Yugoslavia Slobodan Milosevic and American envoy Richard Holbrooke. The agreement ensures the peaceful solution of all problems in Kosovo and Metohija, exclusively by political means and with respect to territorial integrity and sovereignty of the Republic of Serbia and the Federal Republic of Yugoslavia. The agreement also prevents the threat of military intervention.

The Federal Government fully supported the decisions made by the President of the Republic of Serbia Milan Milutinovic and the government of the Republic of Serbia, in the view to implement the agreement.

The Federal Government defined the text of the agreement between the Federal Government of the Federal Republic of Yugoslavia and the OSCE on the OSCE's mission for verification in Kosovo. The Federal Government authorized Foreign Minister Zivadin Jovanovic to sign the agreement with the OSCE Chairman Bronislaw Geremek, Polish Foreign Minister.

As a part of the verification process and the implementation of the Security Council's Resolution 1199, the Federal Republic of Yugoslavia shall permit the observing flights in Kosovo.

The Federal Government thinks the agreement will preserve the peace, not only in Yugoslavia but in the whole region and Europe; it also provides the development of economy, neighbourly relations and comprehensive cooperation in the region.

156 c) Accord Reached by Slobodan Milosevic, President of the FRY, and the UN Special Envoy, Richard Holbrooke, UN Doc. S/1998/953, Annex, 14 October 1998

The Serbian Government endorsed the accord reached by President Milosevic

The Serbian Government held a session on Tuesday chaired by Prime Minister Mirko Marjanovic to discuss a report presented by Serbian President, Milan Milutinovic, on the political talks held by the President of the Federal Republic of Yugoslavia, Slobodan Milosevic, with the Special Envoy of the United States of America, Richard Holbrooke.

President Milutinovic informed the Government of the talks held for several days between President Milosevic and Mr. Holbrooke and Christopher Hill and of the final accord reached on Monday on resolving the problems in Serbia's southern province of Kosovo and Metohija in a peaceful way and by political means.

President Milutinovic presented to the Government a full report on the talks, especially on the interest of the international community in full-scale monitoring of the situation in Kosovo and Metohija.

It has been agreed that the task should be carried out by a mission of the Organization for Security and Cooperation in Europe (OSCE) as the best way of enabling the international community to verify the positive trends under way.

The fact that a positive approach has been adopted is very important, as it will form the basis for a lasting political solution for the autonomy of Kosovo and Metohija within Serbia, in line with the principles of equality of all citizens and ethnic communities living in the area.

In addition, a political framework has been worked out and agreement has been reached on the principles of a political solution and on a timetable framework for its realization, which is an important achievement. The principles are the following:

1. A political approach and a peaceful solution of problems in Kosovo and Metohija, achieved through dialogue, are the only acceptable means for reaching any lasting, just and humane solution to all open issues.

2. Violence and terrorism, as inadmissible means, contrary to all international norms, must stop immediately.

3. Any solution for Kosovo and Metohija must respect the territorial integrity and sovereignty and internationally recognized boundaries of the Federal Republic of Yugoslavia, in full compliance with the basic principles of the Charter of the United Nations, the Helsinki Final Act and the Paris Charter of OSCE.

4. The solution has to be based on the full respect for the equality of all citizens and national communities in Kosovo and Metohija. Full affirmation and equal treatment of their national, confessional and cultural values and historic patrimony should be guaranteed.

5. The future of Kosovo and Metohija lies in peace, equality, integration, economic prosperity and free and common life, not in ethnic, confessional, cultural or any division or isolation.

6. The legal arrangements establishing Kosovo and Metohija's self-governance and the legal frameworks of the Republic of Serbia and the Federal Republic of Yugoslavia are to be harmonized in accordance with international standards and the Helsinki Final Act.

7. Citizens in Kosovo and Metohija shall govern themselves democratically through assemblies and executive and judicial organs of Kosovo and Metohija. Within nine months, there will be free and fair elections for Kosovo and Metohija authorities, including those at the communal level. The Government of the Federal Republic of Yugoslavia hereby invites OSCE to supervise those elections to ensure their openness and fairness.

8. Members of the national communities shall have additional rights in order to preserve and express their national, cultural, religious and linguistic identities in accordance with international standards and the Helsinki Final Act. The national communities shall be legally equal and shall not use their additional rights so as to endanger the rights of other national communities or other rights of citizens.

9. In the context of the political settlement for Kosovo and Metohija, which will devolve many responsibilities to the communal level, police under local-communal direction will be established. These local police, which will be representative of the local population, will be coordinated by administrative organs of Kosovo. The settlement must address the security of all citizens and national communities.

10. No person will be prosecuted in State courts for crimes related to the conflict in Kosovo, except for crimes against humanity and international law, as set forth in chapter XVI of the Federal Penal Code. In order to facilitate full transparency, the State will allow complete, unimpeded access to foreign (including forensic) experts, along with State investigators.

11. The competent organs shall re-examine, with the aim of extraordinary mitigation of the punishments, the sentences of the sentenced members of the national communities in Kosovo and Metohija for criminal offences motivated by political aims.

Timetable

By Wednesday, 14 October, a comprehensive timetable will be agreed upon building on the following elements:

- By 19 October, an agreement on the status of the international presence, including verification, OSCE and other elements;

- By November 2 - the completion of an agreement containing core elements for a political settlement in Kosovo using as a basis the paper proposed by the Contact Group (October 2, 1998);

- By November 9 - the completion of a rules and procedures for elections.

The Serbian Government has fully endorsed the accords that have been reached as they fully preserve the territorial integrity and sovereignty of the country, avert a conflict and lay the conditions for a political dialogue on the basis of the principle that all solutions must be within the framework of the legal systems of the Republic of Serbia and the Federal Republic of Yugoslavia. The Serbian Government decided to propose to the Yugoslav Government to accept the accords that have been reached, the statement says.

157. NATO-FRY, Agreement Providing for the Establishment of an Air Verification Mission over Kosovo, Belgrade, 15 October 1998[1]

The North Atlantic Treaty Organisation, hereafter Called NATO, Represented by General Wesley K. Clark, Supreme Allied Commander, Europe

and

The Federal Republic of Yugoslavia, hereafter Called FRY, Represented by Colonel General Momcilo Perisic, Chief of General Staff of the Army of Yugoslavia

Have agreed on the NATO Kosovo Verification Mission as follows:

Introduction

In order to provide air surveillance to verify compliance by all parties with the provisions of UNSCR 1199, complementing the ground verification to be established by the OSCE, NATO and FRY agree to the establishment of an air surveillance system for Kosovo, to be known as the NATO Kosovo Verification Mission, and agree that NATO will implement it. This document establishes the terms of reference and governing procedures for this NATO Kosovo air verification system. The NATO Kosovo air verification system will be comprised of NATO non-combatant reconnaissance platforms, including U2, unmanned aerial vehicles (UAVs), and low and medium altitude manned reconnaissance platforms such as the P-3. Canberra, DeHaviland-7 ARL and comparably configured non-combatant platforms.

FLIGHT CONTROL REQUIREMENTS

In order to create a cooperative and safe operating environment for the NATO Kosovo air surveillance mission and for the FRY Air Force and Air Defence Forces (FAADF), the following procedures shall apply:

- A mutual Safety Zone encompassing FRY airspace within a radius of 25 km from the contiguous boundary of Kosovo will be established, within which FRY Air Force fighter aircraft and Air Defence Forces will not conduct operations during the period of flight operations by NATO manned non-combatant reconnaissance platforms. This Mutual Safety Zone will be identified for all aircraft as follows: from latitude-longitude to latitude-longitude (to be specifically defined). Additionally, NATO aircraft operating in support of the Kosovo Air Verification Mission will avoid all published instrument approach fixed within Kosovo and the Mutual Safety Zone;

For manned low and medium altitude reconnaissance platforms, NATO flight operations will consist of a defined period to include a thirty-minute safety margin before and after announced NATO flights, and may be conducted at all times within the confines of Kosovo. For U2 and unmanned reconnaissance platforms, flight operations may be conducted at all times and do not require this thirty-minute safety margin;

- In order to permit the FRY air force to comply with this requirement, the NATO flight operations coordinator will provide a weekly schedule of NATO non-combatant reconnaissance platform flight operations. NATO weekly schedules will make all attempts to provide FAADF appropriate time blocks (6-8 hours) to allow for requisite training requirements. In case of an emergent situation or weather and visibility prolbem, NATO may fly any of its non-combatant reconnaissance platforms with a one-hour notice. NATO authorities will contact FAADF liasons immediately to advise of such flights so FAADF fighter aircraft can clear the Kosovo and Mutual Safety Zone airspace immediately;

- Commercial, civilian private aircraft, military air transport and rotary wing flight operations by FRY entities may be operated at any time without restriction, including during the period of NATO non-combatant reconnaissance platform operations. These FRY flight operations may operate anywhere in the sovereign airspace of the FRY. Prior coordination with the NATO Flight Operations Coordinator is not required for these flights: however, FRY flights will be operated to avoid interference with declared NATO flight operations;

- FRY fighter aircraft may fly within Kosovo and the Mutual Safety Zone at all times except when NATO manned low and medium altitude non-combat reconnaissance platforms are operating as described above;

- NATO aircraft will conduct aerial reconnaissance missions on a mutual non-interference basis;

- Airspace entry and exit points for manned non-combatant platforms will be through Albanians and FYROM except if coordinated in advance.

FRY INTEGRATED AIR DEFENCE SYSTEM REQUIREMENTS

During the duration of the NATO Kosovo Verification Mission, the following conditions apply within Kosovo and the Mutual Safety Zone:

- Early warning radars may operate unrestricted at all times;

- All SAMS and air defence weapons (including acquisition, target tracking or other fire control radars, radar-controlled gun and man-portable air defence systems) will either be removed from Kosovo and the established Mutual Safety Zone, or place in cantonment sites and not operated. Cantonment sites will be declared, geographic positions identified, and open for inspection. SAMS Missiles and launchers may remain in deployed sites if separated from their cantoned acquisition, target tracking and fire control radars;

- All SAMs and air defence weapons outside the Mutual Safety Zone must refrain from acquisition, target tracking or otherwise illuminating (except with early warning and air traffic control radars) NATO Kosovo Verification Mission non-combatant reconnaissance platforms;

- Training and maintenance may be conducted on systems precluded from operation with 24-hour notification and approval. Additionally, systems in cantonment areas and deployed sites may be removed to areas outside Kosovo and the Mutual Safety Zone following the same provisions of this agreement;

- No SAMs or air defence weapons not initially identified in the Kosovo and Mutual Safety Zone may be brought into Kosovo.

FORCE PROTECTION

Violations of any provisions of this agreement, to include unauthorized flight or activation of FRY Integrated Air Defence Systems (IADS) within Kosovo and the Mutual Safety Zone, will be immediately arbitrated through appropriate bilateral channels to determine liability and appropriate action to be taken.

COMMAND AND CONTROL

In order to help assure the safe conduct of the NATO Kosovo air verification system, "Air Defence Liaisons" comprised of FRY and NATO representatives will be established at appropriate offices in Belgrade, and at the Combined air Operations Centre (CAOC) in Vincenza, Italy.

---

[1] UN Doc. S/1998/991, Annex, 23 October 1999.

The NATO Kosovo Air Verification Mission air surveillance activities and OSCE Kosovo Verification Mission ground surveillance activities will be coordinated between the OSCE Verification Mission Headquarters and NATO.

STATUS AND CONDITIONS

- The FRY government hereby guarantees the safety and security of the NATO Kosovo Verification Mission and all its members;

- The FRY government and its entities will designate formal liaison officers to work with the NATO Kosovo Verification Mission in Belgrade.

IMPLEMENTATION AND TRANSITION PERIOD

Implementation of this agreement is subject to the following provisions:

- Communications and liaison channels will be established between FAADF in Belgrade and CAOC, Vincenza as soon as possible following conclusion of this agreement;

- U2 and UAV operations may commence within 72-hours of establishing communications and liaison channels;

- Within 15 days, 25 km boundary defining the Mutual Safety Zone will be agreed and identified by both parties on a common reference map;

- Within 15 days, published instrument approach fixes within Kosovo and the Mutual Safety Zone will be identified on a common reference map;

- FAADF will be provided 15 days after concluding this agreement to allow movement and cantonment of air defence systems and establish internal operational procedures of compliance;

- NATO will conduct a flight profile with a manned non-combatant reconnaissance platform prior to full initiation of the Kosovo Air Verification Mission to determine the operational concepts of this agreement. If during this validation profile, flight conduct and safety concerns are identified, NATO and FRY will agree to immediately establish changes to the provisions of this agreement to address the concerns of both parties.

Done at Belgrade on the 15th day of October 1998, in two originals, in the English, French and Serbian languages.

In the event of any dispute on the interpretation of the present Agreement, the English text will be authoritative.

For the North Atlantic Treaty Organisation: General Wesley K. Clark

For the Federal Republic of Yugoslavia: Colonel General Momcilo Perisic

158. UN Security Council Resolution 1203 (1998) of 24 October 1998

The Security Council,

Recalling its resolutions 1160 (1998) of 31 March 1998 and 1199 (1998) of 23 September 1998, and the importance of the peaceful resolution of the problem of Kosovo, Federal Republic of Yugoslavia,

Having considered the reports of the Secretary-General pursuant to those resolutions, in particular his report of 5 October 1998 (S/1998/912),

Welcoming the agreement signed in Belgrade on 16 October 1998 by the Minister of Foreign Affairs of the Federal Republic of Yugoslavia and the Chairman-in-Office of the Organization for Security and Cooperation in Europe (OSCE) providing for the OSCE to establish a verification mission in Kosovo (S/1998/978), including the undertaking of the Federal Republic of Yugoslavia to comply with resolutions 1160 (1998) and 1199 (1998),

Welcoming also the agreement signed in Belgrade on 15 October 1998 by the Chief of General Staff of the Federal Republic of Yugoslavia and the Supreme Allied Commander, Europe, of the North Atlantic Treaty Organization (NATO) providing for the establishment of an air verification mission over Kosovo (S/1998/991, annex), complementing the OSCE Verification Mission,

Welcoming also the decision of the Permanent Council of the OSCE of 15 October 1998 (S/1998/959, annex),

Welcoming the decision of the Secretary-General to send a mission to the Federal Republic of Yugoslavia to establish a first-hand capacity to assess developments on the ground in Kosovo,

Reaffirming that, under the Charter of the United Nations, primary responsibility for the maintenance of international peace and security is conferred on the Security Council,

Recalling the objectives of resolution 1160 (1998), in which the Council expressed support for a peaceful resolution of the Kosovo problem which would include an enhanced status for Kosovo, a substantially greater degree of autonomy, and meaningful self-administration,

Condemning all acts of violence by any party, as well as terrorism in pursuit of political goals by any group or individual, and all external support for such activities in Kosovo, including the supply of arms and training for terrorist activities in Kosovo, and expressing concern at the reports of continuing violations of the prohibitions imposed by resolution 1160 (1998),

Deeply concerned at the recent closure by the authorities of the Federal Republic of Yugoslavia of independent media outlets in the Federal Republic of Yugoslavia, and *emphasizing* the need for these to be allowed freely to resume their operations,

Deeply alarmed and *concerned* at the continuing grave humanitarian situation throughout Kosovo and the impending humanitarian catastrophe, and *re-emphasizing* the need to prevent this from happening,

Stressing the importance of proper coordination of humanitarian initiatives undertaken by States, the United Nations High Commissioner for Refugees and international organizations in Kosovo,

Emphasizing the need to ensure the safety and security of members of the Verification Mission in Kosovo and the Air Verification Mission over Kosovo,

Reaffirming the commitment of all Member States to the sovereignty and territorial integrity of the Federal Republic of Yugoslavia,

Affirming that the unresolved situation in Kosovo, Federal Republic of Yugoslavia, constitutes a continuing threat to peace and security in the region,

Acting under Chapter VII of the Charter of the United Nations,

1. *Endorses* and *supports* the agreements signed in Belgrade on 16 October 1998 between the Federal Republic of Yugoslavia and the OSCE and on 15 October 1998, between the Federal Republic of Yugoslavia and NATO, concerning the verification of compliance by the Federal Republic of Yugoslavia and all others concerned in Kosovo with the requirements of its resolution 1199 (1998), and demands the full and prompt implementation of these agreements by the Federal Republic of Yugoslavia;

2. *Notes* the endorsement by the Government of Serbia of the accord reached by the President of the Federal Republic of Yugoslavia and the United States Special Envoy (S/1998/953, annex), and the public commitment of the Federal Republic of Yugoslavia to complete negotiations on a framework for a political settlement by 2 November 1998, and calls for the full implementation of these commitments;

3. *Demands* that the Federal Republic of Yugoslavia comply fully and swiftly with resolutions 1160 (1998) and 1199 (1998) and cooperate fully with the OSCE Verification Mission in Kosovo and the NATO Air Verification Mission over Kosovo according to the terms of the agreements referred to in paragraph 1 above;

4. *Demands also* that the Kosovo Albanian leadership and all other elements of the Kosovo Albanian community comply fully and swiftly with resolutions 1160 (1998) and 1199 (1998) and cooperate fully with the OSCE Verification Mission in Kosovo;

5. *Stresses* the urgent need for the authorities in the Federal Republic of Yugoslavia and the Kosovo Albanian leadership to enter immedi-

ately into a meaningful dialogue without preconditions and with international involvement, and to a clear timetable, leading to an end of the crisis and to a negotiated political solution to the issue of Kosovo;

6. *Demands* that the authorities of the Federal Republic of Yugoslavia, the Kosovo Albanian leadership and all others concerned respect the freedom of movement of the OSCE Verification Mission and other international personnel;

7. *Urges* States and international organizations to make available personnel to the OSCE Verification Mission in Kosovo;

8. *Reminds* the Federal Republic of Yugoslavia that it has the primary responsibility for the safety and security of all diplomatic personnel accredited to the Federal Republic of Yugoslavia, including members of the OSCE Verification Mission, as well as the safety and security of all international and non-governmental humanitarian personnel in the Federal Republic of Yugoslavia, and calls upon the authorities of the Federal Republic of Yugoslavia, and all others concerned throughout the Federal Republic of Yugoslavia including the Kosovo Albanian leadership, to take all appropriate steps to ensure that personnel performing functions under this resolution and the agreements referred to in paragraph 1 above are not subject to the threat or use of force or interference of any kind;

9. *Welcomes* in this context the commitment of the Federal Republic of Yugoslavia to guarantee the safety and security of the Verification Missions as contained in the agreements referred to in paragraph 1 above, notes that, to this end, the OSCE is considering arrangements to be implemented in cooperation with other organizations, and *affirms* that, in the event of an emergency, action may be needed to ensure their safety and freedom of movement as envisaged in the agreements referred to in paragraph 1 above;

10. *Insists* that the Kosovo Albanian leadership condemn all terrorist actions, *demands* that such actions cease immediately and *emphasizes* that all elements in the Kosovo Albanian community should pursue their goals by peaceful means only;

11. *Demands* immediate action from the authorities of the Federal Republic of Yugoslavia and the Kosovo Albanian leadership to cooperate with international efforts to improve the humanitarian situation and to avert the impending humanitarian catastrophe;

12. *Reaffirms* the right of all refugees and displaced persons to return to their homes in safety, and underlines the responsibility of the Federal Republic of Yugoslavia for creating the conditions which allow them to do so;

13. *Urges* Member States and others concerned to provide adequate resources for humanitarian assistance in the region and to respond promptly and generously to the United Nations Consolidated Inter-Agency Appeal for Humanitarian Assistance Related to the Kosovo crisis;

14. *Calls* for prompt and complete investigation, including international supervision and participation, of all atrocities committed against civilians and full cooperation with the International Tribunal for the former Yugoslavia, including compliance with its orders, requests for information and investigations;

15. *Decides* that the prohibitions imposed by paragraph 8 of resolution 1160 (1998) shall not apply to relevant equipment for the sole use of the Verification Missions in accordance with the agreements referred to in paragraph 1 above;

16. *Requests* the Secretary-General, acting in consultation with the parties concerned with the agreements referred to in paragraph 1 above, to report regularly to the Council regarding implementation of this resolution;

17. *Decides* to remain seized of the matter.

[Adopted by the Security Council at its 3937th meeting, on 24 October 1998 with 13 votes to none with China and the Russian Federation abstaining.]

159. UN, Extract from the Debate of the Security Council Concerning Security Council Resolution 1203 (1998), UN Doc. S/PV. 3937, 24 October 1998[1]

[Members had before them the report of the Secretary-General prepared pursuant to resolutions 1160 (1998) and 1199 (1998) of the Security Council (S/1998/912). Members also had before them a draft resolution submitted by Bahrain, France, Germany, Italy, Japan, Portugal, Slovenia, Sweden, the United Kingdom of Great Britain and Northern Ireland and the United States of America (S/1998/992).][2]

[...]

[2] **Mr. Wyzner** (Poland): [...] I am taking the floor today mainly to present the views of the Polish Chairmanship-in-Office of the Organization for Security and Cooperation in Europe (OSCE). The reason for doing so is the commitment of the organization, as a regional arrangement under the United Nations Charter, to the active pursuit of a settlement of the conflict in Kosovo. We are concerned as well at the unfolding crisis in Kosovo and its dangerous potential ramifications for peace and stability in the region and in Europe, and at the fact that the provisions of Security Council resolutions 1160 (1998) and 1199 (1998) have not been fully complied with.

The OSCE has taken the position that the solution of the Kosovo problem should be based both on respect for the territorial integrity of the Federal Republic of Yugoslavia and on the standards defined in the United Nations Charter as well as the OSCE documents. The OSCE insists that such a solution should take into account the right of the Kosovo Albanians to autonomy and significant self-government, which would be reflected in [3] a special status of the province within the Federal Republic of Yugoslavia.

Among the demands addressed by the OSCE to the authorities of the Federal Republic of Yugoslavia were a cessation of all repression, the initiation of talks on a peaceful resolution of the conflict, international participation in the negotiating process, acceptance of a new mission by the Personal Representative of the Chairman-in-Office for the Federal Republic of Yugoslavia, as well as the return of the OSCE long-term missions in Kosovo, Sanjak and Vojvodina. These demands were included in the OSCE Permanent Council Decision No. 218 of 11 March, which became the platform for the OSCE activities in the Kosovo crisis.

In accordance with Decision No. 218 and Security Council resolutions 1160 (1998) and 1199 (1998), the Chairmanship-in-Office undertook a number of concrete actions in cooperation with international organizations and entities, especially the United Nations, the European Union, the Council of Europe, the Contact Group and others. It is not my intention to recall on this occasion a detailed catalogue of those activities. It seems worth underlining, however, that all of them contributed to the build-up of international solidarity, which is indispensable to bringing effective pressure to bear on the authorities of the Federal Republic of Yugoslavia to change their position. In addition, in the process of implementation of resolution 1 160 (1998), the Chairman-in-Office of the Organization for Security and Cooperation in Europe (OSCE), Minister Geremek, regularly forwarded to the United Nations Secretary-General reports on the situation in Kosovo and on measures taken by the OSCE in this regard. We note with satisfaction that the OSCE information inputs were utilized and included in the periodic reports of the Secretary-General to the Security Council.

---

1 *Only statements which add to the legal analysis or the factual background have been included. Presidential statements not related to substantive issues have been omitted.*

2 *In 1998, membership of the Security Council was as follows: Bahrain, Brazil, China, Costa Rica, France, Gabon, Gambia, Japan, Kenya, Portugal, Russian Federation, Slovenia, Sweden, the United Kingdom of Great Britain and Nothern Ireland, the United States of America. At the invitation of the President the representatives of Germany, Italy, Poland and Ukraine participated in the discussion, without vote, in the discussion in accordance with the Charter and rule 37 of the Council's provisional rules of procedure.*

A strong message sent by the Security Council in its resolution 1199 (1998) allowed for the intensification of efforts by the international community to reach a settlement of the Kosovo conflict. To mention only some of the international endeavours in this regard, I would refer to the significant activity of the North Atlantic Alliance and the Contact Group as well as the painstaking negotiations conducted by the American Envoy, Ambassador Richard Holbrooke.

Thanks to the efforts of the international community, the process of settling the Kosovo dispute entered into a new phase. In a letter to the Secretary-General dated 16 October 1998, issued subsequently as Security Council document S/1998/978, the OSCE Chairman-in-Office informed you, Mr. President, and Mr. Kofi Annan that on that same day in Belgrade he had signed an agreement between the OSCE and the Government of the Federal Republic of Yugoslavia on the establishment of the Kosovo Verification Mission. This agreement, together with the agreement on the North Atlantic Treaty Organization-Kosovo Air Verification Regime, constitutes an important step towards the development of a political framework aimed at ensuring compliance with the demands set out in resolution 1199 (1998).

In the talks with Minister Geremek, the leader of the Kosovo Albanians, Mr. Ibrahim Rugova, in spite of some reservations, welcomed the agreement and expressed the view that the Albanian community in Kosovo would cooperate with the Kosovo Verification Mission. He saw that act as an important step towards enhancing the international presence in Kosovo, which should facilitate negotiations for a political solution to the crisis; the recognition of Albanian community institutions, including local police; and deciding the future of Kosovo.

Soon after the signing of the agreement, the OSCE Chairman-in-Office dispatched to the Federal Republic of Yugoslavia a small, 15-person OSCE technical advance mission to start preparations for the Kosovo Verification Mission operation, the scope of which goes beyond previous OSCE experience. We are pleased to note that this OSCE assessment team has already visited Belgrade and Kosovo, and we also welcome the establishment of a Kosovo Verification Mission support unit in Vienna.

We believe that an effective implementation of the recently concluded agreements must be secured if the process of conflict resolution is to gain momentum. This is but the beginning of an ambitious and difficult undertaking. We are likely to face numerous obstacles and difficulties, possibly even attempts to reverse the process. That is why we must act promptly and with determination. Decisive action is called for also because of the humanitarian factor: the urgent need to avert the impending humanitarian catastrophe among the refugees which may be precipitated by the forthcoming winter.

We are disturbed by the reports of renewed fighting in Kosovo, and we urge both sides to refrain immediately from the further use of force and to search for a peaceful solution.

We trust that the draft resolution which the Security Council is about to adopt will facilitate the [4] implementation of the agreements signed in Belgrade and, by endorsing and supporting them, help to make them effective and ensure the safety and security of international verifiers. These objectives require the direct cooperation and engagement of other organizations, which are duly foreseen in the resolution. [...]

Mr. Yel'chenko (Ukraine): [...] Ukraine also welcomes the signing on 16 October 1998 of the agreement between the Federal Republic of Yugoslavia and the Organization for Security and Cooperation in Europe (OSCE) permitting the OSCE to establish a verification mission in Kosovo, as well as the agreement between the Federal Republic of Yugoslavia and the North Atlantic Treaty Organization (NATO) concerning the Air Verification Mission over Kosovo, which complements the OSCE Verification Mission. We commend the energetic efforts in this regard by the Chairman-in-Office of the OSCE, as well as the tireless efforts of the United States Special Envoy, Mr. Holbrooke. [...]

As the Ministry for Foreign Affairs of Ukraine noted in its statement on 15 October 1998, while "understanding the motivations of NATO's decision of 13 October 1998 on the possibility of the use of military force in Yugoslavia", we are still very hopeful that the latest steps of the Federal Republic of Yugoslavia leadership as to the implementation of Security Council resolution 1199 (1998) will make it possible to avert the use of force, because it could lead to unpredictable consequences. [...]

[A statement by the representative of Bahrain has been omitted.]

[5] **Mr. Soares** (Portugal): The situation in Kosovo is of great concern to the international community. The Council, through its resolutions 1160 (1998) and 1199 (1998), has given a clear response to this concern, of which the draft resolution before us is a logical extension.

We welcome the agreements that have been concluded with the Federal Republic of Yugoslavia to address the critical situation in Kosovo. The draft resolution seeks to ensure that these agreements will be implemented in full. This is, in fact, the number one priority of the draft resolution on which we are about to vote: the endorsement by the Security Council of the North Atlantic Treaty Organization (NATO) and Organization for Security and Cooperation in Europe (OSCE) agreements regarding verification of the commitments that the Government of the Federal Republic of Yugoslavia has made - namely, to take measures to prevent a humanitarian catastrophe, to end the violence against civilians in Kosovo, to allow the return of refugees and displaced persons and to initiate and maintain a dialogue with the Kosovo Albanian community, with a view to finding a political solution to the problems of Kosovo.

[6] Portugal welcomes the readiness of NATO and the OSCE to provide the necessary verification regimes and believes that the Security Council should send, through this draft resolution, a strong signal of support for these Verification Missions and indicate that the safety and security of those unarmed personnel on the ground must never be compromised.

This draft resolution also represents an unambiguous expression of the Council's belief that it is up to the Government of the Federal Republic of Yugoslavia to implement those agreements in full and comply fully with Security Council resolutions.

Mr. Niehaus (Costa Rica) *(interpretation from Spanish)*: Costa Rica has consistently and firmly continued to condemn attacks against the Albanian civilian population in Kosovo, the violation of that population's most fundamental rights and the savage destruction of unarmed small towns and hamlets. Time and again, we have expressed our repudiation of the policy of ethnic cleansing undertaken by the authorities of Serbia and the Federal Republic of Yugoslavia. We are in favour of an international position of political firmness vis-a-vis the Belgrade Government.

In the face of the suffering of the Kosovo population, my delegation voted in favour of Security Council resolutions 1160 (1998) and 1199 (1998). Through these resolutions, we demanded that the Federal Republic of Yugoslavia and the authorities of the Albanian community in Kosovo enter into dialogue without any preconditions, with a view to putting an end to the crisis and finding a negotiated political solution to it. Moreover, we have demanded that the Yugoslav authorities cease all military action in Kosovo which affects the civilian population and that they withdraw all security forces which are being used to repress that population.

Hence, we cannot fail to express our satisfaction at the signing last 16 October of an agreement between the Chairman-in-Office of the Organization for Security and Cooperation in Europe (OSCE) and the Minister for Foreign Affairs of Yugoslavia, with the purpose of establishing a verification mission in Kosovo entrusted with the monitoring of compliance with the demands stipulated in resolutions 1160 (1998) and 1199 (1998), as well as the commitments agreed to by the Yugoslav authorities to comply with the terms of such resolutions. We believe that the Verification Mission will be a key instrument in guaranteeing the peace process in Kosovo, in preventing new violations of human rights and for international humanitarian law in the region.

Thus, the delegation of Costa Rica believes that it is necessary and indispensable for the Security Council to authorize the dispatch of an international observer mission to verify compliance with the obligations agreed to by the Yugoslav authorities in the 16 October agreement.

Moreover, no longer is this question merely a political one. What we have here is a moral and ethical imperative for the international community. Inasmuch as this moral objective leaves no room for doubt, and in that an international presence in Kosovo would take on a high moral character, Costa Rica would never fail to lend its support to a multilateral action aimed at such a noble purpose. That is why we are supporting the draft resolution we have before us.

Nevertheless, having said this, we would like to state some of our misgivings, which are of a legal nature, with regard to certain aspects of this draft resolution. A goal such as this one, which is ethically and morally unquestionable, deserves to be achieved by means of international law. We are not objecting to the goal of the draft resolution, but to its form and lack of clarity, in light of our firm position on absolute respect for international law and the tenets of the Charter.

We believe that any Security Council resolution must be strictly in keeping with international law and with a sound political concept. The adoption of any measure which implies the use of force or military troops must meet all the legal, political and strategic requirements of the Charter and be based on practical experience. Any action which implies the use of force - with the very limited exception of the right of legitimate defence - thus requires clear authorization by the Security Council for each specific case.

We believe these principles to be implicit in the primary responsibility of the Security Council with respect to the maintenance of international peace and security and in the absolute prohibition of the use of force in international relations. The Security Council cannot, nor should it, transfer to others or set aside its primary responsibility for the maintenance of international peace and security. For this reason, we do not believe that the Security Council should, in any case, authorize missions with military troops whose limits and powers are not clearly pre-established or whose mandate may be [7] conditioned to the subsequent decision of other organs or groups of States.

The Security Council alone can determine whether there has been a violation of its resolutions, adopted in the exercise of its mandated powers. Only the Security Council can authorize the use of force to ensure compliance with its resolutions, in exercise of its primary responsibility for the maintenance of international peace and security.

I wish to conclude by repeating that these comments on the law will not stand in Costa Rica's way to lending its support for the draft resolution before us, bearing in mind its profound ethical and humanitarian meaning.

[Statements by the representatives of Sweden, Slovenia, Kenya, Gambia and Japan have been omitted.]

[9] **Mr. Dangue Réwaka** (Gabon) *(interpretation from French)*: The duty of solidarity urged on us by the United Nations Charter implies, especially with regard to situations in which human lives are at risk, that our global Organization is able to act promptly in order to contain threats or to extend the necessary assistance when such threats cannot be contained in time.

For several months the Federal Republic of Yugoslavia has been fighting a secessionist movement in the province of Kosovo that has not hesitated to engage in terrorist acts - acts that are therefore deserving of condemnation. The reprisals that ensued are, in the unanimous opinion of international observers, abominations without parallel. Thousands of homes in many villages have been destroyed by indiscriminate bombardments or by fires set deliberately, forcing hundreds of thousands of women, old people and children to scatter throughout the countryside or to cross borders in search of refuge in neighbouring countries.

All of these excesses have not only caused panic and disarray among the civilian population, but have further worsened the situation in Kosovo, creating the risk, as winter approaches, of a real humanitarian catastrophe.

What should be done? While it is true that this is an internal matter of the Federal Republic of Yugoslavia, it is equally true that the members of the international community, and particularly the United Nations, have a [10] duty and a moral obligation to provide assistance and relief, and to do so without distinction.

We believe that this spirit of solidarity must be demonstrated in similar situations throughout the world. If we act otherwise, will we not be failing to shoulder our responsibilities under the Charter?

For our part, we welcome the tireless efforts that United States and European leaders and the Organization for Security and Cooperation in Europe (OSCE) have made, and are continuing to make, with a view to restoring peace and stability throughout Central and Eastern Europe. Recently, on 16 October, thanks to the perseverance and skill of the United States envoy, Ambassador Richard Holbrooke, those efforts resulted in the conclusion of an agreement authorizing, inter alia, an international verification mission in Kosovo.

Once again diplomacy, which is to say dialogue and negotiation - in other words, peaceful means - has prevailed. As a matter of principle, that is the approach that we most strongly support for the settlement of disputes, both internal and external.

That having been said, experience has shown that the safety of the personnel of missions and humanitarian organizations has often been threatened. We can no longer allow such personnel to be subjected to aggression by the parties to the conflict. That is why the text under consideration contains precautions to prevent such occurrences.

Impelled by all these considerations, my delegation will vote in favour of the draft resolution.

Mr. Amorim (Brazil): Kosovo has become the focus of the same pattern of ethnic violence that has already shattered countless lives throughout the region. Once again, outrage bred by ethnically induced aggression is fuelling radicalism. Once again, the responsibility for having allowed violence to be disseminated falls heavily, although not exclusively, on the leadership of the Federal Republic of Yugoslavia. The Security Council has been trying to articulate a consensus capable of preventing localized clashes from degenerating into a more serious and widespread conflict, even as thousands of civilians are the victims of harassment and dislocation. Resolutions 1160 (1998) and 1199 (1998) were clear signals. The agreements laboriously achieved through diplomacy have now set the stage for a process of reconciliation that should lead to greater autonomy for Albanian Kosovars.

Brazil supports those agreements and remains committed to a peaceful solution to the Kosovo crisis. Our repudiation of all forms of sectarian intolerance requires no elaboration; neither does our adherence to democratic pluralism, with full protection for the rights of minorities. We sincerely hope that a new chapter is being opened in the history of the Federal Republic of Yugoslavia which will allow its social fabric to heal from the traumas of a decade. In order to ensure compliance with the terms and conditions that have been formally accepted, the international community must remain vigilant. In order for the first positive indications to be consolidated into a stable process of confidence-building, adequate pressure remains necessary.

A difficult negotiating process has prevented the Security Council from moving more rapidly on Kosovo after the agreements reached between the Federal Republic of Yugoslavia on the one hand, and the Organization for Security and Cooperation in Europe (OSCE) and the North Atlantic Treaty Organization (NATO) on the other. In its attempt to reach a consensus, the Security Council has often been caught between two opposing tendencies. Some have argued that the Council's role at this stage should not go beyond a mere endorsement of those agreements; others argued in favour of exerting as much pressure as possible, if need be without a clear reference to the Council's prerogatives under the Charter. Of particular concern was the possibility that the Council might be transferring to other organizations its essential role in making the determination on whether or not its resolutions are being complied with.

We believe that before it becomes sufficiently clear that the trend of the past few months has been reversed in Kosovo, the Council cannot allow itself to be seen as showing complacency about non-compliance or even incomplete compliance with its resolutions.

But another important issue is also at stake here, one that transcends the confined limits of Kosovo. We do not wish to raise the question of how regional groups define themselves - which is something for them to decide. As a Member State of the United Nations, however, it is our right - and, indeed, our duty - to defend the Charter. According to the Charter, non-universal organisms may resort to force only on the basis either of the right to legitimate self-defence, as stipulated in Article 51, or through the procedures of Chapter VIII, in particular Article 53, which imposes on them the obligation of seeking Security Council authorization beforehand and [11] abiding by the Council's decision. Tertius non dato. There is no third way.

The integration of non-universal organizations into the wider collective security concept enshrined in the Charter is a serious matter. After having witnessed the rebirth of multilateralism at the end of the cold war, it would be regrettable if we were to slide into a two-tiered international system - a system in which the Security Council would continue to bear primary responsibility for the maintenance of peace and security in most of the world, while it would bear only secondary responsibility in regions covered by special defence arrangements.

After having witnessed certain disturbing signs which would point to a weakening of the Security Council's authority and after long discussions, we note with reassurance that the primary responsibility of the Security Council for the maintenance of international peace and security is reaffirmed. We are glad - and, indeed, grateful to the sponsors - that our suggestions to have a preambular paragraph on this matter was taken on board.

In the light of this reaffirmation and of other changes which satisfied our basic concerns, we will be voting in favour of the draft resolution before us. We would also like to note the helpful assurances given by the sponsors during the informal consultations.

We have finally come to what can be considered an acceptable text. It reconciles a strong political message in accordance with moral and ethical imperatives with what we view as the necessary regard for international law and the United Nations Charter. There can be no more auspicious date than 24 October, when we celebrate the anniversary of the entry into force of the United Nations Charter, to join in the reaffirmation of our respect for its provisions.

Mr. Lavrov (Russian Federation) *(interpretation from Russian)*: In the development of the situation in the Serbian region of Kosovo, Federal Republic of Yugoslavia, a new, important stage has been reached, opening up prospects for a political solution of the Kosovo problem. Thanks to the energetic coordinated efforts of the members of the Contact Group, a real possibility has emerged to stabilize the situation in and around Kosovo. As is well known, Russia has been playing an active role in these developments. I should like to recall that, during the recent visit to Belgrade of the Russian Minister for Foreign Affairs and Defence, the Yugoslav leadership agreed, in principle, to accept a mission of the Organization for Security and Cooperation in Europe (OSCE). The understandings reached by Ambassador Holbrooke, the representative of the Contact Group, with President Milosevic of the Federal Republic of Yugoslavia and the agreements signed on that basis regarding the dispatch of missions to verify the fulfilment by Belgrade and the Kosovar Albanians of the requirements of Security Council resolution 1199 (1998) have created important conditions for progress towards a peaceful, lasting resolution of the conflict in Kosovo on the basis of strict respect for the territorial integrity of the Federal Republic of Yugoslavia. Russia fully supports the Belgrade agreements. We call upon Belgrade to implement them fully, and we intend to play a most active role in the OSCE Verification Mission in Kosovo.

There has clearly been some progress in Belgrade's fulfilment of the requirements contained in Security Council resolutions 1160 (1998) and 1199 (1998). Offensive operations and repressive actions against the civilian population have been ended. The withdrawal of the units of Serbian security forces and of the Yugoslav army to their permanent stations, including outside Kosovo, is continuing. Cooperation between the Serb and Yugoslav authorities and international humanitarian organizations is expanding. The unimpeded access of those organizations to the people in need of assistance is being secured, as is the necessary freedom of movement of international personnel in the territory of Kosovo. These positive shifts have been witnessed, in particular, by the group of diplomatic observers from countries of the European Union, Russia and the United States working in the region. At the same time, much still remains to be done.

The task of the political resolution of the Kosovo problem has always been, and remains, the sole strategic objective of the Contact Group. Even though differences of opinion have sometimes arisen among its members, those differences relate to tactics and methods for moving towards that objective. To some extent, differences of tactical approach also emerged when we were agreeing on the draft resolution that is before us. We are satisfied that in the final analysis, the approach of continuing joint efforts within the framework of the Contact Group in the interests of the peace and stability of the region has prevailed.

Enforcement elements have been excluded from the draft resolution, and there are no provisions in it that would directly or indirectly sanction the automatic use of force, which would be to the detriment of the prerogatives of the Security Council under the Charter.

[12] In the course of the work on the draft resolution, much attention was paid to the question of ensuring the security of the personnel of the Verification Missions in Kosovo. Russia attaches great importance to this issue, especially since a large number of Russian representatives will be working in the OSCE mission. We are satisfied that the authors of the draft, having overcome their hesitations, have clearly stated in paragraph 9 that, in the event of an emergency, measures to ensure the safety of the Verification Missions, including arrangements for evacuating OSCE personnel, will be undertaken strictly in accordance with the procedure provided for in the agreements signed with Yugoslavia. The clarity introduced on this issue provides guarantees against arbitrary and unsanctioned actions.

Nor can one fail to take account of the possible danger to the implementation of the agreements between the OSCE and the Federal Republic of Yugoslavia as a result of actions by the Kosovar Albanians. We are alarmed by news of their continuing failure to comply with the demands of the Security Council. The Kosovar Albanian leadership still has not publicly condemned terrorism. Fighters in the socalled Kosovo Liberation Army have in recent times greatly increased their provocative activities and, as a rule, this is happening precisely in the regions from which Serbian security forces are being withdrawn. In violation of the arms embargo imposed by Security Council resolution 1160 (1998), illegal weapons continue to reach Kosovo and fighters are infiltrating. This creates a real threat of a new outbreak of violence and tension.

As members know, resolution 1160 (1998) was adopted under Chapter VII of the Charter. The draft resolution before us today also makes reference to that chapter. This serves as a reminder to those who are violating the arms embargo, and in particular the prohibition on supplying outside weapons or assistance to the Kosovo terrorists.

We note that paragraph 15 of the draft resolution makes it clear that the embargo shall not apply to equipment for missions established in accordance with the Belgrade agreements.

Also important is the fact that the draft resolution provides for the parties concerned with the implementation of the Belgrade agreements to report regularly to the Security Council on their activities through the Secretary-General. Here the Secretary-General will take account of input from the Federal Republic of Yugoslavia as well. The Security Council will consider the evolution of the situation on the basis of those reports and assessments by the Secretary-General.

At the same time, the draft resolution does not take fully into account the recent positive changes with respect to Belgrade's implementation of the Council's demands. We cannot agree with the one-sided assertion in the preambular part of the text that the unresolved situation in Kosovo constitutes a continuing threat to peace and security in the region.

We regret that the sponsors of the draft resolution refused to delete the portion of the text relating to freedom of operation of media outlets in the Federal Republic of Yugoslavia. I want everyone to be very clear about our position on this matter: for us, freedom of the press is one of the bases of democracy. It is one of the important elements we have achieved in the course of changing our society, and we value it highly. But questions of freedom of the press lie far beyond the powers of the Security Council, and therefore cannot be the object of a Council resolution, especially one adopted under Chapter VII of the Charter. It is other United Nations organs that consider such matters.

We were ready to continue to work on the draft resolution, but the sponsors hurried to bring it to the vote in its present form, which made it impossible to take our continuing concerns into account. In the circumstances, the Russian delegation will abstain in the vote on the draft resolution.

We are convinced that there are no differences of opinion among members of the Security Council on the strategy for action to achieve a peaceful settlement in Kosovo. That strategy, which precludes the granting of carte blanche with respect to the use of force, is reflected in the draft resolution, and we shall not object to its adoption.

We hope that this Council decision will accelerate the implementation of the Belgrade agreements and the dispatch of the OSCE Mission. We also expect the immediate rescission of the NATO decision on the possible use of force, the so-called activation order, which at present remains in force. This is of particular importance with respect to ensuring the safety of OSCE personnel.

In conclusion, I want to reaffirm that Russia will continue to make an active and concrete contribution to the political settlement of the Kosovo problem.

[13] **The President:** [*Speaking in his capacity as representative of the United Kingdom of Great Britain and Northern Ireland.*]

Throughout the Kosovo crisis, the Security Council has set out clearly the international community's concerns and requirements. Security Council resolution 1160 (1998) imposed an arms embargo in response to the use of excessive force by Belgrade security forces and to acts of terrorism, and called for the start of a meaningful political dialogue. Security Council resolution 1199 (1998) called for a ceasefire, the withdrawal of security forces used for civilian repression, cooperation with the international monitoring efforts and steps to improve the humanitarian situation. The situation in Kosovo represents a threat to international peace and security in the region and to human rights, and threatens a humanitarian catastrophe of even greater proportions than now. We are again at a critical stage where it is essential that the Security Council spell out clearly what Milosevic and the Kosovo Albanians must do if a regional disaster is to be averted.

The United Kingdom therefore welcomes today's draft resolution, which places the weight of the Security Council behind the commitments made by President Milosevic to comply with Security Council resolutions 1160 (1998) and 1199 (1998) and with the agreements reached with the Organization for Security and Cooperation in Europe (OSCE) and the North Atlantic Treaty Organization (NATO) providing for the establishment of ground and air verification missions.

It is right that these commitments should be enshrined in a mandatory Chapter VII resolution. President Milosevic's history of unfulfilled commitments over the summer, including those he made personally to President Yeltsin on 16 June, means that we cannot rely on his word. It is actions we must watch, and watch closely. And Milosevic must understand that the international community will not let him get away with token gestures or partial implementation.

The United Kingdom welcomes too the readiness of the OSCE and NATO to respond quickly to implement these agreements. In agreeing to these two missions, President Milosevic has accepted that the international community has a significant role to play in resolving the problems of Kosovo. The presence of the missions in and over Kosovo will be essential in helping to restore peace and security and in providing the reassurance sought by those who have fled their homes to return. As winter approaches, it is essential that the displaced return to their villages if a humanitarian disaster is to be averted. This will not happen unless all concerned in Kosovo adhere strictly to the ceasefire. If the civilian population are to have the confidence to return, the Federal Republic of Yugoslavia and Serbian forces must withdraw to their pre-crisis positions, cease the wanton destruction of homes, crops and livestock and abandon their violent intimidation of the civilian population. The OSCE Verification Mission will, through its intrusive mandate, be able to verify that they do and to report back to the international community if they do not.

The United Kingdom is pleased to be playing its part in making these agreements work. We expect to provide 200 members of the OSCE Mission. We will also provide aircraft for the Air Verification Mission over Kosovo. We will be resolute in following up implementation of these agreements and of the resolutions.

It is imperative that the authorities of the Federal Republic of Yugoslavia, the Kosovo Albanian leadership and all others concerned allow the OSCE Verification Mission to do its job. The Federal Republic of Yugoslavia has guaranteed the freedom of movement of the Mission as well as its safety and security. We shall hold it to these guarantees. No one should be in any doubt that we will use to the full our inherent right to protect our nationals if they are in danger, and the right under this draft resolution to take action to ensure their safety and freedom of movement.

No one should have any doubt: Britain will not stand by and watch a humanitarian disaster unfold in Kosovo. We wholeheartedly endorse the demands made in this draft resolution of the Federal Republic of Yugoslavia and the Kosovo Albanian leadership to cooperate with international efforts to prevent this happening. Again, the United Kingdom is ready to do its share.

This draft resolution and the agreements it endorses also mark the beginning of an accelerated political process. The United Kingdom calls upon the authorities in the Federal Republic of Yugoslavia and the Kosovo Albanian leadership to seize this opportunity to build a new Kosovo based on free elections and the principle of self-government for its people. Failure to do so will not be understood or accepted by the international community. Our message to both sides is, there is a chance for peace, for a better society, for a settled future, for a welcome to Europe and the wider world. Take it.

[*The President put to the vote the draft resolution S/1998/992, which was adopted as Security Council resolution 1203 (1998) with 13 votes to none with China and the Russian Federation abstaining.*]

[14] **Mr. Qin Huasun** (China) *(interpretation from Chinese)*: China welcomes the positive developments on the question of Kosovo, Federal Republic of Yugoslavia. We understand the agreements on the question of Kosovo reached between the Federal Republic of Yugoslavia and the parties concerned and evaluate positively the efforts made by the Government of the Federal Republic of Yugoslavia in alleviating the humanitarian situation in Kosovo and pursuing lasting peace and reconciliation in the region. We are of the view that the international community should try to maintain and promote this momentum towards a peaceful solution of the question of Kosovo.

However, very regrettably, almost at the same time as those agreements were being concluded, a regional organization concerned made the decision to take military actions against the Federal Republic of Yugoslavia and interfere in its internal affairs. More disturbingly, that decision was made unilaterally, without consulting the Security Council or seeking its authorization. Such an irresponsible act is not conducive to the creation of a peaceful atmosphere for dealing with the question of Kosovo and will not help resolve the issue. Furthermore, it has violated the purposes, principles and relevant provisions of the United Nations Charter, as well as international law and widely acknowledged norms governing relations between States. It is a disparagement of and a challenge to the authority of the United Nations and the Security Council and has created an extremely dangerous precedent in international relations. China is gravely concerned about this.

Maintaining the sovereignty and territorial integrity of the Federal Republic of Yugoslavia conforms to the provisions and requirements of the United Nations Charter and is also a shared commitment of the international community. It is on that basis that the question of Kosovo should be resolved. The implementation of the above-mentioned agreements should also proceed on that basis and be completed through full consultation and cooperation with the Federal Republic of Yugoslavia Serbian Government.

In principle, China does not oppose the adoption of a well-focused technical resolution by the Council to endorse the agreements reached between the Federal Republic of Yugoslavia and relevant parties and to encourage peaceful approaches on the question of Kosovo. This is in line with the understandings between the Federal Republic of Yugoslavia and the parties concerned. However, we do not favour the inclusion in the resolution of content beyond the above agreements. We are even more opposed to using Council resolutions to pressure the Federal Republic of Yugoslavia or to interfere in its internal affairs.

The Chinese delegation put forward its amendments during the Council's consultations, among which the request to delete those elements authorizing use of force or threatening to use force was accommodated. We believe that the resolution just adopted does not entail any authorization to use force or to threaten to use force against the Federal Republic of Yugoslavia, nor should it in any way be interpreted as authorizing the use of force or threatening to use force against the Federal Republic of Yugoslavia.

Nonetheless, the resolution just adopted still contains some elements beyond the agreements reached between the Federal Republic of Yugoslavia and parties concerned, including reference to Chapter VII of the Charter and elements of interference in the internal affairs of the Federal Republic of Yugoslavia. To our deep regret, our amendments concerning these questions were not accommodated. Therefore, the Chinese delegation abstained in the voting on the resolution.

[15] **Mr. Burleigh** (United States of America): In our vote today we have taken an important step forward in the search for peace in Kosovo. The agreements which the Security Council has endorsed were negotiated by representatives of the Contact Group and signed by the Organization for Security and Cooperation in Europe (OSCE) and the North Atlantic Treaty Organization (NATO) in the hope that their full implementation, including full compliance by Belgrade, would create an environment in which a peaceful solution could be found.

For too long the voices of reason and moderation in Kosovo have been muffled by repressive political, military and police actions and by those who advocate violence and the use of force over negotiation. Recently, Belgrade has taken steps to silence the independent media, further depriving the people of the Federal Republic of Yugoslavia of the capacity to make their own judgements about events in Kosovo and to accurately assess the actions of their leaders. In this context, we regret that not all members of the Council were able to support this resolution, and in particular its language about the importance of free media to a peaceful resolution of the Kosovo crisis.

The resolution we have adopted demands swift and full compliance by Belgrade with resolutions 1160 (1998) and 1199 (1998) and full cooperation with the OSCE and NATO Verification Missions. It also demands such compliance by the Kosovo Albanians with those resolutions and with the OSCE Verification Mission. We believe this is key to the creation of a climate of trust, which is indispensable to the return of refugees and displaced persons.

The investigations of the International Criminal Tribunal for the Former Yugoslavia into Kosovo are essential to restoring peace and security and must continue with the cooperation of everyone. The Tribunal's jurisdiction over Kosovo was established in resolution 827 (1993) of 25 May 1993 and has been reaffirmed by the Council, most recently in today's resolution. The Council has long been on record as demanding full cooperation with all of the Tribunal's orders, requests for information and investigations.

We must acknowledge that a credible threat of force was key to achieving the OSCE and NATO agreements and remains key to ensuring their full implementation. In addition, no party should be under the misapprehension that it can take any action that would hinder or endanger international verifiers or the personnel of humanitarian organizations.

The NATO allies, in agreeing on 13 October to the use of force, made it clear that they had the authority, the will and the means to resolve this issue. We retain that authority. We will not tolerate the continued violence that has resulted in nearly a quarter of a million refugees and displaced persons and thousands of deaths, and has jeopardized the prospects for peace in the wider Balkans. We reiterate that primary responsibility for the current crisis lies with Belgrade, although we expect full compliance by all parties.

The authorities in Belgrade and the Kosovo Albanians must now take full advantage of the opportunities being created. Neither violence nor repression can achieve a durable settlement. The crisis in Kosovo can and should be resolved through peaceful dialogue and negotiation. A foundation for a settlement now has been laid through the political discussions and shuttle diplomacy endorsed by the Contact Group. All that is required is the political will to move ahead. In our view, that is the only answer. The alternative is more of the same - a constant state of conflict, suffering and growing bitterness, which serves only to threaten peace and stability in the wider Balkan region and beyond.

[A statement by the representative of France has been omitted.]

160. NATO, Statement by the Secretary General Following the Meeting of the North Atlantic Council, 27 October 1998

Two weeks ago, NATO issued an ACTORD for limited air operations and a phased air campaign against Yugoslavia. We took this decision in order to back up diplomatic efforts to achieve peace in Kosovo and open the way for a political solution to the crisis.

From the outset we have insisted on full and unconditional compliance by President Milosevic with United Nations Security Council Resolutions 1199 and 1203. Since the ACTORD was issued, we have continued to put President Milosevic under pressure. General Naumann, SACEUR and I have been to Belgrade to make it clear to him in person that he has no option but to comply. I have also written to President Milosevic twice to stress the gravity of the situation.

It is this pressure and our credible threat to use force which have changed the situation in Kosovo for the better. NATO's unity and resolve have forced the Yugoslav Special Police and military units to exercise restraint and reduce their intimidating presence in Kosovo. We have been able to reduce the level of violence significantly and to achieve a cease-fire which has held, despite some sporadic incidents. This improvement in the security situation in Kosovo has first and foremost allowed an immediate improvement in the humanitarian situation. International relief organisations have re-started their operations in Kosovo. They now have unrestricted access for their convoys. Thousands of displaced persons have returned to their villages. At the same time, the improvement in the security situation is creating the conditions for a meaningful political dialogue to begin between Belgrade and the Kosovar Albanians.

Over the past few days, NATO's aerial surveillance assets and the Kosovo Diplomatic Observer Mission have been verifying whether Mr. Milosevic's actions match the commitments he has made to us.

I am pleased to report that over the past 24 hours, over 4,000 members of the Special Police have been withdrawn from Kosovo. Police and military units that are normally based in Kosovo are now moving back in their barracks together with their heavy weapons. Check points have been dismantled. In addition, most police and military units that are normally based elsewhere in Yugoslavia have left Kosovo. The security forces are returning to the level they were at before the present crisis began.

Despite these substantial steps, NATO's objective remains to achieve full compliance with UNSC Resolutions 1199 and 1203. As a result, we have decided this evening to maintain the ACTORD for limited air operations. Its execution will be subject to a decision and assessments by the North Atlantic Council. We will also maintain our ACTORD for the phased air campaign and will continue our activities under Phase Zero. We have requested our Military Authorities to remain prepared to carry out these air operations should they be necessary and to maintain forces at appropriate readiness levels for the operations under both ACTORDs.

The North Atlantic Council will keep the situation in Kosovo under constant review. If we see evidence of substantial non compliance in the future with UNSC Resolution 1199, then we will be ready to use force. We know that President Milosevic only moves when he is presented with the credible threat of force. The burden of proof of compliance clearly rests with him.

The Kosovar Albanians must equally comply with the UNSC Resolutions and cooperate with the international community. I call on the Kosovar Albanian armed groups to maintain the ceasefire that they have declared.

Our immediate focus will now be on ensuring the effectiveness of the verification regime.

Our NATO verification flights over Kosovo are beginning. We welcome the possible association of Russia and other partner countries in NATO's air verification regime.

NATO and the OSCE have been working closely together to coordinate their activities in carrying out the verification mission. The Alliance is also expediting planning for a NATO force for the extraction of the OSCE verifiers on the ground in Kosovo. We welcome UNSC Resolution 1203 which endorses the establishment of the two verification missions.

Despite the progress we have made, this crisis is far from over. A lot of work remains to be done. It is high time that the two parties in the conflict understand that the international community will not tolerate a continuation of the status quo. There has been too much human suffering. Clearly, a political solution must be found. I urge both sides to take advantage of the opportunity that now exists to move the political process forward and to secure this unique opportunity to work for a better future for Kosovo, and also for Yugoslavia as a whole.

161. NATO Statement on Kosovo, Meeting of the North Atlantic Council in Foreign Ministers Session, Press Communique M-NAC-2(98)143, 8 December 1998

1. NATO's aim has been to contribute to international efforts to stop the humanitarian crisis in Kosovo, end the violence there and bring about a lasting political settlement. NATO's decisions in October made a crucial contribution to the withdrawal of forces of the Federal Republic of Yugoslavia (FRY) from Kosovo and helped to avert a humanitarian disaster. The Alliance's enhanced state of military readiness continues.

2. The security situation in Kosovo remains of great concern to us. Since the beginning of November, violent incidents provoked in some cases by Serbian security forces and in others by armed Kosovar elements have increased tension. These incidents show that both the Belgrade authorities and the armed Kosovar elements have failed to comply fully with the requirements set out in UN Security Council Resolutions 1160, 1199 and 1203. We call upon the armed Kosovar elements to cease and desist from provocative actions and we call upon the FRY and Serbian authorities to reduce the number and visibility of MUP special police in Kosovo and abstain from intimidating behaviour.

3. We insist that both sides maintain scrupulously the ceasefire and comply fully with the UN Security Council resolutions. We also expect them to facilitate the war crimes investigations by the International Criminal Tribunal for the former Yugoslavia (ICTY). In this connection, we deplore the denial of visas to ICTY investigators. Continued violence between FRY and Serbian forces and armed Kosovar elements jeopardises prospects for a political settlement for which an opportunity now exists.

4. We remain firmly convinced that the problems of Kosovo can only be resolved through a process of open and unconditional dialogue between the authorities in Belgrade and representatives of the Kosovar leadership. We therefore strongly urge all parties to move rapidly in a spirit of compromise and accommodation to conclude the negotiating process led by Ambassador Hill in which they are engaged. We reaffirm our support for a political solution which provides an enhanced status for Kosovo, a substantially greater degree of autonomy and meaningful self-administration, and which preserves the territorial integrity of the FRY, and safeguards the human and civil rights of all inhabitants of Kosovo, whatever their ethnic origin. We believe that stability in Kosovo is linked to the democratisation of the FRY and we support those who are genuinely engaged in that process. In this regard, we condemn recent actions taken by President Milosevic to suppress the independent media and political pluralism in Serbia. We welcome the steps the Government of Montenegro has taken to protect the independent media, promote democratic reforms and ensure respect for the rights of all its citizens.

5. We will continue the Alliance's air verification mission, Operation "Eagle Eye", in accordance with the agreement between the FRY and NATO, and communicate periodically to the UN Secretary-General NATO's views on compliance.

6. We intend to cooperate fully with the OSCE Kosovo Verification Mission (KVM). The security and safety of the OSCE verifiers is of the utmost importance to us. We call on the FRY government to meet its responsibilities in this regard, as set out in UNSCRs 1199 and 1203 and the OSCE-FRY agreement of 16th October. We expect the FRY and Serbian authorities, as well as the Kosovar communities, to cooperate fully with the OSCE KVM, in particular by respecting its freedom of movement and right of access and by ensuring that its personnel are not subject to the threat or use of force or interference of any kind. We also expect the FRY and Serbian authorities to continue to allow unhindered access to international relief organisations including by issuing the necessary visas.

7. The North Atlantic Council has authorised an Activation Order (ACTORD) for a NATO-led Extraction Force, Operation "Joint Guarantor". We will quickly deploy the standing elements of this force in the Former Yugoslav Republic of Macedonia[1] to provide the ability to withdraw personnel of the OSCE KVM in an emergency. We greatly appreciate the cooperation and support of the authorities of the former Yugoslav Republic of Macedonia for providing facilities for the basing of NATO forces.

8. We welcome the willingness of Partner countries to join with NATO in contributing to the solution of the Kosovo crisis either by participating in the NATO-led air verification mission or by offering the use of their airspace or other facilities in support of NATO's efforts. We will continue to consult closely with all Partner countries on the Alliance's actions in respect of the Kosovo crisis.

162. FRY, Letter of Federal Foreign Minister Zivadin Jovanovic to the President of the UN Security Council, Mr. Robert Fowler, Belgrade, 1 February 1999

Excellency,

I am writing to you regarding the letter that the Secretary General of NATO addressed to the highest authorities in the Federal Republic of Yugoslavia on 30 January 1999, and regarding the statement by the North Atlantic Council on the Province of Kosovo and Metohija, attached thereto.

---

[1] Turkey recognises the Republic of Macedonia with its constitutional name.

The decision by NATO, as a regional agency, to have its Secretary General authorize air strikes against targets on FRY territory, as well as the position contained in the letter that this was a "final warning", represent an open and clear threat of aggression against the FRY as a sovereign and independent Member State of the United Nations.

Article 53, paragraph 1, of the United Nations Charter stipulates that "...no enforcement action shall be taken under regional arrangements or by regional agencies without the authorization of the Security Council..." In this specific case, the UN Security Council has not authorized NATO to take enforcement action against the FRY. Therefore, NATO's threat directly undermines the sovereignty and territorial integrity of the FRY and flagrantly violates the principles enshrined in the UN Charter, particularly in its Article 2, paragraph 4, and it undercuts the very foundations of the international legal order.

In view of the above, I call on you to inform all Council members of this letter and to convene an emergency session of the Council in order to take appropriate measures available under the Charter to prevent aggression against my country.

I take this opportunity to emphasize once again that the FRY pursues an open policy of peace, good-neighbourly and equal cooperation with all countries and organizations accepting such cooperation; it does not threaten anyone, nor is there any threat from its territory against any side. Consistently following the policy of peaceful settlement of all outstanding issues, the FR of Yugoslavia is a factor of peace and stability in the region. It is determined to protect its legitimate State and national interests, primarily its sovereignty and territorial integrity, in accordance with the principles embodied in the UN Charter, the Final Helsinki Act and the Paris Charter.

163. FRY, Statement of the Federal Government Concerning NATO Decisions, Belgrade, 1 February 1999

1. The decision by the NATO Council to empower its Secretary General to authorize NATO air strikes against targets in the Federal Republic of Yugoslavia represents an open threat of aggression against the sovereignty and territorial integrity of the FRY, as an independent Member State of the United Nations, which is in contravention of the principles enshrined in the United Nations Charter, and in particular its Article 2, paragraph 4.

2. As a regional agency, NATO has no authorization of the Security Council or the right to enforcement action against a sovereign and independent UN Member State, as explicitly stipulated in Article 53 of the UN Charter.

3. Open threats by NATO undermine the fundamental principles of international relations, international peace and security, as well as the very foundations of the international legal order. The Federal Government, therefore, decided to request a meeting of the Security Council in order that appropriate measures under the UN Charter may be taken to prevent an armed aggression against the FR of Yugoslavia.

4. The FRY, as an independent country, pursues a policy of peace and peaceful cooperation; it does not constitute a threat to anyone, nor is there any threat from its territory against any side. In line with these principles, the FRY stands ready to settle all outstanding issues by peaceful political means and to protect resolutely its legitimate State and national interests, and in particular its sovereignty and territorial integrity, in accordance with the UN Charter.

164. FRY, Conclusions of the National Assembly of the Republic of Serbia Concerning NATO Threats of Aggression against FRY and the Participation in Talks in France, Belgrade, 4 February 1999

I

1. The National Assembly condemns in strongest terms the threats of NATO against our country and people. The threats are totally contrary to the proclaimed positions of the international community that it is committed to a peaceful solution of the problems in Kosovo and Metohija and represent an open support to separatists and terrorists.

2. The conduct of NATO represents an open threat of aggression against sovereignty and territorial integrity of the FR of Yugoslavia, as an independent State, one of the founders and a UN Member State, which is a violation of the principles of the Charter of the United Nations, particularly Article 2, para 4 of the UN Charter.

3. NATO is a regional military organization and in Article 53, para 1 of the UN Charter it is expressly stated that no regional arrangements or regional agencies can utilize any enforcement action without the authorization of the Security Council. The UN Security Council has not authorized NATO to undertake enforcement measures against the FR of Yugoslavia and the NATO threat therefore represents a direct violation of the Charter of the United Nations and a threat to the sovereignty and territorial integrity of our country.

4. The National Assembly assess that with such conduct NATO acts in violation of the basic principles of the international relations, the very foundations of the international order and represents a threat to the international peace and security.

5. The FR of Yugoslavia pursues an open policy of peace, good-neighbourliness and equitable cooperation with all countries and organizations accepting such cooperation, it does not pose a threat to anyone nor is there a threat from its territory to anyone. Consistently adhering to the policy of resolving all open questions in a peaceful manner, the FR of Yugoslavia represents a factor of peace and stability in the region. We shall resolutely defend our legitimate State and national interests, above all, the sovereignty and territorial integrity of the country, in accordance with the principles of the Charter of the United Nations, Helsinki Final Act and the Paris Charter.

6. The National Assembly of the Republic of Serbia emphasizes that in the case of aggression against our country, we shall defend the sovereignty and territorial integrity, freedom, independence, lives and property of our citizens - by all available means. We are resolute and united in defending our homeland.

II

1. The Republic of Serbia remains committed to a peaceful political resolution of the problems in Kosovo and Metohija. We are determined to seek ways to resolve the problems through dialogue, while respecting territorial integrity and sovereignty of our country, by ensuring full equality of all citizens and all national communities living in Kosmet.

2. By issuing invitations to negotiations, the Contact Group is knocking at an open door. Serbia and the FR of Yugoslavia have proven that they are committed to the political solution and that they do all they can in order that it be reached in dialogue among all national communities from Kosovo and Metohija.

3. While emphasizing its commitment to peaceful and political solution of the current problems in Kosovo and Metohija, the National Assembly points to major, inadmissible and highly one-sided positions in the conclusions of the Contact Group, inappropriate in relation to a sovereign country.

4. While verbally supporting the sovereignty and territorial integrity of Serbia and the FR of Yugoslavia, at the same time proposals are put forward which threaten and question our sovereignty and integrity, proposing even confederal elements such as an obligatory consent of Kosmet for changes to Kosmet borders and declaration of martial law.

5. From the countries formally supporting the sovereignty and territorial integrity of Serbia and the FR of Yugoslavia at the same time come threats and millions of dollars in financial assistance, arms and equipment to terrorists.

6. It should be particularly condemned that a part of the international community, concerning an internal issue - the right of a State to defend itself from separatism and terrorism - should support the separatists and terrorists and equate a sovereign State with those who seek to destroy that State.

7. It is particularly unacceptable to equate the responsibility of the State organs with that of criminal groups, for the situation in Kosmet.

The legal actions of the State authorities against terrorism cannot be termed repression against civilians, while terrorism in all forms - attacks, murders, kidnapping is termed - as provocations.

8. The international community has failed to grasp what the actions of the so called KLA, as a terrorist organization, are essentially about and does not take measures against it, as is the case when other terrorist organizations in the world are in question.

9. It is unacceptable to downplay the past efforts in seeking a solution by political means and endeavours to recall the agreement between the President of the FRY with the international community, expressed in the positions of the Government of 13 October 1998 and the Agreement with the OSCE of 18 October 1998 and the principles contained therein - that this is an internal issue of a sovereign State; that terrorism and separatism must end; that any solution has to be in line with the *Constitution of the FRY and of the Republic of Serbia and that it* cannot question the sovereignty and territorial integrity of our country.

10. The National Assembly emphasizes the democratic nature of the Joint proposal of the Agreement on the political framework of self-governance in Kosovo and Metohija of 20 November 1998, accepted by all Parliamentary parties in Serbia, as well as the Declaration from Pristina of 25 November 1998, signed by two political parties of Albanians, the representatives of the national communities of Muslims, Turks, Roma, Goranies and Egyptians as well as the representatives of Parliamentary parties from Kosovo and Metohija. It is inadmissible to ignore and discredit the existence of national communities and ethnic groups as well as to recognize the necessity for all national communities living in Kosovo and Metohija to be treated equally.

11. Concerning the demand that "the parties accept the level and nature of international presence deemed appropriate by the international community", the National Assembly wishes to note: the level and nature of the international presence in Kosmet has been ultimately defined in the Agreement between the President of the FRY Slobodan Milosevic and Ambassador Richard Holbrooke and in the Agreement between the Federal Government and the OSCE on the establishment of the OSCE Verification mission in Kosmet in accordance with it.

12. The National Assembly is extremely surprised at the request that "the federal and republican legal frameworks be harmonized with Kosmet interim agreement" since this defies the logic and principles of the constitutional law and would represent a legal and constitutional precedent whereby a broader community would have to adjust to a part of a smaller community.

13. To reduce the rights of other national communities in solutions for Kosmet to some sort of cultural rights is a discrimination and opens up the possibility that concrete solutions be used by the Albanian national community to overrule others, thus directly violating the principles of equality and introducing the existence of first and second class citizens.

14. The National Assembly points out that any demand for a "substantial" or "high degree" self-governance for Kosmet - not only in further negotiations cannot lead to independent Kosovo and Metohija, or a status of a third federal unit, but that this autonomy cannot imply the severance of legal, political and economic ties within the Republic of Serbia.

15. The National Assembly indicates that the so called interim status of Kosmet cannot be either hidden or explicit road towards separatism but a possibility for the signatories to examine the Agreement, after a number of years with a view to promoting its implementation and reviewing the proposals of any signatory for additional measures whose adoption will require the consent of all signatories.

III

1. The National Assembly of the Republic of Serbia emphasizes that the State organs of the Republic of Serbia and the FR of Yugoslavia have done and do all they can to reach a political solution. We fully respect the signed agreements. The OSCE Verification mission in Kosmet has been established to monitor and impartially inform the international community of the situation on the ground. Serbia has nothing to hide in defending its citizens and its territory from separatists and terrorists - verifiers and international community have been granted full and unimpeded access to all parts of Kosovo and Metohija and enabled to monitor the entire situation.

2. The FR of Yugoslavia, as an independent and sovereign State, pursues a policy of peace and peaceful cooperation, it does not threaten anyone or pose a threat to anyone from its territory. In accordance with the above principles, the FR of Yugoslavia stands ready to resolve all open questions by peaceful and political means and to resolutely defend its legitimate State and national interests, particularly sovereignty and territorial integrity in accordance with the Charter of the United Nations.

IV

1. The National Assembly again emphasizes that the cause of the crisis in Kosovo and Metohija is long-standing Albanian separatism, with the ultimate goal of seceding Kosovo and Metohija from Serbia and Yugoslavia. Terrorism has become the ultimate stage of Albanian separatism.

2. This is the major obstacle to the achievement of a political solution. All efforts, offers and good will of the State for them to engage in political dialogue and look for solutions together with others, have been met by the refusal and obstruction of Albanian separatist parties and their leaders. Such position on their part fuelled and encouraged the continuation of the crimes of terrorist gangs. They abused the fact that our State respected the Agreement as well as the presence of the OSCE Verification mission and continued with their crimes.

3. The Republic of Albania has been openly and directly in the function of Albanian separatism and terrorism. Albania has turned into a terrorist State - a base for terrorists and fundamentalists, a centre for training, arming, financing and all other support to their criminal goals towards the FR of Yugoslavia and other countries in the region.

4. A part of the international community has not by a single act unreservedly condemned separatism and terrorism. They have done nothing to prevent the Republic of Albania from being a logistics base of terrorists and separatists in Kosovo and Metohija. The Organization for Security and Cooperation in Europe has not managed even in three months to complete a 2,000-member mission in Kosmet and has not been fully equipped to impartially and accurately inform the international community and international organizations of the true situation on the ground. The fact of the matter is that since the signing of the Agreement and the arrival of verifiers, the terrorism escalated.

5. A part of the international community has all along pursued a policy of double standards preventing any, even the mildest attempt of condemning terrorist gangs by the UN Security Council. Such conduct on the part of the international community actually represents support, assistance and encouragement to separatists and terrorists.

6. By fabricated and inaccurate assessments that the military and police use excessive force, they try to prevent the legitimate forces from defending the people and the State in responding to terrorist acts in an appropriate manner, as the military and police in all countries in the world do in combating this scourge. This is an attempt to reverse the position harmonized with the international community explicitly stating that "state authorities retain the right to respond appropriately to any form of terrorist activities and violation of the law which may endanger the lives and security of citizens and law enforcement authorities".

V

1. Kosovo and Metohija is an internal issue of Serbia which can be resolved only through dialogue of those subjects whose position it affects. Kosovo and Metohija cannot be removed from Serbia. It has been there for centuries and it is the only place it can be in. Kosovo and Metohija is not a testing ground for military and political doctrines in the wake of fabricated charges of the alleged violation of minority and ethnic rights. Kosmet is not under protectorate nor is it a reserve for some new geo-political configurations - Serbia is not giving any grounds for new ultimatums, even if they are made today in the name

of human rights and democracy and other lofty goals which serve nothing but to mask hegemonism.

2. The National Assembly of Serbia once again reaffirms the principles on the basis of which the crisis in Kosovo and Metohija can be resolved successfully, durably and in the interest of all. These are:
- political means and dialogue as the only way to achieve a peaceful and democratic solution of the crisis in Kosovo and Metohija;
- full respect of territorial integrity and sovereignty of Serbia and the FR of Yugoslavia;
- full equality of all citizens, all national communities and ethnic groups in Kosovo and Metohija, without possibility of anyone being overruled;
- solutions harmonized with the Constitutions of Serbia and the FR of Yugoslavia and the international standards in the field of human, civil and the rights of persons belonging to national communities;
- Kosovo and Metohija cannot be granted the status of a republic, but self-governance in line with the highest international standards within Serbia and the FR of Yugoslavia;
- we do not accept any measure which would change territorial integrity and sovereignty or attempt to secede Kosmet from Serbia;
- we do not accept the presence of foreign soldiers in our territory under any pretext of implementing the achieved agreement;

VI

Concerning the invitation of the Contact Group for talks on the problems in Kosovo and Metohija, in France on 6 February 1999, addressed to the Government of the Republic of Serbia:

1. The National Assembly of the Republic of Serbia has decided to accept the invitation for talks because it is a firm commitment of the people and all political parties to fight for peace and because we need to defend Kosovo and Metohija in any place in the world wherever Kosmet may be discussed. By accepting these talks we make another step forward to contribute to resolving the problems in a peaceful manner.

2. The National Assembly hereby authorizes the Government to designate the delegation which will take part in these talks.

165. FRY, Letter of the Yugoslav Foreign Minister Z. Jovanovic Addressed to President of the Security Council of the United Nations, Qin Huasun, Belgrade, 17 March 1999

Excellency,

Referring to my letter of 1 February 1999, concerning open threats of aggression by NATO against the Federal Republic of Yugoslavia, I should like to inform you of some latest developments.

Namely, there has been a build-up of troops and arms by NATO countries, which have been brought in from other parts of Europe and the world, in the immediate neighbourhood of Yugoslavia. According to available reports, more than 10,000 NATO troops have been deployed in the neighbouring Republic of Macedonia, along with 60 tanks, 25 armoured vehicles, several dozen combat helicopters, great many pieces of artillery, including 155mm long-range guns. It has been announced that NATO troops in that neighbouring country will soon increase to over 30,000. There are also reports on military reinforcements as well as the establishment of foreign military bases in other neighbouring countries, in Albania in particular.

Such a build-up of foreign troops and military material, unseen at any time in the post-war period, has been coupled with ultimatums by the highest NATO officials and by individual NATO countries to the effect that they are ready to launch attacks against the FR of Yugoslavia.

We would like to draw the attention of the UN Security Council to such troop and arms build-ups and to undisguised threats of aggression by NATO against Yugoslavia, as a sovereign and independent founding Member State of the United Nations, causing profound concern of the Government and the people of Yugoslavia and posing a threat to peace and security in the region. This is, at the same time, a blatant and flagrant violation of the principles of the UN Charter and the OSCE documents prohibiting the threat or use of force in international relations. As I pointed out in my letter of 1 February, this represents a direct violation of Article 53 para 1 of the UN Charter.

H.E. Mr. Qin Huasun President of the Security Council of the United Nations New York

Also, while issuing open threats of aggression and ultimatums to Yugoslavia, senior NATO officials and those of some NATO countries, on the other hand, are maintaining contacts with, and extending assistance and support for, separatists and terrorists in the Serbian Province of Kosovo and Metohija, an integral part of sovereign Serbia and Yugoslavia. These factors and countries, failed to take steps and measures to cut off the channels of finance, arming, training and infiltration of arms and terrorists into the territory of the FR of Yugoslavia, in breach of and ignoring the obligations under the relevant UN Security Council resolutions, and in particular its resolution 1160 (1998).

The Federal Republic of Yugoslavia pursues an active and peaceful policy; it is committed to good-neighbourly relations, peace and stability in the region; no threat is being posed from its territory nor is it threatening the interests of any other countries, least of all the interests of NATO countries. It is determined to resolve all its internal problems by peaceful political means, in compliance with international standards. This is equally true regarding a political, peaceful solution in Kosovo and Metohija, within the framework of an extensive self-governance and autonomy and equality for all national communities. With this approach and goal as well as a principled and constructive attitude, our delegation is taking part in the meeting, which is currently being held in Paris, France.

Troop and arms build-ups in the neighbourhood of Yugoslavia and open NATO threats cannot be justified on any pretext. This is surely not the way to facilitate the reaching of political agreement. However, there can be no doubt that this is the way to support the opponents of a peaceful political solution, and in particular to encourage the proponents of separatism and terrorism. In case of an attack, the FR of Yugoslavia will act in accordance with its legitimate right to defend itself.

Mr. President,

I call upon you to convene a meeting of the Security Council, so that this body, in line with its primary responsibility for peace and security, could urge NATO to cease its threats of use of force against Yugoslavia, to stop any further build-up of troops and arms in the region and to withdraw those already deployed, which would contribute to the reduction of tensions and elimination of unforeseen threats to peace and security in the region.

Please accept, Excellency, the assurances of my highest consideration. Zivadin Jovanovic

166. FRY, Letter of the Yugoslav Foreign Minister Z. Jovanovic Addressed to Chairman-in-Office of the OSCE, Minister for Foreign Affairs of the Kingdom of Norway, Knut Vollebaek, Belgrade, 17 March 1999

Excellency,

Allow me to draw your attention that there has been a build-up of troops and arms by NATO countries, which have been brought in from other parts of Europe and the world, in the immediate neighbourhood of Yugoslavia. According to available reports, more than 10,000 NATO troops have been deployed in the neighbouring Republic of Macedonia, along with 60 tanks, 250 armoured vehicles, several dozen combat helicopters, great many pieces of artillery, including 155mm long-range guns. It has been announced that NATO troops in that neighbouring country would soon increase to over 30,000. There are also reports on military reinforcements as well as the establishment of foreign military bases in other neighbouring countries, in Albania in particular.

Such a build-up of foreign troops and military equipment, unprecedented in the post-war period, has been coupled with ultimatums by the highest NATO officials and by individual NATO countries to the effect that they are ready to launch attacks against the FR of Yugoslavia.

We would like to draw the attention of the OSCE Member States and particularly of the OSCE Permanent Council to such troop and arms build-ups and to undisguised threats of aggression by NATO against Yugoslavia, as a sovereign and independent founding Member State of the OSCE and the United Nations, causing profound concern of the Government and the people of Yugoslavia and posing a threat to peace and security in the region. This is, at the same time, a blatant and flagrant violation of the principles of the UN Charter and the OSCE documents prohibiting the threat or use of force in international relations.

Also, while issuing open threats and ultimatums to Yugoslavia, senior NATO officials and those of some NATO countries, on the other hand, are maintaining contacts with, and extending assistance and support for, separatists and terrorists in the Serbian Province of Kosovo and Metohija, an integral part of sovereign Serbia and Yugoslavia. These factors and countries failed to take steps and measures to cut off the channels of finance, arming, training and infiltration of arms and terrorists into the territory of the FR of Yugoslavia, in breach of and ignoring the obligations under the relevant UN Security Council resolutions, and in particular its resolution 1160 (1998). My letter of 1 March 1999, to which I expect your esteemed response, refers to this matter.

The Federal Republic of Yugoslavia pursues an active and peaceful policy; it is committed to good-neighbourly relations, peace and stability in the region; no threat is being posed from its territory nor is it threatening the interests of any other countries, least of all the interests of NATO countries. It is determined to resolve all its internal problems by peaceful political means, in compliance with international standards. This is equally true regarding a political, peaceful solution in Kosovo and Metohija, within the framework of an extensive self-governance and autonomy and equality for all national communities. With this approach and goal as well as a principled and constructive attitude, our delegation is taking part in the meeting, which is currently being held in Paris, France.

Troop and arms build-ups in the neighbourhood of Yugoslavia and open NATO threats cannot be justified on any pretext. This is surely not the way to facilitate the reaching of political agreement. However, there can be no doubt that this is the way to support the opponents of a peaceful political solution, and in particular to encourage the proponents of separatism and terrorism, as is clearly evidenced by the developments on the ground. In case of an attack, the FR of Yugoslavia will act in accordance with its legitimate right to defend itself.

Mr. Chairman-in-Office,

I call upon you to convene a meeting of the OSCE Permanent Council, so that this body, in line with its primary responsibility for peace and security, could urge NATO to cease its threats of use of force against Yugoslavia, to stop any further build-up of troops and arms in the region and to withdraw those already deployed, which would contribute to the reduction of tensions and elimination of unforeseen threats to peace and security in the region.

We call upon the OSCE Member States, and particularly our neighbouring States, to show understanding for the efforts by the FR of Yugoslavia to protect its legitimate national and State interests and in particular - not to participate in exercising any pressures of factors outside the Region or in the activities against the FR of Yugoslavia, having in mind the long-standing common interests for peace, stability and cooperation.

Please accept, Excellency, the assurances of my highest consideration. Zivadin Jovanovic

167. NATO, Statement by the North Atlantic Council, Press Release (1999)038, 22 March 1999

In response to Belgrade's continued intransigence and repression, the Secretary General of NATO, to whom the North Atlantic Council had delegated on 30 January the authority to decide on air operations, is completing his consultations with the Allies to this end.

In view of the evolution of the situation on the ground in Kosovo, the North Atlantic Council has also authorised today the Secretary General to decide, subject to further consultations, on a broader range of air operations if necessary.

168. UK, Statement by Defence Minister, Press Release 083/99, Paris, 22 March 1999

At a meeting in Paris today the Defence Ministers of the UK (Mr Robertson), France (M Richard) and Italy (Sr Scognamiglio) discussed Kosovo and said:

"Today is a crucial day for the future of Kosovo,

"Diplomatic efforts to get President Milosevic to see sense are now in their final stage. The three co-negotiators and US envoy Holbrooke are in Belgrade today. We hope they will be successful.

"The time has come for President Milosevic to face up to his responsibilities. The demands of the international community were reiterated in the warning from NATO on 30 January. He must cease offensive military activity in Kosovo immediately. He must reduce force levels to those agreed in October. He must accept the interim settlement negotiated by the international community at Rambouillet including its provisions for civilian and military implementation.

"We hope NATO military action will not be required. But we reaffirm that we are ready, with our NATO Allies, to take whatever measures are necessary to avert a humanitarian catastrophe in Kosovo."

169. UK, Transcript of Statement Given by the Foreign Secretary, Robin Cook, Brussels, 22 March 1999

Good Morning. We have had a very full discussion. I first of all have to say that that discussion was grave and was serious. We are deeply concerned about what is happening on the ground at present within Kosovo. I welcome the fact that Dick Holbrooke has come here for this full consultation and my first message from our meeting to President Milosevic is that this was a meeting that showed total unity. All three of us, myself and my colleagues Hubert Vedrine and Joschka Fischer, fully support Dick Holbrooke's mission and we are at one in the message that he takes. We are also confident that colleagues throughout the European Union will support us in that unity.

The message to President Milosevic is twofold. First of all he now must get down in good faith to reach agreement on the peace accords that we negotiated at Rambouillet, and that must include an international military presence. The events of recent weeks show that the cease-fire will only stick if there is that international guarantee of a cease-fire. But the second message is equally important. He has to stick by the agreement he gave in October not to carry out serious military repression within Kosovo. He cannot expect us to go on talking peace with him while he is making war on the ground in Kosovo and it is equally important that the Kosovo Liberation Army shows restraint also. Hubert Vedrine and I strongly welcomed the decision by the Kosovo Albanians at Paris to sign the peace accords and to give a commitment to demilitarisation. We want to see that commitment honoured in the interim while we press Belgrade also to sign those accords and it is not consistent with the commitment they made for the Kosovo Liberation Army to carry out actions which target Serb civilians.

We very much hope that at this late stage President Milosevic will take this chance to make peace. His record shows he is a brinkman. I think he should clearly understand now he is at the brink and he must now seek a settlement. The only person that can prevent the military action that may follow is President Milosevic. It is down to him as to whether he responds.

4.2 NATO AIR STRIKES

170. NATO, Statement by the Secretary General, Press Release (1999)040, 23 March 1999

Good evening, ladies and gentlemen,

I have just directed SACEUR, General Clark, to initiate air operations in the Federal Republic of Yugoslavia.

I have taken this decision after extensive consultations in recent days with all the Allies, and after it became clear that the final diplomatic effort of Ambassador Holbrooke in Belgrade has not met with success.

All efforts to achieve a negotiated, political solution to the Kosovo crisis having failed, no alternative is open but to take military action.

We are taking action following the Federal Republic of Yugoslavia Government's refusal of the International Community's demands:

- Acceptance of the interim political settlement which has been negotiated at Rambouillet;

- Full observance of limits on the Serb Army and Special Police Forces agreed on 25 October;

- Ending of excessive and disproportionate use of force in Kosovo.

As we warned on the 30 January, failure to meet these demands would lead NATO to take whatever measures were necessary to avert a humanitarian catastrophe.

NATO has fully supported all relevant UN Security Council resolutions, the efforts of the OSCE, and those of the Contact Group.

We deeply regret that these efforts did not succeed, due entirely to the intransigence of the FRY Government.

This military action is intended to support the political aims of the international community.

It will be directed towards disrupting the violent attacks being committed by the Serb Army and Special Police Forces and weakening their ability to cause further humanitarian catastrophe.

We wish thereby to support international efforts to secure Yugoslav agreement to an interim political settlement.

As we have stated, a viable political settlement must be guaranteed by an international military presence.

It remains open to the Yugoslav Government to show at any time that it is ready to meet the demands of the international community.

I hope it will have the wisdom to do so.

At the same time, we are appealing to the Kosovar Albanians to remain firmly committed to the road to peace which they have chosen in Paris. We urge in particular Kosovar armed elements to refrain from provocative military action.

Let me be clear: NATO is not waging war against Yugoslavia.

We have no quarrel with the people of Yugoslavia who for too long have been isolated in Europe because of the policies of their government.

Our objective is to prevent more human suffering and more repression and violence against the civilian population of Kosovo.

We must also act to prevent instability spreading in the region.

NATO is united behind this course of action.

We must halt the violence and bring an end to the humanitarian catastrophe now unfolding in Kosovo.

We know the risks of action but we have all agreed that inaction brings even greater dangers.

We will do what is necessary to bring stability to the region.

We must stop an authoritarian regime from repressing its people in Europe at the end of the 20th century.

We have a moral duty to do so.

The responsibility is on our shoulders and we will fulfil it.

171. NATO, Political and Military Objectives of NATO Action with Regard to the Crisis in Kosovo, Press Release (1999)043, 23 March 1999

NATO's overall political objectives remain to help achieve a peaceful solution to the crisis in Kosovo by contributing to the response of the international community. More particularly, the Alliance made it clear in its statement of 30th January 1999 that its strategy was to halt the violence and support the completion of negotiations on an interim political solution.

Alliance military action is intended to support its political aims. To do so, NATO's military action will be directed towards halting the violent attacks being committed by the VJ and MUP and disrupting their ability to conduct future attacks against the population of Kosovo, thereby supporting international efforts to secure FRY agreement to an interim political settlement.

172. NATO, Press Statement by the Secretary General following the Commencement of Air Operations, Press Release (1999)041, 24 March 1999

I have been informed by SACEUR, General Clark, that at this moment NATO Air Operations against targets in the Federal Republic of Yugoslavia have commenced.

In the last months the international community has spared no efforts to achieve a negotiated solution in Kosovo. But it has not been possible.

Clear responsibility for the air strikes lies with President Milosevic who has refused to stop his violent action in Kosovo and has refused to negotiate in good faith.

The time has now come for action.

Let me reiterate: NATO is not waging war against Yugoslavia.

We have no quarrel with the people of Yugoslavia who for too long have been isolated in Europe because of the policies of their government.

Our actions are directed against the repressive policy of the Yugoslav leadership.

We must stop the violence and bring an end to the humanitarian catastrophe now taking place in Kosovo. We have a moral duty to do so.

NATO's men and women in uniform, who are carrying out this important mission, are among the best in the world. I am confident that they will be successful.

173. FRY, Statement from the Federal Government's Meeting, Belgrade, 25 March 1999

At today's meeting, chaired by Prime Minister Momir Bulatovic, the Federal Government decided to sever diplomatic relations with the governments of the United States, Great Britain, France and Germany.

By the aggression on the Federal Republic of Yugoslavia and the use of enormous military and killing potentials, the governments of the USA, Great Britain and France have degraded and shamed the historical alliance and friendship between the people of the Federal Republic of Yugoslavia and the people of their countries. The German government has hurt the unhealed wounds from the Second World War.

The Federal Government also decided to consider diplomatic and overall relations with other countries that directly or indirectly took part in the aggression on the Federal Republic of Yugoslavia.

The Federal Government gives credit to all governments and countries that express support and solidarity with our people.

The government concluded that all available material resources necessary for armed forces must be at the disposal of Yugoslav Army and Ministry of Internal Affairs. The government made the decision to finance the defence expenses. Therefore it levied the special sales and import taxes. The tax rate is 0,4 % - 6 %. These funds will be put down to special account and will be managed by the Federal Government.

174. NATO, Letter from the Secretary General of NATO to the Secretary-General of the UN, 27 March 1999[1]

I am writing to update you on developments concerning ongoing North Atlantic Treaty Organization (NATO) operations in the Federal Republic of Yugoslavia. During the last few days, an increasing number of reports indicate that security forces of the Federal Republic of Yugoslavia have taken advantage of the absence of international observers and media to commit serious human rights abuses and atrocities against the civilian population, and to plunder and destroy civilian infrastructure and dwellings. This has exacerbated the flow of refugees and internally displaced persons, increased human suffering and led to heightened tension and instability in the region. As a result, I have directed the NATO Supreme Allied Command Europe (SACEUR) to initiate a broader scope of operations to intensify action against the Federal Republic of Yugoslavia forces and compel them to desist from further attacks in Kosovo and to meet the demands of the international community. As I have repeatedly made clear, NATO military actions are intended to support the political aims of the international community. All Allies stand united in this action and in our determination to bring a halt to violence in Kosovo and to prevent further humanitarian catastrophe. I will continue to keep you informed of significant developments.

(Signed) Javier Solana

175. FRY, The Decree on the Assemblies of Citizens during the State of War, Belgrade, 1 April 1999

Article 1: The Assembly of Citizens Act shall be applied during the state of war unless it is otherwise provided by this Act.

Article 2: A public gathering can be convened and held, and persons can appear at the gathering, only with prior permission of the competent organ, irrespective of whether the gathering is held in closed premises or in open air and irrespective of its nature.

The provisions of para 1 of this article are not applied when the public gathering is convened by an organ of the state.

Article 3: A legal person convening or holding a public gathering or appearing at it without a prior permission of a competent organ shall be fined with up to 200 000 new dinars.

For the misdemeanour in para 1 of this article the responsible person of the legal person shall be fined with up to 10 000 new dinars or imprisoned for up to 60 days.

A physical person will be punished for the misdemeanour in para 1 of this article by a fine of up to 10 000 new dinars or by imprisonment of up to 60 days.

Article 4: This Decree shall enter into force on the day of its publication in the Official Gazette of the Republic of Serbia.

Belgrade, 1 April 1999, President of the Republic, Signed: Milan Milutinovic

176. NATO, Statement of the North Atlantic Council Following the Meeting between Representatives of the NATO Member States, the EU Member States, the OSCE CIO, the UNHCR, the Council of Europe and the WEU, Press Release (1999)048, Brussels, 4 April 1999

At the initiative of the EU Presidency and with the agreement of the North Atlantic Council, a timely and constructive meeting was held today at NATO Headquarters in Brussels of representatives of the NATO member states, of the EU member states, the European Commission and ECHO, of the OSCE CiO, of the UNHCR, of the Council of Europe and of the Western European Union. The objective of the meeting was to contribute to the coordination of efforts and to identify concrete measures to address the grave humanitarian crisis brought on by the actions of President Milosevic's forces in Kosovo.

This humanitarian tragedy requires an immediate response. We are ready to work as constructively and efficiently as possible and in coordination with other international organisations and agencies. We welcome and support the statement of the EU Presidency following today's meeting.

The situation in Kosovo and in the region continues to deteriorate further, as a consequence of the continued Yugoslav campaign of ethnic cleansing which has already resulted, according to the UNHCR, in 125,000 refugees in the former Yugoslav Republic of Macedonia[2], 226,000 in Albania and 33,000 in Montenegro. What we have been witnessing over the last few weeks is the climax of a campaign of violence and destruction carried out by Yugoslav Army and Serb police forces.

We have already taken steps to address this humanitarian catastrophe. On 3rd April, we took a series of important decisions which will allow NATO to step in quickly and help with humanitarian efforts both in Albania and in the former Yugoslav Republic of Macedonia.

The Alliance's military forces will engage more actively in refugee relief in the former Yugoslav Republic of Macedonia and Albania, in cooperation and coordination with the relevant humanitarian organisations which are already responding to the crisis, in particular the UNHCR which is the lead international agency in this field.

NATO and its member states are providing shelter, food and logistical support, and are working closely with other international organisations in the provision of humanitarian assistance to the former Yugoslav Republic of Macedonia and Albania. The NATO Commander in the former Yugoslav Republic of Macedonia (representing the Secretary General and the SACEUR) has full authority to coordinate NATO's assistance to the former Yugoslav Republic of Macedonia and has been authorised to use all available NATO forces to assist in humanitarian relief. SACEUR has been authorised to establish a forward headquarters in Albania, in coordination with the Albanian authorities and the UNHCR, in order to assess the humanitarian situation and provide support thereto. The NATO Military Authorities have been tasked to undertake further planning to this end.

The NATO Commanders will continue to initiate action at every opportunity to assist the international humanitarian effort, with the intention of handing over to the UNHCR or other agencies when appropriate. The NATO Commanders will exercise, as necessary, coordination and control of movement on land, sea and in the air.

NATO and its Partners will continue to use the Euro-Atlantic Disaster Response Coordination Centre to assist the coordination of the international humanitarian effort.

The Alliance has informed the member States of the Euro-Atlantic Partnership Council on the outcome of today's meeting.

NATO has agreed to meet on 5th April 1999 at the European Union to continue efforts to coordinate with all relevant agencies.

---

[1] UN Doc. S/1999/360, Annex, 30 March 1999.

[2] Turkey recognises the Republic of Macedonia with its constitutional name.

177. FRY, Statement Carried by Serb Television, 6 April 1999[1]

The FRY [Federal Republic of Yugoslavia] government and the government of the Republic of Serbia at separate sessions passed the following joint statement:

Starting from the agreement between FRY President Slobodan Milosevic and Dr Ibrahim Rugova [leader of Democratic League of Kosovo] in the joint statement signed by them on 1st April 1999, that the problems in Kosmet [Kosovo-Metohija] should be resolved exclusively through peaceful means, and keeping in mind that the further details were worked out of this joint commitment in the meeting between Dr Ibrahim Rugova and FRY Deputy Prime Minister Nikola Sainovic on 5th April 1999, when agreement was reached on the following:

- to work jointly on reaching a political agreement;
- to work jointly on the return of the refugees;

The FRY government and the government of the Republic of Serbia, assessing that there is a need to approach the realization without delay of these commitments, and resolve the most serious problem first, have come to the following joint conclusion:

1. That, in honour of the greatest Christian holiday - Easter - all military and police actions in Kosovo-Metohija against the terrorist organization OVK [Kosovo Liberation Army - UCK] are to cease unilaterally as of 2000 [1800 gmt] on 6th April 1999, in anticipation that such a decision will be construed as a goodwill gesture and a contribution to a peaceful resolution, which is the undisputed wish of the majority of the population of Kosovo-Metohija, regardless of religious or national affiliation.

Also expecting that the extreme elements, respecting the will of the majority of the population, will also refrain from repeating terrorist actions against civilians and the representatives of the authorities.

2. That the representatives of the government, together with the representatives of the Albanians represented by Dr Ibrahim Rugova, prepare a political agreement in the sense that joint work is done on reaching a political agreement with the wish that, first, a simple, temporary agreement be reached that would enable the work of joint bodies of self-government in Kosovo-Metohija of the Albanian and Serbian ethnic communities, and other ethnic communities.

This agreement after a certain period would be the basis for a lasting settlement for a broad autonomy of Kosovo-Metohija within Serbia and Yugoslavia.

3. That, together with the representatives of the Albanians represented by Dr Ibrahim Rugova, they prepare a programme for the return of the refugees with an adequate participation and assistance by the UNHCR and the ICRC.

The FRY government and the government of the Republic of Serbia believe that this way all the current issues in Kosovo-Metohija will be resolved, peace will be stabilized, the refugees returned and self-government established, the equality of the citizens and ethnic communities affirmed and the basis for a lasting solution established.

178. NATO, Statement by the Secretary General, Press Release (1999)049, 6 April 1999

The unilateral ceasefire proposed by the the Federal Republic of Yugoslavia and the government of Serbia is clearly insufficient. Before a ceasefire can be considered President Milosevic must meet the demands established by the international community.

NATO's current military action against the FRY is in support of the political aims of the international community: a peaceful multi-ethnic democratic Kosovo in which all its people live in security.

These aims can be achieved by the return of all refugees and therefore the deployment of an international security presence, the withdrawal of Serb military, police and paramilitary forces, and putting into place a political framework for Kosovo on the basis of the Rambouillet Accords.

179. FRY, The Decree on Internal Affairs during the State of War, 7 April 1999[2]

I. THE BASIC PROVISION

A r t i c l e 1 : The Internal Affairs Act and other rules in the field of internal affairs shall be applied during the state of war unless it is otherwise determined by this Decree.

II. THE PREROGATIVES OF THE MINISTRY OF INTERNAL AFFAIRS

A r t i c l e 2 : The Ministry can restrict the movements (in the further text: detain) any person who disturbs public ordre and peace, speculates on the market under the conditions of the state of war, withdraws merchandise from circulation, creates stocks through the purchase of a large quantities of merchandise with the intention of contraband, raises prices without permission, conditions the purchase of staple food by purchase of other merchandise or by payment in foreign currency, or in any other way disturbs the prescribed currents of the provision of citizens with basic food or merchandise under special regime, as well as in other cases of endangering the security of citizens and the defence and security of the Republic, if it is necessary for the establishment of public order and peace or prevention of danger to defence and security.

Detention of persons may exceed 24 hours if due to insurmountable obstacles there is no possibility to initiate proceedings for misdemeanour of criminal offence.

The decisions on detention of persons according to para 1 of this article shall be enforced by institutions for the enforcement of institutional sanctions.

A r t i c l e 3 : When required by the reasons of the defence of the Republic the Minister may impose the protective measure of compulsory residence on a person representing a danger for the security of the Republic.

The measure from para 1 of this article will remain in force as long as the reasons for it exist, but not longer than 60 days. After this period the person shall be handed over to the organs of the judiciary.

The Ministry shall secure the conditions for the enforcement of the measure referred to in para. 1 of this article.

A r t i c l e 4 : For reasons of security competent officials of the Ministry may at the time of arrest, detention or deprivation of liberty search persons without a search warrant.

Competent officials may, without a search warrant, search persons and their belongings, vehicles and premises in order to determine whether such persons posses without permission arms, ammunition, explosives and other material that can be used for attacks or diversions, merchandise which is under special regime during the state of war, as well as propaganda material with hostile content.

A r t i c l e 5 : When so necessitated by the interests of security and defence of the country competent officials may, on the basis of the decision of their immediate superior, open letters and other postal articles, if there is a well founded reason to believe that they are related to a criminal offence.

A r t i c l e 6 : The competent officials of the Ministry can use firearms if they cannot otherwise prevent the escape of a person found committing a criminal offence which is prosecuted ex officio.

III. LABOR RELATIONS AND DISCIPLINARY RESPONSIBILITY

A r t i c l e 7 : The status of a competent official shall be possessed by all workers in the Ministry of Internal Affairs (in the further text: the Ministry) designated as such by the Minister of Internal Affairs (in the further text: the Minister) or a person empowered by the Minister to do so.

---

[1] Text of report by Serbian TV on 6th April, Source: RTS SAT TV, Belgrade, in Serbo-Croat 1500 gmt 6 Apr 99.

[2] The Official Gazette of The Republic of Serbia, No. 17, 7 April 1999.

Competent officials shall be bound to obey all orders of their superiors issued with the purpose of performing their work, except orders instructing them to commit acts which represent criminal offences.

Article 8: When so demanded by the interest of service the Minister or a person empowered by him/her may transfer a worker of the Ministry or temporarily assign him/her to work in another organisation or unit of the Ministry as long as this is demanded by the interests of the service.

The worker who is transferred or temporarily assigned to another organisation or a unit is bound to report to work immediately.

Article 9: In addition to grave offences provided for in the Act on Civil Servants in the Organs of the State and in the Internal Affairs Act, the following shall also be considered grave violations of working obligations and duties:

1. unwarranted absence or arbitrary departure from a war unit or institution; 2. violation of military secrets, recklessness and insufficient vigilance in the protection of documents or data; 3. failure to submit, or submission of incorrect reports or information, forging of official documents or information and use of forged documents; 4. manifestation of national, racial and religious intolerance and opposition to military, political and economic measures of the organs of the state, which can be conducive to the weakening of the unity in the defence of the country; 5. any other action or omission representing a grave violation of rules and orders or serious neglect and obstruction of the correct and smooth functioning of the service.

In addition to the measures and penalties provided for by the Internal Affairs Act grave violations of the working obligations and duties may be punished by the following:

1. restriction of movement of up to 60 days; 2. degradation to a lower degree or rank for the duration of 1 to 2 years.

The measures and penalties for grave violations of working obligations and duties shall be imposed by the head of the department of the Ministry or a person empowered by him/her, upon the proposal of the immediate superior.

Article 10: Offences against the working obligations which have failed to cause, or could not cause, damaging consequences and which by their nature, conditions under which they have been committed and other circumstances do not represent a grave offence against the rules of service or do not gravely endanger the interest and reputation of the service shall be considered light offences against the working duties.

In addition to the penalties provided for by the Internal Affairs Act the following penalties may be imposed:

1. prohibition to leave the barracks for up to 4 days; 2. restriction of movement for up to 30 days.

The penalties for the light offences against the working duties shall be imposed by the immediate superior in the police war unit.

Article 11: The penalty of restriction of movement in articles 9 and 10 in this Decree will be enforced in the premises of the Ministry.

Article 12: The worker against whom a measure or punishment for the violation of working obligations and duties has been pronounced may submit an appeal according to law. The appeal does not delay the enforcement.

Article 13: Students of the School of Internal Affairs above the age of 16 may be recruited to police units.

IV. FINAL PROVISION

Article 14: This Decree shall enter into force on the day following its publication in the Official Gazette of the Republic of Serbia.

Belgrade, 31 March 1999, President of the Republic, Signed: Milan Milutinović

180. NATO, Statement Issued at the Extraordinary Ministerial Meeting of the North Atlantic Council held at NATO Headquarters, Press Release M-NAC-1(99)51, Brussels, 12 April 1999

1. The crisis in Kosovo represents a fundamental challenge to the values of democracy, human rights and the rule of law, for which NATO has stood since its foundation. We are united in our determination to overcome this challenge.

2. The Federal Republic of Yugoslavia (FRY) has repeatedly violated United Nations Security Council resolutions. The unrestrained assault by Yugoslav military, police and paramilitary forces, under the direction of President Milosevic, on Kosovar civilians has created a massive humanitarian catastrophe which also threatens to destabilise the surrounding region. Hundreds of thousands of people have been expelled ruthlessly from Kosovo by the FRY authorities. We condemn these appalling violations of human rights and the indiscriminate use of force by the Yugoslav government. These extreme and criminally irresponsible policies, which cannot be defended on any grounds, have made necessary and justify the military action by NATO.

3. NATO's military action against the FRY supports the political aims of the international community: a peaceful, multi-ethnic and democratic Kosovo in which all its people can live in security and enjoy universal human rights and freedoms on an equal basis. In this context, we welcome the statement of the UN Secretary-General of 9th April and the EU Council Conclusions of 8th April.

4. NATO's air strikes will be pursued until President Milosevic accedes to the demands of the international community. President Milosevic knows what he has to do. He must:

- ensure a verifiable stop to all military action and the immediate ending of violence and repression;
- ensure the withdrawal from Kosovo of the military, police and paramilitary forces;
- agree to the stationing in Kosovo of an international military presence;
- agree to the unconditional and safe return of all refugees and displaced persons and unhindered access to them by humanitarian aid organisations;
- provide credible assurance of his willingness to work on the basis of the Rambouillet Accords in the establishment of a political framework agreement for Kosovo in conformity with international law and the Charter of the United Nations.

5. Responsibility for the present crisis lies with President Milosevic. He has the power to bring a halt to NATO's military action by accepting and implementing irrevocably the legitimate demands of the international community.

6. We underline that NATO is not waging war against the Federal Republic of Yugoslavia. We have no quarrel with the people of the FRY who for too long have been isolated in Europe because of the policies of their government.

7. We are grateful for the strong and material support we have received from our Partners in the region and more widely in the international community in responding to the crisis.

8. The Alliance shares a common interest with Russia in reaching a political solution to the crisis in Kosovo and wants to work constructively with Russia, in the spirit of the Founding Act, to this end.

9. As a result of President Milosevic's sustained policy of ethnic cleansing, hundreds of thousands of Kosovar people are seeking refuge in neighbouring countries, particularly in Albania and the former Yugoslav Republic of Macedonia. Others remain in Kosovo, destitute and beyond the reach of international relief. These people in Kosovo are struggling to survive under conditions of exhaustion, hunger and desperation. We will hold President Milosevic and the Belgrade leadership responsible for the well-being of all civilians in Kosovo.

10. NATO and its members have responded promptly to this emergency. We have activated with our Partners the Euro-Atlantic Disaster Response Coordination Centre. NATO forces in the former Yugoslav

Republic of Macedonia have constructed emergency accommodation for refugees and have cared for them. NATO troops are also being deployed to Albania to support the humanitarian efforts there and to assist the Albanian authorities in providing a secure environment for them. We will sustain and intensify our refugee and humanitarian relief operations in cooperation with the UNHCR, the lead agency in this field. NATO-led refugee and humanitarian aid airlift operations for both Albania and the former Yugoslav Republic of Macedonia are already under way and they will increase. The steps being taken by NATO and the efforts of other international organisations and agencies, including the European Union, are complementary and mutually reinforcing.

11. We pay tribute to NATO's servicemen and women whose commitment and skill are ensuring the success of NATO's military and humanitarian operations.

12. Atrocities against the people of Kosovo by FRY military, police and paramilitary forces violate international law. Those who are responsible for the systematic campaign of violence and destruction against innocent Kosovar civilians and for the forced deportation of hundreds of thousands of refugees will be held accountable for their actions. Those indicted must be brought before the International Criminal Tribunal for the former Yugoslavia (ICTY) in The Hague in accordance with international law and the relevant resolutions of the United Nations Security Council. Allies reaffirm there can be no lasting peace without justice.

13. NATO has repeatedly stated that it would be unacceptable if the FRY were to threaten the territorial integrity, political independence and security of Albania and the former Yugoslav Republic of Macedonia. We have consulted closely and at a high level with both countries on their specific concerns. We will respond to any challenges by the FRY to the security of Albania and the former Yugoslav Republic of Macedonia stemming from the presence of NATO forces and their activities on their territory.

14. We are concerned over the situation in the Republic of Montenegro. We reaffirm our support for the democratically elected government of President Milo Djukanovic which has accepted tens of thousands of displaced persons from Kosovo. President Milosevic should be in no doubt that any move against President Djukanovic and his government will have grave consequences.

15. The Kosovo crisis underscores the need for a comprehensive approach to the stabilisation of the crisis region in south-eastern Europe and to the integration of the countries of the region into the Euro-Atlantic community. We welcome the EU initiative for a Stability Pact for South-Eastern Europe under the auspices of the OSCE, as well as other regional efforts including the South Eastern Europe Co-operation initiative. We are strengthening the security dialogue between NATO and countries of the region with a view to building a dynamic partnership with them and have tasked the Council in Permanent Session to develop measures to this end. We look forward to a time when the people of Serbia can re-establish normal relations with all the peoples of the Balkans. We want all the countries of south-eastern Europe to enjoy peace and security.

181. NATO, Statement on Kosovo Issued by the Heads of State and Government Participating in the Meeting of the North Atlantic Council in Washington, D.C. on 23rd and 24th April 1999, Press Release S-1(99)62, 23 April 1999

1. The crisis in Kosovo represents a fundamental challenge to the values for which NATO has stood since its foundation: democracy, human rights and the rule of law. It is the culmination of a deliberate policy of oppression, ethnic cleansing and violence pursued by the Belgrade regime under the direction of President Milosevic. We will not allow this campaign of terror to succeed. NATO is determined to prevail.

2. NATO's military action against the Federal Republic of Yugoslavia (FRY) supports the political aims of the international community, which were reaffirmed in recent statements by the UN Secretary-General and the European Union: a peaceful, multi-ethnic and democratic Kosovo where all its people can live in security and enjoy universal human rights and freedoms on an equal basis.

3. Our military actions are directed not at the Serb people but at the policies of the regime in Belgrade, which has repeatedly rejected all efforts to solve the crisis peacefully. President Milosevic must:
- Ensure a verifiable stop to all military action and the immediate ending of violence and repression in Kosovo;
- Withdraw from Kosovo his military, police and para-military forces;
- Agree to the stationing in Kosovo of an international military presence;
- Agree to the unconditional and safe return of all refugees and displaced persons, and unhindered access to them by humanitarian aid organisations; and
- Provide credible assurance of his willingness to work for the establishment of a political framework agreement based on the Rambouillet accords.

4. There can be no compromise on these conditions. As long as Belgrade fails to meet the legitimate demands of the international community and continues to inflict immense human suffering, Alliance air operations against the Yugoslav war machine will continue. We hold President Milosevic and the Belgrade leadership responsible for the safety of all Kosovar citizens. We will fulfill our promise to the Kosovar people that they can return to their homes and live in peace and security.

5. We are intensifying NATO's military actions to increase the pressure on Belgrade. Allied governments are putting in place additional measures to tighten the constraints on the Belgrade regime. These include intensified implementation of economic sanctions, and an embargo on petroleum products on which we welcome the EU lead. We have directed our Defence Ministers to determine ways that NATO can contribute to halting the delivery of war material including by launching maritime operations, taking into account the possible consequences on Montenegro.

6. NATO is prepared to suspend its air strikes once Belgrade has unequivocally accepted the above mentioned conditions and demonstrably begun to withdraw its forces from Kosovo according to a precise and rapid timetable. This could follow the passage of a United Nations Security Council resolution, which we will seek, requiring the withdrawal of Serb forces and the demilitarisation of Kosovo and encompassing the deployment of an international military force to safeguard the swift return of all refugees and displaced persons as well as the establishment of an international provisional administration of Kosovo under which its people can enjoy substantial autonomy within the FRY. NATO remains ready to form the core of such an international military force. It would be multinational in character with contributions from non-NATO countries.

7. Russia has a particular responsibility in the United Nations and an important role to play in the search for a solution to the conflict in Kosovo. Such a solution must be based on the conditions of the international community as laid out above. President Milosevic's offers to date do not meet this test. We want to work constructively with Russia, in the spirit of the Founding Act.

8. The long-planned, unrestrained and continuing assault by Yugoslav military, police and paramilitary forces on Kosovars and the repression directed against other minorities of the FRY are aggravating the already massive humanitarian catastrophe. This threatens to destabilise the surrounding region.

9. NATO, its members and its Partners have responded to the humanitarian emergency and are intensifying their refugee and humanitarian relief operations in close cooperation with the UNHCR, the lead agency in this field, and with other relevant organisations. We will continue our assistance as long as necessary. NATO forces are making a major contribution to this task.

10. We pay tribute to the servicemen and women of NATO whose courage and dedication are ensuring the success of our military and humanitarian operations.

11. Atrocities against the people of Kosovo by FRY military, police and paramilitary forces represent a flagrant violation of international law. Our governments will co-operate with the International Criminal Tribunal for the former Yugoslavia (ICTY) to support investigation of all those, including at the highest levels, responsible for war crimes and crimes against humanity. NATO will support the ICTY in its efforts to secure relevant information. There can be no lasting peace without justice.

12. We acknowledge and welcome the courageous support that states in the region are providing to our efforts in Kosovo. The former Yugoslav Republic of Macedonia and Albania have played a particularly important role, not least in accepting hundreds of thousands of refugees from Kosovo. The states in the region are bearing substantial economic and social burdens stemming from the current conflict.

13. We will not tolerate threats by the Belgrade regime to the security of its neighbours. We will respond to such challenges by Belgrade to its neighbours resulting from the presence of NATO forces or their activities on their territory during this crisis.

14. We reaffirm our support for the territorial integrity and sovereignty of all countries in the region.

15. We reaffirm our strong support for the democratically elected government of Montenegro. Any move by Belgrade to undermine the government of President Djukanovic will have grave consequences. FRY forces should leave the demilitarised zone of Prevlaka immediately.

16. The objective of a free, prosperous, open and economically integrated Southeast Europe cannot be fully assured until the FRY embarks upon the transition to democracy. Accordingly, we express our support for the objective of a democratic FRY which protects the rights of all minorities, including those in Vojvodina and Sandjak, and promise to work for such change through and beyond the current conflict.

17. It is our aim to make stability in Southeast Europe a priority of our transatlantic agenda. Our governments will co-operate urgently through NATO as well as through the OSCE, and for those of us which are members, the European Union, to support the nations of Southeast Europe in forging a better future for their region - one based upon democracy, justice, economic integration, and security co-operation.

182. North Atlantic Council Statement Concerning Bombing of Chinese Embassy, Press Release (1999)076, Brussels, 8 May 1999

Following its meeting this afternoon the North Atlantic Council wishes to express its deep regret for the tragic mistake of the bombing of the Chinese Embassy in Belgrade.

The sincere sympathy and condolences of all members of the Alliance go to the victims, their families and the Chinese government.

NATO never has, and never will, intentionally target civilians. Extraordinary care is taken to avoid damage to other than legitimate military and military-related targets. The bombing of the Chinese Embassy was a deeply regrettable mistake. We continue to review the circumstances surrounding the incident and we will make available any further information as soon as possible.

NATO will continue to pursue its goals: to stop the ethnic cleansing in Kosovo and ensure the Kosovars can return to their homes in peace and security.

NATO is prepared to suspend its air strikes once Belgrade has unequivocally accepted the five key conditions set down by the North Atlantic Council for a peaceful settlement of the conflict.

NATO will continue to support all attempts at a diplomatic solution which respect these conditions. Our mistaken attack against the Chinese Embassy should not diminish or derail these efforts building on the results of the recent G8 meeting.

183. NATO, Statement by the NATO Spokesman on the Korisa Incident, Press Release (1999)079, Brussels, 15 May 1999

Following Serb claims about a NATO attack on the village of Korisa in Kosovo, NATO has conducted an extensive review throughout the night of its operations in that area.

This was a legitimate military target.

The Serb claims of an attack involving cluster bombs against a non-military target are both false.

NATO identified Korisa as a military camp and command post. Military equipment including an armoured personnel carrier and more than ten pieces of artillery were observed at this location. The aircraft observed dug-in military positions at the target before executing the attack.

NATO cannot confirm the casualty figures given by the Serbian authorities, nor the reasons why civilians were at this location at the time of the attack.

NATO deeply regrets accidental civilian casualties that were caused by this attack.

184. NATO, Statement by the Secretary General on Suspension of Air Operations, Brussels, 10 June 1999

A few moments ago I instructed General Wesley Clark to suspend NATO's air operations against Yugoslavia.

I have taken this decision following consultations with the North Atlantic Council and confirmation from SACEUR that the full withdrawal of the Yugoslav security forces from Kosovo has begun. The withdrawal of Yugoslav security forces from Kosovo is taking place in accordance with the Military-Technical Agreement that was concluded between NATO and the Federal Republic of Yugoslavia yesterday evening. It is also consistent with the agreement between the FRY and EU and Russian special envoys of 3 June. I have just written to the Secretary General of the United Nations and the President of the United Nations Security Council to inform them of these developments. I urge all parties to the conflict to seize this opportunity for peace. I call on them to comply with their obligations under the agreements that have been concluded these past days and with all relevant UN Security Council resolutions. The violence must cease immediately. The Yugoslav security forces must withdraw, and all armed Kosovar groups must demilitarize. Violence or non-compliance by any party will not be tolerated. I would like to take this opportunity to salute General Clark, his commanders and all the men and women of Operation Allied Force who have bravely contributed so much to the cause of peace and security for all the people of Kosovo.

Ensemble avec le reste de la communauté internationale, l'OTAN aidera tous les réfugiés et toutes les personnes déplacées à rentrer dans leurs foyers. Nous aiderons tous les habitants du Kosovo - quelque soit leur origine ethnique - à reconstruire une société libre, débarrassée de la répression violente qu'elle a connue pendant si longtemps. Depuis le début de l'opération Force Alliée, j'ai insisté sur le fait que l'OTAN n'a aucun grief contre le peuple de Yougoslavie. J'espère que les Serbes du Kosovo resteront chez eux. Les forces de l'OTAN défendront leurs droits tout autant que les droits des autres communautés ethniques du Kosovo. L'OTAN avance à grands pas dans ses préparatifs pour la KFOR. Dans quelques heures, le Conseil de l'Atlantique Nord se réunira pour approuver formellement le déploiement de forces de l'OTAN au Kosovo. Ces forces créeront un environnement sûr permettant le retour des réfugiés et le processus de reconstruction. Aujourd'hui, une réunion importante se tient à Cologne pour développer un Pacte de Stabilité pour l'Europe du Sud-Est. L'OTAN est prête à contribuer pleinement à cette initiative.

All this would not have been possible without the cohesion and the determination of all Allies. As our air operations against Yugoslavia are now suspended, NATO is ready for its new mission; a mission to bring people back to their homes and to build a lasting and just peace in Kosovo.

4.3 POSSIBLE USE OF NATO GROUND FORCES

185. Press Conference Given by the NATO Secretary General, Mr Javier Solana and the British Prime Minister, Mr Tony Blair, Brussels, 20 April 1999

[Parts not referring to a possible use of NATO ground forces have been omitted]

[...]

Radio Free Europe: There is growing tension on the border between Kosovo and Albania and there are cases where Serbian troops are shelling at Albanian territory. What kind of measures can be taken and what are the options to protect Albania right now from a possible invasion?

Prime Minister: We have made very clear indeed, and let me repeat to you, our belief that any attempt to cause difficulty or damage to Albania, we will do everything we possibly can to prevent and make sure we give proper protection. And I would like to pay tribute to Albania for the unstinting work that it has done in circumstances of very great difficulty to make sure that the refugees are properly looked after. And one of the purposes of the action that we are taking is to make sure that this entire military machine of the Serbs and Milosevic is degraded so he is not able to threaten his neighbours.

Question: NATO has always said it would only go into Kosovo in a permissive environment. Does that permissive environment have to be as a result of a cease-fire and a diplomatic agreement, or could paralysis, immobilisation, weakening of the Serb forces create such an environment, and if so is there any possibility at all of reaching a deal with Milosevic, or does he have to go?

Prime Minister: First of all, there is no question of making some deal or compromise with Milosevic. We have set out our demands and objectives and they will be met in full, because they are the minimum demands that we can in all humanity make, that he gets his forces out of Kosovo, that we have an international military force that goes in and those people are allowed to return to their homes. We have always made clear the difficulties of putting in ground forces as a land force invasion against undegraded organised Serb resistance. We have also equally made it clear that the international military force is there to allow people back to their homes. So it is very important people realise our position on that remains as it is, but of course Milosevic doesn't have some veto on what we do, we have always said that and we make it clear again. The important thing is to make sure that these people are allowed back to the homes that they have been driven out of, as I say at the point of a gun, and our determination to see that through is, as I say, absolute. And of course we have been building up forces in the area precisely so that we can achieve that aim.

Question: (Not interpreted)

Prime Minister: I think, if you will forgive me, the nuances of any answer as such, that I am probably better to rely on your translator rather than my translator.

I agree entirely with what the Secretary General said and the position that he outlined is the position that we have taken throughout, both in relation to ground forces and in relation to NATO strategy in general. If we take a step back for a moment and look at this situation seriously, what is essential is that Milosevic, I think this is perhaps as important as anything else out of the summit that comes to pass in Washington later this week. Milosevic must understand this, that we have embarked upon this action not simply because there is a strategic interest of NATO engaged, there is such an interest and I can make to you all the arguments about how important it is strategically for NATO that we are engaged, but we have embarked on it for a simple humanitarian reason and cause and we are not going to allow Milosevic to get away with this policy of ethnic cleansing, we will defeat that policy.

Now I can't, and I try and put this to you in the most careful and sensitive way since you are all journalists, I can't and I think it is unwise for us to discuss always in every detail every last aspect of military strategy and military planning, but I can assure you our determination to see this through is absolute and we will see it through. So I agree entirely with what the Secretary General said on the BBC and that remains the NATO position.

Mark Laity, BBC: You have talked about the Alliance determination and unity being absolute. Is that unity absolute because you have foreclosed any chance of a ground invasion? Is the real reason that you are relying on air power the fact that you cannot get 19 nations to agree on ground power rather than military necessity?

Prime Minister: No, and can I just point out to you, Mark, first of all that in any event we would be relying on air power at this point in time and it is immensely important that air power is allowed to do its work of diminishing, degrading the military capability, damaging the military capability of Milosevic. Now as for the unity of NATO, there were many people, perhaps including Milosevic himself, who thought at the outset of this campaign that it would only be a matter of days before he could exploit divisions in NATO, pull us apart, remove the cohesion that NATO has. That has not happened and it has not happened partly because of the political will of the government, but it has not happened also because our ordinary citizens, the members of the public, have seen on their television screens night after night the appalling things that have been done to these people. And I know in even the smallest ways, in little communities all over Britain for example, in churches and in local community centres people have given money for the refugees in Kosovo, they have been moved by the humanitarian plight, they are not going to allow this man to prevail. And of course these refugees need immediate humanitarian help, and my goodness one of the extraordinary things that NATO and our armed forces have done is mount a unique humanitarian operation literally within a matter of days, that those people who have given that money and who have seen those refugees, they know this policy cannot prevail and that will keep NATO united through all the coming circumstances. [...]

Question: Last week you had a meeting with the Hungarian Prime Minister, Victor Orman (phon), and according to some reports you were also discussing the possibility of the deployment of ground troops via Hungary if NATO would take such a decision. What do you expect in this regard from Hungary?

Prime Minister: We are very grateful for the help that Hungary has given, we are very grateful for their support in circumstances where of course they are aware, from the ethnic Hungarians living in Vojvadina (phon) of exactly the difficulties of living under the rule of Milosevic. And I am not going into any discussions we had, I don't disclose the disucssions that I have with Prime Ministers, but I think the fact that Hungary and surrounding states have been supportive in this makes a big difference and it is one demonstration of Allied unity that we need to constantly, we need to reflect and we need to engage with. And I am very grateful not just for the words that the Hungarian Prime Minister said last week, but for the way that the Hungarian people have responded, and I know that it is often very easy for us in countries like Britain who are some distance away from this conflict to wish you our words and our declarations, although I hope the fact that our Armed Forces are fighting is some indication that our words are backed up by deeds. But I know for those living literally next door to Milosevic of the problems that are caused and we thank you for your support, that support is greatly valued and it is an integral part of a successful NATO campaign. [...]

186. Edited Transcript of Interview Given by the Prime Minister, Tony Blair, for BBC World Service, Tirana, 18 May 1999

[Parts not referring to a possible use of NATO ground forces have been omitted.]

Interviewer: You visited also a refugee camp today in Elbasan. After all the suffering that you have heard from the refugees themselves in Elbasan and in Macedonia, how urgent do you feel is the decision to commit ground troops?

Prime Minister: Well as we have said before, we keep all options under review and the Secretary General Solana was specifically tasked with that at the Washington NATO Summit. But in the meantime the air campaign has to continue. We are doing immense damage to Milosevic, to his troops. The fact that there were anti-Milosevic demonstrations in two cities yesterday in Serbia is an indication of the success of our campaign. And when I spoke to the refugees at the camp, they had the most terrible stories to tell of humiliation, murder, rape of women, terrible atrocities that have no place in any modern democratic Europe.

Interviewer: The military have suggested that there should be a deployment of ground troops to make sure that the refugees will go back, and the sooner it is, the better it will be before the winter comes. So how long is there a deadline to take the decision?

Prime Minister: Well I don't think we set arbitrary deadlines, but it is important obviously to remember that there is always going to be an implementation force in order to guide the refugees back home, that is part of NATO's demands. And in any event, as I say, Secretary General Solana carries on with his assessment and planning. But it is vitally important that we make sure that the air campaign continues and carries on doing the damage that it is doing. After all, it has done tremendous damage to Milosevic's Air Force, to his command and control, to his lines of supply and communication, and now particularly over the past 2 or 3 weeks we have been immensely successful, probably more than people realise, in doing damage to his tanks and artillery actually on the ground in Kosovo.

Interviewer: The Kosovar Albanians will not trust Milosevic to go back and live under his rule. Would you trust him to sign a negotiation and respect the settlement?

Prime Minister: I don't intend that we start negotiating with Milosevic. We have our demands, they have to be met. And I entirely understand the worries that Kosovar Albanians have if they are returning home under the eye of Serb paramilitaries, police forces and so on. Which is precisely why there has to be an international military force that guides the refugees back home, that allows them security to go back home and that protects them and makes sure that all people in Kosovo, irrespective of their ethnic background or religion, can live in harmony with one another. That is what this whole conflict is about. This isn't a conflict about NATO's power or a desire for territory, it is a battle about decent values of civilisation and we have to make sure that we succeed. [...]

187. Press Conference Given by the NATO Secretary General, Mr Javier Solana and German Chancellor Gerhard Schroeder, Brussels, 19 May 1999

[Parts not referring to a possible use of NATO ground forces have been omitted.]

Chancellor Schroeder: Thank you, Secretary General, ladies and gentlemen.

I had the pleasure to be briefed by the Secretary General and the Chairman of the Military Committee, we do that on a regular basis in a very intensive manner and I would therefore like to use this opportunity to express our trust and confidence in the Military Committee's work, and of course in the Secretary General of NATO.

We talked quite openly about the recent developments and about events that we cannot support, events like the shelling of the Chinese Embassy a couple of days ago. The Secretary General made it very clear that he himself has a great interest in clarifying what happened and why it happened and he again promised to me to see that this investigation makes progress.

This very open and frank approach that we take is the basis for the relationship marked by trust and confidence between the German government and NATO. I have always understood NATO's strategy to be a dual strategy, one element of that dual strategy is the military campaign. The military campaign had to happen, had to take place in order to save people in Kosovo from murder, from being killed, from being displaced and expelled, for preparing the basis for a return of the refugees. But the second element of our strategy has always been the search for a political settlement and that is very much of course in the forefront of my efforts and endeavours, no matter what capacity I have in doing that. It is a dual strategy, a NATO strategy, it is a dual strategy, that is to say the military actions, the air strikes on the one hand, and the search for a diplomatic settlement on the other hand.

Quite frankly I would like to make it very clear that we now slowly realise that the strategy is slowly taking effect, so I think it is not just ... to hear from one or the other that the strategy ought to be altered or to be changed, and this is to do when people talk about sending in ground forces or when they talk about a unilateral pause in the air strikes. My impression is the following. I believe that NATO strategy is slowly taking effect, that we have entered a new stage when it comes to striding for a political solution.

I have made it clear right from the outset that the Russian Special Envoy, Mr Chernomyrdin, he is the Special Envoy of the Russian President and that Special Envoy, the Finnish President, Mr Ahtisaari, should be supported in their endeavours to bring about a diplomatic solution. They complement our endeavours and they are supported by the Vice-Secretary of State of the United States, Mr Talbott.

I believe that we have reason to hope, and I spoke to Mr Ahtisaari only recently, that a diplomatic settlement can only be assisted through those endeavours. I speak as the Federal Chancellor of the Federal Republic of Germany now, but also as the EU Chair. I have made it very clear to the Finnish President that he has our support, not matter whether I speak as the German Chancellor as the EU Presidency and that we wish those talks to be successful. Knowing that you have a few information yourselves, you may also have come to know that Mr Chernomyrdin is going to go to Belgrade very soon and the parties agreed that the talks are to be continued as soon as possible in Moscow. Of course that is not yet enough reason to be jubilant or triumphant, or overly enthusiastic, but I think that it is quite a hopeful signal. We should continue to work towards a political solution, it makes it very clear that the path on which we have set out is a path that will lead towards success in the long run. That is what I believe.

No doubt it will be not that easy for us, we will encounter a few difficult problems too, but we still have to live with the fact that as far as the time frame is concerned, the time axis of which I tend to speak is that people have different views on this, some people say that there should be a pause in the air strikes before we begin to talk about a Security Council Resolution, others think it should be the other way round, and NATO believes it should be the other way round. Right now we could at least agree on that. I believe that we should move closer towards each other on that time axis. Our objective is a Security Council Resolution on the basis of the G8 principles, developed in Bonn a week ago, and I think that we should be able to bring our positions closer as far as the time axis is concerned so that in the end we can harmonise or synchronise our positions so that that problem could be solved in that way.

You will understand I trust that I am a bit more hopeful as far as a political settlement is concerned, a bit more hopeful than I was a week ago, and now again I speak as the German Chancellor and as the EU Chair. We want to do everything we can to use the talks towards a solution that is in line with the principles that we have laid down.

That is basically what I wanted to share with you.

Question: You have said that ground troops are unthinkable, are they unthinkable for Germany or for NATO? And do you feel your position on ground troops is closer to President Clinton's, I assume they are not very close to Tony Blair's?

Chancellor Schroeder: I don't think it is up to me to talk about how far away I am from the position of one or the other of my colleagues. I am not here for commenting on the news, I am responsible for the news, and I think it is right to say that the Federal Government, by the way the Opposition is equally clear on this particular point, rejects the sending of ground forces, that is the German position, the German position supported unanimously by the members of the German Parliament. Of course this is first and foremost a German position. If I understood NATO strategy correctly, and I try to explain it to you, then that position is also the present position of NATO, that is to say the strategy of an Alliance can only be changed if all of the parties involved agree on it, so I trust that NATO strategy is not going to be changed. I say this on the basis of the talks, about which I reported to you. I see no reason whatsoever of a change in our strategy, based on the reports we have had, and you have to guess how far away my position is from the position of another friend.

Question: Are you against a change in that strategy, in NATO's strategy?

Chancellor Schroeder: Yes indeed, I am against any change of NATO strategy, last but not least because I believe that the strategy is slowly beginning, politically too, to take effect.

Mark Laity, BBC News: You have just said that the strategy will not change. There are many military people who believe that air power can achieve very much but it cannot achieve everything. Presumably you believe the only thing that is really unthinkable is to lose the war. If it comes down to a choice between risking losing the war and using ground troops, which would you choose?

Chancellor Schroeder: Please don't try too hard. I will not participate in this specifically British debate on war theories. I think and I trust that we have a good strategy, a strategy that has indeed been successful in some respect and will continue to be successful, and this is why I refuse to participate in such a theoretical debate.

Question: Could I just pursue you on that, Chancellor. When do you think that ground troops might be ..

Chancellor Schroeder: I have said everything that is to be said on this particular issue and you will not get more out of me if you go on pestering me with these questions.

Question: I am not pestering you, you have come to give a press conference, surely journalists have a right to ask the question?

Chancellor Schroeder: Do I look very offended, do I look very angry?

Question: When do you believe the use of ground troops would become thinkable? Under what circumstances should NATO send ground troops into Kosovo?

Chancellor Schroeder: I think I made myself very clear on this. I oppose sending in ground forces and this is very much to do with the fact that NATO strategy, a strategy that we developed together, is slowly beginning to take effect, and it is supporting a political settlement. So of course I understand that you have questions, questions that go in a different direction, but I think it would be wrong if I were to respond in a theoretical manner to theoretical questions, because that would be misinterpreted. I support the present strategy of NATO, I think it is promising, it can give us success, this is why I am against changing it, that once the war is over we have to send in a robust international military presence into Kosovo, that we need it, that we have to have it, is something that is obvious and that again is part and parcel of NATO strategy.

Question: In view of the brutal behaviour of the Serbs, don't you think that that would be reason enough to at least think about sending in ground forces?

Chancellor Schroeder: I have been trying, I have been trying hard, to make it very clear that I am not willing to participate in theoretical debates about what is going to happen if a, b, c. I understand your desire and your need for a new subject, but it is not all that easy I understand to fill the pages of a newspaper day in, day out with news. But please understand why I refuse to participate in this extremely theoretical debate. [...]

Question: Secretary General, you are both representing the two organisations that are taking care of what is going in Kosovo nowadays. Can we say that NATO and the European Union are on the very same line at this moment, because on Monday Foreign Secretary Cook was talking in this very same room about this time about ground troops - that nobody wants to talk about - and at the same time the Ministers of Foreign Affairs of the European Union were having a more diplomatic move, seeing Dr Rugova, President Djukanovic, as well as the Russian Foreign Minister Ivanov. Are you very much on the same line in this moment also?

Chancellor Schroeder: In my eyes they are very much on the same line. You know what counts here is not what is being said by one or the other of my colleagues of the Foreign Ministers, they have every right to speak their minds freely, but what is important is what is the decision taken by the European Union and by NATO. The Secretary General has made it more than clear what NATO's position is, and he will probably want to comment on it, but as far as the EU is concerned, Brussels has taken a decision, a decision by the Heads of State and Government under the Chairmanship of the German Presidency of the EU, we have taken a decision here. And the points decided are identical with the strategy that I explained that is being pursued by NATO. Of course everyone has every right to express his very own view and that might be a different view from the views that we have, but the decisions taken by NATO and by the European Union are more than crystal clear and they are identical.

Mr. Solana: It is a very, very simple, the answer, and the Chancellor has made it very, very clear. The strategy of NATO was very clearly established in Washington at the occasion of the Summit in which a very high percentage of the members are members of the European Union; and reciprocally the meetings in which the decisions were taken at the European Union, a very high percentage of the members were members of NATO. So it would be very difficult to have a different strategy and in particular on something so clear, so dramatic as the crisis in Kosovo. The positions are clear, well established in Washington as far as NATO is concerned, and the European Union summit as far as the European Union is concerned. You should read the texts, the texts are basically word by word exact. [...]

188. Press Conference Given by the NATO Secretary General, Mr Javier Solana and the Italian Prime Minister, Mr Massimo D'Alema, Brussels, 20 May 1999

[Parts not referring to a possible use of NATO ground forces have been omitted.]

Mr D'Alema: [...] This is the meaning of the position taken yesterday by the Italian Parliament and I have come here to illustrate this position to our allies. We are convinced that the military campaign should be closely linked to this political action and effort. We are convinced that if we had an agreed draft, to be submitted to the UN Security Council, the moment you have such a draft resolution agreed, at that time there should, could, be a pause in the bombings to allow a convening of such a meeting and to enable the Security Council to take this deliberation and to verify immediately whether Belgrade is willing to comply with such a UN decision.

Clearly what we suggest is not a unilateral cease-fire, but the possibility that faced with a concrete political perspective, weapons may cease to be used, there might be a pause in the military action to verify whether the conditions are there for a solution. Clearly as far as Italy is concerned, in the case that the Yugoslav government, if the Yugoslav government were not to accept even a UN position, and if the Yugoslav government were not to accept the request of the international community, even when submitted by the UN, if that were so, military action should be resumed in the form that would be jointly decided with our allies. [...]

Question - Mark Laity, BBC: Could I ask you a little more about the references you made to a bombing pause. How have other allies reacted to this proposal for a bombing pause? How long would you propose that bombing pause be to give Belgrade time to react? And if they do not react in a satisfactory way, are the methods, which you refer to as jointly decided, would Italy support the use of ground forces to force their way into Kosovo if Belgrade does not accept the Security Council resolution?

Mr. D'Alema: I very clearly stated already what you have just asked me. However, I will repeat it. We are convinced that a pause in the bombings would become necessary at the time when an agreed draft resolution for the UN Security Council were available, for the time that is useful, that is needed to enable the convening of such a meeting, the adoption of such a resolution and the communication to Belgrade of the resolution itself, and to receive an immediate answer by the Belgrade government. I am convinced that if such an initiative were to occur, this would probably provide the solution. However, I also said that if the Belgrade government were to say no to a decision taken by the United Nations, Italy would be ready to resume military action in whatever forms are agreed with our allies.

Mark Laity: With respect, I asked you how long that drafting, convening, adopting, sending to Belgrade and getting an answer would be - 1 day, 2 days, 3 days? And would Italy, if that was rejected, support the use of ground forces, not what would you support generally but what would your nation specifically support?

Mr D'Alema: I told you as long as it is necessary to perform these operations. Now I am not the Secretary General of the United Nations. How long that process would take is not in my hands. I think that those operations can be performed in a very short time, 72 hours possibly, but I think such a pause in the bombings would have a political meaning and it should be sure for the time needed to perform these operations. I haven't calculated how many hours are needed because this is not my prerogative.

As to your following question, here again I think it is completely wrong, at such a delicate time as the present one, when it is absolutely essential for the Atlantic Alliance to be united, to open up a discussion or to trigger a debate on scenarios which are purely hypothetical and which would only have the purpose of highlighting hypothetical disagreement in a hypothetical future, in an assumed future. It is a totally useless exercise for us, it is a pointless exercise that can be useful only for our adversaries. [...]

189. Edited Transcript of Interview Given by the Foreign Secretary, Robin Cook, and U.S. Secretary of State, Madeleine Albright, for CNN, Washington, 20 May 1999

[Parts not referring to a possible use of NATO ground forces have been omitted.]

Interviewer (Larry King): Foreign Secretary, are you here to sort of bring things together, are you here to interrupt a rift?

Foreign Secretary: Not at all. I am here to keep in touch with my good friend Madeleine Albright and I am here because the United States and the United Kingdom are two of the closest allies in the Alliance and what I have been doing today is demonstrating the solidarity between us, the conviction that we are going to secure our objectives, we are going to take those refugees home under our joint protection and we are both going to be there when it happens.

Interviewer: So the trip has nothing to do with stories that your government and the US government are having differences?

Foreign Secretary: I am glad you asked that, Larry, because I would like to knock it firmly on the head. There is no rift between the United States and the United Kingdom. We are absolutely together, we both share the objectives of NATO, we have both taken part in the campaign and I want to make it clear that that campaign is being successful, we have got to be ready to build on that success.

Interviewer: Madam Secretary, are the stories that Great Britain would like ground troops, or certainly the thought of introducing them, and the United States wouldn't, are they untrue?

Mrs Albright: I think they are because we are totally agreed on the objectives of what we are doing and doing it together. Robin and I spend an inordinate amount of time together, either on the phone or in person, and we are a sign of the way that the Alliance is working and the Alliance is determined to prevail. Our objectives are really very firm and quite simple, and that is that the refugees have to be able to go back, that they will be protected by an international force where NATO is at the core of it, that the Serb forces have to come out and that we have asked the NATO planners to take a look at up-dating assessments of having forces in in either a permissive or a non-permissive environment.

Interviewer: The Daily Telegraph reports that Mr Blair feels so hampered by the United States' position on this that they are urging him that Great Britain should take over this operation. How do you react to that?

Foreign Secretary: First of all it is totally untrue that Mr Blair feels in any way frustrated with his relations with the United States. Bill Clinton and Tony Blair have a very good relationship, they talk regularly.

Interviewer: Where do these stories start though?

Foreign Secretary: Well papers have to write something Larry. But if you wanted to get to the bottom line actually, I think what is impressive about the Alliance throughout these 8 weeks is the unity of the Alliance, the common resolve, the fact that not only have all the Heads of Government signed up to the objectives, but they also signed up that there should be no compromise to those objectives. Can I make one other point, because you talk about Britain taking over the show. It would be impossible for us to do that. America is making an immense contribution to this campaign and I actually do think the American people should take more pride in what their pilots and what their Service people have been doing over the past 8 weeks.

Interviewer: Let's be clear on the question of ground troops. Britain feels exactly, if it comes to that, they should be used, is that what we are saying?

Foreign Secretary: Two priorities: first of all we have got to press ahead with the air campaign, which is making a big impact on the troops on the ground in Kosovo, you know they have lost 400 pieces of tanks, artillery, armoured personnel carriers. No army can continue to take that rate of attrition; and then secondly, whilst we carry on intensifying that campaign, we have got to be prepared and plan ahead so that when the time comes we are ready to go in there and take the refugees back.

Mrs Albright: Let me just say this, we are an Alliance, we are an Alliance of 19 democracies and there is a lot of public discussion, but the most important thing is what we have been saying is that now for 8 weeks this Alliance has been totally united in following through on the air campaign.

Interviewer: What do you think keeps President Milosevic going, when you bombard him every night?

Mrs Albright: I think that partially he is isolated from everything, he only gets the news that he wants to get. The people themselves are subjected to massive propaganda. Do you know that the people in Serbia have not seen photographs or pictures of the kinds of horrors that we have, of people being driven out of their homes, they in fact have been told that these are actors, you know running around in circles.

Foreign Secretary: The people who are being hit during the course of that bombardment, the people of the Yugoslav Army, know exactly what is happening and they are cracking up. There was a very interesting case two days ago when an entire battalion just walked out, walked through the hills back from Kosovo. Now they are carrying a message to the people back home and that message is going to work through. [...]

4.4. LAND OPERATIONS BY THE KLA

190. Morning Briefing by Jamie Shea, NATO Spokesman, Brussels, 23 May 1999

Jamie Shea: I will just give you the quick operational up-date overnight. First of all let me give you the one piece of news that you didn't get in your information sheet this morning, which is that last night we flew 652 sorties, 222 of those were strike sorties and that is strike sorties without air defence, and 79 were strike sorties against air defence, so all in all 301 were strike sorties in the total out of a total of 652, so as you can see somewhat very slightly below 50%. So it was quite an intensive night of air operations and that brings now the number of sorties since the beginning of Operation Allied Force to over 25,000.

As you could see, yesterday we continued to enjoy favourable weather, it was Day 60 of Operation Allied Force and again the focus was very much on the fielded forces of the Yugoslav Army in Kosovo. You have seen that we struck at least 9 armoured vehicles, 10 artillery positions, tanks and other military vehicles. In addition we struck at 3 parked aircraft, 2 SA6 surface to air missile transporters and launcher vehicles, and also a radar site. Other facilities that were attacked that directly support the Serb forces in Kosovo were a command post at Rakovica and ammunition storage sites at Urosevac, Kosovska Mitrovica and Srebscka Mitrovica.

You have seen also that our aircraft attacked petroleum storage sites at Smedorevo and Leskovac. We also attacked TV and radio transmitters and radio relay sites at Kula, Kacanik Bodeva and Preprolac. In addition yesterday evening NATO aircraft struck at a special MUP police depot in Belgrade and an electrical power transformer yard at Obrarnova. Again I am happy to be able to announce that all of the NATO aircraft returned safely to their bases. Today as you know is Day 61 and the operations are already under way.

And as always I end with my usual announcement that there will be the usual press briefing at 3.00 this afternoon. General Jertz doesn't have a day off today so he is going to be back with me then.

Nick: Just a point of detail. The three parked aircraft, do you have any details on what they were? Can we assume they were military aircraft?

Jamie Shea: Yes, I think you can safely assume they were military aircraft but would hope that General Jertz will have the details at 3.00.

Jake: On the barracks, according to our correspondent in Albania, the Kosare barracks has been in KLA hands since 9 April. I am just recalling that this time yesterday you initially said do you mean Kasane? Is it not possible that a spelling mistake has become lodged in the system somewhere?

Jamie Shea: Jake, thanks for that because as I told you yesterday there was some confusion on that, which I readily acknowledge and obviously I asked the military commanders to clear up the confusion. I hope they have done so now, so let me give you what we know now.

The post that we attacked was at Glava, indeed that is what we said in our written morning up-date yesterday. This location is one mile from Kosare, and as you know that is the name that has been used in connection with the incident. But we are talking about one incident at Glava, a command post at Glava. We have been aware of fighting for a long time now between UCK forces and the Yugoslav Army in the area around Glava, but we were not aware that the post had been taken over by the UCK before we struck it. Obviously we missed something here in our targeting and this results from I suppose the necessary confusion that sometimes surrounds military operations. Obviously we want to minimise these kind of errors in identifying targets, but I am not going to pretend that we will ever entirely eliminate them in a very intensive operation such as this.

However, I would like to draw your attention to something which I am sure you have seen already, which is that Hassim Thaqi, the head of the Kosovo Liberation Army interim government for Kosovo did say that this attack by NATO was a technical mistake, so I believe that they understand fully well that of course NATO was not deliberately targeting the Kosovo Liberation Army, and he did say that despite this error NATO should intensify even more its air strikes. So I believe that at least he understands and that it was I am afraid a mistake, a technical error, and not something which results from a deliberate policy.

Jake: Inaudible.

Jamie Shea: Absolutely, Glava, it was one mile away from Kosare at a command post in Glava. I have had the military commanders working all night on that, to be absolutely certain. I would have liked to have been able to clear up the confusion yesterday, obviously I don't want to be the bearer of confusion, rather the bearer of clarity, but anyway that happened and that is the situation today.

Mark Laity - BBC: But what you are saying is that it is the same thing, we are all agreeing on the same building that was hit, it was just that you called it Glava and the KLA called it Kosare?

Jamie Shea: Yes, it is about one mile away and I think Kosare is the main place, but I want to be clear about that, it was a command at Glava, about one mile away.

Mark Laity - BBC: You have been hitting power transformer yards again. I have seen some of the pictures showing the damage, the Serb pictures, and they look different to the original pictures which were quite clearly this graphite bomb and soft bomb. Are you actually hitting them with explosive bombs rather than graphite bombs now.

Jamie Shea: Mark, you will forgive me if I don't give you the details, but I did say yesterday, and I repeat that today, that we are using a mixture of munitions to attack those targets and we are doing this again because this is fundamental to disrupting the military command and control system of the Yugoslav Army. It also obliges Milosevic, or the government, the army, to try to identify back-up systems, it puts pressure on them in terms of the priorities they give to the use of their fuel, whether they want to use the fuel for those back-up systems, either for civilian purposes or for military purposes, but most of the civilian installations, such as hospitals, obviously have back-up electrical transformer systems.

Mark Laity - BBC: Because the obvious Serb response is that they are going to say that NATO said it doesn't target civilians, but this is in effect targeting civilians?

Jamie Shea: We target anything that in our view will add to the worries of the Yugoslav Army and disrupt their operations, but as I say, the important civilian facilities have back-up transformer systems and I think that is demonstrated by the fact that those essential facilities continue to operate. I don't think anybody disputes that, even if the lights go out in terms of street lights and traffic lights for certain periods. But again this forces Belgrade to spend a lot of time, a lot of effort to use its back-up systems, it disrupts the command and control and again anything that we can do to hasten the end of this conflict by convincing Milosevic that his military machine is being degraded is something that we are going to continue to do.

Rick: I have noticed that a lot of times now we are hearing at the bottom of the operational up-date it says that the NATO manned aircraft all returned safely. Does that mean that some of the drones are not returning?

Jamie Shea: It does indeed Rick.

Rick: Do you have numbers on that, and also when you tell us about the strikes on the air defence system, are you noticing that the Serbs are able to fix those systems and get them back up and operational, and how quickly can they do that?

Jamie Shea: First of all on the unmanned aerial reconnaissance vehicles, or UAVs as they are called in the jargon, it is true that in the last couple of weeks we have lost a few of those. I am not sure if I have an overall figure now to give you, but for example we lost a Hunter on 21 May, that was south west of Prizren, we lost another Hunter on 22 May yesterday, although I understand that was successfully recovered. Now the reason for this is clear, these fly at far lower altitudes than our aircraft, they also fly very, very slowly indeed, so they are particularly vulnerable to anti-aircraft fire. The Yugoslav Army knows how valuable these are as reconnaissance and intelligence gathering platforms so clearly they will do whatever they can to take those down, although we have various other means of course as you know of gathering intelligence. So I don't have an exact figure, but clearly that is something there.

On the air defence, I think the fact that we have only had two aircraft come down thus far, with 25,000 sorties flown in 61 days shows that we have been successful at handling that air defence. To be honest with you I think it must be extremely depressing for President Milosevic every morning to be told by his military commanders: "Last night, Mr President, we tried, and we tried, and we tried to shoot down NATO planes but we didn't succeed", and I think this is an important part in demonstrating to Milosevic the effectiveness of NATO's air campaign, not simply the fact that we were able to hit the targets that he prizes the most, but also that he isn't shooting down NATO aircraft. Now we mustn't be complacent about that obviously because there is always the risk in any conflict that planes will be lost, but I think that if you look at the number of sorties again and compare that with previous air operations of this intensity, the safety record if you like is good. And this is not just a question of protecting our pilots, as we have said before. Obviously we want to protect our pilots, we have an obligation, if we are sending them into harms way, to give them the maximum protection we can give them. But it is also an important part of convincing Belgrade that they have to come to terms here, to show them that they are not shooting down our planes. I heard at least from various sources at the beginning of this operation the belief in Belgrade that they would be successful at shooting down about 6% of our aircraft every operation that we flew. Well the fact that that hasn't happened I think is an important means of influencing Belgrade.

Having said that, obviously as we have said, General Jertz has said, they have not got the central command and control any longer to direct operations nation-wide, they are very intelligent people, we know that, they have got a lot of military experience, they have got a very dense and redundant air defence system, and the amount of anti-aircraft fire shows that they are trying very, very hard to shoot down our aircraft.

Douglas Hamilton: I am wondering about this report yesterday that the prison in Mitrovica was emptied out and a lot of men in very bad condition came across the border to Macedonia. It is an old chestnut really, but is there any sign that Podujevo, Kosovska, Mitrovica, that sort of northern sector is being more emptied out than other parts of Kosovo, ie for some sort of end solution in which they get to keep the northern part with the mine and the minerals and the towns up there, is there any sign of that?

Jamie Shea: I don't believe that, Doug, quite frankly. I know that at the moment the ethnic cleansing is mainly in that area, that is Suva Reka as well, but as you know Urosevac in the south has been very comprehensively ethnically cleansed. Prizren, even if the actual physical damage to Prizren in the centre at least is less than in other cities, has been very effectively cleansed of its pre-conflict if you like Albanian population. So I generally think that the pattern is province wide and that doesn't seem to suggest any kind of plan for a partition. We don't quite know what Milosevic is up to, but I wouldn't have thought that. On the contrary, his plan would seem to be to have a solution with a very weak form of autonomy for Kosovo under his control, with maybe some Kosovar Albanians coming back, but far fewer than the pre-conflict population. If you want my opinion, that is more the strategy than the notion of a partition.

Having said that, the prison incident is a disturbing one. As you know, 2,000 apparently have been freed, 500 crossed the border at Kukes yesterday, the UNHCR as you know reported that these people were in extremely poor physical condition, having been put on a starvation diet of bread and water, many of them had broken bones, signs of beatings and the rest. Apparently 1,500, the rest are due to arrive soon. We have to wait to see today if those 1,500 are going to be bussed over like the other 500 yesterday. The good thing however, given our concern about the 225,000 missing men is at least those 2,000 seem to be, well are clearly alive, so that is if I could the positive side to this rather macabre affair and that suggests that one of the things that Milosevic may have been wanting to do by holding these men is either get them to do forced labour on defence fortifications, which has been happening, particularly in the south, or to use them as human shields. But anyway let's see where the other 1,500 are.

John: Coming back to Jake's first question as to when this particular command post changed hands, he said 9 April he had been informed, I didn't hear an answer to that?

Jamie Shea: You didn't hear an answer because I don't think he asked the question, or if he did I apologise for not answering. But I don't know exactly what our information is on when that changed hands, but clearly it did and we have acknowledged that.

John: The incident at Glava raises a question about exactly what nature of contacts are going on between the KLA and NATO. Could you explain how exactly the KLA would be expected to inform NATO of its whereabouts inside Kosovo? And could you comment on some of the press reports from people who were at the Glava post who said that they saw the KLA phoning in coordinants of Serb military positions to NATO air controllers?

Jamie Shea: John, I am not aware of any direct contacts between the UCK and NATO as such. There probably are contacts, we know that, between the UCK and allies, but there is no contact, to my knowledge, between the UCK and the political or military structures of the Alliance. So that is I think my point there.

As for the UCK, obviously we use all of the means at our disposal to monitor their activities, to find out where they are, where they are fighting and the rest, and I often report on that in the briefings. By the way, there is a great deal of fighting going on and the UCK at the moment is trying to push a corridor from Kosare into western Kosovo to provide a logistic supply to the UCK people there who are very short, by the way, of ammunition in western Kosovo but continue to fight on. But again I am not pretending that we are always going to have, despite our best efforts, the total, total, up-to-date information as to when a border post changes hands in what is obviously a very dynamic situation in a very mountainous area.

191. Morning Briefing by Jamie Shea, NATO Spokesman, Brussels, 30 May 1999

[Parts not directly referring to the KLA Land Operations have been omitted.]

Greg: Do you have any information on what is going on at the Morina crossing, that is on the fighting there? Is there really the sense that the KLA is trying to open up the Morina crossing as an in-point to Kosovo? And is NATO - I know NATO is not the Air Force for the KLA - is NATO in any way coordinating its bombing around there to facilitate the KLA action?

Jamie Shea: Greg, as I said the other day, we obviously want to try to get the refugees away from Kukes and Morina up in the north to safer locations because the Serbs have been shelling over the border for several weeks now, and as you know, we have always been worried that one of those shells could land in a refugee camp with appalling consequences. Also, Kukes has been in any case over-crowded. There are water problems there, sanitation problems, and I can tell you that

AFOR, the NATO soldiers, in conjunction with UNHCR, have begun a major evacuation programme which started last week, and I can tell you for example that 2,017 refugees were moved yesterday, 50 of them by helicopter, to camps elsewhere in Albania. So that is one thing that we are doing.

As far as the UCK is concerned, yes the UCK has been trying to open up a further corridor into Kosovo out of Morina and to link up with their existing corridor in the Kosare area. And they have tried to launch a limited offensive there, particularly to come down into the valley from a mountain where they are currently deployed, called Pastrik Mountain, and there has been lots of fighting there. Now again I want to stress that NATO has no formal links with the UCK, we do not co-ordinate. There have been several newspaper reports suggesting that we exchange intelligence and so on. But I have no confirmation of that, but obviously the UCK is able to exploit the fact that Serb forces are immobilised because of NATO air strikes, or they are able to attack those Serb forces which are degraded by NATO air strikes and harass them all the more effectively. But that is an indirect consequence, if you like, of what we are doing and not the result of any formal links between our organisation and theirs. [...]

192. Press Conference by Mr Jamie Shea, NATO Spokesman and Major General Walter Jertz, SHAPE, Brussels, 2 June 1999

[Parts not referring to the KLA land operation have been omitted.]

General Jertz: [...] Yesterday, despite poor weather, which caused cancellation of some air operations, NATO flew almost 600 sorties against strategic and tactical targets, including 197 strike and 70 suppression of enemy air defence sorties. Strategic targets are shown on this slide. They were an air defence command centre, radio relay sites, radio broadcast stations, TV FM relay sites, and an electricity transmission tower. Other strategic targets are shown on the next slide. Ammunition storage sites, refuelling station, one highway, one railway bridge, petroleum storage site. Overall, there was little anti-aircraft activity yesterday, and no Serb aircraft activity at all. Air defence radars as well as early warning radars activity was very light. All NATO aircraft returned safely.

Let us now turn our attention to the operations in Kosovo, where NATO's tactical air strikes against Serb forces in Kosovo increased yesterday. Military targets supporting tactical operations in Kosovo struck included radio relay, Kosovska Mitrovica, border posts, army barracks at Pec, troop staging area, ammunition depot. We also identified and struck two major targets, such as bridges at Tupec and Nacek. These critical bridges sit astride the two main roads of resupply into the area around Mount Pastrik. We deployed NATO aircraft to bring more air power to bear on Serb front-line units in this area, very close to the Kosovo-Albanian border. To maximise air effectiveness, air controllers have set up what they call a hog pen over this area. That means a holding area in the sky for one of our most potent ground attack aircraft, the A10, known as a tank buster. I will come back to that in a minute.

Indications are that Serb forces are also repositioning within Kosovo, most probably to counter reported UCK activity. In turn, NATO air activity over Kosovo has increased as a result of the increase in Serb ground force activity. Yesterday I called it a rich target environment.

Our assessment is that the current Serbian counter-offensive against the UCK around Mount Pastrik, offers NATO the best opportunity so far in the air campaign to hit Serb forces hard. To counter UCK advances, Serbia has had to mobilise and concentrate in this area. Because these forces have had to come out of their camouflage positions they have become more visible to our airborne forward air controllers. Once the forward air controllers spot a target, for example a tank or an APC, they call up NATO strike aircraft circling in the area, and guide them into their attack.

Yesterday, we conducted nearly 150 sorties only around Mount Pastrik. Let me elaborate more on tactical targets in the vicinity of Mount Pastrik. We struck 32 artillery pieces, 9 armoured personnel carriers, 6 armoured vehicles, 4 other military vehicles, 8 mortar positions, revetted positions, and one SA6 surface to air missile site. Initial indications are that we have had a significant impact on the Serbian forces operating in this area. A fuller battle damage assessment of course will have to wait a few more days.

What I have said so far is a testimony to the flexibility of this air operation that we have been able to concentrate our air power so quickly in response to actions on the ground. But bear in mind, the tactical part of NATO's air campaign is very different from the strategic operations that make up the other elements of an air war. Tactical air employment consists of static and dynamic elements. Let me elaborate a little bit on the dynamic elements I just mentioned. The time between a forward air controller spotting a target and the air strike against that target can be, and should be, in a matter of minutes only. Timing of course depends on whatever and whether we have to pull the aircraft off a tanker, or whether there is already one available in a holding pattern over Kosovo. Just think of .... over Grand Canyon.

The pace of bombing is dictated by the pace of the battle on the ground. Yesterday, NATO aircraft carrying out attacks against Serb forces on the Albanian, and close to the Albanian, border unintentionally dropped several bombs just over the border inside Albania. The training and equipment of the pilots involved in NATO's operation over Kosovo is second to none. But as any pilot will be able to tell you, these things which I have just described, can and will happen in an intensive and dynamic tactical air operation of this nature. As I mentioned on several occasions, we do not have direct contact with the Kosovar Albanian forces on the ground. However, they are obviously benefiting indirectly from our success against Serb forces. We carefully watch the ground situation close to the Albanian border. A Serb mechanised brigade based out of Prizren has managed to contain the UCK advance around Mount Pastrik, but by moving down to counter-attack, the Serbs have left some flanks exposed. UCK units in the interior appear to be taking advantage of this, and intensifying guerrilla type operations against Serb forces using classic partisan tactics. We are also getting reports of increased fighting between UCK special forces and Serb ground forces throughout Kosovo. It seems that the Belgrade political and military leadership may have been premature when it claimed victory over the UCK a few days ago.

Ladies and gentlemen, this concludes my portion of the briefing. [...]

Greg Palcott, Fox News: First, General, could you respond to a report in the "Washington Post" today that NATO responded to urgent KLA pleas to attack Serb force positions around Mount Pastrik. That this is, according to the "Washington Post" the first known example of NATO air support for KLA actions; and Jamie could you just update us on your feeling about the situation on diplomacy now that Ahtisaari and Chernomyrdin are headed towards Belgrade?

General Jertz: I read this report also in the "Washington Post" but let me reiterate once again, we are hitting Serb forces around Mount Pastrik because they do come out of their camouflage positions, and that is one of the reasons why we of course identified them much easier than we did before, and why we had the good chance to also hit them. And that is one of the main reasons why we are so successful in this area, and we do attack and we do fight and we do try to destroy Serb military assets wherever we find them, and once again Mount Pastrik, an area where heavy fighting is ongoing, we of course do find much better and much easier what we want to destroy and attack.

Greg: But the NATO strikes were not in response to a KLA call for those strikes in that area?

General Jertz: No they were not, they were not. Because we have enough intelligence and other resources which indicate what's going on on the ground. And once again, those tanks have to move, the artillery pieces have to move, and this gives us a good capability and possibility to really attack those.

Jamie Shea: And where NATO effectively strikes Serb forces, then on the other hand it gives the Kosovo Liberation Army extra opportunities to attack those forces which have been degraded. [...]

Mark Laity, BBC News: [...] And on the matter of the attacks around Mount Pastrik, accepting that you don't have formal contacts with the KLA, are they telling you what they're up to and is there any evidence that they've been hitting, the Serb force have been hitting the KLA very hard by all accounts, causing a lot of casualties, has all the damage you've been doing stopped the VJ counter offensive, the Serb forces counter offensive against the KLA? [...]

General Jertz: Mark, the first part of your question, no, we are not in direct co-ordination with KLA or UCK, I have already mentioned that. Of course, once again, we have the good chance now to find the very many targets in this area and that's why we attacked them, as I already explained. And on the second part, even so I said that they did benefit, UCK did benefit from our air attacks, especially in the area of Mount Pastrik, they didn't get too many positive results so they are obviously drawn back to the border but in other areas the results for the UCK fighting Serb forces are better. Mount Pastrik is not standing very well for the UCK. [...]

Craig Whitney, New York Times: General Jertz, you have said there is no direct contact between the UCK or the KLA and NATO but how does NATO know where the UCK positions are so that it doesn't strike them by mistake? Do you have contact indirectly with them?

General Jertz: Well if I would be cynical I would say unfortunately we did strike one of their command posts just a few weeks ago, just maybe two weeks ago, so that might be a clear indication that we didn't know that they were there, we wouldn't have attacked them. On the other hand, no there is no direct link and for us of course if I would go into more details I would have to tell you exactly on what kind of intelligence orders we are using to know where their forces are which I'm not going to do, at least not here, so I think you understand that.

Jamie Shea: Craig, they are two totally different armed forces. The UCK, to my knowledge, don't have tanks, major armoured vehicles, armoured personnel carriers, major pieces of artillery, so as I say, spot the difference. It's not that hard.

Julie, National Public Radio: You have just detailed all of the allied action around Mount Pastrik, 150 sorties were flown there yesterday. How have the allies contributed to the intensity of the fighting themselves? Is not the alliance getting drawn thicker and thicker into the fighting a) on behalf of the UCK and complicating any sort of peace arrangement and b) intensifying the fighting there at a time when the diplomacy is at such a delicate point?

General Jertz: Let me answer the first question and maybe Jamie can use the second part of this question. The connection you are talking about of course UCK and us, NATO, we do have the same aim. We do want to destroy military and Serb forces on the ground. And then of course that's why I always mention that they are benefiting of our operations of course but that does not mean that we are, as I've always said, we are not the KLA or UCK Air Force and I will repeat it again, we are not. We have by our intelligence sources good information on where the Serb ground forces are and we are going to attack them until we finally reach what Jamie I hope is now answering.

Jamie Shea: Julie, we don't see any contradiction between the diplomacy and the continuing use of NATO air power. Quite the reverse. It's what is going to concentrate Milosevic's mind wonderfully on the diplomacy and I always like to quote from Frederick the Great, my mentor here, he said diplomacy without arms is like music without instruments. [...]

4.5 REPORTS ON THE NATO AIR CAMPAIGN

193. Human Rights Watch, Civilian Deaths in the NATO Air Campaign, February 2000[1]

Summary

PRINCIPAL FINDINGS

Minimizing harm to civilians was central to governmental and public consent for NATO's bombing campaign in the Federal Republic of Yugoslavia-an air war officially justified as humanitarian intervention. The decision to intervene was taken with the awareness that the use of force would be subjected to close scrutiny through the lens of international humanitarian law-and in the court of public opinion.

From the beginning of Operation Allied Force, NATO and allied government and military officials stressed their intent to limit civilian casualties and other harm to the civilian population. The practical fulfilment of this legal obligation and political imperative turned upon a range of decisions relating to targeting, weapons selection, and the means of attack.

Despite precautions, including the use of a higher percentage of precision-guided munitions than in any other major conflict in history, civilian casualties occurred. Human Rights Watch has conducted a thorough investigation of civilian deaths as a result of NATO action. On the basis of this investigation, Human Rights Watch has found that there were ninety separate incidents involving civilian deaths during the seventy-eight day bombing campaign. Some 500 Yugoslav civilians are known to have died in these incidents.

We determined the intended target in sixty-two of the ninety incidents. Military installations account for the greatest number, but nine incidents were a result of attacks on non-military targets that Human Rights Watch believes were illegitimate. (Human Rights Watch is currently preparing a separate report with a full analysis of our legal objections to the choice of certain targets.) These include the headquarters of Serb Radio and Television in Belgrade, the New Belgrade heating plant, and seven bridges that were neither on major transportation routes nor had other military functions.

Thirty-three incidents occurred as a result of attacks on targets in densely populated urban areas (including six in Belgrade). Despite the exclusive use of precision-guided weapons in attacks on the capital, Belgrade experienced as many incidents involving civilian deaths as any other city. In Nis, the use of cluster bombs was a decisive factor in civilian deaths in at least three incidents. Overall, cluster bomb use by the United States and Britain can be confirmed in seven incidents throughout Yugoslavia (another five are possible but unconfirmed); some ninety to 150 civilians died from the use of these weapons.

Thirty-two of the ninety incidents occurred in Kosovo, the majority on mobile targets or military forces in the field. Attacks in Kosovo overall were more deadly-a third of the incidents account for more than half of the deaths. Seven troubling incidents were as a result of attacks on convoys or transportation links. Because pilots' ability to properly identify these mobile targets was so important to avoid civilian casualties, these civilian deaths raise the question whether the fact that pilots were flying at high altitudes may have contributed to these civilian deaths by precluding proper target identification. But insufficient evidence exists to answer that question conclusively at this point.

Another factor in assessing the higher level of civilian deaths in Kosovo is the possible Yugoslav use of civilians for "human shields." There is some evidence that Yugoslav forces used internally displaced civilians as human shields in the village of Korisa on May 13, and may thus share the blame for the eighty-seven deaths there.

In an important development, sensitivity to civilian casualties led to significant changes in weapons use. Widespread reports of civilian casualties from the use of cluster bombs and international criticism of these weapons as potentially indiscriminate in effect led, according to senior U.S. Department of Defense officials interviewed by Human

---

[1] *Used with the permission of HRW. Cannot be reused or reprinted without the expressed written consent of HRW.*

Rights Watch, to an unprecedented (and unannounced) U.S. executive order in the middle of May to cease their further use in the conflict. The White House issued the order only days after civilians were killed by NATO cluster bombs in the city of Nis on May 7. U.S. cluster bomb use did apparently stop at about that time, according to Human Rights Watch observations, although British cluster bomb use continued. Human Rights Watch released its own report on May 11 questioning the civilian effects of cluster bombs and calling for a moratorium on their use.

INTERNATIONAL HUMANITARIAN LAW AND ACCOUNTABILITY

In its investigation Human Rights Watch has found no evidence of war crimes. The investigation did conclude that NATO violated international humanitarian law.[1] Human Rights Watch calls on NATO governments to establish an independent and impartial commission, competent to receive confidential information, that would investigate violations of international humanitarian law and the extent of these violations, and would consider the need to alter targeting and bombing doctrine to ensure compliance with international humanitarian law. Such a commission should issue its findings publicly. Human Rights Watch also calls for NATO to alter its targeting and bombing doctrine in order to bring it into compliance with international humanitarian law.

With respect to NATO violations of international humanitarian law, Human Rights Watch was concerned about a number of cases in which NATO forces:

conducted air attacks using cluster bombs near populated areas;

attacked targets of questionable military legitimacy, including Serb Radio and Television, heating plants, and bridges;

did not take adequate precautions in warning civilians of attacks;

took insufficient precautions identifying the presence of civilians when attacking convoys and mobile targets; and

caused excessive civilian casualties by not taking sufficient measures to verify that military targets did not have concentrations of civilians (such as at Korisa).

One disturbing aspect of the matter of civilian deaths is how starkly the number of incidents and deaths contrasts with official U.S. and Yugoslav statements. U.S. officials, including Secretary of Defense William Cohen, Deputy Secretary of Defense John Hamre, and Gen. Wesley Clark, have testified before Congress and stated publicly that there were only twenty to thirty incidents of "collateral damage" in the entire war. The number of incidents Human Rights Watch has been able to authenticate is three to four times this number. The seemingly cavalier U.S. statements regarding the civilian toll suggest a resistance to acknowledging the actual civilian effects and an indifference to evaluating their causes.

The confirmed number of deaths is considerably smaller than Yugoslav public estimates. The post-conflict casualty reports of the Yugoslav government vary but coincide in estimating a death toll of at least some 1,200 and as many as 5,000 civilians. At the lower end, this is more than twice the civilian death toll of around 500 that Human Rights Watch has been able to verify. In one major incident-Dubrava prison in Kosovo-the Yugoslav government attributed ninety-five civilian deaths to NATO bombing. Human Rights Watch research in Kosovo determined that an estimated nineteen prisoners were killed by NATO bombs on May 21 (three prisoners and a guard were killed in an earlier attack on May 19), but at least seventy-six prisoners were summarily executed by prison guards and security forces subsequent to the NATO attack. The countervailing claims about the civilian death toll underscore the need for full accountability by NATO for its military operations.

THE OBJECTIVE OF THIS REPORT

This report has the limited goal of assessing the number of civilian deaths from NATO attacks, as a step toward assessing NATO forces' compliance with their obligation to make protection of civilians an integral part of any use of military force. The benchmarks to be used for judging NATO's attacks are those of international humanitarian law, also known as the laws of war.

In concentrating on civilian deaths, this report addresses only peripherally the damage to civilian property and infrastructure upon which civilian welfare depends, an issue to be addressed in a later report. Nor does this report address other broad issues which are important for an assessment of the war. These include the obligations of the international community to act effectively to prevent crimes against humanity and war crimes; the legality under international law of NATO's launching the operation; the constraints arising from issues of sovereignty; and the modalities of international consensus and decision-making. The report also does not address the war crimes and crimes against humanity committed by Serbian and Yugoslav forces against ethnic Albanians. These gross violations of international humanitarian law, as well as abuses committed by the Kosovo Liberation Army (KLA), have been documented in numerous Human Rights Watch reports in 1998 and 1999, and continue to be the focus of investigations.

COMPILING AND EVALUATING THE EVIDENCE

A fundamental challenge in the analysis of the war over Kosovo is to distinguish the facts of civilian deaths from the propaganda. In order to investigate civilian deaths resulting from NATO bombing, a Human Rights Watch team conducted a twenty-day bomb damage assessment mission in Serbia (including Vojvodina) and Montenegro in August 1999. The team visited ninety-one cities, towns, and villages, and inspected forty-two of the ninety sites of incidents in which civilian deaths occurred. Human Rights Watch researchers also conducted ongoing investigations inside Kosovo beginning June 12, the day NATO entered the province. While most of this research was on war crimes committed by Serbian and Yugoslav forces against ethnic Albanians, several cases relevant to this report were investigated, including the case of Dubrava prison, and incidents involving refugee convoys. Many of the remaining sites in Kosovo at which NATO attacks resulted in civilian deaths have been visited by independent observers whose findings are on the public record.

The Human Rights Watch team in Serbia and Montenegro met with officials from a dozen ministries in Belgrade, and in other locations met with regional, municipality, factory, and utility representatives. Taking eyewitness testimony and inspecting bomb damage, they were able to verify individual events and assess the veracity of wartime and post-war reporting. Human Rights Watch also met with or requested information from a range of officials of NATO countries, in particular the United States, although little new official information on the bombing incidents apart from official press statements has so far been released.

During the war, the research team compiled a master chronological database from military sources and from Yugoslav media and Internet reports, collating these with press and governmental reporting from the NATO countries. Research also drew upon a variety of bomb damage assessments undertaken by Yugoslav government agencies which, in some cases, have produced meticulous documentation on incidents. In order to assess sometimes contradictory renditions, we reviewed these data sets against other information from Yugoslav sources, while comparing this with information from NATO states, in particular the United States and the United Kingdom.

---

[1] Rules of international humanitarian law arise from international agreements such as the Geneva Conventions, or develop as international customary law. States have an obligation to ensure compliance with all provisions of international humanitarian law, and to suppress all violations. War crimes constitute some of the most serious violations of international humanitarian law, known as grave breaches. These violations give rise to the specific obligation to search for and punish those responsible, regardless of the nationality of the perpetrator or the place where the crime was committed. Examples of war crimes are wilful killing, torture or inhuman treatment of non-combatants, wilfully causing great suffering or serious injury to body or health of non-combatants, or launching an indiscriminate attack in the knowledge that the attack will cause excessive loss of life or injury to civilians.

In the end, Human Rights Watch confirmed ninety incidents involving civilian deaths (see Appendix A). The field mission visited forty-two of the ninety confirmed incident locations and collected primary source information on thirty other incidents. Sufficient corroborating information existed on twenty-two others to recognize their credibility (including five about which NATO has officially confirmed that it attacked nearby targets at the same time). Eight incidents were eliminated altogether because they could not be verified or because the reported civilian deaths were actually deemed to be paramilitary troops or army soldiers (see Appendix C).

NATO has offered explanations for what went wrong or merely confirmed attacks in eighteen incidents. After May 7, when NATO began to publicly release a daily list of fixed targets, it confirmed attacking nearby targets in thirty-one of forty-three incidents that occurred between May 7 and the end of the war. NATO is on record as disputing three of the ninety confirmed incidents; Human Rights Watch was able to verify the authenticity of two of these (the other was in Kosovo) through on-the-ground inspections. Still, with the exception of the highly publicized incidents in which NATO has been forced to offer explanations of what happened (for example, the attacks on the Chinese Embassy, the Djakovica-Decane convoys, and the Grdelica gorge), no information has been released on individual targeting missions, strike aircraft, or pilots.

THE CIVILIAN DEATHS

This report documents civilian deaths in Operation Allied Force. Some 500 Yugoslav civilians were killed in ninety separate incidents over seventy-eight days of bombing, although it must be acknowledged that this evidence may be incomplete. In sixty-nine of ninety incidents, the precise number of victims and the names of the victims are known (see Appendix B). In another seven incidents, the number of victims is known and some of the names have been confirmed. In eleven incidents, the number of victims is known but the names are unknown. In three incidents, the names and precise numbers of victims are unknown.

Human Rights Watch concludes on the basis of evidence available on these ninety incidents that as few as 488 and as many as 527 Yugoslav civilians were killed as a result of NATO bombing. Between 62 and 66 percent of the total registered civilian deaths occurred in just twelve incidents. These twelve incidents accounted for 303 to 352 civilian deaths. These were the only incidents among the ninety documented in which ten or more civilian deaths were confirmed.

Available data on each incident are presented in Appendices A and B. They include descriptions of the physical destruction observed at the forty-two sites visited by Human Rights Watch, accounts by witnesses interviewed at each site and elsewhere in regard to particular incidents, documentation on individual incidents, and other available information compiled from public and private Yugoslav and NATO sources. In each incident report the emphasis is upon the evidence of civilian deaths, although any available evidence concerning the apparent target, the means of the attack, and the resulting physical damage is also presented.

Information drawn from the ninety incident reports allows a general picture to be drawn of the civilian deaths by the time, place, and circumstances in which they occurred. The deaths resulted from attacks on a range of targets, under different circumstances, and using a variety of munitions. Fifty-five of the incidents occurred in Serbia (including five in Vojvodina), three in Montenegro, and thirty-two in Kosovo. But between 278 and 317 of the dead-between 56 and 60 percent of the total number of deaths-were in Kosovo. In Serbia, 201 civilians were killed (five in Vojvodina) and eight died in Montenegro. A third of the incidents-a total of thirty-three-occurred as a result of attacks on targets in densely populated urban areas.

Human Rights Watch was able to determine the intended target in sixty-two of the ninety incidents (68 percent). Of these, the greater number of incidents were caused as a result of attacks on military barracks, headquarters, and depots; thirteen were a result of attacks on bridges (and one tunnel); six resulted from attacks on telecommunications and air defense facilities; five each resulted from attacks on industrial facilities, oil installations, and airfields; and seven were as a result of attacks on convoys or on what were perceived to be military forces in the field. These latter incidents were the most deadly, though two of the ten worst incidents occurred as a result of attacks on bridges.

Almost half of the incidents (forty-three) resulted from attacks during daylight hours, when civilians could have been expected to be on the roads and bridges or in public buildings which may have been targeted. Overall, forty incidents occurred in April, forty-five occurred in May, four in June, and one in March. May 29 saw the most incidents (with five), followed by four on April 14, May 30, and May 31. The pace of the air war peaked at the end of May.

Human Rights Watch was able to determine the weapons involved in the cause of the civilian deaths in only twenty-eight of the ninety incidents. Of these, twenty-one are incidents about which it can be confirmed that precision-guided munitions (PGMs) were used (though there could be others). This includes all of the attacks on bridges or targets in and around the Belgrade area. Cluster bomb use can be positively determined in seven incidents (another five are possible but unconfirmed). In almost all of the other instances, it is impossible to establish the weapon used.

Other than a factual statistical analysis of attacks, insufficient evidence exists to determine the cause of civilian deaths. U.S. Deputy Defense Secretary John Hamre has provided the only analysis regarding the "30 instances of unintended damage" that the Pentagon seems to acknowledge. Of those, he says one third occurred when the target was hit but innocent civilians were killed at the same time. Of the remaining twenty, three were said to be caused by human error when the pilot identified the wrong target, and two were caused by technical malfunction. In the other fourteen instances, the Pentagon has not yet announced whether human error or mechanical failure was responsible.

THE STANDARDS APPLIED

[...]

CONCLUSIONS AND RECOMMENDATIONS

Yugoslav civilian deaths in Operation Allied Force occurred under all circumstances, day and night, during good and bad weather, from the use of "smart" and "dumb" bombs, in attacks on almost every type of target. The number of incidents increased (and peaked) in the last three days of May. During this period, the intensity of the attacks also peaked. This was also a time when the percentage of precision-guided munitions being used by NATO aircraft was declining (due to inventory shortages and cost considerations). Most of the increased bombing effort, particularly in the large number of dumb bombs being dropped by B-1 and B-52 heavy bombers, was taking place in western and southern Kosovo. Attacks at a greater intensity in this area, which was largely depopulated, did not result in any increase in civilian deaths.

Throughout the air war, then, the incidents of civilian deaths per number of strikes seem to have remained fairly constant. Human Rights Watch therefore concludes that civilian deaths in Operation Allied Force were not necessarily related to the pace or intensity of the war, but occurred as a result of decisions regarding target and weapons selection, or were caused by technical malfunction or human error. This suggests that affirmative measures-restrictions on certain daylight attacks, prohibitions on the use of cluster bombs in populated areas, greater care in attacking mobile targets, better target selection-could indeed have been taken to further reduce the level of civilian harm during these military operations.

Five of the ten worst incidents involving civilian deaths (see Table 1 following Appendix C) were attacks on presumed Yugoslav military convoys or transportation routes, four in Kosovo. NATO Gen. Wesley Clark stated after the war that NATO often observed military vehicles moving on roads in Kosovo "intermixed with civilian convoys," particularly during bad weather. This does not exempt NATO from the obligation to take fundamental precautions to focus their effort on military objectives. In fact, after the first two incidents, on April 12 and 14, the civilian deaths led to changes in rules of engagement. While pilots had previously been required to visually identify the military nature of traffic before attacking, after the initial incidents new guidance directed that if military vehicles were intermingled with civilian vehicles, they were not to be attacked.

Similarly, after a mid-day attack on the bridge in the town of Varvarin on May 30 which resulted in civilian deaths (incident no. 81), NATO again provided excuses for the incident but then changed the rules of engagement for attacks on bridges. NATO Spokesman Jamie Shea publicly stated that the alliance had bombed a "legitimate designated military target" and stated that "we take the same precautions at midday as we do at midnight." Yet after the incident at Varvarin, according to Lt. Gen. Michael Short, the air war commander, pilots were directed not to attack bridges during daylight hours, on weekends, on market days, or on holidays. There is no evidence that the daylight timing of the attack at Varvarin (or on many other fixed targets) was critical to the destruction of the target-the attack was not directed specifically against military traffic. Around-the-clock bombing in these and other cases rather seems to have been part of a psychological warfare strategy of harassment undertaken without regard to the greater risk to the civilian population.

With respect to target selection itself, one of the worst incidents of civilian deaths, and certainly the worst in Belgrade, was the bombing of state Serb Radio and Television headquarters in Belgrade on April 23 (incident no. 30). There was considerable disagreement between the United States and French governments regarding the legality and legitimacy of the target, and there was a lively public debate regarding selection of Yugoslav civilian radio and television as a target group. There is no evidence that the radio and television headquarters meet the legal test of military necessity in target selection, as it made no direct contribution to the military effort in Kosovo. In this case, the purpose of the attack again seems to have been more psychological harassment of the civilian population than to obtain direct military effect. The risks involved to the civilian population in undertaking this urban attack grossly outweigh any perceived military benefit.

Another issue of intense public interest in the war is NATO's use of cluster bombs. There are seven confirmed and five likely incidents involving civilian deaths from cluster bomb use by the United States and Britain. Altogether, someninety to 150 civilians died from cluster bomb use. The first confirmed incident was on April 10 (incident no. 14) and the last was on May 13 (incident no. 57). After the technical malfunction of a cluster bomb used in an attack on the urban Nis airfield on May 7 (incident no. 48), the White House quietly issued a directive to restrict cluster bomb use (at least by U.S. forces). Cluster bombs should not have been used in attacks in populated areas, let alone urban targets, given the risks. The use prohibition clearly had an impact on the subsequent civilian effects of the war, particularly as bombing with unguided weapons (which would otherwise include cluster bombs) significantly intensified after this period. Nevertheless, the British air force continued to drop cluster bombs (official chronologies show use at least on May 17, May 31, June 3, and June 4), indicating the need for universal, not national, norms regarding cluster bomb use.

What is striking about the Yugoslav conflict, given the level of intense media coverage and public interest it has received in the United States and abroad, is that there is almost a complete lack of any public accountability by any of the national NATO members for missions undertaken in the NATO alliance's name. Little information has been released on nations or aircraft involved in bombing missions, on specific targets, and there is sparse information on weapons used in individual circumstances.

Human Rights Watch calls on NATO and its individual member states to:

establish an independent and impartial commission, competent to receive confidential information, that would investigate violations of international humanitarian law and the extent of these violations, and would consider the need to alter targeting and bombing doctrine to ensure compliance with international humanitarian law;

alter NATO's targeting and bombing doctrine to reflect the rules of engagement adopted during Operation Allied Force to increase civilian protection, as an important step toward bringing the doctrine fully into compliance with international humanitarian law;

conduct an impartial and independent investigation of the nine incidents which were the result of attacks on inappropriate targets that Human Rights Watch believes were illegitimate. (Human Rights Watch will identify other examples of inappropriate targets in a separate report currently in preparation);

carry out a full review of the compliance with international humanitarian law of the psychological warfare strategy of harassment of the civilian population evident in many of the attacks;

acknowledge and evaluate all instances of civilian deaths and "collateral" damage-and not just some twenty or thirty select incidents-if there is to be a publicly relevant post-war analysis;

declassify all NATO and national operations reports that could establish the precise nature of munitions employed in each attack to enable a comprehensive evaluation of the humanitarian dimension of the use of cluster bombs or other weapons, and suspend the use of cluster bombs until such evaluation has occurred;

release comprehensive information on their operations-including chronologies of attacks, target lists, numbers and types of weapons expended, as well as any analysis or evaluations of the causes of incidents of civilian deaths or damage-that would enable independent observers to carry out a proper analysis of these operations under international humanitarian law; and

examine targeting emphasis and weapons selection during the war and take whatever corrective measures are needed in the future to further minimize the civilian effects of the use of military force.

The Crisis in Kosovo

[...]

Operation Allied Force Attacks

Operation Allied Force was initiated at 7 p.m. GMT (8 p.m. local time in Yugoslavia). Of thirteen (out of nineteen) NATO nations that made aircraft available for the operation (Belgium, Canada, Denmark, France, Germany, Italy, the Netherlands, Norway, Portugal, Spain, Turkey, the United Kingdom, and the United States), eight put their planes in action on the first night. Aircraft from the United States, the United Kingdom, France, Canada, and Spain conducted bombing, carrying out a succession of attack waves with almost exclusively precision-guided munitions (PGMs) against fixed and pre-selected targets. Long-range cruise missiles were fired by the United States and Britain. Though targets were hit throughout Yugoslavia across a mix of target types (for example, airfields, command and control sites, barracks, andheadquarters, particularly of the special police), the initial focus was almost exclusively an effort to neutralize the Yugoslav air defense system. In the first day, NATO hit fifty-three targets, largely air defenses and radar sites.[1]

The mission of Operation Allied Force, in General Clark's words, "was to halt or disrupt a systematic campaign of ethnic cleansing."[2]

---

[1] Dana Priest, "Tensions Grew with Divide over Strategy," Washington Post, September 21, 1999, p. A1.

[2] Gen. Wesley Clark, Remarks to the American Enterprise Institute regarding military action in Yugoslavia, August 31, 1999. See also Testimony before the U.S. Senate Armed Services Committee Hearing on Lessons Learned from Military Operations and Relief Efforts in Kosovo, October 21, 1999. NATO's objectives for the conflict in Kosovo were set out in the Statement issued at the Extraordinary Meeting of the North Atlantic Council held at NATO on April 12, 1999 and were reaffirmed by Heads of State and Government in Washington on April 23, 1999. They included:
- A verifiable stop to all military action and the immediate ending of violence and repression;
- The withdrawal from Kosovo of the military, police, and paramilitary forces;
- The stationing in Kosovo of an international military presence;
- The unconditional and safe return of all refugees and displaced persons

Attacks would be along two lines, a "strategic attack line operating against Serb air defenses, command and control, VJ [Yugoslav Army] and MUP [Ministry of Interior] forces, their sustaining infrastructure, supply routes, and resources," and "a tactical line of operation against the Serb forces deployed in Kosovo and in southern Serbia."[1] The initial attacks against air defenses and command and control elements were intended to "set the conditions for moving on up [the hierarchy of targets] to [include] the forces in the field."[2]

Following the attacks on air defenses and command and control centers, NATO chose targets to isolate Yugoslav forces and constrain their movement. According to Chairman of the Joint Chiefs of Staff Gen. Henry Shelton, this included their "ability to move both horizontally [and] laterally on the battlefield, the road and bridge network, which was key to that, and also...sustainment, particularly the POL [petroleum, oil, and lubricants], to start causing shortages, since this was a predominantly mechanized armored force."[3]

Although there were expectations on the part of some, including evidently many political leaders in NATO governments, that Allied Force would be a short campaign, the U.S. Department of Defense stated that it "made clear to our allied counterparts that Operation Allied Force could well take weeks or months to succeed."[4] Regardless of this post-war claim, NATO operations began with just a limited number of cruise missile and air strikes. The carefully planned "phases" were quickly melded together and expanded to accommodate political and public sensitivities, as well as to escalate the intensity of operations to make progress towards forcing Yugoslav submission. According to U.S. Secretary of Defense William Cohen, "soon after the conflict began, entire classes of targets were delegated for approval by NATO's military commanders. And only certain sets of targets, such as those in downtown Belgrade, in Montenegro and those with a high likelihood of civilian casualties, were reviewed by the allied capitals and by higher political authorities."[5]

At the NATO summit in Washington on April 23, 1999, one month into the air war, alliance leaders decided to intensify the air campaign by expanding the target set to include military-industrial infrastructure, news media, and othertargets considered to be of a strategic nature.[6] More aircraft and weapons were deployed in the theater of operations, and there was an intensification not only in the rate at which targets were hit, but also a shift from an initial eight-hour day to a twenty-four-hours a day campaign.[7]

With an increasing force and greater intensity of attacks, there were also increasing attacks on Yugoslav forces in and around Kosovo. However, by and large, the focus into the second month of bombing continued to be attacks on objects that would cut the supply lines and support infrastructure of the military forces. Not only was poor weather a prohibitive factor in mounting attacks on mobile forces, but NATO had to "learn" the Kosovo geography and the organization of Yugoslav forces. It was many weeks before it was able to track forces on the ground, identify key elements, predict their movements and activities, and attack them in urban settings. Nevertheless, NATO's air attacks, both against "strategic targets" and in the south, slowly had an accumulating impact on Yugoslav military operations. Air activity forced Yugoslav forces to remain largely hidden from view, traveling only under limited circumstances.[8] Over time, attrition of heavy equipment accelerated, peaking at about the last week in May.

In the first month of Operation Allied Force, NATO reported that it averaged around 350 sorties per day, with nearly 130 attack sorties. By the fourth week, it was flying nearly two-and-a-half times the number of attack sorties per day than it flew during the first three weeks.[9] NATO reported in early July that it had flown a total of 37,465 sorties, of which 14,006 were strike and suppression of air defense (SEAD) sorties and 10,808 were strike-attack sorties.[10] By the end of the conflict, NATO had attacked over 900 targets.[11]

As more NATO forces were introduced and the attacks continued, the percentage of PGMs being used also declined. In the early days of Allied Force, "smart" weapons constituted more than 90 percent of the ordnance employed. By mid-May, this had declined to only 10 or 20 percent of the total, with guided weapons constituting about 35 percent of the 26,000 weapons employed throughout the course of the war.[12]

From the very beginning of Operation Allied Force, minimizing civilian casualties was a major declared NATO concern. According to NATO, consideration of civilian casualties was fully incorporated into the planning and targeting process. All targets were "looked at in terms of their military significance in relation to the collateral damage or the unintended consequences that might be there," General Shelton said on April 14. "Then every precaution is made...so that collateral damage is avoided."[13] According to Lt. Gen. Michael Short, "collateral damage drove us to an extraordinary degree. General Clark committed hours of his day dealing with the allies on issues of collateral damage."[14]

Though a couple of dozen incidents would dog NATO throughout the war in its press and propaganda battles with the Yugoslav government, from another perspective, the limitation of "collateral damage" was a political imperative to successful conclusion of an alliance war. In the words of Lt. Gen. Marvin R. Esmond, the senior Air Force operations officer, "NATO's success with precision engagement and minimal collateral damage was a key factor in holding the Alliance firmly together during the bombing."[15]

Documenting and Assessing the Civilian Toll

Because of keen public interest in the civilian toll from Operation Allied Force, Human Rights Watch assumed a major undertaking to document and evaluate the impact and effects of the NATO military operation. Human Rights Watch military consultant William M. Arkin and researcher Bogdan Ivanisevic conducted extensive research into

---

and unhindered

access to them by humanitarian aid organizations; and

- The establishment of a political framework agreement for Kosovo on the basis of the

Rambouillet Accords, in conformity with international law and the Charter of the United Nations.

[1] Special Department of Defense Press Briefing with General Wesley Clark, Supreme Allied Commander, Europe, Topic: Kosovo Strike Assessment Also Participating: Airmen and Analysts from Operation Allied Force and Post-strike Assessment Work, Brussels, Belgium, September 16, 1999.

[2] Testimony of Gen. Henry Shelton, to the U.S. House Armed Services Committee, April 14, 1999.

[3] Hearing of the U.S. Senate Armed Services Committee, Lessons Learned from Military Operations and Relief Efforts in Kosovo, October 14, 1999.

[4] DOD/JCS, Joint Statement on the Kosovo After Action Review, October 14, 1999.

[5] Hearing of the U.S. Senate Armed Services Committee, Lessons Learned from Military Operations and Relief Efforts in Kosovo, October 14, 1999.

[6] DOD/JCS, Joint Statement on the Kosovo After Action Review, October 14, 1999.

[7] U.S. Secretary of Defense William S. Cohen, Remarks as Delivered to the International Institute for Strategic Studies, Hotel del Coronado, San Diego, California, Thursday, September 9, 1999.

[8] DOD/JCS, Joint Statement on the Kosovo After Action Review, October 14, 1999.

[9] Anthony H. Cordesman, "The Lessons and Non-Lessons of the Air and Missile Campaign in Kosovo," CSIS, revised September 29, 1999, p. 17.

[10] Jane's Defense Weekly, July 7, 1999, p. 21.

[11] Statement of the Honorable John J. Hamre, U.S. Deputy Secretary of Defense, before the U.S. House Permanent Select Committee on Intelligence, July 22, 1999.

[12] Gen. Wesley Clark, Remarks to the American Enterprise Institute regarding military action in Yugoslavia, August 31, 1999.

[13] Testimony of Gen. Henry Shelton, to the U.S. House Armed Services Committee, April 14, 1999.

[14] Testimony of Lt. Gen. Michael Short before the U.S. Senate Armed Services Committee Hearing on Lessons Learned from Military Operations and Relief Efforts in Kosovo, October 21, 1999.

[15] Statement of Lt. Gen. Marvin R. Esmond, U.S. Deputy Chief of Staff, Air and Space Operations, United States Air Force, October 19, 1999.

the operation. During the war, they compiled a master chronological database from military sources, Yugoslav media and Internet reports, collating these with press and governmental reporting from the NATO countries. Tanjug (official Yugoslav news agency) and Yugoslav television and radio dispatches were monitored on the Internet and via the Foreign Broadcast Information Service (FBIS) and BBC Summary of World Broadcasts. The researchers corresponded with Yugoslav civil defense, military, and information ministry officials via E-mail, and scoured Yugoslav websites, particularly those maintained by official agencies. They also comprehensively monitored the Yugoslav press from March-June 1999, including: BLIC (Belgrade independent daily), Politika (Belgrade pro-government daily), Politika Ekspres (Belgrade pro-government), Vecernje Novosti (Belgrade pro-government daily), Glas Javnosti (Belgrade independent), Dan (Montenegrin pro-Belgrade/SPS daily), Pobjeda (Montenegrin pro-Podgorica government daily), and Vijesti (Montenegrin independent daily).[1]

Between August 2 and August 20, 1999, Arkin and Ivanisevic conducted a bomb damage assessment mission in Serbia and Montenegro. Human Rights Watch Executive Director Kenneth Roth accompanied the team on August 2-5. In twenty days, the team drove approximately 5,000 kilometers, visited ninety-one cities, towns, and villages, and inspected well over 250 sites (targets, reported targets, areas of civilian damage, stray craters, etc.). They met with officials from a dozen ministries in Belgrade, and in other locations met with regional, municipality, factory, and utility representatives. Taking eyewitness testimony and inspecting bomb damage, they were able to verify individual events and assess the veracity of wartime and post-war reporting.

Human Rights Watch confirmed ninety incidents in which civilians died as a result of NATO bombing (see Appendix A). The field mission visited forty-two of the ninety confirmed incident locations and collected primary source information on thirty other incidents. Sufficient corroborating information existed on twenty-two others to recognize their credibility (including five in which NATO has officially confirmed that it attacked nearby targets at the same time). Eight additional reported and claimed incidents have been eliminated altogether, three because they could not be verified or there was little corroborative reporting,[2] and five because the reported deaths are actually presumed to be paramilitary policemen or soldiers (see Appendix C).[3]

Human Rights Watch has also assessed the veracity of information compiled by the Yugoslav government, including autopsy reports, death certificates, and photographic evidence of bomb damage and casualties. The government's two-volume White Book, NATO Crimes in Yugoslavia, provides information on seventy-five of ninety incidents. Other releases by the Ministry of Foreign Affairs and the Ministry of Health document, in a less comprehensive manner, other aspects of the civilian effects of the bombing. Human Rights Watch also met with representatives of the governmental Committee for Compiling Data on Crimes Against Humanity and International Law, which is compiling dossiers on eachinstance of civilian casualties, as well as the government Reconstruction Commission, which is responsible for repair of the public infrastructure.

The findings of Human Rights Watch's field operation facilitated a critical review of governmental and private reports from both sides of the conflict. Systematic on-site inspections facilitated the cross-checking of information compiled from press and Internet reports, as well as providing the basis for evaluating the detailed reporting on casualties by the Yugoslav government and private agencies. Our inspection of bomb damage and interviews with witnesses, survivors, and others enabled us to assess the accuracy of detailed reporting on deaths and bomb damage produced on the same incidents, for example, by the Yugoslav and other government sources. On the basis of spot-checking in the course of our own field research and correlation with other sources, some of these documentation sets, notably the White Book and the Ministry of Health photographic record, have been found to be largely credible.[4]

Civilian Deaths as a Result of Attacks

Human Rights Watch concludes that as few as 489 and as many as 528 Yugoslav civilians were killed in the ninety separate incidents in Operation Allied Force. In sixty-nine of the ninety incidents, the precise number and the names of the victims are known (see Appendix B). In another nine incidents, the number of victims is known and some of the names have been confirmed. In nine incidents, the number of victims is known but the names are unknown. In three incidents, the names and precise numbers of victims are unknown.[5]

Between 62 and 66 percent of the total registered civilian deaths occurred in just twelve incidents (see Table 1). These twelve incidents accounted for from 303 to 352 civilian deaths, based on the best available information. These were the only incidents among the ninety documented in which ten or more civilian deaths were confirmed.

Information drawn from the ninety incident reports allows a general picture to be drawn of the civilian deaths by the time, place, and circumstances in which they occurred. The deaths resulted from attacks on a range of targets, under different circumstances, and from a variety of munitions. Fifty-five of the incidents occurred in Serbia (including five in Vojvodina), three in Montenegro, and thirty-two in Kosovo. But between 279 and 318 of the dead-between 56 and 60 percent of the total number of deaths-were in Kosovo. In Serbia, 201 civilians were killed (five in Vojvodina) and eight died in Montenegro. A third of the incidents-thirty-three-occurred as a result of attacks on targets in densely populated urban areas.

Human Rights Watch was able to determine the intended target in sixty-two of the ninety incidents (68 percent). Of these, the greater number of incidents was caused as a result of attacks on military barracks, headquarters, and depots; thirteen were a result of attacks on bridges (and one tunnel); six resulted from attacks on telecommunications and air defense facilities; five each resulted from attacks on industrial facilities, oil installations, and airfields; and seven were as a result of attacks on convoys or on what were perceived to be military forces in the field. These latter incidents were the most deadly, while two of the ten worst incidents occurred as a result of attacks on bridges.

Almost half of the incidents (forty-three) resulted from attacks during daylight hours, when civilians could have been expected to be on the roads and bridges or in public buildings which may have been targeted. Overall, forty incidentsoccurred in April, forty-five occurred in May, four in June, and one in March. May 29 saw the most incidents (five), followed by April 14, May 30, and May 31 (four each).

---

[1] These are collectively referred to as "Yugoslav press reports" in footnotes throughout this report and Appendices. When significant individual articles are referenced, they are listed individually.

[2] These are Turkovac near Leskovac (April 11), Kastrat east of Kursumlija (April 26), and Smederevo (May 21).

[3] These are Kursumilija and Prizren (March 25), Nis and Pristina "refugee" camps (March 29), and Stavaljska breza village near Sjenica (April 6). Like army soldiers, paramilitary troops are considered combatants in the context of the Yugoslav war. and as such are excluded from this assessment of civilian (i.e., non-combatant) deaths.

[4] One major exception to the largely credible nature of the government's White Book is the case of Dubrava prison, discussed in this report. It should also be noted that the general accuracy of the documentation contained in the White Book and the Ministry of Health's photographic record concerning civilian casualties and damage to civilian objects contrasts sharply with the sweeping statements made by the Yugoslav government of 1,200 to 5,000 civilian deaths during the war.

[5] There is some uncertainty as to the precise number of civilians killed in about three incidents. These include the April 12 attack on the Djakovica-Klina road (incident no.17), the May 1 attack in Luzane which destroyed the Nis Express bus (incident no. 41), and the May 13 Korisa attacks (incident no. 57). In Djakovica-Klina, where the best information only indicates that "several" civilians were killed, Human Rights Watch uses five civilian deaths as its estimate. In the case of Korisa, reporting of civilian deaths varies from forty-eight to eighty-seven.

Human Rights Watch was able to determine the weapon involved in the cause of the civilian deaths in only twenty-eight of the ninety incidents. Of these, twenty-one are incidents in which it can be confirmed that precision-guided munitions (PGMs) were used (though there could be others). This includes all of the attacks on bridges or targets in and around the Belgrade area. Cluster bomb use can be positively determined in seven incidents (another five are possible but unconfirmed).[1] In almost all of the other instances, we have been unable to establish the weapon used.

Countervailing Claims

One disturbing aspect of the matter of civilian deaths is how starkly the number of incidents and deaths contrasts with official U.S. and Yugoslav statements. Speaking on September 9, 1999, Secretary of Defense William Cohen said: "Of the thousands of bombs that were dropped and the missiles that were fired, nearly all of them hit their intended target. Of all those thousands of weapons that were dropped and expended, approximately 20 had unintended consequences or were not on target."[2] Gen. Wesley Clark, commander of NATO forces, in the war, stated on August 31 that there were just "20 incidents of collateral damage" in the entire war.[3] Deputy Secretary of Defense John Hamre testified before Congress on July 21 that "Out of the 9,300 strikes [sic], we had 30 where we killed people...30 where we had damage we hadn't intended."[4] In October, General Clark again repeated that there had been twenty incidents: "I just want to emphasize the incredible precision of the bombing; the fact that on 78 days, with over 23,000 weapons dropped or fired, there were only 20 incidents of collateral damage...that's an incident rate of less than 1/10th of 1 percent."[5]

However, the number of confirmed deaths is considerably smaller than both U.S. and Yugoslav public estimates. The post conflict casualty reports of the Yugoslav government vary, but coincide in estimating a civilian death toll of at least some 1,200 and as many as 5,700 civilians. On May 22, Margit Savovic, president of Yugoslav Committee for Cooperation with UNICEF said that "more than 1,200 civilians were killed and more than 5,000 [were] wounded."[6] On July 14, Milovan Zivkovic, director of the Federal Office of Statistics, said at press conference that "estimations [of] about 1,200 killed have appeared, and some sources talk about more than 5,000 victims, some go even up to 18,000."[7] According to the BETA independent news agency, Zivkovic also said that the 1,200 number publicized by the Yugoslav Committee for Cooperation with UNICEF pertained only to those killed during the two and a half months of the air campaign. "But the 5,000 and 5,700 numbers are exact as well, only they cover a longer period of time and various ways of losing life," he said.[8] Ambassador Djorde Lopicic, chief of international law at the Ministry of Foreign Affairs (MFA), told Human Rights Watch on August 5, 1999, that 2,000 civilians had died and over 10,000 were injured from NATO bombing. At the lower end, even the 1,200 figures is more than twice the civilian death toll of around 500 that Human Rights Watch has been able to verify for the ninety known incidents involving civilian deaths.

While there have been various pronouncements from the Yugoslav government regarding the number of civilian deaths, NATO has been far more silent. There has been only one informal U.S. government or NATO statement regarding the number of Yugoslav civilian deaths from the bombing. General Joseph W. Ralston, vice chairman of the Joint Chiefs of Staff, said in September that "Despite the weight of bombs dropped, Serbian civilian casualties were amazingly light, estimated at less than 1,500 dead."[9] This estimate is three times the number calculated by Human Rights Watch.

In the thirty instances acknowledged by the Defense Department, Deputy Defense Secretary John Hamre has provided the only analysis regarding the causes of civilian deaths. In Congressional testimony in July he said of the thirty incidents:

one third were instances where we damaged the target we wanted to destroy, but innocent civilians were killed at the same time. You will recall the time one of our electro-optically guided bombs homed in on a railroad bridge just when a passenger train raced to the aim point. We never wanted to destroy that train or kill its occupants. We did want to destroy the bridge and we regret this accident. As I said, 10 of the 30 instances of unintended damage fall in this category. For the remaining 20 instances, 3 were caused by human error that identified the wrong target, and two were caused by mechanical error by our hardware. In 14 instances we have not yet determined whether the unintended damage was caused by human error or mechanical failure. We will determine that to the best of our ability during our after action assessment. The one remaining ... [is the] bombing of the Chinese embassy. ... [It] was unique in that we had a legitimate target that we wanted to hit; the only problem is we had the target located in the wrong building. To my knowledge, this is the only example of this failing in all of our strike operations.[10]

The Standards Applied

[...]

Case Studies of Civilian Deaths

The ninety incidents involving some 500 civilian deaths provide a part of the picture from which to consider NATO's conduct of the war (two subsequent Human Rights Watch reports are planned to look in greater detail at targeting in Operation Allied Force and the use of cluster bombs).[11] At issue is whether NATO effectively adhered to the humanitarian law imperative that the civilian population be protected against dangers arising from military operations. At the core is the principle of civilian immunity from attack and its complementary principle requiring the parties to a conflict to do everything feasible to distinguish civilians from combatants at all times. Several incidents,

---

[1] In three other cases, Yugoslav authorities claimed that civilian casualties were a result of cluster bomb use, but Human Rights Watch could find no evidence to corroborate the claims or found evidence to refute them.

[2] Remarks as Delivered to the International Institute for Strategic Studies by Secretary of Defense William S. Cohen, Hotel del Coronado, San Diego, California, Thursday, September 9, 1999.

[3] Gen. Wesley Clark, Remarks to the American Enterprise Institute regarding military action in Yugoslavia, August 31, 1999.

[4] U.S. Congress, House Permanent Select Committee on Intelligence, Hearing on the Bombing of the Chinese Embassy, July 21, 1999.

[5] Testimony before the U.S. Senate Armed Services Committee Hearing on Lessons Learned from Military Operations and Relief Efforts in Kosovo, October 21, 1999.

[6] "Savovic: Deca cine 30 odsto od ukupno ubijenih civila," [Savovic: Children Make 30 Percent of the Total Number of Killed Civilians], Politika, May 23, 1999, p. 12.

[7] "Temeljno utvrditi posledice agresije," ["To Establish a Full Account of the Consequences of the Aggression"], Politika, July 15, 1999, p. 17. In a report about the same press conference, the independent Danas newspaper quoted Zivkovic as saying that the G-17 group of independent economists had estimated the number of civilians who lost their lives in NATO attacks to be 5,700. "NATO ubio 5.700 civila," [NATO Killed 5,700 Civilians], Danas, July 15, 1999, p. 5.

[8] "Zivkovic: Steta od NATO bombardovanja neprocenjiva," [Zivkovic: Damage Caused by NATO Bombardments Unmeasurable], BETA, July 14, 1999.

[9] Gen. Joseph W. Ralston, Vice Chairman, Joint Chiefs of Staff, AFA Policy Forum: "Aerospace Power and the Use of Force," September 14, 1999.

[10] Statement of the Honorable John J. Hamre, U.S. Deputy Secretary of Defense, before the U.S. House Permanent Select Committee on Intelligence, July 22, 1999.

[11] For an early account of the use of cluster bombs by NATO in the Federal Republic of Yugoslavia and Human Rights Watch's position, see Human Rights Watch, "Ticking Time Bombs: NATO's Use of Cluster Munitions in Yugoslavia," A Human Rights Watch Short Report, vol. 11, no. 6(D), May 1999; and Human Rights Watch, "Cluster Bombs: Memorandum for CCW Delegates," December 16, 1999.

which accounted for a large proportion of civilian deaths, illustrate various problems faced in NATO actions, and are further presented below.

The most dramatic losses of civilian life from the NATO offensive in Kosovo came from attacks on fleeing or traveling refugees confused with military forces. These included repeated attacks on refugees over a twelve-mile stretch of the Djakovica-Decane road in Kosovo, in which seventy-three civilian refugees died (incident no. 19), attacks near Korisa in Kosovo (incident no. 57), in which as many as eighty-seven civilian displaced persons and refugees died, and two incidents involving attacks on civilian buses, at Luzane (incident no. 41) and Savine Vode (incident no. 46). Another dramatic loss of civilian life followed from an attack on Dubrava prison, which caused nineteen deaths (see below).

In these various incidents involving the deaths of Kosovar refugees, the principal issue is whether every feasible precaution was taken to accurately distinguish civilians from combatants. At the same time, there are questions regarding the decisions to attack on the basis of incomplete and/or seriously flawed information. The public statements by NATO spokespersons concerning particular attacks, and the changes in the way attacks were characterized, also bear some analysis, in particular insofar as they may seek to justify attacks in which civilian casualties were clearly excessive.

Moreover, there is a question as to whether NATO's extraordinary efforts to avoid casualties among its pilots precluded low-flying operations that might have helped to identify targets more accurately. This was and continues to be a major issue in the public debate about Operation Allied Force. For many weeks in the initial stages of the war, NATO airplanes were not flying below 15,000 feet. If the height at which the NATO pilots flew had little to do with identification and attack of the target, than the issue is irrelevant. But if precision would have been greater (and civilian casualties lessened) had NATO pilots flown lower, it could be argued that NATO was "obligated" to have its pilots fly lower.[1] In the case of attacks such as those at Djakovica-Decane, in which flying at a higher altitude seems to have impeded a pilot from adequately identifying a target, the conclusion again is that inadequate precautions were taken to avoid civilian casualties.

The incident at Korisa (incident no. 57) also raises important questions of Yugoslav responsibility for some civilian deaths attributed to NATO bombing. In this case, NATO did not apply adequate precautions in executing its airstrikes. But Yugoslav military forces may share the blame for the eighty-seven civilian deaths at Korisa: there is some evidence that displaced Kosovar civilians were forcibly concentrated within a military camp there as a human shield.

Yugoslav responsibility of a more direct kind has been shown for killings at the Dubrava prison that Yugoslav authorities attributed to NATO bombing. Human Rights Watch researchers in Kosovo have found that some seventy-six prisoners there were victims of extrajudicial executions-cold-blooded murder-by Yugoslav forces in the days after NATO bombed the prison. The NATO attack on May 21 was, however, responsible for nineteen deaths at the facility prior to the massacre of prisoners; an earlier NATO attack killed four civilians at the prison (see incidents nos. 60 and 65).[2]

A third of all of the incidents in which civilians died-thirty-three-occurred as a result of attacks on targets in populated urban areas. Six incidents occurred in Belgrade, Nis, and Vranje (the latter two are towns in southern Serbia). Eight towns had two or three incidents each involving civilian deaths: Aleksinac, Cacak, Novi Sad, Surdulica, and Valjevo in Serbia and Vojvodina, and Djakovica, Pristina, and Prizren in Kosovo. The targets in almost all of these attacks were headquarters or military/police barracks and facilities, and/or factories. In these cases there was little doubt as to the apparent objective of the attack, or that these locations constituted lawful military objectives.

In one case, involving the use of cluster bombs in Nis (incident no. 48), the weapon employed was a decisive factor in the civilian deaths. Nis is one of seven confirmed and five likely incidents involving civilian deaths from cluster bomb use. Altogether, some ninety to 150 civilians died from cluster bomb use by the United States and Britain. In the case of the attack on the Nis airfield on May 7, the technical malfunction of the weapon points to the fact that cluster bombs should not be used in attacks in populated areas, let alone on urban targets, given the risks. After the Nis incident, there was a U.S. executive prohibition on further cluster bomb use.[3] Nevertheless, British planes continued to drop cluster bombs, indicating the need for universal, not national, norms regarding cluster bomb use.

In three cases-the bombing of Serb Radio and Television headquarters in Belgrade (incident no. 30), the bombing of the "Marshal Tito" Petrovaradin (Varadinski) Bridge in Novi Sad (incident no. 2), and the bombing of the Belgrade Heating Plant (incident no. 7)-Human Rights Watch questions the legitimacy of the target. Regardless of NATO's legal determination that civilian radio and television were legitimate military objectives because of their role in internal and external propaganda,[4] NATO did not take adequate precautions in warning civilians in the attack on the media headquarters, nor did the attack satisfy the legal requirement in terms of proportionality, given that the center was located in a densely populated urban neighborhood and was staffed twenty-four hours. After strikes on the Belgrade headquarters, moreover, Yugoslav state broadcasters were easily able to move operations to private and makeshift facilities.[5] Similarly, in the case of the 04:35 a.m. attack on the New Belgrade Heating Plant on April 4, in which one civilian (the night watchman) was killed, NATO issued no warning and attacked a target located in an urban area.[6] The risks involved to civilians in undertaking the two Belgrade urban attacks were grossly disproportionate to any perceived military benefit.

The attacks on the Novi Sad bridge and six other bridges in which civilian deaths occurred (Ostruznica, incident no. 37; Trstenik, incident no. 39; Nis, incident no. 51; Vladicin Han, incident no. 55; Pertate, incident no. 71; and Varvarin, incident no. 81) also were of questionable military effect. All are road bridges. Most are urban or town bridges that are not major routes of communications. Human Rights Watch questions individual target selection in the case of these bridges. U.S. military sources have told Human Rights Watch that bridges were often selected for attack for reasons other than their role in transportation (for example, they were conduits for communications cables, or because they were symbolic and psychologically lucrative, such as in the case of the bridge over the Danube in Novi Sad). The destruction of bridges that are not central to transportation arteries or have a purely psychological importance does not satisfy the criterion of making an "effective contribution to military action" or offering a "definite military advantage," the baseline tests for legitimate military targets codified in Protocol I, art. 52. Moreover, the risk in terms of civilian casualties in attacking urban bridges, or in attacking during daylight hours, is "excessive in relation to the concrete and direct military advantage anticipated," the standard of proportionality codified in Protocol I, art. 57.

---

[1] The question as to what extent the military is obligated to expose its own forces to danger in order to limit civilian casualties or damage to civilian objects is examined in William J. Fenrick, "Attacking The Enemy Civilian As A Punishable Offense," Duke Journal of Comparative and International Law, 1997, p. 546, located at http://www.law.duke.edu/ journals/djcil/articles/djcil7p539.htm).

[2] The eighty-seven deaths in Korisa are counted in the Human Rights Watch total of 500; the seventy-six at Dobrava prison are not.

[3] Human Rights Watch discussions with U.S. Air Force and Joint Chiefs of Staff officers, October 1999.

[4] This issue will be discussed in greater detail in Human Rights Watch's upcoming report on targeting in Operation Allied Force.

[5] The second largest broadcast center in Yugoslavia, in Novi Sad, was hit the next day but there were no civilian casualties. Officials told Human Rights Watch that after the attack on Belgrade, RTS evacuated the facility.

[6] Seven oil storage tanks were damaged in the attack, as were the pump house and pouring station on the Sava river.

In one final incident, a pilot targeted a large sanatorium complex in Surdulica in southeastern Serbia (incident no. 79) in what was suggested to be an error, the complex apparently being mistaken for a military installation located in the same town. Other than the Chinese Embassy bombing in Belgrade (incident no. 49), which NATO claimed it had mistakenly identified as the Yugoslav Directorate for Supply and Procurement, this appears to be the only target attacked in error. U.S. officials have elliptically admitted to what happened at Surdulica, but have not mentioned the place name.[1] In another incident of civilian deaths, at Tornik peak in the Zlatibor mountains (incident no. 12), Human Rights Watch has been unable to identify the intended target.

What follows is a discussion of the major legal and policy issues raised in selected incidents (others are discussed in Appendix A).

REFUGEES ON THE DJAKOVICA-DECANE ROAD, KOSOVO

On April 14, during daylight hours, NATO aircraft repeatedly bombed refugee movements over a twelve-mile stretch of road between Djakovica and Decane in western Kosovo, killing seventy-three civilians and injuring thirty-six-deaths Human Rights Watch could document. The attack began at 1:30 p.m. and persisted for about two hours, causing civilian deaths in numerous locations on the convoy route near the villages of Bistrazin, Gradis, Madanaj, and Meja. NATO and U.S. spokespersons initially claimed the target was an exclusively military convoy and that Serb forces may have been responsible for the attacks on civilians. Pentagon spokesman Ken Bacon said that NATO commander Gen. Wesley Clark had received reports that "after the convoy was hit, military people got out and attacked civilians." "The pilots state they attacked only military vehicles," NATO said, adding that the "reported incident will be fully investigated once all mission details have been reviewed." There are also various NATO reports of Serbian deception in placing dead civilians at the site of the bombing. German Defense Minister Rudolf Scharping, in particular, put the blame for civilian casualties on Yugoslav forces.[2]

On April 15 NATO began to backtrack. It said one plane had "apparently" dropped a bomb on a civilian vehicle traveling with a military convoy. The reference to a strictly military convoy was modified: "Serbian police or army vehicles might have been in or near the convoy." NATO acknowledged that it had bombed civilian vehicles by mistake: "Following a preliminary investigation, NATO confirmed that apparently one of its planes dropped a bomb on a civilian vehicle traveling with a convoy yesterday," alliance spokespersons said.

Reporters from U.S. media went to the scene on April 15. They interviewed refugee survivors and observed shattered farm tractors, burned bodies identified as refugees, bomb craters, shrapnel, and bomb remnants with U.S. markings. The refugee column had apparently been divided in two main groups. Over the next few days, NATO wavered from insisting its forces attacked only military vehicles to an explanation that two convoys had been targeted, that the refugees had been at the rear of military columns, and that the civilian death toll was limited. On April 16, NATO spokesman Jamie Shea and Gen. Giuseppe Marini declared that "in one case and one only, we have proof of civilian loss of life. Otherwise, we are sure that we targeted military vehicles."

NATO finally admitted that the pilot of a U.S. F-16 mistakenly fired on what he believed to be military trucks, and expressed "deep regret." Later, on April 19, NATO modified its account of a single pilot's error, declaring that about a dozen planes had been involved in numerous attacks on the two convoys, dropping a total of nine bombs. Convoluted explanations continued for a number of days after the incident; NATO and the United States seemed incapable of reconstructing what had occurred. There were widespread press reports of the use of cluster bombs, which the United States denied.[3]

In addition to the press reporting of this incident and the endless damage control by NATO and U.S. spokespersons, Human Rights Watch obtained extensive forensic details of the incident from the Yugoslav government.[4] No evidence whatsoever was ever produced to indicate Serb responsibility for any of the deaths, though Tanjug reported the deaths of three Serbian "policemen" in the bombings who it said "were securing the safe passage for the convoy."[5] This tends to suggest that military or police were present in the refugee vehicles, but

Human Rights Watch found no basis to support the claim that the convoys themselves were composed of military vehicles.[6]

General Clark stated in September that NATO consistently observed Yugoslav military vehicles moving on roads "intermixed with civilian convoys." After the Djakovica-Decane incident, General Clark says, "we got to be very, very cautious about striking objects moving on the roads.[7] Another NATO officer, Col. Ed Boyle, says: "Because we were so concerned with collateral damage, the CFAC [Combined Forces Air Component Commander] at the time, General [Michael] Short, put out the guidance that if military vehicles were intermingled with civilian vehicles, they were not to be attacked, due to the collateral damage."[8] When this directive was actually issued, and why it may not have served to avoid the subsequent three incidents, remains an important question. Nevertheless, the change in NATO rules of engagement indicates that the alliance recognized that it had taken insufficient precautions in mounting this attack, in not identifying civilians present, and in assuming that the intended targets were legitimate military objectives rather than in positively identifying them.

DISPLACED CIVILIANS IN THE KORISA WOODS, KOSOVO

On May 13, almost a month after the Djakovica-Decane incidents, as many as eighty-seven displaced Kosovar civilians were killed and sixty wounded when bombs were dropped during the night on a refugee camp in a wooded area on the Prizren-Suva Reka road, near the village of Korisa in Kosovo (incident no. 57). There have been various conflicting reports of the number of dead, from 48 to 87.[9] The Yugoslav government claimed the attackers used cluster bombs, and the White Book published by the Ministry of Foreign Affairs includes photographs of the remains of tactical munitions dispensers (TMDs) it says are from the site. NATO spokespersons vociferously denied the use of cluster bombs,[10] and Human Rights Watch has been unable to independently confirm that cluster bombs were indeed used in this attack.

In an official statement on May 15, NATO spokesman Maj. Gen. Walter Jertz acknowledged the attack, deeply regretting any "accidental civilian casualties." He insisted, nonetheless, that the attack was against Yugoslav army forces in the field:

---

1 U.S. Congress, House Permanent Select Committee on Intelligence, Hearing on the Bombing of the Chinese Embassy, July 21, 1999.
2 NATO, SHAPE News Morning Update, April 15, 1999; Reuters, 150059 GMT April 15, 1999.
3 Joie Chen and Jamie McIntyre, "As Serb Force Grows, Limits of Air Attacks Become Apparent," CNN The World Today Broadcast, April 19, 1999; Sarah Chayes, "General Daniel Leaf Explains the Refugee Bombings," National Public Radio, All Things Considered Broadcast, April 19, 1999.
4 FRY Ministry of Foreign Affairs, NATO Crimes in Yugoslavia, vol. 1, pp. 1, 21-26, 32-37; FRY Ministry of Housing, "Photo Documentation of Civilians Who Were Killed By NATO Attacks, from 24.03 until 20.05.1999."
5 Tanjug, Pristina, April 15, 1999.
6 At least two eyewitnesses told Human Rights Watch that the convoy was interspersed with military vehicles. Interviews with Kole Hasanaj, Meja, July 25, 1999, and with Safet Shalaj, Djakovica, July 25, 1999.
7 Special U.S. Department of Defense Press Briefing with Gen. Wesley Clark, Supreme Allied Commander, Europe, Topic: Kosovo Strike Assessment; Also Participating: Airmen and Analysts from Operation Allied Force and Post-Strike Assessment Work, Brussels, Belgium, September 16, 1999.
8 Ibid.
9 FRY Ministry of Foreign Affairs, NATO Crimes in Yugoslavia, vol. II, pp. 1-17. Though the White Book states that there were "only" forty-eight victims in Korisa, Yugoslav and Western press, as well as the U.S. State Department and the U.N. report figures of eighty to eighty-seven victims. Based upon Human Rights Watch investigations and discussions with Western journalists who attempted to reconstruct the incident, it appears that more that forty-eight people definitely died in the Korisa attack. The range of deaths is thus used.
10 Transcript of Backgrounder given by Peter Daniel and Major General Walter Jertz, in Brussels, May 15, 1999.

This was a legitimate military target. The Serb claims of an attack involving cluster bombs against a non-military target are both false. NATO identified Korisa as a military camp and command post. Military equipment including an armored personnel carrier and more than ten pieces of artillery were observed at this location. The aircraftobserved dug-in military positions at the target before executing the attack. NATO cannot confirm the casualty figures given by the Serbian authorities, nor the reasons why civilians were at this location at the time of the attack.[1]

The NATO statement further stressed that military positions had been positively identified and that the bombs employed included laser-guided PGMs and non-guided gravity bombs:

Immediately prior to the attack at 23.30 - 11.30 pm - local time Thursday night an airborne forward air controller confirmed the target, so the identification and attack system of his aircraft, having positively identified the target as what looked like dug in military reveted positions, he dropped two laser guided bombs. Following his attack, he cleared his wingman to also attack the same target using two more laser guided bombs. Approximately 10 minutes later, the third aircraft engaged the target with...six gravity bombs. A total of 10 bombs were dropped on the target.[2]

The same day, Pentagon spokesman Kenneth Bacon said at a news briefing that the incident would be reviewed, but that major changes in operations should not be expected:

This accident at Korisa did not shake NATO's resolve in any way....NATO deeply regrets civilian casualties....We try very hard to avoid these casualties, but combat is inherently dangerous and accidents cannot be avoided...this mission, like every other, will be reviewed, and the airmen and their commanders will learn what they can from it and continue. But I don't anticipate that there will be a sweeping change. We can't cross legitimate military targets off the list, and we won't.[3]

On May 16, a Kosovar refugee who witnessed the NATO strike on Korisa reported to Deutsche Welle that FRY police forced some 600 displaced Kosovars to serve as human shields there before the attack. "We were told something bad would happen to us if we left the place," said the eyewitness, interviewed by the station's Albanian service. He said Serbian police hinted at what was about to happen. "Now you'll see what a NATO attack looks like," the refugee quoted one policeman as saying. The refugee said he finally went to sleep underneath a tractor only to be woken up by explosions and the cries of children and adults. He said he and others managed to scale a two-meter wall surrounding the plot and fled in the direction of the village as Serbian paramilitaries fired bullets around them.[4]

On the basis of available evidence it is not possible to determine positively that Yugoslav police or army troops deliberately forced civilians to group near them, nor to establish the motive for such action. It is not clear, for example, how potential attackers could be expected to have been aware of the refugee concentration in order to be deterred from attacking.

The laws of war expressly forbid shielding. Article 28 of the Geneva Convention IV stipulates that "The presence of a protected person may not be used to render certain points or areas immune from military operations." Geneva Protocol I, article 51(7), elaborates:

The presence or movements of the civilian population or individual civilians shall not be used to render certain points or areas immune from military operations, in particular in attempts to shield military objectives from attacks or to shield, favour or impede military operations. The Parties to the conflict shall not direct the movement of the civilian population or individual civilians in order to attempt to shield military objectives from attacks or to shield military operations.

The Protocol stresses, however, in art. 51(8), that such violations of the laws of war do not in any account release an adversary from obligations to respect civilian immunity. An authoritative new commentary on humanitarian law states: "If one party to a conflict breaks this rule, this does not exempt the other side from the regulations applicable in military attacks....The military commander must therefore take into account the column of refugees used by the adversary as a shield."[5]

For NATO, then, the question is whether its target designation was made with the knowledge that hundreds of displaced civilians were present in this wooded area-there is no evidence to this effect-and secondly, whether sufficient measures were taken to verify that the target had no such concentrations of civilians. On this score, the excessive civilian death toll in what NATO has itself described as a lamentable accident suggests that verification was inadequate.

BOMBING OF THE DUBRAVA PENITENTIARY, KOSOVO

Another case of Yugoslav deception involves civilian deaths and NATO bombing that damaged the large Dubrava penitentiary complex near Istok in Kosovo. According to NATO and former Dubrava prisoners interviewed by Human Rights Watch, Yugoslav Army and police forces were based adjacent to the penitentiary, which was fully operational well into the NATO air campaign, housing common and political criminals serving out their terms.

The Penitentiary Institute Istok, as it was officially called, was hit twice, causing civilian deaths among both prisoners and guards. In the first attack, at 1:15 p.m. on May 19 (incident no. 60), three prisoners and a guard were reported killed. The second attack occurred on May 21 (incident no. 65), in which at least nineteen prisoners were killed. According to a separate investigation undertaken by Human Rights Watch in Kosovo, based upon extensive eyewitness testimony, prisoners were hunted down by Serb police inside the penitentiary walls after the May 21 attack, and some eighty or so prisoners were killed.

The Yugoslav government initially reported nineteen people killed in the Dubrava Penitentiary as a result of the May 21 attack.[6] However, four days later, the Yugoslav press reported from the official Tanjug agency that "in days long bombardment of the Penitentiary Institute Istok, some 100 prisoners died, and some 200 were wounded." On May 27, Tanjug quoted Vladan Bojic, judge in Pec's District Court, saying that ninety-six corpses had been pulled from the ruins. On May 29, the Yugoslav government stated that "The number of casualties in the Correctional Institution in Istok is increasing."[7] On May 30, Tanjug reported a total of ninety-three killed.[8] In July, the Yugoslav government claimed that NATO bombs killed ninety-five inmates and injured 196.[9]

While NATO readily acknowledged the air strikes at Istok and justified the attacks on the grounds that it had targeted military objectives "in the vicinity of a prison,"[10] Human Rights Watch has determined that Yugoslav forces were likely responsible for the majority of deaths which occurred after the bombing. On May 22, according to eyewit-

---

[1] NATO, Subject: Press Release (99) 079, Statement by the NATO Spokesman on the Korisa Incident, May 15, 1999.
[2] Transcript of Backgrounder, May 15, 1999.
[3] Transcript, U.S. Department of Defense News Briefing, May 15, 1999.
[4] Reuters 152249 GMT, May 15, 1999; Kosovo Chronology, Timeline of events 1989-1999 relating to the crisis in Kosovo, released by the Department of State, Washington, DC, June 18, 1999.

[5] Hans-Peter Gasser, "Protection of the Civilian Population," in Dieter Fleck (ed.), The Handbook of Humanitarian Law in Armed Conflicts (Oxford: Oxford University Press, 1995), p. 505, para. 506. Hans-Peter Gasser is a Senior Legal Adviser of the ICRC.
[6] Information provided by Yugoslav civil defense authorities; FRY MFA, NATO raids on manufacturing and civilian facilities on May 21st and in the night between May 21st and 22nd 1999.
[7] FRY Ministry of Foreign Affairs, NATO Raids on Manufacturing and Civilian Facilities on May 29th and in the Night Between May 29th and 30th 1999.
[8] Yugoslav press reports; "Identifikovano 86 mrtvih," DAN, May 27, 1999, p. 2; "Jos sedam leseva," DAN, May 30, 1999.
[9] FRY Ministry of Foreign Affairs, NATO Crimes in Yugoslavia, vol. II, p. 319.
[10] NATO, Operation Allied Force Update, May 22, 1999, 0930 CET. See also Transcript of Press Conference given by Mr. Jamie Shea and Col. Konrad Freytag in Brussels on Saturday, May 22, 1999.

nesses, prison officials ordered the approximately 1,000 prisoners to line up in the prison yard. After a few minutes, they were fired upon, and grenades were thrown at them from the prison walls and guard towers, killing at least seventy people. Over the next twenty-four hours, prison guards, special police, and possibly paramilitaries attacked prisoners who were hiding in the prison's undestroyed buildings, basements, and sewers, killing at least another twelve people.

Journalists who visited the Dubrava prison on May 21, just after the morning bombing, reported seeing deaths on the order of ten or twenty.[1] Serb authorities again opened the prison for journalists on May 24. Reporting for the BBC, Jacky Rowland said it was unclear how the victims in the prison had died:

Walking around the prison we counted forty-four bodies; about half of these appeared to be the victims of the first bombing raid on Friday [May 19], still lying under blankets on the grass. Then we were taken to a room in a damaged cell block where there were twenty-five corpses. The men appeared to be ethnic Albanians, some of them had shaved heads, others had longer hair. A couple of the corpses had their trousers pulled down around their knees. We were told they had died between Friday and Sunday although it was not clear how all of them had met their deaths, nor why they were all in one relatively undamaged room.[2]

The Washington Post, wrote:

This time, the official version-that bombs again were to blame-did not match what reporters saw at the scene, where twenty-five more ethnic Albanian corpses were on display. The corpses were piled in the foyer of a clinic. Except for a ruined dining hall, however, no new bomb damage was visible inside the prison, and none of the newly dead had been crushed, or touched by the concrete dust that covered the dining hall floor.[3]

Post-war visits to the prison by journalists confirmed that prisoners had been killed after the bombing.[4]

In the two attacks on the Dubrava prison, NATO did not apply adequate precautions in executing its airstrikes on nearby military objectives, and therefore must be held accountable for the civilian deaths that occurred as a direct result of those attacks. But Yugoslav forces must be held fully responsible for seventy-six of the claimed ninety-five deaths at Dubrava, as these were prisoners who were executed extrajudicially well after the NATO strikes.

SERB RADIO AND TELEVISION HEADQUARTERS

One of the worst incidents of civilian deaths, and certainly the worst in Belgrade, was the bombing of state Serb Radio and Television (RTS) headquarters in Belgrade on April 23 (incident No. 30). According to military sources, there was considerable disagreement between the United States and French governments regarding the legality and legitimacy of the target, and there was a lively public debate regarding the selection of Yugoslav civilian radio and television as a target group.

The NATO attack was originally scheduled for April 12, but due to French disapproval of the target, it was postponed. According to military, media, and Yugoslav sources, Western news organizations, who were using the facility to forward material from Yugoslavia, were alerted by NATO government authorities that the headquarters would be attacked. Attacks also had to be rescheduled because of rumors that foreign journalists ignored warnings to leave the buildings.[5] When the initial warnings were given to Western media, the Yugoslav government also found out about the intended attack. When the target was finally hit in the middle of the night on April 23, according to RTS and Yugoslav government officials, authorities were no longer taking the threats seriously, given the time that had transpired since the initial warnings. As a consequence, sixteen RTS civilian technicians and workers were killed and sixteen were wounded.

Paragraph 7 of the 1956 ICRC guidelines describing lists of targets that are legitimate military objectives includes "installations of broadcasting and television stations; [and] telephone and telegraph exchanges of fundamental military importance."[6] In a May 13 letter to NATO Secretary-General Javier Solana, Human Rights Watch questioned the legitimacy of the target group in the Yugoslav war. The reasoning was that the system was not "... being used to incite violence (akin to Radio Milles Collines during the Rwandan genocide), which might have justified their destruction. At worst, as far as we know, the Yugoslav government was using them to issue propaganda supportive of its war effort. And, in fact, NATO has stated that it bombed the television facilities because they were being used as a propaganda tool of the Milosevic government." As a consequence, Human Rights Watch believes that "While stopping such propaganda may serve to demoralize the Yugoslav population and undermine the government's political support, neither purpose offers the `concrete and direct' military advantage necessary to make them a legitimate military target."[7]

Even if one could justify legal attacks on civilian radio and television, there does not appear to be any justification for attacking urban studios, as opposed to transmitters. After strikes on the Belgrade and Novi Sad headquarters, Yugoslav state broadcasters were able to easily move operations to other facilities. In this case, target selection was done more for psychological harassment of the civilian population than for direct military effect. The risks involved to the civilian population in undertaking the urban attack thus grossly outweighed any perceived military benefit. What is more, NATO failed to provide clear advance warning of the attacks "whenever possible," as required by Protocol I, art. 57(2).

CLUSTER BOMBS AND CIVILIAN DEATHS

One of the issues of most intense public interest that has emerged from Operation Allied Force is NATO's use of cluster bombs. As noted, there are seven confirmed and five likely incidents involving civilian deaths from cluster bomb use by the United States and Britain. Altogether, some ninety to 150 civilians died from cluster bomb use. The first confirmed incident was on April 10 (incident no. 14) and the last was on May 13 (incident no. 57).

The most serious incident involving civilian deaths and the use of cluster bombs occurred on May 7 in Nis (incident no. 48). The mid-day attack on Nis airfield, which is located inside the urban zone, killed fourteen civilians and injured twenty-eight. Cluster bomb submunitions fell in three widely separated areas: near the Pathology building of the Nis Medical Center in southeast Nis; in the town center near the Nis University Rector's Office, including the area of the central city market place, the bus station near the Nis Fortress, and the "12 February" Health Center; and near a car dealership and the "Nis Express" parking lot across the river from the fortress.

NATO confirmed the attack on Nis airfield,[8] and on May 8, NATO Secretary General Solana confirmed NATO responsibility for the attack, stating that "NATO has confirmed that the damage to the market and clinic was caused by a NATO weapon which missed its tar-

---

[1] Jacky Rowland, "Bombs, Blood and Dark Despair," Scotland on Sunday, May 23, 1999; Paul Watson, "NATO Bombs Ignite Prison Chaos-KLA Officers Reported to be Among Inmates," Toronto Star, May 22, 1999; Associated Press, "NATO Hits Kosovo Jail Again Friday Night," May 21, 1999.
[2] Jacky Rowland, "Istok Prison's Unanswered Questions," BBC World News, May 25, 1999.
[3] Daniel Williams, "Kosovo Revisited: At War's End, Old Places Seen in New Light," Washington Post, June 26, 1999.
[4] Carlotta Gall, "Stench of Horror Lingers in a Prison in Kosovo," New York Times, November 9, 1999.

[5] Human Rights Watch interviews with Air Force and Joint Staff planners. See also Dana Priest, "Bombing by Committee: France Balked at NATO Targets," Washington Post, September 20, 1999, p. A1.
[6] ICRC, Commentary on the Additional Protocols, p. 632, para. 2002, note 3.
[7] Human Rights Watch letter to Javier Solana, May 13, 1999.
[8] NATO (SHAPE), ACE News Release - Press Release 99-05-02, May 8, 1999.

get."[1] According to U.S. Air Force sources, the CBU-87 cluster bomb container failed to open over the airfield but opened right after release from the attacking airplane, projecting submunitions at a great distance into the city.[2]

After the incident in Nis, the White House quietly issued a directive to the Pentagon to restrict cluster bomb use (at least by U.S. forces).[3] Human Rights Watch considers this to have been the right move, but is concerned, given these risks, that cluster bombs were being used in attacks on urban targets in the first place. The mid-May prohibition against the further use of cluster bombs clearly had an impact on the level of civilian deaths as the war continued, particularly as bombing with unguided weapons (which would otherwise include cluster bombs) significantly intensified towards theend of the month. Nevertheless, the British air force continued to drop cluster bombs (official chronologies show use at least on May 17, May 31, June 3, and June 4),[4] indicating the need for universal, not national, norms regarding cluster bomb use.

Appendix A: Incidents Involving Civilian Deaths in Operation Allied Force

[Incidents to which the report refers have been reprinted.]

[...]

April 1

2. In a 4:55-5:30 a.m. attack on the "Marshal Tito" Petrovaradin (Varadinski) Bridge (the so-called "old bridge") across the Danube in Novi Sad in Vojvodina, one civilian is fatally injured. Oleg Nasov (29) dies in late May as a result of injuries sustained in the April 1 attack. A building of the University of Novi Sad is also damaged[5] and the Yugoslav government claims "severe damage" to the roof structure of the Fortress of Petrovaradin and to the Petrovaradin Monastery of the Church of St. Juraj (built in 1714).[6]

Human Rights Watch visited the site (N4515242/E01951302)[7] on August 15, and inspected the damage. Though initial reports stated that there were no casualties in the attack,[8] a posted death notice for Nasov located on the bridge announced that his funeral took place on May 28. The attack, according to U.S. Air Force sources, was undertaken by a B-2 bomber, firing satellite guided Joint Direct Attack Munitions (JDAMs).

[...]

April 4

[...]

7. In a 4:35 a.m. attack on the New Belgrade Heating Plant, one civilian is killed. Night watchman Slobodan Trisic (53) is killed while making his rounds. Six oil storage tanks are hit and a seventh is damaged, and the pump house and pouring station on the Sava river are also destroyed.[9]

Human Rights Watch visited the site ("Beogradske elektrane" on 11 Savski nasip street, N4447904/E02024721) on August 5, inspected the damage, and verified the casualties with authorities at the plant. Authorities provided details relating to the attack and the civilian death. Remains of cruise missiles reportedly used to attack the plant were on display.The Yugoslav government provides forensic detail of the incident in its White Book. Human Rights Watch also received photo documentation of the death from the Ministry of Health.[10]

[...]

April 8

12. In an 4:00-4:10 a.m. attack on telecommunications and/or air defense facilities on Tornik peak in the Zlatibor mountains in central Serbia, three civilians are killed. They are forest ranger Milenko Savic (25) and guards Nedjo Urosevic (31) and Radoje Marjanovic (34).[11] The "Tornik" ski resort and a training facility of the Medical Institute "Cigota" incorporating a children's recreation center and an outpatient clinic are hit. The site is visited shortly afterwards by Judge Momcilo Krivokapic and Deputy Attorney-General Stevan Zrnic.[12] A government report at the time said, "Almost all objects on 2,000 square meters surface are completely destroyed."[13]

Human Rights Watch visited the site on August 7, inspected the damage and interviewed eyewitnesses. Eyewitnesses said that army soldiers were occupying homes and hotels in the area, but that the local population knew little about the functions and activities of the army in the area during the war. The site of the civilian deaths (N4340272/E01938755), a ski lodge at the bottom of the lifts, is more than 2,000 meters from the telecommunications tower on Tornik peak, which was also bombed. The Yugoslav government provides forensic detail of the incident in its White Book. Human Rights Watch also received photo documentation of the deaths from the Ministry of Health.[14]

[...]

April 10

14. In an 11:55 p.m. attack on unidentified targets in the area between Podujevo and Kursumlija on the Serbian-Kosovo border, five are killed and some three are injured near the villages of Merdare and Mirovac. Killed were Bozina Tosovic (30) and his one-year-old daughter Bojana, while Marija Tosovic, his wife, was seriously wounded. Dragan Bubalo (31) from Podujevo, Goran Djukic from Ploce, and Srdjan Cvetkovic are also killed.[15] Politika names five killed: Bojana Tosovic (eleven months), Bozina Tosovic, Dragan Bubalo, Goran Djukic, and Srdjan Cvetkovic.[16] According to the chief of orthopedic surgery at the Djakovica hospital, forty-three people injured at Bistrzin and Meja were admitted to the hospital on April 14.[17]

Yugoslav press accounts state that cluster bombs are responsible for the killings.[18] Cluster bomb submunitions are later observed near the

---

1. Transcript of Press Conference given by the NATO Secretary General, Mr. Javier Solana, in Brussels, on Saturday, May 8, 1999 (including Maj. Gen. Jertz).
2. Human Rights Watch correspondence with a U.S. Air Force officer, November 1999.
3. Human Rights Watch discussions with U.S. Air Force and Joint Chiefs of Staff officers, October 1999.
4. U.K. Ministry of Defense, Royal Air Force, Operation Allied Force News and Downloadable Images (http://www.mod.raf.uk/news/ kosovonews.html).
5. Tanjug, "Chronology of Crimes and Dishonor of NATO," June 5, 1999.
6. Information provided by the Yugoslav Ministry of Information.
7. Human Rights Watch used a Global Positioning System (GPS) receiver to locate precisely targets and areas of civilian damage. These coordinates are derived from on-the-scene readings.
8. Tanjug, "NATO aircraft destroy bridge linking Novi Sad and Petrovaradin," April 1, 1999.
9. FRY, MFA, NATO Crimes in Yugoslavia, vol. I, pp. 355-365; Tanjug, Belgrade, April 4, 1999; Yugoslav press reports; Information provided by Yugoslav civil defense authorities.
10. FRY, MOH, "Photo Documentation of Civilians Who Were Killed By NATO Attacks, from 24.03 until 20.05.1999."
11. FRY, MFA, NATO Crimes in Yugoslavia, vol. I, pp. 411-414; Yugoslav press reports; information provided by the Yugoslav Ministry of Information and Yugoslav civil defense authorities during Operation Allied Force via Email.
12. Information provided by the Yugoslav Ministry of Information and Yugoslav civil defense authorities during Operation Allied Force via Email.
13. "War Against Yugoslavia: Uzice" (www.inet.co.yu/rat/gradovi/uzice/index.html).
14. FRY, MOH, "Photo Documentation of Civilians Who Were Killed By NATO Attacks, from 24.03 until 20.05.1999."
15. FRY, MFA, NATO Crimes in Yugoslavia, vol. I, p. 141; information provided by Yugoslav civil defense authorities.
16. Politika, April 13, 1999, p. 17.
17. Human Rights Watch interview with Dr. Burim Sahatqija, Djakovica, August 4, 1999.
18. Yugoslav press reports.

road from Podujevo to Kursumlija, near the village Merdare.[1] According to a New York Times report, "in Merdare, NATO bombs and anti-personnel cluster bombs demolished four houses early Sunday morning, killing five....A number of pigs and cows were killed and injured....In the fields, there were hundreds of small holes in the earth from detonations, and small green nylon parachutes from what appeared to be NATO anti-personnel cluster bombs, covering an area of about 300 square yards. Large pieces of green painted metal, with yellow stripes, perfectly broken open as if on a seam, lay about the yard. There were large pieces of formed yellow plastic foam and light aluminum containers, with fans like whirligigs, that appeared to have held the small parachutes, with explosives attached...."[2]

The Yugoslav government provides forensic detail of the incident in its White Book. This is the first confirmed instance of civilian deaths resulting from cluster bomb use. Human Rights Watch also received photo documentation of the deaths from the Ministry of Health.[3]

[...]

April 14

19. Between 1:30-3:30 p.m., a refugee convoy is bombed along a twelve mile stretch of road between Djakovica and Decane in Kosovo, killing seventy-three individuals and injuring thirty-six The bombing incidents occur near the villages of Bistrazin, Gradis, Madanaj and Meja in numerous different locations. On April 14, Yugoslav authorities claimed fifty-six dead and thirty-six wounded. On April 15, four additional bodies were discovered. Later the total was increased even more; Yugoslav authorities in the White Book state that seventy-three were killed and thirty-six were wounded. The Committee for Compiling Data on Crimes Against Humanity and International Law says eighty-two dead and fifty injured.[4]

The identified dead are: Ferat Bajrami, Imer Cela, Sali Gjokaj, Skendi Gjokaj, Martin Hasanaj, Lek Hasanaj, Ram Maloku, Arton Maloku, Tazija Pajaziti, Vjollca Pajaziti (18), Violeta Pajaziti (16), Nevrija Pajaziti, Hasan Pajaziti, Flora Pajaziti, Adem Seljmani, Besarde Smajli, Fikrije Sulja, Nerdjivane Zeqiri, eight members of the Ali Ibraj family, four members of the Spend Nuraj family, four members of the Fatmir Nuraj family, and three members of the Sejdi Nuraj family.[5] Tanjug reports three Serbian "policemen who were securing the safe passage for the convoy" were also killed.[6]

The incident ignites a major controversy about NATO bombings. The Pentagon suggests Serb security forces might have attacked civilians after a NATO strike on military vehicles in the convoy. Pentagon spokesman Ken Bacon says NATO commander Gen. Wesley Clark had received reports that "after the convoy was hit, military people got out and attacked civilians." "The pilots state they attacked only military vehicles," NATO says, adding that the "reported incident will be fully investigated once all mission details have been reviewed." There are also various reports emanating from NATO spokesman and militaries of Serbian deception in placing dead civilians at the site of the bombing. German Defense Minister Rudolf Scharping is among those who put the blame on Yugoslav forces.[7]

On April 15, NATO acknowledges that it bombed civilian vehicles by mistake: "Following a preliminary investigation, NATO confirms that apparently one of its planes dropped a bomb on a civilian vehicle traveling with a convoy yesterday." NATO says the attack was made because military vehicles were identified in the area. "Serbian police or army vehicles might have been in or near the convoy," NATO spokesmen state.

On the same day, the AFP correspondent in Kosovo, Aleksandar Mitic, Los Angeles Times correspondent Paul Watson, and two Greek television crew are allowed to go to the scene of the bombing. They find, according to the AFP dispatch, "bodies charred or blown to pieces, tractors reduced to twisted wreckage and houses in ruins." According to Mitic's report, two convoys, one to the north and one to the south of Djakovica, were hit. He quotes one refugee as saying the groups had been bombed three or four times, "the planes circling overhead as if they were following us." The Los Angeles Times reports small craters and bomb remnants found at the scene with U.S. markings, and reports eyewitness accounts of explosions in the air (which the newspaper says indicates the use of cluster bomblets), extensive shrapnel dispersion, and the burned bodies of refugees. Tractors pulling the refugees on wagons were destroyed, suggesting, the Times says, that the infrared heat-seeking "sensors" on the bomblets (sic) mistook the tractors for tanks. Cluster bomb remnants, small craters and destroyed tractors are reportedly found at Meja, about three miles west of Djakovica, and also about nine miles away, east of Djakovica.[8]

Human Rights Watch spoke with two witnesses to the April 14 bombing in Meja, one of whom was seriously injured. Safet Shalaj from Junik had a large scar on his back and leg due to his injuries from the NATO bombing. He said:

It was April 14, around 12:45 p.m. There were seven or eight tractors and some cars. NATO bombed us. It was a civilian convoy with two or three pitzgowers in front and the [Yugoslav] army behind us burning houses. After the bombing they took us into a house with Serbian police. In my tractor, fourteen people died. I'm not angry with NATO. Only that they can now help me find my children.[9]

Kole Hasanaj from Meja told Human Rights Watch:

NATO bombed the convoy on Wednesday, April 14, around 2:00 p.m. It was a convoy from Junik. When the aircraft were in the sky then the military vehicles mixed with the column. I counted twenty-three killed people from the tractors. There were others around, maybe twenty-seven or twenty-eight. NATO bombed five times. No military vehicles were damaged. After the bombing, they [Serb forces] went into the hills. The Albanians stayed in my house for about three hours.[10]

On April 16, NATO spokesman Jamie Shea and Brig. Gen. Giuseppe Marini state that "in one case and one only, we have proof of civilian loss of life. Otherwise, we are sure that we targeted military vehicles." NATO admits that the pilot of a U.S. F-16 fired on what he believed to be military trucks, and expresses "deep regret." There is confirmation that fragments of Mk 82 500 lb. unguided bombs found at the scene were indeed used.[11]

On April 19, a new version of events emerges. NATO admits that about a dozen planes were involved in attacks on more than one convoy, dropping a total of nine bombs. NATO makes public a voice recording of one of the pilots responsible for bombing the first convoy, who says the vehicles in question are "of a military type." As for a second convoy, NATO claims it had been targeted because its "pace and formation were of a typically military nature."

---

1 Information provided by Yugoslav civil defense authorities; FRY MFA, "Aide-Memoire on the Use of Inhumane Weapons in the Aggression of the North Atlantic Treaty Organization Against the Federal Republic of Yugoslavia," May 15, 1999.

2 Steven Erlanger, "NATO Bombs Slam Passenger Train," Seattle Post-Intelligencer, April 13, 1999, p. A1.

3 FRY, MOH, "Photo Documentation of Civilians Who Were Killed By NATO Attacks, from 24.03 until 20.05.1999."

4 Committee for Compiling Data on Crimes Against Humanity and International Law (http://www.gov.yu/cwc/fejmel_nato.htm). Human Rights Watch believes that the White Book figures are accurate, and seventy-three deaths corresponds with almost all the independent press reporting on the incident.

5 FRY, MFA, NATO Crimes in Yugoslavia, vol. I, pp. 1, 21-26, 32-37.

6 Tanjug, Pristina, April 15, 1999.

7 NATO, SHAPE News Morning Update, April 15, 1999; Reuters, 150059 GMT April 1999.

8 Paul Watson, "Cluster Bombs May Be What Killed Refugees," Los Angeles Times, April 17, 1999, p. A1.

9 Human Rights Watch interview with Safet Shalaj, Djakovica, July 25, 1999.

10 Human Rights Watch interview with Kole Hasanaj, Meja, July 25, 1999.

11 FRY, MFA, NATO Crimes in Yugoslavia, vol. I, p. 10.

"This is a very complicated scenario and we will never be able to establish all the exact details," says U.S. Brig. Gen. Daniel Leaf, commander of the 31st Wing at Aviano, Italy, where the F-16s originated. Leaf suggests that after NATO aircraft attacked military vehicles, Serb forces attacked refugees in the rear with cluster bombs and grenades. He denies that NATO used cluster bombs in an attacks in the area.[1]

The news media later reveals that one of the U.S. pilots responsible for the bombings had been warned by a British pilot that the convoy included civilians. NATO later admits that the recording made public on April 19 had no connection with the bombing of the convoys, but was just an example of pilot "chatter."

The Yugoslav government provides forensic detail of the incident in its White Book. Human Rights Watch also received photo documentation of the deaths from the Ministry of Health.[2]

[...]

April 23

30. In a 2:06-2:20 a.m. attack on the Radio Televizija Srbija (RTS) Studio on 1 Aberdareva street in central Belgrade, sixteen are killed and another sixteen are wounded. Killed are: technician Darko Stoimenovski (26), technician Nebojsa Stojanovic (27), security guard Dragorad Dragojevic (27), video mixer Ksenija Bankovic (28), make-up artist Jelica Munitlak (28), security guard Dejan Markovic (30), cameraman Aleksandar Deletic (31), technician Dragan Tasic (31), producer Slavisa Stevanovic (32), program designer Sinisa Medic (33), foreign programming specialist Ivan Stukalo (34), security officer Milan Joksimovic (47), program operator Branislav Jovanovic (50), set decorator Slobodan Jontic (54), mechanic Milovan Jankovic (59), and program director Tomislav Mitrovic (61).[3] The RTS initially reported that morepersons may still be missing who were known to have been inside the building during the bombing,[4] but it is now believed that all bodies have been recovered.

About one hundred journalists and technicians were reported working in the complex when the bombing occurred.[5] Producing and directing rooms and equipment were completely destroyed. There was damage to neighboring buildings, including the "Dusko Radovic" Theater next door.[6]

Human Rights Watch visited the site (N4448615/E02028195) on August 5, inspected the damage to RTS and surrounding buildings and took eyewitness testimony. The damage to the St. Trinity Russian Orthodox and the St. Marco Serbian Orthodox churches consisted on broken windows and other minor effects from the nearby blast. The theater, across a courtyard from the RTS building, received major damage. The Yugoslav government provides forensic detail of the incident in its White Book. Human Rights Watch also received photo documentation of the deaths from the Ministry of Health.[7]

At least one JDAM precision-guided munition (PGM) dropped by a B-2 bomber was used in the attack, according to Air Force sources.

April 29

[...]

37. In 12:58-4:35 a.m. attacks on the Ostruznica highway bridge over the Sava river south of Belgrade, one civilian is killed. Nebojsa Arsic (35) died on the bridge in his car.[8] Both the highway and railroad bridges in Ostruznica were bombed.[9]

Human Rights Watch visited the site (N4444436/02019342) on August 5 and inspected the damage. It also received photo documentation of the death from the Ministry of Health.[10] The Yugoslav government provides forensic detail of the incident in its White Book. A precision-guided munition (PGM) was used in the attack.

April 30

[...]

39. In a 3:15 p.m. attack on the "old bridge"over the Zapadna Morava river in the center of Trstenik in central Serbia, two civilians are killed and fifteen are wounded, one seriously.[11] Dejan Djordjevic (40) and Nadezda Petrickovic (44), both of Grabovac village, are killed on the bridge.[12]

The Yugoslav government provides forensic detail of the incident in its White Book. Human Rights Watch received photo documentation of the deaths from the Ministry of Health.[13] A precision-guided munition (PGM) was used in the attack.

[...]

May 1

41. In a 1:40 p.m. attack on a bridge over the Lab river near the village of Luzane, twelve miles north of Pristina in Kosovo, a bus is hit, killing thirty-nine and injuring thirteen.[14] The "Nis Express" passenger bus is hit on a bridge and plunges into the river.[15] The Yugoslav press reports, quoting Leposava Milicevic (the Serbian Health Minister), that forty-seven passengers are killed and sixteen are heavily wounded.[16] The Yugoslav government reports that "aircraft also bombed the ambulance which came to help the victims when one doctor was injured."[17]

NATO admits destroying a civilian bus, saying that the bus appeared after an attacking aircraft released its weapon against the bridge, which it described as a key military route.[18] NATO's Col. Konrad Freytag said: "Unfortunately, after the weapon's release, a bus crossed on the bridge but was not seen by the pilot whose attention was focused on his aim point during weapon trajectory."

The Yugoslav government provides forensic detail of the incident in its White Book. Human Rights Watch received photo documentation of

---

1. Joie Chen and Jamie McIntyre, "As Serb Force Grows, Limits of Air Attacks Become Apparent," CNN, The World Today broadcast, April 19, 1999; Sarah Chayes, "General Daniel Leaf Explains the Refugee Bombings," NPR, All Things Considered broadcast, April 19, 1999.
2. FRY, MOH, "Photo Documentation of Civilians Who Were Killed By NATO Attacks, from 24.03 until 20.05.1999."
3. FRY, MFA, NATO Crimes in Yugoslavia, vol I, pp. 343-350; FRY, MFA, "Overview of Civilian Destruction in the Territory of the FR of Yugoslavia as a consequence of Barbaric and Criminal NATO Aggression," Belgrade, April 26, 1999; FRY, MFA, "NATO Crimes Against Civilians," May 10, 1999.
4. Yugoslav press reports; Vecernje Novosti, April 25, 1999, p. 3; Politika, April 28, 1999, p. 16; Nedeljni Telegraf, July 21, 1999, p. 7; Information provided by Yugoslav civil defense authorities.
5. Tanjug, "Chronology of Crimes and Dishonor of NATO," June 5, 1999.
6. FRY, MFA, "NATO raids on civilian and industrial facilities in the night between April 22 and 23 1999"; information provided by the Yugoslav Ministry of Information.
7. FRY, MOH, "Photo Documentation of Civilians Who Were Killed By NATO Attacks, from 24.03 until 20.05.1999."
8. FRY, MFA, NATO Crimes in Yugoslavia, vol. II, pp. 334-335.
9. FRY, MFA, "NATO raids on industrial and civilian facilities on April 28 and in the night between April 28 and 29 1999"; "War Against Yugoslavia: Beograd" (www.inet.co.yu/rat/gradovi/beograd/ index.html).
10. FRY, MOH, "Photo Documentation of Civilians Who Were Killed By NATO Attacks, from 24.03 until 20.05.1999."
11. FRY, MFA, "NATO raids on industrial and civilian facilities on April 30th and in the night between April 30 and May 1, 1999"; information provided by Yugoslav civil defense authorities; Tanjug, "Chronology of Crimes and Dishonor of NATO," June 5, 1999.
12. FRY, MFA, NATO Crimes in Yugoslavia, vol. II, p. 340; Yugoslav press reports.
13. FRY, MOH, "Photo Documentation of Civilians Who Were Killed By NATO Attacks, from 24.03 until 20.05.1999."
14. FRY, MFA, NATO Crimes in Yugoslavia, vol. II, pp. 341-346.
15. Yugoslav press reports; FRY, MFA, "NATO raids on civilian and industrial facilities on May 1, and in the night between May 1 and 2, 1999."
16. Pobjeda, May 3, 1999, p. 2; Tanjug, "Chronology of Crimes and Dishonor of NATO," June 5, 1999.
17. FRY, MFA, "NATO Crimes Against Civilians," May 10, 1999.
18. AFP (Brussels), "Lengthening List of NATO Errors," May 4, 1999.

the deaths from the Ministry of Health.[1] A precision-guided munition (PGM) was used in the attack.

[...]

May 3

46. In an attack between 11:45 a.m. and 13:30 p.m. in the area of Savine Vode in northwestern Kosovo, a bus and car are hit, killing seventeen and injuring forty-four civilians. Aircraft hit the "Djakovica Prevoz" bus on its regular Pec-Rozaje route and a VW Golf Jetta car.[2] After being hit by two weapons, the bus burst in flames. Forty-three casualties from the bus and the adjacent automobiles were reported admitted to the Pec hospital.[3] Cluster bomb use is reported.[4]

NATO denied its planes were responsible for the attack, saying that it could find "no evidence" linking it with the incident.[5]

The Yugoslav government provides forensic detail of the incident in its White Book. Human Rights Watch also received photo documentation of cluster bomb remains and of the deaths from the Ministry of Health.[6]

[...]

May 7

48. In an 11:20-11:40 a.m. cluster bomb attack on the Nis airfield in southeast Serbia, fourteen civilians are killed and twenty-eight are wounded. Those killed are Ljiljana Spasic (26), Gordana Sekulic (29), Sasa Miljkovic (33), Dragisa Vucic (35), Bozidar Veljkovic (38), Ljubisa Stancic (48), Aleksandar Deljanin (50), Bozidar Djordjevic (57), Slobodan Stoiljkovic (61), Vera Ilic (65), Zivorad Ilic (71), Gerasim Jovanovski (84), and Trifun Vuckovic (86). Ljiljana Spasic, killed on the corner of Jelene Dimitrijevic and Sumatovacka streets, is nine months pregnant. A fourteenth victim, Milutin Zivkovic (74), dies on May 8.[7]

Cluster bomblets fall in three areas: near the Pathology building of the Nis Medical Center in southeast Nis; in the town center near the Nis University Rector's Office, including the area of the central city market place, the bus station near the Nis Fortress, and the "12 February" Health Center; and near a car dealership and the "Nis Express" parking lot across the river from the fortress. Unexploded bomblets are reported on Ljube Nenadovica St., Sumatovacka St., Franca Rozmana St., and Anete Andrejevic St. It is reported that "there are several hundred unexploded cluster bombs in the city center."[8]

Initial Yugoslav government reports state that fifteen civilians are killed and more than sixty are wounded.[9] Later reports state thirteen civilians are killed and twenty-nine are wounded, eighteen gravely and eleven lightly. The Yugoslav government also reports that 120 housing units are damaged and forty-seven destroyed, and that fifteen passenger cars are also destroyed.[10]

NATO confirms that it attacked the Nis airfield on May 7.[11] There are other reports that the Jugopetrol fuel storage depot in northwest Nis is also targeted.[12] On May 8, NATO Secretary General Solana states that it "NATO has confirmed that the damage to the market and clinic was caused by a NATO weapon which missed its target. This strike was directed against the Nis airfield utilizing cluster munitions. The attack was aimed at destroying Serbian aircraft which were parked on the airfield, air defence systems and support vehicles, targets to which cluster munitions are appropriately suited. Once again of course civilian casualties were never intended and NATO regrets the loss of life and injuries inflicted."

NATO states that U.S. aircraft dropped CBU-87 cluster bombs in the airfield attack. According to NATO Maj. Gen. Walter Jertz says: "I can tell you that we did not target-repeat we did not target-civilian hospitals and we do not target any civilian targets whatsoever." He further states: "We were using cluster bombs on the Nis target because, as I already mentioned, cluster bombs are used in aerial targets where we know that collateral damage could not occur, and it would be speculation if I would continue on the reason why some of the clusters obviously did go astray, maybe because of atechnical malfunction or they could have been inadvertently released."[13] According to U.S. Air Force sources, the intended target was the airfield and the cluster bomb container failed to open over the airfield, but opened right after release, projecting submunitions to a great distance.

Human Rights Watch visited the sites on August 11, inspected the damage and interviewed eyewitnesses. There were two areas where civilians were killed: near the town marketplace on Anete Andrejevic, Sumatovacka, and Jelene Dimitrijevic streets near the Nisava river; and near the Clinical Center on Ljube Nenadovica street. The closest to the airfield is more than 1.5 kilometers from the base perimeter; the Clinical Center is close to six kilometers from the airfield. Eyewitnesses also said that several people were injured at the "12 February" Health Center on Jelene Dimitrijevic street.

Human Rights Watch also observed a small military barracks on the banks of the Nisava river to the west of the October Revolution bridge, and the 3rd Army Headquarters building in downtown Nis at "Yugoslav Army" square in the downtown. Though NATO did not report attacks on these installations, both were extensively bombed, and could have been the objects of attack on May 7 (see also May 8). Nis civil defense officials stated that eight weapons-four "guided bombs," two cluster bombs, and two unexploded bombs-were dropped in Nis on May 7. The Yugoslav government provides forensic detail of the incident in its White Book. Human Rights Watch also received photo documentation of the deaths from the Ministry of Health.[14]

49. In an 11:50 p.m. to midnight attack on what was wrongly identified as the Yugoslav Federal Directorate for Supply and Procurement (Yugoimport FDSP) at 2 Umetnosti Boulevard in New Belgrade, the Chinese Embassy compound is mistakenly hit, killing three and injuring twenty Embassy staff members.[15] The three Chinese nationals

---

1 FRY, MOH, "Photo Documentation of Civilians Who Were Killed By NATO Attacks, from 24.03 until 20.05.1999."
2 FRY, MFA, NATO Crimes in Yugoslavia, vol. II, pp. 349-353; FRY, MFA, "Aide-Memoire on the Use of Inhumane Weapons in the Aggression of the North Atlantic Treaty Organization Against the Federal Republic of Yugoslavia," May 15, 1999.
3 FRY, MFA, "NATO raids on industrial and civilian facilities on May 3 and in the night between May 3 and 4, 1999."
4 FRY, MFA, "Aide-Memoire on the Use of Inhumane Weapons in the Aggression of the North Atlantic Treaty Organization Against the Federal Republic of Yugoslavia," May 15, 1999.
5 AFP (Brussels), "Lengthening List of NATO Errors," May 4, 1999.
6 FRY, MOH, "Photo Documentation of Civilians Who Were Killed By NATO Attacks, from 24.03 until 20.05.1999."
7 FRY, MFA, NATO Crimes in Yugoslavia, vol. II, pp. 118-121; Yugoslav press reports; Vijesti, May 4, 1999, p. 4; BLIC, May 10, 1999, p. 9; Vreme, May 15, 1999, p. 5. Committee for Compiling Data on Crimes Against Humanity and International Law (http://www.gov.yu/cwc/fejmel_nato.htm) says fourteen killed and thirty injured.
8 Yugoslav press reports; "War Against Yugoslavia: Nis" (www.inet.co.yu/rat/gradovi/nis/index.html).
9 FRY, MFA, "NATO Crimes Against Civilians," May 10, 1999; Information Provided by the FRY, MOD.
10 FRY, MFA, "Aide-Memoire on the Use of Inhumane Weapons in the Aggression of the North Atlantic Treaty Organization Against the Federal Republic of Yugoslavia," May 15, 1999.
11 NATO (SHAPE), ACE News Release - Press Release 99-05-02, May 8, 1999.
12 "War Against Yugoslavia: Nis" (www.inet.co.yu/rat/gradovi/nis/ index.html).
13 Transcript of Press Conference given by the NATO Secretary General, Mr. Javier Solana, in Brussels, on Saturday, May 8, 1999 (including Maj. Gen. Jertz).
14 FRY, MOH, "Photo Documentation of Civilians Who Were Killed By NATO Attacks, from 24.03 until 20.05.1999."
15 Oral Presentation by Under Secretary of State Thomas Pickering on June 17 to the Chinese government regarding the Accidental Bombing of the PRC Embassy in Belgrade, released July 6, 1999.

killed include Hi Hinhu (31), Zhu Jing (28), and Shao-Jin Juan (48).[1] At the moment of the attack, fifty people were reported in the embassy buildings.[2]

According to the U.S. government, at 2146 Zulu time (GMT) (about midnight local time in Belgrade) on May 7, 1999, a B-2 dropped five Joint Direct Attack Munitions (JDAM) 2000 lb. GPS-guided bombs on the target designated as the FDSP building but which was, in fact, the Chinese Embassy.[3] According to U.S. government sources, the street address of the FDSP headquarters (the intended target) was known as Bulevar Umetnosti 2 in New Belgrade. During a mid-April "work-up" of the target to prepare a mission folder for the B-2 bomber crew, three maps were used in an attempt to physically locate this address within the neighborhood: two local commercial maps from 1989 and 1996, and one U.S. government (National Imagery and Mapping Agency or NIMA) map produced in 1997. None accurately identified the current location of the Chinese Embassy. CIA Director George Tenet says that there were people at the CIA and at the Department of Defense who had an intimate understanding of the Belgrade environment, but they were not consulted in this process.[4]

Human Rights Watch visited the Chinese Embassy site (N4449483/E02025147) located at Tresnjin cvet street No. 3 on August 4, and inspected the damage and the surrounding area. It also located the location of the FDSP headquarters at Bulevar Umetnosti 2, some 300 meters away from the Chinese Embassy. The Yugoslav government provides forensic detail of the incident in its White Book. Human Rights Watch also received photo documentation of the deaths from the Ministry of Health.[5]

[...]

May 8

51. In a 4:03-4:25 p.m. attack on the concrete "12 February" bridge over the Nisava river in downtown Nis between, two civilians are killed. Initially, it is reported that one person is seriously and ten people are lightly wounded, and damage is caused to the Greek consulate, a car dealership, and the Nis Express parking lot. A city bus on Stanka Paunovica street is also reported hit.[6] Later press reports state that two persons are killed.[7]

A precision-guided munition (PGM) was used in the attack. NATO confirms that it attacked Nis airfield, a "highway bridge" in Nis, and the Nis petroleum storage site on May 8.[8]

Human Rights Watch visited the site (N4319395/E02153439) on August 11, inspected the damage and interviewed eyewitnesses. The bridge is located on Oktobarske Revolucije street, an extension of 12. Februara Boulevard. The Greek consulate is on the north bank of the river, on Kej Mike Paligorica street. The bridge was hit with one weapon, which did damage to the west side of the roadway (the bridge was not further damaged). Another crater from an errant weapon was observed further west on the bank of the Nisava river across from the "Rudo" factory. This crater was close to a small military barracks on the banks of the Nisava river (see comments on May 7). The 3rd Army Headquarters building in downtown Nis at "Yugoslav Army" square is also only a few hundred meters away. It seems possible that the bridge was not the object of the attack (the "highway" bridge reported attacked by NATO is assumed not to be this downtown road bridge). Nis civil defense officials stated that ten weapons-five "missiles" and five "guided bombs"-were dropped in Nis on May 8.

[...]

May 11

[...]

55. In a 9:30 p.m. attack on the Vladicin Han road bridge over the Juzna Morava river in southeast Serbia, two civilians are killed and three are wounded. Gordana Nikolic (18) and Milan Ignjatovic (19) are killed.[9] The bridge in the center of the town, as well as a nearby department store, are destroyed.[10]

A precision-guided munition (PGM) was used in the attack. NATO confirms attacking the Vladicin Han bridge on May 11.[11]

Human Rights Watch visited the site (N4242353/E02203747) on August 12, inspected the damage and interviewed eyewitnesses. Eyewitnesses stated that the bridge was attacked four times on different occasions. The fourth attack was the one which ultimately destroyed the bridge, they said. Milan Ignjatovic and Gordana Nikolic were killed during the first attack. They were some 500 meters away and were knocked down by the blast created by the explosion. Townspeople said that they thought another town bridge was more likely to be attacked (the main one leading to Surdulica). The bridge that was actually attacked was not on the main highway nor was it the access route to the older secondary north-south road in Yugoslavia; it only connects the town center over the banks of the river.

The Yugoslav government provides forensic detail of the incident in its White Book.

[...]

May 13

57. In an 11:50 p.m. attack on Yugoslav Army forces in the field, a refugee camp on the Prizren-Suva Reka primary road, near the village of Korisa in Kosovo, is bombed, killing at least forty-eight and as many as eighty-seven, and injuring as many as sixty.[12]

The Yugoslav government initially reports "at least seventy-nine civilians were killed, and more than fifty wounded," when aircraft attacked a convoy of about 500 ethnic Albanians hiding in the near-by woods.[13] Another Yugoslav government report stated that initial and still incomplete data indicates that eighty-four people were killed and over one hundred were wounded ("Yugoslav citizens of Albanian nationality, mainly women, children and the elderly").[14] Yugoslav and western press reports ultimately put the death toll at eighty-seven, a number repeated by the U.S. State Department.[15] The UN Kosovo

---

1 FRY, MFA, NATO Crimes in Yugoslavia, vol. II, pp. 122-136; FRY, MFA, "NATO Crimes Against Civilians," May 10, 1999.
2 Information Provided by the FRY, MOD.
3 Oral Presentation by Under Secretary of State Thomas Pickering on June 17 to the Chinese government regarding the Accidental Bombing of the PRC Embassy in Belgrade, released July 6, 1999.
4 U.S. Congress, House Permanent Select Committee on Intelligence, Hearing on the Bombing of the Chinese Embassy, July 21, 1999.
5 FRY, MOH, "Photo Documentation of Civilians Who Were Killed By NATO Attacks, from 24.03 until 20.05.1999."
6 FRY, MFA, "Aide-Memoire on the Use of Inhumane Weapons in the Aggression of the North Atlantic Treaty Organization Against the Federal Republic of Yugoslavia," May 15, 1999; "War Against Yugoslavia: Nis" (www.inet.co.yu/rat/gradovi/nis/index.html).
7 Yugoslav press reports; "Dva pesaka poginula na mostu," (Two Pedestrians Died on the Bridge), BLIC, May 10, 1999, p. 9.
8 NATO, Operation Allied Force Update, May 9, 1999.
9 Yugoslav press reports; FRY, MFA, NATO Crimes in Yugoslavia, vol. II, pp. 375-377, incorrectly reports this incident as occurring on May 18.
10 FRY, MFA, "NATO raids on civilian and industrial facilities on may 11 and in the night between May 11 and 12 1999."
11 NATO, Operation Allied Force Update, May 12, 1999, 0900.
12 FRY, MFA, NATO Crimes in Yugoslavia, vol. II, pp. 1-17. Though the White Book states that there were "only" forty-eight victims in Korisa, the Yugoslav and western press cite eighty-seven victims. The Committee for Compiling Data on Crimes Against Humanity and International Law (http://www.gov.yu/cwc/fejmel_nato.htm) says eighty-one killed and seventy injured. Based upon Human Rights Watch investigations, it was clear that the overall impression in Yugoslavia was that more that forty-eight people died in the Korisa attack, nevertheless forty-eight is the latest official figure.
13 FRY, MFA, "NATO raids on manufacturing and civilian facilities on may 14 and in the night between may 14 and 15 1999."
14 FRY, MFA, "Aide-Memoire on the Use of Inhumane Weapons in the Aggression of the North Atlantic Treaty Organization Against the Federal Republic of Yugoslavia," May 15, 1999; FRY, MFA, NATO Crimes in Yugoslavia, vol. II, p. 17.
15 Yugoslav press reports; DAN, May 20, 1999, p. 2; Kosovo Chronology, Timeline of events 1989-1999 relating to the crisis in Kosovo, released by the Department of State, Washington, DC, June 18, 1999.

High Commissioner for Human Rights also quotes eighty civilians killed.[1]

The Yugoslav government also claimed the use of cluster bombs, and the White Book, Volume II, contains photographic evidence of remains of tactical munitions dispensers (TMDs) from the site.[2] Tanjug also reports that NATO used "thermo-vision bombs that develop high temperature of up to 2000 degrees Celsius so that they burn even the stone."[3]

In an official statement on May 15, NATO says:

This was a legitimate military target. The Serb claims of an attack involving cluster bombs against a non-military target are both false. NATO identified Korisa as a military camp and command post. Military equipment including an armoured personnel carrier and more than ten pieces of artillery were observed at this location. The aircraft observed dug-in military positions at the target before executing the attack. NATO cannot confirm the casualty figures given by the Serbian authorities, nor the reasons why civilians were at this location at the time of the attack. NATO deeply regrets accidental civilian casualties that were caused by this attack.[4]

Maj. Gen. Jertz states further that

Immediately prior to the attack at 23.30-11.30 p.m.-local time Thursday night an airborne forward air controller confirmed the target, so the identification and attack system of his aircraft, having positively identified the target as what looked like dug in military reveted positions, he dropped two laser guided bombs. Following his attack, he cleared his wingman to also attack the same target using two more laser guided bombs. Approximately 10 minutes later, the third aircraft engaged the target with gravity bombs, with six gravity bombs. A total of 10 bombs were dropped on the target. Contrary to Serbian reports, I want to be very clear that cluster munitions were not used against these targets.[5]

On May 14, the first rumors emerge that suggest that Serb troops were using civilians as human shields in Korisa. Amnesty International says that Korisa had been under attack by VJ and MUP forces prior to the bombing. On May 15, AFP quotes a spokesman for SHAPE as saying: "The possibility of human shields is one that always exist....But we are not on the ground so we have no way of confirming civilian casualties, their number or why they were there in the first place."[6] Visiting Albania the next day, General Clark said: "We know there is a real threat of human shields all the way through Kosovo."[7] On May 16, a Kosovar refugee who witnessed the NATO strike on Korisa also reported to Deutsche Welle that FRY police forced some 600 displaced Kosovars to serve as human shields there before the attack.[8]

On May 15, Assistant Secretary of Defense Kenneth Bacon also says at the DOD News Briefing that

This accident at Korisa did not shake NATO's resolve in any way. The air campaign will continue with increasing force, particularly against Serb ground forces and police units in Kosovo.... NATO deeply regrets civilian casualties.... We try very hard to avoid these casualties, but combat is inherently dangerous and accidents cannot be avoided. ... This mission, like every other, will be reviewed, and the airmen and their commanders will learn what they can from it and continue. But I don't anticipate that there will be a sweeping change. We can't cross legitimate military targets off the list, and we won't.

The Yugoslav government provides forensic detail of the incident documenting civilian deaths in its White Book. Human Rights Watch also received photo documentation of the deaths from the Ministry of Health.[9]

[...]

May 19

60. In a 1:15 p.m. attack on what NATO claimed were Yugoslav army and police forces near the Dubrava penitentiary near Istok in Kosovo, four civilians are killed and two are injured (see also May 21). Three weapons reportedly hit the penitentiary. Three prisoners and a guard are killed and two prisoners are wounded. The penitentiary administration building and two wings are hit.[10] Tanjug reports "There are fears that the casualty toll will rise, as it is difficult to approach the site, where ruins are being cleared. Material damage is tremendous." Provincial secretary for administration and regulations Jovica Jovanovic said that one of the wounded prisoners is in critical condition. Three penitentiary employees were lightly wounded, he added.[11]

The Vujindol village on the Istok-Zubin Potok road is also reported hit.[12]

NATO states that it attacked an "army facility" in Istok on May 19.[13] NATO spokesman Maj. Gen. Walter Jertz says that the facility was "a militarily significant target...a military security complex." He says that precision-guided munitions were used in the attack.[14]

Among those believed killed by NATO bombing are: Enver Topalli, Abdullah Tahiri, and Gjon Ndrecaj.

[...]

May 21

[...]

65. In an 8:10-10:25 a.m. attack on believed military barracks and assembly areas at Dubrava Penitentiary near Istok in Kosovo, at least nineteen prisoners are killed and more are wounded (see also May 19). The Yugoslav government initially reports nineteen people were killed in the Dubrava Penitentiary, and more than ten were "severely or lightly" wounded. It said that twenty-four missiles were launched causing "huge damage to most of the buildings in the penitentiary perimeter."[15]

On May 25, the Yugoslav press reported from Tanjug that "in days long bombardment of the Penitentiary Institute Istok, some 100 prisoners died, and some 200 were wounded." On May 27, Tanjug quoted Vladan Bojic, judge in Pec's District Court, saying that ninety-six corpses had been pulled from the ruins and that forty wounded are in critical condition. On May 29, the Yugoslav government stated that "The number of casualties in the Correctional Institution in Istok is increasing. Out of 196 people wounded in the vandal bombing of this institution another three persons died, and seven more were taken out

---

1 Report by the High Commissioner for Human Rights on the Situation of Human Rights in Kosovo, Report by the High Commissioner for Human Rights on the Situation of Human Rights in Kosovo, May 31, 1999.
2 FRY, MFA, "Aide-Memoire on the Use of Inhumane Weapons in the Aggression of the North Atlantic Treaty Organization Against the Federal Republic of Yugoslavia," May 15, 1999; FRY, MFA, NATO Crimes in Yugoslavia, vol. II, p. 17.
3 Tanjug, "Chronology of Crimes and Dishonor of NATO," June 5, 1999; Yugoslav press reports.
4 NATO, Subject: Press Release (99) 079, Statement by the NATO Spokesman on the Korisa Incident, May 15, 1999.
5 Transcript of Backgrounder given by Peter Daniel and Major General Walter Jertz, in Brussels, May 15, 1999.
6 SHAPE News Summary and Analysis, May 15, 1999.
7 SHAPE News Morning Update, May 16, 1999.
8 Kosovo Chronology, Timeline of events 1989-1999 relating to the crisis in Kosovo, released by the Department of State, Washington, DC, June 18, 1999.

9 FRY, MOH, "Photo Documentation of Civilians Who Were Killed By NATO Attacks, from 24.03 until 20.05.1999."
10 Human Rights Watch has conducted a separate investigation into the deaths at the Dubrava prison (report forthcoming). In the May 19 attack, according to eyewitnesses, three prisoners were killed. FRY, MFA, "NATO Raids on Manufacturing and Civilian Facilities on May19th and in the Night Between May 19 and 20, 1999," says two prisoners and a guard were killed.
11 Tanjug, "NATO Kills Two, Wounds several in attack on Istok Wednesday," May 20, 1999.
12 Yugoslav press reports.
13 NATO, Operation Allied Force Update, May 20, 1999, 0930 CET.
14 Transcript of NATO Press Conference, May 20, 1999.
15 Information provided by Yugoslav civil defense authorities; FRY, MFA, "NATO raids on manufacturing and civilian facilities on May 21 and in the night between May 21 and 22, 1999."

from under the rubble, while the search for the dead continues."[1] On May 30, Tanjug reports seven more bodies found, bringing the total to ninety-three killed.[2] The White Book eventually states that ninety-five prisoners are killed and over one hundred are wounded at the Dubrava Penitentiary.[3]

NATO declares that "a barracks and assembly area for the VJ and MUP forces that conduct ethnic cleansing operations in Kosovo, in the vicinity of a prison, were struck at Istok" on May 21.[4] On May 22, NATO Spokesman Col. Freytag states that the prison was on the target list as "an unused prison with an airfield with a large military facility used by the military forces, Serbian ground forces and special police." He says that NATO had bombed the "very large complex" twice before and "caused a lot of damage."[5]

Human Rights Watch has determined that Yugoslav forces were likely responsible for the majority of deaths which occurred after the bombing (this accounts for the seeming discrepancy between the estimate of at least 19 quoted here and the Yugoslav claims of ninety-five dead). According to a separate investigation undertaken by Human Rights Watch in Kosovo, based upon extensive eyewitness testimony, prisoners were hunted down inside the penitentiary walls after the May 21 attack, eventually killing another eighty or so prisoners. The bombing on May 21 caused chaos in the facility. The Yugoslav government states that some prisoners tried to escape during this time, and the guards were struggling to maintain order. On May 22, according to eyewitnesses, prison officials ordered the approximately 1,000 prisoners to line up in the prison yard. After a few minutes, they were fired upon, and grenades were thrown at them from the prison walls and guard towers, killing at least seventy people. Over the next twenty-four hours, prison guards, special police, and possibly paramilitaries attacked prisoners who were hiding in the prison's undestroyed buildings, basements, and sewers, killing at least another twelve people. There has been extensive press reporting to substantiate this conclusion in addition to the Human Rights Watch investigation.[6]

Among those believed killed by NATO bombing are: Mehdi Dallosi, Ahmet Hoxha, and Ali Kelmendi.

[...]

May 27

71. In a 1:25 p.m. attack on the Cekavicki bridge over the Jablanica river near Pertate between Leskovac and Lebane in southeastern Serbia, two civilians are killed and one is wounded. Branka Stankovic (55) and Veselka Spasic (59) are killed near the bridge.[7] The bridge is reported hit with three "missiles." The "Grmija" trading company storage facilityis also reported targeted with two "missiles."[8] Later, the Yugoslav government reports a 2:20 p.m. attack on the Cenovacki Bridge on the road to Lebane that kills two civilians, undoubtedly the same incident.[9]

A precision-guided munition (PGM) was used in the attack. NATO confirms attacking the Pertate bridge on May 27.[10]

Human Rights Watch visited the site (N4258001/E02151265) on August 12, inspected the damage and interviewed eyewitnesses. The Yugoslav government provides forensic detail of the incident in its White Book.

[...]

May 30

79. In a midnight attack intended for an ammunition depot in Surdulica in southeastern Serbia, a sanatorium is bombed, and twenty-three civilians are killed and thirty-six are wounded. Milenko Malobabic (16), Rada Malobabic (19), Milena Malobabic (20), Djordje Pavkovic (45), Rada Zigic (52), Bosiljka Malobabic (53), Slavko Popovic (60), Petar Budisavljevic (60), Bogdanka Janjanin (60), Stamen Rangelov (61), Milanka Vuckovic (65), Stana Rasic (66), Desanka Velickovic (67), Bosa Miladinovic (68), Danica Malesevic (68), Nepijal Dragic (70), Dragic Napijalo (70), Dusan Manojlovic (72), Bogdanka Janjanin (74), and Mile Slijepcevic (90) are killed.[11] On June 7, Boris Eremijev (60) from Klisura dies in a hospital in Bosilegrad.[12] The bodies of two more victims, names and ages unknown, were reportedly recovered on August 11.

The Special Hospital for Lung Diseases "Sanatorium" in southeastern Surdulica is hit. The complex includes an home for the aged and a refugee center. Directly hit were three widely separated buildings.[13] Tanjug reports "at least 17 children and helpless old people lost their lives."[14] In all, the Yugoslav government states, twenty civilians are killed and eighty-eight wounded.[15]

NATO reports the bombing of the Surdulica ammunition storage site on May 30.[16] NATO spokesman Col. Konrad Freitag says that aircraft struck an ammunition storage depot and military barracks. "NATO cannot confirm any Serb claims of casualties or collateral damage," he said. On June 1, NATO spokesman Jamie Shea further addresses the Surdulica incident:

when we looked at this incident we clearly saw that the 4 missiles, precision guided missiles, which were fired at the facilities in Surdulica, all hit the target, the military target, the legitimate military target, accurately. There were no errant weapons in this situation.[17]

In July, while testifying before Congress, Deputy Secretary of Defense John Hamre and CIA Director George Tenet address the Surdulica incident. Hamre says: "We did have an instance where we hit a hospital. It was totally an accident. In this case, that was human error that led in this instance where we hit a hospital." Tenet says: "We hit a hospital. We didn't want to do that. That was the case of the pilot got confused and he was off by about a mile and what he thought was his coordinates."[18]

Human Rights Watch visited the site (N4240929/E02209910) on August 12, inspected the damage and interviewed eyewitnesses. Guards at the sanatorium said that they observed NATO aircraft flying

---

[1] FRY, MFA, "NATO Raids on Manufacturing and Civilian Facilities on May 29 and in the Night Between May 29 and 30 1999."
[2] Yugoslav press reports; "Identifikovano 86 mrtvih," (Eighty-six Bodies Identified), DAN, May 27, 1999, p. 2; "Jos sedam leseva," (Seven More Bodies), DAN, May 30, 1999.
[3] FRY, MFA, NATO Crimes in Yugoslavia, vol.II, p. 319.
[4] NATO, Operation Allied Force Update, May 22, 1999, 0930 CET.
[5] Transcript of Press Conference given by Mr. Jamie Shea and Colonel Konrad Freytag in Brussels on Saturday, May 22, 1999.
[6] Jacky Rowland, "Bombs, Blood and Dark Despair," Scotland on Sunday, 23 May 1999; Paul Watson, "NATO Bombs Ignite Prison Chaos-KLA Officers Reported to be Among Inmates," Toronto Star, May 22, 1999; AP, "NATO Hits Kosovo Jail Again Friday Night," May 21, 1999; Jacky Rowland, "Istok Prison's Unanswered Questions," BBC World News, May 25, 1999; Daniel Williams, "Kosovo Revisited: At War's End, Old Places Seen in New Light," Washington Post, June 26, 1999; Carlotta Gall, "Stench of Horror Lingers in a Prison in Kosovo,"New York Times, November 9, 1999.
[7] FRY, MFA, NATO Crimes in Yugoslavia, vol. II, pp. 385-388.
[8] FRY, MFA, "NATO Raids on the Civilian and Manufacturing Facilities on May 27 and in the Night Between May 27 and 28, 1999."

[9] FRY, MFA, "NATO Raids on Manufacturing and Civilian Facilities on May 30 and in the Night Between May 30 and 31, 1999."
[10] NATO, Operation Allied Force Update, May 28, 1999, 09:30 CET.
[11] FRY, MFA, NATO Crimes in Yugoslavia, vol. II, pp. 252-294.
[12] FRY, MFA, "NATO Raids on Manufacturing and Civilian Facilities on June 7 and in the Night Between June 7 and 8, 1999."
[13] FRY, MFA, NATO Crimes in Yugoslavia, vol.II, pp. 252-294; FRY, MFA, "NATO Raids on Manufacturing and Civilian Facilities on May 31 and in the Night Between May 31 and June 1, 1999."
[14] Tanjug, "Chronology of Crimes and Dishonor of NATO," June 5, 1999.
[15] Permanent Mission of the FRY to the UN, "Provisional Assessment," July 3, 1999.
[16] NATO, Operation Allied Force Update, May 31, 1999, 09:30 CET.
[17] Transcript of Press Conference given by Mr. Jamie Shea and Major General Walter Jertz in Brussels on Tuesday, June 1, 1999.
[18] U.S. Congress, House Permanent Select Committee on Intelligence, Hearing on the Bombing of the Chinese Embassy, July 21, 1999.

at a low altitude, and that there was no air defenses active in the area. On August 11, one day before the Human Rights Watch team visited the site, the guards stated that two more corpses were found on the roof of a sanatorium building. Human Rights Watch also inspected a large crater in a field some 400 meters from the sanatorium facility. The Yugoslav government provides forensic detail of the incident in its White Book.

[...]

81. In a 1:00-1:25 p.m. attack on the Varvarin bridge over the Velika Morava river in central Serbia, nine civilians are killed and some forty are wounded. Reported killed are: Sanja Milenkovic (17), Milan Savic (24), Vojkan Stankovic (31), Zoran Marinkovic (33), Stojan Ristic (56), Ruzica Simonovic (60), priest Milivoje Ciric (66), Dragoslav Terzic (68), and Tola Apostolovic (74).[1] Tanjug says local people were attending the town's market on the holiday Svete Trojice when the daylight attack happened at 1 p.m. local time. Witnesses said four cars fell into the river. Rescuers who went to aid of the wounded were hit in a second attack. Tanjug and the Yugoslav government reports eleven killed and at least forty wounded.[2] There is damage to the "Plaza" hotel, the St. Bogordica church, and the municipal assembly building.

On June 2, Tanjug reported that six persons have been listed as missing since the NATO attack. It again reported eleven killed and "about forty" wounded. It states that nine victims had so far been identified.[3]

NATO confirms the attack and states that a precision-guided munition (PGM) was used. Spokesman Jamie Shea said the alliance had bombed a "legitimate designated military target" and stated that "we take the same precautions at midday as we do at midnight." "There is always a cost to defeat an evil," he says. "It never comes free, unfortunately. But the cost of failure to defeat a great evil is far higher."[4]

Human Rights Watch visited the site (N4343444/E02122405) on August 11, inspected the damage and interviewed eyewitnesses. The attack took place in the afternoon on Sunday, the market day. During the first explosion, no one was killed. In the second explosion, some seven minutes later, according to eyewitnesses, people were killed on and around the bridge. Among them was the priest Milivoje Ciric, who, after the first blast, interrupted the service in the nearby St. Bogorodica church, to go to the bridge. Varvarin is located on a secondary road between the main E-75 Nis-Belgrade highway and Krusevac. The bridge that was destroyed was not the main link to the north (which was not bombed); it was only a local bridge.

The Yugoslav government provides forensic detail of the incident in its White Book.

[...]

Appendix B: Civilian Victims of NATO Bombing During Operation Allied Force

[...]

Appendix C: Incidents Involving Unsubstantiated Reports of Civilian Deaths

March 25

In an attack on a Prizren Ministry of Interior (MUP) building or headquarters in Kosovo, Dragan Barac and Dragan Renic are reported killed. Though the Ministry of Health provided photographs of the bodies,[5] they are mentioned nowhere else in the press or the Yugoslav government's White Book and it is doubted whether these two casualties were civilians.

The field (war) headquarters of the 3rd Army in Kursumlija in southern Serbia is hit "on the first night of the campaign and ... badly damaged." According to the British government, "This is the HQ from which the Yugoslav Army is controlling its Kosovo campaign and this will give the Yugoslavs key command and control problems. We know that their army has been badly rattled by this attack."[6] The Yugoslav government initially reports that a refugee center was bombed, killing eleven "refugees" from Bosnia-Herzegovina and Croatia, and wounding twenty-four.[7]

Human Rights Watch was unable to verify Yugoslav claims of civilian casualties in this incident, the bombing of a refugee center, and it suspects that those killed were not refugees but military or MUP personnel. The Kursumlija refugee center incident is not reported in the Yugoslav government White Book, nor does it figure in later Yugoslav compilations.[8] In the May 29, 1999 "espionage" verdict for three Care Australia workers (Steve Pratt, Peter Wallace, and Branko Jelen) handed down by the Military Court of the 1st Army command in Yugoslavia (No. I.K.14/99), the court stated that a March 29 report compiled by Pratt refers to the initial bombing of Kursumlija. In that report, according to the verdict, Pratt stated that "what was hit in Kursumlija and Pristina were not refugee camps, but Army depots and a paramilitary police headquarters."[9]

March 29

Tanjug reports that refugee camps near Nis in southern Serbia and Pristina in Kosovo are "bombed," killing fifteen refugees.[10] The refugee camps are managed by CARE Australia on behalf of the U.N. High Commissioner for Refugees (UNHCR). Steve Pratt of CARE Australia is quoted by Australian ABC radio as saying that his staff could confirm that nine refugees died when NATO hit buildings in Pristina near the agency's refugee centers. Pratt is later arrested by Yugoslav authorities for espionage, and it is later learned that the attacks were actually on police facilities. The Ministry of Health reports that in an attack on the Pristina MUP building on March 29, Radoica Kovac is killed.[11] The death is not reported again in the press, is not mentioned in Yugoslav government compilations, nor in the White Book. Human Rights Watch accordingly concludes that Kovac was likely not a civilian.[12]

April 6

At 8:45 p.m., in an attack on the Sjenica airfield in eastern central Serbia, one person is killed in the village of Stavaljska breza.[13] Civilian buildings were reported struck with cluster bombs at Dubinje in the vicinity of Sjenica causing substantial damage to the management building of the agricultural complex "Pester," as well as to the dairy, workers' accommodation facilities, and a number of auxiliary buildings and motor vehicles. Telephone, power, and water supply lines are reported hit, cutting water and power supply and telephone service.[14]

---

1 FRY, MFA, NATO Crimes in Yugoslavia, vol. II, pp. 400-413; FRY, MFA, "NATO Raids on Manufacturing and Civilian Facilities on May 31 and in the Night Between May 31 and June 1, 1999." Committee for Compiling Data on Crimes Against Humanity and International Law (http://www.gov.yu/cwc/fejmel_nato.htm) says ten killed and sixteen injured.
2 Yugoslav press reports; Tanjug, "Chronology of Crimes and Dishonor of NATO," June 5, 1999; FRY, MFA, "NATO Raids on Manufacturing and Civilian Facilities on May 30 and in the Night Between May 30 and 31, 1999."
3 Tanjug, "Six persons listed as missing after NATO attack on bridge in Vavarin," June 2, 1999.
4 Transcript of Press Conference given by Mr. Jamie Shea and Major General Walter Jertz in Brussels on Tuesday, June 1, 1999.
5 FRY, MOH, "Photo Documentation of Civilians Who Were Killed By NATO Attacks, from 24.03 until 20.05.1999."
6 Statement by Gen. Charles Guthrie. See Briefing By the Secretary of State for Defence, Mr. George Robertson, and the Chief of the Defence Staff, Gen Sir Charles Guthrie, London, March 27, 1999.
7 Yugoslav press reports; FRY, MFA, "Consequences of NATO aggression against the FRY," Belgrade, March 27, 1999.
8 For instance, the incident is not listed on the compilation of the Committee for Compiling Data on Crimes Against Humanity and International Law (http://www.gov.yu/cwc/fejmel_nato.htm).
9 Judgment of the Military Court of the 1st Army Command, I.K. No. 14/99, May 29, 1999.
10 Tanjug, "Chronology of Crimes and Dishonor of NATO," June 5, 1999.
11 FRY, MOH, "Photo Documentation of Civilians Who Were Killed By NATO Attacks, from 24.03 until 20.05.1999."
12 Ibid.
13 Yugoslav press reports.
14 FRY, "Aide-Memoire," May 15, 1999.

The Yugoslav White Book reports the bombing in Dubinje and Sjenica at 8:45 p.m. on April 6, but do not report any civilian casualties.[1] The Yugoslav press states that a "person" was killed in the attack, not a "civilian."[2] Human Rights Watch concludes that it is likely that a member of the military or police was killed.

April 11

Yugoslav authorities claim that in a 5:00 a.m. attack on the village Turekovac near Leskovac in southeastern Serbia, "there were some damages on civilian objects and some civilians have been killed."[3] The Yugoslav White Book mentions the attack, which it says "heavily damaged a large number of family houses," but it does not include any further reports of civilian casualties.[4] Human Rights Watch thus doubts that there were any civilian casualties.

April 26

Tanjug reports that civilians are killed in an attack on a bridge on the outskirt of Kastrat just east of Kursumlija. "The number of civilians killed in Kursumlija as a result of air strikes rose up to 17," Tanjug reports.[5] The incident on April 26 is not mentioned in the Yugoslav government White Book, nor is there any further corroboration or reporting in the Yugoslav press. The Tanjug reference to "up to 17" killed in Kursumlija area likely refers to deaths from attacks on March 25, April 2, and April 10 (see above and Appendix A).

May 21

In an 11:00 a.m. attack on the Smederevo "Jugopetrol" depot in eastern Serbia, seven people are reported killed. The depot is reportedly targeted with three weapons for the sixth time. One weapon hit the grounds of "Trudbenik-Buducnost" factory and the other Godominsko Polje near the Smederevo medium wave (MW) radio transmitter.[6]

NATO reports attacking the petroleum storage facility in Smederevo on May 21,[7] but the Yugoslav government White Book does not mention any civilian deaths in the attack, nor was there any reporting of the deaths in the Yugoslav press. Human Rights Watch visited Smederevo and was able to verify the attack, but could not verify any civilian deaths in this incident.

See also Appendix A, incident 65.

[...]

194. UK, House of Commons, Foreign Affairs Committee, Fourth Report on Kosovo, 7 June 2000

Select Committee on Foreign Affairs - Fourth Report

[...]

International Law

INTRODUCTION

124. The Government has consistently asserted that the military action taken in the Kosovo campaign has been lawful, and that NATO would not have acted outside the principles of international law. The then Minister of State told the Committee that the Government had determined that the action threatened in October 1998 would have been lawful,[8] and the Foreign Secretary was also clear that there was a legal base for the action which began in March 1999.[9] Both Ministers told us that states had the right to use force in the case of "overwhelming humanitarian necessity where, in the light of all the circumstances, a limited use of force is justifiable as the only way to avert a humanitarian catastrophe."[10] A number of difficult questions of law (as well as difficult questions of fact) arise. In considering these questions, the Committee benefited greatly from oral evidence from three international lawyers, as we have already mentioned. Our oral legal witnesses were Professor Christopher Greenwood QC of the London School of Economics, Mr Mark Littman QC (author of Kosovo: Law and Diplomacy)[11] and Professor Vaughan Lowe of Oxford University. Most useful written evidence was also received from Professor Ian Brownlie QC (Oxford University), Professor Christine Chinkin (University of Michigan), Professor Peter Rowe (Lancaster University) and Professor Bruno Simma (Ludwig-Maximilians-Universität, Munich). The Committee also sought the opinion of the Attorney General, but the Attorney declined to give evidence on what he described as a "matter as sensitive as this,"[12] citing the convention of the confidentiality of the Law Officers' advice to Government.

125. These legal questions are not arcane. There is a need for a system of law governing the conduct of states, just as the internal affairs of states should be governed by the rule of law. An agreed system of law is particularly important where the use of force is concerned. It is in the national interest of the United Kingdom that an international order based on law should exist, and that individual states, or groups of states, should not be able to interpret the law perversely in their immediate interest. When the law is clear, there can be a consensus; when there is ambiguity, international stability and the mechanisms of collective security set up through the United Nations are threatened.

Was military intervention legal?

UNITED NATIONS APPROVAL

126. The Charter of the United Nations was described by Professor Simma as "not just one multilateral treaty among others, but an instrument of singular legal weight, something akin to a 'constitution' of the international community."[13] The Charter prohibits the threat or use of force[14] except in self defence[15] or when the Security Council determines that there is a threat to peace, breach of the peace or act of aggression, in which case the Security Council may determine (under Chapter VII) that force should be employed "to maintain or restore international peace and security."[16] The NATO military intervention was patently not an act of self defence,[17] nor was there any specific Security Council authorisation for the operation. As Dr Jones Parry told us, none of the three classic bases for intervention (a UN Security Council Resolution; an invitation to intervene; or self-defence) applied in the case of Kosovo.[18] The FCO told us that it had been clear since June 1998 that China and Russia would veto any authorisation of Chapter VII intervention in Kosovo in the Security Council.[19] Legal authorities, ranging from Professor Brownlie, the sternest critic of the legality of NATO action, to Professor Greenwood, the firmest supporter of legality, agree that the provisions of the UN Charter were thus not complied with. Professor Lowe puts it as follows: "the analysis of the text of the UN Charter...yields no clear justification for the NATO action. On the contrary, it suggests that the action was unlawful."[20] Professor Adam Roberts similarly told us that "in strict terms of black letter international law," NATO's actions were not "demonstrably and beyond any reasonable doubt legal" but equally were not illegal.[21] Professor Reisman, the one jurist in addition to Professor Greenwood who was cited to us by the FCO as believing that NATO's actions were

---

1 FRY, MFA, NATO Crimes in Yugoslavia, vol. I, p. 129.
2 Vecernje Novosti, April 6, 1999, p. 4.
3 Information provided by Yugoslav civil defense authorities.
4 FRY, MFA, NATO Crimes in Yugoslavia, vol. I, p. 141.
5 Tanjug, "Chronology of Crimes and Dishonor of NATO," June 5, 1999.
6 FRY, MFA, "NATO raids on manufacturing and civilian facilities on May 21 and in the night between May 21 and 22, 1999."
7 NATO, Operation Allied Force Update, May 22, 1999, 0930 CET.
8 QA64.
9 QB152.

10 Ev. p. 1.
11 Centre for Policy Studies 1999.
12 Ev. p. 364.
13 P. 18 of the article in the European Journal of International Law 10 (1999). Professor Simma submitted this article as his evidence.
14 Article 2(4).
15 Article 51.
16 Articles 39 and 42.
17 Ev. pp. 137 and 147.
18 QC14.
19 Ev. p. 7.
20 Ev. p. 148.
21 QC172.

lawful,[1] also wrote that Operation Allied Force "did not accord with the design of the UN Charter."[2]

127. There were certainly many actions at the United Nations which could properly be interpreted as supportive of the NATO allies' position:

UNSCR 1199 of September 1998 was agreed under Chapter VII, though it did not authorise "all necessary means."[3] It called for a cease-fire, recognised "the impending humanitarian catastrophe," and affirmed that there was a threat to peace and security;

UNSCR 1203, adopted in October 1998 after the agreement signed in Belgrade following the NATO threat of force, does not condemn the threat of force (and indeed welcomed the agreement secured), and can therefore be taken tacitly to support its use. It again affirms the existence of a threat to peace;

the Security Council rejected (by 12 votes to 3) a draft resolution proposed by Russia on 26 March 1999 which would have condemned NATO military action. The rejection of a proposition that military action should be condemned could be interpreted as approval of that action;[4]

UNSCR 1244 of 10 June 1999 authorised the international security presence in Kosovo to exercise "all necessary means" to fulfill its responsibilities. Again, this could be taken to imply post facto approval of the military action.

As Professor Chinkin put it:[5]

"Arguments for the legality of NATO's actions in the FRY are strengthened by taking all these actions together: the Security Council recognised the situation in Kosovo as warranting Chapter VII action; it imposed such measures as it could get agreement on; prior to the bombing it affirmed the on-going actions of various European organisations, the EU, the OSCE and NATO, that did not involve the use of force; when it could take no stronger measures itself it did not condemn the regional agency that did so act; and subsequent to the action it endorsed the political agreement."

But she remains dubious that these were sufficient grounds to regard NATO's actions as lawful.

UNITING FOR PEACE

128. There is a procedure at the United Nations known as "Uniting for Peace". This can help a blockage in the Security Council to be bypassed by reference to the General Assembly. Uniting for Peace is relevant only when a peace-and-security issue is on the Security Council agenda and the Council is prevented from exercising its "primary responsibility" to deal with it by veto of one of its permanent members. Though Article 12 of the UN Charter bars the General Assembly from making any recommendation in respect of any dispute or situation where the Security Council is exercising its functions, except at Security Council request, a procedural vote to refer a matter to the General Assembly requires the affirmative vote of nine members of the Security Council and is not subject to veto.[6] The Uniting for Peace procedure was used against the United Kingdom and France over their intervention in Suez in 1956. In the case of Kosovo, the General Assembly could have been called into special session and could, by two-thirds majority, have supported military action. Professor Adam Roberts told us that he had suggested this procedure after Rambouillet failed, but had been rebuffed by the FCO, which was uncertain that the two thirds majority would have been achieved, and which regarded the General Assembly as in any case a cumbersome procedure to use since resolutions passed there could not easily be modified.[7] Dr Jones Parry told us that the Government had considered a resort to the General Assembly, but had rejected the option. He pointed out that, though a resolution of the General Assembly would have been particularly persuasive, the UN Charter still specified that military action required Security Council endorsement.[8] Moreover, in some ways a bare two thirds majority would have been less persuasive than the majority (of 12 to three) actually secured in the Security Council on 26 March 1999. There was thus no ready means at the United Nations of securing direct approval for the NATO action in Kosovo. Our conclusion is that Operation Allied Force was contrary to the specific terms of what might be termed the basic law of the international community-the UN Charter, although this might have been avoided if the Allies had attempted to use the Uniting for Peace procedures.

CUSTOMARY INTERNATIONAL LAW: INTERVENTION FOR HUMANITARIAN PURPOSES (HUMANITARIAN INTERVENTION)

129. International law is not, however, static. It develops both through the agreement of new treaties and other international instruments, and through the evolution of customary law. The Charter of the United Nations has been interpreted in different ways in the half century since it was written. As Professor Greenwood pointed out,[9] some parts of the Charter have been conveniently ignored, while, since the end of the Cold War, the provisions of Article 2(7) which forbid intervention in internal affairs of states have been widened to allow such intervention on the grounds that what is happening internally in the state threatens international peace and security.[10] Moreover, it is at least arguable that the preponderant will of the international community ought not to be held to ransom by the exercise of the veto (or threat of the exercise of the veto) by a minority, or indeed only one, of the permanent members of the Security Council. As Professor Greenwood put it, "an interpretation of international law which would forbid intervention to prevent something as terrible as the Holocaust, unless a permanent member could be persuaded to lift its veto, would be contrary to the principles on which modern international law is based as well as flying in the face of the developments of the last fifty years."[11] We also note the fact that a veto by China on 25 February 1999 prevented the Security Council from authorising a six month extension of the term of the UN Preventive Deployment Force (UNPREDEP) in Macedonia. It was commonly believed that this veto was cast because of the establishment of diplomatic relations with Taiwan by Macedonia. One country's veto should not force the international community to sit on the sidelines and watch appalling human rights violations continue unchecked. We discuss the issue of the morality of the intervention, as distinct from its legality, below.[12]

130. Supporters of NATO's position argue that a new right has developed in customary international law-the right of humanitarian intervention. The argument in favour of the existence of this right was set out by Professor Greenwood.[13] First he asserted that states' rights did not take priority over human rights. Second he argued that there was increasing evidence of the exercise of intervention in defence of human rights. Third he pointed to recognition by the Security Council that human rights violations could be a threat to international security. He concluded that "modern customary international law does not exclude all possibility of military intervention on humanitarian grounds by states, or by an organisation like NATO," though he qualified his opinion by saying that two criteria had to be met: the existence, or immediate threat, of "the most serious humanitarian emergency involving large scale loss of life" and military intervention being "the only practicable means by which that loss of life can be ended or pre-

---

1 Ev. p. 174.
2 www.asil.org/kosovo.htm.
3 This is the accepted phrase used by the Security Council to authorise the use of force.
4 QC172. Professor Roberts comments that "an attempt to clearly declare this action illegal failed utterly".
5 Ev. p. 283.
6 If the item is not on the agenda, no transfer of authority is necessary and the General Assembly may, under Article 10 of the Charter, recommend enforcement measures to Members or the Security Council or both. See Keith S. Petersen, 'The Uses of the Uniting for Peace Resolution since 1950,' International Organization, Vol. 13, No. 2 (Spring 1959), 219-232; Sydney D. Bailey and Sam Daws, The Procedure of the UN Security Council, 3rd ed. (Oxford: Clarendon Press, 1998).
7 QC178.
8 QQC63ff.
9 QQC314, 326.
10 Ev. p. 148.
11 Ev. p. 139.
12 See para 137.
13 Ev. pp 139-140.

vented." Dame Pauline Neville-Jones was clear that NATO action had been lawful,[1] and Professor Lowe told us that NATO action (if a breach of a fifty year old Charter) was "consonant with the way international customary law is developing."[2] Professor Reisman put it thus: "when human rights enforcement by military means is required, it should, indeed be the responsibility of the Security Council acting under the Charter. But when the Council cannot act, the legal requirement continues to be to save lives."[3]

131. Professor Greenwood conceded that the right of humanitarian intervention was based on state practice, but that this was state practice which had evolved in the past 10 years since the end of the Cold War.[4] Although the interventions of India in East Pakistan (1971), Vietnam in Cambodia (1978), and Tanzania in Uganda (1979) had the effect of putting an end to massive human rights violations in each case, the intervening states relied ultimately on arguments of self-defence to justify their actions, even if reference was also made to the humanitarian situation. Only the interventions of ECOWAS in Liberia (1990) and the intervention by the USA, the United Kingdom and France in northern Iraq (1992) seem to have been unambiguously humanitarian in their stated aims. Professor Greenwood told us that the very short time scale over which the new practice had been apparent was unsurprising in international law, where a custom could develop much more quickly than in domestic law. Moreover, he argued that customary law formed a much more important part of international law than it did of domestic law.[5]

132. An entirely contrary view is taken by Professor Brownlie, who provided the Committee with an exhaustive review of the authorities, including jurists of twelve nationalities, three of whom had been President of the International Court of Justice. He concluded that "there is very little evidence to support assertions that a new principle of customary law legitimating humanitarian intervention has crystallised."[6] Professor Brownlie's view that the right of humanitarian intervention was at least doubtful was also held by Professor Lowe (who told us that "few lawyers would claim that the 'right' is at present clearly established in international law")[7] and Professor Chinkin (who wrote that she did "not think that state practice is sufficient to conclude definitively that the right to use force for humanitarian reasons has become part of customary international law."[8] We are persuaded that Professor Greenwood was too ambitious in saying that a new customary right has developed. We conclude that, at the very least, the doctrine of humanitarian intervention has a tenuous basis in current international customary law, and that this renders NATO action legally questionable.

HUMANITARIAN INTERVENTION IN SUPPORT OF THE SECURITY COUNCIL

133. Circumvention of the Security Council is a step which cannot be taken lightly, especially when, as Professor Lowe argued,[9] the Security Council has begun to act since the end of the Cold War as it was always intended to act, with Chapter VII invoked over 120 times[10] and few vetos cast. Mr Littman told us of his view that acting without Security Council approval was also contrary to public policy since to do so might lead to more conflict; because the precedent was likely to be abused; and because such action would only be taken by powerful states against less powerful states.[11] To sideline the Council would, in his view, be foolish.[12] But as we have already described, there were many indications of Security Council support for NATO's actions, even if no resolution specifically authorised the use of force.

134. To justify its action the British Government relied not just upon a defence of humanitarian intervention, but a defence of humanitarian intervention in support of the Security Council, if not specifically endorsed by the Council. The Government's position on the legality of Operation Allied Force was in this way clearly set out by the then Defence Secretary on 25 March 1999.[13] He told the House that the Government was "in no doubt that NATO is acting within international law" and that "the use of force...can be justified as an exceptional measure in support of purposes laid down by the UN Secretary, but without the Council's express authorisation, where that is the only means to avert an immediate and overwhelming humanitarian catastrophe." Identical wording was used in evidence to the Committee.[14] This legal justification was described by Professor Lowe as "one of some subtlety"[15] because it wrapped up two separate issues-the criteria on which it might be lawful to intervene, and the manner in which it can be determined whether those criteria have been met. We conclude that, faced with the threat of veto in the Security Council by Russia and China, the NATO allies did all that they could to make the military intervention in Kosovo as compliant with the tenets of international law as possible.

LEGALITY UNDER NATO TREATY

135. There is a further issue about the legality of NATO's actions. There was agreement among our legal witnesses that the North Atlantic Treaty gave no authority for NATO to act for humanitarian purposes.[16] As Professor Chinkin pointed out, Article 5 of the Treaty "provides for the use of force only in collective self-defence" of NATO members.[17] Professor Brownlie also referred to NATO's own wish not to be seen as a regional organisation for the purposes of the United Nations.[18] The Foreign Secretary did not believe that any amendment of the North Atlantic Treaty was necessary, though he accepted that NATO's action in Kosovo had extended the role and function of NATO beyond the terms of the NATO Treaty. He also drew our attention to NATO's new strategic concept which recognises a crisis management responsibility for NATO.[19] Despite this, we certainly would not wish to see NATO taking on a role as a regional arbiter of when humanitarian intervention was appropriate, persuasive as the unanimous support of 19 democratic governments for any action would be. Russia, for one, would be deeply concerned by any arrogation of this role to itself by NATO. We note Professor Simma's view that "legally the Alliance has no greater freedom than its Member States," and agree with him that "the genie of 'NATO self-authorisation' must not be let out of the bottle."[20] Professor Roberts told us that "NATO was not the ideal instrument, it was simply the only one that was there."[21] We recognise the pragmatism of this argument. We accept the view of expert witnesses that the North Atlantic Treaty gives NATO no authority to act for humanitarian purposes, and we recommend that the Government examine whether any new legal instrument is necessary to allow NATO to take action in future in the same manner as it did in Kosovo.

International Court of Justice

136. It would have been possible for the legality of the intervention to have been subject to the judgement of the International Court of Justice. Yugoslavia brought proceedings against several members of NATO, including the United Kingdom, in April 1999. The United

---

1 QC275.
2 QC314.
3 www.asil.org/kosovo.htm.
4 QC309.
5 QC327.
6 Ev. p. 231.
7 Ev. p. 148, QC307.
8 Ev. p. 285.
9 Ev. p. 150.
10 Though Chapter VII invocation does not mean that "all necessary means" were authorised.
11 QQC303-4.
12 QC316.

13 HC Deb, 25 March 1999, Col 616-7.
14 Ev. p. 22 in HC 41, Session 1999-2000, First Report from the Foreign affairs Committee, Annual Report on Human Rights 1999, available on: www.publications.parliament.uk/pa/cm199899/cmselect/cmfaff/100/10001.htm.
15 Ev. p. 148.
16 QQC367-8.
17 Ev. p. 282.
18 Ev. p. 235.
19 QQB206-8.
20 Pages 19 & 20 of the European Journal of International Law (10) 1999.
21 QC182.

Kingdom, decided, however, not to contest the substantive issue but to argue the procedural point that Yugoslavia had accepted the Court's compulsory jurisdiction too late for the United Kingdom to be required to deal with the substantive issue.[1] Dr Jones Parry agreed that this was "a legal technicality."[2] Mr Littman was very critical of this decision because it had, in his view, deprived the world of an authoritative judgement on the legality of humanitarian intervention.[3] Professor Lowe, however, argued that the United Kingdom should not accept jurisdiction in this case because the law in the area was in a state of development, and the International Court might arrest that development.[4] The decision to rely on a technicality to prevent the International Court from deciding the issue does suggest a concern that the judgement would not have been favourable, though this was specifically denied by FCO witnesses, who instead said that the Government had been unwilling to allow the "capricious" use of the Court by the Yugoslavs.[5]

Law and Morality

137. Disputes about international law are not ones which this Committee can resolve, but there is a separate question of morality. Philosophers since Aquinas have wrestled with the issue of when a war is a just war, and many of the issues raised by the Kosovo campaign are germane to that debate. Whether NATO action was lawful is a very different question from whether NATO action was right-a point made by John Sweeney.[6] Professor Simma[7] pointed out that there is a moral, as well as a legal issue at stake:

"Humanitarian interventions involving the threat or use of armed force and undertaken without the mandate or the authorisation of the Security Council will, as a matter of principle, remain in breach of international law. But such a general statement cannot be the last word. Rather, in any instance of humanitarian intervention a careful assessment will have to be made of how heavily such illegality weighs against all the circumstances of a particular concrete case, and of the efforts, if any, undertaken by the parties involved to get 'as close to the law' as possible. Such analyses will influence not only the moral but also the legal judgement in such cases."

As Professor Chinkin put it, "the actions have a legitimacy, if not strict legality under international law."[8] Professor Reisman, while upholding the importance of the rule of law, and clearly discomforted by some aspects of the legality of the Kosovo campaign, pointed to US Supreme Court Justice Holmes's dictum that "a constitution is not a suicide pact."[9] We believe that, while legal questions in international relations are important, law cannot become a means by which universally acknowledged principles of human rights are undermined.

138. To determine whether NATO's action was morally justified, and legally justified under the criteria which NATO set itself, we have to ask whether a humanitarian emergency existed before NATO intervened, and whether a humanitarian catastrophe would have occurred-perhaps over a number of years, rather than being concentrated within the 78 days of the NATO campaign-if intervention had not taken place. We have dealt with these issues elsewhere,[10] and concluded that the answer to both questions is "yes". That being the case, we conclude that NATO's military action, if of dubious legality in the current state of international law, was justified on moral grounds.

The Development of the Law

139. Professor Lowe told us that it was now much more important to develop international law so that actions such as Operation Allied Force would in future be legally acceptable.[11] Ideally, the international community should agree a treaty which would set out the conditions under which humanitarian intervention should be permissible. However, Professor Lowe believed that there was no likelihood of consensus on a treaty text on humanitarian intervention, but that the parameters for action set by NATO as expressed by the then Defence Secretary should become the basis of a new customary law principles. Mr Littman believed that Professor Lowe's view that there was no prospect of a new treaty text indicated that there was no consensus as to the principles of humanitarian intervention, and for that reason it could not be argued that a new custom of international law had arisen. In his view, "a custom can only exist by the general consent of mankind."[12] Professor Greenwood repudiated this argument, pointing to the past failure to agree on the definition of terrorism. He told us that "the fact that states are not prepared to agree on a form of words does not mean that they do not support the principle of humanitarian intervention."[13]

140. Professor Lowe set out his principles for humanitarian intervention as follows:[14]

" prior determination by the Security Council of a grave crisis, threatening international peace and security;

· articulation by the Security Council of specific policies for the resolution of the crisis, the implementation of which can be secured or furthered by armed intervention;

· an imminent humanitarian catastrophe which it is believed can be averted by the use of force and only by the use of force;

· intervention by a multinational force."

A considerable problem for these criteria is the involvement of the Security Council. As Mr Littman pointed out, if "the passing of the non-force resolution[15] would legally open the door to forceful intervention, the states which were opposed to the latter would veto the former."[16] It is certainly likely that China and Russia might not be prepared to allow the Security Council to determine that a country's internal problems were a threat to peace if they felt that a resolution to this effect gave a green light to the use of force somewhere down the line. Professor Lowe's desire to keep the Security Council involved[17] was shared by Professor Greenwood who told us that it was "obviously desirable, where possible" for the Security Council to take action.[18] But the dilemma remains of balancing the problem of potential Security Council paralysis with the danger of having too few hurdles to prevent states from asserting a right of intervention on specious humanitarian grounds. In a subsequent memorandum, Professor Lowe conceded that, if the use of the veto in the Security Council led to stalemate, "the possibility of proceeding on the basis of a similar determination made by a regional organisation might have to be considered."[19]

141. Alternative criteria were set out by Professor Chinkin.[20] These were that:

(i) a gross violation of human rights occurring in the targeted state
(ii) the UN is unable or unwilling to act
(iii) an overwhelming necessity to act

---

[1] When the United Kingdom accepted the compulsory jurisdiction of the International Court, one of the provisos which it made was that it did not accept jurisdiction "where the acceptance of the Court's compulsory jurisdiction on behalf of any other Party to the dispute was deposited or ratified less than twelve months prior to the filing of the application bringing the dispute before the Court."
[2] QC57.
[3] QC336.
[4] QC336.
[5] QC57.
[6] QC175.
[7] P. 6 of the European Journal of International Law (10) 1999.
[8] Ev. p. 288. She also argued (Ev. p. 286) that "if the UN is unwilling or unable to authorise action [when gross violation of human rights occur], there is a moral imperative for some other body to act in its place, preferably through collective action, and such action should not be deemed illegal."
[9] www.asil.org/kosovo.htm.
[10] See paras 122-3.

[11] QC317.
[12] QC369.
[13] QC369.
[14] Ev. pp.149-150.
[15] i.e. Professor Lowe's 'prior determination.
[16] QC316.
[17] QC324.
[18] QC321.
[19] Ev. p. 173.
[20] Ev. pp. 285-6.

(iv) the intervention must be proportionate

The Government is itself pursuing with the United Nations new principles to govern humanitarian intervention. This has been the subject of two important speeches by the Prime Minister-at the Economic Club of Chicago on 22 April 1999, and at the Guildhall on 22 November 1999.[1] Mr Hain, the Minister of State at the FCO, set the British proposals out for us as follows:

" first, any intervention is by definition a failure of prevention. Force should always be the last resort;

· second, the immediate responsibility for halting violence rests with the state in which it occurs;

· but, third, when faced with an immediate and overwhelming humanitarian catastrophe and a government that has demonstrated itself unwilling or unable to prevent it, the international community should take action;

· and finally, any use of force in this context must be collective, proportionate, likely to achieve its objective, and carried out in accordance with international law."[2]

142. We agree entirely with these principles, which contain many of the ideas advanced by Professors Lowe and Chinkin. However, the difficulty remains in the final phrase "carried out in accordance with international law." So far as it is an assertion that the norms such as the Geneva Conventions will be followed, it is not problematic, but this wording is presumably also intended to cover the legal basis on which the action is commenced. The implication is that, when the Security Council refuses to endorse an act of humanitarian intervention, that humanitarian intervention will rest on the very shaky basis of an evolving principle of customary international law which flies in the face of the plain words of the UN Charter. However, if there is no prospect of a new treaty text, then this will have to remain the fig leaf of legal respectability for actions which are generally thought to be morally entirely justified. As Professor Lowe put it in the case of Kosovo, the intervention took place because of "overwhelming moral imperatives and all the NATO states sought desperately to articulate the legal justification which would encapsulate that moral imperative."[3]

143. Of course, NATO's action in Kosovo is itself a precedent. As Professor Greenwood told us, customary international law develops through actions by states.[4] Professor Lowe pointed out[5] that "new rules of customary law emerge when a consistent practice is followed or acquiesced in by states in general", and that if NATO states assert that Operation Allied Force was the exercise of a legal right, "they help to lay the foundations of a legal rule that would entitle all states to act similarly in comparable situations". He amplified his view in a supplementary memorandum.[6] Mr Littman told us that the precedent was not valid because the Kosovo action was not regarded as lawful,[7] but in this view he appears to argue against the whole principle of evolving customary law.

144. The international community will not be obliged to intervene for humanitarian reasons even if it were legally possible for it to do so. As in the case of Rwanda, drawn to our attention by Professor Greenwood,[8] or Chechnya, it may choose not to do so for reasons of practicality or realpolitik. The Government's formulation of "likely to achieve its objective" would cover the case of Chechnya. It will certainly be important that strict criteria such as those set out by the Government are applied before any humanitarian intervention is deemed desirable. Mr Littman quoted[9] a FCO document of 1986 which argues against the right of humanitarian intervention "on prudential grounds" because "the scope for abusing such a right argues strongly against its creation." Professor Greenwood argued that this is not persuasive, because "all rights are capable of being abused."[10] Professor Lowe did not believe that "objective criteria can ever be used to establish without doubt that a particular instance of humanitarian intervention is justifiable", and he conceded that "the danger of abuse is evident."[11] Nevertheless, what will be important is that criteria are devised which would establish with as little doubt as possible when humanitarian intervention is justifiable and when it is not, and that these criteria must not be so flexible as to legitimise one state's intervention in another's internal affairs simply because of an assertion of humanitarian grounds for doing so. We support the FCO in its aim of establishing in the United Nations new principles governing humanitarian intervention. [...]

195. ICTY, Final Report to the Prosecutor by the Committee Established to Review the NATO Bombing Campaign Against the FRY, PR/P.I.S./510-E, 13 June 2000

I. Background and Mandate

1. The North Atlantic Treaty Organization (NATO) conducted a bombing campaign against the Federal Republic of Yugoslavia (FRY) from 24 March 1999 to 9 June 1999. During and since that period, the Prosecutor has received numerous requests that she investigate allegations that senior political and military figures from NATO countries committed serious violations of international humanitarian law during the campaign, and that she prepares indictments pursuant to Article 18(1) & (4) of the Statute.

2. Criticism of the NATO bombing campaign has included allegations of varying weight: a) that, as the resort to force was illegal, all NATO actions were illegal, and b) that the NATO forces deliberately attacked civilian infrastructure targets (and that such attacks were unlawful), deliberately or recklessly attacked the civilian population, and deliberately or recklessly caused excessive civilian casualties in disregard of the rule of proportionality by trying to fight a "zero casualty" war for their own side. Allegations concerning the "zero casualty" war involve suggestions that, for example, NATO aircraft operated at heights which enabled them to avoid attack by Yugoslav defences and, consequently, made it impossible for them to properly distinguish between military or civilian objects on the ground. Certain allegations went so far as to accuse NATO of crimes against humanity and genocide.

3. Article 18 of the Tribunal's Statute provides:

"The Prosecutor shall initiate investigations ex officio or on the basis of information obtained from any source, particularly from Governments, United Nations organs, intergovernmental and non-governmental organizations. The Prosecutor shall assess the information received or obtained and decide whether there is sufficient basis to proceed".

On 14 May 99 the then Prosecutor established a committee to assess the allegations and material accompanying them, and advise the Prosecutor and Deputy Prosecutor whether or not there is a sufficient basis to proceed with an investigation into some or all the allegations or into other incidents related to the NATO bombing.

4. In the course of its work, the committee has not addressed in detail the issue of the fundamental legality of the use of force by NATO members against the FRY as, if such activity was unlawful, it could constitute a crime against peace and the ICTY has no jurisdiction over this offence. (See, however, paras 30 - 34 below). It is noted that the legitimacy of the recourse to force by NATO is a subject before the International Court of Justice in a case brought by the FRY against various NATO countries.

---

1 Available at www.fco.gov.uk/news/speechtext.asp?2316 and www.fco.gov.uk/news/speechtext.asp?3026.
2 Ev. p. 171.
3 QC317.
4 QC311.
5 Ev. p. 149.
6 Ev. p. 172.
7 Ev. p. 166.
8 QC317.
9 Page 3 of Kosovo: Law and Diplomacy.
10 Ev. p. 140.
11 Ev. pp. 172-3.

II. Review Criteria

5. In the course of its review, the committee has applied the same criteria to NATO activities that the Office of the Prosecutor (OTP) has applied to the activities of other actors in the territory of the former Yugoslavia. The committee paid particular heed to the following questions:

a. Are the prohibitions alleged sufficiently well-established as violations of international humanitarian law to form the basis of a prosecution, and does the application of the law to the particular facts reasonably suggest that a violation of these prohibitions may have occurred? and

b. upon the reasoned evaluation of the information by the committee, is the information credible and does it tend to show that crimes within the jurisdiction of the Tribunal may have been committed by individuals during the NATO bombing campaign ?

This latter question reflects the earlier approach in relation to Article 18(1) of the Statute taken by the Prosecutor when asserting her right to investigate allegations of crimes committed by Serb forces in Kosovo (Request by the Prosecutor, Pursuant to Rule 7 bis) (B) that the President Notify the Security Council That the Federal Republic of Yugoslavia Has Failed to Comply With Its Obligations Under Article 29, dated 1 February 1999). The threshold test expressed therein by the Prosecutor was that of "credible evidence tending to show that crimes within the jurisdiction of the Tribunal may have been committed in Kosovo". That test was advanced to explain in what situation the Prosecutor would consider, for jurisdiction purposes, that she had a legal entitlement to investigate. (As a corollary, any investigation failing to meet that test could be said to be arbitrary and capricious, and to fall outside the Prosecutor's mandate). Thus formulated, the test represents a negative cut-off point for investigations. The Prosecutor may, in her discretion require that a higher threshold be met before making a positive decision that there is sufficient basis to proceed under Article 18(1). (In fact, in relation to the situation on the ground in Kosovo, the Prosecutor was in possession of a considerable body of evidence pointing to the commission of widespread atrocities by Serb forces.) In practice, before deciding to open an investigation in any case, the Prosecutor will also take into account a number of other factors concerning the prospects for obtaining evidence sufficient to prove that the crime has been committed by an individual who merits prosecution in the international forum.

III. Work Program

6. The committee has reviewed:

a. documents sent to the OTP by persons or groups wishing the OTP to commence investigations of leading persons from NATO countries,

b. public documents made available by NATO, the US Department of Defense and the British Ministry of Defence,

c. documents filed by the FRY before the ICJ, a large number of other FRY documents, and also the two volume compilation of the FRY Ministry of Foreign Affairs entitled NATO Crimes in Yugoslavia (White Book),

d. various documents submitted by Human Rights Watch including a letter sent to the Secretary General of NATO during the bombing campaign, a paper on NATO's Use of Cluster Munitions, and a report on Civilian Deaths in the NATO Air Campaign,

e. a UNEP study: The Kosovo Conflict: Consequence for the Environment and Human Settlements,

f. documents submitted by a Russian Parliamentary Commission,

g. two studies by a German national, Mr. Ekkehard Wenz, one concerning the bombing of a train at the Grdelica Gorge and the other concerning the bombing of the Djakovica Refugee Convoy,

h. various newspaper reports and legal articles as they have come to the attention of committee members,

i. the response to a letter containing a number of questions sent to NATO by the OTP, and

j. an Amnesty International Report entitled "Collateral Damage" or Unlawful Killings? Violations of the Laws of War by NATO during Operation Allied Force.

7. It should be noted that the committee did not travel to the FRY and it did not solicit information from the FRY through official channels as no such channels existed during the period when the review was conducted. Most of the material reviewed by the committee was in the public domain. The committee has relied exclusively on documents. The FRY submitted to the Prosecutor a substantial amount of material concerning particular incidents. In attempting to assess what happened on the ground, the committee relied upon the Human Rights Watch Report entitled Civilian Deaths in the NATO Air Campaign and upon the documented accounts in the FRY Ministry of Foreign Affairs volumes entitled NATO Crimes in Yugoslavia. The committee also relied heavily on NATO press statements and on the studies done by Mr. Ekkehard Wenz. The information available was adequate for making a preliminary assessment of incidents in which civilians were killed or injured. Information related to attacks on objects where civilians were not killed or injured was difficult to obtain and very little usable information was obtained.

8. To assist in the preparation of an Interim Report, a member of the Military Analysis Team reviewed the documents available in the OTP at the time, that is, all those referred to in paragraph 6 above except the FRY volumes entitled NATO Crimes in Yugoslavia, the HRW report on Civilian Deaths in the NATO Air Campaign, the studies by Mr. Wenz, NATO's response to the letter sent by the OTP to NATO, and the Amnesty International Report. The analyst prepared: a) a list of key incidents, b) a list of civilian residential targets, c) a list of civilian facility targets, d) a list of cultural property targets, e) a list of power facility targets, f) a list of targets the destruction of which might significantly affect the environment, and g) a list of communications targets. Very little information was available concerning the targets in lists (b) through (g).

9. The committee reviewed the above lists and requested the preparation of a file containing all available information on certain particular incidents, and on certain target categories. (It should be noted that the use of the terms "target" or "attack" in this report does not mean that in every case the site in question was deliberately struck by NATO. The terms are convenient shorthand for incidents in which it is alleged that particular locations were damaged in the course of the bombing campaign).

The key incidents and target categories were:

a. the attack on a civilian passenger train at the Grdelica Gorge - 12/4/99 - 10 or more civilians killed, 15 or more injured,

b. the attack on the Djakovica Convoy - 14/4/99 - 70-75 civilians killed, 100 or more injured,

c. the attack on Surdulica, - 27/4/99 - 11 civilians killed, 100 or more injured,

d. the attack on Cuprija - 8/4/99 - 1 civilian killed, 5 injured,

e. the attack on the Cigota Medical Institute - 8/4/99 - 3 civilians killed,

f. the attack on Hotels Baciste and Putnik - 13/4/99 - 1 civilian killed,

g. the attacks on the Pancevo Petrochemical Complex and Fertilizer Company - 15/4/99 and 18/4/99 - no reported civilian casualties,

h. the attack on the Nis Tobbaco Factory - 18/4/99 - no reported civilian casualties,

i. the attack on the Djakovica Refugee Camp - 21/4/99 - 5 civilians killed, 16-19 injured,

j. the attack on a bus at Lu`ane - 1/5/99 39 civilians killed,

k. the attack on a bus at Pec - 3/5/99 - 17 civilians killed, 44 injured,

l. the attack at Korisa village - 13/5/99 - 48-87 civilians killed,

m. the attack on the Belgrade TV and Radio Station - 23/4/99 - 16 civilians killed,

n. the attack on the Chinese Embassy in Belgrade - 7/5/99 - 3 civilians killed, 15 injured,

o. attack on Nis City Centre and Hospital - 7/5/99 - 13 civilians killed, 60 injured,

p. attack on Istok Prison - 21/5/99 - at least 19 civilians killed,

q. attack on Belgrade Hospital - 20/5/99 - 3 civilians killed, several injured,

r. attack on Surdulica Sanatorium - 30/5/99 - 23 killed, many injured,

s. attack on journalists convoy Prizren-Brezovica Road - 31/5/99 - 1 civilian killed - 3 injured

t. attack on Belgrade Heating Plant - 4/4/99, - 1 killed,

u. attacks on Trade and Industry Targets.

10. On 23 July 1999, each committee member was provided with a binder including all available material. The committee members reviewed material in the binders.

11. In addition to reviewing factual information, the committee has also gathered legal materials and reviewed relevant legal issues, including the legality of the use of depleted uranium projectiles, the legality of the use of cluster munitions, whether or not the bombing campaign had an unlawfully adverse impact on the environment, and legal issues related to target selection.

12. The committee prepared an interim report on the basis of its analysis of the legal and factual material available and this was presented to the Prosecutor on 6 December 1999. At the direction of the Prosecutor, the committee then further updated the incident list and prepared a list of general questions and questions related to specific incidents. A letter enclosing the questionnaire and incident list was sent to NATO on 8 February 2000. A general reply was received on 10 May 2000.

13. It has not been possible for the committee to look at the NATO bombing campaign on a bomb by bomb basis and that was not its task. The committee has, however, reviewed public information concerning several incidents, including all the more well known incidents, with considerable care. It has also endeavored to examine, and has posed questions to NATO, concerning all other incidents in which it appears three or more civilians were killed.

In conducting its review, the committee has focused primarily on incidents in which civilian deaths were alleged and/or confirmed. The committee reviewed certain key incidents in depth for its interim report. These key incidents included 10 incidents in which 10 or more civilians were killed. The review by Human Rights Watch revealed 12 incidents in which 10 or more civilians were killed, all of the incidents identified by the committee plus two additional incidents: a) the attack on the Aleksinak "Deligrad" military barracks on 5/5/99 in which 10 civilians were killed and 30 wounded (a bomb aimed at the barracks fell short), and b) the attack on a military barracks in Novi Pazar on 31/5/99 in which 11 civilians were killed and 23 wounded (5 out of 6 munitions hit the target but one went astray). The committee's review of incidents in which it is alleged fewer than three civilians were killed has been hampered by a lack of reliable information.

IV. Assessment
A. GENERAL ISSUES
i. Damage to the Environment

14. The NATO bombing campaign did cause some damage to the environment. For instance, attacks on industrial facilities such as chemical plants and oil installations were reported to have caused the release of pollutants, although the exact extent of this is presently unknown. The basic legal provisions applicable to protection of the environment in armed conflict are Article 35(3) of Additional Protocol I, which states that '[i]t is prohibited to employ methods or means of warfare which are intended, or may be expected, to cause widespread, long-term and severe damage to the natural environment' and Article 55 which states:

1. Care shall be taken in warfare to protect the natural environment against widespread, long-term and severe damage. This protection includes a prohibition of the use of methods or means of warfare which are intended or may be expected to cause such damage to the natural environment and thereby to prejudice the health or survival of the population.

2. Attacks against the natural environment by way of reprisals are prohibited

15. Neither the USA nor France has ratified Additional Protocol I. Article 55 may, nevertheless, reflect current customary law (see however the 1996 Advisory Opinion on the Legality of Nuclear Weapons, where the International Court of Justice appeared to suggest that it does not (ICJ Rep. (1996), 242, para. 31)). In any case, Articles 35(3) and 55 have a very high threshold of application. Their conditions for application are extremely stringent and their scope and contents imprecise. For instance, it is generally assumed that Articles 35(3) and 55 only cover very significant damage. The adjectives 'widespread, long-term, and severe' used in Additional Protocol I are joined by the word 'and', meaning that it is a triple, cumulative standard that needs to be fulfilled.

Consequently, it would appear extremely difficult to develop a prima facie case upon the basis of these provisions, even assuming they were applicable. For instance, it is thought that the notion of 'long-term' damage in Additional Protocol I would need to be measured in years rather than months, and that as such, ordinary battlefield damage of the kind caused to France in World War I would not be covered.

The great difficulty of assessing whether environmental damage exceeded the threshold of Additional Protocol I has also led to criticism by ecologists. This may partly explain the disagreement as to whether any of the damage caused by the oil spills and fires in the 1990/91 Gulf War technically crossed the threshold of Additional Protocol I.

It is the committee's view that similar difficulties would exist in applying Additional Protocol I to the present facts, even if reliable environmental assessments were to give rise to legitimate concern concerning the impact of the NATO bombing campaign. Accordingly, these effects are best considered from the underlying principles of the law of armed conflict such as necessity and proportionality.

16. The conclusions of the Balkan Task Force (BTF) established by UNEP to look into the Kosovo situation are:

"Our findings indicate that the Kosovo conflict has not caused an environmental catastrophe affecting the Balkans region as a whole.

Nevertheless, pollution detected at some sites is serious and poses a threat to human health.

BTF was able to identify environmental 'hot spots', namely in Pancevo, Kragujevac, Novi Sad and Bor, where immediate action and also further monitoring and analyses will be necessary. At all of these sites, environmental contamination due to the consequences of the Kosovo conflict was identified.

Part of the contamination identified at some sites clearly pre-dates the Kosovo conflict, and there is evidence of long-term deficiencies in the treatment and storage of hazardous waste.

The problems identified require immediate attention, irrespective of their cause, if further damage to human health and the environment is to be avoided."

17. The OTP has been hampered in its assessment of the extent of environmental damage in Kosovo by a lack of alternative and corroborated sources regarding the extent of environmental contamination caused by the NATO bombing campaign. Moreover, it is quite possible that, as this campaign occurred only a year ago, the UNEP study may not be a reliable indicator of the long term environmental consequences of the NATO bombing, as accurate assessments regarding the long-term effects of this contamination may not yet be practicable.

It is the opinion of the committee, on the basis of information currently in its possession, that the environmental damage caused during the NATO bombing campaign does not reach the Additional Protocol I threshold. In addition, the UNEP Report also suggests that much of the environmental contamination which is discernible cannot unambiguously be attributed to the NATO bombing.

18. The alleged environmental effects of the NATO bombing campaign flow in many cases from NATO's striking of legitimate military targets compatible with Article 52 of Additional Protocol I such as stores of fuel, industries of fundamental importance for the conduct of

war and for the manufacture of supplies and material of a military character, factories or plant and manufacturing centres of fundamental importance for the conduct of war. Even when targeting admittedly legitimate military objectives, there is a need to avoid excessive long-term damage to the economic infrastructure and natural environment with a consequential adverse effect on the civilian population. Indeed, military objectives should not be targeted if the attack is likely to cause collateral environmental damage which would be excessive in relation to the direct military advantage which the attack is expected to produce (A.P.V. Rogers, "Zero Casualty Warfare," IRRC, March 2000, Vol. 82, pp. 177-8).

19. It is difficult to assess the relative values to be assigned to the military advantage gained and harm to the natural environment, and the application of the principle of proportionality is more easily stated than applied in practice. In applying this principle, it is necessary to assess the importance of the target in relation to the incidental damage expected: if the target is sufficiently important, a greater degree of risk to the environment may be justified.

20. The adverse effect of the coalition air campaign in the Gulf war upon the civilian infrastructure prompted concern on the part of some experts regarding the notion of "military objective." This has prompted some experts to argue that where the presumptive effect of hostilities upon the civilian infrastructure (and consequently the civilian population) is grave, the military advantage conferred by the destruction of the military objective would need to be decisive (see below, paras. 40-41). Similar considerations would, in the committee's view, be warranted where the grave threat to the civilian infrastructure emanated instead from excessive environmental harm resulting from the hostilities. The critical question is what kind of environmental damage can be considered to be excessive. Unfortunately, the customary rule of proportionality does not include any concrete guidelines to this effect.

21. The military worth of the target would need to be considered in relation to the circumstances prevailing at the time. If there is a choice of weapons or methods of attack available, a commander should select those which are most likely to avoid, or at least minimize, incidental damage. In doing so, however, he is entitled to take account of factors such as stocks of different weapons and likely future demands, the timeliness of attack and risks to his own forces (A.P.V. Rogers, ibid, at p. 178). Operational reality is recognized in the Statute of the International Criminal Court, an authoritative indicator of evolving customary international law on this point, where Article 8(b)(iv) makes the infliction of incidental environmental damage an offence only if the attack is launched intentionally in the knowledge that it will cause widespread, long-term and severe damage to the natural environment which would be clearly excessive in relation to the concrete and direct overall military advantage anticipated. The use of the word "clearly" ensures that criminal responsibility would be entailed only in cases where the excessiveness of the incidental damage was obvious.

22. Taken together, this suggests that in order to satisfy the requirement of proportionality, attacks against military targets which are known or can reasonably be assumed to cause grave environmental harm may need to confer a very substantial military advantage in order to be considered legitimate. At a minimum, actions resulting in massive environmental destruction, especially where they do not serve a clear and important military purpose, would be questionable. The targeting by NATO of Serbian petro-chemical industries may well have served a clear and important military purpose.

23. The above considerations also suggest that the requisite mens rea on the part of a commander would be actual or constructive knowledge as to the grave environmental effects of a military attack; a standard which would be difficult to establish for the purposes of prosecution and which may provide an insufficient basis to prosecute military commanders inflicting environmental harm in the (mistaken) belief that such conduct was warranted by military necessity. (In the Hostages case before the Nuremberg Military Tribunals, for instance, the German General Rendulic was acquitted of the charge of wanton devastation on the grounds that although Rendulic may have erred in believing that there was military necessity for the widespread environmental destruction entailed by his use of a 'scorched earth' policy in the Norwegian province of Finnmark, he was not guilty of a criminal act (11 Trials of War Criminals, (1950), 1296)). In addition, the notion of 'excessive' environmental destruction is imprecise and the actual environmental impact, both present and long term, of the NATO bombing campaign is at present unknown and difficult to measure.

24. In order to fully evaluate such matters, it would be necessary to know the extent of the knowledge possessed by NATO as to the nature of Serbian military-industrial targets (and thus, the likelihood of environmental damage flowing from their destruction), the extent to which NATO could reasonably have anticipated such environmental damage (for instance, could NATO have reasonably expected that toxic chemicals of the sort allegedly released into the environment by the bombing campaign would be stored alongside that military target?) and whether NATO could reasonably have resorted to other (and less environmentally damaging) methods for achieving its military objective of disabling the Serbian military-industrial infrastructure.

25. It is therefore the opinion of the committee, based on information currently available to it, that the OTP should not commence an investigation into the collateral environmental damage caused by the NATO bombing campaign.

ii. Use of Depleted Uranium Projectiles

26. There is evidence of use of depleted uranium (DU) projectiles by NATO aircraft during the bombing campaign. There is no specific treaty ban on the use of DU projectiles. There is a developing scientific debate and concern expressed regarding the impact of the use of such projectiles and it is possible that, in future, there will be a consensus view in international legal circles that use of such projectiles violate general principles of the law applicable to use of weapons in armed conflict. No such consensus exists at present. Indeed, even in the case of nuclear warheads and other weapons of mass-destruction - those which are universally acknowledged to have the most deleterious environmental consequences - it is difficult to argue that the prohibition of their use is in all cases absolute. (Legality of Nuclear Weapons, ICJ Rep. (1996), 242). In view of the uncertain state of development of the legal standards governing this area, it should be emphasised that the use of depleted uranium or other potentially hazardous substance by any adversary to conflicts within the former Yugoslavia since 1991 has not formed the basis of any charge laid by the Prosecutor. It is acknowledged that the underlying principles of the law of armed conflict such as proportionality are applicable also in this context; however, it is the committee's view that analysis undertaken above (paras. 14-25) with regard to environmental damage would apply, mutatis mutandis, to the use of depleted uranium projectiles by NATO. It is therefore the opinion of the committee, based on information available at present, that the OTP should not commence an investigation into use of depleted uranium projectiles by NATO.

iii. Use of Cluster Bombs

27. Cluster bombs were used by NATO forces during the bombing campaign. There is no specific treaty provision which prohibits or restricts the use of cluster bombs although, of course, cluster bombs must be used in compliance with the general principles applicable to the use of all weapons. Human Rights Watch has condemned the use of cluster bombs alleging that the high "dud" or failure rate of the submunitions (bomblets) contained inside cluster bombs converts these submunitions into antipersonnel landmines which, it asserts, are now prohibited under customary international law. Whether antipersonnel landmines are prohibited under current customary law is debatable, although there is a strong trend in that direction. There is, however, no general legal consensus that cluster bombs are, in legal terms, equivalent to antipersonnel landmines. It should be noted that the use of cluster bombs was an issue of sorts in the Martic Rule 61 Hearing Decision of Trial Chamber I on 8 March 1996. In that decision the Chamber stated there was no formal provision forbidding the use of cluster bombs as such (para. 18 of judgment) but it regarded the use of the Orkan rocket with a cluster bomb warhead in that particular case as

evidence of the intent of the accused to deliberately attack the civilian population because the rocket was inaccurate, it landed in an area with no military objectives nearby, it was used as an antipersonnel weapon launched against the city of Zagreb and the accused indicated he intended to attack the city as such (paras. 23-31 of judgment). The Chamber concluded that "the use of the Orkan rocket in this case was not designed to hit military targets but to terrorise the civilians of Zagreb" (para. 31 of judgment). There is no indication cluster bombs were used in such a fashion by NATO. It is the opinion of the committee, based on information presently available, that the OTP should not commence an investigation into use of cluster bombs as such by NATO.

iv. Legal Issues Related to Target Selection
a. Overview of Applicable Law

28. In brief, in combat military commanders are required: a) to direct their operations against military objectives, and b) when directing their operations against military objectives, to ensure that the losses to the civilian population and the damage to civilian property are not disproportionate to the concrete and direct military advantage anticipated. Attacks which are not directed against military objectives (particularly attacks directed against the civilian population) and attacks which cause disproportionate civilian casualties or civilian property damage may constitute the actus reus for the offence of unlawful attack under Article 3 of the ICTY Statute. The mens rea for the offence is intention or recklessness, not simple negligence. In determining whether or not the mens rea requirement has been met, it should be borne in mind that commanders deciding on an attack have duties:

a) to do everything practicable to verify that the objectives to be attacked are military objectives,

b) to take all practicable precautions in the choice of methods and means of warfare with a view to avoiding or, in any event to minimizing incidental civilian casualties or civilian property damage, and

c) to refrain from launching attacks which may be expected to cause disproportionate civilian casualties or civilian property damage.

29. One of the principles underlying international humanitarian law is the principle of distinction, which obligates military commanders to distinguish between military objectives and civilian persons or objects. The practical application of this principle is effectively encapsulated in Article 57 of Additional Protocol which, in part, obligates those who plan or decide upon an attack to "do everything feasible to verify that the objectives to be attacked are neither civilians nor civilian objects". The obligation to do everything feasible is high but not absolute. A military commander must set up an effective intelligence gathering system to collect and evaluate information concerning potential targets. The commander must also direct his forces to use available technical means to properly identify targets during operations. Both the commander and the aircrew actually engaged in operations must have some range of discretion to determine which available resources shall be used and how they shall be used. Further, a determination that inadequate efforts have been made to distinguish between military objectives and civilians or civilian objects should not necessarily focus exclusively on a specific incident. If precautionary measures have worked adequately in a very high percentage of cases then the fact they have not worked well in a small number of cases does not necessarily mean they are generally inadequate.

b. Linkage Between Law Concerning Recourse to Force and Law Concerning How Force May Be Used

30. Allegations have been made that, as NATO's resort to force was not authorized by the Security Council or in self-defence, that the resort to force was illegal and, consequently, all forceful measures taken by NATO were unlawful. These allegations justify a brief discussion of the jus ad bellum. In brief, the jus ad bellum regulates when states may use force and is, for the most part, enshrined in the UN Charter. In general, states may use force in self defence (individual or collective) and for very few other purposes. In particular, the legitimacy of the presumed basis for the NATO bombing campaign, humanitarian intervention without prior Security Council authorization, is hotly debated. That being said, as noted in paragraph 4 above, the crime related to an unlawful decision to use force is the crime against peace or aggression. While a person convicted of a crime against peace may, potentially, be held criminally responsible for all of the activities causing death, injury or destruction during a conflict, the ICTY does not have jurisdiction over crimes against peace.

31. The jus in bello regulates how states may use force. The ICTY has jurisdiction over serious violations of international humanitarian law as specified in Articles 2-5 of the Statute. These are jus in bello offences.

32. The precise linkage between jus ad bellum and jus in bello is not completely resolved. There were suggestions by the prosecution before the International Military Tribunal at Nuremberg and in some other post World War II war crimes cases that all of the killing and destruction caused by German forces were war crimes because the Germans were conducting an aggressive war. The courts were unreceptive to these arguments. Similarly, in the 1950's there was a debate concerning whether UN authorized forces were required to comply with the jus in bello as they represented the good side in a battle between good an evil. This debate died out as the participants realized that a certain crude reciprocity was essential if the law was to have any positive impact. An argument that the "bad" side had to comply with the law while the "good" side could violate it at will would be most unlikely to reduce human suffering in conflict.

33. More recently, a refined approach to the linkage issue has been advocated by certain law of war scholars. Using their approach, assuming that the only lawful basis for recourse to force is self defence, each use of force during a conflict must be measured by whether or not it complies with the jus in bello and by whether or not it complies with the necessity and proportionality requirements of self defence. The difficulty with this approach is that it does not adequately address what should be done when it is unclear who is acting in self defence and it does not clarify the obligations of the "bad" side.

34. As a matter of practice, which we consider to be in accord with the most widely accepted and reputable legal opinion, we in the OTP have deliberately refrained from assessing jus ad bellum issues in our work and focused exclusively on whether or not individuals have committed serious violations of international humanitarian law as assessed within the confines of the jus in bello.

c. The Military Objective

35. The most widely accepted definition of "military objective" is that in Article 52 of Additional Protocol I which states in part:

In so far as objects are concerned, military objectives are limited to those objects which by their nature, location, purpose or use make an effective contribution to military action and whose total or partial destruction, capture or neutralization, in the circumstances ruling at the time, offers a definite military advantage.

36. Where objects are concerned, the definition has two elements: (a) their nature, location, purpose or use must make an effective contribution to military action, and (b) their total or partial destruction, capture or neutralization must offer a definite military advantage in the circumstances ruling at the time. Although this definition does not refer to persons, in general, members of the armed forces are considered combatants, who have the right to participate directly in hostilities, and as a corollary, may also be attacked.

37. The definition is supposed to provide a means whereby informed objective observers (and decision makers in a conflict) can determine whether or not a particular object constitutes a military objective. It accomplishes this purpose in simple cases. Everyone will agree that a munitions factory is a military objective and an unoccupied church is a civilian object. When the definition is applied to dual-use objects which have some civilian uses and some actual or potential military use (communications systems, transportation systems, petrochemical complexes, manufacturing plants of some types), opinions may differ. The application of the definition to particular objects may also differ

depending on the scope and objectives of the conflict. Further, the scope and objectives of the conflict may change during the conflict.

38. Using the Protocol I definition and his own review of state practice, Major General A.P.V. Rogers, a former Director of British Army Legal Services has advanced a tentative list of military objectives:

military personnel and persons who take part in the fighting without being members of the armed forces, military facilities, military equipment, including military vehicles, weapons, munitions and stores of fuel, military works, including defensive works and fortifications, military depots and establishments, including War and Supply Ministries, works producing or developing military supplies and other supplies of military value, including metallurgical, engineering and chemical industries supporting the war effort; areas of land of military significance such as hills, defiles and bridgeheads; railways, ports, airfields, bridges, main roads as well as tunnels and canals; oil and other power installations; communications installations, including broadcasting and television stations and telephone and telegraph stations used for military communications. (Rogers, Law on the Battlefield (1996) 37)

The list was not intended to be exhaustive. It remains a requirement that both elements of the definition must be met before a target can be properly considered an appropriate military objective.

39. In 1956, the International Committee of the Red Cross (ICRC) drew up the following proposed list of categories of military objectives:

I. The objectives belonging to the following categories are those considered to be of generally recognized military importance:

(1) Armed forces, including auxiliary or complementary organisations, and persons who, though not belonging to the above-mentioned formations, nevertheless take part in the fighting.

(2) Positions, installations or constructions occupied by the forces indicated in sub-paragraph 1 above, as well as combat objectives (that is to say, those objectives which are directly contested in battle between land or sea forces including airborne forces).

(3) Installations, constructions and other works of a military nature, such as barracks, fortifications, War Ministries (e.g. Ministries of Army, Navy, Air Force, National Defence, Supply) and other organs for the direction and administration of military operations.

(4) Stores of army or military supplies, such as munition dumps, stores of equipment or fuel, vehicles parks.

(5) Airfields, rocket launching ramps and naval base installations.

(6) Those of the lines and means of communications (railway lines, roads, bridges, tunnels and canals) which are of fundamental military importance.

(7) The installations of broadcasting and television stations; telephone and telegraph exchanges of fundamental military importance.

(8) Industries of fundamental importance for the conduct of the war:

(a) industries for the manufacture of armaments such as weapons, munitions, rockets, armoured vehicles, military aircraft, fighting ships, including the manufacture of accessories and all other war material;

(b) industries for the manufacture of supplies and material of a military character, such as transport and communications material, equipment of the armed forces;

(c) factories or plant constituting other production and manufacturing centres of fundamental importance for the conduct of war, such as the metallurgical, engineering and chemical industries, whose nature or purpose is essentially military;

(d) storage and transport installations whose basic function it is to serve the industries referred to in (a)-(c);

(e) installations providing energy mainly for national defence, e.g. coal, other fuels, or atomic energy, and plants producing gas or electricity mainly for military consumption.

(9) Installations constituting experimental, research centres for experiments on and the development of weapons and war material.

II. The following however, are excepted from the foregoing list:

(1) Persons, constructions, installations or transports which are protected under the Geneva Conventions I, II, III, of August 12, 1949;

(2) Non-combatants in the armed forces who obviously take no active or direct part in hostilities.

III. The above list will be reviewed at intervals of not more than ten years by a group of Experts composed of persons with a sound grasp of military strategy and of others concerned with the protection of the civilian population.

(Y. Sandoz, C. Swiniarski, B. Zimmerman, eds., Commentary on the Additional Protocols of 8 June 1977 to the Geneva Conventions of 12 August 1949 (1987) at 632-633.

40. The Protocol I definition of military objective has been criticized by W. Hays Parks, the Special Assistant for Law of War Matters to the U.S. Army Judge Advocate General as being focused too narrowly on definite military advantage and paying too little heed to war sustaining capability, including economic targets such as export industries. (W. Hays Parks, "Air War and the Law of War," 32 A.F.L. Rev. 1, 135-45 (1990)). On the other hand, some critics of Coalition conduct in the Gulf War have suggested that the Coalition air campaign, directed admittedly against legitimate military objectives within the scope of the Protocol I definition, caused excessive long-term damage to the Iraqi economic infrastructure with a consequential adverse effect on the civilian population. (Middle East Watch, Needless Deaths in the Gulf War: Civilian Casualties during the Air Campaign and Violations of the Laws of War (1991); Judith G. Gardam, "Proportionality and Force in International Law," 87 Am. J. Int'l L. 391, 404-10 (1993)).

41. This criticism has not gone unexplored. Françoise Hampson, a British scholar, has suggested a possible refinement of the definition:

In order to determine whether there is a real subject of concern here, it would be necessary to establish exactly what the effect has been of the damage to the civilian infrastructure brought about by the hostilities. If that points to a need further to refine the law, it is submitted that what is needed is a qualification to the definition of military objectives. Either it should require the likely cumulative effect on the civilian population of attacks against such targets to be taken into account, or the same result might be achieved by requiring that the destruction of the object offer a definite military advantage in the context of the war aim. Françoise Hampson, "Means and Methods of Warfare in the Conflict in the Gulf," in P. Rowe, ed., The Gulf War 1990-91 in International and English Law 89 (1983) 100.

42. Although the Protocol I definition of military objective is not beyond criticism, it provides the contemporary standard which must be used when attempting to determine the lawfulness of particular attacks. That being said, it must be noted once again neither the USA nor France is a party to Additional Protocol I. The definition is, however, generally accepted as part of customary law.

43. To put the NATO campaign in context, it is instructive to look briefly at the approach to the military objective concept in history of air warfare. The Protocol I standard was not applicable during World War II. The bomber offensives conducted during that war were conducted with technological means which rendered attacks on targets occupying small areas almost impossible. In general, depending upon the period in the conflict, bomber attacks could be relied upon, at best, to strike within 5 miles, 2 miles or 1 mile of the designated target. The mission for the US/UK Combined Bomber Offensive from the UK was:

"To conduct a joint United States-British air offensive to accomplish the progressive destruction and dislocation of the German military, industrial and economic system, and the undermining of the morale of the German people to a point where their capacity for armed resistance is fatally weakened. This is construed as meaning so weakened as to permit initiation of final combined operations on the Continent."

(A. Verrier, The Bomber Offensive (1968) 330).

The principal specific objectives of the offensive were designated as:

"Submarine construction yards and bases, German aircraft industry, Ball bearings, Oil, Synthetic rubber and tires, Military transport vehicles."[1]

Notwithstanding the designation of specific targets and the attempt, at least by US Army Air Force commanders on occasion, to conduct a precision bombing campaign, for the most part World War II bombing campaigns were aimed at area targets and intended, directly or indirectly, to affect the morale of the enemy civilian population. It is difficult to describe the fire bombing of Hamburg, Dresden and Tokyo as anything other than attacks intended to kill, terrorize or demoralize civilians. Whether or not these attacks could be justified legally in the total war context of the time, they would be unlawful if they were required to comply with Protocol I.

44. Technology, law, and the public consensus of what was acceptable, at least in demonstrably limited conflicts, had evolved by the time of the 1990-91 Gulf Conflict. Technological developments, such as precision guided munitions, and the rapid acquisition of control of the aerospace by coalition air forces significantly enhanced the precision with which targets could be attacked.

Target sets used during the Gulf Conflict were:

"Leadership; Command, Control, and Communications; Strategic Air Defenses; Airfields; Nuclear, Biological, and Chemical Research and Production; Naval Forces and Port Facilities; Military Storage and Production; Railroads and Bridges, Electrical Power; and Oil Refining and Distribution Facilities. Schwarzkopf added the Republican Guard as a category and Scuds soon emerged as a separate target set. After the beginning of Desert Storm, two more categories appeared: fixed surface-to-air missile sites in the KTO and breaching sites for the ground offensive."

(W. Murray, Air War in the Persian Gulf (1995) 32)

45. In the words of the Cohen, Shelton Joint Statement on Kosovo given to the US Senate:

"At the outset of the air campaign, NATO set specific strategic objectives for its use of force in Kosovo that later served as the basis for its stated conditions to Milosevic for stopping the bombing. These objectives were to:

-- Demonstrate the seriousness of NATO's opposition to Belgrade's aggression in the Balkans;

-- Deter Milosevic from continuing and escalating his attacks on helpless civilians and create conditions to reverse his ethnic cleansing; and

-- Damage Serbia's capacity to wage war against Kosovo in the future or spread the war to neighbors by diminishing or degrading its ability to wage military operations...

Phases of the Campaign. Operation Allied Force was originally planned to be prosecuted in five phases under NATO's operational plan, the development of which began in the summer of 1998. Phase 0 was the deployment of air assets into the European theater. Phase 1 would establish air superiority over Kosovo and degrade command and control over the whole of the FRY. Phase 2 would attack military targets in Kosovo and those FRY forces south of 44 degrees north latitude, which were providing reinforcement to Serbian forces into Kosovo. This was to allow targeting of forces not only in Kosovo, but also in the FRY south of Belgrade. Phase 3 would expand air operations against a wide range of high-value military and security force targets throughout the FRY. Phase 4 would redeploy forces as required. A limited air response relying predominantly on cruise missiles to strike selected targets throughout the Phase 1. Within a few days of the start of NATO's campaign, alliance aircraft were striking both strategic and tactical targets throughout Serbia, as well as working to suppress and disrupt the FRY's integrated air defence system.

At the NATO Summit in Washington on April 23, 1999, alliance leaders decided to further intensify the air campaign by expanding the target set to include military-industrial infrastructure, media, and other strategic targets ...."

46. The NATO Internet Report Kosovo One Year On (http://www.nato.int/kosovo/repo 2000, 21 Mar 00) described the targets as:

"The air campaign set out to weaken Serb military capabilities, both strategically and tactically. Strikes on tactical targets, such as artillery and field headquarters, had a more immediate effect in disrupting the ethnic cleansing of Kosovo. Strikes against strategic targets, such as government ministries and refineries, had long term and broader impact on the Serb military machine.

The bulk of NATO's effort against tactical targets was aimed at military facilities, fielded forces, heavy weapons, and military vehicles and formations in Kosovo and southern Serbia...

Strategic targets included Serb air defences, command and control facilities, Yugoslav military (VJ) and police (MUP) forces headquarters, and supply routes".

47. Most of the targets referred to in the quotations above are clearly military objectives. The precise scope of "military-industrial infrastructure, media and other strategic targets" as referred to in the US statement and "government ministries and refineries" as referred to in the NATO statement is unclear. Whether the media constitutes a legitimate target group is a debatable issue. If the media is used to incite crimes, as in Rwanda, then it is a legitimate target. If it is merely disseminating propaganda to generate support for the war effort, it is not a legitimate target.

d. *The Principle of Proportionality*

48. The main problem with the principle of proportionality is not whether or not it exists but what it means and how it is to be applied. It is relatively simple to state that there must be an acceptable relation between the legitimate destructive effect and undesirable collateral effects. For example, bombing a refugee camp is obviously prohibited if its only military significance is that people in the camp are knitting socks for soldiers. Conversely, an air strike on an ammunition dump should not be prohibited merely because a farmer is plowing a field in the area. Unfortunately, most applications of the principle of proportionality are not quite so clear cut. It is much easier to formulate the principle of proportionality in general terms than it is to apply it to a particular set of circumstances because the comparison is often between unlike quantities and values. One cannot easily assess the value of innocent human lives as opposed to capturing a particular military objective.

49. The questions which remain unresolved once one decides to apply the principle of proportionality include the following:

a) What are the relative values to be assigned to the military advantage gained and the injury to non-combatants and or the damage to civilian objects?

b) What do you include or exclude in totaling your sums?

c) What is the standard of measurement in time or space? and

d) To what extent is a military commander obligated to expose his own forces to danger in order to limit civilian casualties or damage to civilian objects?

50. The answers to these questions are not simple. It may be necessary to resolve them on a case by case basis, and the answers may differ depending on the background and values of the decision maker. It is unlikely that a human rights lawyer and an experienced combat commander would assign the same relative values to military advantage and to injury to noncombatants. Further, it is unlikely that military commanders with different doctrinal backgrounds and differing degrees of combat experience or national military histories would always agree in close cases. It is suggested that the determination of relative values must be that of the "reasonable military commander". Although there will be room for argument in close cases, there will be many cases where reasonable military commanders will agree that the injury to noncombatants or the damage to civilian objects was clearly disproportionate to the military advantage gained.

---

[1] A. Verrier, ibid, at 330.

51. Much of the material submitted to the OTP consisted of reports that civilians had been killed, often inviting the conclusion to be drawn that crimes had therefore been committed. Collateral casualties to civilians and collateral damage to civilian objects can occur for a variety of reasons. Despite an obligation to avoid locating military objectives within or near densely populated areas, to remove civilians from the vicinity of military objectives, and to protect their civilians from the dangers of military operations, very little prevention may be feasible in many cases. Today's technological society has given rise to many dual use facilities and resources. City planners rarely pay heed to the possibility of future warfare. Military objectives are often located in densely populated areas and fighting occasionally occurs in such areas. Civilians present within or near military objectives must, however, be taken into account in the proportionality equation even if a party to the conflict has failed to exercise its obligation to remove them.

52. In the Kupreskic Judgment (Case No: IT-95-16-T 14 Jan 2000) the Trial Chamber addressed the issue of proportionality as follows:

"526. As an example of the way in which the Martens clause may be utilised, regard might be had to considerations such as the cumulative effect of attacks on military objectives causing incidental damage to civilians. In other words, it may happen that single attacks on military objectives causing incidental damage to civilians, although they may raise doubts as to their lawfulness, nevertheless do not appear on their face to fall foul per se of the loose prescriptions of Articles 57 and 58 (or of the corresponding customary rules). However, in case of repeated attacks, all or most of them falling within the grey area between indisputable legality and unlawfulness, it might be warranted to conclude that the cumulative effect of such acts entails that they may not be in keeping with international law. Indeed, this pattern of military conduct may turn out to jeopardise excessively the lives and assets of civilians, contrary to the demands of humanity."

This formulation in Kupreskic can be regarded as a progressive statement of the applicable law with regard to the obligation to protect civilians. Its practical import, however, is somewhat ambiguous and its application far from clear. It is the committee's view that where individual (and legitimate) attacks on military objectives are concerned, the mere cumulation of such instances, all of which are deemed to have been lawful, cannot ipso facto be said to amount to a crime. The committee understands the above formulation, instead, to refer to an overall assessment of the totality of civilian victims as against the goals of the military campaign.

v. Casualty Figures

53. In its report, Civilian Deaths in the NATO Air Campaign, Human Rights Watch documented some 500 civilian deaths in 90 separate incidents. It concluded: "on the basis available on these ninety incidents that as few as 488 and as many as 527 Yugoslav civilians were killed as a result of NATO bombing. Between 62 and 66 percent of the total registered civilian deaths occurred in just twelve incidents. These twelve incidents accounted for 303 to 352 civilian deaths. These were the only incidents among the ninety documented in which ten or more civilian deaths were confirmed." Ten of these twelve incidents were included among the incidents which were reviewed with considerable care by the committee (see para. 9 above) and our estimate was that between 273 and 317 civilians were killed in these ten incidents. Human Rights Watch also found the FRY Ministry of Foreign Affairs publication NATO Crimes in Yugoslavia to be largely credible on the basis of its own filed research and correlation with other sources. A review of this publication indicates it provides an estimated total of approximately 495 civilians killed and 820 civilians wounded in specific documented instances. For the purposes of this report, the committee operates on the basis of the number of persons allegedly killed as found in both publications. It appears that a figure similar to both publications would be in the range of 500 civilians killed.

vi. General Assesment of the Bombing Campaign

54. During the bombing campaign, NATO aircraft flew 38,400 sorties, including 10,484 strike sorties. During these sorties, 23, 614 air munitions were released (figures from NATO). As indicated in the preceding paragraph, it appears that approximately 500 civilians were killed during the campaign. These figures do not indicate that NATO may have conducted a campaign aimed at causing substantial civilian casualties either directly or incidentally.

55. The choice of targets by NATO (see paras. 38 and 39 above) includes some loosely defined categories such as military-industrial infrastructure and government ministries and some potential problem categories such as media and refineries. All targets must meet the criteria for military objectives (see para. 28-30 above). If they do not do so, they are unlawful. A general label is insufficient. The targeted components of the military-industrial infrastructure and of government ministries must make an effective contribution to military action and their total or partial destruction must offer a definite military advantage in the circumstances ruling at the time. Refineries are certainly traditional military objectives but tradition is not enough and due regard must be paid to environmental damage if they are attacked (see paras. 14-25 above). The media as such is not a traditional target category. To the extent particular media components are part of the C3 (command, control and communications) network they are military objectives. If media components are not part of the C3 network then they may become military objectives depending upon their use. As a bottom line, civilians, civilian objects and civilian morale as such are not legitimate military objectives. The media does have an effect on civilian morale. If that effect is merely to foster support for the war effort, the media is not a legitimate military objective. If the media is used to incite crimes, as in Rwanda, it can become a legitimate military objective. If the media is the nerve system that keeps a war-monger in power and thus perpetuates the war effort, it may fall within the definition of a legitimate military objective. As a general statement, in the particular incidents reviewed by the committee, it is the view of the committee that NATO was attempting to attack objects it perceived to be legitimate military objectives.

56. The committee agrees there is nothing inherently unlawful about flying above the height which can be reached by enemy air defences. However, NATO air commanders have a duty to take practicable measures to distinguish military objectives from civilians or civilian objectives. The 15,000 feet minimum altitude adopted for part of the campaign may have meant the target could not be verified with the naked eye. However, it appears that with the use of modern technology, the obligation to distinguish was effectively carried out in the vast majority of cases during the bombing campaign.

B. SPECIFIC INCIDENTS

57. In the course of its review, the committee did not come across any incident which, in its opinion, required investigation by the OTP. The five specific incidents discussed below are those which, in the opinion of the committee, were the most problematic. The facts cited in the discussion of each specific incident are those indicated in the information within the possession of the OTP at the time of its review.

i. The Attack on a Civilian Passenger Train at the Grdelica Gorge on 12/4/99

58. On 12 April 1999, a NATO aircraft launched two laser guided bombs at the Leskovac railway bridge over the Grdelica gorge and Juzna Morava river, in eastern Serbia. A 5-carriage passenger train, travelling from Belgrade to Ristovac on the Macedonian border, was crossing the bridge at the time, and was struck by both missiles. The various reports made of this incident concur that the incident occurred at about 11.40 a.m. At least ten people were killed in this incident and at least 15 individuals were injured. The designated target was the railway bridge, which was claimed to be part of a re-supply route being used for Serb forces in Kosovo. After launching the first bomb, the person controlling the weapon, at the last instant before impact, sighted movement on the bridge. The controller was unable to dump the bomb at that stage and it hit the train, the impact of the bomb cutting the second of the passenger coaches in half. Realising the bridge was still intact, the controller picked a second aim point on the bridge at the opposite end from where the train had come and launched the second

bomb. In the meantime the train had slid forward as a result of the original impact and parts of the train were also hit by the second bomb.

59. It does not appear that the train was targeted deliberately. US Deputy Defense Secretary John Hamre stated that "one of our electro-optically guided bombs homed in on a railroad bridge just when a passenger train raced to the aim point. We never wanted to destroy that train or kill its occupants. We did want to destroy the bridge and we regret this accident." The substantive part of the explanation, both for the failure to detect the approach of the passenger train and for firing a second missile once it had been hit by the first, was given by General Wesley Clark, NATO's Supreme Allied Commander for Europe and is here reprinted in full:

"[T]his was a case where a pilot was assigned to strike a railroad bridge that is part of the integrated communications supply network in Serbia. He launched his missile from his aircraft that was many miles away, he was not able to put his eyes on the bridge, it was a remotely directed attack. And as he stared intently at the desired target point on the bridge, and I talked to the team at Aviano who was directly engaged in this operation, as the pilot stared intently at the desired aim point on the bridge and worked it, and worked it and worked it, and all of a sudden at the very last instant with less than a second to go he caught a flash of movement that came into the screen and it was the train coming in.

Unfortunately he couldn't dump the bomb at that point, it was locked, it was going into the target and it was an unfortunate incident which he, and the crew, and all of us very much regret. We certainly don't want to do collateral damage.

The mission was to take out the bridge. He realised when it had happened that he had not hit the bridge, but what he had hit was the train. He had another aim point on the bridge, it was a relatively long bridge and he believed he still had to accomplish his mission, the pilot circled back around. He put his aim point on the other end of the bridge from where the train had come, by the time the bomb got close to the bridge it was covered with smoke and clouds and at the last minute again in an uncanny accident, the train had slid forward from the original impact and parts of the train had moved across the bridge, and so that by striking the other end of the bridge he actually caused additional damage to the train." (Press Conference, NATO HQ, Brussels, 13 April).

General Clark then showed the cockpit video of the plane which fired on the bridge:

"The pilot in the aircraft is looking at about a 5-inch screen, he is seeing about this much and in here you can see this is the railroad bridge which is a much better view than he actually had, you can see the tracks running this way.

Look very intently at the aim point, concentrate right there and you can see how, if you were focused right on your job as a pilot, suddenly that train appeared. It was really unfortunate.

Here, he came back around to try to strike a different point on the bridge because he was trying to do a job to take the bridge down. Look at this aim point - you can see smoke and other obscuration there - he couldn't tell what this was exactly.

Focus intently right at the centre of the cross. He is bringing these two crosses together and suddenly he recognises at the very last instant that the train that was struck here has moved on across the bridge and so the engine apparently was struck by the second bomb." (Press Conference, NATO HQ, Brussels, 13 April).

60. Some doubt has since been cast on this version of events by a comprehensive technical report submitted by a German national, Mr Ekkehard Wenz, which queries the actual speed at which the events took place in relation to that suggested by the video footage of the incident released by NATO. The effect of this report is to suggest that the reaction time available to the person controlling the bombs was in fact considerably greater than that alleged by NATO. Mr. Wenz also suggests the aircraft involved was an F15E Strike Eagle with a crew of two and with the weapons being controlled by a Weapons Systems Officer (WSO) not the pilot.

61. The committee has reviewed both the material provided by NATO and the report of Mr. Wenz with considerable care. It is the opinion of the committee that it is irrelevant whether the person controlling the bomb was the pilot or the WSO. Either person would have been travelling in a high speed aircraft and likely performing several tasks simultaneously, including endeavouring to keep the aircraft in the air and safe from surrounding threats in a combat environment. If the committee accepts Mr. Wenz's estimate of the reaction time available, the person controlling the bombs still had a very short period of time, less than 7 or 8 seconds in all probability, to react. Although Mr Wenz is of the view that the WSO intentionally targeted the train, the committee's review of the frames used in the report indicates another interpretation is equally available. The cross hairs remain fixed on the bridge throughout, and it is clear from this footage that the train can be seen moving toward the bridge only as the bomb is in flight: it is only in the course of the bomb's trajectory that the image of the train becomes visible. At a point where the bomb is within a few seconds of impact, a very slight change to the bomb aiming point can be observed, in that it drops a couple of feet. This sequence regarding the bomb sights indicates that it is unlikely that the WSO was targeting the train, but instead suggests that the target was a point on the span of the bridge before the train appeared.

62. It is the opinion of the committee that the bridge was a legitimate military objective. The passenger train was not deliberately targeted. The person controlling the bombs, pilot or WSO, targeted the bridge and, over a very short period of time, failed to recognize the arrival of the train while the first bomb was in flight. The train was on the bridge when the bridge was targeted a second time and the bridge length has been estimated at 50 meters (Wenz study para 6 g above at p.25). It is the opinion of the committee that the information in relation to the attack with the first bomb does not provide a sufficient basis to initiate an investigation. The committee has divided views concerning the attack with the second bomb in relation to whether there was an element of recklessness in the conduct of the pilot or WSO. Despite this, the committee is in agreement that, based on the criteria for initiating an investigation (see para. 5 above), this incident should not be investigated. In relation to whether there is information warranting consideration of command responsibility, the committee is of the view that there is no information from which to conclude that an investigation is necessary into the criminal responsibility of persons higher in the chain of command. Based on the information available to it, it is the opinion of the committee that the attack on the train at Grdelica Gorge should not be investigated by the OTP.

ii. The Attack on the Djakovica Convoy on 14/4/99

63. The precise facts concerning this incident are difficult to determine. In particular, there is some confusion about the number of aircraft involved, the number of bombs dropped, and whether one or two convoys were attacked. The FRY Ministry of Foreign Affairs Report (White Book) describes the incident as follows:

"On April 14, 1999 [...] on the Djakovica-Prizren road, near the villages of Madanaj and Meja, a convoy of Albanian refugees was targeted three times. Mostly women, children and old people were in the convoy, returning to their homes in cars, on tractors and carts. The first assault on the column of over 1000 people took place while they were moving through Meja village. Twelve persons were killed on that occasion. The people from the convoy scattered around and tried to find shelter in the nearby houses. But NATO warplanes launched missiles on those houses as well, killing another 7 persons in the process. The attack continued along the road beween [the] villages [of] Meja and Bistrazin. One tractor with trailer was completely destroyed. Twenty people out of several of them on the tractor were killed. In the repeated attack on the refugee vehicles, one more person was killed." (Vol 1, p.1)

Total casualty figures seem to converge around 70-75 killed with approximately 100 injured. The FRY publication NATO War Crimes in Yugoslavia states 73 were killed and 36 were wounded.

64. NATO initially denied, but later acknowledged, responsibility for this attack. Assuming the facts most appropriate to a successful prosecution, NATO aircraft flying at 15000 feet or higher to avoid Yugoslav air defences attacked two vehicle convoys, both of which contained civilian vehicles. On 15 April, NATO confirmed that the aircraft had been flying at an altitude of 15,000 feet (approximately 5 km) and that, in this attack, the pilots had viewed the target with the naked eye rather than remotely. The aim of the attack was to destroy Serb military forces, in the area of Djakovica, who had been seen by NATO aircraft setting fire to civilian houses. At a Press Conference of 15 April 1999, NATO claimed that this was an area where the Yugoslav Special Police Forces, the MUP, were conducting ethnic cleansing operations over the preceding days. The road between Prizren and Djakovica served as an important resupply and reinforcement route for the Yugoslav Army and the Special Police.

65. A reconstruction of what is known about the attack reveals that in the hours immediately prior to the attack, at around 1030, NATO forces claimed to have seen a progression of burning villages, and that a series of fires could be seen progressing to the south east. They formed the view that MUP and VJ forces were thus methodically working from the north to the south through villages, setting them ablaze and forcing all the Kosovar Albanians out of those villages. At around 1030, the pilot spotted a three-vehicle convoy near to the freshest burning house, and saw uniformly shaped dark green vehicles which appeared to be troop carrying vehicles. He thus formed the view that the convoy comprised VJ and MUP forces working their way down towards Djakovica and that they were preparing to set the next house on fire. In response, an F-16 bombed the convoy's lead vehicle at approximately 1110; the pilot relayed a threat update and the coordinates of the attack and departed the area to refuel. A second F-16 aircraft appears to have arrived on the scene around 1135, and visually assessed the target area as containing large vehicles which were located near a complex of buildings. A single GBU-12 bomb was dropped at 1148. Contemporaneously, a third aircraft identified a large convoy on a major road south east out of Djakovica and sought to identify the target. The target was verified as a VJ convoy at 1216 and an unspecified number of bombs were dropped at 1219. In the next 15 or so minutes (exact time unspecified), the same aircraft appears to have destroyed one further vehicle in the convoy. Simultaneously, two Jaguar aircraft each dropped 1 GBU-12 bomb each, but both missed their targets. Between 1235 and 1245, the first F-16 aircraft appears to have dropped three further bombs, at least one of which appears to have missed its target.

66. It is claimed by one source (report on file with the OTP) that the Yugoslav TV broadcast of the attack on the Djakovica convoy on 15 April 1999 recorded a conversation between one F-16 pilot involved in the attack and the AWACs. This conversation is alleged to establish both that the attack on the convoy was deliberate and that a UK Harrier pilot had advised the F-16 pilot that the convoy was comprised solely of tractors and civilians. The F-16 pilot was then allegedly told that the convoy was nevertheless a legitimate military target and was instructed to fire on it. This same report also suggests that the convoy was attacked with cluster bombs, indicated by bomb remnants and craters left at the site. However, these claims - both with regard to the foreknowledge of the pilot as to the civilian nature of the convoy and of the weapons used - are not confirmed by any other source.

67. NATO itself claimed that although the cockpit video showed the vehicles to look like tractors, when viewed with the naked eye from the attack altitude they appeared to be military vehicles. They alleged that several characteristics indicated it to be a military convoy including movement, size, shape, colour, spacing and high speed prior to the attack. There had also been reports of Serb forces using civilian vehicles. An analysis of the Serb TV footage of the attack on Djakovica by the OTP indicates that at approximately 1240, some point during the attack, doubt was conveyed that Serb convoys do not usually travel in convoys of that size. However, the on-scene analysis of the convoy appeared to convey the impression that the convoy comprised a mix of military and civilian vehicles. At around 1300, an order appears to have been issued, suspending attacks until the target could be verified.

68. NATO has consistently claimed that it believed the Djakovica convoy to be escorted by Serb military vehicles at the time of the attack. Human Rights Watch has commented on the incident as follows:

"General Clark stated in September that NATO consistently observed Yugoslav military vehicles moving on roads "intermixed with civilian convoys." After the Djakovica-Decane incident, General Clark says, "we got to be very, very cautious about striking objects moving on the roads. Another NATO officer, Col. Ed Boyle, says: "Because we were so concerned with collateral damage, the CFAC [Combined Forces Air Component Commander] at the time, General [Michael] Short, put out the guidance that if military vehicles were intermingled with civilian vehicles, they were not to be attacked, due to the collateral damage." When this directive was actually issued remains an important question. Nevertheless, the change in NATO rules of engagement indicates that the alliance recognized that it had taken insufficient precautions in mounting this attack, in not identifying civilians present, and in assuming that the intended targets were legitimate military objectives rather than in positively identifying them."

69. It is the opinion of the committee that civilians were not deliberately attacked in this incident. While there is nothing unlawful about operating at a height above Yugoslav air defences, it is difficult for any aircrew operating an aircraft flying at several hundred miles an hour and at a substantial height to distinguish between military and civilian vehicles in a convoy. In this case, most of the attacking aircraft were F16s with a crew of one person to fly the aircraft and identify the target. As soon as the crews of the attacking aircraft became aware of the presence of civilians, the attack ceased.

70. While this incident is one where it appears the aircrews could have benefitted from lower altitude scrutiny of the target at an early stage, the committee is of the opinion that neither the aircrew nor their commanders displayed the degree of recklessness in failing to take precautionary measures which would sustain criminal charges. The committee also notes that the attack was suspended as soon as the presence of civilians in the convoy was suspected. Based on the information assessed, the committee recommends that the OTP not commence an investigation related to the Djakovica Convoy bombing.

iii. The Bombing of the RTS (Serbian TV and Radio Station) in Belgrade on 23/4/99

71. On 23 April 1999, at 0220, NATO intentionally bombed the central studio of the RTS (state-owned) broadcasting corporation at 1 Aberdareva Street in the centre of Belgrade. The missiles hit the entrance area, which caved in at the place where the Aberdareva Street building was connected to the Takovska Street building. While there is some doubt over exact casualty figures, between 10 and 17 people are estimated to have been killed.

72. The bombing of the TV studio was part of a planned attack aimed at disrupting and degrading the C3 (Command, Control and Communications) network. In co-ordinated attacks, on the same night, radio relay buildings and towers were hit along with electrical power transformer stations. At a press conference on 27 April 1999, NATO officials justified this attack in terms of the dual military and civilian use to which the FRY communication system was routinely put, describing this as a

"very hardened and redundant command and control communications system [which ...] uses commercial telephone, [...] military cable, [...] fibre optic cable, [...] high frequency radio communication, [...] microwave communication and everything can be interconnected. There are literally dozens, more than 100 radio relay sites around the country, and [...] everything is wired in through dual use. Most of the commercial system serves the military and the military system can be put to use for the commercial system [...]."

Accordingly, NATO stressed the dual-use to which such communications systems were put, describing civilian television as "heavily dependent on the military command and control system and military traffic is also routed through the civilian system" (press conference of 27 April, ibid).

73. At an earlier press conference on 23 April 1999, NATO officials reported that the TV building also housed a large multi-purpose communications satellite antenna dish, and that "radio relay control buildings and towers were targeted in the ongoing campaign to degrade the FRY's command, control and communications network". In a commu-

nication of 17 April 1999 to Amnesty International, NATO claimed that the RTS facilities were being used "as radio relay stations and transmitters to support the activities of the FRY military and special police forces, and therefore they represent legitimate military targets" (Amnesty International Report, NATO/Federal Republic of Yugoslavia: Violations of the Laws of War by NATO during Operation Allied Force, June 2000, p. 42).

74. Of the electrical power transformer stations targeted, one transformer station supplied power to the air defence co-ordination network while the other supplied power to the northern-sector operations centre. Both these facilities were key control elements in the FRY integrated air-defence system. In this regard, NATO indicated that

"we are not targeting the Serb people as we repeatedly have stated nor do we target President Milosevic personally, we are attacking the control system that is used to manipulate the military and security forces."

More controversially, however, the bombing was also justified on the basis of the propaganda purpose to which it was employed:

"[We need to] directly strike at the very central nerve system of Milosovic's regime. This of course are those assets which are used to plan and direct and to create the political environment of tolerance in Yugoslavia in which these brutalities can not only be accepted but even condoned. [....] Strikes against TV transmitters and broadcast facilities are part of our campaign to dismantle the FRY propaganda machinery which is a vital part of President Milosevic's control mechanism."

In a similar statement, British Prime Minister Tony Blair was reported as saying in The Times that the media "is the apparatus that keeps him [Milosevic] in power and we are entirely justified as NATO allies in damaging and taking on those targets" (24 April, 1999). In a statement of 8 April 1999, NATO also indicated that the TV studios would be targeted unless they broadcast 6 hours per day of Western media reports: "If President Milosevic would provide equal time for Western news broadcasts in its programmes without censorship 3 hours a day between noon and 1800 and 3 hours a day between 1800 and midnight, then his TV could be an acceptable instrument of public information."

75. NATO intentionally bombed the Radio and TV station and the persons killed or injured were civilians. The questions are: was the station a legitimate military objective and; if it was, were the civilian casualties disproportionate to the military advantage gained by the attack? For the station to be a military objective within the definition in Article 52 of Protocol I: a) its nature, purpose or use must make an effective contribution to military action and b) its total or partial destruction must offer a definite military advantage in the circumstances ruling at the time. The 1956 ICRC list of military objectives, drafted before the Additional Protocols, included the installations of broadcasting and television stations of fundamental military importance as military objectives (para. 39 above). The list prepared by Major General Rogers included broadcasting and television stations if they meet the military objective criteria (para. 38 above). As indicated in paras. 72 and 73 above, the attack appears to have been justified by NATO as part of a more general attack aimed at disrupting the FRY Command, Control and Communications network, the nerve centre and apparatus that keeps Milosevic in power, and also as an attempt to dismantle the FRY propaganda machinery. Insofar as the attack actually was aimed at disrupting the communications network, it was legally acceptable.

76. If, however, the attack was made because equal time was not provided for Western news broadcasts, that is, because the station was part of the propaganda machinery, the legal basis was more debatable. Disrupting government propaganda may help to undermine the morale of the population and the armed forces, but justifying an attack on a civilian facility on such grounds alone may not meet the "effective contribution to military action" and "definite military advantage" criteria required by the Additional Protocols (see paras. 35-36, above). The ICRC Commentary on the Additional Protocols interprets the expression "definite military advantage anticipated" to exclude "an attack which only offers potential or indeterminate advantages" and interprets the expression "concrete and direct" as intended to show that the advantage concerned should be substantial and relatively close rather than hardly perceptible and likely to appear only in the long term (ICRC Commentary on the Additional Protocols of 8 June 1977, para. 2209). While stopping such propaganda may serve to demoralize the Yugoslav population and undermine the government's political support, it is unlikely that either of these purposes would offer the "concrete and direct" military advantage necessary to make them a legitimate military objective. NATO believed that Yugoslav broadcast facilities were "used entirely to incite hatred and propaganda" and alleged that the Yugoslav government had put all private TV and radio stations in Serbia under military control (NATO press conferences of 28 and 30 April1999). However, it was not claimed that they were being used to incite violence akin to Radio Milles Collines during the Rwandan genocide, which might have justified their destruction (see para. 47 above). At worst, the Yugoslav government was using the broadcasting networks to issue propaganda supportive of its war effort: a circumstance which does not, in and of itself, amount to a war crime (see in this regard the judgment of the International Military Tribunal in Nuremberg in 1946 in the case of Hans Fritzsche, who served as a senior official in the Propaganda ministry alleged to have incited and encouraged the commission of crimes. The IMT held that although Fritzsche clearly made strong statements of a propagandistic nature, it was nevertheless not prepared to find that they were intended to incite the commission of atrocities, but rather, were aimed at arousing popular sentiment in support of Hitler and the German war effort (American Journal of International Law, vol. 41 (1947) 328)). The committee finds that if the attack on the RTS was justified by reference to its propaganda purpose alone, its legality might well be questioned by some experts in the field of international humanitarian law. It appears, however, that NATO's targeting of the RTS building for propaganda purposes was an incidental (albeit complementary) aim of its primary goal of disabling the Serbian military command and control system and to destroy the nerve system and apparatus that keeps Milosevic in power. In a press conference of 9 April 1999, NATO declared that TV transmitters were not targeted directly but that "in Yugoslavia military radio relay stations are often combined with TV transmitters [so] we attack the military target. If there is damage to the TV transmitters, it is a secondary effect but it is not [our] primary intention to do that." A NATO spokesperson, Jamie Shea, also wrote to the Brussels-based International Federation of Journalists on 12 April claiming that OperationAllied Force "target[ed] military targets only and television and radio towers are only struck if they [were] integrated into military facilities ... There is no policy to strike television and radio transmitters as such" (cited in Amnesty International Report, ibid, June 2000).

77. Assuming the station was a legitimate objective, the civilian casualties were unfortunately high but do not appear to be clearly disproportionate.

Although NATO alleged that it made "every possible effort to avoid civilian casualties and collateral damage" (Amnesty International Report, ibid, June 2000, p. 42), some doubts have been expressed as to the specificity of the warning given to civilians by NATO of its intended strike, and whether the notice would have constituted "effective warning ... of attacks which may affect the civililan population, unless circumstances do not permit" as required by Article 57(2) of Additional Protocol I.

Evidence on this point is somewhat contradictory. On the one hand, NATO officials in Brussels are alleged to have told Amnesty International that they did not give a specific warning as it would have endangered the pilots (Amnesty International Report, ibid, June 2000, at p. 47; see also para. 49 above re: proportionality and the extent to which a military commander is obligated to expose his own forces to danger in order to limit civilian casualties or damage). On this view, it is possible that casualties among civilians working at the RTS may have been heightened because of NATO's apparent failure to provide clear advance warning of the attack, as required by Article 57(2).

On the other hand, foreign media representatives were apparently forewarned of the attack (Amnesty International Report, ibid). As Western journalists were reportedly warned by their employers to stay away from the television station before the attack, it would also appear that some Yugoslav officials may have expected that the building was about to be struck. Consequently, UK Prime Minister Tony Blair blamed Yugoslav officials for not evacuating the building, claiming that "[t]hey could have moved those people out of the building. They knew it was a target and they didn't ... [I]t was probably for ... very clear propaganda reasons." (ibid, citing Moral combat - NATO at war, broadcast on BBC2 on 12 March 2000). Although knowledge on the part of Yugoslav officials of the impending attack would not divest NATO of its obligation to forewarn civilians under Article 57(2), it may nevertheless imply that the Yugoslav authorities may be partially responsible for the civilian casualties resulting from the attack and may suggest that the advance notice given by NATO may have in fact been sufficient under the circumstances.

78. Assuming the RTS building to be a legitimate military target, it appeared that NATO realised that attacking the RTS building would only interrupt broadcasting for a brief period. Indeed, broadcasting allegedly recommenced within hours of the strike, thus raising the issue of the importance of the military advantage gained by the attack vis-à-vis the civilian casualties incurred. The FRY command and control network was alleged by NATO to comprise a complex web and that could thus not be disabled in one strike. As noted by General Wesley Clark, NATO "knew when we struck that there would be alternate means of getting the Serb Television. There's no single switch to turn off everything but we thought it was a good move to strike it and the political leadership agreed with us" (ibid, citing "Moral combat, NATO at War," broadcast on BBC2 on 12 March 2000). At a press conference on 27 April 1999, another NATO spokesperson similarly described the dual-use Yugoslav command and control network as "incapable of being dealt with in "a single knock-out blow (ibid)." The proportionality or otherwise of an attack should not necessarily focus exclusively on a specific incident. (See in this regard para. 52, above, referring to the need for an overall assessment of the totality of civilian victims as against the goals of the military campaign). With regard to these goals, the strategic target of these attacks was the Yugoslav command and control network. The attack on the RTS building must therefore be seen as forming part of an integrated attack against numerous objects, including transmission towers and control buildings of the Yugoslav radio relay network which were "essential to Milosevic's ability to direct and control the repressive activities of his army and special police forces in Kosovo" (NATO press release, 1 May 1999) and which comprised "a key element in the Yugoslav air-defence network" (ibid, 1 May 1999). Attacks were also aimed at electricity grids that fed the command and control structures of the Yugoslav Army (ibid, 3 May 1999). Other strategic targets included additional command and control assets such as the radio and TV relay sites at Novi Pazar, Kosovaka and Krusevac (ibid) and command posts (ibid, 30 April). Of the electrical power transformer stations targeted, one transformer station supplied power to the air-defence coordination network while the other supplied power to the northern sector operations centre. Both these facilities were key control elements in the FRY integrated air-defence system (ibid, 23 April 1999). The radio relay and TV transmitting station near Novi Sad was also an important link in the air defence command and control communications network. Not only were these targets central to the Federal Republic of Yugoslavia's governing apparatus, but formed, from a military point of view, an integral part of the strategic communications network which enabled both the military and national command authorities to direct the repression and atrocities taking place in Kosovo (ibid, 21 April 1999).

79. On the basis of the above analysis and on the information currently available to it, the committee recommends that the OTP not commence an investigation related to the bombing of the Serbian TV and Radio Station.

iv. The Attack on the Chinese Embassy on 7/5/99

80. On 7/5/99, at 2350, NATO aircraft fired several missiles which hit the Chinese Embassy in Belgrade, killing 3 Chinese citizens, injuring an estimated 15 others, and causing extensive damage to the embassy building and other buildings in the immediate surrounds. At the moment of the attack, fifty people were reported to have been in the embassy buildings. By the admission of US Government sources, the Chinese Embassy compound was mistakenly hit. The bombing occurred because at no stage in the process was it realised that the bombs were aimed at the Chinese Embassy. The Embassy had been wrongly identified as the Yugoslav Federal Directorate for Supply and Procurement (Yugoimport FDSP) at 2 Umetnosti Boulevard in New Belgrade. The FDSP was deemed by the CIA to be a legitimate target due to its role in military procurement: it was selected for its role in support of the Yugoslav military effort.

81. Under Secretary of State Thomas Pickering offered the following explanation for what occurred:

"The bombing resulted from three basic failures. First, the technique used to locate the intended target - the headquarters of the Yugoslav Federal Directorate for Supply and Procurement (FDSP) - was severely flawed. Second, none of the military or intelligence databases used to verify target information contained the correct location of the Chinese Embassy. Third, nowhere in the target review process was either of the first two mistakes detected. No one who might have known that the targeted building was not the FDSP headquarters - but was in fact the Chinese Embassy - was ever consulted."

According to US Government sources, the street address of the intended target, the FDSP headquarters was known as Bulevar Umetnosti 2 in New Belgrade. During a mid-April "work-up" of the target to prepare a mission folder for the B-2 bomber crew, three maps were used in an attempt to physically locate this address within the neighborhood: two local commercial maps from 1989 and 1996, and one US government (National Imagery and Mapping Agency or NIMA) map produced in 1997. None of these maps had any reference to the FDSP building and none accurately identified the current location of the Chinese Embassy.

82. The root of the failures in target location appears to stem from the land navigation techniques employed by an intelligence officer in an effort to pinpoint the location of the FDSP building at Bulevar Umetnosti 2. The officer used techniques known as "intersection" and "resection" which, while appropriate to locate distant or inaccessible points or objects, are inappropriate for use in aerial targeting as they provide only an approximate location. Using this process, the individual mistakenly determined that the building which we now know to be the Chinese Embassy was the FDSP headquarters. This method of identification was not questioned or reviewed and hence this flaw in the address location process went undetected by all the others who evaluated the FDSP headquarters as a military target. It also appears that very late in the process, an intelligence officer serendipitously came to suspect that the target had been wrongly identified and sought to raise the concern that the building had been mislocated. However, throughout a series of missed opportunities, the problem of identification was not brought to the attention of the senior managers who may have been able to intervene in time to prevent the strike.

83. Finally, reviewing elements in, inter alia, the Joint Staff did not uncover either the inaccurate location of the FDSP headquarters or the correct location of the Chinese Embassy. The data base reviews were limited to validating the target data sheet geographic coordinates and the information put into the data base by the NIMA analyst. Such a circular process did not serve to uncover the original error and highlighted the system's susceptibility to a single point of data base failure. The critical linchpin for both the error in identification of the building and the failure of the review mechanisms was thus the inadequacy of the supporting data bases and the mistaken assumption the information they contained would necessarily be accurate.

84. The building hit was clearly a civilian object and not a legitimate military objective. NATO, and subsequently various organs of the US Government, including the CIA, issued a formal apology, accepted full responsibility for the incident and asserted that the intended target, the Federal Directorate for Supply and Procurement, would have been a legitimate military objective. The USA has formally apologized to the Chinese Government and agreed to pay $28 million in compensation to the Chinese Government and $4.5 million to the families of those killed or injured. The CIA has also dismissed one intelligence officer and reprimanded six senior managers. The US Government also claims to have taken corrective actions in order to assign individual responsibility and to prevent mistakes such as this from occurring in the future.

85. It is the opinion of the committee that the aircrew involved in the attack should not be assigned any responsibility for the fact they were

given the wrong target and that it is inappropriate to attempt to assign criminal responsibility for the incident to senior leaders because they were provided with wrong information by officials of another agency. Based on the information available to it, the committee is of the opinion that the OTP should not undertake an investigation concerning the bombing of the Chinese Embassy.

v. The Attack on Koriša Village on 13/5/99

86. On 14 May 1999, NATO aircraft dropped 10 bombs on the village of Koriša, on the highway between Prizren and Pristina. Much confusion seems to exist about this incident, and factual accounts do not seem to easily tally with each other. As many as 87 civilians, mainly refugees, were killed in this attack and approximately 60 appear to have been wounded. The primary target in this attack was asserted by NATO to be a Serbian military camp and Command Post which were located near the village of Koriša. It appears that the refugees were near the attacked object. However, unlike previous cases where NATO subsequently claimed that an error had occurred in its targeting or its military intelligence sources, NATO spokespersons continued to affirm the legitimacy of this particular attack. They maintained that this was a legitimate military target and that NATO intelligence had identified a military camp and Command Post near to the village of Koriša.

87. According to NATO officials, immediately prior to the attack, the target was identified as having military revetments. The pilot was able to see silhouettes of vehicles on the ground as the attack took place at 2330, when two laser guided bombs were dropped. Ten minutes later, another two laser guided bombs and six gravity bombs were dropped. In a press conference on 15 May, NATO stated that the attack went ahead because the target was confirmed by prior intelligence as being valid and the pilot identified vehicles present. There were never any doubts, from NATO spokespersons, as to the validity of this target.

88. Information about NATO's position on the bombardment of Koriša was released at the press conference on the following day, 15 May. At this conference, General Jertz twice affirmed that the target was, in NATO's opinion, legitimate since military facilities were present at the site:

"As already has been mentioned, it was a legitimate military target. NATO reconnaissance and intelligence orders identified just outside Koriša a military camp and command post, including an armoured personnel carrier and 10 pieces of artillery. Follow-up intelligence confirmed this information as being a valid military target. Immediately prior to the attack at 23.30-11.30 pm - local time Thursday night an airborne forward air controller identified the target, so the identification and attack system of his aircraft, having positively identified the target as what looked like dug-in military reveted positions, he dropped two laser guided bombs. Approximately 10 minutes later, the third aircraft engaged the target with gravity bombs, with six gravity bombs. A total of 10 bombs were dropped on the target."

When questioned about the presence of civilians on the ground, General Jertz indicated:

"What I can say so far is when the pilot attacked the target he had to visually identify it through the attack systems which are in the aircraft, and you know it was by night, so he did see silhouettes of vehicles on the ground and as it was by prior intelligence a valid target, he did do the attack [...] it was a legitimate target. Since late April we knew there were command posts, military pieces in that area and they have been continuously used. So for the pilot flying the attack, it was a legitimate target. But when he is in the target area for attacking, it is his responsibility to make sure that all the cues he sees are the ones which he needs to really attack. And at night he saw the silhouettes of vehicles and that is why he was allowed to attack. Of course, and we have to be very fair, we are talking at night. If there is anybody sleeping somewhere in a house, you would not be able to see it from the perspective of a pilot. But once again, don't misinterpret it. It was a military target which had been used since the beginning of conflict over there and we have all sources used to identify this target in order to make sure that this target was still a valid target when it was attacked." (Emphasis added).

The NATO position thus appears to be that it bombed a legitimate military target, that it knew nothing of the presence of civilians and that none were observed immediately prior to the attack. Indeed, NATO stated that they believed this area to have been completely cleared of civilians. There is some information indicating that displaced Kosovar civilians were forcibly concentrated within a military camp in the village of Koriša as human shields and that Yugoslav military forces may thus be at least partially responsible for the deaths there.

89. The available information concerning this incident is in conflict. The attack occurred in the middle of the night at about 2330. The stated object of the attack was a legitimate military objective. According to NATO, all practicable precautions were taken and it was determined civilians were not present. It appears that a relatively large number of civilians were killed. It also appears these civilians were either returning refugees or persons gathered as human shields by FRY authorities or both. The committee is of the view that the credible information available is not sufficient to tend to show that a crime within the jurisdiction of the Tribunal has been committed by the aircrew or by superiors in the NATO chain of command. Based on the information available to it, the committee is of the opinion that OTP should not undertake an investigation concerning the bombing at Koriša.

V. Recommendations

90. The committee has conducted its review relying essentially upon public documents, including statements made by NATO and NATO countries at press conferences and public documents produced by the FRY. It has tended to assume that the NATO and NATO countries' press statements are generally reliable and that explanations have been honestly given. The committee must note, however, that when the OTP requested NATO to answer specific questions about specific incidents, the NATO reply was couched in general terms and failed to address the specific incidents. The committee has not spoken to those involved in directing or carrying out the bombing campaign. The committee has also assigned substantial weight to the factual assertions made by Human Rights Watch as its investigators did spend a limited amount of time on the ground in the FRY. Further, the committee has noted that Human Rights Watch found the two volume compilation of the FRY Ministry of Foreign Affairs entitled NATO Crimes in Yugoslavia generally reliable and the committee has tended to rely on the casualty figures for specific incidents in this compilation. If one accepts the figures in this compilation of approximately 495 civilians killed and 820 civilians wounded in documented instances, there is simply no evidence of the necessary crime base for charges of genocide or crimes against humanity. Further, in the particular incidents reviewed by the committee with particular care (see paras. 9, and 48-76) the committee has not assessed any particular incidents as justifying the commencement of an investigation by the OTP. NATO has admitted that mistakes did occur during the bombing campaign; errors of judgment may also have occurred. Selection of certain objectives for attack may be subject to legal debate. On the basis of the information reviewed, however, the committee is of the opinion that neither an in-depth investigation related to the bombing campaign as a whole nor investigations related to specific incidents are justified. In all cases, either the law is not sufficiently clear or investigations are unlikely to result in the acquisition of sufficient evidence to substantiate charges against high level accused or against lower accused for particularly heinous offences.

91. On the basis of information available, the committee recommends that no investigation be commenced by the OTP in relation to the NATO bombing campaign or incidents occurring during the campaign.

CHAPTER 5: SETTLEMENT OF THE CRISIS

During the NATO bombing campaign political efforts for a peaceful settlement of the crisis continued. On 6 May 1999, the G8 states agreed on general principles for a solution (*document no. 200*). These principles included, inter alia, the immediate and verifiable end of violence and repression in Kosovo; withdrawal from Kosovo of military, police and paramilitary forces; deployment of an international civil and security presence, endorsed and adopted by a UN Security Council Resolution; establishment of an interim administration to be decided by the UN Security Council; the demilitarisation of the KLA; a political process towards the establishment of an interim political framework agreement providing for substantial self-government within the parameters of the Rambouillet Accords and taking account of the territorial integrity of the FRY.

By end of May 1999 the European Union authorized the Finnish President Ahtisaari to go on a mission to Belgrade together with the Russian Special Envoy Chernomyrdin to negotiate a peace plan based on the G8 principles. The FRY accepted the peace plan on 3 June 1999 (*document no. 204*). Milosevic's acceptance of the plan is said to have been influenced by evidence that Britain and France were actively contemplating a ground force deployment (*documents no. 185-189*).[1] In addition, changes had been made since Rambouillet[2]. The international civil presence in Kosovo was to be deployed under UN rather than NATO auspices. There was no mentioning of KFOR's or NATO's unrestricted passage or unimpeded access throughout the rest of the FRY. While the peace plan took the Rambouillet accords into account for the political process which was to determine Kosovo's final status, it did not provide for a three-year transition period. Through means of secret diplomacy Russia had informed Milosevic that it would not support any further Yugoslav demands. NATO, on the other hand, could point to the fact that the timetable for withdrawing all Yugoslav forces from Kosovo had been reduced from months to days. Furthermore, the peace plan permitted only a small number of Yugoslavian forces back for border control and guard duties.

On 10 June 1999, the UN Security Council passed resolution 1244 (1999) (*document no. 208*). Acting under Chapter VII, the UN Security Council decided that the political solution to the crisis would rest on the general principles adopted on 6 May by the G8 states and the principles contained in the Ahtisaari-Chernomyrdin peace plan.

EU plans for an economic reconstruction of the entire region backed the initiatives for a political settlement of the crisis. In April Germany proposed within the framework of the EU a Stability Pact for South-Eastern Europe (*document no. 196*). The Countries of South-Eastern Europe, the EU, the G8, and the representatives of different international organisations signed the Stability Pact in Cologne on 10 June 1999. The pact aims to achieve "lasting peace, prosperity and stability for South-Eastern Europe ... through a comprehensive and coherent approach to the region". The Pact is supposed to act as a clearing-house and in a co-ordinating role to stimulate activity by international agencies. The Pact has set up three working tables bringing together the various efforts in the region in a manner reminiscent of the CSCE: democratisation and human rights, economic reconstruction, development and cooperation, and security issues. In the field of human rights, leaders of specific task forces have been appointed. The Council of Europe, for instance, is responsible for good governance. Several international organisations are involved in the economic projects: the European Commission, the World Bank, the European Investment Bank, the European Bank for Reconstruction and Development and the OECD. However, the Pact attracts criticism. The Council of Europe, for instance, criticises the Pact for its present structure, since it delays its implementation.[3] In addition to the Pact, the EU pursues the long-term aim to negotiate Stabilisation and Association Agreements with Albania, Bosnia, Croatia, Macedonia and Yugoslavia.

---

[1] NATO, *One Year On - Achievement and Challenge* (2000), p. 26.
[2] Michael MccGwire, 'Why did we bomb Belgrade' (2000) 76 *International Affairs* 1-23 at 11.
[3] Council of Europe, Parliamentary Assembly, Report adopted on 4 April 2000; Available on http://stars.coe.fr/index_e.htm.

196. Germany, A Stability Pact for South-Eastern Europe, 12 April 1999

The pan-European effects of regional conflicts and instability mean that the medidum- and long-term stabilization of South-Eastern Europe is in our foreign, stability and security policy interests. If foreign, security and development policy are to amount to something more than one crisis management cycle after the other, we need to adopt a broad approach of preventive and lasting conflict resolution in the region.

A medium- and long-term policy must aim to prevent violent confrontations emerging in the region, to create lasting conditions for democracy, a market economy and regional cooperation, and to anchor the South-Eastern European countries firmly in the Euro-Atlantic structures. A negotiated solution for Kosovo, and its implementation, present both an opportunity and a prerequisite for such an approach.

The EU Common Strategy for the Western Balkans, commissioned by the Vienna European Council, is of great importance for the stabilization of the region in the medium and long term. Depending on the outcome of efforts to settle the Kosovo crisis, Germany together with its partners in the European Union will also take the initiative (within CFSP) for a Stability Pact for South-Eastern Europe under the auspices of the OSCE. A high-level international opening conference would launch a long-term stabilization process, bringing together the South-Eastern European countries and representatives of the international community at a "South-Eastern Europe Regional Round Table", which would include several more specialized fora (subjects to include border and minority issues, return of displaced persons, economic cooperation, civil societies) as well as talks on arms control. The aim of the stability pact is the conclusion and consistent implementation of bilateral and multilateral agreements as well as domestic accords to surmount political and economic structural deficits, and thus the region's potential for conflict.

I. Causes of the Conflict

Structural shortfalls and unresolved issues in South-Eastern Europe are concentrated mainly, albeit not exclusively, in the partner states of the EU Regional Approach (Albania, Bosnia and Herzegovina, the Federal Republic of Yugoslavia, FYROM, Croatia). The region is heterogeneous in every respect - ethnically, culturally, religiously, linguistically, economically and politically. Nevertheless some potential conflict causes are shared by almost all the aforementioned countries:

- unresolved territorial and minority questions,
- economic backwardness and high levels of economic distortion, due to, inter alia, Titoist economic self-administration, war and reform bottlenecks,
- considerable shortfalls in the democratization process and in building up civil societies,
- reluctance to resort to peaceful conflict settlement mechanisms and to confidence-building measures, and
- underdeveloped regional cooperation structures.es

II. Our Interests

Our interests in South-Eastern Europe are largely in line with those of our partners. These lie primarily in the following areas:

- the containment of violent ethnic conflict, as a pre-requisite for lasting stability all over Europe,
- the reduction of migration motivated by poverty, war, persecution and civil strife,
- the concretization of democracy, as well as human and minority rights, as the aim of a valueled foreign policy,
- the establishment of market economy structures with stable economic growth to close the prosperity gap in Europe,
- economic interests (expandable markets, investment targets), and
- the maintenance of cohesion and credibility of international organizations in which we play an active role (EU, NATO, OSCE, UN).

III. Parameters of Success

A strategy to stabilize the region in the medium and long term must incorporate the following points and criteria:

- An attempt to solve the closely-intertwined and in some cases centuries-old con-flicts at one fell swoop would be doomed to failure. We must launch an effective process which creates the conditions for a stable and peaceful development of South-Eastern Europe through democratization, increasing economic prosperity and strengthening regional cooperation. The building of civil societies, taking particular account of the problems of minorities, plays a pivotal role.

- The countries' responsibility in achieving these goals cannot be replaced by impetus and assistance from outside. To increase this sense of responsibility, incentives should regularly be linked to fulfilling specific requirements.

- It will not be possible to bring lasting peace and stability to South-Eastern Europe if the Federal Republic of Yugoslavia persists in its role as an outsider and cannot be accepted as a negotiating partner by its neighbours (or the international community). Until then, international efforts must focus on consolidating and linking the islands of stability in the region to lay a firm foundation in all countries for the transition of the FRY and the region as a whole to a peaceful, democratic future.

- Any attempt at long term stabilization of the region in the long term must involve the neighbouring countries of the partners of the EU Regional Approach fully, not only because of their geographical proximity, without however burdening the process by additional conflict potential.

- The great heterogeneity of the States in the region requires, on the one hand, that we take on board the interests and problems of individual countries and consider the progress each of them has made in the reform process. On the other hand, the political and structural deficits these countries share require an all-embracing approach. A strategy of stabilization in the medium and long term must combine both approaches so that they complement and strengthen each other.

- The explosive nature of the region was and is, at least in some countries, marked by a readiness to resort to violence and large stocks of weapons to go with it. Efforts to bring stability, as highlighted by the Bosnia-Herzegovina example, must incorporate arms control measures (confidence-building and disarmament) to counter this.

- One of the international community's most important tasks in the region is to defuse the critical playoff between the people's right to self-determination and maintaining the unity of a multi-ethnic state. In this, the principle of the inviolability of borders is to be upheld.

IV. Recommendations and Instruments for Action

Given its particular interest in the stability of the region Germany together with its partners in the EU should lead an effort towards devising a medium- and long-term strategy to stabilize South-Eastern Europe. This strategy should take into account the results of existing Regional Initiatives such as CEI and SECI. Over time however these initiatives should be integrated into the strategy towards a single and comprehensive approach. A common European policy is crucial.

The main players in this field are the EU and the OSCE. For the countries in the region, the EU is the most important political and economic point of orientation (cooperation, rapprochement, membership). The pan-European nature of the OSCE means that, at present, under its auspices alone can a long-term stabilization strategy materialize. All the more so because via the OSCE the involvement of other interested OSCE member States such as the USA and Russia in a stabilization strategy for South-Eastern Europe is ensured.

NATO, the Council of Europe, the United Nations and the International Financial Institutions, in their specific functions, will remain crucial for the stabilization of South-Eastern Europe. It will be a matter of bringing together the stabilization efforts of all those involved to create a web of complementary and mutually enhancing institutions so that the total is greater than the sum of its parts.

1. THE EUROPEAN UNION, PACE-SETTER AND INCENTIVE FOR SOUTH-EASTERN EUROPE TO CONTINUE THE REFORM PROCESS

The EU can, beyond its current instruments (regional approach for Croatia, Bosnia and Herzegovina, the Federal Republic of Yugoslavia, FYROM and Albania, large-scale efforts to reconstruct Bosnia and Herzegovina), do more for the medium- and long-term stabilization of South-Eastern Europe:

- Raising the EU's political visibility and effectiveness in the region: the EU Common Strategy for the Western Balkans (commissioned by the Vienna European Council) involving the neighbouring States; nomination of an EU Special Representative for South-Eastern Europe and/or mandating the new CFSP Special Representative; review of current EU mechanisms.

- Clear and repeated commitment on the part of the EU that the countries in the region have a prospect of acceding, even if the time of accession can not yet be determined. This is not merely based on equality of treatment with the Central and Eastern European States. As developments in the CEE countries have shown, the prospect of EU membership is a key incentive to reform. This is the only way to keep the South-Eastern European countries on the stabilization track in the long term. Once conditions are met (full use of the trade and cooperation agreements, resolution of the minority problems) the EU must be ready to hold out the prospect of association to the countries in question, for example in the case of FYROM.

- EU (CFSP) initiative within the OSCE for a "Stability Pact for South-Eastern Europe" in coordination with EU partners.

2. OSCE - THE STABILITY PACT FOR SOUTH-EASTERN EUROPE

The OSCE must act as an umbrella for a process of medium- and long-term stabilization of South-Eastern Europe. In the medium term, the EU (CFSP) should develop an initiative for a Stability Pact for South-Eastern Europe within the OSCE.

In view of the particular problems in the region, a Stability Pact for South-Eastern Europe should be more broadly-based than the Stability Pact of 1994/95 (Stability Pact Plus) and should cover the whole range of regional crisis factors. A "South-Eastern Europe Regional Round Table" could include several fora or more specialized working groups:

- border and minority issues,
- return of displaced persons and refugees,
- economic questions (strengthening regional cooperation structures/free trade area),
- promoting civil societies by encouraging dialogue between the social elites of the countries concerned.

The aim of these institutionalized regional talks is the conclusion of bilateral and multilateral agreements as well as domestic accords to surmount the political and economic structural deficits and thus the region's potential for conflict.

The Stability Pact for South-Eastern Europe needs initial political impetus in the form of a high-level opening conference. This "starting blocks" conference must mark the break-off point in public perception between reactive crisis management and the launch of a process of active medium and long term stabilization of South-Eastern Europe. It is of course clear that this process can have nothing to do with a 19th century-style "Balkans conference" and that this is not what we intend.

The following aspects must also be taken into account in a Stability Pact for South-Eastern Europe:

- It will not be simple getting all the States of the region round a table, due to the deep-rooted mutual distrust and the unjustified fear of being dictated to by Europe. The European Stability Pact had similar teething problems. The EU, the Council of Europe, NATO and the WEU must therefore encourage participation using a system of incentives and disincentives (clear signals: participation paves the way into the Euro-Atlantic structures, non-participation blocks it off).

- The Stability Pact for South-Eastern Europe will need the additional support of a donor and reconstruction conference. In this case, crisis prevention is also cost prevention. Cross-border and cross-community economic and education programmes, infrastructure investment, projects in the fields of minority protection, institution-building and freedom of the media are essential but do not come for free.

- Arms control is pivotal to the OSCE's comprehensive security concept. Regional approaches in accordance with the Dayton agreement (Annex 1B) have been successfully implemented in two accords (confidence-building in Bosnia and Herzegovina, disarmament agreement for Bosnia and Herzegovina, the Federal Republic of Yugoslavia and Croatia). Now negotiations to establish a regional balance in and around the former Yugoslavia are on the way (Dayton, Annex 1B, Article V). The mandate agreed by the Contact Group and 20 participating States in the region, in view of the experience in Kosovo, provides for the inclusion of paramilitary forces. In the longer term, the aim has to remain the full and equal inclusion of South-Eastern Europe, above all the Federal Republic of Yugoslavia, in the cooperative security structure of the OSCE with its control mechanisms.

- The stabilization process must go hand in hand with establishing and strengthening competitive and internationally-integrated private sectors in the region. This includes, inter alia, support in building up strong SME, encouraging privatization, incentives for international cooperation in the business sector (including EU trade preferences, suitable financing and guarantee facilities). Bilateral development cooperation could act as a catalyst here.

- In the early stages, the Stability Pact for South-Eastern Europe should build on the Royaumont process: (1) the Royaumont process is a Joint Action of the EU, (2) it is the EU's only joint regional cooperation initiative so far, (3) the Federal Republic of Yugoslavia is a full Royaumont member, that is, the Royaumont process could be used as a training ground for the subsequent Stability Pact.

- The Stability Pact should aim to bring under one roof the current initiatives to foster regional cooperation (for example, the South-Eastern Europe Cooperation Initiative - SECI, Central European Initiative etc.).

3. NATO - SECURITY POLICY INTEGRATION AND SUPPORTIVE STABILIZATION

Alongside accession to the EU, the prospect of NATO membership is one of the most important incentives for reform for the countries of South-Eastern Europe. Therefore, it is particularly important that NATO continues its course and keeps the door open to new members in the long term. Similarly, the Alliance should make its current cooperation instruments (EAPC, PfP) accessible to Croatia, Bosnia and Herzegovina and the Federal Republic of Yugoslavia once they meet the conditions.

NATO must retain its presence in South-Eastern Europe in the medium and long term, in conflict prevention and the development of modern security policy thinking (EAPC, PfP), in peace-keeping (SFOR) as well as peace-making.

Thus, the international community's conflict management in the crisis countries in the region must continue to rely on averting bloodshed, with the threat - and as a last resort - the use of force. The military potential of NATO thus remains indispensable to the credibility of western diplomacy in the region. The proposals currently under discussion in the North Atlantic Council aiming at the best use of the opportunities granted by the Euro Atlantic Partnership Council and the Partnership for Peace to enhance stability and security in South Eastern Europe are highly appreciated as a major contribution to this Stability Pact. They give a valuable example how to implement the objectives of this Pact in a practical manner as far as NATO's Partners in the region are concerned. However, any such initiative should be confined to NATO's role and objectives in the field of Security Policy.

V. Civil Society as the Task of Political Micro-Management

Building civil societies is key to a stable and peaceful development in the region. Supporting the gradual social, political and economic change in the countries of South-Eastern Europe must therefore remain the focus of complementary measures to the proposed multilateral stabilization approach. The international community is already active in the following areas:

- building democratic institutions,
- creating a sufficient basis for the livelihood of the vast majority of the population,
- supporting domestic and cross-border return of refugees,
- increasing levels of professionalism and democracy in the armed forces,
- promoting independent media and non-governmental organizations,
- economic and legislative counselling, basic and further training of political and economic leadership, promoting the private sector.

These measures from bilateral and multilateral donors must be continued in the short, medium and long term and be developed into a cooperation approach which focuses on priority areas.

197. U.S. Secretary of State Albright and Russian Foreign Minister Ivanov Joint Press Availability, as Released by the Office of the Spokesman U.S. Department of State, Oslo, 13 April 1999

Foreign Minister Ivanov: Dear ladies and gentlemen, we have finished our meeting, our meeting with the Secretary of State of the United States, Mrs. Albright. The meeting was held in accordance with the agreements reached by our two Presidents, Presidents of our two countries, and the purpose was to set up the general contours of a political settlement in the Balkans to stop the bloodshed and violence. On these issues, Mrs. Albright and I find ourselves in constant contact, and this is understandable since today we are talking not only about the Balkans, but about the future of U.S.-Russian relations.

Our discussion, naturally, was not simple. The positions of Russia, vis-à-vis military actions against Yugoslavia remains unchanged. The most important thing, however, is that in Oslo we proceeded from the common task of finding a way out of this cul-de-sac, and therefore the talk was not so much about what divides Russia and the United States today, as those approaches which would lead us to a settlement.

Now, the common elements in our approaches are quite a few. Russia and the United States really use as a starting point the fact that in the final analysis the Kosovo settlement can be only political. In achieving this goal, the most active role can and should be played by the international community. Naturally, the United States and we maintain also certain differences of opinion. The constant dialogue between our two Presidents and between our Prime Minister and Vice President Gore, and between the Ministers of Foreign Affairs is precisely aimed at reducing these kinds of differences of opinion. That's why I believe that today's meeting between us was very useful and very timely.

We agreed with Mrs. Albright to continue active political and diplomatic efforts in the interest of a political settlement. We also discussed today very timely issues of U.S.-Russian relations and certain other international relations issues, specifically, a Middle East settlement, issues of non-proliferation, disarmament, issue of Iraq. The heads of our two states, as they stressed in the letters which President Yeltsin and President Clinton exchanged just a few days ago, here they stressed the high priority which we attach to U.S.-Russian mutual relations and cooperation in order to achieve international stability.

Secretary Albright: As Foreign Minister Ivanov has said, we have had a very good and useful meeting and we came here today to look for ways to work together to resolve the crisis in Kosovo. The U.S.-Russian relationship has as its foundation our many common interests and shared goals. Simply put, it is in the interest of both our nations to work together whenever we can, and today we have made some important progress.

As the Foreign Minister said, we did talk about a number of other subjects besides Kosovo. He listed them, so I won't go through that again. But as far as Kosovo is concerned, we have reached agreement on many of the basic principles that must be respected in any resolution of the crisis in Kosovo, for example, that there needs to be an immediate and verifiable end of violence and oppression in Kosovo. There has to be withdrawal from Kosovo of military police and paramilitary forces. There has to be unconditional and safe return of all refugees and displaced persons regardless of their ethnicity or religion, and for allowing the international humanitarian organizations unhindered access to fulfill their functions throughout Yugoslavia and, in the first place, in Kosovo.

We will continue to work together to attain a common basis for a resolution of this crisis, and the work we have done today has helped to lay a foundation for a result that we all seek. I think that it is very important that we continue this work together. Foreign Minister Ivanov and I have spent a great deal of time in the last weeks on the telephone with each other. We have wanted to have this face-to-face meeting. We will continue our phone work as well as the possibility, obviously, of meeting again in person. [...]

Question: Mr. Minister, the Secretary ticked off four things which she said there was agreement in principle. She made no mention of an international force. So the question is, is there something in these four points that represents a change in position by the Russian government? Has either government, in fact, changed its position in any way? You, in your search for a diplomatic solution, have you found the U.S. more inclined now to pursue diplomacy? The U.S., in its search for support for you, for what NATO is doing - any change, any place?

Foreign Minister Ivanov: The Secretary of State mentioned the items where we have significant commonality, and there are also a series of additional items. As far as the international presence, this is an issue - one of the most complicated ones today - and we are going to continue discussion of this item. You know that this had been discussed at the negotiations at Rambouillet and during subsequent contacts. And in fact it is complicated, because you know that the leadership of Yugoslavia today comes out against any kind of military presence on the territory of Yugoslavia. At the same time, we talked about an acceptable form of international presence in order to provide conditions for a political settlement would be necessary. Now the form it takes, this is something that we should discuss in the future, and we should work on. I think that the dialogue is the format which allows us to find a way of bringing our positions closer and to find solutions of the most difficult and complicated issues. So that the dialogue between us continues, and we believe the faster we can get out of this cul-de-sac, the better it will be for the situation in the Balkans and in the world as a whole.

Secretary Albright: Could I just continue with that? Let me just say, clearly as Foreign Minister Ivanov has said, this has been one of the difficult aspects of trying to get an agreement. What also has been interesting in our discussions and he pointed out here is that there is agreement that there needs to be some kind of an international presence that would in fact provide the security and the confidence for the refugees to be able to return. What we disagree on, or have not yet reached agreement on, is the character of that kind of a force. As you know, yesterday NATO made some statements about it. And our sense is that it has to have a NATO core with other countries being able to provide other aspects of it, or to work in coordination.

I think that as the Foreign Minister said, this is a subject that we have not yet reached agreement on and is a very central aspect of any final agreement that we come to. But I have to say that I think that what we have managed today is, as has been a part of all our discussions today, is to really have a very frank and important discussion about the pros and cons of various ways of dealing with this issue.

Question: Mr. Minister, have you talked about bringing in other foreign ministers of the G-8 into this format?

Foreign Minister Ivanov: We have a constant contact among and between a whole series of Ministers of Foreign Affairs, both bilateral and multilateral. I think here that nobody should be excluded. Everyone who wishes to participate actively in the search for agreement, a way to get out of the situation, I think we are open to cooperation with every Minister.

Question: Mr. Ivanov, can you say specifically what Russia sees as a (inaudible) of an international force? What it would take for Russia to be part of this force? And, you said you wanted to continue contacts, but when do you see this thing brought to closure? And, would Russia support a UN resolution that would basically back some of the principles that you articulated today?

Foreign Minister Ivanov: I want to clarify our position on the international presence. This position, in one form or another, has already been exposed and said. Any form of international presence requires the agreement of the leadership of Yugoslavia. Therefore, to speak now, about a certain format until or before Belgrade agrees to something like this, this is very complicated. That is why, as far as the resolution of the Security Council of the United Nations, it undoubtedly can be useful and we are in favor of a more active inclusion of the United Nations in the search for finding a way out of this. But any resolution must of necessity, be directed at finding a solution and be achievable. A resolution cannot be adopted just to have something that is adopted. Because, if we see a resolution will help progress toward the settlement, then such a resolution should be adopted.

Question: Have you received any news at all as far as what form NATO, or how NATO is going to be behaving in terms of finding a settlement? And, what is the policy of the alliance?

Foreign Minister Ivanov: Now, in terms of the future activities of NATO, our position in this regard is well-known. We feel that the sooner NATO ceases air strikes, then it will be easier to find a settlement. Yesterday there was a Council of NATO statement, and you all know what the position of NATO is from yesterday's communiqué.

Question: Mr. Minister, do you have or any of your fellow government leaders have any plans to go to Belgrade to talk to Mr. Milosevic about an international presence, and trying to persuade him to accept this?

Foreign Minister Ivanov: Russia tried to make attempts and will continue to attempt to find a way out of this cul-de-sac. If we have to go to Belgrade, we will go to Belgrade. If we have to go to Washington, we will go to Washington. We will go wherever it is necessary. The most important thing is that it promotes finding a settlement.

Question: In a few days, there should be a meeting of Ministers in Japan. Is that possible? Thank you.

Foreign Minister Ivanov: Well, as we said, we are ready for any meeting in any format. Right now, this issue today, we did not discuss it, but when we have a need to do so, I think I and Mrs. Albright will be ready.

Secretary Albright: I think both of us have expressed in any number of ways, our willingness to meet in whatever format. I think that it is so evident from our discussion today that we would like to see a solution to this terrible problem and end of the repression and the violence. We consider it very important to do what we can to bring this about in a way that provides justice.

Question: You mentioned withdrawal of police and military troops. Does that include regular troops as well?

Secretary Albright: Yes, we believe that - our view is that it means that all forces need to come out. Because, as a practical matter, it is very hard to imagine how those forces that have been committing these kinds of atrocities can be there if we want to see the Albanians and those who have been pushed out come back and live in a secure environment where they have the confidence to develop political solutions for their future.

Question: To both Ministers. Have you agreed on something which you are going to be telling us? In other words, is there something else beyond this press conference that you are not telling us? (Laughter)

Foreign Minister Ivanov: Well, I think that we have come to terms on the most important - to continue actively seeking to find a settlement and getting out of this situation. And, we are going to have very active contacts. I think that this really is in the interest of both international stability and the interest of U.S.-Russia relations. We have a certain point of view which we feel is necessary to continue working in order to try to find or get our positions closer. If we manage to do so, we will announce it when the time comes.

Question: Question for Minister Ivanov. You have criticized on many occasions the bombing by NATO, but you have been very silent on the fate of the refugees. And, what has happened in particular to the ethnic Albanians who are still inside Kosovo? Is your government taking measures to ask Belgrade to make it easier to provide international aid for the people inside Kosovo, many of whom seem to be close to starvation?

Foreign Minister Ivanov: I do not know about what you used as sources for my statements but I spoke about it. I said I was against it. And now it continues to be the position of Russia against the military operations of NATO. But at the same time, we are against any forms of violence, irrespective of who. If you noticed, in terms of what President Yeltsin said in his statement, the leadership of Yugoslavia said that it is prepared to provide the opportunity for the return of all refugees, irrespective of ethnicity or religion. This statement was made officially. This process can begin when there is a cessation of military operations of NATO.

Secretary Albright: Let me just add to that that we believe very strongly that it is not the NATO operation that is causing the problems for the refugees. And, in fact, we are convinced that the plans for this kind of ethnic cleansing and expulsion were in place for many months. And, therefore it was essential that NATO take the action it did in order to prevent even greater violence and instability.

Question: Question to Madame Secretary. Could you tell us what is the positive side of today's meeting, in addition to the fact that the meeting took place and in addition to the fact that you agreed to continue your contacts? In other words, do you see any positives here in terms of how Russia's position may have changed?

Secretary Albright: First of all, let me say that there were a number of positive aspects to our meeting. Because, I think it was evident when we talked to each other on the phone that we would like to see a solution to this problem. But, I think in our ability to begin to find areas of commonality, as I mentioned, those that we agreed on. I think we find that there is a narrowing of the differences that we have had. Ultimately, I have very much the sense that, as Foreign Minister Ivanov has said, the common goals of the United States and Russia to try to deal together with a myriad of problems that create instability is something that is the basis of our relationship, and is also very important in the terms of working generally on solutions to problems internationally, as well as in our bilateral relationship.

I think that there was a narrowing of some of the gaps, in terms of the basic principles which I discussed. And, I say this on my behalf, I don't think that there is a sense of one side pressuring the other, but more an honest discussion about how two great nations deal with each other with respect and with a desire to try to solve problems. We obviously look at it from a different perspective. The Foreign Minister has made very clear that Russia has not changed its views about NATO bombing. I made it very clear that I have not changed my views about the ultimate responsibility of Milosevic for all of this and the necessity for a NATO action.

I think that the meeting was a very important one, frankly as all our meetings are. But, this one, I think, really we managed to narrow our differences and will continue to do so for the good of solving this problem.

Foreign Minister Ivanov: Let me add that I think that we made yet one more step forward, maybe not as large as we wanted to, but it is a step forward, and really did quite a bit in today's situation.

198. U.S. Secretary of State Albright and Norwegian Foreign Minister Vollebaek: Joint Press Conference, as Released by the Office of the Spokesman U.S. Department of State, Oslo, 13 April 1999

[Parts not referring directly to the Kosovo crisis have been omitted.]

Question: There have been some reports today that Serb forces have entered Albanian territory and there's been some fighting inside of Albania today. What would be the NATO response and what is the U.S. response to that?

Secretary Albright: First of all, we have not been able to confirm that, and so I can't comment specifically on the incident that you're talking about. But, we have made clear within NATO as well as the United States specifically, that the widening of this conflict by the Serbs to the other countries in the region would have serious consequences.

Question: I was going to ask that question. Let me also ask was there any discussion with the Foreign Minister of Russia regarding that surveillance vessel and was there any discussion of the subject, in any manner or form, of ground troops, even in a hypothetical discussion - his response, what the U.S. view would be?

Secretary Albright: First of all, we have discussed the issue of the vessel many times, and the Russians do know our views on that. We did not discuss ground troops as such. We did talk, obviously, as I said in my press conference with Foreign Minister Ivanov, generally about the character of an international presence in a permissive environment.

Question: Is the U.S. willing to accept an international force in Kosovo under the auspices of the U.N. or the OSCE?

Secretary Albright: What we have said is that in order for the force to be effective - and one that we could support - it has to have a NATO core, so that the NATO command structure can operate to the satisfaction of the military leaders. We have also said that such a core NATO force could have other forces associated with it, in a variety of ways that can be discussed, including, obviously, some component in cooperation with OSCE. These questions are obviously open to discussion, but from our perspective, a core NATO aspect to it is essential because the only way that we would be able to participate is if the NATO command structure is able to operate as it must for military purposes.

Question: You said that NATO must stay its course until its terms are met. Where does that leave any mediation from the Russian side, or negotiations for a settlement for the attack on Kosovo?

Secretary Albright: We made clear yesterday, in the NATO declaration, what it is that President Milosevic has to do. There are five points to that. I will not read them to you again, but basically Milosevic knows what he has to do. I think that this is a NATO document and so the Russians do not agree with the formulation of a NATO document. But, as I said in my earlier press conference, there were a number of principles that are identical to these, in terms of: stopping the fighting and repression; the necessity to withdraw from Kosovo; the military police and paramilitary forces; the need for the safe return of all refugees, and the fact that humanitarian agencies need to have access. So, there was a great deal of similarity in those views. But, I think that we made very clear what it is that NATO is - NATO knows what Milosevic must do. So, we have made that very clear. That is what staying the course means.

Question: Do you, Mr. Vollebaek, rule out U.N. participation or a central U.N. role in a future peacekeeping force in Kosovo as the Secretary now does?

Foreign Minister Vollebaek: I didn't hear Secretary Albright ruling out U.N participation in a peacekeeping force. But what Secretary Albright stressed, and what I think is important, is that it has to have a NATO core. Then we can discuss - but I think it's unfortunately too early - the modalities around this. But when we reach the stage when we can implement the peace plan, I'm certain that we can find a solution to this.

I think, again, if I may repeat also what the Secretary said as a follow-up to the meeting yesterday, it is very important now that Milosevic starts reacting to the offers that he gets, like this meeting today between Foreign Minister Ivanov and Secretary Albright. So, there is a willingness on all sides to try to find a political solution. But, there are certain fundamental demands that have to be met, and he knows them. And, if he can come up with acceptance of a robust international military presence in Kosovo, that will be one of the demands, and a very important one.

Question: Did Mr. Ivanov, in any way, tell you that he or other leading Russian government members are ready to go to Belgrade again to talk to Mr. Milosevic?

Secretary Albright: He, in response to a question during that press conference, said that they would be willing to go, but he didn't say when or with what message. But, I think he indicated clearly that they are prepared to play a role. I think that our discussions show that they are very much determined to try to reach a political solution. We would all like to find a political solution. As I said, about the result of our talks, what to me was very important was that it was possible to narrow our gaps on some of the things where there had been some sense that there were differences.

Question: Did you ask him to go?

Secretary Albright: No, I did not.

Question: Did you and Foreign Minister Ivanov discuss Yugoslavia's wish to join a union with Russia and Belarus?

Secretary Albright: We talked about it, and he said that there were people on both sides in both countries that thought that this was a good idea. And we just generally discussed the fact that there is this phenomenon, but did not comment on it either positively or negatively.

199. Press Statements by Chancellor Mr. Schröder and Russian Special Envoy to the FRY, Mr. Chernomyrdin, Bonn, 29 April 1999

Chancellor Schröder: Ladies and gentlemen, I am greatly pleased that Mr. Chernomyrdin accepted my invitation. As you can well imagine, we focused on the situation in Kosovo and the special mission Mr. Chernomyrdin has assumed at President Yeltsin's request.

The German government expressly welcomes the role Russia has assumed in an attempt to reach a political solution of the conflict in Kosovo. It expressly welcomes the fact that Russia has strengthened its diplomatic and political activities by appointing Mr. Chernomyrdin. We know that a political solution and a lasting peace in this part of Europe as well as reasonable economic development will not be possible without Russia's involvement. We also know that our political desire to involve the UN, particularly the Security Council, more strongly in a political solution will not be possible without Russia.

Of course we are acting on the basis of the positions we helped to decide at the NATO summit in Washington and note in this context that there has been some narrowing of differences in the meantime. Three substantive demands are unrelinquishable:

1. The killing in Kosovo must stop.

2. The refugees must be able to return and must be protected by an international force, the core of which must be provided by NATO.

3. Yugoslav forces - including paramilitary and special police units - must be withdrawn.

When it has been verified that such a withdrawal has begun - and I emphasise: when it has begun - then it would make sense to contemplate a temporary suspension of the air strikes.

I think that as a result of the efforts that have been undertaken by the UN Secretary-General, and as a result of the efforts undertaken by Russia, in particular those of Mr. Chernomyrdin, movement has been created in the direction of a political solution. We have our sights set on this. Germany wants to see a political solution to the conflict. A lasting solution can be secured only on a reliable basis.

Chernomyrdin: Mr. Chancellor, ladies and gentlemen, I would like to begin by expressing my thanks to the Chancellor for the opportunity to meet with him today.

I received an invitation from you right after my appointment to this difficult post. Accordingly, my first visit with regard to this problem is to you. I am very pleased that we were able to discuss this problem at length and in detail. I would like to say to you once again that we will play our role as a mediator very conscientiously as we pursue a settlement of the problem in the Balkans and in Kosovo in particular. I am convinced that this problem merits very serious treatment.

I fully agree that first of all everything possible needs to be done to end the missile and bomb attacks against Kosovo and Yugoslavia. I also fully agree that we need to organise and to undertake everything possible to see to it that the refugees can return to their homes. We believe that in this regard Belgrade is pursuing a policy and moving in a direction so that a safe return can be guaranteed for these refugees. We approve an international presence under the umbrella of the United Nations and that is a very big step - in particular with Russian involvement. This is an initial step, one that engenders hope in us, particularly if the UN Secretary-General, Kofi Annan, is able to become involved with his structures, he being a person who has an enormous amount of experience in dealing with matters of this kind.

We are convinced we will be able to continue to move in this direction. If we can ensure that no missiles or bombs will fall on people's heads, if peace can be restored, then this is the primary objective to be worked towards. We discussed numerous questions today for which we have common approaches for resolving this problem. We hope that this understanding will spread to others and are very much counting on it. We will then be able to secure peace in the Balkans all the more rapidly. - Thank you.

200. G 8, Statement by the Chairman on the Conclusion of the Meeting of the G 8 Foreign Ministers, Petersberg, 6 May 1999

The G 8 Foreign Ministers adopted the following general principles on the political solution to the Kosovo crisis:

- Immediate and verifiable end of violence and repression in Kosovo;

- Withdrawal from Kosovo of military, police and paramilitary forces;

- Deployment in Kosovo of effective international civil and security presences, endorsed and adopted by the United Nations, capable of guaranteeing the achievement of the common objectives;

- Establishment of an interim administration for Kosovo to be decided by the Security Council of the United Nations to ensure conditions for a peaceful and normal life for all inhabitants in Kosovo;

- The safe and free return of all refugees and displaced persons and unimpeded access to Kosovo by humanitarian aid organisations;

A political process towards the establishment of an interim political framework agreement providing for a substantial self-government for Kosovo, taking full account of the Rambouillet accords and the principles of sovereignty and territorial integrity of the Federal Republic of Yugoslavia and the other countries of the region, and the demilitarization of the UCK;

Comprehensive approach to the economic development and stabilization of the crisis region.

In order to implement these principles the G 8 Foreign Ministers instructed their Political Directors to prepare elements of a United Nations Security Council resolution.

The Political Directors will draw up a roadmap on further concrete steps towards a political solution to the Kosovo crises.

The G 8 presidency will inform the Chinese government on the results of today's meeting.

Foreign Ministers will reconvene in due time to review the progress which has beeen achieved up to that point.

201. EU-World Bank Agreement on Economic Co-ordination, IP/99/329, Brussels, 12 May 1999

The World Bank and the European Commission (acting on behalf of the European Union) have agreed a mechanism to co-ordinate the response of the international community to the economic needs of the Balkans as a result of the Kosovo crisis. This agreement is contained in a joint statement signed today in London by World Bank President James Wolfensohn and Yves-Thibault de Silguy, Commissioner responsible for economic, monetary and financial affairs. It follows a decision at a meeting of high-level representatives of governments and international agencies in Washington on 27 April to give the EU and the World Bank joint responsibility to co-ordinate work on assessing the needs and mobilising support for the Balkans region. The Commission and the World Bank have already co-chaired donor meetings for Bulgaria and the Former Yugoslav Republic of Macedonia (FYROM) and there will be further meetings during May on Albania and Bosnia Herzegovina. At all these meetings the regional economic impact of the Kosovo crisis is discussed as well as the economic developments and the needs of the particular country concerned.

The full text of the statement follows:

"At the special high-level meeting of governments and international agencies held in Washington on 27 April to review the international community's response to the Kosovo crisis and its impact on Kosovo's neighbours in the Balkans, the World Bank and the Commission were called upon to co-ordinate needs assessment and modalities for assistance. We have today discussed how to put that mandate into operation.

We have started from the need, broadly endorsed at the meeting in Washington, for a comprehensive regional framework that takes into account the political, humanitarian, economic and social factors including plans for post-conflict reconstruction and recovery so as to ensure stability in the region in the medium term.

The World Bank and the Commission will work closely together, and in close co-operation with the IMF, to ensure that an efficient economic co-ordination mechanism is in operation, in line with the following basic principles, namely, the need to: take fully into account the regional dimension; keep structures light and efficient, and where possible build on existing structures; enhance co-operation among the countries of the region themselves; have a direct and efficient link between political and economic co-ordination, bearing in mind the respective mandates of the institutions.

To put these principles into practice, we have decided to set up immediately a joint office in Brussels and to create a small Task Force composed of officials from the Commission and the World Bank, co-operating closely with the IMF and other major donors. The Task Force, which will meet regularly, will ensure that the regional dimension is fully taken into account, and will co-ordinate four main tasks: donor mobilisation, through high-level donor conferences and donor consultative groups, chaired by the World Bank and the Commission; economic analysis, and the identification and estimation of needs, the definition of strategies and priorities, and the assessment of progress; conditions of support, to ensure the consistency of the criteria on which donor funding would be committed; implementation, mainly on the spot with a local task force in each country, supported by sectoral groups, if appropriate.

It is proposed that the work of the Task Force, especially for major priority setting, the regional dimension and donor mobilisation, will be guided by a high-level group, composed of Messrs Camdessus, de Silguy and Wolfensohn, and the major donors at ministerial level. The role of this group will be reviewed in the light of decisions on the political co-ordination process.

The Task Force will start work immediately. As well as mobilising donor assistance through consultative groups, its first tasks will include establishing, regularly updating and circulating to the donor community: a calendar of events at which the economic impact of the Kosovo crisis will be discussed; an overview of the assessment of the economic impacts and costs; a register of donor assistance, which will include both amounts and type of assistance by country, as well as regional aggregates, so as to help avoid duplication and to identify gaps.

In addition, the World Bank and the Commission plan to call and chair meetings of governments of the region, bilateral donors, multilateral financial and non-financial institutions and other interested parties."

202. EU, Common Position Adopted by the Council on the Basis of Article 15 of the EU Treaty Concerning a Stability Pact for South-Eastern Europe, 1999/345/CFSP, 17 May 1999[1]

The Council of the European Union,

Having regard to the Treaty on European Union, and in particular Article 15 thereof;

Whereas:

(1) on 8 and 26 April 1999 the Council adopted conclusions concerning South-Eastern Europe;

(2) a political solution to the Kosovo crisis must be embedded in a determined effort geared towards stabilising the region as a whole;

(3) a Stability Pact for South-Eastern Europe should be prepared;

(4) such a Stability Pact should be founded on the UN Charter, the principles and commitments of the OSCE, and the relevant treaties and conventions of the Council of Europe, in particular the European Convention on Human Rights;

(5) the European Union should play the leading role in the Stability Pact, the OSCE has a key role to play in fostering security and stability, and the Stability Pact should be developed and implemented in close association with the OSCE;

(6) the European Union, within the framework of the regional approach and beyond, is already active in strengthening democratic and economic institutions in the region through a number of well established programmes;

(7) the European Union will drawn the region closer to the perspective of full integration of these countries into its structures through a new kind of contractual relationship, taking into account the individual situation of each country, with a perspective of European Union membership on the basis of the Treaty of Amsterdam and once the Copenhagen criteria have been met;

(8) the Federal Republic of Yugoslavia should be invited to participate in such a Stability Pact once it has met the necessary conditions,

has adopted this Common Position:

Article 1

1. the European Union will play the leading role in establishing a Stability Pact for South-Eastern Europe.

2. The aim of this Stability Pact is to help ensure cooperation among its participants towards comprehensive measures for the long-term stabilisation, security, democratisation, and economic reconstruction and development of the region, and for the establishment of durable good-neighbourly relations among and between them, and with the international community.

3. The European Union will work to ensure the creation among the participants themselves of a "South-Eastern Europe Regional Table" to carry forwards the Stability Pact.

Article 2

1. In order to further the objectives stated in Article 1 the European Union will convene a conference on South-Eastern Europe.

2. The conference will take place at the level of Foreign Ministers, if possible no later than the end of July 1999. The conference will be held using the Royaumont format (excluding the Federal Republic of Yugoslavia until it has met the conditions of the international community for its participation). In addition, representatives of Canada, Japan, EBRD, EIB, IMF, WB, OECD, UN, NATO, WEU, UNHCR, as well as representatives of regional initiatives will also participate at the conference.

3. The conference will be prepared at a meeting in Königswinter (Petersberg) on 27 May 1999 at the level of senior officials, in the format set out in paragraph 2. With a view to this, work for this conference will be carried forward urgently.

Article 3

1. The European Union will actively support the countries in the region in achieving the objectives on the Stability Pact.

2. The European Union will undertake together with international donors to organise a donors/reconstruction conference for South-Eastern Europe.

Article 4

This Common Position shall take effect on the date of its adoption.

Article 5

This Common Position shall be published in the Official Journal.

Done at Brussels, 17 May 1999. For the Council: The President J. Fischer

203. EU, Statement on Kosovo, Brussels, 31 May 1999[2]

1. The international community continues to exert strong pressure on the Belgrade authorities to reverse their course of action in Kosovo and accept its demands for a political solution. The Council reaffirmed the European Union's full support for the efforts, including a possible mission to Belgrade in the coming days, by the President of Finland, Martti Ahtisaari, on behalf of the European Union, in close cooperation with the United States, Russia and the United Nations. In this regard, the Council expects Belgrade to translate its reported statements into a firm, unambiguous and verifiable commitment to accept the G8 principles and a Security Council resolution. The Presidency will remain in close contact with President Ahtisaari with a view to his attending the European Council in Cologne.

2. The Council welcomed the strong endorsement by the international community of the Stability Pact for South-Eastern Europe and the result of the Petersberg Conference of 27 May. Work should now be carried forward urgently to clear remaining open issues among participants. The European Union looks forward to an early ministerial meeting to adopt the Stability Pact, and welcomed the Presidency's preparations for it.

204. Agreement on the Principles (Peace Plan) to Move towards a Resolution of the Kosovo Crisis Presented to the Leadership of the FRY by the President of Finland, Mr. Ahtisaari, Representing the European Union, and Mr. Chernomyrdin, Special Representative of the President of the Russian Federation, 3 June 1999[3]

Agreement should be reached on the following principles to move towards a resolution of the Kosovo crisis:

1. An immediate and verifiable end of violence and repression in Kosovo.

---

[1] OJ L 133, 28/05/1999 p. 0001 - 0002, 499X0345.

[2] UN.Doc. S/1999/650, Annex, 7 June 1999.
[3] UN Doc. S/1999/649, Annex, 7 June 1999.

2. Verifiable withdrawal from Kosovo of all military police and paramilitary forces according to a rapid timetable.

3. Deployment in Kosovo under United Nations auspices of effective international civil and security presences, acting as may be decided under Chapter VII of the Charter, capable of guaranteeing the achievement of common objectives.

4. The international security presence with substantial North Atlantic Treaty Organization participation must be deployed under unified command and control and authorized to establish a safe environment for all people in Kosovo and to facilitate the safe return to their homes of all displaced persons and refugees.

5. Establishment of an interim administration for Kosovo as a part of the international civil presence under which the people of Kosovo can enjoy substantial autonomy within the Federal Republic of Yugoslavia, to be decided by the Security Council of the United Nations. The interim administration to provide transitional administration while establishing and overseeing the development of provisional democratic self-governing institutions to ensure conditions for a peaceful and normal life for all inhabitants in Kosovo.

6. After withdrawal, an agreed number of Yugoslav and Serbian personnel will be permitted to return to perform the following functions:

- Liaison with the international civil mission and the international security presence;
- Marking/clearing minefields;
- Maintaining a presence at Serb patrimonial sites;
- Maintaining a presence at key border crossings.

7. Safe and free return of all refugees and displaced persons under the supervision of the Office of the United Nations High Commissioner for Refugees and unimpeded access to Kosovo by humanitarian aid organizations.

8. A political process towards the establishment of an interim political framework agreement providing for substantial self-government for Kosovo, taking full account of the Rambouillet accords and the principles of sovereignty and territorial integrity of the Federal Republic of Yugoslavia and the other countries of the region, and the demilitarization of UCK. Negotiations between the parties for a settlement should not delay or disrupt the establishment of democratic self-governing institutions.

9. A comprehensive approach to the economic development and stabilization of the crisis region. This will include the implementation of a stability pact for South-Eastern Europe with broad international participation in order to further promotion of democracy, economic prosperity, stability and regional cooperation.

10. Suspension of military activity will require acceptance of the principles set forth above in addition to agreement to other, previously identified, required elements, which are specified in the footnote below.[1] A military-technical agreement will then be rapidly concluded that would, among other things, specify additional modalities, including the roles and functions of Yugoslav/Serb personnel in Kosovo:

Withdrawal

- Procedures for withdrawals, including the phased, detailed schedule and delineation of a buffer area in Serbia beyond which forces will be withdrawn;

---

[1] Other required elements:
- A rapid and precise timetable for withdrawals, meaning, e.g., seven days to complete withdrawal and air defence weapons withdrawn outside a 25 kilometre mutual safety zone within 48 hours;
- Return of personnel for the four functions specified above will be under the supervision of the international security presence and will be limited to a small agreed number (hundreds, not thousands);
- Suspension of military activity will occur after the beginning of verifiable withdrawals;
- The discussion and achievement of a military-technical agreement shall not extend the previously determined time for completion of withdrawals.

Returning personnel
- Equipment associated with returning personnel;
- Terms of reference for their functional responsibilities;
- Timetable for their return;
- Delineation of their geographical areas of operation;
- Rules governing their relationship to the international security presence and the international civil mission.

205. FRY, Statement from the Federal Government's Meeting, Belgrade, 3 June 1999

At today's meeting, chaired by Prime Minister Momir Bulatovic, the Federal Government fully supported Serbian Parliament's decision to accept the peace proposal suggested by special Russian presidential envoy Victor Chernomyrdin and Finnish President Martti Ahtisaari, the envoy of the European Union and the United Nations.

The government accepted the peace proposal as it guarantees the sovereignty and territorial integrity of the Federal Republic of Yugoslavia, prevents the terrorist and separatist activities and ends the aggression against our country, the sufferings of the population and the destruction of national resources.

The government assesses as especially important the fact that decision-making is being shifted to the United Nations, the basis of the UN Charter.

This decision is another confirmation of the lasting Yugoslavia's orientation towards peace, stability and the resolution of all issues by political means.

206. EU, Presidency Conclusions, Cologne European Council, 3 and 4 June 1999

[Parts not pertinent to the situation in Kosovo have been omitted.]

V. External Relations

KOSOVO

62. The European Council adopted the declaration on Kosovo set out in the Annex.

WESTERN BALKANS

63. Throughout the crisis, the European Union has been in the forefront of efforts to ease the plight of refugees and displaced persons. The European Council reaffirms the willingness of the European Union and its Member States to continue to do their utmost to support the countries in the region and the humanitarian aid organisations in fulfilling their important humanitarian mission. In this connection it welcomes the extraordinary efforts of the countries in the region, particularly Albania and the Former Yugoslav Republic of Macedonia, to grant temporary protection and shelter to the displaced persons in spite of the severe economic and social burden.

64. The European Council emphasises the Union's commitment to regional stability and its pledge to stand by the countries in the region and help shoulder the burden imposed on them by the Kosovo crisis. The European Council recalls the 100 million financial assistance package pledged to countries in the region.

65. The European Council reiterates the European Union's commitment to take a leading role in the reconstruction efforts in Kosovo, and calls on other donors to participate generously in the reconstruction effort. To this end, a clear and effective transitional administration of the province will need to be established in the framework of the political solution. This administration, which could be headed by the European Union, will need to have the authority and capacity to act as a counterpart to the international community, enabling an effective reconstruction and rehabilitation process.

66. The European Council invites the Commission to develop, as a matter of priority, proposals regarding the organisation of reconstruction assistance envisaged, in particular on the appropriate means and

mechanisms to be put in place and the necessary human and financial resources to carry out the process.

67. Conscious of the exceptional effort that will have to be made to reconstruct the region following the end of the crisis and of the necessity to put in place rapidly the most appropriate measures, the European Council invites the Commission to elaborate proposals before the end of June aimed at creating an agency to be charged with the implementation of Community reconstruction programmes. The Council, the European Parliament and the Court of Auditors are called upon to do their utmost to allow the agency to become operational before the end of the summer.

68. In the light of the foreseeable needs the European Council invites the Commission to come forward as soon as possible with proposals for additional human und financial resources for refugee relief and return, including, as appropriate, the mobilisation of the existing 196 million reserve on the current European Community budget, transfer of funds from other budget lines or a proposal for a supplementary budget for 1999. Appropriate solutions will be needed for the following years.

69. The European Council looks forward to adopting a Common Strategy on the Western Balkans, in accordance with the conclusions of the Vienna European Council, and invites the Council to continue to press ahead with the necessary preparations.

70. The European Council confirms the position of the European Union in connection with sports events with the Federal Republic of Yugoslavia. The Council will re-examine the matter after a UN Security Council Resolution has been adopted.

STABILITY PACT FOR SOUTH-EASTERN EUROPE

71. The European Council warmly welcomes the progress made towards defining the Stability Pact for South-Eastern Europe, and looks forward to early agreement at the planned Ministerial meeting to be held in Cologne on 10 June. The Stability Pact will help to enhance peace, stability and prosperity in, and cooperation between, countries in the region. The participation of the Federal Republic of Yugoslavia in this process will be examined in due course, once it has met the conditions of the international community on Kosovo. The settlement of the Kosovo crisis represents a prerequisite. Furthermore, the European Council recalls the necessity for progress in democratic freedoms and respect for the rights of minorities.

72. The European Council reaffirms the readiness of the European Union to draw the countries of this region closer to the prospect of full integration into its structures. This will be done through a new kind of contractual relationship taking into account the individual situations of each country, including progress in regional cooperation, and with a prospect of European Union membership on the basis of the Amsterdam Treaty and fulfilment of the criteria defined at the Copenhagen European Council in June 1993.

73. The European Union will do its utmost to support the Republic of Montenegro under its democratic Government, making it a beneficiary of the Stability Pact process right from the beginning.

74. The European Council emphasises its determination that the European Union should take the lead in the implementation of the Stability Pact. It invites the Council and the Commission to give priority to taking the necessary implementing measures. The Union will actively assist the countries in the region in their efforts to achieve the goals of the Stability Pact. In keeping with its leading role, the European Union will appoint, after consultation with the Chairman-in-Office of the Organisation for Security and Cooperation in Europe and other participants, the Special Coordinator for the Stability Pact.

75. The European Council takes note of the efforts of the Commission and the World Bank in developing a coherent international assistance strategy and in preparing rapidly for a donors conference process for South Eastern Europe, based on a joint realistic assessment of financial means for economic reconstruction of the region in mid- and long term perspective.

76. The European Council confirms its willingness to contribute substantially to the reconstruction efforts and calls upon other donors to join these efforts generously.

77. The European Council reiterates the importance of effective coordination among Commission, International Financial Institutions and bilateral donors. In this context, the Special Coordinator of the Stability Pact will have to play an important role.

[...]

Annex V
EUROPEAN COUNCIL DECLARATION ON KOSOVO

President Ahtisaari, mandated by the European Union, reported to the Heads of State or of Government meeting in Cologne on the mission he had undertaken to Belgrade together with Mr Chernomyrdin, Special Envoy of the President of the Russian Federation.

The Heads of State or of Government congratulated the two emissaries on the success of their demarche. They took note of the Yugoslav authorities' acceptance of the peace plan setting out and detailing the international community's demands.

The Heads of State or of Government acknowledge that there is now a real possibility of achieving a political settlement, the first stage of which is to begin the verifiable withdrawal of all Yugoslav forces from Kosovo. This would enable NATO operations to be suspended. They want this process to be initiated immediately.

They therefore emphasise the urgent need for the adoption of a UN Security Council Resolution authorising the creation of the international security force and the setting up of the provisional international civil administration.

They decided that a draft Resolution will be drafted without delay so that it can be forwarded immediately to the member countries of the Security Council. [...]

207. Military-Technical Agreement between the International Security Force (KFOR) and the Governments of the FRY and the Republic of Serbia, 9 June 1999[1]

Article I: General Obligations

1. The Parties to this Agreement reaffirm the document presented by President Ahtisaari to President Milosevic and approved by the Serb Parliament and the Federal Government on June 3, 1999, to include deployment in Kosovo under UN auspices of effective international civil and security presences. The Parties further note that the UN Security Council is prepared to adopt a resolution, which has been introduced, regarding these presences.

2. The State Governmental authorities of the Federal Republic of Yugoslavia and the Republic of Serbia understand and agree that the international security force ("KFOR") will deploy following the adoption of the UNSCR referred to in paragraph 1 and operate without hindrance within Kosovo and with the authority to take all necessary action to establish and maintain a secure environment for all citizens of Kosovo and otherwise carry out its mission. They further agree to comply with all of the obligations of this Agreement and to facilitate the deployment and operation of this force.

3. For purposes of the agreement, the following expressions shall have the meanings as described below:

a. "The Parties" are those signatories to the Agreement.

b. "Authorities" means the appropriate responsible individual, agency, or organisation of the Parties.

c. "FRY Forces" includes all of the FRY and Republic of Serbia personnel and organisations with a military capability. This includes regular army and naval forces, armed civilian groups, associated paramilitary groups, air forces, national guards, border police, army re-

---
[1] UN Doc. S/1999/682, Annex, 15 June 1999.

serves, military police, intelligence services, federal and Serbian Ministry of Internal Affairs local, special, riot and anti-terrorist police, and any other groups or individuals so designated by the international security force ("KFOR") commander.

d. The Air Safety Zone (ASZ) is defined as a 25-kilometre zone that extends beyond the Kosovo province border into the rest of FRY territory. It includes the airspace above that 25-kilometre zone.

e. The Ground Safety Zone (GSZ) is defined as a 5-kilometre zone that extends beyond the Kosovo province border into the rest of FRY territory. It includes the terrain within that 5-kilometre zone.

f. Entry into Force Day (EIF Day) is defined as the day this Agreement is signed.

4. The purposes of these obligations are as follows:

a. To establish a durable cessation of hostilities, under no circumstances shall any Forces of the FRY and the Republic of Serbia enter into, reenter, or remain within the territory of Kosovo or the Ground Safety Zone (GSZ) and the Air Safety Zone (ASZ) described in paragraph 3, Article I without the prior express consent of the international security force ("KFOR") commander. Local police will be allowed to remain in the GSZ.

The above paragraph is without prejudice to the agreed return of FRY and Serbian personnel which will be the subject of a subsequent separate agreement as provided for in paragraph 6 of the document mentioned in paragraph 1 of this Article.

b. To provide for the support and authorization of the international security force ("KFOR") and in particular to authorize the international security force ("KFOR") to take such actions as are required, including the use of necessary force, to ensure compliance with this Agreement and protection of the international security force ("KFOR"), and to contribute to a secure environment for the international civil implementation presence, and other international organisations, agencies, and non-governmental organisations (details in Appendix B).

Article II: Cessation of Hostilities

1. The FRY Forces shall immediately, upon entry into force (EIF) of this Agreement, refrain from committing any hostile or provocative acts of any type against any person in Kosovo and will order armed forces to cease all such activities. They shall not encourage, organise or support hostile or provocative demonstrations.

2. Phased Withdrawal of FRY Forces (ground): The FRY agrees to a phased withdrawal of all FRY Forces from Kosovo to locations in Serbia outside Kosovo. FRY Forces will mark and clear minefields, booby traps and obstacles. As they withdraw, FRY Forces will clear all lines of communication by removing all mines, demolitions, booby traps, obstacles and charges. They will also mark all sides of all minefields. International security forces' ("KFOR") entry and deployment into Kosovo will be synchronized. The phased withdrawal of FRY Forces from Kosovo will be in accordance with the sequence outlined below:

a. By EIF + 1 day, FRY Forces located in Zone 3 will have vacated, via designated routes, that Zone to demonstrate compliance (depicted on the map at Appendix A to the Agreement). Once it is verified that FRY forces have complied with this subparagraph and with paragraph 1 of this Article, NATO air strikes will be suspended. The suspension will continue provided that the obligations of this agreement are fully complied with, and provided that the UNSC adopts a resolution concerning the deployment of the international security force ("KFOR") so rapidly that a security gap can be avoided.

b. By EIF + 6 days, all FRY Forces in Kosovo will have vacated Zone 1 (depicted on the map at Appendix A to the Agreement). Establish liaison teams with the KFOR commander in Pristina.

c. By EIF + 9 days, all FRY Forces in Kosovo will have vacated Zone 2 (depicted on the map at Appendix A to the Agreement).

d. By EIF + 11 days, all FRY Forces in Kosovo will have vacated Zone 3 (depicted on the map at Appendix A to the Agreement).

e. By EIF +11 days, all FRY Forces in Kosovo will have completed their withdrawal from Kosovo (depicted on map at Appendix A to the Agreement) to locations in Serbia outside Kosovo, and not within the 5 km GSZ. At the end of the sequence (EIF + 11), the senior FRY Forces commanders responsible for the withdrawing forces shall confirm in writing to the international security force ("KFOR") commander that the FRY Forces have complied and completed the phased withdrawal. The international security force ("KFOR") commander may approve specific requests for exceptions to the phased withdrawal. The bombing campaign will terminate on complete withdrawal of FRY Forces as provided under Article II. The international security force ("KFOR") shall retain, as necessary, authority to enforce compliance with this Agreement.

f. The authorities of the FRY and the Republic of Serbia will cooperate fully with international security force ("KFOR") in its verification of the withdrawal of forces from Kosovo and beyond the ASZ/GSZ.

g. FRY armed forces withdrawing in accordance with Appendix A, i.e. in designated assembly areas or withdrawing on designated routes, will not be subject to air attack.

h. The international security force ("KFOR") will provide appropriate control of the borders of FRY in Kosovo with Albania and FYROM (1) until the arrival of the civilian mission of the UN.

3. Phased Withdrawal of Yugoslavia Air and Air Defence Forces (YAADF)

a. At EIF + 1 day, no FRY aircraft, fixed wing and rotary, will fly in Kosovo airspace or over the ASZ without prior approval by the international security force ("KFOR") commander. All air defence systems, radar, surface-to-air missile and aircraft of the Parties will refrain from acquisition, target tracking or otherwise illuminating international security ("KFOR") air platforms operating in the Kosovo airspace or over the ASZ.

b. By EIF + 3 days, all aircraft, radars, surface-to-air missiles (including man-portable air defence systems (MANPADS)) and anti-aircraft artillery in Kosovo will withdraw to other locations in Serbia outside the 25 kilometre ASZ.

c. The international security force ("KFOR") commander will control and coordinate use of airspace over Kosovo and the ASZ commencing at EIF. Violation of any of the provisions above, including the international security force ("KFOR") commander's rules and procedures governing the airspace over Kosovo, as well as unauthorised flight or activation of FRY Integrated Air Defence (IADS) within the ASZ, are subject to military action by the international security force ("KFOR"), including the use of necessary force. The international security force ("KFOR") commander may delegate control of normal civilian air activities to appropriate FRY institutions to monitor operations, deconflict international security force ("KFOR") air traffic movements, and ensure smooth and safe operations of the air traffic system. It is envisioned that control of civil air traffic will be returned to civilian authorities as soon as practicable.

Article III: Notifications

1. This agreement and written orders requiring compliance will be immediately communicated to all FRY forces.

2. By EIF +2 days, the State governmental authorities of the FRY and the Republic of Serbia shall furnish the following specific information regarding the status of all FRY Forces:

a. Detailed records, positions and descriptions of all mines, unexploded ordnance, explosive devices, demolitions, obstacles, booby traps, wire entanglement, physical or military hazards to the safe movement of any personnel in Kosovo laid by FRY Forces.

b. Any further information of a military or security nature about FRY Forces in the territory of Kosovo and the GSZ and ASZ requested by the international security force ("KFOR") commander.

Article IV: Establishment of a Joint Implementation Commission (JIC)

A JIC shall be established with the deployment of the international security force ("KFOR") to Kosovo as directed by the international security force ("KFOR") commander.

Article V: Final Authority to Interpret

The international security force ("KFOR") commander is the final authority regarding interpretation of this Agreement and the security aspects of the peace settlement it supports. His determinations are binding on all Parties and persons.

Article VI: Entry into Force

This agreement shall enter into force upon signature.

Appendices:

A. PHASED WITHDRAWAL OF FRY FORCES FROM KOSOVO

[The map has been omitted.]

B. INTERNATIONAL SECURITY FORCE ("KFOR") OPERATIONS

1. Consistent with the general obligations of the Military Technical Agreement, the State Governmental authorities of the FRY and the Republic of Serbia understand and agree that the international security force ("KFOR") will deploy and operate without hindrance within Kosovo and with the authority to take all necessary action to establish and maintain a secure environment for all citizens of Kosovo.

2. The international security force ("KFOR") commander shall have the authority, without interference or permission, to do all that he judges necessary and proper, including the use of military force, to protect the international security force ("KFOR"), the international civil implementation presence, and to carry out the responsibilities inherent in this Military Technical Agreement and the Peace Settlement which it supports.

3. The international security force ("KFOR") nor any of its personnel or staff shall be liable for any damages to public or private property that they may cause in the course of duties related to the implementation of this Agreement. The parties will agree a Status of Forces Agreement (SOFA) as soon as possible.

4. The international security force ("KFOR") shall have the right:

a. To monitor and ensure compliance with this Agreement and to respond promptly to any violations and restore compliance, using military force if required.

This includes necessary actions to:

1. Enforce withdrawals of FRY forces.

2. Enforce compliance following the return of selected FRY personnel to Kosovo

3. Provide assistance to other international entities involved in the implementation or otherwise authorised by the UNSC.

b. To establish liaison arrangements with local Kosovo authorities, and with FRY/Serbian civil and military authorities.

c. To observe, monitor and inspect any and all facilities or activities in Kosovo that the international security force ("KFOR") commander believes has or may have military or police capability, or may be associated with the employment of military or police capabilities, or are otherwise relevant to compliance with this Agreement.

5. Notwithstanding any other provision of this Agreement, the Parties understand and agree that the international security force ("KFOR") commander has the right and is authorised to compel the removal, withdrawal, or relocation of specific Forces and weapons, and to order the cessation of any activities whenever the international security force ("KFOR") commander determines a potential threat to either the international security force ("KFOR") or its mission, or to another Party. Forces failing to redeploy, withdraw, relocate, or to cease threatening or potentially threatening activities following such a demand by the international security force ("KFOR") shall be subject to military action by the international security force ("KFOR"), including the use of necessary force, to ensure compliance.

208. UN Security Council Resolution 1244 (1999) of 10 June 1999

The Security Council,

Bearing in mind the purposes and principles of the Charter of the United Nations, and the primary responsibility of the Security Council for the maintenance of international peace and security,

Recalling its resolutions 1160 (1998) of 31 March 1998, 1199 (1998) of 23 September 1998, 1203 (1998) of 24 October 1998 and 1239 (1999) of 14 May 1999,

Regretting that there has not been full compliance with the requirements of these resolutions,

Determined to resolve the grave humanitarian situation in Kosovo, Federal Republic of Yugoslavia, and to provide for the safe and free return of all refugees and displaced persons to their homes,

Condemning all acts of violence against the Kosovo population as well as all terrorist acts by any party,

Recalling the statement made by the Secretary-General on 9 April 1999, expressing concern at the humanitarian tragedy taking place in Kosovo,

Reaffirming the right of all refugees and displaced persons to return to their homes in safety,

Recalling the jurisdiction and the mandate of the International Tribunal for the Former Yugoslavia,

Welcoming the general principles on a political solution to the Kosovo crisis adopted on 6 May 1999 (S/1999/516, annex 1 to this resolution) and welcoming also the acceptance by the Federal Republic of Yugoslavia of the principles set forth in points 1 to 9 of the paper presented in Belgrade on 2 June 1999 (S/1999/649, annex 2 to this resolution), and the Federal Republic of Yugoslavia's agreement to that paper,

Reaffirming the commitment of all Member States to the sovereignty and territorial integrity of the Federal Republic of Yugoslavia and the other States of the region, as set out in the Helsinki Final Act and annex 2,

Reaffirming the call in previous resolutions for substantial autonomy and meaningful self-administration for Kosovo,

Determining that the situation in the region continues to constitute a threat to international peace and security,

Determined to ensure the safety and security of international personnel and the implementation by all concerned of their responsibilities under the present resolution, and *acting* for these purposes under Chapter VII of the Charter of the United Nations,

1. *Decides* that a political solution to the Kosovo crisis shall be based on the general principles in annex 1 and as further elaborated in the principles and other required elements in annex 2;

2. *Welcomes* the acceptance by the Federal Republic of Yugoslavia of the principles and other required elements referred to in paragraph 1 above, and demands the full cooperation of the Federal Republic of Yugoslavia in their rapid implementation;

3. *Demands* in particular that the Federal Republic of Yugoslavia put an immediate and verifiable end to violence and repression in Kosovo, and begin and complete verifiable phased withdrawal from Kosovo of all military, police and paramilitary forces according to a rapid timetable, with which the deployment of the international security presence in Kosovo will be synchronized;

4. *Confirms* that after the withdrawal an agreed number of Yugoslav and Serb military and police personnel will be permitted to return to Kosovo to perform the functions in accordance with annex 2;

5. *Decides* on the deployment in Kosovo, under United Nations auspices, of international civil and security presences, with appropriate equipment and personnel as required, and welcomes the agreement of the Federal Republic of Yugoslavia to such presences;

6. *Requests* the Secretary-General to appoint, in consultation with the Security Council, a Special Representative to control the imple-

mentation of the international civil presence, and *further requests* the Secretary-General to instruct his Special Representative to coordinate closely with the international security presence to ensure that both presences operate towards the same goals and in a mutually supportive manner;

7. *Authorizes* Member States and relevant international organizations to establish the international security presence in Kosovo as set out in point 4 of annex 2 with all necessary means to fulfil its responsibilities under paragraph 9 below;

8. *Affirms* the need for the rapid early deployment of effective international civil and security presences to Kosovo, and *demands* that the parties cooperate fully in their deployment;

9. *Decides* that the responsibilities of the international security presence to be deployed and acting in Kosovo will include:

(a) Deterring renewed hostilities, maintaining and where necessary enforcing a ceasefire, and ensuring the withdrawal and preventing the return into Kosovo of Federal and Republic military, police and paramilitary forces, except as provided in point 6 of annex 2;

(b) Demilitarizing the Kosovo Liberation Army (KLA) and other armed Kosovo Albanian groups as required in paragraph 15 below;

(c) Establishing a secure environment in which refugees and displaced persons can return home in safety, the international civil presence can operate, a transitional administration can be established, and humanitarian aid can be delivered;

(d) Ensuring public safety and order until the international civil presence can take responsibility for this task;

(e) Supervising demining until the international civil presence can, as appropriate, take over responsibility for this task;

(f) Supporting, as appropriate, and coordinating closely with the work of the international civil presence;

(g) Conducting border monitoring duties as required;

(h) Ensuring the protection and freedom of movement of itself, the international civil presence, and other international organizations;

10. *Authorizes* the Secretary-General, with the assistance of relevant international organizations, to establish an international civil presence in Kosovo in order to provide an interim administration for Kosovo under which the people of Kosovo can enjoy substantial autonomy within the Federal Republic of Yugoslavia, and which will provide transitional administration while establishing and overseeing the development of provisional democratic self-governing institutions to ensure conditions for a peaceful and normal life for all inhabitants of Kosovo;

11. *Decides* that the main responsibilities of the international civil presence will include:

(a) Promoting the establishment, pending a final settlement, of substantial autonomy and self-government in Kosovo, taking full account of annex 2 and of the Rambouillet accords (S/1999/648);

(b) Performing basic civilian administrative functions where and as long as required;

(c) Organizing and overseeing the development of provisional institutions for democratic and autonomous self-government pending a political settlement, including the holding of elections;

(d) Transferring, as these institutions are established, its administrative responsibilities while overseeing and supporting the consolidation of Kosovo's local provisional institutions and other peace-building activities;

(e) Facilitating a political process designed to determine Kosovo's future status, taking into account the Rambouillet accords (S/1999/648);

(f) In a final stage, overseeing the transfer of authority from Kosovo's provisional institutions to institutions established under a political settlement;

(g) Supporting the reconstruction of key infrastructure and other economic reconstruction;

(h) Supporting, in coordination with international humanitarian organizations, humanitarian and disaster relief aid;

(i) Maintaining civil law and order, including establishing local police forces and meanwhile through the deployment of international police personnel to serve in Kosovo;

(j) Protecting and promoting human rights;

(k) Assuring the safe and unimpeded return of all refugees and displaced persons to their homes in Kosovo;

12. *Emphasizes* the need for coordinated humanitarian relief operations, and for the Federal Republic of Yugoslavia to allow unimpeded access to Kosovo by humanitarian aid organizations and to cooperate with such organizations so as to ensure the fast and effective delivery of international aid;

13. *Encourages* all Member States and international organizations to contribute to economic and social reconstruction as well as to the safe return of refugees and displaced persons, and emphasizes in this context the importance of convening an international donors' conference, particularly for the purposes set out in paragraph 11 (g) above, at the earliest possible date;

14. *Demands* full cooperation by all concerned, including the international security presence, with the International Tribunal for the Former Yugoslavia;

15. *Demands* that the KLA and other armed Kosovo Albanian groups end immediately all offensive actions and comply with the requirements for demilitarization as laid down by the head of the international security presence in consultation with the Special Representative of the Secretary-General;

16. *Decides* that the prohibitions imposed by paragraph 8 of resolution 1160 (1998) shall not apply to arms and related matériel for the use of the international civil and security presences;

17. *Welcomes* the work in hand in the European Union and other international organizations to develop a comprehensive approach to the economic development and stabilization of the region affected by the Kosovo crisis, including the implementation of a Stability Pact for South Eastern Europe with broad international participation in order to further the promotion of democracy, economic prosperity, stability and regional cooperation;

18. *Demands* that all States in the region cooperate fully in the implementation of all aspects of this resolution;

19. *Decides* that the international civil and security presences are established for an initial period of 12 months, to continue thereafter unless the Security Council decides otherwise;

20. *Requests* the Secretary-General to report to the Council at regular intervals on the implementation of this resolution, including reports from the leaderships of the international civil and security presences, the first reports to be submitted within 30 days of the adoption of this resolution;

21. *Decides* to remain actively seized of the matter.

Annex 1

[See document no. 197]

Annex 2

[See document no. 204]

Adopted by the Security Council at its 4011th meeting, on 10 June 1999 with 14 votes to none and China abstaining.

209. UN Extracts from the Debates of the Security Council Concerning Security Council Resolution 1244 (1999), UN Doc. S/PV. 4011, 10 June 1999[1]

[Members of the Council had before them, inter alia, document S/1999/661, which contained the text of a draft resolution submitted by Canada, France, Gabon, Germany, Italy, Japan, the Netherlands, the Russian Federation, Slovenia, Ukraine, the United Kingdom of Great Britain and Northern Ireland and the United States of America. Bahrain had joined as a sponsor of the draft resolution.][2]

[3] **Mr. Jovanović**: The Federal Republic of Yugoslavia, the victim of the unilateral and brutal aggression of the United States of America and other member States of the North Atlantic Treaty Organization (NATO), has had two basic goals: to defend itself from that aggression, which it has done successfully, and to have the resolution of all questions and problems related to Kosovo and Metohija, an integral part of Serbia and the Federal Republic of Yugoslavia, shifted from the track of war and destruction to the track of political decision-making and law.

After the unilateral, unauthorized military action by NATO against the Federal Republic of Yugoslavia - a State Member of the United Nations and a founding Member of the world Organization - which lasted for two and a half months, this question has finally been put on the agenda of the Security Council. Unfortunately, this was done only in the wake of great delays and of many civilian victims, destruction and a humanitarian catastrophe of a size unprecedented in post-war European history.

The aggression was not directed only against the Federal Republic of Yugoslavia but also against all peaceloving peoples and all those standing in the way of attempts to create a unipolar world based on the policy of force and the establishment of global hegemony and domination. In that sense, the systematic destruction of the Federal Republic of Yugoslavia and the killing of innocent civilians, which lasted two and half months, has been a denial of all of the basic principles of the Charter of the United Nations, and in particular of the principles of the settlement of disputes by peaceful means; respect for the sovereign equality of States, regardless of their size and political, economic and military might; non-intervention and non-interference in internal affairs; and the right to choose one's own road to internal development and international position.

As one of the founding Members of the United Nations, the Federal Republic of Yugoslavia issued timely but unsuccessful warnings to, and requested protection from, the Security Council, as the key organ responsible for the maintenance of international peace and security, asking it to stand up to the policy of force and diktat and to engage actively in favour of a peaceful solution to the situation in Kosovo and Metohija.

Under pressure from the countries that spearheaded the aggression against the Federal Republic of Yugoslavia, the Security Council turned a deaf ear to Yugoslavia's repeated requests that the aggression be condemned and stopped. The annals of the world Organization will therefore record the disgraceful fact that during 78 days of ruthless, savage aggression by the most powerful military organization against a small and peaceloving country, the Security Council could not bring itself to condemn and stop the aggressor. This is all the more so since the Federal Republic of Yugoslavia did not attack any of its neighbours, nor did it threaten anyone.

Before and during the aggression, the Federal Republic of Yugoslavia had all along indicated its interest in and readiness for a political solution to the crisis that would respect the territorial integrity and sovereignty of the country and enable the highest level of autonomy in Kosovo and Metohija, guaranteeing full equality for the members of all ethnic groups in accordance with the highest international standards. In that connection, on 6 April 1999, at the very beginning of the aggression by NATO, the Government of the Federal Republic of Yugoslavia and the Republic of Serbia expressed their unequivocal readiness, following the talks between President Milosevic and Mr. Rugova, for a political [4] solution in Kosovo and Metohija to be reached in direct talks between the Government of Serbia and the representatives of the Albanian minority in Kosovo and Metohija.

Also, on 9 May 1999, the Supreme Defence Council took a decision on the beginning of withdrawal of part of the units of the army of Yugoslavia and the special police forces from Kosovo and Metohija, following the elimination of the terrorist Kosovo Liberation Army (KLA). The actions of the Yugoslav security forces in Kosovo and Metohija have been taken within the framework of the legitimate efforts of the Federal Republic of Yugoslavia to stamp out terrorism, aided and abetted from abroad and aimed at causing a sovereign part of the Yugoslav territory to secede. Instead of welcoming that step, NATO intensified the bombing of the Federal Republic of Yugoslavia, thereby causing a mass exodus of the civilian population from Kosovo and Metohija and other parts of the Federal Republic of Yugoslavia.

At the same time, by focusing its raids exclusively on civilian targets, NATO has caused untold suffering to the entire population of the Federal Republic of Yugoslavia. Those who gave and carried out the orders for NATO's aggression against Yugoslavia have over the past 78 days violated all known international conventions in the field of the law of war, human rights and fundamental freedoms. No civilian target was spared by NATO planes. For the first time, NATO designated as legitimate targets hospitals, housing blocks, refugee centres and convoys, media institutions and journalists, prisons, schools, kindergartens, business centres and shopping malls, buses and passenger trains, even foreign diplomatic missions.

Set on intimidating and punishing the entire Yugoslav people, the NATO aggressors have destroyed the economy and the infrastructure, including bridges, roads and railroads, as well as power grids and the country's water supply system. Hundreds of thousands of people are now jobless, and millions are without any income. By destroying pharmaceutical and chemical plants and oil refineries, by bombing national parks and using inhumane weapons, including depleted uranium ammunition, NATO has caused an ecological catastrophe whose consequences will be felt for generations.

On behalf of the Government and people of the Federal Republic of Yugoslavia, I address to you, Mr. President, and to the members of the Security Council the following requests.

First, to point out the responsibility of the NATO member States for flagrantly violating the principles of the Charter of the United Nations and for the unauthorized and brutal bombing of the Federal Republic of Yugoslavia, which resulted in a massive humanitarian catastrophe, the destruction of the civilian infrastructure and the economy of the country, the death of more than 2,000 persons and the wounding of more than 6,000 innocent civilians. Secondly, to stress the moral, political and material obligation of the NATO member States fully to compensate the Federal Republic of Yugoslavia and its citizens within the shortest possible period of time for all the damage caused by the unauthorized and ruthless incessant bombing of the last 78 days. And thirdly, to restore to the Federal Republic of Yugoslavia, a peaceloving and independent country and a founding Member of the United Nations and of many other international organizations, all of its suspended rights in the world Organization, international and financial institutions and in other international organizations and associations, as well as to

---

[1] *Only statements which add to the legal analysis or the factual background have been included. Presidential statements not related to substantive issues have also been omitted.*

[2] *In 1999, membership of the Security Council was as follows: Argentinia, Bahrain, Brazil, Canada, China, France, Gambia, Gabon, Malaysia, Namibia, the Netherlands, Russian Federation, Slovenia, the United Kingdom of Great Britain and Northern Ireland and the United States of America. The Council invited the representatives of Albania, Belarus, Bulgaria, Costa Rica, Croatia, Cuba, Germany, Hungary, the Islamic Republic of Iran, Italy, Japan, Mexico, Norway, the former Yugoslav Republic of Macedonia, Turkey and Ukraine to participate in the discussion without the right to vote, in accordance with the Charter and rule 37 of the Council's provisional rules of procedure. The President also invited Mr. Vladislav Jovanovic (FRY).*

lift all existing sanctions and unilateral restrictions and all other discriminatory measures. I call on the Council to receive this request with understanding and the necessary urgency.

The Federal Republic of Yugoslavia accepted the G-8 principles of 7 May 1999 and the Ahtisaari-Chernomyrdin plan for the political solution of the crisis. In that context, the National Assembly of the Republic of Serbia made on 3 June 1999 the decision regarding the acceptance of that plan, which confirms the territorial integrity of Yugoslavia and a role for the United Nations in the solution of the crisis. The Ahtisaari-Chernomyrdin plan provided for a conclusion of a military-technical agreement determining the timetable and routes for the withdrawal of military and police forces of the Federal Republic of Yugoslavia from Kosovo and Metohija, including the elements for the return of some of them to Kosovo and Metohija.

Instead, we have faced NATO attempts to deploy its troops in Kosovo and Metohija by way of insisting on some political elements without a decision and a mandate from the Security Council. This provides further proof that the aggressor is trying to marginalize and bypass the world Organization, as well as the G-8 principles, with the aim of achieving its final goal of occupying a sovereign part of the Republic of Serbia and the Federal Republic of Yugoslavia.

In order to achieve lasting and stable peace in the region and to reaffirm the roles of the United Nations [5] and the Security Council as the highest bodies for the maintenance of international peace and security, it is necessary to deploy the United Nations peacekeeping mission in Kosovo and Metohija on the basis of a decision of the Security Council and of Chapter VI of the Charter of the United Nations and with the prior and full agreement of the Government of the Federal Republic of Yugoslavia.

In that context, the Security Council draft resolution should contain the following positions: a firm and unequivocal reaffirmation of full respect for the territorial integrity and sovereignty of the Federal Republic of Yugoslavia; a political solution to the situation in Kosovo and Metohija that would be based on broad autonomy, in accordance with the highest international standards, such as the Paris Charter and the Organization for Security and Cooperation in Europe (OSCE) Copenhagen document, ensuring the full equality of all ethnic communities. The solution for Kosovo and Metohija must fall within the legal frameworks of the Republic of Serbia and the Federal Republic of Yugoslavia, which implies that all State and public services in the province, including the organs of law and order, should function according to the Constitutions and laws of the Federal Republic of Yugoslavia and the Republic of Serbia.

The draft resolution should not contain provisions on the International Tribunal, considering that that institution has no jurisdiction over the Federal Republic of Yugoslavia and was not included in the principles of the Ahtisaari-Chernomyrdin plan.

It should contain a condemnation of the NATO aggression against the Federal Republic of Yugoslavia as an act in violation of the Charter of the United Nations and a threat to international peace and security; a reference to the reports of United Nations Under-Secretary-General Sergio Vieira de Mello and United Nations High Commissioner for Human Rights Mary Robinson, which should point to the civilian casualties and material destruction as consequences of the NATO aggression, and a condemnation of the use of inhumane weapons - cluster and graphite bombs and depleted uranium ammunition; a condemnation of the NATO bombing of foreign diplomatic and consular missions in the Federal Republic of Yugoslavia, which represents a violation of international legal norms, especially of the 1973 Convention on the Prevention and Punishment of Crimes against Internationally Protected Persons, including Diplomatic Agents; provisions ensuring unhindered and safe passage of refugees - Yugoslav citizens that left the country because of the NATO aggression - and the procedures and criteria established by the competent Yugoslav Federal Republican authorities and the Office of the United Nations High Commissioner for Refugees; and respect for the Constitution and laws of the Republic of Serbia and the Federal Republic of Yugoslavia as necessary preconditions for the solution of all questions and a successful evolution of the international presence.

The Federal Republic of Yugoslavia firmly believes that the United Nations mission in Kosovo and Metohija, which would include military and civil components, would have to have the mandate and authority of the United Nations and the Security Council. The mandate of the mission should consist of the supervision of the implementation of the comprehensive agreement on Kosovo and Metohija, the withdrawal of Yugoslav military and police forces, the return of refugees and displaced persons and cooperation with international humanitarian organizations in providing assistance to all in need of it. The mission must guarantee full security and equality to all citizens in Kosovo and Metohija, regardless of their religious and national affiliations, and prevent all violence, especially the resurgence of terrorism and separatism. The mission as a whole must be responsible to and report to the Secretary-General, that is, the Security Council of the United Nations. The Federal Republic of Yugoslavia cannot accept a mission that would take over the role of government in Kosovo and Metohija or any form of open or hidden protectorate.

Considering that the NATO aggressors have carried out brutal crimes against the members of all national communities living in Kosovo and Metohija, the Federal Republic of Yugoslavia is, on principle and for other reasons, against the participation in the United Nations mission by the countries that have taken an active part in the aggression. We consider that the mission must reflect equal, regional and political representation which includes participation by countries such as Russia, China, India and non-aligned and developing countries from various regions of the world.

Yugoslavia requests that the commander of the military part and the head of the civil part of the mission be appointed by the Secretary-General of the United Nations on the basis of consultations with the Security Council and the Federal Republic of Yugoslavia as the host country. Also, the commander of the military part and the head of the civilian part of the mission should be directly responsible to the Secretary-General, that is, the Security Council.

[6] The Federal Republic of Yugoslavia considers that the mandate and the duration of the United Nations mission must be limited in time. This includes the possibility of their being renewed after three or six months, on the basis of a decision of the Security Council and with the agreement of the Government of the Federal Republic of Yugoslavia. The attempt to grant an open mandate to the United Nations mission is absolutely unacceptable to the Federal Republic of Yugoslavia, since this would amount to a gross violation of the sovereignty of the Federal Republic of Yugoslavia, which otherwise is being reaffirmed by the proposed draft resolution.

I must note with regret that the draft resolution proposed by the G-8 is yet another attempt to marginalize the world Organization aimed at legalizing post festum the brutal aggression to which the Federal Republic of Yugoslavia has been exposed in the last two and a half months. In doing so, the Security Council and the international community would become accomplices in the most drastic violation of the basic principles of the Charter of the United Nations to date and in legalizing the rule of force rather than the rule of international law.

It is an historic anomaly that the victim of the aggression is being proclaimed guilty by those who are in possession of force and power and are in breach of all norms of international law and civilized behaviour among States, although the entire world public knows very well who is the victim and who is the guilty party.

The solutions which are being tried to be imposed on the Federal Republic of Yugoslavia set a dangerous precedent for the international community and a great encouragement to separatist and terrorist groups all over the world. They provide a broad authority to those who have conducted a total genocidal war against a sovereign and peace-loving country and legitimize the policy of ultimatum and diktat. In sub-item (a) and (b) of operative paragraph 9, the draft resolution requests in all practical terms that the Federal Republic of Yugoslavia renounce a part of its sovereign territory and grant amnesty to terrorists. Furthermore, in operative paragraph 11, the draft resolution establishes a protectorate, provides for the creation of a separate political and economic system in the province and opens up the possibility of the secession of Kosovo and Metohija from Serbia and the Federal Republic of Yugoslavia.

In adopting the present text of the draft resolution, the Security Council would be writing one of the darkest pages of its history. In doing so, the Security Council would not only be instrumental in a de facto dismemberment of a sovereign European State, but would also set a negative precedent with far-reaching consequences for overall international relations, in particular for the position of small and medium-sized developing countries. In that way, the Security Council would in fact support the nefarious theory of limited sovereignty and open the floodgates to the unimpeded intervention and interference of the mighty and powerful in the internal affairs of other States.

By opposing these provisions, the Security Council shall stand up in defence not only of the territorial integrity and sovereignty of the Federal Republic of Yugoslavia, but also of the basic principles of the Charter of the United Nations and international law and, by the same token, of its own authority as the highest organ for the maintenance of international peace and security. [...]

Mr. Andjaba (Namibia): [...] [7] The purposes and principles of the Charter of the United Nations are clear. It is the primary responsibility of the Security Council to maintain international peace and security. All States Members of the United Nations have the obligation to uphold the provisions of the Charter in that regard.

Mr. Lavrov (Russian Federation) *(spoke in Russian)*: Today's draft resolution of the Security Council was prepared by the Ministers for Foreign Affairs of the G-8 on the basis of the principles for a political settlement and peace plan adopted by the leadership of the Federal Republic of Yugoslavia, as well as of the relevant provisions of previous Security Council decisions. The draft resolution's main significance lies in the fact that it restores the Kosovo settlement to the political track along with the central role of the United Nations. This is the only possible way to surmount the crisis in and around the Yugoslav province of Kosovo. It is precisely such an approach to a solution of the Kosovo problem that Russia has always and consistently advocated, seeking the earliest possible end to the unlawful military actions of the North Atlantic Treaty Organization (NATO) against Yugoslavia as an absolute condition for a political settlement and for overcoming the humanitarian catastrophe.

Russia has strongly condemned the NATO aggression against a sovereign State. This action on the part of the Alliance, which was undertaken in violation of the United Nations Charter and in circumvention of the Security Council, has severely destabilized the entire system of international relations based on the primacy of international law. The humanitarian crisis in Kosovo was transformed by the NATO bombing into the most serious humanitarian catastrophe, encompassing not only Kosovo, but all Yugoslavia and the Balkans as a whole. The irreparable harm done to the social and economic development of all Balkan States and to the environment is enormous.

We cannot close our eyes to violations of international humanitarian law, wherever they may take place. However, the tragic consequences of the NATO air strikes clearly show that such violations cannot be countered by even greater lawlessness and the wanton use of violence. It is essential to fight for respect of human rights and norms of international humanitarian law, but solely through political and legal methods on the firm basis of the United Nations Charter and the relevant multilateral instruments.

We are pleased that the members of NATO have finally recognized the utter futility of the war they have unleashed and come to understand that there is no alternative to respecting the Charter prerogatives of the Security Council as the body charged with the primary responsibility for the maintenance of international peace and security. This insight, won at such a heavy price, is clearly reflected in the draft resolution, which puts an end to the military actions of NATO and establishes genuine conditions for the return of refugees and displaced persons.

In addition to clearly reaffirming the commitment of all States to the sovereignty and territorial integrity of the Federal Republic of Yugoslavia, the draft resolution authorizes the deployment in Kosovo, under United Nations auspices, of international civil and security presences with a clearly formulated, concrete mandate. The activities of both presences are to be carried out under the thorough political control of the Security Council, to which the Secretary-General will regularly submit reports on the course of the entire operation. As a matter of principle, it is important that the obligations of the Special Representative of the Secretary-General, who is to be appointed in consultation with the Security Council, should include the overall coordination of all international efforts in Kosovo. This will undoubtedly help enhance their effectiveness.

The draft resolution's reference to Chapter VII of the United Nations Charter relates exclusively to ensuring the safety and security of international personnel and compliance with the provisions of the draft resolution. It does not even hint at the possibility of any use of force [8] beyond the limits of the tasks clearly set out by the Security Council.

The demilitarization of the so-called Kosovo Liberation Army (KLA) and other armed Kosovo Albanian groups is of special importance in terms of achieving a lasting and effective political settlement of the Kosovo crisis. The draft resolution clearly defines this as one of the principal duties of the international security presence. This task must be carried out conclusively, with maximal effectiveness and completely. The KLA must scrupulously comply with all demands made of it by the Security Council and must cease to exist as a military force.

The leadership of the Federal Republic of Yugoslavia should, of course, comply fully with the obligations it has entered into.

Russia supports and is taking an active part in efforts to find a comprehensive approach to the social and economic reconstruction, stabilization and development of the Balkan region. We are convinced that the effectiveness of those efforts will depend directly on full, constructive involvement by all States of the region, including the Federal Republic of Yugoslavia. The United Nations has an important coordinating role to play here. We are certain that the adoption and ensuing adequate implementation of the draft resolution will make a vital contribution to achieving a peaceful, just and long-term solution to the Kosovo crisis under United Nations auspices. The Russian Federation will continue actively to promote the earliest possible achievement of that goal.

The draft resolution has even greater significance, going beyond the framework of the Kosovo problem and the Balkan region. It highlights the urgent need to form a truly multi-polar world order based on the Charter of the United Nations, a world order in which there will be no room for unilateral diktat or attempts at domination by force. Only on such a collective basis can we achieve lasting solutions to the complex problems of today's world.

Mr. Shen Guofang (China) *(spoke in Chinese)*: [...] More than two months ago, without authorization from the Security Council, the United States-led North Atlantic Treaty Organization (NATO) blatantly launched military strikes against the sovereign State of the Federal Republic of Yugoslavia. In taking this action, NATO seriously violated the Charter of the United Nations and norms of international law, and undermined the authority of the Security Council, thus setting an extremely dangerous precedent in the history of international relations.

For over two months, the United States-led NATO has waged an unprecedented and indiscriminate bombing campaign against the Federal Republic of Yugoslavia, killing over 1,000 civilians, injuring thousands and leaving nearly one million displaced persons and refugees. Civilian facilities such as factories, bridges, schools and hospitals have been wantonly destroyed. What is more flagrant is that even the embassy of the People's Republic of China in Yugoslavia, which is under the protection of international conventions, became one of NATO's bombing targets. This war, waged in the name of humanitarianism, has in fact produced the greatest humanitarian catastrophe in post-Second-World-War Europe and has seriously undermined peace and stability in the Balkans. Naturally, it has met with strong international condemnation.

From the very beginning, the Chinese Government and people have made their principled stance clear. We firmly oppose the NATO military action against Yugoslavia and demand that NATO immediately stop all its bombing operations. We stand for peaceful settlement of the question of Kosovo on the basis of respect for the sovereignty and territorial integrity of the Federal Republic of Yugoslavia and guarantees of the legitimate rights and interests of all ethnic groups in the Kosovo region. We are of the view that any proposed solution should take full account of the views of the Federal Republic of Yugoslavia.

Although NATO's bombing has stopped, the damage it has inflicted on the Balkans and the suffering it has brought to the people there cannot possibly disappear soon. Meanwhile, it will give us a lot to ponder for a long time to come.

There are nearly 200 countries and over 2,500 ethnic groups all over the world. The majority of countries are home to multiple ethnic groups, and many countries have ethnic problems; NATO countries are no exception. We have always held that in multiethnic countries there should be equality, unity, harmony and common prosperity among the various ethnic groups. We are not in favour of discrimination against or the oppression of any ethnic group. At the same time, we are also opposed to any act that would create division between different ethnic groups and undermine national unity. Fundamentally speaking, ethnic problems within a State [9] should be settled in a proper manner by its own Government and people, through the adoption of sound policies. They must not be used as an excuse for external intervention, much less used by foreign States as an excuse for the use of force. Otherwise, there will be no genuine security for States and no normal order for the world.

Fifty-four years ago, on 26 June, the Charter of the United Nations was signed in San Francisco. The birth of the United Nations and its Charter reflected the lofty aspirations of peoples that had suffered enormously from two catastrophic world wars, waged for peace, cooperation and development. Over the ensuing years, the purposes and principles of the Charter have withstood the test of time and have become universally recognized basic norms governing contemporary international relations.

History has proved that only by upholding the purposes and principles of the United Nations Charter and by seeking peaceful solutions to regional and international conflicts and disputes through talks and negotiations, without resorting to force, can all States live in harmony and achieve common development; only thus can world peace be maintained and promoted; and only thus can the United Nations play a role in international affairs. Any deviation from or violation of these purposes and principles will lead to rampant power politics, will make it impossible to effectively safeguard regional and international peace, and will damage the sovereignty and independence of countries, especially the small and weak ones, weakening the role of the United Nations and leaving the world with no peace.

Respect for sovereignty and non-interference in each other's internal affairs are basic principles of the United Nations Charter. Since the end of the cold war, the international situation has undergone major changes, but those principles are by no means outdated. On the contrary, they have acquired even greater relevance. At the threshold of the new century, it is even more imperative for us to reaffirm those principles. In essence, the "human rights over sovereignty" theory serves to infringe upon the sovereignty of other States and to promote hegemonism under the pretext of human rights. This totally runs counter to the purposes and principles of the United Nations Charter. The international community should maintain vigilance against it.

The draft resolution before us has failed to fully reflect China's principled stand and justified concerns. In particular, it makes no mention of the disaster caused by NATO bombing in the Federal Republic of Yugoslavia and it has failed to impose necessary restrictions on the invoking of Chapter VII of the United Nations Charter. Therefore, we have great difficulty with the draft resolution. However, in view of the fact that the Federal Republic of Yugoslavia has already accepted the peace plan, that NATO has suspended its bombing in the Federal Republic of Yugoslavia, and that the draft resolution has reaffirmed the purposes and principles of the United Nations Charter, the primary responsibility of the Security Council for the maintenance of international peace and security and the commitment of all Member States to the sovereignty and territorial integrity of the Federal Republic of Yugoslavia, the Chinese delegation will not block the adoption of this draft resolution.

[The president put to vote draft resolution S/1999/661 which was adopted with 14 votes to none and China abstaining as Security Council resolution 1244 (1999).]

Mr. Türk (Slovenia): [...] With this resolution, the Security Council realistically recognizes the existence of the threat to international peace and security and, acting under Chapter [10] VII, provides the legitimacy for the necessary measures of implementation of the resolution.

The resolution provides for comprehensive international military and civilian presences in Kosovo. The mandates of the missions are clear and precise and, at the same time, sufficiently flexible.

The resolution provides for credible military force and authorizes it to use all necessary means to fulfil its mandate. This is a prerequisite for the force to establish a safe and secure environment for the return of refugees and internally displaced persons.

Finally, the resolution delegates overall responsibility for civilian operations to the United Nations, with the specific responsibility of working with all other institutions and organizations so that the operations will be conducted in an integrated manner. We expect the security and civil presences to cooperate towards the same goal and in a mutually supportive manner.

The resolution reaffirms the jurisdiction of the International Criminal Tribunal for the Former Yugoslavia over Kosovo. Full cooperation of all concerned is required. It is our understanding that the personnel of the United Nations Tribunal should be granted immediate and unimpeded access to Kosovo and that they will be provided with the appropriate support and protection by the international security presence.

An important part of the resolution is devoted to humanitarian issues, which will constitute an essential priority in the immediate future - especially the return of refugees and caring for children in the post-conflict period. Slovenia fully supports these provisions and stands ready to strengthen its cooperation in the humanitarian field, including the priority tasks in the activities of demining and other activities in the field of mine action.

The focused character of the resolution and its clear setting of priorities do not mean that the Security Council is neglecting any of the relevant aspects of the Kosovo crisis. In the area of humanitarian action the Security Council remains committed to all the relevant tasks, including those related to the security and safety of humanitarian personnel. In this context, my delegation would like to repeat its concern over the fate of the two Australian aid workers, Steve Pratt and Peter Wallace, who were convicted by a military court of charges that are difficult to reconcile with international standards of humanitarian law and protection of humanitarian workers. We hope that they will be released soon, which would improve the confidence needed for effective humanitarian work.

With regard to the military and security aspects, we would like to emphasize the need for the Federal Republic of Yugoslavia (Serbia and Montenegro) to terminate the state of war in the country immediately. In particular, the state of war and related measures must not be used against the Republic of Montenegro, which has demonstrated a reasoned and constructive approach throughout the conflict, including by accepting and taking care of tens of thousands of internally displaced persons. The pressures exerted by Belgrade against Montenegro under the pretext of military needs must stop. Montenegro has suffered economically, socially and politically as a result of those pressures. We expect that the military presence in Montenegro will be reduced to normal levels. We are concerned that without such a measure the situation in Montenegro could escalate into a new threat to international peace and security in the region.

At the political level, the Federal Republic of Yugoslavia must understand the importance of the normalization of its relations with its neighbours and with other States. The requirements in this domain constitute a large agenda and include normalization and establishment of diplomatic relations, acceptance by the Federal Republic of Yugoslavia of the basic principles of State succession and, above all, a far greater degree of realism. The Federal Republic of Yugoslavia must finally accept the principle of equality with the other successor States that emerged as a result of the dissolution of the former Socialist Federal Republic of Yugoslavia, which ceased to exist many years ago. The Federal Republic of Yugoslavia must thus stop its attempts to create the erroneous impression that it is the continuing Member State of the United Nations and should apply for membership in the United Nations, as expressly required by Security Council resolution 777 (1992) and General Assembly resolution of 47/1. Political wisdom and legality require that this issue be resolved on the basis of the relevant resolutions of the Security Council and the General Assembly.

Let me now reflect in a slightly broader context upon the resolution that was adopted a few moments ago. This is necessary because the resolution adopted today provides the platform for the future engagement of the entire international community in the effort to resolve the Kosovo crisis. Its implications can be seen as belonging, broadly speaking, to two groups. First, the resolution and [11] the tasks that will be necessary for its implementation suggest that there are serious obstacles on the road to peace that will need to be overcome. Let me briefly refer to those obstacles.

Ensuring security in Kosovo means having to create something that did not exist in Kosovo for many years. The Kosovo conflict was not a sudden eruption - it has persisted for decades in different forms, ranging from latent tensions to violent outbursts. This vicious spiral of violence needs to be stopped, and security must become irreversible. The international security presence will therefore face a wide range of tasks reaching beyond the traditional military functions. The willingness and ability to perform these tasks will be an important test of its success.

Complete security will, in turn, require the establishment of an adequate civil administration, a task which presupposes carrying out an ambitious agenda inspired by internationally agreed standards of human rights. The difficulties in securing conditions for the full realization of human rights and fundamental freedoms in Kosovo for all - the Albanians, the Serbs and the others - must not be underestimated. Particular care should be given to the need to prevent any provocation calculated to generate an atmosphere of insecurity or to provoke the emigration from Kosovo of people belonging to the Serb or any other ethnic group.

The fact that basic human rights were denied to the people of Kosovo throughout its past and, most brutally, in the past decade, represents a formidable obstacle to the establishment of normalcy for the future.

Let me repeat that justice will be an essential condition for the durability of peace, and the role of the International Criminal Tribunal for the Former Yugoslavia as an independent criminal court will be indispensable.

The second set of implications relates to the opportunities that the current resolution presents. The success of the international effort in and around Kosovo would show that the international organizations involved in this undertaking are capable of ensuring the essential humanity of the people concerned as well as the preservation of international order and stability, in accordance with the purposes and principles of the United Nations Charter. Success in this specific case would give an example of the balance between the considerations of State sovereignty on the one hand and humanity and international order on the other. It is true that international organizations must be careful in all their efforts and that they must respect international law, including the principle of the sovereignty of States. However, it is at least equally clear that State sovereignty is not absolute and that it cannot be used as a tool of denial of humanity resulting in threats to peace. While the situation in Kosovo last year and early this year escalated to a serious threat to peace, there is now a genuine opportunity to reverse the situation and to create the balance necessary for political stability and durable peace for the future.

Today, the Security Council is resuming its legitimate role in the Kosovo crisis. This is an important beginning. The Council is put to a test of whether it will be able to maintain and strengthen its role as envisaged in the Charter. Success depends primarily on the unity of the Security Council. Determined efforts will be necessary in the implementation of the present resolution. Skilful navigation will be essential so as to avoid the Scylla of the marginalization of the Council and the Charybdis of engaging the Council in micromanagement. With the right decisions in the coming months, the Council will have an opportunity to shape the future of Kosovo and the stability and prosperity of its immediate international environment. Moreover, the Council will have an opportunity to define the patterns of the division of work and new forms of cooperation between the United Nations and the regional organizations concerned. This is an opportunity of great significance.

It is too early today for optimistic conclusions. Now is the time for the restoration of the unity of the Security Council, for the recommitment to its purposes and for the determination to strengthen the efforts to resolve the Kosovo crisis and other crisis situations on the Council's agenda.

Mr. Dejammet (France) *(spoke in French)*: The adoption by the Security Council of this resolution is a decisive step towards settling the crisis in Kosovo. For more than a year the Security Council has been seized of the matter. On several occasions over the course of more than a year it has taken a position on the humanitarian situation in Kosovo and the region and, above all, on the principles that should underpin a political solution. In resolution 1160 (1998), adopted on 31 March 1998, the Security Council imposed an embargo on the sale and supply of arms to the Federal Republic of Yugoslavia, including Kosovo. But it also underlined that the way to defeat violence and terrorism in Kosovo was for the Belgrade authorities to engage in a genuine political process with the Albanian Kosovar community. In resolution 1199 (1998) of 23 September 1998, [12] the Security Council spelt out what was required of the two parties. A third decision, resolution 1203 (1998) of 24 October 1998, made it possible to deploy the Organization for Security and Cooperation in Europe Verification Mission in Kosovo.

Unfortunately, the Belgrade regime refused to comply with the obligations set out in those resolutions. It opposed and rejected outright the efforts of the negotiators at the Rambouillet conference and all other forms of diplomatic intervention, even though, after lengthy negotiations, the political settlement envisaged at Rambouillet laid out a future for Kosovo. The continued and worsening repression of the civilian population compelled the members of the Atlantic Alliance to resort to military means in order to put an end to a senseless and unacceptable policy of destruction and deportation. However, in parallel with that, the members of the Atlantic Alliance continued their efforts with the Russian Federation, with the assistance of the Secretary-General of the United Nations, to identify the bases of a political settlement.

Fortunately, the negotiations conducted so tenaciously by President Ahtisaari of Finland, on behalf of the European Union, by the Russian envoy Mr. Chernomyrdin and by the American envoy Mr. Talbott, yielded results and have made it possible to envisage a peaceful solution. It will still demand a great deal of effort and a great deal of determination. But the resolution just adopted provides us with the legal, political and practical means to restore peace.

Everyone is now aware that this resolution bolsters the authority of the Security Council. It is the Security Council that is deciding on the deployment of civil and security presences in Kosovo under the auspices of the United Nations. It is the Security Council that is authorizing the Member States and the international organizations concerned to establish the international security presence in Kosovo. It is the Security Council that is authorizing the Secretary-General to establish an international civil presence. It is the Security Council that is determining the precise responsibilities entrusted to the international security presence and to the civil presence. The Security Council is requesting the Secretary-General to appoint a special representative to control the implementation of the civil presence and to ensure close coordination with the international security presence. The Security Council will remain in control of the implementation of the peace plan for Kosovo because it is requesting the Secretary-General to report to it regularly on the implementation of the resolution and to include reports from the leadership of the civil and security presences. Those of us who wish to recall the primacy of the Security Council for the maintenance of international peace and security, as established by the Charter, have been satisfied. Everyone deserves gratitude for the steps taken to achieve this result.

The chapter that is now closing has been a painful one. This resolution blazes the way towards peace. It enshrines the reaffirmed authority of the Security Council but also the effective and decisive action taken by regional organizations. It underscores the role of the Secretary-General of the United Nations, but it demands a great deal of Member States. [...]

Mr. van Walsum (Netherlands): The Netherlands has voted for this resolution with a sense of relief. This does not stem from a feeling that we are concluding a military operation we should not have been engaged in. We sincerely hope that the few delegations which have maintained that the North Atlantic Treaty Organization (NATO) air strikes against the Federal Republic of Yugoslavia were a violation of the United Nations Charter will one day begin to realize that the Charter is not the only source of international law.

The Charter, to be sure, is much more specific on respect for sovereignty than on respect for human rights, but since the day it was drafted the world has witnessed a gradual shift in that balance, making respect for human rights more mandatory and respect for sovereignty less absolute. Today, we regard it as a generally accepted rule of international law that no sovereign State has the right to terrorize its own citizens. Only if that shift is a reality can we explain how on 26 March the Russian-Chinese draft resolution branding the NATO air strikes a violation of the Charter could be so decisively rejected by 12 votes to 3.

This is not a time to be triumphant about that. One day, when the Kosovo crisis will be a thing of the past, we hope that the Security Council will devote a debate to the balance between respect for national sovereignty and territorial integrity on the one hand and respect for human rights and fundamental freedoms on the other hand, as well as to the shift to which I referred. This will not be a pro-Western or anti-third-world debate. The shift from [13] sovereignty to human rights spells uncertainty, and we all have our difficulties with it. But the Security Council cannot afford to ignore the phenomenon. Times have changed, and they will not change back. One simply cannot imagine a replay in the twenty-first century of the shameful episode of the 1980s, when the United Nations was apparently more indignant at a Vietnamese military intervention in Cambodia, which almost all Cambodians had experienced as a liberation, than at three years of Khmer Rouge genocide. As a result of that misconception, the large majority of delegations, including my own, allowed the Khmer Rouge to continue to occupy the Cambodian seat in the General Assembly for more than a decade.

Today, 20 years later, it seems inconceivable that respect for national sovereignty and territorial integrity could once more prompt so many States to pursue such a mistaken policy.

Mr. Fowler (Canada) (*spoke in French*): [...] The Council's response today is a recognition of the human dimension of international peace and security. From Rwanda to Kosovo, there is mounting historical evidence which shows how internal conflicts which threaten human security spill over borders and destabilize entire regions. We have learned in Kosovo and from other conflicts that humanitarian and human rights concerns are not just internal matters. Therefore, unlike the delegation of China, Canada considers that such issues can and must be given new weight in the Council's definition of security and in its calculus as to when and how the Council must engage.

We wholeheartedly agree with the Ambassador of the Netherlands that the tensions in the United Nations Charter between state sovereignty on the one hand and the promotion of international peace and security on the other must be more readily reconciled when internal conflicts become internationalized, as in the case of [14] Kosovo. Canada believes that the agreement reached today in the Council is an important step towards a broader definition of security by the international community. [...]

Mr. Burleigh (United States of America): In adopting this resolution today, the Security Council takes a historic step in reversing the campaign of terror, brutality and ethnic cleansing in Kosovo. This resolution will advance a goal that is shared by all members: the goal of returning hundreds of thousands of Kosovars to their homes with security and self-government. The United States is proud to have voted in favour of this milestone in the search for peace and security in Kosovo and the region.

This resolution lays out a concrete plan for ending the humanitarian tragedy in Kosovo and building a better future for its people. Regrettably, its adoption comes much later than it should have. Months of death, destruction and forced displacement of Kosovars could have been avoided if, in Paris last March, the Belgrade authorities had joined the Kosovar Albanians in saying yes to peace and no to war. While we welcome Belgrade's agreement to principles for resolving this crisis, we cannot forget the Federal Republic of Yugoslavia's brutal, pre-planned, systematic campaign of repression and ethnic cleansing carried out against the people of Kosovo in violation of recognized principles of international law. In this resolution, the international community has clearly demonstrated that such policies and such behaviour will not be tolerated. [...]

The resolution addresses all of our key objectives as set out by the North Atlantic Treaty Organization (NATO). Let me reiterate them here. The Federal Republic of Yugoslavia must ensure a verifiable and immediate end to violence and repression in Kosovo; must withdraw from Kosovo all its military police and paramilitary forces; must agree to the stationing in Kosovo of an international security presence with substantial NATO participation and unified command and control; must agree to the unconditional and safe return of all refugees and displaced persons and to unhindered access to such persons by humanitarian aid organizations; and must provide credible assurance of its willingness to engage in a political process aimed at the establishment of an interim political framework agreement providing for substantial self-government for Kosovo, taking full account of the Rambouillet accords.

This resolution establishes an international security force in Kosovo, which will create a safe and secure environment in which the people of Kosovo can return to their homes and rebuild their lives. NATO has signed a military-technical agreement with the Federal Republic of Yugoslavia authorities that specifies the details for the rapid withdrawal of all Federal Republic of Yugoslavia forces from Kosovo and the details of the role and authorities of the international security force (KFOR). The Federal Republic of Yugoslavia authorities have accepted that that international security force, KFOR, will operate with a unified NATO chain of command, under the political direction of the North Atlantic Council, in consultation with non-NATO force contributors.

We welcome in particular the reiteration in this resolution of the strong mandate of the authority and the jurisdiction of the International Tribunal for the Former Yugoslavia over war crimes committed in the former Yugoslavia, including Kosovo, contained in Security Council resolution 1160 (1998). Indeed, paragraph 14 of today's resolution demands full cooperation with the Tribunal.

The Security Council's vote today also sets up a civilian United Nations mission to provide an interim administration for Kosovo. This is a task of great magnitude to which all Member States will need to contribute. It is important to note that this resolution provides for the civil and military missions to remain in place until the Security Council affirmatively decides that conditions exist for their completion. The United States will work to ensure that the people of Kosovo are given the meaningful self-government they deserve, as envisioned in the Rambouillet accords.

The Federal Republic of Yugoslavia has accepted the principles of the Group of Eight foreign ministers and has agreed to withdraw all of its security forces. Only a few will be permitted to return, to perform very specific and limited functions in accordance with the Belgrade principles. All other groups, including the Kosovo Liberation Army, also must end immediately all offensive [15] actions. They must demilitarize as they have agreed, and should turn their energies to building the democratic institutions necessary for their future in the European mainstream. Both sides to this conflict must demonstrate a firm commitment to peace. In this context, we welcome public assurances by the Kosovo Liberation Army that it intends to abide by the terms of the Rambouillet accords.

To all the people of South-Eastern Europe, we say that we will dedicate ourselves to fulfilling the vision of a region that is at peace and integrated fully into the Euro-Atlantic community. We are committed to a robust programme of reconstruction and reconciliation through the European Union's Stability Pact for South-Eastern Europe. [...]

Mr. Hasmy (Malaysia): The resolution the Council has just adopted is the culmination of the strenuous efforts of the international community in the search for lasting peace and stability in Kosovo. This resolution seeks to seal the various peace plans that appear in its annexes. While not wishing to downplay the many potential pitfalls of these plans - as many aspects of their full implementation still remain to be anticipated - my delegation recognizes that they offer real and realistic prospects for an early end to the cataclysmic crisis in and around Kosovo. If the plans are to work - and they must - they require the full and genuine cooperation of all the parties concerned, in particular the Government of the Federal Republic of Yugoslavia's full implementation of and compliance with the provisions of the peace plans and the demands set out in the resolution just adopted. At the same time, there should be strong and unqualified support on the part of the international community to ensure the success of the peace plans.

My delegation is also gratified that the issue has come back to the Council, where it rightly belonged and where it could have been appropriately dealt with had there been a greater sense of unity and common purpose among its members, particularly the permanent members. We hope that the lessons learned from this experience will not be lost and will serve to guide the Council in the conduct of its future work.

My delegation is satisfied that the resolution contains the necessary elements that provide a viable basis for lasting peace and stability in Kosovo and therefore supported it. One of the centrepieces of the resolution pertains to the establishment of the international security and civil presences in Kosovo. The resolution specifies the necessary and critical tasks to be undertaken by the international security and civil presences. My delegation fervently hopes that this collective international mission will be able to discharge its mandates fully, effectively and in a well-coordinated manner. In ensuring the success of this international mission in Kosovo, the international community must be vigilant to any attempt to undermine what has been agreed. Any such attempt must be resolutely resisted. [...]

[16] As we take these tenuous and necessary steps towards a lasting peace in Kosovo, the atrocities and horrors that have been carried out in pursuance of the policy of ethnic cleansing must be addressed as part of any consolidated effort in the implementation of the peace plans. Ethnic cleansing, which reared its ugly head once again in the Balkans, is a crime against humanity and should not be brushed aside out of political expediency. Those responsible for such acts should not be allowed to go unpunished, nor should the victims be denied justice. It is important, therefore, that the work of the International Tribunal for the Former Yugoslavia, whose jurisdiction and mandate are reaffirmed in this resolution, be fully recognized and strongly supported. The work of the Tribunal should, in fact, form part and parcel of the proposed international civil presence in Kosovo. In this regard, the Council's decision, as contained in paragraph 14 of the resolution - which demands full cooperation by all concerned, including the international security presence, with the Tribunal - should be fully implemented. My delegation would have preferred an unequivocal language in this paragraph that would grant the necessary support of this Council to the Tribunal.

Enormous work has already been done by the Tribunal in relation to gross violations of human rights and humanitarian law in Kosovo. Indictments have been made and perhaps more will follow. It is of vital importance for the international community to maintain the credibility of the Tribunal, as well as of this Council, which created it. The arrest and prosecution of indicted war criminals is not only an issue of justice, but one that will have important and long-lasting effects on the process of re-establishing the rule of law and accomplishing reconciliation in Kosovo. It should also serve as a stern warning to would-be perpetrators of crimes against humanity, who should not be allowed to get away with impunity. We strongly believe that, had the international community been more resolute in apprehending the leading indicted war criminals who were responsible for the atrocities in Bosnia and Herzegovina, the ethnic cleansing in Kosovo could have been averted. [...]

Peace in Kosovo and the Balkans as a whole should be viewed as a long-term process and not as a quick-exit strategy from the Balkans by the international community. As part of the international endeavours to nurture peace and to restore normality in Kosovo, efforts towards infrastructure rehabilitation and economic reconstruction must be given immediate and priority attention. In this connection, my delegation is gratified that serious efforts are being made in this direction, particularly by the Office of the United Nations High Commissioner for Refugees (UNHCR) and other United Nations agencies, as well as by the proposed Stability Pact for South-Eastern Europe, which aims at carrying out economic assistance and long-term development in Kosovo and other parts of the southern Balkans. Given the immensity of the humanitarian and reconstruction tasks, there is an obvious need for effective coordination and cooperation between those aid agencies and the members of the international community to avoid unnecessary competition, duplication and wastage of resources.

With regard to the responsibility of the international civil presence, my delegation underscores the paramount importance of the proposed interim administration for Kosovo, which should pave the way for an early settlement of the future status of Kosovo, taking fully into account the political framework proposed in the Rambouillet accords. The root cause of the crisis is clear. The Secretary-General himself stated, in his address to the High-Level Meeting on the crisis in the Balkans, held in Geneva on 14 May 1999:

"Before there was a humanitarian catastrophe in Kosovo, there was a human rights catastrophe. Before there was a human rights catastrophe, there was a political catastrophe: the deliberate, systematic and violent disenfranchisement of the Kosovar Albanian people."

This clearly demonstrates the need to ensure one very fundamental element in the peace settlement: the fulfilment of the legitimate aspirations and expectations of the Kosovar Albanian people, the majority inhabitants of Kosovo. Any departure from this fundamental point will risk unravelling the entire exercise which is being painstakingly put together.

In conclusion, my delegation would like to commend all the efforts of the members of the international community that have been actively engaged in the search for peace in Kosovo, which have brought us to where we are today. We would also like to take this opportunity to express our profound thanks and appreciation to all United Nations agencies and other international and relief [17] organizations, as well as to several Governments, for their role in alleviating the plight of the refugees and displaced persons.

Mr. Fonseca (Brazil): Tensions in Kosovo have been simmering for a decade. In the month of June 1989, a policy shift on the part of the Belgrade authorities towards the ethnic Albanians in Kosovo marked the beginning of a cycle of intolerance in the former Yugoslavia. This shift would eventually lead to destruction and suffering in the Balkans on a scale not seen in Europe since the Second World War. At the core of this tide of violence were the policies of certain leaders who lost the capacity to understand the logic of peace. Instead of seeking unity in diversity, strength in pluralism and accommodation through dialogue, they resorted to discrimination and violence, without realizing, perhaps, that they were sowing the seeds of disruption of their own society.

The Balkan wars of the 1990s have cast a tragic shadow over the expectations raised by the end of the cold war for a world of increased international cooperation for peace and security. They have wreaked havoc in south-eastern Europe and spread discord on a global scale. In dealing with the complex challenges posed by Bosnia and Kosovo, the Security Council has not always been able to devise the most effective strategies to reach its shared objectives of combating ethnic hatred and promoting regional stability.

These have often been times of frustration for those who, like we in Brazil, remain just as firm in their rejection of the instruments of intolerance as they remain committed to preserving and strengthening the authority of the Security Council.

Today we have perhaps reached a turning point. It is with a considerable measure of relief that my Government lends its support to a Security Council resolution that paves the way for the return of refugees to Kosovo under conditions of safety. We trust that these measures will lay the groundwork for putting an end to the enormous suffering that the inhabitants of the region have been subjected to in recent weeks and months. Thousands of lives have been lost. A large number of civilians have died or been wounded. More than a million remain displaced. Those who make it back to their former homes will, for the most part, be returning to destroyed villages. Even if a new regional agenda for cooperation takes hold, it will be years before any semblance of normality can be aspired to.

At the same time - and independent of the moral considerations invoked for these actions, with which we fully identify - problematic precedents have been set in the resort to military force without Security Council authorization. These have neither contributed to upholding the Council's authority nor improved the humanitarian situation.

It is possible to hope that today's meeting will herald a new chapter for the countless Kosovars and others in the region whose lives have been shattered by the ravages of this bloody conflict. It is possible to hope that the Security Council will build upon this day to find a new blend of realism and idealism that will translate itself into greater wisdom and true effectiveness. It is possible to hope, together with the Secretary-General, Mr. Kofi Annan, that, in the future, countries will not have to choose between inaction and genocide, intervention and Council division.

The Security Council and the entire United Nations system are now presented with a historic opportunity to demonstrate their unique capacity for legitimate joint action to promote reconciliation and stability, and to promote peace on the basis of international law. No doubt, the path ahead will be fraught with great challenges as an ambitious programme for a civil and security presence in Kosovo is put into place and a provisional administration for Kosovo is established. But we are confident that this is the correct way for the international community to proceed. As the Security Council resumes its rightful role in the handling of this crisis, there is even scope for hoping that a new inclination to find, within the Council, multilateral solutions to other serious problems affecting world security, will gradually emerge. [...]

The traumatic experiences of the past 10 years will not be easily forgotten. But if an age of hope can now be imagined, it is up to the members of the Security Council, as participants in the only universally recognized organ [18] in the field of peace and security, to ensure that Kosovo is allowed a new beginning. [...]

Sir Jeremy Greenstock (United Kingdom): [...] This Chapter-VII resolution and its annexes clearly set out the key demands of the international community, which Belgrade must satisfy. The interpretation and conditions which the delegation of the Federal Republic of Yugoslavia has attempted to propose have been rejected. The resolution also provides for the deployment of an international civil presence, led by the United Nations, for the continuing work of the International Criminal Tribunal for the former Yugoslavia, and for an effective international security presence to re-establish a safe environment in Kosovo. This force must command the confidence of Kosovo Albanian refugees if they are to return home. That is why NATO has made clear that it will be essential to have a unified NATO chain of command under the political direction of the North Atlantic Council in consultation with non-NATO force contributors. This force, with NATO at its core, will be commanded by a British general. The United Kingdom will provide the leading contribution of at least 13,000 troops.

This resolution applies also in full to the Kosovo Albanians, requiring them to play their full part in the restoration of normal life to Kosovo and in the creation of democratic, self-governing institutions. The Kosovo Albanian people and its leadership must rise to the challenge of peace by accepting the obligations of the resolution, in particular to demilitarize the Kosovo Liberation Army (KLA) and other armed groups. [...]

Mr. Petrella (Argentina) *(spoke in Spanish)*: The resolution just adopted by the Security Council is of [19] singular importance for various reasons. First, it marks the end of a humanitarian tragedy in which the main victims were thousands of innocent civilians whose fundamental human rights were being systematically and persistently violated.

Secondly, it lays the foundation for a definitive political solution to the Kosovo crisis that will respect the sovereignty and territorial integrity of the Federal Republic of Yugoslavia. The rights of minorities and of all the inhabitants of Kosovo, without exception, to live in a climate of peace and tolerance must also be unequivocally recognized.

Thirdly, this resolution confirms the central and irreplaceable role of the United Nations, and in particular that of the Security Council and the Secretary-General at times when there is a need to join efforts in order to maintain international peace and security.

Lastly, it represents an interpretation of the Charter that reflects the current recognition of human rights throughout the international community. [...]

Mr. Buallay (Bahrain) *(spoke in Arabic)*: In adopting this resolution on the situation in Kosovo, the Security Council today finds itself at a historic turning point. Through this action the Council is conferring the international legitimacy necessary to settle this situation, which is both tragic and complex. [...]

[20] **Mr. Dangue Rewaka** (Gabon) *(spoke in French)*: It will be recalled that before 24 March 1999, the Security Council, the Contact Group - consisting of the Ministers for Foreign Affairs of Germany, the United States of America, the Russian Federation, France, Italy and the United Kingdom of Great Britain and Northern Ireland - and the Permanent Council of the Organization for Security and Cooperation in Europe had to strive unceasingly to bring about a lasting political solution to the Kosovo crisis.

For its part, the Security Council adopted resolutions 1160 (1998) of 31 March 1998, 1199 (1998) of 23 September 1998 and 1203 (1998) of 24 October 1998. All of them called, inter alia, for the cessation of hostilities in Kosovo, in the Federal Republic of Yugoslavia, and for the beginning of constructive dialogue with a view to arriving at a political settlement to the Kosovo situation.

Neither the peaceful measures that were advocated nor the condemnation repeatedly expressed by the international community succeeded in curbing the violence in Kosovo. Villages have been destroyed, causing thousands of casualties and displacing hundreds of thousands of people. The confrontations in February and March 1998 in the Drenica region, in the centre of Kosovo, are a vivid illustration of this dramatic situation. Should this tragedy have been allowed to continue? The answer is clearly no.

It is therefore understandable that the regional Powers had to resort to the means they deemed best suited to the situation. The resolution that we have just adopted not only offers fresh prospects for a resolution of the Kosovo conflict and for peace in the Balkan region, it also bolsters the key role of the United Nations, in particular that of the Security Council, in the maintenance of international peace and security.

Indeed, the first preambular paragraph recalls the purposes and principles of the Charter of the United Nations. Paragraphs 6, 10 and 20 clearly spell out the mission entrusted to the Secretary-General of the United Nations in the implementation of this resolution. Likewise, the resolution reaffirms the principles of dialogue, negotiation and peace, which Gabon holds very dear.

For all of those reasons, we co-sponsored the resolution and voted in favour of it.

The President: *[Speaking in his capacity as representative of Gambia.]*

Throughout the crisis over Kosovo, the Security Council has endeavoured to set out clearly the concerns of the international community. The more resolutions and statements the Council adopted on this issue, the more Belgrade brazenly stepped up its repression and violence against the civilian population in Kosovo. Such violence and flagrant violations of human rights have shocked the collective conscience of mankind. The subsequent massive influx of refugees into neighbouring countries and their accounts of the atrocities inflicted on them and their families can leave no one indifferent. The international community could no longer afford the luxury of being a helpless spectator while the policy of ethnic cleansing was going on in Kosovo. It is regrettable that force had to be used to arrive at where we are today. We therefore welcome wholeheartedly the agreements reached a few hours ago for a political settlement of the Kosovo crisis. The delegation of the Gambia always upheld the view that the plight of the refugees and internally displaced persons would persist unless and until the underlying political problems were addressed.

The whole world has a lot to celebrate today. We would, however, guard against euphoria, because there remains a lot of healing to be done. As far as the United Nations - and especially the Security Council - is concerned, it is a happy day, in view of the fact that the issue of Kosovo has divided the Council for so long. At long last, the Security Council is once more able to find unity around this issue and, above all, it is again able to assume its primary responsibility in the maintenance of international peace and security. Its authority has been recognized and restored.

[21] Furthermore, the preponderant role of the Secretary-General has been clearly spelt out. It is high time we gave to Caesar what belongs to Caesar. The resolution that we have just adopted takes on particular importance for my delegation for two reasons. First, it is a comprehensive and well-balanced text - in other words, a blueprint for the peaceful resolution of the Kosovo crisis. Secondly, it recognizes and restores the authority of the Security Council and places it on a firmer footing to tackle other major crisis situations that are still pending. That is the beauty of it, and we therefore voted in favour.

I now resume my functions as President of the Council. [...]

[A statement by the UN Secretary-General has been omitted.]

210. Stability Pact for South Eastern Europe, Cologne, 10 June 1999

I. Participants, Description of Situation

1. We, the Foreign Ministers of the Member States of the European Union, the European Commission, the Foreign Ministers of Albania, Bosnia and Herzegovina, Bulgaria, Croatia, Hungary, Romania, the Russian Federation, Slovenia, the former Yugoslav Republic of Macedonia, Turkey, the United States of America, the OSCE Chairman in Office and the Representative of the Council of Europe representing the participants in today's Conference on South Eastern Europe; and the Foreign Ministers of Canada and Japan, Representatives of the United Nations, UNHCR, NATO, OECD, WEU, International Monetary Fund, the World Bank, the European Investment Bank and the European Bank for Reconstruction and Development, acting within their competences, representing the facilitating States, Organisations and Institutions of today's Conference, as well as the Representatives of the Royaumont process, BSEC, CEI, SECI and SEECP, have met in Cologne on 10 June 1999, in response to the European Union's call to adopt a Stability Pact for South Eastern Europe.

2. The countries of South Eastern Europe recognize their responsibility to work within the international community to develop a shared strategy for stability and growth of the region and to cooperate with each other and major donors to implement that strategy. Seizing the opportunity to address structural shortfalls and unresolved issues will accelerate democratic and economic development in the region.

3. We will strive to achieve the objective of lasting peace, prosperity and stability for South Eastern Europe. We will reach this objective through a comprehensive and coherent approach to the region involving the EU, the OSCE, the Council of Europe, the UN, NATO, the OECD, the WEU, the IFIs and the regional initiatives. We welcome the fact that the European Union and the United States have made support for the Stability Pact a priority in their New Transatlantic Agenda, as well as the fact that the European Union and the Russian Federation have made the Stability Pact a priority in their political dialogue.

4. A settlement of the Kosovo conflict is critical to our ability to reach fully the objectives of the Stability Pact and to work towards permanent, long term measures for a future of peace and inter-ethnic harmony without fear of the resurgence of war.

II. Principles and Norms

5. We solemnly reaffirm our commitment to all the principles and norms enshrined in the UN Charter, the Helsinki Final Act, the Charter of Paris, the 1990 Copenhagen Document and other OSCE documents, and, as applicable, to the full implementation of relevant UN Security Council Resolutions, the relevant conventions of the Council of Europe and the General Framework Agreement for Peace in Bosnia and Herzegovina, with a view to promoting good neighbourly relations.

6. In our endeavours, we will build upon bilateral and multilateral agreements on good neighbourly relations concluded by States in the region participating in the Pact, and will seek the conclusion of such agreements where they do not exist. They will form an essential element of the Stability Pact.

7. We reaffirm that we are accountable to our citizens and responsible to one another for respect for OSCE norms and principles and for the implementation of our commitments. We also reaffirm that commitments with respect to the human dimension undertaken through our membership in the OSCE are matters of direct and legitimate concern to all States participating in the Stability Pact, and do not belong exclusively to the internal affairs of the State concerned. Respect for these commitments constitutes one of the foundations of international order, to which we intend to make a substantial contribution.

8. We take note that countries in the region participating in the Stability Pact commit themselves to continued democratic and economic reforms, as elaborated in paragraph 10, as well as bilateral and regional cooperation amongst themselves to advance their integration, on an individual basis, into Euro-Atlantic structures. The EU Member States and other participating countries and international organisations and institutions commit themselves to making every effort to assist them to make speedy and measurable progress along this road. We reaffirm the inherent right of each and every participating State to be free to choose or change its security arrangements, including treaties of alliance as they evolve. Each participating State will respect the rights of all others

in this regard. They will not strengthen their security at the expense of the security of other States.

III. Objectives

9. The Stability Pact aims at strengthening countries in South Eastern Europe in their efforts to foster peace, democracy, respect for human rights and economic prosperity, in order to achieve stability in the whole region. Those countries in the region who seek integration into Euro-Atlantic structures, alongside a number of other participants in the Pact, strongly believe that the implementation of this process will facilitate their objective.

10. To that end we pledge to cooperate towards:

- preventing and putting an end to tensions and crises as a prerequisite for lasting stability. This includes concluding and implementing among ourselves multilateral and bilateral agreements and taking domestic measures to overcome the existing potential for conflict;

- bringing about mature democratic political processes, based on free and fair elections, grounded in the rule of law and full respect for human rights and fundamental freedoms, including the rights of persons belonging to national minorities, the right to free and independent media, legislative branches accountable to their constituents, independent judiciaries, combating corruption, deepening and strengthening of civil society;

- creating peaceful and good-neighbourly relations in the region through strict observance of the principles of the Helsinki Final Act, confidence building and reconciliation, encouraging work in the OSCE and other fora on regional confidence building measures and mechanisms for security cooperation;

- preserving the multinational and multiethnic diversity of countries in the region, and protecting minorities;

- creating vibrant market economies based on sound macro policies, markets open to greatly expanded foreign trade and private sector investment, effective and transparent customs and commercial/regulatory regimes, developing strong capital markets and diversified ownership, including privatisation, leading to a widening circle of prosperity for all our citizens;

- fostering economic cooperation in the region and between the region and the rest of Europe and the world, including free trade areas; promoting unimpeded contacts among citizens;

- combatting organised crime, corruption and terrorism and all criminal and illegal activities;

- preventing forced population displacement caused by war, persecution and civil strife as well as migration generated by poverty;

- ensuring the safe and free return of all refugees and displaced persons to their homes, while assisting the countries in the region by sharing the burden imposed upon them;

- creating the conditions, for countries of South Eastern Europe, for full integration into political, economic and security structures of their choice.

11. Lasting peace and stability in South Eastern Europe will only become possible when democratic principles and values, which are already actively promoted by many countries in the region, have taken root throughout, including in the Federal Republic of Yugoslavia. International efforts must focus on consolidating and linking areas of stability in the region to lay a firm foundation for the transition of the region as a whole to a peaceful and democratic future.

We declare that the Federal Republic of Yugoslavia will be welcome as a full and equal participant in the Stability Pact, following the political settlement of the Kosovo crisis on the basis of the principles agreed by G8 Foreign Ministers and taking into account the need for respect by all participants for the principles and objectives of this Pact.

In order to draw the Federal Republic of Yugoslavia closer to this goal, respecting its sovereignty and territorial integrity, we will consider ways of making the Republic of Montenegro an early beneficiary of the Pact. In this context, we welcome involvement in our meetings of representatives of Montenegro, as a constituent Republic of the Federal Republic of Yugoslavia. We also note the intention of the European Union and other interested participants to continue to work closely with its democratically elected government.

IV. Mechanisms of the Stability Pact

12. To reach the objectives we have set for ourselves, we have agreed to set up a South Eastern Europe Regional Table. The South Eastern Europe Regional Table will review progress under the Stability Pact, carry it forward and provide guidance for advancing its objectives.

13. The Stability Pact will have a Special Coordinator, who will be appointed by the European Union, after consultation with the OSCE Chairman in Office and other participants, and endorsed by the OSCE Chairman in Office. The Special Coordinator will chair the South Eastern Europe Regional Table and will be responsible for promoting achievement of the Pact's objectives within and between the individual countries, supported by appropriate structures tailored to need, in close cooperation with the governments and relevant institutions of the countries, in particular other interested associated countries of the European Union, as well as relevant international organisations and institutions concerned. The Special Coordinator will provide periodic progress reports to the OSCE, according to its procedures, on behalf of the South Eastern Europe Regional Table.

14. The South Eastern Europe Regional Table will ensure coordination of activities of and among the following Working Tables, which will build upon existing expertise, institutions and initiatives and could be divided into sub-tables:

- Working Table on democratisation and human rights; - Working Table on economic reconstruction, development and cooperation; - Working Table on security issues.

15. Responsibilities for these Working Tables are referred to in the Annex to this document. The Working Tables will address and facilitate the resolution of the issues entrusted to them by arrangements to be agreed at each table.

16. The South Eastern Europe Regional Table and the Working Tables will consist of the participants of the Stability Pact. The facilitator States, Organisations and Institutions as well as the regional initiatives referred to in paragraph 1 of this document are entitled to participate in the Working Tables and in the South Eastern Europe Regional Table if they so wish. Neighbouring and other countries, in particular other interested associated countries of the EU, as well as relevant international organisations and institutions may be invited as participants or observers, as appropriate, and without any ensuing commitment to the future, to the South Eastern Europe Regional Table and/or the Working Tables, in order to contribute to the objectives of the Stability Pact.

V. Roles of and Cooperation Between Participants

17. Work in the Stability Pact should take into account the diversity of the situation of participants. To achieve the objectives of this Pact, we will provide for effective coordination between the participating and facilitating States, international and regional Organisations and Institutions, which have unique knowledge and expertise to contribute to the common endeavour. We look to the active and creative participation by all concerned to bring about the conditions which will enable the countries in the region to seize the opportunity represented by this Pact. Each of the participants will endeavour to ensure that the objectives of the Stability Pact are furthered in their own participation in all relevant international Organisations and Institutions.

ROLE OF THE EU

18. We welcome the European Union's initiative in launching the Stability Pact and the leading role the EU is playing, in cooperation with other participating and facilitating States, international Organisations and Institutions. The launching of the Pact will give a firm European anchorage to the region. The ultimate success of the Pact will depend largely on the efforts of the States concerned to fulfil the objec-

tives of the Pact and to develop regional cooperation through multilateral and bilateral agreements.

19. We warmly welcome the European Union's readiness to actively support the countries in the region and to enable them to achieve the objectives of the Stability Pact. We welcome the EU's activity to strengthen democratic and economic institutions in the region through a number of relevant programmes. We note progress towards the establishment and development of contractual relations, on an individual basis and within the framework of its Regional Approach, between the EU and countries of the region. We take note that, on the basis of the Vienna European Council Conclusions, the EU will prepare a "Common Strategy towards the Western Balkans", as a fundamental initiative.

20. The EU will draw the region closer to the perspective of full integration of these countries into its structures. In case of countries which have not yet concluded association agreements with the EU, this will be done through a new kind of contractual relationship taking fully into account the individual situations of each country with the perspective of EU membership, on the basis of the Amsterdam Treaty and once the Copenhagen criteria have been met. We note the European Union's willingness that, while deciding autonomously, it will consider the achievement of the objectives of the Stability Pact, in particular progress in developing regional cooperation, among the important elements in evaluating the merits of such a perspective.

ROLE OF COUNTRIES IN THE REGION

21. We highly appreciate the contribution and the solidarity of the countries in the region with the efforts of the international community for reaching a peaceful solution on Kosovo. We welcome the efforts so far deployed and results achieved by countries in South Eastern Europe towards democratisation, economic reform and regional cooperation and stability. These countries will be the main beneficiaries of the Pact and recognise that its successful implementation, and the advance towards Euro-Atlantic structures for those seeking it depend decisively on their commitment to implement the objectives of the Pact, in particular on their willingness to cooperate on a bilateral and multilateral level and to promote the objectives of the Pact within their own respective national structures.

ROLE OF THE OSCE

22. We welcome the OSCE's intention, as the only pan-European security organisation and as a regional arrangement under Chapter VIII of the UN Charter and a primary instrument for early warning, conflict prevention, crisis management and post-conflict rehabilitation, to make a significant contribution to the efforts undertaken through the Stability Pact. We reaffirm that the OSCE has a key role to play in fostering all dimensions of security and stability. Accordingly, we request that the Stability Pact be placed under the auspices of the OSCE, and will rely fully on the OSCE to work for compliance with the provisions of the Stability Pact by the participating States, in accordance with its procedures and established principles.

23. We will rely on the OSCE institutions and instruments and their expertise to contribute to the proceedings of the South Eastern Europe Regional Table and of the Working Tables, in particular the Working Table on Democratisation and Human Rights. Their unique competences will be much needed in furthering the aims and objectives of the Stability Pact. We express our intention, in cases requiring OSCE involvement with regard to the observance of OSCE principles in the implementation of the Stability Pact, to resort, where appropriate, to the instruments and procedures of the OSCE, including those concerning conflict prevention, the peaceful settlement of disputes and the human dimension. States parties to the Convention establishing the Court of Conciliation and Arbitration may also refer to the Court possible disputes and ask for the non-binding opinion of the Court.

ROLE OF THE COUNCIL OF EUROPE

24. We welcome the Council of Europe's readiness to integrate all countries in the region into full membership on the basis of the principles of pluralist democracy, human rights and the rule of law. The Council of Europe can make an important contribution to the objectives of the Pact through its parliamentary and intergovernmental organs and institutions, its European norms embodied in relevant legally-binding Conventions, primarily the European Convention of Human Rights (and the Court), its instruments and assistance programmes in the fields of democratic institutions, human rights, law, justice and education, as well as its strong links with civil society. In this context, we take note with great interest of the Council of Europe's Stability Programme for South East Europe to be implemented, together and in close coordination with the countries concerned and other international and regional organisations active in the field.

ROLE OF THE UN, INCLUDING UNHCR

25. We underline the UN's central role in the region for peace and security and for lasting political normalisation, as well as for humanitarian efforts and economic rehabilitation. We strongly support UNHCR's lead agency function in all refugee-related questions, in particular the protection and return of refugees and displaced persons and the crucial role undertaken by WFP, UNICEF, WHO, UNDP, UNHCHR and other members of the UN system. We look forward to the active involvement of relevant UN agencies in the South Eastern Europe Regional Table. We note that the UN Economic Commission for Europe has expertise which can usefully contribute to the proceedings of the Working Tables of the Stability Pact.

ROLE OF NATO

26. We note NATO's decision to increase cooperation with the countries of South Eastern Europe and its commitment to openness, as well as the intention of NATO, the Euro-Atlantic Partnership Council and the Partnership for Peace to work in cooperation with other Euro-Atlantic structures, to contribute to stability and security and to maintain and increase consultations with the countries of the region. We call for their engagement, in conformity with the objectives of the Pact, in regional security cooperation and conflict prevention and management. We welcome these stabilization activities aimed at promoting the objectives of this Pact. The enhanced use of NATO's consultative fora and mechanisms, the development of an EAPC cooperative mechanism and the increased use of Partnership for Peace programmes will serve the objectives of overall stability, cooperation and good-neighbourliness envisaged in the Pact.

The members of NATO and a substantial number of other participants underscore that the Alliance has an important role to play in achieving the objectives of the Pact, noting in particular NATO's recent decisions to reach out to countries of the region.

ROLE OF THE UNITED STATES OF AMERICA

28. Having worked closely with the European Union to launch this Pact, the United States of America will continue to play a leading role in the development and implementation of the Pact, in cooperation with other participants and facilitators. We believe that the active role of the United States underscores the vital importance attached by countries of the region to their integration into Euro-Atlantic structures.

We note the United States' readiness to support this objective, as these countries work to become as strong candidates as possible for eventual membership in Euro-Atlantic institutions. We welcome the ongoing contribution of the United States, including through economic and technical assistance programmes, and through its shared leadership in International financial Institutions, to the States of South Eastern Europe. The United States will coordinate and cooperate with the other donors to ensure the maximum effectiveness of assistance to the region.

ROLE OF THE RUSSIAN FEDERATION

29. Russia has played and continues to play a key role in the region. Russian efforts and contribution to achieving a peaceful solution of conflicts there, in particular of the Kosovo crisis, are appreciated. Having been involved at an early stage in the launching of this Pact, the Russian Federation will continue to play a leading and constructive role in development and implementation of the Pact, in cooperation with the EU, the UN, the OSCE, the Council of Europe, international

economic and financial organisations and institutions, as well as regional initiatives and individual states. The Russian Federation can make a valuable contribution to activities aimed at promoting peace, security and post-conflict cooperation.

Role of the IFIs

30. The IMF, the World Bank, the EBRD and the EIB, as the European Union financing institution, have a most important role to play, in accordance with their specific mandates, in supporting the countries in the region in achieving economic stabilisation, reform, and development of the region. We rely on them to develop a coherent international assistance strategy for the region and to promote sound macroeconomic and structural policies by the countries concerned. We call on these International Financial Institutions to take an active part in the South Eastern Europe Regional Table and the relevant Working Tables.

Role of the OECD

31. We note the OECD's unique strength as a forum for dialogue on medium-term structural policy and best practices. We rely on the OECD in consideration of its well-known competence in dealing with economies in transition and its open dialogue with the countries of South Eastern Europe, to take an active part in the South Eastern Europe Regional Table and to assist in the process of economic reconstruction, the strengthening of good governance and administrative capacities and the further integration of affected States into the European and global economy.

Role of the WEU

32. We welcome the role which the WEU plays in promoting stability in the region. We note in this respect the contribution to security the WEU makes, at the request of the European Union, through its missions in countries in the region.

VI. Regional Initiatives and Organisations

33. We stress our interest in viable regional initiatives and organisations which foster friendly cooperation between neighbouring States. We welcome sub-regional cooperation schemes between participating countries. We will endeavour to ensure cooperation and coordination between these initiatives and the Stability Pact, which will be mutually reinforcing. We will build on their relevant achievements.

34. We note that the Royaumont process has already established a dynamic framework for cooperation in the area of democracy and civil society. Therefore, Royaumont has a key role to play in this area, particularly within the framework of the first Working Table of the Stability Pact.

35. We note the role of the Organization of the Black Sea Economic Cooperation in promoting mutual understanding, improving the overall political climate and fostering economic development in the Black Sea region. Welcoming its engagement to peace, security and stability through economic cooperation, we invite the BSEC to contribute to the implementation of the Stability Pact for South Eastern Europe.

36. We note that the Central European Initiative has established, with countries in the region, a stable and integrated framework of dialogue, coordination and cooperation in the political, economic, cultural and parliamentary fields. On the basis of its experience, it has an important role to play in the framework of the South Eastern Europe Regional Table.

37. We note that the South East Europe Cooperation Initiative (SECI) has developed an innovative approach to economic and infrastructure related cooperation in the region by facilitating joint decision-making by the South Eastern European countries in its areas of activity. As such, it has a key role to play concerning regional economic issues, in particular the removal of disincentives to private investment in the region, in the framework of the Stability Pact.

38. We commend the South Eastern Europe Cooperation Process as a further successful regional cooperation scheme. We encourage its further development and institutionalisation, including the finalisation of its charter on good-neighbourly relations and cooperation.

39. We note the contribution in the security dimension of the South Eastern European Defence Ministers (SEDM) group, which has brought the countries of the region and other nations into a variety of cooperative activities which enhance transparency and mutual confidence, such as the new Multinational Peace-Keeping Force for South East Europe.

40. We expect the proposed Conference on the Adriatic and Ionian Sea region to provide a positive contribution to the region.

VII. International Donor Mobilisation and Coordination Process

41. We reaffirm our strong commitment to support reconstruction, stabilisation and integration for the region, and call upon the international donor community to participate generously. We welcome the progress made by the World Bank and the European Union, through the European Commission, towards establishing a donor coordination process. This process will closely interact with the relevant Working Table, and will identify appropriate modalities to administer and channel international assistance. The World Bank and the European Commission will also be responsible for coordinating a comprehensive approach for regional development and the necessary donors conferences.

VIII. Implementation and Review Mechanisms

42. Effective implementation of this Pact will depend on the development and the strengthening of administrative and institutional capacity as well as civil society in the countries concerned - both at national and local level - in order to reinforce the consolidation of democratic structures and have longer-term benefits for effective administration and absorption of international assistance for the region.

43. The South Eastern Europe Regional Table and the Working Tables will be convened for their inaugural meetings at the earliest possible opportunity at the invitation of the Presidency of the European Union. They will work to achieve concrete results according to agreed timelines, in conformity with the objectives of the Stability Pact. The South Eastern Europe Regional Table will meet periodically, at a level to be determined, to review progress made by the Working Tables. The South Eastern Europe Regional Table will provide guidance to the Working Tables.

Annex

ORGANISATION OF THE SOUTH EASTERN EUROPE REGIONAL TABLE AND THE WORKING TABLES OF THE STABILITY PACT FOR SOUTH EASTERN EUROPE

A. The South Eastern Europe Regional Table will carry forward the Stability Pact by acting as a clearing house for all questions of principle relating to the substance and implementation of the Stability Pact as well as a steering body in the Stability Pact process. The South Eastern Europe Regional Table will provide guidance to the Working Tables.

B. The Working Tables are instruments for maintaining and improving good-neighbourly relations in the region by constructively addressing and facilitating the resolution of the issues entrusted to them. The objectives of the Working Tables will be in particular:

- the discussion of issues in a multilateral framework conducive to the definition of ways to address shortfalls and to the settlement of differences by arrangements and agreements, drawing on the expertise and support of participants as well as facilitator States, Organisations, Institutions and regional initiatives, in particular from the OSCE and the Council of Europe;

- the identification of projects aimed at facilitating the achievement of arrangements, agreements and measures in conformity with the objectives of the Pact. Special attention is to be given to projects which involve two and more countries in the region.

- where necessary, the injection of momentum in areas where further progress should be achieved.

C. Each Working Table will address the following range of issues and will decide, as appropriate, whether the establishment of sub-tables, comprising the participants and facilitators, will be necessary;

- Working Table on democratisation and human rights, which will address:

i. democratisation and human rights, including the rights of persons belonging to national minorities; free and independent media; civil society building; rule of law and law enforcement; institution building; efficient administration and good governance; development of common rules of conduct on border related questions; other related questions of interest to the participants;

ii. refugee issues, including protection and return of refugees and displaced persons;

- Working Table on economic reconstruction, development and co-operation, including economic cooperation in the region and between the region and the rest of Europe and the world; promotion of free trade areas; border-crossing transport; energy supply and savings; deregulation and transparency; infrastructure; promotion of private sector business; environmental issues; sustainable reintegration of refugees; other related questions of interest to the participants, while maintaining the integrity of the donor coordination process;

- Working Table on security issues, which will :

(i) address justice and home affairs, as well as migratory issues; focus on measures to combat organized crime, corruption, terrorism and all criminal and illegal activities, transboundary environmental hazards; other related questions of interest to the participants;

(ii) receive regular information from the competent bodies addressing transparency and confidence- building measures in the region. This Table will also encourage continued implementation of the Dayton/Paris Article IV Arms Control Agreement and progress of the negotiations of Article V, and should consider whether, at an appropriate time, further arms control, security and confidence building measures might be addressed, by the competent bodies, taking into account existing obligations and commitments under the CFE Treaty.

(iii) receive regular information from the competent bodies addressing cooperation on defence/military issues aimed at enhancing stability in the region and among countries in the region, and facilitate the sustained engagement of all concerned to ensure regional security, conflict prevention and management. The work of this Table will complement and be coherent with efforts for the security of this region undertaken by various European and Euro-Atlantic initiatives and structures.

D. The Working Tables will establish work plans in conformity with the objectives of the Stability Pact. Within the range of their competence, they can establish side tables or call meetings and conferences on matters of a specific or sub-regional nature. In this context, special attention is to be given to fostering the exchange between private citizens (in particular youth), societal groups, entrepreneurs and companies as well as non-governmental organisations and their respective counterparts in the various countries of the region. They will, in particular, pay attention to the coherence and consistency of their work with existing activities and seek to promote complementarity and synergy, as well as avoid duplication, with existing activities.

E. The Chairmanship of the Working Tables will be established by the South Eastern Europe Regional Table. The Working Tables will report to the South Eastern Europe Regional Table. The respective chairs of the South Eastern Europe Regional Table and the Working Tables will meet periodically and as necessary to discuss and coordinate the activities of the Working Tables and to monitor progress.

F. The location and timing of the individual Working Tables should be arranged to facilitate, to the extent possible, the attendance of participants who may take part in more than one Working Table, without excluding different Tables developing their own calendars according to their respective dynamics. Tables could take place either in rotation in the countries of the region or at the invitation of individual countries or of the European Union or in Vienna, at the venue of the Permanent Council of the OSCE.

G. The host country, or host organisation, should provide at its expense meeting facilities, such as conference rooms, secretarial assistance and interpretation. The European Union has expressed its readiness to bear such expenses when meetings are held at the seat of its institutions.

211. G 8, Proposals of the G 8 Presidency in the Light of the Discussions on Civilian Implementation in Kosovo, Gürzenich, 10 June 1999

The G 8 Foreign Ministers adopted the following general principles on the civilian aspects of the implementation of an interim peace settlement in Kosovo:

- Integrated civilian implementation structure to maximise effectiveness.

- A Special Representative of the United Nations Secretary-General, as envisaged in paragraph 6 and 10 of the draft United Nations Security Council Resolutions prepared by the G 8 Foreign Ministers on 8 June 1999 should be appointed rapidly to lead the civilian effort.

- Other international organisations with relevant expertise to contribute as part of an integrated structure, with each organisation retaining its own separate accountability.

- A Steering Board to give strategic direction, bringing together the, EU, the UN, the OSCE, the G8-Member States, the organisations involved and a representative of the OIC.

- Close coordination between the civilian and military presences from the outset.

- Civilian implementation structure to be deployed rapidly, as soon as a secure environment has been established.

- A conference of the relevant international organisations to be convened urgently by the United Nations Secretary-General to assign responsibility for the specific areas set out in paragraph 11 of the draft United Nations Security Council Resolutions as prepared by the G 8 Foreign Ministers on 8 June 1999.

- Particular priority to be given to the establishment and deployment of an international civilian police force, and to the training of a locally recruited police force, in order to take on responsibility for civil law and order as soon as possible from KFOR, as envisaged in the MTA of 9 June 1999.

- Given the scale of the reconstruction task, an early donors' conference in which G 8 member states pledge to play a full part.

- The restoration of stability in Kosovo to be part of a wider strategy for regeneration of the region, as set out in the Stability Pact for South Eastern Europe.

212. NATO, Letter from the Secretary General of the North Atlantic Treaty Organization addressed to the UN Secretary-General, 10 June 1999[1]

Yesterday NATO military authorities agreed with the Federal Republic of Yugoslavia (Serbia and Montenegro) on the procedures and modalities for the withdrawal from Kosovo of FRY security forces.

FRY security forces have begun to withdraw from Kosovo in accordance with these agreed procedures and modalities. NATO is monitoring the FRY's compliance closely. Against this background, NATO air operations against the FRY have been suspended.

I look forward to keeping in close touch with you on this matter and the evolution of the overall situation.

(Signed) Javier Solana

---

[1] UN Doc. S/1999/663, Annex, 10 June 1999.

213. FRY, Statement from the Federal Government's Meeting, Belgrade, 11 June 1999

At today's meeting, chaired by Prime Minister Momir Bulatovic, the Federal Government concluded that, by the adoption of the Resolution of the UN Security Council, the brutal aggression of NATO against the Federal Republic of Yugoslavia, is ended. The adoption of the Resolution affirms the territorial integrity and sovereignty of the Federal Republic of Yugoslavia, prevents terrorism and separatism and excludes every possibility of Kosovo's independence.

The government thinks that the country was defended thanks to the unity of the people and its heroism, and especially thanks to the constancy, patriotism and courage of the defenders - army and police.

Our people and our state showed pride and dignity which caused the admiration of all freedom-loving people in the world.

The defence potential and armed forces of the country have been preserved, thanks to the training and extraordinary tactics. The Federal Republic of Yugoslavia will render assistance to all whose relatives gave their lives for the defence of the fatherland.

By the adoption of the Resolution, the United Nations and its Security Council, after three months of passivity, have taken their duties defined by the UN Charter, as they are the only and ultimate authority charged for the protection of peace and security in the world.

The logic of war, destruction and killing has finally yielded to peace and negotiations. The solving of the crisis has been brought back to the international law, which the Federal Government of Yugoslavia pleaded for all the time.

In that way, the environment for political solution in Kosovo and Metohija is created, which will include the autonomy within the legal and constitutional system of Serbia and Yugoslavia; it will guarantee the equality of all citizens and national communities. During the transitional period, the Security Council will assume the responsibility for the protection of all citizens in Kosovo and Metohija, regardless of their nationality. In this way, the safety of all citizens - Serbs, Montenegrins, Albanians, Turks, Romanies, Muslims, and Egyptians - is guaranteed. The military technical agreement excludes the possibility of creating entrance of the so-called KLA. That terrorist organization has never been representing the Kosovo Albanians, who are just the biggest victims of its terrorist and separatist acting.

The FRY, as the victim of the aggression that caused so many deaths and devastation, expects the UN to raise the issue of responsibility for the aggression, crimes against peace and humanity and the suffering of all Yugoslav citizens.

The government thinks that the Security Council's Resolution does not amnesty the aggressors. To that effect, our country expects complete compensation for war damage which is necessary for the restoration of the country. The Federal Republic of Yugoslavia will take steps to restore the consequences of the aggression as soon as possible, and create the conditions for the overall development of the country.

The government decided to form the committee for the cooperation with the UN Mission. The head of the committee is ambassador Nebojsa Vujovic, the assistant of Foreign Minister.

CHAPTER 6: STATEMENTS BY NATO MEMBER STATES

6.1 CANADA

214. Special Debate in the House of Commons, Extracts, 36th Parliament, 1st Session, Hansard 134, 1830-2330, Ottawa/Ontario, 7 October 1998

[Statements that do not add to the legal evaluation or the factual background have been omitted.]

KOSOVO

Hon. Lloyd Axworthy (Minister of Foreign Affairs, Lib.) moved:

That this House take note of the dire humanitarian situation confronting the people of Kosovo and the government's intention to take measures in co-operation with the international community to resolve the conflict, promote a political settlement for Kosovo and facilitate the provision of humanitarian assistance to refugees.

He said: [...] It is a difficult and troubling time as we watch a tragedy unfold in that part of the world. It is one in which I believe Canadians are deeply engaged in seeing how we can try to find a solution. The immediate issue we face of course is the imminent danger to the life and well-being of tens of thousands of people in that area.

The Yugoslav government has a long history of its involvement. It is important to point out that in the late 1980s, 1989 to be exact, it withdrew the autonomous status that Kosovo had enjoyed with the former Yugoslavia. This gave rise to an insurgent movement and after nearly a decade of political repression, it has resulted in open fighting.

We can understand and perhaps could even have accepted the Yugoslav government's need to preserve its own internal security and to defend its borders from outside, which it says is the roots of its campaign of mass military action that it launched last February and March. But it is clear and obvious to anyone who looks at what is taking place that the Yugoslav government has gone way beyond anything that can be justified in terms of those set objectives.

The brutal tactics of the Yugoslav authorities in countering the Kosovo Liberation Army have included shelling civilian populations, burning homes and crops, and the execution of innocent civilians. A couple of quite tragic examples will suffice to make the point.

Just one week ago diplomatic observers visited the village of Gladno Selo, which means hungry village in our language. Virtually every house in that village had been destroyed. No furniture or possessions remained anywhere. It was flattened to the ground. There was no trace of any of the inhabitants of that village.

On the same day villagers in the Vranic area said that an indiscriminate Yugoslav offensive had started a few days earlier with artillery and then infantry backed by mechanized weapon vehicles. Twenty thousand villagers were reportedly driven from their homes into the mountains.

The next day the military informed the villagers that it was safe to return. As their convoy began to work its way back to the village, police, army and others stopped, attacked, searched and looted the convoy. The charred remains of 150 vehicles were later observed along the road to Vranic. Clearly, many people paid the price with their lives.

[Translation]

It is very clear. Canada and the communities must reject terrorism as a means of obtaining independence for Kosovo. We have stated clearly that the solution for Kosovo is independence within Yugoslavia. No peace is possible in the Balkans if the borders can be changed by force.

We invested a lot to prevent that in Bosnia. No one in Canada and in the international community supports the use of violence to achieve political ends.

[1835] We have even less tolerance for the actions of the Government of Yugoslavia, which controls the military, paramilitary and police forces, which in turn are using the government's artillery, tanks and planes to subdue its own people.

[English]

There are times when we have to look at the rules that guide us. There are precedents, conventions, covenants, agreements, documents and treaties, but oftentimes those have to be weighed against the sheer weight of humanity and the suffering that goes along with it.

Clearly, in this case we have the making of a major humanitarian disaster. Aid agencies report that close to 300,000 people have been displaced as a result of the actions of militarists in Yugoslavia and Kosovo. Thirty thousand have become refugees in surrounding countries. The remainder are displaced persons within the republic of Yugoslavia.

We also know that in that part of the world winter is soon approaching. It is just a matter of days before the snow arrives and upward of 50,000 people are living without any form of shelter. I do not think we can afford to wait until they are frozen on the hillsides to resolve to do something, to draw the line on the actions of the government that has made them flee in the first place and put them in this untenable situation.

I want to say that from the outset Canada has attempted to mobilize and energize international action. Last summer we underwent a quite substantial diplomatic campaign in capitals around the world to try to get the United Nations Security Council engaged directly in this issue, with some degree of success. It was through those urgings that the Security Council, which had lain dormant on this issue for a long period time, began to meet.

I also wrote directly to Russian foreign minister Primakov reminding him that as a permanent member of the council and a privileged partner with the Belgrade government, Russia had a special role to play in putting effective pressure on Milosevic.

As many members will recall, when we had the meetings of the G-8 summit in London and Birmingham last spring, there had been a direct commitment by the Russian government to intercede with Milosevic, to ask for the kind of response on the humanitarian basis that was required. As I said, they have that special access. We have made a particular effort to try to have the Russians live up to that kind of commitment and to use whatever special offices they may occupy with the Belgrade people.

I have also just recently repeated the same message to the new foreign minister, Ivanov, just before he travelled to Belgrade this weekend.

I would also like to report that we also sent our special envoy to Belgrade and to Kosovo over this past weekend to begin to undertake direct Canadian representations within that area itself, but not with a great deal of success.

I think these actions are clearly reflective of the combined actions of many other countries that have been introducing envoys, making representations and trying to get a peaceful, political reconciliation or resolution to this dispute.

In September the Security Council adopted a resolution that demanded that Yugoslav forces cease attacking civilians and withdraw forces that were being used to oppress their population, that they should begin meaningful dialogue and negotiations with political leaders in Kosovo with a view to achieving a political settlement, that the Kosovars themselves, the KLA, refrain from violence and also come to the negotiation table, and that there be clear commitments to allow for the delivery of humanitarian assistance and freedom of movement for international observers.

At the same time, there has been an opportunity for organizations like the OSCE and others to send missions in. Again Canada has participated in observer missions within Kosovo in an attempt to provide an international presence and an opportunity to monitor these areas.

[1840] The United States government has made a variety of efforts, including one that is still ongoing with its special envoy to again try to come to grips with the Yugoslav government and the Kosovars to say that there are ways and means of resolving this and the international community is behind them.

It is clear that up to this point the Belgrade government has simply been playing a cat and mouse game with the rest of the world and has been toying with the lives of its own citizens. It has claimed that the Kosovo crisis is purely an internal affair, that there is no violation of human rights, and that it is simply responding to terrorist attacks. This is after close to 15,000 Kosovar refugees have already crossed the border into Albania.

When NATO ministers agreed to prepare a wide range of contingency plans to prevent a spillover into the neighbourhoods of Macedonia, President Milosevic again promised that mediation and peaceful activities would ensue. He had promised President Yeltsin in a widely publicized meeting that he would implement a plan of action so a group of observers could come to Belgrade to start talking about the return of the international community to the OSCE. He agreed to set up centres where displaced persons could seek help.

However, just to show the calumny that takes place, within two weeks of making that commitment, the Yugoslav army intensified shelling and pursued actions which pushed more people out of their homes and their villages. Police routinely denied any kind of access for international observers. Over the summer the tempo of aggression toward its own people had increased.

The Belgrade authorities had clearly decided two things. First, to uproot as many Kosovars as possible, torching their homes, destroying their livelihoods. The price of supporting the insurgents would become too great. It was an act of terrorism. Those the army and the police could not convince, the winter would. Second is very much the point of tonight's debate. It was clear they did not believe the international community would act so decisively to prevent this from happening.

When we look at this record of attempts and efforts to try to come to grips with the situation and the duplicitous responses from the government itself, we can see how those conclusions could be reached. The question is what are the choices and options before us. That is the point of the debate tonight and why we welcome the participation of members of parliament who are speaking on behalf of their constituents.

To focus that debate I turn back to resolution 1199 which was adopted in September and the demands that were made. At the same time those demands were clearly articulated, NATO, which is the only international organization that has the capacity to mobilize any form of international action in the area, also began to prepare plans for air intervention and to implement and look at the contingencies for those plans. As NATO countries identified their contributions, Belgrade again in its cat and mouse game began to moderate its behaviour.

Resolution 1199 has clearly called upon the Yugoslav authorities to meet a series of conditions. As the Secretary General said in his report which was tabled on Monday, those conditions have not been met. He reported that there still continues to be violations of human rights, that there still continues to be transgressions against humanitarian principles and standards, and that any compliance is clearly far from complete.

[1845] While the Security Council continues to wrestle with its problems in trying to come to grips with this issue it is also important that the broader international community of which we are also members begin to look at how it can exert maximum pressure and follow through on the declarations that have been made. It is clear that the Belgrade authorities are not of a mind to negotiate willingly. They must feel the full weight and pressure of the international community to bring them to the table and find a solution. NATO is an important part of this effort.

I have urged NATO colleagues from the outset to look at the broadest possible range of contingencies they can take to promote a resolution with particular emphasis on having a proportionate response using the right modulated measure to suit the condition. NATO has prepared a number of actions to show Milosevic that he has gone too far and must change his ways. These plans include air strikes aimed at the capacity of the Yugoslav army and police to drive people from their homes and to try to use that in a selective way to show they cannot use these forces as a form of intimidation and terror against their own population.

I emphasize that NATO is also looking at ways in which it can create a more secure environment for displaced persons to return to their homes. As the NATO meetings continue to the end of this week we will continue to emphasize the importance of developing those plans and actions that can ensure proper treatment of the displaced persons and the access to humanitarian assistance. It is also clear that NATO must be ready to act. It is also clear that Canada must be able to contribute to its readiness to act. It is also clear that such actions do not come easy. They are difficult and they must be wrestled with. That is why it is very important that we use this opportunity to consult with the House.

I was at United Nations last week for several days, meeting with the Secretary-General and I spoke to members of the Security Council, a body by which we hope some time tomorrow we will be accepted. In the meantime we can only make our representations. I expressed that it is preferable that the Security Council use its article VII mandate to give clear direction. It ought to do that but there is also another reality that one or two permanent members of the Security Council who hold the veto power have said they will refuse to give such a mandate.

That is a tough dilemma. I still expect that tomorrow or the day after there will be further attempts to have the Security Council come to resolution but if not and the veto is exercised or the Security Council itself does not take action, does that mean that we stop and give up and allow the humanitarian tragedy to unfold? That is a dilemma we have to face.

I want to give every assurance that we have made every effort on the phones, in the corridors and in the various embassies around the world the last several days doing everything we possibly can to find a way of ensuring these actions take place within the right context and the right frame. We still have to face the terrible tragedy that we may have to decide that without that clear mandate there is enough legitimacy in resolution 1199 already passed and the clear statement by the Secretary-General that has not been complied with that we would have to contemplate other actions and other measures. These would be considered at NATO council meetings at the end of this week. It is one of those tough choices that have to be made by all of us in this setting. However, under these circumstances we must be reminded of the saying that all it takes for evil to triumph is that the good do nothing.

[1850] I am here in the House this evening to invite members to express themselves on this issue and give us the best of their judgments so that we can take into account, as we go through as a government some difficult decisions in the next three or four days. I hope members will remember that all it takes for evil to triumph is for the good to do nothing.

Mr. Bob Mills (Red Deer, Ref.): Mr. Speaker, I have a number of questions for the minister. I will try to be brief.

I realize how difficult the situation is. I guess the question a lot of people are asking is what are we going to bomb if we bomb something. That is a question we need to ask. We also need to know what happens after that. What are the contingency plans? What are we going to do to help those 270,000 homeless people?

There is also a real concern about the expansion, things like the predicament Russia is in and the impending decision it might make. What will be the reaction the minister would foresee to action by NATO after it has vetoed a potential UN involvement? I could of course also ask about Turkey, Greece and all the other countries but let us just zero in on Russia.

The other thing Canadians want to know is the level of involvement the minister foresees for Canada. What are we actually going to do? We hear about the independent Kosovo. That is what Kosovans want.

Could the minister clarify that he is not looking at that sort of thing?

Hon. Lloyd Axworthy: Mr. Speaker, as I said in my opening remarks, there has been a quite active series of examinations by the NATO council, the strategic command within NATO and the military forces of a series of contingency phases.

I do not think it would be very appropriate for me to outline what the steps would be until the decisions are taken. I can assure the member that one of the clear options would be to use a form of air strikes. Where the targets would be and so on I am not at liberty to discuss. We would hope the clear will and determination that could be shown to use those would mean that they would not have to be used. There is some suggestion that in the past, as we know in Bosnia, when the question of air strikes came up Milosevic did come to the table. That is the kind of equation we are dealing with.

As far as our relation with Russia, again it is not easy. The Russians have made very clear statements. They were in Belgrade just this last weekend. There will be meetings tomorrow in London of the contact group. I was in touch with certain foreign ministers today to talk about that. We would hope that those discussions would lead to discussion with the Russian foreign minister which I hope would lead to a more active and positive contribution in the Security Council itself and the support of a resolution in the Security Council. I cannot say that I am wildly optimistic about that and the time grows short.

[1855] There will be a planned meeting I believe on Friday of the NATO-Russian joint council. Members will recall that when we talked about the NATO expansion there was an agreement to have this joint council that brings NATO and Russia together. I believe there is a meeting planned on Friday before we go into the weekend discussions at the NATO council level.

As for the commitment at the present time, Canada has six CF-18s in the theatre stationed in Italy. They have been part of the contingency planning at this point. It is probably more proper to raise the question with the Minister of Defence who will be here later this evening, but at this point there are no further commitments on that.

It is one of the areas we have been emphasizing during the discussions both at the UN and at NATO that we also see the need for some form of provision for security within Kosovo from the point of view of humanitarian assistance and for assurances of protection of displaced persons. These people are afraid. They are not going to come back to their villages. They are going to freeze. They think when they come back they are going to be hit, and that is the difficulty we face. I have to say to the member for Red Deer that is part of the contingency plan as well.

[Translation]

Mr. Daniel Turp (Beauharnois-Salaberry, BQ): Mr. Speaker, I have three questions for the minister.

In his speech, he referred to the fact that two permanent members of the Security Council could exercise their veto. We all realize that Russia is one of the members, since he said so clearly. Could he tell us which other member he considers likely to exercise its veto and why it would do so?

My second question concerns the work done by the minister's personal representative. I think the minister made a very good choice in calling on James Wright, an official with his department, who is very well liked. I have had the opportunity of working with him on a mission to Bosnia-Herzegovina, and I understand that he has met Yugoslav government officials as well as representatives of the Kosovars. I would like to know what the minister's personal representative had to report and what was the outcome of the discussions he referred to earlier.

Third and last, I would like to know what the minister thinks of a statement made at the start of the week, I think, by someone described as arcane and a notorious warlord, who said, and I quote-

[English]

"We shall not kneel before NATO missiles. We shall not allow ourselves to become enslaved to NATO or any other foreign power"

[Translation]

Is the minister concerned about such statements? Does he think that military intervention under the NATO or UN banner could lead to a dangerous war for the people of Kosovo and the Yugoslavs?

[English]

Hon. Lloyd Axworthy: Mr. Speaker, I thank the hon. member for the questions.

The answer to the first is that reports are that China has also indicated that it would exercise a veto. But I think that again depends on the resolution itself. As I said, there is still some time to play.

As the hon. member knows, because he and I talked about it at length, based on this question of the balance between non-ingérence that is classic under article 2 of the United Nations charter versus the broader humanitarian issue, I will not give a full description at this time but that is one of the major transition issues that we are facing today. How far can the international community go to its international organizations to hold nations accountable to humanitarian standards? That really is the issue which is at stake at this point in time.

[1900] I certainly agree with the hon. member's assessment that Mr. Wright is by far the best and most appropriate person, which is the reason he was there. I have not received written reports, but we have had telephone conversations.

He was able to get access to Belgrade authorities and was able to deal directly with the Kosovar civilian people, not the armed rebels. But he did not have a great deal of success. They do not seem to be willing to change what is going on at this point in time. But we never know. We were there. We were making the case. It was heard and listened to and we can only hope that the cumulative effect of that will perhaps have some influence over the next day or two.

As for the statement that was read, it is somewhat of a threatening statement. It is not unusual. I am not surprised by it. We certainly heard similar kinds of statements when we wrestled with the problems in Bosnia. I do not think it will result in a wider conflict. In fact I still have very much hope that by having debates such as this, by showing that there is some will that is going to be exercised, we may be able to find a political solution by the end of the week. But it has to be accompanied, clearly, not simply by the minuet that has been going on; it has to be accompanied by a much clearer sense of direction and it must be made clear that we are prepared to use the necessary measures.

Before I conclude I want to assure members that we have already, as a concern related to Canadians within Yugoslavia, given warning notices to dependants and the non-essential staff at our embassy. They have been given notice to leave. We will likely maintain a small skeleton staff at the embassy for the duration.

[1920] [...]

Mr. Ted McWhinney (Vancouver Quadra, Lib.): Mr. Speaker, might I address the hon. member for Red Deer and ask him whether I am correct in assuming that his party would authorize the use of armed force involving Canadian forces.

If so, would he relate that to existing Security Council resolutions which are territorialized rather precisely, or would he base it on more general chapter 7, article 51 provisions? In particular, what is his feeling on the use of aerial power? How would he relate that to the protocols additional to the Geneva protocols of 1977?

Mr. Bob Mills: Mr. Speaker, as we have always done in take note debates, we would support the ultimate decision to use military force if dealing with someone like Mr. Milosevic. That is the only thing he understands. We also believe that these questions should be asked and answered. That is what Canadians want to know.

Overall our party and Canadians support our involvement in international situations. Obviously, though, we are responding to a humanitarian need. It is very troubling that the veto will be used. We may end up fulfilling NATO action as opposed to UN action.

That is troubling because I believe it greatly weakens the position of the United Nations. It means that more and more people will challenge its authority. Going outside the UN does nothing but hurt that organization and could ultimately lead to its demise. [...]

[1930] [...]

Hon. Lloyd Axworthy: Mr. Speaker, I will not eat into the hon. member's time but let me say first that resolution 1199 passed by the Security Council does set out very specific conditions that we would want the Belgrade authorities to meet.

Beyond that I think it is important to look at the text of the Secretary-General's report which also indicates that in order to have this occur there would have to be a more active form of international presence. I think that answers the previous questions regarding how to get some form of guarantee, some assurances, particularly to the displaced people, that they can come back. That would have to be part of any discussions and negotiations at the table. There is that combination.

I am not trying to be vague. I think these comments are very helpful. There is still Security Council activity potentially tomorrow, Thursday. There will certainly be NATO meetings beginning on Thursday, Friday and likely Saturday. These types of comments will inform us as we make representation in terms of formulating the ultimate plan that will be decided at the NATO council.

[Translation]

Mr. Daniel Turp (Beauharnois-Salaberry, BQ): [...]

The Bloc Quebecois supports the motion before the House this evening. It supports an initiative aimed at putting an end to the cycle of violence that has really occurred in Kosovo, in the federal republic of Yugoslavia.

[1935] As early as last March, the Bloc Quebecois drew the attention of this House to the urgent need to act before the situation in that region of the Balkans deteriorated. The conflict has been degenerating since March, forcing us today to have an eleventh hour debate as the international community prepares for more aggressive action to pressure President Slobodan Milosevic into honouring his country's commitments under the UN charter.

Canada announced that it would impose sanctions, but the sanctions that were eventually imposed in the spring and summer were quite modest, as the hon. member for Vancouver Quadra and then parliamentary secretary admitted. He even said that these measures were perhaps too modest to deal effectively with the problems at hand. Six months later, we must recognize that the sanctions imposed by Canada and other countries were not successful, and the situation is much worse.

In fact, the kind of soft diplomacy exemplified by these sanctions gave attackers plenty of time to consolidate their positions, while their victims, who are confronted to this situation on a daily basis, are forced into exile as part of a mass exodus. The member for Red Deer mentioned that in excess of 250,000 Kosovars have fled their villages and communes and sought refuge outside their country. They also took refuge in European countries that are neither immediate neighbours nor states likely to provide a safe haven for the victims of the terror imposed by Slobodan Milosevic and his troops in Kosovo.

Economic sanctions are only effective if there is a real political will to demand that the actions of a foreign government which violate human rights be immediately stopped.

The brutal acts of violence and the repression of the Kosovo people by Serbian security forces are now well documented. They have been known for a long time, in fact for too long. These acts of violence and this repression justify a response on the part of the international community, but it must act in a consistent and coherent manner. But, first and foremost, the international community must act before it is too late. Canada must act jointly with other countries, including those that are part of the contact group that the member for Red Deer would like Canada to join-it is not for lack of trying on our part, but this select club simply does not want to invite Canada to join.

Canada must work in partnership with the countries that are members of the contact group, and with the other members of the UN Security Council, to act quickly and decisively, so that a clear and unequivocal message is sent to Mr. Milosevic.

The numerous calls for negotiation made this summer by the Minister of Foreign Affairs and his officials have remained unanswered. These appeals have been fruitless. This is why we must now use a different approach. We must now resort to means other than diplomatic and economic sanctions, because these too have been ineffective.

[1940] It is not that there has been no Security Council intervention, for on March 31, 1998 it adopted resolution 1160, and more recently, on September 23, resolution 1199, to which the minister has referred several times in his speech. Intervention by the Security Council, which has obviously had only limited, if any, effects, now must be more energetic and more significant than ever before.

It is time for the Security Council to act for reasons that are essentially humanitarian in nature. It is time to act, because too many people have been forced into exile, because too many people may be slaughtered. Many have already been the victims of massacres, but many more Kosovars have been driven out of their communes, out of their towns by the killings, rapes, inhuman and degrading treatment, and torture.

Too many fear what is going on in their homeland, and have vivid memories of what went on in Sarajevo, only a few kilometres from the capital of the Republic. Too many women and children, too many young and old people, have chosen exile because winter is approaching and their harvests have been destroyed by this filthy war, a war which has laid waste to village after village, commune after commune, a war which will leave famine in its wake.

Now the people of Kosovo are turning to the international community, to the Security Council itself, for the only ray of hope they have left. The message the international community must send to the Yugoslav Republic and its president must be a clear one: civilian populations must not be abandoned. Efforts must be made to ensure that they are spared further misery.

Above all, the international community must act out of concern for these populations. Its actions must be consistent. The international community must intervene in Kosovo, in the Yugoslav Federal Republic, to ensure that its people have some chance of a better life. Not only must it engage in humanitarian efforts, but now it must go beyond them to contemplate armed retaliation, military action, until peace is restored to this region of the Balkans.

The international community has had to intervene in this region and is still involved in Bosnia, especially in Sarajevo, in certain areas where the Bosnians, the Serbs and the Croats were killing each other and where a threat remains to the lives of all these people.

At the time, however, the international community and Canada were slow to take real action against this constant threat to peace and security by, yet again, Slobodan Milosevic and his Yugoslav government.

We also tried at the time to impose sanctions and to promote a return to diplomacy and dialogue. We hoped these measures would succeed, measures that we thought Slobodan Milosevic would act on. We were forced into military intervention only in the face of the parties' refusal to negotiate a lasting ceasefire.

We considered the problem at the time with blinkers on, intimating that the problem was in Sarajevo and should be settled for Sarajevo, where the conflict was better known, more dramatic, receiving more media attention and more symbolic. Few countries intervening in Bosnia thought that the problem could surface in Kosovo.

[1945] So today, we must consider our intervention in much broader terms to prevent this conflict, once peace is returned to Kosovo, from moving on to Macedonia, as it well might. Kosovo refugees are already on Macedonian territory. Refugees could find themselves in neighbouring regions as well.

The current situation therefore calls for consistent action, a strong humanitarian commitment by UN member countries and by the members of the Security Council and the General Assembly and of NATO, which could implement the provisions of the Security Council. Consistent action is called for.

We must act quickly in concert with our international allies. I understand the dilemma the Minister of Foreign Affairs described. Obviously, the UN Security Council could be prevented from taking action under chapter VII, if Russia and China were to use their veto.

This is a major dilemma, because action taken by the international community, through a group of countries or through NATO, may be construed as illegal under international law. The member for Vancouver Quadra is perfectly aware of the illegal situation the international community would put itself in by acting without the council's approval.

But what the minister is telling us is that the international community, that a group of countries, that NATO may act illegally, because military action is justified in this case.

We have a motion before us, a motion that may be too modest, too timid. There is no mention, in this motion, of the use of armed forces or of Canadian participation through NATO. It only refers to the humanitarian situation facing an increasing number of men, women and children, the well-being of whom we must be concerned with, even though Ottawa is thousands of kilometres away from Kosovo.

The government is asking that we take notice of this terrible situation. It is indeed time Parliament took notice of this situation. The government has announced its intention to take measures. But what measures?

Reform Party members were right to point out that we do not have here, this evening, concrete indications on the measures that Canada favours, or wants to favour, in the debates that will take place at the Security Council, the NATO council and in other forums where this issue will be discussed over the next few hours or days. We are told that these measures seek a diplomatic solution to the problem. This is fine, but what specific measures? What would be Kosovo's status within or outside the Yugoslav Republic? We should consider any solution that respects the wishes of the Kosovo people.

All this seems pretty weak. The motion does not go far enough. It should have been worded in stronger terms, because the daily tragedy of these populations deserves stronger wording.

I will conclude by saying that this is a matter of justice. I am going to quote someone, not George Washington-whom the minister likes to quote, as he did yesterday during a debate on a piece of legislation-but Blaise Pascal, a philosopher whom some of you know and like. Pascal said: "Justice without strength is powerless. Strength without justice is tyrannical. Therefore, both justice and strength must be present and, to that end, we must make sure that what is just is also strong".

In this particular case, justice and strength must be combined to end the tragedy suffered by the people of Kosovo. We must put an end to their tragedy.

[1950] **Mr. Ted McWhinney (Vancouver Quadra, Lib.):** Mr. Speaker, I will take advantage of the legal expertise of the hon. member for Beauharnois-Salaberry.

The possibility was mentioned of a NATO-led intervention. The hon. member is well aware that NATO is a regional association governed by the UN charter, that it is limited by charter imposed conditions regarding the use of armed force.

He will certainly recall that, during the Korean War, the well-known resolution 377(V) passed by the General Assembly was used to compensate for the gaps in international public law.

Does the hon. member think that there is a new category of humanitarian intervention distinct from the charter, or are specific Security Council resolutions necessary before Canadian troops can be sent in?

He is well aware that the resolutions passed for Bosnia apply to a very specific area. What way is there around this legal impasse? Does he have any useful suggestions?

He is also certainly aware that the protocols, additional to the Geneva protocol of 1977, set very tight restrictions on the use of air strikes.

Mr. Daniel Turp: Mr. Speaker, the House wants to hear about international law tonight. How very interesting.

Earlier tonight, the member for Vancouver Quadra had a test question for the member for Red Deer, a very difficult one too. The member for Red Deer gave a very political answer.

I will try to reply to the question using the knowledge we share, which we want to see benefit the House, moreover. There is some value to having expertise and to being willing to share it with one's colleagues during debates such as this.

It is difficult under current international law to claim that force can be used under chapter 7 without the formal approval of the Security Council. The use of force was possible during the Gulf crisis because the Security Council authorized certain states to use force.

Just a few months ago, we debated in this House the potential use of force against Iraq. Members will remember that, on several occasions, I asked the government if it thought that Canada and other states had the authority to use force against Iraq. That question remained unanswered. I know that legal opinions were provided on the subject.

But I think it is difficult to claim, under international law as it currently stands, that the use of force, even in this case, would be consistent with the charter without prior authorization of the Security Council.

On the other hand, are we seeing a customary rule emerge from a practice whereby the states will be able to invoke a breach of the peace to justify an intervention? I think that circumventing the charter by invoking a customary rule that would allow states to intervene in a case like this may be a way to solve the problem.

Article 51 may be the only legal basis that could be used to justify an intervention in this case, even though it would require a very liberal interpretation of that article.

Beyond all that and even as an internationalist, I think we must weigh the good and the bad in this type of situation.

[1955] If we think that an armed intervention is necessary to protect the most fundamental of human rights, if the international community agrees that such an intervention is legitimate, and if the international public is in favour of this intervention, then it is surely justified. Such intervention will free many people from the terror inflicted upon them by individuals who, one day, will hopefully have to appear before an international criminal tribunal and be held accountable for their war crimes and their crimes against humanity before the international community.

[English]

Mr. Chuck Strahl (Fraser Valley, Ref.): Mr. Speaker, I cannot quote Pascal or Washington, but the quote I have dug up is one by the Greek philosopher Pindar who said "the test of any man lies in action". Versions of this have been regurgitated over time.

I do not have the answer for the question I have for the member but I would like to have his comment on it. Why is it that problems in central Europe receive, necessarily, a very high priority at the United Nations but often other equally horrendous human rights abuses in other parts of the world do not seem to grab the United Nations by the throat to say that it is a compelling problem that has to be solved today?

One example I can think of is what is going on in Algeria. According to Amnesty International thousands of people have been massacred in rural areas, and there is not a blink and no resolution. It is a human rights abuse on a grand scale and no one says anything.

In the southern part of Sudan there are Christians and tribal communities that are being actively ethnic cleansed by a Muslim government in this case. It is persecuting people systematically and no one blinks.

There are problems in Angola. We certainly know about the problems in Rwanda and they are entering into more problems in Rwanda, hopefully not as bad as they had. There are hundreds of thousands of refugees from Somalia.

There is systematic and systemic abuses in a large part of the world, a lot in Africa, and the United Nations just does not consider these to be the crisis that it does Kosovo. It is a crisis in Kosovo and that is why we are here. We all agree about that. However, I wonder why this is and I wonder if the member has thought about it.

Regardless of whether it is the Geneva convention, section 77 or Security Council resolutions or whatever technical things, why is it there are so many other areas of the world that the western world remains quiet about but the problem in Kosovo is seizing the world? I have some ideas on why this is happening but I was wondering if the member had any ideas.

I think it is a tragedy that the United Nations and those of us who are concerned about human rights abuses do not treat all human rights abuses as a problem for all of us. Martin Luther King was right when he coined the phrase.

Mr. Daniel Turp: Mr. Speaker, that is a very good question, and a very difficult one to answer. Maybe the simplest answer would be that there are double standards in the international community. There are too many double standards when it comes to human rights and the ways in which the United Nations and other international organizations intervene when there are conflicts. That is the simplest answer.

The more complex answer would be that when human rights abuses bring a real threat to peace and security, that is when there is a drive toward involving the Security Council and other organs of the United Nations.

[2000] That is when it happens. Because there was a severe threat of international peace and security in Bosnia there was an intervention of the international community and there still is. There was also a threat of international peace and security in Somalia, in Africa. The member also mentioned Sudan and Algeria. When there was a very important threat to peace and security in Somalia there was an intervention of the UN.

Maybe because of that the problem of the intervention of the UN in Somalia was created, especially in the eyes of the Americans. That is why there is a very cautious attitude to intervene in Africa. That is very unwise. Africa is a lost continent. It is continent that is sacrificed nowadays. I do not think it should be. We should not accuse the United Nations of that. We should never forget that the United Nations is composed of member states. Those states allow or disallow the intervention of the Security Council.

That is the more complex answer. It does not justify double standards. Once double standards are lifted we will live in a better international community. [...]

Mr. Svend J. Robinson: [...] My colleagues and I in the New Democratic Party support the motion.

[Translation]

As the member for Beauharnois-Salaberry said, we were hoping that it would go further, that it would be stronger, that justice and strength, two fundamental principles, would have been expressed more clearly in this motion. Nevertheless, we support the motion.

[English]

It was last week that this House unanimously spoke with one voice following the terrible atrocities that were brought to light by Human Rights Watch, the massacre of 18 innocent civilians in a forest in the Drenica region. Other members have spoken of this earlier. The House spoke with one voice urging the Government of Yugoslavia, Milosevic and the parties involved to put down arms immediately and start negotiating a solution with the help of international organizations like the United Nations and the OSCE.

It was last week as well, a few days afterward, that Human Rights Watch issued a report that documented the terrible violations of international law showing that the Serbian special police and the Yugoslav army units have executed civilians, systematically destroyed civilian property and attacked humanitarian aid workers.

The director said it has been clear for seven months that the government is conducting a brutal war against civilians in Kosovo. These are war crimes. These are crimes against humanity and yet the Government of Yugoslavia and Milosevic refuse to co-operate with the international tribunal investigating it. They have gone further and have restricted the work of domestic and foreign journalists seeking to report on these terrible atrocities.

These atrocities can also strike home. The hon. member for Churchill spoke with family members in a community that she has the honour of representing who have family in Kosovo who were terribly injured. This strikes home to her and to each of us at a very profoundly human level.

[2005] This has gone on for far too long. We have heard the same threats, the same promises of action in the case of Kosovo that we heard in the case of Bosnia, and there the international community failed terribly. It took three years, 200,000 people who died and too many warnings before finally when spurred by the terrible mortar attack by the Serbs on a crowded marketplace in Sarajevo in August 1995 the west took action.

Tragically that action was not taken by the United Nations. One of the great dilemmas and tragedies of the situation in Kosovo is that we cannot rely on the United Nations in these circumstances to definitely respond to this humanitarian crisis. We cannot assume the Security Council will adopt a resolution that will authorize the kind of firm military response that clearly is warranted and was likely warranted some time ago.

We saw the effects of Serb aggression in Bosnia and now we see them in Kosovo. I witnessed them when I visited Vukovar. I witnessed the Serb aggression on Croatia and its people. I will never forget walking through the ruins of a church in Vukovar and picking up a small piece of wood, the remains of a small wooden cross.

The community of nations has to say that the occurrence of this kind of atrocity is not acceptable. The United Nations' own high commissioner for refugees has estimated that over 280,000 people have been displaced by the fighting since March. This is mostly within Kosovo. Some 50,000 have not found shelter yet. Many others are living in very difficult conditions. Over 700 have died. And with winter fast approaching there is a very real danger of a humanitarian disaster.

I urge the Government of Canada to respond to that disaster, to step up donor funding for reconstruction and winter emergency plans in Kosovo and to provide financial assistance to Montenegro, to Albania and the former Yugoslav republic of Macedonia hosting many of the refugees and which desperately need support as winter fast approaches.

We would prefer a resolution of the United Nations Security Council. We would hope the OSCE, the regional security body in that region, would be able to come to a consensus, but we cannot allow the veto power of Russia and possibly China, the consensus rule of the OSCE to prevent the kind of action that very likely must be taken, the kind of military action that must be taken to save human lives.

Let us be under no illusions about the possible risk to Canadians. Canada has six CF-18 aircraft on the ground in Aviano, Italy, 130 Canadian pilots and ground crew. They are courageous men and women who will be directly affected by the decision our government makes. I am sure that every member of this House wishes those men and women well at this very difficult time. I am sure we all recognize that when we talk about the possibility of military action, it is our sons and daughters who may very well be on the front lines, who may be fired on by those ground to air missiles that the Serbs have threatened to use.

This is a humanitarian disaster. I believe that as Canadians we have an obligation not to stand by but to act. The member for Fraser Valley has spoken at the same time, and rightly so I believe, of the fact that there is certainly a great deal of selectivity in the international response. Of course we are profoundly concerned about the situation in Kosovo and we must recognize that air strikes alone fall far short of what would be a thoughtful and appropriate response. If there is not a presence on the ground, that could exacerbate the situation and make it even more difficult.

[2010] We must remember as well that in whatever military action that may be undertaken innocent people's lives must not be put at risk, whether Yugoslavians, Kosovars or anybody else, but we made the mistake globally of waiting too long in Bosnia and we cannot afford to make that mistake in Kosovo.

The world though has stood by, as the member for Fraser Valley said, in cases of other humanitarian disasters; the genocide in East Timor, a third of the population, 200,000 people, murdered by the Suharto regime. Where is the international outcry on that? Where is Canada's voice on that?

There have been ten resolutions at the United Nations on East Timor and Canada shamefully has either abstained or voted against every one. So the member for Fraser Valley is right. There is a double standard, whether in East Timor, the situation with the Kurds, in Turkey, northern Iraq, Colombia, Sudan.

Again, my colleagues and I in the New Democratic Party support this motion. We desperately hope that Milosevic will come to his senses, pull back, respect the rights of the people of Kosovo to determine their own future, hopefully have the kind of autonomy they had previously, but to respect their rights to self-determination, and that we can avert the continued horrors, because already too many people have died, that would in many respects be totally unacceptable not just to Canadians but to all civilized people should the global community not respond, not just with words but with action. La justice et la force.

Mr. Ted McWhinney (Vancouver Quadra, Lib.): Madam Speaker, there exists a strong possibility after hearing the addresses already in the House that there will be a political consensus. It may be an all-party political consensus within the House. I wonder if he could help us over the next stage and comment on the suggestions by the member for Beauharnois-Salaberry.

There is a new concept of humanitarian intervention which is separate, its origins different, from classic intervention. It is still subject to some limitations. The OSCE is like NATO, a regional security organization and cannot exceed charter conditions and limitations.

Would the hon. member believe either through customary international law or through the General Assembly that we might find an adequate base for Canadian armed intervention if that would arise and also take us over the aerial bombardment issue?

I believe in the war in the gulf he had some difficulties with the compatibility with some of the operations. Can he help us to this next step? Customary law can gallop at the present time. There has been the phrase used, instant customary law. A number of quick precedents can help make new norms.

Can the hon. member help us here? I think there is a good possibility of a political all-party consensus emerging.

Mr. Svend J. Robinson: Mr. Speaker, I think the hon. member for Vancouver Quadra is correct. Certainly as we listen to the debate tonight it appears there is an emerging political consensus around the desirability of hopefully the United Nations with a resolution; if not the United Nations, then certainly the OSCE as the regional body under article VII. Failing that-and I think the member asks a very important question-is there another basis in international law for military intervention?

[2015] Clearly international law is an evolving body of law. There is a clear and demonstrable threat to human life on the massive scale that we have witnessed already in Kosovo. This is not an anticipatory action, as the member is well aware. This is an action in response to brutal war crimes against humanity. Those crimes are well described in international law. If the community of nations in taking action does not exceed what is required to respond to those well documented war crimes against humanity are, I would hope that international law would recognize the justice of that intervention.

It is important at the same time that the intervention not be excessive. It is important that it be based on humanitarian law principles and that there be support and follow up. It is not acceptable to drop bombs, to conduct air strikes, and then what happens next? If there is no support for the Kosovars on the ground, there could be massive retaliation by the Serb military, a situation of complete anarchy could prevail, and it could be counterproductive.

In terms of the international legal basis for action, had the world waited for a new concept of international law in the case of Bosnia as it did in Rwanda to the shame of the international community, I can only imagine the kind of carnage that would have continued to take place. If international law does not provide that base at this point, certainly it may be time to establish that precedent.

Mr. David Price (Compton-Stanstead, PC): [...] [2030] [...] The issue before us is the Yugoslavian province of Kosovo. Slobodan Milosevic is the Serbian leader of Yugoslavia and the evidence suggests that he has ordered the slaughter of thousands of ethnic Albanians. This is not new evidence. The west has known publicly about these atrocities at least since February. Now 200 villages in Kosovo have been destroyed and more than 250,000 people have become refugees. Thousands have been killed.

The west has failed to act, and Canada under this government has done nothing to urge the United Nations or NATO to take action sooner. Only now when the President of the United States and the Prime Minister of Britain decide it is time to take action will the government move. That is not leadership. But then Canadians have not come to expect leadership from this government. From this government they have come to expect excuses.

In Bosnia the European Union looked foolish. In Bosnia the United Nations failed. Only when NATO took action, belated action admittedly, did Milosevic respond. That action was late, but it was tough.

In 1995 air strikes led to the Dayton accords, a fragile settlement that is being monitored by 1,300 Canadian troops to this day.

Kofi Annan, the UN Secretary-General, came out with a statement that condones military action. While the west has been late, it is important this action be taken now.

As some of us have learned, this century's greatest lesson is that if an aggressor is appeased, their appetite only grows. Although leadership on this issue has been lacking, NATO must act now.

But it is not a straightforward issue. Kosovo is a province inside Yugoslavia. Yugoslavia is ruled by Milosevic. Should we be in favour of Kosovo independence at this juncture? This is a classic case of how not to deal with ethnic minorities, but it is certainly a difficult dilemma between self-determination and not breaking up countries.

If only it could be as simple as pointing to Canada as a beacon of how two distinct peoples can live together with occasional debate and heartache, but mostly a great love and respect for each other. If only Milosevic listened to reason the way the people of Quebec and the people of Alberta listen to reason, the Balkans would be a lot safer place.

But Mr. Milosevic is not a reasonable man. By all accounts he is a murderous tyrant who must be dealt with and must be dealt with harshly. NATO has proven that it is the only credible force that can act at this time.

This government talks about taking measures. If these measures do not include helping our NATO allies who will be using force, then my party will have to disagree with the government.

Canada has six CF-18s based at Aviano Air Force Base in Italy. They must be used. There is no reason that I am aware of that Canada could not fly air cover for this mission. If there are reasons why they cannot be used, the minister has to tell the House right now. But there are risks and the government must do all that it can to prepare Canadians for these risks.

First, the CF-18s will be flying over hostile territory. Milosevic has no small force. He has four brigades and will attempt to shoot down any NATO planes. This is a risk, but a risk that Canada must take.

[2035] Second, Milosevic has threatened retaliation against NATO troops anywhere, and that includes Bosnia. As I mentioned earlier, Canada has 1,300 troops in Bosnia. I visited them last spring and they are certainly up to the task but there will be danger. They will be threatened and that is a danger. The government must tell the Canadian public about this danger. The Canadian public must know that Canadians will be part of this operation.

Third, after this bombing, it may be necessary to put troops on the ground. U.S. Secretary of Defence Cohen said yesterday in Washington that might indeed be necessary. He said that if it is done, it will only be European troops. Canada needs to know if that has been agreed to and exactly what role Canada will be playing after the initial bombings.

There are other factors. There is the Russian factor. As the House knows, the Russians are related ethnically and religiously to the Serbs. They have told us that they are against NATO bombing. That is unfortunate, but unfortunately NATO will have to go ahead without their approval. Hopefully they will get on side once the urgency of the matter is made clear to them.

There is another factor that I must make reference to and that is the Clinton factor. The president is weakened because he is under investigation in a legitimate legal inquiry under the U.S. constitution. At this time, in my party's opinion, it is important for our NATO allies to show solidarity more than ever.

While U.S. leadership is essential, if Canada is assertive and plays its role as it should, the world will know that NATO continues to be history's finest example of collective security. And while the situation in Kosovo is certainly a humanitarian crisis, it is also a military situation.

Bosnia showed that NATO was the only credible force Milosevic will respect.

At this time the foreign minister, who has no understanding of the world, is talking about Canada leading the way in calling for total nuclear disarmament, a policy that would have Canada expelled from NATO. Now is the time for this government, this minister of defence to be serious about Canada and the world and live up to its good name.

Canada must play a role of responsibility. It must understand that NATO is the one structure that can make a difference and it must take action with our allies.

My party will stand behind this government if this government stands behind its soldiers.

[...] [2045] [...]

Hon. Arthur C. Eggleton (Minister of National Defence, Lib.): [...] [2050] [...] If NATO decides to take further action, we have military assets in the area that could be made available subject to a decision of this government. We are trying to get the input before we make the decision which is why we are here tonight. We have six CF-18 aircraft and a Hercules air refuelling aircraft that would be provided. We have had discussions accordingly with the supreme allied commander in Europe with respect to that. Upon a final decision by this government and upon a final decision by the NATO those assets and the personnel involved would be made available as part of an operation.

As I said quite clearly in my remarks, if our NATO allies are going to go in there, if action has to be taken, if we cannot come to a diplomatic resolution, Canada expects to be there with its allies.

As far as troops on the ground are concerned, that matter is under active consideration. It would most likely be necessary but it has not yet been finalized. The military authorities of NATO are examining the possibilities, the size, where the operations might take place on the ground. I expect we will be asked to participate in that as well but that is still in the preliminary planning stage. At this point two activation warnings have been given by NATO. Both relate to the possibility of a limited air option, a limited air strike. The other is a phased air campaign. If the first one does not work then there is the possibility of an ever accelerating air campaign.

I reiterate our hope that a diplomatic resolution can be found but we know the history in terms of Mr. Milosevic with respect to Bosnia. We know that air strikes worked there to bring him to the table. As the hon. member indicated a few moments ago, that led to the Dayton accord. If we have to use these means to bring him to the table then, subject to the decision of this government and the decision of NATO, those resources would be made available to do so.

Mr. Gary Lunn (Saanich-Gulf Islands, Ref.): Madam Speaker, I begin by thanking the Minister of National Defence and the Minister of Foreign Affairs for their comments this evening. For the record I support the positions they have stated. I support the use of military intervention. As the minister stated and as somebody said earlier, the only thing Mr. Milosevic understands is being clubbed over the head.

I will add a few comments and some concerns. I understand it is very difficult to get the permission of the UN Security Council. As we know, there are some vetoes likely to be used by Russia and China. They may proceed under a current Security Council resolution or they may end up proceeding under NATO but we will have to let that take its course. I support Canada's involvement there and the use of Canada's military. We have a role to play.

Someone's first question might be why should Canada be there. We have to state from the outset that we have seen the slaughter of thousands and thousands of innocent individuals. We have seen something in the magnitude of 250,000 to 300,000 people driven from their homes. We have seen entire communities burned. This is clearly not acceptable to a civilized nation such as ours. I believe we have a duty to intervene. I do not know if words can describe how bad it is over there. I came back from the Canada-Europe parliamentary meetings in Strasbourg. This was an emergency debate over there. I had an opportunity to speak to many of my colleagues from the European Community. They also expressed exactly what I have stated in this House.

[2055] This is the feeling I had after speaking to some of these people. I will read a few sentences from an article written by Gwynne Dyer on October 4 of this year, very current. It will set the tone. I cannot go very far into it because it becomes unacceptable to read it in the House: "They stripped one woman and cut off her ears, nose and fingers, said a farmer who watched from a hiding as the Serbian police massacred 18 members of the family ranging from 18 months to 95 years old".

I could not go on reading because it gets worse and worse. It makes my stomach turn to realize that this is what is happening over there, that Mr. Milosevic has ordered his officials to carry out these types of tasks. They burned out entire villages.

We have heard the foreign affairs critic for the official opposition talk about his observations driving down the roads and seeing grave after grave and entire villages burnt out.

I believe Canada has a duty to participate. This type of ethnic cleansing is equal to what we have seen and heard of the Holocaust in World War II. It is not acceptable. I think Mr. Milosevic has had ample opportunity to comply with current UN security resolutions and he has elected not to do so.

I do not have the same optimism and I may be mischaracterizing the minister of defence when he says our goal is for a peaceful resolution. I honestly believe he does wish we could achieve that. However, I do not think that is possible with this man we are dealing with. He may even agree with that. I think Canada and the rest of the world have been more than patient with Mr. Milosevic and we now must act as the slaughter of innocent people by the thousands is clearly not acceptable anywhere in the world now or at any other time.

Let us assume we are going to proceed. I support that whether it is under NATO or whether we get a UN security agreement or we have to proceed under an existing one. What happens next? We know there are hundreds of thousands of these families and people who have been driven to the hills. As the minister has correctly stated, winter is fast approaching; 300,000 people left shelterless and homeless.

I think we also have to be prepared as a nation to make a commitment, whether it is the UN or NATO. That has to be followed up after. Yes, the air strikes have to happen. I am not even so sure that we want to bring Milosevic back to the table or we just want to find some place where we can put him. I am not sure whether we can reason with a man like that.

I guess the point I am emphasizing is that we as a nation have to make a long term commitment to ensure that what actions we carry out now are not temporary, that there is an overall plan, a goal we have to achieve. It is a very difficult situation. The Serbs are not prepared to give up the province of Kosovo for all kinds of reasons. Yet it is 90% Albanian. I think we are there for the long haul and hopefully part of a UN force that will be present to ensure the safety of these individuals.

[2100] Hopefully this region could become a republic separate from Serbia. That may be argued against by some of my colleagues. We have had a very interesting debate. Some of them do not think that is achievable, but that in the long term it could not become an independent republic but would have to remain a part of Serbia, with autonomy, as it did prior to 1990.

These are fascinating debates when we look at all the details. However, at the end of the day I would like to offer my encouragement to both ministers who were present tonight. I hope there will be a long term commitment on the part of Canada. I am very pleased to be a part of this debate and to see that everybody is focused on the crisis in Kosovo and looking toward a solution in the near future.

Hon. Charles Caccia (Davenport, Lib.): [...] Several speakers have referred to a NATO intervention. I hope we will not be so naive as to believe that NATO air attacks will solve the problem. They will only strengthen the already rigid and unbearable position taken by the Serbs. Instead, NATO ground forces to protect the entire civilian population would represent the first necessary step.

In that context let us have no elusion. The presence of troops to protect the population may be required for years. Kosovo could turn out to be another Cypress and the presence of troops, be they NATO or the United Nations, may be necessary for many decades to come.

The Council of Europe, where this parliament has, through the Canada-Europe Parliamentary Association, observer status, produced a political report prepared by Andras Bargony of Hungary. It is entitled "Crisis in Kosovo and the situation in the federal Republic of Yugoslavia". The recommendations of the report, adopted two weeks ago by the Assembly of the Council of Europe, include the following elements considered as essential by European parliamentarians in reaching a lasting peaceful solution to the crisis.

[2105] The first element is to guarantee the security of all people living in Kosovo, to be achieved through the withdrawal of the Serbian security forces, the disarmament of armed groups of ethnic Albanians and the deployment of an international peace force.

The second is to give a new political status to Kosovo based on a high level of autonomy within the Yugoslav federation, based on the prerogatives the province enjoyed according to the 1974 constitution of the Socialist Federal Republic of Yugoslavia, adapted of course to the new situation and, where necessary, enlarged.

Thirdly, such status would include the highest possible form of self-government for Kosovo in lawmaking, the executive, the judiciary, public order, economy, education and culture with respect to the rights of Serbs and other minorities living in Kosovo, and finally the direct participation of Kosovo representatives in federal institutions and also through the adoption of democratic reforms.

The fourth element is to give international guarantees, ensuring respect for the future agreement and preventing any attempts to return to the status quo or to secede.

The final element is to introduce democratic reforms implemented through the federal Republic of Yugoslavia, guaranteeing full compliance with the Council of Europe standards concerning the functioning of a democratic political system, the rule of law and the protection of human rights and the rights of national minorities, notably in Kosovo, in Vojvodina and in Sanjak.

It seems to me that these are very sensible proposals made by the Council of Europe, by the assembly and by our European colleagues. The assembly also considered that in the absence of a clear and unequivocal position of the international community the political and military pressure exerted on the two sides to engage in negotiations would remain largely unaffected.

Therefore, it would seem that a clear and unequivocal position of the international community is urgently needed. The future status of Kosovo must be placed at the top of the international agenda. That is quite clear now. The participation of all interested parties, governments and relevant international bodies is essential.

I am sure that everyone will agree tonight that we must not fail the people of Kosovo. We must prove that the international community can intervene in the name of humanity. It is high time that we do so.

[...] [2115] [...]

Mr. Keith Martin (Esquimalt-Juan de Fuca, Ref.): [...] We have heard some discussions today about intervention. It has been proven over the last several decades that the world has been unable or unwilling to deal with conflicts when they occur and only get involved after a huge loss of lives has taken place. From Rwanda to Chechnya, to Cambodia, to the Sudan and to others, the world has sat on its hands while innocent civilians have been slaughtered.

[2135] That is why international law respects, acknowledges and supports intervention by outside powers within the borders of a country if gross human rights abuses are taking place. The reason it supports that is that although we support the integrity of a nation state, international law respects the integrity and safety of people over and above the nation state. In other words, a despot cannot abuse people and expect to go away unscathed.

We collectively have a responsibility to protect people not only on humanitarian grounds but also for very pragmatic reasons. What happens in a conflict half a world away winds up on our own doorstep through increasing demands on our defence budgets, aid budgets and our social programs domestically as people migrate away from an ethnic conflict and wind up as refugees on our shores.

International law respects and supports intervention. The proof in the pudding is when we look at who pays the price. Civilians pay the price. It was not always that way. In World War I 85% of the casualties were soldiers. Wars took place between nation states. In World War II 60% were soldiers. Today 85% of the penalties that are paid in blood, in death and in rape are paid for by innocent unarmed men, women and children. The civilian population pays the price in conflicts that are by and large ethnic conflicts within the boundaries of a country. They generally are not wars between nation states. [...]

Early intervention by identifying the precursors to conflict and having the tools to address them are essential. We should first start with non-military means and then work up to military means.

I was disappointed earlier today. I introduced a private members' motion asking the House of Commons to call on the United Nations to indict Slobodan Milosevic for war crimes and to allow the UNHCR and NGOs free and unfettered access to the refugees in and around Kosovo. I was deeply saddened that the House did not give unanimous consent. I hope the government will take heed of that motion and adopt it as soon as possible.

I am glad we had this debate. We must remember that in the future we cannot allow this genocide in Kosovo or in other country to continue. We must work early and preventatively because the lives of hundreds of thousands of innocent men, women and children are at stake.

Mr. Bill Graham (Toronto Centre-Rosedale, Lib.): [...] [2140] [...] I felt that the member for Red Deer was saying that if we act without the sanction of the United Nations Security Council, which as the foreign minister clearly indicated is probably unlikely because of the position both of Russia and possibly of China, that will cause a great deal of problems for us and for the United Nations in the long run. The member himself was much more aggressive in saying that we must act and we must act now if we are to answer to the humanitarian requirements of this terrible situation.

Can he help us with his view as to how he believes this will impact on the relationship between Canada and the United Nations and other countries in the region if NATO moves in a somewhat more ambiguous area than one that would be given the comfort of a cover of a firm Security Council resolution?

Mr. Keith Martin: [...] He points to the first thing that I think we all desire, which is support from the United Nations. We have a larger commitment here and a larger rationale for involvement: the humanitarian reasons that many members in the House articulated earlier today.

We would like to have the UN involved, but if it is not involved, NATO certainly has the power and the ability to do that. The justification comes within the confines of international law which supports intervention in environments where gross human rights abuses are clearly taking place and in this case where genocide is occurring.

I think NATO has a responsibility. Although as the hon. member mentioned it is slightly out of its purview, NATO is largely responsible for a good segment of the security of Europe. If the situation in Kosovo expands, the expanding conflict would involve Montenegro, Greece, Russia and other nation states in the surrounding area. All those nation states could be involved in the larger conflagration. If that happened, the world simply could not turn a blind eye.

In the larger scheme of things, in an effort to prevent more bloodshed and in an effort to save more lives, while NATO would like to have the UN's tacit involvement, it should go ahead regardless because I think a larger principle is involved. It would add a lot more credibility to the United Nations in its ability to act early to intervene.

With respect to Bosnia, we were far too late in intervening. As a result, 250,000 people were killed and the countryside was laid to waste for generations to come.

If there is any lesson to be learned from recent history, we should look at Bosnia and see the abysmal failure of NATO. If it moves a little further along within the confines of international law to act where it is appropriate, then I think it will be justified in the long term not only within the nation states that participate but also history will take a favourable view to the intervention.

Mr. Bill Graham (Toronto Centre-Rosedale, Lib.): [...] [2145] [...] There is a difference between what is taking place in Kosovo today and what is taking place in Bosnia today. That difference is the fact that in Bosnia some years ago NATO chose to act. We acted with efficiency. We finally were pushed into the situation where we had to do something. We did it. Today, while we have to live with the tremendous situation the member for Red Deer described, to some extent we are seeing a situation where peace, security and civil society are returning. Farmers can till their fields. Children can play. Birds can sing again. There is a chance for life, which does not exist in Kosovo.

Why is there that difference? The difference is, as the minister pointed out in his opening statement, the Yugoslav authorities have a plan to terrorize their own population. That plan is succeeding for one reason and one reason only. It is that there is no credible threat from the international community that will stop them.

Stopping them with resolutions was proven in the Bosnia situation not to be successful. Words are good in parliaments. They are a part of our work. However words will not deal with Slobodan Milosevic. We learned that in Bosnia. He will only be stopped by actions. That was our experience. There is no reason it would not apply here as it applied in Bosnia.

The need to act is clear. All members in the House that I heard speak tonight have echoed that. How to act, however, is less clear. There will be debate and there will be reasonable discussions about how we should act. We know, as the member from Esquimalt and many others have pointed out, that NATO has the capacity to act. The question we must ask ourselves is a reasonable one. What is the legal authority by which NATO will act? If we act without legal authority that is an issue.

I had the privilege of attending the debates of the Organization for Security and Co-operation in Europe, in Copenhagen this summer. We debated a resolution on Kosovo. A strong debate took place between those of us who wanted to ensure there would be a capacity to act and those who were more determined that whatever action would be taken would be taken under legal authority.

[2150] Eventually the OSCE adopted a resolution which provided that military measures should be taken in Kosovo with the explicit endorsement of a relevant UN Security Council resolution.

I opposed that aspect of the resolution when it came up in the OSCE assembly. I would oppose the same approach we are taking tonight. The foreign minister addressed the reason in his remarks. If we depend upon a clear Security Council resolution with Russian and Chinese approval, there is a serious chance it just will not happen.

The member for Red Deer put that in context tonight. We have to look at that as members of parliament who believe in a world society which is governed more and more ỳy the rule of law. The very humanitarian principles we seek to apply tonight are those that create the sense of the world law to which we want to adhere if we are to have a rule of law we can all live within. It would be similar to the rule of law those of us in the House adhere to, wish to adhere to, and wish to build in a world community in the same way we have in our wonderful Canadian society. We must be aware of that.

While the Security Council resolution is important and may put the UN authority in jeopardy if we act without it, we have to face the fact that if we allow the UN Security Council issue to prevent us from acting the UN will lose its authority in the world. It will be eroded to such a point that it will become irrelevant for all of us.

I believe my view echoes that of most members who have spoken tonight. We must prepare to act. It must be a preparation that is credible and determined. It is only this credible and determined action and the ability to deliver it that will provide the Yugoslav authorities with a reason to back down. Only that will bring them to the table. Only that will force them to act. If not, we will see this situation drag on. We will see problems develop in the region that will be worse than those if we do not act.

I met with the Macedonian ambassador today. He told me not to be hasty in this matter. He said that they would be ineffective if precipitous NATO action was taken. I asked him what would happen if this situation were to drag on for another year, what would happen to the communities and societies living on the border of this untenable situation.

That is what the situation will be. It will drag on for years. We will not see 200,000 refugees; we will see 400,000 refugees. Inevitably people will be dragged into the situation. If we do not act now, the worst thing that will happen is that we will have to act a year from now when thousands of lives will have been lost and the situation will be much worse. It is always that way. We are forced to act.

We must deal with Russia's reaction, with Turkey and with Greece. All of this is true. The risk of not acting is worse than the threat of acting. We must act if we are to preserve the moral authority of our situation in a world where we must preserve humanitarian rights in the face of the determination of states to deny rights to their own citizens.

I read a little history as I prepared for my speech tonight. Count Bismarck who subsequently became Prince Bismarck, the chancellor of the German Empire as it was then, said in 1890 "If there is another war in Europe it will come out of some damned silly thing in the Balkans". This is not a damned silly thing we are talking about tonight.

This is a human tragedy. We are on the threshold of the 21st century and nothing has changed.

We owe it to ourselves to act as parliamentarians and as citizens of the world to make a change. Let us pledge in the House tonight that we will act together to make a change. Let us pledge that we will keep the spirit of the House tonight in which all members are saying that we must act. Let us encourage our government to be positive, to act and to end the humanitarian tragedy that we are facing. If we do not act today we will act in the future and it will be worse.

[2155]

Mr. Keith Martin (Esquimalt-Juan de Fuca, Ref.): [...] [T]he problem has been inaction. Since 1890 until now we have seen inaction in the face of gross human rights abuses. There are solutions. The solutions require changing the way in which we think of conflict and changing the way in which we deal with conflict. Essentially it boils down to conflict prevention and how we identify the precursors to conflict and the actions necessary to deal with those conflicts. I suggest we start out with non-military intervention, particularly economic intervention.

Will the hon. member, in his capacity as chairman of the committee of foreign affairs, submit to the Minister of Foreign Affairs the following?

First, we should convene like-minded nations in Ottawa to develop a concerted, united effort to deal with conflict prevention in whichever forum we happen to be in, be it the United Nations, OSCE, OAU, OAS or whatever.

Will he work behind the scenes to support the private member's motion I put forth on that idea and Motion No. 477 that I put forth today to have our country present to the United Nations a proposal to indict Slobodan Milosevic for crimes against humanity and to ensure that refugees in the region around Kosovo will have free access to representatives of the United Nations High Commission for Refugees and other humanitarian NGOs?

[...] [2205] [...]

Hon. Charles Caccia (Davenport, Lib.): [...] As members know, Canada has always preferred that the Security Council pass the resolution that would determine what the world would do with the situation in Kosovo.

We are deeply disappointed that if such a resolution were attempted to be passed Russia would object and possibly China would object. Therefore we find ourselves in a situation where our preferred situation is not going to work. The humanitarian crisis is there nonetheless.

[2210] Winter is setting in and things are get worse actually by the hour in Kosovo. Therefore Canada stands ready to act with NATO.

Mr. Bill Graham (Toronto Centre-Rosedale, Lib.):[...] I recall when the minister was speaking the parliamentary secretary was here as well. He pointed out that the Secretary General's report in respect of the situation in Kosovo had clearly indicated that the conditions which Security Council mandated for an improvement in the situation in Kosovo have not been lived up to.

Would the parliamentary secretary agree with me that if perhaps there is not a formal resolution at least it is clear that within the United Nations situation itself there is a clear opportunity for NATO and Canada to say we must take advantage of this situation and deal with it and that the Secretary-General, by his findings, has indicated that the situation for an imperative intervention is there? Would that be a fair way of putting it?

Mr. Julian Reed: Mr. Speaker, the report of the Secretary-General actually shows that the world is appalled by this situation. When he came back to report that Mr. Milosevic had not undertaken to comply with the Security Council resolution it stands to reason that while NATO may be the one that has to take action, essentially the whole world will be in support of this action. [...]

[The House adjourned]

215. Notes for a Speech by the Honourable Lloyd Axworthy Minister for Foreign Affairs, Ottawa, Ontario, 24 March 1999

The international community today is facing a situation in the heart of Europe, where a government is denying the most basic rights to its people, using disproportionate force to quell dissidence, sending tanks and artillery to destroy villages, taking the lives of innocent civilians, and forcing hundreds of thousands of people out of their homes and into the cold.

For 10 years, now, the world has witnessed the tragedy unfolding in the Balkans. First it was Slovenia, then Croatia and then Bosnia. In the last year, the same pattern of disproportionate violence against civilians from a targeted ethnic group has appeared in Kosovo.

International Efforts: UN, OSCE, Rambouillet

The international community has spared no effort to encourage the Federal Republic of Yugoslavia [FRY] to find a peaceful arrangement with its Albanian Kosovar population. Scores of diplomatic missions were sent to Belgrade and the United Nations Security Council [UNSC], acting under Chapter VII of the UN Charter, issued crucial resolutions that identified the conflict as a threat to peace and security in the region.

Resolutions 1199 and 1203, and the October agreements between the FRY and the Organization for Security and Co-operation in Europe [OSCE] and NATO, impose a clear legal obligation on the FRY to respect a cease-fire, protect the civilian population and limit the deployment of its security forces in Kosovo.

In October, a verification mission under the OSCE was created. Its purpose was not only to monitor the cease-fire but also to build confidence.

Finally, the parties were called to an international peace conference in Rambouillet, where they were asked to give up their maximalist positions and accept an honourable compromise for peace. The Kosovars demonstrated courage and vision by signing the agreement. Only the Yugoslav President held out and refused to depart from his intransigence.

Canada's Actions

Canada has continually pushed for the strongest possible UNSC engagement in the Kosovo issue. During the summer and fall, I instructed Canadian diplomats to urge the UNSC to take action on Kosovo, consistent with the mandate and duty of the Council. As President of the Council in February, our Ambassador chaired many meetings on the situation. We have supported the peace negotiations in Rambouillet. We have been an active participant in the efforts of the OSCE to monitor a cease-fire, engage the parties in dialogue and build confidence.

In March and June 1998, I had announced measures to prompt the FRY to resolve the Kosovo issue: suspension of EDC [Export Development Corporation] credits to the FRY; suspension of discussions on JAT [Yugoslav Airlines] landing rights; suspension of discussions on other bilateral agreements; a ban on investments in Serbia; and a freeze of the assets of the Serbian and FRY governments in Canada. Some of these measures were imposed under the Special Economic Measures Act (SEMA) following a decision of the G-8.

We have also supported the efforts of the international humanitarian agencies. CIDA [the Canadian International Development Agency] has to date disbursed $3.18 million to provide for basic necessities such as food, water, shelter and medical supplies, as follows: UNICEF Preparedness for Kosovo ($430 000); High Commissioner for Refugees ($1.2 million); World Food Program ($300 000); Red Cross ($900 000); and CARE Canada ($350 000).

Failure of Efforts, Humanitarian Disaster

Unfortunately, the diplomatic efforts of the international community did not ultimately succeed. The looming humanitarian disaster caused by the refusal of President Milosevic to accept any peaceful compromise leaves us with very few options. Every day the situation gets worse, and it is the civilian population who suffers. According to the UN High Commissioner for Refugees (UNHCR), over 450 000 people have been displaced by the conflict in Kosovo, including over 260 000 within Kosovo itself. Since March 20, it is estimated that over 25 000 persons were displaced.

As long as it remains unresolved, the conflict in Kosovo threatens to precipitate a humanitarian disaster and destabilize the entire region.

NATO Action, Objectives, Protection of Canadians

Our preference has always been for a diplomatic solution and the diplomatic track has been given every chance to succeed. The continuing oppression in Kosovo by the FRY government, armed forces and police, continuing failure on the part of the Milosevic government to implement the agreements it has made with the OSCE and NATO, and its continuing refusal to act in compliance with the requirements of successive UN Security Council resolutions - developments that have contributed to an increase in tension and are creating a major humanitarian crisis - leave NATO with no choice but to take action.

NATO is ready to act and Canada is ready to participate. The Canadian Forces have six CF-18 aircraft in the region, prepared to contribute to NATO operations.

NATO's objectives are, first, to avert a humanitarian crisis by enforcing compliance with FRY's obligations, including respect for a cease-fire, an end to violence against the civilian population and full observance of limits on FRY security forces as agreed on October 25, 1998, and also to pressure the FRY to sign a peace agreement on Kosovo.

While NATO was preparing for action, we made sure that Canadians living in the FRY were well aware of the situation. All the members of the KVM [Kosovo Verification Mission] have safely left the FRY. So have the Canadian staff of our Embassy in Belgrade, which has temporarily suspended its operations. Before his departure, the Canadian Ambassador was constantly in touch with the Canadians registered with the Embassy. We have advised Canadians to defer all travel to the FRY and those in the country to leave immediately by the safest means possible.

Kosovo and Canadian Foreign Policy: Meaning of Kosovo for Canada

Humanitarian considerations are the main impulse for our action. We cannot stand by while an entire population is displaced, people are killed, villages are burned and looted, and a population is denied its basic rights because it does not belong to the "right" ethnic group. We remain very concerned about potential atrocities. Those responsible for any action against civilians should be aware that they will be held accountable.

Kosovo embodies many aspects of Canada's view of the world. We want a world where rights are respected, a world where peaceful solutions to regional conflicts are negotiated, a world where war criminals do not act in impunity, a world free of landmines. We want to consolidate the multilateral system, which was created to make the world better, in institutions such as the United Nations, the OSCE and NATO.

Thank you.

216. House of Commons Debate on Kosovo, Extracts, 36th Parliament, 1st Session, Hansard 216, 1310-1320, Ottawa/Ontario, 27 April 1999

[1310] **Hon. Arthur C. Eggleton (Minister of National Defence, Lib.):** Madame Speaker, I am pleased to speak to this motion today.

Let me say clearly at the outset that we in Canada, we in the Government, seek peace. As always, we prefer to seek peace through peaceful means. [*Translation*]

In its quest for peace and security, Canada has always favoured diplomacy. [*English*]

Our diplomatic heritage has become a tradition that we further at all opportunities. It is something that we are justifiably proud of. But even our elder statesman of diplomacy, former Prime Minister Lester Pearson - the father of peacekeeping - understood that military force had a necessary role in achieving peace and security. Why? Because sometimes words and threats are not enough. Negotiations require two parties at the table, together believing in what their words and promises can achieve.

We have been and are willing to sit at that table. At this point, President Milosevic is not. Let me remind the House of Mr. Milosevic's appalling track record when it comes to his willingness to negotiate.

In March 1998, the United Nations passed Resolution 1160, calling on all parties to reach a peaceful settlement. This was followed by UN Resolution 1199 in September. It demanded that both sides cease hostilities and improve the rapidly deteriorating humanitarian situation in the region. In October, 1998, backed by the threat of NATO airpower, an agreement was reached that established a cease-fire and allowed for an observer mission, led by the Organization for Security and Cooperation in Europe, to verify compliance. The Agreement also called for strict limits on the deployment of Yugoslav security forces.

Regrettably, and true to form, as we have seen over many years, Mr. Milosevic did not keep his word. Yugoslav forces violated the cease-fire, responded disproportionately to actions by the Kosovo Liberation Army and carried out a campaign against civilians in clear violation of international humanitarian law.

[1315] Despite this gross misconduct, we still gave negotiations another chance. Talks quickly began in Rambouillet, France. These negotiations sought a peaceful solution by balancing the interests and demands of the parties. The interim agreement we reached provided for a high degree of autonomy for Kosovo, but as part of the Federal Republic of Yugoslavia. In the end the Kosovars agreed. They exercised courage and they signed the Agreement. Mr. Milosevic did not. Eleventh-hour efforts by U.S. envoy Richard Holbrooke proved fruitless.

By March 24th, we realized that the diplomatic track to that point in time had run its course. Our patience and our commitment to leave no diplomatic stone unturned was once again rewarded by Mr. Milosevic's unwillingness to honour the agreements he had made, or to seek a peaceful resolution.

I have just described the long history of our diplomatic efforts to stand against Milosevic's tyranny. This crisis represents a fundamental challenge to the values of democracy, human rights and the rule of law. These are values that Canadians have defended in words, but also in deeds - in the First and Second World Wars, in Korea, and more recently, in the Gulf War. They are also values that NATO has upheld since its inception some fifty years ago.

Our military actions are justified. We have been forced to use a military tool because the Federal Republic of Yugoslavia has repeatedly violated United Nations Security Council resolutions. It has spurned attempts to forge a negotiated peace - with catastrophic results to the people of Kosovo. The unrestrained assault by Yugoslav military, police and paramilitary forces on Kosovar civilians has created a massive humanitarian catastrophe and threatens to destabilize the surrounding region. These have been extreme, calculated and criminal policies. They cannot be defended on any grounds.

But let me be clear: the military action against the Federal Republic of Yugoslavia supports the political aims of the international community. Our objective is to foster a return to a peaceful, multi-ethnic and democratic Kosovo in which all of its people can live in security and enjoy universal human rights and freedoms on an equal basis. Canada and its allies are united in this objective.

It is an objective that is supported by the UN Secretary-General and the European Union, and by Russia. Even Russian efforts to seek a negotiated settlement were met with half-hearted concessions and a flagrant disregard for the need to respect basic human rights and international law. However, the Alliance shares a common interest with

Russia in reaching a political solution to the crisis in Kosovo and will work constructively with Russia to this end wherever possible.

We know of the forthcoming mission of my colleague, the Minister of Foreign Affairs, and we wish him well in his efforts to help bring that about.

The international community is united in its ultimate preference for a negotiated settlement in this crisis.

Before I finish, I would like to provide some additional information on the latest developments. As the Prime Minister indicated just a few moments ago, Canada has now received a formal request from NATO to deploy to the Former Yugoslav Republic of Macedonia the military contingent we had identified some months ago as our contribution to the international peace implementation process in Kosovo. We have agreed to this request.

A Canadian peacekeeping force in the Former Yugoslav Republic of Macedonia will consist of up to 800 people and be equipped with about 280 vehicles and eight Griffon helicopters. Its main components will be a reconnaissance squadron, which will be capable of conducting surveillance and security operations in Kosovo. In fact, they will be using some of the latest equipment, such as the Coyote. The helicopter unit, which I mentioned, will carry out airborne surveillance, transport and medical evacuation missions. Also added to this team of about 600 people will be 200 combat engineers.

[1320] Our force will operate as part of a British armoured brigade within the NATO-led Allied Rapid Reaction Corps. That is why we are going to Macedonia. That is where the British brigade is located. These troops and these functions complement and supplement those which the British will be providing. We currently work with them in SFOR in Bosnia and it will be a similar kind of arrangement in Macedonia. The British already have troops in the region, and they are counting on us to be there with them. The Secretary of Defence for the U.K. specifically said that to me in a meeting held last week.

It will take our force up to 60 days, we hope a little less, to reach the Former Yugoslav Republic of Macedonia and become operationally ready. This period is necessary to assemble the required military equipment and logistical supplies, move them by rail to Montreal and then by ship to Europe.

As the Prime Minister pointed out, our Canadian Forces contingent will be part of an international peace implementation force. In other words, they will be peacekeepers. Although a peace settlement has not yet been reached, deploying our people now will serve two important purposes. First, it will allow our force to integrate fully with the British Brigade and to train with them so that they can respond rapidly and effectively when a settlement is reached. Second, our troops will be able to provide immediate support to ongoing humanitarian operations in the region until - and after - a peace settlement is reached.

With our military campaign, we are achieving what we set out to do. The cost of standing idly by is being measured in the lives of our fellow human beings. We have seen so far a callous and ominous disregard for human security. Canada always prefers a diplomatic solution. Our tradition has always been to appeal to the powers of reason and try to achieve peace without the use of force, or even the threat of it.

Although we have gained a deserved reputation as a peacekeeper, no one should forget that we have never and will never shy away from the stronger means if that is what is necessary to pursue peace and human rights. [...]

6.2 FRANCE

217. Statement by M. Lionel Jospin, Prime Minister, in the National Assembly, during Government Question Time, Paris, 23 March 1999

Over the past few months, taking on board the lessons of the tragedy which occurred in Bosnia, President Chirac and the government have taken several initiatives - working with our European friends and our allies and liaising with the Russians - in order to send to the protagonists in the conflict which has developed in Kosovo the necessary messages: to encourage the forces which want peace and a negotiated solution to the conflict, and intimidate, warn in advance those which once again want to find solutions through violence.

With our allies, we sent these extremely clear messages to the Serb authorities who, once again, have not felt able to seek in Kosovo the orderly solution, which, while retaining the integrity of the Yugoslav Federation's borders, would have permitted the solution of internal autonomy, demonstrating that lessons had been learned from the previous tragedies and that these protagonists were starting to be in tune with our times. We sent these same messages to the Kosovars and particularly the KLA whose methods and, very probably, strategic or diplomatic aims we don't share. We are no more in favour of a Greater Albania than we are of a Greater Serbia.

The French authorities, and first and foremost the Foreign Minister, made great efforts to initiate a negotiating process - that of Rambouillet - to try to get a political solution showing that the Serb and Kosovar parties were renouncing violence, fanaticism, excessive nationalism and an ethnically-based approach to problems and, like us, believed that respect for minorities, the quest for compromise through collective negotiations and the exercise of democracy were now what united all the European peoples and nations, including those of the Balkans.

At this moment, as I speak to you, it has to be recognized that this process has not been successful, that the tension on the ground is becoming greater and greater, that the violence is not stopping and, as the President of your Assembly has said, the number of refugees is growing.

Despite the efforts of the French and British co-chairmen, the negotiators, emissaries and members of the Contact Group, Mr Milosevic is showing no sign of positive movement and is still refusing to adhere to the framework of the settlement drawn up in Rambouillet, a political framework now accepted - and this is a factor in the situation - by the Kosovo Albanians.

So the moment is not far off when we shall have to draw all the necessary conclusions from this situation as the international community has consistently and clearly warned the Belgrade authorities. We are in the final phase. In this respect, we are in constant touch with our partners and our allies.

If all the means of persuading the Belgrade authorities to stop their repression and adhere to both the political and military aspects of the Rambouillet Accords are found to be exhausted, France is determined to play its full part in the military action which will have become inevitable and that will involve French and other European forces and not, as has been said, exclusively US forces.

President Chirac and the government share this determination.

In the event of military action, the Defence and Foreign Ministers will be at the disposal of the National Assembly and Senate Foreign Affairs and Defence Committees in order to inform them as soon as it becomes necessary. If the development of the situation so justifies, the government, in agreement with President Chirac, will then take all necessary steps to ensure that both parliamentary assemblies are quickly and fully informed.

France

218. Communiqué by the French Authorities, Paris, 24 March 1999

1. The Belgrade authorities have refused to respond to the demands of the international community: to stop all offensives in Kosovo and adhere to the Rambouillet Accords.

2. By persisting with this attitude during the last-ditch efforts made with him, President Milosevic bears the total responsibility for the consequences resulting from this refusal, of which he was fully warned.

3. All possible political means have been employed to convince the Belgrade authorities to choose a negotiated solution and peace.

These means are today exhausted.

4. Consequently, the President of the Republic, in agreement with the government, has decided on the participation of the French forces in the now inevitable military operations, which are going to be initiated in the framework of the Atlantic Alliance.

5. France, like its partners in the Contact Group, European Union and Atlantic Alliance, is convinced that the framework laid down by the Rambouillet Accords remains the only one which can lead to a fair settlement of the Kosovo crisis.

219. Statement by M. Jacques Chirac, President of the Republic, Berlin, 24 March 1999

I would like to explain to the French people why NATO is going to conduct an operation against the Serb forces of President Milosevic.

I would like to explain to them why I have decided, in full agreement with the government, that the French air force would participate in this operation with the whole Atlantic Alliance.

For too long, the Serb authorities have behaved unacceptably towards the Kosovo Albanians who, let me remind you, make up 90% of that province's population.

The floods of refugees, destruction of villages, murders and massacres bear witness to this. And it is intolerable.

What is at stake today is peace on our soil, peace in Europe - which we are part of too - and human rights.

Britain and France, in agreement with their European, American and Russian partners, took the initiative of holding a peace conference. It took place, as you know, in Rambouillet and tangible results were achieved:

- The Kosovars accepted a status of substantial autonomy for their province; they also agreed that their armed forces would surrender their weapons.

- On the other hand, the Serbs, who had initially given the impression that they accepted the political agreement, rejected it without reason, just as they refused the presence in Kosovo of a military force to ensure both parties' compliance with the Accords.

Furthermore, in violation of the commitments to which he had subscribed, the Serb president has massed 40,000 men and over 300 tanks in the province or on its borders.

Everything has been done to achieve a rational solution, one of peace. One complying with human rights. Everything.

In the face of President Milosevic's unjustifiable and incomprehensible obstinacy, the allies unanimously took the view that there were no longer any other options than to intervene militarily against clearly targeted Serb objectives in order to contain a tragedy which is gradually threatening the stability of the whole Balkan region.

President Milosevic, who bears total responsibility for this situation, must nevertheless know that he can at any moment return to the negotiating table to sign the peace accord.

Because it is a matter of peace on our continent, because it is a matter of human rights on our continent, I know that the French people will understand that we had to act.

220. Ministry of Foreign Affairs, Legal Basis for the Action Taken by NATO, 25 March 1999[1]

NATO's action finds its legitimacy in the authority of the Security Council. The resolutions of the Council concerning the situation in Kosovo (resolution 1199 of 23 September 1998 and 1203 of 24 Ocotober 1998) have been passed under Chapter VII of the United Nations Charter which deals with coercive actions in case of a breach of peace.

These resolutions have established that the deterioration of the situation in Kosovo constitutes a threat to peace and security in the region.

In resolution 1199 the Security Council demands that the authorities in Belgrade:

- immediately cease hostilities and maintain a ceasefire in Kosovo,

- take immediate steps to avert the impending humanitarian catastrophe,

- cease all action by the security forces affecting the civilian population,

- order the withdrawal of security units used for civilian repression,

- make rapid progress in the dialogue with the Kosovo Albanian community with the aim of finding a political solution to the problems of Kosovo.

Resolution 1203 has endorsed the agreements concluded between Jugoslavia on one side and OSCE and NATO on the other side and it has demanded that they will be implemented. The agreements include precise commitments and obligations of the Yugoslav government.

None of these obligations has been observed by Belgrade. All efforts have been taken in order to call upon the Yugoslav government to respect its obligations for the territory and to accept the Rambouillet Agreement. These efforts have been exhausted.

Therefore the recourse to force has become inevitable. It reponds to Belgrade's violation of its international obligations resulting from the resolutions of the United Nations Security Council taken under Chapter VII of the Charter.

221. Speech by M. Lionel Jospin, Prime Minister, to the National Assembly, Paris, 26 March 1999

On Wednesday, 24 March at 18.50 hours, the North Atlantic Treaty Organization launched military operations in the Federal Republic of Yugoslavia. On the decision of the President of the Republic and in agreement with the government, France is participating in them alongside its allies.

As you know, our country has done its utmost to achieve a political solution to the crisis in Kosovo. In vain. Unless we wanted to abdicate our responsibilities and resign ourselves to impotence, the use of force had become inevitable.

When our forces were on the point of being committed, President Chirac addressed the country. You yourselves wanted, legitimately, a Parliamentary debate on the situation in Kosovo. I would willingly have spoken to you immediately. But because I had to be with President Chirac and my fellow Prime Ministers at the very important European Council in Berlin - which concluded early this morning with an agreement - we have organized this debate today.

The government, you may be sure, is keen for Parliament generally to be kept better informed about our country's defence policy, with due regard to constitutional rules and the respective prerogatives of those holding executive and legislative power. In the present situation, this desire for transparency vis-à-vis the nation's representatives is, in my view, especially important. Last Tuesday, during question time, I told you that "the government would take all the necessary steps to ensure that both Parliamentary assemblies are quickly and fully informed about developments in the situation in Kosovo". In line with that commitment, and in addition to reminding you of the facts and describing

---

[1] *Unofficial translation by the editor.*

the French military assets involved, I want to emphasize to you the government's grounds for France's participation in the current operations and the significance it attaches to it.

For ten years now, the Belgrade authorities have been denying the Kosovo Albanians - who make up 90% of that province's population - the exercise of their legitimate rights. In 1989, the abolition of that territory's status of autonomy led to a growing radicalization on both sides. Thus, the growth since 1996 of violent action by extremist movements is the direct consequence of the political and military repression conducted by the Serb government in Kosovo. The vicious circle of violence was triggered: repression, provocation, reprisals, development of guerrilla warfare and urban terrorism and, in retaliation, increased repression.

In February 1998, the Serb forces intervened militarily in the Drenica Valley. The following April, the Serb government rejected any foreign mediation. Summer 1998 saw the launch of an especially bloody offensive, arousing the indignation of the international community. Despite an interim agreement which allowed Kosovo the hope of a degree of autonomy, a new Serb offensive took place in September.

In the face of allied military threats, President Milosevic agreed, last October, to withdraw the Serb special forces, halt actions against the Kosovar population and accept the deployment of 2,000 verifiers from the Organization for Security and Cooperation in Europe. But, after a period of relative calm, the clashes resumed.

This conflict has already claimed nearly 2,000 lives - including very many civilians - and caused hundreds of thousands of people to flee.

Confronted by a situation of such gravity, the Contact Group on the former Yugoslavia - comprising France, Britain, the United States, Russia, Germany and Italy - decided in March 1998 to tackle the Kosovar crisis. Since then, every avenue has been explored: warnings, threats, sanctions, an arms embargo and diplomatic initiatives.

In vain.

In May 1998, the international community facilitated the opening of direct talks between Mr Milosevic and Mr Rugova.

In vain.

These talks were followed by a violent Serb offensive which triggered an escalation of the clashes and wrecked this attempt at a dialogue.

With Christopher Hill, the American envoy, Wolfgang Petritsch, the European envoy, Boris Maiorski, the Russian envoy, and Jacques Huntzinger, the French envoy, there was non-stop shuttle diplomacy at the end of last year and the start of this.

In vain.

On 15 January, in Racak, with the massacre of 45 Albanians, a new degree of horror was reached.

At that point, France and the United Kingdom, with their Contact Group partners, co-chaired and organized the renewed diplomatic effort at the beginning of 1999 - what is known as the "Rambouillet process". Our country spared no effort - and I would like to pay tribute here to the tireless work of our Foreign Minister, M. Hubert Védrine. In the Contact Group France played a driving role in the effort to establish the framework for a balanced political solution respecting the major principles of international law.

In vain.

Indeed, while, finally, on 18 March, the Kosovar delegation signed the whole of the Rambouillet Accords, President Milosevic obstinately refused to do the same, including during the final attempt to persuade him made by Mr Richard Holbrooke on behalf of the Contact Group.

That was the turning point in the crisis.

In fact, President Milosevic had already begun an intensive remilitarization of Kosovo, thereby clearly signalling his choice of violence. Serb forces arrived en masse: 50,000 men with heavy equipment, artillery, tanks. Communication lines were mined to isolate the province; large-scale operations were conducted to reduce the number of areas controlled by the KLA; there was systematic shelling of the villages, causing their inhabitants to flee.

The Yugoslav President has thus chosen to bear the full responsibility for the current political deadlock.

Fifteen months elapsed between the joint letter, signed by Hubert Védrine and Klaus Kinkel on 19 November 1997, calling on President Milosevic to exercise restraint and engage a dialogue with the Kosovo Albanians, and the joint Védrine-Cook letter of 23 February 1999, asking that same Milosevic to sign the Rambouillet draft agreement.

Fifteen months during which the situation in Kosovo itself constantly deteriorated and the crisis spread and worsened. Fifteen months which saw the forced exile of the terrorized population and the destruction of whole villages by the Serb militia in Kosovo. Fifteen months of war and growing risks for the stability of the whole Balkan region.

After the tragic events of Bosnia, the same confrontations, the same mindless action, the same fanaticism, the same hatred were being unleashed. For decades Europe, at any rate our Europe, has been being rebuilt on new foundations of peace, respect for human rights. To accept the flouting of these values on the European Union's doorstep would have meant betraying ourselves. What is at stake in today's conflict is a certain conception of Europe. Do we accept the return of barbarism on our continent or do we rise up against it? For us, the choice is clear.

To serve the law, recourse to force had become inevitable.

To respond to the persistent violation, by Belgrade, of the commitments and obligations laid down by the Security Council,

To confront the grave and repeated violation of the most fundamental human rights.

We had to act. Act before it was too late. The military intervention was absolutely necessary. Because the irrationality of the Yugoslav regime left no other choice; because we could not reconcile ourselves to impotence.

We could not just watch, resignedly, those terrible pictures - the violence against civilians, the villages wiped off the map, the floods of refuges. We could not consent to being stunned witnesses of the preparation of fresh massacres.

Vukovar, Srebrenica, Sarajevo: to that list of martyred cities, we could not stand idly by and watch the addition of Pristina, Klina, Srbica.

It is in the name of freedom and justice that we are intervening militarily. While force not backed by law is always tyranny, law without force sometimes means impotence. As the UN Secretary-General in fact reiterated on Wednesday, "the recourse to force can be legitimate".

The Security Council is the body with the primary responsibility for maintaining international peace and security. As you well know, I am very committed to that primordial responsibility. But because the Council wasn't in a position to enforce its application, because it had become a matter of urgency, it was up to us to shoulder all our responsibilities, particularly in the Atlantic Alliance.

Especially since, when adopting, under Chapter VII of the United Nations Charter - which concerns the recourse to force - resolutions 1160 (of 31 March 1998), 1199 (of 23 September 1998) and 1203 (of 24 October 1998), the Security Council clearly established that the deterioration of the situation in Kosovo was a threat to international peace and security.

Through SCR 1199, in particular, the Security Council demanded that the Belgrade authorities put an end to the hostilities and maintain a ceasefire in Kosovo, that all action by the security forces affecting the civilian population cease and that Belgrade enter immediately into a dialogue with the Albanian community.

Belgrade has complied with none of those resolutions, has fulfilled none of its obligations, has shouldered none of its responsibilities. On the contrary, on several occasions, the Federal Republic of Yugoslavia has, deliberately, flouted the rules of international law.

So our reaction was one about which President Chirac and I had thought long and hard. The present military operation, discussed at length with our European parties and allies, was postponed several times in order to give every chance to negotiation and to Serbia.

We are not at war with the Serb people. We remember their heroic past in the struggle against the Nazi oppression. We are not the enemies of the Serb nation, which is legitimately entitled to be offered a future in a democratic Europe. But we have to face the fact that, today, it is the Belgrade authorities who alone bear the heavy responsibility for the current crisis. It is not a people who are under attack, but a military and repressive machine. It isn't a nation which is being outlawed, but a regime that is obstinately rejecting the rules of the international community.

Ladies and gentlemen,

That is why France decided to participate in the allied military operation being carried out by NATO.

What does it involve?

An air strike, first of all, on military targets with the aim of exerting coercive action against Serbia and reducing its ability to do harm. It is also designed to prevent the risk of the conflict spreading, being exacerbated and of a worsening of the fighting and consequent disorder. Finally, its aim is to bring President Milosevic as quickly as possible to his senses, i.e. to dialogue and peace.

Then, a ground force in Macedonia, initially deployed to protect the OSCE verifiers and whose presence is today contributing to regional stabilization.

Detachments of our three armed forces are engaged.

French air assets in the Adriatic comprise around forty aircraft belonging to the French air force and naval aviation. These aircraft are capable of carrying out a variety of missions, such as ground attack (Mirage 2000 Ds, carrier-borne Super Etendards), air defence (Mirage 2000 Cs) air recce (Jaguars, Mirage IVs and carrier-borne Etendards), electromagnetic intelligence, operational control and combat search and rescue (CSAR).

French airforce assets involved, for the most part based in Italy, include 8 Mirage 2000 Cs, 4 Mirage 2000 Ds, 2 Jaguars, 1 Mirage IV P, 2 C 135 FR tankers, one airborne early warning E3F, 1 C 160 "Gabriel" and 2 Puma CSAR helicopters.

For its part, the Navy is contributing 14 ground attack Super Etendards and 4 recce Etendards from the aircraft carrier Foch. This is accompanied by the naval group made up by the frigate Cassard, the British frigate Somerset integrated in the French group, the replenishment ship Meuse and the nuclear attack submarine Améthyste.

On the ground, forces essentially consisting of European elements have been deployed in Macedonia. Initially consisting of the extraction force for the OSCE verifiers, they have now been supplemented by the first components of a peacekeeping force which had been set up to ensure compliance with the Accords once they had been signed by the parties. Out of the 10,000 men currently in the NATO force in Macedonia, 2,400 are French.

I now come to the military operations.

The first night saw a succession of four phases: first of all cruise missile attacks, then three waves of bombing. Four French Mirage 2000 Ds took part in the first of these raids. The goal was essentially to neutralize the air defence system. During the day on 25 March, the allies kept in flight a significant defensive force and provided powerful air cover over the whole area. Mirages and Super Etendards from the aircraft carrier Foch were involved in this mission. Last night, the strikes resumed following an identical pattern. Again, four of our Mirage 2000 Ds took part in the bombing of a military site. At this very moment, our planes are monitoring the region's airspace.

Ladies and Gentlemen,

France's involvement in this operation is consistent with our values. It is prompted by what makes the very spirit of the Europe we are building: the desire to place respect for individuals at the heart of what our States do, to put an end to the settlement of differences by violence and hatred. Solemnly before you, I pay tribute to the French forces, the military and the civilians, the OSCE volunteers, who are all committed on behalf of France in the service of peace. I know with what professionalism they are taking on their missions, I know too of the risks our soldiers, sailors and airmen are running.

Because of his intransigent attitude, President Milosevic bears the responsibility for the failure of the Rambouillet process. Over and above this, because of all the opportunities, alas missed, which ought to have made it possible to find a political and peaceful outcome to this crisis, he is accountable, before his own people, and before history.

We don't defend terrorism or support the partisans of a Greater Albania, but still less so the militias who are massacring civilians. Our political objective, defined a year ago by the Contact Group, hasn't changed: the establishment of an interim status of substantial autonomy for Kosovo, within the framework of Yugoslavia's existing borders, guaranteed by an international civilian and military presence. The strikes can be halted at any moment if President Milosevic agrees to return to the negotiating table in order to conclude the Rambouillet Accords.

The military operation isn't an end in itself. The reason we decided to conduct it, I repeat, was because there was no longer any other alternative. But we haven't renounced our political objective. We want a Kosovo which is at peace, Kosovars and Serbs who can live together and a Balkan region which is developing, in which democracy is growing stronger and which is becoming a full part of modern Europe. We are ready to help. We shall continue our work with our European and American allies and with the Russians, whom we consider, despite the current disagreements, to be essential partners in Europe.

It is with the determination to ensure compliance with the law, the resolve to restore peace and the aim of returning to a negotiated political solution that we have committed the French armed forces alongside our allies.

The government counts on the support of the whole nation which you represent.

222. Speech by M. Lionel Jospin, Prime Minister, during Question Time in the National Assembly, Paris, 27 April 1999

Since my first speech to the National Assembly on the Kosovo conflict, on 26 March, I have had occasion several times to go back over the purpose and significance of our participation in the military operation against the Serb forces. I have also had regular meetings with the chairmen of your groups and relevant committees. But, after five weeks of the air campaign, it seems useful for us to meet once again to take stock. It is indeed legitimate, in the face of such a tragic crisis, for questions to be asked and I would like to answer them.

I want to emphasize right away that our goals in this conflict remain unchanged, since they are the justification of our intervention. They have a direct bearing on the choice of means adopted. They guide us in the quest for a political solution.

What are these goals?

We want the campaign of repression and ethnic cleansing launched by the Serb authorities in Kosovo to cease.

We want the police, military and paramilitary forces to leave the province where they are committing their atrocities.

We want the refugees and displaced people to return to their land and homes, the Kosovars to be able to live in peace, at home, in Kosovo.

We want the Albanian-speaking population to have a status of autonomy recognizing all their rights and guaranteeing the safety of all Kosovo's inhabitants.

Mr Milosevic and the Serb authorities bear the total responsibility for the current confrontation.

Because of their intransigence during the year-long attempts at negotiation.

Because of their obstinate refusal to grant all Kosovo's inhabitants the political, cultural and social rights at the heart of democracies.

Because of their determination to implement a long-prepared plan to empty Kosovo of its Albanian-speaking inhabitants.

That's why we assigned the allied forces the mission of incapacitating the Serb repressive machine and striking strategic targets in order to use force to pave the way for a political solution.

For that, was it necessary to declare war on Serbia? We aren't waging war on Serbia. To dominate Serbia, to conquer all or part of its territory, to fight the Serb people: no, none of those are our goals. But morally we could not stand by in the face of Belgrade's incessant violations of Security Council commitments and obligations, of serious and repeated attacks on human rights and the prospect of further massacres.

Could we have used other means of pressure? Could we, in reality, have avoided the airstrikes? No one has so far been able to propose a convincing alternative. Once Mr Milosevic had obstinately rejected any negotiated way out - as we saw for the last time in Rambouillet, then in Paris - to have given up on air strikes which had been clearly announced, would have meant guaranteeing the Serb authorities being able to go on doing what they're doing with impunity and resigning ourselves to impotence.

Mr Milosevic is today having to take responsibility for the consequences of his obstinacy, at the cost of very severe destruction in his country already drained of resources and of the opprobrium heaped on him by the international community. It is revealing that, on the world stage, even among those who don't support the military operations, not one country is supporting his actions, no democrat is supporting his regime.

Ought we, conversely, to have opted for a ground operation? Besides the fact that our intention wasn't to wage war on Serbia, that would have been a high-risk gamble. Given the capabilities deployed by Serbia in and around Kosovo, in violation of the October 1998 accords, such a decision would immediately have embroiled us in large-scale military operations with unpredictable consequences.

That option wouldn't have enabled us to prevent the massacres. The time necessary for the preparations and actually carrying out the air and land operations would have left the Serb forces a free hand for too long. The forces prepositioned in Macedonia for the purpose of guaranteeing a peace deal were in fact neither ready, nor equipped for an operation of that kind.

A rushed ground operation would have meant taking considerable risks for our forces without that enabling us to save the refugees. Yet we couldn't wait: we knew that Mr Milosevic's military forces were going to go into action, once the failure of the negotiations was established.

Is the strategy of airstrikes effective? Admittedly, they haven't prevented the continuation of the ethnic cleansing. But what other strategy was capable of doing so?

The ethnic cleansing was planned, decided on and had begun. No strategy could guarantee it being stopped. It was no more possible to stop it through a high-risk ground campaign, which would have seen an extension of the practice of using human shields, or by doing nothing, which would have given free rein to these criminal activities. Wanting peace, without the airstrikes, would have meant having the ethnic cleansing without the bombing, i.e. without the Serb regime paying the price for it.

It is only with time that we'll be able to estimate the effectiveness of the chosen strategy. You know that our determination is total. Mr Milosevic will have to give in.

The imbalance of forces between Serbs and Kosovars - extremely heavily armed military and paramilitary troops on one side, defenceless civilians or lightly armed groups on the other - was blatant. The Alliance intervention has transformed this balance of forces.

We are advancing towards the achievement of our military objectives, despite the restraint we are imposing on ourselves in order to spare civilians as much as possible. The goal of the air campaign is to destroy the Serb air defence systems to ensure our control of the air space. The intention is to reduce the Serb military and repressive capabilities and everything which helps them move around, their command and control structures. The allied planes now dominate the Yugoslav skies during their raids over Serbia and Kosovo. The Serb forces in Kosovo have lost their mobility. Their logistical capabilities are struggling under the blows. The instruments of Serb propaganda are malfunctioning. Let's be wary of precise calculations of the number of tanks, planes, radar installations and command posts destroyed or damaged. The military assessment which matters is that of the cohesion of the Serb war machine. This is being weakened day after day; not fast enough, no doubt, but it is deteriorating. The air reinforcements the Allies are going to deploy will help speed up this deterioration.

So the results we are seeking are twofold: military - to reduce the Serb forces' destructive power - and political - to destroy the pillars underpinning this regime.

So we must have the tenacity and sang-froid to apply this strategy until the regime is made to give way, pull back its militia. Especially because the bombing can stop as soon as Mr Milosevic agrees to the conditions laid down by the international community and, in particular, the United Nations Secretary-General.

In the meantime, how are we coping with the humanitarian problems? The brutal policy of the Serb military and repressive forces in Kosovo has thrown onto the streets, first thousands, then hundreds of thousands of men, women and children. Men are being arbitrarily arrested and summarily executed, women, in as yet unknown numbers, are once again being raped and whole families are being deported after their homes or villages have been looted, devastated and burnt.

According to the UNHCR, there are almost 700,000 refugees, 365,000 of them in Albania, 135,000 in Macedonia and 65,000 in Montenegro. There are over 80,000 more in Bosnia-Herzegovina and Serbia. Several hundred thousand displaced persons are still in very vulnerable situations in Kosovo itself, fleeing the military repression, seeking to protect themselves from the militia's atrocities, trying just to survive. We know that Arkan, the butcher of Bosnia, and his men and other criminals, indicted like him by the International Criminal Court, are again on the rampage.

In Macedonia, the government has finally agreed to open new refugee camp sites, while continuing to encourage the departure of refugees to Albania and other countries - mainly the European Union and Turkey. From now on, the UNHCR and NGOs will be fully able to carry out their work with the refugees. In Albania, the government, which doesn't want the refugees to leave for other countries, has asked the Alliance to organize the relief. To this end, an agreement was signed a few days ago by NATO and the UNHCR.

With the help of our embassies and our armed forces, several of you have been able to go over there and see this tragic situation for yourselves. I myself will be going to Macedonia and Albania at the end of this week.

Our country is playing its full part in the international effort of solidarity. In Macedonia and Albania, France is making military personnel available, deploying hundreds of specialists from its emergency unit, sécurité civile (emergency services dealing with national disasters, etc.) and SAMU (mobile emergency medical service). It is delivering thousands of tonnes of humanitarian relief - food, medicines, tents, essentials - collected in France. In Macedonia, taking over from our soldiers, Action humanitaire francaise is now running, with NGOs, the Stenkovec camp, which is sheltering over 11,000 people. In Albania, France is running several camps; our doctors are operating an epidemiological monitoring system and are about to upgrade the facilities of a hospital in Tirana.

The government has also decided to provide aid directly to the Albanian and Macedonian families who have taken in refugees. Several of you were asking for this: we are currently studying the ways and means of doing it and, in particular, deciding on the most appropriate bilateral or multilateral way of providing effective relief to the host families and States.

With the same aim in mind, France has decided to grant economic and financial aid to the affected countries: teams of experts are going to Tirana and Skopje to determine, working with the relevant governments, which projects need to be financed as a matter of urgency. President Chirac and I will also be able to raise these matters with the Albanian President, Mr Mejdani, who is today in France.

Finally, we have written to the International Monetary Fund and the World Bank to ensure the orderly mobilization of creditor and donor countries. The IMF "Balkans Group" is meeting this very day, in the presence of our Minister for the Economy and Finance. A special meeting of the World Bank will be held on 5 May. With the European Union, we shall be facing up to our responsibilities and providing Albania and Macedonia, and Kosovo's other neighbours, with the aid required by their economies which are being hard hit by the conflict.

In France itself, there has been an exceptional response to the crisis by the people, to which I have already paid tribute. Thanks to our compatriots, over 10,000 tonnes of emergency humanitarian aid have been collected and are being delivered by French aircraft and ships.

Over 10,000 families in France have volunteered to take in refugees. Standing by our decision to allow the temporary stay of families, if this is their wish - this has to be ascertained by the UNHCR - we have to date organized the arrival of over a thousand people in public reception centres. Some of them are going to French families. More will do likewise. We shall do everything we can to help them forget, while they are here, the ordeal they are suffering. When the day comes - and it will - we shall help them go back home to Kosovo.

To achieve this goal, some think that there is a need for a ground intervention, an entry in force into Kosovo. At the Atlantic Alliance summit, which has just been held in Washington, it was clearly stated that this item wasn't on the agenda. I want to tell you here the great reservations my government and - I think I can say - President Chirac have regarding the scenarios which postulate the failure of the airstrikes and subsequent launch of a ground offensive in Kosovo.

Today, that option remains, as was the case a month ago, fraught with dangers. Moving from coercive action based on an air campaign to a ground operation means accepting the inevitability of the involvement of the population and our soldiers in murderous clashes.

It means accepting the inevitability of a war which might not stop in Pristina, but in Belgrade.

It means risking a Balkan-wide conflagration.

It means jeopardizing our relations with Russia and ostracizing a partner who is vital for the political settlement of this crisis.

In any event, the possibility of that type of military engagement on the ground could not be envisaged without the issue being submitted to you. You would be formally consulted in order to give (or withhold) your authorization for such an operation.

That doesn't mean that no military presence in Kosovo can be envisaged. We are well aware that when we achieve - as is our objective - a political solution, such a deployment will be necessary to implement and guarantee it. It will have to be decided on by a Security Council resolution, adopted under Chapter VII of the United Nations Charter. This force will, of course, have to have the necessary assets: it must have sufficient capabilities, a unified chain of command and effective rules of engagement.

Since we know that NATO will have to have its place in that force, I should now like to take about that organization's role in the current conflict and, going beyond that, about our relations with it.

You are familiar with the history of these relations. After the decisions General de Gaulle took in 1966, France went on, outside the integrated command structure, actively cooperating with its Alliance partners. In 1967, the Ailleret-Lemnitzer agreement laid down the conditions of the French commitment to the Alliance. 1991 saw France envisaging changing its relationship with NATO. Closer ties with the integrated structure were to be the necessary prerequisite for the development of a European defence policy. In his second term of office, President Francois Mitterrand opted for a gradual diplomatic process, requiring as many changes on the French side as on NATO's. Francois Mitterrand used to say: "We'll move when NATO changes".

Between 1991 and 1995, seeking to influence the organization of European security, our country asserted the need for a more balanced NATO. The quest, on President Jacques Chirac's initiative, for a new French attitude to NATO did not put an end to that debate.

In the Kosovo conflict, France is playing its full role: that of a respected member of the Alliance. It wasn't dragged into the NATO-led military operations: it shared in the decision with its allies and, after assessing the risks, took the view that there was no longer any possible alternative.

As you know, France is a partner in the conduct of the airstrikes. Our opinion is followed when we oppose an operation. I have no reason to doubt that the same applies to our partners.

It so happened that the fiftieth anniversary of the Atlantic Alliance was held right in the middle of the Kosovo crisis. On Saturday, in Washington, the Atlantic Alliance Heads of State and Government adopted a statement on the conflict. It reaffirms our determination to prevail, in the face of the challenge to our fundamental values: democracy, human rights and the rule of law. The discussion was at the same time straightforward - because there were no differences of opinion between the allies on the points I have just mentioned - and difficult because, of course, the Kosovo crisis has impacted on the definition of the Alliance's new "strategic concept".

In the field of peacekeeping, it has always been our view that it is for the Security Council, in conformity with the United Nations Charter, to authorize the recourse to force in order to maintain or restore peace and international security. While the emergency in Kosovo forced a derogation from the principle - although there were three resolutions - the principle can't be called into question by an exception. Nothing must diminish the strength of the commitments in the United Nations Charter, commitments made by countries which regained their freedom at the end of the last world war.

We recognize, as does the Charter itself, the importance of the regional collective security organizations - of which NATO is one of the most important. We appreciate the Alliance's essential contribution to European security. But we do not wish NATO to turn into a worldwide organization, freeing itself from the universal rules of the United Nations in order to intervene when and where it wishes.

It is this firm view that President Chirac, with the Foreign Affairs and Defence Ministers and in line with the position drawn up jointly with the government, upheld in Washington. It is reflected by the reiteration in the new strategic concept that NATO is "an Alliance of nations committed to the Washington Treaty and the United Nations Charter".

In this context, can we have a European defence? The Kosovo crisis obviously prompts that question. I am pleased to see the extent to which, here, the testing events of today are arousing support for that idea.

The pragmatic path explored in Saint-Malo, described in the Franco-British declaration, must be taken further with our partners. A progressive and practical approach must be adopted at every stage of the development of the CFSP. The EU must be capable of taking, in the intergovernmental framework, decisions on defence and crisis management. This presupposes that it acquire, without unnecessary duplication and liaising with NATO, its own means for assessing situations and autonomous asset planning and the freedom to deploy its capabilities.

The conflict we are confronting together is strengthening our collective resolve. In the quest for a negotiated solution for Kosovo, as in the military intervention, the Fifteen are working and speaking as one. This was clear both at the summit of Heads of State and Government in Brussels on 14 April, and the Washington summit. We are taking advantage of this solidarity in the conflict and in the quest for peace and relaunching the project of a common defence.

But, right now, the top priority is to put an end to the tragedy of Kosovo.

While we remain determined to continue the necessary use of force, we are clearly reaffirming, with our partners, our strong desire to find a diplomatic solution to the current conflict. Because we are democracies and democracies only extremely reluctantly resort to force. Because we have committed ourselves so that peace may reign in Kosovo. Because a lasting peace can be based only on a political agreement enabling the peoples and States of the Balkans to live together.

On the basis of the Rambouillet principles, we are continuing to advocate a solution based on substantial autonomy for Kosovo, within the borders of the Federal Republic of Yugoslavia. We would like a Security Council resolution to underpin this political settlement and provide for an interim administration safeguarded by the deployment of an international security force. We are already working on this, with our Contact Group partners, on the basis of the UN Secretary-General's statement of 8 April, which received the immediate support of France and the European Union. It's also the subject of the discussions we are pursuing with Russia, which must play a major role both in the quest for an agreement and its implementation.

At the beginning of my speech, I mentioned the grounds for our action and its goals. The armed strength of the European and North American countries is today united and working for, not national interests, or a "desire for empire", but justice and human rights.

By imposing, in accordance with these principles, a diplomatic solution securing, not only the return of the Kosovars to their country, an autonomous and democratic Kosovo, but also the peaceful coexistence and prosperity of the peoples of the Balkans who are the primary victims of this conflict, we will demonstrate that we are capable of defining and ensuring the success of a solution worthy of today's Europe.

223. Communique Issued by M. Hubert Vedrine, Minister of Foreign Affairs, Paris, 10 June 1999

The Security Council's adoption of the resolution on Kosovo, which has just taken place, expresses the international community's unity on the principles which have constantly motivated the diplomatic efforts and military action of France and its partners.

France had ceaselessly stressed the essential role of the United Nations in the political settlement of the crisis. The Security Council resolution is the cornerstone of this settlement.

A considerable task awaits us from tomorrow on: to prepare the return of the refugees, in a totally secure environment, put in place institutions which will organize Kosovo's autonomy within the Federal Republic of Yugoslavia and build a peaceful future for all Kosovo's communities.

6.3 GERMANY

224. Deliberations of the *Deutscher Bundestag*, BT *Plenarprotokolle* 13/248, p. 23127, Extracts, Bonn, 16 October 1998[1]

[...]

Dr. Klaus Kinkel, Minister of Foreign Affairs: [...] [23129] Dear colleagues, NATO, that is the 16 member states who have traditionally enjoyed the rule of law, has carefully examined the legal basis for the decision to send troops and for their potential eventual deployment. After it had become clear during the meeting of the Contact Group last week that there won't be a new resolution of the Security Council - yesterday the Russian Foreign Minister Ivanov confirmed this expressly during the meeting of the Contact Group in Paris - NATO Secretary-General Solana summarized the results of the consultations in the NATO Council at 9 October 1998 as follows:

The FRY has not yet fulfilled the urgent demands of the international community despite the UN Security Council resolutions 1160 of 31 March 1998 and 1199 of 23 September 1998 taken under Chapter VII of the UN Charter.

The clear report of the UN Secretary-General on both resolutions has, inter alia, warned of the danger of a humanitarian catastrophe in Kosovo.

The humanitarian emergency situation continues to exist due to the FRY's refusal to take up measures for a peaceful solution.

In the foreseeable future, another resolution of the UN Security Council which would provide for sanctions concerning Kosovo cannot be expected.

UN Security Council Resolution 1199 affirms unambiguously that the deterioration of the situation in Kosovo constitutes a serious threat to peace and security in the region.

Under the exceptional circumstances of the present crisis in Kosovo, as they are described in UN Security Council resolution 1199, the threat to use force and, if necessary, the recourse to force by NATO is justified.

The German government shares this legal opinion with all the other 15 NATO partners. With its decision NATO has not created a new legal instrument, nor did it intend to do so, which could serve as a general authorization for subsequent NATO interventions. NATO's decision must not become a precedent. We must not go the wrong way concerning the UN Security Council's monopoly on the authorization to use force.

However, in Kosovo there is an acute humanitarian emergency situation of a massive scale which requires immediate action. The possibilities for negotiating are exhausted. The use of force is an ultima ratio. The international community has sharply condemned the behaviour of the government in Belgrade through UN Security Council resolution 1199 and through the report of the UN Secretary-General. Therefore, one can state that the threat to use military action aims at the implementation of the unanimously adopted UN Security Council resolution. It is supposed to prevent a humanitarian catastrophe and a further destabilization of the situation in and around Kosovo. [...]

[23130] The UN Security Council will confirm the agreements with the OSCE and NATO as well as the confirmation of self-government by a Security Council resolution in accordance with Chapter VII of the Charter. Thus, the Security Council remains in control of the proceeding.

We aim at a resolution which will provide a clear provision concerning sanctions. Of course, this is very important regarding NATO's activation order. Yesterday, this has been the main issue in the talks of the Contact Group, since there is, of course a connection, which is easily seen. [...]

Dear colleagues, permanent peace and stability in Kosovo will only be attained by comprehensive self-government of Kosovo within the FRY's existing boundaries. Both Belgrade and Pristina have to contribute to this aim. Therefore, the KLA carries a special responsibility.

UN Security Council resolution 1199 demands that the Kosovo Albanians pursue their aims peacefully. We welcome KLA's recent decla-

---

[1] *Unofficial translation by the editor.*

ration on ending violence. On the other hand: those who choose the path of violence have to face energetic measures by the international community.

The Kosovo Albanians must know: The call for the observation of their legitimate human rights and minority rights must not be used to alter existing boundaries.

We have to clearly and distinctly tell the Kosovo Albanian side that the results of dialogue and negotiations can only lead to comprehensive self-government, not to independence. [...] [23135]

Mr. Gerhard Schröder (Minister President of Lower Saxony): [...] [23137] There exists a very important question concerning the legal basis of NATO's decision. [...] I would also have preferred - I will tell you this - a UN mandate with an unambiguous authorization. However, NATO member states are not responsible for the fact that there is no such mandate. Out of regard for Russia and out of regard for the role of the UN it was appropriate not to let the NATO decision depend on a further resolution of the UN Security Council.

Resolution 1199 of 23 September 1999 has been taken under Chapter VII of the UN Charter. The UN Secretary-General has stated that the addressee of the resolution, Milosevic, has not fulfilled its demands. In its decision, NATO refers explicitly to resolution 1199 and to the necessity of preventing a humanitarian catastrophe. NATO - I find it important for all of us - has not authorized itself; NATO acts within the framework of the UN.

Ladies and Gentlemen, I would not like to leave any doubt open, that the UN Charter's exclusive right to authorise the use force and the primary responsibility of the Security Council for the maintenance of international peace and security are indispensable for the development of a world peace order. The new government will act along these principles.

I will not conceal that it has been of some importance to me, when weighing these difficult legal considerations, to look at the results of our friends and allies. When all NATO member states, in the majority of which socialist parties are governing, support NATO's decision and find a sufficient legal basis, it is not compelling for me to presume that all our friends are mistaken and only some of us are right.

Moreover, we have to consider something very important: We could not stick to our attitude, which was first accepted by the American President and other important allies, that the Bundestag could presently not reach a decision for reason of constitutional policy, not constitutional legality, because there are problems of constitutional legitimacy. [23138] After we could not exclude that the German conduct would significantly influence the reaction in Belgrade such a position was no longer feasible. This would have been seen as a German refusal and it would have caused serious damages, difficult to repair, within the alliance and maybe also within the European Union. A failure of the negotiations could have been attributed to us.

The result would have been a disastrous loss of prestige and significance for the Federal Republic of Germany. Nobody can be interested in this. One can ask whether today's decision of the Bundestag is still necessary in the light of the recent developments. This question can definitely still be answered with yes. [...]

Dr. Wolfgang Schäuble (CDU/CSU): [...] [23139] What about a legal basis? A few month ago during comparable debates you still asked: Will you, as a last resort, intervene without authorization of the UN Security Council? How will you differentiate?

I am convinced: [...] The decision of the government, to which the Bundestag shall agree and to which the fraction of the CDU/CSU will agree, is solidly based on constitutional and public international law. I want that there are no doubts about it. I think that the debate on the monopoly for the use of force - which we want; there is no dissent - in public international law is a bit more complicated. We should not give way for illusions. Maybe, in the future, we will have to take other equally difficult decisions.

In a world in which the interrelation of developments has grown stronger - you have talked about the problem of refugees - we still do not have a situation, and maybe will not have in the foreseeable future, a situation comparable to a democratic state under the rule of law, that there really is a monopoly to use force and decision-making institutions which can make majority decisions, which are accepted by the minority; and these decisions, if necessary, can be controlled by courts, and can be enforced because the implementation of these decisions is possible. We do not find this situation on the international level, and we will not find something comparable in due course.

Therefore, on the international level, we have to be careful when we look for a legal basis for decisions in the interest of peace and human rights in this world, which are indivisible, and we have to think about tomorrow when we make a decision today. You have to consider this whenever you make a decision. Therefore, we have said at an early stage [...]: Of course, a clear authorization by the UN Security Council is the best solution - [23140] this has always been beyond dispute. However, there can be a situation in which we have to make such an authorization without any legal reservation - there have been reservations by two permanent members - after due examination and weighing of arguments. We should consider in due time that such a situation for a decision could come along. [...]

I speak about the problem that on the international level we cannot generally renounce the use of military means under very narrow prerequisites, which have to be carefully examined, in order to maintain peace and implement human rights.

This is a situation on the international level which is different from the situation in a free and democratic state under the rule of law and will probably remain so for a long time. [...] Can we intervene in the internal affairs, and the legal affairs of a State? The principle of non-intervention has been weighed against the implementation of human rights.

Since we know from the history of this century that the step to a disturbance of international peace is a small one in questions of public international law, we have to be ready to secure peace and fundamental human rights: by integration, by regionalization, if necessary, by threat to use military force. A threat is only effective if one is ready to realise it in case of doubt; otherwise a threat is ineffective. Therefore, one has to take into account the consequences when making a decision. One should not make a threat which cannot be fulfilled. This is the question. [...] [23141]

Joseph Fischer (Frankfurt) (Bündnis 90/DIE GRÜNEN): [...] It is important for us ... that there is no "self-authorisation" of NATO in this question. I would like to underline, Mr. Kinkel that your statement today that we have an emergency situation, an extraordinary situation, not a precedent - that fact is of great importance to us. We support with conviction the position that we need now a UN resolution with an unambiguous and clear legal basis. [...]

225. Statement Made by Federal Chancellor Gerhard Schröder, Bonn, Press Release, Bonn, 24 March 1999

My fellow countrymen:

NATO began launching air strikes against military targets in Yugoslavia this evening. In doing so, the Alliance wants to stop further serious, systematic human rights violations and prevent a humanitarian catastrophe in Kosovo.

Yugoslavia's President Milosevic is waging a relentless war in Kosovo. In defiance of all warnings, Yugoslav forces have stepped up their terror against the Albanian majority in Kosovo. The international community can no longer watch the human tragedy this has caused in that part of Europe without taking action. We are not waging war. We are however called upon to enforce a peaceful solution in Kosovo even under the use of military means.

This military action is not aimed at the Serbian people. I want to also say this specifically to the Yugoslav nationals living here in Germany. We will do everything possible to avoid losses among the civilian population.

The Yugoslav delegation at the Paris conference rejected even minimal concessions just late last week. This is particularly hard to comprehend in light of the fact that the peace agreement negotiated there did not question Yugoslavia's existence. What is more, the European Union held out the prospect of Belgrade's return to international organizations and a gradual lifting of sanctions in the event that a settlement could be reached.

Belgrade's response was to breach agreements and send further troops to Kosovo. As a result, the use of force became the only means left.

By contrast, the representatives of the Albanian majority signed the Paris peace agreement, documenting to the entire world their willingness to reach a peaceful solution.

This operation is jointly supported by all Alliance partners. By conducting it, we are also defending our common fundamental values of peace, democracy and human rights. We cannot allow these values to be trampled on just one hour by air away from here.

Bundeswehr soldiers are also participating in this NATO mission, as was decided by the German government and the *Deutscher Bundestag* in accordance with the will of a vast majority of the German people.

This was not an easy decision for the German government. After all, this will be the first time that German soldiers will have seen military action since the end of the second world war.

I call upon everyone in Germany here and now to stand by our soldiers in this hour. They and their families ought to know that we will do everything possible to protect them during this difficult and dangerous mission. Nonetheless, we cannot rule out the possibility of danger to life and limb for our soldiers.

I call upon President Milosevic here and now to end the fighting in Kosovo immediately. NATO and the entire international community remain willing to help implement the peace agreement when so desired by the parties to this conflict. The first NATO units, which include 3,000 German soldiers, are standing ready to provide military assistance for safeguarding the necessary ceasefire. Europe reaffirmed its responsibility for the peaceful development of events on the continent at the Berlin summit. Europe speaks with one voice as well when it comes to the difficult mission in Kosovo.

There can be no doubt about our determination to end the killing in Kosovo. It is in the hands of Belgrade's leaders alone to end this NATO operation by deciding in favour of peace.

226. Deliberations of the *Deutscher Bundestag*, BT *Plenarprotokolle* 14/32, p. 2619, Extracts, Bonn, 15 April 1999

[2645] [...] [2647] **Rudolf Scharping, Minister of Defense:** [...][1] Now I turn to questions - legal questions have already been discussed here - which go beyond the day and the special conflict: [...] Does the Helsinki Final Act not state that a single state's human rights situation is not longer an internal affair of the state? Has this not been a major step forward on the way to European integration in the sense that it exchanges, free from violence, sovereignty for the respect of human rights and of rights of minorities?

Is it not the case - it is the case - that the head of states of the nations represented in the UN Security Council have explicitly and unanimously decided that restrictions of a state's sovereignty might be necessary for the implementation of human rights? Is it not the case that the United Nations have adopted the Convention on the Prevention and Punishment of Genocide as early as 9 September 1948. This convention was based on the horrendous experiences of the Second World War. Kofi Annan, as already pointed out, spoke on 9 April about the convention, emphasizing that we stand under the dark cloud of genocide. He added: The UN Security Council must not become a refuge of those who commit the gravest violations of human rights under the pretext of sovereignty.

We should not forget that the European Parliament expressively requested the partners of the European Union on 20 April 1994 to participate in a law creating process in order to develop public international law in a way whereby a state can intervene for humanitarian reasons and for human rights considerations under the following prerequisites: an extraordinary and extremely serious humanitarian emergency situation - present in this case -; a paralysis of the United Nations - sadly also present -; a failure of all other attempts for a solution - we have tried for months to achieve a solution -; a restricted military operation proportional to objectives. I want to tell you that NATO has deployed 50% of its planned attacks during the last ten days because the risk of civil damage could not be estimated or was too high. Even if mistakes were made in single cases what is terrifying and deplorable, I am astonished about the manner of a discussion which only pays lesser attention to thousands of murdered persons because NATO is not able to and does not wish to - thank heaven - develop its propagandistic abilities and means in the same way the regime of Milosevic has done it with its unscrupulous propaganda.

In addition, one of the criteria of the European Parliament was that the operation must be carried out in a way so as not to give rise to a condemnation by the United Nations. The question more pressing will be: Does the sovereignty of a state, in conflict with the other principles of the UN Charter, i.e. the ban on crimes against humanity, permit to violate human rights internally? [2648] Do we not face an objective conflict of aims which we have to reconcile? Can the sovereignty of a single state permit that that state may endanger the sovereignty and integrity of its neighbouring states by the expulsion of an entire segment of its population which is without doubt the case in Macedonia and Albania? [...]

Do we not need as well - I pose this question deliberately - mechanisms in order to overcome the veto of a nuclear power in the UN Security Council? Or are we really willing to accept in the future - whatever these mechanisms will be - that one of a few stabilising elements in this region, i.e. the UN Mission in Macedonia with the name UNPREDEP, has only been blocked by China because Macedonia had been so reckless as to recognize Taiwan under public international law? [...]

Policy Statement delivered by Federal Chancellor Gerhard Schröder in the *Deutscher Bundestag* on the current situation in Kosovo[2]

[2620] Mr President, Ladies and gentlemen,

At the informal meeting of the European Council yesterday in Brussels, attended at my invitation also by the Secretary-General of the United Nations, the Heads of State and Government of the European Union reaffirmed their determination not to tolerate the killings and deportations in Kosovo. They reiterated that to prevent this the use of military force is necessary and justified.

We agreed on how, in cooperation with our partners, a political settlement can be achieved, given the necessary conditions.

I will come back to the results of yesterday's meeting later on.

The Heads of State and Government of the EU support the initiative of the Secretary-General of the United Nations and will press for a resolution to be adopted by the Security Council under Chapter VII of the United Nations Charter.

Ladies and gentlemen,

Never before has a Government of the Federal Republic of Germany faced the tough decision to send German soldiers to participate in a military combat operation undertaken jointly with our partners.

I want therefore to explain once again the reasons we had to take this difficult step.

---

[1] *Unofficial translation by the editor.*

[2] *As taken from the German government server.*

Over the weeks and months before the air strikes began the international community left no stone unturned to bring about a political solution to the conflict.

But President Milosevic time and again deceived his own people, the Albanian majority in Kosovo and the international community.

For months EU Special Envoy Petritsch and his American colleague Hill, later also together with the Russian envoy Mayorski had conducted talks with all parties to the conflict and laid the groundwork for a fair settlement.

At Rambouillet there were weeks of dogged negotiations. The agreement submitted to the parties was intended to safeguard the human rights of the Albanian majority in Kosovo but also Yugoslavia's territorial integrity.

This agreement could and should have been accepted by both parties.

We agreed to a further two-week period to allow concerns raised by the parties to be dealt with. At the end of that period we met for further negotiations in Paris. The Kosovo Albanians finally signed the agreement.

Foreign Minister Fischer as President of the European Council, Russian Foreign Minister Ivanov, OSCE Chairman Vollebaek and last of all once more Richard Holbrooke as United States Special Envoy right up to the end urged Milosevic in Belgrade to accept the agreement.

But the Belgrade leadership let all attempts at mediation founder. While affecting to negotiate peace, they actually continued the campaign of murder and deportation which they have been systematically stepping up in recent weeks.

The campaign of ethnic cleansing we are witnessing today was planned by the Yugoslav Government from the outset. It has cost thousands in Kosovo their lives.

Ladies and gentlemen,

Like everyone in Germany I am shocked by the daily reports on the suffering of the refugees. Images of houses that have been blown up. Refugees and deportees who have terrible tales to tell.

All this is the work of the Yugoslav military and police forces. Deportation and murder had been long under way before NATO's military operation began.

To simply look on while these crimes were being committed would have been cynical and irresponsible. NATO had to respond to the escalation of the use of force. Since the loss of 200,000 lives in the war in Croatia and in Bosnia and Herzegovina, we know Europe would have once more made itself culpable, had it stood idly by.

NATO is a community based on values. It is for those values we are fighting in Kosovo together with our partners. For human rights, freedom and democracy.

In this commitment of ours the issue is also what kind of Europe we want to see in the century to come.

Are we Europeans, having experienced two horrific world wars this century, prepared to allow dictators a free hand to wreak their will in Europe?

The German Government has a clear and consistent approach which we are pursuing together with our partners.

We want to put an end as soon as possible to the humanitarian disaster and the grave and systematic violations of human rights. We want to achieve a peaceful political settlement for Kosovo.

The German Government will continue to stand shoulder to shoulder with its NATO and EU partners, it will not tolerate violence against innocent people.

We clearly must not slacken our efforts to reach a political solution.

In achieving such a solution Russia should play an important role.

The German Government is in close contact with Russia's leaders. We look forward also to an early meeting with the newly appointed Russian envoy for Yugoslavia Chernomyrdin.

I am counting on Russia to play an even greater role in ongoing international efforts to bring about a peaceful solution. That goes also and in particular for Moscow's contribution within the United Nations framework.

The crisis on the Balkans must not be allowed to jeopardize either Europe's or Germany's good relations with Russia.

Russia is an important factor for our continent's security and stability.

We will therefore continue to provide every possible support for the policy of reform on which Russia's leaders are embarked.

Ladies and gentlemen,

It remains our goal to create as soon as possible the conditions for the refugees and deportees to return home in safety.

Yet as long as these conditions do not exist, the priority should be to look after people in the region where they have sought refuge and with which they are linked by language and culture.

Any other policy would make us de facto accomplices of Belgrade's policy of deportation.

Albania and Macedonia are currently bearing the main brunt of the consequences of this ruthless policy.

We cannot leave the neighbouring countries to cope with the problem alone. To help these countries a real effort of international solidarity is vital.

Allow me at this point to pay tribute to all those in Germany who in this hour of need, through donations or in other ways, have demonstrated their solidarity.

The German Government for its part has allocated substantial funds so refugees and deportees can be cared for in the region.

The European Union, too, is making special funds available to relieve the plight of the refugees and prevent a destabilization of the neighbouring countries.

The Bundeswehr has set up an air lift to fly food, tents, blankets and doctors to the region.

We are willing in addition to provide temporary refuge for an appropriate number of refugees here in Germany.

The first refugees have already arrived. They are welcome, they can rely on the solidarity of the German people.

However, we expect our partners in Europe and the Alliance to carry their fair share of the burden as well.

Ladies and gentlemen,

We are concerned by the situation in Montenegro.

We support the democratically elected leadership of this constituent republic of Yugoslavia under President Djukanovic.

At this point, I would like to warn the Belgrade leadership against destabilizing Montenegro. Such a policy would have particularly grave consequences.

Ladies and gentlemen,

I am firmly convinced that only a united front on the part of the entire international community will make Milosevic yield.

Given our German history, we cannot leave any doubt about our reliability, determination and steadfastness.

Germany's integration in the western community of nations is part and parcel of our raison d'être. We do not want a separate lane for Germany.

And we must recognize that Germany's role has changed following the collapse of state socialism. We cannot shirk our responsibility.

German soldiers are engaging in a combat mission for the first time since the end of World War Two. They are carrying out a difficult and dangerous mission. We cannot exclude the possibility of danger to life and limb.

Hence, I would also like to offer my sincere thanks once more to the soldiers and their families.

They should know how much this Parliament appreciates their commitment to humanity and lasting peace.

Ladies and gentlemen,

The German Government and all NATO partners are aware that the current crisis management in Kosovo cannot replace a longer-term stabilization policy for South-Eastern Europe.

Our policy is not directed against the people of Yugoslavia. Rather, we want to give them a prospect for the future as well as the assurance that they belong in Europe.

The Balkans need European help. Yugoslavia, just like Germany after 1945, needs democratisation, economic development and a civil society.

Comprehensive measures for long-term stabilization, security, democratisation and economic reconstruction are essential.

We need a type of Marshall Plan for the Balkans. I know such a plan doesn't come for free. Europe cannot and must not renege on this task.

All countries in the region are entitled to a prospect of moving closer to the European Union. We want to be able to say to all people in the region that they belong in Europe.

We want to win them over to the European model. And we want to help democracy prevail in the Balkans in the long term.

Thus, the German EU Presidency proposed a Stability Pact for the Balkans last week.

For the German Government, this is a real alternative to the fanatical nationalism which has once more brought disaster to the region after all the bitter experience of this century.

To close, let me return to yesterday's meeting of the Heads of State and Government of the European Union. We had an intensive and serious discussion with the UN Secretary-General and reached agreement.

We concluded that:

- In our determination not to tolerate the murders and deportations in Kosovo, we agree that the use of the severest measures, including military action, is both necessary and warranted.

We want a multi-ethnic and democratic Kosovo in which all people can live in peace and security. The Yugoslav authorities must be made aware that we hold them responsible for the safety and well-being of the displaced persons in Kosovo.

- The Heads of State and Government support the Secretary-General's initiative of 9 April outlining the demands of the international community on which they will on no account back down, that is:

Immediate cessation of all use of force, withdrawal of the military, the police and the paramilitary forces, deployment of international military forces as well as the return of all refugees and displaced persons.

It is now up to the Yugoslav authorities to accept the international demands unequivocally and begin the implementation process without delay. This would allow NATO to suspend military action and open the way for a political solution.

- We will push for the adoption of these principles in a United Nations Security Council Resolution under Chapter VII.

- The Heads of State and Government reaffirmed their support for a political agreement on Kosovo, building on what has already been achieved in Rambouillet. They agreed on the main elements of an interim arrangement for Kosovo, to be set up immediately following the end of the conflict. These should include:

- establishment of an international interim administration,

- creation of a police force that reflects the composition of the Kosovo population,

- holding free and fair elections,

- deployment of international security forces to ensure the protection of the whole population of Kosovo.

- There was agreement at the meeting on the prime importance of close cooperation with the Russian Federation, which has a crucial role to play in solving the Kosovo problem.

- The decisions of the General Affairs Council on 8 April regarding humanitarian aid for refugees and displaced persons and support for the countries neighbouring the Federal Republic of Yugoslavia were reaffirmed. These countries can be assured of the solidarity of the European Union and its member states.

- Finally we agreed that the European Union will convene a conference on South-Eastern Europe to decide on comprehensive measures for the long-term stabilization, security, democratisation and economic reconstruction of the region. All countries of the region are entitled to a prospect of moving closer to the European Union.

That is to say: the European Union, NATO and the UN Secretary-General agree upon this assessment of the situation and on the way forward. The German Government will pursue this course with determination.

227. Deliberations of the *Deutscher Bundestag, BT Plenarprotokolle* 14/35, Extracts, p. 2761, Bonn, 22 April 1999

Policy Statement Delivered by Federal Chancellor Gerhard Schröder in the Deutscher Bundestag on the Occasion of the 50th Anniversary of the Founding of the NATO[1]

Gerhard Schröder, Federal Chancellor: This weekend the Heads of State and Government of the NATO member nations will assemble in Washington. Our original intention was to celebrate together a special anniversary: the signing of the North Atlantic Treaty fifty years ago.

Fifty years of NATO, which particularly we Germans cannot rate too highly, has meant fifty years of development in peace, freedom and democracy. In this assessment the key factor is not NATO's military achievements. Right from the outset, and today this is truer than ever, NATO has been an alliance founded on shared values. And given the current world situation, NATO's future is clearly as an alliance committed to peace, democracy and human rights.

We have seen how the threat of strife and armed conflict looms wherever democracy is absent. Wherever dictators seek to impose their will on their own nations as well as their neighbours. It is this recognition that has inspired NATO's action as a defence community. That is why we will not be spending the weekend in jubilant celebration. The war in Kosovo is today at the top of the Alliance's political agenda. Also at the Washington summit therefore the situation in South-East Europe will be the main focus.

If the Alliance's commitment to the values it proclaimed was to mean anything, after all, NATO had to act, it had to confront the *systematic expulsions and mass murder taking place in Kosovo*. The Alliance had to demonstrate it will not abandon a part of Europe to repression and barbarism. [...]

[2763] The international community has left no stone unturned to settle the conflict in Kosovo by diplomatic means. However, all efforts to achieve a peaceful solution foundered in the face of the ruthless intransigence of the leadership in Belgrade. With catastrophe looming, the Alliance finally had no other choice. It had to resort to military action to make Belgrade realize the consequences of the war it was waging on its own people. Having unleashed a brutal campaign against the Albanian majority in Kosovo, the dictator Milosevic had to be shown that the weak have in NATO a strong friend and ally ready and willing to defend their human rights.

By the same token the Alliance is doing its utmost to relieve as far as possible the plight of the refugees. It is giving logistical and financial support to the neighbouring countries most severely affected by the

---

[1] *Translated summary as taken from the German government server.*

refugee exodus. NATO itself has provided emergency accommodation for tens of thousands of refugees.

Lastly, a good many countries - with Germany leading the way - have offered the refugees a temporary home. [...]

The Alliance was and still is - that is important to emphasize - at all times ready to respond to any credible signal: finding a political solution to the conflict is the focus of all our efforts. [...]

NATO has, in agreement with the Secretary-General of the United Nations and also the European Union, set out its conditions for suspending the air-strikes: - an immediate halt to all use of force, - withdrawal of all military forces, special police forces and paramilitary units from Kosovo, - deployment of international security forces so that the refugees can return home without fear. [...]

The German Government supports the initiative outlined by the Secretary-General of the United Nations on 9 April 1999. The political fora of the NATO members and the German Foreign Minister first and foremost are indefatigable in their efforts to seek a political solution and get back to the negotiating table. It is entirely up to the Yugoslav leadership to fully accept the international demands and to act on them without delay.

We remain keen to see Russia play an important part in the search for a peaceful settlement. Lasting peace on the Balkans is, I am convinced, in Russia's own best interest. Our long-term goal must be to ensure democratic and peaceful development throughout the region. That will obviously mean opening up not just a security but also an economic perspective for the countries of South-East Europe. As part of a strategy for the entire region the European Union, the OSCE and NATO will all have a role to play in integrating these countries into the Euro-Atlantic structures.

In participating in the NATO operation in Kosovo, Germany has assumed its share of the overall responsibility. Our contribution is not just a normal expression of Alliance solidarity. As part of the democratic community we Germans, also in the light of our history, have an obligation to stand up for peace and security and against repression, expulsions and the use of force.

We all know our soldiers taking part in this operation are facing considerable personal risk. But also all other Germans involved in the relief effort in the Balkans are daily risking their lives to help the many people there in dire need of help.

[2764] For over forty years the East-West conflict was a fact of life in Europe. Today that is past history. At the Washington summit we will be welcoming three new Alliance members: Poland, the Czech Republic and Hungary. Three countries that just ten years ago were members of the Warsaw Pact. We Germans felt a special commitment towards these three new members. We have not forgotten the prodigious contribution these nations made in bringing about German reunification. Reunification would never have happened, had Germany not been firmly integrated into the Atlantic Alliance.

The opening up of the Alliance to the countries of Central and Eastern Europe is part and parcel of our efforts to build a Europe-wide order of peace. Erstwhile enemies have become partners. Our common aim now is to develop a new strategic vision: an order that will secure peace and stability, founded on precepts of human rights, justice and democratic, social and ecological development.

This also means greater responsibility for Europe. The countries of Europe can only really pull their weight, live up to this responsibility if they evolve a common European security and defence policy. Obviously key elements of the new Strategic Concept will be very much in line with NATO traditions since 1949. Also in future a core function will be defence of the NATO area. At the same time the Alliance will remain the foundation of a stable security environment. And as hitherto the Alliance will remain the central forum for consultation among the Allies.

The revised Strategic Concept will in addition define a new core function. This will be the response to the new challenges facing the Alliance. Given the new threats that have emerged, our paramount goal must be to strengthen security and stability on our continent. The United States involvement, through the Alliance, with Europe as well as its presence there remain crucial to the security of our continent.

Now the East-West conflict has been overcome, it is today plainer than ever that to achieve security, military means alone cannot suffice. A modern security policy must create a nexus between peace and socio-economic development. That is what I understand by good crisis management and effective crisis prevention. And that is why in Kosovo, too, the issue is not simply military victory. To open up a political and economic perspective for the entire region: that is our aim.

In this context Europe is already playing a part commensurate with its greater responsibility for the world. With its willingness to take responsibility for the defence of human rights, legal certainty and respect for the general principles of law, Europe through the Alliance is making its own contribution to the political definition of our continent as a humane Europe, a Europe of human rights.

Soon after the fall of the Iron Curtain, the Alliance extended an offer of extensive cooperation to the former Warsaw Pact countries. A new forum for security policy cooperation was created with the North Atlantic Cooperation Council, since 1997 the Euro-Atlantic Partnership Council. Alongside the Russian Federation and Ukraine, it also includes all the other successor states of the former Soviet Union, as well as the young democracies of Central and Eastern Europe.

The Partnership for Peace, founded in 1994, became the Alliance's most successful programme of all. It was in Bosnia that this partnership faced its first major test. And it passed this test very successfully. Together with Russia and other partners, the Alliance is today ensuring the implementation of the Dayton peace agreement for Bosnia and Herzegovina. The Dayton agreement meant a halt could be called to unspeakable atrocities in this long-suffering country. The deployment of IFOR troops and their continuation as SFOR serves as a perfect example today of NATO's commitment to crisis management.

At the NATO summit, we will adopt a package of initiatives to make the Partnership for Peace even more effective. It will be a matter of further enhancing cooperation between the partner states' armed forces. At the same time we want to extend the civil aspects of the partnership. The Alliance's cross-border cooperation does not just mean being open for dialogue. It also means keeping the door open for new members. The entry of Poland, the Czech Republic and Hungary on 12 March made it clear that NATO was not and is not an exclusive club. We will show interested candidates ways to start their preparations for possible membership now, and give active support as they do so.

We also want to further strengthen the distinctive relationship between NATO and Ukraine. By concluding the Charter on the partnership between NATO and Ukraine in Madrid in 1997, the Alliance underlined the significance of this relationship. The first summit meeting of the NATO-Ukraine Commission will now take place in Washington. There we will emphasize that the Alliance will continue to support the development of a stable, independent Ukraine in the future.

[2765] Whether it is to move closer to membership or, as with Ukraine, to develop a stronger partnership, one aspect is always to the fore: the countries concerned seek military security. But they want and need economic as well as social stability. Both are in NATO's interest. Exporting political stability makes the whole continent a safer place. No one in Europe should regard this process with suspicion. This is particularly true of Russia. The Russian Federation continues to be the Alliance's most important security partner.

Closely involving Russia in the responsibility for European security is a key component of Alliance policy.

The NATO-Russia Permanent Joint Council established by the NATO-Russia Founding Act has proved to be a valuable instrument for dialogue and cooperation. We have succeeded in the last two years in breathing life into the NATO-Russia Permanent Joint Council. This forum has played a key role, particularly in the fields in which the Alliance and Russia did not see eye to eye. Through this cooperation based on trust Russia has been given the opportunity to get to know the

Alliance's ways of thinking and working at first hand. We want to further extend this cooperation. Russia, too, should recognize the opportunities offered by the dialogue in the NATO-Russia Permanent Joint Council, suspended at the end of March. However, Russia for its part must face up to its responsibility to make constructive contributions to establishing European security. And I mean that in particular with regard to solving the Kosovo crisis.

The founding of NATO fifty years ago was a unique, historic move. For the first time, Europe and America, the old and the new world, came together to defend European values, values which have become universal: freedom, democracy and human rights. For the people of Germany and the whole of the European Union, there is no political or cultural alternative to this Western alliance. But the Transatlantic Partnership can only flourish if it takes the increased European responsibility into account. Incidentally, our American friends share this view.

We want a new Europe for the new NATO and we want the new NATO for the new Europe. In recent years, the united Europe has taken momentous steps towards irreversible economic and political unity. With the introduction of the common currency, the euro, a large part of the European Union performed a genuine act of joint sovereignty.

Now Europe faces a twofold challenge: to strengthen and enlarge the Union. A Common Foreign and Security Policy which is worthy of the name and the development of a European Security and Defence Dimension are cornerstones of this process.

The Treaties of Maastricht and Amsterdam open up new scope for action in this field. The European Council will have the competence to establish guidelines for the Western European Union on defence policy matters. In the future, the European Union will need its own political and military decision-making structures. But we certainly do not want to duplicate existing structures. But with my proposal to confer the office of the WEU Secretary General on the High Representative of the Common Foreign and Security Policy, we want to give a clear signal that Europe will also be able to speak with one voice in security and defence policy issues in the future.

We are all agreed within the Alliance that international military operations beyond Alliance borders need to be clearly rooted in international law. Thus I want to say at this point that I respect the arguments of those who maintain that there was no such basis in the case of NATO's operations in Kosovo. But after careful deliberation, I consider the legal basis of NATO's action, that is to contain a humanitarian crisis, to be both valid and sufficient.

International law sets out clear rules with regard to the treatment of refugees and their right to return safely to their homeland. I would like to emphasize that no one wants to detract from the United Nations as an organ of international understanding and crisis management. Quite the opposite. Hence I invited Kofi Annan, the UN Secretary-General, to last week's meeting of European Heads of State and Government in Brussels. And that is why I openly welcome the Secretary-General's readiness to work with us on the peaceful solution to the Kosovo conflict. And I am delighted to be able to welcome Kofi Annan to Berlin for further talks next week.

Respect for the United Nations is undisputed in the Alliance. [2766] NATO is not an Alliance in which one partner imposes his opinion on others. It is and remains a community of shared values. That is why we are partners in this Alliance and accept responsibility within this Alliance. Not because we are forced to. Rather out of firm conviction. And because we know that we can rely on NATO's commitment to our common values. [...]

[2776] **Joseph Fischer, Foreign Minister:**[1] [...] [2778] The present discussion on whether the operation is legally permissible or not is, from my non-juridical, but political point of view, a formal debate. Why? Because the Security Council should simply have acted in the case of Kosovo. I would have been happy, if we had obtained a resolution taken under Chapter VII of the UN Charter. I hope that [2779] now with the involvement of Russia such a resolution will be adopted, since all previous resolutions led to this point. Personally, the question is not about a new strategy for NATO, nor whether an alternative to the UN and their possible reforms has been created, but rather whether the former are prerequisites for a regional security organisation in Europe. To my mind, overextending NATO would endanger these reforms. Therefore, we must debate OSCE and NATO reforms and we must arrive at some essential decisions. [...]

228. Statement by Federal Chancellor Gerhard Schröder, 1 May 1999

Public attention is currently focused on the situation in Kosovo more strongly than on any other topic. No other issue moves people in our country more at the present time than the situation in the Balkans. Together with our partners in NATO we Germans have assumed responsibility to enforce peace, democracy, and human rights in Kosovo. Together with our partners we want to stop the murdering and the expulsions in Kosovo. We want a political solution for a peaceful and democratic Kosovo.

The German government has undertaken every conceivable diplomatic and political initiative in an attempt to achieve this. At the informal summit held in Brussels the EU heads of state and government adopted its proposals and they were made part of the decisions taken at NATO summit in Washington. The German proposal to create a stability pact for the Balkan countries received broad support.

The demands of the international community for resolving the Kosovo conflict are on the table: the withdrawal of Serb military and police forces as well as special units, and the return of the refugees to their homes under the protection of an international peace-keeping force.

6.4 GREECE

229. Greece and the New Millennium: Signposts to a Point of Departure, Speech by the Greek Prime Minister Costas Simitis, Woodrow Wilson School, United States, April 1999

[Parts not referring to the Kosovo crisis have been omitted].
[...]

Strengthening the International Role of Greece
[...]
We work for the rapprochement of the Balkan states with the European Union and we contribute decisively to inter-Balkan co-operation at a multilateral and a bilateral level. We undertake peace and mediation initiatives in the existing crises and we promote investment and economic co-operation projects. Within this context, one of our top priorities is the improvement of our relations with the Former Yugoslav Republic of Macedonia and the constant support of the democratisation process in Albania.

It is in this light that we see our role in the current crisis in Kosovo. In front of our eyes is unfolding a humanitarian tragedy of proportions unseen in Europe since the Second World War. All civilised nations have a duty to help solve the crisis and relieve the plight of the refugees.

As members of NATO we have actively co-operated with our allies on this issue. We have however stated from the beginning that we will not participate in military operations. We are neighbours with Yugoslavia and we would like a political solution. Yugoslavia should give

---
[1] *Unofficial translation by the editor.*

the people of Kosovo a wide measure of autonomy, respect their human rights and seek a peaceful solution to the problem. We have unequivocally condemned the practice of "ethnic cleansing" that Serbia has pursued. One of the tragic results of the crisis is the creation of a large refugee problem. The Greek government has undertaken in this respect a number of initiatives both within NATO and with its European Union partners in order to provide humanitarian relief and help find a political solution. It is of paramount importance to ensure that the refugees remain close to their country of origin.

We believe that the continuing use of force cannot lead to a permanent solution to the Kosovo problem. We have urged our NATO allies to explore the possibilities for a new peace initiative and dialogue between the parties involved. We seek a political solution, we demand that human rights are respected and our goal is the restoration of stability in the region. [...]

230. Press Release by Ministry of Foreign Affairs, Athens, 26 March 1999

Strikes against the Federal Republic of Yugoslavia must stop immediately, Greek Alternate Foreign Minister Yiannos Kranidiotis said last night, adding that otherwise there was a danger of increasing tension and the spreading of the crisis. He furthermore underlined the need for a resumption of diplomatic efforts for the search of a political solution, noting that Greece was in contact with neighbouring countries and its European Union partners stressing this need.

Mr. Kranidiotis announced that Greece intends to raise the issue of the economic consequences of the crisis and the need to seek ways of tackling them at the next EU Council of General Affairs, adding that the European Union should examine the idea of convening an international conference on the economic development of the Balkans. He also said that instructions have been given to Greece's permanent NATO representative, ambassador G. Savaidis, to express Greece's reservations when the issue of NATO's operations passing into the "third phase" is raised.

The "second phase" of the alliance's operations is currently underway and for which the consensus of member-states has been secured with a previous decision. The "third phase" anticipates mass bombings of military targets throughout the entire territory of Yugoslavia. On the question of the "fourth phase", concerning the sending of ground forces, Mr. Kranidiotis said that Greece "is extremely reserved to the point of being negative."

Mr. Kranidiotis had a meeting lasting for about an hour with the Russian Ambassador to Athens Mikhail Bocharnikov in the afternoon with whom he exchanged views on the crisis in Kosovo.

Today, he will be having successive meetings with the ambassadors of Romania, Albania and the Former Yugoslav Republic of Macedonia. US Ambassador to Athens Nicholas Burns has also requested a meeting with M. Kranidiotis. [...]

231. Press Release by Ministry of Foreign Affairs, Athens, 29 March 1999

Greece yesterday relayed to the the U.S. ambassador in Athens its view that there could be no military solution to the Kosovo crisis adding that talks should resume for the finding of a political solution. Foreign Minister George Papandreou and Alternate Foreign Minister Yiannos Kranidiotis held separate meetings yesterday with US Ambassador Nicholas Burns and exchanged views on the Yugoslav crisis. Mr. Papandreou and Mr. Burns held lengthy talks in the afternoon at the latter's request, while diplomatic sources disclosed that the US envoy underlined to the Greek foreign minister the US point of view that NATO should appear and act united regarding the Alliance's strikes against Yugoslavia with the aim of convincing President Slobodan Milosevic to accept the proposed agreement on the strife-torn province of Kosovo. The same sources stated that Mr. Papandreou reiterated to Mr. Burns the Greek government's stance that whatever military solution will create more problems than solve. The diplomatic sources added that Mr. Burns requested from the Greek side to keep its reactions low key, regarding US President Bill Clinton's statements that Greece and Turkey could be drawn into the Kosovo conflict if it worsened, while he reiterated that those statements were misinterpreted. Mr. Kranidiotis, who met earlier in the day with Ambassador Burns, expressed the Greek government's wish to see an end to NATO strikes against Yugoslavia and give diplomacy a new chance. Diplomatic sources said Greece was even considering using its veto if the offensive continued up to the third phase. Greece's permanent representative to NATO has been instructed to keep a close watch on developments. Mr. Burns, who requested the meeting with Mr. Kranidiotis, reiterated the U.S. position that NATO's objective was to convince Yugoslav leader Slobodan Milosevic to concede. He also discussed the issue of coordination between the US and Greece in providing humanitarian assistance for any refugees. According to diplomatic sources, Mr. Burns told the Greek minister that President Clinton's remarks about Greece and Turkey had been misinterpreted. "Mr. Burns told Mr. Kranidiotis that President Clinton did not mean that there could be a war. He meant that the continuation of the Kosovo crisis could intensify and take on wider dimensions in the region but not with the meaning that there would be a military clash between Greece and Turkey," the sources said. Mr. Kranidiotis, however, pointed out that such statements created a climate of insecurity.

6.5 HUNGARY

232. Statement by the Spokesman of the Ministry of Foreign Affairs, Budapest, 24 March 1999

The Ministry of Foreign Affairs deeply regrets that, as a result of the refusal of the Yugoslav leadership, the comprehensive and resolute efforts of the international community aimed at finding a peaceful solution to the Kosovo crisis had failed. NATO air strikes, announced earlier and aimed at forcing a peaceful settlement were subsequently launched on Wednesday evening.

The objective of military action is to force a peaceful solution, to halt the recently renewed Yugoslav military offensive in Kosovo and to prevent further bloodshed, further destabilization in the region and the aggravation of the refugee situation already affecting almost one fourth of the population of Kosovo, that is nearly half a million people.

All responsible states and organizations of the international community had hoped for a peaceful settlement up to the very last moment, and that the Yugoslav leadership would abide by its commitments of October 1998, that is, observance of the cease-fire in Kosovo and the withdrawal of its forces stationed there. The Yugoslav Government did not so.

The draft agreement of the Contact Group outlined a compromise solution for the two parties concerned. The very last diplomatic mediation effort also failed, so the document - signed by the Kosovo Albanians - was not approved by the Yugoslav government. The whole world was aware that missing the chance of political settlement could lead to enforcement by military means, the responsibility for the consequences of which lies with the party refusing to sign the agreement.

In the view of the Ministry of Foreign Affairs the Yugoslav government still has the possibility to meet the demands of the international community, and return to the political solution and give up violence in

Kosovo. Hungary fully shares the objectives of NATO's action and continues to support a lasting settlement through peaceful means.

The Ministry of Foreign Affairs expresses its hope that with due wisdom and foresight the Yugoslav side will realize the indispensable need for a peaceful solution and that the return to a negotiated settlement constitutes the only way out of the current situation.

The Ministry of Foreign Affairs hopes that Belgrade will keep the Kosovo conflict away from the Hungarian border and ethnic Hungarians living in Voivodina.

233. Statement by the Ministry of Foreign Affairs, Budapest, 27 March 1999

Hungary sincerely hopes that, as a result of NATO's firm action, the leadership of the Federal Republic of Yugoslavia will realize without any further delay that the Kosovo crisis can exclusively be solved by returning to the framework elaborated during the negotiations aimed at resolving the crisis.

Hungary deems it unacceptable and condemns the recent atrocities deliberately committed against civilians in Kosovo by the Yugoslav armed forces. Those responsible will have to account for these crimes before the International War Crimes Tribunal set up by the UN Security Council to investigate war crimes in May 1993. Hungary shares NATO's demands that Yugoslav leaders must fully comply with their commitments of October 1998, primarily the observance of cease-fire in Kosovo, and that they must immediately halt their renewed military operations in Kosovo. Unjustified violence against innocent civilians strengthens NATO's resolve to enforce the return to negotiations with as little delay as possible with utmost determination.

The key to settle the Kosovo crisis and to ensure the security and prosperity of the Yugoslav people is exclusively held by the leaders of Yugoslavia.

Hungary believes that the Yugoslav leadership, being aware of the above, will return to a peaceful settlement of the conflict without delay.

Hungary sincerely wishes that, after a negotiated settlement of the Kosovo crisis, relations can be renewed between Hungary and a Yugoslavia which, respecting democracy and human rights, and living in prosperity and in peace with its ethnic minorities, will take its place again in the international community.

6.6 THE NETHERLANDS

234. Statement by the Minister of Foreign Affairs in the Lower House, The Hague, 24 March 1999

As I speak, NATO is due to begin air strikes against military targets in the Federal Republic of Yugoslavia.

It is with the greatest sorrow and disappointment that the Netherlands Government is forced to note that President Milosevic is not prepared to choose the path of peace, a path which is wide open to him. And it will remain open.

The decision to employ military force is one of the most difficult that a politician can face. But in the Government's view, the terrible, unceasing human tragedy in Kosovo leaves us no other choice.

Despite the pain caused by such a decision, I say to you that the intolerable humanitarian disaster unfolding before our eyes strengthens us in our conviction that this is nevertheless the right decision. We did not arrive at this view easily, but we are fully convinced that it is justified.

Over a quarter of a million Kosovars have fled the indiscriminate violence inflicted by Yugoslav troops. The victims are innocent civilians. This situation cannot be allowed to continue. The international community has done everything in its power to make a peaceful solution possible.

The negotiators from the United States, the Russian Federation and the EU have made every possible effort to prevent a humanitarian catastrophe occurring on European soil on the threshold of the 21st century.

These military operations have a political aim: to halt Serb aggression and to compel the Yugoslav government to return to the negotiating table.

235. Speech by Dick Benschop, Released by the Ministry of Foreign Affairs, State Secretary for Foreign Affairs, College of Europe - Natolin, Warsaw, 12 May 1999

[Parts not referring to the situation in Kosovo have been omitted.]
[...]

Kosovo

Images of war are haunting Europe again. Hundreds of thousands of Kosovars have been forced from their homes at gunpoint. Many are trapped inside Kosovo, while countless other refugees have fled to neighbouring countries. Other countries, including Poland and the Netherlands, are also providing shelter for some of these victims of ethnic cleansing.

The use of military force is always the last resort. It is with the greatest of reluctance that the 19 members of NATO decided to start using military means. But there was truly no alternative. We had tried all diplomatic means, at the Rambouillet and Paris conferences. If we had simply shrugged our shoulders and done nothing, we would have been blamed - and justly so - for displaying cynical indifference to the burning villages of Kosovo. Furthermore, it would have been said that the Alliance had outgrown its relevance to security and stability in Europe.

Now, in the midst of this full-scale military campaign, I welcome the support given by the three new member states - and in particular Poland - for the NATO actions that are being carried out as we speak. My country, the Netherlands, is fully involved in the NATO operation, with 20 F-16 fighter jets and other military means. Despite all the "smart bombs" and high-tech intelligence, we have all been sharply reminded that human fallibility remains a significant factor. Like our partners in NATO, we deeply regret the accidental bombing of the Chinese embassy. Unfortunate and deplorable as it is, however, it is no reason to turn our backs to what is going in Serbia and Kosovo.

Tyranny is tyranny, whatever you choose to call it. It must be emphasised that this NATO campaign is not an attack on the Serbian nation, Serbian culture or Serbian national identity. It is a fight against the policies of intolerance towards people with a different religion, race or descent. It is a fight against a regime that is putting the future stability of Europe in jeopardy by flouting all notions of democracy and individual liberty and by pursuing dangerous nationalist policies with the consequences that are clear for all to see: rape, beatings, and ethnic cleansing.

We must stand firm now. We are determined to continue until our objectives are met and Milosevic gives in to our perfectly reasonable demands, and agrees:

- ensure a verifiable stop to all military action and the immediate ending of violence and repression in Kosovo;

- withdraw from Kosovo his military, police and para-military forces;

- agree to the stationing in Kosovo of an international military presence;

- agree to the unconditional and safe return of all refugees and displaced persons, and unhindered access to them by humanitarian aid organisations; and

- provide credible assurance of his willingness to work for the establishment of a political framework agreement based on the Rambouillet accords.

The G-8 have now hammered out an agreement which has drawn Russia on board. We need Russia's support - without Russia there is no hope for a true and lasting peace deal in the Balkans. And despite recent setbacks, we will continue to press for a resolution by the UN Security Council, of which the Netherlands is currently a member.

Stability for the Region

These are the anxieties of today. However, this conflict will end some day soon. When the conflict ends, it will not be enough to ensure that the Kosovars can return to their homes and to provide for their immediate needs. Peace will only prevail if all the people in the region feel safe to continue their lives. Piecemeal solutions will not do. What is called for is a comprehensive Stability Pact for the whole region, which we need to develop now.

It must be a broad political and economic strategy that will encompass the whole of the Balkan region. The EU, Russia and the United States, international financial institutions, other organisations such as the Council of Europe, the OSCE, NATO and the UN and others, have started work on developing such a Pact. It must not be a mere bureaucratic exercise involving institutional ties between various organisations. Rather, it should pool the power of all those involved. It would be counter-productive if Western peacemakers were to be as Balkanised as the region we are trying to pacify. The EU and others involved must coordinate their effort to an unprecedented degree. The Netherlands therefore advocates the appointment of a special coordinator. Another important point is that the Pact must not confine itself to the longer term. We should engage now, including rendering macroeconomic assistance under the right conditions. The Netherlands represents several Balkan countries at the IMF and World Bank. We have already pledged substantial macro-economic assistance to some of them. It is also clear that all these countries need the incentive of an eventual place in the European mainstream to uphold standards of democracy, tolerance and human rights. Unless we remain fully committed, there will be little hope for the region.

A stability imposed from outside cannot endure unless it is backed up in other ways. The region has known imposed stability several times. It has never lasted. In its day, the Ottoman empire acted as a kind of vast refrigerator, rendering dormant all the nationalist tendencies of the region. When the cooling mechanism broke down, old hatred and fears revived. After the Second World War, Marshall Tito's dictatorship provided a similar mechanism. He sought to bring 'brotherhood and unity' to his people, but balanced ethnic interests rather than eradicating them. The break-up of Tito's Yugoslavia unleashed mayhem, and the bloodshed is still continuing. We cannot afford to stand back and allow this to happen again. The goal must therefore be to ensure that the old Balkan animosities are finally consigned to the past. We must de-Balkanise the Balkans.

What do I mean by this? Not to do away with the richness of Balkan cultures and nations, on the contrary. But to overcome the old fear, hatred and rivalry that have haunted the Balkans for too long. Our new cooling device, in the form of the proposed Stability Pact, must make a difference. Its aim should not be to enforce servitude to a stabilising system imposed from the outside, but to provide instruction in the habits of freedom, tolerance and an open society. It should teach conflict resolution, democratisation and, eventually, integration. There is no need for current maps to be redrawn. Rather, all efforts should be concentrated on reversing crucial Balkan failings, such as a lack of democracy and unsound economic policies. Democracy and prosperity, you will say, will not necessarily cure all ills. That is true. But societies that embrace the spirit of democracy and openness, the rule of law, independent institutions and human rights are more likely to win the allegiance of their minorities. And if, in the end, they fail to do so, they are more likely to break up peacefully than with bloodshed and tears.

In many parts of the Western Balkan region, democracy will not come by itself. It must be encouraged, sometimes even imposed, before it can start to grow. But at some point it should gather momentum and continue under its own steam. We need to develop a system to ensure that this happens. Clear incentives with clear requirements in relation to each individual state and nation may help here. There is one requirement, however, which the individual countries in the region cannot fulfil on their own - to get on with their neighbours. In the long run, only a regional deal worked out by the regional powers themselves will endure. Stability, prosperity and democracy in the Balkans will never be secured until effective regional cooperation is established.

Without the Kosovo crisis we would have had a decade or more to ponder these matters in detail. The conflict in Kosovo has created a sense of urgency which forces us to deal with them right now. The Balkan countries may be unlikely to join the European Union in the short term, but they must be an integral part of Europe once again, including their political outlook.

Let me emphasise that I strongly believe that ultimately, Serbia too should be part of this process. The question is not whether Kosovo belongs in Serbia, but rather how Serbia can join the future of a new Europe. Peace will only prevail when all the nations and countries of the region feel secure and can taste the fruits of freedom. I can imagine a free, open, democratic Serbia whose pride would be a constructive factor contributing to the welfare of all. Serbia's destiny, if it is to be a bright one, is no different from that of the rest of the region: integrating with Europe. [...]

6.7 UNITED KINGDOM

236. Memorandum Submitted by the Foreign and Commonwealth Office, Kosovo: Legal Authority for Military Action, 22 January 1999[1]

1. This memorandum responds to the Committee's request for information on the specific legal authority upon which military action in Kosovo would be based, following the Foreign Secretary's answer in the House of Commons on 19 January that:

"Preparations continue and they have not ceased, on what might be the appropriate military response if one is required."

2. The legal basis for any military action would need to be considered in the light of the circumstances at the time. A range of possibilities is conceivable in relation to the situation in Kosovo. Any military action by British forces would have to be lawful under international law.

3. Military forces could be sent to the Federal Republic of Yugoslavia, including Kosovo, in support of a political settlement. This would normally be based upon the agreement of the parties and be backed by a resolution of the United Nations Security Council.

---

[1] House of Commons, Session 1998-1999, Foreign Affairs - Minutes of Evidence taken before the Foreign Affairs Committee, HC 188: 26 January 1999.

4. Circumstances may arise in which military action would be based on the right of individual or collective self-defence recognised in Article 51 of the Charter, including the right to rescue nationals when the local authorities are unable or unwilling to do so. Action might also be based on an authorisation given by the Security Council of the United Nations under Chapter VII of the United Nations Charter.

5. There may also be cases of overwhelming humanitarian necessity where, in the light of all the circumstances, a limited use of force is justifiable as the only way to avert a humanitarian catastrophe.

237. Statement by the Prime Minister, Tony Blair, in the House of Commons, Hansard, HC, vol. 328, col. 161, 23 March 1999

Madam Speaker, with your permission I will make a statement on Kosovo.

As I speak, it is still unclear what the outcome of Mr Holbrooke's talks in Belgrade will be, but there is little cause to be optimistic.

On the assumption they produce no change in President Milosevic's position and the repression in Kosovo by Serb forces continues, Britain stands ready with our NATO allies to take military action.

We do so for very clear reasons. We do so primarily to avert what would otherwise be a humanitarian disaster in Kosovo.

Let me give the House an indication of the scale of what is happening: a quarter of a million Kosovars, more than 10 per cent of the population, are now homeless as a result of repression by Serb forces. 65,000 people have been forced from their homes in the last month, and no less than 25,000 in the four days since peace talks broke down. Only yesterday, 5,000 people in the Srbica area were forcibly evicted from their villages.

Much of the Drenica region of northern Kosovo is being cleared of ethnic Albanians. Every single village the UNHCR observers could see in the Glogovac and Srbica region yesterday were on fire. Families are being uprooted and driven from their homes. There are reports of masked irregulars separating out the men: we don't know what has happened to them. The House will recall that at Srebrenica, they were killed.

Since last summer 2000 people have died. Without the international verification force, there is no doubt the numbers would have been vastly higher.

We act also because we know from bitter experience throughout this century, most recently in Bosnia, that instability and civil war in one part of the Balkans inevitably spills over into the whole of it, and affects the rest of Europe too. Let me remind the House. There are now over 1 million refugees from the former Yugoslavia in the EU.

If Kosovo was left to the mercy of Serbian repression, there is not merely a risk but a probability of re-igniting unrest in Albania; Macedonia de-stabilised; almost certain knock-on effects in Bosnia; and further tension between Greece and Turkey.

There are strategic interests for the whole of Europe at stake. We cannot contemplate, on the doorstep of the EU, a disintegration into chaos and disorder.

And thirdly Madam Speaker, we have made a very plain promise to the Kosovar people. Thousands of them returned to their homes as a result of the ceasefire we negotiated last October. We have said to them and to Mr Milosevic we would not tolerate the brutal suppression of the civilian population. After the massacre at Racak, these threats to Milosevic were repeated. To walk away now would not merely destroy NATO's credibility, more importantly it would be a breach of faith with thousands of innocent civilians. whose only desire is to live in peace and who took us at our word.

I say this to the British people. There is a heavy responsibility on a government when putting our forces into battle, to justify such action. I warn: the potential consequences of military action are serious, both for NATO forces and the people in the region. Their suffering cannot be ended overnight. But in my judgement the consequences of not acting are more serious still for human life and for peace in the long term.

We must act: to save thousands of innocent men, women and children from humanitarian catastrophe, from death, barbarism and ethnic cleansing by a brutal dictatorship; to save the stability of the Balkan region, where we know chaos can engulf all of Europe. We have no alternative but to act and act we will, unless Milosevic even now chooses the path of peace.

Let me recap briefly on the last few months.

Last October, NATO threatened to use force to secure Milosevic's agreement to a cease-fire and an end to the repression that was then in hand. This was successful - at least for a while. Diplomatic efforts, backed by NATO's threat, led to the creation of the 1500 strong Kosovo Verification Mission. A NATO extraction force was established in neighbouring Macedonia in case the monitors got into difficulty.

At the same time, Milosevic gave an undertaking to the US envoy Mr Holbrooke that he would withdraw Serb forces so that their numbers returned to the level before February 1998 - roughly 10,000 internal security troops and 12,000 Yugoslav army troops. Milosevic never fulfilled that commitment, indeed the numbers have gone up. We believe there are some 16,000 internal security and 20,000 Yugoslav army troops now in Kosovo, with a further 8,000 army reinforcements poised just over the border.

In January, NATO warned Milosevic that it would respond if he failed to come into compliance with the October agreements: if the repression continued; and if he frustrated the peace process. Milosevic has failed to meet any of these requirements.

Even then, intense diplomatic efforts have been under way. My Rt Hon Friend the Foreign Secretary, and his French colleague Mr Vedrine, have co-chaired the peace talks in France. There is an agreement now on the table.

Autonomy for Kosovo would be guaranteed, with a democratically-elected Assembly, accountable institutions and locally controlled police forces. After three years Kosovo's status would be reviewed.

The rights of all its inhabitants - including Serbs - would be protected, regardless of their ethnic background.

And the awful conflict that has been a blight on the lives of its peoples could come to an end.

The Kosovo Albanians have signed the peace agreement.

The Serbs have not. They have reneged on the commitments they made on the political texts at Rambouillet. And they refuse to allow a peace-keeping force in Kosovo under NATO command to underpin implementation.

It takes two sides to make peace. So far only one side has shown itself willing to make the commitment. It was Milosevic who stripped Kosovo of its autonomy in 1989. It is Milosevic who is now refusing to tackle a political problem by political means.

NATO action would be in the form of air strikes. It will involve many NATO countries. It has the full support of NATO.

It will have as its minimum objective to curb continued Serbian repression in Kosovo in order to avert a humanitarian disaster. It would therefore target the military capability of the Serb dictatorship. To avoid such action, Milosevic must do what he promised to do last October. End the repression; withdraw his troops to barracks; get them down to the levels agreed; and withdraw from Kosovo the tanks, heavy artillery and other weapons he brought into Kosovo early last year.

He must agree to the proposals set out in the Rambouillet Accords, including a NATO led ground force.

Any attack by Serbian forces against NATO personnel engaged in peace-keeping missions elsewhere in the region would be completely unjustified and would be met with a swift and severe response in self-defence. President Milosevic should be in no doubt about our determination to protect our forces and to deal appropriately with any threats to them.

Mr Holbrooke has made the position of the international community crystal clear to Milosevic. There can be no doubt about what is at stake. The choice is now his.

Milosevic can choose peace for the peoples of Kosovo and an end to the Federal Republic of Yugoslavia's isolation in Europe.

Or he can choose continued conflict and the serious consequences that would follow.

I hope the House will join with me in urging President Milosevic to choose the path of peace; and support NATO and the international community in action should he fail to do so.

238. Statement by the Deputy Prime Minister, John Prescott, in the House of Commons, Hansard, HC, vol. 328, col. 383, 24 March 1999

Earlier this evening, four British aircraft, together with missiles from the submarine HMS Splendid, attacked targets in the Federal republic of Yugoslavia as part of a co-ordinated NATO air strike. Two other aircraft flew supporting missions.

Hon. Members may have heard the Prime Minister's remarks from Berlin earlier this evening, when he said 'I want to pay tribute, at the outset, to our forces. We owe a huge debt to them for their courage, and their professionalism. Tonight, there are families in Britain who will be feeling a real sense of anxiety. They can feel too a real sense of pride at the contribution their loved ones make to peace and stability in Europe.'

I am sure that the House will wish to join me in echoing those sentiments. The UK Harriers operated out of Gioia del Colle in Italy. In addition, attacks were mounted by seven United States Air Force B52 bombers from Fairford in Gloucestershire. The strike in which they participated was a very significant one, involving both air-launched and sea-launched cruise missiles and manned aircraft from the United States, the United Kingdom, France, Canada and Spain. A number of other allied air forces flew supporting missions.

The targets being attacked in this first phase were mainly elements of the Yugoslavian air defence system, but also included a number of Serbian military facilities related to the repression in Kosovo.

The NATO military action, which has the full support of all 19 member states, is intended to support the political aims of the international community. It is justified as an exceptional measure to prevent an overwhelming humanitarian catastrophe.

It is, and will continue to be, directed towards disrupting the violent attacks being committed by the Yugoslav army and the Serbian special police force and weakening their ability to continue their repressive strategy.

Two United Nations Security Council resolutions, 1199 and 1203, underpin our actions. Both demanded that the Serbs cease all actions against the civilian population and withdraw the security units used for civilian repression. Milosevic has been in breach of every single part of those UN resolutions. As the Prime Minister said yesterday, a quarter of a million Kosovars, more than 10 per cent. of the population, are now homeless as a result of repression by Serb forces. Sixty five thousand people have been forced from their homes in the past month, and no less than 25,000 in the days since the peace talks broke down. Families are being uprooted and driven from their homes. There are disturbing reports of the destruction of whole villages. Over the past few days, we have all seen harrowing and unforgettable images on the television and in newspapers. The scenes are more reminiscent of the middle ages than of Europe on the eve of the 21st century.

I would remind the House that the decision to initiate air strikes was taken last night only after it became clear that the final diplomatic effort in Belgrade had not with success and that all efforts to achieve a negotiated political solution to the Kosovo crisis had failed. Over the past year the international community, with Britain at the forefront, has made intensive efforts to seek a peaceful solution. Milosevic has either rejected these approaches or entered into undertakings on which he has subsequently reneged, notably his blatant failure to observe the limits on army and special police numbers in Kosovo. Military force is now the only option.

NATO's position is clear, and was set out in statement of 30 January. We seek to bring an end to the violence in order to avert a humanitarian catastrophe and support the completion of negotiations on an interim political settlement. Three demands were made at the time, all of Which Mr Milosevic has so far rejected: he has not ended his use of excessive and disproportionate force in Kosovo; he has broken the undertaking that he gave last October to reduce Serb forces in Kosovo to pre-February 1998 levels; and he has so far refused to accept the interim political settlement that was negotiated at the peace talks in France earlier this year.

Tonight the NATO alliance-19 nations of which 13 flew their aircraft tonight-has backed its words with action. It has hit hard and it will continue to hit hard until its military objectives are achieved.

What happens next is up to Mr Milosevic. It remains open to him to show at any time that he is ready to meet the demands of the international community. The demands are reasonable: they are an autonomous Kosovo within Serbia and an international military force to underpin the settlement. We hope that the Yugoslav people will understand that this is the only practical basis of moving forward without further bloodshed.

I take this opportunity tonight to address a warning to those in the Yugoslav army and other forces who may be in receipt of orders to repress the Albanians in Kosovo: 'Do not assume that you can carry out such activity with impunity. You have a personal responsibility not to exceed the bounds of international law. You run the risk of being prosecuted by the International Criminal Tribunal for the former Yugoslavia at The Hague if you do so.'

I also address the Kosovar Albanians: 'You have had the courage to commit yourselves to the path of peace. It is imperative that you remain committed to that approach and refrain from provocative actions in the days to come.'

Neither NATO nor the United Kingdom is waging war against the people of Yugoslavia. We will make every effort to avoid civilian casualties. Our objective is to reduce the human suffering and violence against the civilian population of Kosovo. We seek to bring to an end the human tragedy now unfolding. We know the risks of action and we salute the bravery of our service men and women who are undertaking these operations on our behalf. To the families of the brave men and women of our armed forces involved in this action- and indeed to the British people as a whole-I say this: we should remind ourselves that history has proved time and time again that standing up to aggression is the only way to stop such brutal leaders.

As my right hon. Friend the Prime Minister said to the house yesterday: 'If Kosovo was left to the mercy of Serbian repression. There is not merely a risk, but the probability of re-igniting unrest in Albania, of a destabilised Macedonia, of almost certain knock-on effects in Bosnia. and of further tension between Greece and Turkey. Strategic interests for the whole of Europe are at stake.' We, as fellow Europeans, cannot contemplate, on our own doorstep, a disintegration into chaos and disorder.

This is indeed a grave moment. Those who have doubted NATO's resolve have been shown to be wrong. We are prepared to see this through. We do not expect that air attacks will lead to an instant end to the brutality in Kosovo-Yugoslavia has a substantial military machine and is under the control of a ruthless man. But our attacks will make it clear to the president and his security forces that if they continue to use excessive force in Kosovo, they will pay a very high price indeed.

239. Briefing by Mr. George Robertson, Secretary of State for Defence, and Gen Sir Charles Guthrie, Chief of the Defence Staff, 25 March 1999

Mr. Roberston: Good morning. Over the past year the international community, with Britain at the forefront, has made intensive efforts to see a peaceful resolution to the crisis in Kosovo. President Milosevic has either rebuffed the approaches or made deals that he has reneged on. The result, as we have all seen, has been a developing humanitarian catastrophe in which Yugoslav and Serb security forces are destroying whole villages and making tens of thousands homeless. Only yesterday, before we had to embark on the air strikes, the Ministry of the Interior Special Police were reported to be razing villages in central Kosovo and the areas around Pojovevo, Serbicia and Kormorani (phon).

The diplomatic track came to an end on Tuesday this week when Ambassador Holbrooke had a final unsuccessful meeting with Milosevic. Throughout this period NATO has been supporting these initiatives because it was only the credible threat of force which led to the agreements last October which Milosevic ultimately failed to observe.

Seven weeks, on 30 January, the North Atlantic Council reaffirmed its readiness to take action and passed to NATO Secretary General Javier Solana the power to order air strikes against targets in Yugoslav territory in order to underpin international efforts to bring about a resolution. On Tuesday of this week, following the failure of two rounds of talks in France, and after a final round of consultations and with great reluctance, he directed Saceur to begin operations. The military objective of these operations is absolutely clear cut, it is to avert an impending humanitarian catastrophe by disrupting the violent attacks currently being carried out by the Yugoslav security forces against the Kosovar Albanians and to limit their ability to conduct such repression in the future. This action is supported by all 18 NATO states, 13 of which had planes and support assets committed to the operation.

Last night the Air Forces of Belgium, Canada, Denmark, France, Germany, Italy, the Netherlands, Norway, Portugal, Spain, Turkey and the United Kingdom and the United States were all involved in the allied military action. We are in no doubt that NATO is acting within international law and our legal justification rests upon the accepted principle that force may be used in extreme circumstances to avert a humanitarian catastrophe. NATO's action has received support inside the UN Security Council from the United States, France, Argentina, Slovenia, Malaysia, Gambia, Bahrain, the Netherlands and Gabon. Outside of Russia and China, only Namibia disagreed with the military action in the Security Council, and in the wider United Nations we know of only opposition from India and understandably Belarus and the former Republic of Yugoslavia itself.

We believe that military action is clearly justified in the circumstances of Kosovo given the undisputed humanitarian emergency and the rejection by Milosevic of all diplomatic efforts. Yesterday the time came for NATO to act in a clear and determined way and if yesterday Milosevic still doubted the Alliance's resolve, he has now in the damage to his military machine the evidence of our determination to take action to avert a human tragedy in Kosovo. But Milosevic should, even at this late stage, think again and should stop the violence in Kosovo, withdraw his troops and sign the peace accord. And let me make it clear that NATO has the will, the determination and the stomach to see this through and to stop the flow of blood and human misery in Kosovo. So let Mr Milosevic understand this, we will be watching how he behaves and British and allied aircraft will resume their attacks later today unless he stops the violence against the Kosovo population.

The decision to use force was not taken lightly. We are well aware of the considerable risks involved and we salute the bravery of our Servicemen and women who are undertaking these operations on our behalf. But we will not stand idly by and watch a tragedy continue to unfold in our own continent, a tragedy which could all too easily lead to a wider conflict.

Last night NATO backed its words with actions, we hit hard and we shall continue to hit hard until our military objectives are achieved. The Chief of the Defence Staff will shortly say more about the United Kingdom's role in last night's operations, but briefly, 6 British Harriers operating out of Gioia del Colle in Italy took part in the attack, as did HMS Splendid with the Cruise missiles, the first ever British Cruise missiles fired in anger. 7 United States Air Force B52 bombers flying from Fairford in Gloucestershire also participated in the mission, as did aircraft from the 11 other allies that I have mentioned. And I am pleased to say that all allied aircraft returned safely.

This first round of strikes concentrated mainly but not exclusively on Yugoslav air defence systems, thus paving the way for attacks on further targets associated with Belgrade's capability for repression in Kosovo. What happens next is up to President Milosevic. It remains open for him to show at any time that he is willing to meet the demands of the international community. These demands are reasonable and they are in his own country's self-interest and we hope that the Yugoslav people will understand that this is the only practical and humanitarian basis for moving forward without further bloodshed.

We don't expect that air attacks will lead to an instant end to the brutality in Kosovo. We know that Yugoslavia has a substantial military machine, but NATO is prepared to see this through until our military objectives have been achieved and our attacks will make it clear to President Milosevic, and to his security forces, that he and they will pay a very high price for the continued use of excessive force in Kosovo.

Ladies and Gentlemen, I understand that NATO will be giving a briefing later on today on the overall pattern of last night's actions. It will clearly be some time before staff in Brussels can assemble a complete picture of the damage caused by our strikes overnight. However, I will now ask General Sir Charles Guthrie, the Chief of the Defence Staff, to speak about some aspects of Britain's role in last night's operations. [...]

240. Statement by the Foreign Secretary, Robin Cook, in the House of Commons, Hansard, HC, vol. 328, col. 526, 25 March 1999

Madam Speaker, last night NATO forces commenced air strikes against military targets within Yugoslavia. The whole House will wish to salute the courage and professionalism of the British and Allied crews who were in action last night, and will also share the relief of their families at the safe return of all Allied planes.

My Right Honourable Friend the Secretary of State for Defence when he replies to the debate will deal more fully with the details of the military operation. I will open this debate by explaining why that action had become necessary, despite our determined efforts to find a diplomatic solution through negotiation.

The decision to commit service personnel to military action can only be taken with the greatest reluctance. There is no one in this Government who did not want to avoid taking this step, if it had been possible to find a way forward by any alternative avenue. It was with regret that we came to the conclusion that there was no longer any alternative.

Every member state within NATO came to the same conclusion. The decision to hand over to the NATO commanders the power to initiate air strikes was a unanimous one.

Last night eight member states had planes participating in the operation. Others supplied essential back-up to the operation. NATO has demonstrated an impressive unity and resolve. Our best prospect of securing our objectives is through maintaining that unity and resolve.

The solid basis for that unity is our common revulsion at the violent repression which we can witness in Kosovo. Since March last year well over 400,000 people in Kosovo have at some point been driven from their homes. That is about a fifth of the total population. In Britain, the equivalent would be over ten million people. We have seen villages shelled, crops burned, and farm animals slaughtered - not for any legitimate military purpose, but as acts of ethnic hatred.

President Milosevic has been given repeated opportunities over that year to demonstrate he was willing to accept any solution that did not require military action.

In June of last year, he was warned to stop the repression against the civilian population. He did. He stuck to his word for six weeks, and then the killing began again in August.

In October he signed up to the Holbrooke Package. He agreed to reduce his troops in Kosovo to the level before the conflict began, to co-operate with OSCE verification monitors, and to halt military action. He has broken every one of those undertakings.

He not only has more army and security police in and around Kosovo than he is permitted under the Holbrooke package. He has double that number. The OSCE at the end of last week was reluctantly forced to withdraw the verification monitors because of concern for their safety. They were not receiving co-operation from the Belgrade forces, but in its place increasing intimidation.

And worst of all the repression in Kosovo has again been resumed. Two months ago at Racak forty-five men, women and children were murdered. They were executed at close range for no other reason than their ethnic identity.

In the past few days another 25,000 more refugees have been forced to flee their homes. We have all seen the television shots of homes burning while women and children flee on foot not knowing where they may find a safe refuge.

I very much regret that the people of Serbia themselves are denied the same opportunity to see the truth about what their government is really doing in Kosovo. This week President Milosevic closed down B92, the last major independent broadcasting station in Belgrade. It is only able to re-broadcast to other outlets in Serbia through an ISDN line supplied and funded by Britain. Journalists from the station who have interviewed me in recent weeks have been arrested, or are hiding in fear of arrest. President Milosevic's repression in Kosovo is paralleled by his suppression of freedom in Serbia.

I understand fully the motivation of those Honourable Members who would have rather seen this conflict resolved through dialogue and negotiation. I myself would have preferred that. But it is President Milosevic who has frustrated every attempt to find a solution through dialogue.

It is also President Milosevic who has prevented us from finding a solution through the United Nations. Three times in the past year we have sponsored resolutions on Kosovo in the Security Council. Resolutions which called on President Milosevic to halt the conflict, to pull back his troops, and to admit the War Crimes Tribunal to investigate atrocities. He has responded to none of these resolutions. It is President Milosevic, not NATO, who is challenging the authority of the United Nations.

No nation has done more to seek a peaceful settlement for Kosovo than Britain. It was Britain that convened and chaired the Heathrow meeting of the Contact Group which sent Dick Holbrooke last October with a mandate to negotiate a cease-fire. It was Britain which then made a leading contribution to the verification mission to police the supposed cease-fire. It was Britain and France that jointly chaired the peace talks at Rambouillet and in Paris.

As a result of those talks there is a detailed peace plan which is fair to both sides. It would provide Kosovo with its own Assembly, President, laws and internal security. It would also provide full protection for the Serb minority within Kosovo, including an elected body to protect and promote their language, religion and curriculum.

We have reached out to both parties to make peace. I am sorry to say that only one party has reached back. The Kosovar Albanians at Rambouillet promised that they would sign the peace accords after consulting with their people. When we met at Paris they kept their word. They signed up to the peace accords in full, including the commitment to demilitarisation by the Kosovo Liberation Army. They were willing to compromise in the interests of peace.

I regret to say that the Serbian delegation made no attempt at Paris to reach agreement. They took an even harder line than at Rambouillet. My colleague Hubert Vedrine and I took the decision last Friday to suspend the talks, because there was no point in prolonging them while the Serb side was not attempting to negotiate in good faith.

Even then, it was not the last chance we gave President Milosevic for dialogue. Dick Holbrooke went again to Belgrade on Monday to find if there was any way even at that eleventh hour to find a solution through dialogue. When I spoke to him on his return from Belgrade, he told me that he had never found President Milosevic more defiant or less interested in serious dialogue. President Milosevic even insisted that there was no fighting by Serb forces in Kosovo.

We have tried repeatedly, right up to the last minute, to find a way to halt the repression of Kosovar Albanians through negotiation. It was not possible, and the person who made it impossible was President Milosevic.

We were left with no other way of preventing the present humanitarian crisis from becoming a catastrophe than by taking military action to limit the capacity of Milosevic's army to repress the Kosovar Albanians. We will continue with this action until we secure that objective. But President Milosevic can halt it at any time by signalling that he is willing to pull back his troops, to honour the cease-fire he signed in October, and to accept in principle the Rambouillet peace plan.

This morning some of the broadcast media have been interviewing many voices from Belgrade complaining about military attacks on Serbia. It would be helpful for balance if they also reflected the views of the Kosovar Albanians, who have long been pleading for NATO intervention to halt their villages being assaulted by armoured tanks and heavy artillery.

I defy any Honourable Member to meet the Kosovo Albanians, to whom I have talked repeatedly over the past three months, and to tell them that we know what is being done to their families. That we see it every night on the television in our own homes. That in the region we have a powerful fleet of Allied planes. And yet although we know what is happening and we have the power to intervene we have chosen not to do so. Not to have acted, when we knew the atrocities that were being committed, would have been to make ourselves complicit in their repression. That is the first reason why Britain has a national interest in the success of this military action. And there are others.

Our confidence in our own peace and security depends on the credibility of NATO. Last October it was NATO that guaranteed the cease-fire that President Milosevic signed. He has comprehensively shattered that cease-fire. What possible credibility would NATO have the next time our security is challenged if we did not honour that guarantee? The consequences of NATO inaction would be far worse than the result of NATO action.

As a result of the expansion of NATO to include Hungary, NATO now has a common border with Serbia. How can we be committed to securing peace and maintaining the stability of our borders while one of our immediate neighbours is conducting a violent military operation?

It would not have produced a peaceful outcome if we had simply turned a blind eye to the bloodshed and conflict over our border. During the past year President Milosevic has suffered from the delusion that he can defeat the KLA by confronting the whole of the Albanian population. The predictable result is that over the past year the strength of the KLA has grown from a few hundred to approaching twenty thousand. President Milosevic has been their best recruiting sergeant. As a result the conflict is now greater and would have continued to get worse if we had not intervened to curb President Milosevic.

At some point it would have spilled over into the neighbouring countries of the region, and then NATO would have been forced to act, but in circumstances more difficult and more dangerous than now.

We have withdrawn all our diplomatic and other government personnel from the Yugoslavia, and for some time we have warned all other British nationals to leave. There are several thousand British service personnel deployed elsewhere in the region - in Bosnia and in Macedonia. I repeat to the House the clear warning given by the Prime Minister, that any action that targets those personnel will be met with a response that will be swift and severe.

Nor should President Milosevic imagine that he can with impunity take revenge on the Kosovar Albanians. Judge Arbour, the Chief Prosecutor of the War Crimes Tribunal, has confirmed that her remit covers Kosovo. If there are any reprisals in Kosovo through atrocities against the civilian population, we will hold personally responsible not just their field commanders, but also the political leaders who instruct them from Belgrade.

Responsibility for the present position of Yugoslavia lies squarely with President Milosevic. It is his brand of ethnic confrontation which has brought a decade of violence and suffering to the peoples of the Former Yugoslavia.

In the early '90s, he was at war first with Slovenia and then Croatia. The massacres at Vukovar and the merciless bombardment of Dubrovnik were representative of a war driven by ethnic hatred.

In the mid '90s, President Milosevic was the prime player in the war in Bosnia which gave our language the hideous phrase 'ethnic cleansing'. Only after three years of fighting in which a quarter of a million people were killed, did NATO find the resolve to use force.

Now we are seeing exactly the same pattern of ethnic violence being replayed again in Kosovo. The same reports have been emerging this week of masked paramilitaries separating the men of the village from the women and children. We now know what happened next at Srebrenica. All the men were massacred. We cannot allow the same tragedy to be repeated again in Kosovo.

That is why our service personnel were ordered to take action. And that is why this House should back our resolve to halt any more ethnic cleansing being imposed by President Milosevic.

241. Statement by the Prime Minister, Tony Blair, London, 10 June 1999

As you will now know, the Serb withdrawal from Kosovo is under way and NATO has suspended its air campaign. Shortly, with the backing of the United Nations, the entry of military forces into Kosovo, led by the British Army, will begin. As soon as possible afterwards, the first refugees will start their journey home.

There was no yearning on the part of NATO to commence this military action. I feel no sense of triumph now, only the knowledge that our cause was just and was rightly upheld.

We tried hard to avoid conflict. For many months of patient negotiation we strove hard for peace. But we had no serious negotiating partner in Milosevic. Instead he began the policy of ethnic cleansing. We are all familiar with this term, but do not let the familiarity with it blind us to its hideousness. What it meant in reality for hundreds of thousands of innocent people in Kosovo was systematic murder and rape, brutality and barbarism on a scale our continent of Europe thought we had seen the last of in the dark days of World War Two.

We were faced with the moral choice: to let this barbarism happen or to stop it. We chose the right course. In doing so, we knew we could not prevent death and destruction for many people. But Milosevic now knows, and the world now knows, that we will not let racial genocide go on without challenge. We will not see the values of civilisation sacrificed without raising the hand of justice in their defence.

Nothing we say or do now can compensate for the loss of loved ones killed in this conflict. But I believe we can say that they did not die in vain. War is never civilised. The innocent die as well as the guilty. But war can be necessary sometimes to uphold civilisation. And this one was. This war was not fought for Albanians against Serbs. It was not fought for territory. Still less for NATO aggrandisement. It was fought for a fundamental principle necessary for humanity's progress: that every human being, regardless of race, religion or birth, has the inalienable right to live free from persecution.

Milosevic has now given his word that he will withdraw his forces. He has started this withdrawal. But the Balkans is littered with his broken promises. He should have no doubt that NATO will remain vigilant to ensure that this time he complies and does what he says he will do.

I would like to pay tribute to those who have worked with us in this campaign. I want to pay tribute first and foremost, of course, to the courage and professionalism of our own Armed Forces. It is because of them that we have managed to defeat the evil of ethnic cleansing and that the hundreds of thousands of refugees forced to flee their own country can start planning to return home.

It is a testament to their skills that not one British serviceman or woman lost their lives in the NATO action.

But this should not lead anyone to believe that this was a risk-free operation; it was not, nor will it be in the future. There are real dangers ahead. We cannot guarantee there will be no loss of life.

They will enter a land, for instance, where hundreds of thousands of landmines have been scattered indiscriminately. They may face resistance from Serbs angry at their defeat. But I have every confidence in their ability - and that of our allies in this operation - to finish the task in front of them. I believe our forces face these dangers with the country united behind them.

I want to thank our allies in the NATO alliance. Many commentators suggested that this alliance of 19 democracies could not hold together. Indeed Milosevic was banking on this from day one. Today, on day 79, he knows he got that wrong too.

A great deal of the credit for this must go to Javier Solana for his crucial role in coordinating the NATO operation, to the superb and tireless job done by General Wesley Clark as Supreme Allied Commander Europe and his deputy, General Rupert Smith, and by General Mike Jackson in ensuring the detail of the Serb withdrawal and in insuring our forces are ready to replace them in Kosovo. We should give thanks also to President Ahtisaari and to Viktor Chernomyrdin for the role they played.

I want, as British Prime Minister, to thank Robin Cook who worked so brilliantly to build and maintain the international consensus against Milosevic; to George Robertson for his magnificent leadership; and to Clare Short for her strength and intelligence in coordinating Britain's vital contribution to the humanitarian effort.

And I also want us in Europe to say special thanks to the President of the United States of America, Bill Clinton, and to the American people. I have just spoken to Bill Clinton to thank him in person. As ever he gave leadership and vision when it was needed most, steadfast in his support of what was right and, as ever, the American people showed their foresight and imagination in knowing that though this evil of ethnic cleansing was happening far from their shores, they had a duty to help defeat it.

I want to take the opportunity also to send a message to the people of Serbia. Our quarrel was never with you but with the regime that has lied to you about the causes of this conflict, the reasons for NATO's military action, the deliberate killing and ethnic cleansing of hundreds of thousands of your fellow citizens, a regime that, even today, continues to lie to you about their defeat.

Our quarrel is with Milosevic and with the brutal dictatorship which rules you.

Today in Germany, very important discussions are taking place between the Foreign Ministers of the G8 countries, European Union member states, Turkey, the Eastern European democracies and, most important of all, the front-line Balkan states which have suffered so much from Milosevic's destabilisation of their region.

We have pledged to help them rebuild their economies and we will. It will require real commitment and generosity. But it is more than an act of charity. We know that it is essential for the future of all of us who inhabit our shared continent that we work together to build long-term peace and prosperity across Europe.

But until Serbia embraces democracy, until Serbia has a Government which wants to live in peace with its neighbours, Serbia cannot be part of that modern Europe. You cannot expect democracies to prop up dictatorships. We want a modern, democratic Serbia to be part of a modern, democratic Europe. But the choice rests with Serbia.

We intend to start building that new Europe in Kosovo as soon as the first members of KFOR arrive there.

We have made a pledge to the refugees that they will go home to live in peace and security alongside their Serbian neighbours. We intend to deliver that pledge and we want a Kosovo where all people, whether Albanian or Serb, have the same rights and do live together in peace.

As well as helping the Kosovar people rebuild their shattered lives and communities, our forces will gather evidence of war crimes so that those responsible are brought to justice.

We began this campaign with reluctance but with resolve. We end it with no sense of rejoicing.

We cannot rest until the refugees are home. Then, truly, we will be able to say that good has triumphed over evil, justice has overcome barbarism, and the values of civilization have prevailed.

6.8 UNITED STATES OF AMERICA

242. Secretary of State Albright, Remarks on Kosovo as Released by the Office of the Spokesman, Department of State, Washington, D.C., 27 October 1998

Secretary Albright: Good afternoon. I want to speak for a few minutes about Kosovo and what we in NATO have decided today.

Two weeks ago, NATO took the historic step of authorizing the NATO commander to launch air strikes for only the second time in its fifty year history. The Alliance insisted that President Milosevic comply with the repeated political, humanitarian and military demands of the UN Security Council with respect to the treatment of the people of Kosovo. The Alliance made clear that continued failure to comply would result in the use of force. Today the Alliance was able to report that President Milosevic is in very substantial compliance with Security Council Resolution 1199, and that this compliance is sufficient to justify not launching air strikes at this time.

This is an important and welcome development. It would not have happened if we had not combined diplomacy with the threat by NATO to use force. The key now is to ensure that Belgrade sustains compliance and for the parties to make progress towards a political settlement. To these ends, we will continue to pursue diplomacy combined with a credible threat of force.

Let me repeat - NATO's threat to use force if necessary remains.

Over the past two weeks, as a result of NATO's resolve, there have been tangible changes in Serb behavior and in the situation on the ground in Kosovo. Army units brought into Kosovo from outside have been withdrawn. Kosovo-based units are moving back to their garrisons and progress is being made toward placing heavy weapons in storage.

Equally important, we are seeing the withdrawal of thousands of police reinforcements from outside Kosovo and the return of other units to garrisons. Yesterday, the Kosovo Diplomatic Observer Mission witnessed the withdrawal of more than 4,000 Serbian special police, the units responsible for the lion's share of violence.

In addition to the numbers, we have a commitment from Milosevic - that will have to be tested - that remaining units will not engage in the aggressive behavior that has caused so much repression and terror.

Relief agencies are now able to operate without major impediments. Food, blankets and medical kits are being delivered. Although more remains to be done, progress has been made in providing shelter. Thousands of Kosovar Albanians who had been displaced by the violence have already left the mountains to return to their villages and begin rebuilding their lives.

These developments should result in a safer and more secure climate in which those still displaced may also return home. The result, if all goes well, will be the prevention of further humanitarian catastrophe.

It is vital to understand that even if the humanitarian crisis is averted, the political crisis remains. This crisis can only be resolved at the bargaining table. This is a vital point, for not even NATO military force can resolve the tensions, rivalries and disagreements that are at the heart of the problems of Kosovo.

Politically, the Serbs and Kosovar Albanians have resumed a dialogue with the goal of an interim agreement that would give Kosovars democratic self-government, including their own police, and elections supervised by the international community. To support those negotiations, we have also delivered a clear message to the leadership of the Kosovo Liberation Army: there should be no attempt to take military advantage of the Serb pull-back. Neither side can achieve a military victory in Kosovo.

This message is starting to have an effect. In recent days, we've seen a new degree of restraint on the part of the Kosovo Liberation Army, which has been willing to negotiate the disengagement of forces in several key areas. Future progress will be enhanced if Kosovars have confidence that the international community is engaged and determined to prevent a return to repression and terror.

The Kosovo Diplomatic Observer Mission is in the field reporting to ensure that Milosevic is complying with our demands not only on paper, but also on the ground. NATO already has begun air verification missions. Their efforts will soon be augmented by the OSCE's new Kosovo Verification Mission, led by US Ambassador Bill Walker.

I'm not here to tell you today that in Kosovo all is well; it is not. We have made considerable progress over the past ten days, but have to do far more than look at this week's snapshot of events. We must consider Milosevic's track record, his long-standing unwillingness to negotiate seriously and the accumulated barbarity of the past months. Time and again, Milosevic has taken half-steps to avoid the consequences of his actions. We are not interested in further promises, only continued compliance. We assume that Milosevic will act responsibly only when all the other alternatives have been exhausted.

That's why we are maintaining the threat of force and not letting down our guard. That's why today at NATO, we have decided on an integrated package of steps to ensure Milosevic's complete and verifiable compliance with our demands.

This regime will include the following elements:

First, NATO will soon activate the full air verification regime to ensure Serb compliance with the military provisions of the agreement.

Second, I've been working with my NATO counterparts to accelerate planning for a reaction force with forward elements in the Former Yugoslav Republic of Macedonia if the government of Skopje agrees. Its purpose will be to ensure that Alliance forces are on call to respond if needed.

Third, the authority for NATO to launch air strikes remains in place.

And fourth, NATO forces remain prepared to act promptly if and when that is necessary.

Milosevic should be under no illusions. NATO will be overhead and next door. The OSCE will have an intrusive presence on the ground. NATO will remain willing and able to act. NATO military authorities will provide regular assessments for the NATO Council on Milosevic's track record on compliance. These assessments will be developed with inputs from the Kosovo Verification Mission.

We are at a key decision point in the history of the Balkans, as well as of NATO. As events over the past two weeks reflect, we have started to move down the right path for both. For the moment, a humanitarian catastrophe has been averted. But the crisis will remain until there is a political solution that ensures respect for the rights of all the people of Kosovo. We must and we will do all we can to see that the progress continues.

Question: Madame Secretary, even with those new mechanisms, mindful of how many meetings had to be held, how many allies had to be consulted, the trips you had to make, the laborious preparations, should - and it's not hypothetical, given his track record - he should renege on this agreement, would it take a long time for NATO to get to the point again of hitting him, of attacking him, should he violate the agreement; or would there have to be meetings of the Contact Group, all sorts of mechanisms to satisfy? Could he be playing for time?

Secretary Albright: Well, frankly, Barry, what I think is that there has been the best of all possible contact and coordination with the NATO allies. I've spent a lot of time with them on the phone - not so much in an effort to persuade, but in an effort to stay in touch.

I think that because it's not easy to assure and assess all these facts, and there's been a lot of stuff going on with General Clark and General Naumann going to Belgrade - so there's been a lot. What I've found whether they're Contact Group meetings or individual conversations, that we do not have a disagreement about the fact that Milosevic needs to comply nor the fact that the threat of the use of force has been useful in terms of getting the kinds of progress that we have had.

So I do not see any delay. What I'd like to do, because I think it's the clearest, is to read to you from the Solana statement on this that explains how that Act Ord remains in effect. Let me just read this.

"Despite these substantial steps, NATO's objective remains to achieve full compliance with Security Council Resolutions 1199 and 1203. As a result, we have decided this evening to maintain the Act Ord for limited air operations. Its execution will be subject to a decision and assessment by the North Atlantic Council. We will also maintain our Act Ord for the phased air campaign, and will continue our activities under Phase 0. We have requested our military authorities to remain prepared to carry out these air operations, should they be necessary, and to maintain forces at appropriate readiness levels for the operations under both Act Ords."

So it would be my sense, Barry, first of all, that they actually had a choice: they could have suspended the Act.Ords; they didn't do that. What they did was keep them in effect and simply use the fact that we would have to stay in contact and that the execution would be subject to a decision and assessments by the NAC. I think given the kinds of exchanges and interchanges we're having on an hourly basis, that we're all pretty much on the same track.

Question: Madame Secretary, can you address what happens now with Ambassador Hill's talks - the political talks that need to start between the Serbs and the Kosovar Albanians?

Secretary Albright: Well, what's going on now, as you know, is that we have submitted a potential document and we have received comments from the parties. He is working to get them together.

I think that what is interesting is that there is increased cohesion in the Kosovars in terms of coming together to join these talks. We're hoping that this is - as I said, that is the issue that now has to be dealt with; because the political crisis aspect of this has not gone away. We are working with the representatives of all various parts of the Albanian community, the Albanian political groups. We are welcoming their participation as they are indicating increasingly their desire to work with us. That's where we are turning our attention to now.

Some of this has been going on already, Betsy, but we're going to rev it up.

Question: Madame Secretary, given the events in Kosovo in the last six months, as well as Milosevic's role in the Bosnia war, would you favor a serious look at prosecuting him for war crimes?

Secretary Albright: Well, I think that the War Crimes Tribunal is in place, and we have said that it has no statute of limitations and it is pursuing its work.

They have allowed some lower-level officials from the War Crimes Tribunal to go in and begin to investigate. I think that what I think it important - and I have always said this - one, that the trail needs to go wherever it needs to go; and basically, there is no statute of limitations.

Question: Madame Secretary, could you tell us more about this reaction force in Macedonia? First, how big would it be? Would American troops take part in it? And would they be prepared to cross borders?

Secretary Albright: Well, first of all, this is one of the things that I've been talking to my counterparts about - especially the French and British. I think that there have not yet been decisions made about its size.

The US would consider assisting, short of the US deployment of ground combat forces. But as to how it would behave and the size of it, I think are the questions that we are dealing with. It is basically there in an attempt to help stabilize the situation and be at work in coordination with the ARG so that it's an over-the-horizon force.

But the details of it have not - I mean, one of the things that has been happening in NATO, and will be over the next few days, is a request for planning as to how that force would work.

Question: And would Congress have to give specific approval?

Secretary Albright: I think that depending upon - well, first of all, we are always seeking support from Congress. We are basically now looking at what it would do. It would respond in emergencies; it would work with the ARG. And as I've said, we would help in any way we can, short of the deployment of ground combat forces. But we are just exploring this.

Question: Madame Secretary, what kind of a violation by Milosevic, in your mind, would trigger military action by NATO at this point, based on today's developments?

Secretary Albright: Well, I think that what we're looking at now is, we've had some fairly good progress in the last hours, which is that as far as the special police were concerned, there were about 10,000 there before February and 4,000 to 5,000 had been brought into Kosovo. Over 4,000 have departed in the past 48 hours; so there has been movement there.

On the military, there had been about 11,000 in pre-February and the units from Serbia have left Kosovo and returned to Serbia. The remaining 10,000 are returning to garrison, except for border units and three companies that are allowed along lines of communication.

So I think - we're saying very substantial were the words I used in terms of compliance. I think that what we're going to be assessing is if there is a reversal of this movement, the level of it, the speed of it; and more importantly, we would like to see more happen here. So I can't give you specifics, but I think we will know if there is not compliance, which is why we have the KDOM in there and why we have air verification. By the way, I think that Milosevic has, as a result of his actions here, managed to earn himself verification in the air, verification on the ground and forces next door. So we are able to keep track very closely of what he is doing and making sure he will comply.

But there is no one specific instant that I can identify for you. We will know if he is not complying.

Question: Madame Secretary, do you get any sense that President Milosevic has at all come to accept any of the long-term goals set for him by the international community for Kosovo; or is he acting, do you think, purely to escape military action?

Secretary Albright: First of all, it's hard to read his mind. But I do think that it must be evident to him that in the course of the last years, first of all, that he has been isolated from the international community by the outer wall. That can only be removed if there is democratization, if he cooperates with the War Crimes Tribunal and if he can deal with the situation in Kosovo in a way that allows the Kosovars to have some self-government. So he is isolated in that way.

For a leader who kept talking about a greater Serbia, that dream is certainly not coming true. Actually, he started out with Yugoslavia. He doesn't have Croatia, Slovenia, Bosnia-Herzegovina; and Montenegro, within the FRY, is acting more and more independently. Now what has happened, which I think is so important, is that Kosovo - which he kind of saw as his backyard or his own preserve - has now become - the problem has become internationalized. Something that he never allowed before, which was international observers on the ground, he has now said up to 2,000 of this new force under the OSCE will be there to verify.

So I would think that he would begin to get the message that his actions are unacceptable to the international community, and that there is a way for him to reverse course and stop being in denial about what has gone on as far as he is concerned.

I do think, though, again, that it was as a result of the NATO threat of the use of force and the diplomacy that has made him take a very careful look at what is going on. Today's action, which leaves the Act Ord in place and yet recognizes the fact that he has made some movement, I think is exactly the right calibration of what ought to be going on - which is not to remove the threat of the use of force, recognize that something has happened, be very vigilant and understand that we have dealt with a humanitarian catastrophe at this stage but not with the political crisis inside it.

Thank you.

243. President Clinton, Address to the Nation, Washington, D.C., 24 March 1999

My fellow Americans, today our Armed Forces joined our NATO allies in air strikes against Serbian forces responsible for the brutality in Kosovo. We have acted with resolve for several reasons. We act to protect thousands of innocent people in Kosovo from a mounting military offensive. We act to prevent a wider war; to diffuse a powder keg at the heart of Europe that has exploded twice before in this century with catastrophic results. And we act to stand united with our allies for peace. By acting now we are upholding our values, protecting our interests and advancing the cause of peace. Tonight I want to speak to you about the tragedy in Kosovo and why it matters to America that we work with our allies to end it. First, let me explain what it is we are responding to. Kosovo is a province of Serbia, in the middle of southeastern Europe, about 160 miles east of Italy. That's less than the distance between Washington and New York, and only about 70 miles north of Greece. Its people are mostly ethnic Albanian and mostly Muslim. In 1989, Serbia's leader, Slobadan Milosevic, the same leader who started the wars in Bosnia and Croatia, and moved against Slovenia in the last decade, stripped Kosovo of the constitutional autonomy its people enjoyed; thus denying them their right to speak their language, run their schools, shape their daily lives. For years, Kosovars struggled peacefully to get their rights back. When President Milosevic sent his troops and police to crush them, the struggle grew violent. Last fall our diplomacy, backed by the threat of force from our NATO Alliance, stopped the fighting for a while, and rescued tens of thousands of people from freezing and starvation in the hills wherethey had fled to save their lives. And last month, with out allies and Russia, we proposed a peace agreement to end the fighting for good. The Kosovar leaders signed that agreement last week. Even though it does not give them all the want, even though their people were still being savaged, they saw that a just peace is better than a long and unwinnable war.

The Serbian leaders, on the other hand, refused even to discuss key elements of the peace agreement. As the Kosovars were saying "yes" to peace, Serbia stationed 40,000 troops in and around Kosovo in preparation for a major offensive - and in clear violation of the commitments they had made.

Now, they've started moving from village to village, shelling civilians and torching their houses. We've seen innocent people taken from their homes, forced to kneel in the dirt and sprayed with bullets; Kosovar men dragged from their families, fathers and sons together, lined up and shot in cold blood. This is not war in the traditional sense. It is an attack by tanks and artillery on a largely defenseless people, whose leaders already have agreed to peace.

Ending this tragedy is a moral imperative. It is also important to America's national interest. Take a look at this map. Kosovo is a small place, but it sits on a major fault line between Europe, Asia and the Middle East, at the meeting place of Islam and both the Western and Orthodox branches of Christianity. To the south are our allies, Greece and Turkey; to the north, our new democratic allies in Central Europe. And all around Kosovo there are other small countries, struggling with their own economic and political challenges - countries that could be overwhelmed by a large, new wave of refugees from Kosovo. All the ingredients for a major war are there: ancient grievances, struggling democracies, and in the center of it all a dictator in Serbia who has done nothing since the Cold War ended but start new wars and pour gasoline on the flames of ethnic and religious division.

Sarajevo, the capital of neighboring Bosnia, is where World War I began. World War II and the Holocaust engulfed this region. In both wars Europe was slow to recognize the dangers, and the United States waited even longer to enter the conflicts. Just imagine if leaders back then had acted wisely and early enough, how many lives could have been saved, how many Americans would not have had to die.

We learned some of the same lessons in Bosnia just a few years ago. The world did not act early enough to stop that war, either. And let's not forget what happened - innocent people herded into concentration camps, children gunned down by snipers on their way to school, soccer fields and parks turned into cemeteries; a quarter of a million people killed, not because of anything they have done, but because of who they were. Two million Bosnians became refugees. This was genocide in the heart of Europe - not in 1945, but in 1995. Not in some grainy newsreel from our parents' and grandparents' time, but in our own time, testing our humanity and our resolve.

At the time, many people believed nothing could be done to end the bloodshed in Bosnia. They said, well, that's just the way those people in the Balkans are. But when we and our allies joined with courageous Bosnians to stand up to the aggressors, we helped to end the war. We learned that in the Balkans, inaction in the face of brutality simply invites more brutality. But firmness can stop armies and save lives. We must apply that lesson in Kosovo before what happened in Bosnia happens there, too.

Over the last few months we have done everything we possibly could to solve this problem peacefully. Secretary Albright has worked tirelessly for a negotiated agreement. Mr. Milosevic has refused.

On Sunday I sent Ambassador Dick Holbrooke to Serbia to make clear to him again, on behalf of the United States and our NATO allies, that he must honor his own commitments and stop his repression, or face military action. Again, he refused.

Today, we and our 18 NATO allies agreed to do what we said we would do, what we must do to restore the peace. Our mission is clear: to demonstrate the seriousness of NATO's purpose so that the Serbian leaders understand the imperative of reversing course. To deter an even bloodier offensive against innocent civilians in Kosovo and, if necessary, to seriously damage the Serbian military's capacity to harm the people of Kosovo. In short, if President Milosevic will not make peace, we will limit his ability to make war.

Now, I want to be clear with you, there are risks in this military action - risks to our pilots and the people on the ground. Serbia's air defenses are strong. It could decide to intensify its assault on Kosovo, or to seek to harm us or our allies elsewhere. If it does, we will deliver a forceful response.

Hopefully, Mr. Milosevic will realize his present course is self-destructive and unsustainable. If he decides to accept the peace agreement and demilitarize Kosovo, NATO has agreed to help to implement it with a peace-keeping force. If NATO is invited to do so, our troops should take part in that mission to keep the peace. But I do not intend to put our troops in Kosovo to fight a war.

Do our interests in Kosovo justify the dangers to our Armed Forces? I've thought long and hard about that question. I am convinced that the dangers of acting are far outweighed by the dangers of not acting - dangers to defenseless people and to our national interests. If we and our allies were to allow this war to continue with no response, President Milosevic would read our hesitation as a license to kill. There would be many more massacres, tens of thousands more refugees, more victims crying out for revenge.

Right now our firmness is the only hope the people of Kosovo have to be able to live in their own country without having to fear for their own lives. Remember: We asked them to accept peace, and they did. We asked them to promise to lay down their arms, and they agreed. We pledged that we, the United States and the other 18 nations of NATO, would stick by them if they did the right thing. We cannot let them down now.

Imagine what would happen if we and our allies instead decided just to look the other way, as these people were massacred on NATO's doorstep. That would discredit NATO, the cornerstone on which our security has rested for 50 years now.

We must also remember that this is a conflict with no natural national boundaries. Let me ask you to look again at a map. The red dots are towns the Serbs have attacked. The arrows show the movement of refugees - north, east and south. Already, this movement is threatening the young democracy in Macedonia, which has its own Albanian minority and a Turkish minority. Already, Serbian forces have made forays into Albania from which Kosovars have drawn support. Albania is a Greek minority. Let a fire burn here in this area and the flames will spread. Eventually, key U.S. allies could be drawn into a wider conflict, a war we would be forced to confront later - only at far greater risk and greater cost.

I have a responsibility as President to deal with problems such as this before they do permanent harm to our national interests. America has a responsibility to stand with our allies when they are trying to save innocent lives and preserve peace, freedom and stability in Europe. That is what we are doing in Kosovo.

If we've learned anything from the century drawing to a close, it is that if America is going to be prosperous and secure, we need a Europe that is prosperous, secure undivided and free. We need a Europe that is coming together, not falling apart; a Europe that shares our values and shares the burdens of leadership. That is the foundation on which the security of our children will depend.

That is why I have supported the political and economic unification of Europe. That is why we brought Poland, Hungary and the Czech Republic into NATO, and redefined its missions, and reached out to Russia and Ukraine for new partnerships.

Now, what are the challenges to that vision of a peaceful, secure, united, stable Europe? The challenge of strengthening a partnership with a democratic Russia, that, despite our disagreements, is a constructive partner in the work of building peace. The challenge of resolving the tension between Greece and Turkey and building bridges with the Islamic world. And, finally, the challenge of ending instability in the Balkans so that these bitter ethnic problems in Europe are resolved the force of argument, not the force of arms; so that future generations of Americans do not have to cross the Atlantic to fight another terrible war.

It is this challenge that we and our allies are facing in Kosovo. That is why we have acted now - because we care about saving innocent lives; because we have an interest in avoiding an even crueler and costlier war; and because our children need and deserve a peaceful, stable, free Europe.

Our thoughts and prayers tonight must be with the men and women of our Armed Forces who are undertaking this mission for the sake of our values and our children's future. May God bless them and may God bless America.

244. Secretary of State Albright, Press Conference on "Kosovo" as Released by the Office of the Spokesman, Department of State, Washington, D.C., 25 March 1999

Secretary Albright: Good afternoon. In his remarks today and previously, President Clinton has explained why America and our NATO allies made the decision to launch air strikes against the military capacities of the Milosevic regime. NATO Headquarters and the Defense Department are providing more detailed information on the results of last night's operations; but I wanted to take this opportunity to bring you up to date on our diplomatic and humanitarian efforts.

First, we must be clear that there is one reason only that we have moved from diplomacy backed by the threat of force to the use of force backed by diplomacy. That reason is President Milosevic. It is impossible for us to negotiate while he builds up his forces, attacks civilians and torches villages in Kosovo. NATO's actions are intended to further peace and security in Europe and to bring an end to atrocities and a humanitarian crisis.

Now that air strikes have begun, our diplomatic goals are fourfold:

First, ensuring that the necessity for military action is understood around the world;

Second, maintaining the unity of our coalition on planning next steps;

Third, maintaining contact with Russia and making clear that our differences over Kosovo need not disrupt progress on other fronts;

And fourth, remaining in close communication with leaders in the region to address humanitarian concerns, respond to fears, and prevent unpleasant surprises.

We're very pleased with the broad international support NATO actually has achieved. In the past 24 hours, President Clinton has spoken with a great many European leaders. I've been in virtually constant contact with my counterparts in NATO and Contact Group states, as well as the leaders of countries that border Serbia and key members of the UN Security Council. Based on those contacts, I can assure you that the allies are united and supported by many NATO partners behind forceful and sustained NATO action.

As you know, Russia does not agree with our decision to launch military strikes, but Russian leaders deserve credit for the efforts they made to persuade Milosevic to accept the Rambouillet accords. We are and will remain in close touch. Both sides recognize the importance of our relationship and the need to continue to work together on many shared concerns.

Regrettably, Milosevic's forces in Kosovo are today continuing their offensive against civilians, burning and looting and attacking political leaders. Sixty thousand people have been forced to flee their homes in the last five weeks, and that number is increasing daily. We are working with Kosovo's neighbors to help them prepare for a flood of new refugees.

I spoke yesterday with Mrs. Ogata, the UN High Commissioner for Refugees, and assured her that we and our partners are prepared to help in every way possible to care for those who fled for their lives. Here in the Department, Assistant Secretary Julia Taft is leading an interagency group so that we can deal with the humanitarian problems.

These developments are unfortunately exactly what we have come to expect from President Milosevic. They underscore the need for sustained military action to limit the capability of his military to threaten innocent people in Kosovo. I also want to stress that President Milosevic should not attempt to use this crisis to broaden the conflict or spread violence and instability elsewhere in the region. Nor should he attack the democratically-elected government of Montenegro, whose approach to the crisis has been rational and constructive, in stark contrast to that of President Milosevic.

It must be very clear that we will not tolerate attacks on Americans or other foreigners or mistreatment of foreign journalists in Serbia. We hold the authorities in Belgrade responsible for their safety. Finally, let me say again that these strikes are not an end in themselves; rather they are a means we had hoped would not be necessary to an end that is necessary. That goal is peace and stability in Kosovo and throughout the Balkans.

In the days to come, our diplomatic efforts toward that end will continue, and we remind President Milosevic that the accords negotiated at Rambouillet are still on the table. They remain the best hope for a peaceful future in Kosovo and for a return to normalcy for all of the people of the Federal Republic of Yugoslavia.

Thank you.

Question: Madame Secretary, just to be clear about it, please, is there diplomacy going on? You speak of no point of it now unless he's willing to stop some of these things he's been doing. Then you say in the days ahead, we'll try. Is there a channel open; is someone trying - if not the United States - to get, if not negotiations, at least talks going? And are you confident that force can produce the diplomacy, the settlement that you and a lot of the allies seek?

Secretary Albright: Well, first of all, let me say that diplomatic channels remain open. Ambassador Hill is in Skopje, and he made clear upon his departure from Belgrade that he was available if the Serb parties wished to be in contact with him. They know his number; they also know others. So diplomatic channels are open.

I think it is very important to understand that obviously the choice here - President Milosevic can make the choice to have a peaceful settlement. The force that is being used - the objectives of that is in order to deter him from building up this offensive that is going on in Kosovo; and secondly, if he is not deterred, to seriously damage his ability to be able to undertake the horrendous things he has been doing versus the Kosovar people.

I believe that the force that is being used has an important objective, and President Milosevic is the one who can determine whether he is prepared to deal on a peace settlement.

Question: Just a quick follow-up. You now, in the last things you said, you're focusing on one of the two things that the US holds him at fault for - actually what he's doing on the ground. If he relents on the ground - I know you don't want to negotiate with the press in a briefing - but if he should relent on the ground, does that establish a basis for talking to him again, or does he have to signal he accepts the entire package for Kosovo?

Secretary Albright: I think that, first of all, it is essential that he stop what he is doing on the ground. That was one of the points that Ambassador Holbrooke made clear, that he could not continue to have this kind of a build-up and be so threatening.

What we have said is that he needs to, for a peace settlement, embrace the framework of Rambouillet. As I said in my prepared remarks, the accords are on the table.

Question: Madame Secretary, have there been any contacts with the Serbs today? And can you be a little more explicit about how you are trying to get by this problem with the Russians? What kind of conversations have you had? How are you going to bring them back into NATO; have they said that their withdrawal from NATO cooperation is a temporary thing?

Secretary Albright: To the best of my knowledge, Carol, there have been no American Government contacts with Milosevic today. I have actually been talking to Ambassador Chris Hill, who has another problem, which is that the embassy in Skopje has been attacked by an angry mob. Some vehicles were damaged because they entered the compound, but everybody is safe - just as a parenthesis.

On the Russians, let me say, first of all, that we do disagree on the use of force in this event. We did not disagree about the political parts of the Rambouillet document. We have many issues on which we deal in the short, medium and long-term. Both countries, I think - I know, because I've spoken with Prime Minister Ivanov a number of times - are determined to make those immediate short, medium and long-term relationships and objectives - we're determined to continue to working on those. I think we will continue to keep in touch, and I just ask you to note that even now there are some agreements that are being carried out because some of the committees came over as part of the Gore-Primakov Commission; so there have been agreements on health, science and on nuclear issues.

Question: Madame Secretary, you say that the NATO alliance is unified. However, earlier today the Italian Prime Minister made some comments before a meeting of the European Union, in which he said that perhaps the Russian suggestion that the Contact Group should meet is a good one, and that perhaps the time for diplomacy is now. Have you been contacted, or has this Administration had any contact today with the Italian Government? How do you read this? And do you think that perhaps the Contact Group should meet?

Secretary Albright: Well, first of all, let me say that my contacts today - I spoke to Secretary General Solana, and he was well-satisfied with the unity of the allies. They had had a meeting - I don't know whether it was formal or informal - but they had met and he was satisfied. I have not spoken to the Italians today. I will call them.

I think, obviously, as I've said, President Milosevic is the one that can decide if he's ready to talk about peace within the framework of the Rambouillet accords. There will be a time for diplomacy. But I think that this air campaign is going on and it has an objective and it will last as long as necessary.

Question: I'm sorry, just to follow-up - you say that there will be a time for diplomacy, but are you saying that this is not that time right now - that the Contact Group shouldn't meet?

Secretary Albright: There is no indication that there is any change at all in Milosevic's position. As I said to Barry, he knows how to get in touch with us.

Question: Madame Secretary, the media, as you know, is being forced out Serbia pretty much - the Western media, at least - certainly out of Kosovo. Accounts from people on the ground there not in the media sound horrific - refugees being herded into camps, villages being surrounded and shelled, by all accounts looks pretty much like Bosnia and perhaps other places we've seen in Europe this century. The Albanians look to the United States - particularly ethnic Albanians - particularly for protection in this very situation. I'm wondering whether there's anything the United States is prepared to do, NATO is prepared to do other than degrade their air defenses at this point to ease the situation for the thousands of people fleeing there?

Secretary Albright: Well, first of all, I think that your explanation of what is going on is also a good explanation to the American people as to why we have undertaken this action, and very much emphasizes the kinds of points that President Clinton made yesterday about why this was necessary and that we could not stand by and watch this go on.

We are obviously thinking about the front line states. I have been in touch with President Gligorov as well as with the Foreign Minister of Albania. We will stay in very close touch with them. The Secretary General of NATO wrote to the Prime Ministers of Albania, Bulgaria, Romania and Slovenia and to President Gligorov to reiterate NATO's support for the territorial integrity of their countries. In all the letters, Solana emphasized that any Yugoslav threat to the security of these countries would be unacceptable and that the Alliance would view any attack on them with utmost seriousness.

As we have noted previously, there are a number of ways in which Milosevic might respond to the NATO air strikes which are now underway. NATO is formulating detailed plans for reacting to all of these possible scenarios.

We also are, as I mentioned earlier, very much concerned about the outflow of refugees. That is what I talked to Mrs. Ogata about. The US is - I can't now remember the number - upping our assistance, and also talking - it was very convenient - all the Europeans were together yesterday in Berlin. I talked to them sequentially. To each one, I pointed out the importance of assisting economically in some way to deal with the problems that you're talking about.

Question: Madame Secretary, you just used the words today that you want President Milosevic to "embrace the framework of Rambouillet." Should we read that as saying the Rambouillet accords, as signed by the Kosovar Albanians, are negotiable?

Secretary Albright: Are what?

Question: Are negotiable?

Secretary Albright: No, I'm saying that they are on the table and that President Milosevic knows what he has to do. The Kosovar Albanians signed a document. But we had said before that there were technical adjustments. But I'm not going to go into the details of that.

I want to make very clear that the Rambouillet accords are on the table. Milosevic knows what's there. Milutinovic indicated that he favored the political parts of the document. When we were at Rambouillet, he walked that back when they came to Paris, and they have not engaged at all on the implementation parts of it. They have a long way to go, but it's on the table.

Question: Madame Secretary, what do you do if these air strikes continue and Milosevic does not agree to come to the table. Military experts say that these kinds of air strikes without ground troops backing them up rarely are successful. Do you have a plan B?

Secretary Albright: I think that I am very satisfied on the briefings I've had, and I think that the military have laid out a very substantial air campaign. I'm not going to discuss the details of any of that. We believe that it is well planned out, and Milosevic will either have been deterred from undertaking these horrors against the Kosovar people, or his ability to do so will have been seriously damaged, in which case we have helped the ordinary, suffering people of Kosovo to be able to have some respite.

Question: Madame Secretary, in an interview last night you talked about this being an important moment for the 20th Century. I wonder if you could expand on that here. Also, you've talked about how there's concern that this conflict could spread into a wider war. But some historians, who believe we should be involved for humanitarian reasons, don't believe that the area is a powder keg anymore and would spread to a wider conflict. How do you respond to that?

Secretary Albright: Well, first of all, let me say about the moment of the 20th Century. Here we are in 1999, at the end of what historians agree has been the bloodiest century in the history of the world. We know how the blood was created and why it happened. It happened because there were evil dictators or aggressive leaders in countries who felt that their own space was not big enough and that they had to expand it. It took a long time for those with good intentions to understand that without their direct involvement those dictators would be able to not only spread fear among their neighbors, but to systematically murder the people within that they did not like for ethnic reasons.

I believe that as we came out of the era of the Second World War and then the divisions created by the horrors of the Cold War, where Europe was divided and half the people were also not able to live freely, that we have an opportunity now. This is what President Clinton has been talking about - to finally have a Europe that is free and undivided and prosperous. The reason that Americans should care about that is that our own economic prosperity and security is very evidently tied to Europe.

I think that we have an opportunity to learn from the mistakes that our predecessors made, the slowness of responding, of not dealing with wars or problems when they were small and coming in - I am somebody who was liberated by Americans, but I think that if things had been done earlier, not so many lives would have been lost.

I think also, the question that you asked about the Balkans - it has always been a difficult area. World War I started in it; World War II was fought there. All you have to do is look at the map and understand the ethnic composition of these countries. Again, the President, I think, explained very clearly last night the fact that Kosovo itself is made up primarily - 90 percent - of Albanians of Muslim religion, and there are other minorities there. Interestingly enough, the Rambouillet accords protect those minorities and allow them to be able to practice their legitimate rights.

In Albania, there are Greeks; and Macedonia itself is a very complicated country in terms of its ethnic composition - Macedonians and Albanians and a very small Serb minority that has been whipped up today by a Serb political leader. So that ethnic composition is one, I think, that creates difficulties and there have been long-standing rivalries. I think we have an opportunity not to have this spill out beyond control.

Question: Madame Secretary, not only the Italians are calling for a Contact Group meeting, but also the Greeks as early as last night. There are some indications that the French are kind of uneasy with what's going on. Outside of NATO, there are the Chinese and the Russians. You mentioned today - you also mentioned the unrest in Macedonia. Are you concerned at all that the wider conflict that you are seeking to prevent by going in with this bombing may actually occur as a result of it?

Secretary Albright: No, I am not. I think that it is very important for us to carry on this air campaign for as long as it takes to achieve the objectives that I stated earlier, which is to deter Milosevic and to seriously damage his capability. We are in very close touch with the Allies. I will be doing more of that - maybe Jamie [Rubin] can give you a whole list of all the people that I've talked to - but I will continue to do that. NATO is an alliance that operates by consensus and as I've said, I spoke with the Secretary General this morning. It is very clear that the Russians do not agree, and the Chinese do not agree, but they are not in NATO.

Question: Madame Secretary, can you give us a more detailed accounting of what's going on on the ground in Kosovo? Have the Serbs increased their assaults since the air strikes? And are you confident that you really know what's going on on the ground because the international monitors are out?

Secretary Albright: Well, to answer your last question, it's obviously not as clear as it was before. But mainly what we have is a report that there is no lessening of the Serb buildup; not what we had asked for, which was that they needed to get their military back into garrison and to come back into compliance. So there's no evidence of that. There are some reports about torchings and continued harassment of the populations - maybe you can give them a real update - I got a very brief one this morning.

The main thing is that nothing has changed, in that Milosevic - the deter part, I think he has not gotten the message yet.

Question: Madame Secretary, you and others within the Administration have characterized first Bosnia and now Kosovo as a test of the new NATO. Something that makes Kosovo unique is that it is a crisis that unfolds within the borders of a sovereign country. There are also questions about international law. Are these elements that you think make Kosovo a "one off" in the new NATO's mandate? Or in the post-Cold War world are they going to be "one offs," and Kosovo is symptomatic of what NATO will be addressing in the future in these areas?

Secretary Albright: First of all, I think - and it goes to the question I was asked here - we lived in a very different world until the Berlin Wall came down. I think we all know why NATO was founded, and it was founded to deal with a single threat by the Soviet Union and the Warsaw Pact. With the end of both and the fact that NATO, I think, is the most remarkable military alliance of all time and is necessary still, NATO obviously has to change its mission. We have to see what it is that are the major threats that face the NATO countries.

From our estimation, the biggest threat that we have now is the threat of chaos and instability, which comes about as a result - a variety of reasons - but one is ethnic tensions, border disputes, and something that we have said in NATO - the existence of weapons of mass destruction used by terrorists.

I do think that the NATO alliance has great relevancy to the 21st century and the end of the 20th in dealing with what we see now as the major threats. Clearly, Kosovo fits with the fact that here there is an ethnic conflict, which has created huge numbers of displaced people and refugees, an overly large number of massacred people with slit throats. I believe that it is an appropriate thing for NATO to be doing. Milosevic has started a number of wars in the region. It all started with his attacks on Slovenia. We all know his record in Croatia and Bosnia. He has no regard for international borders. I think that his pleading that he is a sovereign country is very much like the child who killed his parents and pleaded that he was an orphan.

Question: Madame Secretary, in your opening statement you mentioned Montenegro. Clearly, you must be very concerned about the threats to Montenegro. Are you concerned enough to offer a security guarantee, either implicit or explicit? And if I could tack on one other little question on this, there seems to be an eclipsing of the Security Council institutionally, NATO has taken over. Instead of referring to the Charter of the United Nations, there are people referring to violations of humanitarian law. Is this because of the disarray and the disunity in the Security Council, or is this part of NATO's new mission?

Secretary Albright: What was the first -

Question: Montenegro.

Secretary Albright: Montenegro. Let me say here we obviously are concerned about Montenegro. We have been in very close touch with Djukanovic. We staunchly support him and other democratic elements. We are concerned about the possibility of civil strife there and we want them to remain calm.

I think that it is very important that the FRY leadership understand that any attempt to either overthrow the democratically-elected government or to create instability would lead to deeper isolation for the Serbs, for the FRY, and escalate the conflict with NATO. So I think that we have made quite clear that they should not get involved there.

Question: A security guarantee, or do you need -

Secretary Albright: Let me just explain on the UN. I think that Secretary General Annan gave a statement yesterday in which he correctly acknowledged that the FRY is responsible for the failure of the international community's efforts to achieve a peaceful settlement. His statement acknowledges that there are times when the use of force is necessary in the pursuit of peace.

The Council has, in fact, been fully involved in issues of Kosovo for over a year, as it has looked at the humanitarian. It's expressed itself several times on the dangers of the situation created by the humanitarian crisis and the dangers that it poses and the threats that it poses to peace and security in the region.

Acting under Chapter 7, the Security Council adopted three resolutions - 1160, 1199 and 1203 - imposing mandatory obligations on the FRY; and these obligations the FRY has flagrantly ignored. So NATO actions are being taken within this framework, and we continue to believe that NATO's actions are justified and necessary to stop the violence.

I think the issue here is one where NATO is operating by consensus and within what we believe are legitimate parameters.

245. President Clinton and Secretary of Defence Cohen, Statement on Kosovo, Released by the White House Office of the Press Secretary, Washington, D.C., 5 April 1999

[...]

Question: Mr. President, do your military share your goals in the operation on Kosovo? We've got there are many, many stories that -

The President: I know that.

Question: - the Pentagon people are not with you.

The President: Let me say, I will answer this question, and then I think we might want Secretary Cohen and General Shelton to answer it, since they're here. And I want to give them a chance to comment.

First, let me say that one of the jobs that the Secretary of Defense and the Chairman of the Joint Chiefs have is to report to me faithfully the view of the Chiefs, the Service Chiefs, the members of the Joint Chiefs of Staff. And they have performed that faithfully, so that when there is a difference of opinion, when there is even a nuance, they have let me know that, as far as I know, in every important matter. Ultimately, after all, I am responsible for all these decisions, and must bear the burden of them, regardless.

Now, in this case, everybody's first choice was diplomacy. Let me remind - let's do a little bit of brief history here. In February of '98, over a year ago, this problem started. We worked on it through diplomacy, and with the threat of NATO force, all the way up until last fall. In October, we finally got an agreement that allowed hundreds of thousands of people to come down out of the hills to avoid starvation and freezing with the pending winter. We all knew - no one was blind to the difficulties of having to carry forward with any kind of military sanctions.

Now, that worked. Then the problems arose again this year. When the talks failed, we had a series of difficult choices. In the end, everybody agreed that of a bunch of bad options, our military campaign was the best available option to show aggressive action, to keep NATO's word, to keep our NATO allies together, and to give us a chance to preserve our objectives.

Secretary Albright made a point - I believe it was yesterday - that I would like to reiterate. We have a lot of tough questions to answer about this operation. And I am quite sure that we cannot answer every one to everyone's satisfaction. But I would far rather be standing here answering these questions with these people talking about this endeavor, than I would to be standing here having you ask me why we are permitting wholesale ethnic slaughter and ethnic cleansing and the creation of hundreds of thousands of refugees and not lifting a finger to do anything about it.

So I recognize that I cannot answer every question to everyone's satisfaction. That is a legitimate question; all the questions are. We are doing the best we can to keep the Alliance together, to be forthright, to be clear and to achieve our objectives. And I believe we will prevail.

Question: Well, are the military with you?

The President: My impression is - and, again, I think I owe it to the Secretary of Defense and General Shelton, to give them a chance to answer, because they're here - that everyone agreed that while there were problems with the air campaign, including the weather, which all of you saw last week, that this was the best available option for us to maximize the possibility of achieving our mission of standing up against ethnic cleansing, fulfilling NATO's commitment, getting the refugees to be able to go back home, live in peace and security and have some autonomy.

So that's what I believe. But I want to - Secretary Cohen? [...]

Secretary Cohen: Let me respond to the question. The President has outlined it exactly right. All of the issues, the military issues were discussed by the Chiefs and amongst the Chiefs, and they looked at the options, knowing that air power had limitations and knowing that there was going to be tough weather, a tough geography and a very robust air defense system.

And so those questions were raised, they were discussed, they were debate within the Armed Services, so to speak, and with the Chiefs in the tank. They came to the conclusion, unanimously that the only option available other than sitting on the sidelines was to pursue the air campaign, given its limitations. There was no doubt or division on that ultimate decision.

That was not only made clear to the President, it was made clear to key members of Congress, as both the Chairman and I briefed House members and Senate members on several occasions, and on each and every occasion, we raised the issues involved in waging a military campaign by air - everyone recognizing its limitations, but ultimately understanding that this country could not sit on the sidelines and watch Slobodan Milosevic slaughter hundreds of thousands of people which he was prepared to do, to drive them into the hills, to starve them, to have them freeze to death - we could simply not maintain any credibility as a moral leader in this world, and certainly not as a leader of the NATO force. So there was no question about the options, and this was the option that they unanimously agreed to.

Question: Mr. Secretary, the President has said again today that he will persist until the objectives are, in fact, achieved. You, yourself, have now said that everyone understood that air power has limitations. If air power has limitations and cannot achieve the objectives, what then? Abandon the objectives?

Secretary Cohen: The President did not say we could not achieve the objective. He laid out three -

Question: - does not have limitations?

Secretary Cohen: He laid out - every military operation has limitations. There is no military operation, including ground forces, which does not have limitations. What the President said at the very beginning was that there are three objectives: number one, that demonstrate resolve on the part of the NATO Alliance. We've done that. Number two, to try and deter Slobodan Milosevic from carrying out his campaign of ethnic cleansing, and failing that, to make him pay a serious substantial price for doing so and to take his military down as best we can through the air power.

Those were the objectives laid out. That is exactly what the Chiefs have signed up to.

Question: Sir, the President said that the Kosovars will be returned to Kosovo under safe and secure conditions - If Milosevic doesn't knuckle under and air power has limitations, how are you going to do it?

246. Secretary of State Albright: Statement before the Senate Foreign Relations Committee, as Released by the Office of the Spokesman, Department of State, Washington, D.C., 20 April 1999

"U.S. and NATO Policy Toward the Crisis in Kosovo"

Good afternoon, Mr. Chairman, and Senators, I am pleased to appear before you concerning U.S. and NATO policy towards the crisis in Kosovo.

My intention is to lay out concisely America's stake in the outcome of this crisis; the events that brought us to this point; the status of our military, diplomatic and humanitarian efforts; and our vision for the future.

As you know, Mr. Chairman, the potential dangers of the situation in Kosovo have been recognized throughout this decade. Slobodan Milosevic first vaulted to prominence by exploiting the fears of ethnic Serbs in this province. A decade ago, he catered to those fears by robbing Kosovo Albanians of their cherished autonomy. For years thereafter, the Kosovo Albanians sought to recover their rights by peaceful means. And in 1992, after fighting had broken out elsewhere in the Balkans, President Bush issued a warning against Serb military repression in Kosovo.

Meanwhile, President Milosevic was the primary instigator in three wars, attacking first Slovenia, then Croatia, and finally triggering a devastating and prolonged conflict in Bosnia.

Early last year, he initiated a more extensive and violent campaign of repression against ethnic Albanians in Kosovo. One result was a humanitarian crisis, as tens of thousands of people fled their homes. A second consequence - unforeseen by him - was the strengthening of the Kosovar Liberation Army (KLA), which contributed to the unrest by committing provocative acts of its own.

With our allies and partners, including Russia, the United States sought to end this cycle of violence by diplomatic means. Last October, President Milosevic agreed to a ceasefire, to the withdrawal of most of his security forces, and to the entry of a verification mission from the OSCE.

It soon became clear, however, that Milosevic never had any intention of living up to this agreement. Instead of withdrawing, his security forces positioned themselves for a new offensive. Early this year, they perpetrated a massacre in the village of Racak. And at Rambouillet, Belgrade rejected a plan for peace that had been accepted by the Kosovo Albanians, and that included provisions for disarming the KLA, and safeguarding the rights of all Kosovars, including ethnic Serbs.

Even while blocking our diplomatic efforts, Milosevic was preparing a barbaric plan for expelling or forcing the total submission of the Kosovo Albanian community. First, his security forces threatened and then forced the withdrawal of the OSCE mission. Then, a new rampage of terror began.

We have all seen the resulting images of families uprooted and put on trains, children crying for parents they cannot find, refugees recounting how loved ones were separated and led away, and ominous aerial photos of freshly-upturned earth.

Behind these images is a reality of people no different in their fundamental rights or humanity than you or me - of children no different than yours or mine - cut off from their homes, deprived of their families, robbed of their dreams. And make no mistake, this campaign of terror was the cause, not the result, of NATO action. It is a Milosevic production.

Today, our values and principles, our perseverance and our strength, are being tested. We must be united at home and with our Allies overseas. The stakes are high. To understand why that is, we need, as President Clinton has repeatedly urged, to consult the map. Kosovo is a small part of a region with large historic importance and a vital role to play in Europe's future.

The region is a crossroads where the Western and Orthodox branches of Christianity and the Islamic world meet. It is where World War I began, major battles of World War II were fought, and the worst fighting in Europe since Hitler's surrender occurred in this decade.

Its stability directly affects the security of our Greek and Turkish allies to the south, and our new allies Hungary, Poland and the Czech Republic to the north. Kosovo itself is surrounded by small and struggling democracies that are being overwhelmed by the flood of refugees Milosevic's ruthless policies are creating.

Today, this region is the critical missing piece in the puzzle of a Europe whole and free. That vision of a united and democratic Europe is critical to our own security. And it cannot be fulfilled if this part of the continent remains wracked by conflict.

Further, Belgrade's actions constitute a critical test of NATO, whose strength and credibility have defended freedom and ensured our security for five decades. To paraphrase Senator Chuck Hagel, today, there is a butcher in NATO's backyard, and we have committed ourselves to stopping him. History will judge us harshly if we fail.

For all of these reasons, NATO's decision to use force against the Milosevic regime was necessary and right. And the conditions the Alliance has set for ending its campaign are clear, just and firm.

There must be a verifiable stop to Serb military action against the people of Kosovo. Belgrade's military, police and paramilitary forces must leave so that refugees can return. An international military presence must be permitted. And the people of Kosovo must be given the democratic self-government they have long deserved.

As President Clinton has said, as long as Milosevic refuses to accept these conditions, NATO's air campaign will continue, and we will seek to destroy as much of Belgrade's military capabilities as we can. Each day, Milosevic's capacity to conduct repression will diminish.

It is evident that the efforts of our courageous military forces are having a significant impact on Milosevic's options and abilities. But that impact is not yet sufficient. We must maintain the pressure until an acceptable outcome is achieved.

At the same time, we will continue to help those in the region cope with the humanitarian disaster Milosevic has created.

We do not know with any certainty how many people are now homeless inside Kosovo, but officials estimate as many as 800,000. Belgrade has made a terrible situation worse by interfering with efforts to provide food and other basic necessities. We are exploring every possible option for helping these people before it is too late. And we welcome efforts by Greek NGOs and the International Committee of the Red Cross to open up a relief lifeline, which we hope will move desperately needed supplies to the population at risk.

In addition to the internally displaced, more than half a million Kosovars have fled the region since the latest violence began. Of these, the vast majority are now in Albania and Macedonia, where the terrain is rugged, the weather harsh and the infrastructure limited. Feverish efforts are underway to build camps and provide services. With local officials, the UNHCR, WHO, UNICEF, our allies and partners, and non-governmental organizations, we are struggling to save lives, maintain health and restore hope.

Thus far, we have contributed $150 million to this effort. Yesterday, the President submitted an emergency supplemental request that includes $386 million in additional State Department and USAID humanitarian assistance funds, and $335 million in Defense Department humanitarian assistance. Last week, NATO approved Operation Allied Harbor, under which 8,000 troops will work with relief agencies in Albania to establish camps, deliver aid and ensure security. The U.S. Information Agency is participating in an effort to provide internal communications facilities at refugee camps in order to help reunify families.

Many of the refugees streaming out of Kosovo have reported Serb war crimes and crimes against humanity. These reported abuses include the widespread and systematic destruction of entire settlements, the burning of homes, the seizure of civilians for use as human shields and human blood banks, the rape of ethnic Albanian women and girls, and the systematic separation and execution of military-aged men.

For example, there have been reports of the killing of 60 men in Kacanik; and of the burial of 24 people at Glavnik, 30 in Lapastica, 150 in Drenica, 34 in Malisevo, 100 in Pristina; and other suspected mass burials at Pusto Selo and Izbica, where refugees reported that victims were first tortured and then burned to death.

There should be no misunderstanding. When it comes to the commission of war crimes or crimes against humanity, "just following orders" is no defense. In the prosecution of such crimes, there is no statute of limitations. And the international war crimes tribunal has rightly indicated that it will follow the evidence no matter where it leads.

The tribunal has already put Milosevic and 12 other FRY or Serbian officials on notice that forces under their command have committed war crimes, and that failure to prosecute those responsible can give rise to criminal charges against them. The United States has publicly identified nine military commanders whose forces may have been involved in the commission of such crimes.

By helping to document refugee accounts, and by compiling and sharing other evidence, we are and will continue to assist the tribunal in its effort to hold perpetrators accountable.

Mr. Chairman, in dealing with Kosovo prior to the last week of March, we were engaged in diplomacy backed by the threat of force. Since that time, we have used diplomacy to back NATO's military campaign.

Our diplomacy has several objectives. The first is to ensure that NATO remains united and firm. To this end, I met with Alliance foreign ministers in Brussels last week. And the President will meet with his counterparts here in Washington at the NATO Summit on Friday and Saturday. To date, we have been heartened by the broad participation and strong support the military campaign has received. In one way or another, every Ally is contributing.

Our unity has been strengthened by the knowledge that Milosevic refused a diplomatic settlement and by revulsion at his campaign of ethnic cleansing. No country in NATO wanted to have to use force against Serbia. But no country in NATO is willing to stand by and accept in Europe the expulsion of an entire ethnic community from its home.

Our second diplomatic objective has been to help leaders in the countries directly affected to cope with the humanitarian crisis, and to prevent a wider conflict. To this end, I have been in regular contact with my counterparts from the region. Their leaders will participate as partners in the NATO Summit. And the President's supplemental request includes $150 million in emergency and project assistance to these nations and to democratic Montenegro.

Our third objective is to work constructively with Russia. We want to continue to make progress in other areas of our relationship, and to bring Russia back into the mainstream of international opinion on Kosovo.

When I met with Foreign Minister Ivanov last week, he was clear about Russia's opposition to the NATO air campaign. But we did agree on the need for an end to the violence and repression in Kosovo; the withdrawal of Serb forces; the return of refugees and internally displaced persons; and unimpeded access for humanitarian aid.

Where we continue to have differences is over the kind of international presence required to achieve these objectives. As I told Foreign Minister Ivanov, after Milosevic's depredations in Kosovo, refugees will not be able to return home unless the protective force is credible, which requires that its core must come from NATO. As in Bosnia, however, we think that Russia could and should play an important role in that force, and we would welcome the participation of NATO's other partner countries, as well.

Our fourth diplomatic objective has been to ensure that NATO's message is understood around the world. We are engaged in a vigorous program of public diplomacy, and have provided information on a regular basis to nations everywhere.

We have been encouraged by strong statements from the European Union and UN Secretary-General Kofi Annan, and by the participation in relief efforts of diverse countries such as Egypt, Jordan and Ukraine.

Moreover, last week, the UN Human Rights Commission in Geneva voted 44 to 1 to condemn Belgrade's campaign of ethnic cleansing in Kosovo and called upon Serb authorities to accept a peace agreement. Supporters of this Resolution came from every continent.

We have also tried to pierce the veil of propaganda and ignorance with which Milosevic has tried to shroud the people of former Yugoslavia. Radio Free Europe, Radio Liberty and other broadcasts are reaching the country 24 hours a day. As President Clinton and other NATO leaders have made clear, our actions are directed against Belgrade's policies, not against the region's people. And our effort to broadcast the truth is designed to counteract Belgrade's Big Lie that the refugees from Kosovo are fleeing NATO and not the Serb forces.

In the days and weeks to come, we will press ahead with our military, diplomatic and humanitarian strategies. Our purpose will be to steadily bring home to Milosevic the reality that this confrontation must end on the terms we have stated.

Our desire is to begin as soon as possible the vital work of returning, reuniting and rebuilding in Kosovo. But we are not interested in a phony settlement based on unverifiable assumptions or Milosevic's worthless word. The only settlement we can accept is one we have the ability to verify and the capability to enforce.

Even as we respond to the crisis in Kosovo, we must also concern ourselves more broadly with the future of the region. The peaceful integration of Europe's north, west and center is well advanced or on track. But, as I said earlier, the continent cannot be whole and free until its southeast corner is also stable.

Some say violence is endemic to this region, and that its people have never and will never get along. Others say that stability is only possible under the crushing weight of a dominant empire such as the Ottoman, Hapsburg and Communist regimes that once held sway.

I am no prophet. Certainly, the scars of the past are still visible. Certainly, the wounds opened by the current devastation will take much time to heal. But the evidence is there in the testimony of average people whether in Zagreb or Tirana, Sarajevo or Skopje, that they are far more interested in plugging into the world economy than in slugging it out with former adversaries.

If you look at the region today, you will see Greeks and Turks operating side by side as NATO Allies; you will see Macedonians and Albanians and Montenegrins answering the humanitarian call. You will see Christians and Muslims and Jews united in their condemnation of the atrocities being committed.

In Bosnia, NATO and its partners are working with ethnic Serbs, Croats and Bosniaks to implement the Dayton Accords. And through our own Southeast European Cooperative Initiative, you will see leaders and citizens from throughout the region engaged in joint efforts and cooperative planning.

The problems that have plagued the Balkans - of competition for resources, ethnic rivalry and religious intolerance - are by no means restricted to that part of the world. Nor does the region lack the potential to rise above them.

During the NATO Summit, the President and our partners will discuss the need for a coordinated effort to consolidate democracy in Southeast Europe, promote economic integration and provide moral and material support to those striving to build societies based on law and respect for the rights and dignity of all.

Our explicit goal should be to transform the Balkans from the continent's primary source of instability into an integral part of the European mainstream. We do not want the current conflict to be the prelude to others; we want to build a solid foundation for a new generation of peace - so that future wars are prevented, economies grow, democratic institutions are strengthened and the rights of all are preserved.

This will require a commitment from us. It will require the involvement of the European Union and the international financial institutions. It will require a continued willingness on the part of local leaders to work together on behalf of the common good. And it will require, ultimately, a change in leadership in Belgrade so the democratic aspirations of the Serb people may be fulfilled and the isolation of the former Yugoslavia can come to an end.

Finally, Mr. Chairman, I would like to add just a few words about the crisis in Kosovo and the future of NATO. For the challenge we currently face has dramatized the need for precisely the kind of adaptations the Alliance has already initiated, and which we will take to a new level at the Summit here in Washington later this week.

In Kosovo, we are responding to a post-Cold War threat to Alliance interests and values. We are seeing the need for military forces that are mobile, flexible, precise and inter-operable. We are seeing the value to the Alliance of its new members and partners. And we are reaffirming the unshakable strength of the trans-Atlantic bond.

Having said that, I want to emphasize that although we are focused now on Kosovo, the future of NATO is a much larger issue. The current fighting notwithstanding, NATO's core mission remains collective self-defense. NATO's relationship to Russia is a key to Europe's future security and will be determined by many factors in addition to Kosovo. The Alliance must be ready to respond to the full spectrum of missions it may face, including the perils posed by weapons of mass destruction. And the United States will continue to welcome efforts to strengthen the European pillar of our Alliance in a way that bolsters overall effectiveness and unity.

I know that your Subcommittee on Europe will be conducting a hearing on these and related issues tomorrow, Mr. Chairman, and I am sure that Assistant Secretary Grossman and his counterpart from the Department of Defense will discuss them in greater depth than I have had the opportunity to do in my remarks this afternoon.

I also understand that the Congressional leadership will host a reception this week for our visitors from NATO countries. I hope that you will thank them for their efforts and stress to them the importance of standing together and standing tall until the current confrontation is settled.

As the President and our military leaders have made clear, this struggle may be long. We can expect days of tragedy for us as well as for the people of the region. But we must not falter and we cannot fail.

By opposing Solobodan Milosevic's murderous rampage, NATO is playing its rightful role as a defender of freedom and security within the Euro-Atlantic region. Because our cause is just, we are united. And because we are united, we are confident that in this confrontation between barbaric killing and necessary force; between vicious intolerance and respect for human rights; between tyranny and democracy; we will prevail. To that essential objective, I pledge the full measure of my own efforts, and respectfully solicit both your wise counsel and support.

247. United States Senate, NATO's 50th Anniversary Summit, Hearing before the Committee on Foreign Relations, One Hundred Sixth Congress, First Session, 21 April 1999

[...]

Prepared Statement of Assistant Secretary Franklin D. Kramer

Mr. Chairman and Members of the Committee:

I welcome the opportunity to appear before you today. Recent events over the past few weeks underscore the vitality of the NATO Alliance, an Alliance designed to achieve peace, freedom, and democracy through a collective strength derived from the robust defense capabilities of its members.

Summit Goals

At the Summit, Allied leaders will approve a revised Strategic Concept that reflects the present and foreseeable security environment and focuses on transforming the defense capabilities of the Alliance to meet the challenges of the 21st century. While collective defense continues to be the core function of the Alliance, future missions should include "out-of-area" contingencies such as Bosnia and Kosovo, which threaten the overall strategic stability of Europe. They should also include readiness to respond to threats such as those posed by weapons of mass destruction (WMD) and by terrorism. Both the fighting in Kosovo as well as the proliferation of chemical, biological and nuclear weapons and the means to deliver them demonstrates that the Alliance must prepare its military capabilities so it can act when required.

As you know, in taking any such NATO action, it is our strong belief that UN Security Council resolutions mandating or authorizing NATO efforts are not required as a matter of international law - and, as the Kosovo situation has shown, that view is widely shared in the Alliance. NATO's actions have been and will remain consistent with the purposes and principles of the United Nations - a proposition reflected in the Washington Treaty itself. The United States will not accept any statement in the new Strategic Concept that would require a UN Security Council resolution for NATO to act. [...]

248. President Clinton, Statement, Released by the White House, Office of the Press Secretary, aboard Air Force One, 25 May 1999

I believe that our air campaign in Kosovo is working and will ultimately succeed in its objective of returning the people of Kosovo to their homes with security and self-government. With that in mind, we are planning with our allies for success. Today, NATO endorsed an updated plan for implementing the peace in Kosovo when its conditions are met.

The force that NATO plans to deploy - KFOR - will deter renewed hostilities and provide the security and confidence the refugees need to return and get on with their lives. To be credible and effective, KFOR will have NATO at its core.

Given the new circumstances, including the enormous humanitarian crisis caused by Mr. Milosevic, KFOR will need to be larger than we originally foresaw. We expect the American contribution to increase proportionately but our European allies will still provide the vast bulk of the force. We also hope that Russia and other non-NATO countries will participate.

The headquarters and leading elements of KFOR are already in the region, where they are helping to relieve the refugee crisis. NATO's military authorities will now work with allied countries to determine what additional forces will be required so that the Alliance is ready when the time comes for the refugees to return. Make no mistake, that time will come, in accordance with the conditions we have repeatedly laid out.

CHAPTER 7: INTERNATIONAL REACTIONS TO THE CRISIS

7.1 UNITED NATIONS

249. Statement of the Secretary-General, Press Release, SG/SM/6938, 24 March 1999

I speak to you at a grave moment for the international community. Throughout the last year, I have appealed on many occasions to the Yugoslav authorities and the Kosovo Albanians to seek peace over war, compromise over conflict, I deeply regret that, in spite of all the efforts made by the international community, the Yugoslav authorities have persisted in their rejection of a political settlement, which would have halted the bloodshed in Kosovo and secured an equitable peace for the population there. It is indeed tragic that diplomacy has failed, but there are times when the use of force may be legitimate in the pursuit of peace. In helping maintain international peace and security, Chapter VIII of the United Nations Charter assigns an important role to regional organizations. But as Secretary-General I have many times pointed out, not just in relation to Kosovo, that under the Charter the Security Council has primary responsibility for maintaining international peace and security - and this is explicitly acknowledged in the North Atlantic Treaty. Therefore the Council should be involved in any decision to resort to the use of force.

250. Extracts from the Debate of the Security Council Concerning Letter dated 24 March 1999 from the Permanent Representative of the Russian Federation to the UN Addressed to the President of the Security Council (S/1999/320), S/PV. 3988, 24 March 1999[1]

[The Council was meeting in response to the request of the Russian Federation (S/1999/320).][2]

[...]

[2] **Mr. Lavrov** (Russian Federation) *(spoke in Russian)*: The Russian Federation is profoundly outraged at the use by the North Atlantic Treaty Organization (NATO) of military force against the Federal Republic of Yugoslavia. In recent weeks, when we were constantly hearing threats - detrimental to the negotiating process - that there would be missile strikes against Serbian positions in Kosovo and other parts of Serbia, the Russian Government strongly proclaimed its categorical rejection of the use of force in contravention of decisions of the Security Council and issued repeated warnings about the long-term harmful consequences of this action not only for the prospects of a settlement of the Kosovo situation and for safeguarding security in the Balkans, but also for the stability of the entire modern multi-polar system of international relations.

Those who are involved in this unilateral use of force against the sovereign Federal Republic of Yugoslavia - carried out in violation of the Charter of the United Nations and without the authorization of the Security Council - must realize the heavy responsibility they bear for subverting the Charter and other norms of international law and for attempting to establish in the world, de facto, the primacy of force and unilateral diktat.

The members of NATO are not entitled to decide the fate of other sovereign and independent States. They must not forget that they are not only members of their alliance, but also Members of the United Nations, and that it is their obligation to be guided by the United Nations Charter, in particular its Article 103, which clearly establishes the absolute priority for Members of the Organization of Charter obligations over any other international obligations.

Attempts to justify the NATO strikes with arguments about preventing a humanitarian catastrophe in Kosovo are completely untenable. Not only are these attempts in no way based on the Charter or other generally recognized rules of international law, but the unilateral use of force will lead precisely to a situation with truly [3] devastating humanitarian consequences. Moreover, by the terms of the definition of aggression adopted by the General Assembly in 1974,

"No consideration of whatever nature, whether political, economic, military or otherwise, may serve as a justification for aggression". (General Assembly resolution 3314 (XXIX), annex, article 5, para. 1)

We certainly do not seek to defend violations of international humanitarian law by any party. But it is possible to combat violations of the law only with clean hands and only on the solid basis of the law. Otherwise lawlessness would spawn lawlessness. It would be unthinkable for a national court in a civilized democratic country to uphold illegal methods to combat crime. Attempts to apply a different standard to international law and to disregard its basic norms and principles create a dangerous precedent that could cause acute destabilization and chaos on the regional and global level. If we do not put an end to this very dangerous trend, the virus of illegal unilateral approaches could spread not merely to other geographical regions but to spheres of international relations other than questions of peace and security.

The fact that NATO has opted to use force in Kosovo raises very serious questions about the sincerity of the repeated assurances that that alliance was not claiming the role of the world's policeman and was prepared to cooperate in the interests of common European security. In the light of this turn of events, we shall draw the appropriate conclusions in our relations and contacts with that organization.

NATO's decision to use military force is particularly unacceptable from any point of view because the potential of political and diplomatic methods to yield a settlement in Kosovo has certainly not been exhausted. The enormous quantity of complicated work done by the international community has now been dealt a very powerful, a very grave and probably an irrevocable blow.

The Russian Federation vehemently demands the immediate cessation of this illegal military action against the Federal Republic of Yugoslavia. We reserve the right to raise in the Security Council the question of the adoption by the Council, under the United Nations Charter, of appropriate measures with respect to this situation, which has arisen as a result of NATO's illegal actions and which poses a clear threat to international peace and security. Today, the President of the Russian Federation, Boris N. Yeltsin, issued the following statement:

"Russia is profoundly outraged by NATO's military action against sovereign Yugoslavia, which is nothing less than an act of open aggression.

---

[1] *Only statement which add to the legal analysis or the factual background have been included. Presidential statements not related to substantive issues have also been omitted.*

[2] *In 1999, the membership of the Security Council was as follows: Argentinia, Bahrain, Brazil, Canada, China, France, Gabon, Gambia, Malaysia, Namibia, the Netherlands, Russian Federation, Slovenia, the United Kingdom of Great Britain and Northern Ireland and the United States of America. The President invited the representatives of Albania, Belarus, Bosnia and Herzegovina, Germany and India to participate in the discussion, without the right to vote, in accordance with the Charter and rule 37 of the Council's provisional rules of procedure. The President also invited Mr. Vladislav Jovanovic (FRY).*

"Only the Security Council can decide on what measures, including the use of force, should be taken to maintain or restore international peace and security. The Security Council did not take such decisions with regard to Yugoslavia. Not only the Charter of the United Nations has been violated; the Founding Act on Mutual Relations, Cooperation and Security Between NATO and The Russian Federation has been violated as well. A dangerous precedent has been created regarding the policy of diktat and force, and the whole of the international rule of law has been threatened.

"We are basically talking about an attempt by NATO to enter the twenty-first century in the uniform of the world's policeman. Russia will never agree to that.

"The Security Council must discuss the situation that has emerged and demand the immediate cessation of NATO's use of force.

"For its part, the leadership of the Russian Federation will review its relationship with NATO as an organization, which has shown disrespect for the fundamental basis of the system of international relations.

"As President and Supreme Commander, I have already given the following instructions: to cut short the visit to the United States of the Chairman of the Government of the Russian Federation, Yevgeny Primakov; to demand an urgent convening of a meeting of the Security Council of the United Nations and to seek an immediate cessation of NATO's military action; to recall to Moscow the chief military representative of the Russian Federation to NATO; to suspend our participation in the Partnership for Peace programme and to end the carrying out of the programme on Russia-NATO partnership; and to postpone talks for the opening of a NATO liaison mission in Moscow.

"I have already appealed to the President of the United States, Bill Clinton, and to the leaders of [4] other NATO member countries to put an immediate end to this military adventure, which threatens the lives of peaceful people and could lead to an explosion of the situation in the Balkans.

"A settlement of the situation in Kosovo, as the settlement of other similar problems, is only possible through negotiations. The quicker they are resumed, the greater the possibility for the international community to find a political settlement to the situation. Russia is prepared to interact with other members of the Contact Group in order to reach that goal.

"Those who decided upon military adventure bear the full responsibility to their peoples and to the world community for the dire consequences of this for international stability.

"If the military conflict increases, then Russia reserves the right to take adequate measures, including military measures, to ensure its own and common European security."

Mr. Burleigh (United States of America): The current situation in Kosovo is of grave concern to all of us. We and our allies have begun military action only with the greatest reluctance. But we believe that such action is necessary to respond to Belgrade's brutal persecution of Kosovar Albanians, violations of international law, excessive and indiscriminate use of force, refusal to negotiate to resolve the issue peacefully and recent military build-up in Kosovo - all of which foreshadow a humanitarian catastrophe of immense proportions.

We have begun today's action to avert this humanitarian catastrophe and to deter further aggression and repression in Kosovo. Serb forces numbering 40,000 are now in action in and around Kosovo. Thirty thousand Kosovars have fled their homes just since 19 March. As a result of Serb action in the last five weeks, there are more than 60,000 new refugees and displaced persons. The total number of displaced persons is approaching a quarter of a million.

The continuing offensive by the Federal Republic of Yugoslavia is generating refugees and creating pressures on neighbouring countries, threatening the stability of the region. Repressive Serb action in Kosovo has already resulted in cross-border activity in Albania, Bosnia and the former Yugoslav Republic of Macedonia. Recent actions by Belgrade also constitute a threat to the safety of international observers and humanitarian workers in Kosovo.

Security Council resolutions 1199 (1998) and 1203 (1998) recognized that the situation in Kosovo constitutes a threat to peace and security in the region and invoked Chapter VII of the Charter. In resolution 1199 (1998), the Council demanded that Serbian forces take immediate steps to improve the humanitarian situation and avert the impending humanitarian catastrophe.

In October 1998, Belgrade entered into agreements and understandings with the North Atlantic Treaty Organization (NATO) and the Organization for Security and Cooperation in Europe (OSCE) to verity its compliance with Security Council demands, particularly on reduction of security forces, cooperation with international observers, cooperation with humanitarian relief agencies and negotiations on a political settlement for substantial autonomy. Belgrade has refused to comply.

The actions of the Federal Republic of Yugoslavia also violate its commitments under the Helsinki Final Act, as well as its obligations under the international law of human rights. Belgrade's actions in Kosovo cannot be dismissed as an internal matter.

For months, Serb actions have led to escalating explosions of violence. It is imperative that the international community take quick measures to avoid humanitarian suffering and widespread destruction, which could exceed that of the 1998 offensive.

I reiterate that we have initiated action today with the greatest reluctance. Our preference has been to achieve our objectives in the Balkans through peaceful means. Since fighting erupted in February 1998, we have been actively engaged in seeking resolution of the conflict through diplomacy under the auspices of the Contact Group backed by NATO. These efforts led to talks in Rambouillet and Paris, which produced a fair, just and balanced agreement. The Kosovar Albanians signed that agreement, but Belgrade rejected all efforts to achieve a peaceful resolution.

We are mindful that violations of the ceasefire and provocations by the Kosovo Liberation Army have also contributed to this situation. However, it is Belgrade's systematic policy of undermining last October's agreements and thwarting all diplomatic efforts to resolve the situation which have prevented a peaceful solution and have led us to today's action.

[5] In this context, we believe that action by NATO is justified and necessary to stop the violence and prevent an even greater humanitarian disaster. As President Clinton said today,

"We and our allies have a chance to leave our children a Europe that is free, peaceful and stable. But we must act now to do that". [...]

[A statement by the representative of Canada has been omitted.]

[6] **Mr. Türk** (Slovenia): The situation being discussed today relates principally to Kosovo. The Security Council has been seized of the situation in Kosovo for about a year now. Throughout this entire period, the situation has been deteriorating and the extent of human suffering and humanitarian problems has been increasing. The threat of the situation in Kosovo to international peace and security has been growing. The Security Council has adopted three resolutions on Kosovo, all of them under Chapter VII of the United Nations Charter. They represent a clear expression of the will of the international community to assist in devising a solution and a framework for action in search of the solution.

Slovenia regrets that the developments in Kosovo have brought the international community to the point at which all diplomatic means have been exhausted and military action in the Federal Republic of Yugoslavia has become inevitable. The constant endeavours of the international community to achieve a diplomatic solution to the crisis and to prevent a humanitarian catastrophe of even greater extent have yielded no results. In view of this tragic moment for the peoples in that part of Europe, we would like to emphasize that the tragedy is the result and consequence of the erroneous policy of the Belgrade Government alone.

The current situation was not inevitable. A diplomatic solution was not impossible. Let me recall that, not long ago, the Council welcomed and supported the negotiating process conducted by the Contact Group in France, which aimed at reaching a political settlement between the parties and at establishing a na. newwork and timetable for that purpose.

Slovenia, for its part, has all along supported a peaceful solution to the Kosovo problem that would include broad autonomy for Kosovo with due respect for the internationally recognized borders of the Federal Republic of Yugoslavia (Serbia and Montenegro). Slovenia, through its Prime Minister, has been actively engaged in the efforts of the international community to achieve this aim. Slovenia supports the agreement prepared by the Contact Group on the basis of the results of extensive discussions with the parties during the course of the second half of 1998. We believe that the political part of the agreement on the autonomy of Kosovo and the part on the implementation of the agreement constitute a whole and provide the only realistic way to stabilize the situation in Kosovo. The interim period of three years would also provide enough time to continue the search for a balanced and long-term solution, as well as for the restoration of and reconciliation among the Serbian and Albanian communities in Kosovo.

Unfortunately, the efforts of the international community were in vain, since the Belgrade Government was not ready to agree to a political solution of the crisis. The military activities and those of the special Serbian police forces in Kosovo against the civilian population have not ceased, despite the numerous demands of the Security Council in its resolutions and despite the commitments made by the Belgrade Government to that effect. On the contrary, in recent months and weeks, the military action against the civilian population has further escalated. The attacks have become more violent, thus causing an even greater humanitarian catastrophe. According to the recent figures published by the Office of the United Nations High Commissioner for Refugees (UNHCR), there are already about half a million refugees and internally displaced persons. This situation represents a case of massive violation of the relevant Security Council resolutions, in particular resolution 1199 (1998) of 23 September 1998, which called for an immediate end to all military activity against the civilian population. The threat to international peace and security in the region is looming large.

Today's meeting is a sombre occasion for various reasons. I wish to emphasize this: It is most deplorable that the Security Council has to meet to discuss the consequences of systematic and brutal violations of its own resolutions. This is the main source of our concern today.

We regret the fact that not all permanent members were willing to act in accordance with their special [7] responsibility for the maintenance of international peace and security under the United Nations Charter. Their apparent absence of support has prevented the Council from using its powers to the full extent and from authorizing the action which is necessary to put an end to the violations of its resolutions.

It is our expectation and belief that the action which is being undertaken will be carried out strictly within the substantive parameters established by the relevant Security Council resolutions. We would also like to express our hope that a peace agreement on Kosovo will be reached in the shortest possible time. We will continue to actively support the endeavours of the international community to achieve a mutually acceptable solution under international supervision.

Mr. Buallay (Bahrain) *(spoke in Arabic)*: Our delegation regrets the recent developments in Kosovo, which have finally led to the use of military force against the forces of the Federal Republic of Yugoslavia. We have long called for a peaceful settlement of the Kosovo crisis through serious and constructive dialogue between the parties to the conflict.

However, the authorities in Belgrade unfortunately insisted on their position and did not seize the opportunity afforded them in Rambouillet. Those authorities insisted on pursuing a policy of repression against the Kosovar Albanian community, a policy that started when those authorities put an end to the autonomy enjoyed by Kosovo until 1989. It would seem as if they have quickly forgotten or disregarded the lessons drawn from the tragic experience of Bosnia and Herzegovina.

It would also seem that the authorities in Belgrade do not want the Balkan region to enjoy the peace and stability so sorely missed by the peoples of the region. The policy of "ethnic cleansing" and the denial of the fundamental rights of the Kosovar Albanians can bring only destruction and instability to the Federal Republic of Yugoslavia. Such a policy has also led to the displacement of thousands of Kosovo inhabitants. There are more than 200,000 displaced persons within Kosovo, in addition to the thousands of others who have sought refuge in neighbouring countries. The problem has indeed become extremely serious, and a humanitarian catastrophe is looming.

Our delegation hopes that the authorities in Belgrade will come to their senses and obey the dictates of reason and logic with a view to achieving peace and stability in the Federal Republic of Yugoslavia and in the Balkan region in general. This can become reality only if they enter into a serious and constructive dialogue and commit to all relevant Security Council resolutions and to cooperation with the international community in order to put an end to the conflict in Kosovo.

Mr. Jagne (Gambia): The situation in Kosovo, in the Federal Republic of Yugoslavia, is a cause of great concern to my delegation. Like all peace-loving nations, we in the Gambia are very much attached to the sacrosanct principle of the peaceful settlement of disputes, as enshrined in the Charter of the United Nations.

Throughout the past year, the international community has deployed a great deal of effort in order to find a peaceful settlement to the question concerning Kosovo. Unfortunately, however, many opportunities to resolve the crisis were missed, for reasons well known to all of us, including the latest talks in Paris.

Meanwhile, the onslaught against the ethnic Albanian community in Kosovo continued unabated. The international community time and again called on the authorities in Belgrade to respect human rights and to cooperate with the international community with a view to settling peacefully the question of greater autonomy for Kosovo, but to no avail.

As far as my delegation is concerned, we cannot remain indifferent to the plight of the murdered people of Kosovo. In recent times, the actions of the Federal Republic of Yugoslavia Government in Kosovo have caused an untold amount of suffering among the Kosovar Albanians and have generated thousands and thousands of refugees and displaced persons.

It is the responsibility of any Government to protect its citizens. We speak with great regret of the fact that the international community had to take the action it took today. Of course, regional arrangements have responsibility for the maintenance of peace and security in their areas. The Security Council, however, has the primary responsibility for the maintenance of international peace and security, as clearly stated in the Charter of the United Nations.

It must be noted, though, that at times the exigencies of a situation demand, and warrant, decisive and immediate action. We find that the present situation in Kosovo deserves such a treatment. The action started today by the international community could have been avoided, for the action could still be prevented. We [8] therefore call on those with whom the responsibility lies to take the necessary action to prevent a continuation of this action before it is too late.

Mr. van Walsum (Netherlands): We have participated in and assumed responsibility for the North Atlantic Treaty Organization (NATO) decision because there was no other solution. As for the Netherlands, this decision was not taken lightly; it was taken with conviction. Responsibility for the NATO action lies squarely with President Milosevic. He is responsible for the large-scale violations of the October agreements with the Organization for Security and Cooperation in Europe (OSCE) and NATO. It is President Milosevic's recourse to violence in Kosovo that has finally convinced us that the impending humanitarian catastrophe, at which the Council expressed its alarm in its resolutions of September and October, could not be averted by peaceful means.

In some capitals, our determination to avoid a humanitarian catastrophe in Kosovo has apparently been underestimated. It goes without saying that a country - or an alliance - which is compelled to take up arms to avert such a humanitarian catastrophe would always prefer to be able to base its action on a specific Security Council resolution. The Secretary-General is right when he observes in his press statement that the Council should be involved in any decision to resort to the use of force. If, however, due to one or two permanent members' rigid interpretation of the concept of domestic jurisdiction, such a resolution is not attainable, we cannot sit back and simply let the humanitarian catastrophe occur. In such a situation we will act on the legal basis we have available, and what we have available in this case is more than adequate.

The Netherlands has been deeply involved in the events in the former Yugoslavia ever since the beginning of the breakup of the Socialist Federal Republic of Yugoslavia on 25 June 1991. In spite of this, we have accepted a situation in which the leading role was played by a Contact Group of which Russia is an important member. Our acceptance of this arrangement was always based on the assumption that Russia had so much influence in Belgrade that it could persuade President Milosevic to accept a reasonable solution. The present state of affairs should convince every delegation that with regard to the problem of Kosovo, the diplomatic means of finding a solution are now exhausted. As stated by the Secretary-General, diplomacy has failed, but there are times when the use of force may be legitimate in the pursuit of peace. The Netherlands feels that this is such a time. [...]

Mr. Enio Cordeiro (Brazil): The Brazilian Government is attentively following the situation in Kosovo and expresses its concern about the most recent developments in the crisis, including the humanitarian aspects. In conformity with its unflinching commitment to the pacific settlement of disputes, the Brazilian Government regrets that the escalation of tensions has resulted in recourse to military action.

Mr. Dejammet (France) *(spoke in French)*: Drawing lessons from the tragedy that took place in Bosnia and Herzegovina, France and its partners in the Contact Group mobilized very early to react to the crisis in Kosovo, the Federal Republic of Yugoslavia. That action was aimed at bringing to an end the violence by the parties and at arriving at a comprehensive settlement of the conflict.

The Security Council also endorsed those concerns, in particular in resolutions 1160 (1998), 1199 (1998) and 1203 (1998), which it adopted in relation to the situation in Kosovo. The Council indicated that in those resolutions it was acting under Chapter VII of the Charter.

In resolutions 1199 (1998) and 1203 (1998), the Security Council affirmed that the deterioration of the situation in Kosovo posed a threat to peace and security in the region. In resolution 1199 (1998), the Council demanded in particular that the Belgrade authorities immediately cease hostilities and maintain a ceasefire in Kosovo; that they take immediate steps to avert the impending humanitarian catastrophe; that they cease all action by the security forces affecting the civilian population and order the withdrawal of security units used for repression of civilians; and that they make rapid progress, in the framework of a dialogue with the Albanian community of Kosovo, towards a political solution to the problems of Kosovo.

In resolution 1203 (1998), the Security Council furthermore endorsed and supported the agreements concluded between the Federal Republic of Yugoslavia and the Organization for Security and Cooperation in Europe on the one hand, and between the Federal Republic of Yugoslavia and the North Atlantic Treaty Organization on the other. The Council demanded the prompt and full implementation of those agreements by the Federal Republic of Yugoslavia. Those agreements [9] included precise commitments and obligations on the part of the Yugoslav Government.

Those obligations were not respected by Belgrade. However, every effort was made to prompt the Yugoslav Government to meet its obligations on the ground and to adhere to the Rambouillet agreements. Those efforts have been exhausted.

In recent weeks we have witnessed, together with the inflexibility of the Belgrade authorities in negotiating a peace agreement, an increase in tension and confrontation, with the massing of a powerful offensive capacity by the Yugoslav army, inspiring fears that there will be a new upsurge of massacres in a community of 2 million people. We cannot abandon that community to violent repression. What is at stake today is peace, peace in Europe - but human rights are also at stake.

The actions that have been decided upon are a response to the violation by Belgrade of its international obligations, which stem in particular from the Security Council resolutions adopted under Chapter VII of the United Nations Charter. The Belgrade authorities must be persuaded that the only way to settle the crisis in Kosovo is for them to halt their military offensives in Kosovo and to accept the framework defined by the Rambouillet agreements.

Mr. Hasmy (Malaysia): The Security Council is meeting today in reaction to the dramatic developments that are now taking place in Kosovo. For the past 13 months the continuing crisis in Kosovo has caused tremendous hardship and suffering to the civilian population in the province. The continued repressive actions on the part of the Yugoslav security forces against the Kosovar Albanian community, which have again intensified during the past few days, have led to tragic humanitarian consequences. Many lives have been lost, while more than half a million Kosovar Albanians have been forced to flee their burning homes and villages and seek refuge elsewhere in Kosovo and in the neighbouring countries.

The violence against the civilian population has been on the increase in recent weeks and days. The intensified terror tactics and military assaults by the Yugoslav forces against the ethnic Albanian community in many parts of the province represent the continuation of a systematic repression by the Yugoslav authorities to drive innocent civilians, especially women and children, out of Kosovo, reminiscent of the policy of ethnic cleansing that was carried out during the dark days of the Bosnian crisis.

According to the Organization for Security and Cooperation in Europe, the current security environment in Kosovo is characterized by a disproportionate use of force, including heavy weaponry, by the Yugoslav authorities against the poorly armed Kosovar Albanians. One thing should be clear: combating the so-called acts of terrorism in Kosovo does not in any way justify gross human rights violations or the failure to respect international norms and international humanitarian law.

The Security Council supported the peace process initiated by the Contact Group back in January this year, which was designed to settle the crisis in Kosovo through peaceful means. My delegation cannot fail to express its appreciation for the strenuous efforts made by the members of the Contact Group, and in particular those that were determined to bring about the success of the peace negotiations in Rambouillet, which resumed in Paris last week. Unfortunately, the outcome of the negotiations was not as the international community had expected. Yugoslavia continues to reject the Rambouillet accords and has rebuffed all efforts to change its mind, while the Kosovar Albanian side has put its signature on them, despite serious reservations on its part. My delegation welcomes the decision by the Kosovar Albanian delegation to sign the Rambouillet accords. By that act, the Kosovar Albanians have chosen the path of peace, instead of continued conflict. That was, indeed, a courageous decision which ought to be commended by the international community and this Council.

My delegation believed that the crisis in Kosovo could have been resolved through dialogue and negotiations predicated on good faith and the necessary political will on the part of the parties concerned. Clearly, the Kosovar Albanian side has demonstrated this good faith and political will but, regrettably, the Yugoslav authorities have not. We had hoped that the intensive diplomatic efforts, culminating in the Rambouillet talks in February, which resumed in Paris last week, including all the efforts made right up to the eleventh hour, to secure an agreement from Belgrade, would succeed in finding a peaceful settlement and thereby avert the catastrophic humanitarian situation now unfolding in Kosovo. Regrettably, the hopes and expectations of the international community were dashed by the continued intransigence of the Yugoslav leadership.

As a matter of principle, my delegation is not in favour of the use or threat of use of force to resolve any conflict situation, regardless of where it occurs. If the use of force is at all necessary, it should be a recourse of last [10] resort, to be sanctioned by the Security Council, which has been vested with primary responsibility for the maintenance of international peace and security. The ongoing conflict in Kosovo could indeed - and will - have international repercussions, given the still volatile situation in some of the neighbouring countries. In any case, the international community cannot afford to stand idly by, given the dimension of the violence on the ground and the worsening humanitarian conditions in Kosovo in the wake of the repressive military actions carried out by the Serbian and Yugoslav authorities.

My delegation would have wished that the crisis in Kosovo could be dealt with directly by the Council. It is regrettable that, given the divisions in the Council on this subject, during the past 13 months it has not been able to address the issue in any meaningful way. It is regrettable that in the absence of a consensus in the Council - thanks, or rather, no thanks, to the irreconcilable differences among permanent members - the Council has been denied the opportunity to firmly and decisively pronounce on this issue, as expected of it by the international community. We regret that in the absence of Council action on this issue it has been necessary for action to be taken outside of the Council.

We are seriously concerned about the current situation on the ground when, with the withdrawal of international observers and the onset of military actions by the North Atlantic Treaty Organization (NATO), the Yugoslav authorities are likely to unleash their preponderant military might upon the poorly armed Albanians in retaliation. If this happens, the humanitarian impact on the Kosovar civilian population will be enormous and tragic indeed. This aspect of the problem must be immediately addressed by the international community and this Council. My delegation joins others in calling for international readiness to provide humanitarian assistance to the Kosovar Albanians.

Mr. Andjaba (Namibia): The current crisis in the Serbian province of Kosovo in particular and in the Federal Republic of Yugoslavia in general is a source of great concern to us. The degree of brutality perpetrated on the civilian population, the massacre of women, children and the elderly, the displacement of people from their homes kidnappings and the wanton destruction of property continue to take place in Kosovo.

What we have been yearning for in the Federal Republic of Yugoslavia, as in any crisis situation, is peace. More violence and destruction cannot salvage peace.

In numerous cases of conflict situations it has been the view of the Security Council - and rightly so - that military action is not the solution, but rather that peaceful means should be resorted to. This principle has been reaffirmed time and time again - and even recently, during the open meeting that the Council convened on Friday, 19 March 1999. It is a principle that we believe should not be used selectively.

My delegation wishes to underscore that military action against the Federal Republic of Yugoslavia may not be the solution. Furthermore, the implications of this action may go beyond the Federal Republic of Yugoslavia, thereby posing a serious threat to peace and security in the region.

Therefore, my delegation appeals for the immediate cessation of the ongoing military action and for the exhausting of all possible avenues for a peaceful resolution of the conflict.

Mr. Dangue Rewaka (Gabon) *(spoke in French)*: The delegation of Gabon has always supported the efforts made by the Contact Group to lead the Federal Republic of Yugoslavia to grant greater autonomy to its Kosovo province.

Like the members of the Contact Group, we have condemned the acts of terrorism committed by the Kosovo Liberation Army. We have also condemned the repressive measures taken against these acts. It is regrettable that all of these condemnations and these appeals aimed at achieving a political solution to the question of Kosovo were not heeded.

In spite of this silence, we would have hoped that the Contact Group would continue to use all its authority to compel the Federal Republic of Yugoslavia to sign the Rambouillet agreement, which gave rise to new hopes for a settlement of the situation in Kosovo.

My Government is in principle opposed to the use of force to settle local or international disputes.

Mr. Petrella (Argentina) *(spoke in Spanish)*: The attacks by the North Atlantic Treaty Organization (NATO) against Serb targets, which are taking place at this moment, are a source of great concern for Argentina.

Since the peaceful settlement of disputes is one of the guiding principles of our foreign policy, we regret that [11] the intransigence of the Belgrade Government has led to this result, which no member of this Council desires.

Argentina reiterates its position regarding the urgent need for strict compliance with Security Council resolutions 1160 (1998) and 1199 (1998), in which the humanitarian abuses in Kosovo were condemned.

Yesterday the Government of Argentina issued a communiqué in which it emphasized the need to create conditions conducive to a lasting peace, within a framework based on respect for human rights and for the principles of the territorial integrity and sovereignty of the Federal Republic of Yugoslavia, as well as greater autonomy for Kosovo and protection of minorities.

We also wish to say that Argentina profoundly regrets the suffering of the innocent civilian population and any other victims that may result from this situation. But, as we indicated at the beginning, the responsibility lies with the Belgrade Government, since the objective of the military action is to avert a humanitarian catastrophe in Kosovo.

Lastly, we wish to make a sincere appeal to the Belgrade Government to return to the path of negotiation.

Sir Jeremy Greenstock (United Kingdom): President Milosevic has been engaged in repression of the Kosovo Albanians since he revoked Kosovo's extensive autonomy almost 10 years ago. During all this time he has declined seriously to pursue a political solution to the problem of Kosovo, a problem that everyone knew would lead to increased tension and that he, as leader of his nation, held the responsibility for remedying. Instead, he has chosen to use brute aggression against a peaceful population. Where is the outrage at that?

Since March last year, Serb violence against the population of Kosovo has increased massively. Over last summer and autumn, Serbian internal security forces and the Yugoslav army embarked on a series of offensives in western and central Kosovo, which were increasingly characterized by wanton destruction of homes, crops and livestock. Over 2,000 people have been killed in Kosovo since March 1998, and Serb scorched-earth tactics have forced over 300,000 people to flee their homes.

Today, President Milosevic is once again repeating the tactics of the summer, forcing people out of their homes and burning entire villages. In the past month alone he has created more than 65,000 new displaced people. While the Kosovo Albanians were signing the Rambouillet accords in Paris last week, Belgrade substantially reinforced its security-force presence in Kosovo and began a new offensive.

The international community - the Security Council, the North Atlantic Treaty Organization (NATO), the Organization for Security and Cooperation in Europe (OSCE), the Contact Group and the United Nations and its agencies - have sought over the past year to persuade Belgrade to end the suffering it has caused and to agree a political settlement with the Kosovo Albanians providing for a substantial degree of self-government but also respecting the territorial integrity of the Federal Republic of Yugoslavia.

In a series of resolutions, most recently resolutions 1199 (1998) and 1203 (1998), the Security Council has called on Belgrade to end actions against the civilian population and withdraw security forces responsible for repression, to cooperate with organizations engaged in humanitarian relief and to pursue a negotiated settlement. But Belgrade has rejected all of the Security Council's demands, and continues to act in defiance of the expressed will of the Council. In these circumstances, when diplomacy has failed, do we react just with further words?

In October, Ambassador Holbrooke negotiated a package with President Milosevic setting up an unarmed OSCE verification mission and a NATO-led air verification mission. President Milosevic also accepted a commitment to reduce his force levels in Kosovo. But President Milosevic tried to expel the head of the OSCE mission. His forces continued to repress, particularly in those areas where the mission was not present. The massacre at Racak showed his contempt for the mission and for the international community as a whole. And his force levels were, and remain, well above the agreed levels.

In recent months the Contact Group and Ambassadors Hill, Mayorsky and Petritsch, on behalf of the United States, the Russian Federation and the European Union, have taken the lead in seeking a negotiated settlement. Several months of painstaking shuttle diplomacy led to the talks in February and March at Rambouillet and at Paris on an interim settlement for Kosovo, underpinned by a NATO-led force: a truly exhaustive process. But President Milosevic refused to engage seriously in negotiations on an agreement. His intransigence led instead to the breakdown of the Rambouillet process. Since the ending of the talks, a [12] further 25,000 people have been forced to flee their homes in the face of pre-planned military action by the Yugoslav army.

In defiance of the international community, President Milosevic has refused to accept the interim political settlement negotiated at Rambouillet, to observe the limits on security-force levels agreed on 25 October, and to end the excessive and disproportionate use of force in Kosovo. Because of his failure to meet these demands, we face a humanitarian catastrophe. NATO has been forced to take military action because all other means of preventing a humanitarian catastrophe have been frustrated by Serb behaviour.

We have taken this action with regret, in order to save lives. It will be directed towards disrupting the violent attacks being perpetrated by the Serb security forces and towards weakening their ability to create a humanitarian catastrophe. In the longer term, the International Criminal Tribunal for the Former Yugoslavia, whose mandate extends to Kosovo, will hold those responsible for violations of international humanitarian law accountable for their actions.

The action being taken is legal. It is justified as an exceptional measure to prevent an overwhelming humanitarian catastrophe. Under present circumstances in Kosovo, there is convincing evidence that such a catastrophe is imminent. Renewed acts of repression by the authorities of the Federal Republic of Yugoslavia would cause further loss of civilian life and would lead to displacement of the civilian population on a large scale and in hostile conditions.

Every means short of force has been tried to avert this situation. In these circumstances, and as an exceptional measure on grounds of overwhelming humanitarian necessity, military intervention is legally justifiable. The force now proposed is directed exclusively to averting a humanitarian catastrophe, and is the minimum judged necessary for that purpose.

The focus of our discussion today is the crisis in Kosovo itself. But Belgrade should be under no illusion that we have taken our eye off the ball elsewhere in the Federal Republic of Yugoslavia. We are watching Serb behaviour closely in relation to Montenegro. We have also noted with dismay that the Federal Telecommunications Ministry, backed by police officers, raided Radio B92 on 24 March, closed the station down and detained its editor-in-chief. We condemn this action aimed at further reducing the right of free speech in Serbia.

Allow me to close with the following appeals to the two sides in the dispute. To the Kosovo Albanians our appeal is that they should remain on the path of peace which they chose by signing the Rambouillet accords in their entirety on 18 March. The United Kingdom urges them to show the utmost restraint in the next crucial days. And to the Federal Republic of Yugoslavia our appeal is that it is not too late to show at any time that they are ready to meet the demands of the international community. I strongly urge them to do so.

The President: [*Spoke in Chinese in his capacity as the representative of China.*]

Today, 24 March, the North Atlantic Treaty Organization (NATO), with the United States in the lead, mobilized its airborne military forces and launched military strikes against the Federal Republic of Yugoslavia, seriously exacerbating the situation in the Balkan region. This act amounts to a blatant violation of the United Nations Charter and of the accepted norms of international law. The Chinese Government strongly opposes this act.

The question of Kosovo, as an internal matter of the Federal Republic of Yugoslavia, should be resolved among the parties concerned in the Federal Republic of Yugoslavia themselves. Settlement of the Kosovo issue should be based on respect for the sovereignty and territorial integrity of the Federal Republic of Yugoslavia and on guaranteeing the legitimate rights and interests of all ethnic groups in the Kosovo region. Recently, the parties concerned have been working actively towards a political settlement of the crisis. We have always stood for the peaceful settlement of disputes through negotiations, and are opposed to the use or threat of use of force in international affairs and to power politics whereby the strong bully the weak. We oppose interference in the internal affairs of other States, under whatever pretext or in whatever form.

It has always been our position that under the Charter it is the Security Council that bears primary responsibility for the maintenance of international peace and security. And it is only the Security Council that can determine whether a given situation threatens international peace and security and can take appropriate action. We are firmly opposed to any act that violates this principle and that challenges the authority of the Security Council.

[13] The Chinese Government vigorously calls for an immediate cessation of the military attacks by NATO against the Federal Republic of Yugoslavia. China calls on the international community and on the parties concerned in the Federal Republic of Yugoslavia to make concerted efforts to stabilize the situation as soon as possible and to defuse the crisis so as to bring peace back to the Balkan region at an early date. [...]

Mr. Lavrov (Russian Federation) *(spoke in Russian)*: I have already said what my position is. Nothing of what I have heard here has changed that position. In any case, the assertion that the traditional basis for the use of force lies beyond the confines of the United Nations Charter is something that I cannot take seriously. I have set forth my position, and it has absolutely not changed.

But I have taken the floor just to make two factual clarifications, as some of my colleagues have mentioned by way of argument certain events that were not quite presented correctly. I would like to make the facts known, particularly given that this is an open, public meeting at which Members of the United Nations that are not members of the Security Council are present. I must therefore clarify two points.

The first point has to do with some colleagues' mention of the fact that Russia is a member of the Contact Group. That is quite correct, but they went on to say that Russia was a co-sponsor of the package of documents of the Contact Group. That is only partially true. The Contact Group adopted a document in London that is the basis of the draft political settlement. It is also true that that document enjoys the full co-sponsorship of the Russian Federation. With regard to the military implementation, the Contact Group never discussed that document, not because the Russian Federation did not want it to be discussed but because our partners in the Contact Group decided to discuss the military aspects of the implementation of the agreement behind our backs, in the North Atlantic Treaty Organization (NATO) and not in the Contact Group. We were discussing this with our partners in the Contact Group and made offers so that questions about the implementation of the agreement would be the subject of co-sponsorship within the Contact Group. That was not done.

So when they say that Russia is a co-sponsor of everything that was rejected by Belgrade, that is not the true situation. Now, I repeat: our Western partners in the Contact Group decided to prepare and discuss the military aspects behind our backs, and Russia had nothing to do with that proposal. It was the choice of our Western partners to do this.

The second clarification that I wanted to make has to do with the statement made by some of our colleagues to the effect that NATO's actions became inevitable because one or two of the permanent members of the Security Council had blocked action in the Council. That is simply not correct, for one simple reason: no proposals on this topic were introduced in the Security Council by anyone. There was never any draft resolution; there were no informal discussions, not even in the corridors - at least not with one permanent member of the Security Council, namely, Russia. Those discussions never took place. I am not saying what the results of those discussions were, but to state now that one or two permanent members of the Security Council blocked action in the Council is simply, diplomatically speaking, not true.

These are the clarifications I wanted to make so that everyone knows what the facts are. [...]

Mr. Jovanovic: Today, the armed forces of the North Atlantic Treaty Organization (NATO) committed a unilateral act of the most brutal and unprovoked aggression against the Federal Republic of Yugoslavia, a sovereign and independent State and a founding Member of the United Nations. The Federal Republic of Yugoslavia has not threatened any country or the peace and security of the region. It has been attacked because it sought to solve an internal problem and used its sovereign right to fight terrorism and prevent the secession of a part of its territory that has always belonged to Serbia and Yugoslavia.

The decision to attack an independent country has been taken outside the Security Council, the sole body responsible, under the Charter of the United Nations, for maintaining international peace and security. This blatant aggression is a flagrant violation of the basic principles of the Charter of the United Nations and is in direct contravention of its Article 53, paragraph 1, which states that,

[14] "no enforcement action shall be taken under regional arrangements or by regional agencies without the authorization of the Security Council".

Today, NATO was unmasked. It ceased to be a defensive military alliance and became an aggressive military alliance, disregarding its own statute, the Charter of the United Nations, and the Paris Charter of the Organization for Security and Cooperation in Europe (OSCE), as well as the system of international relations based on respect for the sovereignty and territorial integrity of States. By bombing massively and indiscriminately the cities and towns of the Federal Republic of Yugoslavia, NATO has become the air force and mercenary of the terrorist Kosovo Liberation Army (KLA).

The United States of America and NATO must assume full responsibility for all consequences of their act of open aggression, both foreseeable and unforeseeable.

By committing the aggression against the Federal Republic of Yugoslavia, NATO has trampled upon international law and the fundamental principles of international relations by endangering peace and security in the world in the most irresponsible and criminal way.

That is why my Government requested, on the basis of Chapter VII of the United Nations Charter, an urgent meeting of the Security Council. We expect and request the Security Council to take immediate action strongly to condemn and stop the aggression against the Federal Republic of Yugoslavia and to protect its sovereignty and territorial integrity. Until this happens, my country has no alternative but to defend its sovereignty and territorial integrity by all means at its disposal, in accordance with Article 51 of the Charter of the United Nations.

The NATO attacks have been made against my country only because Yugoslavia, as a sovereign and independent State, refuses to allow foreign troops to occupy its territory and to reduce its sovereignty. The excuse for this NATO action was the alleged refusal of the Federal Republic of Yugoslavia to sign the so-called agreement, which had neither been endorsed by all members of the Contact Group nor negotiated with my country. The meetings in France were not negotiations about the autonomy of Kosovo and Metohija, but a crude and unprecedented attempt to impose a solution clearly endorsing the separatists' objectives, under pressure, blackmail and the threat of use of force against my country.

The Government of the Federal Republic of Yugoslavia was and is ready to find a political solution. We give it absolute priority, but we cannot agree to the secession of Kosovo and Metohija, either immediately or after the interim period of three years.

Our delegation had submitted a document on the substantial autonomy and genuine self-government of Kosovo and Metohija on the basis of the 10 principles agreed by the Contact Group. That document is signed by all the members of our delegation. It is fully in line with the highest European standards relating to human rights, democracy and multi-ethnicity. As in the past, we remain committed to a reasonable political settlement of the problems in Kosovo and Metohija that respects the sovereignty and territorial integrity of Serbia and Yugoslavia and guarantees the equality of the rights of all citizens and national communities living there.

If the Security Council does not protect a State Member of the United Nations against such aggression, it will undermine the entire system of international peace and security as we know it. The question is: What has happened to the credibility of the Security Council and who is responsible for maintaining international peace and security? Is it the Security Council or the usurper, NATO? The NATO air strikes have already resulted in heavy destruction and great loss of human life. If this aggression is not stopped immediately and unconditionally, its consequences for peace in the world will be catastrophic.

I call on the members of the Security Council to act swiftly and in accordance with the Charter of the United Nations to condemn this act of aggression and to take appropriate measures to stop it immediately and unambiguously so that all problems may be resolved by political means.

The Government of my country extends an urgent appeal to all States to categorically oppose the current aggression of NATO and the United States of America against the Federal Republic of Yugoslavia. If the aggression is not stopped, the precedent of such unpunished aggression will, sooner or later, lead to aggression against a number of other, smaller and medium-sized countries. The real question is: Which country is next?

Sixty-five years ago, the Emperor Haile Selassie, whose country was subjected to aggression by Fascist Italy - as the Federal Republic of Yugoslavia is today [15] by NATO and the United States of America - entered history with his prophetic outcry that the League of Nations and international peace would be fatally wounded if the aggression did not stop. The United Nations is at the crossroads today, as the League of Nations was then. I hope that, this time, the United Nations chooses the right path. [...]

Mr. Martynov (Belarus): Belarus was among the three States that urged, several hours ago, that an immediate meeting of the Security Council be convened. The President of Belarus issued earlier this morning a statement strongly denouncing the decision of the North Atlantic Treaty Organization (NATO) to use military strikes against a sovereign State.

Belarus stresses that the use of military force against Yugoslavia without a proper decision of the only competent international body, which is undoubtedly the United Nations Security Council, as well as any introduction of foreign military contingents against the wish of the Government of Yugoslavia, qualify as an act of aggression, with all ensuing responsibility for its humanitarian, military and political consequences. Under these circumstances, no rationale, no reasoning presented by NATO can justify the unlawful use of military force and be deemed acceptable.

As a United Nations Member, Belarus is extremely disturbed by the fact that the unlawful military action against Yugoslavia means an intentional disregard for the role and responsibility of the Security Council in maintaining international peace and security.

Let us take a moment and some courage to look into the face of truth. Ignoring the primary and principal body for collective decision-making on maintaining international peace and security-and, in fact, the system itself, which was created and nurtured as a result of the Second World War-means obstructing the system, signing it off and effectively destroying it, thereby ignoring the lessons of the bloodiest-ever war, which the leaders of the Member countries, and above all the permanent members of the Security Council, a generation ago vowed to respect.

It was said today that diplomacy failed. But will lethal military force succeed in fine-tuning a delicate political solution? Is a just settlement in Yugoslavia closer today than it was yesterday? Belarus calls for an immediate stop to the use of force against and in sovereign Yugoslavia. It calls also for the immediate resumption of the negotiating process on a peaceful settlement, including through the Contact Group efforts. Belarus also insists on restoring the Charter role of the Security Council in maintaining international peace and security.

We are convinced that even now, even today, opportunities for renewing the political and diplomatic dialogue can and must be found on the basis of the sovereignty and territorial integrity of Yugoslavia and of respect for the rights of its ethnic groups. [...]

Mr. Sharma (India): Earlier today, after it became known that the North Atlantic Treaty Organization (NATO) was contemplating military action against the Federal Republic of Yugoslavia, the Ministry of External Affairs issued the following statement in New Delhi:

"The Government of India has closely been following developments in Kosovo. It recalls its statement of 9 October 1998 and reiterates that the sovereignty and territorial integrity of the international border of the Federal Republic of Yugoslavia is inviolable. That must be fully respected by all States.

"We are of the firm conviction that the resolution of this crisis can only be through peaceful means, through consultation and dialogue, and not through either confrontation or any military action, unilateral or otherwise. In this regard we wish to reaffirm commitments to the United Nations Charter, which clearly stipulates that no enforcement actions shall be undertaken under regional arrangements without the authorization of the Security Council."

The attacks against the Federal Republic of Yugoslavia that started a few hours ago are in clear violation of Article 53 of the Charter. No country, group of countries or regional arrangement, no mater how powerful, can arrogate to itself the right to take arbitrary and unilateral military action against others. That would be a return to anarchy, where might is right. Among the barrage of justifications that we have heard, we have been told that the attacks are meant to prevent violations of [16] human rights. Even if that were to be so, it does not justify unprovoked military aggression. Two wrongs do not make a right.

Article 2, paragraph 7, of the Charter stipulates that nothing contained in it would

"authorize the United Nations to intervene in matters which are essentially within the domestic jurisdiction of any State or shall require the Members to submit such matters to settlement under the present Charter".

Kosovo is recognized as part of the sovereign territory of the Federal Republic of Yugoslavia. Under the application of Article 2, paragraph 7, the United Nations has no role in the settlement of the domestic political problems of the Federal Republic. The only exception laid down by Article 2, paragraph 7, would be the "application of enforcement measures under Chapter VII". The attacks now taking place against the Federal Republic of Yugoslavia have not been authorized by the Council, acting under Chapter VII, and are therefore completely illegal.

What is particularly disturbing is that both international law and the authority of the Security Council are being flouted by countries that claim to be champions of the rule of law and which contain within their number permanent members of the Council, whose principal interest should surely be to enhance rather than undermine the paramountcy of the Security Council in the maintenance of international peace and security.

We have heard that the attack on the Federal Republic of Yugoslavia will be called off if its Government accepts what are described as NATO peacekeeping forces on its territory. In other forums, we, along with the entire membership of the Non-Aligned Movement, have repeatedly said that the United Nations cannot be forced to abdicate its role in peacekeeping and that a peacekeeping operation can be deployed only with the consent of the Government concerned. Quite apart from being a violation of Article 2, paragraph 7, of the Charter, a peacekeeping operation forced upon a reluctant Government or population stands little chance of success. Somalia established that. In Somalia, there was at least the excuse that State authority had crumbled, but that excuse does not even remotely obtain in the Federal Republic of Yugoslavia. What NATO has tried to do is to intimidate a Government through the threat of attack, and now through direct and unprovoked aggression, to accept foreign military forces on its territory. There are several traditional descriptions for this kind of coercion; peacekeeping is not one of them.

We have also heard that these attacks are meant to ensure that events in the Federal Republic do not threaten regional peace and security. In fact, there is a very real danger that these attacks will imperil regional peace and security and spread discord in the Balkans and beyond.

In the interests of peace and security in the region, and if the countries now attacking the Federal Republic of Yugoslavia truly have the interests of all Yugoslavs at heart, this arbitrary, unauthorized and illegal military action should be stopped immediately. Domestic political problems have to be settled peacefully by the parties concerned through consultation and dialogue. Foreign military intervention can only worsen matters. It will solve nothing.

We urge NATO to immediately stop the military action against the Federal Republic of Yugoslavia, and we trust that the Security Council will be able to exert its authority to bring about an early restoration of the peace that was broken earlier today. [...]

[A statement by the representative of Germany speaking as the Presidency of the European Union has been omitted.]

[18] **Mr. Nesho** (Albania): The moment that we are going through is a historic moment for the future of the Balkans, as the international community is intervening in order to stop the humanitarian catastrophe and the tragedy of a nation whose people have been tortured, killed and buried in common graves, a nation that is justly demanding its legitimate rights to freedom and to its very existence - undeniable rights for all peoples. The Albanians of Kosovo, despite all this, made an exemplary decision by respecting the will of the international community and signing the Rambouillet agreement.

For more than 10 years the international community did not succeed in organizing a common action such as the one undertaken today in order to stop the Belgrade regime from creating a new and dangerous crisis in the heart of Europe. The previous inaction was made possible by prolonged discussion as well as by claiming respect for principles - while in reality Europe at the end of the twentieth century witnessed the massacre of Bosnia, of Racak and other places, and more than 300,000 killings and the creation of millions of refugees.

The Republic of Albania totally supports the military action by the North Atlantic Treaty Organization, and we consider it an action in support of peace and stability in the region. My country strongly supports today's action, just as we were in favour of a peaceful solution, which did not seem to come.

Today the international community did not declare war on Serbia, because war had existed there for a long time. But the international community did achieve the first step towards peace, security in the region and the reestablishment of human values and of the principles that are so well expressed in the Charter of the United Nations - principles in which we all believe.

No country that tried to bury the basic Charter principles of peace, security and cooperation, and that commited genocide and crimes against humanity, can expect to receive the protection of the United Nations and the Security Council.

[A statement by the representative of Bosnia and Herzegovina has been omitted.]

[19] **Mr. Türk** (Slovenia): My delegation has listened very carefully to this important discussion relating to a subject which is not an easy one for any among us, and we heard the categorical words uttered by some concerning the question of the use of force by States. It is true that sometimes force is used without an explicit basis in Security Council resolutions. This is not a new phenomenon. It may be different from the kind of perfect world which we would all like to have, but it is a part of reality.

I would like to refer to only one historical example. In 1971, in Asia, a State Member of the United Nations used force in a situation of extreme necessity. That was a case of the use of force without the authorization of the Security Council and without reference to legitimate selfdefence. Nevertheless, the situation of necessity was very widely understood in the international community. I think that the historical lessons that can be drawn from that example should not be completely ignored today.

I would also like to say something about Security Council resolutions: resolutions 1199 (1998) and 1203 (1998), which are applicable law in the case discussed today. The situation in Kosovo is defined by the Security Council as a threat to international peace and security in the region. This defines that situation as something other than a matter which is essentially within the domestic jurisdiction of a State. In other words, Article 2, paragraph 7, of the Charter clearly does not apply.

Of course, resolutions 1199 (1998) and 1203 (1998) could be clearer, and one might have hoped that such resolutions would develop more completely the responsibility of the Security Council for the maintenance of international peace and security. Those of us who participated in the drafting of those resolutions know very well that the original draft texts were intended to do precisely that, and that, because of differences of views among permanent members, it was not possible to provide in those resolutions a sufficiently complete framework to allow for the entire range of measures that might be necessary to address the situation in Kosovo with success. That is another example of an imperfect world.

I would like to make one more point by way of conclusion. The responsibility of the Security Council for international peace and security is a primary responsibility; it is not an exclusive responsibility. It very much depends on the Security Council, and on its ability to develop [20] policies that will make it worthy of the authority it has under the Charter, whether the primacy of its responsibility will actually be the reality of the United Nations. [...]

251. Draft Resolution Submitted by Belarus, the Russian Federation and India, S/1998/328, 26 March 1999

"The Security Council,

"*Recalling* its primary responsibility under the United Nations Charter for the maintenance of international peace and security,

"*Deeply concerned* that the North Atlantic Treaty Organization (NATO) used military force against the Federal Republic of Yugoslavia without the authorization by the Council,

"*Affirming* that such unilateral use of force constitutes a flagrant violation of the United Nations Charter, in particular Articles 2 (4), 24 and 53,

"*Recognizing* that the ban by NATO of civil flights in the airspace of a number of countries in the region constitutes a flagrant violation of the principle of complete and exclusive sovereignty of every State over the airspace above its territory in accordance with article 1 of the Chicago Convention on International Civil Aviation,

"*Recalling* all its relevant resolutions and decisions, in particular the statement of its President of 29 January 1999 (S/PRST/1999/5), in which it, inter alia, expressed the intention to be informed by members of the Contact Group about the progress reached in the negotiations on a political settlement of the situation in Kosovo, Federal Republic of Yugoslavia, and awaiting such a report,

"*Reaffirming* its commitment to the sovereignty and territorial integrity of the Federal Republic of Yugoslavia,

"*Determining* that the use of force by NATO against the Federal Republic of Yugoslavia constitutes a threat to international peace and security,

"*Acting* under Chapters VII and VIII of the Charter,

"1. *Demands* an immediate cessation of the use of force against the Federal Republic of Yugoslavia and urgent resumption of negotiations;

"2. *Decides* to remain actively seized of the matter."

[Not obtaining the required majority the draft resolution was not adopted.]

252. Extracts from the Debates of the Security Council Concerning Draft Resolution S/1999/328, S/PV. 3989, 26 March 1999[1]

[Members of the Council had before them a draft resolution submitted by Belarus and the Russian Federation. India had joined in sponsoring the draft resolution (S/1999/328.)][2]

[...]

[2] **Mr. Fowler** (Canada) *(spoke in French)*: The draft resolution before us today demands an immediate cessation of the hostilities and urgent resumption of negotiations. What has the entire international community been doing since the beginning of the humanitarian crisis in Kosovo if not negotiating urgently and actively in order to avert this escalation? We dispatched many diplomatic missions and special envoys to Belgrade, under the auspices of the United Nations, of the North Atlantic Treaty Organization and of the Organization for Security and Cooperation in Europe. We also engaged on many occasions in bilateral initiatives aimed at convincing President Milosevic of the seriousness of our intentions. [3] We deployed an international monitoring force and organized a major peace conference. The Security Council adopted a number of resolutions and presidential statements precisely asking President Milosevic to put an end to the brutal repression perpetrated against his fellow-citizens. During that process, President Milosevic took advantage of the international community's good intentions to continue and even intensify his tactic of repression in Kosovo - even while negotiations were under way - in obvious violation of the relevant resolutions of the Security Council and of the commitments he undertook last October.

(spoke in English)

Having done so only 36 hours ago, I do not need to reiterate the extent of the humanitarian crisis in Kosovo. I would, however, remind those members of the Council who need reminding that thousands have

---

[1] *Only statements that add to the legal analysis or the factual background have been included. Presidential statements not related to substantive issues have also been omitted.*

[2] *In 1999, membership of the Security Council was as follows: Argentinia, Bahrain, Brazil, Canada, China, France, Gambia, Malaysia, Namibia, the Netherlands, Russian Federation, Slovenia, the United Kingdom of Great Britain and Northern Ireland and the United States of America. The President invited the representatives of Albania, Belarus, Bosnia and Herzegovina, Germany and India as well as Mr. Vladislav Jovanovic (FRY). The representatives of Cuba and Ukraine were also invited to participate in the discussion, without the right to vote, in accordance with the Charter and rule 37 of the Council's provisional rules of procedure.*

died and many hundreds of thousands remain homeless and at the mercy of extremely harsh winter conditions. Hourly their numbers increase; their homes and farms have been looted and burned and their livestock slaughtered.

Those who would support this draft resolution place themselves outside the international consensus, which holds that the time has come to stop the continuing violence perpetrated by the Government of the Federal Republic of Yugoslavia against its own people. Rather than bringing forward this unproductive draft resolution in an attempt to divert attention from the fundamental humanitarian issue, these countries might more usefully have directed their energies towards convincing the leaders in Belgrade to stop the violence against their people and to accept the Rambouillet peace agreement.

As proposed, this draft resolution would serve only to grant President Milosevic free rein to finish the brutal job he started last year and has since continued to such deadly effect, most prominently at Racak.

For these reasons, Canada will vote against this draft resolution.

Mr. Türk (Slovenia): Slovenia will vote against the draft resolution submitted for action by the Security Council today. The text represents, in our opinion, an inadequate attempt to address the situation concerning Kosovo. It takes a selective political view of the situation and lacks the objectivity necessary in a resolution of the Security Council. The draft resolution ignores the fact that several months ago the Security Council declared the situation in Kosovo to be one constituting a threat to peace and security in the region.

Furthermore, the draft resolution ignores the fact that the Security Council has already spelled out the requirements for the removal of that threat and the fact that those requirements were flagrantly violated by the Federal Republic of Yugoslavia (Serbia and Montenegro). The most dangerous among those violations is the ongoing massive military offensive by the military and security forces of the Federal Republic of Yugoslavia, affecting the civilian population in Kosovo.

All these and other obstacles to the implementation of the resolutions adopted by the Security Council under Chapter VII of the United Nations Charter are ignored in the draft resolution. It appears as if the draft resolution were intended to redefine the assessment of the factual situation contained in resolutions 1160 (1998), 1199 (1998) and 1203 (1998). Proceeding from such a fundamentally flawed factual assessment, the text tries to invoke some of the basic norms of the United Nations Charter. The draft resolution fails to address the relevant circumstances and ignores the situation of necessity which has led to the current international military action. Furthermore, the draft resolution does not even address the stated reasons for that military action, let alone provide any argument against those reasons. Instead, in its third preambular paragraph, it describes that action as a "flagrant violation of the United Nations Charter". The political jargon of "flagrant violation" cannot conceal the lack of convincing argument.

Furthermore, the draft resolution completely fails to reflect the practice of the Security Council, which has several times, including on recent occasions, chosen to remain silent at a time of military action by a regional organization aimed at the removal of a regional threat to peace and security. It is true that each case is unique. However, the requirement of consistency in the interpretation and application of the principles and norms of the United Nations Charter demands at least some indication as to the specific justification for the approach proposed by the draft resolution in the present case. Such indication is sadly lacking and, as I mentioned before, cannot be replaced by the strong words we see in the draft resolution.

For these reasons, the delegation of Slovenia will vote against the draft resolution proposed for action today.

[4] Before concluding, I wish to make an additional, general point. The use of force by the Belgrade Government against the civilian population created a situation that made the current military action inevitable. We would have preferred such military action to be fully authorized by the Security Council; however, that was not possible for reasons that we explained during the discussions of the Security Council two days ago. In the present circumstances, it is important to be aware that, according to the Charter, the Security Council has the primary but not exclusive responsibility for the maintenance of international peace and security. At a moment like this, all the Council members have to think hard about what needs to be done to ensure the Council's authority and to make its primary responsibility as real as the Charter requires.

Mr. van Walsum (Netherlands): Just over five months ago, the adoption of Security Council resolution 1203 (1998) was greeted with relief in the Netherlands, because it was felt that with all the pressure applied on Belgrade in that resolution, it should at last be possible to make President Milosevic see reason and accept a peaceful solution to the problem of Kosovo.

The resolution clearly stated that the Security Council was acting under Chapter VII of the Charter of the United Nations. In the resolution, the Security Council expressed its deep alarm at the impending humanitarian catastrophe in Kosovo, emphasizing the need to keep this from happening. It endorsed and supported the agreements signed in Belgrade between the Federal Republic of Yugoslavia and the Organization for Security and Cooperation in Europe and between the Federal Republic of Yugoslavia and the North Atlantic Treaty Organization (NATO) respectively, and demanded the full and prompt implementation of these agreements by the Federal Republic of Yugoslavia.

Being aware of its strong commitment to the sovereignty and territorial integrity of the Federal Republic of Yugoslavia, we were grateful to Russia for having contributed to this pressure being brought to bear on the Yugoslav leadership.

Since then, however, at every critical juncture Russia has somehow succeeded in making the pressure less credible, so that in the end NATO had no choice but to make good on its threat, which was initially meant to bring about a peaceful solution to the Kosovo crisis. It is legitimate to make a threat hoping that it need never be carried out, but ultimately one must also be prepared to bring a threat into effect. The alternative, which we could not seriously contemplate, would have been to sit back and simply let the humanitarian catastrophe occur.

The NATO action, in which we are participating, follows directly from resolution 1203 (1998), in conjunction with the flagrant non-compliance on the part of the Federal Republic of Yugoslavia. Given its complex background, we cannot allow it to be described as unilateral use of force. If the Security Council should now demand an immediate cessation of the NATO action, it would once again - and once again at the initiative of Russia - give the wrong signal to President Milosevic, leading to a further prolongation of the bloodshed in Kosovo.

It is for this reason that the Netherlands will vote against the draft resolution before us.

Mr. Burleigh (United States of America): The United States greatly appreciates the broad support for the North Atlantic Treaty Organization (NATO) shown in the Security Council this past Wednesday and around the world in the past several days. We emphasize that we and our allies began military action only with the greatest reluctance, after all peaceful options had been thoroughly exhausted. By rejecting a peace settlement and escalating its assault on the people of Kosovo - in violation of numerous Security Council resolutions - Belgrade chose the path of war.

Belgrade continues to attack innocent Kosovars. We have received disturbing reports that Federal Republic of Yugoslavia forces are using human shields, that non-combatants are being rounded up in large groups and that some are being summarily executed. Attempts to verify these reports have been obstructed by the Belgrade Government, which has cracked down on independent journalists in Yugoslavia, harassed and expelled international media, and clamped down on independent human rights groups.

Even today Federal Republic of Yugoslavia forces are pressing their offensive against civilians, burning and looting, and attacking Kosovar Albanian political leaders. Some 60,000 people have been forced to flee their homes since the last round of peace talks began in France, and that number is increasing daily. It stands now at more than 250,000 displaced persons - one in 10 of Kosovo's population. This is a humanitarian catastrophe.

Large refugee flows out of Kosovo into neighbouring countries could have a serious and [5] destabilizing effect. The stability of Albania, of Bosnia and Herzegovina, of the former Yugoslav Republic of Macedonia and of the rest of the region is at stake.

These developments justify sustained military action to limit Belgrade's ability to threaten and harm innocent civilians in Kosovo.

I want to be very clear about the following. We appreciate very much the enormous contribution the Russian Federation has made to advance the cause of peace in Kosovo and in the Balkans, in particular in the context of the Contact Group. The Group's efforts to uphold human rights and to negotiate an equitable settlement to the crisis have been endorsed on several occasions by this Council.

The avenue to peace is clear. In resolutions 1199 (1998) and 1203 (1998) the Security Council laid out the steps Belgrade must take to resolve this crisis. Belgrade, however, has chosen to defy repeatedly the will of the international community.

The draft resolution before us today alleges that NATO is acting in violation of the United Nations Charter. This turns the truth on its head. The United Nations Charter does not sanction armed assaults upon ethnic groups, or imply that the international community should turn a blind eye to a growing humanitarian disaster.

NATO's actions are completely justified. They are necessary to stop the violence and to prevent a further deterioration of peace and stability in the region. The authorities of the Federal Republic of Yugoslavia could quickly bring NATO's actions to a halt by ceasing their brutal attacks against the people of Kosovo and moving to a peace agreement.

This draft resolution should be defeated. If adopted, it could only encourage President Milosevic to continue or even to intensify military repression of the civilian population of Kosovo. Furthermore, if adopted, it would damage prospects for a negotiated settlement and make further bloodshed more likely. In short, the draft resolution does nothing to advance the cause of peace in the Balkans, a cause that the international community and the Security Council have worked long and hard to achieve.

Mr. Lavrov *(spoke in Russian)*: At the 24 March Security Council meeting the Russian delegation set forth its principled assessment of the unilateral use of force against the Federal Republic of Yugoslavia by the member countries of the North Atlantic Treaty Organization (NATO). The continuing military action, undertaken under the pretext of preventing a humanitarian catastrophe, has already caused severe humanitarian consequences and done serious damage to the efforts to find a political settlement in Kosovo. This again confirms how justified we were in stating the absolute need for scrupulous compliance by all States with international law.

The attempts, repeated today, to justify this lawlessness cannot be taken seriously, just as one cannot take seriously the statements, bordering on blackmail, that those who vote in favour of the draft resolution will place themselves outside of the consensus. To the contrary: those who vote against it will place themselves in a situation of lawlessness.

With regard to attempts to distort Russia's position, I would like to recall here that today it was precisely Russia that was in favour of convening an urgent meeting of the ministers of the Contact Group if the military action were to cease.

The aggressive military action unleashed by NATO against a sovereign State without the authorization and in circumvention of the Security Council is a real threat to international peace and security and a gross violation of the United Nations Charter and other basic norms of international law. Key provisions of the Charter are being violated, in particular Article 2, paragraph 4, which requires all Members of the United Nations to refrain from the threat or use of force in their international relations, including against the territorial integrity or political independence of any State; Article 24, which entrusts the Security Council with the primary responsibility for the maintenance of international peace and security; Article 53, on the inadmissibility of any enforcement action under regional arrangements or by regional agencies without the authorization of the Security Council; as well as others.

The illegal use of force by NATO not only destabilizes significantly the situation in the Balkans and in Europe as a whole, but it also directly undermines the fundamental bases of the entire modern system of international relations, which is based on the primacy of the United Nations Charter. One's worst fears are now [6] being fulfilled. The virus of lawlessness is spreading to ever more spheres of international relations. The latest example was the ban declared by NATO on any civil aviation flights in the airspace of the Federal Republic of Yugoslavia, Bosnia and Herzegovina, Macedonia and Croatia. In undertaking this ban, NATO decided to control the fate of other States. That is a gross violation of the principle of the exclusive sovereignty of a State over the airspace above its territory, which is enshrined in the article 1 of the Chicago Convention.

The Security Council cannot and should not remain passive in this situation, which, we are profoundly convinced, runs counter to the fundamental interests of the overwhelming majority of States. Accordingly, the Russian Federation submitted, together with the Republic of Belarus and India, a draft resolution for the consideration of the Security Council that contains a demand for the immediate cessation of the use of force against the Federal Republic of Yugoslavia and that calls for an urgent resumption of talks. A solution of precisely this kind should be urgently sought by the international community if it is really interested in preventing unilateral approaches and the prevalence of force in world affairs.

We know that many members of the Security Council are racked with doubts over this vote. What is in the balance now is the question of law and lawlessness. It is a question of either reaffirming the commitment of one's country and people to the basic principles and values of the United Nations Charter, or of tolerating a situation in which gross force dictates realpolitik. Doubts can also been seen on the part of NATO countries. In an editorial dated 25 March, the Financial Times says,

"So far, Governments of NATO countries are apparently united on bombing, but their publics and parliaments are not." ("NATO politics", p. 15)

We do not want to moralize here, but we cannot forget the fact that members of the Security Council bear a special responsibility not only to their peoples but to all Members of the United Nations, upon which decisions of the Council are binding under the Charter. Today's vote is not just on the problem of Kosovo. It goes directly to the authority of the Security Council in the eyes of the world community. Members of the Council cannot ignore the demands that we are now hearing in various parts of the world - made by, among others, the Rio Group, the Council of Defence Ministers of the member countries of the Commonwealth of Independent States and members of the Non-Aligned Movement - to stop the military aggression and to respect international legality.

The capacity of the Security Council to defend the United Nations Charter is key for the future of the United Nations. If the Council cannot do this, then no negotiations or talks about reforming the Council will help.

I will not be asking for the floor after the voting. As I have said, law and lawlessness are in the balance today. It is up to the members of the Security Council to make their choice, which they will do at this public meeting, before the eyes of all the members of the international community, in conditions of full transparency.

[The President put to vote draft resolution S/1999/328. China, Namibia and the Russian Federation voted in favour while the 12 other members of the Council voted against it. Not obtaining the required majority the draft resolution was not adopted.]

Mr. Eldon (United Kingdom): As Sir Jeremy Greenstock set out in detail in the Security Council debate on 24 March, the international community has over the past year made exhaustive efforts to resolve the crisis in Kosovo through negotiation. Every means short of force was used to try to avert the current situation. These efforts have failed because President Milosevic has flouted the demands of the international community, including successive Security Council resolutions, allowed his forces to continue their violent oppression of civilians in Kosovo and ignored all appeals to negotiate a [7] political settlement. He has acted in defiance of the expressed will of the Security Council.

As recognized in Security Council resolutions 1199 (1998) and 1203 (1998), it is Belgrade's policies with regard to Kosovo that have caused the threat to peace and security in the region, not the actions of the North Atlantic Treaty Organization (NATO). In the current circumstances, military intervention is justified as an exceptional measure to prevent an overwhelming humanitarian catastrophe.

Adoption of the draft resolution before us today would simply have signalled to President Milosevic that there was no check on his repressive action in Kosovo. It would have done nothing to avert an imminent humanitarian catastrophe. That is why the United Kingdom voted against it.

As I said earlier, our position was explained in great detail in the Council's debate on 24 March. I do not, therefore, want to go too far into the substance of the draft resolution on which we have just voted in my statement now. But I should refer to the suggestion in the Security Council draft resolution, repeated today by the representative of the Russian Federation, that NATO has banned civil flights over a number of countries in the Balkan region. This is incorrect; NATO has no power to do this. What has actually happened is that NATO advised Croatia, Albania, Macedonia and Bosnia that the NATO air strikes could make their airspace unsafe for civil flights. In the light of that advice, these countries decided to close their airspace to such flights. There has therefore been no breach either of the United Nations Charter or of the Chicago Convention.

Mr. Dejammet (France) *(spoke in French)*: During the formal meeting held by the Security Council on 24 March 1999, my delegation laid out the reasons for France's involvement in the actions under way in the Federal Republic of Yugoslavia.

The Security Council adopted resolutions 1160 (1998), 1199 (1998) and 1203 (1998) under Chapter VII of the United Nations Charter. In resolutions 1199 (1998) and 1203 (1998), the Security Council affirmed that the deterioration of the situation in Kosovo constituted a threat to peace and security in the region. In resolution 1199 (1998), the Security Council made a certain number of demands addressed, in particular, to the Belgrade authorities.

In its resolution 1203 (1998), the Security Council endorsed and supported the agreements concluded between the Federal Republic of Yugoslavia and the Organization for Security and Cooperation in Europe, on the one hand, and between the Federal Republic of Yugoslavia and the North Atlantic Treaty Organization, on the other. The Security Council demanded the full and prompt implementation of these agreements by the Federal Republic of Yugoslavia. These agreements involved specific obligations and commitments on the part of the Yugoslav Government.

These obligations have not been respected by Belgrade. Meanwhile, tension, confrontation and the threat of violent repression have increased. The actions decided upon respond to Belgrade's violation of its international obligations under the resolutions which the Security Council has adopted under Chapter VII of the United Nations Charter.

The draft resolution that was submitted to us runs directly counter to our judgement. That is why France voted against it.

Mr. Petrella (Argentina) *(spoke in Spanish)*: The delegation of Argentina wishes to explain its position in the voting that has just taken place on the draft resolution in document S/1999/328, submitted by the delegations of Belarus and the Russian Federation and co-sponsored by the delegation of India.

In this connection, we wish to state that Argentina's negative vote was based on the vital need to contribute to putting an end to the extremely grave violations of human rights that are taking place in the province of Kosovo, Federal Republic of Yugoslavia. These violations are clearly documented in many reports of the Secretary-General and inspire the many principles that lie at the core of Security Council resolutions 1160 (1998), 1199 (1998) and 1203 (1998).

Argentina also wishes to stress that the fulfilment of the legal norms of international humanitarian law and human rights is a response to universally recognized and accepted values and commitments. The obligation to protect and ensure respect for these rights falls to everyone and cannot and must not be debated. That obligation is all the more urgent given that it has been alleged, witnessed and proven that, in that region, extremely serious international crimes have been [8] committed, including acts of genocide, some of which are being tried in a special tribunal established by this Council.

Since 1992, Argentina has been and remains involved in the Balkans through peacekeeping operations. The position we are taking here is based on our own direct experience, acquired in the field. Ultimately, this position, based on fundamental legal principles and on practical experience, cannot come as a surprise. We cannot accept a draft resolution that fails to mention earlier resolutions of the Security Council on the question of Kosovo, disregards the extremely grave humanitarian context and does not take into account the background and precedents of that region. Any document, statement or - as in this case - draft resolution that does not recognize reality lacks balance. It cannot contribute to a peaceful settlement of the problem and encourages the most negative elements at work in the Federal Republic of Yugoslavia.

For all these reasons, we once again respectfully urge all of those with the capacity to exert influence in the region, in particular the Russian Federation, to pursue their valuable and recognized efforts to put an end to this extremely grave crisis and to arrive at a comprehensive and definitive agreement to restore lasting peace.

We sincerely sympathize with the victims of this situation and we are prepared to do all within our capacity to alleviate their suffering, particularly that of the refugees and displaced persons, many of whom have forever lost their homes.

Mr. Rastam (Malaysia): Malaysia fully subscribes to the fundamental principle of the paramount need to preserve the sanctity of the Charter of the United Nations. The Charter confers upon the Security Council the primary responsibility for the maintenance of international peace and security. Malaysia underlined clearly, when the Council met on Wednesday, that any conflict should be resolved through dialogue and political negotiations and not by the use of force. Force, if at all necessary, should be a recourse of last resort and it should be sanctioned by the Security Council.

It is to our great disappointment that serious efforts at finding a peaceful resolution to the conflict in Kosovo have failed. The Yugoslav leadership bears full responsibility for the failure of those efforts, since it continues to reject the Rambouillet accords and chooses to carry out massive military offensives against the people of Kosovo, even at this very hour. We take serious note of the information provided through the letter of the Secretary-General, dated 25 March 1999 in document S/1999/338, in which the Secretary-General of the North Atlantic Treaty Organization (NATO) states that

"Following the withdrawal of the Kosovo Verification Mission of the Organization for Security and Cooperation in Europe (OSCE) on 20 March, the Federal Republic of Yugoslavia has increased its military activities and is using excessive and wholly disproportionate force, thereby creating a further humanitarian catastrophe". (S/1999/338, p. 2)

The draft resolution has completely ignored this reality.

Malaysia remains gravely concerned at the worsening situation on the ground in Kosovo. The violent repression by the Serbian and Yugoslav security forces against the population in Kosovo has increased dramatically in the past few days. The current Serbian military offensive has resulted in further deaths and destruction. Large numbers of civilians, especially women and children, have been forcibly displaced from their homes and villages. The present action by Serb forces against the Kosovar Albanians is certainly creating an immense humanitarian catastrophe. Such a tragic situation calls for appropriate and prompt action by the international community.

Security Council resolutions 1199 (1998) and 1203 (1998) both invoke Chapter VII of the Charter and recognize that the situation in Kosovo constitutes a threat to international peace and security in the region. In resolution 1199 (1998), the Council had demanded that the Yugoslav authorities take immediate steps to improve the humanitarian situation and avert the impending humanitarian catastrophe. The Council had also, in resolution 1203 (1998), demanded that the same authorities implement fully and promptly the ceasefire agreements signed with NATO on 15 October 1998 and with the OSCE on 16 October 1998.

In its presidential statement of 29 January 1999, the Council welcomed and supported the peace process initiated by the Contact Group, culminating in the Rambouillet accords, which the Kosovar Albanians signed on 18 March 1999. Unfortunately, the Yugoslav leadership not only has failed to comply with the resolutions of the Council, but also continues to reject the Rambouillet accords and rebuff all efforts at finding a political solution to the conflict.

[9] In light of the foregoing, Malaysia had no other option but to vote against the draft resolution, as we have just done.

As we also stated during the meeting last Wednesday, Malaysia would have wished that the crisis in Kosovo could have been dealt with directly and in an effective manner by the Security Council. The outcome of the action that the Council has just taken today, however, demonstrates clearly the serious and irreconcilable differences in the Council. Malaysia therefore regrets that in the absence of Council action on the issue it has been necessary for measures to be taken outside of the Council.

Mr. Buallay (Bahrain) *(spoke in Arabic)*: This meeting has been convened by the Security Council in conditions of extreme urgency. The Belgrade authorities have been given one opportunity after another to reach a peaceful settlement to the problem of Kosovo. The party representing the Kosovar Albanians had agreed to a peaceful settlement at Rambouillet and had signed the agreement. The Serb side, however, refused to sign and has continued to use extreme force in the Kosovo region, causing thousands of casualties and displacing thousands of persons. The result is a humanitarian crisis of tremendous proportions that cannot be resolved without the cooperation of neighbouring States.

In view of this situation, we were not able to vote in favour of the draft resolution before the Council today, because it would have encouraged the Belgrade authorities to continue with their current policy of "ethnic cleansing" and led to more massacres and displacements for the Kosovar Albanians.

The President *(spoke in Chinese)*: I shall now make a statement in my capacity as the representative of China.

The continued military strikes against the Federal Republic of Yugoslavia by the North Atlantic Treaty Organization, with the United States at the lead, has already resulted in severe casualties and damage, and the situation in the Balkan region has seriously deteriorated. The Chinese Government strongly opposes such an act, which constitutes a blatant violation of the principles of the Charter of the United Nations and of international law, as well as a challenge to the authority of the Security Council. We would like to reiterate our strong call for an immediate cessation of this military action, so as to facilitate the restoration of peace in the Balkan region at an early date.

China has always stood for the peaceful settlement of disputes through negotiations. We oppose the use or the threat of use of force in international affairs. We oppose the power politics of the strong bullying the weak. We oppose interference in the internal affairs of other States, under whatever pretext, in whatever form. The Chinese delegation would like to reiterate that the question of Kosovo, being an internal matter of the Federal Republic of Yugoslavia, should be resolved by the parties concerned in the Federal Republic of Yugoslavia among themselves.

The Kosovo issue should be settled on the basis of respect for the sovereignty and territorial integrity of the Federal Republic of Yugoslavia and of a guarantee of the legitimate rights and interests of all the ethnic groups in the Kosovo area.

It was based on the above principles that the Chinese delegation voted in favour of the draft resolution before us. We deeply regret that the Council has failed to adopt this draft, which is in conformity with the basic principles of the Charter of the United Nations and international law. [...]

Mr. Yel'chenko (Ukraine): [...] At the outset, I would like to read the statement issued by the Ministry for Foreign Affairs of Ukraine on 24 March 1999, since it expresses the position of my Government with regard to the subject currently under consideration by the Security Council in a most comprehensive and condensed manner. That statement reads as follows:

[10] "It is with deep concern that Ukraine has received the news about the North Atlantic Treaty Organization (NATO) air strikes against the targets on the territory of the Federal Republic of Yugoslavia.

"Adhering to the norms and principles enshrined in the United Nations Charter, Ukraine considers as inadmissible the use of military force against a sovereign State without the authorization of the United Nations Security Council- the only body entrusted to take such decisions in order to maintain international peace and security.

"At the same time, Belgrade's refusal to sign the agreements elaborated through the mediation of the Contact Group resulted in the breakdown of the negotiating process. Therefore, the provisions of Security Council resolutions 1160 (1998) and 1199 (1998) have not been fully implemented, and that led to the use of force.

"Ukraine urges the parties to the conflict, as well as the international community, to urgently exert additional efforts in order to stop the further escalation of the conflict. It is necessary to return as soon as possible to a peaceful political settlement on the basis of the preservation of the sovereignty and territorial integrity of the Federal Republic of Yugoslavia and the granting of a wide autonomy to Kosovo.

"Ukraine reaffirms its readiness to contribute to the efforts aimed at restoring peace and ensuring stability and respect for human rights, including the rights of national minorities, on the territory of the Federal Republic of Yugoslavia."

That was the statement of the Ministry for Foreign Affairs of Ukraine of 24 March. Even though it was issued as far back as two days ago, all of its provisions remain topical with regard to the current crisis in the centre of Europe. My country has good grounds to be seriously concerned about this crisis, because it is fraught with the danger of unpredictable consequences. We are ready to do everything possible in order to avert such consequences.

That is why Ukraine has already become actively involved in the efforts to stop the crisis and to achieve a peaceful solution of the Kosovo problem. I would like to inform this body, which we still believe bears the primary responsibility for the maintenance of international peace and security, about the current visit to Belgrade by the Foreign Minister of Ukraine, Mr. Tarasyuk, which is under way as we speak. This peacemaking mission, undertaken by the Foreign Minister of Ukraine, is further proof of the sincere aspiration of my country to contribute constructively to the cause of finding a solution to the conflict and to the restoration of peace and stability in the entire Balkan region.

In the course of negotiations with the leadership of the Federal Republic of Yugoslavia, the Ukrainian Foreign Minister will put forward a number of concrete proposals which could lead to the suspension of NATO air strikes against the Federal Republic of Yugoslavia, the resumption of the negotiating process between the parties to the conflict in Kosovo, the return of the Organization for Security and Cooperation in Europe Verification Mission, the settlement of the refugee problem, the preservation of the territorial integrity of the Federal Republic of Yugoslavia and the granting of wide autonomy to Kosovo.

One of the specific proposals to be made by the Foreign Minister of Ukraine is to reconsider the question of the guarantees to secure the political settlement in Kosovo through the deployment there of a multinational peacekeeping force with a composition acceptable to all parties. As soon as I receive information about the results of negotiations in Belgrade, I will immediately make them known to the members of the Security Council.

In the meantime, I would like to emphasize that the sine qua non of any peaceful solution must be full implementation by both the authorities of the Federal Republic of Yugoslavia and the leaders of the Kosovo Albanian community of all the relevant provisions of Security Council resolutions 1160 (1998), 1199 (1998) and 1203 (1998), first of all with regard to the maintenance of an effective ceasefire and withdrawal of Serbian security forces involved in the repressive actions against the population in Kosovo.

I do not want to comment on the results of the vote that has just been taken. I just want to say, on a personal note, that the discussion we have heard reminded me very much of the grim times of the cold war. I sincerely believe that it is not the wish of anyone in this room that those grim times come back. [...]

[11] **Mr. Jovanovic**: My country has been a victim of the brutal unlawful aggression of the North Atlantic Treaty Organization (NATO), led by the United States of America, for the third straight day. The most powerful war machine in the world has made a sovereign and peaceful country and its proud people into a killing field and a testing ground for its most sophisticated weaponry and military games.

Tramping upon each and every principle of international relations, defying the authority of the Security Council of the United Nations and its resolutions and outperforming even the Nazis in its animosity towards and hatred of the Serbian and Montenegrin people, NATO, led by the United States of America, has engaged in a mad orgy of destruction and havoc against one small and peaceloving country. They disgracefully distort the truth about the events in Kosovo and Metohija, openly supporting and assisting separatists and terrorists and demonizing the Serbian people and my country in a shameless attempt to manipulate the world public and provide a cover for their aggression.

By attacking Yugoslavia, NATO aircraft have become the air force and the ally of the terrorist Kosovo Liberation Army (KLA). The NATO aggression has stepped up the KLA terrorist activities, not only against the Yugoslav security forces, but also against civilians, including Albanians. A victim of this aggression, we have no choice but to defend ourselves and preserve our sacred land of Kosovo and Metohija, which is the soul of the Serbian national being. Opposing the aggression, we also uphold the basic principles of the Charter of the United Nations.

The aggression and the massive and reckless bombing campaign is not limited to the so-called military targets alone, but brings death to hundreds of civilians and destroys property. In a callous act, the aggressors did not spare the memorial park in the martyr city of Kragujevac, in which tens of thousands of victims of Nazi genocide from the Second World War are buried, or the museum town of Cetinje, which have no military significance at all. Two camps of Serbian refugees from Croatia and Bosnia and Herzegovina and two student hostels were hit, as well.

For the third time in this century, the Serbian people have been presented with an ultimatum. In 1914, the Habsburgs issued an ultimatum, demanding the Kingdom of Serbia so as to throw its sovereignty underfoot, but the Serbian people rejected it. In 1941, the Axis Powers gave the Kingdom of Yugoslavia an ultimatum to join them or be destroyed. The Serbs refused to capitulate and rejected the ultimatum once again.

Now Yugoslavia is faced with another ultimatum, this time from NATO - from so-called democratic countries. It has been offered two alternatives: either voluntarily to give up a part of its territory or to have it taken away by force. This is the essence of the "solution" for Kosovo and Metohija that was offered by way of an ultimatum at the "negotiations" in France.

The flagrant aggression by NATO countries, led by the United States, cannot be justified on any grounds whatsoever. The fact that they change position and objectives every day is telling proof that they do not believe in what they are saying themselves. If the aggression goes on, the Federal Republic of Yugoslavia will continue to protect its sovereignty and territorial integrity on the basis of Article 51 of the United Nations Charter. However, once the aggression is stopped, we will be ready to resume negotiations about political solutions of the problem in Kosovo and Metohija on the basis of the 10 principles adopted by the Contact Group on 29 January 1999 and the document signed in Paris by the members of our delegation.

By attacking Yugoslavia, NATO has not solved the alleged humanitarian catastrophe in Kosovo and Metohija, which they so maliciously presented as a casus belli; on the contrary, they themselves are creating a catastrophe of enormous proportions for all citizens of Yugoslavia and for peace and stability in the region and beyond.

Their aggression is unjust, illegal, indecent and unscrupulous. The aggressor displays arrogant contempt for the United Nations and its Charter and arrogates the prerogatives of the Security Council as the only organ in charge of maintaining international peace and security. The United Nations should not allow them to rob it of its rights and duties. The Security Council is in a position to prevent this if it strongly condemns the aggression today and requests NATO to stop it immediately and unconditionally.

If the Security Council fails to do so it will be responsible for the breakdown of the present system of international relations. Today the Security Council is not taking only a decision on the fate of my country, but a historic decision on its own future as well. It is up to the Council to decide whether it will retain the responsibility that it bears under the Charter for the maintenance of international peace and security, or whether it will cede [12] that responsibility to NATO. Today, the Council has made its choice. The right of might will be enthroned instead of the might of right. [...]

Mr. Sychou (Belarus) *(spoke in Russian)*: As before, the Republic of Belarus is extremely concerned at the illegal aggressive military action that the North Atlantic Treaty Organization (NATO) is carrying out against the Federal Republic of Yugoslavia. It was because of the primary responsibility that the Security Council bears for the maintenance of international peace and security that the Republic of Belarus was among the States that called for the convening of an emergency meeting of the Council and that joined in sponsoring the draft resolution that was before the Council at this meeting.

The President and the Government of the Republic of Belarus have repeatedly declared their commitment to a peaceful settlement of this conflict. We are convinced that even today opportunities for continuing dialogue can and should be found. It is there that we see the key role of the Security Council pursuant to its powers under the United Nations Charter.

In that connection, we express our profound concern and disappointment at the fact that the draft resolution was not adopted. The Republic of Belarus considers that decision by the Council to be utterly counterproductive. In view of the continuing massive military strikes against a sovereign State, in view of the civilian casualties and in view of all the destruction, it is scarcely possible to accept the arguments put forward by representatives of NATO about the alliance resolving the humanitarian crisis in Kosovo through the use of force. We are firmly convinced that the use of force will not promote stability or put an end to the confrontation between the parties. The decision to use force, which is an extreme measure, may be made only by the Security Council taking into account the views of the States Members of the Organization.

Today, we are witnessing a negative turn of events: the violation of basic principles of international law that make no provision for military intervention for humanitarian purposes. The consequences of these actions cannot be predicted. They threaten to undermine the United Nations system and, indeed, international relations as a whole. The Republic of Belarus again calls on the Security Council to take all necessary steps to put a halt to these NATO military actions and to stop the bloodshed. We also call for the resumption of the work of the Contact Group on the former Yugoslavia, in the interest of the resumption of dialogue between the parties to the conflict and of advancing the peace process in the region. We believe that the present events give the Organization a historic opportunity to demonstrate to the entire world the supremacy of the principles and ideals that are enshrined in the United Nations Charter.

The Republic of Belarus reaffirms its position on the settlement of the Kosovo conflict: it should be based on unconditional respect for the sovereignty and territorial integrity of Yugoslavia and on the non-use of force, in keeping with the rights of all ethnic groups. Scrupulous adherence to those principles alone will guarantee the establishment of a solid, lasting peace in Kosovo. [...]

Mr. Rodriguez Parrilla (Cuba) *(spoke in Spanish)*: With this shameful vote, the Security Council has just missed a historic opportunity. By their vote, Council members have assumed an enormous responsibility.

I wish at the outset to read out a statement issued by the Republic of Cuba on the aggression by the North Atlantic Treaty Organization (NATO). That statement reads as follows:

"Following a series of distressing and highly manipulative political events, prolonged armed clashes, and complex - and hardly transparent - negotiations on the question of Kosovo, the North Atlantic Treaty Organization (NATO) finally launched its heralded brutal air attacks against the Federal Republic of Yugoslavia, whose peoples were the most heroic of those who fought the Nazi hordes in Europe during the Second World War.

"This action, intended to 'punish the Yugoslav Government', is being conducted outside the context of the Security Council, where the main promoter of the aggression, the United States, would have had to face opposed any action that could undermine the prerogatives of that organ under the United Nations Charter with respect to the maintenance of international peace and security. This [13] has thus led to a violation of the norms and principles of international law.

"The war launched by NATO revives mankind's justified fears concerning the emergence of a contemptuous uni-polar system governed by a warlike empire that has declared itself to be the world's policeman and that is capable of dragging its political and military allies into the most foolish of actions. This is similar to what took place early and during the first half of this century with the creation of military blocs that enshrouded Europe in destruction, death and misery, dividing it and weakening it as the United States built up its own economic, political and military might.

"We may well ask whether the use and abuse of force will solve the world's problems and protect the human rights of the innocent people who are dying today because of the missiles and bombs that are falling upon a small country of cultured, civilized Europe.

"The Ministry of Foreign Affairs of the Republic of Cuba vigorously condemns this aggression against Yugoslavia by the North Atlantic Treaty Organization (NATO), under the leadership of the United States, and it denounces the dishonest manoeuvring that has led to the continued imposition of such uncivilized practices on the international political scene in order to satisfy the interests of those seeking to impose their designs on all the States of the globe in the name of a new and unworthy world order, created in their image and likeness.

"During this time of suffering and pain for the peoples of Yugoslavia, Cuba urges the international community to rally its forces in order to put an immediate end to this unjustifiable aggression, to avoid further and even more regrettable losses of innocent life and to allow that nation to resume the peaceful course of negotiations so as to solve its internal problems - matters that depend solely and exclusively on the sovereign will and self-determination of the Yugoslav peoples.

"Cuba expresses its concern that the aggression could, in an unpredictable manner, spread to the other States of the region, either because of the violence itself or because of its unsettling social and human effects.

"The ridiculous attempt to impose solutions by force is incompatible with any civilized reasoning and with the essential principles of international law. The firmness of the positions that are being used to try to justify this new crime only reflects the moral impossibility of sustaining ideas and policies that run counter to the interests of the peoples involved in the conflict and of imposing on them an imperial will. If this course were to be continued, there could be unforeseeable consequences for Europe and for all of humankind."

We are living in a shameful time in which international legality is being violated. Never before has the uni-polar order imposed by the United States been so obvious and so disturbing. When the Security Council serves as its docile instrument, then the United Nations seems to be working, and its foundations - the Charter and international law - seem to be in force, although they are always subject to capricious interpretations and gross manipulation.

Some days ago we were surprised to witness an occasion on which the Security Council refused to authorize an international criminal act by the United States and its accomplices. Today we have witnessed the capitulation of the Security Council. When the Security Council plucks up its courage and refuses to yield to unipolar might, and tries to fulfil the responsibilities that the Charter and the community of nations have entrusted to it, then the super-Power, which does not accept lack of discipline on the part of its subjects, takes matters into its own hands.

The no-flight zones, the missiles striking Kabul, Khartoum, Tripoli, Baghdad and Benghazi, and now Pristina, Pancevo and other cities, remind us of the harsh realities of global disorder. What is going to become of the Security Council, or at least of its remains, after today's vote? What will become of the United Nations?

democracy and transparency, in this high command - the Security Council - everyone's real position becomes painfully clear: the positions of those who play with words in order to conceal hegemonic interests, and of those of us who make up the great majority that is always ignored and always subject to the political pressure of the powerful, because the majority often forgets the weight of our countries when we unite to reclaim our place. If we do not take our rightful place, the United Nations, instead of developing as the emerging [14] government of a global democracy in a globalized and united world, will merely be a crude, repressive instrument of the powerful, as this meeting has made clear.

No one can forget in these tragic circumstances, in which the destiny of us all is at stake, the historic contribution made by the Serbs during the Second World War, when they fought more heroically than any other people against fascism and against the Nazi hordes in occupied Europe. Humankind cannot be stripped of its memory, however intoxicated it may be by technology used to disseminate lies or by television used to promote war. It must be recalled here and now - because it is a fact - that these are the bitter fruits of a conspiracy to destroy Yugoslavia. That is what is at the root of this conflict and of the grave events we are now experiencing.

Some of those who today are brutally bombing in the past conspired and fought to dismember that noble and multi-ethnic country. Today they are punishing some of those they previously promoted. Bombs are not the path to peace. War is no humanitarian solution. History teaches us that only negotiations can build peace. Cuba hopes that - without delay, because every minute costs lives - an end will be put to the armed aggression, and there will be a resumption of negotiations in order to reach a just and lasting peace, as a condition for full respect for the rights and the dignity of all the ethnic groups, peoples and religions of the former Yugoslavia. [...]

Mr. Sacirbey (Bosnia and Herzegovina): The last time we spoke before the Security Council we emphasized in our statement that resorting to the military alternative is never welcome. We would only wish to further proclaim that view. Unfortunately, though, on the basis of events in Kosovo over the last couple of days, we can only come even more surely to the conclusion that military force sometimes is the only alternative left.

We want to join all who believe that the most prompt cessation of all military action is desirable. But have any of the demands made by the Security Council in past resolutions, or the demands of the Contact Group, been accepted? Has Belgrade accepted the peace plan?

Unfortunately the Serbian defence against the North Atlantic Treaty Organization (NATO) has primarily consisted of an intensified campaign against its own civilian population, particularly the Kosovar Albanians. But this goes beyond the issue of courage and morality. It goes to the heart of the only two visible strategies pursued by Belgrade: "Let NATO bomb; we will hurry up to create faits accomplis on the ground by completing the tactic of ethnic cleansing. If some Serbs are hurt, if they have to die, and if more Kosovars are killed, so be it, so much the better."

Does anyone remember the ethnic cleansing and genocide committed against Bosnians? I must say that I feel deeply disturbed, even insulted, when after the experience in Bosnia some rush to condemn military measures to confront Belgrade's continuing resistance to peace and escalated ethnic cleansing campaign. Who are the real victims and who are the victimizers?

Should those rushing to complete ethnic cleansing hope to garner sympathy while the civilian victims of such cleansing wonder if they are being forgotten, or even ignored? Did we learn something from the Bosnia experience, at least gain sensitivity to the victims of genocide?

Let me set aside my moral outrage. Let me turn to the alternatives of realpolitik. Do the supporters of this draft resolution believe that a unilateral end to NATO's action would produce anything positive for Kosovo, for Bosnia and Herzegovina or for the region as a whole? The Belgrade authorities would only then claim a victory, the victory of a brave fighter standing up to the mightiest military force on earth. The new mythology of the Battle of Kosovo, 1999, would be written and the current Belgrade authorities would use this as a revitalized tool, a weapon of war, against the Kosovars, Bosnia and our other neighbours; indeed, as a tool to further enslave the emotions and minds of the Serb people themselves.

If this draft resolution had been adopted or even succeeded in garnering significant support, this would have been a defeat for peace in Bosnia and Herzegovina. Let me emphasize: that would have been a defeat for peace in Bosnia and Herzegovina. We are not here to preach morality, but we are here to plead for the cause of peace in our country and the region as a whole.

Let me take note of one final point - and I am very happy to see that the Secretary-General has been here throughout this entire debate. Like many other Members of the United Nations, we are concerned by the implications of this matter: the NATO military action [15] being undertaken without the sanction of the United Nations Security Council. However, we would be even more concerned and dismayed if the Security Council were blocked and there were no response to the humanitarian crisis and to the legal obligation to confront ethnic cleansing and war crime abuses.

The Security Council has on numerous occasions called for Belgrade to refrain from its disastrous policies in Kosovo. Belgrade has refused to heed the Security Council. Then the Contact Group was given the mandate of bringing peace. The Contact Group made several fair and progressive proposals for peace. The Kosovar Albanians accepted a proposal. Belgrade rejected the peace proposal and actually responded by intensifying its resort to military force against the Albanian Kosovars. Finally, all the Contact Group members except one resorted to the only step available, the step that had been threatened for quite some time against Belgrade's obstinacy.

Is the Security Council now to be used as a marginalized institution to actually block or criticize the only viable response in order to bring peace and to stop vast human rights abuses? Remember, these abuses are themselves the most serious violations of the United Nations Charter. I do not need to cite the Ambassador of Slovenia, Danilo Turk, on this point.

When the war against Bosnia and Herzegovina was being waged, the United Nations was too frequently criticized, even savaged, for its ineffectiveness in stopping the war in Bosnia and Herzegovina - the human rights violations, genocide and aggression that we suffered. Unfortunately, even we were too frequently a part of pointing the finger at the United Nations. For this we would like to apologize to all those who may have misunderstood us in our time of deep need.

Now, in hindsight, it is clear that responsibility in the failures and successes of Bosnia lay with the United Nations Members themselves, particularly the most powerful: the members of the Security Council. The same responsibility now exists with respect to Kosovo. Let us not once again allow the Security Council and the United Nations to be seen as ineffective in, or even as an obstacle to, the necessary steps for peace or, even more so, for stopping the vast human rights abuses.

In the alternative, should we debate here in the Security Council the necessary response to what is going on in Kosovo, to what Belgrade is doing in Kosovo, as we did for Bosnia and Herzegovina for three and a half years? Do we have the luxury of that time? Are we to set aside daily the lives that are being wrecked and lost?

Why does Bosnia and Herzegovina speak before the Security Council today? Well, first of all, let me mention that there is the issue of self-interest. And I would like to correct one point: Bosnia and Herzegovina's airspace is closed on the basis of our own decision. I believe the case with Croatia is the same.

There is also an issue of history. Just before my statement, I heard the representative of Cuba speak of the fight of the Serbs against Nazism. The Bosnians were part of that fight. My uncles died in that fight. The greatest resistance to the Nazis was found in Bosnia. I do not with to see history once again rewritten here on another point.

There is also a moral obligation. We in Bosnia came and pleaded before the Security Council, and then pleaded outside the Security Council to the Contact Group and others, for any salvation, any response. Thanks to many of the countries around this table - France, the United Kingdom, the United States and many others - that response finally came. We say it was late, but it was welcome. We do not wish to see now a response come too late for the Kosovars. We do not wish to see once again a response come late once again for Bosnia, if once again injustice, nationalism and ethnic cleansing are allowed to go undisturbed in our region.

I would be here before the Council if the issue were Sierra Leone or any other situation that deserved its urgent attention.

Unfortunately, in today's world it seems that we cannot hope for the United Nations and the Security Council to always be effective and prompt in bringing peace. That is unfortunately the reality that we deal with. But at least we should not allow the Security Council and the United Nations to be seen as an obstacle. [...]

Mr. Sharma (India): It is a matter of very great concern to us that the attacks of the North Atlantic Treaty Organization (NATO) on the Federal Republic of Yugoslavia continue, with the Security Council reduced to helplessness. As we said in the Council when it met on 24 March, we expected it to exert its authority to bring about an early return of the peace that was broken by the [16] bombing. The draft resolution prepared by the Russian Federation has aims to which we completely subscribe. It calls for an immediate end to this senseless violence and it seeks to re-establish the authority of the Security Council, which has been one of the early victims of NATO's bombing campaign. We therefore joined as a co-sponsor.

We deeply regret that the Council has not adopted this draft. The effect will be to prevent a return of the peace that the international community so dearly wants and which permanent members, three of whom cast vetoes in pursuit of national interests, have a special responsibility to uphold.

It is clear that NATO will not listen to the Security Council. It would appear that it believes itself to be above the law. We find this deeply uncomfortable. In New Delhi earlier today, the External Affairs Minister said that India cannot accept any country's taking on the garb of a world policeman. NATO argues that the Serb police in Kosovo act violently and without any respect for law. Unfortunately, NATO seems to have taken on the persona and the methods of operation of those whose activities it wants to curb.

It is natural to be revolted by violence and to want to put an end to human suffering. However, between nations as within them, populations can be protected, the law upheld and those who break it punished only through legal means. The cure otherwise is as bad as the disease. It is also very rarely effective and often makes things worse. Those who take the law into their hands have never improved civic peace within nations; neither will they help in international relations.

Those who continue to attack the Federal Republic of Yugoslavia profess to do so on behalf of the international community and on pressing humanitarian grounds. They say that they are acting in the name of humanity. Very few members of the international community have spoken in this debate, but even among those who have, NATO would have noted that China, Russia and India have all opposed the violence which it has unleashed. The international community can hardly be said to have endorsed their actions when already representatives of half of humanity have said that they do not agree with what they have done.

Mr. Fowler (Canada): The representative of India made reference to the fact that three vetoes had been cast in this morning's voting. I would simply like to point out, as the representative of a country that is rather sensitive about the issue of the veto, that my understanding is that the rules are very clear. There were no vetoes cast this morning. A veto is cast only when it overrides nine positive votes, and that was not the case this morning.

Mr. Dejammet (France) *(spoke in French)*: I entirely associate myself with the statement just made by the representative of Canada. [...]

253. Statement of the Secretary-General Concerning Kosovo Transmitted to His Excellency Mr. Milosevic, President of the FRY, and to His Excellency Mr. Solana, Secretary General of NATO, S/1999/402 = SG/SM/6952, 9 April 1999

I am deeply distressed by the humanitarian tragedy taking place in Kosovo and in the region, which must be brought to an end. The suffering of innocent civilians should not be further prolonged. In this spirit, I urgently call upon the Yugoslav authorities to undertake the following commitments:

- to end immediately the campaign of intimidation and expulsion of the civilian population;

- to cease all activities of military and paramilitary forces in Kosovo and to withdraw these forces;

- to accept unconditionally the return of all refugees and displaced persons to their homes;

- to accept the deployment of an international military force to ensure a secure environment for the return of refugees and the unimpeded delivery of humanitarian aid; and

- to permit the international community to verify compliance with the undertakings above.

Upon the acceptance by the Yugoslav authorities of the above conditions, I urge the leaders of the North Atlantic Alliance to suspend immediately the air bombardments upon the territory of the Federal Republic of Yugoslavia.

Ultimately, the cessation of hostilities I propose above is a prelude to a lasting political solution to the crisis, which can only be achieved through diplomacy. In this context, I would urge the resumption of talks on Kosovo among all parties concerned at the earliest possible moment.

254. Security Council Debate Concerning Letter Dated 7 May 1999 from the Permanent Representative of China Addressed to the President of the Security Council (S/1999/523), S/PV. 4000, 8 May 1999 [1]

[The Council met in response to a request contained in a letter dated 7 May 1999 from the Permanent Representative of China to the UN addressed to the President of the Security Council (S/1999/523).] [2]

[...]

[2] **Mr. Qin Huasun** (China) *(spoke in Chinese)*: [...] First, I wish to read out a statement issued by the Chinese Government:

"At midnight on 7 May, the North Atlantic Treaty Organization (NATO), led by the United States of America, flagrantly attacked the Embassy of the People's Republic of China in the Federal Republic of Yugoslavia, launching three missiles at it from different angles. The attack resulted in serious damage to the Embassy premises. As of now, two people have died, two are missing and more than 20 injured.

"The flagrant bombing of Yugoslavia by NATO, led by the United States of America, over the past 40 days has already claimed an enormous number of casualties among innocent civilians. Now, NATO has gone so far as to bomb the Chinese Embassy. This action represents a gross violation of China's sovereignty and a flagrant flouting of the Vienna Convention on Diplomatic Relations and the basic norms of international relations, a rare occurrence in the history of diplomacy. The Chinese Government and people express their utmost indignation and severe condemnation of this barbaric action and raise the strongest protest against it.

"NATO, led by the United States, must assume full responsibility for this action. The Chinese Government reserves the right to take further measures."

The working and residence buildings of the Chinese Embassy in Yugoslavia - the entire Embassy from the fifth floor to the basement - have been destroyed by the bombing. Everyone in the Embassy, apart from those who have been sent to the hospital for treatment and some others, has been withdrawn to hotels.

We express our utmost indignation and strong condemnation of this incident. This barbaric action of NATO is a flagrant violation of the Convention on the Prevention and Punishment of Crimes against Internationally Protected Persons, including Diplomatic Agents. Even in times of war, it is internationally recognized that diplomatic institutions are inviolate and diplomats protected. Any threat to the safety of diplomatic [3] personnel is also a serious threat to the maintenance of necessary and normal international relations. This indiscriminate act constitutes a serious breach of the Convention and a crime of war that should be punished. We strongly demand that NATO carry out an investigation of this serious incident and account for it. NATO must assume all responsibility for this.

We reserve our right to take further action. The frenzied bombardment carried out over the last 45 days by NATO, under the leadership of the United States, has already resulted in enormous casualties in-

---

[1] *Only statement that add to the legal analysis or the factual background have been included. Presidential statements not related to substantive issues have also been omitted.*

[2] *In 1999, membership of the Security Council was as follows: Argentinia, Bahrain, Brazil, Canada, China, France, Gambia, Malaysia, Namibia, the Netherlands, Russian Federation, Slovenia, the United Kingdom of Great Britain and Northern Ireland and the United States of America. The President invited the representatives of Albania, Belarus, Cuba, India, Iraq and Ukraine to participate in the discussion, without the right to vote, in accordance with the Charter and rule 37 of the Council's provisional rules of procedure. Mr. Jovanovic (FRY) was also invited to make a statement.*

volving innocent civilians, and now it has gone as far as to violate a diplomatic mission. This is really shocking.

Once again we strongly demand that NATO immediately and unconditionally stop its air strikes against the Federal Republic of Yugoslavia.

Mr. Burleigh (United States of America): We have no confirmation of the facts at this time. The North Atlantic Treaty Organization (NATO) has opened an investigation of the matter. If NATO was responsible for this incident we are deeply sorry. NATO would never target civilians, and NATO would never target an embassy.

But we in this Council must keep our eye on the big picture, and the big picture is this: that one man alone is responsible for this crisis in the Federal Republic of Yugoslavia, and his name is Slobodan Milosevic. NATO is taking action in response to Belgrade's sustained, multiyear, outrageous, unacceptable policies of ethnic cleansing, terrorization and repression of its own citizens in Kosovo. As the world knows, we worked for months and months and months on a negotiated settlement with Mr. Milosevic. He never agreed. And as the world also knows, he triggered a humanitarian catastrophe.

Those are the basic facts and the bottom line. We will continue to press the Federal Republic of Yugoslavia until it agrees to accept NATO's conditions and the G-8 principles. That is the only way out of this current situation.

Again, if NATO is responsible for this, we deeply regret the incident.

I have conveyed my Government's regrets and sincere condolences to Ambassador Qin, and Secretary of State Albright is conveying the same message to the Chinese Foreign Minister.

Mr. Lavrov (Russian Federation) *(spoke in Russian)*: In these unconscionable activities in flagrant violation of the Charter of the United Nations, the North Atlantic Treaty Organization (NATO) is exceeding all limits. Every day we hear reports of further civilian casualties and of destruction of civilian structures, social and economic infrastructure and mass-communications facilities in Yugoslavia. All norms of international law are being flouted.

On 7 May we witnessed a new tragedy: a NATO strike on the Embassy of the People's Republic of China in the Federal Republic of Yugoslavia. Some of its personnel were killed. Serious material damage was done to the mission.

Russia expresses its deepest condolences to the Government of China and to the families of the victims of the NATO strike. We are outraged by this barbaric action. We are outraged and demand an immediate investigation. The Security Council cannot let this go without consequences.

By now it is clear to everyone that NATO's military adventurism bears absolutely no relation to efforts to protect the civilians in Kosovo and to prevent a humanitarian crisis. In fact, it is quite the contrary: the fate of the Kosovars has become entirely incidental, and the humanitarian banner is being used as a cover for NATO's attempts to destroy the present world order, which is based on respect for international law and for the Charter of the United Nations.

This, in fact, is the big picture, not the fact that one single person is responsible for all of this. How many people must be killed, how many people must be left homeless, how many countries must be destabilized in order to punish one single person?

We appeal to the members of NATO to think before it is too late and to immediately halt their military action which has already brought such untold suffering to hundreds of thousands of people, created a humanitarian catastrophe and thrown Europe backwards into the distant past.

It is essential to shift immediately to a political settlement, as was stated once again on 7 May by the Secretary-General. This is what Russia has advocated from the very beginning of the crisis in Kosovo. We have advocated a peaceful settlement within the context of the [4] United Nations, and the Russian leadership has been doing all it can to work towards that end.

This goal can and must be reached. However, a necessary prerequisite is halting the NATO strikes immediately.

Mr. van Walsum (Netherlands): As the representative of a country that participates in the North Atlantic Treaty Organization (NATO) air strikes against the Federal Republic of Yugoslavia, I join the delegation of the United States in expressing our deep regret about the incident involving the Chinese Embassy in Belgrade, likewise on the assumption that the incident will be confirmed to have been caused by NATO action.

Collateral damage is damage caused by bombs or missiles that have gone astray. It is always deplorable, and it is especially disturbing if it entails loss of life among innocent civilians. It is, however, by definition, accidental and not intentional. Accordingly, collateral damage to an embassy building is not essentially different from other collateral damage. As the Embassy was not deliberately targeted, the accident cannot be regarded as a violation of diplomatic immunity, let alone as an attack on the integrity of the country concerned.

All collateral damage is regrettable, and it is a deeply disturbing thought that air strikes in which my country participates have led to loss of life among innocent civilians. It is equally disturbing to realize that Belgrade's ethnic cleansing of Kosovo, which was already well under way by 23 March, has enormously accelerated and intensified since our air strikes began. Yet we do not waver in our conviction that we had no choice but to launch these air strikes after Mr. Milosevic had continued to ignore the Security Council's demands contained in its resolutions of 23 September and 24 October 1998.

The United Nations High Commissioner for Refugees, Mrs. Ogata, has confirmed that last year more than a quarter of all asylum requests in Europe were made by people from Kosovo and that up to 23 March her Office was providing assistance to 400,000 people displaced or otherwise affected by fighting inside the province and to 90,000 refugees and displaced people outside Kosovo.

It is true that here are many more refugees today, but no civilized Government could have foreseen the scope, the meticulous preparation and the sheer ferocity of Belgrade's determination to drive out the ethnic Albanians. We cannot be held responsible for the fact that Mr. Milosevic seized this opportunity to accelerate and try to complete his final solution to the Kosovo problem.

We accept our share of responsibility for the tragic events that are occurring in this conflict, but we totally reject any suggestion of equivalence or even comparison between the accidental casualties caused by our air strikes and the systematic killings, executions, rape, physical abuse, intimidation, harassment and burning of houses, for which the regime in Belgrade must assume full responsibility.

[A statement by the representative of Argentina has been omitted.]

Mr. Dejammet (France) *(spoke in French)*: First of all, the delegation of France wishes to express its [5] profound sympathy to the delegation of China. We extend our condolences to the families of the victims and to the authorities of the People's Republic of China. We also associate ourselves with the regret expressed over the tragic event to which the Embassy of China and its personnel in Belgrade have fallen victim. This event is at the moment the subject of an investigation by the authorities of the North Atlantic Treaty Organization.

France is engaged in an action undertaken with its allies that is aimed at putting an end to the intolerable actions of the authorities of the Federal Republic of Yugoslavia, a policy of deportation that has made it necessary and legitimate to apply the severest measures, including military action.

At the same time, France, which, like all the members of the European Union supports the initiative of the Secretary-General of the United Nations dated 9 April 1999, is working together with its Russian, American, English, Canadian, Italian, German and Japanese partners to develop a political solution. The meeting of Ministers for Foreign Affairs of our eight countries - which was held the day before yesterday, 6 May - made it possible to adopt general principles for a political solution to the Kosovo problem.

Those principles are as follows: immediate and verifiable cessation of violence and repression in Kosovo; withdrawal from Kosovo of the military, police and paramilitary forces; deployment of an international presence in Kosovo an effective civil and security presence endorsed by the United Nations that is able to guarantee the achievement of the shared objectives; establishment of a provisional administration for Kosovo, pursuant to a decision by the Security Council, in order to guarantee conditions that will make it possible for all the inhabitants of Kosovo to lead a normal existence in peace; freedom and security for the return of all refugees and displaced persons and unhindered access by humanitarian organizations to Kosovo; a political process leading to the establishment of an interim political agreement, involving substantial autonomy for Kosovo, that fully takes into account the Rambouillet accords, the principles of the sovereignty and territorial integrity of the Federal Republic of Yugoslavia and the other countries of the region and the demilitarization of the Kosovo Liberation Army; and finally, a comprehensive approach for the stabilization and economic development of the region.

I have cited these principles because it is our desire to arrive at the adoption of a Security Council resolution under Chapter VII that will endorse and adopt these principles for a settlement and that will, we hope, finally make it possible to restore peace and stability to that region in crisis.

Mr. Andjaba (Namibia): It is indeed dismaying and shocking that just when diplomatic efforts are being consolidated towards a much needed political solution, military action continues to be intensified in the Federal Republic of Yugoslavia, which is resulting in the loss of life and destruction of infrastructure.

We would like to recall the recent successful humanitarian visit of the Reverend Jesse Jackson to the Federal Republic of Yugoslavia, which resulted in the release of the American prisoners of war. Furthermore, the Secretary-General of the United Nations undertook a mission to some North Atlantic Treaty Organization (NATO) countries and to Russia. All these efforts were aimed at finding a peaceful solution. More importantly, the statement of the G-8 ministers gave us a flicker of hope.

My delegation has on many occasions underscored the fact that continuation of hostilities in the Federal Republic of Yugoslavia will have unimaginable consequences. Yesterday, the Chinese Embassy in Belgrade was hit. This is a very serious development. Fatalities, serious injuries and missing Chinese diplomats have been reported. We express our profound sympathy and condolences to the Government and people of China. The bombing of the Chinese Embassy could escalate the conflict. We therefore await the results of the reported ongoing investigations by NATO.

My delegation remains convinced that the pain and suffering inflicted on the innocent and unsuspecting Chinese diplomats, as well as other innocents civilians in the Federal Republic of Yugoslavia, could have been avoided if there were political will for a political solution. We believe that it is still possible and necessary to find a timely political solution. It is imperative that the Security Council becomes actively involved in the search for a political solution. Similarly, the Secretary-General must continue to work towards the cessation of hostilities. We therefore reiterate our call for an immediate end to the bombing in the Federal Republic of Yugoslavia. Only then can diplomacy be meaningfully pursued.

Mr. Fowler (Canada): We are assembled tonight to consider a tragic event, one that has occurred in the context of a military action brought about by a nation's [6] abuse of its own people. As the North Atlantic Treaty Organization (NATO) seeks to bring an end to the gross and persistent violence visited upon the Albanian population of the province of Kosovo by a brutal regime in Belgrade, accidents and errors have inevitably and very regrettably occurred. NATO is engaged in an action designed exclusively to stop the Serbian authorities from prosecuting their policy of ethnic cleansing, which has already resulted in two thirds of the population of Kosovo - about a million and a half people - having been expelled from their homes, many suffering much worse fates at the hands of Serb security forces.

Bringing a halt to such action, protecting the people of Kosovo and permitting their safe return are NATO's only purposes. NATO does not attack embassies or target civilians under any circumstances. Canada deeply regrets, therefore, the damage caused to the Embassy of the People's Republic of China in Belgrade, which is apparently the result of NATO's air action. Above all, we are saddened by the death of members of the staff of the Chinese Embassy and by the injuries sustained by many others in this most unfortunate accident.

Just a couple of days ago, Foreign Ministers of the Group of Eight, meeting in Germany, produced a blueprint for a possible settlement of this conflict that, by resolution of the Security Council, would end the persecution of the ethnic Albanian population of Kosovo, see the departure from Kosovo of Serb forces engaged in such nefarious activities, facilitate the return of all Kosovar refugees, guarantee their protection through an international civil and military presence in Kosovo, and thus allow the bombing to be concluded.

For the first time in many weeks we have seen the shape of a possible settlement, and we are anxious to pursue it as vigorously as we can. In the meantime, we express our deepest condolences to the people and Government of China over the deaths and injuries they suffered some hours ago.

[Statements by the representatives of Bahrain, Malaysia, Slovenia, the United Kingdom and a statement made by the President in his capacity as representative of Gabon have been omitted.]

Mr. Jovanovic: The Federal Republic of Yugoslavia sent a timely [8] warning to the Security Council of the unforeseeable consequences of the illegal and brutal aggression of the North Atlantic Treaty Organization (NATO) and requested on a number of occasions that the aggression be stopped immediately. If this legitimate request had been heeded, vast human suffering and material destruction would have been avoided.

My country has been a victim of NATO aggression for 45 days now. NATO attacks have been concentrated primarily on civilian targets, threatening lives, the environment and the basic human rights of the entire population of the country. The principle for selecting allegedly legitimate military targets looks like: hit anything, anytime, anywhere. Using over 1,000 planes, NATO has made over 12,000 sorties thus far, has launched over 3,000 cruise missiles and has dropped more than 10,000 tons of explosives. The tragic toll is 1,200 civilian lives lost and the over 5,000 people wounded, many of whom will remain disabled for life.

Can the lost or ruined life of any human being be cynically called collateral damage? Is this term fitting to describe the deaths of over 100 children brought on by NATO bombs? No mention of collateral damage or incidental killings of people and destruction of property is made in the Geneva Convention of 1949 or in the statutes of the International Criminal Tribunal for the Former Yugoslavia. Human life has no price tag and cannot be compared to anything else. However, the NATO bombs threaten the lives of the entire population of the Federal Republic of Yugoslavia.

Who can live in a country in which houses, bridges, roads, railroads, schools, hospitals, water-supply systems, heating or house appliance plants or public transport are being systematically destroyed? Graphite bombs have short-circuited the power grid of the country, leaving more than 5 million people without power or water and by extension without the most essential provisions. NATO has used weapons banned by international conventions, causing an ecological catastrophe. Over 20,000 cluster bombs have been dropped thus far, while depleted uranium ammunition has also been used. No exception has been made for cultural monuments, cemeteries or memorials to victims of Nazi atrocities in the last war. No army so far has vandalized Serbian medieval monasteries and churches. They survived centuries, eliciting the respect of all except NATO strategists.

The NATO countries, which in their conceit like to think of themselves as standard bearers of democracy and of the right to hold a different opinion, dispatched their planes to drop bombs on television centres in my country, thus committing a crime against freedom of speech and of the media. The buildings of TV Belgrade and TV Novi Sad have been totally destroyed, as well as the Ustje business centre in Belgrade which housed three private television and four radio stations. Scores of television transmitters have been hit too, including the television transmitter on Mount Avala, the largest facility of its kind in Yugoslavia and the beacon above Belgrade which greeted passengers and beckoned to many generations of Yugoslavs from afar that they were coming home at last.

The Federal Republic of Yugoslavia has been committed to a peaceful solution of the crisis in Kosovo and Metohija. I would like to remind members of the Security Council that all activities of the armed forces of the Federal Republic of Yugoslavia in Kosovo and Metohija were unilaterally stopped on 6 April, that the Government of Serbia and Yugoslavia has called on all refugees and displaced persons to return home, guaranteeing them safety and security, and that constructive talks were conducted on a number of occasions between the highest representative of Serbia and Yugoslavia and Dr. Ibrahim Rugova. However, the Federal Republic of Yugoslavia has the right and the duty to protect itself from aggression. The right and the duty are enshrined in the constitution as well as in the Charter of the United Nations and international law.

Yesterday, the aggressors' warplanes targeted and destroyed the Embassy of the People's Republic of China in Belgrade. The Embassy was hit by at least two missiles. According to preliminary information, 26 Embassy staff members were wounded, two very seriously, and two persons were killed. The Embassy building is in the exclusive residential area of New Belgrade. There is no military target around there. The attack is in gross violation of the Geneva Convention of 1949 and of international law. It is, without any doubt, a war crime.

[9] It is more and more evident that NATO is waging a total war against a sovereign country and its people. It is not only Yugoslavia that is targeted, but peace and security in the region as well. The neighbouring countries are already involved in the aggression. The economy of the region is seriously disrupted by the aggression. The main waterway in Europe, the Danube, is out of use. The consequences of the bombing on the region's environment are devastating.

This criminal aggression against Yugoslavia should cease immediately. The Security Council has failed until now to condemn the aggression and to halt the bombing. The entire international legal system is at stake. This morning the Security Council has perhaps the last chance to exercise its duty and reaffirm the authority invested in it by the Charter of the United Nations. [...]

Mr. Sychov (Belarus) *(spoke in Russian)*: [...] The Republic of Belarus strongly condemns the illegal, aggressive military actions by the North Atlantic Treaty Organization (NATO) against the Federal Republic of Yugoslavia. Belarus, which lost every fourth inhabitant in the years of the Second World War, is deeply disturbed to see that the flames of war are heating up again in the centre of Europe. Further escalation of military action, barbaric bombings of industrial, social, cultural and civilian targets and the peaceful population are all assuming horrible proportions. [...]

The military actions of NATO are contrary to many international instruments and to the generally recognized norms of international law. In this connection, we call for a halt to this senseless aggression and for an end to this violation of international law by NATO. As we enter the third millennium, the international community has a special responsibility for the future of our planet. The President of the Republic of Belarus and the Government of my country have frequently declared their commitment to a peaceful settlement of this conflict. We believe that today it is still possible to find a diplomatic solution to the situation with regard to Yugoslavia. In this respect, the Security Council has a key role to play in accordance with its powers under the Charter of the United Nations. The United Nations must show the entire world that the ideals of its Charter are paramount. [...]

Mr. Hasan (Iraq) *(spoke in Arabic)*: At the outset, I would like to express our deep condolences to the people and the Government of the People's Republic of China for the victims of the bombing of the premises of the Chinese Embassy in Belgrade by the North Atlantic Treaty Organization (NATO). We condemn this barbaric act, which violates the United Nations Charter, international law and the rules governing relations between countries. We call for the immediate cessation of NATO's military acts.

The targeting of the Chinese Embassy in Belgrade and, before that, the severe damage inflicted on the Iraqi Embassy in Belgrade, are yet further manifestations of the aggression of the United States, which started a systematic war against all the people of Yugoslavia on 24 March this year, in a flagrant violation of the Charter of the United Nations and the mandate of the Security Council. This aggression coincides with the Anglo American aggression against Iraq, which started on 16 December last year and which is continuing. This clearly demonstrates the pattern of American behaviour, which flouts international law and the rights of nations and peoples. Earlier, there was American aggression against Libya and then against the Sudan. Who knows which peoples of the third world will be the next victims if the international community does not stand up against the tyranny of the American force?

We deeply sympathize with the people of Yugoslavia, which stands steadfast as it witnesses the achievements of generations being destroyed by the American smart bombs that have spared no school, church, mosque or hospital. We have suffered from the systematic destruction of every area of life in our country [10] by the same brute American force. However, we remained steadfast and emerged victorious to rebuild what they destroyed. The people of Yugoslavia will also remain steadfast and emerge victorious.

We call upon countries that love peace, freedom and justice to learn the right lessons from this continued aggression, which is designed to undermine the territorial integrity of countries and to systematically destroy their cultural achievements. We call upon the international community to unify its efforts to stop the brutal use of force immediately and to punish the aggressor. [...]

Mr. Rodríguez Parrilla (Cuba) *(spoke in Spanish)*: [...] The United States and NATO, which refer to civilian dead and wounded as "collateral damage", now cynically declare that the Embassy was not a deliberate target, that it may have been an accident, that they are investigating, that they do not attack civilians and that we must see the "big picture". It is not an accident, but an act of aggression. After one has seen the terrible images traversing the world, there is not much to investigate. Furthermore, there is information that today other civilian targets were bombed.

The Government of the Republic of Cuba forcefully condemns this new act of genocide, which constitutes a flagrant violation of the sovereignty of the People's Republic of China, of the Charter of the United Nations, of international law and of the Geneva Convention.

As Jose Marti said, the truth must be spoken. The Security Council cannot remain impassive and silent, as though it were unaware that the yesterday's bombings and those of the past 45 days have brought death, injury, hunger, desolation and terror to millions of people.

The hundreds of civilians killed, many of them children, the thousands of civilians injured, the passengers burnt to death in the Grdelica gorge train, the dozens of journalists killed in the bombing of the Serbian television station, the children trapped in the mangled iron remains of the refugee convoy on the Djakovica-Pec road and the people who were travelling in the bus on the Luzane bridge may not for now be present in the records and resolutions, but they are present in the consciences of all of those seated around this table and, more importantly, in the consciences of those peoples that feel - rightly, in almost every case - that this place has little to do with their lives and aspirations.

The United States and NATO are deliberately using technologically advanced weapons in order to interrupt the supply of energy for health services, water supply and food production, as though they were unaware that they would cause humanitarian consequences by cutting off electricity, heating, communications, energy and transport, by destroying civilian facilities that provide essential services to the population, information sources and the livelihoods of the population and by engaging in psychological warfare.

Residential buildings, hospitals and health centres, schools, old-age homes, historical monuments, churches, places of worship and works of art have been destroyed. Civilian targets have been intentionally attacked, with prior knowledge that they were occupied by civilians and that those attacks would result in their deaths. This is a gross violation of the Geneva Protocols and international humanitarian law.

How is it possible that the Security Council does not at least call for a cessation of the brutal bombing against the peoples of Yugoslavia when considering this subject? Can anyone believe the refrain that the war is not against the Serbian people? NATO, headed by the United States, is committing acts of genocide. The genocide must stop.

The attacks in recent hours on the Chinese Embassy and on civilian targets show that there has been no progress at all towards a political solution, despite what is being said. Actions speak louder than speeches and papers. How can the Group of 8 agreement be considered acceptable if that agreement begins by ignoring the main cause of the tragedy, which is the NATO bombing? There can be no just or worthwhile agreement unless the aggression, acts of genocide, bombing of civilian targets and the systematic attempt to deprive a nation of its means of subsistence are first brought to an end. [...]

[11] I can assure the Council that the Cuban diplomats who remain in and move around everyday in Belgrade are qualified as witnesses to what is now occurring.

Cuba hopes that the Security Council will act immediately in accordance with its responsibilities and that it will resume its role under these exceptional and emergency circumstances. If it does not do so, the damage to international order, to the collective security of States and to the United Nations will be irreparable. The historical responsibility will be enormous if the Security Council continues to allow itself to be subordinated, sullied and scorned.

It is the task and unique duty of the Security Council to regain the powers and mandates assigned to it by the Charter. Its most urgent and important task is to halt the genocide and stop the NATO bombings. Having accomplished that, its task will then be to find the path towards a just and dignified political solution that respects the sovereignty and territorial integrity of the Federal Republic of Yugoslavia and all the States of the region.

Cuba hopes that the Security Council will neither accept nor endorse any project that is based on force, inequality or pillage; that it will neither accept or endorse a discussion of the elements of a peace process under NATO bombardment; and that it will neither accept nor endorse any agreement before halting the genocide. Failing this, the Security Council will have to be counted not only among the victims, but also among the accomplices. [...]

Mr. Nesho (Albania): [...] We are present here at this emergency meeting of the Security Council to discuss the damage caused to the Chinese Embassy as a result of bombardments in Belgrade against criminal and brutal regime that is killing, massacring, torturing, raping and is committing genocide against the entire Albanian population of Kosovo. The Albanian Government expressed its regrets and condolences to the Chinese Government over this unfortunate incident, believing that that friendly country, China, has always shown maturity and wisdom on the basis of its foreign policy principles and that it is among the countries promoting progress and development in the world.

Albania would not like for this incident to be used as a pushing force for not punishing the medieval regime in Belgrade and for allowing the wave of crime and conflict to spread in Europe and throughout the world. On the contrary, we must make every effort to prevent our civilization from facing a tragic new history.

After 300,000 people were massacred in Bosnia and Herzegovina and millions were deported, we face today the same reality of 1 million Albanians being deported in the same way - homeless, hopeless and massacred together with their children. The only hope for all of them is the action of the North Atlantic Treaty Organization (NATO) to stop their catastrophe and to ensure their safe return to their land.

The incident that happened yesterday may not respect or be in conformity with international agreements, but those agreements have been completely and constantly violated by the Belgrade regime through crimes against humanity, ethnic cleansing and genocide against the Albanians of Kosovo and other peoples, about whose suffering not much has been said in this debate by some of the speakers.

Any action that serves peace, stability and security in the world and saves humanity cannot be limited, but should be supported by all the countries that respect human values and democracy. We believe that NATO, through its action, is trying to preserve the same [12] principles as those of the United Nations Charter, including the maintenance of peace and international security. [...]

[A statement by the representative of India has been omitted.]

Mr. Qin Huasun (China) *(spoke in Chinese)*: [...] However, we have also heard an absurd argument made to the effect that, as the North Atlantic Treaty Organization (NATO) did not intentionally attack the Chinese Embassy and its diplomats, it cannot be charged with violating the Convention on the Prevention and Punishment of Crimes against Internationally Protected Persons, including Diplomatic Agents. We were most astonished by the fact that this remark was made by a senior diplomat.

Facts speak louder than words. Deliberate or not, NATO's action was a blatant flouting of international law. Are we to understand that a killer, merely by arguing that he did not kill deliberately, can escape the punishment of law? I wish to reiterate here that NATO must shoulder full responsibility for its action. [...]

255. UN Security Council Resolution 1239 (1999) of 14 May 1999

The Security Council,

Recalling its resolutions 1160 (1998) of 31 March 1998, 1199 (1998) of 23 September 1998, and 1203 (1998) of 24 October 1998, and the statements of its President of 24 August 1998 (S/PRST/1998/25), 19 January 1999 (S/PRST/1999/2), and 29 January 1999 (S/PRST/1999/5),

Bearing in mind the provisions of the Charter of the United Nations and guided by the Universal Declaration of Human Rights, the international covenants and conventions on human rights, the Conventions and Protocol relating to the Status of Refugees, the Geneva Conventions of 1949 and the Additional Protocols thereto of 1977, as well as other instruments of international humanitarian law,

Expressing grave concern at the humanitarian catastrophe in and around Kosovo, Federal Republic of Yugoslavia, as a result of the continuing crisis,

Deeply concerned by the enormous influx of Kosovo refugees into Albania, the former Yugoslav Republic of Macedonia, Bosnia and Herzegovina, and other countries, as well as by the increasing numbers of displaced persons within Kosovo, the Republic of Montenegro and other parts of the Federal Republic of Yugoslavia,

Stressing the importance of effective coordination of humanitarian relief activities undertaken by States, the United Nations High Commissioner for Refugees (UNHCR) and international organizations in alleviating the plight and suffering of refugees and internally displaced persons,

Noting with interest the intention of the Secretary-General to send a humanitarian needs assessment mission to Kosovo and other parts of the Federal Republic of Yugoslavia,

Reaffirming the territorial integrity and sovereignty of all States in the region,

1. *Commends* the efforts that have been taken by Member States, the United Nations High Commissioner for Refugees (UNHCR) and other international humanitarian relief organizations in providing the urgently needed relief assistance to the Kosovo refugees in Albania, the former Yugoslav Republic of Macedonia and Bosnia and Herzegovina, and urges them and others in a position to do so to contribute resources for humanitarian assistance to the refugees and internally displaced persons;

2. *Invites* the UNHCR and other international humanitarian relief organizations to extend relief assistance to the internally displaced persons in Kosovo, the Republic of Montenegro and other parts of the Federal Republic of Yugoslavia, as well as to other civilians being affected by the ongoing crisis;

3. *Calls* for access for United Nations and all other humanitarian personnel operating in Kosovo and other parts of the Federal Republic of Yugoslavia;

4. *Reaffirms* the right of all refugees and displaced persons to return to their homes in safety and in dignity;

5. *Emphasizes* that the humanitarian situation will continue to deteriorate in the absence of a political solution to the crisis consistent with the principles adopted by the Foreign Ministers of Canada, France, Germany, Italy, Japan, the Russian Federation, the United Kingdom of Great Britain and Northern Ireland and the United States of America on 6 May 1999 (S/1999/516), and *urges* all concerned to work towards this aim;

6. *Decides* to remain actively seized of the matter.

[Adopted by the Security Council at its 4003rd meeting, on 14 May 1999 with 13 votes to none and China abstaining.]

256. Extracts from the Debate of the Security Council Concerning Security Council Resolution 1239 (1999), S/PV. 4003, 14 May 1999[1]

[Members of the Council had before them a draft resolution submitted by Argentina, Bahrain, Bosnia and Herzegovina, Brazil, Egypt, Gabon, Gambia, the Islamic Republic of Iran, Jordan, Kuwait, Malaysia, Morocco, Namibia, Pakistan, Qatar, Saudi Arabia, Senegal, Slovenia, Turkey, the United Arab Emirates and Yemen (S/1999/517).][2]

[...]

[3] **Mr. Buallay** (Bahrain) *(spoke in Arabic):* The situation in Kosovo was caused by a crisis: the displacement of many inhabitants of the region, people who for the most part are Albanians. These displacements were caused by destructive acts by Belgrade, the burning of the houses and property of Albanians, as well as acts of terror, rape and assassination.

The events that have taken place in Kosovo have reminded us of a similar situation: that which took place in Bosnia and Herzegovina.

---

[1] *Only statements that add to the legal analysis or the factual background have been included. Presidential statements not related to substantive issues have also been omitted.*

[2] *In 1999, membership of the Security Council was as follows: Argentinia, Bahrain, Brazil, Canada, China, France, Gambia, Malaysia, Namibia, the Netherlands, Russian Federation, Slovenia, the United Kingdom of Great Britain and Northern Ireland and the United States of America. The Council invited the representatives of Albania, Belarus, Bosnia and Herzegovina, Cuba, Egypt, the Islamic Republic of Iran, Jordan, Kuwait, Morocco, Pakistan, Qatar, Saudi Arabia, Senegal, Turkey, Ukraine, the United Arab Emirates and Yemen to participate in the discussion, without the right to vote, in accordance with the Charter and rule 37 of the Council's provisional rules of procedure. The President also invited Mr. Vladislav Jovanovic (FRY).*

This proves that the Serb authorities have not learned any lessons from what happened in Bosnia. The international community has helped the Croats, Serbs and Bosniacs to achieve international legitimacy, but the excesses that caused the tragedy in Bosnia still remain. The Serb authorities in Belgrade have started to act with the same ferocity as they did in Bosnia, and this has led to the displacement of a large number of people in the region.

We are concerned that, as in Bosnia, there are various forms of displacement in this tragic situation unfolding in Kosovo. There are people who have gone to live in the mountains and people who are lost in various areas. Others are scattered throughout the region. Others still are in border areas waiting for the chance to emigrate. And there are those who are refugees in neighbouring States and States yet further away.

If one wishes to cite figures, according to United Nations sources there are more than 840,000 displaced persons within the Federal Republic of Yugoslavia and more than 700,000 outside that territory. So the total number exceeds 1.5 million people out of a population of two million. This seems to be a way of ridding Kosovo of its population, of destroying its politics, culture and religion.

I don't think we need to go into the military and political factors that have caused this situation in Kosovo, but these factors cannot be separated from the humanitarian crisis. Therefore there is a need for us to try to redress the humanitarian situation - the displacement of the population - and to help the refugees. The situation of a refugee, whoever he may be, touches our hearts.

It is in view of this humanitarian situation that the delegations of Malaysia and Bahrain took the initiative to submit a draft resolution. It has achieved consensus in the Council and in the caucus and other groups of Member States outside of the Council.

The draft resolution was the result of various consultations and was discussed today. The humanitarian efforts are particularly cited in this draft resolution, the purpose of which is two-fold. One goal is to draw the attention of the international community to the humanitarian catastrophe occurring in Kosovo today, a catastrophe that has led to the displacement of thousands of people. The second goal is to make it possible for the Council to review the situation in Kosovo from the humanitarian perspective and to make humanitarian concerns fundamental to the consideration of the military and political aspects of the situation when the Council is ready to do so.

The elements contained in the draft resolution are the same as those found in other United Nations resolutions and in non-United Nations resolutions. They are what is necessary to resolve the problem of refugees. International organizations have a great deal of experience in this field.

The points contained in this draft resolution are as follows. It appeals to States and organizations to contribute resources to help the refugees, facilitating the delivery of assistance and helping the refugees return to their homes after the crisis is over. This humanitarian draft resolution that is now before the Council, while being a simple, caring resolution that does not invite controversy, nonetheless deals with a humanitarian tragedy which has caused the displacement of a large proportion of the Kosovo population.

In keeping with this appeal we call upon Council members to adopt this draft resolution by consensus so that this humanitarian assistance that is so necessary to the refugees can be given to them and so that their situation can be improved pending their return to their homes.

Mr. Hasmy (Malaysia): We are meeting this evening to take action on the draft resolution on the humanitarian situation in and around Kosovo. My delegation is pleased to have played a role, together with [4] Bahrain, in helping move the process forward, culminating in this formal meeting of the Council. We are grateful for the solid support shown by members of the Council, especially those who have contributed important input and sponsored the draft resolution. We are equally grateful to those countries outside of the Council that have joined in sponsoring this draft resolution.

My delegation is strongly of the view that, in the wake of the humanitarian tragedy unfolding in and around Kosovo, it is timely for the Council to pronounce itself on the subject. We feel that the Council should have been able to adopt a draft resolution on the humanitarian issue, after weeks of paralysis in the Council, even as the international community watched in anguish the plight of the refugees and internally displaced persons.

We are, of course, equally concerned over the ongoing conflict in Kosovo. We share the views already expressed by other members of the international community on the need for an early political settlement. Nothing would have pleased my delegation more than the Council's adopting a resolution which addressed the Kosovo issue in a comprehensive fashion. Efforts are being made by many international actors, including the Secretary-General of the United Nations, in that direction. It remains our earnest hope that these efforts will yield tangible results and that the Council will be in a position to address the issue in a comprehensive manner as soon as possible. We remain convinced that the issue can be finally resolved only by way of a political solution.

In the meantime, it is also our conviction that the Council can, and ought to, play a meaningful role by pronouncing itself on an important aspect of the Kosovo crisis - namely, the humanitarian situation, which is characterized by the exodus of hundreds of thousands of refugees and internally displaced persons, who are in a very desperate and traumatized condition in and around Kosovo and other parts of Yugoslavia.

We are of the view that, while there remain fundamental differences among Council members on the political and other aspects of the Kosovo problem, there is universal concern among Council members on the humanitarian tragedy which continues to unfold in and around Kosovo. It is in cognizance of this widely shared concern that the initiative has been taken to bring the issue to the Council for formal action, as a concrete step in the efforts to bring the Kosovo issue to the Council by the least contentious aspect, which should command the support of all members of the Council.

Formal action by the Council on the humanitarian issue in and around Kosovo would be a clear expression of the serious concern of the Council about the humanitarian tragedy which unfolded weeks ago. It would also be an important and positive response to the appeals by the United Nations High Commissioner for Refugees and the Secretary-General for international humanitarian assistance to alleviate the plight of the refugees and internally displaced persons, not only in and around Kosovo, but also in other parts of Yugoslavia. It would be a welcome expression of the Council's strong support and encouragement of the ongoing efforts made by international organizations that are operating in the region. At the same time, the adoption of the draft resolution would be a strong and unequivocal expression of support for the refugees and internally displaced persons, particularly in respect of their right to return to their homes in security and in dignity.

The Council has not been able to address the issue of Kosovo in any meaningful way for a long time now due to a lack of consensus, which, regrettably, led to action being taken outside the Council. This draft resolution represents the first serious attempt on the part of some Council members to bring the Kosovo issue back to the Council in the earnest hope that it could pave the way for the forging of a consensus on the more difficult aspects of the Kosovo problem, thereby reasserting the role of the Council on this issue. In submitting this draft resolution, the sponsors are impelled by a desire to make a contribution to galvanizing international action in addressing the enormous humanitarian tragedy in and around Kosovo. Equally importantly, it represents a modest contribution by these members towards unifying the Council. We earnestly hope that this will indeed be the case.

Mr. Burleigh (United States of America): The United States supports the draft resolution initiated by our Council colleagues from Bahrain and Malaysia. We thank them and express our appreciation for their efforts. Similar thanks go to the other sponsors of the draft resolution.

This draft resolution focuses our attention on the urgent issue at hand in Kosovo and the surrounding region: the plight of hundreds of thousands of refugees and displaced persons, and the critical need to assist the United Nations High Commissioner for Refugees and other humanitarian organizations and workers in their efforts to address this crisis.

[5] Slobodan Milosevic is responsible for the humanitarian crisis. It is his campaign of ethnic cleansing, of burning villages, of executing men, women and children and of rape and intimidation that has caused hundreds of thousands to flee their homes. It is clear how this crisis can be resolved: Belgrade must meet the conditions set out by the North Atlantic Treaty Organization and the principles of the Group of Eight, agreed to at the Foreign Ministers' meeting in Bonn on 6 May. We remain firm in our resolve to continue to exert pressure on Milosevic and his Government to stop their planned, systematic campaign of ethnic cleansing and to permit the return of all refugees and displaced persons to their homes in safety and in security. All of our efforts in Kosovo and the Federal Republic of Yugoslavia are focused on this objective.

The number of Kosovar refugees and displaced persons now exceeds 1 million. Many of the ethnic Albanians in Kosovo have been rendered homeless. The United States has contributed and will continue to contribute to humanitarian relief efforts. My Government is currently building a camp in Fier, Albania, that will house as many as 20,000 Kosovar Albanian refugees. We are working to identify other sites for up to an additional 40,000 refugees. Americans have also opened their doors to these homeless, with the recent arrival of the first of 20,000 Kosovar Albanians for whom we have pledged to provide safe haven. We urge other countries, too, to provide temporary shelter for Kosovar Albanian refugees.

We expect that the Secretary-General's humanitarian mission to the Federal Republic of Yugoslavia will focus on the destruction in Kosovo. The mission can greatly assist in preparing for the return of refugees and internally displaced persons to their homes. The team can also identify the types of humanitarian food and medical assistance that are most urgently needed. In our view, it is essential that this team have unimpeded access throughout its visit.

I would like to conclude by reiterating a statement made by Secretary of State Madeleine Albright at the conclusion of the 6 May meeting of the Foreign Ministers of the Group of Eight. She said,

"by standing together, as we do today, our nations offer an alternate vision to Milosevic's campaign of terror, tyranny and vicious intolerance. We are united in urging Belgrade to choose a future of integration, can to make that future a reality."

[Statements by the representatives of the United Kindgom and Canada have been omitted.]

Mr. Dejammet (France) *(spoke in French)*: [...] [6] The French delegation wishes also particularly to stress the importance of one provision of the draft resolution, that of paragraph 5, which emphasizes that the humanitarian situation will continue to deteriorate in the absence of a political solution to the crisis. We are convinced of this. It is striking that this evening the Council is indicating what the parameters of that political solution must be, by specifying that the solution must be consistent with the principles adopted by the Foreign Ministers of Canada, France, Germany, Italy, Japan, the Russian Federation, the United Kingdom of Great Britain and Northern Ireland and the United States of America on 6 May 1999. Those are the principles that the French delegation set out in its Security Council statement of 8 May. We hope that, as outlined in the draft resolution, these will be endorsed by the Security Council.

For these reasons, the French delegation will vote in favour of the draft resolution.

[A statement by the representative of Gambia has been omitted.]

Mr. Andjaba (Namibia): A crisis is unfolding in Kosovo, Federal Republic of Yugoslavia. What was hoped would be a limited crisis has continued to escalate to frightening proportions. Persecutions, loss of life, destruction of infrastructure and property, as well as environmental damage with possible effect well beyond the borders of the Federal Republic of Yugoslavia, continue. As a result of ethnic cleansing, as well as of the military action of the North Atlantic Treaty Organization (NATO), many refugees are finding themselves in neighbouring countries, as well as in other parts of the Federal Republic of Yugoslavia, far away from [7] their homes, living under deplorable conditions. Similarly, the ongoing military action has severely affected the lives of the people in the Federal Republic of Yugoslavia.

It is in view of the aforementioned that Namibia has joined in co-sponsoring the draft resolution under consideration. We wish to emphasize that the human tragedy, which continues to escalate, is such that a political solution has become even more imperative.

My delegation wishes to underscore that the humanitarian situation in and around Kosovo is not a natural phenomenon. It cannot be addressed in isolation from the political context. We wish to reiterate our position in calling for a cessation of hostilities. Only then can we meaningfully address the humanitarian situation. In this connection, we reiterate that the Security Council should reassert its authority over the situation that is now unfolding in the Federal Republic of Yugoslavia as a whole.

Mr. Qin Huasun (China) *(spoke in Chinese)*: China is deeply disturbed by the current humanitarian crisis in the Balkans and has profound sympathy for the over 700,000 Kosovar refugees who have been left homeless and separated from their loved ones. We have a saying in China: "Nothing on Earth is more precious than human life and no benevolence is greater than that which treasures life." I believe that, to each and every one of us, there is no place like home. The pain of having one's home ravaged can hardly be put into words. We would like to take this opportunity to express our appreciation to the Office of the United Nations High Commissioner for Refugees and other international relief agencies for the tremendous relief work they have done.

What is equally of concern to us is that, bypassing the United Nations and without the authorization of the Security Council, the United States-led North Atlantic Treaty Organization (NATO) has launched military attacks against the Federal Republic of Yugoslavia and thus unleashed a regional war in the Balkans. Over the past 52 days, this war, conducted in the name of humanitarianism, has created the largest humanitarian disaster since the Second World War. Residents within the Federal Republic of Yugoslavia- including Serbs, ethnic Albanians, Hungarians, Slovaks and other ethnic minorities-are living in miserable and inhuman conditions. Oil refineries and chemical plants have been levelled by NATO bombs. As a result, poisonous gas and pollutants are threatening the health and lives of hundreds of millions, especially children, in the Federal Republic of Yugoslavia and Europe at large. All the bridges over the Danube in the Federal Republic of Yugoslavia have been destroyed. Water and electricity supplies have been cut off and television stations seem to have become legitimate bombing targets. The national economy and infrastructure of the Federal Republic of Yugoslavia have been devastated, resulting in a large number of civilian casualties. In this connection, I cannot fail to mention that, even as the Security Council deliberated today on the draft resolution on the Balkans, another tragedy took place in Kosovo. Six missiles launched by NATO hit a refugee camp in south-western Kosovo, causing over 100 deaths and more than 50 injuries. The tragedy was horrific, the area being strewn with dead bodies. These refugees were on their way home. We express shock at this incident. I repeat: We are shocked by this latest incident.

We believe that, in addressing the crisis in various regions in the Balkans, the Security Council should not apply double standards.

While stepping up its bombing campaign against the Federal Republic of Yugoslavia, NATO has brazenly attacked the Chinese Embassy in Belgrade. 8 May 1999 was an extremely painful day that the 1.2 billion Chinese people will never forget. On that day, the United Statesled NATO ferociously attacked the Chinese Embassy in the Federal Republic of Yugoslavia with five missiles. Three people in the Embassy were killed and more than 20 injured. The Embassy building was severely damaged. Such a criminal act is a flagrant encroachment on China's sovereignty and a serious violation of the international law and norms governing international relations. It has aroused great indignation among the Chinese people. The Chinese Government issued a solemn statement that very morning, strongly condemning this barbaric act of NATO. This tragedy shocked the international community and met with worldwide condemnation.

Despite the tragic incident of the bombing of the Chinese Embassy that caused death and injury to Chinese diplomats, NATO is still saying that its air campaign will continue. Such perversity in NATO has outraged the entire world and should be strongly condemned by everyone who has reason and conscience. As a victim, China has every reason, on moral and legal grounds alike, to demand that NATO immediately and unconditionally stop the bombing. Are not the shedding of blood and loss of life of Chinese diplomats tragic enough to restore NATO to sanity? As a permanent member of the Security Council, China shoulders unshirkable responsibilities in upholding justice and safeguarding peace. In our view, [8] it is illogical for NATO to continue with the bombing campaign while talking about the return and relief of refugees. An immediate cessation of NATO's bombing campaign against the Federal Republic of Yugoslavia should be the prerequisite for any political solution to the Kosovo issue and also the minimum condition for alleviating the humanitarian crisis in the Balkans.

For these reasons, the Chinese delegation put forward constructive amendments to the draft resolution and proposed to add to it such words as "there must be an immediate cessation of all military activities". It should be stated that this was called for also in the Non-Aligned Movement's statement of 9 April. However, this important position of the Chinese side was not accepted; we find this most regrettable. We note also that the draft resolution refers to the principles adopted by the Foreign Ministers of the G-8. We cannot accept that the Council has prejudged those principles in its draft resolution without first deliberating on them, and therefore we deem it necessary to express our reservations. On the basis of these considerations, the Chinese delegation has no choice but to abstain in the voting on the draft resolution. [...]

Mr. Granovsky (Russian Federation) *(spoke in Russian)*: The tragic course of events in Yugoslavia since 24 March last has shown convincingly that it is precisely the military action against that sovereign country - which is being conducted by the North Atlantic Treaty Organization (NATO) in circumvention of the Security Council and in violation of the Charter of the United Nations and other generally recognized norms of international law - that has caused this humanitarian catastrophe and has created a real emergency situation in the Balkans region.

For more than a month and a half now, an unprecedented campaign of air strikes by NATO against Yugoslavia has been taking place, whose victims, with grim regularity, are innocent civilians - more than 1,200 so far. There has been much testimony about the severe humanitarian damage caused by the NATO bombing, which dispels the myth that the Alliance is conducting its military operation in the name of high humanitarian ideals.

It is hard to contradict well-known facts. The number of civilians and refugees killed or wounded continues to grow. Systematically and deliberately, the civilian infrastructure of Yugoslavia is being destroyed, and very serious damage is being done to its economy. The whole region is threatened by a huge environmental catastrophe. The material basis for the return of the refugees and the displaced persons to their homes is being destroyed, though NATO proclaims that the resolution of the problem of refugees is one of its main tasks.

It is difficult to remain indifferent in the face of the escalating humanitarian catastrophe in and around Kosovo, Federal Republic of Yugoslavia. It is clear, however, that this is a consequence, not a cause, of the crisis situation. It is precisely with regard to the causes of the humanitarian catastrophe that the Security Council should have spoken out, as a matter of priority, as the organ bearing primary responsibility for the maintenance of international peace and security.

Unfortunately, because of the well-known position of a number of its members, the Council was unable to take a stand on NATO's illegal military action and to demand an immediate halt to the bombing and the return of the Kosovo crisis to the track of a peaceful political settlement. Upon the initiative of the Russian delegation, the draft resolution submitted to the Council took on board an important conclusion: that the humanitarian situation would continue to deteriorate unless - a political settlement to the crisis could be ensured.

Just as important is the urgent appeal to all concerned to make every effort to arrive at this agreement. There is no alternative, and there is a growing [9] understanding of this fact, as was clearly shown by the adoption by the Foreign Ministers of the G-8 of general principles on a political settlement of the Kosovo crisis. The draft resolution, however, did not take into account a number of our other amendments, of which the main one was an appeal for an immediate cessation of the NATO air strikes on Yugoslavia, adamantly supported by Russia and China.

A few days ago, the world was shaken by the barbaric bombing of the Chinese Embassy in Belgrade and the death of several of its staff members. Today we learned of another terrible tragedy, which occurred in the Kosovo village of Korisa as a result of NATO's use of proscribed cluster bombs. At least 50 people died there, primarily women, children and the elderly, and more than 100 were wounded.

As was stressed in the statement published today by the Russian Ministry for Foreign Affairs, Russia, which repeatedly warned NATO's leadership about the dire consequences of the military action against Yugoslavia, strongly condemns this new crime by the Alliance and calls upon the NATO strategists immediately to halt this insanity. A settlement of the Kosovo problem is possible only at the negotiating table.

Unless there is an immediate cessation to the illegal military action by NATO, genuine progress will be impossible, either towards a political settlement of the crisis or to overcome this humanitarian catastrophe. Furthermore, continued bombing could lead to that catastrophe's spreading throughout the entire Balkan region. Unfortunately, this obvious fact was not reflected in the text because of the negative position adopted by a number of Council members.

We must note here that once again, narrow national interests and an unwillingness properly to assess and react to real threats to the physical survival of an entire population of a sovereign State and to the tragic fate of hundreds of thousands of refugees have prevailed over the Charter obligations of certain members of the Council.

Because of the principled nature of our position, the Russian delegation cannot support this text. The Russian Federation, together with its active efforts to promote a peaceful political settlement of the Kosovo crisis, will continue to give whatever humanitarian assistance it can on an impartial, non-discriminatory basis to the needy civilian population in Kosovo, other regions of Yugoslavia and neighbouring States.

[The President put to vote the draft resolution S/1999/517 which was adopted with 13 votes to none with China and the Russian Federation abstaining.]

Mr. Petrella (Argentina) *(spoke in Spanish)*: [...] In our opinion, this resolution sets out to give impetus to specific relief and assistance action, in the affected countries, which definitely include the Federal Republic of Yugoslavia. The statements made two days ago by the United Nations High Commissioner for Human Rights upon visiting the region make further comments unnecessary. [...]

[10] Finally, I wish to call for United Nations staff and other humanitarian workers in the territories and countries involved in this grave conflict to be given the necessary protection in accordance with the relevant international conventions. In this context, we wish respectfully to ask the Yugoslav Government to release the Australian humanitarian workers.

Mr. Moura (Brazil): The humanitarian situation in and around Kosovo is a matter of universal concern. The Security Council is quite aware of the suffering of hundreds of thousands of people in the Balkans. We had hoped, therefore, that the dramatic humanitarian situation in the region would lead to a consensual response on the part of the Council.

The stated purpose of this resolution, which Brazil cosponsored and for which we worked together with the members of the Non-Aligned Movement caucus, was to serve as a bridge between positions and to help build unity within the Council in responding to the crisis in Kosovo. In this respect, we insist both on the linkage between the deterioration of the humanitarian situation and on the absence of a political solution to the crisis and a reaffirmation of the role of the Security Council in the search for that solution.

While we regret that a full convergence of views was not possible over the terms of the resolution, we are pleased that the Council was able to adopt the resolution, the main thrust of which is to support unconditionally the efforts of the United Nations and humanitarian agencies in assisting the needs of the thousands of people in distress all over the region. It does not address the crucial question of a final resolution of the conflict, as the elements for that, unfortunately are not yet in the hands of the Council.

I wish to underline the importance of the step taken tonight by the Council and to express the hope that this expression of common concern will help us achieve in the near future greater involvement by the Security Council in the political resolution of the Kosovo crisis. [...]

Mr. Jovanovic: In its latest ferocious attack, North Atlantic Treaty Organization (NATO) aeroplanes bombed refugees in Korisa, near Prizren, and killed over 80 civilians, predominantly children, women and elderly people who were returning to their homes in Kosovo, in Metohija. Many were wounded, 58 seriously. Is this tragedy going to be once again cynically interpreted as collateral damage of NATO humanitarian bombings? How many more innocent victims have to die before the international community and the Security Council react by condemning and stopping this brutal NATO aggression against Yugoslavia and insisting on a political solution?

The aggression of the North Atlantic Treaty Organization against the Federal Republic of Yugoslavia, now in its fifty-first day, is continuing, expanding and intensifying. It is a gross violation of the Charter of the United Nations and the basic principles of international relations. Notwithstanding many requests by the Government of the Federal Republic of Yugoslavia, the Security Council took no steps to uphold the Charter of the United Nations, to prevent the arrogation of its authority and the violations of international peace and security. Had this legitimate request been heeded, vast human suffering and material destruction would have been avoided.

NATO's campaign of terror and devastation targets civilians, infrastructure and the economy, inflicting a humanitarian catastrophe on the 11 million citizens of the Federal Republic of Yugoslavia. So far more than 1,200 people have been killed and more than 5,000 wounded, while more than 300 schools, dozens of hospitals and a great number of civilian factories, bridges, railways, public roads, churches and cultural and historical monuments have been destroyed. NATO's strikes against downtown Nis and Belgrade have caused many civilian deaths, while entire city blocks, marketplaces, hospitals and even foreign diplomatic missions have been destroyed or damaged. This is telling proof that NATO is perpetrating a deliberate and premeditated genocide in an attempt to intimidate the population and erode its morale, which stands in the way of NATO's conquest and occupation.

[11] NATO bombs have caused an ecological disaster in the Federal Republic of Yugoslavia and in the region. My country has informed many United Nations specialized agencies about this disaster. NATO is increasingly using weapons banned by the Convention on Prohibitions or Restrictions on the Use of Certain Conventional Weapons Which May Be Deemed to Be Excessively Injurious or to Have Indiscriminate Effects, of 10 October 1980. These weapons include cluster bombs, which afflict children the most, depleted uranium ammunition and graphite bombs aimed at short-circuiting the power grid of the country. NATO has caused deliberate, indescribable suffering, especially to the most vulnerable segments of the population, such as pregnant women, babies in incubators, the hospitalized and the elderly.

The most recent estimates put the damage done by NATO bombs at more than $100 billion. The destruction of much of the Yugoslav industry has rendered half a million people jobless, and more than 2 million are without any source of income whatsoever. The indirect damage from the enforced halts in production cannot be calculated.

As we all witnessed, only a few days ago the Embassy of the People's Republic of China in Belgrade also fell prey to this reign of terror and twilight of reason. Three persons were killed, and a large number were wounded. This act of barbarism is without precedent in the recent history of international relations and constitutes a flagrant violation of the 1973 Convention on the Prevention and Punishment of Crimes against Internationally Protected Persons, including Diplomatic Agents.

NATO has flagrantly violated international conventions and covenants on human rights and freedoms, in particular the Geneva Convention relative to the Protection of Civilian Persons in Time of War. In destroying radio and television stations in my country, NATO is trying to prevent the public around the world from being informed about the shameful campaign and is trying to impose its own mendacious propaganda as the only and the whole truth.

NATO has cited its concern for protecting the Albanian national minority from alleged mistreatment and ethnic cleansing by Serbian security forces as a post-facto pretext for its aggression. The best evidence of the fallacy of this claim is the humanitarian situation before and after the NATO bombs began to fall. Refugees took to the roads as soon as the first bomb was dropped. Of all the mayhem wrought to date, one of the worst incidents was on 14 April, when a convoy of refugees returning to their homes in response to a public appeal by the authorities of the Federal Republic of Yugoslavia was struck along the Djacovica road. Seventy-five civilians were killed and more than 40 were wounded. NATO bombs have also hit many refugee camps, killing Serbs expelled from Croatia and Bosnia and Herzegovina. More than 100 people- primarily women, children and the elderly-have been killed in those camps. So these people's sad and sorry exodus ended in a most tragic and careless fashion. Regrettably the draft resolution makes no mention of these tragic consequences of the NATO aggression.

The concern of the Security Council about the humanitarian situation in the Federal Republic of Yugoslavia is justified. However, the attempt to legalize the aggression of the North Atlantic Treaty Organization against my country by means of this so-called humanitarian resolution is unjustified. The bypassing of the Security Council, the body charged with the maintenance of international peace and security, prior to the commencement of the aggression, and the subsequent attempts to get the Council on board in order to legalize the aggression deal a heavy blow to the reputation of the United Nations and sets a dangerous precedent for international relations in general.

The draft resolution must, therefore, contain a demand by the Security Council that the NATO aggression against the Federal Republic of Yugoslavia be stopped immediately and unconditionally. For without addressing the causes, no success will be achieved in addressing the consequences. The sooner this is understood, the quicker the solution will be found for all the problems caused by the unprovoked and unauthorized attack by the United States of America and its NATO confederates against the independent and sovereign Federal Republic of Yugoslavia.

Mr. van Walsum (Netherlands): I would like to comment briefly on the statement of the speaker before me.

The present conflict will one day come to an end, but if Serbia wants to be part of Europe it will at last have to start realizing why it has been subjected to NATO air strikes. One day the Serbian people will have to understand that our intervention on account of the atrocities committed by the Serbian security forces and the Yugoslav army in Kosovo would probably not have been possible if it had not been preceded by almost eight years of ethnic cleansing, carried out in the [12] name of the Serbian nation, first in the Krajina in East Slavonia, then in Bosnia and finally in its ultimate form in Kosovo.

Were it not for our accumulated disgust at this practice, we might not have had the courage to act. [...]

Mr. Kamal (Pakistan): [...] It is shocking that, so soon after Bosnia, we are witnessing yet another campaign of genocide and ethnic cleansing being perpetrated by the same regime. The Belgrade authorities are pursuing systematic and deliberate policies of hatred and intolerance, aimed at decimating and uprooting a whole community for its ethnic origin and beliefs. Only four years ago, while addressing the crisis in Bosnia and Herzegovina, the international community vowed not to allow the recurrence of such a heinous crime against humanity anywhere in the world. The perpetrators of such crimes must not go unpunished.

Pakistan has been closely following the Kosovo situation. The Prime Minister of Pakistan recently visited the refugee camps in Tirana to have first-hand information about the suffering of the innocent Kosovars. As part of the visit to Tirana, he had stopovers in Baku, Rome and Ankara, where he exchanged views with the leaders on the Kosovo crisis. During an official visit to Moscow last month, the Prime Minister held discussions with the Russian leadership on the issue. Also at Pakistan's initiative, a ministerial meeting of the Organization of the Islamic Conference Contact Group on Bosnia and Herzegovina and Kosova was convened in Geneva last month. This meeting adopted a comprehensive declaration on the issue and was followed up by visits to Moscow, Rome, Bonn and Tirana by a ministerial delegation of the Contact Group.

In all these contacts and forums, Pakistan emphasized the need for the Security Council to address the crisis effectively and, in particular, stressed the urgency of establishing a United Nations peacekeeping force in Kosovo. The inability of the Security Council to take effective action and to carry out its Charter responsibility has been a matter of deep concern to us. Its failure to address the issues of international peace and security in the past has only aggravated conflicts and human tragedies, as we in South Asia know well.

We hope that the Security Council will soon address the Kosovo crisis comprehensively and facilitate an early implementation of last week's decision by the Foreign Ministers of the Group of Seven industrialized nations and Russia to establish a United Nations peacekeeping operation in Kosovo. The Security Council must endorse the proposals which, among other things, would pave the way for a verifiable end to violence and ethnic cleansing in Kosovo, the withdrawal of Yugoslav military, police and paramilitary forces, the establishment of an interim administration in the province, the safe and free return of refugees and a political settlement providing self-government for Kosovo. Pakistan has already expressed its willingness to contribute to the United Nations [13] peacekeeping efforts, as and when authorized by the Security Council, in fulfilling its Charter responsibility.

As a sponsor of the resolution, Pakistan supports the measures adopted by the Security Council on the humanitarian crisis in Kosovo. [...]

[Statement by representatives of Quatar and Saudi Arabia have been omitted.]

[14] Mr. Nejad Hosseinian (Islamic Republic of Iran): [...] The people and the Government of the Islamic Republic of Iran were greatly distressed to learn that during the night of 7 May 1999 the Chinese Embassy in Belgrade, Federal Republic of Yugoslavia, came under attack, resulting in loss of life and property damage. We would like to convey our sincere condolences to the Government and the people of the People's Republic of China for the unfortunate loss of the lives of Chinese diplomats. Our condolences go particularly to those families which lost loved ones in this tragedy.

In my capacity as Chairman of the Organization of the Islamic Conference (OIC) Contact Group on Bosnia and Herzegovina and Kosovo, I would like to take this opportunity to express once again the grave concerns not only of the members of the OIC Contact Group but of the whole international community, including the Islamic countries, at the escalating humanitarian tragedy that continues to unfold in and around Kosovo. The plight of the refugee and internally displaced Kosovar

Albanians has shocked the conscience of humanity. We salute the neighbouring countries for so generously shouldering the burden of caring for the refugees. Members of the OIC Contact Group have been responsive to the imperative of burden-sharing at this difficult time and will continue on their course until the refugees and displaced persons return to their homes in peace and safety.

Moreover, the OIC Contact Group is deeply concerned about the ripple effect of the Kosovo crisis. We believe that the continuation of the current Kosovo crisis could endanger the fragile peace and security in other parts of the Balkans. The grave concern of the OIC Contact Group about the forced flight of an increasing number of the Muslims from Sandjak and about their [15] taking refuge in neighbouring countries, mainly in Bosnia and Herzegovina, has been conveyed to the Security Council.

The OIC Contact Group deeply regrets the failure of the Security Council to deal effectively with the crisis in Kosovo and to put an end to the plight of the Albanian Kosovars. Reiterating that the Security Council has the primary responsibility for the maintenance of international peace and security, we hope that the Security Council will accelerate its endeavours in order to carry out its responsibility under the United Nations Charter in an effective manner.

In view of all this, the OIC Contact Group has, since the onset of the crisis, taken a number of initiatives to help to contain the crisis and to find a peaceful solution. To this end, the OIC Contact Group decided in its Ministerial Meeting, held in Geneva on 7 April 1999, to strengthen contacts with all parties concerned, thus trying to promote a peaceful, just and lasting settlement of the Kosovo crisis. In this connection, a high-level delegation of the Contact Group, headed by the Foreign Minister of the Islamic Republic of Iran, in April visited a number of capitals, including Moscow, Bonn, Tirana and Rome. Exchanging views with officials of various countries, the OIC delegation explored ways and means of cooperating at the international level with a view to promoting a peaceful, just and lasting settlement of the Kosovo crisis.

We wish to recall the declaration of the Ministerial Meeting of the OIC Contact Group, held in Geneva on 7 April 1999; to confirm our strong condemnation of the policy of ethnic cleansing perpetrated by the Serbian authorities against the Albanian Kosovars; and to demand an immediate halt to all repressive actions undertaken in Kosovo by the Serbian authorities and the immediate withdrawal of the Serbian military and paramilitary forces from Kosovo.

In its statement dated 22 April 1999, the OIC Contact Group expressed support for the proposals made by the Secretary-General of the United Nations on 9 April, in which he called upon the Yugoslav authorities to undertake five commitments to allow a lasting political solution to be found through diplomacy to the crisis in Kosovo. We also support the latest initiatives of the Secretary-General, including his consultations with concerned officials in various capitals, his appointment of two envoys and the decision to undertake a humanitarian-needs assessment in the Federal Republic of Yugoslavia, starting in Kosovo.

The OIC Contact Group lends its full support to all diplomatic efforts and initiatives in search of a just and durable political solution which would ensure, inter alia, an end to the Yugoslav policy of ethnic cleansing and the swift, safe and unimpeded return of all Kosovar refugees and internally displaced persons to their homes under international protection.

While appreciating the efforts being made by the international community and recalling the mobilization already underway in the Islamic countries to assist the Kosovar refugees, we emphasize the continued necessity of providing humanitarian assistance to the refugees in and around Kosovo with a view to alleviating their sufferings.

In light of the increasing and continuing plight of the refugees and displaced persons in and around Kosovo, the OIC Contact Group decided to lend its full support to the resolution submitted by the Caucus of the Non-Aligned Movement and cosponsored it in order to underline the fact that the worsening humanitarian crisis in and around Kosovo requires immediate and serious international attention. [...]

Mr. Abdelaziz (Egypt) *(spoke in Arabic)*: Faced with a serious escalation of the crisis in Kosovo and the Security Council's inability to take steps to strengthen its credibility in the maintenance of international peace and security that would allow us to achieve a political settlement to end the humanitarian tragedy and the acts of ethnic-cleansing perpetrated by Serb forces against the inhabitants of that province, whatever their ethnic origin, there is an increasing need to support humanitarian action to ease the suffering of refugees and displaced persons, who have been provoked by these events to undertake an exodus.

Egypt is fully convinced that the provision of humanitarian assistance to refugees and displaced persons [16] is within the competence of the Secretary-General. The deterioration of the humanitarian situation in Kosovo and its grave implications for international peace and security; the urgent need for the international community to provide timely humanitarian assistance to the victims of these events throughout the States of the region and to ensure that it reach those for whom it is intended; and the need for a comprehensive assessment by the mission which the Secretary-General has sent are all reasons that have compelled Egypt, together with other States members of the Organization of the Islamic Conference Contact Group on Bosnia and Kosovo, to endorse the resolution which the Security Council has adopted today. We are convinced that it will be supported by all Members of the United Nations.

We believe that the resolution is exclusively humanitarian in its objectives. We wished to distinguish this issue from the current political problems and the various ways and means of solving them, although we made certain amendments aimed at globalizing the resolution so that it might be adopted unanimously. However, despite the urgent humanitarian nature of the resolution, it was delayed for political reasons, albeit without affecting the unanimity of the vote today. The clear message which the sponsors of the resolution - in particular the members of the OIC Contact Group on Bosnia and Kosovo, including Egypt - wish to send to the international community is that the lack of a defined role for the Security Council in the search for a peaceful settlement, engendered by its inability to discharge its responsibilities for international peace and security, cannot justify ignoring the urgent humanitarian situation in the region. Thus, the international community, especially the United Nations, must step up its activities to end the humanitarian suffering of the victims of the situation and of those States that have sheltered a large number of refugees and displaced persons, thereby assuming a significant additional material and logistical burden.

In this regard, we wish to thank the Secretary-General for his particular efforts, as well as the Office of the United Nations High Commissioner for Refugees and the other humanitarian institutions involved.

We hope that the Security Council will be able to overcome its current difficulties and reassert its role in reaching a comprehensive political settlement of the situation in order to guarantee the return; security and wellbeing of all displaced persons and refugees under international control. In the meantime, we appeal to the international community to grant all possible assistance to displaced persons in Kosovo and the States that have suffered in the exodus. We hope that this clear message will meet with the wholehearted approval of the international community. [...]

[Statements by the representatives of Ukraine, Belarus, Cuba and Albania have been omitted.]

[20] **Mr. Hosseini** (Organization of the Islamic Conference): [...] Since the arbitrary termination of the autonomy of Kosovo by the Belgrade authorities in 1989, we, together with the international community, have watched with great distress the Serbian acts of atrocities against the innocent and hard-working people of Kosovo and the campaigns of ethnic cleansing that have been reminiscent of the preceding sinister acts against the population of Bosnia and Herzegovina that were also committed by the Serbs.

Regrettably, the Bosnian experience has failed to teach the Serbs an important lesson of history, which is that when a nation tries to keep another in the ditch, it does so by also staying with it in the ditch.

It is relevant to remind this Council that the Organization of the Islamic Conference (OIC) Contact Group on Bosnia and Herzegovina and Kosova, meeting at the level of Ministers of Foreign Affairs in Geneva last month, regretted that the Security Council has been unable to discharge its responsibility in Kosovo in accordance with the Charter of the United Nations. It reiterated that the Security Council has the primary responsibility for the maintenance of international peace and security, and that in carrying out its duties in accordance with this responsibility, the Council shall be looked upon to act on behalf of the Members of the United Nations.

The ministers expressed their solidarity with the Kosovars in their present hour of need and, among other things, undertook to contribute to the monitoring and peacekeeping operations in Kosovo as part of the international peacekeeping efforts.

Since the Geneva meeting, the diplomatic efforts of the Ministers of Foreign Affairs of the OIC Contact Group, aimed at finding a viable solution to the crisis in Kosovo, have been intense and have led to the Contact Group's support of the resolution just adopted by the [21] Council - a resolution initiated by the Permanent Representatives of Bahrain and Malaysia and presented to the Council by the Permanent Representative of Gambia, all members of the OIC.

The resolution addresses, in particular, the humanitarian aspect of the crisis in Kosovo, which is of crucial concern at this time. By its nature, the resolution allows the Security Council to act in unity and without controversy, which may otherwise have posed possible constraints on its ability to act quickly in the matter in fulfilment of its responsibilities at this grave moment.

The response just demonstrated by members will hopefully be a significant factor in rescuing the people of Kosovo from the agony and suffering they are undergoing at this time.

[A statement by the representative of Slovenia has been omitted.]

257. Extracts of the UN General Assembly General Debate from 20 September 1999 to 2 October 1999

[Presidential statements not related to substantive issues and statements of member states that do not add to the legal evaluation or the factual background have been omitted.]

257a. United Nations General Assembly, 54th Session, 4th Plenary Meeting, 20 September 1999

Agenda item 10

Report of the Secretary-General on the work of the Organization (A/54/1)

[1] **The Secretary-General:** [...] On this occasion, I should like to address the prospects for human security and intervention in the next century. In the light of the dramatic events of the past year, I trust that the Assembly will understand this decision.

As Secretary-General, I have made it my highest duty to restore the United Nations to its rightful role in the pursuit of peace and security, and to bring it closer to the peoples it serves. As we stand at the brink of a new century, this mission continues. But it continues in a world transformed by geopolitical, economic, technological and environmental changes whose lasting significance still eludes us. As we seek new ways to combat the ancient enemies of war and poverty, we will succeed only if we all adapt our Organization to a world with new actors, new responsibilities and new possibilities for peace and progress.

The sovereign state, in its most basic sense, is being redefined by the forces of globalization and international cooperation. The state is now widely understood to be the servant of its people, ant not vice versa. At the same time, individual sovereignty - and by this I mean the human rights and fundamental freedoms of each and every individual, as enshrined in our Charter - has been [2] enhanced by a renewed consciousness of the right of every individual to control his or her own destiny.

These parallel developments - remarkable and in many ways welcome - do not lend themselves to easy interpretations or simple conclusions. They do, however, demand of us a willingness to think anew about how the United Nations responds to the political, human rights and humanitarian crises affecting so much of the world; about the means employed by the international community in situations of need; and about our willingness to act in some areas of conflict while limiting ourselves to humanitarian palliatives in many other crises whose daily toll of death and suffering ought to shame us into action.

Our reflections on these critical questions derive not only from the events of the past year but from a variety of challenges that confront us today, most urgently in East Timor. From Sierra Leone to the Sudan to Angola to the Balkans and to Cambodia, and then to Afghanistan, there are a great number of peoples who need more than just words of sympathy from the international community. They need a real and sustained commitment to help end their cycles of violence and launch them on a safe passage to prosperity.

While the genocide in Rwanda will define for our generation the consequences of inaction in the face of mass murder, the more recent conflict in Kosovo has prompted important questions about the consequences of action in the absence of complete unity on the part of the international community. It has cast in stark relief the dilemma of what has been called "humanitarian intervention": on one side, the question of the legitimacy of an action taken by a regional organization without a United Nations mandate; on the other, the universally recognized imperative of effectively halting gross and systematic violations of human rights with grave humanitarian consequences.

The inability of the international community in the case of Kosovo to reconcile these two equally compelling interests - universal legitimacy and effectiveness in defence of human rights - can be viewed only as a tragedy. It has revealed the core challenge to the Security Council and to the United Nations as a whole in the next century: to forge unity behind the principle that massive and systematic violations of human rights - wherever they may take place - should not be allowed to stand.

The Kosovo conflict and its outcome have prompted a wide debate of profound importance to the resolution of conflicts, from the Balkans to Central Africa to East Asia. And to each side in this critical debate, difficult questions can be posed.

To those for whom the greatest threat to the future of international order is the use of force in the absence of a Security Council mandate, one might ask, not in the context of Kosovo but in the context of Rwanda, if, in those dark days and hours leading up to the genocide, a coalition of States had been prepared to act in defence of the Tutsi population, but did not receive prompt Council authorization, should such a coalition have stood aside and allowed the horror to unfold?

To those for whom the Kosovo action heralded a new era when States and groups of States can take military action outside the established mechanism for enforcing international law, one might ask: is there not a danger of such interventions undermining the imperfect, yet resilient, security system created after the Second World War, and of setting dangerous precedents for future interventions without a clear criterion to decide who might invoke these precedents and in what circumstances?

In response to this turbulent era of crises and interventions, there are those who have suggested that the Charter itself - with its roots in the aftermath of global inter-State war - is ill-suited to guide us in a world of ethnic wars and intra-State violence. I believe they are wrong.

The Charter is a living document whose high principles still define the aspirations of peoples everywhere for lives of peace, dignity and development. Nothing in the Charter precludes a recognition that there are rights beyond borders. Indeed, its very letter and spirit are the affirmation of those fundamental human rights. In short, it is not the deficiencies of the Charter which have brought us to this juncture, but our difficulties in applying its principles to a new era - an era when strictly traditional notions of sovereignty can no longer do justice to the aspirations of peoples everywhere to attain their fundamental freedoms.

The sovereign States that drafted the Charter over a half century ago were dedicated to peace, but experienced in war. They knew the terror of conflict, but knew equally that there are times when the use of force may be legitimate in pursuit of peace. That is why the Charter's own words declare that "armed force shall not be used, F save in the common interest". But what is the common interest? Who shall define it? Who will defend it - under [3] whose authority and with what means of intervention? These are the monumental questions facing us as we enter the new century. While I will not propose specific answers or criteria, I shall identify four aspects of intervention which I believe hold important lessons for resolving future conflicts.

First, it is important to define intervention as broadly as possible, to include actions along a wide continuum from the most pacific to the most coercive. A tragic irony of many of the crises that continue to go unnoticed and unchallenged today is that they could be dealt with by far less perilous acts of intervention than the one we witnessed recently in Yugoslavia. Yet the commitment of the international community to peacekeeping, to humanitarian assistance and to rehabilitation and reconstruction varies greatly from region to region and crisis to crisis.

If the new commitment to intervention in the face of extreme suffering is to retain the support of the world's peoples, it must be, and must be seen to be, fairly and consistently applied, irrespective of region or nation. Humanity, after all, is indivisible. It is also necessary to recognize that any armed intervention is itself a result of the failure of prevention. As we consider the future of intervention, we must redouble our efforts to enhance our preventive capabilities, including early warning, preventive diplomacy, preventive deployment and preventive disarmament.

A recent powerful tool of deterrence has been the actions of the Tribunals for Rwanda and for the former Yugoslavia. In their battle against impunity lies a key to deterring crimes against humanity. With these concerns in mind, I have dedicated the introductory essay of my annual report to exploring ways of moving from a culture of reaction to a culture of prevention. Even the costliest policy of prevention is far cheaper, in lives and in resources, than the least expensive of armed force.

Secondly, it is clear that sovereignty alone is not the only obstacle to effective action in human rights or humanitarian crises. No less significant are the ways in which the States Members of the United Nations define their national interest in any given crisis. Of course, the traditional pursuit of national interest is a permanent feature of international relations and of the life and work of the Security Council. But I believe that as the world has changed in profound ways since the end of the cold war, our conceptions of national interest have failed to follow suit.

A new, more broadly defined, more widely conceived definition of national interest in the new century would, I am convinced, induce States to find far greater unity in the pursuit of such basic Charter value as democracy, pluralism, human rights and the rule of law. A global era requires global engagement. Indeed, in a growing number of challenges facing humanity, the collective interest is the national interest.

Thirdly, in the event that forceful intervention becomes necessary, we must ensure that the Security Council, the body charged with authorizing force under international law, is able to rise to the challenge. As I said during the Kosovo conflict, the choice must not be between, on the one hand, Council unity and inaction in the face of genocide, as in the case of Rwanda and, on the other, Council division and regional action, as in the case of Kosovo. In both cases, the States Members of the United Nations should have been able to find common ground in upholding the principles of the Charter and in acting in defence of our common humanity.

As important as the Council's enforcement power is its deterrent power. Unless it is able to assert itself collectively when the cause is just and when the means are available, its credibility in the eyes of the world may well suffer. If States bent on criminal behaviour know that frontiers are not the absolute defence and if they know that the Security Council will take action to halt crimes against humanity, they will not embark on such a course of action in expectation of sovereign impunity.

The Charter requires the Council to be the defender of the common interest, and unless it is seen to be so in an era of human rights, interdependence and globalization, there is a danger that others could seek to take its place. Let me say that the Council's prompt and effective action in authorizing a multinational force for East Timor reflects precisely the unity of purpose that I have called for today. Already, however, far too many lives have been lost and far too much destruction has taken place for us to rest on our laurels. The hard work of bringing peace and stability to East Timor still awaits us.

Finally, after the conflict is over, in East Timor as everywhere, it is vitally important that the commitment to peace be as strong as the commitment to war. In this situation, too, consistency is essential. Just as our commitment to humanitarian action must be universal if it is to be legitimate, so our commitment to peace can not end with the cessation of hostilities. The aftermath of war [4] requires no less skill, no less sacrifice and no fewer resources in order to forge a lasting peace and avoid a return to violence. The Kosovo Mission and other United Nations missions currently deployed or looming over the horizon present us with just such a challenge.

Unless the United Nations is given the means and the support to succeed, not only the peace, but the war, too, will have been lost. From civil administration and policing to the creation of a civil society capable of sustaining a tolerant, pluralist, prosperous society, the challenges facing our peacekeeping, peacemaking and peace-building missions are immense. But if we are given the means - in Kosovo, in Sierra Leone and in East Timor - we have a real opportunity to break the cycles of violence, once and for all.

We leave a century of unparalleled suffering and violence. Our greatest, most enduring test remains our ability to gain the respect and support of the world's peoples. If the collective conscience of humanity - a conscience which abhors cruelty, renounces injustice and seeks peace for all peoples - cannot find in the United Nations its greatest tribune, there is a grave danger that it will look elsewhere for peace and for justice. If it does not hear in our voices, and see in our actions, reflections of its own aspirations, its needs and its fears, it may soon lose faith in our ability to make a difference.

Just as we have learned that the world cannot stand aside when gross and systematic violations of human rights are taking place, so we have also learned that intervention must be based on legitimate and universal principles if it is to enjoy the sustained support of the world's peoples.

This developing international norm in favour of intervention to protect civilians from wholesale slaughter will no doubt continue to pose profound challenges to the international community. Any such evolution in our understanding of state sovereignty and individual sovereignty will, in some quarters, be met with distrust, scepticism and even hostility. But it is an evolution that we should welcome.

Why? Because, despite its limitations and imperfections, it is testimony to a humanity that cares more, not less, for the suffering in its midst; and a humanity that will do more, and not less, to end it. It is a hopeful sign at the end of the twentieth century. [...]

Agenda item 9
[Statements by the respresentatives of Brazil, South Africa, Algeria and Namibia have been omitted.]

[19] **Address by Mr. Eduard Shevardnadze, President of Georgia**: [...] [23] The Assembly can imagine how disillusioned I was when ethnic purging of the Georgian population occurred, and, by the way, remaining unpunished within my own country. I addressed the Security Council twice with a [24] detailed account and explanation of what

happened, but no substantial progress has yet been made, even in the formulation of its resolutions. Having experienced this disappointment, I believe it should have come as no surprise that I firmly supported the North Atlantic Treaty Organization (NATO) operation in Kosovo, aimed at putting an end to ethnic cleansing, since I viewed that operation as the long-awaited manifestation of a firm stand against evil. At the same time, however, the action in Kosovo must not be interpreted by anyone as even indirect support of aggressive separatism. By no means. I have always believed that aggressive separatism and attempts to manipulate evolving democratic orders by use of force is one of the worst and most dangerous maladies of modern times. [...]

[25] Of course, it is true that the world does respond to some extent to threats as they occur. Individual States and alliances of States do make serious efforts to fight global ailments. Sometimes, as has just happened in Kosovo, they undertake such tasks as a coercion to peace. It is my position that no one has a moral right to denounce NATO for that operation, particularly those who, through their inaction, play into the hands of those who disturb the peace.

Yet this is not precisely what one would call a demonstration of collective responsibility. In such a case several democratic and developed - and therefore powerful - States undertake the stewardship of the rest of the world. Of course, we can only thank them for this. But it would be better for all if those who have undertaken responsibility for the fate of the world carried out their mission within the framework of a mechanism established by the international organizations. We have already proposed to expand the membership of the Security Council and address the issue of veto rights in order to adapt it to present-day requirements. In my view, the almost automatic use of the veto is unacceptable. In the bipolar world this practice largely cancelled out the possibility of conducting peace enforcement operations, because in those years any force represented, to some extent, one pole for the other.

With the end of the cold war, the possiblity of using collective decisions to bring about peace reappeared. The decision taken against the aggression in Kuwait gave many the hope that from then on the Security Council would be bound by shared principles and that an ethical approach would prevail. There were other encouraging episodes as well. But in the case of Kosovo, a new cold breeze seemed to have begun to blow from the Security Council. Despite its humane motivations, the operation carried out by NATO - like any ethical action today - also contained a pragmatic component. Had NATO not intervened in Kosovo, the influx of refugees would inevitably have upset the fragile balance in that extremely important part of Europe. Perhaps a number of States would have been drawn into the conflict. We might even have witnessed a big Balkan war.

In today's world an ethical approach in international politics is justified from a pragmatic standpoint as well. It is from a position of morality that we should act if we want to do good for mankind. Morality should be the basis of our policy, and it should become the pillar of the new thinking of the twenty-first century.

We are encouraged by the Secretary-General's statement that measures to reform the Security Council will be taking place shortly and that the reform will enable us to act in accordance with the norms of international law when addressing regional conflicts in the future. [...]

[26] **Address by Mr. Lionel Jospin, Prime Minister of the French Republic**: [...] [27] The United Nations is undertaking a grand civilizing endeavour, a task that is constantly being challenged but ever necessary. To unite peoples to work together for peace and development, to affirm a body of legal rules framing relations among States and to achieve common standards: that is the goal of the United Nations- a civilizing goal.

That goal is achieved first of all through the peaceful settlement of conflicts. The role of the Security Council in this mission is more vital than ever, a pre-eminence it derives from the Charter. France will recall this fundamental rule as often as necessary. To be sure, there have been circumstances when an urgent humanitarian situation dictated we should act immediately, but such an approach must remain an exception. We must take care, as in the case of Kosovo, to reintegrate this action into the context of the Charter. Our fundamental rule is that it is for the Security Council to resolve crisis situations. For that reason, the North Atlantic Treaty Organization's new strategic concept recalls that the Washington Treaty recognizes the primary responsibility of the Security Council in the maintenance of peace.

Indeed, the universal nature of the Organization is intangible. The United Nations must strive to respond to crises, wherever they may occur. While we have not hesitated to do precisely that in recent years and on several continents, I would like to express regret at the relative timidity of the Organization where Africa is concerned. The extent of the tragedies on that continent requires us to take more resolute action.

Universality is compatible with complementarily in action. In the interests of efficiency, the United Nations must encourage, in every part of the world, regional arrangements among States capable of handling crises in the first instance. Such is the spirit of Chapter VIII of the Charter. Tasks should be realistically shared between the regional organizations and the Security Council without weakening the latter's authority. For instance, my country has, through the RECAMP programme, along with others, strengthened African peacekeeping capabilities through assistance provided under United Nations auspices in cooperation with the Organization of African Unity. [...]

The United Nations mission is not limited to the settlement of conflicts between States. With humankind's growing aspirations for greater freedom and responsibility, this mission extends to the safeguarding of human dignity, within each State and, when necessary - as the Charter allows - against States. State-instigated violence has spawned serious humanitarian crises over the past few years. Civilians have been targeted, whole populations have been forcibly displaced, and refugee camps are not longer secure. This is unacceptable. Consequently, we must uphold the principle of international intervention, under United Nations auspices, to assist the victims.

Every crisis recalls the need for the founding principle of working for peace and for respect for the law and the human person. A case in point is the conflict in Kosovo. Security Council resolution 1244 (1999), which laid down the foundations of the settlement, illustrates these principles and this resolve.

We have at ourselves ambitious objectives: ensuring security for all, organizing reconstruction, ensuring coexistence between communities, transferring authority to local leaders, and promoting democracy and pluralism. The Secretary-General's Special Representative and the KFOR Commander have done remarkable work. Much, however, remains to be done. The atrocities must be stopped, the exodus stemmed and housing built before winter. On the political front, preparations must be made for the future, which will require establishing dialogue between the communities. Elections will, I hope, be held in the year 2000. France has made resolute efforts in this respect, alongside its partners in the European Union, which is providing half the international financing agreed upon by the conference of donors for Kosovo. [...]

[30] **Mr. El-Khatib** (Jordan) *(spoke in Arabic)*: [...] [33] The tragic situation the people of Kosovo were made to experience severely tested the ability of the international community, at the close of this century, to prevent the crimes of ethnic cleansing and the violation of basis human rights from being committed in a most despicable, racist manner. This matter raises extremely serious and complex questions about the role of the United Nations and the limits that separate the right of States to assert their sovereignty without committing mass crimes against helpless unarmed civilians.

There are lessons to be drawn from this bitter human experience. On the one hand, the North Atlantic Treaty Organization's ability to put an end to the criminal acts has given clear evidence to all those who harbor thoughts of rebelling against international law and of committing similar acts that they should not presume that their domestic military strength ensures absolute dominance, including violation of human rights. Upholding the principle of sovereignty should not overturn the obligation to observe human rights and international humanitarian law.

On the other hand, as members of this international Organization, we must look into finding mechanisms that ensure the enhancement of the United Nations and its ability to be the framework that expresses the determination of the international community to prevent such crimes, and to be the umbrella for the coordination and organization of collective international action to achieve that goal.

That situation has demonstrated the need for formulating a new international order for the twenty-first century, in which all peoples can enjoy respect for their diversity and can participate in the formation of a world conscience that ensures their coexistence. Continued progress by peoples in adopting democracy as a way of life makes it urgent to strenghten democracy within the international system. Since the United Nations is the backbone of the world system, it must evolve in such a way that reflects the new realities in the international arena.

Our international community has an urgent need to pause for a real review of the international situation in all its dimensions: political, security, economic, environmental and human rights. We hope that the world summit to be held next year will provide an opportunity for such a review. [...]

257b. United Nations General Assembly, 54th Session, 5th Plenary Meeting, 20 September 1999

[Statements by the representatives of Tanzania, Nicaragua, Colombia, Portugal and Bangladesh have been omitted.]

[17] **Address by Mr. Kjell Magne Bondevik, Prime Minister of the Kingdom of Norway**: [...] [18] But at the same time, there are critics who claim that the United Nations has failed. Of course, many things could have been done better, but we must not forget the many successes and we must not forget that it is we, the Member States, who are responsible for giving the United Nations the mandates to act and the money and the means to succeed. Let us not make the United Nations a scapegoat for our own shortcomings. Instead, we must make sure that the Security Council can fulfil its primary function in international peace and security. We must act in accordance with the United Nations Charter and international law. We must put the United Nations first.

This means enhancing the capacity of the United Nations for conflict prevention, crisis management and long-term development. All Members must meet their financial obligations to our world Organisation and its peace operations. Creating common security is not cost-free. In particular, it is the duty of the most powerful members of the United Nations to set an example for others.

The United Nations must develop further its cooperation with regional organizations. As Chairman-in-Office of the Organization for Security and Cooperation in Europe (OSCE), Norway has been working to build closer relations with the United Nations system. We need constructive interaction between all international, governmental and non-governmental organizations involved in peacekeeping and post-conflict work in Europe and elsewhere.

Kosovo is a tragic example of the complex conflict that we have seen in recent years. Building lasting peace there will require the concerted efforts of all actors involved: the United Nations, the North Atlantic Treaty Organization (NATO), the OSCE, the European Union and others. Our immediate concern is to secure a safe, environment for all the people of Kosovo through credible international presence.

We must promote integration between all the peoples and nations of south-eastern Europe. We must include everyone and isolate no one. This summer, at the Sarajevo Summit, we pledged to make the Stability Pact a key element of our efforts to ensure that democracy, peace and prosperity become firmly rooted all over south eastern Europe.

At the same time, our efforts to build peace in the Balkans must not be made at the expense of the poorest people elsewhere in the world. They should not pay the bill. [...]

[Statements by the representatives of Cambodia, Andorra and the Fiji Islands have been omitted.]

[30] **Mr. Essy** (Côte d'Ivoire) *(spoke in French)*: [...] [31] We hope that the Millenium Summit planned for September 2000 will launch the United Nations into the twenty-first century. It is therefore of great urgency that the plan to enlarge the Security Council be completed. There can be no doubt that by increasing the number of both permanent and non-permanent members, among which Africa will have to have its rightful place, we will also be remedying the lack of political visibility form which the Council has been suffering. The Kosovo crisis revealed the necessity of reaffirming the primacy of the Security Council and hence that of the United Nations. [...]

[32] The prospect of the Organization's soon deploying a peacekeeping force of 20.000 for the implementation of the Lusaka agreement in the Democratic Republic of the Congo is certainly a harbinger of an increase effort of the international community to restore peace and security in Africa. But we should take care that this hope not be dashed, thereby strenghtening the feeling, widely held in African public opinion, that our continent is subject to discriminatory treatment as compared with other regions of the world. What was possible in Kosovo should also be possible in Angola, Congo and Sierra Leone. The reference to the values of democracy and human rights that served as a catalyst for the large-scale action in Kosovo is equally applicable to African populations.

I am fully aware of the reluctance of the great Powers to become involved in complex conflicts whose local protagonists are often difficult to identify and tend to compete with one another, at very great humanitarian cost. Certainly, political prerequisites, especially in the form of cease-fire agreements, are necessary for the deployment of peacekeeping forces, but they are not insurmountable when the Security Council makes use of all the resources offered by the Charter.

The breathing of new life into the principle of peacekeeping operations through the provision of credible deterrent elements and resources should not absolve us of reviewing or of clarifying Chapter VIII on Cooperation between the United Nations and regional arrangements. Too many uncertainties remain on the scope and modalities of such Cooperation and the role that falls to the Security Council in this regard. The Kosovo crisis and military intervention under the auspices of the North Atlantic Treaty Organisation have only increased our doubts and questions in this connection. The promotion of the regional approach to collective security should in no way serve as a pretext for the Security Council's lack of involvement. By reiterating the validity of the principles of the Charter at the dawn of a new millennium, we commit ourselves to establishing better living conditions for future generations, including all the children of Africa. [...]

[34] **Mr. Cook** (United Kingdom): [...] That is why I want to support the excellent opening address by our Secretary-General by focusing my remarks also on what we must do if we are to replace failure to halt war with success in preventing conflict. The harrowing scenes we have witnessed this past year from Kosovo, from Sierra Leone, from East Timor and too may other places underline the urgency of improving our performance in preventing conflicts and also in stopping them once they have started.

I propose five priority areas for action. First, we must tackle the root causes of conflict, starting with the poverty that breeds it. War is becoming a poor man's burden. In the modern world, wealthy nations no longer experience the trauma of conflict on their soil. The soundest basis for peace is prosperity, and the best way we can prevent conflict is by promoting sustainable development. The forthcoming Millennium Assembly must make a reality of the commitment of to halving the proportion of people in extreme poverty and reducing the number of nations in heavy debt.

[35] Secondly, we must promote human rights and good governance. Development of a nation will be more rapid where people have the right to develop their full potential. Conflict is more likely where governments rule without the consent of their people.

Thirdly, we must curb the supply of weapons that fuel conflict. For decades, the United Nations, rightly, has focused on halting the spread of weapons of mass destruction. Yet in truth, in those same decades, the weapons that have killed masses in conflicts have been the most common of small arms. In Friday's debate in the Security Council, we will have the opportunity to take forward action to halt the illegal trade in small arms, to promote regional moratoriums on small arms and to limit arsenals of military firearms to legitimate Government agencies.

Fourthly, we must stop the illegal trade in diamonds and other precious commodities which pay for the small arms - and all too often the mercenaries - which sustain conflict. The markets for these commodities, especially the market in diamonds, are small and tightly located in a few centres. We must encourage cooperation with those who manage those markets to cut off the supply of funds to those who are promoting conflict.

Lastly, I strongly endorse the view expressed by our Secretary-General this morning that we must counter the culture of impunity. Those who break international humanitarian law, from Kosovo to East Timor, must know that they will be held to account by the international community.

The international criminal tribunals have shown what can be done. We must build on their work by getting a permanent international criminal court up and running with all speed.

But we will not always succeed in preventing conflict. We need, therefore, to be better equipped to restore peace when war breaks out. As my Prime Minister, Tony Blair, said in Chicago earlier this year, working out the conditions and identifying the circumstances when it is right in the modern world to intervene is the most pressing problem in foreign policy today. His speech demonstrated that Britain is anxious to play its full part in that debate. Our starting point is that our common interest in preserving the world from major conflict is greater than our individual interests as nations.

Globalisation is the long and rather ugly term which is used to describe how in today's world we are interdependent with each other rather than independent of each other. We are bound together by our strengthening links in trade and investment, in travel and communication. What happens in one country can have a direct impact on the prosperity and the security - even the climate - of countries on the other side of the world.

And we are also bound together by the consequences of conflict. In Britain 90 per cent of the heroin on the streets of our big cities is grown in Afghanistan under cover of the generation-long conflict in that land. In central Africa, the upheavals of population sparked by the mass genocide in Rwanda have destabilised the region and caught up half a dozen countries in the conflicts that have ensued. Across the countries of Europe there are now several hundred thousands of citizens of the former Yugoslavia who have fled to seek sanctuary from the repeated conflicts there. Just as few nations can stand alone in the modern world, there are now few major conflicts which remain only an internal matter with no impact on the rest of the world.

If we are to respond adequately when conflict breaks out, then the United Nations needs to develop three strenghts - credibility, consensus and capacity.

If the United Nations is to have the credibility to press the parties to a conflict to a solution, it must be more representative of the modern world. A small increase in the size of the Security Council would be a modest price to pay for the big increase in its credibility which would come from a more representative permanent membership. [...]

[36] But in Kosovo we discovered that it was less difficult to put together an armed force to end the military violence than to assemble a United Nations police force to keep civil order. Today, therefore, I can announce that Britain will follow up our standby agreement increasing the number of United Kingdom police officers available for United Nations troops. This will include a commitment to a rapid response squad, ready for deployment at short notice when it is urgently needed. We shall also be establishing with the United Nations a flagship training course in Britain to train police from around the world to play their part in our joint missions. [...]

257c. United Nations General Assembly, 54th Session, 6th Plenary Meeting, 21 September 1999

[A statement by the representative of Peru has been omitted.]

[2] **Address by Mr. William J. Clinton, President of the United States of America** [...] [4] The second resolution I hope we will make today is to strengthen the capacity of the international community to prevent and whenever possible to stop outbreaks of mass killing and displacement. This requires, as we all know, shared responsibility, like the one West African nations accepted when they acted to restore peace in Sierra Leone; the one 19 democracies in the North Atlantic Treaty Organization (NATO) embraced to stop ethnic cleansing in Bosnia and in Kosovo; the one that Asian and Pacific nations have now assumed in East Timor, with the strong support of the entire United Nations, including the United States.

Secretary-General Annan spoke for all of us during the Kosovo conflict, and more recently in regard to East Timor, when he said that ethnic cleansers and mass murderers can find no refuge in the United Nations, no source of comfort or justification in its Charter. We must do more to make these words real. Of course, we must approach this challenge with some considerable degree of humility. It is easy to say "never again", but much harder to make it so. Promising too much can be as cruel as caring too little.

But difficulties, dangers and costs are not an argument for doing nothing. When we are faced with deliberate, organized campaigns to murder whole peoples or expel them from their land, the care of victims is important but not enough. We should work to end the violence. Our response in every case cannot and should not be the same. Sometimes collective military force is both appropriate and feasible. Sometimes concerted economic and political pressure combined with diplomacy is a better answer, as it was in making possible the introduction of forces to East Timor. Of course, the way the international community responds will depend on the capacity of countries to act and on their perception of their national interests. NATO acted in Kosovo, for example, to stop a vicious campaign of ethnic cleansing in a place where we had important interests at stake and the ability to act collectively.

The same considerations brought Nigerian troops and their partners to Sierra Leone and Australians and others to East Timor. That is proper - so long as we work together, support each other and do not abdicate our collective responsibility. I know that some are troubled that the United States and others cannot respond to every humanitarian catastrophe in the world. [5] We cannot do everything, everywhere. But simply because we have different interests in different parts of the world does not mean we can be indifferent to the destruction of innocents in any part of the world. That is why we have supported the efforts of Africans to resolve the deadly conflicts that have raged through parts of their continent. It is why we are working with friends in Africa to build the African Crisis Response Initiative, which has trained more than 4,000 peacekeepers from six countries. It is why we are helping establish an international coalition against genocide to bring nations together to stop the flow of money and arms to those who commit crimes against humanity.

There is also a critical need for countries emerging from conflict to build police institutions accountable to people and the law, often with the help of civilian police from other nations. We need international forces with the training to fill the gap between local police and military peacekeepers, as French, Argentine, Italian and other military police have done in Haiti and Bosnia. We will work with our partners and the United Nations to continue to ensure that such forces can deploy when they are needed.

What is the role of the United Nations of in preventing mass slaughter and dislocation? Very large. Even in Kosovo, NATO's actions followed a clear consensus, expressed in several Security Council resolutions, that the atrocities committed by Serb forces were unacceptable and that the international community had a compelling interest in seeing them end. Had we chosen to do nothing in the face of this brutality, I do not believe we would have strengthened the United Nations. Instead we would have risked discrediting everything it stands for.

By acting as we did, we helped to vindicate the principles and purposes of the United Nations Charter to give the United Nations the opportunity it now has to play the central role in shaping Kosovo's future. In the real world, principles often collide and tough choices must be made. The outcome in Kosovo is hopeful. [...]

[A statement by the representative of Zimbabwe has been omitted.]

[9] **Address by Mr. Alvaro Arzú Irigoyen, President of the Republic of Guatemala**

[...] [12] For those same reasons, Guatemala wishes to express its unreserved support for the strengthening of our Organization. We are firmly convinced that the United Nations must be the principal forum responsible for maintaining world peace. That is why we welcome the Security Concil's prompt response to the crisis in East Timor. We believe that United Nations involvement in such situations confirms ist functions as the sole organ competent to decide on the action to be taken in cases where the principle of non-intervention needs to be interpreted with due regard to the existence of violations of international humanitarian law. [...]

[13] **Mr. Ivanov** (Russian Federation) *(spoke in Russian)*: [...] [14] The founding fathers of the United Nations made provision for a law-based response to violations of peace and security. The international community can take also coercive measures, but this should be done in accordance with the Charter and following a decision by the Security Council. Unlawful means can only undermine rightful ends. It is from this very perspective that we assess such doctrines as that of humanitarian intervention. In general, we should take an extremely careful approach to coercive measures; what is more, we must not allow them to turn into a repressive mechanism for influencing States and peoples that are not to the liking of some.

Of course, evolution of the international situation means that it is appropriate for existing rules of international law to be developed and adapted to prevailing conditions, but this should be done through collective discussion and the adoption of appropriate decisions, not as a fait accompli and not working from scratch: it should be based on valid rules of international law. This is precisely what Russia had in mind with its initiative to consider at the Millennium Summit legal aspects of the use of force in international relations in the era of globalization. We invite all countries to a broad and open dialogue on this issue.

Much has been said in recent years about the reform of the United Nations, which is only natural. Life is an evolving process and, as times change, any system will need to be updated. What objectives future reform should pursue is another matter. In our view, reform means, first and foremost, the adoption of a package of measures to enhance the role of the United Nations in the world arena. The Organization should be ready to respond in a timely and appropriate way to the challenges that globalization presents to mankind. We must give serious thought to how to enhance the efficiency of the Security Council and how to make that principal organ of the United Nations more representative through the inclusion of influential new members, including - and this is absolutely indispensable - developing countries. This would help maintain the overall balance in the system of international relations, especially when the use of force, bypassing the Security Council, continues. It is also beyond doubt that preservation of the right of veto of permanent members is indispensable for meaningful and efficient work in the Council.

Generally speaking, the entire system of international organizations needs sensible and responsible reform. At the same time, the United Nations must remain a focal point of the international community's efforts to settle the most burning problems of the day. The issue of strengthening the authority of the United Nations after it has been seriously and painfully tested by the Balkan and Iraq crises is at the very top of the agenda at the current session of the General Assembly. First of all, we must continue strenuous efforts to restore the role of the Security Council in world affairs.

We have managed through joint efforts to bring the settlement of the Kosovo problem back within the legal and political framework of the United Nations. Now we need jointly to strive for strict and consistent implementation of Security Council resolution 1244 (1999). We cannot afford to let the re-emerging political process be undermined again, since that could become a tragedy for all of Europe and could once again bring the world to the brink of catastrophe. Equally urgent is the issue of post-conflict rehabilitation in the Balkans. The United Nations has an important role to play in meeting these challenges as well. [...]

[15] Taking into account the limited resources of the world Organization, and given the high demand for peacekeeping operations, cooperation and division of labour between the United Nations and regional structures has become a priority. It is of fundamental importance that such cooperation should be in strict accordance with Chapter VIII of the Charter and should be fully consistent with the prerogatives of the Security Council. [...]

[16] **Mr. Gbeho** (Ghana): [...] [23] My delegation believes therefore that the time has come for the international community to do in Africa as much as it has done in other areas, particularly the Balkans, to guarantee peace. We have seen in the past few months the kind of resources that the world has been willing and able to mobilize in the Balkans on short notice. We do not see the same response to the tragedies of Africa. African Member States feel discriminated against when the response of the international community to conflicts on the continent continues to be muted or lukewarm. [...]

Ms. Halonen (Finland): [...] The European Union strongly emphasizes civilian crisis management. We hope that it will be more often resorted to as the principal means to manage and solve crises. We will work actively to develop further this concept. The European Union is in the process of improving its crisis management capabilities, keeping in mind that the primary responsibility for the maintenance of international peace and security lies with the United Nations and the Security Council.

Regional organizations have a key role in international security. For their success, cooperation with the United Nations is essential. The European Union thanks the Secretary-General for his efforts to strengthen this cooperation and urges him to continue this work.

The crisis in Kosovo requires concerted efforts. The European Union supports the full implementation of Security Council resolution 1244 (1999). With the adoption of this resolution, the United Nations regained its relevance as far as Kosovo is concerned. We also support the United Nations Interim Administration Mission in Kosovo (UNMIK) and KFOR in their efforts to ensure peace, democracy and security in Kosovo. The United Nations needs the means and cooperation of all to fulfil its mandate.

At the height of the Kosovo crisis the European Union launched the Stability Pact for South-Eastern Europe. Its aim is to address the questions of democracy, human rights, economic reconstruction and security in a comprehensive and durable manner. We would welcome the Federal Republic of Yugoslavia joining the Stability Pact as a full and equal participant and beneficiary. The current regime of Mr. Milosevic is responsible for its present isolation, and we look forward to welcoming democratic change inside Serbia. Meanwhile, we are searching for ways in which Kosovo and the Republic of Montenegro could be made beneficiaries of the Pact.

In Kosovo there is an urgent need to put an end to human suffering. We are concerned about the violence towards minorities, which has resulted in a large number of Serbs and Roma people leaving Kosovo. Urgent restoration of the rule of law is extremely important. [...]

257d. United Nations General Assembly, 54th Session, 7th Plenary Meeting, 21 September 1999

[Statements by representatives of Venezuela and Argentina have been omitted.]

[6] **Address by Mr. Mikuláš Dzurinda, Prime Minister of the Slovak Republic**: [...] [8] Kosovo is the most recent example of the

tragic reality of the present-day Balkans, driven by violence and ethnic hatred, which is not only a product of the region's complicated historical circumstances, but, above all, the result of human rights violations and of the misuse of ethnic differences to reach short-sighted political goals. Slovakia attaches great importance to the political resolution of the Kosovo conflict, and appreciates the efforts of the United Nations, the Secretary-General, the Contact Group, dealing with the former Yugoslavia and regional organizations to this end. We welcomed with great hope the adoption of Security Council resolution 1244 (1999), aimed at creating conditions for building a democratic Kosovo based on respect for the human rights of all citizens, regardless of their ethnic origin and religion, and for all the principles enshrined in Article 2 of the United Nations Charter. [...]

[Statements by the representatives of Mali and Japan have been omitted.]

[17] **Ms. Ferrero-Waldner** (Austria): [...] [18] Most threats to human security have a human rights dimension. This is why a human rights security agenda must include an overall strategy aimed at the strenghtening of a worldwide human rights culture. Recent events in Kosovo or East Timor have shown that the most basic rights cannot be taken for granted. Again and again we will achieve to assert the universality and indivisibility of human rights. We therefore stress the importance of human rights education, which is essential for the promotion and the achievement of stable and harmonious relations within countries and among communities. We must redouble our efforts in support of the United Nations Decade for Human Rights Education. Next year's mid-term evaluation of progress made in the Decade provides an ideal opportunity. Institutions and organizations with specialized expertise in our countries should identify specific ideas for further action on human rights education activities at national level, in foreign policy, and in the context of development cooperation. [...]

[20] The western Balkans, being geographically so close to Austria, will remain in the foreground of Austrian foreign policy. The most burning problem is currently the situation in Kosovo, which merits the joint attention of the international community. I would like to commend the work which has already been carried out by the United Nations Interim Administration Mission in Kosovo (UNMIK) and by KFOR, and the progress realized so far, in spite of such difficult circumstances. True, in the implementation of Security Council resolution 1244 (1999), and in our efforts to bring Kosovo back to normalcy, there are delays and setbacks, in particular the insecurity, the tensions in Kosovo Mitrovica, and the exodus of the majority of Kosovo Serbs and other non-Albanians. Nevertheless, one must not forget the paramount importance of the Kosovo issue for the stability of the whole Balkan area, which is why we must not become discouraged when we meet problems. Rather, we have to understand them as an incentive to redouble our efforts. Yesterday's demilitarization agreement between KFOR and the UCK is, I would say, a very encouraging step in the right direction.

In addition to setting up a functioning civil administration, including police, creating a democratic political atmosphere respectful of human rights, repatriating over 1 million refugees, and reconstructing the infrastructure and the economic life of Kosovo, it is UNMIK's crucial task to facilitate a political process leading to a definite status of the province. This is a very complicated endeavour, which requires sound and prudent preparation. We must not try to rush things, since it is clear that stability and reconciliation have to be established and solidified before we can tackle the final status question.

The same holds true for Montenegro. We must, and we will continue to, support the Montenegrin reform process, and we must not allow forces in Belgrade to undercut those pluralistic and economic improvements. For the Federal Republic of Yugoslavia as a whole, we will continue to work towards democratization, political reform and respect for human and minority rights. Upon such changes - which are not only urgently necessary but which are also yearned for by the Serb and Yugoslav people - Yugoslavia should, and will take its rightful place in the international community. [...]

[A statement by the representative of Ukraine has been omitted.]

[26] **Mr. Benaissa** (Morocco) *(spoke in Arabic)*: [...] [28] Morocco has followed with keen interest the international endeavours aimed at restoring peace in Kosovo and at putting an end to the bloody conflict and ethnic-cleansing campaigns that have claimed the lives of thousands of innocents Kosovars, in blatant violation of international law and of the most fundamental principles of human rights. Given its keen desire to strengthen peace in the region, Morroco has expressed its readiness to participate in KFOR and has made all possible humanitarian efforts to provide material assistance to Kosovar refugees. To this end, it also set up, at the initiave of Her Royal Highness Princess Lalla Meryem, a fund to collect donations for Kosovar children. [...]

[A statement by the representative of Uzbekistan has been omitted.]

[32] **Ms. Lindh** (Sweden): [...] When it comes to intervention to secure peace, regional organizations and arrangements, as well as so-called coalitions of the willing, can have important roles, together with the United Nations, as we have just seen in East Timor. But it is for the Security Council to provide the legal foundation - the mandate - for such action, in particular when force has to be used. Without such a legal foundation, we run the risk of anarchy in international relations, and in fact we undermine the prospects for peace and security; and that long-term perspective must never be lost.

Our responsibility for international peace and security implies that necessary action by the Security Council should not be hindered by a veto. If the Security Council in an urgent situation is paralysed by a vet or a threat of veto, this may undermine the authority and the relevance of the United Nations itself. It also presents the international community with a difficult dilemma.

When human life is threatened on a massive scale, it is not possible to remain passive. Humanitarian intervention has to be assessed on a case-by-case basis, in view of the value at stake and whether all other means have been exhausted. The effects on international law and international security at large have to be considered as well.

As the Secretary-General said yesterday, we must ensure that the Security Council is able to rise to the challenge. It must negotiate in earnest, with creativity and without the threat of veto, to define threats to peace and security at an early stage, and to deal with a crisis before an emergency situation arises. Council action does not necessarily mean the use of force. The use of force almost inevitably causes suffering for the innocent. It should, therefore, only be the last resort. There are many other tools available. The United Nations Charter offers several options.

The most obvious alternative to the use of force is conflict prevention and early action. Member States, in particular the permanent members of the Security Council, must share information on conflict situations and early warning signals with the Secretariat. The Secretary-General should be invited to react to such reports and to propose appropriate and timely action to the Security Council. The United Nations offices in the field and early fact-finding missions dispatched to areas of potential conflict could help the Secretary-General formulate such proposals. Academic institutions and non-governmental organizations could also be helpful in this regard.

[33] The Swedish Government has adopted a programme of action to facilitate and contribute to the prevention of armed conflicts. It is our hope that this action plan will stimulate a debate on how to change the focus from crisis management to early preventive action in order to promote a culture of prevention. [...]

[34] **Mr. Al-Noaimi** (United Arab Emirates) *(spoke in Arabic)*:[...] [37] The international community recently followed the developments of the deplorable events to which the people of Kosovo, particularly the Muslims, were subjected. These events included ethnic and religious cleansing, population displacements and other heinous crimes by Yugoslav and Serbian forces, in blatant violation of international humanitarian law.

The United Arab Emirates, acting on high-level instructions from an informed leadership, was one of the first countries to participate in the international relief operation. Our armed forces, together with the Red Crescent Society and other humanitarian organizations, provided humanitarian, medical, food and development assistance to the people of Kosovo. In addition, military troops from the Emirates participated in the United Nations peacekeeping operation in Kosovo, helping to ensure the return of the refugees to their homes and land, maintain internal security and initiate and develop vital projects such as schools, roads and hospitals. It is essential for international efforts to continue in order to provide the people of Kosovo with security and humanitarian guarantees and enable them to achieve their legitimate aspirations. It is also in the interest of establishing peace and security in the Balkans. [...]

[38] **Mr. Matutes** (Spain) *(spoke in Spanish)*: [...] [40] From the crises the world has lived through this year, we must learn certain lessons. One is without doubt that the political resolution of the crisis in Kosovo has only been possible thanks to the United Nations, which faced an urgent challenge, and on the success or failure of its response depends to a large extent the public image of our Organization. [...]

[Statements by the representatives of Iran, the United Kingdom and the United Arab Emirates have been omitted.]

257e. United Nations General Assembly, 54th Session, 8th Plenary Meeting, 22 September 1999

[Statements by the representatives of Honduras and Paraguay have been omitted.]

[8] **Address by Mrs. Vaira Vike-Freiberga, President of the Republic of Latvia**: [...] [9] Some of the negative feelings about the United Nations stem from excessive expectations. One cannot view the United Nations as a panacea, particularly where decisions on long-lasting regional problems are concerned or when preventive actions on a regional level are long overdue. Yet even in those situations a modern United Nations system is expected to seek earlier and more effective involvement than was the case in South-East Europe, East Timor or the Middle East. It must be stressed that that the painful refugee crisis of Kosovo could not possibly be resolved without the direct involvement of the United Nations and its institutions. But, sadly, the maximum potential of the United Nations cannot always be utilized because of prejudice, lack of political will or perceived political ambitions. Let us not forget that the costs of our reluctance to take action are extremely high: too often our reluctance results in the deaths of innocent people and is the cause of wholesale destruction which may take years and decades to remedy. [...]

[11] **Mr. Fischer** (Germany) *(spoke in German; English text furnished by the delegation)*: [...] Today the question of peacekeeping must be considered under conditions very different to those during the United Nations early years. First, most conflicts today are internal rather than international, as in earlier times. Secondly, the role of the nation State has been considerably relativized by the increased importance of human rights and the globalization of the economy and society. Against this background, the question of peacekeeping arises more and more in an area of tension between traditional State sovereignty and protection of human rights.

What is to be done when entire States collapse and the civilian population is massacred in never-ending civil wars from all sides? What if ethnic tensions in a State are partly provoked by criminal Governments, which then respond with pogroms, mass expulsions and mass murders, even genocide? Should the United Nations then regard State sovereignty as more important than protection of individuals and their rights? Rwanda, Kosovo and East Timor are dramatic examples of this.

In many ways, therefore, the Kosovo conflict represents a turning point. The international community could no longer tolerate a State waging war against its own people and using terror and expulsion as a political instrument. As Secretary-General Kofi Annan said in his brilliant and trail-blazing speech to the fifty-fifth session of the Commission on Human Rights, no Government has the right to use the cover of the principle of State sovereignty to violate human rights.

Non-interference in internal affairs must no longer be misused as a shield for dictators and murderers. The World Conference on Human Rights in Vienna reaffirmed this in 1993, with the approval of all United Nations Member States, with the words:

"the promotion and protection of all human rights is a legitimate concern of the international community". (Vienna Declaration and Programme of Action, I, para. 4)

However, the Kosovo conflict also marks a change of direction in the development of international relations. How will the international community decide in the [12] future - this question has just been raised once more in East Timor - when it comes to preventing massive human rights violations against an entire people? Two developments are conceivable.

A practice of humanitarian interventions could evolve outside the United Nations system. This would be a very problematic development. The intervention in Kosovo which took place in a situation where the Security Council had tied its own hands after all efforts to find a peaceful solution had failed, was intended to provide emergency assistance and, ultimately, to protect the displaced Kosovo Albanians. The unity of the European States and the Western Alliance, as well as various Security Council resolutions, were of crucial significance here. However, this step, which is only justified in this special situation, must not set a precedent for weakening the United Nations Security Council's monopoly on authorising the use of legal international force. Nor must it become a licence to use external force under the pretext of humanitarian assistance. This would open the door to the arbitrary use of power and anarchy and throw the world back to the nineteenth century.

The only solution to this dilemma, therefore, is to further develop the existing United Nations system in such a way that in the future it is able to intervene in good time in cases of very grave human rights violations, but not until all means of settling conflicts peacefully have been exhausted and - this is a crucial point - within a strictly limited legal and controlled framework.

In the twenty-first century the individual and his rights must take a more prominent place alongside the rights of States in the concept of security as defined by the international community. The reform of the Security Council, the central body for safeguarding world peace, must be oriented towards this principle. The Security Council is, in fact, authorised to act, and able to do so, where peace or security are at risk due to internal developments. This has been demonstrated by a long chain of decisions, from the apartheid resolution to the interventions in Iraq, Bosnia and Haiti. However, in Rwanda, Kosovo and the Congo, decision making in the Security Council was blocked, thus rendering it unable to live up to its responsibilities enshrined in the United Nations Charter, with disastrous results for the peoples in question.

These conflicts are a pressing reason, particularly in view of the important Millennium General Assembly, to finally carry out the long-overdue substantial reform of the Security Council. The Security Council must be adapted to the new realities of the global political situation. It must have a more representative composition and, above all, it must be equipped to react to the crises and conflicts of today. Reform must involve enlargement to include both more permanent and non-permanent members, as well as a strengthening of its decision-making powers. As the Assembly knows, Germany has for some time now expressed its willingness to assume more and lasting responsibility in this connection. We stand by this unreservedly.

In the debate on reform we must not avoid the issue of the permanent members' right of veto, a question of key importance for the Security Council's capability to act. The right of veto is regarded by many as outdated in its current form. However, it is a situation with which we have to reckon internationally for a long time to come. How then can decision-making in the Security Council be made more efficient?

According to the Charter, the Security Council acts with the mandate, and on behalf, of all United Nations Member States. But hitherto they have not been entitled to learn why a State has exercised its right of veto. This is not only neither democratic nor transparent, but also makes it easier for States to veto a draft resolution unilaterally for national rather than international interests. The introduction of an obligation for a State to explain to the General Assembly why it is vetoing a draft resolution would make it more difficult to do so and thus bring about substantial progress towards using the right of veto more responsibly. Why should not the General Assembly assume more responsibility in the future, too?

A second approach to making the international peacekeeping system more efficient would be via Chapter VIII of the United Nations Charter, namely by strengthening the regional security systems and redistributing tasks and areas of responsibility among them and the United Nations. It is becoming clear that the regional organizations could be allocated an even greater implementation role. This would also foster the capabilities of regional organizations to engage in security cooperation, as well as their collaboration with the United Nations. However, the primacy of the Security Council remains absolutely essential.

Without reforms in the area of peacekeeping, the Security Council will be circumvented more and more frequently, resulting in the erosion of the Security Council and, ultimately, of the entire United Nations [13] system. The United Nations, one of civilization's greatest achievements this century, as well as the values and principles it represents, would thus be at risk of subsiding into insignificance. We must prevent that. [...]

[15] **Mr. Tang Jiaxuam** (China) *(spoke in Chinese)*: [...] Hegemonism and power politics have manifested themselves in new expressions. Military blocs are being expanded and reinforced, and there is an increasing tendency towards military intervention. Triggered by ethnic, religious and territorial issues, regional conflicts and disputes continue to emerge one after another. [...]

[16] Hegemonism and power politics are the root causes of the turmoil in today's world. The outbreak of war in Kosovo sounded a resounding alarm. A regional military organization, in the name of humanitarianism and human rights, bypassed the United Nations to take large-scale military actions against a sovereign State, thus creating an ominous precedent in international relations. This act was a violation of the United Nations Charter and other universally recognized norms governing international relations. It has eroded the leading role of the United Nations in safeguarding world peace and security and gravely undermined the authority of the United Nations Security Council. During that war, the Chinese Embassy in the Federal Republic of Yugoslavia was bombed, which caused heavy casualties and much loss of property. It was an incident such as has rarely been seen in diplomatic history, and naturally roused the utmost indignation of the entire Chinese people and the strong condemnation of the international community.

As a permanent member of the Security Council China has held a clear and consistent position on the issue of Kosovo. We seek no selfish interests and are only upholding justice. For the sake of peace, we maintain that the Kosovo issue should be resolved through peaceful negotiations on the basis of respect for the sovereignty and territorial integrity of the Federal Republic of Yugoslavia and with guarantees of the legitimate rights and interest of all ethnic groups in Kosovo. We are opposed to the use of force under any pretext. [...]

The first relates to sovereign equality and non-interference in the internal affairs of others. Such arguments as human rights taking precedence over sovereignty and humanitarian intervention seem to be in vogue these days. Some countries have even put such arguments into practice. We believe that it is the sacred duty of all Governments to promote and protect human rights and fundamental freedoms, and that all countries have an obligation to promote and protect the human rights and fundamental freedoms of their own peoples in accordance with the purposes and principles of the United Nations Charter and international human rights instruments, and in the light of their respective national conditions and relevant laws. But as political systems, levels of economic development, history, cultural background and values vary from country to country, it is only natural that countries should have different interpretations and even diverging views on human rights. Countries should engage in dialogue and exchanges on the basis of equality and mutual respect so as to better understand each other, expand common ground and handle their differences properly, rather than resort to confrontation or interference in the internal affairs of others under the pretext of human rights.

The issue of human rights is, in essence, the internal affair of a given country, and should be addressed mainly by the Government of that country through its own efforts. Ours is a diversified world. Each country has the right to choose its own social system, approach to development and values that are suited to its national conditions. The history of China and other developing countries shows that a country's sovereignty is the prerequisite for and the basis of the human rights that the people of that country can enjoy. When the sovereignty of a country is put in jeopardy, its human rights can hardly be protected effectively. Sovereign equality, mutual respect for State sovereignty and non-interference in the internal affairs of others are the basic principles governing international relations today. In spite of the major changes in the post-cold-war international situation, these principles are by no means out of date. Any deviation from or violation of these principles would destroy the universally recognized norms governing international relations, and would lead to the rule of hegemonism; if the notion of "might is right" should prevail, a new gun-boat policy would wreak havoc, the sovereignty and independence by virtue of which some small and weak countries protect themselves would be jeopardized and international peace and stability would be seriously endangered.

The Kosovo crisis has proved that to engage in so-called humanitarian intervention in a sovereign State with neither a mandate from the Security Council nor the prior [17] consent of the country concerned will cause a greater humanitarian catastrophe instead of resolving the problem. In view of this, under the current circumstances, the principles of respect for State sovereignty and non-interference in the internal affairs of others must be effectively strengthened rather than weakened in order to maintain world peace and stability. [...]

[19] **Mr. Dini** (Italy): [...] The last few years of this century have disproved the notion that people and human freedoms take second place to State sovereignty. In Kosovo and East Timor a coalition of States resorted to the use of force, but not for self-seeking national interests, not to defend their borders, not to impose new hegemonies.

The end of the nuclear nightmare has coincided with a rampant proliferation of local conflicts, terrorist acts and traumatic economic and financial crises. Can the end of communism have given peace to former cold-war enemies and conflict to the rest of the world? The cold war brought a precarious, imperfect peace. Was that preferable to the tragic series of conflicts that have embroiled humanity over the past 10 years? The division of Europe helped neutralize tensions throughout the planet. Does this mean that nuclear weapons brought about a period of unprecedented stability, and - as some have suggested, paradoxically - that we should award the Nobel Peace Prize to the bomb? The breakdown of the former international order has created a plethora of new States. Does this mean that dividing the world in two was the only way to grant common citizenship to peoples and religious groups that have never learned the art of peaceful coexistence? The international community now takes military action to deal with tragedies that only a few years ago would have left us indifferent, and yet we are still influenced by military assessments, strategic interests, regional solidarity, public opinion and the magnitude of any human rights violations. How can we act according to more precise rules, based primarily on the duty of States to protect the rights of individuals?

The crises that have broken out in recent years have raised agonizing dilemmas and difficult questions that demand answers. It would be wrong to use the imperfections of the international system as an excuse for inaction. But it would also be wrong to ignore the new demands for certainty and the rule of law: the greatest [20] challenge is how to relate authority to law and lay down codes of conduct and political discipline that reconcile power with legitimacy.

Allow me to articulate a set of principles that could guide our action in the new century. First, we should enhance crisis prevention rather than conflict suppression. Secretary-General Kofi Annan has rightly observed that we must eradicate the cultural and economic causes of conflicts and that a culture of conflict prevention must prevail over the culture of conflict suppression. We know what these causes of conflict are: the huge gap between the living standards and incomes of different classes and nations; the exponential increase in mass migration from poor to rich countries; cultural difference and the conflicts and fanaticism it triggers; criminal acts for the sake of glorifying or even creating a nation. These are the four horsemen of the contemporary Apocalypse.

Secondly, we should use force only as a last resort. Arms should be used to stop criminal behaviour only when economic and political instruments are inapplicable or have failed. Ten years ago, these same instruments brought down totalitarian communism, which was a more formidable enemy than today's tyrants. In the Balkans and in East Timor, peacekeeping operations were launched to address serious, massive and systematic violations of human rights. The decisions to intervene were made after repeated demands that the culprits end a state of illegality; after an exhaustive and fruitless search for a diplomatic solution; and by a group of States rather than by a single Power.

We are living in an age of unfinished wars. In Iraq as in Serbia, authoritarian rulers have been seriously weakened, but they are still in power. How and how much can sanctions be used to replace or complement the use of force? Perhaps we need clearer international strategies and rules that pay heed to the most vulnerable members of society, to the political opposition and to the risk of strengthening despots through sanctions. Our focus should be more on incentives than on sanctions.

Thirdly, we need to define rules. No one knows the size or shape of the next challenge. But our response must be dictated by respect for universal principles rather than by a balance of power. We must beware of conjuring up the spectre of international law as the law of the strongest. We must beware of making some countries more equal than others. To do so would run counter to our best political and cultural traditions, in which the law is meant to protect the weak.

The Western world and the Euro-Atlantic institutions are no threat to anyone's integrity, prosperity and freedom. But we must perfect the instruments that uphold the international rule of law. We must spell out the duties of States. We must create a fully fledged corpus of case law on universal human rights. We must work out rules and procedures that will justify the erosion of sovereignty in the name of global responsibility. This is why every country must make it a priority to ratify the international instruments for safeguarding human rights. I am thinking in particular of the International Criminal Court, which was instituted in Rome in June of last year. These instruments should be reflected in our national legislation and practice. Finally, we should encourage the involvement of our own institutions. It is in this spirit that we have invited the United Nations High Commissioner for Human Rights, Mrs. Mary Robinson, to address the Italian Parliament.

Until human rights are firmly institutionalized, doubts will remain over the relationship between legitimacy and effectiveness. The gradual construction of universal citizenship is a learning process to which we all should contribute. Otherwise we shall be racing towards fragmentation, seeking forms of independence that are not economically viable and that are vulnerable to others' desire for hegemony.

Fourthly, we must learn to appreciate the judgement of others. I would like to quote, in this respect, one of the founding fathers of American democracy, James Madison. He said:

"An attention to the judgement of other nations is important to every government for two reasons. The first one is that, independently of the merits of any particular plan or measure, it is desirable, on various accounts, that it should appear to other nations as the offspring of a wise and honourable policy. The second is that, in doubtful cases, particularly where the national councils may be warped by some strong passion or momentary interests, the presumed or known opinion of the impartial world may be the best guides that can be followed."

Today's world has acquired a new sensitivity. It will no longer tolerate the oppression of the weak. This implies a rethinking of the principles of national sovereignty and non-interference that have governed the community of nations for over three centuries, beginning in Europe. But we must avoid double standards, applying [21] one yardstick to friendly countries and another to those that are not. This is what makes the ultimate sanction of United Nations so indispensable, since an international legal standard cannot - except in exceptional temporary situations - be the prerogative of any single group States.

When we defend the rights of others, we cannot pretend that the lives of our own people are not also at risk. By the same token, it would be inconsistent not to place the same value on other human lives as we do on our own.

Every culture and tradition must be involved in the defence of liberties and freedom. We cannot ignore the regional dimension of human rights, whose inviolable universal character can be enriched by the varieties of historic experiences. But stalemates and the paralysis of intersecting vetoes must be avoided by anchoring even the strongest States to a system of rules and principles, balancing their power against the effectiveness and strength of the international institutions.

Fifthly, we should strengthen the institutions. The aftermath of the cold war has proved that large political and economic groupings can more easily guarantee ethnic coexistence, religious tolerance and economic advancement. This should be kept in mind whenever pressure builds to release the genie of self-determination from the bottle of State sovereignty.

Only the great institutions, whether regional - such as the European Union and the Atlantic Alliance - or universal - such as the United Nations - can close the gap between democratic codification of laws and their effective enforcement. Unless we have a strong institutional network, every peacekeeping operation could end up looking as if we were taking the law into our own hands. Everyone would feel as if he should look out only for his own security, leading to a proliferation of weapons of mass destruction. Therefore, let us resume the disarmament talks, as President Clinton proposed in his statement yesterday, and place our common security on more solid foundations.

There is one lesson to be learned from these years of turmoil: actions to prevent and repress the most serious violations of human rights may take precedence over respect for national sovereignty. No Government can hide behind the shield of its own borders. Legitimacy demands the redefinition of relations between States and the international community. If demands the reformulation of the principle of non-interference, which has sometimes allowed States to neglect their duties towards their citizens. Although the United Nations is an organisation of States, the rights and the ideals it protects are those of individuals.

I have listed some rules that will help redefine coexistence among peoples through the work of the United Nations. We live in a world in which threats against one group immediately affect every other group and impel them to take responsibility, a world in which the concept of non-interference can no longer be invoked to obstruct action in the face of serious violations of fundamental rights. We must ask ourselves how to address all these changes, for the sake of closer and more equitable international cooperation.

Of course, States will continue to have different perceptions of national interests, and there will be a continued need to reconcile them peacefully. But for the United Nations to meet the challenges of the new century, our codes of conduct must be placed within a more solid institutional framework. The United Nations Security Council should be made more representative and democratic in composition, in line with proposals of a number of Member States. All the citizens of the world should be able to identify themselves with the United Nations and feel a part of its decision-making and law-making processes; this for the sake of universal sovereignty, which is not the prerogative of a few, but the right of all. [...]

[A statement by the representative of San Marino has been omitted.]

257f. United Nations General Assembly, 54th Session, 9th Plenary Meeting, 22 September 1999

[...]

[1] **Address by Mr. Ismail Omar Guelleh, President of the Republic of Djibouti**: [...] [15] The Somalis, too, have human rights; they have the same right as others to be protected from opressive, malicious and power-hungry individuals who continually and freely move from one capital to another, raising funds and securing armaments. Although these individuals are responsible for the destruction of their country, for the deaths of tens of thousands of innocent civilians, countless numbers of casualties and for the paralysis that immobilizes the country to this day, the international community did not intervene in Somalia, "to defend humanitarian principles and to stand up for the values of civilization and justice", as one Western leader stated in justifying the Kosovo operation. The United Nations Operation in Somalia was also saddled with ambiguities in its mandate and there was never an intention to rid the country of the warlords.

Furthermore, Kosovo represents a clear case of determined and vigorous action to achieve a specific objective - to drive the marauding Serb army from Kosovo. Furthermore, the United Nations operation in Kosovo is vested with unprecedented power, because the circumstances warrant the exercise of nearly sovereign powers. It has authority over the territory, the people of Kosovo, the legislative and the executive powers of Kosovo, including the administration of the judiciary system. That mandate is a far cry from that in Somalia; but then Somalia is not Kosovo. [...]

[Statements by the representatives of Costa Rica, Suriname, Micronesia and Zambia have been omitted.]

[23] **Address by the Honourable Denzil Douglas, Prime Minister of Saint Kitts and Nevis**: [...] [24] The recent development in Kosovo, the terribly disturbing stories of the human tragedy that befell its people, the injustices that were highlighted during that conflict - all this constitutes a severe limitation in the work of the United Nations.

My Government takes the view that genocidal activity, from whichever sources it emanates, is unacceptable and a violation of international law. The United Nations must therefore be vigilant as it continues its pacification efforts. Now that the job of rebuilding is under way, let us look forward - look forward with hope to an era of peace and reconstruction - and let us hope that what [...]

[A statement by the representative of Pakistan has been omitted.]

[32] **Mr. Papandreou** (Greece): [...] [33] We need to globalize human rights. Do we apply the same standards everywhere, from Kosovo and East Timor to Cyprus and Rwanda? We need to globalize our concept of rights pertaining to human beings. We understand multinationals that support human rights to protect their investments, but who will protect individuals who seek protection from the indignities of the world market?

We need to globalize ethics. From Kosovo to East Timor we have bowed our heads, for we are still ill-equipped to deal with global ethical dilemmas such as those mentioned by the Secretary-General. Can human suffering be subordinated to sovereignty? Can we afford to be inconsistent in the application of military intervention? Is it right to impose trade sanctions on Governments that violate international rules, at the expense of their innocent populations? [...]

[34] The tragic events in Kosovo will be remembered for acts of brutal ethnic cleansing and a military intervention that ensued without the authorization of the Security Council. Today, I encounter individuals who, under pressure, to "close the case of the Balkans", opt to redraw the maps, believing that ethnic isolation, construction new walls and barriers between our peoples of the region, will solve our problems. But it can only compound our problems.

I assure the Assembly that there is no short path, no lazy road if you will, to lasting peace in the Balkans. Consistent with our policy in our region is our belief that borders are sacrosanct. But within them we must do our utmost to protect minorities, democratic procedures and human rights. We must strive to develop the three pillars of the Stability Pact for South-eastern Europe: democracy, security and reconstruction. We need to build democratic institutions, judicial and financial systems, competitive business and free media, things we often take for granted. We need to be aggressive in ensuring that all forms of likely threat to security within and among our countries are dealt with directly, openly and with vigour. The protection of minorities is of fundamental importance. We need, as the Secretary-General has said, a new commitment to the prevention of conflict. We need to provide basic economic help that will fight against the poverty and degradation that lead to ethnic and religious fanaticism.

But more important, we need a total Balkan approach. When I say "total", I mean a coherent and consistent approach by the international community. The Balkans are badly served by mixed signals.

Greece has drawn for itself a creative and effective role in the region. Greece supports all efforts to deepen democracy in the region. A total Balkan approach to democracy, security and reconstruction will pave the way for our neighbours to enter the European Union. Yugoslavia, of course, is also an integral part of this total Balkan approach. So too are Greece's bilateral and trilateral contacts of very close cooperation with Albania, the Former Yugoslav Republic of Macedonia, Bulgaria and Romania. We worked closely together during the recent Kosovo crisis for stability in the region and in providing humanitarian aid to Kosovo refugees.

We believe that in our region there are no good or bad people, just good and bad practices. We have delivered and continue to deliver humanitarian assistance, as major humanitarian problems remain in many parts of Yugoslavia, and peacekeeping forces. We have conducted multilateral diplomacy, and we have promoted every effort that adheres to principles I have just stated without discrimination. Yes, in the total Balkan approach there is room for both the Albanian and the Serbian people. We ask them to dare to have a vision, the same vision: that, [35] one by one, each Balkan country will become part of a united democratic Europe. [...]

[36] **Mr. Petersen** (Denmark): [...] Increasingly we see internal conflicts and blatant violations of human rights and humanitarian law pose a special and serious kind of threat. Terrorism, drug-trafficking and international crime also thrive in a globalized world.

The international community must possess the means and display the resolve to confront such challenges. Our fundamental concerns about human security and human development cannot be met only in a domestic context.

I should like to illustrate these concerns, first, in relation to the Kosovo and East Timor crises and, secondly, with regard to international development cooperation.

Kosovo and East Timor raised serious questions with regard to the classic concepts of State sovereignty, the respect for human rights and the non-use of force in international relations. How do these concepts interrelate? How do they relate to our concern for human security? And what does the interrelationship mean for the role and responsibility of the United Nations and for the Security Council?

The first point to be made is that the international community cannot be idle in the face of gross and systematic violations of human rights. Nor can we stand idly by if the United Nations and its representatives, who have assisted a people in exercising its right to self-determination, are trampled on.

International law finds itself at a crossroads. We have spent the last 50 years developing an impressive body of human rights law, applicable in time of peace as well as during armed conflict, starting with the Universal Declaration of Human Rights. Indeed, there is no shortage of rules. What is lacking is effective implementation of existing rules, in the very last resort through the use of force.

We must now aim at enforcement in order to provide assistance, regardless of frontiers, to the victims of human rights violations. We must show resolve in promoting respect for the rule of law and for the institutions called upon to uphold the rule of law. A broad spectrum of actions is available; the choice of action must depend on the problem we face. The thorny question is whether and when to use military force in the face of an emerging humanitarian catastrophe, such as a planned ethnic cleansing or downright genocide.

It cannot be emphasized too often that a negotiated settlement must remain the primary and ultimate goal of any conflict solution. If, however, all attempts at securing a peaceful solution fail or are brushed aside, the question of whether to use force in one form or another arises. This brings the United Nations Security Council to the forefront. The Council has the primary responsibility for maintaining international peace and security. It has [37] carried out its functions as foreseen in the United Nations Charter in a much more effective and innovative way since the end of the cold war. I am referring, in particular, to the conflicts in relation to Iraq, Bosnia, Haiti, and Albania. A main challenge for the Security Council remains that of reacting effectively against gross and systematic violations of human rights conducted against an entire population.

The Council has interpreted its competence under Chapter VII of the Charter to cover humanitarian situations that shock the conscience of mankind. This augurs well for the victims of brutal oppression and ill for the dictators of today. Oppressors of whole peoples, mass murderers and ethnic cleansers can no longer invoke the shield of national sovereignty. Nor can they expect impunity. The international community has a responsibility to act in the face of a humanitarian tragedy such as the one we witnessed in Kosovo and the one we are witnessing in East Timor.

Unfortunately, the Council was not able to live up to its responsibilities concerning the ethnic cleansing in Kosovo. Should the paralysis of the Council lead to blind acceptance? No; the international community could not stand idly by and watch, while the principle of State sovereignty was misused in Kosovo to violate international humanitarian law.

In this serious situation the decision to launch the North Atlantic Treaty Organization campaign was legitimate and justified. It opened the way to a political solution, bringing the United Nations back into a central role. [...]

We all share the responsibility for enabling the international community to address these issues and for enabling the United Nations to act. Where force has to be resorted to, we have to look to countries possessing that capability. In practical terms, this means that we often have to rely upon countries and organizations in the region.

The Security Council must do its utmost to live up to its primary responsibility for the maintenance of peace, security and humanitarian decency - a primary responsibility that all the Member States have vested in the Security Council in accordance with Article 24 of the Charter.

The Council's permanent members should apply the veto only in matters of vital importance, taking into account their unique responsibility for the interests of the United Nations as a whole. And they should state on what grounds they consider such a situation to be present. [...]

[A statement by the representatives of India and Turkmenistan have been omitted.]

[46] **Mr. Kavan** (Czech Republic): [...] [47] The disintegration of the bipolar world has brought about a transition from confrontation to cooperation given rise to efforts to create a new security architecture, and led to integration processes, particularly on the European continent. However, it has also brought about the resurgence of dormant threats and the emergence of new centers of instability. The Kosovo tragedy and other crises have brought us closer to recognizing the importance of the principle of the personal security of human beings and its guarantees as a precondition of peace and security in the world. The fact that the worst atrocities, which have nothing in common with the civilized world, are still being committed at the end of the twentieth century makes this recognition all the more sad and alarming. In this context, the Czech Republic would express its appreciation and support for the work of the International Tribunal for the Former Yugoslavia.

The Czech Republic is convinced that the international community's efforts should result in just punishment for all the atrocities committed.

The United Kingdom's Secretary of State for Foreign and Commonwealth Affairs, Robin Cook, correctly argued here that we must counter the culture of impunity. All criminals should be held to account. As Secretary-General Kofi Annan said, massive and systematic violations of human rights should not be allowed to stand, wherever they may take place.

Kosovo will be the benchmark for the success achieved by international institutions. Kosovo is now in a period when it is necessary to defend peace, a period in which to achieve political stability and democratization, economic stabilization and a gradual development of the region. The Czech Republic is interested in the region's stability in all respects. That is why it participated, in its capacity as the currently presiding country of the Central European Initiative, in the Stability Pact Summit meeting at Sarajevo and why it will be working towards democratization, economic reconstruction and security in the region. We are, of course, fully aware that this is far easier said than done. The obstacles on the road a numerous and enormous.

The United Nations plays an irreplaceable role in providing for international peace and security. The peaceful resolution of disputes will undoubtedly continue to be one of the main priorities of the United Nations. The Czech Republic therefore attaches great importance to the use of peacekeeping operations in dealing with crisis situations and supports the efforts directed towards their greater efficiency, particularly as regards their rapid deployment. Speed appears to be the key aspect in many cases. However, the United Nations must also have adequate funding to carry out this demanding role effectively; unfortunately, its financial resources are considerably limited at present because of the fact that some Member States fail to honor their financial obligations. The United Nations Interim Administration Mission in Kosovo (UNMIK) has been marked by these problems: the Mission was not financially secured to the degree which would have corresponded with the security situation at hand and with the very difficult task of restoring the civil administration in Kosovo. On the other hand, it was probably the most rapidly deployed mission in the history of the United Nations.

The importance of UNMIK is shown by the fact that, as the highest civilian authority in Kosovo, it coordinates activities of international regional governmental and non-governmental organizations. The Czech Republic greatly appreciates the positive cooperation between UNMIK and KFOR, although it is evident that the international security forces cannot in the long term replace civilian administration and police forces.

A major degree of responsibility lies on the shoulders of the United Nations, and especially on those of the Secretary-General's Special Representative, Mr. Bernard Kouchner, in Kosovo. I had an opportunity to get to know his difficult task at first hand during my visit to Pristina a few days ago. The Secretary-General's Special Representative needs the full support of the international community in his efforts, including the transformation of the UCK into a non-military Kosovo protection corps. The Czech Republic obviously supports all steps and measures which may bring about the establishment of a democratic and multi-ethnic society in Kosovo as stipulated by the Washington North Atlantic Treaty Organization (NATO) Summit. Unfortunately, during my stay in Kosovo I did not come across any convincing evidence that that vision could really be [48] implemented in any foreseeable future - just the contrary. The diminishing number of Serbs in Kosovo, the continuous threats of murder - even to very old Serbian ladies - the rising influence of a mafia, which Mr. Kouchner told me about, the ever-present spirit of revenge, the lack of trained police forces, the absence of local civil administration, the disease of corruption and rivalry between different sectors of the Kosovo Albanians are just some of the obstacles which have to be dealt with decisively in order to prevent the vision of the future from becoming nothing but a never-fulfilled dream.

I wholeheartedly agree with the Secretary-General's unequivocal statement that commitment to humanitarian action must be universal if it is to be legitimate. This means not only that our commitment to peace and stability cannot end with the cessation of hostilities but that we have to be seen to be objective and even-handed towards all ethnic groups, as well as towards all regions. I am glad to note that the recent argument that "East Timor is not Kosovo" was quietly dropped. The Secretary-General has said that humanity, after all, is indivisible; we have to wholeheartedly agree with him. [...]

Peace and security in crisis-ridden areas are also closely related to humanitarian relief, which is provided as a rule to afflicted civilian populations. A radical deterioration in the Security situation may cause a devastating humanitarian crisis, as we have seen in Kosovo. Here, too, there is a need to look at the possibilities of simplifying the United Nations decision-making mechanisms. It is disturbing that, for example, the Office of the United Nations High Commissioner for Refugees did not have sufficient resources and capacities to tackle the humanitarian crisis in that region, which was due mainly to somewhat rigid procedures. [...]

[49] In our view, the United Nations must first of all respond to the changed substance of conflicts in today's world. These are not classical conflicts between States but, in most cases, internal conflicts rather similar to civil wars. The United Nations and the international community in general face the need to clearly define the relationship between national sovereignty and the protection of human rights and ultimately to engage in a discussion on how they should support sensible civilian Governments that keep armed forces under control. In this context, we should clearly focus on the Secretary-General's argument about individual sovereignty and the right of every individual to control his or her own destiny.

Secondly, the urgency of a radical acceleration of the process of United Nations reform, particularly reform of the Security Council, is becoming increasingly evident. The Czech Republic fully supports the Secretary General's reform efforts, and I would like to share the optimism concerning early substantial progress in reform negotiations which Mr. Annan expressed to me during our talks in Prague last July. I have to admit that we consider the results of this year's negotiations, especially those on Security Council reform, to be inadequate. This, of course, corresponds to the role of the United Nations during the initial stages of the Kosovo conflict. The composition of the Security Council requires change. The Czech Republic believes that the number of both permanent and non-permanent members of the Security Council needs to be increased, while representation of developing countries has to be strengthened.

Thirdly, conflict-prevention mechanisms need to be created, and attention should be devoted to questions such as discrimination, poverty, access to raw materials and the arms trade. The arms trade does not include only extensive, elaborate weapons systems. It is the excessive accumulation of hand-held and other small arms which above all requires our tough response, because these personal weapons play a key role in most conflicts. I would like to express my full support for the call by the United Kingdom Foreign Secretary, Robin Cook, to halt the illegal trade in small arms. Cooperation with regional organizations such as the Organization for Security and Cooperation in Europe and the Organization of African Unity, which may be more successful in dealing with conflicts, should also play a role in preventing conflicts. I very much welcome the Secretary-General's emphasis here on moving from a culture of reaction to a culture of prevention.

[50] Fourthly, the role of the United Nations in the area of human rights and as part of a broader concept of human security should be considerably intensified. We welcomed the Secretary-General's personal statement in his address at this year's session of the Commission on Human Rights, in which he said, "I have made human rights a priority in every United Nations programme". This, it seems to me, accurately reflects the importance which the United Nations should give human rights issues in the future. The United Nations should ensure that the universal nature of human rights is accepted and projected as a leading principle for the conduct of the international community. By our joint efforts we should guarantee a dignified and complete life for every individual in the next millennium. It is unacceptable at the threshold of the new millennium to claim that human rights are relative and that their violation by sovereign States on their own territory is solely their internal affair and as such may not be a subject of interest to other members of the international community. If the United Nations were unable publicly to defend the existence of human rights, it would be unable to defend its own existence.

At the same time, let us not forget the Secretary General's warning about the need to ensure universal legitimacy, which he issued in connection with the bombing campaign against Yugoslavia. Incidentally, the new Czech Government has adopted a foreign policy concept which regards human rights as one of its main pillars and which at the same time stresses the desirability of United Nations mandates for peace-enforcing operations.

Fifthly, it is in the vital interest of the United Nations for the world to step into the twenty-first century under the rule of law in international relations. The situation in the former Yugoslavia, including developments in Kosovo, clearly shows the extremely important role already played today by international judicial bodies in enhancing the prestige of international law and its gradual integration into the political decision-making processes. The implementation of international law by the United Nations international judicial bodies has considerable positive influence on how global public opinion perceives the United Nations itself. [...]

257g. United Nations General Assembly, 54th Session, 11th Plenary Meeting, 23 September 1999

[A statement by the representative of Equatorial Guinea has been omitted.]

[4] **Address by The Right Honourable Pakalitha Bethuel Mosili, Prime Minister of Lesotho**: [...] [5] I also wish also to express my satisfaction with the Secretary-General's trenchant report on the work of the Organization. In particular, I concur with his analysis of the moral dilemma that faces the United Nations when the Security Council is unable to act, because of a lack of consensus, in the face of the most heinous human rights violations. In those circumstances, and while conflicts continue unabated in different parts of the world, the capacity of the international conflict-resolution machinery is put to a severe test. Perhaps no conflict has done this as intensely as the one in Kosovo.

The Kosovo crisis represented the very disturbing trend towards the most serious violations of human rights in the form of ethnic cleansing and impunity. After the experience of Bosnia, which is still so fresh in our minds, the world could not be expected to sit back and take no action. It would indeed be a sad comment on the efficacy of the United Nations if the next millenium were to begin under a cloud of tolerance of impunity in the face of acknowledged genocide and other gross violations of human rights. While it is recognized that the conflict was an internal matter of Serbia, the dilemma was whether the world could sit idly by and watch a people being exterminated.

The more difficult questions that Kosovo raises is the one of the role of the Security Council in similar crises. The Charter places responsibility for the maintenance of international peace and security squarely in the hands of the Security Council. That body must therefore discharge this function with seriousness and firmness. It must resist the temptation to view questions of international peace and security through the lenses of national fears and preoccupations. If it is paralyzed by parochial interests, the temptation to take unilateral action increases. The belated submission of the Kosovo issue to the jurisdiction of the Security Council is therefore very welcome, as is the United Nations involvement through its civilian administration. [...]

[Statements by the representatives of Lebanon and Luxembourg have been omitted.]

International Reactions to the Crisis

[17] **Mr. Al-Shaheen** (Kuwait) *(spoke in Arabic)*: [...] [21] Still on the international scene, Kuwait welcomes the peace accord reached between the North Atlantic Treaty Organization and the Federal Republic of Yugoslavia on Kosovo as a first step towards the resolution of the dispute and the return of displaced persons to their homes in Kosovo. This will eventually put an end to the conflict and restore peace and security to the people, who have the right to live in freedom and dignity.

The Balkan crisis, which was precipitated by the Federal Republic of Yugoslavia, has demonstrated once again that the United Nations role is indispensable to the maintenance of international peace and security and for lending legitimacy and credibility to any solutions reached, be it in a regional context or an international one. Kuwait supports and encourages the United Nations to continue its role until all aspects of the crisis have definitively resolved. [...]

[22] **Mr. Opertti** (Uruguay) *(spoke in Spanish)*: [...] [23] There is no longer a place for an elitist international society that freezes obsolete historical periods in time, typical of a dialectic of confrontation measured in terms of the cold war. We must propose new formulas to avoid the effect of blockage that in many cases produces the conspicuous right to veto, granting the Security Council the procedural means to break it and even entrusting the General Assembly, under certain conditions, as proposed by my delegation, with new competencies so that it could be formally informed and its decision be required in situations which demand it, particularly when it concerns cases that could involve the legitimate use of force.

The recent problem in Kosovo, which continues, could serve as a typical example of the aforementioned paralysing effect of the veto in the Security Council, without forgetting the disturbing consequences that effect would have in producing the marginalization of the United Nations system of peace and security, with the resulting questioning of the Organization itself and its real possibilities.

This, naturally, requires the foresight of international law as the sole source of legitimacy, without ignoring the authentic and grave humanitarian situations that are imposed on us by the drama of the real facts at a time when they require a formal framework of timely, legitimate and efficient international action. [...]

[25] **Mr. Kadirgamar** (Sri Lanka): [...] [29] In the unfolding debate on the stand-off between state sovereignty and the rights of individuals being subjected to massive human-rights violations, we must be careful to see that terrorist organizations do not reap the benefit of misplaced sympathy in situations of civil conflict. Those who resort to terror in pursuit of their political objectives must never be permitted or encouraged to believe that unremitting terror will ultimately bring its reward in recognition and results. On the contrary, it is only the recognition that a campaign of terror will put its exponents beyond the pale of civilized discourse that will persuade terrorists to seek other ways of gaining a hearing. [...]

[31] **Mr. Green** (Mexico) *(spoke in Spanish)*: [...] [32] We note with growing concern that, far from disappearing, conflicts have multiplied and their nature has changed as a consequence of the reshuffling of forces in the international arena. Today, these ever-proliferating confrontations are to a great extent internal ones, presenting formidable challenges to an Organization conceived to resolve disputes between States. We still lack clear-cut mandates and a defined consensus on how to address this new state of affairs. This often divides us, not on the ultimate goal - peace - but on the means to achieve it. Given the absence of a new political contract that enjoys the support of all Members of the United Nations, Mexico will continue firmly to maintain that the search for solutions to conflicts, whether they be internal or international, must be in conformity with the letter and the spirit of the San Francisco Charter. Its principles cannot be subjected to interpretations varying with circumstances or to unilateral whims. We cannot allow the authority or the legitimacy of the Organization to be damaged. We cannot accept actions that openly contradict the intentions of the founders and that weaken the rights of the community of States.

Mexico has always maintained that the use of force, even when motivated by the loftiest humanitarian impulses, is no solution; to the contrary, it generates further instability, uncertainty and violence. But my country has shown restraint when the Security Council has acted in strict compliance with Chapter VII of the Charter. Even so, the Mexican Government reiterates the value of the peaceful settlement of disputes and firmly rejects the existence of an alleged right to intervene, particularly when it is proclaimed outside the framework of international law.

This is one of the most pressing challenges that we must face as we move towards the new millennium. Essentially, we are striving to give the United Nations the political underpinning that will enable it to face new threats to peace and security in line with the thinking that inspired the authors of the San Francisco Charter. If we fail, we run the risk of eroding international negotiating tools and of doing precisely what we want to avoid: weakening the Organization.

For these reasons, my delegation invites all Member States to begin an exercise in collective thinking that will enable us to solve the dilemma of humanitarian crises caused by internal conflicts on the one hand and of the capability of the United Nations to respond on the other. This must be an exercise in deep thinking that will lead us to lasting solutions, which will both preserve peace and protect the lives and human rights of those involved in conflicts. [...]

[Statements by the representatives of Indonesia and Turkey have been omitted.]

[39] **Mr. Plesu** (Romania): [...] [40] This way of thinking has lately brought up the issue of humanitarian intervention, human rights and reform of the system of international law. This is a sensitive issue and one full of pitfalls. There are those who say that we would not tolerate legal injustice under the pretext of humanitarian intervention. That is true. Similarly, some say that we should tolerate either social injustice nor crime under the pretext of non-interference in domestic affairs. Undoubtedly respect for human rights is primarily the responsibility of national Governments and State institutions. However, if they do not fulfil this task, there should be an instrument capable of enforcing respect for international standards and there is no better instrument for doing than the United Nations. [...]

[42] **Mr. Dimitrov** (the former Yugoslav Republic of Macedonia): [...] The Kosovo crisis had particularly adverse effects on my country. We had to cope with an enormous influx of refugees, numbering more than 360,000, or 18 per cent of the total population. The Republic of Macedonia entered a rather difficult economic, social and political situation that tended to destabilize it, particularly against the background that the international community reacted with insufficient speed and agility. The damage which the Macedonian economy suffered is enormous, amounting to approximately $ 660 million. A large number of workers were dismissed as a result of lost markets and increased transportation costs. The unemployment rate reached 40 per cent. All of this has negatively affected the already poor economic and social situation. In these circumstances, the citizens of the Republic of Macedonia have demonstrated great humaneness towards the refugees, tolerance and solidarity, but also restraint in the conditions of enormous social, political and economic pressure they were exposed to and whose consequences could have been more dramatic. Finally, we should not forget that there are still 30,000 refugees in the Republic of Macedonia. I urge the Assembly to continue the joint efforts for their safe return to their homes.

At the same time, the peace forces of the North Atlantic Treaty Organization (NATO) for Kosovo were deployed in the Republic of Macedonia in support of the international efforts for a political resolution of the crisis, as were a large number of international governmental and non-governmental organizations.

Macedonia has managed to overcome these hardships, but the consequences are still being felt in the national economy. Financial assistance and support from the international community are indispensable for the recovery of the national economy. It is beyond doubt that compensation for the damage we suffered by making our [43] national capacities available for the resolution of the Kosovo crisis should be an obligation of the international community.

The Macedonian Government highly appreciates the assistance provided by the international community thus far through certain financial institutions or on a bilateral basis. The assistance should continue, which is to say, we expect States to fully carry out the commitments they have undertaken. This is the right moment to write off parts of our external debts as a recognition of the efforts we are making to overcome the crisis. Today, the only thing that the Republic of Macedonia requests is the fulfilment of the promises made by the international community during the crisis.

Even prior to the outbreak of the crisis and the adoption of Security Council resolution 1244 (1999), my country had consistently supported a peaceful and political solution to the Kosovo crisis that would include substantial autonomy within the framework of the Federal Republic of Yugoslavia; respect for the human rights of all living in Kosovo; respect for the inviolability of existing borders; the cessation of hostilities and of repression; the deployment of peace forces; the safe and free return of refugees; the demilitarization of the Kosovo Liberation Army (KLA) and other paramilitary forces; and the economic reconstruction of Kosovo and the region.

I would like to take this opportunity to commend the efforts made fully to implement Security Council resolution 1244 (1999). The Republic of Macedonia, in this respect, will continue to support the United Nations Interim Administration Mission in Kosovo (UNMIK), the European Union, the Organization for Security and Cooperation in Europe, the Council of Europe and all other international governmental and non-governmental organizations. In this context, I would like to recall that on many occasions the Macedonian Government has demonstrated its readiness closely to cooperate with the Secretary-General, Mr. Kofi Annan, with his Special Representative, Mr. Kouchner, and with UNMIK, and that it has offered its good offices.

The Republic of Macedonia strongly supports the Stability Pact for South-Eastern Europe as one of the most important adopted documents for the wider region and for Europe. Furthermore, it is prepared to take an active part in its implementation and to contribute to the reconstruction and stabilization of the region and its speedy integration into European structures. The Stability Pact, through its three pillars, or "working tables", and through the relevant international global and regional institutions, is expected to contribute to a lasting stabilization of the region and to its final integration into European and Euro-Atlantic structures. To this effect, I would like to call upon all of the parties to this extremely important document to mutually reinforce their activities and to enhance their coordination.

I would here like to underscore the strong interest of the Republic of Macedonia in the prompt implementation of the second pillar for economic development and reconstruction. The most important issue linked with its unimpeded functioning and the realization of the desired results - greater inclusion of the Balkans in European economic, political and democratic trends - is the setting up of lasting mechanisms for the necessary fund-raising and the securing of funds to this end. Many United Nations programmes and activities could be used for this purpose. The Republic of Macedonia is interested in seeing the United Nations play a role in this sphere.

The Republic of Macedonia will propose a pertinent draft resolution at this session of the General Assembly that stresses the importance of the prompt consolidation and development of South-Eastern Europe, the importance of the Stability Pact and the need for the full implementation of Security Council resolution 1244 (1999). We are convinced that the draft will be supported by all States Members of the United Nations.

Let us hope that this will be the last crisis in the Balkans or South-Eastern Europe. But to prevent any recurrence of this kind of situation, we will have to defend more successfully democratic principles and values and develop long-term preventive strategies.

I am convinced that the beginning of the next millennium will mark a new era in the history of this area, which has been overburdened with conflicts and therefore needs to focus primarily on its own development and prosperity. In the long run, regional stability can be provided by economic development, democracy, respect of human rights and the rights of national minorities, and bilateral and regional cooperation. However, the best way to guarantee the security of the region and transform it into an area of democracy, development, stability and cooperation is for the countries of the region to join the European Union and the North Atlantic Treaty Organization (NATO) and become fully fledged members.

The Republic of Macedonia is among the countries most affected by the crisis - economically, socially and [44] politically. This has hampered our efforts to build a society that meets the expectations of our people.

Despite the major challenges it has confronted in the past, my country has managed to implement and advance the strategic commitments set out in its foreign policy: integration in the European Union, inclusion in Euro-Atlantic security structures and development of good-neighbourliness.

The success of that policy is reflected in the fact that the Republic of Macedonia was able to stay out of the four armed conflicts which have taken place in the last decade on the territory of the former Yugoslavia. For the first time in the history of the Republic of Macedonia as an independent country, we have been faced with a war on our borders. In such circumstances, the contribution of the peaceful and constructive Macedonian policy to conflict resolution is highly significant. The Republic of Macedonia is fully committed to carrying out the reforms that have been initiated, based on European standards, in the political, economic and democracy fields, with maximum respect for human rights, including minority rights.

That commitment by the Macedonian Government and the results of the reforms have been commended by the international community. That is precisely why the European Union has decided that the Republic of Macedonia should be the first partner in the commencement of negotiations for the conclusion of the Stability and Association Agreement. [...]

257h. United Nations General Assembly, 54th Session, 12th Plenary Meeting, 24 September 1999

[Statements by the representatives of Panama, the Dominican Republic, Senegal and Iran have been omitted.]

[14] **Mr. Pérez Roque** (Cuba) *(spoke in Spanish)*: [...] [15] That is why we so passionately defend respect for the principles of international law, which have guided relations among all of the world's countries for more that half a century. What would we have left to defend ourselves in the future if we poor countries were no longer able to rely on such principles as respect for sovereignty and self-determination, the sovereign equality of all States and non-interference in the internal affairs of other nations? How could we call on the international community to protest a threat against one of our countries if those principles, which are today systematically and flagrantly violated, were to be struck form the Charter of the United Nations?

In a unipolar world, attempts to impose notions such as the limitation of sovereignty, and humanitarian intervention, do not advance international security: they pose a threat to the countries of the Third World, which have neither powerful armies nor nuclear weapons. Such attempts must therefore be brought to an end: they violate the letter and the spirit of the Charter. [...]

[21] **Mr. Tokaer** (Kazakhstan): [...] We believe that the United Nations remains a unique intergovernmental institution that ensures a positive trend in the development of international relations. Kazakhstan calls for a strengthening of the United Nations, the only forum that is universal both in terms of its composition and in terms of the comprehensiveness of its agenda. Only the United Nations has the right to address fundamental issues of peace and security.

The Yugoslav crisis has clearly demonstrated how urgent the issue of strengthening the authority of the United Nations has become. We are becoming increasingly convinced of the need to enhance the responsibility of the Security Council for the maintenance of international peace and security and to make authorization of certain actions its exclusive prerogative.

The nature of many conflicts makes this an especially challenging task. That is why we believe that to be able to adapt to new political realities, the Security Council should enter the twenty-first century renewed and strengthened through the admission of new permanent members, first of all Japan and Germany, as well as non-permanent members representing different regions of the world.

[24] **Mr. Jayakumar** (Singapore): [...] [26] The definition of what is in the legitimate public interest within a specific State or nation is the product of a long historical process, cultural attributes and a level of economic development. It is the basic stuff of most political contests in most States. Consensus is not easy to reach domestically. It certainly will be even more difficult in an international system that is concurrently united and divided by globalization and the end of the cold war.

The international problem is compounded because the expectation that the post-cold-war international system would be multipolar has proved premature. A multipolar world is still more a matter of potential rather than a current reality. This has engendered discomfort.

The war in Kosovo focused such feelings. It threw into brutal relief a trend that has been under way for some time: that the absolute sovereignty of States has to be qualified to require compliance with generally accepted standards of conduct and respect for human rights.

This is not all that novel a notion. The traditional approach of non-interference in domestic affairs was never as absolute in practice as in theory. The doctrine of humanitarian intervention dates from the nineteenth century, when the powerful claimed the right to intervene in the affairs of the weak. The war in Kosovo resonated with such historical memories, thus adding to the discomfort.

It is a fact that sovereignty now coexists uneasily with a different current of international law concerned with the rights of individuals. These trends have not yet been reconciled. But both trends are facts that cannot be wished away. In any case, their logical compatibility is not the real issue.

Notwithstanding Kosovo, it does not appear that the majority of States have much to fear if they treat their citizens well. There are many countries that treat their citizens badly without any suggestion of any sanction harsher than moral disapproval. Concern for human rights has always been selective.

The more critical issue is related but different. The loss of territorial reference points engendered by globalization's mismatch between economic and political geographies and the loss of strategic meaning after the end of the cold war have made most international reactions ad hoc.

We lurch from crisis to crisis, with no clear sense of direction or consistency. Why Kosovo or East Timor and not Africa? Are the rights of humans everywhere not universal? How to choose when to intervene among the all-too-many conflicts? In his statement to the General Assembly this year, the Secretary-General has posed several thoughtful challenges for us: "Nothing in the Charter precludes a recognition that there are rights beyond borders." What the Charter does say is that armed force shall not be used, save in the common interest. The Secretary-General then asked, what is the common interest? Who shall define it? Who will defend it? Under whose authority? With what means of intervention?

I agree with the Secretary-General that these questions will need to be answered and criteria established. Rules and objective criteria for such interventions are urgently needed. Failure to do so will breed uncertainty and instability. If a new balance has to be struck between sovereignty and other values, it should be struck knowingly and with our eyes open. The alternative is to be led, one step at a time, with the best of intentions, by ad hoc solutions.

This will be a major challenge for the international community if the United Nations is to remain relevant in the coming century. This is because we can expect to face many more situations which will pose the dilemma of reconciling State sovereignty with international intervention to redress violations of human rights.

We are all familiar with the pressures of the international media and non-governmental actors. These are realities but provide no satisfactory answers. It is not politically acceptable that questions of international peace and stability should be decided on an ad hoc basis. It is even less acceptable that consensus on the need for more [27] peaceful modes of international cooperation should reflect the preoccupations of a few.

What we need is to replicate on a global scale those conditions that have made the pluralistic societies in advanced economies still capable of collective action. No Government anywhere can rule by coercion alone or lead legitimately merely because it wields supreme power. Resort to coercion or naked power is more often than not taken to be a symptom of failure of government and not its defining feature.

What is required, therefore, on the international stage is what has already been accepted domestically - indeed, insisted upon in the name of democracy: a modest acceptance of the reality of diversity and a nuanced appreciation of the difference between friends, friendly critics and honest disagreements. Persuading those already disoriented by globalization and rapid technological changes requires patient and skilful diplomacy in the artful balance of competing interests.

Despite the handicaps under which it laboured, and for all its imperfections, the United Nations has played a critical role in some of the great world issues of the first four decades of its existence. It eased the pangs of decolonization. It provided a cathartic theatre to vent the most dangerous passions of the cold war. It provided the means for the super-Powers to back down from unwanted confrontations without grievous political costs to either. From time to time, it scored notable successes in peacekeeping operations around the world. At the same time, the United Nations, through its specialized agencies, continues to play a vital developmental role for the majority of its Members.

But the United Nations experiences of the last decade have been less happy. The United Nations has played at best only a very marginal role in the great developments of the closing years of the twentieth century that I have tried to describe. It risks becoming increasingly divorced from the very international realities in which it is inescapably embedded.

Like all organizations of sovereign States, the United Nations can only provide a mechanism for its Members to use for whatever purpose their agreements or disagreements dictate. But the United Nations cannot be just a tool of the few, a repository for issues that no country is willing or knows how to confront, or a convenient scapegoat. The hard fact is that these are the roles that the United Nations has been forced to play in recent years. It cannot continue on this path without permanent damage.

In our century, the trend towards international organization, towards the development of a more predictable pattern of relationships between States and international regimes that transcend individual sovereignties is, I believe, established. There is no going back. Whether we like it or not, the world has become too complex to be dealt with except multilaterally.

But this does not mean that any particular international institution will necessarily play an effective role in the organization of international life in the next century. The United Nations cannot assume that it will survive intact, just by clinging on to structures and processes conceived in 1945. The world has changed dramatically since then. It will continue to do so. The United Nations has no choice but to change in tandem.

This imperative is clear. What is unclear is how the United Nations should change. That is why I have posed more questions than I have provided answers. The process of discussion must start now. The mechanism is at our disposal. The responsibility to use it is ours.

Whether we will engage ourselves in this responsibility quickly enough to make a difference to the United Nations is for us to choose. I do not know how much time we have. I only know that the time left is finite. [...]

Mr. Al-Sahaf (Iraq) *(spoke in Arabic)*: [...] [28] The most dangerous phenomenon witnessed during the present decade, which in the course of this session has become an endeavor orchestrated by a group of Western States, is the advocacy of so-called humanitarian intervention. This doctrine, which has no place in international law, stems from an organized infringement of the most fundamental rules of the present international order, such as sovereignty, political independence, territorial integrity and non-interference in internal affairs. These principles cannot provide a protective shield for grave violations of human rights or for intervention, sometimes with the use of force, in order to protect those rights. No one should be deceived by this doctrine as the new framework for a modern forum of neo-colonialism based on the logic of power.

First of all, we should realize that no situation used as a justification for this doctrine is free from the external political interventions that led in the first place to the emergence of such a situation. Accordingly, it could not be claimed that international responsibility for the situation rests exclusively with the targeted Government. On the other hand, we should also realize that the purposes and principles of the United Nations Charter and the mechanisms of the Organization are not devoid of modalities to deal with any situation of the type advanced to justify this doctrine.

The problem does not lie with the principles, rules and procedures. Rather, it rests with the selfish and unilateral policies of the controlling Powers, whose interests cannot be served by using the United Nations mechanisms established for the correct application of the principles and rules of the Charter, which reflect the joint will and collective interests of the members of the international community. [...]

It is not justifiable to consider the role of the United Nations as marginalized after it has become captive to the views of the controlling Powers in international relations and their selfish interests. Regardless of what the Charter provides in terms of rights, duties and procedures, we are convinced that the doctrine of presumed humanitarian intervention represents a dangerous destructive tool that affects the gains that have accrued through joint efforts in favour of the general international interest, as evidenced by the records of this Organization. The universalization of the concepts of this doctrine would mean the complete denial of the will of the vast majority of States, with the result of destroying the present international order. Iraq joins all delegations which have declared a position contrary to this Western doctrine. We call for joint efforts to confront it. [...]

257i. United Nations General Assembly, 54th Session, 13th Plenary Meeting, 24 September 1999

[A statement by the representative of Guinea has been omitted.]

[4] **Address by Colonel (Retired) Yahya Jammeh, President of the Republic of Gambia**: [...] [8] Whilst it is important to uphold the principle of non-interference in the internal affairs of States, when a State exceeds all bounds and engages in the heinous policy of ethnic cleansing, as in Kosovo, the rest of the international community cannot remain silent. The timely adoption of Security Council resolution 1244(1999) marked a watershed in the history of the conflict, the full implementation of which, we hope, will bring lasting to peace to Kosovo. [...]

[A statement by the representative of Guyana has been omitted.]

[13] **Address by Mr. Janez Drnovsek, Prime Minister of the Republic of Slovenia**: [...] [15] To make matters even worse, the number of civilians killed in these nominally "internal" wars is sharply increasing. A new kind of warfare is developing in which civilians are a primary strategic target. "Ethnic cleansing", massacres and a horrifying variety of war crimes have become weapons for achieving political, economic and military goals. Ethnic, religious, national and social inequalities are frequently used as a smokescreen to hide the reality of massacre and conquest from the rest of the world. Furthermore, these inequalities are exploited by ruthless leaders, who use them as a tool to achieve very concrete aims. We have seen this phenomenon in almost all of the armed conflicts of recent times - in Bosnia and Herzegovina, Kosovo, Rwanda, Sierra Leone, the Democratic Republic of the Congo, Angola, Afghanistan and, most recently, in East Timor.

How should the international community react to gross violations of human rights -violations that amount to threats to international peace and security? When and how can the international community seek to establish that a sovereign Government cannot, or does not want to, prevent a humanitarian catastrophe? When and by what criteria does it decide to use its instruments of enforcement?

All United Nations Member States must think hard about these questions. We are grateful to the Secretary General, who made, at the beginning of this debate, a significant contribution to such thinking.

This turn-of-the-century crime wave cries out for new approaches and new ways of protecting vulnerable civilian populations. Armed conflicts have in fact become a problem for humankind, not just for the nation or nations directly concerned.

The international community must innovate as it seeks to solve these pressing humanitarian problems. Our basic aim has to be human security, and here I mean [16] physical and not just legal security. Slovenia welcomes and participates in the initiatives of like-minded countries which are determined to give full meaning and specific practical expression to the concept of human security. In addition, as one answer to these challenges, new and more sophisticated concepts of peacekeeping operations are being developed. New methods of conflict prevention should also be explored. Preventive diplomacy, preventive deployment, preventive disarmament and post-conflict peace-building are the orders of the day.

We have to ensure respect for human rights. We are firm in our belief that a determined commitment to promote and protect human rights has to be an underlying principle for the activities of the United Nations at the threshold of the new millenium. We have to create conditions for good governance, the rule of law, sustainable development and social justice. All of these tasks and many others require creative thinking and bold action. Solving these thorny problems is a prerequisite for peace and prosperity. This is also the way to prevent conditions which directly feed the flames of the conflicts that I have described. [...]

Finally, in post-conflict situations, such as Kosovo, continued coordinated action by the international community is necessary. It is only by working in concert that the United Nations, regional organizations and other international players can be effective. Only in this way can the difficult goals that have been set be achieved. These goals include bringing political and economic stabilization, democratization, the protection of human rights to the territory in question and establishing a functional legal system there.

The changing nature of armed conflicts is also changing the role of the Security Council as it discharges its primary responsibility for the maintenance of international peace and security. We note the increase readiness and determination of regional organizations to take on their share of responsibility for the maintenance of regional peace and security. As many examples of fruitful collaboration attest, relations between the Security Council and these regional organizations are relations not of competition but rather of cooperation. We therefore commend the increased role of regional organizations under Chapter VIII of the Charter.

Let me continue by presenting some elements that we must consider in any international response to the changing nature of armed conflicts. There is an unacceptably wide - even a growing - gap between the existing norms of international humanitarian and human rights law and common situations on the ground: human rights are frequently and openly violated. Determined and united action by the international community is needed to ensure that the existing norms of human rights are fully observed.

Those who commit war crimes and crimes against humanity must be brought to justice. This is primarily the responsibility of States, which must act both individually through their national systems of justice, and collectively through an effective international justice system. Failure to act is no more and no less than an invitation to those capable of creating new, even more serious cycles of human tragedy to do just that.

Whether there is to be human progress and development depends on the result of this confrontation between the rule of international law and those who stand to benefit directly from lawlessness. International indifference can only reward such people. In this regard, Slovenia attaches particular importance to the need to ensure more effective, comprehensive and efficient delivery of international justice. We are supportive of the two existing United Nations International Criminal Tribunals and of the ongoing process designed to give birth to a permanent International Criminal Court. To this end we have begun the legislative procedures necessary to ratify the Rome Statute. We are also contributing to efforts to complete the mandate of the Preparatory Commission for the International Criminal Court. [...]

[A statement by the representative of Papua New Guinea has been omitted.]

[21] **Mr. van Aartsen** (Netherlands): [...] [22] This leaves me with the central question: Why is the Council often running behind reality? How can we make it catch up with developments?

As I look back at the general debate this week, I think that we are getting very close to identifying the main obstacle. I know that many interventions share a common element - they compare the notion of sovereignty to that of human rights and territorial integrity to humanitarian intervention. To be sure, the question per se is as old as the Charter itself. What is [23] new is the venue. I cannot recall that Foreign Ministers at the General Assembly have talked about this question at any length before. I strongly believe that this issue was bound to surface at this level at some point or another.

In 1945, the architects of this Organization included two contradictory premises: respect for territorial integrity and political independence, on the one hand; and respect for human rights and fundamental freedoms, on the other. The world in those days was ruled by Governments alone, and so the United Nations was made up of States. At the time, the notion of human rights, although grafted onto the Charter with much conviction, was essentially at odds with classical legal thinking. In a way, the tension became even more pronounced at the adoption of the Universal Declaration. After all, for half a millennium the notion of sovereignty had served as the basis of our global political architecture. As the idea was enshrined in the Charter, the founding fathers believed it would stand the test of time. By contrast, the idea of human rights in international relations was, for the most part, a post-war novelty. Indeed, the Charter is much more specific on respect for sovereignty than on respect for human rights.

Since 1945, the world has witnessed a gradual shift in that balance, making respect for human rights more and more mandatory and respect for sovereignty less and less stringent. An elaborate body of international human rights law has come to counterbalance the dictates of paragraphs 4 and 7 of Article 2. Today, human rights have come to outrank sovereignty. Increasingly, the prevailing interpretation of the Charter is that it aims to protect individual human beings, not to protect those who abuse them. Today, we regard it as a generally accepted rule of international law that no sovereign State has the right to terrorize its own citizens. Indeed, if the Charter were to be written today, there would be an Article 2.8 saying that nothing contained in the present Charter shall authorize Member States to terrorize their own people. [...]

Let me go one step further. The blurring of the boundaries of sovereignty does not stop at human rights. In the future, the notion of sovereignty is going to be tested beyond that. Think of decrepit nuclear installations, massive damage to the environment, lack of water or mass marketing of narcotic drugs. Can responsible statesmen afford to wait until the damage is actually done? Or do they in fact have a duty to prevent it? These are questions which, at some point the Security Council will have to be involved in.

It is not the lack of early warning, not the absence of preventive diplomacy, not the veto per se. I call on every politician and every diplomat in this room to accept that the traditional balance between sovereignty and human rights, between the state and the people is shifting. I am convinced this is one of the paramount issues of our time. Momentum is building, and we should seize it. Let us put the issue squarely on the agenda: the agenda of the United Nations, of the Council and of our parliaments at home. I ask the legal community to keep a keen eye on the groundswell that is developing and to be innovative in its thinking. We politicians have a vast responsibility here. We should steer the discussion towards the people instead of the State.

The Security Council should be stronger, not weaker. It should be a credible leader in the maintenance of peace. In order to be credible, it must be consistent, swift and proactive. It must show courage, drive and vision. It must keep changing with the times. It must put people over politics. That is a tall order. Its decision on East Timor gave us hope for the Council's potential. [...]

Mr. Abdulla (Oman) *(spoke in Arabic)*: [...] [26] We have a deep sense of pain for the human tragedy in the Balkans. Reckless policies led to instability, a huge waste of resources, the flight of defenceless people and loss of life and destruction of property. We are thankful for the timely intervention by the North Atlantic Treaty Organization in Kosovo, especially after the failure to carry out the Rambouillet Agreement, to put an end to the pain and suffering of the provinces' inhabitants.

As we praise the human role assumed by the world community in helping the displaced and the refugees in the Balkans, we hope that those great efforts will continue and thus conclude this noble task. We also appreciate the efforts of the Secretary-General to restore peace and stability to the region.

[27] **Mr. Martonyi** (Hungary) *(spoke in French)*: [...] [28] Most conflicts today are not between States, but within States, essentially as major ethnic or religious confrontations that too often lead to humanitarian crises of unprecedented dimensions. Entire ethnic groups and communities and national and linguistic minorities are falling victim to "ethnic cleansing". Dictatorial regimes do not hesitate to resort to nationalist extremism and xenophobia, and to unspeakable violence, exterminating hundreds of thousands of people, terrorizing others in their ancestral lands and expelling millions of people from their homes. We cannot remain indifferent to such acts.

A great debate is therefore going on in the international arena, as demonstrated in this very Hall, about how the world should react to tragic situations involving massive and flagrant violations of human rights at a time when, for all kinds of reasons, our world Organization finds itself paralysed. We are convinced that, given the terrible upheavals we are witnessing throughout the world, the international community cannot fail to respond effectively to this major present-day challenge.

The traditional concept of the principle of national sovereignty is undergoing a progressive evolution in inter-State relations and within multilateral organizations. Because of developments in the area of international law, national sovereignty is becoming less acceptable as a justification for Governments in cases of serious violations within their countries of universally recognized international legal standards. As the Secretary-General rightly said, in our era of globalization the collective interest represents national interests. Fortunately, today the principles of good governance are prevailing and flourishing in an ever-growing number of countries.

In the immediate vicinity of my country, a regime based on extreme nationalism has sparked four wars in the last decade. The international community, albeit after hesitation and delay, took the necessary measures. In the case of Kosovo, it did so with great resolve and consistency. In the wake of the action undertaken to defend universally recognized values, and thanks to the presence of international military forces and the United Nations mission, a fragile peace reigns today in that martyred region, and considerable, increasingly effective efforts are being deployed there with a view to establish peace and stability.

In the light of the events of the past decade in this part of Europe, let us state clearly and unambiguously that it would be pointless to expect democratization in the Federal Republic of Yugoslavia if things remain unchanged in Belgrade. However, a new Serbia, emerging from tragedy and destruction, free of the burdens of the past, would no doubt be able to rely on the understanding and effective assistance of the international community. In this context, we would underscore the importance of the implementation of the judgments of the International Tribunal for the Former Yugoslavia. The Stability Pact, devised with a view to responding to the needs of the countries of South-Eastern Europe, will play a primary role in the rehabilitation and development of the region. It will also contribute to promoting respect for democratic standards and human rights by proposing, inter alia, institutional arrangements aimed at improving relations between majority and minority communities within the region. [...]

[29] The tragic events in Kosovo and East Timor only confirm the universality of human rights and the importace of a timely resolution of conflict by appropriate means. They also demonstrate the value of harmonious cooperation between the United Nations, regional organizations and particular groups of States, a cooperation that is becoming increasingly important in dealing with the diverse and varied conflicts that are erupting - and, unfortunately, will continue to erupt - throughout the world. Hungary is prepared, with its own means, to take part in this great enterprise of safeguarding and restoring international peace and security. [...]

[30] **Mr. Ásgrímsson** (Iceland): [...] [32] Conflicts where the civilian population is expressly targeted are abhorrent and leave scars that take generations to heal. Once again, we have witnessed the emergency of the dark and evil side of human nature in the horrible ethnic cleansing that took place in the recent conflict in Kosovo. It would have been desirable if the United Nations could have played an all-encompassing role in the settlement of that conflict.

In this regard, I would like to endorse the position put forward on humanitarian intervention by the Secretary-General. When a State not only stops protecting the rights of its citizens but turns against them through gross violations of human rights, the international community cannot and should not stand idly by.

Iceland currently holds the chair of the Council of Europe, which encompasses 41 European countries. I would like to take this opportunity to stress the value and importance of close cooperation between the Council and the United Nations in the field of human rights. We have recent samples of such practical cooperation in Kosovo, where the Council of Europe is working together with the United nations and other organizations in fulfilment of Security Council resolution 1244 (1999) and the European Union-led Stability Pact for South Eastern Europe. Referring again to the benefits of prevention, I should say that prevention is at the very centre of the Council of Europe's work on human rights, democracy and the rule of law. [...]

[33] **Mrs. Willi** (Liechtenstein): [...] [34] At the same time, we also have questions, and we notice that others do too. How can we reconcile the role given to the Security Council under the Charter of the United Nations with a "humanitarian intervention" not mandated by the Council? What does this mean for the future of the Security Council and of the Organization as a whole? Are regional organizations to assume a leading role that goes beyond what is contained in Chapter VIII of the Charter? It will be important to discuss these questions, though finding satisfactory answers is certainly difficult.

To our mind, Kosovo has made it very clear once more that the prevention of conflicts must be the key concept in conflict-resolution as well as in other areas. Preventive measures are the best means of saving lives and resources of every kind, and they can be carried out quickly and with discretion. Prevention does not make big news headlines, but it reduces the number of headlines on disasters, of which we continue to see just too many. The potential of prevention is enormous, but its application so far is too modest and far too limited.

We know that there is still reluctance and hesitation, but we feel a sense of urgency, a pressing need to enhance preventive activities and to replace a classical concept o sovereignty - a concept that is outdated in many aspects - with a new one which enables us to tackle situations of potential and actual crisis with determination and efficiency. We thus welcome the report of the Secretary General on the work of the Organization and his very inspiring and timely remarks on a "culture of prevention" We are convinced that this is the right way for the international community to go.

Kosovo has been and somewhat sadly remains a prime example of the need for prevention. Liechtenstein has for several years now promoted ideas and suggestions on preventive approach with regard to problems arising from the application of the right of self-determination. The international community remains stuck in a situation in which the exercise of the right of self-determination which is the prerequisite for the enjoyment of all human rights - is denied because it is misunderstood as a claim to independence and statehood. We all have known for very long, since the adoption by the General Assembly of the Friendly Relations Declaration in 1970, that this is not correct. Self-determination can mean many other things, if exercised in a flexible manner and based on a dialogue between the parties concerned. It does not have to lead to the break-up of States; it should rather facilitate the peaceful coexistence of States and communities which are provided a degree of self-administration or self-governance as an expressive of their right of self-determination.

It is time to free ourselves from biased and obsolete thinking and to recognize that the effective application and exercise of the right of self-determination is the basis for preventing violent disintegration of States as well as internal armed conflicts with all their gruesome aspects and endless human suffering. [...]

[Statements by the representatives of Brunei and Myanmar have been omitted.]

257 j. United Nations General Assembly, 54th Session, 14th Plenary Meeting, 25 September 1999

[Statements by the representatives of Palau, Belarus, Democratic People's Republic of Korea, Burkina Faso and Belgium have been omitted.]

[19] **Mr. Valdés** (Chile) *(spoke in Spanish)*: [...] [20] The crisis in Kosovo revealed one of the most serious weaknesses and contradictions of the United Nations. The policies of ethnic cleansing supported by the Serbian leadership in that region required an immediate and vigorous response by the international community.

It was truly regrettable that our Organization was prevented from the outset from taking action with the vigour that the situation required. It was also regrettable that the solution to the crisis was found outside the appropriate framework of United Nations mechanisms and in contravention of the principles of the Charter. There is clearly a responsibility shared by all the permanent members of the Security Council for the inadequate functioning of the mechanisms of collective security. Once again, it was evident that the veto or the threat of its use can reduce to impotence the world's principal organ of collective security. Once again, it was evident that, when this occurs, a vacuum is created that can lead to the unilateral use of force without the prior authorization of the Security Council.

[A statement by the representative of Malta has been omitted.]

257k. United Nations General Assembly, 54th Session, 15th Plenary Meeting, 25 September 1999

[1] **Address by Mr. Petar Stoyanov (President of the Republic of Bulgaria)**: [...] Some of the developments in our region were not the result of human will. The earthquakes in Turkey and Greece, which

claimed tens of thousands of victims, shook the world. Regrettably, man-made disasters have taken a high toll on our region. The war in Kosovo, the fourth in a row in the former Yugoslavia, has left in its wake a comparable trail of tragedies.

Now that the war is over, there are two things we must do: as soon as possible, repair the damage and alleviate the trauma it has inflicted, and build an infrastructure of security and prosperity that precludes any future repetition of such tragic events.

The international community has in the past set itself similar ambitious tasks. This time, I hope, the experience it has gained has reached the critical mass needed for the achievement of lasting peace settlements in conflict areas.

The consequences of the Kosovo crisis have spilled over the borders of the region. That is why I find it worthwhile to share with the Assembly some conclusions about what was, hopefully, the last war in the Balkans.

With the adoption of Security Council resolution 1244 (1999), the world community has endorsed the political end of the system established by the cold war. That resolution reflected the new international status quo and the understanding that has grown during the past 10 years of the importance of individual security.

[2] Today, the rights and dignity of the human individual, civil freedoms and the international rule of law override even the sovereignty of States. This calls for a new responsibility on the part of the international community for their protection. The resolution also showed the commitment of Security Council members to international stability.

Paradoxical as it may sound, the Kosovo crisis has served as a catalyst of post-bipolar relations and of a new type of political dialogue among States. Significantly, for the first time since the Second World War, four permanent Security Council members are participating in one force - KFOR. Furthermore, they have been involved in peace-keeping operations - something that would have been unthinkable 10 years ago.

The Kosovo crisis has also highlighted the need for change within the United Nations system itself. For example, the world Organization is in serious need of a mechanism for compensating neighbouring States for damage caused by international intervention or sanctions. I raise this issue not only because of the losses sustained by my country during the past eight years from the embargo against Iraq and because of the military conflicts in the former Yugoslavia, but also because this will increase the efficiency and boost the image of the United Nations. It will certainly improve the credibility of United Nations-led operations and provide better motivation for individual countries to participate.

On the other hand, the crisis in Kosovo promoted a new type of relations among international organizations in respect of the protection of human rights. As a result of the crisis, a new kind of interface has been born between the United Nations and the regional organizations in Europe, such as the North Atlantic Treaty Organisation (NATO), the Organisation for Security and Co-operation in Europe, the European Union and regional initiatives such as the Stability Pact for South-Eastern Europe. This has strengthened the role of the United Nations on that continent.

Today, the Balkan people expect the international community to show the same commitment to the future of the region as it did during the crisis. Threats to peace and security should cease to be the only international mobilizing factor, and we must act towards this end.

I am convinced that the developments in the former Yugoslavia have not been due to some peculiar Balkan mentality or to any historic predestination. Half a century ago, Western Europe was embroiled in wars that were no less bloody. The difference is that after the Second World War the nations of Western Europe were rescued at the same time from fascism and communism. This helped them attain a democratic and economic homogeneity that, in turn, enabled victors and vanquished alike to set aside their differences and build their present prosperity while respecting human rights and protecting their national identity.

Unfortunately, a different lot fell to the countries of South-Eastern Europe after the Second World War. States like Greece and Turkey, both NATO members, preserved and built up their potential for liberal-democratic development and a free market, and the rest of the States in the region were forced to become a part of the Soviet communist system.

Today, 10 years after the fall of the Berlin Wall, the Balkans still lack democratic homogeneity. This has been a source of tensions, which, translated into ethnic hatred, are the favoured tool of any totalitarian regime attempting to cling to power. But I am sure it is wrong to apply a common denominator to the whole region. Today Bulgaria, as well as most of the Balkan States, is a country with a working democracy, a free market economy and the rule of law.

An earlier democratic homogenization of South Eastern Europe can be achieved only if the vision for our countries' integration with the rest of the European States is shared by both the Balkan nations and the people of Western Europe. Efforts and perseverance to this end are the safest guarantee for converting the whole of Europe into a continent of peace, stability and prosperity.

This common European vision fully applies to the future Yugoslavia. There is hardly any country that has a higher stake in Yugoslavia's earliest possible integration in the family of democratic Balkan States than Bulgaria. I cannot but share here the concern of the world community at the continuing ethnic tensions in Kosovo, which distance us from the desired state of peace and ethnic tolerance. Six months ago I firmly supported NATO's operation, designed to end ethnic violence against the Albanian population in Kosovo. Today, just as firmly, I oppose ethnic violence against the Serb population in that province.

The Balkans have paid a high price for peace in Kosovo. Today the region needs direct assistance for its reconstruction. The priority beneficiaries should clearly [3] be the hardest-hit countries and areas. Nonetheless, rather than discussing figures and reparations, I believe it would be more productive for both the Balkans and the world to adopt a clear vision for the future of South-Eastern Europe. This future has no alternative but the transformation of the Balkans into an integral part of a united Europe of the next century.

The General Assembly is the right forum to discuss the issue of how this can be done. The path leads through the direct rehabilitation and reconstruction of the Balkans-the best form of assistance for our region being "help for self-help". The Stability Pact for South-Eastern Europe can provide the necessary framework.

We are convinced that the economic prosperity of the region is a vital condition for achieving political stability. We need infrastructure and strategic investment that generate and guarantee more security than any political dialogue. We need the promotion of trade and a maximum involvement of the economic potential of our countries in the reconstruction effort. This will encourage them to cooperage with each other, while opening up the region and transforming it into a natural, organic part of Europe, rather than isolating it.

The crisis in Kosovo will be long over before its effects, such as the blockage of the Danube to shipping, have been eliminated. The international waterway should not become a new line of conflict; we should help it play its natural role of a link rather than allow it to act as a dividing line across Europe. The issue I am raising at this point concerns both the economic damage that has been caused and the very principles of the European architecture since the end of the crisis in Kosovo.

The location of the Balkans at a crossroads has been a curse for its people in the past; in today's globalized world, it is our greatest blessing. The Balkans should serve as a link between Western Europe and Central Asia, the Caucasus and the Caspian Sea. It is one of the most promising regions for the coming century. A case in point is the restoration of the historic silk road, which crosses the whole of Asia and links it to Europe. Restoration will entail huge infrastructure projects and investment which in turn could improve the quality of life of whole nations and regions.

The Balkan nations have already demonstrated a willingness to adopt a new approach in their relations with one another. The various forms of aid which neighbouring States generously offered each other in response to the recent natural disasters were a positive new sign. Another significant fact is the formation of the multinational peace force for South-Eastern Europe, staffed jointly by countries that were enemies earlier this century, including during the cold war. It is an honour for my country that the first headquarters of that force is based in Bulgaria.

I cannot fail to mention here the success of the trilateral initiatives between Bulgaria, Romania and Greece and between Bulgaria, Romania and Turkey for cooperation in combating organized crime and illegal drugs and arms trafficking.

The Kosovo crisis calls for a contemporary rereading of the chronicles of the Balkan wars by all the Balkan peoples: the modern perspective will reveal to them that those wars have done no country in the region any good. The new task facing the political elite is to translate these lessons of history into a lasting commitment to peace and cooperation. Having paid such a high price in suffering and fear, it would be a pity if we failed to leave from our experience. [...]

[Statements by the representatives of El Salvador, Mongolia and Cape Verde have been omitted.]

Mr. Granić (Croatia): [...] [13] Having mentioned the issue of security, allow me to observe that the situation in South-Eastern Europe has come full circle with the return of the epicentre of the crisis to the Federal Republic of Yugoslavia and Kosovo, where it started more than a decade ago. The military intervention of the international community, supported by all the countries of the region, including Croatia, must now be followed up with an appropriate political response. Just as we joined the international community in condemning violations of human rights, it is clear that energies must now be concentrated on building a lasting and just peace. [...]

[16] **Mr. Nguyen Manh Cam** (Viet Nam) *(spoke in French)*: [...] [17] In the past year, the situation in certain regions has faced the international community with the challenge of the politics of diktat practised by a group of countries and regional organizations. The unilateral military attacks against the territorial integrity of sovereign States in the Balkans and the Gulf have set a dangerous precedent in international relations, running counter to the purposes and principles of the United Nations and in violation of the fundamental principles of international law, especially those of respect for the independence, sovereignty and territorial integrity of Member States. This presented a serious challenge to the role and effectiveness of the United Nations, as well as to its legal foundations.

The first lesson to be learned from those events is that it is not possible for the United Nations to build or guarantee peace and security in the world at large or at the regional level unless international law and the United Nations Charter are fully respected and strictly implemented. Secondly, the United Nations can play the role and exert the influence that is commensurate with its magnitude only if, now as well as in the future, it steadfastly upholds the purposes and principles defined at San Francisco 54 years ago and carries out a thorough and in-depth reform of its organizational structure and operation, in order to imbue our Organization with inner strength.

By so doing, the United Nations will be able to prevent any country or regional organization from using a pretext, or a cause such as human rights, for example, to trample on the independence, sovereignty or territorial integrity of another country or to interfere in its internal affairs. By so doing, the United Nations will be able to preserve its important role and to meet the expectations of Member States with respect to preventing policies of dictate and the use or threat of use of force in international relations. And by so doing, the United Nations will be able to help create and foster the climate of lasting peace and security that is needed for the solid, sustainable development that all Member countries need today and will need in the coming century. [...]

[Statements by the representatives of Kenya and Ireland have been omitted.]

[30] **Mr. Idji** (Benin) *(spoke in French)*: [...] [31] The example of Kosovo is there to remind us of the key importance of prompt and determined action on the part of the international community in order to restore and maintain peace. The distressing events in East Timor are another eloquent example of this. [...]

[33] **Mr. Mubanda** (Uganda): [...] [34] I would be remiss if I did not emphasize Uganda's commitment to the observances, in the region, of human rights and fundamental freedoms. In 1994 the world was witness to genocide in Rwanda in which an estimated 1 million people were massacred. A similar act was about to be perpetrated in the Democratic Republic of Congo in the course of 1997 and 1998. Apart from our legitimate concerns about our national security and territorial integrity, Uganda finds it unacceptable that gross violations of the right to life should again be carried out in its neighbourhood or anywhere else in the world.

It is vital for all of us to recognize the sanctity of the right to life. We are glad to note that the evolution of international law on human rights no longer condones country's internal affairs. The principle of non-interference in the internal affairs of States has been so fundamentally eroded that the international community should now openly adopt a definitive convention which will permit instant intervention in cases of massive threats to the right to life. [...]

[36] **Mr. Khalil** (Sudan) *(spoke in Arabic)*: [...] [37] In this Assembly and in the Security Council there have been many discussions and examples regarding the policies of the Ugandan regime and its interventions. A representative of a certain State described the Ugandan President less than a year ago as a new Hitler. This was because of the many interventions and conflicts and the instability that the Ugandan regime has fostered and practised in all its neighbouring countries.

These acts were committed to achieve personal aims that are not recognized by international laws nor by African traditions and norms. We are all aware of these attempts, particularly the most recent, to invade a neighbouring State. Suffice is to say that one item on our agenda is entitled "Armed aggression against the Democratic Republic of Congo".

These practices and policies of the Ugandan President, committed before the eyes of the entire international community, inter alia, to pillage the wealth of certain countries in which his forces had intervened and to transfer such wealth to his personal accounts have been reported in the world's press along with sarcastic reference to the extensive national resources that he wasted in carrying out such adventures. The Sudan, like all Uganda's neighbours, has also suffered from the adventures and the intervention of the Ugandan President in its internal affairs. These actions have all been documented by the Security Council and I do not believe I need to recall them all at this point.

257 l. United Nations General Assembly, 54th Session, 17th Plenary Meeting, 29 September 1999

[...]

[1] **Mr. Mullings** (Jamaica): [...] [3] During the past year, events in the Balkans have raised profound questions about the principle of intervention, the use of force, the scale of military enforcement and the role of the Security Council. The debate on these questions has revealed differing perspectives, elements of consensus and varying positions on the applicable principle of international law. In recent times, we have witnessed atrocities committed as a result of the practice of ethnic cleansing as communities rise up against each other to settle old grievances. We all must continue to condemn these practices and understand the need for some kind of action to halt such excesses which violate international humanitarian norms.

However, the principles of international law affecting the sovereignty of States and the use of force should not be brushed aside. We believe in the adoption of an approach which has the confidence of the international community whereby diplomatic and any necessary enforcement action is taken or authorized by the multilateral institutions entrusted with safeguarding international peace and security. The Security Council has the primary responsibility. It should not be ignored and disregarded in favour of unilateral action on the part of any State or group of States. [...]

[5] **Mr. Geremek** (Poland): [...] In my statement today, I wish to focus on the three issues which, in my view, are at the centre of discussions within this Organisation. These are, first, human freedoms, and in particular the question of rethinking the principle of national sovereignty and non-interference; secondly, current challenges to the United Nations Charter-based system of international security; and thirdly, coping with contradictions of globalization through better international cooperation.

We have recently been witnessing new, painful manifestations of ethnic hatred in Kosovo. Armed clashes have again shaken the north Caucasus. East Timor is another example of intolerance and the folly of violence. We pay homage to the victims of this violence. But the people in all the crisis-stricken areas expect more from us than just words of sympathy.

We should pose ourselves some questions: could these new outbursts of conflict have been prevented? Is there a political will to head them off in the future? If the answer is positive, then what should be done to translate our political commitment into action in a concerted and effective way? How should the system of international relations be improved to give people the hope that they will not be left defenceless in the face of genocide and persecution?

The United Nations Charter-based system of international security was born of the lessons of a devastating world war which started with blatant violations of sovereignty of States. To address this reality, the system of international law and institutions was rightly geared to give those nations a sense of security and to prevent inter-State conflict. Most of today's conflicts, however, are of an intra-State nature. They stem from human rights abuses, social tensions or the collapse of State structures. Can we tackle the new challenges with existing concepts and notions only?

We have come to understand that absolute sovereignty and total non-interference are no longer tenable. There is not, and there cannot be, a sovereign right to ethnic cleansing and genocide. We have learned that what should not be repeated is the unacceptable inaction which occurred in the past, such as in the Rwandan crisis. Rwanda demonstrates what Kosovo might have become had we not intervened in 1999. Kosovo demonstrates what Rwanda might have been had we intervened in 1994. The burden of responsibility is enormous, the lesson clear.

[6] At the same time, we should follow the principle that our responsibility is the same for all ethnic groups. In Kosovo the ethnic cleansing of Albanians by Serbs has been stopped and reversed, but now we witness that the presence of Serbs and Roma in Kosovo is under threat.

In this decade the international community has through its actions - recently in Kosovo and in East Timor - recognized the universal political and moral imperative to act in order to stop gross and systematic violations of human rights.

This recognition, setting aside the distinction between inter- and intra-State conflicts, reflects the spirit of the Charter of the United Nations.

Indeed, the central figure of the system of the United Nations must be the human being - his or her right to a peaceful life, to personal freedom, to a decent existence and dignity. When human life and freedoms are assailed and individual rights brutally violated, then we must not remain indifferent and unconcerned: we cannot stand idle.

The imperative to act raises the question of the right to act. We have recognised that the walls of sovereignty cannot be used to conceal and legitimize the abuse of human rights and fundamental freedoms. Sovereignty cannot mean impunity for genocide and human rights abuses.

Let us all remember that it remains one of the fundamental objectives of the United Nations

"to reaffirm faith in fundamental human rights, in the dignity and worth of the human person, in the equal rights of men and women and of nations large and small".

The primacy of the human person and human rights, however, has to be adequately reflected in the application of international law. This is not an easy task, first, because there are still too many cases where behind hypocritical lip-service to human rights there exist practices of curbing and limiting those rights for the sake of preserving political power; secondly, because the legal framework of intervention, which should ensure the possibility of quick and effective action, is too often distorted by selective and subjective interpretations.

On the one hand, the banner of humanitarian intervention should not be used as a pretext for imposing political control and domination from the outside. We want to make the walls of sovereignty surmountable, but not for all purposes. On the other hand, the principle of humanitarian intervention has to be fairly and consistently applied to avoid double standards.

The development of international law should thus uphold the basic truth that a sustainable, lasting and secure order in international relations can be built only on the freedom of the human being.

The principle of solidarity in international relations should grow in importance, since it also provides the key to the effectiveness of the mission of the United Nations.

Acting for universal observance of human rights while preserving the necessary content of the notion of sovereignty raises the question of the best strategies for humanitarian intervention. We have but to agree that intervention by force is an instrument of last resort. What is preferable is an early and cooperative engagement to correct the practices that give rise to concern. There is no doubt that armed intervention is a sign of the failure of cooperative methods.

We support wholeheartedly the efforts to foster a new culture of prevention. The basis for this philosophy should be the universal recognition that international commitments undertaken by States in the field of human rights are matters of direct and legitimate concern to other States as well before their abuse degenerates into a threat to international peace and security. Human rights do not belong exclusively to the internal affairs of States. [...]

[A statement by the representative of Guinea-Bissau has been omitted.]

[10] **Mr. Kinnon** (New Zealand): [...] [11] It is inevitable that comparison will be made between East Timor and Kosovo. In Kosovo the world saw a grave humanitarian crisis with the Security Council unable to act. In New Zealand's view, collective action to try to put a stop to a humanitarian disaster involving genocide and the most serious crimes against humanity should never be held hostage to the veto. When it is, the Security Council loses its credibility and its relevance. I need hardly reiterate New Zealand's continuing opposition to the veto, voiced since San Francisco in 1945. While it is understandable that national interests will influence how members vote in the Security Council, we have accepted that some narrow interests of any [12] one of five countries should be able to override the will of a clear majority of members.

The adoption by the Security Council of its resolution 1244 (1999) of 10 June, which provided the international community's endorsement of a political solution to the Kosovo conflict, was certainly greeted with much relief in most quarters, including in New Zealand. The resolution was proof, if any were needed, that the United Nations remains, as in East Timor, the indispensable organization. And as the Secretary-General observed at the time, it also gave strong legal underpinning to the task ahead, a task which, he noted, is daunting. The contribution of the dedicated United Nations and specialized agency staff who are now working with little fanfare in Kosovo certainly deserves our recognition.

Both Kosovo and East Timor have put the Security Council to the test. In their own ways they have challenged this Organization's capacity to take effective action in the face of severe difficulties. The world must never again witness horrors such as those in Kosovo whilst the Security Council remains impotent. The case of East Timor shows that the Security Council can react swiftly and effectively when the will exists. For this to be possible, the fullest commitment to support those humanitarian ideals that are the basis of the United Nations Charter remains essential.

[Statements by the representatives of Tunesia, Armenia, Gabon, Saint Vincent and the Grenadines, Congo, Lithuania and Antigua and Barbuda have been omitted.]

257 m. United Nations General Assembly, 54th Session, 18th Plenary Meeting, 30 September 1999

[Statements by the representatives of Belize, Qatar, Mauritius and Congo have been omitted.]

[15] **Mr. Al-Shara'** (Syrian Arab Republic) *(spoke in Arabic)*: [...] [17] Clearly, many are dissatisfied with the use of humanitarian pretexts to launch military intervention outside the framework of the Security Council. It began with the intervention in Somalia in 1992, whose repercussions included the collapse of all State institutions and the carving up of the capital, Mogadishu, among fighting warlords. This trend continued with the intervention in Kosovo, where the fate of the people remains in balance, although the intervention succeeded in supplying the people with medicine and food.

But here it must be said that illegitimate intervention outside the framework of the Security Council is not as bad as completely ignoring dangerous and bloody crises such as those beyond what might be called the line of death and hunger: a line stretching from the Horn of Africa, in the east, to Angola, in the west, and then to Rwanda, Burundi and the Congo. Many suffering Africans who live along this bleeding line and who lack the most basic necessities may well envy the inhabitants of Kosovo, who at least had food and medicine during their ordeal. [...]

[A statement by the representative of the Republic of Korea has been omitted.]

[22] **Mr. Ortíz** (Ecuador) *(spoke in Spanish)*: [...] [25] Over the past year the international community has witnessed an aggravation of regional conflicts: war has left deep scars in various parts of the world. In this context, the United Nations has had to play a special role in resolving international conflicts, and its concerted and decisive action has enabled it to resolve some of the successfully. Nevertheless, strengthening our world Organization's activities in this field must be carried out in such a way that all measures taken under the Charter follow its principles faithfully so that the United Nations keeps the necessary international credibility and continues to be the legitimate mouthpiece and manager for collective action to maintain international peace and security. [...]

Mr. Miller (Barbados): [...] [27] Barbados shares the profound anguish and suffering of the people of Kosovo and was appalled by the barbaric slaughter and the massive displacement of innocent people and the destabilizing effect this has had on neighbouring States. We support the role that the peacekeeping forces are playing in restoring order to Kosovo and providing the conditions for the return of the displaced population to their homes.

[28] We wish to reiterate, together with the members of the Caribbean Community, that military intervention should be authorized by the United Nations Security Council. As a small, defenceless State, we are uncomfortable with the notion that intervention can take place without the prior authorization of the United Nations Security Council. [...]

278 n. United Nations General Assembly, 54th Session, 19th Plenary Meeting, 30 September 1999

[Statements by the representatives of Mozambique, Niger and Nepal have been omitted.]

[16] **Mr. Dorda** (Libyan Arab Jamahiriya) *(spoke in Arabic)*: [...] Colonialism is also returning through direct armed invasion, when necessary, as we have recently witnessed. It is also returning through bilateral sanctions policies enforced through so-called international legitimacy and through selective disarmament or rearmament. Colonialism is returning through the elimination - not the mere violation - of State sovereignty. The slogan that is now more in vogue, "humanitarian intervention", will help erode the little that remains of State sovereignty. That pretext has been completely exposed. If the new Colonialists understood the real meaning of humanity, they would not be producing and stockpiling all kinds of weapons of mass destruction or committing aggression against others. Nor would they be imposing sanctions on countries, as they continue to do, with the aim of [17] humiliating, starving and killing their people. We declare our absolute rejection of intervention under any slogan. [...]

[Statements by the representatives of Yemen, Saint Lucia and Sudan have been omitted]

[32] **Mr. Madani** (Saudi Arabia) *(spoke in Arabic)*: [...] [35] Just when it seemed that the problem of Bosnia and Herzegovina was resolved in accordance with the provisions of the Dayton Accords - which laid the ground for Bosnian independence and sovereignty, paved the way for the return of refugees, provided for the pursuit and arrest of officials responsible for the crimes of ethnic cleansing and genocide, and the establishment of domestic peace - the Balkan region witnessed a crisis in Kosovo no less devastating in its human dimensions than that in its human dimensions than that in Bosnia. Like the Bosnians, the Kosovars were exposed to ethnic cleansing, genocide, repression, intimidation and forced deportation at the hands of Serbian forces as the world watched. Once again, the United Nations faced the problem of dealing with dangerous situation that threatened the entire Balkan region. This situation was reversed only by the intervention of the North Atlantic Treaty Organization forces after Serbia refused to accept the provisions of the Rambouillet agreement.

Resort to military force without a United Nations mandate to resolve such problems might not be the ideal way to settle international crises, but it becomes an unavoidable necessity whenever the Security Council, due to disunity and disagreements between its permanent Members, fails to fulfil its role in maintaining the world peace and security. We hope that this pattern will not be repeated, so that the United Nations may preserve its dignity and integrity.

[A statement by the representative of Sierra Leone has been omitted.]

7.2 EU

258. Presidency Conclusions - Berlin European Council, 24 - 25 March 1999

[...]

Part III - Statements on Kosovo

STATEMENT BY THE EUROPEAN COUNCIL CONCERNING KOSOVO

The European Council is deeply concerned about the failure of the mediation efforts undertaken by Ambassador Holbrooke and the three Rambouillet Process negotiators, Ambassadors Hill, Majorski and Petritsch with the President of the Federal Republic of Yugoslavia, Slobodan Milosevic. The common objective of these efforts was to persuade the Federal Republic of Yugoslavia to accept a ceasefire in the Kosovo and a political solution to the Kosovo conflict, in order to stop a humanitarian catastrophe in Kosovo.

Over one quarter of a million of Kosovars are now homeless because of the repression carried out by Belgrade's security forces. 65000 have been driven from their homes in the last month, 25000 since the peace talks broke down in Paris last Friday. While the Kosovo Albanians signed the Rambouillet Accords, Belgrade's forces poured into Kosovo to start a new offensive. Since the outbreak of hostilities in Kosovo in March 1998 around 440,000 people, more than one fifth of the population of Kosovo, have fled or been displaced. There are new victims every day. The civilian population is the target of the hostilities.

The international community has done its utmost to find a peaceful solution to the Kosovo conflict.

In Rambouillet, and most recently in Paris, intensive efforts have been made after months of preparations to negotiate an agreement for the self-government of Kosovo which is fair for both parties to the conflict and which would ensure a peaceful future for Kosovo Serbs as well as Kosovo Albanians and all other national communities. The draft agreement, which was signed by the Kosovo Albanians in Paris, meets these requirements: on the basis of the sovereignty and territorial integrity of Yugoslavia it assures Kosovo a high degree of self-government, guarantees the individual human rights of all citizens in Kosovo according to the highest European standards, envisages extensive rights for all national communities living in Kosovo and creates the basis for the necessary reconstruction of the war-torn region.

The Yugoslav leadership under President Milosevic has persistently refused to engage seriously in the search for a political solution. It has presented the Yugoslav people with a distorted picture of the issues and course of the negotiations. In addition, the Serb police and Yugoslav Federal Armed Forces have in the last few weeks massively reinforced their presence in Kosovo, thereby further exceeding the ceilings set out in the Holbrooke-Milosevic agreement of 12 October 1998. Finally, the Yugoslav security forces are conducting military operations against the civilian population in Kosovo in contravention of the provisions of UN Security Council resolution 1199.

On the threshold of the 21st century, Europe cannot tolerate a humanitarian catastrophe in its midst.

It cannot be permitted that, in the middle of Europe, the predominant population of Kosovo is collectively deprived of its rights and subjected to grave human rights abuses. We, the countries of the European Union, are under a moral obligation to ensure that indiscriminate behaviour and violence, which became tangible in the massacre at Racak in January 1999, are not repeated. We have a duty to ensure the return to their homes of the hundreds of thousands of refugees and displaced persons. Aggression must not be rewarded. An aggressor must know that he will have to pay a high price. That is the lesson to be learnt from the 20th century.

Nor will the international community tolerate crimes against humanity. Those now persisting with the conflict in Kosovo should not forget that the mandate of The Hague Tribunal covers Kosovo.

They and their leaders will be held personally accountable for their actions.

In the final analysis, we are responsible for securing peace and co-operation in the region. This is the way to guarantee our fundamental European values, i.e. respect for human rights and the rights of minorities, international law, democratic institutions and the inviolability of borders.

Our policy is neither directed against the Yugoslav or Serb population nor against the Federal Republic of Yugoslavia or the Republic of Serbia. It is directed against the irresponsible Yugoslav leadership under President Milosevic. It is directed against security forces cynically and brutally fighting a part of their own population. We want to put an end to these outrages. President Milosevic must stop Serb aggression in Kosovo and sign the Rambouillet Accords, which include a NATO-led implementation force to provide stability.

We urge the Yugoslav leadership under President Milosevic to summon up the courage at this juncture to change radically its own policy. It is not yet too late to stop the internal repression and to accept the international community's mediation efforts. The international community's only objective is to find a political future for the Kosovo, on the basis of the sovereignty and territorial integrity of the Federal Republic of Yugoslavia, which does justice to the concerns and aspirations of all the people in the Kosovo.

The Kosovo Albanians showed their commitment to a peaceful solution by signing the Rambouillet Accords. It is vital that they now show maximum restraint.

We underline that it is not our aim to keep the Federal Republic of Yugoslavia in its self-imposed isolation in Europe and the world. On the contrary, we would like to end the isolation of the Federal Republic of Yugoslavia in Europe. But for this to happen, Milosevic must choose the path of peace in Kosovo and the path of reform and democratisation, including freedom of the media in the whole of Yugoslavia.

STATEMENT BY THE EUROPEAN COUNCIL ON KOSOVO

The European Council in its declaration earlier today set out the efforts which the international community had made to avoid the need for military intervention. We urged the Yugoslav leadership under President Milosevic to summon up the courage at this juncture to change radically its own policy. Now the North Atlantic Alliance is taking action against military targets in the Federal Republic of Yugoslavia in order to put an end to the humanitarian catastrophe in Kosovo.

The Federal Republic of Yugoslavia is now facing the severest consequences, about which it was repeatedly warned, of its failure to work with the international community for a peaceful settlement of the Kosovo crisis. President Milosevic must now take full responsibility for what is happening. It is up to him to stop the military action by immediately stopping his aggression in Kosovo and by accepting the Rambouillet Accords.

259. Special Meeting of the EU General Affairs Council, Conclusions on Kosovo, Luxembourg, 8 April 1999

The Council is appalled by the human tragedy inflicted upon the population of Kosovo by the criminal and barbaric acts being perpetrated by the authorities of the Federal Republic of Yugoslavia and Serbia.

In the face of extreme and criminally irresponsible policies, and repeated violations of UNSC Resolutions the use of severest measures, including military action, has been both necessary and warranted. The North Atlantic Alliance is taking action against military targets in the FRY in order to put an end to the humanitarian catastrophe in Kosovo. The EU emphasises that the responsibility for the armed conflict which is now taking place lies entirely with President Milosevic and his regime, who deliberately worked to destroy the chances of a diplomatic settlement which others strove so hard, and so exhaustively, to bring about. All those who planned, authorised and executed this brutal campaign of forced deportation, torture and murder should be held personally accountable and be brought to justice before the ICTY.

The Council recalled its conclusions of 25 January and 21 February, including on the strengthening of economic sanctions.

President Milosevic knows what he has to do:

- ensure a verifiable stop to all military action and the immediate ending of the killing;

- ensure the withdrawal from Kosovo of the military, police and paramilitary forces;

- agree to the stationing of an international military peacekeeping presence;

- agree to the unconditional return of all deportees and unhindered access to them by humanitarian aid organisations;

- provide credible assurance of his willingness to work on the basis of the Rambouillet agreement in the establishment of a political framework agreement for Kosovo in conformity with international law and the Charter of the United Nations.

The EU will not accept the success of a policy of deportation and destruction of a people for brutal nationalistic purposes.

The Council is deeply concerned about the conditions of displaced persons forced to live in the open within Kosovo. While they remain within the borders of the FRY their humanitarian needs are the responsibility of President Milosevic whom we hold to account for their survival. We deplore the recent closure of the FRY borders to Albania and Macedonia to the refugees. It is just as unacceptable to compel the refugees by force to remain in Kosovo as it is to deport them.

The European Union fully supports the regional refugee concept of the UNHCR as the lead agency to accommodate and assist deportees close to their home, allowing them to return to their places of origin as soon as possible. At the same time, it recognises the need to make the overwhelming task on the ground manageable by providing effective protection as extensively as possible within the region.

The Council recognises that it might also for humanitarian reasons and to avoid destabilising individual host countries in the region of origin, prove necessary in the future to afford displaced persons protection and assistance outside their region of origin on a temporary basis. Any such humanitarian evacuations out of neighbouring area must be based on the voluntary choice of the refugees to be temporarily relocated. In this context, the principle of family unity should also be applied.

In dealing with the consequences of the brutal and criminal deportation of hundreds of thousands of people, active regional solidarity and effective regional cooperation are paramount. In line with its solidarity and in addition to the substantial assistance already provided, the European Union will continue to assist the most affected countries of the region to counter the destabilising effects of the flow of deportees. The Council welcomes the communication by the Commission of 7 April to this effect and urges the speedy implementation of this assistance package for neighbouring governments, in particular in Albania, FYROM and Montenegro. This assistance amounting to up to 250 MEURO involves the mobilisation of the reserves of the Community budget for emergency assistance and includes up to 150 MEURO for the EU humanitarian effort for the victims of the Kosovo crisis and up to 100 MEURO in form of refugee-related support. The Council welcomes the intention of the Commission to work in close coordination with other donors including IFIs to maximise the efficiency of this specific and conditional assistance, inter alia through macro-economic support.

The European Union and its Member States are working with the International Financial Institutions to alleviate the exceptional burdens of the countries most affected.

The European Union remains gravely concerned about the repercussions of the deportee exodus from Kosovo on the stability of the region as a whole.

A political solution to the Kosovo crisis must be embedded in a determined effort geared towards stabilising the region as a whole. South Eastern Europe needs a Stability Pact opening the door to a long term political and economic stabilisation process. Such a broad based strategy could take advantage of existing regional initiatives.

Taking account of the good progress made in the cooperation agreement context the Council invites the European Commission to report, in the context of the regional approach, on the upgrading of the EC's contractual relations with the former Yugoslav Republic of Macedonia including the option of an Association Agreement. The European Union welcomes the efforts of the former Yugoslav Republic of Macedonia to alleviate the plight of the deportees in the country and urges it to intensify these, to ensure humane conditions for all those suffering in this crisis. The EU stressed the obligation of all governments concerned to undertake such transfers of refugees or deportees only in full cooperation with the UNHCR.

The EU notes that the progress in stabilisation and development in Albania will contribute to the further enhancement of EU Albania relations, including programmes towards a future upgrading of contractual relations. The European Union warmly welcomes Albania's stated readiness to accept, in addition to the huge numbers already admitted, additional deportees currently in FYROM and at FYROM's borders. The European Union will give technical and financial advice and assistance to aid Albania as much as possible.

The European Union underlines its concern over the situation in the Republic of Montenegro. It reconfirms its full support for the democratically elected Government of President Milo Djukanovic, as well as its readiness to help Montenegro in coping with the flow of deportees. A part of the package is to be directed to Montenegro for humanitarian and budgetary aid. Any attempt by Belgrade to undermine the democratically elected government of Montenegro will have the most serious consequences.

260. Chairman's Summary of the Deliberations on Kosovo at the Informal Meeting of the Heads of State and Government of the EU in Brussels, 14 April 1999

1. The Heads of State and Government of the European Union had an indepth discussion on the present crisis in Kosovo. The Secretary-General of the United Nations took part in this meeting.

2. The Heads of State and Government reiterate their determination not to tolerate the killings and deportations in Kosovo and believe that the use of severest measures, including military action, has been both necessary and warranted. They will persist in pursuing the goal of a multi-ethnic and democratic Kosovo in which all its people can live in peace and security. The Yugoslav authorities will be held fully responsible for the security and well-being of people displaced in Kosovo.

3. The Heads of State and Government support the initiative of the Secretary-General of 9 April 1999 which sums up the demands of the international community and on which which they cannot compromise: an immediate halt to the use of force, withdrawal of all military and special police forces as well as irregular units, deployment of an international military force and the return of all refugees and displaced persons. They stress that it is now up to the Yugoslav authorities to fully accept the international demands and begin immediately with their implementation. This would permit a suspension of military action by NATO and would pave the way for a political solution.

4. The Heads of State and Government shall initiate the introduction of these principles into a resolution to be adopted by the United Nations Security Council under Chapter VII.

5. The Heads of State and Government recall their support for a political settlement of the Kosovo crisis, based on the Rambouillet acquis which provides for substantial autonomy within the borders of the Federal Republic of Yugoslavia. They have agreed upon the main elements of an interim arrangement for Kosovo, to be established directly after the end of the conflict. They consider the following elements to be essential: - establishment of an international interim administration which the European Union could take over, - creation of a police force that reflects the composition of the population of Kosovo, - holding of free and fair elections, - deployment of international military forces that will guarantee protection for the whole population of Kosovo.

6. The Heads of State and Government stressed the necessity of an active role for the European Union in overcoming the crisis.

7. The Heads of State and Government emphasise the importance they attach to close cooperation with the Russian Federation, whose contribution is indispensable to finding a solution to the Kosovo problem.

8. The Heads of State and Government reaffirm the Conclusions of the General Affairs Council of 8 April 1999 regarding humanitarian assistance for refugees and displaced persons as well as assistance for the neighbouring countries of the Federal Republic of Yugoslavia. These countries can be assured of the solidarity of the European Union and its Member States.

9. The European Union will convene a Conference on South-Eastern Europe to decide upon further comprehensive measures for the long-term stabilisation, security, democratisation and economic reconstruction of the entire region. In this context, the Heads of State and Government underline that all the countries in the region have a prospect for an increasing rapprochement to the European Union.

261. Common Position, Defined by the Council on the Basis of Article J.2 of the EU-Treaty Concerning a Ban on the Supply and Sale of Petroleum and Petroleum Products to the FRY, 1999/273/CFSP, 23 April 1999[1]

The Council of the European Union,

Having regard to the Treaty on European Union, and in particular Article J.2 thereof,

(1) Whereas on 8 April 1999 the Council recalled its conclusions of 25 January and 21 February, including those on the strengthening of economic sanctions;

(2) Whereas on 14 April 1999 the Heads of State Government reiterated their determination not to tolerate the killings and deportations in Kosovo and that the use of the most severe measures is necessary and warranted;

(3) Whereas, in the face of extreme and criminally irresponsible policies by the FRY authorities, the European Union considers it appropriate to prohibit the supply and sale of petroleum and petroleum products to the FRY and to invite the Associated Countries of central and eastern Europe and Cyprus and the EFTA Members of the EEA to do likewise;

(4) Whereas action by the Community is needed in order to implement the measures cited below,

has defined this Common Position:

Article 1

1. The supply and sale of petroleum and petroleum products to the FRY shall be prohibited.

2. The prohibition referred to in paragraph 1 shall not apply to sales or supplies for verified humanitarian purposes, in particular for the needs of internally displaced persons and returnees.

Article 2

The Presidency will request the Associated Countries of central and eastern Europe and Cyprus and the EFTA Members of the EEA to align themselves with this Common Position.

Article 3

This Common Position shall be kept under constant review.

Article 4

This Common Position shall take effect on the date of its adoption.

Article 5

This Common Position shall be published in the Official Journal.

Done at Brussels, 23 April 1999. For the Council: The President J. Fischer[2]

262. Conclusions of the 2173rd Council Meeting, General Affairs, Luxembourg, 26 April 1999

The Council recalled its conclusions of 8 April and expressed its strong and continuing support for maximum pressure from the international community on President Milosevic and his regime to stop their brutal campaign of forced deportation, torture and murder in Kosovo and accept the international community's five demands. It also reaffirmed the EU's commitment to contribute fully to relieving the fate of the hundreds of thousands of refugees and internally displaced persons caused by President Milosevic's policy. The Council also considered the regional implications of the crisis. In particular the Council:

- commended the efforts of the international humanitarian organisations, in particular the UNHCR, which the EU and its members are supporting in every possible way;

- welcomed the Commission's commitment to the speedy implementation of the Council decision of 8 April, on the disbursement of the 150 MEURO of EC assistance for refugee relief and of the 100 MEURO of EC budget support for refugee related expenses to countries in the region;

- following the adoption of a Common Position imposing on the FRY a ban on the delivery of petroleum and petroleum products, reached a political agreement today with a view of its formal entry into force no later than Friday 30 April 1999. In this context the Council welcomed the intention of associated countries to join the EU's oil embargo, and invited third countries to follow suit;

- agreed to extend the existing EU sanctions regime and welcomed the Commission's intention to introduce proposals, on the basis of existing Common Positions where appropriate. The measures to be speedily adopted include:

- a travel ban on President Milosevic, his family, all Ministers/ senior officials of the FRY and Serbian governments, and on persons, included in a specific list, close to the regime whose activities support President Milosevic;

- extension of the scope of the freeze of funds held abroad by the Federal Republic of Yugoslavia and Serbian Governments to cover individuals associated with President Milosevic and companies controlled by, or acting on behalf of the Federal Republic of Yugoslavia and Serbian Governments;

- prohibition of provision of export finance by the private sector further to the existing moratorium on Government-financed export credits set out in Common Position 98/240 of 19 March 1998;

- extension of the investment ban set out in Council Regulation (EC) No. 1607/98;

- widening the scope of the prohibition on the export of equipment for internal repression and its extension to include goods, services, technology and equipment for the purpose of restoring/repairing assets damaged in airstrikes;

- encouragement to Member States and sporting organisations not to organise international sporting events with the participation of the FRY;

- a comprehensive flight ban between the territory of the EU and that of the FRY;

- welcomed the determination of NATO, as expressed in the statement on Kosovo issued by the Washington Summit, to achieve the aims and objectives of the international community;

- emphasised the role of the UN Security Council for a political settlement of the Kosovo crisis and the efforts of UN Secretary-General Kofi Annan;

- extended an invitation to Ibrahim Rugova to address the next session of the General Affairs Council and welcomed the Presidency's intention to invite him and his family to Bonn at an earlier date;

- reiterated its strong support for the democratically elected Government of Montenegro. The Council condemned Belgrade's efforts to undermine its authority and destabilise the Republic. The European Union recalled the assistance it has already provided to Montenegro to help address the problems it faces as a result of the humanitarian catastrophe in Kosovo, and stressed the importance it attaches to the rapid disbursement of assistance, whether from the European Community or from other international agencies. The European Union will additionally consider every opportunity to help Montenegro bear the burdens imposed upon it by the conflict in Kosovo, especially through further financial and economic support. In this regard, the Council welcomed the Commission's measures to assist the Montenegrin economy and instructed its competent bodies to explore the scope for a CFSP Joint Action in support of the democratically elected Government;

- considered the position of the Former Yugoslav Republic of Macedonia and of Albania during the current crisis. It fully recognized the dramatically increased burdens which had been placed on these neighbouring states as a result of ethnic cleansing carried out in Kos-

---

[1] OJ L 108, 27/04/1999, p. 0001 - 0001
[2] See 99/44/CFSP, 28 April 1999.

ovo by President Milosevic's régime. The Council commended the policy of moderation which the governments of the two countries have been pursuing, and expressed its profound appreciation of the sacrifices which they have made in dealing with the huge influx of refugees from Kosovo in recent weeks. The Council agreed that the policies being pursued by the two governments continued to constitute an essential contribution to the security and stability of the region as a whole, and to the wider efforts of the international community to ensure a political settlement which would allow all refugees to return in complete security to Kosovo;

- stressed the particular importance of the European Union's relationship with the Former Yugoslav Republic of Macedonia and with Albania. The Council looked forward to the political dialogue meetings at Ministerial level between the two countries and the EU Troika on 27 April. These will provide an important opportunity to discuss in detail our common approach in addressing the present crisis, and to review the vital contribution which these two countries are making. The Council also welcomed the intention of the European Commission to examine urgently, in the context of the regional approach and the EU contribution to a future Stability Pact, the upgrading of the contractual relations between the European Union and the former Yugoslav Republic of Macedonia and between the European Union and Albania, towards an Association Agreement;

- expressed its determination, in a spirit of solidarity, to continue to provide the necessary financial and economic assistance to the two countries to help them address the burdens posed by the present crisis in the region, noting once again the assistance which the European Union and its member states had already provided;

- looked forward to the adoption of joint statements with the Former Yugoslav Republic of Macedonia and Albania on the occasion of tomorrow's Political Dialogue meetings at ministerial level;

- invited the Commission to report, as soon as possible, on the economic consequences of the crisis on the countries most affected in the region;

- adopted the annexed Declaration in support of Bulgaria and Romania.

The Council agreed to start with the preparation of a Stability Pact for South-Eastern Europe and welcomed the endorsement of the proposed Stability Pact by the international community. Work will now be carried forward urgently within the EU, with the relevant international organisations and regional initiatives, and in particular with the regional states concerned, with a view to the Conference on South-Eastern Europe which will be convened by the European Union in Bonn on 27 May 1999. In this context, the Council also welcomed the forthcoming coordination meeting of relevant international organisations and initiatives in Vienna on 7 May 1999. The Stability Pact will give all Countries in the Balkans region a concrete perspective of stability and integration into Euro-Atlantic structures.

263. Common Position Adopted by the Council on the Basis of Article 15 of the EU-Treaty Concerning Additional Restrictive Measures against the FRY, 1999/318/CFSP, 10 May 1999[1]

The Council of the European Union,

Having regard to the Treaty on European Union, and in particular Article 15 thereof,

(1) Whereas on 8 April 1999 the Council concluded that extreme and criminally irresponsible policies and repeated violations of United Nations Security Council Resolutions by the Federal Republic of Yugoslavia (FRY) had made the use of the most severe measures, including military action, both necessary and warranted;

(2) Whereas on 26 April 1999 the Council expressed its strong and continuing support for maximum pressure on the FRY authorities to accept the five conditions prescribed by the International Community;

(3) Whereas the Council agreed to implement a ban on the sale and supply of petroleum and petroleum products by 30 April 1999 and to extend the European Union sanctions regime by extending the travel bans; extending the scope of the freeze of funds; prohibiting the provision of export finance by the private sector further to the existing moratorium on government-financed export credits; extending the ban on new investments; widening the scope of the prohibition on the export of equipment for internal repression and its extension to include goods, services, technology and equipment for the purpose of restoring or repairing assets damaged in air strikes; discouraging the participation of the FRY in international sporting events; banning all flights between the FRY and the European Community;

(4) Whereas the Union will consider every opportunity to help Montenegro bear the burdens imposed upon it by the conflict in Kosovo;

(5) Whereas the European Union considers the alignment of its Associated Countries of Eastern and Central Europe and Cyprus, and the EFTA countries important to maximise the impact of this Common Position;

(6) Whereas action by the Community is needed in order to implement some of the measures cited below,

has adopted this common position:

Article 1

1. No visas shall be issued for President Milosevic, his family, all Ministers and senior officials of the FRY and Serbian Governments, and for persons close to the regime whose activities support President Milosevic.

2. The visa bans established in Common Positions 98/240/CFSP[2] and 98/725/CFSP[3] are confirmed.

3. The persons listed in the implementing Council Decision have been identified as falling within the scope of the prohibitions identified in paragraphs 1 and 2 and shall be reported for the purposes of non-admission in the territories of the Member States. All updates of the list shall be subject to an implementing decision by the Council.

4. In exceptional cases, exemptions may be made if this would further vital Union objectives and be conducive to political settlement.

Article 2

The scope of the freeze of funds held abroad by the FRY and Serbian Governments will be extended, covering individuals associated with President Milosevic and companies controlled by, or acting on behalf of the FRY and Serbian Governments.

Article 3

The provision of export finance by the private sector to the Government of the FRY, the Government of the Republic of Serbia, a company, institution, undertaking or entity owned or controlled by those governments, or to any person acting on their behalf, will be prohibited.

Article 4

All flights operated commercially or for private purposes between the FRY and the European Community will be banned.

Article 5

No goods, services, technology or equipment will be exported to the FRY suitable for repairing damage caused by air strikes to assets, infrastructure or equipment which enable the Government of the FRY to conduct its policy of internal repression.

---

[1] OJ L 123, 13/05/1999 p. 0001 - 0002, 499X0318.
[2] OJ L 95, 27/03/1998, p. 1.
[3] OJ L 345, 19/12/1998, p. 1.

Article 6

The Presidency will ask the Associated Countries of Eastern and Central Europe and Cyprus and the EFTA Members to align themselves with this Common Position in order to maximise the impact of the above measures.

Article 7

This Common Position will be kept under constant review.

Article 8

This Common Position shall take effect on the date of its adoption.

Article 9

This Common Position shall be published in the Official Journal.

Done at Brussels, 10 May 1999. For the Council: The President H. Eichel

Amendments:

Amended by 400X0056 (OJ L 021 26.01.00 p.4)

Amended by 499X0604 (OJ L 236 07.09.99 p.1)

264. Kosovo: Action by the European Commission, IP/99/319, Brussels, 11 May 1999

Faced by an unusually grave crisis in Europe, the Commission has in recent weeks embarked on a series of measures and preparatory discussions aimed at:

- meeting pressing humanitarian needs;

- providing assistance to neighbouring regions and countries sheltering large numbers of displaced persons and refugees;

- setting up an effective structure to handle the subsequent reconstruction and establishing the requisite coordination machinery with the international financial institutions, and in particular the World Bank;

- helping shape a European strategy for stability in south-eastern Europe.

The Refugee Crisis

REFUGEES IN REGIONS BORDERING ON KOSOVO

Europe is facing a dramatic humanitarian crisis. Though the neighbouring regions of Montenegro, the Former Yugoslav Republic of Macedonia and Albania have been affected most, account must also be taken of displaced persons inside Kosovo.

The Commission's immediate aim has been to employ the Community's resources to address the most pressing needs. It is doing so in close cooperation with the United Nations High Commissioner for Refugees.

With over 700 000 refugees and displaced persons in the region and some 660 000 displaced persons inside Kosovo, the humanitarian situation is becoming increasingly alarming.

The Humanitarian Office (ECHO) has already committed EUR 32 million from its 1999 budget. Now that the budgetary authority has approved a request to transfer funds from the Community's emergency aid reserve to the humanitarian aid chapter, the Commission will shortly be presented with a commitment decision for EUR 150 million, bringing total aid to EUR 182 million. A global plan drawn up for the purpose was unanimously approved by the Humanitarian Aid Committee on 7 May.

This plan covers humanitarian needs arising from the Kosovo crisis until September. The sum of EUR 100 million has been earmarked for financing emergency humanitarian action in the region, in particular by the Red Cross, the UN High Commissioner for Refugees, UNICEF and non-governmental organisations. Events permitting, the remaining EUR 50 million is intended to help refugees and displaced persons return to their places of origin in Kosovo.

Should the crisis continue, even in the event of a negotiated settlement, the funds allocated to date will not be enough to meet humanitarian needs beyond September. The Commission will therefore have to consider whether to seek the mobilisation of the remaining EUR 196 million in the Community budget's emergency aid reserve once the EUR 150 million recently mobilised has been used up.

ECHO has stepped up its presence in the field. Fifteen officials and specialists are currently in Albania, the Former Yugoslav Republic of Macedonia and Montenegro. Ms Bonino visited the region from 6 to 9 May.

COORDINATION BETWEEN MEMBER STATES

To permit the Community budget to help Member States providing temporary shelter for refugees in response to the UNHCR's evacuation pleas, the Council, on 26 April, approved the Commission's proposal for a joint action permitting the use of the EUR 15 million in the European Fund for Refugees. Under the Odysseus programme for cooperation on asylum, immigration and controls at external borders, the Commission will see that the most vulnerable groups, and in particular women who have suffered sexual abuse, receive particular care.

SOLIDARITY WITH REGIONS BORDERING ON KOSOVO

The decision to give priority to sheltering refugees temporarily inside the region requires the Union and its partners to provide special assistance to help neighbouring regions and countries cope with the considerable demands on their budgets.

On 7 April the Council approved the Commission's proposals in this matter. Albania, the Former Yugoslav Republic of Macedonia and Montenegro are likely to be the main beneficiaries of such assistance, but other regions taking in large numbers of refugees could benefit.

The Commission is planning to provide up to EUR 100 million to cover direct costs related to taking in refugees: the cost of ensuring their safety, administrative costs, additional transport, electricity and water-supply costs, etc. A Commission team visited the region from 12 to 17 April to assess needs. On the basis of meetings on the spot and information provided by the countries concerned and the IMF, the Commission proposed that Albania be granted budget aid of EUR 62 million, the Former Yugoslav Republic of Macedonia EUR 25 million and Montenegro EUR 13 million. On 21 April the Commission authorised Mr Van den Broek to decide on financing proposals for these countries.

This aid will only be granted if the countries receiving it fulfil their international obligations, particularly under the Geneva Convention.

To finance this operation, EUR 100 million has been drawn from the following budget headings: EUR 54 million from the Phare reserve, EUR 30 million from the Obnova reserve and EUR 16 million from the TACIS and MEDA headings. The Commission will propose that the appropriations drawn from these budget headings be restored by a supplementary and amending budget: it would not be politically acceptable for needs arising from the Kosovo crisis to be covered by raiding assistance to other countries in the region, and in particular applicant countries, some of which, such as Romania and Bulgaria, are directly affected by the current crisis, or the former Soviet republics and Mediterranean countries.

COPING WITH THE ECONOMIC CONSEQUENCES OF THE CRISIS AND PREPARING FOR RECONSTRUCTION

Though the economic impact of the Kosovo crisis will vary from one country to another, certain questions of regional interest will require a coherent approach, among them trade and infrastructure. Given the complexity of the situation and the need to mobilise all available economic and financial instruments in an effective and complementary manner, close coordination between the main donors is vital. A meeting co-chaired by the IMF and the World Bank in Washington on 27 April called on the World Bank and the Commission to set up the requisite coordination apparatus.

Without creating new structures, the aim is to coordinate existing international initiatives with a minimum of red tape.

On 12 May Mr de Silguy will be meeting the President of the World Bank, Mr James Wolfensohn, in London with a view to finalising and approving this apparatus.

The European Union will play a major role in rebuilding Kosovo and the whole of the Federal Republic of Yugoslavia. As soon as security conditions permit, a large-scale reconstruction programme will be needed to enable refugees and displaced persons gradually to return to the safe areas.

CONTRIBUTING TO STABILITY IN SOUTH-EASTERN EUROPE

The proposal for a stability pact for south-eastern Europe was tabled by the Presidency at the Council meeting of 8 April and confirmed by the European Council on 14 April. Work on this proposal is proceeding in the Council working parties, which expect a substantial contribution from the Commission.

The stability pact is to be established in June at a ministerial conference to be preceded by a high-level meeting in Bonn on 27 May. As matters stand, the meeting will be attended by:

- the Member States and the Commission for the EU;
- the countries of the region: Albania, the Former Yugoslav Republic of Macedonia, Bosnia-Herzegovina, Bulgaria, Croatia, Federal Republic of Yugoslavia (if it fulfils the conditions for its attendance), Hungary, Romania, Slovenia and Turkey;
- the United States, Russia, Canada and Japan;
- representatives of the United Nations, the UN High Commissioner for Refugees, the Council of Europe, NATO and the international financial institutions (IMF, World Bank, EIB and EBRD);
- representatives of various regional initiatives (SECI, BSEC, SEECP, CIS).

The purpose of the pact will be to set up machinery actively contributing to the democratic and economic stabilisation of the region by means of "round tables" on democracy and human rights, reconstruction, economic reform and security. A donor conference for south-eastern Europe is also planned, though a date and arrangements remain to be fixed.

Pending the stability pact, the Commission will have to review the working of contractual relations with some countries of the region against the background of the regional approach developed by the Union since 1996. The Commission intends to spark discussions among the countries concerned in preparation for the drafting by the Community of a common strategy for the Balkans, in accordance with the new provisions inserted in the Treaty at Amsterdam.

7.3 WEU

265. WEU Ministerial Council, Bremen Declaration, Bremen, 11 May 1999

1. Ministers for Foreign Affairs and Defence of the WEU nations met in Bremen on 10 and 11 May 1999.

2. Ministers warmly welcomed the participation of the Ministers of the Czech Republic, Hungary and Poland present for the first time in their new capacity as Associate Members. They issued the attached Declaration on the Associate Membership of the three countries.

3. Ministers had an extended discussion of the implications of the Kosovo crisis for the region. Ministers deplored the catastrophic humanitarian situation in Kosovo and the region. They recalled that the regime in Belgrade had repeatedly rejected all efforts to solve the crisis peacefully.

They emphasized their complete support and full solidarity for EU and NATO on Kosovo. They strongly emphasized that NATO's military action is both necessary and warranted in order to achieve the political objectives of the international community for a peaceful multi-ethnic and democratic Kosovo where all its people can live in security and enjoy universal human rights and freedom on an equal basis. Such a political solution should support the five legitimate demands of the international community.

Ministers expressed their high appreciation for the solidarity of the countries in the region and other Associate Partners with the actions of NATO and the EU.

Ministers welcomed diplomatic efforts for a peaceful solution for the crisis, involving Russia. In this respect they welcomed the results of the meeting of Foreign Ministers of the G8 on 6 May 1999 and expressed the strong hope that these will form the basis of further progress towards such a solution.

Ministers welcomed the EU initiative for a Stability Pact for South-Eastern Europe aiming at lasting peace, democratisation, prosperity, security and stability in the region. They looked forward to the forthcoming meeting of high officials in Bonn on May 27, 1999 to discuss the stability pact and the Conference on South-Eastern Europe to be convened by the EU.

Ministers also welcomed the South-East European Cooperation process as well as other regional efforts.

Ministers fully supported the measures imposed by NATO and the EU preventing weapons and petroleum products from entering the FRY as well as the strengthened sanctions against the FRY, and call on other governments to do the same.

Ministers underlined the importance of the extended mission, on the basis of Article J 4.2 of the Treaty on European Union, of the WEU Multinational Advisory Police Element (MAPE), in supporting the process of stabilisation and democratic reform in Albania. MAPE's enhanced geographical coverage and increased operational mobility will enable MAPE to better respond to the needs of the Albanian authorities in building a police force according to European norms.

Ministers welcomed the launch of the WEU de-mining assistance mission in Croatia (WEUDAM). They underlined that WEUDAM is the first operation conducted by WEU at the request of the EU on the basis of Article J 4.2 of the Treaty on European Union and with EU finance, and looked forward to continued close cooperation with the EU in this respect. They expressed their appreciation for the contribution made by Sweden as lead nation.

Ministers welcomed the general security surveillance mission of the WEU Satellite Centre on the Kosovo region, on the basis of Article J 4.2 of the Treaty on European Union, and the contribution thus being provided to the EU, OSCE and NATO as part of international humanitarian efforts. Lessons learned from the mission shall be taken account of in further work inter alia on a possible WEU participation in a developing multilateral European satellite observation programme.

4. Ministers had an exchange of views on the question of European security and defence in light of the entry into force of the Amsterdam Treaty, of the reflections launched since the Rome Declaration in WEU and following the St. Malo Declaration in the EU, including the Vienna European Council conclusions, and of NATO's Washington Summit. They looked forward to the decisions to be taken in this regard by the European Council in Cologne.

Ministers stressed the importance of continuing to develop European security and defence. This development will serve the interests of all WEU nations. In this context they welcomed the informal reflection mandated in Rome and held at meetings of directors for security policy from Foreign and Defence Ministries which had confirmed:

- the willingness of European nations to strengthen European operational capabilities for Petersberg tasks based on appropriate decision-making bodies and effective military means, within NATO or national and multinational means outside the NATO framework;

- their wish to further develop these structures and capabilities in complementarity with the Atlantic Alliance whilst avoiding unnecessary duplication;

- the need for WEU to be operationally effective with the involvement and participation of all WEU nations in accordance with their status and to continue its cooperation with the EU and NATO, in preparation for any new arrangements which may be agreed in light of ongoing developments.

Ministers decided that the informal reflection should be pursued on this basis.

Ministers took note of the oral report of the Presidency Defence Minister on the informal meeting of EU and European NATO Defence Ministers in Bremen. They welcomed the determination expressed on this occasion to contribute to the development of an effective European defence and security policy and the capability for European crisis management in the scope of Petersberg tasks.

Ministers welcomed the report of the Presidency on the audit of assets and capabilities available for European operations inter alia on the basis of the Special Report prepared in NATO. They asked the Permanent Council to continue the evaluation of the first results contained in the Report. They requested the Permanent Council to carry out phase two of the audit, on the basis of modalities proposed by the Presidency. This shall, in addition to multinational forces, also cover the identification and evaluation of relevant national forces and force capabilities. The results shall be presented to the next Ministerial meeting in Luxembourg.

The findings of this audit should help to identify what changes need to be made to ensure that WEU's operational instruments (Military Staff, Military Committee, Satellite Centre etc) can make a more effective contribution to the mounting of crisis-management missions within the EU framework.

They should also assist nations in identifying areas where national and multinational capabilities need to be strengthened in order to make the conduct of Petersberg operations more effective.

5. Ministers welcomed the entry into force of the Treaty of Amsterdam.

Recalling the invitation of the European Council in Vienna to bring forward the completion of arrangements for enhanced WEU-EU cooperation under the Protocol of Art. 17 of the Treaty on European Union, so that these may come into effect on the Treaty's entry into force, Ministers endorsed the present set of arrangements which had been elaborated in WEU and EU and underlined the need for close dialogue and cooperation at all levels between the two Organisations with a view to the full application of the Amsterdam Treaty.

6. Ministers welcomed the results of the NATO Summit in Washington.

They noted with satisfaction that the key elements for the development of the European Security and Defence Identity within the Alliance, building on the Berlin, Brussels and Birmingham ministerial decisions, are being put in place and that the Alliance reaffirmed its strong commitment to pursue the process of reinforcing its European pillar. In this context, they welcomed the agreement with NATO of a Framework Document on the release of assets to WEU, and of improved consultation arrangements in the event of a WEU-led operation using NATO assets and capabilities.

They appreciated that the Alliance welcomed the new impetus given to the strengthening of a common European policy in security and defence as laid out in paragraphs 8, 9 and 10 of the Washington Summit Communique.

7. Ministers noted with interest the report by the Presidency on the Military Committee meeting held at Berlin on 20 April 1999. In particular, they welcomed the progress made with regard to the organisational structure and functioning of the Military Staff and the decisions taken with a view to improving harmonisation of future military requirements in support of the process of force and armaments planning and subsequently for further developing European military capabilities.

Ministers endorsed the WEU proposal to NATO to incorporate the capabilities of the Associate Partner countries drawn from the PARP process into the Special Report on forces and capabilities available for WEU-led operations. This, as well as their future participation in relevant WEU discussions, would lead to a further enhancement of the role of the Associate Partner countries in the operational development of WEU.

8. Ministers underlined Russia's key role in Europe's security and stability and looked forward towards further developing WEU's relationship with Russia based on enhanced political dialogue and practical cooperation.

Ministers reaffirmed Ukraine's significance as a European partner. They welcomed the discussions with Ukraine on a catalogue of areas for political dialogue and practical cooperation between WEU and Ukraine.

Ministers called on Belarus, Russia and Ukraine to ratify the Open Skies Treaty without further delay.

Ministers expressed their satisfaction with the development of WEU's Mediterranean Dialogue and confirmed their readiness to further enhance cooperation with the non-WEU Mediterranean dialogue partners. The Dialogue contributes to confidence-building and cooperation in the region and reinforces other international efforts, notably the EU Barcelona Process, given additional impetus by the recent Stuttgart Conference, and NATO's Mediterranean dialogue.

Ministers took note with appreciation of the ongoing dialogue between Cyprus[1] and WEU that evolves in line with the development of Cyprus's* links with the European Union, with which negotiations for accession are continuing.

9. Ministers reiterated the importance of continuing the Transatlantic Forum dialogue with decision-making circles in the United States and Canada. They welcomed the initiatives undertaken by the Danish Chair.

10. Ministers attached importance to the contribution of the WEU Assembly and its Committees to the Organisation's work and the ongoing reflection on European security and defence.

11. Ministers welcomed the statement presented by Luxembourg on its programme for its forthcoming Presidency of WEU.

---

[1] Turkey dissociates itself from this reference by reserving its stated position on this issue.

7.4 COUNCIL OF EUROPE

266. Council of Europe, Parliamentary Assembly, Resolution 1182 (1999), Crisis in Kosovo and Situation in the FRY, 30 March 1999

[Extract from the Official Gazette of the Council of Europe - March 1999. Text adopted by the Standing Committee, acting on behalf of the Assembly, on 30 March 1999.]

1. The Assembly highly appreciates the efforts of the Contact Group which led to the holding of the Rambouillet meeting and considers that the Interim Agreement for Peace and Self-Government in Kosovo resulting from this meeting represents a fair and equitable proposal for the solution of the Kosovo conflict.

2. The Assembly fully supports this agreement, which is entirely in line with previous Assembly recommendations on the crisis in Kosovo and the situation in the Federal Republic of Yugoslavia (Recommendations 1360 (1988), 1368 (1998), 1376 (1998), 1384 (1998) and 1397 (1999)).

3. The signing, on 18 March 1999 in Paris, of this agreement by the representatives of the Kosovo Albanians reflects their willingness to compromise and respect the will of the international community.

4. The Assembly regrets that, due to the intransigent policy of the leadership of the Federal Republic of Yugoslavia and the inability of the United Nations Security Council to reach a unanimous decision, military action had to be taken by Nato to prevent a human tragedy in Kosovo.

5. The indiscriminate offensive of the Serb forces in Kosovo has inflicted enormous sufferings on the Albanian civilian population, which could no longer be tolerated.

6. The Assembly stresses that President Milosevic and his government are responsible for this development, thus holding hostage their own country's whole population.

7. The Assembly calls on the Contact Group to intensify its diplomatic efforts to bring the Yugoslav authorities to sign and implement the Rambouillet Interim Agreement, and to put an end to the sufferings inevitably resulting from the Nato military action.

8. The Assembly welcomes the peacemaking mission by the Prime Minister of the Russian Government, Mr Yevgeniy Primakov.

9. The Assembly condemns any ethnic cleansing and stresses the importance of the indisputable right of all inhabitants of Kosovo to return to their original homes.

10. The Assembly calls on the Council of Europe's member states to assist Montenegro and Yugoslavia's neighbouring countries in receiving and accommodating those fleeing the conflict.

11. In this context, the Assembly calls on member states and the international community to urgently organise, in co-operation with the Council of Europe, an international conference on humanitarian aid to refugees and the people of Kosovo as well as to the civilian victims of the present military strikes in the Federal Republic of Yugoslavia.

12. The Assembly reiterates its willingness to help all political forces in the Federal Republic of Yugoslavia that are striving to establish democracy, human rights and the rule of law in the country.

267. Council of Europe, Parliamentary Assembly, Recommendation 1403 (1999), Crisis in Kosovo and Situation in the FRY, 28 April 1999

[Extract from the Official Gazette of the Council of Europe - April 1999. Text adopted by the Assembly on 28 April 1999 (13th Sitting).]

1. The Assembly reiterates the views expressed in its Recommendations 1384 (1998), 1397 (1999), 1400 (1999) and Resolution 1182 (1999) on the crisis in Kosovo and the situation in the Federal Republic of Yugoslavia.

2. It recalls that the provisions of United Nations Security Council Resolutions 1160 (1998), 1199 (1998) and 1203 (1998) and the principles of the proposed Rambouillet Interim Agreement, even if not signed by every party, are the basis for a solution to the crisis in Kosovo.

3. The Assembly reiterates its regret that, due to the uncompromising attitude of the Serb and Yugoslav authorities and the inability of the United Nations Security Council to force them to abide by its relevant resolutions, diplomacy could not put an end to the criminal policy of President Milosevic and resorting to force became inevitable.

4. The Assembly recalls that the Nato decision to take limited military action against the Federal Republic of Yugoslavia was aimed at preventing the already existing human tragedy in Kosovo from worsening and bringing the authorities of the Federal Republic of Yugoslavia to sign the proposed Rambouillet Interim Agreement.

5. So far the military action taken by Nato has not succeeded in stopping the humanitarian tragedy in the region. Since the beginning of the air strikes, the Serb authorities have accelerated ethnic cleansing of Kosovo and increased the risk of spill-over of the crisis into neighbouring countries and of a long war that will destabilise the southern Balkan region even further. The Nato military actions have also caused numerous victims among the civilian population. The Assembly regrets all civilian victims of the conflict and appeals for assistance to them.

6. The Assembly strongly condemns the policy of systematic ethnic cleansing carried out by the Yugoslav military and Serb paramilitary forces in Kosovo which has led to the destruction of entire villages, the killing of innocent civilians, the perpetration of war crimes, particularly the abduction and rape of women as a systematic tool of war, and the expulsion of hundreds of thousands of persons into neighbouring countries.

7. The Assembly holds President Milosevic, the Yugoslav and the Serb leadership responsible for these crimes against humanity.

8. It demands that those responsible for these criminal acts be brought before the International Criminal Tribunal for the Former Yugoslavia. All governments which are in possession of evidence of criminal acts should immediately hand it over to the Tribunal.

9. The Assembly recalls that only democratic reforms implemented throughout the Federal Republic of Yugoslavia, the functioning of a democratic political system, the rule of law and the protection of human rights, including the rights of persons belonging to national minorities, can open the way for gradual and conditional integration of the country into the international community, including membership in the Council of Europe.

10. The Assembly expresses its hope that the Yugoslav and Serb people will be able to succeed with democratic changes and underlines that their participation in the completion of the vision of a peaceful Europe united by shared values is indispensable.

11. The position of the Government of Montenegro in the current conflict and its will to continue the democratic reforms despite the threats by the Serbian authorities should enjoy the full support of the international community.

12. The initiatives taken by the United Nations Secretary General and the European Union in seeking to solve the conflict by diplomatic means deserve the Assembly's full support.

13. The Assembly expresses the hope that the peace initiatives undertaken by the Russian authorities will result in an acceptable political solution to the conflict.

14. It welcomes the commitment of the Social Development Fund of the Council of Europe to make two million euros available for the refugees in the crisis area.

15. The Assembly demands that the Council of Europe, as a pan-European organisation, which according to its statute aims to protect human rights, including the rights of persons belonging to national minorities, pluralistic democracy and the rule of law, should play a more active role in finding a political solution to the crisis.

16. The Assembly notes the lack of unanimity between the Council of Europe member states on the use of force in the search for a solution to the conflict.

17. Therefore, the Assembly recommends that the Committee of Ministers:

i. do its utmost to contribute to reaching a political settlement of the conflict;

ii. make full use of its pan-European nature in order to narrow the gap between its member states on the ways to end the conflict;

iii. ensure that the Council of Europe make available its experience and its resources in its fields of competence in all international efforts to solve the crisis, to overcome its consequences and be associated in negotiations on the future political status of Kosovo;

iv. mobilise the Council of Europe's Social Development Fund to assist the victims of the atrocities being perpetrated in Kosovo and provide them not only with psychological assistance as recommended in the 22 April 1999 declaration of the Committee of Ministers, but also with all necessary care, including, for rape victims, if they so desire, the means to terminate any pregnancies;

v. decide at its next meeting in Budapest to allocate, as an exceptional measure, the unspent balance of the 1998 budget to finance specific activities aimed at assisting refugees and facilitating their return;

vi. urgently adopt a global long-term stability programme for the Balkan region, which also includes the fight against organised crime and corruption;

vii. involve the Council of Europe in programmes for reconstruction of the war-torn region, in particular by jointly organising, without delay, with the European Union, the OSCE and financial institutions, such as the European Bank for Reconstruction and Development, the International Monetary Fund, and the World Bank, a conference involving all countries in the region;

viii. express its support to the government and the people of Montenegro in their efforts to stay out of the crisis and to construct democratic institutions;

ix. open a Council of Europe Secretariat office in "the former Yugoslav Republic of Macedonia" in order to help that country overcome the difficulties it is facing due to the conflict in Kosovo;

x. revise the mandate of the Council of Europe Secretariat office in Albania in order to allow its participation in humanitarian activities;

xi. prepare the opening of a Council of Europe Secretariat office in Pristina with the task of building democratic institutions in Kosovo;

xii. urge the Serb and Yugoslav authorities:

a. to implement in full and without delay United Nations Security Council Resolutions 1160 (1998), 1199 (1998) and 1203 (1998);

b. to withdraw Yugoslav troops and Serb military forces from Kosovo and to put an end to the ethnic cleansing and the destruction of houses and property;

c. to accept the deployment of an international armed peace-keeping force under the mandate of the United Nations or OSCE to ensure the return of refugees and other displaced persons and the respect of human rights in Kosovo;

d. to accept diplomatic efforts with a view to achieving a comprehensive political solution to the conflict in Kosovo, based on broad autonomy for this territory within the Federal Republic of Yugoslavia;

e. to respect strictly the norms of international humanitarian law;

xiii. demand that all governments reaffirm that rape and torture in armed conflicts constitute war crimes and should be treated as crimes against humanity;

xiv. urge all governments to ensure assistance to women and children victims through specific programmes.

268. Council of Europe, Chairman of the Committee of Ministers, Declaration on the Kosovo Crisis, Budapest, 7 May 1999

Fifty years ago the Council of Europe was established with the main aim to secure peace through the development of pluralist democracy, human rights and the rule of law. Today, all basic human rights and fundamental freedoms are massively violated in the conflict related to Kosovo. The Chairman of the Committee of Ministers of the Council of Europe, meeting in Budapest on the occasion of the 50th anniversary of the Organisation, expresses the Committee's deep concern over the tragic developments which have caused terrible suffering for hundreds of thousands of civilian victims.

The Chairman of the Committee of Ministers of the Council of Europe firmly condemns those responsible for the massive deportations and violations of human rights and humanitarian law against the civilian population; they must be brought to justice. In this respect he reiterates the support for the action of the International Criminal Tribunal for the former Yugoslavia in The Hague, established in accordance with international law and relevant resolutions of the United Nations Security Council.

The Chairman of the Committee of Ministers expresses his deep appreciation for the large scale humanitarian assistance from governments, international organisations and NGOs to all civilian victims of the conflict. He calls on all governments and competent international institutions to continue and intensify their humanitarian assistance to refugees and to offer them temporary shelter.

The Chairman expresses support for the efforts of the United Nations Secretary-General in search of a peaceful settlement to the Kosovo crisis in full respect for human rights, the rule of law and the basic principles of international law. He further welcomes the outcome of the G8 Foreign Ministers' meeting on 6 May 1999 and the general principles adopted on the political solution to the Kosovo crisis.

The Chairman reiterates the willingness of the Council of Europe to contribute, in its fields of competence, to the implementation of the political settlement and to political and institutional reconstruction in the region.

The Council of Europe will mobilise all efforts and resources to assist in the restoration of democratic stability and security in South East Europe. The Council of Europe looks forward to the day when all countries of the region will abide by the principles of pluralist democracy, human rights (including the rights of national minorities) and the rule of law, and will fulfil the conditions to become members of the Organisation.

7.5 RUSSIAN FEDERATION AND CIS STATES

269. Speech Delivered by Minister of Foreign Affairs I. S. Ivanov during the Sitting of the State Duma, 27 March 1999[1]

Dear Gennadiy Nicolaievitch, dear Deputies,

The 24th of March will remain one of the darkest dates in the history of Europe. The NATO aggression against sovereign Yugoslavia - and it was an aggression according to all the criteria of international law- seriously overshadowed the end of the 20th century, delivered a hard blow to the affords, undertaken during the last years in order to create a reliable system of European security, caused a serious danger to world peace.

A chilling breath of war comes again from the Balkans.

All of us - the President, the Government, the Federal Council the political parties and social organizations - have to make a deep and comprehensive political analysis of the present situation and to draw concrete conclusions concerning both our international and defence policy. The government has received this task from the president.

But what actually happened?

The basis of the present tragedy lies in the problem of Kosovo, which has deep historical roots. According the 1974 Constitution of the Federal Republic Yugoslavia the autonomous province of Kosovo was granted broad rights, which gave it de facto-equality with other federal

---

[1] Unofficial translation by Mr. Sergey Lagodinsky, Institute for Public International Law, University of Göttingen.

republics. The only difference was - the province did not have a right to leave Serbia.

During the dissolution of SFRY in 1989 a new constitution was introduced in Serbia, which in effect took away from Kosovo all the sovereign rights. All of us know, what it means to grant a people certain rights and then take them away instantly. Exactly from that point the Albanian population began their demonstrations against this loss of rights. Yet Albanians comprise according to various sources 60 to 80 percent of the whole population in Kosovo.

Aware of the severity of the problem, we repeatedly raised the question of a fast political solution in our contacts with Belgrade. In this respect B.N. Yeltsin and E.M. Primakov held talks with the Yugoslavian government several times.

Unfortunately, no necessary steps were made for a political solution to the Kosovo problem. But it is a well known fact - and we have learned it from our own experience - that the longer an ethnic problem remains unresolved and no political resolution is achieved, the easier it is for extremists of different kinds to use the situation for their own profit. This is what happened in Kosovo as well, where a couple of years ago a so called Kosovo Liberation Army appeared, whose goal was the forceful separation of the province from Yugoslavia. These separatists immediately found as their patrons Muslim extremists amongst others. In their efforts to fight separatist and terrorist actions, the Yugoslavian government retaliated with such overwhelming force that the civilian population frequently had to suffer as well. The refugees streams from Kosovo increased.

NATO did not want to lose this occasion, to widen its presence in the Balkans.

For this reason the change of Yugoslavian politics was needed. So the accusation of genocide, was put forward against Yugoslavia, the myth about some humanitarian catastrophe began to be actively spread, etc. To cut it short, the basis for a future intervention was being prepared. The main force moving behind this operation was the USA, who - now has it become obvious - had its own far reaching plans - to use Kosovo as a testing area for an American version of new strategic concept of NATO to impose the political and military demands of the USA.

Of course we had foreseen this development and tried to prevent any military scenario. I have reported several times in the Duma about the steps that Russian did in this context.

Despite all this, the situation reached its climax last fall. The NATO assaults seemed to be inevitable. On the instruction of the President, together with Marshal Sergeiev and representatives of the Administration of the Security Council of the Russian Federation, I left for Belgrade to meet with President Milosevic. At that time we managed to relieve the tension through the deployment of a OSCE mission in Kosovo.

Simultaneously the Yugoslavian government signed two secret agreements with NATO, in which Russia was not involved. One of them dealt with the amount of Yugoslavian armed forces in the region of Kosovo, the other one concerned the flight routes of the NATO planes above Kosovo. Later on NATO used these documents to accuse the Yugoslavian government of violating them, in order to justify NATO's military action.

Taking into account the remaining tension around Kosovo, we initiated another meeting of the Contact Group in London this January, where we managed to prevent the danger of military action and successfully pressed for open negotiations in Rambouillet. I would especially like to thank those Duma parties, who supported our approach and recommended to Belgrade that it should participate in the talks.

The result of the difficult negotiating process was a political document which in our opinion gave us an opportunity to start a peaceful settlement to this problem. According to this document the rights taken away from the Kosovo region were to be restored and their enforcement was to be guaranteed. All these principles were reached on the basis of respect to Yugoslavian integrity and sovereignty. Special provisions of this document dealt with the establishment of a system of local self-government and securing the rights of the population especially the rights of ethnic communities, conducting elections, solving economic problems and organizing the help to these goals.

I would like to stress the fact, that this was a compromise prepared by international mediators taking into account the position of both involved sides and supported by the Contact Group. A much more complicated question regarded the enforcement of this political agreement. Without consulting us, the western negotiators made a suggestion in Rambouillet, which presumed use of police and military units to implement the agreement, where NATO was to play a central role. We categorically refused to acknowledge this idea. We insisted there is and can be no "packages" in connection to the political agreement. As for the implementation, we considered it to be a matter of further negotiations. It must be a Yugoslavian sovereign decision, whether it wishes any international assistance and what kind of assistance it should be.

Unfortunately, the Yugoslavian side did not sign the political agreement. If it had done that, the situation could have developed in a different way. As for the Albanian delegation, it did formally sign in Paris the political document coupled with military and police suggestions. However, at the same time the Albanians made a written reservation, stating that they still remain committed to the aim of secession from the FRY. In fact this reservation disavowed their signature.

Thus it is wrong in all aspects to blame solely Belgrade for the collapse of the negotiating process. Yes, Milosevic is a complicated partner. Yes. The position of the Yugoslavian delegation was not a constructive one during the talks in Rambouillet and in Paris. We frankly told it the government of FRY. But Belgrade never refused to participate in the negotiating process and does not do it now.

While telling you about the negotiating details, I keep asking myself, if our approach was correct, if we have done our best to prevent the bloodshed. Yes, we had been procrastinating the forceful solution, we managed to launch the negotiating process. But nevertheless, we could not prevent NATO aggression against Yugoslavia.

Dear Deputies! The rocket and bombarding attacks on the territory of the Federal Republic Yugoslavia have been lasting for three days. This first act of aggression against an independent state in Europe since the end of the World War II is continuing. Europe has never been so close to severe challenges before. The persons responsible for a decision to start the bombing have been cynically stating that these assaults are aimed to prevent a humanitarian catastrophe in Kosovo. Unfortunately, the whole world can witness now the results of such humanitarian concerns, supported by cruise missiles.

The Russian President, the Government, the Federal Assembly - all have unanimously condemned this open aggression against a sovereign state - a UN-member. Our voice has been heard. To be even more definite: while yesterday hardly anyone dared to support our views, today more and more states are on our side. Interestingly enough, our project of a resolution in the Security Council calling upon an immediate cease of NATO bombardments was supported in particular by such influential countries as India and China. The Indian representative noted that the united opinion of Moscow, Peking and Delhi in this matter, means that more than a half of the Earth population decisively rejects the illegal and dubious military enterprise of NATO. Belarus has been acting with us in a united front. The mood is shifting in the world and in European public opinion. More and more frequently people ask, when will this barbarism stop and what are the real reasons behind it. And this is not a coincidence.

Today not only is Yugoslavia being attacked. The whole world community is being defied. The whole world order created after the World War II is endangered. Whatever reasons are being brought forward by NATO and primarily by American strategists to justify their international tyranny, the real reasons are obvious - to establish such a monopoly world order in the 21st century, where the world's fate would have to be decided from Washington. And that is why, in defending the Yugoslavia's right to sovereignty, we are defending the future of the world and Europe against this new form of neo-colonisation - the so called NATO-colonisation. Having just now accepted three new members, NATO has demonstrated right away its aggressive character. Moreover NATO has for the first time acted ultra vires, using force not for the reason of defence, and not against an aggressor, but against a sovereign state.

Earlier we have heard from our partners the phrase: mutual trust is good, control is better. Now it's our turn to use this principle. If the NATO policy is determined to ignore the UN-Charter and aims at a role of world police, then we will go different ways. As you know, the President made a number of harsh steps to freeze our relations to NATO. We hope these steps to make many people in Brussels reconsider things seriously.

I won't make a secret out of the fact that international relations are now in a very hard phase. It will not be easy to overcome it - the atmosphere of trust and partnership has endured a grave blow.

Realizing these things Russia should not degrade itself by a confrontation any more so by engaging in a shady military enterprise. If somebody hopes, that we will lose control and answer to these violations of the UN-Charter or Final Helsinki Act in a similar way, he has made a mistake. As the President of Russia said: we have to be morally above those, who started all this. Russia has been and Russia remains a reliable and a predictable partner. Nevertheless, we will strive even more energetically to shape a democratic multipolar world, to stop the arms race, to create a reliable European security and stability system, where every state would enjoy a guaranteed and worthy role and where each state would enjoy equal security. We certainly do not close the door for any bilateral contacts to the USA, though our relations are seriously damaged. One should not forget that our countries have gone a long way from opposition to partnership during the last years. Just let me remind you that only in the span of time from 1996 till 1998 seven summits between the Presidents of Russia and the USA, 5 sessions of the bilateral Commission on Economic and Technical Co-operation on the level of Prime Minister/Vice-president as well 22 meetings between the Foreign Ministers have taken place. We should cherish such a valuable political store of experience.

Dear Deputies! The NATO attacks have destroyed the results of long labour work in seeking a political solution in Kosovo. We have lost the positive outcome of Rambouillet and Paris.

A new situation is being created which demands new approaches. However there is no alternative to a political process and a passionate search for mutually acceptable solutions.

That is why Russia directs its efforts primarily to immediate cessation of aggression and stopping the bombings, which has cost so many innocent human lives.

With this aim in mind I have already suggested to my colleagues from the Contact Group that we should urgently meet in Moscow to work out some decisions for a political settlement. The reaction of the European partners is generally positive. Washington still has not agreed.

In this connection I have invited to the Ministry of Foreign Affairs the ambassadors of the Troika states of the European Union and suggested that we should use the political instrument of consultations between Russia and EU for analysing and resolving the situation politically. This instrument is mentioned in the Agreement on Partnership and Co-operation between Russia and the EU. We hope for a positive reaction on our initiative.

On another front we actively get involved to activate the potentials of the UN in this critical situation. I have already mentioned the resolution initiated by Russia. The results of the vote which took place this night were 3 votes "for" and 12 "against". This result was foreseen and should not disappoint us. First of all, I have already cited the Indian representative and this reference can tell us a lot. Second the citizens of the NATO countries will be able to see the actions of their government in a proper perspective. The fact that already 70 per cent of the British population does not support the Kosovo policy of their government is quite revealing. You also know the mood in Italy and Greece who have distanced themselves from their NATO partners. Even in the USA the action is supported by already less than hardly 50 per cent of the population. We are sure that the protest in the world including the NATO countries will grow steadily, if in Brussels they do not change their mind. The hard position taken by Russia contributes to the formation of this public attitude.

In the case that NATO aggression does not immediately stop, Russia will demand an extraordinary session of the UN General Assembly be commenced.

Our country certainly cannot and will not remain indifferent to the great destruction, that Yugoslavia is suffering. Most terribly it is the people, those peaceful civilians, that die. The victims are already counted in hundreds. For this reason the President decided to offer emergency humanitarian aid.

Our diplomatic service has no more important task than assisting the interests of the Russian citizens and securing their safety. We have been taking and still take all the necessary measures to organise an evacuation of the Russians living in FRY who wish to leave.

Our Embassy and other Russian institutions work in an almost military modus to fulfil all their tasks. Their employees deserve our strong support and gratitude for their courage and selflessness.

And something else. We often hear the question, whether Russia has a Balkan strategy at all. I am answering with all the responsibility of my office: of course it has.

Here are the main aspects of this strategy:

- support for stable and secure developments in the Balkans, for turning this region into a stabilizing factor for the whole Europe;

- active participation in the peaceful settlement of the critical situations and local conflicts, as well as on the post-crisis restoration;

- turning the Balkans into a region of mutual co-operation, an interesting market for infrastructure and energy projects;

- involving the states of the region into the Russian efforts to create a "Big Mediterranean" and to secure the freedom of navigation in the Black Sea straits;

- an all-round development of partnerships with all the countries of the region, based on the principles of the UN and OSCE.

This position has been approved by the President of Russia and is consequently implemented.

Dear Deputies! During these days we undertook a number of decisive measures, to stop the aggression and to help the Yugoslavian people at this moment of hardships. We hope for the understanding and support for these actions by the State Duma. We will regularly inform the Russian legislators about our future actions.

270. Statement of Ministry of Foreign Affairs, Press-Release, 29 March 1999[1]

All the advocates of an immediate cessation of bloodshed in the Balkans have highly praised the political position taken by the Latin-American countries - members of the Rio Group- who expressed their deep concern in connection to the air attacks of NATO against Yugoslavia.

One cannot help sharing the deep regret, expressed by this influential regional union regarding the fact, that force is being used in the Balkans in violation of Articles 53 (1) and 54 of the UN-Charter. No less important is the Rio-Group's appeal to all parties, to resume their talks as soon as possible and to reach a definitive settlement securing a solid and durable peace, based on the respect for human rights of every ethnic group and minority in this region as well as for the territorial integrity of the states. We hope, this appeal will be heard by the NATO States.

---

[1] *Unofficial translation by Mr. Sergey Lagodinsky, Institute for Public International Law, University of Göttingen.*

271. Press Conference by Russian Federation Foreign Minister Ivanov and Colonel General Baluyevsky, Chief of Main Operational Directorate, General Staff of the Russian Federation Armed Forces, First Deputy Chief of General Staff, Verbatim Report, Ministry of Foreign Affairs, 2 April 1999

I. S. Ivanov: Russia continues making most active efforts aimed at ending NATO's military action against sovereign Yugoslavia and resuming the negotiating process with a view to a long-term settlement of the situation in Kosovo. As you know, President of the Russian Federation B.N. Yeltsin instructed me yesterday to address a request to the foreign ministers [of the G-8] for holding an urgent meeting where they might map out ways for the earliest possible emergence from the Kosovo crisis. Moreover, the President of Russia stressed that each lost day was bringing new victims and that an immediate action had to be taken.

The initiative undertaken by the Russian leadership has been dictated by the wish to reverse the tragic course of events in connection with Yugoslavia and to bring the settlement process back to the negotiating table. It demonstrates once again Russia's readiness to cooperate with all, let me stress it, with all states, which have a stake in finding a political way out of this situation. We are certain that such an authoritative body as [the G-8] must and can play its weighty and positive role in this context. We expect our partners to duly appreciate this new step made by Russia.

Let me tell you that the first reaction is on the whole a positive one, although there were certain zealous press secretaries, who attempted to give their own off-hand evaluations. I must say that I am in constant contact with the ministers of foreign affairs of most nations, the United States and Europe included. Let me say it once again, the reaction to this initiative is on the whole positive. But some of my opposite numbers have expressed a view that a meeting like this ought to be duly prepared. We subscribe to it too and have started an exchange of views on the possible basis for such discussion to be held within the framework [of the G-8].

The Council of the CIS Heads of State today considered the situation in connection with Yugoslavia. All leaders spoke against the use of force and for a political settlement of the Kosovo problem.

Regrettably, the rocket and bomb strikes delivered against Yugoslavia are in their eighth day. The peoples of that country realize quite well the true aim of this aggression: to bleed white and cause the disintegration of the Union Republic of Yugoslavia. And their reaction to this aggression is unanimous. Indicatively, the bombing raids were unequivocally condemned by the leaders of all opposition forces, in Yugoslavia. There is no one in that country today who would think that the bombing raids are capable of solving the Kosovo problem. Everyone in Yugoslavia is unanimous, including those, who in their time used to disapprove of the policies conducted by the leadership of Yugoslavia, that this is an aggression against Yugoslavia, one against the Yugoslav people. And that people is united today in its effort to rebuff the aggression.

It is quite logical in this connection that an appeal for stopping the NATO strikes has come from Ibrahim Rugova, the acknowledged leader of the Kosovo Albanians. And he is the same man who over the last ten years has epitomized the struggle which the Kosovo Albanians pursued for their rights. Now it becomes clear why he found himself actually debarred from leading the Kosovo delegation at Rambouillet and in Paris.

Upon my arrival to Rambouillet, I had a meeting with both the Yugoslav and the Kosovo delegations. I was extremely surprised to find that all of a sudden, at Rambouillet, Ibrahim Rugova, who all these years had epitomized as it were the Kosovo Albanians' movement, was keeping in the background and actually did not utter a word during our almost one-hour-long talk. Playing the main role in the delegation were individuals, who literally a few days before their travel to Rambouillet had performed, arms in hand, all manner of provocative actions and did not wish to conceal that they were working to separate Kosovo [from Yugoslavia].

It is not accidental either that Ibrahim Rugova accepted direct contacts with the Yugoslav authorities yesterday. Why this took place is now clear, I think, to everyone. The true Kosovo Albanians are far from wishing to have Kosovo separated from Yugoslavia; they are prepared to live in a united state provided, of course, that their legitimate rights are fully respected. As we see it, presenting the problem in this way is fair and Russia will do all in her power to secure full respect for the rights of the Albanian population like for those of other ethnic groups and peoples.

One more thing. This turn of events does not satisfy in any way the Albanian extremists, who have put a stake on the expansion of combat operations in Kosovo. At gunpoint, they are recruiting to their ranks refugees who flee the horrors of war. So, the question is this: Who does NATO support and whose interests does it aspire to defend? Various rumours were put in circulation yesterday right after the meeting between President Slobodan Milosevic and Ibrahim Rugova. I will tell you frankly that we, for example, were surprised to learn that a report was published right away about people in Great Britain officially declaring their full support for the so-called Kosovo Liberation Army. I think, all true plans are becoming increasingly obvious with each passing day: Who supported whom in this conflict and what aims pursued.

It is being claimed that Ibrahim Rugova was forced to accept a meeting with Slobodan Milosevic. I wish to remind you that Ibrahim Rugova arrived by plane from Paris at his own initiative. I wonder, who could force him to do anything in Paris? Themes discussed during their talk were the current situation in Kosovo, the state of the humanitarian situation, and problems connected with the massive exodus of refugees from the territory of the province. To be sure, the sides stated that some considerable material damage had been inflicted on the population of the province since the start of the NATO air operation: Hundreds of citizens had died regardless of their ethnic affiliation, who had nothing to do with the substance of differences existing between the Serbs and the Albanians in Kosovo. Fleeing from bombs, people are forced to leave their homes. The flows of refugees are increasing.

I also would like to draw your attention to the fact that Ibrahim Rugova came up with an initiative on March 31 of this year, asking the United States and Western countries to stop the annihilation of the Kosovo population. The Western media, for some reason, tend to keep silent about it. He refuted rumours about his having been wounded and his house having been burned by Serbs. As you know, there were other conjectures to the effect that part of the Albanian leaders had been either destroyed or persecuted.

Though it is entirely obvious that the attempts to resolve the Kosovo problem by military means are totally without prospect, the NATO leadership in the persons of the Secretary General of NATO and the Joint Force Commander, who personally gave the order to start the aggression, go on saying with maniacal stubbornness that they wish literally to wipe both Yugoslavia and its peoples off the face of the earth. Practically on the daily basis, NATO extends its list of targets, against which strikes are planned to be delivered. A Pentagon spokesman went on record as saying yesterday that the intention was to inflict so much damage on the Serb forces that the price of losses would force President Slobodan Milosevic [to accept peace on NATO's terms]. Considering that people in both the United States and the European nations have much respect for rights, I would like specifically to attract your attention to those words. That is, [at any price] - and there is only one price here, that of human life - to force Slobodan Milosevic to accept peace on NATO's terms. What is it leading to in practice? The list of killed is growing; the number of refugees has topped 160 thousand. Civilian facilities are destroyed in an intentional and systematic manner. The latest case in point is a bombed-out bridge in the city of Novi Sad. The Danube navigation has been disrupted as result and there is a danger of an environmental disaster. I wish to stress in this connection that this already affects the interests of not only Yugoslavia but also of all Danube states, including Austria, Germany, Hungary, and other states using this crucial water artery of Europe. That is, the aggression's consequences are increasingly on the regional scale.

Another circumstance that attracts one's attention is that NATO's air campaign against Yugoslavia is performed almost exclusively by U.S. forces. For this reason, the operation can be called an international one only with a great degree of point-stretching. Despite the tireless attempts to portray it as massive collective efforts, despite the wish to harp all the time on [the unbending Atlantic solidarity] within the framework of NATO, 90 percent of air strikes is delivered by U.S. aircraft and ships. True enough, Norwegian planes took part in air strikes for the first time this night [April 2]. Thus far, I cannot say what it is all about.

And yet, although the total yield of bombs and rockets dropped on Yugoslav cities and villages equals two atomic bombs that fell on Hiroshima, the NATO strategists have failed to achieve their goal. You may easily make certain of it by listening to the daily press conferences held in the NATO headquarters. People there show much skill in avoiding a discussion of the concrete results of those operations. As a consequence, a land operation is being prepared at an accelerated rate and in spite all assurances to the contrary. The Secretary General of NATO, for one, has stated as much. Though you may hear many assurances that this is not so, nor, allegedly, can ever be. And a pretext has been invented to justify such operation - avoiding a humanitarian catastrophe. That is, NATO itself first creates a humanitarian catastrophe through its air strikes, and then launches a land operation in order to head off that same humanitarian catastrophe. Some very "sane" logic.

According to calculations made by the NATO people themselves, a land force numbering 150 to 200 thousand servicemen will be needed to invade Kosovo. An impressive figure! Concrete units and subunits from the United States and other NATO countries are named, which it is planned to use in the operation. Redeployment of the relevant contingents has come under way. The striking force in the land operation is due to be composed of military units from Great Britain and France, which, accordingly, will account for the greatest losses. That such losses are inevitable is well known to NATO generals. Fearing that the Congress will not agree to a direct involvement in hand-to-hand fights, the Americans reserve for themselves a rear-guard role which somehow is strongly reminiscent of one played by detachments designed to keep an invading force from fleeing after a contact with the enemy. It is clear to everyone today that all this barbarity will bring martial glory neither to the NATO arms nor to the NATO strategists. These men in uniform and in mufti are trying to put a brave face on a very sorry game. But it is obvious that their adventure is bankrupt from both the political and military points of view.

Now about the legal aspect of the affair. No matter how hard someone tries to vindicate the NATO actions with reference to some "new" international law concepts or to some allegedly existing limitations of state sovereignty, it must be clear to everyone that the case in point is a direct aggression. We would insistently recommend rereading the resolution on the definition of aggression, approved by the UN General Assembly in 1974. It says everything. And it was passed unanimously, including the votes of those states which are currently perpetrating the aggression. Things, therefore, must be called by their proper names and no one should attempt to mislead the public opinion in his own and other countries. An aggression is taking place with all the ensuing consequences.

Yet another thing. When someone speaks about genocide in Kosovo, and it is the argument which NATO falls back on to justify its use of force, it must be remembered that the 1948 international convention on the fight against genocide does not authorize states to use armed force spontaneously for the prevention of genocide in circumvention of the UN Charter. Quite the contrary. The Convention makes it incumbent on states to urge a relevant UN body to adopt all necessary measures in order to prevent and cut short the acts of genocide. And if an armed force is to be used after all, it is only the UN Security Council that can have such a prerogative; but, as is common knowledge, the NATO countries did not apply to the Security Council. And so, this argument is a soap bubble too. Incidentally, neither the OSCE nor any other international expert organization came up with a conclusion that genocide was perpetrated in Kosovo.

Yet another propaganda campaign is unfolding in the West in connection with Russia sending its reconnaissance ship, The Leman, to the Mediterranean. Assertions are being made - and have been let out to the media - that the ship will well-nigh guide the Yugoslav air defence weapons to NATO aircraft. Someone even goes as far as to allege that she will aid the Yugoslavs in capturing NATO officers and men. Well, what can one say to this? I see you are smiling, but we others find it hard to smile, regrettably, because it is we who have to react to all this. But, speaking seriously, the Defence Minister of Russia, Marshal I.D. Sergeyev, who addressed the last meeting with journalists held here, clearly outlined the missions, which the ship was to pursue. She will operate solely in the interests of Russia's national security. We do not want an escalation of military operations and have called, ever since March 24, for an end to any hostilities and a return to the negotiating table.

Considering that we speak a lot today about the legal underpinnings, I wish to emphasize that our ship makes her voyage in strict conformity with the START-1 Treaty, which envisages that a Side which deploy heavy bombers outside of its national territory has a duty to notify about it the other side via the diplomatic channels. The other side, in turn, has a right to monitor strategic offensive weapons, including the movements of heavy bombers, with the help of its national technical means of verification. In mid-March, the United States notified us about a redeployment of 11 heavy bombers to bases outside of the United States' territory. We, in our turn, following the letter of the START-2 Treaty, took the decision that the monitoring of their movements would be pursued by our verification means, including the reconnaissance ship, The Leman. I want to emphasize it specifically that this step on the part of Russia is fully justified. As is to be regretted, the aggression against Yugoslavia is expanding with each passing day. There is a real threat growing to regional and as a whole to international security. We, as is understood, do not wish to be caught unawares.

A return to the negotiating process is inevitable in events surrounding Kosovo. We are certain of this and have been saying as much since the first day of the aggression. But it will be increasingly harder to do with each passing day. And already now it is necessary that all of us - and Russia has been doing it from the first day - should think about the format and substance of the future agreements.

While we are at it, there should be no illusions: The NATO bombing raids have put paid to the Rambouillet process and the documents it produced. The more so that with each passing day we learn ever more details about who and how mapped them out and what promises were given to those who, with NATO's aid, are attempting, arms in hand, to separate Kosovo from Yugoslavia.

Today, I am focusing on the legal aspects because diplomats have a duty to dispel all manner of speculations only with documents in their hands. In keeping with the 1969 Vienna Convention on International Treaty Law, any [treaty is null and void if its conclusion has been the result of a threat or use of force in violation of the principles of the international law as embodied in the UN Charter]. This means that a different basis is required for successful international talks.

Russia will go on making all the necessary efforts to render such talks possible. We support wide-ranging contacts with all those who are prepared to make their constructive contribution to the solution of this problem. The Prime Minister and I hold regular talks over the telephone with our partners, including the U.S. State Secretary and the foreign ministers of France, Germany, Italy, Great Britain, Greece and other countries. I wish to stress it once again in this room that Russia is prepared to respond to any proposal which would enable a headway to be made. We are making proposals of our own, but we are also open to a consideration of any real, I repeat it, real proposal, not just an ultimatum, which would make it possible to emerge from this situation by way of talks, a situation which is threatening everyone, is threatening the European stability and security. We hope that our partners will soon display a sense of realism, show a constructive approach in their estimate of the situation, and cooperate with us actively in order to find a political settlement. We are calling on our partners for this and will do everything in our power.

272. Declaration Adopted by the Inter-Parliamentary Assembly of States Members of the Commonwealth of Independent States, 3 April 1999[1]

The Inter-Parliamentary Assembly of States Members of the Commonwealth of Independent States (CIS),

Recognizing its shared responsibility for national security and global peace,

Perceiving military operations by the North Atlantic alliance in the territory of sovereign Yugoslavia, without the authorization of the United Nations Security Council, as a challenge to the current system of international relations, and a real threat to peace and stability in Europe and the world in general,

Expressing its deep concern at the risk of another cold war on the planet and of armed inter-State conflicts,

Calls on the parliaments and Governments of the States members of the North Atlantic Alliance to take immediate action to halt military operations in the territory of the Federal Republic of Yugoslavia, a Member of the United Nations,

Considers that missiles and bombs cannot be used as arguments in addressing the complex problems of the modern world and that the letter and spirit of the Charter of the United Nations must be observed, and, accordingly, supports the proposal of the Russian Federation to convene an emergency session of the United Nations General Assembly, and to include the item on the agenda of the Inter-Parliamentary Union, the Parliamentary Assembly of the Council of Europe and the Parliamentary Assembly of OSCE,

Calls on the leadership of Yugoslavia to do its utmost to settle the Kosovo conflict exclusively by peaceful means and on the basis of political dialogue.

The Inter-Parliamentary Assembly of States members of CIS, acting as a consistent proponent of political settlement in situations of crisis, invites parliamentarians throughout the world to take the most resolute action to halt NATO military action and resume the process of negotiations within the framework of the Contact Group, for it is convinced that concerted efforts by the international community to establish peace in Yugoslavia will prevent further tragic developments that could have unpredictable consequences for humanity.

The Inter-Parliamentary Assembly supports the initiative of the Verkhovna Rada (Parliament) of Ukraine and the National Assembly of the Republic of Belarus to propose that parliaments throughout the world designate the year 2000 as the Year of Concord and Consolidation of Good-neighbourliness, with a view to promoting peace, trade, economic, cultural and other international relations.

[Adopted unanimously by parliamentary delegations from the Republic of Armenia, the Republic of Belarus, the Republic of Kazakhstan, the Kyrgyz Republic, the Republic of Moldova, the Russian Federation, the Republic of Tajikistan and Ukraine.]

273. Statement by the Official Representative of the Ministry of Foreign Affairs, 3 April 1999[2]

NATO committed another barbaric act in the Balkans. The centre of Belgrade was bombarded. The fact that the rockets' targets were dangerously close to a hospital complex, a kindergarten and private houses did not stop those who planned and gave this felonious order.

The Russian embassy is situated not far from the place of explosions. Fortunately, no officials were injured. Those in the NATO-capitals should be aware of the heavy consequences for any action that endangers the life of Russian citizens. This expanding NATO aggression has matured into a ruthless war to extinction against the peoples of Yugoslavia. It has already spread over to the neighbour-states, presenting a real threat to regional and international security. In front of the whole world, NATO heavily tramples on generally accepted rules of international law and elementary principles of human morals. The fact, that these NATO actions take place under the slogan of "preventing a humanitarian catastrophe", makes them especially cynical.

This chain of events reveals the strong necessity of quickly stopping the NATO aggression and the desirability of returning to the process of a political settlement. The suggestions of the Russian government on this matter are well known.

There is need for immediate action. Every lost day means new victims and tragedies.

274. Permanent Mission of the Russian Federation to the OSCE, Representation and Request for Information, Vienna, 23 April 1999

The Permanent Mission of the Russian Federation to the Organization for Security and Co-operation in Europe presents its compliments to the Mission of the United States of America to the OSCE and has the honour to draw its attention to the following.

The Russian Federation, referring to paragraph 1 of the section "Human Dimension" of the Concluding Document of the Vienna Meeting 1986 of Representatives of the participating States of the Conference on Security and Co-operation in Europe, Held on the Basis of the Provisions of the Final Act Relating to the Follow-up to the Conference, is forwarding this representation and is requesting information in connection with mass violations of human rights and fundamental freedoms as well as of the humanitarian commitments, arising from the decisions and arrangements adopted within the CSCE/OSCE framework, committed by the North Atlantic Treaty Organization and, in particular by its members, officials and military personnel, in the territory of the Federal Republic of Yugoslavia.

Under the Final Act (section "Questions relating to Security in Europe", Declaration on Principles Guiding Relations between participating States) the United States of America is obliged to respect in good faith human rights and fundamental freedoms, including the freedom of thought, conscience, religion or belief. The United States of America, like all other OSCE participating States, in its actions "should recognize the universal significance of human rights and fundamental freedoms, respect for which is an essential factor for peace, justice and well-being necessary to insure development of friendly relations and co-operation among themselves as among all States". The United States of America has solemnly undertaken to "constantly respect these rights and freedoms in their mutual relations and to endeavour jointly and separately, including in co-operation with the United Nations, to promote universal and effective respect for them". Moreover, the United States of America has undertaken "in the field of human rights and fundamental freedoms to act in conformity with the purposes and principles of the Charter of the United Nations and with the Universal Declaration of Human Rights" and "also fulfill its obligations as set forth in the international declarations and agreements in this field, including inter alia the International Covenants on Human Rights, by which they may be bound". Based on this principle a vast set of humanitarian norms has been worked out within the CSCE/OSCE in regard to which the United States of America has assumed obligations on specific aspects of human rights and fundamental freedoms, including those to which its attention is drawn below in this representation.

The developments in the territory of the Federal Republic of Yugoslavia since March 24 1999 resulted from the aggression of NATO, of

---

[1] UN Doc. A/53/920 - S/1999/461, Annex II, 22 April 1999.
[2] *Unofficial translation by Mr. Sergey Lagodinsky, Institute for Public International Law, University of Göttingen.*

which the United States of America is a member, have pointed out to mass violations of human rights and fundamental freedoms, of commitments assumed in this field by the United States of America and other NATO member States within the CSCE/CSCE, including actions of officials and military personnel.

The Russian Federation demands an immediate cessation of the above violations and expects to receive complete information about all violations of humanitarian norms, committed during NATO's use of force campaign against the Federal Republic of Yugoslavia, including reports on casualties among the civilian population, in particular on the casualties resulted from missile and bomb strikes, destroyed cities, towns and villages, attacks on unprotected cities, villages and dwellings or buildings, or their bombardments by using whatever weapons, on destruction of or damage to religious, charitable, educational, cultural and scientific institutions, historical monuments and literary and scientific works, included in the International Register of Cultural Values under special protection, the damages to the State, private and personal property, loss of benefits, arising from enjoying human rights and fundamental freedoms, including the freedom of thought, conscience, religion and belief and the right to freely receive and disseminate information. Within the framework of this Note Verbale the Russian Federation expects to receive properly documented data on all circumstances connected with the above mentioned violations in the course of military actions of NATO against the Federal Republic of Yugoslavia, as well as a complete list of objects, which have become the targets of NATO actions, and the assessment of the inflicted damage and, correspondingly, the amount of reparations.

The Russian Federation expects the submission of information requested in this representation within the time limits established by the decisions of CSCE/OSCE.

Without prejudice to the above the Russian Federation requests the information and explanations, including the ones in connection with actions of officials and military personnel of the United States of America concerning the situations and concrete cases which follow below.

1. In accordance with paragraph 1 of Article 20 of the International Covenant on Civil and Political Rights, of December 16, 1966 "Any propaganda for war shall be prohibited by law". Statements of officials and representatives of the military of the United States of America, its citizens, within the NATO organs, emphasise the necessity to continue and intensify military actions against the Federal Republic of Yugoslavia and lead them to the "final victory", which means the propaganda for war. In addition to the above requested information the Russian Federation expects to receive information on the existing legislative prohibition in to exercise propaganda for war and, if such a prohibition exists, then the information on legal procedures to stop propaganda for war by the officials and military personnel of the United States of America.

2. A selected list of enterprises and objects of infrastructure destroyed or damaged as a result of the NATO bombings is contained in the Annex attached herewith. The Russian Federation expects to receive a documented information on each and every position of the above mentioned list, as well as an information on supposed actions to restore them.

3. The NATO aggression against the Federal Republic of Yugoslavia right away brought about a humanitarian catastrophe, of which all the peoples of this State, representatives of all the ethnic communities and confessions without exclusion have become victims. The use of force by NATO caused the necessity for the constitutional Yugoslav authorities to declare a state of war with corresponding limitations of human rights and fundamental freedoms and adopt protective measures on its territory within the framework of legitimate self-defence. The strikes of NATO resulted in a considerable increase in the number of displaced persons and refugees of various nationalities, have caused especially grave consequences for the population of Kosovo. Thus, the actions of the member states of NATO, including the United States of America, have led to the greatest humanitarian disaster in Europe after the end of the second world war. In this context any justifications of motives of "prevention of humanitarian catastrophe" look unacceptable: the guilty of the humanitarian catastrophe try to whitewash themselves by references to the humanitarian disaster. Whatever these of those officials say, it is precisely after late March 24, that is after the start of the NATO strikes that these terrible sufferings and distress of the Yugoslav population, and first of all of ethnic Albanians, have taken place and begun a dramatic upsurge in the number of the refugees and displaced persons, who found themselves without means of existence and minimal conditions of safety in locations of their residence. According to UNHCR estimation, compared to the period before March 24, when figures of internally displaced persons who fled their regions of permanent residence amounted to 200 000 people, following the start of NATO air strikes only the amount of refugees exceeded half a million. Quantity features of internally displaced persons as s result of the NATO military action simply cannot be counted whatsoever.

The Russian Federation expects to receive the information and explanations concerning political, legal and material responsibility of the United States of America for the humanitarian catastrophe in the Federal Republic of Yugoslavia, the consequences of which have touched upon neighbouring States.

4. It is common knowledge that residents of the Yugoslav cities, townships and villages voluntarily and openly stand out as "living shield" of buildings and structures dear to them. For example, citizens of Belgrade and Novi Sad went out on the bridges, which are cultural monuments of the all-European importance. Workers of the "Zastava" automobile plant did not vacate it even at night. Nevertheless these and other objects have become targets for the NATO strikes. The NATO members, which include the United States of America, have demonstrated disregard for human life, their readiness not to stop irrespective of any number of victims considered as merely a "collateral damage, which is impossible to avoid".

The deliberate strikes of NATO against the objects with a known presence of population there run flagrantly counter to Article 3 of the Universal Declaration of Human Rights, which reads: "Everyone has the right to life, liberty and security of person". Rejecting the right to life, liberty and security of person for all the peoples of Yugoslavia, members of NATO, including the United States of America, commit the most serious violation of international law and obligations assumed within the framework of the Human Dimension of the CSCE/OSCE.

5. The destruction of houses of peaceful residents undermines the fundamental principles fixed in Article 17 (20) of the Universal Declaration of Human Rights and Article 9.6 of the Document of the Copenhagen Meeting of the Conference on the Human Dimension of the CSCE.

6. Systematic destruction of basic public facilities, including district heating and power plants, highways and hospitals, entails a drastic lowering of the standard of living of the civil population, i.e. violates the right to the standard of living, including food, clothing, medical care and necessary social services, that is adequate for the health and well-being, as laid down in Article 25 of the Universal Declaration of Human Rights. Furthermore, that can seriously impede a future return of refugees and internally displaced persons.

7. Violations mentioned in paragraph 6 above disrupt the conditions under which women and children can expect to get a special protection provided for in Article 25 (2) of the Universal Declaration of the Human Rights. The obligation of the participating States "to accord particular attention to the recognition of the rights of the child, his civil rights and his personal freedoms, his economic, social and cultural rights, and his right to special protection against all forms of violence", established in Article 13 of the CSCE Copenhagen Document, as well as in Articles 3, 6, 16, 19 (1), 24 (1), 27 (1), 28 and 39 of the Convention on the Rights of the Child.

8. The Russian Federation expects that the OSCE participating States, which are members of NATO, will - in accordance with paragraph 7 of Section C of the Document adopted by the CSCE Bonn Conference (1990) on economic co-operation in Europe - fully meet

their commitments in terms of assessing the impact of the ecological stress on the population of the Federal Republic of Yugoslavia by providing data on consequences of the pollution of the environment and damage inflicted on the health of the population in the result of the destruction of chemical plants and drug factories, oil warehouses and pipe-lines, and the use, in the course of air raids on Yugoslavia, of ammunition containing radio-active substances.

9. Systematic destruction and demolition of radio- and TV transmitters on the territory of the Federal Republic of Yugoslavia, including Kosovo, violate the right to freely get and disseminate information, laid down in Article 19 of the Universal Declaration of Human Rights, Article 19 (2) of the International Covenant on Civil and Political Rights, Article 17 of the Convention on the Rights of the Child, Article 9.1, Part II of the CSCE Copenhagen Document, Article 10 (1) of the European Convention for the Protection of Human Rights and Fundamental Freedoms; and endanger the life of journalists, which runs counter the commitment of the participating States "to take all feasible measures to protect journalists engaged in dangerous professional missions particularly in cases of armed conflicts", as laid down in paragraph 34 of the Document of the Moscow Meeting of the CSCE Conference on Human Dimension.

One-sided and biased coverage of the developments in Yugoslavia by the NATO States' mass media, deliberate blackout on damage inflicted on civil facilities, including destruction of historical and cultural monuments, and tendentious interpretation of the Yugoslav authorities' position openly run counter the provisions of the Helsinki Final Act (Section 2 - Information, paragraphs a) and b)) which provide for the commitment of the participating States "to promote the improvement of the dissemination of filmed and broadcast information... and to this end... encourage the wider showing and broadcasting of a greater variety of recorded and filmed information from the other participating States", as well as "... favour co-operation among public or private, national or international radio and television organizations, in particular through the exchange of both.... radio and television programmes". Clearly, the installation along the perimeter of the FRY borders of powerful relay stations waging anti-Yugoslav propaganda with simultaneous "jamming" by military force broadcasting of Yugoslav television and radio services, constitutes a gross violation of the principle of free access to information embodied in the aforementioned documents of the OSCE, the United Nations and the Council of Europe.

Broadcasted by information agencies of NATO countries statements and declarations of some leaders of the NATO States appealing to overthrow the legally elected leadership of Yugoslavia are unlawful and most inflammatory. Moreover, such a goal has been recently presented nearly a major one from the perspective of the NATO-launched military operation against the FRY. This sort of statements cannot but be considered as a direct interference in the internal affairs of the sovereign State.

10. On April 12 a.c. the NATO aircraft hit and destroyed after two deliberate raids a passenger train which was crossing a bridge near the village of Crdelica (320 km south of Belgrade), that resulted in 10 civilians killed and 16 wounded. This information, as known, was confirmed on April 13 by W. Clark, NATO's supreme commander in Europe at a briefing at NATO headquarters in Brussels.

On April 14 a.c. the NATO planes intentionally bombed and struck two convoys of ethnic Albanian refugees, who were travelling in tractors and cars down a road between Djakovica and Prizren (southwestern part of Kosovo, Federal Republic of Yugoslavia). As a result of that brutal action estimated over 80 people were killed. The information was acknowledged by US Defence Secretary W. Cohen on April 15 before the Senate Armed Services Committee of the US Congress.

The Russian Federation identifies the above-mentioned instances as a flagrant violation by NATO countries, including the United States of America, of human rights and other humanitarian norms on the territory of the Federal Republic of Yugoslavia and recalls that in accordance with section VI, paragraph 49 of the CSCE Helsinki Document 1992 "those who violate international humanitarian law are held personally accountable".

The Russian Federation requests hereby from the United States of America information on the following: what personal responsibility has been or will be borne on those of civil and military personnel who are directly or indirectly involved in the above violations; how the United States of America estimates victims among civilian population caused by actions of NATO countries; what damage has been inflicted on the economy of the Federal Republic of Yugoslavia; what measures and when NATO members, including the United States of America, are going to undertake to cease and correct clear, gross and continuing violations of their commitments within the Human Dimension, norms of international law, as well as how NATO countries, including the United States of America, plan to reimburse economic and other damages to the Federal Republic of Yugoslavia and to its citizens after the cessation of military activities against this sovereign State-member of the OSCE.

The Permanent Mission avails itself of this opportunity to renew to the Mission of the United States of America the assurances of its highest consideration.

Vienna, April 23, 1999

[The Annex "Selected List of Enterprises and Objects of Infrastructure Destroyed or Damaged in a Result of the NATO Bombings" has been omitted.]

275. Permanent Mission of the Russian Federation to the OSCE, Statement by Russian Foreign Ministry Representative, 23 April 1999

The Russian side is consistently pursuing the course, approved by Russian Federation President Boris Yeltsin, towards achieving most fast a political settlement of the Kosovo crisis on a just and longterm basis. This work is being done along numerous vectors - from high-level bilateral contacts and mediation missions to broad activities in the field of multilateral diplomacy and the activization of the possibilities of the international organizations of which Russia is a member to bring about peace on the Balkans.

The Organization for Security and Cooperation in Europe plays a key role in that process. For the past quarter-century, special instruments for interaction in crisis situations have been worked out within the framework of that Organization. One of them - the mechanism for consultations and cooperation with respect to unusual military activities, as provided for by the 1994 Vienna document - has already been enacted by Belarus in connection with the NATO aggression on the Balkans. Russia on its part, while appraising highly and supporting the move made by Minsk, forwarded on April 21, 1999, in keeping with the mechanism adopted at the first meeting of the OSCE Council in 1991 in Berlin for consultations and cooperation with respect to emergency situations, official inquiries to the NATO member-states. In them, it states, specifically, the obvious, gross and continuing violation by the countries of the North Atlantic Treaty of at least seven of the ten founding principles of international relations set forth in the Helsinki Final Act. They include the principles of sovereign equality, respect for the rights inherent in sovereignty, non-use of force or a threat of force, the territorial integrity of states, a peaceful settlement of disputes, non-interference in internal affairs, respect for human rights, and fulfilment in good faith of international law obligations.

To be sure, it is impossible to find any international law justification of the NATO strikes. The Russian side qualifies the forcible actions with respect to the Federal Republic of Yugoslavia, undertaken in circumvention of the generally accepted and imperative norms of international law, as an aggression with the ensuing consequences of responsibility for it. All the references by NATO representatives and the Alliance member-states to Chapter VII of the U.N. Charter, an "intervention in the interest of overcoming a humanitarian catastrophe," "counteraction to the policy of genocide," etc. are far-fetched and are refuted by the first serious analysis of their correspondence to the legal norms and practice of international relations, primarily to the U.N. Charter and the decisions and obligations within the OSCE.

The developments in Yugoslavia after March 24, 1999 have shown that it was the NATO military operations that have provoked the current humanitarian catastrophe and created a truly emergency situation on the Balkans. The Russian Federation demands that NATO should stop and recall its obligations, the moral, ethical and democratic values we all have agreed to respect and follow as a basis for building a new Europe in the 21st century - a Europe which is peaceful, democratic, flourishing and free from any divisions. We hope that the addressees will give us an adequate answer within the period of 48 hours, as provided for by the Berlin mechanism. We believe that this enquiry gives the NATO member-states a chance to have a fresh look at their deeds and practically come back to the observation of the norms and principles of international law.

The setting in motion on April 23 of the OSCE human dimension mechanism should give a serious political impulse in the same direction. In keeping with the Final Act of the 1986 Vienna meeting of representatives of the CSCE member-states, the Russian side has forwarded a notification and an information enquiry in connection with the mass violations of human rights and fundamental freedoms, as well as the humanitarian obligations ensuing from the decisions and agreements reached within the CSCE/OSCE, perpetrated by NATO, its members, officials and military personnel on the territory of the Federal Republic of Yugoslavia. Specific reference was made to the facts of the destruction by NATO aircraft of a passenger train on April 12 and of two convoys of Albanian refugees on April 14, which resulted in the death of dozens of civilians. This, just as NATO's purposeful strikes on facilities where civilians were present, is in glaring contradiction with Article 3 of the Universal Declaration of Human Rights, which says: "Each person has the right to life, freedom and personal immunity." The reasoning within the Alliance that human losses are a "side damage which cannot be avoided" is unacceptable, cynical and amoral. Who in NATO has defined the limits of that "side damage" and do such limits generally exist for the Alliance?

The enquiries state, with reference to concrete international documents, the violations by NATO of such documents as a result of actions, such as the systematic destruction of Yugoslav towns and settlements, the homes of peaceful citizens, life-supporting, economic and ecological facilities in the Federal Republic of Yugoslavia. All this may lead to a full collapse of life in Yugoslavia, to new sufferings by the population, primarily elderly people, women and children. Moreover, the material base and conditions for a return of refugees and displaced persons to the place of their permanent residence are being destroyed, though it is a solution to the problem of refugees that is declared one of the main missions of the Alliance. The declarations by some leaders of the Alliance member-states who call for the removal from power of Yugoslavia's legitimately elected leaders look unlawful and highly firebranding. The media coverage of developments in Yugoslavia in the NATO countries is one-sided and biased. The damage inflicted on the country is purposefully hushed up or considerably underestimated. Simultaneously, radio and TV transmitters are being systematically damaged or destroyed on the territory of Yugoslavia in violation of the right to free access to and dissemination of information. Finally - and this arouses special concern - NATO's belligerent calls for stepping up the armed actions and continuing them to "the victorious end" are a blatant violation of Article 20 (1) of the International Covenant on Civilian and Political Rights, which declares: "All war propaganda shall be prohibited by law."

On the basis of these facts, as well as the accords that have been reached in the OSCE at the highest level, i.e. with the participation of the heads of state and government of the NATO members, to the effect "that those who violate international humanitarian rights, shall bear personal responsibility for their actions," the Russian Federation has demanded information as to what kind of responsibility has been borne or shall be borne by the persons who, directly or indirectly, are involved in the above-mentioned violations. From the NATO countries, we expect their assessments of the casualties among the civilian population as a result of the Alliance's actions and the damage that has been done to Yugoslavia's economy. We would also like to know what measures, and when the NATO members intend to take to cease and rectify the obvious gross and continuing violations of the commitments that they took upon themselves, how they plan to reimburse the economic and other losses inflicted upon Yugoslavia and its citizens after the termination of the armed actions against that sovereign state - a member of the OSCE.

Once again, this is a reminder: the Kosovo crisis, just as any other similar situation, cannot be solved by resorting to power methods. Violence breeds violence. The attainment of a lasting and just peace in the 21st century is possible only by employing peaceful means, by patient, painstaking and, if necessary, protracted political and diplomatic work. It is towards this end that Russia's foreign policy is oriented, and we appeal to all the rest of the members of the international community to work towards this objective.

276. Statement of the Ministry of Foreign Affairs, 14 May 1999[1]

Russia, who Repeatedly Warned the NATO Administration about the Gravest Consequences of Military Actions against Yugoslavia, Decidedly Condemns the new Crime of the Alliance

For one and a half months the NATO air force has been carrying out an unparalleled bombardment of Yugoslavian territory, where peaceful citizens have become ominously the victims of such actions. The number of casualties exceeded 1200 people.

Several days ago the world was shocked by the barbaric bombing of the Embassy of China in Belgrade and by the death of its officials. Today we were confronted with another terrible tragedy, occurring in the Kosovo village of Korisa (Prisren-community). As a result of the use of the forbidden so called cluster bombs by the NATO aviation, at least 50 People, mainly women, children and senior adults were killed there and more than 100 were injured.

Russia, who repeatedly warned the NATO administration about the gravest consequences of military actions against Yugoslavia, vehemently condemns this new crime of the Alliance. We summon upon NATO strategists immediately to stop this insanity. The settlement of the Kosovo problem is only possible at the negotiating table.

277. Statement of the Ministry of Foreign Affairs, 20 May 1999[1]

The building of the neuro-surgical department in the clinical center of 'Dragisha Mishovich' was destroyed, and the pediatric and gynaecologic departments considerably damaged by the direct hit of two rockets during the course of NATO's most massive air-raid in Belgrade last night. As a result of the bombings three patients were killed and two women and several medical employees injured. The NATO bombs have also damaged the residence of the Swedish Ambassador to FRY.

Russia declares once again its condemnation of these felonious actions by the air force of the Alliance. The gravest consequences of the bomb assaults for the Yugoslavian population have become an everyday reality. The air raid on the Clinical Center in Belgrade is a most grave violation of the Geneva Conventions on protection of victims of war.

We protest such actions and once again call upon the administration of NATO and all the state-members of the Alliance to change their mind and seriously consider political negotiations aimed at the settlement of the Kosovo problem. We are convinced - there is no alternative, and this conclusion the NATO strategist must also clearly realize.

---

[1] *Unofficial translation by Mr. Sergey Lagodinsky, Institute for Public International Law, University of Göttingen.*

7.6 CHINA

278. Vice Premier and Foreign Minister Qian Qichen on the Question of Kosovo (FRY), PRO 4/98, 13 March 1998

[Parts not referring to the situation in Kosovo have been omitted.]

Question: What is China's position on the question of Kosovo? Now some countries are attempting to put this question, an internal matter of Yugoslavia, under UN Security Council discussion, in the absence of such a request from the Federal Republic of Yugoslavia. How does China view such an act?

Answer: We are very much concerned about the bloodshed in Kosovo. Kosovo is part of the territory of Yugoslavia. The Government of the Federal Republic of Yugoslavia and the Government of Serbia have the responsibility as well as the capability to handle it properly. I am of the view that this issue falls within the sovereignty of Yugoslavia and is essentially its internal matter. At the Balkans where ethnic relations are very complicated, the legitimate rights and interests of all ethnic groups should be duly protected, and at the same time, cautions should be exercised to guard against splittist activities by extremist elements. Imprudence on this matter may trigger regional chaos, or even conflict, plaguing large areas in the region. We hope that measures to be taken by the international community on this matter will, on the one hand, be conducive to peace and stability in the region, and on the other hand, avoid interfering in the internal affairs of a certain country.

Question: Now some people believe that arms embargo on Yugoslavia can at the very least prevent further bloodshed. Is China going to vote against such an embargo?

Answer: Arms embargo can be one way out, because weapons are seen everywhere in the region now. During the chaos not long ago in Albania, almost everybody had a weapon. That had been extremely dangerous. The European Union is now moving towards an arms embargo, but this question is so far not discussed by the UN. We believe that UN discussion of this matter is not very appropriate. We can well foresee that arms embargo on Yugoslavia will not by itself solve the whole problem. A more suitable solution must be figured out to resolve this issue through peaceful means, instead of with bloodshed.

279. Statement by Foreign Ministry Spokesman, PR 12/98, 25 October 1998

China's Foreign Ministry Spokesman Tang Guoqiang said on 25 October that China will continue to work with the international community on a peaceful settlement to the Kosovo issue. Some progress has recently been made on the Kosovo issue and China understands and welcomes the agreement reached between Yugoslavia and the parties concerned, Tang said. However, certain regional organizations have unilaterally decided on a military action without consulting the UN Security Council. This irresponsible action, he added, is not in line with the actual conditions and runs counter to the principles outlined in the UN Charter and in international laws and sets a dangerous precedent in international relations.

In principle, China does not oppose the Security Council passing a technical resolution to endorse the agreement reached between Yugoslavia and the parties concerned, Tang said, but the draft proposed by some countries includes authorizing the use of force against Yugoslavia and interferring in the internal affairs of a sovereign state. China has made it clear that it will not accept the contents and has tabled amendment proposals, Tang said, and China has pointed out that it will have to veto the draft if the authorization of force is not deleted. China's proposals were adopted on the whole, he said, so it did not prevent the draft resolution from passing, although some of the wording is still unsatisfactory, Tang said.

China reiterates that the sovereignty and territorial integrity of a country should not be infringed upon and its right to choose its own path of development should be respected, he said. China opposes any interference in another country's internal affairs under any pretext whatever and the use of force or the threat of use of force in international affairs.

280. Ambassador Qin Huasun, Permanent Representative of PRC Talks to the Press at the UN on the Question of Kosovo, 23 March 1999

Recently, the development of events in Kosovo is causing concerns and worries to all peace-loving peoples around the world. The question of Kosovo is an internal matter of the Federal Republic of Yugoslavia (FRY). The Chinese Government believes that it should be settled politically through dialogues, on the basis of respect for the sovereignty and territorial integrity of FRY and the guarantee of the legitimate rights and interests of the ethnic groups in the region. Any military action against FRY without the authorization of UN Security Council will be a severe violation of the UN Charter and established principles of international law. Such action will not be accepted by the international community. We urge the relevant parties to adopt a restrained, patient and flexible attitude and continue to seek a proper and fair settlement of the issue of Kosovo through negotiations.

7.7 JAPAN

281. Statement by Foreign Minister Masahiko Koumura, 25 March 1999

1. Despite the tireless diplomatic efforts by the United States and various European countries, an agreement could not be reached at the Paris peace talks on Kosovo because of the uncompromising attitude of the government of the Federal Republic of Yugoslavia. It is extremely regrettable that that has led to the current situation.

2. The government of the Federal Republic of Yugoslavia adamantly refuses to accept the proposed peace agreement while at the same time continuing to take actions in violation of the relevant United Nations Security Council Resolutions. Japan understands NATO's use of force as measures that had to be taken to prevent humanitarian catastrophe of further increase in victims. Japan is presently following the development of the situation with great concern.

3. It is essential to have a peace agreement between the two parties, the government of the Federal Republic of Yugoslavia and the Kosovo Albanians, to ultimately resolve this issue. Japan strongly urges the government of the Federal Republic of Yugoslavia to immediately accept the peace agreement proposed by the Contact Group.

282. Archives on Press Conferences by the Press Secretary, 27 April 1999

1. The challenge facing the international community in Kosovo is to put an end to the systematic repression and massive forced expulsion of the civilian population in Kosovo as soon as possible, and to change this region from a region of war and confusion to that of peace and prosperity.

2. In order to meet these challenges, it is necessary to first realize an early political solution to the Kosovo crisis. United Nations Secretary-General Kofi Annan has already announced the conditions to end hostilities in Kosovo. Japan strongly hopes that the government of the Federal Republic of Yugoslavia will accept the international community's demands as reflected by the Secretary-General's statement. The acceptance will bring about a suspension of NATO's use of military force and pave a path to peace. As a member of the G8, Japan will continue to contribute to achieving a political solution.

3. Japan has decided to provide assistance worth approximately 200 million dollars, taking into account the report prepared by the Ministry of Foreign Affairs' survey mission. The details are as follows.

(1) First, for refugee assistance, Japan will add 25 million dollars to the 15 million dollars which has already been announced and provide 40 million dollars in total to the United Nations High Commissioner for Refugees (UNHCR) and other international organizations. Furthermore, as material assistance, Japan will provide 10,000 blankets and 5,000 sleeping mats to the United Nations High Commissioner for Refugees (UNHCR) on top of the 1,000 tents that have already been provided.

(2) Second, as assistance to the neighboring countries which have been accepting a large number of refugees, Japan will provide 30 million dollars worth of grant aid to Macedonia and Albania. Japan will additionally provide 30 million dollars, which will make the total amount to be provided to these countries 60 million dollars over the next two years. In addition to financial assistance, Japan will send medical specialists and other support staff and also provide related medical equipment, as assistance to medical and other fields.

(3) Third, once a peace agreement is reached, Japan will provide approximately 100 million dollars to the "Human Security Fund" at the UN, initiated by Prime Minister Obuchi, and to other Funds to primarily assist the rehabilitation of Kosovo and the return of refugees.

(4) Fourth, for both the government and Japanese NGOs to act in unison, Japan will provide financial support to assistance activities carried out by Japanese NGOs. Japan will also provide assistance which will enable Japanese volunteers to participate in activities conducted by international humanitarian organizations.

4. The situation in Kosovo remains fluid. Japan will consider further assistance measures as the situation develops in the future.

7.8 OTHERS

283. El Salvador, Statement, Press Release 82/99, San Salvador, 24 March 1999[1]

The government of the Republic of El Salvador deplores that the intransigence and the lack of compliance of the President of the FRY, Slobodan Milosevic, has forced NATO to resort to force in the Balkan peninsula.

In this respect, El Salvador supports the military actions, which NATO has employed with the aim to prevent any further aggression, repression and death as well as to guarantee peace and security in the zone.

Likewise, the Salvadorian government deplores that the diplomatic efforts and negotiations in Rambouillet have failed; nonetheless, the government recognizes that, if the international community does not act by military means in this moment, this will only support the continual killing of innocent persons and the forced displacement for racial reasons; facts that must be inacceptable at the beginning of the new century.

The Salvadorian government is confident that the actions which have begun today will allow the establishment of a durable and secure peace in the region.

284. India, Official Spokesman's Statement, New Delhi, 24 March 1999

The Government of India has closely been following developments in Kosovo. It recalls its statement of October 9, 1998 and reiterates that the sovereignty and territorial integrity of the international border of the Federal Republic of Yugoslavia is inviolable. That must be fully respected by all states.

We are of the firm conviction that the resolution of this crisis can only be through peaceful means; through consultation and dialogue, and not through either confrontation or any military action, unilateral or otherwise. In this regard we wish to reaffirm commitments to the UN Charter, which clearly stipulates that no enforcement actions shall be undertaken under regional arrangements without the authorisation of the Security Council.

285. Mexico, Statement of Foreign Minister, NUM. 121/99, Tlatelolco, D.F., 24 March 1999[2]

In relation to the air strikes which NATO has commenced today against Serbian targets, the Foreign Office has stated its concern about the fact that no peaceful solution has been found for the differences that exist between the parties involved in the Kosovo conflict. Likewise, it deplores the recourse to the use of force in the Balkans without the explicit consent of the UN Security Council - the organ responsible for the maintenance of international peace and security.

The Mexican Government expresses its firm conviction that the primary instruments for the solution of a conflict must be dialogue and negotiations and it calls upon all parties to resume the pending negotiations as soon as possible in order to reach a lasting and solid peace, which is founded on the respect for the human rights of all ethnic groups in the region as well as on the territorial integrity of states.

286. The Philippines, Statement, Press Release No. 74-99, 24 March 1999

The Government of the Republic of the Philippines has always viewed the situation in Kosovo with deep concern. For this reason, we have welcomed all efforts to mediate a lasting peace in that embattled province. We also note the grave humanitarian situation and crisis in Kosovo, where over 300,000 people have already been displaced from their homes over the past few months.

---

[1] *Unofficial translation by Dr. J. Martinez Soria, Institute for Public International Law, University of Göttingen.*

[2] *Unofficial translation by Dr. J. Martinez Soria, Institute for Public International Law, University of Göttingen.*

The recent increase in violence in that province, coupled with the decision by NATO to conduct military operations against Yugoslavia, lead us to view the situation with increasing concern. We therefore hope that NATO's action shall not lead to an escalation of violence, which has already claimed so many innocent lives in Kosovo.

We continue to hold the firm belief that peace should still be mediated in Kosovo and, in this regard, strongly urge all parties to this conflict to negotiate a political solution.

287. Egypt, Statement by Foreign Minister Moussa, Cairo, 25 March 1999

Foreign Minister Amre Moussa stated today that Egypt has been following the developments in Kosovo with deep concern. Commenting on recent developments in Kosovo, the Foreign Minister iterated that no people, government or, indeed, any human being could accept what has been happening to individuals and the people of Kosovo. He added that such a breech of human rights is a grave and dangerous matter that is both unjustifiable and unacceptable. Moussa added that dealing with this issue falls within the jurisdiction of the United Nations and the Security Council.

Moussa pointed out that it was both necessary and essential for the parties to accept mediation and the proposed initiatives for resolving this situation and that Serb refusal to do so has led to the current situation. He added that Egypt continues to follow developments and hopes for an end to this serious problem through the acceptance of the settlement presented to both parties and was accepted by the Kosovo Albanians. Moussa reiterated that a negotiated agreement should be reached and that such an agreement is the only way of resolving this problem that has become one of the most grave human rights problems in Europe.

288. India, Official Spokesman's Statement, New Delhi, 25 March 1999

The Government of India expresses its serious concern over NATO air strikes on the territory of the Federal Republic of Yugoslavia. Such unilateral moves, even if taken as regional initiatives, but without due authorisation of the United Nations Security Council, seriously undermine the authority of the entire United Nations System. The Government holds that the air strikes are in violation of the UN Charter, also that they amount to interfering in the internal affairs of a country.

The present crisis in Kosovo can only be resolved through peaceful means and a solution found within the framework of the national sovereignty and territorial integrity of the Federal Republic of Yugoslavia. The Government of India also expresses its concern about the possibility of the conflict spreading. Besides, this demonstration of NATO's extra territorial engagement is a development that can only cause anxiety.

We would urge that all military actions be brought to a halt; that peace be given a chance; and that the Federal Republic of Yugoslavia, a fellow member of the Non-Aligned, be enabled to resolve its internal issues internally.

289. Republic of Korea, Comment by a Foreign Ministry Official, 25 March 1999

1. The Government of the Republic of Korea regrets that despite diplomatic efforts for a peaceful resolution of the situation in Kosovo, the failure of the related party to accept the Interim Peace Agreement proposed by the Contact Group has led to today's military action.

2. The ROK Government hopes that peace and stability will be established in Kosovo with the acceptance of the Agreement by the related party without delay.

3. The ROK Government expresses its concern over the safety and well-being of the civilian people in Kosovo.

290. Rio Group, Communiqué, 25 March 1999[1]

The countries members of the Rio Group express their anxiety about the commencement of air strikes by the North Atlantic Treaty Organization against Serbian military targets and, in particular, their concern that no peaceful means of solving, in conformity with international law, the existing dispute among the various parties to the conflict in Kosovo has been found.

The Rio Group therefore calls on all parties to resume, as soon as possible, talks with a view to achieving a comprehensive and final settlement with a view to re-establishing a stable and lasting peace based on respect for the human rights of all ethnic groups and minorities in the region, and on the territorial integrity of States.

The Rio Group also regrets the recourse to the use of force in the Balkan region in contravention of the provisions of Article 53, paragraph 1, and Article 54 of the Charter of the United Nations, which state "... no enforcement action shall be taken under regional arrangements or by regional agencies without the authorization of the Security Council" and "the Security Council shall at all times be kept fully informed of activities undertaken or in contemplation under regional arrangements or by regional agencies for the maintenance of international peace and security".

291. Singapore, Response by the Foreign Minister to Questions from Journalists in Rome, 25 March 1999

It is unfortunate that a negotiated diplomatic solution could not be reached to resolve the Kosovo crisis. We urge the Yugoslav government to put an end to the crisis immediately by working with all the parties concerned towards a peaceful resolution of the conflict. The people of Kosovo have suffered greatly and Singapore would like to see a quick end to the conflict.

292. South Africa, Statement Issued by the Department of Foreign Affairs, Pretoria, 25 March 1999

The South African Government has noted with grave concern the current military action against the sovereign state of the Federal Republic of Yugoslavia. This is in violation of the United Nations Charter and accepted norms of international law and it has exacerbated the situation in the Balkans.

The South African Government would like to stress the need to resolve disputes by peaceful means and in this context it strongly emphasises the primary responsibility of the United Nations Security Council in the maintenance of international peace and security. The erosion of the United Nations Charter and the authority of the United Nations Security Council cannot be tolerated by the international community.

The South African Government further calls on all parties to the conflict to respect United Nations Security Council resolutions 1199 and 1203 and to actively explore a diplomatic solution in this regard.

293. Israel, Foreign Minister Sharon, Statement, Communicated by Foreign Minister's Spokesman, 2 April 1999

Foreign Minister Ariel Sharon, today (Friday), 2.4.99, clarified his position that the terrible human tragedy taking place in Yugoslavia, and particularly in Kosovo, must be drawn to an immediate close.

Sharon added that he takes a harsh view of all acts of murder, injury or deportation directed against innocent civilians. "As steadfast friends of the United States, we expect that the United States and the NATO forces will do everything possible in order to end the suffering of the innocent, and to bring about the resumption of negotiations between the parties."

---

[1] UN Doc. A/53/884 - S/1999/347, Annex, 26 March 1999.

The Foreign Minister added that, as in the past, Israel is rendering assistance to the casualties. "This is our moral responsibility as Jews, and the consistent policy of the State of Israel."

294. Malaysia, Statement by Datuk Seri Syed Hamid Albar, Minister of Foreign Affairs, Kuala Lumpur, 2 April 1999

Malaysia is gravely concerned at the worsening situation on the ground in Kosovo arising out of the continued refusal by the regime in Belgrade to engage seriously in a search for a political solution. Its continued military operations and repressive policies against the civilian population in Kosovo are equally unacceptable. These actions represent a continued affront to the provisions of relevant UN Security Council resolutions and international standards of civilised behaviour.

2. The unfolding situation has become a humanitarian catastrophe, involving crimes of genocide and ethnic cleansing. Malaysia would like to reiterate that the International Criminal Tribunal for the Former Yugoslavia be mandated to try crimes committed on the territory of Kosovo, including those perpetrated in the current campaign of terror staged by the Belgrade regime against the people of Kosovo.

3. The Malaysian Permanent Representative in the United Nations has, over the weekend, been working closely with other members of the OIC Contact Group on Bosnia and Herzegovina and Kosovo in New York to address the tragic situation in Kosovo. The Contact Group has expressed alarm at the continuing pattern of well organized, armed and systematic violence against the ethnic Albanian population of Kosovo. These include summary executions, destruction of civilian housing and other inhuman acts against women, children and the elderly.

4. As a follow-up to the meeting of the Contact Group in New York, I have this morning spoken with the Foreign Minister of Iran, as Iran is the current Chairman of the OIC, on the deteriorating situation unfolding in Kosovo. We have agreed that a Ministerial-level meeting of the OIC Contact Group should meet as soon as possible to be seized with the situation and to exchange views on the best ways to achieve a political solution and bring an end to the tragedy in Kosovo.

5. The atrocities being perpetrated against the people in Kosovo had been nothing short of tragic. It is equally tragic that diplomacy did not succeed in finding a peaceful resolution to the Kosovo issue and bringing an end to the suffering of the people there. While Malaysia accepts the fact that urgent action was needed to address the humanitarian catastrophe which had befallen the people of Kosovo, we hope the UN Security Council will be allowed ultimately to address this breach of international peace and take appropriate action.

6. The humanitarian dimensions of the Kosovo saga is monumental. The suffering of the people there is immense. Their needs are great and numerous. These must be addressed.

295. Islamic Conference on Bosnia and Herzegovina and Kosovo, Statement and Declaration by the Contact Group of the Organization of the Islamic Conference (OIC) on Bosnia and Herzegovina and Kosovo, 7 April 1999[1]

The Ministers for Foreign Affairs of the OIC Contact Group on Bosnia and Herzegovina and Kosova, meeting on 7 April 1999 in Geneva to review the recent developments in Kosova:

- Guided by the principles and purposes of the Charter of the United Nations, the Charter of the Organization of the Islamic Conference, the Universal Declaration of Human Rights, the International Covenants on Human Rights, the Convention on the Rights of the Child, the Geneva Conventions of 12 August 1949 and the Additional Protocols of 1977, as well as other instruments of international humanitarian law;

- Take note of the statement of the OIC Contact Group on Bosnia and Herzegovina and Kosova in New York;

- Urge the immediate implementation of the elements contained in the draft resolution of OIC on the situation of human rights in Kosova presented before the fifty-fifth session of the Commission on Human Rights which:
  - Stipulates that the Kosovars must be allowed to freely determine their own political future;
  - Strongly condemns the policy of ethnic cleansing perpetrated by the Serbian authorities against the Albanian Kosovars;
  - Demands an immediate halt to all repressive actions undertaken in Kosova by the Serbian authorities and the immediate withdrawal of the Serbian military and paramilitary forces from Kosova;
  - Calls upon the international community to bring to international criminal justice the perpetrators of ethnic cleansing and all other crimes against humanity in Kosova;
  - Demands also that the Serbian authorities immediately sign and implement the Rambouillet Accords;
  - Appeals to the international community to extend all humanitarian assistance to the refugees and internally displaced persons inside and outside Kosova;

- Regret that the Security Council has been unable to discharge its responsibility in this case, in accordance with the Charter of the United Nations, and reiterate that the Security Council has the primary responsibility for the maintenance of international peace and security and that, in carrying out its duties under this responsibility, the Security Council shall act on behalf of the Members of the United Nations;

- Express their solidarity with the Kosovars and Bosniac national minorities in Sanjak region;

- Decide to establish contacts with all parties concerned at the appropriate time and further enhance their cooperation with the International Contact Group and its members as well as Kosova political leadership with the view to promote a peaceful, just and lasting settlement of the Kosova crisis and to dispatch a high-level delegation for talks with them;

- Undertake to contribute to the monitoring and peacekeeping operations in Kosova as part of international peacekeeping effort;

- Appreciate all the assistance being provided by the OIC countries to Kosovars and refugees, including the receipt of thousands of refugees from Kosova and provision of humanitarian assistance to them;

- While appreciating the efforts being made, appeal to the international community to extend all humanitarian assistance to the refugees and internally displaced persons in and outside Kosova with the view to alleviate their suffering, and request the neighbouring countries and the international community to continue to receive the Kosova refugees;

- Underscore the right of all refugees and internally displaced persons to return to their homes in safety and honour, preventing any measures taken by the Serbian authorities to evacuate the region of its original people and, in this context, demand that compensation and reparation be given to all the victims of the Serbian repression by the Serbian authorities;

- Decide to urgently mobilize humanitarian assistance for the Kosovar victims, including refugees and internally displaced persons;

- Decide also to set up a coordination group of the Permanent Representatives of the OIC Contact Group in Geneva to coordinate OIC assistance to Kosova and interact with the humanitarian agencies involved to be briefed on actions taken by the concerned agencies;

- Strongly appeal to all OIC members and to the international community as a whole to stay firm to all their commitments regarding the full implementation of all aspects of the peace process in Bosnia and Herzegovina, particularly unimpeded implementation of annex VII - Return of refugees and displaced persons to their homes of origin;

- Support the present efforts of the Office of the High Representative and the Stabilization Force to protect the peace process in Bosnia and Herzegovina in all its aspects.

---

[1] UN Doc. S/1999/394, Annex, 7 April 1999.

296. Malaysia, Speech by YB Datuk Dr. Leo Michael Toyad, Deputy Minister of Foreign Affairs at the Emergency Ministerial Meeting of the OIC Contact Group, Geneva, 7 April 1999

His Excellency Dr. Kamal Kharrazi, Minister of Foreign Affairs of the Islamic Republic of Iran and Chairman of the OIC Ministerial Level Contact Group, Honourable Foreign Ministers, His Excellency Dr. Azzeddine Laraki, Secretary General of the OIC, Ladies and Gentemen,

Malaysia views with great importance this meeting which has been convened on the initiative of His Excellency President Khatami of the Islamic Republic of Iran. This is no ordinary meeting. It is intended as a fully considered, timely and effective response towards arresting mankind's greatest tragedy which is unfolding in Kosovo.

Foreign Minister Datuk Seri Syed Hamid Albar has asked me to convey his deepest apologies for his inability to be present personally at this important meeting. If not for his prior commitments involving official visits to two other brother countries, he would have been coming out with ideas and initiatives that would stop a most despicable and murderous affront to humanity.

Malaysia does not view the acts of cruelty, violence and crime against humanity that are being perpetrated in Kosovo as acts against any specific group, ethnic or religious sect, but as one against humanity.

The atrocities being committed to secure such hegemony have been nothing short of tragic. It is equally tragic that diplomacy has, thus far, failed to find a peaceful resolution to the Kosovo issue or to end the suffering of the Kosovar people.

Malaysia has consistently advocated a peaceful resolution of international disputes through negotiations and non-use of force. In this specific case, we are of the view that urgent action involving some force has been necessary. We trust that beyond this phase the UN Security Council will be allowed ultimately to address this breach of international peace.

Present day events in Kosovo suggest that Slobodan Milosevic is bent, against all the voices of reason and even the vexatious Nato strikes, to reverse history and indulge in a virtual policy of earth-scorching to eliminate a people from their rightful place of abode.

A fully armed, well-equipped and well planned operation inspired and led by Milosevic has been allowed to take its course without any resistance. The reason for the lack of resistance is not a lack of will on the part of the Kosovar people. They have trusted in the international community and have lived in peace without equipping themselves for this most horrendous eventuality.

Malaysia is encouraged that the international community, including OIC member countries, is determined to take a united, unambiguous and clear stand to bring about some modicum of normalcy to Kosovo. Clearly there are no other options. An unmistakable message has to be sent to Milosevic that this murderous rampage must stop.

The message is that the intenational community will not allow this brutal dictator to get on with this vile ethnic war. Over one million Kosovar Albanians have been either forced out of their country or are internally displaced persons.

The Belgrade regime has long lost its credibility. Its recent offer of a unilateral ceasefire is certainly not enough. This meeting should send a clear message that there must be a total and complete withdrawal of all Serbian police and other security forces from Kosovo; there must also be guarantees to be put in place to permit for the stationing of an international monitoring and military force, and there must be clear arrangements that will allow for the creation of conditions for the return of all refugees and other internally displaced persons to their homes in Kosovo in safety and honour, and to rebuild their lives.

Albanian Kosovo leaders, including Ibrahim Rogova, presently held hostage by the genocidal regime must be allowed to leave Kosovo to meet with members of the international community. Any so-called agreement extracted under those circumstances cannot be considered as valid.

The OIC and the international community should renew and continue to reiterate these demands.

The Belgrade regime after having committed this unforgettable and unforgivable crime against humanity, cannot now be given the opportunity to continue to hood-wink the international community over some dubious call for settlement of the conflict. That initiative for a comprehensive, lasting and durable settlement must remain with the international community.

Malaysia, in the meantime, remains concerned that over 1 million people of Kosovo have been forced to face the ravages of the elements as they seek shelter in the neighbouring countries or within Kosovo. The speed and scale of the refugee flow and the situation of the internally displaced persons is indeed mind-boggling.

Malaysia urges the international community, and particularly OIC member countries, to contribute generously towards providing immediate relief to these refugees and displaced persons. Malaysia, on its part, has also initiated a fund to coordinate assistance on a countrywide level.

Excellencies, Ladies and Gentlemen,

We in Malaysia are convinced that the situation in Kosovo is a most dangerous and threatening one. It is a crime against humanity. The worst may yet to come. It calls for concerted and clear action. This is not the time for declarations and exhortations. What we need is immediate action to stop the madness that Milosevic had unleashed on an unsuspecting, unarmed and most peaceful people. I am confident that with the combined resolve and effort that all our countries are making this madness can be stopped.

Thank you.

297. Pakistan, Statement by the Foreign Minister at the Emergency Ministerial Meeting of the OIC Contact Group, Geneva, 7 April 1999

Mr. Chairman, Honourable Secretary General and Excellencies,

As we gather here today in an emergency session of the Contact Group, a human tragedy is taking place in the centre of Europe. Even before the close of this "bloody century", we are witnessing, once again, in this continent, systematic and deliberate policies of hatred and intolerance aimed at decimating and uprooting a whole community for its religious beliefs causing great human suffering and misery.

I should like to thank the Islamic Republic of Iran for its leadership in calling for this emergency session. I also thank the OIC Secretary General for his letter addressed to the Yugoslav President conveying the anger and indignation of the Muslim world at the policies and actions of the Serbian authorities in Kosovo. The Kosovo situation is of direct concern to the OIC as the victims of the tragedy are primarily Muslims.

Prime Minister Nawaz Sharif is of the view that all Muslim countries must take immediate steps to bring to an end this continuing tragedy which not only affects a people but also violates fundamental principles of justice and human rights. In a letter to President Khatami, the Prime Minister had called for urgent consultations so that the OIC may address the Kosovo crisis effectively, and thereby facilitate a quick end to the Kosovo tragedy. We hope today's meeting will lead to the OIC playing an active role in bringing the Kosovo crisis to an end.

Mr. Chairman,

We have been following the recent developments in Kosovo with increasing concern and dismay. The Serbian repression of the Kosovo Albanian Muslims, who constitute 90 percent of the population of Kosovo intensified since Kosovo's autonomy was revoked in 1990. The Kosovo Albanians launched a legitimate movement against Serbian repression a few years ago. The Security Council in successive resolutions expressed concern over the Kosovar situation, called for cessation

International Reactions to the Crisis

of hostilities and a political solution and authorized OSCE to monitor the situation. The Security Council resolutions and other international efforts for a peaceful solution were thwarted by Serbian intransigence.

While their desire for independence has been clearly enunciated by their leadership, the Kosovo people, nevertheless, accepted the Rambouillet Agreement brokered by the six nation Contact Group. The Serbians refused to accept the Agreement. Following the failure of the efforts by the Contact Group for a political solution, the NATO air strikes are being carried-out to prevent further violations of human rights in Kosovo and a humanitarian catastrophe. The Serbs, however, remain undeterred. The Serbian forces have launched a massive and planned campaign of repression, killing, and ethnic cleansing in Kosovo.

There is documented evidence of the pre-meditated and systematic manner in which the Serbian authorities have carried out their policy of ethnic cleansing, ethnic engineering and identity elimination. The Serbians obviously only want the land and not the people. The trainloads of people arriving in Macedonia and the thousands pouring into Albania, after being ordered at gunpoint to leave their homes and hearths, is happening before the world's eyes. Thousands are stranded in a no-man's land with no shelter, little food and increasing inability of the host countries to receive them. More than one third of the Kosovar population has been forced out of its country. The humanitarian situation can no longer be described as a crisis - it is a humanitarian catastrophe. In this context, we deeply appreciate the efforts made by the neighbouring countries and the international community for providing sanctuary to the Kosovars.

While those fleeing from Serbian repression into neighbouring countries continue to suffer, the fate of those left behind may be worse. Their physical safety is in doubt. They are left confronted with the terrible choice of losing their lives or fleeing from their ancestral lands. The existence of the Kosovars as a people is under threat. According to western military accounts, the Serbs may be only a few days from achieving their objective of "cleansing" the entire region of its Muslim inhabitants. The Serbian policy of ethnic cleansing is so comprehensive and premeditated that in order to prevent the return of refugees, their identity papers including even the number plates of the vehicles have been retained at the Kosovo border by the Serbian forces.

The international community has responded to the Kosovo crisis through diplomatic efforts, and now through military strikes. All efforts have yet failed to stop the genocidal policies of the Serbian authorities. The NATO strikes have also proved insufficient thus far. The OIC must play an effective role diplomatically and, if necessary, in mobilizing international consensus for other means to address this humanitarian catastrophe. The OIC was able to manifest its solidarity with the people of Bosnia Herzegovina. Kosovo is yet another test case of our ability to assist our brethren who are the victims of violence and aggression.

The OIC can play a role in the humanitarian, political and military areas. I would like to submit for consideration of the meeting some specific suggestions in all these areas.

One, in order to deal with the immediate humanitarian crisis facing the Kosovars, a coordination group of our Permanent Representatives in Geneva should be set-up to inter-act with the agencies involved, especially the UNHCR. The Coordination Group should be briefed of the actions taken by the concerned agencies. It should also act as an assistance mobilization group to deal with the immediate humanitarian crisis.

Two, the OIC should offer to contribute experts to investigate human rights violations of the Kosovars. These violations should be promptly and comprehensively documented so as to bring to justice the perpetrators of the crimes against humanity.

Three, the OIC must categorically come forward to express solidarity with the people of Kosovo, demanding immediate acceptance of the Rambouillet accords by Belgrade. Further delay and the continuation of Serb atrocities will seriously erode the validity of the Accords. The OIC must assist the international community in ensuring that a solution acceptable to the Kosovars is found. The solution must ensure the return of the refugees and returnees to their homes in safety and honour, and include assurances of reparations and compensation to all the victims.

Four, the OIC Contact Group should coordinate with the Kosovar representatives to ascertain the assistance that can be provided to them in their diplomatic efforts to achieve a just political settlement. For this purpose, it should also interact with the Western Contact Group on behalf of the OIC countries.

Five, demarches must be made on behalf of the OIC Contact Group in all capitals of members of the Security Council. The Security Council must carry out its principal responsibility of maintenance of peace and security in the world.

Six, Prime Minister Nawaz Sharif has suggested to President Khatami that a high level mission of the OIC should visit Brussels and Moscow to urge for action to end the Kosovo tragedy. It is essential that we also maintain close contacts both with members of NATO as well as with the Russian Federation which exercises considerable influence with the Serb authorities. In addition, we believe that our contact group in Geneva should also visit the neighbouring countries to examine the humanitarian situation and make concrete suggestions to alleviate the sufferings of the people.

Seven, if the Serb repression and brutal campaign at pushing the Kosovars out of their homeland continues, the OIC should consider how it can supplement the on-going military effort to stop the Serb aggression against the Kosovar people. OIC should ask the UN Security Council to take effective action. If the situation demands, Pakistan will be ready to commit its military troops as part of an international peace keeping effort.

Eight, the Islamic Ummah must come together in assisting the victims of the tragedy through the Hilal-e-Ahmar and other humanitarian agencies. We should immediately despatch relief goods, food, medicines and doctors to the region to help the refugees.

Pakistan has already sent a plane load of relief goods, mainly tents and blankets, for the Kosovar refugees in Albania. We have decided to follow it up with further consignments of relief goods. We will also send a contingent of Doctors and medical personnel to the area to help the refugees.

Mr. Chairman,

The Kosovars need our help and assistance at this tragic moment in their history. We cannot be passive spectators while our Kosovar brothers are being killed and brutally expelled from their homeland. We cannot allow the elimination of an entire Muslim community. It is the hope of my Government that the OIC will respond effectively to this grave challenge facing the Muslim world.

298. Movement of Non-Aligned Countries, Statement, Geneva, 9 April 1999[1]

The Non-Aligned Movement, reaffirming the Movement's commitment to the sovereignty, territorial integrity and political independence of all States, and reaffirming the Non-Aligned Movement's principles and the sanctity of the Charter of the United Nations, is deeply alarmed at the worsening crisis in Kosovo, Federal Republic of Yugoslavia, and the Balkan region.

The Non-Aligned Movement reaffirms that the primary responsibility for the maintenance of international peace and security rests with the United Nations Security Council.

The Non-Aligned Movement is deeply concerned by the deteriorating humanitarian situation in Kosovo, and other parts of the Federal Republic of Yugoslavia, and the displacement, both internal and to neighbouring countries, of vast numbers of the Kosovo civilian population. In this regard, the Non-Aligned Movement urges the Secretary-General to intensify the role of the United Nations in alleviating the

---
[1] UN Doc. S/1999/451, Annex, 21 April 1999.

suffering of the displaced persons and refugees who are fleeing Kosovo, and to investigate all abuses of human rights.

The Non-Aligned Movement calls for an immediate cessation of all hostilities, and the swift and safe return of all refugees and displaced persons.

The Non-Aligned Movement firmly believes that the urgent resumption of diplomatic efforts, under the auspices of the United Nations and the relevant Security Council resolutions, 1199 (1998) and 1203 (1998), constitutes the only basis for a peaceful, just and equitable solution to the conflict.

299. Sri Lanka, Ministry of Foreign Affairs, Press Release, 16 April 1999

The Government of Sri Lanka views with deep concern the deteriorating situation in Kosovo and other parts of the Federal Republic of Yugoslavia, and particularly the reports concerning the practice of ethnic cleansing and the contrived exodus of civilians based on the unacceptable concepts of ethnic exclusiveness and secession. Sri Lanka deplores these practiced whenever and whenever they occur, not least because a ruthless terrorist group, the LTTE, has subjected people of different ethnic and religious communities in Sri Lanka to such abhorrent practices aimed at achieving an ethnically segregated separate state.

In view of the grave humanitarian situation in Kosovo, Sri Lanka voted for the resolution on the situation in Kosovo, which was adopted early this week at the ongoing session of the Commission o Human Rights in Geneva. The resolution calls for a series of strong measures to address, stabilize and resolve the situation. Sri Lanka, as a member of the Non-Aligned Movement, also believes that the struggle against terrorism would be most effective when carried out in pursuance of the collective will of the international community, in full conformity with the principles of the UN Charter and respect for the sovereignty and territorial integrity of all States.

300. Islamic Conference on Bosnia and Herzegovina and Kosovo, Statement and Declaration by the Contact Group of the Organization of the Islamic Conference on Bosnia and Herzegovina and Kosovo, 22 April 1999[1]

Recalling the Declaration of the Ministerial Meeting of the OIC Contact Group on Bosnia and Herzegovina and Kosova adopted on 7 April 1999 in Geneva (S/1999/394, annex), the OIC Contact Group expresses support for the proposals of the Secretary-General of 9 April 1999, as contained in S/1999/402, concerning the deeply distressing tragedy in Kosova and in which the Secretary-General called upon the Yugoslav authorities to undertake five commitments to allow for a lasting political solution to be found for the crisis in Kosova through diplomacy.

The OIC Contact Group welcomes the fact that, in the informal consultations of the Security Council on 19 April 1999, the Secretary-General reiterated the commitments he had sought from the Yugoslav authorities and tried "to promote consensus in the Security Council" with a view to enabling the United Nations to fulfil its obligation under the Charter and finding "a diplomatic solution aimed at ensuring lasting peace and stability in the region".

In this context, the OIC Contact Group lends full support to the Secretary-General for his initiatives and diplomatic efforts in search of a just and durable political solution which would ensure, inter alia, an end to the Yugoslav policy of ethnic cleansing and the swift, safe and unimpeded return of all Kosovar refugees and internally displaced persons under international protection throughout Kosova.

---

[1] UN Doc. S/1999/468, Annex, 22 April 1999.

301. Cuba, Excerpts From the Speech Made by Comrade Fidel Castro at a Mass Rally in the University of Havana, 4 May 1999

[...]

There is another more important conflict. Presently, brutal and destructive air strikes are taking place in the very heart of Europe, which are causing devastation, death and terror in a population of millions. Religious and ethnic conflicts have been considerably aggravated and thus hundreds of thousands of men, women and children, also horrified by the bombs and the war, are massively migrating.

On the eve of the next millenium Europe, - that is, NATO and its members, the United States of America included - is involved in what can be described, whether they like it or not, as genocide. That is what results from depriving one million people from electricity and heating services, overnight and in mid winter. Also from cutting off all communications, sources of energy and transportation; destroying non-military facilities providing crucial services to all the population and tearing to pieces all the means of life created by a nation. Such destructive frenzy, either by mistake or recklessness, is directly killing or injuring thousands of civilians while trying to submit them by the destruction of their mass media and the intensification of the psychological warfare with overpowering technology and bombs. Unquestionably, this is a major genocide.

Europe is involved in a conflict hazardous to itself and the world. An extremely serious precedent is being set in defiance of international law and the United Nations Organization, and resulting in an increasingly complicated the situation.

We are of the view that in such a predicament only a political, and not a military, solution is possible based on respect for the rights of every nation in that region, and every religion, ethnic group and culture: a solution for both, Serbians and Kosovars. I am deeply convinced that the problem cannot be solved by force, that the military technology will crash against the will of any people determined to fight. I firmly believe that when the people are willing to fight - and this is how I feel about our own people, too- no power, regardless of its might, can throw them down on their knees.

In the case of Serbia, the aggressor thought it would be a simple walk, a three days adventure, that the Serbians would surrender to the first bombs. Forty days have already passed and thousands and thousands of bombs have been dropped, however, we do not perceive any symptom of weakness in their will to fight. This we know by keeping in touch, through cell phones, - the only means of communication- with three Cuban diplomats in Belgrade who relate to us what is happening there every day and after every night of Dantesque bombing.

We are told by those diplomats about the extraordinary morale of the Serbian people, in general, and particularly the people in Belgrade where planes are constantly flying at low altitude, thundering in the sky, terrorizing and causing traumas in children - hundreds of thousands, millions of children and adolescents afflicted perhaps for life - youth, women and elders affected by the noise of the explosions and the constant attacks, whose growing viciousness is also announced. Once again I insist that that path will not lead to the solution of the problem. I firmly believe that there is no other choice, for anybody, but to work toward a political solution which is possible on the basis of common sense and rationality.

From the beginning of the attacks we realized that they would be useless and would only bring about a catastrophe.

We are aware of the history of World War II, the nazi invasion of Yugoslavia and that people's long resistance. This time the aggressors do not even want to use ground forces since they believe that their smart bombs and guided missiles can solve the problem. But, the problem cannot be resolved with missiles, bombs or ground troops because when the people are determined to fight they do so everywhere, from all directions, and every house may become a fortress, every man or woman a combatant. It is not a matter of armored divisions, artillery groups, air or navy war fleets.

We know very well how we would conduct a struggle in our country under similar conditions and so do millions of people here; all those methods would be useless. This country cannot be conquered by anyone; no one can conquer a country that is willing to fight. It is wrong to try to conquer it. It already happened in Vietnam where the Americans understood it only when they had lost over 50 thousand lives and killed 4 million Vietnamese. Well, now, they are in a similar situation there, and one that can become more complicated if the Serbians everywhere give their support to the Serbians inside Serbia. Then, the political situation in Russia would become untenable because the ethnic bonds between both peoples are very strong.

Other peoples will draw their own conclusions. I think the Russians are drawing theirs - after all that has happened to them in the past and all that can still happen to them in the future- when they see the numberless bombs dropped by a military alliance driven increasingly arrogant, haughty and furious by an unexpected resistance. Europe and NATO have become the hostages of a subjective factor: the decision the Serbians might adopt - or not- to resist to the end, although it is to be assumed that after such destruction they are not going to be much inclined to give up. What is happening there was obvious to us from the beginning. This does not mean that we are against anybody's rights; we support both, the rights of the Serbians and the Kosovars' rights.

When we were recently informed that Guantanamo Naval Base would be used to accommodate 20 thousand Kosovar refugees, we immediately agreed, and I think it is the first time that we have agreed with anything the United States of America has done in that base. It is not that they requested our permission or agreement, actually they simply were kind enough to communicate to us that they would do that. They explained their purposes, they said it would be for a limited period of time while the conflict was settled, and so on. The least they expected - they do not know this country- was our reply.

We said that we did not only agree that 20 thousand Kosovar refugees were sheltered there but also that we were willing to cooperate as much as possible in providing care for those refugees, that we offered our hospital services if required, our doctors and any other cooperation within our capabilities.

Finally, they were not sent in and it was a clever thing to rectify that decision because they would have been much criticized. The truth is that none of the NATO countries, which have dropped so many bombs there, really want to receive refugees. There is much xenophobia and selfishness in the West. They had said they would receive from 80 thousand to a 100 thousand but they have only received a few thousands because they do not want to have Kosovar refugees in their own territories, so they have done nothing significant. Anyway, it was a political mistake but we were informed and we said that we agreed.

There is something else. There is this international humanitarian organization known as the Saint Egidious Community which cares for refugees; it sustains relations with the Catholic Church and works mostly in supportive actions every time there are refugee problems.

Although we strongly condemn the brutal and genocidal attacks against the Serbian people, we also share in the suffering of the hundreds of thousands of refugees dragged to such condition by a series of longstanding factors, not only historic in nature but also associated to the disintegration of Yugoslavia, a country that had lived in peace for 40 years after World War II.

Those who disintegrated Yugoslavia and stirred up the national ethnic and religious conflicts are greatly responsible for what is happening there now. Many of Europe's statesmen and public figures are aware of Europe's responsibility in that process. Those who so lightly agreed to use all their sophisticated and overwhelming military technology against what was left of the former Yugoslavia bear a great responsibility for what is going on there and the misery of those hundreds of thousands of refugees.

As for solutions, we advocate solutions for all the parties involved: refugees, citizens of Kosovo, Serbians and people of other nationalities living there, and all the nations that make up what is left of Yugoslavia today. That is, from the humane point of view our sympathies are with all the suffering people there. In this token, when several weeks ago, in the first days of April, we were visited by leaders of the Saint Egidious Community and they explained to us what they were doing to provide care and assistance to those distressed refugees, for which purpose they had about 30 medical doctors, - this happened a few weeks ago but I have not mentioned it before, I am doing it for the first time- we said to them: Look, we do not have abundant resources but we have a human asset. If you needed medical personnel to care for those hundreds of thousands of refugees living in deprived camps, our country would be willing to contribute with one thousand physicians, absolutely free of charge, to care for the Kosovar refugees. (Applause)

Based on a longstanding experience we know that language is not a barrier. A six months old baby speaks no language at all, however, he/she can be care for by a doctor. This offer we made to the leaders of the Saint Egidious Community on the night of April 5, that is, 12 days after the onset of the NATO attacks.

302. Egypt, Statement by Foreign Minister Amre Moussa, Cairo, 8 May 1999

Stating to media men today, Foreign Minister Amre Moussa pointed out that the G-8 agreement that was reached in Bonn with regards to the political settlement of the Kosovo crisis was appropriate, since the agreement will obviously be referred to the United Nations, whereby the Security Council would issue the relevant resolution. He added that this would suggest resumption of work and implementation of agreed-upon elements within the framework of the United Nations.

"The Security Council's resolution would be very important", Moussa said, "Since the Council is the main body of the United Nations that is responsible for maintaining international peace and security and upholding the presence of an international force".

Moreover, Moussa described the new agreement as a step ahead and that it is based on very reasonable items, pointing out the importance that the United Nations would have an effective role whether with regards to the return of refugees in peace and security, the administration of the Kosovo province or regarding the special force that would be assigned to protect this framework.

In another question, Moussa replied that the items specified in the latest agreement are close to the initiative launched by the UN Secretary-General - a matter that reflects proximity of views of the G-8 Group, the international community and the UN Secretary-General.

303. The Philippines, Statement, Press Release No. 109-99, 10 May 1999

We are deeply saddened by NATO's bombing by mistake last Saturday of the Embassy of the People's Republic of China in Belgrade, the capital city of the Federal Republic of Yugoslavia.

We offer our sympathies and prayers to all the innocent victims of this unfortunate incident and their families.

This incident should all the more convince the parties involved in the Kosovo conflict, as well as Russia and China, to intensify efforts towards a diplomatic solution to the Kosovo issue which would substantially provide a role for the United Nations Secretary General.

The Philippine Government welcomes the new initiatives undertaken by NATO and Russia to end the conflict in Kosovo, and allow the return of hundreds of thousands of Kosovar Albanian refugees under the protection of an international armed force. We believe that the use of force is not a desirable option to resolve any conflict or issue, but we also feel that such inhuman policies as genocide and ethnic cleansing should have no place in our civilized world and must be strongly opposed.

304. Egypt, Statement by Foreign Minister Moussa, Cairo, 15 May 1999

Foreign Minister Amre Moussa today stated that the Kosovo crisis is a multidimensional issue, since peaceful efforts continue to be exerted alongside military operations. "We cannot be fully convinced which of the two methods shall apply unless we resort to the Security Council", Moussa confirmed, adding that the proposal, or rather the agreement that was reached at the last G-8 Summit should have been presented to the Security Council and that the Serbian forces should have withdrawn from Kosovo, however, discussions are still going on.

Regarding his viewpoint towards Russia's peaceful pursuits and how they are to be considered within the initiatives launched by the United Nations, Moussa said that after the participation of Russia in the latest G-8 Summit and her approval of the main outlines raised with relation to the resolution of the crisis, Russia has been reiterating the same views of NATO members, namely the importance of introducing a political solution. This solution should be based on the pullout of Serbian forces and police, the presence of international troops operating under the UN flag, placement of an international administration as well as ensuring a secured return of refugees, following up of reconstruction processes and disarmament of militias.

On whether it is important that Russia's attempts should be pursued in coordination with those of the other parties, Moussa remarked that work should continue in order to reach a peaceful solution and that this should be agreed upon among the other parties within the framework of the United Nations.

On whether Egypt's willingness to take part in the peace keeping forces in Kosovo would depend on the nature of these forces and whether they will operate under the UN flag, Moussa elaborated that Egypt has been one of the most effective participants in previous peace keeping forces such as the one in Bosnia. However, Moussa added that this issue is yet to be discussed.

305. Zimbabwe, Foreign Affairs Minister, Hon. Mudenge's Address at a Reception in Honour of the Visiting Chinese Foreign Minister, 14 January 2000

Honourable Minister Tang Jiaxuan

[...]

Honourable Minister, we enter the new millennium against a background of disturbing developments on the international scene. Since the end of the cold war, our world has witnessed the phenomenon of unipolarity and a tendency by the big and powerful to resort to unilateral actions in international affairs. New noxious notions of political and diplomatic "social banditry" masquerading under the guise of humanitarianism are being propounded to justify outmoded and discredited policies of domination, interference and interventionism. These dangerous notions are propagated by latter day "diplomatic Robinhoods" who have arrogated to themselves the "right" to intervene wherever and whenever their selective morality and or selfish national interests beckon them, without any reference whatsoever to the United Nations or other established framework of international law. Thus, the United Nations, the principal custodian of international peace and security is often undermined and sidelined on issues falling within its remit. This is a prescription for chaos in international relations. It must be resisted by all peace loving countries. The concept of "Humanitarian intervention" has been put forward to justify interference in the internal affairs of other countries. This new doctrine is meant to enlarge existing conventions on such matters as "crimes against humanity", including genocide which are already covered by existing international instruments. The new concept of "humanitarian intervention" is much wider and rather vague. We have seen it selectively invoked to violate the sovereignty of small and weak countries. Contrast the developments in Kosovo and Chechnya. It is this selectivity that we object to. When some rights are violated in certain situations we see intervention but when many other human rights in the Declaration of Human and Peoples' Rights are regularly violated in many other places no action is taken. While some have advocated this principle out of a genuine concern for the weak and oppressed the powerful have exploited it to justify their global adventurism in order to promote their national interests. "We are now living in a truly global village where human rights violations anywhere is human rights violations everywhere," we are counselled. This sounds well and good provided it is consistently applied in a just and fair democratic order of which our current so called "global village" is not. We must agree on which "human rights" can be a basis for intervention; on who shall determine that; what criteria shall be used in order to avoid present day Rambo-like interventionism.

Distinguished guests, can we expect justice and fairness from a global order where the dominant actors are self-appointed and might and not right is the law? Can we seriously expect justice from an international order where we not only have selective morality but where some powerful states claim extra-territorial jurisdiction? These matters require that we debate and exchange views regularly and that is one of the reasons I welcome your visit to Zimbabwe.

So long as the major instruments of global governance remain undemocratic and unrepresentative in their membership and decision-making processes, justice and fairness will forever remain elusive. Noble principles such as "humanitarian intervention" must emanate from a democratic and enlarged Security Council, which takes cognisance of the interests of all or else it will always be manipulated to camouflage the selfish interests of the strong. Furthermore, they must emanate from a global order where all, including the weakest, are equal before the law of nations and none, even the strongest, are above it. Above all they must proceed from a global order where all, rich or poor, weak or strong have a say in the decisions that affect our global village. [...]

CHAPTER 8: COURT ACTION WITH REGARD TO THE KOSOVO CRISIS

8.1 The International Court of Justice (ICJ)

On 28 April 1999, the FRY submitted a request for the indication of provisional measures against Belgium, Canada, France, Germany, Italy, the Netherlands, Portugal, Spain, the United Kingdom, and the United States of America (*document no. 306*). A day later the FRY submitted an application accusing these states that by taking part in the air strikes against the FRY, they had infringed upon their obligation not to use force and that by taking part in the training, arming, financing, equipping, and supplying of the KLA they had violated their obligation to non-intervention (*document no. 307*). In addition, the FRY raised claims concerning breaches of international humanitarian law, environmental law, basic human rights, freedom of navigation on international rivers, and allegations of genocide. Only four days before filing the application the FRY had accepted the compulsory jurisdiction of the International Court of Justice according to Art. 36 para. 2 of the ICJ-Statute.

Oral pleadings were held from 10 May 1999 to 12 May 1999 (*document no. 308*). By the order of 2 June 1999 (*document no. 309*), the Court rejected the request for the indication of provisional measures. The question of prima facie jurisdiction of the Court was decisive for the order. Depending on a legal obligations of the different respondent parties the ICJ examined various bases for jurisdiction: The question of reservations *ratione temporis* according to Art. 36 para. 2 of the ICJ-Statute was taken into consideration in the cases against Belgium, Canada, the Netherlands, and Portugal. Yugoslavia had accepted the compulsory jurisdiction of the Court making a reservation *ratione temporis*. The majority of the judges agreed that the request was essentially directed against the air strikes against the territory of the FRY. The air strikes, taken as a whole, formed the legal dispute which had arisen before the date of the acceptance of the compulsory jurisdiction of the Court by the FRY. Even though the dispute continued since that date, each individual air attack could not give rise to a separate subsequent dispute. Furthermore, Yugoslavia had not demonstrated that new disputes, distinct from the initial ones, had arisen since that date.[1] In the cases against the UK and Spain, the Court examined a different kind of reservation. The prerequisite of both declarations is that the acceptance of the Court's compulsory jurisdiction must have been deposited 12 months prior to the filing of an application. Since Yugoslavia only instituted proceedings 4 days after the deposition of the declaration of acceptance these conditions for the exclusion of the Court's jurisdiction were satisfied.[2] In addition, the Court considered Art. IX of the Convention on the Prevention and Punishment of the Crime of Genocide. In eight cases, the Court held that the acts attributed by the FRY to the respondents did not fall under the provisions of the Genocide convention. The Court stressed that an element of intent to commit genocide on a group as such was absent.[3]

In the cases of Belgium and the Netherlands, the FRY also tried to base jurisdiction on judicial settlement in the second round of oral argument, i.e. Art. 4 of the Convention on Conciliation, Judicial Settlement and Arbitration between Belgium and the Kingdom of Yugoslavia of 25 March 1930 and Art. 4 of the Treaty of Judicial Settlement, Arbitration and Conciliation between the Netherlands and the Kingdom of Yugoslavia of 11 March 1931. The ICJ rejected the presentation as belated. Therefore, the Court could not examine the argument without the consent of the respondents because this would "seriously jeopardizes the principle of procedural fairness and the sound arbitration of justice."[4]

In the cases of Spain and the USA, the Court found no basis for jurisdiction because both states had made a reservation to Art. IX of the Genocide Convention. Neither had Yugoslavia objected to the reservation nor was such a reservation explicitly prohibited by the Convention.[5] The ICJ decided the cases against Spain and the USA had to be removed from its list.[6] In the other eight cases it held that its findings did not prejudge questions relating to the admissibility of the application or relating to the merits.[7]

The Order against Belgium also touched shortly upon the question of the legal status of the FRY which is still controversial under international law. Belgium, like most UN members, officially disputes the continuation of the SFRY. They take the view that the SFRY has ceased to exist and claim that it must apply again to the UN for membership which it has not yet done. The FRY, on the other hand, contends that the pertinent General Assembly resolution 47/1 of 22 September 1992 did not terminate nor suspend the FRY's membership in the UN. While the ICJ stated that there was no need for it to decide the question, Judge Oda argued against it[8] and the Yugoslav Judge ad hoc Kreca affirmed the membership of the FRY.[9] The question remains of interest since Chapter VII powers of the Security Council are binding only for UN member States. Thus, it remains to be examined how imposing Chapter VII measures on a State which is allegedly no longer a member of the UN can be justified.

Finally, the Court stated that it was "profoundly concerned with the use of force in Yugoslavia" and that "under the present circumstances such use raises very serious issues of international law".[10] It further emphasised that "all parties appearing before it must act in conformity with their obligations under the United Nations Charter and other rules of international law, including humanitarian law."[11]

---

[1] ICJ, Legality of the Use of Force (Yugoslavia v. Belgium), ICJ Reports 1999, paras. 28-29.
[2] Ibid., paras. 23-25.
[3] Ibid., para. 40.
[4] Ibid., para. 44.
[5] Ibid., paras. 21-28.
[6] Ibid., para. 34.
[7] Ibid., para. 46.
[8] Separate opinion of Judge Oda, Legality of the Use of Force (Yugoslavia v. Belgium), ICJ Reports 1999, Part II para. 3.
[9] Dissenting opinion of Judge Kreca, Legality of the Use of Force (Yugoslavia v. Belgium), ICJ Reports 1999, Part III 8.
[10] ICJ, Legality of the Use of Force (Yugoslavia v. USA), ICJ Reports 1999, para. 17.
[11] Ibid., para. 19.

8.2 International Criminal Tribunal for the Former Yugoslavia (ICTY)

On 22 February 1993 by UN Security Council resolution 780 (1993), the UN Security Council decided to establish an International Tribunal for the Persecution of Persons Responsible for Serious Violations of International Humanitarian Law Committed in the Territory of the Former Yugoslavia since 1991 (ICTY) while the conflict in the FRY was still continuing. On 25 May 1993, a statute for the Tribunal was adopted by UN Security Council resolution 808 (1993). The first judges were elected on 17 September 1993, and the Tribunal commenced its work in The Hague on 17 November 1993. The Tribunal consists of three organs: the Chambers, the Office of the Prosecutor and the Registry. It now has three Trial Chambers each composed of three judges, and an Appeals Chamber, consisting of five judges. It currently has a budget of nearly $ 100 million and employs more than 700 staff members. [1]

The Tribunal's authority belongs to the enforcement powers of the Security Council under Chapter VII. The Tribunal has jurisdiction over persons responsible for serious violations of international humanitarian law (Art. 1 of the Statute) committed in the territory of the former Yugoslavia since 1991. Serious violations of international humanitarian law include grave breaches of the Geneva Conventions of 1949 (Art. 2), violations of the laws or customs of war (Art. 3), genocide (Art. 4), and crimes against humanity (Art. 5). Those committing the acts, as well as those organising and ordering their commissioning may be held responsible (Art.7).

In regard to Kosovo, the Tribunal reacted quickly to the reports of the initial massacres of Kosovo Albanians in the Drenica region (*documents no.48*). In a statement of 10 March 1998, the Prosecutor affirmed her opinion that the jurisdiction of the Tribunal "is ongoing and covers the recent violence in Kosovo." (*document no. 312*). Regardless of the legal status that Kosovo enjoyed under the Yugoslav constitution during the break-up of the SFRY, it is covered by the ICTY's geographical jurisdiction. Likewise, the temporal jurisdiction is considered to be a settled issue. Since there is no express end to the competence *ratione temporis*, it is up to the Security Council to decide that the ICTY has served its purpose which it has not yet done.[2]

On 7 July 1998, the Prosecutor informed the Contact Group that she believes an "armed conflict" within the meaning of public international law exists in Kosovo. She also emphasized that the jurisdiction of the Court includes crimes committed by persons on both sides of the conflict. This point of view contrasts the FRY's position that the KLA should be considered merely as a terrorist group.

The UN Security Council confirmed the jurisdiction of the Tribunal over Kosovo in its Resolution 1160 (1998) (*document no. 65*) and urged the Prosecutor to begin gathering information about violence in Kosovo. In Resolution 1199 (1998) (*document no. 89*) the Council called upon the authorities of the FRY as well as upon the leaders of the Kosovo Albanian community to cooperate fully with the prosecutor. While until October 1998, the ICTY had been able to gather evidence on the ground in Kosovo, the FRY then refused to issue visas for the investigators. It claimed that "the Tribunal has no jurisdiction to conduct investigations in Kosovo" (*document no. 314*). The Prosecutor's reaction to the refusal was firm. She stated that the jurisdiction was not conditional upon the consent of the FRY's authorities, but that it was up to the ICTY judges to interpret such jurisdiction and for the UN Security Council to modify or expand it. She forwarded a letter to President Milosevic informing him that it was her intention to resume investigations in Kosovo and to personally visit the areas where some of the alleged crimes had been committed (*document no. 315*). The continuing refusal of the FRY to cooperate with the Tribunal caused the Security Council to adopt Resolution 1207 (1998) of 17 November 1998, which called again upon the FRY and the Kosovo Albanian community to cooperate fully with the Tribunal (*document no. 316*). The conflict culminated when border guards denied the Chief Prosecutor access to the FRY, when she tried to enter Kosovo from Macedonia after the Racak incident.

On 22 May 1999, the ICTY issued an indictment and arrest warrant against Milosevic, the President of the FRY, Milutinovic, the President of Serbia, Sainovic, Deputy Prime Minister of the FRY, Ojdanic, Chief of Staff of the Yugoslav Army and Stojiljkovic, Minister of Internal Affairs of Serbia. (*document no. 319*) The indictment was the first in the history of the Tribunal directed against a head of State during an ongoing armed conflict. The indictment alleges that, between 1 January and late May 1999, the indictees planned, instigated, ordered and committed a campaign of terror and violence directed at Kosovo Albanian civilians living in Kosovo. The indictees undertook the operations with the objective of removing a substantial portion of the Kosovo Albanian population from Kosovo in an effort to ensure continued Serbian control over the province. Forces under the control of the five accused have, in a systematic manner, deported, murdered and persecuted the Kosovo Albanian civilian population on political, racial or religious grounds. The five indictees, thus, have committed crimes against humanity, i.e. deportation punishable under Art. 5 (d), murder punishable under Art. 5 (a) and persecution on political, racial, or religious grounds punishable under Art. 5 (h) of the Statute of the Tribunal, and they have violated the laws or customs of war through murder according to Art. 3 of the Statute of the Tribunal and recognised by Art. 3 (1) (a) of the Geneva Conventions. Specifically, the five indictees are charged with the murder of over 340 persons identified by name in an annex to the indictment.[3]

With regard to crimes being committed since the establishment of UNMIK the Prosecutor of the ICTY has stated that the Office of the Prosecutor of the ICTY has neither the mandate, nor the resources, to function, as the primary investigative and prosecutorial agency for all criminal acts committed on the territory of Kosovo. The investigation and prosecution of offences, which may fall outside the scope of the jurisdiction are the responsibility of UNMIK. However, the Prosecutor assumes that there may be matters that may potentially have a relationship to crimes within the purview of the ICTY, i.e. crimes with a factual and legal basis that may link the offence to the armed conflict in Kosovo (*document no. 322*).

On 10 November 1999, the Chief Prosecutor reported to the UN Security Council that during five months of investigation by forensic specialists the Tribunal has received reports of 11,334 bodies in 529 gravesites. Approximately, 195 of those sites had so far been examined with 2,108 bodies exhumed. She announced that 300 mass graves would need to be examined in 2000.[4]

---

[1] Report of the International Tribunal for the Persecution of Persons Responsible for Serious Violations of International Humanitarian Law Committed in the Territory of the Former Yugoslavia since 1991, UN Doc. A/54/187 of 25 August 1999, p. 9 para. 2.

[2] Sonja Boelaert-Suominen, 'The International Criminal Tribunal for the Former Yugoslavia and the Kosovo conflict', International Review of the Red Cross No. 837, pp. 217-252; see http://www.icrc.org. p. 6.

[3] ICTY, Indictment of Slobodan Milosevic and others, 24 May 1999, para. 100.

[4] UN Security Council, Press Release, SC/6749 of 10 November 1999, 4063rd Meeting of the Security Council.

International Reactions to the Crisis

8.1 INTERNATIONAL COURT OF JUSTICE (ICJ)

[A complete account of the proceedings before the International Court of Justice can be found in the internet: http://www.icj-cij.org. The case against Belgium has been selected due to the variety of legal questions which have been brought up.]

306. Request for the Indication of Provisional Measures Concerning the Application of the Federal Republic of Yugoslavia against the Kingdom of Belgium for Violation of the Obligation not to Use Force, Belgrade, 28 April 1999 (Extracts)

On the basis of Article 73 of the Rules of the Court, I submit:

Request for the Indication of Provisional Measures Concerning the Application of the Federal Republic of Yugoslavia against the Kingdom of Belgium for Violation of the Obligation not to Use Force

REASONS

The Federal Republic of Yugoslavia is exposed to acts of use of force by which the Kingdom of Belgium has violated its international obligations not to resort to threat or use of force against another State, not to intervene in the internal affairs of another State and not to violate the sovereignty of another State, to protect civilians and civilian objects in time of war, to protect the environment, as well as those relating to free navigation on international rivers, to the fundamental rights and liberties of the individual, to the ban on the use of prohibited weapons and on deliberate infliction on ethnic groups conditions of life calculated to bring about physical destruction of the group.

Both military and civilian targets came under attack in the air strikes launched against the Federal Republic of Yugoslavia.

There are many casualties, including a large number of civilian deaths. Even residential areas have been attacked. Countless dwellings have been destroyed. Enormous damage has been caused to schools, hospitals, radio and television stations, institutions and cultural monuments as well as to places of worship. Many bridges, roads and railway lines have also been destroyed. Industrial facilities have not been spared either. Attacks on oil refineries and chemical plants have had serious environmental effects on some cities, towns and villages in the Federal Republic of Yugoslavia. The bombing of oil refineries and oil storage tanks as well as chemical plants is bound to produce massive pollution of the environment, posing a threat to human life, plants and animals. The use of weapons containing depleted uranium warheads is having far-reaching consequences for human health.

From the onset of the bombing of the Federal Republic of Yugoslavia, over 10 000 attacks were made against the territory of the Federal Republic of Yugoslavia. In air strikes were used: 806 warplanes (of which over 530 combat planes) and 206 helicopters stationed in 30 airbases (situated in 5 states) and aboard 6 warships in the Adriatic Sea. More than 2,500 cruise missiles were launched and over 7,000 tons of explosives were dropped.

About 1000 civilians, including 19 children, were killed and more than 4,500 sustained serious injuries, e.g.:

- in Doganovici village, near Urosevac, the following children were killed from a cluster bomb: Endon (3), Fisnik (9), Osman (13), Burim (14) and Vajdet (15) Kodzan. In addition, two boys were wounded and taken to hospital;

- in Kursumlija: 13 dead (among them Veroljub Stevanovic) and 25 wounded (among them Dobrivoje Grcic, Milan Jankovic and Milovan Ognjenovic);

- in village of Velika Dobranja, a six-year old Arta Lugic was killed while three other children named Egzon, Neom and Arijeta were seriously wounded;

- in Pancevo: 2 dead (Dusan Bogosavljev and Mirko Dmitrovic) and 4 wounded;

- in Cacak: one dead (Mileva Kuveljic) and 7 wounded;

- in Kragujevac: over 120 workers were wounded during an attack on the car factory "Zastava";

- in Vranje: two dead (Goran Eminovic and Milica Grujic) and 23 wounded;

- in Aleksinac: 12 dead (among them Jovan Radojicic, Sofija Radojicic, Vojislav Jovanovic, Radojka Jovanovic, Dragomir Miladinovic, Snezana Miladinovic and Velimir Stankovic) and more than 40 wounded (among them Ljubica Miladinovic, Slobodan Mladenovic, Bogomir Arsic, Gvozden Milivojevic, Dragoljub Todorovic, Branislava Stevanovic, Veroljub Milutinovic, Vukica Miladinovic, Marko Miladinovic, Dijana Miladinovic, Dragica Milivojevic, Branko Stevanovic, Boban Stojanovic, Vesna Stojanovic, Srboljub Stojanovic, Marija Stojanovic, Verica Miletic, Slavimir Miletic, Dusan Miletic, Stefan Miletic, Ruica Sljivic, Zagorka Marinkovic, Srbislav Stefanovic, Natasa Stefanovic, Vesna Stefanovic, Radmila Projovic, Ljiljana Milutinovic, Nadezda Zivadinovic, Dragoljub Milosevic, Desanka Rakocevic, Slavoljub Rakocevic, Bratislav Zivadinovic, Zagorka Todorovic, Vukasin Djokic, Vladimir Jankovic, Jorgovan Bankovic, Goran Stojkovic and Todor Petric);

- in the village of Nagavac, Orahovac municipality: 11 dead (among them Cazim Krasnici, Mahmut Krasnici, Hisen Zunici and Hisni Eljsani) and 5 wounded (Zade Eljsani, Valentina Krasnici, Siresa Krasnici, Ridvan Berisa and Edonis Gasi);

- in Pristina: 10 dead (among them Adem Berisa, Radovan Aleksic, Dejan Vitkovic, and Gasi family - Mesud, Dijana, Dea, Rea and Denis) and 8 wounded;

- Grdelicka gorge: 55 killed (among them Zoran Jovanovic, Petar Mladenovic, Verka Mladenovic and Jasmina Veljkovic) and 16 wounded;

- attack on two refugee columns, with four cruise missiles, on the Djakovica-Prizren road: 75 killed (Martin Hasanaj, Lek Hasanaj, Salji Djokaj, Skendi Djokaj, and Pajaziti family - Razija, Vjolca, Violeta, Nevrija, Hastar and Fljora, Ram Maljoku, Arton Maljoku, Fikrija Sulja, Imer Celja, Ferat Bajrami, Nerdjivane Zajciri and Bersad Smailji) and 100 wounded, of whom 26 critically (among them Dzafer Mazreku, Sokolj Bajrami, Sahe Smailji, Zoja Curi, Semsije Smajli, Skumbin Sulja, Teuta Sulja, Isljam Cuni, Ljabinot Sulja, Ardijan Sulja, Zoje Tahiraj);

- in the village of Srbica: 10 killed, among whom 7 children;

- Belgrade suburb of Batajnica: a three year old girl Milica Rakic was killed, and five civilians wounded;

- in Nis: in the attack on apartment buildings one civilian was killed while 11 wounded;

- in Pristina: in the attack on the Provincial Government building in the suburb of Grmija, one civilian was killed while 2 were wounded;

- in Djakovica: in the attack on a refugee settlement housing Serb refugees from the Republic of Croatia, 10 refugees were killed and 16 wounded;

- in Belgrade: in the attack on Radio Television of Serbia office building, 15 employees were been killed and 17 wounded.

Three million children are endangered in the Federal Republic of Yugoslavia as a result of war and bombing.

After these military attacks hundreds of thousands of citizens have been exposed to poisonous gases which can have lasting consequences for the health of the entire population and the environment.

After the destruction of the Petrovaradin bridge, Novi Sad and Petrovaradin were cut off water supply (600 000 people) since the main and city pipeline was built into the bridge. About one million citizens in our country are short of water supply due to the bombing.

About 500 000 workers became jobless due to the total destruction of industrial facilities all around the country. Two million citizens have no means of living and are unable to ensure minimum means of sustenance.

The road and railway network, in particular road and railway bridges, most of which have been destroyed or damaged beyond repair, suffered extensive destruction. The targets of attacks were:

BRIDGES

[...]

RAILWAY STATIONS

[...]

ROADS AND TRANSPORTERS

[...]

AIRPORTS

[...]

The air strikes have so far destroyed or damaged all over the Federal Republic of Yugoslavia several thousand economic facilities and dwellings. In the Leskovac region alone, over 3,500 industrial facilities and dwellings were either destroyed or damaged.

The devastation was particularly manifest in Pristina, Novi Sad, Aleksinac, Djakovica, Prokuplje, Gracanica, Cuprija, etc. Housing blocks on the outskirts of Belgrade - Kijevo Knezevac, Batajnica, Jakovo, Borca, as well as the area around Pancevo, were under attack.

INDUSTRY AND TRADE

The Kingdom of Belgium is taking part in attacks targeting the factories and industrial facilities directly catering for the needs of the population, among which are:

[...]

REFINERIES AND WAREHOUSES

storing liquid raw materials and chemicals intended for oil and chemical industry, were hit in Pancevo, Novi Sad, Sombor and elsewhere, causing large contamination of soil and the air:

[...]

AGRICULTURE

[...]

HOSPITALS AND HEALTH CARE CENTRES

The aviation of the Kingdom of Belgium also targeted many hospitals and health-care institutions, which have been partially damaged or totally destroyed, including:

[...]

SCHOOLS (MORE THAN 200 FACILITIES)

Over 2000 schools, faculties and facilities for students and children were damaged or destroyed (over 25 faculties, 10 colleges, 45 secondary and 90 elementary schools, 8 student dormitories, as well as a number of kindergartens), including:

[...]

PUBLIC AND HOUSING FACILITIES (TENS OF THOUSANDS)

[...]

INFRASTRUCTURE

[...]

TELECOMMUNICATIONS: TV TRANSMITTERS

[...]

CULTURAL-HISTORICAL MONUMENTS AND RELIGIOUS SHRINES

Medieval Monasteries and Religious Shrines:

[...]

Cultural-Historical Monuments and Museums:

[...]

The acts described above caused death, physical and mental harm to the population of the Federal Republic of Yugoslavia; huge devastation; heavy pollution of the environment, so that the Yugoslav population is deliberately imposed conditions of life calculated to bring about physical destruction of the group, in whole or in part.

Possible consequences in case requested measures are not adopted

If the proposed measure were not to be adopted, there will be new losses of human life, further physical and mental harm inflicted on the population of the FR of Yugoslavia, further destruction of civilian targets, heavy environmental pollution and further physical destruction of the people of Yugoslavia.

Requested measures

The Government of the Federal Republic of Yugoslavia request the Court to order the next measure:

The Kingdom of Belgium shall cease immediately its acts of use of force and shall refrain from any act of threat or use of force against the Federal Republic of Yugoslavia.

The Government of the FR of Yugoslavia reserves the right to amend and supplement this Request.

Belgrade, 28 April 1999

(Signed) Rodoljub Etinski, Agent for the Federal Republic of Yugoslavia

307. Legality of Use of Force (Yugoslavia v. Belgium), Application Instituting Proceedings Filed in the Registry of the Court on 29 April 1999 (Extracts)

[The Declaration on the acceptance by the Federal Republic of Yugoslavia of the compulsory jurisdiction of the International Court of Justice as well as the related cover letters have been omitted.]

LEGALITY OF USE OF FORCE (YUGOSLAVIA V. BELGIUM)

[...]

III. Application of the Federal Republic of Yugoslavia

On the basis of Article 40 of the Statute of the International Court of Justice and Article 38 of the Rules of the Court, I submit the following: "Application of the Federal Republic of Yugoslavia against the Kingdom of Belgium for Violation of the Obligation Not to Use Force".

SUBJECT OF THE DISPUTE

The subject-matter of the dispute are acts of The Kingdom of Belgium by which it has violated its international obligation banning the use of force against another State, the obligation not to intervene in the internal affairs of another State, the obligation not to violate the sovereignty of another State, the obligation to protect the civilian population and civilian objects in wartime, the obligation to protect the environment, the obligation relating to free navigation on international rivers, the obligation regarding fundamental human rights and freedoms, the obligation not to use prohibited weapons, the obligation not to deliberately inflict conditions of life calculated to cause the physical destruction of a national group.

LEGAL GROUNDS FOR JURISDICTION OF THE COURT

The Government of the Federal Republic of Yugoslavia invokes Article 36, para 2 of the Statute of the International Court of Justice as well as Article 9 of the Convention on the Prevention and Punishment of the Crime of Genocide.

CLAIM

The Government of the Federal Republic of Yugoslavia requests the International Court of Justice to adjudge and declare:

- by taking part in the bombing of the territory of the Federal Republic of Yugoslavia, The Kingdom of Belgium has acted against the Federal Republic of Yugoslavia in breach of its obligation not to use force against another State;

- by taking part in the training, arming, financing, equipping and supplying terrorist groups, i.e. the so-called "Kosovo Liberation Army", The Kingdom of Belgium has acted against the Federal Republic of Yugoslavia in breach of its obligation not to intervene in the affairs of another State;

- by taking part in attacks on civilian targets, The Kingdom of Belgium has acted against the Federal Republic of Yugoslavia in breach of its obligation to spare the civilian population, civilians and civilian objects;

- by taking part in destroying or damaging monasteries, monuments of culture, The Kingdom of Belgium has acted against the Federal Republic of Yugoslavia in breach of its obligation not to commit any act of hostility directed against historical monuments, works of art or places of worship which constitute cultural or spiritual heritage of people;

- by taking part in the use of cluster bombs, The Kingdom of Belgium has acted against the Federal Republic of Yugoslavia in breach of its obligation not to use prohibited weapons, i.e. weapons calculated to cause unnecessary suffering;

- by taking part in the bombing of oil refineries and chemical plants, The Kingdom of Belgium has acted against the Federal Republic of Yugoslavia in breach of its obligation not to cause considerable environmental damage;

- by taking part in the use of weapons containing depleted uranium, The Kingdom of Belgium has acted against the Federal Republic of Yugoslavia in breach of its obligation not to use prohibited weapons and not to cause far-reaching health and environmental damage;

- by taking part in killing civilians, destroying enterprises, communications, health and cultural institutions, The Kingdom of Belgium has acted against the Federal Republic of Yugoslavia in breach of its obligation to respect the right to life, the right to work, the right to information, the right to health care as well as other basic human rights;

- by taking part in destroying bridges on international rivers, The Kingdom of Belgium has acted against the Federal Republic of Yugoslavia in breach of its obligation to respect freedom of navigation on international rivers;

- by taking part in activities listed above, and in particular by causing enormous environmental damage and by using depleted uranium, The Kingdom of Belgium has acted against the Federal Republic of Yugoslavia in breach of its obligation not to deliberately inflict on a national group conditions of life calculated to bring about its physical destruction, in whole or in part;

- The Kingdom of Belgium is responsible for the violation of the above international obligations;

- The Kingdom of Belgium is obliged to stop immediately the violation of the above obligations vis-a-vis the Federal Republic of Yugoslavia;

- The Kingdom of Belgium is obliged to provide compensation for the damage done to the Federal Republic of Yugoslavia and to its citizens and juridical persons.

The Federal Republic of Yugoslavia reserves the right to submit subsequently accurate evaluation of the damage.

FACTS UPON WHICH THE CLAIM IS BASED

The Government of The Kingdom of Belgium, together with the Governments of other Member States of NATO, took part in the acts of use of force against the Federal Republic of Yugoslavia by taking part in bombing targets in the Federal Republic of Yugoslavia. In bombing the Federal Republic of Yugoslavia military and civilian targets were attacked. Great number of people were killed, including a great many civilians. Residential houses came under attack. Numerous dwellings were destroyed. Enormous damage was caused to schools, hospitals, radio and television stations, cultural and health institutions and to places of worship. A large number of bridges, roads and railway lines were destroyed. Attacks on oil refineries and chemical plants have had serious environmental effects on cities, towns and villages in the Federal Republic of Yugoslavia. The use of weapons containing depleted uranium is having far-reaching consequences for human life. The above-mentioned acts are deliberately creating conditions calculated at the physical destruction of an ethnic group, in whole or in part. The Government of The Kingdom of Belgium is taking part in the training, arming, financing, equipping and supplying the so-called "Kosovo Liberation Army".

LEGAL GROUNDS ON WHICH THE CLAIM IS BASED

The above acts of the Government of Belgium represent a gross violation of the obligation not to use force against another State. By financing, arming, training and equipping the so-called "Kosovo Liberation Army", support is given to terrorist groups and the secessionist movement in the territory of the Federal Republic of Yugoslavia in breach of the obligation not to intervene in the internal affairs of another State. In addition, the provisions of the Geneva Convention of 1949 and of the Additional Protocol No. 1 of 1977 on the protection of civilians and civilian objects in time of war have been violated. The obligation to protect the environment has also been breached. The destruction of bridges on the Danube is in contravention of the provisions of Article 1 of the 1948 Convention on free navigation on the Danube. The provisions of the International Covenant on Civil and Political Rights and of the International Covenant on Economic, Social and Cultural Rights of 1966 have also been breached. Furthermore, the obligation contained in the Convention on the Prevention and Punishment of the Crime of Genocide not to impose deliberately on a national group conditions of life calculated to bring about the physical destruction of the group has been breached. Furthermore, the activities in which The Kingdom of Belgium is taking part are contrary to Article 53, para 1 of the Charter of the United Nations.

The Government of the FR of Yugoslavia reserves the right to amend and supplement this Application.

(Signed) Rodoljub Etinski, Agent for the Federal Republic of Yugoslavia

308. Belgium, Oral Pleading in the Case "Legality of the Use of Force", CR 99/15 (translation), 10 May 1999

[...]

I. Facts and Past History
BACKGROUND

May I remind you that in 1974 the province of Kosovo was granted wide-ranging autonomy, but that in 1989 this autonomy was abruptly abolished by Mr. Milosevic's régime. In 1992, as you know, the inception of the Federal Republic of Yugoslavia was proclaimed, and at the beginning of 1998 events began to accelerate: clashes between the Kosovo Albanians and the Serbs became more and more frequent. The massacres and the ethnic cleansing began.

It was at this point that the Security Council became involved. Allow me to recall the three resolutions.

SECURITY COUNCIL RESOLUTION OF 31 MARCH 1998 - RESOLUTION 1160 (1998)

The Security Council resolution of 31 March 1998 - resolution 1160 - was taken under Chapter VII of the Charter of the United Nations. The resolution noted a threat to international peace and security and condemned the use of excessive force by Serbian police forces against civilians and peaceful demonstrators in Kosovo.

The Security Council urged a political solution to the question, and demanded substantially increased autonomy for Kosovo. The resolution contained conditions very similar to those subsequently laid down by NATO: the initiation of meaningful, peaceful dialogue; the withdrawal of police units and military and paramilitary forces; allowing humanitarian organizations to gain access to the areas where refugees were in distress; a mission to Kosovo by the United Nations High Commissioner on Human Rights.

The Federal Republic of Yugoslavia ignored the resolution. The situation continued to deteriorate.

SECURITY COUNCIL RESOLUTION OF 23 SEPTEMBER 1998 - RESOLUTION 1199 (1998)

There was the report of the Secretary-General, written pursuant to the Security Council resolution which I quoted just now. Following on from the report of the Secretary-General, a second resolution was adopted, resolution 1199 (1998), the second resolution of 23 September 1998.

Once again, the indiscriminate use of force was condemned. However, a very important form of wording was used in the resolution. The Security Council was alarmed, let me emphasize, "at the impending humanitarian catastrophe". This is very important for our legal reasoning later in this statement.

The impending humanitarian catastrophe noted by the Security Council

Still under Chapter VII of the Charter, the Security Council reiterated the demands made in the previous resolution.

Then came the report of the Secretary-General of the United Nations two months later, pursuant to that resolution on the situation in Kosovo. What did the Secretary-General of the United Nations say? He said that fighting was continuing and that the Federal Republic of Yugoslavia continued to ignore the resolution, in flagrant breach of the previous resolution. The Secretary-General noted that a further 20,000 people had been displaced, that increasingly civilians had become the main target in the conflict and that there were still 200,000 displaced people inside Kosovo, as recorded by the High Commissioner for Refugees.

AGREEMENTS OF OCTOBER 1998

Thus the situation deteriorated. Then came the agreements of October 1998, which were mentioned this morning: (a) Milosevic-Holbrooke Agreement (S/1998.953); (b) Agreement between NATO and the Federal Republic of Yugoslavia; (c) Agreement between NATO and the Federal Republic of Yugoslavia; (d) Agreement between the Federal Republic of Yugoslavia and the Organization for Security and Cooperation in Europe. The Secretary-General of the United Nations nevertheless noted, in the reports quoted in the memorandum which we filed, that there were "alarming signs that there was a risk of the situation deteriorating".

SECURITY COUNCIL RESOLUTION OF 24 OCTOBER 1998 - RESOLUTION 1203 (1998)

And it was following this observation that the third resolution was taken: Security Council resolution 1203 of 24 October of the same year. Still under Chapter VII of the Charter: the finding of a threat to international peace and security arising from the situation in Kosovo. Once again, that very important form of wording appeared in the resolution, the impending humanitarian catastrophe; the Security Council expressed its alarm at the impending humanitarian catastrophe.

The Security Council recalled that the Federal Republic of Yugoslavia had undertaken publicly to bring negotiations for a political settlement of the question to a successful conclusion, and it reiterated its previous resolutions which had been ignored by the Federal Republic of Yugoslavia.

The situation became worse. In January the massacres resumed. There was a new report of the Secretary-General, dated 29 January, two months before NATO's armed intervention. What did the Secretary-General say?

He stated that three resolutions had been addressed to the Federal Republic of Yugoslavia and urged it to meet its commitments. Yet the massacres continued and on 29 January the Secretary-General of the United Nations noted a major change in the character of the violence in Kosovo. What was happening? The massacres were becoming generalized.

From that time onwards they covered almost the entire territory of Kosovo and above all they began to target the élite, the intelligentsia, all the intellectuals who advocated a spirit of openness and tolerance became the target of a campaign of fear; watch out, they were told: the population as a whole is being terrorized, including the elite and the intellectuals.

MASSACRE OF RACAK

Then came the massacre at Racak, the sombre event which shocked the conscience of the civilized world. On 15 January 1999, 45 Kosovar civilians were killed. The Yugoslav troops (paramilitary forces) entered the village on 15 January and when they left the next day, 16 January, 45 civilians, including women and children, were found massacred. An autopsy mission established that responsibility for the massacre lay with the military or paramilitary forces of the Federal Republic of Yugoslavia.

POSITION OF NATO

On 30 January, the NATO Council expressed the view that the Kosovo crisis remained a threat to peace, and NATO called on the Parties to start negotiations at Rambouillet; at the same time, in view of the catastrophic deterioration in the situation, it authorized its Secretary-General to order airstrikes on military - I stress, military - objectives in the Federal Republic of Yugoslavia.

CONTACT GROUP

The Rambouillet negotiations were then getting under way. You know what happened at Rambouillet; you know that the Kosovars signed the agreement and that the Federal Republic of Yugoslavia refused to do so.

REPORT FROM THE UNITED NATIONS SECRETARY-GENERAL

This brought us to the brink of armed intervention. On 17 March 1999, the United Nations Secretary-General issued a further report in which he stated that there had been deliberate killings of civilians, summary executions, brutality to prisoners and kidnappings. On 17 March the Secretary-General's report stated that 211,000 persons were displaced within Kosovo, and put at 25,000 the number of persons displaced to Montenegro. He observed that the Serbian forces were still flagrantly violating the Security Council resolutions referred to above.

ACTION BY NATO

On 24 March 1999, the NATO Secretary-General, using powers properly conferred, started the intervention. With what objectives? - peace, multiethnicity, democracy for a Kosovo in which all the members of the Kosovo community, whatever their racial, ethnic or religious origin, can live in peace, in compliance with fundamental human rights. The conditions set out by NATO for halting the airstrikes that had begun were the following, and they were to remain unchanged, subject to the decisions taken at the G-8 summit, which I shall describe below:

(i) end of all military action in Kosovo;

(ii) withdrawal of military forces;

(iii) acceptance of an international military presence in Kosovo;

(iv) return of all refugees and displaced persons to their homes; humanitarian aid organizations to be allowed access to these refugees;

(v) assurances given by the Federal Republic of Yugoslavia of its will to achieve a political settlement of the crisis.

If you look carefully at these conditions you will find that they are quite close, I repeat, to the conditions which had already been stipulated by the Security Council.

REJECTION OF THE RESOLUTION PROPOSED TO THE SECURITY COUNCIL BY THE RUSSIAN DELEGATION

There is one last salient point to which I wish to bring your attention: on 26 March, two days after operations started, the Russian Representative laid before the Security Council a draft resolution condemning NATO armed intervention as contrary to the United Nations Charter. That proposal was thrown out by twelve votes to three, and if you read the discussions preceding the adoption of the relevant resolution you will find this said: "Immediate cessation of NATO action would once again send the wrong message to President Milosevic, which could well prolong bloodshed in Kosovo".

Further systematic, large-scale and flagrant violations of human rights in Kosovo

The systematic, large-scale and flagrant violations of human rights in Kosovo continued. I may cite a recent report from the Human Rights Commission released in April, which describes extensive ethnic cleansing.

POSITION OF THE G-8

Then came the G-8 summit. The decision was taken on 6 May. G-8 comprises, as you know, not only some of the NATO powers but also Russia and Japan. It adopted a decision for a peaceful settlement of the conflict largely in line - give or take minor discrepancies - with the substance of the conditions laid down by NATO.

I have summarized the facts. What do these facts signify? Contempt for decisions taken by the highest international agencies; time-wasting manoeuvring; and a systematic policy of purging and repression of the Albanian minority in Kosovo, to say nothing of other serious violations of human rights committed by the Yugoslav authorities.

II. The Request for Provisional Measures

I turn now to the attitude of the Government of the Kingdom of Belgium to the problem of provisional measures. The Kingdom of Belgium takes the view that the conditions for the indication of provisional measures have not been met.

In the first place, your Court has no prima facie jurisdiction.

Secondly, the urgency of the matter has not been established.

Thirdly, the imminence of irreparable harm and the risk of aggravation of the dispute have not been established either.

LACK OF PRIMA FACIE JURISDICTION

I begin with the question of the Court's prima facie jurisdiction. The request is based on Article 36, paragraph 2, of your Statute. But, I hardly need to say this, Mr. President, the Court's jurisdiction is governed by Article 36, paragraph 2, of your Statute. And the declaration provided for in that paragraph can be made only by States which are ipso jure full parties to your Court's Statute, as provided in Article 93 of the United Nations Charter. The crucial question arising, in order to determine whether or not this recognition of your Court's jurisdiction is valid, is the issue of whether the Federal Republic of Yugoslavia can claim to have retained the status of United Nations Member enjoyed by the former Federative Socialist Republic of Yugoslavia. There is no doubt whatever that the answer is "no". Allow me to recall briefly the background.

When the Federative Socialist Republic of Yugoslavia broke up, all the other Member States - Slovenia, Croatia, Bosnia-Herzegovina and Macedonia - applied for United Nations membership because these republics took the view that none of them could claim continuity with the former State of Yugoslavia. Thus they quite rightly took the view that they were the successor States of the former Federative Socialist Republic of Yugoslavia and that they accordingly needed to apply for membership of the United Nations. They were admitted, but the Federal Republic of Yugoslavia itself made no such application. Why? The Federal Republic of Yugoslavia has always taken the view that it was the sole successor of the former Federative Socialist Republic of Yugoslavia. Does the international community agree? Does the United Nations agree? No. On 22 September 1992, in a very important resolution (47/1) the UN General Assembly voted overwhelmingly, by 127 votes to 6, with 26 abstentions, for a resolution recommended by the Security Council which I quote, all these resolutions can be quoted. What does the General Assembly say in this resolution? It says that the Federal Republic of Yugoslavia cannot claim the membership status enjoyed by the former Republic of Yugoslavia. Thus, to take a seat at the United Nations, of which it is not a Member, it "should apply for membership". The resolution is quite clear.

On 28 October 1996, the permanent representatives of Slovenia, Croatia, Bosnia-Herzegovina and Macedonia again wrote to the United Nations Secretary-General stating that the Federal Republic of Yugoslavia could not claim the succession of the former Socialist Republic (Doc. A/51/564-S/1996/885, quoted by Mr. Wood). On this point, the Member States of the European Union, and of the Islamic Conference, and the United States, all agreed with the view taken by the United Nations bodies.

Also, Mr. President, Members of the Court, the clearest evidence that the Federal Republic of Yugoslavia is not the successor of the former Yugoslavia is provided by the Federal Republic of Yugoslavia itself in a declaration made by that country's Foreign Minister on 22 September 1992 to the General Assembly, when he said: "I hereby formally request membership in the United Nations on behalf of the new Yugoslavia, whose Government I represent" (Doc. A/47/PV.7,p. 149, quoted by Mr. Wood).

If you are already a Member, why apply for membership? Here, the Foreign Minister recognized, as demanded by the Assembly General, that an application had to be made. But merely applying does not suffice; what is required is that the relevant United Nations bodies decide on the basis of Article 4 of the Charter to admit the Federal Republic of Yugoslavia to the Organization. No such decision has ever been taken, and the relevant United Nations bodies - the Security Council and the General Assembly - have never altered their 1992 decision, to the effect that the Federal Republic of Yugoslavia cannot claim to be the successor of the former Yugoslavia. Specialized international agencies agree: the Universal Postal Union and the Governing Body of the International Labour Office also agree, so does the World Health Organization. Our conclusion must be that, as the Federal Republic of Yugoslavia is not a Member of United Nations, it is not party to your Statute either, and, this being so, it could not properly, under Article 36, paragraph 2, of that instrument, declare that it recognizes your Court's jurisdiction. Manifestly, in the absence of such recognition, you have no jurisdiction to entertain this request.

THE ALLEGED JURISDICTION OF YOUR COURT UNDER ARTICLE IX OF THE CONVENTION ON THE PREVENTION AND PUNISHMENT OF THE CRIME OF GENOCIDE

The second head of the Court's jurisdiction relied on by the Federal Republic of Yugoslavia is Article IX of the Convention on the Prevention and Punishment of the Crime of Genocide.

Mr. President, Members of the Court, this is nothing but a procedural device and the Kingdom of Belgium will show you why. It is a blatant abuse of the procedure. Before you can entertain a request or declare the Court prima facie competent on the basis of this ground of jurisdiction, it is necessary that the issue raised concerns the interpretation or the application of the Convention. You said so yourselves in your Order of 8 April 1993: you stated that the Court has jurisdiction:

"to the extent that the subject-matter of the dispute relates to 'the interpretation, application or fulfilment' of the Convention, including disputes 'relating to the responsibility of a State for genocide or for any of the other acts enumerated in article III' of the Convention" (para. 26).

CONCLUSION AS TO THE JURISDICTION OF YOUR COURT

Thus the issue in the dispute must pertain to the scope of the Convention, which is determined by the concept of "genocide" [acts of genocide]. To charge Belgium with genocide in this case is an abuse of the Court's procedure and lacking in any serious basis. For genocide to exist - and the Convention itself defines it - there must be intent, the intent to destroy some or all of an ethnic, racial or religious population. I defy the Federal Republic of Yugoslavia to produce any evidence whatever of such intention, real or apparent. No such evidence has been offered. It is quite clear that the situation lies outside the scope of the Genocide Convention and consequently, prima facie, there is not the slightest ground of jurisdiction here either. It is perfectly clear that you do not have jurisdiction on the basis of this Convention.

THE ISSUE OF URGENCY

The alleged urgency of the matter is contradicted by the facts: this morning the applicant State - I was listening carefully - itself recognized this. We were told that "as early as October 1998, NATO had threatened the use of force". This is true. The parties agree on this. But why then was the Court's jurisdiction not recognized then and provisional measures already requested? The threat of force is, ex hypothesi, just as illegal as the use of force. Why wait?

On 30 January 1999, the NATO Council, I may remind the Court, publicly authorized its Secretary-General to launch air strikes; still your Court's jurisdiction was not recognized. The air strikes were in fact launched on 24 March, your Court's jurisdiction was still not recognized. Only at the end of April, with the system under mounting pressure, did the Yugoslav authorities, with a purely tactical manoeuvre, decide to recognize your Court's jurisdiction in the hope of securing temporary relief.

THE ABSOLUTE AND COMPELLING NEED FOR THE CURRENT ARMED OPERATION

As regards the intervention, the Kingdom of Belgium takes the view that the Security Council's resolutions which I have just cited provide an unchallengeable basis for the armed intervention. They are clear, and they are based on Chapter VII of the Charter, under which the Security Council may determine the existence of any threat to international peace and security. But we need to go further and develop the idea of armed humanitarian intervention. NATO, and the Kingdom of Belgium in particular, felt obliged to intervene to forestall an ongoing humanitarian catastrophe, acknowledged in Security Council resolutions. To safeguard what? To safeguard, Mr. President, essential values which also rank as jus cogens. Are the right to life, physical integrity, the prohibition of torture, are these not norms with the status of jus cogens? They undeniably have this status, so much so that international instruments on human rights (the European Human Rights Convention, the agreements mentioned above) protect them in a waiver clause (the power of suspension in case of war of all human rights except right to life and integrity of the individual): thus they are absolute rights, from which we may conclude that they belong to the jus cogens. Thus, NATO intervened to protect fundamental values enshrined in the jus cogens and to prevent an impending catastrophe recognized as such by the Security Council. There is another important feature of NATO's action: NATO has never questioned the political independence and the territorial integrity of the Federal Republic of Yugoslavia - the Security Council's resolutions, the NATO decisions, and the press releases have, moreover, consistently stressed this. Thus this is not an intervention against the territorial integrity or independence of the former Republic of Yugoslavia. The purpose of NATO's intervention is to rescue a people in peril, in deep distress. For this reason the Kingdom of Belgium takes the view that this is an armed humanitarian intervention, compatible with Article 2, paragraph 4, of the Charter, which covers only intervention against the territorial integrity or political independence of a State.

There is no shortage of precedents. India's intervention in Eastern Pakistan; Tanzania's intervention in Uganda; Vietnam in Cambodia, the West African countries' interventions first in Liberia and then in Sierra Leone. While there may have been certain doubts expressed in the doctrine, and among some members of the international community, these interventions have not been expressly condemned by the relevant United Nations bodies. These precedents, combined with Security Council resolutions and the rejection of the draft Russian resolution on 26 March, which I have already referred to, undoubtedly support and substantiate our contention that the NATO intervention is entirely legal. Allow me to remind the Court of the three features of the intervention which have been noted by the international authorities, in this case the Security Council; there was a humanitarian catastrophe, recognised by the Security Council, imminent danger, i.e., a situation constituting a threat to peace as noted by the Security Council resolution; and the power responsible for this - as is made clear in the three Security Council resolutions - is the Federal Republic of Yugoslavia.

The intervention is of a quite exceptional character, prompted by entirely objective criteria. In the circumstances do we need to add another consideration, the tendency in contemporary international law towards a steadily greater protection of minorities? We are accused of encroaching on sovereignty, but the Government of the Kingdom of Belgium would like to quote a passage from a speech given by Mr. Kofi Annan, United Nations Secretary-General, on 30 April last, at the University of Michigan. Mr. Annan said "no Government has the right to hide behind national sovereignty in order to violate the human rights or fundamental freedoms of its peoples", and headded a very important point, "Emerging slowly, but I believe surely is an international norm against the violent repression of minorities that will and must take precedence over concerns of State sovereignty".

NATO's action has had and still has a further dimension. The aim is to protect a distressed population in the throes of a humanitarian catastrophe, but there is also a need to safeguard the stability of an entire region, for the Security Council resolutions have also noted that the behaviour of the Federal Republic of Yugoslavia in Kosovo was generating a threat to international peace and security by impairing the stability of the whole area. This is a case of a lawful armed humanitarian intervention for which there is a compelling necessity. And, Mr. President, Members of the Court, if we have failed to convince you that what has been taking place is armed humanitarian intervention justified by international law, the Government of the Kingdom of Belgium will also plead, in the alternative, that there is a state of necessity.

THE STATE OF NECESSITY

The notion of a state of necessity, which is enshrined in all branches of the law, is unquestionably acknowledged in international law; and the draft Article 33 proposed by the International Law Commission reflects this.

Allow me to suggest a definition to the Court: what is a state of necessity? A state of necessity is the cause which justifies the violation of a binding rule in order to safeguard, in face of grave and imminent peril, values which are higher than those protected by the rule which has been breached. Let me review the elements of this definition one at a time and set them against the case we are dealing with today.

First, what rule has been breached? We do not accept that any rule has been breached. However, for the sake of argument, let us say that it is the rule prohibiting the use of force. Where is the imminent peril, the grave and imminent peril? There it was - no doubt about it - at the time of the armed intervention; there it is still, the humanitarian catastrophe recorded in the resolutions of the Security Council - an impending peril. What are the higher values which this intervention attempts to safeguard? They are rights of jus cogens. It is the collective security of an entire region. And the final element of a state of necessity, I almost forgot, is that the acts must be proportionate; the intervention must be proportional to the threat. The intervention is wholly in proportion to the gravity of the peril; it is limited to aerial bombardments directed solely and exclusively against the war machine of the aggressor and against its military-industrial complex.

The Court will see that this is a use of force which is utterly unlike the parallel drawn this morning by one of my esteemed opponents; a parallel with what was the diktats of the Nazi régime to its peaceful neighbours. The Kingdom of Belgium regrets to have to say that it finds such a parallel totally unacceptable, and apt to shock the civilized legal conscience. The situation is the total reverse. It is we, the member countries of NATO, democratic countries with freely elected governments, who find ourselves confronted by a régime which rejects the most fundamental values of humanity.

THE BALANCE OF THE INTERESTS CONCERNED

I now return to a further element, to another criterion determining the granting of provisional measures, namely the balance of the interests concerned.

When the Court grants provisional measures, it may direct such measures against a single one of the States in dispute or it may address them bilaterally to both parties. It is very difficult to speculate as to what your decision will be. However, let us assume that the Court were to indicate provisional measures against both the applicant and the respondent State. You would hinder the humanitarian action but you would not stop severe and massive violations of fundamental rights from continuing in Kosovo.

Indeed, it is abundantly clear that the Federal Republic of Yugoslavia cares not one whit for the decisions of international agencies, be they political bodies, the Security Council, the General Assembly or even your Court. Let me just remind you of your own Orders: Orders dated 8 April 1993, 13 September 1993. Two Orders indicating provisional measures against the Federal Republic of Yugoslavia in the case of Bosnia against Yugoslavia. What became of these Orders? Were they complied with? Were the provisional measures implemented? There are grave doubts on this score. Thus, the Court has indicated provisional measures against the Federal Republic of Yugoslavia, and it is known that Yugoslavia cheerfully ignores them, utterly ignores them, ignores these international decisions. You would run the risk of hampering an ongoing humanitarian operation which meets a desperate need. To indicate provisional measures is likely to be far more damaging than to refuse to do so. And at this point the Kingdom of Belgium respectfully urges the Court to weigh up the balance of the interests concerned.

WHETHER THE ALLEGED ACTS MAY BE IMPUTED TO THE KINGDOM OF BELGIUM

A further important point is whether the acts alleged against the Kingdom of Belgium are properly imputable to it, even if only apparently so. There has been talk of destruction, of damage to the environment, of the use of prohibited weapons, but nowhere have we seen evidence establishing prima facie that such facts are imputable to the military forces of the Kingdom of Belgium. In fact, the measures requested of the Court today serve a purely political and tactical objective. It is a tactical step designed to hinder initiatives under way at international level.

THE PURELY POLITICAL PURPOSE OF THE REQUEST FOR PROVISIONAL MEASURES

Moreover, if the Court were to order provisional measures in this case, it would run the risk of prejudging the merits of the case. For let us see how the request of the applicant State is worded: "The Kingdom of Belgium shall cease immediately its acts of use of force and shall refrain from any act of threat or use of force against the Federal Republic of Yugoslavia." Yet this request, based on the premise that the acts concerned are illegal, necessarily prejudges their legality.

The measures as formulated are vague, so vague that it may be asked whether they are compatible with the concept of provisional measures. Once again, I repeat, a tactical, short-term advantage is being sought.

Let me sum up. Mr. President, Members of the Court, your jurisprudence on provisional measures is restrictive; the Court does not grant provisional measures lightly. Undoubtedly, in the past the Court has granted provisional measures in cases of armed conflict, that is true. However, the Kingdom of Belgium would point out that the case before you is fundamentally different from previous cases.

In the case of the Respondent, the Kingdom of Belgium, as I have sought to show, it cannot seriously be alleged that it has any intention whatsoever of committing genocide, or that it is actually committing genocide. Quite the reverse. We are therefore dealing with a case which is fundamentally different from the case of Bosnia against Yugoslavia, which the Court heard in 1990 [sic].

Nor are we dealing with a frontier dispute or a case of assistance to rebels with the intention of destabilizing a régime, something which might constitute a threat to the security of the region. There is much more than that in this case. The Court is dealing with an intervention to save an entire population in peril, a population which is the victim of severe, widespread violations of its rights, rights which have the status of a norm of jus cogens. Were the Court to order this humanitarian policing action to stop, it would magnify the catastrophe and would create irreparable damage within this persecuted group of the population, damage which would be far more serious than that which NATO is inflicting on the aggressor's military-industrial complex and its war machine. It would weaken humanitarian action that is providing assistance to persons in danger. It would give a precious breathing space to a destructive system which is now on its knees. The Court would fall into the trap, and this is the risk, of becoming the instrument of a cunning strategist which is using all sorts of delaying tactics in order to escape its international commitments and to pursue its evil ends. The Court would render justice by refusing any kind of provisional measure. And the cause of human rights and of contemporary international law, the champion of the weak and the oppressed, would be enhanced. On-going military pressure on the oppressor, and recent diplomatic initiatives undertaken as a result of the G-8 summit, are converging. Pressure must be maintained, and continuing military pressure is a condition sine qua non of establishing peace in the region. [...]

Mrs. Foucart-Kleynen: Mr. President, Members of the Court,

For all the reasons put forward by counsel, the Kingdom of Belgium requests the Court, without prejudice to the merits of the case:

- to declare the request for provisional measures submitted by the Federal Republic of Yugoslavia inadmissible on the grounds that the Court has not even a shred of jurisdiction to hear the case;

and, in any event,

- to state that there are no grounds for the indication of provisional measures:

first, because there is no trace of any element in the jurisprudence of the Court or in the general principles of international law which might justify provisional measures; and

second, because of the serious effects which such measures would have on the outcome of the humanitarian crisis instigated by the Federal Republic of Yugoslavia in Kosovo and in neighbouring countries. [...]

309. ICJ Case Concerning the Legality of Use of Force, Request for the Indication of Provisional Measures, Order, 2 June 1999

309 a) Belgium

Present: Vice-President Weeramantry, Acting President; President Schwebel; Judges Oda, Bedjaoui, Guillaume, Ranjeva, Herczegh, Shi, Fleischhauer, Koroma, Vereshchetin, Higgins, Parra-Aranguren, Kooijmans; Judges ad hoc Kreca, Duinslaeger; Registrar Valencia-Ospina.

The International Court of Justice,

Composed as above,

After deliberation,

Having regard to Articles 41 and 48 of the Statute of the Court and to Articles 73 and 74 of the Rules of Court,

Having regard to the Application by the Federal Republic of Yugoslavia (hereinafter "Yugoslavia") filed in the Registry of the Court on 29 April 1999, instituting proceedings against the Kingdom of Belgium (hereinafter "Belgium") "for violation of the obligation not to use force",

Makes the following Order:

1. Whereas in that Application Yugoslavia defines the subject of the dispute as follows:

"The subject-matter of the dispute are acts of the Kingdom of Belgium by which it has violated its international obligation banning the use of force against another State, the obligation not to intervene in the internal affairs of another State, the obligation not to violate the sovereignty of another State, the obligation to protect the civilian population and civilian objects in wartime, the obligation to protect the environment, the obligation relating to free navigation on international rivers, the obligation regarding fundamental human rights and freedoms, the obligation not to use prohibited weapons, the obligation not to deliberately inflict conditions of life calculated to cause the physical destruction of a national group";

2. Whereas in the said Application Yugoslavia refers, as a basis for the jurisdiction of the Court, to Article 36, paragraph 2, of the Statute of the Court and to Article IX of the Convention on the Prevention and Punishment of the Crime of Genocide, adopted by the General Assem-

bly of the United Nations on 9 December 1948 (hereinafter the "Genocide Convention");

3. Whereas in its Application Yugoslavia states that the claims submitted by it to the Court are based upon the following facts:

"The Government of the Kingdom of Belgium, together with the Governments of other Member States of NATO, took part in the acts of use of force against the Federal Republic of Yugoslavia by taking part in bombing targets in the Federal Republic of Yugoslavia. In bombing the Federal Republic of Yugoslavia military and civilian targets were attacked. Great number of people were killed, including a great many civilians. Residential houses came under attack. Numerous dwellings were destroyed. Enormous damage was caused to schools, hospitals, radio and television stations, cultural and health institutions and to places of worship. A large number of bridges, roads and railway lines were destroyed. Attacks on oil refineries and chemical plants have had serious environmental effects on cities, towns and villages in the Federal Republic of Yugoslavia. The use of weapons containing depleted uranium is having far-reaching consequences for human life. The above-mentioned acts are deliberately creating conditions calculated at the physical destruction of an ethnic group, in whole or in part. The Government of the Kingdom of Belgium is taking part in the training, arming, financing, equipping and supplying the so-called 'Kosovo Liberation Army'";

and whereas it further states that the said claims are based on the following legal grounds:

"The above acts of the Government of Belgium represent a gross violation of the obligation not to use force against another State. By financing, arming, training and equipping the so-called 'Kosovo Liberation Army', support is given to terrorist groups and the secessionist movement in the territory of the Federal Republic of Yugoslavia in breach of the obligation not to intervene in the internal affairs of another State. In addition, the provisions of the Geneva Convention of 1949 and of the Additional Protocol No. 1 of 1977 on the protection of civilians and civilian objects in time of war have been violated. The obligation to protect the environment has also been breached. The destruction of bridges on the Danube is in contravention of the provisions of Article 1 of the 1948 Convention on free navigation on the Danube. The provisions of the International Covenant on Civil and Political Rights and of the International Covenant on Economic, Social and Cultural Rights of 1966 have also been breached. Furthermore, the obligation contained in the Convention on the Prevention and Punishment of the Crime of Genocide not to impose deliberately on a national group conditions of life calculated to bring about the physical destruction of the group has been breached. Furthermore, the activities in which the Kingdom of Belgium is taking part are contrary to Article 53, paragraph 1, of the Charter of the United Nations";

4. Whereas the claims of Yugoslavia are formulated as follows in the Application:

"The Government of the Federal Republic of Yugoslavia requests the International Court of Justice to adjudge and declare:

- by taking part in the bombing of the territory of the Federal Republic of Yugoslavia, the Kingdom of Belgium has acted against the Federal Republic of Yugoslavia in breach of its obligation not to use force against another State;

- by taking part in the training, arming, financing, equipping and supplying terrorist groups, i.e. the so-called 'Kosovo Liberation Army', the Kingdom of Belgium has acted against the Federal Republic of Yugoslavia in breach of its obligation not to intervene in the affairs of another State;

- by taking part in attacks on civilian targets, the Kingdom of Belgium has acted against the Federal Republic of Yugoslavia in breach of its obligation to spare the civilian population, civilians and civilian objects;

- by taking part in destroying or damaging monasteries, monuments of culture, the Kingdom of Belgium has acted against the Federal Republic of Yugoslavia in breach of its obligation not to commit any act of hostility directed against historical monuments, works of art or places of worship which constitute cultural or spiritual heritage of people;

- by taking part in the use of cluster bombs, the Kingdom of Belgium has acted against the Federal Republic of Yugoslavia in breach of its obligation not to use prohibited weapons, i.e. weapons calculated to cause unnecessary suffering;

- by taking part in the bombing of oil refineries and chemical plants, the Kingdom of Belgium has acted against the Federal Republic of Yugoslavia in breach of its obligation not to cause considerable environmental damage;

- by taking part in the use of weapons containing depleted uranium, the Kingdom of Belgium has acted against the Federal Republic of Yugoslavia in breach of its obligation not to use prohibited weapons and not to cause far-reaching health and environmental damage;

- by taking part in killing civilians, destroying enterprises, communications, health and cultural institutions, the Kingdom of Belgium has acted against the Federal Republic of Yugoslavia in breach of its obligation to respect the right to life, the right to work, the right to information, the right to health care as well as other basic human rights;

- by taking part in destroying bridges on international rivers, the Kingdom of Belgium has acted against the Federal Republic of Yugoslavia in breach of its obligation to respect freedom of navigation on international rivers;

- by taking part in activities listed above, and in particular by causing enormous environmental damage and by using depleted uranium, the Kingdom of Belgium has acted against the Federal Republic of Yugoslavia in breach of its obligation not to deliberately inflict on a national group conditions of life calculated to bring about its physical destruction, in whole or in part;

- the Kingdom of Belgium is responsible for the violation of the above international obligations;

- the Kingdom of Belgium is obliged to stop immediately the violation of the above obligations vis-à-vis the Federal Republic of Yugoslavia;

- the Kingdom of Belgium is obliged to provide compensation for the damage done to the Federal Republic of Yugoslavia and to its citizens and juridical persons";

and whereas, at the end of its Application, Yugoslavia reserves the right to amend and supplement it;

5. Whereas on 29 April 1999, immediately after filing its Application, Yugoslavia also submitted a request for the indication of provisional measures pursuant to Article 73 of the Rules of Court; and whereas that request was accompanied by a volume of photographic annexes produced as "evidence";

6. Whereas, in support of its request for the indication of provisional measures, Yugoslavia contends inter alia that, since the onset of the bombing of its territory, and as a result thereof, about 1,000 civilians, including 19 children, have been killed and more than 4,500 have sustained serious injuries; that the lives of three million children are endangered; that hundreds of thousands of citizens have been exposed to poisonous gases; that about one million citizens are short of water supply; that about 500,000 workers have become jobless; that two million citizens have no means of livelihood and are unable to ensure minimum means of sustenance; and that the road and railway network has suffered extensive destruction; whereas, in its request for the indication of provisional measures, Yugoslavia also lists the targets alleged to have come under attack in the air strikes and describes in detail the damage alleged to have been inflicted upon them (bridges, railway lines and stations, roads and means of transport, airports, industry and trade, refineries and warehouses storing liquid raw materials and chemicals, agriculture, hospitals and health care centres, schools, public buildings and housing facilities, infrastructure, telecommunications, cultural-historical monuments and religious shrines); and whereas Yugoslavia concludes from this that:

"The acts described above caused death, physical and mental harm to the population of the Federal Republic of Yugoslavia; huge devastation; heavy pollution of the environment, so that the Yugoslav population is deliberately imposed conditions of life calculated to bring about physical destruction of the group, in whole or in part";

7. Whereas, at the end of its request for the indication of provisional measures, Yugoslavia states that

"If the proposed measure were not to be adopted, there will be new losses of human life, further physical and mental harm inflicted on the population of the FR of Yugoslavia, further destruction of civilian targets, heavy environmental pollution and further physical destruction of the people of Yugoslavia";

and whereas, while reserving the right to amend and supplement its request, Yugoslavia requests the Court to indicate the following measure:

"The Kingdom of Belgium shall cease immediately its acts of use of force and shall refrain from any act of threat or use of force against the Federal Republic of Yugoslavia";

8. Whereas the request for the indication of provisional measures was accompanied by a letter from the Agent of Yugoslavia, addressed to the President and Members of the Court, which read as follows:

"I have the honour to bring to the attention of the Court the latest bombing of the central area of the town of Surdulica on 27 April, 1999 at noon resulting in losses of lives of civilians, most of whom were children and women, and to remind of killings of peoples in Kursumlija, Aleksinac and Cuprija, as well as bombing of a refugee convoy and the Radio and Television of Serbia, just to mention some of the well-known atrocities. Therefore, I would like to caution the Court that there is a highest probability of further civilian and military casualties.

Considering the power conferred upon the Court by Article 75, paragraph 1, of the Rules of Court and having in mind the greatest urgency caused by the circumstances described in the Requests for provisional measure of protection I kindly ask the Court to decide on the submitted Requests proprio motu or to fix a date for a hearing at earliest possible time";

9. Whereas on 29 April 1999, the day on which the Application and the request for the indication of provisional measures were filed in the Registry, the Registrar sent to the Belgian Government signed copies of the Application and of the request, in accordance with Article 38, paragraph 4, and Article 73, paragraph 2, of the Rules of Court; and whereas he also sent to that Government copies of the documents accompanying the Application and the request for the indication of provisional measures;

10. Whereas on 29 April 1999 the Registrar informed the Parties that the Court had decided, pursuant to Article 74, paragraph 3, of the Rules of Court, to hold hearings on 10 and 11 May 1999, where they would be able to present their observations on the request for the indication of provisional measures;

11. Whereas, pending the notification under Article 40, paragraph 3, of the Statute and Article 42 of the Rules of Court, by transmittal of the printed bilingual text of the Application to the Members of the United Nations and other States entitled to appear before the Court, the Registrar on 29 April 1999 informed those States of the filing of the Application and of its subject-matter, and of the filing of the request for the indication of provisional measures;

12. Whereas, since the Court includes upon the bench no judge of Yugoslav nationality, the Yugoslav Government has availed itself of the provisions of Article 31 of the Statute of the Court to choose Mr. Milenko Kreca to sit as judge ad hoc in the case; and whereas no objection to that choice was raised within the time-limit fixed for the purpose pursuant to Article 35, paragraph 3, of the Rules of Court; whereas, since the Court includes upon the bench no judge of Belgian nationality, the Belgian Government has availed itself of the provisions of Article 31 of the Statute of the Court to choose Mr. Patrick Duinslaeger to sit as judge ad hoc in the case; whereas, within the time-limit fixed for the purpose pursuant to Article 35, paragraph 3, of the Rules of Court, Yugoslavia, referring to Article 31, paragraph 5, of the Statute, objected to that choice; and whereas the Court, after due deliberation, found that the nomination of a judge ad hoc by Belgium was justified in the present phase of the case;

13. Whereas, at the public hearings held between 10 and 12 May 1999, oral observations on the request for the indication of provisional measures were presented by the Parties:

On behalf of Yugoslavia: Mr. Rodoljub Etinski, Agent, Mr. Ian Brownlie, Mr. Paul J. I. M. de Waart, Mr. Eric Suy, Mr. Miodrag Mitic, Mr. Olivier Corten;

On behalf of Belgium: Mrs. Raymonde Foucart, Agent, Mr. Rusen Ergec;

14. Whereas, by letter of 12 May 1999, the Agent of Yugoslavia submitted to the Court a "Supplement to the Application" of his Government, which read as follows:

"Using the right reserved by the Application of the Federal Republic of Yugoslavia against the Kingdom of Belgium for violation of the obligation not to use force, filed to the International Court of Justice on 29 April 1999, I supplement its part related to the grounds of jurisdiction of the Court, which should now read as follows:

'The Government of the Federal Republic of Yugoslavia invokes Article 36, paragraph 2 of the Statute of the International Court of Justice as well as Article IX of the Convention on the Prevention and Punishment of the Crime of Genocide and Article 4 of the Convention of Conciliation, Judicial Settlement and Arbitration between the Kingdom of Yugoslavia and Belgium, signed at Belgrade on 25 March 1930 and in force since 3 September 1930'";

whereas, at the start of the afternoon session of the hearing of 12 May 1999, the Vice-President of the Court, acting President, made the following statement:

"In the light of the new bases of jurisdiction invoked today by Yugoslavia ... the Court wishes to inform the Parties that it will give its consideration to any observations of Belgium ... in regard to the admissibility of the additional grounds invoked";

and whereas at the said afternoon session of 12 May 1999 Belgium made various observations on the admissibility of the Yugoslav "Supplement to the Application", and on the new basis of jurisdiction invoked therein;

15. Whereas, in this phase of the proceedings, the Parties presented the following submissions:

On behalf of Yugoslavia: "[T]he Court [is asked] to indicate the following provisional measure: [T]he Kingdom of Belgium ... shall cease immediately the acts of use of force and shall refrain from any act of threat or use of force against the Federal Republic of Yugoslavia";

On behalf of Belgium: "For all the reasons put forward . . ., the Kingdom of Belgium requests the Court, without prejudice to the merits of the case,

To declare the request for provisional measures submitted by the Federal Republic of Yugoslavia inadmissible on the ground that the Court has no prima facie jurisdiction to hear the case, and, in any event,

To find that it should not indicate provisional measures on the ground, first,

Of the absence of any prima facie evidence which, according to the jurisprudence of the Court and to the general principles of international law, could justify provisional measures and, second,

Of the serious effects which such measures would have on the outcome of the humanitarian crisis caused by the Federal Republic of Yugoslavia in Kosovo and in neighbouring countries."

16. Whereas the Court is deeply concerned with the human tragedy, the loss of life, and the enormous suffering in Kosovo which form the background of the present dispute, and with the continuing loss of life and human suffering in all parts of Yugoslavia;

17. Whereas the Court is profoundly concerned with the use of force in Yugoslavia; whereas under the present circumstances such use raises very serious issues of international law;

18. Whereas the Court is mindful of the purposes and principles of the United Nations Charter and of its own responsibilities in the maintenance of peace and security under the Charter and the Statute of the Court;

19. Whereas the Court deems it necessary to emphasize that all parties appearing before it must act in conformity with their obligations under the United Nations Charter and other rules of international law, including humanitarian law;

20. Whereas the Court, under its Statute, does not automatically have jurisdiction over legal disputes between States parties to that Statute or between other States to whom access to the Court has been granted; whereas the Court has repeatedly stated "that one of the fundamental principles of its Statute is that it cannot decide a dispute between States without the consent of those States to its jurisdiction" (East Timor, Judgment, I.C.J. Reports 1995, p. 101, para. 26); and whereas the Court can therefore exercise jurisdiction only between States parties to a dispute who not only have access to the Court but also have accepted the jurisdiction of the Court, either in general form or for the individual dispute concerned;

21. Whereas on a request for provisional measures the Court need not, before deciding whether or not to indicate them, finally satisfy itself that it has jurisdiction on the merits of the case, yet it ought not to indicate such measures unless the provisions invoked by the applicant appear, prima facie, to afford a basis on which the jurisdiction of the Court might be established;

22. Whereas in its Application Yugoslavia claims, in the first place, to found the jurisdiction of the Court upon Article 36, paragraph 2, of the Statute; whereas each of the two Parties has made a declaration recognizing the compulsory jurisdiction of the Court pursuant to that provision; whereas Yugoslavia's declaration was deposited with the Secretary-General of the United Nations on 26 April 1999, and that of Belgium on 17 June 1958 (together with the instrument of ratification);

23. Whereas Yugoslavia's declaration is formulated as follows:

"I hereby declare that the Government of the Federal Republic of Yugoslavia recognizes, in accordance with Article 36, paragraph 2, of the Statute of the International Court of Justice, as compulsory ipso facto and without special agreement, in relation to any other State accepting the same obligation, that is on condition of reciprocity, the jurisdiction of the said Court in all disputes arising or which may arise after the signature of the present Declaration, with regard to the situations or facts subsequent to this signature, except in cases where the parties have agreed or shall agree to have recourse to another procedure or to another method of pacific settlement. The present Declaration does not apply to disputes relating to questions which, under international law, fall exclusively within the jurisdiction of the Federal Republic of Yugoslavia, as well as to territorial disputes.

The aforesaid obligation is accepted until such time as notice may be given to terminate the acceptance";

and whereas the declaration of Belgium reads as follows:

"1. I declare on behalf of the Belgian Government that I recognize as compulsory ipso facto and without special agreement, in relation to any other State accepting the same obligation, the jurisdiction of the International Court of Justice, in conformity with Article 36, paragraph 2, of the Statute of the Court, in legal disputes arising after 13 July 1948 concerning situations or facts subsequent to that date, except those in regard to which the parties have agreed or may agree to have recourse to another method of pacific settlement.

This declaration is made subject to ratification. It shall take effect on the day of deposit of the instrument of ratification for a period of five years. Upon the expiry of that period, it shall continue to have effect until notice of its termination is given";

24. Whereas, under the terms of its declaration, Yugoslavia limits ratione temporis its acceptance of the Court's compulsory jurisdiction to "disputes arising or which may arise after the signature of the present Declaration, with regard to the situations or facts subsequent to this signature"; whereas Belgium has based no argument on this provision; but whereas the Court must nonetheless consider what effects it might have prima facie upon its jurisdiction in this case;

25. Whereas, according to Yugoslavia, "[t]he issue before the Court is that of interpreting a unilateral declaration of acceptance of its jurisdiction, and thus of ascertaining the meaning of the declaration on the basis of the intention of its author"; whereas Yugoslavia contends that the text of its declaration "allows all disputes effectively arising after 25 April 1999 to be taken into account"; whereas, referring to bombing attacks carried out by NATO member States on 28 April, 1 May, 7 May and 8 May 1999, Yugoslavia states that, "[i]n each of these cases, which are only examples, [it] denounced the flagrant violations of international law of which it considered itself to have been the victim", and the "NATO member States denied having violated any obligation under international law"; whereas Yugoslavia asserts that "each of these events therefore gave rise to 'a disagreement on a point of law or fact', a disagreement ... the terms of which depend in each case on the specific features of the attack" in question; whereas Yugoslavia accordingly concludes that, since these events constitute "instantaneous wrongful acts", there exist "a number of separate disputes which have arisen" between the Parties "since 25 April relating to events subsequent to that date"; and whereas Yugoslavia argues from this that "[t]here is no reason to exclude prima facie the Court's jurisdiction over disputes having effectively arisen after 25 April, as provided in the text of the declaration"; and whereas Yugoslavia adds that to exclude such disputes from the jurisdiction of the Court "would run entirely counter to the manifest and clear intention of Yugoslavia" to entrust the Court with the resolution of those disputes;

26. Whereas Yugoslavia has accepted the Court's jurisdiction ratione temporis in respect only, on the one hand, of disputes arising or which may arise after the signature of its declaration and, on the other hand, of those concerning situations or facts subsequent to that signature (cf. Right of Passage over Indian Territory, Merits, Judgment, I.C.J. Reports 1960, p. 34); whereas, in order to assess whether the Court has jurisdiction in the case, it is sufficient to decide whether, in terms of the text of the declaration, the dispute brought before the Court "arose" before or after 25 April 1999, the date on which the declaration was signed;

27. Whereas Yugoslavia's Application is entitled "Application of the Federal Republic of Yugoslavia against the Kingdom of Belgium for Violation of the Obligation Not to Use Force"; whereas in the Application the "subject of the dispute" (emphasis added) is described in general terms (see paragraph 1 above); but whereas it can be seen both from the statement of "facts upon which the claim is based" and from the manner in which the "claims" themselves are formulated (see paragraphs 3 and 4 above) that the Application is directed, in essence, against the "bombing of the territory of the Federal Republic of Yugoslavia", to which the Court is asked to put an end;

28. Whereas it is an established fact that the bombings in question began on 24 March 1999 and have been conducted continuously over a period extending beyond 25 April 1999; and whereas the Court has no doubt, in the light, inter alia, of the discussions at the Security Council meetings of 24 and 26 March 1999 (S/PV. 3988 and 3989), that a "legal dispute" (East Timor (Portugal v. Australia), I.C.J. Reports 1995, p. 100, para. 22) "arose" between Yugoslavia and the Respondent, as it did also with the other NATO member States, well before 25 April 1999 concerning the legality of those bombings as such, taken as a whole;

29. Whereas the fact that the bombings have continued after 25 April 1999 and that the dispute concerning them has persisted since that date is not such as to alter the date on which the dispute arose; whereas each individual air attack could not have given rise to a separate subsequent dispute; and whereas, at this stage of the proceedings, Yugoslavia has not established that new disputes, distinct from the initial one, have

arisen between the Parties since 25 April 1999 in respect of subsequent situations or facts attributable to Belgium;

30. Whereas, as the Court recalled in its Judgment of 4 December 1998 in the case concerning Fisheries Jurisdiction (Spain v. Canada),

"It is for each State, in formulating its declaration, to decide upon the limits it places upon its acceptance of the jurisdiction of the Court: '[t]his jurisdiction only exists within the limits within which it has been accepted' (Phosphates in Morocco, Judgment, 1938, P.C.I.J., Series A/B, No. 74, p. 23)" (I.C.J. Reports 1998, para. 44);

and whereas, as the Permanent Court held in its Judgment of 14 June 1938 in the Phosphates in Morocco case (Preliminary Objections), "it is recognized that, as a consequence of the condition of reciprocity stipulated in paragraph 2 of Article 36 of the Statute of the Court", any limitation ratione temporis attached by one of the Parties to its declaration of acceptance of the Court's jurisdiction "holds good as between the Parties" (Phosphates in Morocco, Judgment, 1938, P.C.I.J., Series A/B, No. 74, p. 10); whereas, moreover, as the present Court noted in its Judgment of 11 June 1988 in the case concerning the Land and Maritime Boundary between Cameroon and Nigeria (Cameroon v. Nigeria), "[a]s early as 1952, it held in the case concerning Anglo-Iranian Oil Co. that, when declarations are made on condition of reciprocity, 'jurisdiction is conferred on the Court only to the extent to which the two Declarations coincide in conferring it' (I.C.J. Reports 1952, p. 103)" (I.C.J. Reports 1998, p. 298, para. 43); and whereas it follows from the foregoing that the declarations made by the Parties under Article 36, paragraph 2, of the Statute do not constitute a basis on which the jurisdiction of the Court could prima facie be founded in this case;

31. Whereas Belgium contends that the Court's jurisdiction in this case cannot in any event be based, even prima facie, on Article 36, paragraph 2, of the Statute, for, under this provision, only "States parties to the ... Statute" may subscribe to the optional clause for compulsory jurisdiction contained therein; and whereas, referring to United Nations Security Council resolutions 757 (1992) of 30 May 1992 and 777 (1992) of 19 September 1992, and to United Nations General Assembly resolutions 47/1 of 22 September 1992 and 48/88 of 20 December 1993, it contends that "the Federal Republic of Yugoslavia is not the continuator State of the former Socialist Federal Republic of Yugoslavia as regards membership of the United Nations", and that, not having duly acceded to the Organization, it is in consequence not a party to the Statute of the Court and cannot appear before the latter;

32. Whereas Yugoslavia, referring to the position of the Secretariat, as expressed in a letter dated 29 September 1992 from the Legal Counsel of the Organization (doc. A/47/485), and to the latter's subsequent practice, contends for its part that General Assembly resolution 47/1 "[neither] terminate[d] nor suspend[ed] Yugoslavia's membership in the Organization", and that the said resolution did not take away from Yugoslavia "[its] right to participate in the work of organs other than Assembly bodies";

33. Whereas, in view of its finding in paragraph 30 above, the Court need not consider this question for the purpose of deciding whether or not it can indicate provisional measures in the present case;

34. Whereas in its Application Yugoslavia claims, in the second place, to found the jurisdiction of the Court on Article IX of the Genocide Convention, which provides:

"Disputes between the Contracting Parties relating to the interpretation, application or fulfilment of the present Convention, including those relating to the responsibility of a State for genocide or for any of the other acts enumerated in article III, shall be submitted to the International Court of Justice at the request of any of the parties to the dispute";

and whereas in its Application Yugoslavia states that the subject of the dispute concerns inter alia "acts of the Kingdom of Belgium by which it has violated its international obligation ... not to deliberately inflict conditions of life calculated to cause the physical destruction of a national group"; whereas, in describing the facts on which the Application is based, Yugoslavia states: "The above-mentioned acts are deliberately creating conditions calculated at the physical destruction of an ethnic group, in whole or in part"; whereas, in its statement of the legal grounds on which the Application is based, Yugoslavia contends that "the obligation ... not to impose deliberately on a national group conditions of life calculated to bring about the physical destruction of the group has been breached"; and whereas one of the claims on the merits set out in the Application is formulated as follows:

"by taking part in activities listed above, and in particular by causing enormous environmental damage and by using depleted uranium, the Kingdom of Belgium has acted against the Federal Republic of Yugoslavia in breach of its obligation not to deliberately inflict on a national group conditions of life calculated to bring about its physical destruction, in whole or in part";

35. Whereas Yugoslavia contends moreover that the sustained and intensive bombing of the whole of its territory, including the most heavily populated areas, constitutes "a serious violation of Article II of the Genocide Convention"; whereas it argues that "the pollution of soil, air and water, destroying the economy of the country, contaminating the environment with depleted uranium, inflicts conditions of life on the Yugoslav nation calculated to bring about its physical destruction"; whereas it asserts that it is the Yugoslav nation as a whole and as such that is targeted; and whereas it stresses that the use of certain weapons whose long-term hazards to health and the environment are already known, and the destruction of the largest part of the country's power supply system, with catastrophic consequences of which the Respondent must be aware, "impl[y] the intent to destroy, in whole or in part, the Yugoslav national group as such;

36. Whereas for its part Belgium argues that the Genocide Convention can be invoked only "where there is a dispute relating to a matter coming within the scope of the Convention," and that, in order for the said Article to be applicable, "the claims submitted by the Applicant must relate, even indirectly or tenuously, to the concept of genocide"; whereas, with reference to the definition of genocide contained in Article II of the Convention, Belgium stresses that "it is impossible to discern any intention on the part of the Kingdom of Belgium to destroy, in whole or in part, any national, ethnic, racial or religious group coming under the jurisdiction of the Federal Republic of Yugoslavia, or even any appearance of such alleged intention"; and whereas Belgium asserts that "the NATO operation is in no sense directed against the population of the Federal Republic of Yugoslavia, but ... against that country's military machine and military-industrial complex"; and whereas Belgium accordingly concludes "that, since the claims of the Federal Republic of Yugoslavia manifestly fall totally outside the scope of the Convention, [the Court] has no prima facie jurisdiction to consider Yugoslavia's Application on the basis of the said Convention";

37. Whereas it is not disputed that both Yugoslavia and Belgium are parties to the Genocide Convention without reservation; and whereas Article IX of the Convention accordingly appears to constitute a basis on which the jurisdiction of the Court might be founded to the extent that the subject-matter of the dispute relates to "the interpretation, application or fulfilment" of the Convention, including disputes "relating to the responsibility of a State for genocide or for any of the other acts enumerated in article III" of the said Convention;

38. Whereas, in order to determine, even prima facie, whether a dispute within the meaning of Article IX of the Genocide Convention exists, the Court cannot limit itself to noting that one of the Parties maintains that the Convention applies, while the other denies it; and whereas in the present case the Court must ascertain whether the breaches of the Convention alleged by Yugoslavia are capable of falling within the provisions of that instrument and whether, as a consequence, the dispute is one which the Court has jurisdiction ratione materiae to entertain pursuant to Article IX (cf. Oil Platforms (Islamic Republic of Iran v. United States of America), Preliminary Objection, Judgment, I.C.J. Reports 1996 (II), p. 810, para. 16);

39. Whereas the definition of genocide set out in Article II of the Genocide Convention reads as follows:

"In the present Convention, genocide means any of the following acts committed with intent to destroy, in whole or in part, a national, ethnical, racial or religious group, as such:

(a) Killing members of the group;

(b) Causing serious bodily or mental harm to members of the group;

(c) Deliberately inflicting on the group conditions of life calculated to bring about its physical destruction in whole or in part;

(d) Imposing measures intended to prevent births within the group;

(e) Forcibly transferring children of the group to another group";

40. Whereas it appears to the Court, from this definition, "that [the] essential characteristic [of genocide] is the intended destruction of 'a national, ethnical, racial or religious group'" (Application of the Convention on the Prevention and Punishment of the Crime of Genocide, Provisional Measures, Order of 13 September 1993, I.C.J. Reports 1993, p. 345, para. 42); whereas the threat or use of force against a State cannot in itself constitute an act of genocide within the meaning of Article II of the Genocide Convention; and whereas, in the opinion of the Court, it does not appear at the present stage of the proceedings that the bombings which form the subject of the Yugoslav Application "indeed entail the element of intent, towards a group as such, required by the provision quoted above" (Legality of the Threat or Use of Nuclear Weapons, Advisory Opinion, I.C.J. Reports 1996 (I), p. 240, para. 26);

41. Whereas the Court is therefore not in a position to find, at this stage of the proceedings, that the acts imputed by Yugoslavia to the Respondent are capable of coming within the provisions of the Genocide Convention; and whereas Article IX of the Convention, invoked by Yugoslavia, cannot accordingly constitute a basis on which the jurisdiction of the Court could prima facie be founded in this case;

42. Whereas after it had filed its Application Yugoslavia further invoked, as a basis for the Court's jurisdiction in this case, Article 4 of the Convention of Conciliation, Judicial Settlement and Arbitration, between Belgium and Kingdom of Yugoslavia, signed in Belgrade on 25 March 1930; whereas Yugoslavia's "Supplement to the Application", in which it invoked this new basis of jurisdiction, was presented to the Court in the second round of oral argument (see paragraph 14 above); and whereas Yugoslavia gave no explanation of its reasons for filing this document at this stage of the proceedings;

43. Whereas Belgium, referring to Article 38, paragraph 2, of the Rules of Court, argues as follows:

"It follows clearly that it is unacceptable, as in this case, to introduce a new ground in extremis supplementing an essential point in the arguments on the prima facie jurisdiction of the Court. Moreover, we may ask ourselves why the Federal Republic of Yugoslavia, which is deemed to be aware of the treaties to which it claims now to have succeeded, thought it unnecessary, contrary to the requirement of the principle of the sound administration of justice and of the provisions of Article 38 which I have just cited, to include this ground when filing its Application";

and whereas Belgium accordingly asks the Court, "primarily, to strike this ground from the proceedings"; whereas Belgium contends "in the alternative" "that the Convention of 1930 confers jurisdiction not on [the] Court, but on the PCIJ", and whereas it contends that Article 37 of the Statute is without effect here; and whereas Belgium states "in the further alternative ... that, under the terms of [the] Convention [of 1930], recourse to the PCIJ is a subsidiary remedy", and whereas it points out that Yugoslavia "has failed to exhaust the preliminary procedures whose exhaustion is a necessary condition for seisin of the PCIJ";

44. Whereas the invocation by a party of a new basis of jurisdiction in the second round of oral argument on a request for the indication of provisional measures has never before occurred in the Court's practice; whereas such action at this late stage, when not accepted by the other party, seriously jeopardizes the principle of procedural fairness and the sound administration of justice; and whereas in consequence the Court cannot, for the purpose of deciding whether it may or may not indicate provisional measures in the present case, take into consideration the new title of jurisdiction which Yugoslavia sought to invoke on 12 May 1999;

45. Whereas the Court has found above that it had no prima facie jurisdiction to entertain Yugoslavia's Application, either on the basis of Article 36, paragraph 2, of the Statute or of Article IX of the Genocide Convention; and whereas it has taken the view that it cannot, at this stage of the proceedings, take account of the additional basis of jurisdiction invoked by Yugoslavia; and whereas it follows that the Court cannot indicate any provisional measure whatsoever in order to protect the rights claimed by Yugoslavia in its Application.

46. Whereas, however, the findings reached by the Court in the present proceedings in no way prejudge the question of the jurisdiction of the Court to deal with the merits of the case or any questions relating to the admissibility of the Application, or relating to the merits themselves; and whereas they leave unaffected the right of the Governments of Yugoslavia and Belgium to submit arguments in respect of those questions;

47. Whereas there is a fundamental distinction between the question of the acceptance by a State of the Court's jurisdiction and the compatibility of particular acts with international law; the former requires consent; the latter question can only be reached when the Court deals with the merits after having established its jurisdiction and having heard full legal arguments by both parties;

48. Whereas, whether or not States accept the jurisdiction of the Court, they remain in any event responsible for acts attributable to them that violate international law, including humanitarian law; whereas any disputes relating to the legality of such acts are required to be resolved by peaceful means, the choice of which, pursuant to Article 33 of the Charter, is left to the parties;

49. Whereas in this context the parties should take care not to aggravate or extend the dispute;

50. Whereas, when such a dispute gives rise to a threat to the peace, breach of the peace or act of aggression, the Security Council has special responsibilities under Chapter VII of the Charter;

51. For these reasons,

The Court,

(1) By twelve votes to four,

Rejects the request for the indication of provisional measures submitted by the Federal Republic of Yugoslavia on 29 April 1999;

In Favour: President Schwebel; Judges Oda, Bedjaoui, Guillaume, Ranjeva, Herczegh, Fleischhauer, Koroma, Higgins, Parra-Aranguren, Kooijmans; Judge ad hoc Duinslaeger;

Against: Vice-President Weeramantry, Acting President; Judges Shi, Vereshchetin; Judge ad hoc Kreca;

(2) By fifteen votes to one,

Reserves the subsequent procedure for further decision.

In Favour: Vice-President Weeramantry, Acting President; President Schwebel; Judges Bedjaoui, Guillaume, Ranjeva, Herczegh, Shi, Fleischhauer, Koroma, Vereshchetin, Higgins, Parra-Aranguren, Kooijmans; Judges ad hoc Kreca, Duinslaeger;

Against: Judge Oda.

Done in English and in French, the French text being authoritative, at the Peace Palace, The Hague, this second day of June, one thousand nine hundred and ninety-nine, in three copies, one of which will be placed in the archives of the Court and the others transmitted to the Government of the Federal Republic of Yugoslavia and the Government of the Kingdom of Belgium, respectively.

(Signed) Christopher G. Weeramantry, Vice-President.

(Signed) Eduardo Valencia-Ospina, Registrar.

Judge Koroma appends a declaration to the Order of the Court.

Judges Oda, Higgins, Parra-Aranguren and Kooijmans append separate opinions to the Order of the Court.

Vice-President Weeramantry, Acting President, Judges Shi and Vereshchetin, and Judge ad hoc Kreca append dissenting opinions to the Order of the Court.

(Initialled) C.G.W. (Initialled) E.V.O.

[Declarations, Separate and Dissenting Opinions have been omitted.]

309 b) United States of America (Extracts)

[Only the line of reasoning leading to the removal of the case from the list has been reprinted.]

[...]

21. Whereas in its Application Yugoslavia claims, in the first place, to found the jurisdiction of the Court upon Article IX of the Genocide Convention, which provides:

"Disputes between the Contracting Parties relating to the interpretation, application or fulfilment of the present Convention, including those relating to the responsibility of a State for genocide or for any of the other acts enumerated in article III, shall be submitted to the International Court of Justice at the request of any of the parties to the dispute";

whereas it is not disputed that both Yugoslavia and the United States are parties to the Genocide Convention; but whereas, when the United States ratified the Convention on 25 November 1988, it made the following reservation:

"That with reference to Article IX of the Convention, before any dispute to which the United States is a party may be submitted to the jurisdiction of the International Court of Justice under this Article, the specific consent of the United States is required in each case.";

22. Whereas the United States contends that "[its] reservation [to Article IX] is clear and unambiguous"; that "[t]he United States has not given the specific consent [that reservation] requires [and] ... will not do so"; and that Article IX of the Convention cannot in consequence found the jurisdiction of the Court in this case, even prima facie; whereas the United States also observed that reservations to the Genocide Convention are generally permitted; that its reservation to Article IX is not contrary to the Convention's object and purpose; and that, "[s]ince ... Yugoslavia did not object to the ... reservation, [it] is bound by it"; and whereas the United States further contends that there is no "legally sufficient ... connection between the charges against the United States contained in the Application and [the] supposed jurisdictional basis under the Genocide Convention"; and whereas the United States further asserts that Yugoslavia has failed to make any credible allegation of violation of the Genocide Convention, by failing to demonstrate the existence of the specific intent required by the Convention to "destroy, in whole or in part, a national, ethnical, racial or religious group, as such", which intent could not be inferred from the conduct of conventional military operations against another State.

23. Whereas Yugoslavia disputed the United States interpretation of the Genocide Convention, but submitted no argument concerning the United States reservation to Article IX of the Convention;

24. Whereas the Genocide Convention does not prohibit reservations; whereas Yugoslavia did not object to the United States reservation to Article IX; and whereas the said reservation had the effect of excluding that Article from the provisions of the Convention in force between the Parties;

25. Whereas in consequence Article IX of the Genocide Convention cannot found the jurisdiction of the Court to entertain a dispute between Yugoslavia and the United States alleged to fall within its provisions; and whereas that Article manifestly does not constitute a basis of jurisdiction in the present case, even prima facie;

26. Whereas in its Application Yugoslavia claims, in the second place, to found the jurisdiction of the Court on Article 38, paragraph 5, of the Rules of Court, which reads as follows:

"5. When the applicant State proposes to found the jurisdiction of the Court upon a consent thereto yet to be given or manifested by the State against which such application is made, the application shall be transmitted to that State. It shall not however be entered in the General List, nor any action be taken in the proceedings, unless and until the State against which such application is made consents to the Court's jurisdiction for the purposes of the case";

27. Whereas the United States observes that it "has not consented to jurisdiction under Article 38, paragraph 5, [of the Rules of Court] and will not do so";

28. Whereas it is quite clear that, in the absence of consent by the United States, given pursuant to Article 38, paragraph 5, of the Rules, the Court cannot exercise jurisdiction in the present case, even prima facie; [....]

34. For these reasons,

The Court,

(1) By twelve votes to three,

Rejects the request for the indication of provisional measures submitted by the Federal Republic of Yugoslavia on 29 April 1999;

In Favour: Vice-President Weeramantry, Acting President; President Schwebel; Judges Oda, Bedjaoui, Guillaume, Ranjeva, Herczegh, Fleischhauer, Koroma, Higgins, Parra-Aranguren, Kooijmans;

Against: Judges Shi, Vereshchetin; Judge ad hoc Kreca;

(2) By twelve votes to three,

Orders that the case be removed from the List.

In Favour: Vice-President Weeramantry, Acting President; President Schwebel; Judges Oda, Bedjaoui, Guillaume, Ranjeva, Herczegh, Shi, Fleischhauer, Koroma, Higgins, Kooijmans;

Against: Judges Vereshchetin, Parra-Aranguren; Judge ad hoc Kreca.

[Declarations, Separate and Dissenting Opinions have been omitted.]

310. Russian Federation, Statement by the Ministry of Foreign Affairs, Press Release, 2 June 1999[1]

[...] The reasons for the generally negative attitude of the Court towards the request of Yugoslavia to order provisional measures seem to lie to not an inconsiderable extent in the personal composition of the Court. Five out of 15 of its permanent members are citizens of the NATO States. Four other judges from NATO States took part in the court examination as judges from the responding party.[2] Under such circumstances all the procedural mistakes (which instantly influence judicial decisions) were interpreted by the majority of the court against Yugoslavia.

311. FRY, Statement from the Federal Government's Meeting, Belgrade, 6 June 1999

At today's meeting, the Federal Government expressed concern at the decision of the International Court of Justice to turn down the requests for the end of bombardment, due to formalistic reasons related to the Court's jurisdiction. The government believes the other states are disappointed too, as well as the international law public.

The government is familiar with the decisions of the International Court of Justice and points at the fact that the refusal of ten countries - aggressors to accept the competence of the International Court of

---

[1] *Unofficial translation by Mr. Sergey Lagodinsky, Institute for Public International Law, University of Göttingen.*
[2] Judges ad hoc.

Justice and to settle the dispute on the legality of the bombing of Yugoslav territory, clearly shows that they know the aggression is illegal and criminal, and that therefore they would lose the case.

It is absolutely clear that the members of NATO have violated the UN Charter and the basis of the international law, that they have committed the biggest crimes against peace and humanity, genocide, war crimes, and that they have to hold responsibility. Some points of view of the International Court of Justice are in accordance with it:

The Court has expressed its deep concern because of the use of force in Yugoslavia. It has emphasized that all sides are obliged to act in accordance with the UN Charter and international and humanitarian law. Regardless of whether the states recognize the Court's competence, they are responsible for the acts of violation of international law. The Court appealed on all sides to settle the dispute by peaceful means. The message of the Court is absolutely clear.

8.2 INTERNATIONAL CRIMINAL TRIBUNAL FOR THE FORMER YUGOSLAVIA (ICTY)

312. ICTY, Statement by the Prosecutor, CC/PIO/302-E, The Hague, 10 March 1998

The Prosecutor of the International Criminal Tribunal for the Former Yugoslavia has in the past made it a practice not to comment on ongoing investigations. However, recent events in Kosovo are on exceptional circumstance and the Prosecutor wishes to point out that the Statue of the Tribunal, which was adopted by the United Nations Security Council in May 1993, empowers the Tribunal to prosecute persons responsible for serious violations of international humanitarian law committed in the territory of the former Yugoslavia since 1991. This jurisdiction is ongoing and covers the recent violence in Kosovo. In this regard, the Prosecutor is currently gathering information and evidence in relation to the Kosovo incidents and will continue to monitor any subsequent developments. Following her recent visit to Belgrade, the Prosecutor expects the full co-operation of the authorities of the Federal Republic of Yugoslavia in respect of investigations into the Kosovo situation.

313. U.S. Department of State, Office of the Spokesman, Press Statement by James P. Rubin, Spokesman, 15 July 1998

The United States is deeply concerned about the safety of the civilian population in Kosovo, both Albanian and Serb. We have condemned on numerous occasions the use of excessive force by Serbian security forces, particularly when directed indiscriminately against Kosovar Albanian civilians. We are also, however, concerned about attacks against Serbian civilians in Kosovo by Albanian extremist groups, including the Kosovo Liberation Army (UCK).

In recent weeks a number of Serb civilians have reportedly been kidnapped by armed Albanian groups. There can be no excuse for such actions. The civilian population of Kosovo should not be subject to armed attack or intimidation.

Those holding civilian hostages should release them immediately and without condition.

In this context we would note that the chief prosecutor for the ICTY has determined that the situation in Kosovo should be considered an "armed conflict" under international law. The prosecutor will investigate potential war crimes by both sides. The United States believes hostage-taking and the kidnapping of civilians would be grounds for inquiry for ICTY investigators.

314. ICTY, Statement by the Office of the Prosecutor, CC/PIU/351-E, The Hague, 7 October 1998

Up until the last few weeks, the Prosecutor has been undertaking investigations in relation to the events in Kosovo without any obstruction on the part of the Belgrade authorities. A team has just returned from Kosovo and it was the Prosecutor's intention to supplement this team with other investigators. That has not been possible because for the first time the Belgrade authorities had not issued visas in time for these other investigators to travel to Yugoslavia.

On Friday of last week the Prosecutor's staff in Belgrade sought an explanation from the Belgrade authorities as to why these visas had not been issued.

In response the representative of the Foreign Ministry indicated that the official position of the Federal Republic of Yugoslavia (FRY) regarding the Tribunal and Kosovo is that the Tribunal has no jurisdiction to conduct investigations in Kosovo and the Tribunal will not be allowed to do so.

It was further stated by the Ministry, that the Prosecutor's investigations in Kosovo represented a violation of the FRY's sovereignty. The Prosecutor's investigators would be allowed to move around in Kosovo but would not be permitted to conduct investigations. If such investigations were carried out in Kosovo, the FRY might reconsider its existing co-operation with the Tribunal and in particular might reconsider the agreement relating to the Prosecutor's Liaison Office in Belgrade.

The Prosecutor finds the position of the FRY Government to be totally unacceptable. Such a position ignores not only the express terms of the Tribunal's Statue, but also with various United Nations Security Council resolutions and Presidential Statements which unequivocally state that the Tribunal does in fact have jurisdiction over Kosovo.

For instance, UN SC Resolution 1160, which was adopted on 31 March 1998, recognised the ICTY's mandate on Kosovo. The relevant wording of that Resolution is as follows:

"Acting under Chapter VII of the UN Charter:...the Security Council.....

17. Urges the Office of the Prosecutor of the International Tribunal established pursuant to resolution 827 (1993) of 25 May 1993 to begin gathering information related to the violence in Kosovo that may fall within its jurisdiction, and notes that the authorities of the Federal Republic of Yugoslavia have an obligation to co-operate with the Tribunal ..."

Further UN SC Resolution 1199, which was adopted on 23 September 1998, noted that:

"...the communication by the Prosecutor of the International Tribunal for the Former Yugoslavia to the Contact Group on 7 July 1998, expressing the view that the situation in Kosovo represents an armed conflict within the terms of the mandate of the Tribunal;..."

and acting under Chapter VII of the Charter of the United Nations the Security Council:

"...13. Calls upon the authorities of the Federal Republic of Yugoslavia, the leaders of the Kosovo Albanian community and all others concerned to co-operate fully with the Prosecutor of the International Tribunal for the Former Yugoslavia in the investigation of possible violations within the jurisdiction of the Tribunal;..."

Further, in response President McDonald's briefing to the Security Council last Friday, the President of the Security Council stated publicly that the Security Council reaffirmed the authority and jurisdiction of the International Tribunal over matters within its competence throughout the territory of the former Yugoslavia.

The Prosecutor believes that it is in the best interest of the FRY and of all people in Kosovo and Serbia, to allow the Prosecutor's investigator's to fulfill their duties and thus to contribute to the establishment of the full truth about the conflict in Kosovo and the prosecution of those responsible for the crimes falling within the Tribunal's jurisdiction, as requested by the UN Security Council.

In conclusion, the Prosecutor intends to pursue her investigations into the events in Kosovo and urges the authorities of the FRY to reconsider their position and to comply with its international obligations to co-operate fully with the Tribunal and the Prosecutor's investigations.

315. ICTY, Statement by the Prosecutor, CC/PIU/353-E, The Hague, 15 October 1998

"Following reports that the US envoy Mr Richard Holbrooke was not able to obtain any concessions from President Milosevic on Tuesday regarding the jurisdiction of this Tribunal over events in Kosovo, I wish to make a strong and unequivocal statement regarding this Tribunal's jurisdiction.

On 25 May 1993 the United Nations Security Council passed resolution 827 which created this Tribunal, giving it jurisdiction to prosecute persons responsible for Crimes Against Humanity and War Crimes, as well as other serious violations of international humanitarian law, committed in the territory of the former Yugoslavia since 1991, which includes Kosovo. Consistent with the initial resolution, the Security Council has since reaffirmed this jurisdiction in resolutions 1160 of 31 March 1998 and 1199 of 23 September 1998.

The jurisdiction of this Tribunal is not conditional upon President Milosevic's consent, nor is it dependent on the outcome of any negotiations between him and anyone else. It is for the Judges of this Tribunal to interpret such jurisdiction and for the Security Council to modify or expand.

Today I have forwarded a letter to President Milosevic informing him that it is my intention to resume investigations in Kosovo at the earliest opportunity. In respect of the next investigative mission to Kosovo, it is my intention to lead the team, which will include the Deputy Prosecutor, senior staff in my Office, together with eight other members of my team which is investigating crimes falling within this Tribunal's jurisdiction that have allegedly occurred in Kosovo during 1998.

I have also informed President Milosevic that is my intention to visit the areas where some of the alleged crimes have been committed, to meet with government and other officials, and to meet with other organisations which may assist my investigations. In accordance with normal practice investigators will also gather any relevant evidence and interview potential witnesses.

Finally, I have sought an assurance from President Milosevic that visas will be forthcoming to enable my investigations in Kosovo to continue forthwith."

316. UN Security Council Resolution 1207 (1998) of 17 November 1998

The Security Council,

Recalling all its previous relevant resolutions concerning the conflicts in the former Yugoslavia, in particular resolution 827 (1993) of 25 May 1993,

Recalling also the statement by its President of 8 May 1996 (S/PRST/1996/23),

Recalling further the General Framework Agreement for Peace in Bosnia and Herzegovina and the Annexes thereto (S/1995/999, annex), in particular its Article IX and its Annex 1-A, Article X,

Having considered the letters of the President of the International Tribunal for the Former Yugoslavia to the President of the Security Council of 8 September 1998 (S/1998/839), 22 October 1998 (S/1998/990) and 6 November 1998 (S/1998/1040),

Deploring the continued failure of the Federal Republic of Yugoslavia to cooperate fully with the Tribunal, as described in those letters,

Reaffirming the commitment of all Member States to the sovereignty and territorial integrity of the Federal Republic of Yugoslavia,

Acting under Chapter VII of the Charter of the United Nations,

1. *Reiterates* its decision that all States shall cooperate fully with the Tribunal and its organs in accordance with resolution 827 (1993) and the Statute of the Tribunal, including the obligation of States to comply with requests for assistance or orders issued by a Trial Chamber under Article 29 of the Statute, to execute arrest warrants transmitted to them by the Tribunal, and to comply with its requests for information and investigations;

2. *Calls again upon* the Federal Republic of Yugoslavia, and all other States which have not already done so, to take any measures necessary under their domestic law to implement the provisions of resolution 827 (1993) and the Statute of the Tribunal, and affirms that a State may not invoke provisions of its domestic law as justification for its failure to perform binding obligations under international law;

3. *Condemns* the failure to date of the Federal Republic of Yugoslavia to execute the arrest warrants issued by the Tribunal against the three individuals referred to in the letter of 8 September 1998, and demands the immediate and unconditional execution of those arrest warrants, including the transfer to the custody of the Tribunal of those individuals;

4. *Reiterates* its call upon the authorities of the Federal Republic of Yugoslavia, the leaders of the Kosovo Albanian community and all others concerned to cooperate fully with the Prosecutor in the investigation of all possible violations within the jurisdiction of the Tribunal;

5. *Requests* the President of the Tribunal to keep the Council informed about the implementation of this resolution for the Council's further consideration;

6. *Decides* to remain seized of the matter.

[Adopted by the Security Council at its 3944th meeting, on 17 November 1998]

317. ICTY, The Prosecutor v. Slobodan Milosevic, Milan Milutinovic, Nikola Sainovic, Dragoljub Ojdanovic, Vlajko Stojiljkovic, Presentation of an Indictment for Review and Application for Warrants of Arrest and for Related Orders, 22 May 1999

The International Criminal Tribunal for the Former Yugoslavia

Case No. IT- 99-37-I

The Office of the Prosecutor

Louise Arbour, Prosecutor

The Prosecutor

v.

Slobodan Milosevic, Milan Milutinovic, Nikola Sainovic, Dragoljub Ojdanovic, Vlajko Stojiljkovic

I, Louise Arbour, Prosecutor, pursuant to my authority under Rule 47 of the Rules of Procedure and Evidence, having determined that there is sufficient evidence to provide reasonable grounds for believing that the abovenamed persons have committed crimes within the jurisdiction of the Tribunal, forward herewith an indictment against them, together with the attached supporting material, for confirmation by a Judge of the Tribunal.

This indictment is the first in the history of this Tribunal to charge a Head of State during an on-going armed conflict with the commission of serious violations of international humanitarian law. Bringing the accused to trial will therefore raise enforcement issues not hitherto encountered by this institution. Accordingly, I request that, upon confirmation, a number of specific orders be made concerning arrest warrants, the delayed public disclosure of the indictment, and the seizure of assets.

1. First, I ask that, pursuant to Rule 55, an order be made that a certified copy of the warrant of arrest for each of the accused be transmitted by the Registrar to the authorities of the Federal Republic of Yugoslavia, addressed to Mr. Zoran Knezevic, Federal Minister of Justice, Belgrade. In the situation where the President of the Federal Republic of Yugoslavia and senior government and military officials stand accused of crimes requiring that they be taken into custody and transferred to the International Tribunal for trial, I consider that the most appropriate course of action is to address the certified copies of the warrants to the Federal Minister of Justice.

2. Second, although each of the accused resides in the Federal Republic of Yugoslavia, and that is where they were last known to be and are likely to be found, I also request that an order be made, pursuant to Rule 55(D), that certified copies of each of the said warrants be transmitted by the Registrar to all States. I consider this necessary because it is reasonable to believe that, upon indictment, some or all of the accused may attempt to seek refuge outside the territory of the Federal Republic of Yugoslavia. These accused should be subject to immediate arrest and transfer to the Tribunal, regardless of where they may try to go. The same order should instruct the Registrar also to transmit certified copies of each of the said warrants to the International Criminal Police Organisation (INTERPOL).

3. Third, I request that an order be made pursuant to Rules 53(A), 53(C), 54 and 55(D), that (a) there be no public disclosure of the indictment and arrest warrants until 12 noon (The Hague time) on Thursday, 27 May 1999, subject to the notification by the Prosecutor to appropriate authorities as discussed below; (b) that the transmission by the Registrar of certified copies of the said warrants also be delayed until 12 noon (The Hague time) on Thursday, 27 May 1999; and (c) that there be no public disclosure of the supporting materials, the Review of the Indictment or the present Application until the arrest of the accused.

4. Finally, I request that an order be made under Rule 54, that each State make enquiries to discover whether any of the accused have assets located in their territory, and that any State finding such assets adopt provisional measures to freeze such assets, without prejudice to the rights of third parties, until the accused are taken into custody.

5. In relation to my third request listed above, the accused in this indictment are leaders occupying some of the highest positions in the Federal Republic of Yugoslavia and the Republic of Serbia. Together and individually they have enormous power over the territory and resources and have all the apparatus of State control at their disposal. They may have power and influence beyond the borders of the Federal Republic of Yugoslavia. Their reaction to the publication of this indictment is unpredictable. A number of my staff are active in the region. They and others are currently exposed to the risk of intimidation or reprisals. In particular, a United Nations Mission, which includes a member of my staff known to the Yugoslav authorities, is presently in the Federal Republic of Yugoslavia on a fact-finding mission. This mission is scheduled to depart the Federal Republic of Yugoslavia at 08:00 hours on Thursday, 27 May 1999. Other United Nations agencies, governments, and humanitarian agencies from the international community have many staff dealing with refugees and displaced persons at or near the borders of the Federal Republic of Yugoslavia. The publication of this indictment may have security implications for them. A delay in publication until 12 noon on that date, however, will allow my Office; and others, to take steps to minimise these risks.

6. In relation to my final request listed above, the indictment alleges that, on a large scale, property was unlawfully taken from homes of the victims, and that many victims were robbed of money and other valuables. The destination of this property is presently unknown, but my investigations will continue in order to attempt to establish whether the accused obtained such property or proceeds.

7. Rule 98 ter provides that if a Trial Chamber finds the accused guilty of a crime and concludes from the evidence that unlawful taking of property was associated with it, a Trial Chamber shall make a specific finding to that effect in its judgement. Rule 105 makes provision for the restitution of the property or the proceeds thereof, and allows a Trial Chamber to order provisional measures for the preservation and protection of the property or proceeds, including property or proceeds in the hands of third parties not otherwise connected with the crime of which the convicted person has been found guilty. At an earlier stage of proceedings, Rule 61(D) makes similar provision for a Trial Chamber to order States to take provisional measures to freeze the assets of the accused, without prejudice to the rights of third parties.

8. Moreover, Rules 39 and 54, which deal with the making of orders by a Judge of the Tribunal, are worded in general terms, and place no limit on the types of order that may be made. Provisional measures are designed to protect the ability of the Tribunal ultimately to do justice in the case. They are by their nature temporary, and do not permanently divest accused persons of their assets. It therefore appears appropriate for provisional measures to freeze assets to be available to a single Judge of the Tribunal. Further, it may be thought logical for such measures to be available to the Tribunal at an early stage in proceedings, when the accused are still at large, and when, in the full knowledge that they are indicted, they are in a position both to use their assets to escape being arrested and brought to justice, and to take steps to disperse or otherwise dispose of their assets in an attempt to disguise them or place them beyond the reach of the Tribunal. Although no express provision is made in the Rules for such an order by a single Judge of the Tribunal, the principle of the freezing of assets of an accused is an accepted part of the procedure of the Tribunal, a step regarded as necessary to preserve the Tribunal's ability to impose the penalties set out in Article 24 of the Statute. In all the circumstances, I therefore consider it appropriate to request an order locating and freezing any assets of the accused in this case.

9. In accordance with existing practice, I attach proposed drafts of the orders sought.

Louise Arbour, Prosecutor

Dated this twenty second day of May 1999; At The Hague, The Netherlands

318. ICTY, The Prosecutor v. Slobodan Milosevic, Milan Milutinovic, Nikola Sainovic, Dragoljub Ojdanovic, Vlajko Stojiljkovic, Decision on Review of Indictment and Application for Consequential Orders, 24 May 1999

Before a Judge of a Trial Chamber

Before: Judge David Hunt

Registrar: Mrs Dorothee de Sampayo Garrido-Nijgh

Decision of: 24 May 1999

Prosecutor
v.
Slobodan Milosevic, Milan Milutinovic, Nikola Sainovic, Dragoljub Ojdanic & Vlajko Stojiljkovic

The Office of the Prosecutor:

Louise Arbour, Prosecutor

I. Introduction

1. Pursuant to Article 19 of the International Tribunal's Statute and Rule 47 of the Rules of Procedure and Evidence, the Prosecutor has submitted for review an indictment naming Slobodan Milosevic, Milan Milutinovic, Nikola Sainovic, Dragoljub Ojdanic and Vlajko Stojiljkovic. Each of the accused is charged with crimes against humanity,

in accordance with Article 5 of the Statute, involving persecution, deportation and murder. Murder is also charged against each accused as a violation of the laws or customs of war, in accordance with Article 3 of the Statute, on the basis that it is recognised as such by common Article 3(1)(a) of the Geneva Conventions of 1949.

II. Review and Confirmation of the Indictment

2. The indictment comes before me as a judge of a Trial Chamber, in accordance with Articles 18 and 19 of the Statute. Article 19 provides that if, after such review of the indictment, I am satisfied that a prima facie case has been established by the Prosecutor, I am to confirm the indictment. Rule 47(E) requires me, for the purpose of confirming the indictment, to examine also any supporting material which the Prosecutor may forward pursuant to Rule 47(B). The purpose of Rule 47(E) is not to permit the supporting material to fill in any gaps which may exist in the material facts pleaded in the indictment.[1] It is to ensure that there is evidence to support the material facts so pleaded, so that the confirming judge is acting, in effect, as a grand jury (or a committing magistrate) in the common law system or as a juge d'instruction in some civil law systems.[2]

3. The joint operation of Article 19 and Rule 47(E) is, therefore, that I must be satisfied that the material facts pleaded in the indictment establish a prima facie case and that there is evidence available which supports those material facts. The structure of the Rules of Procedure and Evidence makes it clear that the confirming judge is concerned only with the substance of the indictment, and not with its form.[3]

4. A prima facie case on any particular charge exists in this situation where the material facts pleaded in the indictment constitute a credible case which would (if not contradicted by the accused) be a sufficient basis to convict him of that charge.[4]

5. The events upon which the indictment is based are alleged to have taken place in the Autonomous Province of Kosovo in the southern part of the Republic of Serbia, a constituent republic of the Federal Republic of Yugoslavia, between 1 January and late April 1999. At the commencement of that period, almost 90% of the population of that Province was Albanian, and the remainder were Serbs.

6. The military forces of the Federal Republic of Yugoslavia, the police force of Serbia, some police units from the Federal Republic of Yugoslavia and associated paramilitary units are alleged during that period to have engaged, in concert, in a widespread and systematic series of offensives against many predominately Kosovo Albanian towns and villages. The general pattern of the offensive was that Kosovo Albanian residents of these towns and villages were ordered to leave their homes, upon threats of death. After they left, the property they had left behind was stolen and their homes were destroyed or rendered uninhabitable by fire. They were forced to join convoys of similarly displaced Kosovo Albanians on route to the borders between Kosovo and neighbouring countries. They were physically mistreated. In many instances, the Kosovo Albanian men who had been displaced were separated from the women and children and they were killed. At the border, the property they had with them was stolen, including their identification papers and motor vehicles. In some cases, the villages were initially shelled and Kosovo Albanians were killed in the shelling.

7. These forces from the Federal Republic of Yugoslavia and Serbia are also alleged to have deliberately shot and killed unarmed Kosovo Albanians, including women and children, on a number of occasions during this period. This happened at the villages of Racak (where fortyfive Kosovo Albanians were killed), Velika Krusa (where 105 Kosovo Albanians were killed and their bodies burnt), Izbica (where 130 Kosovo Albanians were killed) and other villages. It is alleged that approximately 740,000 Kosovo Albanian civilians were forcibly deported from Kosovo, and that approximately 385 identified Kosovo Albanians were murdered.

8. The indictment alleges that these operations targeting Kosovo Albanians were undertaken with the objective of removing a substantial portion of the Kosovo Albanian population from Kosovo, in an effort to ensure continued Serbian control over the Province. If these pleaded facts are accepted, they establish that the forces from the Federal Republic of Yugoslavia and Serbia persecuted the Kosovo Albanian civilian population on political, racial or religious grounds, and that there was both deportation and murder, constituting crimes against humanity and violations of the laws or customs of war.

9. The five accused are alleged to be criminally responsible for the actions of those forces upon two bases -

(a) their individual responsibility, having planned, instigated, ordered or otherwise aided and abetted their planning, preparation or execution (Article 7.1), and

(b) in relation to four of them (the accused Sainovic being excepted), their superior authority, having known or had reason to know that their subordinates were about to commit such acts or had done so but having failed to take the necessary and reasonable measures to prevent such acts or to punish those subordinates who did those acts (Article 7.3).

The subordinates were the members of the military forces of the Federal Republic of Yugoslavia, the police force of Serbia, the police units from the Federal Republic of Yugoslavia and the associated paramilitary units. The case against each of the accused is built upon both their legal and their de facto relationship with those forces.

10. During the relevant period, the military forces of the Federal Republic of Yugoslavia were under the control of, inter alia -

(1) The accused Milosevic, as the President of the Federal Republic of Yugoslavia and the Supreme Commander of the Armed Forces of the Federal Republic of Yugoslavia (known as the VJ) with the power to implement the National Defence Plan decided by the Supreme Defence Council in compliance with the decisions of that Council (of which he was the President).

(2) The accused Milutinovic, as the President of Serbia and as such a member of the Supreme Defence Council, participating in the decisions concerning the activities of the VJ.

(3) The accused Ojdanic, as Chief of the General Staff of the VJ, with the power to command the VJ as required.

11. During the relevant period (or a substantial part thereof), the police force of Serbia was under the control of, inter alia -

(1) The accused Milosevic, as President of the Federal Republic of Yugoslavia, having command authority of republic and federal police units subordinated to the VJ during a declared state of imminent threat of war or a declared state of war. (A declaration of a state of imminent threat of war was proclaimed on 23 March 1999, and of a state of war the next day.)

(2) The accused Milutinovic, as the President of Serbia with power, during a declared state of imminent threat of war or a declared state of war, to enact measures for the governance of the republic.

(3) The accused Stojiljkovic, as Minister of Internal Affairs of Serbia, and responsible for the enforcement of the laws of the republic, including the activities of the police.

12. During the relevant period (or a substantial part thereof), the police units from the Federal Republic of Yugoslavia were under the control of, inter alia, the accused Milosevic, for the reasons set out in the last paragraph. He also exercised an extensive de facto control over

---

[1] Prosecutor v Krnojelac, Case IT-97-25-PT, Decision on the Defence Preliminary Motion on the Form of the Indictment, 24 Feb 1999, at para 15.

[2] Prosecutor v Kordic, Case IT-95-14-I, Decision on the Review of the Indictment, 10 Nov 1995 (Judge Gabrielle Kirk McDonald), at p 3.

[3] Prosecutor v Krnojelac, Case IT-97-25-PT, Decision on Prosecutor's Response to Decision of 24 February 1999, 20 May 1999, at para 11 footnote 11. Rule 72(A) gives to the Trial Chamber the jurisdiction to deal with the form of the indictment.

[4] Prosecutor v Kordic, Case IT-95-14-I, Decision on the Review of the Indictment, 10 Nov 1995 (Judge Gabrielle Kirk McDonald), at p 3, adopting the Report of the International Law Commission, UN Document A/49/10 (1994), at 95.

both federal and Serbian institutions (including the police) nominally within the competence of the respective Governments or Assemblies.

13. During the relevant period, the paramilitary units worked in association with, and in concert with, the other forces from the Federal Republic of Yugoslavia and Serbia, and at their direction.

14. In addition, during the relevant period the accused Milosevic was the primary person on behalf of the Federal Republic of Yugoslavia and Serbia with whom the international community had negotiated in the continuing conflict in the Balkans, as he had been since 1989, including the negotiations with representatives of the North Atlantic Treaty Organisation (NATO) and the Organisation for Security and Co-operation in Europe (OSCE) conducted in October 1998, from which an "Agreement on OSCE Kosovo Verification Mission" was signed on 16 October 1998. The accused Milutinovic was also a significant person with whom the international community had negotiated, as he had been since 1995, and he had been present at the international negotiations for peace in Kosovo held at Rambouillet, France, in February 1999.

15. Although the accused Sainovic has not been charged with superior authority, it is significant that, as Deputy Prime Minister of the Federal Republic of Yugoslavia, he was designated by the accused Milosevic as his representative in relation to the Kosovo situation. Diplomats and other international officials were directed to speak to him concerning that subject. He signed the "Clark-Naumann agreement" in October 1998, which provided for the partial withdrawal of forces of the Federal Republic of Yugoslavia and Serbia from Kosovo, a limitation on the introduction of additional forces and equipment into the area, and the deployment of unarmed OSCE verifiers. He was a member of the Serbian delegation to the negotiations at Rambouillet. As with most cases where an accused is charged with both individual responsibility (not including the actual commission of the crimes himself) and superior authority, the relationship of the accused to those who did commit those crimes is directly relevant to the issue whether he did plan, instigate, order or otherwise aid and abet in the planning, preparation or execution of those crimes. The absence of any legal relationship between the accused Sainovic and those persons in the present case no doubt explains why he has not been charged with superior authority, but it does not detract from the issue of his individual responsibility in the circumstances outlined in this paragraph.

16. This has been a very brief outline of what I understand to be the prosecution case. The supporting material is very much more detailed than may be suggested by that outline.

17. After reviewing and considering the indictment and the supporting material forwarded by the Prosecutor, and after hearing the Prosecutor in person, I am satisfied that the material facts pleaded establish a prima facie case in respect of each and every count of the indictment and that there is evidence available which supports those material facts. I am satisfied that the requirements of Article 19 and Rule 47 have been complied with. Accordingly, I confirm the indictment submitted for review.

III. Consequential Orders

18. The Prosecutor seeks a number of consequential orders. Article 19 provides that, if requested by the Prosecutor to do so, I may issue such orders and warrants for the arrest, detention, surrender or transfer of persons, or such other orders, as may be required for the conduct of the trial.

(A) EXECUTION OF ARREST WARRANTS

19. Upon confirmation of an indictment, the judge confirming it may issue an arrest warrant,[1] and such warrant must include an order for the prompt transfer of the accused to the Tribunal upon his or their arrest.[2] A certified copy of the arrest warrant is then transmitted by the Registrar to, inter alia, the national authorities of the State in whose territory or under whose jurisdiction resides, or was last known to be or is believed by the Registrar to be likely to be found.[3]

20. In the present case, the Prosecutor seeks an order that the warrants of arrest of the accused be transmitted by the Registrar to the Federal Republic of Yugoslavia, addressed to Mr Zoran Knezevic, Federal Minister of Justice, Belgrade. As the accused Milosevic is the Head of State of the Federal Republic of Yugoslavia, and as the other accused are senior government and military figures of the Federal Republic, the Prosecutor says, the Federal Minister of Justice is the most appropriate person in authority in the Federal Republic to execute those warrants. I agree. I accept that such an order should be made in this case.

21. In the light of the possibility that some or all of the accused may seek refuge outside the territory of the Federal Republic of Yugoslavia, the Prosecutor also seeks an order, pursuant to Rule 55(D), that certified copies of each of the warrants are to be transmitted by the Registrar to all States Members of the United Nations and to the Confederation of Switzerland.

22. Rule 61(D) permits the issue of international arrest warrants to be transmitted to all such States, but only where the arrest warrant issued pursuant to Rule 55 has not been executed within a reasonable time, and such international warrants may be issued only by a Trial Chamber. It is nevertheless argued that the power to transmit certified copies of the arrest warrant pursuant to Rule 55(D) is a wide one, and that it is expressly not limited to transmission only to those national authorities of the States or territories where the accused resides or is believed to reside. In any event, it is argued, the procedure permitted by Rule 55(D) of transmitting certified copies of the original arrest warrant is not the same as the issue of international arrest warrants pursuant to Rule 61(D). Rule 54 permits a judge of the Tribunal to issue such orders as may be necessary for the purposes of the preparation or conduct of the trial. There can be no trial until the accused is arrested. The orders sought would assist in ensuring the arrest of the accused.

23. I accept the Prosecutor's argument, and that the order sought pursuant to Rule 55(D) should be made in this case. States Members of the United Nations are bound to comply without undue delay with any order of the Tribunal for the arrest or detention of any person,[4] but it is not suggested that the Confederation of Switzerland is similarly bound. The transmission of the certified copy of the warrants to be sent to the Confederation of Switzerland should therefore be expressed in terms of a request for assistance rather than an order.

24. For the same reason, the Prosecutor seeks a similar order that certified copies of the arrest warrant are to be transmitted by the Registrar to the Prosecutor herself so that she may use those certified copies to seek the assistance of the International Criminal Police Organisation (INTERPOL), pursuant to Rule 39, by circulating those certified copies under its "Red Notice" procedure. Again, I accept that such an order should be made in this case.

25. Because of the sheer bulk involved in transmitting the certified copies of the arrest warrants to all those nominated if, as Rule 55(C) would otherwise require, each arrest warrant must be accompanied by a certified copy of the indictment and the statement of the accused's rights translated into a language understood by the accused, I order pursuant to Rule 55(D) that the arrest warrants need no be so accompanied in this case.

(B) FREEZING THE ASSETS OF THE ACCUSED

26. The Prosecutor seeks orders that each of the States Members of the United Nations -

(i) make inquiries to discover whether any of the accused have assets located in their territory, and

---

[1] Rules of Procedure and Evidence, Rule 47(H).
[2] Rule 55(A).
[3] Rule 55(D).
[4] Statute, Article 29.2.

(ii) if any such assets are found, adopt provisional measures to freeze those assets, without prejudice to the rights of third parties, until the accused are taken into custody.

It is pointed out that the indictment alleges that property was unlawfully taken from the homes of victims and that many victims were robbed of money and other valuables.

27. The application was initially based solely upon Rule 54, which gives power to a judge (as well as to a Trial Chamber) to issue such orders as may be necessary for the preparation or conduct of the trial. As earlier stated, there can be no trial until the accused is arrested - so, the argument went, any order which assists in ensuring the arrest of the accused may be made by a judge pursuant to Rule 54. Freezing the assets of the accused, the Prosecutor submitted, may be done for two distinct purposes - for the purpose of granting restitution of property or payment from its proceeds (which may be ordered by a Trial Chamber pursuant to Rule 105 after conviction, subject to appropriate findings having been made in the judgment pursuant to Rule 98ter), and also for the purpose of preventing an accused who is still at large from using those assets to evade arrest and from taking steps to disguise his assets or putting them beyond the reach of the Tribunal.

28. The apparent width of the powers given to a judge by Rule 54, however, may perhaps be somewhat limited by the fact that Rule 61(D) gives power to a Trial Chamber (but not to a judge) to grant such relief for the same reasons at a slightly later stage, where the arrest warrant has not been executed within a reasonable time. But no such limitation can be placed upon the power given to the confirming judge by Article 19.2 of the Statute in much the same terms as Rule 54, and incorporated in Rule 47(H)(i). The application then proceeded upon the basis of Article 19.2.

29. In the situation where the Federal Republic of Yugoslavia has consistently, in breach of its legal obligations, ignored the Tribunal's orders to arrest persons who have been indicted to stand trial before the Tribunal, and who are living within its territory, and where the Tribunal has no police force of its own to execute its warrants, I accept that it is of the utmost importance that every permissible step be taken which will assist in effecting the arrest of those who shelter in the Federal Republic of Yugoslavia or who otherwise seek to evade arrest. I agree that the orders sought should be made in this case.

(C) A NON-DISCLOSURE ORDER

30. Lastly, the Prosecutor has sought orders -

(i) pursuant to Rules 54 and 55(D), that the transmission of the warrants and certified copies thereof be delayed until 12 noon (The Hague time) on Thursday, 27 May 1999;

(ii) pursuant to Rule 53, that there be no disclosure of the indictment, the accompanying material or the confirmation and orders made until the same time, subject to certain nominated exceptions; and

(iii) also pursuant to Rule 53, that there be no disclosure of the supporting material forwarded by her pursuant to Rule 47(B) until the arrest of all the accused.

Rule 55(D) makes the transmission by the Registrar of certified copies of the arrest warrants for execution subject to any order of a judge of a Trial Chamber. Rule 54 gives power to a judge of Trial Chamber to make such orders as may be necessary for the preparation of the trial. Rule 53 limits the power of the Tribunal to make an order for non-disclosure to where there are exceptional circumstances and where it is in the interests of justice that the order be made. Such orders for non-disclosure are usually sought and made where the disclosure of the indictment would enable the accused named in it to take steps to evade arrest.

31. The Prosecutor has put forward a number of reasons which are said to justify the first and second orders being made. The availability of both orders may be considered together.

32. I accept that the various accused in this case hold the highest positions of power within the Federal Republic of Yugoslavia and the Republic of Serbia and that, together and individually, they wield enormous power over their territories and their resources, with all the apparatus of State at their disposal. I also accept that their reaction to the indictment is unpredictable. I accept too that a number of the Prosecutor's staff are active in the area over which the accused exert such enormous power and that they would be exposed to the serious risk of reprisals and intimidation if the indictment is disclosed immediately. I consider that the need to give an opportunity to the Office of the Prosecutor to minimise those risks is a legitimate consideration in determining whether it is in the interests of justice to make a non-disclosure order for the short period sought.

33. The same is true of the serious risk of reprisals and intimidation against many other persons within the Federal Republic of Yugoslavia or at or near to its borders - the United Nations Mission presently there on a fact-finding mission and the staffs there of other United Nations and Governmental agencies and of the humanitarian agencies from the international community dealing with refugees and displaced persons - as well as such risk against the personnel of various Governments presently engaged there and elsewhere in seeking a resolution of the current armed conflict. The disclosure of the indictment would have serious security implications for all of them which can be reduced, and hopefully minimised, if there is a short delay in the disclosure of the indictment to enable precautionary measures to be taken.

34. It is clearly in the interests of justice that there be a delay in the disclosure of the indictment and the other documents to enable steps to be taken to protect all of these people from the risk of such reprisals. There could be no doubt that all these circumstances are exceptional.

35. No submission has been made that the impact of such disclosure on the current attempts to resolve the armed conflict in the Kosovo Province is a relevant matter to be considered in determining whether it is in the interests of justice to order non-disclosure. The safety of those personnel involved in the attempts to resolve that armed conflict is a legitimate consideration in relation to the interests of justice, but the possible political and diplomatic consequences of the indictment are not the same thing. There is a clear and substantial distinction to be drawn between what may be relevant to the well known and accepted discretion of prosecuting authorities as to whether an indictment should be presented and what may be relevant to this Tribunal's discretion as to whether an order should be made for the non-disclosure of that indictment once it has been presented and confirmed. In view of the opinion which I have already expressed, that a non-disclosure order for a short period is justified to enable security measures to be taken in relation to those at risk of intimidation or reprisals, it is unnecessary for me to determine whether the impact of the public disclosure of the indictment upon the peace process itself is also a consideration which is relevant to the exercise of my discretion to make a non-disclosure order pursuant to Rule 53. It is sufficient for me to say that such impact is not a matter which I have considered in determining the application made for non-disclosure in this case.

36. The Prosecutor has informed me that the United Nations Mission is presently scheduled to depart from the Federal Republic of Yugoslavia at 8.00 am on Thursday, 27 May. The limit on the public non-disclosure order until 12 noon on that day was suggested as an appropriate one in the light of that fact. I accept that an order for that period of time (just short of seventytwo hours) is reasonable in this case. I also accept that it is reasonable for the Prosecutor herself, in her discretion, to notify the Secretary-General of the United Nations and the Governments whose personnel or staff are at risk of reprisals or intimidation of the presentation and confirmation of the indictment and the issue of the arrest warrants, so that precautionary security measures may be taken for the safety of those so at risk (including the staff of the humanitarian agencies earlier referred to). I will make such orders accordingly.

37. As to the third order sought - that there be no disclosure of the accompanying material until the arrest of all the accused, the Prosecutor says that the enormous power which the accused, together and individually, wield over the territories in which many of the witnesses still live puts those witnesses in grave danger of physical harm if they are identified before all of the accused are arrested. I am prepared to make such an order at this stage. It may need to be varied if one or

more but not all of the accused are arrested, when steps might be devised at that stage for the protection of the identity of the witnesses so that the accused who have been arrested can be made aware of the case against them.

IV. Disposition

38. For the foregoing reasons,

1. I confirm each count of the indictment submitted by the Prosecutor against each accused.

2. I make the following orders:

(1) That certified copies of the warrants of arrest for each accused be transmitted by the Registrar to -

(a) the Federal Republic of Yugoslavia, addressed to Mr Zoran Knezevic, Federal Minister of Justice, Belgrade;

(b) all States Members of the United Nations;

(c) the Confederation of Switzerland; and

(d) the Prosecutor,

as soon as practicable after 12 noon (The Hague time) on Thursday, 27 May 1999, but not before, unless otherwise ordered.

(2) That the Registrar is not required to have a copy of the indictment or a statement of the rights of the accused accompany the certified copies of the warrants transmitted in accordance with the previous order.

(3) That, with the exception that the Prosecutor may, in her discretion, notify the Secretary-General of the United Nations and the Governments whose personnel or staff are at risk of reprisals or intimidation, there be no disclosure of the indictment, the review and confirmation of the indictment, the arrest warrants or the Prosecutor's application dated 22 May 1999 during the period ending at 12 noon (The Hague time) on Thursday, 27 May 1999, unless otherwise ordered.

(4) That there be no disclosure of the supporting material forwarded by the Prosecutor pursuant to Rule 47(B) until the arrest of all of the accused.

(5) That all States Members of the United Nations make inquiries to discover whether the accused (or any of them) have assets located in their territory and, if so, adopt provisional measures to freeze such assets, without prejudice to the rights of third parties, until the accused are taken into custody.

3. I grant liberty to apply to me without further formal application for any variation of the orders made, at any time prior to 12 noon on Thursday, 27 May 1999.

Done in English and French, the English version being authoritative.
Dated this 24th day of May 1999; At The Hague; The Netherlands
Judge David Hunt
[Seal of the Tribunal]

319. ICTY, Indictment of Slobodan Milosevic and others, 24 May 1999

The International Criminal Tribunal for the Former Yugoslavia

The Prosecutor of the Tribunal
Against
Slobodan Milosevic, Milan Milutinovic, Nikola Sainovic, Dragoljub Ojdanic, Vlajko Stojiljkovic

Indictment

The Prosecutor of the International Criminal Tribunal for the former Yugoslavia, pursuant to her authority under Article 18 of the Statute of the Tribunal, charges:

Slobodan Milosevic, Milan Milutinovic, Nikola Sainovic, Dragoljub Ojdanic, Vlajko Stojiljkovic

with Crimes Against Humanity and Violations of the Laws or Customs of War as set forth below:

Background

1. The Autonomous Province of Kosovo and Metohija is located in the southern part of the Republic of Serbia, a constituent republic of the Federal Republic of Yugoslavia (hereinafter FRY). The territory now comprising the FRY was part of the former Socialist Federal Republic of Yugoslavia (hereinafter SFRY). The Autonomous Province of Kosovo and Metohija is bordered on the north and north-west by the Republic of Montenegro, another constituent republic of the FRY. On the south-west, the Autonomous Province of Kosovo and Metohija is bordered by the Republic of Albania, and to the south, by the Former Yugoslav Republic of Macedonia. The capital of the Autonomous Province of Kosovo and Metohija is Pristina.

2. In 1990 the Socialist Republic of Serbia promulgated a new Constitution which, among other things, changed the names of the republic and the autonomous provinces. The name of the Socialist Republic of Serbia was changed to the Republic of Serbia (both hereinafter Serbia); the name of the Socialist Autonomous Province of Kosovo was changed to the Autonomous Province of Kosovo and Metohija (both hereinafter Kosovo); and the name of the Socialist Autonomous Province of Vojvodina was changed to the Autonomous Province of Vojvodina (hereinafter Vojvodina). During this same period, the Socialist Republic of Montenegro changed its name to the Republic of Montenegro (hereinafter Montenegro).

3. In 1974, a new SFRY Constitution had provided for a devolution of power from the central government to the six constituent republics of the country. Within Serbia, Kosovo and Vojvodina were given considerable autonomy including control of their educational systems, judiciary, and police. They were also given their own provincial assemblies, and were represented in the Assembly, the Constitutional Court, and the Presidency of the SFRY.

4. In 1981, the last census with near universal participation, the total population of Kosovo was approximately 1,585,000 of which 1,227,000 (77%) were Albanians, and 210,000 (13%) were Serbs. Only estimates for the population of Kosovo in 1991 are available because Kosovo Albanians boycotted the census administered that year. General estimates are that the current population of Kosovo is between 1,800,000 and 2,100,000 of which approximately 85-90% are Kosovo Albanians and 5-10% are Serbs.

5. During the 1980s, Serbs voiced concern about discrimination against them by the Kosovo Albanian-led provincial government while Kosovo Albanians voiced concern about economic underdevelopment and called for greater political liberalisation and republican status for Kosovo. From 1981 onwards, Kosovo Albanians staged demonstrations which were suppressed by SFRY military and police forces of Serbia.

6. In April 1987, Slobodan MILOSEVIC, who had been elected Chairman of the Presidium of the Central Committee of the League of Communists of Serbia in 1986, travelled to Kosovo. In meetings with local Serb leaders and in a speech before a crowd of Serbs, Slobodan MILOSEVIC endorsed a Serbian nationalist agenda. In so doing, he broke with the party and government policy which had restricted nationalist expression in the SFRY since the time of its founding by Josip Broz Tito after the Second World War. Thereafter, Slobodan MILOSEVIC exploited a growing wave of Serbian nationalism in order to strengthen centralised rule in the SFRY.

7. In September 1987 Slobodan MILOSEVIC and his supporters gained control of the Central Committee of the League of Communists of Serbia. In 1988, Slobodan MILOSEVIC was re-elected as Chairman of the Presidium of the Central Committee of the League of Communists of Serbia. From that influential position, Slobodan MILOSEVIC was able to further develop his political power.

8. From July 1988 to March 1989, a series of demonstrations and rallies supportive of Slobodan MILOSEVIC's policies - the so-called "Anti-Bureaucratic Revolution" - took place in Vojvodina and Montenegro. These protests led to the ouster of the respective provincial and republican governments; the new governments were then supportive of, and indebted to, Slobodan MILOSEVIC.

9. Simultaneously, within Serbia, calls for bringing Kosovo under stronger Serbian rule intensified and numerous demonstrations addressing this issue were held. On 17 November 1988, high-ranking Kosovo Albanian political figures were dismissed from their positions within the provincial leadership and were replaced by appointees loyal to Slobodan MILOSEVIC. In early 1989, the Serbian Assembly proposed amendments to the Constitution of Serbia which would strip Kosovo of most of its autonomous powers, including control of the police, educational and economic policy, and choice of official language, as well as its veto powers over further changes to the Constitution of Serbia. Kosovo Albanians demonstrated in large numbers against the proposed changes. Beginning in February 1989, a strike by Kosovo Albanian miners further increased tensions.

10. Due to the political unrest, on 3 March 1989, the SFRY Presidency declared that the situation in the province had deteriorated and had become a threat to the constitution, integrity, and sovereignty of the country. The government then imposed "special measures" which assigned responsibility for public security to the federal government instead of the government of Serbia.

11. On 23 March 1989, the Assembly of Kosovo met in Pristina and, with the majority of Kosovo Albanian delegates abstaining, voted to accept the proposed amendments to the constitution. Although lacking the required two-thirds majority in the Assembly, the President of the Assembly nonetheless declared that the amendments had passed. On 28 March 1989, the Assembly of Serbia voted to approve the constitutional changes effectively revoking the autonomy granted in the 1974 constitution.

12. At the same time these changes were occurring in Kosovo, Slobodan MILOSEVIC further increased his political power when he became the President of Serbia. Slobodan MILOSEVIC was elected President of the Presidency of Serbia on 8 May 1989 and his post was formally confirmed on 6 December 1989.

13. In early 1990, Kosovo Albanians held mass demonstrations calling for an end to the "special measures." In April 1990, the SFRY Presidency lifted the "special measures" and removed most of the federal police forces as Serbia took over responsibility for police enforcement in Kosovo.

14. In July 1990, the Assembly of Serbia passed a decision to suspend the Assembly of Kosovo shortly after 114 of the 123 Kosovo Albanian delegates from that Assembly had passed an unofficial resolution declaring Kosovo an equal and independent entity within the SFRY. In September 1990, many of these same Kosovo Albanian delegates proclaimed a constitution for a "Republic of Kosovo." One year later, in September 1991, Kosovo Albanians held an unofficial referendum in which they voted overwhelmingly for independence. On 24 May 1992, Kosovo Albanians held unofficial elections for an assembly and president for the "Republic of Kosovo."

15. On 16 July 1990, the League of Communists of Serbia and the Socialist Alliance of Working People of Serbia joined to form the Socialist Party of Serbia (SPS), and Slobodan MILOSEVIC was elected its President. As the successor to the League of Communists, the SPS became the dominant political party in Serbia and Slobodan MILOSEVIC, as President of the SPS, was able to wield considerable power and influence over many branches of the government as well as the private sector. Milan MILUTINOVIC and Nikola SAINOVIC have both held prominent positions within the SPS. Nikola SAINOVIC was a member of the Main Committee and the Executive Council as well as a vice-chairman; and Milan MILUTINOVIC successfully ran for President of Serbia in 1997 as the SPS candidate.

16. After the adoption of the new Constitution of Serbia on 28 September 1990, Slobodan MILOSEVIC was elected President of Serbia in multi-party elections held on 9 and 26 December 1990; he was re-elected on 20 December 1992. In December 1991, Nikola SAINOVIC was appointed a Deputy Prime Minister of Serbia.

17. After Kosovo's autonomy was effectively revoked in 1989, the political situation in Kosovo became more and more divisive. Throughout late 1990 and 1991 thousands of Kosovo Albanian doctors, teachers, professors, workers, police and civil servants were dismissed from their positions. The local court in Kosovo was abolished and many judges removed. Police violence against Kosovo Albanians increased.

18. During this period, the unofficial Kosovo Albanian leadership pursued a policy of non-violent civil resistance and began establishing a system of unofficial, parallel institutions in the health care and education sectors.

19. In late June 1991 the SFRY began to disintegrate in a succession of wars fought in the Republic of Slovenia (hereinafter Slovenia), the Republic of Croatia (hereinafter Croatia), and the Republic of Bosnia and Herzegovina (hereinafter Bosnia and Herzegovina). On 25 June 1991, Slovenia declared independence from the SFRY, which led to the outbreak of war; a peace agreement was reached on 8 July 1991. Croatia declared its independence on 25 June 1991, leading to fighting between Croatian military forces on the one side and the Yugoslav People's Army (JNA), paramilitary units and the "Army of the Republic of Srpska Krajina" on the other.

20. On 6 March 1992, Bosnia and Herzegovina declared its independence, resulting in wide scale war after 6 April 1992. On 27 April 1992, the SFRY was reconstituted as the FRY. At this time, the JNA was re-formed as the Armed Forces of the FRY (hereinafter VJ). In the war in Bosnia and Herzegovina, the JNA, and later the VJ, fought along with the "Army of Republika Srpska" against military forces of the Government of Bosnia and Herzegovina and the "Croat Defence Council." Active hostilities ceased with the signing of the Dayton peace agreement in December 1995.

21. Although Slobodan MILOSEVIC was the President of Serbia during the wars in Slovenia, Croatia and Bosnia and Herzegovina, he was nonetheless the dominant Serbian political figure exercising de facto control of the federal government as well as the republican government and was the person with whom the international community negotiated a variety of peace plans and agreements related to these wars.

22. Between 1991 and 1997 Milan MILUTINOVIC and Nikola SAINOVIC both held a number of high ranking positions within the federal and republican governments and continued to work closely with Slobodan MILOSEVIC. During this period, Milan MILUTINOVIC worked in the Foreign Ministry of the FRY, and at one time was Ambassador to Greece; in 1995, he was appointed Minister of Foreign Affairs of the FRY, a position he held until 1997. Nikola SAINOVIC was Prime Minister of Serbia in 1993 and Deputy Prime Minister of the FRY in 1994.

23. While the wars were being conducted in Slovenia, Croatia and Bosnia and Herzegovina, the situation in Kosovo, while tense, did not erupt into the violence and intense fighting seen in the other countries. In the mid-1990s, however, a faction of the Kosovo Albanians organised a group known as Ushtria Clirimtare e Kosovës (UCK) or, known in English as the Kosovo Liberation Army (KLA). This group advocated a campaign of armed insurgency and violent resistance to the Serbian authorities. In mid-1996, the KLA began launching attacks primarily targeting FRY and Serbian police forces. Thereafter, and throughout 1997, FRY and Serbian police forces responded with forceful operations against suspected KLA bases and supporters in Kosovo.

24. After concluding his term as President of Serbia, Slobodan MILOSEVIC was elected President of the FRY 15 July 1997, and assumed office on 23 July 1997. Thereafter, elections for the office of the President of Serbia were held; Milan MILUTINOVIC ran as the SPS candidate and was elected President of Serbia on 21 December 1997. In 1996, 1997 and 1998, Nikola SAINOVIC was re-appointed Deputy Prime Minister of the FRY. In part through his close alliance with Milan MILUTINOVIC, Slobodan MILOSEVIC was able to retain his influence over the Government of Serbia.

25. Beginning in late February 1998, the conflict intensified between the KLA on the one hand and the VJ, the police forces of the FRY, police forces of Serbia, and paramilitary units (all hereinafter forces of the FRY and Serbia), on the other hand. A number of Kosovo Albani-

ans and Kosovo Serbs were killed and wounded during this time. Forces of the FRY and Serbia engaged in a campaign of shelling predominantly Kosovo Albanian towns and villages, widespread destruction of property, and expulsions of the civilian population from areas in which the KLA was active. Many residents fled the territory as a result of the fighting and destruction or were forced to move to other areas within Kosovo. The United Nations estimates that by mid-October 1998, over 298,000 persons, roughly fifteen percent of the population, had been internally displaced within Kosovo or had left the province.

26. In response to the intensifying conflict, the United Nations Security Council (UNSC) passed Resolution 1160 in March 1998 "condemning the use of excessive force by Serbian police forces against civilians and peaceful demonstrators in Kosovo," and imposed an arms embargo on the FRY. Six months later the UNSC passed Resolution 1199 (1998) which stated that "the deterioration of the situation in Kosovo, Federal Republic of Yugoslavia, constitutes a threat to peace and security in the region." The Security Council demanded that all parties cease hostilities and that "the security forces used for civilian repression" be withdrawn.

27. In an attempt to diffuse tensions in Kosovo, negotiations between Slobodan MILOSEVIC, and representatives of the North Atlantic Treaty Organisation (NATO), and the Organisation for Security and Co-operation in Europe (OSCE) were conducted in October 1998. An "Agreement on the OSCE Kosovo Verification Mission" was signed on 16 October 1998. This agreement and the "Clark-Naumann agreement," which was signed by Nikola SAINOVIC, provided for the partial withdrawal of forces of the FRY and Serbia from Kosovo, a limitation on the introduction of additional forces and equipment into the area, and the deployment of unarmed OSCE verifiers.

28. Although scores of OSCE verifiers were deployed throughout Kosovo, hostilities continued. During this period, a number of killings of Kosovo Albanians were documented by the international verifiers and human rights organisations. In one such incident, on 15 January 1999, 45 unarmed Kosovo Albanians were murdered in the village of Racak in the municipality of Stimlje/Shtime.

29. In a further response to the continuing conflict in Kosovo, an international peace conference was organised in Rambouillet, France beginning on 7 February 1999. Nikola SAINOVIC, the Deputy Prime Minister of the FRY, was a member of the Serbian delegation at the peace talks and Milan MILUTINOVIC, President of Serbia, was also present during the negotiations. The Kosovo Albanians were represented by the KLA and a delegation of Kosovo Albanian political and civic leaders. Despite intensive negotiations over several weeks, the peace talks collapsed in mid-March 1999.

30. During the peace negotiations in France, the violence in Kosovo continued. In late February and early March, forces of the FRY and Serbia launched a series of offensives against dozens of predominantly Kosovo Albanian villages and towns. The FRY military forces were comprised of elements of the 3rd Army, specifically the 52nd Corps, also known as the Pristina Corps, and several brigades and regiments under the command of the Pristina Corps. The Chief of the General Staff of the VJ, with command responsibilities over the 3rd Army and ultimately over the Pristina Corps, is Colonel General Dragoljub OJDANIC. The Supreme Commander of the VJ is Slobodan MILOSEVIC.

31. The police forces taking part in the actions in Kosovo are members of the Ministry of Internal Affairs of Serbia in addition to some units from the Ministry of Internal Affairs of the FRY. All police forces employed by or working under the authority of the Ministry of Internal Affairs of Serbia are commanded by Vlajko STOJILJKOVIC, Minister of Internal Affairs of Serbia. Under the FRY Act on the Armed Forces, those police forces engaged in military operations during a state of war or imminent threat of war are subordinated to the command of the VJ whose commanders are Colonel General Dragoljub OJDANIC and Slobodan MILOSEVIC.

32. Prior to December 1998, Slobodan MILOSEVIC designated Nikola SAINOVIC as his representative for the Kosovo situation. A number of diplomats and other international officials who needed to speak with a government official regarding events in Kosovo were directed to Nikola SAINOVIC. He took an active role in the negotiations establishing the OSCE verification mission for Kosovo and he participated in numerous other meetings regarding the Kosovo crisis. From January 1999 to the date of this indictment, Nikola SAINCOVIC has acted as the liaison between Slobodan MILOSEVIC and various Kosovo Albanian leaders.

33. Nikola SAINOVIC was most recently re-appointed Deputy Prime Minister of the FRY on 20 May 1998. As such, he is a member of the Government of the FRY, which, among other duties and responsibilities, formulates domestic and foreign policy, enforces federal law, directs and co-ordinates the work of federal ministries, and organises defence preparations.

34. During their offensives, forces of the FRY and Serbia acting in concert have engaged in a well-planned and co-ordinated campaign of destruction of property owned by Kosovo Albanian civilians. Towns and villages have been shelled, homes, farms, and businesses burned, and personal property destroyed. As a result of these orchestrated actions, towns, villages, and entire regions have been made uninhabitable for Kosovo Albanians. Additionally, forces of the FRY and Serbia have harassed, humiliated, and degraded Kosovo Albanian civilians through physical and verbal abuse. The Kosovo Albanians have also been persistently subjected to insults, racial slurs, degrading acts based on ethnicity and religion, beatings, and other forms of physical mistreatment.

35. The unlawful deportation and forcible transfer of thousands of Kosovo Albanians from their homes in Kosovo involved well-planned and co-ordinated efforts by the leaders of the FRY and Serbia, and forces of the FRY and Serbia, all acting in concert. Actions similar in nature took place during the wars in Croatia and Bosnia and Herzegovina between 1991 and 1995. During those wars, Serbian military, paramilitary and police forces forcibly expelled and deported non-Serbs in Croatia and Bosnia and Herzegovina from areas under Serbian control utilising the same method of operations as have been used in Kosovo in 1999: heavy shelling and armed attacks on villages; widespread killings; destruction of non-Serbian residential areas and cultural and religious sites; and forced transfer and deportation of non-Serbian populations.

36. On 24 March 1999, NATO began launching air strikes against targets in the FRY. The FRY issued decrees of an imminent threat of war on 23 March 1999 and a state of war on 24 March 1999. Since the air strikes commenced, forces of the FRY and Serbia have intensified their systematic campaign and have forcibly expelled hundreds of thousands of Kosovo Albanians.

37. In addition to the forced expulsions of Kosovo Albanians, forces of the FRY and Serbia have also engaged in a number of killings of Kosovo Albanians since 24 March 1999. Such killings occurred at numerous locations, including but not limited to, Bela Crkva, Mali Krusa/Krushe e Vogel - Velika Krusa/ Krushe e Mahde, Dakovica/ Gjakovë, Crkovez/ Padalishte, and Izbica.

38. The planning, preparation and execution of the campaign undertaken by forces of the FRY and Serbia in Kosovo, was planned, instigated, ordered, committed or otherwise aided and abetted by Slobodan MILOSEVIC, the President of the FRY; Milan MILUTINOVIC, the President of Serbia; Nikola SAINOVIC, the Deputy Prime Minister of the FRY; Colonel General Dragoljub OJDANIC, the Chief of the General Staff of the VJ; and Vlajko STOJILJKOVIC, the Minister of Internal Affairs of Serbia.

39. By 20 May 1999, over 740,000 Kosovo Albanians, approximately one-third of the entire Kosovo Albanian population, were expelled from Kosovo. Thousands more are believed to be internally displaced. An unknown number of Kosovo Albanians have been killed in the operations by forces of the FRY and Serbia.

The Accused

40. Slobodan MILOSEVIC was born on 20 August 1941 in the town of Pozarevac in present-day Serbia. In 1964 he received a law degree from the University of Belgrade and began a career in management and banking. Slobodan MILOSEVIC held the posts of deputy director and later general director at Tehnogas, a major gas company until 1978. Thereafter, he became president of Beogradska banka (Beobanka), one of the largest banks in the SFRY and held that post until 1983.

41. In 1983 Slobodan MILOSEVIC began his political career. He became Chairman of the City Committee of the League of Communists of Belgrade in 1984. In 1986 he was elected Chairman of the Presidium of the Central Committee of the League of Communists of Serbia and was re-elected in 1988. On 16 July 1990, the League of Communists of Serbia and the Socialist Alliance of Working People of Serbia were united; the new party was named the Socialist Party of Serbia (SPS), and Slobodan MILOSEVIC was elected its President. He holds the post of President of the SPS as of the date of this indictment.

42. Slobodan MILOSEVIC was elected President of the Presidency of Serbia on 8 May 1989 and re-elected on 5 December that same year. After the adoption of the new Constitution of Serbia on 28 September 1990, Slobodan MILOSEVIC was elected to the newly established office of President of Serbia in multi-party elections held on 9 and 26 December 1990; he was re-elected on 20 December 1992.

43. After serving two terms as President of Serbia, Slobodan MILOSEVIC was elected President of the FRY on 15 July 1997 and he began his official duties on 23 July 1997. At all times relevant to this indictment, Slobodan MILOSEVIC has held the post of President of the FRY.

44. Milan MILUTINOVIC was born on 19 December 1942 in Belgrade in present-day Serbia. Milan MILUTINOVIC received a degree in law from Belgrade University.

45. Throughout his political career, Milan MILUTINOVIC has held numerous high level governmental posts within Serbia and the FRY. Milan MILUTINOVIC was a deputy in the Socio-Political Chamber and a member of the foreign policy committee in the Federal Assembly; he was Serbia's Secretary for Education and Sciences, a member of the Executive Council of the Serbian Assembly, and a director of the Serbian National Library. Milan MILUTINOVIC also served as an ambassador in the Federal Ministry of Foreign Affairs and as the FRY Ambassador to Greece. He was appointed the Minister of Foreign Affairs of the FRY on 15 August 1995. Milan MILUTINOVIC is a member of the SPS.

46. On 21 December 1997, Milan MILUTINOVIC was elected President of Serbia. At all times relevant to this indictment, Milan MILUTINOVIC has held the post of President of Serbia.

47. Nikola SAINOVIC was born on 7 December 1948 in Bor, Serbia. He graduated from the University of Ljubljana in 1977 and holds a Master of Science degree in Chemical Engineering. He began his political career in the municipality of Bor where he held the position of President of the Municipal Assembly of Bor from 1978 to 1982.

48. Throughout his political career, Nikola SAINOVIC has been an active member of both the League of Communists and the Socialist Party of Serbia (SPS). He held the position of Chairman of the Municipal Committee of the League of Communists in Bor. On 28 November 1995, Nikola SAINOVIC was elected a member of the SPS's Main Committee and a member of its Executive Council. He was also named president of the Committee to prepare the SPS Third Regular Congress (held in Belgrade on 2-3 March 1996). On 2 March 1996 Nikola SAINOVIC was elected one of several vice chairmen of the SPS. He held this position until 24 April 1997.

49. Nikola SAINOVIC has held several positions within the governments of Serbia and the FRY. In 1989, he served as a member of the Executive Council of Serbia's Assembly and Secretary for Industry, Energetics and Engineering of Serbia in 1989. He was appointed Minister of Mining and Energy of Serbia on 11 February 1991, and again on 23 December 1991. On 23 December 1991, he was also named Deputy Prime Minister of Serbia. Nikola SAINOVIC was appointed Minister of the Economy of the FRY on 14 July 1992, and again on 11 September 1992. He resigned from this post on 29 November 1992. On 10 February 1993, Nikola SAINOVIC was elected Prime Minister of Serbia.

50. On 22 February 1994, Nikola SAINOVIC was appointed Deputy Prime Minister of the FRY. He was re-appointed to this position in three subsequent governments: on 12 June 1996, 20 March 1997 and 20 May 1998. Slobodan MILOSEVIC designated Nikola SAINOVIC as his representative for the Kosovo situation. Nikola SAINOVIC chaired the commission for co-operation with the OSCE Verification Mission in Kosovo, and was an official member of the Serbian delegation at the Rambouillet peace talks in February 1999. At all times relevant to this indictment, Nikola SAINOVIC has held the post of Deputy Prime Minister of the FRY.

51. Colonel General Dragoljub OJDANIC was born on 1 June 1941 in the village of Ravni, near Uzice in what is now Serbia. In 1958, he completed the Infantry School for Non-Commissioned Officers and in 1964, he completed the Military Academy of the Ground Forces. In 1985, Dragoljub OJDANIC graduated from the Command Staff Academy and School of National Defence with a Masters Degree in Military Sciences. At one time he served as the Secretary for the League of Communists for the Yugoslav National Army (JNA) 52nd Corps, the precursor of the 52nd Corps of the VJ now operating in Kosovo.

52. In 1992, Colonel General Dragoljub OJDANIC was the Deputy Commander of the 37th Corps of the JNA, later the VJ, based in Uzice, Serbia. He was promoted to Major General on 20 April 1992 and became Commander of the Uzice Corps. Under his command, the Uzice Corps was involved in military actions in eastern Bosnia during the war in Bosnia and Herzegovina. In 1993 and 1994 Dragoljub OJDANIC served as Chief of the General Staff of the First Army of the FRY. He was Commander of the First Army between 1994 and 1996. In 1996, he became Deputy Chief of the General Staff of the VJ. On 26 November 1998, Slobodan MILOSEVIC appointed Dragoljub OJDANIC Chief of General Staff of the VJ, replacing General Momcilo Perisic. At all times relevant to this indictment, Colonel General Dragoljub OJDANIC has held the post of Chief of the General Staff of the VJ.

53. Vlajko STOJILJKOVIC was born in Mala Krsna, in Serbia. He graduated from the University of Belgrade with a law degree, and then was employed at the municipal court. Thereafter, he became head of the Inter-Municipal Secretariat of Internal Affairs in Pozarevac. Vlajko STOJILJKOVIC has served as director of the PIK firm in Pozarevac, vice-president and president of the Economic Council of Yugoslavia, and president of the Economic Council of Serbia.

54. By April 1997, Vlajko STOJILJKOVIC became Deputy Prime Minister of the Serbian Government and Minister of Internal Affairs of Serbia. On 24 March 1998, the Serbian Assembly elected a new Government, and Vlajko STOJILJKOVIC was named Minister of Internal Affairs of Serbia. He is also a member of the main board of the SPS. At all times relevant to this indictment, Vlajko STOJILJKOVIC, has held the post of Minister of Internal Affairs.

Superior Authority

55. Slobodan MILOSEVIC was elected President of the FRY on 15 July 1997, assumed office on 23 July 1997, and remains President as of the date of this indictment.

56. As President of the FRY, Slobodan MILOSEVIC functions as President of the Supreme Defence Council of the FRY. The Supreme Defence Council consists of the President of the FRY and the Presidents of the member republics, Serbia and Montenegro. The Supreme Defence Council decides on the National Defence Plan and issues decisions concerning the VJ. As President of the FRY, Slobodan MILOSEVIC has the power to "order implementation of the National Defence Plan" and commands the VJ in war and peace in compliance with decisions made by the Supreme Defence Council. Slobodan

MILOSEVIC, as Supreme Commander of the VJ, performs these duties through "commands, orders and decisions."

57. Under the FRY Act on the Armed Forces of Yugoslavia, as Supreme Commander of the VJ, Slobodan MILOSEVIC also exercises command authority over republican and federal police units subordinated to the VJ during a state of imminent threat of war or a state of war. A declaration of imminent threat of war was proclaimed on 23 March 1999, and a state of war on 24 March 1999.

58. In addition to his de jure powers, Slobodan MILOSEVIC exercises extensive de facto control over numerous institutions essential to, or involved in, the conduct of the offences alleged herein. Slobodan MILOSEVIC exercises extensive de facto control over federal institutions nominally under the competence of the Assembly or the Government of the FRY. Slobodan MILOSEVIC also exercises de facto control over functions and institutions nominally under the competence of Serbia and its autonomous provinces, including the Serbian police force. Slobodan MILOSEVIC further exercises de facto control over numerous aspects of the FRY's political and economic life, particularly the media. Between 1986 and the early 1990s, Slobodan MILOSEVIC progressively acquired de facto control over these federal, republican, provincial and other institutions. He continues to exercise this de facto control to this day.

59. Slobodan MILOSEVIC's de facto control over Serbian, SFRY, FRY and other state organs has stemmed, in part, from his leadership of the two principal political parties that have ruled in Serbia since 1986, and in the FRY since 1992. From 1986 until 1990, he was Chairman of the Presidium of the Central Committee of the League of Communists in Serbia, then the ruling party in Serbia. In 1990, he was elected President of the Socialist Party of Serbia, the successor party to the League of Communists of Serbia and the Socialist Alliance of the Working People of Serbia. The SPS has been the principal ruling party in Serbia and the FRY ever since. Throughout the period of his Presidency of Serbia, from 1990 to 1997, and as the President of the FRY, from 1997 to the present, Slobodan MILOSEVIC has also been the leader of the SPS.

60. Beginning no later than October 1988, Slobodan MILOSEVIC has exercised de facto control over the ruling and governing institutions of Serbia, including its police force. Beginning no later than October 1988, he has exercised de facto control over Serbia's two autonomous provinces - Kosovo and Vojvodina - and their representation in federal organs of the SFRY and the FRY. From no later than October 1988 until mid-1998, Slobodan MILOSEVIC also exercised de facto control over the ruling and governing institutions of the Montenegro, including its representation in all federal organs of the SFRY and the FRY.

61. In significant international negotiations, meetings and conferences since 1989, Slobodan MILOSEVIC has been the primary interlocutor with whom the international community has negotiated. He has negotiated international agreements that have subsequently been implemented within Serbia, the SFRY, the FRY, and elsewhere on the territory of the former SFRY. Among the conferences and international negotiations at which Slobodan MILOSEVIC has been the primary representative of the SFRY and FRY are: The Hague Conference in 1991; the Paris negotiations of March 1993; the International Conference on the Former Yugoslavia in January 1993; the Vance-Owen peace plan negotiations between January and May 1993; the Geneva peace talks in the summer of 1993; the Contact Group meeting in June 1994; the negotiations for a cease fire in Bosnia and Herzegovina, 9-14 September 1995; the negotiations to end the NATO bombing in Bosnia and Herzegovina, 14-20 September 1995; and the Dayton peace negotiations in November 1995.

62. As the President of the FRY, the Supreme Commander of the VJ, and the President of the Supreme Defence Council, and pursuant to his de facto authority, Slobodan MILOSEVIC is responsible for the actions of his subordinates within the VJ and any police forces, both federal and republican, who have committed the crimes alleged in this indictment since January 1999 in the province of Kosovo.

63. Milan MILUTINOVIC was elected President of Serbia on 21 December 1997, and remains President as of the date of this indictment. As President of Serbia, Milan MILUTINOVIC is the head of State. He represents Serbia and conducts its relations with foreign states and international organisations. He organises preparations for the defence of Serbia.

64. As President of Serbia, Milan MILUTINOVIC is a member of the Supreme Defence Council of the FRY and participates in decisions regarding the use of the VJ.

65. As President of Serbia, Milan MILUTINOVIC, in conjunction with the Assembly, has the authority to request reports both from the Government of Serbia, concerning matters under its jurisdiction, and from the Ministry of the Internal Affairs, concerning its activities and the security situation in Serbia. As President of Serbia, Milan MILUTINOVIC has the authority to dissolve the Assembly, and with it the Government, "subject to the proposal of the Government on justified grounds," although this power obtains only in peacetime.

66. During a declared state of war or state of imminent threat of war, Milan MILUTINOVIC, as President of Serbia, may enact measures normally under the competence of the Assembly, including the passage of laws; these measures may include the reorganisation of the Government and its ministries, as well as the restriction of certain rights and freedoms.

67. In addition to his de jure powers, Milan MILUTINOVIC exercises extensive de facto influence or control over numerous institutions essential to, or involved in, the conduct of the crimes alleged herein. Milan MILUTINOVIC exercises de facto influence or control over functions and institutions nominally under the competence of the Government and Assembly of Serbia and its autonomous provinces, including but not limited to the Serbian police force.

68. In significant international negotiations, meetings and conferences since 1995, Milan MILUTINOVIC has been a principal interlocutor with whom the international community has negotiated. Among the conferences and international negotiations at which Milan MILUTINOVIC has been a primary representative of the FRY are: preliminary negotiations for a cease fire in Bosnia and Herzegovina, 15-21 August 1995; the Geneva meetings regarding the Bosnian cease fire, 7 September 1995; further negotiations for a cease fire in Bosnia and Herzegovina, 9-14 September 1995; the negotiations to end the NATO bombing in Bosnia and Herzegovina, 14-20 September 1995; the meeting of Balkan foreign ministers in New York, 26 September 1995; and the Dayton peace negotiations in November 1995. Milan MILUTINOVIC was also present at the negotiations at Rambouillet in February 1999.

69. As the President of Serbia, and a member of the Supreme Defence Council, and pursuant to his de facto authority, Milan MILUTINOVIC is responsible for the actions of any of his subordinates within the VJ and within any police forces who have committed the crimes alleged in this indictment since January 1999 within the province of Kosovo.

70. Colonel General Dragoljub OJDANIC was appointed Chief of the General Staff of the VJ on 26 November 1998. He remains in that position as of the date of this indictment. As Chief of the General Staff of the VJ, Colonel General Dragoljub OJDANIC commands, orders, instructs, regulates and otherwise directs the VJ, pursuant to acts issued by the President of the FRY and as required to command the VJ.

71. As Chief of the General Staff of the VJ, Colonel General Dragoljub OJDANIC determines the organisation, plan of development and formation of commands, units and institutions of the VJ, in conformity with the nature and needs of the VJ and pursuant to acts rendered by the President of the FRY.

72. In his position of authority, Colonel General Dragoljub OJDANIC also determines the plan for recruiting and filling vacancies within the VJ and the distribution of recruits therein; issues regulations concerning training of the VJ; determines the educational plan and

advanced training of professional and reserve military officers; and performs other tasks stipulated by law.

73. As Chief of the General Staff of the VJ, Colonel General Dragoljub OJDANIC - or other officers empowered by him - assigns commissioned officers, non-commissioned officers and soldiers, and promotes non-commissioned officers, reserve officers, and officers up to the rank of colonel. In addition, Colonel General Dragoljub OJDANIC nominates the president, judges, prosecutors, and their respective deputies and secretaries, to serve on military disciplinary courts.

74. Colonel General Dragoljub OJDANIC carries out preparations for the conscription of citizens and mobilisation of the VJ; co-operates with the Ministries of Internal Affairs of the FRY and Serbia and the Ministry of Defence of the FRY in mobilising organs and units of Ministries of Internal Affairs; monitors and, proposes measures to correct problems encountered during, and informs the Government of the FRY and the Supreme Defence Council about the implementation of the aforementioned mobilisation.

75. As the Chief of the General Staff of the VJ, Colonel General Dragoljub OJDANIC is responsible for the actions of his subordinates within the VJ and for the actions of any federal and republican police forces, which are subordinated to the VJ, who have committed crimes since January 1999 within the province of Kosovo.

76. Vlajko STOJILJKOVIC was named Minister of Internal Affairs of Serbia on 24 March 1998. As head of a Serbian government ministry, Vlajko STOJILJKOVIC is responsible for the enforcement of laws, regulations and general acts promulgated by Serbia's Assembly, Government or President.

77. As Minister of Internal Affairs of Serbia, Vlajko STOJILJKOVIC directs the work of the Ministry of Internal Affairs and its personnel. He determines the structure, mandate and scope of operations of organisational units within the Ministry of Internal Affairs. He is empowered to call up members of the Ministry of Internal Affairs reserve corps to perform duties during peace time, and to prevent activities threatening Serbia's security. The orders which he and Ministry of Internal Affairs superior officers issue to Ministry of Internal Affairs personnel are binding unless they constitute a criminal act.

78. As Minister of Internal Affairs of Serbia, Vlajko STOJILJKOVIC has powers of review over decisions and acts of agents for the Ministry. He considers appeals against decisions made in the first instance by the head of an organisational unit of the Ministry of Internal Affairs. Moreover, he is empowered to decide appeals made by individuals who have been detained by the police.

79. On 8 April 1999, as Minister of Internal Affairs of Serbia, Vlajko STOJILJKOVIC's powers during the state of war were expanded to include transferring Ministry employees to different duties within the Ministry for as long as required.

80. As Minister of Internal Affairs of Serbia, Vlajko STOJILJKOVIC is responsible for ensuring the maintenance of law and order in Serbia. As Minister of Internal Affairs, he is responsible for the actions of his subordinates within the police forces of the Ministry of Internal Affairs of Serbia who have committed crimes since January 1999 in the province of Kosovo.

General Allegations

81. At all times relevant to this indictment, a state of armed conflict existed in Kosovo in the FRY.

82. All acts and omissions charged as crimes against humanity were part of a widespread or systematic attack directed against the Kosovo Albanian civilian population of Kosovo in the FRY.

83. Each of the accused is individually responsible for the crimes alleged against him in this indictment, pursuant to Article 7(1) of the Tribunal Statute. Individual criminal responsibility includes committing, planning, instigating, ordering or aiding and abetting in the planning, preparation or execution of any crimes referred to in Articles 2 to 5 of the Tribunal Statute.

84. In as much as he has authority or control over the VJ and police units, other units or individuals subordinated to the command of the VJ in Kosovo, Slobodan MILOSEVIC, as President of the FRY, Supreme Commander of the VJ and President of the Supreme Defence Council, is also, or alternatively, criminally responsible for the acts of his subordinates, including members of the VJ and aforementioned employees of the Ministries of Internal Affairs of the FRY and Serbia, pursuant to Article 7(3) of the Tribunal Statute.

85. In as much as he has authority or control over police units of the Ministry of Internal Affairs, the VJ, or police units, other units or individuals subordinated to the command of the VJ in Kosovo, Milan MILUTINOVIC, as President of the Serbia and a member of the Supreme Defence Council, is also, or alternatively, criminally responsible for the acts of his subordinates, including aforementioned employees of the Ministry of Internal Affairs of Serbia, pursuant to Article 7(3) of the Tribunal Statute.

86. In as much as he has authority or control over the VJ and police units, other units or individuals subordinated to the command of the VJ in Kosovo, Colonel General Dragoljub OJDANIC, as Chief of the General Staff of the VJ, is also, or alternatively, criminally responsible for the acts of his subordinates, including members of the VJ and aforementioned employees of the Ministries of Internal Affairs of Serbia and the FRY, pursuant to Article 7(3) of the Tribunal Statute.

87. In as much as he has authority or control over employees of the Ministry of Internal Affairs, including any other regular or mobilised police units, Vlajko STOJILJKOVIC, as Minister of Internal Affairs of Serbia, is also, or alternatively, criminally responsible for the acts of his subordinates, including employees of the Ministry of Internal Affairs of Serbia, pursuant to Article 7(3) of the Tribunal Statute.

88. A superior is responsible for the acts of his subordinate(s) if he knew or had reason to know that his subordinate(s) was/were about to commit such acts or had done so and the superior failed to take the necessary and reasonable measures to prevent such acts or to punish the perpetrators thereof.

89. The general allegations contained in paragraphs 81 through 88 are re-alleged and incorporated into each of the charges set forth below.

Charges

COUNTS 1 - 4 Crimes against Humanity Violations of the Laws or Customs of War

90. Beginning in January 1999 and continuing to the date of this indictment, Slobodan MILOSEVIC, Milan MILUTINOVIC, Nikola SAINOVIC, Dragoljub OJDANIC, and Vlajko STOJILJKOVIC planned, instigated, ordered, committed or otherwise aided and abetted in a campaign of terror and violence directed at Kosovo Albanian civilians living in Kosovo in the FRY.

91. The campaign of terror and violence directed at the Kosovo Albanian population was executed by forces of the FRY and Serbia acting at the direction, with the encouragement, or with the support of Slobodan MILOSEVIC, Milan MILUTINOVIC, Nikola SAINOVIC, Dragoljub OJDANIC, and Vlajko STOJILJKOVIC. The operations targeting the Kosovo Albanians were undertaken with the objective of removing a substantial portion of the Kosovo Albanian population from Kosovo in an effort to ensure continued Serbian control over the province. To achieve this objective, the forces of the FRY and Serbia, acting in concert, have engaged in well-planned and co-ordinated operations as described in paragraphs 92 through 98 below.

92. The forces of the FRY and Serbia, have in a systematic manner, forcibly expelled and internally displaced hundreds of thousands of Kosovo Albanians from their homes across the entire province of Kosovo. To facilitate these expulsions and displacements, the forces of the FRY and Serbia have intentionally created an atmosphere of fear and oppression through the use of force, threats of force, and acts of violence.

93. Throughout Kosovo, the forces of the FRY and Serbia have looted and pillaged the personal and commercial property belonging to

Kosovo Albanians forced from their homes. Policemen, soldiers, and military officers have used wholesale searches, threats of force, and acts of violence to rob Kosovo Albanians of money and valuables, and in a systematic manner, authorities at FRY border posts have stolen personal vehicles and other property from Kosovo Albanians being deported from the province.

94. Throughout Kosovo, the forces of the FRY and Serbia have engaged in a systematic campaign of destruction of property owned by Kosovo Albanian civilians. This has been accomplished through the widespread shelling of towns and villages; the burning of homes, farms, and businesses; and the destruction of personal property. As a result of these orchestrated actions, villages, towns, and entire regions have been made uninhabitable for Kosovo Albanians.

95. Throughout Kosovo, the forces of the FRY and Serbia have harassed, humiliated, and degraded Kosovo Albanian civilians through physical and verbal abuse. Policemen, soldiers, and military officers have persistently subjected Kosovo Albanians to insults, racial slurs, degrading acts, beatings, and other forms of physical mistreatment based on their racial, religious, and political identification.

96. Throughout Kosovo, the forces of the FRY and Serbia have systematically seized and destroyed the personal identity documents and licenses of vehicles belonging to Kosovo Albanian civilians. As Kosovo Albanians have been forced from their homes and directed towards Kosovo's borders, they have been subjected to demands to surrender identity documents at selected points en route to border crossings and at border crossings into Albania and Macedonia. These actions have been undertaken in order to erase any record of the deported Kosovo Albanians' presence in Kosovo and to deny them the right to return to their homes.

97. Beginning on or about 1 January 1999 and continuing until the date of this indictment, the forces of the FRY and Serbia, acting at the direction, with the encouragement, or with the support of Slobodan MILOSEVIC, Milan MILUTINOVIC, Nikola SAINOVIC, Dragoljub OJDANIC, and Vlajko STOJILJKOVIC have perpetrated the actions set forth in paragraphs 92 through 96, which have resulted in the forced deportation of approximately 740,000 Kosovo Albanian civilians. These actions have been undertaken in all areas of Kosovo, and these means and methods were used throughout the province, including the following municipalities:

a. Dakovica/Gjakovë: On or about 2 April 1999, forces of the FRY and Serbia began forcing residents of the town of Dakovica/Gjakovë to leave. Forces of the FRY and Serbia spread out through the town and went house to house ordering Kosovo Albanians from their homes. In some instances, people were killed, and most persons were threatened with death. Many of the houses and shops belonging to Kosovo Albanians were set on fire, while those belonging to Serbs were protected. During the period from 2 to 4 April 1999, thousands of Kosovo Albanians living in Dakovica/Gjakovë and neighbouring villages joined a large convoy, either on foot or driving in cars, trucks and tractors, and moved to the border with Albania. Forces of the FRY and Serbia directed those fleeing along pre-arranged routes, and at police checkpoints along the way most Kosovo Albanians had their identification papers and license plates seized. In some instances, Yugoslav army trucks were used to transport persons to the border with Albania.

b. Gnjilane/Gjilan: Forces of the FRY and Serbia entered the town of Prilepnica/Përlepnicë on or about 6 April 1999, and ordered residents to leave saying that the town would be mined the next day. The townspeople left and tried to go to another village but were turned back by police. On 13 April 1999, residents of Prilepnica/Përlepnicë were again informed that the town had to be evacuated by the following day. The next morning, the Kosovo Albanian residents left in a convoy of approximately 500 vehicles and headed to the Macedonian border. Shortly after the residents left, the houses in Prilepnica/Përlepnicë were set on fire. Kosovo Albanians in other villages in Gnjilane/Gjilan municipality were also forced from their homes, and were made to join another convoy to the Macedonian border. Along the way, some men were taken from the convoy and killed along the road. When the Kosovo Albanians reached the border, their identification papers were confiscated.

c. Kosovska Mitrovica/Mitrovicë: In late March 1999, forces of the FRY and Serbia began moving systematically through the town of Kosovska Mitrovica/Mitrovicë. They entered the homes of Kosovo Albanians and ordered the residents to leave their houses at once and to go to the bus station. Some houses were set on fire forcing the residents to flee to other parts of the town. Over a two week period the forces of the FRY and Serbia continued to expel the Kosovo Albanian residents of the town. During this period, properties belonging to Kosovo Albanians were destroyed and Kosovo Albanians were robbed of money, vehicles, and other valuables. A similar pattern was repeated in other villages in the Kosovska Mitrovica/Mitrovicë municipality, where Kosovo Albanians were forced from their homes, followed by the destruction of their villages by forces of the FRY and Serbia. The Kosovo Albanian residents of the municipality were forced to join convoys going to the Albanian border. En route to the border, Serb soldiers, policemen, and military officers robbed them of valuables and seized their identity documents.

d. Orahovac/Rahovec: On the morning of 25 March 1999, forces of the FRY and Serbia surrounded the village of Celine with tanks and armoured vehicles. After shelling the village, troops entered the village and systematically looted and pillaged everything of value from the houses. Most of the Kosovo Albanian villagers had fled to a nearby forest before the army and police arrived. On 28 March, a number of Serb police forced the thousands of people hiding in the forest to come out. After marching the civilians to a nearby village, the men were separated from the women and were beaten, robbed, and had all of their identity documents taken from them. The men were then marched to Prizren and eventually forced to go to the Albanian border.

On 25 March 1999, a large group of Kosovo Albanians went to a mountain near the village of Nagafc, also in Orahovac/Rahovec municipality, seeking safety from attacks on nearby villages. Forces of the FRY and Serbia surrounded them and on the following day, ordered the 8,000 people who had sought shelter on the mountain to leave. The Kosovo Albanians were forced to go to a nearby school and then they were forcibly dispersed into nearby villages. After three or four days, the forces of the FRY and Serbia entered the villages, went house to house and ordered people out. Eventually, they were forced back into houses and told not to leave. Those who could not fit inside the houses were forced to stay in cars and tractors parked nearby. On 2 April 1999, the forces of the FRY and Serbia started shelling the villages, killing a number of people who had been sleeping in tractors and cars. Those who survived headed for the Albanian border. As they passed through other Kosovo Albanian villages, which had been destroyed, they were taunted by Serb soldiers. When the villagers arrived at the border, all their identification papers were taken from them.

e. Pec/Pejë: On 27 and 28 March 1999, in the city of Pec/Pejë, forces of the FRY and Serbia went from house to house forcing Kosovo Albanians to leave. Some houses were set on fire and a number of people were shot. Soldiers and police were stationed along every street directing the Kosovo Albanians toward the town centre. Once the people reached the centre of town, those without cars or vehicles were forced to get on buses or trucks and were driven to the town of Prizren. Outside Prizren, the Kosovo Albanians were forced to get off the buses and walk approximately 40 kilometres to the Albanian border where they were ordered to turn their identification papers over to Serb policemen.

f. Pristina/Prishtinë: On or about 1 April 1999, Serbian police went to the homes of Kosovo Albanians in the city of Pristina/Prishtinë and forced the residents to leave in a matter of minutes. During the course of these forced expulsions, a number of people were killed. Many of those forced from their homes went directly to the train station, while others sought shelter in nearby neighbourhoods. Hundreds of ethnic Albanians, guided by Serb police at all the intersections, gathered at the train station and then were loaded onto overcrowded trains or buses after a long wait where no food or water was provided. Those on the trains went as far as General Jankovic, a village near the Macedonian border. During the train ride many people had their identification papers taken from them. After getting off the trains, the Kosovo Albanians were told by the Serb police to walk along the tracks into Macedonia since the surrounding land had been mined. Those who tried to hide in Pristina/Prishtinë were expelled a few days later in a similar fashion.

During the same period, forces of the FRY and Serbia entered the villages of Pristina/Prishtinë municipality where they beat and killed many Kosovo Albanians, robbed them of their money, looted their property and burned their homes. Many of the villagers were taken by truck to Glogovac in the municipality of Lipljan/Lipjan. From there, they were transported to General Jankovic by train and walked to the Macedonian border. Others, after making their way to the town of Urosevac/Ferizaj, were ordered by the Serb police to take a train to General Jankovic, from where they walked across the border into Macedonia.

g. Prizren: On 25 March 1999 the village of Pirana was surrounded by forces of the FRY and Serbia, tanks and various military vehicles. The village was shelled and a number of the residents were killed. Thereafter, police entered the village and burned the house of Kosovo Albanians. After the attack, the remaining villagers left Pirana and went to surrounding villages. Some of the Kosovo Albanians fleeing toward Srbica were killed or wounded by snipers. Serb forces then launched an offensive in the area of Srbica and shelled the villages of Reti e Utlet, Reti and Randobrava. Kosovo Albanian villagers were forced from their homes and sent to the Albanian border. From 28 March 1999, in the city of Prizren itself, Serb policemen went from house to house, ordering Kosovo Albanian residents to leave. They were forced to join convoys of vehicles and persons travelling on foot to the Albanian border. At the border all personal documents were taken away by Serb policemen.

h. Srbica/Skenderaj: On or about 25 March 1999, the villages of Vojnik, Lecina, Klladernica, Turiqevc Broje and Izbica were destroyed by shelling and burning. A group of approximately 4,500 Kosovo Albanians from these villages gathered outside the village of Izbica where members of the forces of the FRY and Serbia demanded money from the group and separated the men from the women and children. A large number of the men were then killed. The surviving women and children were moved as a group towards Vojnik and then on to the Albanian border.

i. Suva Reka/Suharekë: On the morning of 25 March 1999, forces of the FRY and Serbia surrounded the town of Suva Reka/Suharekë. During the following days, police officers went from house to house, threatening Kosovo Albanian residents, and removing many of the people from their homes at gunpoint. The women, children and elderly were sent away by the police and then a number of the men were killed by the Forces of the FRY and Serbia. The Kosovo Albanians were forced to flee making their way in trucks, tractors and trailers towards the border with Albania. While crossing the border, they had all their documents and money taken.

On 31 March 1999, approximately 80,000 Kosovo Albanians displaced from villages in the Suva Reka/Suharekë municipality gathered near Bellanice. The following day, forces of the FRY and Serbia shelled Bellanice, forcing the displaced persons to flee toward the Albanian border. Prior to crossing the border, they had all their identification documents taken away.

j. Urosevac/Ferizaj: During the period between 4 and 14 April 1999, forces of the FRY and Serbia shelled the villages of Softaj, Rahovica, Zltara, Pojatista, Komoglava and Sojevo, killing a number of residents. After the shelling, police and military vehicles entered the villages and ordered the residents to leave. After the villagers left their houses, the soldiers and policemen burned the houses. The villagers that were displaced joined in a convoy to the Macedonian border. At the border, all of their documents were taken.

98. Beginning on or about 1 January 1999 and continuing until the date of this indictment, forces of the FRY and Serbia, acting at the direction, with the encouragement, or with the support of Slobodan MILOSEVIC, Milan MILUTINOVIC, Nikola SAINOVIC, Dragoljub OJDANIC, and Vlajko STOJILJKOVIC, have murdered hundreds of Kosovo Albanian civilians. These killings have occurred in a widespread or systematic manner throughout the province of Kosovo and have resulted in the deaths of numerous men, women, and children. Included among the incidents of mass killings are the following:

a. On or about 15 January 1999, in the early morning hours, the village of Racak (Stimlje/Shtime municipality) was attacked by forces of the FRY and Serbia. After shelling by the VJ units, the Serb police entered the village later in the morning and began conducting house-to-house searches. Villagers, who attempted to flee from the Serb police, were shot throughout the village. A group of approximately 25 men attempted to hide in a building, but were discovered by the Serb police. They were beaten and then were removed to a nearby hill, where the policemen shot and killed them. Altogether, the forces of the FRY and Serbia killed approximately 45 Kosovo Albanians in and around Racak. (Those persons killed who are known by name are set forth in Schedule A, which is attached as an appendix to this indictment.)

b. On or about 25 March 1999, forces of the FRY and Serbia attacked the village of Bela Crkva (Orahovac/Rahovec municipality). Many of the residents of Bela Crkva fled into a streambed outside the village and sought shelter under a railroad bridge. As additional villagers approached the bridge, a Serbian police patrol opened fire on them killing 12 persons, including 10 women and children. The police then ordered the remaining villagers out of the streambed, at which time the men were separated from the women and small children. The police ordered the men to strip and then systematically robbed them of all valuables. The women and children were then ordered to leave. The village doctor attempted to speak with the police commander, but he was shot and killed, as was his nephew. The other men were then ordered back into the streambed. After they complied, the police opened fire on the men, killing approximately 65 Kosovo Albanians. (Those persons killed who are known by name are set forth in Schedule B which is attached as an appendix to the indictment.)

c. On or about 25 March 1999, the villages of Velika Krusa and Mali Krusa/ Krushe e Mahde and Krushe e Vogel (Orahovac/Rahovec municipality) were attacked by forces of the FRY and Serbia. Village residents took refuge in a forested area outside Velika Krusa/ Krushe e Mahde, where they were able to observe the police systematically looting and then burning the villagers' houses. On or about the morning of 26 March 1999, Serb police located the villagers in the forest. The police ordered the women and small children to leave the area and to go to Albania. The police then searched the men and boys and took their identity documents, after which they were made to walk to an uninhabited house between the forest and Mali Krusa/ Krushe e Vogel. Once the men and boys were assembled inside the house, the Serb police opened fire on the group. After several minutes of gunfire, the police piled hay on the men and boys and set fire to it in order to burn the bodies. As a result of the shootings and the fire, approximately 105 Kosovo Albanian men and boys were killed by the Serb police. (Those persons killed who are known by name are set forth in Schedule C which is attached as an appendix to this indictment.)

d. On or about the evening of 26 March 1999, in the town of Dakovica/Gjakovë, Serb gunmen came to a house on Ymer Grezda Street. The women and children inside the house were separated from the men, and were ordered to go upstairs. The Serb gunmen then shot and killed the 6 Kosovo Albanian men who were in the house. (The names of those killed are set forth in Schedule D which is attached as an appendix to this indictment.)

e. On or about 27 March 1999, in the morning hours, forces of the FRY and Serbia attacked the village of Crkolez/Padalishte (Istok/Istog municipality). As the forces entered the village, they fired on houses and on villagers who attempted to flee. Eight members of the Beke IMERAJ family were forced from their home and were killed in front of their house. Other residents of Crkolez/Padalishte were killed at their homes and in a streambed near the village. Altogether, forces of the FRY and Serbia killed approximately 20 Kosovo Albanians from Crkolez/Padalishte. (Those persons killed who are known by name are set forth in Schedule E which is attached as an appendix to this indictment.)

f. On or about 27 March 1999, FRY and Republic of Serbia forces attacked the village of Izbica (Srbica/Skenderaj municipality). Several thousand village residents took refuge in a meadow outside the village. On or about 28 March 1999, forces of the FRY and Serbia surrounded the villagers and then approached them, demanding money. After valuables were stolen by the soldiers and policemen, the men were separated from the women and small children. The men were then further divided into two groups, one of which was sent to a nearby hill, and the other of which was sent to a nearby streambed. Both groups of men were then fired upon by the forces of the FRY and Serbia, and approximately 130 Kosovo Albanian men were killed. (Those persons killed who are known by name are set forth in Schedule F which is attached as an appendix to this indictment.)

g. On or about the early morning hours of 2 April 1999, Serb police launched an operation against the Qerim district of Dakovica/Gjakovë. Over a period of several hours, Serb police forcibly entered houses of Kosovo Albanians in the Qerim district, killing the occupants, and then setting fire to the buildings. In the basement of a house on Millosh Gilic Street, the Serb police shot the 20 occupants and then set the house on fire. As a result of the shootings and the fires set by the Serb police, 20 Kosovo Albanians were killed, of whom 19 were women and children. (The names of those killed are set forth in Schedule G which is attached as an appendix to this indictment.)

99. Beginning on or about 1 January 1999 and continuing until the date of this indictment, the forces of the FRY and Serbia, acting at the direction, with the encouragement, or with the support of Slobodan MILOSEVIC, Milan MILUTINOVIC, Nikola SAINOVIC, Dragoljub OJDANIC, and Vlajko STOJILJKOVIC, have utilised the means and methods set forth in paragraphs 92 through 98 to execute a campaign of persecution against the Kosovo Albanian civilian population based on political, racial, or religious grounds.

100. By these actions Slobodan MILOSEVIC, Milan MILUTINOVIC, Nikola SAINOVIC, Dragoljub OJDANIC, and Vlajko STOJILJKOVIC planned, instigated, ordered, committed or otherwise aided and abetted the planning, preparation or execution of:

COUNT 1 (DEPORTATION)

Count 1: Deportation, a CRIME AGAINST HUMANITY, punishable under Article 5(d) of the Statute of the Tribunal.

COUNT 2 (MURDER)

Count 2: Murder, a CRIME AGAINST HUMANITY, punishable under Article 5 (a) of the Statute of the Tribunal.

COUNT 3 (MURDER)

Count 3: Murder, a VIOLATION OF THE LAWS OR CUSTOMS OF WAR, punishable under Article 3 of the Statute of the Tribunal and recognised by Article 3(1)(a) (murder) of the Geneva Conventions.

COUNT 4 (PERSECUTIONS)

Count 4: Persecutions on political, racial and religious grounds, a CRIME AGAINST HUMANITY, punishable under Article 5(h) of the Statute of the Tribunal.

Louise Arbour Prosecutor

22 May 1999 The Hague, The Netherlands

[Schedule A Persons Known by Name Killed at Racak - 15 January 1999, Schedule B Persons Known by Name Killed at Bela Crkva - 25 March 1999, Schedule C Persons Known by Name Killed at Velika Krusa/Krushe e Mahde - Mali Krusa/Krushe e Vogel - 26 March 1999, Schedule D Persons Killed at Dakovica /Gjakove - 26 March 1999, Schedule E Persons Known by Name Killed at Crkolez/Padalishtë - 27 March 1999, Schedule F Persons Known by Name Killed at Izbica - 28 March 1999 and Schedule G Persons Killed at Dakovica / Gjakovë - 2 April 1999 have been omitted.]

320. Russian Federation, Statement by the Ministry of Foreign Affairs, 27 May 1999[1]

The information about the intention of the prosecutor of the International Criminal Tribunal on Former Yugoslavia (ICTY) L. Arbour to indicte the President of the Federal Republic Yugoslavia S. Milosevic was received in Moscow with deep concern.

The ICTY was established in 1993 through the decision of the Security Counsel to detect and punish the persons responsible for mass murder and other large-scale violations of international humanitarian law, committed in the territory of the former Yugoslavia.

Regarding the intention to initiate a criminal procedure against S. Milosevic under the present circumstances it is absolutely obvious that this step cannot be considered in any light other than politically motivated.

Such acts on behalf of ICTY, which have already happened before, seriously undermine the credibility of this organ of the Security Counsel of the UN.

In practice, if the before mentioned indictment by the prosecutor is issued, it will only create additional obstacles on the way towards settling the situation in Yugoslavia and challenge even more the persistent efforts, undertaken now to work out a political solution.

The Russian side intends to continue its active search for a fast political solution of the conflict concerning Yugoslavia, including participation of S. Milosevic.

321. Russian Federation, Statement of the Ministry of Foreign Affairs, 27 May 1999[1]

The decision of the prosecutor of the International Criminal Tribunal for the Former Yugoslavia L. Arbour to indicte five high political and military leaders of the Federal Republic Yugoslavia, including its President and the President of Serbia, cannot be interpreted in any way, other than as an action motivated by political concerns. Most surprising is the haste with which the prosecutor has conducted the investigation and drew her categorical conclusions. Yet it is quite obvious, that taking into account the present situation in and around Yugoslavia such decisions require special thoroughness and scrupulousness. It can be hardly considered coincidental, that this step was made in the moment, when the negotiations around the settlement of Kosovo problem enter its most decisive phase. As a result the whole negotiating process becomes more difficult. At the same time, L. Arbour demonstrates an amazing passiveness in the face of the obvious fact of NATO aggression against Yugoslavia and looks indifferently at the results of the two months incessant bombing. She is in no way moved by the death of hundreds of innocent people, the destruction of the economic and social infrastructure of the country, the ruining of historic monuments and the threat of an ecological catastrophe. Is it not a task of a prosecutor to find out who gives the orders to launch such massive assaults, leading to such terrible results? Unfortunately, L. Arbour is absolutely silent on all these question, which can hardly prove her objectivity. Russia will continue its efforts aiming at a just political settlement, for which it will continue to cooperate with all necessary partners including those in Yugoslavia. This approach also corresponds to the Russian role in settling the present Balkan crises recognized by the whole international community.

322. ICTY, Statement by the Prosecutor, PR/P.I.S./437-E, The Hague, 29 September 1999

1. The Prosecutor of the International Criminal Tribunal for the former Yugoslavia (ICTY) will investigate crimes committed during the armed conflict in Kosovo and she will vigorously prosecute those responsible before the Trial Chambers at The Hague. These investiga-

---

[1] *Unofficial translation by Mr. Sergey Lagodinsky, Institute for Public International Law, University of Göttingen.*

tions and prosecutions have to be conducted within the scope of the statutory jurisdiction of the International Tribunal; in accordance with the prosecution strategy adopted by the Office of the Prosecutor (OTP); and as a function of the resources available to the OTP. This statement is intended to make the position of the Prosecutor clear, respecting how she will carry out her mandate in Kosovo.

2. In light of the factors just mentioned, the primary focus of the OTP must be the investigation and prosecution of the five leaders of the Federal Republic of Yugoslavia and the Republic of Serbia, who have already been indicted, and who are alleged to be responsible for the crimes described in the indictment. This involves gathering additional evidence relating to what occurred on the ground in Kosovo during the time period relevant to the indictment, and collecting further evidence respecting the chain of command and responsibility linking the accused to what happened on the ground during that time period. This will be done, in order to add to the existing evidentiary foundation supporting the indictment.

3. OTP ICTY investigative resources must also necessarily be applied, in relation to other high level civilian, police, and military leaders, of whichever party to the conflict who may be held responsible for crimes committed during the armed conflict in Kosovo.

4. The OTP ICTY may investigate and prosecute other individuals, on a case by case basis, who may have committed particularly serious crimes during the course of the armed conflict. The Prosecutor may also investigate and prosecute, on a case by case basis, perpetrators of sexual violence committed in relation to the armed conflict in Kosovo.

5. Under the Statute establishing the ICTY, the International Tribunal has the power to prosecute persons for grave breaches of the Geneva Conventions of 1949, for violations of the laws and customs of war, for genocide, and for crimes against humanity. With the exception of genocide, a prerequisite to the prosecution of persons charged with committing the crimes falling within the jurisdiction of the International Tribunal is the existence of an armed conflict at the time of the commission of the crimes (and, in the case of grave breaches, the existence of an international armed conflict). In the Tadic case, the ICTY Appeals Chamber said, in part, "an armed conflict exists whenever there is resort to armed force between States or protracted armed violence between governmental authorities and organized armed groups or between such groups within a State. International humanitarian law applies from the initiation of such armed conflicts and extends beyond the cessation of hostilities until a general conclusion of peace is reached; or, in the case of internal conflicts, a peaceful settlement is achieved." The Appeals Chamber also required, for a crime to fall within the jurisdictional scope of ICTY, that "a sufficient nexus must be established between the alleged offence and the armed conflict which gives rise to the applicability of international humanitarian law." It is difficult to prejudge the matter of jurisdiction, and so the Prosecutor will continue to examine the factual and legal basis that may link offences to the armed conflict in Kosovo. Nevertheless, the limits of jurisdiction cannot be ignored, and must be taken into account along with a prosecution strategy that properly focuses on leadership investigative targets, as well as perpetrators of particularly serious crimes or sexual violence in relation to the armed conflict. The Prosecutor must also make a realistic appraisal of the resources that she has available to her to carry out her mandate under the ICTY Statute.

6. In light of the above considerations, it is clear that OTP ICTY has neither the mandate, nor the resources, to function, as the primary investigative and prosecutorial agency for all criminal acts committed on the territory of Kosovo. The investigation and prosecution of offences, which may fall outside the scope of the jurisdiction described above is properly the responsibility of UNMIK, through UNCivPol and the newly formed civilian police in Kosovo, assisted by KFOR. To ensure that the OTP ICTY and the agencies just mentioned are operating within their proper spheres, it will be helpful for an effective liaison to be maintained between them and the OTP. This should enable the Prosecutor to be kept informed about the nature and status of investigations being conducted by UNMIK (UNCivPol and the civilian police force), assisted by KFOR, into matters that may potentially have a relationship to crimes within the purview of the ICTY.

7. Continuing liaison with ICTY is important, because the Security Council provided for concurrent jurisdiction in the International Tribunal and in national courts to prosecute persons for crimes within the scope of the ICTY Statute. Therefore, the judicial authorities in Kosovo have the competence to judge those accused of crimes of the sort that come within the jurisdiction of the International Tribunal. In appropriate cases, which must be determined on a case by case basis, it is open to the International Tribunal to request national courts to defer to its competence, in accordance with the Statute of the Tribunal and its Rules of Procedure and Evidence (the Rules).

8. The Prosecutor will carry out her mandate in a vigilant and responsive manner, in accordance with the criteria described above.

CHAPTER 9: IMPLEMENTATION OF THE PRINCIPLES FOR A POLITICAL SOLUTION OF THE CONFLICT

By resolution 1244 (1999) (*document no. 208; see Chapter 5*) the UN Security Council authorised member States and relevant international organisations to set up an international security presence - KFOR - and decided that its responsibilities would include preventing renewed hostilities, demilitarising the KLA, and establishing a safe environment for the return of the refugees as well as for the operation of an international civil presence. The deployment of KFOR was synchronised with the departure of the Serbian security forces. By 20 June 1999, the Serb withdrawal was complete and KFOR established in Kosovo. On the same day, NATO Secretary General Solana announced that, in accordance with the Military Technical Agreement (*document no. 207*), he had formally terminated the air campaign (*document no. 328*). Neither Resolution 1244 (1998) nor its annexes regulated the Russian participation in KFOR. During further talks the Russian government refused to place its troops under the command of NATO but suggested to create a separate Russian sector. The Russian Federation intended to deny freedom of operation to the NATO forces throughout its sector. On 11 June 1999 before the arrival of NATO forces, Russian forces occupied the Pristina airfield. the incident increased the tensions between the NATO states and the Russian Federation. The Agreement on Russian Participation in KFOR concluded in Helsinki on 18 June 1999 resolved the dispute about the airfield and regulated, inter alia, the maximal Russian deployment (*document no. 326*). However, the agreement did not grant a separate sector to the Russian forces.

UN Security Council resolution 1244 (1999) also vested the Secretary-General with the power to establish in Kosovo an interim international civilian administration. Two days later, the UN Secretary-General presented to the Council a detailed plan for the United Nations Interim Administration Mission in Kosovo (UNMIK) (*document no. 324*). On 12 July, in his follow-up report to the Council, the Secretary-General outlined a comprehensive plan for the UN-led international civil operation in Kosovo (*document no. 332*).

The Security Council has bestowed upon the UN Mission authority over the territory of Kosovo, including all legislative and executive powers, as well as the administration of the judiciary. Among its key tasks, UNMIK will promote the establishment of substantial autonomy and self-government in Kosovo, perform basic civilian administrative functions, facilitate a political process to determine Kosovo's future status, support the reconstruction of key infrastructure as well as humanitarian and disaster relief, maintain civil law and order, promote human rights, and assure the safe and unimpeded return of all refugees and displaced persons to Kosovo.

With UNMIK a UN mission has been framed in which other multilateral organisations are full partners under UN leadership. There are four sectors concerned with implementing the rehabilitation and reform of Kosovo: civil administration, under the UN itself; humanitarian assistance, led by the office of the UNHCR; democratisation and institution-building, led by the OSCE and economic reconstruction, managed by the EU.[1] The mission is headed by the Special Representative of the UN Secretary-General, Dr. Bernard Kouchner (France), who assumed office on 15 July 1999.

It is planned that UNMIK will exercise its functions in five phases. In Phase I, the Mission will establish administrative structures and provide emergency assistance. In the second phase it will focus on providing social services and the consolidation of the rule of law. In addition, it will prepare for the elections of a Kosovo Transitional Authority which will be held during Phase III. In Phase IV UNMIK will assist in setting up provisional institutions for democratic self-government. The concluding phase will oversee the transfer of authority from Kosovo's provisional institutions to institutions under a political settlement. Under Phase I UNMIK has built up the administration of Kosovo since June 1999. Through the Kosovo Transitional Council (KTC), over which UN presides, the involvement of local leaders in the interim administration and the decision-making process is ensured (*documents no. 332, 334, 338*). It meets regularly once a week. This body brings together all major political parties and ethnic groups. On 15 December 1999, three Kosovo Albanian political leaders signed an agreement to set up the Kosovo-UNMIK Joint Interim Administrative Structure (JIAS). The agreement sets up 14 joint Administrative Departments, subsequently increased to 19, each to be co-headed by a representative of UNMIK and a Kosovo representative. It installs an Interim Administrative Council which will define the policies and recommend new regulations and amendments to current law. The Council is composed of 8 members - the three Kosovo Albanian leaders and an as of yet unnamed Kosovo Serb, plus four UNMIK members.

The Special Representative of the UN Secretary-General has the right to issue legislative acts in the form of regulations for the performance of the duties entrusted to the interim administration under UN Security Council resolution 1244 (1999) (*documents no. 339 - 346*). On 12 December 1999, the Special Representative of the Secretary-General announced a regulation making UNMIK regulations the primary law of Kosovo and relegating the law in force in Kosovo on 22 March 1989 to a subsidiary level (*document no. 346*). Furthermore, a new penal code is being drafted by Kosovar legal experts with the help of the Council of Europe. All these laws must conform to international human rights standards.

In regard to humanitarian activities UNHCR organised the return of 810,000 people who had been living in camps or with host families in Albania, the Former Yugoslav Republic of Macedonia, Montenegro, Bosnia and Herzegovina and other countries during the NATO air strikes. However, UNHCR reports that an estimated 180,000 displaced Serb and Roma people have moved from Kosovo to Serbia and Montenegro. Between 80,000 and 130,000 of these internally displaced persons are believed to have left Kosovo since the end of NATO air strikes and the deployment of KFOR in Kosovo in June 1999.

These developments coincide with concerns about the security situation for Kosovo Serbs, Roma and other minority groups as stated by the UN Secretary-General in his report of 23 December 1999. Despite the efforts of KFOR and UNMIK, "the level and nature of violence in Kosovo, especially against vulnerable minorities, remains unacceptable" according to the report (*document no. 338*).

With a view to the economic reconstruction there have been two donor conferences held in July and November 1999 in Brussels to cover the budgetary deficits presented by UNMIK, the immediate basic needs identified by UN agencies and the immediate requirements for reconstruction.

---

[1] See for instance, EU, Council Joint Action Concerning the Installation of the Structures of UNMIK, 1999/522/CFSP/ of 29 July 1999.

Concerning the KLA an agreement was reached on 20 September 1999 to demilitarise and transform the KLA, according to the Undertaking of 20 June (*document no. 227*) and the regulation of 20 September issued by Head of UNMIK on the creation of a Kosovo Protection Corps (*document no. 343*). The Kosovo Protection Corps is a multi-ethnic civilian emergency corps modelled after the French *Sécurité Civile*. UNMIK created the corps to respond to disasters, undertake search and rescue missions, provide humanitarian aid, help demining, and to contribute to rebuilding the infrastructure and local communities. The UN has political authority over the Kosovo Protection Corps, but KFOR will actively monitor and supervise it.

The OSCE is also active within the framework of UNMIK. By decision of the OSCE Permanent Council, the OSCE-KVM ceased to exist as of 9 June 1999 (*document no. 323*) and was replaced by a transitional OSCE Task Force for Kosovo, which had to prepare the deployment of a further OSCE mission into Kosovo and which continued to assess the human rights situation there. This task force was succeeded by the OSCE Mission in Kosovo set up by decision of the OSCE Permanent Council of 1 July 1999 (*documents no. 330, 331*). Referring to UN Security Council resolution 1244 (1999), the Permanent Council decided that the OSCE would, within the overall framework of UNMIK "take the lead role in matters relating to institution- and democracy-building and human rights". According to its mandate the Mission cooperates with other relevant international and non-governmental organisations in its task, such as the UNHCR, the UN High Commissioner for Human Rights, the European Union and the Council of Europe. Pursuant to its mandate, the OSCE is responsible for training judges, prosecutors, civil administration and police, furthering the development of civil society, non-governmental organisations and political parties, supporting media development, organising and supervising elections, monitoring, protecting, and promoting human rights.

While the reconstruction of Kosovo advances, the international community has continuously applied pressure on Milosevic and his regime. The EU, for instance, continues to maintain its system of economic sanctions (*documents no. 347, 350, 352, 353*), so long as it holds that the government of the FRY violates UN Security Council resolutions. The EU states that the FRY pursues "criminally irresponsible policies" which constitute serious violations of human rights and international humanitarian law. In order to support democratic forces in the FRY, the EU does not only exclude Kosovo but also the Republic of Montenegro from its sanction regime.

9.1 INTERNATIONAL CIVIL AND SECURITY PRESENCE IN KOSOVO

323. OSCE, Permanent Council, PC. EC/296/Corr., 8 June 1999

The Permanent Council decides that:

The OSCE Kosovo Verification Mission will cease to exist from 9 June 1999. From the same date a transitional OSCE Task Force for Kosovo will be established, pending a decision on future tasks for the OSCE in Kosovo. The tasks of the OSCE Task Force will be the following:

- To prepare for the deployment to Kosovo of available and relevant OSCE assets as soon as this may be required;
- To assist in planning and preparation for new tasks which the OSCE may take on as part of a new international presence in Kosovo;
- To carry out preparatory visits and activities in Kosovo in order to facilitate the entry of a future OSCE Mission to Kosovo as soon as conditions allow;
- To co-operate, as required, with the UN and other international organizations in on-going activities relevant to possible future OSCE tasks in Kosovo, in particular registration and documentation of refugees;
- To continue assessing the human rights situation in Kosovo.

The Permanent Council tasks the Secretary General to take all measures necessary for the closure of the KVM, and authorizes him to transfer resources previously allocated to the KVM to the OSCE Task Force and:

(a) To incur obligations to the extent required for the fulfilment of the tasks of the OSCE Task Force, but not exceeding the residual portion of the spending authority previously granted, following the implementation of all necessary measures to close the KVM;

(b) To continue making use of the existing Post Table authorized by PC Decisions Nos. 266 and 282;

(c) To make use of the physical assets previously acquired for the use of the KVM.

[233rd Plenary Meeting PC Journal No. 233, Agenda item 1 Decision No. 296. Corrected reissue incorporating amendment regarding date of issue.]

324. UN, Report of the Secretary-General Prepared pursuant to Paragraph 10 of Security Council Resolution 1244 (1999), UN Doc. S/1999/672, 12 June 1999

I. Introduction

1. The present report is submitted pursuant to paragraph 10 of Security Council resolution 1244 (1999), in which the Council authorized the Secretary-General, with the assistance of the relevant international organizations, to establish an international civil presence in Kosovo in order to provide an interim administration for Kosovo under which the people of Kosovo can enjoy substantial autonomy. In paragraph 11 of the resolution, the Council enumerated the main responsibilities of the interim administration. This report presents a preliminary operational concept for the overall organization of the civil presence, which will be known as the United Nations Interim Administration Mission in Kosovo (UNMIK). A more detailed concept will be submitted to the Security Council in connection with the request, in paragraph 20 of resolution 1244 (1999), that the Secretary-General report on implementation of the resolution within 30 days. That document will be based on a report by the advance Headquarters team to be deployed shortly in Kosovo.

II. Overall Structure of the Mission

2. It is apparent that in order to fulfil the provisions of Security Council resolution 1244 (1999) effectively, the structure of the Mission must ensure that all activities of the international community in Kosovo are carried out in an integrated manner with a clear chain of command. The Mission will rely on the capabilities and expertise of the various international organizations that will participate, while maintaining coherence and effectiveness.

3. Accordingly, UNMIK will be headed by a Special Representative of the Secretary-General, appointed by the Secretary-General in consultation with the Security Council. The Special Representative of the Secretary-General will have overall authority to manage the Mission and coordinate the activities of all United Nations agencies and other international organizations operating as part of UNMIK. The Special Representative will also be responsible for facilitating a political process designed to determine the future political status of Kosovo, taking into account the Rambouillet accords, as specified in paragraph 11 (e).

4. The Special Representative of the Secretary-General, who will be appointed at the rank of Under-Secretary-General, will be supported in his work by a Chief of Staff and various units, including units for political and legal advice, military liaison, liaison with the International Tribunal for the Former Yugoslavia and relations with the mass media.

5. The Special Representative of the Secretary-General will be assisted in his tasks by four Deputy Special Representatives of the Secretary-General. Each will be responsible for one major component of the Mission. In order to ensure that the institutional capacities of the agencies cooperating with the United Nations are pooled for optimal effectiveness on the ground, each component will be assigned to an agency which would take the lead role in a particular area, as follows:

(a) Interim civil administration: the United Nations;

(b) Humanitarian affairs: the Office of the United Nations High Commissioner for Refugees (UNHCR);

(c) Institution-building: the Organization for Security and Cooperation in Europe (OSCE);

(d) Reconstruction: the European Union.

The Deputy Special Representative of the Secretary-General for Interim Civil Administration will also serve as the Principal Deputy Special Representative and officiate as Chief of Mission in the absence of the Special Representative. A preliminary description of the structure of the Mission is annexed to the present report.

6. The Special Representative of the Secretary-General will appoint an Executive Committee whose membership will include the four Deputy Special Representatives. The Executive Committee will assist the Special Representative in fulfilling his responsibilities. It is expected that the agency with the overall responsibility for a particular component will draw upon the capacities and expertise of other organizations on the ground and coordinate their work to maximum advantage.

7. It is imperative that UNMIK and the international security presence coordinate their activities closely to ensure that both the military and the civilian presences operate in a mutually supportive manner towards the same goals, as required by paragraphs 6 and 9 (f) of resolution 1244 (1999). To this end, effective arrangements will be established for regular consultations between the Special Representative of the Secretary-General and the Commander of the international security presence. The Special Representative's staff will include a Military Liaison Unit to facilitate day-to-day relations with the international security presence and to ensure that effective liaison with the military is established for all aspects of the Mission's work.

III. Role and Responsibilities of the Components

Interim Civil Administration

8. The interim civil administration component of the Mission, under the United Nations, will comprise three main offices, namely, a Police Commissioner, an Office for Civil Affairs, and an Office for Judicial Affairs.

9. The Police Commissioner's staff will consist of the following:

(a) An International Civilian Police Unit to oversee the civilian police operation and to establish and supervise a Kosovo Police Force;

(b) A Special Police Unit for crowd control and other special police functions;

(c) An International Border Police Unit.

It is recalled that resolution 1244 (1999) stipulates, in paragraph 9 (d), that the international security presence will initially be responsible for public safety and order. When the civil presence takes over, as envisaged in paragraph 11 (i), and in view of the Mission's executive responsibilities for law and order, consideration will have to be given to arming the police.

10. The Office for Civil Affairs will be responsible for overseeing and, where necessary, conducting a number of civil affairs functions, such as the civil service and economic and budgetary affairs, as well as supporting the restoration and provision in the short run of basic public services, such as public health, education, utilities, transport and telecommunications.

11. The Office for Judicial Affairs will be responsible for the organization and oversight of the judicial system, authenticating legal documentation and related activities.

Humanitarian Affairs

12. Paragraph 11 (k) of resolution 1244 (1999) stipulates that the principal function of UNMIK in the humanitarian area is to ensure the safe and unimpeded return of all refugees and displaced persons to their homes in Kosovo. Other functions are likely to include protection of and assistance to minority groups. As foreseen in paragraph 11 (h), the humanitarian affairs component, led by UNHCR, will also coordinate, with other international organizations and non-governmental organizations, the provision of humanitarian and disaster relief aid. UNMIK will establish, as soon as possible, a Mine Action Centre to deal with the threat posed to the returnees and internally displaced persons by landmines and unexploded ordnance.

Institution-Building

13. The task of institution-building, for which OSCE will be the lead agency, might comprise four main functions, the final structure to be decided in consultation with OSCE:

(a) Human resources capacity-building, in the areas of justice, police and public administration;

(b) Democratization and governance;

(c) Human rights monitoring and capacity-building;

(d) Conduct and monitoring of elections.

Strengthening the institutions of civil society, especially independent indigenous media, would also be central to these tasks.

Reconstruction

14. The tasks of reconstruction would be led by the European Union, and should be aimed at rebuilding the physical, economic and social infrastructure and systems of Kosovo and supporting the reactivation of public services and utilities. The range of tasks would be decided in consultation with the European Union. These could include near-term projects in the area of agriculture and markets, and activities relating to commerce; activities to re-establish essential public services and develop programmes for economic recovery; and longer-term capital projects in the areas of housing, utilities, transportation and communications. Every effort should be made to avoid the creation of a gap between humanitarian relief and rehabilitation and longer-term reconstruction. The overall plan for Kosovo should take into account the reconstruction and stabilization plans for the wider region.

IV. Observations

15. The structure described above on a preliminary basis represents, in my judgement, the optimum for an effective and integrated international civil presence in Kosovo, which can fulfil the provisions of Security Council resolution 1244 (1999) with the assistance of relevant international organizations, under the leadership of the United Nations. Consultations are being undertaken with the organizations concerned to refine this concept further. Without prejudice to the role and authority of the Security Council, it would be my intention, as in other operations, to consult regularly with Governments and organizations in a position to assist me in the discharge of the responsibilities entrusted to me by the Council.

16. It is clearly an essential requirement for the success of UNMIK that the people of Kosovo be included fully and effectively in its work, in particular that of the interim administration, so that the transition to self-governing institutions is both smooth and timely. Community leaders and professionals can make immediate and significant contributions in judicial affairs, governance and the provision of public services. UNMIK intends to establish from the start a system of advisory mechanisms and implementation committees which will fully engage the local population.

17. I have informed the President of the Security Council of my intention to appoint Mr. Sergio Vieira de Mello as my Special Represen-

tative, on an interim basis. The deployment of UNMIK is under way. Humanitarian agencies have deployed along with the first contingent of the international security presence and have begun to provide humanitarian relief. An advance core headquarters has been assembled at Skopje and will be deployed in Kosovo at the earliest opportunity.

18. I would welcome an early indication from the Security Council that this concept of operations for UNMIK meets with its general approval. A more detailed report and cost estimates will be submitted, in accordance with the usual procedures, once the advance team has completed its initial assessment on the ground and the necessary consultations with the participating agencies have been held.

325. NATO, Initial Report on the International Security Force (KFOR) Operations (12-15 June 1999), 17 June 1999[1]

1. Status of the Deployment of the International Security Force (KFOR):

(a) KFOR deployment continued throughout Zone 1 (see attached map) 6 days after the military technical agreement was signed. All the brigades of KFOR are now deployed in their initial area of responsibilities. As provided for in the military technical agreement, KFOR deployment in Kosovo is being synchronized with the phased withdrawal of forces of the Federal Republic of Yugoslavia. The withdrawal of the Federal Republic of Yugoslavia forces from Kosovo continues with two thirds of personnel and equipment being cleared of Zone 1. In general, the Yugoslav Army and the Ministry of the Interior Police are respecting the timetable in the military technical agreement, however, logistic and maintenance difficulties may well delay their withdrawal in the days ahead.

(b) The deployment of the Italian and German Brigades to western Kosovo on the border with Albania has reduced tension in the area and allowed the Yugoslav Army/Ministry of the Interior Police to withdraw with minimal interference from the Kosovar Albanian population. Convoys from Pec and Pristina were escorted by KFOR to deter attacks. The deployment of United States forces (Task Force Falcon) has been advanced and they have assumed responsibility for the Kacanik defile. The French Framework Brigade has advanced westward towards the area around Gnjilane. The French Framework Brigade movement has been somewhat constrained by the constant stream of withdrawing Yugoslav Army/Ministry of the Interior Police vehicles, but they have established excellent liaison with the Yugoslav Army and Ministry of the Interior Police in Gnjilane.

(c) Four United Kingdom Armoured Brigade conducted an extensive patrol programme throughout their area of responsibility to include Pristina without incident. The situation remains tense with incidents of violence between Kosovar Albanians and Kosovar Serbs. The visible presence of KFOR troops is proving to deter violence. Overall, the operation is proceeding as planned.

(d) Liaison with Yugoslav Army and Ministry of the Interior Police commanders in Zones 2 and 3 has started in preparation for phase 2 and phase 3 deployments. Yugoslav Army and Ministry of the Interior Police forces are withdrawing at a steady pace, but their operations have been hampered by traffic congestion, a lack of fuel, and concerns over UCK attacks. The future pace of the withdrawal could also be determined by the availability of heavy equipment transport owing to maintenance problems in the Yugoslav forces resulting from the operational pace of the past several months. The Yugoslav Army is currently using about 22 heavy equipment transports to move armour and heavy equipment out of the Province. Federal Republic of Yugoslavia air defence units are continuing to withdraw from Kosovo in compliance with the military technical agreement, but owing to logistical and communications difficulties, they were unable to meet their 12 June deadline. Isolated clashes between departing Yugoslav Army/Ministry of the Interior Police and UCK elements, as well as burning and looting by departing Yugoslav Army/Ministry of the Interior Police forces continue to be reported. In some cases, Kosovar Albanian villagers fired on withdrawing Federal Republic of Yugoslavia units. In general, the Yugoslav Army and Ministry of the Interior Police are in compliance with the military technical agreement. However, in the western region of Kosovo, they are unwilling to depart until North Atlantic Treaty Organization forces fill the vacuum between them and the UCK. The UCK established a border control point at Globocica along Kosovo's border with the Former Yugoslav Republic of Macedonia.* UCK uniformed personnel stopped traffic and demanded identity cards and raised the Albanian flag in place of the Federal Republic of Yugoslavia's flag.

(e) Monday, 14 June 1999, was marred by three incidents, two of which directly involved KFOR troops. In Prizren, two Serbs riding in a passenger car opened fire on German troops with automatic weapons as they drove towards the German soldiers. In self-defence, the soldiers returned fire, killing the driver and wounding the passenger. One of the German soldiers was slightly injured in the exchange of gunfire. In Pristina, British troops shot and killed a Ministry of the Interior Police policeman after he began shooting at the troops. The policeman was warned to stop, but he ignored the warning. In Stimle, just south of Pristina, an unknown assailant shot two German journalists. One of the journalists was killed instantly and the other died later in a British military facility. In Skopje, despite the efforts of our KFOR medical personnel, KFOR released press statements on the shootings, notified Federal Republic of Yugoslavia authorities and urged all sides to cooperate and avoid confrontation.

2. Overall Progress of Withdrawal of Serb Military, Police and Paramilitary Forces and Demilitarization of other Forces:

(a) Progress of Serb withdrawal. Yugoslav Army/Ministry of the Interior Police appear to be making every effort to comply with the timelines contained in the military technical agreement, nonetheless, there have been a few technical problems and these may lead to some elements not achieving full withdrawal within the required timelines. As of 14 June 1999, approximately half of the Serbian forces had been withdrawn from Kosovo.

(b) Progress of demilitarization of other forces. To date there has been very little progress in the demilitarization of other forces. On a few occasions, UCK fighters handed over their weapons voluntarily in order to return to their homes.

326. US - Russian Federation, Agreement on Russian Participation in KFOR, Helsinki, 18 June 1999

Agreed Points on Russian Participation in KFOR

It is agreed by the Secretary of Defense of the United States and the Minister of Defense of the Russian Federation:

To accept the Agreed Principles attached (attachment 1) as the basis for Russian participation in the international peacekeeping force (KFOR) in full compliance with UNSC Resolution 1244.

To provide for participation of one to two Russian battalions operating in Kosovska Kamenica in the US sector according to the attached command and control model (attachment 2). A Russian officer will serve as the Representative to the Sector Commander for Russian Forces.

Additionally, the US will recommend that NATO agree that Russian forces also participate in the KFOR forces deployed in the German and French sectors, also according to the command and control model (attachment 2), specifically that Russia provide one to two battalions to be part of the KFOR force in the German sector, to operate in the area near Malisevo, and one battalion to the KFOR force in the French sector, to operate in the area near Lausa both areas as shown on the attached map (attachment 3). A German company and a French company will also operate in the Malisevo and Lausa areas respectively.

---

[1] UN Doc. S/1999/692, Annex, 17 June 1999.

Establishment of an Interim Administration

Russian officers will serve as Representatives for Russian Forces to the sector commanders in the German and French sectors, respectively.

The total Russian deployment in Kosovo will not exceed five battalions with a total strength not exceeding 2850 troops, plus up to 750 troops for the airfield and logistics base operation combined, plus 16 liaison officers. The level of Russian participation will be reduced in proportion to reductions in the overall size of KFOR.

To resolve the Pristina (Slatina) airfield issues on the basis of the allocation of responsibilities described in attachments 4 and 5.

All KFOR participants will have access to the airfield, under procedures to be established by KFOR. Details to be determined by Commander, KFOR in consultation with Russian representatives.

That Russia will have the right to establish a logistics base with an appropriate site security in the vicinity of the town of Kosovo Polje, as agreed with COMKFOR, to support Russian forces in KFOR.

To send a Russian military representative to SHAPE and to augment his staff and expand his responsibilities to include Russian participation in KFOR, and to establish liaison and planning cells at AFSOUTH and KFOR as rapidly as possible in accordance with attachment 6.

To convene consultations as soon as possible to develop details for implementation of these agreements.

That these points, including determination on which sector the Russians will participate in, will be confirmed by the NAC for NATO and by the Government of the Russian Federation. The scheme of deployment of the Russian of KFOR may be reviewed and adjusted in the light of the prevailing circumstances by mutual agreement of the confirming parties, keeping in mind all aspects of a continued, appropriate Russian presence.

All command arrangements will preserve the principle of unity of command. It is understood that the Russian contingent in Kosovo will be under the political and military control of the Russian Command.

[signed] For the Department of Defense of the United States of America

[signed] For the Ministry of Defense of the Russian Federation

Attachment 1
AGREED PRINCIPLES FOR RUSSIAN PARTICIPATION IN THE INTERNATIONAL SECURITY FORCE (KFOR) FOR KOSOVO

Subject to political review and approval by NATO and Russian authorities, the following principles are accepted as the basis for Russian participation in a military effective peace enforcement operation in Kosovo:

1. Common Mission/Purpose: Under the mandate of UNSCR 1244 taken under Chapter VII of the UN Charter and according to the principles therein, and within the framework of the Military Technical Agreement between KFOR and the Federal Republic of Yugoslavia, KFOR will deploy to establish a secure environment for the return of refugees and Internally Displaced Persons and to monitor, and if necessary enforce, compliance with the Military Agreement and the demilitarization of the KLA. The participation of all national contingents in KFOR will be based on OPLAN 10413, Operation Joint Guardian.

2. Common Rules of Engagement: All contingents of KFOR will accepts and operate under common rules of engagement to be applied impartially in all areas toward all parties without exception.

3. Unity of Command: All command arrangements will preserve the principle of unity of command. This presumes that the Russian side exercises full political and military control over the Russian exception.

4. Single Airspace Management: All contingents of KFOR will operate under KFOR-established airspace and airfield management controls in accordance with agreements.

5. Single System of Ground movement Control: All ground movement will be conducted under the KFOR movement control procedures in accordance with agreements. To this end, a Russian liaison group will be created for communication and co-ordination, in accordance with the attached Liaison Arrangements for Russian forces in KFOR.

6. Intelligence Sharing and Exchange: Conduct as under IFOR and SFOR. Tactical mission-oriented information will be exchanged on an agreed basis.

7. Co-ordinated Public Information Process: Conducted as under IFOR and SFOR. Public Information messages will be co-ordinated and public information products exchanged.

8. Single System to Co-ordinate National Logistics and KFOR Base Support: KFOR may assist in co-ordinating national logistics operations among national contingents. All contingents of KFOR are responsible for their financial and logistics commitments.

9. KFOR Freedom of Manoeuvre and Operation: In the case where a sector commander, or a commander of a national contingent within a sector, declines to accept an order from the KFOR commander, COMKFOR will have full authority to order other KFOR forces, from that sector, or any other sector, to carry out the mission, and those other forces will have full freedom of manoeuvre and operation throughout the sector in question, including the zone of responsibility of the sector commander or national contingent commander, who declined to accept the order.

10. Command Structure: The command structure depicted on the attached chart (Russian Participation in KFOR) will be the command structure for Russian participation in KFOR.

[Attachments 2 und 3 which contain a chart and a map have been omitted.]

Attachment 4
ALLOCATION OF RESPONSIBILITIES BETWEEN RF ARMED FORCES AND KFOR AT THE PRISTINA (SLATINA) AIRFIELD.

Overall direction for the operation of the airfield and airspace in the KFOR AOR will be provided by the Director of Kosovo Air Operations working for the KFOR Commander.

The Chief of the Airfield, who carries out the functions enumerated in point 1 below, is a Russian officer, while the Chief of Air Movement, who carries out the function enumerated in point 2 below, is a representative of NATO. They will carry out their functions in the name of the Director of Air Operations in Kosovo and KFOR Commander.

1. The Armed Forces of the Russian Federation will be responsible for: Airfield Security Airport Space Allocation Ramp Management Runway Inspection / Maintenance Taxiway Inspection / Maintenance / FOD Airfield Lighting Public Works / Utilities Protocol (Including linguistics) Public Affairs General Purpose Transportation General Purpose Vehicle Maintenance / Fuels Aircraft Fuels / Refuelling for Russian aircraft

2. The Representative of NATO will be responsible for Approach Control Tower Services (includes Ground Control) Flight Planning / NOTAMs TERPs (if / as required) Weather NAVAIDs Approach Lighting Aerial Port Operations (Cargo and Passenger) Aircraft Fuels /Refuelling for non-Russian aircraft Crash / Fire Protection

In each of the created functions assigned to NATO, a group of Russian representatives will be created. Detailed development of plans for these representatives will be accomplished after the Russian aviation group arrives at Pristina Airfield.

The number of Russian Federation Armed Forces for performing their assigned tasks shall be determined on the basis of NATO-accepted standards.

Attachment 5
TIME TABLE FOR THE PREPARATION FOR FUNCTIONS AND INITIATION OF OPERATIONS OF THE PRISTINA (SLATINA AIRFIELD)

[A graphic of tentative time line for bringing Slatina Airfield into operation has been omitted.]

Events:

- Obtain Hungary's clearance for overflight of its territory for initial flights; remove all obstacles at the airfield; give UK access to all parts of airfield.

Implementation of the Principles for a Political Solution of the Conflict

- Arrival, in no more than six IL76 aircraft, of Russian administrative team and essential airfield equipment. Arrival, in no more than six IL76 equivalent aircraft, of NATO air movement personnel and equipment. No further flights into the airfield until general opening.

- Work in preparation for the start of the operation of the airbase.

- Upon certification of the airfield for operation, begin routine air operations and provide access for all KFOR forces to the airfield with consent of COMKFOR. US/NATO will assist in obtaining clearances for further Russian overflight of foreign airspace with respect to deployment to Kosovo and back consistent with the Cohen / Sergeyev Agreed points on Russian Participation in KFOR.

- Delivery of necessary equipment and Russian airfield teams (detachments).

- Deployment of airfield equipment to support full scale functioning.

Attachment 6
LIAISON ARRANGEMENTS FOR PARTICIPATION OF RUSSIAN FORCES IN KFOR

The following detail the agreed liaison arrangements for Russian Forces in KFOR:

a. Russia will return the Russian Military Representative to SHAPE, augment his staff and expand their responsibilities to include Russian participation in KFOR. The Russian representation will consist of up to 10 officers.

b. Russia will establish a liaison group with HQ AFSOUTH. The Russian liaison group will consist of three officers.

c. Russia will temporarily establish a liaison group with CAOC to co-ordinate the initial strategic deployment of Russia's peacekeeping contingent.

d. Russia will establish a military representative at KFOR HQs for matters pertaining to the planning and employment of Russian peacekeeping contingent in KFOR:

1. for planning (3-4 officers) 2. for support (3-4 officers) 3. for co-ordination of Russian activities in KFOR brigade zones (2-3) officers per zone where Russian Peacekeeping contingent are located)

327. NATO - KLA, Undertaking of Demilitarisation and Transformation by the KLA, 20 June 1999

1. This Undertaking provides for a ceasefire by the UCK, their disengagement from the zones of conflict, subsequent demilitarisation and reintegration into civil society. In accordance with the terms of UNSCR 1244 and taking account of the obligations agreed to at Rambouillet and the public commitments mady by the Kosovar Albanian Rambouillet delegation.

2. The UCK undertake to renounce the use of force to comply with the directions of the Commander of the international security force in Kosovo (COMKFOR), and where applicable the bead of the interim civil administration for Kosovo, and to resolve peacefully any questions relating to the implementation of this undertaking.

3. The UCK agree that the International Security Presence (KFOR) and the international civil presence will continue to deploy and operate without hindrance within Kosovo and that KFOR has the authority to take all necessary action to establish and maintain a secure environment for all citizens of Kosovo and otherwise carry out its mission.

4. The UCK agrees to comply with all of the obligations of this Undertaking and to ensure that with immediate effect all UCK forces in Kosovo and in neighbouring countries will observe the provisions of this Undertaking, will refrain from all hostile or provocative acts, hostile intent and freeze military movement in either direction across International borders or the boundary between Kosovo and other parts of the FRY, or any other actions inconsistent with the spirit of UNSCR 1244. The UCK in Kosovo agree to commit themselves publicly to demilitarise in accordance with paragraphs 22 and 23, refrain from activities which jeopardise the safety of international governmental and non-governmental personnel including KFOR, and to facilitate the deployment and operation of KFOR.

5. For purposes of this Undertaking, the following expressions shall have the meanings as described below :

a. The UCK includes all personnel and organisations within Kosovo, currently under UCK control, with a military or paramilitary capability and any other groups or individuals so designated by Commander KFOR (COMKFOR)

b. " FRY Forces " includes all of the FRY and Republic of Serbia personnel and organisations with a military capability. This includes regular army and naval forces, armed civilian groups, associated paramilitary groups, air forces, national guards, border police, army reserves, military police, intelligence services, Ministry of Internal Affairs, local, special, riot and anti-terrorist police, and any other groups or individuals so designated by Commander KFOR (COMKFOR).

c. The Ground Safety Zone (GSZ) is defined as a 5-kilometre zone that extends beyond the Kosovo province border into the rest of FRY territory. It includes the terrain within that 5-kilometre zone.

d. Prohibited weapons are any weapon 12.7mm or larger, any anti-tank or anti-aircraft weapons, grenades, mines or explosives, automatic and long barrelled weapons.

6. The purpose of this Undertaking are as follows :

a. To establish a durable cessation of hostilities.

b. To provide for the support and authorisation of the KFOR and in particular to authorise the KFOR to take such actions as are required, including the use of necessary force in accordance with KFOR's rules of engagement, to ensure compliance with this Undertaking and protection of the KFOR, and to contribute to a secure environment for the international civil implementation presence, and other international organisations, agencies, and non-governmental organisations and the civil populace.

7. The actions of the UCK shall be in accordance with this Undertaking. " The KFOR " commander in consultation, where appropriate, with the interim civil administrator will be the final authority regarding the interpretation of this Undertaking and the security aspects of the peace settlement it supports. His determinations will be binding on all parties and persons.

Cessation of Hostilities

8. With immediate effect on signature the UCK agrees to comply with this Undertaking and with the directions of COMKFOR. Any forces which fall to comply with this Undertaking or with the directions of COMKFOR will be liable to military action as deemed appropriate by COMKFOR.

9. With immediate effect on signature of this Undertaking all hostile acts by the UCK will cease. The UCK Chief of General Staff undertakes to issue clear and precise instructions to all units and personnel under his command, to ensure contact with the FRY force is avoided and to comply fully with the arrangements for bringing this Undertaking into effect. He will make announcements immediately following final signature of this Undertaking, which will be broadcast regularly through all appropriate channels to assist in ensuring that instructions to maintain this Undertaking reach all the forces under his command and are understood by the public in general.

10. The UCK undertakes and agrees in particular :

a. To cease the firing of all weapons and use of explosive devices.

b. Not to place any mines, barriers or checkpoints, nor maintain any observation posts or protective obstacles.

c. The destruction of buildings, facilities or structures is not permitted. It shall not engage in any military, security, or training related activities, including ground or air defence operations, in or over Kosovo or GSZ, without the prior express approval of COMKFOR.

d. Not to attack, detain or intimidate any civilians in Kosovo, nor shall they attack, confiscate or violate the property of civilians in Kosovo.

11. The UCK agrees not to conduct any reprisals, counter-attacks, or any unilateral actions in response to violations of the UNSCR 1244 and other extant agreements relating to Kosovo. This in no way denies the right of self-defence.

12. The UCK agrees not to interfere with those FRY personnel that return to Kosovo to conduct specific tasks as authorised and directed by COMKFOR.

13. Except as approved by COMKFOR, the UCK agrees that its personel in Kosovo will not carry weapons of any type :

a. Within 2 kilometres of VJ and MUP assembly areas ;

b. Within 2 kilometres of the main roads and the towns upon them listed at Appendix A ;

c. Within 2 kilometres of external borders of Kosovo ;

d. In any other areas designated by COMKFOR

14. Within 4 days of signature of this Undertaking :

a. The UCK will close all fighting positions, entrenchments, and checkpoints on roads, and mark their minefields and booby traps.

b. The UCK Chief of General Staff shall report in writing completion of the above requirement to COMKFOR and continue to provide weekly detailed written status reports until demilitarisation, as detailed in the following paragraphs, is complete.

Cross-Border Activity

15. With immediate effect the UCK will cease the movement of armed bodies into neighbouring countries. All movement of armed bodies into Kosovo will be subject to the prior approval of COMKFOR.

Monitoring the Cessation of Hostilities

16. The authority for dealing with breaches of this Undertaking rests with COMKFOR. He will monitor and maintain and if necessary enforce the cessation of hostilities.

17. The UCK agrees to co-operate fully with KFOR and the interim civil administration for Kosovo. The chief of the General Staff of the UCK will ensure that prompt and appropriate action is taken to deal with any breaches of this Undertaking by his forces as directed by COMKFOR.

18. Elements of KFOR will be assigned to maintain contact with the UCK and will be deployed to its command structure and bases.

19. KFOR will establish appropriate control at designated crossing points into Albania and the FYROM.

Joint Implementation Commission (JIC)

20. A JIC will be established in Pristina within 4 days of the signature of this Undertaking. The JIC will be chaired by COMKFOR and will comprise the senior commanders of KFOR and the UCK, and a representative from the interim civil administration for Kosovo.

21. The JIC will meet as often as required by COMKFOR throughout the implementation of this Undertaking. It may be called without prior notice and representation by the UCK is expected at a level appropriate with the rank of the KFOR chairman. Its functions will include :

a. Ensuring compliance with agreed arrangements for the security and activities of all forces ;

b. The investigation of actual or threatened breaches of his Undertaking ;

c. Such other tasks as may be assigned to it by COMKFOR in the interests of maintaining the cessation of hostilities.

Demilitarisation and transformation

22. The UCK will follow the procedures established by COMKFOR for the phased demilitarisation, transformation and monitoring of UCK forces in Kosovo and for further regulation of their activities. They will not train or organise parades without the authorithy of COMKFOR.

23. The UCK agrees to the following timetable which will commence from the signature of this Undertaking:

a. Within 7 days, the UCK shall establish secure weapons storage sites, which shall be registered with and verified by the KFOR;

b. Within 7 days the UCK will clear their minefields and booby traps, vacate their fighting positions and transfer to assembly areas as agreed with COMKFOR at the JIC. Thereafter only personnel authorised by COMKFOR and senior Officers of the UCK with their close protection personnel not exceeding 3, carrying side arms only, will be allowed outside the assembly areas.

c. After 7 days automatic small arms weapons not stored in the registered weapons storage sites can only be held inside the authorised assembly areas.

d. After 29 days, the retention of any non automatic long barrelled weapons shall be subject to authorisation by COMKFOR.

e. Within 30 days, subject to arrangements by COMKFOR, if necessary, all UCK personnel, who are not of local origin, whether or not they are legally within Kosovo, including individual advisors, freedom fighters, trainers, volunteers, and personnel from neighbouring and other States, shall be withdrawn from Kosovo.

f. Arrangements for control of weapons are as follows :

i. Within 30 days the UCK shall store in the registered weapons storage sites all prohibited weapons with the exception of automatic small arms. 30 per cent of their total holdings of automatic small arms weapons will also be stored in these sites at this stage. Ammunition for the remaining weapons should be withdrawn and stored at an approved site authorised by COMKFOR separate from the assembly areas at the same time.

ii. At 30 days it shall be illegal for UCK personnel to possess prohibited weapons, with the exception of automatic small arms within assembly areas, and unauthorised long barrelled weapons. Such weapons shall be subject to confiscation by the KFOR.

iii. Within 60 days a further 30 per cent of automatic small arms, giving a total of 60 per cent of the UCK holdings, will be stored in the registered weapons storage sites.

iv. Within 90 days all automatic small arms weapons will be stored in the registered weapons storage sites. Thereafter their possession by UCK personnel will be prohibited and such weapons will be subject to confiscation by KFOR.

g. From 30 days until 90 days the weapons storage sites will be under joint control of the UCK and KFOR under procedures approved by COMKFOR at the JIC. After 90 days KFOR will assume full control of these sites.

h. Within 90 days all UCK forces will have completed the processes for their demilitarisation and are to cease wearing either military uniforms or insignia of the UCK.

i. Within 90 days the Chief of General Staff UCK shall confirm compliance with the above restrictions in writing to COMKFOR.

24. The provisions of this Undertaking enter into force with immediate effect of its signature by the Kosovar Albanian representative(s).

25. The UCK intends to comply with the terms of the United Nations Security Council Resolution 1244, and in this context that the international community should take due and full account of the contribution of the UCK during the Kosovo crisis and accordingly give due consideration to :

a. Recognition that, while the UCK and its structures are in the process of transformation, it is committed to propose individual current members to participate in the administration and police forces of Kosovo, enjoying special consideration in view of the expertise they have developed.

b. The formation of an Army in Kosovo on the lines of the US National Guard in due course as part of a political process designed to determine Kosovo's future status, taking into account the Rambouillet Accord.

26. This Undertaking is provided in English and Albanian and if there is any doubt as to the meaning of the text the English version has precedence.

[Appendix A has been omitted.]

328. NATO, Letter from the Secretary General Addressed to the UN Secretary-General, 20 June 1999[1]

I am writing to follow up on my letter of 10 June 1999 (S/1999/663), in which I informed you of the suspension of NATO's air campaign subsequent to the successful conclusion of a military technical agreement between NATO military authorities and the Federal Republic of Yugoslavia (Serbia and Montenegro). I have received confirmation from the Supreme Allied Commander Europe, General Clark, that all uniformed Federal Republic of Yugoslavia and Serbian Security Forces have withdrawn from Kosovo as of today in conformity with the military technical agreement. The Alliance's limited air response and phased air campaign has therefore been terminated.

I will keep you informed of further significant developments.

(Signed) Javier Solana

329. Council of Europe, Parliamentary Assembly, Recommendation 1414 (1999), Crisis in Kosovo and Situation in the FRY, 23 June 1999

[Extract from the Official Gazette of the Council of Europe - June 1999. Text adopted by the Assembly on 23 June 1999 (21st Sitting).]

1. The Assembly welcomes the agreement on a political solution to the Kosovo crisis based on the principles proposed by the G8, and the resulting withdrawal of Yugoslav military, police and paramilitary forces from Kosovo. It further welcomes the adoption of United Nations Security Council (UNSC) Resolution 1244 (1999), deciding the deployment in Kosovo of an international civil and security presence.

2. The Assembly pays tribute to the diplomatic efforts undertaken by the President of Finland, Mr Ahtisaari, as special representative of the European Union, Mr Chernomyrdin, special envoy of Russia's President Yeltsin, and Mr Talbott, US Deputy Secretary of State. It deeply regrets, however, that the Yugoslav authorities only accepted a political solution following the intensive use of military force by Nato.

3. The Assembly notes that, under UNSC Resolution 1244, the Kosovo Military Implementation Force (KFOR) is ensuring a security presence and that the United Nations Secretary General is setting up, on an interim basis, a civil presence, the UN Interim Administration Mission in Kosovo (UNMIK), led by Mr Sergio Vieira de Mello as the United Nations Secretary General's Special Representative.

4. The Assembly considers that the reconstruction of Kosovo and the establishment of democratic self-governing institutions will be an immense and difficult task, which will require an enormous and concerted effort by all states and international organisations involved. The Council of Europe has an important contribution to make together with other organisations such as the UNHCR, the UNIFEM, the OSCE and the European Union, and should therefore be properly represented in the UNMIK.

5. The Assembly considers that the voluntary, orderly return and reintegration of refugees and internally displaced persons in safety and security constitute an essential element of the reconstruction of Kosovo. The efforts undertaken by UNHCR and other intergovernmental and non-governmental organisations should be widely supported and generously financed by Council of Europe member states.

6. The Assembly expresses its horror at the mounting evidence of mass executions and other atrocities such as the systematic violation of women's dignity, carried out by Yugoslav forces in Kosovo. It strongly supports the efforts of the International Criminal Tribunal for the Former Yugoslavia to collect evidence and bring those responsible to justice.

7. The Assembly is deeply concerned about the mass urgent departure of the Kosovo Serbian population. These people should be guaranteed adequate protection.

8. The Assembly considers that there can be no stability in the region before genuine democratic reforms take place in the Federal Republic of Yugoslavia. However, this will not be possible as long as Mr Milosevic and other indicted war criminals remain in power. The Assembly therefore calls on the people of the Federal Republic of Yugoslavia openly to support such reforms. Besides providing humanitarian assistance, the international community should also support democratic forces and the free media.

9. The Assembly, in this context, welcomes and supports the courageous position taken by the Government of Montenegro during the conflict. As its policy is to be a catalyst for change within the whole Federal Republic of Yugoslavia, the Government of Montenegro should be able to count on the full support, and material assistance, of the international community.

10. The Assembly is highly appreciative of the political contribution from Albania and "the former Yugoslav Republic of Macedonia", neighbours of the Federal Republic of Yugoslavia, to safeguarding peace and stability in the region. These countries have dealt with the heavy burden of the crisis with exemplary calmness and generosity. The Assembly suggests that co-operation with Albania and "the former Yugoslav Republic of Macedonia" and the aid to be channelled to them under the Stability Pact for South-Eastern Europe be priority issues.

11. The Assembly welcomes the adoption, at the initiative of the European Union, of the Stability Pact for South-Eastern Europe, in Cologne on 10 June 1999, with the Council of Europe as a full participant. The Organisation, including the Parliamentary Assembly, should now play a major role in its implementation, notably as regards democratisation and human rights.

12. The Assembly notes with satisfaction the adoption by the Committee of Ministers of a stability programme for south-eastern Europe, which contains both urgent action to assist returning refugees and displaced persons, and other civilian victims of the Kosovo conflict in the region, as well as longer term measures for the establishment of democratic institutions.

13. The Assembly considers that the Congress of Local and Regional Authorities has an important role to play in the establishment of local self-government in Kosovo, and welcomes the proposals made by the Congress in this respect.

14. The Assembly urges the Kosovo Liberation Army (KLA) to implement fully the agreement with KFOR signed on 21 June 1999 requiring the KLA to disarm within ninety days. The Assembly condemns all attacks against the Serb civilian population as well as the threats made against the Russian component of the security presence. The KLA should refrain from acts of vengeance and work together with all political forces of the Kosovo Albanian population in the establishment of democratic institutions. Representatives of the Serbian population of Kosovo should be enabled and encouraged to participate fully in this process.

15. The Assembly calls on the International Criminal Tribunal for the Former Yugoslavia to investigate the crimes allegedly committed by members of the KLA and to act accordingly.

16. Therefore, the Assembly:

A. Resolves to organise a conference on the Parliamentary contribution to the implementation of the Stability Pact, to be held in the region in the coming months.

B. Recommends that the Committee of Ministers :

i. concerning the implementation of the UNSC Resolution 1244, ensure:

a. the proper representation of the Council of Europe in UNMIK at the level of Deputy Special Representative and an active role in the fields concerning human rights, and in particular children's rights, local self-government, legal affairs, democratisation, rehabilitation of women victims of rape, civil affairs, and, in particular, culture and education, human resources and governance;

b. a leading role for the Council of Europe as regards:

---

[1] UN Doc. S/1999/702, Annex, 21 June 1999.

- the monitoring of the human rights situation;
- the establishment of the Office of Ombudsman;
- the development of political parties;
- the training of judges;
- the reform of curricula and the educational system;

ii. consider the opening of a Council of Europe office in Belgrade as soon as possible, with the task of contributing to the achievement of Council of Europe standards in the Federal Republic of Yugoslavia;

iii. adapt its own stability programme to the new situation in Kosovo, to include the opening of a Council of Europe Office in Pristina;

iv. ensure a major contribution by the Council of Europe in the implementation of the Stability Pact, notably as regards Working Tables I (Democratisation and Human Rights) and III (Security Issues).

330. OSCE, Permanent Council, Decision No. 305, PC. DEC/305, 1 July 1999

The Permanent Council,

Referring to United Nations Security Council Resolution 1244 of 10 June 1999 and to the report by the Secretary-General of the United Nations of 12 June 1999 (S/1999/672),

Determined that the OSCE will contribute to the implementation of UNSC Resolution 1244, in particular the relevant parts of operative paragraph 11 of this resolution,

Decides that:

- The transitional OSCE Task Force for Kosovo, established by the Permanent Council on 8 June (PC.DEC/296) will cease to exist from 1 July 1999;
- The OSCE Mission in Kosovo is established from the same date.

The OSCE Mission in Kosovo will constitute a distinct component within the overall framework of the United Nations Interim Administration Mission in Kosovo (UNMIK).

The OSCE Mission in Kosovo will, within this overall framework, take the lead role in matters relating to institution- and democracy-building and human rights. It will co-operate closely with other relevant organizations - intergovernmental and, as appropriate, non-governmental - in the planning and implementation of its tasks.

The OSCE Mission in Kosovo will concentrate its work in the following interrelated areas:

1. Human resources capacity-building, including the training of a new Kosovo police service within a Kosovo Police School which it will establish and operate, the training of judicial personnel and the training of civil administrators at various levels, in co-operation, inter alia, with the Council of Europe;

2. Democratization and governance, including the development of a civil society, non-governmental organizations, political parties and local media;

3. Organization and supervision of elections;

4. Monitoring, protection and promotion of human rights, including, inter alia, the establishment of an Ombudsman institution, in co-operation, inter alia, with the UNHCHR;

5. Such tasks which may be requested by the Secretary-General of the United Nations or his Special Representative, which are consistent with the UNSC Resolution 1244 and approved by the Permanent Council.

The OSCE Mission in Kosovo will in its work be guided by the importance of bringing about mutual respect and reconciliation among all ethnic groups in Kosovo and of establishing a viable multi-ethnic society where the rights of each citizen are fully and equally respected.

The OSCE Mission in Kosovo will be established for an initial period until 10 June 2000, with the possibility of prolongations as decided by the Permanent Council.

The Head of the OSCE Mission in Kosovo will be appointed by the Chairman-in-Office and will report to the Chairman-in-Office and to the Permanent Council in accordance with established OSCE rules and procedures. The Head of Mission will assist the Special Representative of the Secretary-General of the United Nations in his tasks.

The Permanent Council requests the Secretary General urgently to present a budget proposal for the OSCE Mission in Kosovo.

Pending a decision on the budget for the OSCE Mission in Kosovo, the Permanent Council tasks the Secretary General to take all measures necessary for the closure of the OSCE Task Force, and authorizes him to transfer resources previously allocated to the OSCE Task Force to the OSCE Mission in Kosovo and:

(a) To incur obligations to the extent required for the fulfilment of the tasks of the OSCE Mission, but not exceeding the residual portion of the spending authority previously granted, following the implementation of all necessary measures to close the OSCE Task Force;

(b) To continue making use of the existing Post Table authorized by Permanent Council Decisions Nos. 266 and 282;

(c) To make use of the physical assets previously acquired for the use of the OSCE Task Force.

237th Plenary Meeting, PC Journal No. 237, Agenda item 2

331. OSCE, Permanent Council, Decision No. 306, PC. DEC/306, 1 July 1999

The Permanent Council,

Welcoming the adoption by the Cologne Ministerial Conference on 10 June 1999 of the Stability Pact for South Eastern Europe, launched at the initiative of the European Union, as well as the European Union's leading role in co-operation with other participating and facilitating States, international organizations and institutions,

Sharing the principles, norms and objectives on which the Stability Pact is established,

Reaffirming that the OSCE has a key role to play in fostering stab*ility and security across the OSCE area,*

Determined to make a significant contribution to the efforts undertaken through the Stability Pact,

Decides:

- To place the Stability Pact for South Eastern Europe under the auspices of the OSCE and to work for compliance with the provisions of the Stability Pact by the participating States, in accordance with its procedures and established principles;

- To make use of OSCE institutions and instruments and their expertise to contribute to the proceedings of the South Eastern Europe Regional Table and of the Working Tables;

- To work closely with the EU, the Council of Europe, the UN, NATO, the OECD, the WEU, the IFIs, the regional initiatives as well as the countries of South Eastern Europe to achieve the objectives set out in the Stability Pact.

The OSCE stands ready to host meetings of the Working Tables of the Stability Pact at the venue of its Permanent Council. The Special Coordinator of the Stability Pact will provide periodic progress reports to the OSCE according to its procedures, on behalf of the South Eastern Europe Regional Table.

The Permanent Council requests the Chairman-in-Office:

- To ensure the appropriate follow-up by the OSCE of its decision to place the Stability Pact under its auspices;

- To promote further the development of the regional dimension of the OSCE's efforts in South Eastern Europe, including through the use of the mechanisms of the Stability Pact;

- To report regularly to the Permanent Council on the OSCE's work within the framework of the Stability Pact as well as on progress made concerning the development of the regional dimension of the OSCE's own efforts in the region.

237th Plenary Meeting PC Journal No. 237, Agenda item 3

332. UN, Report of the Secretary-General on the United Nations Interim Administration Mission in Kosovo, UN Doc. S/1999/779, 12 July 1999

I. Introduction

1. The Security Council, by its resolution 1244 (1999) of 10 June 1999, authorized the Secretary-General, with the assistance of the relevant international organizations, to establish an international civil presence in Kosovo, Federal Republic of Yugoslavia, in order to provide an interim administration in Kosovo under which the people of Kosovo can enjoy substantial autonomy. In my report to the Security Council of 12 June 1999 (S/1999/672), I presented a preliminary concept for the United Nations Interim Administration Mission in Kosovo (UNMIK). The current report is issued pursuant to paragraph 20 of resolution 1244 (1999), in which the Council requested me to report to it on the implementation of the resolution. The report contains a comprehensive framework of the United Nations-led international civil operation in Kosovo, and is based on the assessment conducted by the advance team of UNMIK.

2. In order to provide an initial overview of the scope of the challenge, the report first gives a brief description of the current security, political and humanitarian situation, as well as of the state of the administrative and public services infrastructure and the economy. Second, it gives a comprehensive account of the steps undertaken by the UNMIK advance team, which had to assess, plan and act at the same time. Third, it outlines in greater detail the authority and competencies of UNMIK as provided for in Security Council resolution 1244 (1999). Fourth, it sets out the structure of the Mission and the relationship between UNMIK and the international organizations which will be taking a lead role in its four components, namely the United Nations, the European Union (EU), and the Organization for Security and Co-operation in Europe (OSCE). Fifth, the complex range of activities is described which will be carried out by each component. Finally, a preliminary plan is provided of the phases of implementation of the mandated task and objectives.

3. On 2 July 1999, I appointed Bernard Kouchner as my Special Representative. I also appointed Jock Covey as Principal Deputy Special Representative, Dominique Vian as Deputy Special Representative for interim civil administration, Dennis McNamara as Deputy Special Representative for humanitarian affairs, Daan Everts as Deputy Special Representative for institution-building, and Joly Dixon as Deputy Special Representative for reconstruction.

II. Situation on the Ground

A. SECURITY AND POLITICAL SITUATION

4. Following the deployment in Kosovo on 12 June 1999 of the international security presence known as KFOR, the Yugoslav army and the Serbian security forces began their withdrawal from the province in accordance with the schedule established by the military-technical agreement between the Federal Republic of Yugoslavia (Serbia and Montenegro) and the North Atlantic Treaty Organization (NATO) military authorities (see S/1999/682, annex). This withdrawal was completed by 20 June 1999. On 21 June 1999, the Kosovo Liberation Army (KLA) signed an undertaking on demilitarization, received by KFOR, which established the modalities and the schedule for the demilitarization of the KLA.

5. The general situation in Kosovo has been tense but is stabilizing. The KLA has rapidly moved back into all parts of Kosovo, in particular the south-west, and a large number of Kosovo Serbs have left their homes for Serbia. While the first wave of Kosovo Serb departures was prompted by security concerns rather than by actual threats, a second wave of departures resulted from an increasing number of incidents committed by Kosovo Albanians against Kosovo Serbs. In particular, high profile killings and abductions, as well as looting, arsons and forced expropriation of apartments, have prompted departures. This process has now slowed down, but such cities as Prizren and Pec are practically deserted by Kosovo Serbs, and the towns of Mitrovica and Orahovac are divided along ethnic lines.

6. The security problem in Kosovo is largely a result of the absence of law and order institutions and agencies. Many crimes and injustices cannot be properly pursued. Criminal gangs competing for control of scarce resources are already exploiting this void. While KFOR is currently responsible for maintaining both public safety and civil law and order, its ability to do so is limited due to the fact that it is still in the process of building up its forces. The absence of a legitimate police force, both international and local, is deeply felt, and therefore will have to be addressed as a matter of priority.

7. There are, nevertheless, signs that the situation could be improved with a view to creating an environment to facilitate the return of all Kosovo civilians to their homes. The most important confidence-building mechanism in the medium term will be the involvement, on a consultative basis, of political leaders of all communities in the decision-making processes of UNMIK.

B. HUMANITARIAN SITUATION

8. The humanitarian consequences of the conflict on the people of Kosovo have been profound. Out of a population estimated in 1998 to number 1.7 million, almost half (800,000) have sought refuge in neighbouring Albania, the former Yugoslav Republic of Macedonia and Montenegro during the past year. While estimates vary, up to 500,000 persons may have been internally displaced. Many internally displaced persons (IDPs) are in worse health than the refugees, having spent weeks in hiding without food or shelter. Many refugees and IDPs bear the scars of psychological trauma as well as physical abuse.

9. As of 8 July 1999, more than 650,000 refugees had returned to Kosovo through a combination of spontaneous and Office of the United Nations High Commissioner for Refugees (UNHCR)-assisted movement. This leaves an estimated 150,000 persons in neighbouring regions and countries, 90,000 evacuees in third countries and an unknown number of asylum-seekers. Those who have not returned home will continue to require a high level of assistance in their country of asylum and upon eventual return. Within Kosovo, a still unknown number of individuals remain outside their homes. The past weeks have also witnessed an exodus of members of minority groups, primarily Serbs, into Montenegro and Serbia, where according to the Yugoslav Red Cross, approximately 58,000 displaced persons have registered for assistance.

10. Despite the hardship endured over the last three months, the health and nutritional status of both the remaining and returning population, with some limited exceptions, has not deteriorated significantly. However, the pace and scope of rehabilitation efforts in the shelter, water and sanitation sectors will have a direct impact on the population's health status as winter approaches. Widespread damage to community-level facilities of the former parallel system does raise concern about access to basic services in the near term.

C. STATE OF PUBLIC SERVICES AND ADMINISTRATION

11. The level of damage suffered during the recent conflict varies markedly across the province. Much of northern Kosovo remains virtually untouched by the hostilities, while such towns as Pec, Djakovica and Mitrovica sustained massive damage. Surveys to determine the state of public administration structures and the provision of utilities have been undertaken by UNMIK, with the assistance of a United Nations disaster assessment and coordination team and teams from the Council of Europe.

12. Neither of Kosovo's two power generation stations are currently functioning, leaving the province dependent on links with Serbia, Montenegro and the former Yugoslav Republic of Macedonia for its electrical energy. The supply of coal from the open cast mine is blocked by the breakdown of local distribution networks. Water distribution problems have plagued Pristina. The principal problems impeding water distribution in Pristina are the lack of maintenance, the failure to pay salaries and the inadequate supply of electricity to pumping stations.

13. The public service structures of Kosovo are largely inoperative due to a combination of neglect, war damage and the departure of

trained staff. The municipalities are functioning inadequately or not at all. While water and electricity are usually available, the telephone lines are down, schools are not open and there is practically no public transport service. According to an assessment by the Council of Europe, the judiciary is not functioning since many of its previous Kosovo Serb staff have recently departed, and Kosovo Albanian or other personnel either have not yet returned to Kosovo or have not yet been identified.

14. The payment of public service salaries needs to be urgently addressed since government funding for municipalities has not been provided since March 1999. As an interim measure, salaries for electrical workers will be paid by UNMIK for the next three months from funds donated by the United Kingdom and United States Governments. Additional funds, however, are urgently required to address arrears and recurrent costs in other sectors until UNMIK is able to raise income through local taxation and excise duties.

15. With no refuse disposal since March 1999 and with widespread pollution of wells and other water sources, there is a significant risk to public health throughout Kosovo. The initial assessment of health services indicates that material damage to these facilities is less serious than expected, though their status varies by municipality. Most hospitals are functioning, but patient care has been compromised by serious political disputes about the future management structure and the reintegration of Kosovo Albanian staff. The Kosovo Serbs, who have had a disproportionately important role in managing public services, are now frequently excluded or intimidated into leaving Kosovo, creating a skills gap. This major problem of reintegrating technical staff from both communities is common in most sectors.

D. ECONOMIC SITUATION

16. The immediate economic outlook for Kosovo is precarious. Well into summer, much of Kosovo's rich agricultural land lies fallow, a grave situation for a territory that relies heavily on agriculture for its livelihood. The industrial and manufacturing sector has been severely debilitated by a long-standing lack of capital investment, and by damage caused by the conflict and in some cases by the departure of Kosovo Serb managers and staff. While an encouraging revival of commercial activity is evident, significant economic activity will continue to be hampered by the existing system of discriminatory property rights, lack of commercial or industrial finance, currency instability and other impediments. Payments systems and the financial services sector are largely non-functional. At present, much of Kosovo's current economic activity is confined to trading of scarce goods and services at inflated prices.

III. Activities of the Advance Team

17. The Special Representative ad interim, Sergio Vieira de Mello, arrived at Pristina on 13 June 1999, one day after the initial deployment of KFOR. The bulk of the UNMIK advance team was deployed in Kosovo within subsequent days. Upon deployment, UNMIK established close working relations with KFOR and various international organizations on the ground, including the International Criminal Tribunal for the former Yugoslavia (ICTY), the International Committee of the Red Cross (ICRC) and non-governmental organizations. UNMIK has also maintained regular contacts with local representatives of the Federal Republic of Yugoslavia in Pristina. In order to enhance an early international police presence, unarmed civilian police officers were redeployed from the United Nations Mission in Bosnia and Herzegovina. On 3 July 1999, the first international police were deployed in a liaison capacity to five locations in Kosovo.

18. On 20 June 1999, the Special Representative a.i. issued a statement in which he indicated that in accordance with Security Council resolution 1244 (1999), he would perform the executive functions of government during the transitional period until new legitimate authorities were established. To avert a violent takeover of public institutions, he has emphasized that there cannot be any changes in authority in such institutions without UNMIK's expressed approval. He further indicated his intention to appoint international administrators at the regional and municipal levels, and has taken the initial steps to re-establish a multi-ethnic and democratic judicial system in Kosovo. As an emergency measure, he has issued three decrees, one establishing a Joint Advisory Council for judicial appointments, a second appointing its members, and a third appointing four prosecutors, two investigating judges and a three-judge panel approved by the Judicial Panel. Additional candidates are currently being reviewed for appointment in the coming week.

19. In his regular contacts with federal representatives, as well as local political leaders, the Special Representative has urged them to demonstrate restraint and tolerance. At the functional level, UNMIK has established joint civilian commissions (JCCs) to facilitate the process of a mediated and controlled transition to integrated public institutions and to address such contentious issues as administration and staffing of various public facilities. This initiative was welcomed. JCCs have been established in the areas of health, universities, education and culture, municipalities and governance, post and telecommunications, and power. Representatives of Kosovo Albanian and Kosovo Serb communities participate in the councils chaired by UNMIK regional administrators. However, a continuing departure of Serb professionals and managers due to intimidation and a lack of confidence could undermine the work of the Commissions.

20. At the political level, consultations are continuing for the formation of the Kosovo Transitional Council, which will provide a mechanism for enhancing cooperation between UNMIK and the people of Kosovo, restore confidence between the communities and identify candidates for interim administration structures at all levels. This broadly representative body, which will be composed of representatives of all main ethnic and political groups in Kosovo, is intended to ensure participation of the people of Kosovo in the decisions and actions of UNMIK. It will be chaired by the Special Representative, and will provide him with advice, be a sounding board for proposed decisions and help to elicit support for those decisions among all major political groups. In addition to facilitating the work of UNMIK, the Kosovo Transitional Council will promote democratization and institution-building.

21. UNMIK immediately took steps to communicate with the people of Kosovo and the international community via all available media. Daily broadcasts were inaugurated on a private radio station, reaching a significant portion of the territory. While no newspapers are currently being published in Kosovo, direct contact has been established with the few publications in circulation in the territory. UNMIK has consistently provided information to the international press corps in Kosovo, which serves both Kosovo and international audiences. The lack of functioning media in the territory is, however, a major obstacle to UNMIK's work.

22. With the assistance of KFOR, UNMIK has prevented some unauthorized takeovers of media facilities. UNMIK also instituted procedures governing the start-up of new radio broadcasting operations, pending the establishment of a regulatory framework under the civil administration.

23. Initial civil affairs operations began at Pristina on 14 June, at Prizren on 16 June, at Pec on 4 July and at Mitrovica and Gnjiliane on 5 July 1999. Regional administrators have now been deployed in all five regions, and links have been established with local leaders to ensure continuation of basic services and the reduction of tension.

24. UNMIK and KFOR have established close working relationships and have put in place a comprehensive structure of coordination mechanisms, including daily meetings of the Special Representative and the KFOR Commander. UNMIK liaises closely with KFOR to assist the latter in implementing its responsibility for ensuring public safety in Kosovo. This includes responding both to ordinary crimes and to politically motivated incidents, such as attempts by certain Kosovo Albanian groups to take over local government offices, hospitals and media facilities.

25. UNMIK has deployed military liaison officers to the headquarters of KFOR and to the five KFOR multinational brigades. KFOR

representatives take part, as necessary, in the work of UNMIK, while UNMIK, in turn, participates in KFOR's Joint Implementation Commission (JIC), which liaises with the Federal Republic of Yugoslavia's armed forces and the KLA. As UNMIK continues its deployment, these initial coordination mechanisms will expand, particularly at the regional and municipal levels.

26. In close cooperation with KFOR, UNMIK has undertaken various confidence-building measures aimed at restraining Kosovo Albanians and reassuring Kosovo Serbs. On 2 July 1999, in response to harassment and attacks against minority groups, the Special Representative brought together Kosovo Serb and Kosovo Albanian leaders to agree on concrete measures to enhance security. This was the first time such a meeting had occurred. The two sides issued a joint statement on security calling, inter alia, for the creation of a joint crisis task force involving Kosovo Albanians, Kosovo Serbs, UNMIK and KFOR. The joint statement on security was immediately broadcast over Radio Pristina and video coverage of the event was widely broadcast.

27. Following reports of the deliberate destruction of documentation, UNMIK, with the assistance of KFOR, has taken measures to secure official records stored in administrative buildings.

28. UNMIK has closely cooperated with ICTY and provided support for its activities. ICTY is engaged in the collection of evidence, including the processing of crime scene sites throughout Kosovo, to support existing and new indictments. New sites are being discovered almost daily and are being secured by KFOR until they can be documented. By 1 July 1999, over 150 crime scene sites had been reported by KFOR.

29. Supported by the United Nations Mine Action Service and the United Nations Office for Project Services (UNOPS), UNMIK's mine action team has begun setting up the mine action programme for Kosovo, the first step of which is the establishment of the United Nations Mine Action Coordination Centre (UNMACC). This Centre is being mobilized and is already coordinating emergency mine action activities in Kosovo with its various partners, including United Nations agencies, in particular the United Nations Children's Fund (UNICEF), KFOR, NGOs, commercial companies and international organizations, in order to ensure that all available resources are being used efficiently and effectively in support of the UNHCR return programme.

30. UNMIK and KFOR have also worked closely to coordinate mine action efforts. Early consultations resulted in the expeditious establishment, with the support of the Geneva International Center for Humanitarian Demining, of a shared information management system for mine action that will contain all mine and unexploded ordnance (UXO)-related information on Kosovo. The database, which has initially been set up at KFOR headquarters, will be transferred to UNMACC as soon as the latter is fully operational. Other cooperative efforts between KFOR and UNMIK mine action staff include the development of maps showing the mine/UXO suspected and confirmed areas, the sharing of technical information on the mine/UXO threat, and the sharing of mine information received from the Yugoslav army and KLA sources.

31. The principal United Nations humanitarian agencies - UNHCR, the World Food Programme (WFP), UNICEF and the World Health Organization (WHO) - as well as the International Organization for Migration (IOM), ICRC and the International Federation of the Red Cross (IFRC) have established representative offices at Pristina and are operating in all regions. Over 45 NGOs, along with major bilateral donors, have committed personnel and resources to meet the immediate relief needs of the people of Kosovo. The first humanitarian convoy, led by UNHCR, arrived at Pristina on 13 June 1999, within hours of KFOR securing the road from the former Yugoslav Republic of Macedonia border to the city. A base and warehouse were established, and efforts were made to reach vulnerable groups of internally displaced persons. UNHCR has established a regular supply and distribution system, and is also in the process of establishing a number of legal advice centres throughout Kosovo. An organized repatriation programme to selected areas inside Kosovo where security is reasonably assured has begun.

32. UNHCR, as the lead agency for humanitarian assistance in Kosovo, has organized a series of multisectoral and inter-agency assessments to identify the most urgent needs and areas for winterization programmes. WFP is conducting helicopter missions to locate and provide immediate assistance to displaced persons inside Kosovo. As of 8 July 1999, WFP had delivered over 5,723 tons of basic commodity items and emergency rations to Kosovo, of which 3,000 tons have already been distributed. WHO, UNICEF and a consortium of NGOs have initiated a rapid village assessment programme to provide details on the state of roads, populations, water and sanitation, food supplies, shelter and the availability of local services and utilities. UNICEF has initiated a mine awareness campaign, and has distributed over 220,000 mine awareness leaflets throughout Kosovo through its NGO partners.

33. UNMIK continues to build working-level relationships with the other organizations that form part of the integrated mission structure. OSCE has established a mission task force to assess needs on the ground and establish its larger organizational presence. It has provided assistance in identifying judges, and has set up a local skills database for use by the interim civil administration. It has also loaned personnel to UNMIK on a temporary basis to support efforts to protect important documentation. Human rights monitors have worked closely with KFOR on actions to protect and promote human rights. OSCE has identified a site for establishing a police training academy and preparations to begin training police cadets are under way.

34. The head of the European Union advance team of the Task Force for Reconstruction arrived at Pristina on 28 June 1999 to meet with UNMIK personnel and begin the process of joint planning for reconstruction and economic recovery. An initial damage assessment mission commissioned by the EU is currently under way.

IV. Authority and Competencies of the Mission

35. The Security Council, in its resolution 1244 (1999), has vested in the interim civil administration authority over the territory and people of Kosovo. All legislative and executive powers, including the administration of the judiciary, will, therefore, be vested in UNMIK.

36. In implementing its mandate in the territory of Kosovo, UNMIK will respect the laws of the Federal Republic of Yugoslavia and of the Republic of Serbia insofar as they do not conflict with internationally recognized human rights standards or with regulations issued by the Special Representative in the fulfilment of the mandate given to the United Nations by the Security Council. In the same vein, the UNMIK interim civil administration will respect the existing institutions to the extent that they are compatible with its mandate. Arrangements will be entered into with the Federal Republic of Yugoslavia in order to facilitate UNMIK activities in territories of the Federal Republic of Yugoslavia outside Kosovo.

37. Any movable or immovable property, including monies, bank accounts and any property of or registered in the name of the Federal Republic of Yugoslavia or the Republic of Serbia or any of its organs which is in the territory of Kosovo will be administered by UNMIK.

38. In exercising their functions, all persons undertaking public duties or holding public office in Kosovo will be required to observe internationally recognized human rights standards, and shall not discriminate against any person on any grounds, such as sex, race, colour, language, religion, political or other opinion, national, ethnic or social origin, association with a national community, property, birth or other status.

39. The authority vested in UNMIK will be exercised by the Special Representative. He will be empowered to regulate within the areas of his responsibilities laid down by the Security Council in its resolution 1244 (1999). In doing so, he may change, repeal or suspend existing laws to the extent necessary for the carrying out of his functions, or where existing laws are incompatible with the mandate, aims and purposes of the interim civil administration.

40. The Special Representative will also have the authority to appoint any person to perform functions in the interim civil administration in Kosovo, including the judiciary, and to remove such persons if their service is found to be incompatible with the mandate and the purposes of the interim civil administration. Such authority shall be exercised in accordance with the existing laws, as specified previously, and any regulations issued by UNMIK. In exercising this function, the Special Representative will endeavour to have all elements of Kosovo society appropriately represented and to respect the requirements and procedures for appointments and nominations provided for under local law. He shall, furthermore, promote the independence of the judicial system as the guarantor of the rule of law.

41. In the performance of the duties entrusted to UNMIK, the Special Representative will, as necessary, issue legislative acts in the form of regulations. Such regulations will remain in force until repealed by UNMIK or suspended by rules issued by the Kosovo Transitional Authority once it is established (see para. 114 below).

42. In its resolution 1244 (1999), the Security Council requests UNMIK to protect and promote human rights in Kosovo. In assuming its responsibilities, UNMIK will be guided by internationally recognized standards of human rights as the basis for the exercise of its authority in Kosovo. UNMIK will embed a culture of human rights in all areas of activity, and will adopt human rights policies in respect of its administrative functions.

V. Structure of the Mission

43. In order to fulfil the provisions of Security Council resolution 1244 (1999) effectively, the structure of UNMIK must ensure that all of its activities in Kosovo are carried out in an integrated manner with a clear chain of command. The Mission will be composed of four main components led by the United Nations (civil administration), UNHCR (humanitarian), OSCE (institution-building) and the EU (reconstruction). Each of these components will rely on the capabilities and expertise of the lead organization, as well as that of various other international organizations and agencies. While maintaining coherence and effectiveness, the lead organization will incorporate its own respective command structures.

44. The Special Representative of the Secretary-General as the head of UNMIK, is the highest international civilian official in Kosovo. He will enjoy the maximum civilian executive powers envisaged and vested in him by the Security Council in its resolution 1244 (1999), and will also be the final authority on their interpretation. In accordance with Security Council resolution 1244 (1999), the Special Representative will facilitate a political process designed to determine Kosovo's future status, taking into account the Rambouillet accords.

45. In view of the complexities of the UNMIK mission and the multifaceted tasks it will be required to perform, it was imperative to appoint a Principal Deputy Special Representative, who will assist the Special Representative in directing and managing UNMIK and will also ensure a coordinated and integrated approach by all of the Mission's four components. Each of the four components will be headed by a deputy special representative, drawn from the international organization which will have the lead responsibility in a particular area.

46. The deputy special representatives will report directly to the Special Representative on the implementation of their tasks, and will also be responsible for ensuring the effective coordination of all activities, both of UNMIK and its partners, within their areas of designated responsibility. While the deputy special representatives have overall responsibility for activities falling under their authority, the Special Representative will retain the ability to direct activities to ensure the coherent implementation of the tasks assigned to the mission.

47. An Executive Committee whose membership will include the Principal Deputy Special Representative and the four deputy special representatives, will be chaired by the Special Representative. The Executive Committee will assist the Special Representative in fulfilling his responsibilities, and will be the main instrument through which he will control the implementation of UNMIK's objectives. Through the Executive Committee, he will oversee tasks relating to effective mission integration, such as the setting of implementation priorities, the phasing and designation of tasks, ensuring effective coordination with outside agencies, especially KFOR, and the setting of overall mission policy.

48. The Executive Committee will be assisted by a Joint Planning Group (JPG), which will be chaired by the Principal Deputy Special Representative. JPG will be composed of senior planning staff from each lead organization. The main tasks of JPG will be to ensure consistency of plans between the components, in particular links between emergency relief and longer-term reconstruction activities, as well as between interim civil administration and institution-building. KFOR will be invited to designate a senior representative to work with JPG on military-civilian issues. Representatives of other agencies will be invited to participate when necessary.

49. The Special Representative will have an Executive Office headed by a Director to assist him in his duties. The Office will include senior staff to advise the Special Representative on legal, political and economic matters. A senior human rights adviser will ensure a proactive approach on human rights in all UNMIK activities and ensure the compatibility of regulations issued by UNMIK with international human rights standards. There will also be a gender advisory unit to provide guidance on how to mainstream gender issues into the mandate and activities of the various components. UNMIK will require a substantial administration component in order to support it administratively and logistically.

50. A Chief Military Officer, who will head the UNMIK Military Liaison Office, will also be assigned to the Special Representative. The Military Liaison Office will deploy officers to KFOR at the headquarters, regional and multinational brigade levels. The military liaison officers will also provide military advice to the UNMIK components, assist in assessing threats to the security of the international civilian personnel, and provide advice on such matters to UNMIK and its partners.

51. UNMIK will have a substantial unified public information programme. Its public information activities will support all aspects of its mandate. The Public Information Division will be comprised of an office of the Director, a spokesperson's office, units for radio and television, print and publication production, mass information and outreach, the Internet and media monitoring, and will be responsible for the overall management of a radio production facility.

52. It is also foreseen that UNMIK will have liaison offices, including military liaison officers, at Skopje, Tirana, and subject to the agreement of the Federal Republic of Yugoslavia, at Podgorica. The existing liaison office at Belgrade will also support UNMIK. The liaison offices will address issues affecting the mission and assist the Special Representative in his contacts with authorities in those capitals.

VI. Main Components of the Mission

53. Under the direction of the Special Representative, the four components of UNMIK will act in an integrated manner to attain the objectives set out in paragraph 11 of Security Council resolution 1244 (1999). The allocation of tasks set out below cannot, therefore, be perceived as being exclusive to one or another of the components.

A. CIVIL ADMINISTRATION COMPONENT

54. The civil administration functions of UNMIK, led by the United Nations, will be divided into functional departments as set out below.

1. Public administration/civil affairs

55. The civil administration component will establish the multi-ethnic governmental structures essential for the sustainable delivery of public services where and as long as required.

56. UNMIK will make maximum use of skilled former or current public employees, irrespective of ethnicity. They will be integrated into the interim civil administrative structure as quickly as possible. The guiding principles for integration are capability, the level of local confidence enjoyed by the individuals, efficiency and integrity. As the

integration of trained staff proceeds and their capacity increases, the level of day-to-day executive control exercised by UNMIK should diminish.

57. Small teams of international staff with professional experience in the various facets of public administration (ranging from management of health services to post and telecommunications) will contribute to the provision of public services throughout Kosovo, oversee service implementation, and undertake or direct the administration. Qualified public service advisers will give guidance on the implementation of sectoral policies in the municipalities of the region.

58. In the municipalities, UNMIK public administration staff will oversee the implementation of policy directives, report on the effectiveness of local bodies and use executive authority, where necessary. They will also provide advice to KFOR and justice officials operating in the region.

59. In the field of education, there is a continuing pressing need to align the Serb and Kosovo Albanian systems. Under the supervision of the civil administration and with advice from international organizations and NGOs, curricula, the standardization of exams, the recognition of degrees, and the financing and supervision of schools should be determined jointly by representatives of all communities. This would imply the recognition of both education systems on the basis of their fulfilment of certain standards and, where possible, integration.

2. Police

60. Two main goals will define UNMIK's law and order strategy in Kosovo: provision of interim law enforcement services, and the rapid development of a credible, professional and impartial Kosovo Police Service (KPS). To achieve these goals, UNMIK will deploy international police personnel, commanded by a UNMIK Police Commissioner who will report to the Special Representative through the Deputy Special Representative for Interim Civil Administration. UNMIK's international police personnel will be deployed to the five Kosovo regions. It will consist of three separate elements: civilian police (1,800 officers), special units (10 formed units of about 115 officers each) and border police (205 officers). The functions of the three elements will change over three distinct phases.

61. In the first phase, KFOR will be responsible for ensuring public safety and order until the international civil presence can take responsibility for this task. Until the transfer of that responsibility, UNMIK's civilian police will advise KFOR on policing matters and establish liaison with local and international counterparts. The special police units under UNMIK control will also establish liaison with local and international counterparts and protect United Nations installations, if needed. UNMIK border police will advise KFOR units stationed at the border.

62. In the second phase, once UNMIK has taken over responsibility for law and order from KFOR, UNMIK civilian police will carry out normal police duties and will have executive law enforcement authority. At that time, UNMIK civilian police will be armed. To the extent that trained local police become available through the police academy under UNMIK's institution-building component, UNMIK civilian police will initiate on-the-job training, advising and monitoring. UNMIK special police units will carry out public order functions, such as crowd control and area security. The special police units will also provide support for UNMIK civilian police and protect UNMIK installations. At that time, it would be preferable for any special police unit previously under KFOR command to be transferred to UNMIK authority so as to avoid two units with similar mandates in the same theatre. The United Nations border police will ensure compliance with immigration laws and other border regulations. KFOR will continue to support UNMIK in these efforts, as required.

63. A cadre of local community liaison officers will be employed as soon as possible to serve as an interface between UNMIK civilian police and the population, assist in the assessment of the law and order situation, and demonstrate early local engagement with UNMIK policing tasks. Community liaison officers will exercise no police powers, and will undergo a basic skills and standards course at the police academy. They will be hired strictly on a limited-term basis, although they will be given due consideration for subsequent selection to the permanent Kosovo police service.

64. UNMIK will begin developing a professional Kosovo Police Service immediately, recruiting candidates on the basis of stringent standards for selection and conduct ongoing screening and background checks. This will be done jointly by UNMIK police leadership and personnel responsible for the police academy. KPS will have to be representative of the different ethnic communities of the municipalities in which it serves. Training for selected candidates will include basic training organized in the police academy, as well as field training under the supervision and guidance of UNMIK civilian police. Background screening and critical assessment of the performance of KPS officers will be ongoing, and the Police Commissioner will retain full discretion, under the authority of the Special Representative, to dismiss or discipline KPS officers. UNMIK civilian police will, moreover, maintain the capacity and authority to conduct independent investigations of alleged human rights violations or other misconduct by the members of KPS. It will also be responsible for developing an effective and transparent command structure for KPS in accordance with international standards of democratic policing.

65. In the third phase, once properly trained and selected local police in sufficient strength are available, UNMIK will transfer responsibilities for law and order and border policing functions to the Kosovo Police Service. At that time, UNMIK civilian and border police will revert to training, advising and monitoring functions. UNMIK special police units might still be needed as a backup.

3. Judicial affairs

66. There is an urgent need to build genuine rule of law in Kosovo, including through the immediate re-establishment of an independent, impartial and multi-ethnic judiciary. Politically motivated and ethnically one-sided appointments, removals and training led to a judiciary in which, out of 756 judges and prosecutors in Kosovo, only 30 were Kosovo Albanians. The exodus of Kosovo Serbs has accelerated the collapse of the judicial system. The daily arrests of criminals by KFOR and the need to bring to justice those who are suspected of having committed the most serious crimes, including war crimes, amplifies the urgency of these issues. This is a fundamental challenge for UNMIK. Only a fully functioning independent and multi-ethnic judicial system will address the existing security concerns in Kosovo and build public confidence. Where justice can be seen to be done, it will also make an important contribution to reconciliation in Kosovo.

67. Under its civil administration component, UNMIK will have a Judicial Affairs Office, with four major areas of responsibility: the administration of courts, prosecution services and prisons; the development of legal policies; the review and drafting of legislation, as necessary, for the goals and purposes of UNMIK; and the assessment of the quality of justice in Kosovo, including training requirements.

68. The establishment of an independent and multi-ethnic judiciary requires immediate action. For an interim period, the judges and prosecutors appointed by the emergency judicial panel will hold office until a newly created judicial commission can conduct a Kosovo-wide selection process. In view of the knowledge required in the domestic judicial system, UNMIK will continue to fill the judiciary and the prosecution service with professionals recruited from among local lawyers.

69. Generally, newly appointed judges should receive continuous training, particularly in the area of the law and application of international instruments on human rights, in particular the Universal Declaration of Human Rights, the 1966 International Convention on Civil and Political Rights, the 1966 International Covenant on Economic, Social and Cultural Rights, and the European Convention on the Protection of Human Rights and Fundamental Freedoms and its Protocols. In addition, it will be important to provide immediate "quick start" training programmes in domestic and international law for those Kosovo Albanian lawyers who were trained during the time of the "parallel institutions" or were banned from practising their profession in the past

decade. These efforts will be supplemented by the dissemination of international instruments in local languages.

70. UNMIK will also establish a technical advisory commission on the structure and administration of the judiciary and the prosecution service. This commission will provide advice on such matters as the territorial jurisdiction of existing courts and the workload of judges and prosecutors with a view to rationalization and possible reduction in the number of judges and prosecutors, and salaries. The commission shall also be composed of both local and international experts and make recommendations to the Judicial Affairs Office within two months of its establishment.

71. As an initial step, UNMIK will re-establish the Supreme Court of Kosovo, which was abolished in 1991, to hear, inter alia, appeals against decisions of the current five district courts in Kosovo. Similarly, a General Prosecutor's Office will be re-established.

72. UNMIK'S Judicial Affairs Office will also re-establish and reform the correctional system in Kosovo, in a legal and operational framework that is consistent with international prison standards. Due to the exodus of most of the prison staff and the transfer of prisoners to facilities in Serbia and Montenegro, the prisons in Kosovo are literally empty at the moment. UNMIK will recruit, select and train new as well as former staff of these prisons, applying the highest international standards regarding prisons and human rights. As an immediate step, a thorough assessment of the existing correctional facilities will be conducted, and an initial contingent of prison wardens will be deployed to fill the current vacuum.

73. The establishment of strong and independent judges and prosecutors associations in Kosovo is an additional and essential institutional safeguard for building and securing an independent judiciary. At the same time, UNMIK will sponsor the revival of the Kosovo Bar Association to help identify and build legal capacities and further support the creation of an effective judiciary.

74. UNMIK is also planning to establish a legal aid scheme to facilitate equal access to courts and ensure the provision of legal assistance, where required, in particular in property cases and domestic war crimes cases, which may constitute a significant portion of all cases in the near future. This effort will be complemented by disseminating information on the legal system in general and the legal rights of the individual in particular.

75. UNMIK will initiate a process to amend current legislation in Kosovo, as necessary, including criminal laws, the law on internal affairs and the law on public peace and order, in a way consistent with the objectives of Security Council resolution 1244 (1999) and internationally recognized human rights standards.

76. UNMIK will address on a priority basis the problem of identification and documentation of all people in Kosovo, particularly returnees and IDPs. This process will contribute to maintaining law and order, facilitate the restoration of social services and help to resolve a number of potential legal problems, including property rights. As a priority, UNMIK will attempt to locate and secure key documents as well as record books and archives. The reissue of obligatory documents will become crucial for voter registration and elections. UNMIK will need to establish a team of international and national experts for these tasks. Addressing issues of documentation will also serve as a confidence-building and reconciliation measure since it will address the problem of illegal immigrants and the fears of Kosovo residents whose records, and personal and property documents, have been seized or destroyed.

77. Serious violations of property rights in Kosovo have occurred before, during and after the military conflict. There are indications that irregular property transactions were conducted in the years prior to the conflict, discriminating against Kosovo Albanians. The rapid return of Kosovo Albanians and the need for alternative accommodation for those who have lost their property, as well as the displacement of large numbers of the Serbian population, have led to an increasing number of cases of violation of tenure and occupancy rights. There are reports of illegal occupation of land and property in areas left by departing Albanian and Serbian local residents, as well as indications that criminal groups may be taking control of vacant housing and property in flagrant violation of the legitimate rights of the original owners and occupants.

78. The continuation of these incidents is reinforcing divisions, and will hinder peace-building efforts and the establishment of democratic institutions in Kosovo. Loss of records and irregular property transactions in recent years preclude a transparent process of property restitution. UNMIK, with the support of other international organizations and agencies, will establish a standard registry of property claims; redress legal measures on property taken in recent years and that in any way discriminate against any ethnic group; and rebuild the property and cadastral records. UNMIK will also establish a court to review property disputes.

B. INSTITUTION-BUILDING COMPONENT

79. The tasks of the institution-building component of the UNMIK mission, which will be led by OSCE, will include assisting the people of Kosovo in strengthening the capacity of local and central institutions and civil society organizations, as well as promoting democracy, good governance and respect for human rights. It will also include organizing elections. Given the recent history of the region, much work will be required to establish the foundations of a free, pluralist and multi-ethnic society.

1. Democratization and institution-building

80. As an immediate priority, UNMIK will work with other international organizations to identify the needs of local civil administrators and provide them with the required training as quickly as possible. It will also facilitate the awareness and involvement of citizens in social and political change in Kosovo by strengthening the development of local citizens, women's and youth groups, and professional, cultural and other associations. Existing structures will be preserved to the maximum extent possible. UNMIK will also undertake programmes to facilitate conditions that support pluralistic political party structures, political diversity and a healthy democratic political climate.

81. Over the longer term, UNMIK will develop an integrated approach to the strengthening of governance structures through the training of government officials and executive and administrative officers in procedures of democratic governance.

82. UNMIK has the unprecedented opportunity to lay the foundation for democratic and professional media in Kosovo. At present, there is a serious lack of objective information. While a few newspapers are in circulation in Kosovo, there is a near vacuum in the sphere of electronic media. UNMIK will support the emergence of independent media and will monitor compliance with international media standards. The Special Representative will appoint a media regulatory commission to manage the frequency spectrum, establish broadcast and press codes of conduct, and issue licences.

83. In facing the challenge of fostering the development of independent media in Kosovo, UNMIK will promote a media culture based on democratic principles. To create a framework for this purpose, the Special Representative intends to establish an independent media board, which will include representatives of the media and civil society. The board will, inter alia, identify reconstruction priorities for media infrastructure.

2. Elections

84. In accordance with paragraph 11 (c) of Security Council resolution 1244 (1999), UNMIK will organize and oversee the development of provisional institutions for democratic and autonomous self-government pending a political settlement. This includes the holding of elections. In order to prepare an environment in which free, fair and multi-ethnic elections can be held, UNMIK will conduct wide-ranging activities related to confidence-building, reconciliation and the restoration of democratic political organizations and institutions. A key element of this process will be the design and implementation of a comprehensive voter registration, which will be closely linked to the civic identification process. It will also be necessary to conduct a census of

Kosovo citizens residing in the province as well as refugees and displaced persons. These will be an immense challenge given the level of displacement and the destruction of public records.

3. Human rights

85. To strengthen the rule of law in Kosovo, UNMIK will develop mechanisms to ensure that the police, courts, administrative tribunals and other judicial structures are operating in accordance with international standards of criminal justice and human rights. Any concerns will be brought to the attention of UNMIK civilian police, the Judicial Affairs Office or the independent commission on judicial appointments, as appropriate.

86. UNMIK will also ensure that ICRC and other relevant organizations have unimpeded access to detention facilities in Kosovo. The treatment of detainees, the standard of prison facilities and the running of prison facilities will be monitored for compliance with international standards. UNMIK will also ensure the identification and subsequent dissolution of illegal detention facilities in Kosovo.

87. UNMIK will have a core of human rights monitors and advisors who will have unhindered access to all parts of Kosovo to investigate human rights abuses and ensure that human rights protection and promotion concerns are addressed through the overall activities of the mission. Human rights monitors will, through the Deputy Special Representative for Institution-building, report their findings to the Special Representative. The findings of human rights monitors will be made public regularly and will be shared, as appropriate, with United Nations human rights mechanisms, in consultation with the Office of the United Nations High Commissioner for Human Rights. UNMIK will provide a coordinated reporting and response capacity.

88. A particularly acute human rights problem in Kosovo is uncertainty about the whereabouts of family members who have gone missing during the conflict. Abductions have also occurred after the conflict ended. UNMIK will support the efforts of ICRC and ICTY on this issue, and the Special Representative will use his executive authority to directly intervene, when necessary, on the issue of missing persons. UNMIK will also undertake efforts to build and support local human rights capacity, based on experience within Kosovo civil society.

89. Recognizing that a strong system of human rights protection offers accessible and timely mechanisms for the independent review, redress and appeal of non-judicial actions, an ombudsperson institution will be established in Kosovo. It will receive, inter alia, complaints regarding the abuse, if any, of authority by the Interim Civil Administration and any emerging local institutions and any non-state actors claiming or exercising authority. The Ombudsperson's office will consist of national ombudspersons, supported by national and international professional staff.

90. The Ombudsperson, to be appointed by the Special Representative, will have jurisdiction over allegations of human rights by any person or entity in Kosovo, and will have the authority to conduct, either on its own initiative or in response to an allegation by any person or entity, its own investigations. It will take all necessary action to address those violations, including by directly intervening with relevant authorities, which will be required to respond within a time limit as prescribed by the Ombudsperson. The Ombudsperson will make recommendations to these authorities, including on the compatibility of domestic laws and regulations with recognized international standards. The Ombudsperson will provide a regular report to the Special Representative and make its findings public.

C. HUMANITARIAN COMPONENT

91. The humanitarian component will be led by UNHCR. The success of the humanitarian aspects of the Kosovo operation will depend on how quickly and accurately a clear needs assessment can be conducted and translated into action, utilizing funds provided by the international donor community. It is essential that humanitarian activities be closely coordinated with those devoted to reconstruction.

1. Humanitarian assistance

92. The priority for the humanitarian community is to ensure that adequate shelter, food, clean water, medical assistance and employment will be available to meet the needs of the growing number of returnees inside Kosovo itself. In collaboration with developmental partners, the United Nations system agencies are also preparing programmes for the longer-term rehabilitation, reconstruction and development of the region.

93. In the coming weeks, UNHCR will design and implement a protection strategy to address the protection needs of returning refugees and IDPs, as well as Croatian Serb refugees and the Serb and Roma ethnic minorities in Kosovo. Humanitarian programmes will also target urgent and essential infrastructure repairs and short-term rebuilding efforts to ensure that the population at large are prepared for the approaching winter. UNHCR will also provide for the transport and distribution of materials that will be used to provide shelter to families whose houses were largely destroyed.

94. IFRC, complemented by IOM, will work with Kosovo's Red Cross structure to support activities aimed at longer-term rehabilitation of health services, agriculture, village water systems, hospital training and psycho-social support.

95. WFP and NGOs will continue to furnish food supplies from stocks in Albania and the former Yugoslav Republic of Macedonia, and are establishing a supply line from Thessaloniki via Skopje into Kosovo. Daily deliveries of bread are also supplied from Kukes in Albania to Djakovica in western Kosovo.

96. WHO, UNICEF and NGOs have commenced the distribution of drug kits throughout Kosovo.

97. The Food and Agriculture Organization of the United Nations (FAO) is currently assessing the region's agricultural needs in the coming months. The means will be provided to enable farmers to protect livestock and make provision for the autumn planting.

98. The success and efficiency of the humanitarian operation will depend on a coordinated and coherent approach. To this end, UNHCR has established an inter-agency coordination unit with direct support from the Office for the Coordination of Humanitarian Affairs of the United Nations Secretariat.

2. Mine action

99. UNMACC will plan mine action activities and act as the point of contact and coordination between the various mine action partners, including KFOR, United Nations agencies and international organizations, NGOs and commercial companies. During the initial emergency phase, UNMACC will focus on mine action in support of humanitarian relief, the repatriation and resettlement of refugees and IDPs, and the deployment of UNMIK. This includes setting up an information management system for mine action database, defining the scope of the mine/UXO threat, mobilising mine action resources, conducting mine action liaison and planning with KFOR, planning and coordinating the efforts of the humanitarian mine action resources in support of the UNHCR return plan, and responding to other humanitarian needs.

100. In the longer term, UNMACC will coordinate mine action support for the reconstruction of Kosovo; assist local authorities in the development of a comprehensive and integrated mine action plan; disseminate, manage and collect mine/UXO-related information; develop technical and safety standards; and perform quality assurance management tasks. In performing these functions, UNMACC will investigate the feasibility of utilizing indigenous and other mine action capabilities and retain the option of contracting for this purpose. UNMACC will also coordinate a Kosovo-wide, initial survey of the mine and unexploded ordnance threat in order to determine the scope of the problem and establish priorities for the allocation of available and anticipated mine action resources. The information management system for mine action that has been set up at KFOR headquarters, will be transferred to UNMACC as soon as the latter is fully operational.

D. RECONSTRUCTION COMPONENT

101. UNMIK has an obligation to promote peace and prosperity in Kosovo and to facilitate the development of an economic life that brings better prospects for the future. In paragraph 11 (g) of its resolution 1244 (1999), the Security Council mandates UNMIK to support the reconstruction of key infrastructure and other economic and social systems. This component of the mission will be led by the European Union.

102. The main functions of the reconstruction component will be to plan and monitor the reconstruction of Kosovo; prepare and evaluate policies in the economic, social and financial fields; and to coordinate between the various donors and international financial institutions in order to ensure that all financial assistance is directed towards the priorities indicated by UNMIK. Since policies in the economic, social and financial fields will, in many cases, have a bearing on the work of the other components of UNMIK, it is important that these policies be properly coordinated within UNMIK.

103. The Special Representative will seek to create a viable, market-based economy and to develop a comprehensive approach to the economic and social development of Kosovo, taking into account, inter alia, the Stability Pact for Southeastern Europe. Under his direction, UNMIK will consult with representatives of Kosovo communities, the United Nations Development Programme (UNDP) and other relevant United Nations organizations, and will seek the advice and guidance of international financial institutions in order to develop a comprehensive programme for the economic and social stabilization and development of Kosovo. Such a programme will map the institutional framework which should prevail in the medium term, and will elaborate policy actions which are compatible with it.

104. As an urgent priority, UNMIK will thoroughly assess the existing legal, financial, and fiscal structure and capacities in order to put in place policies for the recovery, development and future integration of Kosovo into a healthy and expanding regional economy in Southeastern Europe. Among others, these policies will encompass trade and commercial issues, currency and monetary issues, and a banking system.

105. Reconstruction and economic recovery of Kosovo will occur in three overlapping phases, which will encompass immediate humanitarian relief, reconstruction and rehabilitation, and the creation of a viable market economy and equitable social system.

106. In addition to humanitarian measures, which remain an urgent necessity, the rehabilitation of essential services (power, water, sanitation, health education) and infrastructure require immediate attention. In this regard, an emergency programme to maintain the payroll and recurring costs of essential services in the Interim Civil Administration is of particular urgency, pending development of a system for revenue generation. Other priority needs in the short term include restarting local economic activities (including small and medium enterprise development) and the restoration of social protection systems.

107. Pending the finalization of a programme for stabilization and development, it will be of paramount importance that these basic service and support activities start as soon as possible and target resident populations, returnees, internally displaced persons and other war-affected and vulnerable populations alike. These short-term activities should be identified, planned and implemented in conjunction with resettlement measures, the establishment of interim civil administrative structures, and institution-building activities.

108. Projects in the long-term category will include investment in capital infrastructure as well as human resources development. These projects will be selected on the basis of assessments of inherent future revenue potential conducted by the international financial institutions or other appropriate international institutions. Financial support will be obtained with the assistance of foreign donors in the first instance and from domestic sources, including public revenue collection. As a general consideration, foreign financial assistance should take into consideration Kosovo's economic size and absorptive capacity. Disproportionately large inflows of funds risk distorting the structure of the Kosovo economy.

109. With respect to international assistance, the European Community (EC) and the World Bank will organize an initial donor conference on 28 July 1999, to cover relief as well as urgent reconstruction requirements. This will be followed in the coming months by donor pledging conferences for reconstruction requirements.

VII. General Strategy

110. The work of UNMIK will be conducted in five integrated phases. The first phase will focus on the establishment and consolidation of UNMIK's authority and the creation of interim UNMIK-managed administrative structures. To ensure participation from the outset, local consultative bodies will be established at both the political and the functional levels. Deployment of international civilian police liaison officers with KFOR public security units will be accelerated. The provision of emergency assistance to returning refugees and the internally displaced will also be a major priority, as will the early commencement of shelter reconstruction to ensure completion before the onset of winter. Basic public services will be restored and maintained, and capacity-building activities, including police and judicial training, will be carried out.

111. UNMIK will also develop a phased plan for economic recovery and development. UNMIK will need to develop expenditure priorities bearing in mind both reconstruction and social needs, as well as the most appropriate division of responsibility between central and local authorities. Customs revenue will represent one of the most important sources of finance to meet public expenditures in the short term. As soon as UNMIK can deploy civilian customs agents at Kosovo's international borders, it will commence collection of customs revenues for use to meet Kosovo public spending needs.

112. UNMIK will aim at the establishment and maintenance of a viable, self-sustaining economy covering, inter alia, public finance, trade and commerce, currency and monetary policies, customs, and fiscal as well as banking issues.

113. Once conditions of basic stability have been achieved, the second phase of UNMIK's efforts will be directed towards the administration of social services and utilities, and the consolidation of the rule of law. UNMIK will continue to encourage the revival of broadly representative political activity and political expression, including through assistance to the formation of political party structures. It will also encourage the strengthening and deepening of civil society through, inter alia, the revival of print and broadcast media and the promotion of reconciliation at the grass-roots level. These efforts will have as their goal the promotion of harmonious relations between all ethnic communities within Kosovo. In this phase, it is expected that there will be intensive efforts to build, and where possible restore, basic economic structures, such as payments systems, public finances and hard budget constraints, so as to promote economic and social development as well as to make donor assistance efforts effective and sustainable. During the latter stages of phase two, it is expected that provisional transfer of executive authority for the management and administrative functions of specific sectors, such as health and education, could begin at the local and possibly regional levels. Preparations will also begin for the conduct of elections.

114. Once sufficient progress has been made towards the goals set for the second phase, UNMIK will move into the third phase. The emphasis during this phase will be the finalization of preparations for and the conduct of elections to what may be termed the Kosovo Transitional Authority. This will require UNMIK to ensure the necessary preconditions for free and unfettered political expression, free assembly, and campaigning by parties and candidates, including through equitable access to the media. This will also involve UNMIK-managed or conducted voter registration, electoral training, and monitoring of votes and ballot-counting. During this phase, administrative and economic revival will continue and deepen. Local revenue generation should increasingly replace international assistance. It is envisaged that

efforts to facilitate the political process designed to determine Kosovo's future status, taking into account the Rambouillet accords, will be intensified during this phase of UNMIK's work.

115. In the fourth phase, UNMIK will oversee and, as necessary, assist elected Kosovo representatives in their efforts to organize and establish provisional institutions for democratic and autonomous self-government. As these are established, UNMIK will transfer its remaining administrative responsibilities while overseeing and supporting the consolidation of Kosovo's local provisional institutions.

116. A concluding fifth phase will depend on a final settlement and the dispositions made therein. As provided for in paragraph 11 (f) of Security Council resolution 1244 (1999), in a final stage UNMIK would oversee the transfer of authority from Kosovo's provisional institutions to institutions established under a political settlement.

VIII. Observations

117. The adoption of Security Council resolution 1244 (1999) and the deployment of KFOR and UNMIK has marked the end of a tragic chapter in the history of the people of Kosovo. The task before the international community is to help the people of Kosovo to rebuild their lives and heal the wounds of conflict. Reconciliation will be a long and slow process. Patience and persistence will be needed to carry it through.

118. The concept outlined in the present report to implement this challenging mandate is a novel one. Four international organizations and agencies will be working together in one operation under one leadership. None of them would be able to span the wide range of complex activities on its own. Setting up an interim administration, providing humanitarian relief, building democratic institutions and restoring an entire economy would go beyond the competence and capabilities of just one organization. The cooperation of the lead agencies and those other organizations which will contribute to the four components will set a precedent for the future.

119. During the interim period, UNMIK will endeavour to promote, in cooperation with KFOR, an atmosphere of security and safety that will enable all refugees and internally displaced persons, regardless of their ethnicity, to return freely to their homes and live there in conditions in which the highest standards of human rights and fundamental freedoms are respected. It will, furthermore, endeavour to create conditions of normalcy in Kosovo under which all peoples can enjoy the benefits of democracy and self-governance. UNMIK will ensure at an early stage the involvement of local leaders in the interim administration through the Kosovo Transitional Council and sectoral joint consultative committees. Nobody can be excluded from this process. I strongly encourage all ethnic communities and parties in Kosovo to demonstrate restraint and tolerance and fully cooperate with the international community in the implementation of tasks defined by the Security Council in its resolution 1244 (1999). I wish to remind them that the only legitimate path to any future political settlement for Kosovo is through the mechanisms envisioned in Council resolution 1244 (1999). I also urge the Government of the Federal Republic of Yugoslavia to cooperate fully with the provisions of that resolution.

120. The Security Council has mandated the United Nations with an unprecedented challenge in Kosovo. To meet this challenge and fulfil the responsibilities entrusted to the Organization, significant financial resources and personnel, including experts in various fields, will be required immediately. As indicated above, the situation on the ground in some areas remains tense, and I am particularly concerned about the continued harassment and lack of security of minority groups in Kosovo. The full deployment of KFOR and UNMIK personnel will undoubtedly contribute to the easing of these tensions. In order to create a climate of law and order, UNMIK must rapidly deploy international police throughout Kosovo. I commend those Governments which have offered police personnel for this purpose and appeal to other Member States to urgently place police officers at UNMIK's disposal. Their early arrival is essential if we are to stem the tendency towards lawlessness which is taking hold in some areas. I also count on the Security Council's support on this matter.

121. If we are to succeed to establishing the rule of law as the basis for the development of democratic institutions, it is also vital to rapidly revive the judicial penal systems of Kosovo. Reconciliation will not begin until those suspected of committing the most serious crimes, especially war crimes, are brought to justice. I appeal to Member States to place at UNMIK's disposal sufficient resources in terms of personnel and experts to meet the tremendous needs in this area.

122. The strong and committed financial backing of the donor community will enable relief agencies to continue humanitarian assistance to all those in need in Kosovo. The Office for the Coordination of Humanitarian Affairs will shortly present to donors a Consolidated Inter-agency Appeal that will outline funding requirements to enable agencies and their partners to move forward with the implementation of humanitarian operations in Kosovo. At this stage, the priority humanitarian need is for the rehabilitation of shelter. Efforts must begin immediately if people whose homes were damaged or destroyed during the war are to be protected from the oncoming winter.

123. Aside from humanitarian assistance, there is a broad variety of urgent needs in the aftermath of the Kosovo conflict. Most essential is the payment of local salaries in the public sector. I commend those Governments that have already provided funding for salaries, and appeal to other Member States to make available the far greater resources required. If we are not able to meet this requirement, we will face a collapse of the public sector in Kosovo which will have tremendous implications for social order and jeopardize the success of the Interim Administration. A long-term commitment in reconstruction and restoration will also be required. A Trust Fund established in the Office of the Special Representative will provide a temporary facility through which such needs can be met. I commend those Governments which have already contributed to this Fund and appeal to other Member States urgently to make available the necessary resources.

124. In order to achieve its goals, it is essential that all components of UNMIK act in a fully integrated manner and speak with one voice. Consultations with the EU and OSCE regarding modalities of their participation in the integrated structure of the United Nations Interim Administration Mission in Kosovo are continuing, and I will inform the Council of their results accordingly.

125. I will also inform the Council of the financial implications of the present report in due course.

126. The United Nations welcomes the opportunity to rise to the challenge of restoring peace, security, good governance and development to the shattered society of Kosovo. Such a mission goes to the heart of the purposes and principles of the Organization. Its effectiveness in responding to them is, however, dependent on prompt and strong support from the Council and Member States.

127. In conclusion, I would like to thank my Special Representative ad interim, Sergio Vieira de Mello, and the advance team of UNMIK personnel for the exceptional work they have done, under very difficult conditions, in establishing the mission and planning for its future. I would also like to pay tribute to all those international organizations, including KFOR, OSCE, the Council of Europe and the EU, for their assistance and cooperation in this collaborative effort.

333. EU, Council Joint Action Concerning the Installation of the Structures of the United Nations Mission in Kosovo (UNMIK), 1999/522/CFSP, 29 July 1999[1]

The Council of the European Union,

Having regard to the Treaty on European Union, and in particular Article 14 thereof,

Whereas:

---

[1] OJ L 201, 31/07/1999 p. 0001 - 0001, 499X0522.

(1) United Nations Security Council Resolution 1244 (1999) of 10 June 1999 establishes the principle of organisation of the civil administration in Kosovo (UNMIK), headed by a Special Representative of the United Nations Secretary-General;

(2) The Special Representative of the United Nations Secretary-General will be assisted in his duties by four Deputy Special Representatives, each responsible for one major component of the United Nations Mission;

(3) The United Nations Secretary-General wished to entrust the task of economic reconstruction, rehabilitation and development of Kosovo to the European Union; on 19 July 1999 the Council welcomed the rapid deployment of the fourth UNMIK component and the UN Secretary-General's appointment of Mr Dixon as Deputy Special Representative on 2 July 1999,

has adopted this joint action:

Article 1

The European Union shall ensure the installation of the UNMIK component which it has been made responsible for and notes the UN Secretary-General's appointment of Mr Joly Dixon as head of that component.

Article 2

1. The financial reference amount to cover the cost of the task referred to in Article 1 shall be EUR 910000 for the period to 31 December 1999.

2. The amount referred to in paragraph 1 is intended to finance the infrastructure and current expenditure of the UNMIK component entrusted to the European Union, including the travel and subsistence expenses and daily allowances of seconded staff and the salaries of local staff.

3. Member States and institutions of the European Union may propose the secondment of staff to the UNMIK component entrusted to the Union. The remuneration of staff so seconded shall be covered by the Member State or institution concerned respectively.

Article 3

This Joint Action shall apply from 2 July to 31 December 1999.

Article 4

This Joint Action shall be published in the Official Journal.

Done at Brussels, 29 July 1999. For the Council: The President T. Halonen

Amendments: Applic. extended by 400X0175 (OJ L 055 29.02.00 p.78)

334. UN, Report of the Secretary-General on the United Nations Interim Administration Mission in Kosovo, UN Doc. S/1999/987, 16 September 1999

I. Introduction

1. In my report to the Security Council of 12 July 1999 (S/1999/779), I gave an overview of the scope of the challenges facing the United Nations Interim Administration Mission in Kosovo (UNMIK) and the Mission's plan to undertake its mandated task and objectives. The current report is issued pursuant to paragraph 20 of resolution 1244 (1999) of 10 June 1999, which requested me to report to the Council at regular intervals on the implementation of the resolution, and covers developments in Kosovo, Federal Republic of Yugoslavia, since my report of 12 July 1999.

II. Overview

2. Since its deployment, UNMIK has made significant progress. It has established structures at various levels that allow the people of Kosovo to provide expertise and to share responsibility and accountability for the development and future of the province. Foremost amongst these structures is the Kosovo Transitional Council (KTC), which meets on a weekly basis under the leadership of my Special Representative. This body brings together all major political parties and ethnic groups. Its establishment has given Kosovo residents an opportunity to have a direct input into the UNMIK decision-making process and to achieve consensus on a broad range of issues related to civil administration, institution-building and essential services, thereby creating a climate where participation in democratic processes is the norm.

3. The establishment of the Kosovo Transitional Council is an initial step towards the creation of a framework of wider and more inclusive democratic structures covering all aspects of life in Kosovo. To broaden the inclusive nature of the Council and to give it greater responsibility for the administration of Kosovo, my Special Representative has proposed the creation within it of four directorates covering housing, health, education and public utilities. The directorates would be chaired by two co-directors, one of whom would be an UNMIK representative, with the other drawn from the local community. The local director would be selected based upon criteria such as experience, technical expertise and ethnic and political balance. These directorates will have the merit of involving the people of Kosovo in decision-making on these important issues.

4. The level and nature of violence in Kosovo, especially against vulnerable minorities, remains a major concern. Measures taken to address this problem are having a positive effect, but continued vigilance is necessary. KFOR deserves great credit for its efforts to provide a secure environment under extremely difficult conditions. The deployment of over 1,100 United Nations civilian police has also had an important effect. In addition, in response to the efforts of my Special Representative, senior Kosovo Albanian personalities, including the leadership of the Kosovo Liberation Army (KLA), have voiced increasingly forthright public positions on tolerance and security for minorities. Senior KLA figures have denied KLA involvement in attacks and called for non-Albanians to remain in Kosovo and repeatedly affirmed their commitment to human rights, tolerance and diversity. However, although these statements are a positive step, they seem, so far, to have had little effect in preventing attacks against minorities, the cessation of which would encourage Serbs and others to remain in Kosovo.

5. Hardening Serb attitudes towards Kosovo Albanians, driven in part by outside extremists, are helping to radicalize Albanians in Mitrovica. Tensions also continue in Orahovac where local Albanian residents are blocking the deployment of KFOR troops.

6. Around 4,000 of the 10,000 registered KLA combatants remain in assembly areas awaiting demilitarization, which KFOR expects to be completed by 19 September 1999. To be effective, arrangements for demilitarization must provide a future for former combatants, most of whom have a deep apprehension about their future. Opportunities to join the new police, fire and civil services, as well as registration of KLA members for civilian employment by the International Office of Migration (IOM), are useful but are not sufficient to absorb the bulk of KLA manpower. At the very least, unemployed and resentful former soldiers are a potential source of instability as the international community attempts to build a stable political system in Kosovo. In light of the foregoing, KFOR, in close consultation with my Special Representative, is developing a concept for demobilization of the KLA, offering individual members an opportunity to participate in a disciplined, professional, multi-ethnic civilian emergency corps. In accordance with its mandate, KFOR will provide day-to-day direction of the corps. The UNMIK civil administration component will continue to maintain responsibility for overall civil emergency management.

7. Significant problems have resulted from the as yet unresolved questions related to property rights. These are reinforcing ethnic divisions and complicating the process of return. As I noted in my report of 12 July 1999 (S/1999/779, para. 78), UNMIK, with the support of other international organizations and agencies, intends to establish a standard registry of property claims; redress legal measures on property taken in recent years that in anyway discriminate against any

ethnic group; and rebuild the property and cadastral records. A mechanism will also be established to review property disputes.

III. Humanitarian Situation

8. UNMIK, with the Office of the United Nations High Commissioner for Refugees (UNHCR) as the lead agency, is cooperating closely with the main United Nations humanitarian agencies - the World Food Programme (WFP), the United Nations Children's Fund (UNICEF) and the World Health Organization (WHO) - as well as IOM, the International Committee of the Red Cross (ICRC) and the International Federation of Red Cross Societies (IFRC). Strong links have also been established with the many non-governmental organizations and bilateral donors that have established a presence in Kosovo.

9. As of 4 September 1999, more than 770,000 refugees had returned to Kosovo through a combination of spontaneous and UNHCR-assisted movements. Awaiting return are an estimated 44,400 persons in neighbouring regions and countries, 37,000 evacuees in third countries and an unknown number of asylum-seekers. There is no accurate figure for the number of internally displaced persons, although it is estimated to be as high as 500,000.

10. In the period since mid-June 1999, non-Albanian groups, primarily Serbs and Roma, have been targets for harassment, intimidation and attacks. As a result, many have left Kosovo. According to the Yugoslav Red Cross, approximately 150,000 displaced persons have registered for assistance in Serbia and Montenegro since mid-June 1999. Freedom of movement for those who remain is extremely limited and, in some cases, virtually non-existent. In effect, non-Albanians are restricted from making use of public facilities such as hospitals or visiting shops and markets. UNHCR, humanitarian non-government organizations and KFOR have distributed assistance, including medical assistance, to these individuals in their homes or villages. As a last resort, UNHCR has been assisting people in urgent, life-threatening situations to leave Kosovo, as well as assisting transfers of vulnerable groups for purposes of family reunification. Efforts are, however, being made to create acceptable conditions for the return of those who have left temporarily.

11. Housing surveys have been conducted in more than 90 per cent of the war-affected villages. An estimated 50,000 houses are beyond repair and another 50,000 have sustained damage of up to 50 per cent, but are repairable. One of the most urgent tasks to be completed before winter is the temporary rehabilitation of the 50,000 repairable houses. UNHCR's emergency rehabilitation programme is designed to provide at least one warm and dry room for the duration of winter until more sustainable reconstruction can take place in spring. In excess of 55,000 shelter kits are being provided by UNHCR and international agencies; heating stoves will also be provided. These measures are being complemented by the provision of prefabricated shelters and direct repairs, as well as cash subsidies to enable residents to purchase supplies locally that can be used to improve the quality of weather-proofing or to winterize an additional room. Concurrent with housing rehabilitation are measures to restore public utilities, which remain precarious.

12. Should all these measures be fully implemented, the vast majority of the population would be housed, albeit temporarily, during the winter months. The occupants of the 50,000 houses that are beyond repair will, however, require alternative accommodation. Most are already living with host families and it is expected that they will stay with them throughout the winter. These host families are provided with support and additional programmes are under consideration. However, the enormous difficulties with winterization make it highly unlikely that all measures will be in place by the start of the cold season. A number of contingency measures are being developed in case additional capacity is needed, including the identification of temporary community shelters and distribution of 15,000 heated, all-season tents that can accommodate about 90,000 people.

13. One priority area of concern is targeted assistance for women and children. UNHCR, UNICEF and international and local non-government organizations are implementing a series of projects under a "Kosovo Women's Initiative". Activities include psychosocial and community support, including counselling and skills development programmes; special health-care services to promote the needs of women and children; and, micro-finance and income-generation projects. IFRC, complemented by IOM, is working with Kosovo's Red Cross structure to support activities aimed at longer-term rehabilitation of health services, agriculture, village water systems, hospital training and psychosocial support. WHO is closely involved in the rehabilitation of the health sector.

14. The UNMIK Mine Action Coordination Centre is the focal point for the coordination of mine action activities in Kosovo. Under an integrated mine action programme, developed in close cooperation with various partners, including United Nations agencies, KFOR, ICRC, non-governmental organizations and commercial companies, 1.1 million square metres of land have been demined or cleared of unexploded ordnance. It is estimated that it will take more than two years to completely clear Kosovo of mines. Clearance priorities continue to target shelter reconstruction, the restoration of essential services and infrastructure, the rehabilitation of key installations and mined areas that pose an immediate humanitarian problem. Sixteen mine clearance organizations have been funded by various donors to undertake mine clearance tasks. Complementing mine action activities include mine-awareness programmes undertaken by 12 organizations at the provincial and community levels. Additionally, a mine victim surveillance programme is under way to identify victim assistance and rehabilitation requirements, as well as to determine clearance priorities.

IV. Civil Administration

15. UNMIK faces two simultaneous challenges: preparing for an interim administration and taking emergency measures to restore essential services. The orderly arrangements necessary for a credible interim administration, including consistency with international standards of efficiency, accountability and transparency, will take time to design, fund and implement. To fill critical administrative and economic gaps in the short term, UNMIK must, therefore, design and implement emergency measures in virtually every sector.

16. These emergency measures, as well as the establishment of more permanent ones, are being implemented by civil administration teams of international staff with professional expertise in a range of public administration functions. These staff are deployed in Pristina, the five regions of Kosovo and in 18 of the province's 29 municipalities. The other 11 municipalities are covered through visits by designated civil administration officers from the regions or from larger municipalities in their vicinity. Activities are closely coordinated with KFOR.

A. PROVISION OF PUBLIC SERVICES

17. The civil administration component of UNMIK, working in close cooperation with KFOR, and acting largely through joint civilian commissions, has achieved considerable progress in the re-establishment of public services and utilities. The main post and telecommunications office and five sub-offices in Pristina have been reopened. The rubbish collection and disposal system has also been restored in the city and efforts are under way to revive services in the five regions. The United Nations trust fund for small-scale "quick impact" projects that will help the people of Kosovo return to normal life is operational and has already disbursed more than US$ 900,000. Following the restoration of the electricity power lines with the former Yugoslav Republic of Macedonia and Albania, the electricity system in Kosovo is currently capable of meeting two-thirds of the expected winter demand. Work is continuing, under the supervision of an international company, to ensure that the electricity system can meet full demand. Encouraging progress has been made in the reintegration of workers in the Kosovo Railway Enterprise where 350 Serbs have rejoined the workforce, among them, 120 individuals who have returned from Serbia. This represents the first time that Serbs who had left Kosovo have returned to their homes and jobs. Work is also continuing to revive the social welfare system.

18. To ensure the continuation of public services and to provide a minimum living standard for public employees, UNMIK is in the

process of paying stipends to health workers, fire-fighters, judges, customs officers and education workers. Payments of stipends will be extended to all other categories of public employees. This is a temporary measure pending the development of a public service pay mechanism.

19. With European Union (EU) assistance, UNMIK has established, on an emergency basis, a customs system in Kosovo. Customs and excise duties as well as sales tax and exemptions have been established by a regulation issued by my Special Representative (all regulations issued to date by my Special Representative are attached in the annex to this report). All exports are exempt from customs duties. On 3 September 1999, customs duties collection began at the Djeneral Jankovic international border crossing with Kosovo and the former Yugoslav Republic of Macedonia. Customs operations at the other four international border crossings will begin in the coming weeks. To facilitate the customs operation, Kosovo importers and exporters have been registered and preparations are under way for the registration of commercial companies by the end of September 1999.

20. The personal identification documents of many Kosovo residents that were destroyed or lost in the conflict must be replaced, not least in order to establish a pre-electoral census. To respond to a growing request by the population, and to contribute to the battle against criminality and trafficking, the civil administration component should begin issuing temporary identification cards to residents by 30 October 1999, with the hope of completing the process by mid-2000. To facilitate this process, every effort will be made to draw on existing data banks, including the information compiled by WFP on nearly 1,300,000 Kosovo Albanians and UNHCR's refugee registration system.

21. Under UNMIK coordination, more than 400 schools, only two of which are ethnically mixed, reopened for over 100,000 children on 1 September 1999. A key UNMIK goal is to enable the completion of the 1998-1999 academic year, which was disrupted by the conflict, and to prepare for the coming school year. At the tertiary level, UNMIK will ensure that all staff and students of both the Serb and Albanian educational systems have access to all faculties to prepare for and conduct examinations. Currently, minority students and staff, including Serbs, have been denied access to some educational facilities.

22. To support the resumption of schooling, 263 schools are currently under repair and most will become functional in October 1999. UNMIK is also obtaining printing paper for textbooks, school furniture and supplies and winterized tents for sites where school buildings have been completely destroyed. KFOR and UNMIK have made the necessary arrangements to provide security to staff and students at all educational institutions.

B. ESTABLISHMENT OF MULTI-ETHNIC GOVERNMENTAL STRUCTURES

23. Four joint civilian commissions, under UNMIK's leadership or co-leadership, are currently operating in the health, education, energy and public utilities and post and telecommunications sectors. Two of the commissions are multi-ethnic, but no Kosovo Serbs have yet agreed to join the other two. Following my Special Representative's decision to begin establishing directorates for some aspects of public administration (see para. 3 above), it is intended that the health and education commissions will be replaced by such directorates, which will exercise executive powers under the authority of my Special Representative.

24. By the first week in September, civil administration officers were chairing or supervising the work of the senior municipal bodies in 9 of Kosovo's 29 municipalities. In all nine municipalities, the municipal body advises the UNMIK administrator on municipal administration matters. In some cases, the municipal body also carries out management and technical functions. All of Kosovo's municipalities are functioning to varying degrees and by the end of the month all will be under direct civil administration supervision.

C. POLICE

25. As stated in my report of 12 July 1999 (S/1999/779), the Mission's international police component will consist of three separate elements: civilian police, special units and border police.

26. UNMIK's civilian police has expanded its presence in Kosovo, concentrating resources first on the city of Pristina and its surrounding region, where approximately one third of the crimes reported in Kosovo occur. UNMIK civilian police will extend law enforcement operations to each of the four other regions in turn with preparations for operations in the Prizren region already under way. In Pristina, UNMIK police have taken over authority for police investigations for the city and are conducting the full range of police activities in the city's four main police districts. Patrolling and protection is now expanding to the entire Pristina region. Three police sub-stations, operating on a 24-hour basis, have been set up in high crime areas to address, in particular, the ongoing pattern of violence directed against the Serb and Roma population. Joint patrols are undertaken with KFOR, which has deployed an additional 200 soldiers for patrolling duties in the city.

27. UNMIK police are also operating a small police detention facility in Pristina. This is the only civilian detention facility in Kosovo and it serves the short-term demands of UNMIK pending the re-establishment of full correctional functions. The urgent need to increase the capacity of detention and corrections facilities is presently a high priority, and will depend upon timely financial and logistical support from contributing Governments. An appropriate detention facility has already been identified at Istok and emergency repairs have ensured that it can receive up to 170 prisoners. Further repairs and refurbishment are, however, required. It is anticipated that this facility will be partially functional by the end of September 1999. UNMIK civilian police will provide, on an emergency basis, staffing to maintain security at the prison. It is, however, imperative that international prison officers be urgently provided to take on this role.

28. Eighty-two UNMIK police officers have been deployed at the major border crossings with Albania and the former Yugoslav Republic of Macedonia. Officers assigned to UNMIK's Border Police division are currently conducting vehicle checks, as well as control of passports and other personal documents. Joint border patrols with KFOR are being carried out and UNMIK is conducting further surveys to identify border security priorities. Effective border control will be crucial to preventing smuggling and reducing organized crime activities in Kosovo. It is becoming evident that a greater number of border police than initially envisaged will be required to perform these tasks and my Special Representative has recommended an increase in the number of officers from 205 to 364.

29. In addition to 169 unarmed International Police Task Force (IPTF) monitors temporarily transferred from the United Nations Mission in Bosnia and Herzegovina (UNMIBH), UNMIK has deployed over 1,100 civilian police officers from 25 nations. Most of the remaining UNMIK civilian police should be deployed by 15 October 1999. However, even at full deployment, the ratio of police to inhabitants will remain well below the norm of that in other countries. It is clear, therefore, that more international police are needed until sufficient numbers of newly trained Kosovo Police Service officers are available. My Special Representative estimates that a significant increase in the number of civilian police officers may be required. The exact additional requirements are still being determined. Additional human rights and legal advisers are also urgently required within the UNMIK police structure. As regards the Special Police Units, intensive efforts are continuing to ensure their early deployment so that they may provide support for UNMIK civilian police. I hope that Member States will urgently provide the necessary personnel for this task.

30. Development of the future Kosovo Police Service, which will operate under the authority and control of the UNMIK Police Commissioner, is proceeding rapidly through close cooperation between the UNMIK civil administration and the institution-building component led by the Organization for Security and Cooperation in Europe (OSCE). The latter component is responsible for establishing and

managing the Kosovo Police Service training school in Vucitrn, which inducted the first multi-ethnic class of 200 cadets on 7 September 1999. These first 200 cadets were selected from more than 19,500 applicants, 400 of whom were short-listed, interviewed and vetted by UNMIK civilian police and the training school personnel. The recruitment and selection process was fully transparent and extensive consultation with concerned groups and parties was undertaken by the Police Commissioner prior to the final class selection. Unfortunately, despite various confidence-building measures undertaken by UNMIK, Serb cadets remain concerned about their security. Candidates who successfully complete the training school will be deployed for field training under the control of UNMIK civilian police officers starting in mid-October.

D. JUDICIAL AFFAIRS

31. In my previous report, I outlined the organization of the Judicial Affairs Office, including its four areas of responsibility - two in operational areas and two in policy development. The latter two deal with the development of legal policies and the review and drafting of legislation. In view of the interrelationship of these functions with those of the legal adviser to my Special Representative, it has been decided to incorporate these functions within the legal adviser's office. Consequently, the Judicial Affairs Office will focus on operational issues, including the administration of courts, prosecution services and prisons.

32. UNMIK, in consultation with a Joint Advisory Council, has appointed 36 judges and 12 prosecutors on a provisional basis. The majority are Kosovo Albanian, but Serbs, Muslims, Roma and Turks are also represented. Of the seven Serb judges appointed, two have left Kosovo. An Advisory Judicial Commission has been created with the task of recommending suitable candidates for appointment on a permanent basis as judges and prosecutors. A Technical Advisory Commission has also been established to advise UNMIK on the structure and administration of the judiciary and prosecution services and to make recommendations for the establishment of the Supreme Court of Kosovo. Pending the establishment of the Supreme Court, an ad hoc court of appeal will serve as a higher court.

33. A review, conducted by legal experts from the Council of Europe, is under way on four major bodies of law applicable in Kosovo, including the criminal codes, the criminal procedure code and the laws on internal affairs and public peace and order. The review, which will be completed by October 1999, will make recommendations to bring the laws in line with international human rights standards and regulations, resolution 1244 (1999) and UNMIK regulations. Kosovo legal professionals will also participate in the review.

V. Institution-Building

34. The Organization for Security and Cooperation in Europe (OSCE) is in the lead in respect of the institution-building tasks of UNMIK described below.

A. MEDIA AFFAIRS

35. A new public broadcasting service, known as Radio-Television Kosovo, is being developed by the institution-building component. In the interim, Radio Pristina is operating under international supervision and has been broadcasting programmes since 28 June 1999 in the Albanian, Serbian and Turkish languages. A legal framework is currently under preparation for its operations removing it from direct political control. Once this framework is in place, Radio-Television Kosovo will operate under its own management.

B. DEMOCRATIZATION

36. To encourage the development of political parties and to provide support for their activities, political party support centres are being established. These centres will provide telephone, facsimile and computer support, on a shared basis, to all Kosovo political parties. The first five facilities will open in September, with five more to follow in October. In addition, the development of local non-governmental organizations is supported through the coordination of training assistance so that local organizations can improve their project development skills and publicize their activities in a more effective manner. Assistance will also be provided to other representative bodies in Kosovo.

C. HUMAN RIGHTS

37. Human rights monitors, working closely with the humanitarian component and the Office of the United Nations High Commissioner for Human Rights (UNHCHR), are active throughout Kosovo. In several instances, monitors have intervened with the KLA to secure the release of abducted Serbs in Gnjilane and Orahovac. In addition to human rights monitoring, a human rights training unit has been set up to provide training to local human rights organizations. Programmes in monitoring, investigating and reporting on human rights issues and intervention will be conducted. The unit will also coordinate with the Council of Europe and international and local non-government organizations in training local human rights defenders in international standards and mechanisms. Work is also continuing on the establishment of an ombudsman's office. At least 2,000 persons are believed to be missing from or within Kosovo. A focal point for issues related to missing persons has also been established within the institution-building component and works closely with ICRC and the International Commission on Missing Persons. The issue of missing persons is a highly sensitive and important problem for the people of Kosovo and it is being addressed by the Kosovo Transitional Council, which has established a subcommission for this purpose.

D. JUDICIAL ISSUES

38. The institution-building component provides support to the operations of the judicial system. An emergency judicial system was initiated on 30 June 1999 with the opening of the District Court in Pristina. Other courts have been established in Prizren, Pec, Gnjilane and Mitrovica. To supplement these, two mobile courts are in operation, which have, since 2 July 1999, reviewed 248 cases involving 552 persons. The institution-building component is also involved in the selection of judges and prosecutors and has, so far, interviewed 526 individuals, of whom 48 have been selected.

VI. Economic Reconstruction

39. With the European Union (EU) in the lead for the rehabilitation and reconstruction tasks of UNMIK, economic activity in Kosovo has restarted rapidly, even if only partially, in areas such as retail trade, agriculture and basic services. This is, however, insufficient to overcome the effects of conflict and years of neglect and under-investment. As a result, domestic output remains limited and there is the continuing prospect of serious economic hardship for many, which will be compounded by the effects of the coming winter. To encourage external investment, transparent procedures, structures and licensing arrangements, which will also help to undermine organized crime in Kosovo, are being developed.

40. The first priority in economic reconstruction is the resumption of basic public utilities. This has been largely achieved; the most urgent repairs are under way and financing for power sector operations through the winter has been secured. Despite this, the power, water and heating sectors remain highly precarious. Another high priority, the restoration of telecommunications, will require several months to show results.

41. UNMIK has put into place the first of the basic institutions and legal frameworks needed for a normally functioning economy. An economic policy board has been established, co-chaired by the Deputy Special Representative for Reconstruction and an eminent Kosovo economist, and including a broad range of local economic expertise.

42. In the areas of payments and banking, a regulation permitting unrestricted use of foreign currencies in transactions, alongside the Yugoslav dinar, was issued. Work is well advanced in designing a modern payments system and a private banking sector that will both be conducive to economic development and tightly regulated to protect its depositors. The establishment of the basic legal framework for this will be done by regulations approved by my Special Representative, taking into account the recommendations of the economic policy board. This is expected to be completed shortly. Thereafter, the envisaged meas-

ures are designed to make the greatest possible use of existing infrastructure and skills so as to be operational as soon as possible. A basic payments system should be operational shortly and banking activity should begin well before the end of the year.

43. A major milestone in public finance was the establishment of a customs administration and the initiation, in early September 1999, of revenue collection. UNMIK is also developing a Central Fiscal Agency (CFA) that will prepare and implement a provisional Kosovo budget. This exercise is under way in collaboration with the civil administration. It will establish a systematic means of setting spending priorities and matching expenditure to local and donor resources. The Central Fiscal Agency will act to assure international donors that requests for additional funding are based on a solid assessment of requirements and that funds will be allocated through a fully transparent budgetary procedure. Currently, Kosovo's public revenue base consists only of customs and excise duties and sales taxes on imported goods. The introduction of further simple taxes is foreseen for next year in order to ensure that the Kosovo public sector is self-sustaining as soon as possible.

44. UNMIK is developing priorities for reconstruction and an investment framework. The priority areas are housing, infrastructure, agriculture and reviving industry. For the revival of industry, there are two main themes. First, the modernization and reconstruction of existing industry, which will require capital and extensive training. Second, the promotion of new industry, especially small and medium-sized firms, which will require both technical assistance and micro-credit facilities.

VII. Observations

45. UNMIK has made important strides over the past 12 weeks. Today's Kosovo bears little resemblance to that of mid-June 1999; most refugees are home, the informal economy is thriving and efforts are under way to restore law and order as well as security throughout the province. However, Kosovo's future is not yet secured and there remains a threat that these gains might be reversed if UNMIK is unable to address three pressing challenges in the coming weeks and months.

46. First, is the establishment and cementing of the rule of law and the authority of UNMIK. This is essential for the retention of a multi-ethnic Kosovo and for the creation of conditions necessary for those who have left Kosovo to return. The international community must make it clear to extremists that it cannot and will not tolerate ethnically motivated murders and violence. It must also make it clear to the Kosovo political leadership that they must make far greater efforts to restrain and redirect the emotions unleashed by the conflict. The international community must also redouble its own efforts to provide a secure environment, especially for Kosovo's vulnerable minorities. Towards this end, an increase in the UNMIK civilian police strength, rapid deployment of international civilian police officers and the development of the Kosovo Police Service are essential. In the longer term, it will be important to ensure the development of the Service as a pluralistic, multi-ethnic and depoliticized body that enjoys the confidence of all in Kosovo. This will require continuing international involvement through both formal and informal training and support. Equal attention must be paid to the judiciary and the penal system. All bodies must conform to internationally accepted human rights standards in order to enjoy both the confidence and respect of the people of Kosovo.

47. The second pressing priority is the provision of temporary winterized accommodation for the almost 350,000 people in need. Most at risk are those who live in rural or high altitude communities. Most of the damaged and destroyed houses cannot be permanently repaired before winter, nor is it within the scope or capacity of humanitarian agencies to do this work. The emergency rehabilitation programme is thus aimed at ensuring that all residents have at least temporary housing until next spring. Attention must also be directed towards the rehabilitation of public utilities. As winter approaches, Kosovo has only two thirds of its winter electricity requirements and, despite repairs, the electricity system remains fragile. International support is vital. In addition, early planning for longer-term reconstruction and development will be crucial to ensure a smooth transition from the current emergency relief phase. It is essential that humanitarian activities be closely coordinated with those devoted to reconstruction.

48. Third, to ensure the future stability of Kosovo, it is important that the international community ensure the demobilization of the KLA and other armed elements. Sufficient funds and resources should be provided to enable former combatants to find opportunities for employment. Without such support, there is a real threat that former fighters may become an obstacle to the implementation of resolution 1244 (1999) by refusing to disarm or by engaging in criminal activities. Either situation would have negative consequences for the international community's efforts to build a secure, multi-ethnic and democratic society in Kosovo.

49. In addition to the increased security and political measures taken by the international community, it is the establishment of the Kosovo Transitional Council and the active involvement, on a consultative basis, of political and local leaders in the executive functions of UNMIK that is expected to provide the most important confidence-building mechanism in the medium term for the improvement of the overall situation in Kosovo. I strongly encourage all ethnic communities to participate constructively in this body, as the only path to a future political settlement in Kosovo lies in cooperation with UNMIK and adherence to the provisions of resolution 1244 (1999).

50. The support given by the international community to UNMIK has underpinned the Mission's progress. If the gains made are not to be eroded, the international community must continue to offer consistent and long-term political, material and financial support to the Mission. Of critical importance to the Mission's success will be the provision of voluntary contributions to fund the salaries of local public servants and other public activities pending receipt of sufficient monies within the Kosovo budget. I urgently appeal to all Member States to contribute generously to the United Nations trust fund set up for this purpose.

335. Council of Europe, Committee of Ministers, Reply to Recommendation 1414 (1999), 17 September 1999

[Adopted at the 678th meeting of the Ministers' Deputies (8-9 September 1999).]

In replying to Recommendation 1414 (1999) of the Parliamentary Assembly on the crisis in Kosovo and the situation in the Federal Republic of Yugoslavia [paragraph 16.b], the Committee of Ministers draws the Assembly's attention to the following:

As part of the Council of Europe's contribution to the implementation of UN Security Council Resolution 1244, the Committee of Ministers authorised the Secretariat to follow up the planning and implementation of a series of proposals in its specific fields of competence. In this context a Secretariat delegation visited Pristina at the beginning of August to discuss with the various UNMIK branches, the modalities of the Council of Europe contribution.

As regards implementation of the UN Security Council Resolution 1244 on Kosovo, the Council of Europe has already played a very active role in its specific fields of competence. Council of Europe experts have assisted in the drafting of the UN Secretary-General's report to the Security Council of 12 July, in particular in the fields of local administration and organisation of the judiciary. On the basis of the report, the Council of Europe has offered the deployment of several experts on long-term missions to assist UNMIK in the fields of human rights, organisation of the judiciary, local government, civil society, inter alia. A particular attention is paid to the compatibility of the legislation and regulations in Kosovo with European norms. At the request of the Special Representative, a group of Council of Europe experts is examining the compatibility of the applicable penal laws with European norms. Legal advisors appointed by the Council of Europe will occupy significant positions within UNMIK, in particular to assist the newly-created "Joint Advisory Council on Legislative matters". Specific Council of Europe missions have been sent to Kosovo to study the issues of women (in particular victims of rape) and University matters with a view to defining possible Council of Europe action. The Joint UNICEF/Council of Europe project on psycho-social support to children victims of the conflict initiated in Albania in now pursued in Kosovo.

As regards the monitoring of human rights, a training Seminar for human rights NGOs based on the experience in Albania and "the former Yugoslav Republic of Macedonia", took place in Pristina on 17-19 August; discussions are under way concerning the organisation of a Joint Council of Europe/UN High Commissioner for Human rights/OSCE/European Commission training Seminar for human rights monitors in Kosovo. The Council of Europe has proposed several experts to staff the Ombudsman Support Unit set up within UNMIK; in addition a legal expertise of the Ombudsman institution is being organised with the participation of Venice Commission and Council of Europe experts.

Council of Europe experts have been involved from the outset in the various aspects of the organisation of an independent judiciary, including the training of judges; the Council of Europe has offered to UNMIK the placement of several advisers in the field of curriculum development and supervision of the training of judges and prosecutors. In the field of education a Council of Europe delegation visited Pristina in August to examine the situation of the University and to define possibilities of action.

At this stage, the Committee of Ministers has not decided on the possible setting up of a Council of Europe Office in Belgrade; this question could be considered in the more general context of the Council of Europe relations with the Federal Republic of Yugoslavia. However, the Committee of Ministers has authorised the Secretariat to establish an Office in Pristina primarily concerned with the relations and communications with UNMIK. The Pristina Office is operational since 23 August; it has already assisted in the organisation of various missions to Kosovo, including visits by parliamentary delegations.

Finally, as regards the issue of the future status of the Kosovo, the Venice Commission stands ready to assist. An advisor on constitutional matters could be appointed in Pristina for this purpose.

On the separate question of the Stability Pact for South East Europe, the Committee of Ministers, following the endorsement of its own Stability Programme at the Ministerial Session in Budapest on 7 May 1999, has fixed the general lines of its contribution to the Stability Pact for South East Europe. This contribution was presented at the Summit of the Pact in Sarajevo on 30 July 1999. Discussions are under way concerning the structure of the different working tables, in particular as regards Working Table I (Democratisation and Human rights) and its Chairmanship.

336. Council of Europe, Parliamentary Assembly, Recommendation 1422 (1999), Southeastern Europe Following the Kosovo Conflict: Political Situation, 23 September 1999

[Extract from the Official Gazette of the Council of Europe - September 1999. Text adopted by the Assembly on 23 September (30th Sitting).]

1. The Assembly welcomes the recognition in the Sarajevo Summit declaration of 30 July 1999 of the Council of Europe's important role in the implementation of the Stability Pact for Southeastern Europe.

2. The Assembly welcomes the appointment of Mr Max Van der Stoel, current OSCE High Commissioner on National Minorities, and a former outstanding member of the Parliamentary Assembly of the Council of Europe, as Chairman of the Stability Pact's Working Table 1 on democratisation and human rights. To emphasise the Council of Europe's particular responsibility in this field, it should be ensured that a person nominated by the Council of Europe be closely associated with the Chairman.

3. The Assembly recalls that its Political Affairs Committee will organise a conference on the parliamentary contribution to the Stability Pact in Sofia on 26 November 1999.

4. The Assembly reiterates its position that the basis for the normalisation of the situation in Kosovo should be full and strict implementation of the United Nations Security Council Resolution 1244 and considers the establishment of normal conditions for the operation of all components of KFOR as an important prerequisite for the progress of the political settlement.

5. As regards the Kosovo conflict, while understanding the gravity of the events that may have provoked it, the Assembly strongly condemns the organised and systematic violence against the remaining Serb and Roma populations, and other minority groups, and the continuing criminal destruction of Orthodox cultural heritage. The United Nations civil police should become fully operational as soon as possible. Regrouping of the population at risk for security reasons should not lead to permanent segregation.

6. The Assembly again calls on the Kosovo Liberation Army (KLA) to comply with KFOR's demand for its disarmament. It further calls on all Kosovo Albanian political forces to publicly and unequivocally condemn violence against Serbs, Roma and other minority groups.

7. The Assembly considers that there is a genuine need to establish democratically elected local institutions by next summer. However, it is essential that all ethnic groups can participate in free and fair local elections.

8. The Assembly fully supports the setting up of a training institute to train future administrative staff in Kosovo, to which the Council of Europe could make a major contribution through its experience and know-how in the field of local democracy.

9. The Assembly believes that lasting peace and democratic stability in the area can only be achieved if appropriate cultural and educational policies are rapidly put in place. These should exclude ethnic hatred and promote democratic values, respect for human rights and cultural difference. The reconstruction of civil society, with special reference to young people, is just as important as the reconstruction of cultural heritage.

10. The Assembly welcomes the recent opening of a Council of Europe office in Pristina. The office should be given maximum political and material support to enable it to ensure an appropriate and effective Council of Europe contribution to the work of the United Nations Mission in Kosovo. An early visit by the new Secretary-General to Pristina would be a clear demonstration of such support.

11. The Assembly further welcomes the detailed proposals concerning the Council of Europe's contribution to UNMIK, notably as regards human rights standards as well as local government, police, judicial, and media issues. In this respect, the Assembly emphasises the paramount importance of rendering the standards contained in the European Convention on Human Rights and relevant case-law directly applicable in Kosovo.

12. The Assembly again expresses its support for all democratic forces in the Federal Republic of Yugoslavia and urges them to work together more closely.

13. The Assembly endorses the recent decision of the European Union to lift sanctions against Kosovo and Montenegro. While supporting international pressure on the Yugoslav authorities to meet democratic standards, it considers that the oil embargo against Serbia should also be lifted for political and humanitarian reasons.

14. International assistance to meet the basic needs of the Serbian people, including energy, should be provided, with any consequent necessary adjustments to sanctions. Further hardship, especially during the coming winter, would only weaken the democratic forces and consolidate the position of the current regime in Belgrade.

15. The Assembly expresses its support for the policy and democratic reforms of the Government of Montenegro. Immediate large-scale economic assistance is essential if popular support for these policies is to be strengthened.

16. The Assembly takes note of the proposals by the Montenegrin authorities to redefine the constitutional framework of the Federal Republic of Yugoslavia. It welcomes the decision of the Montenegrin authorities to consult the Council of Europe's Venice Commission on their proposals.

17. For these reasons, the Assembly:

a. resolves:

i. to set up task forces:

- to assist forthwith the electoral process in Kosovo;
- to support co-operation between the political parties in Kosovo;
- to contribute to the work of the new local institutions;
- to work on the reconstruction of the educational system;

ii. to strengthen dialogue with the democratic forces in the Federal Republic of Yugoslavia.

b. recommends that the Committee of Ministers:

i. welcome, on behalf of the Organisation, the chairmanship of Mr Van der Stoel of Working Table 1 of the Stability Pact and request that a person nominated by the Council of Europe be closely associated with the Chairman;

ii. draw up proposals for action in the fields of culture, education - in particular history teaching - and the media for immediate implementation in Kosovo and, more generally, in the area as a whole;

iii. as regards Kosovo, ensure that the Council of Europe's proposals for assistance to the United Nations Mission in Kosovo (UNMIK) be given adequate political support, also through the representatives of Council of Europe member states at the United Nations;

iv. ensure Council of Europe involvement in the process of voter registration for the future local elections in Kosovo;

v. increase its political, financial and technical support for effective and concrete action to be undertaken by the Council of Europe office in Pris?tina;

vi. open similar Council of Europe offices in Podgorica and Belgrade.

337. The Kosovo Protection Corps, Commander Kosovo Force's Statement of Principles, 23 September 1999

The members of the Kosovo Protection Corps will act in accordance with the United Nations Security Council Resolution 1244(1999) of 10 June 1999.

The members of the Kosovo Protection Corps will act in accordance with the Undertaking of Demilitarisation and Transformation by the UCK offered on 21 June 1999.

The Members of the Kosovo Protection Corps are resolved to provide a disciplined and effective emergency service.

They therefore agree to this Statement of Principles.

Article 1: Purpose

1. The Kosovo Protection Corps is to provide assistance to the United Nations Mission In Kosovo in the event of natural disaster or similar emergency, in the reconstruction of the Kosovo civilian infrastructure and other assistance as may from time to time be requested by the United Nations Mission In Kosovo.

2. The Kosovo Protection Corps is consistent with the process outlined in the Undertaking on Demilitarisation and Transformation signed on 21 June 1999.

3. *Mission*. The Kosovo Protection Corps shall be the only multidisciplinary, multi-ethnic, indigenous emergency service agency that will undertake to:

a. Respond to any disaster affecting the population and territory of Kosovo.

b. Conduct search and rescue operations.

c. Assist in rebuilding the infrastructure and community of Kosovo.

d. Provide assistance to the United Nations Mission in Kosovo and Kosovo Force when required.

e. Perform ceremonial duties.

in order to serve all the people of Kosovo in keeping with the transition to a democratic and free society.

4. The Mission of the Kosovo Protection Corps may only be changed by the Special Representative of the Secretary General.

Article 2: Principles

1. The Kosovo Protection Corps in pursuit of the purpose stated in Article 1 of this Statement of Principles, shall act in accordance with the following principles:

a. The Kosovo Protection Corps will exist to serve all of the people of Kosovo. It will be politically neutral, and its members will neither serve in public office nor hold any office or positions in political parties whether voluntary or paid.

b. The Kosovo Protection Corps shall comply with internationally recognised human rights agreements in all aspects including recruitment, retention, career progression and in the activities of the Kosovo Protection Corps. There shall be no discrimination against any person on grounds of race, sex, colour, language, religion, political or other opinion, national or ethnic or social origin or association with a national community, property, birth or other status.

c. Nothing contained in this Statement of Principles shall authorise or permit the Kosovo Protection Corps to intervene or concern itself with, as an organisation or through its membership, any matter other than those specified in this Statement of Principles.

d. Any member of the Kosovo Protection Corps who breaches the principles and regulations contained in this Statement of Principles or the United Nations Mission in Kosovo Regulation 1999/8 may be dismissed from the Corps and may be subject to criminal prosecution.

e. Members of the Kosovo Protection Corps may only operate outside the boundaries of the Province of Kosovo with the authority of the Special Representative of the Secretary General.

Article 3: Composition

1. The strength of the Kosovo Protection Corps will be about 5000 members, of which 3000 will be permanent members and the remainder reserve members. Up to 100 locally employed personnel may also be employed.

2. Recruiting to the Kosovo Protection Corps will be on an individual basis and will be carried out by the Kosovo Force and the Kosovo Protection Corps transitional leadership under the authority of the Special Representative of the Secretary General. A significant portion of the Kosovo Protection Corps will initially come from the leadership and ranks of the demilitarised UCK and the remainder from the civilian population at large.

3. The Kosovo Protection Corps is to be recruited and based on multi-ethnic, non-sectarian principles. No specific religious, ethnic or gender quotas will be applied; however, continued international support will depend upon continued evidence of an organisation that mirrors the Province's ethnic balance.

4. Every member of the Kosovo Protection Corps will wear a uniform; the pattern of the uniform and its badges and emblems will be in accordance with that which has been approved by the Commander Kosovo Force. The official badge of the Kosovo Protection Corps is at Annex D. Members of the Kosovo Protection Corps may not wear any other form of uniform. They may wear their uniforms whilst off duty and at home if they so wish; however, any evidence of misuse of this privilege will result in the uniform only being worn on duty.

5. The Kosovo Protection Corps will issue an identification card of an approved design to every member of the Kosovo Protection Corps under the supervision of the Commander Kosovo Force. This identification card must be carried at all times.

Article 4: Command Status

1. Commander Kosovo Force will exercise day to day supervision of the Kosovo Protection Corps within the framework of the Mission.

2. No formed body of the Kosovo Protection Corps may be used outside its regional boundaries without the express permission of the Commander Kosovo Force.

3. Commander Kosovo Protection Corps will employ the Corps in accordance with Commander Kosovo Force's direction.

4. Commanders of the Kosovo Force multinational brigades will exercise supervision over and, consistent with the requirements of a secure environment, provide security for any tasking of the Kosovo Protection Corps within their areas. Multinational brigades will provide assistance to operational deployments of the Kosovo Protection Corps within means and capabilities.

Article 5: Organisation

1. The Kosovo Protection Corps is to consist of one Central Headquarters, six regional headquarters and task groups, one Guard and Rapid Reaction Group, seven central support or service support group sincluding Communications, Engineer, Environmental and Chemical Protection, Air Search and Rescue, Medical, Transport and Supply, and Maintenance, and two training colleges. The structure of the Kosovo Protection Cods is shown at Annex A to this Statement of Principles. Changes to this structure can only be authorised by the Special Representative of the Secretary General.

2. The Kosovo Force will, within means and capabilities, provide Training and Advisory Teams to the Kosovo Protection Corps, at its Central Headquarters and six regional headquarters.

3. The administrative locations for the key components of the Kosovo Protection Corps may not be changed without the authority of Commander Kosovo Force.

Article 6: Training and Assistance

1. All training for the Kosovo Protection Corps will be planned by Commander Kosovo Protection Corps and will be approved by Commander Kosovo Force.

2. All aid, equipment and assistance provided to the Kosovo Protection Corps by the International Community must be authorised by the Special Representative of the Secretary General and Commander Kosovo Force.

3. The Kosovo Protection Corps will maintain liaison links with other public service organisations such as the civil fire, police, electricity, water and forestry departments as well as key international humanitarian organisations that could require specialised emergency assistance.

Article 7: Equipment

1. The equipment of the UCK is to be made available for use by the Kosovo Protection Corps. Specific arrangements for weapons are covered in Article 8.1.f.

2. All equipment issued to the Kosovo Protection Corps for the purpose of fulfilling its Mission is to be accounted for at the Kosovo Protection Corps Central Headquarters. Where such equipment is issued down to regional task groups, similar accounting procedures are to be in place.

3. A rolling annual stock take of equipment is to be completed. Quarterly returns are to be submitted to the Deputy Special Representative of the Secretary General for Civil Administration, via the Kosovo Protection Corps chain of command.

Article 8: Self Defence

Every member of the Kosovo Protection Corps has the inherent right of self defence. To clarify this, the following guidelines apply:

a. Every member of the Kosovo Protection Corps who is attacked, or minimum force as is necessary in the circumstances to defend himself.

b. No member of the Kosovo Protection Corps has the right to use force to defend another person, unless the member has been specifically authorised by the Special Representative of the Secretary General to protect that person.

c. Force can never be used unless necessary and then only minimum force can be used.

d. Minimum force can include lethal force but only if life is in imminent danger and no alternative action can be taken.

e. No member of the Kosovo Protection Corps will be permitted to carry arms of any kind unless authorised to do so by the Special Representative of the Secretary General.

f. 2000 weapons in total are held in trust for the Kosovo Protection Corps. 200 will be in use at any one time for:

(a) Guarding of installations.

(b) Security when units are deployed.

Issuance of these weapons will be specifically authorised by Commander Kosovo Force and their use by the Kosovo Protection Corps will be in accordance with Kosovo Force guidelines.

g. The remaining 1800 weapons held for the Kosovo Protection Corps will be stored within Kosovo Force secure weapons facilities to which authorised Kosovo Protection Corps members will have privileged access in order to exercise joint control.

h. Additionally:

(1) Weapons (sidearms) may be carried by authorised officers for personal protection, as authorised by the Commander Kosovo Force, using his delegated authority from the UNMIK Police Commissioner. Such authorisations will be limited to a period of one year and will be subject to review at the Special Representative of the Secretary General's discretion.

(2) Ceremonial units will carry de-commissioned bolt action weapons.

(3) Close protection units will carry sidearms or automatic short barrelled weapons for close protection of key members of the Kosovo Protection Corps.

i. Weapons will be made available to the Kosovo Protection Corps for training.

Article 9: Supplemental Arrangements

1. The Special Representative of the Secretary General shall make such supplemental arrangements to this Statement of Principles which may from time to time be required. When concluded, such arrangements will be annexed to and shall form part of this Statement of Principles and shall have the same force and effect as this Statement of Principles.

Article 10: Amendments

1. Any part of this Statement of Principles may be amended or modified by the Special Representative to the Secretary General.

(signed) M D Jackson, Lieutenant General, Commander Kosovo Force

Accepted By: (signed), Agim Çeku, Lieutenant General

[The Annexes A. Authorised Structure of the Kosovo Protection Corps, B. Kosovo Protection Corps Key Tasks, C. Kosovo Protection Corps Locations, D. Kosovo Protection Corps Official Badge have been omitted.]

338. UN, Report of the Secretary-General on the United Nations Interim Administration Mission in Kosovo, UN Doc. S/1999/1250, 23 December 1999

I. Introduction

1. The present report is submitted pursuant to Security Council reso-

establish the United Nations Interim Administration Mission in Kosovo (UNMIK) for an initial period of 12 months. In paragraph 20 of that resolution, the Council requested me to report at regular intervals on the implementation of the mandate of UNMIK. The current report covers the activities of UNMIK and developments in Kosovo, Federal Republic of Yugoslavia, since my last report of 16 September (S/1999/987).

II. Overview

2. During the reporting period, UNMIK made progress in involving the population of Kosovo in the provisional administration of the province. The agreement on the establishment of a Kosovo-UNMIK Joint Interim Administrative Structure was an important step in this direction. During the period, the process of demilitarization of the Kosovo Liberation Army (KLA) by KFOR was completed and the process of transforming former soldiers commenced. The establishment of the Kosovo Protection Corps (KPC) was instrumental in this regard. Several encouraging steps were also taken to establish democratic and unified political movements. At the same time, the number of attacks on Kosovo Serbs and other ethnic minorities remained high and continued to be the overriding human rights issue in Kosovo.

A. Political Situation

3. The Kosovo Transitional Council (KTC) continued to meet on a weekly basis under the chairmanship of my Special Representative. However, the Kosovo Serb representatives on the Council, Bishop Artemije and Mr. Trajkovic, withdrew from the body on 22 September in protest at the establishment of KPC, which they view as the KLA in disguise, and the deteriorating security situation. Furthermore, Mr. Veton Surroi has stated that he was withdrawing from the political field in general and Mr. Thaci also temporarily suspended his participation in KTC. KTC has, however, continued to convene with Kosovo Albanian, Bosniac and Turkish participation. The Kosovo Serb representatives are being provided with the minutes of all Council meetings and my Special Representative maintains contact with them with the aim of bringing them back into KTC. At the same time, the Joint Security Committee has kept its regular schedule of weekly meetings with Kosovo Serb participation.

4. As mentioned in my last report (S/1999/987), UNMIK has also established other consultative mechanisms through which the local population and leadership have been able to participate in the decision-making of the interim administration by providing expert guidance and advice to UNMIK on specific issues, for example in the fields of legislative matters, humanitarian affairs, economic policy, health, education, energy and public utilities. Further efforts will be made to ensure that these forums encompass all relevant groups within Kosovo and include women, who are currently inadequately represented.

5. In a significant development on 15 December, the leaders of the Kosovo Democratic Progress Party (PPDK), the Democratic League of Kosovo (LDK) and the United Democratic Movement (LDB) agreed to participate in the establishment by UNMIK of a Kosovo-UNMIK Joint Interim Administrative Structure. The structure, which will respect resolution 1244 (1999) and the executive and legislative authority of my Special Representative, will involve all communities of Kosovo in the provisional administration. It will be composed of an Interim Administrative Council which will make recommendations for amendments to the Applicable Law and for new regulations, as well as propose policy guidelines for Administrative Departments in applying the Applicable Law. The Administrative Departments will perform the administrative tasks to implement the policy guidelines formulated by the Interim Administrative Council. At the municipal level, administration will be entrusted to an Administrative Board appointed and headed by the UNMIK Municipal Administrator.

6. Under the 15 December agreement, KTC will maintain its consultative role and will be enlarged to better reflect the pluralistic nature of Kosovo's population. If a majority of the KTC members disagree with a decision or position of the Interim Administrative Council, it will be able to propose a different solution to my Special Representative, who shall take the final decision. Finally, as part of the agreement, all parallel structures within Kosovo are to be transformed and progressively integrated, to the extent possible, into the Joint Administrative Structure.

7. Since my previous report, there has been a consolidation of the representation of the Kosovo Albanian and Kosovo Serb political parties. On 14 October, the two main political figures of the former KLA joined forces and announced the formation of the Kosovo Democratic Progress Party (PPDK). Mr. Thaci will serve as President. Mr. Mahmuti, the former head of the Party of Democratic Unity (PBD), was named as one of the two Vice-Presidents and Mr. Kuci, the former international relations officer of the parallel Albanian university in Pristina, was named as the other. Two major political parties now dominate the Kosovo Albanian political scene, the new PPDK and the Democratic League of Kosovo (LDK), headed by Dr. Rugova. Both parties have engaged in extensive efforts to gain influence among the local population and to establish a presence throughout Kosovo.

8. A Kosovo Serb National Council (SNC) was established on 18 October, spearheaded and chaired by Bishop Artemije. Mr. Trajkovic was elected Chairman of the Executive Council of SNC. Some local Kosovo Serb leaders, primarily those from Mitrovica, have yet to join the Council. SNC has criticized both KFOR and UNMIK for the precarious security situation facing Kosovo Serbs, but vowed to continue cooperation with the international presence in Kosovo. SNC has also expressed its opposition to the current leadership of the Federal Republic of Yugoslavia, whose authorities' influence has increased among some parts of the Kosovo Serb population, primarily owing to the persisting lack of security. UNMIK continues to maintain contacts with the Federal Republic of Yugoslavia through regular meetings with its Committee for Cooperation in Kosovo.

B. Demilitarization and Transformation of the KLA

9. As indicated in my previous report (S/1999/987), demilitarization of the KLA was scheduled to be completed by 19 September. In order to ensure an effective demilitarization process, KFOR, in close consultation with my Special Representative, developed a concept for demobilization which offered individual members of the KLA an opportunity to participate in a disciplined, professional, multi-ethnic civilian emergency corps. The proposal to create a Kosovo Protection Corps (KPC) was an integral part of the demobilization process and was an essential factor in securing support for the demilitarization of the KLA.

10. Demilitarization of the KLA was successfully completed on 20 September with the signing of UNMIK regulation No. 1999/8, which authorized the establishment of KPC, and the issuance of a "Statement of Principles" by the Commander of KFOR. Under regulation No. 1999/8, KPC will operate under the authority of my Special Representative while KFOR will provide day-to-day operational direction to the Corps in accordance with policies and priorities established by my Special Representative. KPC, which will consist of up to 3,000 active and 2,000 reserve members, will not have any role in law enforcement or the maintenance of law and order. It will be used exclusively for civil emergencies, search and rescue, demining projects and rebuilding infrastructure and housing. At least 10 per cent of both active and reserve members shall comprise individuals from minority groups.

11. During the reporting period, recruitment for KPC was, with the concurrence of UNMIK, initiated by the International Organization for Migration (IOM). Potential candidates were provided with cards identifying them as applicants for KPC and an extensive screening process of all applicants, involving police checks, was initiated. Provisional KPC headquarters were also identified in each region. In addition, some 1,400 members of the Corps began working on winterization and environmental clean-up projects.

12. Since my previous report, a number of security incidents and crimes have taken place which reportedly involved former members of the KLA and potential members of KPC. In one incident, a large arsenal of weapons was found in the possession of two potential KPC members. Some potential KPC members also attempted to exercise unauthorized and unacceptable police functions.

13. On 9 November, following strong representations by KFOR and UNMIK to Kosovo Albanian leaders about reports of participation of

former KLA members and potential KPC members in criminal activity, the provisional Commander of KPC, General Agim Ceku, and the rest of his senior staff issued a written communiqué condemning criminal acts committed by individuals carrying provisional KPC identity cards. The communiqué, which was also published in the local press, encouraged members of the public to notify KPC headquarters of inappropriate behaviour of persons wearing "KPC" uniforms. The communiqué stressed that members of KPC found to be violating the laws or the norms and regulations of KPC would be expelled, and appropriate legal action taken against them. Since then, UNMIK police have arrested several potential KPC members for illegal and criminal activities. In addition, KFOR has carried out a series of raids on former KLA assembly areas and offices as part of a wider campaign to ensure that potential KPC leaders and members understand that there will be no tolerance for unauthorized weapons and criminal activities by Corps members.

14. Following certification by my Special Representative that the necessary funding is available for the establishment and maintenance of the Corps and KFOR confirmation of compliance with the relevant provisions of resolution 1244 (1999), KPC will be formally established by a ceremony to be held in the near future. Both KFOR and UNMIK will ensure that any acts of non-compliance with its mandate will be swiftly and firmly dealt with.

C. SECURITY SITUATION

15. A number of serious security incidents have heightened the tension and security concerns in Kosovo. Such incidents have targeted both the local population and members of the international community. This heightened insecurity was, in a most tragic way, underlined by the murder on 11 October of Valentin Krumov, a newly arrived UNMIK international staff member. A number of members of the international community in Kosovo also appear to have been targeted and subjected to burglary, harassment, intimidation and threats of violence. In addition, Mr. Trajkovic, a member of KTC, was shot through the door of his apartment on 1 November. This incident was the first attack on a senior political representative since the arrival of UNMIK and KFOR in Kosovo.

16. The number of attacks on Kosovo Serbs and members of other ethnic minorities in Kosovo remains high and continues to be the overriding human rights issue in Kosovo. KTC has issued several statements condemning attacks against minorities as well as attacks against political leaders and the incitement of violence through the media. Nevertheless, Serbs, Roma and, increasingly, Slavic Muslims have been the victims of killings, abductions, illegal arrests, arbitrary detentions, beatings, threats and harassment. Ethnic Albanians have also been targeted, on suspicion of collaboration with Yugoslav authorities; because they are in possession of property desired by other members of the local population; or as a result of organized crime. The security situation of women in Kosovo also remains precarious, with an increasing number of abductions of young women.

17. Members of ethnic minorities continue to suffer severe restrictions on their freedom of movement. They also continue to concentrate in areas with other members of their communities and to form ethnic enclaves in which they have more mobility. In Pristina, the estimated remaining 300 to 600 Kosovo Serbs are frightened to go out and are mostly confined to their homes. During the last two months, freedom of movement was impeded on several occasions by roadblocks which were dismantled by KFOR, sometimes with the help of UNMIK police or the local population.

18. A growing number of juveniles have been suspected of committing serious crimes in Kosovo. The province does not yet have a juvenile court or a functioning juvenile detention facility. As a result, a de facto impunity may be developing, as criminal elements are using juveniles, who are not subject to detention, to commit crimes and to harass minorities.

19. There are signs that organized criminal elements are reinforcing their position and activities in Kosovo. These activities appear to include protection rackets, smuggling, extortion, gambling and sale of narcotics. There are also indications of prostitution and trafficking in persons and human organs. The presence of organized crime directly contributes to instability and undermines efforts to establish the rule of law in Kosovo.

D. STATUS OF THE MISSION

20. All components of UNMIK are now better staffed. The Office of my Special Representative now includes a Human Rights Unit and a Gender Unit; the latter will ensure that gender is mainstreamed throughout all UNMIK activities. The Executive Committee, which brings together on a daily basis my Special Representative, his Principal Deputy and the four Deputy Special Representatives heading the four components of UNMIK, has confirmed itself as an important and useful coordination mechanism. Furthermore, the Joint Planning Group (JPG) has been meeting regularly and has promoted and enhanced cross-component coordination across a wide spectrum of policy and operational issues, including transformation of KPC, information management, border control, utilities management and joint UNMIK/KFOR security issues. A working group has been formed, under the supervision of JPG, consisting of planners from the four components, UNMIK police, KFOR and the Office of my Special Representative, which will develop a strategic plan for UNMIK.

III. Humanitarian Affairs

21. The Office of the United Nations High Commissioner for Refugees (UNHCR) is the lead organization for the humanitarian activities of UNMIK. UNHCR cooperates closely with other United Nations partners such as the World Food Programme (WFP), the United Nations Children's Fund (UNICEF) and the World Health Organization (WHO), as well as with the International Organization for Migration (IOM), the International Committee of the Red Cross (ICRC), the International Federation of Red Cross and Red Crescent Societies (IFRC) and over 250 international and 45 local non-governmental organizations (NGOs). A Humanitarian Community Information Centre has been established to facilitate information exchange and coordination.

A. RETURNS

22. At least 810,000 refugees have now returned to their homes in Kosovo. Of these, 110,000 returned in an organized manner, mostly with the assistance of UNHCR and IOM. It is estimated that over 25,500 refugees, including Serbs and Roma, remain in neighbouring countries. Approximately 40 per cent of the 96,000 refugees evacuated from the former Yugoslav Republic of Macedonia under the Humanitarian Evacuation Programme remain in third countries. As of 1 November, the Yugoslav Red Cross and local authorities indicated that the total number of registered internally displaced persons from Kosovo in both Serbia and Montenegro stood at some 243,000. UNHCR is conducting a joint registration exercise with the Federal Republic of Yugoslavia authorities in Montenegro and Serbia, which will verify the number of persons who have left Kosovo. The exercise will be finalized early next year. Out of an estimated 5,000 Croatian and Bosnian refugees present in Kosovo before the North Atlantic Treaty Organization (NATO) air strikes, only some 600 remain.

23. There has been an increase in the number of returns to Kosovo of Kosovo Serbs from Serbia proper and Montenegro. While some returnees are making temporary visits to ascertain whether it is safe enough to return home, others are returning to mono-ethnic villages that are safer than their places of origin in areas of mixed ethnicity. UNHCR is not encouraging returns of minority populations at the current stage as the necessary preconditions, in particular a safe and secure environment, are not yet in place. Efforts are, however, made to ensure that those who do return receive the necessary protection and humanitarian assistance.

B. PROTECTION OF MINORITIES

24. Security concerns, restricted movement, discrimination, lack of access to public services, especially education, medical/health care and pensions have been determining factors in the departure of Kosovo Serbs and other non-Albanian groups from Kosovo.

25. An inter-agency Ad Hoc Task Force on Minorities meets on a weekly basis to coordinate efforts aimed at protecting and assisting minorities. The major challenge is to ensure the physical safety of all residents. Creative methods for increasing security, such as installation of emergency calling devices in homes, reinforcement of doors and the establishment of a hotline between agencies, KFOR and UNMIK police are being implemented. Particular attention has also been paid to promoting unhindered and non-discriminatory access of minorities to food, health care, education and other public services. The Humanitarian component has also designed a special distribution network for needy minority groups, as well as interim systems for providing medical care to minority groups who are otherwise denied access.

26. Other initiatives include facilitating contact between community leaders, organized "go and see" visits for displaced minorities to their home areas and the provision of satellite phones to minorities living in isolated enclaves to enhance communication. Freedom of movement has improved with the commencement in October of a shuttle bus programme, with security provided by KFOR, between minority enclaves and, from these, to destinations outside Kosovo. The programme also permits non-Albanians, many of whom have not been able to leave their homes for security reasons, to meet family and visit doctors and shops. The programme was temporarily suspended after an attack in Pec, on 27 October, on a humanitarian convoy of 155 Kosovo Serbs leaving for Montenegro. Nobody was seriously injured in the incident, but at least 15 cars were burned.

27. In life-threatening situations or particularly vulnerable circumstances, UNHCR has resorted to evacuating minorities to Serbia and Montenegro. Some 487 individuals have so far benefited from this protection measure.

28. Since mid-September, the Civil Administration component has also appointed Civil Affairs Minority Officers to reside on a permanent basis in selected villages/communities in Kosovo. The aim of this initiative is to contribute to a further improvement of security in areas where minorities reside, to extend the provision of essential administrative services and to facilitate access to essential public services. The initiative also aims at facilitating contacts with different local and international actors in support of reconstruction and revitalization of the local economy.

C. SHELTER AND WINTERIZATION

29. The international community has been working on a priority basis to provide emergency housing rehabilitation in Kosovo. As indicated in my last report (S/1999/987, para. 11), the emergency rehabilitation programme is designed to provide at least one warm and dry room for the duration of winter until more sustainable reconstruction may take place in spring. UNHCR, the European Community's Humanitarian Office (ECHO) and the United States Office for Disaster Assistance (OFDA) have distributed over 42,600 (out of 57,100), basic emergency shelter kits. This programme was augmented by the provision of 4,200 UNHCR hard-roofing kits which will support an estimated 12,600 families. OFDA is providing materials for another 5,900 roofs. As a complement to these efforts, UNMIK has, with the support of the Governments of France and Japan, launched a small-scale winterization programme aimed at repairing some 3,000 houses through the provision of building materials and/or cash to house owners selected by municipal housing commissions. The Government of Japan has also funded 500 prefabricated houses, which will be put up in Pec and North Mitrovica.

30. Most of the occupants of the 50,000 houses beyond repair in Kosovo are already living with host families and are expected to remain with them throughout the winter. UNMIK will support a targeted host family assistance programme. UNMIK has also identified temporary community shelters for some 12,000 people as a contingency measure. Over 5,000 homeless people are already living in the shelters. If the range of solutions can be fully applied, the vast majority of the population should be housed during the winter, albeit temporarily.

31. The Humanitarian component and the United States Agency for International Development (USAID) are also distributing 45,000 multi-purpose stoves (for heating and cooking). Other humanitarian actors are distributing additional stoves. The need for stoves this winter should be covered. UNHCR, IOM and ECHO have provided over 87,000 cubic metres of firewood for extremely vulnerable families, and for those who cannot collect firewood because of the risk of mines. UNMIK, together with IOM, is also providing 15,000 cubic metres of firewood and 9,800 tonnes of coal with Japanese funding. WFP and Food-for-Peace have already pre-positioned up to four months of food stocks for villages considered to be inaccessible during winter.

32. The problems faced by organizations bringing humanitarian cargo through the Blace border crossing with the former Yugoslav Republic of Macedonia worsened during the reporting period. Taxes have been levied on trucks transiting that country and cumbersome customs procedures have become time-consuming. As a consequence, there were very long delays for trucks waiting to enter Kosovo, which affected the delivery of food, relief items and shelter material. Concerted efforts have been made to address the situation over the past two months and, following the recent visit of my Special Representative to Skopje, some progress has been achieved in clearing the backlog of vehicles at the border crossing.

D. MINE ACTION

33. There have been over 405 mine-related casualties, including 79 fatalities, since June 1999. As people prepared for the winter, firewood collection has increased the number of casualties. The Mine Action Programme, coordinated by the United Nations Mine Action Coordination Centre, focused on clearing as many mines as possible before winter began. To date, over 16,000 houses and 770 schools have been cleared of mines. In addition, 2,700 cluster bombs, 2,400 anti-personnel mines and over 2,000 anti-tank mines have been cleared from public places. A community-based mine-awareness programme has been established throughout the province, which includes training of mine-awareness educators. A programme has also been established to ensure that victims have access to appropriate medical facilities that can provide immediate care, rehabilitation and psychosocial support.

IV. Civil Administration

34. The United Nations is the lead organization in the civil administration component of UNMIK. Although the Mission is yet to be fully staffed, the critical mass necessary to accomplish all-important tasks is being reached. There are now UNMIK administrators in all 29 municipalities and five regions; their powers have been established by UNMIK regulation No. 1999/14 of 21 October. These administrators form the backbone of UNMIK's work in the regions and municipalities and their presence has enhanced the Mission's credibility as the Interim Administration authority. At the same time, while all efforts are being made to strengthen local administration at the municipal level, the task has not been easy owing to the prevailing ethnic tensions as well as continued acts of violence, intimidation and extortion against minorities.

35. The limited UNMIK presence in the regions and municipalities during the early stages of the Mission has allowed parallel local structures to take root in some areas. These structures, mainly affiliated with the former KLA, are competing with UNMIK for interim administration authority through such illegal activities as tax collection and certification. My Special Representative has taken measures to make it widely known that UNMIK is the only legitimate authority in Kosovo. Additionally, an institutional framework common to all municipalities has been established which includes an administrative body, under UNMIK chairmanship, tasked with carrying out administrative tasks and executing policies and a consultative body ensuring representation of as broad a spectrum of the population as possible. The objective is to incorporate individuals who participate in parallel structures in the municipal administration as well as persons from other political parties and representatives of minorities.

A. SECTORAL DEVELOPMENTS

36. Through the generous contributions of Member States and the efforts of United Nations specialized agencies, funds and programmes

as well as non-governmental organizations, basic health care services in Kosovo have resumed. The Joint Civil Commission on Health, composed of international, Kosovo Albanian and Kosovo Serb representatives, has established task forces on health policy and planning, human resources development, drugs and medical supplies and control of communicable diseases. General policy guidelines to direct primary health care, family practice and nursing education have also been issued by UNMIK.

37. All hospitals in Kosovo are now functioning under the direction of international management teams that were appointed to fill the vacuum created as a result of the departure of the former managers. The immunization programme that was interrupted by the conflict has resumed with the support of the Kosovo Institute of Public Health, WHO, UNICEF and several non-governmental organizations. Steps to implement environmental hygiene (particularly food) control and regulate the import, sale and distribution of drugs have been initiated. Winterization of health facilities, mainly done by NGOs under UNMIK's guidance, is under way.

38. There are currently no multi-ethnic hospitals in Kosovo. UNMIK is engaged in intensive efforts to re-establish such facilities, including in North Mitrovica which is a majority Serb area. These efforts have, however, not yet borne fruit. In the interim, measures have been undertaken, such as the establishment of a surgical unit in the predominantly Kosovo Serb area of Gracanica, in order to improve access to emergency health care for minorities.

39. The school year commenced on 25 October without any major incidents, with the great majority of primary and secondary schools opening, and with over 300,000 children attending. One third of the 700 schools targeted for reconstruction were completed before the first day of the school year. It is expected that the remaining schools will be completed by the end of the year. UNMIK has also commenced payment of stipends to teachers and should shortly complete the printing of textbooks in the Albanian, Serbian, Bosniac and Turkish languages. Humanitarian agencies have provided school equipment and supplies, including 18,000 school desks and 36,000 chairs distributed by UNICEF, and 185,000 school bags, complete with notebooks and writing supplies, supplied by UNHCR and UNICEF. Priorities now include heating for schools and access to education by minority children.

40. The majority of schools in Kosovo are now in Albanian-majority areas. As a result, many Serb and Roma parents have not registered their children at schools owing to security concerns. The widespread inability of ethnic communities to organize schooling for their children in their mother tongue has increased their feeling of insecurity. Once security can be guaranteed, UNMIK will strive to establish integrated schools attended by children of all ethnic groups. Exceptional measures have been taken, including the temporary allocation of the Plementina and Bresje schools to Serb pupils, to ensure access to schooling for Serb pupils.

41. Problems of access continue to plague the University of Pristina and the Faculty of Technology, Metallurgy and Mining in north Mitrovica, the latter being a flashpoint for violent demonstrations.

42. The Joint Civil Commission on Education continues to hold regular meetings, without the participation of Serb representatives, to discuss all education-related matters.

43. The transport sector is in bad repair owing to poor infrastructure, lack of investment and maintenance and some destruction during the conflict. Under the guidance of UNMIK's Kosovo Transport Authority, a task force has been established to form the central structures necessary for the sustainable development of the transport sector. While the European Union will fund urgent repairs to the two major axes, long-term needs for road repairs and rebuilding of bridges will require substantial funding, for a total estimated cost of 170 million euros. Several donors are providing funds to restore and upgrade the long-neglected railway system in Kosovo.

44. On 15 October 1999, Pristina airport opened for limited commercial traffic. Five airlines were granted permission by UNMIK to operate flights. However, following the crash of the WFP plane on 12 November, resulting in the tragic deaths of 24 passengers and crew members, UNMIK and KFOR, in accordance with a preliminary recommendation from the air accident investigation authority, suspended all civilian flights in and out of Pristina on 20 November. UNMIK has contacted the International Civil Aviation Organization (ICAO), among others, for assistance to ensure that the airport meets civilian safety standards. Substantial funding (an estimated 40 million euros) will be needed to upgrade the airport to conform to international standards.

45. UNMIK regulation No. 1999/9 of 24 September established a Fuel Supervisory Board to issue licences for the import, transport, distribution and sale of petroleum products. The regulation was issued so as to secure the reliable provision of fuel to Kosovo; to bring the black market in fuel products under control; to introduce a reasonable amount of competition and investment in the market; and to provide legitimate administration of the two publicly owned fuel companies in Kosovo, Beopetrol and Jugopetrol. Applications for licences will be dealt with once the complex issues relating to publicly owned fuel companies, as well as legal and economic aspects of the issuance of licences, are resolved.

46. Regulation No. 1999/12 of 14 October established the Kosovo Post and Telecommunications (PTK) as a separate juridical entity and authorized it to provide services and provisionally administer the existing telecommunication assets of Telecom Serbia in Kosovo. An initial evaluation of the fixed telephone network has revealed that distribution needs to be restored in most places. Delays in the restoration, however, can be expected owing to difficulties in undertaking outdoor work during the winter.

47. UNMIK has issued an international tender inviting bids for the establishment of a Global System for Mobiles (GSM) in Kosovo. Bids received were reviewed by the Mission and, on 12 November, the Joint Civil Commission on Telecommunications selected a French company, Alcatel, for this purpose. The company will provide telecommunications services in Kosovo within 12 weeks of signing the contract. This decision provoked intense debate in Kosovo and criticism from some personalities, mainly for economic and political reasons. On 17 December, the contract was signed in Paris for the turnkey supply of the GSM network. Under the agreement, Alcatel will install a mobile network with a capacity of 100,000 lines in Kosovo. The first phase of the project should be launched this month and should provide a network for the seven main cities of Kosovo within 12 weeks.

48. The Universal Postal Union (UPU) has consented to UNMIK's issuing of postage stamps, denominated in deutsche mark, in Kosovo. UNMIK postage stamps have been designed and the Government of France has agreed to print the initial requirement free of charge. An agreement of principle has also been reached with UPU on the establishment of an international sorting centre and international routes. The European Union has agreed to provide start-up equipment, including vehicles, workstations and other assorted items. Selected post offices have opened and limited delivery of mail is under way.

49. A policy on agricultural rehabilitation of the farming sector has been prepared with the full participation of local experts and NGOs. Meanwhile, the pig farm component of the Agrokosovo complex in Kosovo Polje is under reactivation, both for agro-industrial considerations and to provide a livelihood to members of the Serb minority.

50. Deforestation has become a major concern in Kosovo as the population has been using firewood to make up for the inadequate electricity supply. UNMIK and the Food and Agriculture Organization of the United Nations (FAO) have developed a two-phased project to address this problem. The first (emergency) phase will organize the firewood supply for the coming winter and launch plans for reforestation and forest control. The second phase will focus on institution-building in agroforestry policy and services, as well as forestry management. However, funding for the project has not yet been secured.

51. UNMIK is scheduled to begin the registration of Kosovo residents in the near future. The legal basis for registration will be included in a regulation now under preparation. Once registered, all eligible

residents will be entered in a central database and will receive an UNMIK-issued, tamper-proof identity card. Compulsory temporary motor vehicle registration began on 30 November 1999, in accordance with UNMIK regulation 1999/15 of 21 October. All motor vehicles will be registered for an initial one-year period with newly designed UNMIK licence plates. The temporary registration will remain in place until a more permanent system is devised. Birth, death and marriage certificates are now being issued, under the UNMIK logo, in all 29 municipalities.

52. UNMIK, in close cooperation with the United Nations Centre for Human Settlements (Habitat), has established a mechanism to regularize residential housing and property rights (regulation No. 1999/23 of 15 November). This includes the establishment of an independent Housing and Property Directorate and a Housing and Property Claims Commission which will perform a variety of functions, including analysing the relevant laws, allocating and administering available housing stock and the settlement of disputes. At the same time, an inventory of all cadastral offices in Kosovo is being carried out as a basis for the development of a new cadastral information system. Meanwhile, regional administrators have been authorized to temporarily allocate vacant housing to homeless people on humanitarian grounds. My Special Representative has also, through regulation No. 1999/10 of 13 October, repealed discriminatory legislation affecting housing and rights to property that were contrary to international human rights standards.

53. Payment of Kosovo public service employees has been a high priority for UNMIK. Pending the introduction of a salary structure, UNMIK decided to pay stipends to eligible public service employees. In order to maintain a level of compensation that could be sustained within limited resources, a three-tier monthly rate structure of DM 300 for executives, DM 200 for professionals and DM 100 for support staff was adopted across the board for all public employees. The programme is expected to continue until the end of the year, at a total cost of some DM 50 million, after which a proper salary structure is expected to be in place. Four rounds of payment are envisaged, each of which involves a payment of over 70,000 stipends amounting to over DM 12 million. Public employees in different sectors have voiced strong dissatisfaction with the amount of the stipend, with some threatening to strike.

B. Judicial Affairs

54. One of UNMIK's priorities has been the establishment of an effective, impartial and independent judiciary. To this end, the Institution-Building and Civil Administration components have worked together closely on the Emergency Judicial System. A total of 572 interviews have been conducted for the local judiciary database. A total of 328 judges and prosecutors and 238 lay judges have been recommended for appointment by the Advisory Judicial Commission. However, the Emergency Judicial System at present has only 47 judges and prosecutors - 41 Kosovo Albanians, 4 Muslims (Bosniac), 1 Roma and 1 Turk - following the resignation of 6 Kosovo Serb judges for security reasons and the departure of another to Serbia. Reportedly, judges, prosecutors and lawyers, particularly those belonging to ethnic minorities, have been threatened. As a result, preserving a multi-ethnic judiciary in Kosovo is becoming increasingly difficult.

55. UNMIK regulation No. 1999/1 of 10 June 1999 provided, inter alia, that the laws in force in Kosovo prior to 24 March 1999 should continue to apply in the province, insofar as they did not contravene internationally recognized human rights standards. The local judicial community has been extremely reluctant to apply these laws, especially Serbian criminal law, which is viewed to have been part and parcel of the revocation of Kosovo's prior autonomous status and an instrument of oppression since then. Judges and prosecutors in Kosovo have interpreted regulation No. 1999/1 to include laws in force until March 1989. Given the acute and urgent need for functioning courts, my Special Representative determined that regulation 1999/1 should be amended so as to give explicit legal validity to the practices followed by the courts.

56. Accordingly, regulations Nos. 1999/24 and 1999/25 were adopted on 12 December 1999. In essence, these regulations state that the applicable law in Kosovo will be the regulations promulgated by the Special Representative, including subsidiary rules, and the law in force in Kosovo on 22 March 1989. Federal law will continue to apply in any situation governed neither by UNMIK regulations nor the law in force in Kosovo as at 22 March 1989. This includes the law of criminal procedure. Serbian law will apply only in rare cases where the applicable law or Federal law fails to cover a given situation or subject matter. In no case will laws be applied that contravene, in any aspect, internationally recognized standards of human rights.

57. In criminal trials, the defendant will have the benefit of the most favourable provision in the laws in force in Kosovo between 22 March 1989 and the date of issuance of the new regulation. This accords with section 7 of the European Convention for the Protection of Human Rights and Fundamental Freedoms. A transitional provision has also been included to ensure that legal actions taken under UNMIK regulation No. 1999/1 remain valid.

58. Two teams of penal management experts have completed a comprehensive assessment of the requirements for the nine detention centres located in Pristina, Lipljan, Pec, Prizren, Gnjilane, Istok, Mitrovica, Camp Bondsteel and Smahozina. These centres are currently being run by KFOR, with the exception of those at Pristina and Mitrovica, which are operated by UNMIK police, and the detention centre in Prizren, which was transferred to the UNMIK Kosovo Correctional Service on 29 November. The detention centres at Istok and Lipljan will come under civilian control early next year. The remaining facilities will follow throughout the year.

59. Former local employees of the correctional facilities, including wardens and correctional officers, will form the basis for the re-establishment of the Kosovo Correctional Service. These staff will function under the supervision of international experts. Training of selected staff for ISTOK prison began on 30 November at the Kosovo Police Service School.

60. As UNMIK assumes temporary responsibilities for the management and security of detention centres, it will need material resources to ensure that the basic humanitarian needs of the detainees are met and that their basic human rights are respected. However, current resource levels are already strained and will become further stretched as KFOR hands over primary detention authority to UNMIK in additional areas of Kosovo.

C. UNMIK Police

61. The ability of UNMIK to effectively address the law and order challenge in Kosovo is dependent on an early and full deployment of international police officers. In this regard, in the addendum to my previous report (S/1999/987/Add.1), I recommended that the number of United Nations police officers in UNMIK be increased to 4,718. The Security Council took note of my recommendation. In the light of the continued precarious security situation in Kosovo, my Special Representative has emphasized the urgency of bringing the UNMIK police to its full strength as soon as possible in order to improve both the law and order and the human rights situation in the province.

62. As of 13 December, there were only 1,817 UNMIK police in the mission area, including 149 border police deployed at international border crossings and at Pristina airport. Also included in the total number are 78 civilian police transferred from the United Nations Mission in Bosnia and Herzegovina (UNMIBH), all of whom have now been authorized by their Governments to participate in UNMIK under its executive policing mandate. Owing to logistic and other constraints, none of the 10 formed Special Police units have yet arrived in the mission area. Two special police companies, out of a total authorized strength of 10 companies, are now expected to arrive in January.

63. UNMIK police have now assumed full law-enforcement authority in the Pristina and Prizren regions. In Mitrovica, Gnjilane and Urosevac municipality, they have assumed full investigative responsibility. UNMIK police also manage the Mitrovica detention centre and

operate 39 police stations, five border police stations (including the airport), five regional headquarter facilities and the main police headquarters. Plans are under way for the establishment of 21 police substations throughout Kosovo. At present, some 70 per cent of the Kosovo population lives in areas in which UNMIK police have assumed law-enforcement responsibility.

64. Crime statistics are now being tracked and maintained in conjunction with KFOR as well as autonomously by UNMIK police. KFOR and UNMIK police are working at the political and operational levels to address the issue of illegal police stations, illegal detention facilities and persons illegally acting in a law-enforcement capacity. In addition, UNMIK police, in close coordination with KFOR, are preparing mechanisms for enhancing criminal intelligence and combating organized crime in Kosovo.

65. UNMIK's current policing resources are being stretched by the multiple non-police tasks which police officers are required to fulfil in the absence of other appropriate personnel. These tasks include guarding of official buildings and detention facilities and providing escorts to large money transfers within Kosovo. The lack of equipment and logistic support for UNMIK police also continues to hamper many crucial policing functions, particularly in the areas of forensic analysis and information management systems.

66. In view of the current operational constraints facing UNMIK police and in order to successfully establish law and order and gain the confidence of the Kosovo public, it has become imperative that a larger number of Kosovo Police Service officers be assigned as soon as possible to work for the UNMIK police. Having analysed numerous options, including the possibility of speeding up the basic training of cadet officers of the Kosovo Police Service, UNMIK police are now developing plans to recruit a significant number of former Kosovo police officers expelled by the Federal Government in 1989 and 1990. These officers will receive specially designed and focused training in democratic policing standards and human rights which will allow them to be deployed on an accelerated basis. In this way, it is hoped that the number of Kosovo Police Service officers working under UNMIK command can be substantially increased in the relatively near future.

67. The success of UNMIK police, as part of the overall justice system, will, however, remain dependent on the establishment of an effective, impartial and independent judiciary. The continuing absence of functioning courts in Kosovo seriously hampers the effectiveness of UNMIK police, and diminishes public confidence in them. It is hoped that the recent appointment of 400 judges and the decision on the applicable law will improve the effectiveness of the functioning judicial system.

V. Institution Building

68. The Organization for Security and Cooperation in Europe (OSCE) is the lead organization in the institution-building tasks of UNMIK. The Institution-Building component has a total of 14 field offices throughout Kosovo and five regional centres.

A. DEMOCRATIZATION

69. A Political Party Service Centre designed to promote the development of mature, democratic political parties in Kosovo was opened in Pristina on 6 October. The Centre currently provides offices for 13 political parties and one coalition. The parties have welcomed this initiative and most of them have taken possession of their offices and started their regular work. Preparations are under way for the opening of political party service centres in the regions. Besides working with political parties, the Democratization Department has cultivated contacts with a wide range of representatives of NGOs and other members of civil society in Kosovo. A development programme for local NGOs is in place which includes material and logistical support as well as capacity-building and the improvement of fund-raising abilities.

B. HUMAN RIGHTS

70. Human rights violations against minorities, in particular Kosovo Serbs, have continued, including killings, abductions, threats, beatings, discrimination in access to basic public services and grenade attacks against property. Reports of abduction of ethnic Serbs seem to have declined, although this may be linked to the general trend of diminishing Serb populations in areas with a Kosovo Albanian majority. Most of the missing-person cases reported since the end of the conflict have not been solved. Since my last report, five Serbs from the Serb quarter in Orahovac were reported missing on their way to the Montenegrin border after they stopped in Djakovica; another 49-year-old Serb man was reported missing by his wife; a Serb was reportedly kidnapped at the Mitrovica battery factory; and in Gracanica, the body of a Serb male who had been missing since 28 October was found on 4 November.

71. Particularly disturbing is the persistent targeting of the elderly. On 31 October, in Prizren, a 79-year-old Serb man was badly beaten in front of his house near the United Nations building. UNMIK police arrested two suspects in connection with this attack. A similar incident took place on 2 November when a 60-year-old Serb woman was beaten by young Kosovo Albanians. In September, a 95-year-old man was found killed in his house, bound and gagged. Two Serb women in their eighties were brutally beaten in the Zupa region in October. In the Gnjilane area, a 72-year-old Serb man reported that he had been threatened with a knife and severely beaten by a group of six Albanians near the village of Donja Bitinja. Again in the Zupa region, seven elderly Serbs, the last residents of their village, had to abandon their homes and flee to the security of the Orthodox seminary in Prizren.

72. Roma and Muslim Slavs also suffer abuses. Both communities face accusations by Kosovo Albanians of having collaborated with the Serb authorities during the conflict. Three bodies, believed to be Roma, were found in a trash dump in a village near Podujevo on 25 October, apparently killed "execution style". In Djakovica, a hand grenade was thrown inside a Roma house, killing one female and seriously injuring another. In Prizren, two unidentified bodies, allegedly Roma, were found. Two Roma women were raped in Prizren, allegedly by an Albanian male. Three Roma houses were burned down in Urosevac. Elsewhere, four grenades were thrown into the compounds of Slavic Muslims in Dragash in a single eight-day period in October. In Pec, a Muslim Slav male was killed and another wounded by unknown perpetrators. In a separate incident, a Muslim Slav boy was killed after Kosovo Albanians accused his family of burning their houses during the war. A Muslim Slav and a Kosovo Albanian were reportedly detained and beaten at a self-proclaimed "KLA police station" in Pec.

73. Kosovo Albanians have also been the target of violence and intimidation. A local leader of the Democratic League of Kosovo (LDK) in Srbica was killed "execution style" after he was abducted on 2 November by unknown perpetrators. Other recent incidents of intimidation and harassment against moderates or followers of LDK may indicate growing inter-Albanian political tension.

74. The beating to death of a woman by her husband on 28 October also highlighted the problem of domestic violence in Kosovo. This issue, as well as the trafficking of women for prostitution, have been identified by grass-roots organizations as one of the main problems affecting women in Kosovo.

75. Arson and grenade attacks against the property of minorities and their cultural symbols also continued to be reported. In Gnjilane, a grenade was launched towards an Orthodox church on 4 November. The explosion injured a Serb man and damaged a nearby house. On 8 November, an Orthodox church in Gornja Zakut, in the region of Pristina, was destroyed in an arson attack.

76. At least five people were killed and dozens injured during the weekend of 27 to 28 November, which marked celebrations of "Albanian Flag Day". In some areas, the situation deteriorated significantly, resulting in violent attacks against Kosovo Serbs. In Prizren, four Serb homes were burned during the weekend. In Pristina, three elderly Kosovo Serbs were assaulted by a large crowd. The man was shot dead and the two women were severely beaten. In yet another serious incident on 17 December, unidentified persons opened automatic weapon fire on the patrons of a Serb café in the Serb quarter of Orahovac and threw hand grenades into the café before fleeing the scene. Eight Serbs

were wounded in the attack, one of whom subsequently died from his injuries.

77. The issue of Kosovo Albanians detained in Serbian prisons remains a major concern. An ICRC civilian prison census confirmed that 1,970 Kosovo Albanians were officially held. Unconfirmed reports indicate that some people may be detained at military installations. The Kosovo Transitional Council Commission on Prisoners and Detainees, composed of Kosovo Albanian and Kosovo Serb human rights lawyers and advocates, met four times since the beginning of October. The Commission, which is chaired by the Office of the United Nations High Commissioner on Human Rights, is working towards the resolution of all cases concerning those deprived of their liberty, including Kosovo Albanian detainees, who were transferred to prisons in Serbia, and on behalf of those who have reportedly been kidnapped or abducted, or have been registered as missing in Kosovo since February 1998, including Kosovo Serbs. Some 300 Kosovar Albanian prisoners have been released by the Belgrade authorities since the summer. However, there is growing concern at reports that some prisoners are being released after paying prison officials or other intermediaries in Serbia.

78. On 6 December, the Institution-Building component (OSCE) released two reports documenting human rights violations in Kosovo before and after the arrival of KFOR and UNMIK. The documents generated great interest and showed that the human rights situation in the province needs careful monitoring. On 10 and 11 December, the Institution-Building component organized and held the first International Human Rights Conference in Pristina. The Conference, which was well received, coincided with International Human Rights Day and provided members of all ethnic communities in Kosovo with the opportunity to discuss their situation and problems with leading international experts.

C. RULE OF LAW

79. The Rule of Law Division includes a Legal Community Support Section which aims to identify the needs of the legal community. The section has already identified relevant actors within the community, on both local and international levels. Although several local initiatives to organize Kosovo lawyers have been taken, there does not yet exist an operational consolidated Kosovo Bar Association.

80. The Council of Europe has completed its review of certain criminal laws and codes applicable in Kosovo. It has recommended that certain provisions be suspended and that others be amended, so as to be compatible with internationally recognized human rights standards. At the invitation of the Council, members of the Joint Advisory Council on Legislative Matters and a representative of UNMIK met with international experts in Strasbourg on 28 and 29 October to discuss cooperation in the area of legal reform in Kosovo. After the meeting, the Committee of Ministers of the Council of Europe decided that the Council should make its experts available to provide training in the field of law in support of and in coordination with UNMIK.

81. Training symposia were held in Pristina for the newly appointed local judges, prosecutors and defence counsel. The symposia, which included Kosovo Serb participants, provided an opportunity to discuss a wide variety of issues with international experts. These judicial training efforts were made possible through collaboration with the Council of Europe, the American Bar Association and staff of other UNMIK components. The symposia are the first stage of a plan to establish a permanent Judicial Training Institute, with an international director.

82. Representatives of the International Tribunal for the Former Yugoslavia attended the training symposia, during which issues such as local prosecution of war crimes were also addressed. As a result of the interest expressed by Kosovo judges and prosecutors, the judicial training section is now preparing a seminar concentrating on war crimes for the Kosovo judiciary. The Legal System Monitoring Section is following the judicial proceedings against individuals accused of war crimes and currently in pre-trial detention. A strategy for building institutional judicial capacity that can handle certain war crimes prosecutions in the local courts is being developed.

83. The Ombudsman Support Section, together with the Commission for Democracy through Law (the Venice Commission), the Council of Europe and others, continued to work to establish the Ombudsman Institute in Kosovo. The expert group agreed that the Ombudsman Institute would be set up primarily to protect the rights and freedoms of all legal entities in Kosovo, by monitoring the activity of the Interim Civil Administration and emerging local institutions prior to and following provisional elections. Consideration is also being given to the feasibility of monitoring non-State actors claiming or exercising authority in Kosovo. The expert group agreed that, during an interim period, the Ombudsman should be an international expert assisted by at least two local deputies.

84. A growing atmosphere of fear imperils efforts to create the rule of law in Kosovo. Witnesses to human rights violations frequently refuse to provide information to the police, or if they do, later retract their testimony or do not appear for court hearings. Judges and prosecutors have received threats demanding that they not pursue investigations against certain suspects or that they release them, despite compelling incriminating evidence gathered by KFOR or UNMIK police. Impunity is emerging as a problem which undermines the substantial efforts to build an independent legal system and a police force that respects human rights.

D. POLICE EDUCATION AND DEVELOPMENT

85. The inaugural class of the future Kosovo Police Service graduated from the Kosovo Police Service School on 16 October. Of the 173 graduating officers, 156 were Albanians and 17 were non-Albanians (8 Kosovo Serbs, 3 Muslim Slavs, 3 Roma and 3 Turks). There were 39 female graduates. Seventy-nine per cent of the graduates had either a military or a police background. Upon graduation, the officers began their field training with UNMIK police field training officers. The second police course started on 29 November. The class includes a total of 178 students: 135 Kosovo Albanians, 29 Kosovo Serbs, 7 Kosovo Turks and 6 Muslim Slavs and 1 Roma. Thirty-two members of the class are female.

E. ELECTIONS

86. In accordance with paragraph 11 (c) of resolution 1244 (1999), UNMIK has been actively studying the feasibility of holding municipal elections in Kosovo in 2000. Mayors and other local officials would be elected for limited terms and to limited responsibilities within the province. In order to hold elections as early as possible, the Institution-Building and Civil Administration components have agreed to form a Registration Task Force with the objective of jointly planning, resourcing and executing a joint civil and voters registration, including registration of Kosovo residents outside the province. The registration process, which is scheduled to begin early next year, is expected to be completed in June 2000. The UNMIK Department of Elections, with the help of experts from other OSCE missions and the United Nations, has also been addressing the procedural aspects of municipal elections. Issues under consideration include the evidential and residential criteria for enfranchisement and the locality where voters can cast a ballot (previous or current place of residence). An assessment of documentation available in the 29 municipalities of Kosovo has shown that the majority of Kosovo residents may be able to produce either personal documents or evidence (such as cadastral records) of their habitual residence in Kosovo. Work has commenced on drafting election regulations and organizing the required institutional framework. A decision on the timing of the elections is still under consideration. A decision on the timing of the elections will be determined by a variety of factors, including the speed with which the civil and voters registrations can be completed.

F. MEDIA AFFAIRS

87. On 19 September, Radio-Television Kosovo transmitted its first television programme. This public, independent broadcasting service enjoys broad local support and international endorsement. The European Broadcasting Union has been subcontracted to produce this satel-

lite emergency programme for public television. The Government of Norway, through the OSCE Chairman-in-Office, provided initial funding for the project. The transformation of public broadcasting was further advanced with the closing of Radio Pristina on 31 October and the opening of Radio Kosovo on 1 November. As Radio-Television Kosovo is entirely dependent on voluntary contributions, budgetary constraints dictated a reduction of staff and a change in the programme schedule. At the same time, general agreement was reached that UNMIK's "Blue Sky Radio" should become part of Radio-Television Kosovo. Blue Sky staff are now training Radio Kosovo staff.

88. A Temporary Media Commissioner for Kosovo, who is an international UNMIK/ OSCE staff member, has been appointed by my Special Representative. He is charged with formulating a plan for a licensing and regulatory authority in order to bring direction to the still disorganized media environment in Kosovo. Currently, existing radio and television stations, as well as those planning to commence operations, are required to apply for temporary broadcasting licences.

89. With the addition of two prominent local journalists, the Kosovo Media Policy Advisory Board expanded its membership to seven. The Board's only Kosovo Serb member, however, left Kosovo for Montenegro. Efforts are under way to identify a new Kosovo Serb member, along with new members drawn from Kosovo's Turkish and Bosniac communities.

90. The issue of codes of practice for the print and broadcast media continue to be contentious. Although the Media Policy Advisory Board favours such codes, many journalists and press freedom groups do not. UNMIK and KFOR representatives have formed a Joint Consultative Committee and also met informally to discuss, among other things, the advisability of such codes and the enforcement mechanisms for potential infractions.

VI. Economic Reconstruction

91. The European Union is the lead organization for the rehabilitation and economic reconstruction tasks of UNMIK.

A. Kosovo Budget

92. As part of the development of a transparent and efficient fiscal process, UNMIK regulation No. 1999/16, which establishes a Central Fiscal Authority (CFA), was signed and went into force on 6 November. The Authority will be responsible for overall financial management of the Kosovo Consolidated Budget, including its preparation and the monitoring of its execution.

93. The budget for the interim administration of UNMIK for 1999, the Kosovo Consolidated Budget is set out in regulation No. 17 of 6 November. Expenditures total some DM 125 million. Some DM 38 million will be raised from tax revenue, with DM 87 million to be sought from donor grants. Of this latter figure, some DM 34 million has already been received through the United Nations Trust Fund of which DM 27.4 million has been spent on paying stipends to the local public service employees. Full support for the Kosovo budget would permit continuous stipend payments, payment of operating costs and assistance payments to the needy.

94. Projections for the 2000 budget are nearing completion. As both wage and employment levels were higher than earlier targets, the anticipated deficit is somewhat higher than the earlier estimate. UNMIK will continue to work on decreasing the total budget requirements, through such measures as reducing wage levels, rationalizing employee numbers and introducing user charges.

95. A donor conference, held in Brussels on 17 November, to discuss Kosovo's medium-term reconstruction programme, resulted in pledges of over US$ 1 billion until the end of 2000. Of this amount, $88 million was pledged for budgetary support for 1999 and 2000, $47 million for peace implementation activities and $18 million for humanitarian activities.

96. UNMIK local customs officers, under the guidance of international customs experts, collect customs and excise and sales tax at two international border posts. Revenue estimates show consistent trends. Collections for the three taxes have shown a slight decline from earlier figures and amount to approximately DM 1.9 million per week, for a total of DM 28.2 million by 17 December.

97. UNMIK completed the recruitment of an additional 25 local customs officers. In addition, the customs post at the Pristina airport and at Globocica at the border with the former Yugoslav Republic of Macedonia will soon become operational. UNMIK has now addressed the question of establishing additional designated tax posts for the collection of excise and sales taxes to be levied on the consumption and sale of goods. For the 2000 budget, there will be specific revenue targets established for a range of utilities such as electricity, public heating, water supply, post, telecommunications and other municipal-level charges such as building and work permits.

98. UNMIK is now regularly using customs and tax revenues as well as donor funding for expenses incurred by the interim administration. Expenditures have increased rapidly during the past month. The process developed for the comprehensive expenditure control procedure is in operation and the administration is processing expenditures from the 1999 budget in accelerating quantities.

B. Financial System

99. The Supervisory Board for Payment Operations has been established, pursuant to UNMIK regulation No. 1999/11 of 13 October. The Board will begin a phased reorganization of the former Payments Bureau, which includes integrating the bureau into the Banking and Payment Authority (regulation No. 1999/20 of 15 November). The reorganization will boost the efficiency of deutsche mark transactions and, over time, shift most payments services to the banking system. The six members of the Governing Board of the Banking and Payment Authority of Kosovo were appointed on 1 December 1999. The first applications for banking licences and for non-bank, microfinance institutions have already been received. The first bank is expected to begin full operations in January 2000.

C. Power and Water Sector

100. The restoration of basic public services such as electricity, water and waste disposal remains a fundamental task of UNMIK. Urgent action is being undertaken to ensure minimal disruption of power during the harsh winter months. One of the two units at the Kosovo-B power station was restarted as planned on 23 November and is generating about 240 MW of electricity. The Kosovo-A power station is generating 290 MW, bringing the total to 530 MW. This compares with the target of 650 MW. Repairs and maintenance continue on the second unit at Kosovo-B, which will come on-stream in mid-December, increasing supply by roughly a further 240 MW. The district heating system in Pristina has also been repaired and is currently working at 50 per cent capacity. Additionally, plans are under way to repair the smaller district heating systems in Mitrovica and Djakovica. Despite the partial restoration of electrical power to Pristina, many municipalities could still face a severe shortage of electricity, which threatens to deprive large parts of Kosovo of electrical heating during the winter months. Urgent work is therefore under way to repair distribution lines so as to link up to as many communities as possible.

101. Assessment of the damage to the water systems has revealed that, in some municipalities, the provision of water has deteriorated to alarming levels and potable water has become scarce. Measures are being taken to prevent the interruption of the water supply by providing back-up generators to priority areas.

102. The Kosovo Power Company is being managed by Kosovars with oversight and advice from an international management team. The company has set tariffs for electricity consumption in consultation with the international management team and UNMIK and bills will be distributed in the second week of December. Agreement has also been reached between the Pristina Regional Water Board and UNMIK on the tariffs to be charged for users.

103. A meeting of regional power companies on energy exchanges was held in Athens from 11 to 13 October. Representatives of companies from Albania, Bosnia and Herzegovina, Bulgaria, Greece, the former Yugoslav Republic of Macedonia, Serbia and Montenegro and

Romania participated, together with a member of the British Trade International management team from the Kosovo Power Company. A further meeting was held in November in Skopje.

D. ENTERPRISE SECTOR

104. UNMIK has defined a comprehensive strategy for private-sector development. This strategy has three goals. First, it will promote the growth and development of the privately owned enterprises already within the official economy and encourage new start-ups. Secondly, it will embrace the parallel economy and bring it within the official economy through a combination of inducements and requirements. Thirdly, it will transfer the potentially viable public enterprises to private ownership. To give effect to this strategy, UNMIK will create a regulatory framework and build the institutions that allow a market economy to flourish.

105. UNMIK has begun to implement this strategy in a number of areas while addressing the important issue of ownership and legal status of enterprises. It has also developed a business registration system to create a tax revenue base. Furthermore, it is defining a legal and regulatory framework suitable for a market economy. In the public enterprise sector, it is devising liquidation procedures for non-viable enterprises and privatization strategies for viable enterprises.

106. The scheme for revitalizing some enterprises in the construction sector envisages a series of about 10 contracts for managerial/technical assistance and a small injection of working capital for restarting the activity. Firms have been identified which have manifested their agreement to prepare letters of expression of interest for investment in some strategic medium-sized enterprises. Investors will be requested to elaborate and implement a comprehensive business plan for the revitalization of those enterprises and to put in the necessary investment in return for a concession/licence for the exploitation of the assets of the companies.

107. The Trepca complex is an important component of the Kosovo economy which has major social and political implications. An industrial strategy has been identified for the revitalization of the Trepca mines which would subdivide its main component parts into separate entities. A number of issues are currently being addressed, covering the legal status of the company, possible ways to handle different parts of the combine and the issue of liabilities.

108. The successful implementation of this strategy requires the wide-ranging involvement of all levels of Kosovo society. Consultations have started with economic policy experts and business representatives to develop a consensus on needed reforms. Once the policies are set, UNMIK will develop a comprehensive public education programme to ensure public and political support for its policies. The effort will be aimed at the general public in order to help bring its expectation levels in line with the current realities and to convey and explain the salient points of the new structure of the economy.

VII. Observations

109. The four components of UNMIK have made good progress in implementing their mandate since the adoption of resolution 1244 (1999) six months ago on 10 June 1999. The demilitarization and ongoing transformation of the former KLA marked an important step forward. The gradual consolidation of both the Kosovo Albanian and the Kosovo Serb political actors may initially complicate the reconciliation process, but in the longer term may also augur well for a more stable and democratic Kosovo. Critical challenges nonetheless remain.

110. During my visit to Kosovo on 13 and 14 October, one of the most frequently raised concerns was the precarious security situation for Kosovo Serbs, Roma and other minority groups in the province. Despite the concerted efforts of KFOR and UNMIK police, the level and nature of the violence in Kosovo, especially against vulnerable minorities, remains unacceptable. I underlined this message in my meetings with political leaders of all ethnic groups. In my meeting with the Kosovo Transition Council, which both Serb representatives (Bishop Artemije and Mr. Trajkovic) attended, I emphasized the need for all leaders to advocate and help to create a tolerant society in which all people can live without fear. I again urge all political leaders in Kosovo and the local population to stop the violence, intimidation and harassment.

111. The international community must also do better. KFOR and UNMIK police have redoubled their efforts, but more resources are needed. I would like to emphasize the need to ensure the rapid deployment of international police officers and to give support to the Kosovo Police Service. Furthermore, the authority of UNMIK must be cemented and the judiciary and penal system must be strengthened. Crimes must be prosecuted in order to establish the rule of law in Kosovo. The involvement in criminal and unofficial law-enforcement activities of former members of the KLA and members of the Kosovo Protection Corps and the Kosovo Police Service risks undermining the future authority of those bodies and will not be tolerated. A strong response is needed in order to address the problem of unofficial law-enforcement actors that have been reported to operate in the area. These structures must be dismantled and authority must rest only within legitimate bodies within the Joint Administrative Structure. All these efforts are, however, critically dependent on the support of the Kosovo political leadership, which must commit itself fully and irreversibly to peace, reconciliation, tolerance and respect for the rule of law.

112. The onset of winter in Kosovo represents another key challenge. While the humanitarian community has made all possible efforts to ensure that the population of Kosovo is prepared for the cold months, the international community must remain focused on the need for temporary winterized accommodation and the related issue of the rehabilitation of public utilities. The current problems at the border with the former Yugoslav Republic of Macedonia must be urgently resolved if winterization efforts are not to be compromised.

113. Work has already begun to coordinate humanitarian activities with rehabilitation and reconstruction efforts. An immediate priority is to develop detailed planning for the reconstruction of private housing after the winter. Another priority is to develop an effective social system which can address the needs of vulnerable persons following the end of the emergency phase of humanitarian assistance. The involvement of United Nations programmes and agencies in this process will be necessary.

114. The success of UNMIK depends in large part upon full and consistent support by Member States. This support is needed not only for project-oriented programmes, but also for the recurrent costs of the local administration. Resources will have to be made available by Member States on a voluntary basis in order to defray essential public expenditures, including the payroll of Kosovo's civil servants. I urge Member States to demonstrate their support by ensuring that the Kosovo Consolidated Budget succeeds. The recent pledges made at the Brussels donor conference on 17 November are encouraging but must be followed up with the urgent provision of the promised funds. Without donor assistance, the budget will not be sustainable. As a consequence, public utilities will suffer and public-sector wages will not be paid. Social unrest might follow. The people of Kosovo need support at this critical juncture.

115. As noted in my last report (S/1999/987), there is a clear need to share responsibility with the local population for the decision-making process of the interim administration. I welcome, therefore, the recent agreement on the establishment of a Joint Administrative Structure in Kosovo. This structure, which was the result of long negotiations, is an important step towards engaging the population in the interim administration of the province. It is my hope that all peoples of Kosovo, including the Kosovo Serbs, will join in this endeavour under the leadership of my Special Representative.

116. In conclusion, I would like to commend all international and local staff of UNMIK for their efforts in support of United Nations activities in Kosovo. In conclusion, I would like to pay tribute to Vladimir Krumov as well as to the victims of the World Food Programme plane crash on 12 November, who all lost their lives trying to bring peace and stability to Kosovo.

Implementation of the Principles for a Political Solution of the Conflict

Annex
Composition of the police component of the United Nations, Interim Administration Mission in Kosovo (as at 13 December 1999)
Present number of participating countries: 41

	Main head-quarters	Pristina	Prizren	Gnjilane	Pec	Mitrovica	Kosovo Police Service	Border police	Induction training Staff	New Arr.	Total
Argentina	7	4		2	1	12	2	9	1		38
Austria	6	21	10	4				3	1		45
Bangladesh	2	9	3			2	2		1		19
Belgium										5	5
Bulgaria	7	16		6	2	12	1	5			49
Canada	18	20		1		17	1	6	6		69
Czech Republic		3						3			6
Denmark	4			3		10			3		20
Egypt		20	20	10		10		1			61
Estonia	1	3							1		5
Fiji	2	25			2			4			33
Finland	1	1									2
France	2		10			66					78
Germany	16	20	107	2			6	41	1		192
Ghana	1	27				5	1		1		35
Hungary	3	3	4								10
Iceland						2					2
Italy	3	11	10		14			8			46
Jordan	1	21		4	9	10	1	2	1		49
Kenya		19							1		20
Kyrgyzstan		2									2
Lithuania		3		4			2				9
Malaysia	6		39				3				48
Netherlands	1										1
Nigeria		1	6	5							12
Pakistan	5	36	1	2	3	9	4	6			66
Philippines			13					10			23
Poland	1			8							9
Portugal	3	3		4	1				1	13	25
Romania	4	14				4	3		1		26
Russian Federation	17	47				5	4	12	3		88
Senegal		8	4			4					16
Spain	7	22			3		2	2	1		37
Sweden	13	15	4		3			4	5		44
Tunisia						5					5
Turkey	8	20	6	10			1	4			49
Ukraine	5	2	3	5	4	6		5			30
United Kingdom	1	57								2	60
United States	33	147	57	85	29	36	21	34	3		446
Zambia		14									14
Zimbabwe		8	8	8							24
Subtotal	178	622	305	155	78	216	53	159	31	20	1817
Total											1817

[Text of UNMIK regulations has been omitted; see Chapter 9.2]

9.2. REGULATIONS OF THE UN INTERIM ADMINISTRATION MISSION IN KOSOVO (UNMIK)

339. UNMIK/REG/1999/1, On the Authority of the Interim Administration in Kosovo, 25 July 1999

The Special Representative of the Secretary-General,

Recalling resolution 1244 (1999) of 10 June 1999, whereby the United Nations Security Council, acting under Chapter VII of the Charter of the United Nations, authorized the Secretary-General, with assistance of relevant international organizations, to establish an international civil presence in Kosovo, known as the United Nations Interim Administration Mission in Kosovo (UNMIK), in order to provide an interim administration in Kosovo with the mandate as described in the resolution;

Acting pursuant to the authority given to him under United Nations Security Council resolution 1244 (1999) of 10 June 1999, and for the purpose of establishing and maintaining the interim administration in the territory of Kosovo;

Hereby promulgates the following:

Section 1: Authority of the Interim Administration

All legislative and executive authority with respect to Kosovo, including the administration of the judiciary, is vested in UNMIK and is exercised by the Special Representative of the Secretary-General.

The Special Representative of the Secretary-General may appoint any person to perform functions in the civil administration in Kosovo, including the judiciary, or remove such person. Such functions shall be exercised in accordance with the existing laws, as specified in section 3, and any regulations issued by UNMIK.

Section 2: Observance of Internationally Recognized Standards

In exercising their functions, all persons undertaking public duties or holding public office in Kosovo shall observe internationally recognized human rights standards and shall not discriminate against any person on any ground such as sex, race, color, language religion, political or other opinion, national, ethnic or social origin, association with a national community, property, birth or other status.

Section 3: Applicable Law in Kosovo

The laws applicable in the territory of Kosovo prior to 24 March 1999 shall continue to apply in Kosovo insofar as they do not conflict with standards referred to in section 2, the fulfilment of the mandate given to UNMIK under United Nations Security Council resolution 1244 (1999), or the present or any other regulation issued by UNMIK.

Section 4: Regulations Issued by UNMIK

In the performance of the duties entrusted to the interim administration under United Nations Security Council resolution 1244 (1999), UNMIK will, as necessary, issue legislative acts in the form of regulations. Such regulations will remain in force until repealed by UNMIK or superseded by such rules as are subsequently issued by the institutions established under a political settlement, as provided for in United Nations security Council resolution 1244 (1999).

Section 5: Entry into Force and Promulgation of Regulations Issued by UNMIK

5.1. UNMIK regulations shall be approved and signed by the Special Representative of the Secretary-General. They shall enter into force upon the date specified therein.

5.2. UNMIK regulations shall be issued in Albanian, Serbian and English. In case of divergence, the English text shall prevail. The regulations shall be published in a manner that ensures their wide dissemination by public announcement and publication.

5.3. UNMIK regulations shall bear the symbol UNMIK/REG/, followed by the year of issuance and the issuance number of that year. A register of the regulations shall indicate the date of promulgation, the subject matter and amendments or changes thereto or the repeal or suspension thereof.

Section 6: State Property

UNMIK shall administer movable or immovable property, including monies, bank accounts, and other property of, or registered in the name of the Federal Republic of Yugoslavia or the Republic of Serbia or any of its organs, which is in the territory of Kosovo.

Section 7: Entry into Force

The present regulation shall be deemed to have entered into force as of 10 June 1999, the date of adoption by the United Nations Security Council of resolution 1244 (1999).

Dr. Bernard Kouchner, Special Representative of the Secretary-General

340. UNMIK/REG/1999/2, On the Prevention of Access by Individuals and Their Removal to Secure Public Peace and Order, 12 August 1999

The Special Representative of the Secretary-General,

Acting pursuant to the authority given to him under United Nations Security Council resolution 1244 (1999) of 10 June 1999, and for the purpose of maintaining public peace and order in the territory of Kosovo;

Hereby promulgates the following:

Section 1: Temporary Removal and Prevention of Access

1.1. The relevant law enforcement authorities may temporarily remove a person from a location, or prevent access by a person to a location, if this is necessary in the opinion of the law enforcement authorities and in light of the prevailing circumstances on the scene, to prevent a threat to public peace and order.

1.2. A threat to public peace and order may be posed by any act that jeopardizes:

(a) the rule of law;

(b) the human rights of individuals;

(c) public and private property;

(d) the unimpeded functioning of public institutions.

1.3. The relevant law enforcement authorities may temporarily remove a person from a location, or prevent access by a person to a location, if this is necessary in the opinion of the law enforcement authorities and in light of the prevailing circumstances on the scene, to prevent interference with the carrying out of the duties of the fire department, the delivery of first aid, or any other emergency activity.

Section 2: Temporary Detention

2.1. The relevant law enforcement authorities may temporarily detain a person, if this is necessary in the opinion of the law enforcement authorities and in light of the prevailing circumstances on the scene, to remove a person from a location, or to prevent access by a person to a location in accordance with section 1 of the present regulation.

2. 2. The detention may last only so long as necessary to carry out the actions specified in section 1 of the present regulation and in any case no longer than 12 hours.

Section 3: Entry into Force

The present regulation shall enter into force on 12 August 1999.

Bernard Kouchner, Special Representative of the Secretary-General

341. UNMIK/REG/1999/5, On the Establishment of an Ad Hoc Court of Final Appeal and an Ad Hoc Office of the Public Prosecutor, 4 September 1999

The Special Representative of the Secretary General,

Pursuant to the authority given to him under United Nations Security Council Resolution 1244 (1999) of 10 June 1999,

Taking into account United Nations Interim Administration Mission in Kosovo (UNMIK) Regulation No. 1999/1 of 25 July 1999 on the Authority of the Interim Administration in Kosovo,

For the purpose of enhancing the administration of justice in Kosovo pending a more thorough review,

Hereby promulgates the following:

Section 1: Court of Final Appeal

There shall be established, ad hoc, a Court of final appeal, which shall have the powers of the Supreme Court which exercised jurisdiction in Kosovo, as regards appeals against decisions of District Courts in the sphere of criminal law and also as regards detention terms.

1.2. The Court shall be composed of five judges including the President of the Court. The Special Representative of the Secretary General shall appoint the judges, including the President, following consultations with the Joint Advisory Council on Provisional Judicial Appointments. Additional judges also may be appointed if required, following the same procedure.

Section 2: Public Prosecutor's Office

A Chief Public Prosecutor and a deputy Public Prosecutor shall be appointed, ad hoc, to discharge the duties prescribed by law for the Public Prosecutor's Office in Kosovo. They shall be appointed by the Special Representative of the Secretary General following consultations with the Joint Advisory Council on Provisional Judicial Appointments.

Section 3: Criteria for Selection and Appointment of the Judges and the Prosecutor

The candidates selected for appointment as judges of the Court and as Prosecutors shall satisfy the following criteria:

a) have served for at least twelve years as a judge or Public Prosecutor;

b) be of high moral character, impartiality and integrity;

c) not have a criminal record;

d) not have participated in discriminatory measures or applied any repressive law or have implemented any dictatorial policies;

e) not be registered with any political party or otherwise engaged in political activity;

Section 4: Appointment and Term of Office

Upon appointment, each judge shall subscribe to the following oath or solemn declaration before the Special Representative of the Secretary-General:

"I swear (or solemnly declare) that I will perform my duties and exercise my powers as a judge of the ad hoc Court of Final Appeal honourably, faithfully, impartially and conscientiously."

4.2. Upon appointment, each Prosecutor shall subscribe to the following oath or solemn declaration before the Special Representative of the Secretary-General:

"I swear (or solemnly declare) that I will perform my duties and exercise my powers as a Prosecutor honourably, faithfully, impartially and conscientiously."

4.3. The Special Representative of the Secretary-General may remove a judge or the Prosecutor from office on any of the following grounds:

failure to meet the criteria specified in section 3 of the present regulation; physical or mental incapacity which is likely to be permanent or prolonged; serious misconduct; failure in the due execution of office; or having been placed, by personal conduct or otherwise in a position incompatible withthe due execution of office.

If the Special Representative of the Secretary-General becomes aware of evidence that indicates that a judge or a Prosecutor has failed to comply with his or her obligations under the present regulation the Special Representative of the Secretary-General shall inform the judge or Prosecutor of the charge and consider his or her response before taking any action other than temporary suspension of the judge or Prosecutor pending resolution of the charge. The Special Representative of the Secretary-General after consultation with the Joint Advisory Council on Provisional Judicial Appointments may remove the judge or Prosecutor from office if he considers that the charge is established.

Section 5: Procedure

Depending on the nature of the issue to be considered, the Court shall sit in a panel of three judges or five judges.

Section 6: Term of Office

The Court shall function and the Prosecutors shall exercise their respective duties until the Supreme Court of Kosovo is re-established.

Section 7: Honorarium and Facilities

7.1. The honorarium to be paid to the judges and to the Prosecutors shall be determined by the Special Representative of the Secretary-General.

7.2. The facilities required for the functioning of the Court and of the Prosecutor's office shall be provided by the Special Representative of the Secretary-General.

Section 8: Applicable Law

This regulation shall supersede any provision in the applicable laws relating to the appointment and removal from office of judges of the Court and of Prosecutors which is inconsistent with it.

Section 9: Final Provision

This regulation shall enter into force on 4 September 1999.

Bernard Kouchner, Special Representative of the Secretary-General

342. UNMIK/REG/1999/7, On Appointment and Removal From Office of Judges and Prosecutors, 7 September 1999

The Special Representative of the Secretary-General,

Pursuant to the authority given to him under United Nations Security Council Resolution 1244 (1999) of 10 June 1999,

Taking into account United Nations Interim Administration Mission in Kosovo (UNMIK) Regulation No. 1999/1 of 25 July 1999 on the Authority of the Interim Administration in Kosovo,

For the purpose of establishing an independent and multi-ethnic judiciary in Kosovo,

Hereby promulgates the following:

Section 1: The Advisory Judicial Commission

1.1 The Advisory Judicial Commission (hereinafter called the Commission) is hereby established to advise the Special Representative of the Secretary-General on matters related to the appointment of judges and prosecutors as required, as well as on complaints, if any, against any judge or prosecutor. Upon request from the Special Representative of the Secretary-General, the Commission may tender advice on other issues related to the judicial system.

1.2 The Commission shall be independent in the exercise of its functions.

Section 2: Composition

2.1 The Commission shall be composed of eight local and three international experts. The composition of the Commission shall be multi-ethnic and reflect varied legal expertise. Both local and international members of the Commission shall be distinguished legal professionals meeting the highest standards of efficiency, competence and integrity. They shall be independent and impartial. They shall not hold public office or any other position incompatible with their functions as members of the Commission.

The individual members shall be selected and appointed by the Special Representative of the Secretary-General in accordance with the above principles after appropriate consultations.

Section 3: Appointment and Term of Office

Upon appointment, each member of the Commission shall subscribe to a solemn oath or declaration before the Special Representative of the Secretary-General. The form of the oath or declaration shall be as follows:

"I solemnly declare and promise to discharge the functions entrusted to me by UNMIK regulation 1999/7 of 7 September 1999 strictly according to its terms and not to seek or accept instructions in regard to the performance of these duties from any source other than the Special Representative of the Secretary-General".

If the Special Representative of the Secretary-General becomes aware of evidence that indicates that a member of the Commission has failed to comply with his or her obligations under the present regulation the Special Representative of the Secretary-General shall inform the member of the charge and consider the member's response before taking any action other than temporary suspension of the member pending resolution of the charge. The Special Representative of the Secretary-General may remove the member from office if he considers that the charge is established.

The term of office of the members of the Commission shall be one year. This term may be renewed.

Section 4: Procedural Issues

4.1 The Commission shall adopt its rules of procedure.

The Commission may as necessary form committees for the efficient discharge of its Duties.

The Commission shall convene meetings as required or upon request by the Special Representative of the Secretary-General.

Section 5: Functions and Objectives

The Commission shall invite, by public announcement, applications of legal professionals in Kosovo for service as judges or prosecutors. It shall review the individual applications and make its recommendation in writing to the Special Representative of the Secretary-General on candidates indicating the reasons therefor.

5.2 In reviewing individual applications, the Commission members shall be guided by UNMIK's goal to establish a professional, independent, impartial and multi-ethnic judiciary and prosecution service.

Section 6: Criteria for Selection of Candidates

Applicants for service as judges or prosecutors shall satisfy the following criteria:

Have a university degree in law;

Have passed the examination for candidates for the judiciary, or, in the case of applicants for the position of a judge in the Minor Offences Court, have passed the professional examination;

be of high moral integrity;

not have a criminal record;

not have participated in discriminatory measures, or applied any repressive law or have implemented dictatorial policies;

not be registered with any political party or otherwise engage in political activity.

Except in the case of positions in the Minor Offences Court, applicants should have relevant work experience in the field of law, i.e. three years for the position of a Municipal Court judge (or prosecutor) or of a judge of Minor Offences Appeals body, seven years for the position of a District Court judge (or prosecutor) and four years for the position of a Commercial Court judge.

Section 7: Appointment and Removal from Office of Judges and Prosecutors

The Special Representative of the Secretary-General shall appoint judges and prosecutors taking into account the recommendation of the Commission under section 5.1 above.

A judge or prosecutor shall not hold any other public or administrative office or engage in any occupation of a professional nature, whether remunerative or not, or otherwise engage in any activity incompatible with his or her functions.

A complaint regarding a judge shall be referred to the Special Representative of the Secretary-General, who shall consult the Commission. After investigating the complaint, the Commission shall make an appropriate recommendation to the Special Representative of the Secretary-General, bearing in mind that no judge may be removed from office except on the ground of:

a) physical or mental incapacity which is likely to be permanent or prolonged;

b) serious misconduct;

c) failure in the due execution of office; or

d) having been placed, by personal conduct or otherwise, in a position incompatible

with the due execution of office.

The above procedure shall also be followed mutatis mutandis in the case of a complaint against a prosecutor.

The Special Representative of the Secretary-General may remove from office a judge or prosecutor after taking into account the recommendation of the Commission under section 7.3 or 7.4 above.

Section 8: Emoluments and Facilities

The honorarium to be paid to the members of the Commission shall be determined by the Special Representative of the Secretary-General.

The facilities required for the functioning of the Commission shall be provided by theSpecial Representative of the Secretary-General.

Section 9: Applicable Law

This regulation shall supersede any provision in the applicable laws relating to the appointment and removal from office of judges and prosecutors which is inconsistent with it.

Section 10: Final and Transitional Provisions

10.1 This regulation shall enter into force on 7 September 1999.

UNMIK emergency decrees 1999/1, 1999/2 are hereby repealed. However, judges,prosecutors and other judicial personnel provisionally appointed pursuant to these decrees shall continue to hold office until their respective terms expire.

Bernard Kouchner, Special Representative of the Secretary-General

343. UNMIK/REG/1999/8, On the Establishment of the Kosovo Corps, 20 September 1999

The Special Representative of the Secretary-General,

Acting pursuant to the authority given to him under United Nations Security Council resolution 1244 (1999) of 10 June 1999,

Hereby promulgates the following:

Section 1: Establishment of the Kosovo Corps

1.1 The Kosovo Corps shall be established as a civilian emergency service agency, the tasks of which shall be to:

provide disaster response services;

perform search and rescue;

provide a capacity for humanitarian assistance in isolated areas;

assist in demining; and

contribute to rebuilding infrastructure and communities.

1.2 The Kosovo Corps shall not have any role in law enforcement or the maintenance of law and order.

Section 2: Organization of the Kosovo Corps

2.1 The Kosovo Corps shall consist of active members, up to maximum of three thousand, as well as reserve members, up to a maximum of two thousand, who may be called upon when required.

Members of the Kosovo Corps shall be individually recruited on the basis of professional criteria required for the functions to be performed. In keeping with the multi-ethnic character of the Kosovo Corps, at least ten percent of both active and reserve members shall comprise individuals from minority groups.

2.3 The Special Representative of the Secretary-General shall have final authority over the selection and appointment of members of the Kosovo Corps and shall have the authority to dismiss such members on appropriate grounds.

2.4 The Kosovo Corps shall not take part in any political activity, nor shall members of the Kosovo Corps hold public office or actively engage in political affairs.

Section 3: Functioning of the Kosovo Corps

The Kosovo Corps shall operate under the authority of the Special Representative of the Secretary-General. KFOR shall provide day-to-day operational direction to the Kosovo Corps in accordance with policies and priorities established by the Special Representative of the Secretary-General.

Section 4: Entry into Force

The present regulation shall enter into force when the Special Representative of the Secretary-General determines that necessary funding is available for the establishment and maintenance of the Kosovo Corps and COMKFOR confirms compliance with the relevant provisions of Security Council resolution 1244 (1999).

Bernard Kouchner, Special Representative of the Secretary-General

344. UNMIK/REG/1999/14, On the Appointment of Regional and Municipal Administrators, 21 October 1999

The Special Representative of the Secretary-General,

Pursuant to the authority given to him under United Nations Security Council Resolution 1244 (1999) of 10 June 1999,

Taking into account United Nations Interim Administration Mission in Kosovo (UNMIK) Regulation No. 1999/1 of 25 July 1999 on the Authority of the Interim Administration in Kosovo,

For the purpose of the efficient administration of Kosovo,

Hereby promulgates the following:

Section 1: Regional Administrators

The Special Representative of the Secretary-General shall appoint, and may transfer or replace, a Regional Administrator for each of the five regions of Kosovo (Pristina, Pec, Mitrovica, Prizren, and Gnjilane) to act on his behalf.

The Regional Administrators shall report to the Deputy Special Representative of the Secretary-General for Civil Administration, who shall ensure the implementation of the present regulation.

Section 2: Authority and Functions of Regional Administrators

2.1 The Regional Administrators shall control, discharge or otherwise supervise the functions entrusted to public services and local government bodies in the respective regions and may require that those services or bodies seek his or her prior approval for specific decisions or initiatives.

2.2 The Regional Administrators may appoint advisory bodies in their respective regions that shall advise the Regional Administrator in the discharge of his or her functions.

2.3 The Regional Administrators shall oversee and coordinate the activities of UNMIK staff in their regions.

Section 3: Municipal Administrators

3.1 The Regional Administrators shall supervise Municipal Administrators for the municipalities in their respective regions.

The Municipal Administrators shall control, discharge or otherwise supervise the functions entrusted to public services and local government bodies in the respective municipalities and Municipal Administrators may require that those services and bodies seek his or her prior approval for specific decisions or initiatives. In particular, the Municipal Administrators shall:

Reactivate or establish and oversee, as the case may be, administrative structures,

institutions and enterprises, falling within the jurisdiction of the municipality, to carry out government activities at a municipal level, including revenue generating activities and systems of financial management and control;

Reactivate or establish and oversee modalities for local participation in the decision making process pending elections; and Coordinate international assistance at the municipal level.

Section 4: Implementation

The Special Representative of the Secretary-General may issue administrative directions in connection with the implementation of the present Regulation.

Section 5: Applicable Law

The provisions of the applicable laws relating to regional and municipal administration regulation shall apply subject to the provisions of the present regulation.

Section 6: Entry into Force

This Regulation shall enter into force on 21 October 1999.

Bernard Kouchner, Special Representative of the Secretary-General

345. UNMIK/REG/1999/16, On the Establishment of the Central Fiscal Authority of Kosovo and Other Related Matters, 6 November 1999

The Special Representative of the Secretary-General,

Pursuant to the authority given to him under United Nations Security Council Resolution 1244 (1999) of 10 June 1999,

Taking into account United Nations Interim Administration Mission in Kosovo (UNMIK) Regulation No. 1999/1 of 25 July 1999 on the Authority of the Interim Administration in Kosovo,

For the purposes of establishing the Central Fiscal Authority in Kosovo and other related matters,

Hereby promulgates the following:

Section 1: Central Fiscal Authority

The Central Fiscal Authority, acting under the authority of the Special Representative of the Secretary-General, is responsible for the overall financial management of the Kosovo Budget and the budgets under the responsibility of the municipalities, which together form the Kosovo Consolidated Budget. This budget will be developed, adopted and executed separately from the budget of the United Nations Interim Administration Mission in Kosovo (UNMIK) that is adopted by the General Assembly of the United Nations.

Section 2: Functions

2.1 The Central Fiscal Authority, having consulted the responsible central and municipal spending authorities, shall make recommendations to the Special Representative of the Secretary-General concerning:

a) formulation of an overall fiscal strategy for the Kosovo Consolidated Budget, in the light of macroeconomic conditions and the effect that fiscal policy may have on economic conditions;

b) development of a public revenue and expenditure programme for the Kosovo Consolidated Budget and formulation of plans for the control and execution of spending under that revenue and expenditure programme;

c) formulating policies for the raising and collection of revenues including, but not limited to, direct and indirect taxes, customs and excise taxes, sales taxes, service charges and donor contributions;

d) controlling and executing the raising of revenues and spending under the Kosovo Consolidated Budget;

e) the establishment of appropriate internal audit arrangements for the Kosovo Consolidated Budget; and,

f) managing the bank accounts of the Kosovo Consolidated Fund.

2.2 The Central Fiscal Authority shall:

develop the Kosovo Consolidated Budget and present this budget to the Special Representative of the Secretary-General for approval and adoption by regulation;

ensure that the budgets of the Municipalities are developed, approved and executed by Municipal Administrators in a manner consistent with assessed macroeconomic conditions and with the Kosovo Consolidated Budget;

record and report to the Special Representative of the Secretary-General on expenditures and revenues of the Kosovo Consolidated Budget;

arrange for the establishment of an information technology environment to support the functions; and, perform any other functions necessary for the above mentioned activities.

Section 3: Head of the Central Fiscal Authority

3.1 The Special Representative of the Secretary-General shall appoint the Head of the Central Fiscal Authority who, as chief executive officer under the day to day supervision of the Deputy Special Representative of the Secretary-General for Economic Reconstruction, Recovery and Development, shall be responsible for managing the Central Fiscal Authority and ensuring that the functions entrusted to it are implemented.

3.2 The Head of the Central Fiscal Authority shall staff, organize and administer the Central Fiscal Authority and shall issue administrative instructions and operating guidelines relating to administration of the Kosovo Consolidated Budget and on any matters pertaining to the functions of the Central Fiscal Authority.

Section 4: Kosovo Consolidated Budget Accounts

4.1 Except as otherwise determined the Special Representative of the Secretary-General, the fiscal year is a year of 12 months, starting on first January and ending on thirty-first December of each calendar year.

4.2 The Head of the Central Fiscal Authority shall open and maintain one or more bank accounts for the receipt, custody, payment or transmission of moneys raised or received relating to the Kosovo Consolidated Budget.

4.3 Moneys raised or received shall constitute the Kosovo Consolidated Fund, irrespective of whether such monies are initially received into Cash Payment Offices of the Public Payment Service of Kosovo or into bank accounts. With regard to moneys received from the UN Trust Fund for the UN Interim Administration in Kosovo, allocation and reporting arrangements with regard to the transfer shall be entered into by the Controller of the United Nations and the Special Representative of the Secretary-General.

4.4 No expenditure shall be made from the Kosovo Consolidated Fund except by means of appropriations contained in a regulation promulgated by the Special Representative of the Secretary-General.

Section 5: Independent Audit

The Special Representative of the Secretary-General shall ensure that appropriate independent audit arrangements are established for the Kosovo Consolidated Budget. The auditors shall report to the Secretary-General.

Section 6: Personnel and Employment Policy

The Head of the Central Fiscal Authority shall implement non-discriminatory personnel policies designed to ensure that the composition of the staff of the CFA reflects the multi-ethnic character of communities of Kosovo.

Section 7: Applicable Law

The present regulation shall supersede any provision in the applicable laws which are inconsistent with it.

Section 8: Implementation

The Special Representative of the Secretary-General may issue administrative directions in connection with the implementation of the present regulation

Section 9: Entry into Force

The present regulation shall enter into force on 6 November 1999.

Bernard Kouchner, Special Representative of the Secretary-General

346. UNMIK/REG/1999/24, On the Law Applicable in Kosovo, 12 December 1999

The Special Representative of the Secretary-General,

Pursuant to the authority given to him under United Nations Security Council Resolution 1244 (1999) of 10 June 1999,

Taking into account United Nations Interim Administration Mission in Kosovo (UNMIK) Regulation No. 1999/1 of 25 July 1999 on the Authority of the Interim Administration in Kosovo,

For the purposes of defining the law applicable in Kosovo,

Hereby promulgates the following:

Section 1: Applicable Law

1. The law applicable in Kosovo shall be:

a. The regulations promulgated by the Special Representative of the Secretary-General and subsidiary instruments issued thereunder; and

b. The law in force in Kosovo on 22 March 1989.

In case of a conflict, the regulations and subsidiary instruments issued thereunder shall take precedence.

2. If a court of competent jurisdiction or a body or person required to implement a provision of the law, determines that a subject matter or situation is not covered by the laws set out in section 1 of the present regulation but is covered by another law in force in Kosovo after 22 March 1989 which is not discriminatory and which complies with section 3 of the present regulation, the court, body or person shall, as an exception, apply that law.

3. In exercising their functions, all persons undertaking public duties or holding public office in Kosovo shall observe internationally recognized human rights standards, as reflected in particular in:

The Universal Declaration of Human Rights of 10 December 1948;

The European Convention for the Protection of Human Rights and Fundamental Freedoms of 4 November 1950 and the Protocols thereto;

The International Covenant on Civil and Political Rights of 16 December 1966 and the Protocols thereto;

The International Covenant on Economic, Social and Cultural Rights of 16 December 1966;

The Convention on the Elimination of All Forms of Racial Discrimination of 21 December 1965;

The Convention on Elimination of All Forms of Discrimination Against Women of 17 December 1979;

The Convention Against Torture and Other Cruel, Inhumane or Degrading Treatment or Punishment of 17 December 1984;

The International Convention on the Rights of the Child of 20 December 1989.

4. No person undertaking public duties or holding public office in Kosovo shall discriminate against any person on any ground such as sex, race, colour, language, religion, political or other opinion, natural, ethnic or social origin, association with a national community, property, birth or other status. In criminal proceedings, the defendant shall have the benefit of the most favourable provision in the criminal laws which were in force in Kosovo between 22 March 1989 and the date of the present regulation.

5. Capital punishment is abolished.

Section 2: Implementation

Courts in Kosovo may request clarification from the Special Representative of the Secretary-General in connection with the implementation of the present regulation. The Special Representative of the Secretary-General shall provide such clarification for the consideration of the courts in the exercise of their functions.

Section 3: Entry into Force

The present regulation shall be deemed to have entered into force as of 10 June 1999.

Bernard Kouchner, Special Representative of the Secretary-General

9.3 INTERNATIONAL CONTRIBUTION TO THE IMPLEMENTATION OF THE KOSOVO SETTLEMENT

347. EC Council Regulation No 1294/1999 Concerning a Freeze of Funds and a Ban on Investment in Relation to the FRY and Repealing Regulations (EC) No 1295/98 and (EC) No 1607/98, 15 June 1999 [1]

The Council of the European Union,

Having regard to the Treaty establishing the European Community, and in particular Articles 60 and 301;

Having regard to Common Position 98/326/CFSP of 7 May 1998 defined by the Council on the basis of Article J.2 of the Treaty on European Union concerning the freezing of funds held abroad by the Governments of the Federal Republic of Yugoslavia (FRY) and the Republic of Serbia[2], Common Position 98/374/CFSP of 8 June 1998 defined by the Council on the basis of Article J.2 of the Treaty on European Union concerning the prohibition of new investment in Serbia[3], as well as to Common Position 1999/318/CFSP of 10 May 1999 adopted by the Council on the basis of Article 15 of the Treaty on European Union concerning additional restrictive measures against the Federal Republic of Yugoslavia[4],

Having regard to the proposal from the Commission;

Whereas:

(1) The continued violation by the Governments of the Federal Republic of Yugoslavia and the Republic of Serbia of the relevant United Nations Security Council resolutions and the pursuance of extreme and criminally irresponsible policies, including repression against citizens, constitute serious violations of human rights and international humanitarian law;

(2) An extension of the scope of the present legal framework concerning the freezing of funds held abroad by the Governments of the Federal Republic of Yugoslavia and the Republic of Serbia, and concerning the prohibition of new investment in the Republic of Serbia will significantly increase the pressure on those governments;

(3) Therefore, the scope of the provisions of this legal framework should be extended to cover certain assets, other than funds and financial resources, which may generate funds or other financial resources for the governments concerned, and to cover companies, undertakings, institutions and entities owned or controlled by those governments, as well as persons acting for or on behalf of those governments, as well as the acquiring or extending of a participation in, ownership of or control of real estate or companies, undertakings, institutions or entities which are owned or controlled by the Government of the Federal Republic of Yugoslavia or of the Republic of Serbia;

(4) The measures contained in this Regulation should be proportionate to the objectives pursued by the Council with regard to the Kosovo crisis and the measures should not lead to severe damage to the interests of the Community;

(5) There is a need to provide for certain specific exemptions;

(6) A procedure should be laid down for amending the Annexes to this Regulation and for granting specific authorisations to avoid serious damage to industry, companies or the interests of the Community;

(7) Circumvention of this Regulation should be countered by an adequate system of information, and where appropriate, remedial measures, including additional Community legislation;

(8) Competent authorities of the Member States should, where necessary, be empowered to ensure compliance with this Regulation;

(9) It is desirable that sanctions for violations of the provisions of this Regulation can be imposed as of the date of entry into force of this Regulation;

(10) There is a need for the Commission and Member States to inform each other of the measures taken under this Regulation and of other relevant information at their disposal in connection with this Regulation;

(11) For reasons of transparency and simplicity the main provisions of Council Regulations (EC) No 1295/98[5] and No 1607/98[6] have been incorporated into this Regulation, and, therefore those Regulations can be repealed,

Has adopted this Regulation:

Article 1

For the purpose of this Regulation:

1. Government of the FRY means: the Government of the Federal Republic of Yugoslavia, at any level, its agencies, bodies or organs, and companies, undertakings, institutions and entities owned or controlled by that Government, including all financial institutions and State-owned and socially-owned entities organised in the Federal

---

[1] OJ L 153, 19/06/1999 p. 0063 - 0082, 399R1294.
[2] OJ L 143, 14/05/1998, p. 1.
[3] OJ L 165, 10/06/1998, p. 1.
[4] OJ L 123, 13/05/1999, p. 1.
[5] OJ L 178, 23/06/1998, p. 33.
[6] OJ L 209, 25/07/1998, p. 16.

Republic of Yugoslavia as of 26 April 1999, any successors to such entities, and their respective subsidiaries and branches, wherever located, and any persons acting or purporting to act for or on behalf of any of the foregoing;

2. Government of the Republic of Serbia means: the Government of the Republic of Serbia, at any level, its agencies, bodies or organs, and companies, undertakings, institutions and entities owned or controlled by that Government, including all financial institutions and State-owned and socially-owned entities organised in the Republic of Serbia as of 26 April 1999, any successors to such entities, and their respective subsidiaries and branches, wherever located, and any persons acting or purporting to act for or on behalf of any of the foregoing;

3. Funds means: financial assets and economic benefits of any kind, including, but not necessarily limited to, cash, cheques, claims on money, drafts, money orders and other payment instruments; deposits with financial institutions or other entities, balances on accounts, debts and debt obligations; publicly and privately traded securities and debt instruments, including stocks and shares, certificates representing securities, bonds, notes, warrants, debentures, derivatives contracts; interest, dividends or other income on or value accruing from or generated by assets; credit, right of set-off, guarantees, performance bonds or other financial commitments; letters of credit, bills of lading, bills of sale; documents evidencing an interest in funds or financial resources, and any other instrument of export-financing;

4. Freezing of funds means: preventing any move, transfer, alteration, use of or dealing with funds in any way that would result in any change in their volume, amount, location, ownership, possession, character, destination or other change that would enable the use of the funds, including portfolio management;

5. Owning a company, undertaking, institution or entity means: being in possession of 50 % or more of the proprietary rights of a company, undertaking, institution or entity or having a majority interest therein;

6. Controlling a company, undertaking, institution or entity means any of:

(a) having the right to appoint or remove a majority of the members of the administrative, management or supervisory body of a company, undertaking, institution or entity;

(b) having appointed solely as a result of the exercise of one's voting rights a majority of the members of the administrative, management or supervisory bodies of a company, undertaking, institution or entity who have held office during the present and previous financial year;

(c) controlling alone, pursuant to an agreement with other shareholders in or members of a company, undertaking, institution or entity, a majority of shareholders' or members' voting rights in that company, undertaking, institution or entity;

(d) having the right to exercise a dominant influence over a company, undertaking, institution or entity, pursuant to an agreement entered into with that company, undertaking, institution or entity, or to a provision in its Memorandum or Articles of Association, where the law governing that company, undertaking, institution or entity permits its being subject to such agreement or provision;

(e) having the power to exercise the right to exercise a dominant influence referred to at (d), without being the holder of that right;

(f) having the right to use all or part of the assets of a company, undertaking, institution or entity;

(g) managing a company, undertaking, institution or entity on a unified basis, while publishing consolidated accounts;

(h) sharing jointly and severally the financial liabilities of a company, undertaking, institution or entity, or guaranteeing them.

Article 2

1. Any person listed in Annex I to this Regulation shall be deemed to be a person acting or purporting to act for or on behalf of the Government of the FRY or the Government of the Republic of Serbia.

2. Companies, undertakings, institutions or entities, located, registered or incorporated outside the territory of the Federal Republic of Yugoslavia and listed in Annex II to this Regulation, shall be deemed to be owned or controlled by the Government of the FRY or the Government of the Republic of Serbia.

3. In cases where a natural or legal person holds or acquires well-founded evidence that a person, company, undertaking, institution or entity is covered by the definitions of Governments of the FRY or Government of the Republic of Serbia but does not appear on the lists of Annexes I or II, such person shall, before entering into any commercial transaction or activity covered by Articles 3, 4, 5 or 7 with that person, undertaking, institution or entity, submit the evidence to the competent authorities of the Member States listed in Annex III. The competent authorities will examine all evidence made available to them. If the competent authorities consider the evidence made available as insufficient and are not able to confirm in writing within five working days after the said submission that the intended transaction or activity is prohibited under this Regulation, the transaction or the activity will not constitute a violation of this Regulation.

Article 3

Except as permitted under the provisions of Articles 7 and 8:

1. All funds held outside the territory of the Federal Republic of Yugoslavia and belonging to the Government of the FRY and/or to the Government of the Republic of Serbia shall be frozen.

2. No funds shall be made available, directly or indirectly, to or for the benefit of, either or both, those Governments.

Article 4

1. It shall be prohibited to acquire any new or extend any existing participation in, ownership of or control of real estate, a company, undertaking, institution or entity:

- located, registered or incorporated within the Republic of Serbia, or

- wherever else located, registered or incorporated, and owned or controlled by the Government of the FRY or the Government of the Republic of Serbia,

in exchange or not, for the supply or provision of tangible or intangible goods, services or technology (including patents), capital, debt relief or other financial resources.

2. It shall also be prohibited to engage in or continue activities facilitating, promoting or otherwise enabling the acquisition or extension of a participation in, ownership of or control over such real estate, companies, undertakings, institutions or entities.

Article 5

1. The participation, knowingly and intentionally, in related activities, the object or effect of which is, directly or indirectly, to circumvent the provisions of Articles 3 and 4 shall be prohibited.

2. Any information that the provisions of this Regulation are being, or have been circumvented shall be notified to the competent authorities of the Member States as listed in Annex III and/or the Commission.

Article 6

Without prejudice to the Community rules concerning confidentiality and to the provisions of Article 284 of the Treaty, the competent authorities of the Member States shall have the power to require banks, other financial institutions, insurance companies, and other bodies and persons to provide all relevant information necessary for ensuring compliance with this Regulation.

Article 7

1. Article 3 shall not apply to funds exclusively used for the following purposes and on the following conditions:

(a) Payment of current expenses, including salaries of local staff, of embassies, consular posts or diplomatic missions of the Government of the Federal Republic of Yugoslavia or the Government of the Republic of Serbia within the Community;

(b) Transfers from the Community to natural persons resident in the Federal Republic of Yugoslavia of social security or pension payments as well as the transfer of other payments to protect entitlements in the area of social insurance where these transfers are made into separate bank accounts established exclusively for this purpose and where the private recipient has immediate access to the funds in the convertible currency thus transferred;

(c) Payments of taxes, compulsory insurance premiums and fees for public utility services such as gas, water, electricity and telecommunications to be paid in the Community by persons, companies, undertakings, institutions or entities listed in Annexes I and II and resident or located or registered or incorporated within the Community;

(d) Payments of normal salaries, including compulsory redundancy payments, except bonuses and other irregular payments by companies, undertakings, institutions or entities listed in Annex II and located or registered or incorporated within the Community to employees employed at the date of entry into force of this Regulation by these companies, undertakings, institutions or entities, on the condition:

(i) that such salaries are paid into accounts held with banks or financial institutions within the Community, and

(ii) that the salary of each employee is at the rate applicable during the six months preceding the date of entry into force of this Regulation without prejudice to salary increases obtained in collective bargaining agreements, and

(iii) in case of replacement of any employee that the new employee is paid at the same rate of salary as that of the employee being replaced;

(e) Payments related to projects in support of democratisation, humanitarian and educational activities and independent media carried out by the Community and/or the Member States.

2. Article 3(2) shall not apply to:

(a) Payments in cash in Yugoslav dinars or any of the currencies of the Member States, in denominations to the value of no more than EUR 150, within the territory of the Republic of Yugoslavia;

(b) Payments of debts due to the Government of the FRY or the Government of the Republic of Serbia incurred before the entry into force of this Regulation (with the exception of bank guarantees, performance bonds, bid bonds and similar instruments), and the execution of payment orders received from outside the Community, on the condition that these payments are made into frozen accounts held by those Governments with bank or financial institutions within the Community;

(c) Payments for essential transit services provided by the Federal Republic of Yugoslavia and Serbia on the condition that provision of these services takes place at the average rate applicable during the six months before the entry into force of this Regulation and applied on a non-discriminatory basis.

3. Notwithstanding Articles 4 and 3(2), the acquisition of new or the extension of existing participation in, or ownership of, or control of real estate located in the Community shall be allowed only if the transaction meets the following conditions:

(a) the payment for the acquisition or extension of the participation, ownership or control is made into a separate frozen account held by the former owner of the real estate with a bank or financial institution within the Community;

(b) the price at which the participation in, ownership of or control of the real estate concerned is acquired or extended is in conformity with the value as determined by an appropriately authorised independent valuer;

(c) the seller of the ownership of, control of or participation in the real estate is a legal person listed in Annex II;

(d) the said seller does not hold or has no access to other funds;

(e) the purpose of the sale is solely to acquire funds to cover expenses mentioned under paragraph (1) above.

4. For any payment made under paragraphs 1, 2 and 3, conclusive evidence of the fulfilment of the conditions and the purposes shall be kept available for one year for inspection by the competent authorities listed in Annex III.

Article 8

1. In accordance with the provisions of Article 9, the Commission shall be empowered:

(a) to amend Annexes I and II;

(b) to grant authorisations, if not granting an authorisation would cause serious damage to industry, companies or the interests of the Community:

(i) to unfreeze funds or make funds available for the benefit of the Government of the FRY or the Government of the Republic of Serbia;

(ii) to acquire or extend a participation in, ownership of or control over real estate, a company, undertaking, institution or entity referred to in Article 4.

2. Any request by a legal or natural person for an authorisation referred to in paragraph 1 (b), or for an amendment of Annexes I or II, shall be made to the Commission through the appropriate competent authorities of the Member States, listed in Annex III.

3. For the purposes of implementing this Regulation, the Commission shall be empowered, on the basis of information supplied by Member States, to amend Annex III.

Article 9

1. For the purposes of the implementation of Article 8(1) and (2), the Commission shall be assisted by the Committee composed of the representatives of the Member States and chaired by the representative of the Commission, established under Council Regulation (EC) No 2271/96[1], in accordance with the following provisions.

2. The representative of the Commission shall submit to the committee a draft of the measures to be taken. The Committee shall deliver the opinion on the draft within a time limit, which the chairman may lay down according to the urgency of the matter. The opinion shall be delivered by the majority laid down in Article 205 (2) of the Treaty in the case of decisions, which the Council is required to adopt on a proposal from the Commission. The votes of the representatives of the Member States within the Committee shall be weighted in the manner set out in that Article. The chairman shall not vote.

3. (a) The Commission shall adopt measures which shall apply immediately.

(b) However, if these measures are not in accordance with the opinion of the committee, they shall be communicated by the Commission to the Council forthwith. In that event:

- the Commission shall defer application of the measures which it has decided for 10 working days from the date of such communication,

- the Council, acting by a qualified majority, may take a different decision within the time-limit referred to in the preceding indent.

Article 10

The Committee referred to in Article 9 may examine technical questions concerning the application of this Regulation, which may be raised either by the chairman or by a representative of a Member State.

Article 11

The Commission and the Member States shall inform each other of the measures taken under this Regulation and supply each other with the relevant information at their disposal in connection with this Regulation, in particular information received in accordance with Articles 2, 5, 6 and 8, and in respect of violation and enforcement problems or judgments handed down by national courts.

---

1 OJ L 209, 25/07/1998, p. 16.

Article 12

Each Member State shall determine the sanctions to be imposed where the provisions of this Regulation are infringed. Such sanctions shall be effective, proportionate and dissuasive.

Pending the adoption, where necessary, of any legislation to this end, the sanctions to be imposed where the provisions of this Regulation are infringed shall be those determined by the Member States in accordance with Article 6 of Regulation (EC) No 1295/98 or Article 3 of Regulation (EC) No 1607/98.

Article 13

Regulations (EC) No 1295/98 and No 1607/98 shall be repealed.

Article 14

This Regulation shall apply:
- within the territory of the Community including its airspace,
- on board any aircraft or any vessel under the jurisdiction of a Member State,
- to any person elsewhere who is a national of a Member State,
- to any body which is incorporated or constituted under the law of a Member State.

Article 15

This Regulation shall enter into force on the day of its publication in the Official Journal of the European Communities.

This Regulation shall be binding in its entirety and directly applicable in all Member States.

Done at Luxembourg, 15 June 1999. For the Council: The President K.-H. Funke

Amendments:

Amended by 399R1970 (OJ L 244 16.09.99 p.39)

Amended by 399R2756 (OJ L 331 23.12.99 p.43)

[Annex I: Persons acting or purporting to act for or on behalf of the Governments of the Federal Republic of Yugoslavia (FRY) or the Republic of Serbia and Annex II: Companies, undertakings, institutions or entities owned or controlled by the Governments of the Federal Republic of Yugoslavia or the Republic of Serbia (not located in the Federal Republic of Yugoslavia) have been omitted.]

348. G-8 Statement on Regional Issues, 20 June 1999[1]

[Parts not referring to Kosovo have been omitted.]

Kosovo

We welcome the decisive steps already taken and now under way to end violence and repression in Kosovo, to establish peace and to provide for the safe and free return of all refugees and displaced persons to their homes. In this regard, we particularly welcome the adoption on 10 June of Security Council resolution 1244 (1999), and commend the intensive efforts of our Foreign Ministers and others, including the Special Envoys of the European Union and the Russian Federation, to restore peace and security.

We reaffirm strong support for the international civil and security presences in accordance with resolution 1244 (1999). We welcome the leadership of the United Nations in the international civil presence, and pledge to collaborate closely to ensure the United Nations success in carrying out its complex mission. We also welcome the agreement reached between NATO and the Russian Federation on the international security presence, and the relevant military technical agreement. In that regard, we insist that all parties to the conflict in Kosovo respect the ceasefire and fully abide by the terms of resolution 1244 (1999) and the military technical agreement concerning the withdrawal of all Yugoslav and Serb military, police and paramilitary forces from Kosovo and the demilitarization of the Kosovo Liberation Army and other armed Kosovo Albanian groups.

We expect all residents of Kosovo to contribute to the creation of a democratic, multi-ethnic Kosovo. The return of refugees and displaced persons to their homes, and the assurance of security for all persons, including Serb and all other minorities in Kosovo, will be high priorities of the international community. To ensure the well-being of the refugees and displaced persons, their return must be undertaken in a safe, orderly and organized fashion. We will work cooperatively with each other, the United Nations, the European Union, the Organization for Security and Cooperation in Europe (OSCE) and other international organizations to facilitate safe return, including demining.

We will fully cooperate with the work of the International Tribunal for the Former Yugoslavia. We affirm our commitment to a meeting of the international donor community in July to address short-term humanitarian and other needs for Kosovo, and a subsequent meeting in the autumn after a full assessment of needs has been made pursuant to the assistance coordination process chaired by the European Commission and the World Bank.

We stress the importance of the civil implementation and, given the key role the G-8 has played in the Kosovo crisis, we invite our Foreign Ministers to review on a regular basis the progress achieved thus far in this process and to provide further guidance.

South-Eastern Europe Stability Pact and Donor Coordination

We welcome the adoption of the Stability Pact on 10 June in Cologne, an initiative of the European Union, which will continue to play the leading role. This Stability Pact has launched a process for south-eastern Europe with the objective of a positive mid- and long-term perspective for the countries in the region to achieve lasting peace as well as political and economic stability. We note that countries in the region participating in the Stability Pact commit themselves to continued democratic and economic reforms, as well as bilateral and regional cooperation among themselves to advance their integration, on an individual basis, into Euro-Atlantic structures. We consider this stabilization process to be one of the major political and economic challenges ahead of us.

We declare our readiness to take strong action to achieve all the objectives of the Stability Pact. In regard to the above, the Federal Republic of Yugoslavia must demonstrate a full commitment to all of the principles and objectives of the Pact.

We emphasize that, in achieving the goals of the Stability Pact, the countries of the region bear a primary responsibility. Assistance from outside can help, but not replace the countries' own efforts. Therefore we call on the countries of south-eastern Europe to cooperate with each other and within the international community to develop a shared strategy for the stability and growth of the region. In recognition of the principle of fair burden sharing, we also call on the international donor community to take the necessary measures to give the countries in the region a strong signal of active international support and solidarity, and to organize donor conferences as early as feasible.

We welcome the progress made through the chairmanship of the European Commission and the World Bank towards establishing a donor coordination process to develop a coherent international assistance strategy for the region, opening the door for all donor opportunities, as well as to mobilize additional financial support for reconstruction, regional integration, economic recovery and reform and to promote sound macroeconomic and structural policies by the countries concerned. This process will be guided by the High-level Steering Group, in which the Special Coordinator of the Stability Pact will play an important role.

The High-level Steering Group will be chaired jointly by the European Commission and the World Bank and include the Special Coordinator of the Stability Pact, the International Monetary Fund, the European Investment Bank and the European Bank for Reconstruction and Development, which will be active in the region, plus one United

---

[1] UN Doc. S/1999/711, Annex, 24 June 1999.

Nations representative and the Finance Ministers of major donor countries and, where appropriate, development ministers. [...]

349. EU, 2192nd Council Meeting, General Affairs, Luxembourg, 21-22 June 1999

[...]

Western Balkans
KOSOVO - CONCLUSIONS

The Council warmly welcomed the adoption of UN Security Council Resolution (UNSCR) 1244, the full withdrawal of all Serb security forces, the end of NATO's air campaign, as well as the deployment of KFOR and the steps under way to establish the interim civil administration for Kosovo.

The Council attached the highest importance to all parties cooperating fully with KFOR and UNMIK (UN Interim Administration Mission in Kosovo) in the implementation of UNSCR 1244. It urged the Kosovo Liberation Army to fully comply with UNSCR 1244, to honour the commitments it has made to NATO and to refrain from acts of violence against the Serb population. It also reiterated its call to all Kosovo Albanian factions to work together, on the basis of UNSCR 1244, for the future of their people.

The Council expects all residents of Kosovo to contribute to the creation of a democratic, multi-ethnic Kosovo. The return of refugees and displaced persons to their homes, and the assurance of security for all people in Kosovo, as well as bringing to justice the perpetrators of atrocities are high priorities of the international community. The Council was alarmed by the exodus of the Serb population from Kosovo and urged all Serb residents of Kosovo to return to their homes.

The Council attached the greatest importance to active and constructive Russian participation in the international community's efforts to restore security, stability and respect for human rights in Kosovo. Accordingly it welcomed the agreement on Russian participation in KFOR.

The Council noted that UNMIK was deploying in Pristina in order to fulfil its mandate set out by the United Nations, and emphasised that the EU would participate fully in the integrated structure with a substantial presence. The EU recalled its expectation that, in recognition of the major contribution to the stabilisation of Kosovo that the EU and its member States are making, an EU national be appointed as Special Representative of the Secretary General.

The Council invited the Presidency, together with the Commission, to convey to the UN Secretary-General EU views on the mission and on the contribution the EU expects to make in assisting it to fulfil its mandate. The EU will shortly designate the head of the fourth pillar responsible for economic affairs and reconstruction.

The Council heard a report on the Commission's orientations on reconstruction in Kosovo, as well as on the creation of an agency to be charged with the implementation of Community reconstruction programmes and welcomed its intention to commence speedily the reconstruction process in Kosovo within the overall UNMIK effort in close cooperation with the International Financial Institutions. It noted that a damage assessment mission will be dispatched to the region, and invited the Commission to report further to the Council on reconstruction needs for the region, including the need for supplementary budget resources.

The Council welcomed the Commission's action to mobilise, for humanitarian assistance, the existing 196 MEURO reserve on the current European Community budget. In the light of the foreseeable needs, it invited the Commission to come forward, as soon as possible, with proposals for additional human and financial resources for refugee relief, return and reconstruction, including, as appropriate, transfer of funds from other budget lines or a proposal for a supplementary budget for 1999. Appropriate solutions will be needed for the following years.

The Council called on the Yugoslav authorities to release the three CARE aid workers jailed by a military Court in Belgrade on 29 May.

The Council condemned the mass killings of mostly civilian inhabitants of Kosovo. It emphasised the resolve of the Member States of the European Union to cooperate fully with ICTY (International Criminal Tribunal for the former Yugoslavia) and to meet their obligations under relevant UNSCRs, particularly as regards the arrest warrants issued on 24 May 1999.

Conclusions on the Development of a Comprehensive Policy Based on the Commission Communication on "The Stabilisation and Association Process for Countries of South-Eastern Europe"
GENERAL CONCLUSIONS

1. The Council notes that work has begun in the competent bodies with a view to formulating a comprehensive policy on the basis of the Communication by the Commission on the "Stabilisation and Association Process for the Countries of South Eastern Europe". This new process will be based on the existing Regional Approach and reaffirms the European Union's resolve to take up the challenge and responsibility to contribute to stability of the region. However, the objectives of this process can only be achieved if the peoples and governments of the region take active responsibility and make determined efforts. Ultimately, the future of the region lies in the hands of its peoples and governments. This process will help enable the countries in the region to create lasting peace, democracy, stability and prosperity, which are also central goals of the Stability Pact on South-Eastern Europe. In this context, the Council recalled the Conclusions by the European Council of 4 June 1999 in Cologne, in particular paragraph 72 thereof. The Council emphasises that the Stabilisation and Association process will also be a contribution to the future EU Common Strategy towards the Western Balkans.

2. The stabilisation and association process will focus on Albania, Bosnia and Herzegovina, Croatia, the Federal Republic of Yugoslavia, the Former Yugoslav Republic of Macedonia and on regional cooperation in South-Eastern Europe.

3. In the framework of its comprehensive policy on South-Eastern Europe, the European Union will introduce a new dimension to its relations to the region, namely the offer to the five countries - in return for compliance with the relevant conditions - of a tailor-made category of contractual relations: Stabilisation and Association Agreements (SAAs). These agreements will be available for all the countries and will provide a more advanced relationship. These agreements will take into account the specific and evolving situation of each country and will be gradually introduced in light of the ability of each country to meet reciprocal, contractual obligations, as well as of its effective contribution to regional cooperation.

4. The Stabilisation and Association process will include, as appropriate:

- Stabilisation and Association Agreements;

- Autonomous Trade Measures and other economic and trade relations;

- Economic and financial assistance, inter alia PHARE assistance, OBNOVA assistance, budgetary assistance and balance of payment support;

- Assistance for democratisation and civil society;

- Humanitarian aid for refugees, returnees and other persons of concern;

- Cooperation in justice and home affairs;

- Development of political dialogue.

The success of the stabilisation process will depend on the efforts made by each country to make full use of the support offered as well as on an effective combination of the various instruments listed above.

5. On autonomous trade measures in general, the Council confirms that the existing system of autonomous trade preferences, adjusted and enhanced as necessary, will remain important until contractual relations are established. It notes the Commission's intention, in the future, to split the existing system of autonomous trade preferences into separate trade preferences for each country in order to ensure a transparent and equitable share of these preferences between these countries, and to prepare possible future negotiations for Stabilisation and Association Agreements.

6. The Council confirms, that its policy on conditionality of 29 April 1997 will continue to apply to the granting of autonomous trade preferences, PHARE assistance as well as to contractual relations. It is important that the objective criteria of the Regional Approach are applied in a way which provides the necessary incentives for each country to make progress in the Stabilisation and Association process.

7. The Council notes that the Commission will continue to prepare regular reports on compliance with the policy on conditionality of 29 April 1997. The Council expects to undertake its next conditionality review in November 1999. The Council charges its competent bodies to examine a review mechanism covering the instruments of the Stabilisation and Association process.

COUNTRY SPECIFIC CONCLUSIONS

8. The Council reviewed the performances by the countries of the region in the light of the conditions set out in the Council conclusions of 29 April 1997 as well as of 31 May 1999. In this context, the Communication by the Commission on a Stabilisation and Association process for countries of South Eastern Europe has been taken into account.

Albania

9. There has been progress regarding the respect for democratic principles, human rights and market economy reform. However, large parts of the country remains marked by a lack of public order and security. The dialogue between the Government and the Democratic Party has contributed to an improvement of the domestic, political climate in Albania. The country has dealt admirably with the massive refugee influx from Kosovo and has cooperated efficiently with international organisations.

10. PHARE and other Community assistance will be continued with a view to achieving further progress in stabilisation, recovery, economic reform and democratisation in this country as well as to enhancing regional co-operation. The EU will continue, in particular, to support the re-establishment of a viable Albanian police in co-operation with the strengthened WEU Mission and, to enhance its Customs Assistance Mission, on the basis of the amended Customs Code. Budgetary assistance for refugee-related expenses is being provided. The Council welcomes the Commission's intention to implement, without delay, balance of payment support adopted recently and that macro-economic developments will be monitored closely by the Commission and the IFIs.

11. In accordance with its Conclusions of 26 April and 31 May 1999, the Council welcomes that the Commission will prepare, as soon as possible, a report on the feasibility of the opening of negotiations for a Stabilisation and Association Agreement with Albania. In the light of discussions on this report in Council, the Commission will then be invited to present recommendations for negotiating directives. In the interim, contractual relations will continue, based on the 1992 Cooperation Agreement and the connected Declaration on Political Dialogue, will be continued, and new working parties (on infrastructure and agriculture) will be established. The Council welcomes that the Commission, in accordance with its Conclusions of 9 November 1998, has presented a proposal aiming at the upgrading the bilateral trade regime towards regional standards. It instructs its competent bodies to examine it with a view to an early adoption by the Council.

Bosnia and Herzegovina

[...]

Croatia

[...]

Federal Republic of Yugoslavia

18. Today, the Federal Republic of Yugoslavia does not fulfil the relevant conditions for Autonomous Trade Measures, PHARE assistance or the Association and Stabilisation Agreement. Progress in respecting democratic freedoms and the rights of persons belonging to national minorities are key conditions to be met. In any event, progress in Kosovo will be important.

19. The Council will continue to support the Republic of Montenegro under its democratically elected Government.

Former Yugoslav Republic of Macedonia

20. The Former Yugoslav Republic of Macedonia continues to confirm its maturity with regard to democratic progress, separation of powers and protection of human rights. The continued presence of the "Democratic Party of Albanians" in the new Government demonstrates the willingness to develop a multiethnic and pluralistic society. The country has come under tremendous strain through the effects of the Kosovo crisis. The efforts made in coping with a massive refugee influx are commendable. The country should continue to fully cooperate with and grant access to international organisations and NGOs.

21. The country will continue to benefit from Community assistance, notably in the framework of PHARE. The eligibility of the former Yugoslav Republic of Macedonia for additional PHARE multi-beneficiary programmes will be determined on a case-by-case basis, taking into account their consistence with and value-added to the National Programme. Budgetary assistance for refugee-related expenses is being provided.

22. The Council notes the positive record achieved so far, as well as the country's compliance with the relevant conditions. It welcomes that, in accordance with its Conclusions of 8 and 26 April and 31 May 1999, the Commission has presented its report on the feasibility of the opening of negotiations for a Stabilisation and Association Agreement with this country. The Council instructs its competent bodies to examine this report for its next session with a view to invite the Commission to present a formal recommendation for negotiating directives. The Council takes note, that in that case, the Commission will present a formal recommendation for negotiating directives before the end of July. In the interim, the Cooperation Agreement and the Agreement in the Field of Transport will continue to be implemented, and relations will intensify in that framework and in the framework of the Political Dialogue.

European Community Monitor Mission

CONCLUSIONS

The Council emphasises the necessity to review the activities of ECMM in the light of changed circumstances in the region.

The Council instructs its competent bodies to review the role and mandate of the ECMM and invites the Commission to consult the current as well as the two preceding Presidencies on the cost and management of ECMM with a view to submitting, by the end of October 1999, relevant information on future costs and configuration of ECMM.

Furthermore, the Council and the Commission have agreed to make all efforts to identify, by the end of October 1999, wherever possible, savings of current Common Foreign Security Policy expenditure as well as the scope for transferring such expenditure to first pillar financing, where an EC legal basis exists. The forthcoming revision of the OBNOVA Regulation will be a first opportunity to pursue this actively.

The Council will decide, by the end of 1999, on the future of ECMM including questions of legal base and financing in the light of these reviews.

Humanitarian Situation in Kosovo

The Council heard a report by Commissioner BONINO on the latest developments concerning the humanitarian situation of Albanian Kosovars returning to their homes, both internally displaced persons as well as refugees located in Albania and FYROM. She also reported on the situation resulting from the exodus of Serbs from Kosovo.

350. EU, Council Common Position Amending Common Position 1999/273/CFSP Concerning a Ban on the Supply and Sale of Petroleum and Petroleum Products to the FRY, and Common Position 1999/318/CFSP Concerning Additional Restrictive Measures against the FRY, 1999/604/CFSP, 3 September 1999[1]

The Council of the European Union,

Having regard to the Treaty on European Union, and in particular Article 15 thereof,

Whereas:

(1) On 23 April 1999 the Council adopted Common Position 1999/273/CFSP concerning a ban on the supply and sale of petroleum and petroleum products to the Federal Republic of Yugoslavia (FRY)[2] and on 10 May 1999 Common Position 1999/318/CFSP concerning additional restrictive measures against the Federal Republic of Yugoslavia[3];

(2) On 19 July 1999 the Council recalled its support for the democratically elected government of President Djukanovic in Montenegro and for the Republic of Montenegro's political and economic reform programme, and underlined the necessity to speedily exempt Kosovo and Montenegro from the oil embargo and other sanctions;

(3) Article 1 of Common Position 1999/273/CFSP and Article 4 of Common Position 1999/318/CFSP should be amended accordingly;

(4) The European Union considers the alignment of the Associated Countries of Central and Eastern Europe, Cyprus, Malta and the EFTA countries important to maximise the impact of this Common Position;

(5) Corresponding expeditious action by the Community is needed in order to implement the measures cited below,

has adopted this Common Position:

Article 1

The following paragraph shall be added to Article 1 of Common Position 1999/273/CFSP:

"3. The prohibition referred to in paragraph (1) will not apply to the supply and sale of petroleum and petroleum products to the Province of Kosovo or the Republic of Montenegro for the purpose of activity carried on in, or operated from Montenegro or Kosovo, without prejudice to the applicability of this Article with regard to the rest of the Federal Republic of Yugoslavia."

Article 2

The following paragraph shall be added to Article 4 of Common Position 1999/318/CFSP: "The prohibition referred to above will not apply to flights operated for commercial or private purposes between the Community and the Republic of Montenegro or the Province of Kosovo by non-Yugoslav carriers and Montenegro airlines, without prejudice to the applicability of this Article with regard to the rest of the Federal Republic of Yugoslavia."

Article 3

The Presidency will request the Associated Countries of Central and Eastern Europe, Cyprus, Malta and the EFTA Members to align themselves with this Common Position.

Article 4

This Common Position shall take effect on the date of its adoption.

Article 5

This Common Position shall be published in the Official Journal.

Done at Brussels, 3 September 1999. For the Council: The President T. Halonen

351. Council of Europe, Parliamentary Assembly, Recommendation 1423 (1999), Southeastern Europe Following the Kosovo Conflict: Economic Reconstruction and Renewal, 23 September 1999

[Extract from the Official Gazette of the Council of Europe - September 1999. Text adopted by the Assembly on 23 September 1999 (30th Sitting).]

1. In the aftermath of the Kosovo conflict it is urgent for all of Europe, together with the rest of the world, to engage in the economic reconstruction and renewal of Southeastern Europe, a region vital to the continent's overall peace and stability.

2. With this in mind, the Assembly welcomes the speedy international response to the need for post-conflict reconstruction, as manifested both in the sizeable assistance pledged to Kosovo by numerous countries at the Brussels donor conference on 28 July 1999, and at the conference on the Stability Pact for Southeastern Europe held in Sarajevo on 30 July 1999.

3. The Assembly, referring in particular to its Recommendation 1414 (1999) on the crisis in Kosovo and the situation in the Federal Republic of Yugoslavia and its Resolution 1184 (1999) on the need for intensified economic co-operation in Southeastern Europe, calls on the Committee of Ministers to ensure that the reconstruction effort is built on the following principles:

i. Comprehensiveness, in that it must encompass the entire region, from conflict-torn Kosovo to a Federal Republic of Yugoslavia under a new democratic regime to all the countries in Southeastern Europe directly or indirectly affected by the Kosovo conflict as well as those conflicts preceding it;

ii. Renewal, in that all the countries of Southeastern Europe must seize the opportunity presented by the conflict to open a new chapter in their relations, and in that the reconstruction must bring about thoroughgoing structural reform leading to a market-oriented economy and a modernisation of infrastructure and industry;

iii. Correct phasing of assistance, covering successively humanitarian aid, water and energy, infrastructure repair including educational facilities, environmental clean-up, macro-economic stabilisation and regional integration;

iv. The closest possible co-ordination between international institutions and programmes involved;

v. Long-term commitment by the international community and by the countries concerned;

vi. Democracy, human rights and the rule of law, all of which must pervade the entire project.

Kosovo

4. The Assembly welcomes the rapid establishment of the United Nations Interim Administration Mission in Kosovo (UNMIK), the appointment of a United Nations Special Representative and the creation of a High Level Steering Group for enlisting and channelling emergency assistance. It calls on the Committee of Ministers to ensure full support by all parties concerned for these institutions in their difficult mission.

5. In order to fulfil the economic aims of United Nations Security Council Resolution 1244 on the situation relating to Kosovo, assistance to the province must focus on:

---

[1] OJ L 236, 07/09/1999 p. 0001 - 0001, 499X0604.
[2] OJ L 108, 27.4.1999, p. 1.
[3] OJ L 123, 13.5.1999, p. 1.

i. emergency assistance to support the return of refugees and displaced persons, including housing reconstruction, and in particular the construction of some 30 000 prefabricated houses before the onset of winter;

ii. the establishment of a civil administration capable of ensuring the advent of democracy, the rule of law and the protection of all citizens;

iii. an assessment of the damage incurred from the conflict and the practical organisation of the reconstruction effort, including the necessary institutional basis;

iv. priorities for public spending and the creation of a stable environment for investment, private sector development, banking, external trade, currency and macro-economic measures;

v. technical and financial assistance to local authorities in order to overcome urgent needs following the conflict, such as disposal of rubble and treatment of municipal waste, water purification for drinking water supplies and waste water treatment;

vi. the establishment of a land ownership system and a regional land register, as a precondition for land use planning and economic development in Kosovo;

vii. the renewal of infrastructure, in particular the road network, telecommunications network and postal service, and the production and distribution of electricity;

viii. the urgent detection and elimination of anti-personnel mines scattered throughout the territory of Kosovo.

Most affected neighbouring countries and the overall region

6. The Assembly notes the major economic disruptions caused by the conflict to countries neighbouring the Federal Republic of Yugoslavia and to Southeastern Europe as a whole. Of particular concern is the collapse of transport on and across the Danube due to destroyed bridges - a disruption which has particularly affected Danube basin countries and those linked up with them, such as Ukraine and Moldova. It is essential that these countries not only be assisted in their efforts to repair the damage still being done to their economies, but that they are also given the firm prospect of timely economic integration with other parts of Europe, notably the European Union. For humanitarian reasons, it is also imperative to remove the debris of destroyed bridges before the onset of the winter, for they can have a serious damming effect on the flow of the river, which could result in flooding in the Vojvodina region (Federal Republic of Yugoslavia), Croatia and southern Hungary.

7. The Assembly reiterates its support for the Stability Pact for Southeastern Europe, which it welcomes as a broad political framework which, if rightly used and supported by the countries in the region, will facilitate regional integration and development. The Assembly calls on the Committee of Ministers:

i. to envisage urgent measures to re-establish international navigation on the Danube River, given its importance as the major waterway and transport link used for economic development and trade in central and Southeastern Europe;

ii. to assess, within the framework of the Stability Pact, the long-term external financing needs of the countries concerned, fully involving in particular the European Union and the World Bank as well as other international financial institutions concerned;

iii. to lay particular emphasis on a plan for intensified Southeast European economic co-operation, which alone can ensure that assistance leads to sustainable growth. Such a plan should include structural reform; measures to facilitate trade and border crossings; repair and renewal of trans-European transport links and other infrastructure, preferably through projects involving several countries simultaneously and using, wherever possible, companies from the region, and applying procedures of environmental impact assessment;

iv. to ensure privileged access to the more economically advanced European countries for exports from the region, such as through preferential unilateral trade agreements, in particular with the European Union and EFTA;

v. to work in favour of the conclusion of a multilateral free trade agreement involving as many countries in the region as possible, as well as the members of the Central European Free Trade Agreement (CEFTA);

vi. to make a comprehensive damage assessment on the state of the environment and to provide financial and technical assistance to the countries in the region in order to establish a strict and transparent environmental monitoring system, notably for compiling data on water quality in the Danube basin.

8. The Assembly urges the European Union to take steps without delay to ensure that produce donated in the framework of humanitarian operations be exempt from quota regulations.

9. The Assembly resolves fully to use its special position as a parliamentary forum for international organisations such as the OECD, the EBRD, the World Bank, the IMF, the United Nations Economic Commission for Europe and the WTO in order to monitor their efforts on behalf of Southeastern Europe.

10. Finally, the Assembly recalls the important position of the Federal Republic of Yugoslavia in Southeastern Europe and states its belief that complete economic recovery is not possible in the region without reconstruction also in that country under a new democratic regime. It calls on all Council of Europe member states to work together in favour of such an outcome and, as soon as it is reached, to provide that country with assistance going beyond the humanitarian assistance immediately required, by involving it fully in the Southeast European reconstruction project, in particular as concerns economic reform and infrastructure repair and environmental clean-up following the Kosovo conflict.

352. EC Council Regulation No 2111/1999 Prohibiting the Sale and Supply of Petroleum and Certain Petroleum Products to Certain Parts of the FRY and Repealing Regulation (EC) No 900/1999, 4 October 1999[1]

The Council of the European Union,

Having regard to the Treaty establishing the European Community, and in particular Article 301 thereof,

Having regard to Council Common Position 1999/604/CFSP of 3 September 1999, amending Common Position 1999/273/CFSP concerning a ban on the supply and sale of petroleum and petroleum products to the Federal Republic of Yugoslavia (FRY), and Common Position 1999/318/CFSP concerning additional restrictive measures against the Federal Republic of Yugoslavia[2]

Having regard to the proposal from the Commission,

Whereas:

(1) The Government of the Federal Republic of Yugoslavia ("FRY") has continued to violate United Nations Security Council Resolutions and to pursue extreme and criminally irresponsible policies, including repression against its own citizens, which constitute serious violations of human rights and international humanitarian law, and Common Position 1999/273/CFSP[3] provided that the supply and sale of petroleum and petroleum products to the FRY should be prohibited; however, Council Common Position 1999/604/CFSP provides that that prohibition should not apply to the sale and supply of such products to the Province of Kosovo and the Republic of Montenegro;

(2) The prohibition of selling, supplying or exporting petroleum and petroleum products to the FRY falls within the scope of the Treaty establishing the European Community;

---

[1] OJ L 258, 05/10/1999 p. 0012 - 0018, 399R2111.
[2] OJ L 236, 07/09/1999, p. 1.
[3] OJ L 108, 27/04/1999, p. 1.

(3) Therefore, and particularly with a view to avoiding distortion of competition, Community legislation is necessary for the implementation of this prohibition as far as the territory of the Community is concerned; for the purposes of this Regulation such territory is deemed to encompass the territories of the Member States to which the Treaty establishing the European Community is applicable, under the conditions laid down in that Treaty;

(4) To that end the Council adopted on 29 April 1999 a Regulation (EC) No 900/1999 prohibiting the sale and supply of petroleum and certain petroleum products to the Federal Republic of Yugoslavia (FRY)[1]

(5) The developments with regard to the FRY permit a partial lifting of the embargo imposed by Regulation (EC) No 900/1999;

(6) Such partial lifting should not prejudice the remaining applicability of Regulation (EC) No 900/1999 with regard to the FRY;

(7) For reasons of transparency and simplicity, the provisions of Regulation (EC) No 900/1999 should be incorporated in this Regulation, and that Regulation should be repealed,

has adopted this Regulation:

Article 1

It shall be prohibited, knowingly and intentionally, to:

(a) sell, supply or export, directly or indirectly, petroleum and petroleum products listed in Annex I, whether or not originating in the Community, to any person or body in the FRY or to any person or body for the purpose of any business carried on in, or operated from, the territory of the FRY;

(b) ship products referred to in point (a) to the territory of the FRY;

(c) participate in related activities the object or the effect of which is to promote the transactions or activities referred to in points (a) and (b).

Article 2

1. Notwithstanding the provisions of Article 1, the competent authorities may authorise:

(a) the sale, supply, export or shipment of products listed in Annex I for the use of diplomatic and consular missions of the Member States in the FRY as well as for the use of an international military peace-keeping presence;

(b) on a case-by-case basis and subject to the consultation procedure set out in paragraph 2, the sale, supply or export of the products listed in Annex I if conclusive evidence is given to these authorities that the sale, supply or export serves strictly humanitarian purposes.

2. The competent authorities of a Member State which intend to authorise a sale, supply or export in accordance with paragraph 1(b) shall notify to the competent authorities of the other Member States and to the Commission the grounds on which they intend to authorise the sale, supply or export concerned.

If, within one working day after the receipt of the said notification, a Member State or the Commission has given notice to the other Member States or the Commission of conclusive evidence that the intended sale, supply or export will not serve the indicated humanitarian purposes, the Commission will convene within one working day of the said notice a meeting with the Member States in order to consult on the relevant evidence.

The Member State which intends to authorise the sale, supply or export shall take a decision with regard to this authorisation only when no objections have been raised or after the consultations on the conclusive evidence have taken place at the meeting convened by the Commission. In case of an authorisation, the Member State concerned shall notify to the other Member States and the Commission the grounds on which its decision to authorise has been taken.

Article 3

1. Notwithstanding the provisions of Article 1, the competent authorities may authorise the sale, supply or export, directly or indirectly, of petroleum and petroleum products listed in Annex I to any person or body for the purpose of any business carried on in, or operated from, the territory of the Federal Republic of Yugoslavia, and the shipment to the territory of the Federal Republic of Yugoslavia, provided that conclusive evidence is presented to these authorities that:

(a) the petroleum and petroleum products sold, supplied or exported are shipped from the Community to the Republic of Montenegro or the Province of Kosovo without transiting through other parts of the Republic of Serbia; and

(b) the petroleum and petroleum products shall not leave the territory of the Republic of Montenegro or the Province of Kosovo for any destination elsewhere in the Republic of Serbia.

Any authorisation should be made in accordance with the model set out in Annex II.

2. A declaration by the relevant bodies designated by the Special Representative of the United Nations Secretary General for the Province of Kosovo or by the competent authorities of the Republic of Montenegro listed in Annex III, in accordance with the model set out in Annex IV, shall be conclusive evidence for the purpose of any authorisation pursuant to paragraph 1.

3. With regard to each territory concerned and until such time as the names and addresses of its relevant body or competent authority to be listed in Annex III will have been published in the Official Journal of the European Communities, a competent authority of a Member State shall not grant a prior authorisation before it has requested the competent authorities of the other Member States and the Commission to give their comments on the evidence presented, which, if any, shall be given within a period of five working days after sending the request. After these five days and on the basis of the comments received or any other information obtained in the meantime, the competent authority concerned shall take a decision in respect of the granting of an authorisation, and notify the Commission and the other Member States of this decision.

Article 4

Article 1 shall not apply as regards sales, supplies, exports or shipments to the forces in which the Member States participate, operating in the FRY.

Article 5

Each Member State shall determine the sanctions to be imposed where the provisions of this Regulation are infringed. Such sanctions shall be effective, proportionate and dissuasive.

Pending the adoption, where necessary, of any legislation to this end, the sanctions to be imposed where the provisions of this Regulation are infringed shall be those determined by the Member States in accordance with Article 5 of Council Regulation (EC) No 926/98 of 27 April 1998 concerning the reduction of certain economic relations with the Federal Republic of Yugoslavia[2].

Article 6

The Commission and the Member States shall inform each other of the measures taken under this Regulation and shall supply each other with other relevant information at their disposal in connection with this Regulation, such as violation and enforcement problems or judgments handed down by national courts.

Member States shall notify the competent authorities of other Member States and the Commission of any authorisations for sale, supply, or export or shipment granted in accordance with Article 3(1).

---

[1] OJ L 114, 01/05/1999, p. 7.

[2] OJ L 130, 01/05/1998, p. 1.

Article 7

The Commission shall establish the list of competent authorities referred to in Articles 2 and 3(1) on the basis of relevant information provided by the Member States. The Commission shall publish this list and any changes to it in the Official Journal of the European Communities.

The Commission shall establish and, if necessary, amend the list of competent authorities of the Republic of Montenegro referred to in Article 3(2).

The Commission shall establish and, if necessary, amend the list of relevant bodies designated by the Special Representative of the United Nations Secretary-General for the Province of Kosovo referred to in Article 3(2).

The Commission shall amend if necessary the models of prior authorisation and prior final destination declaration referred to Article 3(1) and (2). The Commission shall publish any changes to this list and these models in the Official Journal of the European Communities.

Article 8

Regulation (EC) No 900/1999 is hereby repealed and replaced by the provisions of this Regulation. Any reference to Articles of that Regulation shall be construed as reference to the corresponding Article of this Regulation.

Article 9

This Regulation shall apply within the territory of the Community, including its air space and on board any aircraft or any vessel under the jurisdiction of a Member State and to any person elsewhere who is a national of a Member State and any body which is incorporated or constituted under the law of a Member State.

Article 10

This Regulation shall enter into force on the day of its publication in the Official Journal of the European Communities.

This Regulation shall be binding in its entirety and directly applicable in all Member States.

Done at Luxembourg, 4 October 1999. For the Council: The President K. Häkämies

[Annex I: Petroleum and petroleum products referred to in Article 1, Annex II, ANNEX III: List of relevant bodies in the Province of Kosovo and competent authorities of the Republic of Montenegro, referred to in Article 3(2) and Annex IV have been omitted.]

Amendments:
Amended by 300R0607 (OJ L 073 22.03.00, p.2)
Amended by 300R0303 (OJ L 035 10.02.00 p.8)
Amended by 399R2421 (OJ L 294 16.11.99 p.7)

353. EC Council Regulation No 2151/1999 Imposing a Ban on Flights between the Territories of the Community and the FRY other than the Republic of Montenegro or the Province of Kosovo, and Repealing Regulation (EC) No 1064/1999, 11 October 1999[1]

The Council of the European Union,

Having regard to the Treaty establishing the European Community, and in particular Article 301 thereof,

Having regard to Common Position 99/318/CFSP adopted by the Council on the basis of Article 15 of the Treaty on European Union concerning additional restrictive measures against the Federal Republic of Yugoslavia[2],

Having regard to the proposal from the Commission,

Whereas:

(1) The government of the Federal Republic of Yugoslavia (FRY) has continued to violate United Nations Security Council resolutions and to pursue extreme and criminally irresponsible policies, including repression against its own citizens, which constitute serious violations of human rights and international humanitarian law;

(2) Therefore, all flights between the territory of the Community and that of the Federal Republic of Yugoslavia other than the Republic of Montenegro or the Province of Kosovo should be prohibited;

(3) This prohibition should not apply, under certain conditions, to Montenegro Airlines;

(4) This measure falls under the scope of the Treaty establishing the European Community;

(5) Therefore, and notably with a view to avoiding distortion of competition, Community legislation is necessary for the implementation of this measure, whereas as far as the territory of the Community is concerned; such territory is deemed to encompass, for the purposes of this Regulation, the territories of the Member States to which the Treaty establishing the European Community is applicable, under the conditions laid down in that Treaty;

(6) There is a need to allow emergency landings and ensuring take-offs, and to allow exceptions for flights which serve strictly humanitarian purposes;

(7) There is a need for the Commission and Member States to inform each other of the measures taken under this Regulation and of other relevant information at their disposal in connection with this Regulation;

(8) For reasons of transparency and simplicity, the provisions of Council Regulation (EC) No 1064/1999 of 21 May 1999 imposing a ban on flights between the European Community and Federal Republic of Yugoslavia, and repealing Regulation (EC) No 1901/98[3] should be incorporated in this Regulation, and that Regulation should be repealed,

has adopted this Regulation:

Article 1

It shall be prohibited to take off from or land in the territory of the Community for:

(a) any aircraft operated, directly or indirectly, by a Yugoslav carrier, that is a carrier having its principal place of business or its registered office in the Federal Republic of Yugoslavia (FRY);

(b) any aircraft registered in the FRY; and

(c) any civil aircraft, that is an aircraft operated for commercial or private purposes, if it has taken off from or is destined to land in the territory of the FRY.

Article 2

1. All operating authorisations for scheduled air services between any point in the territory of the Community and any point in the FRY are hereby revoked and no new operating authorisations for such services shall be granted.

2. All authorisations for charter flights, be they individual or series flights, between any point in the territory of the Community and any point in the FRY are hereby revoked and no new authorisations for such flights shall be granted.

3. No new operating authorisations shall be granted or existing ones renewed enabling aircraft that are either registered in the FRY or operated by Yugoslav carriers, to fly to or from airports in the Community.

Article 3

1. Article 1 shall not apply to emergency landings and ensuing take-offs.

2. Notwithstanding Articles 1 and 2, the competent authorities of the Member States may authorise on a case-by-case basis and subject to

---

[1] OJ L 264, 12/10/1999 p. 0003 - 0008, 399R2151.
[2] OJ L 123, 13/05/1999, p. 1. Common Position amended by Common Position 1999/604/CFSP (OJ L 236, 7.9.1999, p. 1).
[3] OJ L 129, 22/05/1999, p. 27.

the consultation procedure of paragraph 3, that civil aircraft take off from or land in the territory of the Community, if conclusive evidence is given to these authorities that the flight to or from the territory of the FRY serves strictly humanitarian purposes.

3. The competent authorities of a Member State which intend to authorise a take off or landing in accordance with paragraph 2 shall notify to the competent authorities of the Member States and to the Commission the grounds on which they intend to authorise the take off or landing concerned.

If, within one working day after the receipt of the said notification, a Member State or the Commission has given notice to the other Member States or the Commission of conclusive evidence that the intended flight will not serve the indicated humanitarian purposes, the Commission will convene within one working day of the said notice a meeting with the Member States in order to consult on the relevant evidence.

The Member State which intends to authorise the take off or landing shall only take a decision with regard to this authorisation when either no objections have been raised, or after the consultations on the conclusive evidence have taken place at the meeting convened by the Commission. Where an authorisation is granted after such meeting, the Member State concerned shall notify to the other Member States and the Commission the grounds on which its decision to authorise has been taken.

4. Nothing in this Regulation shall be construed as limiting the right of any aircraft to fly over the territories of the Community and the FRY for transit purposes in accordance with applicable regulations.

Article 4

1. Notwithstanding Articles 1 and 2, the competent authorities listed in Annex I may authorise individual or series flights with civil aircraft as defined in Article 1(c) between the territories of the Community and the FRY, on the condition that:

(a) the aircraft used for these flights:

- are not registered in the FRY and are operated by Montenegro Airlines or by a carrier which is not a Yugoslav carrier as defined in Article 1(a); or

- are registered in the FRY and listed in Annex II, either as aircraft used by the government of Montenegro or the relevant bodies designated by the Special Representative of the UN Secretary-General for the Province of Kosovo, for non-commercial purposes, or as aircraft used by Montenegro Airlines for commercial purposes;

and

(b) the point of departure of flights, intermediate points and points of final destination in the FRY are located only in the Republic of Montenegro or the Province of Kosovo.

2. Authorisations granted under this Article shall cease to be valid if:

(a) in cases of flights to or from points in the Province of Kosovo, payments for the provision of essential services necessary for the normal execution of these flights are made to others than the providers of these services listed in Annex III, the level of such payments does not correspond to the average rates applicable for such services during the six month period before 19 June 1999 or such rates are applied on a discriminatory basis; or

(b) in cases of flights to or from points in the Republic of Montenegro, payments for the provision of essential services necessary for the normal execution of these flights, other than Air Traffic Control Services provided by the competent bodies of the FRY, are not made into the account of the competent authorities of the Republic of Montenegro, listed in Annex III, the level of such payments does not correspond to the average rates applicable during the six month period before 19 June 1999 or such rates are applied on a discriminatory basis.

3. For the purpose of this Regulation, Air Traffic Control services provided by the competent bodies of the FRY and essential services necessary for the normal execution of authorised flights provided by the entities listed in Annex III shall be deemed to be essential transit services referred to in Article 7(2)(c) of Regulation (EC) No 1294/1999[1].

Article 5

Participation, knowingly and intentionally, in related activities, the object or effect of which is, directly or indirectly, to circumvent Articles 1 and 2 shall be prohibited.

Article 6

Each Member State shall determine the sanctions to be imposed where the provisions of this Regulation are infringed. Such sanctions must be effective, proportionate and dissuasive.

Pending the adoption, where necessary, of any legislation to this end, the sanctions to be imposed where the provisions of this Regulation are infringed shall be those determined by the Member States in accordance with Article 5 of Regulation (EC) No 1901/98[2] or Article 6 of Regulation (EC) No 1064/1999.

Article 7

The Commission and the Member States shall inform each other of the measures taken under this Regulation and supply each other with any other relevant information at their disposal in connection with this Regulation, such as breaches and enforcement problems, judgments handed down by national courts or decisions of relevant international fora.

Article 8

Regulation (EC) No 1064/1999 shall be repealed and replaced by the provisions of this Regulation. Any reference to Articles of that Regulation shall be construed as a reference to the corresponding Article of this Regulation.

Article 9

The Commission shall be empowered to:

(a) amend the list of competent authorities contained in Annex I on the basis of relevant information provided by the Member States;

(b) amend the list of aircraft registered in the FRY and operated by Montenegro Airlines, the Government of Montenegro or the relevant bodies designated by the Special Representative of the UN Secretary-General for the Province of Kosovo, on the basis of relevant information provided by this government or these bodies;

(c) publish and, if necessary, modify, the list of competent authorities of the Republic of Montenegro and of the relevant bodies and the essential service providers in the Province of Kosovo designated or identified as appropriate by the Special Representative of the United Nations Secretary-General for the Province of Kosovo.

The Commission shall publish these lists and any changes thereto in the Official Journal of the European Communities.

Article 10

This Regulation shall apply:

(a) within the territory of the Community including its airspace,

(b) on board any aircraft or any vessel under the jurisdiction of a Member State,

(c) to any person elsewhere who is a national of a Member State, and

(d) to any body which is incorporated or constituted under the law of a Member State.

Article 11

This Regulation shall enter into force on the day of its publication in the Official Journal of the European Communities.

This Regulation shall be binding in its entirety and directly applicable in all Member States.

---

[1] OJ L 153, 19/06/1999, p. 63. Regulation as amended by Commission Regulation (EC) No 1970/99 (OJ L 244, 16.9.1999, p. 39).
[2] OJ L 248, 08/09/1998, p. 7. Regulation as amended by Regulation (EC) No 214/1999 (OJ L 23, 30.1.1999, p. 6).

Done at Luxembourg, 11 October 1999. For the Council: The President T. Halonen

[Annex I: List of competent authorities referred to in Article 3, Annex II: List of aircraft registered in the FRY referred to in Article 4 and Annex III have been omitted.]

Amendments:
Suspended by 300R0607 (OJ L 073 22.03.00 p.4)

354. Council of Europe, Final Communique of the 105th Session of the Committee of Ministers of the Council of Europe, Strasbourg, 4 November 1999

The Committee of Ministers held its 105th Session in Strasbourg on 3 and 4 November 1999. Ministers discussed the Council of Europe's contribution to the implementation of the Kosovo settlement and the Stability Pact for South Eastern Europe, as a follow-up to decisions taken at their 104th meeting (Budapest, 7 May 1999) and UN Security Council Resolution 1244. The Ministers gave the action taken by the Council in the region their full support and agreed a political message to the Federal Republic of Yugoslavia.

At the Secretary General's invitation, an informal meeting was held on 3 November, in the presence of the President of the Parliamentary Assembly, with Mr Bernard Kouchner, the UN Secretary-General's Special Representative in Kosovo. Ministers also discussed the same subject on 4 November with the Parliamentary Assembly in the framework of the annual enlarged Joint Committee.

The Chairman of the Committee of Ministers, Mr Halldór Ásgrímsson, Minister for Foreign Affairs of Iceland, noted that the discussions on Kosovo placed the emphasis on humanitarian considerations and the need for a political settlement. The Ministers reiterated their support for the action undertaken by the Council of Europe in cooperation with UNMIK to implement UN Security Council Resolution 1244, as well for the Organisation's specific contribution, in the fields of its competence, to the Stability Pact for South Eastern Europe. The substance of the discussion is resumed in the following paragraphs.

The Ministers emphasised their determination to do everything possible to contribute to the success of the two processes at present under way, and to strengthen the Council of Europe's contribution to the international community's co-ordinated effort to promote democratic stability in South-East Europe. They reaffirmed the Council's mission to bring together all countries of Europe which share a commitment to pluralist democracy, human rights and the rule of law, and to a society based on tolerance and mutual respect.

In this spirit, the Ministers decided that the Organisation should pursue its contribution to implementation of the Kosovo settlement and the Stability Pact, and in particular:

- step up its activities in Kosovo in support of and in co-ordination with the United Nations as well as the OSCE and the European Union, in particular by making its experts available to provide professional training in the fields of law, police work, human rights, the fight against racism, intolerance and xenophobia, local democracy, the media and psycho-social assistance for children traumatised by the war. They re-iterated the need to contribute effectively to a democratic and multi-ethnic society in Kosovo, the Federal Republic of Yugoslavia, as called for, inter alia, in UN Security Council Resolution 1244. They stressed the importance of an on-the-spot presence of the Council of Europe, including through the Office opened in Pristina.

- press ahead with implementation of the Council of Europe's programme for democratic stability in South-East Europe, adopted in Budapest on 7 May 1999, and increase the Organisation's contribution to the Stability Pact through active participation in the "working tables" on democratisation and human rights, on economic reconstruction, development and co-operation and on security issues - justice and home affairs.

Ministers recalled that the Summit of States and Organisations participating in the Stability Pact, meeting in Sarajevo on 30 July, had called on "the people of the Federal Republic of Yugoslavia to embrace democratic change and to work actively for regional reconciliation". They expressed the hope that the Federal Republic of Yugoslavia will soon fulfil the conditions necessary to become a full participant in the Stability Pact. The Ministers affirmed their willingness, once the requirements of the Council of Europe, based on its standards and principles, have been met, to consider the application of the Federal Republic of Yugoslavia for membership of the Organisation, in accordance with standard procedures for all new applicants, in a positive spirit. They expressed their hope that this process will enable the people of the Federal Republic of Yugoslavia to take their place as members of the European family.

Ministers noted the current situation with regard to the candidature of Bosnia and Herzegovina. They encouraged its authorities to continue to take the measures necessary to fulfil the conditions required for membership so that this can be granted at the earliest possible moment.

Ministers agreed that the Council of Europe's specific contribution to stability in South-East Europe lies in particular in the fields of protection of minorities, the establishment of non-judicial machinery for the protection of human rights, legal co-operation, the fight against corruption, organised crime and terrorism, support for independent media, the development of local democracy, transfrontier co-operation and education, culture and youth. They urged countries in the region to accede rapidly to the legal instruments developed by the Council of Europe in these fields.

CHRONOLOGICAL LIST OF DOCUMENTS

DATE	TEXT	DOCUMENT
1974	The Constitution of the Socialist Federal Republic of Yugoslavia	No. 1
1974	Constitution of the Socialist Republic of Serbia	No. 2
1974	Constitution of the Socialist Autonomous Province of Kosovo	No. 3
1989	Amendments of the Serbian Constitution	No. 4
28 June 1989	Speech by Slobodan Milosevic at the Central Celebration Marking the 600th Anniversary of the Battle of Kosovo, Gazimestan	No. 7
28 September 1990	The Constitution of the Socialist Republic of Serbia	No. 5
18 October 1991	Peace Conference on Yugoslavia, Carrington Draft Paper, "Arrangements for a General Settlement", UN Doc. S/23169, Annex VI	No. 50 a)
18 October 1991	Peace Conference on Yugoslavia, Carrington Draft Paper, "Treaty Provisions for the Convention", UN Doc. S/23169, Annex VII	No. 50 b)
22 October 1991	Statement Made by the People's Assembly of Albania	No. 9
22 December 1991	Peace Conference on Yugoslavia, Letter from Dr. Rugova to Lord Carrington	No. 50 c)
27 April 1992	The Constitution of the Federal Republic of Yugoslavia	No. 6
27 June 1992	EU, European Council in Lisbon 26-27 June 1992: Conclusions of the Presidency, DOC/92/3	No. 51
27 August 1992	London International Conference on the Former Yugoslavia, Co-Chairman's Paper on Serbia and Montenegro	No. 50 d)
28 August 1992	UN Commission on Human Rights, Report on the Situation of Human Rights in the Former Yugoslavia, UN Doc. E/CN.4/1992/S-1/9	No. 23
11 November 1992	UN, Report of the Secretary-General on the International Conference on the Former Yugoslavia, UN Doc. S/24795	No. 50 e)
18 December 1992	UN General Assembly Resolution 47/147, Situation of Human Rights in the Territory of the Former Yugoslavia	No. 12
23 February 1993	UN Commission on Human Rights, Resolution 1993/7, Situation of Human Rights in the Territory of the Former Yugoslavia	No. 30
26 February 1993	UN Commission on Human Rights, Report on the Situation of Human Rights in the Territory of the Former Yugoslavia Submitted by Mr. Tadeusz Mazowiecki, Special Rapporteur of the Commission on Human Rights, pursuant to Commission Resolution 1992/S-1/1 of 14 August 1992, UN Doc. A/48/92-S/25341, paras. 153-171	No. 24
30 March 1993	UN, Report of the UN Secretary-General on the International Conference of the Former Yugoslavia, Recent Activities of the Working Groups, UN Doc. S/25490	No. 50 f)
9 August 1993	UN Security Council Resolution 855 (1993)	No. 52
17 November 1993	UN Commission on Human Rights, Fifth Periodic Report on the Situation of Human Rights in the Territory of the Former Yugoslavia Submitted by Mr. Tadeusz Mazowiecki, Special Rapporteur of the Commission on Human Rights, pursuant to Paragraph 32 of Commission Resolution 1993/7 of 24 February 1993, UN Doc. E/CN.4/1994/47, paras. 188-205	No. 25
20 December 1993	Violations of Human Rights in the Republic of Bosnia and Herzegovina, the Republic of Croatia and the FRY (Serbia and Montenegro), UN General Assembly Resolution 48/153	No. 13
9 March 1994	UN Commission on Human Rights, Resolution 1994/76, Situation of Human Rights in Kosovo	No. 31
4 November 1994	UN Commission on Human Rights, Ninth Periodic Report on the Situation of Human Rights in the Territory of the Former Yugoslavia Submitted by Mr. Tadeusz Mazowiecki, Special Rapporteur of the Commission on Human Rights, pursuant to Commission Resolution 1994/72 of 9 March 1994 and ECOSOC Decision 1994/262 of 22 July 1994, UN Doc. A/49/641-S/1994/1252, paras. 162-203	No. 26
23 December 1994	Situation of Human Rights in Kosovo, UN General Assembly Resolution 49/204	No. 14
18 December 1995	Letter from the Charge d'affaires a.i. of the Permanent Mission of Yugoslavia to the United Nations Addressed to the Secretary-General	No. 10
22 December 1995	Situation of Human Rights in Kosovo, UN General Assembly Resolution 50/190	No. 15
14 March 1996	UN Commission on Human Rights, Situation of Human Rights in the Territory of the Former Yugoslavia, Report Submitted by Ms Elisabeth Rehn, Special Rapporteur of the Commission on Human Rights pursuant to Commission Resolution 1995/89, UN Doc. E/CN.4/1996/63, paras. 140-149, 162-180	No. 27
1 September 1996	St. Egidio Education Agreement	No. 8 a)
1 October 1996	EU, 1950th Council Meeting, General Affairs, PRES/96/253, Luxembourg	No. 53

Chronological List of Documents

DATE	TEXT	DOCUMENT
11 November 1996	Letter from the Chargé d'affaires a.i. of the Permanent Mission of Yugoslavia to the United Nations Addressed to the Secretary-General	No. 11
12 December 1996	Situation of Human Rights in Kosovo, UN General Assembly Resolution 51/111	No. 16
12 December 1996	Situation of Human Rights in Bosnia and Herzegovina, the Republic of Croatia and the FRY (Serbia and Montenegro), UN General Assembly Resolution 51/116	No. 17
10 September 1997	UN Commission on Human Rights, Situation of Human Rights in the Territory of the Former Yugoslavia: Two Trials of Kosovo Albanians Charged with Offences against the State in the FRY in 1997, Report Submitted by the Special Rapporteur, Ms Elisabeth Rehn, pursuant to Paragraph 42 (c) of Commission Resolution 1997/57, UN Doc. E/CN.4/1998/9	No. 28
24 September 1997	Contact Group of Foreign Ministers, Statement on Kosovo, New York	No. 54
12 December 1997	Situation of Human Rights in Kosovo, UN General Assembly Resolution 52/139	No. 18
12 December 1997	Situation of Human Rights in Bosnia and Herzegovina, the Republic of Croatia and the FRY (Serbia and Montenegro), UN General Assembly Resolution 52/147	No. 19
1998	Amnesty International Report 1998: FRY: For the Period January - December 1997	No. 47
8 January 1998	Contact Group Meeting, Statement on Kosovo, Washington, D.C	No. 97
25 February 1998	Contact Group Meeting, Statement on Kosovo, Moscow	No. 55
3 March 1998	EU, Declaration by the Presidency on behalf of the European Union Concerning the Upsurge of Violence in Kosovo, 98/18/CFSP, Brussels	No. 56
9 March 1998	Contact Group Meeting, Statement on Kosovo, London	No. 57
10 March 1998	Countries of South Eastern Europe, Joint Declaration of the Ministers of Foreign Affairs of Countries of South-Eastern Europe Concerning the Situation in Kosovo, Sofia	No. 58
10 March 1998	ICTY, Statement by the Prosecutor, CC/PIO/302-E, The Hague	No. 312
11 March 1998	FRY, Declaration by Milan Milutinovic, President of the Republic of Serbia on the Political Process Initiated for Kosovo and Metohija	No. 59
11 March 1998	OSCE, Permanent Council, Decision No. 218, PC. DEC/218/98	No. 98
13 March 1998	China, Vice Premier and Foreign Minister Qian Qichen on the Question of Kosovo (FRY), PRO4/98	No. 278
18 March 1998	Council of Europe, Parliamentary Assembly, Recommendation 1360 (1998), Crisis in Kosovo	No. 60
19 March 1998	EU, Common Position Defined by the Council on the Basis of Article J.2 of the EU Treaty on Restrictive Measures against the FRY, 98/240/CFSP	No. 61
24 March 1998	Agreed Measures for the Implementation of the Agreement on Education of 1 September 1996, Belgrade	No. 8 b)
24 March 1998	FRY, Declaration of the Parliament of Serbia on National Unity	No. 62
25 March 1998	Contact Group, Statement on Kosovo, Bonn	No. 63
30/31 March 1998	EU, 2078th Council Meeting, General Affairs, PRES/98/86, Brussels	No. 64
31 March 1998	UN Security Council Resolution 1160 (1998)	No. 65
31 March 1998	UN, Extracts from the Debates of the Security Council Concerning Security Council Resolution 1160 (1998), UN Doc. S/PV. 3868	No. 66
2 April 1998	FRY, Letter by the President of the FRY to the Presidents of the Republic of Serbia, of the Serbian Government and of the Assembly of Serbia, on the Referendum whether or not Foreign Representatives Should be Involved in Dealing with the Problem of Kosovo	No. 67
22 April 1998	Council of Europe, Parliamentary Assembly, Recommendation 1368 (1998), Latest Developments in the FRY and the Situation in Kosovo	No. 68
22 April 1998	UN Commission on Human Rights, Resolution 1998/79, Situation of Human Rights in Bosnia and Herzegovina, the Republic of Croatia and the FRY	No. 32
27 April 1998	EU, 2085th Council Meeting, General Affairs, PRES/98/109, Luxembourg	No. 69
27 April 1998	EC Council Regulation No 926/98 Concerning the Reduction of Certain Economic Relations with the FRY	No. 70
29 April 1998	Contact Group, Statement, Rome	No. 71
30 April 1998	UN, Report of the Secretary-General Prepared pursuant to Security Council Resolution 1160 (1998), UN Doc. S/1998/361	No. 116
7 May 1998	EU, Common Position Defined by the Council on the Basis of Article J.2 of the EU Treaty Concerning the Freezing of Funds Held Abroad by the FRY and Serbian Governments, 98/326/CFSP	No. 72
12 May 1998	WEU, Ministerial Council, Rhodes Declaration, Rhodes	No. 73
28 May 1998	NATO, Statement on Kosovo Issued at the Ministerial Meeting of the North Atlantic Council, Press Release M-NAC-1(98)61, Luxembourg	No. 152

Chronological List of Documents

DATE	TEXT	DOCUMENT
4 June 1998	UN, Report of the Secretary-General Prepared pursuant to Security Council Resolution 1160 (1998), UN Doc. S/1998/470	No. 117
8 June 1998	EU, Common Position Defined by the Council on the Basis of Article J.2 of the EU Treaty Concerning the Prohibition of New Investment in Serbia, 98/374/CFSP	No. 74
11 June 1998	EU, Declaration by the European Union on Kosovo, 98/56/CFSP	No. 75
11 June 1998	NATO, Statement on Kosovo Issued at the Meeting of the North Atlantic Council in Defence Ministers Session, Press Release M-NAC-D-1(98)77	No. 153
12 June 1998	Contact Group, Statement Issued Following a Meeting of the Foreign Ministers of the Contact Group and the Foreign Ministers of Canada and Japan, London	No. 76
15/16 June 1998	EU, Cardiff European Council, Presidency Conclusions, DOC/98/10	No. 77
16 June 1998	FRY - Russian Federation, Joint Declaration Signed in Moscow by President Yeltsin and President Milošević, Moscow	No. 78
22 June 1998	EC Council Regulation No. 1295/98 on Freezing of Funds Held Abroad of FRY and Republic of Serbia	No. 79
24 June 1998	Council of Europe, Parliamentary Assembly, Recommendation 1376 (1998), Crisis in Kosovo and the Situation in the FRY	No. 80
29 June 1998	EU, Council Common Position, Ban on Flights by Yugoslav Carriers between FRY and the EC	No. 81
29 June 1998	EU, 2111th Council Meeting, General Affairs, PRES/98/227, Luxembourg	No. 82
2 July 1998	UN, Report of the Secretary-General Prepared pursuant to Security Council Resolution 1160 (1998), UN Doc. S/1998/608,	No. 118
8 July 1998	Contact Group, Statement, Bonn	No. 83
13 July 1998	EU, 2113th Council Meeting, General Affairs, PRES/98/240 Brussels	No. 84
15 July 1998	U.S. Department of State, Office of the Spokesman, Press Statement by James P. Rubin, Spokesman	No. 313
20 July 1998	EU, Declaration by the Presidency on behalf of the European Union on Recent Fighting in Kosovo, 98/77/CFSP, Brussels	No. 85
24 July 1998	EC Council Regulation No. 1607/98 on Prohibition of New Investment in Republic of Serbia	No. 86
5 August 1998	UN, Report of the Secretary-General Prepared pursuant to Security Council Resolution 1160 (1998), UN Doc. S/1998/712	No. 119
24 August 1998	UN Security Council, Presidential Statement, S/PRST/1998/25	No. 87
4 September 1998	UN, Report of the Secretary-General Prepared pursuant to Security Council Resolution 1160 (1998), UN Doc. S/1998/834	No. 120
7 September 1998	EC Council Regulation No. 1901/98, Ban on Flights of Yugoslav Carriers between FRY & EC	No. 88
23 September 1998	UN Security Council Resolution 1199 (1998)	No. 89
23 September 1998	UN, Extracts from the Debate of the Security Council Concerning Security Council Resolution 1199 (1998), UN Doc. S/PV. 3930	No. 90
24 September 1998	Council of Europe, Parliamentary Assembly, Recommendation 1384 (1998), Crisis in Kosovo and Situation in the FRY	No. 91
24 September 1998	NATO, Statement by the Secretary General following the ACTWARN Decision, Vilamoura	No. 154
October 1998	Human Rights Watch: FRY: Humanitarian Law Violations in Kosovo, Extracts	No. 48
1 October 1998	First Hill Draft Agreement for a Settlement of the Crisis in Kosovo	No. 93 a)
3 October 1998	UN, Report of the Secretary-General Prepared pursuant to Security Council Resolutions 1160 (1998) and 1199 (1998), UN Doc. S/1998/912,	No. 121
7 October 1998	Canada, Special Debate in the House of Commons, Extracts, 36th Parliament, 1st Session, Hansard 134, 1830-2330, Ottawa/Ontario	No. 214
7 October 1998	ICTY, Statement by the Office of the Prosecutor, CC/PIU/351-E, The Hague	No. 314
13 October 1998	Holbrooke Agreement - FRY, Statement by President, Slobodan Milosevic, on the Accords to Resolve the Problems in Kosovo and Metohija in a Peaceful Way and by Political Means	No. 156 a)
13 October 1998	NATO, Statement by the Secretary General Following Decision on the ACTORD, NATO HQ	No. 155
14 October 1998	Holbrooke Agreement - FRY, Statement from the Federal Government's Meeting, Belgrade	No. 156 b)
14 October 1998	Holbrooke Agreement, Accord Reached by Slobodan Milosevic, President of the FRY, and the UN Special Envoy, Richard Holbrooke, UN Doc. S/1998/953, Annex	No. 156 c)
15 October 1998	ICTY, Statement by the Prosecutor, CC/PIU/353-E, The Hague	No. 315

Chronological List of Documents

DATE	TEXT	DOCUMENT
15 October 1998	NATO-FRY, Agreement Providing for the Establishment of an Air Verification Mission over Kosovo, Belgrade	No. 157
15 October 1998	OSCE, Permanent Council, Decision No. 259, PC. DEC/259/98	No. 99
16 October 1998	Germany, Deliberations of the *Deutscher Bundestag, BT Plenarprotokolle* 13/248, p. 23127, Extracts, Bonn	No. 224
16 October 1998	OSCE-FRY, Agreement on the OSCE Kosovo Verification Mission	No. 100
24 October 1998	UN Security Council Resolution 1203 (1998)	No. 158
24 October 1998	UN, Extract from the Debate of the Security Council Concerning Security Council Resolution 1203 (1998), UN Doc. S/PV. 3937	No. 159
25 October 1998	China, Statement by Chinese Foreign Ministry Spokesman, PR 12/98	No. 279
25 October 1998	OSCE, Permanent Council, Decision No. 263, PC. DEC/263/98	No. 101
27 October 1998	EU, Declaration by the European Union on a Comprehensive Approach to Kosovo, 98/128/CFSP, Brussels	No. 92
27 October 1998	NATO, Statement by the Secretary General Following the Meeting of the North Atlantic Council	No. 160
27 October 1998	U.S., Secretary of State Albright, Remarks on Kosovo as Released by the Office of the Spokesman U.S. Department of State, Washington, D.C	No. 242
1 November 1998	Revised Hill Proposal	No. 93 b)
3 November 1998	Statement on Fundamental Principles for a Settlement of the Kosovo Question Issued by the Government of the Republic of Kosovo	No. 93 c)
12 November 1998	UN, Report of the Secretary-General Prepared pursuant to Security Council Resolutions 1160 (1998), 1199 (1998) and 1203 (1998), UN Doc. S/1998/1068	No. 122
17 November 1998	UN Security Council Resolution 1207 (1998)	No. 316
17 November 1998	WEU, Ministerial Council, Rome Declaration, Rome	No. 94
20 November 1998	FRY, Joint Proposal of the Agreement on the Political Framework of Self-Governance in Kosovo and Metohija, Belgrade	No. 93 d)
25 November 1998	FRY, Declaration on Support of the Joint Proposal of the Agreement on the Political Frameworks of Self-Governance in Kosovo and Metohija, Belgrade	No. 95
1 December 1998	FRY, Government Memorandum on the Situation in the Autonomous Province of Kosovo and Metohija, Belgrade	No. 102
2 December 1998	Third Hill Draft Proposal for a Settlement of the Crisis in Kosovo	No. 93 e)
3 December 1998	FRY, Declaration by the Federal Assembly, Belgrade	No. 96
4 December 1998	UN, Report of the Secretary-General Prepared pursuant to Resolutions 1160 (1998), 1199 (1998) and 1203 (1998), UN Doc. S/1998/1147	No. 123
8 December 1998	NATO Statement on Kosovo, Meeting of the North Atlantic Council in Foreign Ministers Session, Press Communique M-NAC-2(98)143	No. 161
9 December 1998	Situation of Human Rights in Bosnia and Herzegovina, the Republic of Croatia and the FRY (Serbia and Montenegro), UN General Assembly Resolution 53/163	No. 20
9 December 1998	Situation of Human Rights in Kosovo, UN General Assembly Resolution 53/164	No. 21
24 December 1998	UN, Report of the Secretary-General Prepared pursuant to Security Council Resolutions 1160 (1998), 1199 (1998) and 1203 (1998), UN Doc. S/1998/1221	No. 124
January 1999	Human Rights Watch: Report on the Massacre in Racak	No. 104
17 January 1999	FRY, Statement by the President of the Republic of Serbia, Milan Milutinovic	No. 105
18 January 1999	FRY, Statement by the Federal Government	No. 106
18 January 1999	UNHCR Press Release, Kosovo: Ogata Condemns Atrocities, Appeals for Access	No. 107
19 January 1999	UN Security Council, Presidential Statement, New York City, UN Doc. S/PRST/1999/2	No. 108
20 January 1999	UN Commission on Human Rights, Situation of Human Rights in the Former Yugoslavia, Report of Mr. Jiri Dienstbier, Special Rapporteur of the Commission on Human Rights on the Situation of Human Rights in Bosnia and Herzegovina, the Republic of Croatia and the FRY, UN Doc. E/CN.4/1999/42	No. 29
20 January 1999	EU, Statement of the Presidency of the European Union on the Racak Massacre, PRES/99/14, Brussels	No. 109
20 January 1999	EU, Letter of the German Minister for Foreign Affairs on behalf of the European Union to Milosevic	No. 110
21 January 1999	FRY, Statement from the Session of the Federal Government	No. 112
21 January 1999	OSCE Troika, Press Release No. 10/99	No. 111
22 January 1999	Contact Group, Chairman's Conclusions, London	No. 113

Chronological List of Documents

DATE	TEXT	DOCUMENT
22 January 1999	UK, Memorandum Submitted by the Foreign and Commonwealth Office, Kosovo: Legal Authority for Military Action	No. 236
26 January 1999	Islamic Group, Statement on the Situation in Kosovo, New York	No. 114
26 January 1999	U.S. Secretary of State Albright and Russian Foreign Minister Ivanov, Joint Statement, Moscow	No. 127
27 January 1999	Final Hill Proposal	No. 93 f)
28 January 1999	NATO, Statement to the Press by Secretary General, Press Release (1999)011, Brussels	No. 128
28 January 1999	UN Secretary-General, Statement of Kofi Annan to the North Atlantic Council, Brussels	No. 129
29 January 1999	Contact Group, Chairman's Conclusions, London	No. 130
29 January 1999	UN Security Council, Presidential Statement, UN Doc. S/PRST/1999/5	No. 131
30 January 1999	Contact Group Negotiators' Proposal	No. 133
30 January 1999	NATO, Statement by the North Atlantic Council, Press Release 99 (12)	No. 132
30 January 1999	UN, Report of the Secretary-General Prepared pursuant to Security Council Resolutions 1160 (1998), 1199 (1998) and 1203 (1998), UN Doc. S/1999/99	No. 125
1 February 1999	FRY, Letter of Federal Foreign Minister Zivadin Jovanovic to the President of the UN Security Council, Mr. Robert Fowler, Belgrade	No. 162
1 February 1999	FRY, Statement of the Federal Government Concerning NATO Decisions, Belgrade	No. 163
1 February 1999	UK, Statement by the Foreign Secretary, Mr. Robin Cook, to the House of Commons	No. 134
4 February 1999	FRY, Conclusions of the National Assembly of the Republic of Serbia Concerning NATO Threats of Aggression against FRY and the Participation in Talks in France, Belgrade	No. 164
6 February 1999	Joint Press Conference by Mr. Vedrine and Mr. Cook, Rambouillet	No. 135
11 February 1999	Statement of the Delegation Designated by the Government of the Republic of Serbia, at the Meeting in Rambouillet, Rambouillet	No. 136
14 February 1999	Contact Group Meeting, Chairman's Conclusions, Paris	No. 137
19 February 1999	EU, Declaration by the Presidency on behalf of the European Union, 99/15/CFSP, Brussels	No. 138
19 February 1999	NATO, Statement by the Secretary General on behalf of the North Atlantic Council, Press Release (99)020	No. 139
20 February 1999	Conclusions of the Contact Group, Rambouillet	No. 140
23 February 1999	Interim Agreement for Peace and Self-Government in Kosovo, Rambouillet	No. 141
23 February 1999	Contact Group, Rambouillet Accords: Co-Chairmen's Conclusions, Rambouillet	No. 142
23 February 1999	EU, Statement of the Presidency on behalf of the European Union on the Conclusion of the Rambouillet Conference	No. 145
23 February 1999	NATO, Statement by the Secretary General, Press Release (99)21	No. 146
23 February 1999	UN Security Council's Statement to the Press, Rambouillet	No. 143
23 February 1999	UN Secretary-General, Press Release, UN Doc. SG/SM/6902	No. 144
24 February 1999	UK, Statement by the Foreign Secretary, Mr. Robin Cook, House of Commons	No. 147
24 February 1999 - 4 March 1999	UNHCR Country Updates - Former Yugoslavia: 24 February 1999 - 4 March 1999, UN Inter-Agency Humanitarian Situation Report: Kosovo Population Movements	No. 41
26 February 1999	U.S. Department of State: Serbia-Montenegro Country Report on Human Rights Practices for 1998, Released by the Bureau of Democracy, Human Rights, and Labor	No. 45
14 - 21 March 1999	UNHCR Country Updates - Former Yugoslavia: 14 - 21 March 1999, UN Inter-Agency Humanitarian Situation Report: Kosovo	No. 42
15 March 1999	Kosovo Delegation Letter of Agreement Addressed to the French and British Foreign Ministers	No. 148
17 March 1999	FRY, Letter of the Yugoslav Foreign Minister Z. Jovanovic Addressed to President of the Security Council of the United Nations, Qin Huasun, Belgrade	No. 165
17 March 1999	FRY, Letter of the Yugoslav Foreign Minister Z. Jovanovic Addressed to Chairman-in-Office of the OSCE, Minister for Foreign Affairs of the Kingdom of Norway, Knut Vollebaek, Belgrade	No. 166
17 March 1999	Report of the EU Forensic Expert Team on the Racak Incident	No. 115
17 March 1999	UN, Report of the Secretary-General Prepared pursuant to Security Council Resolutions 1160 (1998), 1199 (1998) and 1203 (1998), UN Doc. S/1999/293	No. 126
18 March 1999	FRY, Agreement for Self-Government in Kosmet, Paris	No. 149
19 March 1999	Declaration of the Co-Chairmen Hubert Vedrine and Robin Cook, Paris	No. 150
19 March 1999	OSCE, Kosovo Verification Mission, Press Release No. 24/99, Oslo	No. 103

Chronological List of Documents

DATE	TEXT	DOCUMENT
22 March 1999	FRY, Letter of Yugoslav President Milosevic to the British and French Foreign Minister	No. 151
22 March 1999	NATO, Statement by the North Atlantic Council, Press Release (1999)038	No. 167
22 March 1999	United Kingdom, Statement by Defence Minister, Press Release 083/99, Paris	No. 168
22 March 1999	United Kingdom, Transcript of Statement Given by the Foreign Secretary, Robin Cook, Brussels	No. 169
23 March 1999	China, Ambassador Qin Huasun, Permanent Representative of PRC Talks to the Press at the UN on the Question of Kosovo	No. 280
23 March 1999	France, Statement by M. Lionel Jospin, Prime Minister, in the National Assembly, during Government Question Time, Paris	No. 217
23 March 1999	NATO, Statement by the Secretary General, Press Release (1999)040	No. 170
23 March 1999	NATO, Political and Military Objectives of NATO Action with Regard to the Crisis in Kosovo, Press Release (1999)043	No. 171
23 March 1999	UK, Statement by the Prime Minister, Tony Blair, in the House of Commons, Hansard, HC, vol. 328, col. 161	No. 237
24 March 1999	Canada, Notes for a Speech by the Honourable Lloyd Axworthy Minister for Foreign Affairs, Ottawa, Ontario	No. 215
24 March 1999	El Salvador, Statement, Press Release 82/99, San Salvador	No. 283
24 March 1999	France, Communiqué by the French Authorities, Paris	No. 218
24 March 1999	France, Statement by M. Jacques Chirac, President of the Republic, Berlin	No. 219
24 March 1999	Germany, Statement Made by Federal Chancellor Gerhard Schröder, Bonn, Press Release, Bonn	No. 225
24 March 1999	Hungary, Statement by the Spokesman of the Ministry of Foreign Affairs, Budapest	No. 232
24 March 1999	India, Official Spokesman's Statement, New Delhi	No. 284
24 March 1999	Mexico, Statement of Foreign Minister, NUM. 121/99, Tlatelolco, D.F	No. 285
24 March 1999	NATO, Press Statement by the Secretary General following the Commencement of Air Operations, Press Release (1999)041	No. 172
24 March 1999	The Netherlands, Statement by the Minister of Foreign Affairs in the Lower House, The Hague	No. 234
24 March 1999	The Philippines, Statement, Press Release No. 74-99	No. 286
24 March 1999	UK, Statement by the Deputy Prime Minister, John Prescott, in the House of Commons, Hansard, HC, vol. 328, col. 383	No. 238
24 March 1999	UN, Statement of the Secretary-General, Press Release, UN Doc. SG/SM/6938	No. 249
24 March 1999	UN, Extracts from the Debate of the Security Council Concerning Letter dated 24 March 1999 from the Permanent Representative of the Russian Federation to the UN Addressed to the President of the Security Council (S/1999/320), UN Doc. S/PV. 3988	No. 250
24 March 1999	U.S., President Clinton, Address to the Nation, Washington, D.C	No. 243
24 - 25 March 1999	EU, Presidency Conclusions - Berlin European Council	No. 258
25 March 1999	Egypt, Statement by Foreign Minister Moussa, Cairo	No. 287
25 March 1999	France, Ministry of Foreign Affairs, Legal Basis for the Action Taken by NATO	No. 220
25 March 1999	FRY, Statement from the Federal Government's Meeting, Belgrade	No. 173
25 March 1999	India, Official Spokesman's Statement, New Delhi	No. 288
25 March 1999	Japan, Statement by Foreign Minister Masahiko Koumura	No. 281
25 March 1999	Republic of Korea, Comment by a Foreign Ministry Official	No. 289
25 March 1999	Rio Group, Communiqué	No. 290
25 March 1999	Singapore, Response by the Foreign Minister to Questions from Journalists in Rome	No. 291
25 March 1999	South Africa, Statement Issued by the Department of Foreign Affairs, Pretoria	No. 292
25 March 1999	UK, Briefing by Mr. George Robertson, Secretary of State for Defence, and Gen Sir Charles Guthrie, Chief of the Defence Staff	No. 239
25 March 1999	UK, Statement by the Foreign Secretary, Robin Cook, in the House of Commons, Hansard, HC, vol. 328, col. 526	No. 240
25 March 1999	U.S., Secretary of State Albright, Press Conference on "Kosovo" as Released by the Office of the Spokesman, U.S. Department of State, Washington, D.C	No. 244
26 March 1999	France, Speech by M. Lionel Jospin, Prime Minister, to the National Assembly, Paris	No. 221
26 March 1999	Greece, Press Release by Ministry of Foreign Affairs, Athens	No. 230
26 March 1999	UN, Draft Resolution Submitted by Belarus, the Russian Federation and India, S/1998/328	No. 251

Chronological List of Documents

DATE	TEXT	DOCUMENT
26 March 1999	UN, Extracts from the Debates of the UN Security Council Concerning Draft Resolution S/1999/328, S/PV. 3989	No. 252
26 March 1999	UN High Commissioner for Human Rights, Statement by the UN High Commissioner for Human Rights	No. 35
27 March 1999	Hungary, Statement by the Ministry of Foreign Affairs of the Republic of Hungary, Budapest	No. 233
27 March 1999	NATO, Letter from the Secretary General of NATO to the Secretary-General of the UN	No. 174
27 March 1999	Russian Federation, Speech Delivered by Minister of Foreign Affairs I. S. Ivanov during the Sitting of the State Duma	No. 269
29 March 1999	Greece, Press Release by Ministry of Foreign Affairs, Athens	No. 231
29 March 1999	Russian Federation, Statement of Ministry of Foreign Affairs, Press-Release	No. 270
30 March 1999	Council of Europe, Parliamentary Assembly, Resolution 1182 (1999), Crisis in Kosovo and Situation in the FRY	No. 266
April 1999	Greece and the New Millennium: Signposts to a Point of Departure, Speech by the Greek Prime Minister Costas Simitis, Woodrow Wilson School, United States	No. 229
1 April 1999	FRY, The Decree on the Assemblies of Citizens during the State of War, Belgrade	No. 175
2 April 1999	Israel, Foreign Minister Sharon, Statement, Communicated by Foreign Minister's Spokesman	No. 293
2 April 1999	Malaysia, Statement by Datuk Seri Syed Hamid Albar, Minister of Foreign Affairs, Kuala Lumpur	No. 294
2 April 1999	Russian Federation, Press Conference by Russian Federation Foreign Minister Ivanov and Colonel General Baluyevsky, Chief of Main Operational Directorate, General Staff of the Russian Federation Armed Forces, First Deputy Chief of General Staff, Verbatim Report, Ministry of Foreign Affairs	No. 271
3 April 1999	CIS States, Declaration Adopted by the Inter-Parliamentary Assembly of States Members of the Commonwealth of Independent States	No. 272
3 April 1999	Russian Federation, Statement by the Official Representative of the Ministry of Foreign Affairs	No. 273
4 April 1999	NATO, Statement of the North Atlantic Council Following the Meeting between Representatives of the NATO Member States, the EU Member States, the OSCE CIO, the UNHCR, the Council of Europe and the WEU, Press Release (1999)048, Brussels	No. 176
5 April 1999	U.S., President Clinton and Secretary of Defence Cohen, Statement on Kosovo, Released by the White House Office of the Press Secretary, Washington, D.C.	No. 245
6 April 1999	FRY, Statement Carried by Serb Television	No. 177
6 April 1999	NATO, Statement by the Secretary General, Press Release (1999)049	No. 178
7 April 1999	FRY, The Decree on Internal Affairs during the State of War	No. 179
7 April 1999	Islamic Conference on Bosnia and Herzegovina and Kosovo, Statement and Declaration by the Contact Group of the Organization of the Islamic Conference (OIC) on Bosnia and Herzegovina and Kosovo	No. 295
7 April 1999	Malaysia, Speech by YB Datuk Dr. Leo Michael Toyad, Deputy Minister of Foreign Affairs of Malaysia at the Emergency Ministerial Meeting of the OIC Contact Group, Geneva	No. 296
7 April 1999	Pakistan, Statement by the Foreign Minister of Pakistan at the Emergency Ministerial Meeting of the OIC Contact Group, Geneva	No. 297
8 April 1999	EU, Special Meeting of the EU General Affairs Council, Conclusions on Kosovo, Luxembourg	No. 259
9 April 1999	Movement of Non-Aligned Countries, Statement, Geneva	No. 298
9 April 1999	UN High Commissioner for Human Rights, Briefing on Situation of Human Rights in Kosovo, Geneva	No. 36
9 April 1999	UN, Statement of the Secretary-General Concerning Kosovo Transmitted to His Excellency Mr. Milosevic, President of the FRY, and to His Excellency Mr. Solana, Secretary General of NATO, UN Doc. S/1999/402 = SG/SM/6952	No. 253
12 April 1999	Germany, A Stability Pact for South-Eastern Europe	No. 196
12 April 1999	NATO, Statement Issued at the Extraordinary Ministerial Meeting of the North Atlantic Council held at NATO Headquarters, Press Release M-NAC-1(99)51, Brussels	No. 180
13 April 1999	UN Commission on Human Rights, Resolution 1999/2, Situation of Human Rights in Kosovo	No. 33
13 April 1999	U.S. Secretary of State Albright and Russian Foreign Minister Ivanov Joint Press Availability, as Released by the Office of the Spokesman U.S. Department of State, Oslo	No. 197
13 April 1999	U.S. Secretary of State Albright and Norwegian Foreign Minister Vollebaek: Joint Press Conference, as Released by the Office of the Spokesman U.S. Department of State, Oslo	No. 198

Chronological List of Documents

DATE	TEXT	DOCUMENT
14 April 1999	EU, Chairman's Summary of the Deliberations on Kosovo at the Informal Meeting of the Heads of State and Government of the EU in Brussels	No. 260
15 April 1999	Germany, Deliberations of the *Deutscher Bundestag, BT Plenarprotokolle* 14/32, p. 2619, Extracts, Bonn	No. 226
16 April 1999	Sri Lanka, Ministry of Foreign Affairs, Press Release	No. 299
20 April 1999	Press Conference Given by the NATO Secretary General, Mr Javier Solana and the British Prime Minister, Mr Tony Blair, Brussels	No. 185
20 April 1999	U.S., Secretary of State Albright: Statement before the Senate Foreign Relations Committee, as Released by the Office of the Spokesman U.S. Department of State, Washington, D.C.	No. 246
21 April 1999	U.S. Senate, NATO's 50th Anniversary Summit, Hearing before the Committee on Foreign Relations, One Hundred Sixth Congress, First Session	No. 247
22 April 1999	Germany, Deliberations of the *Deutscher Bundestag, BT Plenarprotokolle* 14/35, Extracts, p. 2761, Bonn	No. 227
22 April 1999	Islamic Conference on Bosnia and Herzegovina and Kosovo, Statement and Declaration by the Contact Group of the Organization of the Islamic Conference on Bosnia and Herzegovina and Kosovo	No. 300
22 April 1999	UN High Commissioner for Human Rights, Report on Situation of Human Rights in Kosovo, FRY, HC/K224, Geneva	No. 37
23 April 1999	EU, Common Position, Defined by the Council on the Basis of Article J.2 of the EU-Treaty Concerning a Ban on the Supply and Sale of Petroleum and Petroleum Products to the FRY, 1999/273/CFSP	No. 261
23 April 1999	NATO, Statement on Kosovo Issued by the Heads of State and Government Participating in the Meeting of the North Atlantic Council in Washington, D.C. on 23rd and 24th April 1999, Press Release S-1(99)62	No. 181
23 April 1999	Russian Federation, Permanent Mission of the Russian Federation to the OSCE, Representation and Request for Information, Vienna	No. 274
23 April 1999	Russian Federation, Permanent Mission of the Russian Federation to the OSCE, Statement by Russian Foreign Ministry Representative	No. 275
23 April 1999	UN Commission on Human Rights, Resolution 1999/18, The Situation of Human Rights in the FRY (Serbia and Montenegro), the Republic of Croatia and Bosnia and Herzegovina	No. 34
26 April 1999	EU, Conclusions of the 2173rd Council Meeting, General Affairs, Luxembourg	No. 262
27 April 1999	Canada, House of Commons Debate on Kosovo, Extracts, 36th Parliament, 1st Session, Hansard 216, 1310-1320, Ottawa/Ontario	No. 216
27 April 1999	France, Speech by M. Lionel Jospin, Prime Minister, during Question Time in the National Assembly, Paris	No. 222
27 April 1999	Japan, Archives on Press Conferences by the Press Secretary	No. 282
27 April 1999	Medecins Sans Frontieres: Survey Data on Mass Expulsions from Kosovo, A Survey of the Kosovar Refugees at Rosaye, Montenegro, Vincent Brown, MSF/Epicentre, Rosaye	No. 49
28 April 1999	Council of Europe, Parliamentary Assembly, Recommendation 1403 (1999), Crisis in Kosovo and Situation in the FRY	No. 267
28 April 1999	I.C.J., Request for the Indication of Provisional Measures Concerning the Application of the Federal Republic of Yugoslavia against the Kingdom of Belgium for Violation of the Obligation not to Use Force, Belgrade (Extracts)	No. 306
29 April 1999	I.C.J. Legality of Use of Force (Yugoslavia v. Belgium), Application Instituting Proceedings Filed in the Registry of the Court (Extracts)	No. 307
29 April 1999	Press Statements by Chancellor Mr. Schröder and Russian Special Envoy to the FRY, Mr. Chernomyrdin, Bonn	No. 199
30 April 1999	UN High Commissioner for Human Rights, Report on the Human Rights Situation involving Kosovo, HC/K304, Geneva	No. 38
May 1999	U.S., Erasing History: Ethnic Cleansing in Kosovo, Report Released by the U.S. Department of State, Washington, D.C.	No. 46
1 May 1999	Germany, Statement by Federal Chancellor Gerhard Schröder	No. 228
4 May 1999	Cuba, Excerpts From the Speech Made by Comrade Fidel Castro at a Mass Rally in the University of Havana	No. 301
5 May 1999	UNHCR, Briefing by Mrs Sadako Ogata to the UN Security Council, New York	No. 43
6 May 1999	G 8, Statement by the Chairman on the Conclusion of the Meeting of the G 8 Foreign Ministers, Petersberg	No. 200
7 May 1999	Council of Europe, Chairman of the Committee of Ministers, Declaration on the Kosovo Crisis, Budapest	No. 268

Chronological List of Documents

DATE	TEXT	DOCUMENT
8 May 1999	UN Security Council Debate Concerning Letter Dated 7 May 1999 from the Permanent Representative of China Addressed to the President of the Security Council (S/1999/523), UN Doc. S/PV. 4000	No. 254
8 May 1999	North Atlantic Council Statement Concerning Bombing of Chinese Embassy, Press Release (1999)076, Brussels	No. 182
8 May 1999	Egypt, Statement by Foreign Minister Amre Moussa, Cairo	No. 302
10 May 1999	EU, Common Position Adopted by the Council on the Basis of Article 15 of the EU-Treaty Concerning Additional Restrictive Measures against the FRY, 1999/318/CFSP	No. 263
10 May 1999	I.C.J., Belgium, Oral Pleading in the Case "Legality of the Use of Force", CR 99/15 (translation)	No. 308
10 May 1999	The Philippines, Statement, Press Release No. 109-99	No. 303
11 May 1999	EU, Kosovo: Action by the European Commission, IP/99/319, Brussels	No. 264
11 May 1999	WEU Ministerial Council, Bremen Declaration, Bremen	No. 265
12 May 1999	EU-World Bank Agreement on Economic Co-ordination, IP/99/329, Brussels	No. 201
12 May 1999	The Netherlands, Speech by Dick Benschop, Released by Netherlands Ministry of Foreign Affairs, State Secretary for Foreign Affairs, College of Europe - Natolin, Warsaw	No. 235
14 May 1999	Russian Federation, Statement of the Ministry of Foreign Affairs	No. 276
14 May 1999	UN Security Council Resolution 1239 (1999)	No. 255
14 May 1999	UN, Extracts from the Debate of the Security Council Concerning Security Council Resolution 1239 (1999), Un Doc. S/PV. 4003	No. 256
15 May 1999	Egypt, Statement by Foreign Minister Moussa, Cairo	No. 304
15 May 1999	NATO, Statement by the NATO Spokesman on the Korisa Incident, Press Release (1999)079, Brussels	No. 183
17 May 1999	EU, Common Position Adopted by the Council on the Basis of Article 15 of the EU Treaty Concerning a Stability Pact for South-Eastern Europe, 1999/345/CFSP	No. 202
18 May 1999	UK, Edited Transcript of Interview Given by the Prime Minister, Tony Blair, for BBC World Service, Tirana	No. 86
19 May 1999	Press Conference Given by the NATO Secretary General, Mr Javier Solana and German Chancellor Gerhard Schroeder, Brussels	No. 187
20 May 1999	Press Conference Given by the NATO Secretary General, Mr Javier Solana and the Italian Prime Minister, Mr Massimo D'Alema, Brussels	No. 188
20 May 1999	Edited Transcript of Interview Given by the Foreign Secretary, Robin Cook, and US Secretary of State, Madeleine Albright, for CNN, Washington	No. 189
20 May 1999	Russian Federation, Statement of the Ministry of Foreign Affairs	No. 277
22 May 1999	ICTY, The Prosecutor v. Slobodan Milosevic, Milan Milutinovic, Nikola Sainovic, Dragoljub Ojdanovic, Vlajko Stojiljkovic, Presentation of an Indictment for Review and Application for Warrants of Arrest and for Related Orders	No. 317
23 May 1999	Morning Briefing by Jamie Shea, NATO Spokesman, Brussels	No. 190
24 May 1999	ICTY, The Prosecutor v. Slobodan Milosevic, Milan Milutinovic, Nikola Sainovic, Dragoljub Ojdanovic, Vlajko Stojiljkovic, Decision on Review of Indictment and Application for Consequential Orders	No. 318
24 May 1999	ICTY, Indictment of Slobodan Milosevic and others	No. 319
25 May 1999	U.S., President Clinton, Statement, Released by the White House, Office of the Press Secretary, aboard Air Force One	No. 248
27 May 1999	Russian Federation, Statement by the Ministry of Foreign Affairs	No. 320
27 May 1999	Russian Federation, Statement of the Ministry of Foreign Affairs	No. 321
30 May 1999	Morning Briefing by Jamie Shea, NATO Spokesman, Brussels	No. 191
31 May 1999	EU, Statement on Kosovo, Brussels	No. 203
31 May 1999	UN High Commissioner for Human Rights, Report on the Situation of Human Rights in Kosovo, FRY, UN Doc. E/CN.4/2000/7	No. 39
2 June 1999	I.C.J., Case Concerning the Legality of Use of Force, Request for the Indication of Provisional Measures, Order	No. 309
2 June 1999	Press Conference by Mr Jamie Shea, NATO Spokesman and Major General Walter Jertz, SHAPE, Brussels	No. 192
2 June 1999	Russian Federation, Statement by the Ministry of Foreign Affairs, Press Release	No. 310

Chronological List of Documents

DATE	TEXT	DOCUMENT
3 June 1999	Agreement on the Principles (Peace Plan) to Move towards a Resolution of the Kosovo Crisis Presented to the Leadership of the FRY by the President of Finland, Mr. Ahtisaari, Representing the European Union, and Mr. Chernomyrdin, Special Representative of the President of the Russian Federation	No. 204
3 June 1999	FRY, Statement from the Federal Government's Meeting, Belgrade	No. 205
3 and 4 June 1999	EU, Presidency Conclusions, Cologne European Council	No. 206
6 June 1999	FRY, Statement from the Federal Government's Meeting, Belgrade	No. 311
8 June 1999	OSCE, Permanent Council, PC. EC/296/Corr	No. 323
9 June 1999	Military-Technical Agreement between the International Security Force (KFOR) and the Governments of the FRY and the Republic of Serbia	No. 207
10 June 1999	France, Communique Issued by M. Hubert Vedrine, Minister of Foreign Affairs, Paris	No. 223
10 June 1999	G 8, Proposals of the G 8 Presidency in the Light of the Discussions on Civilian Implementation in Kosovo, Gürzenich	No. 211
10 June 1999	NATO, Statement by the Secretary General on Suspension of Air Operations, Brussels	No. 184
10 June 1999	NATO, Letter from the Secretary General of the North Atlantic Treaty Organization addressed to the UN Secretary-General	No. 212
10 June 1999	Stability Pact for South Eastern Europe, Cologne	No. 210
10 June 1999	UK, Statement by the Prime Minister, Tony Blair, London	No. 241
10 June 1999	UN Security Council Resolution 1244 (1999)	No. 208
10 June 1999	UN Extracts from the Debates of the Security Council Concerning Security Council Resolution 1244 (1999), UN Doc. S/PV. 4011	No. 209
11 June 1999	FRY, Statement from the Federal Government's Meeting, Belgrade	No. 213
12 June 1999	UN, Report of the Secretary-General Prepared pursuant to Paragraph 10 of Security Council Resolution 1244 (1999), UN Doc. S/1999/672	No. 324
15 June 1999	EC Council Regulation No 1294/1999 Concerning a Freeze of Funds and a Ban on Investment in Relation to the FRY and Repealing Regulations (EC) No 1295/98 and (EC) No 1607/98	No. 347
17 June 1999	NATO, Initial Report on the International Security Force (KFOR) Operations (12-15 June 1999)	No. 325
18 June 1999	US - Russian Federation, Agreement on Russian Participation in KFOR, Helsinki	No. 326
20 June 1999	G-8 Statement on Regional Issues	No. 348
20 June 1999	NATO - KLA, Undertaking of Demilitarisation and Transformation by the KLA	No. 327
20 June 1999	NATO, Letter from the Secretary General Addressed to the UN Secretary-General	No. 328
21-22 June 1999	EU, 2192nd Council Meeting, General Affairs, Luxembourg	No. 349
23 June 1999	Council of Europe, Parliamentary Assembly, Recommendation 1414 (1999), Crisis in Kosovo and Situation in the FRY	No. 329
1 July 1999	OSCE, Permanent Council, Decision No. 305, PC. DEC/305	No. 330
1 July 1999	OSCE, Permanent Council, Decision No. 306, PC. DEC/306	No. 331
12 July 1999	UN, Report of the Secretary-General on the United Nations Interim Administration Mission in Kosovo, UN Doc. S/1999/779	No. 332
25 July 1999	UNMIK/REG/1999/1, On the Authority of the Interim Administration in Kosovo	No. 339
29 July 1999	EU, Council Joint Action Concerning the Installation of the Structures of the United Nations Mission in Kosovo (UNMIK), 1999/522/CFSP	No. 333
12 August 1999	UNMIK/REG/1999/2, On the Prevention of Access by Individuals and Their Removal to Secure Public Peace and Order	No. 340
3 September 1999	EU, Council Common Position Amending Common Position 1999/273/CFSP Concerning a Ban on the Supply and Sale of Petroleum and Petroleum Products to the FRY, and Common Position 1999/318/CFSP Concerning Additional Restrictive Measures against the FRY, 1999/604/CFSP	No. 350
4 September 1999	UNMIK/REG/1999/5, On the Establishment of an Ad Hoc Court of Final Appeal and an Ad Hoc Office of the Public Prosecutor	No. 341
7 September 1999	UNMIK/REG/1999/7, On Appointment and Removal From Office of Judges and Prosecutors	No. 342
7 September 1999	UN High Commissioner for Human Rights, Report on the Situation of Human Rights in Kosovo, FRY, UN Doc. E/CN.4/2000/10	No. 40
16 September 1999	UN, Report of the Secretary-General on the United Nations Interim Administration Mission in Kosovo, UN Doc. S/1999/987	No. 334

Chronological List of Documents

DATE	TEXT	DOCUMENT
17 September 1999	Council of Europe, Committee of Ministers, Reply to Recommendation 1414 (1999)	No. 335
20 September 1999 - 2 October 1999	Extracts of the UN General Assembly General Debate	No. 257
20 September 1999	UNMIK/REG/1999/8, On the Establishment of the Kosovo Corps	No. 343
23 September 1999	Council of Europe, Parliamentary Assembly, Recommendation 1422 (1999), Southeastern Europe Following the Kosovo Conflict: Political Situation	No. 336
23 September 1999	Council of Europe, Parliamentary Assembly, Recommendation 1423 (1999), Southeastern Europe Following the Kosovo Conflict: Economic Reconstruction and Renewal	No. 351
23 September 1999	The Kosovo Protection Corps, Commander Kosovo Force's Statement of Principles	No. 337
29 September 1999	ICTY, Statement by the Prosecutor, PR/P.I.S./437-E, The Hague	No. 322
4 October 1999	EC Council Regulation No 2111/1999 Prohibiting the Sale and Supply of Petroleum and Certain Petroleum Products to Certain Parts of the FRY and Repealing Regulation (EC) No 900/1999	No. 352
11 October 1999	EC Council Regulation No 2151/1999 Imposing a Ban on Flights between the Territories of the Community and the FRY other than the Republic of Montenegro or the Province of Kosovo, and Repealing Regulation (EC) No 1064/1999	No. 353
15 October 1999	UNHCR, Numbers of Refugees Displaced from Kosovo 23 March - 9 June 1999, Geneva	No. 44
21 October 1999	UNMIK/REG/1999/14, On the Appointment of Regional and Municipal Administrators	No. 344
4 November 1999	Council of Europe, Final Communique of the 105th Session of the Committee of Ministers of the Council of Europe, Strasbourg	No. 354
6 November 1999	UNMIK/REG/1999/16, On the Establishment of the Central Fiscal Authority of Kosovo and Other Related Matters	No. 345
12 December 1999	UNMIK/REG/1999/24, On the Law Applicable in Kosovo	No. 346
17 December 1999	Situation of Human Rights in Kosovo, UN General Assembly Resolution 54/183	No. 22
23 December 1999	UN, Report of the Secretary-General on the United Nations Interim Administration Mission in Kosovo, UN Doc. S/1999/1250	No. 338
14 January 2000	Zimbabwe, Foreign Affairs Minister, Hon. Mudenge's Address at a Reception in Honour of the Visiting Chinese Foreign Minister	No. 305
February 2000	Human Rights Watch, Civilian Deaths in the NATO Air Campaign	No. 193
7 June 2000	UK, House of Commons, Foreign Affairs Committee, Fourth Report on Kosovo	No. 194
13 June 2000	ICTY, Final Report to the Prosecutor by the Committee Established to Review the NATO Bombing Campaign Against the FRY, PR/P.I.S./510-E	No. 195

Select Bibliography

1. Governmental and Non-Governmental Publications

Amnesty International, *A Background: A Crisis Waiting to Happen* (June 1998)

Amnesty International, *Violence in Drenica, February - April 1998* (June 1998)

Amnesty International, *Deaths in Custody, Torture and Ill-Treatment* (June 1998)

Amnesty International, *Unfair Trials and Abuses of Due Process* (June 1998)

Médicins Sans Frontières, *Kosovo Refugee Crisis - One Year Lager* (March 2000)

NATO, Lord Robertson of Port Ellen, Secretary General of NATO: *Kosovo - One Year On - Achievement and Challenge* (2000)

OSCE, *Kosovo/Kosova - As Seen, As Told: An Analysis of the Human Rights Findings of the OSCE Kosovo Verification Mission, October 1998 to June 1999*

OSCE, *Situation of Ethnic Minorities in Kosovo, July 1999 - June 2000*

OSCE, *The Kosovo Judicial System, November 1999 - March 2000*

UK Ministry of Defence, Lord Robertson of Port Ellen, Secretary of State for Defence, *Kosovo - An Account of the Crisis* (1999)

UNEP, *Kosovo Conflict: Consequences for the Environment and Human Settlements* (1999)

UNHCR, *The Kosovo Refugee Crisis - UNHCR's Emergency Preparedness and Response: An Independent Evaluations* (2000)

U.S. Department of State, *Ethnic Cleansing in Kosovo: An Accounting* (December 1999)

U.S. Department of State, *Kosovo Judicial Assessment, Mission Report* (April 2000)

2. Books

Amdam, Bernard, *La guerre du Kosovo* (Bruxelles 1999)

Campbell, Greg, *The Road to Kosovo: A Balkan Diary* (Boulder, Colorado, Westview Press 1999)

Hibbert, Reginald, *The Kosovo Question: Origins, Present Complications and Prospects* (London: David Davies Memorial Inst. of Internat. Studies 1999)

Littman, Mark, *Kosovo - Law and Diplomacy* (Centre for Policy Studies, London 1999)

Loquai, Heinz, *Der Kosovo-Konflikt - Wege in einen vermeidbaren Krieg: die Zeit von Ende November 1997 bis März 1999* (Baden-Baden 2000)

Lutz, Dieter S., *Der Kosovo-Krieg: Rechtliche und rechtsethische Aspekte* (Baden-Baden 2000)

Malcolm, Noel, *Kosovo: A Short History* (London 1998)

Mertus, Julie, *Kosovo - How Myths and Truths Started a War* (Berkeley, California, University of California Press 1999)

Saxer, Urs, *Kosovo und das Völkerrecht: Ein Konfliktmanagement im Spannungsfeld von Menschenrechten, kollektiver Sicherheit und Unilateralismus* (Basel 1999)

Schmid, Thomas (ed.), *Krieg im Kosovo* (Reinbek 1999)

Weller, Marc, *The Crisis in Kosovo: 1989 - 1999: From the Dissolution of Yugoslavia to Rambouillet and the Outbreak of Hostilities* (Cambridge: Documents and Analysis Publ. Ltd. 1999)

Weller, Marc, *The Kosovo Conflict: Forced Displacement, the Conduct and Termination of Hostilities and the Renewed Search for a Settlement* (Cambridge: Documents and Analysis, Publ. Ltd. 1999)

3. Articles

Baggett, Ted, 'Human Rights Abuses in Yugoslavia: To Bring an End to Political Oppression, the International Community Should Assist in Establishing an Independent Kosovo' (1999) 27 *Georgia Journal of International & Comparative Law* pp. 457-476

Bekker, Peter H.F./Borgen, Christopher J.,'World Court Rejects Yugoslav Requests to Enjoin Ten NATO Members from Bombing Yugoslavia' *ASIL Insights* No. 36

Boelaert-Suominen, Sonja, 'The International Criminal Tribunal for the Former Yugoslavia and the Kosovo Conflict' (2000) *International Review of the Red Cross* No. 837 pp. 217-252

Bothe, Michael/Martenczuk, Bernd, 'Die NATO und die Vereinten Nationen nach dem Kosovo-Konflikt: Eine völkerrechtliche Standortbestimmung' (1999) 47 *Vereinte Nationen* pp. 125-132

Select Bibliography

Burger, James A., 'International Humanitarian Law and the Kosovo Crisis: Lessons Learned or to be Learned' (2000) *International Review of the Red Cross* No. 837 pp. 129-145

Caccamo, Domenico, 'Kosovo: vincitori e vinti' (1999) 66 *Rivista di studi politici internazionali* pp. 361-406

Carpentier, Chantal, 'Qu'appelle-t-on menace contre la paix dans les résolutions sur le Kosovo?' (1999) 101 *Revue politique et parlementaire* pp. 35-40

Cassese, Antonio, 'Ex iniuria ius oritur: Are We Moving towards International Legitimation of Forcible Humanitarian Countermeasures in the World Community?' (1999) 10 *European Journal of International Law* pp. 23-30

Charney, Jonathan I., 'Anticipatory Humanitarian Intervention in Kosovo' (1999) 93 *American Journal of International Law* pp. 834-841

Chinkin, Christine M., 'Kosovo: A "Good" or "Bad" War?' (1999) 93 *American Journal of International Law* pp. 841-847

Defarges, Moreau, 'Le Kosovo ne sera pas indépendant' (1999) 55 *Défense nationale* pp. 73-79

Dobrkovic, Nina, 'Ethnic Problems and Solutions: Is the South Tyrol Model Applicable to Kosovo? A Comment from Belgrade' (1998) 11 *Humanitäres Völkerrecht-Informationsschriften* pp. 250-251

Duursma, Jorri C., 'Justifying NATO's Use of Force in Kosovo?' 12 (1999) *Leiden Journal of International Law* pp. 287-295

Falk, Richard A., 'Kosovo, World Order, and the Future of International Law' 93 (1999) *American Journal of International Law* pp. 847-857

Franck, Thomas M., 'Lessons of Kosovo' (1999) 93 *American Journal of International Law* pp. 857-860

Garcia, Thierry, 'Interventions humanitaires et maintien de la paix - La mission d'administration intérimaire des Nations Unies au Kosovo' (2000) 104 *Revue générale de droit international public* pp. 61-72

Gnesotto, Nicole, 'L'OTAN et l'Europe à la lumière du Kosovo' (1999) 64 *Politique étrangère* pp. 207-218

Greco, Ettore, 'The OSCE's Kosovo Verification Mission: a Preliminary Assessment' (1998) 4 *International Peacekeeping* pp. 115-118

Heintze, Hans-Joachim, 'Die völkerrechtliche Verantwortlichkeit der Föderativen Republik Jugoslawien und die Massenflucht aus dem Kosovo' (1999) 37 *Association for the Study of the World Refugee Problem: Bulletin* pp. 9-15

Henkin, Louis, 'Kosovo and the Law of "Humanitarian Intervention"' (1999) 93 *American Journal of International Law* pp. 824-828

Hilpold, Peter, 'Sezession und humanitäre Intervention - völkerrechtliche Instrumente zur Bewältigung innerstaatlicher Konflikte?' (1999) 54 *Austrian Journal of Public and International Law* pp. 529-602

Hummer, Waldemar/Mayr-Singer, Jelka, 'Der Kosovo-Krieg vor dem Internationalen Gerichtshof' (2000) 54 *Neue Justiz* pp. 113-119

Hürner, R. G., 'Kosovo after the Dayton Agreement' (1997) 50 *Studia diplomatica* pp. 71-77

Ipsen, Knut, 'Der Kosovo - Illegal? Gerechtfertigt? Entschuldbar?' (1999) 74 *Die Friedens-Warte* pp. 19-23

Kamp, Karl-Heinz, 'L'OTAN après le Kosovo: Ange de paix ou gendarme du monde?' (1999) 64 *Politique étrangère* pp. 245-256

Kessedjian, Catherine, 'Introduction: La legalite de l'intervention de l'OTAN au Kosovo' (1999) 1 *International Law Forum* pp.147-148

Kirgis, Frederic L., 'The Kosovo Situation and NATO Military Action' *ASIL Insight* No. 30

Klein, Eckart/Schmahl, Stefanie, 'Die neue NATO-Strategie und ihre völkerrechtlichen und verfassungsrechtlichen Implikationen' 1999 *Recht und Politik* pp. 198-209

Köck, Heribert Franz, 'Legalität und Legitimität der Anwendung militärischer Gewalt - Betrachtungen zum Gewaltmonopol der Vereinten Nationen und seinen Grenzen' (1999) 54 *Austrian Journal of Public and International Law* pp.133 -160

Lange, Christian, 'Zu Fragen der Rechtmäßigkeit des NATO-Einsatzes im Kosovo' (1999) 26 *Europäische Grundrechte Zeitschrift* pp. 313-316

Laubach, Birgit, 'Angriffkrieg oder Humanitäre Intervention' (1999) 32 *Zeitschrift für Rechtspolitik* pp. 276-278

Lavrov, Sergej, 'On the Ground: Russian Diplomats in Kosovo' (1999) 45 *International Affairs* pp. 15-24

Leurdijk, Dick A., 'Kosovo: A Case of "Coercive Diplomacy"' (1999) 10 *Helsinki monitor* pp. 8-18

Lupis, Alexander, 'Assessing the Mandate of the OSCE Kosovo Verification Mission Proposed at Rambouillet: An Insider's Perspective from the OSCE Mission to Bosnia and Herzegovina' (1999) 10 *Helsinki monitor* pp. 18-29

Momtaz, Djamchid, 'NATO's "Humanitarian Intervention" in Kosovo and the Prohibition of the Use of Force' (2000) *International Review of the Red Cross* No. 837 pp. 89-102

Nation, Robert C., 'US Policy and the Kosovo Crisis' (1998) 33 *The International Spectator* pp. 23-39

O'Connell, Mary Ellen, 'The UN, NATO, and International Law After Kosovo' (2000) 22 *Human Rights Quarterly* pp. 57-89

Pellet, Alain, 'La guerre du Kosovo - Le fait rattrape par le droit' (1999) 1 *International Law Forum* pp.160-165

Pradetto, August, 'Die NATO, humanitäre Intervention und Völkerrecht' (1999) 49 *Aus Politik und Zeitgeschichte* pp. 26-38

Select Bibliography

Pradetto, August, 'NATO-Intervention in Kosovo? Kein Eingreifen ohne UN-Mandat' (1998) 53 *Internationale Politik* pp. 41-46

Reisman, Michael W., 'Kosovo's Antinomies' (1999) 93 *American Journal of International Law* pp. 860-862

Reuter, Jens, 'Die internationale Gemeinschaft und der Krieg in Kosovo' (1998) 47 *Südost-Europa* pp. 281-297

Reuter, Jens, 'Kosovo 1998, (1998) 4 *OSCE Yearbook* pp. 183-194

Rittberger, Volker, 'Die NATO in den Fallstricken des Kosovo-Konflikts' (1999) 74 *Die Friedens-Warte* pp. 24-32

Salla, Michael, 'Kosovo, Non-Violence and the Break-Up of Yugoslavia' (1995) 26 *Security Dialogue* pp. 427-438

Schreuer, Christoph, 'Is there a Legal Basis for the NATO Intervention in Kosovo?' (1999) 1 *International Law Forum* pp. 151-154

Schrijver, Nico, 'NATO in Kosovo: Humanitarian Intervention Turns into Von Clausewitz War' (1999) 1 *International Law Forum* pp. 155-159

Simma, Bruno, 'NATO, the UN and the Use of Force: Legal Aspects' (1999) 10 *European Journal of International Law* pp. 1-22

Thürer, Daniel, 'Der Kosovo-Konflikt im Lichte des Völkerrechts: Von drei - echten und scheinbaren – Dilemmata' (2000) 38 *Archiv des Völkerrechts* pp. 1-22

Thürer, Daniel, 'Die NATO-Einsätze in Kosovo und das Völkerrecht: Spannungsfeld zwischen Gewaltverbot und Menschenrechten' in: Lutz, Dieter (ed.), *Der Kosovo-Krieg: rechtliche und rechtsethische Aspekte* pp. 129-133

Tomuschat, Christian, 'Völkerrechtliche Aspekte des Kosovo-Konflikts' (1999) 74 *Die Friedens-Warte* pp. 33-37

Valticos, Nicolas, 'Les droits de l'homme, le droit international et l'intervention militaire en Yougoslavie' (2000) 104 *Revue générale de droit international public* pp. 5-18

Ward, Benjamin, 'The Failure to Protect Minorities in Post-War Kosovo, (2000) 11 *Helsinki monitor* pp. 37-47

Wedgwood, Ruth, 'NATO's Campaign in Kosovo' (1999) 93 *American Journal of International Law* pp. 828-834

Weller, Marc, 'The Rambouillet Conference on Kosovo' (1999) 75 *International Affairs* pp. 211-251

Wilms, Heinrich, 'Der Kosovo-Einsatz und das Völkerrecht' (1999) 32 *Zeitschrift für Rechtspolitik* pp. 227-229

Zappala, Salvatore, 'Nuovi sviluppi in tema di uso della forza armata in relazione alle vicende del Kosovo' (1999) 82 *Rivista di diritto internazionale* pp. 975-1004

INDEX

Ahtisaari-Chernomyrdin peace proposal 360, 361, 362, 367
Albania
    flow of weapons to Kosovo 149, 213, 296
    statements on Kosovo 431, 444
Argentina 373, 428, 435, 448
Arms control 121
Arms embargo 130, 207, 293, 296, 365, 491
    by UN 122, 128-129
    Russian position 131
Asylum to Kosovo Albanians 146
Austria 457
Autonomy 118, 120, 128, 144, 259, 278, 301, 364 see also Kosovo, status of; self-government
    restauration of 16
    under the 1974 constitution 2
    under the 1994 Serbian constitution 5

Bahrain 373, 426, 436, 445
Belarus 430, 437, 443
Benin 471
Bosnia and Herzegovina 136, 439
Brazil 130, 295, 373, 427, 448
Bulgaria 469

Canada
    political initiatives 380, 390
    statements on Kosovo 380-392, 432, 442
Chile 469
China
    bombing of Chinese embassy 440-444
    statements on Kosovo 153, 297, 368, 429, 447, 491
Clinton doctrine 455
Cluster bombs 327, 343, 490
Collateral damage 441
Conference on Yugoslavia 118-120
    Special Group on Kosovo 119
Conflict prevention 454
Contact Group
    and Rambouillet Conference 255, 256, 260, 278
    on Milosevic-Yeltsin meeting 147
    Russian position 122
    statements on Kosovo 121, 126, 140, 143, 147, 187, 197, 223
Costa Rica 294
Côte d'Ivoire 454
Council of Europe 388
    FRY request for membership 138, 583
    on NATO air strikes 481
    statements on Kosovo 125, 138, 145, 154, 480, 538, 553, 554, 578, 583
Crimes against humanity 83
Croatia 471
Cuba 438, 443, 465, 497
Czech Republic 462

Danube Commission 209
Declaration of independence 118
Denmark 461
Depleted Uranium, use of 343, 504
Displacement of population 46, 50, 54, 252
Djibouti 461
Drenica region, killings 41, 92-97, 124, 125, 221, 385

Education 11, 28, 29, 30, 119, 120, 210
Egypt 137, 450, 493, 498, 499
El Salvador 492

Escalation of the conflict 244, 250, 256, 257, 299
Ethnic cleansing 25, 42, 44, 47, 82, 132, 421, 436
EU
    and Rambouillet 260, 279
    and UNMIK 548, 576
    EC Monitor Mission 577
    EC relations with FRY 139
    financial assistance to the Balkans 361
    humanitarian assistance 475, 476
    on Milosevic-Yeltsin meeting 147
    polices on South-Eastern Euope 576
    report on situation in Kosovo 200
    sanctions 125, 140-142, 144, 146, 149, 150, 476, 477, 578, 579, 581
    statements on Kosovo 120, 121, 127, 133, 139, 142, 143, 147-149, 154, 361, 362, 456, 473
    statements on Racak 195
    travel ban on Milosevic 476
    withdrawal of diplomatic staff from FRY 260

Federal Republic of Yugoslavia (FRY)
    and Rambouillet 259
    cease-fire offer 306
    democratisation process 147
    membership in the UN 512
    on ICJ proceedings 514
    on Rambouillet Conference 286
    position of 186, 190
    proposals for a political solution 166, 186, 190, 280, 301, 306
Former Yugoslav Republic of Macedonia 464
France 370, 392-398, 435, 446, 453

G 8 492
    on Interim Administration 378
    proposals for political settlement 359, 367, 441, 442
    Russian initiatives 485
    statements on Kosovo 359, 575
Gabon 295, 373, 428
Gambia 374, 426, 467
1949 Geneva Conventions 318, 504
    Additional Protocol No. 1 344, 504
1948 Genocide Convention 486, 506, 512, 514
Georgia 452
Germany
    and Stability Pact for South-Eastern Europe 354 see also Stability Pact for South-Eastern Europe
    statements on Kosovo 135, 398-404, 458
Ghana 456
González mission 128, 130, 133, 143, 144, 288
Greece 136, 461
    statements on Kosovo 404, 405
Guatemala 456

Hill process 155-185, 257, 414
    responses 165, 166
Holbrooke Agreement 289-291
Human rights
    and sovereignty 369-373, 400, 451, 453, 458, 459, 466, 470-472
    see also UN Charter, Art. 2 (7)
Human rights situation 219, 222, 228
    after establishment of UNMIK 61
    arbitrary detentions 58, 73, 102-103, 245, 251
    arbitrary executions 46, 47, 50, 85, 100
    arbitrary interference with privacy 75
    arbitrary killings 56, 228
    discriminatory measures 15-22, 40

ethnic minorities in Kosovo 61, 64
extrajudicial killings 25, 71
forcible disappearances 101
housing evictions 28
in Serbia-Montenegro 71
monitoring of 15-18, 137, 147, 187, 224, 230
    access 41, 43, 80, 122, 123, 129, 143, 147, 148, 152, 205, 210, 213
political prisoners 40, 41
repressions by Serbian authorities 15-17, 19
respect for civil rights 76, 79, 216
responsibility for violations 20
restrictions on media 105, 107
Special Rapporteur of the Commission on Human Rights 16, 18, 19, 25-39, 42, 45
    Yugoslav refusal of field office 29
torture 27, 29, 51, 59, 72, 91
treatment of women 46, 47, 51, 57, 85
unfair trials 31, 74, 90, 228, 234, 240, 245, 251
use of language 28

Human rights violations
threat to peace 385

Humanitarian assistance 219, 223, 240, 252, 444, 445
under UNMIK 546

Humanitarian intervention 410, 469
and UN 338, 397
anticipation 386
by regional organisation 433, 451, 507
under UN Security Council mandate 383, 385, 453, 458, 464
development of law 339, 400
unilateral 384-389, 432, 451, 456-460, 464, 465, 472, 489, 499, 507
    and UN 389
    customary law 337, 384

Humanitarian law
armed conflict 515
damage to the environment 342
military objectives 344, 346
principle of proportionality 346
violations by NATO 318, 342-352

Hungary 468

Iceland 469
ILC Draft State Responsibility
Art. 33 507
India 431, 439, 492, 493
Indiscriminate use of force by Serbian authorities 75, 93-100, 122, 125, 142, 143, 250
Interim administration 361, 365, 372, 475
Internally displaced persons 21, 53, 65, 66, 84, 222, 227, 246
return of 234, 238
International Committee of the Red Cross (ICRC) 152
access 142
International Court of Justice
jurisdiction 506, 511, 514
order 508
proceedings 502-515
1966 International Covenant on Civil and Political Rights 488, 489, 504
International Criminal Tribunal for the Former Yugoslavia
access to Kosovo 44, 197, 515
indictment of Milosevic 516-529
investigations after 10 June 1999 529, 542
jurisdiction over Kosovo 42, 44, 48, 364, 367, 372, 515, 516
report on NATO bombing 340-352
Russian position 529
International Monetary Fund 359
Intervention 504

Iran 137, 449
Iraq 443, 467
Israel 493
Italy 459

Jamaica 471
Japan 129, 491

Kazakhstan 465
KDOM 238
KFOR
depoyment 534
establishment 365, 371, 373
military-technical agreement with FRY 362, 364
negotiations on presence in Kosovo 357, 358, 361
preparation 359
Russian participation 534
KLA
abductions 38
condemnation of terrorist acts 122, 132, 142, 145, 146, 152, 295
demilitarisation 359, 361, 365, 368, 373, 536, 549, 557
land operations 314-317
paramilitary tribunals 235
violations of humanitarian law 108-110
Kosovo
1974 Constitution 7
as internal matter of FRY 132, 134, 153, 295, 301, 431, 436, 491
democratisation 545, 552, 562, 563
economic situation 541
independence of 12, 129, 136, 140, 259, 301, 384 see also Kosovo, status of
reconstruction 547, 552, 564, 578
security situation 204, 210, 227, 239
self-government 260, 261, 290, 359, 361 see also autonomy, Kosovo, status of
situation of Serb minority 457, 470, 540, 558, 562
status of 121, 148, 154, 155-185, 186, 187, 258, 262
threat to international peace 129, 130, 153, 297, 394, 427, 432
Kosovo Protection Corps 555, 569
Kosovo Transitional Council 549, 557
Kosovo Verification Mission 155, 187, 191, 292, 294, 297, 301
agreement on 188, 189
withdrawal 191
Kuwait 464

Landmines 100, 228, 559
Latvia 458
Lesotho 463
Liechtenstein 469

Malaysia 372, 427, 435, 445, 494, 495
Mexico 464, 492
Military operations by Serbian authorities 42, 43
Montenegro 139, 146, 216, 370, 419, 457, 475, 476
Morocco 457

Namibia 368, 428, 442, 446
NATO
ACTORD 289, 298
ACTWARN 289
air strikes 304, 309, 381, 396
    after action reports 317-352
    bombing of Chinese embassy 309, 351, 440, 490, 498
    bombing of Serbian TV station 349
    civilian deaths 51, 60, 317, 336, 367, 481, 488, 502, 504
    initiation 304
    Korisa incident 309, 325, 352, 448, 490

military issues 419
   suspension 309, 358, 362, 379, 398, 412, 423
   termination 538
Air Verification Mission 292-294
and humanitarian assistance 305, 308
and Rambouillet Conference 254, 256, 258, 279
coordination with international organisations 305
ground forces 310-313, 387, 388, 396, 397, 416, 486
military action
   aggression 300, 302, 367, 430, 437, 443, 482, 486, 489
   and UN 336, 368
   authorisation by UN Security Council 336, 337, 423, 435, 436, 486
   Canadian participation 382, 386, 387, 388
   French participation 395
   implicit *post facto* approval 336
   justification 307, 308, 391, 393, 409, 415, 420, 425, 433, 435, 455, 474
   legality of 336, 338, 404
   political aims 304, 305, 308, 371, 395, 406, 420
   response by FRY 299, 300, 302, 304, 366, 379, 430, 437, 442, 448
   Russian position 356, 359, 424
   violation of UN Charter 471, 493
regional organisation 300, 384, 386, 397, 433
support to monitoring 208
threat to use force 254, 256, 288-303, 408, 413, 491
Netherlands 371, 406, 426, 433, 449, 468
New Zealand 472
Norway 454

Oman 468
Organization of the Islamic Conference (OIC) 197, 450, 494, 497
OSCE (CSCE)
   head of KVM, persona non grata 193, 194, 196
   Kosovo Verification Mission 237
   long-term mission to Kosovo 17, 19-21, 40, 120, 122, 144, 214 *see also* UN Security Council resolutions 855 (1993), 1160 (1998)
   measures taken by 201, 206, 210, 213, 224, 230, 241
   statement on Kosovo 293

Pakistan 449, 495
Paris conference 191, 280, 286
Philippines 492
Poland 472
Portugal 294

Racak incident 192-199, 245, 251
   report of EU Forensic Expert Team 197-199
Rambouillet Conference 258-280
   deployment of ground forces 258
   Kosovo delegation 280
   preparation 253-257
   Rambouillet accords 261-278, 365, 372, 418, 474
      freedom of movement for KFOR 275, 483
      signature 280, 286
Refugees 85, 111, 212, 218, 222, 227, 246, 361
   humanitarian assistance 52, 65, 67, 68
   influx of 231, 236, 242
   refugee crisis 46, 68, 305, 396, 445, 446, 478, 488
   return of 19, 61, 361, 540, 550, 558
   violations of the rights of 52
Republic of Korea 493
Romania 464
Russian Federation
   agreement to political solution 360
   bombing of Chinese embassy 441

   initiatives at OSCE 487-489
   on human rights violations by NATO 487
   on implementation of UNSC resolutions 202
   proposals for political settlement 484
   statements on Kosovo 131, 153, 296, 434, 447, 456, 482, 490

Saint Kitts and Nevis 461
Self-determination 386, 469
Singapore 466, 493
Slovac Republic 456
Slovenia 369, 433, 467
South Africa 493
Spain 458
Spillover effect 12, 136, 141, 225, 231, 237, 242, 358, 487
Sri Lanka 464
St' Egidio Education Agreement 11-12, 18, 19, 41, 121, 122, 123, 125, 127, 128, 206
Stability Pact for South-Eastern Europe 354, 356, 360, 362, 365, 374-378, 475, 479, 575
State of necessity 507
Sudan 471
Sweden 457

The Balkans
   economic development 359
   situation on 470
   stability of 407
The Philippines 498
Turkey 136

Uganda 471
Ukraine 436
UN
   involvement in peaceful settlement 357, 358, 361, 362, 475, 476
UN Charter
   Art. 2 (4) 300, 434
   Art. 2 (7) 131, 337, 431, 432 *see also* Human Rights and sovereignty
   Art. 12 337
   Art. 24 434, 462
   Art. 39 137
   Art. 51 384
   Art. 53 300, 302, 431, 434, 484, 493, 504
   Art. 54 493
   Chapter VII 131, 134, 384, 394, 419, 431, 462
   Chapter VII, resolutions taken under 128, 151, 153, 292 296, 364, 368, 369, 394 *see also* Kosovo, threat to peace
   Chapter VIII 453, 454, 456, 459, 467
UN Commission on Human Rights
   resolutions on Kosovo 40-45
UN General Assembly 24
   debates 451-473
   resolutions 15-23
      377 (V) 337, 384
UN High Commissioner for Human Rights 45-64
   Kosovo Emergency Operation 54
   on NATO military actions 45, 48, 53
   role after 10 June 1999 60
UN High Commissioner for Refugees 65-70
UN Interim Administration Mission in Kosovo (UNMIK) 61, 462, 532
   applicable law in Kosovo 567, 571
   authority of 567
   competence 542
   judicial affairs 544, 552, 554, 561, 568
   Kosovo Protection Corps 569
   police 551, 561, 567
   public administration 543, 570

public services 540, 550, 559
structure 543
UN Mission to FRY 228
UN Secretary-General
on humanitarian intervention 451
on Kosovo 440
on NATO air strikes 424
reports 199-253
UN Security Council
and national interest 452, 455, 466, 472
authorisation to use force 295, 296, 297, 373, 381, 384, 398, 399, 422, 428
Committee established pursuant to resolution 1160 (1998) 233
debates 129, 153, 293, 366, 424
draft resolution by Russia 432, 483
on ICTY 516
on Racak 195
on Rambouillet Conference 256, 278
presidential statements 150, 195, 256
primary responsibility 368, 370, 372-374, 399, 424, 426, 431, 453, 454, 462-465, 492, 493, 496
reform 453, 456, 458, 463
resolutions
  855 (1993) 17, 120
  1160 (1998) 17, 128, 203
  1199 (1998) 151, 393, 398, 399
  1203 (1998) 292, 393
  1207 (1998) 516
  1239 (1999) 444
  1244 (1999) 364
  monitoring of implementation 203, 211, 226, 238, 248, 250
veto 382-387, 390, 426, 428, 456, 458, 472
UNHCR 239
coordination with KVM 240
United Arab Emirates 457
United Kingdom
on Rambouillet Conference 279
political initiatives 411
statements on Kosovo 132, 153, 257, 297, 407-413, 428, 435, 454
United States of America 132, 154
bombing of Chinese embassy 441
statements on Kosovo 298, 413-423, 425, 433, 455
UNPREDEP 122, 288, 289
Uruguay 464
Use of force 434, 436, 451, 464, 471, 493, 502, 503

Vienna Convention on Law of Treaties 486
Viet Nam 471

War crimes 44, 83, 86
WEU 209, 479
statements on Kosovo 141, 185
Withdrawal of FRY forces 538, 540
World Bank 359, 478, 575

For EU product safety concerns, contact us at Calle de José Abascal, 56–1°, 28003 Madrid, Spain or eugpsr@cambridge.org.

www.ingramcontent.com/pod-product-compliance
Ingram Content Group UK Ltd.
Pitfield, Milton Keynes, MK11 3LW, UK
UKHW050800060825
461487UK00021B/1753